Rand McNally

GOODE'S WORLD ATLAS

18th EDITION

EDITOR

Edward B. Espenshade, Jr.

*Professor Emeritus of Geography
Northwestern University*

SENIOR CONSULTANT

Joel L. Morrison

United States Geological Survey

RAND McNALLY

Chicago • New York • San Francisco

D0731332

Goode's World Atlas

Copyright © 1990 by Rand McNally & Company
Sixth printing, revised 1992

Copyright © 1922, 1923, 1932, 1933, 1937, 1939,
1943, 1946, 1949, 1954, 1957, 1960, 1964, 1970, 1974,
1978, 1982, 1986 by Rand McNally & Company
Formerly *Goode's School Atlas*
Made in U.S.A.

Library of Congress Catalog Card Number 89-40419

This publication, or parts thereof, may not be reproduced
in any form by photographic, electrostatic, mechanical, or
any other method, for any use, including information storage
and retrieval, without the prior written permission
from the publisher.

Photo credits:
Figures 22, 23 - United States Geological Survey;
Figures 1, 2, 18, 19, 20 - National Aeronautics and
Space Administration

CONTENTS

Introduction [vii–xvi]

vii Geography and Maps / Geographic Education / Organization of the Atlas / Cartographic Communication / Map Data

ix Map Scale

x Map Projections

xiii Remotely Sensed Imagery

xiv Landsat

xv SPOT

xv High-Altitude Imagery

xvi Earth–Sun Relations and World Time Zones

World Thematic Maps [1–54]

1 Introduction

2 Political

4 Physical

6 Landforms

8 Climatic Regions

10 Surface Temperature Regions / January Normal Temperature

11 Normal Annual Range in Temperature / July Normal Temperature

12 January Pressure and Predominant Winds / Precipitation November 1 to April 30

13 July Pressure and Predominant Winds / Precipitation May 1 to October 31

14 Annual Precipitation and Ocean Currents
    INSETS: Variability of Annual Precipitation / Zones of Precipitation

16 Natural Vegetation

18 Soils

20 Population Density

22 Birth Rate / Death Rate

23 Natural Increase / Urbanization

24 Gross Domestic Product / Literacy

25 Languages / Religions

26 Nutrition • Calorie Supply / Protein Consumption

27 Health • Population per Physician / Life Expectancy

28 Predominant Economies

30 Major Agricultural Regions

32 Wheat / Tea, Rye

33 Maize (Corn) / Coffee, Oats

34 Barley, Cacao / Rice, Millet and Grain Sorghum

35 Potatoes, Cassava / Cane Sugar, Beet Sugar

36 Fruits / Tobacco, Fisheries

37 Vegetable Oils

38 Natural Fibers / Man-made Fibers

39 Cattle / Swine

40 Sheep / Forest Regions

41 Rubber, Grapes / Precious Metals

42 Copper / Tin, Bauxite

43 Lead / Zinc

44 Iron Ore and Ferroalloys

45 Steel / Manufacturing

46 Mineral Fertilizers / Fertilizer Use

47 Energy Production / Energy Consumption

48 Mineral Fuels

50 Nuclear and Geothermal Power / Water Power

51 Exports / Imports

52 Land and Ocean Transportation

54 Political and Military Alliances / Economic Alliances

Regional Maps [55–213]

55 Introduction and Legend

NORTH AMERICA [56–118]

56 Northern Lands and Seas Scale 1:60,000,000

57 North America • Energy / Water Resources / Natural Hazards / Landforms

58 North America • Annual Precipitation / Vegetation / Population / Economic, Minerals

59 North America • Environments Scale 1:36,000,000

60 United States and Canada • Environments Scale 1:12,000,000

62 United States and Canada • Physiography Scale 1:12,000,000

64 United States and Canada • Precipitation / Glaciation

65 United States and Canada • Climate

66 United States and Canada • Natural Vegetation

68 United States • Water Resources

69 United States and Canada • Minerals

70 United States and Canada • Population

71 United States • Demographic / Education

72 United States • Economics / Health

73 United States • Labor Structure / Westward Expansion

74 United States and Canada • Types of Farming / Manufacturing

75 United States and Canada • Transportation

76 North America Scale 1:40,000,000

77 Canada • Cities and Environs Scale 1:1,000,000 Montréal / Québec / Toronto / Ottawa / Calgary / Winnipeg / Edmonton

CONTENTS, *continued*

78 Canada *Scale 1:12,000,000*
INSET: Newfoundland *Same scale*

80 Southwestern Canada *Scale 1:4,000,000*

82 South-Central Canada *Scale 1:4,000,000*

84 Southeastern Canada *Scale 1:4,000,000*

86 Northern New England, Eastern Gateway of Canada, and Newfoundland *Scale 1:4,000,000*
INSET: Boston *Scale 1:1,000,000*

88 Hawaii • Annual Precipitation / Vegetation / Population / Environments

89 Alaska *Scale 1:12,000,000*
INSET: Aleutian Islands *Same scale*

90 United States of America *Scale 1:12,000,000*
INSETS: Hawaii *Same scale* / Oahu *Scale 1:3,400,000*
Alaska *Scale 1:36,000,000*

92 Northeastern U.S.A. *Scale 1:4,000,000*

94 United States • Cities and Environs *Scale 1:1,000,000*
New York / Providence / Atlanta / New Orleans / Baltimore–Washington / Philadelphia / Norfolk / Birmingham / Milwaukee–Chicago / Detroit / Buffalo / Cleveland / Pittsburgh / Cincinnati / Indianapolis / Louisville

96 Northern Interior U.S.A. *Scale 1:4,000,000*

98 Northwestern U.S.A. *Scale 1:4,000,000*

100 United States and Canada • Cities and Environs *Scale 1:1,000,000*
Victoria–Seattle–Tacoma / San Francisco–Oakland / Portland / Vancouver / Los Angeles / Salt Lake City / Dallas–Ft. Worth / San Antonio / St. Louis / Kansas City / Duluth / Sault Ste. Marie / Minneapolis–St. Paul

102 Southwestern U.S.A. *Scale 1:4,000,000*
INSET: San Diego *Scale 1:1,000,000*

104 Central U.S.A. *Scale 1:4,000,000*

106 Western Gulf Region of U.S.A. and Part of Mexico *Scale 1:4,000,000*
INSET: Houston–Galveston *Scale 1:1,000,000*

108 Southeastern U.S.A. *Scale 1:4,000,000*

110 Gulf and Caribbean Lands *Scale 1:16,000,000*
INSETS: Panama Canal *Scale 1:1,000,000*
Puerto Rico and Virgin Islands *Scale 1:4,000,00*
St. Thomas *Scale 1:500,000*

112 Mexico • Central *Scale 1:4,000,000*
INSET: Mexico City *Scale 1:1,000,000*

114 Central America *Scale 1:4,000,000*
INSETS: Yucatan Peninsula / Leeward and Windward Islands *Same scale*

116 West Indies • Western *Scale 1:4,000,000*
INSET: Havana *Scale 1:1,000,000*

118 Middle America • Ethnic / Political

SOUTH AMERICA [119–126]

119 South America • Energy / Peoples / Natural Hazards / Landforms

120 South America • Annual Precipitation / Vegetation / Population / Economic, Minerals

121 South America • Environments *Scale 1:36,000,000*

122 South America *Scale 1:40,000,000*

123 South America • Cities and Environs *Scale 1:4,000,000*
São Paulo–Rio de Janeiro / Santiago / Buenos Aires–Montevideo

124 South America • Northern *Scale 1:16,000,000*
INSETS: Caracas / Medellín–Bogotá–Cali *Scale 1:4,000,000*

126 South America • Southern *Scale 1:16,000,000*
INSETS: Buenos Aires / Rio de Janeiro *Scale 1:1,000,000*

EUROPE [127–166]

127 Europe • Energy / Natural Hazards

128 Europe • Annual Precipitation / Vegetation

129 Europe • Population / Minerals

130 Europe • Environments *Scale 1:16,000,000*

132 Europe • Physiography *Scale 1:16,000,000*
INSETS: Physiographic Provinces / Europe During the Ice Age

134 Europe • Languages *Scale 1:16,500,000*

136 Europe and Western Asia *Scale 1:16,000,000*

138 England • Central Manufacturing Region / London *Scale 1:1,000,000*

139 Europe • Cities and Environs *Scale 1:1,000,000*
Amsterdam–The Hague–Rotterdam–Antwerp–Brussels / Berlin / Hamburg / Vienna / Munich

140 Western Europe *Scale 1:10,000,000*

142 Mediterranean Lands *Scale 1:10,000,000*

144 British Isles and North Sea Lands *Scale 1:4,000,000*
INSET: Shetland Islands, Orkney Islands *Same scale*

146 Southern Scandinavia and the East Baltic Republics *Scale 1:4,000,000*

148 Central Europe *Scale 1:4,000,000*

150 France *Scale 1:4,000,000*
INSETS: Marseille / Paris / Ruhr *Scale 1:1,000,000*

152 Spain and Portugal *Scale 1:4,000,000*
INSETS: Madrid / Lisbon / Naples / Rome *Scale 1:1,000,000*

154 Italy and the Balkans *Scale 1:4,000,000*
INSET: Crete *Same scale*

156 Belarus, Ukraine, and Western Russia *Scale 1:4,000,000*

158 Northern Eurasia *Scale 1:20,000,000*

160 Eastern Europe and Asia Minor *Scale 1:10,000,000*

162 Siberia *Scale 1:16,000,000*

164 Russia • Ural Industrial Area *Scale 1:4,000,000*
INSETS: Moscow / St. Petersburg *Scale 1:1,000,000*

165 Northern Eurasia • Population / Economic, Minerals

166 Northern Eurasia • Ethnic
Middle East • Ethnic

ASIA [167–192]

167 Asia • Energy / Natural Hazards

168 Asia • Annual Precipitation / Population

169 Asia • Vegetation / Economic, Minerals

170 Asia • Environments *Scale 1:36,000,000*

171 Asia • Political

172 Asia *Scale 1:40,000,000*
INSETS: Lebanon, Israel, West Jordan / The Singapore Region *Scale 1:4,000,000*

174 Asia • Southwestern *Scale 1:16,000,000*
INSETS: Khyber Pass *Scale 1:4,000,000*
Sri Lanka (Ceylon) *Scale 1:16,000,000*
India • Political *Scale 1:40,000,000*

176 Middle East *Scale 1:12,000,000*

178 India *Scale 1:10,000,000*
INSETS: Calcutta / Bombay *Scale 1:1,000,000*
Major Languages / Economic and Land Use

180 China and Japan *Scale 1:16,000,000*

182 Part of Eastern China *Scale 1:4,000,000*

183 China • Economic, Minerals / Population
INSETS: Guangzhou / Shanghai *Scale 1:1,000,000*

184 China • Eastern *Scale 1:10,000,000*
INSET: Beijing *Scale 1:1,000,000*

186 Korea and Japan *Scale 1:10,000,000*

187 Southern Japan *Scale 1:4,000,000*
INSETS: Ōsaka−Kōbe−Kyōto / Tōkyō−Yokohama *Scale 1:1,000,000*

188 Indonesia and the Philippines *Scale 1:16,000,000*
INSET: Northern Philippines *Scale 1:4,000,000*

190 Pacific Ocean *Scale 1:50,000,000*

192 Pacific Islands • Western Samoa−American Samoa / Palau / Truk / Okinawa *Scale: 1:4,000,000*
Solomon Islands / Fiji / New Caledonia−Vanuatu *Scale 1:8,000,000*

AUSTRALIA [193−199]

193 Australia and New Zealand • Energy / Natural Hazards

194 Australia • Annual Precipitation / Vegetation / Population / Economic, Minerals / Transportation / Water

195 Australia and New Zealand • Environments *Scale 1:36,000,000*
INSETS: Melbourne / Sydney *Scale 1:1,000,000*

196 Australia and New Zealand *Scale 1:16,000,000*

198 Australia • Southeastern *Scale 1:8,000,000*

199 New Zealand *Scale 1:6,000,000*
INSETS: Land Use
Auckland / Wellington *Scale 1:1,000,000*

AFRICA [200−213]

200 Africa • Political Change / Peoples / Natural Hazards / Landforms

201 Africa • Annual Precipitation / Vegetation / Population / Economic, Minerals

202 Africa • Environments *Scale 1:36,000,000*

203 Africa *Scale 1:40,000,000*

204 Africa • Northern *Scale 1:16,000,000*
INSETS: Azores / Cape Verde *Same scale*

206 Africa • Southern *Scale 1:16,000,000*
INSETS: Cape Town / Johannesburg−Pretoria *Scale 1:1,000,000*
Southeastern South Africa *Scale 1:4,000,000*

208 Africa • Western *Scale 1:10,000,000*

210 Africa • Central *Scale 1:10,000,000*

212 Africa • Northeast and Regional
Somalia *Scale 1:16,000,000*
Lower Nile Valley *Scale 1:4,000,000*
Suez Canal *Scale 1:1,000,000*
Northeastern South Africa *Scale 1:4,000,000*

213 Antarctica *Scale 1:60,000,000*

Plate Tectonics and Ocean Floor Maps [214−221]

214 Earth Plate Tectonics

215 Continental Drift / Ocean Floor Maps

216 Atlantic Ocean Floor *Scale 1:44,000,000*

218 Pacific Ocean Floor *Scale 1:58,000,000*

220 Indian Ocean Floor *Scale 1:46,000,000*

221 Arctic Ocean Floor / Antarctic Ocean Floor *Scale 1:60,000,000*

Major Cities Maps *Scale 1:300,000* [222−240]

222 Introduction and Legend

223 Montréal / Toronto / Boston

224 New York

225 Baltimore / Washington / Philadelphia / Cleveland

226 Buffalo / Pittsburgh / Detroit

227 San Francisco / Chicago

228 Los Angeles

229 Mexico City / Havana / Lima / Buenos Aires

230 Caracas / Santiago / Rio de Janeiro / São Paulo

231 London

232 Ruhr Area

233 Liverpool / Manchester / Paris

234 Berlin / Madrid / Milan / Lisbon / Barcelona

235 St. Petersburg / Moscow / Rome / Athens / Vienna / İstanbul / Budapest

236 Calcutta / Delhi / Bombay / Singapore / Beijing

237 Shanghai / Seoul / Victoria / T'aipei / Kyōto / Bangkok / Manila / Tehrān / Jakarta / Ho Chi Minh City (Saigon)

238 Tōkyō−Yokohama / Ōsaka−Kōbe

239 Sydney / Melbourne

240 Lagos / Kinshasa and Brazzaville / Cairo / Johannesburg

Geographical Tables and Indexes [241−368]

241 World Political Information Table

246 World Comparisons

247 Principal Cities of the World

248 Glossary of Foreign Geographical Terms

249 Abbreviations of Geographical Names and Terms

249 Pronunciation of Geographical Names

250 Pronouncing Index

367 Subject Index

368 Sources

ACKNOWLEDGMENTS

This is the eighteenth edition of the Rand McNally *Goode's World Atlas* which was first published more than sixty years ago. The name of Dr. J. Paul Goode, the original editor and distinguished cartographer who designed the early editions, has been retained to affirm the high standards which all those who have participated in the preparation of the atlas during these years have sought to attain.

Through the years, general-reference maps coverage has been expanded; the number of thematic maps has been increased and their subject range broadened; and systematic improvements in symbolism, cartographic presentation, and map production and printing have been incorporated.

The eighteenth edition continues this tradition, and includes twenty new thematic maps. World maps have been added on military and economic alliances, precious metals and use of fertilizers. Eight new United States maps depict health and economic conditions. New population, economic and ethnic maps for the Soviet Union have been compiled. Other thematic maps include ethnic maps for the Middle East and Gulf and Caribbean Lands, and water resources and transportation maps for Australia. New reference maps include a page on the Pacific Islands.

Thematic maps, statistics, graphs, and various tables have been revised to incorporate the latest available data. The major city maps have been placed at the end of the reference map section, a list of source materials, and an index to thematic topics (subject index) have been added in response to suggestions from users of the atlas. These additions and other revisions reflect the editors' and publisher's commitment to increasing the usefulness and quality of each edition of the Rand McNally *Goode's World Atlas*, thus maintaining it as a standard among world atlases.

Sources

Every effort was made to assemble the latest and most authentic source materials to use in this edition. In the general physical-political maps, data from national and state surveys, recent military maps, and hydrographic charts were utilized. Source materials for the specialized maps were even more varied (See the partial list of sources at the end of the atlas). They included both published and unpublished items in the form of maps, descriptions in articles and books, statistics, and correspondence with geographers and others. To the various agencies and organizations, official and unofficial, that cooperated, appreciation and thanks are expressed. Noteworthy among these organizations and agencies were: The United Nations (for demographic and trade statistics); the Food and Agriculture Organization of The United Nations (for production statistics on livestock, crops, and forest products and for statistics on world trade); the Population Reference Bureau (for population data); the Office of the Geographer, Department of State (for the map "Surface Transport Facilities" and other items); the office of Foreign Agricultural Relations, Department of Agriculture (for information on crop and livestock production and distribution); the Bureau of Mines, Department of the Interior (for information on mineral production); various branches of the national military establishment and the Weather Bureau, Department of Commerce (for information on temperature, wind, pressure, and ocean currents); the Maritime Commission and the Department of Commerce (for statistics on ocean trade); the American Geographical Society (for use of its library and permission to use the Miller cylindrical projection); the University of Chicago Press, owners of the copyright (for permission to use Goode's Homolosine equal-area projection);the McGraw-Hill Book Company (for cooperation in permitting the use of Glenn Trewartha's map of climatic regions and Petterssen's diagram of zones of precipitation); the Association of American Geographers (for permission to use Richard Murphy's map of landforms); and publications of the World Bank (for nutrition, health, and economic information).

Some additional sources of specific data and information are as follows: World Oil (for oil and gas data); International Labour Organisation (for labor statistics); International Road Federation (for transportation data); Miller Freeman Publications, Inc. (for data on coal, copper, tin, and iron ore); Organisation for Economic Co-operation and Development (for data on ocean transportation and uranium); and Textile Economics Bureau, Inc. (for data on fibers).

Other Acknowledgments

The variety and complexity of the problems involved in the preparation of a world atlas make highly desirable the participation of specialists in the fields concerned. In the preparation of the new edition of the Rand McNally *Goode's World Atlas*, the editors have been ably assisted by several such experts. They express their deep appreciation and thanks to all of them.

They are particularly indebted to the following experts who have cooperated over the years: A.W. Kuchler, Department of Geography, University of Kansas; Richard E. Murphy, late professor of geography, University of New Mexico, Erwin Raisz, late cartographer, Cambridge, Massachusetts; Glenn T. Trewartha, late professor of geography, University of Wisconsin; Derwent Whittlesey, late professor of geography, Harvard University; and Bogdan Zaborski, professor emeritus of geography, University of Ottawa.

The editors thank the entire Cartographic and Design staff of Rand McNally & Company for their continued outstanding contributions.

EDWARD B. ESPENSHADE, JR.
JOEL L. MORRISON

INTRODUCTION

Geography and Maps

The study of geography is the study of the location, description, and interrelations of the earth's features — its people, landforms, climate, and natural resources. In fact, anything on the earth is fair game for geographic inquiry, and mapping. Helping to answer the questions of *where* something is, and *why* it is there, is fundamental to any geographic study.

Maps, photographs, and images based on radar and the electromagnetic spectrum increase one's ability to study the earth. They enable geographers and other earth scientists to record information about the earth through time and to examine and study areas of the earth's surface far too large to view firsthand.

Geographic Education

There are five fundamental themes of geography that help people organize and understand information about the earth. The maps in *Goode's World Atlas* present information that is essential for applying these themes. The themes are as follows:

Theme 1. **Location: Absolute and Relative.** Maps show where places are located in absolute terms, such as latitude and longitude, and where they are in relation to other places — their relative location. By locating and graphically portraying places and things, maps reveal the patterns of the earth's diverse landscape.

Theme 2. **Place: Physical and Human Characteristics.** Maps provide useful information about the physical and human characteristics of places. Landform maps show the surface features of the earth. Climate and natural vegetation maps may be compared to reveal how vegetation responds to climatic conditions. Human characteristics include those effects people have on places. Population maps show the density and distribution of people, while maps of language and religion provide information about cultural characteristics.

Theme 3. **Relationships Within Places: People Interacting with the Environment.** People interact with the natural environment, and the extent to which they alter the environment can be studied by viewing maps. The maps in the atlas provide information about current and past conditions of the environment and are useful in making informed decisions about the future effects of people on the land.

Theme 4. **Movement: Interactions Between Places.** The movement of people and products between places results in networks that span the earth. The dynamics of global interdependence are illustrated by maps that show the movement of commodities from places of production to places of consumption. Maps in the atlas depict highways, air traffic corridors, and shipping lanes that use the world's rivers, lakes, and oceans.

Theme 5. **Regions: How They Form and Change.** A *region* is a part of the earth's surface that displays similar characteristics in terms of selected criteria. Climates, nations, economies, languages, religions, diets, and urban areas are only a few of the topics that can be shown regionally on maps. The region is the basic unit of geographic study. It makes the complex world more readily understandable by organizing the earth according to selected criteria, allowing the similarities and differences from place to place to be studied and understood more fully.

Organization of the Atlas

The maps in *Goode's World Atlas* are grouped into four parts, beginning with *World Thematic Maps*, portraying the distribution of climatic regions, raw materials, landforms, and other major worldwide features. The second part is the *Regional Maps* section and main body of the atlas. It provides detailed reference maps for all inhabited land areas on a continent-by-continent basis. Thematic maps of the continents are also contained in this part. The third part is devoted to *Plate Tectonics and Ocean Floor Maps*. In the fourth part, *Major Cities Maps*, the focus is on individual cities and their environs all mapped at a consistent scale.

Geographical tables, an index of places, a subject index, and list of sources complete the atlas. The tables provide comparative data, a glossary of foreign geographical terms, and the index of places — a universal place-name pronouncing index for use with the reference maps.

Cartographic Communication

To communicate information through a map, cartographers must assemble the geographic data, use their personal perception of the world to select the relevant information, and apply graphic techniques to produce the map. Readers must then be able to interpret the mapped data and relate it to their own experience and need for information. Thus, the success of any map depends on both the cartographer's and the map reader's knowledge and perception of the world and on their common understanding of a map's purpose and limitations.

The ability to understand maps and related imagery depends first on the reader's skill at recognizing how a curved, three-dimensional world is symbolized on a flat, two-dimensional map. Normally, we view the world horizontally (that is, our line of vision parallels the horizon), at an eye level about five and one-half to six feet above the ground. Images appear directly in front and to either side of us, with our eyes encompassing all details as nonselectively as a camera. Less frequently, when we are atop a high platform or in an airplane, we view the world obliquely, as shown in *Figure 1*, in which both vertical and horizontal facets of objects can be seen. And only those persons at very high altitudes will view the world at a vertical angle (*Figure 2*). Yet maps are based on our ability to visualize the world from an overhead, or vertical, perspective.

A map differs from a purely vertical photograph in two important respects. First, in contrast to the single focal point of a photograph, a map is created as if the viewer were directly overhead at all points (See *Figure 3*). Second, just as our brains select from the myriad items in our field of vision those objects of interest or importance to us, so each map presents only those details necessary for a particular purpose — a map is not an inventory of all that is visible. Selectivity is one of a map's most important and useful characteristics.

Skill in reading maps is basically a matter of practice, but a fundamental grasp of cartographic principles and the symbols, scales, and projections commonly employed in creating maps is essential to comprehensive map use.

Map Data

When creating a map, the cartographer must select the objects to be shown, evaluate their relative importance, and find some way to simplify their form. The combined process is called *cartographic generalization*. In attempting to generalize data, the cartographer is limited by the purpose of the map, its scale, the methods used to produce it, and the accuracy of the data.

Figure 1.   Oblique aerial photograph of New York City.

Figure 2.   High-altitude vertical photograph of New York City area.

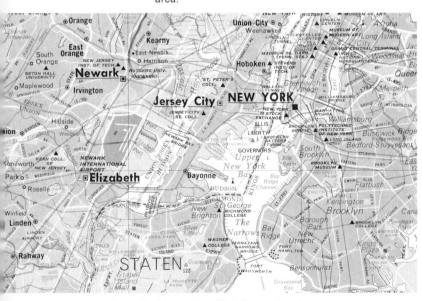

Figure 3.   Map of New York City and environs.

Cartographic generalization consists of simplification, classification, symbolization, and induction.

Simplification involves omitting details that will clutter the map and confuse the reader. The degree of simplification depends on the purpose and scale of the map. If the cartographer is creating a detailed map of Canada and merely wants to show the location of the United States, he or she can draw a simplified outline of the country. However, if the map requires a precise identification of the states in New England and the Great Lakes region, the mapmaker will have to draw a more detailed outline, still being careful not to distract the reader from the main features of the Canadian map.

Classification of data is a way of reducing the information to a form that can be easily presented on a map. For example, portraying precise urban populations in the United States would require using as many different symbols as there are cities. Instead, the cartographer groups cities into population categories and assigns a distinct symbol to each one. With the help of a legend, the reader can easily decode the classifications (for an example, see page 51).

Symbolization of information depends largely on the nature of the original data. Information can be *nominal* (showing differences in kind, such as land versus water, grassland versus forest); or *ordinal* (showing relative differences in quantities as well as kind, such as *major* versus *minor* ore deposits); or *interval* (degrees of temperature, inches of rainfall) or *ratio* (population densities), both expressing quantitative details about the data being mapped.

Cartographers use various shapes, colors, or patterns to symbolize these categories of data, and the particular nature of the information being communicated often determines how it is symbolized. Population density, for example, can be shown by the use of small dots or different intensities of color. However, if nominal data is being portrayed—for instance, the desert and fertile areas of Egypt—the mapmaker may want to use a different method of symbolizing the data, perhaps pattern symbols. The color, size, and style of type used for the different elements on a map are also important to symbolization.

Induction is the term cartographers use to describe the process whereby more information is represented on a map than is actually supplied by the original data. For instance, in creating a rainfall map, a cartographer may start with precise rainfall records for relatively few points on the map. After deciding the interval categories into which the data will be divided (e.g., thirty inches or more, fifteen to thirty inches, under fifteen inches), the mapmaker infers from the particular data points that nearby places receive the same or nearly the same amount of rainfall and draws the lines that distinguish the various rainfall regions accordingly. Obviously, generalizations arrived at through induction can never be as precise as the real-world patterns they represent. The map will only tell the reader that all the cities in a given area received about the same amount of rainfall; it will not tell exactly how much rain fell in any particular city in any particular time period.

Cartographers must also be aware of the map reader's perceptual limitations and preferences. During the past two decades, numerous experiments have helped determine how much information readers actually glean from a map and how symbols, colors, and shapes are recognized and interpreted. As a result, cartographers now have a better idea of what kind of rectangle to use; what type of layout or lettering suggests qualities such as power, stability, movement; and what colors are most appropriate.

Map Scale

Since part or all of the earth's surface may be portrayed on a single page of an atlas, the reader's first question should be: What is the relation of map size to the area represented? This proportional relationship is known as the *scale* of a map.

Scale is expressed as a ratio between the distance or area on the map and the same distance or area on the earth. The map scale is commonly represented in three ways: (1) as a simple fraction or ratio called the representative fraction, or RF; (2) as a written statement of map distance in relation to earth distance; and (3) as a graphic representation or a bar scale. All three forms of scale for distances are expressed on Maps A–D.

The RF is usually written as 1:62,500 (as in Map A), where 1 always refers to a unit of distance on the map. The ratio means that 1 centimeter or 1 millimeter or 1 foot on the map represents 62,500 centimeters or millimeters or feet on the earth's surface. The units of measure on both sides of the ratio must always be the same.

Maps may also include a *written statement* expressing distances in terms more familiar to the reader. In Map A the scale 1:62,500 is expressed as being (approximately) 1 inch to 1 mile; that is, 1 inch on the map represents roughly 1 mile on the earth's surface.

The *graphic scale* for distances is usually a bar scale, as shown in Maps A–D. A bar scale is normally subdivided, enabling the reader to measure distance directly on the map.

An *area scale* can also be used, in which one unit of area (square inches, square centimeters) is proportional to the same square units on the earth. The scale may be expressed as either $1:62,500^2$ or 1 to the square of 62,500. Area scales are used when the transformation of the globe to the flat map has been made so that areas are represented in true relation to their respective area on the earth.

When comparing map scales, it is helpful to remember that the *larger* the scale (see Map A) the smaller the area represented and the greater the amount of detail that a map can include. The *smaller* the scale (see Maps B, C, D) the larger the area covered and the less detail that can be presented.

Large-scale maps are useful when readers need such detailed information as the location of roadways, major buildings, city plans, and the like. On a smaller scale, the reader is able to place cities in relation to one another and recognize other prominent features of the region. At the smallest scale, the reader can get a broad view of several states and an idea of the total area. Finer details cannot be shown.

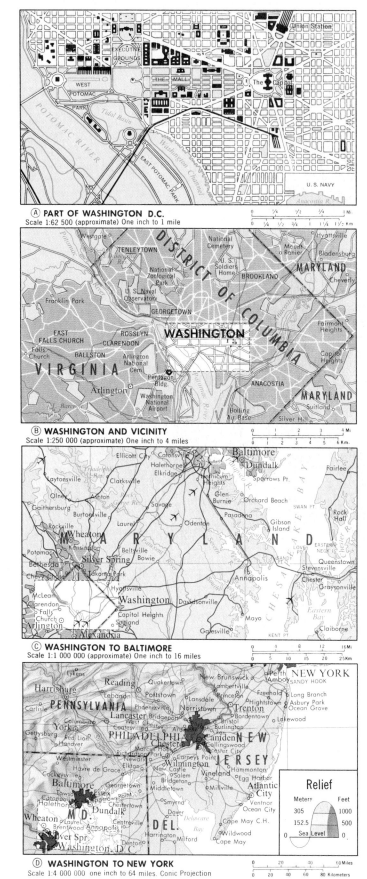

Ⓐ **PART OF WASHINGTON D.C.**
Scale 1:62 500 (approximate) One inch to 1 mile

Ⓑ **WASHINGTON AND VICINITY**
Scale 1:250 000 (approximate) One inch to 4 miles

Ⓒ **WASHINGTON TO BALTIMORE**
Scale 1:1 000 000 (approximate) One inch to 16 miles

Ⓓ **WASHINGTON TO NEW YORK**
Scale 1:4 000 000 one inch to 64 miles. Conic Projection

Map Projections

Every cartographer is faced with the problem of transforming the curved surface of the earth onto a flat plane with a minimum of distortion. The systematic transformation of locations on the earth (spherical surface) to locations on a map (flat surface) is called projection.

It is not possible to represent on a flat map the spatial relationships of angle, distance, direction, and area that only a globe can show faithfully. As a result, projection systems inevitably involve some distortion. On large-scale maps representing a few square miles, the distortion is generally negligible. But on maps depicting large countries, continents, or the entire world, the amount of distortion can be significant. Some maps of the Western Hemisphere, because of their projection, incorrectly portray Canada and Alaska as larger than the United States and Mexico, while South America looks considerably smaller than its northern neighbors.

One of the more practical ways map readers can become aware of projection distortions and learn how to make allowances for them is to compare the projection grid of a flat map with the grid of a globe. Some important characteristics of the globe grid are found listed on page xii.

There are an infinite number of possible map projections, all of which distort one or more of the characteristics of the globe in varying degrees. The projection system that a cartographer chooses depends on the size and location of the area being projected and the purpose of the map. In this atlas, most of the maps are drawn on projections that give a consistent area scale; good land and ocean shape; parallels that are parallel; and as consistent a linear scale as possible throughout the projection.

The transformation process is actually a mathematical one, but to aid in visualizing this process, it is helpful to consider the earth reduced to the scale of the intended map and then projected onto a simple geometric shape—a cylinder, cone, or plane. These geometric forms are then flattened to two dimensions to produce cylindrical, conic, and plane projections (see Figures 4, 5, and 6). Some of the projection systems used in this atlas are described on the following pages. By comparing these systems with the characteristics of a globe grid, readers can gain a clearer understanding of map distortion.

Mercator: This transformation—bearing the name of a famous sixteenth century cartographer—is conformal; that is, land masses are represented in their true shapes. Thus, for every point on the map, the angles shown are correct in every direction within a limited area. To achieve this, the projection increases latitudinal and longitudinal distances away from the equator. As a result, land *shapes* are correct, but their *areas* are distorted. The farther away from the equator, the greater the area distortion. For example, on a Mercator map, Alaska appears far larger than Mexico, whereas in fact Mexico's land area is greater. The Mercator projection is used in nautical navigation, because a line connecting any two points gives the compass direction between them. (See Figure 4.)

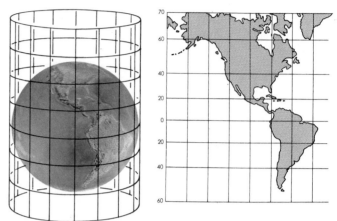

Figure 4. Mercator Projection (right), based upon the projection of the globe onto a cylinder.

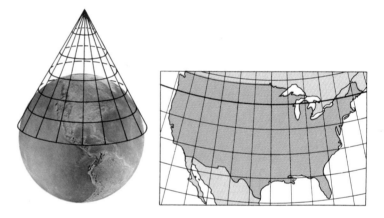

Figure 5. Projection of the globe onto a cone and a resultant Conic Projection.

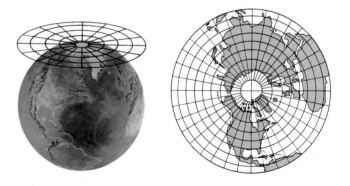

Figure 6. Lambert Equal-Area Projection (right), which assumes the projection of the globe onto a plane surface.

Conic: In this transformation—a globe projected onto a tangent cone—meridians of longitude appear as straight lines, and lines of latitude appear as parallel arcs. The parallel of tangency (that is, where the cone is presumed to touch the globe) is called a standard parallel. In this projection, distortion increases in bands away from the standard parallel. Conic projections are helpful in depicting middle-latitude areas of east-west extension. (See Figure 5.)

Lambert Equal Area *(polar case):* This projection assumes a plane touching the globe at a single point. It shows true distances close to the center (the tangent point) but increasingly distorted ones away from it. The equal-area quality (showing land areas in their correct proportion) is maintained throughout; but in regions away from the center, distortion of shape increases. (See Figure 6.)

Miller Cylindrical: O. M. Miller suggested a modification to the Mercator projection to lessen the severe area distortion in the higher latitudes. The Miller projection is neither conformal nor equal-area. Thus, while shapes are less accurate than on the Mercator, the exaggeration of *size* of areas has been somewhat decreased. The Miller cylindrical is useful for showing the entire world in a rectangular format. (See Figure 7.)

Mollweide Homolographic: The Mollweide is an equal-area projection; the least distorted areas are ovals centered just above and below the center of the projection. Distance distortions increase toward the edges of the map. The Mollweide is used for world-distribution maps where a pleasing oval look is desired along with the equal-area quality. It is one of the bases used in the Goode's Interrupted Homolosine projection. (See Figure 8.)

Sinusoidal, or Sanson-Flamsteed: In this equal-area projection the scale is the same along all parallels and the central meridian. Distortion of shapes is less along the two main axes of the projection but increases markedly toward the edges. Maps depicting areas such as South America or Africa can make good use of the Sinusoidal's favorable characteristics by situating the land masses along the central meridian, where the shapes will be virtually undistorted. The Sinusoidal is also one of the bases used in the Goode's Interrupted Homolosine. (See Figure 9.)

Goode's Interrupted Homolosine: An equal-area projection, Goode's is composed of the Sinusoidal grid from the equator to about 40° N and 40° S latitudes; beyond these latitudes, the Mollweide is used. This grid is interrupted so that land masses can be projected with a minimum of shape distortion by positioning each section on a separate central meridian. Thus, the shapes as well as the sizes of land masses are represented with a high degree of fidelity. Oceans can also be positioned in this manner. (See Figure 10.)

Robinson: This projection was designed for Rand McNally to present an uninterrupted and visually correct map of the earth. It maintains overall shape and area relationships without extreme distortion and is widely used in classrooms and textbooks. (See Figure 11.)

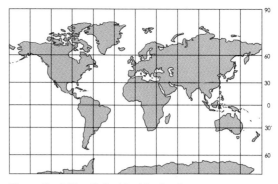

Figure 7. Miller Cylindrical Projection.

Figure 8. Mollweide Homolographic Projection.

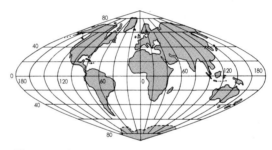

Figure 9. Sinusoidal Projection.

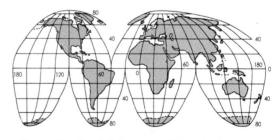

Figure 10. Goode's Interrupted Homolosine Projection.

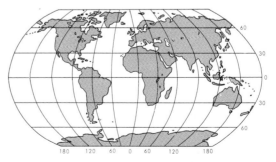

Figure 11. Robinson Projection.

Bonne: This equal-area transformation is mathematically related to the Sinusoidal. Distances are true along all parallels and the central meridian. Farther out from the central meridian, however, the increasing obliqueness of the grid's angles distorts shape and distance. This limits the area that can be usefully projected. Bonne projections, like conics, are best employed for relatively small areas in middle latitudes. (See Figure 12.)

Conic with Two Standard Parallels: The linear scale of this projection is consistent along two standard parallels instead of only one as in the simple conic. Since the spacing of the other parallels is reduced somewhat between the standard parallels and progressively enlarged beyond them, the projection does not exhibit the equal-area property. Careful selection of the standard parallels, however, provides good representation of limited areas. Like the Bonne projection, this system is widely used for areas in middle latitudes. (See Figure 13.)

Polyconic: In this system, the globe is projected onto a series of strips taken from tangent cones. Parallels are nonconcentric circles, and each is divided equally by the meridians, as on the globe. While distances along the straight central meridian are true, they are increasingly exaggerated along the curving meridians. Likewise, general representation of areas and shapes is good near the central meridian but progressively distorted away from it. Polyconic projections are used for middle-latitude areas to minimize all distortions and were employed for large-scale topographic maps. (See Figure 14.)

Lambert Conformal Conic: This conformal transformation system usually employs two standard parallels. Distortion increases away from the standard parallels, being greatest at the edges of the map. It is useful for projecting elongated east-west areas in the middle latitudes and is ideal for depicting the forty-eight contiguous states. It is also widely used for aeronautical and meteorological charts. (See Figure 15.)

Lambert Equal Area *(oblique and polar cases):* This equal-area projection can be centered at any point on the earth's surface, perpendicular to a line drawn through the globe. It maintains correct angles to all points on the map from its center (point of tangency), but distances become progressively distorted toward the edges. It is most useful for roughly circular areas or areas whose dimensions are nearly equal in two perpendicular directions.

The two most common forms of the Lambert projection are the oblique and the polar, shown in Figures 6 and 16. Although the meridians and parallels for the forms are different, the distortion characteristics are the same.

Important characteristics of the globe grid

1. All meridians of longitude are equal in length and meet at the Poles.
2. All lines of latitude are parallel and equally spaced on meridians.
3. The length, or circumference, of the parallels of latitude decreases as one moves from the equator to the Poles. For instance, the circumference of the parallel at 60° latitude is one-half the circumference of the equator.
4. Meridians of longitude are equally spaced on each parallel, but the distance between them decreases toward the Poles.
5. All parallels and meridians meet at right angles.

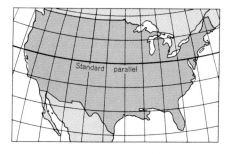

Figure 12. Bonne Projection.

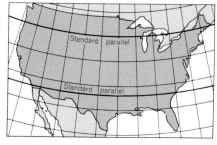

Figure 13. Conic Projection with Two Standard Parallels.

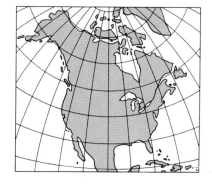

Figure 14. Polyconic Projection.

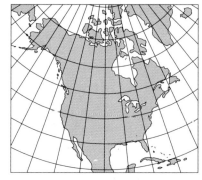

Figure 15. Lambert Conformal Conic Projection.

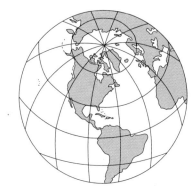

Figure 16. Lambert Equal-Area Projection (oblique case).

Remotely Sensed Imagery

Recent technological advances have greatly expanded our ability to "see" surface features on the earth. *Remote sensing* can be defined as gathering and recording from a distance information about many types of geographic features. Human beings have been using a form of remote sensing for thousands of years. To gather information about terrain, people have climbed trees or hilltops and used their eyes, ears, and even their sense of smell to detect what lay in the distance. Now, with highly sophisticated cameras and electronic sensing equipment as our remote sensors, we can learn a great deal more about our world than we have been able to gather with our physical senses.

Remote sensing is based on two fundamental principles. First, each type of surface material (rock, soil, vegetation) absorbs and reflects solar energy in a characteristic manner. In addition, a certain amount of internal energy is emitted by each surface. Remote-sensing instruments can detect this absorbed, reflected, and emitted energy and produce photographs or images.

Second, while the human eye is sensitive to only a small portion of the electromagnetic spectrum (shown as A in the top illustration of Figure 17), remote-sensing instruments can work in longer and shorter wavelengths, generally in the infrared and radar, or microwave, regions. These areas of the spectrum are often referred to as bands.

In remote-sensing photography, the most commonly used bands, in addition to those in the visible spectrum, are the near-infrared bands of 0.7 to 0.8μ (micrometers) and 0.8 to 1.1μ. Infrared photography has proved invaluable in studying agricultural areas. Since healthy plants reflect a considerable amount of near-infrared light, high-altitude photographs using this band of the spectrum can detect diseased vegetation before the problem is visible to the naked eye.

Multispectral photographic techniques are also being used. In this type of remote sensing, reflected energy from a surface is isolated into a number of given wavelength bands (shown in the bottom illustration of Figure 17). Each band can be separately recorded on film, or bands can be recorded simultaneously. These restricted wavelengths include a blue band of 0.4 to 0.5μ, a green band of 0.5 to 0.6μ, and a red band of 0.6 to 0.7μ. Scientists can select various band widths in order to highlight certain features within an area. The photographs in Figure 18 demonstrate the different effects that multispectral photography can produce and the types of information that can be revealed.

Thermal infrared (shown as B in the top illustration in Figure 17) and radar, or microwave, (shown as C) have also been important for gathering geographical data. Thermal imagery records the temperatures of surface features and is collected through electronic sensing instruments, not by cameras. These images show "hot spots" in lakes, rivers, and coastal areas where waste discharges are affecting the water temperature. Thermal-infrared sensing can also pick up animal populations that may be camouflaged to the naked eye. Heat loss from buildings can also be measured.

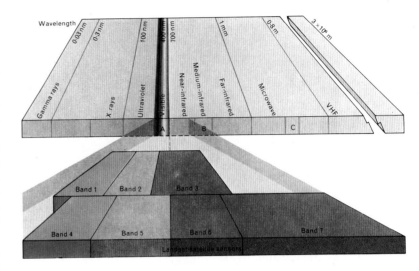

Figure 17. Top: The electromagnetic spectrum.

Bottom: Visible portion of the spectrum.

0.7 to 0.8μ band: Black-and-white, infrared.

0.8 to 0.9μ band: Black-and-white, infrared.

0.5 to 0.8 μ band: Color infrared.

0.4 to 0.7μ band: Color.

0.6 to 0.7μ band: Black-and-white, visible.

0.5 to 0.6μ band: Black-and-white, visible.

Figure 18. Images taken over Lake Mead, Nevada, by a multispectral camera. Each of the images has been derived from a different wavelength band of the spectrum.

Figure 19. Landsat (satellite) image of southeastern Colorado.

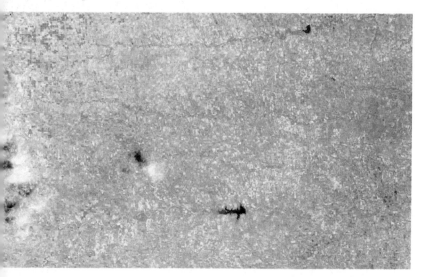

Figure 20. Landsat (satellite) image of western Kansas.

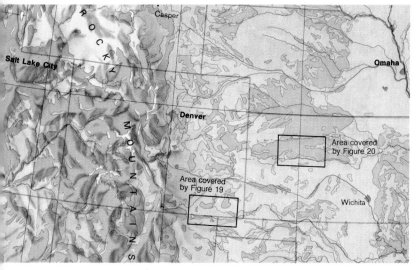

Figure 21. Land use (environment) map derived by using information from the satellite images in Figures 19 and 20.

There are several types of electronic sensors of proven utility in use today.

One type, a scanner, is utilized in the Landsat series of satellites as discussed below. The images are gathered electronically by sensors that scan the terrain directly beneath the satellite and record energy from individual areas on the ground. The size of these areas is determined by the spot size, or resolution capacity, of the optical scanner on board the satellite. The smallest individual area distinguished by the scanner is called a picture element, or *pixel*.

A second type of electronic sensor in use and of importance to cartographers is the multiple linear array, MLA. A MLA is a stationary set of individual charged coupled devices, CCD. Rows or arrays of CCDs systematically (time sequenced) record energy from the ground over which the array passes. Each recording by a CCD results in a pixel. The SPOT satellite discussed below utilizes MLAs.

Whether from a scanner or a CCD the pixels are recorded as digits and transmitted to a ground receiving station. The digits represent brightness values and are stored in a computer as arrays, one for each band of the electromagnetic spectrum being sensed. The digits can be electronically manipulated to produce false color pictures like those shown in *Figure 19* and *Figure 20*. This form of data gathering has a number of advantages over conventional aircraft photography. Chiefly, the digits can be computer enhanced to bring out specific features more clearly and reveal subtle changes that may not appear on a conventional photograph of the same area. Additionally the stability of the satellite platform is far greater than that of an aircraft.

Radar differs from other sensing methods in that a signal is sent out by the sensor, and the intensity of the reflected "echo" is recorded electronically. (The images may then be printed as a photograph.) Radar has the advantage of being unaffected by weather conditions, and in areas with persistent cloud cover it has proved to be the most reliable sensor available. This type of remote sensing can record surface relief features with remarkable accuracy.

Landsat

Perhaps the most well-known examples of satellite remotely sensed imagery are the pictures created from data gathered by the Landsat satellites, originally known as ERTS (Earth Resource Technology Satellite). Since 1972 when Landsat 1 was launched a continuous coverage of the earth has been recorded. As of this writing Landsats 4 and 5 (improved versions of Landsat 3) are orbiting the earth and returning valuable data. Landsat 5 is in a sun-synchronous orbit at an altitude of 705 kilometers. It has a repeat cycle of 16 days and carries a multispectral scanner producing four bands of 80 meter resolution data (two visible and two near-infrared bands). Landsat 5 also carries a Thematic Mapper sensor which produces six bands of 30 meter resolution data and one thermal band with 120 meter resolution.

Each MSS Landsat pixel covers about an acre of the earth's surface, with approximately 7,800,000 pixels composing each image. (An image covers 115 × 115 mi. or 185 × 185 km.) Scientists are still discovering new uses for Landsat images. The uniform orbits of the Landsat satellites allow for repeated coverage of the same terrain. As a result, the sensors can detect changes in veg-

etation, and farming patterns; damage resulting from disasters; and erosion patterns, and levels of some pollutants. Landsat images have been particularly helpful to cartographers in correcting existing maps or creating new ones, as the striking resemblance between the environmental map (Figure 21) and the two pictures above it shows.

SPOT

The *Systeme Probatoire d'Observation de la terre, SPOT*, is a satellite launched in 1984 in a sun-synchronous orbit at 909 kilometers by a combination of government and private organizations in France. The SPOT satellite uses MLA technology to produce 20 meter resolution imagery from three bands of the electro-magnetic spectrum: 0.50-0.59, 0.61-0.68, and 0.79-0.89μ. SPOT also provides a black-and-white image at 10 meter resolution from 0.51-0.73μ of the spectrum. The data from the SPOT satellite are the best resolution available to the citizenry of the world today. Scientists are using SPOT imagery for many of the same purposes that Landsat data have been used. Combinations of SPOT and Landsat data have also proven valuable.

High-Altitude Imagery

Cartographers also benefit from the increased use of high-altitude photography. *Figure 22* is a good example of an infrared photograph taken with a high-altitude camera mounted in an aircraft. The imagery gathered is limited by the sensitivity of the film, which can record only in the 0.3 to 1.1μ range of the spectrum. Even within this range, and using only black-and-white film, the data collected can be used to generate highly accurate 1:24,000-scale topographic maps, such as the one shown in *Figure 23*. Side benefits of this form of photography can be the production of orthophotomaps and digital elevation models (DEM). A DEM is composed of a set of equally spaced surface elevations for an area of the earth.

Although *Goode's World Atlas* does not contain topographic maps, they are used as a reference source for the volume. High-altitude photography makes it possible to update such features as highway networks, extent of metropolitan areas, the shape and flow of rivers and lakes, ocean currents, and ice formations.

Recent and future technological advances in collecting geographic information promise to make the cartographer's job somewhat easier. More important, these advances will allow us to give the atlas user more-detailed and up-to-date knowledge about our world and the impact of human activity around the globe.

EDWARD B. ESPENSHADE, JR.
JOEL L. MORRISON

Figure 22. High-altitude infrared image of the Goodland, Kansas, area.

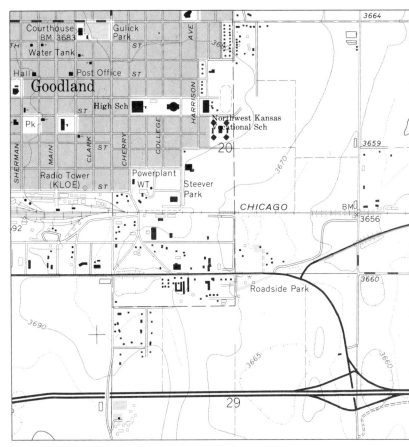

Figure 23. 1:24,000 United States Geological Survey map of the Goodland, Kansas, area.

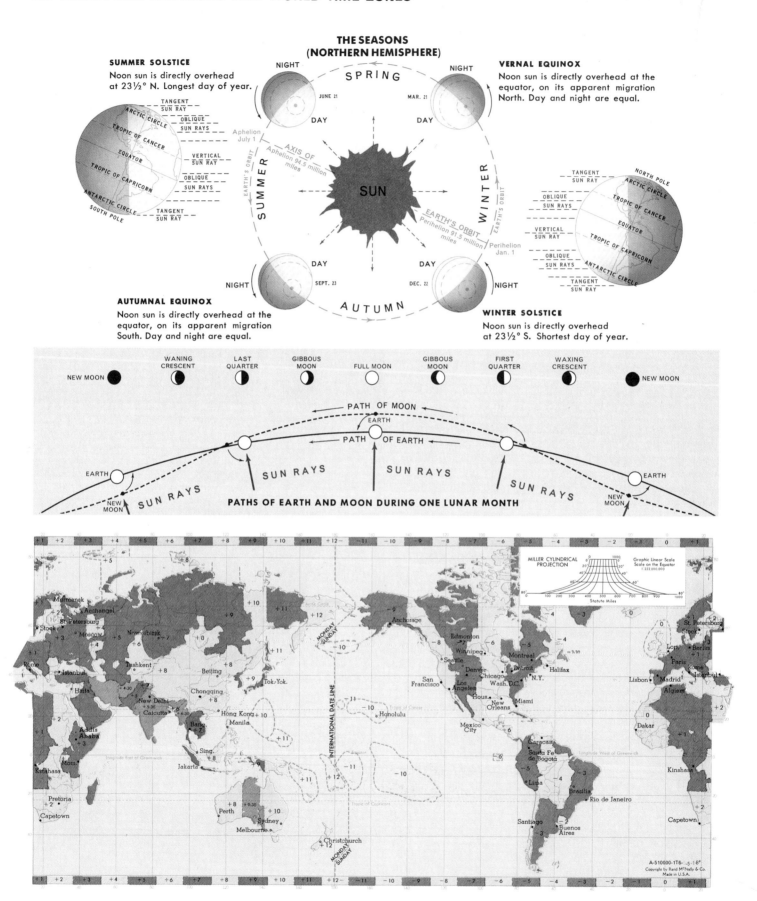

THE SEASONS (NORTHERN HEMISPHERE)

SUMMER SOLSTICE
Noon sun is directly overhead at 23½° N. Longest day of year.

VERNAL EQUINOX
Noon sun is directly overhead at the equator, on its apparent migration North. Day and night are equal.

AUTUMNAL EQUINOX
Noon sun is directly overhead at the equator, on its apparent migration South. Day and night are equal.

WINTER SOLSTICE
Noon sun is directly overhead at 23½° S. Shortest day of year.

PATHS OF EARTH AND MOON DURING ONE LUNAR MONTH

Time Zones

The surface of the earth is divided into 24 time zones. Each zone represents 15° of longitude or one hour of time. The time of the initial, or zero, zone is based on the central meridian of Greenwich and is adopted eastward and westward for a distance of 7½° of longitude. Each of the zones in turn is designated by a number representing the hours (+ or −) by which its standard time differs from Greenwich mean time. These standard time zones are indicated by bands of orange and yellow. Areas which have a fractional deviation from standard time are shown in an intermediate color. The irregularities in the zones and the fractional deviations are due to political and economic factors.

(Revised to 1989. After U.S. Defense Mapping Agency)

WORLD THEMATIC MAPS

This section of the atlas consists of more than sixty thematic maps presenting world patterns and distributions. Together with accompanying graphs, these maps communicate basic information on mineral resources, agricultural products, trade, transportation, and other selected aspects of the natural and cultural geographical environment.

A thematic map uses symbols to show certain characteristics of, generally, one class of geographical information. This "theme" of a thematic map is presented upon a background of basic locational information—coastline, country boundaries, major drainage, etc. The map's primary concern is to communicate visually basic impressions of the distribution of the theme. For instance, on page 39 the distribution of cattle shown by point symbols impresses the reader with relative densities—the distribution of cattle is much more uniform throughout the United States than it is in China, and cattle are more numerous in the United States than in China.

Although it is possible to use a thematic map to obtain exact values of a quantity or commodity, it is not the purpose intended, any more than a thematic map is intended to be used to give precise distances from New York to Moscow. If one seeks precise statistics for each country, he may consult the bar graph on the map or a statistical table.

The map on this page is an example of a special class of thematic maps called cartograms. The cartogram assigns to a named earth region an area based on some value other than land surface area. In the cartogram below the areas assigned are proportional to their countries' populations and tinted according to their rate of natural increase. The result of mapping on this base is a meaningful way of portraying this distribution since natural increase is causally related to existing size of population. On the other hand, natural increase is not causally related to earth area. In the other thematic maps in this atlas, relative earth sizes have been considered when presenting the distributions.

Real and hypothetical geographical distributions of interest to man are practically limitless but can be classed into point, line, area, or volume information relative to a specific location or area in the world. The thematic map, in communicating these fundamental classes of information, utilizes point, line, and area symbols. The symbols may be employed to show *qualitative* differences (differences in *kind*) of a certain category of information and may also show *quantitative* differences in the information (differences in *amount*). For example, the natural-vegetation map (page 16) was based upon information gathered by many observations over a period of time. It utilizes area symbols (color and pattern) to show the difference in the *kind* of vegetation as well as the extent. Quantitative factual information was shown on the annual-precipitation map, page 14, by means of isohyets (lines connecting points of equal rainfall). Also, area symbols were employed to show the intervals between the lines. In each of these thematic maps, there is one primary theme, or subject; the map communicates the information far better than volumes of words and tables could.

One of the most important aspects of the thematic-map section is use of the different maps to show comparisons and relationships among the distributions of various types of geographical information. For example, the relationship of dense population (page 20) to areas of intensive subsistence agriculture (page 30) and to manufacturing and commerce (page 28) is an important geographic concept.

The statistics communicated by the maps and graphs in this section are intended to give an idea of the relative importance of countries in the distributions mapped. The maps are not intended to take the place of statistical reference works. No single year affords a realistic base for production, trade, and certain economic and demographic statistics. Therefore, averages of data for three or four years have been used. Together with the maps, the averages and percentages provide the student with a realistic idea of the importance of specific areas.

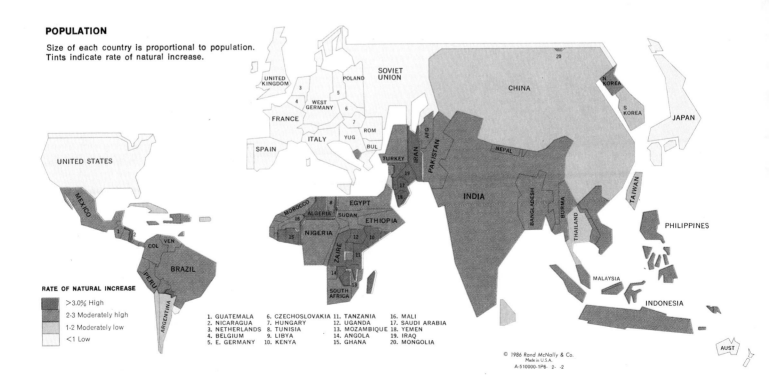

POPULATION

Size of each country is proportional to population.
Tints indicate rate of natural increase.

RATE OF NATURAL INCREASE

- >3.0% High
- 2-3 Moderately high
- 1-2 Moderately low
- <1 Low

1. GUATEMALA	6. CZECHOSLOVAKIA	11. TANZANIA	16. MALI
2. NICARAGUA	7. HUNGARY	12. UGANDA	17. SAUDI ARABIA
3. NETHERLANDS	8. TUNISIA	13. MOZAMBIQUE	18. YEMEN
4. BELGIUM	9. LIBYA	14. ANGOLA	19. IRAQ
5. E. GERMANY	10. KENYA	15. GHANA	20. MONGOLIA

© 1986 Rand McNally & Co.
Made in U.S.A.
A-510000-1P6- 2- -2

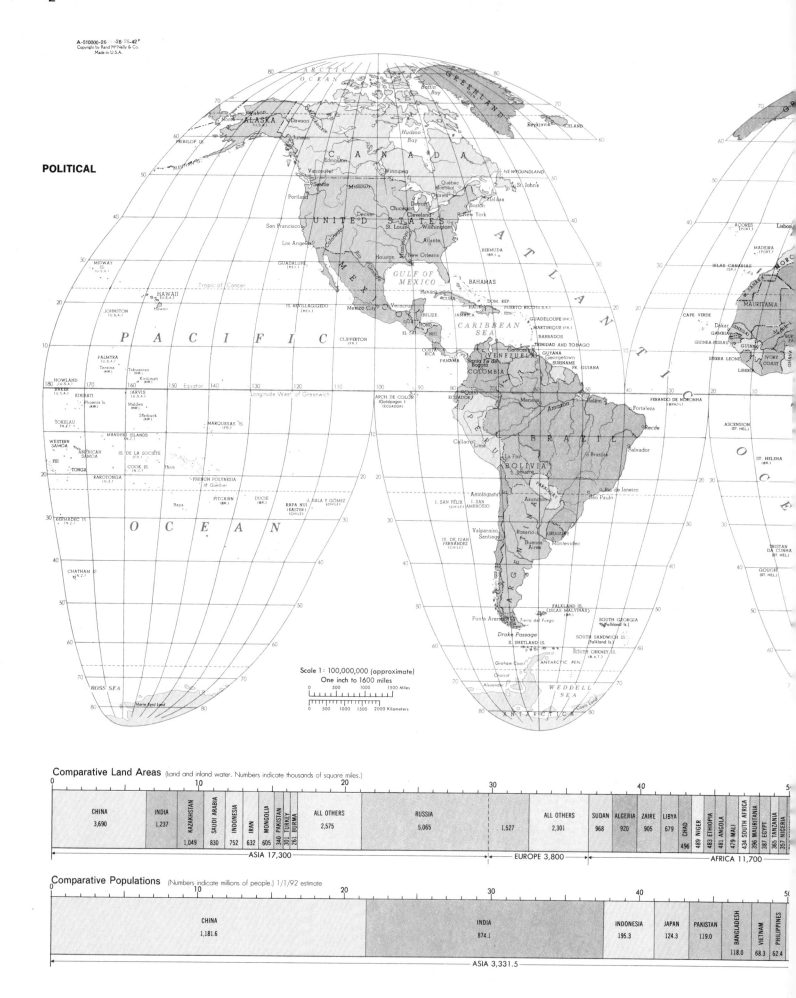

2

A-510000-26 -26-26-42 P
Copyright by Rand M°Nally & Co.
Made in U.S.A.

POLITICAL

Scale 1 : 100,000,000 (approximate)
One inch to 1600 miles
0   500   1000   1500 Miles
0   500 1000 1500 2000 Kilometers

Comparative Land Areas (land and inland water. Numbers indicate thousands of square miles.)

| CHINA 3,690 | INDIA 1,237 | KAZAKHSTAN 1,049 | SAUDI ARABIA 830 | INDONESIA 752 | IRAN 632 | MONGOLIA 605 | PAKISTAN 340 | TURKEY 301 | BURMA 261 | ALL OTHERS 2,575 | RUSSIA 5,065 | 1,527 | ALL OTHERS 2,301 | SUDAN 968 | ALGERIA 920 | ZAIRE 905 | LIBYA 679 | CHAD 496 | NIGER 489 | ETHIOPIA 483 | ANGOLA 481 | MALI 479 | SOUTH AFRICA 434 | MAURITANIA 396 | EGYPT 387 | TANZANIA 365 | NIGERIA 357 |

ASIA 17,300 — EUROPE 3,800 — AFRICA 11,700

Comparative Populations (Numbers indicate millions of people.) 1/1/92 estimate

| CHINA 1,181.6 | INDIA 874.1 | INDONESIA 195.3 | JAPAN 124.3 | PAKISTAN 119.0 | BANGLADESH 118.0 | VIETNAM 68.3 | PHILIPPINES 62.4 |

ASIA 3,331.5

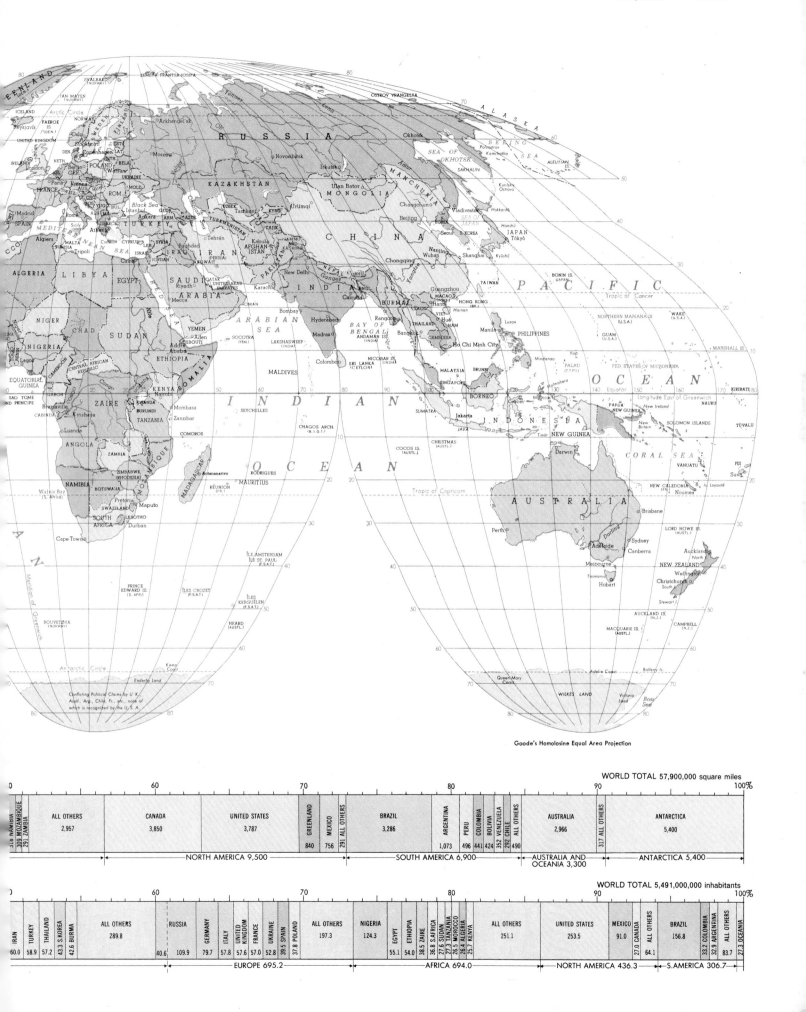

Goode's Homolosine Equal Area Projection

A-510000-76 -413-24
Copyright by Rand McNally & Co.
Made in U.S.A.

PHYSICAL

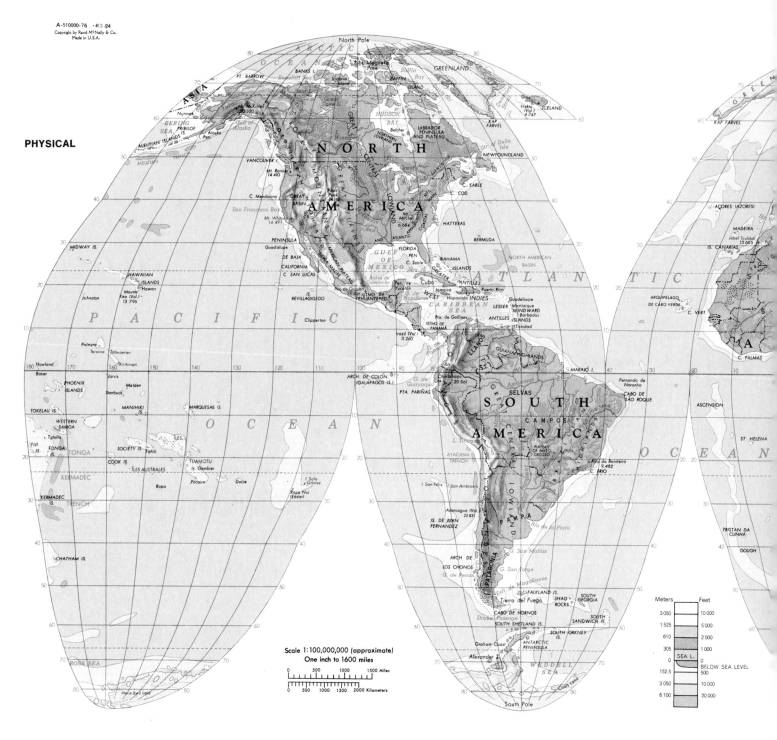

Scale 1:100,000,000 (approximate)
One inch to 1600 miles

Meters	Feet
3 050	10 000
1 525	5 000
610	2 000
305	1 000
0	SEA L.
	BELOW SEA LEVEL
152.5	500
3 050	10 000
6 100	20 000

Land Elevations in Profile

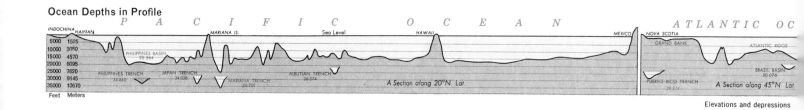

Ocean Depths in Profile

Elevations and depressions

For Glossary of Foreign Geographical Terms see page 248

Goode's Homolosine Equal Area Projection

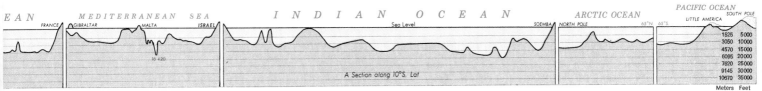

are given in feet

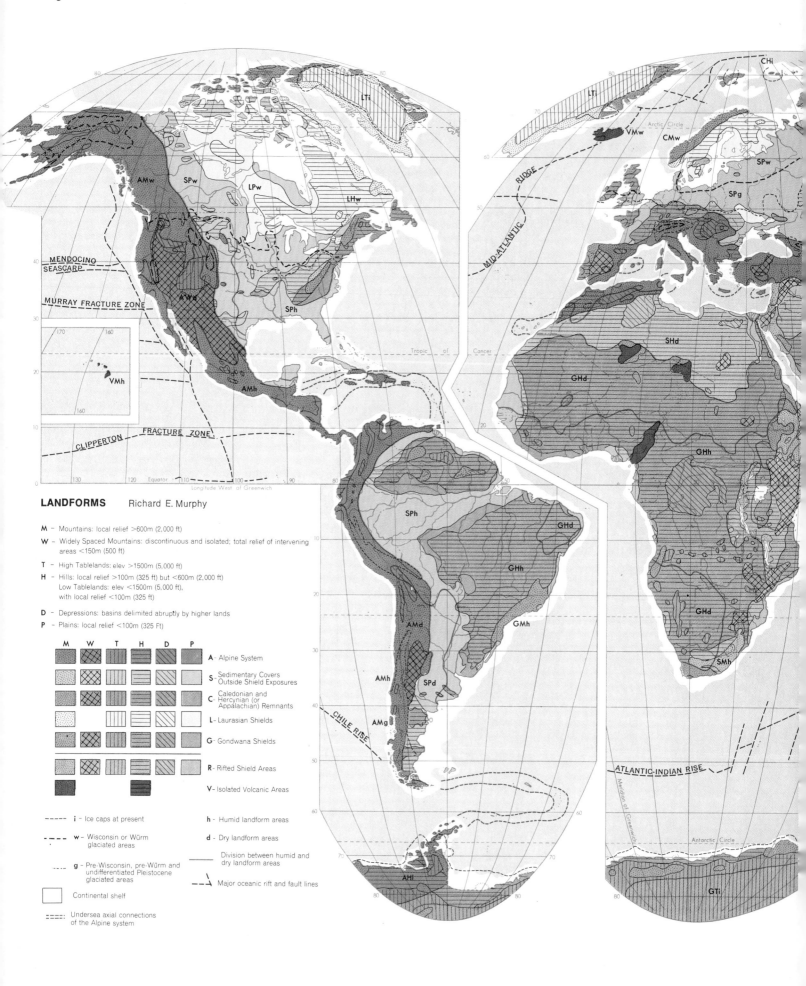

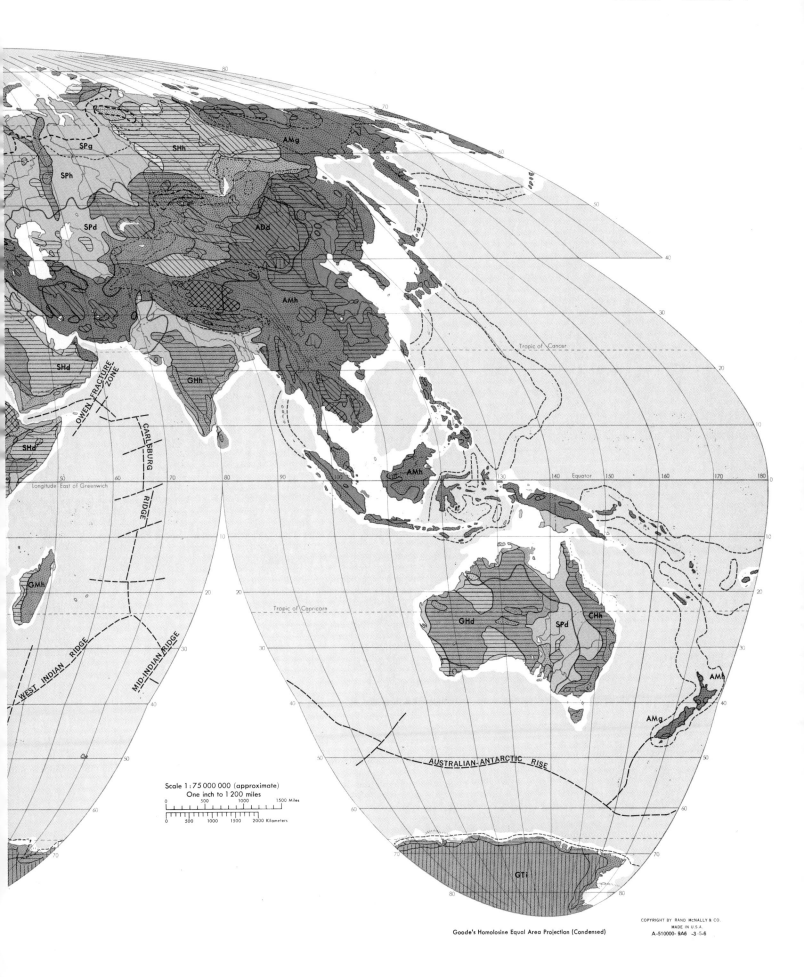

SPg

SHh

AMg

SPh

SPd

ADd

AMh

SHd

Tropic of Cancer

GHh

SHd

OWEN FRACTURE ZONE

CARLSBURG RIDGE

Equator

AMh

Longitude East of Greenwich

GMh

Tropic of Capricorn

WEST INDIAN RIDGE

MID-INDIAN RIDGE

GHd

SPd

CHh

AMh

AMg

AUSTRALIAN-ANTARCTIC RISE

Scale 1:75 000 000 (approximate)
One inch to 1 200 miles

| 0 | 500 | 1000 | 1500 Miles |

| 0 | 500 | 1000 | 1500 | 2000 Kilometers |

GTi

COPYRIGHT BY RAND McNALLY & CO.
MADE IN U.S.A.
A-510000-9A6 -3-5-6

Goode's Homolosine Equal Area Projection (Condensed)

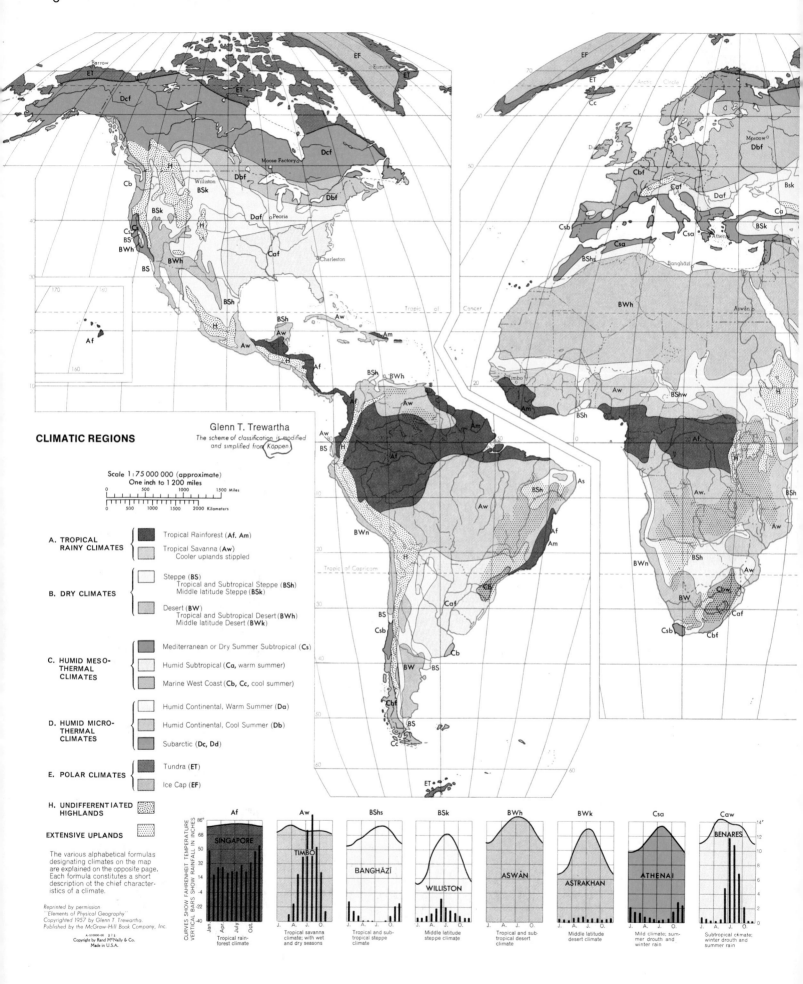

8

CLIMATIC REGIONS

Glenn T. Trewartha
*The scheme of classification is modified
and simplified from Köppen*

Scale 1:75 000 000 (approximate)
One inch to 1 200 miles

0   500   1000   1500 Miles
0   500   1000   1500   2000 Kilometers

A. TROPICAL RAINY CLIMATES
Tropical Rainforest (**Af, Am**)
Tropical Savanna (**Aw**)
Cooler uplands stippled

B. DRY CLIMATES
Steppe (**BS**)
Tropical and Subtropical Steppe (**BSh**)
Middle latitude Steppe (**BSk**)
Desert (**BW**)
Tropical and Subtropical Desert (**BWh**)
Middle latitude Desert (**BWk**)

C. HUMID MESO-THERMAL CLIMATES
Mediterranean or Dry Summer Subtropical (**Cs**)
Humid Subtropical (**Ca**, warm summer)
Marine West Coast (**Cb, Cc**, cool summer)

D. HUMID MICRO-THERMAL CLIMATES
Humid Continental, Warm Summer (**Da**)
Humid Continental, Cool Summer (**Db**)
Subarctic (**Dc, Dd**)

E. POLAR CLIMATES
Tundra (**ET**)
Ice Cap (**EF**)

H. UNDIFFERENTIATED HIGHLANDS

EXTENSIVE UPLANDS

The various alphabetical formulas
designating climates on the map
are explained on the opposite page.
Each formula constitutes a short
description ot the chief characteristics of a climate.

Reprinted by permission.
"Elements of Physical Geography"
Copyrighted 1957 by Glenn T. Trewartha.
Published by the McGraw-Hill Book Company, Inc.

A-510000-66 2°5
Copyright by Rand McNally & Co.
Made in U.S.A.

CURVES SHOW FAHRENHEIT TEMPERATURE
VERTICAL BARS SHOW RAINFALL IN INCHES

Af — SINGAPORE
Tropical rain-
forest climate

Aw — TIMBO
Tropical savanna
climate; with wet
and dry seasons

BShs — BANGHĀZĪ
Tropical and sub-
tropical steppe
climate

BSk — WILLISTON
Middle latitude
steppe climate

BWh — ASWÂN
Tropical and sub-
tropical desert
climate

BWk — ASTRAKHAN
Middle latitude
desert climate

Csa — ATHENAI
Mild climate; sum-
mer drouth and
winter rain

Caw — BENARES
Subtropical climate;
winter drouth and
summer rain

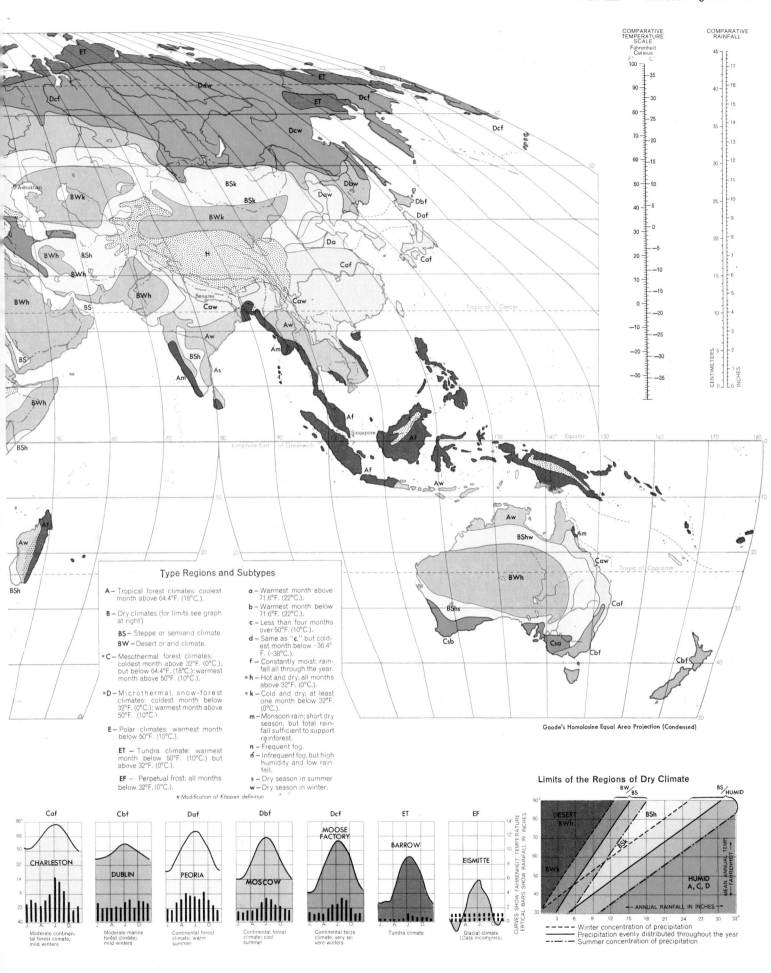

COMPARATIVE
TEMPERATURE
SCALE
Fahrenheit
Celsius

COMPARATIVE
RAINFALL

Goode's Homolosine Equal Area Projection (Condensed)

Type Regions and Subtypes

A — Tropical forest climates: coolest month above 64.4°F. (18°C.).

B — Dry climates (for limits see graph at right)

BS — Steppe or semiarid climate.

BW — Desert or arid climate.

*C — Mesothermal forest climates: coldest month above 32°F. (0°C.); but below 64.4°F. (18°C.); warmest month above 50°F. (10°C.).

*D — Microthermal, snow-forest climates: coldest month below 32°F. (0°C.); warmest month above 50°F. (10°C.).

E — Polar climates: warmest month below 50°F. (10°C.).

ET — Tundra climate: warmest month below 50°F. (10°C.) but above 32°F. (0°C.).

EF — Perpetual frost: all months below 32°F. (0°C.).

a — Warmest month above 71.6°F. (22°C.).

b — Warmest month below 71.6°F. (22°C.).

c — Less than four months over 50°F. (10°C.).

d — Same as "c," but coldest month below −36.4° F. (−38°C.).

f — Constantly moist; rainfall all through the year.

*h — Hot and dry; all months above 32°F. (0°C.).

*k — Cold and dry; at least one month below 32°F. (0°C.).

m — Monsoon rain; short dry season, but total rainfall sufficient to support rainforest.

n — Frequent fog.

ń — Infrequent fog, but high humidity and low rainfall.

s — Dry season in summer.

w — Dry season in winter.

* Modification of Köppen definition

Limits of the Regions of Dry Climate

DESERT BWh

BWk

BSh

BSk

HUMID A, C, D

MEAN ANNUAL TEMP. FAHRENHEIT

ANNUAL RAINFALL IN INCHES

- - - Winter concentration of precipitation
——— Precipitation evenly distributed throughout the year
—·—· Summer concentration of precipitation

CURVES SHOW FAHRENHEIT TEMPERATURE
VERTICAL BARS SHOW RAINFALL IN INCHES

Caf
CHARLESTON
Moderate continental forest climate; mild winters.

Cbf
DUBLIN
Moderate marine forest climate; mild winters.

Daf
PEORIA
Continental forest climate; warm summer.

Dbf
MOSCOW
Continental forest climate; cool summer.

Dcf
MOOSE FACTORY
Continental taiga climate; very severe winters.

ET
BARROW
Tundra climate.

EF
EISMITTE
Glacial climate (Data incomplete).

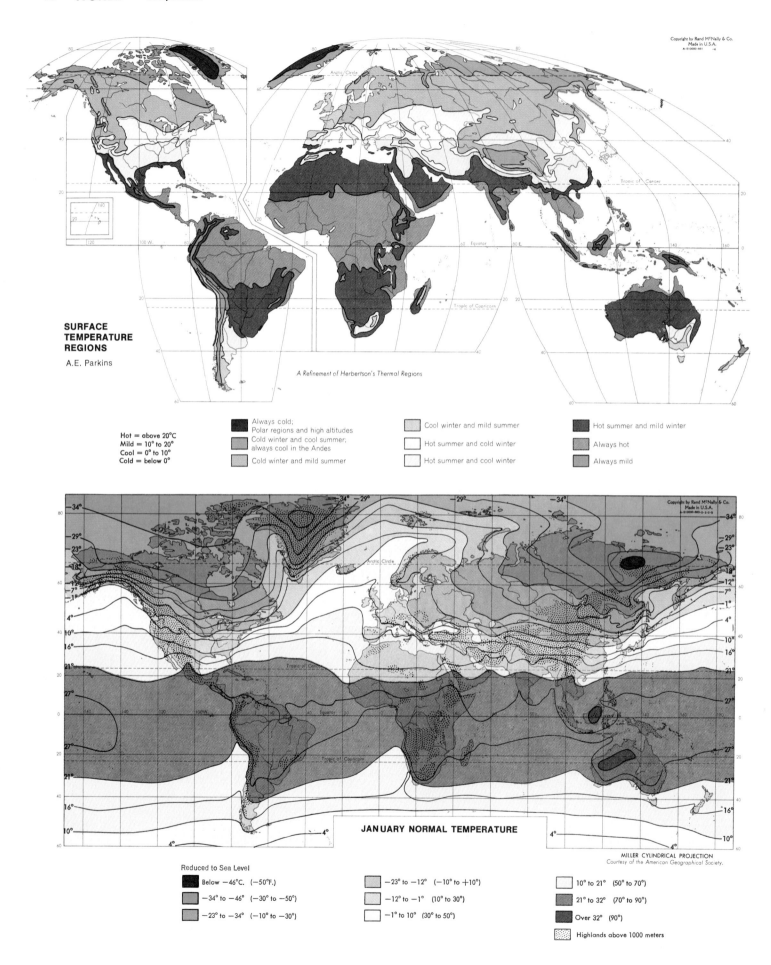

Copyright by Rand McNally & Co.
Made in U.S.A.
A-510000-661 -4

**SURFACE
TEMPERATURE
REGIONS**

A.E. Parkins

A Refinement of Herbertson's Thermal Regions

Hot = above 20°C
Mild = 10° to 20°
Cool = 0° to 10°
Cold = below 0°

Always cold;
Polar regions and high altitudes

Cold winter and cool summer;
always cool in the Andes

Cold winter and mild summer

Cool winter and mild summer

Hot summer and cold winter

Hot summer and cool winter

Hot summer and mild winter

Always hot

Always mild

Copyright by Rand McNally & Co.
Made in U.S.A.
A-510000-663-2-2-3-5

JANUARY NORMAL TEMPERATURE

MILLER CYLINDRICAL PROJECTION
Courtesy of the American Geographical Society.

Reduced to Sea Level

Below −46°C. (−50°F.)

−34° to −46° (−30° to −50°)

−23° to −34° (−10° to −30°)

−23° to −12° (−10° to +10°)

−12° to −1° (10° to 30°)

−1° to 10° (30° to 50°)

10° to 21° (50° to 70°)

21° to 32° (70° to 90°)

Over 32° (90°)

Highlands above 1000 meters

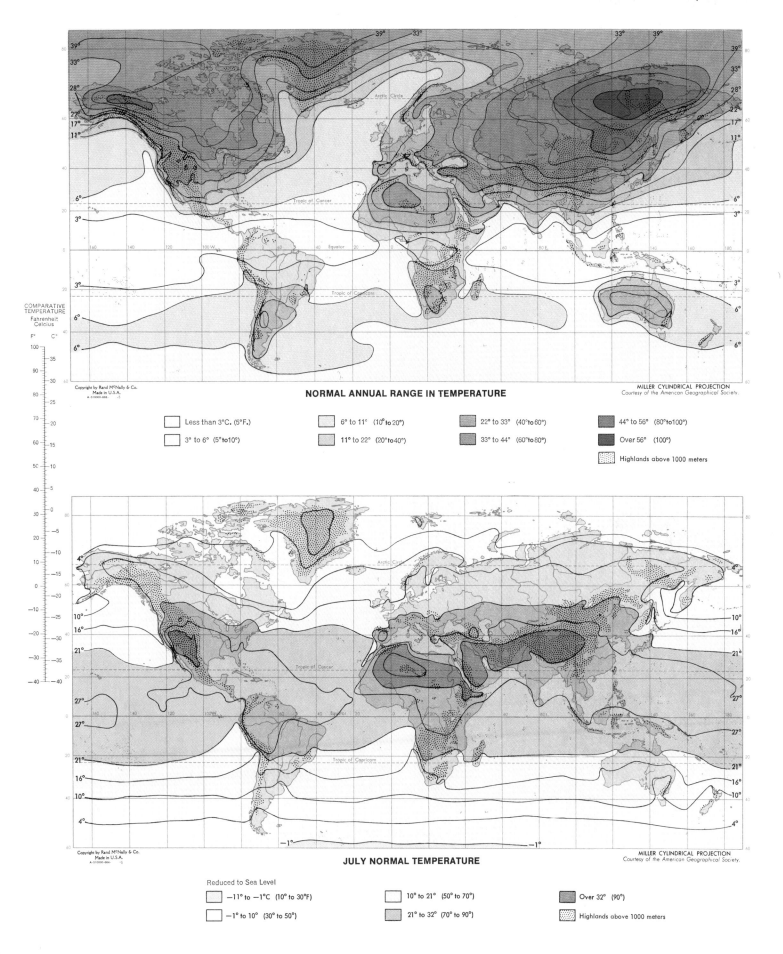

COMPARATIVE
TEMPERATURE
Fahrenheit
Celcius

NORMAL ANNUAL RANGE IN TEMPERATURE

Copyright by Rand McNally & Co.
Made in U.S.A.

MILLER CYLINDRICAL PROJECTION
Courtesy of the American Geographical Society.

☐ Less than 3°C. (5°F.)	☐ 6° to 11° (10° to 20°)
☐ 3° to 6° (5° to 10°)	☐ 11° to 22° (20° to 40°)

22° to 33° (40° to 60°)   44° to 56° (80° to 100°)

33° to 44° (60° to 80°)   Over 56° (100°)

Highlands above 1000 meters

JULY NORMAL TEMPERATURE

Copyright by Rand McNally & Co.
Made in U.S.A.

MILLER CYLINDRICAL PROJECTION
Courtesy of the American Geographical Society.

Reduced to Sea Level

☐ −11° to −1°C (10° to 30°F)	☐ 10° to 21° (50° to 70°)
☐ −1° to 10° (30° to 50°)	☐ 21° to 32° (70° to 90°)

Over 32° (90°)

Highlands above 1000 meters

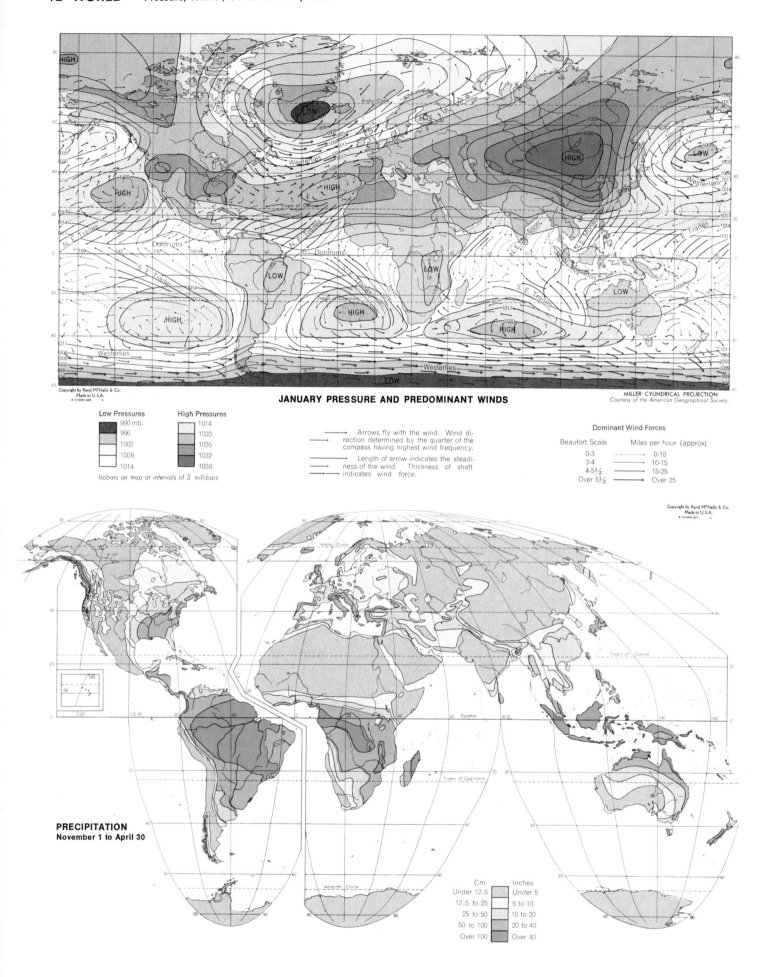

JANUARY PRESSURE AND PREDOMINANT WINDS

MILLER CYLINDRICAL PROJECTION
Courtesy of the American Geographical Society.

Copyright by Rand McNally & Co.
Made in U.S.A.
A-510000-665   4

Low Pressures		High Pressures	
	990 mb.		1014
	996		1020
	1002		1026
	1008		1032
	1014		1038

Isobars on map at intervals of 3 millibars

→ Arrows fly with the wind. Wind direction determined by the quarter of the compass having highest wind frequency.

→ Length of arrow indicates the steadiness of the wind. Thickness of shaft indicates wind force.

Dominant Wind Forces

Beaufort Scale	Miles per hour (approx)
0-3	0-10
3-4	10-15
4-5½	15-25
Over 5½	Over 25

Copyright by Rand McNally & Co.
Made in U.S.A.
A-510000-661   4

PRECIPITATION
November 1 to April 30

Cm.	Inches
Under 12.5	Under 5
12.5 to 25	5 to 10
25 to 50	10 to 20
50 to 100	20 to 40
Over 100	Over 40

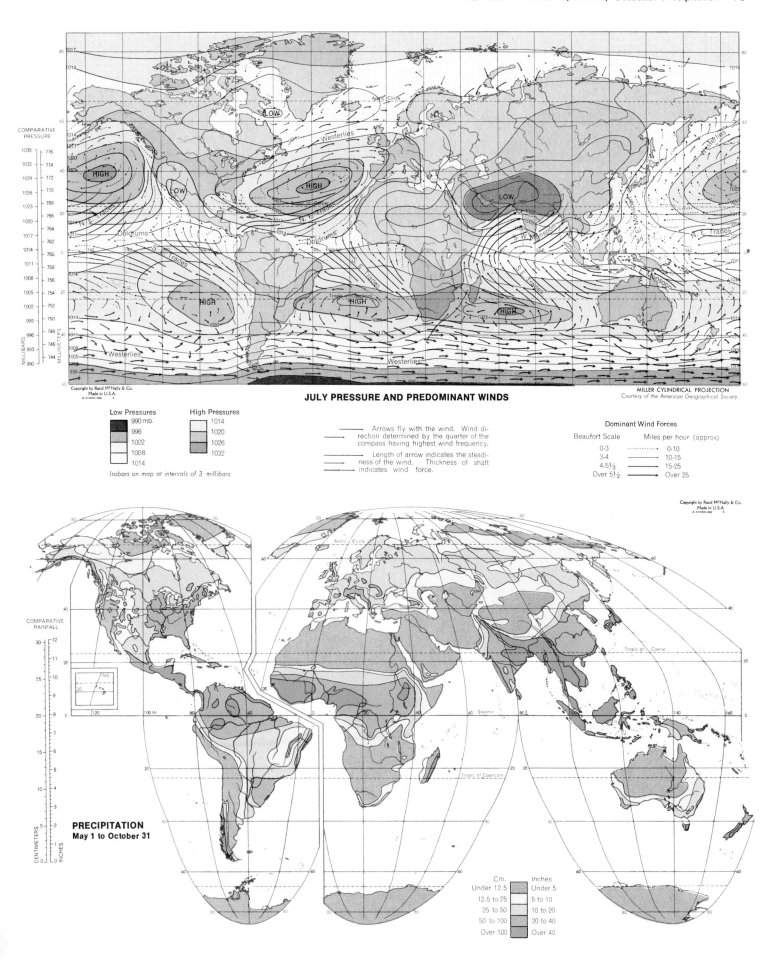

Copyright by Rand McNally & Co.
Made in U.S.A.
A-510000-666   4

JULY PRESSURE AND PREDOMINANT WINDS

MILLER CYLINDRICAL PROJECTION
Courtesy of the American Geographical Society.

COMPARATIVE PRESSURE

Low Pressures	High Pressures
990 mb.	1014
996	1020
1002	1026
1008	1032
1014	

Isobars on map at intervals of 3 millibars

Arrows fly with the wind. Wind direction determined by the quarter of the compass having highest wind frequency.

Length of arrow indicates the steadiness of the wind. Thickness of shaft indicates wind force.

Dominant Wind Forces

Beaufort Scale	Miles per hour (approx)
0-3	0-10
3-4	10-15
4-5½	15-25
Over 5½	Over 25

Copyright by Rand McNally & Co.
Made in U.S.A.
A-510000-666   4

COMPARATIVE RAINFALL

PRECIPITATION
May 1 to October 31

Cm.	Inches
Under 12.5	Under 5
12.5 to 25	5 to 10
25 to 50	10 to 20
50 to 100	20 to 40
Over 100	Over 40

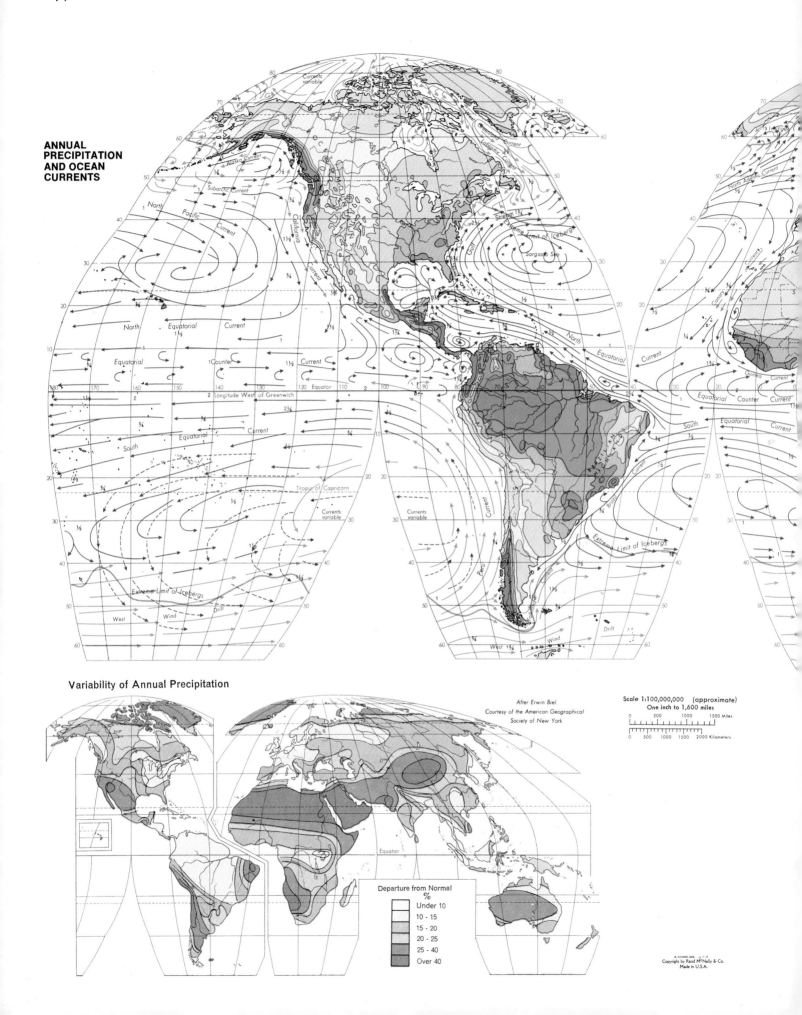

14

ANNUAL
PRECIPITATION
AND OCEAN
CURRENTS

Variability of Annual Precipitation

After Erwin Biel.
Courtesy of the American Geographical
Society of New York

Scale 1:100,000,000 (approximate)
One inch to 1,600 miles

Departure from Normal
%
Under 10
10 - 15
15 - 20
20 - 25
25 - 40
Over 40

Copyright by Rand McNally & Co.
Made in U.S.A.

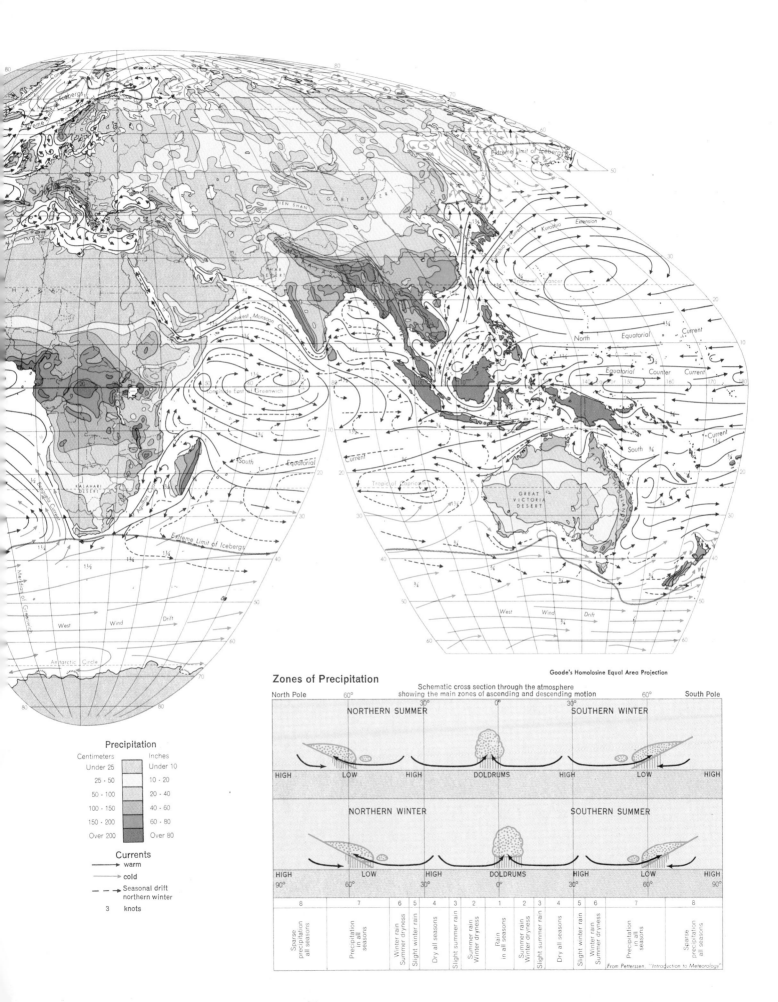

Goode's Homolosine Equal Area Projection

Zones of Precipitation

Schematic cross section through the atmosphere
showing the main zones of ascending and descending motion

North Pole   60°   30°   0°   30°   60°   South Pole

NORTHERN SUMMER   SOUTHERN WINTER

| HIGH | LOW | HIGH | DOLDRUMS | HIGH | LOW | HIGH |

NORTHERN WINTER   SOUTHERN SUMMER

| HIGH | LOW | HIGH | DOLDRUMS | HIGH | LOW | HIGH |
| 90° | 60° | 30° | 0° | 30° | 60° | 90° |

8	7	6	5	4	3	2	1	2	3	4	5	6	7	8
Sparse precipitation all seasons	Precipitation in all seasons	Winter rain Summer dryness	Slight winter rain	Dry all seasons	Slight summer rain	Summer rain Winter dryness	Rain in all seasons	Summer rain Winter dryness	Slight summer rain	Dry all seasons	Slight winter rain	Winter rain Summer dryness	Precipitation in all seasons	Sparse precipitation all seasons

From Petterssen, "Introduction to Meteorology"

Precipitation

Centimeters	Inches
Under 25	Under 10
25 - 50	10 - 20
50 - 100	20 - 40
100 - 150	40 - 60
150 - 200	60 - 80
Over 200	Over 80

Currents

→ warm
→ cold
– – – Seasonal drift northern winter

3   knots

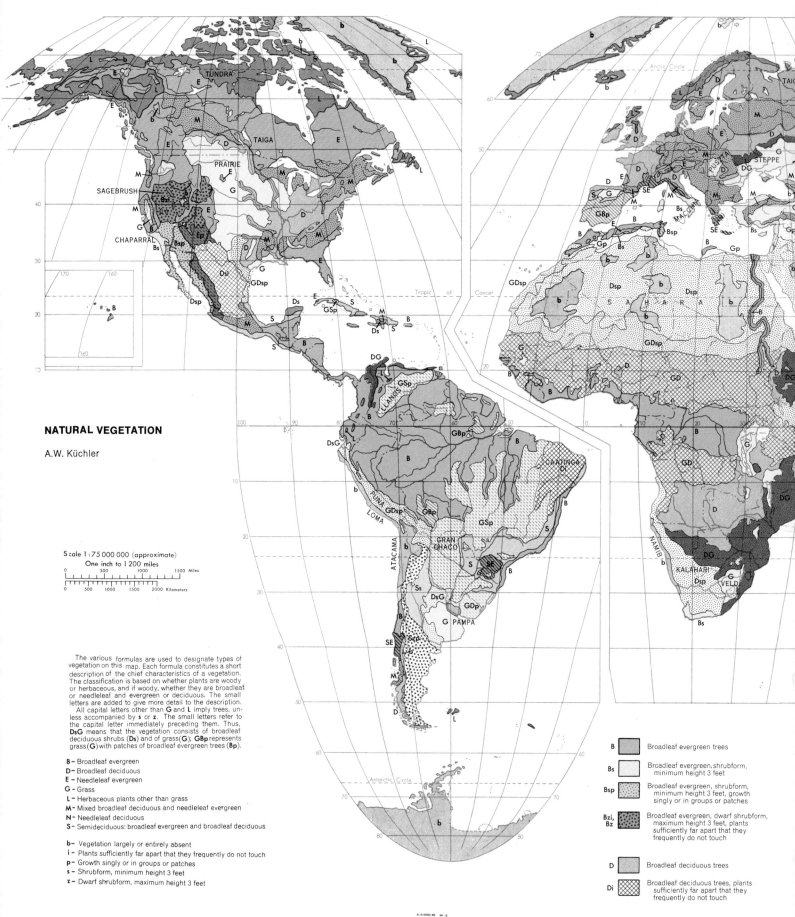

NATURAL VEGETATION

A.W. Küchler

Scale 1:75 000 000 (approximate)

One inch to 1 200 miles

| 0 | 500 | 1000 | 1500 Miles |
| 0 | 500 | 1000 | 1500 | 2000 Kilometers |

The various formulas are used to designate types of vegetation on this map. Each formula constitutes a short description of the chief characteristics of a vegetation. The classification is based on whether plants are woody or herbaceous, and if woody, whether they are broadleaf or needleleaf and evergreen or deciduous. The small letters are added to give more detail to the description.

All capital letters other than **G** and **L** imply trees, unless accompanied by **s** or **z**. The small letters refer to the capital letter immediately preceding them. Thus, **DsG** means that the vegetation consists of broadleaf deciduous shrubs (**Ds**) and of grass (**G**); **GBp** represents grass (**G**) with patches of broadleaf evergreen trees (**Bp**).

B – Broadleaf evergreen
D – Broadleaf deciduous
E – Needleleaf evergreen
G – Grass
L – Herbaceous plants other than grass
M – Mixed broadleaf deciduous and needleleaf evergreen
N – Needleleaf deciduous
S – Semideciduous: broadleaf evergreen and broadleaf deciduous

b – Vegetation largely or entirely absent
i – Plants sufficiently far apart that they frequently do not touch
p – Growth singly or in groups or patches
s – Shrubform, minimum height 3 feet
z – Dwarf shrubform, maximum height 3 feet

B	Broadleaf evergreen trees
Bs	Broadleaf evergreen, shrubform, minimum height 3 feet
Bsp	Broadleaf evergreen, shrubform, minimum height 3 feet, growth singly or in groups or patches
Bzi, Bz	Broadleaf evergreen, dwarf shrubform, maximum height 3 feet, plants sufficiently far apart that they frequently do not touch
D	Broadleaf deciduous trees
Di	Broadleaf deciduous trees, plants sufficiently far apart that they frequently do not touch

A-510000-86
Copyright by Rand McNally & Co.
Made in U.S.A.

TUNDRA

TAIGA

N

E

E

L

L

L

L

B

N

E

M

G

Bp

ND

E

E

M

Ds

Dsp

D

D

D

Ep

GOBI

TAKLA MAKAN

b

Gp

b

Bz

D

D

Bz

B

M

Ep

Gp

M

b

Bs

M

b

Dsp

Gp

b

SE

TERAI

G

GSp

S

B

Dzp

D

DBs

S

D

DsG

B

D

M

B

Dj

S

B

B

D

B

Bs

GBp

M

G

G

Bs

Dsp

B

B

B

B

Gsp

GBp

GSp

S

S

B

Tropic of Cancer

Equator

Longitude East of Greenwich

Tropic of Capricorn

B

GSp

Bs

B

B

GBp

G

B

b

Gp

Bp

Gp

SE

b

SsG

Bs

B

GBp

Bs

GBp

MALLEE

B

B

M

M

D

G

b

S

G

B

B

Goode's Homolosine
Equal Area Projection
(Condensed)

Ds	Broadleaf deciduous, shrubform, minimum height 3 feet	**E**	Needleleaf evergreen trees	**GDsp**	Grass and other herbaceous plants Broadleaf deciduous, shrubform, minimum height 3 feet, growth singly or in groups or patches	**S**	Semideciduous: broadleaf evergreen and broadleaf deciduous trees
Dsi	Broadleaf deciduous, shrubform, minimum height 3 feet, plants sufficiently far apart that they frequently do not touch	**Ep**	Needleleaf evergreen trees, growth singly or in groups or patches	**GSp**	Grass and other herbaceous plants Semideciduous: broadleaf evergreen and broadleaf deciduous trees, growth singly or in groups or patches	**Ss**	Semideciduous: broadleaf evergreen and broadleaf deciduous, shrubform, minimum height 3 feet
sp	Broadleaf deciduous, shrubform, minimum height 3 feet, growth singly or in groups or patches	**G**	Grass and other herbaceous plants	**L**	Herbaceous plants other than grass	**SsG**	Semideciduous: broadleaf evergreen and broadleaf deciduous, shrubform, minimum height 3 feet Grass and other herbaceous plants
zp	Broadleaf deciduous, dwarf shrubform, maximum height 3 feet, growth singly or in groups or patches	**Gp**	Grass and other herbaceous plants, growth singly or in groups or patches	**M**	Mixed: broadleaf deciduous and needleleaf evergreen trees	**Szp**	Semideciduous: broadleaf evergreen and broadleaf deciduous, dwarf shrub-form, maximum height 3 feet, growth singly or in groups or patches
sG	Broadleaf deciduous, shrubform, minimum height 3 feet Grass and other herbaceous plants	**GBp**	Grass and other herbaceous plants Broadleaf evergreen trees, growth singly or in groups or patches	**N**	Needleleaf deciduous trees	**SE**	Semideciduous: broadleaf evergreen and broadleaf deciduous trees Needleleaf evergreen trees
DG	Broadleaf deciduous trees Grass and other herbaceous plants	**GD**	Grass and other herbaceous plants Broadleaf deciduous trees	**ND**	Needleleaf deciduous trees Broadleaf deciduous trees		
DBs	Broadleaf deciduous trees Broadleaf evergreen, shrubform, minimum height 3 feet	**GDp**	Grass and other herbaceous plants Broadleaf deciduous trees, growth singly or in groups or patches			**b**	Vegetation largely or entirely absent

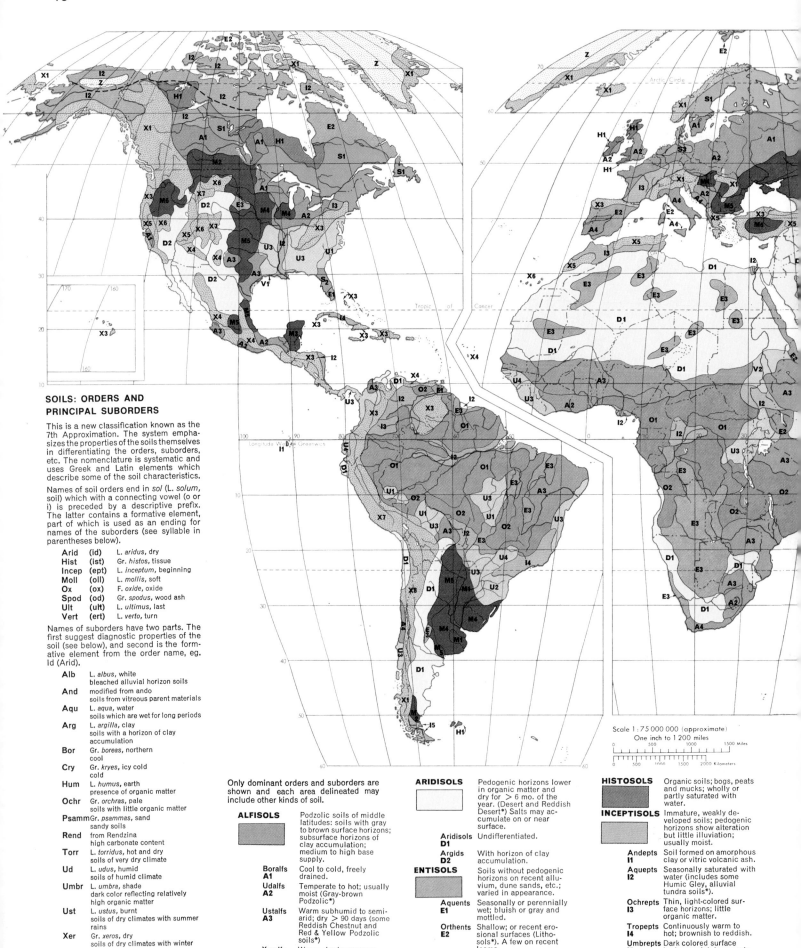

SOILS: ORDERS AND PRINCIPAL SUBORDERS

This is a new classification known as the 7th Approximation. The system emphasizes the properties of the soils themselves in differentiating the orders, suborders, etc. The nomenclature is systematic and uses Greek and Latin elements which describe some of the soil characteristics.

Names of soil orders end in *sol* (L. *solum*, soil) which with a connecting vowel (o or i) is preceded by a descriptive prefix. The latter contains a formative element, part of which is used as an ending for names of the suborders (see syllable in parentheses below).

Arid	(id)	L. *aridus*, dry
Hist	(ist)	Gr. *histos*, tissue
Incep	(ept)	L. *inceptum*, beginning
Moll	(oll)	L. *mollis*, soft
Ox	(ox)	F. *oxide*, oxide
Spod	(od)	Gr. *spodus*, wood ash
Ult	(ult)	L. *ultimus*, last
Vert	(ert)	L. *verto*, turn

Names of suborders have two parts. The first suggest diagnostic properties of the soil (see below), and second is the formative element from the order name, eg. Id (Arid).

Alb	L. *albus*, white bleached alluvial horizon soils
And	modified from ando soils from vitreous parent materials
Aqu	L. *aqua*, water soils which are wet for long periods
Arg	L. *argilla*, clay soils with a horizon of clay accumulation
Bor	Gr. *boreas*, northern cool
Cry	Gr. *kryes*, icy cold cold
Hum	L. *humus*, earth presence of organic matter
Ochr	Gr. *orchras*, pale soils with little organic matter
Psamm	Gr. *psammas*, sand sandy soils
Rend	from Rendzina high carbonate content
Torr	L. *torridus*, hot and dry soils of very dry climate
Ud	L. *udus*, humid soils of humid climate
Umbr	L. *umbra*, shade dark color reflecting relatively high organic matter
Ust	L. *ustus*, burnt soils of dry climates with summer rains
Xer	Gr. *xeros*, dry soils of dry climates with winter rains

Only dominant orders and suborders are shown and each area delineated may include other kinds of soil.

ALFISOLS
Podzolic soils of middle latitudes: soils with gray to brown surface horizons; subsurface horizons of clay accumulation; medium to high base supply.

Boralfs A1	Cool to cold, freely drained.
Udalfs A2	Temperate to hot; usually moist (Gray-brown Podzolic*)
Ustalfs A3	Warm subhumid to semi-arid; dry > 90 days (some Reddish Chestnut and Red & Yellow Podzolic soils*)
Xeralfs A4	Warm, dry in summer; moist in winter.

ARIDISOLS
Pedogenic horizons lower in organic matter and dry for > 6 mo. of the year. (Desert and Reddish Desert*) Salts may accumulate on or near surface.

Aridisols D1	Undifferentiated.
Argids D2	With horizon of clay accumulation.

ENTISOLS
Soils without pedogenic horizons on recent alluvium, dune sands, etc.; varied in appearance.

Aquents E1	Seasonally or perennially wet; bluish or gray and mottled.
Orthents E2	Shallow; or recent erosional surfaces (Lithosols*). A few on recent loams.
Psamments E3	Sandy soils on shifting and stabilized sands.

HISTOSOLS
Organic soils; bogs, peats and mucks; wholly or partly saturated with water.

INCEPTISOLS
Immature, weakly developed soils; pedogenic horizons show alteration but little illuviation; usually moist.

Andepts I1	Soil formed on amorphous clay or vitric volcanic ash.
Aquepts I2	Seasonally saturated with water (includes some Humic Gley, alluvial tundra soils*).
Ochrepts I3	Thin, light-colored surface horizons; little organic matter.
Tropepts I4	Continuously warm to hot; brownish to reddish.
Umbrepts I5	Dark colored surface horizons; rich in organic matter; medium to low base supply.

Scale 1:75 000 000 (approximate)
One inch to 1 200 miles

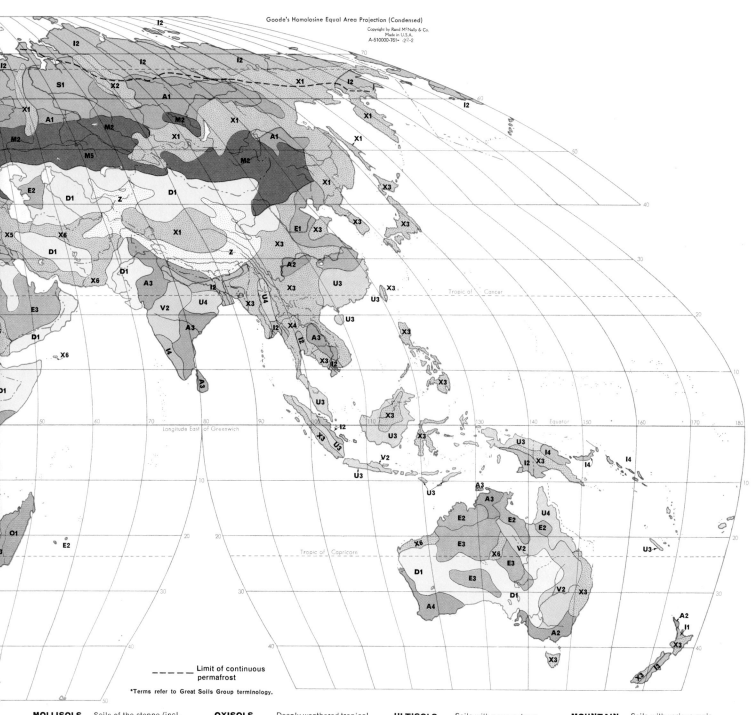

Goode's Homolosine Equal Area Projection (Condensed)
Copyright by Rand McNally & Co.
Made in U.S.A.
A-510000-761- -2-2-2

———— Limit of continuous permafrost

*Terms refer to Great Soils Group terminology.

MOLLISOLS	Soils of the steppe (incl. Chernozem and Chestnut soils*). Thick, black organic rich surface horizons and high base supply.
Albolls **M1**	Seasonally saturated with water; light gray subsurface horizon.
Borolls **M2**	Cool or cold (incl. some Chernozem, Chestnut and Brown soils*).
Rendolls **M3**	Formed on highly calcareous parent materials (Rendzina*).
Udolls **M4**	Temperate to warm; usually moist (Prairie soils*).
Ustolls **M5**	Temperate to hot; dry for > 90 days (incl. some Chestnut and Brown soils*).
Xerolls **M6**	Cool to warm; dry in summer; moist in winter.

OXISOLS	Deeply weathered tropical and subtropical soils (Laterites*); rich in sesquioxides of iron and aluminum; low in nutrients; limited productivity without fertilizer.
Orthox **O1**	Hot and nearly always moist.
Ustox **O2**	Warm or hot; dry for long periods but moist > 90 consecutive days.

SPODOSOLS	Soils with a subsurface accumulation of amorphous materials overlaid by a light colored, leached sandy horizon.
Spodosols **S1**	Undifferentiated (mostly high latitudes).
Aquods **S2**	Seasonally saturated with water; sandy parent materials.
Humods **S3**	Considerable accumulation of organic matter in subsurface horizon.
Orthods **S4**	With subsurface accumulations of iron, aluminum and organic matter (Podzols*).

ULTISOLS	Soils with some subsurface clay accumulation; low base supply; usually moist and low inorganic matter; usually moist and low in organic matter; can be productive with fertilization.
Aquults **U1**	Seasonally saturated with water; subsurface gray or mottled horizon.
Humults **U2**	High in organic matter; dark colored; moist, warm to temperate all year.
Udults **U3**	Low in organic matter; moist, temperate to hot (Red-Yellow Podzolic; some Reddish-Brown Lateritic soils*).
Ustults **U4**	Warm to hot; dry > 90 days.

VERTISOLS	Soils with high content of swelling clays; deep, wide cracks in dry periods dark colored.
Uderts **V1**	Usually moist; cracks open < 90 days.
Usterts **V2**	Cracks open > 90 days; difficult to till (Black tropical soils*).

MOUNTAIN SOILS	Soils with various moisture and temperature regimes; steep slopes and variable relief and elevation; soils vary greatly within short distance.

X1 Cryic great groups of Entisols, Inceptisols and Spodosols.

X2 Boralfs and Cryic groups of Entisols and Inceptisols.

X3 Udic great groups of Alfisols, Entisols and Ultisols; Inceptisols.

X4 Ustic great groups of Alfisols, Entisols, Inceptisols, Mollisols and Ultisols.

X5 Xeric great groups of Alfisols, Entisols, Inceptisols, Mollisols and Ultisols.

X6 Torric great groups of Entisols; Aridisols.

X7 Ustic and cryic great groups of Alfisols, Entisols; Inceptisols and Mollisols; ustic great groups of Ultisols; cryic great groups of Spodosols.

X8 Aridisols; torric and cryic great groups of Entisols, and cryic great groups of Spodosols and Inceptisols.

z	Areas with little or no soil; icefields, and rugged mountain.

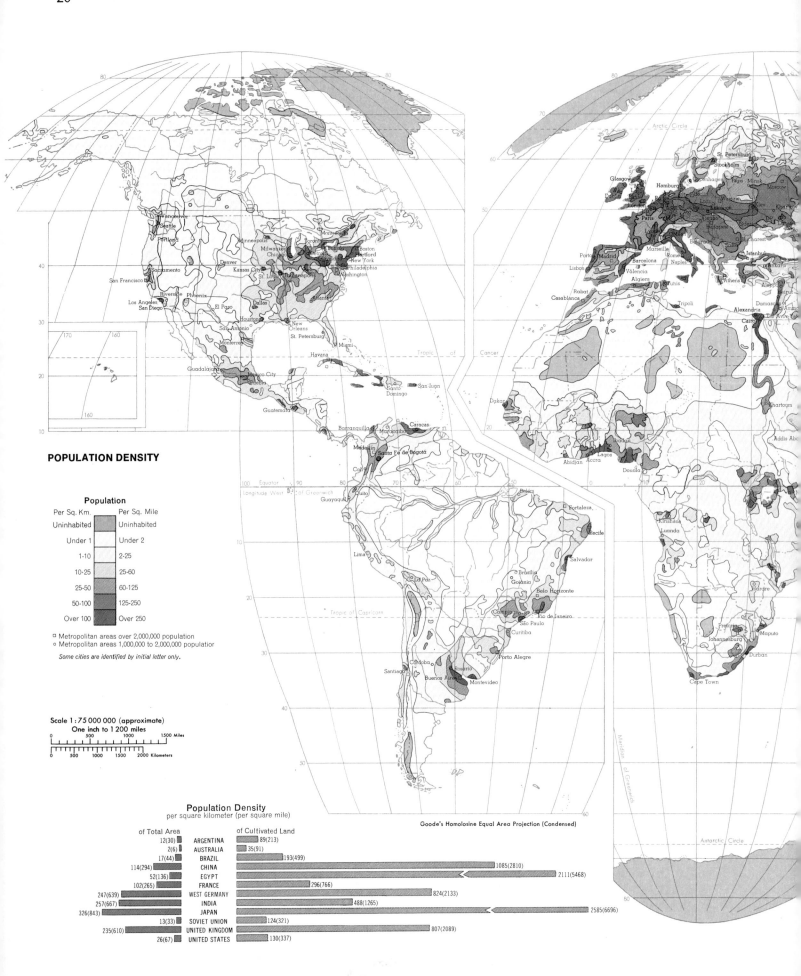

20

POPULATION DENSITY

Population

Per Sq. Km.		Per Sq. Mile
Uninhabited		Uninhabited
Under 1		Under 2
1-10		2-25
10-25		25-60
25-50		60-125
50-100		125-250
Over 100		Over 250

□ Metropolitan areas over 2,000,000 population
○ Metropolitan areas 1,000,000 to 2,000,000 population

Some cities are identified by initial letter only.

Scale 1:75 000 000 (approximate)
One inch to 1 200 miles

| 0 | 500 | 1000 | 1500 Miles |

| 0 | 500 | 1000 | 1500 | 2000 Kilometers |

Goode's Homolosine Equal Area Projection (Condensed)

Population Density
per square kilometer (per square mile)

of Total Area		of Cultivated Land
12(30)	ARGENTINA	89(213)
2(6)	AUSTRALIA	35(91)
17(44)	BRAZIL	193(499)
114(294)	CHINA	1085(2810)
52(136)	EGYPT	2111(5468)
102(265)	FRANCE	296(766)
247(639)	WEST GERMANY	824(2133)
257(667)	INDIA	488(1265)
326(843)	JAPAN	2585(6696)
13(33)	SOVIET UNION	124(321)
235(610)	UNITED KINGDOM	807(2089)
26(67)	UNITED STATES	130(337)

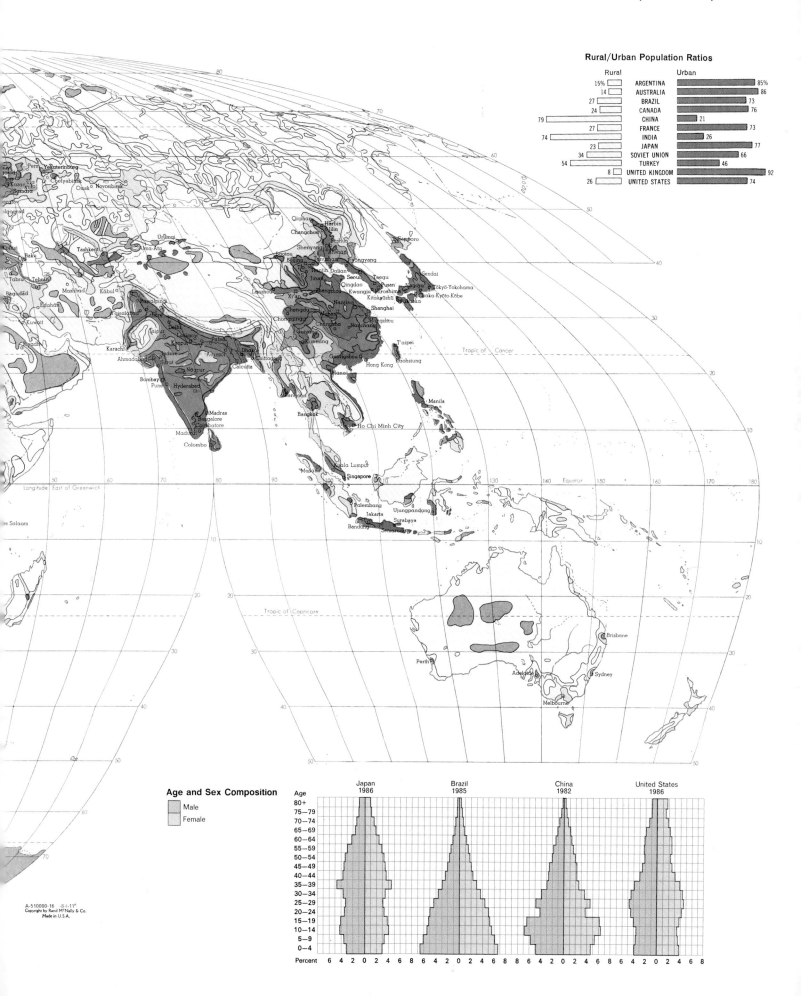

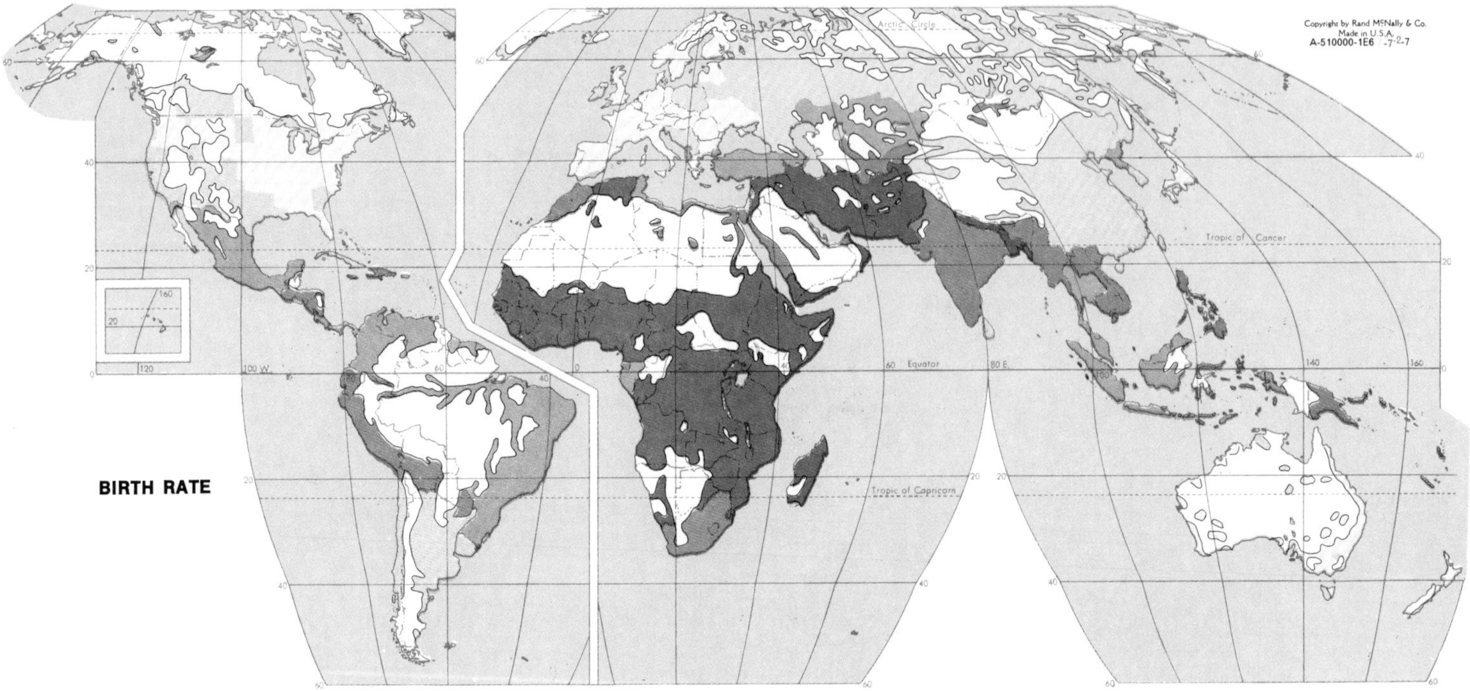

BIRTH RATE

Copyright by Rand McNally & Co.
Made in U.S.A.
A-510000-1E6 .-7-2-7

Birth Rate (Crude)
per 1,000 population

- Over 40 High
- 32-40 Moderately high
- 24-32 Moderately low

World Av.
27 →

- 16-24 Low
- Under 16 Very low
- Uninhabited or sparsely populated

Life Expectancy at Birth

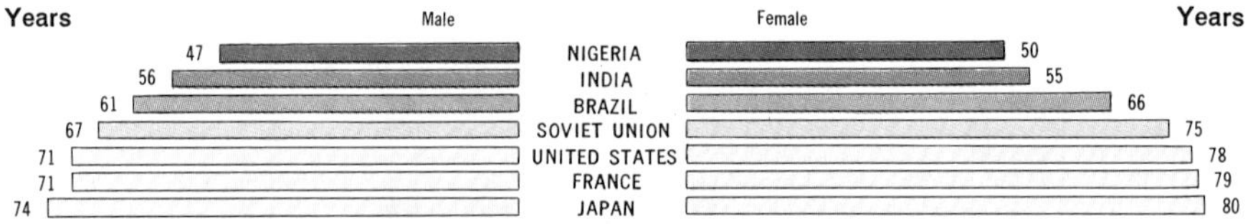

Years	Male		Female	Years
47	NIGERIA		50	
56	INDIA		55	
61	BRAZIL		66	
67	SOVIET UNION		75	
71	UNITED STATES		78	
71	FRANCE		79	
74	JAPAN		80	

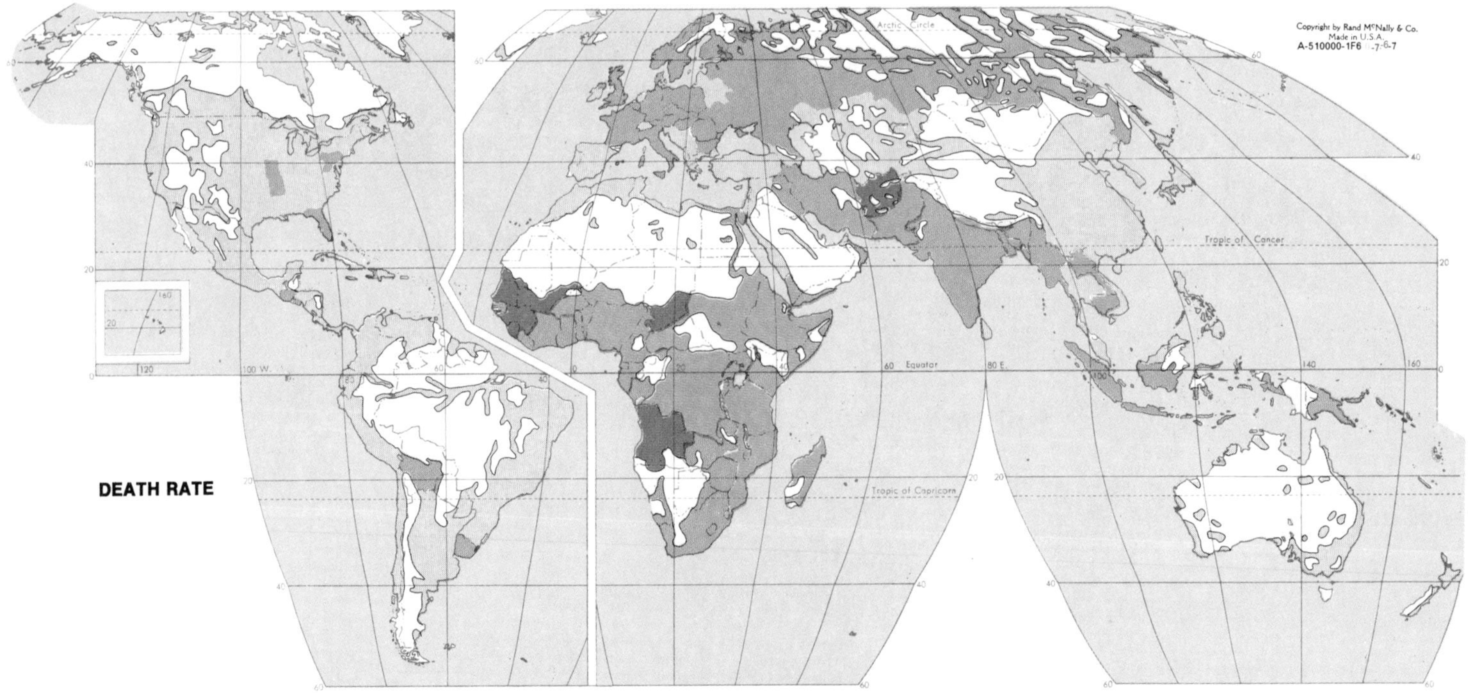

DEATH RATE

Copyright by Rand McNally & Co.
Made in U.S.A.
A-510000-1F6 .-7-6-7

Death Rate (Crude)
per 1,000 population

- Over 20 High
- 15-20 Moderately high
- 10-15 Moderately low

World Av.
10 →

- Under 10 Low
- Uninhabited or sparsely populated

Infant Mortality Rate
Deaths under one year per 1,000 live births

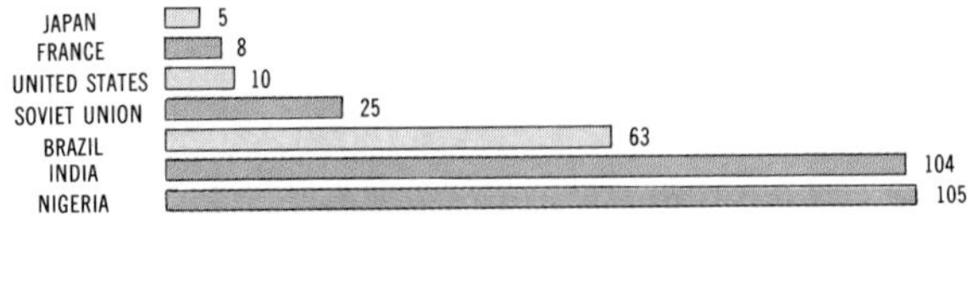

JAPAN	5
FRANCE	8
UNITED STATES	10
SOVIET UNION	25
BRAZIL	63
INDIA	104
NIGERIA	105

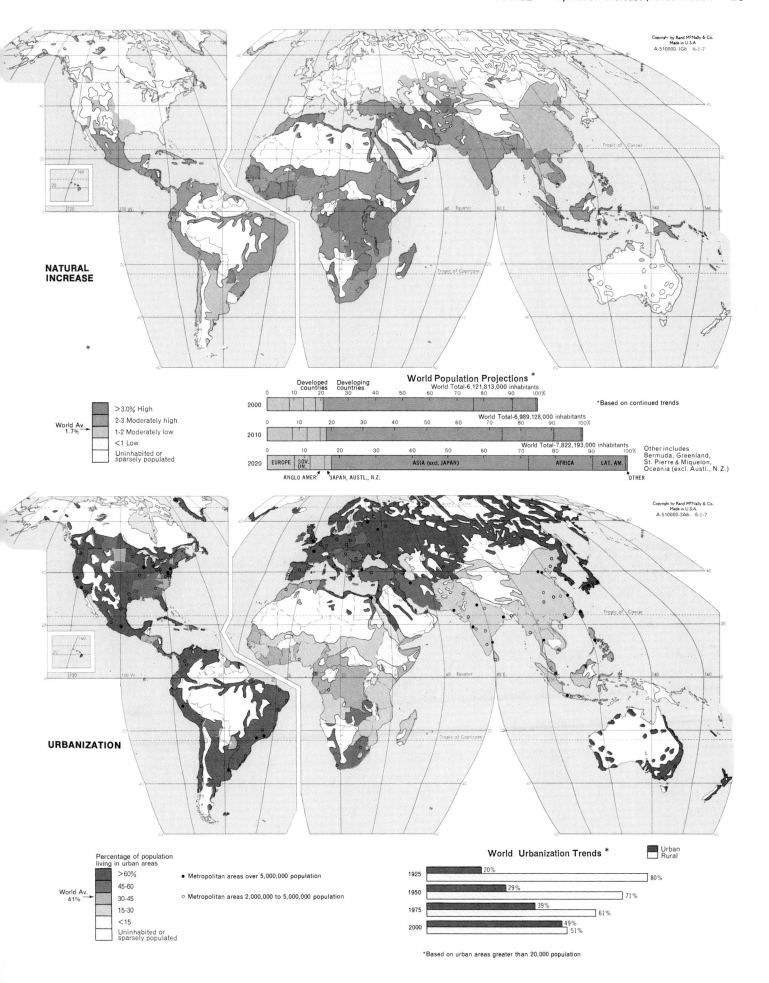

Copyright by Rand McNally & Co.
Made in U.S.A
A-510000-1G6 -6-2-7

NATURAL INCREASE

World Population Projections *

World Total-6,121,813,000 inhabitants

Developed countries   Developing countries

2000

*Based on continued trends

World Total-6,989,128,000 inhabitants

2010

World Total-7,822,193,000 inhabitants

2020 | EUROPE | SOV. UN. | ASIA (excl. JAPAN) | AFRICA | LAT. AM. |

ANGLO AMER.   JAPAN, AUSTL., N.Z.   OTHER

Other includes
Bermuda, Greenland,
St. Pierre & Miquelon,
Oceania (excl. Austl., N.Z.)

World Av.
1.7% →

	>3.0% High
	2-3 Moderately high
	1-2 Moderately low
	<1 Low
	Uninhabited or sparsely populated

Copyright by Rand McNally & Co.
Made in U.S.A
A-510000-3A6- -6-2-7

URBANIZATION

Percentage of population
living in urban areas

World Av. →
41%

	>60%
	45-60
	30-45
	15-30
	<15
	Uninhabited or sparsely populated

● Metropolitan areas over 5,000,000 population

○ Metropolitan areas 2,000,000 to 5,000,000 population

World Urbanization Trends *

■ Urban □ Rural

1925   20%   80%

1950   29%   71%

1975   39%   61%

2000   49%   51%

*Based on urban areas greater than 20,000 population

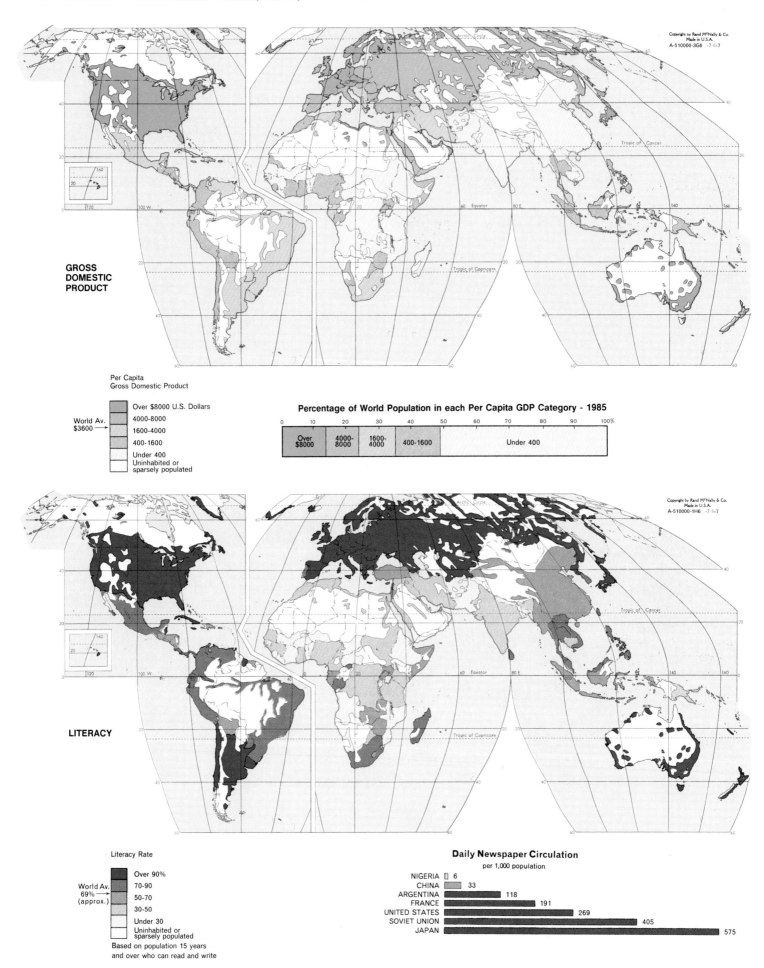

GROSS DOMESTIC PRODUCT

Per Capita
Gross Domestic Product

World Av.
$3600 →

- Over $8000 U.S. Dollars
- 4000-8000
- 1600-4000
- 400-1600
- Under 400
- Uninhabited or sparsely populated

Percentage of World Population in each Per Capita GDP Category - 1985

| Over $8000 | 4000-8000 | 1600-4000 | 400-1600 | Under 400 |

LITERACY

Literacy Rate

World Av.
69%
(approx.) →

- Over 90%
- 70-90
- 50-70
- 30-50
- Under 30
- Uninhabited or sparsely populated

Based on population 15 years
and over who can read and write

Daily Newspaper Circulation
per 1,000 population

NIGERIA	6
CHINA	33
ARGENTINA	118
FRANCE	191
UNITED STATES	269
SOVIET UNION	405
JAPAN	575

Copyright by Rand McNally & Co.
Made in U.S.A.
A-510000-3G6 -7-6-7

Copyright by Rand McNally & Co.
Made in U.S.A.
A-510000-1H6 -7-6-7

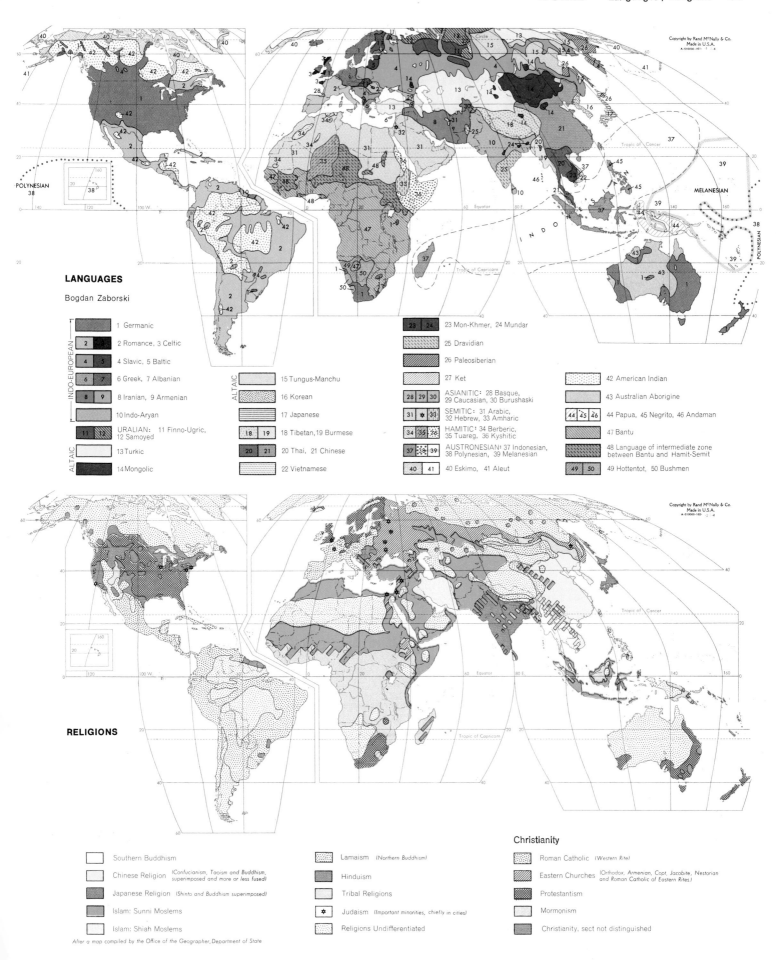

LANGUAGES

Bogdan Zaborski

INDO-EUROPEAN
- 1 Germanic
- 2 Romance, 3 Celtic
- 4 Slavic, 5 Baltic
- 6 Greek, 7 Albanian
- 8 Iranian, 9 Armenian
- 10 Indo-Aryan

URALIAN: 11 Finno-Ugric, 12 Samoyed

ALTAIC
- 13 Turkic
- 14 Mongolic
- 15 Tungus-Manchu
- 16 Korean
- 17 Japanese
- 18 Tibetan, 19 Burmese
- 20 Thai, 21 Chinese
- 22 Vietnamese

- 23 Mon-Khmer, 24 Mundar
- 25 Dravidian
- 26 Paleosiberian
- 27 Ket
- **ASIANITIC:** 28 Basque, 29 Caucasian, 30 Burushaski
- **SEMITIC:** 31 Arabic, 32 Hebrew, 33 Amharic
- **HAMITIC:** 34 Berberic, 35 Tuareg, 36 Kyshitic
- **AUSTRONESIAN:** 37 Indonesian, 38 Polynesian, 39 Melanesian
- 40 Eskimo, 41 Aleut

- 42 American Indian
- 43 Australian Aborigine
- 44 Papua, 45 Negrito, 46 Andaman
- 47 Bantu
- 48 Language of intermediate zone between Bantu and Hamit-Semit
- 49 Hottentot, 50 Bushmen

RELIGIONS

- Southern Buddhism
- Chinese Religion (Confucianism, Taoism and Buddhism, superimposed and more or less fused)
- Japanese Religion (Shinto and Buddhism superimposed)
- Islam: Sunni Moslems
- Islam: Shiah Moslems

- Lamaism (Northern Buddhism)
- Hinduism
- Tribal Religions
- ✡ Judaism (Important minorities, chiefly in cities)
- Religions Undifferentiated

Christianity
- Roman Catholic (Western Rite)
- Eastern Churches (Orthodox, Armenian, Copt, Jacobite, Nestorian and Roman Catholic of Eastern Rites)
- Protestantism
- Mormonism
- Christianity, sect not distinguished

After a map compiled by the Office of the Geographer, Department of State

Copyright by Rand McNally & Co. Made in U.S.A.

CALORIE SUPPLY

Note: Size of each country is proportional to population

Calorie supply per capita
(percentage of requirements*)

≥120% Well above requirements
110 to 120 Above requirements
100 to 110 Adequate nutrition
90 to 100 Some malnutrition
<90 Serious malnutrition and/or hunge

n.a. Data not available

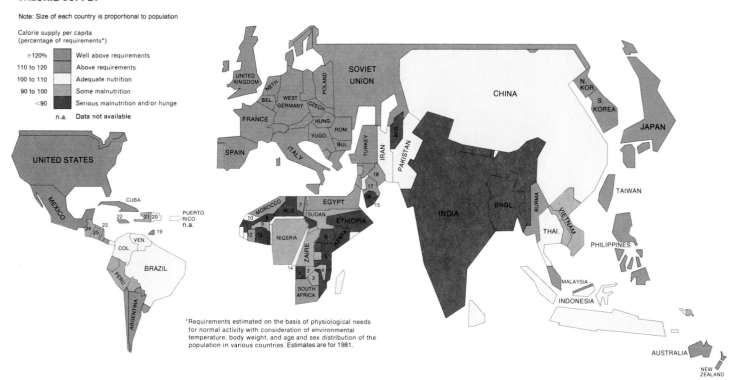

*Requirements estimated on the basis of physiological needs
for normal activity with consideration of environmental
temperature, body weight, and age and sex distribution of the
population in various countries. Estimates are for 1981.

1. ANGOLA	6. UGANDA	11. GUINEA	16. YEMEN	21. HAITI
2. ZAMBIA	7. TUNISIA	12. IVORY COAST	17. SAUDI ARABIA	22. JAMAICA
3. ZIMBABWE	8. MALI	13. GHANA	18. IRAQ	23. HONDURAS
4. MALAWI	9. BURKINA FASO	14. CAMEROON	19. TRIN. & TOBAGO	24. GUATEMALA
5. TANZANIA	10. SENEGAL	15. P.D.R. YEMEN	20. DOM. REPUBLIC	25. EL SALVADOR

© Rand McNally & Co.
Made in U.S.A.
A-510000-1V6 -3-3-3

PROTEIN CONSUMPTION

Note: size of each country is proportional to population

n.a. Data not available

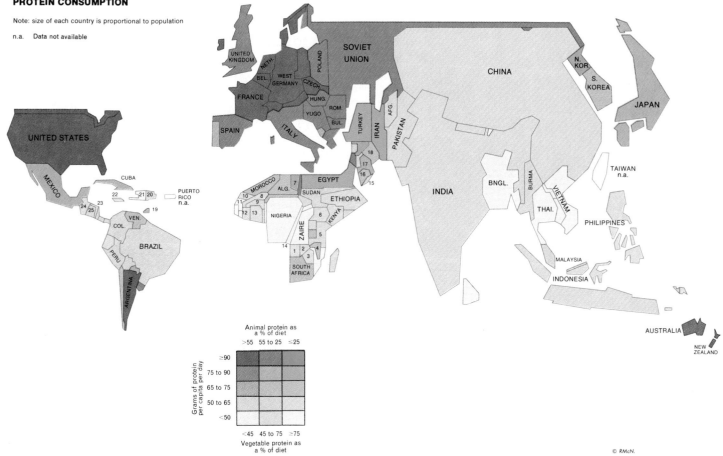

Animal protein as
a % of diet
>55 55 to 25 ≤25

Grams of protein
per capita per day
≥90
75 to 90
65 to 75
50 to 65
<50

<45 45 to 75 ≥75
Vegetable protein as
a % of diet

© RMcN.

PHYSICIANS

Note: Size of each country is proportional to population

Population per physician

- <1000
- 1000 to 6000
- 6000 to 18000
- ≥18000

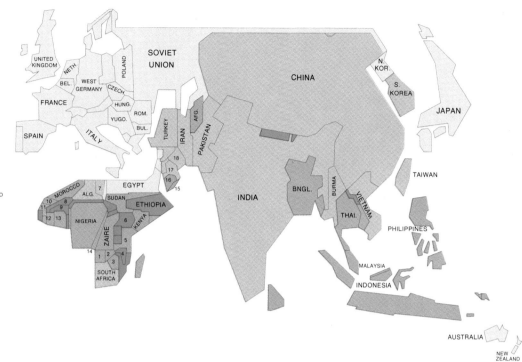

1. ANGOLA	6. UGANDA	11. GUINEA	16. YEMEN	21. HAITI
2. ZAMBIA	7. TUNISIA	12. IVORY COAST	17. SAUDI ARABIA	22. JAMAICA
3. ZIMBABWE	8. MALI	13. GHANA	18. IRAQ	23. HONDURAS
4. MALAWI	9. BURKINA FASO	14. CAMEROON	19. TRIN. & TOBAGO	24. GUATEMALA
5. TANZANIA	10. SENEGAL	15. P.D.R. YEMEN	20. DOM. REPUBLIC	25. EL SALVADOR

© Rand McNally & Co.
Made in U.S.A.
A-510000-1L6- -0-3-3

LIFE EXPECTANCY

Note: Size of each country is proportional to population

Life expectancy at birth

- ≥70 years
- 60 to 70
- 50 to 60
- <50

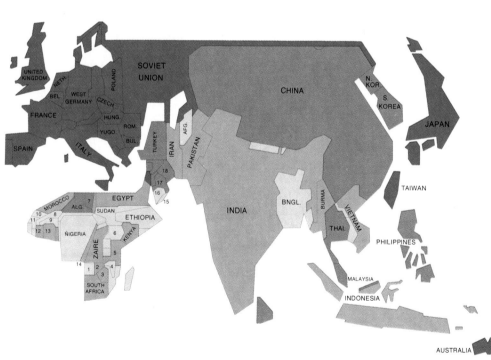

Deaths by Age Group as a % of Total Deaths

DEVELOPING COUNTRIES: Low Income (excluding China and India)*

INDUSTRIAL MARKET COUNTRIES*

Life Expectancy at Birth

DEVELOPING: Low income*	61 years
DEVELOPING: Lower-middle income*	59
DEVELOPING: Upper-middle income*	67
OIL EXPORTING*	64
INDUSTRIAL MARKET*	76

*as defined by the World Bank

© Rand McNally & Co.
Made in U.S.A.
A-510000-1M6 -1-1-1

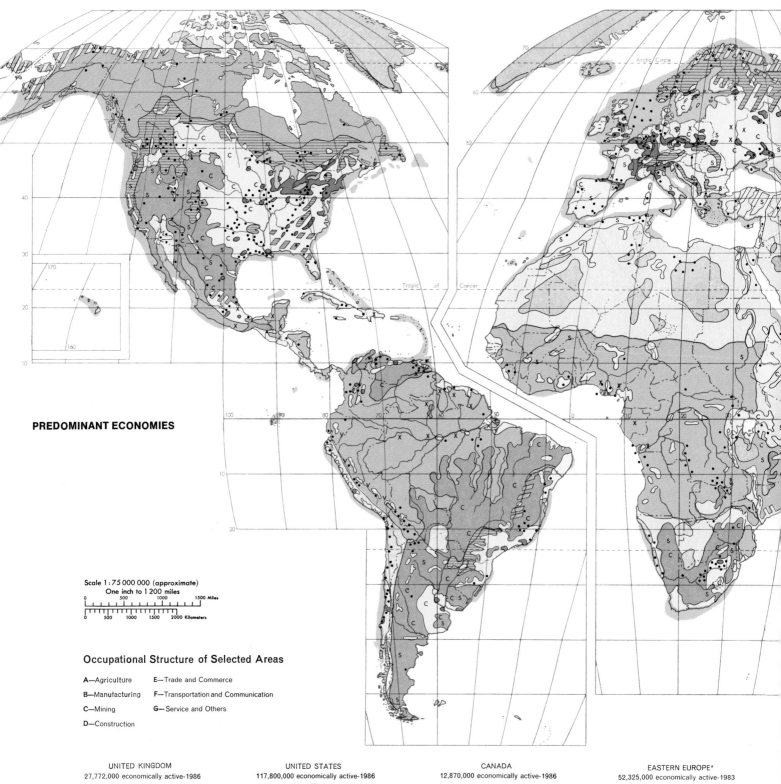

PREDOMINANT ECONOMIES

Scale 1 : 75 000 000 (approximate)
One inch to 1 200 miles

0   500   1000   1500 Miles

0   500   1000   1500   2000 Kilometers

Occupational Structure of Selected Areas

A—Agriculture   E—Trade and Commerce

B—Manufacturing   F—Transportation and Communication

C—Mining   G—Service and Others

D—Construction

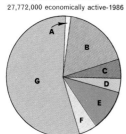

UNITED KINGDOM
27,772,000 economically active-1986

UNITED STATES
117,800,000 economically active-1986

CANADA
12,870,000 economically active-1986

EASTERN EUROPE*
52,325,000 economically active-1983

A-510000-36-6-6-5-6
Copyright by Rand McNally & Co.
Made in U.S.A.

*Includes Bulgaria, Czechoslovakia, East Germany,
Hungary, Poland, and Romania

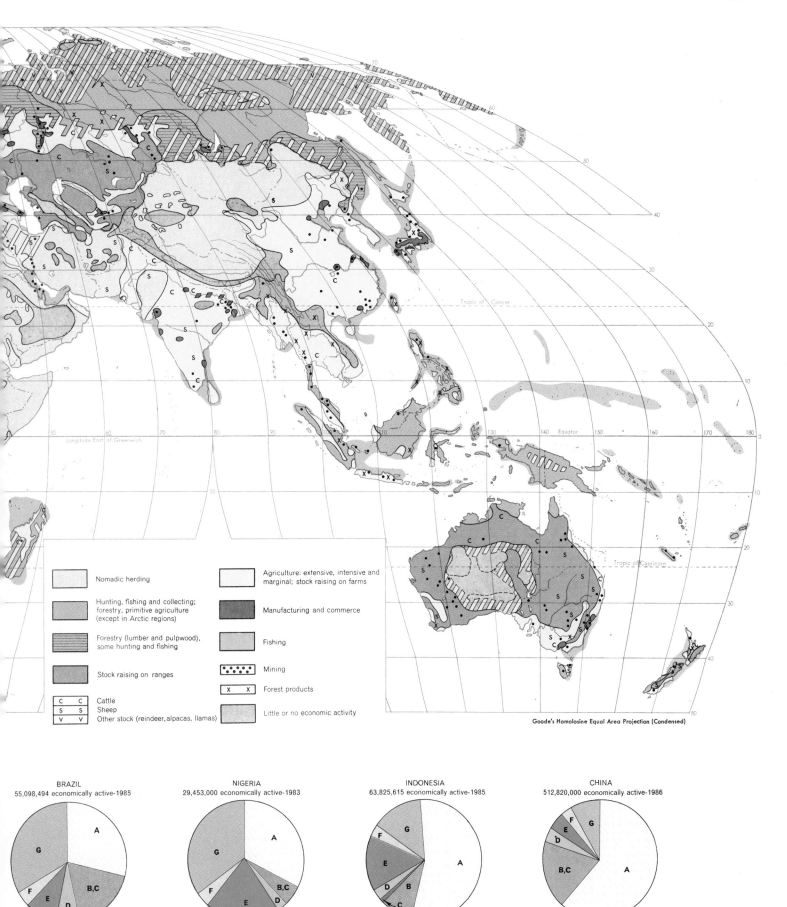

Nomadic herding

Hunting, fishing and collecting; forestry, primitive agriculture (except in Arctic regions)

Forestry (lumber and pulpwood), some hunting and fishing

Stock raising on ranges

C C	Cattle
S S	Sheep
V V	Other stock (reindeer, alpacas, llamas)

Agriculture: extensive, intensive and marginal; stock raising on farms

Manufacturing and commerce

Fishing

Mining

Forest products

Little or no economic activity

Goode's Homolosine Equal Area Projection (Condensed)

BRAZIL
55,098,494 economically active-1985

NIGERIA
29,453,000 economically active-1983

INDONESIA
63,825,615 economically active-1985

CHINA
512,820,000 economically active-1986

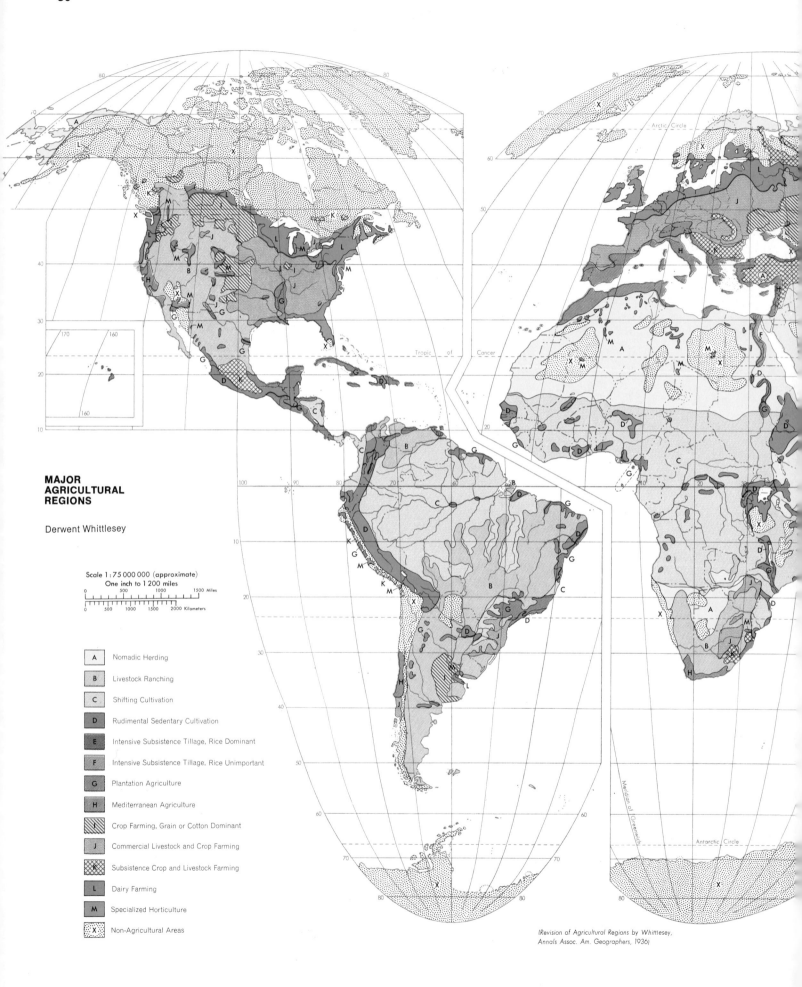

**MAJOR
AGRICULTURAL
REGIONS**

Derwent Whittlesey

Scale 1 : 75 000 000 (approximate)
One inch to 1 200 miles

A	Nomadic Herding
B	Livestock Ranching
C	Shifting Cultivation
D	Rudimental Sedentary Cultivation
E	Intensive Subsistence Tillage, Rice Dominant
F	Intensive Subsistence Tillage, Rice Unimportant
G	Plantation Agriculture
H	Mediterranean Agriculture
I	Crop Farming, Grain or Cotton Dominant
J	Commercial Livestock and Crop Farming
K	Subsistence Crop and Livestock Farming
L	Dairy Farming
M	Specialized Horticulture
X	Non-Agricultural Areas

(Revision of Agricultural Regions by Whittlesey,
Annals Assoc. Am. Geographers, 1936)

Goode's Homolosine Equal Area Projection (Condensed)

A-510000-562.2-3.4'
Copyright by Rand McNally & Co.
Made in U.S.A.

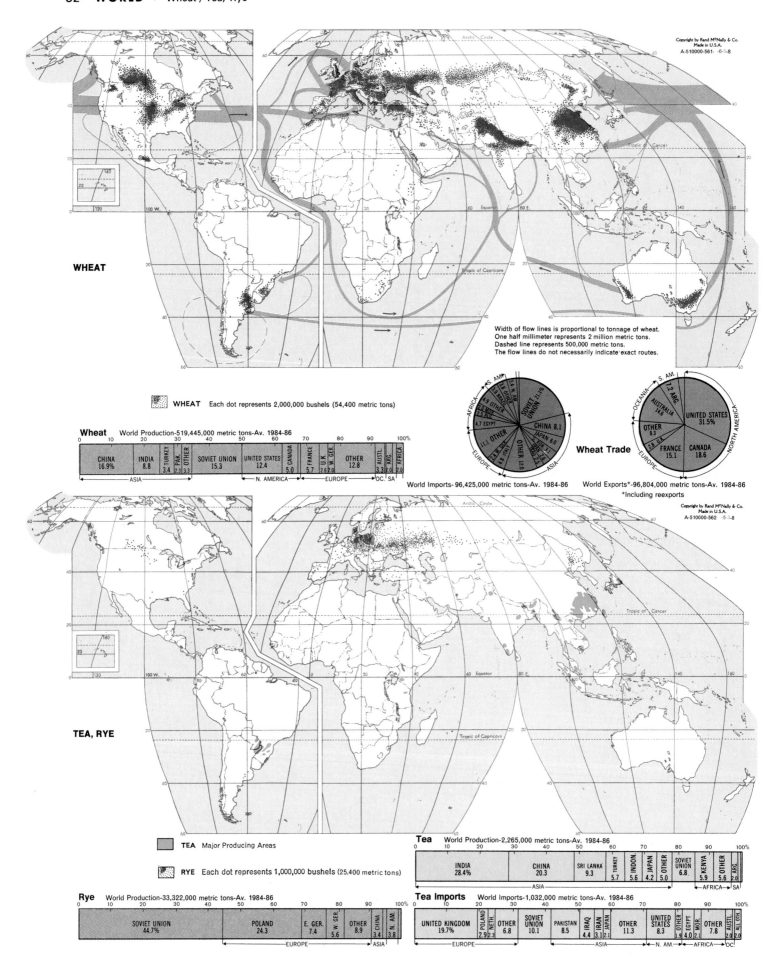

Copyright by Rand McNally & Co.
Made in U.S.A.
A-510000-561- -6-5-8

WHEAT

Width of flow lines is proportional to tonnage of wheat.
One half millimeter represents 2 million metric tons.
Dashed line represents 500,000 metric tons.
The flow lines do not necessarily indicate exact routes.

WHEAT Each dot represents 2,000,000 bushels (54,400 metric tons)

Wheat Trade

Wheat World Production-519,445,000 metric tons-Av. 1984-86

CHINA 16.9%	INDIA 8.8	TURKEY 3.4	PAK. 2.3	OTHER 3.3	SOVIET UNION 15.3	UNITED STATES 12.4	CANADA 5.0	FRANCE 5.7	U.K. 2.6	W.GER. 2.8	OTHER 12.8	AUSTL. 3.3	ARG. 2.0	AFRICA 2.0

World Imports- 96,425,000 metric tons-Av. 1984-86   World Exports*-96,804,000 metric tons-Av. 1984-86
*Including reexports

Copyright by Rand McNally & Co.
Made in U.S.A.
A-510000-562 -5-3-8

TEA, RYE

TEA Major Producing Areas

RYE Each dot represents 1,000,000 bushels (25,400 metric tons)

Tea World Production-2,265,000 metric tons-Av. 1984-86

INDIA 28.4%	CHINA 20.3	SRI LANKA 9.3	TURKEY 5.7	INDON. 5.6	JAPAN 4.2	OTHER 5.0	SOVIET UNION 6.8	KENYA 5.6	OTHER 5.6	ARG. 2.0

Rye World Production-33,322,000 metric tons-Av. 1984-86

SOVIET UNION 44.7%	POLAND 24.3	E. GER. 7.4	W.GER. 5.6	OTHER 8.9	CHINA 3.4	N. AM. 3.8

Tea Imports World Imports-1,032,000 metric tons-Av. 1984-86

UNITED KINGDOM 19.7%	POLAND 2.9	NETH. 2.3	OTHER 6.8	SOVIET UNION 10.1	PAKISTAN 8.5	IRAQ 4.4	IRAN 3.1	JAPAN 2.1	OTHER 11.3	UNITED STATES 8.3	OTHER 1.9	EGYPT 4.0	MOR. 2.1	OTHER 7.8	AUSTL. 2.0	ALL OTH. 2.0

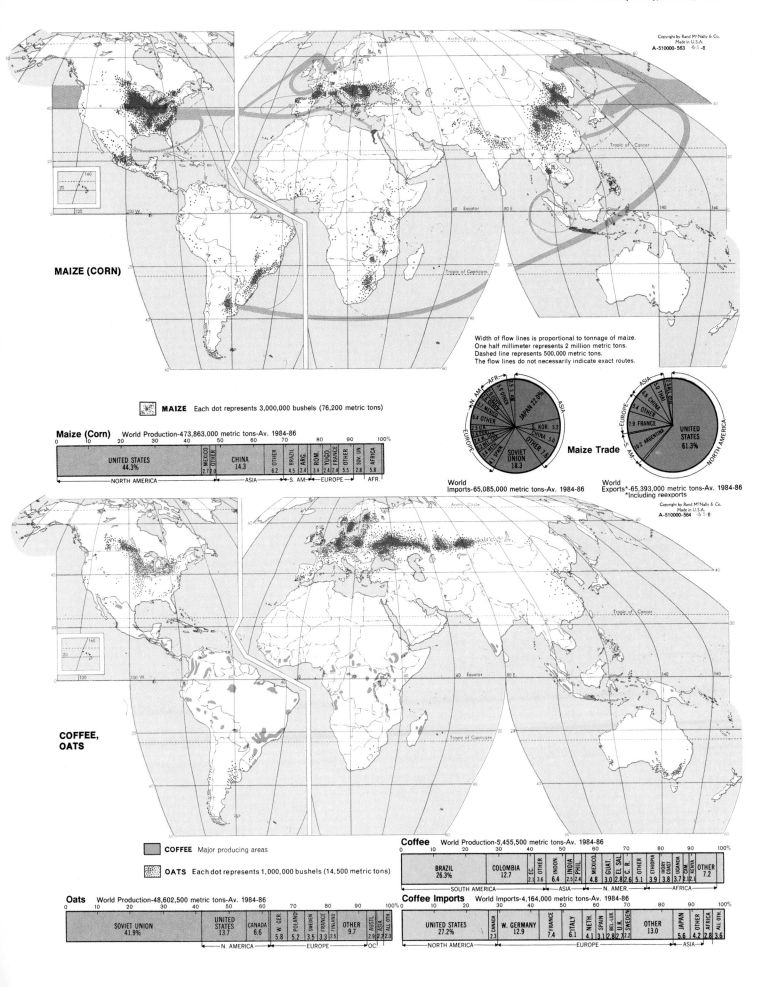

Copyright by Rand M\Nally & Co.
Made in U.S.A.
A-510000-563 -6-5 -8

MAIZE (CORN)

Width of flow lines is proportional to tonnage of maize.
One half millimeter represents 2 million metric tons.
Dashed line represents 500,000 metric tons.
The flow lines do not necessarily indicate exact routes.

MAIZE Each dot represents 3,000,000 bushels (76,200 metric tons)

Maize (Corn) World Production-473,863,000 metric tons-Av. 1984-86

UNITED STATES 44.3%	MEXICO 2.7	OTHER 2.0	CHINA 14.3	OTHER 6.2	BRAZIL 4.5	ARG. 2.4	ROM. 3.4	YUGO 2.4	FRANCE 2.4	OTHER 5.5	SOV. UN 2.8	AFRICA 5.8
NORTH AMERICA			ASIA		S. AM		EUROPE					AFR.

Maize Trade

World
Imports-65,085,000 metric tons-Av. 1984-86

World
Exports*-65,393,000 metric tons-Av. 1984-86
*Including reexports

Copyright by Rand M\Nally & Co.
Made in U.S.A.
A-510000-564 -5 5-8

COFFEE, OATS

COFFEE Major producing areas

OATS Each dot represents 1,000,000 bushels (14,500 metric tons)

Coffee World Production-5,455,500 metric tons-Av. 1984-86

BRAZIL 26.3%	COLOMBIA 12.7	EC. 2.1	OTHER 3.6	INDON. 6.4	INDIA 2.5	PHIL. 2.4	MEXICO. 4.8	GUAT. 3.0	EL SAL 2.8	C. R. 2.6	OTHER 5.1	ETHIOPIA 3.9	IVORY COAST 3.8	UGANDA 3.7	CAM 2.2	KENYA 2.1	OTHER 7.2
SOUTH AMERICA				ASIA			N. AMER.					AFRICA					

Oats World Production-48,602,500 metric tons-Av. 1984-86

SOVIET UNION 41.9%	UNITED STATES 13.7	CANADA 6.6	W. GER. 5.8	POLAND 5.2	SWEDEN 3.5	FRANCE 3.3	FINLAND 2.5	OTHER 9.7	AUSTL. 2.9	ASIA 2.2	ALL OTH. 2.3
	N. AMERICA		EUROPE						OC.		

Coffee Imports World Imports-4,164,000 metric tons-Av. 1984-86

UNITED STATES 27.2%	CANADA 2.3	W. GERMANY 12.9	FRANCE 7.4	ITALY 6.1	NETH. 4.1	SPAIN 3.1	BEL.-LUX. 2.8	U.K. 2.7	SWEDEN 2.5	OTHER 13.0	JAPAN 5.6	OTHER 4.2	AFRICA 2.8	ALL OTH. 3.6
NORTH AMERICA		EUROPE									ASIA	

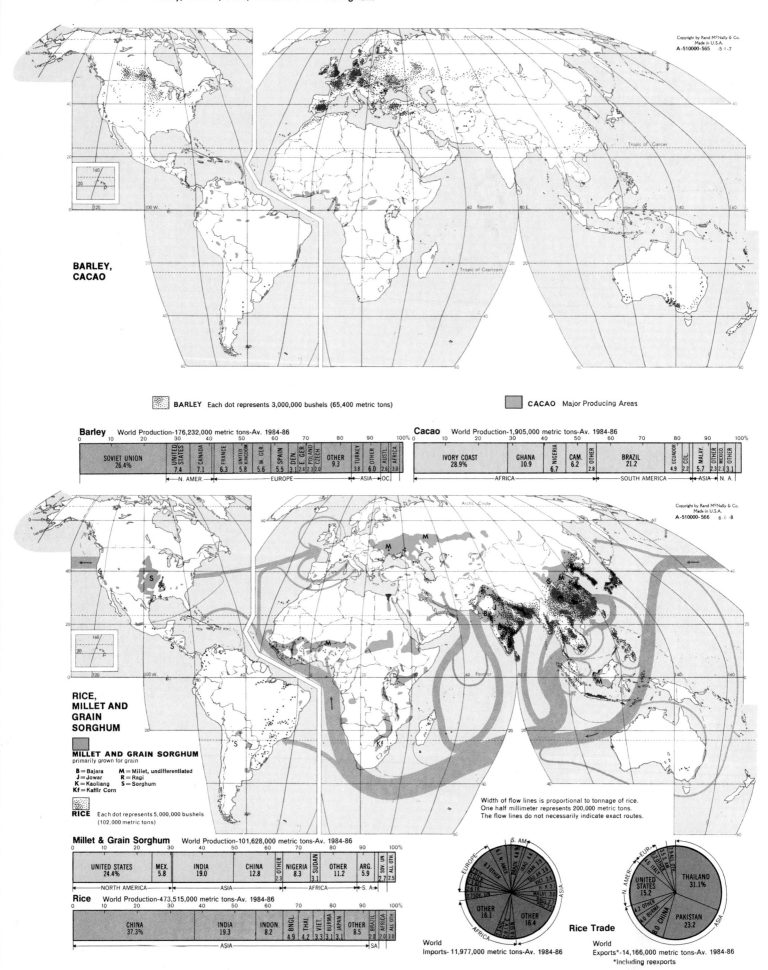

Copyright by Rand McNally & Co.
Made in U.S.A.
A-510000-565 -5-4-7

**BARLEY,
CACAO**

BARLEY Each dot represents 3,000,000 bushels (65,400 metric tons)

CACAO Major Producing Areas

Barley World Production-176,232,000 metric tons-Av. 1984-86

SOVIET UNION 26.4%	UNITED STATES 7.4	CANADA 7.1	FRANCE 6.3	UNITED KINGDOM 5.8	W. GER. 5.6	SPAIN 5.5	DEN. 3.1	E. GER. 2.4	POLAND 2.3	CZECH 2.3	OTHER 9.3	TURKEY 3.8	OTHER 6.0	AUSTL. 2.6	AFRICA 3.0

N. AMER. — EUROPE — ASIA — OC

Cacao World Production-1,905,000 metric tons-Av. 1984-86

IVORY COAST 28.9%	GHANA 10.9	NIGERIA 6.7	CAM. 6.2	OTHER 2.8	BRAZIL 21.2	ECUADOR 4.9	COL. 2.2	MALAY. 5.7	OTHER MEXICO 2.d	OTHER 3.1

AFRICA — SOUTH AMERICA — ASIA — N. A.

Copyright by Rand McNally & Co.
Made in U.S.A.
A-510000-566 6-6-8

**RICE,
MILLET AND
GRAIN
SORGHUM**

MILLET AND GRAIN SORGHUM
primarily grown for grain

B = Bajara   M = Millet, undifferentiated
J = Jowar   R = Ragi
K = Kaoliang   S = Sorghum
Kf = Kaffir Corn

RICE Each dot represents 5,000,000 bushels
(102,000 metric tons)

Width of flow lines is proportional to tonnage of rice.
One half millimeter represents 200,000 metric tons.
The flow lines do not necessarily indicate exact routes.

Millet & Grain Sorghum World Production-101,628,000 metric tons-Av. 1984-86

UNITED STATES 24.4%	MEX. 5.8	INDIA 19.0	CHINA 12.8	OTHER 2.3	NIGERIA 8.3	SUDAN 3.1	OTHER 11.2	ARG. 5.9	SOV UN 2.7 ALL OTH

NORTH AMERICA — ASIA — AFRICA — S. A.

Rice World Production-473,515,000 metric tons-Av. 1984-86

CHINA 37.3%	INDIA 19.3	INDON. 8.2	BNGL. 4.9	THAI. 4.2	VIET. 3.3	BURMA 3.1	JAPAN 3.1	OTHER 8.5	BRAZIL 2.0 AFRICA 2.0 ALL OTH 3.0

ASIA — SA

Rice Trade

World
Imports- 11,977,000 metric tons-Av. 1984-86

World
Exports*-14,166,000 metric tons-Av. 1984-86
*Including reexports

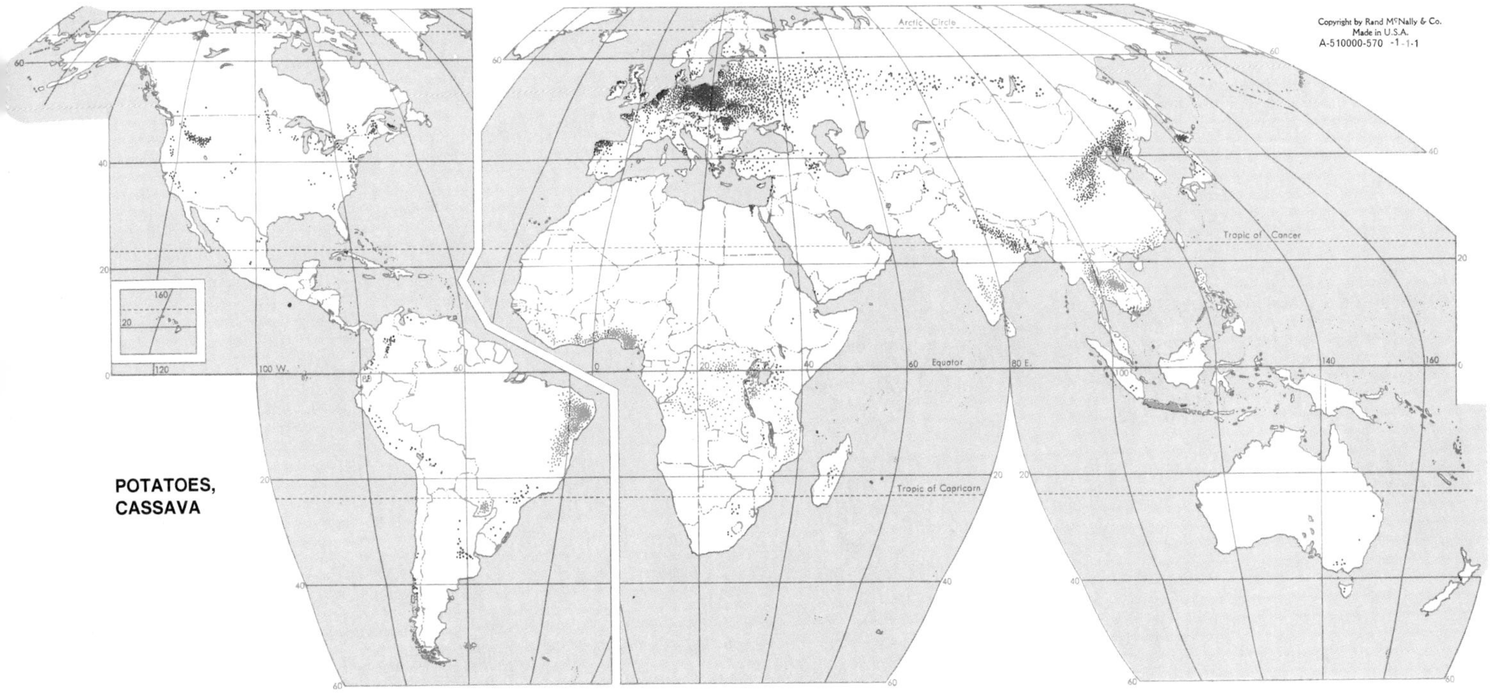
POTATOES,
CASSAVA
Arctic Circle
Tropic of Cancer
Equator
Tropic of Capricorn
100 W.
80 E.
Copyright by Rand McNally & Co.
Made in U.S.A.
A-510000-570 -1-1-1

POTATOES Each dot represents 100,000 metric tons

CASSAVA Each dot represents 100,000 metric tons

Potatoes World Production-306,984,000 metric tons-Av. 1984-86

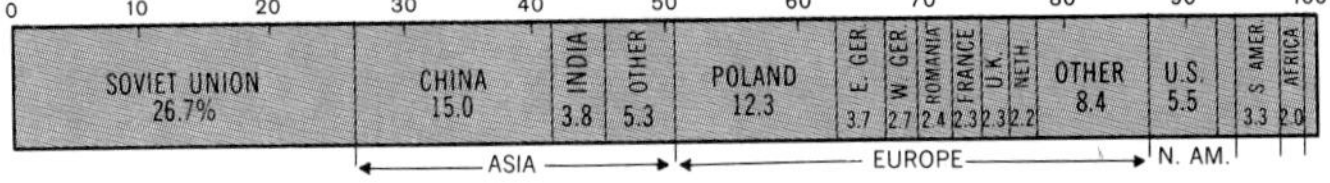
0 10 20 30 40 50 60 70 80 90 100%
SOVIET UNION 26.7%
CHINA 15.0
INDIA 3.8
OTHER 5.3
POLAND 12.3
E. GER. 3.7
W. GER. 2.7
ROMANIA 2.4
FRANCE 2.3
U.K. 2.3
NETH. 2.2
OTHER 8.4
U.S. 5.5
S. AMER. 3.3
AFRICA 2.0
ASIA
EUROPE
N. AM.

Cassava World Production-134,869,000 metric tons-Av. 1984-86

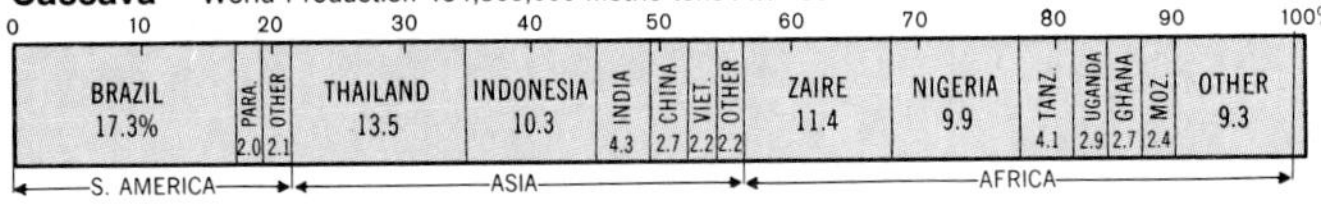
0 10 20 30 40 50 60 70 80 90 100%
BRAZIL 17.3%
PARA. 2.0
OTHER 2.1
THAILAND 13.5
INDONESIA 10.3
INDIA 4.3
CHINA 2.7
VIET. 2.2
OTHER 2.2
ZAIRE 11.4
NIGERIA 9.9
TANZ. 4.1
UGANDA 2.9
GHANA 2.7
MOZ. 2.4
OTHER 9.3
S. AMERICA
ASIA
AFRICA

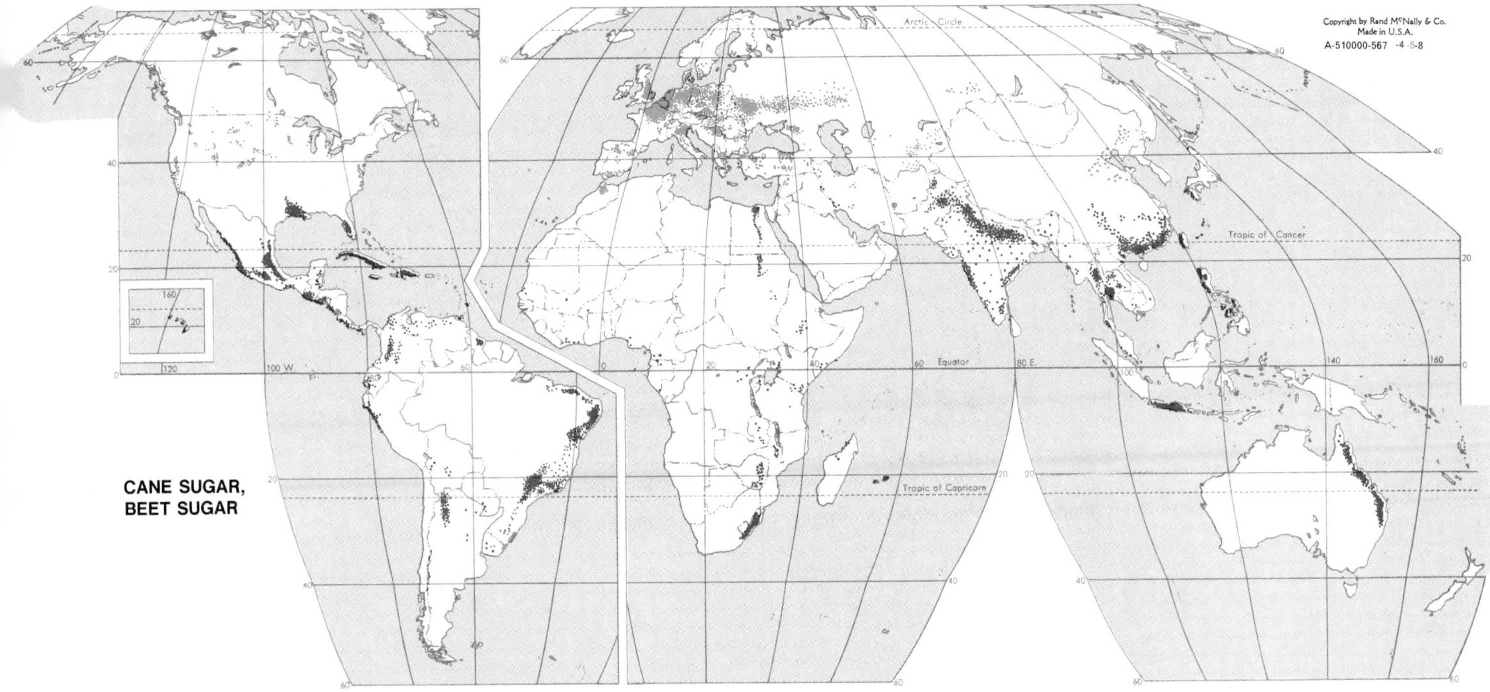
CANE SUGAR,
BEET SUGAR
Arctic Circle
Tropic of Cancer
Equator
Tropic of Capricorn
100 W.
80 E.
Copyright by Rand McNally & Co.
Made in U.S.A.
A-510000-567 -4-5-8

CANE SUGAR Each dot represents 20,000 metric tons

BEET SUGAR Each dot represents 20,000 metric tons

Cane Sugar World Production- 61,955,000 metric tons-Av. 1984-86

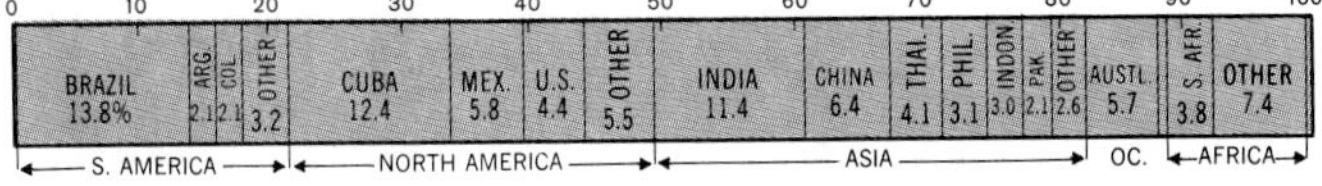
0 10 20 30 40 50 60 70 80 90 100%
BRAZIL 13.8%
ARG. 2.1
COL. 2.1
OTHER 3.2
CUBA 12.4
MEX. 5.8
U.S. 4.4
OTHER 5.5
INDIA 11.4
CHINA 6.4
THAI. 4.1
PHIL. 3.1
INDON. 3.0
PAK. 2.1
OTHER 2.6
AUSTL. 5.7
S. AFR. 3.8
OTHER 7.4
S. AMERICA
NORTH AMERICA
ASIA
OC.
AFRICA

Beet Sugar World Production-37,347,000 metric tons-Av. 1984-86

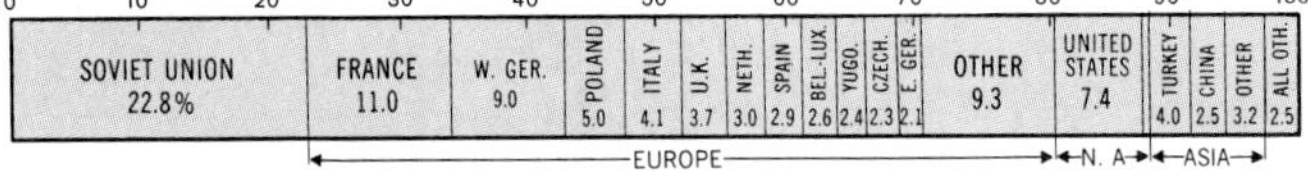
0 10 20 30 40 50 60 70 80 90 100%
SOVIET UNION 22.8%
FRANCE 11.0
W. GER. 9.0
POLAND 5.0
ITALY 4.1
U.K. 3.7
NETH. 3.0
SPAIN 2.9
BEL.-LUX. 2.6
YUGO. 2.4
CZECH. 2.3
E. GER. 2.1
OTHER 9.3
UNITED STATES 7.4
TURKEY 4.0
CHINA 2.5
OTHER 3.2
ALL OTH. 2.5
EUROPE
N. A
ASIA

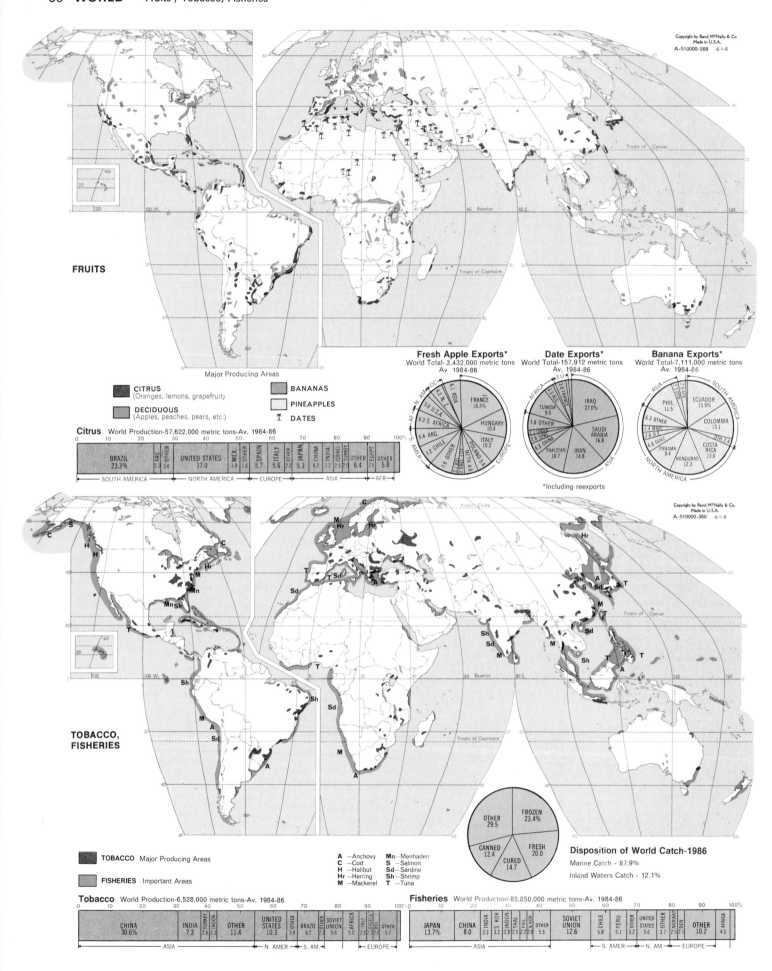

FRUITS

Major Producing Areas

CITRUS
(Oranges, lemons, grapefruit)

DECIDUOUS
(Apples, peaches, pears, etc.)

BANANAS

PINEAPPLES

DATES

Citrus World Production–57,622,000 metric tons–Av. 1984-86

BRAZIL 23.3%	ARG. 2.3	OTHER 3.6	UNITED STATES 17.0	MEX. 3.9	OTHER 2.6	SPAIN 5.7	ITALY 5.6	JAPAN 5.3	CHINA 4.2	INDIA 3.3	ISRAEL 2.0	TURKEY 2.0	OTHER 6.4	EGYPT	OTHER 5.8

SOUTH AMERICA — NORTH AMERICA — EUROPE — ASIA — AFR.

Fresh Apple Exports*
World Total- 3,432,000 metric tons
Av. 1984-86

FRANCE 18.3%
HUNGARY 10.4
ITALY 10.2
POLAND 5.4
NETH. 4.8
OTHER
BUL.
7.6 OTHER
7.2 CHILE
6.4 ARG.
6.3 S. AFRICA
5.8 U.S.A.
4.2 N.Z.
6.1 ASIA

Date Exports*
World Total-157,912 metric tons
Av. 1984-86

IRAQ 22.0%
SAUDI ARABIA 16.8
IRAN 14.8
PAKISTAN 10.7
CHINA 4.3
SYRIA 2.8
OMAN 2.9
OTHER 5.8
TUNISIA 9.6
ALG. 3.5
FRANCE 3.8

Banana Exports*
World Total-7,111,000 metric tons
Av. 1984-86

ECUADOR 15.9%
COLOMBIA 13.1
COSTA RICA 13.0
OTH. 2.4
HONDURAS 12.3
PANAMA 9.4
GUAT. 4.8
U.S. 2.6
MART. 2.4
PHIL. 11.5
OTHER 6.3

*Including reexports

TOBACCO, FISHERIES

TOBACCO Major Producing Areas

FISHERIES Important Areas

A —Anchovy
C —Cod
H —Halibut
Hr —Herring
M —Mackerel
Mn —Menhaden
S —Salmon
Sd —Sardine
Sh —Shrimp
T —Tuna

FROZEN 23.4%
OTHER 29.5
CANNED 12.4
CURED 14.7
FRESH 20.0

Disposition of World Catch-1986

Marine Catch - 87.9%

Inland Waters Catch - 12.1%

Tobacco World Production–6,528,000 metric tons–Av. 1984-86

CHINA 30.6%	INDIA 7.3	TURKEY 2.6	INDON. 2.3	OTHER 11.4	UNITED STATES 10.3	OTHER 3.4	BRAZIL 6.2	SOVIET UNION 5.6	AFRICA 5.0	GREECE 3.2	BUL.	OTHER 5.7

ASIA — N. AMER.— S. AM.— EUROPE

Fisheries World Production–85,850,000 metric tons–Av. 1984-86

JAPAN 13.7%	CHINA 8.0	INDIA 3.3	S. KOR 3.2	INDON. 2.8	THAI. 2.2	N. KOR 2.0	OTHER 5.5	SOVIET UNION 12.6	CHILE 5.8	PERU 5.1	OTHER 3.2	UNITED STATES 5.6	OTHER 3.7	NORWAY 2.5	DEN. 2.1	OTHER 10.2	AFRICA 4.5

ASIA — S. AMER.— N. AM.— EUROPE

Copyright by Rand McNally & Co.
Made in U.S.A.
A-510000-569 -6-4-8

Copyright by Rand McNally & Co.
Made in U.S.A.
A-510000-360 -6-5-8

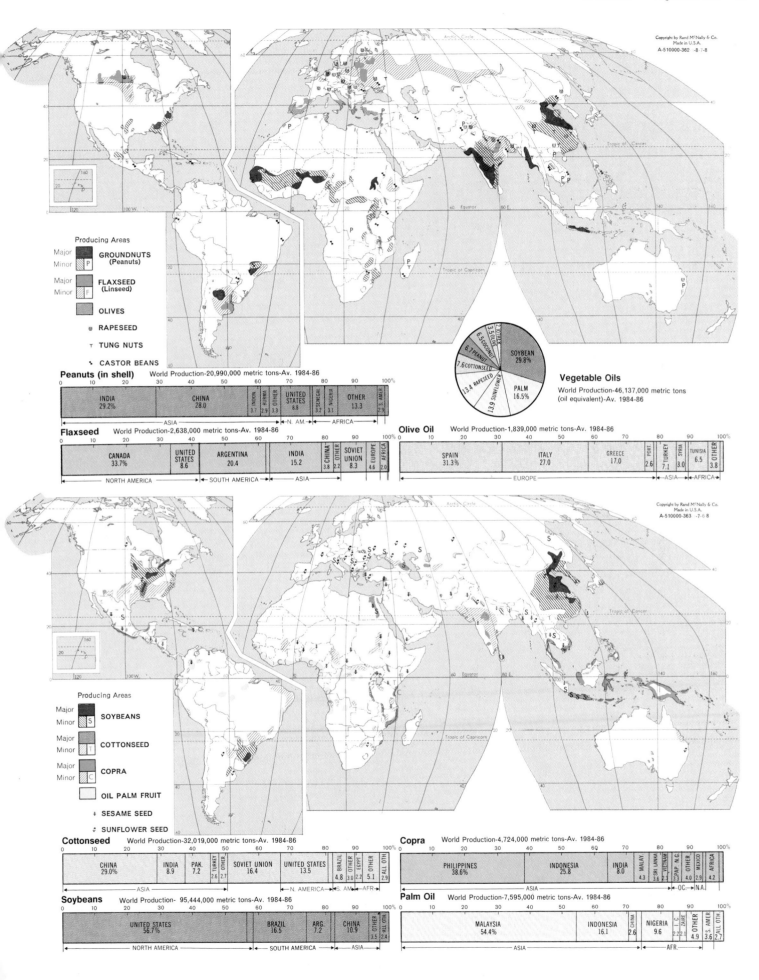

Copyright by Rand McNally & Co.
Made in U.S.A.
A-510000-362 -8-7-8

Producing Areas

Major / Minor GROUNDNUTS (Peanuts) — P

Major / Minor FLAXSEED (Linseed) — F

OLIVES

ᵚ RAPESEED

ᴛ TUNG NUTS

⚹ CASTOR BEANS

Vegetable Oils

World Production-46,137,000 metric tons
(oil equivalent)-Av. 1984-86

Pie chart: SOYBEAN 29.8%, PALM 16.5%, 13.9 SUNFLOWER, 13.4 RAPESEED, 7.6 COTTONSEED, 6.7 PEANUT, 6.5 COCONUT, 3.5 OLIVE, 2.0 OTHER

Peanuts (in shell)   World Production-20,990,000 metric tons-Av. 1984-86

| 0 | 10 | 20 | 30 | 40 | 50 | 60 | 70 | 80 | 90 | 100% |

| INDIA 29.2% | CHINA 28.0 | INDIA 3.7 | BURMA 2.9 | OTHER 3.3 | UNITED STATES 8.8 | SENEGAL 3.2 | NIGERIA 3.1 | OTHER 13.3 | S. AMER. 2.9 |

ASIA — N. AM. — AFRICA

Flaxseed   World Production-2,638,000 metric tons-Av. 1984-86

| 0 | 10 | 20 | 30 | 40 | 50 | 60 | 70 | 80 | 90 | 100% |

| CANADA 33.7% | UNITED STATES 8.6 | ARGENTINA 20.4 | INDIA 15.2 | CHINA 3.8 | SOVIET UNION 8.3 | EUROPE 4.6 | AFRICA 2.0 |

NORTH AMERICA — SOUTH AMERICA — ASIA

Olive Oil   World Production-1,839,000 metric tons-Av. 1984-86

| 0 | 10 | 20 | 30 | 40 | 50 | 60 | 70 | 80 | 90 | 100% |

| SPAIN 31.3% | ITALY 27.0 | GREECE 17.0 | PORT. 2.6 | TURKEY 7.1 | SYRIA 3.0 | TUNISIA 6.5 | OTHER 3.8 |

EUROPE — ASIA — AFRICA

Copyright by Rand McNally & Co.
Made in U.S.A.
A-510000-363 -7-6-8

Producing Areas

Major / Minor SOYBEANS — S

Major / Minor COTTONSEED — T

Major / Minor COPRA — C

OIL PALM FRUIT

⚵ SESAME SEED

☙ SUNFLOWER SEED

Cottonseed   World Production-32,019,000 metric tons-Av. 1984-86

| 0 | 10 | 20 | 30 | 40 | 50 | 60 | 70 | 80 | 90 | 100% |

| CHINA 29.0% | INDIA 8.9 | PAK. 7.2 | TURKEY 2.6 | OTHER 2.7 | SOVIET UNION 16.4 | UNITED STATES 13.5 | BRAZIL 4.8 | EGYPT 3.0 | OTHER 5.1 | ALL OTH 2.9 |

ASIA — N. AMERICA — S. AM. — AFR.

Copra   World Production-4,724,000 metric tons-Av. 1984-86

| 0 | 10 | 20 | 30 | 40 | 50 | 60 | 70 | 80 | 90 | 100% |

| PHILIPPINES 38.6% | INDONESIA 25.8 | INDIA 8.0 | MALAY. 4.3 | SRI LANKA 3.6 | VIETNAM 4.2 | PAP. N.G. 4.0 | MEXICO 2.9 | AFRICA 4.2 |

ASIA — OC. — N.A.

Soybeans   World Production- 95,444,000 metric tons-Av. 1984-86

| 0 | 10 | 20 | 30 | 40 | 50 | 60 | 70 | 80 | 90 | 100% |

| UNITED STATES 56.7% | BRAZIL 16.5 | ARG. 7.2 | CHINA 10.9 | OTHER 3.5 | ALL OTH 2.4 |

NORTH AMERICA — SOUTH AMERICA — ASIA

Palm Oil   World Production-7,595,000 metric tons-Av. 1984-86

| 0 | 10 | 20 | 30 | 40 | 50 | 60 | 70 | 80 | 90 | 100% |

| MALAYSIA 54.4% | INDONESIA 16.1 | CHINA 2.6 | NIGERIA 9.6 | I.C. 2.2 | ZAIRE 2.1 | OTHER 4.9 | S. AMER. 3.6 | ALL OTH 2.7 |

ASIA — AFR.

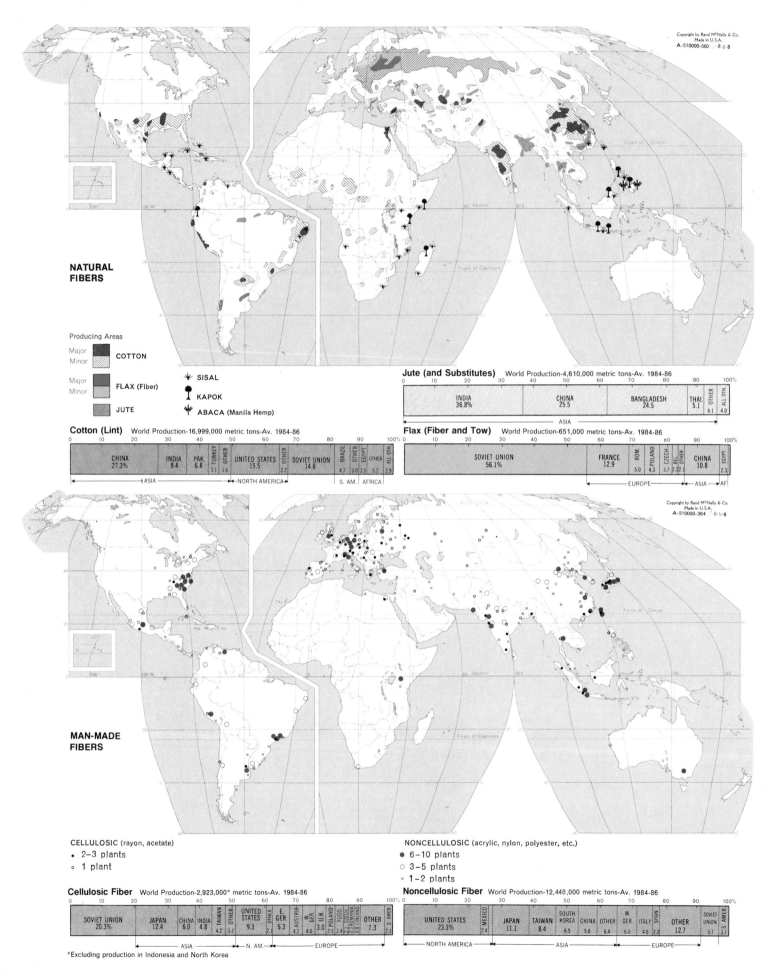

Copyright by Rand McNally & Co.
Made in U.S.A.
A-510000-560 · 8·8·8

NATURAL FIBERS

Producing Areas

Major		COTTON
Minor		
Major		FLAX (Fiber)
Minor		
		JUTE

SISAL
KAPOK
ABACA (Manila Hemp)

Jute (and Substitutes) • World Production-4,610,000 metric tons-Av. 1984-86

0	10	20	30	40	50	60	70	80	90	100%

INDIA 36.8%	CHINA 25.5	BANGLADESH 24.5	THAI. 5.1	OTHER 4.1	ALL OTH. 4.0

ASIA

Cotton (Lint) • World Production-16,999,000 metric tons-Av. 1984-86

0	10	20	30	40	50	60	70	80	90	100%

CHINA 27.3%	INDIA 8.4	PAK. 6.8	TURKEY 3.1	OTHER 3.6	UNITED STATES 15.5	OTHER 2.2	SOVIET UNION 14.8	BRAZIL 4.7	OTHER 3.0	EGYPT 2.5	OTHER 5.2	ALL OTH 2.9

ASIA — NORTH AMERICA — S. AM. AFRICA

Flax (Fiber and Tow) • World Production-651,000 metric tons-Av. 1984-86

0	10	20	30	40	50	60	70	80	90	100%

SOVIET UNION 56.1%	FRANCE 12.9	ROM. 5.0	POLAND 4.3	CZECH. 3.7	BEL. 2.2	OTHER 2.1	CHINA 10.8	EGYPT 2.3

EUROPE — ASIA — AF

Copyright by Rand McNally & Co.
Made in U.S.A.
A-510000-364 · 6·5·8

MAN-MADE FIBERS

CELLULOSIC (rayon, acetate)
- • 2–3 plants
- ○ 1 plant

NONCELLULOSIC (acrylic, nylon, polyester, etc.)
- ● 6–10 plants
- ○ 3–5 plants
- × 1–2 plants

Cellulosic Fiber • World Production-2,923,000* metric tons-Av. 1984-86

0	10	20	30	40	50	60	70	80	90	100%

SOVIET UNION 20.3%	JAPAN 12.4	CHINA 6.0	INDIA 4.8	TAIWAN 4.2	OTHER 3.2	UNITED STATES 9.3	OTHER 2.1	E. GER. 5.3	AUSTRIA 4.2	W. GER. 4.0	U.K. 3.0	POLAND 2.5	CZECH. 2.1	FINLAND 7.0	OTHER 7.3	S. AMER. 2.3

ASIA — N. AM. — EUROPE

Noncellulosic Fiber • World Production-12,448,000 metric tons-Av. 1984-86

0	10	20	30	40	50	60	70	80	90	100%

UNITED STATES 23.3%	MEXICO 2.4	JAPAN 11.1	TAIWAN 8.4	SOUTH KOREA 6.5	CHINA 5.6	OTHER 6.4	W. GER. 6.0	ITALY 4.5	SPAIN 2.2	OTHER 12.7	SOVIET UNION 5.7	S. AMER. 3.1

NORTH AMERICA — ASIA — EUROPE

*Excluding production in Indonesia and North Korea

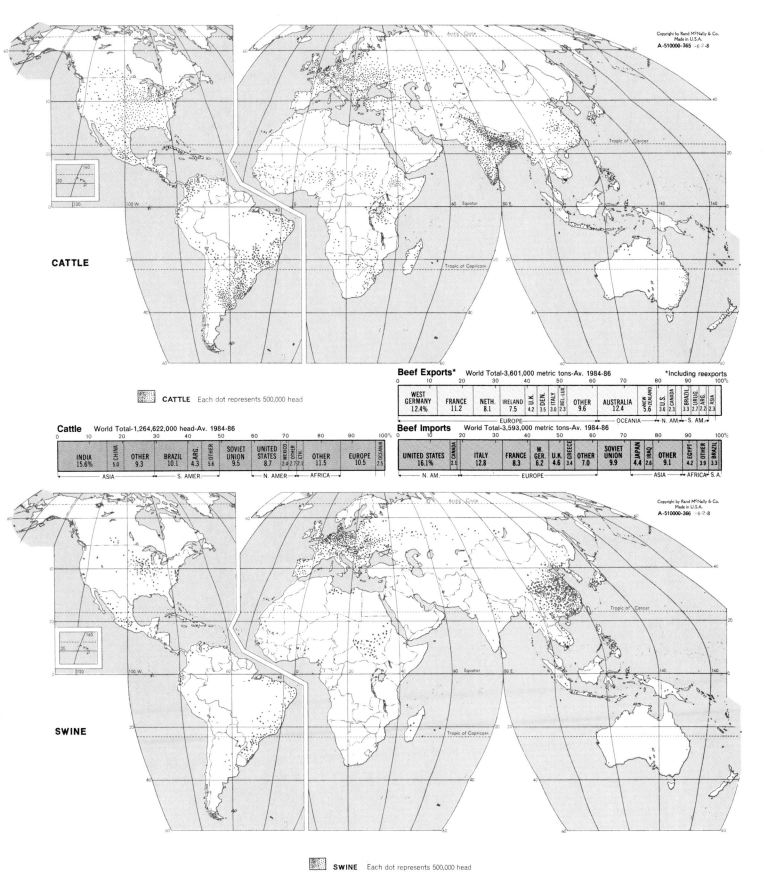

Copyright by Rand McNally & Co.
Made in U.S.A.
A-510000-365 -6-2-8

CATTLE

⬛ **CATTLE** Each dot represents 500,000 head

Cattle World Total-1,264,622,000 head-Av. 1984-86

0	10	20	30	40	50	60	70	80	90	100%
INDIA 15.6%	CHINA 5.0	OTHER 9.3	BRAZIL 10.1	ARG. 4.3	OTHER 5.6	SOVIET UNION 9.5	UNITED STATES 8.7	MEXICO 2.4 / OTHER 2.7 / ETH. 2.1	OTHER 11.5	EUROPE 10.5 / OCEANIA 2.5

‹— ASIA —› ‹—— S. AMER. ——› ‹— N. AMER. —› ‹— AFRICA —›

Beef Exports* World Total-3,601,000 metric tons-Av. 1984-86   *Including reexports

0	10	20	30	40	50	60	70	80	90	100%
WEST GERMANY 12.4%	FRANCE 11.2	NETH. 8.1	IRELAND 7.5	U.K. 4.2	DEN. 3.5	ITALY 3.0	BEL-LUX. 2.3	OTHER 9.6	AUSTRALIA 12.4	NEW ZEALAND 5.6 / U.S. 3.6 / CANADA 2.3 / BRAZIL 3.3 / URUG. 2.7 / ARG. 2.2 / ASIA 2.3

‹———————————— EUROPE ————————————› ‹— OCEANIA —› ‹N. AM.› ‹S. AM.›

Beef Imports World Total-3,593,000 metric tons-Av. 1984-86

0	10	20	30	40	50	60	70	80	90	100%
UNITED STATES 16.1%	CANADA 2.1	ITALY 12.8	FRANCE 8.3	W. GER. 6.2	U.K. 4.6	GREECE 3.4	OTHER 7.0	SOVIET UNION 9.9	JAPAN 4.4 / IRAQ 2.6	OTHER 9.1	EGYPT 4.2 / OTHER 3.9 / BRAZIL 3.3

‹— N. AM. —› ‹———————— EUROPE ————————› ‹— ASIA —› ‹AFRICA› ‹S.A.›

Copyright by Rand McNally & Co.
Made in U.S.A.
A-510000-366 -6-2-8

SWINE

⬛ **SWINE** Each dot represents 500,000 head

Swine World Total-834,168,000 head-Av. 1984-86

0	10	20	30	40	50	60	70	80	90	100%
CHINA 38.5%	OTHER 7.7	SOVIET UNION 9.4	U.S. 6.5	MEXICO 2.3 / OTHER 2.4	BRAZIL 3.9	OTHER 2.3 / W. GER. 2.9 / POLAND 2.1	OTHER 16.4	SUDAN 2.4 / OTHER 2.3

‹———————————— ASIA ————————————› ‹— N. AM. —› ‹S. A.› ‹—— EUROPE ——› ‹AFR.›

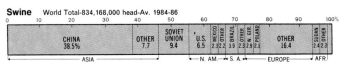

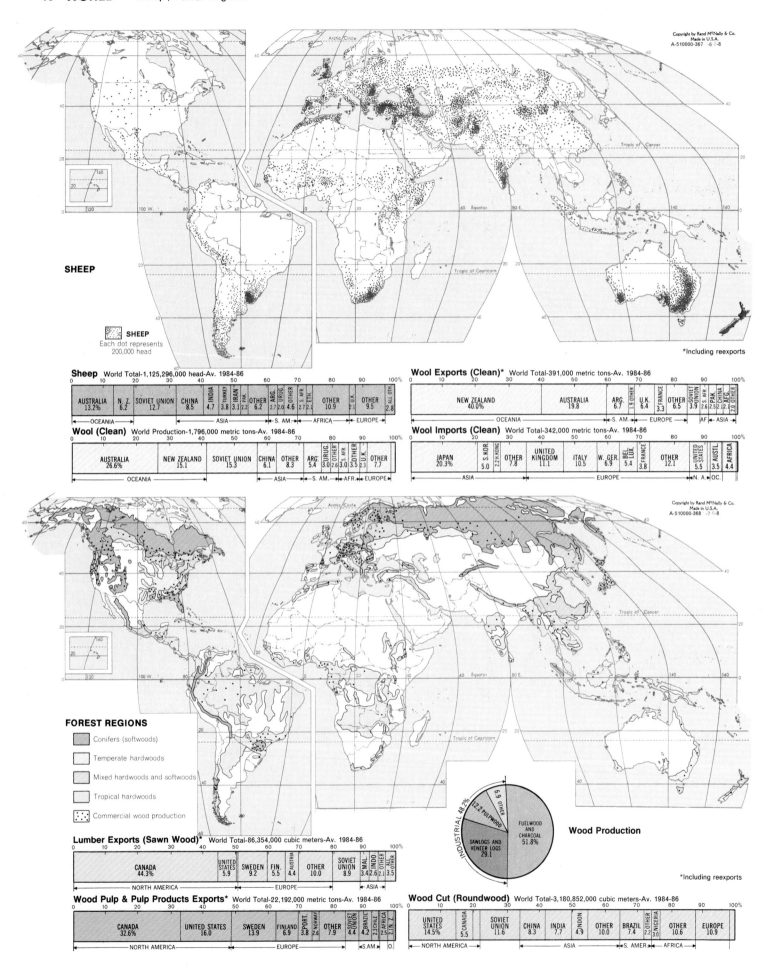

SHEEP

SHEEP
Each dot represents
200,000 head

*Including reexports

Sheep World Total-1,125,296,000 head-Av. 1984-86

AUSTRALIA 13.2%	N. Z. 6.2	SOVIET UNION 12.7	CHINA 8.5	INDIA 4.7	TURKEY 3.8	IRAN 3.1	PAK. 2.2	OTHER 6.2	ARG. 2.7	URUG. 2.0	OTHER 4.6	S. AFR. 2.7	ETH. 2.1	OTHER 10.9	U.K. 2.1	OTHER 9.5	ALL OTH. 2.8

OCEANIA — ASIA — S. AM. — AFRICA — EUROPE

Wool (Clean) World Production-1,796,000 metric tons-Av. 1984-86

AUSTRALIA 26.6%	NEW ZEALAND 15.1	SOVIET UNION 15.3	CHINA 6.1	OTHER 8.3	ARG. 5.4	URUG. 3.0	OTHER 2.6	S. AFR. 3.0	OTHER 3.5	U.K. 2.3	OTHER 7.7

OCEANIA — ASIA — S. AM. — AFR. — EUROPE

Wool Exports (Clean)* World Total-391,000 metric tons-Av. 1984-86

NEW ZEALAND 40.0%	AUSTRALIA 19.8	ARG. 6.7	OTHER 1.9	U.K. 6.4	FRANCE 3.3	OTHER 6.5	SOVIET UNION 3.9	S. AFR. 2.6	PAK. 2.5	CHINA 2.1	AFG. 2.1	OTHER 2.0

OCEANIA — S. AM. — EUROPE — AF. — ASIA

Wool Imports (Clean) World Total-342,000 metric tons-Av. 1984-86

JAPAN 20.3%	S. KOR. 5.0	H. KONG 2.2	OTHER 7.8	UNITED KINGDOM 11.1	ITALY 10.5	W. GER. 6.9	BEL. LUX. 5.4	FRANCE 3.8	OTHER 12.1	UNITED STATES 5.5	AUSTL 3.5	AFRICA 4.4

ASIA — EUROPE — N. A. — OC.

FOREST REGIONS

- Conifers (softwoods)
- Temperate hardwoods
- Mixed hardwoods and softwoods
- Tropical hardwoods
- Commercial wood production

Wood Production

INDUSTRIAL 48.2%
6.9 OTHER
12.2 PULPWOOD
SAWLOGS AND VENEER LOGS 29.1
FUELWOOD AND CHARCOAL 51.8%

*Including reexports

Lumber Exports (Sawn Wood)* World Total-86,354,000 cubic meters-Av. 1984-86

CANADA 44.3%	UNITED STATES 5.9	SWEDEN 9.2	FIN. 5.5	AUSTRIA 4.4	OTHER 10.0	SOVIET UNION 8.9	MAL. 3.4	INDO. 2.6	OTHER 2.1	ALL OTHER 3.5

NORTH AMERICA — EUROPE — ASIA

Wood Pulp & Pulp Products Exports* World Total-22,192,000 metric tons-Av. 1984-86

CANADA 32.6%	UNITED STATES 16.0	SWEDEN 13.9	FINLAND 6.9	PORT. 3.8	NORWAY 2.6	OTHER 7.9	SOVIET UNION 4.4	BRAZIL 4.2	CHILE 2.3	AFRICA 2.1	N. Z. 2.1

NORTH AMERICA — EUROPE — S.AM. — O.

Wood Cut (Roundwood) World Total-3,180,852,000 cubic meters-Av. 1984-86

UNITED STATES 14.5%	CANADA 5.5	SOVIET UNION 11.6	CHINA 8.3	INDIA 7.7	INDON. 4.9	OTHER 10.0	BRAZIL 7.4	NIGERIA 3.0	OTHER 2.2	OTHER 10.6	EUROPE 10.9

NORTH AMERICA — ASIA — S. AMER. — AFRICA

Copyright by Rand McNally & Co.
Made in U.S.A.
A-510000-367 -6-2-8

Copyright by Rand McNally & Co.
Made in U.S.A.
A-510000-368 -7-6-8

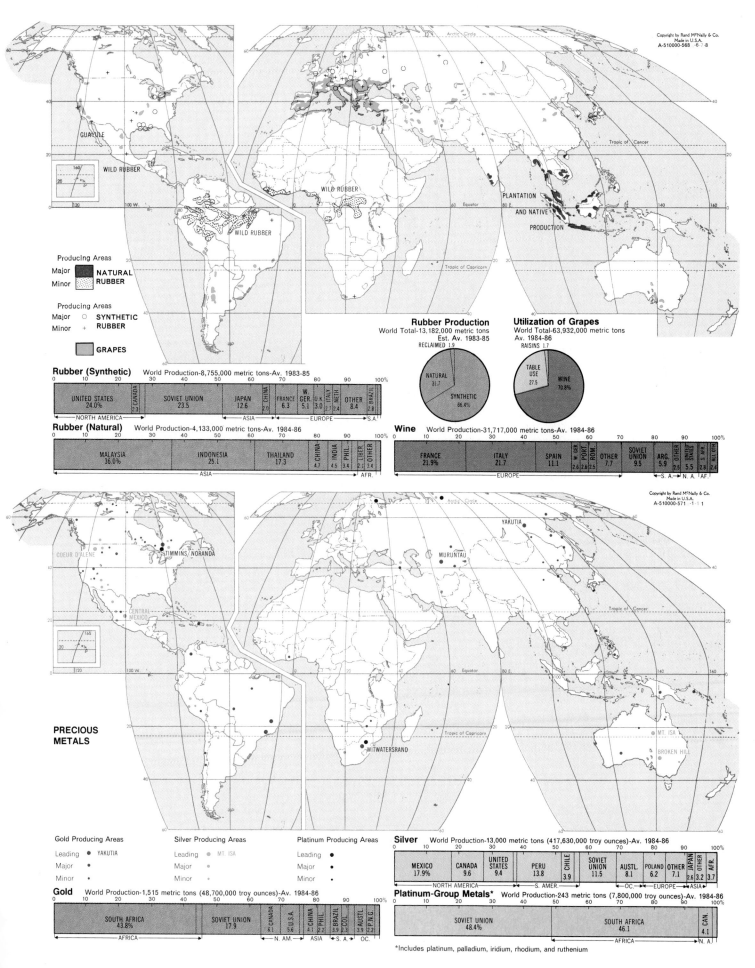

Copyright by Rand McNally & Co.
Made in U.S.A.
A-510000-568 -6-7-8

GUAYULE

WILD RUBBER

WILD RUBBER

WILD RUBBER

PLANTATION
AND NATIVE
PRODUCTION

Producing Areas
Major NATURAL
Minor RUBBER

Producing Areas
Major ○ SYNTHETIC
Minor + RUBBER

GRAPES

Rubber Production
World Total-13,182,000 metric tons
Est. Av. 1983-85
RECLAIMED 1.9
NATURAL 31.7
SYNTHETIC 66.4%

Utilization of Grapes
World Total-63,932,000 metric tons
Av. 1984-86
RAISINS 1.7
TABLE USE 27.5
WINE 70.8%

Rubber (Synthetic)
World Production-8,755,000 metric tons-Av. 1983-85

UNITED STATES 24.0%	CANADA 2.3	SOVIET UNION 23.5	JAPAN 12.6	CHINA 2.0	FRANCE 6.3	W. GER. 5.1	U.K. 3.0	ITALY 2.7	NETH. 2.1	OTHER 8.4	BRAZIL 2.8

NORTH AMERICA — ASIA — EUROPE — S.A.

Rubber (Natural)
World Production-4,133,000 metric tons-Av. 1984-86

MALAYSIA 36.0%	INDONESIA 25.1	THAILAND 17.3	CHINA 4.7	INDIA 4.5	PHIL. 3.4	LIBER. 3.4	OTHER

ASIA — AFR.

Wine
World Production-31,717,000 metric tons-Av. 1984-86

FRANCE 21.9%	ITALY 21.7	SPAIN 11.1	W. GER. 2.6	PORT. 2.6	ROM. 2.5	OTHER 7.7	SOVIET UNION 9.5	ARG. 5.9	OTHER	UNITED STATES 5.5	S. AFR. 2.8	ALL OTH. 2.4

EUROPE — S.A. — N.A. — AF.

Copyright by Rand McNally & Co.
Made in U.S.A.
A-510000-571 -1-1-1

YAKUTIA

COEUR D'ALENE

TIMMINS/NORANDA

MURUNTAU

CENTRAL
MEXICO

MT. ISA

BROKEN HILL

WITWATERSRAND

PRECIOUS
METALS

Gold Producing Areas
Leading ● YAKUTIA
Major ●
Minor ·

Silver Producing Areas
Leading ● MT. ISA
Major ●
Minor ·

Platinum Producing Areas
Leading ●
Major ●
Minor ·

Silver
World Production-13,000 metric tons (417,630,000 troy ounces)-Av. 1984-86

MEXICO 17.9%	CANADA 9.6	UNITED STATES 9.4	PERU 13.8	CHILE 3.9	SOVIET UNION 11.5	AUSTL. 8.1	POLAND 6.2	OTHER 7.1	JAPAN 2.6	OTHER 3.2	AFR. 3.7

NORTH AMERICA — S. AMER. — OC. — EUROPE — ASIA

Gold
World Production-1,515 metric tons (48,700,000 troy ounces)-Av. 1984-86

SOUTH AFRICA 43.8%	SOVIET UNION 17.9	CANADA 6.1	U.S.A. 5.6	CHINA 3.9	PHIL. 2.2	BRAZIL 2.3	COL. 3.9	AUSTL. 3.9	P.N.G. 2.2

AFRICA — N. AM. — ASIA — S. A. — OC.

Platinum-Group Metals*
World Production-243 metric tons (7,800,000 troy ounces)-Av. 1984-86

SOVIET UNION 48.4%	SOUTH AFRICA 46.1	CAN. 4.1

AFRICA — N. A.

*Includes platinum, palladium, iridium, rhodium, and ruthenium

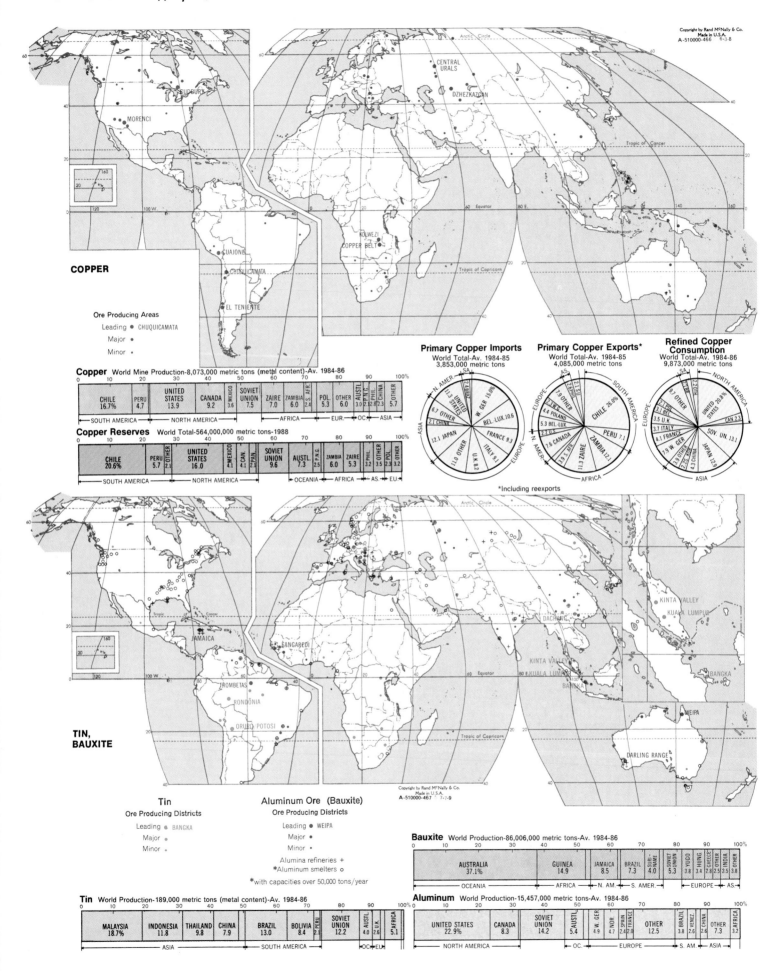

COPPER

Ore Producing Areas
- Leading ● CHUQUICAMATA
- Major ●
- Minor ・

Copper World Mine Production-8,073,000 metric tons (metal content)-Av. 1984-86

CHILE 16.7%	PERU 4.7	UNITED STATES 13.9	CANADA 9.2	MEXICO 3.6	SOVIET UNION 7.5	ZAIRE 7.0	ZAMBIA 6.0	S. AFR. 2.4	POL. 5.3	OTHER 6.0	AUSTL. 3.0	P.N.G. 2.8	CHINA 2.3	OTHER 5.7
SOUTH AMERICA		NORTH AMERICA				AFRICA			EUR.		OC.	ASIA		

Copper Reserves World Total-564,000,000 metric tons-1988

CHILE 20.6%	PERU 5.7	OTHER 2.1	UNITED STATES 16.0	MEXICO 4.1	CAN. 4.1	JAPAN 2.1	SOVIET UNION 9.6	AUSTL. 7.3	P.N.G. 2.5	ZAMBIA 6.0	ZAIRE 5.3	PHIL. 3.2	OTHER 3.5	POL. 2.3	EU. 3.2
SOUTH AMERICA			NORTH AMERICA					OCEANIA		AFRICA		AS.		EU.	

Primary Copper Imports
World Total-Av. 1984-85
3,853,000 metric tons

Primary Copper Exports*
World Total-Av. 1984-85
4,085,000 metric tons

Refined Copper Consumption
World Total-Av. 1984-86
9,873,000 metric tons

*Including reexports

TIN, BAUXITE

Tin
Ore Producing Districts
- Leading ● BANGKA
- Major ●
- Minor ・

Aluminum Ore (Bauxite)
Ore Producing Districts
- Leading ● WEIPA
- Major ●
- Minor ・
- Alumina refineries +
- *Aluminum smelters ○

*with capacities over 50,000 tons/year

Bauxite World Production-86,006,000 metric tons-Av. 1984-86

AUSTRALIA 37.1%	GUINEA 14.9	JAMAICA 8.5	BRAZIL 7.3	SURI-NAME 4.0	SOVIET UNION 5.3	YUGO. 3.8	HUNG. 3.4	GREECE 2.8	OTHER 2.5	INDIA 2.5	OTHER 3.8
OCEANIA	AFRICA	N. AM.	S. AMER.		EUROPE					AS.	

Tin World Production-189,000 metric tons (metal content)-Av. 1984-86

MALAYSIA 18.7%	INDONESIA 11.8	THAILAND 9.8	CHINA 7.9	BRAZIL 13.0	BOLIVIA 8.4	PERU 2.1	SOVIET UNION 12.2	AUSTL. 4.0	U.K. 2.6	AFRICA 5.1
ASIA				SOUTH AMERICA				OC.	EU.	

Aluminum World Production-15,457,000 metric tons-Av. 1984-86

UNITED STATES 22.9%	CANADA 8.3	SOVIET UNION 14.2	AUSTL. 5.4	W. GER. 4.9	NOR. 4.7	SPAIN 2.4	FRANCE 2.0	OTHER 12.5	BRAZIL 3.8	VENEZ. 2.6	CHINA 2.6	OTHER 7.3	AFRICA 3.2
NORTH AMERICA			OC.	EUROPE					S. AM.		ASIA		

Copyright by Rand McNally & Co.
Made in U.S.A.
A-510000-466   6-3-8

Copyright by Rand McNally & Co.
Made in U.S.A.
A-510000-467   7-7-9

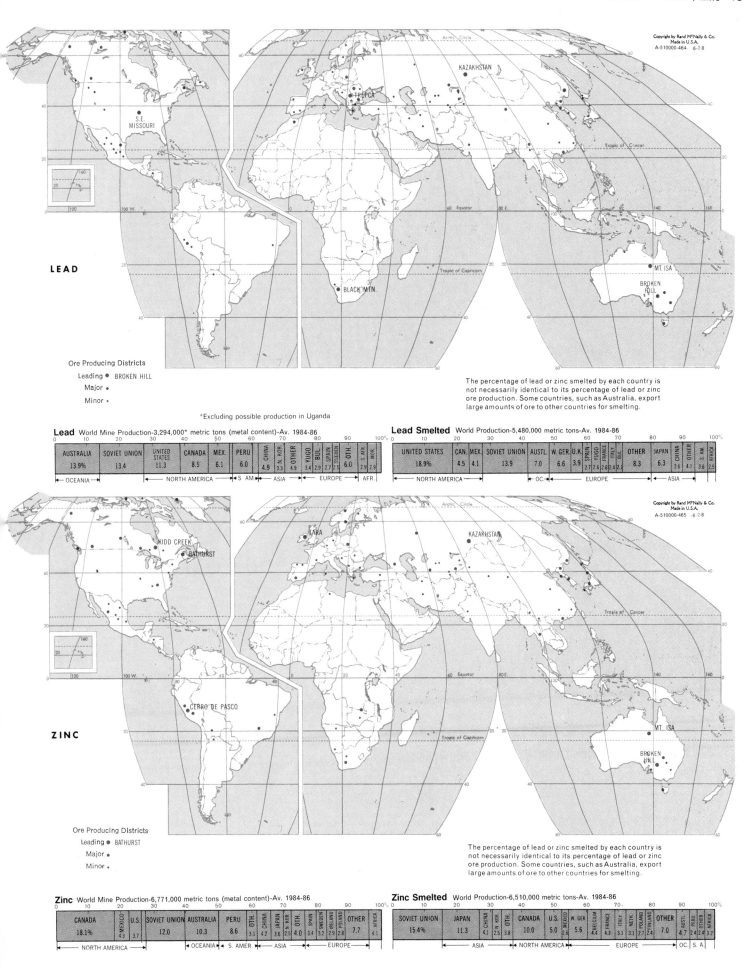

Copyright by Rand McNally & Co.
Made in U.S.A.
A-510000-464 6-2-8

LEAD

KAZAKHSTAN

TREPCA

S.E. MISSOURI

BLACK MTN.

MT. ISA

BROKEN HILL

Ore Producing Districts

Leading ● BROKEN HILL

Major ●

Minor ·

*Excluding possible production in Uganda

The percentage of lead or zinc smelted by each country is not necessarily identical to its percentage of lead or zinc ore production. Some countries, such as Australia, export large amounts of ore to other countries for smelting.

Lead World Mine Production-3,294,000* metric tons (metal content)-Av. 1984-86

AUSTRALIA 13.9%	SOVIET UNION 13.4	UNITED STATES 11.3	CANADA 8.5	MEX. 6.1	PERU 6.0	CHINA 4.9	N. KOR. 4.9	OTHER 4.0	YUGO 3.4	BUL. 2.9	SPAIN 2.7	SWEDEN 2.9	OTH. 6.0	S. AFR. 2.9	MOR. 2.9

← OCEANIA → ← NORTH AMERICA → ← S. AM → ← ASIA → ← EUROPE → ← AFR. →

Lead Smelted World Production-5,480,000 metric tons-Av. 1984-86

UNITED STATES 18.9%	CAN. 4.5	MEX. 4.1	SOVIET UNION 13.9	AUSTL. 7.0	W. GER. 6.6	U.K. 3.9	YUGO 2.7	FRANCE 2.9	ITALY 2.9	BUL. 2.8	OTHER 8.3	JAPAN 6.3	CHINA 3.6	OTHER 4.1	S. AM. 3.6	AFRICA 2.5

← NORTH AMERICA → ← OC. → ← EUROPE → ← ASIA →

Copyright by Rand McNally & Co.
Made in U.S.A.
A-510000-465 6-2-8

ZINC

TARA

KIDD CREEK

BATHURST

KAZAKHSTAN

CERRO DE PASCO

MT. ISA

BROKEN HILL

Ore Producing Districts

Leading ● BATHURST

Major ●

Minor ·

The percentage of lead or zinc smelted by each country is not necessarily identical to its percentage of lead or zinc ore production. Some countries, such as Australia, export large amounts of ore to other countries for smelting.

Zinc World Mine Production-6,771,000 metric tons (metal content)-Av. 1984-86

CANADA 18.1%	MEXICO 4.3	U.S. 3.7	SOVIET UNION 12.0	AUSTRALIA 10.3	PERU 8.6	OTH. 3.1	CHINA 4.2	JAPAN 3.6	N. KOR. 2.5	OTH. 4.0	SPAIN 3.4	SWEDEN 3.2	IRELAND 2.9	POLAND 2.8	OTHER 7.7	AFRICA 4.1

← NORTH AMERICA → ← OCEANIA → ← S. AMER → ← ASIA → ← EUROPE →

Zinc Smelted World Production-6,510,000 metric tons-Av. 1984-86

SOVIET UNION 15.4%	JAPAN 11.3	CHINA 4.1	N. KOR. 3.8	OTH. 3.8	CANADA 10.0	U.S. 5.0	MEXICO 4.3	W. GER. 5.6	BELGIUM 4.4	FRANCE 3.1	ITALY 3.1	NETH. 2.7	POLAND 2.7	FINLAND 2.4	OTHER 7.0	AUSTL. 4.7	PERU 2.4	OTHER 2.4	AFRICA 3.2

← ASIA → ← NORTH AMERICA → ← EUROPE → ← OC. → ← S. A. →

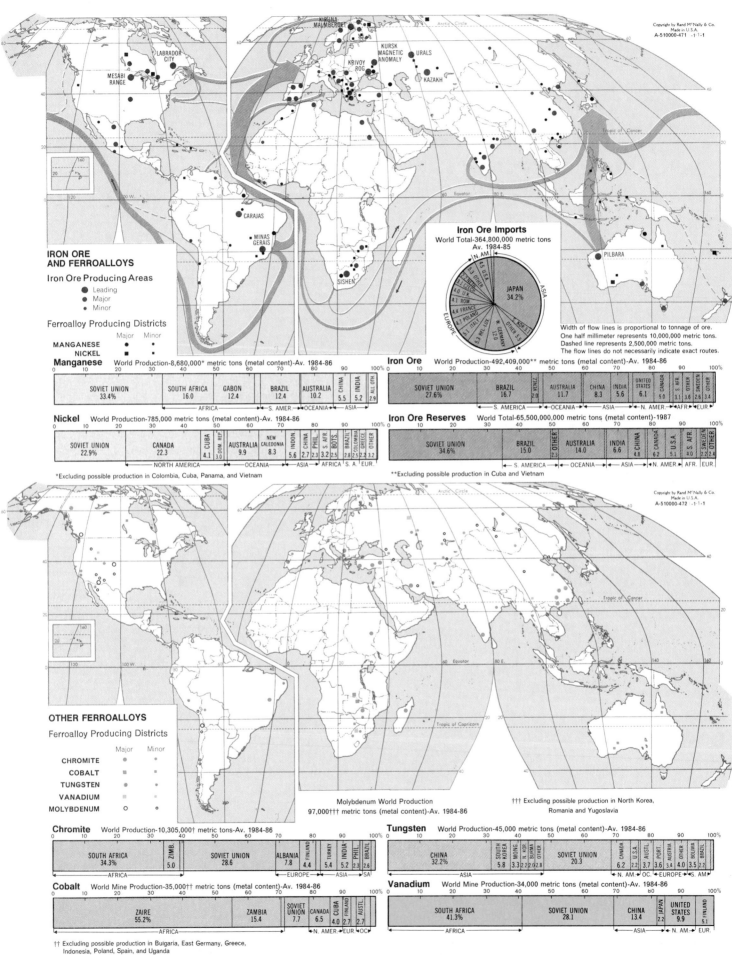

Copyright by Rand McNally & Co.
Made in U.S.A.
A-510000-471 -1-1-1

KIRUNA-MALMBERGET

LABRADOR CITY

MESABI RANGE

KURSK MAGNETIC ANOMALY
URALS
KRIVOY ROG
KAZAKH

Arctic Circle

Tropic of Cancer

Equator

CARAJAS

MINAS GERAIS

SISHEN

PILBARA

IRON ORE AND FERROALLOYS

Iron Ore Producing Areas
- Leading
- Major
- Minor

Ferroalloy Producing Districts

	Major	Minor
MANGANESE		
NICKEL		

Iron Ore Imports
World Total-364,800,000 metric tons
Av. 1984-85

N. AM.
5.3 OTHER
5.3 U.S.A.
ASIA
JAPAN 34.2%
4.0 CZECH.
4.0 U.K.
4.1 ROM
4.4 FRANCE
4.7 POLAND
5.1 ITALY
BEL. LUX.
5.2 W. GERMANY
S. KOR 3.1
OTHER 3.5
12.0
EUROPE

Width of flow lines is proportional to tonnage of ore.
One half millimeter represents 10,000,000 metric tons.
Dashed line represents 2,500,000 metric tons.
The flow lines do not necessarily indicate exact routes.

Manganese
World Production-8,680,000* metric tons (metal content)-Av. 1984-86

0	10	20	30	40	50	60	70	80	90	100%
SOVIET UNION 33.4%			SOUTH AFRICA 16.0	GABON 12.4	BRAZIL 12.4	AUSTRALIA 10.2	CHINA 5.5	INDIA 5.2	ALL OTH 2.9	

AFRICA — S. AMER. — OCEANIA — ASIA

Iron Ore
World Production-492,409,000** metric tons (metal content)-Av. 1984-86

0	10	20	30	40	50	60	70	80	90	100%
SOVIET UNION 27.6%			BRAZIL 16.7	VENEZ 2.0	AUSTRALIA 11.7	CHINA 8.3	INDIA 5.6	UNITED STATES 6.1	CANADA 5.0	S. AFR. 3.1	OTHER 3.6	SWEDEN 2.6	OTHER 3.4

S. AMERICA — OCEANIA — ASIA — N. AMER. — AFR. — EUR.

Nickel
World Production-785,000 metric tons (metal content)-Av. 1984-86

0	10	20	30	40	50	60	70	80	90	100%
SOVIET UNION 22.9%		CANADA 22.3	CUBA 4.1	DOM. REP 3.0	AUSTRALIA 9.9	NEW CALEDONIA 8.3	INDON 5.6	CHINA 2.7	S. AFR. 3.2	BOTS. 2.5	BRAZIL 2.5	COLOMBIA	GREECE 2.2	OTHER

NORTH AMERICA — OCEANIA — ASIA → AFRICA S.A. EUR.

Iron Ore Reserves
World Total-65,500,000,000 metric tons (metal content)-1987

0	10	20	30	40	50	60	70	80	90	100%
SOVIET UNION 34.6%			BRAZIL 15.0	OTHER	AUSTRALIA 14.0	INDIA 6.6	CHINA 4.8	CANADA 6.2	U.S.A. 5.1	S. AFR.	SWEDEN 2.5	OTHER 2.4

S. AMERICA — OCEANIA — ASIA — N. AMER. — AFR. — EUR.

*Excluding possible production in Colombia, Cuba, Panama, and Vietnam

**Excluding possible production in Cuba and Vietnam

Copyright by Rand McNally & Co.
Made in U.S.A.
A-510000-472 -1-1-1

Arctic Circle
Tropic of Cancer
Equator
Tropic of Capricorn

OTHER FERROALLOYS

Ferroalloy Producing Districts

	Major	Minor
CHROMITE		
COBALT		
TUNGSTEN		
VANADIUM		
MOLYBDENUM		

Molybdenum World Production
97,000††† metric tons (metal content)-Av. 1984-86

††† Excluding possible production in North Korea, Romania and Yugoslavia

Chromite
World Production-10,305,000† metric tons-Av. 1984-86

0	10	20	30	40	50	60	70	80	90	100%
SOUTH AFRICA 34.3%			ZIMB. 5.0	SOVIET UNION 28.6		ALBANIA 7.8	FIN. 4.4	TURKEY 5.4	INDIA 5.2	PHIL 2.3	BRAZIL 2.6

AFRICA — EUROPE — ASIA — SA

Tungsten
World Production-45,000 metric tons (metal content)-Av. 1984-86

0	10	20	30	40	50	60	70	80	90	100%
CHINA 32.2%			SOUTH KOREA 5.8	MONG. 3.3	N. KOR 2.2	BURMA 2.0	OTHER 2.8	SOVIET UNION 20.3		CANADA 6.2	U.S.A. 3.7	AUSTL 3.6	PORT. 3.4	AUSTRIA 4.0	BOLIVIA 3.5	BRAZIL 2.2

ASIA — N. AM. OC. EUROPE — S. AM

Cobalt
World Mine Production-35,000†† metric tons (metal content)-Av. 1984-86

0	10	20	30	40	50	60	70	80	90	100%
ZAIRE 55.2%					ZAMBIA 15.4	SOVIET UNION 7.7	CANADA 6.5	CUBA 4.0	FINLAND 2.7	AUSTL 2.7	

AFRICA — N. AMER. EUR. OC

Vanadium
World Mine Production-34,000 metric tons (metal content)-Av. 1984-86

0	10	20	30	40	50	60	70	80	90	100%
SOUTH AFRICA 41.3%				SOVIET UNION 28.1		CHINA 13.4	JAPAN 2.2	UNITED STATES 9.9	FINLAND 5.1

AFRICA — ASIA — N. AM. EUR.

†† Excluding possible production in Bulgaria, East Germany, Greece, Indonesia, Poland, Spain, and Uganda

† Excluding possible production in Bulgaria, China, and North Korea

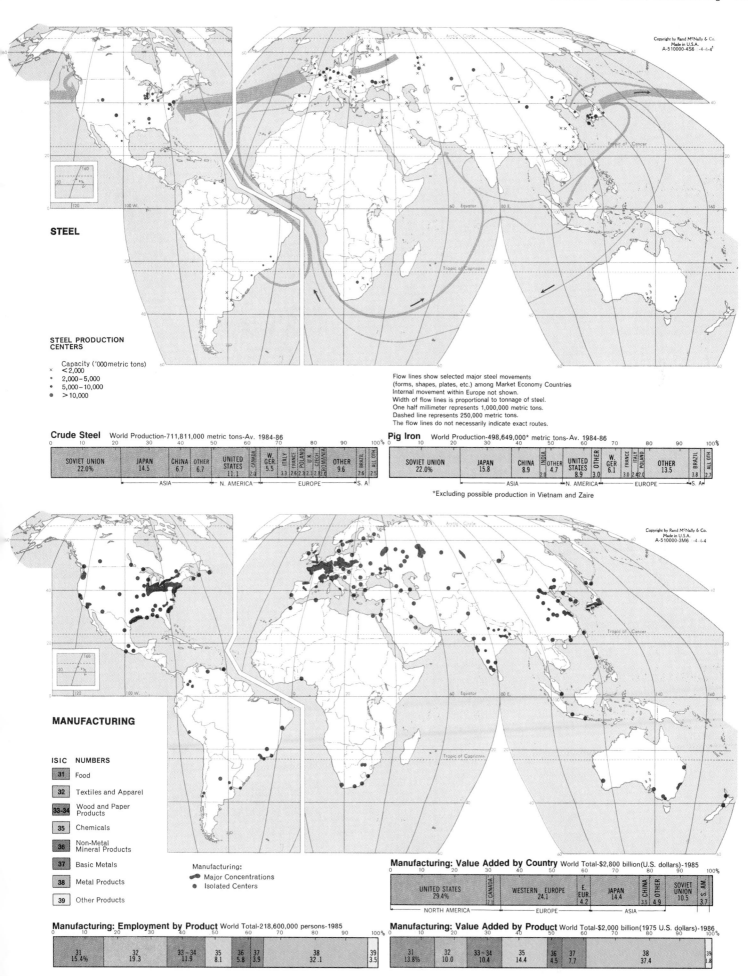

STEEL

STEEL PRODUCTION CENTERS

Capacity ('000 metric tons)
× <2,000
• 2,000–5,000
• 5,000–10,000
● >10,000

Flow lines show selected major steel movements
(forms, shapes, plates, etc.) among Market Economy Countries
Internal movement within Europe not shown.
Width of flow lines is proportional to tonnage of steel.
One half millimeter represents 1,000,000 metric tons.
Dashed line represents 250,000 metric tons.
The flow lines do not necessarily indicate exact routes.

Crude Steel World Production-711,811,000 metric tons-Av. 1984-86

SOVIET UNION 22.0%	JAPAN 14.5	CHINA 6.7	OTHER 6.7	UNITED STATES 11.1	CANADA 2.0	W. GER. 5.5	ITALY 3.3	FRANCE 2.6	POLAND 3.2	U.K. 2.1	CZECH. 2.1	ROMANIA 2.0	OTHER 9.6	BRAZIL 2.6	ALL OTH. 2.5

ASIA — N. AMERICA — EUROPE — S. A.

Pig Iron World Production-498,649,000* metric tons-Av. 1984-86

SOVIET UNION 22.0%	JAPAN 15.8	CHINA 8.9	INDIA 2.0	OTHER 4.7	UNITED STATES 8.9	OTHER 3.0	W. GER 6.1	FRANCE 3.0	ITALY 2.2	POLAND 2.0	OTHER 13.5	BRAZIL 3.8	ALL OTH. 2.7

ASIA — N. AMERICA — EUROPE — S. A.

*Excluding possible production in Vietnam and Zaire

MANUFACTURING

ISIC NUMBERS

31	Food
32	Textiles and Apparel
33–34	Wood and Paper Products
35	Chemicals
36	Non-Metal Mineral Products
37	Basic Metals
38	Metal Products
39	Other Products

Manufacturing:
━ Major Concentrations
● Isolated Centers

Manufacturing: Value Added by Country World Total-$2,800 billion(U.S. dollars)-1985

UNITED STATES 29.4%	CANADA 2.1	WESTERN EUROPE 24.1	E. EUR. 4.2	JAPAN 14.4	CHINA 3.5	OTHER 4.9	SOVIET UNION 10.5	S. AM. 3.7

NORTH AMERICA — EUROPE — ASIA

Manufacturing: Employment by Product World Total-218,600,000 persons-1985

31 15.4%	32 19.3	33–34 11.9	35 8.1	36 5.8	37 3.9	38 32.1	39 3.5

Manufacturing: Value Added by Product World Total-$2,000 billion(1975 U.S. dollars)-1986

31 13.8%	32 10.0	33–34 10.4	35 14.4	36 4.5	37 7.7	38 37.4	39 1.8

Copyright by Rand McNally & Co.
Made in U.S.A.
A-510000-4S6 -4-4-4'

Copyright by Rand McNally & Co.
Made in U.S.A.
A-510000-3M6 -4-4-4

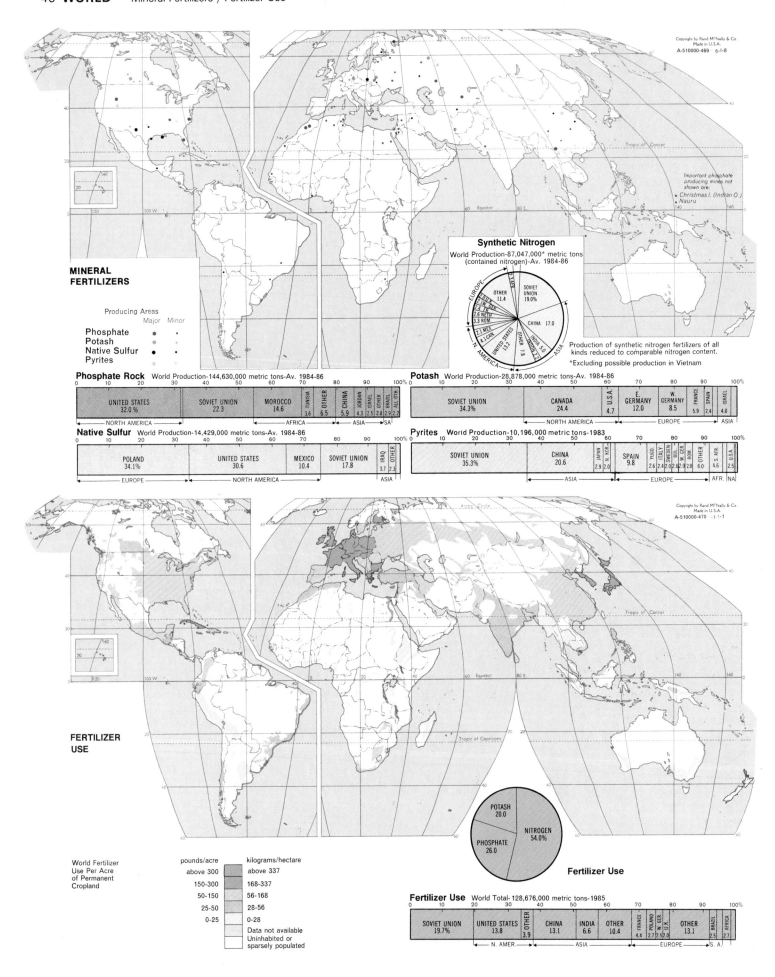

Copyright by Rand McNally & Co.
Made in U.S.A.
A-510000-469 6-6-8

Important phosphate producing mines not shown are:
• *Christmas I. (Indian O.)*
• *Nauru*

MINERAL FERTILIZERS

Producing Areas
Major Minor

Phosphate
Potash
Native Sulfur
Pyrites

Synthetic Nitrogen

World Production-87,047,000* metric tons
(contained nitrogen)-Av. 1984-86

EUROPE
OTHER 11.4
SOVIET UNION 19.0%
CHINA 17.0
INDIA 5.0
INDON 2.1
OTHER 7.8
UNITED STATES 13.2
CAN 4.1
MEX 2.1
ROM 3.3
NETH 2.6
W. GER 2.4
POL 2.4
N. AMERICA
ASIA

Production of synthetic nitrogen fertilizers of all kinds reduced to comparable nitrogen content.
*Excluding possible production in Vietnam

Phosphate Rock World Production-144,630,000 metric tons-Av. 1984-86

0	10	20	30	40	50	60	70	80	90	100%
UNITED STATES 32.0 %			SOVIET UNION 22.3		MOROCCO 14.6		TUNISIA 3.6	OTHER 6.5	CHINA 5.9	JORDAN 4.3	ISRAEL 2.5	OTHER 2.8	BRAZIL 2.9	ALL OTH. 2.2

NORTH AMERICA ←→ AFRICA ←→ ASIA ←→ SA

Native Sulfur World Production-14,429,000 metric tons-Av. 1984-86

0	10	20	30	40	50	60	70	80	90	100%
POLAND 34.1%		UNITED STATES 30.6		MEXICO 10.4	SOVIET UNION 17.8		IRAQ 3.7	OTHER 2.3

EUROPE ←→ NORTH AMERICA ←→ ASIA

Potash World Production-28,878,000 metric tons-Av. 1984-86

0	10	20	30	40	50	60	70	80	90	100%
SOVIET UNION 34.3%			CANADA 24.4		U.S.A. 4.7	E. GERMANY 12.0	W. GERMANY 8.5	FRANCE 5.9	SPAIN 2.4	ISRAEL 4.0

NORTH AMERICA ←→ EUROPE ←→ ASIA

Pyrites World Production-10,196,000 metric tons-1983

0	10	20	30	40	50	60	70	80	90	100%
SOVIET UNION 35.3%			CHINA 20.6		JAPAN 2.9	N. KOR. 2.0	SPAIN 9.8	YUGO. 2.6	ITALY 2.4	SWEDEN 2.0	BUL. 2.0	W. GER 2.0	ROM 2.0	OTHER 6.0	S. AFR. 4.6	U.S.A. 2.5

ASIA ←→ EUROPE ←→ AFR. | NA

Copyright by Rand McNally & Co.
Made in U.S.A.
A-510000-470 -1-1-1

FERTILIZER USE

World Fertilizer Use Per Acre of Permanent Cropland

pounds/acre	kilograms/hectare	
above 300	above 337	
150-300	168-337	
50-150	56-168	
25-50	28-56	
0-25	0-28	
	Data not available	
	Uninhabited or sparsely populated	

Fertilizer Use

POTASH 20.0
NITROGEN 54.0%
PHOSPHATE 26.0

Fertilizer Use World Total-128,676,000 metric tons-1985

0	10	20	30	40	50	60	70	80	90	100%
SOVIET UNION 19.7%		UNITED STATES 13.8	OTHER 3.9	CHINA 13.1	INDIA 6.6	OTHER 10.4	FRANCE 4.4	POLAND 2.7	W. GER. 2.0	U.K. 2.0	OTHER 13.1	BRAZIL 2.5	AFRICA 2.7

N. AMER. ←→ ASIA ←→ EUROPE ←→ S. A.

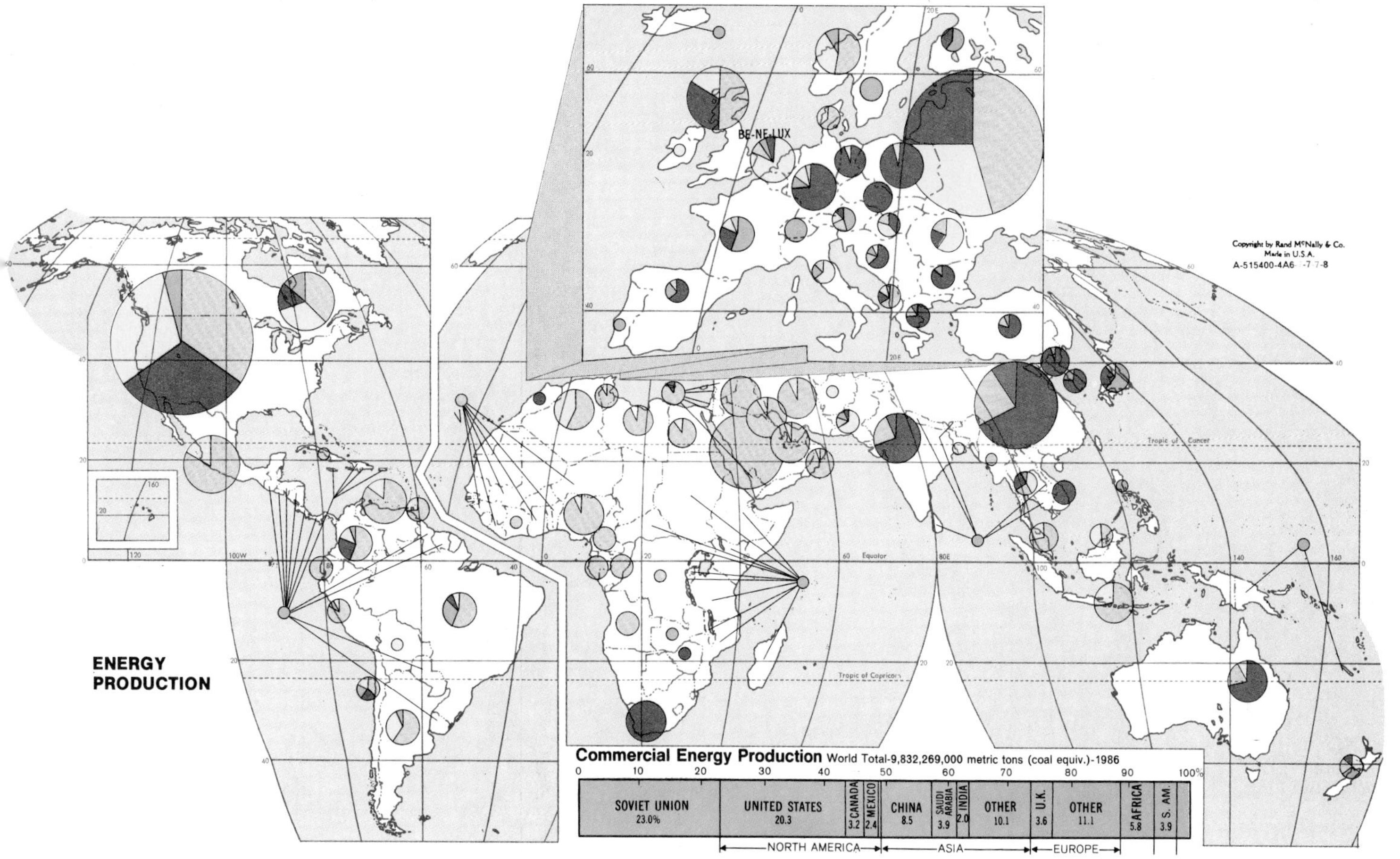
BE-NE-LUX
Tropic of Cancer
Equator
Tropic of Capricorn
ENERGY PRODUCTION
Commercial Energy Production World Total-9,832,269,000 metric tons (coal equiv.)-1986
0 10 20 30 40 50 60 70 80 90 100%
SOVIET UNION 23.0%
UNITED STATES 20.3
CANADA 3.2
MEXICO 2.4
CHINA 8.5
SAUDI ARABIA 3.9
INDIA 2.0
OTHER 10.1
U.K. 3.6
OTHER 11.1
AFRICA 5.8
S. AM. 3.9
NORTH AMERICA
ASIA
EUROPE
Copyright by Rand McNally & Co. Made in U.S.A. A-515400-4A6 -7-7-8

Composition of Energy

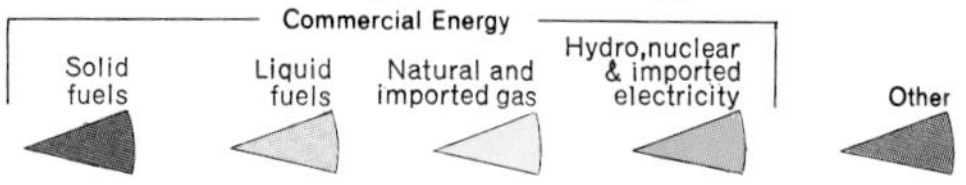
Commercial Energy
Solid fuels
Liquid fuels
Natural and imported gas
Hydro,nuclear & imported electricity
Other

Volume of Energy in millions of metric tons (Coal equivalent)—1986

1,000-2,500
500-1,000
250-500
100-250
40-100
5-40
0-5

Volume data is not shown separately for countries with less than 1 million metric tons (coal equivalent).

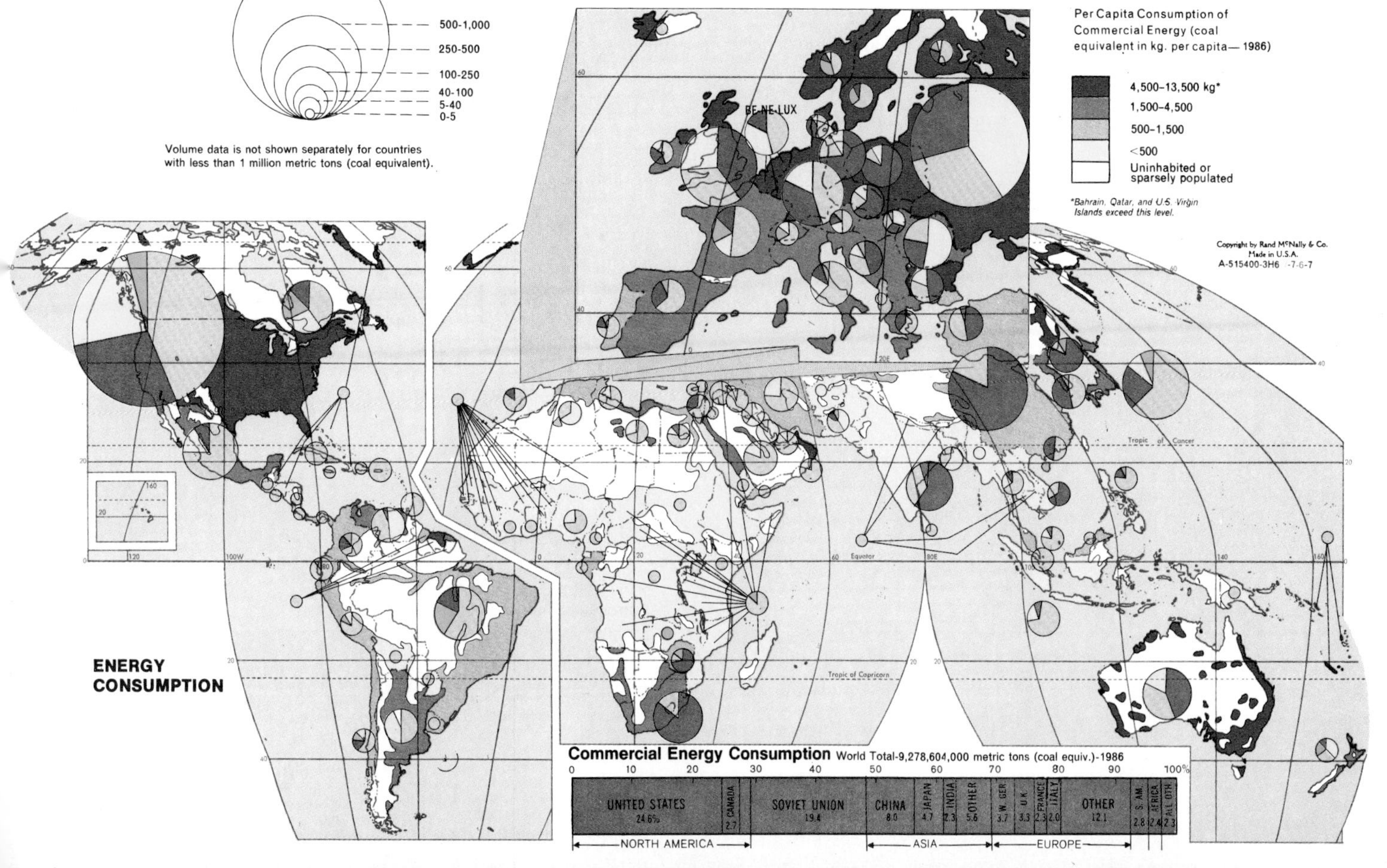
Per Capita Consumption of Commercial Energy (coal equivalent in kg. per capita—1986)
4,500-13,500 kg*
1,500-4,500
500-1,500
<500
Uninhabited or sparsely populated
*Bahrain, Qatar, and U.S. Virgin Islands exceed this level.
BE-NE-LUX
Tropic of Cancer
Equator
Tropic of Capricorn
ENERGY CONSUMPTION
Commercial Energy Consumption World Total-9,278,604,000 metric tons (coal equiv.)-1986
0 10 20 30 40 50 60 70 80 90 100%
UNITED STATES 24.6%
CANADA 2.7
SOVIET UNION 19.4
CHINA 8.0
JAPAN 4.7
INDIA 2.3
OTHER 5.6
W. GER. 3.7
U.K. 3.3
FRANCE 2.3
ITALY 2.0
OTHER 12.1
S. AM. 2.8
AFRICA 2.4
ALL OTH. 2.3
NORTH AMERICA
ASIA
EUROPE
Copyright by Rand McNally & Co. Made in U.S.A. A-515400-3H6 -7-6-7

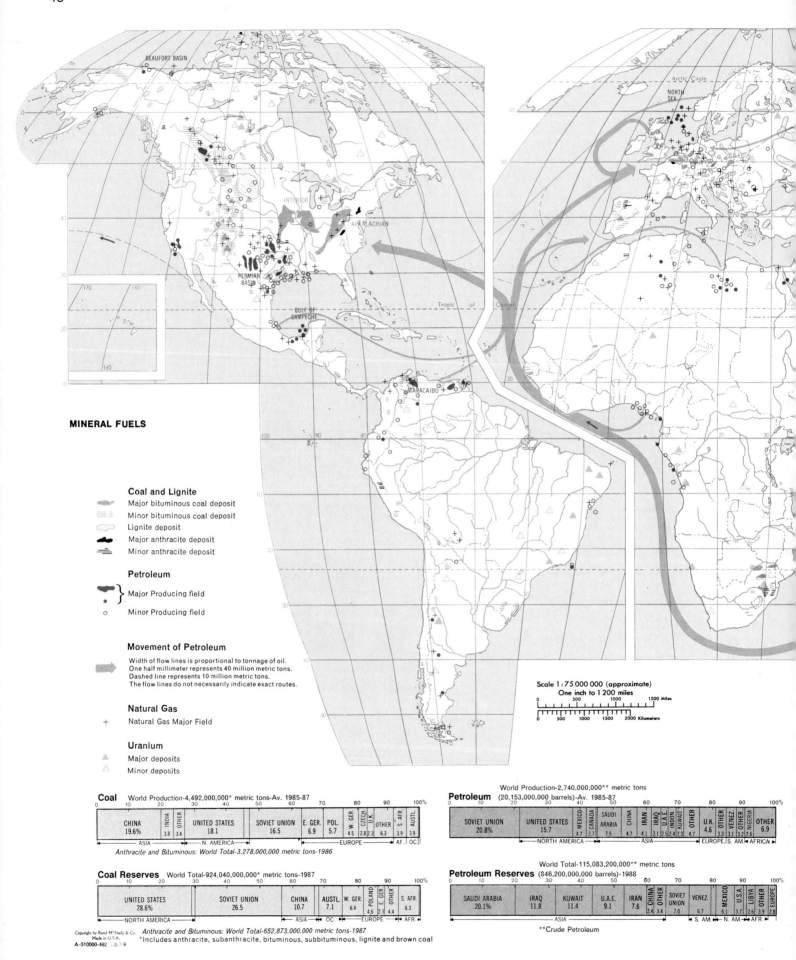

48

BEAUFORT BASIN

Arctic Circle

NORTH SEA

INTERIOR

APPALACHIAN

PERMIAN BASIN

GULF OF CAMPECHE

Tropic of Cancer

MARACAIBO

MINERAL FUELS

Coal and Lignite

Major bituminous coal deposit
Minor bituminous coal deposit
Lignite deposit
Major anthracite deposit
Minor anthracite deposit

Petroleum

Major Producing field

○ Minor Producing field

Movement of Petroleum

Width of flow lines is proportional to tonnage of oil.
One half millimeter represents 40 million metric tons.
Dashed line represents 10 million metric tons.
The flow lines do not necessarily indicate exact routes.

Natural Gas

+ Natural Gas Major Field

Uranium

▲ Major deposits

△ Minor deposits

Scale 1:75 000 000 (approximate)
One inch to 1 200 miles

0 500 1000 1500 Miles

0 500 1000 1500 2000 Kilometers

Coal World Production-4,492,000,000* metric tons-Av. 1985-87

0	10	20	30	40	50	60	70	80	90	100%

| CHINA 19.6% | INDIA 3.8 | OTHER 3.4 | UNITED STATES 18.1 | SOVIET UNION 16.5 | E. GER. 6.9 | POL. 5.7 | W. GER. 4.5 | CZECH. 2.8 | U.K. 2.3 | OTHER 6.3 | S. AFR. 3.9 | AUSTL. 3.9 |

←——ASIA——→ ←—N. AMERICA—→ ←————————EUROPE————————→ AF. OC.

Anthracite and Bituminous: World Total-3,278,000,000 metric tons-1986

Coal Reserves World Total-924,040,000,000* metric tons-1987

0	10	20	30	40	50	60	70	80	90	100%

| UNITED STATES 28.6% | SOVIET UNION 26.5 | CHINA 10.7 | AUSTL. 7.1 | W. GER. 6.4 | POLAND 4.6 | E. GER. 4.4 | OTHER | S. AFR. 6.3 |

←—NORTH AMERICA—→ ←—ASIA—→ OC. ←——EUROPE——→ AFR.

Anthracite and Bituminous: World Total-652,873,000,000 metric tons-1987
*Includes anthracite, subanthracite, bituminous, subbituminous, lignite and brown coal

Petroleum World Production-2,740,000,000** metric tons
(20,153,000,000 barrels)-Av. 1985-87

0	10	20	30	40	50	60	70	80	90	100%

| SOVIET UNION 20.8% | UNITED STATES 15.7 | MEXICO 4.7 | CANADA 4.1 | SAUDI ARABIA 7.5 | CHINA 4.7 | IRAN 4.1 | IRAQ 3.1 | U.A.E. 2.5 | INDON. 2.4 | KUWAIT 2.3 | OTHER 4.7 | U.K. 4.6 | OTHER 3.3 | VENEZ. 3.1 | OTHER 3.2 | NIGERIA 2.6 | OTHER 6.9 |

←——————NORTH AMERICA——————→ ←——————————ASIA——————————→ EUROPE IS. AM AFRICA

World Total-115,083,200,000** metric tons

Petroleum Reserves (846,200,000,000 barrels)-1988

0	10	20	30	40	50	60	70	80	90	100%

| SAUDI ARABIA 20.1% | IRAQ 11.8 | KUWAIT 11.4 | U.A.E. 9.1 | IRAN 7.6 | CHINA 2.4 | OTHER 3.4 | SOVIET UNION 7.0 | VENEZ. 6.7 | MEXICO 6.1 | U.S.A. 3.2 | LIBYA 2.6 | OTHER 3.9 | EUROPE 2.8 |

←————————————————————ASIA————————————————————→ ←S. AM.→ ←N. AM.→ AFR.

**Crude Petroleum

Copyright by Rand McNally & Co.
Made in U.S.A.
A-510000-462 —8-7-9

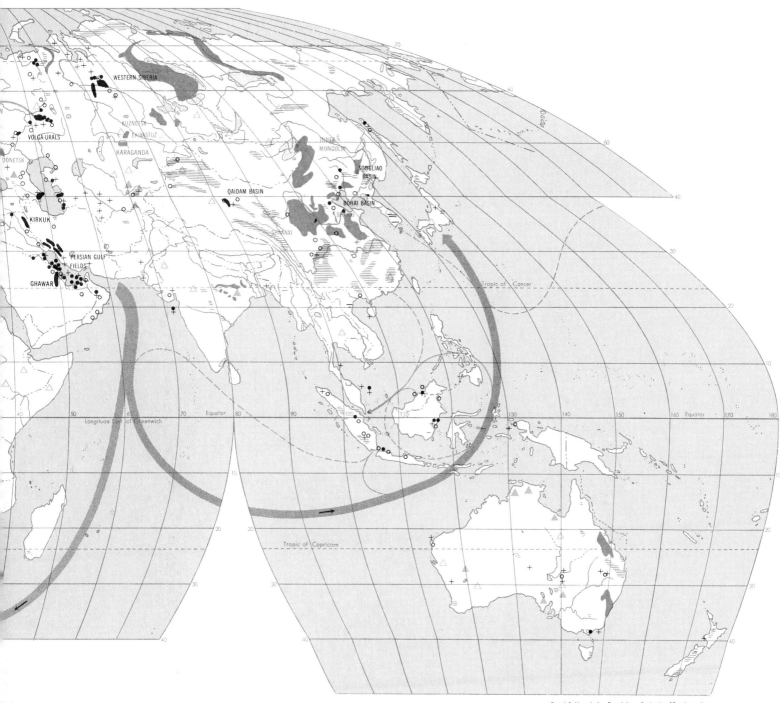

Goode's Homolosine Equal Area Projection (Condensed)

Natural Gas World Production-1,820,000,000,000 cubic meters-Av. 1985-87

SOVIET UNION 37.7%	UNITED STATES 25.3	CAN. 4.5	NETH. 4.1	U.K. 2.5	ROMANIA 2.0	OTHER 5.5	ALGERIA 2.2	ASIA 9.6	S. AMER. 2.7

NORTH AMERICA — EUROPE — AF.

Natural Gas Reserves World Total-108,500,000,000,000 cubic meters-1988

SOVIET UNION 37.8%	IRAN 12.9	U.A.E. 5.2	QATAR 4.2	SAUDI AR. 3.8	INDON. 2.1	OTHER 7.5	U.S.A. 4.9	CANADA 2.7	MEXICO 2.0	NORWAY 2.9	OTHER 3.7	ALGERIA 2.8	OTHER 3.2	VENEZ. 2.5

ASIA — N. AMER. — EUR. | AFR. | SA

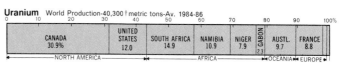

Uranium World Production-40,300 †metric tons-Av. 1984-86

CANADA 30.9%	UNITED STATES 12.0	SOUTH AFRICA 14.9	NAMIBIA 10.9	NIGER 7.9	GABON 2.3	AUSTL. 9.7	FRANCE 8.8

NORTH AMERICA — AFRICA — OCEANIA — EUROPE

†Excluding possible production in China, India, Israel, Soviet Union, and Eastern Europe

Uranium Reserves World Total-2,395,000 metric tons†† -1985

AUSTRALIA 22.0%	UNITED STATES 16.6	CANADA 8.9	SOUTH AFRICA 15.0	NIGER 7.6	NAMIBIA 5.0	OTHER 3.1	BRAZIL 6.8	SYRIA 3.3	OTHER 2.8	FRANCE 2.8	OTHER 4.9

OCEANIA — NORTH AMERICA — AFRICA — S. AM. — ASIA | EUROPE

††Excluding possible reserves in China, Cuba, North Korea, Mongolia, Vietnam, Soviet Union, and Eastern Europe

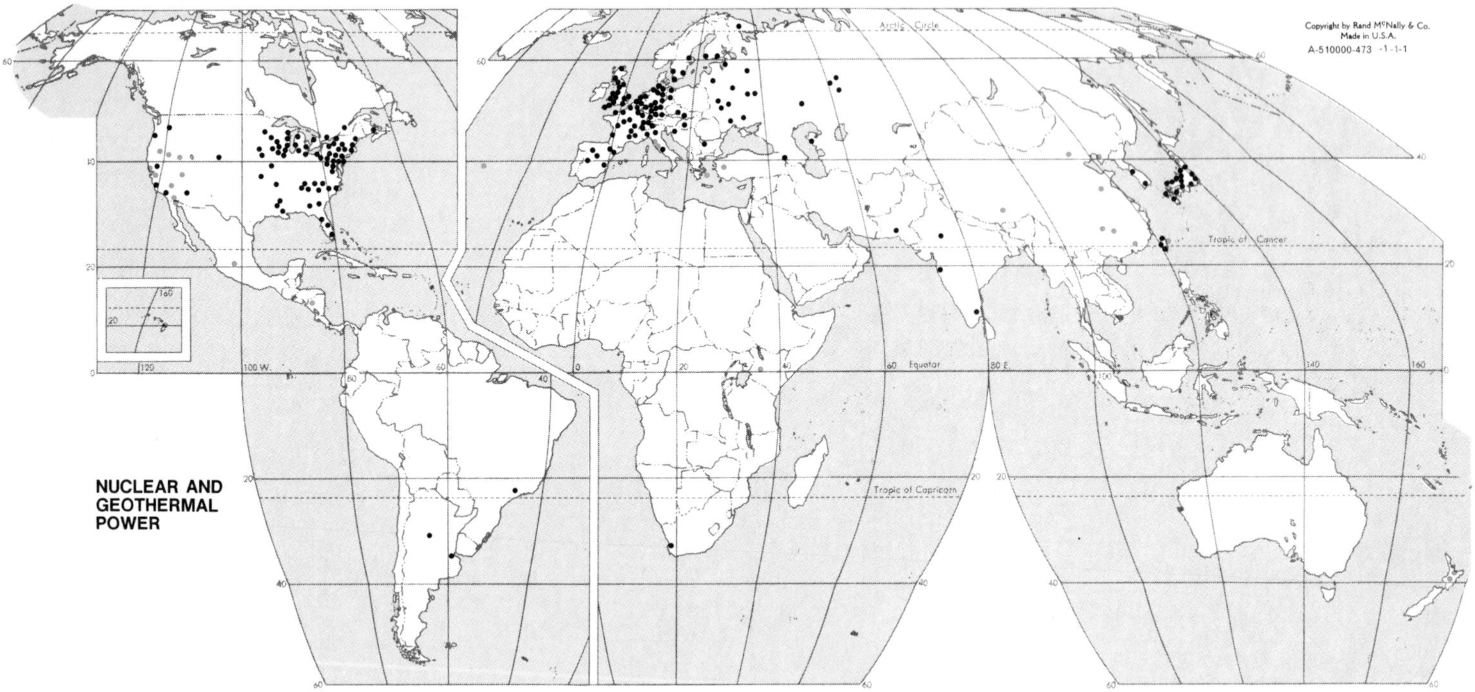

Copyright by Rand McNally & Co.
Made in U.S.A.
A-510000-473 -1-1-1

**NUCLEAR AND
GEOTHERMAL
POWER**

Energy Producing Plants
• Nuclear
• Geothermal

Geothermal Electricity World Production-25,000,000,000 kwt. hrs.-1986

0	10	20	30	40	50	60	70	80	90	100%

UNITED STATES 49.1%					MEXICO 6.9	EL SAL. 2.9	ITALY 11.0	YUGO. 10.7	JAPAN 6.2	N. Z. 4.7	AUSTL. 3.3

NORTH AMERICA ———————— EUROPE ———— ASIA — OC.

Nuclear Electricity World Production-1,529,000 million kwt. hrs.-1986

0	10	20	30	40	50	60	70	80	90	100%

UNITED STATES 27.1%	CAN. 4.7	FRANCE 15.8	W. GER. 7.8	SWE. 4.6	U.K. 3.9	BEL. 2.6	SPAIN 2.4	OTHER 7.0	JAPAN 11.0	OTHER 2.2	SOVIET UNION 10.5

NORTH AMERICA ——————— EUROPE ——————— ASIA ————

Solar Electricity World Production-9,700,000 kwt. hrs.-1984

0	10	20	30	40	50	60	70	80	90	100%

UNITED STATES 53.9%						SOUTH AFRICA 14.4	NORWAY 10.3	ITALY 6.0	AUS. 3.4	JAPAN 6.7	CHINA 2.1

NORTH AMERICA ———————— AFRICA ———— EUROPE —— ASIA —

Copyright by Rand McNally & Co.
Made in U.S.A.
A-510000-468 -4-5-8

**WATER
POWER**

U.S.

INDIA,
PAKISTAN
& SRI LANKA

INDONESIA

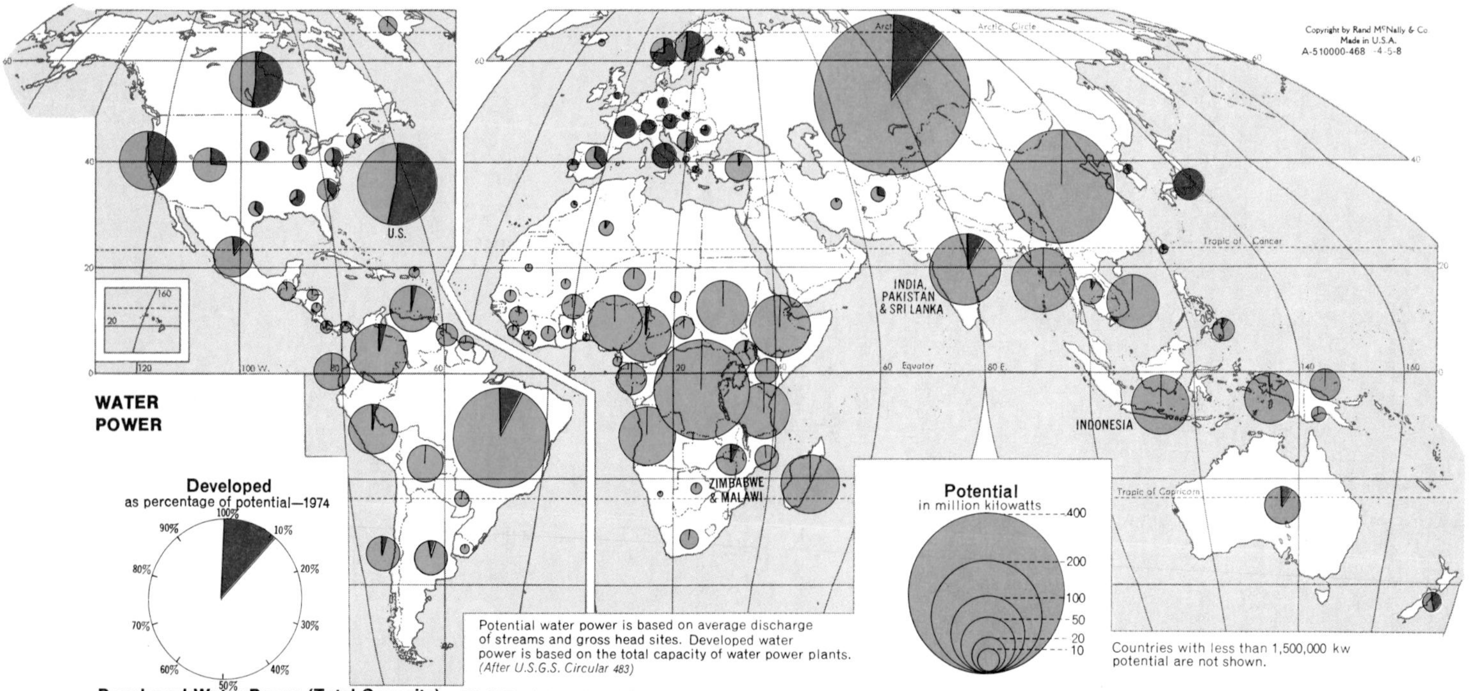

ZIMBABWE
& MALAWI

Developed
as percentage of potential—1974

100%
90% 10%
80% 20%
70% 30%
60% 40%
50%

Potential water power is based on average discharge
of streams and gross head sites. Developed water
power is based on the total capacity of water power plants.
(After U.S.G.S. Circular 483)

Potential
in million kilowatts

—400
—200
—100
—50
—20
—10

Countries with less than 1,500,000 kw
potential are not shown.

Developed Water Power (Total Capacity) World Total-564,259,000 kilowatts-1986

0	10	20	30	40	50	60	70	80	90	100%

UNITED STATES 14.9%	CANADA 10.1	SOVIET UNION 11.0	BRAZIL 6.7	OTHER 4.1	JAPAN 6.2	CHINA 4.8	INDIA 2.8	OTHER 4.3	NORWAY 4.2	FRANCE 4.0	ITALY 3.2	SWEDEN 2.8	SWITZ. 2.0	OTHER 9.4	AFRICA 2.9	OCEANIA 2.0

NORTH AMERICA ———— S. AMER. — ASIA ———— EUROPE ————

All Electricity World Production-9,899,000 million kwt. hrs.-1986

0	10	20	30	40	50	60	70	80	90	100%

UNITED STATES 26.1%	CAN. 4.7	SOVIET UNION 16.2	JAPAN 6.8	CHINA 4.5	INDIA 2.0	OTHER 4.9	W. GER. 4.0	FRANCE 3.5	U.K. 3.0	OTHER 15.0	BRAZIL 2.1	AFRICA 2.2	ALL OTH.

NORTH AMERICA ————— ASIA ———— EUROPE ——— S.A.

Potential Water Power World Total-2,724,044,000 kilowatts—1962

0	10	20	30	40	50	60	70	80	90	100%

SOVIET UNION 14.7%	CHINA 8.1	BURMA 3.4	IND.PK.& SRI LAN. 3.2	INDON. 2.8	S. VIET 2.5	OTHER ASIA 5.5	ZAIRE 6.6	ANGOLA 2.9	MAL. 2.9	OTHER AFRICA 12.7	BRAZIL 6.6	COL. 2.8	OTHER S. AMERICA 7.9	U.S. 4.5	CANADA 2.6	OTHER 4.9	EUROPE 4.1	OCEANIA

ASIA ——————— AFRICA ——— S. AMERICA — N. AM.

Hydroelectricity World Production-1,991,000 million kwt. hrs.-1986

0	10	20	30	40	50	60	70	80	90	100%

CANADA 15.6%	UNITED STATES 14.8	SOVIET UNION 10.8	BRAZIL 9.2	OTHER 5.1	CHINA 5.0	JAPAN 4.3	INDIA 2.7	OTHER 3.6	NOR. 4.8	FRANCE 3.1	SWEDEN 3.0	ITALY 2.5	OTHER 9.7	AFRICA 2.1	ALL OTH. 2.5

NORTH AMERICA ———— S. AMERICA — ASIA ———— EUROPE ————

Major Direction of Trade

EXPORTS TO

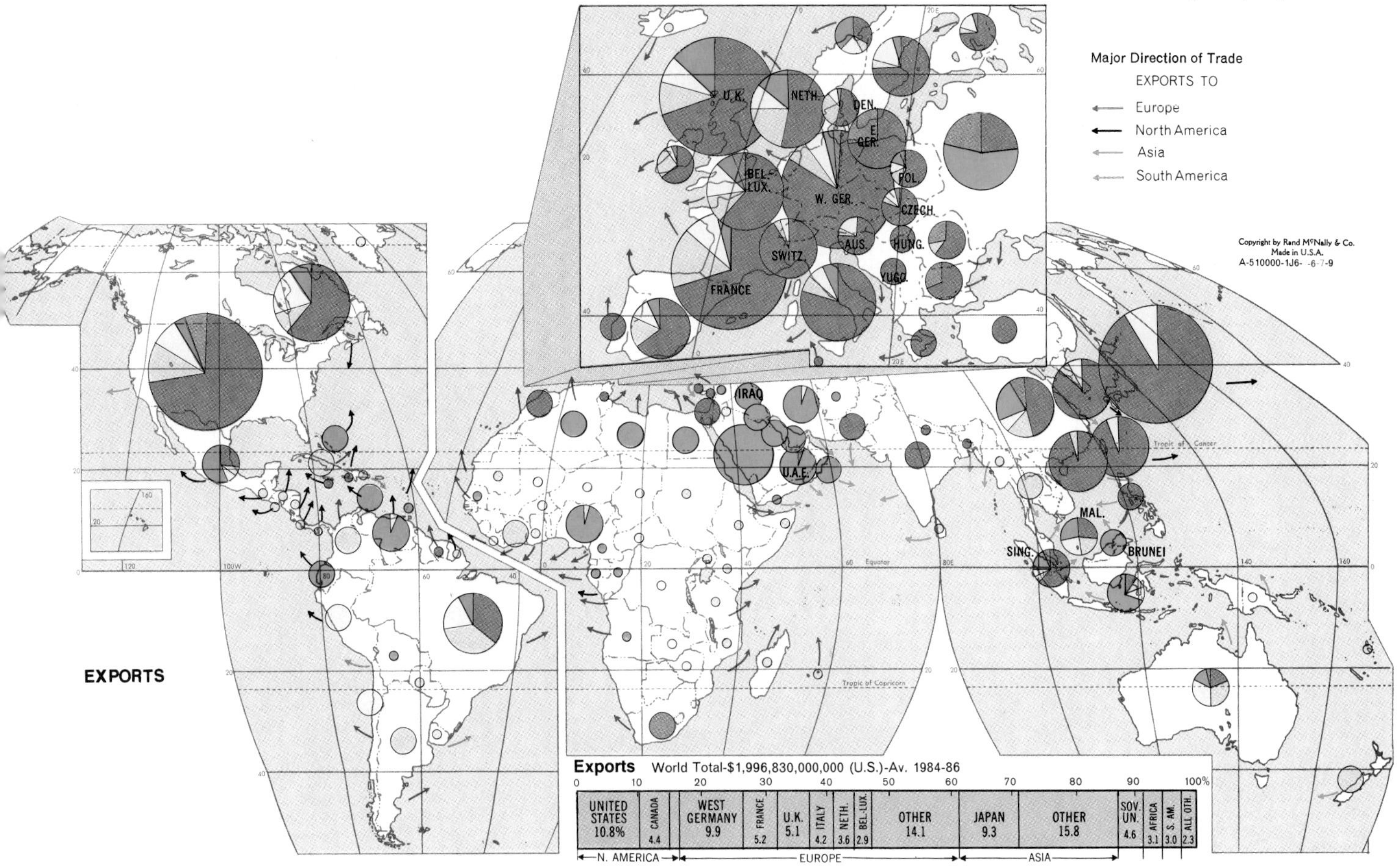

→ Europe
→ North America
→ Asia
→ South America

Copyright by Rand McNally & Co.
Made in U.S.A.
A-510000-1J6- -6-7-9

EXPORTS

Exports World Total-$1,996,830,000,000 (U.S.)-Av. 1984-86

0	10	20	30		40	50	60	70	80		90			100%
UNITED STATES 10.8%	CANADA 4.4	WEST GERMANY 9.9	FRANCE 5.2	U.K. 5.1	ITALY 3.6	NETH. 4.2	BEL-LUX. 2.9	OTHER 14.1	JAPAN 9.3	OTHER 15.8	SOV. UN. 4.6	AFRICA 3.1	S. AM. 3.0	ALL OTH 2.3

← N. AMERICA → ← EUROPE → ← ASIA →

Volume of Trade
(in millions of U.S. dollars-Av. 1984-86)

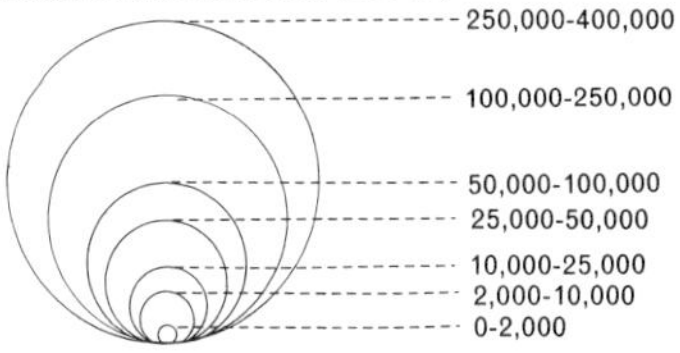

----------- 250,000-400,000

----------- 100,000-250,000

----------- 50,000-100,000
----------- 25,000-50,000
----------- 10,000-25,000
----------- 2,000-10,000
----------- 0-2,000

United States: Exports-216,000; Imports-363,000
If volume of trade is less than 10 billion dollars,
color indicates major class only. If no symbol is
shown, volume of trade is less than 400 million dollars.

Composition of Trade

Manufactured Articles | Food, bev. & tobacco | Raw Materials | Fuel & Related Prod. | All other or undifferentiated

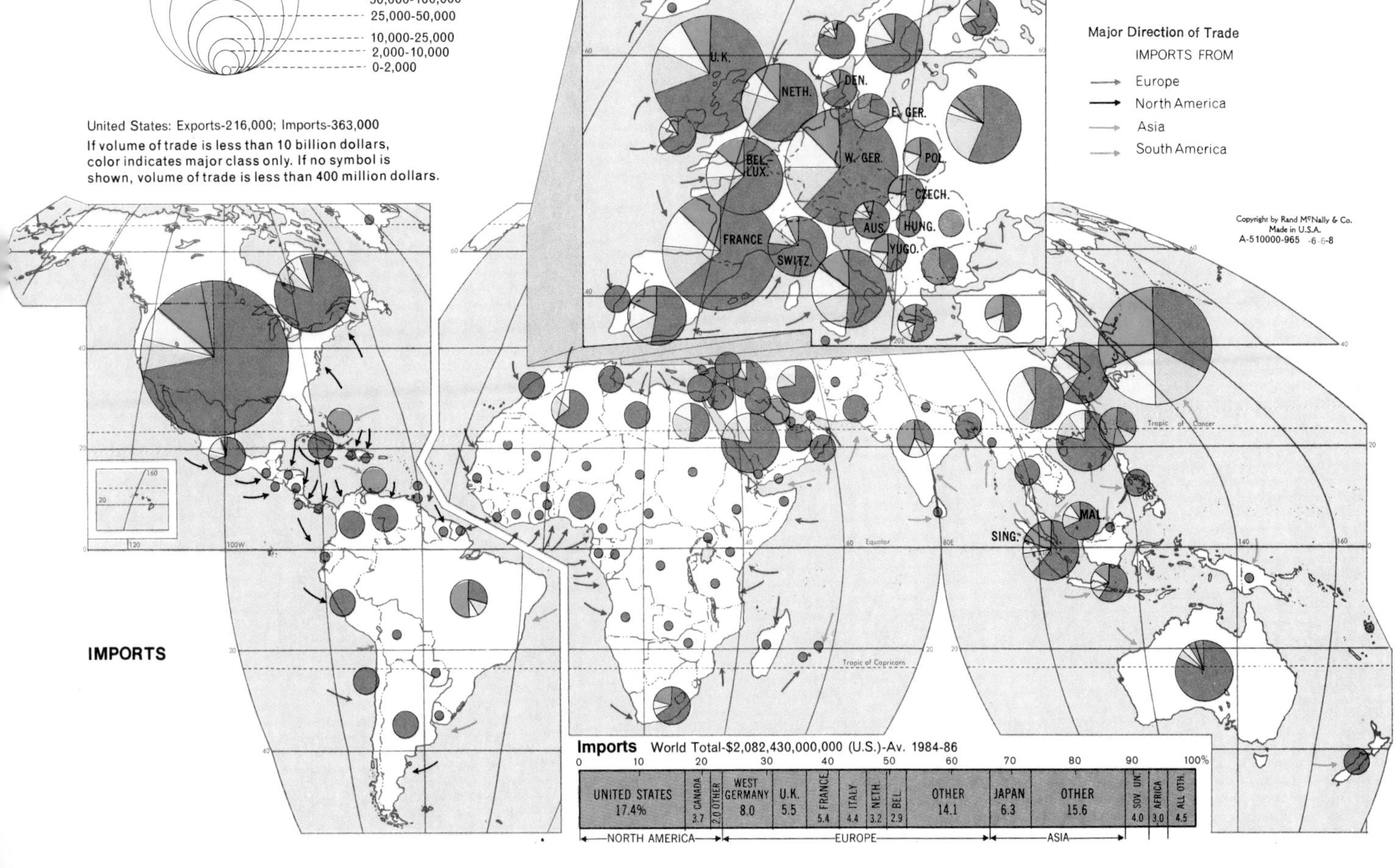

Major Direction of Trade

IMPORTS FROM

→ Europe
→ North America
→ Asia
→ South America

Copyright by Rand McNally & Co.
Made in U.S.A.
A-510000-965 -6-6-8

IMPORTS

Imports World Total-$2,082,430,000,000 (U.S.)-Av. 1984-86

0	10	20	30	40	50	60	70		80		90			100%
UNITED STATES 17.4%	CANADA 3.7	OTHER 2.0	WEST GERMANY 8.0	U.K. 5.5	FRANCE 5.4	ITALY 4.4	NETH. 3.2	BEL. 2.9	OTHER 14.1	JAPAN 6.3	OTHER 15.6	SOV UN 4.0	AFRICA 3.0	ALL OTH 4.5

← NORTH AMERICA → ← EUROPE → ← ASIA →

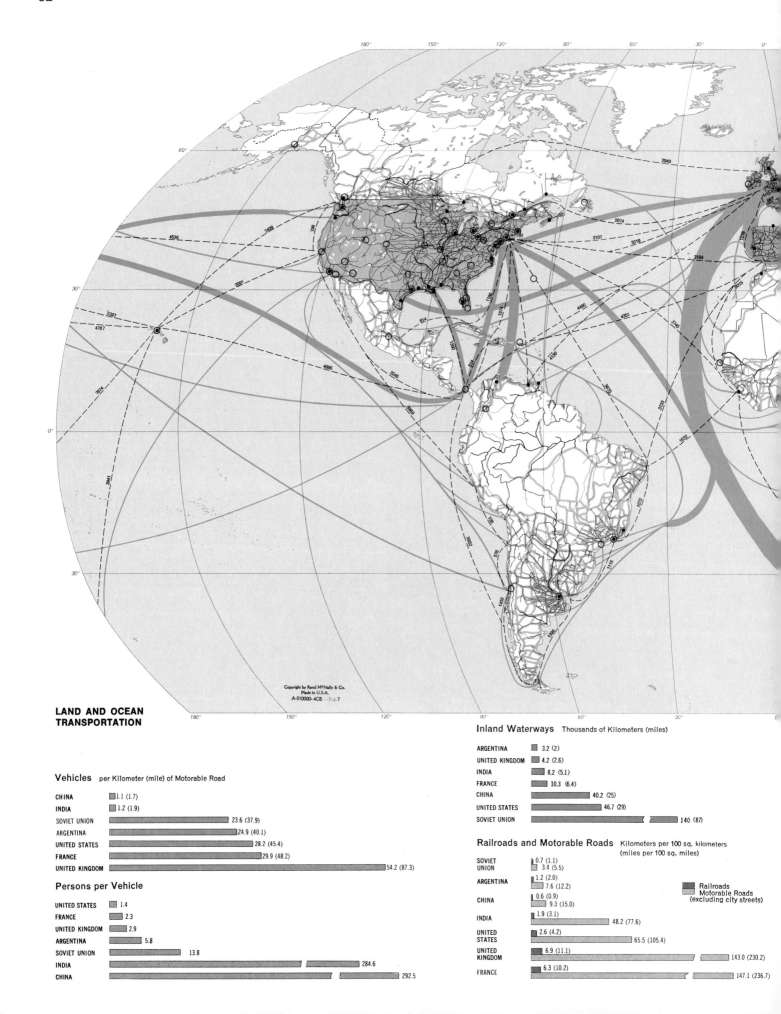

52

**LAND AND OCEAN
TRANSPORTATION**

Copyright by Rand McNally & Co.
Made in U.S.A.
A-510000- 4C6 -7-4-7

Vehicles per Kilometer (mile) of Motorable Road

CHINA	1.1 (1.7)
INDIA	1.2 (1.9)
SOVIET UNION	23.6 (37.9)
ARGENTINA	24.9 (40.1)
UNITED STATES	28.2 (45.4)
FRANCE	29.9 (48.2)
UNITED KINGDOM	54.2 (87.3)

Persons per Vehicle

UNITED STATES	1.4
FRANCE	2.3
UNITED KINGDOM	2.9
ARGENTINA	5.8
SOVIET UNION	13.8
INDIA	284.6
CHINA	292.5

Inland Waterways Thousands of Kilometers (miles)

ARGENTINA	3.2 (2)
UNITED KINGDOM	4.2 (2.6)
INDIA	8.2 (5.1)
FRANCE	10.3 (6.4)
CHINA	40.2 (25)
UNITED STATES	46.7 (29)
SOVIET UNION	140 (87)

Railroads and Motorable Roads Kilometers per 100 sq. kilometers (miles per 100 sq. miles)

	Railroads / Motorable Roads (excluding city streets)
SOVIET UNION	0.7 (1.1)
	3.4 (5.5)
ARGENTINA	1.2 (2.0)
	7.6 (12.2)
CHINA	0.6 (0.9)
	9.3 (15.0)
INDIA	1.9 (3.1)
	48.2 (77.6)
UNITED STATES	2.6 (4.2)
	65.5 (105.4)
UNITED KINGDOM	6.9 (11.1)
	143.0 (230.2)
FRANCE	6.3 (10.2)
	147.1 (236.7)

Railroads
Motorable Roads
(excluding city streets)

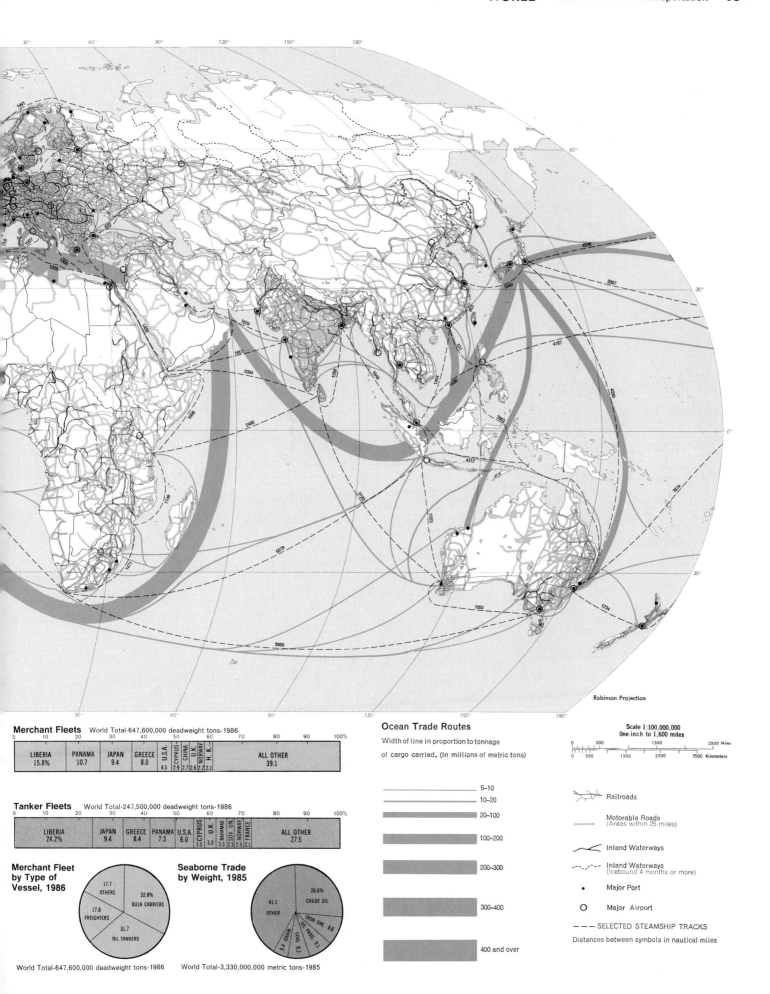

Robinson Projection

Merchant Fleets World Total-647,600,000 deadweight tons-1986

0	10	20	30	40	50	60	70	80	90	100%

| LIBERIA 15.8% | PANAMA 10.7 | JAPAN 9.4 | GREECE 8.0 | U.S.A. 4.5 | CYPRUS 2.9 | CHINA 2.7 | U.K. 2.6 | NORWAY 2.2 | H.K. 2.1 | ALL OTHER 39.1 |

Tanker Fleets World Total-247,500,000 deadweight tons-1986

0	10	20	30	40	50	60	70	80	90	100%

| LIBERIA 24.2% | JAPAN 9.4 | GREECE 8.4 | PANAMA 7.3 | U.S.A. 6.0 | CYPRUS 3.5 | U.K. 3.3 | BAHAMAS 3.3 | SOV. UN. 2.5 | NORWAY 2.5 | FRANCE 2.1 | ALL OTHER 27.5 |

Merchant Fleet by Type of Vessel, 1986

- 32.8% BULK CARRIERS
- 31.7 OIL TANKERS
- 17.8 FREIGHTERS
- 17.7 OTHERS

World Total-647,600,000 deadweight tons-1986

Seaborne Trade by Weight, 1985

- 26.6% CRUDE OIL
- 9.6 IRON ORE
- 9.1 OIL PROD.
- 8.2 COAL
- 5.4 GRAIN
- 41.1 OTHER

World Total-3,330,000,000 metric tons-1985

Ocean Trade Routes

Width of line in proportion to tonnage of cargo carried. (In millions of metric tons)

	5–10
	10–20
	20–100
	100–200
	200–300
	300–400
	400 and over

Scale 1:100,000,000
One inch to 1,600 miles

Railroads

Motorable Roads
(Areas within 25 miles)

Inland Waterways

Inland Waterways
(Icebound 4 months or more)

• Major Port

O Major Airport

— — — SELECTED STEAMSHIP TRACKS

Distances between symbols in nautical miles

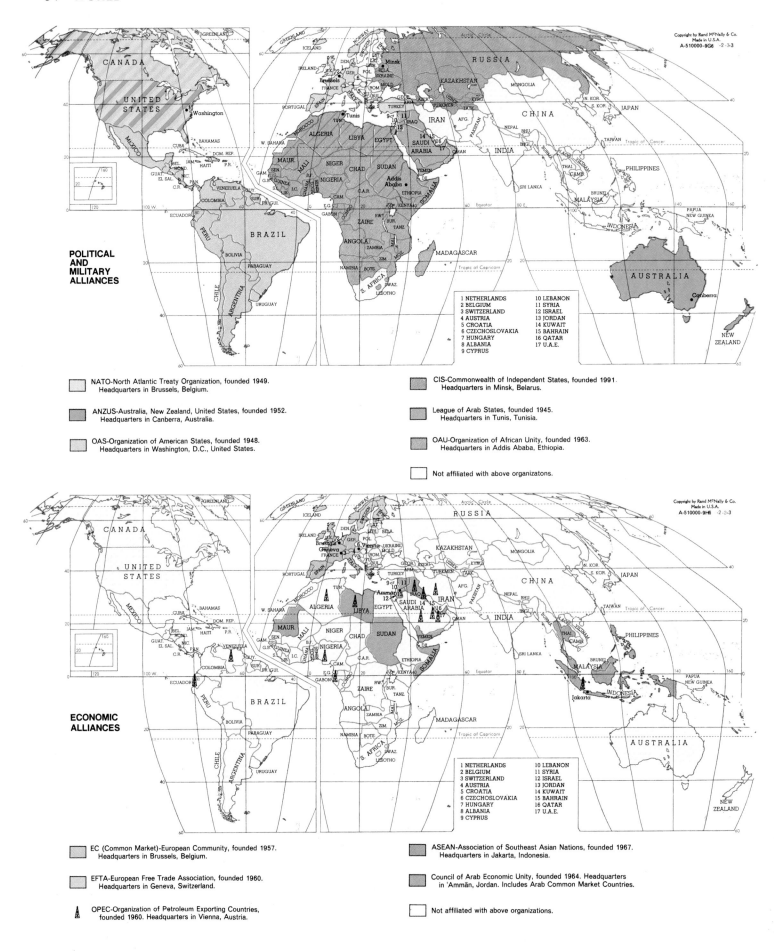

POLITICAL AND MILITARY ALLIANCES

1 NETHERLANDS	10 LEBANON
2 BELGIUM	11 SYRIA
3 SWITZERLAND	12 ISRAEL
4 AUSTRIA	13 JORDAN
5 CROATIA	14 KUWAIT
6 CZECHOSLOVAKIA	15 BAHRAIN
7 HUNGARY	16 QATAR
8 ALBANIA	17 U.A.E.
9 CYPRUS	

NATO-North Atlantic Treaty Organization, founded 1949. Headquarters in Brussels, Belgium.

ANZUS-Australia, New Zealand, United States, founded 1952. Headquarters in Canberra, Australia.

OAS-Organization of American States, founded 1948. Headquarters in Washington, D.C., United States.

CIS-Commonwealth of Independent States, founded 1991. Headquarters in Minsk, Belarus.

League of Arab States, founded 1945. Headquarters in Tunis, Tunisia.

OAU-Organization of African Unity, founded 1963. Headquarters in Addis Ababa, Ethiopia.

Not affiliated with above organizatons.

ECONOMIC ALLIANCES

1 NETHERLANDS	10 LEBANON
2 BELGIUM	11 SYRIA
3 SWITZERLAND	12 ISRAEL
4 AUSTRIA	13 JORDAN
5 CROATIA	14 KUWAIT
6 CZECHOSLOVAKIA	15 BAHRAIN
7 HUNGARY	16 QATAR
8 ALBANIA	17 U.A.E.
9 CYPRUS	

EC (Common Market)-European Community, founded 1957. Headquarters in Brussels, Belgium.

EFTA-European Free Trade Association, founded 1960. Headquarters in Geneva, Switzerland.

OPEC-Organization of Petroleum Exporting Countries, founded 1960. Headquarters in Vienna, Austria.

ASEAN-Association of Southeast Asian Nations, founded 1967. Headquarters in Jakarta, Indonesia.

Council of Arab Economic Unity, founded 1964. Headquarters in 'Ammān, Jordan. Includes Arab Common Market Countries.

Not affiliated with above organizations.

REGIONAL MAPS

Basic continental and regional coverage of the world's land areas is provided by the following section of physical-political reference maps. The section falls into a continental arrangement: North America, South America, Europe, Asia, Australia, and Africa. (Introducing each regional reference-map section are basic thematic maps and the environment maps.)

To aid the student in acquiring concepts of the relative sizes of continents and of some of the countries and regions, uniform scales for comparable areas were used so far as possible. Continental maps are at a uniform scale of 1:40,000,000. In addition, most of the world is covered by a series of regional maps at scales of 1:16,000,000 and 1:12,000,000.

Maps at 1:10,000,000 provide even greater detail for parts of Europe, Africa, and Southeast Asia. The United States, parts of Canada, and much of Europe are mapped at 1:4,000,000. Seventy-six urbanized areas are shown at 1:1,000,000. The new, separate metropolitan-area section contains larger-scale maps of selected urban areas.

Many of the symbols used are self-explanatory. A complete legend below provides a key to the symbols on the reference maps in this atlas.

General elevation above sea level is shown by layer tints for altitudinal zones, each of which has a different hue and is defined by a generalized contour line. A legend is given on each map, reflecting this color gradation.

The surface configuration is represented by hill-shading, which gives the three-dimensional impression of landforms. This terrain representation is superimposed on the layer tints to convey a realistic and readily visualized impression of the surface. The combination of altitudinal tints and hill-shading best shows elevation, relief, steepness of slope, and ruggedness of terrain.

If the world used one alphabet and one language, no particular difficulty would arise in understanding place-names. However, some of the people of the world, the Chinese and the Japanese, for example, use nonalphabetic languages. Their symbols are transliterated into the Roman alphabet. In this atlas a "local-name" policy generally was used for naming cities and towns and all local topographic and water features. However, for a few major cities the Anglicized name was preferred and the local name given in parentheses, for instance, Moscow (Moskva), Vienna (Wien), Cologne (Köln). In countries where more than one official language is used, a name is in the dominant local language. The generic parts of local names for topographic and water features are self-explanatory in many cases because of the associated map symbols or type styles. A complete list of foreign generic names is given in the Glossary, on page 248.

Place-names on the reference maps are listed in the Pronouncing Index, which is a distinctive feature of Goode's World Atlas.

Physical-Political Reference Map Legend

Cultural Features

Political Boundaries

- International (over water) (Demarcated, Undemarcated, and Administrative)
- Disputed de facto
- Claim Boundary
- Indefinite or Undefined
- Secondary, State, Provincial, etc. (over water)
- Parks, Indian Reservations
- City Limits
- Urbanized Areas
- Neighborhoods, Sections of City

Populated Places

- ⊙ 1,000,000 and over
- ◎ 250,000 to 1,000,000
- ⊙ 100,000 to 250,000
- • 25,000 to 100,000
- ° 0 to 25,000
- TŌKYŌ National Capitals
- Boise Secondary Capitals

Note: On maps at 1:20,000,000 and smaller the town symbols do not follow the specific population classification shown above. On all maps, type size indicates the relative importance of the city.

Transportation

- Railroads
- Railroads On 1:1,000,000 scale maps
- Railroad Ferries
- Roads
- Major / Other On 1:1,000,000 scale maps
- Major / Other On 1:4,000,000 scale maps
- On other scale maps
- Caravan Routes
- ✈ Airports

Other Cultural Features

- Dams
- Pipelines
- ▲ Points of Interest
- ∴ Ruins

Land Features

- △ Peaks, Spot Heights
- = Passes
- Sand
- Contours

Water Features

Lakes and Reservoirs

- Fresh Water
- Fresh Water: Intermittent
- Salt Water
- Salt Water: Intermittent

Other Water Features

- Salt Basins, Flats
- Swamps
- Ice Caps and Glaciers
- Rivers
- Intermittent Rivers
- Aqueducts and Canals
- Ship Channels
- Falls
- Rapids
- Springs
- △ Water Depths
- Fishing Banks
- Sand Bars
- Reefs

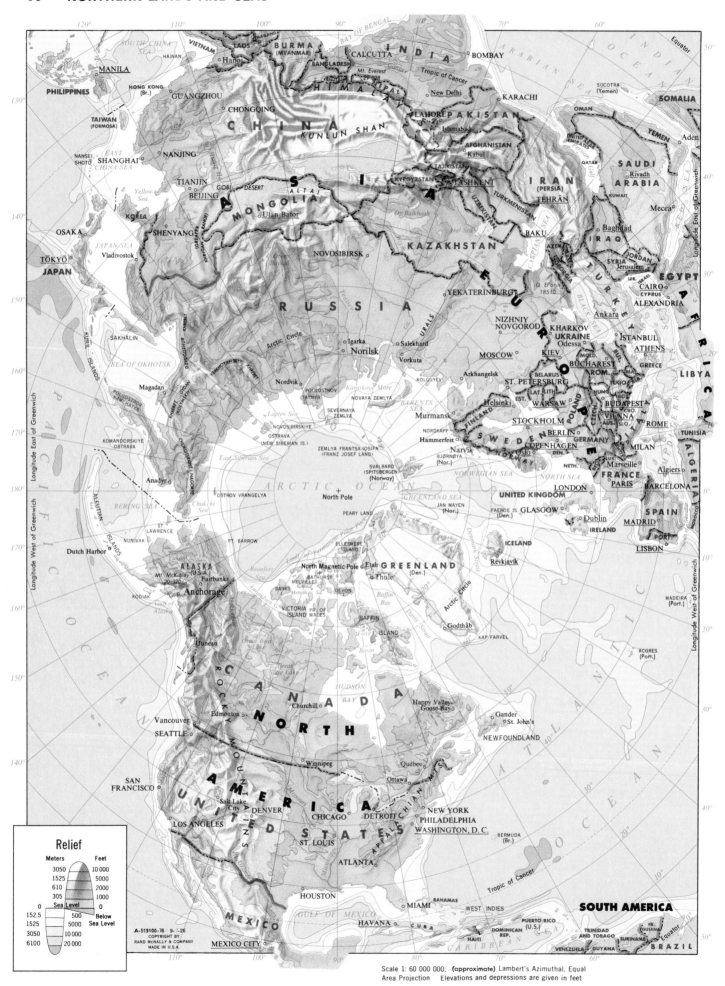

Relief

Meters	Feet
3050	10 000
1525	5000
610	2000
305	1000
0 Sea Level	0
152.5	500 Below
1525	5000 Sea Level
3050	10 000
6100	20 000

A-519100-76   9-1-26
COPYRIGHT BY
RAND M¢NALLY & COMPANY
MADE IN U.S.A.

Scale 1: 60 000 000; (approximate) Lambert's Azimuthal, Equal
Area Projection   Elevations and depressions are given in feet

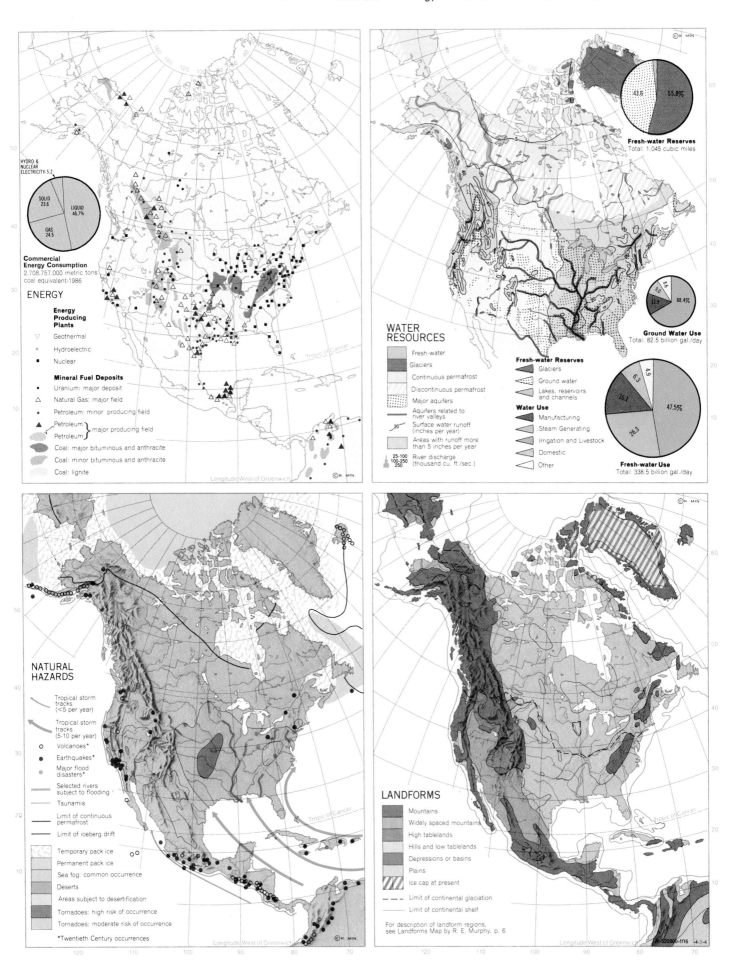

ENERGY

HYDRO. & NUCLEAR ELECTRICITY-5.2

SOLID 23.6
LIQUID 46.7%
GAS 24.5

Commercial Energy Consumption
2,708,757,000 metric tons
coal equivalent-1986

Energy Producing Plants
▽ Geothermal
• Hydroelectric
■ Nuclear

Mineral Fuel Deposits
• Uranium: major deposit
△ Natural Gas: major field
• Petroleum: minor producing field
▲ Petroleum } major producing field
   Petroleum }
Coal: major bituminous and anthracite
Coal: minor bituminous and anthracite
Coal: lignite

WATER RESOURCES

Fresh-water
Glaciers
Continuous permafrost
Discontinuous permafrost
Major aquifers
Aquifers related to river valleys
—20— Surface water runoff (inches per year)
Areas with runoff more than 5 inches per year
River discharge (thousand cu. ft./sec.)
25-100
100-250
250

Fresh-water Reserves
Total: 1,045 cubic miles
43.5 / 55.8%

Fresh-water Reserves
◣ Glaciers
◣ Ground water
◣ Lakes, reservoirs and channels

Water Use
◣ Manufacturing
◣ Steam Generating
◣ Irrigation and Livestock
◣ Domestic
◣ Other

Ground Water Use
Total: 82.5 billion gal./day
8.6 / 9.0 / 13.9 / 68.4%

Fresh-water Use
Total: 338.5 billion gal./day
4.9 / 6.3 / 15.1 / 26.3 / 47.5%

NATURAL HAZARDS

Tropical storm tracks (<5 per year)
Tropical storm tracks (5-10 per year)
○ Volcanoes*
● Earthquakes*
● Major flood disasters*
Selected rivers subject to flooding
Tsunamis
Limit of continuous permafrost
Limit of iceberg drift
Temporary pack ice
Permanent pack ice
Sea fog: common occurrence
Deserts
Areas subject to desertification
Tornadoes: high risk of occurrence
Tornadoes: moderate risk of occurrence

*Twentieth Century occurrences

LANDFORMS

Mountains
Widely spaced mountains
High tablelands
Hills and low tablelands
Depressions or basins
Plains
Ice cap at present

— — Limit of continental glaciation
—— Limit of continental shelf

For description of landform regions,
see Landforms Map by R. E. Murphy, p. 6

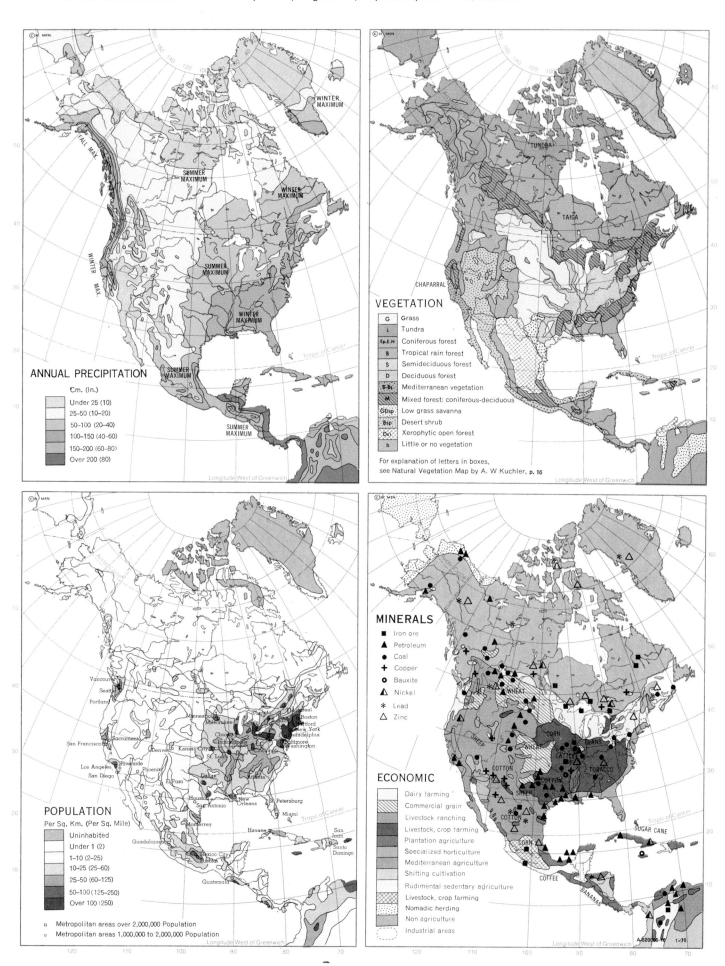

ANNUAL PRECIPITATION

WINTER MAXIMUM

FALL MAX

SUMMER MAXIMUM

WINTER MAXIMUM

WINTER MAX.

SUMMER MAXIMUM

WINTER MAXIMUM

SUMMER MAXIMUM

SUMMER MAXIMUM

Tropic of Cancer

Longitude West of Greenwich

Cm. (In.)

- Under 25 (10)
- 25–50 (10–20)
- 50–100 (20–40)
- 100–150 (40–60)
- 150–200 (60–80)
- Over 200 (80)

VEGETATION

TUNDRA

TAIGA

CHAPARRAL

Tropic of Cancer

Longitude West of Greenwich

G	Grass
L	Tundra
Ep.E.N	Coniferous forest
B	Tropical rain forest
S	Semideciduous forest
D	Deciduous forest
B–Bs	Mediterranean vegetation
M	Mixed forest: coniferous-deciduous
GDsp	Low grass savanna
Bsp	Desert shrub
Dc1	Xerophytic open forest
b	Little or no vegetation

For explanation of letters in boxes,
see Natural Vegetation Map by A. W Kuchler, **p. 16**

POPULATION

Vancouver
Seattle
Portland
San Francisco
Sacramento
Los Angeles
Riverside
San Diego
Phoenix
El Paso
Denver
Kansas City
St. Louis
Dallas
Houston
San Antonio
New Orleans
Minneapolis
Milwaukee
Chicago
Indianapolis
Cincinnati
Atlanta
St Petersburg
Miami
Toronto
Detroit
Buffalo
Montreal
Boston
Hartford
New York
Philadelphia
Baltimore
Washington
Monterrey
Guadalajara
Mexico City
Puebla
Guatemala
Havana
San Juan
Santo Domingo

Tropic of Cancer

Per Sq. Km. (Per Sq. Mile)

- Uninhabited
- Under 1 (2)
- 1–10 (2–25)
- 10–25 (25–60)
- 25–50 (60–125)
- 50–100 (125–250)
- Over 100 (250)

□ Metropolitan areas over 2,000,000 Population
○ Metropolitan areas 1,000,000 to 2,000,000 Population

Longitude West of Greenwich

MINERALS

- ■ Iron ore
- ▲ Petroleum
- ● Coal
- + Copper
- ○ Bauxite
- △ Nickel
- ✳ Lead
- △ Zinc

WHEAT
CORN
BEANS
CATTLE
TOBACCO
WHEAT
SHEEP
COTTON
COTTON
SHEEP
COTTON
CORN
COFFEE
SUGAR CANE
BANANAS

Tropic of Cancer

ECONOMIC

- Dairy farming
- Commercial grain
- Livestock ranching
- Livestock, crop farming
- Plantation agriculture
- Specialized horticulture
- Mediterranean agriculture
- Shifting cultivation
- Rudimental sedentary agriculture
- Livestock, crop farming
- Nomadic herding
- Non agriculture
- Industrial areas

Longitude West of Greenwich

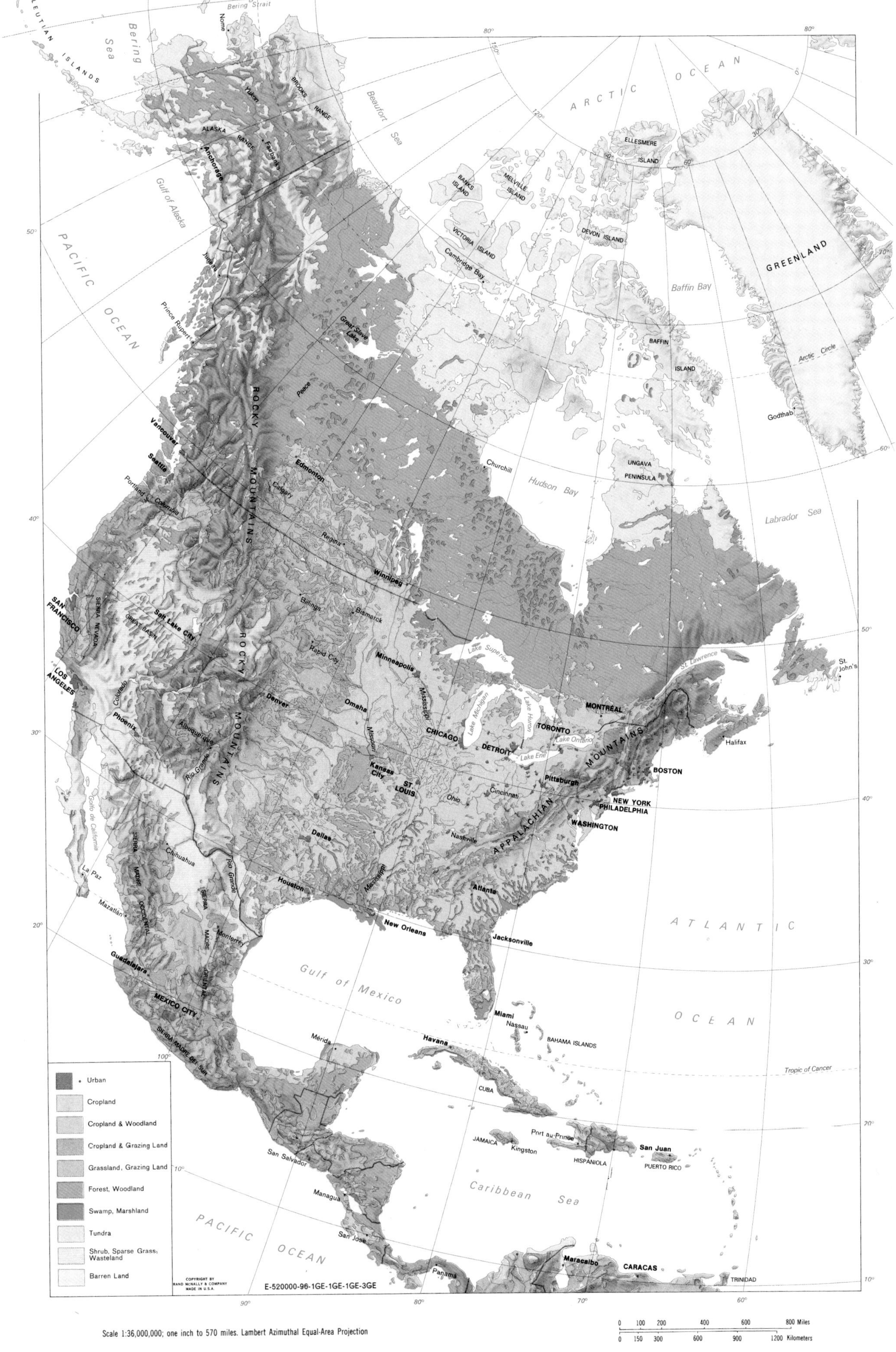

ARCTIC OCEAN

ALEUTIAN ISLANDS
Bering Strait
Nome
Bering Sea
Gulf of Alaska
PACIFIC OCEAN

Anchorage
ALASKA RANGE
BROOKS RANGE
Yukon
Fairbanks
Beaufort Sea

ELLESMERE ISLAND
BANKS ISLAND
MELVILLE ISLAND
DEVON ISLAND
VICTORIA ISLAND
Cambridge Bay
GREENLAND
Baffin Bay
BAFFIN ISLAND
Arctic Circle
Godthåb

ROCKY MOUNTAINS
Prince Rupert
Peace
Great Slave Lake
Churchill
Hudson Bay
UNGAVA PENINSULA
Labrador Sea

Vancouver
Seattle
Portland
Columbia
Edmonton
Calgary
Regina
Winnipeg

SAN FRANCISCO
SIERRA NEVADA
GREAT BASIN
Salt Lake City
Billings
Bismarck
Rapid City
Minneapolis
Lake Superior

LOS ANGELES
Colorado
Denver
Omaha
Missouri
Mississippi
CHICAGO
Lake Michigan
Lake Huron
Lake Ontario
Lake Erie
DETROIT
TORONTO
MONTREAL
St. Lawrence
St. John's

Phoenix
Albuquerque
Rio Grande
Kansas City
ST. LOUIS
Ohio
Cincinnati
Pittsburgh
APPALACHIAN MOUNTAINS
BOSTON
NEW YORK
PHILADELPHIA
WASHINGTON
Halifax

Chihuahua
SIERRA MADRE OCCIDENTAL
Dallas
Nashville
Atlanta

La Paz
Golfo de California
Mazatlán
Monterrey
SIERRA MADRE ORIENTAL
Houston
Mississippi
New Orleans
Jacksonville

Guadalajara
Gulf of Mexico
Miami
Nassau
BAHAMA ISLANDS

MEXICO CITY
SIERRA MADRE DEL SUR
Mérida
Havana
Tropic of Cancer

CUBA
ATLANTIC OCEAN

San Salvador
Port au Prince
JAMAICA
Kingston
HISPANIOLA
San Juan
PUERTO RICO

Managua
San Jose
Panama
Caribbean Sea
TRINIDAD
Maracaibo
CARACAS

PACIFIC OCEAN

Legend

- • Urban
- Cropland
- Cropland & Woodland
- Cropland & Grazing Land
- Grassland, Grazing Land
- Forest, Woodland
- Swamp, Marshland
- Tundra
- Shrub, Sparse Grass, Wasteland
- Barren Land

COPYRIGHT BY
RAND McNALLY & COMPANY
MADE IN U.S.A.

E-520000-96-1GE-1GE-1GE-3GE

Scale 1:36,000,000; one inch to 570 miles. Lambert Azimuthal Equal-Area Projection

0 100 200 400 600 800 Miles
0 150 300 600 900 1200 Kilometers

Moosonee
James Bay
Gulf of St. Lawrence
St. Lawrence
Thunder Bay
Lake Superior
Quebec
Halifax
Duluth
Sudbury
45°
MONTREAL
Bangor
65°
Minneapolis
Lake Huron
Lake Michigan
TORONTO
Lake Ontario
BOSTON
Mississippi
Milwaukee
Buffalo
40°
DETROIT
Lake Erie
Cleveland
NEW YORK
CHICAGO
Pittsburgh
PHILADELPHIA
APPALACHIAN MOUNTAINS
WASHINGTON
Indianapolis
Cincinnati
Kansas City
Ohio
Norfolk
35°
Missouri
ST. LOUIS
Roanoke
PLATEAU
Nashville
Charlotte
OZARK
ATLANTIC OCEAN
Arkansas
Memphis
Little Rock
Mississippi
Atlanta
70°
Birmingham
Charleston
Red
Jacksonville
30°
75°
Tallahassee
Houston
New Orleans
Tampa
Gulf of Mexico
Miami
Nassau
25°

Legend:
- Urban
- Cropland
- Cropland & Woodland
- Cropland & Grazing Land
- Grassland, Grazing Land
- Forest, Woodland
- Swamp, Marshland
- Shrub, Sparse Grass, Wasteland
- Barren Land

Scale 1:12,000,000; one inch to 190 miles. Polyconic Projection

0   50   100   200   300   400 Miles
0   75   150   300   450   600 Kilometers

PHYSIOGRAPHIC DIVISIONS

1 Pacific Mountain System
2 Intermontane Plateaus
3 Rocky Mountain System
4 Interior Plains
5 Ozark-Ouachita Highlands
6 Gulf-Atlantic Plain
7 Appalachian Highlands
8 Laurentian Upland (Canadian Shield)
9 Hudson Bay Lowland

0	25	50	75	100	200	300	400	500 Miles

0	50	100	200	400	600	800 Kilometers

Scale 1: 12 000 000; One inch to 190 miles.   POLYCONIC PROJECTION

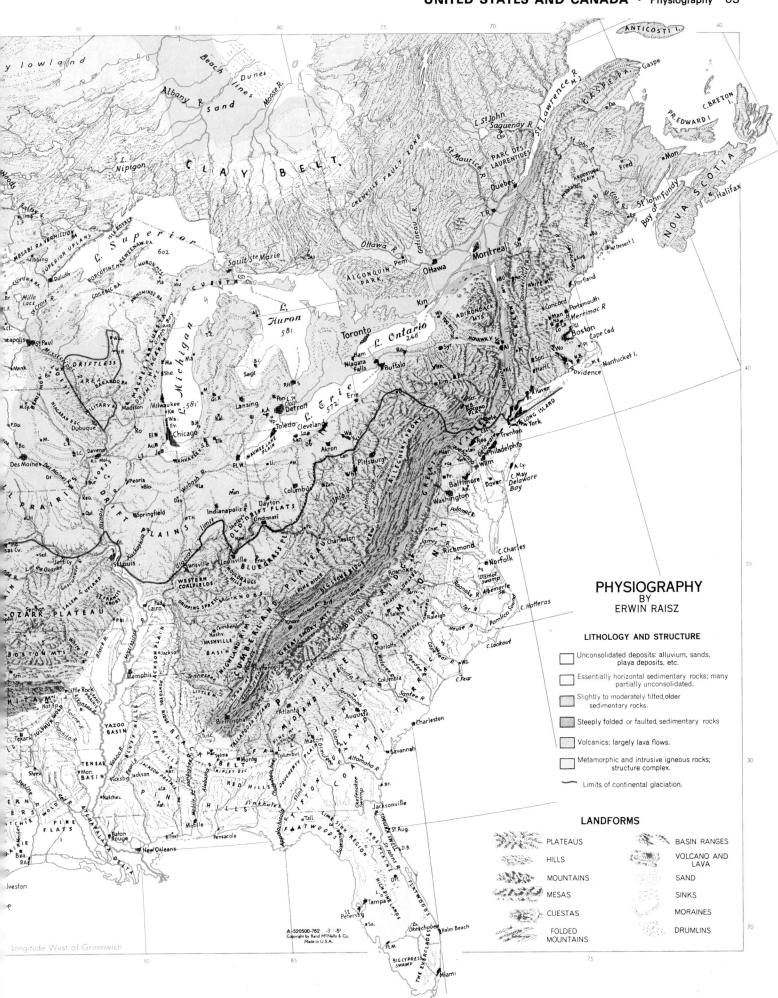

PHYSIOGRAPHY
BY
ERWIN RAISZ

LITHOLOGY AND STRUCTURE

- Unconsolidated deposits: alluvium, sands, playa deposits, etc.
- Essentially horizontal sedimentary rocks; many partially unconsolidated.
- Slightly to moderately tilted, older sedimentary rocks.
- Steeply folded or faulted, sedimentary rocks
- Volcanics; largely lava flows.
- Metamorphic and intrusive igneous rocks; structure complex.
- — Limits of continental glaciation.

LANDFORMS

- PLATEAUS
- HILLS
- MOUNTAINS
- MESAS
- CUESTAS
- FOLDED MOUNTAINS
- BASIN RANGES
- VOLCANO AND LAVA
- SAND
- SINKS
- MORAINES
- DRUMLINS

Longitude West of Greenwich

A-520500-762 -3 1-52
Copyright by Rand McNally & Co.
Made in U.S.A.

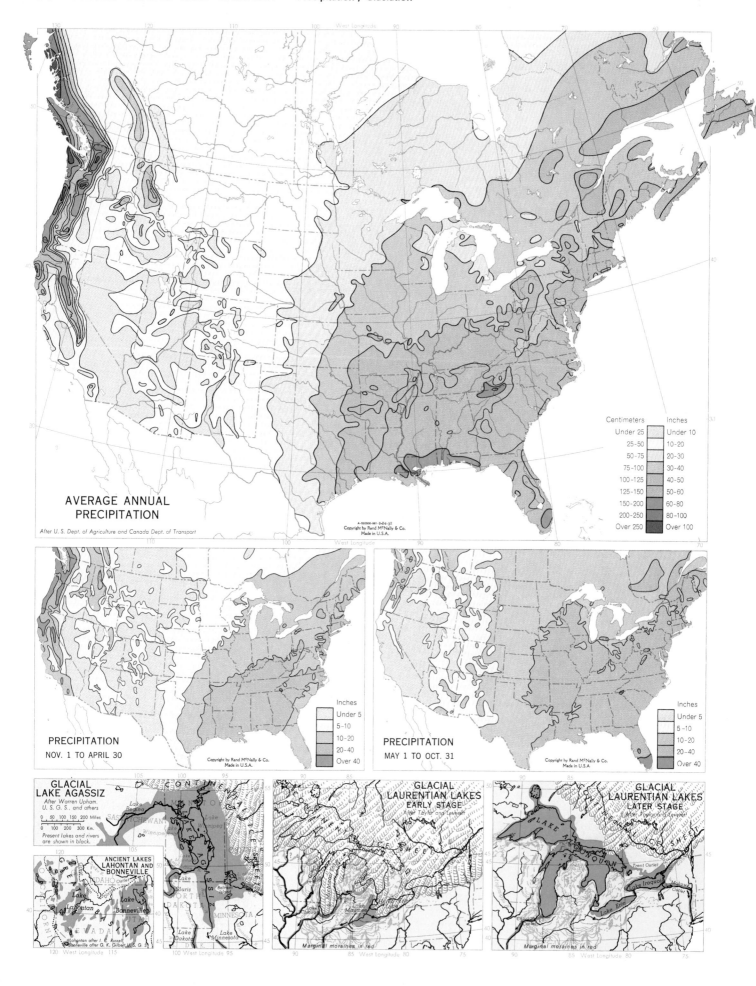

AVERAGE ANNUAL
PRECIPITATION

After U. S. Dept. of Agriculture and Canada Dept. of Transport

A-520500-961-2-2-a-32
Copyright by Rand M°Nally & Co.
Made in U.S.A.

Centimeters	Inches
Under 25	Under 10
25–50	10–20
50–75	20–30
75–100	30–40
100–125	40–50
125–150	50–60
150–200	60–80
200–250	80–100
Over 250	Over 100

PRECIPITATION

NOV. 1 TO APRIL 30

Copyright by Rand M°Nally & Co.
Made in U.S.A

Inches
Under 5
5–10
10–20
20–40
Over 40

PRECIPITATION

MAY 1 TO OCT. 31

Copyright by Rand M°Nally & Co.
Made in U.S.A

Inches
Under 5
5–10
10–20
20–40
Over 40

GLACIAL
LAKE AGASSIZ
After Warren Upham.
U. S. G. S., and others

0 50 100 150 200 Miles
0 100 200 300 Km.

Present lakes and rivers
are shown in black.

ANCIENT LAKES
LAHONTAN AND
BONNEVILLE

Lahontan after I. C. Russell
Bonneville after G. K. Gilbert, U. S. G. S.

GLACIAL
LAURENTIAN LAKES
EARLY STAGE
After Taylor and Leverett

Marginal moraines in red

GLACIAL
LAURENTIAN LAKES
LATER STAGE
After Taylor and Leverett

Marginal moraines in red

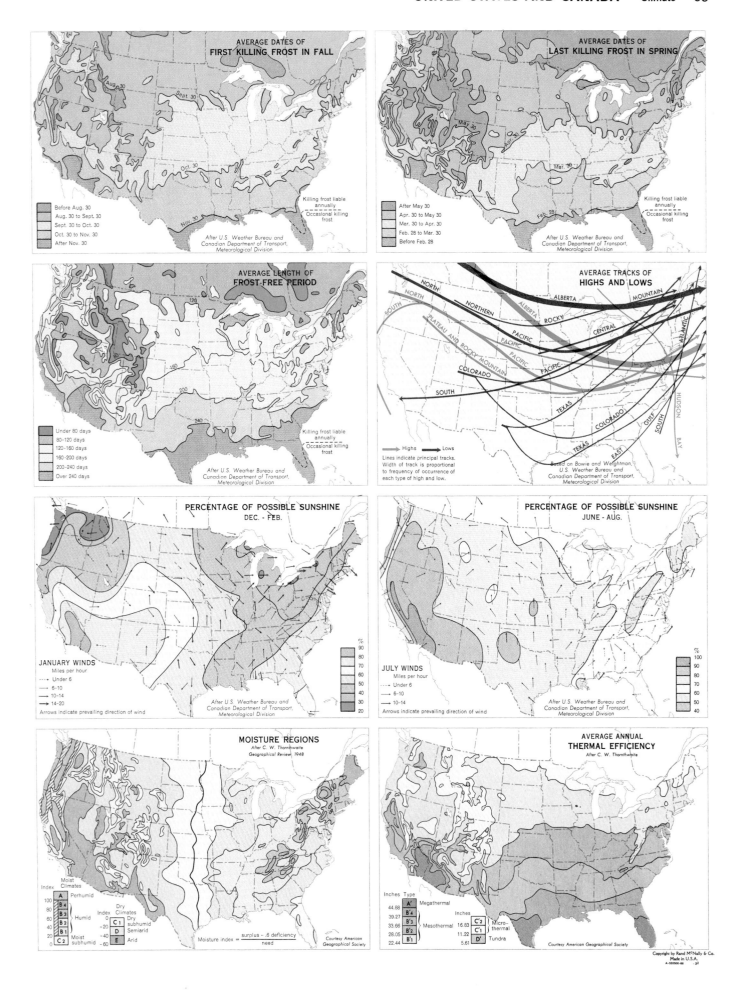

AVERAGE DATES OF FIRST KILLING FROST IN FALL

Before Aug. 30
Aug. 30 to Sept. 30
Sept. 30 to Oct. 30
Oct. 30 to Nov. 30
After Nov. 30

Killing frost liable annually
Occasional killing frost

After U.S. Weather Bureau and Canadian Department of Transport, Meteorological Division

AVERAGE DATES OF LAST KILLING FROST IN SPRING

After May 30
Apr. 30 to May 30
Mar. 30 to Apr. 30
Feb. 28 to Mar. 30
Before Feb. 28

Killing frost liable annually
Occasional killing frost

After U.S. Weather Bureau and Canadian Department of Transport, Meteorological Division

AVERAGE LENGTH OF FROST-FREE PERIOD

Under 80 days
80-120 days
120-160 days
160-200 days
200-240 days
Over 240 days

Killing frost liable annually
Occasional killing frost

After U.S. Weather Bureau and Canadian Department of Transport, Meteorological Division

AVERAGE TRACKS OF HIGHS AND LOWS

Highs
Lows

Lines indicate principal tracks. Width of track is proportional to frequency of occurrence of each type of high and low.

Based on Bowie and Weightman, U.S. Weather Bureau and Canadian Department of Transport, Meteorological Division

PERCENTAGE OF POSSIBLE SUNSHINE DEC. - FEB.

JANUARY WINDS
Miles per hour
Under 6
6-10
10-14
14-20
Arrows indicate prevailing direction of wind

%
90
80
70
60
50
40
30
20

After U.S. Weather Bureau and Canadian Department of Transport, Meteorological Division

PERCENTAGE OF POSSIBLE SUNSHINE JUNE - AUG.

JULY WINDS
Miles per hour
Under 6
6-10
10-14
Arrows indicate prevailing direction of wind

%
100
90
80
70
60
50
40

After U.S. Weather Bureau and Canadian Department of Transport, Meteorological Division

MOISTURE REGIONS
After C. W. Thornthwaite
Geographical Review, 1948

Index
Moist Climates
100 A   Perhumid
80   B4
     B3   Humid
60   B2
40   B1
20   C2   Moist
0   C1   subhumid

Dry Climates
Index
0   C1   Dry subhumid
-20 D   Semiarid
-40 E   Arid
-60

Moisture index = surplus − .6 deficiency / need

Courtesy American Geographical Society

AVERAGE ANNUAL THERMAL EFFICIENCY
After C. W. Thornthwaite

Inches Type
44.88   A'   Megathermal
39.27   B'4
33.66   B'3   Mesothermal
28.05   B'2
22.44   B'1

Inches
16.83   C'2   Microthermal
11.22   C'1
5.61   D'   Tundra

Courtesy American Geographical Society

Copyright by Rand McNally & Co.
Made in U.S.A.
A-520500-66   32

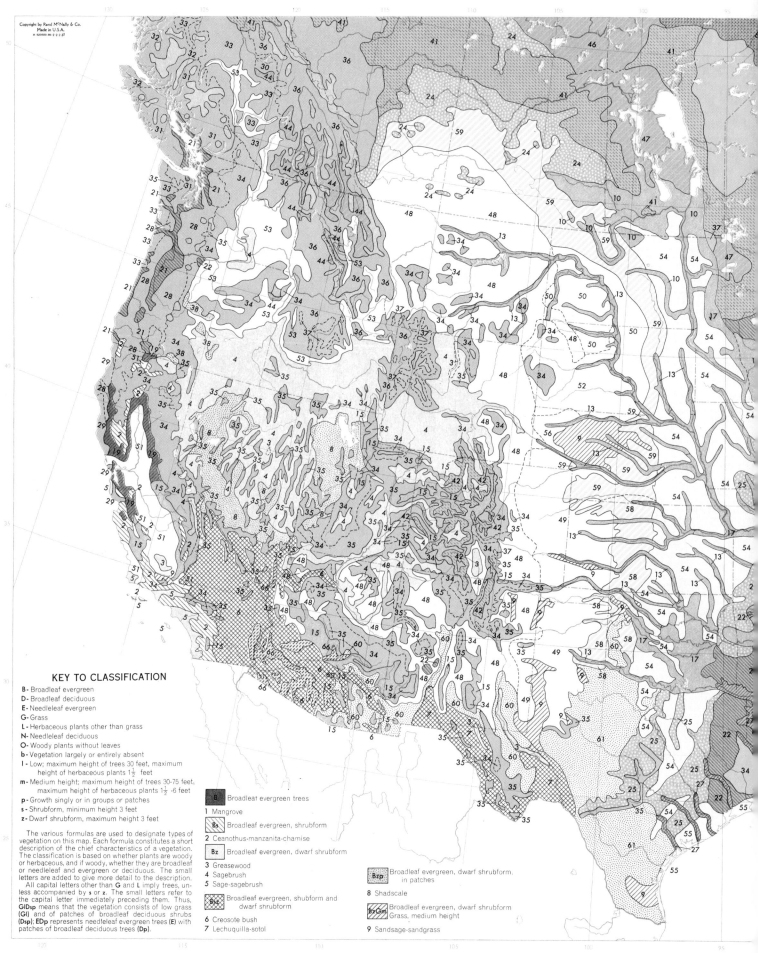

Copyright by Rand McNally & Co.
Made in U.S.A.
A-520500-86-2-2-2-32

KEY TO CLASSIFICATION

B - Broadleaf evergreen
D - Broadleaf deciduous
E - Needleleaf evergreen
G - Grass
L - Herbaceous plants other than grass
N - Needleleaf deciduous
O - Woody plants without leaves
b - Vegetation largely or entirely absent
l - Low; maximum height of trees 30 feet, maximum
    height of herbaceous plants $1\frac{1}{2}$ feet
m - Medium height; maximum height of trees 30-75 feet,
    maximum height of herbaceous plants $1\frac{1}{2}$ -6 feet
p - Growth singly or in groups or patches
s - Shrubform, minimum height 3 feet
z - Dwarf shrubform, maximum height 3 feet

The various formulas are used to designate types of
vegetation on this map. Each formula constitutes a short
description of the chief characteristics of a vegetation.
The classification is based on whether plants are woody
or herbaceous, and if woody, whether they are broadleaf
or needleleaf and evergreen or deciduous. The small
letters are added to give more detail to the description.

All capital letters other than G and L imply trees, unless accompanied by s or z. The small letters refer to
the capital letter immediately preceding them. Thus,
GlDsp means that the vegetation consists of low grass
(Gl) and of patches of broadleaf deciduous shrubs
(Dsp); EDp represents needleleaf evergreen trees (E) with
patches of broadleaf deciduous trees (Dp).

B Broadleaf evergreen trees

1 Mangrove

Bs Broadleaf evergreen, shrubform

2 Ceanothus-manzanita-chamise

Bz Broadleaf evergreen, dwarf shrubform

3 Greasewood
4 Sagebrush
5 Sage-sagebrush

Bsz Broadleaf evergreen, shubform and
      dwarf shrubform

6 Creosote bush
7 Lechuquilla-sotol

Bzp Broadleaf evergreen, dwarf shrubform,
      in patches

8 Shadscale

BzGm Broadleaf evergreen, dwarf shrubform
       Grass, medium height

9 Sandsage-sandgrass

0 25 50 75 100   200   300   400   500 Miles

0 50 100   200   400   600   800 Kilometers

Scale 1:14 000 000;   One inch to 220 miles.

NATURAL VEGETATION

BY A. W. KÜCHLER

Based on "A Physiognomic Classification of Vegetation"
Annals of the Assoc. of American Geographers, Vol. 39, September, 1949

D Broadleaf deciduous trees

10 Aspen-oak
11 Beech-maple
12 Beech-tulip tree-maple-basswood
13 Cottonwood-willow
14 Maple-basswood
15 Oak
16 Oak-ash-maple
17 Oak-hickory
18 Oak-tulip tree

DB Broadleaf deciduous trees
Broadleaf evergreen trees

19 Oak-madrone

DE Broadleaf deciduous trees
Needleleaf evergreen trees

20 Maple-yellow birch-hemlock-pine
21 Oak-Douglas fir
22 Oak-pine
23 Maple-beech-hemlock

D / Gmp Broadleaf deciduous trees
Grass, medium height, in patches

24 Aspen-needle grass-wheat grass
25 Oak-hickory-bluestem

DN Broadleaf deciduous trees
Needleleaf deciduous trees

26 Bay trees-bald cypress
27 Tupelo-gum-bald cypress

E Needleleaf evergreen trees

28 Douglas fir
29 Douglas fir-redwood
30 Hemlock-arbor vitae
31 Hemlock-arbor vitae-Douglas fir
32 Hemlock-arbor vitae-fir
33 Hemlock-spruce
34 Pine
35 Pine-juniper
36 Pine-spruce
37 Spruce-fir

Esp Needleleaf evergreen, shrubform,
in patches

38 Juniper

EDp Needleleaf evergreen trees
Broadleaf deciduous trees, in patches

39 Douglas fir-pine-aspen
40 Pine-spruce-birch
41 Spruce-aspen
42 Spruce-fir-aspen
43 Spruce-poplar-birch

EN Needleleaf evergreen trees
Needleleaf deciduous trees

44 Hemlock-arbor vitae-Douglas fir-larch
45 Pine-bald cypress
46 Pine-spruce-larch
47 Spruce-larch

Gl Grass, low

48 Grama grass
49 Grama grass-buffalo grass
50 Grama grass-needle grass
51 Needle grass-blue grass
52 Wheat grass
53 Wheat grass-blue grass

Gm Grass, medium height

54 Bluestem
55 Broom grass-water grass
56 Marsh grass
57 Saw grass

Gml Grass, medium and low height

58 Bluestem-bunch grass
59 Needle grass-wheat grass

Gl / Dsp Grass, low
Broadleaf deciduous, shrubform, in patches

60 Bunch grass-oak

Gm / Dsp Grass, medium height
Broadleaf deciduous, shrubform, in patches

61 Mesquite grass-mesquite

L Herbaceous plants other than grass

62 Lichens, etc.

LEp Herbaceous plants other than grass
Needleleaf evergreen trees, in patches

63 Lichens-spruce

LEp / Np Herbaceous plants other than grass
Needleleaf evergreen trees, in patches
Needleleaf deciduous trees, in patches

64 Lichens-spruce-larch

N Needleleaf deciduous trees

65 Bald cypress

Op Woody plants without leaves, in patches

66 Palo verde-cacti-ocotillo

b Vegetation largely or entirely absent

LAMBERT CONFORMAL CONIC PROJECTION

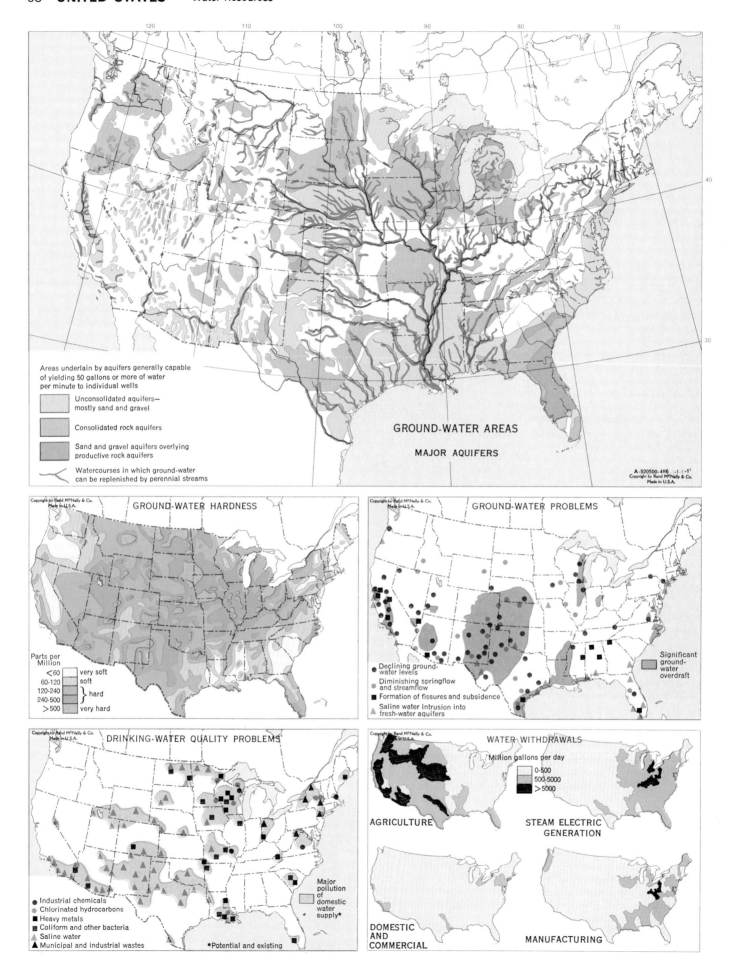

Areas underlain by aquifers generally capable
of yielding 50 gallons or more of water
per minute to individual wells

Unconsolidated aquifers—
mostly sand and gravel

Consolidated rock aquifers

Sand and gravel aquifers overlying
productive rock aquifers

Watercourses in which ground-water
can be replenished by perennial streams

GROUND-WATER AREAS

MAJOR AQUIFERS

A-520500-4H6 -1-1-1¹
Copyright by Rand McNally & Co.
Made in U.S.A.

GROUND-WATER HARDNESS

Parts per
Million
<60   very soft
60-120   soft
120-240   } hard
240-500
>500   very hard

Copyright by Rand McNally & Co.
Made in U.S.A.

GROUND-WATER PROBLEMS

Declining ground-
water levels
Diminishing springflow
and streamflow
Formation of fissures and subsidence
Saline water intrusion into
fresh-water aquifers

Significant
ground-
water
overdraft

Copyright by Rand McNally & Co.
Made in U.S.A.

DRINKING-WATER QUALITY PROBLEMS

Industrial chemicals
Chlorinated hydrocarbons
Heavy metals
Coliform and other bacteria
Saline water
Municipal and industrial wastes

Major
pollution
of
domestic
water
supply*

*Potential and existing

Copyright by Rand McNally & Co.
Made in U.S.A.

WATER WITHDRAWALS

Million gallons per day
0-500
500-5000
>5000

AGRICULTURE

STEAM ELECTRIC
GENERATION

DOMESTIC
AND
COMMERCIAL

MANUFACTURING

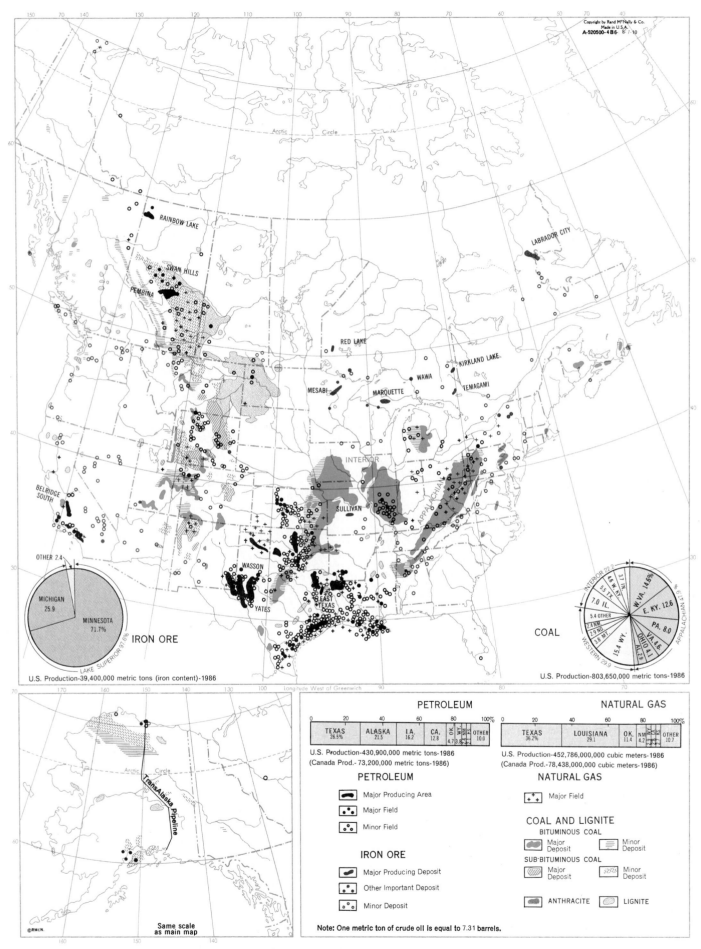

Copyright by Rand McNally & Co.
Made in U.S.A.
A-520500-4 B6- 8-7-10

RAINBOW LAKE

LABRADOR CITY

SWAN HILLS

PEMBINA

RED LAKE

KIRKLAND LAKE

MESABI
MARQUETTE
WAWA
TEMAGAMI

INTERIOR

BELRIDGE
SOUTH

SULLIVAN

APPALACHIAN

WASSON

OTHER 2.4

MICHIGAN
25.9

MINNESOTA
71.7%

EAST
TEXAS

YATES

LAKE SUPERIOR 97.6%

IRON ORE

U.S. Production-39,400,000 metric tons (iron content)-1986

COAL

INTERIOR 22.2
4.6 W. KY.
3.7 IN.
5.5 TX.
7.0 IL.
5.4 OTHER
2.4 UT
2.9 ND
3.8 MT.
15.4 WY.
WESTERN 29.9
AL 2.9
OHIO 4.1
VA. 4.6
PA. 8.0
E. KY. 12.6
W. VA. 14.6%
APPALACHIAN 47.9

U.S. Production-803,650,000 metric tons-1986

Longitude West of Greenwich

Arctic Circle

Trans-Alaska Pipeline

©RMCN.

Same scale
as main map

PETROLEUM

TEXAS 26.5%	ALASKA 21.5	LA. 16.2	CA. 12.8	OK. 4.7	WY. 3.8	KS. NM	OTHER 10.0

U.S. Production-430,900,000 metric tons-1986
(Canada Prod.-73,200,000 metric tons-1986)

NATURAL GAS

TEXAS 36.2%	LOUISIANA 29.1	O.K. 11.4	NM 4.2	KS	WY	OTHER 10.7

U.S. Production-452,786,000,000 cubic meters-1986
(Canada Prod.-78,438,000,000 cubic meters-1986)

PETROLEUM

- Major Producing Area
- Major Field
- Minor Field

IRON ORE

- Major Producing Deposit
- Other Important Deposit
- Minor Deposit

NATURAL GAS

- Major Field

COAL AND LIGNITE

BITUMINOUS COAL
- Major Deposit
- Minor Deposit

SUB-BITUMINOUS COAL
- Major Deposit
- Minor Deposit

- ANTHRACITE
- LIGNITE

Note: One metric ton of crude oil is equal to 7.31 barrels.

Scale 1: 32 000 000; One inch to 500 miles.   LAMBERT CONFORMAL CONIC PROJECTION

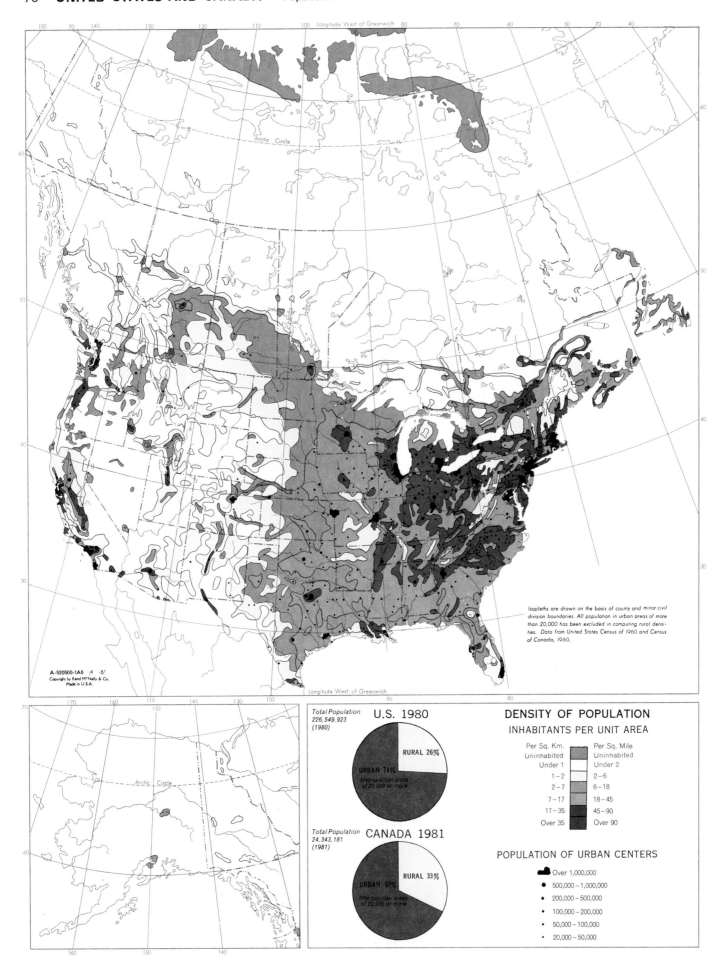

Isopleths are drawn on the basis of county and minor civil division boundaries. All population in urban areas of more than 20,000 has been excluded in computing rural densities. Data from United States Census of 1960 and Census of Canada, 1960.

A-520500-1A6 :4 -5¹
Copyright by Rand McNally & Co.
Made in U.S.A.

Total Population
226,549,923
(1980)

U.S. 1980

RURAL 26%

URBAN 74%
Metropolitan areas
of 20,000 or more

Total Population
24,343,181
(1981)

CANADA 1981

RURAL 33%

URBAN 67%
Metropolitan areas
of 20,000 or more

DENSITY OF POPULATION
INHABITANTS PER UNIT AREA

Per Sq. Km.	Per Sq. Mile
Uninhabited	Uninhabited
Under 1	Under 2
1–2	2–6
2–7	6–18
7–17	18–45
17–35	45–90
Over 35	Over 90

POPULATION OF URBAN CENTERS

Over 1,000,000
500,000 – 1,000,000
200,000 – 500,000
100,000 – 200,000
50,000 – 100,000
20,000 – 50,000

Scale 1: 32 000 000; One inch to 500 miles.   LAMBERT CONFORMAL CONIC PROJECTION

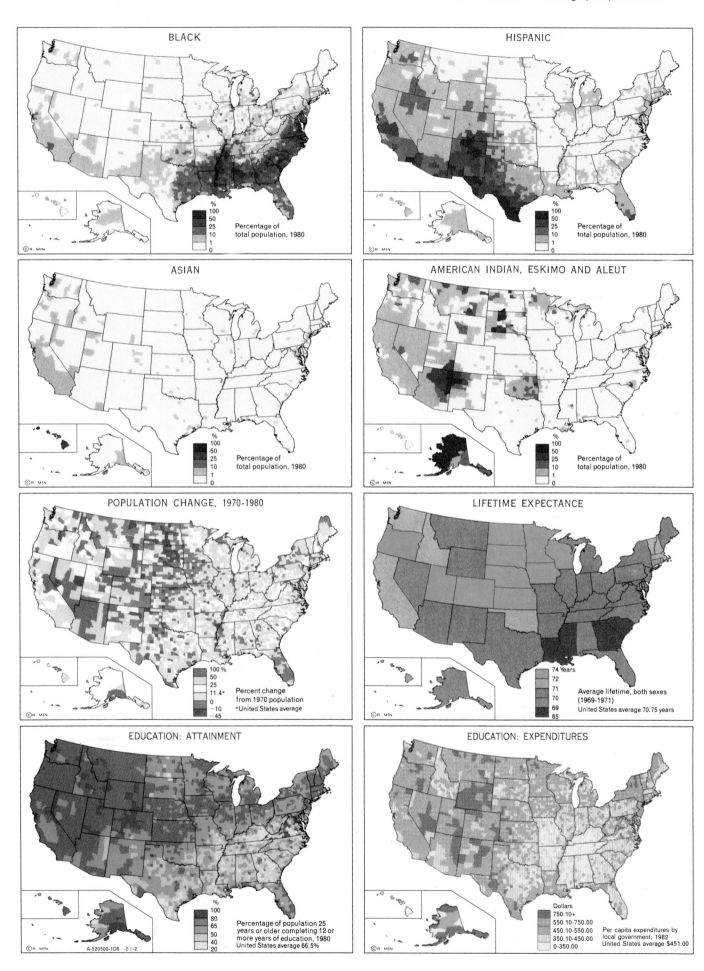

BLACK

Percentage of
total population, 1980

%
100
50
25
10
1
0

HISPANIC

Percentage of
total population, 1980

%
100
50
25
10
1
0

ASIAN

Percentage of
total population, 1980

%
100
50
25
10
1
0

AMERICAN INDIAN, ESKIMO AND ALEUT

Percentage of
total population, 1980

%
100
50
25
10
1
0

POPULATION CHANGE, 1970-1980

100 %
50
25
11.4*
0
−10
−45

Percent change
from 1970 population
*United States average

LIFETIME EXPECTANCE

74 Years
72
71
70
69
65

Average lifetime, both sexes
(1969-1971)
United States average 70.75 years

EDUCATION: ATTAINMENT

%
100
80
65
50
40
20

Percentage of population 25
years or older completing 12 or
more years of education, 1980
United States average 66.5%

A-520500-1D6   -2-2-2

EDUCATION: EXPENDITURES

Dollars
750.10+
550.10-750.00
450.10-550.00
350.10-450.00
0-350.00

Per capita expenditures by
local government, 1982
United States average $451.00

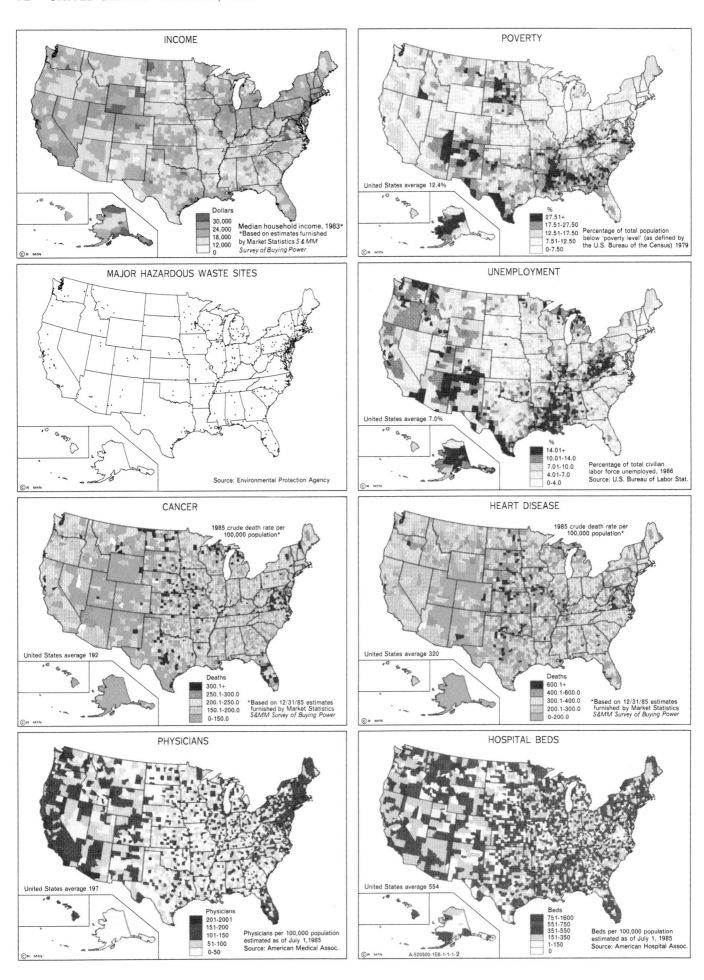

INCOME

Dollars
- 30,000
- 24,000
- 18,000
- 12,000
- 0

Median household income, 1983*
*Based on estimates furnished by Market Statistics *S & MM Survey of Buying Power*

POVERTY

United States average 12.4%

%
- 27.51+
- 17.51-27.50
- 12.51-17.50
- 7.51-12.50
- 0-7.50

Percentage of total population below 'poverty level' (as defined by the U.S. Bureau of the Census) 1979

MAJOR HAZARDOUS WASTE SITES

Source: Environmental Protection Agency

UNEMPLOYMENT

United States average 7.0%

%
- 14.01+
- 10.01-14.0
- 7.01-10.0
- 4.01-7.0
- 0-4.0

Percentage of total civilian labor force unemployed, 1986
Source: U.S. Bureau of Labor Stat.

CANCER

1985 crude death rate per 100,000 population*

United States average 192

Deaths
- 300.1+
- 250.1-300.0
- 200.1-250.0
- 150.1-200.0
- 0-150.0

*Based on 12/31/85 estimates furnished by Market Statistics *S&MM Survey of Buying Power*

HEART DISEASE

1985 crude death rate per 100,000 population*

United States average 320

Deaths
- 600.1+
- 400.1-600.0
- 300.1-400.0
- 200.1-300.0
- 0-200.0

*Based on 12/31/85 estimates furnished by Market Statistics *S&MM Survey of Buying Power*

PHYSICIANS

United States average 197

Physicians
- 201-2001
- 151-200
- 101-150
- 51-100
- 0-50

Physicians per 100,000 population estimated as of July 1, 1985
Source: American Medical Assoc.

HOSPITAL BEDS

United States average 554

Beds
- 751-1600
- 551-750
- 351-550
- 151-350
- 1-150
- 0

A-520500-1E6-1-1-1-2

Beds per 100,000 population estimated as of July 1, 1985
Source: American Hospital Assoc.

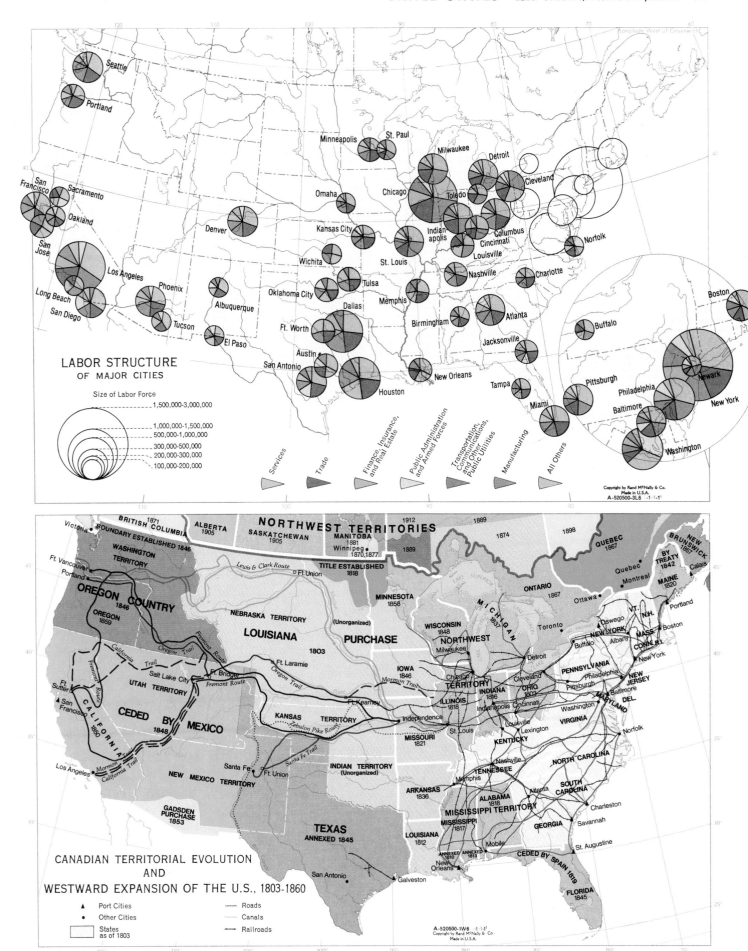

LABOR STRUCTURE
OF MAJOR CITIES

Size of Labor Force

1,500,000-3,000,000
1,000,000-1,500,000
500,000-1,000,000
300,000-500,000
200,000-300,000
100,000-200,000

Services Trade Finance, Insurance, and Real Estate Public Administration and Armed Forces Transportation, Communications, and Other Public Utilities Manufacturing All Others

Copyright by Rand McNally & Co.
Made in U.S.A.
A-520500-3L6 -1-1-1'

CANADIAN TERRITORIAL EVOLUTION
AND
WESTWARD EXPANSION OF THE U.S., 1803-1860

▲ Port Cities   Roads
● Other Cities   Canals
☐ States   Railroads
  as of 1803

A-520500-1W6 -1-1-1'
Copyright by Rand McNally & Co.
Made in U.S.A.

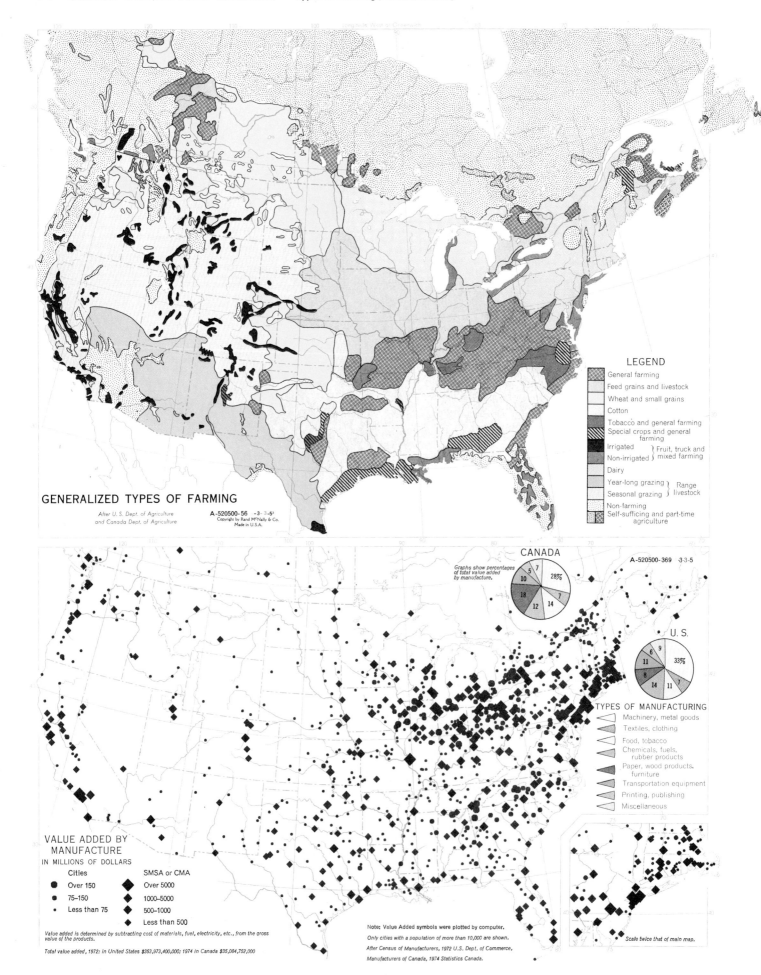

GENERALIZED TYPES OF FARMING

After U. S. Dept. of Agriculture
and Canada Dept. of Agriculture

A-520500-56 -3-3-5³
Copyright by Rand McNally & Co.
Made in U.S.A.

LEGEND

General farming
Feed grains and livestock
Wheat and small grains
Cotton
Tobacco and general farming
Special crops and general farming
Irrigated } Fruit, truck and
Non-irrigated } mixed farming
Dairy
Year-long grazing } Range
Seasonal grazing } livestock
Non-farming
Self-sufficing and part-time agriculture

CANADA

A-520500-369 -3-3-5

Graphs show percentages
of total value added
by manufacture.

5 7 28%
10
18 7
12 14

U.S.

6 9
11 33%
8
14 11 7

TYPES OF MANUFACTURING

Machinery, metal goods
Textiles, clothing
Food, tobacco
Chemicals, fuels, rubber products
Paper, wood products, furniture
Transportation equipment
Printing, publishing
Miscellaneous

VALUE ADDED BY MANUFACTURE

IN MILLIONS OF DOLLARS

Cities
● Over 150
• 75–150
· Less than 75

SMSA or CMA
◆ Over 5000
◆ 1000–5000
◆ 500–1000
◆ Less than 500

Value added is determined by subtracting cost of materials, fuel, electricity, etc., from the gross value of the products.

Total value added, 1972: in United States $353,973,400,000; 1974 in Canada $35,084,752,000

Note: Value Added symbols were plotted by computer.
Only cities with a population of more than 10,000 are shown.
After Census of Manufacturers, 1972 U.S. Dept. of Commerce,
Manufacturers of Canada, 1974 Statistics Canada.

Scale twice that of main map.

Scale 1: 28 000 000; One inch to 440 miles.   LAMBERT CONFORMAL CONIC PROJECTION

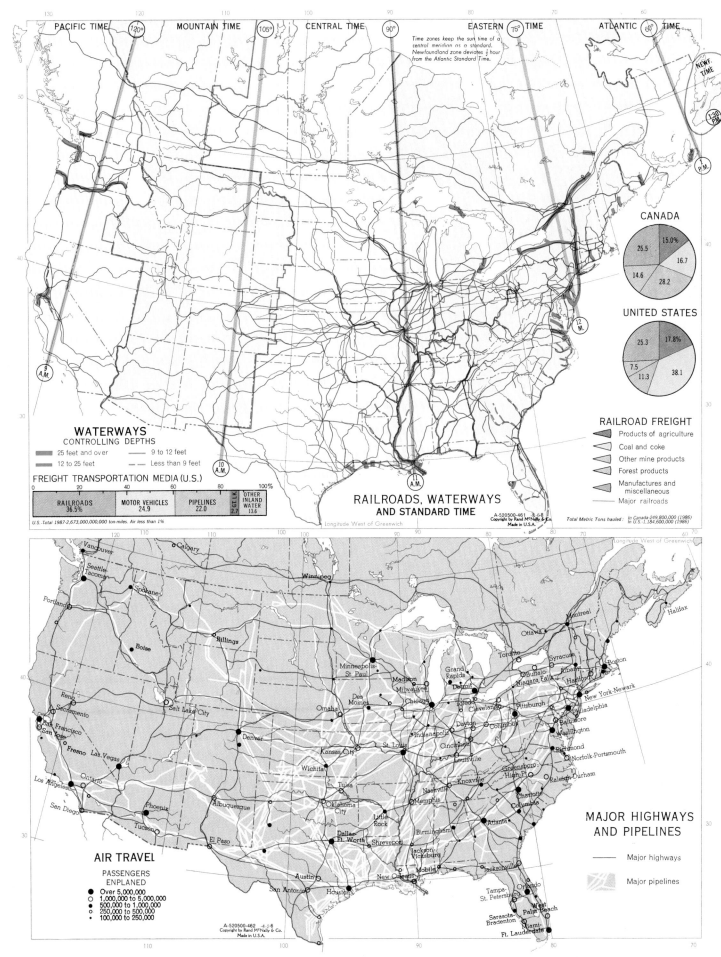

PACIFIC TIME | MOUNTAIN TIME | CENTRAL TIME | EASTERN TIME | ATLANTIC TIME

Time zones keep the sun time of a central meridian as a standard. Newfoundland zone deviates ½ hour from the Atlantic Standard Time.

CANADA

UNITED STATES

RAILROAD FREIGHT
Products of agriculture
Coal and coke
Other mine products
Forest products
Manufactures and miscellaneous
Major railroads

Total Metric Tons hauled: In Canada–249,800,000 (1986)
In U.S.–1,184,600,000 (1986)

WATERWAYS
CONTROLLING DEPTHS
25 feet and over
12 to 25 feet
9 to 12 feet
Less than 9 feet

FREIGHT TRANSPORTATION MEDIA (U.S.)

0	20	40	60	80	100%
RAILROADS 36.5%	MOTOR VEHICLES 24.9	PIPELINES 22.0	G.L.K. 2.7	OTHER INLAND WATER 13.6	

U.S.-Total 1987-2,673,000,000,000 ton-miles. Air less than 1%

RAILROADS, WATERWAYS
AND STANDARD TIME

A-520500-461 8-6-8
Copyright by Rand McNally & Co.
Made in U.S.A.

Longitude West of Greenwich

AIR TRAVEL
PASSENGERS ENPLANED
● Over 5,000,000
○ 1,000,000 to 5,000,000
• 500,000 to 1,000,000
○ 250,000 to 500,000
· 100,000 to 250,000

MAJOR HIGHWAYS
AND PIPELINES
Major highways
Major pipelines

A-520500-462 4-2-6
Copyright by Rand McNally & Co.
Made in U.S.A.

Scale 1: 28 000 000; One inch to 440 miles. LAMBERT CONFORMAL CONIC PROJECTION

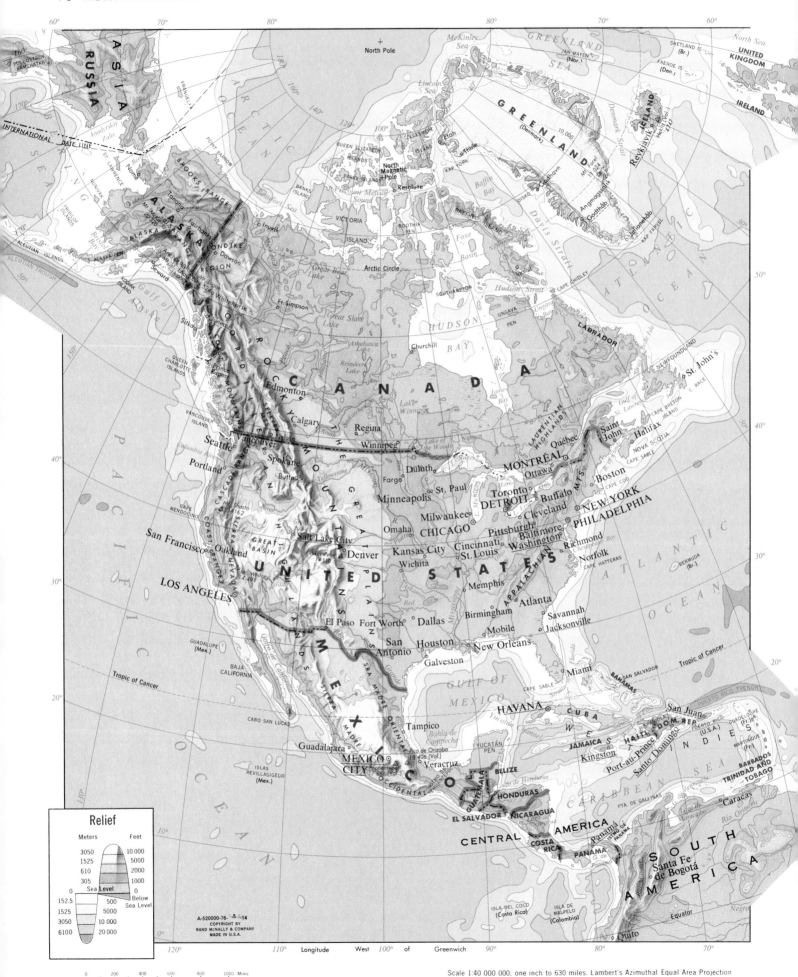

Relief

Meters	Feet
3050	10 000
1525	5000
610	2000
305	1000
0 Sea Level	0 Below Sea Level
152.5	500
1525	5000
3050	10 000
6100	20 000

A-520000-76- -5- -14
COPYRIGHT BY
RAND McNALLY & COMPANY
MADE IN U.S.A.

0 200 400 600 800 1000 Miles

0 400 800 1200 1600 Kilometers

Scale 1:40 000 000; one inch to 630 miles. Lambert's Azimuthal Equal Area Projection
Elevations and depressions are given in feet

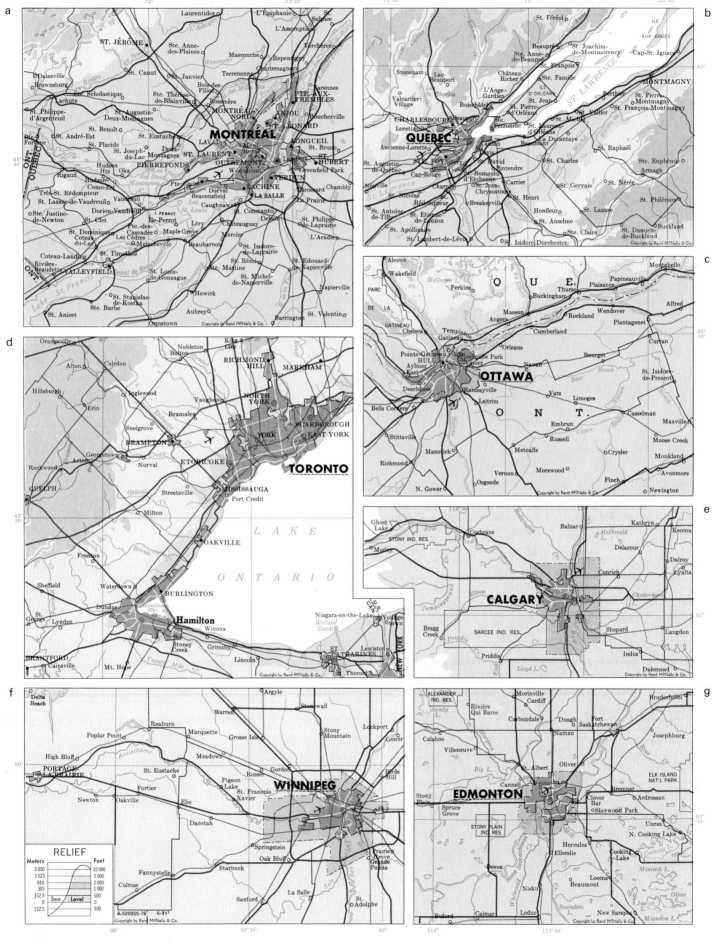

a

74°   73°30'

Laurentides
L'Épiphanie
Sulpice
L'Assomption
ST. JÉRÔME
Ste. Anne-des-Plaines
Mascouche
Repentigny
Verchères
St. Canut
St. Janvier
Terrebonne
Charlemagne
Dalesville
Bois-des-Filion
Brownsburg
Ste. Scholastique
Ste. Thérèse-de-Blainville
Rosemère
PTE.-AUX-TREMBLES
Lachute
St. Augustin-d'Argenteuil
Deux-Montagnes
St. Eustache
MONTRÉAL-NORD
ANJOU
Boucherville
St. Philippe-d'Argenteuil
St. Benoît
Ste. Thérèse
ST. LÉONARD
St. André-Est
ST. LAURENT
MONTRÉAL
St. Placide
St. Joseph-du-Lac
OUTREMONT
LONGUEUIL
Oka
Deux-Montagnes
Mont-Royal
ST. HUBERT
Hudson Hts.
WESTMOUNT
St. Bruno
Rigaud
Como-Est
PIERREFONDS
Greenfield Park
Très-St. Rédempteur
Hudson
VERDUN
Dorval
LACHINE
Brossard Chambly
St. Lazare-de-Vaudreuil
Beaconsfield
LA SALLE
La Prairie
Dorion-Vaudreuil
Vaudreuil
Caughnawaga
St. Constant
St. Justine-de-Newton
Île-Perrot
Léry
Delson
St. Clet
Pte.-des-Cascades
Châteauguay
St. Philippe-de-Laprairie
St. Dominique
Les Cèdres
Maple Grove
Mercier
L'Acadie
Coteau-du-Lac
Melocheville
Beauharnois
St. Isidore-de-Laprairie
Coteau-Landing
St. Timothée
Ste. Martine
St. Rémi
St. Michel-de-Napierville
Rivière-Beaudette
VALLEYFIELD
St. Louis-de-Gonzague
Howick
St. Édouard-de-Napierville
Napierville
St. Stanislas-de-Kostka
Aubrey
St. Anicet
Ste. Barbe
Ormstown
Barrington St. Valentin

Copyright by Rand McNally & Co.

b

71°30'   71°   70°30'

St. Féréol
ÎLE AUX GRUES
Stoneham
Ste. Anne-de-Beaupré
St. Joachim-de-Montmorency
Cap-St. Ignace
Beaupré
Château-Richer
St. François
MONTMAGNY
Lac-Beauport
St. Famille
Berthier
St. Pierre-Montmagny
Valcartier-Village
L'Ange-Gardien
ÎLE D'ORLÉANS
St. Pierre-d'Orléans
St. Michel
St. François-Montmagny
CHARLESBOURG
Boischatel
St. Jean
St. Vallier
Loretteville
Beauport
Ste. Pétronille
St. Laurent-d'Orléans
La Durantaye
St. Raphaël
Ancienne-Lorette
QUEBEC
Sillery
St. David
St. Charles
Ste. Euphémie
St. Augustin-de-Quebec
STE. FOY
Lauzon
Romauld
Bintendre
Armagh
Cap-Rouge
Charny
St. Jean-Chrysostome
Carrier
St. Gervais
St. Nérée
Neuville
St. Nicolas
St. Henri
St. Philémon
St. Antoine-de-Tilly
St. Étienne-de-Lauzon
Breakeyville
Honfleur
St. Lazare
St. Apollinaire
St. Anselme
Buckland
St. Lambert-de-Lévis
Ste. Claire
St. Damien-de-Buckland
S. Isidore Dorchester

Copyright by Rand McNally & Co.

c

Alcove
Montebello
Wakefield
Perkins
McGregor L.
Papineauville
PARC DE LA GATINEAU
Thurso
Plaisance
Buckingham
Alfred
Chelsea
Masson
Wendover
Angers
Rockland
Plantagenet
Templeton
Curran
Gatineau
Orleans
Pointe-Gatineau
HULL
Cumberland
St. Isidore-de-Prescott
Rockcliffe Park
Aylmer
East
Vanier
Navan
Bourget
Deschênes
OTTAWA
Bells Corners
Ramsayville
Vars
Limoges
Casselman
Leitrim
Maxville
Stittsville
Embrun
Russell
Moose Creek
Manotick
Metcalfe
Crysler
Monkland
Richmond
Morewood
Avonmore
N. Gower
Vernon
Finch
Osgoode
Newington

Copyright by Rand McNally & Co.

d

80°   King City   79°30'
Orangeville
Nobleton
Bolton
Alton
Caledon
RICHMOND HILL
MARKHAM
Hillsburgh
Inglewood
Vaughan
Erin
NORTH YORK
Bramalea
Snelgrove
SCARBOROUGH
BRAMPTON
YORK
EAST YORK
Georgetown
Acton
ETOBICOKE
Rockwood
Norval
TORONTO
GUELPH
Streetsville
MISSISSAUGA
Milton
Port Credit

LAKE

OAKVILLE
Freelton
ONTARIO
Sheffield
Waterdown
St. George
BURLINGTON
Lynden
Dundas
Hamilton Hbr.
Niagara-on-the-Lake
Youngstown
Hamilton
Winona
CAN.
U.S.
BRANTFORD
Stoney Creek
Grimsby
Lewiston
Cainsville
Mt. Hope
Lincoln
ST. CATHARINES
NEW YORK
Welland Canal
Twenty Mile Cr.
Thorold

Copyright by Rand McNally & Co.

e

114°30'   114°
Ghost Lake
Balzac
Kathryn
STONY IND. RES.
Bow
Cochrane
McDonald L.
Keoma
Morley
Delacour
Dalroy
Conrich
Lyalta
CALGARY
Elbow
Chestermere L.
Bragg Creek
Shepard
Langdon
Priddis
SARCEE IND. RES.
Cr.
Indus
Priddis
Lloyd L.
Dalemead

Copyright by Rand McNally & Co.

f

Delta Beach
Argyle
Warren
Stonewall
Reaburn
Lockport
Poplar Point
Marquette
Grosse Isle
Stony Mountain
Gonor
High Bluff
Meadows
PORTAGE LA PRAIRIE
St. Eustache
Pigeon Lake
Birds Hill
Fortier
Gordon
Rosser
WINNIPEG
Newton
Oakville
Elie
St. François Xavier
Dacotah
Springstein
Prairie Grove
Oak Bluff
Grande Pointe
Fannystelle
Starbuck
Culross
Sanford
St. Adolphe
La Salle

RELIEF

Meters		Feet
3 050		10 000
1 525		5 000
610		2 000
305		1 000
0	Sea Level	500
152.5		0
152.5		500

A-520055-76   6-11²

Copyright by Rand McNally & Co.

98°   97°30'   97°

g

ALEXANDER IND. RES.
Morinville
Cardiff
Bruderheim
Sandy L.
Rivière Qui Barre
Duagh
Fort Saskatchewan
Carbondale
Calahoo
Namao
Josephburg
Villeneuve
Big L.
St. Albert
Oliver
Stony Plain
Cannell
Bremner
Spruce Grove
EDMONTON
Clover Bar
Ardrossan
ELK ISLAND NAT'L PARK
STONY PLAIN IND. RES.
Sherwood Park
Uncas
N. Cooking Lake
Hercules
Cooking Lake
Devon
Ellerslie
Looma
Nisku
Beaumont
Cooking L.
Ministik L.
Buford
Calmar
New Sarepta
Oliver
Leduc
Miquelon L.

Copyright by Rand McNally & Co.

114°   113°30'

Scale 1:1 000 000; One inch to 16 miles.
Elevations and depressions are given in feet.

0 2 4 6 8 10 12 14 16 18 20 22 24 Miles
0 4 8 12 16 20 24 28 32 36 40 Kilometers

For larger scale coverage of
Montréal and Toronto see page 223.

Continued on pages 90-91

Scale 1: 12 000 000; one inch to 190 miles. Conic Projection

Elevations and depressions are given in feet

Longitude West of Greenwich

a

Relief

Meters		Feet
3050		10 000
1525		5000
610		2000
305		1000
152.5		500
0	Sea Level	0
152.5		500
1525		5000
3050		10 000

A-520200-76- 9-9-18
COPYRIGHT BY
RAND MCNALLY & COMPANY
MADE IN U.S.A.

0 25 50 75 100   200   300   400   500 Miles

0   100   200   400   600   800 Kilometers

PACIFIC OCEAN

BRITISH COLUMBIA

COAST MOUNTAINS

PACIFIC RANGES

VANCOUVER ISLAND RANGES

QUEEN CHARLOTTE ISLANDS

QUEEN CHARLOTTE RANGES

Dixon Entrance

Hecate Strait

Queen Charlotte Sound

Queen Charlotte Strait

Strait of Juan de Fuca

UNITED STATES
CANADA

Relief

Meters		Feet
3050		10 000
1525		5000
610		2000
305		1000
152.5		500
0	Sea Level	0
152.5		500
1525		5000

A-520220-76   6-72
COPYRIGHT BY
RAND McNALLY & COMPANY
MADE IN U.S.A.

Continued on pages 98-99

Longitude West of Greenwich

Scale 1:4 000 000; one inch to 64 miles. Conic Projection
Elevations and depressions are given in feet.

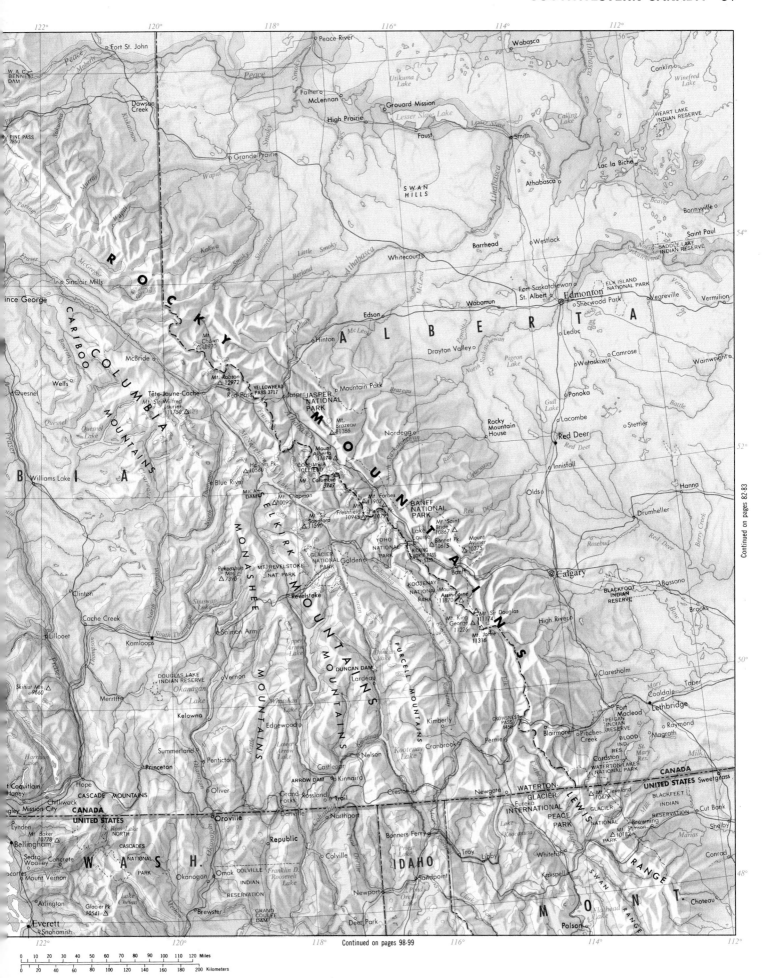

Continued on pages 82-83

Continued on pages 98-99

0 10 20 30 40 50 60 70 80 90 100 110 120 Miles

0   20   40   60   80   100   120   140   160   180   200 Kilometers

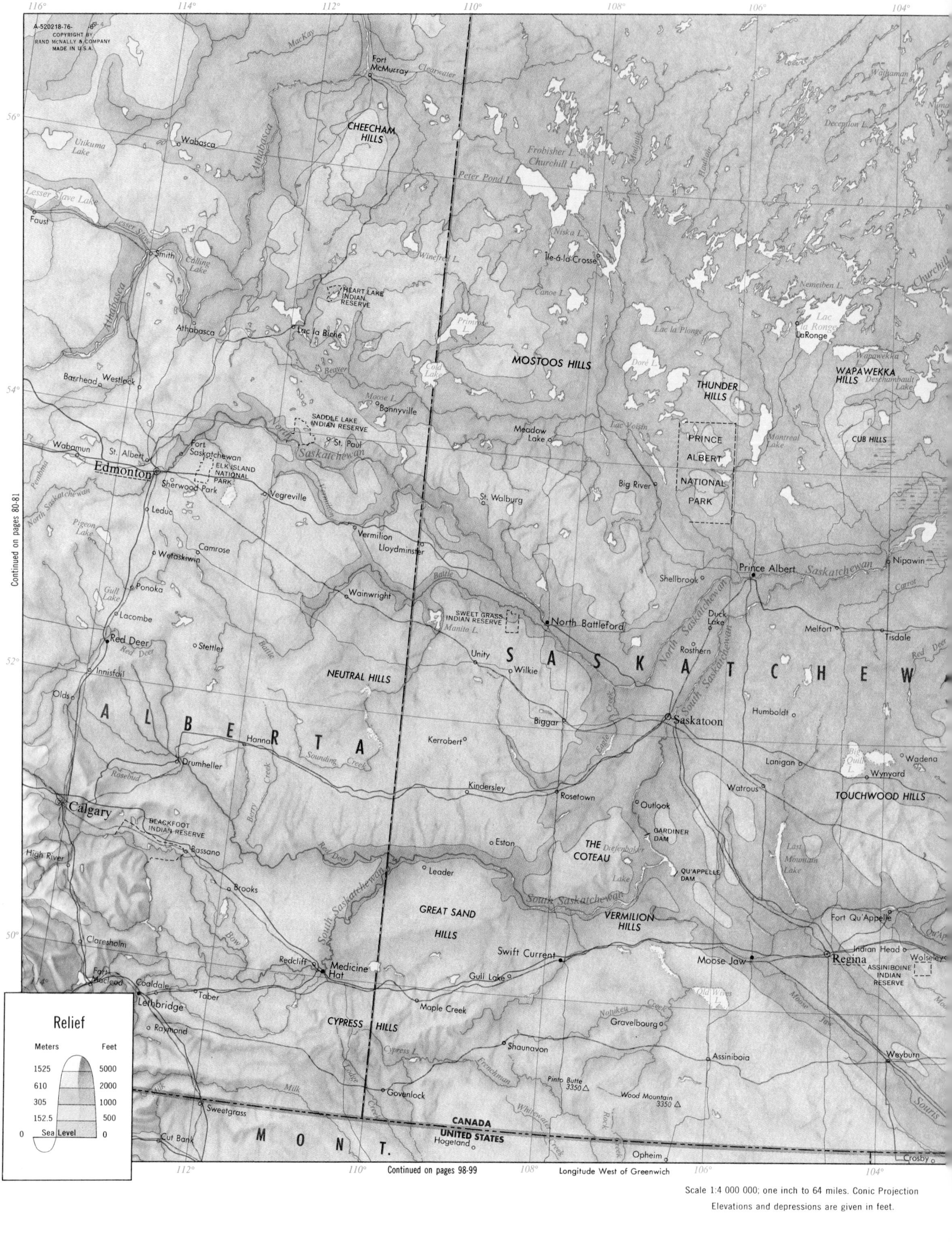

A-520218-76-
COPYRIGHT BY
RAND McNALLY & COMPANY
MADE IN U.S.A.

116° 114° 112° 110° 108° 106° 104°

56°

54°

52°

50°

Continued on pages 80-81

ALBERTA

SASKATCHEWAN

Fort McMurray
Clearwater

CHEECHAM HILLS

MacKay

Wabasca

Utikuma Lake

Lesser Slave Lake

Faust

Athabasca

Calling Lake

Smith

HEART LAKE INDIAN RESERVE

Lac la Biche

Beaver

Athabasca

Batrhead Westlock

Bonnyville
Moose L.

SADDLE LAKE INDIAN RESERVE

Wabamun St. Albert
Fort Saskatchewan

St. Paul

Edmonton

ELK ISLAND NATIONAL PARK

Sherwood Park

Vegreville

Pigeon Lake

Leduc

Camrose

Wetaskiwin

Gull Lake

Ponoka

Lacombe

Red Deer
Red Deer

Stettler

Innisfail

Olds

NEUTRAL HILLS

Hanna

Sounding Creek

Kerrobert

Calgary

Drumheller

Rosebud

BLACKFOOT INDIAN RESERVE

Bassano

Burnt Creek

High River

Bow

Brooks

Leader

Claresholm

Fort Macleod

Redcliff **Medicine Hat**

Coaldale

Taber

Lethbridge

Raymond

GREAT SAND HILLS

CYPRESS HILLS

Sweetgrass

Milk

Govenlock

Cut Bank
Hogeland

M O N T.

Peter Pond L.

Winefred L.

Primrose

Cold Lake

MOSTOOS HILLS

Île-à-la-Crosse

Canoe L.

Meadow Lake

North Saskatchewan

St. Walburg

Big River

Vermilion
Lloydminster

Battle

Wainwright

SWEET GRASS INDIAN RESERVE
Manito L.

North Battleford

Unity

Wilkie

Biggar

Saskatoon

Kindersley

Rosetown

Eston

Outlook

THE COTEAU

GARDINER DAM

Diefenbaker L.

Swift Current

South Saskatchewan

Gull Lake

Maple Creek

Cypress L.

Shaunavon

Frenchman

Pinto Butte
3350 △

Wood Mountain
3350 △

Frobisher L.
Churchill L.

Niska L.

Doré L.

Lac la Plonge

THUNDER HILLS

Lac Voisin

PRINCE ALBERT NATIONAL PARK

Shellbrook

Nemeiben L.

Lac la Ronge

LaRonge

WAPAWEKKA HILLS
Wapawekka L.

Montreal Lake

CUB HILLS

Prince Albert Saskatchewan

Nipawin

North Saskatchewan

Duck Lake

Rosthern

Melfort

Tisdale

Red Deer

Humboldt

Lanigan

Big Quill L.

Wadena

Wynyard

Watrous

TOUCHWOOD HILLS

Last Mountain Lake

QU'APPELLE DAM

VERMILION HILLS

Fort Qu'Appelle

Moose Jaw

Regina

Indian Head

Wolseley

ASSINIBOINE INDIAN RESERVE

Gravelbourg

Assiniboia

Weyburn

CANADA
UNITED STATES

Opheim

Crosby

112° 110° 108° 106° 104°

Continued on pages 98-99

Longitude West of Greenwich

Relief

Meters		Feet
1525		5000
610		2000
305		1000
152.5		500
0	Sea Level	0

Scale 1:4 000 000; one inch to 64 miles. Conic Projection
Elevations and depressions are given in feet.

HUDSON BAY

York Factory
Port Nelson
Thibaudeau
Amery

56°

Reindeer L.

Lynn Lake
South Indian Lake
Southern Indian L.

Sherridon
Snow Lake
Wabowden

Flin Flon

Thompson
Pikwitonei
Sipiwesk

M A N I T O B A

54°

ROSS ISLAND
Norway House

Opasquia

The Pas
Moose Lake

BIG MOSSY POINT

Cedar

Grand Rapids
LAKE
LONG POINT

Hudson Bay

Lake
Winnipegosis
WINNIPEG

52°

PORCUPINE
Hart Mountain
△ 2700
HILLS

BIRCH I.

REINDEER ISLAND
Berens River
BERENS ISLAND

Swan River

MacDowell

Sturgeon Bay

Anama Bay

O N T A R I O

Canora
Kamsack

DUCK MOUNTAIN
Winnipegosis

Gypsumville

MOOSE I.

Baldy Mountain
2727

Yorkton
Roblin
Dauphin

PEGUIS INDIAN RESERVE

BLACK I.

Red Lake

Melville
Russell

HECLA

Bissett

RIDING
RIDING MOUNTAIN
NATIONAL PARK
MOUNTAIN

ELK ISLAND
Lake Winnipeg

FORT ALEXANDER INDIAN RESERVE

Esterhazy

Lake Manitoba

Gimli
Pine Falls

Sioux Lookout

50°

Minnedosa
Neepawa

Selkirk
Beauséjour

Dryden

Moosomin
Rivers
Portage-la-Prairie

Winnipeg

Kenora
Dymett

Virden
Brandon

AULNEAU PENINSULA

Mose Mtn.
2730 △
WHITE BEAR INDIAN RESERVE

Souris
Wawanesa

Steinbach

Manor

Carman

Morris

Lake of the Woods

BIGSBY

Oxbow
Melita
Boissevain

Morden
Winkler
Altona

Emerson
Pembina

Rainy River
Fort Frances
International Falls
VOYAGEURS NAT'L PARK

CANADA
UNITED STATES
N. DAK.
MINNESOTA
Hannah
Badger

102°
100°
98°
Continued on pages 96-97
96°
94°

0 10 20 30 40 50 60 70 80 90 100 110 120 Miles
0 20 40 60 80 100 120 140 160 180 200 Kilometers

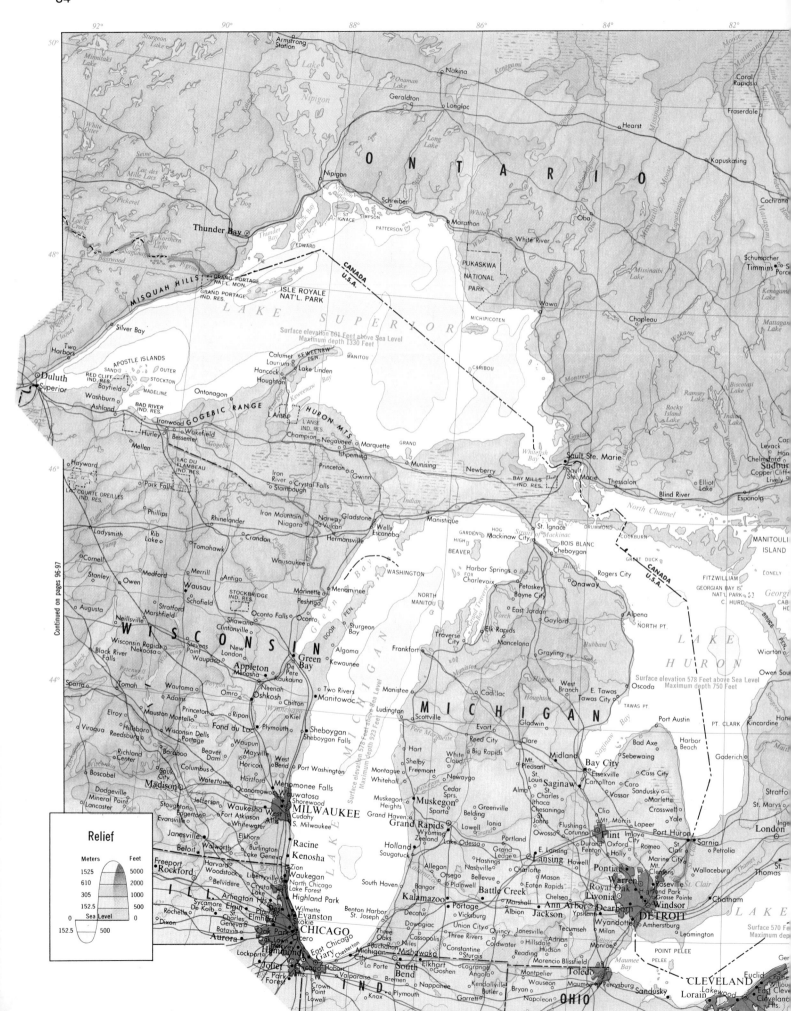

A-520221-76 6-7/11²
COPYRIGHT BY
RAND McNALLY & COMPANY
MADE IN U.S.A.

Continued on pages 86-87

Continued on pages 92-93

Scale 1:4 000 000; one inch to 64 miles. Conic Projection
Elevations and depressions are given in feet

0 10 20 30 40 50 60 70 80 90 100 110 120 Miles

0 20 40 60 80 100 120 140 160 180 200 Kilometers

Continued on pages 92-93

Scale 1:4 000 000; one inch to 64 miles. Conic Projection
Elevations and depressions are given in feet.

Longitude West of Greenwich

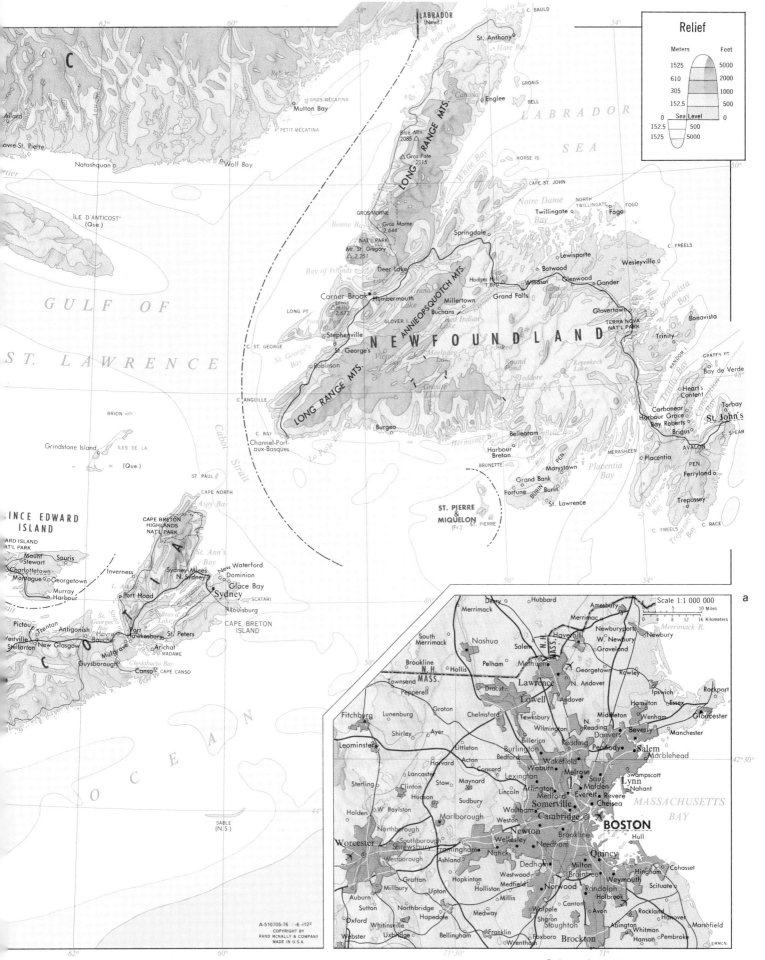

Relief

Meters	Feet
1525	5000
610	2000
305	1000
152.5	500
0	Sea Level	0
152.5	500
1525	5000

Scale 1:1 000 000

For larger scale coverage of Boston see page 223.

A-510705-76

COPYRIGHT BY
RAND McNALLY & COMPANY
MADE IN U.S.A.

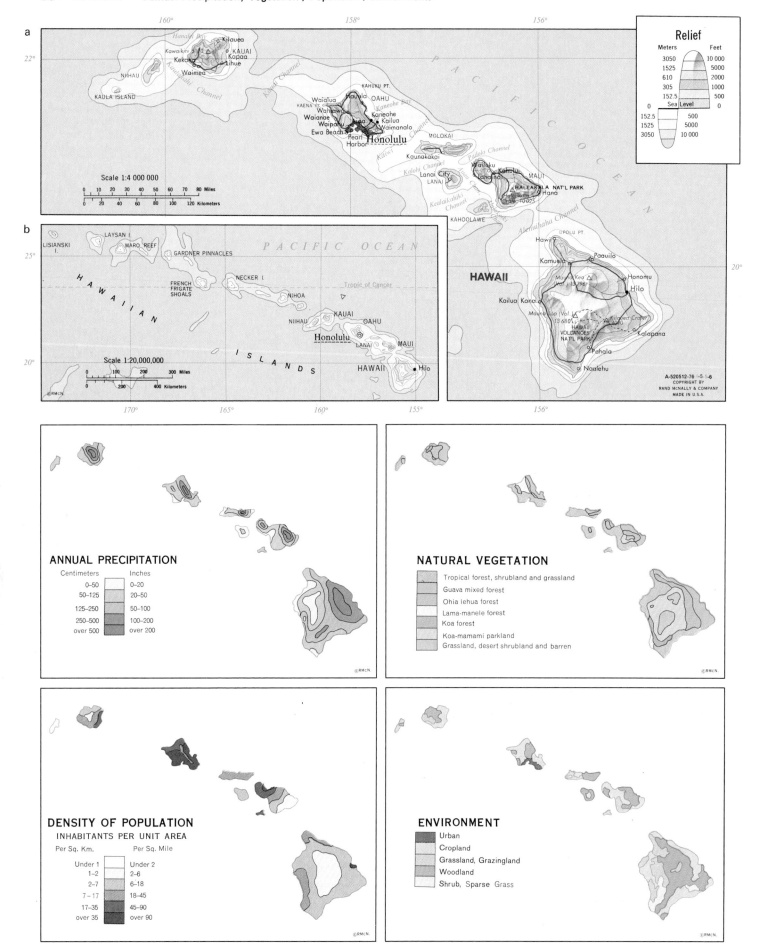

a

Relief

Meters		Feet
3050		10 000
1525		5000
610		2000
305		1000
152.5		500
	Sea Level	
0		0
152.5		500
1525		5000
3050		10 000

Scale 1:4 000 000

b

Scale 1:20,000,000

A-520512-76 -5-5-6
COPYRIGHT BY
RAND McNALLY & COMPANY
MADE IN U.S.A.

ANNUAL PRECIPITATION

Centimeters		Inches
0–50		0–20
50–125		20–50
125–250		50–100
250–500		100–200
over 500		over 200

NATURAL VEGETATION

Tropical forest, shrubland and grassland

Guava mixed forest

Ohia lehua forest

Lama-manele forest

Koa forest

Koa-mamami parkland

Grassland, desert shrubland and barren

DENSITY OF POPULATION

INHABITANTS PER UNIT AREA

Per Sq. Km.		Per Sq. Mile
Under 1		Under 2
1–2		2–6
2–7		6–18
7–17		18–45
17–35		45–90
over 35		over 90

ENVIRONMENT

Urban

Cropland

Grassland, Grazingland

Woodland

Shrub, Sparse Grass

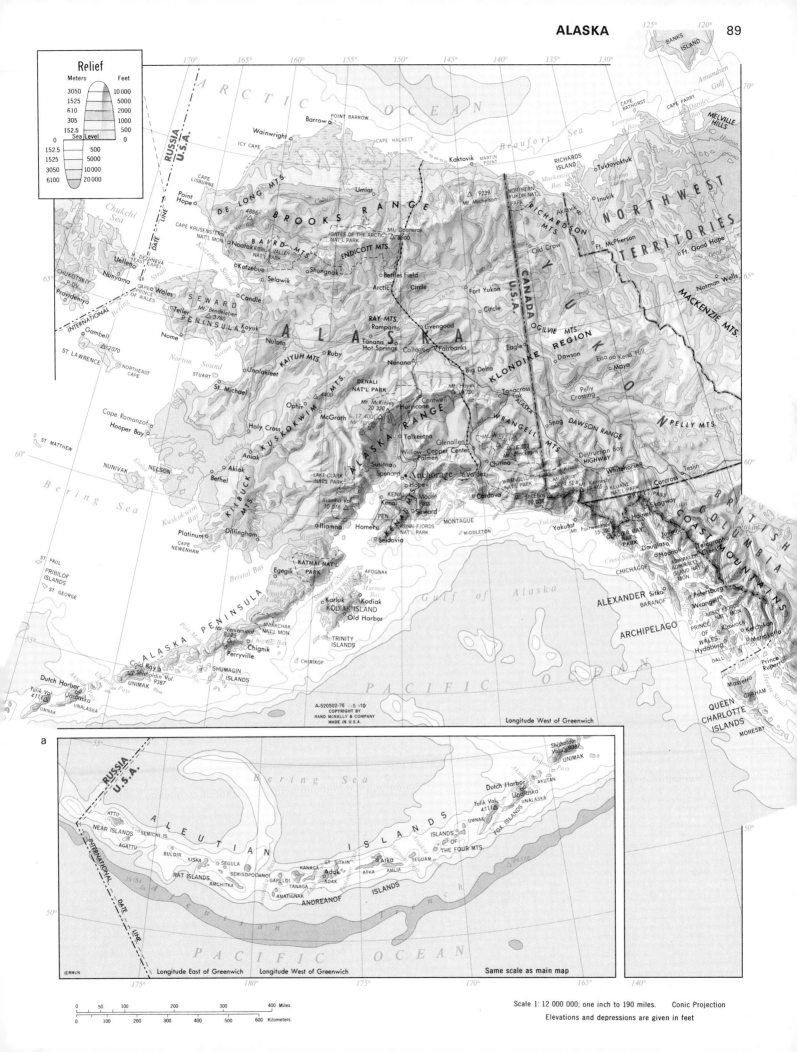

Relief

Meters	Feet
3050	10 000
1525	5000
610	2000
305	1000
152.5	500
0	Sea Level
152.5	500
1525	5000
3050	10 000
6100	20 000

A-520502-76   -5 -10
COPYRIGHT BY
RAND McNALLY & COMPANY
MADE IN U.S.A.

Longitude West of Greenwich

a

Longitude East of Greenwich   Longitude West of Greenwich   Same scale as main map

0   50   100   200   300   400 Miles
0   100   200   300   400   500   600 Kilometers

Scale 1: 12 000 000; one inch to 190 miles.   Conic Projection

Elevations and depressions are given in feet

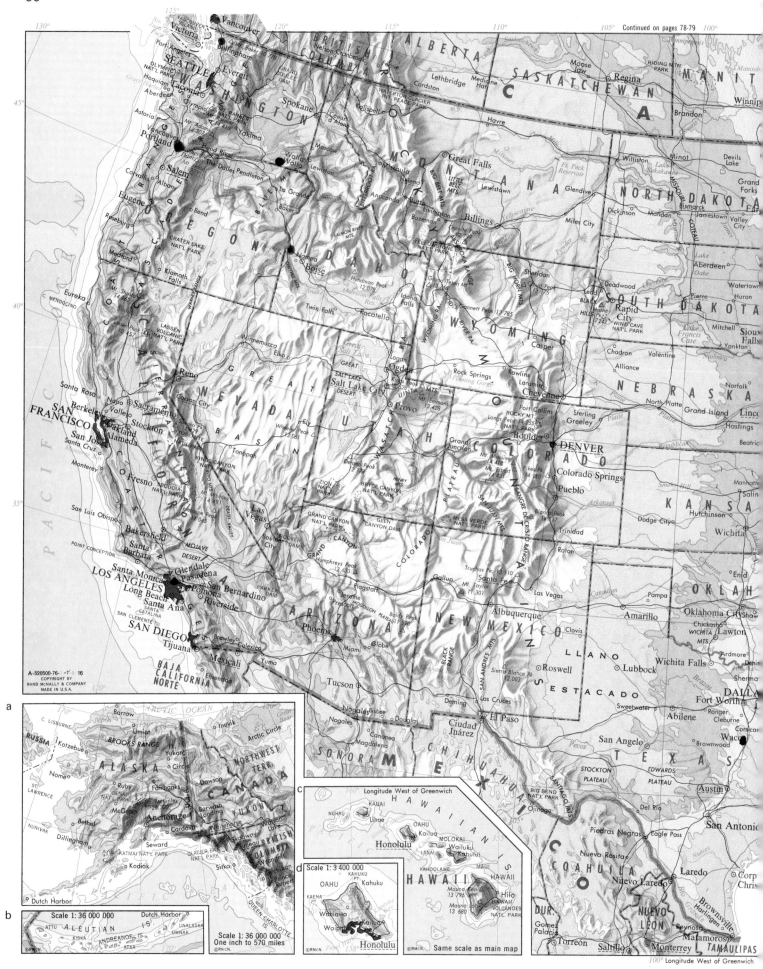

Continued on pages 78-79

a

b   Scale 1: 36 000 000   Dutch Harbor

Scale 1: 36 000 000
One inch to 570 miles
©R.M.C.N.

c   Longitude West of Greenwich

d   Scale 1: 3 400 000

Same scale as main map

Honolulu

A-520500-76- -7¹⁹ 16
COPYRIGHT BY
RAND McNALLY & COMPANY
MADE IN U.S.A.

Scale 1:12 000 000; one inch to 190 miles. Polyconic Projection
Elevations and depressions are given in feet

100° Longitude West of Greenwich

Relief

Meters	Feet
3050	10 000
1525	5000
610	2000
305	1000
152.5	500
0 Sea Level	0
	Below
152.5	500 Sea Level
1525	5 000
3050	10 000
6100	20 000

0 25 50 75 100   200   300   400   500 Miles
0   100   200   400   600   800 Kilometers

Cities and Towns

0 to 50,000 ∘   500,000 to 1,000,000 ◉

50,000 to 500,000 ⊙   1,000,000 and over

Continued on pages 96-97

Continued on pages 108-109

Longitude West of Greenwich

Cities and Towns	
0 to 50,000	500,000 to 1,000,000
50,000 to 500,000	1,000,000 and over

Scale 1:4 000 000; one inch to 64 miles. Conic Projection
Elevations and depressions are given in feet

Continued on pages 84-85

Relief

Meters		Feet
1525		5000
610		2000
305		1000
152.5		500
0	Sea Level	0
152.5		500
1525		5000
3050		10 000

A-520596-76
COPYRIGHT BY
RAND McNALLY & COMPANY
MADE IN U.S.A.

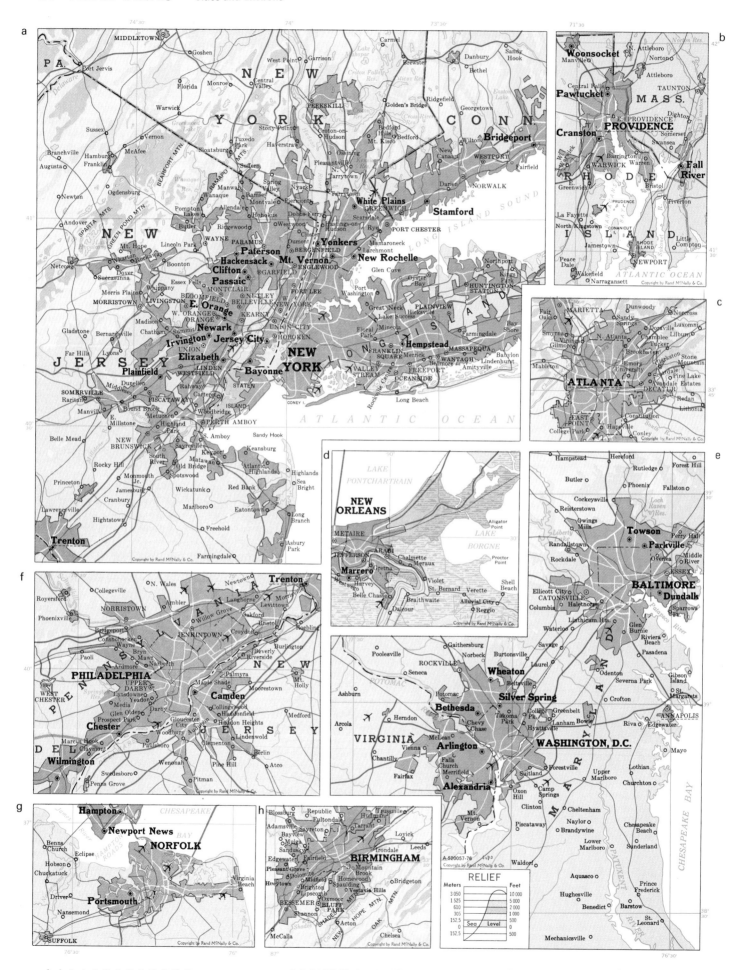

Scale 1:1 000 000; One inch to 16 miles.
Elevations and depressions are given in feet.

For larger scale coverage of New York, Baltimore,
Washington, D.C. and Philadelphia see pages 224 and 225.

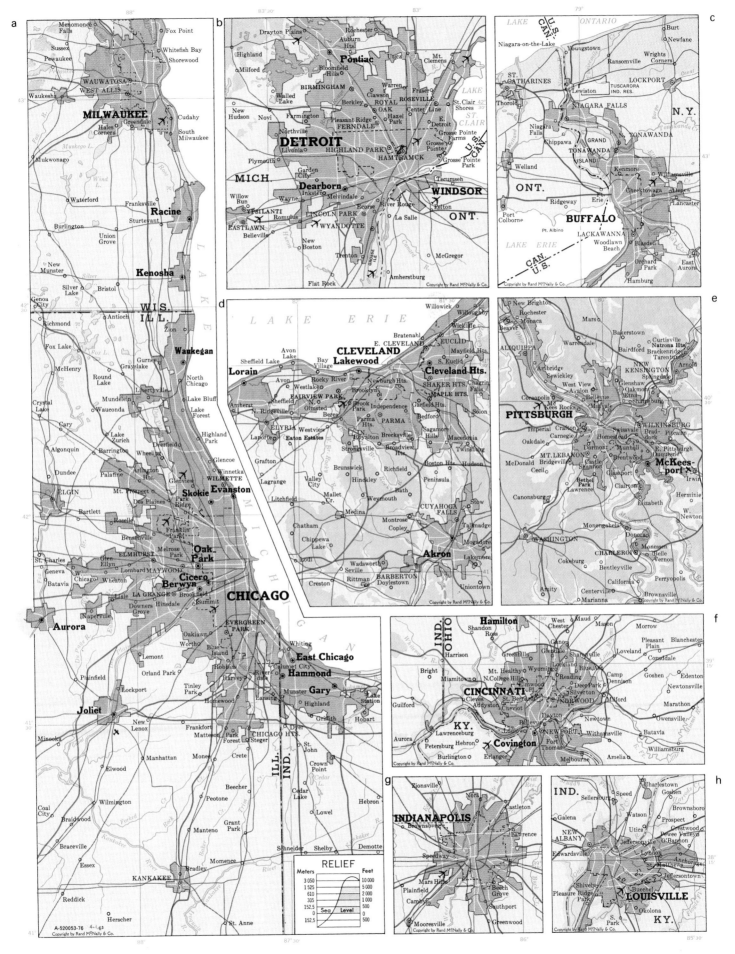

Copyright by Rand McNally & Co.

Scale 1:1 000 000; One inch to 16 miles.
Elevations and depressions are given in feet.

RELIEF

Meters		Feet
3 050		10 000
1 525		5 000
610		2 000
305		1 000
152.5		500
	Sea Level	0
152.5		500

For larger scale coverage of Cleveland, Buffalo, Pittsburgh, Detroit and Chicago see pages 225-227.

A-520053-76 4-4-63
Copyright by Rand McNally & Co.

Miles
0 2 4 6 8 10 12 14 16 18 20 22 24

Kilometers
0 4 8 12 16 20 24 28 32 36 40

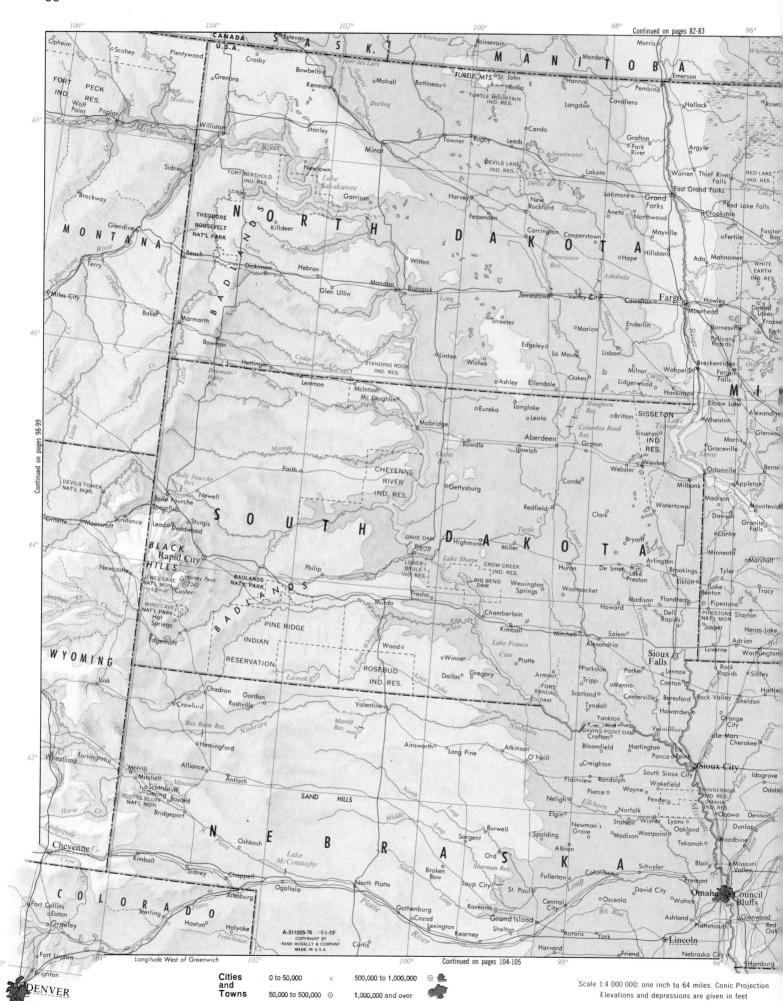

Continued on pages 82-83

Continued on pages 98-99

Continued on pages 104-105

Longitude West of Greenwich

DENVER

Cities and Towns

0 to 50,000 ○
50,000 to 500,000 ⊙
500,000 to 1,000,000 ◎
1,000,000 and over

A-511005-76 -9-8-13⁵
COPYRIGHT BY
RAND M9NALLY & COMPANY
MADE IN U.S.A.

Scale 1:4 000 000; one inch to 64 miles. Conic Projection
Elevations and depressions are given in feet

ONTARIO

Lake of the Woods

LAKE SUPERIOR
Surface elev. 600 Feet above Sea Level
Maximum depth 1333 Feet

CANADA
U.S.A.

ISLE ROYALE NAT'L PARK

Thunder Bay

MINNESOTA

WISCONSIN

IOWA

ILLINOIS

IND.

MICHIGAN

LAKE MICHIGAN
Surface elevation 579 Feet above Sea Level
Maximum depth 870 Feet

Duluth
Superior

MINNEAPOLIS St. Paul
St. Louis Park

MILWAUKEE
West Allis

CHICAGO
E. Chicago
Gary
Hammond

Green Bay
Appleton
Oshkosh
Fond du Lac
Madison
La Crosse

Des Moines
Waterloo
Cedar Rapids
Davenport
Rock Island
Moline

Dubuque
Rockford
Elgin
Aurora
Joliet

Racine
Kenosha
Waukegan
Evanston
Oak Park
Cicero

Muskegon
Grand Rapids
Kalamazoo

Sault Ste. Marie

Marquette

Continued on pages 92-93

Continued on pages 104-105

Relief

Meters		Feet
1525		5000
610		2000
305		1000
152.5		500
0	Sea Level	0
152.5		500

0 20 40 60 80 100 120 Miles
0 20 40 60 80 100 120 140 160 180 200 Kilometers

120° Continued on pages 80-81

BRITISH COLUMBIA
CANADA
U.S.A.

Strait of Georgia
VANCOUVER ISLAND
Nanaimo
Ladysmith
Duncan
Esquimalt
Victoria
CAPE FLATTERY
MAKAH IND. RES.
Strait of Juan de Fuca
Port Angeles
Port Townsend

N. Vancouver
Vancouver
New Westminster
Steveston
Blaine
Lynden
Chilliwack
Bellingham
SAN JUAN ISLANDS
Anacortes
Sedro Woolley
Concrete
Newhalem
Mt. Baker 10,778
Ross Lake
Oroville
Grand Forks
Rossland
Trail
Northport
Porthill
Bonners Ferry
Troy
Libby
CABINET MTS.
Lake Koocanusa

OLYMPIC MTS.
OLYMPIC NATIONAL PARK
Mt. Olympus 7965
QUINAULT IND. RES.
Moclips
Hoquiam
Aberdeen
Cosmopolis
Montesano
Elma
Shelton
Grays Harbor
Raymond
South Bend
Willapa Bay
Ilwaco

Mount Vernon
Arlington
TULALIP IND. RES.
Everett
Snohomish
Monroe
Kirkland
Bellevue
SEATTLE
Bremerton
Renton
Tacoma
Lakewood Center
Auburn
Enumclaw
Puyallup
Carbonado
Centralia
Chehalis

Glacier Peak 10,541
Lake Chelan
Chelan
Leavenworth
Cashmere
Wenatchee
Cascade Tunnel
Roslyn
Cle Elum
Ellensburg
WENATCHEE MTS.
ROCK ISLAND DAM
Waterville
Mansfield
GRAND COULEE DAM
WELLS DAM
Columbia

Rufus Woods Lake
Okanogan
COLVILLE IND. RES.
Franklin D. Roosevelt Lake
Republic
Colville
Chewelah
KALISPEL IND. RES.
Newport
Sandpoint
Lake Pend Oreille
Priest Lake

WASHINGTON

Davenport
Spokane
SPOKANE IND. RES.
Deer Park
Medical Lake
Cheney
Opportunity
Coeur d'Alene
Spirit Lake
Kellogg
Wallace
Mullan
Thompson Falls

Cosmopolis
Mt. Rainier 14,410
MOUNT RAINIER NATIONAL PARK
Mt. Saint Helens 8307
Yakima
YAKIMA INDIAN RESERVATION
Toppenish
Sunnyside
Mt. Adams 12,276
Ephrata
Moses Lake
MOSES LAKE
Ritzville
Odessa
Crab Cr.
Potholes Res.
Priest Rapids Lake
PRIEST RAPIDS DAM
Goldendale

Castle Rock
Longview
Kelso
Kalama
Rainier
Saint Helens
Astoria
Warrenton
Seaside
Columbia R.

Lewis R.
Merwin Lake
Vancouver
Camas
Washougal
Hood River
BONNEVILLE DAM
THE DALLES
THE DALLES DAM
Wasco
JOHN DAY DAM
Mt. Hood 11,239

Hillsboro
Forest Grove
Tillamook
Tillamook Bay
Milwaukie
Portland
Lake Oswego
Oregon City
W. Linn
Gresham
Newberg
McMinnville
Sheridan
Dallas
Woodburn
Silverton
Salem
Independence
Albany
Lebanon
Corvallis
Toledo
Newport

Mt. Jefferson 10,497
WARM SPRINGS IND. RES.
Detroit Lake
Green Peter Lake
Lake Simtustus
Lake Billy Chinook
Deschutes R.

OREGON

LOWER MONUMENTAL DAM
LOWER GRANITE DAM
Richland
Pasco
Kennewick
Prosser
Walla Walla
Wallula
ICE HARBOR DAM
McNARY DAM
Milton-Freewater
Pendleton
Pomeroy
LITTLE GOOSE DAM
Clarkston
Lewiston
NEZ PERCE IND. RES.
Asotin
Winchester
Nez Perce
Dayton
Waitsburg

Colfax
Palouse
Pullman
Moscow
Elk River
Tekoa
St. Maries
COEUR D'ALENE IND. RES.
Dworshak Res.

CLEARWATER MOUNTAINS
Grangeville

BLUE MOUNTAINS
Elgin
Wallowa
Enterprise
La Grande
Union
WALLOWA MTS.
HELLS CANYON
New Meadows
Baker
Brownlee Res.
Oxbow

Heppner
Condon
John Day R.
N. Fork
Middle Fork

IDAHO
SALMON RIVER

Eugene
Springfield
McKenzie R.
Cougar Res.
Lookout Point Lake
Hills Creek Lake
Cottage Grove
Reedsport
North Bend
Coos Bay
Coquille
Bandon
Myrtle Point
CAPE BLANCO
Roseburg
Diamond Peak 8744
Crescent Lake
Waldo Lake
Wickiup Res.
Crane Prairie Res.
Bend
Prineville
Prineville Res.
Crooked R.

GREAT SANDY DESERT
HARNEY BASIN
Burns
Warm Sprs. Res.
Malheur Lake
Harney Lake
Lake
Beulah Res.
Vale
Ontario
Payette
Weiser
Payette R.

Emmett
Caldwell
Nampa
Boise
Lucky Peak Lake
Arrowrock Res.
OWYHEE MTS.
Owyhee R.
Lake Owyhee
Jordan Cr.
Mountain Home
Glenns Ferry
SNAKE

Grants Pass
Medford
Ashland
OREGON CAVES NAT'L MON.
Mt. McLoughlin 9495
CRATER LAKE NATIONAL PARK
Crater Lake
Mt. Scott 8926
Upper Klamath Lake
Klamath Falls
Lake Abert
Swan Lake
Lake Sumner
Silver R.
Donner und Blitzen R.
STEENS MTN.

Lakeview
WARNER MTS.
Goose Lake
Upper Lake
Lower Lake
Clear Lake Res.
FORT McDERMITT IND. RES.
DUCK VALLEY IND. RES.
PINE FOREST RA.

Brookings
Crescent City
Happy Camp
Yreka
Weed
Mt. Shasta 14,162
Dunsmuir
HOOPA VALLEY IND. RES.
KLAMATH MTS.
Lower Klamath Lake
LAVA BEDS NAT'L MON.
Tule Lake
Alturas
Eagle Peak 9892
Lower Lake

CALIFORNIA

Arcata
Fieldbrook
Eureka
Humboldt Bay
Fortuna
Scotia
Ferndale
CAPE MENDOCINO
Weaverville
Redding
Anderson
LASSEN VOLCANIC NATIONAL PARK
Lassen Peak (Vol.) 10,457
Eagle Lake
SMOKE CREEK DESERT

NEVADA
BLACK ROCK DESERT
Winnemucca
Battle Mountain
Rye Patch Res.
Paradise Valley
Midas
Tuscarora
SANTA ROSA RA.
INDEPENDENCE MTS.
SUMMIT LAKE IND. RES.
Elko
Wells
Gooding
Strike Res.
Bruneau R.

PACIFIC OCEAN

COAST RANGE
CASCADE RANGE

48°
46°
44°
42°
124°
122°
120°
118°
116°

Continued on pages 102-103

Longitude West of Greenwich

A-520597-76
COPYRIGHT BY
RAND McNALLY & COMPANY
MADE IN U.S.A.

Scale 1: 4,000,000; one inch to 64 miles. Conic Projection
Elevations and depressions are given in feet

Continued on pages 82-83
Continued on pages 96-97
Continued on pages 102-103

ALBERTA
CANADA
U.S.A.
SASKATCHEWAN

WATERTON-GLACIER
INTERNATIONAL
PEACE PARK

BLACKFEET
IND. RES.

FORT PECK
IND. RES.

N. DAK.

MONTANA

R O C K Y

SWAN RANGE

LEWIS RANGE

BITTERROOT RANGE

FLATHEAD
INDIAN
RESERVATION

NATIONAL
BISON RANGE

BIG BELT MTS.

LITTLE BELT MTS.

CRAZY MTS.

BIG HOLE NAT'L
BATTLEFIELD

PIONEER MTS.

Homer
Youngs Peak
10 621

M O U N T A I N S

ABSAROKA RANGE

CUSTER
BATTLEFIELD
NAT'L MON.

NORTHERN CHEYENNE
IND. RES.

CROW IND. RES.

BIGHORN MOUNTAINS

DEVILS TOWER
NAT'L MON.

Cloud Peak
13 167

Electric Peak
10 992

Mt. Washburn
10 243

YELLOWSTONE

NATIONAL

PARK

7733 ft. above
sea level

Shoshone
Lake

Yellowstone Lake

W I N D

R I V E R

R A N G E

GRAND TETON
NAT'L PARK

Grand Teton
13 770

Gros Ventre

Garnett Peak
13 804

Fremont
Peak 13 745

WIND RIVER
IND. RES.

W Y O M I N G

WYOMING RANGE

GREAT DIVIDE
BASIN

HOLE MTS.

LEMHI RANGE

BEAVERHEAD MTS.

LOST RIVER RA.

Borah Pk.
12 662

Boulder Peak
10 981

Hyndman Peak
12 009

CRATERS OF
THE MOON
NAT'L MON.

SNAKE RIVER PLAIN

Meade Peak
9957

FORT HALL
IND. RES.

UTAH

GREAT
SALT LAKE
DESERT

Great
Salt
Lake

UINTA MTS.

Kings Peak
13 528

Mt. Emmons
13 440

UINTAH AND OURAY
IND. RES.

DINOSAUR
NAT'L MON.

COLO.

PARK RANGE

Flaming
Gorge
Res.

FT. BELKNAP
IND. RES.

ROCKY BOYS
IND. RES.

Continued on pages 102-103

Relief

Meters		Feet
3050		10000
1525		5000
610		2000
305		1000
152.5		500
0	Sea Level	0
1525		500

0   20   40   60   80   100   120 Miles
0   20   40   60   80 100 120 140 160 180 200 Kilometers

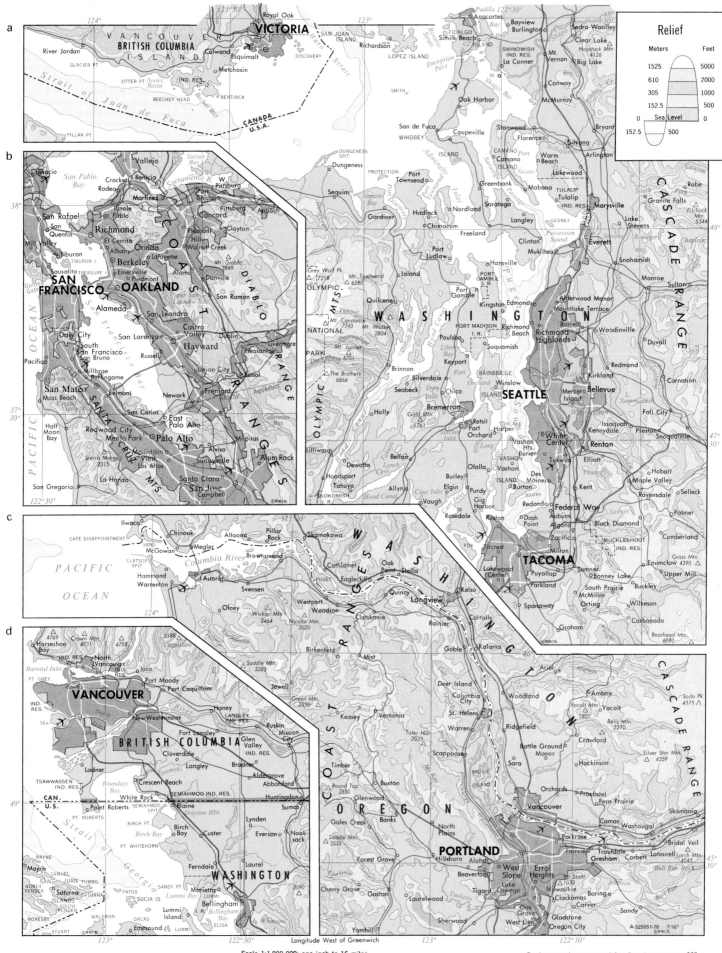

Scale 1:1 000 000; one inch to 16 miles.
Elevations and depressions are given in feet.

For larger scale coverage of San Francisco see page 227.

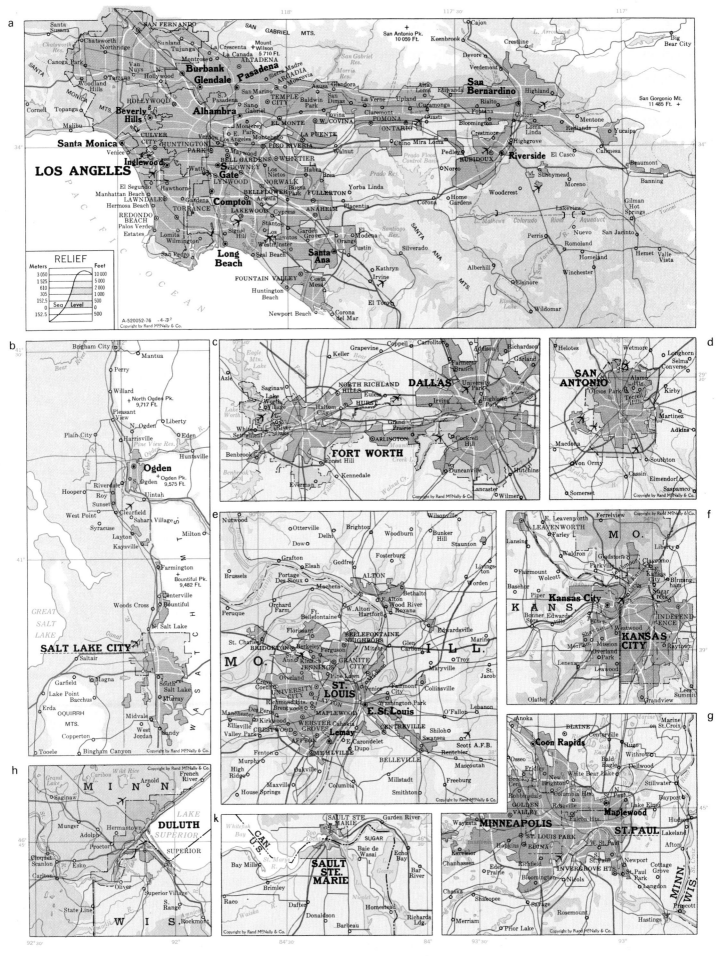

a

Santa
Susana
Chatsworth
Chatsworth
Res.
Canoga Park
Cornell
Topanga
Malibu
San
Susana
SAN FERNANDO
Sunland
Tujunga
La Crescenta
La Canada
Mount
Wilson
5,710 Ft.
ALTADENA
San Antonio Pk.
10,059 Ft.
Keenbrook
Cajon
L. Arrowhead
Crestline
Big
Bear City
Bear
City
Northridge
Van
Nuys
Tarzana
Woodland
Hills
Hollywood
Burbank
Glendale **Pasadena**
SAN GABRIEL MTS.
San Antonio Pk.
Devore
Verdemont
San Bernardino
Highland
San Gorgonio Mt.
11,485 Ft. +
**Beverly
Hills**
Alhambra
HOLLYWOOD
Pasadena
San Marino
ARCADIA
Sierra
Madre
Monrovia
Glendora
Azusa
Alta
Loma
Etiwanda
Cucamonga
Rialto
Fontana
Colton
Highland
Mentone
Santa Monica
Venice
CULVER
CITY
HUNTINGTON
PARK
TEMPLE
CITY
San
Gabriel
Sano
Monterey
El Monte
Baldwin
Park
La Verne
Claremont
POMONA
Upland
Guasti
ONTARIO
Bloomington
Crestmore
Loma
Linda
Highgrove
Redlands
Yucaipa
Los Angeles
Inglewood
El Segundo
Manhattan Beach
Hermosa Beach
REDONDO
BEACH
Palos Verdes
Estates
Hawthorne
LAWNDALE
Gardena
TORRANCE
Lomita
Wilmington
San Pedro
Vernon
Maywood
S.
Gate
Lynwood
Compton
LAKEWOOD
Signal
Hill
Los Nietos
Montebello
PICO RIVERA
BELL GARDENS
DOWNEY
NORWALK
BELLFLOWER
Buena
Park
Artesia
Cypress
Los
Alamitos
Stanton
Garden
Grove
WHITTIER
Walnut
La Puente
W. COVINA
Habra
Brea
FULLERTON
Yorba Linda
Placentia
ANAHEIM
Chino Mira Loma
Norco
Corona
Home
Gardens
Pedley
Prado Flood
Control Basin
RUBIDOUX
Riverside
El Casco
Calimesa
Beaumont
Banning
Moreno
Sunnymead
Woodcrest
Perris
Lakeview
Gilman
Hot
Springs
**Long
Beach**
Seal Beach
Westminster
Los
Alamitos
El
Modena
Orange
Tustin
**Santa
Ana**
Silverado
SANTA
ANA
MTS.
Alberhill
Nuevo
Romoland
Homeland
San Jacinto
Hemet
Winchester
Valle
Vista
FOUNTAIN VALLEY
Huntington
Beach
Costa
Mesa
Kathryn
Irvine
El Toro
Elsinore
Lake
Wildomar
Newport Beach
Corona
del Mar

RELIEF
Meters Feet
3,050 10,000
1,525 5,000
610 2,000
305 1,000
152.5 500
0 Sea Level 0
152.5 500

A-520052-76   -4-3
Copyright by Rand McNally & Co.

b
Brigham City
Mantua
Perry
Willard
North Ogden Pk.
9,717 Ft.
N. Ogden
Pleasant
View
Liberty
Plain City
Harrisville
Eden
Huntsville
Pine View Res.
Ogden
Ogden Pk.
9,575 Ft.
Hooper
Riverdale
Roy
Sunset
Uintah
West Point
Clearfield
Sahara Village
Layton
Kaysville
Milton
Farmington
Bountiful Pk.
9,482 Ft.
Centerville
Bountiful
GREAT
SALT
LAKE
Woods Cross
N. Salt Lake
SALT LAKE CITY
Saltair
Garfield
Magna
Lake Point
Bacchus
Erda
Copperton
OQUIRRH
MTS.
Midvale
South
Salt Lake
Murray
West
Jordan
Sandy
Tooele
Bingham Canyon
WASATCH

c
Eagle
Mtn.
Lake
Keller
Grapevine
Coppell
Carrollton
Addison
Richardson
Garland
Azle
Saginaw
Lake
Worth
NORTH RICHLAND
HILLS
Euless
DALLAS
Farmers
Branch
University
Park
Highland
Park
Irving
White
Settlement
River
Oaks
Haltom
City
HURST
Grand
Prairie
Benbrook
FORT WORTH
ARLINGTON
Cockrell
Hill
Duncanville
Forest Hill
Everman
Kennedale
Lancaster
Wilmer
Hutchins
Copyright by Rand McNally & Co.

d
Helotes
Wetmore
Longhorn
Selma
Converse
**San
Antonio**
Alamo
Hts.
Olmos Park
Terrell
Hills
Kirby
Martinez
Adkins
Macdona
Von Ormy
Southton
Cassin
Elmendorf
Saspamco
Somerset
Copyright by Rand McNally & Co.

e
Nutwood
Otterville
Delhi
Brighton
Woodburn
Wilsonville
Dow
Grafton
Elsah
Godfrey
Fosterburg
Bunker
Hill
Staunton
Brussels
Portage
Des Sioux
Machens
ALTON
Bethalto
Worden
Orchard
Farm
Ft.
Bellefontaine
W. Alton
E. Alton
Wood River
Roxana
Livingston
Peruque
Florissant
BELLEFONTAINE
NEIGHBORS
Edwardsville
Marine
St. Charles
BRIDGETON
Berkeley
Ferguson
GRANITE
CITY
Mitchell
Glen
Carbon
Troy
St.
Jacob
Maryville
Dardenne
JENNINGS
Pine Lawn
Venice
Fairmont
Collinsville
St.
Peters
Overland
UNIVERSITY
CITY
**ST.
LOUIS**
CLAYTON
Washington Park
O'Fallon
Lebanon
Manchester
Des Peres
Richmond Hts.
Brentwood
MAPLEWOOD
E. St. Louis
Ellisville
Kirkwood
WEBSTER
GROVES
Cahokia
Centreville
Shiloh
Valley Park
CRESTWOOD
AFFTON
Lemay
E. Carondelet
Swansea
Scott A.F.B.
Fenton
MEHLVILLE
Dupo
BELLEVILLE
Murphy
Oakville
Rentchler
Mascoutah
High
Ridge
Columbia
Millstadt
Freeburg
House Springs
Maxville
Smithton
Copyright by Rand McNally & Co.

f
E. Leavenworth
Ferrelview
LEAVENWORTH
Farley
M O.
Lansing
Waldron
Gladstone
Liberty
Fairmount
Wolcott
Parkville
Claycomo
Basehor
Piper
Edwardsville
Kansas City
Birmingham
Sugar
Creek
Bonner
Springs
K A N S.
Shawnee
**KANSAS
CITY**
**INDEPEND-
ENCE**
Lenexa
Merriam
Mission
Overland
Park
Leawood
Raytown
Olathe
Grandview
Lee's
Summit
Copyright by Rand McNally & Co.

g
Anoka
BLAINE
Marine
on St. Croix
Coon Rapids
Centerville
Hugo
Withrow
Dellwood
Osseo
Fridley
Bald
Eagle
White Bear Lake
Brooklyn
Cen.
New
Brighton
Columbia Hts.
Stillwater
Robbinsdale
GOLDEN
VALLEY
Roseville
Maplewood
Lake Elmo
Bayport

h
Grand
Lake
Wild Rice
L.
Caribou
French
River
Copyright by Rand McNally & Co.
M I N N.
Arnold
Saginaw
DULUTH
LAKE
SUPERIOR
Munger
Hermantown
Adolph
SUPERIOR
Proctor
Cloquet
Scanlon
Esko
Oliver
Superior Village
Carlton
R. Range
State Line
Rockmont
W I S.

k
Whitefish
Bay
SAULT STE.
MARIE
Garden River
CAN.
U.S.
Soo
Sugar
Bay Mills
Baie
de Wasai
Echo
Bay
**SAULT
STE.
MARIE**
Bar
River
Raco
Dafter
Brimley
Donaldson
Barbeau
Homestead
Richards
Ldg.
Copyright by Rand McNally & Co.

Wayzata
BLAINE
MINNEAPOLIS
St. Louis
Falcon Hts.
ST. PAUL
Excelsior
St. Paul Park
Hopkins
ST. LOUIS PARK
EDINA
W. St. Paul
Newport
Cottage
Grove
Chanhassen
Eden
Prairie
Richfield
S.
St. Paul
Afton
Chaska
Bloomington
INVERGROVE HTS.
Nicols
St. Paul
Park
Langdon
Shakopee
Savage
Lakeland
M I N N.
W I S.
Prior Lake
Rosemount
Merriam
Hastings

0 2 4 6 8 10 12 14 16 18 20 22 24
Miles
0 4 8 12 16 20 24 28 32 36 40
Kilometers

Scale 1:1 000 000; One inch to 16 miles.
Elevations and depressions are given in feet.

For larger scale coverage
of Los Angeles see page 228.

Continued on pages 98-99

Scale 1:4 000 000; one inch to 64 miles. Conic Projection
Elevations and depressions are given in feet

Longitude West of Greenwich

SAN DIEGO

Scale 1:1 000 000

0   5   10 Miles

0 4 8 12 16 Kilometers

A-520599-76   -8-8-13
COPYRIGHT BY
RAND MCNALLY & COMPANY
MADE IN U.S.A.

0   20   40   60   80   100   120 Miles

0 20 40 60 80 100 120 140 160 180 200 Kilometers

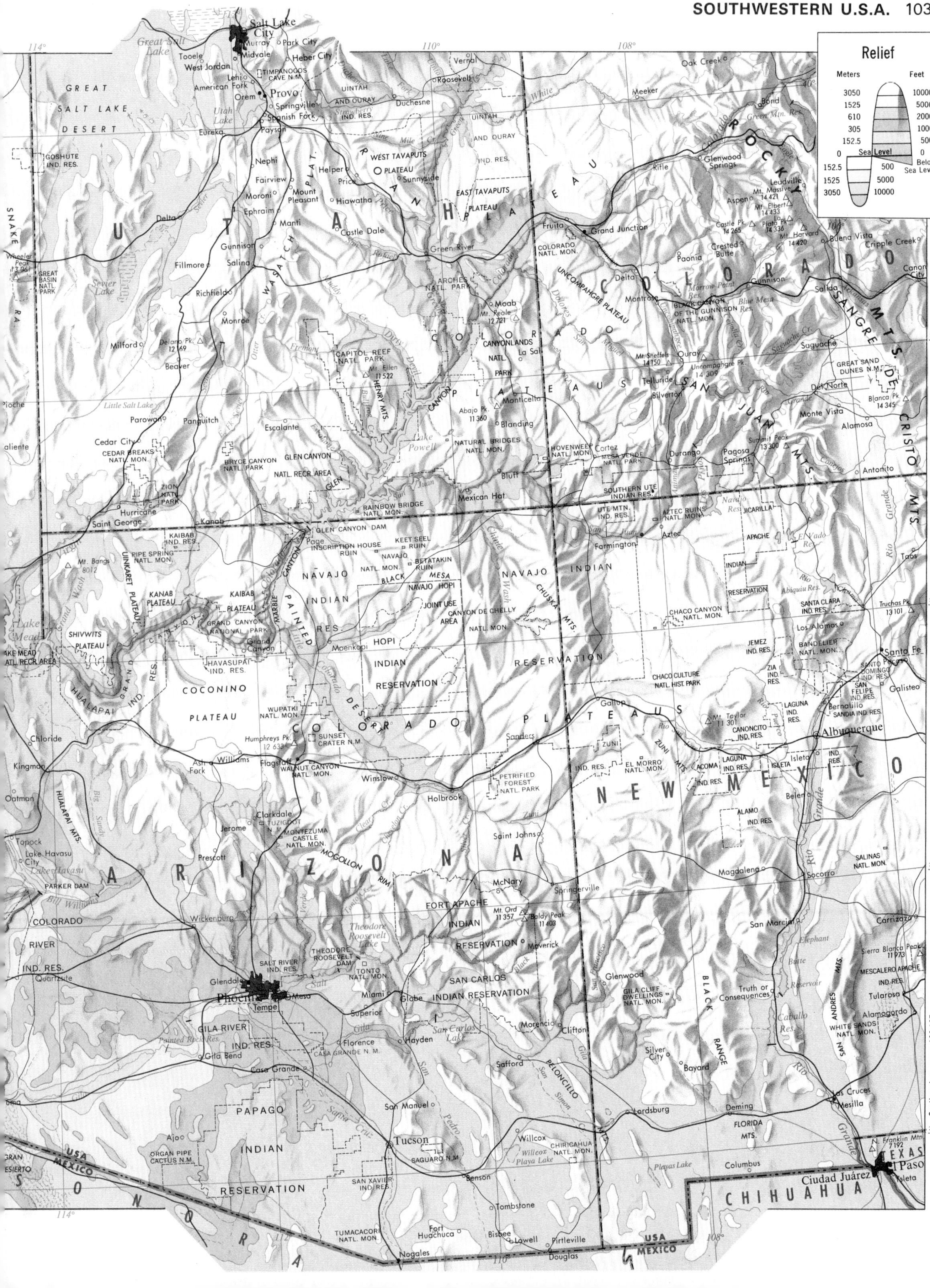

Relief

Meters	Feet
3050	10000
1525	5000
610	2000
305	1000
152.5	500
0	Sea Level
	0
152.5	500 Below Sea Level
1525	5000
3050	10000

Continued on pages 104-105
Continued on pages 106-107

Salt Lake City
Tooele
Murray
Park City
West Jordan
Midvale
Heber City
Lehi
American Fork
TIMPANOGOS CAVE N.M.
Provo
Orem
Springville
Spanish Fork
Utah Lake
Payson
Eureka
Nephi
Delta
Fairview
Moroni
Mount Pleasant
Ephraim
Manti
Gunnison
Salina
Fillmore
Richfield
Monroe
Milford
Beaver
Delano Pk. 12 169
Parowan
Panguitch
Escalante
Cedar City
CEDAR BREAKS NATL. MON.
ZION NATL. PARK
BRYCE CANYON NATL. PARK
Hurricane
Saint George
Kanab
Kanarraville
GREAT SALT LAKE DESERT
GREAT SALT LAKE
GOSHUTE IND. RES.
Wheeler Pk. 13 063
GREAT BASIN NATL. PARK
Sevier Lake
Little Salt Lake
Pioche
Caliente

UINTAH AND OURAY IND. RES.
Vernal
Roosevelt
Duchesne
WEST TAVAPUTS PLATEAU
EAST TAVAPUTS PLATEAU
Helper
Price
Sunnyside
Hiawatha
Castle Dale
Green River
WASATCH PLATEAU
CAPITOL REEF NATL. PARK
Mt. Ellen 11 522
HENRY MTS.
Abajo Pk. 11 360
GLEN CANYON NATL. RECR. AREA
Lake Powell
NATURAL BRIDGES NATL. MON.
RAINBOW BRIDGE NATL. MON.
GLEN CANYON DAM
Page
Mexican Hat
Bluff

UINTAH AND OURAY IND. RES.
Meeker
Rifle
Glenwood Springs
ROCKY
Oak Creek
Bond
Green Mtn. Res.
Leadville 14 421
Mt. Massive 14 421
Aspen
Castle Pk. 14 265
Mt. Elbert 14 433
Mt. Harvard 14 420
Buena Vista
Cripple Creek
Fruita
Grand Junction
COLORADO NATL. MON.
Delta
Paonia
Crested Butte
Montrose
UNCOMPAHGRE PLATEAU
BLACK CANYON OF THE GUNNISON NATL. MON.
Morrow Point Res.
Blue Mesa Res.
Gunnison
Salida
Canon City
Moab
Mt. Peale 12 721
CANYONLANDS NATL. PARK
La Sal
COLORADO PLATEAUS
Monticello
Blanding
Mt. Sneffels 14 150
Ouray
Uncompahgre Pk. 14 309
Telluride
Silverton
SAN JUAN MTS.
Saguache
GREAT SAND DUNES N.M.
Del Norte
Monte Vista
Alamosa
Blanca Pk. 14 345
Summit Peak 13 300
Antonito
SANGRE DE CRISTO MTS.

HOVENWEEP NATL. MON.
Cortez
MESA VERDE NATL. PARK
Durango
Pagosa Springs
SOUTHERN UTE INDIAN RES.
UTE MTN. IND. RES.
AZTEC RUINS NATL. MON.
Aztec
Farmington
CHACO CANYON NATL. MON.
JICARILLA
APACHE
INDIAN
RESERVATION
El Vado Res.
Abiquiu Res.
SANTA CLARA IND. RES.
Truchas Pk. 13 101
Los Alamos
JEMEZ IND. RES.
BANDELIER NATL. MON.
ZIA IND. RES.
Santa Fe
SANTO DOMINGO
SAN FELIPE IND. RES.
Galisteo
Bernalillo
SANDIA IND. RES.
Albuquerque

KAIBAB IND. RES.
PIPE SPRING NATL. MON.
Mt. Bangs 8012
UINKARET PLATEAU
KANAB PLATEAU
KAIBAB PLATEAU
Lake Mead
LAKE MEAD NATL. RECR. AREA
SHIVWITS PLATEAU
HUALAPAI IND. RES.
GRAND CANYON NATIONAL PARK
Grand Canyon
MARBLE CANYON
HAVASUPAI IND. RES.
COCONINO PLATEAU
INSCRIPTION HOUSE RUIN
KEET SEEL RUIN
BETATAKIN RUIN
NAVAJO NATL. MON.
BLACK MESA
NAVAJO INDIAN RES.
Moenkopi
HOPI INDIAN RESERVATION
NAVAJO HOPI JOINT USE AREA
CANYON DE CHELLY NATL. MON.
CHUSKA MTS.
NAVAJO INDIAN RESERVATION
PAINTED DESERT
CHACO CANYON NATL. MON.
CHACO CULTURE NATL. HIST. PARK
Gallup
ACOMA IND. RES.
Mt. Taylor 11 301
CANONCITO IND. RES.
LAGUNA IND. RES.
ZUNI IND. RES.
ZUNI MTS.
EL MORRO NATL. MON.
Zuni
ISLETA IND. RES.
Isleta
Belen

Chloride
Kingman
Oatman
HUALAPAI MTS.
Topock
Lake Havasu City
Lake Havasu
PARKER DAM
Bill Williams
COLORADO RIVER IND. RES.
Quartzsite
Bouse
Humphreys Pk. 12 633
SUNSET CRATER N.M.
Flagstaff
Ash Fork
Williams
WALNUT CANYON NATL. MON.
WUPATKI NATL. MON.
Winslow
Holbrook
PETRIFIED FOREST NATL. PARK
Sanders
Clarkdale
TUZIGOOT N.M.
Jerome
Prescott
MONTEZUMA CASTLE NATL. MON.
MOGOLLON RIM
Saint Johns
McNary
Springerville
FORT APACHE INDIAN RESERVATION
Mt. Ord 11 357
Baldy Peak 11 403
Maverick
Wickenburg
THEODORE ROOSEVELT LAKE
THEODORE ROOSEVELT DAM
TONTO NATL. MON.
SALT RIVER IND. RES.
Glendale
Phoenix
Tempe
Mesa
Miami
Globe
SAN CARLOS INDIAN RESERVATION
San Carlos Lake
Superior
GILA RIVER IND. RES.
Hayden
Florence
Gila Bend
CASA GRANDE N.M.
Casa Grande
San Manuel
PAPAGO INDIAN RESERVATION
Ajo
ORGAN PIPE CACTUS N.M.
Tucson
SAN XAVIER IND. RES.
SAGUARO N.M.
Benson
Tombstone
TUMACACORI NATL. MON.
Fort Huachuca
Nogales
Bisbee
Lowell
Pirtleville
Douglas
Willcox
Willcox Playa Lake
CHIRICAHUA NATL. MON.

COLORADO RIVER IND. RES.
Glenwood
GILA CLIFF DWELLINGS NATL. MON.
Morenci
Clifton
Silver City
Bayard
Safford
BLACK RANGE
ALAMO IND. RES.
SALINAS NATL. MON.
Socorro
Magdalena
San Marcial
Carrizozo
Elephant Butte Res.
Truth or Consequences
Caballo Res.
SAN ANDRES MTS.
WHITE SANDS NATL. MON.
Tularosa
Alamogordo
MESCALERO APACHE IND. RES.
Sierra Blanca Peak 11 973
Las Cruces
Mesilla
Deming
Lordsburg
FLORIDA MTS.
Columbus
Franklin Mtn. 7192
El Paso
Ciudad Juárez
Isleta

UTAH
COLORADO
ARIZONA
NEW MEXICO
TEXAS
SNAKE RA.
WASATCH PLATEAU
UINTA
UINTAH PLATEAU
CANYON PLATEAUS
COLORADO PLATEAUS
Rio Grande
COLORADO RIVER
SONORA
CHIHUAHUA
USA MEXICO

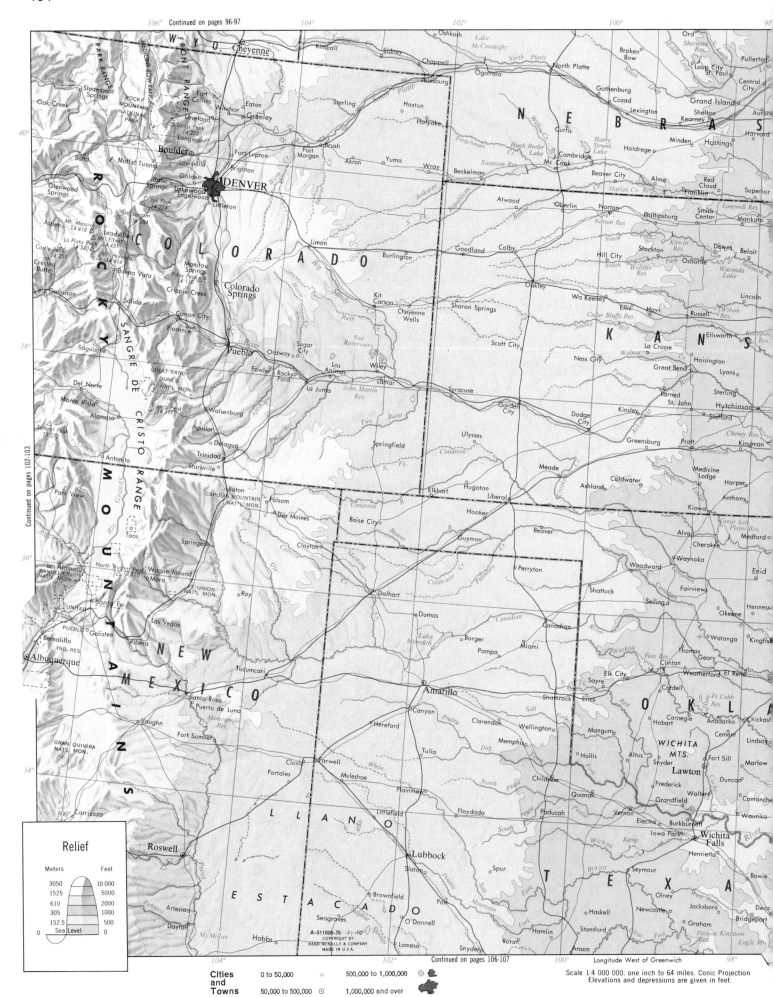

Continued on pages 96-97

106°   104°   102°   100°   98°

W Y O.

Cheyenne

N E B R A S

40°

Oak Creek
Steamboat
Springs
Yampa
PARK RANGE
MEDICINE BOW RANGE
FRONT RANGE
ROCKY MOUNTAIN NATIONAL PARK
Fort Collins
Windsor
Eaton
Greeley
Loveland
Longs Peak 14 255
Longmont
Boulder
Bond
Moffat Tunnel
Louisville
Brighton
Fort Lupton
Brush
Fort Morgan
Akron
Yuma
Wray
Sidney
Ogallala
North Platte
Julesburg
Chappell
Kimball
Oshkosh
Lake McConaughy
North Platte
Broken Bow
Loup City
St. Paul
Ord
Sherman Res.
Middle Loup
Fullerton
Central City
Aurora
Gothenburg
Cozad
Lexington
Grand Island
Shelton
Kearney
Minden
Hastings
Harvard

Glenwood Springs
Idaho Springs
Grays Peak 14 274
Golden
Lakewood
Engelwood
DENVER
Littleton
Bijou Cr.
Limon
Beaver Cr.
Republican
Holyoke
Benkelman
Mc Cook
Hugh Butler Lake
Cambridge
Frenchman
Curtis
Swanson Res.
Harry Strunk Lake
Holdrege
Beaver City
Alma
Franklin
Harlan Co. Res.
Red Cloud
Superior
Lovewell Res.

38°
Aspen
Mt. Massive 14 418
Mt. Elbert 14 431
Leadville
Mt. Lincoln 14 284
La Plata Peak 14 340
Mt. Harvard 14 414
Castle Peak 14 259
Crested Butte
Gunnison
Buena Vista
Salida
Canon City
Florence
Pueblo
Manitou Springs
Pikes Peak 14 110
Colorado Springs
Cripple Creek
C O L O R A D O
Kit Carson
Cheyenne Wells
Burlington
Goodland
Colby
Oakley
Wa Keeney
Sharon Springs
Scott City
Ness City
Hill City
Stockton
Osborne
Downs
Beloit
Waconda Lake
Solomon
Lincoln
Wilson Res.
K A N S A S
Norton
Phillipsburg
Smith Center
Mankato
Norton Res.
Oberlin
Atwood
Kirwin Res.
Webster Res.
Cedar Bluffs Res.
Smoky
Hays
Russell
Ellsworth
Kanopolis Res.

Saguache
ROCKY MOUNTAINS
SANGRE DE CRISTO RANGE
GREAT SAND DUNES NAT'L MON.
Huerfano
Blanca Peak 14 317
Walsenburg
Aguilar
Delagua
Trinidad
Starkville
Fowler
Rocky Ford
Ordway
Sugar City
Las Animas
Lamar
La Junta
John Martin Res.
Wiley
Nee Reservoirs
Rush Cr.
Horse Cr.
Syracuse
Garden City
Dodge City
Greensburg
Pratt
Kinsley
Larned
St. John
Great Bend
Hoisington
Lyons
Sterling
Hutchinson
Stafford
La Crosse
Walnut
Pawnee
Arkansas
Ninnescah
Cheney Res.
Kingman

Del Norte
Monte Vista
Saguache
Alamosa
Summit Peak 13 272
Park View
Conejos
Antonito
Continued on pages 102-103
Springfield
Ulysses
Meade
Coldwater
Ashland
Medicine Lodge
Harper
Anthony
Kiowa
Cimarron

36°
Los Alamos
BANDELIER NAT'L MON.
North Truchas Peak 13 110
Wagon Mound
Mora
Raton
CAPULIN MOUNTAIN NAT'L MON.
Folsom
Des Moines
Clayton
Boise City
Elkhart
Hugoton
Liberal
Hooker
Guymon
Beaver
Woodward
Waynoka
Fairview
Enid
Cherokee
Medford
Alva
Great Salt Plains Res.

Taos
Springer
Roy
UNION NAT'L MON.
Dalhart
Perryton
Coldwater Cr.
Palo Duro Cr.
Mustang Cr.
Carrizo Cr.
Shattuck
Seiling
Okeene
Kingfisher
Watonga
Hennessey
Thomas
Geary
Clinton
Weatherford
El Reno

N E W
Santa Fe
UNITED PUEBLO IND. RES.
Galisteo
Las Vegas
Ribera
Santa Rosa
Puerto de Luna
Dumas
Borger
Pampa
Miami
Lake Meredith
Canadian
Canadian River
Washita
Foss Res.
Cordell
Elk City
Sayre
Ft. Cobb Res.
Carnegie
Anadarko
Cement
Chickasha
Lindsay

Bernalillo
IND. RES.
PUEBLO
Albuquerque
M E X I C O
Tucumcari
Santa Rosa
Amarillo
Canyon
Shamrock
Erick
Hobart
Mangum
Altus
O K L A.
WICHITA MTS.
Fort Sill
Lawton
Duncan
Comanche
Marlow

34°
GRAN QUIVIRA NAT'L MON.
Vaughn
Fort Sumner
Hereford
Clarendon
Wellingtono
Memphis
Hollis
Quanah
Vernon
Frederick
Grandfield
Walters
Waurika

Carrizozo
Clovis
Portales
Farwell
Muleshoe
Tulia
Plainview
Childress
Paducah
Electra
Iowa Park
Burkburnett
Olney
Wichita Falls
Henrietta
Bowie

Roswell
Bernalillo
M O U N T A I N S
Lubbock
Slaton
Littlefield
Floydada
Spur
Post
L L A N O
Seymour
Kemp
Jacksboro
Graham
Possum Kingdom Res.
Eagle Mt.

Artesia
Dayton
McMillan
Hobbs
Seagroves
O'Donnell
Brownfield
E S T A C A D O
Lamesa
Snyder
Rotan
Hamlin
Anson
Stamford
Newcastle
Bridgeport
T E X A S
Brazos
Double Mountain Fork

Pecos
Penasco
Honda

A-511006-76 -7;-10³
COPYRIGHT BY
RAND McNALLY & COMPANY
MADE IN U.S.A.

Continued on pages 106-107

Longitude West of Greenwich

Relief

Meters		Feet
3050		10 000
1525		5000
610		2000
305		1000
152.5		500
0	Sea Level	0

Cities and Towns

0 to 50,000   ○   500,000 to 1,000,000   ◎

50,000 to 500,000   ⊙   1,000,000 and over

Scale 1:4 000 000; one inch to 64 miles. Conic Projection
Elevations and depressions are given in feet.

CHICAGO
Aurora

Continued on pages 96-97

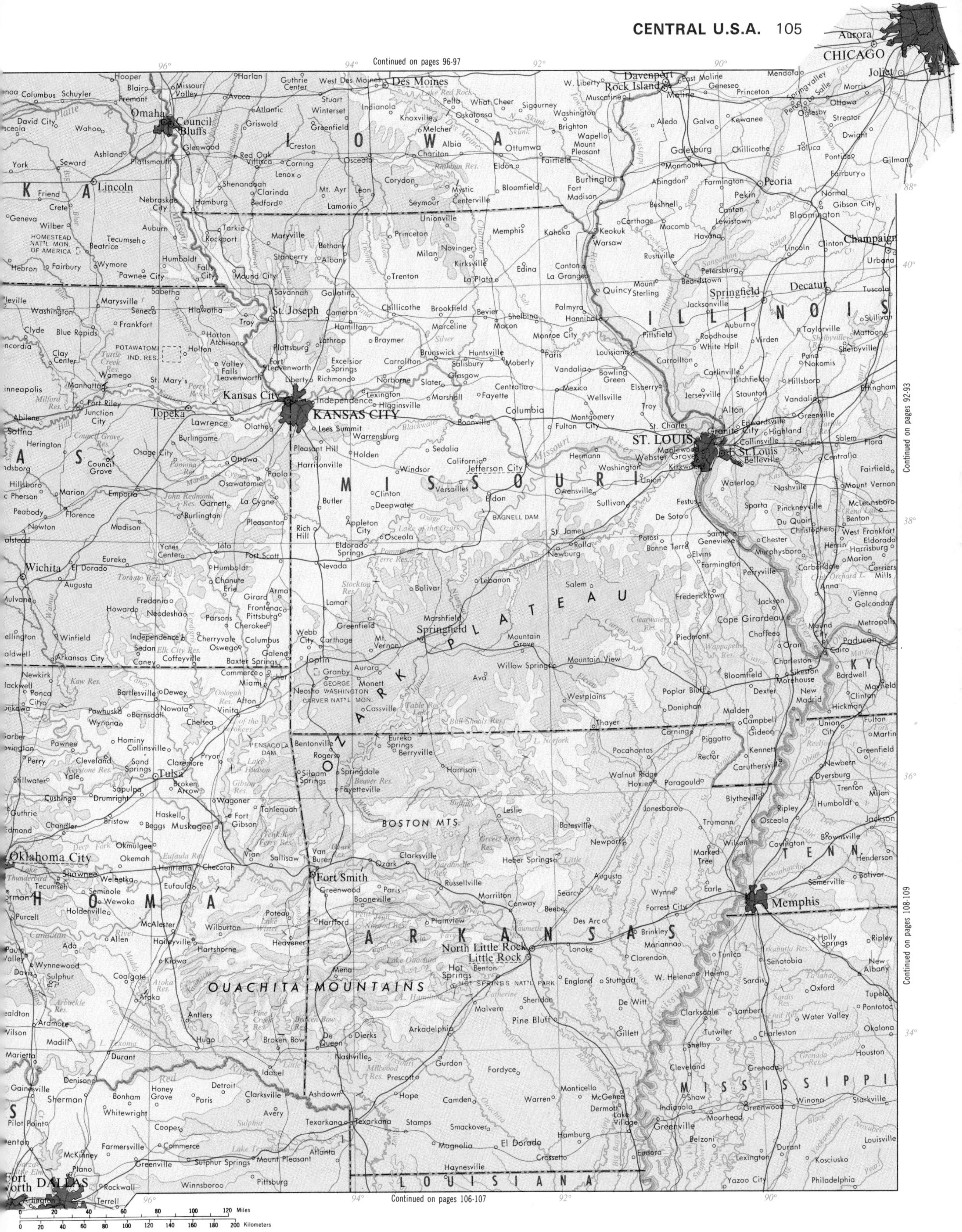

Continued on pages 92-93

Continued on pages 108-109

IOWA

ILLINOIS

KANSAS

MISSOURI

OKLAHOMA

ARKANSAS

TENN.

MISSISSIPPI

LOUISIANA

KY.

Des Moines
Davenport
Rock Island
East Moline
Joliet

Omaha
Council Bluffs

Lincoln

Topeka

Kansas City
KANSAS CITY

St. Joseph

Wichita

Tulsa

Oklahoma City

Fort Worth DALLAS

DALLAS

ST. LOUIS
St. Louis
Granite City
Belleville

Springfield

Jefferson City

Columbia

Memphis

Fort Smith

Little Rock
North Little Rock

OZARK PLATEAU

BOSTON MTS.

OUACHITA MOUNTAINS

GEORGE WASHINGTON CARVER NAT'L MON.

HOT SPRINGS NAT'L PARK

BAGNELL DAM

Lake of the Ozarks

Bull Shoals Res.

Red River

Peoria
Champaign
Urbana
Decatur
Springfield
Bloomington
Normal
Quincy
Hannibal
Cape Girardeau
Cairo
Paducah

96°   94°   92°   90°   88°

40°
38°
36°
34°

0   20   40   60   80   100   120 Miles
0   20   40   60   80   100   120   140   160   180   200 Kilometers

Continued on pages 106-107

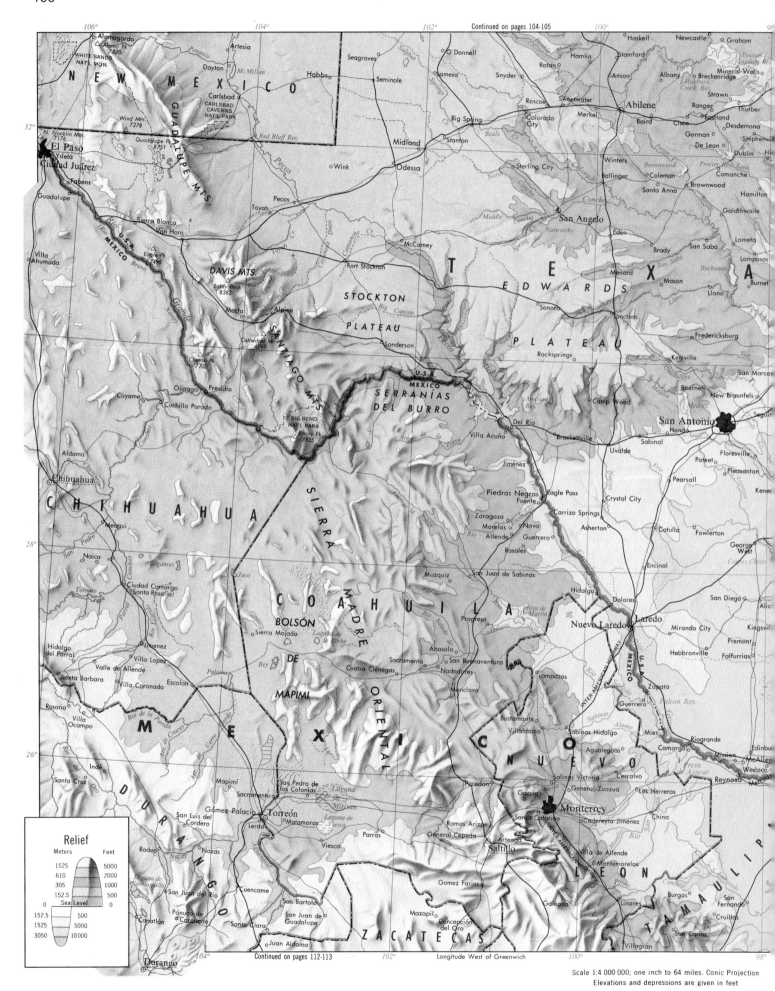

Continued on pages 104-105

106°   104°   102°   100°   98°

NEW MEXICO

White Sands Nat'l Mon.

Alamogordo
Alamo Pk. 7820
Artesia
Penasco
Dayton
McMillan
Seagraves
O'Donnell
Haskell
Newcastle
Graham
Hobbs
Seminole
Lamesa
Rotan
Hamlin
Stamford
Mineral Wells

Carlsbad
Carlsbad Caverns Nat'l Park
Snyder
Roscoe
Sweetwater
Abilene
Ranger
Eastland
Thurber
Strawn
Possum Kingdom Res.

Wind Mtn. 7278
Guadalupe Pk. 8751
Red Bluff Res.
Big Spring
Colorado City
Merkel
Baird
Clsee
Gorman
Desdemona
Stephenville
Dublin

N. Franklin Mtn. 7176
Toyah
Pecos
Stanton
Midland
Odessa
Sterling City
Winters
Ballinger
Coleman
Santa Anna
Comanche
Hamilton

El Paso
Ysleta
Ciudad Juárez
Fabens
Guadalupe

32°

Van Horn
Sierra Blanca
Wink
North Concho
San Angelo
Eden
Brady
San Saba
Lometa
Lampasas
Burnet

Eagle Pk. 7496
DAVIS MTS.
Baldy Peak 8382
McCamey
Fort Stockton
Middle Concho
Sonora
Menard
Mason
Llano
Buchanan

Marfa
Alpine
STOCKTON PLATEAU
Sanderson
Big Canyon
EDWARDS
PLATEAU
Junction
Fredericksburg

Cathedral Mt. 6860
SANTIAGO MTS.
Chinati Pk. 7730
Rocksprings
Kerrville
San Marcos

Ojinaga
Presidio
U.S.A.
MEXICO
SERRANÍAS
DEL BURRO
Amistad Res.
Camp Wood
Boerne
New Braunfels
Seguin

Coyame
Cuchillo Parado
BIG BEND NAT'L PARK
Emory Pk. 7835
Arroyo de la Torre
Del Rio
Villa Acuña
Brackettville
San Antonio
Hondo
Floresville

30°

Aldama
Chihuahua
Jiménez
Uvalde
Sabinal
Poteet
Pleasanton
Kenec

Piedras Negras
Fuente
Crystal City
Pearsall

Meoqui
CHIHUAHUA
SIERRA
Zaragoza
Morelos
Nava
Eagle Pass
Carrizo Springs
Asherton
Cotulla
Fowlerton
George West

Naica
Allende
Guerrero
Encinal

28°

San Pedro
Gigantes
Jaco
Rosales
Muzquiz
San Juan de Sabinas
Hidalgo
Dolores
San Diego
Alic

Ciudad Camargo
Santa Rosalía
MADRE
Toronto
Progreso
Presa de Don Martin
Nuevo Laredo
Laredo
Mirando City
Kingsville
Premont

Hidalgo del Parral
Jiménez
COAHUILA
Sierra Mojada
Laguna de la Leche
Abasolo
Sacramento
San Buenaventura
Nadadores
Monclova
Lampazos
Zapata
Guerrero
Falcon Res.
Hebbronville
Falfurrias

Valle de Allende
Villa López
BOLSÓN
DE
Cuatro Ciénegas
Bustamante
Mier
Camargo
Riogrande
Edinbu
McAllen

Santa Bárbara
Villa Coronado
Escalón
Paloma
MAPIMI
ORIENTAL
Villaldama
Sabinas Hidalgo
Weslaco
Reynosa

26°

Rosario
Villa Ocampo
Rio de la Panda
Rey
Aguaguas
Garcia
Salinas Victoria
Cerralvo
Los Herreras

Santa Cruz
Inde
NUEVO
Paredón
General Zuazua
China

MEXICO

Mapimí
Sacramento
San Pedro de las Colonias
Laguna de Mayran
Salinas Victoria
Garcia
Monterrey
Santa Catarina
Cadereyta Jiménez

Gómez Palacio
Torreón
Lerdo
Matamoros
Laguna de Viesca
Ramos Arizpe
General Cepeda
Arteaga
Villa de Alende
Montemorelos

Rodeo
Nazas
Cuencamé
Viesca
Parras
Saltillo
Gómez Farías

Santa Clara
San Juan del Rio
San Bartolo
Concepción del Oro
Galeana
Linares
Burgos
San Fernando

Canatlán
Pánuco de Coronado
San Juan de Guadalupe
Mazapil
ZACATECAS
Villagrán
Cruillas

DURANGO
Juan Aldama
TAMAULIPAS

Durango
Continued on pages 112-113
104°   102°   100°   98°
Longitude West of Greenwich

Relief

Meters	Feet
1525	5000
610	2000
305	1000
152.5	500
0 Sea Level	0
152.5	500
1525	5000
3050	10000

Scale 1:4 000 000; one inch to 64 miles. Conic Projection
Elevations and depressions are given in feet

Continued on pages 104-105

ARK.

MISSISSIPPI

LOUISIANA

Continued on pages 108-109

Main map place names:

Denton, McKinney, Farmersville, Greenville, Sulphur Springs, Mount Pleasant, Atlanta, Haynesville, Lake Providence, Yazoo City, Canton

Fort Worth, DALLAS, Plano, Rockwall, Winnsboro, Pittsburg, Vivian, Homer, Bastrop, Forest, Ross Barnette Res.

Weatherford, Arlington, Wills Point, Terrell, Kaufman, Marshall, Jefferson, Bossier City, Minden, Arcadia, Rustono, Monroe, Rayville, Delhi, Tallulah, Vicksburg, Jackson, Pelahatchie

Granbury, Waxahachie, Mineola, Longview, Kilgore, Shreveport, Eros, Jonesboro, Winnsboro, Port Gibson, Hazlehurst, Crystal Springs

Cleburne, Ennis, Mabank, Tyler, Carthage, Henderson, Mansfield, Coushatta, Winnfield, Jonesville, Vidalia, Natchez, Fayette, Brookhaven, Sumrall, Collins

Itasca, Italy, Corsicana, Athens, Timpson, Center, Natchitoches, Colfax, Catahoula, Ferriday, Norfield, McComb, Columbia

Meridian, Hillsboro, Hubbard, Palestine, Rusk, Jacksonville, Nacogdoches, San Augustine, Fisher, Peason, Alexandria, Pineville, Marksville, Gloster, Magnolia, Tylertown, Lumberton

Waco, Mexia, Teague, Elkhart, Oakwood, Ratcliff, Lufkin, Hemphill, Leesville, Lecompte, McNary, Woodville, Kentwood, Franklinton, Poplarville, Bogalusa

Gatesville, McGregor, Marlin, Mart, Groesbeck, Buffalo, Crockett, Groveton, Wiergate, Jasper, Fullerton, Glenmora, Bunkie, Jackson, Amite, Picayune

Moody, Bremond, Marquez, Madisonville, Trinity, Newton, De Ridder, Elizabeth, Oakdale, Ville Platte, Melville, New Roads, Hammond, Covington

Temple, Calvert, Hearne, Huntsville, Woodville, Merryville, Longville, Kinder, Eunice, Opelousas, Baton Rouge, Madisonville, Bay St. Louis

Belton, Cameron, Bartlett, Bryan, Willis, Conroe, Kirbyville, De Quincy, Lake Charles, Jennings, Crowley, Lafayette, White Castle, Donaldsonville, Lutcher, Kenner, Slidell

Taylor, Rockdale, Caldwell, Navasota, Cleveland, Vinton, Ged, Lake Arthur, Rayne, St. Martinville, New Iberia, Plaquemine, Napoleonville, Metairie, New Orleans, Gretna

Austin, Round Rock, Elgin, Somerville, Brenham, Hempstead, Dayton, Liberty, Beaumont, Orange, Gueydan, Abbeville, Jeanerette, Thibodaux, Houma, Port Sulphur

Bastrop, Smithville, Giddings, Bellville, Sealy, HOUSTON, Port Neches, Port Arthur, Sabine, Franklin, Patterson, Morgan City

Lockhart, Luling, Columbus, Eagle Lake, Richmond, Alvin, Texas City, Port Bolivar, Galveston, High Island

Gonzales, Hallettsville, Wharton, West Columbia, Angleton, Bay City, Freeport

Nixon, Yoakum, El Campo, Edna, Palacios

Yorktown, Cuero, Victoria, Port Lavaca, Matagorda

Goliad, Beeville, Skidmore, Refugio, Rockport, Aransas Pass, Corpus Christi, Sinton, Portland

Raymondville, Harlingen, San Benito, Brownsville, Matamoros, Padre Island, Laguna Madre

GULF OF MEXICO

Inset map (a):

Scale 1:1 000 000

HOUSTON, Crosby, Sheldon, Highlands, Mont Belvieu, Wallisville, Hankamer, Anahuac

West University Place, Bellaire, Jacinto City, Galena Pk., Channelview, Baytown

Missouri City, Pasadena, South Houston, Genoa, La Porte

Pearland, Seabrook, Kemah, Smith Point, High Island

Arcola, Friendswood, League City, Dickinson, Bolivar Peninsula

Manvel, Alvin, Algoa, Alta Loma, Texas City, La Marque, Port Bolivar

Sandy Point, Hitchcock, Liverpool, Galveston

Danbury, Angleton, GALVESTON ISLAND, GULF OF MEXICO

WEST BAY, GALVESTON BAY, EAST BAY

Scale 1:1 000 000
0   5   10 Miles
0 4 8 12 16 Kilometers

Legend:

Cities and Towns		
0 to 50,000	○	500,000 to 1,000,000
50,000 to 500,000	⊙	1,000,000 and over

A-511007-76-
COPYRIGHT BY
RAND McNALLY & COMPANY
MADE IN U.S.A.

0 20 40 60 80 100 120 Miles
0 20 40 60 80 100 120 140 160 180 200 Kilometers

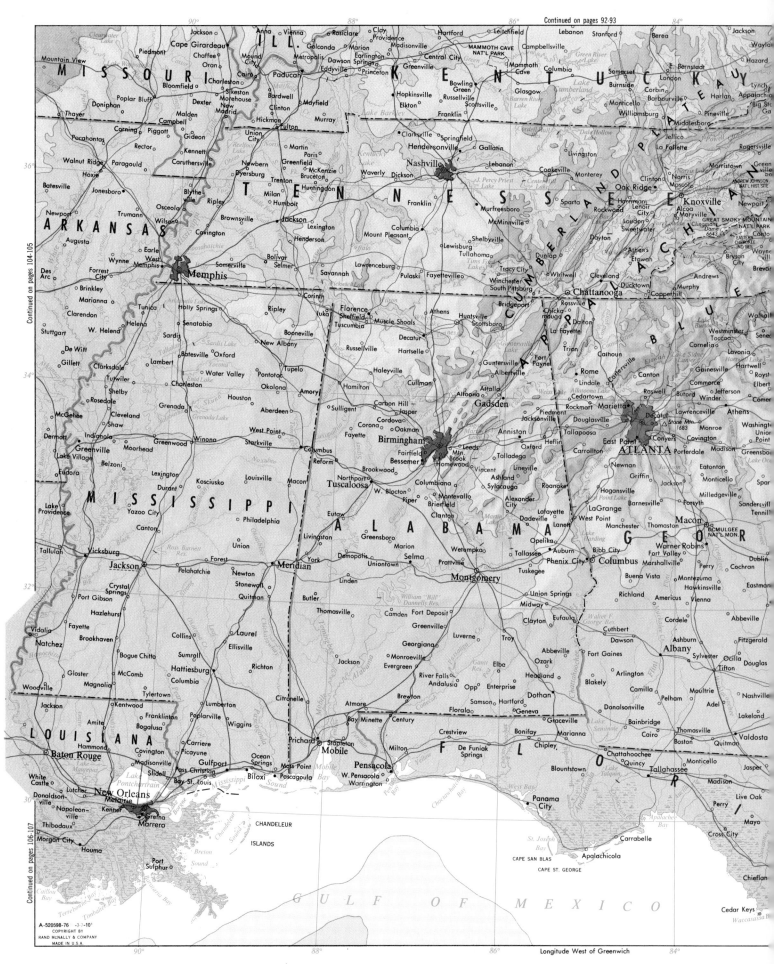

Continued on pages 92-93

Continued on pages 104-105

Continued on pages 106-107

GULF OF MEXICO

A-520598-76 -7-7-10'
COPYRIGHT BY
RAND McNALLY & COMPANY
MADE IN U.S.A.

Longitude West of Greenwich

Scale 1:4 000 000; one inch to 64 miles. Conic Projection
Elevations and depressions are given in feet

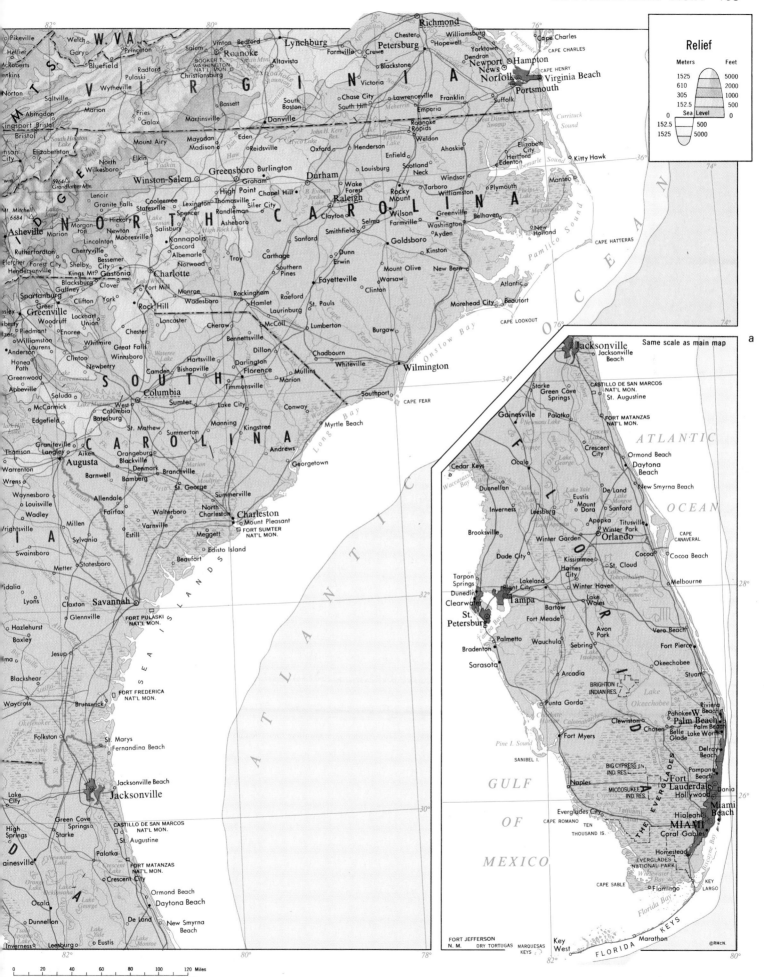

Relief

Meters	Feet
1525	5000
610	2000
305	1000
152.5	500
0	Sea Level 0
152.5	500
1525	5000

Same scale as main map

a

Scale 1:16 000 000; one inch to 250 miles. Polyconic Projection
Elevations and depressions are given in feet

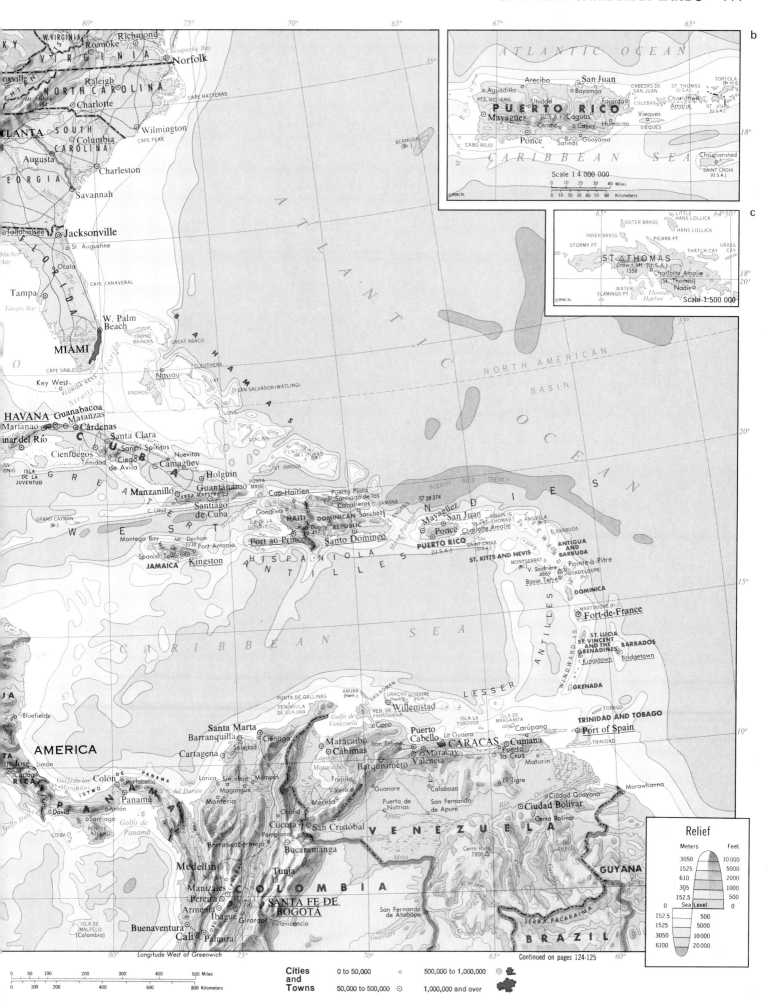

b

ATLANTIC OCEAN

Arecibo · San Juan
Aguadilla · Bayamon · TORTOLA (Br. to I.)
PTA. HIGUERO · Utuado · CABEZAS DE · ST. THOMAS
SAN JUAN · (U.S.A.) · Charlotte
PUERTO RICO · Fajardo · Amalie · ST. JOHN
Mayagüez · (U.S.A.) · Caguas · CULEBRA · (U.S.A.)
Coamo · Cayey · Humacao · Vieques
VIEQUES

Ponce · Salinas · Guayama · 18°

Scale 1:4 000 000
0 10 20 30 40 Miles
0 10 20 30 40 50 60 Kilometers

CARIBBEAN SEA · Christiansted
SAINT CROIX
(U.S.A.)
©RMcN

c

LITTLE
HANS LOLLICK · 64°50'
OUTER BRASS · HANS LOLLICK
INNER BRASS · PICARA PT. · 65°
STORMY PT. · THATCH CAY · GRASS
CAY
ST. THOMAS
Crown Mt. (U.S.A.) · 18°
1558 · Charlotte Amalie · 20'
(St. Thomas)
WATER · Nadir
FLAMINGO PT. · St. Thomas
©RMcN · Harbor · Scale 1:500 000

Relief

Meters	Feet
3050	10 000
1525	5000
610	2000
395	1000
152.5	500
Sea Level	0
152.5	500
1525	5000
3050	10 000
6100	20 000

Continued on pages 124-125

0 50 100 200 300 400 500 Miles
0 100 200 300 400 600 800 Kilometers

Longitude West of Greenwich

Cities and Towns

0 to 50,000 ○ · 500,000 to 1,000,000 ◎
50,000 to 500,000 ⊙ · 1,000,000 and over

Continued on pages 106-107

Relief

Meters		Feet
3050		10 000
1525		5000
610		2000
305		1000
152.5		500
0	Sea Level	0
152.5		500
1525		5000
3050		10 000

A-531695-76
COPYRIGHT BY
RAND McNALLY & COMPANY
MADE IN U.S.A.

Longitude West of Greenwich

Cities and Towns

0 to 50,000   50,000 to 500,000   500,000 to 1,000,000   1,000,000 and over

Scale 1:4 000 000; one inch to 64 miles. Conic Projection
Elevations and depressions are given in feet

a

Inset map (Mexico City region)

Morelos
Nicolás Romero
Cahuacán
Cuautitlán
Tutitlán
Tecamac
Teotihuacán
Acolman
Chiconautla
Tepexpan
Otumba
Pyramids of Teotihuacán
Apan
HIDALGO
Calpulalpan
TLAXCALA
Nanacamilpa

San Bartolo
Ixtlahuaca
Cerro La Catedral 13 000 △
Atizapán
Tepetlaoxtoc
San Jerónimo
Texcoco

M É X I C O

Jiquipilco
Mazatla
Tlalnepantla
Lago de Texcoco (Dry Lake)
Coatlinchán

Temoaya
Atzcapotzalco
Naucalpan
Gustavo A. Madero
MEXICO CITY
Chicoloapan

Mimiapan
Chimalpa
Ixtacalco
Ixtapalapa
Los Reyes
Ayotla
Río Frío
Texmelucan

PUEBLA

Toluca
Cuajimalpa
Huixquilucan
Lerma
Villa Obregón Contreras
San Andrés
Xochimilco
Tláhuac
Ixtapaluca
INTER-AMERICAN HY

Capultitlán
Metepec
Mexicalcingo
Cerro Muneca 12 655
Tlalpan
Coyoacán
Chalco

Almoloya
Ajusco
Cerro Ajusco 12 850
Topilejo
Tecómitl
Milpa Alta
Tlalmanalco
Iztaccíhuatl 17 343

Nevado de Toluca △ 14 409
Coatepec
Oxtotepec
Tenango
Amecameca

Tenango
Tres Cumbres
Huitzilac
Ozumba
Volcán Popocatépetl 17 887

Scale 1:1 000 000
Tepoztlán
Tlalnepantla
Tlayacapan

0   5   10 Miles
0 4 8 12 16 Kilometers

M O R E L O S

©RMcN.
Cuernavaca

Main map

Laguna Almagre
-24°

Tropic of Cancer
-22°

PTA. JEREZ

Laguna de San Andres

Tamira
Ciudad Madero
Tampico
Villa Cuauhtémoc
Tampico Alto

Laguna Tamiahua
CABO ROJO
BARRECIFE BLANQUILLA
ISLA DE LOBOS

Jluama
Tancoco
Alamo
Túxpan
Tamiahua
ARRECIFE TANQUIJO
ARRECIFE TÚXPAN

GULF OF MEXICO

Tihuatlán
Poza Rica
Gutiérrez Zamora
Furbero
Tecolutla
Coyutla
Nautla
Coxquihui
ytlalpan
Cuelzalón del Progreso
Tlapacoyan
Vega de Alatorre

apoaxtla
Atempan
Jalacingo
Teziutlán
Altotonga
Misantla

Las Vigas
Naolinco
Perote
△ 14 048
Jalapa Enríquez
PUNTA ZEMPOALA

Libres
Teocelo
Coatepec
Antigua Veracruz

manitla
Jilotepec
Veracruz

San Juan Ixtenco
Huatusco
ARRECIFE CABEZA

Ciudad Serdán
Pico de Orizaba (Vol.) △ 18 406
Coscomatepec
Acatzingo de Hidalgo
Orizaba
Córdoba
Medellín

oyatempan
Heroica Nogales
Alvarado

Tlacotepec
Maltrata
Omealca
Cotaxtla
Tlalixcoyan

B A H Í A   D E   C A M P E C H E

YUCATÁN
Sisal
Húnucmá
Maxcanú
Halachó

Lerma
Campeche
-20°

Seybaplaya
Champotón
Pustunich

C A M P E C H E

Sabancuy
Chicbul
Mamantel

San Pedro
ISLA DEL CARMEN
Laguna de Términos
Ciudad del Carmen

Tehuacan
Ajalpan
Zoquitlán
San Gabriel Chilac
Chazumba
Huatla de Jiménez
Ojitlán (S. Lucas)

San Martín (Vol.) △ 6000
PTA. ZAPOTLÁN
PUNTA FONTERA
Frontera
Paraíso
Allende
MEXICO
GUATEMALA

Tlacotálpan
Santiago Tuxtla
San Andrés Tuxtla
Catemaco
del Carmen
Comalcalco
Jalpa

Cosamaloápan
Chacaltianguis
Pajapan
Coatzacoalcos (Puerto México)
Cunduacán
Palizada

S Miguel
Teotitlán del Camino
Jalapa de Díaz (San Felipe)
Tuxtepec
Tesecheacan
Soteapan
Cosoleacaque
Cárdenas
Villahermosa
Balancán
Emiliana Zapata

Tepelmeme
Coixtlahuaca
Cuicatlán
Playa Vicente
San Juan Evangelista
Sayula
Texistepec
Minatitlán
Jalpa
Huimanguillo
Tacotalpa
San Carlos
Palenque
Tenosique

Huajuapan de León
Nochixtlán (Asunción)
Jesús Carranza
Puebla Vieja
Pichucalco
Chapultenango
Yajalón
Bachajón

azulpan
Tejupan (Santiago)
Progreso
Talea de Castro (San Miguel)
Villa Alta (San Ildefonso)
Presa de Malpaso
Tecpatán
Pantepec
Simojovel
Ococingo

Teposcolula (Pedro y San Pablo)
Ixtlán de Juárez
Hidalgo Yalalag
Zacatepec (Santiago)
Berriozabal
Compainalá
Jitotol

Tlaxiaco Sta. María Asunción
Mazatlán (San Juan)
Guichicovi (San Juan)
Ozocoautla
Tuxtla Gutiérrez
Bohom
Cancuc
Oxchuc
M E S E T A   D E   A G U A   E S C O N D I D A

herrero
Chalcatongo
Yosonútí (Sta. Cruz)
San Mateo (Etlatongo)
Zaachila
Tlacolula de Matamoros
Oaxaca de Juárez
9400
Ciudad de las Casas
Chiapa de Corzo
Acala
Teopisca

bujía Sta. Cruz
Zimatlán de Alvarez
Ocotlán de Morelos
Taviche
INTER-AMERICAN HY
Ixtepec
Ixtaltepec (Asunción)
Zanatepec (Sto. Domingo)
Cintalapa
Las Cruces
Suchiapa
Amatenango
Las Rosas

ozailtlán (Sta. María)
emilpec
Sola de Vega (S. Miguel)
Ejutla de Crespo
Jalapa del Marqués
Juchitán de Zaragoza
Ixtepec
Tapanatepec
8202 △
Villa Flores
Venustiano Carranza
Socoltenango
Comitán

S I E R R A   D E   O A X A C A
Miahuatlán
Las Vacas
Tehuantepec Sto. Domingo
Ixhuatán (San Francisco)
Arriaga
La Concordia
Trinitaria
SA. CUCHUMATANES

Loxicha (Sta. Catarina)
Pluma Hidalgo
Salina Cruz
Laguna Superior
Laguna Inferior
Mar Muerto
Tonalá
S I E R R A   M A D R E
C O R D.   D E   C H I A P A S
GUATEMALA
Cuauhtémoc
Jacatenango

Pochutla (San Pedro)
Puerto Ángel
Golfo de Tehuantepec
Mapastepec
-16°

I S T M O   D E   T E H U A N T E P E C
T A B A S C O
C H I A P A S
D E L   S U R

0   20   40   60   80   100   120 Miles
0 20 40 60 80 100 120 140 160 180 200 Kilometers

For larger scale coverage of Mexico City see page 229.

Continued on pages 114-115

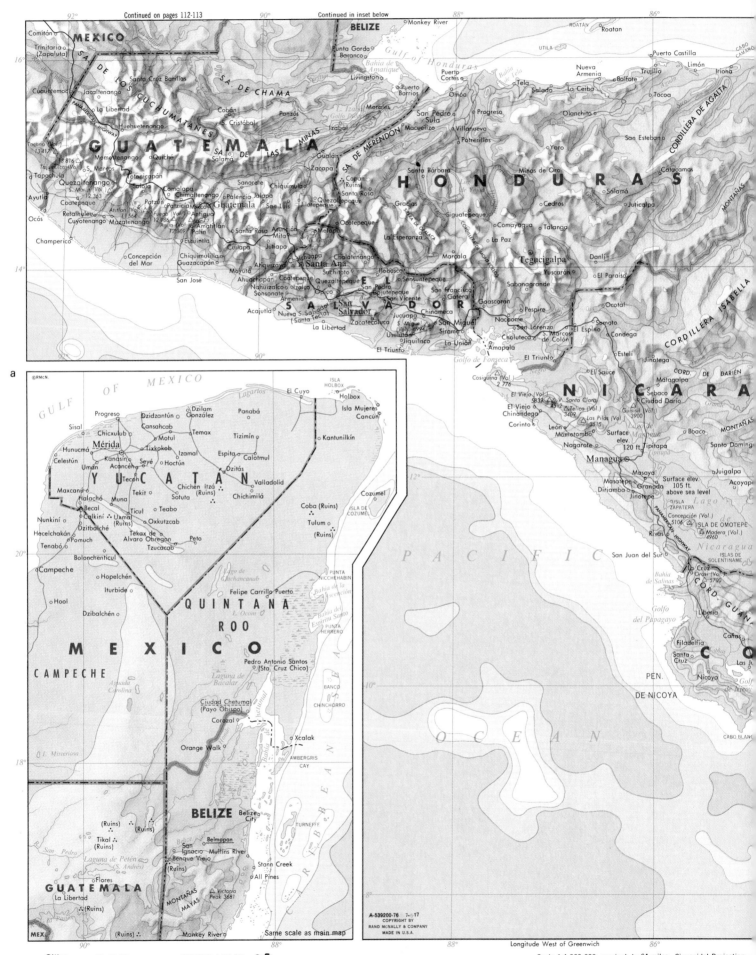

Continued on pages 112-113
Continued in inset below

Cities
and
Towns

0 to 50,000   500,000 to 1,000,000
50,000 to 500,000   1,000,000 and over

Scale 1:4 000 000; one inch to 64 miles. Sinusoidal Projection

Elevations and depressions are given in feet

Longitude West of Greenwich

Longitude West of Greenwich

ANGUILLA (Br.)
ST. MARTIN (Neth. and Fr.)
ST. BARTHÉLEMY (Fr.)
SABA (Neth.)
Codrington o   BARBUDA
ST. EUSTATIUS (Neth.)
Mt. Misery △   ST. KITTS
4314
Basseterre
ST. KITTS AND NEVIS
Charlestown △ Nevis Peak
3596
NEVIS
St. Johns
Boggy Peak △   **ANTIGUA**
1330   **AND BARBUDA**
REDONDA ⊙

Relief

Meters		Feet
3050		10 000
1525		5000
610		2000
305		1000
152.5		500
Sea Level		
152.5		500
1525		5000
3050		10 000

b

PUNTA PATUCA

OLÓN

Cabo Gracias a Dios

CAYOS MISKITO

L E E W A R D

MONTSERRAT (Br.)
Plymouth o △ Soufrière (Vol.)
3002

POINTE DE LA GRANDE VIGIE
GRANDE TERRE
Ste. Rose   Le Moule
DESIRADE (Fr.)
Pointe-à-Pitre o
Ste. Anne   PETITE TERRE (Fr.)
BASSE TERRE   **GUADELOUPE**
Grande Soufrière (Vol.)4869 △ Capesterre (Fr.)
Basse Terre   **MARIE GALANTE** (Fr.)
Grand Bourg
LES SAINTES IS.

C A R I B B E A N

ISLA DE PROVIDENCIA (Colombia)

Portsmouth o △ Morne Diablotin
4 747
St. Joseph
DOMINICA
Roseau o

Dominica Channel

SAN ANDRÉS (Colombia)
CAYOS DE ESE

Mt. Pelée (Vol.)
4800
St. Pierre △ △ Trinité
Pitons du Carbet 3960
Fort-de-France   Le François
Le Marin   **MARTINIQUE** (Fr.)
POINTE D'ENFER

LITTLE CORN
GREAT CORN (Nicaragua)
CAYOS DE ALBUQUERQUE (Colombia)

St. Lucia Channel

Castries
Morne Gimie △ **ST. LUCIA**
3145
Soufrière o

S E A

Lone Star
Puerto Cabezas

Laguna Caratasca
Laguna Huaunta
Prinzapolca

Huaunta

C O S T A   D E   M O S Q U I T O S

Rama

ISLA DE LA CIERVO

Bluefields

PUNTA MICO

St. Vincent Passage

Mt. Soufrière
4048
ST. VINCENT
Kingstown   **AND THE GRENADINES**
BEQUIA
MUSTIQUE
CANOUAN

NORTH POINT
BARBADOS
Mt. Hillaby
1104
Bathsheba
Bridgetown
SOUTH POINT

W I N D W A R D   I S.

A T L A N T I C   O C E A N

C A R I B B E A N   S E A

an Carlos

Bahia de San Juan del Norte

San Juan del Norte (Greytown)

T H E   G R E N A D I N E S

CARRIACOU

Mt. St. Catherine
2749
St. George's o △ Grenville
GRENADA

©RMcN

Same scale as main map

San Ramón   Guapiles
Espírta   Alajuela   Heredia   Caira
Sintonas o   San José   Turrialba
Irazú (Vol.)   Matina
Cartago   Paraíso   Limón

PUNTA CAHUITA

R I C A
C O R D I L L E R A
Parrita
Quepos
Cerro Chirripó
PUNTA QUEPOS   12 530
San Isidro
Cerro Kámuk
11 694
Buenos Aires
Cerro Echandi
10 394
D E   T A L A M A N C A

Puerto Cortés

Bahia de Coronada

ISLA DE CAÑO   **PENÍNSULA**
Puerto Jiménez   **DE OSA**

CABO MATAPALO

PUNTA BURICA

Golfito
La Cuesta

Guabito
Bocas del Toro   Almirante
PUNTA CHIRIQUI
Chiriquí Grande
Boquete
Volcán Barú
11 410
Concepción
David
Horconcitos
Remedios
Las Palmas   Santiago
Soná
Río de Jesús
PENÍNSULA   Chitré o   Los Santos
DE AZUERO   Las Tablas

ESCUDO DE VERAGUAS

Golfo de los Mosquitos

PUNTA MANZANILLO   Nombre de Dios   El Porvenir
Portobelo   PUNTA SAN BLAS
Mandinga   Golfo de San Blas
Colón   C. Brewster
Gatun   Silver City   3018
Chepo
Lago Gatún   North Gamboa
Balboa Heights   Balboa o
Panamá
Chorrera   Bahia de Panamá

ISTMO DE PANAMÁ

CORD. DE SAN BLAS
A   M
A
SERRANÍA DEL DARIÉN

CABO TIBURÓN

PUNTA CHAME
Bejuco
Penonomé   ARCHIPIÉLAGO
C. de Santa   Antón   DE LAS PERLAS
Catalina   Nata o
5249   Río Hato   San Miguel
SERRANÍA   Aguadulce   ISLA DEL REY
DE TABASARÁ   C. Negro 4429
ISLA DE SAN JOSÉ   La Palma

Bahia San Miguel   Garachiné o
El Real

Golfo de Parita

PUNTA GARACHINÉ

Golfo de Panamá

Bahia Charco de Azul

ISLA COIBA

ISLA CEBACO

PUNTA MARIATO

PUNTA MALA

ISLA JICARÓN

COLOMBIA

0	20	40	60	80	100	120 Miles
0	20 40 60 80	100 120 140	160 180	200 Kilometers		

116

Scale 1:1 000 000

HAVANA
(La Habana)

GULF OF MEXICO

Playa de Guanabo
Cojimar
Guanabacoa
Regla
Playa de Santa Fé
Campo Florido
Baracoa
San Francisco de Paula
Marianao
Arroya Arena
Cotorro
Calabazar
Bauta
Rancho Boyeros
Managua
Cuatro Caminos
Caimito del Guayabal
Santiago de las Vegas
San José de las Lajas
Bejucal
La Sabina
Buenaventura
Lago de Ariguanabo
Ceiba del Agua
San Antonio de los Baños
San Antonio de las Vegas
△ 950
©rmcn

JAMES PT.
Governor's Harbour
PALMETTO PT
ELEUTHERA
Corpum Bay
Rock Sound
EUTHERA PT.
LITTLE SAN SALVADOR
CAT
Arthur's Town
NORTHEAST PT.
Old Bight
HAWKS NEST PT.
COLUMBUS PT.
GREAT GUANA CAY
CONCEPTIÓN
ARBY
LEE STOCKING
Rolleville
CAPE STA. MARIA
RUM CAY
GREAT EXUMA
George Town
LITTLE EXUMA
HOG CAY
LONG
Clarence Town
JUMENTO CAYS
Man of War Channel
WATER CAY
FLAMINGO CAY
CAP VERDE
JAMAICA CAY
SEAL CAYS
FORTUNE
DIANA BANK
FISH CAY
NURSE CAY
OCHINOS BANKS
RACCOON CAY
GREAT RAGGED
CASTLE
MIRA POR VOS ISLETS
CAY VERDE
COLUMBUS BANK
CAY STA. DOMINGO

B A H A M A S

A T L A N T I C

O C E A N

SAN SALVADOR
(WATLING)
(Columbus, Oct. 12, 1492)
SOUTHWEST PT.

Tropic of Cancer

SAMANA OR ATWOOD CAY
BIRD ROCK
CROOKED
NORTHEAST PT.
PLANA OR FLAT CAYS
The Bight of Acklins
ACKLINS
MAYAGUANA
Abraham's Bay
SALINA PT.
Mira por Vos Passage
Crooked Island Passage
Mayaguana Passage

BROWN BANK
HOGSTY REEF
LITTLE INAGUA
NORTHEAST PT.
PALMETTO PT.
Ocean Bight
GREAT INAGUA
The Lake
Matthew Town
South Bay
Man of War Bay

Caicos Passage
PROVIDENCIALES
NORTH CAICOS
GRAND CAICOS
CAPE COMETE
EAST CAICOS
WEST CAICOS
CAICOS IS.
(Br.)
CAICOS BANK
GRAND TURK
Grand Turk
TURKS IS. (Br.)
SOUTH CAICOS
WEST SAND SPIT
AMBERGRIS CAYS
SALT CAY
SEAL CAYS
Turks I. Passage
Mouchoir Passage
MOUCHOIR BANK

SILVER BANK

Gibara
CABO LUCRECIA
Banes
Bahía de Nipe
Antilla
Holguín
OLGUÍN
Mayari
Sagua de Tánamo
CUCHILLA OF TOA
Baracoa
SANTIAGO DE CUBA
GUANTÁNAMO
SA. DE PURIAL
PUNTA MAÍSI
Alto Songo
Caney
Palma Soriano
San Luis
Guantánamo
Yateras
Santiago de Cuba
Naval Station (U.S.A.)
Bahía de Guantánamo

Windward Passage

Silver Bank Passage
NAVIDAD BANK

ILE DE LA TORTUE
Canal de la Tortue
Port de Paix
Le Borgne
Cap-Haïtien
CABO ISABELA
Monte Cristi
Puerto Plata
CAP ST. NICOLAS
Le Môle
Limbé
Fort Liberté
Dajabón
CORDILLERA SEPTENTRIONAL
Pico Diego de Ocampo
CABO FRANCES VIEJO
PTE. PLATEFORME
Grande Rivière du Nord
Ouanaminthe
Mao
Santiago Rodriguez
VEGA
Gasper Hernández
Guayubin
Santiago de los Caballeros
Moca
San Francisco de Macoris
Nagua
Gonaïves
Vallière
Salcedo
CABO SAMANÁ
CAP ST. NICOLAS
St-Michel de l'Atalaye
Hinche
Mt. Mira
Pico Duarte
Jarabacoa
Bahía Escocesa
Sánchez
Bahía de Samaná
GOLFE DES GONAÏVES
St. Marc
Pic Bonhomme
CORDILLERA CENTRAL
Riva
Sabana de la Mar
CABO SAN RAFAEL
POINT OUEST
ILE DE LA GONÂVE
Mirebalais
Cotui
Cevicos
Hato Mayor
CORDILLERA ORIENTAL
Miches
Canal du Sud
Lascahobas
Bonao
Bayaguana
Los Llanos
Seibo
HAITI
Port-au-Prince
DOMINICAN REPUBLIC
Higüey
Jérémie
ILE GRANDE CAYEMITE
Anse à Veau
Léogane
Pétionville
SIERRA DE NEIBA
San Juan
Monte Plata
La Romana
CAP DAME MARIE
Anse d'Hainault
MASSIF DE LA HOTTE
Miragoâne
Petit Goave
MASSIF DE LA SELLE
Neiba
Azua
San Cristóbal
S. Pedro de Macoris
CATALINA
CAP DES IROIS
Pico de Macaya
Aquin
Duvergé
Barahona
Bani
Santo Domingo
SAONA
Tiburon
Coteaux
Les Cayes
Jacmel
Belle-Anse
SIERRA DE BAHORUCO
Enriquillo
PTA. PALENQUE
Roche à Bateau
ILE A VACHE
POINTE À GRAVOIS
CABO FALSO
Oviedo
H I S P A N I O L A
FORMIGAS BANK
NAVASSA (U.S.A.)
MORANT PT.
Port Antonio
BEATA
CABO BEATA
ALTO VELO

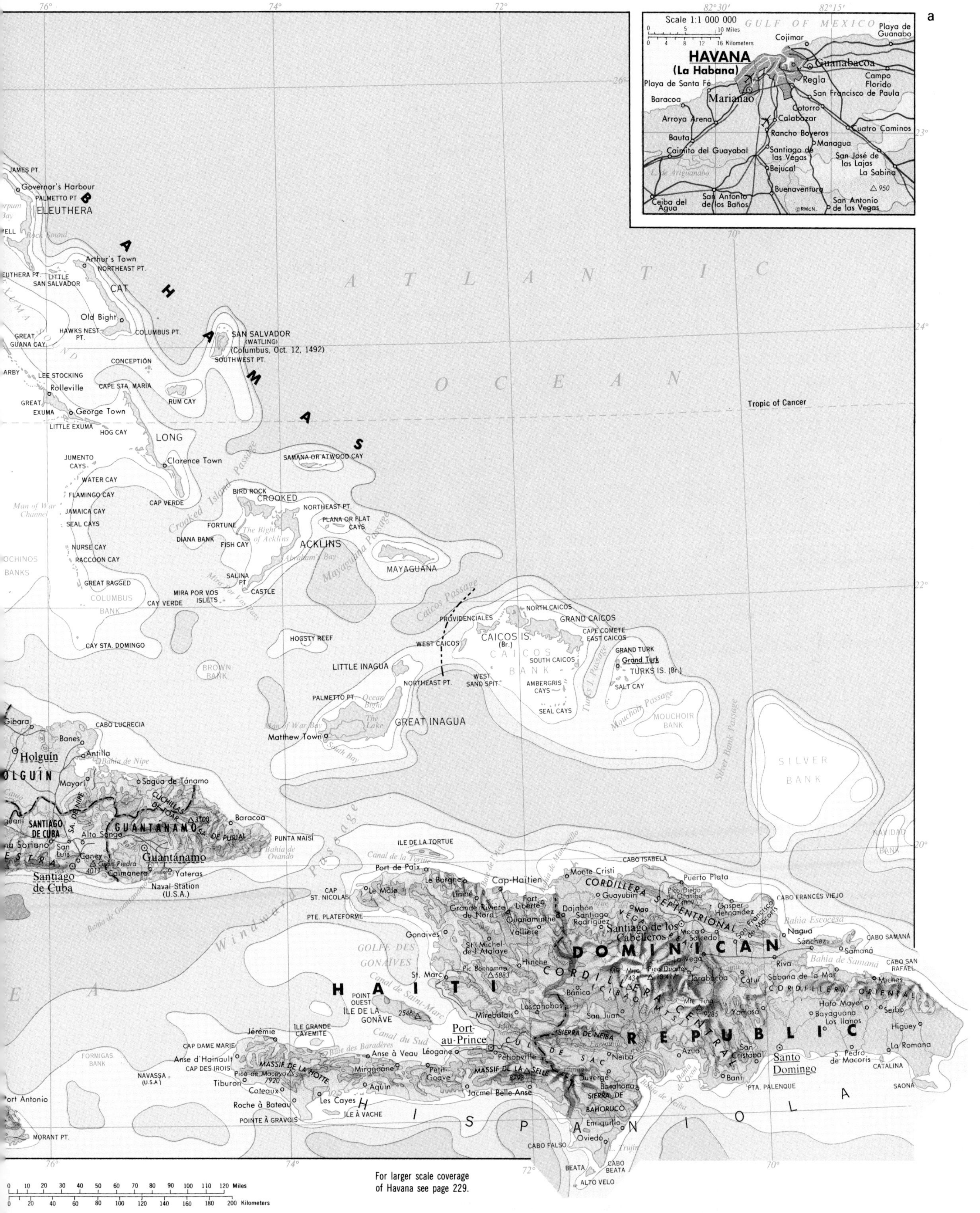

For larger scale coverage of Havana see page 229.

0 10 20 30 40 50 60 70 80 90 100 110 120 Miles
0 20 40 60 80 100 120 140 160 180 200 Kilometers

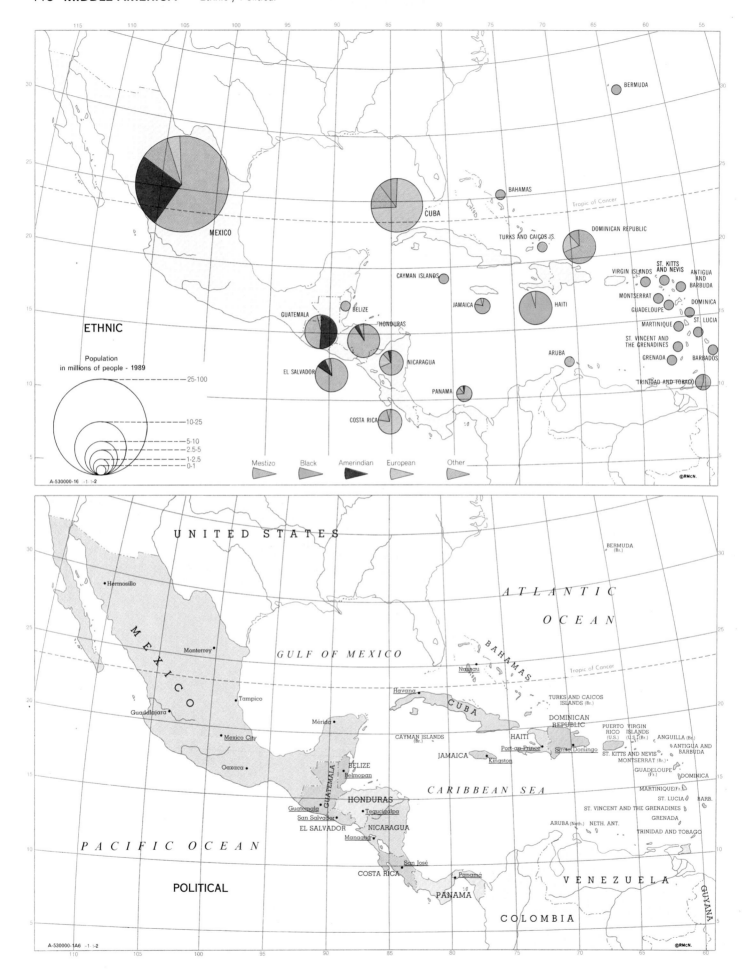

ETHNIC

Population
in millions of people - 1989

25-100

10-25

5-10
2.5-5
1-2.5
0-1

Mestizo   Black   Amerindian   European   Other

BERMUDA

MEXICO

BAHAMAS

CUBA

TURKS AND CAICOS IS.

DOMINICAN REPUBLIC

CAYMAN ISLANDS

VIRGIN ISLANDS

ST. KITTS
AND NEVIS

ANTIGUA
AND
BARBUDA

GUATEMALA

BELIZE

HONDURAS

JAMAICA

HAITI

MONTSERRAT

GUADELOUPE

DOMINICA

MARTINIQUE

ST. LUCIA

EL SALVADOR

NICARAGUA

ARUBA

ST. VINCENT AND
THE GRENADINES

GRENADA

BARBADOS

PANAMA

TRINIDAD AND TOBAGO

COSTA RICA

A-530000-16 -1- -1--2

©RMcN.

UNITED STATES

BERMUDA
(Br.)

ATLANTIC

OCEAN

Hermosillo

M E X I C O

Monterrey

GULF OF MEXICO

BAHAMAS

Tropic of Cancer

Nassau

Tampico

TURKS AND CAICOS
ISLANDS (Br.)

Guadalajara

Havana

CUBA

DOMINICAN
REPUBLIC

Mérida

CAYMAN ISLANDS
(Br.)

PUERTO VIRGIN
RICO   ISLANDS
(U.S.) (U.S.)(Br.)

ANGUILLA (Br.)

Mexico City

HAITI

ANTIGUA AND
BARBUDA

Port-au-Prince

Santo Domingo

ST. KITTS AND NEVIS

Oaxaca

JAMAICA

Kingston

MONTSERRAT (Br.)

GUADELOUPE
(Fr.)

DOMINICA

BELIZE

Belmopan

CARIBBEAN SEA

MARTINIQUE(Fr.)

GUATEMALA

HONDURAS

ST. LUCIA

BARB.

Guatemala

Tegucigalpa

ST. VINCENT AND THE GRENADINES

San Salvador

EL SALVADOR

NICARAGUA

ARUBA (Neth.) NETH. ANT.

GRENADA

Managua

TRINIDAD AND TOBAGO

PACIFIC OCEAN

San José

V E N E Z U E L A

COSTA RICA

Panamá

POLITICAL

PANAMA

GUYANA

COLOMBIA

A-530000-1A6 -1- -1--2

©RMcN.

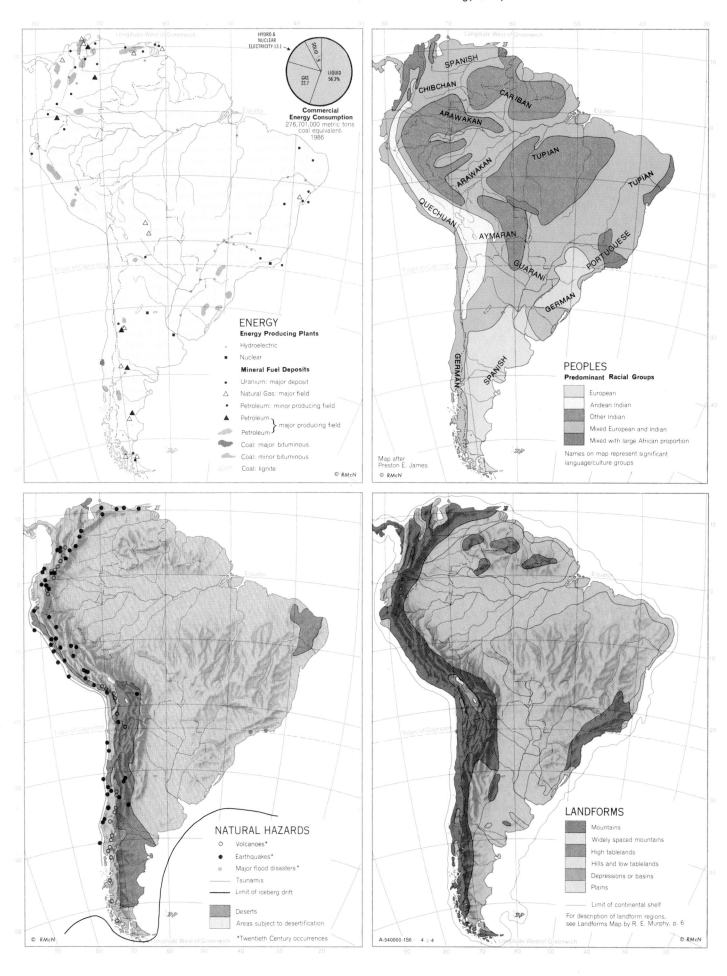

HYDRO. &
NUCLEAR
ELECTRICITY-13.1

SOLID
9

GAS
22.7

LIQUID
56.3%

**Commercial
Energy Consumption**
276,701,000 metric tons
coal equivalent-
1986

ENERGY
Energy Producing Plants

▪ Hydroelectric

■ Nuclear

Mineral Fuel Deposits

△ Uranium: major deposit

△ Natural Gas: major field

● Petroleum: minor producing field

▲ Petroleum } major producing field

Petroleum }

Coal: major bituminous

Coal: minor bituminous

Coal: lignite

© RMcN

PEOPLES
Predominant Racial Groups

European

Andean Indian

Other Indian

Mixed European and Indian

Mixed with large African proportion

Names on map represent significant
language/culture groups

Map after
Preston E. James

© RMcN

SPANISH
CHIBCHAN
CARIBAN
ARAWAKAN
ARAWAKAN
TUPIAN
TUPIAN
QUECHUAN
AYMARAN
GUARANI
PORTUGUESE
GERMAN
GERMAN
SPANISH

NATURAL HAZARDS

○ Volcanoes*

● Earthquakes*

● Major flood disasters *

Tsunamis

Limit of iceberg drift

Deserts

Areas subject to desertification

*Twentieth Century occurrences

© RMcN

LANDFORMS

Mountains

Widely spaced mountains

High tablelands

Hills and low tablelands

Depressions or basins

Plains

Limit of continental shelf

For description of landform regions,
see Landforms Map by R. E. Murphy, p. 6

A-540000-1S6   4 ⑤ 4

© RMcN

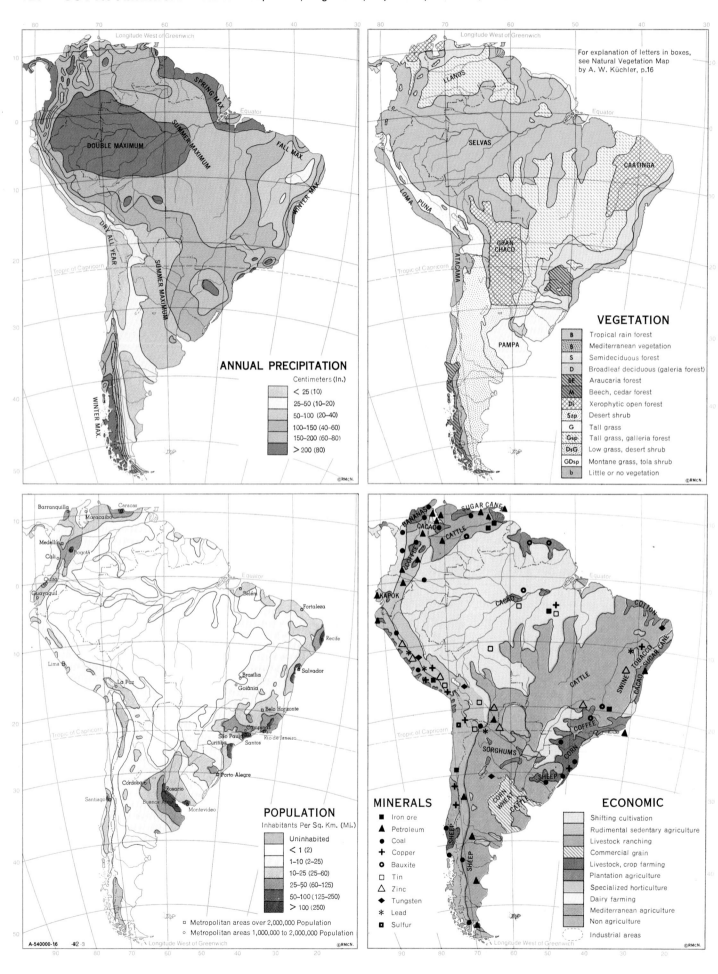

ANNUAL PRECIPITATION

Centimeters (In.)

	< 25 (10)
	25–50 (10–20)
	50–100 (20–40)
	100–150 (40–60)
	150–200 (60–80)
	> 200 (80)

VEGETATION

For explanation of letters in boxes, see Natural Vegetation Map by A. W. Küchler, p.16

B	Tropical rain forest
B	Mediterranean vegetation
S	Semideciduous forest
D	Broadleaf deciduous (galeria forest)
BE	Araucaria forest
M	Beech, cedar forest
Di	Xerophytic open forest
Szp	Desert shrub
G	Tall grass
Gsp	Tall grass, galleria forest
DsG	Low grass, desert shrub
GDsp	Montane grass, tola shrub
b	Little or no vegetation

POPULATION

Inhabitants Per Sq. Km. (Mi.)

	Uninhabited
	< 1 (2)
	1–10 (2–25)
	10–25 (25–60)
	25–50 (60–125)
	50–100 (125–250)
	> 100 (250)

▫ Metropolitan areas over 2,000,000 Population
○ Metropolitan areas 1,000,000 to 2,000,000 Population

MINERALS

■	Iron ore
▲	Petroleum
●	Coal
+	Copper
◉	Bauxite
□	Tin
△	Zinc
◆	Tungsten
✳	Lead
▣	Sulfur

ECONOMIC

	Shifting cultivation
	Rudimental sedentary agriculture
	Livestock ranching
	Commercial grain
	Livestock, crop farming
	Plantation agriculture
	Specialized horticulture
	Dairy farming
	Mediterranean agriculture
	Non agriculture
	Industrial areas

A-540000-16   -82-3

Urban

Cropland

Cropland & Woodland

Cropland & Grazing Land

Grassland, Grazing Land

Forest, Woodland

Swamp, Marshland

Shrub, Sparse Grass;
Wasteland

Barren Land

Scale 1:36,000,000; one inch to 570 miles. Lambert Azimuthal Equal-Area Projection

0 100 200   400   600   800 Miles

0 150 300   600   900   1200 Kilometers

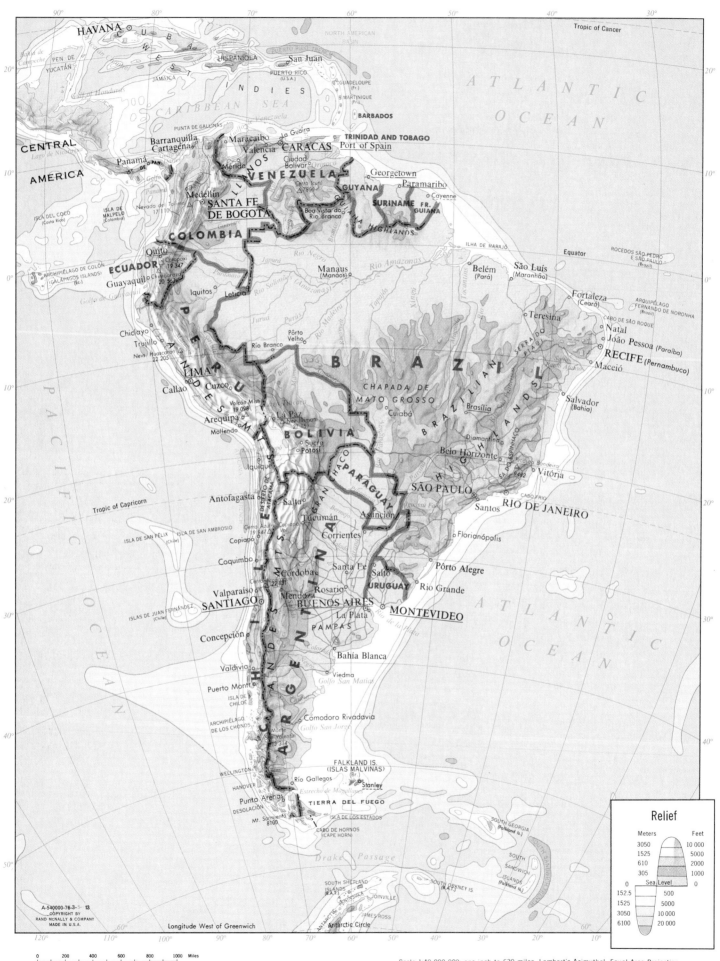

Scale 1:40 000 000; one inch to 630 miles. Lambert's Azimuthal, Equal Area Projection
Elevations and depressions are given in feet

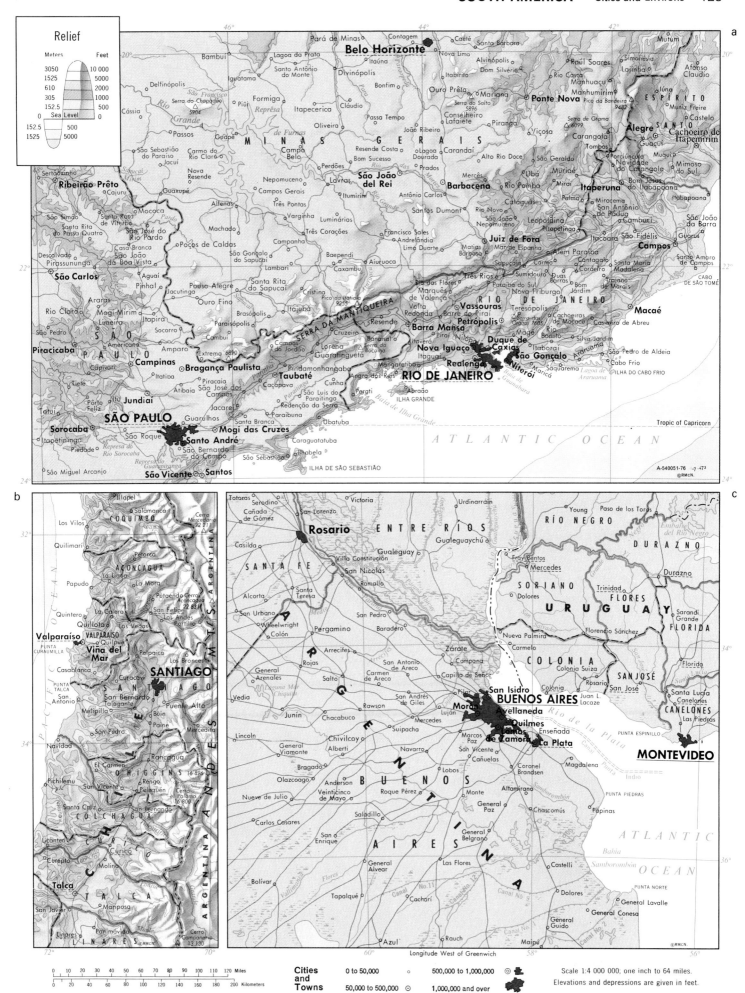

a

Relief

Meters	Feet
3050	10 000
1525	5000
610	2000
305	1000
152.5	500
0	Sea Level	0
152.5	500
1525	5000

Pará de Minas · Contagem · Caeté
Bambuí · Lagoa da Prata · **Belo Horizonte** · Santa Bárbara · Mutum
Iguatama · Santo Antônio do Monte · Nova Lima · Alvinópolis · Simonésia · Afonso Cláudio
Delfinópolis · Divinópolis · Itabirito · Dom Silvério · Rio Casca · Manhuaçu · Manhumirim · Lajinha · **ESPÍRITO**
Cássia · Formiga · Itapecerica · Cláudio · Bonfim · Ouro Prêto · Mariana · **Ponte Nova** · Pica da Bandeira 9482 · Iúna · Muniz Freire
Serra do Chapadão 5904 · Piuí · Passa Tempo · Conselheiro Lafaiete · Piranga · Serra de Grama · **Alegre** · **Santo** · Castelo
Passos · Guapé · Oliveira · Bom Sucesso · São Geraldo · Carangola · Serra de Grama 6099 · Viçosa · Porciúncula · **Cachoeiro de Itapemirim**
São Sebastião do Paraíso · Carmo do Rio Claro · Campo Belo · Resende Costa · Carandaí · Alto Rio Doce · Dourada · Muqui
Sertãozinho · Jacuí · Nova Resende · Perdões · Mercês · Uba · Mirai · **Itaperuna** · Bom Jesus do Itabapoana · Mimoso do Sul
Ribeirão Prêto · Cajuru · Guaxupé · Lavras · Nepomuceno · Antônio Carlos · Rio Pomba · Leopoldina · Miracema · Itapoana
São Simão · Mococa · Altenas · Campos Gerais · Itumirim · Santos Dumont · **Barbacena** · Nova Nepomuceno · Palma · San Antônio de Pádua · Itacoara · São Fidélis
Santa Rosa de Viterbo · Três Pontas · Varginha · Luminárias · Francisco Sales · Andrelândia · Matias Barbosa · Além Paraíba · Cantagalo · Santa Maria Madalena · **Campos**
Casa Branca · São José do Rio Pardo · Machado · Três Corações · Baependi · Lima Duarte · Mar de Espanha · Cordeiro · Trajano de Morais · Santo Amaro de Campos
Descalvado · Poços de Caldas · Campanha · Caxambu · **Juiz de Fora** · **RIO DE JANEIRO** · CABO DE SÃO TOMÉ
Pirassununga · São Gonçalo do Sapucaí · Santa Rita do Sapucaí · Cristina · Pica da Itatiaia 9255 · Três Rios · Sumidouro · Nova Friburgo · Duas Barras
São Carlos · Lambari · Itajubá · Marquês de Valença · Paraíba do Sul · Bom Jardim
Rio Claro · Pinhal · Pouso Alegre · Ouro Fino · Brasópolis · Resende · **Vassouras** · Teresópolis · Casimiro de Abreu
Araras · Mogi-Mirim · Itapira · Jacutinga · Cambuí · Lorena · Barra do Piraí · **Petrópolis** · Cachoeiras de Macacu · São Pedro de Aldeia
Limeira · Amparo · Extrema 6890 · Campos do Jordão · Volta Redonda · **Barra Mansa** · Magé · Silva Jardim
São Pedro · Socorro · Bragança Paulista · Cruzeiro · Guaratinguetá · Bananal · Pirai · Nilópolis · **Duque de Caxias** · Itaboraí · Araruama · Cabo Frio
Piracicaba · Capivari · Itatiba · Paraisópolis · **Campinas** · Piracaia · **Nova Iguaçu** · **São Gonçalo** · Saquarema · ILHA DO CABO FRIO
Tietê · Itapetininga · São José dos Campos · Caçapava · Pindamonhangaba · **Taubaté** · Itaverá · Itaguaí · **Realengo** · **Niterói** · Maricá · Lagoa de Araruama
Pôrto Feliz · Atibaia · Jacareí · São Luis do Paraitinga · Paraty · Mangaratiba · Baía de Guanabara
Jundiaí · Guarulhos · Santa Branca · Redenção da Serra · Abraão · ILHA GRANDE · Tropic of Capricorn
Sorocaba · São Roque · **Mogi das Cruzes** · Ubatuba · Parati · **ATLANTIC OCEAN**
SÃO PAULO · Caraguatatuba · A-540051-76 -7 -473 ©RMcN
Itapetininga · Piedade · São Bernardo do Campo · **Santo André** · São Sebastião
Represa do Rio Sorocaba · Represa do Guarapiranga · São Vicente · Ilhabela
São Miguel Arcanjo · **São Vicente** · **Santos** · ILHA DE SÃO SEBASTIÃO

b

COQUIMBO · Illapel · Salamanca · Cerro Mercedario 22 211
Los Vilos · Quilimarí · **ACONCAGUA** · **ARGENTINA**
Papudo · Petorca · La Ligua · La Mora · Putaendo Cerro Aconcagua 22 831
Quintero · La Calera · San Felipe · Los Andes · Portillo
Valparaíso · **VALPARAÍSO** · Quillota · Las Vegas · Los Broncos
PUNTA CURAUMILLA · **Viña del Mar** · Quilpué · Polpaico
Casablanca · Curacaví · **SANTIAGO**
PUNTA TALCA · San Bernardo · Talagante · Puente Alto
San Antonio · Melipilla · Boin · Paine
San Pedro · **MTS.**
Navidad · Rancagua
Pichilemu · El Carmen · O'HIGGINS 16 896 · Cerro Palomo 16 800
San Vicente · Rengo · Peleguín
Santa Cruz · **COLCHAGUA** · San Fernando
Licantén · **CURICÓ** · Curicó · Teno
Corepto · Molina
Talca · Cerro Companario 13 330
San Javier · Panimávida
Linares · **LINARES**

c

Totoras · Serodino · Victoria · Urdinarrain · Young · Paso de los Toros
Cañada de Gómez · San Lorenzo · **RÍO NEGRO** · Embalse del Río Negro
Rosario · **ENTRE RÍOS** · **DURAZNO**
Casilda · Villa Constitución · Gualeguay · Gualeguaychú · Fray Bentos · Mercedes · Durazno · Trinidad
SANTA FE · San Nicolás · **SORIANO** · **FLORES**
Alcorta · Ramallo · Dolores · **URUGUAY** · Sarandí Grande
San Urbano · Santa Teresa · **FLORIDA**
Wheelwright · San Pedro · Nueva Palmira · Florencio Sánchez
Pergamino · Baradero · Zárate · Carmelo · **COLONIA** · Florida
Colón · Arrecifes · Campana · Colonia Suiza · **SAN JOSÉ**
General Arenales · Rojas · San Antonio de Areco · Capilla del Señor · Colonia · Rosario · San José
Vedia · Salto · Carmen de Areco · Pilar · **San Isidro** · Juan L. Lacaze · Santa Lucía · **CANELONES**
Junín · Rawson · San Andrés de Giles · **BUENOS AIRES** · **Moron** · **CANELONES** · Las Piedras
Chacabuco · Luján · Mercedes · **Avellaneda** · Río de la Plata
Lincoln · Suipacha · Marcos Paz · **Quilmes** · Ensenada · **Lomas de Zamora** · **La Plata** · PUNTA ESPINILLO
General Viamonte · Chivilcoy · Cañuelas · PUNTA PIEDRAS
Bragado · Alberti · Navarro · Lobos · Monte · **MONTEVIDEO**
Olazcoaga · Veinticinco de Mayo · Roque Pérez · Coronel Brandsen · Magdalena · Altamirano · Papinas
Nueve de Julio · Saladillo · General Paz · Chascomús
Anderson · **BUENOS** · PUNTA PIEDRAS
Carlos Casares · Las Flores · Castelli · **ATLANTIC**
Bolívar · General Alvear · **AIRES** · Coronel Brandsen · General Guido · Bahía Samborombón · **OCEAN**
Tapalqué · Cachari · General Lavalle
Azul · Rauch · Maipú · General Conesa
Longitude West of Greenwich

Cities and Towns

0 to 50,000 · 500,000 to 1,000,000
50,000 to 500,000 · 1,000,000 and over

Scale 1:4 000 000; one inch to 64 miles.
Elevations and depressions are given in feet.

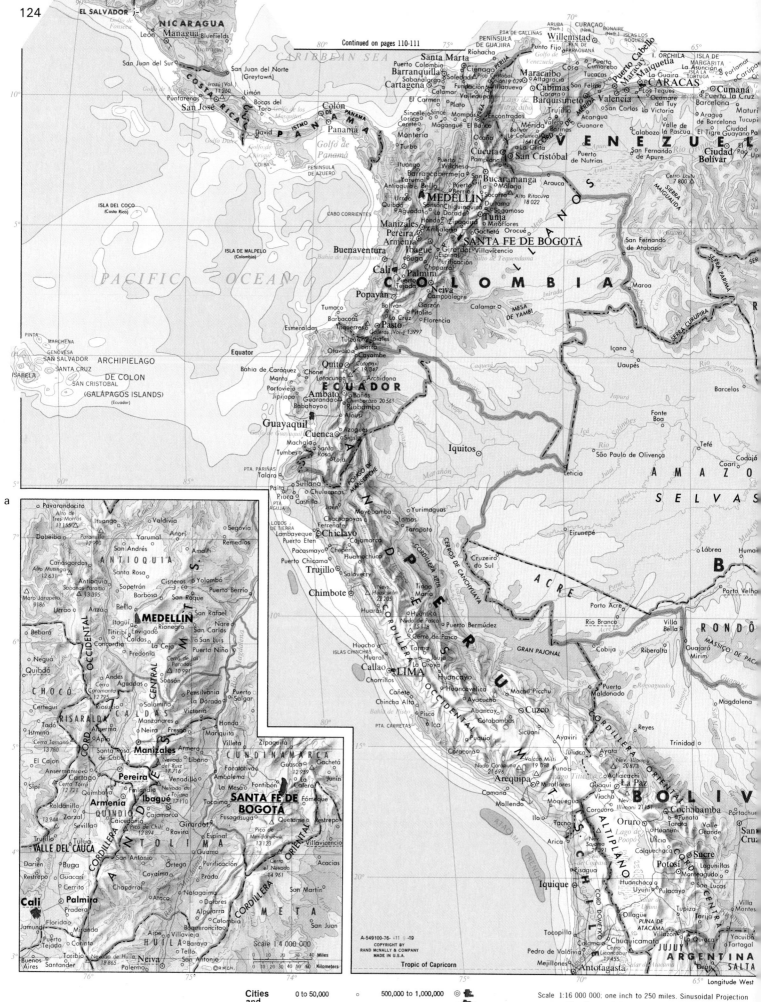

124

Continued on pages 110-111

EL SALVADOR

NICARAGUA

León Managua Bluefields

San Juan del Sur

San Juan del Norte (Greytown)

Puntarenas Irazú 11,260 Limón

COSTA RICA

San José

Bocas del Toro

David P A N A M A Panamá

Colón

ISTMO DE PANAMA

Golfo de Panamá

PENINSULA DE AZUERO

CABO CORRIENTES

CARIBBEAN SEA

PENÍNSULA DE GUAJIRA PTA. DE GALLINAS ARUBA (Neth.) CURAÇAO (Neth.) BONAIRE (Neth.) ISLAS LOS ROQUES LA ORCHILA

Willemstad

Santa Marta Riohacha

Puerto Colombia Punto Fijo Coro Puerto Cabello La Guaira Maiquetía

Barranquilla Sabanalarga Ciénaga PEN. DE PARAGUANÁ Tucacas Maracay

Cartagena Soledad Pico Cristóbal Fundación Villanueva Cabimas Altagracia San Felipe Valencia

El Carmen Plato Calamar Maracaibo Barquisimeto

Sincelejo Sincé Mompós El Banco

Lorica Cereté Magangué Encontrados Trujillo Acarigua

Montería Turbo Ituango Bolívar MÉRIDA Barinas Guanare

Puerto Berrio Ocaña La Grita Calabozo

Antioquia Bello Cúcuta Pamplona San Cristóbal Puerto de Nutrias

Quibdó Aguadas Bucaramanga Málaga Arauca

MEDELLIN Sonsón Chiquinquirá Alto Ritacuva 18,022

Manizales Ambalema Honda La Dorada Sogamoso

Pereira Tunja Miraflores Orocué

Armenia Zipaquirá Gachetá

Ibagué Buga SANTA FE DE BOGOTÁ Villavicencio

Cali Girardot Espinal San Fernando de Atabapo

Palmira Purificación Chaparral Salto de Tequendama

COLOMBIA

Popayán Neiva Campoalegre

Tumaco Bolívar Pitalito Calamar

Barbacoas La Cruz Florencia MESA DE YAMBÍ

Esmeraldas Túquerres Pasto Inirida

Galeras (Vol.) 13,997

Tulcán Ipiales

Otavalo Ibarra Cayambe

Quito Chone Archidona

Latacunga Cotopaxi 19,347

ECUADOR

Manta Ambato Baños

Portoviejo Guaranda Chimborazo 20,561

Jipijapa Babahoyo Riobamba

Guayaquil Alausí

Cuenca Azogues Sigsig

Machala Loja

Santa Rosa

Tumbes

Talara PTA. PARIÑAS

Sullana Chulucanas

Paita Piura Castilla

PTA. AGUJA Jaén Moyobamba Yurimaguas

LOBOS DE TIERRA Chochapoyas Lamas Tarapoto

Lambayeque Ferreñafe Cajamarca

Puerto Eten Chiclayo

Pacasmayo Chepén Huamachuco

Puerto Chicama Tingo María

Trujillo Salaverry

Chimbote Nev. Huascarán 22,205

Casma Huaraz Huánuco Puerto Bermúdez

Huacho Cerro de Pasco

ISLAS CHINCHAS Huaral La Oroya Tarma GRAN PAJONAL

Callao Huancayo

LIMA Jauja

Chorrillos Huancavelica Ayacucho Macha Picchu

Cañete Abancay Cuzco

Chincha Alta Pisco Ica Cotabambas

PTA. CARRETAS Sicuani

Puquio Ayaviri

BAHÍA DE PISCO Coracora

PERU

IQUITOS

Leticia

AMAZO

SELVAS

Içana

Uaupés

SIERRA PARIMA

SIERRA CURUPIRA

São Paulo de Olivença

Tefé Codajás Coari

Fonte Boa

Eirunepé

Cruzeiro do Sul

Lábrea Humai

ACRE

B

RONDÔ

Pôrto Velho

Porto Acre

Rio Branco

Cobija Villa Bella

Riberalta

Guajará Mirim

MASSIÇO DE PACAÁS

Reyes Trinidad

Puerto Maldonado

Rogoaguado Puerto Heath

Magdalena

BOLIV

Juliaca Achacachi La Paz

Puno Viacha

Arequipa Nev. Illampú 21,157

Camaná Lago Titicaca Guaqui Cochabamba

Mollendo Corocoro Oruro Punata Valle Grande

Moquegua Nev. Sajama 21,391 Challapata Uncía

Ilo Viacha Colquechaca Sucre Lagunillas

Tacna ALTIPLANO Potosí Monteagudo

Arica Lago de Poopó Uyuni Pulacayo San Lucas

Pisagua Huanchaca 20,873 Tupiza Tarija

Iquique Chuquicamata

PUNA DE ATACAMA Villazón

Tocopilla Ollagüe Quiaca

Cobija Calama Yacuiba Tartagal

Pedro de Valdivia JUJUY

Mejillones ARGENTINA SALTA

Antofagasta

A-549100-76- -11 9 -19
COPYRIGHT BY
RAND McNALLY & COMPANY
MADE IN U.S.A.

Tropic of Capricorn

PACIFIC OCEAN

ISLA DEL COCO (Costa Rica)

ISLA DE MALPELO (Colombia)

Buenaventura Bahía de Buenaventura

PINTA MARCHENA GENOVESA

SAN SALVADOR SANTA CRUZ

ISABELA SAN CRISTOBAL

ARCHIPIELAGO DE COLON (GALÁPAGOS ISLANDS) (Ecuador)

Equator

Bahía de Caráquez

Golfo de Guayaquil

ATACAMA TRENCH

Inset a:

a

Pavarandocito Alto de Tres Morros 11,155 Ituango Valdivia

Dabeiba Paramillo 12,990 Yarumal Anorí Segovia Remedios

Cañasgordas San Andrés ANTIOQUIA Amalfi

Alto Musinga 12,631 Santa Rosa Yolombó

Antioquia Sobanas-Páramo 9,395 Cisneros

Mar Jarapeta 9,186 Sopetrán Barbosa Puerto Berrío

Urrao Anzá Bello San Roque

Bebará OCCIDENTAL Itagüí Rionegro Nare San Luis

Neguá Caldas San Rafael

Quibdó Concordia La Ceja Puerto Niño

CHOCÓ Cerro de las Paradas 10,991 Puerto Salgar

Certegui Andes Aguadas Sonsón

Cerro Caramanta 12,725 Salamina

Tadó Riosucio Pensilvania La Dorada

Istmina Anserma Apía Manzanares Victoria Honda

Cerro Tamaná 13,780 Neira Fresno

Sipí CALDAS Mariquita

RISARALDA Santa Rosa de Cabal Líbano Villeta Zipaquirá

El Cajón CORD. Manizales Armero Guasca Gachetá

Ansermanuevo Nevado del Ruiz 17,716 CUNDINAMARCA

Cartago Cerro Torrá 12,721 Facatativá Junín

Quimbaya Finlandia Nevado del Tolima 17,110 La Mesa Fontibón La Calera

Roldanillo Pereira Venadillo

QUINDÍO Ambalema Tocaima SANTA FE DE BOGOTÁ

13,944 Zarzal Armenia Ibagué Fusagasugá

Trujillo Sevilla Caicedonia Cajamarca Girardot Quetame Restrepo

VALLE DEL CAUCA Tuluá Pico de Chili 12,894 Rovira Espinal Pico de Mendanueva 13,123

Darién CORDILLERA Guacarí San Antonio Villavicencio

Restrepo Buga Ortega Coyaima Cerro El Nevado 14,961

Cerrito Chaparral Prada Acacías

Cali Palmira TOLIMA Natagaima META

Jamundí Pradera Ataco Dolores

Florida Miranda Alpujarra CORDILLERA ORIENTAL

Puerto Tejada Corinto Colombia San Martín

Buenos Aires Toribio Nevado de Huila 18,865 HUILA Villavieja Aipe San Juan

Santander Baraya

Neiva Palermo Tello San Antonio

Scale 1:4,000,000
0 10 20 30 40 Miles
0 10 20 30 40 50 60 Kilometers
©R.McN.

Cities and Towns
0 to 50,000
50,000 to 500,000
500,000 to 1,000,000
1,000,000 and over

Scale 1:16,000,000; one inch to 250 miles. Sinusoidal Projection
Elevations and depressions are given in feet

Longitude West

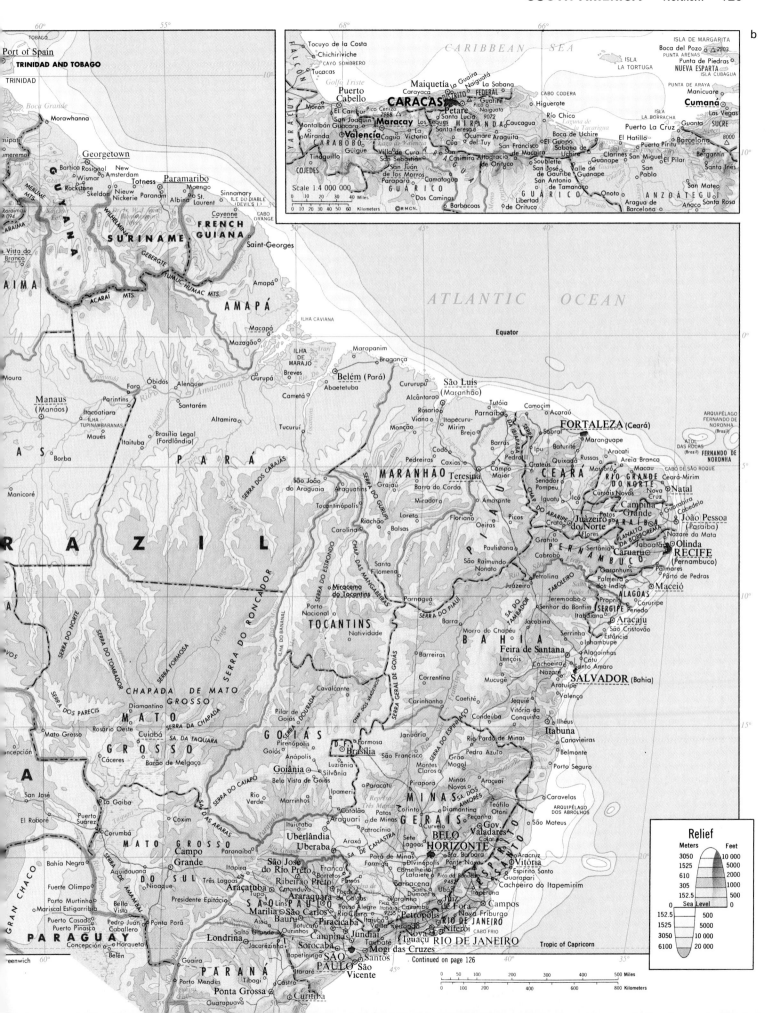

Continued on page 126

Continued on pages 124-125

BOLIVIA

PARAGUAY

GRAN CHACO

CHACO

BRASIL

MINAS GERAIS

BELO HORIZONTE

SÃO PAULO

PARANÁ

SANTA CATARINA

RIO GRANDE DO SUL

PORTO ALEGRE

RIO DE JANEIRO

URUGUAY

MONTEVIDEO

BUENOS AIRES

ARGENTINA

CHILE

SANTIAGO

Asunción

LA PAMPA

MENDOZA

RÍO NEGRO

CHUBUT

SANTA CRUZ

PATAGONIA

TIERRA DEL FUEGO

CABO DE HORNOS (CAPE HORN)

PACIFIC OCEAN

ATLANTIC OCEAN

FALKLAND IS. (ISLAS MALVINAS) (Br.) (Claimed by Argentina) Stanley

Relief

Meters		Feet
3050		10 000
1525		5000
610		2000
305		1000
152.5		500
Sea Level		0
152.5	500	Below Sea Level
1525	5000	
3050	10 000	
6100	20 000	

0 50 100 200 300 400 500 Miles
0 100 200 300 400 600 800 Kilometers

Scale 1:16 000 000 one inch to 250 miles. Sinusoidal Projection
Elevations and depressions are given in feet

a

BUENOS AIRES

RÍO DE LA PLATA

Scale 1:1 000 000
0 2 4 8 12 16 Miles
0 4 8 12 16 Kilometers

b

SERRA DAS ARARAS

RIO DE JANEIRO

RIO DE JANEIRO

Niterói

Baia de Guanabara

Petrópolis

Nova Iguaçu

Scale 1:1 000 000
0 5 10 Miles
0 4 8 12 16 Kilometers

A-549200-76 -11-7-12
COPYRIGHT BY
RAND McNALLY & COMPANY
MADE IN U.S.A.

Longitude West of Greenwich

For larger scale coverage of Buenos Aires, Rio de Janeiro, and São Paulo see pages 229 and 230.

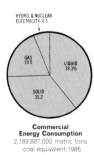

HYDRO & NUCLEAR
ELECTRICITY 6.5

GAS
19.0

LIQUID
39.3%

SOLID
35.2

**Commercial
Energy Consumption**
2,189,887,000 metric tons
coal equivalent-1986

ENERGY

Energy Producing Plants

▽ Geothermal

• Hydroelectric

■ Nuclear

Mineral Fuel Deposits

• Uranium: major deposit

△ Natural Gas: major field

• Petroleum: minor producing field

▲ Petroleum } major producing field
Petroleum }

Coal: major bituminous and anthracite

Coal: minor bituminous and anthracite

Coal: lignite

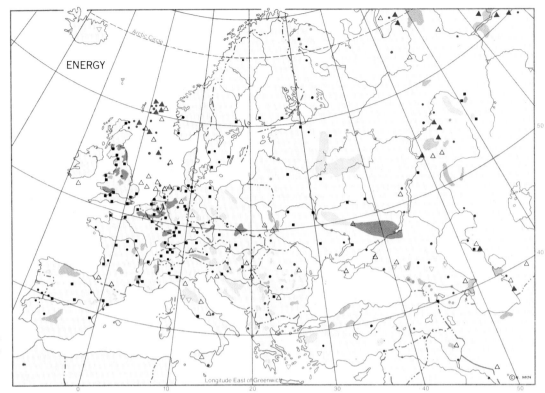

NATURAL HAZARDS

○ Volcanoes*

● Earthquakes*

● Major flood disasters*

Tsunamis

Limit of iceberg drift

Temporary pack ice

Areas subject to desertification

*Twentieth Century occurrences

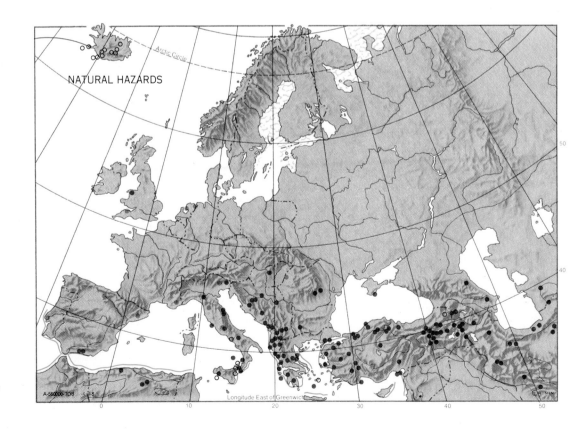

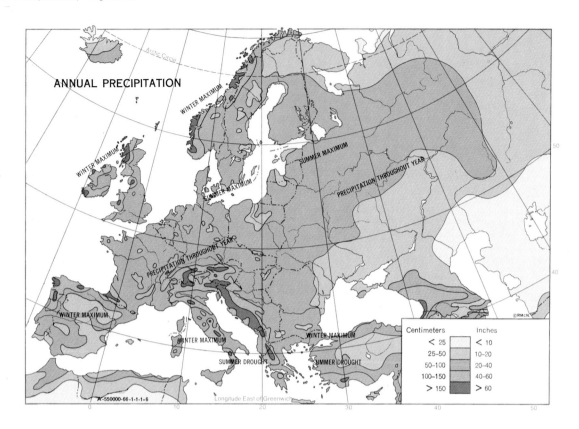

ANNUAL PRECIPITATION

Centimeters		Inches
< 25		< 10
25–50		10–20
50–100		20–40
100–150		40–60
> 150		> 60

A-550000-66-1-1-1-6

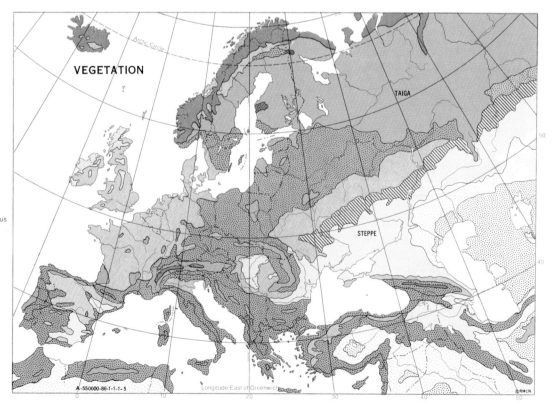

VEGETATION

E	Coniferous forest
B,Bs	Mediterranean vegetation
M	Mixed forest: coniferous-deciduous
S	Semi-deciduous forest
D	Deciduous forest
BG	Wooded steppe
G	Grass (steppe)
Gp	Short grass
Dsp	Desert shrub
L	Heath and moor
L	Alpine vegetation, tundra
b	Little or no vegetation

For explanation of letters in boxes,
see Natural Vegetation Map
by A. W. Kuchler, **p. 16**

A-550000-86-1-1-1-5

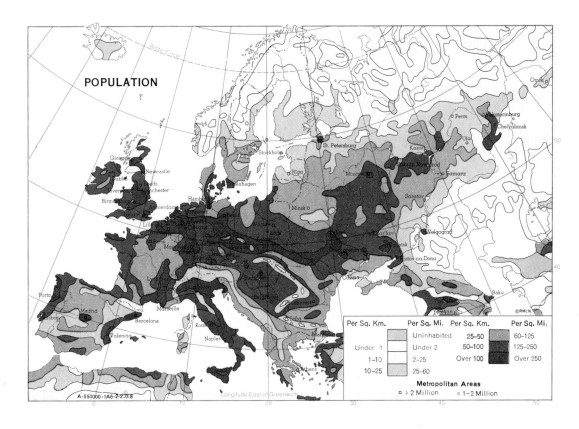

POPULATION

Per Sq. Km.	Per Sq. Mi.	Per Sq. Km.	Per Sq. Mi.
	Uninhabited	25–50	60–125
Under 1	Under 2	50–100	125–250
1–10	2–25	Over 100	Over 250
10–25	25–60		

Metropolitan Areas

□ > 2 Million   ○ 1–2 Million

A-550000-1A6-2-2-0-8

Longitude East of Greenwich

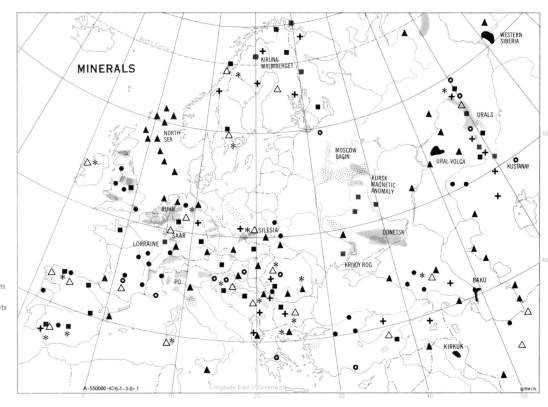

MINERALS

MINERALS

	Industrial areas
	Major coal deposits
	Major petroleum deposits
	Lignite deposits
▲	Minor petroleum deposits
●	Minor coal deposits
■	Major iron ore
■	Minor iron ore
✳	Lead
◉	Bauxite
△	Zinc
✛	Copper

WESTERN SIBERIA

KIRUNA-MALMBERGET

NORTH SEA

MOSCOW BASIN

URALS

URAL-VOLGA

KUSTANAY

KURSK MAGNETIC ANOMALY

RUHR

SAAR

SILESIA

LORRAINE

DONETSK

PO

KRIVOY ROG

BAKU

KIRKUK

A-550000-4D6-1-3-0-7

Longitude East of Greenwich

130

Legend:
- Urban
- Cropland
- Cropland & Woodland
- Cropland & Grazing Land
- Grassland, Grazing Land
- Forest, Woodland
- Swamp, Marshland
- Tundra
- Shrub, Sparse Grass, Wasteland (pattern)
- Barren Land
- Oasis

Longitude West of Greenwich   0°   Longitude East of Greenwich

Scale 1: 16,000,000; one inch to 250 miles. Conic Projection

0 50 100 200 300 400 500 Miles

0 100 200 400 600 800 Kilometers

40°
50°
60°
70°
60°
80°
50°
40°
30°

Nar'yan-Mar
Novosibirsk
Ob'
Ob'
Irtysh
Omsk
White Sea
Archangelsk
URALS
YEKATERINBURG
Karaganda
Perm'
Vologda
Kirov
Balkhash
Kama
Volga
Kazan'
Ufa
Magnitogorsk
Nizhniy
Novgorod
Orsk
Samara
Kzyl-Orda
MOSCOW
Volga
Syr-Dar'ya
Tula
PESKI
KYZYLKUM
Saratov
Ural
Aral
Sea
DEPRESSION
Amu Dar'ya
VOLGOGRAD
CASPIAN
Kiev
Khar'kov
Don
Volga
PESKI KARAKUMY
Astrakhan'
Dnepropetrovsk
Donetsk
MANYCH
DEPRESSION
Dnepr
Caspian
Ashkhabad
Odessa
Krasnodar
CAUCASUS
BAKU
Sea
Black   Sea
TBILISI
Yerevan
İSTANBUL
ELBURZ MTS.
Ankara
TEHRAN
DASHT-E-KAVIR
30°
Kerman
TOROS AĞLARI
Tigris
ZAGROS
Nicosia
Euphrates
Baghdad
MOUNTAINS
CYPRUS
Beirut
Abādān
30°
40°
50°

A-550000-36
2GE   GE   -10GE
COPYRIGHT BY
RAND MCNALLY & COMPANY
MADE IN U.S.A.

COPYRIGHT BY
RAND McNALLY & COMPANY
MADE IN U.S.A.
A-650000-762-1-1-2-2³

Scale 1:16 000 000; one inch to 250 miles. Conic Projection
Elevations and depressions are given in feet.

EUROPE LANGUAGES
BY
BOGDAN ZABORSKI

Scale 1:16,500,000; one inch to 260 miles Conic Projection

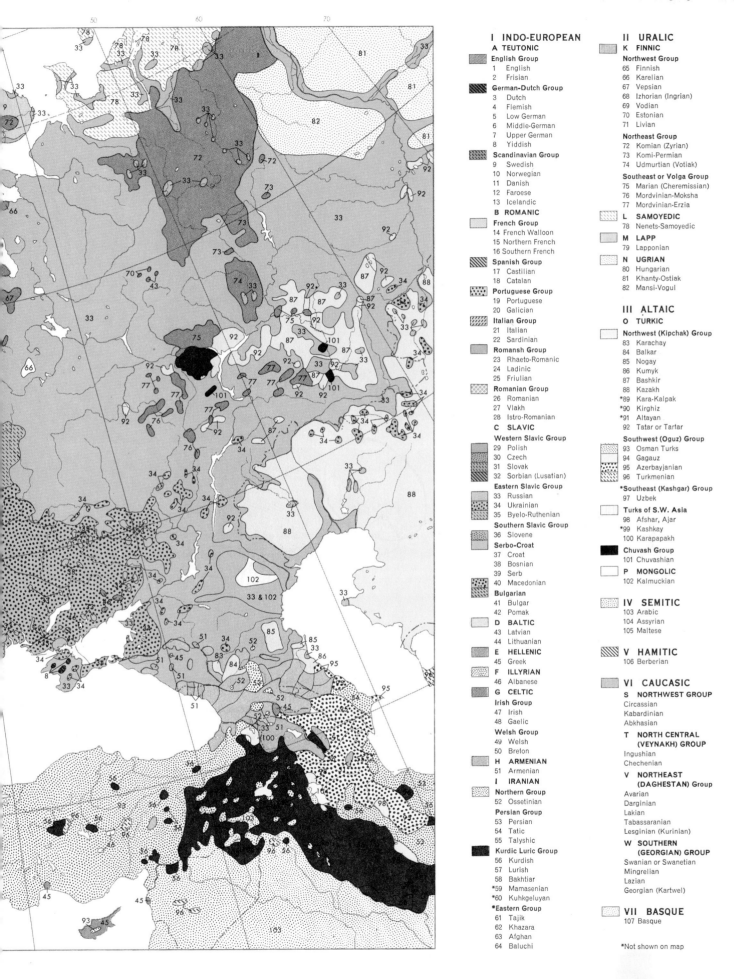

I INDO-EUROPEAN
A TEUTONIC
English Group
1   English
2   Frisian
German-Dutch Group
3   Dutch
4   Flemish
5   Low German
6   Middle-German
7   Upper German
8   Yiddish
Scandinavian Group
9   Swedish
10   Norwegian
11   Danish
12   Faroese
13   Icelandic
B ROMANIC
French Group
14   French Walloon
15   Northern French
16   Southern French
Spanish Group
17   Castilian
18   Catalan
Portuguese Group
19   Portuguese
20   Galician
Italian Group
21   Italian
22   Sardinian
Romansh Group
23   Rhaeto-Romanic
24   Ladinic
25   Friulian
Romanian Group
26   Romanian
27   Vlakh
28   Istro-Romanian
C SLAVIC
Western Slavic Group
29   Polish
30   Czech
31   Slovak
32   Sorbian (Lusatian)
Eastern Slavic Group
33   Russian
34   Ukrainian
35   Byelo-Ruthenian
Southern Slavic Group
36   Slovene
Serbo-Croat
37   Croat
38   Bosnian
39   Serb
40   Macedonian
Bulgarian
41   Bulgar
42   Pomak
D BALTIC
43   Latvian
44   Lithuanian
E HELLENIC
45   Greek
F ILLYRIAN
46   Albanese
G CELTIC
Irish Group
47   Irish
48   Gaelic
Welsh Group
49   Welsh
50   Breton
H ARMENIAN
51   Armenian
I IRANIAN
Northern Group
52   Ossetinian
Persian Group
53   Persian
54   Tatic
55   Talyshic
Kurdic Luric Group
56   Kurdish
57   Lurish
58   Bakhtiar
*59   Mamasenian
*60   Kuhkgeluyan
*Eastern Group
61   Tajik
62   Khazara
63   Afghan
64   Baluchi

II URALIC
K FINNIC
Northwest Group
65   Finnish
66   Karelian
67   Vepsian
68   Izhorian (Ingrian)
69   Vodian
70   Estonian
71   Livian
Northeast Group
72   Komian (Zyrian)
73   Komi-Permian
74   Udmurtian (Votiak)
Southeast or Volga Group
75   Marian (Cheremissian)
76   Mordvinian-Moksha
77   Mordvinian-Erzia
L SAMOYEDIC
78   Nenets-Samoyedic
M LAPP
79   Lapponian
N UGRIAN
80   Hungarian
81   Khanty-Ostiak
82   Mansi-Vogul

III ALTAIC
O TURKIC
Northwest (Kipchak) Group
83   Karachay
84   Balkar
85   Nogay
86   Kumyk
87   Bashkir
88   Kazakh
*89   Kara-Kalpak
*90   Kirghiz
*91   Altayan
92   Tatar or Tartar
Southwest (Oguz) Group
93   Osman Turks
94   Gagauz
95   Azerbayjanian
96   Turkmenian
*Southeast (Kashgar) Group
97   Uzbek
Turks of S.W. Asia
98   Afshar, Ajar
*99   Kashkay
100   Karapapakh
Chuvash Group
101   Chuvashian
P MONGOLIC
102   Kalmuckian

IV SEMITIC
103   Arabic
104   Assyrian
105   Maltese

V HAMITIC
106   Berberian

VI CAUCASIC
S NORTHWEST GROUP
Circassian
Kabardinian
Abkhasian
**T NORTH CENTRAL
(VEYNAKH) GROUP**
Ingushian
Chechenian
**V NORTHEAST
(DAGHESTAN) Group**
Avarian
Darginian
Lakian
Tabassaranian
Lesginian (Kurinian)
**W SOUTHERN
(GEORGIAN) GROUP**
Swanian or Swanetian
Mingrelian
Lazian
Georgian (Kartwel)

VII BASQUE
107   Basque

*Not shown on map

Brian Holden has "marry me !!"

Continued on pages 204-205

Relief

Meters	Feet
3050	10 000
1525	5000
610	2000
305	1000
152.5	500
Sea Level	Sea Level
152.5	500
1525	5000
3050	10 000

Below Sea Level

Scale 1: 16 000 000; one inch to 250 miles. Conic Projection
Elevations and depressions are given in feet

Longitude West of Greenwich   Longitude East of Greenwich

| 0 | 50 | 100 | 200 | 300 | 400 | 500 Miles |
| 0 | 100 | 200 | 400 | 600 | 800 Kilometers |

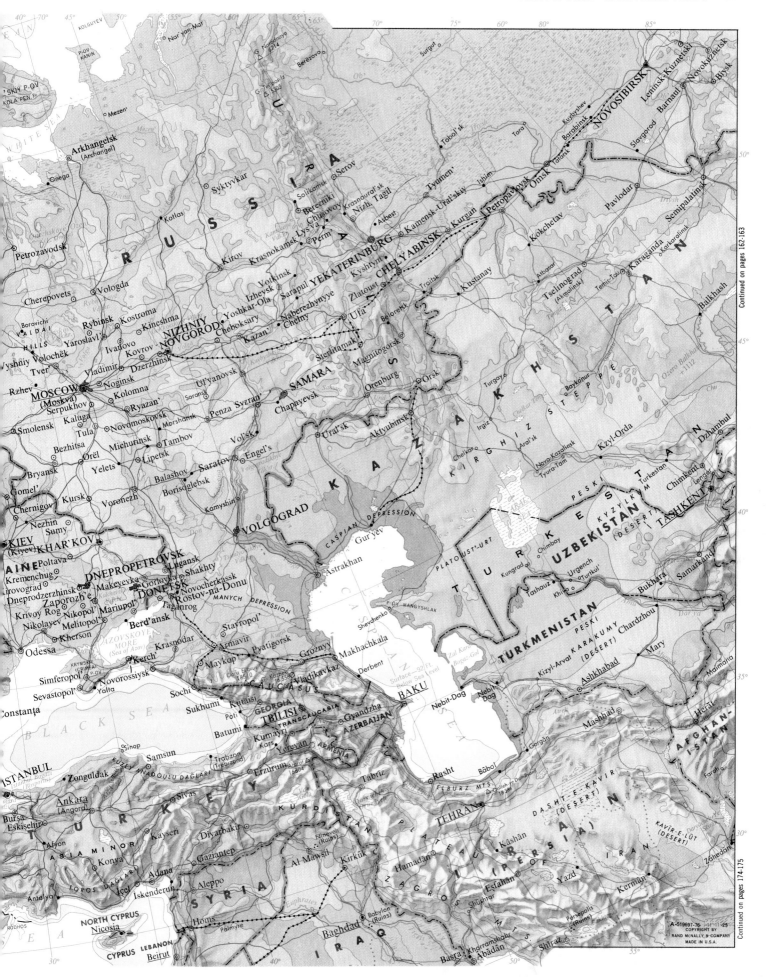

Continued on pages 162-163

Continued on pages 174-175

A-519697-76
COPYRIGHT BY
RAND MCNALLY & COMPANY
MADE IN U.S.A.

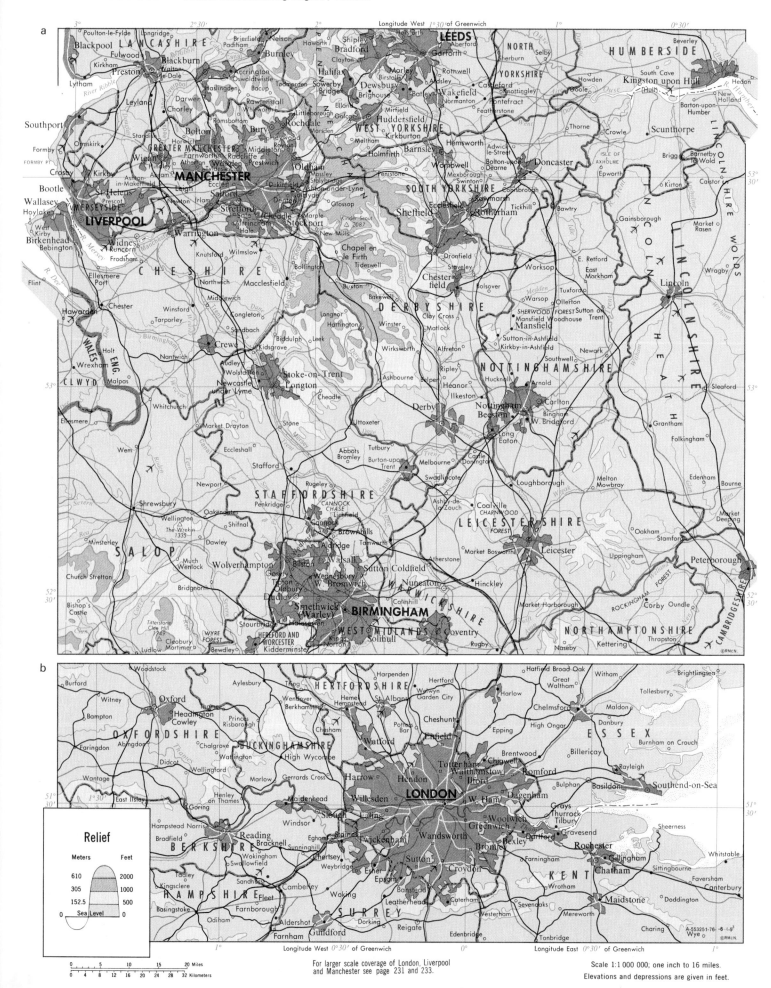

a

Longitude West 1°30′ of Greenwich

Blackpool L A N C A S H I R E
Poulton-le-Fylde Longridge Brierfield Nelson Haworth Shipley Horsforth **LEEDS** Aberford NORTH
Fulwood Kirkham Padiham Clayton Bradford Garforth Sherburn Selby YORKSHIRE Beverley
Lytham Preston Blackburn Accrington Oswaldtwistle Burnley Haworth Morley Rothwell Castleford Knottingley Howden Goole South Cave Kingston upon Hull
Leyland Chorley Darwen Haslingden Rawtenstall Tedmorden Sowerby Dewsbury Batley Wakefield Normanton Pontefract Featherstone (Hull) Barton-upon-Humber New Holland Hedon
Southport Ormskirk Standish Horwich Bolton Ramsbottom Bury Whitworth Littleborough Golcar Mirfield WEST YORKSHIRE Kirkburton Hemsworth Adwick-le-Street Thorne Crowle Scunthorpe Epworth
Formby GREATER MANCHESTER Wigan Farnworth Radcliffe Prestwich Rochdale Heywood Middleton Oldham Huddersfield Meltham Holmfirth Barnsley Wombwell Mexborough Swinton Bolton-upon-Dearne Doncaster ISLE OF AXHOLME Brigg Barnetby le Wold
Crosby Kirkby Ashton-in-Makerfield Atherton Walkden Salford MANCHESTER Mossley Stalybridge Penistone SOUTH YORKSHIRE Conisbrough Bawtry Kirton Caistor
Bootle St Helens Leigh Newton-le-Willows Irlam Eccles Denton Dukinfield Hyde Ashton-under-Lyne Glossop Sheffield Ecclesfield Rawmarsh Tickhill Gainsborough Market Rasen
Wallasey MERSEYSIDE Prescot Warrington Sale Altrincham Cheadle Stockport Marple Kinder Scout 2087 Rotherham LINCOLNSHIRE WOLDS
Hoylake **LIVERPOOL** West Kirby Widnes Runcorn Hale New Mills Chapel en le Frith Tideswell Dronfield Staveley Worksop E. Retford East Markham Wragby
Birkenhead Bebington Frodsham Knutsford Wilmslow Bollington Buxton Bakewell Chesterfield Bolsover Tuxford Sleaford
WALES Flint Ellesmere Port Northwich Macclesfield Winster DERBYSHIRE Clay Cross Warsop SHERWOOD FOREST Sutton on Trent Lincoln
ENG. Hawarden Chester Winsford Middlewich Congleton Hartington Matlock Mansfield Woodhouse Mansfield Newark
CLWYD Holt Tarporley Sandbach Leek Wirksworth Alfreton Sutton-in-Ashfield Kirkby-in-Ashfield Southwell
Wrexham Malpas Nantwich Crewe Kidsgrove Biddulph Ashbourne Belper Ripley NOTTINGHAMSHIRE Hucknall Arnold
Ellesmere Whitchurch Audley Wolstanton Newcastle under Lyme Stoke-on-Trent Longton Cheadle Derby Ilkeston Heanor Nottingham Beeston Carlton Bingham W. Bridgford Grantham
Wem Market Drayton Stone Uttoxeter Long Eaton Folkingham
Shrewsbury Eccleshall Abbots Bromley Tutbury Burton-upon-Trent Melbourne Castle Donington Edenham Bourne
SALOP Wellington Newport Stafford Rugeley Swadlincote Ashby-de-la-Zouch Loughborough Melton Mowbray Market Deeping
The Wrekin 1335 Shifnal Penkridge CANNOCK CHASE Lichfield Coalville CHARNWOOD FOREST Oakham Stamford
Minsterley Dawley Cannock Brownhills Tamworth LEICESTERSHIRE Uppingham Peterborough
Much Wenlock Wolverhampton Aldridge Walsall Sutton Coldfield Atherstone Market Bosworth Leicester ROCKINGHAM FOREST Corby Oundle
Bishop's Castle Bridgnorth Bilston Wednesbury W. Bromwich WARWICKSHIRE Nuneaton Hinckley Market Harborough NORTHAMPTONSHIRE
Church Stretton Dudley Tipton Oldbury Smethwick (Warley) **BIRMINGHAM** Coleshill Rugby Kettering Thrapston
Titterstone Clee Hill 1749 Stourbridge Halesowen WEST MIDLANDS Coventry Naseby
Cleobury Mortimer WYRE FOREST HEREFORD AND WORCESTER Kings Norton Solihull
Ludlow Bewdley Kidderminster

b

Woodstock Harpenden Hatfield Broad Oak Witham Brightlingsea
Burford Witney Oxford Aylesbury Tring HERTFORDSHIRE Hertford Welwyn Garden City Harlow Great Waltham Tollesbury
Bampton Headington Cowley Princes Risborough Wendover Hemel Hempstead St Albans Cheshunt Epping Chelmsford Maldon ESSEX
OXFORDSHIRE Abingdon Chalgrove BUCKINGHAMSHIRE Chesham Watford Potters Bar Enfield High Ongar Danbury Burnham on Crouch
Faringdon Wallingford Watlington High Wycombe Billericay Rayleigh
Didcot Marlow Gerrards Cross Harrow Hendon Tottenham Walthamstow Ilford Romford Brentwood Bulphan Basildon Southend-on-Sea
Wantage Henley on Thames Maidenhead Willesden **LONDON** W. Ham Dagenham Grays Thurrock Tilbury
East Ilsley Goring Slough Ealing Greenwich Woolwich Bexley Dartford Gravesend Sheerness
Hampstead Norris Windsor Staines Twickenham Wandsworth Bromley KENT Rochester Whitstable
Bradfield Reading Egham Sutton Croydon Farningham Gillingham Chatham Sittingbourne Faversham Canterbury
BERKSHIRE Bracknell Chertsey Weybridge Esher Epsom Caterham Wrotham Maidstone
Wokingham Sunninghill Banstead SURREY Sevenoaks Doddington
HAMPSHIRE Swallowfield Camberley Woking Leatherhead Westerham Charing
Tadley Sandhurst Dorking Edenbridge Wye
Kingsclere Fleet Farnborough Waking Reigate Tonbridge
Basingstoke Aldershot SURREY Guildford Farnham Odiham

Relief

Meters	Feet
610	2000
305	1000
152.5	500
0	Sea Level

0   5   10   15   20 Miles
0 4 8 12 16 20 24 28 32 Kilometers

For larger scale coverage of London, Liverpool and Manchester see page 231 and 233.

Longitude West 0°30′ of Greenwich   0°   Longitude East 0°30′ of Greenwich

Scale 1:1 000 000; one inch to 16 miles.
Elevations and depressions are given in feet.

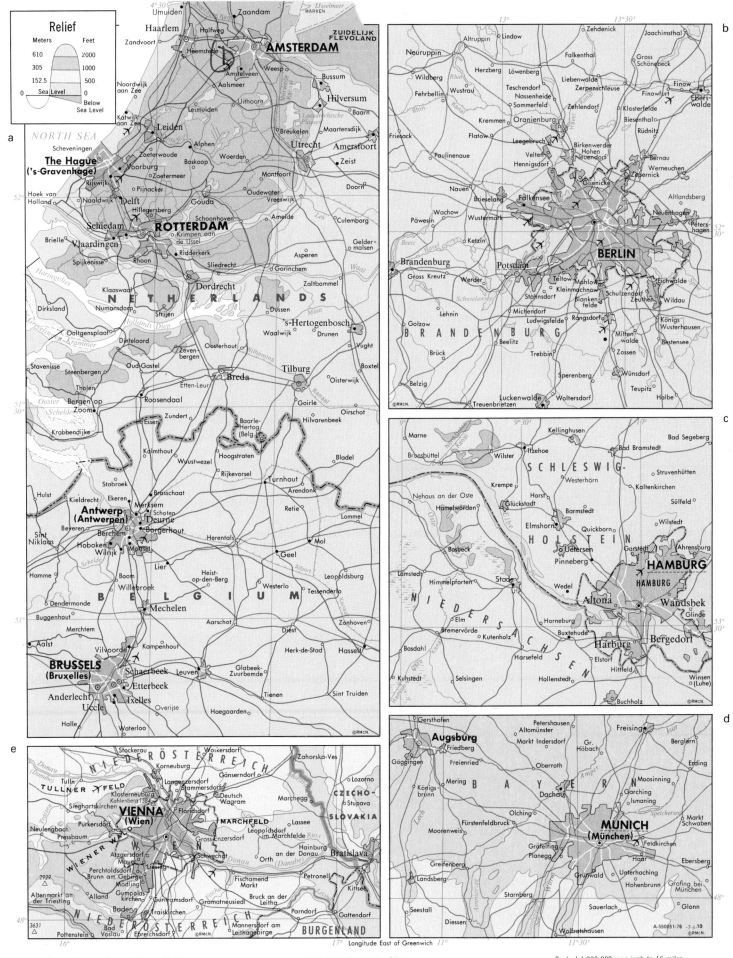

Relief

Meters	Feet
610	2000
305	1000
152.5	500
0	Sea Level
	Below Sea Level

NORTH SEA

AMSTERDAM

The Hague ('s-Gravenhage)

ROTTERDAM

NETHERLANDS

BELGIUM

Antwerp (Antwerpen)

BRUSSELS (Bruxelles)

BERLIN

BRANDENBURG

SCHLESWIG-HOLSTEIN

HAMBURG

NIEDERSACHSEN

VIENNA (Wien)

NIEDERÖSTERREICH

CZECHO-SLOVAKIA

Bratislava

BURGENLAND

Augsburg

BAYERN

MUNICH (München)

For larger scale coverage of Berlin and Vienna see pages 234 and 235.

Longitude East of Greenwich

0   5   10   15   20 Miles
0   4   8   12   16   20   24   28   32 Kilometers

Scale 1:1 000 000; one inch to 16 miles.
Elevations and depressions are given in feet.

Continued on pages 160-161

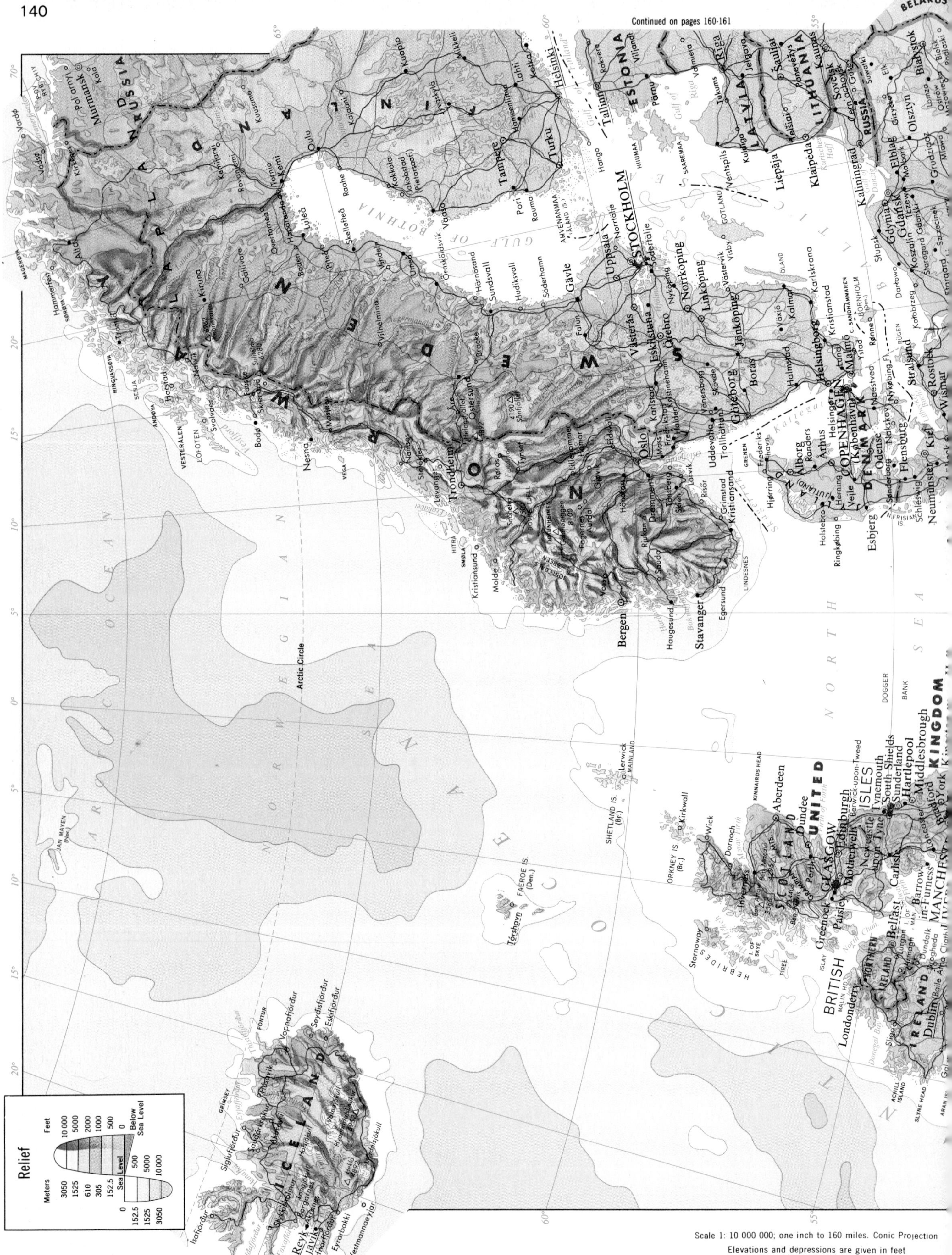

BELARUS

RUSSIA

L A P L A N D

F I N L A N D

Murmansk · Kola

Vardø
Vadsø
Kirkenes
Hammerfest
Alta
SØRØYA
Karasjok
MAGERØYA
Honningsvåg

Pol'arnyj
Nikel'

Ivalo
Kittilä
Muonio
Kuusamo
Kuolo
Kemijärvi
Rovaniemi

Tornio
Kemi
Oulu
Raahe
Kokkola
(Karleby)
Jakobstad
(Pietarsaari)
Vaasa

Kajaani
Iisalmi
Kuopio
Joensuu
Jyväskylä

Helsinki
Lahti
Tampere
Turku
Pori
Rauma

ESTONIA
Tallinn
Pärnu
Viljandi

LATVIA
Riga
Liepāja
Ventspils

LITHUANIA
Kaunas
Klaipėda
Šiauliai

Kaliningrad
RUSSIA
Białystok

Gdańsk
Gdynia
Elbląg
Olsztyn

S W E D E N

N O R W A Y

STOCKHOLM
Uppsala
Gävle
Söderhamn
Sundsvall
Hudiksvall
Härnösand
Örnsköldsvik
Umeå
Skellefteå
Luleå
Boden
Piteå
Kiruna
Gällivare
Jokkmokk

Östersund
Sundsvall
Falun
Borlänge
Västerås
Eskilstuna
Örebro
Norrköping
Linköping
Jönköping
Nyköping
Visby
GOTLAND
Kalmar
ÖLAND
Karlskrona
Kristianstad
Växjö
Halmstad
Helsingborg
Malmö
Göteborg
Borås

Oslo
Drammen
Hamar
Lillehammer
Gjøvik
Kongsvinger
Fredrikstad
Halden
Larvik
Skien
Risør
Arendal
Grimstad
Kristiansand
Egersund
Stavanger
Haugesund
Bergen

Trondheim
Levanger
Steinkjer
Namsos
Mosjøen
Mo i Rana
Nesna
Bodø
Narvik
Svolvær
LOFOTEN
VESTERÅLEN
ANDØYA
Harstad
Tromsø
Hammerfest

Ålesund
Molde
Kristiansund
SMØLA
HITRA
Florø

DENMARK
COPENHAGEN
(København)
Helsingør
Roskilde
Næstved
Odense
Svendborg
Nyborg
Kolding
Esbjerg
Ringkøbing
Holstebro
Herning
Vejle
Horsens
Århus
Randers
Ålborg
Frederikshavn
Hjørring

Flensburg
Kiel
Neumünster
Rostock
Wismar
Stralsund
RÜGEN

NORTH SEA

DOGGER BANK

UNITED KINGDOM

SCOTLAND
Aberdeen
Dundee
Edinburgh
Glasgow
Greenock
Paisley
Perth
Stirling
Motherwell
Stornoway
HEBRIDES
SKYE
TIREE
ISLAY
Wick
Dornoch
Inverness
Kirkwall
ORKNEY IS. (Br.)
SHETLAND IS. (Br.)
Lerwick
MAINLAND

Newcastle upon Tyne
South Shields
Sunderland
Hartlepool
Middlesbrough
Carlisle
Barrow-in-Furness
ISLE OF MAN
Belfast
NORTHERN IRELAND
Londonderry
BRITISH ISLES
IRELAND
Dublin
Drogheda
Dundalk
Sligo

FAEROE IS. (Den.)
Tórshavn

JAN MAYEN (Nor.)

N O R W E G I A N   S E A

A R C T I C   O C E A N

Arctic Circle

I C E L A N D
Reykjavík
Hafnarfjörður
Keflavík
Akureyri
Seyðisfjörður
Eskifjörður
Vopnafjörður
Siglufjörður
Ísafjörður
GRÍMSEY

GULF OF BOTHNIA

ÅLAND IS.

GULF OF FINLAND

Scale 1: 10 000 000; one inch to 160 miles. Conic Projection
Elevations and depressions are given in feet

Relief

Meters	Feet	
3050	10 000	
1525	5000	
610	2000	
305	1000	
152.5	500	
0	Sea Level	
152.5	500	Below Sea Level
1525	5000	
3050	10 000	

Continued on pages 140-141

Scale 1:10 000 000; one inch to 160 miles. Bonne's Projection
Elevations and depressions are given in feet

Relief

Meters	Feet
3050	10000
1525	5000
610	2000
305	1000
152.5	500
0 Sea Level	0
	Below
152.5	500 Sea Level
1525	5000
3050	10000

A-558300-76
COPYR.
RAND McNALLY & COMPANY
MADE IN U.S.A.

Longitude West of Greenwich 0° Longitude East of Greenwich

Continued on pages 160-161

BLACK SEA

AZOVSKOYE MORE
(Sea of Azov)

RUSSIA

KATOWICE
POLAND
UKRAINE
DONETSK
Rostov-na-Donu
GEORGIA

MOLDOVA
ROMANIA
HUNGARY

BUDAPEST
BUCHAREST
Constanţa

CROATIA
BOSNIA AND
HERCEGOVINA
Belgrade
(Beograd)

YUGOSLAVIA
Sofia
(Sofiya)
BULGARIA
Varna (Stalin)

Sevastopol'

İSTANBUL
MACEDONIA

ALBANIA
Tirane

ASIA MINOR
TURKEY
Ankara
(Angora)

Thessaloniki

AEGEAN
SEA

GREECE

IONIAN
SEA

IONIAN
ISLANDS

ATHENS
Piraiévs
(Athínai)

SYRIA
Aleppo

NORTH
CYPRUS

The Turkish Republic of Northern Cyprus
unilaterally declared its independence
on Nov. 15, 1983.

Nicosia

CYPRUS
Limassol

Tarábulus
(Tripoli)
LEBANON
Beirut

Damascus
(Dimashq)

CRETE

Areas occupied by Israel since 1967

ISRAEL
Tel Aviv-Yafo
Jerusalem
Gaza
JORDAN

MEDITERRANEAN SEA

Dumyāt
Port Said
(Būr Saʻīd)

ALEXANDRIA
(Al Iskandarīyah)

CAIRO
(Al Qāhirah)
Suez (As Suways)

SINAI
PEN.

SAUDI
ARABIA

Banghāzī
BARQAH
(CYRENAICA)

LIBYAN
PLATEAU

EGYPT

MUNKHAFAD
AL
QATTĀRAH

LIBYA
DESERT

RED
SEA

LIBYAN DESERT

0 50 100 150 200 250 300 Miles
0   100   200   300   400   500 Kilometers

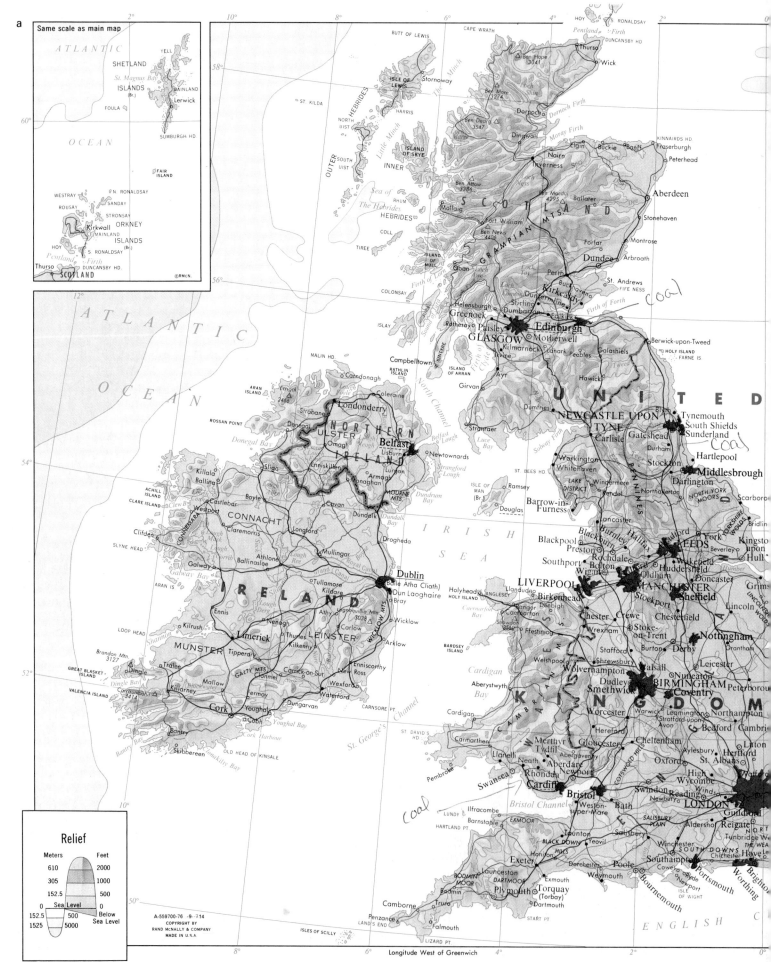

Continued on pages 146-147

Continued on pages 148-149

Continued on pages 150-151

Longitude East of Greenwich

0 10 20 30 40 50 60 70 80 90 100 110 120 Miles
0 20 40 60 80 100 120 140 160 180 200 Kilometers

NORWEGIAN SEA

SMØLA
Kristiansund
Averøya
Molde
Ålesund
Andalsnes
GURSKØY
Floro
BREMANGERLANDET
STORA SOTRA
Bergen
Osøyra
BØMLO
Haugesund
Kopervik
KARMØY
Skudeneshavn
Stavanger
Sandnes
Egersund
Farsund
LINDESNES
Flekkefjord
Mandal
Kristiansand

Trondheim
Orkanger
Støren
Stjørdalshalsen
Selbusjøen
Oppdal
Snøhetta 7500
DOVRE FJELL
TROLLHEIMEN
JOSTEDALSBREEN
JOTUNHEIMEN
Galdhøpiggen 8100
Glittertinden 8084
Leikanger
Vikøyri
Gudvangen
Flåm
Dale
Voss
Eidfjord
Odda
Sauda
Tau
Tveitsund
Dalen
Notodden
Rjukan
Tinnsjø
Skien
Porsgrunn
Brevik
Langesund
Kragerø
Risør
Tvedestrand
Arendal
Grimstad
Lillesand

NORWAY

Lærdalsøyri
Fagernes
Aurdal
Lillehammer
Moelv
Hamar
Mjøsa
Gjøvik
Raufoss
Skreia
Gol
Gulsvik
Hønefoss
Vickersund
Svelvik
Kongsberg
Holmestrand
Horten
Tønsberg
Sandefjord
Larvik
Moss
Sarpsborg
Fredrikstad
Halden

Oslo
Oslofjorden
Drammen
Drøbak
Holmsbu
Lillestrøm
Øyeren
Mysen
Strømstad
Grebbestad
Fjällbacka

Sylarna 5781
Helagsfjället 5892
Storsjö
Tynset
Røros
Fermunden
Savalen
Aursunden
Gaula

Östersund
Ragunda
Kramfors
HEMSÖN
Härnösand
Bräcke
Ånge
Fränsta
Stöde
Sundsvall
ALNÖN
Njurunda
Ramsjö
Sveg
Sånfjället 4190
(NATIONAL PARK)
TÖFSINGDALENS (NATIONAL PARK)
Städjan 3711
Ljusdal
Hudiksvall
Enånger
Bollnäs
Söderhamn
Älvdalen
Mora
Orsa
Lima
Rättvik
Ockelbo
Leksand
Falun
Storvik
Gävle
Gävlebukten
GRÄSÖ
Öregrund
Östhammar
Borlänge
Säter
Ludvika
Hedemora
Smedjebacken
Avesta
Krylbo
Tierp
Vattholma
Kopparberg
Sala
Heby
Uppsala
Rimbo
Sigtuna
Lindesberg
Köping
Tillberga
Västerås
Enköping
SWEDEN

Filipstad
Nora
Forshaga
Kil
Karlstad
Karlskoga
Arboga
Torshälla
Strängnäs
Sundbyberg
STOCKHOLM
Vaxholm
Mariefred
Södertälje
Arvika
Sunne
Charlottenberg
Kongsvinger
Eidsvoll
Elverum
Filsa
Rena
Ossjøen
Torsby
Åmål
Säffle
Kristinehamn
Hallsberg
Örebro
Eskilstuna
Malmköping
Askersund
Katrineholm
Flen
Trosa
DRNO
Nynäshamn
Mellerud
Mariestad
Töreboda
Motala
Vadstena
Norrköping
Söderköping
Bråviken
Nyköping
Uddevalla
Vänersborg
Lidköping
Skara
Skövde
Vara
Falköping
Tidaholm
Hjo
Skänninge
Mjölby
Linköping
Åtvidaberg
Valdemarsvik
Gränna
Tranås
Gamleby
Västervik
GOTLAND
Visby
Klintehamn
Lysekil
Marstrand
Kungälv
Göteborg
Mölndal
Alingsås
Ulricehamn
Huskvarna
Jönköping
Nässjö
Vimmerby
Eksjö
Figeholm
Oskarshamn
Monsterås
Kungsbacka
Varberg
Falkenberg
Oskarström
Halmstad
Borås
Vetlanda
Virserum
Värnamo
ÖLAND
Borgholm
Alvesta
Ljungby
Växjö
Nybro
Kalmar
Mörbylånga
Laholm
Bastad
Markaryd
Älmhult
Tingsryd
Ängelholm
Klippan
Hässleholm
Ronneby
Karlshamn
Karlskrona
Helsingborg
Kristianstad
Åhus
Hanöbukten
Landskrona
Eslöv
Hörby
Sölvesborg
Lund
Copenhagen (København)
Malmö
Skurup
Tomelilla
Simrishamn
SANDHAMMAREN
Svedala
Skanör
Falsterbo
Trelleborg
Ystad
BORNHOLM (Den.)
Allinge
Rønne
Svaneke
Neksø

SKAGERRAK
Grenen
Skagen
Hirtshals
Frederikshavn
Sæby
Brønderslev
LÆSØ
ANHOLT
KATTEGAT
Thisted
Ålborg
Nørresundby
Nibe
Løgstør
Nykøbing
Hobro
Mariager
Randers
Grenå
MORS
Lemvig
Struer
Skive
Viborg
Ebeltoft
Holstebro
Silkeborg
Århus
Skanderborg
Ringkøbing
RINGKØBING FJORD
Herning
Horsens
SAMSØ
Nykøbing
Kalundborg
Holbæk
Roskilde
DENMARK
Varde
Vejle
Fredericia
SJÆLLAND
Esbjerg
FANØ
Kolding
Middelfart
Bogense
Slagelse
Ringsted
Køge
Køge Bugt
Ribe
Haderslev
Odense
Assens
Nyborg
Korsør
Næstved
RØMØ
Åbenrå
ALS
Fåborg
Svendborg
Rudkøbing
Nakskov
Maribo
Nykøbing
Vordingborg
MØN
FALSTER
LOLLAND
LANGELAND
ÆRØ
SYLT
FÖHR
Tønder
Sønderborg
Flensburg
SCHLESWIG
Husum
Schleswig
Eckernförde
Kiel
Kiel Bay
FEHMARN
Gedser
RÜGEN
KAP ARKONA
Sassnitz
Bergen
Stralsund
Greifswald
Barth
Warnemünde
Rostock
Wismar
Lübeck
Cuxhaven
Neumünster
Neustadt in Holstein
Rendsburg
Heide
Tönning
HOLSTEIN
Elbe
GERMANY
Wolgast
Świnoujście
Kamień Pomorski
Pomeranian Bay
Kołobrzeg
Darłowo
Ustka
Słupsk
Lębork
Wejherowo
Gdynia
Sopot
POLAND
Łeba

NORTH SEA
NISSUM FJORD
JYLLAND
NORTH FRISIAN ISLANDS

BALTIC SEA

A-559195-76 12.8 -15
COPYRIGHT BY
RAND MCNALLY & COMPANY
MADE IN U.S.A.

Relief

Meters		Feet
1525		5000
610		2000
305		1000
152.5		500
0	Sea Level	0
152.5		500 Below Sea Level

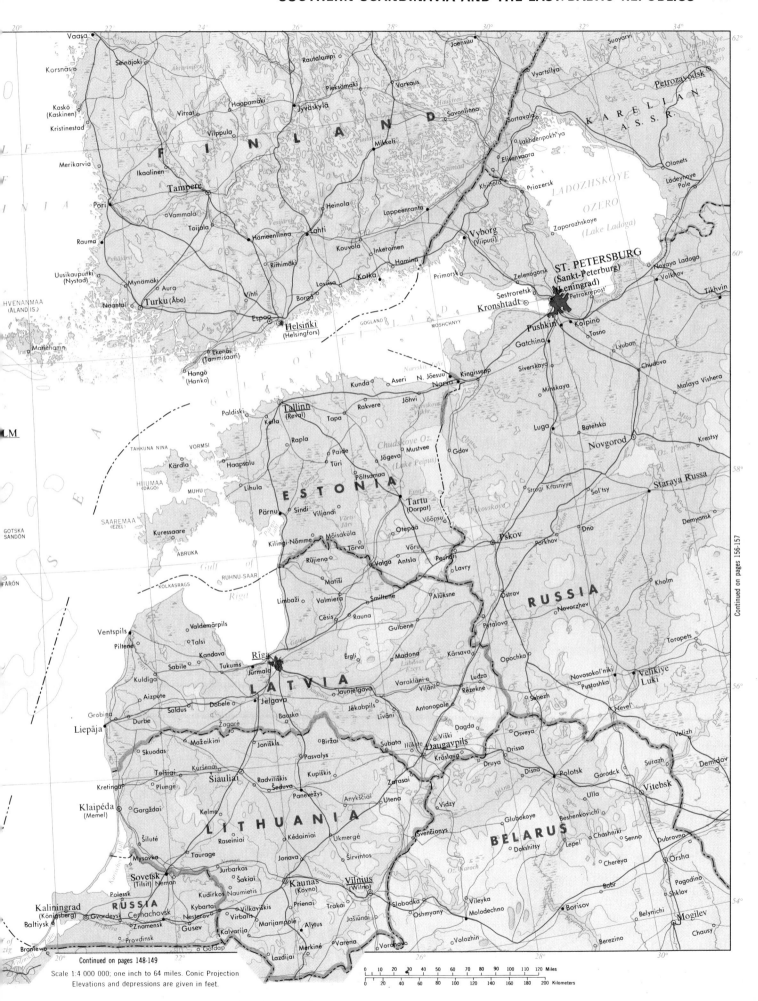

Continued on pages 156-157

Continued on pages 148-149

Scale 1:4 000 000; one inch to 64 miles. Conic Projection
Elevations and depressions are given in feet.

| 0 | 10 | 20 | 30 | 40 | 50 | 60 | 70 | 80 | 90 | 100 | 110 | 120 Miles |

| 0 | 20 | 40 | 60 | 80 | 100 | 120 | 140 | 160 | 180 | 200 Kilometers |

Continued on pages 146-147

DENMARK

NORTH SEA

BALTIC

FRISIAN ISLANDS

NETHERLANDS

SCHLESWIG-HOLSTEIN

MECKLENBURG

POMERANIA

AMSTERDAM

HAMBURG

Bremerhaven
Bremen
Delmenhorst

LÜNEBURGER HEIDE

NIEDERSACHSEN

Kiel
Neumünster
Lübeck
Rostock
Wismar
Schwerin
Stralsund
Greifswald

Hannover
Braunschweig
Wolfsburg

Berlin
Potsdam
BRANDENBURG
Frankfurt an der Oder

G E R M A N Y

DÜSSELDORF
ESSEN
Dortmund
COLOGNE (Köln)
Bonn
NORDRHEIN
WESTFALEN

Magdeburg
Dessau
Halle
Leipzig
Dresden
Görlitz

THÜRINGEN
Erfurt
Weimar
Jena
Gera
Chemnitz
Zwickau
ERZGEBIRGE

FRANKFURT AM MAIN
Wiesbaden
Mainz
Darmstadt
Offenbach

HESSEN

Würzburg
Bamberg
Bayreuth

Nürnberg
Fürth
Erlangen

PRAGUE (Praha)

C Z E C H Y

(BOHEMIA)

MANNHEIM
Heidelberg
Karlsruhe

STUTTGART
Esslingen
Pforzheim
Tübingen
Reutlingen
Ulm

B A Y E R N
(BAVARIA)

Regensburg
Ingolstadt

Augsburg
MUNICH (München)

Brno

FRANCE

Strasbourg

Freiburg
Basel

S W I T Z E R L A N D

Zürich
Bern

OBERÖSTERREICH

Linz

Salzburg

VIENNA (Wien)

A U S T R I A

Innsbruck

Graz

SLOVENIA

Maribor

CROATIA

Continued on pages 150-151

Continued on pages 154-155

Longitude East of Greenwich

Scale 1:4 000 000; one inch to 64 miles. Conic Projection
Elevations and depressions are given in feet.

Continued on pages 146-147

Continued on pages 156-157

Relief

Meters	Feet
3050	10 000
1525	5000
610	2000
305	1000
152.5	500
0 Sea Level	0
	Below Sea Level

SEA

Puck
Wejherowo
Hel
Gdynia
Sopot
Baltiysk
Gulf of Danzig
Gdańsk (Danzig)
Lębork
Kościerzyna
Tczew
Malbork
Starogard Gdański
Czersk
Elbląg
Grudziądz
Kwidzyn
Iława
Ostróda
Olsztyn
Mrągowo
Toruń
Chełmno
Brodnica
Nidzica
Szczytno
Pisz
Ełk
Augustów
Suwałki
Gołdap
Grajewo
Kolno
Łomża
Białystok

Kaliningrad (Königsberg)
RUSSIA
Cernachovsk
Gusev
Sovetsk (Tilsit)
Jurbarkas
Šakiai
Kaunas (Kovno)
Kudirkos (Kovno)
Naumiestis
Vilkaviškis
Marijampole
Kalvarija
Prienai
LITHUANIA
Trakai
Vilnius
Merkine
Varena
Alytus

BELARUS
Minsk
Molodechno
Volozhin
Oshmyany
Slutsk
Baranovichi
Slonim
Ruzhany

Grodno
Wasilków
Knyszyn
Sokółka
Krynki

WARSAW (Warszawa)
Łódź
KATOWICE
Kraków
BUDAPEST
Wrocław
Opole

POLAND
GALICIA
CARPATHIAN MOUNTAINS
SLOVAKIA (SLOVENSKO)
HUNGARY
UKRAINE
ROMANIA
TRANSYLVANIA
MOLDOVA
BUKOVINA
RUTHENIA
MASURIA

HIGH TATRA MTS.
NIZKE TATRY
GÓRY ŚWIĘTOKRZYSKIE

Lublin
Radom
Kielce
Tarnów
Rzeszów
Przemyśl
L'vov
Ternopol
Ivano-Frankovsk
Chernovtsy
Uzhgorod
Mukachevo
Košice
Miskolc
Debrecen
Oradea
Cluj-Napoca
Tîrgu-Mureş
Sibiu
Braşov
Timişoara
Arad
Szeged
Pécs

YUGO

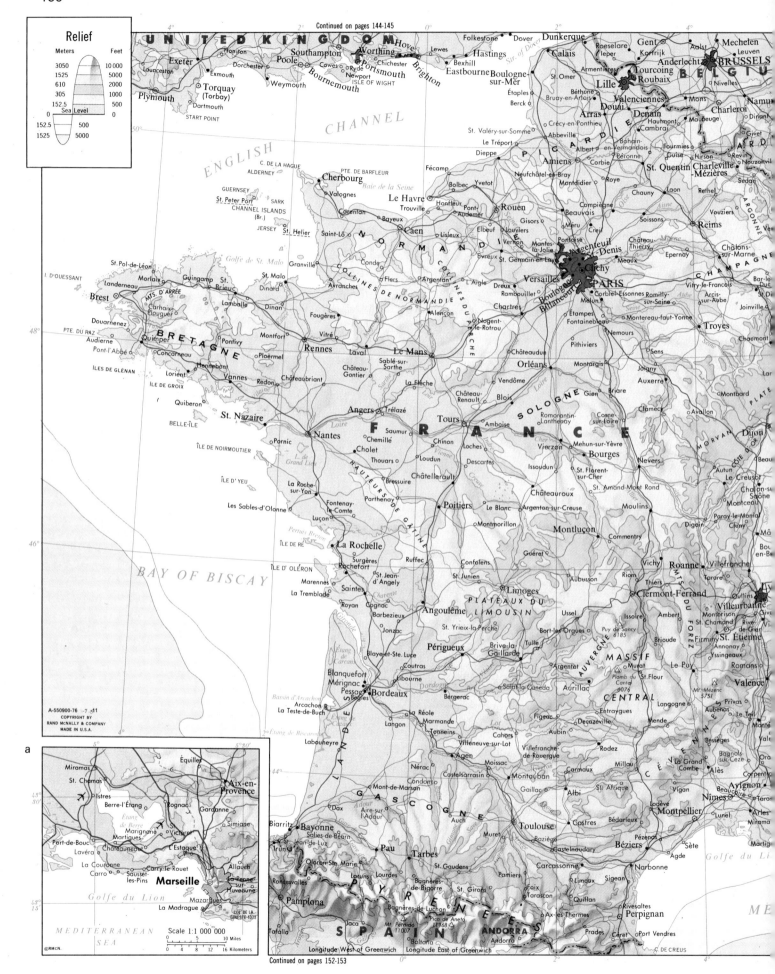

150

Continued on pages 144-145

Relief

Meters	Feet
3050	10 000
1525	5000
610	2000
305	1000
152.5	500
Sea Level	0
152.5	500
1525	5000

UNITED KINGDOM

Honiton · Worthing Hove · Folkestone · Dover Dunkerque · Roeselare · Gent · Aalst · Mechelen
Exeter · Dorchester · Southampton · Chichester · Portsmouth · Brighton · Lewes · Hastings · Calais · Ieper · Kortrijk · Anderlecht · BRUSSELS · Leuven
Exmouth · Poole · Bournemouth · Cowes · Ryde · Newport · ISLE OF WIGHT · Bexhill · Eastbourne · Boulogne-sur-Mer · Armentières · Tourcoing · Roubaix · BELGIUM
Torquay (Torbay) · Weymouth · Étaples · Béthune · Bruay-en-Artois · Lille · Valenciennes · Mons · Nivelles · Charleroi
Plymouth · Dartmouth · Berck · Arras · Douai · Denain · Hautmont · Maubeuge · Dinant
START POINT · St. Valéry-sur-Somme · Crécy-en-Ponthieu · Cambrai · Givet

CHANNEL

ENGLISH

C. DE LA HAGUE · ALDERNEY · PTE. DE BARFLEUR · Fécamp · Bolbec · Yvetot · Neufchâtel-en-Bray · Montdidier · Roye · St. Quentin · Charleville-Mézières · Sedan
GUERNSEY · Cherbourg · Valognes · Baie de la Seine · Le Havre · Honfleur · Pont-Audemer · Rouen · Beauvais · Compiègne · Chauny · Laon · Rethel · Vouziers
St. Peter Port · SARK · Carentan · Trouville · Gisors · Meru · Creil · Soissons · Reims · Châlons-sur-Marne
CHANNEL ISLANDS · Saint-Lô · Bayeux · Caen · Lisieux · Elbeuf · Louviers · Vernon · Mantes-la-Jolie · Pontoise · Château-Thierry · Epernay · Bar-le-Duc
(Br.) · JERSEY · St. Helier · Conde · Flers · Argentan · L'Aigle · Dreux · Évreux · St. Germain-en-Laye · Clichy · PARIS · Meaux · Arcis-sur-Aube · Joinville
Granville · Avranches · Alençon · Nogent-le-Rotrou · Chartres · Versailles · Boulogne-Billancourt · Melun · Corbeil-Essonnes · Romilly-sur-Seine · Vitry-le-François · Chaumont
St. Pol-de-Léon · Landerneau · Morlaix · Guingamp · St. Brieuc · St. Malo · Dinard · Fougères · Vitré · Châteaudun · Pithiviers · Fontainebleau · Montereau-faut-Yonne · Troyes
Brest · Carhaix-Plouguer · Lamballe · Dinan · Montfort · Laval · Le Mans · Orléans · Montargis · Sens · Joigny · Auxerre · Montbard
Douarnenez · Quimper · Pontivy · Ploërmel · Rennes · Sablé-sur-Sarthe · La Flèche · Vendôme · Blois · Gien · Briare · Clamecy · Avallon · Dijon
Audierne · Pont-l'Abbé · Hennebont · Vannes · Redon · Châteaubriant · Angers · Trélazé · Tours · Amboise · Vierzon · Bourges · Nevers · Autun · Le Creusot · Chalon-sur-Saône
Concarneau · Lorient · Quiberon · St. Nazaire · Nantes · Saumur · Chinon · Loches · Mehun-sur-Yèvre · St. Florent-sur-Cher · Moulins · Paray-le-Monial · Cluny · Mâcon
Pornic · Cholet · Thouars · Bressuire · Châtellerault · Issoudun · Châteauroux · St. Amand-Mont Rond · Digoin
La Roche-sur-Yon · Fontenay-le-Comte · Parthenay · Poitiers · Le Blanc · Argenton-sur-Creuse · Montluçon · Commentry · Vichy · Roanne · Villefranche
Les Sables-d'Olonne · Luçon · Niort · Ruffec · Confolens · Guéret · Aubusson · Thiers · Clermont-Ferrand · Villeurbanne
La Rochelle · Surgères · St. Jean-d'Angély · St. Junien · Limoges · Ussel · Riom · Issoire · Ambert · St. Chamond · St. Étienne · Firminy
Rochefort · Saintes · Cognac · Angoulême · St. Yrieix-la-Perche · Brive-la-Gaillarde · Tulle · Bort-les-Orgues · Murat · Le Puy · Romans · Valence
Marennes · La Tremblade · Royan · Barbezieux · Jonzac · Périgueux · Argentat · St. Flour · Aurillac · Mende · Aubenas
Blaye-Ste.-Luce · Coutras · Libourne · Bergerac · Sarlat-la-Canéda · Figeac · Decazeville · Langogne · Privas
Blanquefort · Mérignac · Pessac · Bègles · Bordeaux · La Réole · Marmande · Tonneins · Cahors · Rodez · Millau · Bagnols-sur-Ceze · Alès
Arcachon · La Teste-de-Buch · Langon · Villeneuve-sur-Lot · Aubin · Villefranche-de-Rouergue · Vigan · Avignon · Nîmes
Labouheyre · Agen · Nérac · Moissac · Carmaux · Castelsarrasin · Montauban · Albi · St. Affrique · Lodève · Lunel · Montpellier · Arles · Mirama
Mont-de-Marsan · Condom · Gaillac · Béziers · Sète · Martig
Dax · Aire-sur-l'Adour · Auch · Muret · Toulouse · Castres · Castelnaudary · Pézenas · Agde
Biarritz · Bayonne · Salies-de-Béarn · Jean-de-Luz · Pau · Tarbes · Baziège · Carcassonne · Narbonne
Irun · Oloron-Ste.-Marie · St. Gaudens · Pamiers · Limoux · Sigean
Roncesvalles · Lourdes · Bagnères-de-Bigorre · St. Girons · Foix · Quillan · Rivesaltes · Perpignan
Pamplona · Bagnères-de-Luchon · Tarascon · Ax-les-Thermes · Prades · Céret · Port Vendres · C. DE CREUS
Jaca · Mt. Perdido · Pico de Aneta · ANDORRA

SPAIN

Dieppe · Le Tréport · Abbeville · Albert · Bohain-en-Vermandois · Fourmies · Hirson · Neuzonvil
Amiens · Corbie · Péronne · Guise

PICARDIE

NORMANDIE · COLLINES DE NORMANDIE · COLLINES DU PERCHE

BRETAGNE · MTS. D'ARRÉE

PTE. DU RAZ · ÎLES DE GLÉNAN · ÎLE DE GROIX · BELLE-ÎLE · ÎLE DE NOIRMOUTIER · ÎLE D'YEU

FRANCE · SOLOGNE · CÔTE D'OR · MORVAN · PLATE

HAUTEURS DE GÂTINE

BAY OF BISCAY · PERTUIS BRETON · ÎLE DE RÉ · ÎLE D'OLÉRON

PLATEAUX DU LIMOUSIN · AUVERGNE · Puy de Sancy 6185 · MASSIF · CENTRAL · MTS. DU FOREZ

Plomb du Cantal 6075 · Mt. Mézenc 5751

Étang de Carcans · Bassin d'Arcachon · Étang d'Hourtin · Étang de Biscarrosse

LANDE · GASCOGNE · CÉVENNES · Mt. Mézenc

PYRÉNÉES · Mt. Perdido 11 168 · Pico de Aneta 11 007 · Boltaña

Golfe de St. Malo · L. de Grand Lieu · Gironde · Dordogne · Lot · Adour

I. D'OUESSANT · ÎLE D'OUESSANT

Golfe du Lion · MÉDITERRANEE

Continued on pages 152-153

Longitude West of Greenwich · Longitude East of Greenwich

A-550900-76 -7- -11
COPYRIGHT BY
RAND McNALLY & COMPANY
MADE IN U.S.A.

a

Miramas · St. Chamas · Istres · Équilles · Aix-en-Provence
Berre-l'Étang · Rognac · Gardanne · Simiane
Étang de Berre · Marignane · Vitrolles · Allauch
Port-de-Bouc · Martigues · Châteauneuf · L'Estaque · La Penne-sur-Huveaune
Lavéra · La Couronne · Carry-le-Rouet · Sausset-les-Pins · Marseille
Carro · Allauch
Golfe du Lion · Mazargues · COL DE LA GINESTE 1035
La Madrague

MEDITERRANEAN SEA

®RMCN.

Scale 1:1 000 000

0 · 5 · 10 Miles
0 · 4 · 8 · 12 · 16 Kilometers

Scale 1:4 000 000; one inch to 64 miles. Conic Projection
Elevations and depressions are given in feet

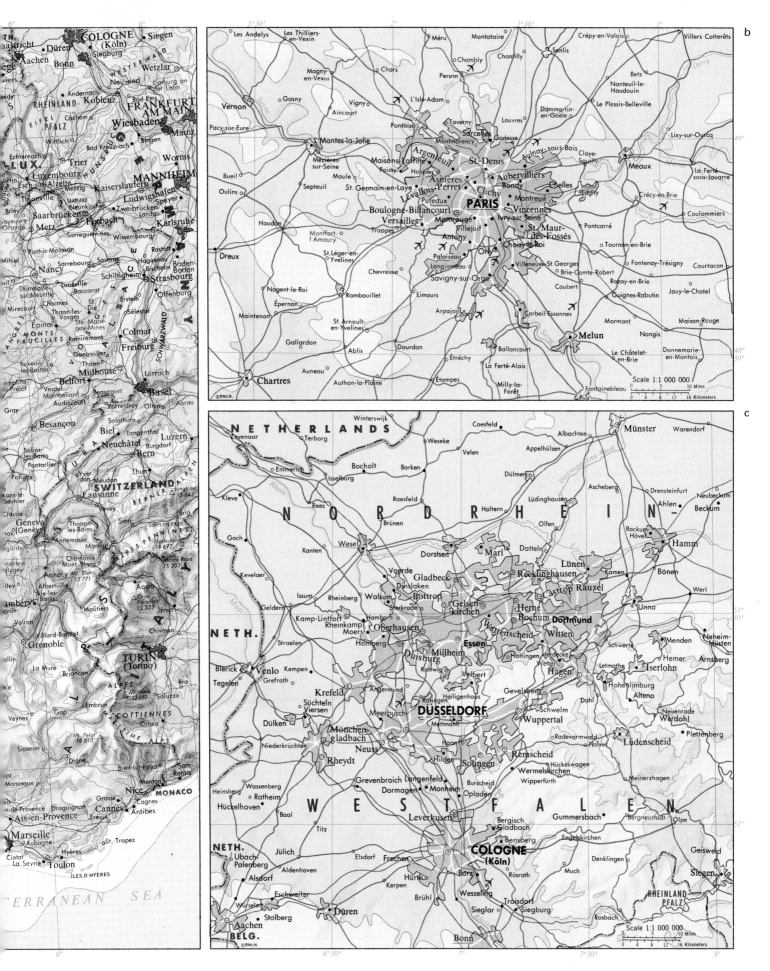

b

c

For larger scale coverage of Dusseldorf
and Paris see pages 232 and 233.

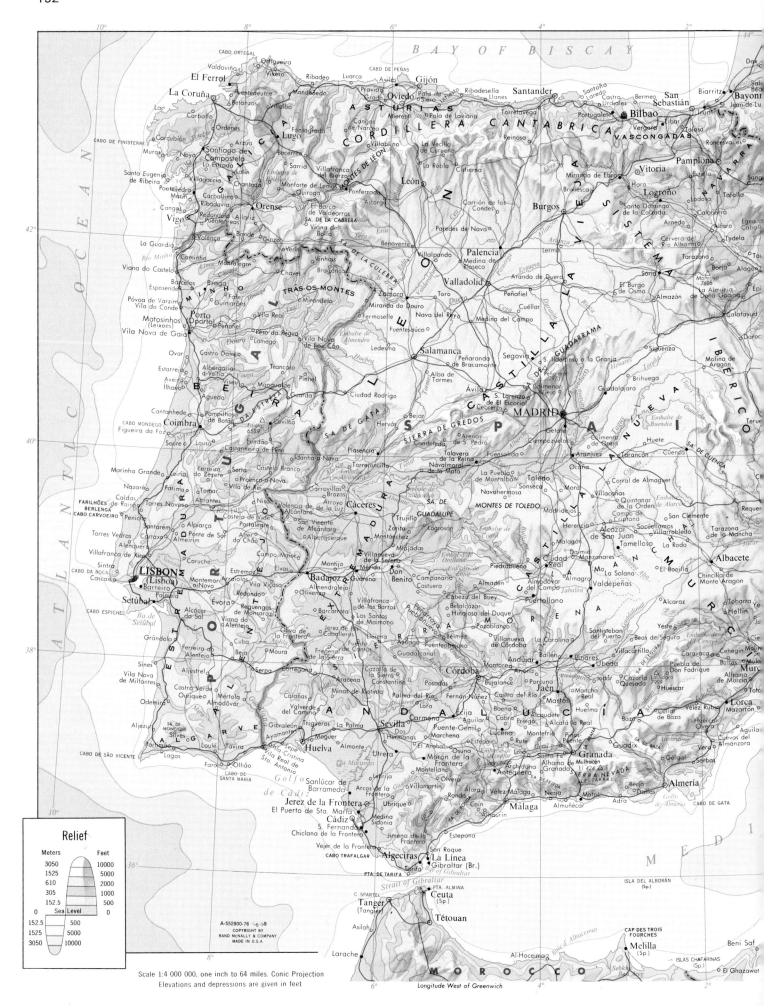

Relief

Meters		Feet
3050		10000
1525		5000
610		2000
305		1000
152.5		500
0	Sea Level	0
152.5		500
1525		5000
3050		10000

A-552900-76 -6-59
COPYRIGHT BY
RAND McNALLY & COMPANY
MADE IN U.S.A.

Scale 1:4 000 000, one inch to 64 miles. Conic Projection
Elevations and depressions are given in feet

Longitude West of Greenwich

Continued on pages 150-151

Main map (Spain / France / Mediterranean)

FRANCE

de Marsan · Condom · Gaillac · Albi · Arles
Verdun · Lodève · Montpellier · Miramas
l'Adour · Auch · Toulouse · Castres · Bédarieux · Pézenas · Mèze · Sète · Mattiques
Pau · Tarbes · Muret · Baziège · Castelnaudary · Béziers · Agde
Oloron- · Lourdes · St. Gaudens · Pamiers · Narbonne
Ste. Marie · Bagnères- · St. Girans · Foix · Limoux · Sigean · Golfe du Lion
Larens · de-Bigorre · Ax-les-Thermes · Quillan · Rivesaltes
Puerto de · Bagnères- · Pique d'Estats · Perpignan
Somport · de-Luchon · 10,020 · Prades · Ceret · Port Vendres
MT. PERDIDO · Pico de Aneto · ANDORRA · Andorra · CABO DE CREUS
Baltaña · 159 · PYRENEES
SA. DE · Huesca · Ripoll · Olot · Golfo de Rosas
GUARA · La Bisbal
Barbastro · Berga · Manlleu · Gerona
Monzón · Vich · San Feliú de Guixols
Tamarite · Balaguer · Manresa · Calella
ragoza · de Litera · Tárrega · Igualada · Granollers · Mataró
Lérida · Borjas Blancas · Tarrasa · Sabadell · Badalona
Fraga · Villafranca · Montblanch · Valls · BARCELONA
Caspe · del Panadés
Alcañiz · Gandesa · Reus · Villanueva y Geltrú
Calanda · Tortosa · Tarragona
CABO DE TORTOSA
Morella · Amposta
Alcanar · Vinaroz · BALEARIC SEA
San Mateo · Benicarló
DE IGUAR · Torreblanca · BALEARES · MENORCA
Peñagolosa · ISLANDS (MINORCA)
5952 · ISLAS · Ciudadela · Mahón
del Cid · Castellón de la Plana · Pollensa · Ba. de Alcudia
Onda · COLUMBRETES · Sóller · La Puebla
segorbe · Villarreal · Burriana · Inca · BALEARIC
Vall de Uxó · Golfo · Palma · Manacor
Sagunto · de · Lluchmayor · Felanitx
Liria · Santañy
Torrente · Valencia · Ba. de Palma · CAPE SALINAS
Catarroja · MALLORCA · CABRERA
Alcira · Sueca · de · (MAJORCA)
Cullera
Játiva · Valencia
Gandía · Oliva · IBIZA
Ontinent · (IVIZA)
Alcoy · Pego · Denia · San Antonio Abad
Cocentaina · Jávea · Sta. Eulalia del Río
Villena · Jijona · Villajoyosa · Ibiza
Monóvar · CABO DE LA NAO · FORMENTERA
elda · Alcoy
villente · Alicante
Orihuela · Elche
Segura · MEDITERRANEAN SEA
Torrevieja
Mar Menor
La Unión · CABO DE PALOS
artagena · Cartagena

Algiers
(El Djazair) · Boudouaou
Delles
Cherchell · Boufarik · El Arba
Ténès · El Affroun · Tamdyya · El Boulaida · Boukk
Carnot · Melyang · Bou
Ech Cheliff · Sour el Ghozlane
Sidi Aissa
Mestghanem · Oued Rhiou · Qasr el Boukhar · ATLAS MOUNTAINS
CAP FERRAT · Arzew
Oran · Ghilizane · ALGERIA
(Wahran) · Oued Tlelat · El Mohammadia · Mouaskar · Aïn Wessara
Temouchent · Stizet · Ksar · Chellala · Bouira-Sahary
Tihert · Zahrez Chergui

Longitude East of Greenwich

Scale bars (miles / kilometers)

For larger scale coverage of Lisbon, Madrid, and Rome see pages 234 and 235.

a — MADRID (Scale 1:1 000 000)

S. Lorenzo de El Escorial · SA. DEL HOYO · Colmenar Viejo · Fuente el Saz
4606 · Galapagar · Algete
El Escorial · S. Sebastián de los Reyes · Alcobendas
El Pardo · Barajas
Valdemorillo · Las Rozas de Madrid · Fuencarral · de Madrid · Torrejón de Ardoz · Alcalá de Henares
Pozuelo de Alarcón · MADRID · Vicálvaro · S. Fernando de Henares
Brunete · Alcorcón · Vallecas · Campo Real
Villaviciosa de Odón · Leganés · Móstoles · Getafe · Arganda
Navalcarnero · Canal del Manzanares · Valdilecha · Carabaña
Parla · Pinto · Morata de Tajuña · Tielmes
S. Martín de la Vega · Perales de Tajuña

b — LISBON (Scale 1:1 000 000)

Mafra · Cheleiros · Alhandra · Alverca · Samora Correia
São João das Lampas · Montelavar · Almargem do Bispo
Colares · Sintra · Loures · Odivelas · Sacavém · a Moscavide
CABO DA ROCA · Queluz · Amadora · Alcochete
Alcabideche · Barcarena · Carnaxide
Estoril · Cascais · Oeiras · LISBON (Lisboa) · Montijo
ATLANTIC OCEAN · Costa de Caparica · Barreiro · Moita · Pinhal Novo
Seixal · Altos Vedros
Coina · Palmela
Setúbal
Ba. de Setúbal
Sesimbra · Comporta
CABO ESPICHEL · Rio Sado

c — NAPLES (Scale 1:1 000 000)

Frattamaggiore · Acerra · Nola · Avellino
Afragola · Pomigliano d'Arco · Monteforte Irpino
Marano di Napoli · Somma Vesuviana
NAPLES (Napoli) · Vesuvio 4190 · S. Giuseppe Vesuviano 3710
Pozzuoli · Portici · Sarno · Mercato
Bacoli · C. MISENO · Torre del Greco · S. Severino
I. DI PROCIDA · Procida · Torre Annunziata · Nocera Inf.
Forio 2585 · Ischia · Pompeii Ruins · Angri · Cava dei Tirreni
I. D'ISCHIA · Golfo di Napoli · Castellammare di Stabia · Gragnano · Salerno
TYRRHENIAN SEA · Sorrento · 4734 · Amalfi
I. DI CAPRI · 1932 · Capri · PUNTA CAMPANELLA · Golfo di Salerno

d — ROME (Scale 1:1 000 000)

Pyrgi · Caere · Veio · Monterotondo
Cerveteri · Mentana · Guidonia
Ladispoli · ROME (Roma) · Tivoli · Villa Adriana
VATICAN CITY · Zagarolo
Fregene · Frascati
Fiumicino · Marino · COLLI ALBANI 3114
Ostia Antica · Albano Laziale · Genzano di Roma
Lido di Roma · Laurentum · Pomezia · Velletri
TYRRHENIAN SEA · AGRO PONTINO · Aprilia · Cisterna di Latina
Lanuvio
Anzio · Nettuno

Continued on pages 148-149
Continued on pages 150-151

BRENNER PASS

AUSTRIA

SWITZERLAND

CARNIC ALPS

Merano
Bressanone
Lienz
Villach
Klagenfurt
Dravograd
Murska Sobota
Maribor
Ptuj
Čakovec

RHAETIAN ALPS
Bolzano
Pieve di Cadore
Tolmezzo
KARAWANKEN
Kranj
Celje
Koprivnica
Szigetvár

Jungfrau
13 642
St. Moritz
ALPI LEPONTINE
TRENTINO-ALTO ADIGE
DOLOMITI
FRIULI-VENEZIA GIULIA
Idrija
Kobarid
Škofja Loka
LJUBLJANA
SLOVENIA
Krško
Brežice
Virovitica
Bjelovar

Sion
Locarno
Lecco
Sondrio
Trento
Feltre
Belluno
Vittorio
Pordenone
Udine
Gorizia
Monfalcone
Postojna
Cerknica
Zagreb
Čazma
Kutina

Matterhorn
Bellinzona
Como
Bergamo
Tirano
Rovereto
Schio
Conegliano
San Vito al Tagliamento
G. of Trieste
Trieste
Rijeka (Fiume)
Karlovac
Sisak
Petrinja
Slavonska Požega

Monte Rosa
15 203
Varallo
Varese
Cantù
Rovato
Bassano del Grappa
Vicenza
Citadella
Mestre
Pirano
ISTRA
Pazin
Poreč
CROATIA
Bosanska Dubica
Bosanski Novi
Prijedor

Gran Paradiso
13 323
Biella
Monza
Brescia
Chiari
Padova (Padua)
Este
Venice (Venezia)
Gulf of Venice
Pula
KRK
Krk
Senj
Bihać

Levanna
11 860
Novara
MILAN (Milano)
Legnano
Magenta
Cremona
Mantova (Mantua)
Rovigo
Chioggia
Cavarzere
Rovinj
CRES
RAB
Bosanski Petrovac
Ključ

Aosta
Busto Arsizio
Gallarate
Lodi
Crema
Codogno
Adria
Copparo
LOŠINJ
Veli Lošinj
PAG
Gospić
Banja Luka

Borgomanero
Vercelli
Abbiategrasso
Vigevano
Pavia
Piacenza
Guastalla
Viadana
Ferrara
Comacchio
MOLAT
Karlobag
Gračac
BOSNA

TURIN (Torino)
Chivasso
Trino
Mortara
Casale
Monferrato
Parma
Reggio nell'Emilia
Carpi
Modena
Valli di Comacchio
DUGI OTOK
Zadar
Benkovac
Knin
Glamoč
Donji Vakuf

Pinerolo
Chieri
Asti
Alessandria
Tortona
Voghera
Casalmaggiore
Borgo Val di Taro
Pontremoli
Bologna
Ravenna
Lugo
Imola
Faenza
Forlì
Cesena
Rimini

Carmagnola
Saluzzo
Acqui
Novi Ligure
Alba
Genoa (Genova)
EMILIA ROMAGNA
Firenzuola
San Marino
Pesaro
Fano
Senigallia
Ancona

Fossano
Cuneo
Mondovì
Savona
Rapallo
Chiavari
Sestri Levante
La Spezia
Carrara
Massa
Viareggio
Lucca
Pistoia
Prato
Florence (Firenze)
Pesia
Copannori
Urbino
Fossombrone
Jesi
Osimo
Recanati
Macerata
Fermo

MARITIME ALPS
FRANCE
Albenga
Imperia
S. Remo
Ventimiglia
MONACO
Nice
LIGURIAN SEA
ISOLA DI GORGONA
Pisa
Pontedera
Empoli
Montevarchi
Arezzo
Città di Castello
Gubbio
Fabriano
MARCHE
San Benedetto del Tronto

DINARA

ADRIATIC

CAPRAIA
ISOLA DI CAPRARA
Volterra
Siena
Poggibonsi
Cortona
Perugia
Assisi
Foligno
Spoleto
Ascoli Piceno
Trogir
Šibenik
Split
DALMATIA
SOLTA
BRAČ
HVAR
VIS
BIŠEVO
KORČULA
LASTOVO

C. CORSE
Bastia
Piombino
Portoferraio
ISOLA D'ELBA
PIANOSA
Grosseto
Massa Marittima
Montepulciano
TOSCANA
Orvieto
UMBRIA
Terni
Rieti
Teramo
Penne
Pescara
PALAGRUŽA (Yugo.)

Calvi
Corte
Mt. Cinto
8828
I. DI MONTECRISTO
I. DEL GIGLIO
Orbetello
Lago di Bolsena
Viterbo
L'Aquila
Mt. Corno 9554
Chieti
Vasto
PIANOSA
ISOLE TREMITI

CORSICA (Fr.)
Ajaccio
Mt. Incudine
6962
I. DI GIANNUTRI
Tarquinia (Corneto)
Civitavecchia
C. Linaro
Tivoli
ABRUZZI
Avezzano
Sulmona
Mt. 9163
MOLISE
Agnone
Termoli
Vieste
TESTA DEL GARGANO
Monte Sant'Angelo
San Marco

Santene
Porto-Vecchio
Bonifacio
Strait of Bonifacio
VATICAN CITY
ROME (Roma)
Frascati
Albano Laziale
Guidonia
Frosinone
Sora
Cassino
Isernia
Larino
Lucera
Campobasso
San Severo
Manfredonia
Golfo di Manfredonia
Foggia

CAPRARA PT.
ASINARA
Golfo dell'Asinara
Tempio Pausania
Olbia
Aprilia
Velletri
Ferentino
Minturno
Gaeta
Capua
Benevento
Ariano
Lavello
Spinazzola
Gravina
Altamura
Cerignola
Andria
Barletta
Trani
Molfetta
Bari

Porto Torres
Sassari
Ozieri
C. COMINO
Anzio
Sabaudia
Terracina
Golfo di Gaeta
ISOLE PONZIANE
Santa Maria Capua
Caserta
Aversa
Avellino
Potenza
Matera
Corato
Bitonto

Alghero
Bonorva
Nuoro
Dorgali
Golfo di Orosei
ISOLA D'ISCHIA
NAPLES (Napoli)
Pozzuoli
Vesuvio 4190
Salerno
CAMPANIA
Altamura
BASILICATA
Taranto

Bosa
Cuglieri
SARDINIA (It.)
Punta la Marmora 6017
Lanusei
TYRRHENIAN SEA
I. DI CAPRI
Torre del Greco
Sorrento
Golfo di Salerno
Eboli
Consilina
Pisticci
Moliterno

Oristano
Golfo di Oristano
Arborea
Villacidro
Iglesias
Carloforte
I. DI S. PIETRO
I. DI S. ANTIOCO
Cagliari
Quartu Sant'Elena
C. CARBONARA
C. SPARTIVENTO
Golfo di Policastro
Castrovillari
Corigliano
Rossano
CALABRIA
Cosenza
San Giovanni in Fiore

a

AKRA SPATHA
Kólpos Kissámou
AEGEAN SEA
DIA
Iráklion (Candia)
AKRA SIDHEROS
Same scale as main map
Golfo di Sant'Eufemia
STROMBOLI (VOL.)
Vibo Valentia
Catanzaro

Kíssamos
Khaniá
Réthimnon
CRETE (Greece)
Neápolis
Sitía
ISOLE EOLIE
FILICUDI
SALINA
LIPARI
PANAREA
VATICANO
Polistena
Palmi
Caulonia
Siderno Marina

Khóra Sfakíon
CRETE
Áno Viánnos
Ierápetra
VULCANO
ALICUDI
Milazzo
Messina
Reggio di Calabria
C. SPARTIVENTO

MEDITERRANEAN SEA
AKRA LÍTHINON
GÁVDHOS
I. DI USTICA
Carini
Palermo
Monreale
Bagheria
Cefalù
Termini
Mistretta
Taormina
Acireale
Catania

Trapani
ISOLE EGADI
Alcamo
Partinico
Corleone
Salemi
Lercara Friddi
Leonforte
Adrano
Mt. Etna 10 902
Paternò

Marsala
Mazara del Vallo
Castelvetrano
Sciacca
Agrigento
Canicattì
Caltanissetta
Piazza Armerina
Caltagirone
Augusta
SICILY (It.)
Enna
Gela

Scale 1:4 000 000; one inch to 64 miles. Conic Projection
Elevations and depressions are given in feet

Relief

Feet	Meters
5000	1525
2000	610
1000	305
500	152.5
Sea Level 0	0
500	152.5

Continued on pages 146-147

Cities and Towns

0 to 50,000   500,000 to 1,000,000

50,000 to 500,000   1,000,000 and over

Scale 1:4 000 000; one inch to 64 miles. Conic Projection
Elevations and depressions are given in feet

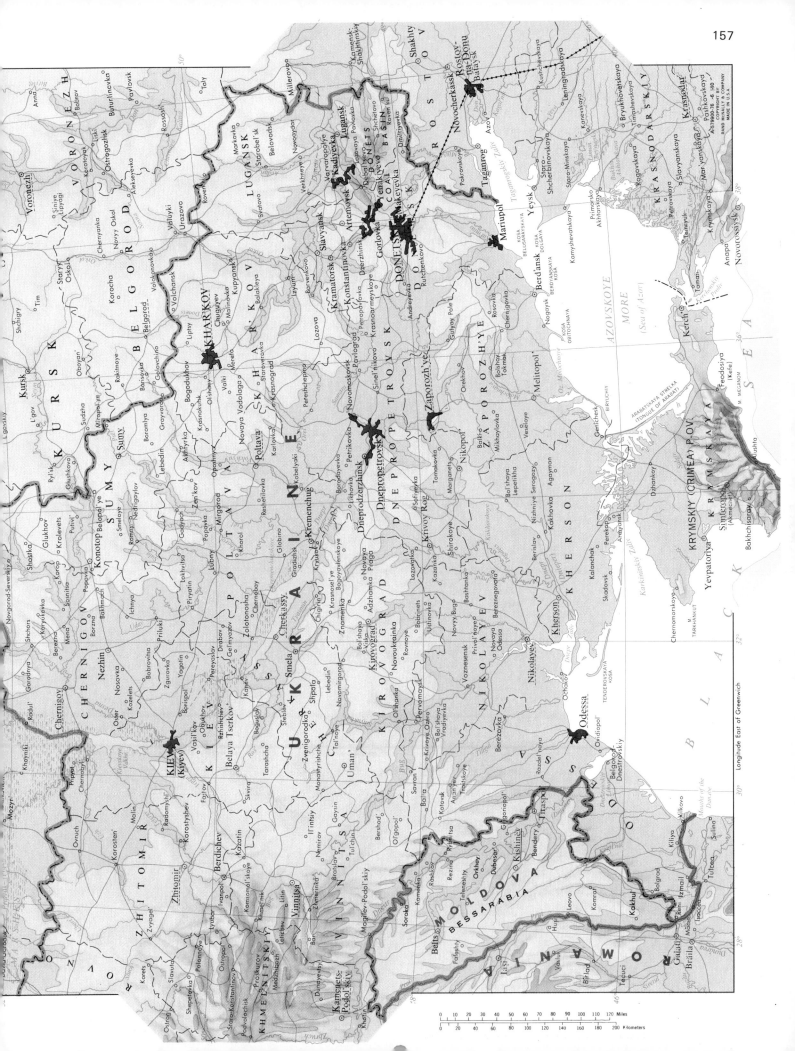

Scale 1:20 000 000; one inch to 315 miles.
Lambert's Azimuthal, Equal Area Projection
Elevations and depressions are given in feet

Cities
and
Towns

0 to 50,000   500,000 to 1,000,000
50,000 to 500,000   1,000,000 and over

Relief

Feet
10000
5000
2000
1000
500
0
Sea Level
500
5000
10000

Meters
3050
1525
610
305
152.5
0
Sea Level
152.5
1525
3050

0   50   100   150   200   250   300 Miles
0   100   200   300   400   500 Kilometers

Continued on pages 140-141

Scale 1:10 000 000; one inch to 160 miles. Conic Projection

Elevations and depressions are given in feet.

Continued on pages 142-143

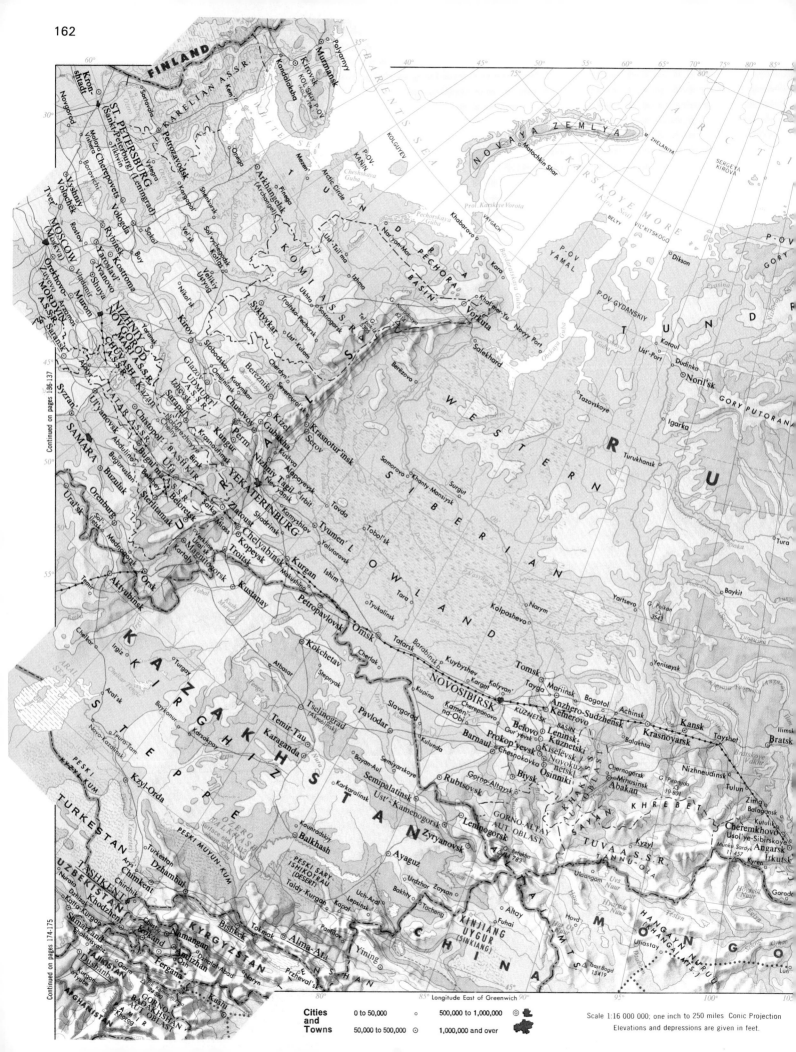

FINLAND

KARELIAN A.S.S.R.

Murmansk
Polyarnny
Kirovsk
KOL'SKIY P-OV

BARENTS SEA

NOVAYA ZEMLYA
M. ZHELANIYA
Matochkin Shar
KARSKOYE MORE
SERGEYA KIROVA

Kron-
shtadt
ST. PETERSBURG
(Sankt-Peterburg) (Leningrad)
Novgorod

KOLGUYEV
P-OV KANIN

KARA
P-OV YAMAL
Dikson

T U N D R A

Murmansk

ARCTIC

GORY

KARSKOYE MORE

Arctic Circle

Nar'yan-Mar
PECHORA BASIN
Vorkuta

Salekhard

Ust'-Port
Dudinka
Noril'sk

TUNDRA

GORY PUTORANA

MOSCOW
(Moskva)
Tver'
Vyshniy Volochëk

NIZHNIY NOVGOROD
MARI A.S.S.R.
CHUVASH A.S.S.R.

KOMI A.S.S.R.

Syktyvkar

Ukhta

W E S T E R N

S I B E R I A N

L O W L A N D

Turukhansk

R U

Igarka

Tazovskoye

Surgut

Khanty-Mansiysk

YEKATERINBURG
Perm
Nizhny Tagil

Chelyabinsk
Magnitogorsk

U R A L

Tyumen'
Tobol'sk

Omsk

Kolpashevo

Narym

Baykit

G. Polkan
3543

SAMARA
UDMURT A.S.S.R.
TATAR A.S.S.R.
BASHKIR A.S.S.R.

Ufa

Orenburg

Aktyubinsk

Kurgan
Petropavlovsk

Tomsk

NOVOSIBIRSK

Tatarsk

Kuybyshev

Kemerovo
Anzhero-Sudzhensk
Achinsk
Kansk
Krasnoyarsk

Tayshet
Bratsk

Yeniseysk

ARAL SEA

K A Z A K H

K I R G I Z

S T E P P E

Kokchetav

Pavlodar

Barnaul
Biysk

Kuznetsk
BASIN

Abakan
Minusinsk

Nizhneudinsk

Tulun

Zima

TURKESTAN

UZBEKISTAN
TASHKENT

PESKI KYZYL-KUM

Kzyl-Orda

Karaganda

Balkhash

Semipalatinsk
Ust'-Kamenogorsk
Zyryanovsk
Leninogorsk

GORNO-ALTAY
AUT. OBLAST

KHAKASS
AUT. OBLAST

TUVA A.S.S.R.
TANNU-OLA

Kyzyl

Cheremkhovo
Usol'ye-Sibirskoye
Angarsk
Irkutsk

Bishkek
Alma-Ata

KYRGYZSTAN

Yining

XINJIANG
UYGUR
(SINKIANG)

C H I N A

M O N G O

HANGAYN NURUU
(HANGAY-MTS.)

Dushanbe

TAJIKISTAN

GORNO-
BADAKHSHAN
AUT. OBLAST

AFGHANISTAN

Kashi

Continued on pages 136-137

Continued on pages 174-175

85° Longitude East of Greenwich 90°

**Cities
and
Towns**

0 to 50,000
50,000 to 500,000
500,000 to 1,000,000
1,000,000 and over

Scale 1:16 000 000; one inch to 250 miles Conic Projection
Elevations and depressions are given in feet.

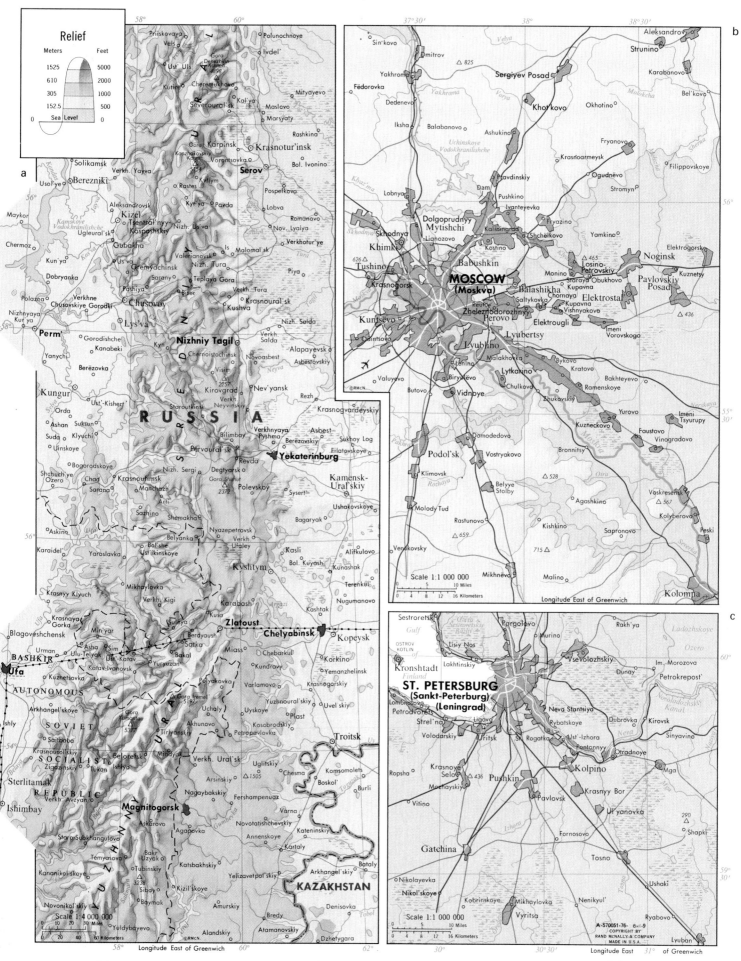

Relief

Meters	Feet
1525	5000
610	2000
305	1000
152.5	500
0 Sea Level	0

a

b

c

RUSSIA

Perm'

Yekaterinburg

Chelyabinsk

Ufa

BASHKIR AUTONOMOUS SOVIET SOCIALIST REPUBLIC

Magnitogorsk

KAZAKHSTAN

Scale 1:4 000 000

MOSCOW (Moskva)

Scale 1:1 000 000

Longitude East of Greenwich

ST. PETERSBURG (Sankt-Peterburg) (Leningrad)

Kronshtadt

Scale 1:1 000 000

Longitude East of Greenwich

A-570051-76- 6- 9
COPYRIGHT BY
RAND MNALLY & COMPANY
MADE IN U.S.A.

Longitude East of Greenwich

Cities and Towns

0 to 50,000	○	500,000 to 1,000,000 ◎
50,000 to 500,000	⊙	1,000,000 and over

For larger scale coverage of Moscow and St. Petersburg see page 235.

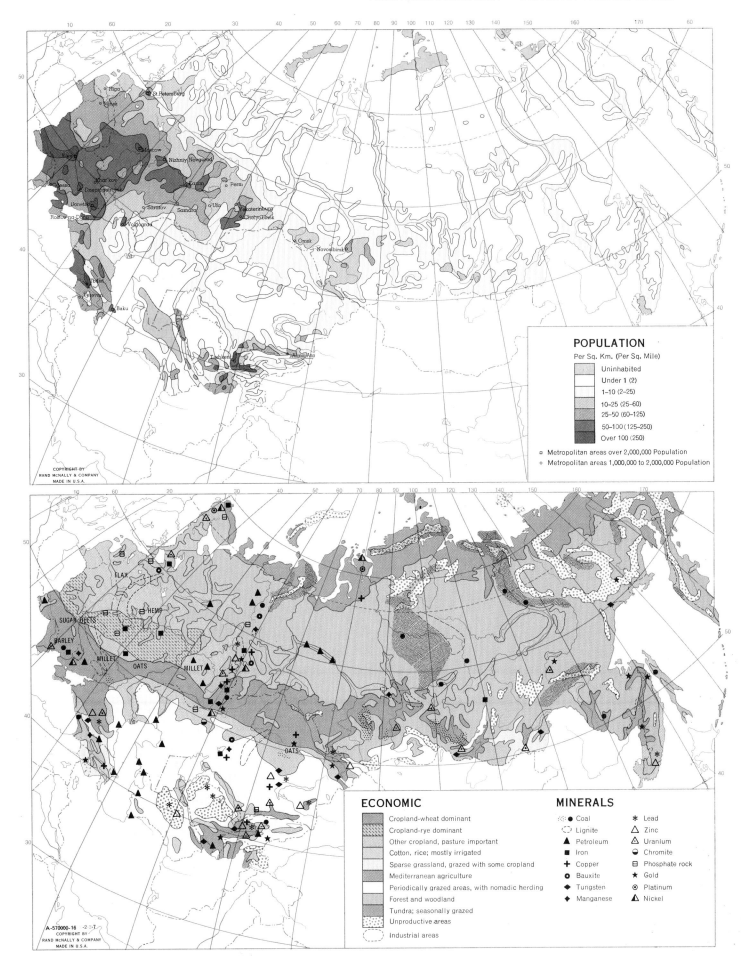

POPULATION

Per Sq. Km. (Per Sq. Mile)

- Uninhabited
- Under 1 (2)
- 1–10 (2–25)
- 10–25 (25–60)
- 25–50 (60–125)
- 50–100 (125–250)
- Over 100 (250)

▫ Metropolitan areas over 2,000,000 Population

○ Metropolitan areas 1,000,000 to 2,000,000 Population

COPYRIGHT BY
RAND McNALLY & COMPANY
MADE IN U.S.A.

ECONOMIC

- Cropland-wheat dominant
- Cropland-rye dominant
- Other cropland, pasture important
- Cotton, rice; mostly irrigated
- Sparse grassland, grazed with some cropland
- Mediterranean agriculture
- Periodically grazed areas, with nomadic herding
- Forest and woodland
- Tundra; seasonally grazed
- Unproductive areas
- Industrial areas

MINERALS

- ● Coal
- ◌ Lignite
- ▲ Petroleum
- ■ Iron
- ✚ Copper
- ◎ Bauxite
- ◆ Tungsten
- ◆ Manganese
- ✳ Lead
- △ Zinc
- △ Uranium
- ◖ Chromite
- ▤ Phosphate rock
- ★ Gold
- ◉ Platinum
- △ Nickel

A-570000-16 -2-3-7
COPYRIGHT BY
RAND McNALLY & COMPANY
MADE IN U.S.A.

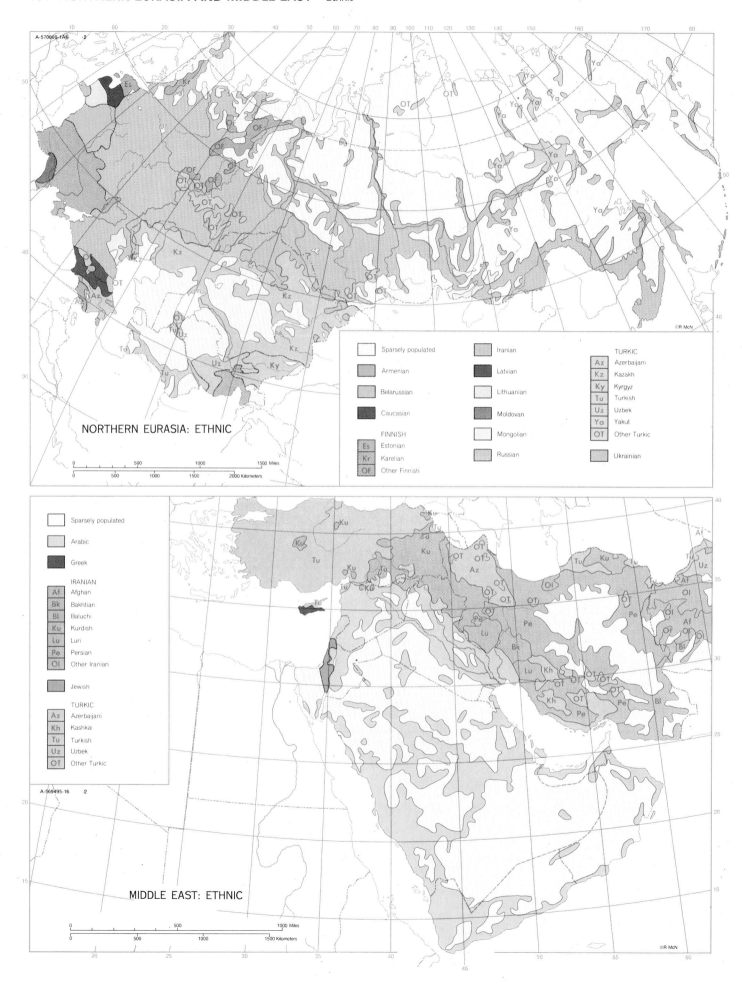

NORTHERN EURASIA: ETHNIC

MIDDLE EAST: ETHNIC

Sparsely populated
Armenian
Belarussian
Caucasian

FINNISH
Es Estonian
Kr Karelian
OF Other Finnish

Iranian
Latvian
Lithuanian
Moldovan
Mongolian
Russian

TURKIC
Az Azerbaijani
Kz Kazakh
Ky Kyrgyz
Tu Turkish
Uz Uzbek
Ya Yakut
OT Other Turkic

Ukrainian

Sparsely populated
Arabic
Greek

IRANIAN
Af Afghan
Bk Bakhtiari
Bl Baluchi
Ku Kurdish
Lu Luri
Pe Persian
OI Other Iranian

Jewish

TURKIC
Az Azerbaijani
Kh Kashkai
Tu Turkish
Uz Uzbek
OT Other Turkic

0   500   1000   1500 Miles
0   500   1000   1500   2000 Kilometers

0   500   1000 Miles
0   500   1000   1500 Kilometers

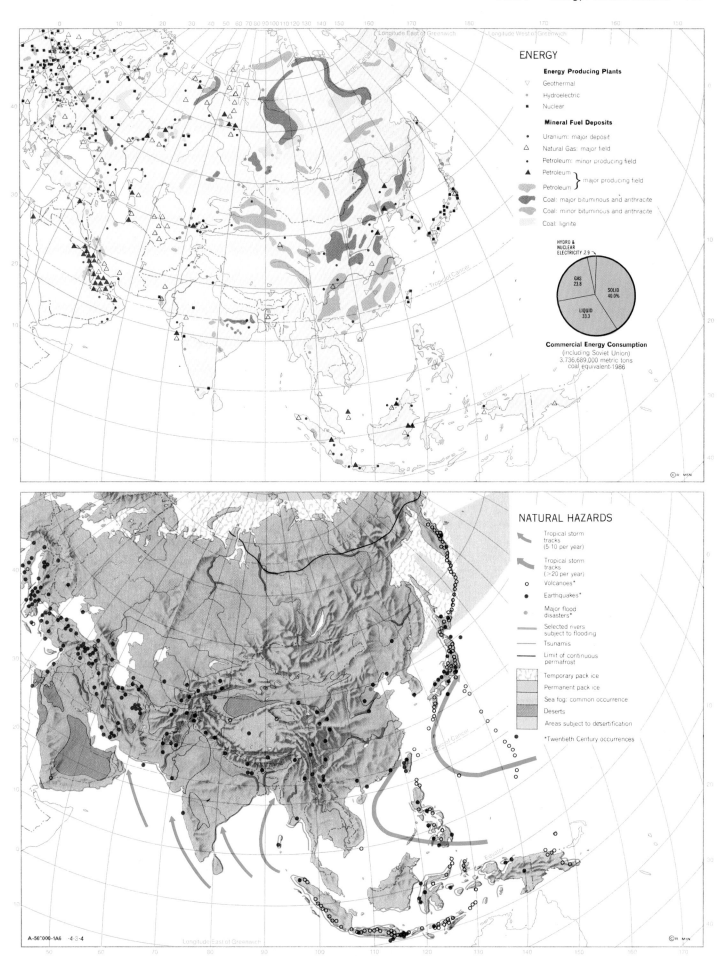

ENERGY

Energy Producing Plants

▽ Geothermal
● Hydroelectric
■ Nuclear

Mineral Fuel Deposits

• Uranium: major deposit
△ Natural Gas: major field
• Petroleum: minor producing field
▲ Petroleum: major producing field
▲ Petroleum } major producing field
    Coal: major bituminous and anthracite
    Coal: minor bituminous and anthracite
    Coal: lignite

HYDRO &
NUCLEAR
ELECTRICITY 2.9

GAS
23.8

SOLID
40.0%

LIQUID
33.3

Commercial Energy Consumption
(including Soviet Union)
3,736,689,000 metric tons
coal equivalent-1986

NATURAL HAZARDS

⬆ Tropical storm
  tracks
  (5-10 per year)

⬆ Tropical storm
  tracks
  (>20 per year)

○ Volcanoes*

● Earthquakes*

● Major flood
  disasters*

━ Selected rivers
  subject to flooding

━ Tsunamis

━ Limit of continuous
  permafrost

    Temporary pack ice

    Permanent pack ice

    Sea fog: common occurrence

    Deserts

    Areas subject to desertification

● *Twentieth Century occurrences

A-56?000-1A6 -4-3-4

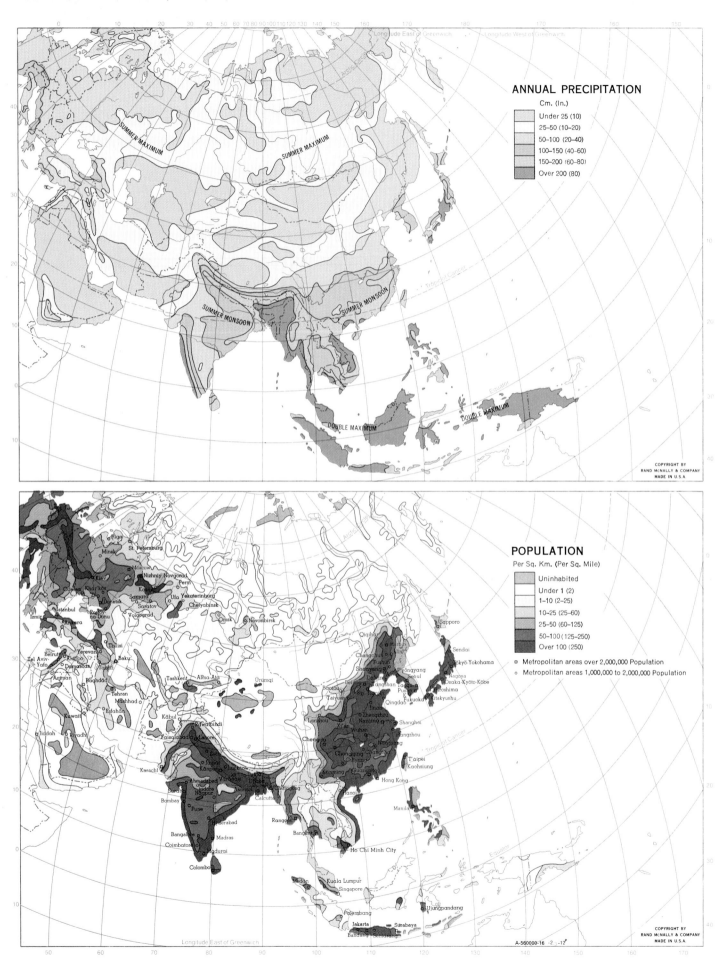

ANNUAL PRECIPITATION

Cm. (In.)

Under 25 (10)
25–50 (10–20)
50–100 (20–40)
100–150 (40–60)
150–200 (60–80)
Over 200 (80)

COPYRIGHT BY
RAND MCNALLY & COMPANY
MADE IN U.S.A.

POPULATION

Per Sq. Km. (Per Sq. Mile)

Uninhabited
Under 1 (2)
1–10 (2–25)
10–25 (25–60)
25–50 (60–125)
50–100 (125–250)
Over 100 (250)

▫ Metropolitan areas over 2,000,000 Population
◦ Metropolitan areas 1,000,000 to 2,000,000 Population

COPYRIGHT BY
RAND MCNALLY & COMPANY
MADE IN U.S.A.

A-560000-16 -2 -12

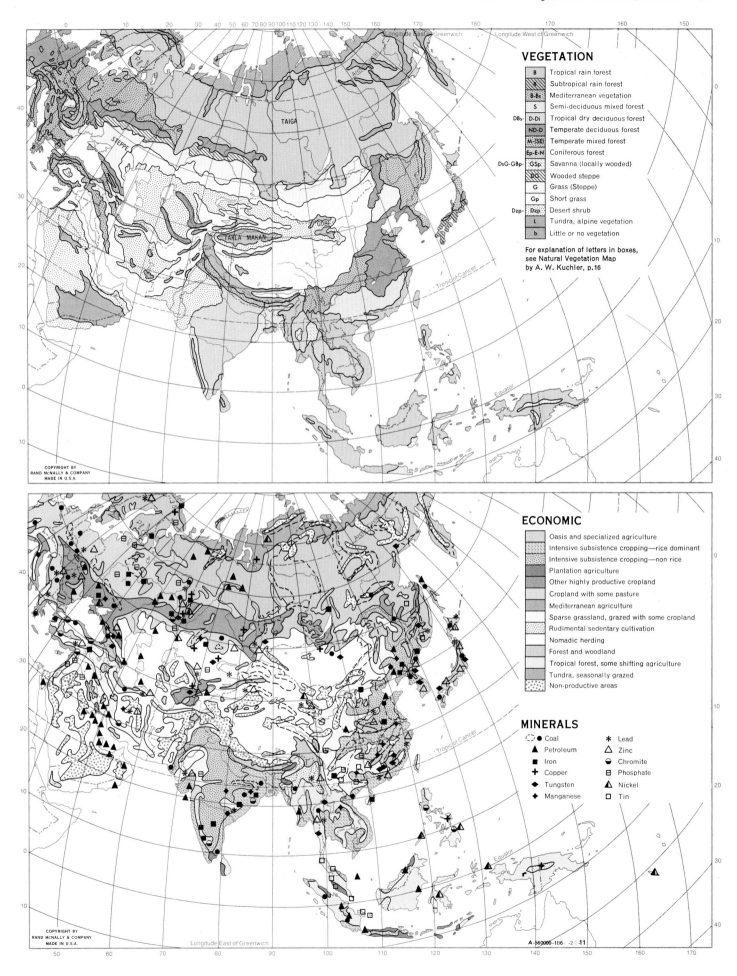

VEGETATION

	B	Tropical rain forest
	b	Subtropical rain forest
	B-Bs	Mediterranean vegetation
	S	Semi-deciduous mixed forest
DBs-	D-Di	Tropical dry deciduous forest
	ND-D	Temperate deciduous forest
	M-(SE)	Temperate mixed forest
	Ep-E-N	Coniferous forest
DsG-GBp-	GSp	Savanna (locally wooded)
	DG	Wooded steppe
	G	Grass (Steppe)
	Gp	Short grass
Dzp-	Dzp	Desert shrub
	L	Tundra, alpine vegetation
	b	Little or no vegetation

For explanation of letters in boxes,
see Natural Vegetation Map
by A. W. Kuchler, p.16

COPYRIGHT BY
RAND MCNALLY & COMPANY
MADE IN U.S.A.

ECONOMIC

	Oasis and specialized agriculture
	Intensive subsistence cropping—rice dominant
	Intensive subsistence cropping—non rice
	Plantation agriculture
	Other highly productive cropland
	Cropland with some pasture
	Mediterranean agriculture
	Sparse grassland, grazed with some cropland
	Rudimental sedentary cultivation
	Nomadic herding
	Forest and woodland
	Tropical forest, some shifting agriculture
	Tundra, seasonally grazed
	Non-productive areas

MINERALS

⬭ ●	Coal		∗	Lead
▲	Petroleum		△	Zinc
■	Iron		◗	Chromite
✛	Copper		⊟	Phosphate
◆	Tungsten		◮	Nickel
✦	Manganese		☐	Tin

COPYRIGHT BY
RAND MCNALLY & COMPANY
MADE IN U.S.A.

A-560000-1B6 -2-11

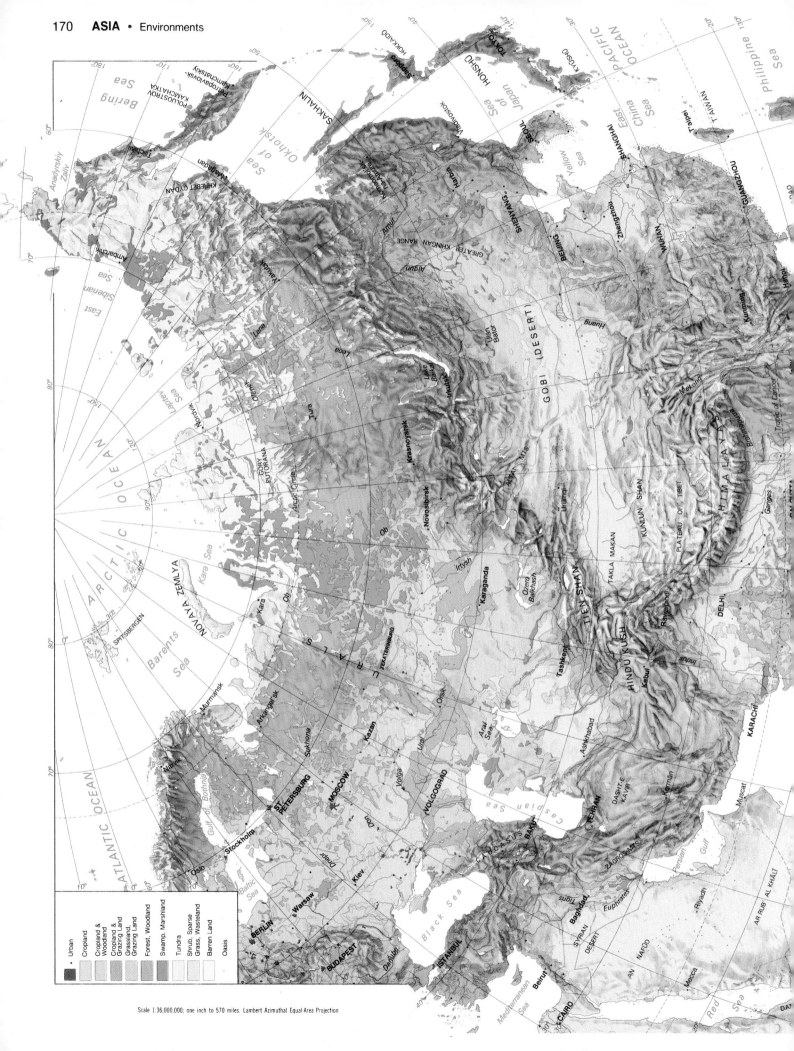

Scale 1:36,000,000; one inch to 570 miles. Lambert Azimuthal Equal-Area Projection

South China Sea

MINDANAO
Cebu
Celebes Sea
Manado
CELEBES
Ujung Pandang
Java Sea
BORNEO
Kota Kinabalu
Kuching
JAKARTA
JAVA
SUMATRA
Medan
SINGAPORE
HO CHI MINH CITY
BANGKOK
Mekong
Rangoon
Salween
Andaman Sea
Bay of Bengal
Equator
SRI LANKA
MADRAS
Colombo
Callcut
WESTERN GHATS
EASTERN GHATS
BOMBAY
Arabian Sea
INDIAN OCEAN
Aden
Gulf of Aden
Berbera

A-560000-36 -4- -43
COPYRIGHT BY
RAND M9NALLY & COMPANY
MADE IN U.S.A.

| 0 | 100 | 200 | 400 | 600 | 800 Miles |

| 0 | 150 | 300 | 600 | 900 | 1200 Kilometers |

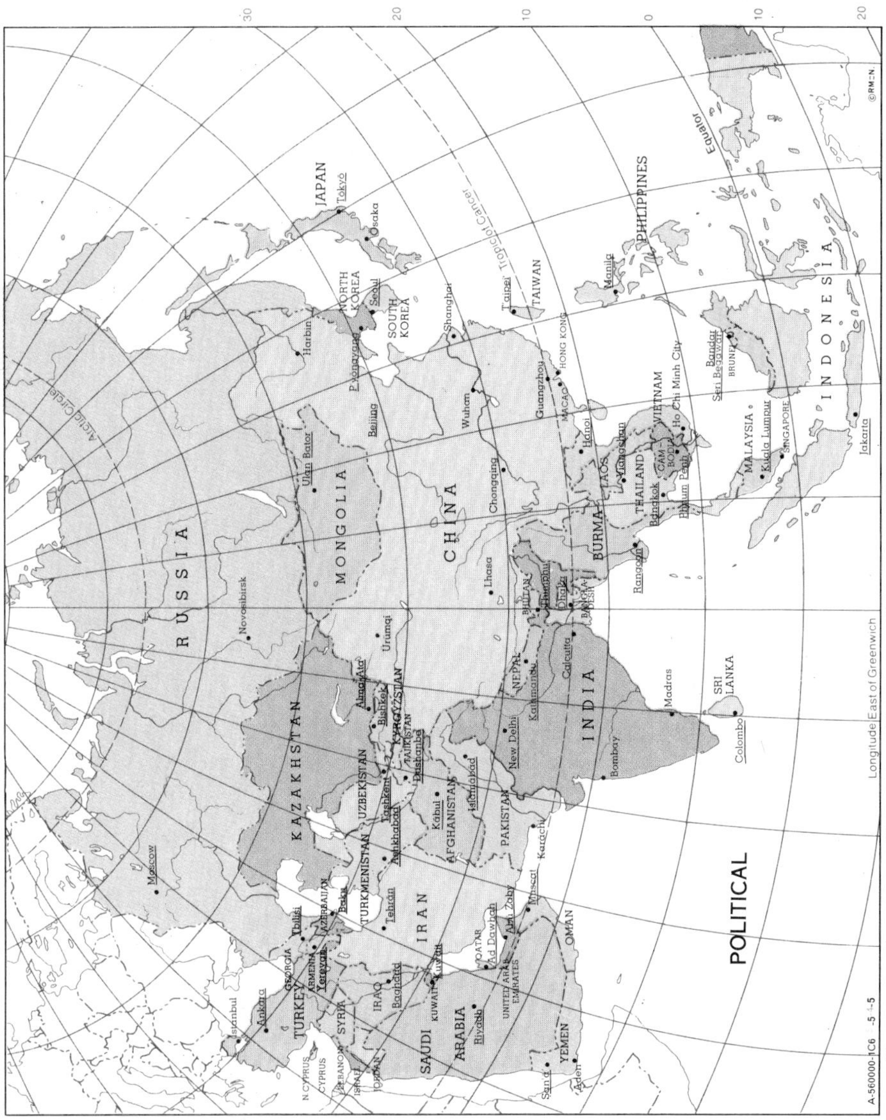

POLITICAL

JAPAN
Tōkyō
Ōsaka
NORTH KOREA
Pyongyang
SOUTH KOREA
Seoul
RUSSIA
Novosibirsk
MONGOLIA
Ulan Bator
Harbin
CHINA
Beijing
Shanghai
Urumqi
Wuhan
Chongqing
Guangzhou
HONG KONG
MACAO
TAIWAN
Taipei
PHILIPPINES
Manila
Moscow
KAZAKHSTAN
Almaty
UZBEKISTAN
KYRGYZSTAN
TAJIKISTAN
TURKMENISTAN
Ashkhabad
Tashkent
Dushanbe
Bishkek
Lhasa
NEPAL
Kathmandu
BHUTAN
BANGLADESH
Dhaka
Calcutta
INDIA
New Delhi
Bombay
Madras
SRI LANKA
Colombo
BURMA
Rangoon
THAILAND
Bangkok
LAOS
Vientiane
CAMB.
Phnom Penh
VIETNAM
Ho Chi Minh City
MALAYSIA
Kuala Lumpur
SINGAPORE
BRUNEI
Bandar Seri Begawan
INDONESIA
Jakarta
Equator
AFGHANISTAN
Kabul
PAKISTAN
Islamabad
Karachi
IRAN
Tehran
GEORGIA
ARMENIA
AZERBAIJAN
Baku
Tbilisi
Yerevan
TURKEY
Ankara
Istanbul
CYPRUS
N. CYPRUS
LEBANON
Beirut
SYRIA
ISRAEL
Damascus
JORDAN
IRAQ
Baghdad
KUWAIT
Kuwait
SAUDI ARABIA
Riyadh
BAHRAIN
QATAR
UNITED ARAB EMIRATES
Ad Dawhah
Abu Zaby
OMAN
Muscat
YEMEN
Aden
Sanaa
Tropic of Cancer
Longitude East of Greenwich

A-560000-1C6 -5- -5

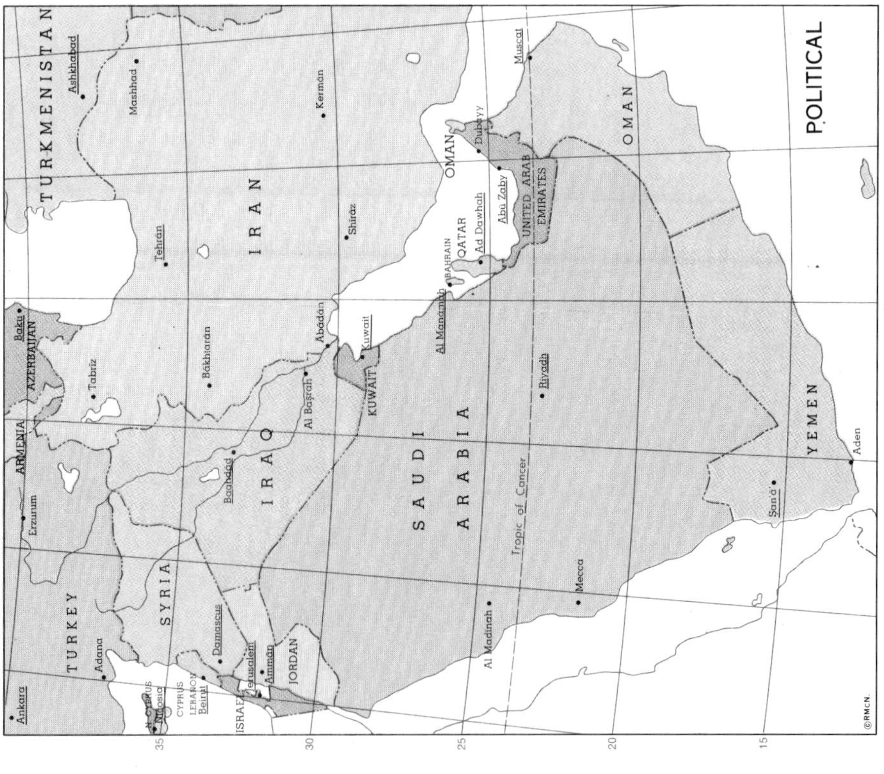

POLITICAL

TURKMENISTAN
Ashkhabad
ARMENIA
AZERBAIJAN
Baku
Tabriz
IRAN
Mashhad
Kerman
Tehran
Shiraz
Bakhtaran
Abadan
IRAQ
Erzurum
Basrah
Al Basrah
KUWAIT
Kuwait
OMAN
QATAR
BAHRAIN
Al Manamah
Ad Dawhah
Dubayy
Abu Zaby
UNITED ARAB EMIRATES
OMAN
Muscat
SAUDI ARABIA
Riyadh
Mecca
Al Madinah
Tropic of Cancer
YEMEN
Aden
Sanaa
SYRIA
TURKEY
Ankara
Adana
CYPRUS
LEBANON
Beirut
ISRAEL
Jerusalem
Damascus
JORDAN
Amman

©RMcN

172

Continued on page 203

Relief

Meters	Feet
3050	10 000
1525	5000
610	2000
305	1000
Sea Level	0
152.5	500 Below Sea Level
1525	5000
3050	10 000
6100	20 000

A-519695-76
COPYRIGHT BY
RAND McNALLY & COMPANY
MADE IN U.S.A.

Longitude East of Greenwich

Scale 1:40 000 000; one inch to 630 miles. Lambert's Azimuthal, Equal Area Projection
Elevations and depressions are given in feet

Longitude 35° East of Greenwich 36°

a

CYPRUS

Néa Páfos
Episkopi
Lemesos
AKR. GÁTAS
AKR. PIDALION
Lárnax Kólpos Lárnakos

MEDITERRANEAN

SEA

Ⓐ Golan Heights area. Occupied by Israel since 1967.
Unilaterally annexed by Israel, 1981.

Ⓑ West Bank area. Unilaterally annexed by
Jordan, 1950. Occupied by Israel since 1967.
Status to be determined.

Ⓒ Gaza Strip. Occupied by Israel since 1967.
Status to be determined.

Port Said (Būr Sa'īd)

Khalīj aṭ Ṭīnah

Daphnae
(Ruins)
Ismailia
(Al Ismā'īlīyah)

Ṭarābulus
(Tripoli)
Al Qusayr
Al Hirmil
Al Batrūn
Zgharṭā
Amyūn
Jubayl (Byblos)
Jūniyah
Ba'labakk
Beirut
(Bayrūt)
Zaḥlah
Ad Dāmūr
Az Zabdānī
Ŝaydā
(Sidon)
Jazzīn
Damascus
Dūmā
(Dimashq)
Rāshayyā
Ŝūr
(Tyre)
Marj 'Uyūn
Al Kiswah
Tibnīn
Qiryat Shemona
Al Qunayṭirah
Naharīyya
Ḥare Meron 1967
Ẑefat
Al Sanamayn
'Akko
As Suwaydā'
Haifa
(Ḥefa)
Ṭeverya
Nazeret
Dar'ā
Nazerat
'Afula
Irbid
Bet She'an
Al Maṭraq
SYRIA
Ḥadera
Jenīn
Jarash
Netanya
Ṭolkarm
Shechem
(Ruins)
Herzliyya
Nābulus
Petaḥ Tiqwa
As Ŝalṭ
Tel Aviv-Yafo
Az Zarqā'
Rishon leẔiyyon
Reḥovot
Lod
Arīḥa
(Jericho)
Amman
Ashdod
Jerusalem
Ma'dabā
Bet
Leḥem
Zuwayzā
Ashqelon
Qiryat
(Bethlehem)
Gat
Al Khalīl
Dhibān
Gaza
(Hebron)
(Ghazzah)
Khān Yūnus
Be'er Sheva
Maḥaṭṭat al
Rafah
Arad
Qaṭrānah
Al Mazra'ah
Al 'Arīsh
Dimona
Al Karak
Sedom
Al Mazār
Rummānah
Ḥorvot Shivta
(Ruins)
Al Qanṭarah
Qeẑi'ot
At Ṭafīlah
Al Qusaymah
Maḥaṭṭat Jurf
ad Darāwīsh
Al Qusaymah
NEGEV
Ash Shawbak
Ra's Abū Qurūn JABAL
Petra
Fā'id
3578 △ YU'ALLIQ
Ruins
Wādī Mūsā
Ma'ān
Great Bitter
Lake
QA' AL JAFR
Süez
(As Suways)
An Nakhl
EGYPT
Ra's an Naqb
Mitla Pass
Al Kuntillah
Elat
Al 'Aqabah
Maḥaṭṭat
'Aqabat al Ḥijāzīyah
Ath Thamad
△ 3513
Jabal Ramm
5755
△ Mahaṭṭat al
Ramlah
4136
JABAL
Al Mudawwarah
JALĀLAH
AL BAHRĪYAH
JABAL AT TĪH
3789 △
Bi'r Za'farānah
JABAL AL 'AJMAH
Ra's al Junaynah
4833 △
5335
SAUDI ARABIA
JABAL AL JALĀLAT
Abū Zanīmah
Nuwaybi' al
Scale 1:4 000 000
AL QIBLĪYAH
SINAI PEN
Muzayyinah
JABAL MAZHAFAH
0 10 20 30 40 50 Miles
(SHIBH JAZĪRAT SĪNĀ')
6232 △
0 20 40 60 80 Kilometers
© RMcN

JORDAN

b

Kuala Lumpur
Kelang
SELANGOR
Kuala Klawang
Gunong Telapa
Telok Datok
3915 △ Burok
NEGERI SEMBILAN
Sepang
Rantau
Bahau
Port Dickson
Seremban
Rompin
Rembau
Tampin
Gemas
CAPE RACHADO
Alor Gajah
Jasin
MELAKA
Segamat
Gunong Besar
Mr. Ophir
3403
Melaka
4187 △
Labis
(Malacca)
Panchor
Paloh
Bandar
JOHOR
Maharani
Keluang
Gunong Blumut
3312 △
Batu
Rengam
Pahat
Ayer
Layang Layang
Hitam
Jumrah
RUPAT
Teluklecak
Pontian Kechil
Kota Tinggi
Dumai
Johor
Bahru
Bengkalis
BENGKALIS
Bukitbatu
Ketamputih
KARIMUN
Pinggir
Kudap
SINGAPORE
TANJONG PIAI
SINGAPORE
Telesung
BATAM
Minas
1837 △
KARIMUN
△ 341
BESAR
INDONESIA
Tebingtinggi
KEPULAUAN RIAU
BINTAN
SUMATRA
PADANG
Tanjungbalai
Tanjungpinang
118 △
RANGSANG
REMPANG
Buatan
Siaksriinderapura
KUNDUR
Serangung
RIAU
Baranpauh

PAHANG

TIOMAN
Gunong Kajang
3444
Padang Endau
PEMANGGIL
AUR
Mersing
2002 △
TINGGI
MALAYSIA
MALAY
PENINSULA
SOUTH
CHINA
SEA
Scale 1:4 000 000
0 10 20 30 40 50 Miles
0 20 40 60 80 Kilometers
TANJONG RAMUNIA
TANJUNG
BERAKIT
© RMcN

NORTH AMERICA
M. DEZHNEVA
(EAST CAPE)
Bering Str.
PRIBILOF IS.
(U.S.A.)
ST. LAWRENCE
WRANGELYA
(WRANGEL)
CHUKOTSKIY POV.
KORYAKSKIY KHREBET
Arctic Circle
ALEUTIAN ISLANDS
(U.S.A.)
ALEUTIAN TRENCH
West Longitude
East Longitude
East Longitude
Yakutsk
Okhotsk
Petropavlovsk-Kamchatsky
KAMCHATKA
P-OV KAMCHATKA
M. LOPATKA
KOMANDORSKIYE OSTROVA
(Sov. Union)
KHREBET DZHUGDZHUR
STANOVOY KHREBET
SEA OF OKHOTSK
SAKHALIN
KURIL ISLANDS
(Sov. Union)
Komsomolsk
HOKKAIDO TRENCH
Blagoveshchensk
Sovetskaya Gavan
Hakodate
Khabarovsk
SIKHOTE ALIN
Vladivostok
Sendai
Nerchinsk
STANOVOY KHREBET
MANCHURIA
HARBIN
CHANGCHUN
Jilin
SEA OF JAPAN
HONSHŪ
TOKYO
SHENYANG
KOREA
KYOTO
YOKOHAMA
Zhangjiakou
Pyongyang
NORTH
KOBE
OSAKA
BEIJING
SEOUL
KYOTO
SOUTH
KITAKYŪSHŪ
SHIKOKU
Nagasaki
TIANJIN
Jinan
Dalian
KYŪSHŪ
TAIYUAN
QINGDAO
NANSEI SHOTŌ
XI'AN
NANJING
SHANGHAI
QIN LING
EAST
CHINA
WUHAN
SEA
Yichang
Tropic of Cancer
Changsha
NAN LING
TAIPEI
Fuzhou
Taiwan Strait
TAIWAN
(FORMOSA)
GUANGZHOU
Xiamen
Shantou
HONG KONG
Wuzhou
(Br.)
Macao
BABUYAN IS.
(Port.)
HAINAN DAO
LUZON
Quezon City
MANILA
PHILIPPINES
SAMAR
MINDORO
LEYTE
HO CHI
PANAY
NEGROS
PHILIPPINE
MINH CITY
PALAWAN
TRENCH
(Saigon)
MINDANAO
MUI BAI BUNG
Kota Kinabalu
SULU IS.
Sandakan
Equator
HALMAHERA
CELEBES SEA
NEW
GUINEA
BRUNEI
BORNEO
CELEBES
Kuching
MALAYSIA
SINGAPORE
INDONESIA

0 200 400 600 800 1000 Miles
0 400 800 1200 1600 Kilometers

BLACK SEA

Istanbul Boğazı (Bosporus)
Marmara Denizi
ISTANBUL
Mitilini
İzmir
Bergama
Kütahya
Bursa
Eskişehir
Ankara
Zonguldak
Kastamonu
Sinop
Samsun
Merzifon
Çorum
Yozgat
Tokat
Sivas
Giresun
Trabzon
RÓDHOS
Aydın
Isparta
Muğla
Afyon
Konya
Kayseri
Kahramanmaraş
TOROS DAĞLARI
Antalya
Icel
Tarsus
Adana
İskenderun
Antakya
Malatya
Elâzığ
Diyarbakır
Urfa
Gaziantep
Siverek
Mardin
Cizre

T U R K E Y

CAUCASUS MTS
RUSSIA
Groznyy
Fort Shevchenko
Vladikavkaz
Makhachkala
Snevchenko
MANGYSHLAK
KAZAK
ARAL SEA
UZBEKISTAN
Kungrad
Chimbay
Nukus
Turtkul
Khiva
Bukhara
PESKI KYZYLK (DESERT)
Kutaisi
Poti
Batumi
GEORGIA
Tbilisi
Leninakan
Kars
ARMENIA
Yerevan
AZERBAIJAN
Gyandzha
Baku
Derbent
CASPIAN SEA
PLATO UST-URT
Zal Kara-Bogaz-Gol
TURKMENISTAN
Nebit-Dag
Ashkhabad
Chardzhou
Mary
KOPPEH DAGH
Bojnurd
KURDISTAN
Erzurum
Erzincan
Van
Tabriz
Ardabil
Lenkoran
Bandar-e Anzali
Rasht
Bandar-e Torkeman
Gorgan
Emamshahr
Neyshabur
Mashhad
Meymaneh
AFGHA
Herat
PARO

Nicosia
NORTH CYPRUS
CYPRUS
MEDITERRANEAN SEA
Al Mawşil
As Sulaymaniyah
Irbil
Kirkūk
Orūmiyeh
Zanjān
Sanandaj
Qazvin
Qal'eh-ye
ELBURZ MTS
TEHRAN
Damāvand
Dāmghān
Ferdows
Bajestan
Qayen
Birjand

Ṭarābulus (Tripoli)
LEBANON
Beirut
Şaydā (Sidon)
ISRAEL
Haifa
Tel Aviv-Yafo
Jerusalem
Gaza
Ladhiqiyah (Latakia)
Hims
Hamah
Dayr az Zawr
Al Furat
SYRIA
Palmyra (Ruins)
Abū Kamāl
Tikrit
Nineveh
Aleppo
Damascus (Dimashq)
As Suwayda
Amman
Ar Ramādī
BAGHDAD
Karbalā
An Najaf
Babylon (Ruins)
Hamadān
Bakhtarān
Qom
Arāk
Borūjerd
Kāshān
Dezfūl
Shūshtar
Masjed-e Soleymān
Esfahān
Qomsheh
Yazd
Bāfq
PLATEAU OF IRAN
DASHT-E KAVIR DESERT
Daryācheh-ye Namak

I R A N

Areas occupied by Israel since 1967
Rashīd
Damietta
Port Saïd
ALEXANDRIA (Al Iskandariyah)
CAIRO (Al Qāhirah)
Suez (As Suways)
SINAI
PEN Elat
JORDAN
Ma'ān
Al 'Aqabah
GULF OF SUEZ
Jabal Shār
Al Jawf
Sakākah
Rafha
An Nāşiriyah
Al Başrah
Khorramshahr
Ābādān
Bandar-e Khomeyni
Ahvāz
KUWAIT
Kuwait (Al Kuwayt)
Al Qaysūmah
Shiraz
Kāzerūn
Borāzjān
Bandar-e Būshehr
Persepolis (Ruins)
Kermān
Zāhedān
CHAGAI HILL
Khāsh
Bampūr
Rigān

EGYPT
Bür Safājah
Al Qusayr
RA'S BANAS
Taymā
Khaybar
Jabal Radwa
Al Madinah (Medina)
Unayzah
Sudair
Ash Shaqrā
Al Hufūf
Ad Dammam
Az Zahrān (Dhahran)
Al Qatif
BAHRAIN
Al Manāmah
QATAR
Ad Dawhah
Abū Zaby
UNITED ARAB EMIRATES
Al Buraymi
JABAL AL AKHDAR
Matrah
Muscat
GULF OF OMAN
Bandar Beheshtī
Gwādar
Jāsk
Bandar-e 'Abbās
Qeshm
QESHM
Str. of Hormuz
Bandar-e Lengeh

S A U D I
A R A B I A
N A J D
AL HASĀ
AD DAHNĀ
AN NAFŪD
JABAL SHAMMAR
Hā'il
Buraydah
Riyadh (Ar Riyāḍ)
AL AFLAJ
Ad Dilam
AD DAHY
JABAL TUWAYQ
Al Mubarraz
NAFŪD
AR RUB' AL KHĀLĪ
OMAN
AL MAŞIRAH
RA'S AL HADD
RA'S AL MADRAKAH

Tropic of Cancer
Yanbu'
Jiddah
Mecca (Makkah)
Al Ṭā'if
Al Khurmah
Al Lidām
Qal'at Bīshah
Wādī ad Dawāsir
AL ASĪR
Abha
Al Qunfudhah

SUDAN
Bür Sūdān
Sawākin
Ṭawkar
Kassalā
Keren
Mitsiwa (Massawa)
Akordat
Asmera
Adi Ugri
ETHIOPIA
Ed
Beylul
DAHLAK ARCH
KAMARĀN
Al Luḥayyah
Al Hudaydah
Al Mukhā (Mocha)
YEMEN
Madīnat ash Sha'b
Aden ('Adan)
DJIBOUTI
Djibouti
Seylac
Berbera
SOMALIA
Tadjoura
Aysha
JAZĀ'IR FARASAN
Qīzān
Abū 'Arish
Şa'dah
San'ā
NAJRAN
RAMLAT AS SAB'ATAYN
Shibām
Say'ūn
Tarīm
HADRAMAWT
Mirbāt
RA'S FARTAK
Sayḥūt
Ash Shiḥr
Al Mukallā
Shuqrah
GULF OF ADEN
SUQUTRA (SOCOTRA) (Yemen)
Hadibu
KHŪRYĀN-MŪRYĀN (Oman)
Caluula
CASEYR
Lass Qoray

PERSIAN GULF
RA'S AT TANNŪRAH

Continued on pages 204-205

Continued on pages 204-205

Relief

Meters		Feet
3050		10 000
1525		5000
610		2000
305		1000
152.5		500
0	Sea Level	0
152.5		500	Below Sea Level
1525		5000
3050		10 000

A-569400-76   18-14-33
COPYRIGHT BY
RAND McNALLY & COMPANY
MADE IN U.S.A.

Longitude East of Greenwich

Scale 1:16 000 000; one inch to 250 miles. Polyconic Projection
Elevations and depressions are given in feet

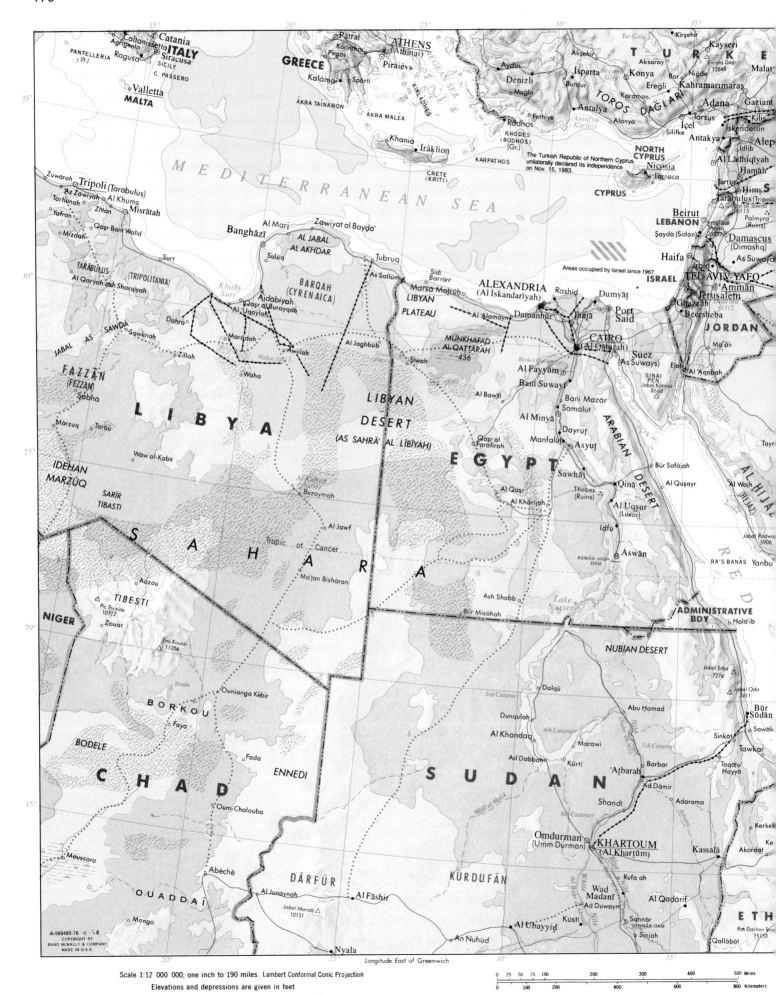

Scale 1:12 000 000; one inch to 190 miles. Lambert Conformal Conic Projection

Elevations and depressions are given in feet

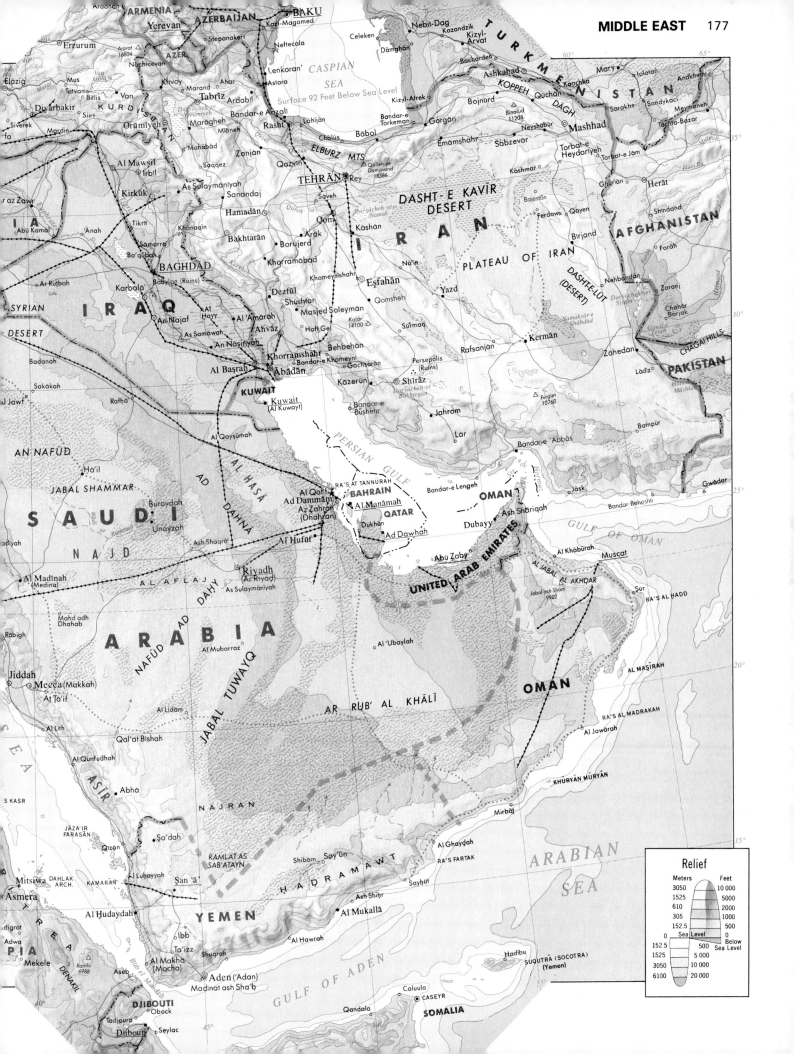

ARMENIA
AZERBAIJAN
BAKU
 Araratlan
Yerevan
Erzurum
AZER.
Kazi-Magomed
Nachicevan
Neftecala
Ararat
16804
Nebit-Dag
Kazandzik
Kizyl-
Arvat
Celeken
TURKMENISTAN
Dämghän
Bacharden
Ashkabad
Kaachka
Mary
Ioloton
Andkhvoy
Elazig
Mus
Van
Gölü
Bitlis
Lenkoran'
CASPIAN
SEA
Astara
KOPPEH
Quchan
Bojnurd
Sarakhs
Sandykaci
Meymaneh
Tatvan
Van
Surface 92 Feet Below Sea Level
Kizyl-Atrek
DAGH
Binalud
11208
Neyshäbür
Torbat-e
Tachta-Bazar
Diyarbakir
Ardabil
Bandar-e Anzali
Bandar-e
Torkeman
Gorgan
Mashhad
Siverek
KURDSTAN
Tabriz
Marand
Ahar
Rasht
Lahijan
Chälüs
Babol
Emämshahr
Sabzevär
Torbat-e
Heydariyeh
Torbat-e Jäm
fa
Mardin
Orümiyeh
Mahabad
Zanjan
ELBURZ MTS
Qolleh-ye
Damavand
18386
Kashmar
Ghurian
Herät
r az Zawr
Saqqez
Qazvin
Rey
Qaleh-ye
TEHRÄN
Bajestän
Ferdows
Qayen
Shindand
Abü Kamal
'Änah
As Sulaymäniyah
Sanandaj
Hamadän
Saveh
DASHT-E KAVIR
DESERT
AFGHANISTAN
Tikrit
Khänaqin
Qom
IRAN
Birjand
Samarra
Bakhtarän
Arak
Kashan
PLATEAU OF IRAN
Ferdows
Farah
SYRIAN
Ba'qubah
Khorramäbäd
Borüjerd
Na'in
DASHT-E-LÜT
(DESERT)
Nehbandän
IRAQ
BAGHDAD
Babylon (Ruins)
Khomeynishahr
Eşfahän
Yazd
Zaranj
Karbalä
Dezfül
Shüshtar
Qomsheh
Chähär
Borjak
DESERT
Ar Rutbah
Al
Hayy
Masjed Soleyman
Kalär
14100
Persepolis
(Ruins)
Kermän
Zähedän
CHAGAI HILLS
An Najaf
Ahväz
Haft Gel
Behbehän
Sürmaq
Rafsanjän
Lädiz
PAKISTAN
An Näşiriyah
As Samäwah
Khorramshahr
Bandar-e Khomeyni
Gachsärän
Shiräz
Persepolis
Furgun
10760
Badanah
Khorramshahr
Al Başrah
Äbädän
Kazerün
Daryächeh-ye
Bakhtegan
Bampür
Sakakah
KUWAIT
Kuwait
(Al Kuwayt)
Bandar-e
Büshehr
Jahrom
Bandar-e 'Abbas
Al Jawf
Rafha
Al Qayşümah
Lär
Jäsk
Bandar Beheshti
AN NAFUD
Ha'il
AD
DAHNA
AL HASA
PERSIAN GULF
RA'S AT TANNURAH
Gwadar
JABAL SHAMMAR
Buraydah
Al Qatif
Ad Dammäm
BAHRAIN
Al Manämah
Bandar-e Lengeh
OMAN
Unayzah
Az Zahrän
(Dhahran)
QATAR
Ash Shäriqah
SAUDI
Ash Shaqrä
Al Hufüf
Dukhan
Ad Dawhah
Dubayy
Al Khäbürah
Muscat
adiyah
NAJD
AL AFLAJ
Riyadh
(Ar Riyäd)
As Sulaymäniyah
Abü Zaby
UNITED ARAB EMIRATES
AL JABAL
AL AKHDAR
Jabal ash Sham
9902
Sür
Al Madinah
(Medina)
AD
DAHY
Al 'Ubaylah
RA'S AL HADD
Rabigh
Al Mubarraz
OMAN
Mahd adh
Dhahab
NAFÜD
ARABIA
AL MAŞIRAH
Jiddah
Mecca (Makkah)
At Ta'if
Al Lidam
JABAL
TUWAYQ
AR RUB' AL KHALI
RA'S AL MADRAKAH
Al Lith
Qal'at Bishah
Al Jawärah
Al Qunfudhah
Mirbat
OMAN
ASIR
Abha
NAJRAN
KHÜRYÄN MÜRYÄN
JÄZA'IR
FARASÄN
Sa'dah
Mitsiwa
DAHLAK
ARCH.
KAMARAN
RAMLAT AS
SAB'ATAYN
Shibam
Say'ün
Al Ghaydah
RA'S FARTAK
ARABIAN
Qizan
Al Luhayyah
Şan'ä
SEA
Asmera
Al Hudaydah
YEMEN
HADRAMAWT
Sayhüt
PIA
Ibb
Al Hawrah
Mekele
Ta'izz
Shuqrah
Al Mukalla
Ash Shihr
Ramlu
6988
Al Makha
(Mocha)
Aden ('Adan)
Madinat ash Sha'b
Hadibu
SUQUTRÄ (SOCOTRA)
(Yemen)
DENAKIL
DJIBOUTI
Bab el Mandab
GULF OF ADEN
Caluula
digrat
Tadjoura
Obock
SOMALIA
CASEYR
PIA
Djibouti
Seylac
Qandala

Relief

Meters		Feet
3050		10 000
1525		5000
610		2000
305		1000
152.5		500
0	Sea Level	0
		Below
152.5		500 Sea Level
1525		5 000
3050		10 000
6100		20 000

a

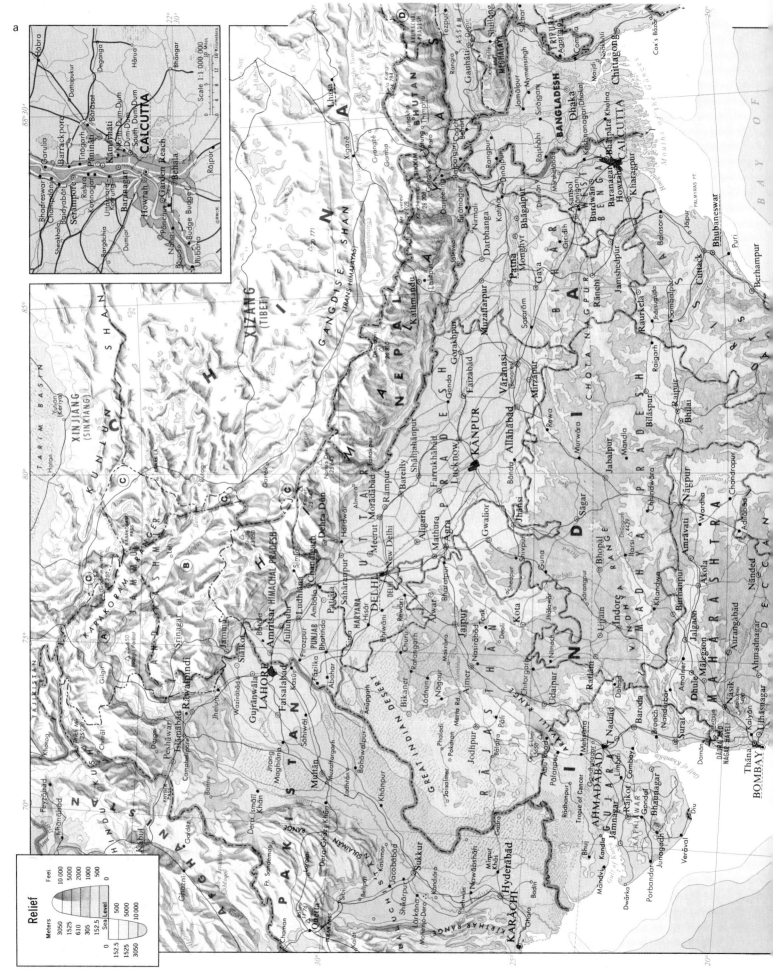

Scale 1:10 000 000; one inch to 160 miles. Lambert Conformal Conic Projection
Elevations and depressions are given in feet

For larger scale coverage of Bombay
and Calcutta see page 236.

Continued on pages 162-163

Continued on pages 174-175

Scale 1:16 000 000; one inch to 250 miles. Polyconic Projection
Elevations and depressions are given in feet

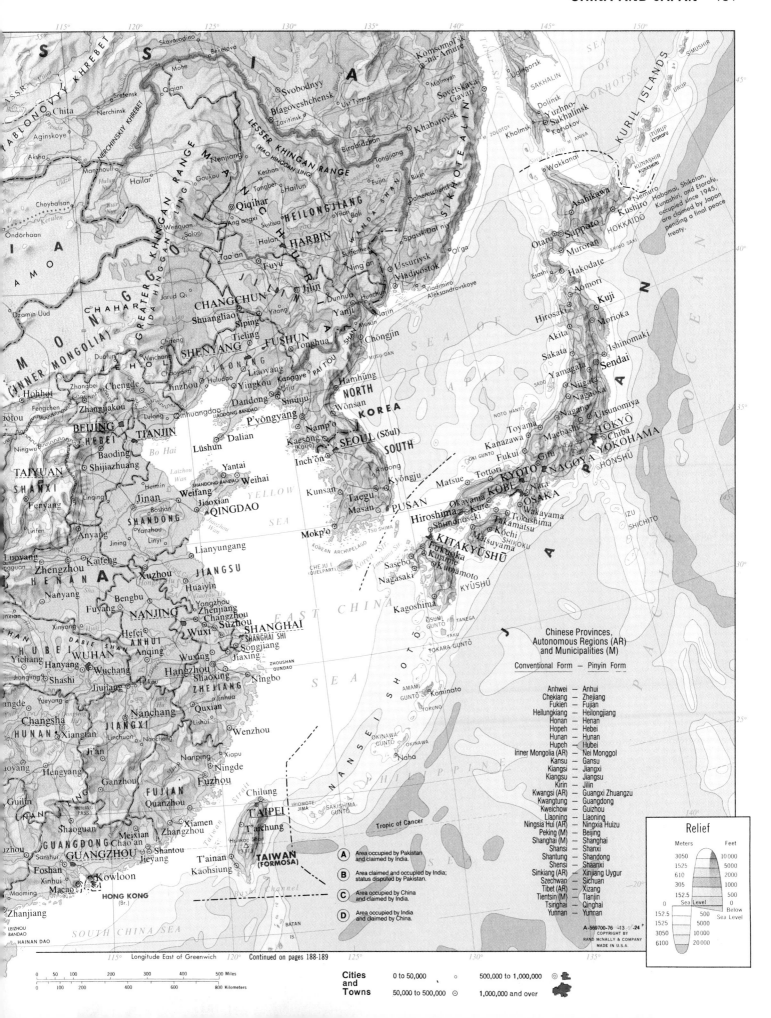

Chinese Provinces,
Autonomous Regions (AR)
and Municipalities (M)

Conventional Form — Pinyin Form

Conventional	Pinyin
Anhwei	Anhui
Chekiang	Zhejiang
Fukien	Fujian
Heilungkiang	Heilongjiang
Honan	Henan
Hopeh	Hebei
Hunan	Hunan
Hupeh	Hubei
Inner Mongolia (AR)	Nei Monggol
Kansu	Gansu
Kiangsi	Jiangxi
Kiangsu	Jiangsu
Kirin	Jilin
Kwangsi (AR)	Guangxi Zhuangzu
Kwangtung	Guangdong
Kweichow	Guizhou
Liaoning	Liaoning
Ningsia Hui (AR)	Ningxia Huizu
Peking (M)	Beijing
Shanghai (M)	Shanghai
Shansi	Shanxi
Shantung	Shandong
Shensi	Shaanxi
Sinkiang (AR)	Xinjiang Uygur
Szechwan	Sichuan
Tibet (AR)	Xizang
Tientsin (M)	Tianjin
Tsinghai	Qinghai
Yunnan	Yunnan

(A) Area occupied by Pakistan and claimed by India.

(B) Area claimed and occupied by India; status disputed by Pakistan.

(C) Area occupied by China and claimed by India.

(D) Area occupied by India and claimed by China.

Hobomai, Shikoton, Kunashiri, and Etorofu, occupied since 1945, are claimed by Japan pending a final peace treaty.

A-569700-76-43-24
COPYRIGHT BY
RAND McNALLY & COMPANY
MADE IN U.S.A.

Relief

Meters	Feet
3050	10 000
1525	5000
610	2000
305	1000
152.5	500
0 Sea Level	0 Sea Level
	Below
152.5	500
1525	5000
3050	10 000
6100	20 000

Continued on pages 188-189

Longitude East of Greenwich

0	50	100	200	300	400	500 Miles
0	100	200	400	600		800 Kilometers

Cities and Towns

0 to 50,000 ○	500,000 to 1,000,000 ◎
50,000 to 500,000 ⊙	1,000,000 and over

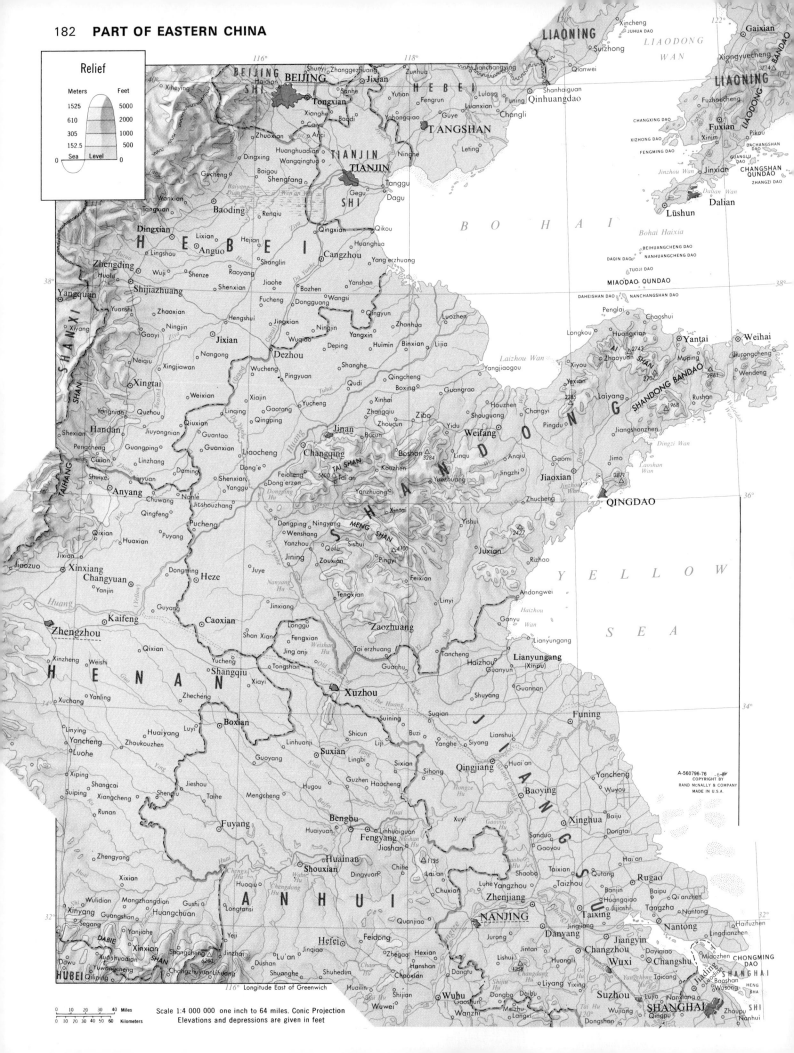

Relief

Meters	Feet
1525	5000
610	2000
305	1000
152.5	500
0 Sea	Level 0

Scale 1:4 000 000 one inch to 64 miles. Conic Projection
Elevations and depressions are given in feet

0 10 20 30 40 Miles
0 10 20 30 40 50 60 Kilometers

116° Longitude East of Greenwich

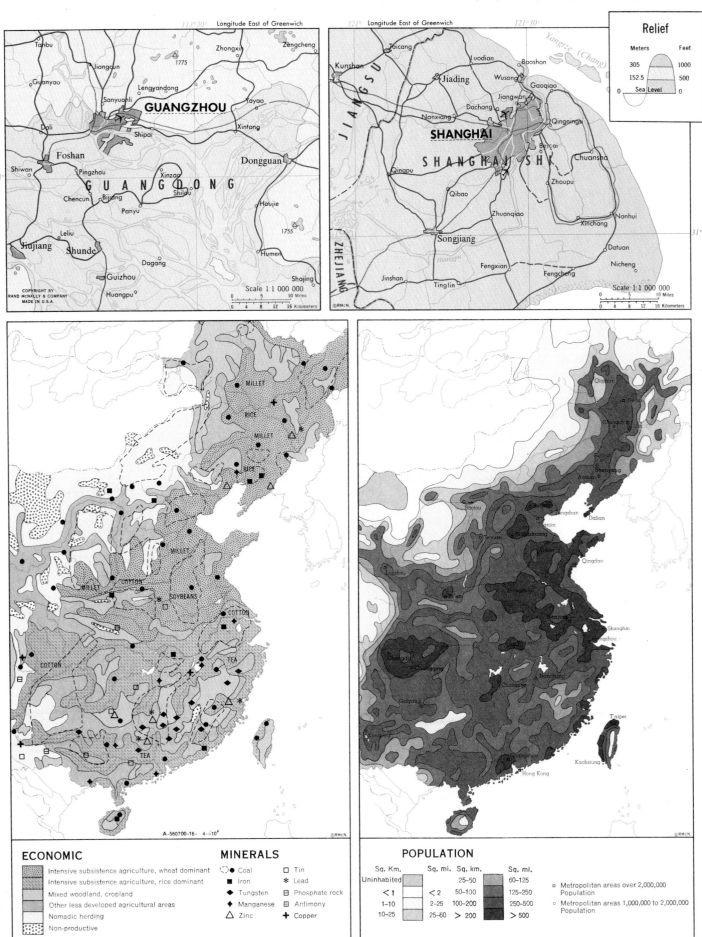

GUANGZHOU

Tanbu · Zhongxin · Zengcheng
Jiangcun · 1775
Guanyao · Lengyandong · Yayao
Sanyuanli · **GUANGZHOU** · Xintang
Dali · Shipai
Foshan · Dongguan
Shiwan · Pingzhou · Xinzao
G U A N G D O N G · Shilou · Houjie
Chencun · Bijiang · Panyu
Leliu · 1755 · Humen
Shunde · Dagang
Hujiang · Guizhou · Shajing
Huangpu

23°

Longitude East of Greenwich 113°30'

COPYRIGHT BY
RAND MCNALLY & COMPANY
MADE IN U.S.A.

Scale 1:1 000 000
0 · 5 · 10 Miles
0 · 4 · 8 · 12 · 16 Kilometers

SHANGHAI

Taicang · Luodian · Baoshan · Yangtze (Chang)
Kunshan · Wusong
Jiading · Gaoqiao
Nanxiang · Dachang · Jiangwan
J I A N G S U · Qingningsi
SHANGHAI · Beicai · Chuansha
Qingpu · **SHANGHAI SHI** · Zhoupu
Qibao · Zhuanqiao · Xinchang · Nanhui
Songjiang · Fengxian · Fengcheng · Datuan · Nicheng
Jinshan · Tinglin
Z H E J I A N G

31°

Longitude East of Greenwich 121° · 121°30'

Scale 1:1 000 000
0 · 5 · 10 Miles
0 · 4 · 8 · 12 · 16 Kilometers

Relief
Meters		Feet
305		1000
152.5		500
0	Sea Level	0

A-560700-16- 4-/-10°

ECONOMIC

- Intensive subsistence agriculture, wheat dominant
- Intensive subsistence agriculture, rice dominant
- Mixed woodland, cropland
- Other less developed agricultural areas
- Nomadic herding
- Non-productive

MINERALS

- ● Coal
- ■ Iron
- ◆ Tungsten
- ◆ Manganese
- △ Zinc
- □ Tin
- ✳ Lead
- ⊟ Phosphate rock
- ⊞ Antimony
- ✛ Copper

POPULATION

Sq. Km.	Sq. mi.	Sq. km.	Sq. mi.
Uninhabited		25–50	60–125
<1	< 2	50–100	125–250
1–10	2–25	100–200	250–500
10–25	25–60	> 200	> 500

- □ Metropolitan areas over 2,000,000 Population
- ○ Metropolitan areas 1,000,000 to 2,000,000 Population

For larger scale coverage
of Shanghai see page 237.

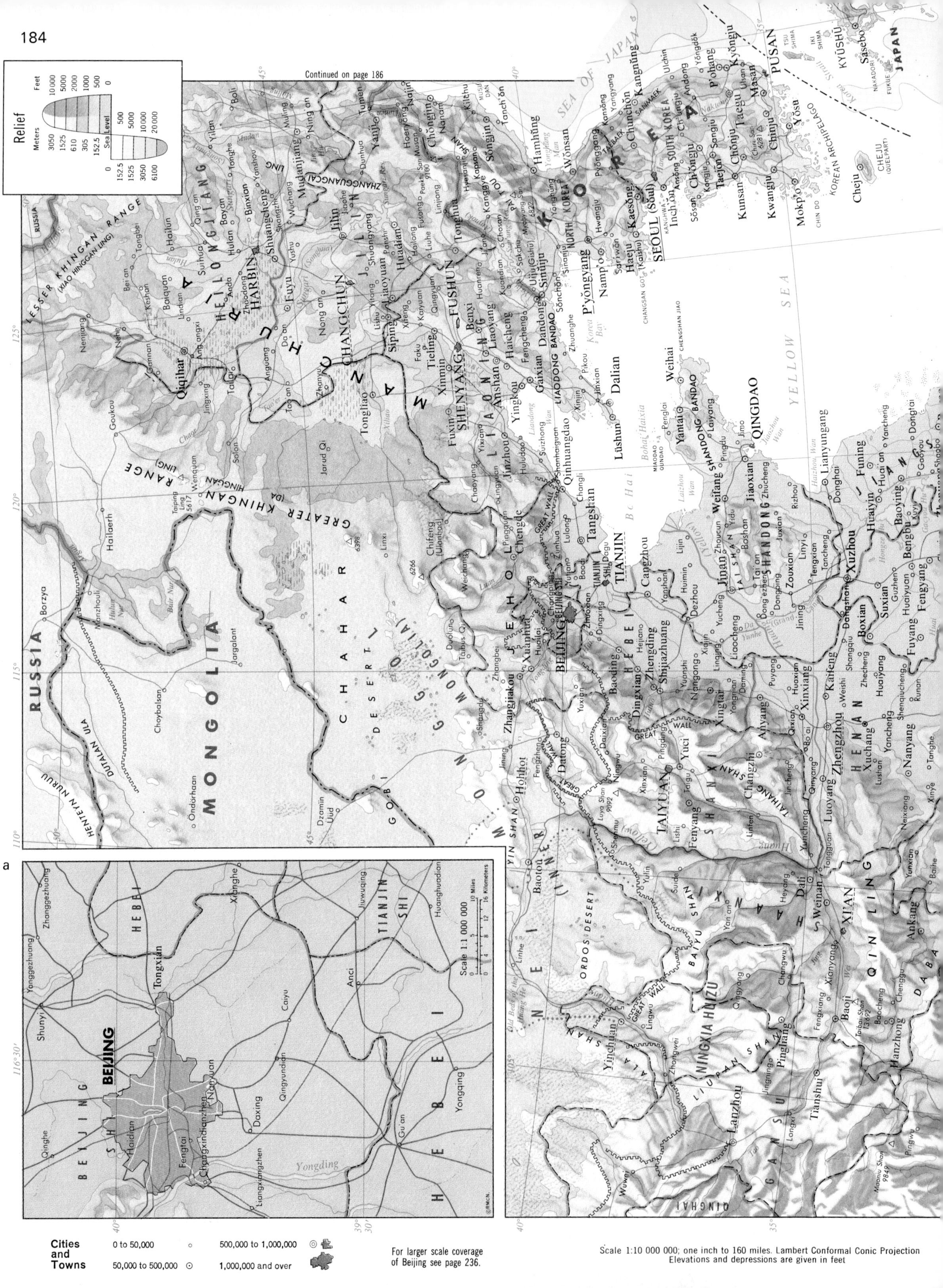

Continued on page 186

Relief

| Feet | 10000 | 5000 | 2000 | 1000 | 500 | 0 |
| Meters | 3050 | 1525 | 610 | 305 | 152.5 | Sea level |

| 500 | 5000 | 10000 | 20000 |
| 152.5 | 1525 | 3050 | 6100 |

a

Cities and Towns

0 to 50,000 ○
50,000 to 500,000 ⊙
500,000 to 1,000,000 ◎
1,000,000 and over

For larger scale coverage of Beijing see page 236.

Scale 1:10 000 000; one inch to 160 miles. Lambert Conformal Conic Projection
Elevations and depressions are given in feet

Scale 1:1 000 000

Major labels visible on map:

RUSSIA, MONGOLIA, KOREA, NORTH KOREA, SOUTH KOREA, JAPAN, KYŪSHŪ, CHINA, HEILONGJIANG, JILIN, LIAONING, INNER MONGOLIA (NEI MONGGOL), HEBEI, SHANDONG, SHANXI, SHAANXI, HENAN, GANSU, NINGXIA HUIZU, QINGHAI, CHAHAR, JEHOL

SEA OF JAPAN, YELLOW SEA, Bo Hai, Korea Strait, Tsushima Strait

LESSER KHINGAN RANGE (XIAO HINGGAN LING), GREATER KHINGAN RANGE (DA HINGGAN LING), YIN SHAN, TAIHANG SHAN, QIN LING, DABA SHAN, LIUPAN SHAN, BAIYU SHAN, ORDOS DESERT, GOBI DESERT

Cities: Harbin, Qiqihar, Changchun, Shenyang, Fushun, Anshan, Dalian, Lüshun, Beijing, Tianjin, Tangshan, Qinhuangdao, Baoding, Shijiazhuang, Taiyuan, Datong, Jinan, Qingdao, Weifang, Yantai, Weihai, Xuzhou, Kaifeng, Zhengzhou, Luoyang, Lanzhou, Tianshui, Baoji, Xian, Hanzhong, Ankang, Hohhot, Baotou, Yinchuan

Korea: Seoul (Sŏul), P'yŏngyang, Namp'o, Kaesong, Hamhŭng, Wŏnsan, Sinŭiju, Chŏngjin, Pusan, Taegu, Taejŏn, Kwangju, Mokp'o, Inch'ŏn, Cheju, Cheju Do

Beijing inset: BEIJING, HEBEI, TIANJIN SHI, Tongxian, Haidian, Fengtai, Shunyi, Daxing, Yongding, Qinghe

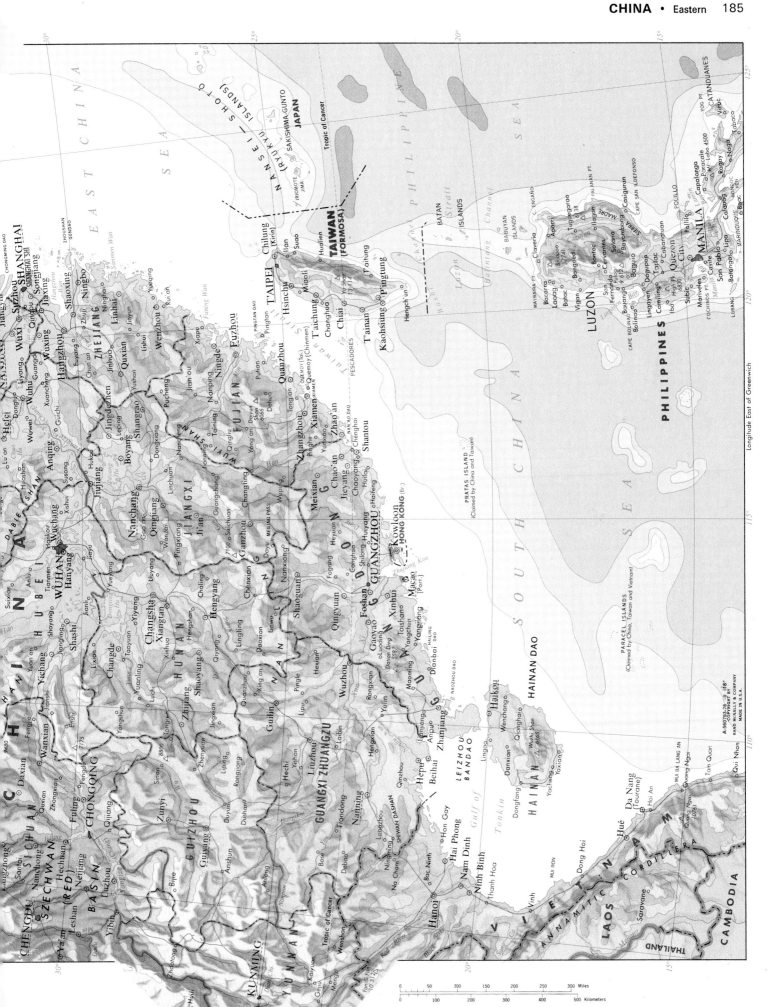

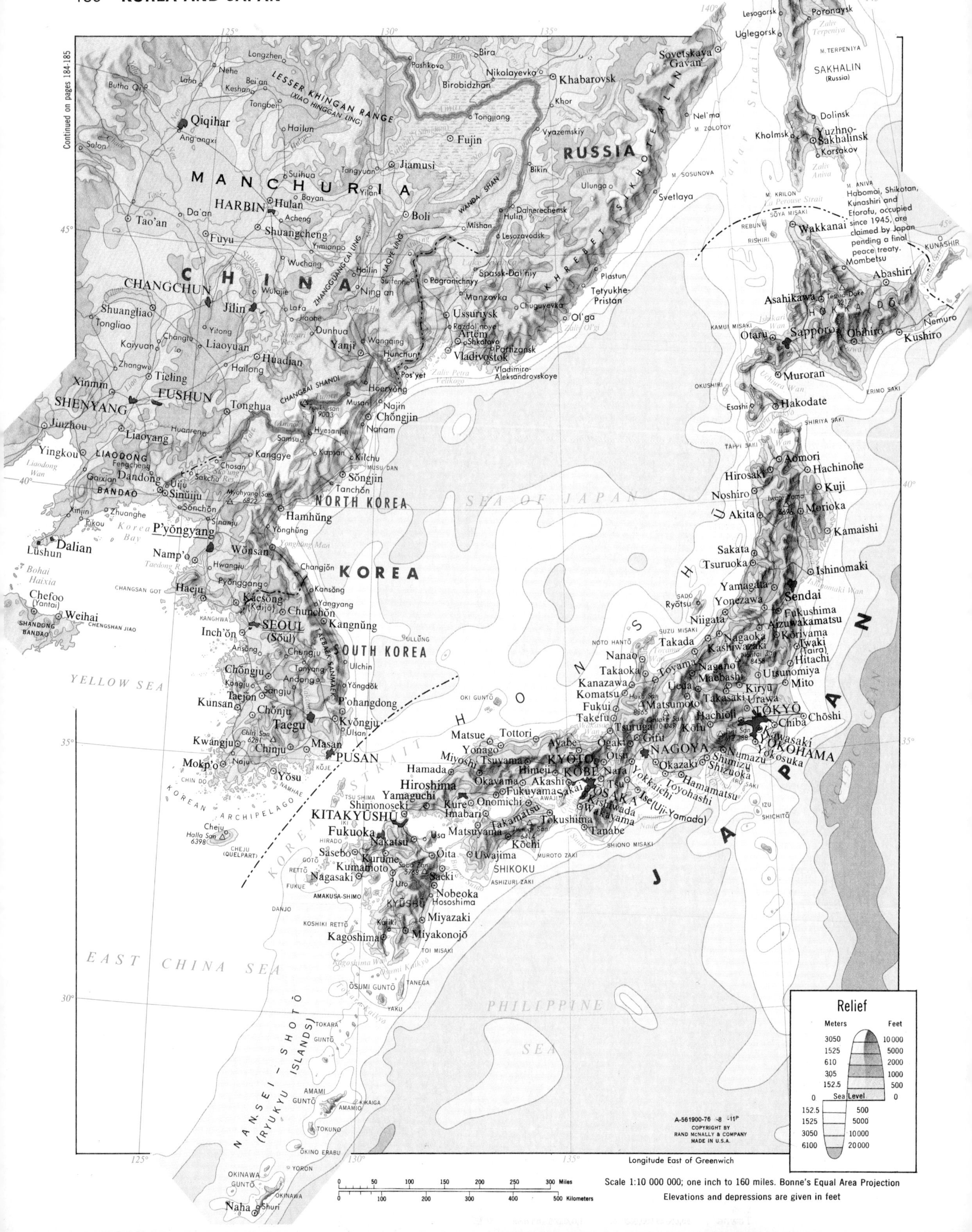

Continued on pages 184-185

Lesogorsk Poronaysk
Uglegorsk M. TERPENIYA
Zaliv
Terpeniya
SAKHALIN
(Russia)
Dolinsk
Kholmsk Yuzhno-
Sakhalinsk
Korsakov
Zaliv
Aniva

Nehe Longzhen
Butha Qi Laba Bei'an Pashkovo
Keshan Tongbei Bira Nikolayevka
Salon Hailun Birobidzhan Khabarovsk
Qiqihar Suihua Jiamusi
Ang'angxi Bayan Khor
Tao'an Da'an Hulan Acheng Yilan Tongjiang
MANCHURIA Fujin
HARBIN Hulan Vyazemskiy
Tangyuan
Shuangcheng Bikin
Wuchang Boli
CHINA Hailin Mishan Dalnerechensk
Yitong Lafa Jiaohe Hulin Lesozavodsk
CHANGCHUN Wulajie Ning'an Spassk-Dal'niy
Shuangliao Jilin Dunhua Suifenhe Pogranichnyy Plastun
Tongliao Changtu Yanji Manzovka
Kaiyuan Hailong Wangqing Razdol'noye Chuguyevka Tetyukhe-
Zhangwu Tieling Huadian Hunchun Shkotovo Pristan
Xinmin FUSHUN Tonghua Hoeryong Pos'yet Artëm Ol'ga
SHENYANG Huanren Musan Najin Vladivostok Zaliv Ol'ga
Jiuzhou Liaoyang Najin Vladimiro-
Yingkou Baekdu-san Chongjin Aleksandrovskoye
LIAODONG Fengcheng 9003 Nanam SEA OF JAPAN
Gaixian Dandong Samsu
Xinjin Zhuanghe Sinuiju Hyesanjin Kilchu MUSU-DAN
Pikou Uiju Kanggye Kapsan
Chosan Sakchu Songjin
Dalian Sonchon Tanchon
Lüshun Myohyang San Hamhung
Korea 6822
Bay P'YONGYANG NORTH KOREA Wonsan
Chefoo Namp'o Hwangju Changjon
(Yantai) Haeju Pyonggang Kangnung
Weihai KOREA Kaesong Chunchon
SHANDONG (Kaijo) Kangnung
BANDAO SEOUL Yangyang
(Soul) Kangnung
Inch'on Chungju Ullung
YELLOW SEA Chongju Tanyang
Kongju Andong Yongdok
Taejon Sangju
Kunsan Chonju Kyongju OKI GUNTO
Kwangju Taegu Ulsan
Mokp'o Naju Chinju Masan
PUSAN
KOREAN ARCHIPELAGO
Cheju
Halla San
6398
CHEJU
(QUELPART)

SEA OF JAPAN

Wakkanai RISHIRI
REBUN Asahikawa HOKKAIDO
Otaru Sapporo Obihiro Abashiri
Muroran Kushiro
Esashi Hakodate ERIMO SAKI
SHIRIYA SAKI
TAPPI SAKI
Aomori Hachinohe
Hirosaki Kuji
Noshiro Morioka
Akita Kamaishi
Sakata Ishinomaki
Tsuruoka Yamagata Sendai
Yonezawa Fukushima
SADO Niigata Aizuwakamatsu
Ryotsu Koriyama
Takada Nagaoka Iwaki (Taira)
Nagano Hitachi
Takaoka Maebashi Mito
Toyama Kiryu
Kanazawa Matsumoto Takasaki Urawa
Komatsu Ueda Utsunomiya
Fukui Nagano Hachioji TOKYO
Takefu Gifu Kofu Choshi
Tsuruga Ogaki Chiba
Matsue Tottori Ayabe Otsu NAGOYA Yokohama
Miyoshi Tsuyama KYOTO Okazaki Yokosuka
Yonago Himeji KOBE Nara
Hamada Okayama Akashi OSAKA Shizuoka
Yamaguchi Kure Onomichi Wakayama Hamamatsu
Hiroshima Imabari Takamatsu Tanabe
Shimonoseki Matsuyama Tokushima
KITAKYUSHU Usa Kochi
Fukuoka Nakatsu SHIKOKU
Hirado Oita Uwajima
Sasebo Kurume Saeki
Kumamoto Uto Nobeoka
Nagasaki Hososhima
AMAKUSA-SHIMO Miyazaki
KYUSHU Miyakonojo
Kagoshima
KOSHIKI RETTO
EAST CHINA SEA
OSUMI GUNTO TANEGA
YAKU
PHILIPPINE SEA

NANSEI-SHOTO
(RYUKYU ISLANDS)
TOKARA GUNTO
AMAMI GUNTO
AMAMI
TOKUNO
OKINAWA GUNTO
OKINAWA Shuri
Naha
OKINO ERABU
YORON

RUSSIA
KHREBET SIKHOTE-ALIN
LESSER KHINGAN RANGE (XIAO HINGGAN LING)

Habomai, Shikotan,
Kunashiri and
Etorofu, occupied
since 1945, are
claimed by Japan
pending a final
peace treaty.
Mombetsu KUNASHIR
Nemuro

Longitude East of Greenwich

Scale 1:10 000 000; one inch to 160 miles. Bonne's Equal Area Projection
Elevations and depressions are given in feet

A-561900-76 -8 -11P
COPYRIGHT BY
RAND M°NALLY & COMPANY
MADE IN U.S.A.

Relief
Meters Feet
3050 10 000
1525 5000
610 2000
305 1000
152.5 500
0 Sea Level 0
152.5 500
1525 5000
3050 10 000
6100 20 000

0 50 100 150 200 250 300 Miles
0 100 200 300 400 500 Kilometers

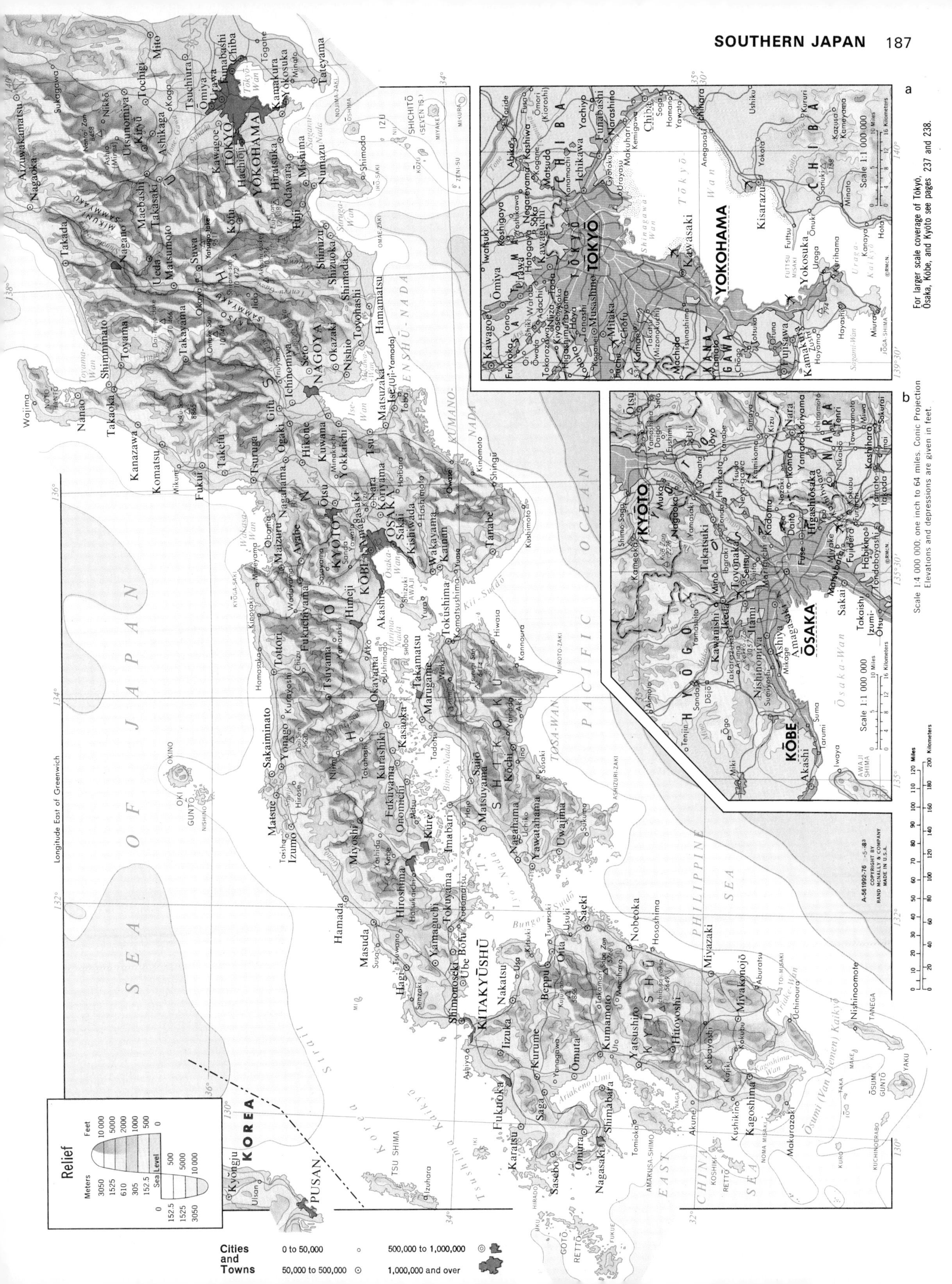

a

For larger scale coverage of Tōkyo,
Ōsaka, Kōbe, and Kyōto see pages 237 and 238.

Scale 1:1 000 000

b

Scale 1:4 000 000; one inch to 64 miles. Conic Projection
Elevations and depressions are given in feet.

Scale 1:1 000 000

Relief

Meters	Feet
3050	10 000
1525	5000
610	2000
305	1000
152.5	500
0	Sea Level 0
152.5	500
1525	5000
3050	10 000

Cities and Towns

0 to 50,000   500,000 to 1,000,000
50,000 to 500,000   1,000,000 and over

A-561992-76   COPYRIGHT BY
RAND McNALLY & COMPANY
MADE IN U.S.A.

S E A   O F   J A P A N

P A C I F I C   O C E A N

PHILIPPINE SEA

EAST CHINA SEA

KOREA

PUSAN

KYŪSHŪ

SHIKOKU

KITAKYŪSHŪ

NAGOYA

TŌKYŌ

YOKOHAMA

KYŌTO

ŌSAKA

KŌBE

Longitude East of Greenwich

Scale 1:16 000 000; one inch to 250 miles. Polyconic Projection
Elevations and depressions are given in feet

Relief

Meters	Feet
3050	10 000
1525	5000
610	2000
305	1000
152.5	500
Sea Level	
152.5	500
1525	5000
3050	10 000
6100	20 000

A-569800-76 8-10-25P
COPYRIGHT BY
RAND MCNALLY & COMPANY
MADE IN U.S.A.

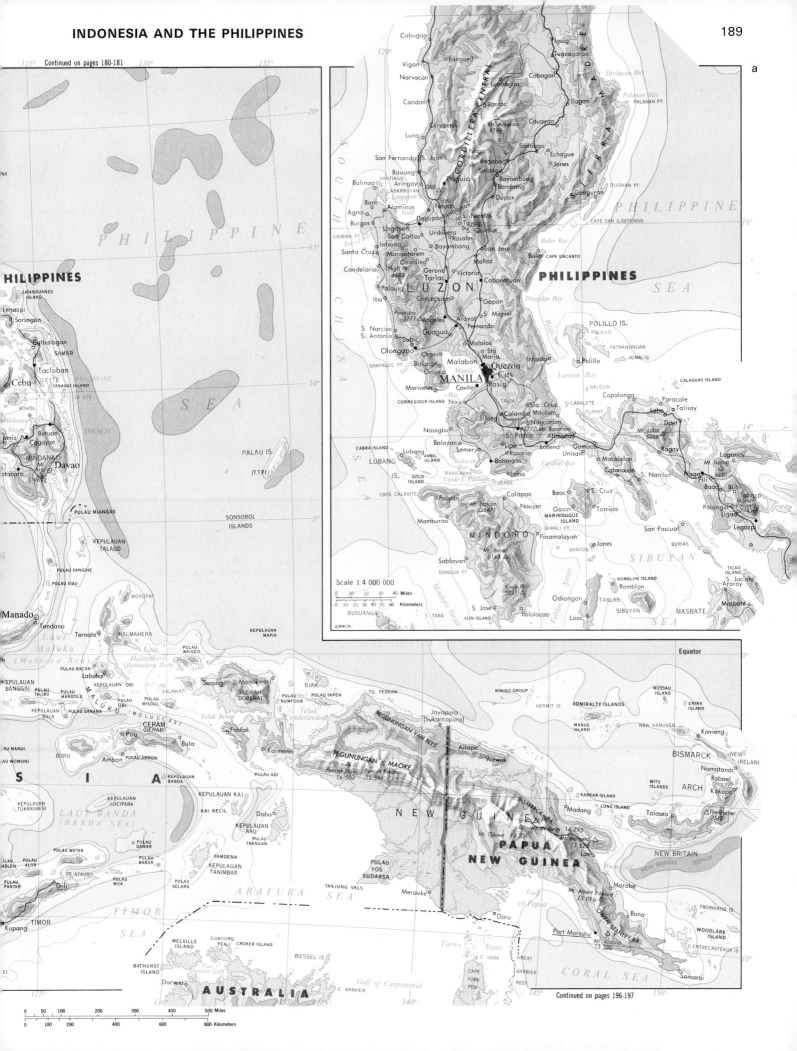

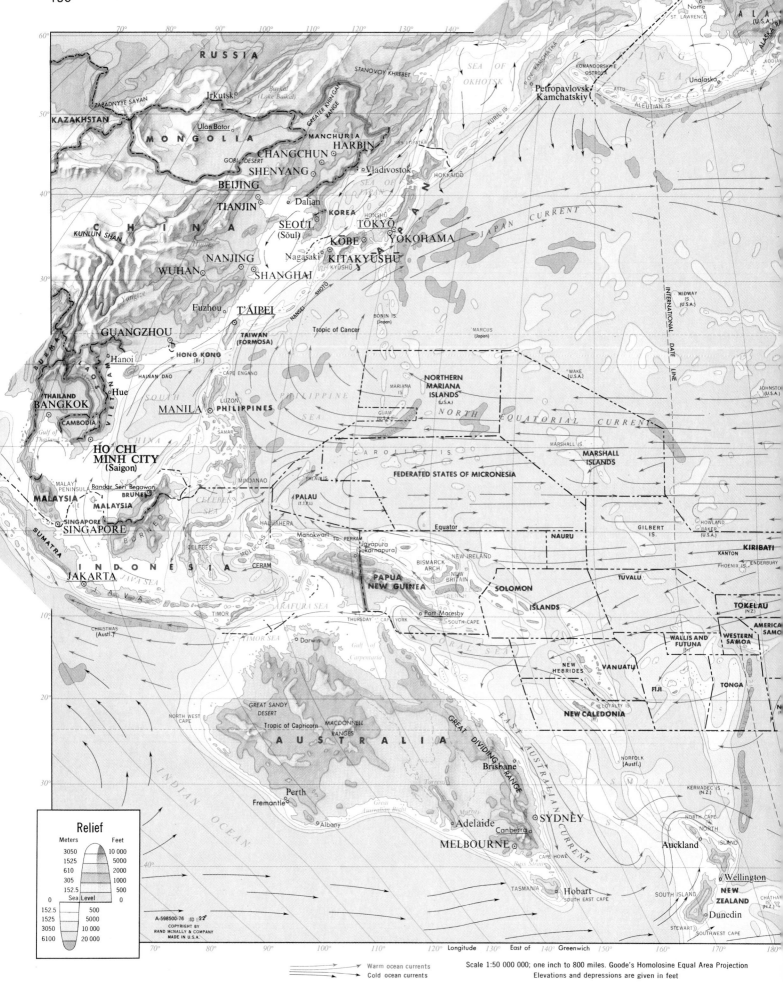

Relief

Meters	Feet
3050	10 000
1525	5000
610	2000
305	1000
152.5	500
0	Sea Level	0
152.5	500
1525	5000
3050	10 000
6100	20 000

A-598500-76   40   22°
COPYRIGHT BY
RAND McNALLY & COMPANY
MADE IN U.S.A.

Warm ocean currents
Cold ocean currents

Scale 1:50 000 000; one inch to 800 miles. Goode's Homolosine Equal Area Projection
Elevations and depressions are given in feet

a

Scale 1:4 000 000

0 10 20 30 40 Miles
0 10 20 30 40 50 60 Kilometers

GULF OF ALASKA

Sitka
Prince Rupert

CANADIAN ROCKY MOUNTAINS

Vancouver
Victoria
SEATTLE
Portland

CASCADE RA.
COAST RANGES
SIERRA NEVADA

Salt Lake City

SAN FRANCISCO

CALIFORNIA CURRENT

LOS ANGELES
SAN DIEGO

UNITED STATES

ST. LOUIS

Missouri
Mississippi

New Orleans
Galveston

CABO SAN LUCAS
Mazatlan

MEXICO
SIERRA MADRE OCCIDENTAL

Tampico

ISLAS REVILLAGIGEDO (Mex.)

MEXICO CITY
Veracruz

Acapulco

BELIZE
GUAT.
HOND.
EL SAL.
NICARAGUA
Guatemala
Managua
COSTA RICA
Colón Panamá
PANAMA

CARIBBEAN SEA

Honolulu
HAWAIIAN IS (U.S.A.)

NORTH EQUATORIAL CURRENT

Buenaventura

PALMYRA (U.S.A.)
TABUAERAN
KIRITIMATI

EQUATORIAL COUNTER CURRENT

ARCHIPIÉLAGO DE COLÓN (GALÁPAGOS IS.) (Ecuador)

Quito
ECUADOR
Guayaquil

COLOMBIA

MALDEN

SOUTH EQUATORIAL CURRENT

MANIHIKI IS
COOK ISLANDS (N.Z.)

MARQUESAS IS.

AITUTAKI
RAROTONGA

SOCIETY IS.
TAHITI
ÎLES TUAMOTU

FRENCH POLYNESIA

PITCAIRN (Br.)
PITCAIRN DUCIE

RAPA NUI (EASTER) (Chile)

I. SALA Y GÓMEZ (Chile)

I. SAN FÉLIX (Chile)
I. SAN AMBROSIO (Chile)

LIMA
Callao

Arequipa
Mollendo
ATACAMA TRENCH
Iquique

PERU CURRENT

Antofagasta

Coquimbo

Valparaíso

ISLAS DE JUAN FERNÁNDEZ (Chile)
SANTIAGO

Concepción

CHILE
ANDES
ARGENTINA

Valdivia

Puerto Montt
CHILOE

Bahía Blanca

Punta Arenas
Estrecho De Magallanes
CABO DE HORNOS

WEST WIND DRIFT

0 500 1000 1500 2000 Miles
0 1000 2000 3000 Kilometers

170° 160° 150° Longitude 140° West of 130° Greenwich 120° 110° 100° 90° 80° 60° 50°

HAWAII (U.S.A.)

Hanalei Bay
Kilauea
Kawaikini 5170
KAUAI
Waimea
Lihue
NIIHAU
Kaulakahi Channel
©RMCN

Waialua
OAHU
KAENA PT.
Waianae
Waipahu
Aiea
Waimanalo
Ewa
Honolulu
Kaneohe Bay
KAHUKU PT.

Kaiwi Channel

MOLOKAI
Kaunakakai
Halawa
Kalohi Channel
LANAI
Pailolo Channel
Wailuku Pauwela
Lahaina
Kahului
Keokea HALEAKALA NAT'L PARK
MAUI
Haleakala Crater
Hana
KAHOOLAWE
Kealaikahiki Channel
Auau Channel

Alenuihaha Channel

UPOLU PT.
Hawi
Paauilo
Waimea
Laupahoehoe
Mauna Kea 13796
Honomu
Kailua
Hilo
Mauna Loa 13680
HAWAII
Ohia
Kilauea Crater 4090
Hookena
Kalapana
Pahala
NAT'L PARK
HAWAII VOLCANOES
Kalae

GULF OF MEXICO

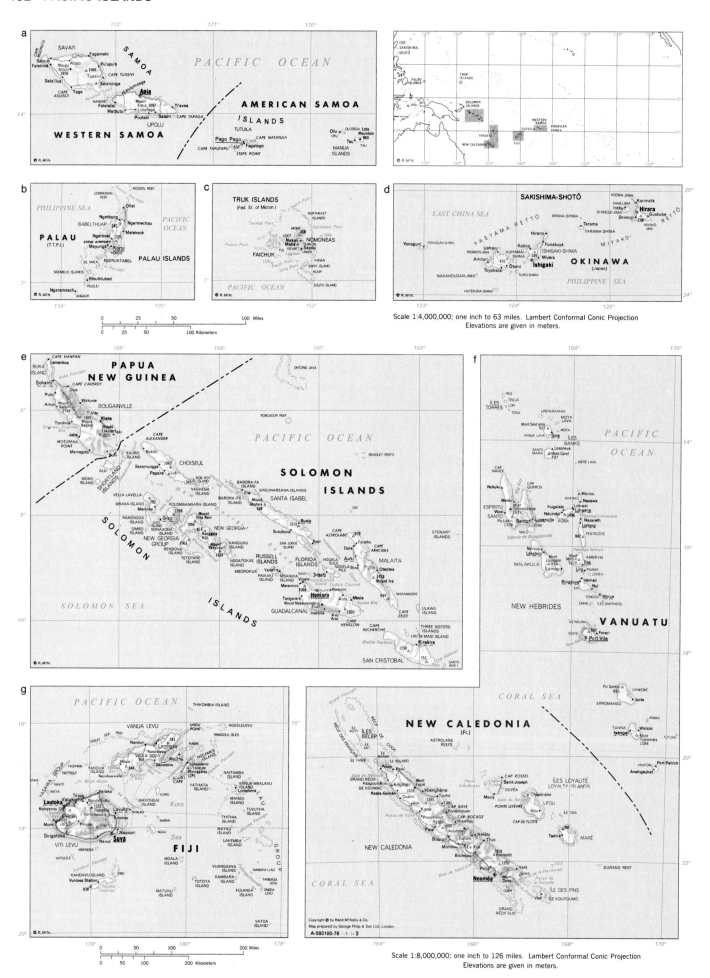

Scale 1:4,000,000; one inch to 63 miles. Lambert Conformal Conic Projection
Elevations are given in meters.

Scale 1:8,000,000; one inch to 126 miles. Lambert Conformal Conic Projection
Elevations are given in meters.

Copyright © by Rand McNally & Co.
Map prepared by George Philip & Son Ltd, London.
A-593100-76 -1-1- 2

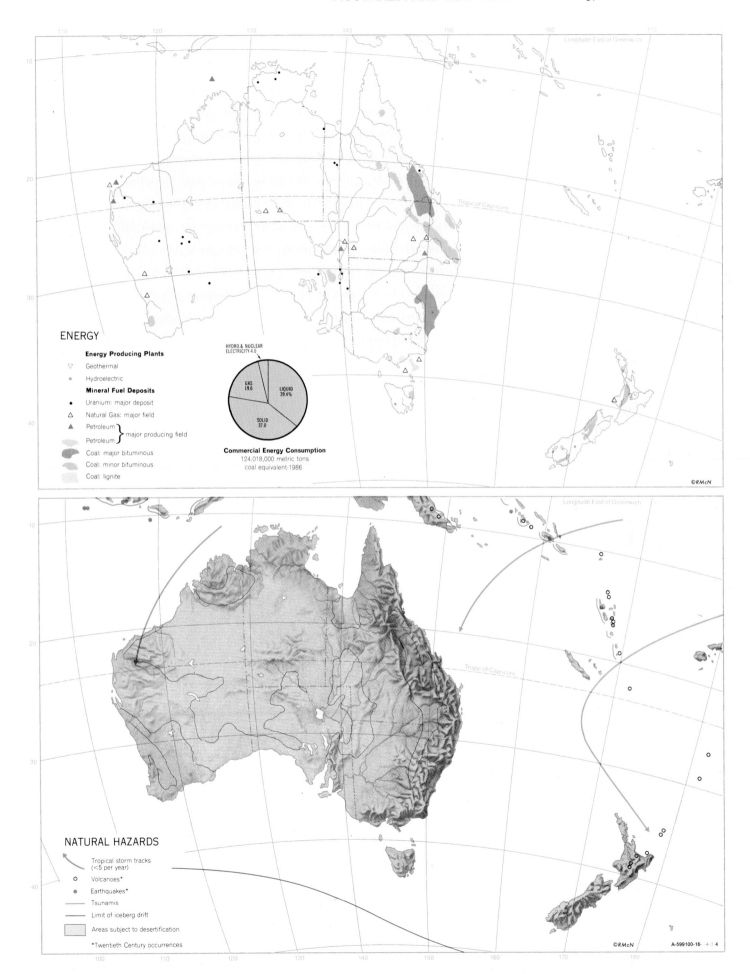

ENERGY

Energy Producing Plants

▽ Geothermal

• Hydroelectric

Mineral Fuel Deposits

• Uranium: major deposit

△ Natural Gas: major field

▲ Petroleum ⎱
⎰ major producing field
Petroleum ⎰

Coal: major bituminous

Coal: minor bituminous

Coal: lignite

HYDRO & NUCLEAR
ELECTRICITY-4.0

GAS
19.6

LIQUID
39.4%

SOLID
37.0

Commercial Energy Consumption
124,018,000 metric tons
coal equivalent-1986

©RMcN

NATURAL HAZARDS

↝ Tropical storm tracks
   (<5 per year)

○ Volcanoes*

• Earthquakes*

—— Tsunamis

—— Limit of iceberg drift

▨ Areas subject to desertification

*Twentieth Century occurrences

©RMcN   A-599100-16- 4-3 4

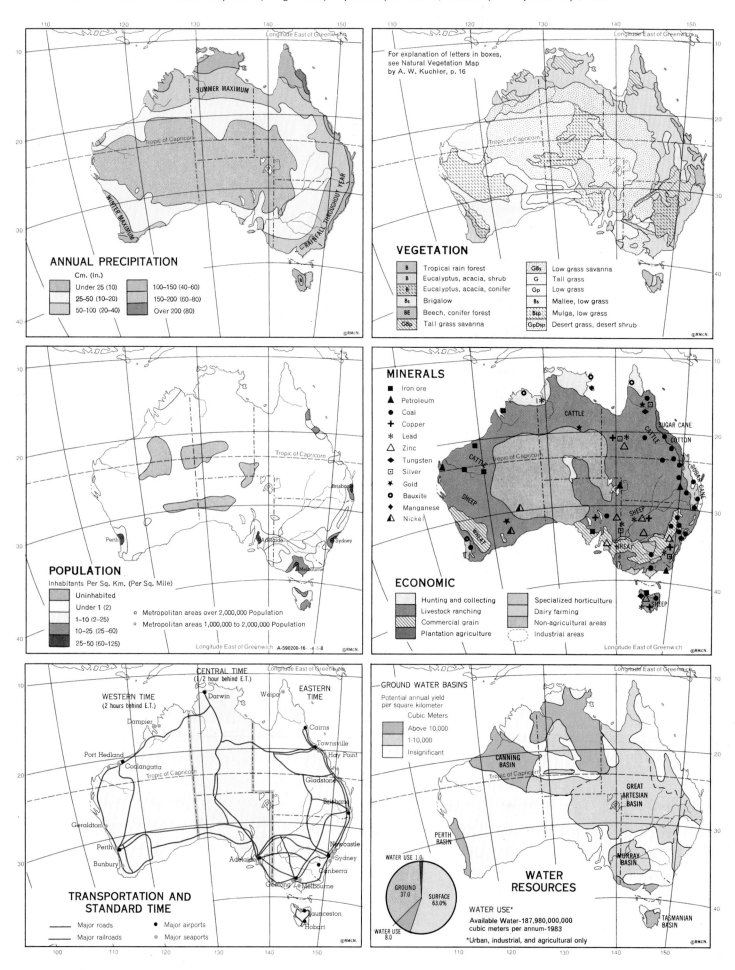

ANNUAL PRECIPITATION

Cm. (In.)

- Under 25 (10)
- 25–50 (10–20)
- 50–100 (20–40)
- 100–150 (40–60)
- 150–200 (60–80)
- Over 200 (80)

SUMMER MAXIMUM
WINTER MAXIMUM
RAINFALL THROUGHOUT YEAR

VEGETATION

For explanation of letters in boxes,
see Natural Vegetation Map
by A. W. Kuchler, p. 16

- B — Tropical rain forest
- B — Eucalyptus, acacia, shrub
- B — Eucalyptus, acacia, conifer
- Bs — Brigalow
- BE — Beech, conifer forest
- GBp — Tall grass savanna
- GBs — Low grass savanna
- G — Tall grass
- Gp — Low grass
- Bs — Mallee, low grass
- Bsp — Mulga, low grass
- GpDsp — Desert grass, desert shrub

POPULATION

Inhabitants Per Sq. Km. (Per Sq. Mile)

- Uninhabited
- Under 1 (2)
- 1–10 (2–25)
- 10–25 (25–60)
- 25–50 (60–125)

▫ Metropolitan areas over 2,000,000 Population
○ Metropolitan areas 1,000,000 to 2,000,000 Population

MINERALS

- ■ Iron ore
- ▲ Petroleum
- ● Coal
- + Copper
- ✳ Lead
- △ Zinc
- ◆ Tungsten
- ▢ Silver
- ✶ Gold
- ◉ Bauxite
- ◆ Manganese
- ▲ Nickel

ECONOMIC

- Hunting and collecting
- Livestock ranching
- Commercial grain
- Plantation agriculture
- Specialized horticulture
- Dairy farming
- Non-agricultural areas
- Industrial areas

TRANSPORTATION AND STANDARD TIME

CENTRAL TIME
(1/2 hour behind E.T.)
WESTERN TIME
(2 hours behind E.T.)
EASTERN TIME

— Major roads
— Major railroads
● Major airports
● Major seaports

WATER RESOURCES

GROUND WATER BASINS

Potential annual yield
per square kilometer
Cubic Meters

- Above 10,000
- 1–10,000
- Insignificant

CANNING BASIN
GREAT ARTESIAN BASIN
PERTH BASIN
MURRAY BASIN
TASMANIAN BASIN

WATER USE 1.0
GROUND 37.0
SURFACE 63.0%
WATER USE 8.0

WATER USE*
Available Water–187,980,000,000
cubic meters per annum–1983

*Urban, industrial, and agricultural only

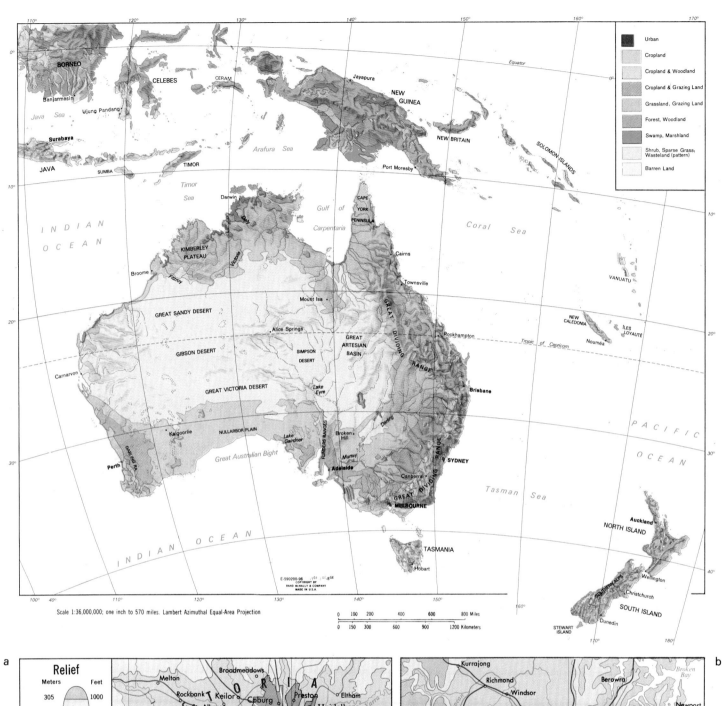

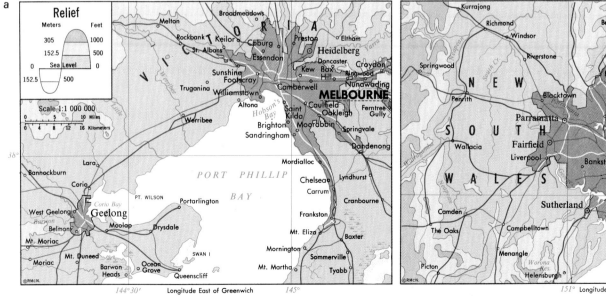

Scale 1:16 000 000; one inch to 250 miles. Lambert's Azimuthal, Equal Area Projection

Elevations and depressions are given in feet

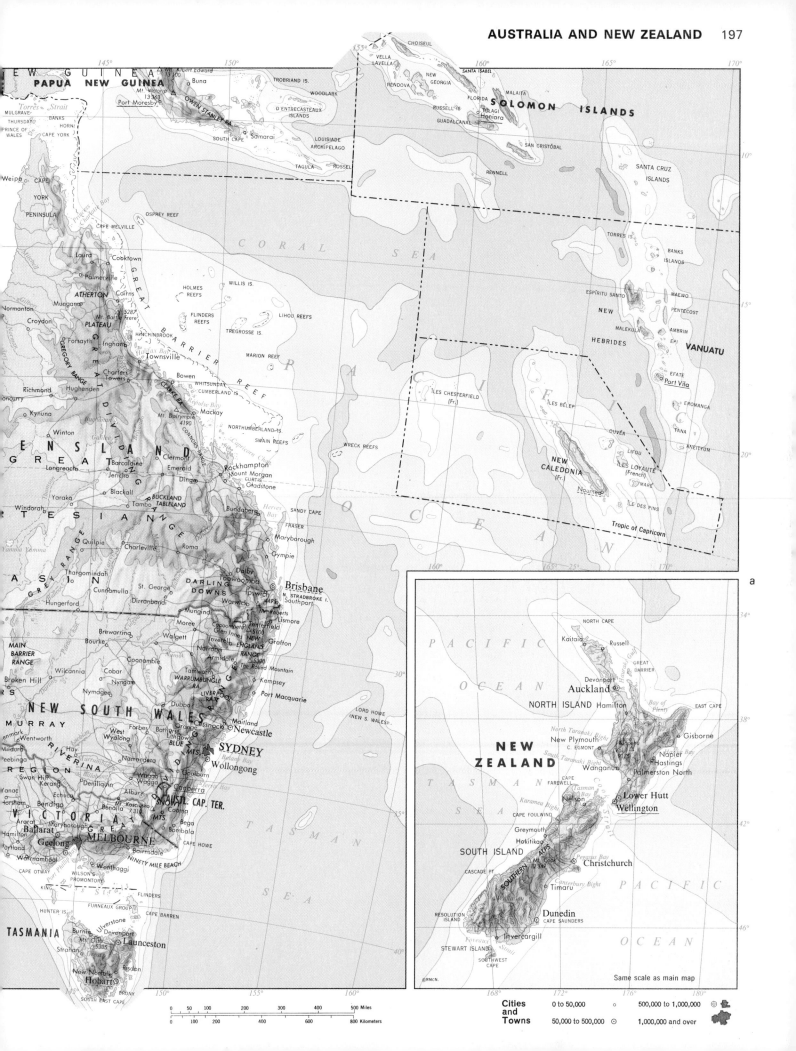

NEW GUINEA
PAPUA NEW GUINEA
Mt. Albert Edward 13100
Buna
Mt. Victoria 13363
Port Moresby
OWEN STANLEY RA.
TROBRIAND IS.
WOODLARK
CHOISEUL
VELLA LAVELLA
NEW GEORGIA
RENDOVA
SANTA ISABEL
FLORIDA
RUSSELL IS.
TULAGI
Honiara
MALAITA
SOLOMON ISLANDS

Torres Strait
THURSDAY
BANKS
HORN I.
PRINCE OF WALES
CAPE YORK
SOUTH CAPE
Samarai
D'ENTRECASTEAUX ISLANDS
LOUISIADE ARCHIPELAGO
TAGULA
ROSSEL
GUADALCANAL
SAN CRISTÓBAL
RENNELL
SANTA CRUZ ISLANDS

Weipa
CAPE YORK PENINSULA
Princess Charlotte Bay
OSPREY REEF
TORRES IS.
BANKS ISLANDS

C O R A L   S E A

Laura
Cooktown
CAPE MELVILLE
HOLMES REEFS
WILLIS IS.
ESPÍRITU SANTO
MAEWO
Normanton
Mungana
Palmerville
ATHERTON PLATEAU
Cairns
Mt. Bartle Frere 5287
FLINDERS REEFS
LIHOU REEFS
NEW HEBRIDES
MALEKULA
PENTECOST
AMBRIM
EPI
Croydon
Forsayth
Ingham
HINCHINBROOK I.
TREGROSSE IS.
VANUATU
Kynuna
Richmond
Hughenden
Charters Towers
Halifax Bay
Townsville
MARION REEF
EFATE
Port Vila
Winton
Mt. Dalrymple 4190
Bowen
WHITSUNDAY
CUMBERLAND IS.
Repulse Bay
Mackay
ÎLES CHESTERFIELD (Fr.)
ÎLES BÉLEP
EROMANGA
Barcaldine
Jericho
Clermont
Emerald
Dingo
NORTHUMBERLAND IS.
SWAIN REEFS
OUVÉA
TANA
ANEITYUM
Longreach
Blackall
Rockhampton
Mount Morgan
CURTIS
Gladstone
WRECK REEFS
NEW CALEDONIA (Fr.)
LIFOU
ÎLES LOYAUTÉ (French)
MARE
Yaraka
Tambo
BUCKLAND TABLELAND
Capricorn Chan.
Nouméa
ÎLE DES PINS
Windorah
Quilpie
Bundaberg
Hervey Bay
SANDY CAPE
Tropic of Capricorn
FRASER I.
Maryborough
Charleville
Roma
Gympie

P A C I F I C   O C E A N

Thargomindah
Cunnamulla
St. George
DARLING DOWNS
Dalby
Toowoomba
Brisbane
Ipswich
N. STRADBROKE I.
Southport
Hungerford
Dirranbandi
Warwick
Mungindi
Stanthorpe
Tenterfield
Lismore
Moree
Inverell
Glen Innes
NEW ENGLAND RANGE
Grafton
Brewarrina
Walgett
Narrabri
Armidale
The Round Mountain 5300
Bourke
Coonamble
Tamworth
WARRUMBUNGLE RA.
Kempsey
Port Macquarie
MAIN BARRIER RANGE
Wilcannia
Cobar
Nyngan
LIVERPOOL RA.
LORD HOWE I. (NEW S. WALES)
Broken Hill
Nymagee
Dubbo
NEW SOUTH WALES
Forbes
Orange
Bathurst
Cessnock
Maitland
Newcastle
MURRAY
West Wyalong
Lithgow
BLUE MTS.
SYDNEY
RIVERINA REGION
Hay
Narrandera
Wagga Wagga
Cootamundra
Wollongong
Mildura
Swan Hill
Kerang
Albury
Canberra
AUSTL. CAP. TER.
VICTORIA
Bendigo
Benalla
Mt. Kosciusko 7316
Cooma
GREAT
Bega
Ararat
Maryborough
Bombala
CAPE HOWE
Ballarat
Geelong
MELBOURNE
Bairnsdale
NINETY MILE BEACH
CAPE OTWAY
WILSON'S PROMONTORY
Warrnambool
Wonthaggi
KING I.
FLINDERS I.
FURNEAUX GROUP

T A S M A N   S E A

TASMANIA
Burnie
Devonport
HUNTER IS.
Ulverstone
CAPE BARREN
Strahan
Launceston
Mt. Ossa 5305
New Norfolk
Hobart
BRUNY I.
SOUTH EAST CAPE

0	50	100	200	300	400	500 Miles
0	100	200	400	600	800 Kilometers

New Zealand inset

a

NORTH CAPE
Kaitaia
Russell
PACIFIC OCEAN
GREAT BARRIER
Devonport
Auckland
NORTH ISLAND
Hamilton
Bay of Plenty
EAST CAPE
North Taranaki Bight
New Plymouth
C. EGMONT
South Taranaki Bight
Gisborne
NEW ZEALAND
Wanganui
Napier
Hastings
Palmerston North
CAPE FAREWELL
Nelson
Lower Hutt
Wellington
T A S M A N   S E A
Karamea Bight
CAPE FOULWIND
Greymouth
Hokitika
Cook Strait
SOUTH ISLAND
SOUTHERN ALPS
Mt. Cook 12349
Christchurch
CASCADE PT.
Canterbury Bight
Timaru
RESOLUTION ISLAND
Dunedin
CAPE SAUNDERS
Invercargill
Foveaux Strait
STEWART ISLAND
SOUTHWEST CAPE

Same scale as main map

Cities and Towns	0 to 50,000	○	500,000 to 1,000,000	◎
	50,000 to 500,000	⊙	1,000,000 and over	⬤

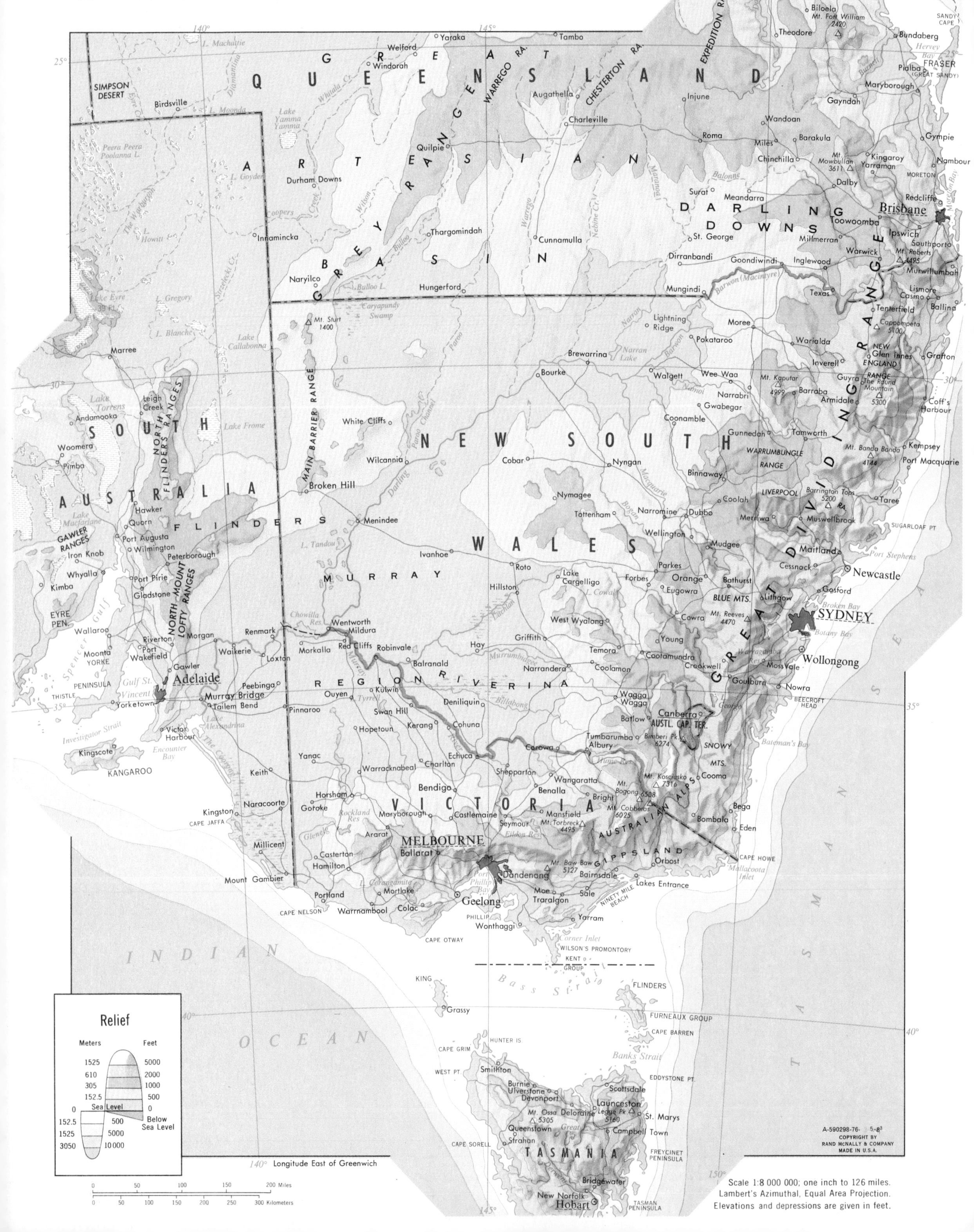
QUEENSLAND
GREAT ARTESIAN BASIN
GREY RANGE
WARREGO RA.
CHESTERTON RA.
EXPEDITION RA.
DARLING DOWNS
SIMPSON DESERT
SOUTH AUSTRALIA
NEW SOUTH WALES
VICTORIA
TASMANIA
FLINDERS RANGES
NORTH FLINDERS RANGES
NORTH MOUNT LOFTY RANGES
MAIN BARRIER RANGE
GAWLER RANGES
MURRAY
MURRAY REGION
RIVERINA
GREAT DIVIDING RANGE
NEW ENGLAND RANGE
WARRUMBUNGLE RANGE
LIVERPOOL RA.
BLUE MTS.
SNOWY MTS.
AUSTRALIAN ALPS
GIPPSLAND
AUSTL. CAP. TER.
EYRE PEN.
YORKE PENINSULA
KANGAROO
INDIAN OCEAN
TASMAN SEA
Bass Strait
Gladstone
Biloela
Mt. Fort William 2420
Theodore
Bundaberg
SANDY CAPE
Hervey Bay
FRASER (GREAT SANDY)
Pialba
Maryborough
Gayndah
Injune
Wandoan
Roma
Miles
Barakula
Chinchilla
Mt. Mowbullan 3611
Kingaroy
Yarraman
Gympie
Nambour
MORETON
Moreton Bay
Dalby
Redcliffe
Brisbane
Toowoomba
Ipswich
Southport
Surat
Meandarra
Balonne
Millmerran
Warwick
Mt. Roberts 4495
Murwillumbah
St. George
Dirranbandi
Goondiwindi
Inglewood
Mungindi
Barwon (Macintyre)
Texas
Lismore
Casino
Ballina
Tenterfield
Cappompeta 5100
Yaraka
Tambo
Welford
Windorah
Augathella
Charleville
Quilpie
Durham Downs
Thargomindah
Cunnamulla
Innamincka
Naryilco
Hungerford
Bulloo L.
Caryapundy Swamp
Birdsville
L. Machattie
L. Moonda
Lake Yamma Yamma
Peera Peera Poolanna L.
L. Goyder
Coopers Creek
L. Howitt
Lake Eyre 39 Ft.
L. Gregory
L. Blanche
Lake Callabonna
Mt. Sturt 1400
Marree
Lake Torrens
Leigh Creek
Andamooka
Lake Frome
Woomera
Pimba
Lake Macfarlane
Hawker
Quorn
Port Augusta
Wilmington
Iron Knob
Peterborough
Whyalla
Port Pirie
Kimba
Gladstone
Wallaroo
Moonta
Riverton
Port Wakefield
Morgan
Renmark
Waikerie
Loxton
Gawler
Adelaide
Gulf St. Vincent
Spencer Gulf
THISTLE
Yorketown
Murray Bridge
Tailem Bend
Peebinga
Pinnaroo
Lake Alexandrina
Victor Harbour
Investigator Strait
Kingscote
Encounter Bay
The Coorong
Keith
Kingston
CAPE JAFFA
Naracoorte
Millicent
Mount Gambier
Lightning Ridge
Moree
Pokataroo
Warialda
Brewarrina
Narran Lake
Bourke
Walgett
Wee Waa
Inverell
Glen Innes
Grafton
Guyra
The Round Mountain 5300
Mt. Kaputar 4999
Barraba
Armidale
Coff's Harbour
Narrabri
Gwabegar
Namoi
Coonamble
White Cliffs
Gunnedah
Tamworth
Mt. Banda Banda 4144
Kempsey
Port Macquarie
Wilcannia
Cobar
Nyngan
Binnaway
Broken Hill
Barrington Tops 5200
Taree
Nymagee
Coolah
Tottenham
Narromine
Dubbo
Merriwa
Muswellbrook
SUGARLOAF PT
Menindee
L. Tandou
Wellington
Mudgee
Maitland
Port Stephens
Ivanhoe
Roto
Parkes
Cessnock
Newcastle
Lake Cargelligo
Forbes
Orange
Bathurst
Gosford
L. Cowal
Eugowra
Hillston
Lithgow
Broken Bay
SYDNEY
Botany Bay
Mt. Reeves 4470
Cowra
West Wyalong
Young
Chowilla Res.
Wentworth
Mildura
Red Cliffs
Robinvale
Hay
Griffith
Temora
Morkalla
Balranald
Murrumbidgee
Cootamundra
Crookwell
Wollongong
Moss Vale
Narrandera
Coolamon
Goulburn
Nowra
BEECROFT HEAD
Ouyen
Kulwin
Tyrrell
Deniliquin
Billabong
Wagga Wagga
Canberra
Lachlan
Swan Hill
Kerang
Cohuna
Batlow
Hopetoun
Bimberi Pk. 6274
Tumbarumba
Albury
Corowa
Hume Res.
Bateman's Bay
Yanac
Warracknabeal
Charlton
Echuca
Shepparton
Wangaratta
Benalla
Bright
Mt. Kosciusko 7316
Cooma
Mt. Bogong 6508
Bendigo
Horsham
Goroke
Rockland Res.
Maryborough
Castlemaine
Seymour
Mansfield
Mt. Cobberas 6025
Mt. Torbreck 4495
Eildon Res.
Bega
Bombala
Eden
Glenelg
Ararat
MELBOURNE
Ballarat
Casterton
Hamilton
Mt. Baw Baw 5127
Orbost
CAPE HOWE
Mallacoota Inlet
Dandenong
Bairnsdale
Lakes Entrance
Port Phillip Bay
L. Corangamite
Portland
Mortlake
Geelong
Moe
Traralgon
Sale
NINETY MILE BEACH
CAPE NELSON
Warrnambool
Colac
PHILLIP
Wonthaggi
Yarram
CAPE OTWAY
Corner Inlet
WILSON'S PROMONTORY
KENT GROUP
KING
FLINDERS
Grassy
FURNEAUX GROUP
CAPE BARREN
HUNTER IS.
CAPE GRIM
Banks Strait
WEST PT.
Smithton
EDDYSTONE PT.
Burnie
Ulverstone
Devonport
Scottsdale
Launceston
Mt. Ossa 5305
Deloraine
Legge Pk. 5160
St. Marys
Queenstown
Great L.
Campbell Town
Strahan
CAPE SORELL
FREYCINET PENINSULA
Bridgewater
Derwent
New Norfolk
Hobart
TASMAN PENINSULA
25°
30°
35°
40°
140°
145°
150°
140° Longitude East of Greenwich
Relief
Meters
Feet
1525
5000
610
2000
305
1000
152.5
500
0
Sea Level
0
Below Sea Level
152.5
500
1525
5000
3050
10 000
0 50 100 150 200 Miles
0 50 100 150 200 250 300 Kilometers
A-590298-76- 5-8
COPYRIGHT BY RAND McNALLY & COMPANY MADE IN U.S.A.
Scale 1:8 000 000; one inch to 126 miles.
Lambert's Azimuthal, Equal Area Projection.
Elevations and depressions are given in feet.

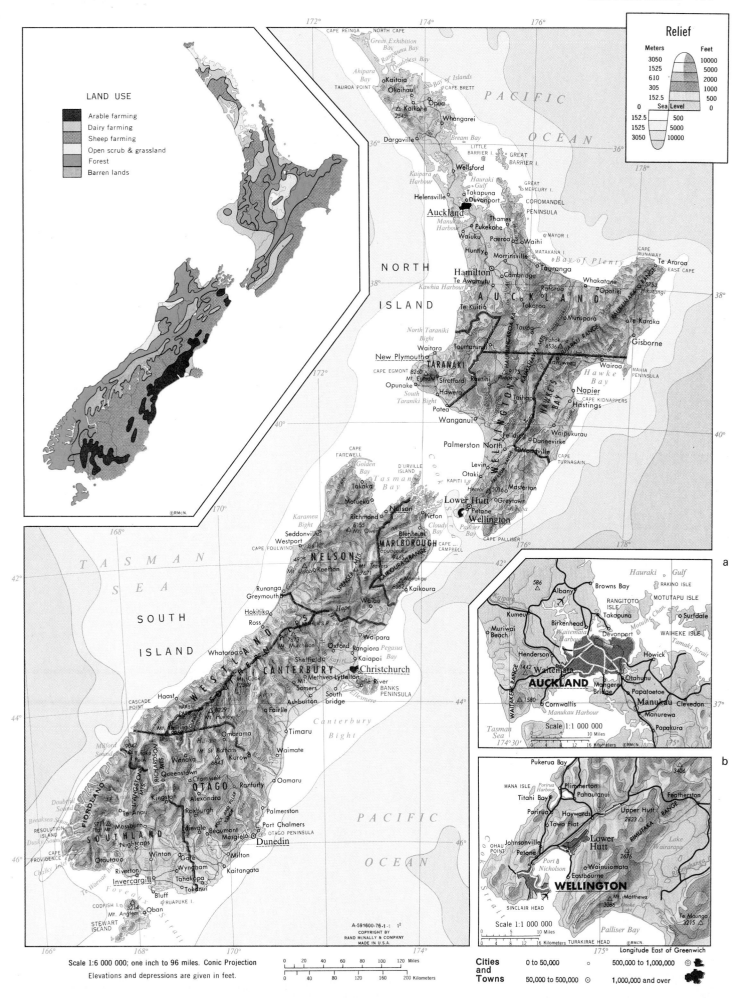

Relief

Meters		Feet
3050		10000
1525		5000
610		2000
305		1000
152.5		500
0	Sea Level	0
152.5		500
1525		5000
3050		10000

LAND USE

- Arable farming
- Dairy farming
- Sheep farming
- Open scrub & grassland
- Forest
- Barren lands

©RMcN.

PACIFIC OCEAN

NORTH ISLAND

AUCKLAND

TASMAN SEA

SOUTH ISLAND

PACIFIC OCEAN

Scale 1:6 000 000; one inch to 96 miles. Conic Projection
Elevations and depressions are given in feet.

| 0 | 20 | 40 | 60 | 80 | 100 | 120 Miles |
| 0 | 40 | 80 | 120 | 160 | 200 Kilometers |

A-591600-76-1 1²
COPYRIGHT BY
RAND McNALLY & COMPANY
MADE IN U.S.A.

a

AUCKLAND

Hauraki Gulf

Scale 1:1 000 000

| 0 | | 10 Miles |
| 0 | 4 8 12 | 16 Kilometers | ©RMcN.

b

WELLINGTON

Lower Hutt

Scale 1:1 000 000

| 0 | | 10 Miles |
| 0 | 4 8 12 | 16 Kilometers | ©RMcN.

Longitude East of Greenwich

Cities and Towns

0 to 50,000	○	500,000 to 1,000,000	◎
50,000 to 500,000	⊙	1,000,000 and over	■

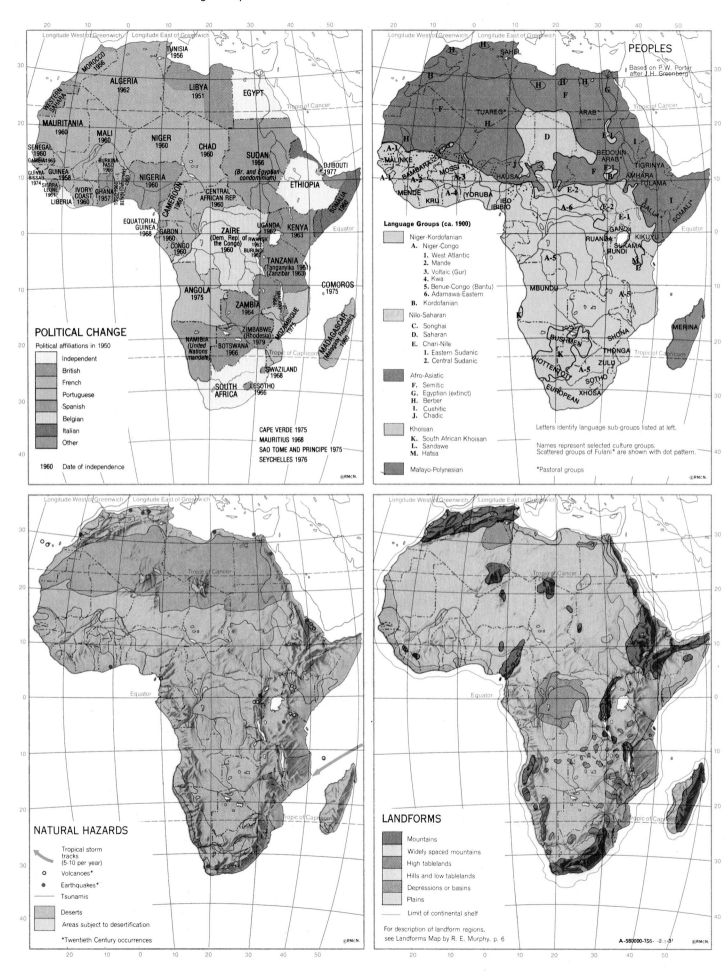

POLITICAL CHANGE

Political affiliations in 1950

- Independent
- British
- French
- Portuguese
- Spanish
- Belgian
- Italian
- Other

1960 Date of independence

CAPE VERDE 1975
MAURITIUS 1968
SAO TOME AND PRINCIPE 1975
SEYCHELLES 1976

WESTERN SAHARA
MOROCCO 1956
TUNISIA 1956
ALGERIA 1962
LIBYA 1951
EGYPT
MAURITANIA 1960
MALI 1960
NIGER 1960
CHAD 1960
SUDAN 1956 (Br. and Egyptian condominium)
DJIBOUTI 1977
SENEGAL 1960
GAMBIA 1965
GUINEA-BISSAU 1974
GUINEA 1958
SIERRA LEONE 1961
LIBERIA 1960
IVORY COAST 1960
GHANA 1957
BURKINA FASO 1960
BENIN (TOGO) 1960
NIGERIA 1960
CAMEROON 1960
CENTRAL AFRICAN REP. 1960
ETHIOPIA
SOMALIA 1960
EQUATORIAL GUINEA 1968
GABON 1960
CONGO 1960
ZAIRE (Dem. Rep. of the Congo) 1960
UGANDA 1962
RWANDA 1962
BURUNDI 1962
KENYA 1963
TANZANIA (Tanganyika 1961) (Zanzibar 1963)
COMOROS 1975
ANGOLA 1975
ZAMBIA 1964
MALAWI 1964
MOZAMBIQUE 1975
MADAGASCAR (Malagasy Republic) 1960
NAMIBIA (United Nations mandate)
ZIMBABWE (Rhodesia) 1979
BOTSWANA 1966
SWAZILAND 1968
SOUTH AFRICA
LESOTHO 1966

PEOPLES

Based on P.W. Porter after J.H. Greenberg

Language Groups (ca. 1900)

Niger-Kordofanian
- A. Niger-Congo
  1. West Atlantic
  2. Mande
  3. Voltaic (Gur)
  4. Kwa
  5. Benue-Congo (Bantu)
  6. Adamawa-Eastern
- B. Kordofanian

Nilo-Saharan
- C. Songhai
- D. Saharan
- E. Chari-Nile
  1. Eastern Sudanic
  2. Central Sudanic

Afro-Asiatic
- F. Semitic
- G. Egyptian (extinct)
- H. Berber
- I. Cushitic
- J. Chadic

Khoisan
- K. South African Khoisan
- L. Sandawe
- M. Hatsa

Malayo-Polynesian

Letters identify language sub-groups listed at left.

Names represent selected culture groups.
Scattered groups of Fulani* are shown with dot pattern.

*Pastoral groups

NATURAL HAZARDS

↗ Tropical storm tracks (5-10 per year)
○ Volcanoes*
● Earthquakes*
— Tsunamis

Deserts
Areas subject to desertification

*Twentieth Century occurrences

LANDFORMS

- Mountains
- Widely spaced mountains
- High tablelands
- Hills and low tablelands
- Depressions or basins
- Plains

— Limit of continental shelf

For description of landform regions,
see Landforms Map by R. E. Murphy, p. 6

A-580000-1S6- -2.1-91

©RMcN.

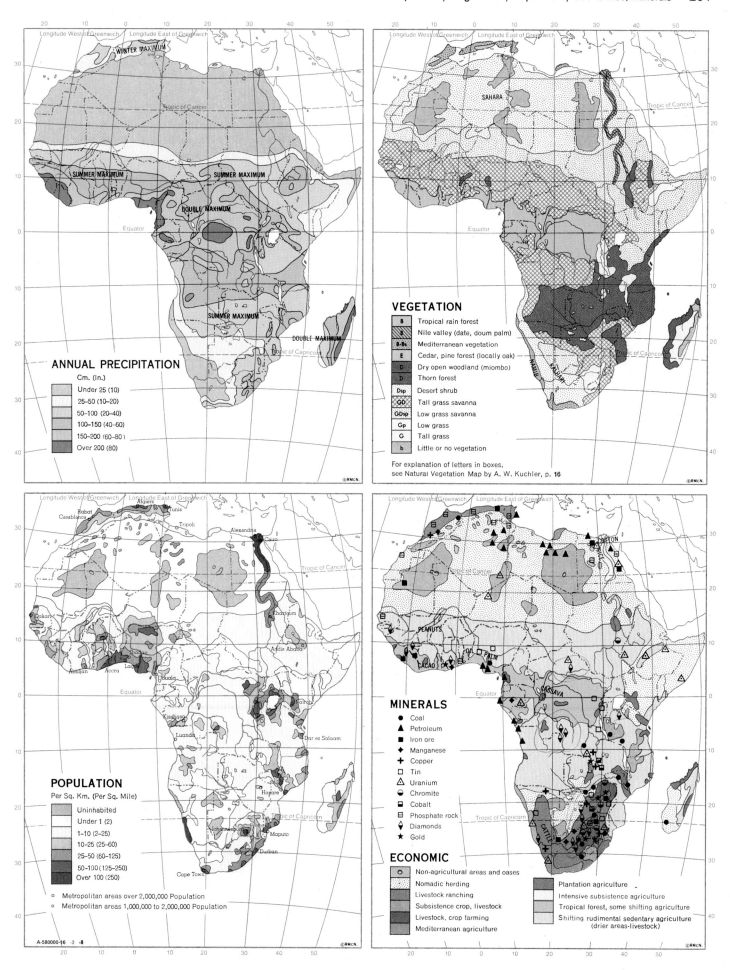

ANNUAL PRECIPITATION

Cm. (In.)

	Under 25 (10)
	25–50 (10–20)
	50–100 (20–40)
	100–150 (40–60)
	150–200 (60–80)
	Over 200 (80)

VEGETATION

B	Tropical rain forest
B	Nile valley (date, doum palm)
B-Bs	Mediterranean vegetation
E	Cedar, pine forest (locally oak)
D	Dry open woodland (miombo)
D	Thorn forest
Dsp	Desert shrub
GD	Tall grass savanna
GDsp	Low grass savanna
Gp	Low grass
G	Tall grass
b	Little or no vegetation

For explanation of letters in boxes,
see Natural Vegetation Map by A. W. Kuchler, p. 16

POPULATION

Per Sq. Km. (Per Sq. Mile)

	Uninhabited
	Under 1 (2)
	1–10 (2–25)
	10–25 (25–60)
	25–50 (60–125)
	50–100 (125–250)
	Over 100 (250)

▫ Metropolitan areas over 2,000,000 Population
◦ Metropolitan areas 1,000,000 to 2,000,000 Population

A-580000-16 -3 -8

MINERALS

● Coal
▲ Petroleum
■ Iron ore
◆ Manganese
✛ Copper
☐ Tin
△ Uranium
◖ Chromite
⊟ Cobalt
⊞ Phosphate rock
◇ Diamonds
★ Gold

ECONOMIC

⊙	Non-agricultural areas and oases
	Nomadic herding
	Livestock ranching
	Subsistence crop, livestock
	Livestock, crop farming
	Mediterranean agriculture
	Plantation agriculture
	Intensive subsistence agriculture
	Tropical forest, some shifting agriculture
	Shifting rudimental sedentary agriculture (drier areas-livestock)

ATLANTIC OCEAN

MADRID

CORSICA
ROME
SARDINIA

Black Sea
ISTANBUL
BAKU
Caspian Sea

M e d i t e r r a n e a n   S e a

SICILY
Athens
CRETE
CYPRUS
Beirut

TEHRĀN

Algiers
Tunis
MALTA

TĪGRIS
Baghdad
Euphrates

Casablanca

ATLAS   MOUNTAINS
Tripoli

Alexandria
SYRIAN DESERT

AN NAFŪD

CANARY ISLANDS

GRAND ERG OCCIDENTAL
GRAND ERG ORIENTAL

CAIRO
ARABIAN DESERT

Riyadh

El Aaiun

Tropic of Cancer

S   A   H   A   R   A

Nile
Lake Nasser
Mecca

AHAGGAR
Tamenghest

LIBYAN DESERT

NUBIAN DESERT

Red Sea

ADRAR
DES IFOGHAS

TIBESTI

Tombouctou

ENNEDI
Nile

Khartoum
Asmera

DANAKIL
Aden
Gulf of Aden

Dakar
Bamako
Niger
Lake Chad
Al-Fāshir
White Nile
Blue Nile
Berbera

Kano
N'Djamena
Addis Ababa

Freetown
Niger
Mountain Nile

Lake Volta
Yaoundé
Bangui
Uele

Abidjan
Lagos

Gulf of Guinea
Congo (Zaire)
Kisangani

Lake Victoria
Nairobi

Equator

Congo (Zaire)

INDIAN OCEAN

Ubangi

Muqdisho

Kasai

Kinshasa
Lake Tanganyika
Dar es Salaam

Luanda
COMORO ISLANDS

ATLANTIC OCEAN
Lubumbashi
Lake Nyasa
Moçambique

Lusaka
Blantyre

Zambezi
Mozambique Channel

Harare
MADAGASCAR
Antananarivo

NAMIB DESERT
Windhoek
KALAHARI DESERT
Limpopo

Tropic of Capricorn

Orange
Johannesburg

Orange
Durban
INDIAN OCEAN

Cape Town

■ Urban
Cropland
Cropland & Woodland
Cropland & Grazing Land
Grassland, Grazing Land
Forest, Woodland
Swamp, Marshland
Shrub, Sparse Grass, Wasteland (pattern)
Barren Land
• Oasis

E-580000-96-
COPYRIGHT BY
RAND McNALLY & COMPANY
MADE IN U.S.A.

Scale 1:36,000,000; one inch to 570 miles. Lambert Azimuthal Equal-Area Projection

0   100   200   400   600   800 Miles

0   150   300   600   900   1200 Kilometers

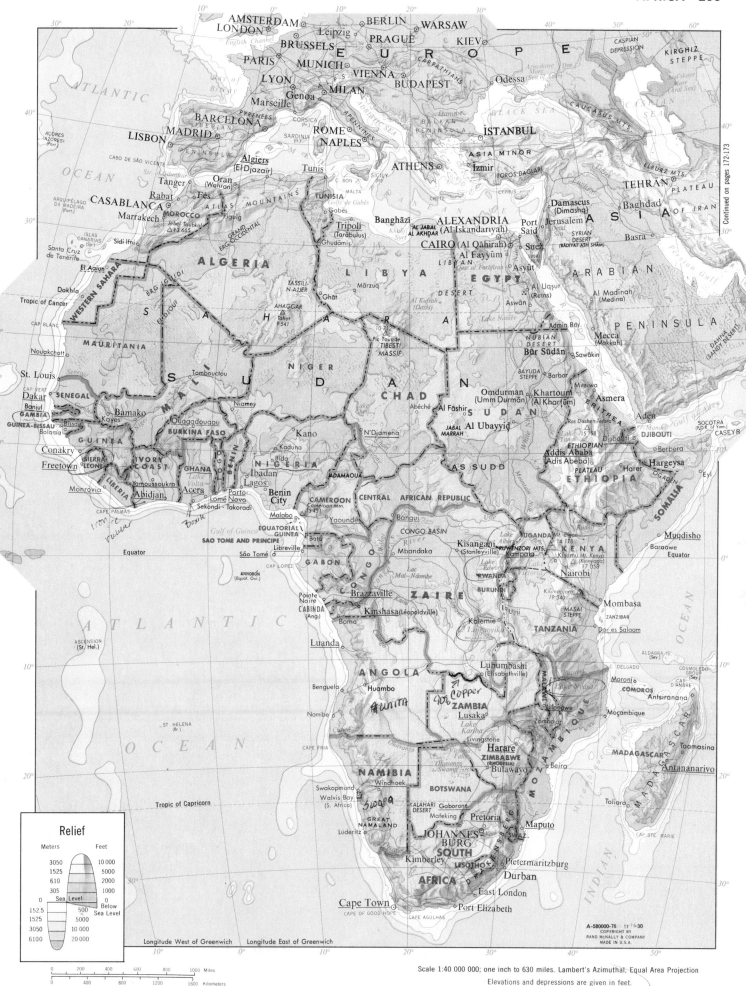

Continued on pages 172-173

Relief

Meters		Feet
3050		10 000
1525		5000
610		2000
305		1000
0	Sea Level	0
		Below
152.5		Sea Level
1525		500
3050		5000
6100		10 000
		20 000

Longitude West of Greenwich   Longitude East of Greenwich

0   200   400   600   800   1000 Miles
0   400   800   1200   1600 Kilometers

Scale 1:40 000 000; one inch to 630 miles. Lambert's Azimuthal, Equal Area Projection

Elevations and depressions are given in feet.

A-580000-76
COPYRIGHT BY
RAND McNALLY & COMPANY
MADE IN U.S.A.

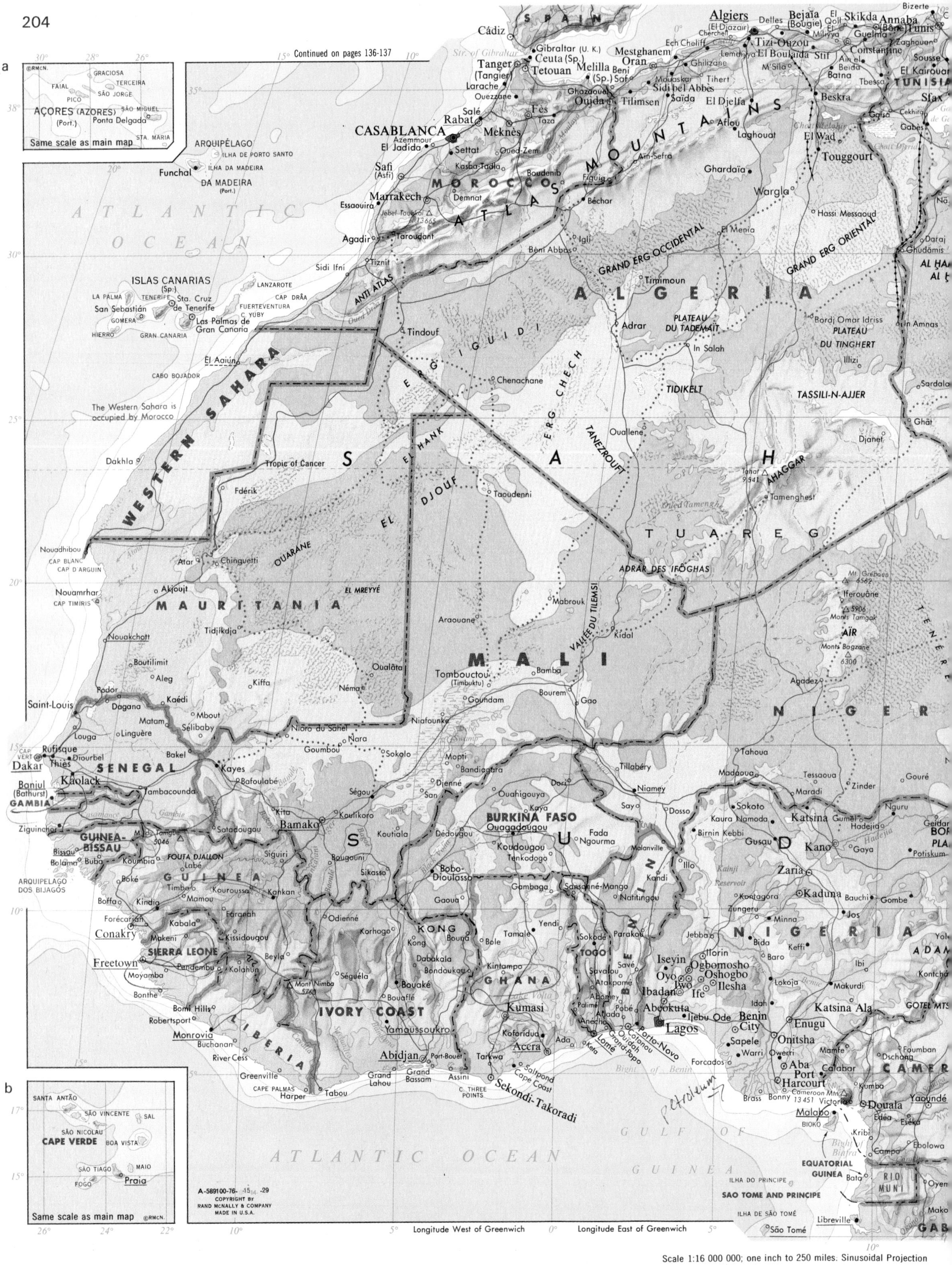

a

AÇORES (AZORES)
(Port.)
GRACIOSA
FAIAL TERCEIRA
PICO SÃO JORGE
SÃO MIGUEL
Ponta Delgada STA. MARIA
Same scale as main map

Continued on pages 136-137

ARQUIPÉLAGO
ILHA DE PORTO SANTO
Funchal
ILHA DA MADEIRA
DA MADEIRA
(Port.)

S P A I N
Cádiz
Gibraltar (U.K.)
Str. of Gibraltar
Ceuta (Sp.)
Tanger (Tangier)
Tetouan Melilla (Sp.)
Larache Beni
Ouezzane

Algiers (El Djazair) Delles Bejaïa (Bougie) El Qoll Skikda Bizerte Annaba (Bône)
Ech Cheliff Cherchell Tizi-Ouzou Stif Guelma TUNIS Tunis
Mestghanem Oran Muaskar Tihert M'Sila Batna El Kairouan Sousse
Sidi-bel-Abbes Saïda El Djelfa Aïn Beïda Tbessa Sfax

CASABLANCA
Rabat Salé
El Jadida Meknès
Settat Fés
Safi (Asfi) Oued-Zem Taza
Kasba-Tadla
Boudenib

Laghouat El Wad
Aflou Touggourt
Ghardaïa Wargla
Béchar Hassi Messaoud
Figuig In Amnas Ghdâmis
AL HAM
AI S

MOROCCO A T L A S M O U N T A I N S A L G E R I A

Marrakech
Essaouira Demnat
Jebel Toubkal 13665
Agadir Taroudant
Tiznit Béni Abbas
Igli

GRAND ERG OCCIDENTAL
Timimoun
Adrar
PLATEAU DU TADEMAÏT
In Salah

GRAND ERG ORIENTAL
Bordj Omar Idriss
PLATEAU DU TINGHERT
Illizi

ISLAS CANARIAS (Sp.)
LA PALMA TENERIFE LANZAROTE
San Sebastián Sta. Cruz de Tenerife CAP DRÂA FUERTEVENTURA
GOMERA Las Palmas de Gran Canaria CAP JUBY
HIERRO GRAN CANARIA

CABO BOJADOR
El Aaiún

ANTI ATLAS
Sidi Ifni
Tindouf

E R G I G U I D I
E R G C H E C H

TIDIKELT
TASSILI-N-AJJER
Ghat
Ouallene
Djanet

The Western Sahara is occupied by Morocco

W E S T E R N S A H A R A

Dakhla
Tropic of Cancer
Fdérik
El Hank
TANEZROUFT
Taoudenni
AHAGGAR
Tahat 9541
Tamenghest

S A H A R A
S A H A R A

Nouadhibou
CAP BLANC
CAP D'ARGUIN
Atar Chinguetti
OUARANE
EL DJOUF

T U A R E G
ADRAR DES IFÓGHAS
Mt. Gréboun 4562
Iferouâne
AÏR
Monts Tamgak
Monts Bogzane 6300

Nouamrhar
CAP TIMIRIS
Akjoujt
EL MREYYÉ
Mabrouk
VALLÉE DU TILEMSI
Kidal
Agadez

M A U R I T A N I A
Nouakchott
Tidjikdja
Boutilimit
Aleg
Kiffa
Néma
Araouane
Tombouctou (Timbuktu)
Bamba
M A L I

N I G E R

Saint-Louis
Podor
Dagana
Matam
Sélibaby
Nioro du Sahel
Niafounké
Goundam
Bourem
Gao
Tahoua
Tessaoua
Zinder
Gouré
Nguru

Louga
Rufisque
CAP VERT
Dakar
Thiès Diourbel
Kaédi
Mbout
Linguère
Nara
Goumbou
Mopti Bandiagara
Douentza
Tillabéry
Madaoua
Maradi
Katsina

SENEGAL
Kaolack
Tambacounda
Kayes
Bafoulabé
Ségou
Dienné
San
Ouahigouya
Kaya
Niamey
Dosso
Sokoto
Kaura Namoda
Gumel

Banjul (Bathurst)
GAMBIA
Ziguinchor
GUINEA-BISSAU
Bissau
Bolama
ARQUIPÉLAGO DOS BIJAGÓS

Kita
Koulikoro
Bamako
Satadougou
Siguiri
Kouroussa
BURKINA FASO
Ouagadougou
Dédougou
Koudougou
Tenkodogo
Dori
Fada N'Gourma
Say
Malanville
Kandi
Birnin Kebbi
Gusau
Illo
Gaya
D Kano
Zaria

FOUTA DJALLON
Labé
Tougué
GUINEA
Boké
Kindia
Conakry
Forécariah
Mamou
Faranah
Kankan
SIERRA LEONE
Freetown
Makeni

Sikasso
Bougouni
Koutiala
Bobo-Dioulasso
Gaoua
Gambaga
Sansanné-Mango
Natitingou
Kontagora
Minna
Bida
Katagum
Bauchi
Gombe
BO
PLA

S O U D A N

Kabala
Kissidougou
Beyla
Odienné
Korhogo
KONG
Bouna
Tamale
Yendi
Sokodé
Parakou
Jebba
N I G E R I A
Kaduna
Zungeru

KONG
Kong
Dabakala
Bondoukou
Bole
Kintampo
TOGO
Lokoja
Keffi
Baro
Ibi

Pendembu
Kolahun
Séguéla
Bouaflé
GHANA
Savalou
Abomey
Iseyin
Ilorin
Ogbomosho
Oshogbo
Ilesha
Ife
Oyo
ADAM

Moyamba
Bonthe
Mont Nimba 5748
Bouaké
Kumasi
Koforidua
Iwo Ibadan
Abeokuta
Benin City
Enugu
Onitsha
Mamfe
Foumban
CAMER

Bomi Hills
Robertsport
LIBERIA
Monrovia
Buchanan
IVORY COAST
Yamoussoukro
Abidjan
Accra
Ada
Anécho
Lagos
Porto-Novo
Ijebu Ode
Sapele
Warri
Owerri
Aba
Calabar
Dschang

River Cess
Greenville
Harper
CAPE PALMAS
Tabou
Grand Lahou
Grand Bassam
Assini
Tarkwa
Cape Coast
Sekondi-Takoradi
Saltpond
C. THREE POINTS
Lomé
Keta
Forcados
Brass
Port Harcourt
Bonny
Calabar 13451 Cameroon Mtn.
Victoria
Douala
Yaoundé
Eséka
Edéa
Kribi
EQUATORIAL GUINEA
Malabo
BIOKO
RIO MUNI
Oyen
GAB

A T L A N T I C O C E A N
GULF OF GUINEA
Bight of Benin
Bight of Biafra

SÃO TOMÉ AND PRINCIPE
ILHA DO PRINCIPE
ILHA DE SÃO TOMÉ
São Tomé
Libreville

Petroleum

b

SANTA ANTÃO
SÃO VICENTE SAL
SÃO NICOLAU BOA VISTA
CAPE VERDE
SÃO TIAGO MAIO
FOGO Praia
Same scale as main map

A-589100-76- -45 -14 -29
COPYRIGHT BY
RAND McNALLY & COMPANY
MADE IN U.S.A.

Longitude West of Greenwich Longitude East of Greenwich

Scale 1:16 000 000; one inch to 250 miles. Sinusoidal Projection
Elevations and depressions are given in feet

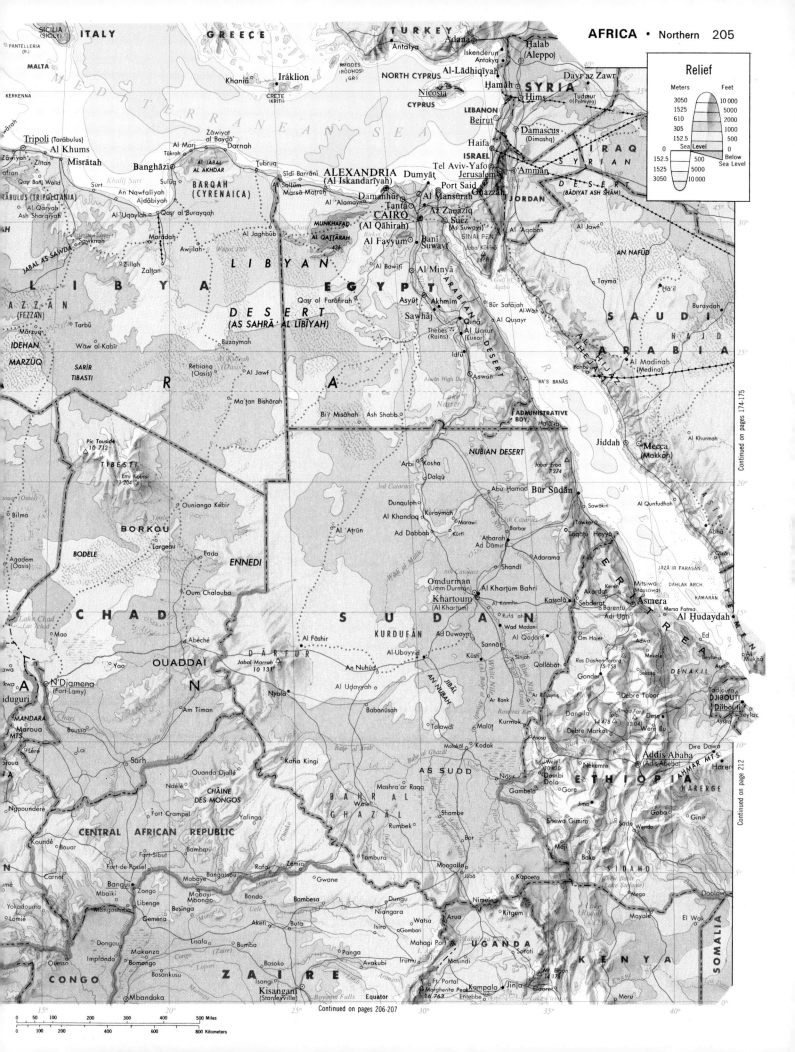

Relief

Meters	Feet
3050	10 000
1525	5000
610	2000
305	1000
152.5	500
0 Sea Level	0
152.5	500
1525	5000
3050	10 000

Below Sea Level

SICILIA (SICILY)
PANTELLERIA (It.)
MALTA
KERKENNA
ITALY
GREECE
TURKEY
Antalya
Adana
Iskenderun
Antakya
Halab (Aleppo)
Dayr az Zawr
Khaniá
Iráklion
RHODES (RÓDHOS) (GR.)
CRETE (KRÍTI)
NORTH CYPRUS
Nicosia
CYPRUS
Al-Lādhiqīyah
Ḥamāh
SYRIA
Ḥimṣ
Tudmur (Palmyra)
LEBANON
Beirut
Damascus (Dimashq)
IRAQ
SYRIAN DESERT (BĀDIYAT ASH SHĀM)
MEDITERRANEAN SEA

Tripoli (Ṭarābulus)
Al Khums
Zāwiyah
Zlitan
Misrātah
Qaṣr Banī Walīd
Banghāzī
Zāwiyat al Baydā
Tūkrah
Al Marj
Darnah
Tubruq
Sīdī Barrānī
Sallūm
Marsá Maṭrūḥ
ALEXANDRIA (Al Iskandarīyah)
Dumyāṭ
Port Said
Haifa
Tel Aviv-Yafo
Jerusalem
Ghazzah
Amman
ISRAEL
JORDAN
Al 'Aqabah
Al Jawf
AN NAFŪD

RABULUS (TRIPOLITANIA)
Surt
Khalīj Surt
BARQAH (CYRENAICA)
AL JABAL AL AKHDAR
Sulūq
An Nawfalīyah
Ajdābiyah
Al Uqaylah
Qaṣr al Burayqah
Al Qaryah
Ash Sharqīyah
Marādah
Awjilah
Al Jaghbūb
Al 'Alamayn
Damanhūr
Tanta
Az Zaqāzīq
Suez (As Suways)
SINAI PEN.
Jabal Katrīnah
Al Fayyūm
Banī Suwayf
Taymā
Ḥā'il
Buraydah

JABAL AS SAWDA
Sawknah
Zillah
Zaltan
MUNKHAFAD AL QATTĀRAH 436
Birkat Qārūn
CAIRO (Al Qāhirah)
LIBYAN
EGYPT
ARABIAN
Al Bawīṭī
Al Minyā
SAUDI ARABIA
NAJD

FEZZÁN (FEZZAN)
AZZAN
Tarbū
Wāw al-Kabīr
DESERT (AS SAHRĀ' AL LĪBĪYAH)
Buzaymah
Qaṣr al Farāfirah
Asyūṭ
Akhmīm
Sawhāj
Qinā
Bur Safājah
Al Qusayr
AL ḤIJAZ
Al Madīnah (Medina)
IDEHAN MARZŪQ
Marzūq
SARĪR TIBASTI
Rebiana (Oasis)
Al Kufrah
Al Jawf
Thebes (Ruins)
Al Uqsur (Luxor)
Idfū
Yanbu'
DESERT

Ma'tan Bishārah
Bi'r Misāḥah
Ash Shabb
Aswān
Aswān High Dam
Lake Nasser
RA'S BĀNĀS

Pic Touside 10 712
TIBESTI
Emi Koussi 11 204
Ma'ṭan Bishārah
ADMINISTRATIVE BDY.
Halā'ib
Jiddah
Mecca (Makkah)
Al Khurmah

BORKOU
BODELE
Ouanga Kébir
Largeau
Fada
ENNEDI
Al 'Aṭrūn
Arbi
Kosha
Dalqū
NUBIAN DESERT
Jabal Erba 7 274
Abu Ḥamad
Bur Sūdān
Sawākin
Al Qunfudhah
Abhā
JĀZ ĪR FARASĀN
3rd Cataract
Dunqulah
Al Khandaq
Kuraymah
Marawi
5th Cataract
Barbar
Taqātu Hayyā
Qizān
DAHLAK ARCH.
KAMARĀN

Agadem (Oasis)
Bilma
LAKE CHAD Lac Tchad
Mao
Abéché
OUADDAÏ
CHAD
Ad Dabbah
Kūrtī
Aṭbarah
Ad Dāmir
Adarama
Shandī
6th Cataract
Omdurman (Umm Durman)
Al Kharṭūm Bahri
Khartoum (Al Khartūm)
Al Kāmilīn
Kassalā
Akordat
Keren
Mitsiwa (Massawa)
Asmera
ERITREA
Mersa Fatma
Al Hudaydah

N'Djamena (Fort-Lamy)
MANDARA MTS.
Maroua
Bousso
SUDAN
KURDUFĀN
DĀRFŪR
Jabal Marrah 10 131
Al Fāshir
An Nuhūd
Al-Ubayyid
Ad Duwaym
Rufā'ah
Wad Madani
Al Qadārif
Om Hajer
Sebderat
Adi Ugri
Barentu
Adwa
Mekele
Ras Dashen Terara 15 158
Gonder
DENAKIL

Léré
Lai
Sarh
Am Timan
Nyala
Babanūsah
Talawdī
Malūṭ
An Rank
Sinjah
Qallābāt
Debre Tabor
Amba Farit 14 478
Dangila
Adwa
AHMAR MTS.
HARERGE
Djibouti
DJIBOUTI
Aysha
Seylac

Ngaoundéré
Bouar
Fort-Sibut
CENTRAL AFRICAN REPUBLIC
Bambari
CHÂINE DES MONGOS
Yalinga
BAHR AL GHAZĀL
Mashra'ar Raqq
AS SUDD
Nāṣir
Gambela
ETHIOPIA
Jima
Goba
SIDAMO
Ginir
Dire Dawa
Harer
Nekemte
Addis Ababa (Adis Abeba)
Debre Markos
Were Ilu
Dese
Asosa
Maji
Shewa Gimira

Bangui
Mbaïki
Zongo
Libenge
Bondo
Gemena
Busing
Akeli
Buta
Isiro
Gombari
Watsa
Niangara
Dungu
Arua
Kitgum
Soroti
UGANDA
Gulu
KENYA
Moyale
El Wak
SOMALIA
Doolow
Mega
Lake Stefanie
Baka
Gore
Dembi Dolo

Yokadouma
Lomié
Ouessa
CONGO
Impfondo
Dongou
Makanza
Bomongo
Mbandaka
Basankusu
Bumba
Lisala
Bomengo
ZAIRE
Basoko
Kisangani (Stanleyville)
Panga
Avakubi
Irumu
Mahagi Port
Masindi
Ft. Portal
Margherita Peak 16 763
Kampala
Jinja
Entebbe
Eldoret
Meru
Equator

Continued on pages 174-175
Continued on page 212
Continued on pages 206-207

0 50 100 200 300 400 500 Miles
0 100 200 400 600 800 Kilometers

Continued on pages 204-205

A T L A N T I C   O C E A N

G A B O N

C O N G O

Brazzaville

Pointe-Noire

CABINDA

Kinshasa
(Leopoldville)

Z A I R E

T A N Z A N

Luanda

A N G O L A

K A T A N G A

Lobito
Benguela

Kolwezi

Lubumbashi
(Elisabethville)

Ndola

Z A M B I A

BAROTSELAND

Lusaka

Harare (Salisbury)

Z I M B A B W E

(RHODESIA)

Bulawayo

CAPRIVI STRIP

O W A M B O

N A M I B I A

DAMARALAND

Windhoek

Walvis Bay
(S. Africa)

Tropic of Capricorn

B O T S W A N A

K A L A H A R I

D E S E R T

VENDA

KRUGER

TRANSVAAL

BOPHUTHATSWANA

Pretoria

JOHANNESBURG

GREAT NAMALAND

**ORANGE FREE
STATE**

Kimberley

Bloemfontein

LESOTHO

Maseru

NATAL

KWAZULU

Pietermaritzburg

Durban

S O U T H   A F R I C A

BUSHMANLAND

CAPE

GREAT KARROO

TRANSKEI

CISKEI

East London

LITTLE KARROO

Cape Town

Port Elizabeth

CAPE OF GOOD HOPE

CAPE AGULHAS

The "Homelands" (Bophuthatswana, Ciskei,
Transkei, Venda) were unilaterally created
by South Africa and are not
internationally recognized.

1 Bophuthatswana
2 Ciskei
3 Transkei
4 Venda

A-589200-76- 13 11-28
COPYRIGHT BY
RAND MCNALLY & COMPANY
MADE IN U.S.A.

Inset a — Cape Town:

**CAPE
TOWN**
MOUILLE PT.

ROBBENEILAND

Bloubergstrand

Durbanville

Milnerton

Table
Bay

Parow   Bellville

Camps Bay

Goodwood

Pinelands

Kuilsrivier

Nuweland

Wynberg

Ottery

**CAPE
FLATS**

Houtbaai

Muizenberg

SEAL ISLAND

Vishoek

Valsbaai
(False Bay)

Kommetjie

Simonstad

Swartkop
2229

ATLANTIC OCEAN

SMITSWINKEL
VLAKTE

KAAPPUNT

CAPE OF GOOD HOPE

Scale 1:1 000 000

0   10 Miles
0   4   8   12   16 Kilometers

Scale 1:16 000 000; one inch to 250 miles. Sinusoidal Projection
Elevations and depressions are given in feet

0   50   100   200   300   400   500 Miles
0   100   200   400   600   800 Kilometers

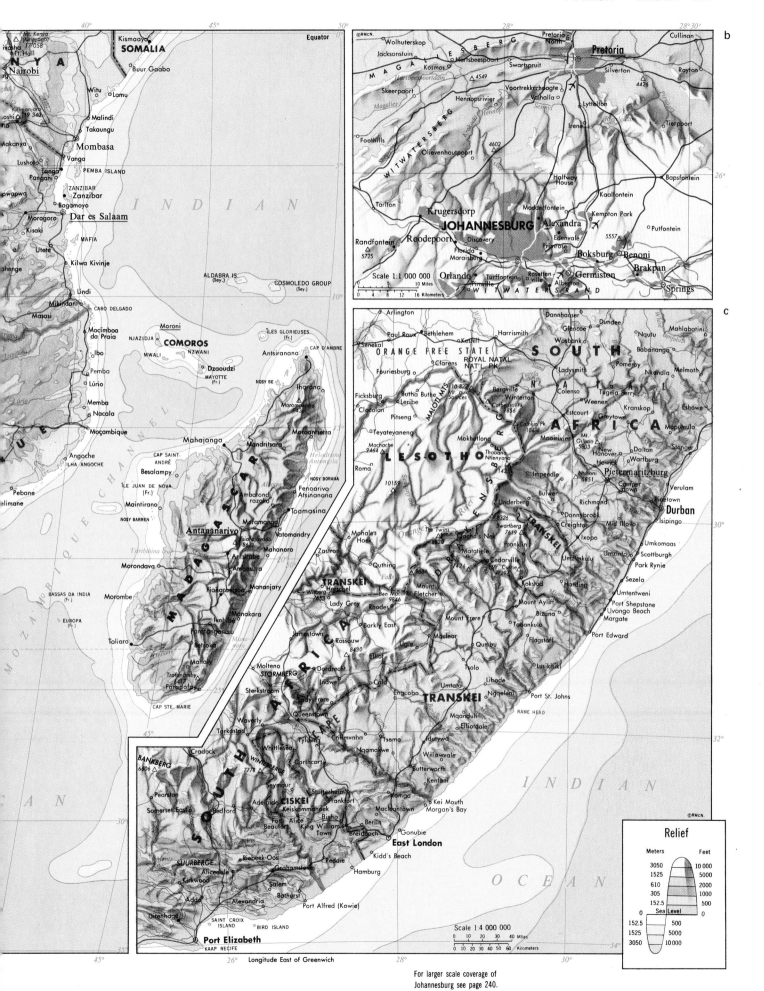

SOMALIA
Nairobi
Kismaayo
Buur Gaabo
Witu
Lamu
Takaungu
Mombasa
Vanga
PEMBA ISLAND
Tanga
ZANZIBAR
Zanzibar
Bagamoyo
Dar es Salaam
Morogoro
Kisaki
MAFIA
Utete
Kilwa Kivinje

I N D I A N

Lindi
Mikindani
CABO DELGADO
Masasi
Mocímboa
da Praia
NJAZIDJA
Moroni
ÎLES GLORIEUSES
(Fr.)
Ibo
COMOROS
NZWANI
MWALI
CAP D'AMBRE
Pemba
MAYOTTE
Dzaoudzi
(Fr.)
Antsiranana
Lúrio
NOSY BE
Memba
Iharana
Nacala
Moçambique
Maromokotro
Maroantsetra
Angoche
Mahajanga
Mandritsara
ILHA ANGOCHE
CAP SAINT-ANDRÉ
NOSY BORAHA
Helodrano
Antongila
Besalampy
ÎLE JUAN DE NOVA
(Fr.)
Fenoarivo
Afsinanana
Pebane
Ambatondrazaka
Toamasina
NOSY BARREN
Maintirano
Moramanga
ANTANANARIVO
Vatomandry
limane
Antsirabe
Mahanoro
Morondava
Ambositra
BASSAS DA INDIA
(Fr.)
Mananjary
Fianarantsoa
EUROPA
(Fr.)
Manakara
Ivohibe
Morombe
Fotadrevo
Mahaly
Farafangana
Toliara
Betroka
Ihosy
Ampanihy
CAP STE. MARIE

M O Z A M B I Q U E   C H A N N E L

MADAGASCAR

O C E A N

Wolhuterskop
Pretoria
North
Cullinan
Jacksonstuin
Pretoria
Kosmos
Hartsbeespoort
Swartspruit
Silverton
Rayton
Skeerpoort
4549
Voortrekkerhoogte
Hennopsrivier
Valhalla
Lyttelton
Tierpoort
Foothills
4602
Olievenhoutpoort
Irene
Halfway
House
26°
Tarlton
Kaalfontein
Bapsfontein
Krugersdorp
Moddarfontein
Kempton Park
JOHANNESBURG
Alexandra
Putfontein
Randfontein
Roodepoort
Discovery
Edenvale
5557
Florida
Primrose
Boksburg
Benoni
5725
Maraisburg
Germiston
Brakpan
Scale 1:1 000 000
Orlando
Turffontein
Rosetten-
ville
Alberton
Springs
0   5   10 Miles
0 4 8 12 16 Kilometers
Pimville
WITWATERSRAND

Arlington
Dannhauser
Dundee
Mahlabatini
Paul Roux
Bethlehem
Glencoe
Nqutu
Harrismith
Wasbank
Babanango
Senekal
Kestell
S O U T H
Pomeroy
Nkandla
Melmoth
ORANGE FREE STATE
Clarens
Ladysmith
Fouriesburg
ROYAL NATAL
NAT'L PK.
Tugela Ferry
Eshowe
Ficksburg
Leribe
MALOTI
10 822 Mt. aux
Sources
Bergville
Winterton
Cathedral Pk.
Colenso
Weenen
Kranskop
Clocolan
Butha Buthe
7856
Estcourt
Greytown
Mapumulo
Pitseng
Mooirivier
Mt.
Gilboa
New
Hanover
Dalton
Teyateyaneng
Cathkin Pk.
10 438
5803
Wartburg
Stanger
Machache
Mokhotlong
LESOTHO
Thabana
Ntlenyana
Howick
9464
1423
Nthoni
Pietermaritzburg
10159
Roma
Impendle
5851
Verulam
Bulwer
Richmond
Camper-
down
Underberg
Donnybrook
Pinetown
Durban
Mohale's
The Twins
Creighton
Mid Illovo
Isipingo
Hoek
Qacha's Nek
Ixopo
Umkomaas
Zastron
9326
Swartberg
Franklin
Umzinto
Scottburgh
Matatiele
7619
Park Rynie
Quthing
Cedarville
Kokstad
Harding
Sezela
9684
Mt. Currie
Umtentweni
Mount
9292
Port Shepstone
TRANSKEI
Fletcher
Mount Ayliff
Bizana
Uvongo Beach
Herschel
8846
Rhodes
Margate
Lady Grey
Mount Frere
Tabankulu
Port Edward
Barkly East
Maclear
Qumbu
Flagstaff
Jamestown
Ugie
Rossouw
8430
Tsolo
Libode
Elliot
Cala
Qumbu
Ngqeleni
Port St. Johns
Dordrecht
Engcobo
TRANSKEI
Indwe
Umtata
RAME HEAD
Lady Frere
Mqanduli
Queenstown
Tsomo
Idutywa
Elliotdale
Waverly
Cofimvaba
Tarkastad
Tylden
Ngamakwe
Willowvale
Cradock
Whittlesea
Cathcart
Butterworth
BANKBERG
WINTERBERG
Komga
Kentani
6406
7778
Stutterheim
Seymour
Frankfort
Kei Mouth
Adelaide
CISKEI
Macleantown
Morgan's Bay
Pearston
Keiskammahoek
Bedford
Bisho
Berlin
Somerset East
Fort
Beaufort
Alice
King William
Town
Breidbach
East London
SUURBERGE
Riebeek-Oos
Gonubie
Aliceldale
Peddie
Kidd's Beach
Kirkwood
Salem
Addo
Grahamstown
Hamburg
Alexandria
Bathurst
Uitenhage
Port Alfred (Kowie)
SAINT CROIX
ISLAND
BIRD ISLAND
Port Elizabeth
KAAP RECIFE
Scale 1:4 000 000
0 10 20 30 40 Miles
0 10 20 30 40 50 60 Kilometers
Longitude East of Greenwich

Relief

Meters		Feet
3050		10 000
1525		5000
610		2000
305		1000
152.5		500
0	Sea Level	0
152.5		500
1525		5000
3050		10 000

For larger scale coverage of
Johannesburg see page 240.

WESTERN SAHARA

ADRAR SOTUF

PUNTILLA NEGRA

CABO BARBAS

Fdérik
Kediet Ijill

Tichia

Nouadhibou

CAP BLANC

ÎLE TIDRA

CAP TIMIRIS

Nouamrhar

MAKTEÏR

OUARANE

EL DJOUF

SAHARA

Taoudenni

TANEZROUFT N-AHNET

Bordj le Prieur

MAURITANIA

ADÂFER EL ABIOD

EL MREYYE

AKLÉ 'ÂOUÂNA

AZAOUAD

Timetrine Monts

Aguelhok

Araouane

VALLÉE DU TILEMSI

Anefis in-n-Datane

Akjoujt

Sebkha de N'Drhamcha

Nouakchott

Tidjikdja

AOUKÂR

M A L I

Moudjéria

IRIGUI

Lac Faguibine

Tombouctou
(Timbuktu)

Taoussa

TRARZA

Aleg

Kiffa

Ayoun el Atrous

Néma

Lac Do

Niger

Gao

Ansongo

Rosso

Dagana

Kaédi

Senegal

Matam

Balé

Léré

Lac Débo

Macina

Hombori

Douentza

Ayor

Saint-Louis

Louga

Linguère

Ranérou

Nioro du Sahel

Goumbou

Kogoni

Kona

S   U   D   A

Aribinda

CAP VERT

Thiès

Touba

FERLO

Naye

Kayes

Diéma

Didiéni

Mopti

Koro

Djibo

Téra

Dani

Rufisque

Dakar

Diourbel

SENEGAL

PARC NATIONAL DE LA BOUCLE DU BAOULÉ

Banamba

Ségou

San

Ouahigouya

Kaya

CAPE SAINT MARY

Kaolack

Sokone

Tambacounda

Bafoulabé

Koulouguidi

Kita

Koulikoro

Bla

Djibasso

BURKINA   FASO

Tougan

Nyou

Kantchari

British Naval Base

Banjul
(Bathurst)

GAMBIA

Kolda

Médina Gonasse

Goumbati
1 368

PARC NATIONAL DU NIOKOLO KOBA

Satadougou

Bamako

Sido

Zangasso

Koudougou

Ouarkoye

Boromo

Ouagadougou

Toécé

Tenkodogo

Léo

Pô

Fada Ngourma

Madjori

Batia

PARC NATION. DE LA PENDJARI

Dapango

Kantchari

Bignona

CAP ROXO

Ziguinchor

Koundara

Manyabá

Massif Du Tamgué 5 046

Danea

Labé

Siguiri

Badogo

Kouálé

Sikasso

Banfara

Boho Dioulasso

Lawra

Walewále

Bolgatanga

Gushiago

Niamtougou

Yendi

Bassari

GUINEA-BISSAU

Bissau

Sao João

ARQUIPÉLAGO DOS BIJAGÓS

Eticoga

Kabot

Tombadonkéa

Téhmélé

Dabola

Dinguiraye

GUINEA

Kouroussa

Kankan

Tingréla

Niélé

Ferkéssédougou

PARK NATIONAL DE BOUNA

Bouna

Bole

Wa

White Volta

Tamale

Boffa

Fria

Kindia

Mamou

Faranah

Kissidougou

Kénouané
Pic De Tio 4 934

Odienné

Boundiali

Korhogo

Niakaramandougou

Bio Gorge

Kintampo

Forêt Classée Du Fazao
Djebobo 2 873

Blitta

Sokodé

Conakry

SIERRA   Forécariah

Makeni

Binturani
Tingi
6 080

Sankanbirwa

Beyla

Touba

Séguéla

Katiola

Bondoukou

Wenchi

Sunyani

GHANA

Techiman

Mampong

Ejura

Agogo

Hohoé

Palime

TOGO

Freetown

LEONE

Luntar

Moyamba

Bo

Kenema

Pendembu

Vahama

Biankouma

Man

Mount Kahoué 3 658

Daloa

Bouaflé

Yamoussoukro

Dimbokro

Abengourou

Kumasi

Kwahu Plateau

Nkawkaw

Akwatia

Begoro

Atakpamé

Lomé

CAPE SAINT P

IVORY   COAST

Bonthe

SHERBRO ISLAND

TURNERS PENINSULA

CAPE MOUNT

Robertsport

Brewerville

Nzérékoré
Tomomy
MT. NIMBA NAT PARK
5 748

Sanniquellie

Danané

Gbarnga

Guiglo

Duékoué

Gagnoa

Divo

Agboville

Adzopé

Bibiani

Obuasi

Dunkwa

Oda

Nyakrom

Tarkwa

Prestea

Koforidua

Nsawam

Accra

Tema

Winneba

Anloga

LIBERIA

Monrovia

Buchanan

Tchien

Duabo

Mont Niénokoué 2 044

Gagnoa

Abidjan

Aboisso

Grand-Bassam

Esiama

Cape Coast

Sekondi-Takoradi

Greenville

Sassandra

Lagune Tadio

Lagune Ébrié

CAPE THREE POINTS

Harper

Tabou

CAPE PALMAS

GULF   OF   G

Copyright by Rand McNally & Co.
Made in U.S.A.
A-589400-76   2- -9

Relief

Meters		Feet
3050		10 000
1525		5000
610		2000
305		1000
152.5		500
0	Sea Level	0
152.5		500
1525		5000
3050		10 000

Scale 1:10,000,000;   one inch to 160 miles. Lambert Azimuthal Equal Area Projection
Elevations and depressions are given in feet.

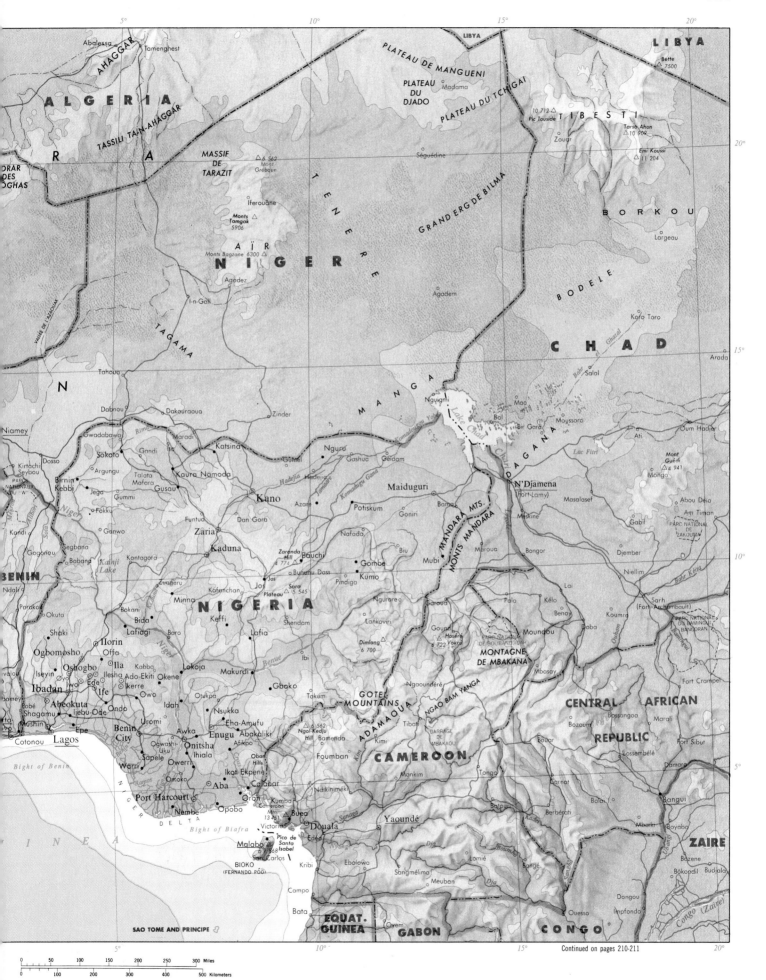

Continued on pages 210-211

Continued on pages 208-209

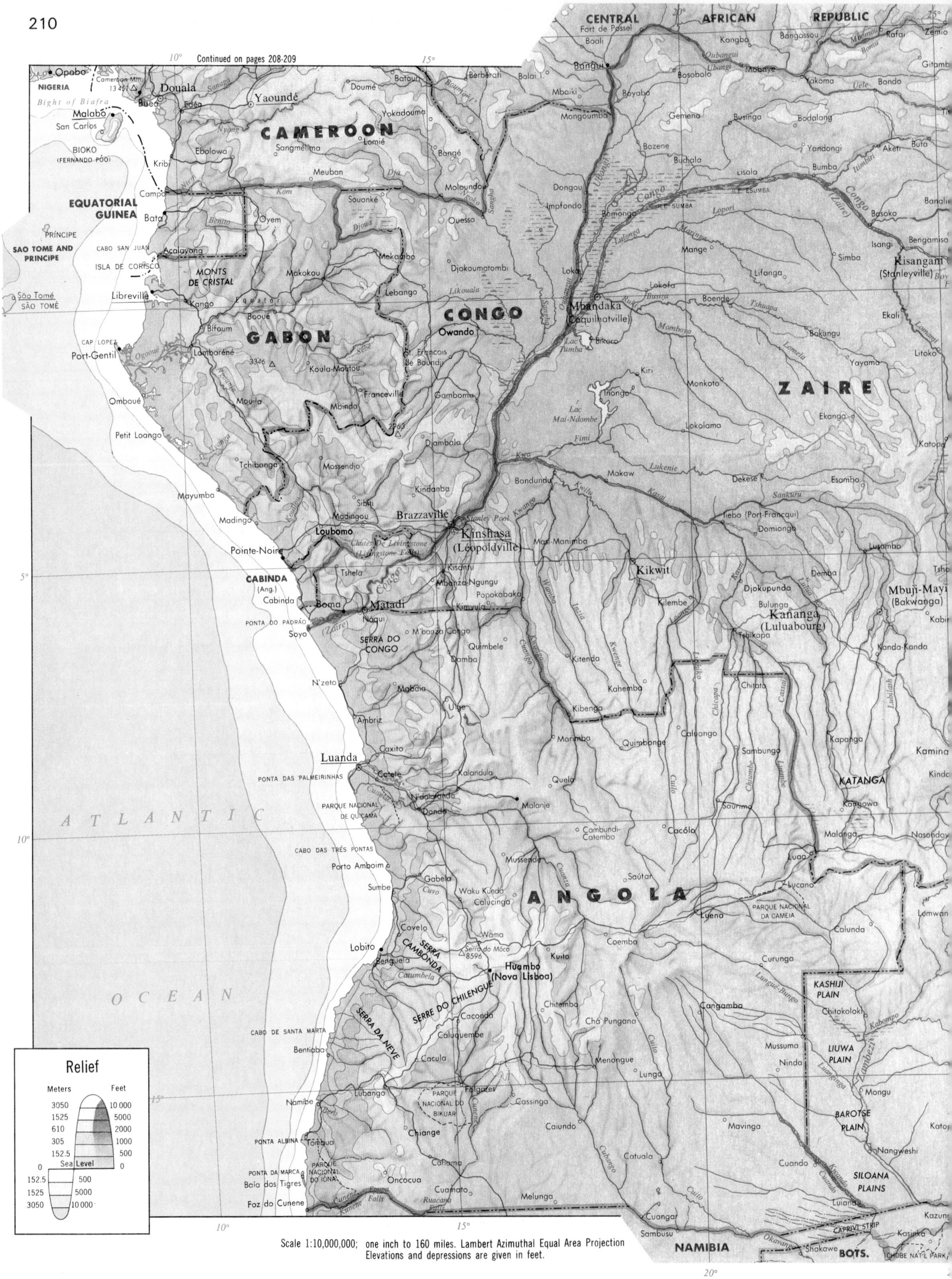

CENTRAL AFRICAN REPUBLIC
Fort de Possel
Boali
Bangui
Kongbo
Bangassou
Zemio

NIGERIA
Opobo
Cameroon Mtn. 13,451
Douala
Buea
Bight of Biafra
Malabo
San Carlos
BIOKO
(FERNANDO PÓO)
Kribi

EQUATORIAL GUINEA
Bata
Campo
Acalayong
CABO SAN JUAN
ISLA DE CORISCO

SAO TOME AND PRINCIPE
PRÍNCIPE
São Tomé
SÃO TOMÉ

CAMEROON
Yaoundé
Edéa
Ebolowa
Sangmélima
Meuban
Doumé
Lomié
Batouri
Yokadouma
Bangé
Souanké
Ouesso
Moloundou
Dongou
Impfondo
Bomongo
Bozene
Lisala
Bumba
Buchala
Businga
Bodalang
Yandongi
Akeri
Buta
Gemena

GABON
Libreville
Kango
MONTS DE CRISTAL
Makokou
Lebango
Booué
Bifoum
3326
Koula-Moutou
Franceville
Mbinda
Mouila
Lambaréné
CAP LOPEZ
Port-Gentil
Omboué
Petit Loango
Tchibanga
Mossendjo
Sibiti
Madingou
Loubomo
Madinga
Mayumba

CONGO
Owando
St. François
de Boundji
Gamboma
Djambala
Kindanba
Brazzaville
Stanley Pool
Chutes De Livingstone
(Livingstone Falls)
Kinshasa
(Léopoldville)
Bandundu

ZAIRE
Mbandaka
(Coquilhatville)
Lac Tumba
Bikoro
Kiri
Inongo
Monkoto
Lac Mai-Ndombe
Lokolama
Boende
Bokungu
Yayama
Ekoli
Ekanga
Litoko
Kisangani
(Stanleyville)
Isangi
Basoko
Lifanga
Lokofa
Mange
Simba
Banalia
Kwa
Fimi
Dekese
Iebo (Port-Francqui)
Domiongo
Lusambo
Esombo
Kikwit
Masi-Manimba
Demba
Mbuji-Mayi
(Bakwanga)
Kananga
(Luluabourg)
Tshikapa
Kanda-Kanda
Kapanga
Kamina
KATANGA
Kamiowa

CABINDA (Ang.)
Cabinda
PONTA DO PADRÃO
Soyo
Boma
Matadi
Nóqui
SERRA DO CONGO
M'banza Congo
Mbanza-Ngungu
Popokabaka
Kimvula
Kitenda
Kahemba
Kibenga
Chitato

ANGOLA
N'zeto
Ambriz
Uge
Maquela
Quimbonge
Caluango
Sambungo
Calunda
Luanda
Catete
Kalandula
Quela
Malanje
Cambundi-Catembo
Cacólo
Malanga
Nasondoy
PONTA DAS PALMEIRINHAS
Ndalatando
Dondo
PARQUE NACIONAL DE QUICAMA
CABO DAS TRÊS PONTAS
Porto Amboim
Mussende
Saútar
Luau
Lucano
Lomwan
Sumbe
Gabela
Waku Kunda
Calucinga
Cuvo
Luena
Coemba
Curunga
PARQUE NACIONAL DA CAMEIA
Covelo
Lobito
Benguela
SERRA CAMBONDA
Wàma
Serra do Môco
8596
Kuito
Huambo
(Nova Lisboa)
Chitemba
Chá Pungana
Cangamba
Mussuma
KASHIJI PLAIN
Chitokolokh
LIUWA PLAIN
Ninda
Catumbela
SERRE DO CHILENGUE
SERRA DA NEVE
Caconda
Caluquembe
Cacula
Chitemba
Menongue
Lunga
Mavinga
CABO DE SANTA MARTA
Bentiaba
Lubango
PARQUE NACIONAL DO BIKUAR
Cassinga
Caiundo
Cuando
Cuangar
BAROTSE PLAIN
Mongu
Namibe
Chiange
Caconda
Cahama
Catuala
SILOANA PLAINS
Luiana
PONTA ALBINA
Tombua
PARQUE NACIONAL DO IONA
Oncocua
Cuamato
Melunga
Cuangar
Sambusu
PONTA DA MARCA
Baía dos Tigres
Foz do Cunene
Ruacana Falls

NAMIBIA
CAPRIVI STRIP
BOTS.
CHOBE NAT'L PARK

ATLANTIC OCEAN

Relief

Meters		Feet
3050		10 000
1525		5000
610		2000
305		1000
152.5		500
0	Sea Level	0
152.5		500
1525		5000
3050		10 000

Scale 1:10,000,000; one inch to 160 miles. Lambert Azimuthal Equal Area Projection
Elevations and depressions are given in feet.

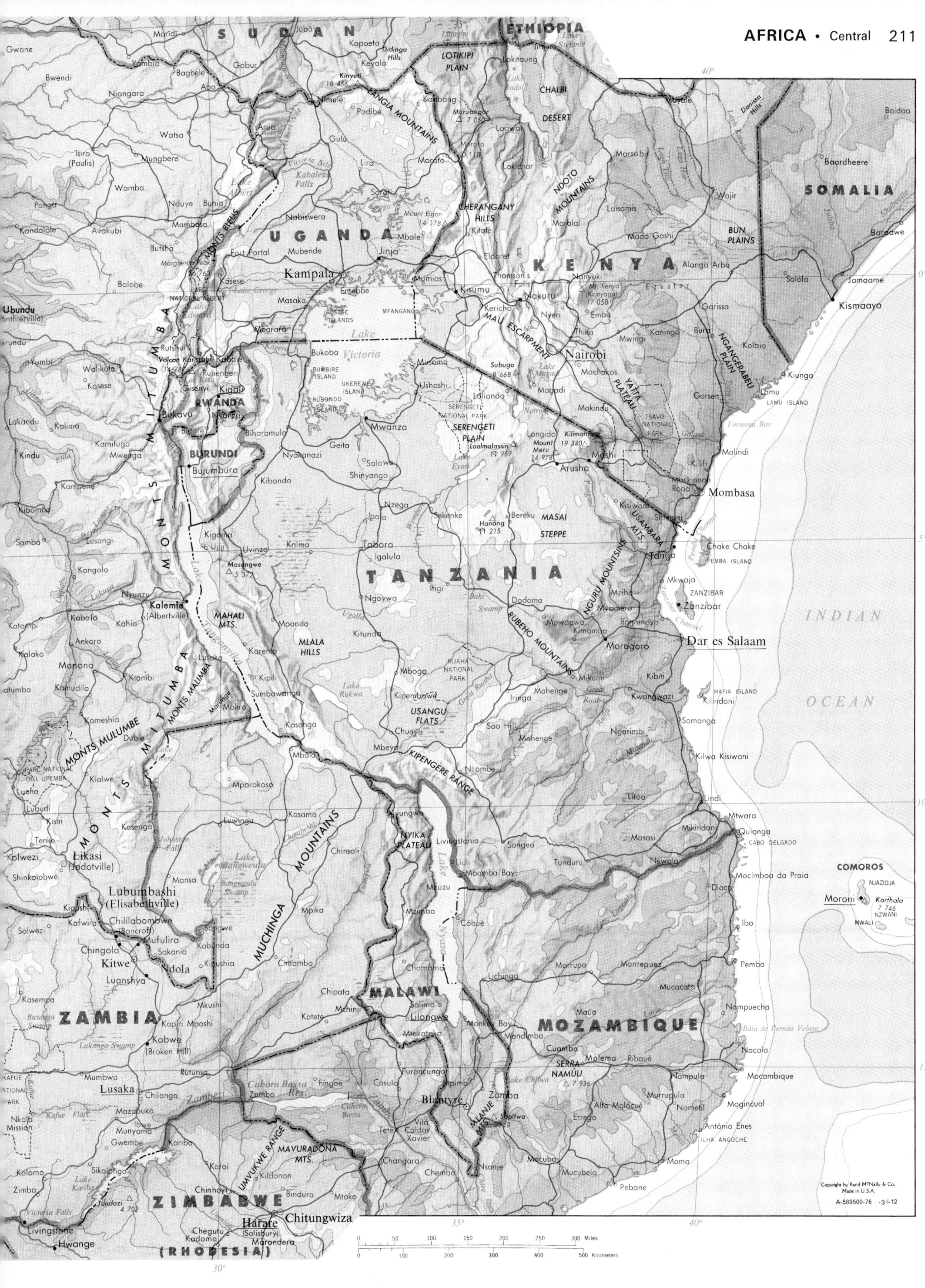

SUDAN
ETHIOPIA

Gwane
Maridi
Jūbā
Kapoeta
Didinga Hills
Keyala
Lake Turkana
Lake Stefanie

Bwendi
Yambio
Bagbele
Ama
Nimule
LOTIKIPI PLAIN
Lokitaung
Lokichar

Niangara
Nzara
Gobur
Kinyeti 10 456
Kabong
Lake Rudolf
CHALBI DESERT
Danisa Hills

Watsa
Isiro (Paulis)
Mungbere
Arua
Gulu
Lira
Moroto
Lodwar
Marsabit
Wajir
Baidoa
Baardheere

Panga
Mambasa
Avakubi
Nabiswera
Mount Elgon 14 178
Mbale
Eldoret
Mado Gashi
BUN PLAINS
SOMALIA
Baraawe

Wamba
Butsha
Fort Portal
Mubende
Jinja
Kitale
Thomson's Falls
Nanyuki
Mt. Kenya/Kirinyaga 17 058
Alanga Arba
Garissa
Sotik
Jamaame

Balobe
Kampala
Entebbe
Masaka
Kisumu
Kericho
Nakuru
Nyeri
Thika
Mwingi
Kaninga
Buro
Kolbio
Kismaayo

Ubundu (Ponthierville)
UGANDA
KENYA
Nairobi
Machakos
Garsen
Kiunga
LAMU ISLAND

Yumbi
Walikale
Kasese
Mbarara
Bukoba
Musoma
Ushashi
Subugo 8 668
Lake Magadi
Makindu
TSAVO NATIONAL PARK
Lamu
Formosa Bay

RWANDA
Lake Victoria
SERENGETI NATIONAL PARK
SERENGETI PLAIN
Loolmalassin 11 969
Longido
Kilimanjaro Mount Meru 14 978 19 340
Moshi
Arusha

BURUNDI
Bujumbura
Nyakanazi
Geita
Mwanza
Shinyanga
Kilifi
Malindi

MONTS MITUMBA
Kigoma
Ujiji
Tabora
Igalula
Nzega
Ipala
Sekenke
Bereku
MASAI STEPPE
Mombasa

TANZANIA
Dodoma
Mpwapwa
Morogoro
Dar es Salaam
ZANZIBAR
Zanzibar

MAHALI MTS.
MLALA HILLS
Mpanda
Kitunda
RUAHA NATIONAL PARK
Iringa
Mahenge
Kibiti
MAFIA ISLAND
INDIAN OCEAN

Sumbawanga
Mbeya
USANGU FLATS
KIPENGERE RANGE
Njombe
Songea
Tunduru
Masasi
Lindi
Mtwara

ZAMBIA
Kasama
MUCHINGA MOUNTAINS
NYIKA PLATEAU
Livingstonia
Mzuzu
COMOROS

Lubumbashi (Elisabethville)
Ndola
Kitwe
Lilongwe
MALAWI
MOZAMBIQUE
Nampula

Lusaka
Kabwe (Broken Hill)
Blantyre
Zomba
SERRA NAMÚLI

ZIMBABWE
(RHODESIA)
Harare (Salisbury)
Chitungwiza
Tete
Mocambique

Victoria Falls
Livingstone

Copyright by Rand McNally & Co.
Made in U.S.A.
A-589500-76   -34-12

0   50   100   150   200   250   300 Miles
0   100   200   300   400   500 Kilometers

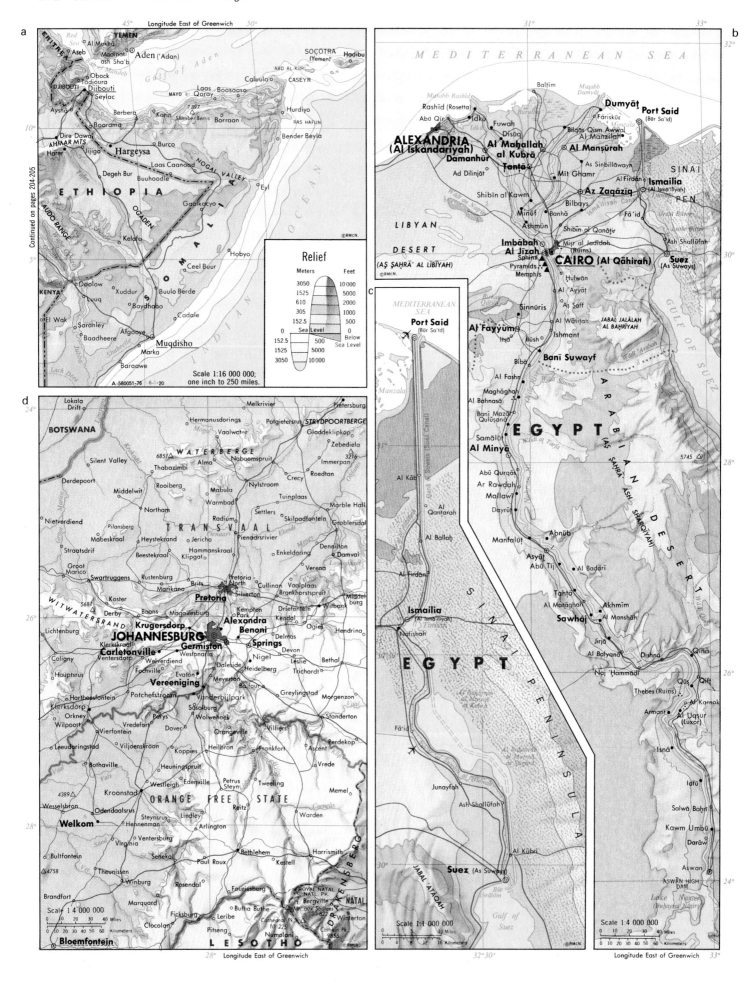

a

Longitude East of Greenwich

YEMEN
Red Sea
Aseb
Al Mukhā
Madīnat ash Sha'b
Aden ('Adan)
SOCOTRA (Yemen)
Hadību
Gulf of Aden
ABD AL-KŪRĪ
CASEYR
Calula
Boosaaso
RAS HAFUN
Hurdiyo
Bender Beyla
Eyl
Obock
Tadjoura
DJIBOUTI
Djibouti
Seylac
Aysha
AHMAR MTS.
Harer
Dire Dawa
Jijiga
Hargeysa
Berbera
Karin
ShimberBerris 7,897
Borraan
Laas Qoray
MAYD I.
Buhoodle
Laas Caanood
NOGAL VALLEY
Degeh Bur
ETHIOPIA
OGADEN
Gaalkacyo
Kelafo
Hobyo
KENYA
AUDO RANGE
Deelow
Luuq
Xuddur
Baydhabo
Ceel Buur
Cadale
El Wak
Saranley
Afgooye
Buulo Berde
Bardheere
SOMALIA
Muqdisho
Marka
Baraawe
Shubeelle
Jubba
Lach Dera
INDIAN OCEAN
Continued on pages 204-205

Scale 1:16 000 000;
one inch to 250 miles.
A-560051-76   6-5-20

Relief

Meters		Feet
3050		10 000
1525		5000
610		2000
305		1000
152.5		500
0	Sea Level	0
152.5		500 Below
1525		5000 Sea Level
3050		10000

b

MEDITERRANEAN SEA
Baltīm
Maşabb Dumyāt
Maşabb Rashīd
Rashīd (Rosetta)
Dumyāt
Port Said (Būr Sa'īd)
Abū Qīr
Idkū
Fuwah
Fāriskūr
Al Manzilah
Burullus
Disūq
Bilqās Qism Awwal
SINAI
ALEXANDRIA (Al Iskandarīyah)
Al Maḩallah al Kubrā
Al Manşūrah
As Sinbillāwayn
Al Firdān
Ismailia (Al Ismā'īlīyah)
Damanhūr
Tantā
Mīt Ghamr
PEN.
Ad Dilinjāt
Shibīn al Kawm
Az Zaqāzīq
Fā'id
Great Bitter Lake
Minūf
Banhā
Ismā'īlīyah Canal
Ashmūn
Shibīn al Qanāţir
Little Bitter Lake
LIBYAN
Ash Shallūfah
DESERT
Imbābah
Al Jīzah
Mişr al Jadīdah (Ruins)
Suez (As Suways)
(AŞ ŞAḨRĀ' AL LĪBĪYAH)
Sphinx
CAIRO (Al Qāhirah)
Pyramids
Memphis
Hulwān
Al 'Ayyāţ
As Şaff
Sinnūris
Al Wāsiţah
JABAL JALĀLAH AL BAḨRĪYAH
Birkat Qārūn
Al Fayyūm
Iţsā
Būsh
Ishmant
GULF OF SUEZ
Biba
Banī Suwayf
Wadi 'Arābah
Al Fashn
Maghāghah
Wadī Sannūr
Banī Mazār
Qulūşanā
Al Bahnasā
EGYPT
ARABIAN
Samālūţ
Wadī aţ Ţarfā
Al Minyā
(AŞ ŞAḨRĀ' ASH SHARQĪYAH)
5745
Abū Qurqāş
Ar Rawdah
DESERT
Mallawī
Dayrūţ
Abnūb
Manfalūţ
Asyūţ
Abū Tīj
Al Badārī
Ţahţā
Al Matāghah
Akhmīm
Sawhāj
Al Manshāh
Jirjā
Al Balyanā
Dishnā
Qinā
Naj' Ḩammādī
Qūs
Qifţ
Thebes (Ruins)
Armant
Al Karnak
Al Uqşur (Luxor)
Isnā
Idfū
Salwā Baḩrī
Kawm Umbū
Darāw
Aswān
ASWĀN HIGH DAM
Lake Nasser (Buḩayrat Nāşir)

c

MEDITERRANEAN SEA
Port Said (Būr Sa'īd)
Al Manzala
Qanā al Suwais (Suez Canal)
Al Kāb
Al Qantarah
Al Ballāh
Al Firdān
Ismailia (Al Ismā'īlīyah)
Nafīshah
SINAI PENINSULA
EGYPT
Junayfah
Ash Shallūfah
Al Kubrī
Suez (As Suways)
JABAL ATAQAH
Gulf of Suez

Scale 1:1 000 000
0   4   8   16 Kilometers
0   4   8   16 Miles

Scale 1:4 000 000
0 10 20 30 40 Miles
0 10 20 30 40 50 60 Kilometers

d

BOTSWANA
Lokala Drift
Melkrivier
Pietersburg
Hermanusdorings
Potgietersrus
STRYDPOORTBERGE
Silent Valley
6851
WATERBERGE
Vaalwater
Thabazimbi
Alma
Zebediela
Gladdeklipkop
3216
Derdepoort
Middelwit
Rooiberg
Nylstroom
Immerpan
Roedtan
Crecy
Nietverdiend
Pilansberg
Mabula
Tuinplaas
Marble Hall
Northam
Warmbad
Settlers
Skilpadfontein
Groblersdal
Groot Marico
Mabeskraal
Radium
TRANSVAAL
Heystekrand
Jericho
Hammanskraal
Klipgat
Dennilton
Damval
Straatsdrif
Beestekraal
Pienaarsrivier
Verena
Losoplaas
Swartruggens
Rustenburg
Brits
Pretoria-North
Enkeldoring
Witbank
Middelburg
Koster
Marikana
Silverton
Cullinan
Vaalplaas
Bronkhorstspruit
WITWATERSRAND
5681
Derby
Boons
Magaliesburg
Pretoria
Kempton Park
Driefontein
Ogies
Hendrina
Lichtenburg
Krugersdorp
Alexandra
Kendal
Coligny
JOHANNESBURG
Benoni
Delmas
Devon
Carletonville
Germiston
Springs
Nigel
Leslie
Bethal
Hauptrust
Venterspost
Westonaria
Daleside
Heidelberg
Trichardt
Klerksdorp
Fochville
Evaton
Meyerton
Balfour
Greylingstad
Morgenzon
Orkney
Wolverdiend
Vereeniging
Vanderbijlpark
Standerton
Wilpoort
Potchefstroom
Sasolburg
Villiers
Ascent
Perdekop
Leeudoringstad
Vierfontein
Dover
Orangeville
Frankfort
Vrede
Memel
Wesselsbron
Vredefort
Koppies
Heilbron
Warden
4389
Bothaville
Parys
Edenville
Tweeling
ORANGE FREE STATE
Kroonstad
Lindley
Reitz
Welkom
Odendaalsrus
Steynsrus
Hennenman
Arlington
Harrismith
Bultfontein
Virginia
Ventersburg
Bethlehem
Kestell
DRAKENSBERG
NATAL
Brandfort
Theunissen
Winburg
Senekal
Paul Roux
Rosendal
Fouriesburg
ROYAL NATAL NATL. PK.
Bergvitte
Marquard
Clocolan
Ficksburg
Leribe
Winterton
Cathkin Pk
Mt. aux Sources 10 822
Cathédral Pk 10 226
9856
Bloemfontein
Butha Buthe
Pitseng
LESOTHO
Numolani

Scale 1:4 000 000
0 10 20 30 40 Miles
0 10 20 30 40 50 60 Kilometers

28°   Longitude East of Greenwich

Relief

Meters	Feet
3050	10 000
1525	5000
610	2000
305	1000
0 Sea Level	0
152.5	500 Below
1525	5000 Sea Level
3050	10 000
6100	20 000

A-594000-76 4- 16
COPYRIGHT BY
RAND MCNALLY & COMPANY
MADE IN U.S.A.

ANTARCTICA IN PROFILE
SECTION ALONG LINE AB

Scale 1: 60 000 000; (approximate)
Lambert's Azimuthal, Equal Area Projection
Elevations and depressions are given in feet

PLATE TECTONICS AND OCEAN FLOOR MAPS

Plate Tectonics

Maps and atlases portray the position of the land and water masses and the surface features of the earth. In general they answer the question *where?* The plate tectonic theory of the earth's actions relates the physics of the earth's subsurface and its surface to explain *how* and *why* the surface features are where they are.

Stated concisely, the theory presumes the lithosphere—the outside crust and uppermost mantle of the earth—is divided into six major rigid plates and several smaller platelets that move relative to one another. The position and names of the plates are shown on the map below.

The motor that drives the plates is found deep in the mantle. The theory states that because of temperature differences in the mantle, slow convection currents circulate. Where two molten currents converge and move upward, they separate, causing the crustal plates to bulge and move apart in midoceanic regions. Lava wells up at these points to cause ridges and volcanic activity. The plates grow larger by accretion along these midocean regions, cause vast regions of the crust to move apart, and force different plates to move into one another. As the plates do so, they are destroyed at subduction zones, where the plates are consumed downward to form deep ocean trenches. Movement along these zones prompts earthquakes as well as changes in the coastline. Further movement results as plates slide past one another along transcurrent faults. The diagrams to the right illustrate the processes.

The overall result of tectonic movements is that the crustal plates move slowly and inexorably as relatively rigid entities, carrying the continents along with them. It is now accepted that the continents have moved and changed their positions during the past millions of years. The sequence of this continental drifting is illustrated on the following page. It begins with a single landmass, called the supercontinent of Pangaea, and the ancestral ocean, the Panthalassa Ocean. Pangaea first split into a northern landmass called Laurasia and a southern block called Gondwanaland and subsequently into the continents we map today.

Subduction Zone

Ocean Ridge Zone

World-Wide Distribution of Tectonic Plates

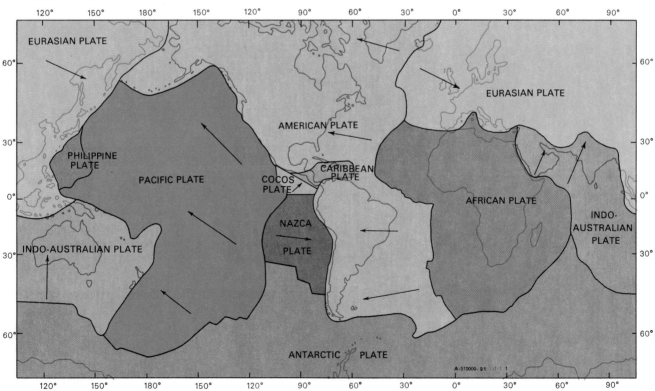

Credit: adapted from a drawing by Scripps Institution of Oceanography

Copyright © by Rand McNally & Company   All Rights Reserved

Continental Drift

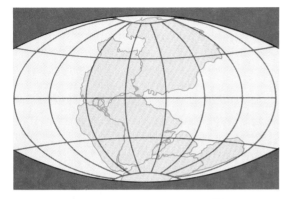

225 million years ago the supercontinent of Pangaea exists and Panthalassa forms the ancestral ocean. Tethys Sea separates Eurasia and Africa.

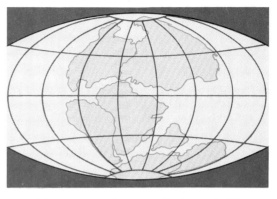

180 million years ago Pangaea splits, Laurasia drifts north. Gondwanaland breaks into South America/Africa, India, and Australia/Antarctica.

65 million years ago ocean basins take shape as South America and India move from Africa and the Tethys Sea closes to form the Mediterranean Sea.

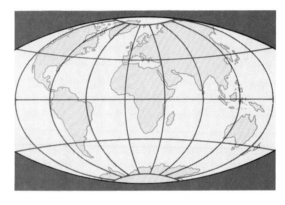

The present day: India has merged with Asia, Australia is free of Antarctica, and North America is free of Eurasia.

Ocean Floor Maps

The maps in this section convey an impression of the physical nature of the world's ocean floors. In general, the colors are those thought to exist on the ocean floors. For continental shelves or shallow inland seas, gray-green is used to correspond to terrigenous oozes, sediments washed from the continental areas. In deeper parts of the oceans, calcareous oozes derived from the skeletons of marine life appear in white, and the fine mud from land is red. In the Atlantic, materials accumulate relatively rapidly, have a high iron content, and thus are brighter red than elsewhere. Slower sedimentation in the Pacific and Indian oceans results in more manganese and hence darker colors. Undersea ridges are shown in black to suggest recent upswelling of molten rock. Small salt-and-pepper patches portray areas where manganese nodules are found. Around certain islands, white is used to show coral reefs. Differences in subsurface form are shown by relief-shading.

Many different features on the ocean floor are recognizable. Towering mountain ranges, vast canyons, broad plains, and a variety of other physiographic forms exceed in magnitude those found on the continents. One of the more pronounced is the Mid-Atlantic Ridge, a chain of mountains bisecting the Atlantic Ocean. One distinct characteristic of this ridge is a trough that runs along the entire center, in effect producing twin ridge lines. Away from the center there are parallel and lower crests, while at right angles to the crests are numerous fracture zones.

Measurements of temperature and magnetism indicate that the troughs in the Mid-Atlantic Ridge are younger than the paralleling crests, whose ages increase with distance from the center. It is believed that the central troughs mark a line where molten materials from the earth's interior rise to the ocean floor, where they form gigantic plates that move slowly apart. Where the plates meet certain continental areas or island chains, they plunge downward to replenish inner-earth materials and form trenches of profound depths. Along the northern and western edges of the Pacific Ocean, several lines of such gutters include some of the deepest known spots—Mariana Trench, Tonga Trench, Kuril Trench. Deep trenches also parallel the western coasts of Central and South America, the northern coasts of Puerto Rico and the Virgin Islands, and other coastal areas. Other identifiable features include the great sub-marine canyons that lead from the edges of the continents; seamounts that rise above the ocean floors; and the continental shelves, which appear to be underwater extensions of landmasses and which vary in shape from narrow fringes to broad plains.

Scale 1:44,000,000; one inch to 700 miles (approx.)
Modified Cylindrical Projection   ▽ Depths in meters.

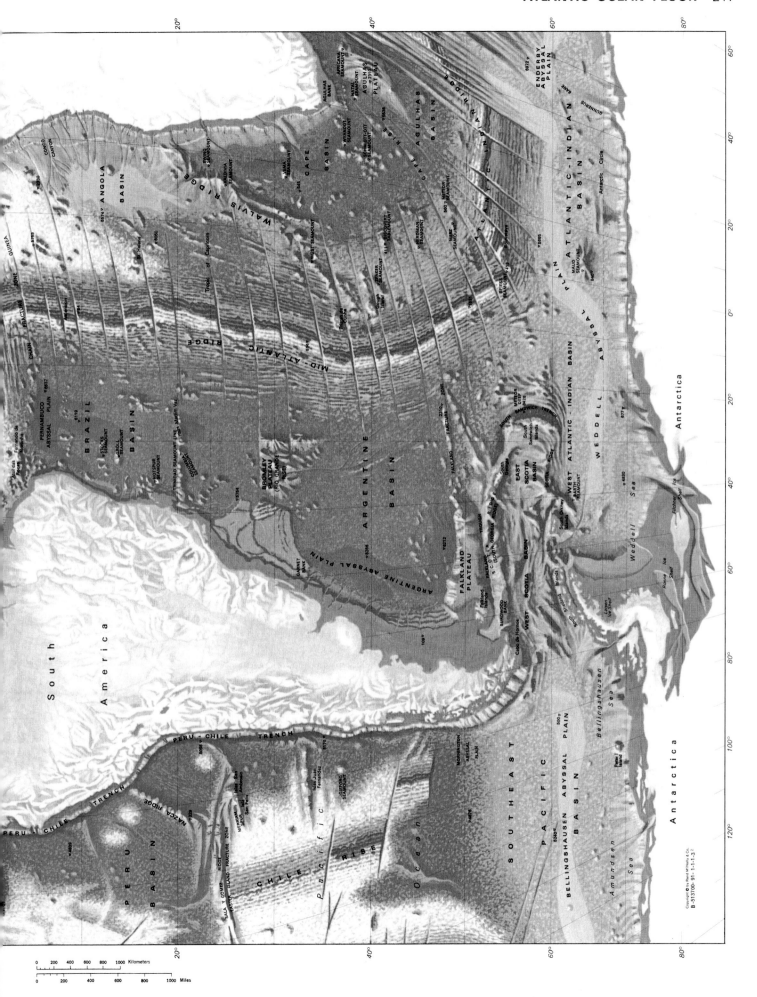

Copyright © by Rand McNally & Co.
B-513700- 91- 1-1-3

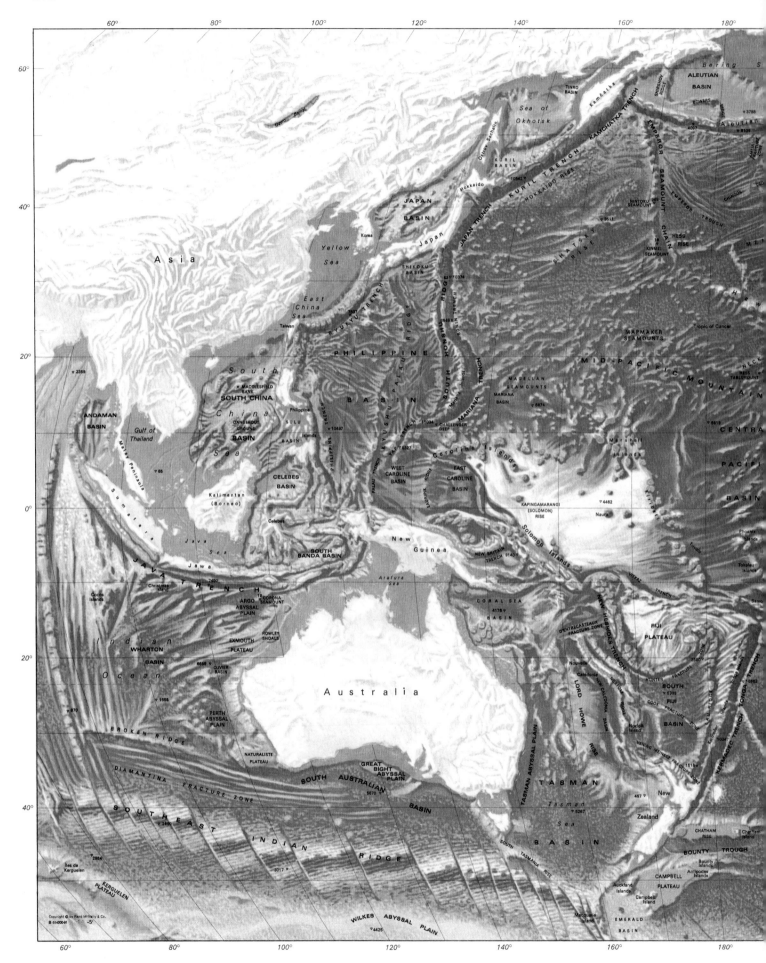

Scale 1:58 000 000; one inch to 900 miles (approx.)
Modified Cylindrical Projection   ▽ Depths in meters.

Labels visible on the map:

North margin / Arctic region:
Hudson Bay · Great Lakes · LABRADOR BASIN · North America · NORTH AMERICAN BASIN

Aleutian / Alaska region:
EUTIAN TRENCH · ALEUTIAN ABYSSAL PLAIN · VEYOR FRACTURE ZONE · KODIAK GUYOT (SEAMOUNT) · ALASKA ABYSSAL PLAIN · ▽3828 · ▽5257 · TUFTS ABYSSAL PLAIN

West / central Pacific:
MUSICIANS SEAMOUNTS · ▽6298 · MURRAY FRACTURE ZONE · 5120 · PIONEER FRACTURE ZONE · ▽1765 · ▽3008 · DELGADA FAN · MONTEREY FAN · CASCADIA FRACTURE ZONE · MENDOCINO FRACTURE ZONE · GORDA BLANCO · MOLOKAI FRACTURE ZONE · HAWAIIAN FRACTURE ZONE · PENSACOLA SEAMOUNT · 1057 · BAJA CALIFORNIA SEAMOUNT PROVINCE · Isla de Guadelupe · PEDRO TRENCH

Equatorial Pacific:
EAST PACIFIC BASIN · CLARION FRACTURE ZONE · 490 · ▽4808 · ▽5720 · CLIPPERTON FRACTURE ZONE · 5349 ▽ · Equator · Christmas Island · CHRISTMAS RIDGE · MOLOKAI RIDGE · Line Islands

Southwest Pacific:
▽5029 · Îles Marquises · ▽5485 · MARQUESAS FRACTURE ZONE · ▽7314 · Îles de la Société · Tahiti · Îles Tuamotu · Cook Islands · Îles Tubai · Tropic of Capricorn · ▽1088 · Rapa · Pitcairn Island · SOUTHWEST PACIFIC BASIN · ▽4756 · ELTANIN FRACTURE ZONE · 3977 ▽ · 1447 · ▽4978 · 5249

East Pacific Rise region:
SUITCASE SEAMOUNTS · RIVERA FRACTURE ZONE · Islas de Revillagigedo · MATHEMATICIANS RIDGE · Isla Clipperton · GERMAINE BANK · SIQUEIROS FRACTURE ZONE · CLIPPERTON FRACTURE ZONE · EAST PACIFIC RISE (ALBATROSS CORDILLERA) · GALAPAGOS FRACTURE ZONE · 5851 ▽ · 20 · MIDDLE AMERICA TRENCH · GUATEMALA BASIN · ▽4095 · GALAPAGOS RISE · COCOS RIDGE · Galapagos Islands · Isla del Malpelo · PANAMA BASIN · CARNEGIE RIDGE

South America margin:
PERU BASIN · BAUER FRACTURE ZONE · ▽4289 · ▽4525 · NAZCA RIDGE · 329 · 5068 ▽ · PERU-CHILE TRENCH · South America

Southeast Pacific:
EASTER ISLAND FRACTURE ZONE · SALA Y GOMEZ RIDGE · Sala y Gomez · Isla de Pascua (Easter Island) · Isla San Felix · Isla San Ambrosio · CHILE BASIN · ▽3841 · Islas Juan Fernandez · GIFFORD SEAMOUNT · CHALLENGER FRACTURE ZONE · FERNANDEZ FRACTURE ZONE · EAST PACIFIC RISE (ALBATROSS CORDILLERA) · CHALLENGER RISE · SOUTHEAST PACIFIC BASIN

Gulf of Mexico / Caribbean:
Gulf of Mexico · MEXICO BASIN · SIGSBEE KNOLLS ▽4023 · Mexico · CAMPECHE BANK · WEST FLORIDA SHELF · BLAKE PLATEAU · ▽5399 · CAYMAN TRENCH · Caribbean Sea · BEATA RIDGE

Atlantic / southern margin:
Atlantic Ocean · ▽109 · FALKLAND PLATEAU · 50° · Falkland Islands · SCOTIA RIDGE (SOUTH GEORGIA RIDGE) · WEST SCOTIA BASIN

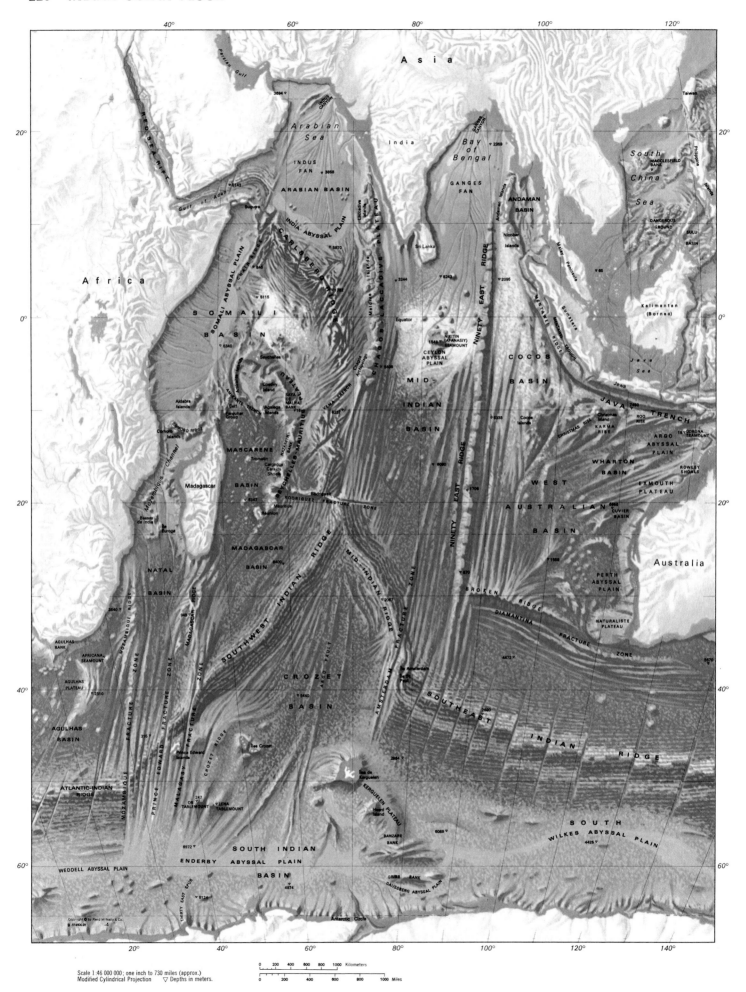

Scale 1:46 000 000; one inch to 730 miles (approx.)
Modified Cylindrical Projection   ▽ Depths in meters.

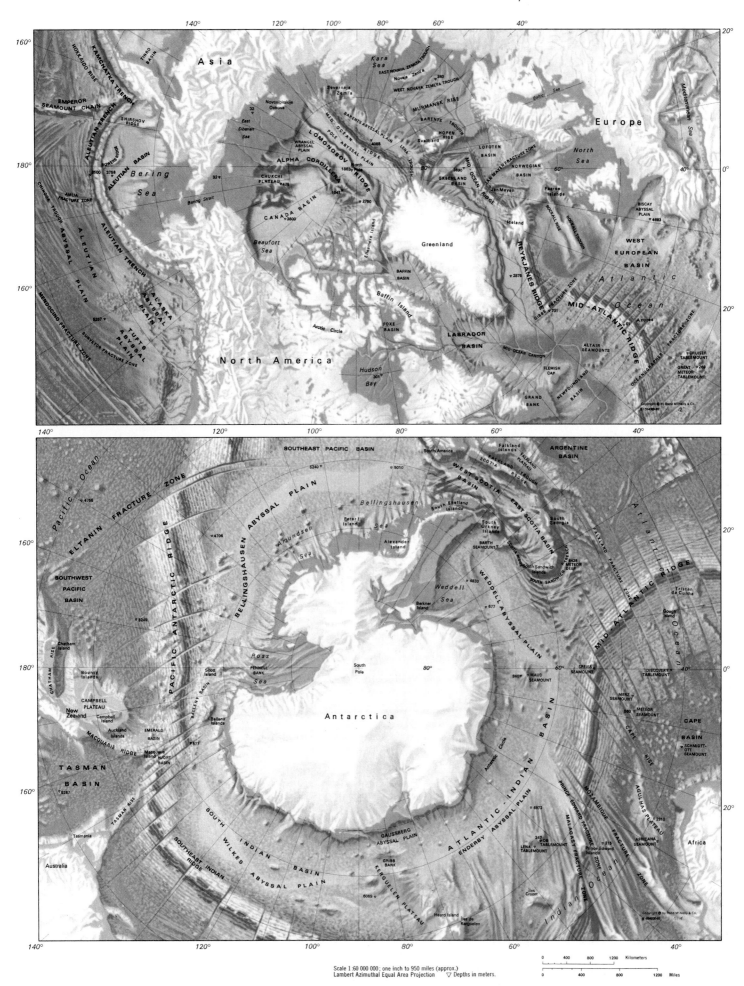

Scale 1:60 000 000; one inch to 950 miles (approx.).
Lambert Azimuthal Equal Area Projection   ▽ Depths in meters.

MAJOR CITIES MAPS

This section consists of 62 maps of the world's most populous metropolitan areas. In order to make comparison easier, all the metropolitan areas are shown at the same scale, 1:300,000.

Detailed urban maps are an important reference requirement for a world atlas. The names of many large settlements, towns, suburbs, and neighborhoods can be located on these large-scale maps. From a thematic standpoint the maps show generalized land-use patterns. Included were the total urban extent, major industrial areas, parks, public land, wooded areas, airports, shopping centers, streets, and railroads. A special effort was made to portray the various metropolitan areas in a manner as standard and comparable as possible. (For the symbols used, see the legend below.)

Notable differences occur in the forms of cities. In most of North America these forms were conditioned by a rectangular pattern of streets; land-use zones (residential, commercial, industrial) are well defined. The basic structure of most European cities is noticeably different and more complex; street patterns are irregular and zones are less well defined. In Asia, Africa, and South America the form tends to be even more irregular and complex. Widespread dispersion of craft and trade activities has lessened zonation, there may be cities with no identifiable city centers, and sometimes there may be dual centers (old and modern). Higher population densities result in more limited, compact urban places in these areas of the world.

Inhabited Localities

The symbol represents the number of inhabitants within the locality

- · 0—10,000
- ○ 10,000—25,000
- ◉ 25,000—100,000
- ▣ 100,000—250,000
- ▨ 250,000—1,000,000
- ■ >1,000,000

The size of type indicates the relative economic and political importance of the locality

Écommoy	
Trouville	**St.-Denis**
Lisieux	**PARIS**

Hollywood ■	Section of a City,
Westminster	Neighborhood
Northland ■	
Center	Major Shopping Center

 Urban Area (area of continuous industrial, commercial, and residential development)

 Major Industrial Area

 Wooded Area

Political Boundaries

International (First-order political unit)

━ ▪ ━ ▪ ━ Demarcated, Undemarcated, and Administrative

━ ━ ━ ━ Demarcation Line

Internal

▦▦▦▦ State, Province, etc. (Second-order political unit)

━━━━ County, Oblast, etc. (Third-order political unit)

···━··· Okrug, Kreis, etc. (Fourth-order political unit)

- - - - - City or Municipality (may appear in combination with another boundary symbol)

Capitals of Political Units

BUDAPEST	Independent Nation
Recife	State, Province, etc.
White Plains	County, Oblast, etc.
Iserlohn	Okrug, Kreis, etc.

Transportation

Road

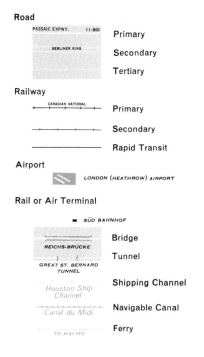

PASSAIC EXPWY. (I-80)	Primary
BERLINER RING	Secondary
	Tertiary

Railway

CANADIAN NATIONAL	Primary
	Secondary
	Rapid Transit

Airport

LONDON (HEATHROW) AIRPORT

Rail or Air Terminal

■ SÜD BAHNHOF

REICHS-BRÜCKE	Bridge
GREAT ST. BERNARD TUNNEL	Tunnel
Houston Ship Channel	Shipping Channel
Canal du Midi	Navigable Canal
TO MALMÖ	Ferry

Hydrographic Features

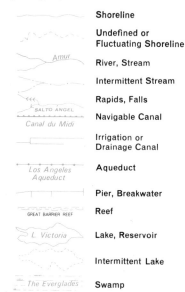

	Shoreline
	Undefined or Fluctuating Shoreline
Amur	River, Stream
	Intermittent Stream
SALTO ANGEL	Rapids, Falls
Canal du Midi	Navigable Canal
	Irrigation or Drainage Canal
Los Angeles Aqueduct	Aqueduct
	Pier, Breakwater
GREAT BARRIER REEF	Reef
L. Victoria	Lake, Reservoir
	Intermittent Lake
The Everglades	Swamp

Miscellaneous Cultural Features

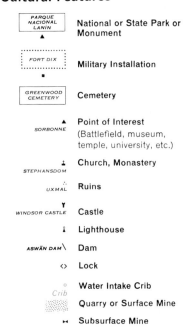

PARQUE NACIONAL LANIN ▲	National or State Park or Monument
FORT DIX ▪	Military Installation
GREENWOOD CEMETERY	Cemetery
▲ SORBONNE	Point of Interest (Battlefield, museum, temple, university, etc.)
⚓ STEPHANSDOM	Church, Monastery
∴ UXMAL	Ruins
♜ WINDSOR CASTLE	Castle
⚑	Lighthouse
ASWÄN DAM \	Dam
<>	Lock
○ Crib	Water Intake Crib
⠿	Quarry or Surface Mine
◄	Subsurface Mine

Topographic Features

Mt. Kenya 5199 △ Elevation Above Sea Level

Elevations are given in meters

⋆ Rock

A N D E S Mountain Range, Plateau,
KUNLUNSHANMAI Valley, etc.

BAFFIN ISLAND Island

POLUOSTROV KAMČATKA Peninsula, Cape, Point, etc.
CABO DE HORNOS

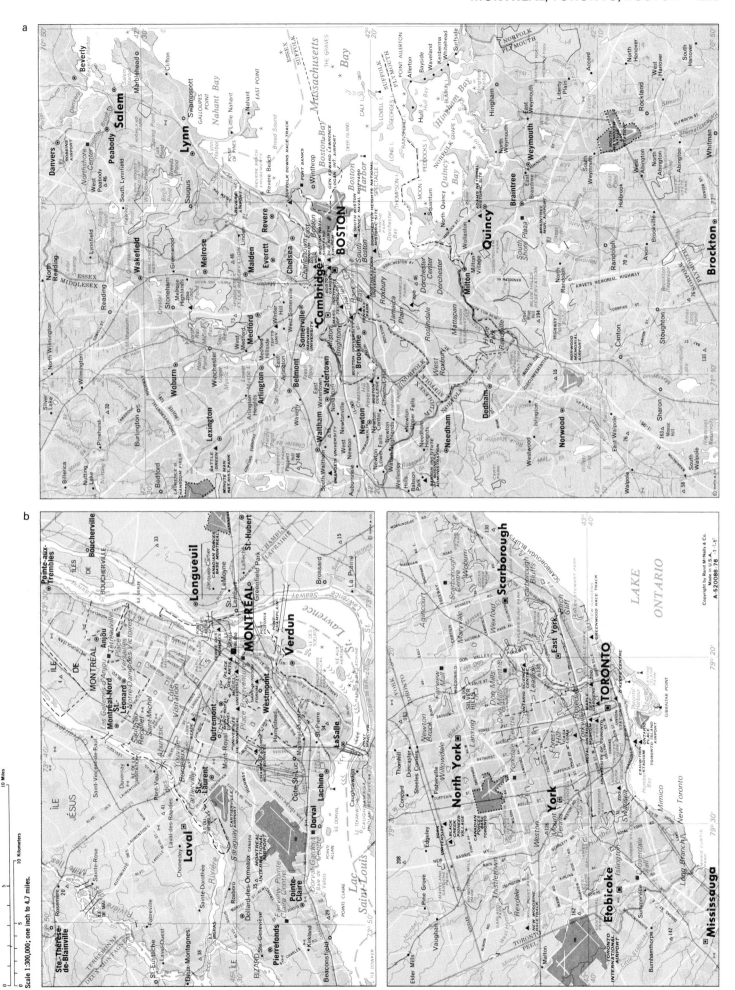

a

b

c

Copyright by Rand McNally & Co.
Made in U.S.A.
A-520086-76 -1`-1°

Scale 1:300,000; one inch to 4.7 miles.

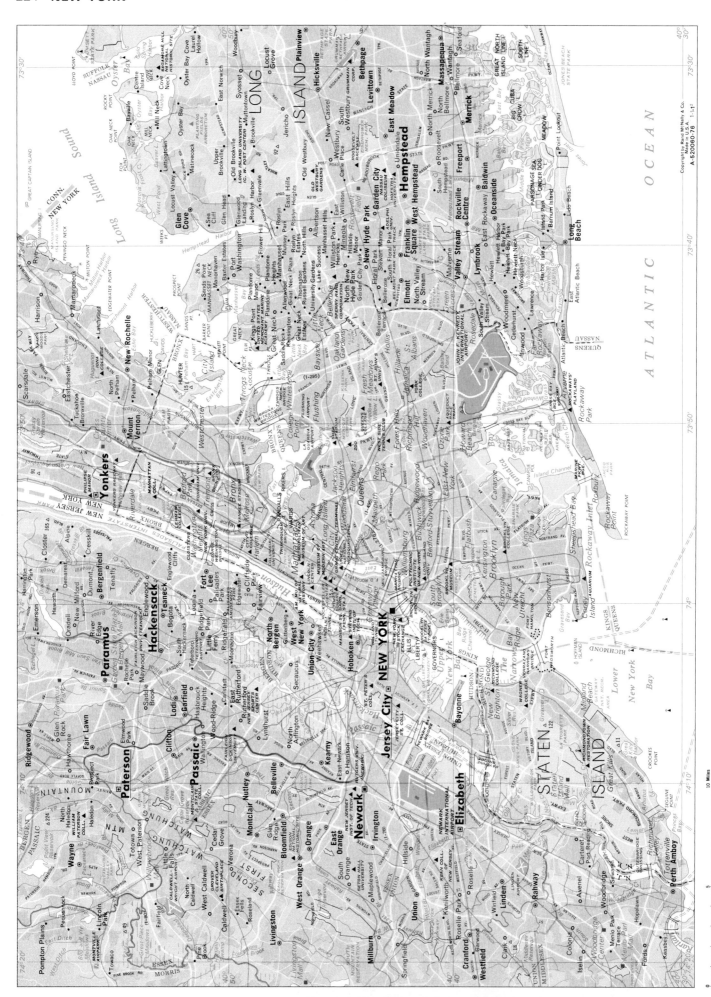

Scale 1:300,000; one inch to 4.7 miles.

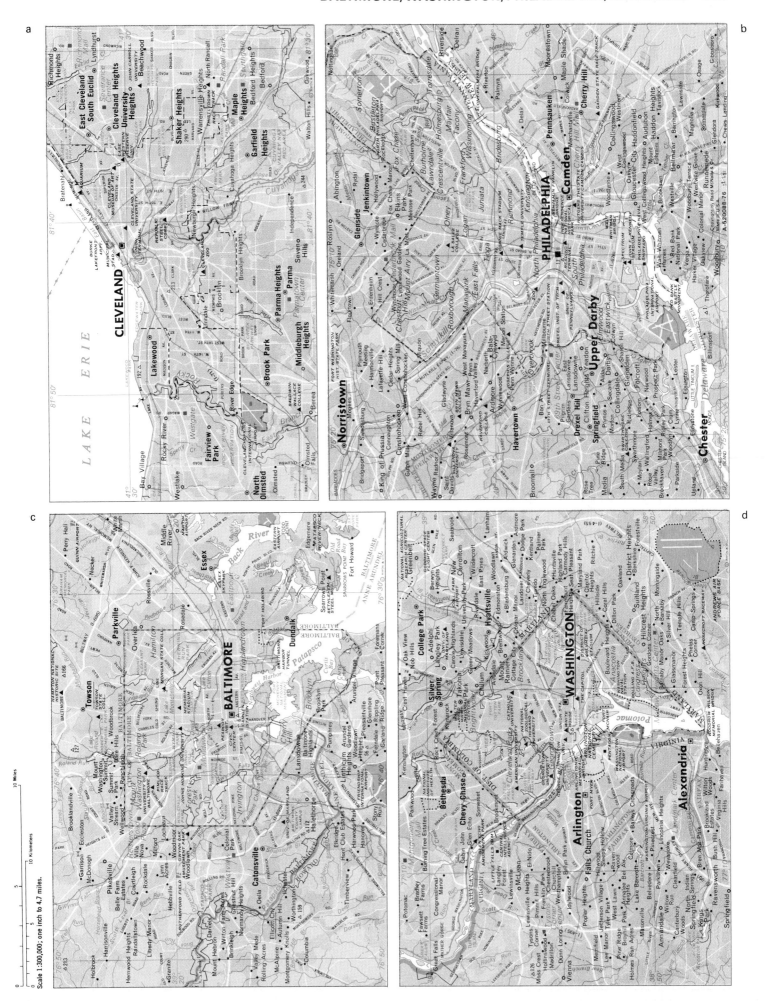

a

b

c

d

Scale 1:300,000; one inch to 4.7 miles.

10 Miles

10 Kilometers

a

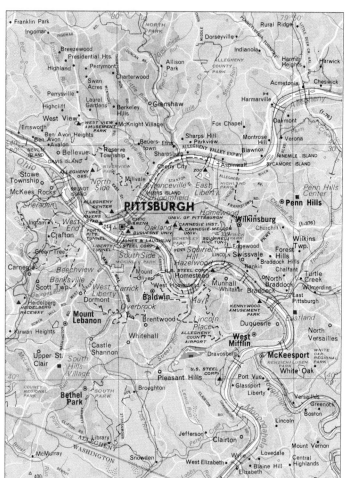

b

c

Scale 1:300,000; one inch to 4.7 miles.

Copyright by Rand McNally & Co.
Made in U.S.A.
A-520089-76   -1-1-1

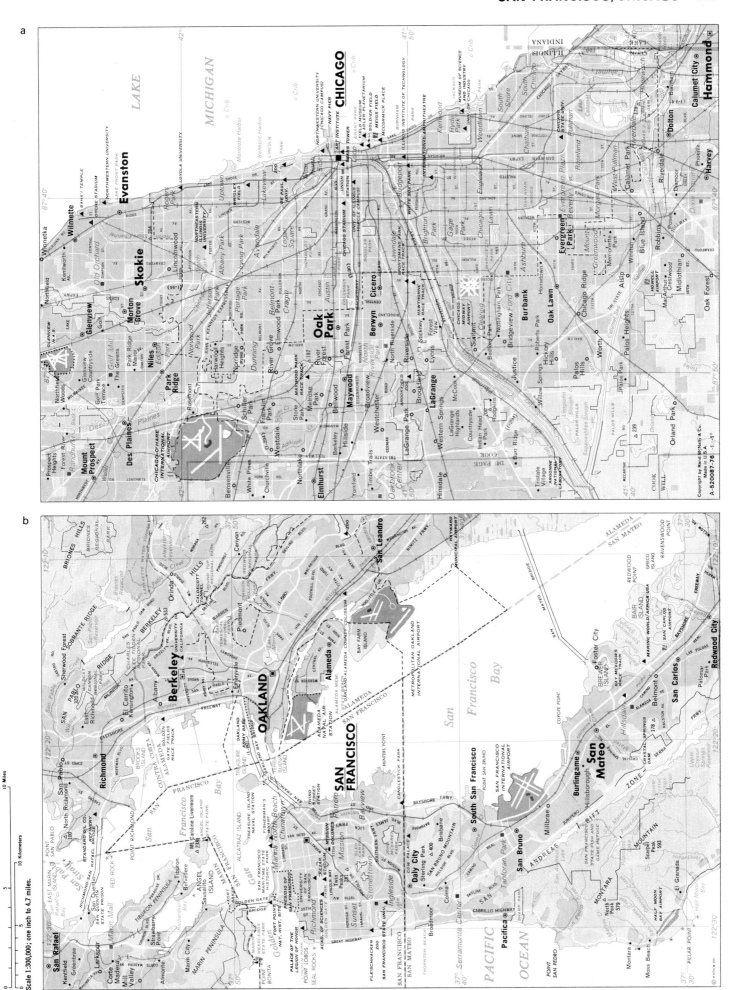

a

Copyright by Rand McNally & Co.
Made in U.S.A.
A-520087-76 -1; -1²

b

Scale 1:300,000; one inch to 4.7 miles.

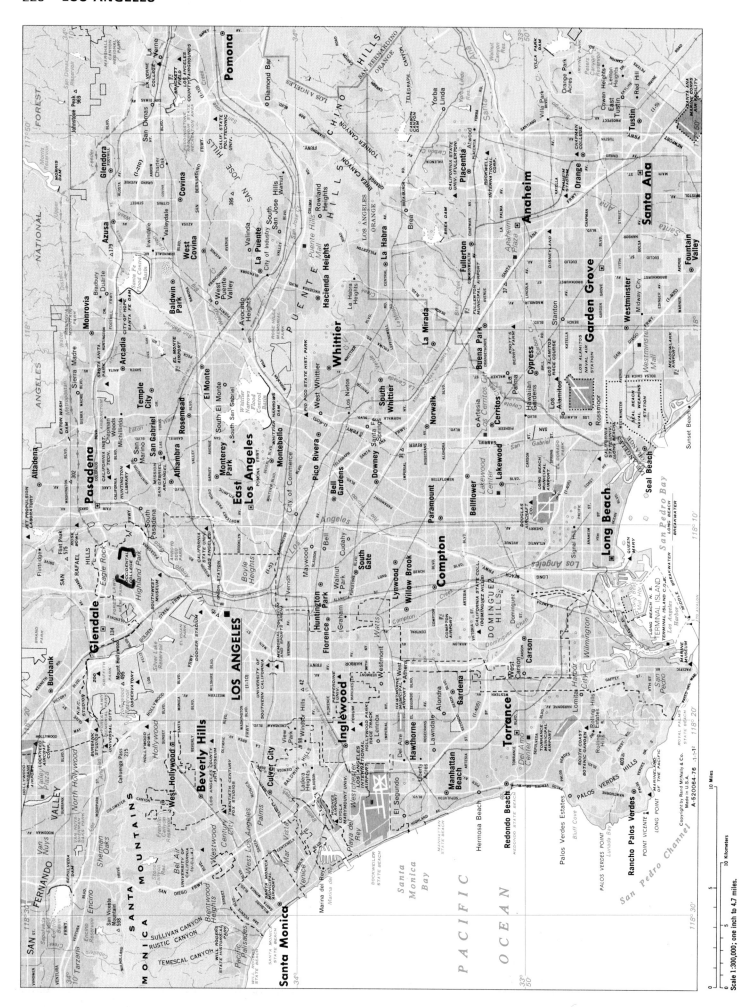

Copyright by Rand McNally & Co.
Made in U.S.A.
A-520064-76 -1-1-1²

Scale 1:300,000; one inch to 4.7 miles.

a

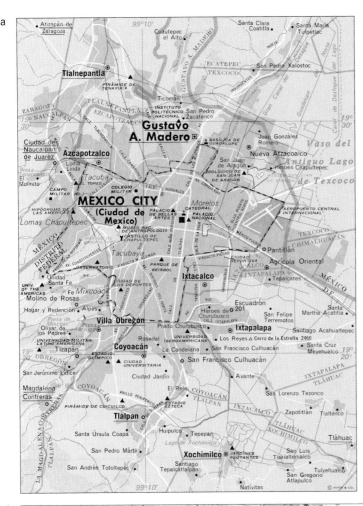

b

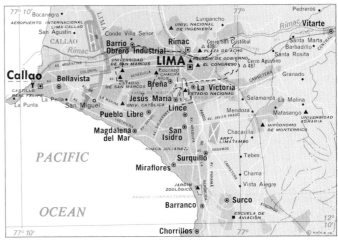
c

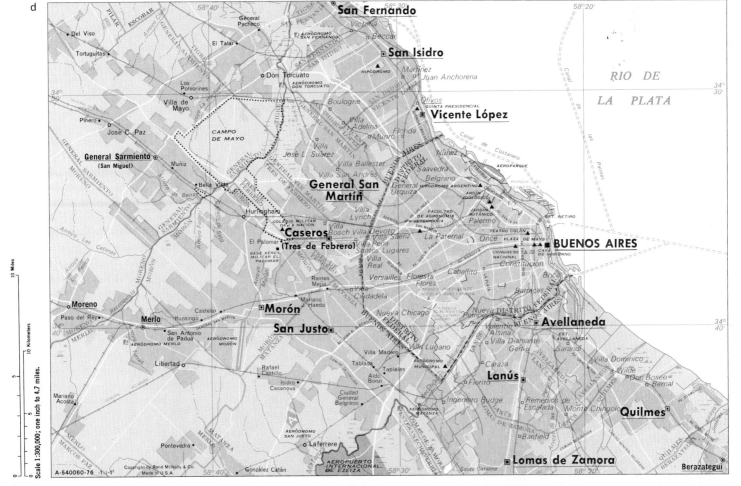
d

Scale 1:300,000; one inch to 4.7 miles.

A-540060-76 -1- -1²

Copyright by Rand McNally & Co.
Made in U.S.A.

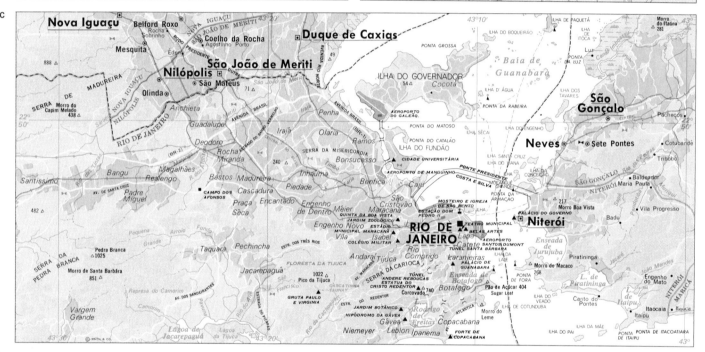

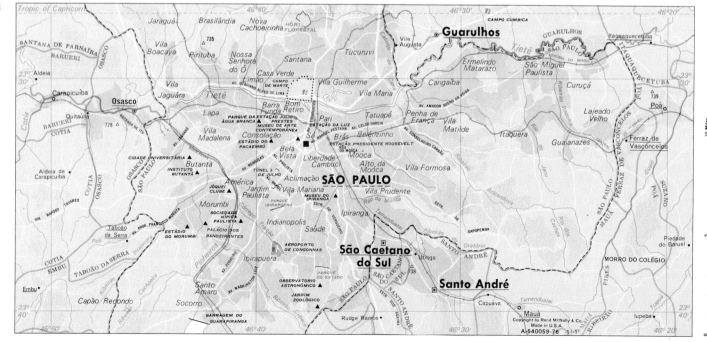

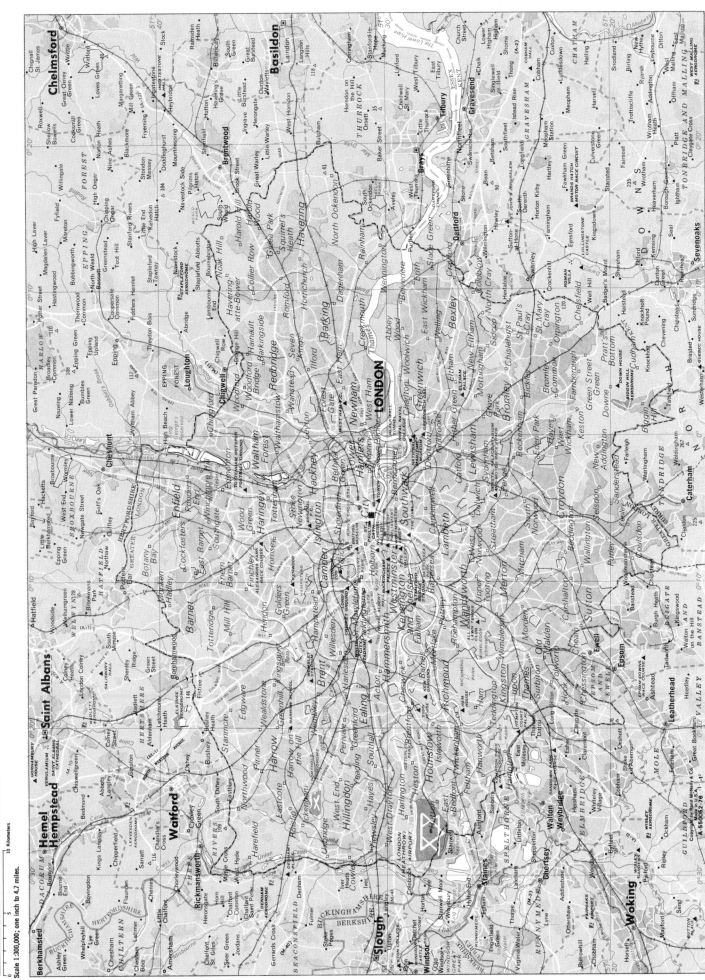

Scale 1:300,000; one inch to 4.7 miles.

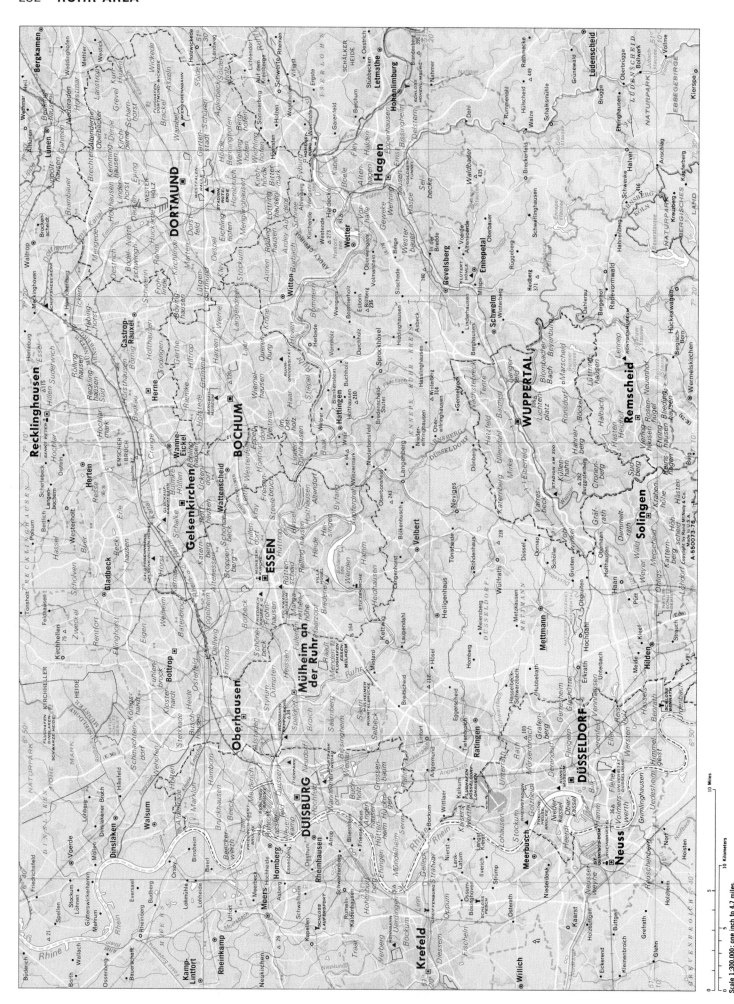

Copyright by Rand McNally & Co.
A-550073-76

Scale 1:300,000; one inch to 4.7 miles.

a

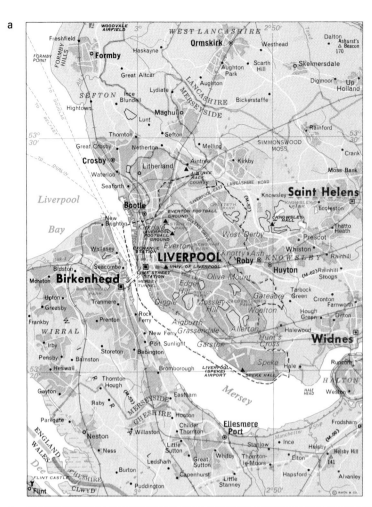

b

c

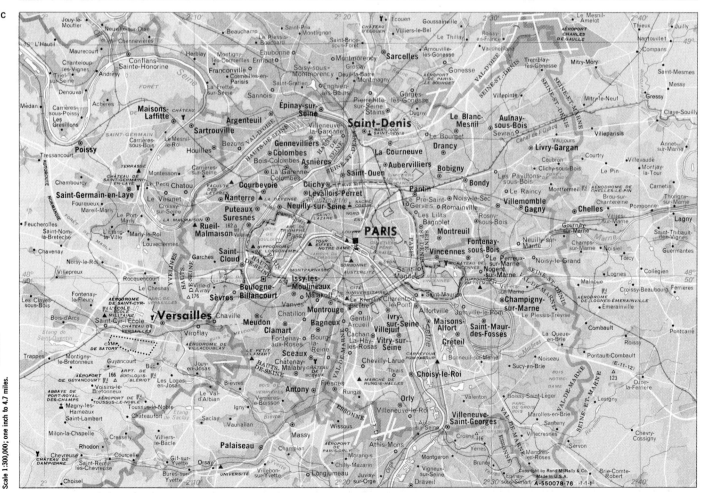

Scale 1:300,000; one inch to 4.7 miles.

a

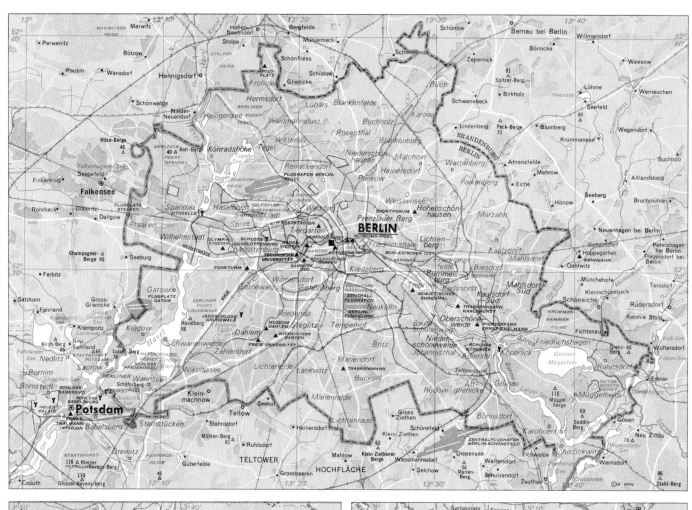

b

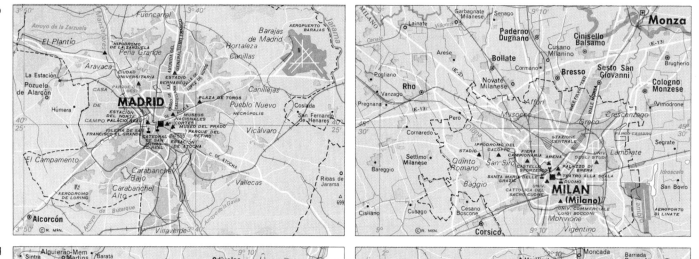

c

d

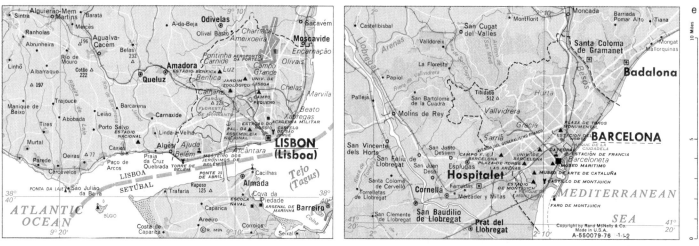

e

Scale 1:300,000; one inch to 4.7 miles.

Copyright by Rand McNally & Co.
Made in U.S.A.
A-550079-76 -1-L-2

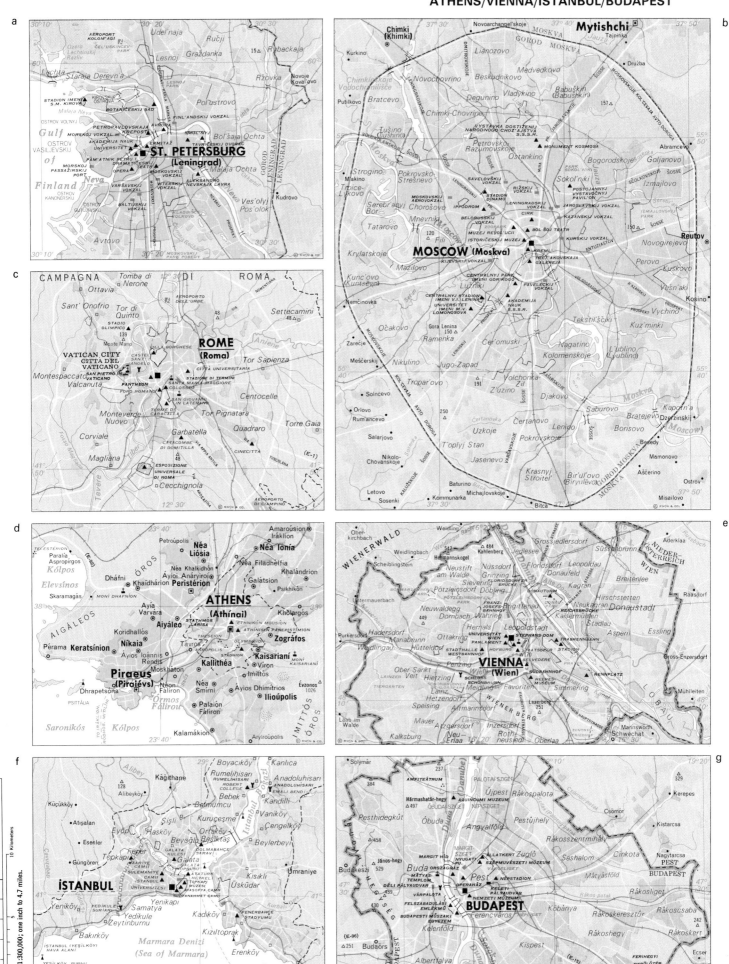

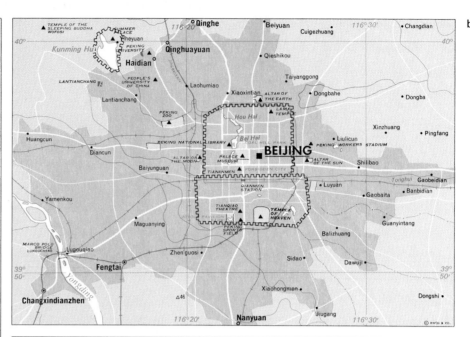

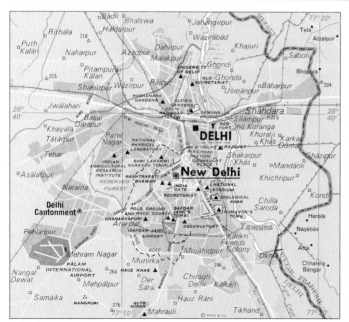

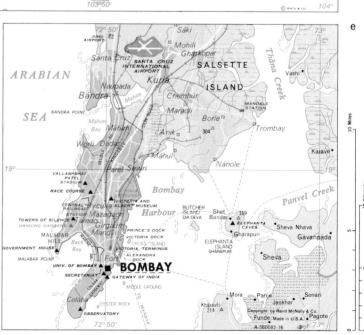

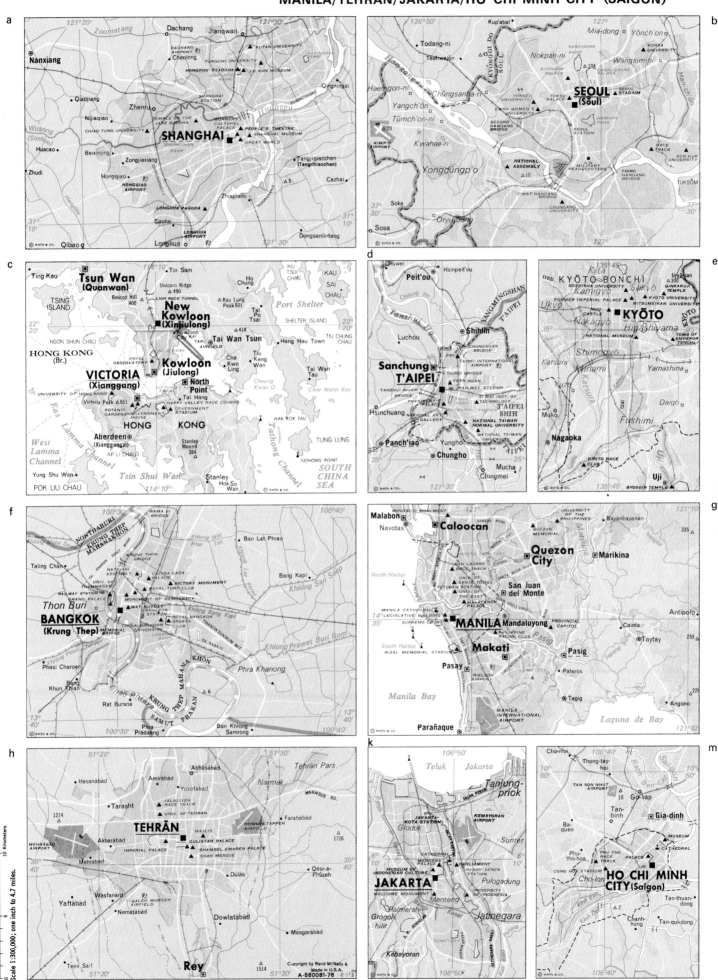

a

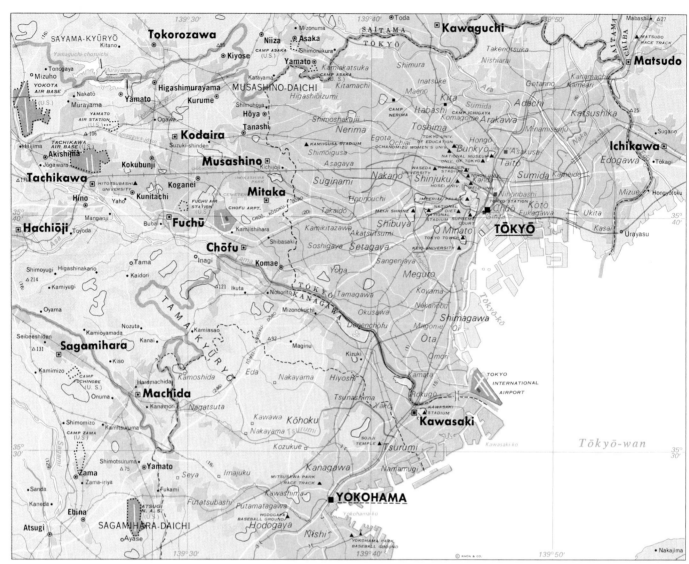

b

Copyright by Rand McNally & Co.
Made in U.S.A.
A-560080-76   -1-1-²

Scale 1:300,000; one inch to 4.7 miles.

a

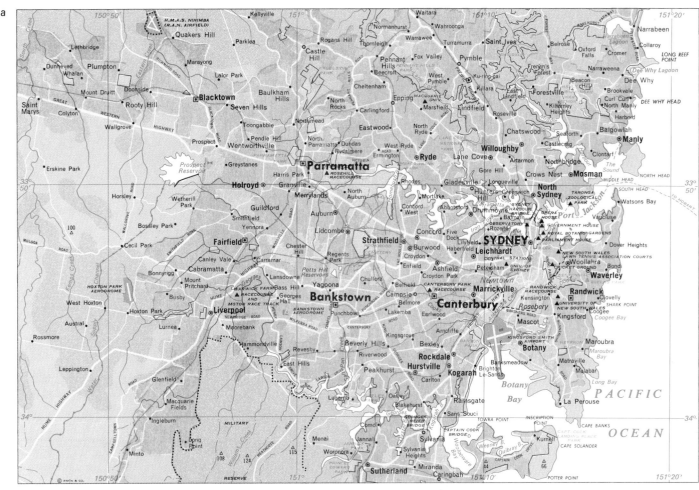

b

a

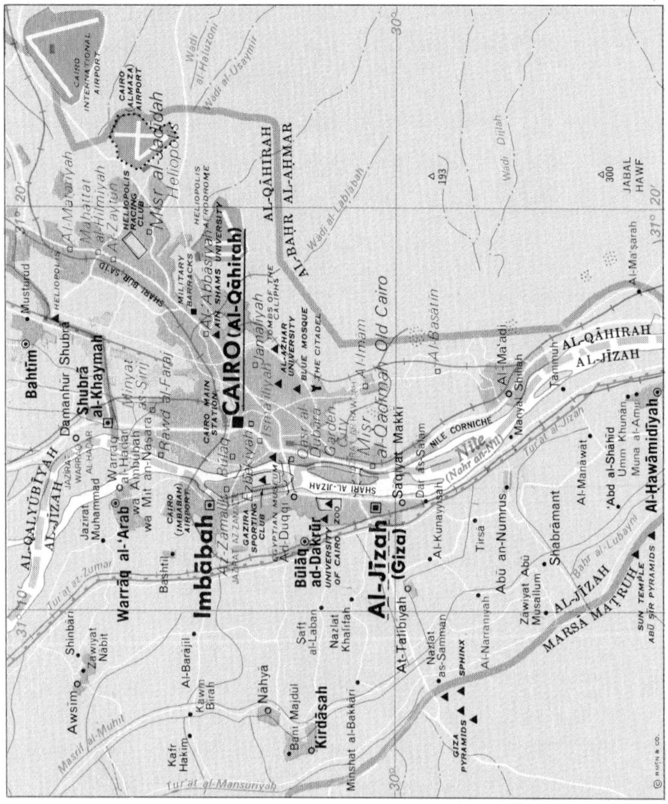

b

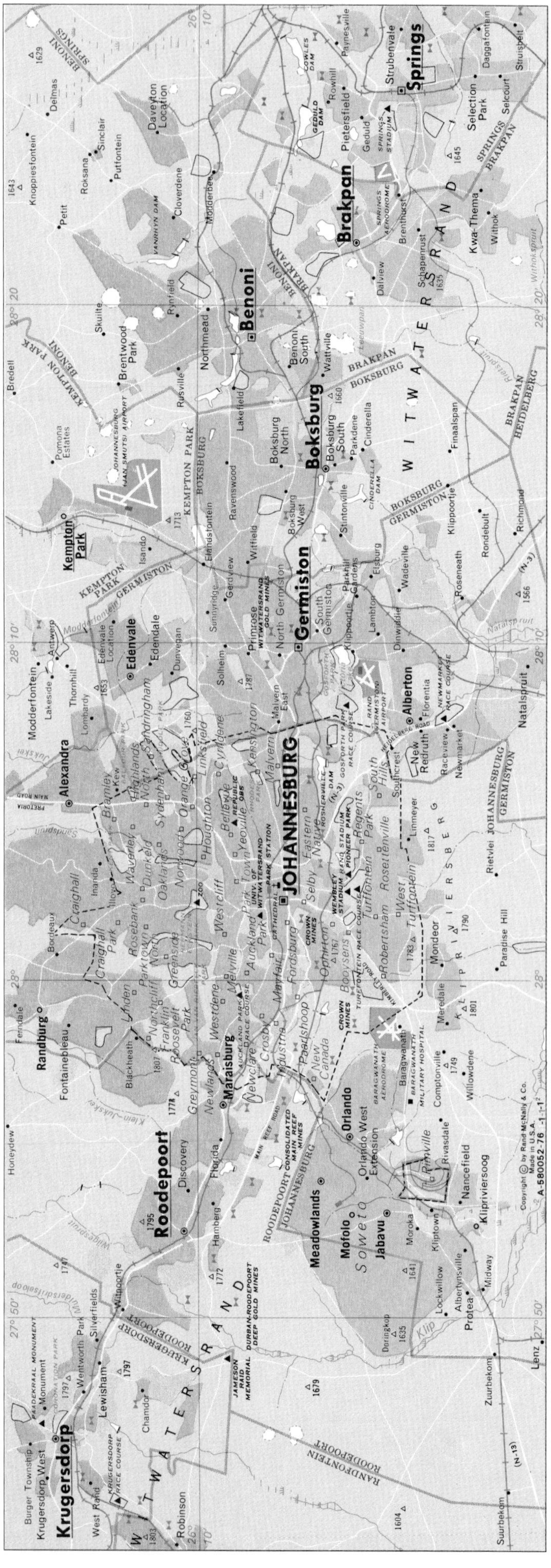

Scale 1:300,000; one inch to 4.7 miles.

c

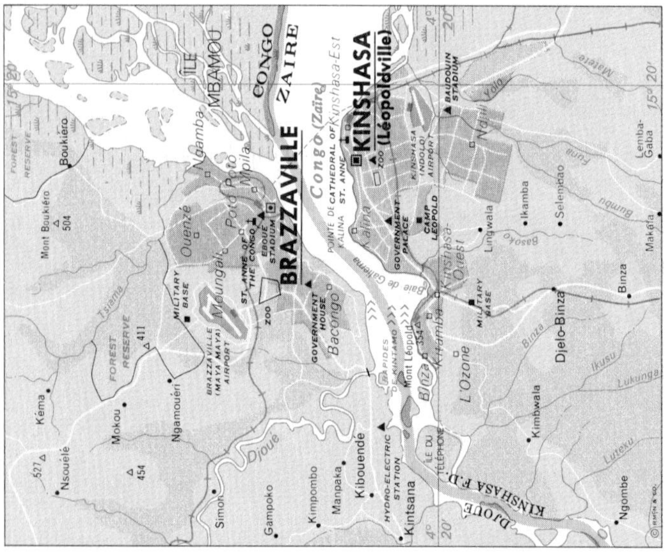

d

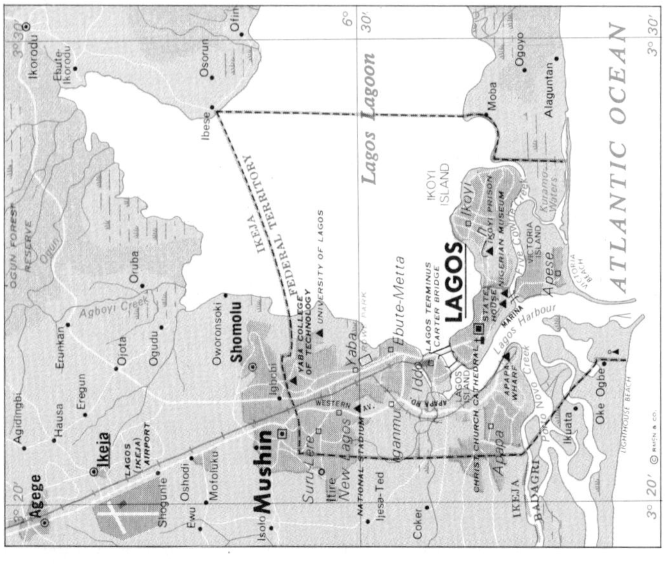

WORLD POLITICAL INFORMATION TABLE

This table gives the area, population, population density, political status, capital, and predominant languages for every country in the world. The political units listed are categorized by political status in the form of government column of the table, as follows: A—independent countries; B—internally independent political entities which are under the protection of another country in matters of defense and foreign affairs; C—colonies and other dependent political units; and D—the major administrative subdivisions of Australia, Canada, China, the Soviet Union,

the United Kingdom, and the United States. For comparison, the table also includes the continents and the world. A key to abbreviations of country names appears on page 249. All footnotes to this table appear on page 245.

The populations are estimates for January 1, 1992, made by Rand McNally on the basis of official data, United Nations estimates, and other available information. Area figures include inland water.

REGION OR POLITICAL DIVISION	Area Sq. Mi.	Est. Pop. 1/1/92	Pop. Per. Sq. Mi.	Form of Government and Ruling Power		Capital	Predominant Languages
Afars and Issas see Djibouti							
† Afghanistan	251,826	16,880,000	67	Republic	A	Kābul	Dari, Pashto, Uzbek, Turkmen
Africa	11,700,000	694,000,000	59				
Alabama	52,423	4,099,000	78	State (U.S.)	D	Montgomery	English
Alaska	656,424	560,000	0.9	State (U.S.)	D	Juneau	English, indigenous
† Albania	11,100	3,352,000	302	Socialist republic	A	Tiranë	Albanian, Greek
Alberta	255,287	2,499,000	9.8	Province (Canada)	D	Edmonton	English
† Algeria	919,595	26,360,000	29	Socialist republic	A	Algiers (El Djazaïr)	Arabic, Berber dialects, French
American Samoa	77	49,000	636	Unincorporated territory (U.S.)	C	Pago Pago	Samoan, English
Andorra	175	54,000	309	Coprincipality (Spanish and French protection)	B	Andorra	Spanish, French
† Angola	481,354	10,425,000	22	Socialist republic	A	Luanda	Portuguese, indigenous
Anguilla	35	7,000	200	Dependent territory (U.K. protection)	B	The Valley	English
Anhui	53,668	58,250,000	1,085	Province (China)	D	Hefei	Chinese (Mandarin)
Antarctica	5,400,000		1				
† Antigua and Barbuda	171	64,000	374	Parliamentary state	A	St. John's	English, local dialects
† Argentina	1,073,400	32,860,000	31	Republic	A	Buenos Aires	Spanish, English, Italian, German, French
Arizona	114,006	3,780,000	33	State (U.S.)	D	Phoenix	English
Arkansas	53,182	2,383,000	45	State (U.S.)	D	Little Rock	English
Armenia	11,506	3,360,000	292	Republic	A	Yerevan	Armenian, Azerbaijani, Russian
Aruba	75	64,000	853	Self-governing territory (Netherlands protection)	B	Oranjestad	Dutch, Papiamento, English, Spanish
Ascension	34	1,000	29	Dependency (St. Helena)	C	Georgetown	English
Asia	17,300,000	3,331,500,000	193				
† Australia	2,966,155	17,420,000	5.9	Federal parliamentary state	A	Canberra	English, indigenous
Australian Capital Territory	927	294,000	317	Territory (Australia)	D	Canberra	English
† Austria	32,377	7,681,000	237	Federal republic	A	Vienna (Wien)	German
Azerbaijan	33,436	7,170,000	214	Republic	A	Baku	Azerbaijani, Russian, Armenian
† Bahamas	5,382	260,000	48	Parliamentary state	A	Nassau	English, Creole
† Bahrain	267	546,000	2,045	Monarchy	A	Al Manāmah	Arabic, English, Farsi, Urdu
† Bangladesh	55,598	118,000,000	2,122	Islamic republic	A	Dhaka	Bangla, English
† Barbados	166	257,000	1,548	Parliamentary state	A	Bridgetown	English
Beijing (Peking)	6,487	11,700,000	1,804	Autonomous city (China)	D	Beijing (Peking)	Chinese (Mandarin)
† Belarus	80,155	10,390,000	130	Republic	A	Minsk	Byelorussian, Russian
Belau see Palau							
† Belgium	11,783	9,932,000	843	Constitutional monarchy	A	Brussels (Bruxelles)	Dutch (Flemish), French, German
† Belize	8,866	232,000	26	Parliamentary state	A	Belmopan	English, Spanish, Garifuna, Mayan
† Benin	43,475	4,914,000	113	Republic	A	Porto-Novo and Cotonou	French, Fon, Adja, indigenous
Bermuda	21	60,000	2,857	Dependent territory (U.K.)	C	Hamilton	English
† Bhutan	17,954	1,614,000	90	Monarchy (Indian protection)	B	Thimphu	Dzongkha, Tibetan and Nepalese dialects
† Bolivia	424,165	7,243,000	17	Republic	A	La Paz and Sucre	Spanish, Quechua, Aymara
Bophuthatswana [2]	15,641	3,500,000	224	National state (South African protection)	B	Mmabatho	Tswana
Bosnia and Hercegovina	19,741	4,519,000	229	Republic	A	Sarajevo	Serb, Croat, Albanian
† Botswana	224,711	1,345,000	6.0	Republic	A	Gaborone	English, Tswana
† Brazil	3,286,488	156,750,000	48	Federal republic	A	Brasília	Portuguese, Spanish, English, French
British Columbia	365,948	3,106,000	8.5	Province (Canada)	D	Victoria	English
British Indian Ocean Territory	23		1	Dependent territory (U.K.)	C		English
† Brunei	2,226	411,000	185	Monarchy	A	Bandar Seri Begawan	Malay, English, Chinese
† Bulgaria	42,823	8,902,000	208	Republic	A	Sofia (Sofiya)	Bulgarian
† Burkina Faso	105,869	9,510,000	90	Provisional military government	A	Ouagadougou	French, indigenous
† Burma (Myanmar)	261,228	42,615,000	163	Provisional military government	A	Rangoon (Yangon)	Burmese, indigenous
† Burundi	10,745	5,924,000	551	Provisional military government	A	Bujumbura	French, Kirundi, Swahili
California	163,707	30,680,000	187	State (U.S.)	D	Sacramento	English
† Cambodia	69,898	8,543,000	122	Socialist republic	A	Phnum Pénh (Phnom Penh)	Khmer, French
† Cameroon	183,569	11,550,000	63	Republic	A	Yaoundé	English, French, indigenous
† Canada	3,849,674	26,985,000	7.0	Federal parliamentary state	A	Ottawa	English, French
† Cape Verde	1,557	393,000	252	Republic	A	Praia	Portuguese, Crioulo
Cayman Islands	100	28,000	280	Dependent territory (U.K.)	C	Georgetown	English
† Central African Republic	240,535	2,990,000	12	Republic	A	Bangui	French, Sango, Arabic, indigenous
Ceylon see Sri Lanka							
† Chad	495,755	5,178,000	10	Republic	A	N'Djamena	Arabic, French, indigenous
Channel Islands	75	143,000	1,907	Dependent territory (U.K.)	C		English, French
† Chile	292,135	13,395,000	46	Republic	A	Santiago	Spanish
† China (excl. Taiwan)	3,689,631	1,181,580,000	320	Socialist republic	A	Beijing (Peking)	Chinese dialects
Christmas Island	52	2,300	44	External territory (Australia)	C	The Settlement	English, Chinese, Malay
Ciskei [2]	2,996	2,500,000	834	National state (South African protection)	B	Bisho	English, Xhosa, Afrikaans
Cocos (Keeling) Islands	5.4	700	130	Part of Australia			English, Cocos-Malay, Malay
† Colombia	440,831	33,170,000	75	Republic	A	Santa Fe de Bogotá	Spanish
Colorado	104,100	3,356,000	32	State (U.S.)	D	Denver	English
† Comoros (excl. Mayotte)	863	484,000	561	Federal Islamic republic	A	Moroni	Arabic, French, Shaafi Islam (Swahili), Malagasy
† Congo	132,047	2,344,000	18	Socialist republic	A	Brazzaville	French, indigenous
Connecticut	5,544	3,336,000	602	State (U.S.)	D	Hartford	English
Cook Islands	91	18,000	198	Self-governing territory (New Zealand protection)	B	Avarua	English, Malay-Polynesian languages
† Costa Rica	19,730	3,151,000	160	Republic	A	San José	Spanish
Croatia	21,829	4,800,000	220	Republic	A	Zagreb	Croat, Serb
† Cuba	42,804	10,785,000	252	Socialist republic	A	Havana (La Habana)	Spanish
† Cyprus	2,276	713,000	313	Republic	A	Nicosia (Levkosía)	Greek, English
Cyprus, North [3]	1,295	192,000	148	Republic	A	Nicosia (Lefkoşa)	Turkish

REGION OR POLITICAL DIVISION	Area Sq. Mi.	Est. Pop. 1/1/92	Pop. Per. Sq. Mi.	Form of Government and Ruling Power	Capital	Predominant Languages
† Czechoslovakia	49,382	15,755,000	319	Federal republic .... A	Prague (Praha)	Czech, Slovak, Hungarian
Delaware	2,489	679,000	273	State (U.S.) .... D	Dover	English
† Denmark	16,638	5,154,000	310	Constitutional monarchy .... A	Copenhagen (København)	Danish
District of Columbia	68	611,000	8,985	Federal district (U.S.) .... D	Washington	English
† Djibouti	8,958	351,000	39	Republic .... A	Djibouti	French, Somali, Afar, Arabic
† Dominica	305	87,000	285	Republic .... A	Roseau	English, French
† Dominican Republic	18,704	8,124,000	434	Republic .... A	Santo Domingo	Spanish
† Ecuador	109,484	10,880,000	99	Republic .... A	Quito	Spanish, Quechua, indigenous
† Egypt	386,662	55,105,000	143	Socialist republic .... A	Cairo (Al Qāhirah)	Arabic
Ellice Islands see Tuvalu				....		....
† El Salvador	8,124	5,473,000	674	Republic .... A	San Salvador	Spanish, Nahua
England	50,363	48,015,000	953	Administrative division (U.K.) .... D	London	English
† Equatorial Guinea	10,831	384,000	35	Republic .... A	Malabo	Spanish, indigenous, English
† Estonia	17,413	1,606,000	92	Republic .... A	Tallinn	Estonian, Russian
† Ethiopia	483,123	54,040,000	112	Socialist republic .... A	Addis Ababa	Amharic, Tigrinya, Orominga, Arabic
Europe	3,800,000	695,200,000	183			
Faeroe Islands	540	48,000	89	Self-governing territory (Danish protection) B	Tórshavn	Danish, Faroese
Falkland Islands [4]	4,700	2,000	0.4	Dependent territory (U.K.) C	Stanley	English
† Fiji	7,078	747,000	106	Republic .... A	Suva	English, Fijian, Hindustani
† Finland	130,559	5,001,000	38	Republic .... A	Helsinki (Helsingfors)	Finnish, Swedish
Florida	65,758	13,360,000	203	State (U.S.) .... D	Tallahassee	English
† France (excl. Overseas Departments)	211,208	57,010,000	270	Republic .... A	Paris	French
French Guiana	35,135	104,000	3.0	Overseas department (France) C	Cayenne	French
French Polynesia	1,544	198,000	128	Overseas territory (France) C	Papeete	French, Tahitian, Chinese
Fujian	46,332	30,840,000	666	Province (China) .... D	Fuzhou	Chinese dialects
† Gabon	103,347	1,088,000	11	Republic .... A	Libreville	French, Fang, indigenous
† Gambia	4,127	889,000	215	Republic .... A	Banjul	English, Malinke, Wolof, Fula, indigenous
Gansu	173,746	23,275,000	134	Province (China) .... D	Lanzhou	Chinese (Mandarin), Mongolian, Tibetan dialects
Georgia	59,441	6,657,000	112	State (U.S.) .... D	Atlanta	English
Georgia	26,911	5,550,000	206	Republic .... A	Tbilisi	Georgian, Russian, Armenian
† Germany	137,822	79,710,000	578	Federal republic .... A	Berlin and Bonn	German
† Ghana	92,098	15,865,000	172	Provisional military government .... A	Accra	English, Akan, indigenous
Gibraltar	2.3	31,000	13,478	Dependent territory (U.K.) C	Gibraltar	English, Spanish
Gilbert Islands see Kiribati				....		....
Great Britain see United Kingdom				....		....
† Greece	50,962	10,285,000	202	Republic .... A	Athens (Athínai)	Greek
Greenland	840,004	57,000	0.1	Self-governing territory (Danish protection) B	Godthåb	Danish, Greenlandic, Inuit dialects
† Grenada	133	98,000	737	Parliamentary state .... A	St. George's	English, French
Guadeloupe (incl. Dependencies)	687	346,000	504	Overseas department (France) C	Basse-Terre	French, Creole
Guam	209	147,000	703	Unincorporated territory (U.S.) C	Agana	English, Chamorro, Tagalog
Guangdong	68,726	63,800,000	928	Province (China) .... D	Guangzhou (Canton)	Chinese dialects, Miao-Yao
Guangxi Zhuangzu	91,236	44,310,000	486	Autonomous region (China) .... D	Nanning	Chinese dialects, Thai, Miao-Yao
† Guatemala	42,042	9,386,000	223	Republic .... A	Guatemala	Spanish, indigenous
Guernsey (incl. Dependencies)	30	58,000	1,933	Bailiwick (Channel Islands) C	St. Peter Port	English, French
† Guinea	94,926	7,553,000	80	Provisional military government .... A	Conakry	French, indigenous
† Guinea-Bissau	13,948	1,036,000	74	Republic .... A	Bissau	Portuguese, Crioulo, indigenous
Guizhou	65,637	33,795,000	515	Province (China) .... D	Guiyang	Chinese (Mandarin), Thai, Miao-Yao
† Guyana	83,000	748,000	9.0	Republic .... A	Georgetown	English, indigenous
Hainan	13,127	7,090,000	540	Province (China) .... D	Haikou	Chinese, Min, Tai
† Haiti	10,714	6,361,000	594	Republic .... A	Port-au-Prince	Creole, French
Hawaii	10,932	1,133,000	104	State (U.S.) .... D	Honolulu	English, Hawaiian, Japanese
Hebei	73,359	62,860,000	857	Province (China) .... D	Shijiazhuang	Chinese (Mandarin)
Heilongjiang	181,082	37,690,000	208	Province (China) .... D	Harbin	Chinese dialects, Mongolian, Tungus
Henan	64,479	87,670,000	1,360	Province (China) .... D	Zhengzhou	Chinese (Mandarin)
Holland see Netherlands				....		....
† Honduras	43,277	5,342,000	123	Republic .... A	Tegucigalpa	Spanish, indigenous
Hong Kong	414	5,874,000	14,188	Chinese territory under British administration C	Victoria (Hong Kong)	Chinese (Cantonese), English
Hubei	72,356	56,360,000	779	Province (China) .... D	Wuhan	Chinese dialects
Hunan	81,081	63,810,000	787	Province (China) .... D	Changsha	Chinese dialects, Miao-Yao
† Hungary	35,920	10,555,000	294	Republic .... A	Budapest	Hungarian
† Iceland	39,769	261,000	6.6	Republic .... A	Reykjavík	Icelandic
Idaho	83,574	1,065,000	13	State (U.S.) .... D	Boise	English
Illinois	57,918	11,575,000	200	State (U.S.) .... D	Springfield	English
† India (incl. part of Jammu and Kashmir)	1,237,062	874,150,000	707	Federal republic .... A	New Delhi	English, Hindi, Telugu, Bengali, indigenous
Indiana	36,420	5,615,000	154	State (U.S.) .... D	Indianapolis	English
† Indonesia	752,410	195,300,000	260	Republic .... A	Jakarta	Indonesian, Javanese, Sundanese, Madurese, other indigenous
Iowa	56,276	2,801,000	50	State (U.S.) .... D	Des Moines	English
† Iran	632,457	60,000,000	95	Islamic republic .... A	Tehrān	Farsi, Turkish, Kurdish, Arabic, English, French
† Iraq	169,235	19,915,000	118	Republic .... A	Baghdād	Arabic, Kurdish, Assyrian, Armenian
† Ireland	27,137	3,484,000	128	Republic .... A	Dublin (Baile Átha Cliath)	English, Irish Gaelic
Isle of Man	221	64,000	290	Self-governing territory (U.K. protection) .. B	Douglas	English, Manx Gaelic
† Israel (excl. Occupied Areas)	8,019	4,393,000	548	Republic .... A	Jerusalem (Yerushalayim)	Hebrew, Arabic, Yiddish
Israeli Occupied Areas [5]	2,947	1,789,000	607	None		Arabic, Hebrew, English
† Italy	116,324	57,830,000	497	Republic .... A	Rome (Roma)	Italian
† Ivory Coast	124,518	13,240,000	106	Republic .... A	Abidjan and Yamoussoukro [6]	French, indigenous
† Jamaica	4,244	2,501,000	589	Parliamentary state .... A	Kingston	English, Creole
† Japan	145,870	124,270,000	852	Constitutional monarchy .... A	Tōkyō	Japanese
Jersey	45	85,000	1,889	Bailiwick (Channel Islands) C	St. Helier	English, French
Jiangsu	39,614	69,830,000	1,763	Province (China) .... D	Nanjing (Nanking)	Chinese dialects
Jiangxi	64,325	39,110,000	608	Province (China) .... D	Nanchang	Chinese dialects
Jilin	72,201	25,760,000	357	Province (China) .... D	Changchun	Chinese (Mandarin), Mongolian, Korean
† Jordan (excl. West Bank)	35,135	3,485,000	99	Constitutional monarchy .... D	'Ammān	Arabic
Kansas	82,282	2,517,000	31	State (U.S.) .... D	Topeka	English
Kazakhstan	1,049,156	16,880,000	16	Republic .... A	Alma-Ata	Kazakh, Russian, German, Ukrainian
Kentucky	40,411	3,727,000	92	State (U.S.) .... D	Frankfort	English
† Kenya	224,961	25,695,000	114	Republic .... A	Nairobi	English, Swahili, indigenous
Kiribati	313	72,000	230	Republic .... A	Bairiki	English, Gilbertese
† Korea, North	46,540	22,250,000	478	Socialist republic .... A	Pyŏngyang	Korean
† Korea, South	38,230	43,305,000	1,133	Republic .... A	Seoul (Sŏul)	Korean
† Kuwait	6,880	2,244,000	326	Constitutional monarchy .... A	Kuwait	Arabic, English
Kyrgyzstan	76,641	4,385,000	57	Republic .... A	Bishkek	Kirghiz, Russian, Uzbek
† Laos	91,429	4,158,000	45	Socialist republic .... A	Viangchan (Vientiane)	Lao, French, Thai, indigenous

REGION OR POLITICAL DIVISION	Area Sq. Mi.	Est. Pop. 1/1/92	Pop. Per. Sq. Mi.	Form of Government and Ruling Power		Capital	Predominant Languages
† Latvia	24,595	2,737,000	111	Republic	A	Rīga	Latvian, Russian
† Lebanon	4,015	3,409,000	849	Republic	A	Beirut (Bayrūt)	Arabic, French, Armenian, English
† Lesotho	11,720	1,824,000	156	Constitutional monarchy	A	Maseru	English, Sesotho, Zulu, Xhosa
Liaoning	56,255	41,590,000	739	Province (China)	A	Shenyang	Chinese (Mandarin), Mongolian
† Liberia	38,250	2,776,000	73	Republic	A	Monrovia	English, indigenous
† Libya	679,362	4,416,000	6.5	Socialist republic	A	Tripoli (Ṭarābulus)	Arabic
† Liechtenstein	62	28,000	452	Constitutional monarchy	A	Vaduz	German
† Lithuania	25,174	3,767,000	150	Republic	A	Vilnius	Lithuanian, Russian, Polish
Louisiana	51,843	4,251,000	82	State (U.S.)	D	Baton Rouge	English
† Luxembourg	998	390,000	391	Constitutional monarchy	A	Luxembourg	French, Luxembourgish, German
Macao	6.6	448,000	67,879	Chinese territory under Portuguese administration	C	Macao	Portuguese, Chinese (Cantonese)
Macedonia	9,928	2,120,000	214	Republic	A	Skopje	Macedonian, Albanian
† Madagascar	226,658	12,380,000	55	Republic	A	Antananarivo	Malagasy, French
Maine	35,387	1,252,000	35	State (U.S.)	D	Augusta	English
† Malawi	45,747	9,523,000	208	Republic	A	Lilongwe	Chichewa, English, Tombuka
† Malaysia	129,251	18,200,000	141	Federal constitutional monarchy	A	Kuala Lumpur	Malay, Chinese dialects, English, Tamil
† Maldives	115	230,000	2,000	Republic	A	Male	Divehi
† Mali	478,767	8,438,000	18	Republic	A	Bamako	French, Bambara, indigenous
† Malta	122	357,000	2,926	Republic	A	Valletta	English, Maltese
Manitoba	250,947	1,129,000	4.5	Province (Canada)	D	Winnipeg	English
† Marshall Islands	70	49,000	700	Republic (U.S. protection)	A	Majuro (island)	English, Malay-Polynesian languages, Japanese
Martinique	425	347,000	816	Overseas department (France)	C	Fort-de-France	French, Creole
Maryland	12,407	4,895,000	395	State (U.S.)	D	Annapolis	English
Massachusetts	10,555	6,107,000	579	State (U.S.)	D	Boston	English
† Mauritania	395,956	2,028,000	5.1	Provisional military government	A	Nouakchott	Arabic, French, indigenous
† Mauritius (incl. Dependencies)	788	1,085,000	1,377	Parliamentary state	A	Port Louis	English, Creole, Bhojpuri, Hindi
Mayotte [7]	144	77,000	535	Territorial collectivity (France)	C	Dzaoudzi and Mamoudzou [6]	French, Swahili (Mahorian)
† Mexico	756,066	91,000,000	120	Federal republic	A	Mexico City (Ciudad de México)	Spanish, indigenous
Michigan	96,810	9,423,000	97	State (U.S.)	D	Lansing	English
† Micronesia, Federated States of	271	109,000	402	Republic (U.S. protection)	A	Kolonia	English, Malay-Polynesian languages
Midway Islands	2.0	500	250	Unincorporated territory (U.S.)	C		English
Minnesota	86,943	4,459,000	51	State (U.S.)	D	St. Paul	English
Mississippi	48,434	2,604,000	54	State (U.S.)	D	Jackson	English
Missouri	69,709	5,200,000	75	State (U.S.)	D	Jefferson City	English
Moldova	13,012	4,440,000	341	Republic	A	Kishinev	Moldavian, Russian, Ukrainian
Monaco	0.7	30,000	42,857	Constitutional monarchy	A	Monaco	French, English, Italian, Monegasque
† Mongolia	604,829	2,278,000	3.8	Socialist republic	A	Ulan Bator (Ulaanbaatar)	Khalkha Mongol, Kazakh, Russian, Chinese
Montana	147,046	806,000	5.5	State (U.S.)	D	Helena	English
Montenegro	5,333	647,000	121	Republic (Yugoslavia)	D	Titograd	Serb, Albanian
Montserrat	39	13,000	333	Dependent territory (U.K.)	C	Plymouth	English
† Morocco (excl. Western Sahara)	172,414	26,470,000	154	Constitutional monarchy	A	Rabat	Arabic, Berber dialects, French
† Mozambique	308,642	15,460,000	50	Republic	A	Maputo	Portuguese, indigenous
Myanmar see Burma							
† Namibia (excl. Walvis Bay)	317,818	1,548,000	4.9	Republic	A	Windhoek	Afrikaans, English, German, indigenous
Nauru	8.1	9,000	1,111	Republic	A	Yaren District	Nauruan, English
Nebraska	77,358	1,615,000	21	State (U.S.)	D	Lincoln	English
Nei Monggol (Inner Mongolia)	456,759	22,685,000	50	Autonomous region (China)	D	Hohhot	Mongolian
† Nepal	56,827	19,845,000	349	Constitutional monarchy	A	Kathmandu	Nepali, Maithali, Bhojpuri, other indigenous
† Netherlands	16,133	15,065,000	934	Constitutional monarchy	A	Amsterdam and The Hague ('s-Gravenhage)	Dutch
Netherlands Antilles	309	190,000	615	Self-governing territory (Netherlands protection)	B	Willemstad	Dutch, Papiamento, English
Nevada	110,567	1,257,000	11	State (U.S.)	D	Carson City	English
New Brunswick	28,355	743,000	26	Province (Canada)	D	Fredericton	English, French
New Caledonia	7,358	174,000	24	Overseas territory (France)	C	Nouméa	French, Malay-Polynesian languages
Newfoundland	156,649	591,000	3.8	Province (Canada)	D	St. John's	English
New Hampshire	9,351	1,138,000	122	State (U.S.)	D	Concord	English
New Hebrides see Vanuatu							
New Jersey	8,722	7,850,000	900	State (U.S.)	D	Trenton	English
New Mexico	121,598	1,550,000	13	State (U.S.)	D	Santa Fe	English, Spanish
New South Wales	309,500	5,930,000	19	State (Australia)	D	Sydney	English
New York	54,475	18,260,000	335	State (U.S.)	D	Albany	English
† New Zealand	103,519	3,463,000	33	Parliamentary state	A	Wellington	English, Maori
† Nicaragua	50,054	3,805,000	76	Republic	A	Managua	Spanish, English, indigenous
† Niger	489,191	8,113,000	17	Provisional military government	A	Niamey	French, Hausa, Djerma, indigenous
† Nigeria	356,669	124,300,000	349	Provisional military government	A	Lagos and Abuja [6]	English, Hausa, Fulani, Yorbua, Ibo, indigenous
Ningxia Huizu	25,637	4,845,000	189	Autonomous region (China)	D	Yinchuan	Chinese (Mandarin)
Niue	100	1,800	18	Self-governing territory (New Zealand protection)	B	Alofi	English, Malay-Polynesian languages
Norfolk Island	14	2,600	186	External territory (Australia)	C	Kingston	English, Norfolk
North America	9,500,000	436,300,000	46				
North Carolina	53,821	6,770,000	126	State (U.S.)	D	Raleigh	English
North Dakota	70,704	644,000	9.1	State (U.S.)	D	Bismarck	English
Northern Ireland	5,452	1,596,000	293	Administrative division (U.K.)	D	Belfast	English
Northern Mariana Islands	184	46,000	250	Commonwealth (U.S. protection)	B	Saipan (island)	English, Malay-Polynesian languages
Northern Territory	519,771	160,000	0.3	Territory (Australia)	D	Darwin	English, indigenous
Northwest Territories	1,322,910	54,000		Territory (Canada)	D	Yellowknife	English, indigenous
† Norway (incl. Svalbard and Jan Mayen)	149,412	4,286,000	29	Constitutional monarchy	A	Oslo	Norwegian, Lapp
Nova Scotia	21,425	920,000	43	Province (Canada)	D	Halifax	English
Oceania (incl. Australia)	3,300,000	27,300,000	8.3				
Ohio	44,828	10,980,000	245	State (U.S.)	D	Columbus	English
Oklahoma	69,903	3,169,000	45	State (U.S.)	D	Oklahoma City	English
† Oman	82,030	1,562,000	19	Monarchy	A	Muscat	Arabic, English, Baluchi, Urdu, Indian dialects
Ontario	412,581	9,820,000	24	Province (Canada)	D	Toronto	English
Oregon	98,386	2,895,000	29	State (U.S.)	D	Salem	English
† Pakistan (incl. part of Jammu and Kashmir)	339,732	119,000,000	350	Federal Islamic republic	A	Islāmābād	English, Urdu, Punjabi, Pashto, Sindhi, Saraiki
Palau (Belau)	196	15,000	77	Part of Trust Territory of the Pacific Islands	B	Koror	English, Palauan
† Panama	29,157	2,503,000	86	Republic	A	Panamá	Spanish, English, indigenous

REGION OR POLITICAL DIVISION	Area Sq. Mi.	Est. Pop. 1/1/92	Pop. Per. Sq. Mi.	Form of Government and Ruling Power	Capital	Predominant Languages
† Papua New Guinea	178,704	3,960,000	22	Parliamentary state .... A	Port Moresby	English, Motu, Pidgin, indigenous
† Paraguay	157,048	4,871,000	31	Republic........................ A	Asunción	Spanish, Guarani
Pennsylvania	46,058	12,042,000	261	State (U.S.) .... D	Harrisburg	English
† Peru	496,225	22,585,000	46	Republic........................ A	Lima	Quechua, Spanish, Aymara
† Philippines	115,831	62,380,000	539	Republic........................ A	Manila	English, Pilipino, Tagalog
Pitcairn (incl. Dependencies)	19	40	2.1	Dependent territory (U.K.) C	Adamstown	English, Tahitian
† Poland	120,728	37,840,000	313	Republic........................ A	Warsaw (Warszawa)	Polish
† Portugal	35,516	10,410,000	293	Republic........................ A	Lisbon (Lisboa)	Portuguese
Prince Edward Island	2,185	134,000	61	Province (Canada) .... D	Charlottetown	English
Puerto Rico	3,515	3,528,000	1,004	Commonwealth (U.S. protection) .... B	San Juan	Spanish
† Qatar	4,416	532,000	120	Monarchy .... A	Doha	Arabic, English
Qinghai	277,994	4,725,000	17	Province (China).................. D	Xining	Tibetan dialects, Mongolian, Turkish dialects, Chinese (Mandarin)
Quebec	594,860	6,911,000	12	Province (Canada) .... D	Québec	French, English
Queensland	666,876	2,981,000	4.5	State (Australia) .... D	Brisbane	English
Reunion	969	613,000	633	Overseas department (France) C	Saint-Denis	French, Creole
Rhode Island	1,545	1,019,000	660	State (U.S.) .... D	Providence	English
Rhodesia see Zimbabwe	....	....	....			
† Romania	91,699	23,465,000	256	Republic........................ A	Bucharest (Bucureşti)	Romanian, Hungarian, German
† Russia	6,592,849	150,505,000	23	Republic........................ A	Moscow (Moskva)	Russian, Tatar, Ukrainian
† Rwanda	10,169	8,053,000	792	Provisional military government ...... A	Kigali	French, Kinyarwanda
St. Helena (incl. Dependencies)	121	7,000	58	Dependent territory (U.K.) C	Jamestown	English
† St. Kitts and Nevis	104	42,000	404	Parliamentary state .... A	Basseterre	English
† St. Lucia	238	155,000	651	Parliamentary state .... A	Castries	English, French
St. Pierre and Miquelon	93	6,000	65	Territorial collectivity (France) C	Saint-Pierre	French
† St. Vincent and the Grenadines	150	115,000	767	Parliamentary state .... A	Kingstown	English, French
San Marino	24	23,000	958	Republic........................ A	San Marino	Italian
† Sao Tome and Principe	372	130,000	349	Republic........................ A	São Tomé	Portuguese, Fang
Saskatchewan	251,866	1,052,000	4.2	Province (Canada) .... D	Regina	English
† Saudi Arabia	830,000	16,690,000	20	Monarchy .... A	Riyadh (Ar Riyāḍ)	Arabic
Scotland	30,414	5,125,000	169	Administrative division (U.K.) .... D	Edinburgh	English, Scots Gaelic
† Senegal	75,951	7,569,000	100	Republic........................ A	Dakar	French, Wolof, indigenous
Serbia	34,116	9,975,000	292	Republic (Yugoslavia) .... D	Belgrade	Serb, Albanian, Hungarian, Bulgarian
† Seychelles	175	69,000	394	Republic........................ A	Victoria	English, French, Creole
Shaanxi	79,151	34,030,000	430	Province (China).................. D	Xi'an (Sian)	Chinese (Mandarin)
Shandong	59,074	87,550,000	1,482	Province (China).................. D	Jinan	Chinese (Mandarin)
Shanghai	2,394	13,705,000	5,725	Autonomous city (China)............ D	Shanghai	Chinese (Wu)
Shanxi	60,232	29,895,000	496	Province (China).................. D	Taiyuan	Chinese (Mandarin)
Sichuan	220,078	114,970,000	522	Province (China).................. D	Chengdu	Chinese (Mandarin), Tibetan dialects, Miao-Yao
† Sierra Leone	27,925	4,330,000	155	Republic........................ A	Freetown	English, Krio, indigenous
† Singapore	246	3,062,000	12,447	Republic........................ A	Singapore	Chinese (Mandarin), English, Malay, Tamil
Slovenia	7,819	1,989,000	254	Republic........................ A	Ljubljana	Slovene
† Solomon Islands	10,954	353,000	32	Parliamentary state .... A	Honiara	English, Malay-Polynesian languages
† Somalia	246,201	6,823,000	28	Provisional military government ...... A	Mogadishu (Muqdisho)	Arabic, Somali, English, Italian
† South Africa (incl. Walvis Bay)	433,680	36,765,000	85	Republic........................ A	Pretoria, Cape Town, and Bloemfontein	Afrikaans, English, Zulu, Xhosa, other indigenous
South America	6,900,000	306,700,000	44			
South Australia	379,925	1,465,000	3.9	State (Australia) .... D	Adelaide	English
South Carolina	32,007	3,559,000	111	State (U.S.) .... D	Columbia	English
South Dakota	77,121	673,000	8.7	State (U.S.) .... D	Pierre	English
South Georgia	1,450	¹	....	Dependent territory (U.K.) C	Grytviken Harbour	English
South West Africa see Namibia	....	....	....			
† Spain	194,885	39,465,000	203	Constitutional monarchy .... A	Madrid	Spanish (Castilian), Catalan, Galician, Basque
Spanish North Africa [8]	12	137,000	11,417	Five possessions (Spain) C		Spanish, Arabic, Berber dialects
Spanish Sahara see Western Sahara	....	....	....			
† Sri Lanka	24,962	17,530,000	702	Socialist republic .... A	Colombo and Sri Jayawardenapura	English, Sinhala, Tamil
† Sudan	967,500	27,630,000	29	Islamic republic .... A	Khartoum (Al Kharṭūm)	Arabic, indigenous, English
† Suriname	63,251	405,000	6.4	Republic........................ A	Paramaribo	Dutch, Sranan Tongo, English, Hindustani, Javanese
† Swaziland	6,704	875,000	131	Monarchy .... A	Mbabane and Lobamba	English, siSwati
† Sweden	173,732	8,581,000	49	Constitutional monarchy .... A	Stockholm	Swedish
Switzerland	15,943	6,804,000	427	Federal republic .... A	Bern (Berne)	German, French, Italian, Romansch
† Syria	71,498	13,210,000	185	Socialist republic .... A	Damascus (Dimashq)	Arabic, Kurdish, Armenian, Aramaic, Circassian
Taiwan	13,900	20,785,000	1,495	Republic........................ A	T'aipei	Chinese dialects
Tajikistan	55,251	5,210,000	94	Republic........................ A	Dushanbe	Tajik, Uzbek, Russian
† Tanzania	364,900	27,325,000	75	Republic........................ A	Dar es Salaam and Dodoma [6]	English, Swahili, indigenous
Tasmania	26,178	463,000	18	State (Australia) .... D	Hobart	English
Tennessee	42,146	4,959,000	118	State (U.S.) .... D	Nashville	English
Texas	268,601	17,355,000	65	State (U.S.) .... D	Austin	English, Spanish
† Thailand	198,115	57,200,000	289	Constitutional monarchy .... A	Bangkok (Krung Thep)	Thai, indigenous
Tianjin (Tientsin)	4,363	9,100,000	2,086	Autonomous city (China)............ D	Tianjin (Tientsin)	Chinese (Mandarin)
† Togo	21,925	3,880,000	177	Republic........................ A	Lomé	French, indigenous
Tokelau	4.6	1,700	370	Island territory (New Zealand) C		English, Tokelauan
Tonga	290	103,000	355	Constitutional monarchy .... A	Nuku'alofa	Tongan, English
Transkei [2]	16,816	4,200,000	250	National state (South African protection) . B	Umtata	Xhosa, Afrikaans
† Trinidad and Tobago	1,980	1,293,000	653	Republic........................ A	Port of Spain	English, Hindi, French, Spanish
Tristan da Cunha	40	300	7.5	Dependency (St. Helena) C	Edinburgh	English
† Tunisia	63,170	8,367,000	132	Republic........................ A	Tunis	Arabic, French
† Turkey	300,948	58,850,000	196	Republic........................ A	Ankara	Turkish, Kurdish, Arabic
Turkmenistan	188,456	3,615,000	19	Republic........................ A	Ashkhabad	Turkmen, Russian, Uzbek, Kazakh
Turks and Caicos Islands	193	12,000	62	Dependent territory (U.K.) C	Grand Turk	English
Tuvalu	10	9,000	900	Parliamentary state .... A	Funafuti	Tuvaluan, English
† Uganda	93,104	18,485,000	199	Republic........................ A	Kampala	English, Luganda, Swahili, indigenous
† Ukraine	233,090	52,800,000	227	Republic........................ A	Kiev	Ukrainian, Russian
† United Arab Emirates	32,278	2,459,000	76	Federation of monarchs .... A	Abū Ẓaby (Abu Dhabi)	Arabic, English, Farsi, Hindi, Urdu
† United Kingdom	94,248	57,630,000	611	Constitutional monarchy .... A	London	English, Welsh, Gaelic
† United States	3,787,425	253,510,000	67	Federal republic .... A	Washington	English, Spanish
Upper Volta see Burkina Faso	....	....	....			
† Uruguay	68,500	3,130,000	46	Republic........................ A	Montevideo	Spanish
Utah	84,904	1,757,000	21	State (U.S.) .... D	Salt Lake City	English
Uzbekistan	172,742	20,325,000	118	Republic........................ A	Tashkent	Uzbek, Russian, Kazakh, Tajik, Tatar
† Vanuatu	4,707	153,000	33	Republic........................ A	Port-Vila	Bislama, English, French
Vatican City	0.2	800	4,000	Ecclesiastical city-state .... A	Vatican City	Italian, Latin
Venda [2]	2,393	925,000	387	National state (South African protection) . B	Thohoyandou	Afrikaans, English, Venda

REGION OR POLITICAL DIVISION	Area Sq. Mi.	Est. Pop. 1/1/92	Pop. Per. Sq. Mi.	Form of Government and Ruling Power	Capital	Predominant Languages
† Venezuela	352,145	20,430,000	58	Federal republic . . . . A	Caracas	Spanish, indigenous
Vermont	9,615	583,000	61	State (U.S.) . . . . D	Montpelier	English
Victoria	87,877	4,455,000	51	State (Australia) . . . . D	Melbourne	English
† Vietnam	128,066	68,310,000	533	Socialist republic . . . . A	Hanoi	Vietnamese, French, Chinese, English, Khmer, indigenous
Virginia	42,769	6,333,000	148	State (U.S.) . . . . D	Richmond	English
Virgin Islands (U.S.)	133	103,000	774	Unincorporated territory (U.S.) C	Charlotte Amalie	English, Spanish, Creole
Virgin Islands, British	59	14,000	237	Dependent territory (U.K.) C	Road Town	English
Wake Island	3.0	200	67	Unincorporated territory (U.S.) C	. . . .	English
Wales	8,019	2,894,000	361	Administrative division (U.K.) . . . . D	Cardiff	English, Welsh Gaelic
Wallis and Futuna	98	17,000	173	Overseas territory (France) C	Mata-Utu	French, Uvean, Futunan
Washington	71,303	4,984,000	70	State (U.S.) . . . . D	Olympia	English
Western Australia	975,101	1,672,000	1.7	State (Australia) . . . . D	Perth	English
Western Sahara	102,703	200,000	1.9	Occupied by Morocco C	. . . .	Arabic
† Western Samoa	1,093	192,000	176	Constitutional monarchy . . . . A	Apia	English, Samoan
West Virginia	24,231	1,775,000	73	State (U.S.) . . . . D	Charleston	English
Wisconsin	65,503	4,964,000	76	State (U.S.) . . . . D	Madison	English
Wyoming	97,818	448,000	4.6	State (U.S.) . . . . D	Cheyenne	English
Xinjiang Uygur (Sinkiang)	617,764	15,715,000	25	Autonomous region (China) . . . . D	Ürümqi	Turkish dialects, Mongolian, Tungus, English
Xizang (Tibet)	471,045	2,245,000	4.8	Autonomous region (China) . . . . D	Lhasa	Tibetan dialects
† Yemen	205,356	11,825,000	58	Republic . . . . A	San'ā'	Arabic
† Yugoslavia	39,449	10,622,000	269	Federal socialist republic . . . . A	Belgrade (Beograd)	Serbo-Croatian, Albanian, Hungarian
Yukon Territory	186,661	26,000	0.1	Territory (Canada) . . . . D	Whitehorse	English, Inuktitut, indigenous
Yunnan	152,124	38,875,000	256	Province (China) . . . . D	Kunming	Chinese (Mandarin), Tibetan dialects, Khmer, Miao-Yao
† Zaire	905,446	38,475,000	42	Republic . . . . A	Kinshasa	French, Kikongo, Lingala, Swahili, Tshiluba
† Zambia	290,586	8,201,000	28	Republic . . . . A	Lusaka	English, Tonga, Lozi, other indigenous
Zhejiang	39,305	45,255,000	1,151	Province (China) . . . . D	Hangzhou	Chinese dialects
† Zimbabwe	150,873	9,748,000	65	Republic . . . . A	Harare (Salisbury)	English, ChiShona, SiNdebele
WORLD	57,900,000	5,491,000,000	95	. . . .	. . . .	. . . .

† Member of the United Nations (1991).
. . . None, or not applicable.
(1) No permanent population.
(2) Bophuthatswana, Ciskei, Transkei, and Venda are not recognized by the United Nations.
(3) North Cyprus unilaterally declared its independence from Cyprus in 1983.
(4) Claimed by Argentina.
(5) Includes West Bank, Golan Heights, and Gaza Strip.
(6) Future capital.
(7) Claimed by Comoros.
(8) Comprises Ceuta, Melilla, and several small islands.

WORLD COMPARISONS

General Information

Equatorial diameter of the earth, 7,926.38 miles.
Polar diameter of the earth, 7,899.80 miles.
Mean diameter of the earth, 7,917.52 miles.
Equatorial circumference of the earth, 24,901.46 miles.
Polar circumference of the earth, 24,855.34 miles.
Mean distance from the earth to the sun, 93,020,000 miles.
Mean distance from the earth to the moon, 238,857 miles.
Total area of the earth, 197,000,000 square miles.

Highest elevation on the earth's surface, Mt. Everest, Asia, 29,028 feet.
Lowest elevation on the earth's land surface, shores of the Dead Sea, Asia, 1,312 feet below sea level.
Greatest known depth of the ocean, southwest of Guam, Pacific Ocean, 35,810 feet.
Total land area of the earth (incl. inland water and Antarctica), 57,900,000 square miles.

Area of Africa, 11,700,000 square miles.
Area of Antarctica, 5,400,000 square miles.
Area of Asia, 17,300,000 square miles.
Area of Europe, 3,800,000 square miles.
Area of North America, 9,500,000 square miles.
Area of Oceania (incl. Australia) 3,300,000 square miles.
Area of South America, 6,900,000 square miles.
Population of the earth (est.1/1/92), 5,491,000,000.

Principal Islands and Their Areas

ISLAND	Area (Sq. Mi.)
Baffin I., Can.	195,928
Banks I., Can.	27,038
Borneo (Kalimantan), Asia	287,300
Bougainville, Papua New Guinea	3,600
Cape Breton I., Can.	3,981
Celebes (Sulawesi), Indon.	73,057
Ceram (Seram), Indon.	7,191
Corsica, France	3,352
Crete, Greece	3,189
Cuba, N.A.	42,800
Cyprus, Asia	3,572
Devon I., Can.	21,331
Ellesmere I., Can.	75,767
Flores, Indon.	5,502
Great Britain, U.K.	88,795
Greenland, N.A.	840,000
Guadalcanal, Solomon Is.	2,060
Hainan Dao, China	13,100
Hawaii, U.S.	4,034
Hispaniola, N.A.	29,300
Hokkaidō, Japan	32,245
Honshū, Japan	89,176
Iceland, Europe	39,800
Ireland, Europe	32,600
Jamaica, N.A.	4,200
Java (Jawa), Indon.	51,038
Kodiak I., U.S.	3,670
Kyūshū, Japan	17,129
Leyte, Philippines	2,785
Long Island, U.S.	1,377
Luzon, Philippines	40,420
Madagascar, Africa	227,000
Melville I., Can.	16,274
Mindanao, Philippines	36,537
Mindoro, Philippines	3,759
Negros, Philippines	4,907
New Britain, Papua New Guinea	14,093
New Caledonia, Oceania	6,252
Newfoundland, Can.	42,031
New Guinea, Asia-Oceania	309,000
New Ireland, Papua New Guinea	3,500
North East Land, Norway	6,350
North I., New Zealand	44,274
Novaya Zemlya, Russia	31,900
Palawan, Philippines	4,550
Panay, Philippines	4,446
Prince of Wales I., Can.	12,872
Puerto Rico, N.A.	3,500
Sakhalin, Russia	29,500
Samar, Philippines	5,100
Sardinia, Italy	9,301
Shikoku, Japan	7,258
Sicily, Italy	9,926
Somerset I., Can.	9,570
Southampton I., Can.	15,913
South I., New Zealand	57,870
Spitsbergen, Norway	15,260
Sri Lanka, Asia	24,900
Sumatra (Sumatera), Indon.	182,860
Taiwan, Asia	13,900
Tasmania, Austl.	26,200
Tierra del Fuego, S.A.	18,600
Timor, Indon.	5,743
Vancouver I., Can.	12,079
Victoria I., Can.	83,897
Vrangelya (Wrangel), Russia	2,800

Principal Lakes, Oceans, Seas, and Their Areas

LAKE Country	Area (Sq. Mi.)
Arabian Sea	1,492,000
Aral Sea, Kazakhstan-Uzbekistan	24,700
Arctic Ocean	5,400,000
Athabasca, L., Can.	3,064
Atlantic Ocean	31,800,000
Balkhash, Ozero, (L.) Kazakhstan	7,100
Baltic Sea, Eur.	163,000
Baykal, Ozero, (L. Baikal) Russia	12,200
Bering Sea, Asia-N.A.	876,000
Black Sea, Eur.-Asia	178,000
Caribbean Sea, N.A.-S.A.	1,063,000
Caspian Sea, Asia-Europe	143,240
Chad, L., Cameroon-Chad-Nig.	6,300
Erie, L., Can.-U.S.	9,910
Eyre, L., Austl.	3,700
Gairdner, L., Austl.	1,700
Great Bear Lake, Can.	12,095
Great Salt Lake, U.S.	1,680
Great Slave Lake, Can.	11,030
Hudson Bay, Can.	475,000
Huron, L., Can.-U.S.	23,000
Indian Ocean	28,900,000
Japan, Sea of, Asia	389,000
Koko Nor, (Qinghai Hu) China	1,650
Ladozhskoye Ozero, (L. Ladoga) Russia	683
Manitoba, L., Can.	1,785
Mediterranean Sea, Eur.-Afr.-Asia	967,000
Mexico, Gulf of, N.A.	596,000
Michigan, L., U.S.	22,300
Nicaragua, Lago de, Nic.	3,150
North Sea, Eur.	222,000
Nyasa, L., Malawi-Mozambique-Tanz.	11,150
Onezhskoye Ozero, (L. Onega) Russia	3,753
Ontario, L., Can.-U.S.	7,540
Pacific Ocean	63,800,000
Red Sea, Afr.-Asia	169,000
Rudolf, L., Ethiopia-Kenya	2,473
Superior, L., Can.-U.S.	31,700
Tanganyika, L., Afr.	12,350
Titicaca, Lago, Bol.-Peru	3,200
Torrens, L., Austl.	2,300
Vänern, (L.) Swe.	2,156
Van Gölü, (L.) Tur.	1,420
Victoria, L., Ken.-Tan.-Ug.	26,820
Winnipeg, L., Can.	9,416
Winnipegosis, L., Can.	2,075
Yellow Sea, China-Korea	480,000

Principal Mountains and Their Heights

MOUNTAIN Country	Elev. (Ft.)
Aconcagua, Cerro, Argentina	22,831
Annapurna, Nepal	26,504
Antofalla, Volcán, Argentina	20,013
Api, Nepal	23,399
Apo, Mt., Philippines	9,692
Ararat, Turkey	16,804
Ayers Rock, Australia	2,844
Barú, Volcán, Panama	11,410
Belukha, Gol'tsy, Kazakhstan-Russia	14,783
Bia, Phu, Laos	9,252
Blanc, Mont, France-Italy	15,771
Blanca Pk., Colorado, U.S.	14,317
Bolívar (La Columna), Venezuela	16,411
Borah Pk., Idaho, U.S.	12,662
Cameroon Mtn., Cameroon	13,451
Carrauntoohil, Ireland	3,414
Chimborazo, Ecuador	20,561
Chirripó, Cerro, Costa Rica	12,530
Colima, Nevado de, Mexico	13,993
Cook, Mt., New Zealand	12,349
Cotopaxi, Ecuador	19,347
Cristóbal Colón, Pico, Colombia	19,029
Damāvand, Qolleh-ye, Iran	18,386
Dhaulāgiri, Nepal	26,810
Duarte, Pico, Dominican Rep.	10,417
Dychtau, gora, Russia	17,073
Egmont, Mt., New Zealand	8,260
Elbert, Mt., Colorado, U.S.	14,431
El'brus, Gora, Russia	18,510
Elgon, Mt., Kenya-Uganda	14,178
eNjesuthi, South Africa	11,306
Erciyeş Daği, Turkey	12,848
Etna, Mt., Italy	10,902
Everest, Mt., China-Nepal	29,028
Fairweather, Mt., Alaska-Canada	15,300
Finsteraarhorn, Switzerland	14,022
Foraker, Mt., Alaska, U.S.	17,400
Fuji-san, Japan	12,388
Gannett Pk., Wyoming, U.S.	13,785
Gasherbrum, China-Pakistan	26,470
Gerlachovský Stít, Czechoslovakia	8,710
Giluwe, Mt., Papua New Guinea	14,331
Glittertinden, Norway	8,084
Gongga Shan, China	24,790
Grand Teton Mtn., Wyoming, U.S.	13,766
Grossglockner, Austria	12,461
Gunnbjørn Fjeld, Greenland	12,139
Hadūr Shu'ayb, Yemen	12,336
Haleakala Crater, Hawaii, U.S.	10,025
Haltiatunturi, Finland-Norway	4,357
Hekla, Iceland	4,892
Hkakabo Razi, Burma	19,296
Hood, Mt., Oregon, U.S.	11,239
Huascarán, Nevado, Peru	22,205
Huila, Nevado de, Colombia	18,865
Hvannadalshnúkur, Iceland	6,952
Illampu, Nevado, Bolivia	20,873
Illimani, Nevado, Bolivia	21,151
Iztaccíhuatl, Mexico	17,343
Jaya, Puncak, Indonesia	16,503
Jungfrau, Switzerland	13,642
K2 (Godwin Austen), China-Pakistan	28,250
Kāmet, China-India	25,447
Kānchenjunga, India- Nepal	28,208
Karisimbi, Volcan, Rwanda-Zaire	14,787
Kātrīnā, Jabal, Egypt	8,668
Kebnekaise, Sweden	6,962
Kenya, Mt., Kenya	17,058
Kerinci, Gunung, Indonesia	12,467
Kilimanjaro, Tanzania	19,340
Kinabalu, Gunong, Malaysia	13,455
Klyuchevskaya, Russia	15,584
Kommunizma, Pik, Tajikistan	24,590
Korab, Albania-Macedonia	9,026
Kosciusko, Mt., Australia	7,316
Koussi, Emi, Chad	11,204
Kula Kangri, Bhutan	24,784
Lassen Pk., California, U.S.	10,457
Llullaillaco, Volcán, Argentina-Chile	22,057
Logan, Mt., Canada	19,524
Longs Pk., Colorado, U.S.	14,255
Makālu, China-Nepal	27,825
Margherita Pk., Zaire-Uganda	16,763
Markham, Mt., Antarctica	14,272
Maromokotro, Madagascar	9,436
Matterhorn, Italy-Switzerland	14,692
Mauna Kea, Hawaii, U.S.	13,796
Mauna Loa, Hawaii, U.S.	13,680
McKinley, Mt., Alaska, U.S.	20,320
Meru, Mt., Tanzania	14,978
Misti, Volcán, Peru	19,098
Mitchell, Mt., North Carolina, U.S.	6,684
Moldoveanu, Romania	8,343
Mulhacén, Spain (continental)	11,424
Musala, Bulgaria	9,596
Muztag, China	25,338
Muztagata, China	24,757
Namjagbarwa Feng, China	25,446
Nanda Devi, India	25,645
Nānga Parbat, Pakistan	26,650
Narodnaya, Gora, Russia	6,214
Neblina, Pico da, Brazil-Venezuela	9,888
Nevis, Ben, United Kingdom	4,406
Ojos del Salado, Nevado, Argentina-Chile	22,615
Ólimbos, Cyprus	6,401
Ólimbos, Greece	9,570
Orizaba, Pico de, Mexico	18,406
Orohena, Mont, French Polynesia	7,352
Paektu san, North Korea-China	9,003
Paricutín, Mexico	9,213
Parnassós, Greece	8,061
Pelée, Montagne, Martinique	4,800
Pico, Cape Verde	9,281
Pidurutalagala, Sri Lanka	8,281
Pikes Pk., Colorado, U.S.	14,110
Pissis, Monte, Argentina	22,241
Pobedy, pik, China-Russia	24,406
Popocatépetl, Volcán, Mexico	17,887
Pulog, Mt., Philippines	9,606
Rainier, Mt., Washington, U.S.	14,410
Ras Dashen Terara, Ethiopia	15,158
Rinjani, Gunung, Indonesia	12,224
Rosa, Monte, Italy-Switzerland	15,203
Ruapehu, New Zealand	9,175
St. Elias, Mt., Alaska, U.S.-Canada	18,008
Sajama, Nevado, Bolivia	21,463
Sawdā', Qurnat as, Lebanon	10,114
Scafell Pikes, England, U.K.	3,210
Semeru, Gunung, Indonesia	12,060
Shām, Jabal ash, Oman	9,902
Shasta, Mt., California, U.S.	14,162
Snowdon, Wales, U.K.	3,560
Tahat, Algeria	9,541
Tajumulco (Vol.), Guatemala	13,816
Tirich Mīr, Pakistan	25,230
Tomanivi (Victoria), Fiji	4,341
Toubkal, Jebel, Morocco	13,665
Triglav, Slovenia	9,393
Trikora, Puncak, Indonesia	15,584
Tupungato, Portezuelo de, Argentina-Chile	22,310
Turquino, Pico de, Cuba	6,496
Vesuvio (Vesuvius), Italy	4,190
Victoria, Mt., Papua New Guinea	13,238
Vinson Massif, Antarctica	16,864
Waddington, Mt., Canada	13,260
Washington, Mt., New Hampshire, U.S.	6,288
Weisshorn, Switzerland	14,783
Whitney, Mt., California, U.S.	14,491
Wilhelm, Mt., Papua New Guinea	14,793
Wrangell, Mt., Alaska, U.S.	14,163
Xixabangma Feng (Gosainthan), China	26,286
Zugspitze, Austria-Germany	9,721

Principal Rivers and Their Lengths

RIVER Continent	Length (Mi.)
Albany, N.A.	610
Aldan, Asia	1,412
Amazonas-Ucayali, S.A.	4,000
Amu Darya, Asia	1,578
Amur, Asia	2,744
Amur-Argun, Asia	2,761
Araguaia, S.A.	1,400
Arkansas, N.A.	1,459
Athabasca, N.A.	765
Brahmaputra, Asia	1,770
Branco, S.A.	580
Brazos, N.A.	900
Canadian, N.A.	906
Churchill, N.A.	1,000
Colorado, N.A. (U.S.-Mex.)	1,450
Columbia, N.A.	1,200
Congo (Zaïre), Africa	2,900
Cumberland, N.A.	720
Danube, Europe	1,776
Darling, Australia	864
Dnepr, (Dnieper) Europe	1,400
Dnestr, (Dniestr) Europe	840
Don, Europe	1,162
Elbe, Europe	720
Euphrates, Asia	1,510
Fraser, N.A.	851
Ganges, Asia	1,560
Gila, N.A.	630
Godāvari, Asia	930
Green, N.A.	730
Huang, (Yellow) Asia	3,395
Indus, Asia	1,800
Irrawaddy, Asia	1,300
Juruá, S.A.	1,250
Kama, Europe	1,122
Kasai, Africa	1,338
Kolyma, Asia	1,323
Lena, Asia	2,700
Limpopo, Africa	1,100
Loire, Europe	625
Mackenzie, N.A.	2,635
Madeira, S.A.	2,013
Magdalena, S.A.	950
Marañón, S.A.	1,000
Mekong, Asia	2,600
Meuse, Europe	575
Mississippi, N.A.	2,348
Mississippi-Missouri, N.A.	3,740
Missouri, N.A.	2,315
Murray, Australia	1,566
Negro, S.A.	1,300
Neman, Europe	582
Niger, Africa	2,600
Nile, Africa	4,145
North Platte, N.A.	618
Ob'-Irtysh, Asia	3,362
Oder, Europe	565
Ohio, N.A.	981
Oka, Europe	900
Orange, Africa	1,300
Orinoco, S.A.	1,600
Ottawa, N.A.	790
Paraguay, S.A.	1,610
Paraná, S.A.	2,800
Parnaíba, S.A.	850
Peace, N.A.	1,195
Pechora, Europe	1,124
Pecos, N.A.	735
Pilcomayo, S.A.	1,550
Plata-Paraná, S.A.	3,030
Purús, S.A.	1,860
Red, N.A.	1,270
Rhine, Europe	820
Rhône, Europe	500
Rio Grande, N.A.	1,885
Roosevelt, S.A.	950
St. Lawrence, N.A.	800
Salado, S.A.	900
Salween, (Nu) Asia	1,750
São Francisco, S.A.	1,988
Saskatchewan-Bow, N.A.	1,205
Sava, Europe	585
Snake, N.A.	1,038
Sungari, (Songhua) Asia	1,140
Syr Dar'ya, Asia	1,370
Tagus, Europe	625
Tarim, Asia	1,328
Tennessee, N.A.	652
Tigris, Asia	1,180
Tisa, Europe	607
Tobol, Asia	989
Tocantins, S.A.	1,640
Ucayali, S.A.	1,220
Ural, Asia	1,509
Uruguay, S.A.	1,025
Verkhnyaya Tunguska, (Angara) Asia	1,105
Vilyuy, Asia	1,647
Volga, Europe	2,194
White, N.A. (Ar.-Mo.)	720
Wisła (Vistula), Europe	630
Xiang, Asia	930
Xingu, S.A.	1,230
Yangtze, (Chang) Asia	3,900
Yellowstone, N.A.	671
Yenisey, Asia	2,543
Yukon, N.A.	1,770
Zambezi, Africa	1,700

PRINCIPAL CITIES OF THE WORLD

City	Population
Abidjan, Ivory Coast	1,950,000
Accra, Ghana (1,250,000)	859,640
Addis Ababa, Ethiopia (1,760,000)	1,686,300
Adelaide, Australia (1,036,747)	12,340
Ahmadābād, India (2,400,000)	2,059,725
Aleppo (Halab), Syria (1,275,000)	1,261,000
Alexandria (Al Iskandarīyah), Egypt (3,350,000)	2,917,327
Algiers (El Djazaïr), Algeria (2,547,983)	1,507,241
Alma-Ata, Kazakhstan (1,190,000)	1,128,000
'Ammān, Jordan (1,450,000)	936,300
Amsterdam, Netherlands (1,860,000)	696,500
Ankara (Angora), Turkey (2,650,000)	2,553,209
Anshan, China	1,330,000
Antwerp (Antwerpen), Belgium (1,100,000)	479,748
Asunción, Paraguay (700,000)	477,100
Athens (Athínai), Greece (3,027,331)	885,737
Atlanta, Georgia, U.S. (2,833,511)	394,017
Auckland, New Zealand (850,000)	149,046
Baghdād, Iraq	3,841,268
Baku, Azerbaijan (2,020,000)	1,150,000
Baltimore, Maryland, U.S. (2,382,172)	736,014
Bandung, Indonesia (1,800,000)	1,633,000
Bangalore, India (2,950,000)	2,476,355
Bangkok (Krung Thep), Thailand (6,450,000)	5,716,779
Barcelona, Spain (4,040,000)	1,714,355
Beijing (Peking), China (7,200,000)	6,710,000
Beirut, Lebanon (1,675,000)	509,000
Belém, Brazil (1,200,000)	1,116,578
Belfast, N. Ireland, U.K. (685,000)	303,800
Belgrade (Beograd), Yugoslavia (1,400,000)	1,130,000
Belo Horizonte, Brazil (2,950,000)	2,114,429
Berlin, Germany (3,825,000)	3,352,848
Bilbao, Spain (985,000)	384,733
Birmingham, England, U.K. (2,675,000)	1,013,995
Bombay, India (9,950,000)	8,243,405
Bonn, Germany (570,000)	282,190
Boston, Massachusetts, U.S. (4,171,643)	574,283
Brasília, Brazil	1,567,709
Bremen, Germany (800,000)	535,058
Brisbane, Australia (1,273,511)	744,828
Brussels (Bruxelles), Belgium (2,385,000)	136,920
Bucharest (București), Romania (2,275,000)	1,989,823
Budapest, Hungary (2,565,000)	2,016,132
Buenos Aires, Argentina (10,750,000)	2,922,829
Buffalo, New York, U.S. (1,189,288)	328,123
Cairo (Al Qāhirah), Egypt (9,300,000)	6,052,836
Calcutta, India (11,100,000)	3,305,006
Cali, Colombia (1,400,000)	1,350,565
Canberra, Australia (271,362)	247,194
Cape Town, South Africa (1,790,000)	776,617
Caracas, Venezuela (3,600,000)	1,816,901
Cardiff, Wales, U.K. (625,000)	262,313
Casablanca, Morocco (2,475,000)	2,139,204
Changchun, China (2,000,000†)	1,822,000
Chelyabinsk, Russia (1,325,000)	1,143,000
Chengdu, China (2,960,000†)	1,884,000
Chicago, Illinois, U.S. (8,065,633)	2,783,726
Chittagong, Bangladesh (1,391,877)	980,000
Chongqing (Chungking), China (2,890,000†)	2,502,000
Cincinnati, Ohio, U.S. (1,744,124)	364,040
Cleveland, Ohio, U.S. (2,759,823)	505,616
Cologne (Köln), Germany (1,760,000)	937,482
Colombo, Sri Lanka (2,050,000)	683,000
Columbus, Ohio, U.S. (1,377,419)	632,910
Copenhagen (København), Denmark (1,685,000)	466,723
Curitiba, Brazil (1,700,000)	1,279,205
Dakar, Senegal	1,447,642
Dalian (Lüda), China	2,280,000
Dallas, Texas, U.S. (3,885,415)	1,006,877
Damascus (Dimashq), Syria (1,950,000)	1,326,000
Dar es Salaam, Tanzania	1,300,000
Delhi, India (7,200,000)	4,884,234
Denver, Colorado, U.S. (1,848,319)	467,610
Detroit, Michigan, U.S. (4,665,236)	1,027,974
Dhaka (Dacca), Bangladesh (3,430,312)	2,365,695
Dnepropetrovsk, Ukraine (1,600,000)	1,179,000
Donetsk, Ukraine (2,200,000)	1,110,000
Dresden, Germany (670,000)	518,057
Dublin (Baile Átha Cliath), Ireland (1,140,000)	502,749
Durban, South Africa (1,550,000)	634,301
Düsseldorf, Germany (1,190,000)	569,641
Edinburgh, Scotland, U.K. (630,000)	433,200
Essen, Germany (4,950,000)	620,594
Florence (Firenze), Italy (640,000)	425,835
Fortaleza, Brazil (1,825,000)	1,582,414
Frankfurt am Main, Germany (1,855,000)	625,258
Fukuoka, Japan (1,750,000)	1,160,440
Fushun, China	1,290,000
Gdańsk (Danzig), Poland (909,000)	461,500
Geneva (Génève), Switzerland (460,000)	165,404
Genoa (Genova), Italy (805,000)	727,427
Glasgow, Scotland, U.K. (1,800,000)	695,630
Guadalajara, Mexico (2,325,000)	1,626,152
Guangzhou (Canton), China (3,420,000†)	3,100,000
Guatemala, Guatemala (1,400,000)	1,057,210
Guayaquil, Ecuador (1,580,000)	1,572,615
Hamburg, Germany (2,225,000)	1,603,070
Hannover, Germany (1,000,000)	498,495
Hanoi, Vietnam (1,500,000)	1,089,000
Harare, Zimbabwe (890,000)	681,000
Harbin, China	2,710,000
Hartford, Connecticut, U.S. (1,085,837)	139,739
Havana (La Habana), Cuba (2,125,000)	2,036,800
Helsinki, Finland (1,040,000)	490,034
Hiroshima, Japan (1,575,000)	1,044,118
Ho Chi Minh City (Saigon), Vietnam (3,600,000)	3,169,000
Hong Kong, Hong Kong (4,770,000)	1,175,860
Honolulu, Hawaii, U.S. (836,231)	365,272
Houston, Texas, U.S. (3,711,043)	1,630,553
Hyderābād, India (2,750,000)	2,187,262
Ibadan, Nigeria	1,144,000
Indianapolis, Indiana, U.S. (1,249,822)	731,327
Irkutsk, Russia	626,000
İstanbul, Turkey (7,550,000)	6,748,435
İzmir, Turkey (1,900,000)	1,762,849
Jakarta, Indonesia (10,000,000)	9,200,000
Jerusalem, Israel (530,000)	493,500
Jiddah, Saudi Arabia	1,300,000
Jinan, China (2,140,000†)	1,546,000
Johannesburg, South Africa (3,650,000)	632,369
Kābul, Afghanistan	1,424,400
Kānpur, India (1,875,000)	1,481,789
Kansas City, Missouri, U.S. (1,566,280)	435,146
Kaohsiung, Taiwan (1,845,000)	1,342,797
Karāchi, Pakistan (5,300,000)	4,901,627
Kathmandu, Nepal (320,000)	235,160
Katowice, Poland (2,778,000)	365,800
Kawasaki, Japan (*Tōkyō)	1,088,624
Kazan', Russia (1,140,000)	1,094,000
Khar'kov, Ukraine (1,940,000)	1,611,000
Khartoum (Al Kharṭūm), Sudan (1,450,000)	476,218
Kiev, Ukraine (2,900,000)	2,587,000
Kingston, Jamaica (770,000)	646,400
Kinshasa, Zaire	3,000,000
Kitakyūshū, Japan (1,525,000)	1,056,402
Kōbe, Japan (*Ōsaka)	1,410,834
Kowloon, Hong Kong (*Hong Kong)	774,781
Kuala Lumpur, Malaysia (1,475,000)	919,610
Kunming, China (1,550,000†)	1,310,000
Kuwait (Al Kuwayt), Kuwait (1,375,000)	44,335
Kyōto, Japan (*Ōsaka)	1,479,218
Lagos, Nigeria (3,800,000)	1,213,000
Lahore, Pakistan (3,025,000)	2,707,215
Lanzhou, China (1,420,000†)	1,297,000
La Paz, Bolivia	992,592
Leeds, England, U.K. (1,540,000)	445,242
Leipzig, Germany (700,000)	545,307
Liège, Belgium (750,000)	200,891
Lille, France (1,020,000)	168,424
Lima, Peru (4,608,010)	371,122
Lisbon (Lisboa), Portugal (2,250,000)	807,167
Liverpool, England, U.K. (1,525,000)	538,809
Łódź, Poland (1,061,000)	851,500
London, England, U.K. (11,100,000)	6,574,009
Los Angeles, California, U.S. (14,531,529)	3,485,398
Louisville, Kentucky, U.S. (952,662)	269,063
Luanda, Angola	1,459,900
Lucknow, India (1,060,000)	895,721
Lyon, France (1,275,000)	413,095
Madras, India (4,475,000)	3,276,622
Madrid, Spain (4,650,000)	3,102,846
Managua, Nicaragua	682,000
Manchester, England, U.K. (2,775,000)	437,612
Manila, Philippines (6,800,000)	1,587,000
Mannheim, Germany (1,400,000)	300,468
Maracaibo, Venezuela	890,643
Marseille, France (1,225,000)	874,436
Mecca (Makkah), Saudi Arabia	550,000
Medan, Indonesia	2,110,000
Medellín, Colombia (2,095,000)	1,468,089
Melbourne, Australia (3,039,100)	55,300
Memphis, Tennessee, U.S. (981,747)	610,337
Mexico City, Mexico (14,100,000)	8,831,079
Miami, Florida, U.S. (3,192,582)	358,548
Milan (Milano), Italy (3,750,000)	1,495,260
Milwaukee, Wisconsin, U.S. (1,607,183)	628,088
Minneapolis, Minnesota, U.S. (2,464,124)	368,383
Minsk, Belarus (1,650,000)	1,589,000
Monterrey, Mexico (2,015,000)	1,090,009
Montevideo, Uruguay (1,550,000)	1,251,647
Montréal, Canada (2,921,357)	1,015,420
Moscow (Moskva), Russia (13,100,000)	8,769,000
Munich (München), Germany (1,955,000)	1,211,617
Nagoya, Japan (4,800,000)	2,116,381
Nāgpur, India (1,302,066)	1,219,461
Nairobi, Kenya	1,505,000
Nanjing, China	2,390,000
Naples (Napoli), Italy (2,875,000)	1,204,211
Netzahualcóyotl, Mexico (*Mexico City)	1,341,230
Newcastle upon Tyne, England, U.K. (1,300,000)	199,064
New Delhi, India (*Delhi)	273,036
New Kowloon, Hong Kong (*Hong Kong)	1,526,910
New Orleans, Louisiana, U.S. (1,238,816)	496,938
New York, New York, U.S. (18,087,251)	7,322,564
Nizhniy Novgorod, Russia (2,025,000)	1,438,000
Novosibirsk, Russia (1,600,000)	1,436,000
Nürnberg, Germany (1,030,000)	480,078
Odessa, Ukraine (1,185,000)	1,115,000
Oklahoma City, Oklahoma, U.S. (958,839)	444,719
Omsk, Russia (1,175,000)	1,148,000
Ōsaka, Japan (16,450,000)	2,636,249
Oslo, Norway (720,000)	452,415
Ottawa, Canada (819,263)	300,763
Panamá, Panama (770,000)	411,549
Paris, France (9,775,000)	2,078,900
Perm', Russia (1,160,000)	1,091,000
Perth, Australia (1,158,387)	82,413
Philadelphia, Pennsylvania, U.S. (5,899,345)	1,585,577
Phnum Pénh (Phnom Penh), Cambodia	700,000
Phoenix, Arizona, U.S. (2,122,101)	983,403
Pittsburgh, Pennsylvania, U.S. (2,242,798)	369,879
Port-au-Prince, Haiti (880,000)	797,000
Portland, Oregon, U.S. (1,477,895)	437,319
Porto (Oporto), Portugal (1,225,000)	327,368
Porto Alegre, Brazil (2,600,000)	1,272,121
Prague (Praha), Czechoslovakia (1,325,000)	1,215,656
Pretoria, South Africa (960,000)	443,059
Providence, Rhode Island, U.S. (1,141,510)	160,728
Pune, India (1,775,000)	1,203,351
Pusan, South Korea (3,800,000)	3,773,000
P'yŏngyang, North Korea (1,600,000)	1,283,000
Qingdao, China	1,300,000
Qiqihar, China (1,330,000†)	1,180,000
Québec, Canada (603,267)	164,580
Quezon City, Philippines (*Manila)	1,632,000
Quito, Ecuador (1,300,000)	1,137,705
Rabat, Morocco (980,000)	518,616
Rangoon (Yangon), Burma (2,800,000)	2,705,039
Rāwalpindi, Pakistan (1,040,000)	457,091
Recife, Brazil (2,625,000)	1,287,623
Rīga, Latvia (1,005,000)	915,000
Rio de Janerio, Brazil (10,150,000)	5,603,388
Riyadh, Saudi Arabia	1,250,000
Rome (Roma), Italy (3,175,000)	2,815,457
Rosario, Argentina (1,045,000)	938,120
Rostov-na-Donu, Russia (1,165,000)	1,020,000
Rotterdam, Netherlands (1,110,000)	576,300
St. Louis, Missouri, U.S. (2,444,099)	396,685
St. Paul, Minnesota, U.S. (*Minneapolis)	272,235
St. Petersburg (Leningrad), Russia (5,825,000)	4,465,000
Salt Lake City, Utah, U.S. (1,072,227)	159,936
Salvador, Brazil (2,050,000)	1,804,438
Samara, Russia (1,505,000)	1,257,000
San Antonio, Texas, U.S. (1,302,099)	935,933
San Diego, California, U.S. (2,949,000)	1,110,549
San Francisco, California, U.S. (6,253,311)	723,959
San José, Costa Rica (670,000)	278,600
San Juan, Puerto Rico (1,775,260)	424,600
San Salvador, El Salvador (920,000)	462,652
Santa Fe de Bogotá, Colombia (4,260,000)	3,982,941
Santiago, Chile (4,100,000)	232,667
Santo Domingo, Dominican Rep.	1,313,172
São Paulo, Brazil (15,175,000)	10,063,110
Sapporo, Japan (1,900,000)	1,542,979
Saratov, Russia (1,155,000)	905,000
Seattle, Washington, U.S. (2,559,164)	516,259
Seoul (Sŏul), South Korea (15,850,000)	10,522,000
Shanghai, China (9,300,000)	7,220,000
Shenyang (Mukden), China (4,370,000†)	3,910,000
Singapore, Singapore (3,025,000)	2,685,400
Sofia (Sofiya), Bulgaria (1,205,000)	1,119,152
Stockholm, Sweden (1,550,000)	672,187
Stuttgart, Germany (1,925,000)	562,658
Surabaya, Indonesia	2,345,000
Sydney, Australia (3,623,550)	9,800
Taegu, South Korea	2,207,000
T'aipei, Taiwan (6,130,000)	2,637,100
Taiyuan, China (1,980,000†)	1,700,000
Tashkent, Uzbekistan (2,325,000)	2,073,000
Tbilisi, Georgia (1,460,000)	1,260,000
Tegucigalpa, Honduras	551,606
Tehrān, Iran (7,500,000)	6,042,584
Tel Aviv-Yafo, Israel (1,735,000)	317,800
The Hague ('s-Gravenhage), Netherlands (770,000)	443,900
Tianjin (Tientsin), China (5,540,000†)	4,950,000
Tiranë, Albania	255,700
Tōkyō, Japan (27,700,000)	8,354,615
Toronto, Canada (3,427,168)	612,289
Tripoli (Tarābulus), Libya	990,697
Tunis, Tunisia (1,225,000)	596,654
Turin (Torino), Italy (1,550,000)	1,035,565
Ufa, Russia (1,100,000)	1,083,000
Ulan Bator, Mongolia	548,400
Valencia, Spain (1,270,000)	743,933
Valparaíso, Chile (675,000)	265,355
Vancouver, Canada (1,380,729)	431,147
Venice (Venezia), Italy (420,000)	88,700
Vienna (Wien), Austria (1,875,000)	1,482,800
Vladivostok, Russia	648,000
Volgograd (Stalingrad), Russia (1,360,000)	999,000
Warsaw (Warszawa), Poland (2,323,000)	1,651,200
Washington, D.C., U.S. (3,923,574)	609,909
Wellington, New Zealand (350,000)	137,495
Winnipeg, Canada (625,304)	594,551
Wuhan, China	3,570,000
Wuppertal, Germany (830,000)	371,283
Xi'an, China (2,580,000†)	2,210,000
Yekaterinburg, Russia (1,620,000)	1,367,000
Yerevan, Armenia (1,315,000)	1,199,000
Yokohama, Japan (*Tōkyō)	2,992,926
Zagreb, Croatia	697,925
Zhengzhou, China (1,580,000†)	1,150,000
Zurich, Switzerland (860,000)	342,861

Metropolitan area populations are shown in parentheses.
*City is located within the metropolitan area of another city; for example, Kyōto, Japan is located in the Ōsaka metropolitan area.
†Population of entire municipality or district, including rural area.

GLOSSARY OF FOREIGN GEOGRAPHICAL TERMS

Annam	Annamese
Arab	Arabic
Bantu	Bantu
Bur	Burmese
Camb	Cambodian
Celt	Celtic
Chn	Chinese
Czech	Czech
Dan	Danish
Du	Dutch
Fin	Finnish
Fr	French
Ger	German
Gr	Greek
Hung	Hungarian
Ice	Icelandic
India	India
Indian	American Indian
Indon	Indonesian
It	Italian
Jap	Japanese
Kor	Korean
Mal	Malayan
Mong	Mongolian
Nor	Norwegian
Per	Persian
Pol	Polish
Port	Portuguese
Rom	Romanian
Rus	Russian
Siam	Siamese
So. Slav	Southern Slavonic
Sp	Spanish
Swe	Swedish
Tib	Tibetan
Tur	Turkish
Yugo	Yugoslav

å, Nor., Swe ... brook, river
aa, Dan., Nor ... brook
aas, Dan., Nor ... ridge
āb, Per ... water, river
abad, India, Per ... town, city
ada, Tur ... island
adrar, Berber ... mountain
air, Indon ... stream
akrotírion, Gr ... cape
älf, Swe ... river
alp, Ger ... mountain
altipiano, It ... plateau
alto, Sp ... height
archipel, Fr ... archipelago
archipiélago, Sp ... archipelago
arquipélago, Port ... archipelago
arroyo, Sp ... brook, stream
ås, Nor., Swe ... ridge
austral, Sp ... southern
baai, Du ... bay
bab, Arab ... gate, port
bach, Ger ... brook, stream
backe, Swe ... hill
bad, Ger ... bath, spa
bahía, Sp ... bay, gulf
bahr, Arab ... river, sea, lake
baia, It ... bay, gulf
baía, Port ... bay
baie, Fr ... bay, gulf
bajo, Sp ... depression
bak, Indon ... stream
bakke, Dan., Nor ... hill
balkan, Tur ... mountain range
bana, Jap ... point, cape
banco, Sp ... bank
bandar, Mal., Per. ... town, port, harbor
bang, Siam ... village
bassin, Fr ... basin
batang, Indon., Mal ... river
ben, Celt ... mountain, summit
bender, Arab ... harbor, port
bereg, Rus ... coast, shore
berg, Du., Ger., Nor., Swe. ... mountain, hill
bir, Arab ... well
birkat, Arab ... lake, pond, pool
bit, Arab ... house
bjaerg, Dan., Nor ... mountain
bocche, It ... mouth
boğazı, Tur ... strait
bois, Fr ... forest, wood
boloto, Rus ... marsh
bolsón, Sp. ... flat-floored desert valley
boreal, Sp ... northern
borg, Dan., Nor., Swe ... castle, town
borgo, It ... town, suburb
bosch, Du ... forest, wood
bouche, Fr ... river mouth
bourg, Fr ... town, borough
bro, Dan., Nor., Swe ... bridge
brücke, Ger ... bridge
bucht, Ger ... bay, bight
bugt, Dan., Nor., Swe ... bay, gulf
bulu, Indon ... mountain
burg, Du., Ger ... castle, town
buri, Siam ... town
burun, burnu, Tur ... cape
by, Dan., Nor., Swe ... village
caatinga, Port. (Brazil) ... open brushland
cabezo, Sp ... summit
cabo, Port., Sp ... cape
campo, It., Port., Sp ... plain, field
campos, Port. (Brazil) ... plains
cañón, Sp ... canyon
cap, Fr ... cape
capo, It ... cape
casa, It., Port., Sp ... house
castello, It., Port ... castle, fort
castillo, Sp ... castle
càte, Fr ... hill
çay, Tur ... stream, river
cayo, Sp ... rock, shoal, islet
cerro, Sp ... mountain, hill
champ, Fr ... field
chang, Chn ... village, middle
château, Fr ... castle
chen, Chn ... market town
chiang, Chn ... river
chott, Arab ... salt lake
chou, Chn. ... capital of district; island
chu, Tib ... water, stream
cidade, Port ... town, city
cima, Sp ... summit, peak
città, It ... town, city
ciudad, Sp ... town, city
cochilha, Port ... ridge
col, Fr ... pass
colina, Sp ... hill
cordillera, Sp ... mountain chain
costa, It., Port., Sp ... coast
côte, Fr ... coast
cuchilla, Sp ... mountain ridge
dağ, Tur ... mountain(s)
dake, Jap ... peak, summit
dal, Dan., Du., Nor., Swe ... valley
dan, Kor ... point, cape
danau, Indon ... lake
dar, Arab ... house, abode, country
darya, Per ... river, sea
dasht, Per ... plain, desert
deniz, Tur ... sea
désert, Fr ... desert
deserto, It ... desert
desierto, Sp ... desert
détroit, Fr ... strait
dijk, Du ... dam, dike
djebel, Arab ... mountain
do, Kor ... island
dorf, Ger ... village
dorp, Du ... village
duin, Du ... dune
dzong, Tib. ... fort, administrative capital
eau, Fr ... water
ecuador, Sp ... equator
eiland, Du ... island
elv, Dan., Nor ... river, stream
embalse, Sp ... reservoir
erg, Arab ... dune, sandy desert
est, Fr., It ... east
estado, Sp ... state
este, Port., Sp ... east
estrecho, Sp ... strait
étang, Fr ... pond, lake
état, Fr ... state
eyjar, Ice ... islands
feld, Ger ... field, plain
festung, Ger ... fortress
fiume, It ... river
fjäll, Swe ... mountain
fjärd, Swe ... bay, inlet
fjeld, Nor ... mountain, hill
fjord, Dan., Nor ... fiord, inlet
fjördur, Ice ... fiord, inlet
fleuve, Fr ... river
flod, Dan., Swe ... river
flói, Ice ... bay, marshland
fluss, Ger ... river
foce, It ... river mouth
fontein, Du ... a spring
forêt, Fr ... forest
fors, Swe ... waterfall
forst, Ger ... forest
fos, Dan., Nor ... waterfall
fu, Chn ... town, residence
fuente, Sp ... spring, fountain
fuerte, Sp ... fort
furt, Ger ... ford
gang, Kor ... stream, river
gangri, Tib ... mountain
gat, Dan., Nor ... channel
gàve, Fr ... stream
gawa, Jap ... river
gebergte, Du ... mountain range
gebiet, Ger ... district, territory
gebirge, Ger ... mountains
ghat, India ... pass, mountain range
gobi, Mong ... desert
gol, Mong ... river
göl, gölü, Tur ... lake
golf, Du., Ger ... gulf, bay
golfe, Fr ... gulf, bay
golfo, It., Port., Sp ... gulf, bay
gomba, gompa, Tib ... monastery
gora, Rus., So. Slav ... mountain
góra, Pol ... mountain
gorod, Rus ... town
grad, Rus., So. Slav ... town
guba, Rus ... bay, gulf
gundung, Indon ... mountain
guntō, Jap ... archipelago
gunung, Mal ... mountain
haf, Swe ... sea, ocean
hafen, Ger ... port, harbor
haff, Ger ... gulf, inland sea
hai, Chn ... sea, lake
hama, Jap ... beach, shore
hamada, Arab ... rocky plateau
hamn, Swe ... harbor
hāmūn, Per ... swampy lake, plain
hantō, Jap ... peninsula
hassi, Arab ... well, spring
haus, Ger ... house
haut, Fr ... summit, top
hav, Dan., Nor ... sea, ocean
havn, Dan., Nor ... harbor, port
havre, Fr ... harbor, port
háza, Hung ... house, dwelling of
heim, Ger ... hamlet, home
hem, Swe ... hamlet, home
higashi, Jap ... east
hisar, Tur ... fortress
hissar, Arab ... fort
ho, Chn ... river
hoek, Du ... cape
hof, Ger ... court, farmhouse
höfn, Ice ... harbor
hoku, Jap ... north
holm, Dan., Nor., Swe ... island
hora, Czech ... mountain
horn, Ger ... peak
hoved, Dan., Nor ... cape
hsien, Chn ... district, district capital
hu, Chn ... lake
hügel, Ger ... hill
huk, Dan., Swe ... point
hus, Dan., Nor., Swe ... house
île, Fr ... island
ilha, Port ... island
indsö, Dan., Nor ... lake
insel, Ger ... island
insjö, Swe ... lake
irmak, irmagi, Tur ... river
isla, Sp ... island
isola, It ... island
istmo, It., Sp ... isthmus
järvi, jaur, Fin ... lake
jebel, Arab ... mountain
jima, Jap ... island
jökel, Nor ... glacier
joki, Fin ... river
jökull, Ice ... glacier
kaap, Du ... cape
kai, Jap ... bay, gulf, sea
kaikyō, Jap ... channel, strait
kalat, Per ... castle, fortress
kale, Tur ... fort
kali, Mal ... creek, river
kand, Per ... village
kang, Chn ... mountain ridge; village
kap, Dan., Ger ... cape
kapp, Nor., Swe ... cape
kasr, Arab ... fort, castle
kawa, Jap ... river
kefr, Arab ... village
kei, Jap ... creek, river
ken, Jap ... prefecture
khor, Arab ... bay, inlet
khrebet, Rus ... mountain range
kiang, Chn ... large river
king, Chn ... capital city, town
kita, Jap ... north
ko, Jap ... lake
köbstad, Dan ... market-town
kol, Mong ... lake
kólpos, Gr ... gulf
kong, Chn ... river
kopf, Ger ... head, summit, peak
köpstad, Swe ... market-town
körfezi, Tur ... gulf
kosa, Rus ... spit
kou, Chn ... river mouth
köy, Tur ... village
kraal, Du. (Africa) ... native village
ksar, Arab ... fortified village
kuala, Mal ... bay, river mouth
kuh, Per ... mountain
kum, Tur ... sand
kuppe, Ger ... summit
küste, Ger ... coast
kyo, Jap ... town, capital
la, Tib ... mountain pass
labuan, Mal ... anchorage, port
lac, Fr ... lake
lago, It., Port., Sp ... lake
lagoa, Port ... lake, marsh
laguna, It., Port., Sp ... lagoon, lake
lahti, Fin ... bay, gulf
län, Swe ... county
landsby, Dan., Nor ... village
liehtao, Chn ... archipelago
liman, Tur ... bay, port
ling, Chn ... pass, ridge, mountain
llanos, Sp ... plains
loch, Celt. (Scotland) ... lake, bay
loma, Sp ... long, low hill
lough, Celt. (Ireland) ... lake, bay
machi, Jap ... town
man, Kor ... bay
mar, Port., Sp ... sea
mare, It., Rom ... sea
marisma, Sp ... marsh, swamp
mark, Ger ... boundary, limit
massif, Fr ... block of mountains
mato, Port ... forest, thicket
me, Siam ... river
meer, Du., Ger ... lake, sea
mer, Fr ... sea
mesa, Sp ... flat-topped mountain
meseta, Sp ... plateau
mina, Port., Sp ... mine
minami, Jap ... south
minato, Jap ... harbor, haven
misaki, Jap ... cape, headland
mont, Fr ... mount, mountain
montagna, It ... mountain
montagne, Fr ... mountain
montaña, Sp ... mountain
monte, It., Port., Sp. ... mount, mountain
more, Rus., So. Slav ... sea
morro, Port., Sp ... hill, bluff
mühle, Ger ... mill
mund, Ger ... mouth, opening
mündung, Ger ... river mouth
mura, Jap ... township
myit, Bur ... river
mys, Rus ... cape
nada, Jap ... sea
nadi, India ... river, creek
naes, Dan., Nor ... cape
nafud, Arab ... desert of sand dunes
nagar, India ... town, city
nahr, Arab ... river
nam, Siam ... river, water
nan, Chn., Jap ... south
näs, Nor., Swe ... cape
nez, Fr ... point, cape
nishi, nisi, Jap ... west
njarga, Fin ... peninsula
nong, Siam ... marsh
noord, Du ... north
nor, Mong ... lake
nord, Dan., Fr., Ger., It., Nor., Swe ... north
norte, Port., Sp ... north
nos, Rus ... cape
nyasa, Bantu ... lake
ö, Dan., Nor., Swe ... island
occidental, Sp ... western
ocna, Rom ... salt mine
odde, Dan., Nor ... point, cape
oeste, Port., Sp ... west
oka, Jap ... hill
oost, Du ... east
oriental, Sp ... eastern
óros, Gr ... mountain
ost, Ger., Swe ... east
öster, Dan., Nor., Swe ... eastern
ostrov, Rus ... island
oued, Arab ... river, stream
ouest, Fr ... west
ozero, Rus ... lake
pää, Fin ... mountain
padang, Mal ... plain, field
pampas, Sp. (Argentina) ... grassy plains
pará, Indian (Brazil) ... river
pas, Fr ... channel, passage
paso, Sp ... mountain pass, passage
passo, It., Port. ... mountain pass, passage, strait
patam, India ... city, town
pei, Chn ... north
pélagos, Gr ... open sea
pegunungan, Indon ... mountains
peña, Sp ... rock
peresheyek, Rus ... isthmus
pertuis, Fr ... strait
peski, Rus ... desert
pic, Fr ... mountain peak
pico, Port., Sp ... mountain peak
piedra, Sp ... stone, rock
ping, Chn ... plain, flat
planalto, Port ... plateau
planina, Yugo ... mountains
playa, Sp ... shore, beach
pnom, Camb ... mountain
pointe, Fr ... point
polder, Du., Ger ... reclaimed marsh
polje, So. Slav ... plain, field
poluostrov, Rus ... peninsula
pont, Fr ... bridge
ponta, Port ... point, headland
ponte, It., Port ... bridge
pore, India ... city, town
porthmós, Gr ... strait
porto, It., Port ... port, harbor
potamós, Gr ... river
p'ov, Rus ... peninsula
prado, Sp ... field, meadow
presqu'île, Fr ... peninsula
proliv, Rus ... strait
pu, Chn ... commercial village
pueblo, Sp ... town, village
puerto, Sp ... port, harbor
pulau, Indon ... island
punkt, Ger ... point
punt, Du ... point
punta, It., Sp ... point
pur, India ... city, town
puy, Fr ... peak
qal'a, qal'at, Arab ... fort, village
qasr, Arab ... fort, castle
rann, India ... wasteland
ra's, Arab ... cape, head
reka, Rus., So. Slav ... river
represa, Port ... reservoir
rettō, Jap ... island chain
ría, Sp ... estuary
ribeira, Port ... stream
riberão, Port ... river
rio, It., Port ... stream, river
río, Sp ... river
rivière, Fr ... river
roca, Sp ... rock
rt, Yugo ... cape
rūd, Per ... river
saari, Fin ... island
sable, Fr ... sand
sahara, Arab ... desert, plain
saki, Jap ... cape
sal, Sp ... salt
salar, Sp ... salt flat, salt lake
salto, Sp ... waterfall
san, Jap., Kor ... mountain, hill
sat, satul, Rom ... village
schloss, Ger ... castle
sebkha, Arab ... salt marsh
see, Ger ... lake, sea
şehir, Tur ... town, city
selat, Indon ... stream
selvas, Port. (Brazil) ... tropical rain forests
seno, Sp ... bay
serra, Port ... mountain chain
serranía, Sp ... mountain ridge
seto, Jap ... strait
severnaya, Rus ... northern
shahr, Per ... town, city
shan, Chn ... mountain, hill, island
shatt, Arab ... river
shi, Jap ... city
shima, Jap ... island
shōtō, Jap ... archipelago
si, Chn ... west, western
sierra, Sp ... mountain range
sjö, Nor., Swe ... lake, sea
sö, Dan., Nor ... lake, sea
söder, södra, Swe ... south
song, Annam ... river
sopka, Rus ... peak, volcano
source, Fr ... a spring
spitze, Ger ... summit, point
staat, Ger ... state
stad, Dan., Du., Nor., Swe. ... city, town
stadt, Ger ... city, town
stato, It ... state
step', Rus ... treeless plain, steppe
straat, Du ... strait
strand, Dan., Du., Ger., Nor., Swe ... shore, beach
stretto, It ... strait
strom, Ger ... river, stream
ström, Dan., Nor., Swe. ... stream, river
stroom, Du ... stream, river
su, suyu, Tur ... water, river
sud, Fr., Sp ... south
süd, Ger ... south
suidō, Jap ... channel
sul, Port ... south
sund, Dan., Nor., Swe ... sound
sungai, sungei, Indon., Mal ... river
sur, Sp ... south
syd, Dan., Nor., Swe ... south
tafelland, Ger ... plateau
take, Jap ... peak, summit
tal, Ger ... valley
tanjung, tanjong, Mal ... cape
tao, Chn ... island
târg, târgul, Rom ... market, town
tell, Arab ... hill
teluk, Indon ... bay, gulf
terra, It ... land
terre, Fr ... earth, land
thal, Ger ... valley
tierra, Sp ... earth, land
tō, Jap ... east; island
tonle, Camb ... river, lake
top, Du ... peak
torp, Swe ... hamlet, cottage
tsangpo, Tib ... river
tsi, Chn ... village, borough
tso, Tib ... lake
tsu, Jap ... harbor, port
tundra, Rus ... treeless arctic plains
tung, Chn ... east
tuz, Tur ... salt
udde, Swe ... cape
ufer, Ger ... shore, riverbank
ujung, Indon ... point, cape
umi, Jap ... sea, gulf
ura, Jap ... bay, coast, creek
ust'ye, Rus ... river mouth
valle, It., Port., Sp ... valley
vallée, Fr ... valley
valli, It ... lake
vár, Hung ... fortress
város, Hung ... town
varoš, So. Slav ... town
veld, Du ... open plain, field
verkh, Rus ... top, summit
ves, Czech ... village
vest, Dan., Nor., Swe ... west
vik, Swe ... cove, bay
vila, Port ... town
villa, Sp ... town
villar, Sp ... village, hamlet
ville, Fr ... town, city
vostok, Rus ... east
wad, wādī, Arab. ... intermittent stream
wald, Ger ... forest, woodland
wan, Chn., Jap ... bay, gulf
weiler, Ger ... hamlet, village
westersch, Du ... western
wüste, Ger ... desert
yama, Jap ... mountain
yarimada, Tur ... peninsula
yug, Rus ... south
zaki, Jap ... cape
zaliv, Rus ... bay, gulf
zapad, Rus ... west
zee, Du ... sea
zemlya, Rus ... land
zuid, Du ... south

ABBREVIATIONS OF GEOGRAPHICAL NAMES AND TERMS

Afg.	Afghanistan
Afr.	Africa
Ak., U.S.	Alaska, U.S.
Al., U.S.	Alabama, U.S.
Alb.	Albania
Alg.	Algeria
Am. Sam.	American Samoa
And.	Andorra
Ang.	Angola
Ant.	Antarctica
Antig.	Antigua and Barbuda
aq.	Aqueduct
Ar., U.S.	Arkansas, U.S.
Arg.	Argentina
Arm.	Armenia
arpt.	Airport
Aus.	Austria
Austl.	Australia
Az., U.S.	Arizona, U.S.
Azer.	Azerbaijan
b.	Bay, Gulf, Inlet, Lagoon
Bah.	Bahamas
Bahr.	Bahrain
Barb.	Barbados
B.A.T.	British Antarctic Territory
Bdi.	Burundi
Bel.	Belgium
Bela.	Belarus
Bhu.	Bhutan
bk.	Undersea Bank
bldg.	Building
Bngl.	Bangladesh
Bol.	Bolivia
Boph.	Bophuthatswana
Bos.	Bosnia and Hercegovina
Bots.	Botswana
Braz.	Brazil
Bru.	Brunei
bt.	Bight
Bul.	Bulgaria
Burkina	Burkina Faso
c.	Cape, Point
Ca., U.S.	California, U.S.
Cam.	Cameroon
Camb.	Cambodia
can.	Canal
Can.	Canada
Cay. Is.	Cayman Islands
Cen. Afr. Rep.	Central African Republic
clf.	Cliff, Escarpment
co.	County, Parish
Co., U.S.	Colorado, U.S.
Col.	Colombia
Com.	Comoros
cont.	Continent
Cook Is.	Cook Islands
C.R.	Costa Rica
Cro.	Croatia
cst.	Coast, Beach
Ct., U.S.	Connecticut, U.S.
C.V.	Cape Verde
Cyp.	Cyprus
Czech.	Czechoslovakia
d.	Delta
D.C., U.S.	District of Columbia, U.S.
De., U.S.	Delaware, U.S.
Den.	Denmark
dep.	Dependency, Colony
depr.	Depression
dept.	Department, District
des.	Desert
Dji.	Djibouti
Dom.	Dominica
Dom. Rep.	Dominican Republic
Ec.	Ecuador
educ.	Educational Facility
El Sal.	El Salvador
Eng., U.K.	England, U.K.
Eq. Gui.	Equatorial Guinea
Est.	Estonia
est.	Estuary
Eth.	Ethiopia
Eur.	Europe
Faer. Is.	Faeroe Islands
Falk. Is.	Falkland Islands
Fin.	Finland
fj.	Fjord
Fl., U.S.	Florida, U.S.
for.	Forest, Moor
Fr.	France
Fr. Gu.	French Guiana
Fr. Poly.	French Polynesia
F.S.A.T.	French Southern and Antarctic Territory
Ga., U.S.	Georgia, U.S.
Gam.	Gambia
Geor.	Georgia
Ger.	Germany
Grc.	Greece
Gren.	Grenada
Grnld.	Greenland
Guad.	Guadeloupe
Guat.	Guatemala
Gui.	Guinea
Gui.-B.	Guinea-Bissau
Guy.	Guyana

Hi., U.S.	Hawaii, U.S.
hist.	Historic Site, Ruins
hist. reg.	Historic Region
H.K.	Hong Kong
Hond.	Honduras
Hung.	Hungary
i.	Island
Ia., U.S.	Iowa, U.S.
I.C.	Ivory Coast
ice	Ice Feature, Glacier
Ice.	Iceland
Id., U.S.	Idaho, U.S.
Il., U.S.	Illinois, U.S.
In., U.S.	Indiana, U.S.
Indon.	Indonesia
I. of Man	Isle of Man
I.R.	Indian Reservation
Ire.	Ireland
is.	Islands
Isr.	Israel
Isr. Occ.	Israeli Occupied Areas
isth.	Isthmus
Jam.	Jamaica
Jord.	Jordan
Kaz.	Kazakhstan
Kir.	Kiribati
Ks., U.S.	Kansas, U.S.
Kuw.	Kuwait
Ky., U.S.	Kentucky, U.S.
Kyrg.	Kyrgyzstan
l.	Lake, Pond
La., U.S.	Louisiana, U.S.
Lat.	Latvia
Leb.	Lebanon
Leso.	Lesotho
Lib.	Liberia
Liech.	Liechtenstein
Lith.	Lithuania
Lux.	Luxembourg
Ma., U.S.	Massachusetts, U.S.
Mac.	Macedonia
Madag.	Madagascar
Malay.	Malaysia
Marsh. Is.	Marshall Islands
Mart.	Martinique
Maur.	Mauritania
May.	Mayotte
Md., U.S.	Maryland, U.S.
Me., U.S.	Maine, U.S.
Mex.	Mexico
Mi., U.S.	Michigan, U.S.
Micron.	Micronesia, Federated States of
Mn., U.S.	Minnesota, U.S.
Mo., U.S.	Missouri, U.S.
Mol.	Moldova
Mong.	Mongolia
Monts.	Montserrat
Mor.	Morocco
Moz.	Mozambique
Ms., U.S.	Mississippi, U.S.
Mt., U.S.	Montana, U.S.
mth.	River Mouth or Channel
mtn.	Mountain
mts.	Mountains
Mwi.	Malawi
N.A.	North America
N.C., U.S.	North Carolina, U.S.
N. Cal.	New Caledonia
N. Cyp.	North Cyprus
N.D., U.S.	North Dakota, U.S.
Ne., U.S.	Nebraska, U.S.
neigh.	Neighborhood
Neth.	Netherlands
Neth. Ant.	Netherlands Antilles
N.H., U.S.	New Hampshire, U.S.
Nic.	Nicaragua
Nig.	Nigeria
N. Ire., U.K.	Northern Ireland, U.K.
N.J., U.S.	New Jersey, U.S.
N. Kor.	North Korea
N.M., U.S.	New Mexico, U.S.
N. Mar. Is.	Northern Mariana Islands
Nmb.	Namibia
Nor.	Norway
Nv., U.S.	Nevada, U.S.
N.Y., U.S.	New York, U.S.
N.Z.	New Zealand
o.	Ocean
Oc.	Oceania
Oh., U.S.	Ohio, U.S.
Ok., U.S.	Oklahoma, U.S.
Or., U.S.	Oregon, U.S.
p.	Pass
Pa., U.S.	Pennsylvania, U.S.
Pac. Is.	Pacific Islands, Trust Territory of the
Pak.	Pakistan
Pan.	Panama
Pap. N. Gui.	Papua New Guinea
Para.	Paraguay
pen.	Peninsula
Phil.	Philippines
Pit.	Pitcairn
pl.	Plain, Flat

plat.	Plateau, Highland
Pol.	Poland
Port.	Portugal
P.R.	Puerto Rico
prov.	Province, Region
pt. of i.	Point of Interest
r.	River, Creek
Reu.	Reunion
rec.	Recreational Site, Park
reg.	Physical Region
rel.	Religious Institution
res.	Reservoir
rf.	Reef, Shoal
R.I., U.S.	Rhode Island, U.S.
Rom.	Romania
Rw.	Rwanda
S.A.	South America
S. Afr.	South Africa
Sau. Ar.	Saudi Arabia
S.C., U.S.	South Carolina, U.S.
sci.	Scientific Station
Scot., U.K.	Scotland, U.K.
S.D., U.S.	South Dakota, U.S.
Sen.	Senegal
sea feat.	Undersea Feature
Sey.	Seychelles
S. Ga.	South Georgia
Sing.	Singapore
S. Kor.	South Korea
S.L.	Sierra Leone
Slo.	Slovenia
S. Mar.	San Marino
Sol. Is.	Solomon Islands
Som.	Somalia
Sp. N. Afr.	Spanish North Africa
Sri L.	Sri Lanka
St. Hel.	St. Helena
St. K./N.	St. Kitts and Nevis
St. Luc.	St. Lucia
St. P./M.	St. Pierre and Miquelon
strt.	Strait, Channel, Sound
S. Tom./P.	Sao Tome and Principe
St. Vin.	St. Vincent and the Grenadines
Sur.	Suriname
Sval.	Svalbard
sw.	Swamp, Marsh
Swaz.	Swaziland
Swe.	Sweden
Switz.	Switzerland
Tai.	Taiwan
Taj.	Tajikistan
Tan.	Tanzania
T./C. Is.	Turks and Caicos Islands
ter.	Territory
Thai.	Thailand
Tn., U.S.	Tennessee, U.S.
trans.	Transportation Facility
Trin.	Trinidad and Tobago
Tun.	Tunisia
Tur.	Turkey
Turk.	Turkmenistan
Tx., U.S.	Texas, U.S.
U.A.E.	United Arab Emirates
Ug.	Uganda
U.K.	United Kingdom
Ukr.	Ukraine
Ur.	Uruguay
U.S.	United States
Ut., U.S.	Utah, U.S.
Uzb.	Uzbekistan
Va., U.S.	Virginia, U.S.
val.	Valley, Watercourse
Vat.	Vatican City
Ven.	Venezuela
V.I., Br.	Virgin Islands, British
Viet.	Vietnam
V.I.U.S.	Virgin Islands (U.S.)
vol.	Volcano
Vt., U.S.	Vermont, U.S.
Wa., U.S.	Washington, U.S.
Wi., U.S.	Wisconsin, U.S.
W. Sah.	Western Sahara
W. Sam.	Western Samoa
wtfl.	Waterfall
W.V., U.S.	West Virginia, U.S.
Wy., U.S.	Wyoming, U.S.
Yugo.	Yugoslavia
Zam.	Zambia
Zimb.	Zimbabwe
Zam.	Zambia

PRONUNCIATION OF GEOGRAPHICAL NAMES

Key to the Sound Values of Letters and Symbols Used in the Index to Indicate Pronunciation

ă-ăt; băttle
ă-fĭnăl; ăppeal
ā-rāte; elāte
â-senâte; inanimâte
ä-ärm; cälm
à-àsk; bàth
ȧ-sofȧ; mȧrine (short neutral or indeterminate sound)
â-fâre; prepâre
ch-choose; church
dh-as th in other; either
ē-bē; ēve
ê-êvent; crêate
ĕ-bĕt; ĕnd
ĕ-recĕnt (short neutral or indeterminate sound)
ē-cratēr; cindēr
g-gō; gāme
gh-guttural g
ĭ-bĭt; wĭll
ĭ-(short neutral or indeterminate sound)
ī-rīde; bīte
ᴋ-guttural k as ch in German ich
ng-sing
ŋ-baŋk; liŋger
ɴ-indicates nasalized preceding vowel
ŏ-nŏd; ŏdd
ŏ-cŏmmit; cŏnnect
ō-ōld; bōld
ô-ôbey; hôtel
ô-ôrder; nôrth
oi-boil
ōō-fōōd; rōōt
ȯ-as oo in foot; wood
ou-out; thou
s-soft; so; sane
sh-dish; finish
th-thin; thick
ū-pūre; cūre
ů-ůnite; ůsůrp
û-ûrn; fûr
ŭ-stŭd; ŭp
ŭ-circŭs; sŭbmit
ü-as in French tu
zh-as z in azure
'-indeterminate vowel sound

In many cases the spelling of foreign geographic names does not even remotely indicate the pronunciation to an American, i.e., Słupsk in Poland is pronounced swȯpsk; Jujuy in Argentina is pronounced hōōhwē'; La Spezia in Italy is lä-spē'zyä.

This condition is hardly surprising, however, when we consider that in our own language Worcester, Massachusetts, is pronounced wȯs'tēr; Sioux City, Iowa, sōō si'tĭ; Schuylkill Haven, Pennsylvania, skōōl'kĭl hā-vĕn; Poughkeepsie, New York, pŏ-kĭp'sĕ.

The indication of pronunciation of geographic names presents several peculiar problems:

1. Many foreign tongues use sounds that are not present in the English language and which an American cannot normally articulate. Thus, though the nearest English equivalent sound has been indicated, only approximate results are possible.

2. There are several dialects in each foreign tongue which cause variation in the local pronunciation of names. This also occurs in identical names in the various divisions of a great language group, as the Slavic or the Latin.

3. Within the United States there are marked differences in pronunciation, not only of local geographic names, but also of common words, indicating that the sound and tone values for letters as well as the placing of the emphasis vary considerably from one part of the country to another.

4. A number of different letters and diacritical combinations could be used to indicate essentially the same or approximate pronunciations.

Some variation in pronunciation other than that indicated in this index may be encountered, but such a difference does not necessarily indicate that either is in error, and in many cases it is a matter of individual choice as to which is preferred. In fact, an exact indication of pronunciation of many foreign names using English letters and diacritical marks is extremely difficult and sometimes impossible.

PRONOUNCING INDEX

This universal index includes in a single alphabetical list approximately 34,000 names of features that appear on the reference maps. Each name is followed by a page reference and geographical coordinates.

Abbreviation and Capitalization Abbreviations of names on the maps have been standardized as much as possible. Names that are abbreviated on the maps are generally spelled out in full in the index. Periods are used after all abbreviations regardless of local practice. The abbreviation "St." is used only for "Saint". "Sankt" and other forms of this term are spelled out.

Most initial letters of names are capitalized, except for a few Dutch names, such as "'s-Gravenhage". Capitalization of noninitial words in a name generally follows local practice.

Alphabetization Names are alphabetized in the order of the letters of the English alphabet. Spanish *ll* and *ch*, for example, are not treated as distinct letters. Furthermore, diacritical marks are disregarded in alphabetization — German or Scandinavian ä or ö are treated as a or o.

The names of physical features may appear inverted, since they are always alphabetized under the proper, not the generic, part of the name, thus: "Gibraltar, Strait of". Otherwise every entry, whether consisting of one word or more, is alphabetized as a single continuous entity. "Lakeland," for example, appears after "La Crosse" and before "La Salle." Names beginning with articles (Le Havre, Den Helder, Al Manāmah, Ad Dawhah) are not inverted. Names beginning "St.", "Ste." and "Sainte" are alphabetized as though spelled "Saint."

In the case of identical names, towns are listed first, then political divisions, then physical features.

Generic Terms Except for cities, the names of all features are followed by terms that represent broad classes of features, for example, Mississippi, r. or Alabama, state. A list of all abbreviations used in the index is on page 249.

Country names and names of features that extend beyond the boundaries of one country are followed by the name of the continent in which each is located. Country designations follow the names of all other places in the index. The locations of places in the United States and the United Kingdom are further defined by abbreviations that indicate the state or political division in which each is located.

Pronunciations Pronunciations are included for most names listed. An explanation of the pronunciation system used appears on page 249.

Page References and Geographical Coordinates The geographical coordinates and page references are found in the last columns of each entry.

Page references to two-page maps always refer to the left-hand page. If a page contains several maps or insets, a lowercase letter identifies the specific map or inset.

Latitude and longitude coordinates for point features, such as cities and mountain peaks, indicate the locations of the symbols. For extensive areal features, such as countries or mountain ranges, or linear features, such as canals and rivers, locations are given for the position of the type as it appears on the map.

PLACE (Pronunciation)	PAGE	Lat. °	Long. °
A			
Aachen, Ger. (ä′kĕn)	140	50.46N	6.07E
Aalen, Ger. (ä′lĕn)	148	48.49N	10.08E
Aalsmeer, Neth.	139a	52.16N	4.44E
Aalst, Bel.	144	50.58N	4.00E
Aarau, Switz. (ärou)	140	47.22N	8.03E
Aarschot, Bel.	139a	50.59N	4.51E
Aba, Nig.	204	5.06N	7.21E
Aba, Zaire	210	3.52N	30.14E
Ābādān, Iran (ä′bä́-dän′)	174	30.15N	48.30E
Abaetetuba, Braz. (ä′bä́-tĕ-tōō′bä)	124	1.44S	48.45W
Abajo Peak, mtn., Ut., U.S. (ä-bä′hō)	102	37.51N	109.28W
Abakaliki, Nig.	208	6.21N	8.06E
Abakan, Russia (ŭ-bá-kän′)	158	53.43N	91.28E
Abakan, r., Russia	162	53.00N	91.06E
Abancay, Peru (ä-bän-kä′ē)	124	13.44S	72.46W
Abashiri, Japan (ä-bä-shē′rē)	186	44.00N	144.13E
Abasolo, Mex.	106	27.13N	101.25W
Abasolo, Mex. (ä-bä-sō′lō)	112	24.05N	98.24W
Abaya, Lake, l., Eth. (ä-bä′yä)	204	6.24N	38.22E
'Abbāsābād, Iran	237h	35.44N	51.25E
'Abbāsah, Tur'at al, can., Egypt	212c	30.45N	32.15E
Abbeville, Fr. (áb-vēl′)	140	50.08N	1.49E
Abbeville, Al., U.S. (ăb′é-vĭl)	108	31.35N	85.15W
Abbeville, Ga., U.S.	108	31.53N	83.23W
Abbeville, La., U.S.	106	29.59N	92.07W
Abbeville, S.C., U.S.	108	34.09N	82.25W
Abbey Wood, neigh., Eng., U.K.	231	51.29N	0.08E
Abbiategrasso, Italy (äb-byä′tä-gräs′sō)	154	45.23N	8.52E
Abbots Bromley, Eng., U.K. (ăb′ŭts brŭm′lė)	138a	52.49N	1.52W
Abbotsford, Can. (ăb′ŭts-fērd)	100d	49.03N	122.17W
Abbots Langley, Eng., U.K.	231	51.43N	0.25W
'Abd al Kūrī, i., Yemen (ăbd-ĕl-kó′rė)	212a	12.12N	51.00E
'Abd al-Shāhīd, Egypt	240a	29.55N	31.13E
Abdulino, Russia (äb-dò-lē′nò)	160	53.42N	53.40E
Abengourou, I.C.	208	6.44N	3.29W
Abeokuta, Nig. (ä-bá-ō-kōō′tä)	204	7.10N	3.26E
Abercorn, *see* Mbala, Zam.	206	8.50S	31.22E
Aberdare, Wales, U.K. (äb-ēr-dâr′)	144	51.45N	3.35W
Aberdeen, Scot., U.K.	136	57.10N	2.05W
Aberdeen, Ms., U.S. (ăb-ēr-dēn′)	108	33.49N	88.33W
Aberdeen, S.D., U.S.	90	45.28N	98.29W
Aberdeen, Wa., U.S.	90	47.00N	123.48W
Abergavenny, Wales, U.K. (ăb′ēr-gá-vĕn′ĭ)	144	51.45N	3.05W
Abert, Lake, l., Or., U.S. (a′bĕrt)	98	42.39N	120.24W
Aberystwyth, Wales, U.K. (ä-bĕr-ĭst′wĭth)	144	52.25N	4.04W
Abidjan, I.C. (ä-bēd-zhäN′)	204	5.19N	4.02W
Abiko, Japan (ä-bē-kō)	187a	35.53N	140.01E
Abilene, Ks., U.S. (ăb′ĭ-lēn)	104	38.54N	97.12W
Abilene, Tx., U.S.	90	32.25N	99.45W
Abingdon, Eng., U.K.	138b	51.38N	1.17W
Abingdon, Il., U.S. (ăb′ĭng-dŭn)	96	40.48N	90.21W
Abingdon, Va., U.S.	108	36.42N	81.57W
Abington, Ma., U.S. (ăb′ĭng-tŭn)	87a	42.07N	70.57W
Abington, Pa., U.S.	225b	40.07N	75.08W
Abiquiu Reservoir, res., N.M., U.S.	102	36.26N	106.42W
Abitibi, l., Can. (ăb-ĭ-tĭb′ĭ)	78	48.27N	80.20W
Abitibi, r., Can.	78	49.30N	81.10W
Abkhaz Autonomous Soviet Socialist Republic, , Geor.	160	43.10N	40.45E
Ablis, Fr. (á-blē′)	151b	48.31N	1.50E
Ablon-sur-Seine, Fr.	233c	48.43N	2.25E
Abnūb, Egypt (äb-nōōb′)	212b	27.18N	31.11E
Abóbada, Port.	234d	38.43N	9.20W
Abohar, India	178	30.12N	74.13E
Aboisso, I.C.	208	5.28N	3.12W
Abomey, Benin (áb-ò-mā′)	204	7.11N	1.59E
Abony, Hung. (ŏ′bô-ny′)	148	47.12N	20.00E
Åbo, *see* Turku, Fin.	136	60.28N	22.12E
Abou Deïa, Chad	208	11.27N	19.17E
Abra, r., Phil. (ä′brä)	189a	17.16N	120.38E
Abraão, Braz. (äbrä-ouN′)	123a	23.10S	44.10W
Abraham's Bay, b., Bah.	116	22.20N	73.50W
Abram, Eng., U.K. (ā′brăm)	138a	53.31N	2.36W
Abramcevo, Russia	235b	55.50N	37.50E
Abrantes, Port. (á-brän′tĕs)	152	39.28N	8.13W
Abridge, Eng., U.K.	231	51.39N	0.07E
Abrolhos, Arquipélago dos, is., Braz.	124	17.58S	38.40W
Abruka, i., Est. (á-brò′ká)	146	58.09N	22.30E
Abruzzi e Molise, hist. reg., Italy	154	42.10N	13.55E
Absaroka Range, mts., U.S. (äb-sä-rō-ká)	90	44.50N	109.47W
Abū an-Numrus, Egypt	240a	29.57N	31.12E
Abū Arīsh, Sau. Ar. (ä-bōō ä-rēsh′)	174	16.48N	43.00E
Abū Dhabi, *see* Abū Ẓaby, U.A.E.	174	24.15N	54.28E
Abū Hamad, Sudan (ä′bōō hä′-mĕd)	204	19.37N	33.21E
Abū Kamāl, Syria	174	34.45N	40.46E
Abunã, r., S.A. (ä-bōō-nä′)	124	10.25S	67.00W
Abū Qīr, Egypt (ä′bōō kēr′)	212b	31.18N	30.06E
Abū Qurūn, Ra's, mtn., Egypt	173a	30.22N	33.32E
Aburatsu, Japan (ä′bò-rät′sōō)	187	31.33N	131.20E
Abu Road, India	174	24.38N	72.45E
Abū Şīr Pyramids, hist., Egypt	240a	29.54N	31.12E
Abū Tīj, Egypt	212b	27.03N	31.19E
Abū Ẓaby, U.A.E.	174	24.15N	54.28E
Abū Zanīmah, Egypt	173a	29.03N	33.08E
Abyy, Russia	158	68.24N	134.00E
Acacias, Col. (ä-kä′sēäs)	124a	3.59N	73.44W
Acadia National Park, rec., Me., U.S. (á-kā′dǐ-á)	90	44.19N	68.01W
Acajutla, El Sal. (ä-kä-hōōt′lä)	114	13.37N	89.50W
Acala, Mex. (ä-kä′lä)	112	16.38N	92.49W
Acalayong, Eq. Gui.	210	1.05N	9.40E
Acámbaro, Mex. (ä-käm′bä-rō)	112	20.03N	100.42W
Acancéh, Mex. (ä-kän-sě′)	114a	20.50N	89.27W
Acapetlahuaya, Mex. (ä-kä-pĕt′lä-hwä′yä)	112	18.24N	100.04W
Acaponeta, Mex. (ä-kä-pò-nä′tá)	112	22.31N	105.25W
Acaponeta, r., Mex.	112	22.47N	105.23W
Acapulco, Mex. (ä-kä-pōōl′kō)	110	16.49N	99.57W
Acaraí Mountains, mts., S.A.	124	1.30N	57.40W
Acarigua, Ven. (ä-kä-rē′gwä)	124	9.29N	69.11W
Acatlán de Osorio, Mex. (ä-kät-län′dä ō-sō′rē-ō)	112	18.11N	98.04W
Acatzingo de Hidalgo, Mex.	112	18.58N	97.47W
Acayucan, Mex. (ä-kä-yōō′kän)	112	17.56N	94.55W
Accord, Ma., U.S.	223a	42.10N	70.53W
Accoville, W.V., U.S. (ăk′kò-vĭl)	92	37.45N	81.50W
Accra, Ghana (ä′krä)	204	5.33N	0.13W
Accrington, Eng., U.K. (ăk′rǐng-tŭn)	138a	53.45N	2.22W
Acerra, Italy (ä-chĕ′r-rä)	153c	40.42N	14.22E
Achachachi, Bol. (ä-chä-kä′chě)	124	16.11S	68.32W
Achill Island, i., Ire. (ä-chĭl′)	140	53.55N	10.05W
Achinsk, Russia (ä-chěnsk′)	162	56.13N	90.32E
Acireale, Italy (ä-chě-rä-ä′lä)	154	37.37N	15.12E
Acklins, i., Bah. (ăk′lĭns)	110	22.30N	73.55W
Acklins, The Bight of, bt., Bah.	116	22.35N	74.20W
Acolman, Mex. (ä-kōl-má′n)	113a	19.38N	98.56W
Acoma Indian Reservation, I.R., N.M., U.S.	102	34.52N	107.40W
Aconcagua, prov., Chile (ä-kōn-kä′gwä)	123b	32.20S	71.00W
Aconcagua, r., Chile	123b	32.43S	70.53W
Aconcagua, Cerro, mtn., Arg.	126	32.38S	70.00W
Açores (Azores), is., Port.	203	37.44N	29.25W
Acoyapa, Nic. (ä-kò-yä′pä)	114	11.54N	85.11W
Acqui, Italy (äk′kwē)	154	44.41N	8.22W
Acre, state, Braz. (ä′krä)	124	8.40S	70.45W
Acre, r., S.A.	124	10.33S	68.34W
Acton, Can.	77d	43.38N	80.02W
Acton, Al., U.S. (äk′tŭn)	94h	33.21N	86.49W
Acton, Ma., U.S.	87a	42.29N	71.26W
Acton, neigh., Eng., U.K.	231	51.30N	0.16W
Actopan, Mex. (äk-tò-pän′)	112	20.16N	98.57W
Actópan, r., Mex. (äk-tò′pän)	112	19.25N	96.31W
Acuitzio del Canje, Mex. (ä-kwēt′zē-ō dĕl kän′hä)	112	19.28N	101.21W
Acul, Baie de l', b., Haiti (ä-kōōl′)	116	19.55N	72.20W

ăt; fīnal; rāte; senâte; ärm; àsk; sofá; fâre; ch-choose; dh-as th in other; bē; ėvent; bĕt; recĕnt; crātēr; g-gō; gh-guttural g; bĭt; ī-short neutral; rīde; ĸ-guttural k as ch in German ich:

PLACE (Pronunciation)	PAGE	Lat. °'	Long. °'
Ada, Mn., U.S. (ā'dŭ)	96	47.17N	96.32W
Ada, Oh., U.S.	92	40.45N	83.45W
Ada, Ok., U.S.	104	34.45N	96.43W
Ada, Yugo. (ä'dä)	154	45.48N	20.06E
Adachi, Japan	187a	35.50N	39.36E
Adachi, neigh., Japan	238a	35.45N	139.48E
Adak, Ak., U.S. (ă-dăk')	89a	56.50N	176.48W
Adak, i., Ak., U.S.	89a	51.40N	176.28W
Adak Strait, strt., Ak., U.S.	89a	51.42N	177.16W
Adamaoua, mts., Afr.	204	6.30N	11.50E
Adams, Ma., U.S. (ăd'ămz)	92	42.35N	73.10W
Adams, Wi., U.S.	96	43.55N	89.48W
Adams, r., Can.	80	51.30N	119.20W
Adams, Mount, mtn., Wa., U.S.	90	46.15N	121.19W
Adamsville, Al., U.S. (ăd'ămz-vĭl)	94h	33.36N	86.57W
Adana, Tur. (ä'dä-nä)	174	37.05N	35.20E
Adapazari, Tur. (ä-dä-pä-zä'rē)	142	40.45N	30.20E
Adarama, Sudan (ä-dä-rä'mä)	204	17.11N	34.56E
Adda, r., Italy (äd'dä)	154	45.43N	9.31E
Ad Dabbah, Sudan	204	18.04N	30.58E
Ad Dahnā, des., Sau. Ar.	174	26.05N	47.15E
Ad-Dāmir, Sudan (ad-dä'mĕr)	204	17.38N	33.57E
Ad Dammān, Sau. Ar.	174	26.27N	49.59E
Ad Dāmūr, Leb.	173a	33.44N	35.27E
Ad Dawhah, Qatar	174	25.02N	51.28E
Ad Dilam, Sau. Ar.	174	23.47N	47.03E
Ad Dilinjāt, Egypt	212b	30.48N	30.32E
Addington, Eng., U.K.	231	51.18N	0.23E
Addis Ababa, Eth.	204	9.00N	38.44E
Addison, Tx., U.S. (ă'dĭ-sŭn)	101c	32.58N	96.50W
Addlestone, Eng., U.K.	231	51.22N	0.30W
Addo, S. Afr. (ădō)	207c	33.33S	25.43E
Ad Duwaym, Sudan (dō-ām')	204	13.56N	32.22E
Addyston, Oh., U.S. (ăd'ē-stŭn)	95f	39.09N	84.42W
Adel, Ga., U.S. (ā-dĕl')	108	31.08N	83.55W
Adelaide, Austl. (ăd'ē-lād)	196	34.46S	139.08E
Adelaide, S. Afr. (ăd-ĕl'ād)	207c	32.41S	26.07E
Adelaide Island, i., Ant.	213	67.15S	68.40W
Adelphi, Md., U.S.	225d	39.00N	76.58W
Aden ('Adan), Yemen (ä'dĕn)	174	12.48N	45.00E
Aden, Gulf of, b.	174	11.45N	45.45E
Aderklaa, Aus.	235e	48.17N	16.32E
Adi, Pulau, i., Indon. (ä'dē)	188	4.25S	133.52E
Adige, r., Italy (ä'dē-jā)	142	46.38N	10.43E
Adigrat, Eth.	176	14.17N	39.28E
Adilābād, India (ŭ-dĭl-ä-băd')	178	19.47N	78.30E
Adirondack Mountains, mts., N.Y., U.S. (ăd-ĭ-rŏn'dăk)	90	43.45N	74.40W
Adis Abeba, *see* Addis Ababa, Eth.	204	9.00N	38.44E
Adi Ugri, Eth. (ä-dē ōō'grē)	204	14.54N	38.52E
Adjud, Rom. (ăd'zhŏd)	148	46.05N	27.12E
Adkins, Tx., U.S.	101d	29.22N	98.18W
Adlershof, neigh., Ger.	234a	52.26N	13.33E
Admiralty, i., Ak., U.S.	89	57.50N	133.50W
Admiralty Inlet, Wa., U.S. (ăd'mĭrăl-tē)	100a	48.10N	122.45W
Admiralty Island National Monument, rec., Ak., U.S.	89	57.50N	137.30W
Admiralty Islands, is., Pap. N. Gui.	188	1.40S	146.45E
Ado-Ekiti, Nig.	208	7.38N	5.12E
Adolph, Mn., U.S. (ā'dolf)	101h	46.47N	92.17W
Ādoni, India	178	15.42N	77.18E
Adour, r., Fr. (à-dōōr')	140	43.43N	0.38W
Adra, Spain (ä'drä)	152	36.45N	3.02W
Adrano, Italy (ä-drä'nō)	154	37.42N	14.52E
Adrar, Alg.	204	27.53N	0.15W
Adria, Italy (ä'drē-ä)	154	45.03N	12.01E
Adrian, Mi., U.S. (ā'drĭ-ăn)	92	41.55N	84.00W
Adrian, Mn., U.S.	96	43.39N	95.56W
Adrianople, *see* Edirne, Tur.	136	41.41N	26.35E
Adriatic Sea, sea, Eur.	136	43.30N	14.27E
Adwa, Eth.	204	14.02N	38.58E
Adwick-le-Street, Eng., U.K. (ăd'wĭk-lē-strēt')	138a	53.35N	1.11W
Adycha, r., Russia (ä'dĭ-chà)	162	66.11N	136.45E
Adzhamka, Ukr. (àd-zhäm'kà)	156	48.33N	32.28E
Adz'va, r., Russia (ädz'vå)	160	67.00N	59.20E
Aegean Sea, sea (ē-jē'ăn)	136	39.04N	24.56E
Affton, Mo., U.S.	101e	38.33N	90.20W
Afghanistan, nation, Asia (ăf-găn-ĭ-stăn')	174	33.00N	63.00E
Afgooye, Som. (äf-gô'ĭ)	212a	2.08N	45.08E
Afikpo, Nig.	208	5.53N	7.56E
Aflou, Alg. (ä-flōō')	204	33.59N	2.04E
Afognak, i., Ak., U.S. (ä-fŏg-nák')	89	58.28N	151.35W
Afonso Claudio, Braz. (äl-fōn'sō-klou'dēō)	123a	20.05S	41.05W
Afragola, Italy (ä-frá'gō-lä)	153c	40.40N	14.19E
Africa, cont.	203	10.00N	22.00E
Afton, Mn., U.S. (ăf'tŭn)	101g	44.54N	92.47W
Afton, Ok., U.S.	104	36.42N	94.56W
Afton, Wy., U.S.	98	42.42N	110.52W
'Afula, Isr. (ä-fōō'lá)	173a	32.36N	35.17E
Afyon, Tur. (ä-fē-ōn)	174	38.45N	30.20E
Agadem, Niger (ä'gà-dĕm)	204	16.50N	13.17E
Agadez, Niger (ä'gà-dĕs)	204	16.58N	7.59E
Agadir, Mor. (ä-gà-dēr)	204	30.30N	9.37W
Agalta, Cordillera de, mts., Hond. (kôr-dēl-yĕ'rä-dĕ-ä-gä'l-tä)	114	15.15N	85.42W
Agapovka, Russia (ä-gä-pôv'kä)	164a	53.18N	59.10E
Agartala, India	178	23.53N	91.22E
Agāshi, India	179b	19.28N	72.46E
Agashkino, Russia (á-gäsh'kĭ-nō)	164b	55.18N	38.13E
Agattu, i., Ak., U.S. (á'gä-tōō)	89a	52.14N	173.40E
Agayman, Ukr. (à-gä-ē-män')	156	46.39N	34.20E
Agboville, I.C.	208	5.56N	4.13W
Agdam, Azer. (ág'dám)	160	40.00N	47.00E
Agde, Fr. (ägd)	150	43.19N	3.30E
Agege, Nig.	240d	6.37N	3.20E

PLACE (Pronunciation)	PAGE	Lat. °'	Long. °'
Agen, Fr. (á-zhäN')	140	44.13N	0.31E
Agincourt, neigh., Can.	223c	43.48N	79.17W
Aginskoye, Russia (ä-hĭn'skô-yĕ)	158	51.15N	113.15E
Agno, Phil. (äg'nō)	189a	16.07N	119.49E
Agno, r., Phil.	189a	15.42N	120.28E
Agnone, Italy (än-yō'nā)	154	41.49N	14.23E
Agogo, Ghana	208	6.47N	1.04W
Agostinho Pôrto, Braz.	230c	22.47S	43.23W
Agra, India (ä'grä)	174	27.18N	78.00E
Ağri, Tur.	160	39.50N	43.10E
Agri, r., Italy (ä'grē)	154	40.15N	16.21E
Agrícola Oriental, Mex.	229a	19.24N	99.05W
Agrínion, Grc. (á-grē'nyôn)	142	38.38N	21.06E
Agua, vol., Guat. (ä'gwä)	114	14.28N	90.43W
Agua Blanca, Río, r., Mex. (rē'ō-ä-gwä-blä'n-kä)	112	21.46N	102.54W
Agua Brava, Laguna de, l., Mex.	112	22.04N	105.40W
Agua Caliente Indian Reservation, I.R., Ca., U.S. (ä'gwä kal-yĕn'tä)	102	33.50N	116.24W
Aguada, Cuba (ä-gwä'dă)	116	22.25N	80.50W
Aguada, l., Mex.	114a	18.46N	89.40W
Aguadas, Col. (ä-gwä'dàs)	124	5.37N	75.27W
Aguadilla, P.R. (ä-gwä-dēl'yä)	111b	18.27N	67.10W
Aguadulce, Pan. (ä-gwä-dōōl'sā)	114	8.15N	80.33W
Agua Escondida, Meseta de, plat., Mex.	112	16.54N	91.35W
Agua Fria, r., Az., U.S. (ä'gwä frē-ä)	102	33.43N	112.22W
Aguai, Braz. (ägwä-ē')	123a	22.04S	46.57W
Agualeguas, Mex. (ä-gwä-lä'gwäs)	106	26.19N	99.33W
Agualva-Cacém, Port.	234d	38.46N	9.18W
Aguán, r., Hond. (ä-gwá'n)	114	15.22N	87.00W
Aguanaval, r., Mex. (á-guä-nä-väl')	106	25.12N	103.28W
Aguanus, r., Can. (á-gwä'nŭs)	86	50.45N	62.03W
Aguascalientes, Mex. (ä'gwäs-käl-yĕn'tās)	110	21.52N	102.17W
Aguascalientes, state, Mex.	112	22.00N	102.18W
Águeda, Port. (ä-gwä'dă)	152	40.36N	8.26W
Águeda, r., Eur. (ä-gē-dä)	152	40.50N	6.44W
Aguelhok, Mali	208	19.28N	0.52E
Aguilar, Spain	152	37.32N	4.39W
Aguilar, Co., U.S. (ä-gē-lär')	104	37.24N	104.38W
Aguilas, Spain (ä-gē-läs)	142	37.26N	1.35W
Aguililla, Mex. (ä-gē-lēl-yä)	112	18.44N	102.44W
Aguililla, r., Mex.	112	18.30N	102.48W
Aguja, Punta, c., Peru (pŭn'tà á-gōō' hä)	124	6.00S	81.15W
Agulhas, Cape, c., S. Afr. (ä-gōōl'yäs)	206	34.47S	20.00E
Agusan, r., Phil. (ä-gōō'sän)	188	8.12N	126.07E
Ahaggar, mts., Alg. (á-hà-gär')	204	23.14N	6.00E
Ahar, Iran	176	38.28N	47.04E
Ahlen, Ger. (ä'lĕn)	148	51.45N	7.52E
Ahlenberg, Ger.	232	51.25N	7.28E
Ahmadābād, India (ŭ-mĕd-ä-băd')	174	23.04N	72.38E
Ahmadnagar, India (ä'mûd-nû-gûr)	174	19.09N	74.45E
Ahmar Mountains, mts., Eth.	204	9.22N	42.00E
Ahoskie, N.C., U.S. (ä-hŏs'kē)	108	36.15N	77.00W
Ahrensburg, Ger. (ä'rĕns-bŏrg)	139c	53.40N	10.14E
Ahrensfelde, Ger.	234a	52.35N	13.35E
Ahrweiler, Ger. (är'vī-lĕr)	148	50.34N	7.05E
Ähtärinjärvi, l., Fin.	146	62.46N	24.25E
Ahuacatlán, Mex. (ä-wä-kät-län')	112	21.05N	104.28W
Ahuachapán, El Sal. (ä-wä-chä-pän')	114	13.57N	89.53W
Ahualulco, Mex. (ä-wä-lōōl'kō)	112	20.43N	103.57W
Ahuatempan, Mex. (ä-wä-tĕm-pän)	112	18.11N	98.02W
Ahuntsic, neigh., Can.	223b	45.33N	73.39W
Åhus, Swe. (ô'hōs)	146	55.56N	14.19E
Ahvāz, Iran	174	31.15N	48.54E
Ahvenanmaa (Åland), is., Fin. (ä'vĕ-nàn-mô) (ô'lănd)	140	60.36N	19.55E
Aiea, Hi., U.S.	88a	21.18N	157.52W
Aigburth, neigh., Eng., U.K.	233a	53.22N	2.55W
Aiken, S.C., U.S. (ā'kĕn)	108	33.32N	81.43W
Aimorès, Serra dos, mts., Braz. (sĕ'r-rä-dôs-ī-mō-rĕ's)	124	17.40S	42.38W
Aimoto, Japan (ī-mô-tō)	187b	34.59N	135.09E
Aincourt, Fr. (ăN-kōō'r)	151b	49.04N	1.47E
Aïn el Beïda, Alg.	204	35.57N	7.25E
Ainsworth, Eng., U.K.	233b	53.35N	2.22W
Ainsworth, Ne., U.S. (ānz'wûrth)	96	42.32N	99.51W
Aïn Témouchent, Alg. (ä'ēntĕ-mōō-shaN')	142	35.20N	1.23W
Aintree, Eng., U.K.	233a	53.29N	2.56W
Aïn Wessara, Alg. (ĕn ōō-sä-rá)	152	35.25N	2.50E
Aipe, Col. (ī'pĕ)	124a	3.13N	75.15W
Aïr, mts., Niger	204	18.00N	8.30E
Aire, r., Eng., U.K.	138a	53.42N	1.00W
Aire-sur-l'Adour, Fr. (âr)	150	43.42N	0.17W
Airhitam, Selat, strt., Indon.	173b	0.58N	102.38E
Airport West, Austl.	239b	37.44S	144.53E
Ai Shan, mts., China (äī'shän)	182	37.27N	120.35E
Aisne, r., Fr. (ĕn)	140	49.28N	3.32E
Aitape, Pap. N. Gui. (ä-ē-tä'på)	188	3.00S	142.10E
Aitkin, Mn., U.S. (āt'kĭn)	96	46.32N	93.43W
Aitolikón, Grc. (å-tō'lĭ-kôn)	154	38.27N	21.21E
Aitos, Bul. (ä-ē'tôs)	154	42.42N	27.17E
Aitutaki, i., Cook Is. (ī-tōō-tä'kē)	190	19.00S	162.00W
Aiud, Rom. (ä'ē-ŏd)	142	46.19N	23.40E
Aiuruoca, Braz. (äē'ōō-rōōō'-kà)	123a	21.57S	44.36W
Aiuruoca, r., Braz.	123a	22.11S	44.35W
Aix-en-Provence, Fr. (ĕks-prō-vàNs)	140	43.32N	5.27E
Aix-les-Bains, Fr. (ĕks'-lā-băN')	150	45.42N	5.56E
Aiyáleo, Grc.	235d	37.59N	23.41E
Aiyina, Grc.	154	37.43N	23.35E
Aiyina, i., Grc.	154	37.43N	23.35E
Aiyion, Grc.	154	38.13N	22.04E
Aizpute, Lat. (ä'ēz-pōō-tĕ)	146	56.44N	21.37E
Aizuwakamatsu, Japan	186	37.27N	139.51E
Ajaccio, Fr. (ä-yät'chō)	136	41.55N	8.42E
Ajalpan, Mex. (ä-häl'pän)	112	18.21N	97.14W
Ajana, Austl. (ăj-ăn'ĕr)	196	28.00S	114.45E

PLACE (Pronunciation)	PAGE	Lat. °'	Long. °'
Ajdābiyah, Libya	204	30.56N	20.16E
Ajjer, Tassili-n-, plat., Alg.	204	25.40N	6.57E
Ajmah, Jabal al, mts., Egypt	173a	29.12N	34.03E
Ajman, U.A.E.	174	25.15N	54.30E
Ajmer, India (ŭj-mēr')	174	26.26N	74.42E
Ajo, Az., U.S. (ä'hō)	102	32.20N	112.55W
Ajuchitlán del Progreso, Mex. (ä-hōō-chet-lån)	112	18.11N	100.32W
Ajuda, neigh., Port.	234d	38.43N	9.12W
Ajusco, Mex. (ä-hōō's-kō)	113a	19.13N	99.12W
Ajusco, Cerro, mtn., Mex. (sĕ'r-rô-ä-hōō's-kō)	113a	19.12N	99.16W
Akaishi-dake, mtn., Japan (ä-kī-shē dä'kä)	187	35.30N	138.00E
Akashi, Japan (ä'kä-shē)	186	34.38N	134.59E
Akbarābād, Iran	237h	35.41N	51.21E
Aketi, Zaire (ä-kå-tē)	204	2.44N	23.46E
Akhaltsikhe, Geor. (äkä'l-tsĭ-kĕ)	160	41.40N	42.50E
Akhdar, Al Jabal al, mts., Libya	204	32.00N	22.00E
Akhḑar, Al Jabal al, mts., Oman	174	23.30N	56.43W
Akhelóös, r., Grc. (ä-hĕ'lô-ōs)	154	38.45N	21.26E
Akhisar, Tur. (äk-hĭs-sär')	142	38.58N	27.58E
Akhtarskaya, Bukhta, b., Russia (bōōk'tä àk-tär'skà-yà)	156	45.53N	38.22E
Akhtopol, Bul. (äk'tô-pōl)	154	42.08N	27.54E
Akhtyrka, Ukr. (äk-tür'kà)	160	50.18N	34.53E
Akhunovo, Russia (ä-kû'nô-vô)	164a	54.13N	59.36E
Aki, Japan (ä'kē)	187	33.31N	133.51E
Akiak, Ak., U.S. (äk'yàk)	89	61.00N	161.02W
Akimiski, i., Can. (ä-kĭ-mĭ'skĭ)	78	52.54N	80.22W
Akishima, Japan	238a	35.41N	139.22E
Akita, Japan (ä'kē-tä)	180	39.40N	140.12E
Akjoujt, Maur.	204	19.45N	14.23W
'Akko, Isr.	173a	32.56N	35.05E
Aklavik, Can. (äk'lä-vĭk)	78	68.28N	135.26W
'Aklé'Âouâna, dunes, Afr.	208	18.07N	6.00W
Ako, Japan (ä'kô)	187	34.44N	134.22E
Akola, India (à-kō'lä)	174	20.47N	77.00E
Akordat, Eth.	204	15.34N	37.54E
Akpatok, i., Can. (äk'pà-tŏk)	78	60.30N	67.10W
Akranes, Ice.	140	64.18N	21.40W
Akron, Co., U.S. (ăk'rŭn)	104	40.09N	103.14W
Akron, Oh., U.S.	90	41.05N	81.30W
Akropolis, pt. of i., Grc.	235d	37.58N	23.43E
Aksaray, Tur. (äk-sá-rī')	142	38.30N	34.05E
Akşehir, Tur. (äk'shâ-hēr)	142	38.20N	31.20E
Akşehir Gölü, l., Tur.	174	38.40N	31.30E
Aksha, Russia (äk'shà)	158	50.28N	113.00E
Aksu, China (ä-kü-sōō)	180	41.29N	80.15E
Aktyubinsk, Kaz. (äk'tyōō-bĕnsk)	158	50.20N	57.00E
Akune, Japan (ä'kô-nå)	187	32.03N	130.16E
Akureyri, Ice. (ä-kô-rå'rē)	140	65.39N	18.01W
Akutan, i., Ak., U.S. (ä-kōō-tän')	89a	53.58N	169.54W
Akwatia, Ghana	208	6.04N	0.49W
Alabama, state, U.S. (ăl-à-băm'à)	90	32.50N	87.30W
Alabama, r., Al., U.S.	90	31.20N	87.39W
Alabat, i., Phil. (ä-lä-bät')	189a	14.14N	122.05E
Alacam, Tur. (ä-lä-chäm')	160	41.30N	35.40E
Alacranes, Cuba (ä-lä-krä'nås)	116	22.45N	81.35W
Al Aflaj, des., Sau. Ar.	174	24.00N	44.47E
Alagôas, state, Braz. (ä-lä-gō'äzh)	124	9.50S	36.33W
Alagoinhas, Braz. (ä-lä-gō-ēn'yäzh)	124	12.13S	38.12W
Alagón, Spain (ä-lä-gōn')	152	41.46N	1.07W
Alagón, r., Spain	152	39.53N	6.42W
Alaguntan, Nig.	240d	6.26N	3.30E
Alahuatán, r., Mex. (ä-lä-wä-tä'n)	112	18.30N	100.00W
Alajuela, C.R. (ä-lä-hwa'lä)	114	10.01N	84.14W
Alajuela, Lago, l., Pan.	110a	9.15N	79.34W
Alakol', l., Kaz.	162	45.45N	81.13E
Alalakeiki Channel, strt., Hi., U.S. (ä-lä-lä-kā'kē)	88a	20.40N	156.30W
Al 'Alamayn, Egypt	204	30.53N	28.52E
Al 'Amārah, Iraq	176	31.50N	47.09E
Alameda, Ca., U.S. (ăl-à-mā'dà)	90	37.46N	122.15W
Alameda, r., Ca., U.S.	100b	37.36N	122.02W
Alaminos, Phil. (ä-lä-mē'nôs)	189a	16.09N	119.58E
Al 'Amirīyah, Egypt	142	31.01N	29.52E
Alamo, Mex. (ä'lä-mō)	112	20.55N	97.41W
Alamo, Ca., U.S. (ă'là-mō)	100b	37.51N	122.02W
Alamo, Nv., U.S. (ă'là-mō)	102	37.22N	115.10W
Alamo, r., Mex. (ä'lä-mô)	106	26.33N	99.35W
Alamogordo, N.M., U.S. (ăl-à-mō-gôr'dō)	102	32.55N	106.00W
Alamo Heights, Tx., U.S. (ă'là-mō)	101d	29.28N	98.27W
Alamo Indian Reservation, I.R., N.M., U.S.	102	34.30N	107.30W
Alamo Peak, mtn., N.M., U.S. (ă'là-mō pēk)	106	32.50N	105.55W
Alamosa, Co., U.S. (ăl-à-mō'sà)	102	37.25N	105.50W
Åland, *see* Ahvenanmaa, is., Fin.	140	60.36N	19.55E
Alandskiy, Russia (ä-länt'skĭ)	164a	52.14N	59.48E
Alanga Arba, Kenya	210	0.07N	40.25E
Alanya, Tur.	142	36.40N	32.10E
Alaotra, l., Madag. (ä-lä-ō'trà)	206	17.15S	48.17E
Alapayevsk, Russia (ä-lä-pä'yĕfsk)	158	57.50N	61.35E
Al 'Aqabah, Jord.	174	29.32N	35.00E
Alaquines, Mex. (ä-lä-kē'nås)	112	22.07N	99.35W
Al 'Arīsh, Egypt (a-rēsh')	173a	31.08N	33.48E
Alaska, state, U.S. (à-lăs'kà)	90a	64.00N	150.00W
Alaska, Gulf of, b., Ak., U.S.	89	57.42N	147.40W
Alaska Highway, trans., Ak., U.S.	89	63.00N	142.00W
Alaska Peninsula, pen., Ak., U.S.	89	55.50N	162.10W
Alaska Range, mts., Ak., U.S.	89	62.00N	152.18W
Al 'aṭrūn, Sudan	204	18.13N	26.44E
Alatyr', Russia (ä'lä-tür)	158	54.55N	46.30E
Alba, Italy (äl'bä)	154	44.41N	8.02E
Albacete, Spain (äl-bä-thā'tä)	142	39.00N	1.49W

ng-sing; ŋ-baŋk; N-nasalized n; nŏd; cŏmmit; ōld; ôbey; ôrder; oi-boil; fōōd; ŏ-as oo in foot; ou-out; s-soft; sh-dish; th-thin; pūre; ůnite; ûrn; stŭd; circŭs; ü-as in French tu; '-indeterminate vowel.

PLACE (Pronunciation)	PAGE	Lat. °′	Long. °′
Albachten, Ger. (äl-bä'ĸ-tĕn)	151c	51.55N	7.31E
Alba de Tormes, Spain (äl-bȧ dā tôr'mās)	152	40.48N	5.28W
Alba Iulia, Rom. (äl-bä yōō'lyȧ)	142	46.05N	23.32E
Albani, Colli, hills, Italy	153d	41.46N	12.45E
Albania, nation, Eur. (ăl-bā'nĭ-ȧ)	136	41.45N	20.00E
Albano, Lago, l., Italy (lä'-gō äl-bä'nō)	153d	41.45N	12.44E
Albano Laziale, Italy (äl-bä'nō lät-zē-ä'lā)	154	41.44N	12.43E
Albany, Austl. (ôl'bȧ-nĭ)	196	35.00S	118.00E
Albany, Ca., U.S.	100b	37.54N	122.18W
Albany, Ga., U.S.	90	31.35N	84.10W
Albany, Mo., U.S.	104	40.14N	94.18W
Albany, N.Y., U.S.	90	42.40N	73.50W
Albany, Or., U.S.	90	44.38N	123.06W
Albany, r., Can.	78	51.45N	83.30W
Albany Park, neigh., Il., U.S.	227a	41.58N	87.43W
Al-Barājīl, Egypt	240a	30.04N	31.09E
Al Başrah, Iraq	174	30.35N	47.59E
Al Batrūn, Leb. (bä-trōōn')	173a	34.16N	35.39E
Albemarle, N.C., U.S. (ăl'bē-märl)	108	35.24N	80.36W
Albemarle Sound, strt., N.C., U.S.	90	36.00N	76.17W
Albenga, Italy (äl-bĕŋ'gä)	154	44.04N	8.13E
Alberche, r., Spain (äl-bĕr'chȧ)	152	40.08N	4.19W
Alberga, The, r., Austl. (ăl-bŭr'gȧ)	196	27.15S	135.00E
Albergaria-a-Velha, Port.	152	40.47N	8.31W
Alberhill, Ca., U.S. (ăl'bĕr-hĭl)	101a	33.43N	117.23W
Albert, Fr. (ȧl-bâr')	150	50.00N	2.49E
Albert, l., Afr. (ăl'bērt) (äl-bâr')	204	1.50N	30.40E
Albert, Parc National, rec., Zaire	210	0.05N	29.30E
Alberta, prov., Can. (ăl-bŭr'tȧ)	78	54.33N	117.10W
Alberta, Mount, mtn., Can.	80	52.18N	117.28W
Albert Edward, Mount, mtn., Pap. N. Gui. (ăl'bērt ĕd'wērd)	188	8.25S	147.25E
Albertfalva, neigh., Hung.	235g	47.27N	19.02E
Alberti, Arg. (äl-bĕ'r-tē)	123c	35.01S	60.16W
Albert Kanaal, can., Bel.	139a	51.07N	5.07E
Albert Lea, Mn., U.S. (ăl'bērt lē')	96	43.38N	93.24W
Albert Nile, r., Ug.	210	3.25N	31.35E
Alberton, Can. (ăl'bēr-tŭn)	86	46.49N	64.04W
Alberton, S. Afr.	207b	26.16S	28.08E
Albertson, N.Y., U.S.	224	40.46N	73.39W
Albertville, Fr. (ȧl-bêr-vēl')	150	45.42N	6.25E
Albertville, Al., U.S. (ăl'bērt-vĭl)	108	34.15N	86.10W
Albertville, see Kalemie, Zaire	206	5.56S	29.12E
Albi, Fr. (äl-bē')	140	43.54N	2.07E
Albia, Ia., U.S. (ăl-bĭ-ȧ)	96	41.01N	92.44W
Albina, Sur. (äl-bē'nä)	124	5.30N	54.33W
Albina, Ponta, c., Ang.	210	15.51S	11.44E
Albino, Point, c., Can. (äl-bē'nō)	95c	42.50N	79.05W
Albion, Austl.	239b	37.47S	144.49E
Albion, Mi., U.S. (ăl'bĭ-ŭn)	92	42.15N	84.50W
Albion, Ne., U.S.	96	41.42N	98.00W
Albion, N.Y., U.S.	92	43.15N	78.10W
Alboran, Isla del, i., Spain (ē's-lä-dĕl-äl-bō-rä'n)	136	35.58N	3.02W
Ålborg, Den. (ôl'bŏr)	136	57.02N	9.55E
Albuquerque, N.M., U.S. (ăl-bŭ-kûr'kē)	90	35.05N	106.40W
Albuquerque, Cayos de, is., Col.	114	12.12N	81.24W
Alburquerque, Spain (äl-bōōr-kĕr'kä)	152	39.13N	6.58W
Albury, Austl. (ôl'bĕr-ē)	196	36.00S	147.00E
Alcabideche, Port. (äl-kȧ-bē-dā'chȧ)	153b	38.43N	9.24W
Alcácer do Sal, Port. (äl-kä'sĕr dō säl')	152	38.24N	8.33W
Alcalá de Henares, Spain (äl-kä-lä' dā ā-na'rās)	153a	40.29N	3.22W
Alcalá la Real, Spain (äl-kä-lä'lä rā-äl')	152	37.27N	3.57W
Alcamo, Italy (äl'kȧ-mō)	154	37.58N	13.03E
Alcanadre, r., Spain (äl-kä-nä'drȧ)	152	41.41N	0.18W
Alcanar, Spain (äl-kä-när')	152	40.35N	0.27E
Alcañiz, Spain (äl-kän-yēth')	142	41.03N	0.08W
Alcântara, Braz. (äl-kän'tȧ-rȧ)	124	2.17S	44.29W
Alcântara, neigh., Port.	234d	38.42N	9.10W
Alcaraz, Spain (äl-kä-räth')	152	38.39N	2.28W
Alcaudete, Spain (äl-kou-dhä'tā)	152	37.38N	4.05W
Alcázar de San Juan, Spain (äl-kä'thär dā sän hwän')	142	39.22N	3.12W
Alcira, Spain (ä-thē'rä)	152	39.09N	0.26W
Alcoa, Tn., U.S. (ăl-kō'ȧ)	108	35.45N	84.00W
Alcobendas, Spain (äl-kō-bĕn'dȧs)	153a	40.32N	3.39W
Alcochete, Port. (äl-kō-chä'ta)	153b	38.45N	8.58W
Alcorcón, Spain	153a	40.22N	3.50W
Alcorta, Arg. (ȧl-kôr'tä)	123c	33.32S	61.08W
Alcova Reservoir, res., Wy., U.S. (ăl-kō'vȧ)	98	42.31N	106.33W
Alcove, Can. (ăl-kōv')	77c	45.41N	75.55W
Alcoy, Spain (äl-koi')	142	38.42N	0.30W
Alcudia, Bahía de, b., Spain (bä-ē'ä-dē-äl-kōō-dhē'ȧ)	152	39.48N	3.20E
Aldabra Islands, is., Sey. (äl-dä'brä)	206	9.16S	46.17E
Aldama, Mex.	106	28.50N	105.54W
Aldama, Mex. (äl-dä'mä)	112	22.54N	98.04W
Aldan, Russia	158	58.46N	125.19E
Aldan, r., Russia	158	63.00N	134.00E
Aldan Plateau, plat., Russia	162	57.42N	130.28E
Aldanskaya, Russia	158	61.52N	135.29E
Aldeia, Braz.	230d	23.30S	46.51E
Aldenham, Eng., U.K.	231	51.40N	0.21W
Aldenhoven, Ger. (ăl'dĕn-hō'vĕn)	151c	50.54N	6.18E
Aldenrade, neigh., Ger.	232	51.31N	6.44E
Aldergrove, Can. (ôl'dēr-grōv)	100d	49.03N	122.28W
Alderney, i., Guernsey (ôl'dēr-nĭ)	150	49.43N	2.11W
Aldershot, Eng., U.K. (ôl'dēr-shŏt)	144	51.14N	0.46W
Alderson, W.V., U.S. (ôl-dēr-sŭn)	92	37.40N	80.40W
Alderwood Manor, Wa., U.S. (ôl'dēr-wŏŏd măn'ŏr)	100a	47.49N	122.18W
Aldridge-Brownhills, Eng., U.K.	138a	52.38N	1.55W
Aledo, Il., U.S. (ȧ-lē'dō)	104	41.12N	90.47W
Aleg, Maur.	204	17.03N	13.55W
Alegre, Braz. (ȧlĕ'grĕ)	123a	20.41S	41.32W
Alegre, r., Braz.	126b	22.22S	43.34W
Alegrete, Braz. (ä-lā-grā'tā)	126	29.46S	55.44W
Aleksandrov, Russia (ä-lyĕk-sän' drôf)	160	56.24N	38.45E
Aleksandrovsk, Russia	158	51.02N	142.21E
Aleksandrovsk, Russia (ä-lyĕk-sän'drôfsk)	164a	59.11N	57.36E
Aleksandrów Kujawski, Pol. (ä-lĕk-säh'drōōv kōō-yav'skē)	148	52.54N	18.45E
Alekseyevka, Russia (ä-lyĕk-sā-yĕf'kȧ)	156	50.39N	38.40E
Aleksin, Russia (ä-lyĕk-sĭn)	156	54.31N	37.07E
Aleksinac, Yugo. (ȧ-lyĕk-sē-nȧk')	154	43.33N	21.42E
Alemán, Presa, res., Mex. (prä'sä-lē-mȧ'n)	112	18.20N	96.35W
Alem Paraíba, Braz. (ä-lĕ'm-pȧ-rȧē'bȧ)	123a	21.54S	42.40W
Alençon, Fr. (ȧ-läN-sôN')	140	48.26N	0.08E
Alenquer, Braz. (ä-lĕŋ-kĕr')	124	1.58S	54.44W
Alenquer, Port.	152	39.04N	9.01W
Alentejo, hist. reg., Port. (ä-lĕŋ-tä'zhō)	152	38.05N	7.45W
Alenuihaha Channel, strt., Hi., U.S. (ä'lā-nōō-ē-hä'hä)	88a	20.20N	156.05W
Aleppo, Syria (ȧ-lĕp-ō)	174	36.10N	37.18E
Alès, Fr. (ä-lĕs')	140	44.07N	4.06E
Alessandria, Italy (ä-lĕs-sän'drē-ä)	142	44.53N	8.35E
Ålesund, Nor. (ô'lĕ-sŏŏn')	146	62.28N	6.14E
Aleutian Islands, is., Ak., U.S. (ȧ-lu'shăn)	90b	52.40N	177.30W
Aleutian Trench, deep	89a	50.40N	177.10E
Alevina, Mys, c., Russia	158	58.49N	151.44E
Alexander Archipelago, is., Ak., U.S. (ăl-ĕg-zăn'dēr)	89	57.05N	138.10W
Alexander City, Al., U.S.	108	32.55N	85.55W
Alexander Indian Reserve, I.R., Can.	77g	53.47N	114.00W
Alexander Island, i., Ant.	213	71.00S	71.00W
Alexandra, S. Afr. (ăl-ex-ăn'drȧ)	212d	26.07S	28.07E
Alexandria, Austl. (ăl-ĕg-zăn'drĭ-ȧ)	196	19.00S	136.56E
Alexandria, Can.	84	45.50N	74.35W
Alexandria, Egypt	204	31.12N	29.58E
Alexandria, Rom.	154	43.55N	25.21E
Alexandria, S. Afr. (ăl-ĕx-ăn-drĭ-ȧ)	207c	33.40S	26.26E
Alexandria, In., U.S.	92	40.20N	85.20W
Alexandria, La., U.S.	90	31.18N	92.28W
Alexandria, Mn., U.S.	96	45.53N	95.23W
Alexandria, S.D., U.S.	96	43.39N	97.45W
Alexandria, Va., U.S. (ăl-ĕg-zăn'drĭ-ȧ)	90	38.50N	77.05W
Alexandria Bay, N.Y., U.S.	92	44.20N	75.55W
Alexandroúpolis, Grc.	142	40.41N	25.51E
Alfaro, Spain (äl-färō)	152	42.08N	1.43W
Al-Fāshir, Sudan (fä'shēr)	204	13.38N	25.21E
Al Fashn, Egypt	212b	28.47N	30.53E
Al Fayyūm, Egypt	204	29.14N	30.48E
Alfenas, Braz. (äl-fĕ'nȧs)	123a	21.26S	45.55W
Alfiós, r., Grc.	154	37.33N	21.50E
Al Firdān, Egypt (fer-dän')	212b	30.43N	32.20E
Alfortville, Fr.	233c	48.49N	2.25E
Alfred, Can. (ăl'frĕd)	77c	45.34N	74.52W
Alfreton, Eng., U.K. (ăl'fēr-tŭn)	138a	53.06N	1.23W
Algarve, hist. reg., Port. (äl-gär'vĕ)	152	37.15N	8.12W
Algeciras, Spain (äl-hä-thē'räs)	152	36.08N	5.25W
Algeria, nation, Afr. (ăl-gē'rĭ-ȧ)	204	28.45N	1.00E
Algés, Port.	234d	38.42N	9.13W
Algete, Spain (äl-hä'tä)	153a	40.36N	3.30W
Al Ghaydah, Yemen	176	16.12N	52.15E
Alghero, Italy (äl-gâ'rō)	142	40.32N	8.22E
Algiers, Alg. (ăl-jērs)	204	36.51N	2.56E
Algoa, Tx., U.S. (ăl-gō'ȧ)	107a	29.24N	95.11W
Algoma, Wa., U.S.	100a	47.17N	122.15W
Algoma, Wi., U.S.	96	44.38N	87.29W
Algona, Ia., U.S.	96	43.04N	94.11W
Algonac, Mi., U.S. (ăl'gō-năk)	92	42.35N	82.30W
Algonquin, Il., U.S. (ăl-gŏŋ'kwĭn)	95a	42.10N	88.17W
Algonquin Provincial Park, rec., Can.	90	45.50N	78.20W
Alhama de Granada, Spain (äl-hä'mä)	152	37.00N	3.59W
Alhama de Murcia, Spain	152	37.50N	1.24W
Alhambra, Ca., U.S. (ăl-hăm'brȧ)	101a	34.05N	118.08W
Al Ḩammān, Egypt	142	30.46N	29.42E
Alhandra, Port. (äl-yän'drȧ)	153b	38.55N	9.01W
Alhaurín, Spain (ä-lou-rēn')	152	36.40N	4.40W
Al Ḩawāmidīyah, Egypt	240a	29.54N	31.15E
Al Ḩawrah, Yemen	176	13.49N	47.37E
Al Ḩawţah, Yemen	174	15.58N	48.26E
Al Ḩayy, Iraq	176	32.10N	46.03E
Al Ḩijāz, reg., Sau. Ar.	174	23.45N	39.08E
Al Hirmil, Leb.	173a	34.23N	36.22E
Alhos Vedros, Port. (äl'yōs'vā'drōs)	153b	38.39N	9.02W
Alhucemas, Baie d', b., Afr.	152	35.18N	3.50W
Al Ḩudaydah, Yemen	174	14.43N	43.03E
Al Hufūf, Sau. Ar.	174	25.15N	49.43E
Al Ḩulwān, Egypt (hĕl'wän)	212b	29.51N	31.20E
Aliákmon, r., Grc. (äl-ē-äk'mōn)	142	40.26N	22.17E
Alibori, r., Benin	208	11.40N	2.55E
Alicante, Spain (ä-lē-kän'tä)	142	38.20N	0.30W
Alice, S. Afr. (ăl-ĭs)	207c	32.47S	26.51E
Alice, Tx., U.S. (ăl'ĭs)	106	27.45N	98.04W
Alice, Punta, c., Italy (ä-lē'chĕ)	154	39.23N	17.10E
Alice Arm, Can.	80	55.29N	129.29W
Alicedale, S. Afr. (ăl'ĭs-dāl)	207c	33.18S	26.04E
Alice Springs, Austl. (ăl'ĭs)	196	23.38S	133.56E
Alicudi, i., Italy (ä-lē-kōō'dē)	154	38.34N	14.21E
Alifkulovo, Russia (ä-lĭf-kŭ'lô-vô)	164a	55.57N	62.06E
Alīgarh, India (ä-lē-gŭr')	174	27.58N	78.08E
Al-Imām, neigh., Egypt	240a	30.01N	31.15E
Alingsås, Swe. (ä'lĭŋ-sôs)	146	57.57N	12.30E
Alipore, neigh., India	236a	22.31N	88.18E
Aliquippa, Pa., U.S. (ăl-ĭ-kwĭp'ȧ)	95e	40.37N	80.15W
Al Iskandarīyah, see Alexandria, Egypt	212b	31.12N	29.58E
Aliwal North, S. Afr. (ä-lē-wäl')	206	31.09S	28.26E
Al Jafr, Qa'al, pl., Jord.	173a	30.15N	36.24E
Al Jaghbūb, Libya	204	29.46N	24.32E
Al Jawārah, Oman	176	18.55N	57.17E
Al Jawf, Libya	204	24.14N	23.15E
Al Jawf, Sau. Ar.	174	29.45N	39.30E
Aljezur, Port. (äl-zhä-zōōr')	152	37.18N	8.52W
Al Jīzah, Egypt	212b	30.01N	31.12E
Al Jufrah, oasis, Libya	204	29.30N	15.16E
Al Junaynah, Sudan	176	13.27N	22.27E
Aljustrel, Port. (äl-zhōō-strĕl')	152	37.44N	8.23W
Al Kāb, Egypt	212c	30.56N	32.19E
Al Kāmilīn, Sudan (käm-lēn')	204	15.09N	33.06E
Al Karak, Jord. (kĕ-räk')	173a	31.11N	35.42E
Al Karnak, Egypt (kär'nak)	212b	25.42N	32.43E
Al Khābūrah, Oman	174	23.45N	57.30E
Al Khalīl, Isr. Occ.	173a	31.31N	35.07E
Al Khandaq, Sudan (kän-dăk')	204	18.38N	30.29E
Al Khārijah, Egypt	176	25.26N	30.33E
Al Khums, Libya	204	32.35N	14.10E
Al Khurmah, Sau. Ar.	174	21.37N	41.44E
Al Kiswah, Syria	173a	33.31N	36.13E
Alkmaar, Neth. (älk-mär')	144	52.39N	4.42E
Al Kufrah, oasis, Libya	204	24.45N	22.45E
Al-Kunayyisah, Egypt	240a	29.59N	31.11E
Al Kuntillah, Egypt	173a	29.59N	34.42E
Al Kuwayt, Kuw. (kōō-wit)	174	29.04N	47.59E
Al Lādhiqīyah, Syria	174	35.32N	35.51E
Allagash, r., Me., U.S. (ăl'ȧ-găsh)	86	46.50N	69.24W
Allāhābād, India (ŭl-ŭ-hä-bäd')	174	25.32N	81.53E
All American Canal, can., Ca., U.S. (âl ȧ-mĕr'ĭ-kăn)	102	32.43N	115.12W
Alland, Aus.	139e	48.04N	16.05E
Allariz, Spain (äl-yä-rēth')	142	42.10N	7.48W
Allatoona Lake, res., Ga., U.S. (ăl'ȧ-tōōn'ȧ)	108	34.05N	84.57W
Allauch, Fr. (ä-lē'ō)	150a	43.21N	5.30E
Allaykha, Russia (ä-lī'ĸȧ)	158	70.32N	148.53E
Allegan, Mi., U.S. (ăl'ē-găn)	92	42.30N	85.55W
Allegany Indian Reservation, I.R., N.Y., U.S. (ăl-ē-gā'nĭ)	92	42.05N	78.55W
Allegheny, r., Pa., U.S.	92	41.10N	79.20W
Allegheny Front, mtn., U.S.	92	38.12N	80.03W
Allegheny Mountains, mts., U.S.	90	37.35N	81.55W
Allegheny Plateau, plat., U.S.	92	39.00N	81.15W
Allegheny Reservoir, res., U.S.	92	41.50N	78.55W
Allen, Ok., U.S. (ăl'ĕn)	104	34.51N	96.26W
Allen, Lough, l., Ire. (lŏk ăl'ĕn)	144	54.07N	8.09W
Allendale, N.J., U.S. (ăl'ĕn-dāl)	94a	41.02N	74.08W
Allendale, S.C., U.S.	108	33.00N	81.19W
Allende, Mex.	106	28.20N	100.50W
Allende, Mex. (äl-yĕn'dā)	112	18.23N	92.49W
Allen Park, Mi., U.S.	226c	42.15N	83.13W
Allentown, Pa., U.S. (ălĕn-toun)	90	40.35N	75.30W
Alleppey, India (ȧ-lĕp'ē)	175c	9.33N	76.22E
Aller, r., Ger. (äl'ĕr)	148	52.43N	9.50E
Allerton, Ma., U.S.	223a	42.18N	70.53W
Allerton, neigh., Eng., U.K.	233a	53.22N	2.53W
Alliance, Ne., U.S. (ȧ-lī'ăns)	90	42.06N	102.53W
Alliance, Oh., U.S.	92	40.55N	81.10W
Al Līdām, Sau. Ar.	174	20.45N	44.12E
Allier, r., Fr. (ȧ-lyā')	150	46.43N	3.03E
Alligator Point, c., La., U.S. (al'ĭ-gā-tēr)	94d	30.57N	89.41W
Allinge, Den. (äl'ĭŋ-ĕ)	146	55.16N	14.48E
Allison Park, Pa., U.S.	226b	40.34N	79.57W
Al Līth, Sau. Ar.	176	20.09N	40.16E
All Pines, Belize (ôl pīnz)	114a	16.55N	88.15W
Allston, neigh., Ma., U.S.	223a	42.22N	71.08W
Al Luḩayyah, Yemen	174	15.58N	42.48E
Alluvial City, La., U.S.	94d	29.51N	89.42W
Allyn, Wa., U.S. (ăl'ĭn)	100a	47.23N	122.51W
Alma, Can.	78	48.29N	71.42W
Alma, Can. (ăl'mȧ)	86	45.36N	64.59W
Alma, S. Afr.	212d	24.30S	28.05E
Alma, Ga., U.S.	108	31.33N	82.31W
Alma, Mi., U.S.	92	43.25N	84.40W
Alma, Ne., U.S.	104	40.08N	99.21W
Alma, Wi., U.S.	96	44.21N	91.57W
Alma-Ata, Kaz. (ăl'mȧ ȧ'tȧ)	158	43.19N	77.08E
Al Mabrak, val., Sau. Ar.	173a	29.16N	35.12E
Almada, Port. (äl-mä'dä)	153b	38.40N	9.09W
Almadén, Spain (äl-mȧ-dhän)	152	38.47N	4.50W
Al Madīnah, Sau. Ar.	174	24.26N	39.42E
Al Mafraq, Jord.	173a	32.21N	36.13E
Almagre, Laguna, l., Mex. (lä-gō'nä-äl-mä'grĕ)	112	23.48N	97.45W
Almagro, Spain (äl-mä'grō)	152	38.52N	3.41W
Al Maḩallah al Kubrā, Egypt	212b	30.58N	31.10E
Al Manāmah, Bahr.	174	26.01N	50.33E
Al-Manāwāt, Egypt	240a	29.55N	31.14E
Almanor, Lake, l., Ca., U.S. (ăl-măn'ôr)	102	40.11N	121.20W
Almansa, Spain (äl-män'sä)	152	38.52N	1.09W
Al Manshāh, Egypt	212b	26.31N	31.46E
Almansor, r., Port. (äl-män-sôr)	152	38.41N	8.27W
Al Manşūrah, Egypt	204	31.02N	31.25E
Al Manzilah, Egypt (män'za-la)	212b	31.09N	32.05E
Almanzora, r., Spain (äl-män-thō'rä)	152	37.20N	2.25W
Al Marāghah, Egypt	212b	26.41N	31.35E
Almargem do Bispo, Port. (äl-mär-zhĕN)	153b	38.51N	9.16W
Al-Marj, Libya	204	32.44N	21.08E
Al Maşīrah, i., Oman	174	20.43N	58.58E
Al Mawşil, Iraq	174	36.00N	42.53E
Almazán, Spain (äl-mä-thän')	152	41.30N	2.33W
Al Mazār, Jord.	173a	31.04N	35.41E
Al Mazra'ah, Jord.	173a	31.17N	35.33E
Almeirim, Port. (äl-māī-rēN')	152	39.13N	8.31W
Almelo, Neth. (äl'mē-lō)	144	52.20N	6.42E
Almendra, Embalse de, res., Spain	152	41.15N	6.10W

ăt; finăl; rāte; senāte; ärm; ȧsk; sofȧ; fâre; ch-choose; dh-as th in other; bē; ēvent; bĕt; recĕnt; cratēr; g-gō; gh-guttural g; bĭt; ĭ-short neutral; rīde; ĸ-guttural k as ch in German ich;

PLACE (Pronunciation)	PAGE	Lat. °'	Long. °'
Almendralejo, Spain (äl-män-drä-lā'hō)	152	38.43N	6.24W
Almería, Spain (äl-mā-rē'ä)	136	36.52N	2.28W
Almería, Golfo de, b., Spain (gôl-fô-dĕ-äl-māī-reɴ')	152	36.45N	2.26W
Älmhult, Swe. (älm'hōōlt)	146	56.35N	14.08E
Almina, Punta, c., Mor. (äl-mē'nä)	152	35.58N	5.17W
Al Minyā, Egypt	204	28.06N	30.45E
Almirante, Pan. (äl-mē-rän'tā)	114	9.18N	82.24W
Almirante, Bahía de, b., Pan.	114	9.22N	82.07W
Almirós, Grc.	154	39.13N	22.47E
Almodóvar del Campo, Spain (äl-mō-dhō'vär)	152	38.43N	4.10W
Almoloya, Mex. (äl-mō-lō'yä)	112	19.32N	99.44W
Almoloya, Mex.	113a	19.11N	99.28W
Almonte, Can. (äl-mŏn'tė)	84	45.15N	76.15W
Almonte, Spain (äl-mōn'tā)	152	37.16N	6.32W
Almonte, r., Spain	152	39.35N	5.50W
Almora, India	174	29.20N	79.40E
Al Mubarraz, Sau. Ar.	174	22.31N	46.27E
Al Mudawwarah, Jord.	173a	29.20N	36.01E
Al Mukhā (Mocha), Yemen (mō'kä)	174	13.11N	43.20E
Almuñécar, Spain (äl-mōōn-yā'kär)	152	36.44N	3.43W
Alnön, i., Swe.	146	62.20N	17.39E
Aloha, Or., U.S. (ä'lò-hä)	100c	45.29N	122.52W
Alondra, Ca., U.S.	228	33.54N	118.19W
Alor, Pulau, i., Indon. (ä'lôr)	188	8.07S	125.00E
Álora, Spain (ä'lò-rä)	152	36.49N	4.42W
Alor Gajah, Malay.	173b	2.23N	102.13E
Alor Setar, Malay. (ä'lôr stär)	188	6.10N	100.16E
Alouette, r., Can. (ä-lōō-ĕt')	100d	49.16N	122.32W
Alpena, Mi., U.S. (äl-pē'nȧ)	90	45.05N	83.30W
Alpes Cotiennes, mts., Eur.	150	44.46N	7.02E
Alphen, Neth.	139a	52.07N	4.38E
Alpiarça, Port. (äl-pyär'sȧ)	152	39.38N	8.37W
Alpine, N.J., U.S.	224	40.56N	73.56W
Alpine, Tx., U.S. (ăl'pīn)	106	30.21N	103.41W
Alps, mts., Eur. (ălps)	136	46.18N	8.42E
Alpujarra, Col. (äl-pōō-ĸä'rá)	124a	3.23N	74.56W
Al Qadārif, Sudan	204	14.03N	35.11E
Al Qāhirah, *see* Cairo, Egypt	204	30.00N	31.17E
Al Qanṭarah, Egypt	212c	30.51N	32.20E
Al Qaryah Ash Sharqīyah, Libya	204	30.36N	13.13E
Al Qaṣr, Egypt	176	25.42N	28.53E
Al Qaṭīf, Sau. Ar.	174	26.30N	50.00E
Al Qayṣūmah, Sau. Ar.	174	28.15N	46.20E
Al Qunaytirah, Syria	173a	33.09N	35.49E
Al Qunfudhah, Sau. Ar.	174	19.08N	41.05E
Al Quṣaymah, Egypt	173a	30.40N	34.23E
Al Quṣayr, Egypt	204	26.14N	34.11E
Al Qusayr, Syria	173a	34.32N	36.33E
Als, i., Den. (äls)	146	55.06N	9.40E
Alsace, hist. reg., Fr. (äl-sá's)	150	48.25N	7.24E
Alsip, Il., U.S.	227a	41.40N	87.44W
Altadena, Ca., U.S. (ăl-tă-dē'nä)	101a	34.12N	118.08W
Alta Gracia, Arg. (äl'tä grä'sē-a)	126	31.41S	64.19W
Altagracia, Ven.	124	10.42N	71.34W
Altagracia de Orituco, Ven.	125b	9.53N	66.22W
Altai Mountains, mts., Asia (äl'tī')	180	49.11N	87.15E
Alta Loma, Ca., U.S. (ăl'tă lō'mä)	101a	34.07N	117.35W
Alta Loma, Tx., U.S. (ăl'tȧ lō-mȧ)	107a	29.22N	95.05W
Altamaha, r., Ga., U.S. (ôl-tá-mȧ-hô')	108	31.50N	82.00W
Altamira, Braz. (äl-tä-mē'rä)	124	3.13S	52.14W
Altamira, Mex.	112	22.25N	97.55W
Altamirano, Arg. (äl-tä-mė-rä'nō)	126	35.26S	58.12W
Altamura, Italy (äl-tä-mōō'rä)	142	40.40N	16.35E
Altar of Heaven, pt. of i., China	236b	39.53N	116.25E
Altar of the Earth, rel., China	236b	39.57N	116.24E
Altar of the Moon, rel., China	236b	39.55N	116.20E
Altar of the Sun, rel., China	236b	39.54N	116.27E
Altavista, Va., U.S. (ăl-tä-vĭs'tȧ)	108	37.08N	79.14W
Altay, China (äl-tä)	180	47.52N	86.50E
Altenburg, Ger. (äl-tĕn-bōōrgh)	148	50.59N	12.27E
Altenderne Oberbecker, neigh., Ger.	232	51.35N	7.33E
Altenessen, neigh., Ger.	232	51.29N	7.00E
Altenhagen, neigh., Ger.	232	51.22N	7.28E
Altenmarkt an der Triesting, Aus.	139e	48.02N	16.00E
Altenvoerde, Ger.	232	51.18N	7.22E
Alter do Chão, Port. (äl-tĕr'dò shäɴ'ōɴ)	152	39.13N	7.38W
Altiplano, pl., Bol. (äl-tē-plá'nō)	124	18.38S	68.20W
Altlandsberg, Ger. (ält länts'bĕrgh)	139b	52.34N	13.44E
Altlünen, Ger.	232	51.38N	7.31E
Altmannsdorf, neigh., Aus.	235e	48.10N	16.20E
Alto, La., U.S. (ăl'tō)	106	32.21N	91.52W
Alto da Moóca, neigh., Braz.	230d	23.34S	46.35W
Alto Marañón, Río, r., Peru (rē'ō-ȧl'tô-mä-rän-yō'n)	124	8.18S	77.13W
Altomünster, Ger. (äl'tō-mün'stĕr)	139d	48.24N	11.16E
Alton, Can. (ôl'tŭn)	77d	43.52N	80.05W
Alton, Il., U.S.	90	38.53N	90.11W
Altona, Austl.	195a	37.52S	144.50E
Altona, Can.	82	49.06N	97.33W
Altona, Ger. (äl'tō-nȧ)	139c	53.33N	9.54E
Altona North, Austl.	239b	37.50S	144.51E
Altoona, Al., U.S. (ăl-tōō'nȧ)	108	34.01N	86.15W
Altoona, Pa., U.S.	90	40.25N	78.25W
Altoona, Wa., U.S.	100c	46.16N	123.39W
Alto Rio Doce, Braz. (äl'tô-rē'ō-dō'sĕ)	123a	21.02S	43.23W
Alto Songo, Cuba (äl-fō-sôŋ'gō)	116	20.10N	75.45W
Altotonga, Mex. (ál-tō-tôŋ'gä)	112	19.44N	97.13W
Alto Velo, i., Dom. Rep. (äl-tō-vĕ'lō)	116	17.30N	71.35W
Altrincham, Eng., U.K. (ôl'trĭng-ăm)	138a	53.18N	2.21W
Altruppin, Ger. (ält rōō'ppēn)	139b	52.56N	12.50E
Altun Shan, mts., China (äl-tòn shän)	180	36.58N	85.09E
Alturas, Ca., U.S. (ăl-tōō'rȧs)	98	41.29N	120.33W
Altus, Ok., U.S. (ăl'tŭs)	104	34.38N	99.20W
Al 'Ubaylah, Sau. Ar.	176	21.59N	50.57E
Al-Uḍayyah, Sudan	204	12.06N	28.16E

PLACE (Pronunciation)	PAGE	Lat. °'	Long. °'
Alūksne, Lat. (ä'lòks-nĕ)	160	57.24N	27.04E
Alumette Island, i., Can. (ȧ-lü-mĕt')	84	45.50N	77.00W
Alum Rock, Ca., U.S.	100b	37.23N	121.50W
Al 'Uqaylah, Libya	204	30.15N	19.07E
Al Uqṣur, Egypt	204	25.38N	32.59E
Alushta, Ukr. (ä'lsh-tȧ)	156	44.39N	34.23E
Alva, Ok., U.S. (ăl'vȧ)	104	36.46N	98.41W
Alvanley, Eng., U.K.	233a	53.16N	2.45W
Alvarado, Mex. (äl-vä-rä'dhō)	112	18.48N	95.45W
Alvarado, Luguna de, l., Mex. (lä-gò'nä-dĕ-äl-vä-rà'dò)	112	18.44N	95.45W
Älvdalen, Swe. (ĕlv'dä-lĕn)	146	61.14N	14.04E
Alverca, Port. (al-vĕr'kȧ)	153b	38.53N	9.02W
Alvesta, Swe. (äl-vĕs'tä)	146	56.55N	14.29E
Alvin, Tx., U.S. (ăl'vĭn)	107a	29.25N	95.14W
Alvinópolis, Braz. (äl-vēnō'pō-lės)	123a	20.07S	43.03W
Alviso, Ca., U.S. (äl-vī'sō)	100b	37.26N	121.59W
Al Wajh, Sau. Ar.	174	26.15N	36.32E
Alwar, India (ŭl'wŭr)	174	27.39N	76.39E
Al Wāsiṭah, Egypt	212b	29.21N	31.15E
Alytus, Lith. (ä'lė-tòs)	146	54.25N	24.05E
Amacuzac, r., Mex. (ä-mä-kōō-zák)	112	18.00N	99.03W
Amadeus, l., Austl. (ăm-ȧ-dē'ŭs)	196	24.30S	131.25E
Amadjuak, l., Can. (ä-mädj'wăk)	78	64.50N	69.20W
Amadora, Port.	153b	38.45N	9.14W
Amagasaki, Japan (ä'mä-gä-sä'kė)	187	34.43N	135.25E
Ama Keng, Sing.	236c	1.24N	103.42E
Amakusa-Shimo, i., Japan (ämä-kōō'sä shē-mō)	186	32.24N	129.35E
Åmål, Swe. (ô'môl)	146	59.05N	12.40E
Amalfi, Col. (ä'mȧ'l-fē)	124a	6.55N	75.04W
Amalfi, Italy (ä-mä'l-fē)	153c	40.23N	14.36E
Amaliás, Grc. (ȧ-măl'yȧs)	154	37.48N	21.23E
Amalner, India	178	21.07N	75.06E
Amambai, Serra de, mts., S.A.	124	20.06S	57.08W
Amami, i., Japan	180	28.10N	129.55E
Amapala, Hond. (ä-mä-pä'lä)	114	13.16N	87.39W
Amarante, Braz. (ä-mä-rän'tä)	124	6.17S	42.43W
Amargosa, r., Ca., U.S. (ȧ'mär-gō'sȧ)	102	35.55N	116.45W
Amarillo, Tx., U.S. (ăm-ȧ-rĭl'ō)	90	35.14N	101.49W
Amaro, Mount, mtn., Italy (ä-mä'rō)	142	42.07N	14.07E
Amaroúsion, Grc.	235d	38.03N	23.49E
Amasya, Tur. (ä-mä'sė-ȧ)	142	40.40N	35.50E
Amatenango, Mex. (ä-mä-tä-naŋ'gō)	112	16.30N	92.29W
Amatignak, i., Ak., U.S. (ä-mȧ'tė-näk)	89a	51.12N	178.30W
Amatique, Bahía de, b., N.A. (bä-ē'ä-dē-ä-mä-tē'kā)	114	15.58N	88.50W
Amatitlán, Guat. (ä-mä-tė-tlän')	114	14.27N	90.39W
Amatlán de Cañas, Mex. (ä-mät-län'dā kän-yäs)	112	20.50N	104.22W
Amazonas, state, Braz. (ä-mä-thō'näs)	124	4.15S	64.30W
Amazonas, Rio (Amazon), r., S.A. (rē'ō-ä-mä-thō'näs)	124	2.03S	53.18W
Ambāla, India (ŭm-bä'lŭ)	174	30.31N	76.48E
Ambalema, Col. (äm-bä-lā'mä)	124	4.47N	74.45W
Ambarchik, Russia (ŭm-bär'chĭk)	158	69.39N	162.18E
Ambarnāth, India	179b	19.12N	73.10E
Ambato, Ec. (äm-bä'tō)	124	1.15S	78.30W
Ambatondrazaka, Madag.	206	17.58S	48.43E
Amberg, Ger. (äm'bĕrgh)	148	49.26N	11.51E
Ambergris Cay, i., Belize (ăm'bĕr-grēs kāz)	114a	18.04N	87.43W
Ambergris Cays, is., T./C. Is.	116	21.20N	71.40W
Ambérieu-en-Bugey, Fr. (äɴ-bā-rē-u')	150	45.57N	5.21E
Ambert, Fr. (äɴ-bĕr')	150	45.32N	3.41E
Ambil Island, i., Phil. (äm'bēl)	189a	13.51N	120.25E
Ambler, Pa., U.S. (ăm'blēr)	94f	40.09N	75.13W
Amboise, Fr. (äɴ-bwăz')	150	47.25N	0.56E
Ambon, Indon.	188	3.45S	128.17E
Ambon, Pulau, i., Indon.	188	4.50S	128.45E
Ambositra, Madag. (äɴ-bò-sē'trȧ)	206	20.31S	47.28E
Amboy, Il., U.S. (ăm'boi)	92	41.41N	89.15W
Amboy, Wa., U.S.	100c	45.55N	122.27W
Ambre, Cap d', c., Madag.	206	12.06S	49.15E
Ambridge, Pa., U.S. (ăm'brĭdj)	95e	40.36N	80.13W
Ambrim, i., Vanuatu	196	16.25S	168.15E
Ambriz, Ang.	206	7.50S	13.06E
Amchitka, i., Ak., U.S. (ăm-chĭt'kȧ)	89a	51.25N	178.10E
Amchitka Passage, strt., Ak., U.S.	89a	51.30N	179.36W
Amealco, Mex. (ä-mä-äl'kō)	112	20.12N	100.08W
Ameca, Mex. (ä-mĕ'kä)	110	20.34N	104.02W
Amecameca, Mex. (ä-mȧ-kä-mä'kä)	112	19.06N	98.46W
Ameide, Neth.	139a	51.57N	4.57E
Ameixoera, neigh., Port.	234d	38.47N	9.10W
Ameland, i., Neth.	144	53.29N	5.54E
Amelia, Oh., U.S. (ȧ-mēl'yȧ)	95f	39.01N	84.12W
American, South Fork, r., Ca., U.S. (ȧ-mĕr'ĭ-kăn)	102	38.43N	120.45W
Americana, Braz. (ä-mĕ-rē-kä'nȧ)	123a	22.46S	47.19W
American Falls, Id., U.S. (ȧ-mĕ-ĭ-kăn)	98	42.45N	112.53W
American Falls Reservoir, res., Id., U.S.	90	42.56N	113.18W
American Fork, Ut., U.S.	102	40.20N	111.50W
American Highland, plat., Ant.	213	72.00S	79.00E
American Samoa, dep., Oc.	2	14.20S	170.00W
Americus, Ga., U.S. (ȧ-mĕr'ĭ-kŭs)	90	32.04N	84.15W
Amersfoort, Neth. (ä'mĕrz-fōrt)	139a	52.08N	5.23E
Amersham, Eng., U.K.	231	51.40N	0.38W
Amery, Can. (ā'mēr-ė)	78	56.34N	94.03W
Amery, Wi., U.S.	96	45.19N	92.24W
Ames, Ia., U.S. (āmz)	96	42.00N	93.36W
Amesbury, Ma., U.S. (āmz'bĕr-ė)	87a	42.51N	70.56W
Amfissa, Grc. (ȧm-fĭ'sȧ)	154	38.32N	22.26E
Amga, Russia (ŭm-gä')	158	61.08N	132.09E
Amga, r., Russia	162	61.41N	133.11E
Amgun', r., Russia	162	52.30N	138.00E
Amherst, Can. (ăm'hĕrst)	78	45.49N	64.14W
Amherst, N.Y., U.S.	226a	42.58N	78.48W

PLACE (Pronunciation)	PAGE	Lat. °'	Long. °'
Amherst, Oh., U.S.	95d	41.24N	82.13W
Amherst, i., Can.	84	44.08N	76.45W
Amiens, Fr. (ä-myäɴ')	140	49.54N	2.18E
Amirante Islands, is., Sey.	4	6.02S	52.30E
Amisk Lake, l., Can.	82	54.35N	102.13W
Amistad Reservoir, res., N.A.	106	29.20N	101.00W
Amite, La., U.S. (ă-mēt')	106	30.43N	90.32W
Amite, r., La., U.S.	106	30.45N	90.48W
Amity, Pa., U.S. (ăm'ĭ-tĭ)	95e	40.02N	80.11W
Amityville, N.Y., U.S. (ăm'ĭ-tĭ-vĭl)	94a	40.41N	73.24W
Amlia, i., Ak., U.S. (ȧ'mlēä)	89a	52.00N	173.28W
'Ammān, Jord. (äm'mȧn)	174	31.57N	35.57E
Ammersee, l., Ger. (äm'mĕr)	139d	48.00N	11.08E
Amnicon, r., Wi., U.S. (ăm'nė-kŏn)	101h	46.35N	91.56W
Amorgós, i., Grc. (ä-môr'gōs)	142	36.47N	25.47E
Amory, Ms., U.S. (āmō-rē)	108	33.58N	88.27W
Amos, Can. (ā'mŭs)	78	48.31N	78.04W
Amoy, *see* Xiamen, China	180	24.30N	118.10E
Amparo, Braz. (äm-pá'-rô)	123a	22.43S	46.44W
Amper, r., Ger. (äm'pĕr)	139d	48.18N	11.32E
Amposta, Spain (äm-pōs'tä)	152	40.42N	0.34E
Amqui, Can.	86	48.28N	67.28W
Amrāvati, India	174	20.58N	77.47E
Amritsar, India (ŭm-rĭt'sŭr)	174	31.43N	74.52E
Amstelveen, Neth.	139a	52.18N	4.51E
Amsterdam, Neth. (äm-stĕr-däm')	136	52.21N	4.52E
Amsterdam, N.Y., U.S. (ăm'stĕr-dăm)	92	42.55N	74.10W
Amsterdam, Île, i., F.S.A.T.	213	37.52S	77.32E
Amstetten, Aus. (äm'stĕt-ĕn)	148	48.09N	14.53E
Am Timan, Chad (äm'tė-män')	204	11.18N	20.30E
Amu Darya, r., Asia (ä-mò-dä'rēä)	158	38.30N	64.00E
Amukta Passage, strt., Ak., U.S. (ä-mōōk'tȧ)	89a	52.30N	172.00W
Amundsen Gulf, b., Can. (ä'mŭn-sĕn)	78	70.17N	123.28W
Amundsen Sea, sea, Ant.	213	72.00S	110.00W
Amungen, l., Swe.	146	61.07N	16.00E
Amur, r., Asia	158	49.00N	136.00E
Amurskiy, Russia (ä-mûr'skĭ)	164a	52.35N	59.36E
Amurskiy, Zaliv, b., Russia (zä'lĭf ä-mòr'skĭ)	186	43.20N	131.40E
Amusgos, Mex.	112	16.39N	98.09W
Amuyao, Mount, mtn., Phil. (ä-mōō-yä'ō)	189a	17.04N	121.09E
Amvrakikos Kólpos, b., Grc.	154	39.00N	21.00E
Amyun, Leb.	173a	34.18N	35.48E
Anabar, r., Russia (ăn-ȧ-băr')	162	71.15N	113.00E
Anaco, Ven. (ä-nȧ'kô)	125b	9.29N	64.27W
Anaconda, Mt., U.S. (ăn-ȧ-kŏn'dȧ)	90	46.07N	112.55W
Anacortes, Wa., U.S. (ăn-ȧ-kôr'tĕz)	100a	48.30N	122.37W
Anacostia, neigh., D.C., U.S.	225d	38.52N	76.59W
Anadarko, Ok., U.S. (ăn-ȧ-där'kō)	104	35.05N	98.14W
Anadyr', Russia (ŭ-nȧ-dĭr')	158	64.47N	177.01E
Anadyr, r., Russia	162	65.30N	172.45E
Anadyrskiy Zaliv, b., Russia	158	64.10N	178.00W
'Ānah, Iraq	176	34.28N	41.56E
Anaheim, Ca., U.S. (ăn'ȧ-hīm)	101a	33.50N	117.55W
Anahuac, Tx., U.S. (ä-nä'wăk)	107a	29.46N	94.41W
Ānai Mudi, mtn., India	178	10.10N	77.00E
Anama Bay, Can.	82	51.56N	98.05W
Ana María, Cayos, is., Cuba	116	21.25N	78.50W
Anambas, Kepulauan, is., Indon. (ä-näm-bäs)	188	2.41N	106.38E
Anamosa, Ia., U.S. (ăn-ȧ-mō'sȧ)	96	42.06N	91.18W
Anan'yev, Ukr. (ȧ-nä'nyĕf)	160	47.43N	29.59E
Anapa, Russia (ȧ-nä'pä)	160	44.54N	37.19E
Anápolis, Braz. (ä-nä'pō-lės)	124	16.17S	48.47W
Añatuya, Arg. (ȧ-nyä-tōō'yȧ)	126	28.22S	62.45W
Anchieta, Braz. (ȧn-chyĕ'tä)	126b	22.49S	43.24W
Ancholme, r., Eng., U.K. (ăn'chŭm)	138a	53.28N	0.27W
Anchorage, Ak., U.S. (ăŋ'kĕr-ȧj)	90a	61.12N	149.48W
Anchorage, Ky., U.S.	95h	38.16N	85.32W
Anci, China (än-tsŭ)	182	39.31N	116.41E
Ancienne-Lorette, Can. (äɴ-syĕn' lō-rĕt')	77b	46.48N	71.21W
Ancon, Pan. (ăŋ-kōn')	110a	8.55N	79.32W
Ancona, Italy (än-kō'nä)	136	43.37N	13.32E
Ancud, Chile (äŋ-kōōdh')	126	41.52S	73.45W
Ancud, Golfo de, b., Chile (gôl-fō-dĕ-äŋ-kōōdh')	126	41.15S	73.00W
Anda, China	184	46.20N	125.20E
Åndalsnes, Nor.	146	62.33N	7.46E
Andalucia, hist. reg., Spain (än-dä-lōō-sē'ä)	152	37.35N	5.40W
Andalusia, Al., U.S. (ăn-dȧ-lōō'zhĭȧ)	108	31.19N	86.19W
Andaman Islands, is., India (ăn-dȧ-măn')	188	11.38N	92.17E
Andaman Sea, sea, Asia	188	12.44N	95.45E
Andarax, r., Spain	152	37.00N	2.40W
Anderlecht, Bel. (än'dĕr-lĕkt)	139a	50.49N	4.16E
Andernach, Ger. (än'dĕr-näk)	148	50.25N	7.23E
Anderson, Arg. (ȧ'n-dĕr-sōn)	123c	35.15S	60.15W
Anderson, Ca., U.S. (ăn'dĕr-sŭn)	98	40.28N	122.19W
Anderson, In., U.S.	92	40.05N	85.50W
Anderson, S.C., U.S.	90	34.30N	82.40W
Anderson, r., Can.	78	68.32N	125.12W
Andes Mountains, mts., S.A. (ăn'dēz) (än'dās)	122	13.00S	75.00W
Andheri, neigh., India	179b	19.08N	72.50E
Andhra Pradesh, state, India	174	16.00N	79.00E
Andikíthira, i., Grc.	142	35.50N	23.20E
Andizhan, Uzb. (än-dĕ-zhän')	158	40.45N	72.22E
Andong, S. Kor. (än'dŭng')	180	36.31N	128.42E
Andongwei, China (än-dòŋ-wā)	182	35.08N	119.19E
Andorra, And. (än-dŏr'rä)	152	42.38N	1.30E
Andorra, nation, Eur.	136	42.30N	2.00E
Andover, Ma., U.S. (ăn'dō-vēr)	87a	42.39N	71.08W
Andover, N.J., U.S.	94a	40.59N	74.45W
Andøya, i., Nor. (änd-ûė)	140	69.12N	14.58E
Andreanof Islands, is., Ak., U.S. (än-drā-ä'nôf)	90b	51.10N	177.00W

PLACE (Pronunciation)	PAGE	Lat. °′	Long. °′
Andrelândia, Braz. (än-drĕ-lá'n-dyà)	123a	21.45s	44.18w
Andrésy, Fr.	233c	48.59n	2.04e
Andrew Johnson National Historic Site, rec., Tn., U.S. (ăn'drōō jŏn'sŭn)	108	36.15n	82.55w
Andrews, N.C., U.S. (ăn'drōōz)	108	35.12n	83.48w
Andrews, S.C., U.S.	108	33.25n	79.32w
Andrews Air Force Base, pt. of i., Md., U.S.	225d	38.48n	76.52w
Andreyevka, Ukr. (än-drâ-yĕf'kà)	156	48.03n	37.03e
Andria, Italy (än'drê-ä)	142	41.17n	15.55e
Andros, Grc. (án'dhròs)	154	37.50n	24.54e
Ándros, i., Grc. (án'dròs)	142	37.59n	24.55e
Androscoggin, r., Me., U.S. (ăn-drŭs-kŏg'ĭn)	86	44.25n	70.45w
Andros Island, i., Bah. (ăn'drŏs)	110	24.30n	78.00w
Anefis i-n-Darane, Mali	208	18.03n	0.36e
Anegasaki, Japan (ä'nâ-gä-sä'kê)	187a	35.29n	140.02e
Aneityum, i., Vanuatu (ä-nâ-ē'tê-ŭm)	196	20.15s	169.49e
Aneta, N.D., U.S. (ă-nē'tȧ)	96	47.41n	97.57w
Aneto, Pico de, mtn., Spain (pê'kō-dĕ-ä-nĕ'tō)	136	42.35n	0.38e
Angamacutiro, Mex. (än'gä-mä-kōō-tē'rō)	112	20.08n	101.44w
Angangueo, Mex. (än-gäŋ'gwâ-ō)	112	19.36n	100.18w
Ang'angxi, China (äŋ-äŋ-shyē)	180	47.05n	123.58e
Angarsk, Russia	158	52.48n	104.15e
Ånge, Swe. (ông'ā)	146	62.31n	15.39e
Angel, Salto, wtfl., Ven. (säl'tō-á'n-hĕl)	124	5.44n	62.27w
Ángel de la Guarda, i., Mex. (á'n-hĕl-dĕ-lä-gwä'r-dä)	110	29.30n	113.00w
Angeles, Phil. (än'hâ-läs)	189a	15.09n	120.35e
Ängelholm, Swe. (ĕng'ĕl-hôlm)	146	56.14n	12.50e
Angelina, r., Tx., U.S. (ăn-jê lē'nȧ)	106	31.30n	94.53w
Angels Camp, Ca., U.S. (ān'jĕls kămp')	102	38.03n	120.33w
Angerhausen, neigh., Ger.	232	51.23n	6.44e
Ångermanälven, r., Swe.	140	64.10n	17.30e
Angermund, Ger. (án'ngĕr-mŭnd)	151c	51.20n	6.47e
Angermünde, Ger. (äng'ĕr-mûn-dĕ)	148	53.02n	14.00e
Angers, Can. (äN-zhā')	77c	45.31n	75.29w
Angers, Fr.	150	47.29n	0.36w
Angkor, hist., Kam. (äng'kôr)	188	13.52n	103.50e
Anglesey, i., Wales, U.K. (ăŋ'g'l-sê)	144	53.35n	4.28w
Angleton, Tx., U.S. (aŋ'g'l-tŭn)	107a	29.10n	95.25w
Angmagssalik, Grnld. (äŋ-mà'sá-lĭk)	76	65.40n	37.40w
Angoche, Ilha, i., Moz. (ê'lä-än-gō'chå)	206	16.20s	40.00e
Angol, Chile (aŋ-gōl')	126	37.47s	72.43w
Angola, In., U.S. (ăŋ-gō'lȧ)	92	41.35n	85.00w
Angola, nation, Afr.	206	14.15s	16.00e
Angono, Phil.	237g	14.31n	121.08e
Angora, *see* Ankara, Tur.	174	39.55n	32.50e
Angoulême, Fr. (äŋ'gōō-lâm')	150	45.40n	0.09e
Angra dos Reis, Braz. (aŋ'grä dōs rā'ēs)	123a	23.01s	44.17w
Angri, Italy (ä'n-grê)	153c	40.30n	14.35e
Anguang, China (än-gůäŋ)	184	45.28n	123.42e
Anguilla, dep., N.A.	110	18.15n	62.54w
Anguilla Cays, is., Bah. (äŋ-gwĭl'ȧ)	116	23.30n	79.35w
Anguille, Cape, c., Can. (äŋ-gē'yĕ)	86	47.55n	59.25w
Anguo, China (än-gwò)	182	38.27n	115.19e
Angyalföld, neigh., Hung.	235g	47.33n	19.05e
Anholt, i., Den. (än'hŏlt)	146	56.43n	11.34e
Anhui, prov., China (än-hwā)	180	31.30n	117.15e
Aniak, Ak., U.S. (ä-nyà'k)	89	61.32n	159.35w
Aniakchak National Monument, rec., Ak., U.S.	89	56.50n	157.50w
Anik, neigh., India	236e	19.02n	72.53e
Animas, r., Co., U.S. (ä'nê-mås)	102	37.03n	107.50w
Anina, Rom. (ä-nē'nä)	154	45.03n	21.50e
Anita, Pa., U.S. (á-nē'ȧ)	92	41.05n	79.00w
Aniva, Mys, c., Russia (mĭs á-nē'vá)	186	46.08n	143.13e
Aniva, Zaliv, b., Russia (zä'lĭf á-nē'vá)	186	46.30n	143.00e
Anjou, Can.	77a	45.37n	73.33w
Ankang, China (än-käŋ)	180	32.38n	109.10e
Ankara, Tur. (än'kȧ-rȧ)	174	39.55n	32.50e
Anklam, Ger. (än'kläm)	148	53.52n	13.43e
Ankoro, Zaire (äŋ-kō'rō)	206	6.45s	26.57e
Anloga, Ghana	208	5.47n	0.50e
Anlong, China (än-loŋ)	184	25.01n	105.32e
Anlu, China (än'lōō')	184	31.18n	113.40e
Ann, Cape, c., Ma., U.S. (ăn)	92	42.40n	70.40w
Anna, Russia (än'ä)	156	51.31n	40.27e
Anna, Il., U.S. (ăn'ȧ)	104	37.28n	89.15w
Annaba, Alg.	204	36.57n	7.39e
Annaberg-Bucholz, Ger. (än'ä-bĕrgh)	148	50.35n	13.02e
An Nafūd, des., Sau. Ar.	174	28.30n	40.30e
An Najaf, Iraq (än nä-jäf')	174	32.00n	44.25e
An Nakhl, Egypt	173a	29.55n	33.45e
Annamese Cordillera, mts., Asia	188	17.34n	105.38e
Annandale, Va., U.S.	225d	38.50n	77.12w
Annapolis, Md., U.S. (ă-năp'ô-lĭs)	90	39.00n	76.25w
Annapolis Royal, Can.	86	44.45n	65.31w
Ann Arbor, Mi., U.S. (ăn är'bĕr)	90	42.15n	83.45w
An-Narrānīyah, Egypt	240a	29.58n	31.10e
An Nāşirīyah, Iraq	174	31.08n	46.15e
An Nawfalīyah, Libya	204	30.57n	17.38e
Annecy, Fr. (án sē')	150	45.54n	6.07e
Annemasse, Fr. (än'mäs')	150	46.09n	6.13e
Annen, neigh., Ger.	232	51.27n	7.22e
Annenskoye, Kaz. (ä-nĕn'skô-yĕ)	164a	53.09n	60.25e
Annet-sur-Marne, Fr.	233c	48.56n	2.43e
Annette Island, i., Ak., U.S.	80	55.13n	131.30w
An Nhon, Viet.	188	13.55n	109.00e
Annieopsquotch Mountains, mts., Can.	86	48.37n	57.17w
Anniston, Al., U.S. (ăn'ĭs-tŭn)	90	33.39n	85.47w
Annobón, i., Eq. Gui.	203	2.00s	3.30e
Annonay, Fr. (ån'ĭs-tsiŭn)	150	45.16n	4.36e
Annotto Bay, Jam. (än-nō'tō)	116	18.15n	76.45w
An Nuhūd, Sudan	204	12.39n	28.18e
Anoka, Mn., U.S. (ȧ-nō'kȧ)	101g	45.12n	93.24w
Anori, Col. (á-nō'rê)	124a	7.01n	75.09w
Áno Viánnos, Grc.	154a	35.02n	25.26e
Anpu, China (än-pōō)	180	21.28n	110.00e
Anqiu, China (än-chyò)	182	36.26n	119.12e
Ansbach, Ger. (äns'bäk)	148	49.18n	10.35e
Anschlag, Ger.	232	51.10n	7.29e
Anse à Veau, Haiti (äNs' ä-vō')	116	18.30n	73.25w
Anse d'Hainault, Haiti (äNs'dĕnō)	116	18.30n	74.25w
Anserma, Col. (á'n-sĕ'r-mà)	124a	5.13n	75.47w
Ansermanuevo, Col. (á'n-sĕ'r-má-nwĕ'vō)	124a	4.47n	75.59w
Anshan, China	184	41.00n	123.00e
Anshun, China (än-shōōn')	180	26.12n	105.50e
Anson, Tx., U.S. (ăn'sŭn)	106	32.45n	99.52w
Anson Bay, b., Austl.	196	13.10s	130.00e
Ansŏng, S. Kor. (än'sŭng')	186	37.00n	127.12e
Ansongo, Mali	208	15.40n	0.30e
Ansonia, Ct., U.S. (ăn-sōnĭ-ȧ)	92	41.20n	73.05w
Antakya, Tur. (än-täk'yä)	174	36.20n	36.10e
Antalya, Tur. (än-tä'lê-ä) (ä-dä'lê-ä)	142	37.00n	30.50e
Antalya Körfezi, b., Tur.	142	36.40n	31.20e
Antananarivo, Madag.	206	18.51s	47.40e
Antarctica, cont.	213	80.15s	127.00e
Antarctic Peninsula, pen., Ant.	213	70.00s	65.00w
Antelope Creek, r., Wy., U.S. (ăn'tê-lōp)	98	43.29n	105.42w
Antequera, Spain (än-tĕ-kĕ'rä)	142	37.01n	4.34w
Anthony, Ks., U.S. (ăn'thô-nê)	104	37.08n	98.01w
Anthony Peak, mtn., Ca., U.S.	102	39.51n	122.58w
Anti Atlas, mts., Mor.	204	28.45n	9.30w
Antibes, Fr. (äN-tēb')	150	43.36n	7.12e
Anticosti, Île d', i., Can. (ăn-tĭ-kŏs'tê)	78	49.30n	62.00w
Antigo, Wi., U.S. (ăn'tĭ-gō)	96	45.09n	89.11w
Antigonish, Can. (ăn-tĭ-gô-nêsh')	86	45.35n	61.55w
Antigua, Guat. (än-tē'gwä)	110	14.32n	90.43w
Antigua, r., Mex.	112	19.16n	96.36w
Antigua and Barbuda, nation, N.A.	110	17.15n	61.15w
Antigua Veracruz, Mex. (än-tē'gwä vā-rä-krōōz')	112	19.18n	96.17w
Antilla, Cuba (än-tē'lyä)	116	20.50n	75.50w
Antímano, neigh., Ven.	230a	10.28n	66.59w
Antioch, Ca., U.S. (ăn'tĭ-ŏk)	100b	38.00n	121.48w
Antioch, Il., U.S.	95a	42.29n	88.06w
Antioch, Ne., U.S.	96	42.05n	102.36w
Antioquia, Col. (än-tê-ō'kêä)	124	6.34n	75.49w
Antioquia, dept., Col.	124a	6.48n	75.42w
Antlers, Ok., U.S. (ănt'lērz)	104	34.14n	95.38w
Antofagasta, Chile (än-tô-fä-gäs'tä)	126	23.32s	70.21w
Antofalla, Salar de, pl., Arg. (sà-lär'de àn'tō-fä'lä)	126	26.00s	67.52w
Antón, Pan. (än-tōn')	110	8.24n	80.15w
Antongila, Helodrano, b., Madag.	206	16.15s	50.15e
Antônio Carlos, Braz. (än-tō'nêô-kà'r-lôs)	123a	21.19s	43.45w
António Enes, Moz. (än-to'nyō ĕn'ĕs)	206	16.14s	39.58e
Antonito, Co., U.S. (ăn-tô-nē'tō)	104	37.04n	106.01w
Antonopole, Lat. (än'tô-nô-pō lyĕ)	146	56.19n	27.11e
Antony, Fr.	151b	48.45n	2.18e
Antsirabe, Madag. (änt-sê-rä'bā)	206	19.49s	47.16e
Antsiranana, Madag.	206	12.18s	49.16e
Antsla, Est. (änt'slȧ)	146	57.49n	26.29e
Antuco, vol., S.A. (än-tōō'kō)	126	37.30s	72.30w
Antwerp, Bel.	136	51.13n	4.24e
Antwerp, S. Afr.	240b	26.06s	28.10e
Antwerpen, *see* Antwerp, Bel.	136	51.13n	4.24e
Anūpgarh, India (ŭ-nòp'gŭr)	178	29.22n	73.20e
Anuradhapura, Sri L. (ŭ-nōō'rä-dŭ-pōō'rŭ)	175c	8.24n	80.25e
Anxi, China (än-shyē)	180	40.36n	95.49e
Anyang, China (än'yäng)	180	36.05n	114.22e
Anykščiai, Lith. (anīksh-chä'ē)	146	55.34n	25.04e
Anzhero-Sudzhensk, Russia (än'zhâ-rô-sòd'zhĕnsk)	158	56.08n	86.08e
Anzio, Italy (änt'zê-ō)	154	41.28n	12.39e
Anzoátegui, dept., Ven. (án-zòá'tĕ-gê)	125b	9.38n	64.45w
Aoba, i., Vanuatu	192f	15.25s	167.50e
Aomori, Japan (äô-mō'rê)	180	40.45n	140.52e
Aosta, Italy (ä-ôs'tä)	154	45.45n	7.20e
Aouk, Bahr, r., Afr. (ä-ōk')	204	9.30n	20.45e
Aoukâr, reg., Maur.	208	18.00n	9.40w
Apalachicola, Fl., U.S. (ăp-ȧ-lăch-ĭ-kō'lȧ)	108	29.43n	84.59w
Apan, Mex. (ä-pà'n)	112	19.43n	98.27w
Apango, Mex. (ä-päŋ'gō)	112	17.41n	99.22w
Apaporis, r., S.A. (ä-pä-pō'rĭs)	124	0.48n	72.32w
Aparri, Phil. (ä-pär'rē)	188	18.15n	121.40e
Apasco, Mex. (ä-pà's-kō)	112	20.33n	100.43w
Apatin, Yugo. (ŏ'pō-tĭn)	154	45.40n	19.00e
Apatzingán de la Constitución, Mex.	112	19.07n	102.21w
Apeldoorn, Neth. (ä'pĕl-dōōrn)	140	52.14n	5.55e
Apese, neigh., Nig.	240d	6.25n	3.25e
Apía, Col. (ä-pē'ä)	124a	5.07n	75.58w
Apia, W. Sam.	192a	13.50s	171.44w
Apipilulco, Mex. (ä-pĭ-pĭ-lōōl'kō)	112	18.09n	99.40w
Apishapa, r., Co., U.S. (ăp-ĭ-shä'pȧ)	104	37.40n	104.08w
Apizaco, Mex. (ä-pê-zä'kō)	112	19.18n	98.11w
Aplerbeck, neigh., Ger.	232	51.29n	7.33e
Apo, Mount, mtn., Phil. (ä'pō)	188	6.56n	125.05e
Apopka, Fl., U.S. (ä-pŏp'kȧ)	109a	28.37n	81.30w
Apopka, Lake, l., Fl., U.S.	109a	28.38n	81.50w
Apoquindo, Chile	230b	33.24s	70.32w
Apostle Islands, is., Wi., U.S. (ä-pŏs'l)	96	47.05n	90.55w
Appalachia, Va., U.S. (ăpȧ-lăch'ĭ-ȧ)	108	36.54n	82.49w
Appalachian Mountains, mts., N.A. (ăp-ȧ-lăch'ĭ-ȧn)	90	37.20n	82.00w
Appalachicola, r., Fl., U.S. (ăpȧ-lăch'ĭ-cōlä)	90	30.11n	85.00w
Äppelbo, Swe. (ĕp-ĕl-bōō)	146	60.30n	14.02e
Appelhülsen, Ger. (ä'pĕl-hül'sĕn)	151c	51.55n	7.26e
Appennino, mts., Italy (äp-pĕn-nē'nô)	136	43.48n	11.06e
Appleton, Mn., U.S. (ăp'l-tŭn)	96	45.10n	96.01w
Appleton, Wi., U.S.	90	44.14n	88.27w
Appleton City, Mo., U.S.	104	38.10n	94.02w
Appomattox, r., Va., U.S. (ăp-ô-măt'ŭks)	108	37.22n	78.09w
Aprília, Italy (ȧ-prē'lyȧ)	154	41.36n	12.40e
Apsheronskiy Poluostrov, pen., Azer.	160	40.20n	50.30e
Apt, Fr. (äpt)	150	43.54n	5.19e
Apure, r., Ven. (ä-pōō'rä)	124	8.08n	68.46w
Apurimac, r., Peru (ä-pōō-rê-mäk')	124	11.39s	73.48w
Aqaba, Gulf of, b. (ä'kà-bà)	174	28.30n	34.40e
Aqabah, Wādī al, r., Egypt	173a	29.48n	34.05e
Aquasco, Md., U.S. (ȧ'gwă'scô)	94e	38.35n	76.44w
Aquidauana, Braz. (ä-kê-däwä'nä)	124	20.24s	55.46w
Aquin, Haiti (ä-kăn')	116	18.20n	73.25w
Ara, r., Japan (ä-rä)	187a	35.40n	139.52e
Arab, Baḩr al, r., Sudan	204	9.46n	26.52e
'Arabah, Wādī, val., Egypt	212b	29.02n	32.10e
Arabatskaya Strelka (Tongue of Arabat), spit, Ukr.	156	45.50n	35.05e
Arabi, La., U.S.	94d	29.58n	90.01w
Arabian Desert, des., Egypt (ȧ-rā'bĭ-ăn)	204	27.06n	32.49e
Arabian Sea, sea (ȧ-rā'bĭ-ăn)	172	16.00n	65.15e
Aracaju, Braz. (ä-rä'kä-zhōō')	124	11.00s	37.01w
Aracati, Braz. (ä-rä'kä-tē')	124	4.31s	37.41w
Araçatuba, Braz. (ä-rä-sá-tōō'bä)	124	21.14s	50.19w
Aracena, Spain	152	37.53n	6.34w
Aracruz, Braz. (ä-rä-krōō's)	124	19.58s	40.11w
'Arad, Isr.	173a	31.20n	35.15e
Arad, Rom. (ŏ'rŏd)	142	46.10n	21.18e
Arafura Sea, sea (ä-rä-fōō'rä)	188	8.40s	130.00e
Aragon, hist. reg., Spain (ä-rä-gōn')	152	40.55n	0.45w
Aragón, r., Spain	152	42.35n	1.10w
Aragua, dept., Ven. (ä-rä'gwä)	125b	10.00n	67.05w
Aragua de Barcelona, Ven.	124	9.29n	64.48w
Araguaía, r., Braz. (ä-rä-gwä'yä)	124	8.37s	49.43w
Araguari, Braz. (ä-rä-gwä'rê)	124	18.43s	48.03w
Araguatins, Braz. (ä-rä-gwä-tēns)	124	5.41s	48.04w
Aragüita, Ven. (ärá-gwē'tá)	125b	10.13n	66.28w
Araj, oasis, Egypt (ä-räj')	142	29.05n	26.51e
Arāk, Iran	174	34.08n	49.57e
Arakan Yoma, mts., Burma (ŭ-rŭ-kŭn'yō'mà)	174	19.51n	94.13e
Arakawa, neigh., Japan	238a	35.47n	139.44e
Arakhthos, r., Grc. (är'äк-thôs)	154	39.10n	21.05e
Arakpur, neigh., India	236d	28.35n	77.10e
Aral Sea, sea, Asia	158	45.17n	60.02e
Aral'sk, Kaz. (ȧ-rälsk')	158	46.47n	62.00e
Aralsor, l., Kaz. (ä-räl'sôr')	160	49.00n	48.20e
Aramberri, Mex. (ä-räm-bĕr-rē')	112	24.05n	99.47w
Aranda, Sierra, mts., Spain	152	37.17n	3.28w
Aranda de Duero, Spain (ä-rän'dä dā dwā'rō)	152	41.43n	3.45w
Arandas, Mex. (ä-rän'däs)	112	20.43n	102.18w
Aran Island, i., Ire. (ăr'ăn)	144	54.58n	8.33w
Aran Islands, is., Ire.	140	53.04n	9.59w
Aranjuez, Spain (ä-rän-hwāth')	142	40.02n	3.24w
Aransas Pass, Tx., U.S. (ȧ-răn'sȧs pȧs)	106	27.55n	97.09w
Araouane, Mali	204	18.54n	3.33w
Arapkir, Tur. (ä-räp-kēr')	142	39.00n	38.10e
Araraquara, Braz. (ä-rä-rä-kwá'rä)	124	21.47s	48.08w
Araras, Braz. (ä-rá'räs)	123a	22.21s	47.22w
Araras, Serra das, mts., Braz. (sĕ'r-rä-däs-ä-rá'räs)	124	18.03s	53.23w
Araras, Serra das, mts., Braz.	126	23.30s	53.00w
Araras, Serra das, mts., Braz.	126b	22.24s	43.15w
Ararat, Austl. (ăr'ărăt)	196	37.17s	142.56e
Ararat, mtn., Tur.	174	39.50n	44.20e
Arari, l., Braz. (ä-rá'rē)	124	0.30s	48.50w
Araripe, Chapada do, hills, Braz. (shä-pä'dä-dô-ä-rä-rē'pĕ)	124	5.55s	40.42w
Araruama, Braz. (ä-rä-rōō-ä'mä)	123a	22.53s	42.19w
Araruama, Lagoa de, l., Braz.	123a	23.00s	42.15w
Aras, r., Asia (á-räs)	174	39.15n	47.10e
Aratuípe, Braz. (ä-rä-tōō-ē'pĕ)	124	13.12s	38.58w
Arauca, Col. (ä-rou'kä)	124	6.56n	70.45w
Arauca, r., S.A.	124	7.13n	68.43w
Aravaca, neigh., Spain	234b	40.28n	3.46w
Aravalli Range, mts., India (ä-rä'vŭ-lê)	174	24.15n	72.40e
Araya, Punta de, c., Ven. (pŭn'tä-dĕ-ä-rä'yä)	125b	10.40n	64.15w
Arayat, Phil. (ä-rä'yät)	189a	15.10n	120.44e
'Arbi, Sudan	204	20.36n	29.57e
Arboga, Swe. (är-bō'gä)	146	59.26n	15.50e
Arborea, Italy (är-bō-rē'ä)	154	39.50n	8.36e
Arbroath, Scot., U.K. (är-brōth')	144	56.36n	2.25w
Arcachon, Fr. (är-кä-shôn')	140	44.39n	1.12w
Arcachon, Bassin d', Fr. (bä-sĕn' där-kä-shôn')	150	44.42n	1.50w
Arcadia, Ca., U.S. (är-kā'dĭ-ȧ)	101a	34.08n	118.02w
Arcadia, Fl., U.S.	109a	27.12n	81.51w
Arcadia, La., U.S.	106	32.33n	92.56w
Arcadia, Wi., U.S.	96	44.15n	91.30w
Arcata, Ca., U.S. (är-kā'tȧ)	98	40.54n	124.05w
Arc de Triomphe, pt. of i., Fr.	233c	48.53n	2.17e
Arc Dome Mountain, mtn., Nv., U.S. (ärk dōm)	102	38.51n	117.21w
Arcelia, Mex. (är-sā'lê-ä)	112	18.19n	100.14w
Archbald, Pa., U.S. (ärch'bôld)	92	41.30n	75.35w
Arches National Park, Ut., U.S. (är'ches)	102	38.45n	109.35w
Archidona, Ec. (är-chê-do'nä)	124	1.01s	77.49w
Archidona, Spain (är-chê-dō'nä)	152	37.08n	4.24w
Arcis-sur-Aube, Fr. (är-sēs'sûr-ōb')	150	48.31n	4.04e
Arco, Id., U.S. (är'kō)	98	43.39n	113.15w
Arcola, Tx., U.S. (är'cōlä)	107a	29.30n	95.28w
Arcola, Va., U.S. (är'cōlä)	94e	38.57n	77.32w

ăt; finăl; rāte; senåte; ärm; åsk; sofȧ; fâre; ch-choose; dh-as th in other; bē; êvent; bĕt; recĕnt; cratẽr; g-gō; gh-guttural g; bĭt; ĭ-short neutral; rīde; к-guttural k as ch in German ich;

PLACE (Pronunciation)	PAGE	Lat. °′	Long. °′
Arcos de la Frontera, Spain (är'kōs-dā-lä-frôn-tā'rä)	152	36.44N	5.48W
Arctic Ocean, o.	56	85.00N	170.00E
Arcueil, Fr. (ärk'tīk)	233c	48.48N	2.20E
Arda, r., Bul. (är'dä)	154	41.36N	25.18E
Ardabīl, Iran	174	38.15N	48.00E
Ardahan, Tur. (är-dȧ-hän')	160	41.10N	42.40E
Ardatov, Russia (är-dȧ-tôf')	160	54.58N	46.10E
Ardennes, mts., Eur. (ȧr-dĕn')	140	50.01N	5.12E
Ardey, neigh., Ger.	232	51.26N	7.23E
Ardila, r., Eur. (är-dē'lȧ)	152	38.10N	7.15W
Ardmore, Md., U.S.	225d	38.56N	76.52W
Ardmore, Ok., U.S. (ärd'mōr)	90	34.10N	97.08W
Ardmore, Pa., U.S.	94f	40.01N	75.18W
Ardrossan, Can. (är-dros'ȧn)	77g	53.33N	113.08W
Ardsley, Eng., U.K. (ärdz'lē)	138a	53.43N	1.33W
Åre, Swe.	140	63.12N	13.12E
Arecibo, P.R. (ä-rȧ-sē'bō)	111b	18.28N	66.45W
Areeiro, Port.	234d	38.39N	9.12W
Areia Branca, Braz. (ä-rē'yä-brä'n-kä)	124	4.58S	37.02W
Arena, Point, c., Ca., U.S. (ä-rā'nȧ)	102	38.57N	123.40W
Arenas, Punta, c., Ven. (pōn'tä-rē'näs)	125b	10.57N	64.24W
Arenas de San Pedro, Spain	152	40.12N	5.04W
Arendal, Nor. (ä'rĕn-däl)	146	58.29N	8.44E
Arendonk, Bel.	139a	51.19N	5.07E
Arequipa, Peru (ä-rȧ-kē'pä)	124	16.27S	71.30W
Arezzo, Italy (ä-rĕt'sō)	142	43.28N	11.54E
Arga, r., Spain (är'gä)	152	42.35N	1.55W
Arganda, Spain (är-gän'dä)	153a	40.18N	3.27W
Argazi, l., Russia (är'gä-zĭ)	164a	55.24N	60.37E
Argazi, r., Russia	164a	55.33N	57.30E
Argentan, Fr. (ȧr-zhäN-täN')	150	48.45N	0.01W
Argentat, Fr. (ȧr-zhäN-tä')	150	45.07N	1.57E
Argenteuil, Fr. (är-zhäN-tû'y')	150	48.56N	2.15E
Argentina, nation, S.A. (är-jĕn-tē'nȧ)	126	35.30S	67.00W
Argentino, l., Arg. (är-κĕn-tē'nō)	126	50.15S	72.45W
Argenton-sur-Creuse, Fr. (är-zhäN'tôN-sür-krôs)	150	46.34N	1.28E
Argolikos Kólpos, b., Grc.	154	37.20N	23.00E
Argonne, mts., Fr. (ä'r-gôn)	150	49.21N	5.54E
Argos, Grc. (är'gŏs)	154	37.38N	22.45E
Argostólion, Grc. (är-gŏs-tô'lē-ŏn)	154	38.10N	20.30E
Arguello, Point, c., Ca., U.S. (är-gwāl'yō)	102	34.35N	120.40W
Arguin, Cap d', c., Maur.	204	20.28N	17.46W
Argun', r., Asia (ȧr-gōōn')	158	50.00N	119.00E
Argungu, Nig.	208	12.45N	4.31E
Argyle, Can. (är'gīl)	77f	50.11N	97.27W
Argyle, Mn., U.S.	96	48.21N	96.48W
Århus, Den. (ôr'hōōs)	140	56.09N	10.10E
Ariakeno-Umi, b., Japan (ä-rē'ä-κä'nō ōō'nē)	187	33.03N	130.18E
Ariake-Wan, b., Japan (ä'rē-ä'kä wän)	187	31.19N	131.15E
Ariano, Italy (ä-rē-ä'nō)	154	41.09N	15.11E
Ariari, r., Col. (ä-ryä'rē)	124a	3.34N	73.42W
Aribinda, Burkina	208	14.14N	0.52W
Arica, Chile (ä-rē'kä)	124	18.34S	70.14W
Arichat, Can. (ä-rĭ-shät')	86	45.31N	61.01W
Ariège, r., Fr. (ȧ-rē-ĕzh')	150	43.26N	1.29E
Ariel, Wa., U.S. (ā'rĭ-ĕl)	100c	45.57N	122.34W
Arieşul, r., Rom. (ä-rē-ä'shōl)	148	46.25N	23.15E
Ariguanabo, Lago de, l., Cuba (lä'gō-dē-ä-rē-gwä-nä'bō)	117a	22.52N	82.33W
Arikaree, r., Co., U.S. (ă-rĭ-kȧ-rē')	104	39.51N	102.18W
Arima, Japan (ä'rē-mä')	187b	34.48N	135.16E
Aringay, Phil. (ä-rĭŋ-gä'ē)	189a	16.25N	120.20E
Arino, neigh., Japan	238b	34.50N	135.14E
Arinos, r., Braz. (ä-rē'nōzh)	124	12.09S	56.49W
Aripuanã, r., Braz. (ȧ-rē-pwän'yȧ)	124	7.06S	60.29W
'Arīsh, Wādī al, r., Egypt (ȧ-rēsh')	173a	30.36N	34.07E
Aristazabal Island, i., Can.	80	52.30N	129.20W
Arizona, state, U.S. (ăr-ĭ-zō'nȧ)	90	34.00N	113.00W
Arjona, Spain (är-hō'nä)	152	37.58N	4.03W
Arka, r., Russia	162	60.45N	142.30E
Arkabutla Lake, res., Ms., U.S. (är-kȧ-būt'lȧ)	108	34.48N	90.00W
Arkadelphia, Ar., U.S. (är-kȧ-dĕl'fĭ-ȧ)	104	34.06N	93.05W
Arkansas, state, U.S. (är'kăn-sô) (är-kăn'sȧs)	90	34.50N	93.40W
Arkansas, r., U.S.	90	37.30N	97.00W
Arkansas City, Ks., U.S.	104	37.04N	97.02W
Arkhangelsk (Archangel), Russia (ȧr-κän'gĕlsk)	158	64.30N	40.25E
Arkhangel'skiy, Kaz. (är-kän-gĕl'skĭ)	164a	52.52N	61.53E
Arkhangel'skoye, Russia (är-kän-gĕl'skô-yĕ)	164a	54.25N	56.48E
Arklow, Ire. (ärk'lō)	144	52.47N	6.10W
Arkonam, India (är-kō-näm')	178	13.05N	79.43E
Arlanza, r., Spain (är-län-thä')	152	42.08N	3.45W
Arlanzón, r., Spain (är-län-thōn')	152	42.12N	3.58W
Arlberg Tunnel, trans., Aus. (ärl'bĕrgh)	148	47.05N	10.15E
Arles, Fr. (ärl)	150	43.42N	4.38E
Arlington, S. Afr.	212d	28.02S	27.52E
Arlington, Ga., U.S. (är'lĭng-tun')	108	31.25N	84.42W
Arlington, Ma., U.S.	87a	42.26N	71.13W
Arlington, S.D., U.S. (är'lĕng-tŭn)	96	44.23N	97.09W
Arlington, Tx., U.S. (ár'lĭng-tŭn)	101c	32.44N	97.07W
Arlington, Vt., U.S.	92	43.05N	73.05W
Arlington, Va., U.S.	94e	38.55N	77.10W
Arlington, Wa., U.S.	100a	48.11N	122.08W
Arlington Heights, Il., U.S. (är'lĕng-tŭn-hī'ts)	95a	42.05N	87.59W
Arlington National Cemetery, pt. of i., Va., U.S.	225d	38.53N	77.04W
Arltunga, Austl. (ärl-tŏŋ'gȧ)	196	23.19S	134.45E
Arma, Ks., U.S. (är'mȧ)	104	37.34N	94.43W
Armagh, Can. (är-mä') (är-mäκ')	77b	46.45N	70.36W
Armagh, N. Ire., U.K.	140	54.21N	6.25W
Armant, Egypt (är-mänt')	212b	25.37N	32.32E
Armaro, Col. (är-mȧ'rō)	124a	4.58N	74.54W
Armavir, Russia (år-mȧ-vĭr')	158	45.00N	41.00E
Armenia, Col. (år-mē'nē*ȧ*)	124	4.33N	75.40W
Armenia, El Sal. (är-mä'nē-ä)	114	13.44N	89.31W
Armenia, nation, Asia	158	41.00N	44.39E
Armentières, Fr. (år-mäN-tyâr')	150	50.43N	2.53E
Armeria, Río de, r., Mex. (rē'ō-dĕ-är-mȧ-rē'ä)	112	19.36N	104.10W
Armherstburg, Can. (ärm'hĕrst-bōōrgh)	84	42.06N	83.06W
Armidale, Austl. (är'mĭ-dāl)	196	30.27S	151.50E
Armour, S.D., U.S. (är'mẽr)	96	43.18N	98.21W
Armstrong Station, Can. (ärm'strŏng)	78	50.21N	89.00W
Armyansk, Ukr. (ärm'yȧnsk)	156	46.06N	33.42E
Arnedo, Spain (är-nä'dō)	152	42.12N	2.03W
Arnhem, Neth. (ärn'hĕm)	140	51.58N	5.56E
Arnhem, Cape, c., Austl.	196	12.15S	137.00E
Arnhem Land, reg., Austl. (ärn'hĕm-lănd)	196	13.15S	133.00E
Arno, r., Italy (ä'r-nō)	142	43.30N	11.00E
Arnold, Eng., U.K. (är'nŭld)	138a	53.00N	1.08W
Arnold, Mn., U.S. (år'nŭld)	101h	46.53N	92.06W
Arnold, Pa., U.S.	95e	40.35N	79.45W
Arnprior, Can. (ärn-prī'ẽr)	84	45.25N	76.20W
Arnsberg, Ger. (ärns'bĕrgh)	151c	51.25N	8.02E
Arnstadt, Ger. (ärn'shtät)	148	50.51N	10.57E
Aroab, Nmb. (är-ō-ȧb)	206	25.40S	19.45E
Aroostook, r., Me., U.S. (ȧ-rōs'tŏk)	86	46.44N	68.15W
Aroroy, Phil. (ä-rō-rō'ē)	189a	12.30N	123.24E
Arpajon, Fr. (är-pȧ-jō'n)	151b	48.35N	2.15E
Arpoador, Ponta do, c., Braz. (pô'n-tä-dō-är'pôä-dō'r)	126b	22.59S	43.11W
Arraiolos, Port. (är-rī-ō'lōzh)	152	38.47N	7.59W
Arran, Island of, Scot., U.K. (ă'răn)	144	55.25N	5.25W
Ar Rank, Sudan	204	11.45N	32.53E
Arras, Fr. (ȧ-räs')	140	50.21N	2.40E
Ar Rawḍah, Egypt	212b	27.47N	30.52E
Arrecifes, Arg. (är-rȧ-sē'fās)	123c	34.03S	60.05W
Arrecifes, r., Arg.	123c	34.07S	59.50W
Arrée, Monts d', mts., Fr. (är-rā')	150	48.27N	4.00W
Arriaga, Mex. (är-rēä'gä)	112	16.15N	93.54W
Arrone, r., Italy	153d	41.57N	12.17E
Arrow Creek, r., Mt., U.S. (ăr'ō)	98	47.29N	109.53W
Arrowhead, Lake, l., Ca., U.S. (lăk ăr'ōhĕd)	101a	34.17N	117.13W
Arrowrock Reservoir, res., Id., U.S. (ăr'ō-rŏk)	98	43.40N	115.30W
Arroya Arena, Cuba (är-rō'yä-rĕ'nä)	117a	23.01N	82.30W
Arroyo de la Luz, Spain (är-rō'yō-dĕ-lä-lōō'z)	152	39.39N	6.46W
Arroyo Seco, Mex. (är-rō'yō sä'kō)	112	21.31N	99.44W
Ar Rub' al Khālī, des., Asia	174	20.00N	51.00E
Ar Rutbah, Iraq	176	33.02N	40.17E
Arsen'yev, Russia	158	44.13N	133.32E
Arsinskiy, Russia (är-sĭn'skĭ)	164a	53.46N	59.54E
Árta, Grc. (är'tȧ)	142	39.08N	21.02E
Artarmon, Austl.	239a	33.49S	151.11E
Arteaga, Mex. (är-tä-ä'gä)	106	25.28N	100.50W
Artëm, Russia (*ȧ*r-tyôm')	158	43.28N	132.29E
Artemisa, Cuba (är-tȧ-mē'sä)	116	22.50N	82.45W
Artëmovsk, Ukr. (*ȧ*r-tyôm'ôfsk)	160	48.37N	38.00E
Arteria, Ca., U.S.	228	33.52N	118.05W
Artesia, N.M., U.S. (är-tē'sĭ-*ȧ*)	104	32.44N	104.23W
Arthabaska, Can.	84	46.03N	71.54W
Arthur's Town, Bah.	116	24.40N	75.40W
Arti, Russia (är'tĭ)	164a	56.20N	58.38E
Artibonite, r., N.A. (är-tē-bō-nē'tä)	116	19.00N	72.25W
Artigas, neigh., Ven.	230a	10.30N	66.56W
Aru, Kepulauan, is., Indon.	188	6.20S	133.00E
Arua, Ug. (ä'rōō-ä)	204	3.01N	30.55E
Aruba, i., Aruba (ä-rōō'bȧ)	110	12.29N	70.00W
Arunachal Pradesh, state, India	174	27.35N	92.56E
Arundel Gardens, Md., U.S.	225c	39.13N	76.37W
Arundel Village, Md., U.S.	225c	39.13N	76.36W
Arusha, Tan. (ȧ-rōō'shä)	206	3.22S	36.41E
Arvida, Can.	78	48.26N	71.11W
Arvika, Swe. (är-vē'kȧ)	146	59.41N	12.35E
Arzamas, Russia (är-zä-mäs')	160	55.20N	43.52E
Arziw, Alg.	142	35.50N	0.20W
Arzua, Spain (är-thōō'ä)	152	42.54N	8.19W
Aš, Czech. (äsh')	148	50.12N	12.13E
Asahi-Gawa, r., Japan (ȧ-sä'hē-gä'wä)	187	35.01N	133.40E
Asahikawa, Japan	180	43.50N	142.09E
Asaka, Japan (ä-sä'kä)	187a	35.47N	139.36E
Asālafpur, neigh., India	236d	28.38N	77.05E
Asansol, India	174	23.45N	86.58E
Asbest, Russia (äs-bĕst')	160	57.02N	61.28E
Asbestos, Can. (ăs-bĕs'tŏs)	84	45.49N	71.52W
Asbestovskiy, Russia	164a	57.46N	61.23E
Asbury Park, N.J., U.S. (ăz'bĕr-ĭ)	94a	40.13N	74.01W
Ascención, Bahía de la, b., Mex.	114a	19.39N	87.30W
Ascensión, Mex. (äs-sĕn-sē-ōn')	112	24.21N	99.54W
Ascension, i., St. Hel. (ȧ-sĕn'shŭn)	203	8.00S	13.00W
Ascent, S. Afr. (äs-ĕnt')	212d	27.14S	29.06E
Aschaffenburg, Ger. (ä-shäf'ĕn-bŏrgh)	148	49.58N	9.12E
Ascheberg, Ger. (ä'shĕ-bĕrg)	151c	51.47N	7.38E
Aschersleben, Ger. (äsh'ĕrs-lā-bĕn)	148	51.46N	11.28E
Ascoli Piceno, Italy (äs'kō-lēpē-chā'nō)	154	42.50N	13.55E
Aseb, Eth.	204	12.52N	43.39E
Asenovgrad, Bul.	154	42.00N	24.49E
Aseri, Est. (ȧ'sĕ-rĭ)	146	59.26N	26.58E
Asha, Russia (ä'shä)	164a	55.01N	57.17E
Ashabula, l., N.D., U.S. (ăsh'ȧ-bū-lä)	96	47.07N	97.51W
Ashan, Russia (ä'shän)	164a	57.08N	56.25E
Ashbourne, Eng., U.K. (ăsh'bŭrn)	138a	53.01N	1.44W
Ashburn, Ga., U.S. (ăsh'bŭrn)	108	31.42N	83.42W
Ashburn, Va., U.S.	94e	39.02N	77.30W
Ashburton, r., Austl. (ăsh'bûr-tŭn)	196	22.30S	115.30E
Ashby-de-la-Zouch, Eng., U.K. (ăsh'bĭ-dē-lȧ zōōsh')	138a	52.44N	1.23W
Ashdod, Isr.	173a	31.46N	34.39E
Ashdown, Ar., U.S. (ăsh'doun)	104	33.41N	94.07W
Asheboro, N.C., U.S. (ăsh'bŭr-ô)	108	35.41N	79.50W
Asherton, Tx., U.S. (ăsh'ẽr-tŭn)	106	28.26N	99.45W
Asheville, N.C., U.S. (ăsh'vĭl)	90	35.35N	82.35W
Ashfield, Austl.	239a	33.53S	151.08E
Ashford, Eng., U.K.	231	51.26N	0.27W
Ash Fork, Az., U.S.	102	35.13N	112.29W
Ashikaga, Japan (ä'shē-kä'gȧ)	187	36.22N	139.26E
Ashiya, Japan (ä'shē-yä')	187	33.54N	130.40E
Ashiya, Japan	187b	34.44N	135.18E
Ashizuri-Zaki, c., Japan (ä-shē-zō-rē zä-kē)	186	32.43N	133.04E
Ashkhabad, Turk. (ŭsh-kä-bät')	158	37.57N	58.23E
Ashland, Al., U.S. (ăsh'lȧnd)	108	33.15N	85.50W
Ashland, Ks., U.S.	104	37.11N	99.46W
Ashland, Ky., U.S.	92	38.25N	82.40W
Ashland, Me., U.S.	86	46.37N	68.26W
Ashland, Ma., U.S.	87a	42.16N	71.28W
Ashland, Ne., U.S.	96	41.02N	96.23W
Ashland, Oh., U.S.	92	40.50N	82.15W
Ashland, Or., U.S.	98	42.12N	122.42W
Ashland, Pa., U.S.	92	40.45N	76.20W
Ashland, Wi., U.S.	90	46.34N	90.55W
Ashley, N.D., U.S. (ăsh'lē)	96	46.03N	99.23W
Ashley, Pa., U.S.	92	41.15N	75.55W
Ashley Green, Eng., U.K.	231	51.44N	0.35W
Ashmūn, Egypt (ȧsh-mōōn')	212b	30.19N	30.57E
Ashqelon, Isr. (äsh'kĕ-lōn)	173a	31.40N	34.36E
Ash Shabb, Egypt (shĕb)	204	22.34N	29.52E
Ash Shallūfah, Egypt (shäl'lō-fȧ)	212b	30.09N	32.33E
Ash Shaqrā', Sau. Ar.	174	25.10N	45.08E
Ash Shāriqah, U.A.E.	176	25.22N	55.23E
Ash Shawbak, Jord.	173a	30.31N	35.35E
Ash Shiḥr, Yemen	174	14.45N	49.32E
Ashtabula, Oh., U.S. (ăsh-tȧ-bū'lȧ)	90	41.55N	80.50W
Ashtead, Eng., U.K.	231	51.19N	0.18W
Ashton, Id., U.S. (ăsh'tŭn)	98	44.04N	111.28W
Ashton-in-Makerfield, Eng., U.K. (ăsh'tŭn-ĭn-māk'ẽr-fēld)	138a	53.29N	2.39W
Ashton-under-Lyne, Eng., U.K. (ăsh'tŭn-ŭn-dẽr-līn')	138a	53.29N	2.04W
Ashuanipi, l., Can. (ăsh-wȧ-nĭp'ĭ)	78	52.40N	67.42W
Ashukino, Russia (ȧ-shōō'kĭnô)	164b	56.10N	37.57E
Asia, cont.	172	50.00N	100.00E
Asia Minor, reg., Tur. (ā'zh*ȧ*)	136	38.18N	31.18E
Asientos, Mex. (ä-sē-ĕn'tōs)	112	22.13N	102.05W
Asilah, Mor.	152	35.30N	6.05W
Asinara, i., Italy	154	41.02N	8.22E
Asinara, Golfo dell', b., Italy (gôl'fō-dĕl-ä-sē-nä'rä)	154	40.58N	8.28E
Asīr, reg., Sau. Ar. (ä-sēr')	174	19.30N	42.00E
Askarovo, Russia (äs-kä-rô'vô)	164a	53.21N	58.32E
Askersund, Swe. (äs'kĕr-sŏnd)	146	58.43N	14.53E
Askino, Russia (äs'kĭ-nô)	164a	56.06N	56.29E
Asmera, Eth. (äs-mä'rä)	204	15.17N	38.56E
Asnieres, Fr. (ä-nyâr')	151b	48.55N	2.18E
Asosa, Eth.	204	10.13N	34.28E
Asotin, Wa., U.S. (*ȧ*-sō'tĭn)	98	46.19N	117.01W
Aspen, Co., U.S. (ăs'pĕn)	102	39.15N	106.55W
Asperen, Neth.	139a	51.52N	5.07E
Aspern, neigh., Aus.	235e	48.13N	16.29E
Aspinwall, Pa., U.S.	226b	40.30N	79.55W
Aspy Bay, b., Can. (ăs'pē)	86	46.55N	60.25W
Aş Şaff, Egypt	212b	29.33N	31.23E
As Sallūm, Egypt	204	31.35N	25.05E
As Salt, Jord.	173a	32.02N	35.44E
Assam, state, India (ăs-săm')	174	26.00N	91.00E
As Samāwah, Iraq	176	31.18N	45.17E
Asseln, neigh., Ger.	232	51.32N	7.35E
Assens, Den. (äs'sĕns)	146	55.16N	9.54E
As Sinbillāwayn, Egypt	212b	30.53N	31.37E
Assini, I.C. (ȧ-sē-nē')	204	4.52N	3.16W
Assiniboia, Can.	78	49.38N	105.59W
Assiniboine, r., Can. (ă-sĭn'ĭ-boin)	82	50.03N	97.57W
Assiniboine, Mount, mtn., Can.	80	50.52N	115.39W
Assis, Braz. (ä-sē's)	124	22.39S	50.21W
Assisi, Italy	142	43.04N	12.37E
As-Sudd, reg., Sudan	204	8.45N	30.45E
As Sulaymānīyah, Iraq	174	35.47N	45.23E
As Sulaymānīyah, Sau. Ar.	176	24.09N	46.19E
As Suwaydā', Syria	174	32.41N	36.41E
Astakós, Grc. (äs-tä-kōs)	154	38.42N	21.00E
Astara, Azer.	160	38.30N	48.50E
Asti, Italy (äs'tē)	142	44.54N	8.12E
Astipálaia, i., Grc.	142	36.31N	26.19E
Astley Bridge, Eng., U.K.	233b	53.36N	2.26W
Astorga, Spain (äs-tôr'gä)	152	42.28N	6.03W
Astoria, Or., U.S. (ăs-tō'rĭ-*ȧ*)	90	46.11N	123.51W
Astoria, neigh., N.Y., U.S.	224	40.46N	73.55W
Astrakhan', Russia (äs-trȧ-kän')	158	46.15N	48.00E
Astrida, Rw. (äs-trē'd*ȧ*)	206	2.37S	29.48E
Asturias, hist. reg., Spain (äs-tōō'ryäs)	152	43.21N	6.00W
Asunción, Para. (ä-sōōn-syōn')	126	25.25S	57.30W
Asunción, *see* Ixtaltepec, Mex.	112	16.33N	95.04W
Asunción Mita, Guat. (ä-sōōn-syō'n-mē'tä)	114	14.19N	89.43W
Asunción, *see* Nochistlán, Mex.	112	21.23N	102.52W
Aswān, Egypt (ä-swän')	204	24.05N	32.57E
Aswān High Dam, dam, Egypt	204	23.58N	32.53E
Atacama, Desierto de, des., Chile (dĕ-syĕ'r-tō-dĕ-ä-tä-kä'mä)	122	23.50S	69.00W
Atacama, Puna de, plat., Bol. (pōō'nä-dĕ-ä-tä-kȧ'mä)	124	21.35S	66.58W

ng-sing; ŋ-baŋk; N-nasalized n; nŏd; cŏmmit; ōld; ōbey; ôrder; oi-boil; fōōd; ŏ-as oo in foot; ou-out; s-soft; sh-dish; th-thin; pūre; ůnite; ûrn; stŭd; circŭs; ü-as in French tu; '-indeterminate vowel.

PLACE (Pronunciation)	PAGE	Lat. °′	Long. °′
Atacama, Puna de, reg., Chile (pōō′nä-dĕ-ātä-kà′mä)	126	23.15S	68.45W
Atacama, Salar de, l., Chile (sà-lär′dĕ-ätä-kà′mä)	126	23.38S	68.15W
Atacama Trench, deep	122	25.00S	71.30W
Ataco, Col. (ä-tà′kō)	124a	3.36N	75.22W
Atacora, Chaîne de l', mts., Benin	208	10.15N	1.15E
Atā 'itah, Jabal al, mtn., Jord.	173a	30.48N	35.19E
Atamanovskiy, Russia (ä-tä-mä′nôv-skĭ)	164a	52.15N	60.47E
'Atāqah, Jabal, mts., Egypt	212c	29.59N	32.20E
Atar, Maur. (ä-tär′)	204	20.45N	13.16W
Atascadero, Ca., U.S. (ăt-ăs-kȧ-dâ′rō)	102	35.29N	120.40W
Atascosa, r., Tx., U.S. (ăt-ăs-kō′sȧ)	106	28.50N	98.17W
Atauro, Ilha de, i., Indon. (dĕ-ä-tä′ōō-rō)	188	8.20S	126.15E
Atbara, r., Afr.	204	17.14N	34.27E
'Aṭbarah, Sudan (ät′bȧ-rä)	204	17.45N	33.15E
Atbasar, Kaz. (ät′bä-sär′)	158	51.42N	68.28E
Atchafalaya, r., La., U.S.	106	30.53N	91.51W
Atchafalaya Bay, b., La., U.S. (ăch-ȧ-fȧ-lī′ȧ)	106	29.25N	91.30W
Atchison, Ks., U.S. (ăch′ĭ-sŭn)	90	39.33N	95.08W
Atco, N.J., U.S. (ăt′kō)	94f	39.46N	74.53W
Atempan, Mex. (ä-tĕm-pà′n)	112	19.49N	97.25W
Atenguillo, r., Mex. (ä-tĕn-gĕ′l-yō)	112	20.18N	104.35W
Athabasca, Can. (ăth-ȧ-băs′kȧ)	78	54.43N	113.17W
Athabasca, l., Can.	78	59.04N	109.10W
Athabasca, r., Can.	78	57.30N	112.00W
Athens (Athínai), Grc.	154	38.00N	23.38E
Athens, Al., U.S. (ăth′ĕnz)	108	34.47N	86.58W
Athens, Ga., U.S.	90	33.55N	83.24W
Athens, Oh., U.S.	92	39.20N	82.10W
Athens, Pa., U.S.	92	42.00N	76.30W
Athens, Tn., U.S.	108	35.26N	84.36W
Athens, Tx., U.S.	106	32.13N	95.51W
Atherstone, Eng., U.K. (ăth′ĕr-stŭn)	138a	52.34N	1.33W
Atherton, Eng., U.K. (ăth′ĕr-tŭn)	138a	53.32N	2.29W
Atherton Plateau, plat., Austl. (ădh-ĕr-tŏn)	196	17.00S	144.30E
Athi, r., Kenya (ä′tē)	206	2.43S	38.30E
Athínai, see Athens, Grc.	136	38.00N	23.38E
Athis-Mons, Fr.	233c	48.43N	2.24E
Athlone, Ire. (ăth-lōn′)	140	53.24N	7.30W
Athos, mtn., Grc. (ăth′ŏs)	154	40.10N	24.15E
Ath Thamad, Egypt	173a	29.41N	34.17E
Athy, Ire. (ȧ-thī)	144	52.59N	7.08W
Ati, Chad	208	13.13N	18.20E
Atibaia, Braz. (ä-tē-bà′yȧ)	123a	23.08S	46.32W
Atikonak, l., Can.	78	52.34N	63.49W
Atimonan, Phil. (ä-tē-mō′nän)	189a	13.59N	121.56E
Atiquizaya, El Sal. (ä′tē-kē-zä′yä)	114	14.00N	89.42W
Atitlan, vol., Guat. (ä-tē-tlän′)	114	14.35N	91.11W
Atitlan, Lago, l., Guat. (ä-tē-tlän′)	114	14.38N	91.23W
Atizapán, Mex. (ä′tē-zà-pän′)	113a	19.33N	99.16W
Atka, Ak., U.S. (ăt′kȧ)	89a	52.18N	174.18W
Atka, i., Ak., U.S.	90b	51.58N	174.30W
Atkarsk, Russia (ät-kärsk′)	160	51.50N	45.00E
Atkinson, Ne., U.S. (ăt′kĭn-sŭn)	96	42.32N	98.58W
Atlanta, Ga., U.S. (ăt-lăn′tȧ)	90	33.45N	84.23W
Atlanta, Tx., U.S.	104	33.09N	94.09W
Atlantic, Ia., U.S. (ăt-lăn′tĭk)	96	41.23N	94.58W
Atlantic, N.C., U.S.	108	34.54N	76.20W
Atlantic Beach, N.Y., U.S.	224	40.35N	73.44W
Atlantic City, N.J., U.S.	90	39.20N	74.30W
Atlantic Highlands, N.J., U.S.	94a	40.25N	74.04W
Atlantic Ocean, o.	4	5.00S	25.00W
Atlas Mountains, mts., Afr. (ăt′lăs)	204	31.22N	4.57W
Atliaca, Mex. (ät-lē-ä′kä)	112	17.38N	99.24W
Atlin, l., Can. (ăt′lĭn)	78	59.34N	133.20W
Atlixco, Mex. (ät-lēz′kō)	112	18.52N	98.27W
Atmore, Al., U.S. (ăt′mōr)	108	31.01N	87.31W
Atoka, Ok., U.S. (ȧ-tō′kȧ)	104	34.23N	96.07W
Atoka Reservoir, res., Ok., U.S.	104	34.30N	96.05W
Atotonilco el Alto, Mex.	112	20.35N	102.32W
Atotonilco el Grande, Mex.	112	20.17N	98.41W
Atoui, r., Afr. (ȧ-tōō-ē′)	204	21.00N	15.32W
Atoyac, Mex. (ä-tô-yäk′)	112	20.01N	103.28W
Atoyac, r., Mex.	112	18.35N	98.16W
Atoyac, r., Mex.	112	16.27N	97.28W
Atoyac de Alvarez, Mex. (ä-tô-yäk′dā äl′vä-rāz)	112	17.13N	100.29W
Atoyatempan, Mex. (ä-tō′yà-tĕm-pän′)	112	18.47N	97.54W
Atrak, r., Asia	174	37.45N	56.30E
Ätran, r., Swe.	146	57.02N	12.43E
Atrato, Río, r., Col. (rē′ō-ä-trä′tō)	124	7.15N	77.18W
Atsugi, Japan	238a	35.27N	139.22E
Atta, India	236d	28.34N	77.20E
Aṭ Ṭafīlah, Jord. (tä-fē′la)	173a	30.50N	35.36E
Aṭ Ṭā'if, Sau. Ar.	174	21.03N	41.00E
At-Ṭalibīyah, Egypt	240a	30.00N	31.11E
Attalla, Al., U.S. (ȧ-tăl′yȧ)	108	34.01N	86.05W
Attawapiskat, r., Can. (ăt′ȧ-wȧ-pĭs′kăt)	78	52.31N	86.22W
Attersee, l., Aus.	148	47.57N	13.25E
Attica, N.Y., U.S. (ăt′ĭ-kȧ)	92	42.55N	78.15W
Attleboro, Ma., U.S. (ăt′′l-bŭr-ô)	94b	41.56N	71.15W
Attow, Ben, mtn., Scot., U.K. (bĕn ăt′tô)	144	57.15N	5.25W
Attoyac Bay, Tx., U.S. (ă-toi′yăk)	106	31.45N	94.23W
Attu, i., Ak., U.S. (ăt-tōō′)	90b	53.08N	173.18E
Aṭ Ṭūr, Egypt	142	28.09N	33.47E
Aṭ Ṭurayf, Sau. Ar.	174	31.32N	38.30E
Åtvidaberg, Swe. (ôt-vē′dà-bĕrgh)	146	58.12N	15.55E
Atwood, Ks., U.S. (ăt′wŏŏd)	104	39.48N	101.06W
Atzalpur, India	236d	28.43N	77.21E
Atzcapotzalco, Mex. (ät′zkä-pō-tzäl′kō)	112	19.29N	99.11W
Atzgersdorf, Aus.	139e	48.10N	16.17E
Auau Channel, strt., Hi., U.S. (ä′ò-ä′ò)	88a	20.55N	156.50W
Aubagne, Fr. (ō-băn′y′)	150	43.18N	5.34E
Aube, r., Fr. (ōb)	150	48.42N	3.49E
Aubenas, Fr. (ōb-nä′)	150	44.37N	4.22E
Aubervilliers, Fr. (ō-bĕr-vē-yā′)	151b	48.54N	2.23E
Aubin, Fr. (ō-băɴ′)	150	44.29N	2.12E
Aubrey, Can. (ô-brē′)	77a	45.08N	73.47W
Auburn, Austl.	239a	33.51S	151.02E
Auburn, Al., U.S. (ô′bŭrn)	108	32.35N	85.26W
Auburn, Ca., U.S.	102	38.52N	121.05W
Auburn, Il., U.S.	104	39.36N	89.46W
Auburn, In., U.S.	92	41.20N	85.05W
Auburn, Me., U.S.	90	44.04N	70.24W
Auburn, Ma., U.S.	87a	42.11N	71.51W
Auburn, Ne., U.S.	104	40.23N	95.50W
Auburn, N.Y., U.S.	92	42.55N	76.35W
Auburn, Wa., U.S.	100a	47.18N	122.14W
Auburndale, Ma., U.S.	223a	42.21N	71.22W
Auburn Heights, Mi., U.S.	95b	42.37N	83.13W
Aubusson, Fr. (ō-bü-sôɴ′)	150	45.57N	2.10E
Auch, Fr. (ōsh)	140	43.38N	0.35E
Aucilla, r., Fl., U.S. (ô-sĭl′ȧ)	108	30.15N	83.55W
Auckland, N.Z. (ôk′lănd)	197a	36.53S	174.45E
Auckland Islands, is., N.Z.	2	50.30S	166.30E
Auckland Park, neigh., S. Afr.	240b	26.11S	28.00E
Aude, r., Fr. (ōd)	150	42.55N	2.08E
Audenshaw, Eng., U.K.	233b	53.28N	2.08W
Audierne, Fr. (ō-dyĕrn′)	150	48.02N	4.31W
Audincourt, Fr. (ō-dăn-kōōr′)	150	47.30N	6.49E
Audley, Eng., U.K. (ôd′lĭ)	138a	53.03N	2.18W
Audo Range, mts., Eth.	212a	6.58N	41.18E
Audubon, Ia., U.S. (ô′dŏŏ-bŏn)	96	41.43N	94.57W
Audubon, N.J., U.S.	94f	39.54N	75.04W
Aue, Ger. (ou′ē)	148	50.35N	12.44E
Auf dem Schnee, neigh., Ger.	232	51.26N	7.25E
Augathella, Austl. (ôr′gȧ′thē-lȧ)	198	25.49S	146.40E
Aughton, Eng., U.K.	233a	53.32N	2.56W
Augrabiesvalle, wtfl., S. Afr.	206	28.30S	20.00E
Augsburg, Ger. (ouks′bŏŏrgh)	140	48.23N	10.55E
Augusta, Ar., U.S. (ô-gŭs′tȧ)	104	35.16N	91.21W
Augusta, Ga., U.S.	90	33.26N	82.00W
Augusta, Ks., U.S.	104	37.41N	96.58W
Augusta, Ky., U.S.	92	38.45N	84.00W
Augusta, Me., U.S.	90	44.19N	69.42W
Augusta, N.J., U.S.	94a	41.07N	74.44W
Augusta, Wi., U.S.	96	44.40N	91.09W
Augustow, Pol. (ou-gŏŏs′tŏŏf)	148	53.52N	23.00E
Auki, Sol.Is.	192e	8.46S	160.42E
Aulnay-sous-Bois, Fr. (ō-nĕ′sōō-bwä′)	151b	48.56N	2.30E
Aulne, r., Fr. (ōn)	150	48.08N	3.53W
Auneau, Fr. (ō-nĕü)	151b	48.28N	1.45E
Auob, r., Afr. (ä′wŏb)	206	25.00S	19.00E
Aur, i., Malay.	173b	2.27N	104.51E
Aura, Fin.	146	60.38N	22.32E
Aurangābād, India (ou-rŭŋ-gä-bäd′)	174	19.56N	75.19E
Aurdal, Nor. (äür-däl)	140	60.54N	9.24E
Aurès, Massif de l', mts., Alg.	142	35.16N	5.53E
Aurillac, Fr. (ō-rē-yák′)	140	44.57N	2.27E
Aurora, Can.	84	43.59N	79.25W
Aurora, Il., U.S. (ô-rō′rȧ)	90	41.45N	88.18W
Aurora, In., U.S.	95f	39.04N	84.55W
Aurora, Mn., U.S.	96	47.31N	92.17W
Aurora, Mo., U.S.	104	36.58N	93.42W
Aurora, Ne., U.S.	104	40.54N	98.01W
Aursunden, l., Nor. (äûr-sûndĕn)	146	62.42N	11.10E
Au Sable, r., Mi., U.S. (ô-sä′b′l)	92	44.40N	84.25W
Ausable, r., N.Y., U.S.	92	44.25N	73.50W
Austerlitz, trans., Fr.	233c	48.50N	2.22E
Austin, Mn., U.S. (ôs′tĭn)	96	43.40N	92.58W
Austin, Nv., U.S.	102	39.30N	117.05W
Austin, Tx., U.S.	90	30.15N	97.42W
Austin, neigh., Il., U.S.	227a	41.54N	87.45W
Austin, l., Austl.	196	27.45S	117.30E
Austin Bayou, Tx., U.S. (ôs′tĭn bī-ōō′)	107a	29.17N	95.21W
Austral, Austl.	239a	33.56S	150.48E
Australia, nation, Oc.	196	25.00S	135.00E
Australian Alps, mts., Austl.	198	37.10S	147.55E
Australian Capital Territory, , Austl. (ôs-trā′lĭ-ăn)	196	35.30S	148.40E
Austria, nation, Eur. (ôs′trĭ-ȧ)	136	47.15N	11.53E
Authon-la-Plaine, Fr. (ō-tō′ɴ-lä-plĕ′n)	151b	48.27N	1.58E
Autlán, Mex. (ä-ōōt-län′)	110	19.47N	104.24W
Autun, Fr. (ō-tŭɴ′)	150	46.58N	4.14E
Auvergne, mts., Fr. (ō-vĕrn′y′)	150	45.12N	2.31E
Auxerre, Fr. (ō-sâr′)	140	47.48N	3.32E
Ava, Mo., U.S. (ā′vȧ)	104	36.56N	92.40W
Avakubi, Zaire (ä-vä-kōō′bē)	204	1.20N	27.34E
Avallon, Fr. (ȧ-vȧ-lôɴ′)	150	47.30N	3.58E
Avalon, Ca., U.S.	102	33.21N	118.22W
Avalon, Pa., U.S. (ăv′ȧ-lŏn)	95e	40.31N	80.05W
Aveiro, Port. (ä-vā′rō)	142	40.38N	8.38W
Avelar, Braz. (ä′vĕ-lä′r)	126b	22.20S	43.25W
Aveley, Eng., U.K.	231	51.30N	0.16E
Avellaneda, Arg. (ä-vĕl-yä-nä′dhä)	126	34.40S	58.23W
Avellino, Italy (ä-vĕl-lē′nō)	154	40.40N	14.46E
Avenel, N.J., U.S.	224	40.35N	74.17W
Averøya, i., Nor. (ävĕr-ûē)	146	63.40N	7.16E
Aversa, Italy (ä-vĕr′sä)	154	40.58N	14.13E
Avery, Tx., U.S. (ā′vĕr-ĭ)	104	33.34N	94.46W
Avesta, Swe. (ä-vĕs′tä)	146	60.16N	16.09E
Aveyron, r., Fr. (ä-vâ-rôɴ)	150	44.07N	1.45E
Avezzano, Italy (ä-våt-sä′nō)	154	42.03N	13.27E
Avigliano, Italy (ä-vēl-yä′nō)	154	40.45N	15.44E
Avignon, Fr. (ȧ-vē-nyôɴ′)	140	43.55N	4.50E
Ávila, Spain (ä-vē-lä)	152	40.39N	4.42W
Avilés, Spain (ä-vē-lās′)	142	43.33N	5.55W
Avoca, Ia., U.S. (ȧ-vō′kȧ)	104	41.29N	95.16W
Avocado Heights, Ca., U.S.	228	34.03N	118.00W
Avon, Ct., U.S. (ā′vŏn)	92	41.40N	72.50W
Avon, Ma., U.S. (ā′vŏn)	87a	42.08N	71.03W
Avon, Oh., U.S.	95d	41.27N	82.02W
Avon, r., Eng., U.K. (ā′vŭn)	144	52.05N	1.55W
Avondale, Ga., U.S.	94c	33.47N	84.16W
Avondale Heights, Austl.	239b	37.46S	144.51E
Avon Lake, Oh., U.S.	95d	41.31N	82.01W
Avonmore, Can. (ä′vōɴ-mōr)	77c	45.11N	74.58W
Avon Park, Fl., U.S. (ā′vŏn pärk′)	109a	27.35N	81.29W
Avranches, Fr. (ȧ-vränsh′)	150	48.43N	1.34W
Awaji-Shima, i., Japan	186	34.32N	135.02E
Awe, Loch, l., Scot., U.K. (lŏk ôr)	144	56.22N	5.04W
Awjilah, Libya	204	29.07N	21.21E
Awsīm, Egypt	240a	30.07N	31.08E
Ax-les-Thermes, Fr. (äks′lā tĕrm′)	150	42.43N	1.50E
Axochiapan, Mex. (äks-ō-chyä′pän)	112	18.29N	98.49W
Ay, r., Russia	160	55.55N	57.55E
Ayabe, Japan (ä′yä-bĕ)	186	35.16N	135.17E
Ayachi, Arin', mtn., Mor.	142	32.29N	4.57W
Ayacucho, Arg. (ä-yä-kōō′chō)	126	37.05S	58.30W
Ayacucho, Peru	124	13.12S	74.03W
Ayaguz, Kaz. (ä-yà-gōōz′)	158	48.00N	80.12E
Ayamonte, Spain (ä-yä-mō′n-tĕ)	142	37.14N	7.28W
Ayan, Russia (à-yän′)	158	56.26N	138.18E
Ayase, Japan	238a	35.26N	139.26E
Ayata, Bol. (ä-yä′tä)	124	15.17S	68.43W
Ayaviri, Peru (ä-yä-vē′rē)	124	14.46S	70.38W
Aydar, r., Eur. (ī-där′)	156	49.15N	38.48E
Ayden, N.C., U.S. (ā′dĕn)	108	35.27N	77.25W
Aydın, Tur. (āīy-dĕn)	174	37.40N	27.40E
Ayer, Ma., U.S. (âr)	87a	42.33N	71.36W
Ayer Hitam, Malay.	173b	1.55N	103.11E
Ayiassos, Grc.	154	39.06N	26.25E
Ayía Varvára, Grc.	235d	37.59N	23.39E
Áyion Óros (Mount Athos), hist. reg., Grc.	154	40.20N	24.15E
Ayíos Evstrátios, i., Grc.	142	39.30N	24.58E
Ayíou Orous, Kólpos, b., Grc.	154	40.15N	24.00E
Aylesbury, Eng., U.K. (ālz′bĕr-ĭ)	144	51.47N	0.49W
Aylmer, l., Can. (āl′mĕr)	78	64.27N	108.22W
Aylmer, Mount, mtn., Can.	80	51.19N	115.26W
Aylmer East, Can. (āl′mĕr)	84	45.24N	75.50W
Ayo el Chico, Mex. (ä′yō el chē′kō)	112	20.31N	102.21W
Ayon, i., Russia (ī-ôn′)	158	69.50N	168.40E
Ayorou, Niger	208	14.44N	0.55E
Ayotla, Mex. (ä-yōt′lä)	113a	19.18N	98.55W
Ayoun el Atrous, Maur.	208	16.40N	9.37W
Ayr, Scot., U.K. (âr)	144	55.27N	4.40W
Aysha, Eth.	204	10.48N	42.32E
Ayutla, Guat. (ȧ-yōōt′lä)	114	14.44N	92.11W
Ayutla, Mex.	112	20.09N	104.20W
Ayutla, Mex.	112	16.50N	99.16W
Ayvalık, Tur. (āīy-wä-lĭk)	142	39.19N	26.40E
Azādpur, neigh., India	236d	28.43N	77.11E
Azaouad, reg., Mali	208	18.00N	3.20W
Azaouak, Vallée de l', val., Afr.	208	15.50N	3.10E
Azare, Nig.	208	11.40N	10.11E
Azemmour, Mor. (ȧ-zē-mōōr′)	204	33.20N	8.21W
Azerbaijan, nation, Asia	158	40.30N	47.30E
Azle, Tx., U.S. (ăz′lē)	101c	35.54N	97.33W
Azogues, Ec. (ä-sō′gās)	124	2.47S	78.45W
Azores, see Açores, is., Port.	203	37.44N	29.25W
Azov, Russia (ȧ-zôf′) (ä-zôf)	160	47.07N	39.19E
Azov, Sea of, see Azovskoye More, sea, Eur.	158	46.00N	36.20E
Azovskoye More (Sea of Azov), sea, Eur.	158	46.00N	36.20E
Aztec, N.M., U.S. (ăz′tĕk)	102	36.40N	108.00W
Aztec Ruins National Monument, rec., N.M., U.S.	102	36.50N	108.00W
Azua, Dom. Rep. (ä′swä)	116	18.30N	70.45W
Azuaga, Spain (ä-thwä′gä)	152	38.15N	5.42W
Azucar, Presa de, res., Mex.	106	26.06N	98.44W
Azuero, Península de, pen., Pan.	110	7.30N	80.34W
Azufre, Cerro (Copiapó), mtn., Chile	126	27.10S	69.00W
Azul, Arg. (ä-sōōl′)	126	36.46S	59.51W
Azul, Cordillera, mts., Peru	124	7.15S	75.30W
Azul, Sierra, mts., Mex.	112	23.20N	98.28W
Azusa, Ca., U.S. (ȧ-zōō′sȧ)	101a	34.08N	117.55W
Az Zahrān (Dhahran), Sau. Ar.	174	26.13N	50.00E
Az-Zamālik, neigh., Egypt	240a	30.04N	31.13E
Az Zaqāzīq, Egypt	204	30.36N	31.36E
Az Zarqā', Jord.	173a	32.03N	36.07E
Az Zāwiyah, Libya	204	32.28N	11.55E

B

PLACE (Pronunciation)	PAGE	Lat. °′	Long. °′
Baadheere, Som.	212a	2.13N	42.24E
Baak, Ger.	232	51.25N	7.10E
Baal, Ger. (bäl)	151c	51.02N	6.17E
Baao, Phil. (bä′ō)	189a	13.27N	123.22E
Baarle-Hertog, Bel.	139a	51.26N	4.57E
Baarn, Neth.	139a	52.12N	5.18E
Babaeski, Tur. (bä′bä-ĕs′kĭ)	154	41.25N	27.05E
Babahoyo, Ec. (bä-bä-ō′yō)	124	1.56S	79.24W
Babana, Nig.	208	10.36N	3.50E
Babanango, S. Afr.	207c	28.24S	31.11E
Babanūsah, Sudan	204	11.30N	27.55E
Babar, Pulau, i., Indon. (bä′bär)	188	7.50S	129.15E

ăt; finȧl; rāte; senāte; ärm; ȧsk; sofȧ; fâre; ch-choose; dh-as th in other; bē; ēvent; bĕt; recĕnt; cratēr; g-gō; gh-guttural g; bĭt; ĭ-short neutral; rīde; ĸ-guttural k as ch in German ich;

PLACE (Pronunciation)	PAGE	Lat. °′	Long. °′
Bābarpur, neigh., India	236d	28.41N	77.17E
Bab-el-Mandeb, strt. (băb'ĕl män-dĕb')	174	13.17N	42.49E
Babelsberg, neigh., Ger.	234a	52.24N	13.05E
Babelthuap, i., Palau	192b	7.30N	134.36E
Babia, Arroyo de la, r., Mex.	106	28.26N	101.50W
Babine, r., Can.	80	55.10N	127.00W
Babine Lake, l., Can. (băb'ēn)	78	54.45N	126.00W
Bābol, Iran	174	36.30N	52.48E
Babson Park, Ma., U.S.	223a	42.18N	71.23W
Babushkin, Russia	156	55.52N	37.42E
Babushkin, Russia (bä'bòsh-kĭn)	162	51.47N	106.08W
Babuyan Islands, is., Phil. (bä-bōō-yän')	188	19.30N	122.38E
Babyak, Bul. (bäb'zhàk)	154	41.59N	23.42E
Babylon, N.Y., U.S. (băb'ĭ-lŏn)	94a	40.42N	73.19W
Babylon, hist., Iraq	174	32.15N	45.23E
Bacalar, Laguna de, l., Mex. (lä-gōō-nä-dĕ-bä-kä-lär')	114a	18.50N	88.31W
Bacan, Pulau, i., Indon.	188	0.30S	127.00E
Bacarra, Phil. (bä-kär'rä)	184	18.22N	120.40E
Bacău, Rom.	142	46.34N	27.00E
Baccarat, Fr. (bá-ká-rá')	150	48.29N	6.42E
Bacchus, Ut., U.S. (băk'ŭs)	101b	40.40N	112.06W
Bachajón, Mex. (bä-chä-hōn')	112	17.08N	92.18W
Bachu, China (bä-chōō)	180	39.50N	78.23E
Back, r., Can.	78	65.30N	104.15W
Bačka Palanka, Yugo. (bäch'kä pälän-kä)	154	45.14N	19.24E
Bačka Topola, Yugo. (bäch'kä tô'pô-lä')	154	45.48N	19.38E
Back Bay, India (băk)	179b	18.55N	72.45E
Back Bay, neigh., Ma., U.S.	223a	42.21N	71.05W
Backstairs Passage, strt., Austl. (băk-stârs')	196	35.50S	138.15E
Bac Lieu, Viet.	188	9.45N	105.50E
Bac Ninh, Viet. (bäk'nēn'')	184	21.10N	106.02E
Baco, Mount, mtn., Phil. (bä'kô)	189a	12.50N	121.11E
Bacoli, Italy (bä-kō-lē')	153c	40.33N	14.05E
Bacolod, Phil. (bä-kō'lôd)	188	10.42N	123.03E
Bacongo, neigh., Congo	240c	4.18S	15.16E
Bácsalmás, Hung. (bäch'ôl-mäs)	148	46.07N	19.18E
Bacup, Eng., U.K. (băk'ŭp)	138a	53.42N	2.12W
Bad, r., S.D., U.S. (băd)	96	44.04N	100.58W
Badajoz, Spain (bä-dhä-hōth')	142	38.52N	6.56W
Badalona, Spain (bä-dhä-lō'nä)	152	41.27N	2.15E
Badanah, Sau. Ar.	174	30.49N	40.45E
Bad Axe, Mi., U.S. (băd' ăks)	92	43.50N	82.55W
Bad Bramstedt, Ger. (bät bräm'shtĕt)	139c	53.55N	9.53E
Baden, Aus. (bä'dĕn)	148	48.00N	16.14E
Baden, Switz.	148	47.28N	8.17E
Baden-Baden, Ger. (bä'dĕn-bä'dĕn)	140	48.46N	8.11E
Baden Württemberg, hist. reg., Ger. (bä'dĕn vür'tĕm-bĕrgh)	148	48.38N	9.00E
Bad Freienwalde, Ger. (bät frī'ĕn-väl'dĕ)	148	52.47N	14.00E
Badger's Mount, Eng., U.K.	231	51.20N	0.09E
Bad Hersfeld, Ger. (bät hĕrsh'fĕlt)	148	50.53N	9.43E
Badīn, Pak.	178	24.47N	69.51E
Bad Ischl, Aus. (bät ĭsh''l)	148	47.46N	13.37E
Bad Kissingen, Ger. (bät kĭs'ĭng-ĕn)	148	50.12N	10.05E
Bad Kreuznach, Ger. (bät kroits'näk)	148	49.52N	7.53E
Badlands, reg., N.D., U.S. (băd' lănds)	96	46.43N	103.22W
Badlands, reg., S.D., U.S.	96	43.43N	102.36W
Badlands National Park, S.D., U.S.	96	43.56N	102.37W
Badlāpur, India	179b	19.12N	73.12E
Bādli, India	236d	28.45N	77.09E
Badogo, Mali	208	11.02N	8.13W
Bad Oldesloe, Ger. (bät ōl'dĕs-lōĕ)	148	53.48N	10.21E
Bad Reichenhall, Ger. (bät rī'kĕn-häl)	148	47.43N	12.53E
Bad River Indian Reservation, I.R., Wi., U.S. (băd)	96	46.41N	90.36W
Bad Segeberg, Ger. (bät sĕ'gĕ-bōōrgh)	139c	53.56N	10.18E
Bad Tölz, Ger. (bät tûltz)	148	47.46N	11.35E
Badulla, Sri L.	178	6.55N	81.07E
Bad Vöslau, Aus.	139e	47.58N	16.13E
Badwater Creek, r., Wy., U.S. (băd'wô-tēr)	98	43.13N	107.55W
Baena, Spain (bä-ā'nä)	142	37.38N	4.20W
Baependi, Braz. (bä-å-pĕn'dĭ)	123a	21.57S	44.51W
Baerl, Ger.	232	51.29N	6.41E
Baffin Bay, b., N.A. (băf'ĭn)	76	72.00N	65.00W
Baffin Bay, b., Tx., U.S.	106	27.11N	97.35W
Baffin Island, i., Can.	76	67.20N	71.00W
Bāfq, Iran (bäfk)	174	31.48N	55.23E
Bafra, Tur. (bäf'rä)	142	41.30N	35.50E
Bagabag, Phil. (bä-gä-bäg')	189a	16.38N	121.16E
Bāgalkot, India	178	16.14N	75.40E
Bagamoyo, Tan. (bä-gä-mō'yō)	206	6.26S	38.54E
Bagaryak, Russia (bá-gár-yäk')	164a	56.13N	61.32E
Bagbele, Zaire	210	4.21N	29.17E
Baghdād, Iraq (bagh-dăd') (băg'dăd)	174	33.14N	44.22E
Bagheria, Italy (bä-gå-rē'ä)	154	38.03N	13.32E
Bagley, Mn., U.S. (băg'lē)	96	47.31N	95.24W
Bagnara, Italy (bän-yä'rä)	154	38.17N	15.52E
Bagnell Dam, Mo., U.S. (băg'nĕl)	104	38.13N	92.40W
Bagnères-de-Luchon, Fr. (bän-yâr' dē-lu chôɴ')	150	42.46N	0.36E
Bagneux, Fr.	233c	48.48N	2.18E
Bagnolet, Fr.	233c	48.52N	2.25E
Bagnols-sur-Ceze, Fr. (bä-nyôl')	150	44.09N	4.37E
Bago, Burma	188	17.17N	96.29E
Bagoé, r., Mali (bá-gō'å)	204	12.22N	6.34W
Baguio, Phil. (bä-gē-ō')	188	16.24N	120.36E
Bagzane, Monts, mtn., Niger	204	18.40N	8.40E
Bahamas, nation, N.A. (bå-hä'mås)	110	26.15N	76.00W
Bahau, Malay.	173b	2.48N	102.25E
Bahāwalpur, Pak. (bŭ-hä'wŭl-pōōr)	174	29.29N	71.41E
Bahia, state, Braz.	124	11.05S	43.00W
Bahía, Islas de la, i., Hond. (ē's-läs-dĕ-lä-bä-ē'ä)	110	16.15N	86.30W
Bahía Blanca, Arg. (bä-ē'ä blän'kä)	126	38.45S	62.07W
Bahía de Caráquez, Ec. (bä-e'ä dä kä-rä'kĕz)	124	0.45S	80.29W
Bahía Negra, Para. (bä-ē'ä nä'grä)	124	20.11S	58.05W
Bahi Swamp, sw., Tan.	210	6.05S	35.10E
Bahoruco, Sierra de, mts., Dom. Rep. (sē-ĕ'r-rä-dĕ-bä-ō-rōō'kô)	116	18.10N	71.25W
Bahrain, nation, Asia (bä-rān')	174	26.15N	51.17E
Bahr al Ghazāl, hist. reg., Sudan (bär ĕl ghä-zäl')	204	7.56N	27.15E
Bahrīyah, oasis, Egypt (bá-hå-rē'yä)	142	28.34N	29.01E
Bahtīm, Egypt	240a	30.08N	31.17E
Baía dos Tigres, Ang.	210	16.36S	11.43E
Baia Mare, Rom. (bä'yä mä'rā)	142	47.40N	23.35E
Baidyabāti, India	178a	22.47N	88.21E
Baie-Comeau, Can.	86	49.13N	68.10W
Baie de Wasai, Mi., U.S. (bā dē wä-sä'ē)	101k	46.27N	84.15W
Baie-Saint Paul, Can. (bā'sănt-pôl')	78	47.27N	70.30W
Baigou, China (bī-gō)	182	39.08N	116.02E
Baihe, China (bī-hŭ)	184	32.30N	110.15E
Bai Hu, l., China (bī-hōō)	182	31.22N	117.38E
Baiju, China (bī-jyōō)	182	33.04N	120.17E
Baikal, Lake, see Baykal, Lake, l., Russia	158	53.00N	109.28E
Bailén, Spain (bä-ê-lān')	152	38.05N	3.48W
Băileşti, Rom. (bă-ĭ-lĕsh'tê)	154	44.01N	23.21E
Baileys Crossroads, Va., U.S.	225d	38.51N	77.08W
Bainbridge, Ga., U.S. (bān'brĭj)	108	30.52N	84.35W
Bainbridge Island, i., Wa., U.S.	100a	47.39N	122.32W
Bainchipota, India	236a	22.52N	88.16E
Baipu, China (bī-pōō)	182	32.15N	120.47E
Baiquan, China (bī-chyuäŋ)	184	47.22N	126.00E
Baird, Tx., U.S. (bârd)	106	32.22N	99.28W
Bairdford, Pa., U.S. (bârd'fōrd)	95e	40.37N	79.53W
Baird Mountains, mts., Ak., U.S.	89	67.35N	160.10W
Bairnsdale, Austl. (bârnz'dāl)	196	37.50S	147.39E
Baïse, r., Fr. (bä-ēz')	150	43.52N	0.23E
Baiyang Dian, l., China (bī-yäŋ-dĭĕn)	182	39.00N	115.45E
Baiyunguan, China	236b	39.54N	116.19E
Baiyu Shan, mts., China (bī-yōō shän)	184	37.02N	108.30E
Baja, Hung. (bŏ'yŏ)	148	46.11N	18.55E
Baja California Norte, state, Mex. (bä-hä)	110	30.15N	117.25W
Baja California Sur, state, Mex.	110	26.00N	113.30W
Bajo, Canal, can., Spain	153a	40.36N	3.41W
Bakal, Russia (bä'kál)	164a	54.57N	58.50E
Baker, Mt., U.S. (bā'kēr)	98	46.21N	104.12W
Baker, Or., U.S.	90	44.46N	117.52W
Baker, i., Oc.	2	1.00N	176.00W
Baker, l., Can.	78	63.51N	96.10W
Baker, Mount, mtn., Wa., U.S.	90	48.46N	121.52W
Baker Creek, r., Il., U.S.	95a	41.13N	87.47W
Bakersfield, Ca., U.S. (bā'kĕrz-fēld)	90	35.23N	119.00W
Bakerstown, Pa., U.S. (bā'kerz-toun)	95e	40.39N	79.56W
Baker Street, Eng., U.K.	231	51.30N	0.21E
Bakewell, Eng., U.K. (bāk'wĕl)	138a	53.12N	1.40W
Bakhchisaray, Ukr. (bàκ'chĕ-sà-rī')	156	44.46N	33.54E
Bakhmach, Ukr. (bàκ-mäch')	156	51.09N	32.47E
Bakhtarān, Iran	174	34.01N	47.00E
Bakhtegan, Daryācheh-ye, l., Iran	174	29.29N	54.31E
Bakhteyevo, Russia	164b	55.35N	38.32E
Bakırköy, neigh., Tur.	235f	40.59N	28.52E
Bako, Eth. (bä'kō)	204	5.47N	36.39E
Bakony, mts., Hung. (bå-kōn'y')	148	46.57N	17.30E
Bakoye, r., Afr. (bà-kô-yē')	204	12.47N	9.35W
Bakr Uzyak, Russia (bákr ōōz'yák)	164a	52.59N	58.43E
Baku, Azer. (bà-kōō')	158	40.28N	49.45E
Bakwanga, see Mbuji-Mayi, Zaire	210	6.09S	23.28E
Balabac Island, i., Phil. (bä'lä-bäk)	188	8.00N	116.28E
Balabac Strait, strt., Asia	188	7.23N	116.30E
Ba'labakk, Leb.	173a	34.00N	36.13E
Balabanovo, Russia (bá-lá-bä'nô-vô)	164b	56.10N	37.44E
Bala-Cynwyd, Pa., U.S.	225b	40.00N	75.14W
Balagansk, Russia (bä-lä-gänsk')	162	53.58N	103.09E
Balaguer, Spain (bä-lä-gĕr')	152	41.48N	0.50E
Balakhta, Russia (bá'lák-tá')	158	55.22N	91.43E
Balakleya, Ukr. (bá'lá-klā'yá)	156	49.28N	36.51E
Balakovo, Russia (bá'lá-kô'vô)	160	52.00N	47.40E
Balancán, Mex. (bä-läŋ-kän')	112	17.47N	91.32W
Balanga, Phil. (bä-läŋ'gä)	189a	14.41N	120.31E
Ba Lang An, Mui, c., Viet.	184	15.18N	109.10E
Balashikha, Russia (bá-lä'shĭ-ká)	164b	55.48N	37.58E
Balashov, Russia (bá-lá-shôf')	160	51.30N	43.00E
Balasore, India (bä-lá-sōr')	174	21.38N	86.59E
Balassagyarmat, Hung. (bô'lôsh-shô-dyôr'môt)	148	48.04N	19.19E
Balaton Lake, l., Hung. (bô'lô-tôn)	142	46.47N	17.55E
Balayan, Phil. (bä-lä-yän')	189a	13.56N	120.44E
Balayan Bay, b., Phil.	189a	13.46N	120.46E
Balboa Heights, Pan. (bäl-bô'ä)	114	8.59N	79.33W
Balboa Mountain, mtn., Pan.	110a	9.05N	79.44W
Balcarce, Arg. (bäl-kär'sā)	126	37.49S	58.17W
Balchik, Bul.	154	43.24N	28.13E
Bald Eagle, Mn., U.S. (bôld ē'g'l)	101g	45.06N	93.01W
Bald Eagle Lake, l., Mn., U.S.	101g	45.08N	93.03W
Baldock Lake, l., Can.	82	56.33N	97.57W
Baldwin, N.Y., U.S.	224	40.39N	73.37W
Baldwin, Pa., U.S.	226b	40.23N	79.58W
Baldwin Park, Ca., U.S. (bôld'wĭn)	101a	34.05N	117.58W
Baldwinsville, N.Y., U.S. (bôld'wĭns-vĭl)	92	43.10N	76.20W
Baldy Mountain, mtn., Can.	82	51.28N	100.44W
Baldy Peak, mtn., Az., U.S. (bôl'dē)	90	33.55N	109.35W
Baldy Peak, mtn., Tx., U.S. (bôl'dē pēk)	106	30.38N	104.11W
Baleares, Islas, is., Spain (e's-läs bä-lĕ-ä'rĕs)	136	39.25N	1.28E
Balearic Islands, see Baleares, Islas, is., Spain	136	39.25N	1.28E
Balearic Sea, sea, Spain (băl-ē-ăr'ĭk)	152	39.40N	1.05E
Baleine, Grande Rivière de la, r., Can.	78	55.00N	75.30W
Baler, Phil. (bä-lar')	189a	15.46N	121.33E
Baler Bay, b., Phil.	189a	15.51N	121.40E
Balesin, i., Phil.	189a	14.28N	122.10E
Baley, Russia (bål-yä')	162	51.29N	116.12E
Balfate, Hond. (bäl-fä'tē)	114	15.48N	86.24W
Balfour, S. Afr. (băl'fōr)	212d	26.41S	28.37E
Balgowlah, Austl.	239a	33.48S	151.16E
Bali, i., Indon. (bä'lē)	188	8.00S	115.22E
Bālihāti, India	236a	22.44N	88.19E
Balıkeşir, Tur. (balĭk'ĭysĭr)	160	39.40N	27.50E
Balikpapan, Indon. (bä'lĕk-pä'pän)	188	1.13S	116.52E
Balintang Channel, strt., Phil. (bä-lĭn-täng')	188	19.50N	121.08E
Balizhuang, China	236b	39.52N	116.28E
Balkan Mountains, see Stara Planina, mts., Bul.	136	42.50N	24.45E
Balkh, Afg. (bälk)	174	36.48N	66.50E
Balkhash, Kaz. (bál-käsh')	158	46.58N	75.00E
Balkhash, Ozero, l., Kaz.	158	45.58N	72.15E
Balki, Ukr. (bäl'kĭ)	156	47.22N	34.56E
Ballabhpur, India	236a	22.44N	88.21E
Ballancourt, Fr. (bä-äɴ-kōr')	151b	48.31N	2.23E
Ballarat, Austl. (băl'å-răt)	196	37.37S	144.00E
Ballard, l., Austl. (băl'ård)	196	29.15S	120.45E
Ballater, Scot., U.K. (bäl'å-tēr)	144	57.05N	3.06W
Ballenato, Punta, c., Cuba	229b	23.06N	82.30W
Balleny Islands, is., Ant. (băl'ĕ nē)	213	67.00S	164.00E
Ballina, Austl. (băl-ĭ-nă')	198	28.50S	153.35E
Ballina, Ire.	144	54.06N	9.05W
Ballinasloe, Ire. (băl'ĭ-nå-slō')	144	53.20N	8.09W
Ballinger, Tx., U.S. (băl'ĭn-jēr)	106	31.45N	99.58W
Ballston Spa, N.Y., U.S. (bôls'tŭn spä')	92	43.05N	73.50W
Ballygunge, neigh., India	236a	22.31N	88.21E
Balmain, Austl.	239a	33.51S	151.11E
Balmazújváros, Hung. (bôl'mŏz-ōō'y'vä'rôsh)	148	47.35N	21.23E
Balobe, Zaire	210	0.05N	28.00E
Balonne, r., Austl. (băl-ōn')	196	27.00S	149.10E
Bālotra, India	178	25.56N	72.12E
Balranald, Austl. (băl'-rån-åld)	198	34.42S	143.30E
Balsam, l., Can. (bôl'såm)	84	44.30N	78.50W
Balsas, Braz. (bäl'säs)	124	7.09S	46.04W
Balsas, r., Mex.	110	18.00N	101.00W
Balta, Ukr. (bäl'tà)	160	47.57N	29.38E
Baltic Sea, sea, Eur. (bôl'tĭk)	136	55.20N	16.50E
Baltīm, Egypt (bål-tēm')	212b	31.33N	31.04E
Baltimore, Md., U.S. (bôl'tĭ-môr)	90	39.20N	76.38W
Baltiysk, Russia (bäl-tēysk')	146	54.40N	19.55E
Baluarte, Río del, Mex. (rē'ō-dĕl-bä-lōō'r-tē)	112	23.09N	105.42W
Baluchistān, hist. reg., Asia (bá-lò-chĭ-stän')	174	27.30N	65.30E
Balwyn, Austl.	239b	37.49S	145.05E
Balzac, Can. (bôl'zăk)	77e	51.10N	114.01W
Bama, Nig.	208	11.30N	13.41E
Bamako, Mali (bä-mä-kō')	204	12.39N	8.00W
Bambang, Phil. (bäm-bäng')	189a	16.24N	121.08E
Bambari, Cen. Afr. Rep. (bäm-bá-rē)	204	5.44N	20.40E
Bamberg, Ger. (bäm'bĕrgh)	140	49.53N	10.52E
Bamberg, S.C., U.S. (băm'bûrg)	108	33.17N	81.04W
Bamenda, Cam.	208	5.56N	10.10E
Bamingui, r., Cen. Afr. Rep.	208	7.35N	19.45E
Bampton, Eng., U.K. (băm'tŭn)	138b	51.42N	1.33W
Bampūr, Iran (bŭm-pōōr')	174	27.15N	60.22E
Bam Yanga, Ngao, mts., Cam.	208	8.20N	14.40E
Banahao, Mount, mtn., Phil. (bä-nä-hä'ô)	189a	14.04N	121.45E
Banalia, Zaire	210	1.33N	25.20E
Banamba, Mali	208	13.33N	7.27W
Bananal, Braz. (bä-nä-näl')	123a	22.42S	44.17W
Bananal, Ilha do, i., Braz. (ē'lä-dô-bä-nä-näl')	124	12.09S	50.27W
Banās, r., India (bän-äs')	174	25.20N	75.20E
Banās, Ra's, c., Egypt	204	23.48N	36.39E
Banat, reg., Rom. (bä-nät')	154	45.35N	21.05E
Banbidian, China	236b	39.54N	116.32E
Bancroft, Can. (băn'krôft)	78	45.05N	77.55W
Bancroft, see Chililabombwe, Zam.	210	12.18S	27.43E
Bānda, India (bän'dä)	174	25.36N	80.21E
Banda, Kepulauan, is., Indon.	188	4.40S	129.56E
Banda, Laut (Banda Sea), sea, Indon.	188	6.05S	127.28E
Banda Aceh, Indon.	188	5.10N	95.10E
Banda Banda, Mount, mtn., Austl. (băn'då băn'då)	198	31.09S	152.15E
Bandama Blanc, r., I.C. (bän-dä'mä)	208	6.15N	5.00W
Bandar Beheshtī, Iran	174	25.18N	60.45E
Bandar-e 'Abbās, Iran (bän-där' áb-bäs')	174	27.04N	56.22E
Bandar-e Būshehr, Iran	174	28.48N	50.53E
Bandar-e Lengeh, Iran	174	26.44N	54.47E
Bandar-e Torkeman, Iran	174	37.05N	54.08E
Bandar Maharani, Malay. (bän-där' mä-hä-rä'nē)	173b	2.02N	102.34E
Bandar Seri Begawan, Bru.	188	5.00N	114.59E
Bande, Spain	152	42.02N	7.58W
Bandeira, Pico da, mtn., Braz. (pē'kô dä bän dā'rä)	124	20.27S	41.47W
Bāndel, India	236a	22.56N	88.22E
Bandelier National Monument, rec., N.M., U.S. (băn-dĕ-lēr')	102	35.50N	106.45W
Banderas, Bahía de, b., Mex. (bä-ē'ä dĕ bän-dĕ'räs)	112	20.38N	105.35W
Bandirma, Tur. (bän-dĭr'må)	142	40.25N	27.50E
Bandon, Or., U.S. (băn'dŭn)	98	43.06N	124.25W
Bāndra, India	179b	19.04N	72.49E
Bandundu, Zaire	206	3.18S	17.20E
Bandung, Indon.	188	7.00S	107.22E

ng-sing; ŋ-baŋk; ɴ-nasalized n; nŏd; cŏmmit; ōld; ôbey; ôrder; oi-boil; fōōd; ò-as oo in foot; ou-out; s-soft; sh-dish; th-thin; pūre; ůnite; ûrn; stŭd; circŭs; ü-as in French tu; '-indeterminate vowel.

PLACE (Pronunciation)	PAGE	Lat. °′	Long. °′
Banes, Cuba (bä'näs)	116	21.00N	75.45W
Banff, Can. (bănf)	78	51.10N	115.34W
Banff, Scot., U.K.	144	57.39N	2.37W
Banff National Park, rec., Can.	78	51.38N	116.22W
Bánfield, Arg. (bà'n-fyě'ld)	126a	34.44S	58.24W
Banfora, Burkina	208	10.38N	4.46W
Bangalore, India (băŋ'gá'lôr)	174	13.03N	77.39E
Bangassou, Cen. Afr. Rep. (bäɴ-gà-sōō')	204	4.47N	22.49E
Bangeta, Mount, mtn., Pap. N. Gui.	188	6.20S	147.00E
Banggai, Kepulauan, is., Indon. (bäng-gī')	188	1.05S	123.45E
Banggi, Pulau, i., Malay.	188	7.12N	117.10E
Banghāzī, Libya	204	32.07N	20.04E
Bangka, i., Indon. (bäŋ'kȧ)	188	2.24S	106.55E
Bangkalan, Indon. (bäng-kȧ-län')	188	6.07S	112.50E
Bang Khun Thian, Thai.	237f	13.42N	100.28E
Bangkok, Thai.	188	13.50N	100.29E
Bangladesh, nation, Asia	174	24.15N	90.00E
Bangong Co, l., Asia (bäŋ-gôŋ tswo)	178	33.40N	79.30E
Bangor, Wales, U.K. (băŋ'ŏr)	144	53.13N	4.05W
Bangor, Me., U.S. (băn'gẽr)	90	44.47N	68.47W
Bangor, Mi., U.S.	92	42.20N	86.05W
Bangor, Pa., U.S.	92	40.55N	75.10W
Bangs, Mount, mtn., Az., U.S. (băngs)	102	36.45N	113.50W
Bangu, neigh., Braz.	230c	22.52S	43.27W
Bangued, Phil. (bän-gād')	189a	17.36N	120.38E
Bangui, Cen. Afr. Rep. (bäɴ-gē')	204	4.22N	18.35E
Bangweulu, Lake, l., Zam. (băng-wė-ōō'lōō)	206	10.55S	30.10E
Bangweulu Swamp, sw., Zam.	210	11.25S	30.10E
Bani, Dom. Rep. (bä'-nė)	116	18.15N	70.25W
Bani, Phil. (bä'nē)	189a	16.11N	119.51E
Bani, r., Mali	204	13.00N	5.30W
Bánica, Dom. Rep. (bä'-nē-kä)	116	19.00N	71.35W
Banī Majdūl, Egypt	240a	30.02N	31.07E
Banī Mazār, Egypt	176	28.29N	30.48E
Banister, r., Va., U.S. (băn'ĭs-tẽr)	108	36.45N	79.17W
Banī Suwayf, Egypt	204	29.05N	31.06E
Banja Luka, Bos. (bän-yä-lōō'kȧ)	142	44.45N	17.11E
Banjarmasin, Indon. (bän-jẽr-mä'sėn)	188	3.18S	114.32E
Banjin, China (bän-jyĭn)	182	32.23N	120.14E
Banjul, Gam.	204	13.28N	16.39W
Bankberg, mts., S. Afr. (bȧŋk'bûrg)	207c	32.18S	25.15E
Banks, Or., U.S. (bănks)	100c	45.37N	123.07W
Banks, i., Austl.	196	10.10S	143.08E
Banks, Cape, c., Austl.	195b	34.01S	151.17E
Banks Island, i., Can.	76	73.00N	123.00W
Banks Island, i., Can.	80	53.25N	130.10W
Banks Islands, is., Vanuatu	196	13.38S	168.23E
Banksmeadow, Austl.	239a	33.58S	151.13E
Banks Peninsula, pen., N.Z.	199	43.45S	172.20E
Banks Strait, strt., Austl.	198	40.45S	148.00E
Bankstown, Austl.	195b	33.55S	151.02E
Ban Lat Phrao, Thai.	237f	13.47N	100.36E
Bann, r., N. Ire., U.K. (băn)	144	54.50N	6.29W
Banning, Ca., U.S. (băn'ĭng)	101a	33.56N	116.53W
Bannockburn, Austl.	195a	38.03S	144.11E
Bannu, Pak.	178	33.03N	70.39E
Baños, Ec. (bä'-nyỏs)	124	1.30S	78.22W
Banská Bystrica, Czech. (bän'skä bė'strė-tzä)	140	48.46N	19.10E
Bansko, Bul. (bän'skō)	154	41.51N	23.33E
Banstala, India	236a	22.32N	88.25E
Banstead, Eng., U.K. (băn'stĕd)	138b	51.18N	0.09W
Banton, i., Phil. (bän-tōn')	189a	12.54N	121.55E
Bantry, Ire. (băn'trĭ)	144	51.39N	9.30W
Bantry Bay, b., Ire.	144	51.25N	10.09W
Banyak, Kepulauan, is., Indon.	188	2.08N	97.15E
Banyuwangi, Indon. (bän-jỏ-wäŋ'gė)	188	8.15S	114.15E
Baocheng, China (bou-chŭŋ)	184	33.15N	106.58E
Baodi, China (bou-dē)	184	39.44N	117.19E
Baoding, China (bou-dĭŋ)	180	38.52N	115.31E
Baoji, China (bou-jyē)	184	34.10N	106.58E
Baoshan, China (bou-shän)	180	25.14N	99.03E
Baoshan, China	182	31.25N	121.29E
Baotou, China (bou-tō)	180	40.28N	110.10E
Baoying, China (bou-yĭŋ)	184	33.14N	119.20E
Bapsfontein, S. Afr. (băps-fŏn-tān')	207b	26.01S	28.26E
Ba 'qūbah, Iraq	176	33.45N	44.38E
Ba-queo, Viet.	237m	10.48N	106.38E
Baqueroncito, Col. (bä-kĕ-rô'n-sē-tỏ)	124a	3.18N	74.40W
Bara, India	236a	22.46N	88.17E
Baraawe, Som.	212a	1.20N	44.00E
Barabinsk, Russia (bȧ'rȧ-bĭnsk)	162	55.18N	78.00E
Baraboo, Wi., U.S. (bâr'ȧ-bōō)	96	43.29N	89.44W
Baracoa, Cuba (bä-rä-kō'ä)	116	20.20N	74.25W
Baracoa, Cuba	117a	23.03N	82.34W
Baradères, Baie des, b., Haiti (bä-rä-dâr')	116	18.35N	73.35W
Baradero, Arg. (bä-rä-dĕ'ŏ)	123c	33.50S	59.30W
Baragwanath, S. Afr.	240b	26.16S	27.59E
Barahona, Dom. Rep. (bä-rä-ô'nä)	116	18.15N	71.10W
Barajas de Madrid, Spain (bä-rä'häs dā mä-drēdh')	153a	40.28N	3.35W
Baranagar, India	178	22.38N	88.25E
Baranco, Belize (bä-räŋ'kō)	114	16.01N	88.55W
Baranof, i., Ak., U.S. (bä-rä'nôf)	89	56.48N	136.08W
Baranovichi, Bela. (bä'rä-nỏ-vē'chė)	158	53.08N	25.59E
Baranpauh, Indon.	173b	0.40N	103.28E
Barão de Melgaço, Braz. (bä-roun-dĕ-mĕl-gä'sỏ)	124	16.12S	55.48W
Bārāsat, India	178a	22.42N	88.29E
Bārasat, India	236a	22.51N	88.22E
Barataria Bay, b., La., U.S.	106	29.13N	89.50W
Baraya, Col. (bä-rȧ'yä)	124a	3.10N	75.04W
Barbacena, Braz. (bär-bä-sā'nȧ)	124	21.15S	43.46W
Barbacoas, Col. (bär-bä-kō'äs)	124	1.39N	78.12W
Barbacoas, Ven. (bä-bä-kô'ás)	125b	9.30N	66.58W
Barbados, nation, N.A. (bär-bā'dōz)	110	13.30N	59.00W
Barbar, Sudan	204	18.11N	34.00E
Barbastro, Spain (bär-bäs'trō)	152	42.05N	0.05E
Barbeau, Mi., U.S. (bȧr-bō')	101k	46.17N	84.16W
Barberton, S. Afr.	206	25.48S	31.04E
Barberton, Oh., U.S. (bär'bẽr-tŭn)	95d	41.01N	81.37W
Barbezieux, Fr. (bärb'zyû')	150	45.30N	0.11W
Barbosa, Col. (bär-bô'-sȧ)	124a	6.26N	75.19W
Barboursville, W.V., U.S. (bär'bẽrs-vĭl)	92	38.20N	82.20W
Barbourville, Ky., U.S.	108	36.52N	83.58W
Barbuda, i., Antig. (bär-bōō'dȧ)	110	17.45N	61.15W
Barcaldine, Austl. (bär'kôl-dīn)	196	23.33S	145.17E
Barcarrota, Spain (bär-kär-rō'tä)	152	38.31N	6.50W
Barcellona, Italy (bä-chĕl-lō'nä)	154	38.07N	15.15E
Barcelona, Spain (bär-thȧ-lō'nä)	136	41.25N	2.08E
Barcelona, Ven. (bär-sȧ-lō'nä)	124	10.09N	64.41W
Barcelos, Braz. (bär-sĕ'lỏs)	124	1.04S	63.00W
Barcelos, Port. (bär-thâ'lōs)	152	41.34N	8.39W
Barcroft, Lake, res., Va., U.S.	225d	38.51N	77.09W
Bardawīl, Sabkhat al, b., Egypt	173a	31.20N	33.24E
Bardejov, Czech. (bär'dyĕ-yôf)	148	49.18N	21.18E
Bardsey Island, i., Wales, U.K. (bärd'sė)	144	52.45N	4.50W
Bardstown, Ky., U.S. (bärds'toun)	92	37.50N	85.30W
Bardwell, Ky., U.S. (bärd'wĕl)	108	36.51N	88.57W
Bare Hills, Md., U.S.	225c	39.23N	76.40W
Bareilly, India	174	28.21N	79.25E
Barents Sea, sea, Eur. (bä'rĕnts)	158	72.14N	37.28E
Barentu, Eth. (bä-rĕn'tōō)	204	15.06N	37.39E
Barfleur, Pointe de, c., Fr. (bȧr-flûr')	150	49.43N	1.17W
Barguzin, Russia (bär'gōō-zĭn)	158	53.44N	109.28E
Bar Harbor, Me., U.S. (bär här'bẽr)	86	44.22N	68.13W
Bari, Italy (bä'rē)	136	41.08N	16.53E
Barinas, Ven. (bä-rē'näs)	124	8.36N	70.14W
Baring, Cape, c., Can. (bâr'ĭng)	78	70.07N	119.48W
Barisan, Pegunungan, mts., Indon. (bä-rė-sän')	188	2.38S	101.45E
Bariti Bil, l., India	236a	22.48N	88.26E
Barito, r., Indon. (bä-rē'tō)	188	2.10S	114.38E
Barka, r., Afr.	204	16.44N	37.34E
Barking, neigh., Eng., U.K.	231	51.33N	0.06E
Barkingside, neigh., Eng., U.K.	231	51.36N	0.05E
Barkley Sound, strt., Can.	80	48.53N	125.20W
Barkly East, S. Afr. (bärk'lē ēst)	207c	30.58S	27.37E
Barkly Tableland, plat., Austl. (bär'klė)	196	18.15S	137.05E
Barkol, China (bär-kûl)	180	43.43N	92.50E
Bar-le-Duc, Fr. (bär-lē-dük')	150	48.47N	5.05E
Barlee, l., Austl. (bär-lē')	196	29.45S	119.00E
Barletta, Italy (bär-lĕt'tä)	142	41.19N	16.20E
Barmen, neigh., Ger.	232	51.17N	7.13E
Barmstedt, Ger. (bärm'shtĕt)	139c	53.47N	9.46E
Barnaul, Russia (bŭr-nä-ōl')	158	53.18N	83.23E
Barnes, neigh., Eng., U.K.	231	51.28N	0.15W
Barnesboro, Pa., U.S. (bärnz'bẽr-ỏ)	92	40.45N	78.50W
Barnesville, Ga., U.S. (bärnz'vĭl)	108	33.03N	84.10W
Barnesville, Mn., U.S.	96	46.38N	96.25W
Barnesville, Oh., U.S.	92	39.55N	81.10W
Barnet, Vt., U.S. (bär'nĕt)	92	44.20N	72.00W
Barnetby le Wold, Eng., U.K. (bär'nĕt-bĭ)	138a	53.34N	0.26W
Barnett Harbor, b., Bah.	116	25.40N	79.20W
Barnsdall, Ok., U.S. (bärnz'dôl)	104	36.38N	96.14W
Barnsley, Eng., U.K. (bärnz'lĭ)	138a	53.33N	1.29W
Barnstaple, Eng., U.K. (bärn'stā-p'l)	144	51.06N	4.05W
Barnston, Eng., U.K.	233a	53.21N	3.05W
Barnum Island, N.Y., U.S.	224	40.36N	73.39W
Barnwell, S.C., U.S. (bärn'wĕl)	108	33.14N	81.23W
Baro, Nig. (bä'rō)	204	8.37N	6.25E
Baroda, India (bär-rō'dä)	174	22.21N	73.12E
Barotse Plain, pl., Zam.	210	15.50S	22.55E
Barqah (Cyrenaica), hist. reg., Libya	204	31.09N	21.45E
Barquisimeto, Ven. (bär-kē-sė-mā'tō)	124	10.04N	69.16W
Barra, Braz. (bär'rä)	124	11.04S	43.11W
Barraba, Austl.	198	30.22S	150.36E
Barracas, neigh., Arg.	229d	34.38S	58.22W
Barrackpore, India	178a	22.46N	88.21E
Barra do Corda, Braz. (bär'rä dỏ cōr-dä)	124	5.33S	45.13W
Barra Funda, neigh., Braz.	230d	23.31S	46.39W
Barra Mansa, Braz. (bär'rä män'sä)	123a	22.35S	44.09W
Barrancabermeja, Col. (bär-räŋ'kä-bēr-mā'hä)	124	7.06N	73.49W
Barrancas, Chile	230b	33.27S	70.46W
Barranco, Peru	229c	12.09S	77.02W
Barranquilla, Col. (bär-rän-kēl'yä)	124	10.57N	75.00W
Barras, Braz. (bä'r-räs)	124	4.13S	42.14W
Barre, Vt., U.S. (bär'ė)	92	44.15N	72.30W
Barreiras, Braz. (bär-rā'räs)	124	12.13S	44.59W
Barreiro, Port. (bär-rē'ė-rỏ)	142	38.39N	9.05W
Barren, r., Ky., U.S.	108	37.00N	86.20W
Barren, Cape, c., Austl. (băr'ĕn)	196	40.20S	149.00E
Barren, Nosy, is., Madag.	206	18.18S	43.57E
Barren River Lake, res., Ky., U.S.	108	36.45N	86.02W
Barretos, Braz. (bär-rā'tỏs)	124	20.40S	48.36W
Barrhead, Can. (băr'ĭd)	78	54.08N	114.24W
Barriada Pomar Alto, Spain	234e	41.29N	2.14E
Barrie, Can. (băr'ĭ)	78	44.25N	79.45W
Barrington, Can. (bă-rĕng-tŏn)	77a	45.07N	73.35W
Barrington, Il., U.S.	95a	42.09N	88.08W
Barrington, N.J., U.S.	225b	39.52N	75.04W
Barrington, R.I., U.S.	94b	41.44N	71.16W
Barrington Tops, mtn., Austl.	198	32.00S	151.25E
Barrio Obrero Industrial, prov., Peru	229c	12.04S	77.04W
Bar River, Can. (bär)	101k	46.27N	84.02W
Barron, Wi., U.S. (băr'ŭn)	96	45.24N	91.51W
Barrow, Ak., U.S. (băr'ō)	90a	71.20N	156.00W
Barrow, i., Austl.	196	20.50S	115.00E
Barrow, r., Ire. (bă-rō)	144	52.35N	7.05W
Barrow, Point, c., Ak., U.S.	89	71.20N	156.00W
Barrow Creek, Austl.	196	21.23S	133.55E
Barrow-in-Furness, Eng., U.K.	140	54.10N	3.15W
Barstow, Ca., U.S. (bär'stō)	102	34.53N	117.03W
Barstow, Md., U.S.	94e	38.32N	76.37W
Barth, Ger. (bärt)	148	54.20N	12.43E
Bartholomew Bayou, r., U.S. (bär-thŏl'ō-mū bī-ōō')	104	33.53N	91.45W
Barthurst, Can. (bär-thûrst')	78	47.38N	65.40W
Bartica, Guy. (bär'tĭ-kȧ)	124	6.23N	58.32W
Bartin, Tur. (bär'tĭn)	142	41.35N	32.12E
Bartle Frere, Mount, mtn., Austl. (bärt''l frēr')	196	17.30S	145.46E
Bartlesville, Ok., U.S. (bär'tlz-vĭl)	104	36.44N	95.58W
Bartlett, Il., U.S. (bärt'lĕt)	95a	41.59N	88.11W
Bartlett, Tx., U.S.	106	30.48N	97.25W
Barton, Vt., U.S. (bär'tŭn)	92	44.45N	72.05W
Barton-upon-Humber, Eng., U.K. (bär'tŭn-ŭp'ŏn-hŭm'bẽr)	138a	53.41N	0.26W
Bartoszyce, Pol. (bär-tỏ-shĭ'tsȧ)	148	54.15N	20.50E
Bartow, Fl., U.S. (bär'tō)	109a	27.51N	81.50W
Baruta, Ven.	230a	10.26N	66.53W
Barvenkovo, Ukr. (bär'vĕn-kô'vỏ)	156	48.55N	36.59E
Barwon, r., Austl. (bär'wŭn)	196	30.00S	147.30E
Barwon Heads, Austl.	195a	38.17S	144.29E
Barycz, r., Pol. (bä'rĭch)	148	51.30N	16.38E
Basai Dārāpur, neigh., India	236d	28.40N	77.08E
Basankusu, Zaire (bä-sän-kōō'sōō)	204	1.14N	19.45E
Basbeck, Ger. (bäs'bĕk)	139c	53.40N	9.11E
Basdahl, Ger. (bäs'däl)	139c	53.27N	9.00E
Basehor, Ks., U.S. (bās'hôr)	101f	39.08N	94.55W
Basel, Switz. (bä'z'l)	140	47.32N	7.35E
Bashee, r., Transkei (bă-shē')	207c	31.47S	28.25E
Bashi Channel, strt., Asia (bäsh'ė)	180	21.20N	120.22E
Bashkir Autonomous Soviet Socialist Republic, Russia (bȧsh-kēr')	160	54.12N	57.15E
Bashtanka, Ukr. (bȧsh-tän'kȧ)	156	47.32N	32.31E
Bashtīl, Egypt	240a	30.05N	31.11E
Basilan Island, i., Phil.	188	6.37N	122.07E
Basildon, Eng., U.K.	144	51.35N	0.25E
Basilicata, hist. reg., Italy (bä-zē-lė-kä'tä)	154	40.30N	15.55E
Basin, Wy., U.S. (bā'sĭn)	98	44.22N	108.02W
Basingstoke, Eng., U.K. (bā'zĭng-stōk)	138b	51.14N	1.06W
Baška, Cro. (bäsh'ka)	154	44.58N	14.44E
Baskale, Tur. (bäsh-kä'lĕ)	160	38.10N	44.00E
Baskatong, Réservoir, res., Can.	84	46.50N	75.50W
Baskunchak, l., Russia	160	48.20N	46.40E
Basoko, Zaire (bȧ-sō'kō)	204	0.52N	23.50E
Basra, *see* Al Başrah, Iraq	174	30.35N	47.59E
Bassano, Can. (bäs-sän'ō)	78	50.47N	112.28W
Bassano del Grappa, Italy	154	45.46N	11.44E
Bassari, Togo	208	9.15N	0.47E
Bassas da India, i., Reu. (bäs'säs dä ĕn'dė-ȧ)	206	21.23S	39.42E
Basse Terre, Guad. (bȧs' târ')	110	16.00N	61.43W
Basseterre, St. K./N.	115b	17.20N	62.42W
Basse Terre, i., Guad.	115b	16.10N	62.14W
Bassett, Va., U.S. (băs'sĕt)	108	36.45N	81.58W
Bass Hill, Austl.	239a	33.54S	151.00E
Bass Islands, is., Oh., U.S. (băs)	92	41.40N	82.50W
Bass Strait, strt., Austl.	196	39.40S	145.40E
Basswood, l., N.A. (băs'wŏod)	96	48.10N	91.36W
Båstad, Swe. (bỏ'stät)	146	56.26N	12.46E
Bastia, Fr. (bäs'tē-ä)	140	42.43N	9.27E
Bastogne, Bel. (bäs-tỏn'y')	144	50.02N	5.45E
Bastrop, La., U.S. (băs'trŭp)	106	32.47N	91.55W
Bastrop, Tx., U.S.	106	30.08N	97.18W
Bastrop Bayou, Tx., U.S.	107a	29.07N	95.22W
Bāsudebpur, India	236a	22.49N	88.25E
Bata, Eq. Gui. (bä'tä)	204	1.51N	9.45E
Batabano, Golfo de, b., Cuba (gôl-fō-dĕ-bä-tä-bä'nỏ)	116	22.10N	83.05W
Batāla, India	178	31.54N	75.18E
Bataly, Kaz. (bȧ-tä'lĭ)	164a	52.51N	62.03E
Batam, i., Indon. (bä-täm')	173b	1.03N	104.00E
Batang, China (bä-täŋ)	180	30.08N	99.00E
Batangas, Phil. (bä-tän'gäs)	188	13.45N	121.04E
Batan Islands, is., Phil. (bä-tän')	188	20.58N	122.20E
Bátaszék, Hung. (bä'tá-sĕk)	148	46.07N	18.40E
Batavia, Il., U.S. (bȧ-tā'vĭ-ȧ)	95a	41.51N	88.18W
Batavia, N.Y., U.S.	92	43.00N	78.15W
Batavia, Oh., U.S.	95f	39.05N	84.10W
Bataysk, Russia (bȧ-tīsk')	160	47.08N	39.44E
Bătdâmbâng, Kam. (bát-tȧm-bäng')	188	13.14N	103.15E
Batenbrock, neigh., Ger.	232	51.31N	6.57E
Batesburg, S.C., U.S. (bāts'bûrg)	108	33.53N	81.34W
Batesville, Ar., U.S. (bāts'vĭl)	104	35.46N	91.39W
Batesville, In., U.S.	92	39.15N	85.15W
Batesville, Ms., U.S.	108	34.17N	89.55W
Batetska, Russia (bȧ-tĕ'tskȧ)	156	58.36N	30.21E
Bath, Can. (bȧth)	86	46.31N	67.36W
Bath, Eng., U.K.	140	51.24N	2.20W
Bath, Me., U.S.	86	43.54N	69.50W
Bath, N.Y., U.S.	92	42.25N	77.20W
Bath, Oh., U.S.	95d	41.11N	81.38W
Bathsheba, Barb.	115b	13.13N	60.30W
Bathurst, Austl. (băth'ŭrst)	196	33.28S	149.30E
Bathurst, S. Afr. (băt-hûrst)	207c	33.26S	26.53E
Bathurst, i., Austl.	196	11.19S	130.13E
Bathurst, Cape, c., Can. (bȧth'ŭrst)	78	70.33N	127.55W
Bathurst, *see* Banjul, Gam.	204	13.28N	16.39W
Bathurst Inlet, b., Can.	78	68.10N	108.00W
Batia, Benin	208	10.54N	1.29E
Batley, Eng., U.K. (băt'lĭ)	138a	53.43N	1.37W
Batna, Alg. (bät'nä)	204	35.41N	6.12E
Baton Rouge, La., U.S. (băt'ŭn rōōzh')	90	30.28N	91.10W
Battersea, neigh., Eng., U.K.	231	51.28N	0.10W
Batticaloa, Sri L.	178	7.40N	81.10E

ăt; finȧl; rāte; senāte; ärm; ȧsk; sofȧ; fâre; ch-choose; dh-as th in other; bē; ėvent; bĕt; recĕnt; cratẽr; g-gō; gh-guttural g; bĭt; ĭ-short neutral; rīde; ᴋ-guttural k as ch in German ich;

PLACE (Pronunciation)	PAGE	Lat. °'	Long. °'
Battle, r., Can.	82	52.20N	111.59W
Battle Creek, Mi., U.S. (băt''l krēk')	90	42.20N	85.15W
Battle Ground, Wa., U.S. (băt''l ground)	100c	45.47N	122.32W
Battle Harbour, Can. (băt''l här'bẽr)	78	52.17N	55.33W
Battle Mountain, Nv., U.S.	98	40.40N	116.56W
Battonya, Hung. (bät-tô'nyä)	148	46.17N	21.00E
Batu, Kepulauan, is., Indon. (bä'tōō)	188	0.10S	98.00E
Batumi, Geor. (bŭ-tōō'mē)	158	41.40N	41.30E
Batu Pahat, Malay.	188	1.51N	102.56E
Batupanjang, Indon.	173b	1.42N	101.35E
Bauang, Phil. (bä'wäng)	189a	16.31N	120.19E
Bauchi, Nig. (bà-ōō'chē)	204	10.19N	9.50E
Bauerschaft, Ger.	232	51.34N	6.33E
Bauerstown, Pa., U.S.	226b	40.30N	79.59W
Baukau, neigh., Ger.	232	51.33N	7.12E
Bauld, Cape, c., Can.	79a	51.38N	55.25W
Baulkham Hills, Austl.	239a	33.46S	151.00E
Baumschulenweg, neigh., Ger.	234a	52.28N	13.29E
Bāuria, India	178a	22.29N	88.08E
Bauru, Braz. (bou-rōō')	124	22.21S	48.57W
Bauska, Lat. (bou'skà)	146	56.24N	24.12E
Bauta, Cuba (bá'ōō-tä)	117a	22.59N	82.33W
Bautzen, Ger. (bout'sĕn)	140	51.11N	14.27E
Bavaria, *see* Bayern, state, Ger.	148	49.00N	11.16E
Baw Baw, Mount, mtn., Austl.	198	37.50S	146.17E
Bawean, Pulau, i., Indon. (bá'vē-än)	188	5.50S	112.40E
Bawtry, Eng., U.K. (bôtrĭ)	138a	53.26N	1.01W
Baxley, Ga., U.S. (băks'lĭ)	108	31.47N	82.22W
Baxter, Austl. (băks'tẽr)	195a	38.12S	145.10E
Baxter Springs, Ks., U.S. (băks'tẽr springs')	104	37.01N	94.44W
Bay, Laguna de, l., Phil. (lä-gōō'nä dā bä'ē)	189a	14.24N	121.13E
Bayaguana, Dom. Rep. (bä-yä-gwä'nä)	116	18.45N	69.40W
Bay al Kabīr, Wadi, val., Libya	142	29.52N	14.28E
Bayambang, Phil. (bä-yäm-bäng')	189a	15.50N	120.26E
Bayamo, Cuba (bä-yä'mō)	116	20.25N	76.35W
Bayamón, P.R.	111b	18.27N	66.13W
Bayan, China (bä-yän)	184	46.00N	127.20E
Bayan-Aul, Kaz. (bä'yän-oul')	158	50.43N	75.37E
Bayard, Ne., U.S. (bā'ẽrd)	96	41.45N	103.20W
Bayard, N.M., U.S.	102	32.45N	108.07W
Bayard, W.V., U.S.	92	39.15N	79.20W
Bayburt, Tur. (bä'ĭ-bŏort)	160	40.15N	40.10E
Bay City, Mi., U.S. (bā)	90	43.35N	83.55W
Bay City, Tx., U.S.	106	28.59N	95.58W
Baydaratskaya Guba, b., Russia	160	69.20N	66.10E
Bay de Verde, Can.	86	48.05N	52.54W
Baydhabo, Som.	212a	3.19N	44.20E
Baydrag, r., Mong.	180	46.09N	98.52E
Bayern (Bavaria), hist. reg., Ger. (bī'ĕrn) (bá-vâ-rĭ-á)	148	49.00N	11.16E
Bayeux, Fr. (bá-yû')	140	49.19N	0.41W
Bayfield, Wi., U.S. (bā'fēld)	96	46.48N	90.51W
Bayford, Eng., U.K.	231	51.46N	0.06W
Baykal, Ozero (Lake Baikal), l., Russia	158	53.00N	109.28E
Baykal'skiy Khrebet, mts., Russia	158	53.30N	107.30E
Baykit, Russia (bī-kēt')	158	61.43N	96.39E
Baykonur, Kaz. (bī-kô-nōōr')	158	47.46N	66.11E
Baymak, Russia (bȧy'mäk)	164a	52.35N	58.21E
Bay Mills, Mi., U.S. (bā mĭlls)	101k	46.27N	84.36W
Bay Mills Indian Reservation, I.R., Mi., U.S.	96	46.19N	85.03W
Bay Minette, Al., U.S. (bā'mĭn-ĕt')	108	30.52N	87.44W
Bayombong, Phil. (bä-yôm-bŏng')	189a	16.28N	121.09E
Bayonne, Fr. (bá-yôn')	136	43.28N	1.30W
Bayonne, N.J., U.S. (bā-yōn')	94a	40.40N	74.07W
Bayou Bodcau Reservoir, res., La., U.S. (bī'yōō bŏd'kō)	90	32.49N	93.22W
Bay Park, N.Y., U.S.	224	40.38N	73.40W
Bayport, Mn., U.S. (bā'pōrt)	101g	45.02N	92.46W
Bayramiç, Tur.	154	39.48N	26.35E
Bayreuth, Ger. (bī-roit')	148	49.56N	11.35E
Bay Ridge, neigh., N.Y., U.S.	224	40.37N	74.02W
Bay Roberts, Can. (bā rŏb'ẽrts)	86	47.36N	53.16W
Bays, Lake of, l., Can. (bās)	84	45.15N	79.00W
Bay Saint Louis, Ms., U.S. (bā' sânt lōō'ĭs)	108	30.19N	89.20W
Bay Shore, N.Y., U.S. (bā' shôr)	94a	40.44N	73.15W
Bayside, Ma., U.S.	223a	42.18N	70.53W
Bayside, neigh., N.Y., U.S.	224	40.46N	73.46W
Bayswater, Austl.	239b	37.51S	145.16E
Bayswater North, Austl.	239b	37.49S	145.17E
Bayt Lahm, Isr. Occ. (bĕth'lē-hĕm)	173a	31.42N	35.13E
Baytown, Tx., U.S. (bā'town)	107a	29.44N	95.01W
Bayview, Al., U.S. (bā'vū)	94h	33.34N	86.59W
Bayview, Wa., U.S.	100a	48.29N	122.28W
Bayview, neigh., Ca., U.S.	227b	37.44N	122.23W
Bay Village, Oh., U.S. (bā)	95d	41.29N	81.56W
Bayville, N.Y., U.S.	224	40.54N	73.33W
Baza, Spain (bä'thä)	142	37.29N	2.46W
Baza, Sierra de, mts., Spain	152	37.19N	2.48W
Bazar-Dyuzi, mtn., Azer. (bä'zár-dyōōz'ĕ)	160	41.20N	47.40E
Bazaruto, Ilha do, i., Moz. (bá-zá-rō'tō)	206	21.42S	36.10E
Bazièges, Fr.	150	43.25N	1.41E
Be, Nosy, i., Madag.	206	13.14S	47.28E
Beach, N.D., U.S. (bēch)	96	46.55N	104.00W
Beachwood, Oh., U.S.	225a	41.29N	81.30W
Beachy Head, c., Eng., U.K. (bēchē hĕd)	144	50.40N	0.25E
Beacon, N.Y., U.S. (bē'kŭn)	92	41.30N	73.55W
Beacon Hill, Austl.	239a	33.45S	151.15E
Beacon Hill, China	237c	22.21N	114.09E
Beaconsfield, Can. (bē'kŭnz-fēld)	77a	45.26N	73.51W
Beals Creek, r., Tx., U.S. (bēls)	106	32.10N	101.14W
Bean, Eng., U.K.	231	51.25N	0.17E
Bear, r., U.S.	98	42.17N	111.42W

PLACE (Pronunciation)	PAGE	Lat. °'	Long. °'
Bear, r., Ut., U.S.	101b	41.28N	112.10W
Bear Brook, r., Can.	77c	45.24N	75.15W
Bear Creek, Mt., U.S. (bâr krēk)	98	45.11N	109.07W
Bear Creek, r., Al., U.S. (bâr)	108	34.27N	88.00W
Bear Creek, r., Tx., U.S.	101c	32.56N	97.09W
Beardstown, Il., U.S. (bērds'toun)	104	40.01N	90.26W
Bearfort Mountain, mtn., N.J., U.S. (bē'fōrt)	94a	41.08N	74.23W
Bearhead Mountain, mtn., Wa., U.S. (bâr'hĕd)	100a	47.01N	121.49W
Bear Lake, l., Can.	82	55.08N	96.00W
Bear Lake, l., Id., U.S.	98	41.56N	111.10W
Bear River Range, mts., U.S.	98	41.50N	111.30W
Beas de Segura, Spain (bā'äs dā sä-gōō'rä)	152	38.16N	2.53W
Beata, i., Dom. Rep. (bĕ-ä'tä)	116	17.40N	71.40W
Beata, Cabo, c., Dom. Rep. (ká'bô-bĕ-ä'tä)	116	17.40N	71.20W
Beato, neigh., Port.	234d	38.44N	9.06W
Beatrice, Ne., U.S. (bē'ȧ-trĭs)	90	40.16N	96.45W
Beatty, Nv., U.S. (bēt'ē)	102	36.58N	116.48W
Beattyville, Ky., U.S. (bēt'ē-vĭl)	92	37.35N	83.40W
Beaucaire, Fr. (bō-kâr')	150	43.49N	4.37E
Beaucourt, Fr. (bō-kōōr')	150	47.30N	6.54E
Beaufort, N.C., U.S. (bō'fĕrt)	108	34.43N	76.40W
Beaufort, S.C., U.S.	108	32.25N	80.40W
Beaufort Sea, sea, N.A.	89	70.30N	138.40W
Beaufort West, S. Afr.	206	32.20S	22.45E
Beauharnois, Can. (bō-är-nwä')	84	45.23N	73.52W
Beaumont, Can.	77b	46.50N	71.01W
Beaumont, Can.	77g	53.22N	113.18W
Beaumont, Ca., U.S. (bō'mŏnt)	101a	33.57N	116.57W
Beaumont, Tx., U.S.	90	30.05N	94.06W
Beaune, Fr. (bōn)	150	47.02N	4.49E
Beauport, Can. (bō-pôr')	77b	46.52N	71.11W
Beauséjour, Can.	78	50.04N	96.33W
Beauvais, Fr. (bō-vĕ')	150	49.25N	2.05E
Beaver, Ok., U.S. (bē'vẽr)	104	36.46N	100.31W
Beaver, Pa., U.S.	95e	40.42N	80.18W
Beaver, Ut., U.S.	102	38.15N	112.40W
Beaver, i., Mi., U.S.	92	45.40N	85.30W
Beaver, r., Can.	78	54.20N	111.10W
Beaver City, Ne., U.S.	104	40.08N	99.52W
Beaver Creek, r., Co., U.S.	104	39.42N	103.37W
Beaver Creek, r., Ks., U.S.	104	39.44N	101.05W
Beaver Creek, r., Mt., U.S.	96	46.45N	104.18W
Beaver Creek, r., Wy., U.S.	96	43.46N	104.25W
Beaver Dam, Wi., U.S.	96	43.29N	88.50W
Beaverhead, r., Mt., U.S.	98	45.25N	112.35W
Beaverhead Mountains, mts., Mt., U.S. (bē'vẽr-hĕd)	98	44.33N	112.59W
Beaver Indian Reservation, I.R., Mi., U.S.	92	45.40N	85.30W
Beaverton, Or., U.S. (bē'vẽr-tŭn)	100c	45.29N	122.49W
Bebek, neigh., Tur.	235f	41.04N	29.02E
Bebington, Eng., U.K. (bē'bĭng-tŭn)	138a	53.20N	2.59W
Beccar, neigh., Arg.	229d	34.28S	58.31W
Bečej, Yugo. (bĕ'chā)	154	45.36N	20.03E
Béchar, Alg.	204	31.39N	2.14W
Becharof, l., Ak., U.S. (bĕk-á-rôf)	89	57.58N	156.58W
Becher Bay, b., Can. (bēch'ẽr)	100a	48.18N	123.37W
Beckenham, neigh., Eng., U.K.	231	51.24N	0.02W
Beckley, W.V., U.S. (bĕk'lĭ)	92	37.40N	81.15W
Bédarieux, Fr. (bā-dá-ryû')	150	43.36N	3.11E
Beddington, neigh., Eng., U.K.	231	51.22N	0.08W
Beddington Creek, r., Can. (bĕd'ĕng tŭn)	77e	51.14N	114.13W
Bedford, Can. (bĕd'fẽrd)	84	45.10N	73.00W
Bedford, S. Afr.	207c	32.43S	26.19E
Bedford, Eng., U.K.	140	52.10N	0.25W
Bedford, In., U.S.	92	38.50N	86.30W
Bedford, Ia., U.S.	96	40.40N	94.41W
Bedford, Ma., U.S.	87a	42.30N	71.17W
Bedford, N.Y., U.S.	94a	41.12N	73.38W
Bedford, Oh., U.S.	95d	41.23N	81.32W
Bedford, Pa., U.S.	92	40.05N	78.20W
Bedford, Va., U.S.	108	37.19N	79.27W
Bedford Heights, Oh., U.S.	225a	41.22N	81.30W
Bedford Hills, N.Y., U.S.	94a	41.14N	73.41W
Bedford Park, Il., U.S.	227a	41.46N	87.49W
Bedford Park, neigh., N.Y., U.S.	224	40.52N	73.53W
Bedford-Stuyvesant, neigh., N.Y., U.S.	224	40.41N	73.55W
Bedmond, Eng., U.K.	231	51.43N	0.25W
Bedok, Sing.	236c	1.19N	103.57E
Beebe, Ar., U.S. (bē'bē)	104	35.04N	91.54W
Beecher, Il., U.S. (bē'chŭr)	95a	41.20N	87.38W
Beechey Head, c., Can. (bē'chĭ hĕd)	100a	48.19N	123.40W
Beech Grove, In., U.S. (bēch grōv)	95g	39.43N	86.05W
Beechview, neigh., Pa., U.S.	226b	40.25N	80.02W
Beeck, neigh., Ger.	232	51.29N	6.44E
Beeckerwerth, neigh., Ger.	232	51.29N	6.41E
Beecroft Head, c., Austl. (bē'krŭft)	198	35.03S	151.15E
Beelitz, Ger. (bē'lētz)	139b	52.14N	12.59E
Be'er Sheva53, Isr. (bēr-shē'bȧ)	173a	31.15N	34.48E
Be'er Sheva53, r., Isr.	173a	31.23N	34.30E
Beestekraal, S. Afr.	212d	25.22S	27.34E
Beeston, Eng., U.K. (bēs't'n)	138a	52.55N	1.11W
Beetz, r., Ger. (bětz)	139b	52.28N	12.37E
Beeville, Tx., U.S. (bē'vĭl)	106	28.24N	97.44W
Bega, Austl. (bā'gȧ)	196	36.50S	149.49E
Beggs, Ok., U.S. (bĕgz)	104	35.46N	96.06W
Bègles, Fr. (bĕ'gl')	150	44.47N	0.34W
Begoro, Ghana	208	6.23N	0.23W
Behala, India	178a	22.31N	88.19E
Behbehān, Iran	176	30.35N	50.14E
Behm Canal, can., Ak., U.S.	80	55.41N	131.35W
Bei, r., China (bā)	183a	22.54N	113.08E

PLACE (Pronunciation)	PAGE	Lat. °'	Long. °'
Bei'an, China (bā-än)	184	48.05N	126.26E
Beicai, China (bā-tsī)	183b	31.12N	121.33E
Beifei, r., China (bā-fā)	182	33.14N	117.03E
Beihai, China (bā-hī)	180	21.30N	109.10E
Beihuangcheng Dao, i., China (bā-hůäŋ-chŭŋ dou)	182	38.23N	120.55E
Beijing, China	180	39.55N	116.23E
Beijing Shi, China (bā-jyĭŋ shr)	184	40.07N	116.00E
Beira, Moz. (bā'rȧ)	206	19.45S	34.58E
Beira, hist. reg., Port. (bĕ'y-rä)	152	40.38N	8.00W
Beirut, Leb. (bā-rōōt')	174	33.53N	35.30E
Beiyuan, China	236b	40.01N	116.24E
Beja, Port. (bā'zhä)	142	38.03N	7.53W
Béja, Tun.	142	36.52N	9.20E
Bejaïa (Bougie), Alg.	204	36.46N	5.00E
Bejar, Spain	152	40.25N	5.43W
Bejestān, Iran	174	34.30N	58.22E
Bejucal, Cuba (bā-hōō-käl')	116	22.56N	82.23W
Bejuco, Pan. (bĕ-kōō'kō)	114	8.37N	79.54W
Békés, Hung. (bā'kāsh)	148	46.45N	21.08E
Békéscsaba, Hung. (bā'kāsh-chô'bô)	142	46.39N	21.06E
Beketova, Russia (bĕkĕ-to'vá)	162	53.23N	125.21E
Bela Crkva, Yugo. (bĕ'lä tsĕrk'vä)	154	44.53N	21.25E
Bel Air, Va., U.S.	225d	38.52N	77.10W
Bel Air, neigh., Ca., U.S.	228	34.05N	118.27W
Belalcázar, Spain (bāl-á-kä'thär)	152	38.35N	5.12W
Belarus, nation, Eur.	158	53.30N	25.33E
Belas, Port.	234d	38.47N	9.16W
Bela Vista, neigh., Braz.	230d	23.33S	46.38W
Bela Vista de Goiás, Braz.	124	16.57S	48.47W
Belawan, Indon. (bā-lä'wán)	188	3.43N	98.43E
Belaya, r., Russia (byĕ'lĭ-yá)	160	52.30N	56.15E
Belaya Tserkov', Ukr. (byĕ'lĭ-yá tsĕr'kôf)	160	49.48N	30.09E
Belcher Islands, is., Can. (bĕl'chĕr)	78	56.20N	80.40W
Belding, Mi., U.S. (bĕl'dĭng)	92	43.05N	85.25W
Belebey, Russia (byĕ'lĕ-bā'ĭ)	160	54.00N	54.10E
Belém, Braz. (bā-lĕn')	124	1.18S	48.27W
Belém, neigh., Port.	234d	38.42N	9.12W
Belén, Para. (bā-lān')	126	23.30S	57.09W
Belen, N.M., U.S. (bĕ-lān')	102	34.40N	106.45W
Belènzinho, neigh., Braz.	230d	23.32S	46.35W
Bélep, Îles, is., N. Cal.	196	19.30S	164.00E
Belëv, Russia (byĕl'yĕf)	160	53.49N	36.06E
Belfair, Wa., U.S. (bĕl'far)	100a	47.27N	122.50W
Belfast, N. Ire., U.K.	136	54.36N	5.45W
Belfast, Me., U.S. (bĕl'fást)	86	44.25N	69.01W
Belfast, Lough, b., N. Ire., U.K. (lŏk bĕl'fást)	144	54.45N	6.00W
Belford Roxo, Braz.	126b	22.46S	43.24W
Belfort, Fr. (bā-fôr')	140	47.40N	7.50E
Belgaum, India	174	15.57N	74.32E
Belgium, nation, Eur. (bĕl'jĭ-ŭm)	136	51.00N	2.52E
Belgorod, Russia (byĕl'gŭ-rŭt)	160	50.36N	36.32E
Belgorod, prov., Russia	156	50.40N	36.42E
Belgorod-Dnestrovskiy, Ukr. (byĕl'gŭ-rŭd nyĕs-trôf'skĕ)	160	46.09N	30.19E
Belgrade (Beograd), Yugo.	136	44.48N	20.32E
Belgrano, neigh., Arg.	229d	34.34S	58.28W
Belgrave, Austl.	239b	37.55S	145.21E
Belhaven, N.C., U.S. (bĕl'hā-vĕn)	108	35.33N	76.37W
Belington, W.V., U.S. (bĕl'ĭng-tŭn)	92	39.00N	79.55W
Belitung, i., Indon.	188	3.30S	107.30E
Belize, nation, N.A.	110	17.00N	88.40W
Belize, r., Belize	114a	17.16N	88.56W
Belize City, Belize (bĕ-lēz')	110	17.31N	88.10W
Bel'kovo, Russia (byĕl'kô-vô)	164b	56.15N	38.49E
Bel'kovskiy, i., Russia (byĕl-kôf'skĭ)	162	75.45N	137.00E
Bell, Ca., U.S.	228	33.58N	118.11W
Bell, i., Can. (bĕl)	86	50.45N	55.35W
Bell, r., Can.	84	49.25N	77.15W
Bella Bella, Can.	80	52.10N	128.07W
Bella Coola, Can.	80	52.22N	126.46W
Bellaire, Oh., U.S. (bĕl-âr')	92	40.00N	80.45W
Bellaire, Tx., U.S.	107a	29.43N	95.28W
Bellary, India (bĕl-lä'rē)	174	15.15N	76.56E
Bella Union, Ur. (bĕ'l-yà-ōō-nyō'n)	126	30.18S	57.26W
Bella Vista, Arg.	126	28.35S	58.53W
Bella Vista, Arg. (bä'lyá vēs'tá)	126	27.07S	65.14W
Bella Vista, Arg.	126a	34.35S	58.41W
Bellavista, Chile	230b	33.31S	70.37W
Bella Vista, Para.	124	22.16S	56.14W
Bellavista, Peru	229c	12.04S	77.08W
Belle-Anse, Haiti	116	18.15N	72.00W
Belle Bay, b., Can. (bĕl)	86	47.35N	55.15W
Belle Chasse, La., U.S. (bĕl shäs')	94d	29.52N	90.00W
Belle Farm Estates, Md., U.S.	225c	39.23N	76.45W
Bellefontaine, Oh., U.S. (bel-fōn'tán)	92	40.25N	83.50W
Bellefontaine Neighbors, Mo., U.S.	101e	38.46N	90.13W
Belle Fourche, S.D., U.S. (bĕl' fōōrsh')	96	44.28N	103.50W
Belle Fourche, r., Wy., U.S.	96	44.29N	104.40W
Belle Fourche Reservoir, res., S.D., U.S.	96	44.51N	103.44W
Bellegarde, Fr. (bĕl-gärd')	150	46.06N	5.50E
Belle Glade, Fl., U.S. (bĕl glăd)	109a	26.39N	80.37W
Bellehaven, Va., U.S.	225d	38.47N	77.04W
Belle-Île, i., Fr. (bĕlēl')	140	47.15N	3.30W
Belle Isle, Strait of, strt., Can.	78	51.35N	56.30W
Belle Mead, N.J., U.S. (bĕl mēd)	94a	40.28N	74.40W
Belleoram, Can.	86	47.31N	55.25W
Belle Plaine, Ia., U.S. (bĕl plān')	96	41.52N	92.19W
Bellerose, N.Y., U.S.	224	40.44N	73.43W
Belle Vernon, Pa., U.S. (bĕl vŭr'nŭn)	95e	40.08N	79.52W
Belleville, Can. (bĕl'vĭl)	84	44.15N	77.25W
Belleville, Il., U.S.	101e	38.31N	89.59W
Belleville, Ks., U.S.	104	39.49N	97.37W
Belleville, Mi., U.S.	95b	42.12N	83.29W
Belleville, N.J., U.S.	94a	40.47N	74.09W
Bellevue, Ia., U.S. (bĕl'vū)	96	42.14N	90.26W

ng-sing; ŋ-baŋk; N-nasalized n; nŏd; cŏmmit; ōld; ôbey; ôrder; oi-boil; fōōd; ŏŏ-as oo in foot; ou-out; s-soft; sh-dish; th-thin; pūre; ûnite; ûrn; stŭd; circŭs; ü-as in French tu; '-indeterminate vowel.

PLACE (Pronunciation)	PAGE	Lat. °'	Long. °'
Bellevue, Ky., U.S.	95f	39.06N	84.29W
Bellevue, Mi., U.S.	92	42.30N	85.00W
Bellevue, Oh., U.S.	92	41.15N	82.45W
Bellevue, Pa., U.S.	95e	40.30N	80.04W
Bellevue, Wa., U.S.	100a	47.37N	122.12W
Belley, Fr. (bĕ-lē')	150	45.46N	5.41E
Bellflower, Ca., U.S. (bĕl-flou'ẽr)	101a	33.53N	118.08W
Bell Gardens, Ca., U.S.	101a	33.59N	118.11W
Bellingham, Ma., U.S. (bĕl'ĭng-hăm)	87a	42.05N	71.28W
Bellingham, Wa., U.S.	90	48.46N	122.29W
Bellingham Bay, b., Wa., U.S.	100d	48.44N	122.34W
Bellingshausen Sea, sea, Ant. (bĕl'ingz houz'n)	213	72.00S	80.30W
Bellinzona, Switz. (bĕl-ĭn-tsō'nä)	148	46.10N	9.09E
Bellmawr, N.J., U.S.	225b	39.51N	75.06W
Bellmore, N.Y., U.S. (bĕl-mōr)	94a	40.40N	73.31W
Bello, Col. (bĕ'l-yô)	124	6.20N	75.33W
Bello, Cuba	229b	23.07N	82.24W
Bellow Falls, Vt., U.S. (bĕl'ōz fôls)	92	43.10N	72.30W
Bellpat, Pak.	178	29.08N	68.00E
Bell Peninsula, pen., Can.	78	63.50N	81.16W
Bells Corners, Can.	77c	45.20N	75.49W
Bells Mountain, mtn., Wa., U.S. (bĕls)	100c	45.50N	122.21W
Belluno, Italy (bĕl-lōō'nō)	154	46.08N	12.14E
Bell Ville, Arg. (bĕl vēl')	126	32.33S	62.36W
Bellville, S. Afr.	206a	33.54S	18.38E
Bellville, Tx., U.S. (bĕl'vĭl)	106	29.57N	96.15W
Bellwood, Il., U.S.	227a	41.53N	87.52W
Bélmez, Spain (bĕl'mĕth)	152	38.17N	5.17W
Belmond, Ia., U.S. (bĕl'mŏnd)	96	42.49N	93.37W
Belmont, Ca., U.S.	100b	37.34N	122.18W
Belmont, Ma., U.S.	223a	42.24N	71.10W
Belmonte, Braz. (bĕl-mōn'tå)	124	15.58S	38.47W
Belmopan, Belize	110	17.15N	88.47W
Belmore, Austl.	239a	33.55S	151.05E
Belogorsk, Russia	158	51.09N	128.32E
Belo Horizonte, Braz. (bĕ'lôre-sô'n-tĕ)	124	19.54S	43.56W
Beloit, Ks., U.S. (bē-loit')	104	39.26N	98.06W
Beloit, Wi., U.S.	90	42.31N	89.04W
Belomorsk, Russia (byĕl-ô-môrsk')	160	64.30N	34.42E
Belopol'ye, Ukr. (byĕ'lô-pôl'yĕ)	160	51.10N	34.19E
Beloretsk, Russia (byĕ'lō-rĕtsk)	160	53.58N	58.25E
Belosarayskaya, Kosa, c., Ukr.	156	46.43N	37.18E
Belot, Cuba	229b	23.08N	82.19W
Belovo, Russia (byĕ'lŭ-vû)	162	54.25N	86.18E
Belovodsk, Ukr. (byĕ-lŭ-vôdsk')	156	49.12N	39.36E
Beloye, l., Russia	160	60.10N	38.05E
Belozersk, Russia (byĕ-lŭ-zyôrsk')	160	60.00N	38.00E
Belper, Eng., U.K. (bĕl'pẽr)	138a	53.01N	1.28W
Belt, Mt., U.S. (bĕlt)	98	47.11N	110.58W
Belt Creek, r., Mt., U.S.	98	47.19N	110.58W
Belton, Tx., U.S. (bĕl'tŭn)	106	31.04N	97.27W
Belton Lake, l., Tx., U.S.	106	31.15N	97.35W
Belts, Mol.	160	47.47N	27.57E
Beltsville, Md., U.S. (belts-vĭl)	94e	39.03N	76.56W
Belukha, Gora, mtn., Asia	158	49.47N	86.23E
Belvedere, Ca., U.S.	227b	37.52N	122.28W
Belvedere, Va., U.S.	225d	38.50N	77.10W
Belvedere, neigh., Eng., U.K.	231	51.29N	0.09E
Belvedere, pt. of i., Aus.	235e	48.11N	16.23E
Belvidere, Il., U.S. (bĕl-vē-dēr')	96	42.14N	88.52W
Belvidere, N.J., U.S.	92	40.50N	75.05W
Belyando, r., Austl. (bĕl-yän'dō)	196	22.09S	146.48E
Belyanka, Russia (byĕl'yán-ká)	164a	56.04N	59.16E
Belynichi, Bela. (byĕl-ĭ-nĭ'chĭ)	156	54.02N	29.42E
Belyy, Russia (byĕ'lē)	160	55.52N	32.58E
Belyy, i., Russia	158	73.19N	72.00E
Belyye Stolby, Russia (byĕ'lĭ-ye stôl'bĭ)	164b	55.20N	37.52E
Belzig, Ger. (bĕl'tsēg)	139b	52.08N	12.35E
Belzoni, Ms., U.S. (bĕl-zō'nē)	108	33.09N	90.30W
Bembe, Ang. (bĕn'bĕ)	206	7.00S	14.20E
Bembézar, r., Spain (bĕm-bā-thär')	152	38.00N	5.18W
Bemidji, Mn., U.S. (bē-mĭj'ĭ)	96	47.28N	94.54W
Bena Dibele, Zaire (bĕn'á dē-bĕ'lē)	206	4.00S	22.49E
Benalla, Austl. (bĕn-ăl'á)	196	36.30S	146.00E
Benares, see Vārānasi, India	174	25.25N	83.00E
Benavente, Spain (bā-nä-vĕn'tā)	142	42.01N	5.43W
Ben Avon, Pa., U.S.	226b	40.31N	80.05W
Benbrook, Tx., U.S. (bĕn'brŏŏk)	101c	32.41N	97.27W
Benbrook Reservoir, res., Tx., U.S.	101c	32.35N	97.30W
Bend, Or., U.S. (bĕnd)	90	44.04N	121.17W
Bendeleben, Mount, mtn., Ak., U.S. (bĕn-dĕl-bĕn)	89	65.18N	163.45W
Bender Beyla, Som.	212a	9.40N	50.45E
Bendery, Mol. (bĕn-dyĕ're)	160	46.49N	29.29E
Bendigo, Austl. (bĕn'dĭ-gō)	196	36.39S	144.20E
Benedict, Md., U.S. (bĕnĕ'dĭct)	94e	38.31N	76.41W
Benešov, Czech. (bĕn'ĕ-shôf)	148	49.48N	14.40E
Benevento, Italy (bā-nā-vĕn'tō)	142	41.08N	14.46E
Benfica, neigh., Braz.	230c	22.53S	43.15W
Benfica, neigh., Port.	234d	38.45N	9.12W
Bengal, Bay of, b., Asia (bĕn-gôl')	172	17.30N	87.00E
Bengamisa, Zaire	210	0.57N	25.10E
Bengbu, China (bŭŋ-bōō)	180	32.52N	117.22E
Bengkalis, Indon. (bĕng-kä'lĭs)	188	1.29N	102.06E
Bengkulu, Indon.	188	3.46S	102.18E
Benguela, Ang. (bĕn-gĕl'á)	206	12.35S	13.25E
Beni, r., Bol. (bā'nē)	124	13.41S	67.30W
Béni-Abbas, Alg. (bā'nē ä-bĕs')	204	30.11N	2.13W
Benicia, Ca., U.S. (bē-nĭsh'ĭ-á)	100b	38.03N	122.09W
Benin, nation, Afr.	204	8.00N	2.00E
Benin, r., Nig. (bĕn-ēn')	208	5.55N	5.15E
Benin, Bight of, bt., Afr.	204	5.30N	3.00E
Benin City, Nig.	204	6.19N	5.41E
Beni Saf, Alg. (bā'nē säf')	204	35.23N	1.20W
Benito, r., Eq. Gui.	210	1.35N	10.45E
Benkelman, Ne., U.S. (bĕn-kĕl-măn)	104	40.05N	101.35W
Benkovac, Cro. (bĕn'kō-váts)	154	44.02N	15.41E
Bennettsville, S.C., U.S. (bĕn'ĕts vĭl)	108	34.35N	79.41W
Bennettswood, Austl.	239b	37.51S	145.07E
Benninghofen, neigh., Ger.	232	51.29N	7.31E
Bennington, Vt., U.S. (bĕn'ĭng-tŭn)	92	42.55N	73.15W
Benns Church, Va., U.S. (bĕnz' chûrch')	94g	36.47N	76.35W
Benoni, S. Afr. (bĕ-nō'nĭ)	206	26.11S	28.19E
Benoni South, S. Afr.	240b	26.13S	28.18E
Benoy, Chad	208	8.59N	16.19E
Benque Viejo, Belize (bĕn-kĕ bĭĕ'hō)	114a	17.07N	89.07W
Benrath, neigh., Ger.	232	51.10N	6.52E
Bensberg, Ger.	151c	50.58N	7.09E
Bensenville, Il., U.S. (bĕn'sĕn-vĭl)	95a	41.57N	87.56W
Bensheim, Ger. (bĕns-hīm)	148	49.42N	8.38E
Benson, Az., U.S. (bĕn-sŭn)	102	32.00N	110.20W
Benson, Mn., U.S.	96	45.18N	95.36W
Bentiaba, Ang.	210	14.15S	12.21E
Bentleigh, Austl.	239b	37.55S	145.02E
Bentleyville, Pa., U.S. (bent'lē vĭl)	95e	40.07N	80.01W
Benton, Can.	86	45.59N	67.36W
Benton, Ar., U.S. (bĕn'tŭn)	104	34.34N	92.34W
Benton, Ca., U.S.	102	37.44N	118.22W
Benton, Il., U.S.	92	38.00N	88.55W
Benton Harbor, Mi., U.S. (bĕn'tŭn här'bẽr)	92	42.05N	86.30W
Bentonville, Ar., U.S. (bĕn'tŭn-vĭl)	104	36.22N	94.11W
Benue, r., Afr. (bā'nōō-å)	204	8.00N	8.00E
Benut, r., Malay.	173b	1.43N	103.20E
Benwood, W.V., U.S. (bĕn-wŏod)	92	39.55N	80.45W
Benxi, China (bŭn-shyē)	184	41.25N	123.50E
Beograd, see Belgrade, Yugo.	136	44.48N	20.32E
Beppu, Japan (bĕ'pōō)	187	33.16N	131.30E
Bequia Island, i., St. Vin. (bĕk-ē'ä)	115b	13.00N	61.08W
Berakit, Tanjung, c., Indon.	173b	1.16N	104.44E
Berat, Alb. (bĕ-răt')	154	40.43N	19.59E
Berau, Teluk, b., Indon.	188	2.22S	131.40E
Berazategui, Arg. (bĕ-rä-zá'tĕ-gē)	126a	34.46S	58.14W
Berbera, Som. (bûr'bûr-á)	212a	10.25N	45.05E
Berbérati, Cen. Afr. Rep.	208	4.16N	15.47E
Berchum, Ger.	232	51.23N	7.32E
Berck, Fr. (bĕrk)	150	50.26N	1.36E
Berd'ansk, Ukr.	160	46.45N	36.47E
Berdichev, Ukr. (bĕr-dē'chĕf)	158	49.53N	28.32E
Berdyanskaya, Kosa, c., Ukr. (kō-sä' bĕ-dyän'skä-yä)	156	46.38N	36.42E
Berdyaush, Russia (bĕr'dyáûsh)	164a	55.10N	59.12E
Berea, Ky., U.S. (bē-rē'á)	108	37.30N	84.19W
Berea, Oh., U.S.	95d	41.22N	81.51W
Beregovo, Ukr. (bĕ'rĕ-gô-vô)	148	48.13N	22.40E
Bereku, Tan.	210	4.27S	35.44E
Berens, r., Can. (bĕrĕnz)	82	52.15N	96.30W
Berens Island, i., Can.	82	52.18N	97.40W
Berens River, Can.	78	52.22N	97.02W
Beresford, S.D., U.S. (bĕr'ĕs-fẽrd)	96	43.05N	96.46W
Berettyóújfalu, Hung. (bĕ'rĕt-tyō-ōō'y'fō-lōō)	148	47.14N	21.33E
Berëza, Bela. (bĕ-rā'zá)	148	52.29N	24.59E
Berezhany, Ukr. (bĕr-yĕ'zhá-nĕ)	148	49.25N	24.58E
Berezina, r., Bela. (bĕr-yĕ'zē-ná)	156	53.20N	29.05E
Berezino, Bela. (bĕr-yä'zē-nô)	156	53.51N	28.54E
Berezna, Ukr. (bĕr-yôz'ná)	156	51.32N	31.47E
Bereznegovata, Ukr.	156	47.19N	32.58E
Berezniki, Russia (bĕr-yôz'nyē-kē)	160	59.25N	56.46E
Berëzovka, Russia	164a	57.35N	57.19E
Berëzovka, Ukr. (bĕr-yôz'óf-ká)	156	47.12N	30.56E
Berëzovo, Russia (bĭr-yô'zē-vû)	158	64.10N	65.10E
Berëzovskiy, Russia (bĕr-yô'zôf-skĭ)	164a	56.54N	60.47E
Berga, Spain (bĕr'gä)	152	42.05N	1.52E
Bergama, Tur. (bĕr'gä-mä)	174	39.08N	27.09E
Bergamo, Italy (bĕr'gä-mō)	142	45.43N	9.41E
Bergantin, Ven. (bĕr-gän-tē'n)	125b	10.04N	64.23W
Bergedorf, Ger. (bĕr'gē-dôrf)	139c	53.29N	10.12E
Bergen, Ger. (bĕr'gĕn)	148	54.26N	13.26E
Bergen, Nor.	136	60.24N	5.20E
Bergenfield, N.J., U.S.	94a	40.55N	73.59W
Bergen op Zoom, Neth.	144	51.29N	4.16E
Bergerac, Fr. (bĕr-zhĕ-rák')	140	44.49N	0.28E
Bergfelde, Ger.	234a	52.40N	13.19E
Berghausen, Ger.	232	51.18N	7.17E
Bergholtz, N.Y., U.S.	226a	43.06N	78.53W
Bergisch-Born, Ger.	232	51.09N	7.15E
Bergisch Gladbach, Ger. (bĕrg'ĭsh-glät'bäk)	151c	50.59N	7.08E
Bergkamen, Ger.	232	51.38N	7.38E
Berglern, Ger. (bĕrgh'lĕrn)	139d	48.24N	11.55E
Bergneustadt, Ger.	151c	51.01N	7.39E
Bergville, S. Afr. (bĕrg'vĭl)	207c	28.46S	29.22E
Berhampur, India	174	19.19N	84.48E
Bering Sea, sea (bē'rĭng)	190	58.00N	175.00W
Bering Strait, strt.	90a	64.50N	169.50W
Berislav, Ukr. (byĕr'ĭ-sláf)	156	46.49N	33.24E
Berja, Spain (bĕr'hä)	152	36.50N	2.56W
Berkeley, Ca., U.S. (bûrk'lĭ)	90	37.52N	122.17W
Berkeley, Il., U.S.	227a	41.53N	87.55W
Berkeley, Mo., U.S.	101e	38.45N	90.20W
Berkeley Hills, Pa., U.S.	226b	40.32N	80.00W
Berkeley Springs, W.V., U.S. (bûrk'lĭ springz)	92	39.40N	78.10W
Berkhamsted, Eng., U.K. (bĕk'hám'stĕd)	138b	51.44N	0.34W
Berkhamsted, Eng., U.K.	231	51.46N	0.35W
Berkley, Mi., U.S. (bûrk'lĭ)	95b	42.30N	83.10W
Berkovitsa, Bul. (bĕ-kō'vē-tsá)	154	43.14N	23.08E
Berkshire, co., Eng., U.K.	138b	51.23N	1.07W
Berland, r., Can.	80	54.00N	117.10W
Berlenga, is., Port. (bĕr-lĕn'gázh)	152	39.25N	9.33W
Berlin, Ger. (bĕr-lēn')	136	52.31N	13.28E
Berlin, S. Afr. (bẽr-lĭn)	207c	32.53S	27.36E
Berlin, N.H., U.S. (bûr-lĭn)	92	44.25N	71.10W
Berlin, N.J., U.S.	94f	39.47N	74.56W
Berlin, Wi., U.S. (bûr-lĭn')	96	43.58N	88.58W
Berlin-Tempelhof, Zentral Flughafen, arpt., Ger.	234a	52.29N	13.25E
Bermejo, r., S.A. (bĕr-mā'hō)	126	25.05S	61.00W
Bermeo, Spain (bĕr-mā'yō)	152	43.23N	2.43W
Bermuda, dep., N.A.	110	32.20N	65.45W
Bern, Switz. (bĕrn)	136	46.55N	7.25E
Bernal, Arg. (bĕr-näl')	126a	34.43S	58.17W
Bernalillo, N.M., U.S. (bĕr-nä-lē'yō)	102	35.20N	106.30W
Bernard, l., Can. (bẽr-närd')	92	45.45N	79.25W
Bernardsville, N.J., U.S. (būr nârds'vĭl)	94a	40.43N	74.34W
Bernau, Ger. (bĕr'nou)	148	52.40N	13.35E
Bernburg, Ger. (bĕrn'bŏorgh)	148	51.48N	11.43E
Berndorf, Aus. (bĕrn'dôrf)	148	47.57N	16.05E
Berne, In., U.S. (bûrn)	92	40.40N	84.55W
Berner Alpen, mts., Switz.	148	46.29N	7.30E
Bernier, i., Austl. (bĕr-nēr')	196	24.58S	113.15E
Bernina, Pizzo, mtn., Eur.	148	46.23N	9.58E
Bero, r., Ang.	210	15.10S	12.20E
Beroun, Czech. (bā'rōn)	148	49.57N	14.03E
Berounka, r., Czech. (bĕ-rōn'ká)	148	49.53N	13.40E
Berowra, Austl.	195b	33.36S	151.10E
Berre, Étang de, l., Fr. (ā-tôn' dĕ bâr')	150a	43.27N	5.07E
Berre-l'Étang, Fr. (bâr'lā-tôn')	150a	43.28N	5.11E
Berriozabal, Mex. (bā'rēō-zä-bäl')	112	16.47N	93.16W
Berriyyane, Alg.	142	32.50N	3.49E
Berry Creek, r., Can.	82	51.15N	111.40W
Berryessa, r., Ca., U.S. (bĕ'rĭ ĕs'á)	102	38.35N	122.33W
Berry Islands, is., Bah.	116	25.40N	77.50W
Berryville, Ar., U.S. (bĕr'ē-vĭl)	104	36.21N	93.34W
Bershad', Ukr. (byĕr'shät)	156	48.22N	29.31E
Berthier, Can.	77b	46.56N	70.44W
Bertlich, Ger.	232	51.37N	7.04E
Bertrand, r., Wa., U.S. (bûr'trănd)	100d	48.58N	122.31W
Berwick, Pa., U.S. (bûr'wĭk)	92	41.05N	76.10W
Berwick-upon-Tweed, Eng., U.K. (bûr'ĭk)	140	55.45N	2.01W
Berwyn, Il., U.S. (bûr'wĭn)	95a	41.49N	87.47W
Berwyn Heights, Md., U.S.	225d	38.59N	76.54W
Besalampy, Madag. (bĕz-ä-lám-pē')	206	16.48S	44.40E
Besançon, Fr. (bĕ-sän-sôn)	140	47.14N	6.02E
Besar, Gunong, mtn., Malay.	173b	2.31N	103.09E
Besed', r., Eur. (byĕ'syĕt)	156	52.58N	31.36E
Besedy, Russia	235b	55.37N	37.47E
Beshenkovichi, Bela. (byĕ'shĕn-kōvē'chĭ)	156	55.04N	29.29E
Beskid Mountains, mts., Eur.	148	49.23N	19.00E
Beskra, Alg.	204	34.52N	5.39E
Beskudnikovo, neigh., Russia	235b	55.52N	37.34E
Besós, r., Spain	234e	41.25N	2.12E
Bessarabia, hist. reg., Mol.	156	47.00N	28.30E
Bességes, Fr. (bĕ-sĕzh')	150	44.20N	4.07E
Bessemer, Al., U.S. (bĕs'ê-mẽr)	94h	33.24N	86.58W
Bessemer, Mi., U.S.	96	46.29N	90.04W
Bessemer City, N.C., U.S.	108	35.16N	81.17W
Bestensee, Ger. (bĕs'tĕn-zā)	139b	52.15N	13.39E
Betanzos, Spain (bĕ-tän'thōs)	152	43.18N	8.14W
Betatakin Ruin, Az., U.S. (bĕt-á-tăk'ĭn)	102	36.40N	110.29W
Bethal, S. Afr. (bĕth'ăl)	212d	26.27S	29.28E
Bethalto, Il., U.S. (bá-thál'tō)	101e	38.54N	90.03W
Bethanien, Nmb.	206	26.20S	16.10E
Bethany, Mo., U.S.	104	40.15N	94.04W
Bethel, Ak., U.S. (bĕth'ĕl)	90a	60.50N	161.50W
Bethel, Ct., U.S.	94a	41.22N	73.24W
Bethel, Vt., U.S.	92	43.50N	72.40W
Bethel Park, Pa., U.S.	95e	40.19N	80.02W
Bethesda, Md., U.S. (bĕ-thĕs'dá)	94e	39.00N	77.10W
Bethlehem, S. Afr.	206	28.14S	28.18E
Bethlehem, Pa., U.S. (bĕth'lē-hĕm)	92	40.40N	75.25W
Bethlehem, see Bayt Lahm, Isr. Occ.	173a	31.42N	35.13E
Bethnal Green, neigh., Eng., U.K.	231	51.32N	0.03W
Bethpage, N.Y., U.S.	224	40.45N	73.29W
Béthune, Fr. (bā-tün')	150	50.32N	2.37E
Betroka, Madag. (bĕ-trōk'á)	206	23.13S	46.17E
Betsham, Eng., U.K.	231	51.25N	0.19E
Bet She'an, Isr.	173a	32.30N	35.30E
Betsiamites, Can.	78	48.57N	68.36W
Betsiamites, r., Can.	86	49.11N	69.20W
Betsiboka, r., Madag. (bĕt-sĭ-bō'ká)	206	16.47S	46.45E
Bettles Field, Ak., U.S. (bĕt'tŭls)	89	66.58N	151.48W
Betwa, r., India (bĕt'wá)	174	25.00N	78.00E
Betz, Fr. (bĕ)	151b	49.09N	2.58E
Beveren, Bel.	139a	51.13N	4.14E
B. Everett Jordan Lake, res., N.C., U.S.	108	35.45N	79.00W
Beverly, Ma., U.S.	87a	42.34N	70.53W
Beverly, N.J., U.S.	94f	40.03N	74.56W
Beverly Hills, Austl.	239a	33.57S	151.05E
Beverly Hills, Ca., U.S.	101a	34.05N	118.24W
Beverly Hills, Mi., U.S.	226c	42.32N	83.15W
Bevier, Mo., U.S. (bē-vẽr')	104	39.44N	92.36W
Bewdley, Eng., U.K. (būd'lĭ)	138a	52.22N	2.19W
Bexhill, Eng., U.K. (bĕks'hĭl)	144	50.49N	0.25E
Bexley, Austl.	239a	33.57S	151.08E
Bexley, Eng., U.K. (bĕks'ly)	138b	51.26N	0.09E
Beyenburg, neigh., Ger.	232	51.15N	7.18E
Beyla, Gui. (bā'lá)	204	8.41N	8.37W
Beylerbeyi, neigh., Tur.	235f	41.03N	29.03E
Beylul, Eth.	204	13.15N	42.21E
Beyoğlu, neigh., Tur.	235f	41.02N	28.59E
Beypazari, Tur. (bā-pá-zä'rĭ)	142	40.10N	31.40E
Beyşehir, Tur.	160	38.00N	31.45E
Beysugskiy, Liman, b., Russia (lĭ-män' bĕy-sōōg'skĭ)	156	46.07N	38.35E
Bezhetsk, Russia (byĕ-zhĕtsk')	160	57.46N	36.40E
Bezhitsa, Russia (byĕ-zhĭ'tsá)	160	53.19N	34.18E
Béziers, Fr. (bā-zyā')	140	43.21N	3.12E
Bezons, Fr.	233c	48.56N	2.13E

ăt; finăl; rāte; senåte; ärm; åsk; sofá; fâre; ch-choose; dh-as th in other; bē; êvent; bĕt; recĕnt; cratẽr; g-gō; gh-guttural g; bĭt; ĭ-short neutral; rīde; ĸ-guttural k as ch in German ich;

PLACE (Pronunciation)	PAGE	Lat. °′	Long. °′
Bhadreswar, India	178a	22.49N	88.22E
Bhāgalpur, India (bä′gŭl-pōr)	174	25.15N	86.59E
Bhalswa, neigh., India	236d	28.44N	77.10E
Bhamo, Burma (bŭ-mō′)	174	24.00N	96.15E
Bhāngar, India	178a	22.30N	88.36E
Bharatpur, India (bērt′pōr)	174	27.21N	77.33E
Bhatinda, India (bŭ-tĭn-dȧ)	174	30.19N	74.56E
Bhātpāra, India	174	22.52N	88.24E
Bhaunagar, India (bäv-nŭg′ŭr)	174	21.45N	72.58E
Bhayandar, India	179b	19.20N	72.50E
Bhilai, India	178	21.14N	81.23E
Bhīma, r., India (bē′mȧ)	174	18.00N	74.45E
Bhiwandi, India	179b	19.18N	73.03E
Bhiwāni, India	178	28.53N	76.08E
Bhopāl, India (bō-päl)	174	23.20N	77.25E
Bhopura, India	236d	28.42N	77.20E
Bhubaneswar, India (bō-bû-năsh′vûr)	174	20.21N	85.53E
Bhuj, India (bōōj)	174	23.22N	69.39E
Bhutan, nation, Asia (bōō-tän′)	174	27.15N	90.30E
Biafra, Bight of, bt., Afr.	204	4.05N	7.10E
Biak, i., Indon. (bē′äk)	188	1.00S	136.00E
Biała Podlaska, Pol. (byä′wä pōd-läs′kä)	148	52.01N	23.08E
Białograd, Pol.	148	54.00N	16.01E
Bialystok, Pol. (byä-wĭs′tōk)	136	53.08N	23.12E
Biankouma, I.C.	208	7.44N	7.37W
Biarritz, Fr. (byä-rēts′)	140	43.27N	1.39W
Bibb City, Ga., U.S. (bĭb′ sĭ′tē)	108	32.31N	84.56W
Biberach, Ger. (bē′bērăk)	148	48.06N	9.49E
Bibiani, Ghana	208	6.28N	2.20W
Bic, Can. (bĭk)	86	48.22N	68.42W
Bickerstaffe, Eng., U.K.	233a	53.32N	2.50W
Bickley, neigh., Eng., U.K.	231	51.24N	0.03E
Bicknell, In., U.S. (bĭk′nĕl)	92	38.45N	87.20W
Bicske, Hung. (bĭsh′kē)	148	47.29N	18.38E
Bida, Nig. (bē′dä)	204	9.05N	6.01E
Biddeford, Me., U.S. (bĭd′ē-fērd)	86	43.29N	70.29W
Biddulph, Eng., U.K. (bĭd′ŭlf)	138a	53.07N	2.10W
Bidston, Eng., U.K.	233a	53.24N	3.05W
Biebrza, r., Pol. (byĕb′zhȧ)	148	53.18N	22.25E
Biel, Switz. (bēl)	148	47.09N	7.12E
Bielefeld, Ger. (bē′lē-fĕlt)	140	52.01N	8.35E
Biella, Italy (byĕl′lä)	154	45.34N	8.05E
Bielsk Podlaski, Pol. (byĕlsk pŭd-lä′skĭ)	140	52.47N	23.14E
Bien Hoa, Viet.	188	10.59N	106.49E
Bienville, Lac, l., Can.	78	55.32N	72.45W
Biesenthal, Ger. (bē′sĕn-täl)	139b	52.46N	13.38E
Bièvres, Fr.	233c	48.45N	2.13E
Biferno, r., Italy (bē-fĕr′nō)	154	41.49N	14.46E
Bifoum, Gabon	210	0.22S	10.23E
Biga, Tur. (bē′ghȧ)	154	40.13N	27.14E
Big Bay de Noc, Mi., U.S. (bĭg bā dē nok′)	96	45.48N	86.41W
Big Bayou, Ar., U.S. (bĭg′bī′yōō)	104	33.04N	91.28W
Big Bear City, Ca., U.S. (bĭg bâr)	101a	34.16N	116.51W
Big Belt Mountains, mts., Mt., U.S. (bĭg bĕlt)	90	46.53N	111.43W
Big Bend Dam, S.D., U.S. (bĭg bĕnd)	96	44.11N	99.33W
Big Bend National Park, rec., Tx., U.S.	90	29.15N	103.15W
Big Black, r., Ms., U.S. (bĭg blăk)	108	32.05N	90.49W
Big Blue, r., Ne., U.S. (bĭg blōō)	104	40.53N	97.00W
Big Canyon, Tx., U.S. (bĭg kăn′yŭn)	106	30.27N	102.19W
Big Creek, r., Oh., U.S.	225a	41.27N	81.41W
Big Cypress Indian Reservation, I.R., Fl., U.S.	109a	26.19N	81.11W
Big Cypress Swamp, sw., Fl., U.S. (bĭg sī′prĕs)	109a	26.02N	81.20W
Big Delta, Ak., U.S. (bĭg dĕl′tȧ)	89	64.08N	145.48W
Big Fork, r., Mn., U.S. (bĭg fôrk)	96	48.08N	93.47W
Biggar, Can.	78	52.04N	108.00W
Biggin Hill, neigh., Eng., U.K.	231	51.18N	0.04E
Big Hole, r., Mt., U.S. (bĭg hōl)	98	45.53N	113.15W
Big Hole National Battlefield, Mt., U.S. (bĭg hōl băt′′l-fēld)	98	45.44N	113.35W
Bighorn, r., U.S.	90	45.30N	108.00W
Bighorn Lake, res., Mt., U.S.	98	45.00N	108.10W
Bighorn Mountains, mts., U.S. (bĭg hôrn)	90	44.47N	107.40W
Big Island, i., Can.	82	49.10N	94.40W
Big Lake, Wa., U.S. (bĭg lāk)	100a	48.24N	122.14W
Big Lake, l., Can.	77g	53.35N	113.47W
Big Lake, l., Wa., U.S.	100a	48.24N	122.14W
Big Lost, r., Id., U.S. (lôst)	98	43.56N	113.38W
Big Mossy Point, c., Can.	82	53.45N	97.50W
Big Muddy, r., Il., U.S.	92	37.50N	89.00W
Big Muddy Creek, r., Mt., U.S. (bĭg mŭd′ĭ)	98	48.53N	105.02W
Bignona, Sen.	208	12.49N	16.14W
Big Porcupine Creek, r., Mt., U.S. (pôr′kū-pīn)	98	46.38N	107.04W
Big Quill Lake, l., Can.	78	51.55N	104.22W
Big Rapids, Mi., U.S. (bĭg răp′ĭdz)	92	43.40N	85.30W
Big River, Can.	78	53.50N	107.01W
Big Sandy, r., Az., U.S. (bĭg sănd′ē)	102	34.59N	113.36W
Big Sandy, r., Ky., U.S.	92	38.15N	82.35W
Big Sandy, r., Wy., U.S.	98	42.08N	109.35W
Big Sandy Creek, r., Co., U.S.	104	39.08N	103.36W
Big Sandy Creek, r., Mt., U.S.	98	48.20N	110.08W
Bigsby Island, i., Can.	82	49.04N	94.35W
Big Sioux, r., U.S. (bĭg sōō)	96	44.34N	97.00W
Big Spring, Tx., U.S. (bĭg sprĭng)	106	32.15N	101.28W
Big Stone, l., Mn., U.S. (bĭg stōn)	96	45.29N	96.40W
Big Stone Gap, Va., U.S.	108	36.50N	82.50W
Big Sunflower, r., Ms., U.S. (sŭn-flou′ēr)	108	32.57N	90.40W
Big Timber, Mt., U.S. (bĭg′tĭm-bēr)	98	45.50N	109.57W
Big Wood, r., Id., U.S. (bĭg wŏd)	98	43.02N	114.30W
Bihār, state, India (bē-hâr′)	178	23.48N	84.57E
Biharamulo, Tan. (bē-hä-rä-mōō′lō)	206	2.38S	31.20E
Bihorului, Munții, mts., Rom.	148	46.37N	22.37E
Bijagós, Arquipélago dos, is., Gui.-B.	204	11.20N	17.10W
Bijāpur, India	178	16.53N	75.42E
Bijeljina, Bos.	154	44.44N	19.15E
Bijelo Polje, Yugo. (bē′yĕ-lō pô′lyĕ)	154	43.02N	19.48E
Bijiang, China (bē-jyän)	183a	22.57N	113.15E
Bijie, China (bē-jyĕ)	184	27.20N	105.18E
Bijou Creek, r., Co., U.S. (bē′zhōō)	104	39.41N	104.13W
Bīkaner, India (bĭ-kä′nûr)	174	28.07N	73.19E
Bikin, Russia (bē-kēn′)	186	46.41N	134.29E
Bikin, r., Russia	186	46.37N	135.55E
Bikoro, Zaire (bē-kō′rō)	206	0.45S	18.07E
Bikuar, Parque Nacional do, rec., Ang.	210	15.07S	14.40E
Bilāspur, India (bē-läs′pōōr)	174	22.08N	82.12E
Bilauktaung, mts., Asia	188	14.40N	98.50E
Bilbao, Spain (bĭl-bä′ō)	136	43.12N	2.48W
Bilbays, Egypt	212b	30.26N	31.37E
Bileća, Bos. (bē′lĕ-chä)	154	42.52N	18.26E
Bilecik, Tur. (bē-lĕd-zhĕk′)	142	40.10N	29.58E
Bilé Karpaty, mts., Czech.	148	48.53N	17.35E
Biłgoraj, Pol. (bēw-gō′rī)	148	50.31N	22.43E
Bilimbay, Russia (bē′lĭm-bȧy)	164a	56.59N	59.53E
Billabong, r., Austl. (bĭl′ȧ-bông)	196	35.15S	145.20E
Billerica, Ma., U.S. (bĭl′rĭk-ȧ)	87a	42.33N	71.16W
Billericay, Eng., U.K.	138b	51.38N	0.25E
Billings, Mt., U.S. (bĭl′ĭngz)	90	45.47N	108.29W
Billingsport, N.J., U.S.	225b	39.51N	75.14W
Bill Williams, r., Az., U.S. (bĭl-wĭl′yumz)	102	34.10N	113.50W
Bilma, Niger (bēl′mä)	204	18.41N	13.20E
Biloxi, Ms., U.S. (bĭ-lŏk′sĭ)	90	30.24N	88.50W
Bilqās Qism Awwal, Egypt	212b	31.14N	31.25E
Bimberi Peak, mtn., Austl. (bĭm′bĕrĭ)	198	35.45S	148.50E
Binalonan, Phil. (bē-nä-lô′nän)	189a	16.03N	120.35E
Bingen, Ger. (bĭn′gĕn)	148	49.57N	7.54E
Bingham, Eng., U.K. (bĭng′ăm)	138a	52.57N	0.57W
Bingham, Me., U.S.	86	45.03N	69.51W
Bingham Canyon, Ut., U.S.	101b	40.33N	112.09W
Bingham Farms, Mi., U.S.	226c	42.32N	83.16W
Binghamton, N.Y., U.S. (bĭng′ăm-tŭn)	90	42.05N	75.55W
Bingo-Nada, b., Japan (bĭn′gō nä-dä)	187	34.06N	133.14E
Binjai, Indon.	188	3.59N	108.00E
Binnaway, Austl. (bĭn′ă-wā)	198	31.42S	149.22E
Binsheim, Ger.	232	51.31N	6.42E
Bintan, i., Indon. (bĭn′tän)	173b	1.09N	104.43E
Bintimani, mtn., S.L.	208	9.13N	11.07W
Bintulu, Malay. (bēn′tōō-lōō)	188	3.07N	113.06E
Binxian, China (bĭn-shyän)	182	37.27N	117.58E
Binxian, China	184	45.40N	127.20E
Bio Gorge, val., Ghana	208	8.30N	2.05W
Bioko (Fernando Póo), i., Eq. Gui.	204	3.35N	7.45E
Bira, Russia (bē′rȧ)	186	49.00N	133.18E
Bira, r., Russia	186	48.55N	132.25E
Birātnagar, Nepal (bĭ-rät′nŭ-gŭr)	178	26.35N	87.18E
Birch, Eng., U.K.	233b	53.34N	2.13W
Birch Bay, Wa., U.S. (bûrch)	100d	48.55N	122.45W
Birch Bay, b., Wa., U.S.	100d	48.55N	122.52W
Birch Island, i., Can.	82	52.25N	99.55W
Birch Mountains, mts., Can.	78	57.36N	113.10W
Birch Point, c., Wa., U.S.	100d	48.57N	122.50W
Bird Island, i., S. Afr. (bērd)	207c	33.51S	26.21E
Bird Rock, i., Bah. (bûrd)	116	22.50N	74.20W
Birds Hill, Can. (bûrds)	77f	49.58N	97.00W
Birdsville, Austl. (bûrdz′vĭl)	196	25.50S	139.31E
Birdum, Austl. (bûrd′ŭm)	196	15.45S	133.25E
Birecik, Tur. (bē-rĕd-zhĕk′)	142	37.10N	37.50E
Bir Gara, Chad	208	13.11N	15.58E
Bīrjand, Iran (bēr′jänd)	174	33.07N	59.16E
Birkenfeld, Or., U.S.	100c	45.59N	123.20W
Birkenhead, Eng., U.K. (bûr′kĕn-hĕd)	144	53.23N	3.02W
Birkenwerder, Ger. (bēr′kĕn-vĕr-dĕr)	139b	52.41N	13.22E
Birkholz, Ger.	234a	52.38N	13.34E
Bîrlad, Rom.	142	46.15N	27.43E
Birling, Eng., U.K.	231	51.19N	0.25E
Birmingham, Eng., U.K.	136	52.29N	1.53W
Birmingham, Al., U.S. (bûr′mĭng-häm)	90	33.31N	86.49W
Birmingham, Mi., U.S.	95b	42.32N	83.13W
Birmingham, Mo., U.S.	101f	39.10N	94.22W
Birmingham Canal, can., Eng., U.K.	138a	53.07N	2.40W
Bi′r Misāhah, Egypt	204	22.16N	28.04E
Birnin Kebbi, Nig.	204	12.32N	4.12E
Birobidzhan, Russia (bē′rō-bē-jän′)	158	48.42N	133.28E
Birsk, Russia (bĭrsk)	158	55.25N	55.30E
Birstall, Eng., U.K. (bûr′stôl)	138a	53.44N	1.39W
Biryuchiy, i., Ukr. (bĭr-yōō′chĭ)	160	46.07N	35.12E
Biryulëvo, Russia (bēr-yōōl′yō-vō)	164b	55.35N	37.39E
Biryusa, r., Russia (bēr-yōō′sä)	162	56.43N	97.30E
Bi′r Za′farānah, Egypt	173a	29.07N	32.38E
Biržai, Lith. (bēr-zhä′ē)	146	56.11N	24.45E
Bisbee, Az., U.S. (bĭz′bē)	90	31.30N	109.55W
Biscay, Bay of, b., Eur. (bĭs′kā′)	136	45.19N	3.51W
Biscayne Bay, b., Fl., U.S. (bĭs-kān′)	109a	25.22N	80.15W
Bischeim, Fr. (bĭsh′hīm)	150	48.40N	7.48E
Biscotasi Lake, l., Can.	84	47.20N	81.55W
Biser, Russia (bē′sĕr)	164a	58.24N	58.54E
Biševo, is., Yugo. (bē′shĕ-vō)	154	42.58N	15.50E
Bishkek, Kyrg.	158	42.49N	74.42E
Bisho, Ciskei	206	32.50S	27.20E
Bishop, Ca., U.S. (bĭsh′ŭp)	102	37.22N	118.25W
Bishop, Tx., U.S.	106	27.35N	97.46W
Bishop's Castle, Eng., U.K. (bĭsh′ŏps käs′l)	138a	52.29N	2.57W
Bishopville, S.C., U.S. (bĭsh′ŭp-vĭl)	108	34.11N	80.13W
Bismarck, N.D., U.S. (bĭz′märk)	90	46.48N	100.46W
Bismarck Archipelago, is., Pap. N. Gui.	188	3.15S	150.45E
Bismarck Range, mts., Pap. N. Gui.	188	5.15S	144.15E
Bissau, Gui.-B. (bē-sa′ōō)	208	11.51N	15.35W
Bissett, Can.	82	51.01N	95.45W
Bissingheim, neigh., Ger.	232	51.24N	6.49E
Bistineau, l., La., U.S. (bĭs-tĭ-nō′)	106	32.19N	93.45W
Bistrita, Rom. (bĭs-trĭt-sȧ)	142	47.09N	24.29E
Bistrita, r., Rom.	148	47.08N	25.47E
Bitlis, Tur. (bĭt-lēs′)	174	38.30N	42.00E
Bitola, Mac. (bē′tô-lä) (mô′nä-stĕr)	136	41.02N	21.22E
Bitonto, Italy (bē-tôn′tō)	154	41.08N	16.42E
Bitter Creek, r., Wy., U.S. (bĭt′ēr)	98	41.36N	108.29W
Bitterfeld, Ger. (bĭt′ēr-fĕlt)	148	51.39N	12.19E
Bittermark, neigh., Ger.	232	51.27N	7.28E
Bitterroot, r., Mt., U.S.	98	46.28N	114.10W
Bitterroot Range, mts., U.S. (bĭt′ēr-ōōt)	90	47.15N	115.13W
Bityug, r., Russia (bĭt′yōōg)	156	51.23N	40.33E
Biu, Nig.	208	10.35N	12.13E
Biwabik, Mn., U.S. (bē-wä′bĭk)	96	47.32N	92.24W
Biwa-ko, l., Japan (bē-wä′kō)	187	35.03N	135.51E
Biya, r., Russia (bĭ′yȧ)	162	52.22N	87.28E
Biysk, Russia (bēsk)	158	52.32N	85.28E
Bizana, Transkei (bĭz-änä)	207c	30.51S	29.54E
Bizerte, Tun. (bē-zĕrt′)	204	37.23N	9.52E
Bjelovar, Cro. (byĕ-lō′vär)	154	45.54N	16.53E
Bjørnafjorden, fj., Nor.	146	60.11N	5.26E
Bla, Mali	208	12.57N	5.46W
Black, l., Mi., U.S. (blăk)	92	45.25N	84.15W
Black, l., N.Y., U.S.	92	44.30N	75.35W
Black, r., Asia	188	21.00N	103.30E
Black, r., Can.	84	49.20N	81.15W
Black, r., U.S.	104	35.47N	91.22W
Black, r., Az., U.S.	102	33.35N	109.35W
Black, r., N.Y., U.S.	92	43.45N	75.20W
Black, r., S.C., U.S.	108	33.55N	80.10W
Black, r., Wi., U.S.	96	44.07N	90.56W
Blackall, Austl. (blăk′ŭl)	196	24.23S	145.37E
Black Bay, b., Can. (blăk)	84	48.36N	88.32W
Blackburn, Austl.	239b	37.49S	145.09E
Blackburn, Eng., U.K. (blăk′bûrn)	144	53.45N	2.28W
Blackburn Mount, mtn., Ak., U.S.	89	61.50N	143.12W
Black Butte Lake, res., Ca., U.S.	102	39.45N	122.20W
Black Creek Pioneer Village, bldg., Can.	223c	43.47N	79.32W
Black Diamond, Wa., U.S. (dī′mŭnd)	100a	47.19N	122.00W
Black Down Hills, hills, Eng., U.K. (blăk′doun)	144	50.58N	3.19W
Blackduck, Mn., U.S. (blăk′dŭk)	96	47.41N	94.33W
Blackfeet Indian Reservation, I.R., Mt., U.S.	98	48.40N	113.00W
Blackfoot, Id., U.S. (blăk′fŏt)	98	43.11N	112.23W
Blackfoot, r., Mt., U.S.	98	46.53N	113.33W
Blackfoot Indian Reservation, I.R., Mt., U.S.	98	48.49N	112.53W
Blackfoot Indian Reserve, I.R., Can.	80	50.45N	113.00W
Blackfoot Reservoir, res., Id., U.S.	98	42.53N	111.23W
Black Forest, see Schwarzwald, for., Ger.	148	47.54N	7.57E
Black Hills, mts., U.S.	90	44.08N	103.47W
Black Island, i., Can.	82	51.10N	96.30W
Black Lake, Can.	84	46.02N	71.24W
Blackley, neigh., Eng., U.K.	233b	53.31N	2.13W
Black Mesa, Az., U.S. (blăk măsȧ)	102	36.33N	110.40W
Blackmore, Eng., U.K.	231	51.41N	0.19E
Blackmud Creek, r., Can. (blăk′mŭd)	77g	53.28N	113.34W
Blackpool, Eng., U.K. (blăk′pōōl)	144	53.49N	3.02W
Black Range, mts., N.M., U.S.	90	33.15N	107.55W
Black River, Jam. (blăk′)	116	18.00N	77.50W
Black River Falls, Wi., U.S.	96	44.18N	90.51W
Black Rock, Austl.	239b	37.59S	145.01E
Black Rock Desert, des., Nv., U.S. (rŏk)	98	40.55N	119.00W
Blacksburg, S.C., U.S. (blăks′bûrg)	108	35.09N	81.30W
Black Sea	136	43.01N	32.16E
Blackshear, Ga., U.S. (blăk′shĭr)	108	31.20N	82.15W
Black Springs, Austl.	239b	37.46S	145.19E
Blackstone, Va., U.S. (blăk′stōn)	108	37.04N	78.00W
Black Sturgeon, r., Can. (stû′jŭn)	84	49.12N	88.41W
Blacktown, Austl. (blăk′toun)	195b	33.47S	150.55E
Blackville, Can. (blăk′vĭl)	86	46.44N	65.50W
Blackville, S.C., U.S.	108	33.21N	81.19W
Black Volta (Volta Noire), r., Afr.	204	11.30N	4.00W
Black Warrior, r., Al., U.S. (blăk wŏr′ĭ-ēr)	108	32.37N	87.42W
Blackwater, r., Ire. (blăk-wô′tēr)	144	52.05N	9.02W
Blackwater, r., Mo., U.S.	104	38.53N	93.22W
Blackwater, r., Va., U.S.	108	37.07N	77.10W
Blackwell, Ok., U.S. (blăk′wĕl)	104	36.47N	97.19W
Bladel, Neth.	139a	51.22N	5.15E
Bladensburg, Md., U.S.	225d	38.56N	76.55W
Blagodarnoye, Russia (blä′gô-där-nō′yĕ)	160	45.00N	43.30E
Blagoevgrad, Bul.	154	42.01N	23.06E
Blagoveshchensk, Russia (blä′gŏ-vyĕsh′chĕnsk)	158	50.16N	127.47E
Blagoveshchensk, Russia	164a	55.03N	56.00E
Blaine, Mn., U.S. (blān)	101g	45.11N	93.14W
Blaine, Wa., U.S.	100d	48.59N	122.49W
Blaine, W.V., U.S.	92	39.25N	79.10W
Blaine Hill, Pa., U.S.	226b	40.16N	79.53W
Blair, Ne., U.S. (blâr)	96	41.33N	96.09W
Blairmore, Can.	80	49.38N	114.25W
Blairsville, Pa., U.S. (blârs′vĭl)	92	40.30N	79.40W
Blake, i., Wa., U.S. (blāk)	100a	47.37N	122.28W
Blakehurst, Austl.	239a	33.59S	151.07E
Blakely, Ga., U.S. (blāk′lē)	108	31.22N	84.55W
Blanc, Cap, c., Afr.	204	20.39N	18.08W
Blanc, Mont, mtn., Eur. (môn blän)	136	45.50N	6.53E
Blanca, Bahía, b., Arg. (bä-ē′ä-blän′kä)	126	39.30S	61.00W
Blanca Peak, mtn., Co., U.S. (blăŋ′kȧ)	90	37.36N	105.22W
Blanche, r., Can.	77c	45.34N	75.38W
Blanche, Lake, l., Austl. (blănch)	198	29.20S	139.12E
Blanchester, Oh., U.S. (blăn′chĕs-tēr)	95f	39.18N	83.58W
Blanco, r., Mex.	112	24.05N	99.21W
Blanco, r., Mex.	112	18.42N	96.03W

ng-sing; ŋ-baŋk; N-nasalized n; nŏd; cŏmmit; ōld; ōbey; ôrder; oi-boil; fōōd; ŏ-as oo in foot; ou-out; s-soft; sh-dish; th-thin; pūre; ůnite; ûrn; stŭd; circŭs; ü-as in French tu; ′-indeterminate vowel.

PLACE (Pronunciation)	PAGE	Lat. °′	Long. °′
Blanco, Cabo, c., Arg. (blăŋ'kō)	126	47.08S	65.47W
Blanco, Cabo, c., C.R. (kä'bō-blăŋ'kō)	114	9.29N	85.15W
Blanco, Cape, c., Or., U.S. (blăn'kō)	98	42.53N	124.38W
Blancos, Cayo, i., Cuba (kä'yō-blăŋ'kōs)	116	23.15N	80.55W
Blanding, Ut., U.S.	102	37.40N	109.31W
Blankenburg, neigh., Ger.	234a	52.35N	13.28E
Blankenfelde, Ger. (blän'kĕn-fĕl-dĕ)	139b	52.20N	13.24E
Blankenfelde, neigh., Ger.	234a	52.37N	13.23E
Blankenstein, Ger.	232	51.24N	7.14E
Blanquefort, Fr.	150	44.53N	0.38W
Blanquilla, Arrecife, i., Mex. (är-rē-sē'fē-blän-kē'l-yä)	112	21.32N	97.14W
Blantyre, Mwi. (blăn-tīyr)	206	15.47S	35.00E
Blasdell, N.Y., U.S. (blāz'dĕl)	95c	42.48N	78.51W
Blato, Cro. (blä'tō)	154	42.55N	16.47E
Blawnox, Pa., U.S.	226b	40.29N	79.52W
Blaye-et-Sainte Luce, Fr. (blā'ā-sănt-lüs')	150	45.08N	0.40W
Blażowa, Pol. (bwä-zhō'vä)	148	49.51N	22.05E
Bleus, Monts, mts., Zaire	210	1.10N	30.10E
Bliersheim, Ger.	232	51.23N	6.43E
Blind River, Can. (blīnd)	78	46.10N	83.09W
Blissfield, Mi., U.S. (blĭs-fēld)	92	41.50N	83.50W
Blithe, r., Eng., U.K. (blīth)	138a	52.22N	1.49W
Blitta, Togo	208	8.19N	0.59E
Block, i., R.I., U.S. (blŏk)	92	41.05N	71.35W
Bloedel, Can.	80	50.07N	125.23W
Bloemfontein, S. Afr. (blōōm'fŏn-tān)	206	29.09S	26.16E
Blois, Fr. (blwä)	140	47.36N	1.21E
Blombacher Bach, neigh., Ger.	232	51.15N	7.14E
Blood Indian Reserve, I.R., Can.	80	49.30N	113.10W
Bloomer, Wi., U.S. (blōōm'ēr)	96	45.07N	91.30W
Bloomfield, In., U.S. (blōōm'fēld)	92	39.00N	86.55W
Bloomfield, Ia., U.S.	96	40.44N	92.21W
Bloomfield, Mo., U.S.	104	36.54N	89.55W
Bloomfield, Ne., U.S.	96	42.36N	97.40W
Bloomfield, N.J., U.S.	94a	40.48N	74.12W
Bloomfield Hills, Mi., U.S.	95b	42.35N	83.15W
Bloomfield Village, Mi., U.S.	226c	42.33N	83.15W
Blooming Prairie, Mn., U.S. (blōōm'ĭng prâ'rĭ)	96	43.52N	93.04W
Bloomington, Ca., U.S. (blōōm'ĭng-tŭn)	101a	34.04N	117.24W
Bloomington, Il., U.S.	90	40.30N	89.00W
Bloomington, In., U.S.	92	39.10N	86.35W
Bloomington, Mn., U.S.	101g	44.50N	93.18W
Bloomsburg, Pa., U.S. (blōōmz'bûrg)	92	41.00N	76.25W
Blossburg, Al., U.S. (blŏs'bûrg)	94h	33.38N	86.57W
Blossburg, Pa., U.S.	92	41.45N	77.00W
Bloubergstrand, S. Afr.	206a	33.48S	18.28E
Blountstown, Fl., U.S. (blŭnts'tun)	108	30.24N	85.02W
Bludenz, Aus. (blōō-dĕnts')	148	47.09N	9.50E
Blue Ash, Oh., U.S. (blōō ăsh)	95f	39.14N	84.23W
Blue Earth, Mn., U.S. (blōō ûrth)	96	43.38N	94.05W
Blue Earth, r., Mn., U.S.	96	43.55N	94.16W
Bluefield, W.V., U.S. (blōō'fēld)	108	37.15N	81.11W
Bluefields, Nic. (blōō'fēldz)	110	12.03N	83.45W
Blue Island, Il., U.S.	95a	41.39N	87.41W
Blue Mesa Reservoir, res., Co., U.S.	102	38.25N	107.00W
Blue Mosque, rel., Egypt	240a	30.02N	31.15E
Blue Mountain, mtn., Can.	86	50.28N	57.11W
Blue Mountains, mts., Austl.	196	33.35S	149.00E
Blue Mountains, mts., Jam.	116	18.05N	76.35W
Blue Mountains, mts., U.S.	90	45.15N	118.50W
Blue Mud Bay, b., Austl. (bōō mŭd)	196	13.20S	136.45E
Blue Nile, r., Afr.	204	12.30N	34.00E
Blue Rapids, Ks., U.S. (blōō răp'ĭdz)	104	39.40N	96.41W
Blue Ridge, mtn., U.S. (blōō rĭj)	90	35.30N	82.50W
Blue River, Can.	78	52.05N	119.17W
Blue River, r., Mo., U.S.	101f	38.55N	94.33W
Bluff, Ut., U.S.	102	37.18N	109.34W
Bluff Park, Al., U.S.	94h	33.24N	86.52W
Bluffton, In., U.S. (blŭf-tŭn)	92	40.40N	85.15W
Bluffton, Oh., U.S.	92	40.50N	83.55W
Blumenau, Braz. (blōō'mĕn-ou)	126	26.53S	48.58W
Blumut, Gunong, mtn., Malay.	173b	2.03N	103.34E
Blyth, Eng., U.K. (blīth)	144	55.03N	1.34W
Blythe, Ca., U.S.	102	33.37N	114.37W
Blytheville, Ar., U.S. (blīth'vĭl)	104	35.55N	89.51W
Bo, S.L.	208	7.56N	11.21W
Boac, Phil.	189a	13.26N	121.50E
Boaco, Nic. (bō-ä'kō)	114	12.24N	85.41W
Bo'ai, China (bwo-ī)	184	35.10N	113.08E
Boa Vista, i., C.V. (bō-ä-vēsh'tà)	204b	16.01N	23.52W
Boa Vista do Rio Branco, Braz.	124	2.46N	60.45W
Bobbingworth, Eng., U.K.	231	51.44N	0.13E
Bobĕrka, Ukr. (bō'bĕr-kà)	148	49.36N	24.18E
Bobigny, Fr.	233c	48.54N	2.27E
Bobo Dioulasso, Burkina (bō'bō-dyōō-lás-sō')	204	11.12N	4.18W
Bobr, Bela. (bô'b'r)	156	54.19N	29.11E
Bóbr, r., Pol. (bŭ'br)	148	51.44N	15.13E
Bobrinets, Ukr. (bô'brē-nyĭts)	156	48.04N	32.10E
Bobrov, Russia (bŭb-rôf')	160	51.07N	40.01E
Bobrovitsa, Ukr. (bŭb-rô'vē-tsá)	156	50.43N	31.27E
Bobruysk, Bela. (bŏ-brōō'ĭsk)	160	53.07N	29.13E
Boca, neigh., Arg.	229d	34.38S	58.21W
Boca del Pozo, Ven. (bô-kä-dĕl-pô'zō)	125b	11.00N	64.21W
Boca de Uchire, Ven. (bô-kä-dĕ-ōō-chē'rĕ)	125b	10.09N	65.27W
Bocaina, Serra da, mtn., Braz. (sĕ'r-rä-dä-bô-kä'ē-nä)	123a	22.47S	44.39W
Bocanegra, Peru	229c	12.01S	77.07W
Bocas, Mex. (bō'käs)	112	22.29N	101.03W
Bocas del Toro, Pan. (bō'käs dĕl tō'rō)	114	9.24N	82.15W
Bochnia, Pol. (bōk'nyä)	148	49.58N	20.28E
Bocholt, Ger. (bō'kōlt)	151c	51.50N	6.37E
Bochum, Ger.	148	51.29N	7.13E
Böckel, neigh., Ger.	232	51.13N	7.12E

PLACE (Pronunciation)	PAGE	Lat. °′	Long. °′
Bockum, Ger.	232	51.20N	6.44E
Bockum, neigh., Ger.	232	51.21N	6.38E
Bockum-Hövel, Ger. (bō'kōm-hû'fĕl)	151c	51.41N	7.45E
Bodalang, Zaire	210	3.14N	22.14E
Bodaybo, Russia (bō-dī'bō)	158	57.12N	114.46E
Bodele, depr., Chad (bō-då-lā')	204	16.45N	17.05E
Bodelschwingh, neigh., Ger.	232	51.33N	7.22E
Boden, Swe.	140	65.51N	21.29E
Bodensee, l., Eur. (bō'dĕn zā)	136	47.48N	9.22E
Bodmin, Eng., U.K. (bŏd'mĭn)	144	50.29N	4.45W
Bodmin Moor, Eng., U.K. (bŏd'mĭn mōr)	144	50.36N	4.43W
Bodrum, Tur.	160	37.10N	27.07E
Boende, Zaire (bō-ĕn'då)	206	0.13S	20.52E
Boerne, Tx., U.S. (bō'ērn)	106	29.49N	98.44W
Boesmans, r., S. Afr.	207c	33.29S	26.09E
Boeuf, r., U.S. (bĕf)	106	32.23N	91.57W
Boffa, Gui. (bôf'á)	204	10.10N	14.02W
Bōfu, Japan (bō'fōō)	187	34.03N	131.35E
Bogalusa, La., U.S. (bō-gá-lōō'sá)	106	30.48N	89.52W
Bogan, r., Austl. (bō'gĕn)	198	32.10S	147.40E
Bogense, Den. (bō'gĕn-sĕ)	146	55.34N	10.09E
Boggy Peak, mtn., Antig. (bŏg'ĭ-pēk)	115b	17.03N	61.50W
Bogodukhov, Ukr. (bō-gō-dōō'kôf)	160	50.10N	35.31E
Bogong, Mount, mtn., Austl.	198	36.50S	147.15E
Bogor, Indon.	188	6.45S	106.45E
Bogoroditsk, Russia (bō-gō'rô-dĭtsk)	156	53.48N	38.06E
Bogorodsk, Russia	160	56.02N	43.40E
Bogorodskoje, neigh., Russia	235b	55.49N	37.44E
Bogorodskoye, Russia (bô-gô-rôd'skô-yĕ)	164a	56.43N	56.53E
Bogota, N.J., U.S.	224	40.53N	74.02W
Bogotá, see Santa Fe de Bogotá, Col.	124	4.36N	74.05W
Bogotol, Russia (bŏ'gō-tōl)	158	56.15N	89.45E
Bogoyavlenskoye, Ukr. (bŏ'gō-yäf'lĕn-skō'yĕ)	156	48.46N	33.19E
Boguchar, Russia (bō'gō-chär)	160	49.40N	41.00E
Bogue Chitto, Ms., U.S. (nôr'fēld)	108	31.26N	90.25W
Boguete, Pan. (bō-gĕ'tĕ)	114	8.54N	82.29W
Boguslav, Ukr. (bō'gō-slăf)	156	49.34N	30.51W
Bo Hai, b., China	180	38.30N	120.00E
Bohai Haixia, strt., China (bwo-hī hī-shyä)	184	38.05N	121.40E
Bohain-en-Vermandois, Fr. (bō-ăN-ŏN-vâr-män-dwä')	150	49.58N	3.22E
Bohemia, see Čechy, hist. reg., Czech.	148	49.51N	13.55E
Bohemian Forest, mts., Eur. (bō-hē'mĭ-ăn)	136	49.35N	12.27E
Böhnsdorf, neigh., Ger.	234a	52.24N	13.33E
Bohol, i., Phil. (bō-hōl')	188	9.28N	124.35E
Bohom, Mex. (bō-ō'm)	112	16.47N	92.42W
Boiestown, Can. (boiz'toun)	86	46.27N	66.25W
Bois Blanc, i., Mi., U.S. (boi' blăŋk)	92	45.45N	84.30W
Boischâtel, Can. (bwä-shä-tĕl')	77b	46.54N	71.08W
Bois-Colombes, Fr.	233c	48.55N	2.16E
Bois-des-Filion, Can. (bōō-ä'dĕ-fē-yōN')	77a	45.40N	73.46W
Boise, Id., U.S. (boi'zē)	90	43.38N	116.12W
Boise, r., Id., U.S.	98	43.43N	116.30W
Boise City, Ok., U.S.	104	36.42N	102.30W
Boissevain, Can. (bois'văn)	78	49.14N	100.03W
Boissy-Saint-Léger, Fr.	233c	48.45N	2.31E
Bojador, Cabo, c., W. Sah.	204	26.21N	16.08W
Bojnūrd, Iran	174	37.29N	57.13E
Bokani, Nig.	208	9.26N	5.13E
Boknafjorden, fj., Nor.	140	59.12N	5.37E
Boksburg, S. Afr. (bŏks'bûrgh)	207b	26.13N	28.15E
Boksburg North, S. Afr.	240b	26.12S	28.15E
Boksburg South, S. Afr.	240b	26.14S	28.15E
Boksburg West, S. Afr.	240b	26.13S	28.14E
Bokungu, Zaire	210	0.41S	22.19E
Bol, Chad	208	13.28N	14.43E
Bolai I, Cen. Afr. Rep.	208	4.20N	17.21E
Bolama, Gui.-B. (bō-lä'mä)	204	11.34S	15.41W
Bolan, mtn., Pak. (bō-län')	178	30.13N	67.09E
Bolaños, Mex. (bō-län'yōs)	112	21.40N	103.48W
Bolaños, r., Mex.	112	21.26N	103.54W
Bolan Pass, p., Pak.	174	29.50N	67.10E
Bolbec, Fr. (bōl-bĕk')	150	49.37N	0.26E
Bole, Ghana (bō'lå)	204	9.02N	2.29W
Bolesławiec, Pol. (bō-lĕ-slä'vyĕts)	148	51.15N	15.35E
Bolgatanga, Ghana	208	10.46N	0.52W
Bolgrad, Ukr. (bŏl-grát)	160	45.41N	28.38E
Boli, China (bwo-lē)	180	45.40N	130.38E
Bolinao, Phil. (bō-lē-nä'ō)	189a	16.24N	119.53E
Bolívar, Arg. (bō-lē'vär)	126	36.15S	61.05W
Bolívar, Col.	124	1.46N	76.58W
Bolivar, Mo., U.S. (bŏl'ĭ-vȧr)	104	37.37N	93.22W
Bolivar, Tn., U.S.	108	35.14N	88.56W
Bolívar (La Columna), mtn., Ven.	124	8.44N	70.54W
Bolivar Peninsula, pen., Tx., U.S. (bŏl'ĭ-vȧr)	107a	29.25N	94.40W
Bolivia, nation, S.A. (bō-lĭv'ĭ-á)	124	17.00S	64.00W
Bölkenbusch, Ger.	232	51.21N	7.06E
Bolkhov, Russia (bŏl-kôf')	160	53.27N	35.59E
Bollate, Italy	234c	45.33N	9.07E
Bollensdorf, Ger.	234a	52.31N	13.43E
Bollin, r., Eng., U.K. (bŏl'ĭn)	138a	53.18N	2.11W
Bollington, Eng., U.K. (bôl'ĭng-tŭn)	138a	53.18N	2.06W
Bollington, Eng., U.K.	233b	53.22N	2.25W
Bollnäs, Swe. (bôl'nĕs)	146	61.22N	16.20E
Bollwerk, Ger.	232	51.10N	7.35E
Bolmen, l., Swe. (bôl'mĕn)	146	56.58N	13.25E
Bolobo, Zaire (bō'lō-bō)	206	2.14S	16.18E
Bologna, Italy (bō-lōn'yä)	136	44.30N	11.18E
Bologoye, Russia (bō-lō-gô'yĕ)	160	57.52N	34.02E
Bolonchenticul, Mex. (bō-lōn-chĕn-tē-kōō'l)	114a	20.03N	89.47W
Bolondrón, Cuba (bō-lōn-drōn')	116	22.45N	81.25W

PLACE (Pronunciation)	PAGE	Lat. °′	Long. °′
Bol'šaja Ochta, neigh., Russia	235a	59.57N	30.25E
Bolseno, Lago di, l., Italy (lä'gō-dē-bōl-sā'nō)	154	42.35N	11.40E
Bol'shaya Anyuy, r., Russia	162	67.58N	161.15E
Bol'shaya Chuya, r., Russia	162	58.15N	111.40E
Bol'shaya Kinel', r., Russia	160	53.20N	52.40E
Bol'shaya Lepetikha, Ukr. (bŏl-shá'yá'lyĕ'pyĕ-tē'ká)	156	47.11N	33.58E
Bol'shaya Viska, Ukr. (vĭs-kä')	156	48.34N	31.54E
Bol'shaya Vradiyevka, Ukr. (vrá-dyĕf'ká)	156	47.51N	30.38E
Bol'she Ust'ikinskoye, Russia (bôl'she ôs-tyĭ-kĕn'skô-yĕ)	164a	55.58N	58.18E
Bol'shoy Begichëv, i., Russia	158	74.30N	114.40E
Bol'shoye Ivonino, Russia (ĭ-vô'nĭ-nô)	164a	59.41N	61.12E
Bol'shoy Kuyash, Russia (bôl'-shôy kōō'yásh)	164a	55.52N	61.07E
Bolshoy Tokmak, Ukr. (bŏl-shôy' tôk-mäk')	156	47.17N	35.48E
Bol'shoy Uzen', r.	160	49.50N	49.35E
Bol'šoj Teatr, bldg., Russia	235b	55.46N	37.37E
Bolsover, Eng., U.K. (bōl'zō-vēr)	138a	53.14N	1.17W
Boltaña, Spain (bōl-tä'nä)	152	42.28N	0.03E
Bolton, Can. (bōl'tŭn)	77d	43.53N	79.44W
Bolton, Eng., U.K.	144	53.35N	2.26W
Bolton-upon-Dearne, Eng., U.K. (bōl'tŭn-ŭp'ŏn-dûrn)	138a	53.31N	1.19W
Bolu, Tur. (bō'lō)	142	40.45N	31.45E
Bolva, r., Russia (bôl'vä)	156	53.30N	34.30E
Bolvadin, Tur. (bōl-vä-dēn')	142	38.50N	30.50E
Bolzano, Italy (bōl-tsä'nō)	142	46.31N	11.22E
Boma, Zaire (bō'mä)	206	5.51S	13.03E
Bombala, Austl. (bŭm-bä'lă)	196	36.55S	149.07E
Bombay, India (bŏm-bā')	174	18.58N	72.50E
Bombay Harbour, b., India	179b	18.55N	72.52E
Bomi Hills, Lib.	204	7.00N	11.00W
Bom Jardim, Braz. (bôn zhär-dēN')	123a	22.10S	42.25W
Bom Jesus do Itabapoana, Braz.	123a	21.08S	41.51W
Bømlo, i., Nor. (bûmlō)	146	59.47N	4.57E
Bommerholz, Ger.	232	51.23N	7.18E
Bommern, neigh., Ger.	232	51.25N	7.20E
Bomongo, Zaire	204	1.22N	18.21E
Bom Retiro, neigh., Braz.	230d	23.32S	46.38W
Bom Sucesso, Braz. (bôn-sōō-sĕ'sō)	123a	21.02S	44.44W
Bomu, see Mbomou, r., Afr.	204	4.50N	24.00E
Bon, Cap, c., Tun. (bôN)	142	37.04N	11.13E
Bon Air, Pa., U.S.	225b	39.58N	75.19W
Bonaire, i., Neth. Ant. (bō-nâr')	124	12.10N	68.15W
Bonavista, Can. (bō-nȧ-vĭs'tȧ)	79a	48.39N	53.07W
Bonavista Bay, b., Can.	79a	48.45N	53.20W
Bond, Co., U.S. (bŏnd)	104	39.53N	106.40W
Bondi, Austl.	239a	33.53S	151.17E
Bondo, Zaire (bôn'dō)	162	3.49N	23.40E
Bondoc Peninsula, pen., Phil. (bōn-dŏk')	189a	13.24N	122.30E
Bondoukou, I.C. (bŏn-dōō'kōō)	204	8.02N	2.48W
Bonds Cay, i., Bah. (bŏnds kē)	116	25.30N	77.45W
Bondy, Fr.	151b	48.54N	2.28E
Bone, Teluk, b., Indon.	188	4.09S	121.00E
Bône, see Annaba, Alg.	204	36.57N	7.39E
Bonete, Cerro, mtn., Arg. (bô'nĕtĕh çĕrrō)	126	27.50S	68.35W
Bonfim, Braz. (bôN-fē'N)	123a	20.20S	44.15W
Bongor, Chad	208	10.17N	15.22E
Bonham, Tx., U.S. (bŏn'ăm)	104	33.35N	96.09W
Bonhomme, Pic, mtn., Haiti	116	19.10N	72.20W
Bonifacio, Fr. (bō-nē-fä'chō)	154	41.23N	9.10E
Bonifacio, Strait of, strt., Eur.	142	41.14N	9.02E
Bonifay, Fl., U.S. (bŏn-ĭ-fā')	108	30.46N	85.40W
Bonin Islands, is., Japan (bō'nĭn)	190	26.30N	141.00E
Bonn, Ger. (bŏn)	136	50.44N	7.06E
Bonne Bay, b., Can. (bŏn)	86	49.33N	57.55W
Bonners Ferry, Id., U.S. (bŏnērz fĕr'ĭ)	98	48.41N	116.19W
Bonner Springs, Ks., U.S. (bŏn'ēr sprĭngz)	101f	39.04N	94.52W
Bonne Terre, Mo., U.S. (bŏn târ')	104	37.55N	90.32W
Bonnet Peak, mtn., Can. (bŏn'ĭt)	80	51.26N	115.53W
Bonneuil-sur-Marne, Fr.	233c	48.46N	2.29E
Bonneville Dam, dam, U.S. (bōn'ē-vĭl)	98	45.37N	121.57W
Bonny, Nig. (bŏn'ē)	204	4.29N	7.13E
Bonny Lake, Wa., U.S. (bŏn'ē lăk)	100a	47.11N	122.11W
Bonnyrigg, Austl.	239a	33.54S	150.54E
Bonnyville, Can. (bŏnē-vĭl)	80	54.16N	110.44W
Bonorva, Italy (bō-nôr'vä)	154	40.26N	8.46E
Bonsucesso, neigh., Braz.	230c	22.52S	43.15W
Bonthain, Indon. (bōn-tīn')	188	5.30S	119.52E
Bonthe, S.L.	204	7.32N	12.30W
Bontoc, Phil. (bōn-tŏk')	189a	17.10N	121.01E
Booby Rocks, is., Bah. (bōō'bĭ rŏks)	116	23.55N	77.00W
Booker T. Washington National Monument, rec., Va., U.S. (bŏk'ēr tē wŏsh'ĭng-tŭn)	108	37.07N	79.45W
Boom, Bel.	139a	51.05N	4.22E
Boone, Ia., U.S. (bōōn)	96	42.04N	93.51W
Booneville, Ar., U.S. (bōōn'vĭl)	104	35.09N	93.54W
Booneville, Ky., U.S.	92	37.25N	83.40W
Booneville, Ms., U.S.	108	34.37N	88.35W
Boons, S. Afr.	212d	25.59S	27.15E
Boonton, N.J., U.S. (bōōn'tŭn)	94a	40.54N	74.24W
Boonville, In., U.S.	92	38.00N	87.15W
Boonville, Mo., U.S.	104	38.57N	92.44W
Boorama, Som.	212a	10.05N	43.08E
Boosaaso, Som.	212a	11.19N	49.10E
Boothbay Harbor, Me., U.S. (bōōth'bā här'bēr)	86	43.51N	69.39W
Boothia, Gulf of, b., Can. (bōō'thĭ-ȧ)	78	69.04N	86.04W
Boothia Peninsula, pen., Can.	76	73.30N	95.00W
Boothstown, Eng., U.K.	233b	53.30N	2.25W
Bootle, Eng., U.K. (bōōt'l)	138a	53.29N	3.02W

PLACE (Pronunciation)	PAGE	Lat. °′	Long. °′
Booysens, neigh., S. Afr.	240b	26.14S	28.01E
Bophuthatswana, nation, Afr.	206	26.00S	25.35E
Bor, Sudan (bôr)	204	6.13N	31.35E
Bor, Tur. (bōr)	160	37.50N	34.40E
Boraha, Nosy, i., Madag.	206	16.58S	50.15E
Borah Peak, mtn., Id., U.S. (bō'rä)	98	44.12N	113.47W
Borås, Swe. (bō'rōs)	140	57.43N	12.55E
Borāzjān, Iran (bō-räz-jän')	174	29.13N	51.13E
Borba, Braz. (bôr'bä)	124	4.23S	59.31W
Borbeck, neigh., Ger.	232	51.29N	6.57E
Borborema, Planalto da, plat., Braz. (plä-nàl'tō-dä-bôr-bō-rĕ'mä)	124	7.35S	36.40W
Bordeaux, Fr. (bôr-dō')	136	44.50N	0.37W
Bordeaux, S. Afr.	240b	26.06S	28.01E
Bordentown, N.J., U.S. (bôr'dĕn-toun)	92	40.05N	74.40W
Bordj-bou-Arréridj, Alg. (bôrj-bōō-à-rā-rēj')	142	36.03N	4.48E
Bordj Omar Idriss, Alg.	204	28.06N	6.34E
Borehamwood, Eng., U.K.	231	51.40N	0.16W
Borgarnes, Ice.	140	64.31N	21.40W
Borger, Tx., U.S. (bôr'gẽr)	104	35.40N	101.23W
Borgholm, Swe. (bôrg-hōlm')	146	56.52N	16.40E
Borgne, l., La., U.S. (bôrn'y')	106	30.03N	89.36W
Borgomanero, Italy (bôr'gō-mä-nâ'rō)	154	45.40N	8.28E
Borgo Val di Taro, Italy (bô'r-zhō-väl-dē-tä'rō)	154	44.29N	9.44E
Boring, Or., U.S. (bōring)	100c	45.26N	122.22W
Borislav, Ukr. (bō'rĭs-lôf)	148	49.17N	23.24E
Borisoglebsk, Russia (bŏ-rē sō-glyĕpsk')	158	51.20N	42.00E
Borisov, Bela. (bŏ-rē'sôf)	160	54.16N	28.33E
Borisovka, Russia (bŏ-rē-sôf'kà)	160	50.38N	36.00E
Borispol', Ukr. (bo-rĭs'pol)	156	50.17N	30.54E
Borivli, India	179b	19.15N	72.48E
Borja, Spain (bôr'hä)	152	41.50N	1.33W
Borjas Blancas, Spain (bō'r-käs-blä'n-käs)	152	41.29N	0.53E
Borken, Ger. (bōr'kĕn)	151c	51.50N	6.51E
Borkou, reg., Chad (bôr-kōō')	204	18.11N	18.28E
Borkum, i., Ger. (bōr'kōōm)	148	53.31N	6.50E
Borlänge, Swe. (bôr-lĕŋ'gĕ)	146	60.30N	15.24E
Borle, neigh., India	236e	19.02N	72.55E
Borneo, i., Asia	188	0.25N	112.39E
Bornholm, i., Den. (bôrn-hôlm)	136	55.16N	15.15E
Bornim, neigh., Ger.	234a	52.26N	13.00E
Bornstedt, neigh., Ger.	234a	52.25N	13.02E
Borodayevka, Ukr.	156	48.44N	34.09E
Boromlya, Ukr. (bŏ-rôm''l-yä)	156	50.36N	34.58E
Boromo, Burkina	208	11.45N	2.56W
Borough Green, Eng., U.K.	231	51.17N	0.19E
Borough Park, neigh., N.Y., U.S.	224	40.38N	74.00W
Borovan, Bul. (bō-rō-vän')	154	43.24N	23.47E
Borovichi, Russia (bō-rō-vē'chē)	158	58.22N	33.56E
Borovsk, Russia (bô'rôvsk)	156	55.13N	36.26E
Borraan, Som.	212a	10.38N	48.30E
Borracha, Isla la, i., Ven. (ē's-lä-lä-bôr-rà'chä)	125b	10.18N	64.44W
Borroloola, Austl. (bŏr-rō-lōō'là)	196	16.15S	136.19E
Borshchëv, Ukr. (bôrsh-chyôf')	148	48.47N	26.04E
Borth, Ger.	232	51.36N	6.33E
Bort-les-Orgues, Fr. (bôr-lā-zôrg)	150	45.26N	2.26E
Borūjerd, Iran	174	33.45N	48.53E
Borzna, Ukr. (bôrz'nà)	160	51.15N	32.26E
Borzya, Russia (bôrz'yà)	158	50.37N	116.53E
Bosa, Italy (bō'sä)	154	40.18N	8.34E
Bosanska Dubica, Bos. (bō'sän-skä dōō'bĭt-sä)	154	45.10N	16.49E
Bosanska Gradiška, Bos. (bō'sän-skä grä-dĭsh'kä)	154	45.08N	17.15E
Bosanski Novi, Bos. (bō's sän-skĭ nō'vē)	154	45.00N	16.22E
Bosanski Petrovac, Bos. (bō'sän-skĭ pĕt'rō-väts)	154	44.33N	16.23E
Bosanski Šamac, Bos. (bō'sän-skĭ shä'màts)	154	45.03N	18.30E
Boscobel, Wi., U.S. (bŏs'kō-bĕl)	96	43.08N	90.44W
Bose, China (bwo-sŭ)	184	24.00N	106.38E
Boshan, China (bwo-shan)	180	36.32N	117.51E
Boskol', Kaz. (bås-kôl')	164a	53.45N	61.17E
Boskoop, Neth.	139a	52.04N	4.39E
Boskovice, Czech. (bŏs'kō-vē-tsĕ)	148	49.26N	16.37E
Bosna, r., Yugo.	154	44.19N	17.54E
Bosnia and Hercegovina, nation, Eur.	154	44.15N	17.30E
Bosobolo, Zaire	210	4.11N	19.54E
Bosporus, see İstanbul Boğazi, strt., Tur.	174	41.10N	29.10E
Bossangoa, Cen. Afr. Rep.	208	6.29N	17.27E
Bossier City, La., U.S. (bŏsh'ẽr)	106	32.31N	93.42W
Bossley Park, Austl.	239a	33.52S	150.54E
Bostanci, neigh., Tur.	235f	40.57N	29.05E
Bosten Hu, l., China (bwo-stŭn hōō)	180	42.06N	88.01E
Boston, Ga., U.S. (bôs'tŭn)	108	30.47N	83.47W
Boston, Ma., U.S.	90	42.15N	71.07W
Boston, Pa., U.S.	226b	40.18N	79.49W
Boston Bay, b., Ma., U.S.	223a	42.22N	70.54W
Boston Garden, pt. of i., Ma., U.S.	223a	42.22N	71.04W
Boston Harbor, b., Ma., U.S.	223a	42.20N	70.58W
Boston Heights, Oh., U.S.	95d	41.15N	81.30W
Boston Mountains, mts., Ar., U.S.	90	35.46N	93.32W
Botafogo, neigh., Braz.	230c	22.57S	43.11W
Botafogo, Enseada de, b., Braz.	230c	22.57S	43.10W
Botany, Austl.	239a	33.57S	151.12E
Botany Bay, neigh., Eng., U.K.	231	51.41N	0.07W
Botany Bay, b., Austl. (bŏt'à-nĭ)	196	33.58S	151.11E
Botevgrad, Bul.	154	42.54N	23.41E
Bothaville, S. Afr. (bō'tä-vĭl)	212d	27.24S	26.38E
Bothell, Wa., U.S. (bŏth'ĕl)	100a	47.46N	122.12W
Bothnia, Gulf of, b., Eur. (bŏth'nĭ-à)	136	63.40N	21.30E
Botoşani, Rom. (bō-tō-shàn'ĭ)	148	47.46N	26.40E
Botswana, nation, Afr. (bŏtswănă)	206	22.10S	23.13E
Bottineau, N.D., U.S. (bŏt-ĭ-nō')	96	48.48N	100.28W
Bottrop, Ger. (bŏt'trŏp)	148	51.31N	6.56E
Botwood, Can. (bŏt'wŏŏd)	79a	49.08N	55.21W
Bötzow, Ger.	234a	52.39N	13.08E
Bouafle, I.C. (bŏŏ-à-flā')	204	6.59N	5.45W
Bouar, Cen. Afr. Rep. (bōō-är)	204	5.57N	15.36E
Bou Areg, Sebkha, Mor.	152	35.09N	3.02W
Boubandjidah, Parc National de, rec., Cam.	208	8.20N	14.40E
Boucherville, Can. (bōō-shà-vĕl')	77a	45.37N	73.27W
Boucherville, Îles de, is., Can.	223b	45.37N	73.28W
Boudenib, Mor. (bōō-dĕ-nĕb')	204	32.14N	3.04W
Boudette, Mn., U.S. (bōō-dĕt)	96	48.42N	94.34W
Boudouaou, Alg.	152	36.44N	3.25E
Boufarik, Alg. (bōō-fà-rēk')	152	36.35N	2.55E
Bougainville, i., Pap. N. Gui.	192e	6.00S	155.00E
Bougainville Trench, deep (bōō-găN-vēl')	190	7.00S	152.00E
Bougie, see Bejaïa, Alg.	204	36.46N	5.00E
Bougouni, Mali (bōō-gōō-nē')	204	11.27N	7.30W
Bouïra, Alg. (boo-ē'rà)	142	36.25N	3.55E
Bouïra-Sahary, Alg. (bwē-rà sà'ä-rē)	152	35.16N	3.23E
Bouka, r., Gui.	208	11.05N	10.40W
Boukiéro, Congo	240c	4.12S	15.18E
Boulder, Austl. (bōl'dẽr)	196	31.00S	121.40E
Boulder, Co., U.S.	90	40.02N	105.19W
Boulder, r., Mt., U.S.	98	46.10N	112.07W
Boulder City, Nv., U.S.	90	35.57N	114.50W
Boulder Peak, mtn., Id., U.S.	98	43.53N	114.33W
Boulogne, neigh., Arg.	229d	34.31S	58.34W
Boulogne-Billancourt, Fr. (bōō-lôn'y'-bē-yäN-kōōr')	150	48.50N	2.14E
Boulogne-sur-Mer, Fr. (bōō-lôn'y-sür-mâr')	140	50.44N	1.37E
Boumba, r., Cam.	208	3.20N	14.40E
Bouna, I.C. (bōō-nä')	204	9.16N	3.00W
Bouna, Parc National de, rec., I.C.	208	9.20N	3.35W
Boundary Bay, b., N.A. (boun'dà-rĭ)	100d	49.03N	122.59W
Boundary Peak, mtn., Nv., U.S.	102	37.52N	118.20W
Bound Brook, N.J., U.S. (bound brŏŏk)	94a	40.34N	74.32W
Bountiful, Ut., U.S. (boun'tĭ-fŏŏl)	101b	40.55N	111.53W
Bountiful Peak, mtn., Ut., U.S. (boun'tĭ-fŏŏl)	101b	40.58N	111.49W
Bounty Islands, is., N.Z.	4	47.42S	179.05E
Bourail, N. Cal.	192f	21.34S	165.30E
Bourem, Mali (bōō-rĕm')	204	16.43N	0.15W
Bourg-en-Bresse, Fr. (bōōr-gĕN-brĕs')	140	46.12N	5.13E
Bourges, Fr. (bōōrzh)	140	47.06N	2.22E
Bourget, Can. (bōōr-zhĕ')	77c	45.26N	75.09W
Bourg-la-Reine, Fr.	233c	48.47N	2.19E
Bourgoin, Fr. (bōōr-gwăN')	150	45.46N	5.17E
Bourke, Austl. (bŭrk)	196	30.10S	146.00E
Bourne, Eng., U.K. (bōrn)	138a	52.46N	0.22W
Bournebridge, Eng., U.K.	231	51.38N	0.11E
Bourne End, Eng., U.K.	231	51.45N	0.32W
Bournemouth, Eng., U.K. (bôrn'mŭth)	144	50.44N	1.55W
Bou Saâda, Alg. (bōō-sä'dä)	142	35.13N	4.17E
Bousso, Chad (bōō-sō')	204	10.33N	16.45E
Boutilimit, Maur.	204	17.30N	14.54W
Bouvetøya, i., Ant.	2	55.00S	3.00E
Bövinghausen, neigh., Ger.	232	51.31N	7.19E
Bow, r., Can. (bō)	78	50.35N	112.15W
Bowbells, N.D., U.S. (bō'bĕls)	96	48.50N	102.16W
Bowdle, S.D., U.S. (bōd''l)	96	45.28N	99.42W
Bowdon, Eng., U.K.	233b	53.23N	2.22W
Bowen, Austl. (bō'ĕn)	196	20.02S	148.14E
Bowie, Md., U.S. (bōō'ĭ) (bō'ē)	94e	38.59N	76.47W
Bowie, Tx., U.S.	104	33.34N	97.50W
Bowling Green, Ky., U.S. (bōlĭng grēn)	90	37.00N	86.26W
Bowling Green, Mo., U.S.	104	39.19N	91.09W
Bowling Green, Oh., U.S.	92	41.25N	83.40W
Bowman, N.D., U.S. (bō'măn)	96	46.11N	103.23W
Bowron, r., Can. (bō'rŭn)	80	53.20N	121.10W
Boxelder Creek, r., Mt., U.S. (bŏks'ĕl-dẽr)	96	45.35N	104.28W
Box Elder Creek, r., Mt., U.S.	98	47.17N	108.37W
Box Hill, Austl.	195a	37.49S	145.08E
Boxian, China (bwo shyĕn)	184	33.52N	115.47E
Boxing, China (bwo-shyĭŋ)	182	37.09N	118.08E
Boxmoor, Eng., U.K.	231	51.45N	0.29W
Boxtel, Neth.	139a	51.40N	5.21E
Boyabo, Zaire	210	3.43N	18.46E
Boyacıköy, neigh., Tur.	235f	41.06N	29.02E
Boyang, China (bwo-yäŋ)	184	29.00N	116.42E
Boyer, r., Can. (boi'ẽr)	77b	46.45N	70.56W
Boyer, r., Ia., U.S.	96	41.45N	95.36W
Boyle, Ire. (boil)	144	53.59N	8.15W
Boyne, r., Ire. (boin)	144	53.40N	6.40W
Boyne City, Mi., U.S.	92	45.15N	85.05W
Boyoma Falls, wtfl., Zaire	204	0.30N	25.12E
Boysen Reservoir, res., Wy., U.S.	98	43.19N	108.11W
Bozcaada, Tur. (bōz-cä'dä)	154	39.50N	26.05E
Bozca Ada, i., Tur.	154	39.50N	26.00E
Bozeman, Mt., U.S. (bōz'măn)	90	45.41N	111.00W
Bozene, Zaire	210	2.56N	19.12E
Bozhen, China (bwo-jŭn)	182	38.05N	116.35E
Bozoum, Cen. Afr. Rep.	208	6.19N	16.23E
Bra, Italy (brä)	154	44.41N	7.52E
Bracciano, Lago di, l., Italy (lä'gō-dē-brä-chä'nō)	154	42.05N	12.00E
Bracebridge, Can. (brās'brĭj)	84	45.05N	79.20W
Braceville, Il., U.S. (brās'vĭl)	95a	41.13N	88.16W
Bräcke, Swe. (brĕk'kĕ)	140	62.44N	15.28E
Brackenridge, Pa., U.S. (brăk'ĕn-rĭj)	95e	40.37N	79.44W
Brackettville, Tx., U.S. (brăk'ĕt-vĭl)	106	29.19N	100.24W
Braço Maior, mth., Braz.	124	11.00S	51.00W
Braço Menor, mth., Braz. (brä'zō-mĕ-nō'r)	124	11.38S	50.00W
Bradano, r., Italy (brä-dä'nō)	154	40.43N	16.22E
Braddock, Pa., U.S. (brăd'ŭk)	95e	40.24N	79.52W
Braddock Hills, Pa., U.S.	226b	40.25N	79.51W
Bradenburger Tor, pt. of i., Ger.	234a	52.31N	13.23E
Bradenton, Fl., U.S. (brā'dĕn-tŭn)	109a	27.28N	82.35W
Bradfield, Eng., U.K. (brăd'fēld)	138b	51.25N	1.08W
Bradford, Eng., U.K. (brăd'fẽrd)	140	53.47N	1.44W
Bradford, Oh., U.S.	92	40.10N	84.30W
Bradford, Pa., U.S.	92	42.00N	78.40W
Bradley, Il., U.S. (brăd'lĭ)	95a	41.09N	87.52W
Bradner, Can. (brăd'nẽr)	100d	49.05N	122.26W
Bradshaw, Eng., U.K.	233b	53.36N	2.24W
Brady, Tx., U.S. (brā'dĭ)	106	31.09N	99.21W
Braga, Port. (brä'gä)	142	41.20N	8.25W
Bragado, Arg. (brä-gä'dō)	126	35.07S	60.28W
Bragança, Braz. (brä-gän'sä)	124	1.02S	46.50W
Bragança, Port.	152	41.48N	6.46W
Bragança Paulista, Braz. (brä-gän'sä-pä'ōō-lē's-tà)	126	22.58S	46.31W
Bragg Creek, Can. (brăg)	77e	50.57N	114.35W
Brahmaputra, r., Asia (brä'mà-pōō'trà)	174	26.45N	92.45E
Brāhui, mts., Pak.	174	28.32N	66.15E
Braidwood, Il., U.S. (brād'wŏŏd)	95a	41.16N	88.13W
Brăila, Rom. (brē'ēlà)	136	45.15N	27.58E
Brainerd, Mn., U.S. (brān'ẽrd)	96	46.20N	94.09W
Braintree, Ma., U.S. (brān'trē)	87a	42.14N	71.00W
Braithwaite, La., U.S. (brīth'wīt)	94d	29.52N	89.57W
Brakpan, S. Afr. (brăk'păn)	207b	26.15S	28.22E
Bralorne, Can. (brā'lôrn)	80	50.47N	122.49W
Bramalea, Can.	77d	43.48N	79.41W
Bramhall, Eng., U.K.	233b	53.22N	2.10W
Brampton, Can. (brămp'tŭn)	84	43.41N	79.46W
Branca, Pedra, mtn., Braz. (pĕ'drä-brà'N-kä)	126b	22.55S	43.28W
Branchville, N.J., U.S. (brănch'vĭl)	94a	41.09S	74.44W
Branchville, S.C., U.S.	108	33.17N	80.48W
Branco, r., Braz. (brăŋ'kō)	124	2.21N	60.38W
Brandberg, mtn., Nmb.	206	21.15S	14.15E
Brandenburg, Ger. (brän'dĕn-bŏŏrgh)	140	52.25N	12.33E
Brandenburg, hist. reg., Ger.	148	52.12N	13.31E
Brandfort, S. Afr. (brăn'd-fôrt)	212d	28.42S	26.29E
Brandon, Can. (brăn'dŭn)	78	49.50N	99.57W
Brandon, Vt., U.S.	92	43.45N	73.05W
Brandon Mountain, mtn., Ire. (brăn-dŏn)	144	52.15N	10.12W
Brandywine, Md., U.S. (brăndĭ'wīn)	94e	38.42N	76.51W
Branford, Ct., U.S. (brăn'fẽrd)	92	41.15N	72.50W
Braniewo, Pol. (brä-nyĕ'vō)	148	54.23N	19.50E
Brańsk, Pol. (brän' sk)	148	52.44N	22.51E
Brantford, Can. (brănt'fẽrd)	84	43.09N	80.17W
Bras d'Or Lake, l., Can. (brä-dôr')	86	45.52N	60.50W
Brasília, Braz. (brä-sē'lvä)	124	15.49S	47.39W
Brasilia Legal, Braz.	124	3.45S	55.46W
Brasópolis, Braz. (brä-sō'pō-lēs)	123a	22.30S	45.36W
Braşov, Rom.	142	45.39N	25.35E
Brass, Nig. (brăs)	204	4.28N	6.28E
Brasschaat, Bel. (bräs'kät)	139a	51.19N	4.30E
Bratcevo, neigh., Russia	235b	55.51N	37.24E
Bratenahl, Oh., U.S. (bră'tĕn-ôl)	95d	41.34N	81.36W
Bratislava, Czech. (brä'tĭs-lä-vä)	136	48.09N	17.07E
Bratsk, Russia (brätsk)	158	56.10N	102.04E
Bratskoye Vodokhranilishche, res., Russia	158	56.10N	102.05E
Bratslav, Ukr. (brät'slàf)	156	48.48N	28.59E
Brattleboro, Vt., U.S. (brăt''l-bŭr-ō)	92	42.50N	72.35W
Braunau, Aus. (brou'nou)	148	48.15N	13.05E
Braunschweig, Ger. (broun'shvīgh)	140	52.16N	10.32E
Bråviken, r., Swe.	146	58.40N	16.40E
Brawley, Ca., U.S. (brô'lĭ)	90	32.59N	115.32W
Bray, Ire. (brā)	144	53.10N	6.05W
Braybrook, Austl.	239b	37.47S	144.51E
Braymer, Mo., U.S. (brā'mẽr)	104	39.34N	93.47W
Brays Bay, Tx., U.S. (brās'bĭ'yōō)	107a	29.41N	95.33W
Brazeau, r., Can.	80	52.55N	116.10W
Brazeau, Mount, mtn., Can. (brä-zō')	80	52.33N	117.21W
Brazil, In., U.S. (brà-zĭl')	92	39.30N	87.00W
Brazil, nation, S.A.	124	9.00S	53.00W
Brazilian Highlands, mts., Braz. (brà zĭl yàn hī-lándz)	122	14.00S	48.00W
Brazos, r., Tx., U.S. (brä'zōs)	90	33.10N	98.50W
Brazos, Clear Fork, r., Tx., U.S.	106	32.56N	99.14W
Brazos, Double Mountain Fork, r., Tx., U.S.	104	33.23N	101.21W
Brazos, Salt Fork, r., Tx., U.S. (sôlt fôrk)	104	33.20N	101.57W
Brazzaville, Congo (brà-zà-vēl')	206	4.16S	15.17E
Brčko, Bos. (bẽrch'kō)	154	44.54N	18.46E
Brda, r., Pol. (bẽr-dä)	148	53.18N	17.55E
Brea, Ca., U.S. (brē'à)	101a	33.55N	117.54W
Breakeyville, Can.	77b	46.40N	71.13W
Brechten, neigh., Ger.	232	51.35N	7.28E
Breckenridge, Mn., U.S. (brĕk'ĕn-rĭj)	96	46.17N	96.35W
Breckenridge, Tx., U.S.	106	32.46N	98.53W
Breckerfeld, Ger.	232	51.16N	7.28E
Brecksville, Oh., U.S. (brĕks'vĭl)	95d	41.19N	81.38W
Břeclav, Czech. (brzhĕl'làf)	148	48.46N	16.54E
Breda, Neth. (brā-dä')	144	51.35N	4.47E
Bredasdorp, S. Afr. (brā'das-dôrp)	206	34.15S	20.00E
Bredbury, Eng., U.K.	233b	53.25N	2.06W
Bredell, S. Afr.	240b	26.05S	28.17E
Bredeney, neigh., Ger.	232	51.24N	6.59E
Bredenscheid-Stüter, Ger.	232	51.22N	7.11E
Bredy, Russia (brĕ'dĭ)	164a	52.25N	60.23E
Breezewood, Pa., U.S.	226b	40.34N	80.03W
Bregenz, Aus. (brā'gĕnts)	148	47.30N	9.46E
Bregovo, Bul. (brĕ'gō-vō)	154	44.07N	22.45E

ng-sing; ŋ-baŋk; N-nasalized n; nŏd; cŏmmit; ōld; ôbey; ôrder; oi-boil; fōōd; ŏŏ-as oo in foot; ou-out; s-soft; sh-dish; th-thin; pūre; ûnite; ûrn; stŭd; circŭs; ü-as in French tu; '-indeterminate vowel.

PLACE (Pronunciation)	PAGE	Lat. °′	Long. °′
Breidafjördur, b., Ice.	140	65.15N	22.50W
Breidbach, S. Afr. (brĕd'băk)	207c	32.54S	27.26E
Breil-sur-Roya, Fr. (brĕ'y')	150	43.57N	7.36E
Breitscheid, Ger.	232	51.22N	6.52E
Brejo, Braz. (brå'zhò)	124	3.33S	42.46W
Bremangerlandet, i., Nor.	146	61.51N	4.25E
Bremen, Ger. (brā-mĕn)	136	53.05N	8.50E
Bremen, In., U.S. (brē'mĕn)	92	41.25N	86.05W
Bremerhaven, Ger. (brām-ĕr-hä'fĕn)	140	53.33N	8.38E
Bremerton, Wa., U.S. (brĕm'ĕr-tŭn)	98	47.34N	122.38W
Bremervörde, Ger. (brĕ'mĕr-fûr-dĕ)	139c	53.29N	9.09E
Bremner, Can. (brĕm'nĕr)	77g	53.34N	113.14W
Bremond, Tx., U.S. (brĕm'ŭnd)	106	31.11N	96.40W
Breña, Peru	229c	12.04S	77.04W
Brenham, Tx., U.S. (brĕn'ăm)	106	30.10N	96.24W
Bren Mar Park, Md., U.S.	225d	38.48N	77.09W
Brenner Pass, p., Eur. (brĕn'ĕr)	140	47.00N	11.30E
Brentford, neigh., Eng., U.K.	231	51.29N	0.18W
Brenthurst, S. Afr.	240b	26.16S	28.23E
Brentwood, Eng., U.K. (brĕnt'wòd)	144	51.37N	0.18E
Brentwood, Md., U.S.	92	39.00N	76.55W
Brentwood, Mo., U.S.	101e	38.37N	90.21W
Brentwood, Pa., U.S.	95e	40.22N	79.59W
Brentwood Heights, neigh., Ca., U.S.	228	34.04N	118.30W
Brentwood Park, S. Afr.	240b	26.08S	28.18E
Brescia, Italy (brā'shä)	142	45.33N	10.15E
Bressanone, Italy (brĕs-sä-nō'nä)	154	46.42N	11.40E
Bresso, Italy	234c	45.32N	9.11E
Bressuire, Fr. (grĕ-swēr')	150	46.49N	0.14W
Brest, Bela.	158	52.06N	23.43E
Brest, Fr. (brĕst)	136	48.24N	4.30W
Brest, prov., Bela.	156	52.30N	26.50E
Bretagne, hist. reg., Fr. (brĕ-tän'yĕ)	150	48.00N	3.00W
Breton, Pertuis, strt., Fr. (pâr-twĕ'brĕ-tôN')	150	46.18N	1.43W
Breton Sound, strt., La., U.S. (brĕt'ŭn)	108	29.38N	89.15W
Breukelen, Neth.	139a	52.09N	5.00E
Brevard, N.C., U.S. (brē-värd')	108	35.14N	82.45W
Breves, Braz. (brā'vĕzh)	124	1.32S	50.13W
Brevik, Nor. (brĕ'vêk)	146	59.04N	9.39E
Brewarrina, Austl. (brōō-ĕr-rē'nȧ)	196	29.54S	146.50E
Brewer, Me., U.S. (brōō'ĕr)	86	44.46N	68.46W
Brewerville, Lib.	208	6.26N	10.47W
Brewster, N.Y., U.S. (brōō'stĕr)	94a	41.23N	73.38W
Brewster, Cerro, mtn., Pan. (sĕ'r-rô-brōō'stĕr)	114	9.19N	79.15W
Brewton, Al., U.S. (brōō'tŭn)	108	31.06N	87.04W
Brežice, Slo. (brĕ'zhê-tsĕ)	154	45.55N	15.37E
Breznik, Bul. (brĕs'nêk)	154	42.44N	22.55E
Briancon, Fr. (brē-äN-sôN')	150	44.54N	6.39E
Briare, Fr. (brē-är')	150	47.40N	2.46E
Bridal Veil, Or., U.S. (brīd'ȧl vāl)	100c	45.33N	122.10W
Bridge Point, c., Bah. (brĭj)	116	25.35N	76.40W
Bridgeport, Al., U.S. (brĭj'pôrt)	108	34.55N	85.42W
Bridgeport, Ct., U.S.	90	41.12N	73.12W
Bridgeport, Il., U.S.	92	38.40N	87.45W
Bridgeport, Ne., U.S.	96	41.40N	103.06W
Bridgeport, Oh., U.S.	92	40.00N	80.45W
Bridgeport, Pa., U.S.	94f	40.06N	75.21W
Bridgeport, Tx., U.S.	104	33.13N	97.46W
Bridgeport, neigh., Il., U.S.	227a	41.51N	87.39W
Bridgeton, Al., U.S. (brĭj'tŭn)	94h	33.27N	86.39W
Bridgeton, Mo., U.S.	101e	38.45N	90.23W
Bridgeton, N.J., U.S.	92	39.30N	75.15W
Bridgetown, Barb. (brĭj' toun)	110	13.08N	59.37W
Bridgetown, Can.	86	44.51N	65.18W
Bridgeview, Il., U.S.	227a	41.45N	87.48W
Bridgeville, Pa., U.S. (brĭj'vĭl)	95e	40.22N	80.07W
Bridgewater, Austl. (brĭj'wô-tĕr)	198	42.50S	147.28E
Bridgewater, Can.	78	44.23N	64.31W
Bridgnorth, Eng., U.K. (brĭj'nôrth)	138a	52.32N	2.25W
Bridgton, Me., U.S. (brĭj'tŭn)	86	44.04N	70.45W
Bridlington, Eng., U.K. (brĭd'lĭng-tŭn)	144	54.06N	0.10W
Brie-Comte-Robert, Fr. (brē-kôNt-ĕ-rō-bâr')	151b	48.42N	2.37E
Brielle, Neth.	139a	51.54N	4.08E
Brierfield, Eng., U.K. (brī'ĕr fēld)	138a	53.49N	2.14W
Brierfield, Al., U.S. (brī'ĕr-fēld)	108	33.01N	86.55W
Brier Island, i., Can. (brī'ĕr)	86	44.16N	66.24W
Brieselang, Ger. (brē'zĕ-läng)	139b	52.36N	12.59E
Briey, Fr. (brē-ĕ')	150	49.15N	5.57E
Brig, Switz. (brēg)	140	46.17N	7.59E
Brigg, Eng., U.K. (brĭg)	138a	53.33N	0.29W
Brigham City, Ut., U.S. (brĭg'ăm)	101b	41.31N	112.01W
Brighouse, Eng., U.K. (brĭg'hous)	138a	53.42N	1.47W
Bright, Austl. (brīt)	198	36.43S	147.00E
Bright, In., U.S. (brīt)	95f	39.13N	84.51W
Brightlingsea, Eng., U.K. (brī't-lĭng-sē)	138b	51.50N	1.00E
Brightmoor, neigh., Mi., U.S.	226c	42.24N	83.14W
Brighton, Austl.	195a	37.55S	145.00E
Brighton, Eng., U.K.	140	50.47N	0.07W
Brighton, Al., U.S. (brī'tŭn)	94h	33.27N	86.56W
Brighton, Co., U.S.	104	39.58N	104.49W
Brighton, Il., U.S.	101e	39.03N	90.08W
Brighton, Ia., U.S.	96	41.11N	91.47W
Brighton, neigh., Ma., U.S.	223a	42.21N	71.08W
Brighton Indian Reservation, I.R., Fl., U.S.	109a	27.05N	81.25W
Brighton Le-Sands, Austl.	239a	33.58S	151.09E
Brightwood, neigh., D.C., U.S.	225d	38.58N	77.02W
Brigittenau, neigh., Aus.	235e	48.14N	16.22E
Brihuega, Spain (brê-wā'gä)	152	40.32N	2.52W
Brilyn Park, Va., U.S.	225d	38.54N	77.10W
Brimley, Mi., U.S. (brĭm'lē)	101k	46.24N	84.34W
Brindisi, Italy (brēn'dē-zē)	136	40.38N	17.57E
Brinje, Cro. (brēn'yĕ)	154	45.00N	15.08E
Brinkleigh, Md., U.S.	225c	39.18N	76.50W
Brinkley, Ar., U.S. (brĭŋk'lĭ)	104	34.52N	91.12W
Brinnon, Wa., U.S. (brĭn'ŭn)	100a	47.41N	122.54W
Brion, i., Can. (brē-ôN')	86	47.47N	61.29W
Brioude, Fr. (brē-ōōd')	150	45.18N	3.22E
Brisbane, Austl. (brĭz'bån)	198	27.30S	153.10E
Brisbane, Ca., U.S.	227b	37.41N	122.24W
Bristol, Eng., U.K.	140	51.29N	2.39W
Bristol, Ct., U.S. (brĭs'tŭl)	92	41.40N	72.55W
Bristol, Pa., U.S.	94f	40.06N	74.51W
Bristol, R.I., U.S.	94b	41.41N	71.14W
Bristol, Tn., U.S.	90	36.35N	82.10W
Bristol, Vt., U.S.	92	44.10N	73.00W
Bristol, Va., U.S.	90	36.36N	82.00W
Bristol, Wi., U.S.	95a	42.32N	88.04W
Bristol Bay, b., Ak., U.S.	89	58.05N	158.54W
Bristol Channel, strt., Eng., U.K.	140	51.20N	3.47W
Bristow, Ok., U.S. (brĭs'tō)	104	35.50N	96.25W
British Columbia, prov., Can. (brĭt'ĭsh kŏl'ŭm-bĭ-ȧ)	78	56.00N	124.53W
British Isles, is., Eur.	136	54.00N	4.00W
Brits, S. Afr.	212d	25.39S	27.47E
Britstown, S. Afr. (brĭts'toun)	206	30.30S	23.40E
Britt, Ia., U.S. (brĭt)	96	43.05N	93.47W
Britton, S.D., U.S. (brĭt'ŭn)	96	45.47N	97.44W
Brive-la-Gaillarde, Fr. (brēv-lä-gī-yärd'ĕ)	140	45.10N	1.31E
Briviesca, Spain (brê-vyās'kȧ)	152	42.34N	3.21W
Brno, Czech. (b'r'nô)	136	49.18N	16.37E
Broa, Ensenada de la, b., Cuba	116	22.30N	82.00W
Broach, India	178	21.47N	72.58E
Broad, r., Ga., U.S. (brôd)	108	34.15N	83.14W
Broad, r., N.C., U.S.	108	35.38N	82.40W
Broadheath, Eng., U.K.	233b	53.24N	2.21W
Broadley Common, Eng., U.K.	231	51.45N	0.04E
Broadmeadows, Austl. (brôd'mĕd-ōz)	195a	37.40S	144.53E
Broadmeadows, Austl.	239b	37.40S	144.54E
Broadmoor, Ca., U.S.	227b	37.41N	122.29W
Broadview Heights, Oh., U.S. (brôd'vū)	95d	41.18N	81.41W
Brockenscheidt, Ger.	232	51.38N	7.25E
Brockport, N.Y., U.S. (brŏk'pōrt)	92	43.15N	77.55W
Brockton, Ma., U.S. (brŏk'tŭn)	87a	42.04N	71.01W
Brockville, Can. (brŏk'vĭl)	78	44.35N	75.40W
Brockway, Mt., U.S. (brŏk'wā)	98	47.24N	105.41W
Brodnica, Pol. (brôd'nĭt-sȧ)	148	53.16N	19.26E
Brody, Ukr. (brô'dĭ)	160	50.05N	25.10E
Broich, neigh., Ger.	232	51.25N	6.51E
Broken Arrow, Ok., U.S. (brō'kĕn ăr'ō)	104	36.03N	95.48W
Broken Bay, b., Austl.	198	33.34S	151.20E
Broken Bow, Ne., U.S. (brō'kĕn bō)	96	41.24N	99.37W
Broken Bow, Ok., U.S.	104	34.02N	94.43W
Broken Hill, Austl. (brōk'ĕn)	196	31.55S	141.35E
Broken Hill, *see* Kabwe, Zam.	206	14.27S	28.27E
Bromall, Pa., U.S.	225b	39.59N	75.22W
Bromborough, Eng., U.K.	233a	53.19N	2.59W
Bromley, Eng., U.K. (brŭm'lĭ)	138b	51.23N	0.01E
Bromley Common, neigh., Eng., U.K.	231	51.22N	0.03E
Bromptonville, Can. (brŭmp'tŭn-vĭl)	84	45.30N	72.00W
Brønderslev, Den. (brŭn'dĕr-slĕv)	146	57.15N	9.56E
Bronkhorstspruit, S. Afr.	212d	25.50S	28.48E
Bronnitsy, Russia (brô-nyĭ'tsĭ)	156	55.26N	38.16E
Bronson, Mi., U.S. (brŏn'sŭn)	92	41.55N	85.15W
Bronte Creek, r., Can.	77d	43.25N	79.53W
Bronx, neigh., N.Y., U.S.	224	40.49N	73.56W
Bronxville, N.Y., U.S.	224	40.56N	73.50W
Brood, r., S.C., U.S. (brōōd)	108	34.46N	81.25W
Brookfield, Il., U.S. (bròk'fēld)	95a	41.49N	87.51W
Brookfield, Mo., U.S.	104	39.45N	93.04W
Brookhaven, Ga., U.S. (bròk'hāv'n)	94c	33.52N	84.21W
Brookhaven, Ms., U.S.	108	31.35N	90.26W
Brookhaven, Pa., U.S.	225b	39.52N	75.23W
Brookings, Or., U.S. (bròk'ĭngs)	98	42.04N	124.16W
Brookings, S.D., U.S.	96	44.18N	96.47W
Brookland, neigh., D.C., U.S.	225d	38.56N	76.59W
Brooklandville, Md., U.S.	225c	39.26N	76.41W
Brooklawn, N.J., U.S.	225b	39.53N	75.08W
Brookline, Ma., U.S. (bròk'lĭn)	87a	42.20N	71.08W
Brookline, N.H., U.S.	87a	42.44N	71.37W
Brooklyn, Oh., U.S. (bròk'lĭn)	95d	41.26N	81.44W
Brooklyn, neigh., Md., U.S.	225c	39.14N	76.36W
Brooklyn Center, Mn., U.S.	101g	45.05N	93.21W
Brooklyn Heights, Oh., U.S.	225a	41.24N	81.40W
Brooklyn Park, Md., U.S.	225c	39.14N	76.36W
Brookmans Park, Eng., U.K.	231	51.43N	0.12W
Brookmont, Md., U.S.	225d	38.57N	77.07W
Brook Park, Oh., U.S. (bròk)	95d	41.24N	81.50W
Brooks, Can.	80	50.35N	111.53W
Brooks Range, mts., Ak., U.S. (bròks)	90a	68.20N	159.00W
Brook Street, Eng., U.K.	231	51.37N	0.17E
Brooksville, Fl., U.S. (bròks'vĭl)	109a	28.32N	82.28W
Brookvale, Austl.	239a	33.46S	151.17E
Brookville, In., U.S. (bròk'vĭl)	92	39.20N	85.00W
Brookville, Ma., U.S.	223a	42.08N	71.01W
Brookville, N.Y., U.S.	224	40.49N	73.35W
Brookville, Pa., U.S.	92	41.10N	79.00W
Brookwood, Al., U.S. (bròk'wòd)	108	33.15N	87.17W
Broome, Austl. (brōōm)	196	18.00S	122.15E
Brossard, Can.	77a	45.26N	73.28W
Brothers, is., Bah. (brŭd'hĕrs)	116	26.05N	79.00W
Broughton, Pa., U.S.	226b	40.21N	79.59W
Broumov, Czech. (brōō'môf)	148	50.33N	15.55E
Brou-sur-Chantereine, Fr.	233c	48.53N	2.38E
Brown Bank, bk.	116	21.30N	74.35W
Brownfield, Tx., U.S. (broun'fēld)	104	33.11N	102.16W
Browning, Mt., U.S. (broun'ĭng)	98	48.37N	113.05W
Brownsboro, Ky., U.S. (brounz'bô-rô)	95h	38.22N	85.30W
Brownsburg, Can. (brouns'bûrg)	77a	45.40N	74.24W
Brownsburg, In., U.S.	95g	39.51N	86.23W
Brownsmead, Or., U.S. (brounz'-mēd)	100c	46.13N	123.33W
Brownstown, In., U.S. (brounz'toun)	92	38.50N	86.00W
Brownsville, Pa., U.S. (brounz'vĭl)	95e	40.01N	79.53W
Brownsville, Tn., U.S.	108	35.35N	89.15W
Brownsville, Tx., U.S.	90	25.55N	97.30W
Brownville Junction, Me., U.S. (broun'vĭl)	86	45.20N	69.04W
Brownwood, Tx., U.S. (broun'wòd)	90	31.44N	98.58W
Brownwood, l., Tx., U.S.	106	31.55N	99.15W
Broxbourne, Eng., U.K.	231	51.45N	0.01W
Brozas, Spain (brō'thäs)	152	39.37N	6.44W
Bruce, Mount, mtn., Austl. (brōōs)	196	22.35S	118.15E
Bruce Peninsula, pen., Can.	84	44.50N	81.20W
Bruceton, Tn., U.S. (brōōs'tŭn)	108	36.02N	88.14W
Bruchmühle, Ger.	234a	52.33N	13.47E
Bruchsal, Ger. (bròk'zäl)	148	49.08N	8.34E
Bruck, Aus. (bròk)	148	47.25N	15.14E
Bruck, Aus.	148	48.01N	16.47E
Brück, Ger. (brük)	139b	52.12N	12.45E
Bruckhausen, neigh., Ger.	232	51.29N	6.44E
Bruderheim, Can. (brōō'dĕr-hīm)	77g	53.47N	112.56W
Brugge, Bel.	140	51.13N	3.05E
Brügge, Ger.	232	51.13N	7.34E
Brugherio, Italy	234c	45.33N	9.18E
Brühl, Ger. (brül)	151c	50.49N	6.54E
Bruneau, r., Id., U.S. (brōō-nō')	98	42.47N	115.43W
Brunei, nation, Asia (brò-nī')	188	4.52N	113.38E
Brünen, Ger. (brü'nĕn)	151c	51.43N	6.41E
Brunete, Spain (brōō-nā'tā)	153a	40.24N	4.00W
Brunette, i., Can. (brò-nĕt')	86	47.16N	55.54W
Brunn am Gebirge, Aus. (brōōn'äm gĕ-bĭr'gĕ)	139e	48.07N	16.18E
Brunoy, Fr.	233c	48.42N	2.30E
Brunsbüttel, Ger. (bròns'büt-tĕl)	139c	53.58N	9.10E
Brunswick, Austl.	239b	37.46S	144.58E
Brunswick, Ga., U.S. (brŭnz'wĭk)	90	31.08N	81.30W
Brunswick, Me., U.S.	86	43.54N	69.57W
Brunswick, Md., U.S.	92	39.20N	77.35W
Brunswick, Mo., U.S.	104	39.25N	93.07W
Brunswick, Oh., U.S.	95d	41.14N	81.50W
Brunswick, Península de, pen., Chile	126	53.25S	71.15W
Bruny, i., Austl. (brōō'nē)	196	43.30S	147.50E
Brush, Co., U.S. (brŭsh)	104	40.14N	103.40W
Brusque, Braz. (brōō's-kōōĕ)	126	27.15S	48.45W
Brussels, Bel.	136	50.51N	4.21E
Brussels, Il., U.S. (brŭs'ĕls)	101e	38.57N	90.36W
Bruxelles, *see* Brussels, Bel.	136	50.51N	4.21E
Bryan, Oh., U.S. (brī'ăn)	92	41.25N	84.30W
Bryan, Tx., U.S.	106	30.40N	96.22W
Bryansk, Russia	158	53.15N	34.22E
Bryansk, prov., Russia	156	52.43N	32.25E
Bryant, S.D., U.S. (brī'ănt)	96	44.35N	97.29W
Bryant, Wa., U.S.	100a	48.14N	122.10W
Bryce Canyon National Park, rec., Ut., U.S. (brīs)	90	37.35N	112.15W
Bryn Mawr, Pa., U.S. (brĭn mår')	94f	40.02N	75.20W
Bryson City, N.C., U.S. (brīs'ŭn)	108	35.25N	83.25W
Bryukhovetskaya, Russia (b'ryŭk'ô-vyĕt-skä'yä)	156	45.56N	38.58E
Buala, Sol.Is.	192e	8.08S	159.35E
Buatan, Indon.	173b	0.45N	101.49E
Buba, Gui.-B. (bōō'bȧ)	204	11.39N	14.58W
Buc, Fr.	233c	48.46N	2.08E
Bucaramanga, Col. (bōō-kä'rä-mäŋ'gä)	124	7.12N	73.14W
Buccaneer Archipelago, is., Austl. (bŭk-ȧ-nēr')	196	16.05S	122.00E
Buch, neigh., Ger.	234a	52.38N	13.30E
Buchach, Ukr. (bò'chȧch)	148	49.04N	25.25E
Buchanan, Lib. (bû-kăn'ăn)	204	5.57N	10.02W
Buchanan, Mi., U.S.	92	41.50N	86.25W
Buchanan, l., Austl. (bû-kân'nŏn)	196	21.40S	145.00E
Buchanan, l., Tx., U.S. (bû-kăn'ăn)	106	30.55N	98.40W
Buchans, Can.	86	48.49N	56.52W
Bucharest, Rom.	136	44.23N	26.10E
Buchholz, Ger. (bōōk'hōltz)	139c	53.19N	9.53E
Buchholz, Ger.	234a	52.35N	13.47E
Buchholz, neigh., Ger.	232	51.23N	6.46E
Buchholz, neigh., Ger.	234a	52.36N	13.26E
Buck Creek, r., In., U.S. (bŭk)	95g	39.43N	85.58W
Buckhannon, W.V., U.S. (bŭk-hăn'ŭn)	92	39.00N	80.10W
Buckhaven, Scot., U.K. (bŭk-hā'v'n)	144	56.10N	3.10W
Buckhorn Island State Park, pt. of i., N.Y., U.S.	226a	43.03N	78.59W
Buckie, Scot., U.K. (bŭk'ĭ)	144	57.40N	2.50W
Buckingham, Can. (bŭk'ĭng-ăm)	77c	45.35N	75.25W
Buckingham, can., India (bŭk'ĭng-ăm)	178	15.18N	79.50E
Buckingham Palace, pt. of i., Eng., U.K.	231	51.30N	0.08W
Buckinghamshire, co., Eng., U.K.	138b	51.45N	0.48W
Buckland, Can. (bŭk'lănd)	77b	46.37N	70.33W
Buckland Tableland, reg., Austl.	196	24.31S	148.00E
Buckley, Wa., U.S. (buk'lē)	100a	47.10N	122.02W
Buckow, neigh., Ger.	234a	52.25N	13.26E
Bucksport, Me., U.S. (bŭks'pôrt)	86	44.35N	68.47W
Buctouche, Can. (bük-tōōsh')	86	46.28N	64.43W
Bucun, China (bōō-tsòn)	182	36.38N	117.26E
București, *see* Bucharest, Rom.	136	44.23N	26.10E
Bucyrus, Oh., U.S. (bû-sī'rŭs)	92	40.50N	82.55W
Buda, neigh., Hung.	235g	47.30N	19.02E
Budakeszi, Hung.	235g	47.31N	18.56E
Budaörs, Hung.	235g	47.27N	18.58E
Budapest, Hung. (bōō'dȧ-pĕsht')	136	47.30N	19.05E
Budberg, Ger.	232	51.32N	6.38E
Büderich, Ger.	232	51.37N	6.34E
Budge Budge, India	178a	22.28N	88.08E
Budjala, Zaire	210	2.39N	19.42E
Buea, Cam.	208	4.09N	9.14E
Buechel, Ky., U.S. (bē-chûl')	95h	38.12N	85.38W
Bueil, Fr. (bwā')	151b	48.55N	1.27E

ăt; finȧl; rāte; senåte; ärm; åsk; sofȧ; fâre; ch-choose; dh-as th in other; bē; êvent; bĕt; recĕnt; cratĕr; g-gō; gh-guttural g; bĭt; ĭ-short neutral; rīde; K-guttural k as ch in German ich;

PLACE (Pronunciation)	PAGE	Lat. °′	Long. °′
Buena Park, Ca., U.S. (bwā'nȧ pärk)	101a	33.52N	118.00W
Buenaventura, Col. (bwā'nä-vĕn-to͞o'rȧ)	124	3.46N	77.09W
Buenaventura, Cuba	117a	22.53N	82.22W
Buenaventura, Bahía de, b., Col.	124	3.45N	79.23W
Buena Vista, Co., U.S. (bū'nȧ vĭs'tȧ)	104	38.51N	106.07W
Buena Vista, Ga., U.S.	108	32.15N	84.30W
Buena Vista, Va., U.S.	92	37.45N	79.20W
Buena Vista, Bahía, b., Cuba (bä-ē'ä-bwĕ-nä-vē's-tä)	116	22.30N	79.10W
Buena Vista Lake Bed, l., Ca., U.S. (bū'nȧ vĭs'tȧ)	102	35.14N	119.17W
Buendia, Embalse de, res., Spain	152	40.30N	2.45W
Buenos Aires, Arg. (bwā'nōs ī'rās)	126	34.20S	58.30W
Buenos Aires, Col.	124a	3.01N	76.34W
Buenos Aires, C.R.	114	9.10N	83.21W
Buenos Aires, prov., Arg.	126	36.15S	61.45W
Buenos Aires, l., S.A.	126	46.30S	72.15W
Buer, neigh., Ger.	232	51.36N	7.03E
Buffalo, Mn., U.S. (buf'ȧ lō)	96	45.10N	93.50W
Buffalo, N.Y., U.S.	90	42.54N	78.51W
Buffalo, Tx., U.S.	106	31.28N	96.04W
Buffalo, Wy., U.S.	98	44.19N	106.42W
Buffalo, r., S. Afr.	207c	28.35S	30.27E
Buffalo, r., Ar., U.S.	104	35.56N	92.58W
Buffalo, r., Tn., U.S.	108	35.24N	87.10W
Buffalo Bayou, Tx., U.S.	107a	29.46N	95.32W
Buffalo Creek, r., Mn., U.S.	96	44.46N	94.28W
Buffalo Harbor, b., N.Y., U.S.	226a	42.51N	78.52W
Buffalo Head Hills, hills, Can.	78	57.16N	116.18W
Buford, Can. (bū'fŭrd)	77g	53.15N	113.55W
Buford, Ga., U.S. (bū'fẽrd)	108	34.05N	84.00W
Bug, r., Eur. (bo͞og)	148	52.29N	21.20E
Bug, r., Ukr. (bo͝ok)	160	48.12N	30.13E
Buga, Col. (bo͞o'gä)	124	3.54N	76.17W
Buggenhout, Bel.	139a	51.01N	4.10E
Buglandsfjorden, l., Nor.	146	58.53N	7.55E
Bugojno, Bos. (bo͝o-gō ĭ nō)	154	44.03N	17.28E
Bugul'ma, Russia (bo͝o-gòl'mȧ)	158	54.40N	52.40E
Buguruslan, Russia (bo͝o-go͝o-ròs-làn')	158	53.30N	52.32E
Buhi, Phil. (bo͞o'ê)	189a	13.26N	123.31E
Buhl, Id., U.S. (būl)	98	42.36N	114.45W
Buhl, Mn., U.S.	96	47.28N	92.49W
Buin, Chile (bo͝o-ēn')	123b	33.44S	70.44W
Buinaksk, Russia (bo͝o'ê-näksk)	160	42.40N	47.20E
Buir Nur, l., Asia (bo͞o-ēr no͞or)	180	47.50N	117.00E
Bujalance, Spain (bo͞o-hä-län'thä)	152	37.54N	4.22W
Bujumbura, Bdi.	210	3.23S	29.22E
Buka Island, i., Pap. N. Gui.	192e	5.15S	154.35E
Bukama, Zaire (bo͞o-kä'mä)	206	9.08S	26.00E
Bukavu, Zaire	206	2.30S	28.52E
Bukhara, Uzb. (bo͝o-kä'rä)	158	39.31N	64.22E
Bukittbatu, Indon.	173b	1.25N	101.58E
Bukit Panjang, Sing.	236c	1.23N	103.46E
Bukit Timah, Sing.	236c	1.20N	103.47E
Bukittinggi, Indon.	188	0.25S	100.28E
Bukoba, Tan.	206	1.20S	31.49E
Bukovina, hist. reg., Ukr. (bo͝o-kō'vĭ-nȧ)	148	48.06N	25.20E
Bula, Indon. (bo͞o'lä)	188	3.00S	130.30E
Bulalacao, Phil. (bo͞o-lȧ-lä'kä-ō)	189a	12.30N	121.20E
Bulawayo, Zimb. (bo͞o-lȧ-wä'yō)	206	20.12S	28.43E
Buldir, i., Ak., U.S. (bŭl dĭr)	89a	52.22N	175.50E
Bulgaria, nation, Eur. (bo͝ol-gā'rĭ-ă)	136	42.12N	24.13E
Bulim, Sing.	236c	1.23N	103.43E
Bulkley Ranges, mts., Can. (bŭlk'lê)	80	54.30N	127.30W
Bullaque, r., Spain (bo͝o-lä'kå)	152	39.15N	4.13W
Bullas, Spain (bo͞ol'yäs)	152	38.07N	1.48W
Bullfrog Creek, r., Ut., U.S. (bŭl'drŏg')	102	37.45N	110.55W
Bull Harbour, Can. (här'bẽr)	80	50.45N	127.55W
Bull Head, mtn., Jam.	116	18.10N	77.15W
Bull Run, r., Or., U.S. (bo͝ol)	100c	45.26N	122.11W
Bull Run Reservoir, res., Or., U.S.	100c	45.29N	122.11W
Bull Shoals Reservoir, res., U.S. (bo͝ol shōlz)	90	36.35N	92.57W
Bulmke-Hüllen, neigh., Ger.	232	51.31N	7.06E
Bulpham, Eng., U.K. (bo͝ol'făn)	138b	51.33N	0.21E
Bultfontein, S. Afr. (bo͝olt'fōn-tān')	212d	28.18S	26.10E
Bulun, Russia (bo͞o-lōn')	158	70.48N	127.27E
Bulungu, Zaire (bo͞o-lo͞oŋ'go͞o)	210	6.04S	21.54E
Bulwer, S. Afr. (bo͝ol-wẽr)	207c	29.49S	29.48E
Bumba, Zaire (bo͝om'bȧ)	204	2.11N	22.28E
Bumbire Island, i., Tan.	210	1.40S	32.05E
Bumbles Green, Eng., U.K.	231	51.44N	0.02E
Buna, Pap. N. Gui. (bo͞o'nȧ)	188	8.58S	148.38E
Bunbury, Austl. (bŭn'bŭrĭ)	196	33.25S	115.45E
Bundaberg, Austl. (bŭn'dȧ-bûrg)	196	24.45S	152.18E
Bundoora, Austl. (Chan.)	239b	37.42S	145.04E
Bunguran Utara, Kepulauan, is., Indon.	188	3.22N	108.00E
Bunia, Zaire	210	1.34N	30.15E
Bunker Hill, Il., U.S. (bŭnk'ẽr hĭl)	101e	39.03N	89.57W
Bunker Hill Monument, pt. of i., Ma., U.S.	223a	42.22N	71.04W
Bunkie, La., U.S. (bŭŋ'kĭ)	106	30.55N	92.10W
Bun Plains, pl., Kenya	210	0.55N	40.35E
Bununu Dass, Nig.	208	10.00N	9.31E
Buona Vista, Sing.	236c	1.16N	103.47E
Buor-Khaya, Guba, b., Russia	162	71.45N	131.00E
Buor Khaya, Mys, c., Russia	158	71.47N	133.22E
Bura, Kenya	210	1.06S	39.57E
Buraydah, Sau. Ar.	174	26.23N	44.14E
Burbank, Ca., U.S. (bûr'bănk)	101a	34.11N	118.19W
Burco, Som.	212a	9.20N	45.45E
Burdekin, r., Austl. (bûr'dê-kĭn)	196	19.22S	145.07E
Burdur, Tur. (bo͞or-do͝or')	142	37.50N	30.15E
Burdwān, India (bo͝od-wän')	174	23.29N	87.53E
Bureinskiy, Khrebet, mts., Russia	158	51.15N	133.30E
Bures-sur-Yvette, Fr.	233c	48.42N	2.10E
Bureya, Russia (bo͝orā'ȧ)	158	49.55N	130.00E
Bureya, r., Russia (bo͝o-rā'yä)	162	51.00N	131.15E
Burford, Eng., U.K. (bûr-fẽrd)	138b	51.46N	1.38W
Burg, Ger.	232	51.08N	7.09E
Burgas, Bul. (bo͝or-gäs')	142	42.29N	27.30E
Burgas, Gulf of, b., Bul.	142	42.30N	27.40E
Burgaw, N.C., U.S. (bûr'gô)	108	34.31N	77.56W
Burgdorf, Switz. (bo͝org'dôrf)	148	47.04N	7.37E
Burgenland, prov., Aus.	139e	47.58N	16.57E
Burgeo, Can.	86	47.36N	57.34W
Burger Township, S. Afr.	240b	26.05S	27.46E
Burgess, Va., U.S.	92	37.53N	76.21W
Burgh Heath, Eng., U.K.	231	51.18N	0.13W
Burgos, Mex. (bo͝or'gōs)	106	24.57N	98.47W
Burgos, Phil.	189a	16.03N	119.52E
Burgos, Spain (bo͞o'r-gōs)	142	42.20N	3.44W
Burgsvik, Swe. (bo͝orgs'vĭk)	146	57.04N	18.18E
Burhānpur, India (bo͝or'hän-po͞or)	174	21.26N	76.08E
Burholme, neigh., Pa., U.S.	225b	40.03N	75.05W
Burias Island, i., Phil. (bo͞o'rê-äs)	189a	12.56N	122.56E
Burias Pass, strt., Phil. (bo͞o'rê-äs)	189a	13.04N	123.11E
Burica, Punta, c., N.A. (po͞o'n-tä-bo͞o'rē-kä)	114	8.02N	83.12W
Burien, Wa., U.S. (bū'rĭ-ĕn)	100a	47.28N	122.20W
Burin, Can. (bûr'ĭn)	79a	47.02N	55.10W
Burin Peninsula, pen., Can.	86	47.00N	55.40W
Burkburnett, Tx., U.S. (bûrk-bûr'nĕt)	104	34.04N	98.35W
Burke, Vt., U.S. (bûrk)	92	44.40N	72.00W
Burke Channel, strt., Can.	80	52.07N	127.38W
Burketown, Austl. (bûrk'toun)	196	17.50S	139.30E
Burkina Faso, nation, Afr.	204	13.00N	2.00W
Burley, Id., U.S. (bûr'lĭ)	98	42.31N	113.48W
Burley, Wa., U.S.	100a	47.25N	122.38W
Burli, Kaz.	164a	53.36N	61.55E
Burlingame, Ca., U.S. (bûr'lĭn-găm)	100b	37.35N	122.22W
Burlingame, Ks., U.S.	104	38.45N	95.49W
Burlington, Can. (bûr'lĭng-tŭn)	84	43.19N	79.48W
Burlington, Co., U.S.	104	39.17N	102.26W
Burlington, Ia., U.S.	90	40.48N	91.05W
Burlington, Ks., U.S.	104	38.10N	95.46W
Burlington, Ky., U.S.	95f	39.01N	84.44W
Burlington, Ma., U.S.	87a	42.31N	71.13W
Burlington, N.J., U.S.	94f	40.04N	74.52W
Burlington, N.C., U.S.	108	36.05N	79.26W
Burlington, Vt., U.S.	90	44.30N	73.15W
Burlington, Wa., U.S.	100a	48.28N	122.20W
Burlington, Wi., U.S.	95a	42.41N	88.16W
Burma (Myanmar), nation, Asia (bûr'mȧ)	172	21.00N	95.15E
Burnaby, Can.	78	49.14N	122.58W
Burnage, Eng., U.K.	233b	53.26N	2.12W
Burnet, Tx., U.S. (bûrn'ĕt)	106	30.46N	98.14W
Burnham, Il., U.S.	227a	41.39N	87.34W
Burnham on Crouch, Eng., U.K. (bûrn'ăm-ŏn-krouch)	138b	51.38N	0.48E
Burnhamthorpe, Can.	223c	43.37N	79.36W
Burnie, Austl. (bûr'nê)	196	41.15S	146.05E
Burning Tree Estates, Md., U.S.	225d	39.01N	77.12W
Burnley, Eng., U.K. (bûrn'lê)	144	53.47N	2.19W
Burns, Or., U.S. (bûrnz)	98	43.35N	119.05W
Burnside, Ky., U.S. (bûrn'sīd)	108	36.57N	84.33W
Burns Lake, Can. (bûrnz lăk)	78	54.14N	125.46W
Burnsville, Can. (bûrnz'vĭl)	86	47.44N	65.07W
Burnt, r., Or., U.S. (bûrnt)	98	44.26N	117.53W
Burntwood, r., Can.	82	55.53N	97.30W
Burrard Inlet, b., Can. (bûr'ȧrd)	100d	49.19N	123.15W
Burr Gaabo, Som.	206	1.14N	51.47E
Burriana, Spain (bo͞or-rê-ȧ'nä)	142	39.53N	0.05W
Burro, Serranías del, mts., Mex. (sĕr-rä-nē'ȧs dĕl bo͞o'r-rō)	106	29.39N	102.07W
Burrowhill, Eng., U.K.	231	51.21N	0.36W
Burr Ridge, Il., U.S.	227a	41.46N	87.55W
Bursa, Tur. (bo͞or'sȧ)	174	40.10N	28.10E
Būr Safājah, Egypt	204	26.57N	33.56E
Burscheid, Ger. (bo͞or'shīd)	151c	51.05N	7.07E
Būr Sūdān, Sudan (so͞o-dȧn')	204	19.30N	37.10E
Burt, N.Y., U.S. (bûrt)	95c	43.19N	78.45W
Burt, l., Mi., U.S. (bûrt)	92	45.25N	84.45W
Burton, Eng., U.K.	233a	53.16N	3.01W
Burton, Wa., U.S. (bûr'tŭn)	100a	47.24N	122.28W
Burton, Lake, res., Ga., U.S.	108	34.46N	83.40W
Burtonsville, Md., U.S. (bûrtŏns-vil)	94e	39.07N	76.57W
Burton-upon-Trent, Eng., U.K. (bŭr'tŭn-ŭp'-ŏn-trĕnt)	144	52.48N	1.37W
Buru, i., Indon.	188	3.30S	126.30E
Burullus, l., Egypt	212b	31.20N	30.58E
Burundi, nation, Afr.	206	3.00S	29.30E
Burwell, Ne., U.S. (bûr'wĕl)	96	41.46N	99.08W
Burwood, Austl.	239b	37.51S	145.06E
Bury, Eng., U.K. (bĕr'ĭ)	138a	53.36N	2.17W
Buryat Autonomous Soviet Socialist Republic, Russia	158	55.15N	112.00E
Bury Saint Edmunds, Eng., U.K. (bĕr'ĭ-sānt ĕd'mŭndz)	144	52.14N	0.44E
Burzaco, Arg. (bo͞or-zȧ'kō)	126a	34.50S	58.23W
Busanga Swamp, sw., Zam.	210	14.10S	25.50E
Busby, Austl.	239a	33.54S	150.53E
Buschhausen, neigh., Ger.	232	51.30N	6.51E
Būsh, Egypt (bo͞osh)	212b	29.13N	31.08E
Bushey, Eng., U.K.	231	51.39N	0.22W
Bushey Heath, Eng., U.K.	231	51.38N	0.20W
Bush Hill, Va., U.S.	225d	38.48N	77.07W
Bushmanland, hist. reg., S. Afr. (bo͝osh-măn lănd)	206	29.15S	18.45E
Bushnell, Il., U.S. (bo͝osh'nĕl)	104	40.33N	90.28W
Bushwick, neigh., N.Y., U.S.	224	40.42N	73.55W
Businga, Zaire (bō-sĭŋ'gȧ)	204	3.20N	20.53E
Busira, r., Zaire	210	0.05S	19.20E
Busk, Ukr. (bo͞o'sk)	148	49.58N	24.39E
Busselton, Austl. (bûs'l-tŭn)	196	33.40S	115.30E
Bussum, Neth.	139a	52.16N	5.10E
Bustamante, Mex. (bo͞os-tȧ-män'tȧ)	106	26.34N	100.30W
Bustleton, neigh., Pa., U.S.	225b	40.05N	75.02W
Busto Arsizio, Italy (bo͞os'tō är-sēd'zê-ō)	154	45.47N	8.51E
Busuanga, i., Phil. (bo͞o-swäŋ'gä)	189a	12.20N	119.43E
Buta, Zaire (bo͞o'tȧ)	204	2.48N	24.44E
Butha Buthe, Leso. (bo͞o-thȧ-bo͞o'thȧ)	207c	28.49S	28.16E
Butler, Al., U.S. (bŭt'lẽr)	108	32.05N	88.10W
Butler, In., U.S.	92	41.25N	84.50W
Butler, Md., U.S.	94e	39.32N	76.46W
Butler, N.J., U.S.	94a	41.00N	74.20W
Butler, Pa., U.S.	92	40.50N	79.55W
Butovo, Russia (bo͝o-tô'vô)	164b	55.33N	37.36E
Butsha, Zaire	210	0.57N	29.13E
Buttahatchee, r., Al., U.S. (bŭt-ȧ-hăch'ê)	108	34.02N	88.05W
Butte, Mt., U.S. (būt)	90	46.00N	112.31W
Butterworth, Transkei (bŭ tẽr'wûrth)	207c	32.20S	28.09E
Büttgen, Ger.	232	51.12N	6.36E
Butt of Lewis, c., Scot., U.K. (bŭt ŏv lū'ĭs)	144	58.34N	6.15W
Butuan, Phil. (bo͞o-to͞o'än)	188	8.40N	125.33E
Buturlinovka, Russia (bo͞o-to͞o'lê-nôf'ka)	160	50.47N	40.35E
Buuhoodle, Som.	212a	8.15N	46.20E
Buulo Berde, Som.	212a	3.53N	45.30E
Buxtehude, Ger.	139c	53.29N	9.42E
Buxton, Eng., U.K. (bŭks't'n)	138a	53.15N	1.55W
Buxton, Or., U.S.	100c	45.41N	123.11W
Buy, Russia (bwē)	158	58.30N	41.48E
Büyükmenderes, r., Tur.	174	37.50N	28.20E
Buzău, Rom. (bo͞o-zĕ'ò)	154	45.09N	26.51E
Buzău, r., Rom.	156	45.17N	27.22E
Buzaymah, Libya	204	25.14N	22.13E
Buzi, China (bo͞o-dz)	182	33.48N	118.13E
Buzuluk, Russia (bo͝o-zo͝o-lo͝ok')	158	52.50N	52.10E
Bwendi, Zaire	210	4.01N	26.41E
Byala, Bul.	154	43.26N	25.44E
Byala Slatina, Bul. (byä'la slä'tēnä)	154	43.26N	23.56E
Byblos, *see* Jubayl, Leb.	173a	34.07N	35.38E
Byculla, neigh., India	236e	18.58N	72.49E
Bydgoszcz, Pol. (bĭd'gôshch)	140	53.07N	18.00E
Byelorussia, *see* Belarus, nation, Eur.	158	53.30N	25.33E
Byesville, Oh., U.S. (bīz-vĭl)	92	39.55N	81.35W
Byfang, neigh., Ger.	232	51.24N	7.06E
Byfleet, Eng., U.K.	231	51.20N	0.29W
Bygdin, l., Nor. (bügh-dên')	146	61.24N	8.31E
Byglandsfjord, Nor. (bügh'länds-fyôr)	146	58.40N	7.49E
Bykhovo, Bela.	156	53.32N	30.15E
Bykovo, Russia (bĭ-kô'vô)	164b	55.38N	38.05E
Byrranga, Gory, mts., Russia	162	74.15N	94.28E
Bytantay, r., Russia (byän'täy)	162	68.15N	132.15E
Bytom, Pol. (bĭ'tŭm)	140	50.21N	18.55E
Bytosh', Russia (bĭ-tôsh')	156	53.48N	34.06E
Bytow, Pol. (bĭ'tŭf)	148	54.10N	17.30E

C

PLACE (Pronunciation)	PAGE	Lat. °′	Long. °′
Cabagan, Phil. (kä-bä-gän')	189a	17.27N	121.50E
Cabalete, i., Phil. (kä-bä-lā'tå)	189a	14.19N	122.00E
Caballito, neigh., Arg.	229d	34.37S	58.27W
Caballones, Canal de, strt., Cuba (kä-nä'l-dĕ-kä-bäl-yô'nĕs)	116	20.45N	79.20W
Caballo Reservoir, res., N.M., U.S. (kä-bä-lyō')	102	33.00N	107.20W
Cabanatuan, Phil. (kä-bä-nä-twän')	189a	15.30N	120.56E
Cabano, Can. (kä-bä-nō')	86	47.41N	68.54W
Cabarruyan, i., Phil. (kä-bä-ro͞o'yän)	189a	16.21N	120.10E
Cabedelo, Braz. (kä-bē-dā'lò)	124	6.58S	34.49W
Cabeza, Arrecife, i., Mex.	112	19.07N	95.52W
Cabeza del Buey, Spain (kȧ-bā'thä dĕl bwā')	152	38.43N	5.18W
Cabimas, Ven. (kä-bē'mäs)	124	10.21N	71.27W
Cabinda, Ang.	206	5.33S	12.12E
Cabinda, hist. reg., Ang. (kä-bĭn'dȧ)	206	5.10S	10.00E
Cabinet Mountains, mts., Mt., U.S. (kăb'ĭ-nĕt)	98	48.13N	115.52W
Cabin John, Md., U.S.	225d	38.58N	77.09W
Cabo Frio, Braz. (kä'bō-frē'ô)	123a	22.53S	42.02W
Cabo Frio, Ilha do, Braz. (ē'lä-dō-kä'bō frē'ō)	123a	23.01S	42.00W
Cabo Gracias a Dios, Hond. (kȧ'bô-grä-syäs-ä-dyô's)	114	15.00N	83.13W
Cabonga, Réservoir, res., Can.	84	47.25N	76.35W
Cabora Bassa Reservoir, res., Moz.	206	15.45S	32.00E
Cabot Head, c., Can. (kăb'ŭt)	84	45.15N	81.20W
Cabot Strait, strt., Can. (kăb'ŭt)	79a	47.35N	60.00W
Cabra, Spain (käb'rä)	152	37.28N	4.29W
Cabra, i., Phil.	189a	13.55N	119.55E
Cabramatta, Austl.	239a	33.54S	150.56E
Cabrera, i., Spain (kä-brā'rä)	152	39.08N	2.57E
Cabrera, Sierra de la, mts., Spain	152	42.15N	6.45W
Cabriel, r., Spain (kä-brē-ĕl')	152	39.25N	1.20W
Cabrillo National Monument, rec., Ca., U.S. (kä-brēl'yō)	102a	32.41N	117.03W
Cabuçu, r., Braz. (kä-bo͞o'-so͞o)	126b	22.57S	43.36W
Cabugao, Phil. (kä-bo͞o'gä-ō)	189a	17.48N	120.28E
Čačak, Yugo. (chä'chák)	154	43.51N	20.22E

ng-sing; ŋ-baŋk; ɴ-nasalized n; nŏd; cŏmmit; ōld; ôbey; ôrder; oi-boil; fo͞od; o͝o-as oo in foot; ou-out; s-soft; sh-dish; th-thin; pūre; ûnite; ûrn; stŭd; circŭs; ü-as in French tu; '-indeterminate vowel.

PLACE (Pronunciation)	PAGE	Lat. °′	Long. °′
Caçapava, Braz. (kä'sä-pá'vä)	123a	23.05S	45.52W
Cáceres, Braz. (ká'sĕ-rĕs)	124	16.11S	57.32W
Cáceres, Spain (ká'thā-rās)	142	39.28N	6.20W
Cachan, Fr.	233c	48.48N	2.20E
Cachapoal, r., Chile (kä-chä-pô-ä'l)	123b	34.23S	70.19W
Cache, r., Ar., U.S. (kásh)	104	35.24N	91.12W
Cache Creek, Can.	80	50.48N	121.19W
Cache Creek, r., Ca., U.S. (kásh)	102	38.53N	122.24W
Cache la Poudre, r., Co., U.S. (kásh lá po͞od'r')	104	40.43N	105.39W
Cachi, Nevados de, mtn., Arg. (nĕ-vá'dôs-dĕ-kä'chē)	126	25.05S	66.40W
Cachinal, Chile (kä-chē-näl')	126	24.57S	69.33W
Cachoeira, Braz. (kä-shô-ā'rä)	124	12.32S	38.47W
Cachoeirá do Sul, Braz. (kä-shô-ā'rä-dô-so͞o'l)	126	30.02S	52.49W
Cachoeiras de Macacu, Braz. (kä-shô-ā'räs-dĕ-mä-kà'ko͞o)	123a	22.28S	42.39W
Cachoeiro de Itapemirim, Braz.	124	20.51S	41.06W
Cacilhas, Port.	234d	38.41N	9.09W
Cacólo, Ang.	210	10.07S	19.17E
Caconda, Ang. (kä-kōn'dä)	206	13.43S	15.06E
Cacouna, Can.	86	47.54N	69.31W
Cacula, Ang.	210	14.29S	14.10E
Cadale, Som.	212a	2.45N	46.15E
Caddo, l., La., U.S. (kăd'ō)	106	32.37N	94.15W
Cadereyta, Mex. (kä-dā-rā'tä)	112	20.42N	99.47W
Cadereyta Jimenez, Mex. (kä-dā-rā'tä hē-mā'näz)	106	25.36N	99.59W
Cadi, Sierra de, mts., Spain (sē-ĕ'r-rä-dĕ-kä'dē)	152	42.17N	1.34E
Cadillac, Mi., U.S. (kăd'ĭ-lăk)	92	44.15N	85.25W
Cadishead, Eng., U.K.	233b	53.25N	2.26W
Cádiz, Spain (ká'dēz)	136	36.34N	6.20W
Cadiz, Ca., U.S. (kā'dĭz)	102	34.33N	115.30W
Cadiz, Oh., U.S.	92	40.15N	81.00W
Cádiz, Golfo de, b., Spain (gôl-fô-dĕ-ká'dēz)	142	36.50N	7.00W
Caen, Fr. (käN)	140	49.13N	0.22W
Caernarfon, Wales, U.K.	140	53.08N	4.17W
Caernarfon Bay, b., Wales, U.K.	144	53.09N	4.56W
Cagayan, Phil. (kä-gä-yän')	188	8.13N	124.30E
Cagayan, r., Phil.	188	16.45N	121.55E
Cagayan Islands, is., Phil.	188	9.40N	120.30E
Cagayan Sulu, i., Phil. (kä-gä-yän so͞o'lo͞o)	188	7.00N	118.30E
Cagli, Italy (käl'yē)	154	43.35N	12.40E
Cagliari, Italy (käl'yä-rē)	136	39.16N	9.08E
Cagliari, Golfo di, b., Italy (gôl-fô-dē-käl'yä-rē)	142	39.08N	9.12E
Cagnes, Fr. (kän'y')	150	43.40N	7.14E
Cagua, Ven. (kä'gwä)	125b	10.12N	67.27W
Caguas, P.R. (kä'gwäs)	111b	18.12N	66.01W
Cahaba, r., Al., U.S. (ká hä-bä)	108	32.50N	87.15W
Cahama, Ang. (kä-á'mä)	206	16.17S	14.19E
Cahokia, Il., U.S. (kå-hō'kĭ-å)	101e	38.34N	90.11W
Cahora-Bassa, wtfl., Moz.	210	15.40S	32.50E
Cahors, Fr. (kå-ôr')	140	44.27N	1.27E
Cahuacán, Mex. (kä-wä-kä'n)	113a	19.38N	99.25W
Cahuita, Punta, c., C.R. (po͞o'n-tä-kä-wē'tå)	114	9.47N	82.41W
Caibarién, Cuba (kī-bä-rē-ĕn')	116	22.35N	79.30W
Caicedonia, Col. (kī-sĕ-dô-nēä)	124a	4.21N	75.48W
Caicos Bank, bk. (kī'kōs)	116	21.35N	72.00W
Caicos Islands, is., T./C. Is.	110	21.45N	71.50W
Caicos Passage, strt., N.A.	116	21.55N	72.45W
Caillou Bay, b., La., U.S. (kå-yo͞o')	106	29.07N	91.00W
Caimanera, Cuba (kī-mä-nā'rä)	116	20.00N	75.10W
Caiman Point, c., Phil. (kī'mán)	189a	15.56N	119.33E
Caimito, r., Pan. (kä-ē-mē'tô)	110a	8.50N	79.45W
Caimito del Guayabal, Cuba (kä-ē-mē'tō-dĕl-gwä-yä-bä'l)	117a	22.57N	82.36W
Cairns, Austl. (kârnz)	196	17.02S	145.49E
Cairo, C.R. (kī'rō)	114	10.06N	83.47W
Cairo, Egypt	204	30.00N	31.17E
Cairo, Ga., U.S. (kā'rō)	108	30.48N	84.12W
Cairo, Il., U.S.	90	36.59N	89.11W
Caistor, Eng., U.K. (kâs'tĕr)	138a	53.30N	0.20W
Caiundo, Ang.	210	15.46S	17.28E
Caiyu, China (tsī-yo͞o)	182	39.39N	116.36E
Cajamarca, Col. (kä-kä-má'r-kä)	124a	4.25N	75.25W
Cajamarca, Peru (kä-hä-mär'kä)	124	7.16S	78.30W
Čajniče, Bos. (chī'nĭ-chĕ)	154	43.32N	19.04E
Cajon, Ca., U.S. (kă-hōn')	101a	34.18N	117.28W
Çajuru, Braz. (kå-zho͞o'ro͞o)	123a	21.17S	47.17W
Čakovec, Cro. (chá'kō-vĕts)	154	46.23N	16.27E
Cala, S. Afr. (cä-lå)	207c	31.33S	27.41E
Calabar, Nig. (kăl-å-bär')	204	4.57N	8.19E
Calabazar, Cuba (kä-lä-bä-zä'r)	117a	23.02N	82.25W
Calabozo, Ven. (kä-lä-bō'zō)	124	8.48N	67.27W
Calabria, hist. reg., Italy (kä-lä'brē-ä)	154	39.26N	16.23E
Calafat, Rom. (kå-lå-fát')	154	43.59N	22.56E
Calaguas Islands, is., Phil. (kä-läg'wäs)	189a	14.30N	123.06E
Calahoo, Can. (kă-lå-ho͞o')	77g	53.42N	113.58W
Calahorra, Spain (kä-lä-ôr'rä)	142	42.18N	1.58W
Calais, Fr. (kå-lĕ')	136	50.56N	1.51E
Calais, Me., U.S.	90	45.11N	67.15W
Calama, Chile (kä-lä'mä)	126	22.17S	68.58W
Calamar, Col. (kä-lä-mär')	124	10.24N	75.00W
Calamar, Col.	124	1.55N	72.33W
Calamba, Phil. (kä-läm'bä)	189a	14.12N	121.10E
Calamian Group, is., Phil. (kä-lä-myän')	188	12.14N	118.38E
Calañas, Spain (kä-län'yäs)	152	37.41N	6.52W
Calanda, Spain	152	40.53N	0.20W
Calapan, Phil. (kä-lä-pän')	189a	13.25N	121.11E
Călăraşi, Rom. (kŭ-lŭ-rásh'ĭ)	142	44.09N	27.20E
Calatayud, Spain (kä-lä-tä-yo͞odh')	142	41.23N	1.37W
Calauag Bay, b., Phil.	189a	14.07N	122.10E
Calaveras Reservoir, res., Ca., U.S. (kăl-å-vĕr'ǎs)	100b	37.29N	121.47W
Calavite, Cape, c., Phil. (kä-lä-vē'tä)	189a	13.29N	120.00E
Calcasieu, r., La., U.S. (kăl'kå-shū)	106	30.22N	93.08W
Calcasieu Lake, l., La., U.S.	106	29.58N	93.08W
Calcutta, India (kăl-kŭt'å)	174	22.32N	88.22E
Caldas, Col. (ká'l-däs)	124a	6.06N	75.38W
Caldas, dept., Col.	124a	5.20N	75.38W
Caldas da Rainha, Port. (käl'däs dä rīn'yǎ)	152	39.25N	9.08W
Calder, r., Eng., U.K. (kôl'dĕr)	138a	53.39N	1.30W
Caldera, Chile (käl-dá'rä)	126	27.02S	70.53W
Calder Canal, can., Eng., U.K.	138a	53.48N	2.25W
Caldwell, Id., U.S. (kôld'wĕl)	98	43.40N	116.43W
Caldwell, Ks., U.S.	104	37.04N	97.36W
Caldwell, N.J., U.S.	224	40.51N	74.17W
Caldwell, Oh., U.S.	92	39.40N	81.30W
Caldwell, Tx., U.S.	106	30.30N	96.40W
Caledon, Can. (kăl'ē-dǒn)	77d	43.52N	79.59W
Caledonia, Mn., U.S. (kăl-ē-dō'nĭ-å)	96	43.38N	91.31W
Calella, Spain (kä-lĕl'yä)	152	41.37N	2.39E
Calera Victor Rosales, Mex. (kä-lā'rä-vē'k-tôr-rô-sá'lĕs)	112	22.57N	102.42W
Calexico, Ca., U.S. (kå-lĕk'sĭ-kō)	90	32.41N	115.30W
Calgary, Can. (kăl'gå-rĭ)	78	51.03N	114.05W
Calhariz, neigh., Port.	234d	38.44N	9.12W
Calhoun, Ga., U.S. (kăl-ho͞on')	108	34.30N	84.56W
Cali, Col. (kä'lē)	124	3.26N	76.30W
Calicut, India (kăl'ĭ-kŭt)	174	11.19N	75.49E
Caliente, Nv., U.S. (käl-yĕn'tä)	102	37.38N	114.30W
California, Mo., U.S. (kăl-ĭ-fôr'nĭ-å)	104	38.38N	92.38W
California, Pa., U.S.	95e	40.03N	79.53W
California, state, U.S.	90	38.10N	121.20W
California, Golfo de, b., Mex. (gôl-fô-dĕ-kä-lē-fôr-nyä)	110	30.30N	113.45W
California Aqueduct, aq., Ca., U.S.	102	37.10N	121.10W
California-Los Angeles, University of (U.C.L.A.), educ., Ca., U.S.	228	34.04N	118.26W
Călimani, Munţii, mts., Rom.	148	47.05N	24.47E
Calimere, Point, c., India	178	10.20N	80.20E
Calimesa, Ca., U.S. (kă-lĭ-mā'så)	101a	34.00N	117.04W
Calipatria, Ca., U.S. (kăl-ĭ-pát'rĭ-å)	102	33.03N	115.30W
Calkini, Mex. (käl-kē-nē')	112	20.21N	90.06W
Callabonna, Lake, l., Austl. (căla'bŏn å)	198	29.35S	140.28E
Callao, Peru (käl-yä'ō)	124	12.02S	77.07W
Calling, l., Can. (kôl'ĭng)	80	55.15N	113.12W
Calmar, Can. (kăl'mär)	77g	53.16N	113.49W
Calmar, Ia., U.S.	96	43.12N	91.54W
Caloocan, Phil.	237g	14.39N	120.59E
Caloosahatchee, r., Fl., U.S. (kå-loo-så-hăch'ē)	109a	26.45N	81.41W
Calotmul, Mex. (kä-lôt-mo͞ol)	114a	20.58N	88.11W
Calpulalpan, Mex. (käl-po͞o-läl'pän)	112	19.35N	98.33W
Caltagirone, Italy (käl-tä-jē-rō'nå)	142	37.14N	14.32E
Caltanissetta, Italy (käl-tä-nē-sĕt'tä)	142	37.30N	14.02E
Caluango, Ang.	210	8.21S	19.40E
Calucinga, Ang.	210	11.18S	16.12E
Calumet, Mi., U.S. (kå-lū-mĕt')	96	47.15N	88.29W
Calumet, Lake, l., Il., U.S.	95a	41.43N	87.36W
Calumet City, Il., U.S.	95a	41.37N	87.33W
Calumet Park, Il., U.S.	227a	41.44N	87.33W
Calumet Sag Channel, can., Il., U.S.	227a	41.42N	87.57W
Calunda, Ang.	210	12.06S	23.23E
Caluquembe, Ang.	210	13.47S	14.44E
Caluula, Som.	212a	11.53N	50.40E
Calvert, Tx., U.S. (kăl'vērt)	106	30.59N	96.41W
Calvert Island, i., Can.	78	51.35N	128.00W
Calvi, Fr. (käl'vē)	154	42.33N	8.35E
Calvillo, Mex. (käl-vēl'yō)	112	21.51N	102.44E
Calvinia, S. Afr. (kăl-vĭn'ĭ-å)	206	31.20S	19.50E
Cam, r., Eng., U.K. (kăm)	144	52.15N	0.05E
Camagüey, Cuba (kä-mä-gwā')	110	21.25N	78.00W
Camagüey, prov., Cuba	116	21.30N	78.10W
Camajuani, Cuba (kä-mä-hwä'nē)	116	22.25N	79.50W
Camano, Wa., U.S. (kä-mä'no)	100a	48.10N	122.32W
Camano Island, i., Wa., U.S.	100a	48.11N	122.29W
Camargo, Mex. (kä-mär gō)	106	26.19N	98.49W
Camarón, Cabo, c., Hond. (kå'bô-kä-mä-rōn')	114	16.06N	85.05W
Camas, Wa., U.S. (kăm'ǎs)	100c	45.36N	122.24W
Camas Creek, r., Id., U.S.	98	44.10N	112.09W
Camatagua, Ven. (kä-mä-tá'gwä)	125b	9.49N	66.55W
Ca Mau, Mui, c., Viet.	188	8.36N	104.43E
Cambay, India (kăm-bā')	178	22.22N	72.39E
Camberwell, Austl.	239b	37.50S	145.04E
Cambodia, nation, Asia	188	12.15N	104.00E
Cambonda, Serra, mts., Ang.	210	12.10S	14.15E
Camborne, Eng., U.K. (kăm'bôrn)	144	50.15N	5.28W
Cambrai, Fr. (käN-brĕ')	140	50.10N	3.15E
Cambrian Mountains, mts., Wales, U.K. (kăm'brĭ-ăn)	144	52.05N	4.05W
Cambridge, Can.	84	43.22N	80.19W
Cambridge, Eng., U.K. (kām'brĭj)	140	52.12N	0.11E
Cambridge, Md., U.S.	92	38.35N	76.10W
Cambridge, Ma., U.S.	87a	42.23N	71.07W
Cambridge, Mn., U.S.	96	45.35N	93.14W
Cambridge, Ne., U.S.	104	40.17N	100.10W
Cambridge, Oh., U.S.	92	40.00N	81.35W
Cambridge Bay, Can.	78	69.15N	105.00W
Cambridge City, In., U.S.	92	39.45N	85.15W
Cambridgeshire, co., Eng., U.K.	138a	52.26N	0.19W
Cambuci, Braz. (käm-bo͞o'sē)	123a	21.35S	41.54W
Cambuci, neigh., Braz.	230d	23.34S	46.37W
Cambundi-Catembo, Ang.	210	10.09S	17.31E
Camby, In., U.S. (kăm'bē)	95g	39.40N	86.19W
Camden, Austl.	195b	34.03S	150.42E
Camden, Al., U.S. (kăm'dĕn)	108	31.58N	87.15W
Camden, Ar., U.S.	104	33.36N	92.49W
Camden, Me., U.S.	86	44.11N	69.05W
Camden, N.J., U.S.	90	39.56N	75.06W
Camden, S.C., U.S.	108	34.14N	80.37W
Camden, neigh., Eng., U.K.	231	51.33N	0.10W
Cameia, Parque Nacional da, rec., Ang.	210	11.40S	21.20E
Cameron, Mo., U.S. (kăm'ĕr-ŭn)	104	39.44N	94.14W
Cameron, Tx., U.S.	106	30.52N	96.57W
Cameron, W.V., U.S.	92	39.40N	80.35W
Cameron Hills, hills, Can.	78	60.13N	120.20W
Cameroon, nation, Afr.	204	5.48N	11.00E
Cameroon Mountain, mtn., Cam.	204	4.12N	9.11E
Camiling, Phil. (kä-mē-lĭng')	189a	15.42N	120.24E
Camilla, Ga., U.S. (kå-mĭl'å)	108	31.13N	84.12W
Caminha, Port. (kä-mĭn'yå)	152	41.52N	8.44W
Camoçim, Braz. (kä-mô-sēN')	124	2.56S	40.55W
Camooweal, Austl.	196	20.00S	138.13E
Campana, Arg. (käm-pä'nä)	123c	34.10S	58.58W
Campana, i., Chile (käm-pän'yä)	126	48.20S	75.15W
Campanario, Spain (kä-pä-nä'rē-ō)	152	38.51N	5.36W
Campanella, Punta, c., Italy (pō'n-tä-käm-pä-nĕ'lä)	153c	40.20N	14.21E
Campanha, Braz. (käm-pän-yän')	123a	21.51S	45.24W
Campania, hist. reg., Italy (käm-pän'yä)	154	41.00N	14.40E
Campbell, Ca., U.S. (kăm'bĕl)	100b	37.17N	121.57W
Campbell, Mo., U.S.	104	36.29N	90.04W
Campbell, is., N.Z.	2	52.30S	169.00E
Campbellfield, Austl.	239b	37.41S	144.57E
Campbellpore, Pak.	178	33.49N	72.24E
Campbell River, Can.	78	50.01N	125.15W
Campbellsville, Ky., U.S. (kăm'bĕlz-vĭl)	108	37.19N	85.20W
Campbellton, Can. (kăm'bĕl-tŭn)	78	48.00N	66.40W
Campbelltown, Austl. (kăm'bĕl-toun)	195b	34.04S	150.49E
Campbelltown, Scot., U.K. (kăm'b'l-toun)	144	55.25N	5.50W
Camp Dennison, Oh., U.S. (dĕ'nĭ-sǒn)	95f	39.12N	84.17W
Campeche, Mex. (käm-pā'chå)	110	19.51N	90.32W
Campeche, state, Mex.	110	18.55N	90.20W
Campeche, Bahía de, b., Mex. (bä-ē'ä-dĕ-käm-pā'chä)	110	19.30N	93.40W
Campechuela, Cuba (käm-på-chwā'lä)	116	20.15N	77.15W
Camperdown, S. Afr. (kăm'pĕr-doun)	207c	29.44S	30.33E
Campina Grande, Braz. (käm-pē'nä grän'dĕ)	124	7.15S	35.49W
Campinas, Braz. (käm-pē'näzh)	124	22.53S	47.03W
Camp Indian Reservation, I.R., Ca., U.S. (kămp)	102	32.39N	116.26W
Campo, Cam. (käm'pō)	204	2.22N	9.49E
Campoalegre, Col. (kä'm-pô-ălĕ'grĕ)	124	2.34N	75.20W
Campobasso, Italy (käm'pô-bäs'sō)	154	41.35N	14.39E
Campo Belo, Braz.	123a	20.52S	45.15W
Campo de Criptana, Spain (käm'pō dä krēp-tä'nä)	152	39.24N	3.09W
Campo Florido, Cuba (kä'm-pō flô-rē'dō)	117a	23.07N	82.07W
Campo Grande, Braz. (käm-pò grän'dĕ)	124	20.28S	54.32W
Campo Grande, Braz.	126b	22.54S	43.33W
Campo Grande, neigh., Port.	234d	38.45N	9.09W
Campo Maior, Braz. (käm-pò mä-yôr')	124	4.48S	42.12W
Campo Maior, Port.	152	39.03N	7.06W
Campo Real, Spain (käm'pô rå-äl')	153a	40.21N	3.23W
Campos, Braz. (kä'm-pôs)	124	21.46S	41.19W
Campos do Jordão, Braz. (kä'm-pôs-dô-zhôr-dou'N)	123a	22.45S	45.35W
Campos Gerais, Braz. (kä'm-pôs-zhĕ-ráēs)	123a	21.17S	45.43W
Camps Bay, S. Afr. (kămps)	206a	33.57S	18.22E
Campsie, Austl.	239a	33.55S	151.06E
Camp Springs, Md., U.S. (cămp sprĭngz)	94e	38.48N	76.55W
Camp Springs, Md., U.S.	225d	38.48N	76.55W
Camp Wood, Tx., U.S. (kămp wŏd)	106	29.39N	100.02W
Camrose, Can. (kăm-rōz)	78	53.01N	112.50W
Camu, r., Dom. Rep. (kä'mo͞o)	116	19.05N	70.15W
Canada, nation, N.A. (kăn'å-då)	78	50.00N	100.00W
Canada Bay, b., Can.	86	50.43N	56.10W
Cañada de Gómez, Arg. (kä-nyä'dä-dĕ-gô'mĕz)	126	32.49S	61.24W
Canadian, Tx., U.S. (kå-nā'dĭ-ǎn)	104	35.54N	100.24W
Canadian, r., U.S.	90	35.30N	102.30W
Canajoharie, N.Y., U.S. (kăn-å-jō-hăr'ē)	92	42.55N	74.35W
Çanakkale, Tur. (chä-näk-kä'lĕ)	142	40.10N	26.26E
Çanakkale Boğazi (Dardanelles), strt., Tur.	142	40.05N	25.50E
Canandaigua, N.Y., U.S. (kăn-ǎn-dā'gwå)	92	42.55N	77.20W
Canandaigua, l., N.Y., U.S.	92	42.45N	77.20W
Cananea, Mex. (kä-nä-nĕ'ä)	110	31.00N	110.20W
Canarias, Islas (Canary Is.), is., Spain (ē's-läs-kä-nä'ryäs)	203	29.15N	16.30W
Canarreos, Archipiélago de los, is., Cuba	116	21.35N	82.20W
Canarsie, neigh., N.Y., U.S.	224	40.38N	73.53W
Canary Islands, *see* Canarias, Islas, is., Spain	203	29.15N	16.30W
Cañas, C.R. (kä'-nyäs)	114	10.26N	85.06W
Cañas, r., C.R.	114	10.20N	85.21W
Cañasgordas, Col. (kä'nyäs-gô'r-däs)	124a	6.44N	76.01W
Canastota, N.Y., U.S. (kăn-ås-tō'tå)	92	43.05N	75.45W
Canastra, Serra de, mts., Braz. (sĕ'r-rä-dĕ-kä-nä's-trä)	124	19.53S	46.57W
Canatlán, Mex. (kä-nät-län')	106	24.30N	104.45W
Canaveral, Cape, c., Fl., U.S.	90	28.30N	80.23W
Canavieiras, Braz. (kä-ná-vē-ā'räs)	124	15.40S	38.49W
Canberra, Austl. (kăn'bĕr-å)	196	35.21S	149.10E
Canby, Mn., U.S. (kăn'bĭ)	96	44.43N	96.15W

ăt; finǎl; rāte; senåte; ärm; åsk; sofå; fâre; ch-choose; dh-as th in other; bē; ēvent; bĕt; recĕnt; cratĕr; g-gō; gh-guttural g; bĭt; ĭ-short neutral; rīde; K-guttural k as ch in German ich;

PLACE (Pronunciation)	PAGE	Lat. °'	Long. °'
Canchyuaya, Cerros de, mts., Peru (sĕ′r-rôs-dĕ-kän-chōō-à′īä)	124	7.30S	74.30W
Cancuc, Mex. (kän-kōōk)	112	16.58N	92.17W
Cancún, Mex.	114a	21.25N	86.50W
Candelaria, Cuba (kän-dĕ-lä′ryä)	116	22.45N	82.55W
Candelaria, Phil. (kän-då-lä′rê-ä)	189a	15.39N	119.55E
Candelaria, r., Mex. (kän-dĕ-lä-ryä)	112	18.25N	91.21W
Candeleda, Spain (kän-dhå-lä′dhä)	152	40.09N	5.18W
Candia, see Iráklion, Grc.	136	35.20N	25.10E
Candle, Ak., U.S. (kăn′d'l)	89	65.00N	162.04W
Cando, N.D., U.S. (kăn′dō)	96	48.27N	99.13W
Candon, Phil. (kän-dōn′)	189a	17.13N	120.26E
Canelones, Ur. (kä-nĕ-lô-nĕs)	123c	34.32S	56.19W
Canelones, dept., Ur.	123c	34.34S	56.15W
Cañete, Peru (kän-yā′tå)	124	13.06S	76.17W
Caney, Cuba (kä-nā′) (kā′nĭ)	116	20.05N	75.45W
Caney, Ks., U.S. (kā′nĭ)	104	37.00N	95.57W
Caney Fork, r., Tn., U.S.	108	36.10N	85.50W
Cangamba, Ang.	206	13.40S	19.54E
Cangas, Spain (kän′gäs)	152	42.15N	8.43W
Cangas de Narcea, Spain (kä′n-gäs-dĕ-när-sĕ-ä)	152	43.08N	6.36W
Cangzhou, China (tsäŋ-jō)	184	38.21N	116.53E
Caniapiscau, l., Can.	78	54.10N	71.13E
Caniapiscau, r., Can.	78	57.00N	68.45W
Canicatti, Italy (kä-nê-kät′tē)	154	37.18N	13.58E
Canillas, neigh., Spain	234b	40.28N	3.38W
Canillejas, neigh., Spain	234b	40.27N	3.37W
Cañitas, Mex. (kän-yē′täs)	112	23.38N	102.44W
Cannell, Can.	77g	53.35N	113.38W
Cannelton, In., U.S. (kăn′ĕl-tŭn)	92	37.55N	86.45W
Cannes, Fr. (kån)	140	43.34N	7.05E
Canning, Can. (kăn′ĭng)	86	45.09N	64.25W
Cannock, Eng., U.K. (kăn′ŭk)	138a	52.41N	2.02W
Cannock Chase, reg., Eng., U.K. (kăn′ŭk chās)	138a	52.43N	1.54W
Cannon, r., Mn., U.S. (kăn′ŭn)	96	44.18N	93.24W
Cannonball, r., N.D., U.S. (kăn′ŭn-bâl)	96	46.17N	101.35W
Caño, Isla de, i., C.R. (ĕ′s-lä-dĕ-kä′nō)	114	8.38N	84.00W
Canoga Park, Ca., U.S. (kä-nō′gȧ)	101a	34.07N	118.36W
Canoncito Indian Reservation, I.R., N.M., U.S.	102	35.00N	107.05W
Canon City, Co., U.S. (kăn′yŭn)	104	38.27N	105.16W
Canonsburg, Pa., U.S. (kăn′ŭnz-bûrg)	95e	40.16N	80.11W
Canoochee, r., Ga., U.S. (kȧ-nōō′chê)	108	32.25N	82.11W
Canora, Can. (kȧ-nōr′ȧ)	78	51.37N	102.26W
Canosa, Italy (kä-nō′sä)	154	41.14N	16.03E
Canouan, i., St. Vin.	115b	12.44N	61.10W
Cansahcab, Mex.	114a	21.11N	89.05W
Canso, Can. (kăn′sō)	86	45.20N	61.00W
Canso, Cape, c., Can.	86	45.21N	60.46W
Canso, Strait of, strt., Can.	86	45.37N	61.25W
Cantabrica, Cordillera, mts., Spain	136	43.05N	6.05W
Cantagalo, Braz. (kän-tä-gá′lo)	123a	21.59S	42.22W
Cantanhede, Port. (kän-tän-yā′dȧ)	152	40.22N	8.35W
Canterbury, Austl.	239a	33.55S	151.07E
Canterbury, Austl.	239b	37.49S	145.05E
Canterbury, Eng., U.K. (kăn′tĕr-bĕr-ê)	144	51.17N	1.06E
Canterbury Bight, bt., N.Z.	197a	44.15S	172.08E
Canterbury Woods, Va., U.S.	225d	38.49N	77.15W
Cantiles, Cayo, i., Cuba (ky-ō-kän-tē′lås)	116	21.40N	82.00W
Canto do Pontes, Braz.	230c	22.58S	43.04W
Canton, Ga., U.S.	108	34.13N	84.29W
Canton, Il., U.S.	104	40.34N	90.02W
Canton, Ma., U.S.	87a	42.09N	71.09W
Canton, Ms., U.S.	108	32.36N	90.01W
Canton, Mo., U.S.	104	40.08N	91.33W
Canton, N.C., U.S.	108	35.32N	82.50W
Canton, Oh., U.S.	90	40.50N	81.25W
Canton, Pa., U.S.	92	41.50N	76.45W
Canton, S.D., U.S.	96	43.17N	96.37W
Canton, see Guangzhou, China	180	23.07N	113.15E
Cantu, Italy (kän-tōō′)	154	45.43N	9.09E
Cañuelas, Arg. (kä-nyōĕ′-läs)	123c	35.03S	58.45W
Canyon, Ca., U.S.	227b	37.49N	122.09W
Canyon, Tx., U.S. (kăn′yŭn)	104	34.59N	101.57W
Canyon, r., Wa., U.S.	100a	48.09N	121.48W
Canyon De Chelly National Monument, rec., Az., U.S.	102	36.14N	110.00W
Canyon Ferry Lake, res., Mt., U.S.	98	46.33N	111.37W
Canyonlands National Park, Ut., U.S.	102	38.10N	110.00W
Caoxian, China (tsou shyĕn)	182	34.48N	115.33E
Capalonga, Phil. (kä-pä-lôŋ′gä)	189a	14.20N	122.30E
Capannori, Italy (kä-pän′nô-rē)	154	43.50N	10.30E
Capão Redondo, neigh., Braz.	230d	23.40S	46.46W
Caparica, Port.	234d	38.40N	9.12W
Capaya, r., Ven. (kä-pä-ĭä)	125b	10.28N	66.15W
Cap-Chat, Can. (kȧp-shä′)	78	48.02N	65.20W
Cap-de-la-Madeleine, Can. (kȧp dē lȧ mȧ-d'lĕn′)	84	46.23N	72.30W
Cape, prov., S. Afr. (kāp)	206	31.50S	21.15E
Cape Breton, i., Can. (kāp brĕt′ŭn)	86	45.48N	59.50W
Cape Breton Highlands National Park, Can.	78	46.45N	60.45W
Cape Charles, Va., U.S. (kāp chärlz)	108	37.13N	76.02W
Cape Coast, Ghana	204	5.05N	1.15W
Cape Fear, r., N.C., U.S. (kāp fēr)	90	35.00N	79.00W
Cape Flats, pl., S. Afr. (kāp flăts)	206a	34.01S	18.37E
Cape Girardeau, Mo., U.S. (jē-rär-dō′)	90	37.17N	89.32W
Cape Krusenstern National Monument, rec., Ak., U.S.	89	67.30N	163.40W
Cape May, N.J., U.S. (kāp mā)	92	38.55N	74.50W
Cape May Court House, N.J., U.S.	92	39.05N	75.00W
Capenhurst, Eng., U.K.	233a	53.15N	2.57W
Cape Romanzof, Ak., U.S. (rō′ män zôf)	89	61.50N	165.45W
Capesterre, Guad.	115b	16.02N	61.37W
Cape Tormentine, Can.	86	46.08N	63.47W
Cape Town, S. Afr. (kāp toun)	206	33.48S	18.28E
Cape Verde, nation, Afr.	204b	15.48N	26.02W
Cape York Peninsula, pen., Austl. (kāp yôrk)	196	12.30S	142.35E
Cap-Haïtien, Haiti (kȧp ȧ-ē-syăn′)	110	19.45N	72.15W
Capilla de Señor, Arg. (kä-pēl′yä dā sän-yôr′)	123c	34.18S	59.07W
Capitachouane, r., Can.	84	47.50N	76.45W
Capitol Heights, Md., U.S.	225d	38.53N	76.55W
Capitol Reef National Park, Ut., U.S. (kăp′ĭ-tŏl)	102	38.15N	111.10W
Capitol View, Md., U.S.	225d	39.01N	77.04W
Capivari, Braz. (kä-pē-vȧ′rê)	123a	22.59S	47.29W
Capivari, r., Braz.	126b	22.39S	43.19W
Capoompeta, mtn., Austl. (kȧ-pōōm-pē′tȧ)	196	29.15S	152.12E
Capraia, i., Italy (kä-prä′yä)	142	43.02N	9.51E
Caprara Point, c., Italy (kä-prä′rä)	154	41.08N	8.20E
Capreol, Can.	84	46.43N	80.56W
Caprera, i., Italy (kä-prā′rä)	154	41.12N	9.28E
Capri, Italy	153c	40.18N	14.16E
Capri, Isola di, i., Italy (ē′-sō-lä-dē-kä′prē)	153c	40.19N	14.10E
Capricorn Channel, strt., Austl. (kăp′rĭ-kôrn)	196	22.27S	151.24E
Caprivi Strip, hist. reg., Nmb.	206	18.00S	22.00E
Cap-Rouge, Can. (kȧp rōōzh′)	77b	46.45N	71.21W
Cap-Saint Ignace, Can. (kĭp săn-tē-nyȧs′)	77b	47.02N	70.27W
Captain Cook Bridge, pt. of i., Austl.	239a	34.00S	151.08E
Capua, Italy (kä′pwä)	142	41.07N	14.14E
Capuáva, Braz.	230d	23.39S	46.29W
Capulhuac, Mex. (kä-pōl-hwäk′)	112	19.33N	99.43W
Capulin Mountain National Monument, rec., N.M., U.S. (kȧ-pū′lĭn)	104	36.15N	103.58W
Capultitlán, Mex. (kä-pōō′l-tē-tlà′n)	113a	19.15N	99.40W
Caputh, Ger.	234a	52.21N	13.00E
Caquetá (Japurá), r., S.A.	124	0.20S	73.00W
Caraballeda, Ven.	230a	10.37N	66.50W
Carabaña, Spain (kä-rä-bän′yä)	153a	40.16N	3.15W
Carabanchel Alto, neigh., Spain	234b	40.22N	3.45W
Carabanchel Bajo, neigh., Spain	234b	40.23N	3.47W
Carabelle, Fl., U.S. (kăr′ȧ-bĕl)	108	29.50N	84.40W
Carabobo, dept., Ven. (kä-rä-bô′-bô)	125b	10.07N	68.06W
Caracal, Rom. (kȧ-rȧ-kȧl′)	154	44.06N	24.22E
Caracas, Ven. (kä-rä′käs)	124	10.30N	66.58W
Carácuaro de Morelos, Mex. (kä-rä′kwä-rō-dĕ-mō-rĕ-lōs)	112	18.44N	101.04W
Caraguatatuba, Braz. (kä-rä-gwä-tȧ-tōō′bä)	123a	23.37S	45.26W
Carajás, Serra dos, mts., Braz. (sĕ′r-rä-dôs-kä-rä-zhá′s)	124	5.58S	51.45W
Caramanta, Cerro, mtn., Col. (sĕ′r-rô-kä-rä-mà′n-tä)	124a	5.29N	76.01W
Carangola, Braz. (kä-rán′gō′lä)	123a	20.46S	42.02W
Carapicuíba, Braz.	230d	23.31S	46.50W
Caraquet, Can. (kä-rȧ-kĕt′)	78	47.48N	64.57W
Carata, Laguna, l., Nic. (lä-gò′nä-kä-rä′tä)	114	13.59N	83.41W
Caratasca, Laguna, l., Hond. (lä-gò′nä-kä-rä-täs′kä)	114	15.20N	83.45W
Caravaca, Spain (kä-rä-vä′kä)	152	38.05N	1.51W
Caravelas, Braz. (kȧ-rä-vĕl′äzh)	124	17.46S	39.06W
Carayaca, Ven. (kȧ-rä-ĭá′kä)	125b	10.32N	67.07W
Caràzinho, Braz. (kä-rä′zē-nyō)	126	28.22S	52.33W
Carballino, Spain (kär-bäl-yē′nō)	142	42.26N	8.04W
Carballo, Spain (kär-bäl′yō)	152	43.13N	8.40W
Carbet, Pitons du, mtn., Mart.	115b	14.40N	61.05W
Carbon, r., Wa., U.S. (kär′bŏn)	100a	47.06N	122.08W
Carbonado, Wa., U.S. (kär-bō-nä′dō)	100a	47.05N	122.03W
Carbonara, Cape, c., Italy (kär-bō-nä′rä)	142	39.08N	9.33E
Carbondale, Can. (kär′bŏn-dāl)	77g	53.45N	113.32W
Carbondale, Il., U.S.	92	37.42N	89.12W
Carbondale, Pa., U.S.	92	41.35N	75.30W
Carbonear, Can. (kär-bō-nēr′)	86	47.45N	53.14W
Carbon Hill, Al., U.S. (kär′bŏn hĭl)	108	33.53N	87.34W
Carcagente, Spain (kär-kä-hĕn′tä)	152	39.09N	0.29W
Carcans, Étang de, l., Fr. (ā-tän-dĕ-kär-kän)	150	45.12N	1.00W
Carcassonne, Fr. (kȧr-kȧ-sôn′)	140	43.12N	2.23E
Carcross, Can. (kär′krŏs)	78	60.18N	134.54W
Cárdenas, Cuba (kär′då-näs)	110	23.00N	81.10W
Cárdenas, Mex. (ká′r-dĕ-näs)	112	17.59N	93.23W
Cárdenas, Mex.	112	22.01N	99.38W
Cárdenas, Bahía de, b., Cuba (bä-ē′ä-dĕ-kär′dā-näs)	116	23.10N	81.10W
Cardiff, Can. (kär′dĭf)	77g	53.46N	113.36W
Cardiff, Wales, U.K.	140	51.30N	3.18W
Cardigan, Wales, U.K. (kär′dĭ-găn)	140	52.05N	4.40W
Cardigan Bay, b., Wales, U.K.	140	52.35N	4.40W
Cardston, Can. (kärds′tŭn)	78	49.12N	113.18W
Carei, Rom. (kä-rĕ′)	148	47.42N	22.28E
Carentan, Fr. (kä-rôn-tän′)	150	49.19N	1.14W
Carey, Oh., U.S. (kā′rê)	92	40.55N	83.25W
Carey, l., Austl. (kâr′ē)	196	29.20S	123.35E
Carhaix-Plouguer, Fr. (kär-ĕ′)	150	48.17N	3.37W
Caribbean Sea, sea (kăr-ĭ-bē′ăn)	110	14.30N	75.30W
Caribe, Arroyo, r., Mex. (är-ro′ï-kä-rē′bĕ)	112	18.18N	90.38W
Cariboo Mountains, mts., Can. (kă′rĭ-bōō)	78	53.00N	121.00W
Caribou, Me., U.S.	86	46.51N	68.01W
Caribou, i., Can.	84	47.22N	85.42W
Caribou Lake, l., Mn., U.S.	101h	46.54N	92.16W
Caribou Mountains, mts., Can.	78	59.20N	115.30W
Caringbah, Austl.	239a	34.03S	151.08E
Carinhanha, Braz. (kä-rĭ-nyän′yä)	124	14.14S	43.44W
Carini, Italy (kä-rē′nē)	154	38.09N	13.10E
Carinthia, see Kärnten, prov., Aus.	148	46.55N	13.42E
Carleton Place, Can. (kärl′tŭn)	84	45.15N	76.10W
Carletonville, S. Afr.	212d	26.20S	27.23E
Carlingford, Austl.	239a	33.47S	151.03E
Carlinville, Il., U.S. (kär′lĭn-vĭl)	104	39.16N	89.52W
Carlisle, Eng., U.K. (kär-līl′)	136	54.54N	3.03W
Carlisle, Ky., U.S.	92	38.20N	84.00W
Carlisle, Pa., U.S.	92	40.10N	77.15W
Carloforte, Italy (kär′lō-fôr-tȧ)	154	39.11N	8.28E
Carlos Casares, Arg. (kär-lôs-kä-sá′rĕs)	126	35.38S	61.17W
Carlow, Ire. (kär′lō)	144	52.50N	7.00W
Carlsbad, N.M., U.S. (kärlz′băd)	106	32.24N	104.12W
Carlsbad Caverns National Park, rec., N.M., U.S.	106	32.08N	104.30W
Carlstadt, N.J., U.S.	224	40.50N	74.06W
Carlton, Eng., U.K. (kärl′tŭn)	138a	52.58N	1.05W
Carlton, Mn., U.S.	101h	46.40N	92.26W
Carlton Center, Mi., U.S. (kärl′tŭn sĕn′tĕr)	92	42.45N	85.20W
Carlyle, Il., U.S. (kärlīl′)	104	38.37N	89.23W
Carmagnolo, Italy (kär-mä-nyô′lä)	154	44.52N	7.48E
Carman, Can. (kär′mȧn)	78	49.32N	98.00W
Carmarthen, Wales, U.K. (kär-mär′thĕn)	144	51.50N	4.20W
Carmaux, Fr. (kȧr-mō′)	150	44.05N	2.09E
Carmel, N.Y., U.S. (kär′mĕl)	94a	41.25N	73.42W
Carmelo, Ur. (kär-mĕ′lo)	123c	33.59S	58.15W
Carmen, Isla del, i., Mex. (ē′s-lä-dĕl-kȧ′r-mĕn)	112	18.43N	91.40W
Carmen, Laguna del, l., Mex. (lä-gò′nä-dĕl-kȧ′r-mĕn)	112	18.15N	93.26W
Carmen de Areco, Arg. (kär′mĕn′ dā ä-rā′kō)	123c	34.21S	59.50W
Carmen de Patagones, Arg. (kȧ′r-mĕn-dĕ-pä-tä-gô′nĕs)	126	41.00S	63.00W
Carmi, Il., U.S. (kär′mī)	92	38.05N	88.10W
Carmo, Braz. (kȧ′r-mô)	123a	21.57S	42.45W
Carmo do Rio Clara, Braz. (kȧ′r-mô-dô-rē′ô-klä′rä)	123a	20.57S	46.04W
Carmona, Spain	152	37.28N	5.38W
Carnarvon, Austl. (kär-när′vŭn)	196	24.45S	113.45E
Carnarvon, S. Afr.	206	31.00S	22.15E
Carnation, Wa., U.S. (kär-nā′shŭn)	100a	47.39N	121.55W
Carnaxide, Port. (kär-nä-shē′dĕ)	153b	38.44N	9.15W
Carndonagh, Ire. (kärn-dō-nä′)	144	55.15N	7.15W
Carnegie, Ok., U.S. (kär-nĕg′ĭ)	104	35.06N	98.38W
Carnegie, Pa., U.S.	95e	40.24N	80.06W
Carnegie Institute, pt. of i., Pa., U.S.	226b	40.27N	79.57W
Carnetin, Fr.	233c	48.54N	2.42E
Carneys Point, N.J., U.S. (kär′nēs)	92	39.45N	75.25W
Carnic Alps, mts., Eur.	140	46.43N	12.38E
Carnide, neigh., Port.	234d	38.46N	9.11W
Carnot, Alg. (kär nō′)	152	36.15N	1.40E
Carnot, Cen. Afr. Rep.	204	5.00N	15.52E
Carnsore Point, c., Ire. (kärn′sôr)	144	52.10N	6.16W
Caro, Mi., U.S. (kâ′rō)	92	43.30N	83.25W
Carolina, Braz. (kä-rô-lē′nä)	124	7.26S	47.16W
Carolina, S. Afr. (kăr-ô-lī′nȧ)	206	26.07S	30.09E
Carolina, l., Mex. (kä-rō-lē′nä)	114a	18.41N	89.40W
Caroline Islands, is., Oc.	4	8.00N	140.00E
Caroni, r., Ven. (kä-rō′nē)	124	5.49N	62.57W
Carora, Ven. (kä-rō′rä)	124	10.09N	70.12W
Carpathians, mts., Eur. (kär-pā′thĭ-ăn)	136	49.23N	20.14E
Carpaţii Meridionali (Transylvanian Alps), mts., Rom.	136	45.30N	23.30E
Carpentaria, Gulf of, b., Austl. (kär-pĕn-târ′ĭ-ȧ)	196	14.45S	138.50E
Carpentras, Fr. (kär-pän-träs′)	150	44.04N	5.01E
Carpi, Italy	154	44.48N	10.54E
Carrara, Italy (kä-rä′rä)	142	44.05N	10.05E
Carrauntoohil, Ire. (kä-răn-tōō′ĭl)	144	52.01N	9.48W
Carretas, Punta, c., Peru (pōō′n-tä-kär-rĕ′tĕ′rȧs)	124	14.15S	76.25W
Carriacou, i., Gren.	115b	12.28N	61.20W
Carrick-on-Sur, Ire. (kăr′-ĭk)	144	52.20N	7.35W
Carrier, Can. (kăr′ĭ-ĕr)	77b	46.43N	71.05W
Carriere, Ms., U.S. (kȧ-rēr′)	108	30.37N	89.37W
Carrières-sous-Bois, Fr.	233c	48.57N	2.07E
Carrières-sous-Poissy, Fr.	233c	48.57N	2.03E
Carrières-sur-Seine, Fr.	233c	48.55N	2.11E
Carriers Mills, Il., U.S. (kăr′ĭ-ĕrs)	92	37.40N	88.40W
Carrington, Eng., U.K.	233b	53.26N	2.24W
Carrington, N.D., U.S. (kăr′ĭng-tŭn)	96	47.26N	99.06W
Carr Inlet, Wa., U.S. (kăr ĭn′lĕt)	100a	47.20N	122.42W
Carrion Crow Harbor, b., Bah. (kăr′ĭŭn krō)	116	26.35N	77.55W
Carrión de los Condes, Spain (kär-rê-ōn′ dā lōs kōn′dås)	152	42.20N	4.35W
Carrizo Creek, r., N.M., U.S. (kär-rē′zō)	104	36.22N	103.39W
Carrizo Springs, Tx., U.S.	106	28.32N	99.51W
Carrizozo, N.M., U.S. (kär-rê-zō′zō)	102	33.40N	105.55W
Carroll, Ia., U.S. (kăr′ŭl)	96	42.03N	94.51W
Carrollton, Ga., U.S. (kăr-ŭl-tŭn)	108	33.35N	85.05W
Carrollton, Il., U.S.	104	39.18N	90.22W
Carrollton, Ky., U.S.	92	38.45N	85.15W
Carrollton, Mi., U.S.	92	43.30N	83.55W
Carrollton, Mo., U.S.	104	39.21N	93.29W
Carrollton, Oh., U.S.	92	40.35N	81.10W
Carrollton, Tx., U.S.	101c	32.58N	96.53W
Carrols, Wa., U.S. (kăr′ŭlz)	100c	46.05N	122.51W
Carrot, r., Can.	82	53.12N	103.50W
Carry-le-Rouet, Fr. (kä-rē′lĕ-rō-ā′)	150a	43.20N	5.10E
Carsamba, Tur. (chär-shäm′bä)	142	41.05N	36.40E
Carshalton, neigh., Eng., U.K.	231	51.22N	0.10W
Carson, Ca., U.S.	228	33.50N	118.16W
Carson, r., Nv., U.S. (kär′sŭn)	102	39.15N	119.25W
Carson City, Nv., U.S.	90	39.10N	119.45W
Carsondale, Md., U.S.	225d	38.57N	76.50W

ng-sing; ŋ-baŋk; n-nasalized n; nŏd; cŏmmit; ōld; ôbey; ôrder; oi-boil; fōōd; ò-as oo in foot; ou-out; s-soft; sh-dish; th-thin; pūre; ûnite; ûrn; stŭd; circŭs; ü-as in French tu; ′-indeterminate vowel.

PLACE (Pronunciation)	PAGE	Lat. °′	Long. °′
Carson Sink, Nv., U.S.	102	39.51N	118.25W
Cartagena, Col. (kär-tä-hä'nä)	124	10.30N	75.40W
Cartagena, Spain (kär-tä-ĸĕ'nä)	136	37.46N	1.00W
Cartago, Col. (kär-tä'gō)	124a	4.44N	75.54W
Cartago, C.R.	110	9.52N	83.56W
Cartaxo, Port. (kär-tä'shō)	152	39.10N	8.48W
Carteret, N.J., U.S. (kär'tē-ret)	94a	40.35N	74.13W
Cartersville, Ga., U.S. (kär'tērs-vĭl)	108	34.09N	84.47W
Carthage, Tun.	204	37.04N	10.18E
Carthage, Il., U.S. (kär'thåj)	104	40.27N	91.09W
Carthage, Mo., U.S.	104	37.10N	94.18W
Carthage, N.Y., U.S.	92	44.00N	75.45W
Carthage, N.C., U.S.	108	35.22N	79.25W
Carthage, Tx., U.S.	106	32.09N	94.20W
Carthcart, S. Afr. (cärth-cȧ't)	207c	32.18S	27.11E
Cartwright, Can. (kärt'rīt)	78	53.36N	57.00W
Caruaru, Braz. (kä-rò-å-rōō')	124	8.19S	35.52W
Carúpano, Ven. (kä-rōō'pä-nō)	124	10.45N	63.21W
Caruthersville, Mo., U.S. (kȧ-rŭdh'ērz-vĭl)	104	36.09N	89.41W
Carver, Or., U.S. (kärv'ēr)	100c	45.24N	122.30W
Carvoeiro, Cabo, c., Port. (kå'bō-kär-vō-ĕ'y-rō)	152	39.22N	9.24W
Cary, Il., U.S. (kă'rē)	95a	42.13N	88.14W
Casablanca, Chile (kä-sä-bläŋ'kä)	123b	33.19S	71.24W
Casablanca, Mor.	204	33.32N	7.41W
Casa Branca, Braz. (kå'sä-brå'ɴ-kä)	123a	21.47S	47.04W
Casa Grande, Az., U.S. (kä'sä grän'dä)	102	32.50N	111.45W
Casa Grande National Monument, rec., Az., U.S.	102	33.00N	111.33W
Casale Monferrato, Italy (kä-sä'lä)	154	45.08N	8.26E
Casalmaggiore, Italy (kä-säl-mäd-jō'rā)	154	45.00N	10.24E
Casa Loma, pt. of i., Can.	223c	43.41N	79.25W
Casamance, r., Sen. (kä-sä-mäɴs')	204	12.30N	15.00W
Cascade Mountains, mts., N.A.	80	49.10N	121.00W
Cascade Point, c., N.Z. (kăs-kād')	197a	43.59S	168.23E
Cascade Range, mts., N.A.	90	42.50N	122.20W
Cascade Tunnel, trans., Wa., U.S.	98	47.41N	120.53W
Cascais, Port. (käs-kȧ-ēzh)	152	38.42N	9.25W
Case Inlet, Wa., U.S. (kās)	100a	47.22N	122.47W
Caseros, Arg. (kä-sā'rōs)	126a	34.35S	58.34W
Caserta, Italy (kä-zĕr'tä)	154	41.04N	14.21E
Casey, Il., U.S. (kā'sĭ)	92	39.20N	88.00W
Caseyr, c., Som.	212a	11.55N	51.30E
Cashmere, Wa., U.S. (kăsh'mĭr)	98	47.30N	120.28W
Casiguran, Phil. (käs-sē-gōō'rän)	189a	16.15N	122.10E
Casiguran Sound, strt., Phil.	189a	16.02N	121.51E
Casilda, Arg. (kä-sē'l-dä)	126	33.02S	61.11W
Casilda, Cuba	116	21.50N	80.00W
Casimiro de Abreu, Braz. (kä'sē-mē'ro-dĕ-å-brĕ'ōō)	123a	22.30S	42.11W
Casino, Austl. (kȧ-sē'nō)	198	28.35S	153.10E
Casiquiare, r., Ven. (kä-sē-kyä'rä)	124	2.11N	66.15W
Caspe, Spain (käs'på)	152	41.18N	0.02W
Casper, Wy., U.S. (kăs'pēr)	90	42.51N	106.18W
Caspian Depression, depr. (kăs'pĭ-ȧn)	158	47.40N	52.35E
Caspian Sea, sea	158	40.00N	52.00E
Cass, W.V., U.S. (kăs)	92	38.25N	79.55W
Cass, l., Mn., U.S.	96	47.23N	94.28W
Cassai (Kasai), r., Afr. (kä-sä'ē)	206	11.30S	21.00E
Cass City, Mi., U.S. (kăs)	92	43.35N	83.10W
Casselman, Can. (kăs''l-mȧn)	77c	45.18N	75.05W
Casselton, N.D., U.S. (kăs''l-tŭn)	96	46.53N	97.14W
Cássia, Braz. (kå'syä)	123a	20.36S	46.53W
Cassin, Tx., U.S. (kăs'ĭn)	101d	29.16N	98.29W
Cassinga, Ang.	206	15.05S	16.15E
Cassino, Italy (käs-sē'nō)	142	41.30N	13.50E
Cass Lake, Mn., U.S. (kăs)	96	47.23N	94.37W
Cassopolis, Mi., U.S. (kă-sŏ'pō-lĭs)	92	41.55N	86.00W
Cassville, Mo., U.S. (kăs'vĭl)	104	36.41N	93.52W
Castanheira de Pêra, Port. (käs-tän-yā'rä-dĕ-pĕ'rä)	152	40.00N	8.07W
Castellammare di Stabia, Italy	153c	40.26N	14.29E
Castellbisbal, Spain	234e	41.29N	1.59E
Castelli, Arg. (kås-tĕ'zhē)	123c	36.07S	57.48W
Castellón de la Plana, Spain (käs-tĕl-yō'n-dĕ-lä-plä'nä)	142	39.59N	0.05W
Castelnaudary, Fr. (kås'tĕl-nō-dá-rē')	150	43.20N	1.57E
Castelo, Braz. (käs-tĕ'lô)	123a	20.37S	41.13W
Castelo Branco, Port. (käs-tä'lò bräŋ'kò)	142	39.48N	7.37W
Castelo de Vide, Port. (käs-tä'lò dĭ vē'dĭ)	152	39.25N	7.25W
Castelsarrasin, Fr. (kås'tĕl-sà-rà-zăɴ')	150	44.03N	1.05E
Castelvetrano, Italy (käs'tĕl-vē-trä'nō)	154	37.43N	12.50E
Castilla, Peru (käs-tē'l-yä)	124	5.18S	80.40W
Castilla La Nueva, hist. reg., Spain (käs-tē'lyä lä nwä'vä)	152	39.15N	3.55W
Castilla La Vieja, hist. reg., Spain (käs-tē'lyä lä vyā'hä)	152	40.48N	4.24W
Castillo de San Marcos National Monument, rec., Fl., U.S. (käs-tē'lyä de-sän mär-kōs)	108	29.55N	81.25W
Castle, i., Bah. (kås''l)	116	22.05N	74.20W
Castlebar, Ire. (kås''l-bär)	144	53.55N	9.15W
Castlecrag, Austl.	239a	33.48S	151.13E
Castle Dale, Ut., U.S. (kås'l dāl)	102	39.15N	111.00W
Castle Donington, Eng., U.K. (dŏn'ĭng-tŭn)	138a	52.50N	1.21W
Castleford, Eng., U.K. (kås'l-fērd)	138a	53.43N	1.21W
Castlegar, Can. (kås''l-gär)	80	49.19N	117.40W
Castle Hill, Austl.	239a	33.44S	151.00E
Castlemaine, Austl. (kås''l-mān)	198	37.05S	144.10E
Castle Peak, mtn., Co., U.S.	102	39.00N	106.50W
Castle Rock, Wa., U.S. (kås''l-rŏk)	98	46.17N	122.53W
Castle Rock Flowage, res., Wi., U.S.	96	44.03N	89.48W
Castle Shannon, Pa., U.S. (shăn'ŭn)	95e	40.22N	80.02W
Castleton, Eng., U.K.	233b	53.35N	2.11W

PLACE (Pronunciation)	PAGE	Lat. °′	Long. °′
Castleton, In., U.S. (kås''l-tŏn)	95g	39.54N	86.03W
Castor, r., Can. (kăs'tôr)	77c	45.16N	75.14W
Castor, r., Mo., U.S.	104	36.59N	89.53W
Castres, Fr. (kås'tr')	150	43.36N	2.13E
Castries, St. Luc. (kås-trē')	115b	14.01N	61.00W
Castro, Braz. (käs'trò)	124	24.56S	50.00W
Castro, Chile (käs'tro)	126	42.27S	73.48W
Castro Daire, Port. (käs'trò dīr'ĭ)	152	40.56N	7.57W
Castro del Río, Spain (käs-trò-dĕl rē'ō)	152	37.42N	4.28W
Castrop Rauxel, Ger. (käs'trōp rou'ksĕl)	151c	51.33N	7.19E
Castro Urdiales, Spain (käs'trō òr-dyā'lās)	142	43.23N	3.11W
Castro Valley, Ca., U.S.	100b	37.42N	122.05W
Castro Verde, Port. (käs-trō vĕr'dē)	152	37.43N	8.05W
Castrovillari, Italy (käs'trō-vēl-lyä'rē)	154	39.48N	16.11E
Castuera, Spain (käs-tò-ā'rä)	152	38.43N	5.33W
Casula, Moz.	210	15.25S	33.40E
Cat, i., Bah.	116	24.30N	75.30W
Catacamas, Hond. (kä-tä-kä'mäs)	114	14.52N	85.55W
Cataguases, Braz. (kä-tä-gwá'sĕs)	123a	21.23S	42.42W
Catahoula, l., La., U.S. (kăt-ȧ-hō'lȧ)	106	31.35N	92.20W
Catalão, Braz. (kä-tä-louɴ')	124	18.09S	47.42W
Catalina, i., Dom. Rep. (kä-tä-lē'nä)	116	18.20N	69.00W
Cataluña, hist. reg., Spain	152	41.23N	0.50E
Cataluña, Museo de Arte de, bldg., Spain	234e	41.23N	2.09E
Catamarca, Arg. (kä-tä-mä'r-kä)	126	28.29S	65.45W
Catamarca, prov., Arg. (kä-tä-mär'kä)	126	27.15S	67.15W
Catanaun, Phil. (kä-tä-nä'wän)	189a	13.36N	122.20E
Catanduanes Island, i., Phil. (kä-tän-dwä'nĕs)	188	13.55N	125.00E
Catanduva, Braz. (kä-tän-dōō'vä)	124	21.12S	48.47W
Catania, Italy (kä-tä'nyä)	136	37.30N	15.09E
Catania, Golfo di, b., Italy (gòl-fō-dē-kä-tä'nyä)	154	37.24N	15.28E
Catanzaro, Italy (kä-tän-dzä'rō)	142	38.53N	16.34E
Catarroja, Spain (kä-tär-rō'hä)	152	39.24N	0.25W
Catawba, r., N.C., U.S. (kȧ-tô'bȧ)	108	35.25N	80.55W
Catbalogan, Phil. (kät-bä-lō'gän)	188	11.45N	124.52E
Catemaco, Mex. (kä-tä-mä'kō)	112	18.26N	95.06W
Catemaco, Lago, l., Mex. (lä'gô-kä-tä-mä'kō)	112	18.23N	95.04W
Caterham, Eng., U.K. (kā'tēr-ŭm)	138b	51.16N	0.04W
Catete, Ang. (kä-tĕ'tĕ)	206	9.06S	13.43E
Catete, neigh., Braz.	230c	22.55S	43.10W
Catford, neigh., Eng., U.K.	231	51.27N	0.01W
Cathedral Mountain, mtn., Tx., U.S. (kȧ-thē'drȧl)	106	30.09N	103.46W
Cathedral Peak, mtn., Afr. (kȧ-thē'drȧl)	207c	28.53S	29.04E
Catherine, Lake, l., Ar., U.S. (kă-thēr-ĭn)	104	34.26N	92.47W
Cathkin Peak, mtn., Afr. (kăth'kĭn)	206	29.08S	29.22E
Cathlamet, Wa., U.S. (kăth-lăm'ĕt)	100c	46.12N	123.22W
Catia, neigh., Ven.	230a	10.31N	66.57W
Catlettsburg, Ky., U.S. (kăt'lĕts-bûrg)	92	38.20N	82.35W
Catoche, Cabo, c., Mex. (kä-tô'chĕ)	110	21.30N	87.15W
Catonsville, Md., U.S. (kā'tŭnz-vĭl)	94e	39.16N	76.45W
Catorce, Mex. (kä-tôr'sā)	112	23.41N	100.51W
Catskill, N.Y., U.S. (kăts'kĭl)	92	42.15N	73.50W
Catskill Mountains, mts., N.Y., U.S.	90	42.20N	74.35W
Cattaraugus Indian Reservation, I.R., N.Y., U.S. (kăt'tȧ-rȧ-gŭs)	92	42.30N	79.05W
Catu, Braz. (kä-tōō)	124	12.26S	38.12W
Catuala, Ang.	210	16.29S	19.03E
Catumbela, r., Ang. (kä'tŏm-bĕl'ä)	210	12.40S	14.10E
Cauayan, Phil. (kou-ä'yän)	189a	16.56N	121.46E
Cauca, r., Col. (kou'kä)	124	7.30N	75.26W
Caucagua, Ven. (käò-kà'gwä)	125b	10.17N	66.22W
Caucasus, mts.	158	43.20N	42.00E
Cauchon Lake, l., Can. (kô-shōn')	82	55.25N	96.30W
Caughnawaga, Can.	77a	45.24N	73.41W
Caulfield, Austl.	195a	37.53S	145.03E
Caulonia, Italy (kou-lō'nyä)	154	38.24N	16.22E
Cauquenes, Chile (kou-kā'nās)	126	35.54S	72.14W
Caura, r., Ven. (kou'rä)	124	6.48N	64.40W
Causapscal, Can.	86	48.22N	67.14W
Caution, Cape, c., Can. (kô'shŭn)	80	51.10N	127.47W
Cauto, r., Cuba (kou'tō)	116	20.33N	76.20W
Cauvery, r., India	174	12.00N	77.00E
Cava, Braz. (kà'vä)	126b	22.41S	43.26W
Cava de' Tirreni, Italy (kä'vä-dĕ-tēr-rĕ'nē)	153c	40.27N	14.43E
Cávado, r., Port. (kä-vä'dō)	152	41.43N	8.08W
Cavalcante, Braz. (kä-väl-kän'tä)	124	13.45S	47.33W
Cavalier, N.D., U.S. (kăv-ȧ-lēr')	96	48.45N	97.39W
Cavally, r., Afr.	208	4.40N	7.30W
Cavan, Ire. (kăv'ȧn)	144	54.01N	7.00W
Cavarzere, Italy (kä-vär'dzā-rā)	154	45.08N	12.06E
Cavendish, Vt., U.S. (kăv'ĕn-dĭsh)	92	43.25N	72.35W
Caviana, Ilha, i., Braz. (kä-vyä'nä)	124	0.45N	49.33W
Cavite, Phil. (kä-vē'tä)	189a	14.30N	120.54E
Caxambu, Braz. (kä-shä'm-bōō)	124	22.00S	44.45W
Caxias, Braz. (kä'shē-äzh)	124	4.48S	43.16W
Caxias, Port.	234d	38.42N	9.16W
Caxias do Sul, Braz. (kä'shē-äzh-dò-sōō'l)	126	29.13S	51.03W
Caxito, Ang. (kä-shē'tò)	206	8.33S	13.36E
Cayambe, Ec. (kå-īä'm-bĕ)	124	0.03N	79.09W
Cayenne, Fr. Gu. (kā-ĕn')	124	4.56N	52.18W
Cayetano Rubio, Mex. (kä-yĕ-tà-nô-rōō'byō)	112	20.37N	100.21W
Cayey, P.R.	111b	18.05N	66.12W
Cayman Brac, i., Cay. Is. (kī-măn' brák)	116	19.45N	79.50W
Cayman Islands, dep., N.A.	116	19.30N	80.30W
Cay Sal Bank, bk. (kē-säl)	116	23.55N	80.20W
Cayuga, l., N.Y., U.S. (kā-yōō'gȧ)	92	42.35N	76.35W
Cazalla de la Sierra, Spain	152	37.55N	5.48W

PLACE (Pronunciation)	PAGE	Lat. °′	Long. °′
Cazaux, Étang de, l., Fr. (ā-täɴ' dĕ kä-zō')	150	44.32N	0.59W
Cazenovia, N.Y., U.S. (kăz-ē-nō'vĭ-ȧ)	92	42.55N	75.50W
Cazenovia Creek, r., N.Y., U.S.	95c	42.49N	78.45W
Čazma, Cro. (chäz'mä)	154	45.44N	16.39E
Cazombo, Ang. (kä-zō'm-bō)	206	11.54S	22.52E
Cazones, r., Mex. (kä-zō'nĕs)	112	20.37N	97.28W
Cazones, Ensenada de, b., Cuba (ĕn-sĕ-nä-dä-dĕ-kä-zō'nås)	116	22.05N	81.30W
Cazones, Golfo de, b., Cuba (gôl-fô-dĕ-kä-zō'nås)	116	21.55N	81.15W
Cazorla, Spain (kä-thôr'lä)	152	37.55N	2.58W
Cea, r., Spain (thā'ä)	152	42.18N	5.10W
Ceará-Mirim, Braz. (sā-ä-rä'mē-rē'ɴ)	124	6.00S	35.13W
Cebaco, Isla, i., Pan. (ē's-lä-sā-bä'kō)	114	7.27N	81.08W
Cebolla Creek, r., Co., U.S. (sē-bōl'yä)	102	38.15N	107.10W
Cebreros, Spain (sē-brĕ'rōs)	152	40.28N	4.28W
Cebu, Phil. (sā-bōō')	188	10.22N	123.49E
Čecchignola, neigh., Italy	235c	41.49N	12.29E
Čechy (Bohemia), hist. reg., Czech.	148	49.51N	13.55E
Cecil, Pa., U.S. (sē'sĭl)	95e	40.20N	80.10W
Cecil Park, Austl.	239a	33.52S	150.51E
Cedar, r., Ia., U.S.	96	42.23N	92.07W
Cedar, r., Wa., U.S.	100c	45.56N	122.32W
Cedar, West Fork, r., Ia., U.S.	96	42.49N	93.10W
Cedar Bayou, Tx., U.S.	107a	29.54N	94.58W
Cedar Breaks National Monument, rec., Ut., U.S.	102	37.35N	112.55W
Cedarbrook, Pa., U.S.	225b	40.05N	75.10W
Cedarburg, Wi., U.S. (sē'dēr bûrg)	96	43.23N	88.00W
Cedar City, Ut., U.S.	102	37.40N	113.10W
Cedar Creek, r., N.D., U.S.	96	46.05N	102.10W
Cedar Falls, Ia., U.S.	96	42.31N	92.29W
Cedar Grove, N.J., U.S.	224	40.51N	74.14W
Cedar Heights, Pa., U.S.	225b	40.05N	75.17W
Cedarhurst, N.Y., U.S.	224	40.38N	73.44W
Cedar Keys, Fl., U.S.	108	29.06N	83.03W
Cedar Lake, In., U.S.	95a	41.22N	87.27W
Cedar Lake, l., In., U.S.	95a	41.23N	87.25W
Cedar Lake, res., Can.	78	53.10N	100.00W
Cedar Rapids, Ia., U.S.	90	42.00N	91.43W
Cedar Springs, Mi., U.S.	92	43.15N	85.40W
Cedartown, Ga., U.S. (sē'dēr-toun)	108	34.00N	85.15W
Cedarville, S. Afr. (cēdȧr'vĭl)	207c	30.23S	29.04E
Cedral, Mex. (sā-dräl')	112	23.47N	100.42W
Cedros, Hond. (sā'drōs)	114	14.36N	87.07W
Cedros, i., Mex.	110	28.10N	115.10W
Ceduna, Austl. (sē-dò'nȧ)	196	32.15S	133.55E
Ceel Buur, Som.	212a	4.35N	46.40E
Cega, r., Spain (thā'gä)	152	41.25N	4.27W
Cegléd, Hung. (tsă'glād)	148	47.10N	19.49E
Ceglie, Italy (chĕ'lyĕ)	154	40.39N	17.32E
Cehegín, Spain (thā-ā-hēn')	152	38.05N	1.48W
Ceiba del Agua, Cuba (sā'bä-dĕl-ä'gwä)	117a	22.53N	82.38W
Cekhira, Tun.	204	34.17N	10.00E
Celaya, Mex. (sā-lä'yä)	110	20.33N	100.49W
Celebes (Sulawesi), i., Indon.	188	2.15S	120.30E
Celebes Sea, sea, Asia	188	3.45N	121.52E
Celestún, Mex. (sĕ-lĕs-tōō'n)	114a	20.57N	90.18W
Celina, Oh., U.S. (sēlĭ'na)	92	40.30N	84.35W
Celje, Slo. (tsĕl'yĕ)	154	46.13N	15.17E
Celle, Ger. (tsĕl'ĕ)	140	52.37N	10.05E
Cement, Ok., U.S. (sē-mĕnt')	104	34.56N	98.07W
Cenderawasih, Teluk, b., Indon.	188	2.20S	135.30E
Ceniza, Pico, mtn., Ven. (pē'kô-sĕ-nē'zä)	125b	10.24N	67.26W
Center, Tx., U.S. (sĕn'tēr)	106	31.50N	94.10W
Center Hill Lake, res., Tn., U.S. (sĕn'tēr-hĭl)	108	36.02N	86.00W
Center Line, Mi., U.S. (sĕn'tēr līn)	95b	42.29N	83.01W
Centerville, Ia., U.S. (sĕn'tēr-vĭl)	96	40.44N	92.48W
Centerville, Mn., U.S.	101g	45.10N	93.03W
Centerville, Pa., U.S.	95e	40.02N	79.58W
Centerville, S.D., U.S.	96	43.07N	96.56W
Centerville, Ut., U.S.	101b	40.55N	111.53W
Centocelle, neigh., Italy	235c	41.53N	12.34E
Central, Cordillera, mts., Bol. (kôr-dĕl-yĕ'rä-sĕn-trä'l)	124	19.18S	65.29W
Central, Cordillera, mts., Col.	124a	3.58N	75.55W
Central, Cordillera, mts., Dom. Rep.	116	19.05N	71.30W
Central, Cordillera, mts., Phil. (kôr-dēl-yĕ'rä-sĕn-träl)	189a	17.05N	120.55E
Central African Republic, nation, Afr.	204	7.50N	21.00E
Central America, reg., N.A. (ä-mĕr'ĭ-kȧ)	110	10.45N	87.15W
Central City, Ky., U.S. (sĕn'trȧl)	108	37.15N	87.09W
Central City, Ne., U.S. (sĕn'trȧl sĭ'tĭ)	96	41.07N	98.00W
Central Falls, R.I., U.S. (sĕn'trȧl fôlz)	94b	41.54N	71.23W
Central Highlands, Pa., U.S.	226b	40.16N	79.50W
Centralia, Il., U.S. (sĕn-trā'lĭ-ȧ)	92	38.35N	89.05W
Centralia, Mo., U.S.	104	39.11N	92.07W
Centralia, Wa., U.S.	98	46.42N	122.58W
Central Intelligence Agency, pt. of i., Va., U.S.	225d	38.57N	77.09W
Central Park, pt. of i., N.Y., U.S.	224	40.47N	73.58W
Central Plateau, plat., Russia	160	55.00N	33.30E
Central Valley, N.Y., U.S.	94a	41.19N	74.07W
Centre Island, N.Y., U.S.	224	40.54N	73.32W
Centreville, Il., U.S. (sĕn'tēr-vĭl)	101e	38.33N	90.06W
Centreville, Md., U.S.	92	39.05N	76.05W
Centro Simón Bolívar, pt. of i., Ven.	230a	10.30N	66.55W
Century, Fl., U.S. (sĕn'tū-rĭ)	108	30.57N	87.15W
Century City, neigh., Ca., U.S.	228	34.03N	118.26W
Ceram (Seram), i., Indon.	188	2.45S	129.30E
Céret, Fr.	150	42.29N	2.47E
Cerignola, Italy (chā-rē-nyô'lä)	154	41.16N	15.55E
Cerknica, Slo. (tsĕr'knē-tsä)	154	45.48N	14.21E
Čern'achovsk, Russia (chĕr-nyä'kôfsk)	160	54.38N	21.49E
Čer'omuski, neigh., Russia	235b	55.41N	37.35E

ăt; finȧl; rāte; senāte; ärm; åsk; sofȧ; fâre; ch-choose; dh-as th in other; bē; ēvent; bĕt; recĕnt; cratēr; g-gō; gh-guttural g; bĭt; ĭ-short neutral; rīde; ĸ-guttural k as ch in German ich;

PLACE (Pronunciation)	PAGE	Lat. °'	Long. °'
Cerralvo, Mex. (sěr-räl'vō)	106	26.05N	99.37W
Cerralvo, i., Mex.	110	24.00N	109.59W
Cerrito, Col. (sěr-rē'-tô)	124a	3.41N	76.17W
Cerritos, Mex. (sěr-rē'tôs)	112	22.26N	100.16W
Cerro de Pasco, Peru (sěr'rō dā päs'kō)	124	10.45S	76.14W
Cerro Gordo, Arroyo de, r., Mex. (är-rô-yō-dě-sě'r-rô-gôr-dō)	106	26.12N	104.06W
Čertanovo, neigh., Russia	235b	55.38N	37.37E
Certegui, Col. (sěr-tě'gē)	124a	5.21N	76.35W
Cervantes, Phil. (sěr-vän'täs)	189a	16.59N	120.42E
Cervera del Río Alhama, Spain	152	42.02N	1.55W
Cerveteri, Italy (chěr-vě'tě-rē)	153d	42.00N	12.06E
Cesano Boscone, Italy	234c	45.27N	9.06E
Cesena, Italy (chě'sě-nä)	154	44.08N	12.16E
Çēsis, Lat. (sā'sĭs)	146	57.19N	25.17E
Česká Lípa, Czech. (chěs'kä lē'pa)	148	50.41N	14.31E
České Budějovice, Czech. (chěs'kā bōō'dyě-yô-vēt-sě)	140	49.00N	14.30E
Českomoravská Vysočina, hills, Czech.	148	49.21N	15.40E
Český Těšín, Czech.	148	49.43N	18.22E
Çeşme, Tur. (chěsh'mě)	154	38.20N	26.20E
Cessnock, Austl.	196	32.58S	151.15E
Cestos, r., Lib.	208	5.40N	9.25W
Cetinje, Yugo. (tsět'in-yě)	136	42.23N	18.55E
Ceuta, Sp. N. Afr. (thā-ōō'tä)	204	36.04N	5.36W
Cévennes, reg., Fr. (sā-věn')	140	44.20N	3.48E
Ceylon, see Sri Lanka, nation, Asia	175c	8.45N	82.30E
Chabot, Lake, l., Ca., U.S. (sha'bŏt)	100b	37.44N	122.06W
Chacabuco, Arg. (chä-kä-bōō'kō)	123c	34.37S	60.27W
Chacaltianguis, Mex. (chä-käl-tē-äŋ'gwēs)	112	18.18N	95.50W
Chacao, Ven.	230a	10.30N	66.51W
Chachapoyas, Peru (chä-chä-poi'yäs)	124	6.16S	77.48W
Chaco, prov., Arg. (chä'kō)	126	26.00S	60.45W
Chaco Culture National Historic Park, rec., N.M., U.S. (chä'kō)	102	36.05N	108.00W
Chad, Russia (chăd)	164a	56.33N	57.11E
Chad, nation, Afr.	204	17.48N	19.00E
Chad, Lake, l., Afr.	204	13.55N	13.40E
Chadbourn, N.C., U.S. (chăd'bŭrn)	108	34.19N	78.55W
Chadderton, Eng., U.K.	233b	53.33N	2.08W
Chadron, Ne., U.S. (chăd'rŭn)	90	42.50N	103.10W
Chadstone, Austl.	239b	37.53S	145.05E
Chadwell Saint Mary, Eng., U.K.	231	51.29N	0.22E
Chafarinas, Islas, is., Sp. N. Afr.	152	35.08N	2.20W
Chaffee, Mo., U.S. (chăf'ē)	104	37.10N	89.39W
Chāgal Hills, hills, Afg.	174	29.15N	63.28E
Chagodoshcha, r., Russia (chä-gō-dôsh-chä)	156	59.08N	35.13E
Chagres, r., Pan. (chä'grěs)	114	9.18N	79.22W
Chagrin, r., Oh., U.S. (shȧ'grĭn)	95d	41.34N	81.24W
Chagrin Falls, Oh., U.S. (shȧ'grĭn fôls)	95d	41.26N	81.23W
Chahar, hist. reg., China (chä-här)	180	44.25N	115.00E
Chahār Borjak, Afg.	176	30.17N	62.03E
Chakdaha, India	236a	22.28N	88.20E
Chake Chake, Tan.	210	5.15S	39.46E
Chalatenango, El Sal. (chäl-ä-tě-näŋ'gō)	114	14.04N	88.54W
Chalbi Desert, des., Kenya	210	3.40N	36.50E
Chalcatongo, Mex. (chäl-kä-tôŋ'gō)	112	17.04N	97.41W
Chalchihuites, Mex. (chäl-chē-wē'tås)	112	23.28N	103.57W
Chalchuapa, El Sal. (chäl-chwä'pä)	114	14.01N	89.39W
Chalco, Mex. (chäl-kō)	113a	19.15N	98.54W
Chaldon, Eng., U.K.	231	51.17N	0.07W
Chaleur Bay, b., Can. (shȧ-lûr')	78	47.58N	65.33W
Chalfant, Pa., U.S.	226b	40.25N	79.52W
Chalfont Common, Eng., U.K.	231	51.38N	0.33W
Chalfont Saint Giles, Eng., U.K.	231	51.38N	0.34W
Chalfont Saint Peter, Eng., U.K.	231	51.37N	0.33W
Chalgrove, Eng., U.K. (chăl'grôv)	138b	51.38N	1.05W
Chaling, China (chä'lĭng)	184	27.00N	113.31E
Chalk, Eng., U.K.	231	51.26N	0.25E
Chalmette, La., U.S. (shăl-mět')	94d	29.57N	89.57W
Châlons-sur-Marne, Fr. (shȧ-lôɴ'sür-märn)	140	48.57N	4.23E
Chalon-sur-Saône, Fr.	140	46.47N	4.54E
Chaltel, Cerro, mtn., S.A. (sě'r-rô-chäl'těl)	126	48.10S	73.18W
Chālūs, Iran	176	36.38N	51.26E
Chama, Rio, r., N.M., U.S. (chä'mä)	102	36.19N	106.31W
Chama, Sierra de, mts., Guat. (sē-ě'r-rä-dě-chä-mä)	114	15.48N	90.20W
Chamama, Mwi.	210	12.55S	33.43E
Chaman, Pak. (chŭm-än')	174	30.58N	66.21E
Chambal, r., India (chŭm-bäl')	174	24.30N	75.30E
Chamberlain, S.D., U.S. (chām'běr-lĭn)	96	43.48N	99.21W
Chamberlain, l., Me., U.S.	86	46.15N	69.10W
Chambersburg, Pa., U.S. (chām'běrz-bûrg)	92	40.00N	77.40W
Chambéry, Fr. (shäm-bā-rē')	140	45.35N	5.54E
Chambeshi, r., Zam.	210	10.35S	31.20E
Chamblee, Ga., U.S. (chăm-blē')	94c	33.55N	84.18W
Chambly, Can. (shäɴ-blē')	77a	45.27N	73.17W
Chambly, Fr.	151b	49.11N	2.14E
Chambord, Can.	78	48.22N	72.01W
Chambourcy, Fr.	233c	48.54N	2.03E
Chame, Punta, c., Pan. (pö'n-tä-chä'mȧ)	114	8.41N	79.27W
Chamelecón, r., Hond. (chä-mě-lě-kô'n)	114	15.09N	88.42W
Chamo, l., Eth.	204	5.58N	37.00E
Chamonix-Mont-Blanc, Fr. (shȧ-mō-nē')	150	45.55N	6.50E
Champagne, reg., Fr. (shäm-pän'yē)	150	48.53N	4.48E
Champaign, Il., U.S. (shăm-pān')	90	40.10N	88.15W
Champdāni, India	178a	22.48N	88.21E
Champerico, Guat. (chăm-pā-rē'kō)	114	14.18N	91.55W
Champigny-sur-Marne, Fr.	233c	48.49N	2.31E
Champion, Mi., U.S. (chăm'pĭ-ŭn)	96	46.30N	87.59W
Champlain, Lake, l., N.A. (shăm-plān')	90	44.45N	73.20W
Champlan, Fr.	233c	48.43N	2.16E
Champlitte-et-le-Prálot, Fr. (shäɴ-plēt')	150	47.38N	5.28E
Champotón, Mex. (chäm-pō-tōn')	112	19.21N	90.43W
Champotón, r., Mex.	112	19.19N	90.15W
Champs-sur-Marne, Fr.	233c	48.51N	2.36E
Chāmrāil, India	236a	22.38N	88.18E
Chañaral, Chile (chän-yä-räl')	126	26.20S	70.46W
Chandannagar, India	236a	22.51N	88.21E
Chandeleur Islands, is., La., U.S. (shăn-dě-lōōr')	108	29.53N	88.35W
Chandeleur Sound, strt., La., U.S.	108	29.47N	89.08W
Chandīgarh, India	174	30.51N	77.13E
Chandler, Can. (chăn'dlēr)	78	48.21N	64.41W
Chandler, Ok., U.S.	104	35.42N	96.52W
Chandler's Cross, Eng., U.K.	231	51.40N	0.27W
Chandrapur, India	174	19.58N	79.21E
Changane, r., Moz.	206	22.42S	32.46E
Changara, Moz.	210	16.54S	33.14E
Changchun, China (chäŋ-chón)	180	43.55N	125.25E
Changdang Hu, l., China (chäŋ-däŋ hōō)	182	31.37N	119.29E
Changde, China (chäŋ-dŭ)	180	29.00N	111.38E
Changdian, China	236b	40.01N	116.32E
Changhua, Tai. (chäng'hwä')	184	24.02N	120.32E
Changi, Sing.	236c	1.23N	103.59E
Changjŏn, N. Kor. (chäng'jŭn')	186	38.40N	128.05E
Changli, China (chäŋ-lē)	184	39.46N	119.10E
Changning, China (chäŋ-nĭŋ)	180	24.34N	99.49E
Changping, China (chäŋ-pĭŋ)	184	40.12N	116.10E
Changqing, China (chäŋ-chyĭŋ)	182	36.33N	116.42E
Changsan Got, c., N. Kor.	186	38.06N	124.50E
Changsha, China (chäŋ-shä)	180	28.20N	113.00E
Changshan Qundao, is., China (chäŋ-shän chyōn-dou)	182	39.08N	122.26E
Changshu, China (chäŋ-shōō)	182	31.40N	120.45E
Changting, China	184	25.50N	116.18E
Changwu, China (chäng'wōō')	184	35.12N	107.45E
Changxindianzhen, China (chäŋ-shyĭn-dĭěn-jŭn)	184a	39.49N	116.12E
Changxing Dao, i., China (chäŋ-shyĭŋ dou)	182	39.38N	121.10E
Chang, see Yangtze, r., China	180	30.30N	117.25E
Changyi, China (chäŋ-yē)	182	36.51N	119.23E
Changyuan, China (chyäŋ-yuän)	182	35.10N	114.41E
Changzhi, China (chäŋ-jr)	184	35.58N	112.58E
Changzhou, China (chäŋ-jō)	180	31.47N	119.56E
Changzhuyuan, China (chäŋ-jōō-yuän)	182	31.33N	115.17E
Chanhassen, Mn., U.S. (shăn'hăs-sěn)	101g	44.52N	93.32W
Chanh-hung, Viet.	237m	10.43N	106.41E
Channel Islands, is., Eur. (chăn'ěl)	136	49.15N	3.30W
Channel Islands, is., Ca., U.S.	102	33.30N	119.15W
Channel-Port-aux-Basques, Can.	78	47.35N	59.11W
Channelview, Tx., U.S. (chănĕlvū)	107a	29.46N	95.07W
Chantada, Spain (chän-tä'dä)	152	42.38N	7.36W
Chanteloup-les-Vignes, Fr.	233c	48.59N	2.02E
Chanthaburi, Thai.	188	12.37N	102.04E
Chantilly, Fr. (shäɴ-tē-yē')	151b	49.12N	2.30E
Chantilly, Va., U.S. (shăn'tĭlē)	94e	38.53N	77.26W
Chantrey Inlet, b., Can. (chăn-trē)	78	67.49N	95.00W
Chanute, Ks., U.S. (shȧ-nōōt')	90	37.41N	95.27W
Chany, l., Russia (chä'nē)	158	54.15N	77.31E
Chao'an, China (chou-än)	180	23.48N	116.35E
Chao Hu, l., China	180	31.45N	116.59E
Chao Phraya, r., Thai.	188	16.13N	99.33E
Chaor, r., China (chou-r)	184	47.20N	121.40E
Chaoshui, China (chou-shwā)	182	37.43N	120.56E
Chaoxian, China (chou shyěn)	182	31.37N	117.50E
Chaoyang, China	180	41.32N	120.20E
Chaoyang, China (chou-yäŋ)	184	23.18N	116.32E
Chapada, Serra da, mts., Braz. (sě'r-rä-dä-shä-pä'dä)	124	14.57S	54.34W
Chapadão, Serra do, mtn., Braz. (sě'r-rä-dô-shä-pȧ-dou'ɴ)	123a	20.31S	46.20W
Chapala, Mex. (chä-pä'lä)	112	20.18N	103.10W
Chapala, Lago de, l., Mex. (lä'gô-dě-chä-pä'lä)	110	20.14N	103.02W
Chapalagana, r., Mex. (chä-pä-lä-gȧ'nä)	112	22.11N	104.09W
Chaparral, Col. (chä-pär-rá'l)	124	3.44N	75.28W
Chapayevsk, Russia (châ-pī'ěfsk)	160	53.00N	49.30E
Chapel Hill, N.C., U.S. (chăp''l hĭl)	108	35.55N	79.05W
Chapel Oaks, Md., U.S.	225d	38.54N	76.55W
Chapeltown, Eng., U.K.	233b	53.38N	2.24W
Chaplain, l., Wa., U.S. (chăp'lĭn)	100a	47.58N	121.50W
Chapleau, Can. (chăp-lō')	78	47.43N	83.28W
Chapman, Mount, mtn., Can. (chăp'mȧn)	80	51.50N	118.20W
Chapman's Bay, b., S. Afr. (chăp'mȧns bā)	206a	34.06S	18.17E
Chapman Woods, Ca., U.S.	228	34.08N	118.05W
Chappell, Ne., U.S. (chă-pěl')	96	41.06N	102.29W
Chapultenango, Mex. (chä-pōl-tě-näŋ'gō)	112	17.19N	93.08W
Chapultepec, Castillo de, hist., Mex.	229a	19.25N	99.11W
Chá Pungana, Ang.	210	13.44S	18.39E
Charcas, Mex. (chär'käs)	112	23.09N	101.09W
Charco de Azul, Bahía, b., Pan.	114	8.14N	82.45W
Chardzhou, Turk. (chěr-jô'ō)	158	38.52N	63.37E
Charente, r., Fr. (shȧ-räɴt')	150	45.48N	0.28W
Charenton-le-Pont, Fr.	233c	48.49N	2.25E
Chari, r., Afr. (shä-rē')	208	12.45N	14.55E
Charing, Eng., U.K. (chă'rĭng)	138b	51.13N	0.49E
Chariton, Ia., U.S. (châr'ĭ-tŭn)	96	41.02N	93.16W
Chariton, r., Mo., U.S.	104	40.24N	92.38W
Charlemagne, Can. (shärl-mäny')	77a	45.43N	73.29W
Charleroi, Bel. (shár-lē-rwä')	140	50.25N	4.35E
Charleroi, Pa., U.S. (shär'lē-roi)	95e	40.08N	79.54W
Charles, Cape, c., Va., U.S. (chärlz)	92	37.05N	75.48W
Charlesbourg, Can. (shärl-bōōr')	77b	46.51N	71.16W
Charles City, Ia., U.S. (chärlz)	96	43.03N	92.40W
Charles de Gaulle, Aéroport, arpt., Fr.	233c	49.00N	2.34E
Charleston, Il., U.S. (chärlz'tŭn)	92	39.30N	88.10W
Charleston, Ms., U.S.	108	34.00N	90.02W
Charleston, Mo., U.S.	104	36.53N	89.20W
Charleston, S.C., U.S.	90	32.47N	79.56W
Charleston, W.V., U.S.	90	38.20N	81.35W
Charlestown, St. K./N.	115b	17.10N	62.32W
Charlestown, In., U.S. (chärlz'toun)	95h	38.46N	85.39W
Charleville, Austl. (chär'lē-vĭl)	196	26.16S	146.28E
Charleville Mézières, Fr. (shärl-věl')	150	49.48N	4.41E
Charlevoix, Mi., U.S. (shär'lē-voi)	92	45.20N	85.15W
Charlevoix, Lake, l., Mi., U.S.	96	45.17N	85.43W
Charlotte, Mi., U.S. (shär'lŏt)	92	42.35N	84.50W
Charlotte, N.C., U.S.	90	35.15N	80.50W
Charlotte Amalie, V.I.U.S. (shär-lŏt'ĕ ä-mä'lĭ-á)	110	18.21N	64.54W
Charlotte Harbor, b., Fl., U.S.	109a	26.49N	82.00W
Charlotte Lake, l., Can.	80	52.07N	125.30W
Charlottenberg, Swe. (shär-lŭt'ĕn-běrg)	146	59.53N	12.17E
Charlottenburg, neigh., Ger.	234a	52.31N	13.16E
Charlottenburg, Schloss, hist., Ger.	234a	52.31N	13.14E
Charlottesville, Va., U.S. (shär'lŏtz-vĭl)	90	38.00N	78.25W
Charlottetown, Can. (shär'lŏt-toun)	78	46.14N	63.08W
Charlotte Waters, Austl. (shär'lŏt)	196	26.00S	134.50E
Charlton, neigh., Eng., U.K.	231	51.29N	0.02E
Charmes, Fr. (shärm)	150	48.23N	6.19E
Charneca, neigh., Port.	234d	38.47N	9.08W
Charnwood Forest, for., Eng., U.K. (chärn'wŏŏd)	138a	52.42N	1.15W
Charny, Can. (shär-nē')	77b	46.43N	71.16W
Chars, Fr. (shär)	151b	49.09N	1.57E
Chārsadda, Pak. (chŭr-sä'dä)	175a	34.17N	71.43E
Charters Towers, Austl. (chär'tērz)	196	20.03S	146.20E
Charterwood, Pa., U.S.	226b	40.33N	80.00W
Chartres, Fr. (shärt'r')	140	48.26N	1.29E
Chascomús, Arg. (chäs-kō-mōōs')	126	35.32S	58.01W
Chase City, Va., U.S. (chās)	108	36.45N	78.27W
Chashniki, Bela. (chäsh'nyĕ-kē)	156	54.51N	29.08E
Chaska, Mn., U.S. (chăs'kȧ)	101g	44.48N	93.36W
Châteaudun, Fr. (shä-tō-däɴ')	150	48.04N	1.23E
Châteaufort, Fr.	233c	48.44N	2.06E
Château-Gontier, Fr. (chȧ-tō'gôɴ'tyā')	150	47.48N	0.43W
Châteauguay, Can. (chȧ-tō-gā)	77a	45.22N	73.45W
Châteauguay, r., N.A.	77a	45.13N	73.51W
Châteauneaut, Fr.	150a	43.23N	5.11E
Château-Renault, Fr. (shȧ-tō-rē-nō')	150	47.36N	0.57E
Château-Richer, Can. (shȧ-tō'rē-shā')	77b	47.00N	71.01W
Châteauroux, Fr. (shȧ-tō-rōō')	140	46.47N	1.39E
Château-Thierry, Fr. (shȧ-tō'ty-ěr-rē')	150	49.03N	3.22E
Châtellerault, Fr. (shä-těl-rō')	140	46.48N	0.31E
Châtenay-Malabry, Fr.	233c	48.46N	2.17E
Chatfield, Mn., U.S. (chăt'fēld)	96	43.50N	92.10W
Chatham, Can.	78	47.02N	65.28W
Chatham, Can. (chăt'ȧm)	78	42.25N	82.10W
Chatham, Eng., U.K. (chăt'ŭm)	144	51.23N	0.32E
Chatham, N.J., U.S. (chăt'ȧm)	94a	40.44N	74.23W
Chatham, Oh., U.S.	95d	41.06N	82.01W
Chatham Islands, is., N.Z.	2	44.00S	178.00W
Chatham Sound, strt., Can.	80	54.32N	130.35W
Chatham Strait, strt., Ak., U.S.	89	57.00N	134.40W
Châtillon, Fr.	233c	48.48N	2.17E
Chatou, Fr.	233c	48.54N	2.09E
Chatpur, neigh., India	236a	22.36N	88.23E
Chatswood, Austl.	239a	33.48S	151.12E
Chatsworth, Ca., U.S. (chătz'wûrth)	101a	34.16N	118.36W
Chatsworth Reservoir, res., Ca., U.S.	101a	34.15N	118.41W
Chattahoochee, Fl., U.S. (chăt-tȧ-hōō' chē)	108	30.42N	84.47W
Chattahoochee, r., U.S.	90	32.00N	85.10W
Chattanooga, Tn., U.S. (chăt-ȧ-nōō'gȧ)	90	35.01N	85.15W
Chattooga, r., Ga., U.S. (chă-tōō'gȧ)	108	34.47N	83.13W
Chaudière, r., Can. (shō-dyěr')	84	46.26N	71.10W
Chaumont, Fr. (shō-môɴ')	140	48.08N	5.07E
Chaunskaya Guba, b., Russia	162	69.15N	170.00E
Chauny, Fr. (shō-nē')	150	49.40N	3.09E
Chau-phu, Viet.	188	10.49N	104.57E
Chausy, Bela. (chou'sĭ)	156	53.57N	30.58E
Chautauqua, l., N.Y., U.S. (shȧ-tô'kwȧ)	92	42.10N	79.25W
Chavaniga, Russia	160	66.02N	37.50E
Chavenay, Fr.	233c	48.51N	1.59E
Chaves, Port. (chä'vězh)	152	41.44N	7.30W
Chaville, Fr.	233c	48.48N	2.10E
Chavinda, Mex. (chä-vē'n-dä)	112	20.01N	102.27W
Chazumba, Mex. (chä-zōm'bä)	112	18.11N	97.41W
Cheadle, Eng., U.K. (chē'd'l)	138a	52.59N	1.59W
Cheadle Hulme, Eng., U.K.	233b	53.22N	2.12W
Cheam, neigh., Eng., U.K.	231	51.21N	0.13W
Cheat, W.V., U.S. (chēt)	92	39.35N	79.40W
Cheb, Czech. (κěb)	148	50.05N	12.23E
Chebarkul', Russia (chě-bär-kûl')	164a	54.59N	60.22E
Cheboksary, Russia (chyě-bôk-sä'rě)	160	56.00N	47.20E
Cheboygan, Mi., U.S. (shě-boi'gȧn)	92	45.40N	84.30W
Chech, Erg, des., Alg.	204	24.45N	2.07W
Chechen', i., Russia (chyěch'ěn)	160	44.00N	48.10E
Checotah, Ok., U.S. (chě-kō'tȧ)	104	35.27N	95.32W
Chedabucto Bay, b., Can. (chěd-ȧ-bŭk-tō)	86	45.23N	61.10W
Cheduba Island, i., Burma	188	18.45N	93.01E
Cheecham Hills, hills, Can. (chēē'hăm)	82	56.20N	111.10W
Cheektowaga, N.Y., U.S. (chēk-tō-wä'gȧ)	95c	42.54N	78.46W
Cheetham Hill, neigh., Eng., U.K.	233b	53.31N	2.15W
Chefoo, see Yantai, China	180	37.32N	121.22E
Chegutu, Zimb.	206	18.18S	30.10E
Chehalis, Wa., U.S. (chě-hā'lĭs)	98	46.39N	122.58W
Chehalis, r., Wa., U.S.	98	46.47N	123.17W
Cheju, S. Kor. (chě'jōō')	186	33.29N	126.40E
Cheju (Quelpart), i., S. Kor.	186	33.20N	126.25E

ng-sing; ŋ-baŋk; ɴ-nasalized n; nŏd; cŏmmit; ōld; ôbey; ôrder; oi-boil; fōōd; ŏ-as oo in foot; ou-out; s-soft; sh-dish; th-thin; pūre; ûnite; ûrn; stŭd; circŭs; ü-as in French tu; '-indeterminate vowel.

PLACE (Pronunciation)	PAGE	Lat. °′	Long. °′
Chekalin, Russia (chĕ-kä′lĭn)	156	54.05N	36.13E
Chela, Serra da, mts., Ang. (sĕr′rȧ dä shä′lȧ)	206	15.30S	13.30E
Chelan, Wa., U.S. (chė-lăn′)	98	47.51N	119.59W
Chelan, Lake, l., Wa., U.S.	98	48.09N	120.20W
Chelas, neigh., Port.	234d	38.45N	9.07W
Cheleiros, Port. (shĕ-la′rōzh)	153b	38.54N	9.19W
Chéliff, r., Alg. (shā-lēf)	204	36.00N	2.00E
Chelkar, Kaz. (chyĕl′kär)	158	47.52N	59.41E
Chelkar, l., Kaz.	160	50.30N	51.30E
Chelkar Tengiz, l., Kaz. (chyĕl′kär tĕn′yēz)	158	48.20N	63.45E
Chelles, Fr.	151b	48.53N	2.36E
Chełm, Pol. (ĸĕlm)	140	51.08N	23.30E
Chełmno, Pol. (ĸĕlm′nō)	148	53.20N	18.25E
Chelmsford, Can.	84	46.35N	81.12W
Chelmsford, Eng., U.K. (chĕlm′s-fẽrd)	144	51.44N	0.28E
Chelmsford, Ma., U.S.	87a	42.36N	71.21W
Chelsea, Austl.	195a	38.05S	145.08E
Chelsea, Can.	77c	45.30N	75.46W
Chelsea, Al., U.S. (chĕl′sė)	94h	33.20N	86.38W
Chelsea, Ma., U.S.	87a	42.23N	71.02W
Chelsea, Mi., U.S.	92	42.20N	84.00W
Chelsea, Ok., U.S.	104	36.32N	95.23W
Cheltenham, Eng., U.K. (chĕlt′n*ŭ*m)	144	51.57N	2.06W
Cheltenham, Md., U.S. (chĕltĕn-hăm)	94e	38.45N	76.50W
Chelva, Spain (chĕl′vä)	152	39.43N	1.00W
Chelyabinsk, Russia (chĕl-yä-bėnsk′)	158	55.10N	61.25E
Chelyuskin, Mys, c., Russia (chĕl-yōs′-kĭn)	158	77.45N	104.45E
Chemba, Moz.	210	17.08S	34.52E
Chembūr, neigh., India	236e	19.04N	72.54E
Chemnitz, Ger.	140	50.48N	12.53E
Chemung, r., N.Y., U.S. (shė-mŭng)	92	42.20N	77.25W
Chĕn, Gora, mtn., Russia	158	65.13N	142.12E
Chenāb, r., Asia (chė-nāb)	174	30.30N	71.30E
Chenachane, Alg. (shĕ-nȧ-shän′)	204	26.14N	4.14W
Chencun, China (chŭn-tsòn)	183a	22.58N	113.14E
Cheney, Wa., U.S. (chē′nå)	98	47.29N	117.34W
Chengde, China (chŭŋ-dŭ)	180	40.50N	117.50E
Chengdong Hu, l., China (chŭŋ-dôŋ hōō)	182	32.22N	116.32E
Chengdu, China (chŭŋ-dōō)	180	30.30N	104.10E
Chenggu, China (chŭŋ-gōō)	184	33.05N	107.25E
Chenghai, China (chŭŋ-hī)	184	23.22N	116.40E
Chengshan Jiao, c., China (jyou chŭŋ-shän)	184	37.28N	122.40E
Chengxi Hu, l., China (chŭŋ-shyē hōō)	182	32.31N	116.04E
Chenies, Eng., U.K.	231	51.41N	0.32W
Chennevières, Fr.	233c	49.00N	2.07E
Chenxian, China (chŭn-shyĕn)	184	25.40N	113.00E
Chepén, Peru (chĕ-pĕ′n)	124	7.17S	79.24W
Chepo, Pan. (chā′pō)	114	9.12N	79.06W
Chepo, r., Pan.	114	9.10N	78.36W
Cher, r., Fr. (shâr)	140	47.14N	1.34E
Cherán, Mex. (chā-rän′)	112	19.41N	101.54W
Cherangany Hills, hills, Kenya	210	1.25N	35.20E
Cheraw, S.C., U.S. (chē′rô)	108	34.40N	79.52W
Cherbourg, Fr. (shär-bòr′)	136	49.39N	1.43W
Cherdyn′, Russia (chĕr-dyĕn′)	158	60.25N	56.32E
Cheremkhovo, Russia (chĕr′yĕm-kô-vō)	158	52.58N	103.18E
Cherëmukhovo, Russia (chĕr-yĕ-mû-kô-vô)	164a	60.20N	60.00E
Cherepanovo, Russia (chĕr′yĕ pä-nô′vō)	158	54.13N	83.22E
Cherepovets, Russia (chĕr-yĕ-pô′vyĕtz)	158	59.08N	37.59E
Chereya, Bela. (chĕr-ā′yä)	156	54.38N	29.16E
Chergui, i., Tun.	142	34.50N	11.40E
Chergui, Chott ech, l., Alg. (chĕr gē)	142	34.12N	0.10W
Cherikov, Bela. (chĕ′rē-kôf)	156	53.34N	31.22E
Cherkassy, Ukr. (chĕr-kȧ′sĭ)	156	49.26N	32.03E
Cherkassy, prov., Ukr.	156	48.58N	30.55E
Cherlak, Russia (chĭr-läk′)	158	54.04N	74.28E
Chermoz, Russia (chĕr-môz′)	160	58.47N	56.08E
Chern′, Russia (chĕrn)	156	53.28N	36.49E
Chërnaya Kalitva, r., Russia (chôr′nȧ yȧ kȧ-lēt′vȧ)	156	50.15N	39.16E
Chernigov, Ukr. (chĕr-nē′gôf)	160	51.23N	31.15E
Chernigov, prov., Ukr. (chĕr-nē′gôf)	156	51.28N	31.18E
Chernigovka, Ukr.	156	47.08N	36.20E
Chernobay, Ukr. (chĕr-nō-bī′)	156	49.41N	32.24E
Chernobyl′, Ukr. (chĕr-nō-bĭl′)	156	51.17N	30.14E
Chernogorsk, Russia (chĕr-nŏ-gôrsk′)	162	54.01N	91.07E
Chernoistochinsk, Russia (chĕr-nôy-stô′chĭnsk)	164a	57.44N	59.55E
Chernomorskoye, Ukr. (chĕr-nō-môr′skô-yĕ)	160	45.29N	32.43E
Chernovtsy, Ukr.	158	48.18N	25.56E
Chernyanka, Russia (chĕrn-yäŋ′kä)	156	50.56N	37.48E
Cherokee, Ia., U.S. (chĕr-ō-kē′)	96	42.43N	95.33W
Cherokee, Ks., U.S.	104	37.21N	94.50W
Cherokee, Ok., U.S.	104	36.44N	98.22W
Cherokee Lake, res., Tn., U.S.	108	36.22N	83.22W
Cherokees, Lake of the, res., Ok., U.S. (chĕr-ō-kēz′)	90	36.32N	95.14W
Cherokee Sound, Bah.	116	26.15N	76.55W
Cherry City, Pa., U.S.	226b	40.29N	79.58W
Cherryfield, Me., U.S. (chĕr′ĭ-fēld)	86	44.37N	67.56W
Cherry Grove, Or., U.S.	100c	45.27N	123.15W
Cherry Hill, N.J., U.S.	225b	39.55N	75.01W
Cherry Hill, neigh., Md., U.S.	225c	39.15N	76.38W
Cherryvale, Ks., U.S.	104	37.16N	95.33W
Cherryville, N.C., U.S. (chĕr′ĭ-vĭl)	108	35.32N	81.22W
Cherskogo, Khrebet, mts., Russia	158	67.15N	140.00E
Chertsey, Eng., U.K.	138b	51.24N	0.30W
Cherven′, Bela. (chĕr′vyĕn)	156	53.43N	28.26E
Chervonoye, l., Bela. (chĕr-vô′nô-yĕ)	156	52.24N	28.12E
Chesaning, Mi., U.S. (chĕs′ȧ-nĭng)	92	43.10N	84.10W
Chesapeake, Va., U.S. (chĕs′ȧ-pēk)	94g	36.48N	76.16W
Chesapeake Bay, b., U.S.	90	38.20N	76.15W
Chesapeake Beach, Md., U.S.	94e	38.42N	76.33W
Chesham, Eng., U.K. (chĕsh′*ŭ*m)	138b	51.41N	0.37W
Chesham Bois, Eng., U.K.	231	51.41N	0.37W
Cheshire, Mi., U.S. (chĕsh′ĭr)	92	42.25N	86.00W
Cheshire, co., Eng., U.K.	138a	53.16N	2.30W
Chëshskaya Guba, b., Russia	158	67.25N	46.00E
Cheshunt, Eng., U.K.	138b	51.43N	0.02W
Chesma, Russia (chĕs′mȧ)	164a	53.50N	60.42E
Chesnokovka, Russia (chĕs-nŏ-kôf′kȧ)	158	53.28N	83.41E
Chessington, neigh., Eng., U.K.	231	51.21N	0.18W
Chester, Eng., U.K. (chĕs′tẽr)	144	53.12N	2.53W
Chester, Il., U.S.	104	37.54N	89.48W
Chester, Pa., U.S.	94f	39.51N	75.22W
Chester, Pa., U.S.	225b	39.51N	75.21W
Chester, S.C., U.S.	108	34.42N	81.11W
Chester, Va., U.S.	108	37.20N	77.24W
Chester, W.V., U.S.	92	40.35N	80.30W
Chesterbrook, Va., U.S.	225d	38.55N	77.09W
Chesterfield, Eng., U.K. (chĕs′tẽr-fēld)	144	53.14N	1.26W
Chesterfield, Îles, is., N. Cal.	196	19.38S	160.08E
Chesterfield Inlet, Can.	78	63.19N	91.11W
Chesterfield Inlet, b., Can.	78	63.59N	92.09W
Chestermere Lake, l., Can. (chĕs′tē-mēr)	77e	51.03N	113.45W
Chesterton, In., U.S. (chĕs′tẽr-t*ŭ*n)	92	41.35N	87.05W
Chestertown, Md., U.S. (chĕs′tẽr-toun)	92	39.15N	76.05W
Chestnut Hill, Md., U.S.	225c	39.17N	76.47W
Chestnut Hill, Ma., U.S.	223a	42.20N	71.10W
Chesuncook, l., Me., U.S. (chĕs′*ŭ*n-kòk)	86	46.03N	69.40W
Cheswick, Pa., U.S.	226b	40.32N	79.47W
Chetek, Wi., U.S. (chĕ′tĕk)	96	45.18N	91.41W
Chetumal, Bahía de, b., N.A. (bä-ē-ä dĕ chĕt-ōō-mäl′)	110	18.07N	88.05W
Chevelon Creek, r., Az., U.S. (shĕv′ȧ-lŏn)	102	34.35N	111.00W
Chevening, Eng., U.K.	231	51.18N	0.08E
Cheverly, Md., U.S.	225d	38.55N	76.55W
Chevilly-Larue, Fr.	233c	48.46N	2.21E
Cheviot, Oh., U.S. (shĕv′ĭ-*ŭ*t)	95f	39.10N	84.37W
Chevreuse, Fr. (shĕ-vrûz′)	151b	48.42N	2.02E
Chevy Chase, Md., U.S. (shĕvĭ chās)	94e	38.58N	77.06W
Chevy Chase View, Md., U.S.	225d	39.01N	77.05W
Chew Bahir, Afr. (stĕf-a-nē)	204	4.46N	37.31E
Chewelah, Wa., U.S. (chē-wē′lä)	98	48.17N	117.42W
Cheyenne, Wy., U.S. (shī-ĕn′)	90	41.10N	104.49W
Cheyenne, r., U.S.	90	44.20N	102.15W
Cheyenne River Indian Reservation, I.R., S.D., U.S.	96	45.07N	100.46W
Cheyenne Wells, Co., U.S.	104	38.46N	102.21W
Chhalera Bāngar, India	236d	28.33N	77.20E
Chhināmor, India	236a	22.48N	88.18E
Chhindwāra, India	178	22.08N	78.57E
Chiai, Tai. (chĭ′ī′)	184	23.28N	120.28E
Chiange, Ang.	210	15.45S	13.48E
Chiang Mai, Thai.	188	18.38N	98.44E
Chiang Rai, Thai.	188	19.53N	99.48E
Chiapa, Río de, r., Mex.	114	16.00N	92.20W
Chiapa de Corzo, Mex. (chė-ä′pä dā kôr′zō)	112	16.44N	93.01W
Chiapas, state, Mex. (chė-ä′päs)	110	17.10N	93.00W
Chiapas, Cordilla de, mts., Mex. (kôr-dēl-yĕ′rä-dĕ-chyà′räs)	112	15.55N	93.15W
Chiari, Italy (kyä′rē)	154	45.31N	9.57E
Chiasso, Switz.	148	45.50N	8.57E
Chiautla, Mex. (chyä-ōōt′lȧ)	112	18.16N	98.37W
Chiavari, Italy (kyä-vä′rē)	154	44.18N	9.21E
Chiba, Japan (chē′bȧ)	180	35.37N	140.08E
Chiba, dept., Japan	187a	35.47N	140.02E
Chibougamau, Can. (chē-bōō′gä-mou)	78	49.57N	74.23W
Chibougamau, l., Can.	84	49.53N	74.21W
Chicago, Il., U.S. (shĭ-kô-gō) (chĭ-kä′gō)	90	41.49N	87.37W
Chicago, North Branch, r., Il., U.S.	227a	41.53N	87.38W
Chicago Heights, Il., U.S.	95a	41.30N	87.38W
Chicago Lawn, neigh., Il., U.S.	227a	41.47N	87.41W
Chicago-O′Hare International Airport, arpt., Il., U.S.	227a	41.59N	87.54W
Chicago Ridge, Il., U.S.	227a	41.42N	87.47W
Chicago Sanitary and Ship Canal, can., Il., U.S.	227a	41.42N	87.58W
Chicapa, r., Afr. (chė-kä′pȧ)	206	7.45S	20.25E
Chicbul, Mex. (chēk-bōō′l)	112	18.45N	90.56W
Chic-Chocs, Monts, mts., Can.	78	48.38N	66.37W
Chichagof, i., Ak., U.S. (chė-chä′gôf)	89	57.50N	137.00W
Chichancanab, Lago de, l., Mex. (lä′gō-dĕ-chē-chän-kä-nä′b)	114a	19.50N	88.28W
Chichén Itzá, hist., Mex.	114a	20.40N	88.35W
Chichester, Eng., U.K. (chĭch′ĕs-tẽr)	144	50.50N	0.55W
Chichimilá, Mex. (chē-chē-mē′lä)	114a	20.36N	88.14W
Chichiriviche, Ven. (chē-chē-rē-vē-chĕ)	125b	10.56N	68.17W
Chickamauga, Ga., U.S. (chĭk-ȧ-mô′gȧ)	108	34.50N	85.15W
Chickamauga Lake, res., Tn., U.S.	108	35.18N	85.22W
Chickasawhay, r., Ms., U.S. (chĭk-ȧ-sô′wā)	108	31.45N	88.45W
Chickasha, Ok., U.S. (chĭk′ȧ-shā)	90	35.04N	97.56W
Chiclana de la Frontera, Spain (chė-klä′nä)	152	36.25N	6.09W
Chiclayo, Peru (chė-klä′yō)	124	6.46S	79.50W
Chico, Ca., U.S. (chē′kō)	102	39.43N	121.51W
Chico, Wa., U.S.	100a	47.37N	122.43W
Chico, r., Arg.	126	44.30S	66.00W
Chico, r., Arg.	126	49.15S	69.30W
Chico, r., Phil.	189a	17.33N	121.24E
Chicoloapan, Mex. (chė-kō-lwä′pän)	113a	19.24N	98.54W
Chiconautla, Mex.	113a	19.39N	99.01W
Chicontepec, Mex. (chė-kōn′tĕ-pĕk′)	112	20.58N	98.08W
Chicopee, Ma., U.S. (chĭk′ō-pē)	92	42.10N	72.35W
Chicoutimi, Can. (shē-kōō′tē-mē′)	78	48.26N	71.04W
Chicxulub, Mex. (chēk-sōō-lōō′b)	114a	21.10N	89.30W
Chiefland, Fl., U.S. (chēf′lȧnd)	108	29.30N	82.50W
Chiemsee, l., Ger. (ĸēm zā)	148	47.58N	12.20E
Chieri, Italy (kyâ′rē)	154	45.03N	7.48E
Chieti, Italy (kyĕ′tē)	142	42.22N	14.22E
Chifeng, China (chr-fŭŋ)	180	42.18N	118.52E
Chigirin, Ukr. (chė-gē′rĕn)	156	49.02N	32.39E
Chignall Saint James, Eng., U.K.	231	51.46N	0.25E
Chignanuapan, Mex. (chē′g-ŋä-nwä-pà′n)	112	19.49N	98.02W
Chignecto Bay, b., Can. (shĭg-nĕk′tō)	86	45.33N	64.50W
Chignik, Ak., U.S. (chĭg′nĭk)	89	56.14N	158.12W
Chignik Bay, b., Ak., U.S.	89	56.18N	157.22W
Chigu Co, l., China (chr-gōō tswo)	178	28.55N	91.47E
Chigwell, Eng., U.K.	138b	51.38N	0.05E
Chigwell Row, Eng., U.K.	231	51.37N	0.07E
Chihe, China (chr-hŭ)	182	32.32N	117.57E
Chihuahua, Mex. (chė-wä′wä)	110	28.37N	106.06W
Chihuahua, state, Mex.	110	29.00N	107.30W
Chikishlyar, Turk. (chė-kėsh-lyär′)	160	37.40N	53.50E
Chilanga, Zam.	210	15.34S	28.17E
Chilapa, Mex. (chė-lä′pä)	112	17.34N	99.14W
Chilchota, Mex. (chēl-chō′tä)	112	19.40N	102.04W
Chilcotin, r., Can. (chĭl-kō′tĭn)	80	52.20N	124.15W
Childer Thornton, Eng., U.K.	233a	53.17N	2.57W
Childress, Tx., U.S. (chĭld′rĕs)	104	34.26N	100.11W
Chile, nation, S.A. (chē′lā)	126	35.00S	72.00W
Chilecito, Arg. (chė-lå-sē′tō)	126	29.06S	67.25W
Chilengue, Serra do, mts., Ang.	210	13.20S	15.00E
Chilibre, Pan. (chė-lē′brĕ)	110a	9.09N	79.37W
Chililabombwe, Zam.	210	12.18S	27.43E
Chilka, l., India	178	19.26N	85.42E
Chilko, r., Can. (chĭl′kō)	80	51.53N	123.53W
Chilko Lake, l., Can.	80	51.20N	124.05W
Chillán, Chile (chēl-yän′)	126	36.44S	72.06W
Chillicothe, Il., U.S. (chĭl-ĭ-kŏth′ė)	92	41.55N	89.30W
Chillicothe, Mo., U.S.	104	39.46N	93.32W
Chillicothe, Oh., U.S.	92	39.20N	83.00W
Chilliwack, Can. (chĭl′ĭ-wăk)	78	49.10N	121.57W
Chillum, Md., U.S.	225d	38.58N	76.59W
Chilly-Mazarin, Fr.	233c	48.42N	2.19E
Chiloé, Isla de, i., Chile	126	42.30S	73.55W
Chilpancingo, Mex. (chēl-pän-sēŋ′gō)	110	17.32N	99.30W
Chilton, Wi., U.S. (chĭl′t*ŭ*n)	96	44.00N	88.12W
Chilung, Tai. (chĭ′lung)	180	25.02N	121.48E
Chilwa, Lake, l., Afr.	206	15.12S	36.30E
Chimacum, Wa., U.S. (chĭm′ä-k*ŭ*m)	100a	48.01N	122.47W
Chimalpa, Mex. (chē-mäl′pä)	113a	19.26N	99.22W
Chimaltenango, Guat. (chė-mäl-tå-näŋ′gō)	114	14.39N	90.48W
Chimaltitan, Mex. (chėmäl-tē-tän′)	112	21.36N	103.50W
Chimbay, Uzb. (chĭm-bī′)	158	43.00N	59.44E
Chimborazo, mtn., Ec. (chėm-bō-rä′zō)	124	1.35S	78.45W
Chimbote, Peru (chėm-bō′tå)	124	9.02S	78.33W
Chimkent, Kaz. (chĭm-kĕnt)	158	42.17N	69.42E
Chimki-Chovrino, neigh., Russia	235b	55.51N	37.30E
China, Mex. (chē′nä)	106	25.43N	99.13W
China, nation, Asia (chī′nȧ)	180	36.45N	93.00E
Chinameca, El Sal. (Chē-nä-mā′kä)	114	13.31N	88.18W
Chinandega, Nic. (chē-nän-dā′gä)	114	12.38N	87.08W
Chinati Peak, mtn., Tx., U.S. (chĭ-nä′tē)	106	29.56N	104.29W
Chinatown, neigh., Ca., U.S.	227b	37.48N	122.26W
Chincha Alta, Peru (chĭn′chä äl′tä)	124	13.24S	76.04W
Chinchas, Islas, is., Peru (ė′s-läs-chē′n-chäs)	124	11.27S	79.05W
Chinchilla, Austl. (chĭn-chĭl′ȧ)	198	26.44S	150.36E
Chinchorro, Banco, bk., Mex. (bä′n-kō-chēn-chō′r-rō)	114a	18.43N	87.25W
Chincilla de Monte Aragon, Spain	152	38.54N	1.43W
Chinde, Moz. (shėn′dĕ)	206	17.39S	36.34E
Chin Do, i., S. Kor.	186	34.30N	125.43E
Chindwin, r., Burma (chĭn-dwĭn)	174	23.30N	94.34E
Chingford, neigh., Eng., U.K.	231	51.38N	0.01E
Chingmei, Tai.	237d	24.59N	121.32E
Chingola, Zam. (chĭng-gōlä)	206	12.32S	27.52E
Chinguar, Ang. (chĭng-gär)	206	12.35S	16.15E
Chinguetti, Maur. (chēŋ-gĕt′ė)	204	20.34N	12.34W
Chinhoyi, Zimb.	206	17.22S	30.12E
Chinju, S. Kor. (chĭn′jōō)	186	35.13N	128.10E
Chinko, r., Cen. Afr. Rep. (shĭn′kō)	204	6.37N	24.31E
Chinmen, *see* Quemoy, Tai.	184	24.30N	118.20E
Chino, Ca., U.S. (chē′nō)	101a	34.01N	117.42W
Chinon, Fr. (shē-nôN′)	150	47.09N	0.13E
Chinook, Mt., U.S. (shĭn-ok′)	98	48.35N	109.15W
Chinsali, Zam.	210	10.34S	32.03E
Chinteche, Mwi. (chĭn-tĕ′chĕ)	206	11.48S	34.14E
Chioggia, Italy (kyôd′jä)	154	45.12N	12.17E
Chipata, Zam.	206	13.39S	32.40E
Chipera, Moz. (zhė-pĕ′rä)	206	15.16S	32.30E
Chipley, Fl., U.S. (chĭp′lĭ)	108	30.45N	85.33W
Chipman, Can. (chĭp′m*ă*n)	86	46.11N	65.53W
Chipola, r., Fl., U.S. (chĭ-pō′lȧ)	108	30.40N	85.14W
Chippawa, Can. (chĭp′ė-wä)	95c	43.03N	79.03W
Chipperfield, Eng., U.K.	231	51.42N	0.29W
Chippewa, r., Mn., U.S. (chĭp′ė-wä)	96	45.07N	95.41W
Chippewa, r., Wi., U.S.	96	45.07N	91.19W
Chippewa Falls, Wi., U.S.	96	44.55N	91.26W
Chippewa Lake, Oh., U.S.	95d	41.04N	81.54W
Chipping Ongar, Eng., U.K.	231	51.43N	0.15E
Chipstead, Eng., U.K.	231	51.18N	0.10W
Chipstead, Eng., U.K.	231	51.17N	0.09E
Chiputneticook Lakes, l., N.A. (chĭ-pŏt-nĕt′ĭ-kòk)	86	45.47N	67.45W
Chiquimula, Guat. (chē-kė-mōō′lä)	114	14.47N	89.31W
Chiquimulilla, Guat. (chē-kē-mōō-lē′l-yä)	114	14.08N	90.23W
Chiquinquira, Col. (chė-kēŋ′kė-rä′)	124	5.33N	73.49W
Chirāgh Delhi, neigh., India	236d	28.32N	77.14E
Chirala, India	178	15.52N	80.22E

ăt; finăl; rāte; senåte; ärm; åsk; sofȧ; fâre; ch-choose; dh-as th in other; bē; ėvent; bĕt; recĕnt; cratẽr; g-gō; gh-guttural g; bĭt; ĭ-short neutral; rīde; ĸ-guttural k as ch in German ich;

PLACE (Pronunciation)	PAGE	Lat. °′	Long. °′
Chirchik, Uzb. (chĭr-chēk′)	162	41.28N	69.18E
Chire (Shire), r., Afr.	210	17.15S	35.25E
Chiricahua National Monument, rec., Az., U.S. (chĭ-rä-cä′hwä)	102	32.02N	109.18W
Chirikof, i., Ak., U.S. (chĭ′rĭ-kôf)	89	55.50N	155.35W
Chiriquí, Punta, c., Pan. (pō′n-tä-chē-rē-kē′)	114	9.13N	81.39W
Chiriquí Grande, Pan. (chē-rē-kē′ grän′dä)	114	8.57N	82.08W
Chiri San, mtn., S. Kor. (chĭ′rĭ-sän′)	186	35.20N	127.39E
Chiromo, Mwi.	206	16.34S	35.13E
Chirpan, Bul.	142	42.12N	25.19E
Chirripó, Río, r., C.R.	114	9.50N	83.20W
Chisasibi, Can.	78	53.40N	78.58W
Chisholm, Mn., U.S. (chĭz′ŭm)	96	47.28N	92.53W
Chislehurst, neigh., Eng., U.K.	231	51.25N	0.04E
Chistopol′, Russia (chĭs-tô′pôl-y′)	158	55.21N	50.37E
Chiswellgreen, Eng., U.K.	231	51.44N	0.22W
Chiswick, neigh., Eng., U.K.	231	51.29N	0.16W
Chita, Russia (chē-tá′)	158	52.09N	113.39E
Chitambo, Zam.	210	12.55S	30.39E
Chitato, Ang.	210	7.20S	20.47E
Chitembo, Ang.	210	13.34S	16.40E
Chitina, Ak., U.S. (chĭ-tē′ná)	89	61.28N	144.35W
Chitokoloki, Zam.	210	13.50S	23.13E
Chitorgarh, India	178	24.59N	74.42E
Chitrāl, Pak. (chē-träl′)	174	35.58N	71.48E
Chittagong, Bngl. (chĭt-á-gông′)	174	22.26N	90.51E
Chitungwiza, Zimb.	206	17.51S	31.05E
Chiumbe, r., Afr. (chē-ŏom′bå)	206	9.45S	21.00E
Chivasso, Italy (kē-väs′sō)	154	45.13N	7.52E
Chivhu, Zimb.	206	18.59S	30.58E
Chivilcoy, Arg. (chē-vēl-koi′)	126	34.51S	60.03W
Chixoy, r., Guat. (chē-κoi′)	114	15.40N	90.35W
Chizu, Japan (chē-zōō′)	187	35.16N	134.15E
Chloride, Az., U.S. (klō′rīd)	102	35.25N	114.15W
Chmielnik, Pol. (κmyĕl′nēk)	148	50.36N	20.46E
Choa Chu Kang, Sing.	236c	1.22N	103.41E
Choapa, r., Chile (chō-á′pä)	123b	31.56S	70.48W
Chobham, Eng., U.K.	231	51.21N	0.36W
Choctawhatchee, r., Fl., U.S.	108	30.37N	85.56W
Choctawhatchee Bay, b., Fl., U.S. (chôk-tô-hăch′ē)	108	30.15N	86.32W
Chodziez, Pol. (κôj′yĕsh)	148	52.59N	16.55E
Choele Choel, Arg. (chô-ĕ′lĕ-chôĕ′l)	126	39.14S	65.46W
Chōfu, Japan (chō′fōō′)	187a	35.39N	139.33E
Chōgo, Japan (chō-gō)	187a	35.25N	139.28E
Choisel, Fr.	233c	48.41N	2.01E
Choiseul, i., Sol.Is. (shwä-zûl′)	196	7.30S	157.30E
Choisy-le-Roi, Fr.	151b	48.46N	2.25E
Chojnice, Pol. (κoi-nē-tsĕ)	148	53.41N	17.34E
Cholet, Fr. (shō-lĕ′)	140	47.06N	0.54W
Cho-lon, neigh., Viet.	237m	10.46N	106.40E
Cholula, Mex. (chō-lōō′lä)	112	19.04N	98.19W
Choluteca, Hond. (chō-lōō-tā′kä)	114	13.18N	87.12W
Choluteco, r., Hond.	114	13.34N	86.59W
Cho-moi, Viet.	237m	10.51N	106.38E
Chomutov, Czech. (kō′mō-tôf)	148	50.27N	13.23E
Chona, r., Russia (chō′nä)	162	60.45N	109.15E
Chone, Ec. (chō′nē)	124	0.48S	80.06W
Chŏngjin, N. Kor. (chŭng-jĭn′)	180	41.48N	129.46E
Chŏngju, S. Kor. (chŭng-jōō′)	186	36.35N	127.30E
Chongming Dao, i., China (chôŋ-mĭŋ dou)	184	31.40N	122.30E
Chong Pang, Sing.	236c	1.26N	103.50E
Chongqing, China (chôŋ-chyĭŋ)	180	29.38N	107.30E
Chŏnju, S. Kor. (chŭn-jōō′)	186	35.48N	127.08E
Chonos, Archipiélago de los, is., Chile	126	44.35N	76.15W
Chorley, Eng., U.K. (chôr′lĭ)	138a	53.40N	2.38W
Chorleywood, Eng., U.K.	231	51.39N	0.31W
Chorlton-cum-Hardy, Eng., U.K.	233b	53.27N	2.17W
Chornaya, neigh., Russia	164b	55.45N	38.04E
Chorošovo, neigh., Russia	235b	55.47N	37.28E
Chorrera de Managua, Cuba	229b	23.02N	82.19E
Chorrillos, Peru (chôr-rē′l-yōs)	124	12.17S	76.55W
Chortkov, Ukr. (chôrt′kôf)	148	49.01N	25.48E
Chosan, N. Kor. (chō-sän′)	186	40.44N	125.48E
Chosen, Fl., U.S. (chō′z′n)	109a	26.41N	80.41W
Chōshi, Japan (chō′shē)	186	35.40N	140.55E
Choszczno, Pol. (chôsh′chnô)	148	53.10N	15.25E
Chota Nagpur, plat., India	178	23.40N	82.50E
Choteau, Mt., U.S. (shō′tō)	98	47.51N	112.10W
Chowan, r., N.C., U.S. (chô-wän′)	108	36.13N	76.46W
Chowilla Reservoir, res., Austl.	198	34.05S	141.20E
Chown, Mount, mtn., Can. (choun)	80	53.24N	119.22W
Choybalsan, Mong.	180	47.50N	114.15E
Christchurch, N.Z. (krīst′chûrch)	197a	43.30S	172.38E
Christian, i., Can. (krĭs′chăn)	84	44.50N	80.00W
Christiansburg, Va., U.S. (krĭs′chănz-bûrg)	108	37.08N	80.25W
Christiansted, V.I.U.S.	111b	17.45N	64.44W
Christmas Island, dep., Oc.	188	10.35S	105.40E
Christopher, Il., U.S. (krĭs′tô-fēr)	104	37.58N	89.04W
Chrudim, Czech. (κrōō′dyĕm)	148	49.57N	15.46E
Chrzanów, Pol. (κzhä′nôf)	148	50.08N	19.24E
Chuansha, China (chůän-shä)	183b	31.12N	121.41E
Chubut, prov., Arg. (chò-bōōt′)	126	44.00S	69.15W
Chubut, r., Arg. (chò-bōōt′)	126	43.05S	69.00W
Chuckatuck, Va., U.S. (chŭck á-tŭck)	94g	36.51N	76.35W
Chucunaque, r., Pan. (chōō-kōō-nä′kå)	114	8.36N	77.48W
Chudovo, Russia (chò′dò-vò)	156	59.03N	31.56E
Chudskoye Ozero, l., Eur. (chòt′skô-yĕ)	160	58.43N	26.45E
Chuguchak, hist. reg., China (chōō′gōō-chäk′)	180	46.09N	83.58E
Chuguyev, Ukr. (chōō′gò-yĕf)	160	49.52N	36.40E
Chuguyevka, Russia (chò-gōō′yĕf-ká)	186	43.58N	133.49E
Chugwater Creek, r., Wy., U.S. (chŭg′wô-tēr)	96	41.43N	104.54W
Chukot National Okrug, , Russia	162	68.15N	170.00E
Chukotskiy Poluostrov, pen., Russia	158	66.12N	175.00W
Chukotskoye Nagor′ye, mts., Russia	158	66.00N	166.00E
Chula Vista, Ca., U.S. (chōō′lá vĭs′tá)	102a	32.38N	117.05W
Chulkovo, Russia (chōōl-kô vô)	164b	55.33N	38.04E
Chulucanas, Peru	124	5.13S	80.13W
Chulum, r., Russia	162	57.52N	84.45E
Chumikan, Russia (chōō-mē-kän′)	158	54.47N	135.09E
Chun′an, China (chòn-än)	184	29.38N	119.00E
Chunchŏn, S. Kor. (chòn-chŭn′)	186	37.51N	127.46E
Chungju, S. Kor. (chŭng′jōō′)	186	37.00N	128.19E
Chŭngsanha-ri, neigh., S. Kor.	237b	37.35N	126.54E
Chunya, Tan.	210	8.32S	33.25E
Chunya, r., Russia (chòn′yä′)	162	61.45N	101.28E
Chuquicamata, Chile (chōō-kē-kä-mä′tä)	126	22.08S	68.57W
Chur, Switz. (kōōr)	140	46.51N	9.32E
Churchill, Can. (chûrch′ĭl)	78	58.50N	94.10W
Churchill, Pa., U.S.	226b	40.27N	79.51W
Churchill, Va., U.S.	225d	38.54N	77.10W
Churchill, r., Can.	78	58.00N	95.00W
Churchill, Cape, c., Can.	78	59.07N	93.50W
Churchill Falls, wtfl., Can.	78	53.35N	64.27W
Churchill Lake, l., Can.	82	56.12N	108.40W
Churchill Peak, mtn., Can.	78	58.10N	125.14W
Church Street, Eng., U.K.	231	51.26N	0.28E
Church Stretton, Eng., U.K. (chûrch strĕt′ŭn)	138a	52.32N	2.49W
Churchton, Md., U.S.	94e	38.49N	76.33W
Churu, India	178	28.22N	75.00E
Churumuco, Mex. (chōō-rōō-mōō′kō)	112	18.39N	101.40W
Chuska Mountains, mts., Az., U.S. (chŭs-kå)	102	36.21N	109.11W
Chusovaya, r., Russia (chōō-sô-vä′yá)	160	58.08N	58.35E
Chusovoy, Russia (chōō-sô-vôy′)	158	58.18N	57.50E
Chust, Uzb. (chòst)	158	41.05N	71.28E
Chuvash Autonomous Soviet Socialist Republic, Russia (chōō′vásh)	160	55.45N	46.00E
Chuviscar, r., Mex. (chōō-vēs-kär′)	106	28.34N	105.36W
Chuwang, China (chōō-wäŋ)	182	36.08N	114.53E
Chuxian, China (chōō shyĕn)	184	32.19N	118.19E
Chuxiong, China (chōō-shyòŋ)	180	25.19N	101.34E
Cicero, Il., U.S. (sĭs′ēr-ō)	95a	41.50N	87.46W
Cide, Tur. (jē′dĕ)	142	41.50N	33.00E
Ciechanów, Pol. (tsyĕ-kä′nòf)	148	52.52N	20.39E
Ciego de Avila, Cuba (syä′gō dā ä′vē-lä)	110	21.50N	78.45W
Ciego de Avila, prov., Cuba	116	22.00N	78.40W
Ciempozuelos, Spain (thyĕm-pō-thwā′lōs)	152	40.09N	3.36W
Ciénaga, Col. (syā′nä-gä)	124	11.01N	74.15W
Cienfuegos, Cuba (syĕn-fwā′gōs)	110	22.10N	80.30W
Cienfuegos, prov., Cuba	116	22.15N	80.40W
Cienfuegos, Bahía, b., Cuba (bä-ē′ä-syĕn-fwā′gōs)	116	22.00N	80.35W
Ciervo, Isla de la, i., Nic. (ē′s-lä-dĕ-lä-syĕ′r-vô)	114	11.56N	83.20W
Cieszyn, Pol. (tsyĕ′shĕn)	148	49.47N	18.45E
Cieza, Spain (thyā′thä)	152	38.13N	1.25W
Cigüela, r., Spain	152	39.53N	2.54W
Cihuatlán, Mex. (sē-wä-tlà′n)	112	19.13N	104.36W
Cihuatlán, r., Mex.	112	19.11N	104.30W
Cijara, Embalse de, res., Spain	152	39.25N	5.00W
Cilician Gates, p., Tur.	160	37.30N	35.30E
Cimarron, r., U.S. (sĭm-á-rōn′)	90	36.26N	98.27W
Cimarron, r., Co., U.S.	104	37.13N	102.30W
Cîmpina, Rom.	154	45.08N	25.47E
Cîmpulung, Rom.	142	45.15N	25.03E
Cîmpulung Moldovenesc, Rom.	148	47.31N	25.36E
Cinca, r., Spain (thēŋ′kä)	152	42.09N	0.08E
Cincinnati, Oh., U.S. (sĭn-sĭ-nát′ĭ)	90	39.08N	84.30W
Cinco Balas, Cayos, is., Cuba (kä′yōs-thēŋ′kō bä′läs)	116	21.05N	79.25W
Cinderella, S. Afr.	240b	26.15S	28.16E
Cinisello Balsamo, Italy	234c	45.33N	9.13E
Cinkota, neigh., Hung.	235g	47.31N	19.14E
Cintalapa, Mex. (sēn-tä-lä′pä)	112	16.41N	93.44W
Cinto, Monte, mtn., Fr. (chēn′tō)	140	42.24N	8.54E
Circle, Ak., U.S. (sûr′k′l)	90a	65.49N	144.22W
Circleville, Oh., U.S. (sûr′k′lvĭl)	92	39.35N	83.00W
Cirebon, Indon.	188	6.50S	108.33E
Ciri Grande, r., Pan. (sē′rē-grá′n′dĕ)	110a	8.55N	80.04W
Cisco, Tx., U.S. (sĭs′kō)	106	32.23N	98.57W
Ciskei, nation, Afr.	206	32.50S	27.00E
Cisliano, Italy	234c	45.27N	8.59E
Cisneros, Col. (sēs-nĕ′rôs)	124a	6.33N	75.05W
Cisterna di Latina, Italy (chēs-tĕ′r-nä-dē-lä-tē′nä)	153d	41.36N	12.53E
Cistierna, Spain (thēs-tyĕr′nä)	152	42.48N	5.08W
Citronelle, Al., U.S. (cĭt-rô′nēl)	108	31.05N	88.15W
Cittadella, Italy (chēt-tä-dĕl′lä)	154	45.39N	11.51E
Città di Castello, Italy (chēt-tä′dē käs-tĕl′lō)	154	43.27N	12.17E
City College of New York, pt. of i., N.Y., U.S.	224	40.49N	73.57W
City Island, neigh., N.Y., U.S.	224	40.51N	73.47W
City of Baltimore, Md., U.S.	225d	39.18N	76.37W
City of Commerce, Ca., U.S.	228	33.59N	118.08W
City of Industry, Ca., U.S.	228	34.01N	117.57W
City of London, neigh., Eng., U.K.	231	51.31N	0.05W
City of Westminster, neigh., Eng., U.K.	231	51.30N	0.09W
Ciudad Altamirano, Mex. (syōō-dä′d-äl-tä-mē-rä′nō)	112	18.24N	100.38W
Ciudad Bolívar, Ven. (syōō-dhädh′ bô-lē′vär)	124	8.07N	63.41W
Ciudad Camargo, Mex.	110	27.42N	105.10W
Ciudad Chetumal, Mex.	110	18.30N	88.17W
Ciudad Darío, Nic. (syōō-dhädh′dä′rē-ō)	114	12.44N	86.08W
Ciudad de la Habana, prov., Cuba	116	23.20N	82.10W
Ciudad de las Casas, Mex. (syōō-dä′d-dĕ-lä-kà′säs)	110	16.44N	92.39W
Ciudad del Carmen, Mex. (syōō-dä′d-dĕl-kà′r-mĕn)	110	18.39N	91.49W
Ciudad del Maíz, Mex. (syōō-dhädh′del mä-ēz′)	112	22.24N	99.37W
Ciudad Deportive, rec., Mex.	229a	19.24N	99.06W
Ciudadela, Spain (thyōō-dhä-dhā′lä)	152	40.00N	3.52E
Ciudad Fernández, Mex. (syōō-dhädh′fĕr-nän′dĕz)	112	21.56N	100.03W
Ciudad García, Mex. (syōō-dhädh′gär-sē′ä)	110	22.39N	103.02W
Ciudad General Belgrano, Arg.	229d	34.44S	58.32W
Ciudad Guayana, Ven.	124	8.30N	62.45W
Ciudad Guzmán, Mex. (syōō-dhädh′gòz-män)	110	19.40N	103.29W
Ciudad Hidalgo, Mex. (syōō-dä′d-ē-dä′l-gô)	112	19.41N	100.35W
Ciudad Juárez, Mex. (syōō-dhädh hwä′räz)	110	31.44N	106.28W
Ciudad Madero, Mex. (syōō-dä′d-mä-dĕ′rô)	112	22.16N	97.52W
Ciudad Mante, Mex. (syōō-dä′d-mán′tĕ)	110	22.34N	98.58W
Ciudad Manual Doblado, Mex. (syōō-dä′d-män-wäl′dō-blä′dō)	112	20.43N	101.57W
Ciudad Obregón, Mex. (syōō-dhädh-ô-brĕ-gô′n)	110	27.40N	109.58W
Ciudad Real, Spain (thyōō-dhädh′rā-äl′)	152	38.59N	3.55W
Ciudad Rodrigo, Spain (thyōō-dhädh′rô-drē′gō)	142	40.38N	6.34W
Ciudad Serdán, Mex. (syōō-dä′d-sĕr-dá′n)	112	18.58N	97.26W
Ciudad Universitaria, educ., Spain	234b	40.27N	3.44W
Ciudad Victoria, Mex. (syōō-dhädh′vēk-tō′rē-ä)	110	23.43N	99.09W
Civitavecchia, Italy (chē′vē-tä-vĕk′kyä)	154	42.06N	11.49E
Cixian, China (tsē shyĕn)	182	36.22N	114.23E
Clackamas, Or., U.S. (klăc-kå′măs)	100c	45.25N	122.34W
Claire, l., Can. (klâr)	78	58.33N	113.16W
Clair Engle Lake, l., Ca., U.S.	98	40.51N	122.41W
Clairton, Pa., U.S. (klărt′ŭn)	95e	40.17N	79.53W
Clamart, Fr.	233c	48.48N	2.16E
Clanton, Al., U.S. (klăn′tŭn)	108	32.50N	86.38W
Clare, Mi., U.S. (klâr)	92	43.50N	84.45W
Clare Island, i., Ire.	144	53.46N	10.00W
Claremont, Eng., U.K.	231	51.21N	0.22W
Claremont, Ca., U.S. (klâr′mŏnt)	101a	34.06N	117.43W
Claremont, N.H., U.S. (klâr′mŏnt)	92	43.20N	72.20W
Claremont, W.V., U.S.	92	37.55N	81.00W
Claremore, Ok., U.S. (klâr′mōr)	104	36.16N	95.37W
Claremorris, Ire. (klâr-mŏr′ĭs)	144	53.46N	9.05W
Clarence Strait, strt., Austl. (klăr′ĕns)	196	12.15S	130.05E
Clarence Strait, strt., Ak., U.S.	80	55.25N	132.00W
Clarence Town, Bah.	116	23.05N	75.00W
Clarendon, Ar., U.S. (klâr′ĕn-dŭn)	104	34.42N	91.17W
Clarendon, Tx., U.S.	104	34.55N	100.52W
Clarens, S. Afr. (clâ-rĕns)	207c	28.34S	28.26E
Claresholm, Can. (klâr′ĕs-hōlm)	78	50.02N	113.35W
Clarinda, Ia., U.S. (klå-rĭn′då)	96	40.42N	95.00W
Clarines, Ven. (klä-rē′nĕs)	125b	9.57N	65.10W
Clarion, Ia., U.S. (klăr′ĭ-ŭn)	96	42.43N	93.45W
Clarion, Pa., U.S.	92	41.10N	79.25W
Clark, N.J., U.S.	224	40.38N	74.19W
Clark, S.D., U.S. (klärk)	96	44.52N	97.45W
Clark, Point, c., Can.	84	44.05N	81.50W
Clarkdale, Az., U.S. (klärk-dāl)	102	34.45N	112.05W
Clarke City, Can.	78	50.12N	66.38W
Clarke Range, mts., Austl.	196	20.30S	148.00E
Clark Fork, r., Mt., U.S.	98	47.50N	115.35W
Clarksburg, W.V., U.S. (klärkz′bûrg)	90	39.15N	80.20W
Clarksdale, Ms., U.S. (klärks-dāl)	108	34.10N	90.31W
Clark's Harbour, Can. (klärks)	86	43.26N	65.38W
Clarks Hill Lake, res., U.S. (klärk-hĭl)	90	33.50N	82.35W
Clarkston, Ga., U.S. (klärks′tŭn)	94c	33.49N	84.15W
Clarkston, Wa., U.S.	98	46.24N	117.01W
Clarksville, Ar., U.S. (klärks-vĭl)	104	35.28N	93.26W
Clarksville, Tn., U.S.	108	36.30N	87.23W
Clarksville, Tx., U.S.	104	33.37N	95.02W
Clatskanie, Or., U.S.	100c	46.04N	123.11W
Clatskanie, r., Or., U.S. (klăt-skā′nē)	100c	46.06N	123.11W
Clatsop Spit, Or., U.S. (klăt-sŏp)	100c	46.13N	124.04W
Cláudio, Braz. (klou′-dĕō)	123a	20.26S	44.44W
Claveria, Phil. (klä-vå-rē′ä)	184	18.38N	121.08E
Clawson, Mi., U.S. (klô′s′n)	95b	42.32N	83.09W
Claxton, Ga., U.S. (klăks′tŭn)	108	32.07N	81.54W
Clay, Ky., U.S. (klā)	108	37.28N	87.50W
Clay Center, Ks., U.S. (klā sĕn′tēr)	104	39.23N	97.08W
Clay City, Ky., U.S. (klā sĭ′tĭ)	92	37.50N	83.55W
Claycomo, Mo., U.S. (kla-kō′mo)	101f	39.12N	94.30W
Clay Cross, Eng., U.K. (klā krŏs)	138a	53.10N	1.25W
Claye-Souilly, Fr. (klĕ-sōō-yē′)	151b	48.56N	2.43E
Claygate, Eng., U.K.	231	51.22N	0.20W
Claygate Cross, Eng., U.K.	231	51.16N	0.19E
Claymont, De., U.S. (klā-mŏnt)	94f	39.48N	75.28W
Clayton, Eng., U.K.	138a	53.47N	1.49W
Clayton, Al., U.S. (klā′tŭn)	108	31.52N	85.25W
Clayton, Ca., U.S.	100b	37.56N	121.56W
Clayton, Mo., U.S.	101e	38.39N	90.20W
Clayton, N.M., U.S.	104	36.26N	103.12W
Clayton, N.C., U.S.	108	35.40N	78.27W
Clear, l., Ca., U.S.	102	39.05N	122.50W
Clear Boggy Creek, r., Ok., U.S. (klēr bŏg′ĭ krēk)	104	34.21N	96.22W
Clear Creek, r., Az., U.S.	102	34.40N	111.05W
Clear Creek, r., Tx., U.S.	107a	29.34N	95.13W

ng-sing; ŋ-baŋk; ɴ-nasalized n; nŏd; cŏmmit; ōld; ôbey; ôrder; oi-boil; fōōd; ŏŏ-as oo in foot; ou-out; s-soft; sh-dish; th-thin; pūre; ůnite; ûrn; stŭd; circŭs; ü-as in French tu; ′-indeterminate vowel.

PLACE (Pronunciation)	PAGE	Lat. °'	Long. °'
Clear Creek, r., Wy., U.S.	98	44.35N	106.20W
Clearfield, Pa., U.S. (klēr-fēld)	92	41.00N	78.25W
Clearfield, Ut., U.S.	101b	41.07N	112.01W
Clear Hills, Can.	78	57.11N	119.20W
Clearing, neigh., Il., U.S.	227a	41.47N	87.47W
Clear Lake, Ia., U.S.	96	43.09N	93.23W
Clear Lake, Wa., U.S.	100a	48.27N	122.14W
Clear Lake Reservoir, res., Ca., U.S.	98	41.53N	121.00W
Clearwater, Fl., U.S. (klēr-wô'tēr)	109a	27.43N	82.45W
Clearwater, r., Can.	80	52.00N	120.10W
Clearwater, r., Can.	80	52.00N	114.50W
Clearwater, r., Can.	82	56.10N	110.40W
Clearwater, r., Id., U.S.	98	46.27N	116.33W
Clearwater, Middle Fork, r., Id., U.S.	98	46.10N	115.48W
Clearwater, North Fork, r., Id., U.S.	98	46.34N	116.08W
Clearwater, South Fork, r., Id., U.S.	98	45.46N	115.53W
Clearwater Mountains, mts., Id., U.S.	98	45.56N	115.15W
Cleburne, Tx., U.S. (klē'bŭrn)	90	32.21N	97.23W
Cle Elum, Wa., U.S. (klē ĕl'ŭm)	98	47.12N	120.55W
Clementon, N.J., U.S. (klē'mĕn-tŭn)	94f	39.49N	75.00W
Cleobury Mortimer, Eng., U.K. (klēō-bĕr'ĭ môr'tĭ-mēr)	138a	52.22N	2.29W
Clermont, Austl. (klēr'mŏnt)	196	23.02S	147.46E
Clermont, Can.	84	47.45N	70.20W
Clermont-Ferrand, Fr. (klĕr-môɴ'fĕr-räɴ')	136	45.47N	3.03E
Cleveland, Ms., U.S. (klēv'lănd)	108	33.45N	90.42W
Cleveland, Oh., U.S.	90	41.30N	81.42W
Cleveland, Ok., U.S.	104	36.18N	96.28W
Cleveland, Tn., U.S.	108	35.09N	84.52W
Cleveland, Tx., U.S.	106	30.18N	95.05W
Cleveland Heights, Oh., U.S.	95d	41.30N	81.35W
Cleveland Museum of Art, pt. of i., Oh., U.S.	225a	41.31N	81.37W
Cleveland Park, neigh., D.C., U.S.	225d	38.56N	77.04W
Cleveland Peninsula, pen., Ak., U.S.	80	55.45N	132.00W
Cleves, Oh., U.S. (klē'vĕs)	95f	39.10N	84.45W
Clew Bay, b., Ire. (klōō)	144	53.47N	9.45W
Clewiston, Fl., U.S. (klē'wĭs-tŭn)	109a	26.44N	80.55W
Clichy, Fr. (klē-shē')	150	48.54N	2.18E
Clichy-sous-Bois, Fr.	233c	48.55N	2.33E
Clifden, Ire. (klĭf'dĕn)	144	53.31N	10.04W
Cliffside Park, N.J., U.S.	224	40.49N	73.59W
Clifton, Az., U.S. (klĭf'tŭn)	102	33.05N	109.20W
Clifton, Ma., U.S.	223a	42.29N	70.53W
Clifton, N.J., U.S.	94a	40.52N	74.09W
Clifton, S.C., U.S.	108	35.00N	81.47W
Clifton, Tx., U.S.	106	31.45N	97.31W
Clifton Forge, Va., U.S.	92	37.50N	79.50W
Clifton Heights, Pa., U.S.	225b	39.56N	75.18W
Clinch, r., Tn., U.S. (klĭnch)	108	36.30N	83.19W
Clingmans Dome, mtn., U.S. (klĭng'măns dōm)	108	35.37N	83.26W
Clinton, Can. (klĭn-'tŭn)	78	51.05N	121.35W
Clinton, Il., U.S.	92	40.10N	88.55W
Clinton, In., U.S.	92	39.40N	87.25W
Clinton, Ia., U.S.	96	41.50N	90.13W
Clinton, Ky., U.S.	108	36.39N	88.56W
Clinton, Md., U.S.	94c	38.46N	76.54W
Clinton, Ma., U.S.	87a	42.25N	71.41W
Clinton, Mo., U.S.	104	38.23N	93.46W
Clinton, N.C., U.S.	108	34.58N	78.20W
Clinton, Ok., U.S.	104	35.31N	98.56W
Clinton, S.C., U.S.	108	34.27N	81.53W
Clinton, Tn., U.S.	108	36.05N	84.08W
Clinton, Wa., U.S.	100a	47.59N	122.22W
Clinton, r., Mi., U.S.	95b	42.36N	83.00W
Clinton-Colden, l., Can.	78	63.58N	106.34W
Clintonville, Wi., U.S. (klĭn'tŭn-vĭl)	96	44.37N	88.46W
Clio, Mi., U.S. (klē'ō)	92	43.10N	83.45W
Cloates, Point, c., Austl. (klōts)	196	22.47S	113.45E
Clocolan, S. Afr.	212d	28.56S	27.35E
Clonakilty Bay, b., Ire. (klŏn-ȧ-kĭltē)	144	51.30N	8.50W
Cloncurry, Austl. (klŏn-kŭr'ē)	196	20.58S	140.42E
Clonmel, Ire. (klŏn-mĕl)	144	52.21N	7.45W
Clontarf, Austl.	239a	33.48S	151.16E
Cloquet, Mn., U.S. (klō-kā')	101h	46.42N	92.28W
Closter, N.J., U.S. (klōs'tēr)	94a	40.58N	73.57W
Cloud Peak, mtn., Wy., U.S. (kloud)	90	44.23N	107.11W
Clover, S.C., U.S. (klō'vēr)	108	35.08N	81.08W
Clover Bar, Can. (klō'vēr bär)	77g	53.34N	113.20W
Cloverdale, Can.	100d	49.06N	122.44W
Cloverdale, Ca., U.S. (klō'vēr-dāl)	102	38.47N	123.03W
Cloverdene, S. Afr.	240b	26.09S	28.22E
Cloverport, Ky., U.S. (klō'vēr pōrt)	92	37.50N	86.35W
Clovis, N.M., U.S. (klō'vĭs)	90	34.24N	103.11W
Cluj-Napoca, Rom.	136	46.46N	23.34E
Clun, r., Eng., U.K. (klŭn)	138a	52.25N	2.56W
Cluny, Fr. (klü-nē')	150	46.27N	4.40E
Clutha, r., N.Z. (klōō'thȧ)	197a	45.52S	169.30E
Clwyd, co., Wales, U.K.	138a	53.01N	2.59W
Clyde, Ks., U.S.	104	39.34N	97.23W
Clyde, Oh., U.S.	92	41.15N	83.00W
Clyde, r., Scot., U.K.	144	55.35N	3.50W
Clyde, Firth of, b., Scot., U.K. (fûrth ŏv klīd)	144	55.28N	5.01W
Côa, r., Port. (kō'ä)	152	40.28N	6.55W
Coacalco, Mex. (kō-ä-käl'kō)	113a	19.37N	99.06W
Coachella, Canal, can., Ca., U.S. (kō'chĕl-lȧ)	102	33.15N	115.25W
Coahuayana, Río de, r., Mex. (rē'ō-dē-kō-ä-wä-yä'nä)	112	19.00N	103.33W
Coahuayutla, Mex. (kō'ä-wĭ-yōōt'lä)	112	18.19N	101.44W
Coahuila, state, Mex. (kō-ä-wē'lä)	110	27.30N	103.00W
Coal City, Il., U.S. (kōl sĭ'tĭ)	95a	41.17N	88.17W
Coalcomán, Río de, r., Mex. (rē'ō-dē-kō-äl-kō-män')	112	18.45N	103.15W
Coalcomán, Sierra de, mts., Mex.	112	18.30N	102.45W
Coalcomán de Matamoros, Mex.	112	18.46N	103.10W
Coaldale, Can. (kōl'dāl)	80	49.43N	112.37W
Coalgate, Ok., U.S. (kōl'gāt)	104	34.44N	96.13W
Coal Grove, Oh., U.S. (kōl grōv)	92	38.20N	82.40W
Coal Hill Park, rec., China	236b	39.56N	116.23E
Coalinga, Ca., U.S. (kō-ȧ-lĭŋ'gȧ)	102	36.09N	120.23W
Coalville, Eng., U.K. (kōl'vĭl)	138a	52.43N	1.21W
Coamo, P.R. (kō-ä'mō)	111b	18.05N	66.21W
Coari, Braz. (kō-är'ē)	124	4.06S	63.10W
Coast Mountains, mts., N.A. (kōst)	78	54.10N	128.00W
Coast Ranges, mts., U.S.	90	41.28N	123.30W
Coatepec, Mex.	112	19.26N	96.56W
Coatepec, Mex. (kō-ä-tā-pĕk)	112	19.23N	98.44W
Coatepec, Mex.	113a	19.08N	99.25W
Coatepeque, El Sal.	114	13.56N	89.30W
Coatepeque, Guat. (kō-ä-tȧ-pā'kȧ)	114	14.40N	91.52W
Coatesville, Pa., U.S. (kōts'vĭl)	92	40.00N	75.50W
Coatetelco, Mex. (kō-ä-tȧ-tĕl'kō)	112	18.43N	99.17W
Coaticook, Can. (kō'tĭ-kŏŏk)	84	45.10N	71.55W
Coatlinchán, Mex. (kô-ä-tlē'n-chä'n)	113a	19.26N	98.52W
Coats, i., Can. (kōts)	78	62.23N	82.11W
Coats Land, reg., Ant.	213	74.00S	30.00W
Coatzacoalcos, Mex.	110	18.09N	94.26W
Coatzacoalcos, r., Mex.	112	17.40N	94.41W
Coba, hist., Mex. (kô'bä)	114a	20.23N	87.23W
Cobalt, Can. (kō'bôlt)	78	47.21N	79.40W
Cobán, Guat. (kō-bän')	110	15.28N	90.19W
Cobar, Austl.	196	31.28S	145.50E
Cobberas, Mount, mtn., Austl. (cŏ-bĕr-ăs)	198	36.45S	148.15E
Cobequid Mountains, mts., Can.	86	45.35N	64.10W
Cobh, Ire. (kôv)	136	51.52N	8.09W
Cobham, Eng., U.K.	231	51.23N	0.24E
Cobija, Bol. (kô-bē'hä)	124	11.12S	68.49W
Cobourg, Can. (kō'bōrgh)	78	43.55N	78.05W
Cobre, r., Jam. (kō'brā)	116	18.05N	77.00W
Coburg, Austl.	195a	37.45S	144.58E
Coburg, Ger. (kō'bōōrg)	148	50.16N	10.57E
Cocentaina, Spain (kō-thån-tä-ē'nȧ)	152	38.44N	0.27W
Cochabamba, Bol.	124	17.24S	66.09W
Cochin, India (kō-chĭn')	178	9.58N	76.19E
Cochinos, Bahía, b., Cuba (bä-ē'ä-kô-chē'nōs)	116	22.05N	81.10W
Cochinos Banks, bk.	116	22.20N	76.15W
Cochiti Indian Reservation, I.R., N.M., U.S.	102	35.37N	106.20W
Cochran, Ga., U.S. (kŏk'răn)	108	32.23N	83.23W
Cochrane, Can.	77e	51.11N	114.28W
Cochrane, Can. (kŏk'răn)	78	49.01N	81.06W
Cockburn, i., Can. (kŏk-bûrn)	84	45.55N	83.25W
Cockeysville, Md., U.S. (kŏk'ĭz-vĭl)	94e	39.30N	76.40W
Cockfosters, neigh., Eng., U.K.	231	51.39N	0.09W
Cockrell Hill, Tx., U.S. (kŏk'rĕl)	101c	32.44N	96.53W
Coco, r., N.A.	110	14.55N	83.45W
Coco, Cayo, i., Cuba (kä'-yō-kô'kô)	116	22.30S	78.30W
Coco, Isla del, i., C.R. (ē's-lä-dĕl-kô-kô)	110	5.33N	87.02W
Cocoa, Fl., U.S. (kō'kō)	109a	28.21N	80.44W
Cocoa Beach, Fl., U.S.	109a	28.20N	80.35W
Cocoli, Pan. (kŏ-kŏ'lē)	110a	8.58N	79.36W
Coconino, Plateau, plat., Az., U.S. (kō kō nē'nō)	102	35.45N	112.28W
Cocos (Keeling) Islands, is., Oc. (kō'kōs) (kē'lĭng)	2	11.50S	90.50E
Coco Solito, Pan. (kô-kô-sō-lē'tô)	110a	9.21N	79.53W
Cocotá, neigh., Braz.	230c	22.49S	43.11W
Cocula, Mex. (kō-kōō'lä)	112	20.23N	103.47W
Cocula, r., Mex.	112	18.17N	99.45W
Cod, Cape, pen., Ma., U.S.	90	41.42N	70.15W
Codajás, Braz. (kō-dä-häzh')	124	3.44S	62.09W
Codera, Cabo, c., Ven. (kä'bô-kō-dĕ'rä)	125b	10.35N	66.06W
Codogno, Italy (kô-dō'nyō)	154	45.08N	9.43E
Codrington, Antig. (kŏd'rĭng-tŭn)	115b	17.39N	61.49W
Cody, Wy., U.S. (kō'dĭ)	98	44.31N	109.02W
Coelho da Rocha, Braz.	126b	22.47S	43.23W
Coemba, Ang.	210	12.08S	18.05E
Coesfeld, Ger. (kûs'fĕld)	151c	51.56N	7.10E
Coeur d'Alene, Id., U.S. (kûr dȧ-lān')	90	47.43N	116.35W
Coeur d'Alene, r., Id., U.S.	98	47.26N	116.35W
Coeur d'Alene Indian Reservation, I.R., Id., U.S.	98	47.18N	116.45W
Coeur d'Alene Lake, l., Id., U.S.	98	47.32N	116.39W
Coffeyville, Ks., U.S. (kŏf'ĭ-vĭl)	90	37.01N	95.38W
Coff's Harbour, Austl.	198	30.20S	153.10E
Cofimvaba, Transkei (căfĭm'vä-bȧ)	207c	32.01S	27.37E
Coghinas, r., Italy (kō'gē-nás)	154	40.31N	9.00E
Cognac, Fr. (kōn-yak')	140	45.41N	0.22W
Cohasset, Ma., U.S. (kō-hăs'ĕt)	87a	42.14N	70.48W
Cohoes, N.Y., U.S. (kō-hōz')	92	42.50N	73.40W
Coig, r., Arg. (kô'ĕk)	126	51.15N	71.00W
Coimbatore, India (kô-ēm-bȧ-tôr')	174	11.03N	76.56E
Coimbra, Port. (kō-ēm'brä)	136	40.14N	8.23W
Coín, Spain (kō-ēn')	152	36.40N	4.45W
Coina, Port. (kō-ē'nȧ)	153b	38.35N	9.03W
Coina, r., Port. (kō'y-nä)	153b	38.35N	9.02W
Coipasa, Salar de, pl., Bol. (sä-lä'r-dē-koi-pä'-sä)	124	19.12S	69.13W
Coixtlahuaca, Mex. (kō-ēks'tlä-wä'kä)	112	17.42N	97.17W
Cojedes, dept., Ven. (kô-kē'dĕs)	125b	9.50N	68.21W
Cojimar, Cuba (kō-hē-mär')	117a	23.10N	82.19W
Cojutepeque, El Sal. (kô-hô-tē-pā'kȧ)	114	13.45N	88.50W
Cokato, Mn., U.S. (kō-kā'tō)	96	45.03N	94.11W
Cokeburg, Pa., U.S. (kōk bûgh)	95e	40.06N	80.03W
Coker, Nig.	240d	6.29N	3.20E
Colāba, neigh., India	236e	18.54N	72.48E
Colac, Austl. (kŏ'lăc)	198	38.25S	143.40E
Colares, Port. (kō-lä'rĕs)	153b	38.47N	9.27W
Colatina, Braz. (kō-lä-tē'nä)	124	19.33S	40.42W
Colby, Ks., U.S. (kōl'bĭ)	104	39.23N	101.04W
Colchagua, prov., Chile (kôl-chȧ'gwä)	123b	34.42S	71.24W
Colchester, Eng., U.K. (kōl'chĕs-tēr)	144	51.52N	0.50E
Coldblow, neigh., Eng., U.K.	231	51.26N	0.10E
Cold Lake, l., Can. (kōld)	82	54.33N	110.05W
Coldwater, Ks., U.S. (kōld'wô-tēr)	104	37.14N	99.21W
Coldwater, Mi., U.S.	92	41.55N	85.00W
Coldwater, r., Ms., U.S.	108	34.25N	90.12W
Coldwater Creek, r., Tx., U.S.	104	36.10N	101.45W
Coleman, Tx., U.S. (kōl'mȧn)	106	31.50N	99.25W
Colenso, S. Afr. (kŏ-lĕnz'ô)	207c	28.48S	29.49E
Coleraine, N. Ire., U.K.	144	55.08N	6.40W
Coleraine, Mn., U.S. (kōl-rān')	96	47.16N	93.29W
Coleshill, Eng., U.K. (kōlz'hĭl)	138a	52.30N	1.42W
Colfax, Ia., U.S. (kōl'făks)	96	41.40N	93.13W
Colfax, La., U.S.	106	31.31N	92.42W
Colfax, Wa., U.S.	98	46.53N	117.21W
Colhué Huapi, l., Arg. (kôl-wä'ôä'pē)	126	45.30S	68.45W
Coligny, S. Afr.	212d	26.20S	26.18E
Colima, Mex. (kōlē'mä)	110	19.13N	103.45W
Colima, state, Mex.	112	19.10N	104.00W
Colima, Nevado de, mtn., Mex. (nĕ-vä'dô-dĕ-kô-lē'mä)	110	19.30N	103.38W
Coll, i., Scot., U.K. (kōl)	144	56.42N	6.23W
College, Ak., U.S.	89	64.43N	147.50W
College Park, Ga., U.S. (kŏl'ĕj)	94c	33.39N	84.27W
College Park, Md., U.S.	94e	38.59N	76.58W
College Point, neigh., N.Y., U.S.	224	40.47N	73.51W
Collegeville, Pa., U.S. (kŏl'ĕj-vĭl)	94f	40.11N	75.27W
Collie, Austl. (kŏl'ē)	196	33.20S	116.20E
Collier Bay, b., Austl. (kŏl-yēr)	196	15.30S	123.30E
Collier Row, neigh., Eng., U.K.	231	51.36N	0.10E
Collingdale, Pa., U.S.	225b	39.55N	75.17W
Collingswood, N.J., U.S. (kŏl'ĭngz-wŏŏd)	94f	39.54N	75.04W
Collingwood, Austl.	239b	37.48S	145.00E
Collingwood, Can.	84	44.30N	80.20W
Collins, Ms., U.S. (kŏl'ĭns)	108	31.40N	89.34W
Collinsville, Il., U.S. (kŏl'ĭnz-vĭl)	101e	38.41N	89.59W
Collinsville, Ok., U.S.	104	36.21N	95.50W
Colmar, Fr. (kôl'mär)	140	48.03N	7.25E
Colmenar de Oreja, Spain (kôl-mä-när' dāōrä'hä)	152	40.06N	3.25W
Colmenar Viejo, Spain (kôl-mä-när'vyā'hō)	152	40.40N	3.46W
Colnbrook, Eng., U.K.	231	51.29N	0.31W
Colney Heath, Eng., U.K.	231	51.44N	0.15W
Colney Street, Eng., U.K.	231	51.42N	0.20W
Cologne, Ger.	136	50.56N	6.57E
Cologno Monzese, Italy	234c	45.32N	9.17E
Colombes, Fr.	233c	48.55N	2.15E
Colombia, Col. (kô-lôm'bē-ä)	124a	3.23N	74.48W
Colombia, nation, S.A.	124	3.30N	72.30W
Colombo, Sri L. (kô-lôm'bō)	175c	6.58N	79.52E
Colón, Arg. (kō-lōn')	123c	33.55S	61.08W
Colón, Cuba (kō-lō'n)	116	22.45N	80.55W
Colón, Mex. (kō-lōn')	112	20.46N	100.02W
Colón, Pan. (kō-lō'n)	110	9.22N	79.54W
Colón, Archipiélago de, is., Ec.	124	0.10S	87.45W
Colón, Montañas de, mts., Hond. (môn-tä'n-yäs-dē-kō-lō'n)	114	14.58N	84.39W
Colonail Park, Md., U.S.	225c	39.19N	76.45W
Colonia, N.J., U.S.	224	40.35N	74.18W
Colonia, Ur. (kō-lō'nē-ä)	126	34.27S	57.50W
Colonia, dept., Ur.	123c	34.08S	57.50W
Colonial Manor, N.J., U.S.	225b	39.51N	75.09W
Colonia Suiza, Ur. (kô-lô'nēä-sōē'zä)	123c	34.17S	57.15W
Colonna, Capo, c., Italy	154	39.02N	17.15E
Colonsay, i., Scot., U.K. (kŏl-ŏn-sā')	144	56.08N	6.08E
Coloradas, Lomas, Arg. (lô'mäs-kō-lō-rä'däs)	126	43.30S	68.00W
Colorado, state, U.S.	90	39.30N	106.55W
Colorado, r., N.A.	90	36.00N	113.30W
Colorado, r., Tx., U.S.	90	30.08N	97.33W
Colorado, Río, r., Arg.	126	38.30S	66.00W
Colorado City, Tx., U.S. (kŏl-ô-rä'dō sĭ'tĭ)	106	32.24N	100.50W
Colorado National Monument, rec., Co., U.S.	102	39.00N	108.40W
Colorado Plateau, plat., U.S.	90	36.20N	109.25W
Colorado River Aqueduct, aq., Ca., U.S.	102	33.38N	115.43W
Colorado River Indian Reservation, I.R., Az., U.S.	102	34.03N	114.02W
Colorados, Archipiélago de los, is., Cuba	116	22.25N	84.25W
Colorado Springs, Co., U.S. (kŏl-ō-rä'dō)	90	38.49N	104.48W
Colosseo, hist., Italy	235c	41.54N	12.29E
Colotepec, r., Mex. (kô-lô'tē-pĕk)	112	15.56N	96.57W
Colotlán, Mex. (kō-lō-tlän')	112	22.06N	103.14W
Colotlán, r., Mex.	112	22.09N	103.17W
Colquechaca, Bol. (kōl-kā-chä'kä)	124	18.47S	66.02W
Colstrip, Mt., U.S. (kōl'strip)	98	45.54N	106.38W
Colton, Ca., U.S. (kōl'tŭn)	101a	34.04N	117.20W
Columbia, Il., U.S. (kô-lŭm'bĭ-ȧ)	101e	38.26N	90.12W
Columbia, Ky., U.S.	108	37.06N	85.15W
Columbia, Md., U.S.	94e	39.15N	76.51W
Columbia, Ms., U.S.	108	31.15N	89.49W
Columbia, Mo., U.S.	90	38.55N	92.19W
Columbia, Pa., U.S.	92	40.00N	76.25W
Columbia, S.C., U.S.	90	34.00N	81.00W
Columbia, Tn., U.S.	108	35.36N	87.02W
Columbia, r., N.A.	78	46.00N	120.00W
Columbia, Mount, mtn., Can.	80	52.09N	117.25W
Columbia City, In., U.S.	92	41.10N	85.30W
Columbia City, Or., U.S.	100c	45.53N	112.49W
Columbia Heights, Mn., U.S.	101g	45.03N	93.15W
Columbia Icefield, ice., Can.	80	52.08N	117.26W

PLACE (Pronunciation)	PAGE	Lat. °′	Long. °′
Columbia Mountains, mts., N.A.	80	51.30N	118.30W
Columbiana, Al., U.S. (kō-ŭm-bĭ-ă'nȧ)	108	33.10N	86.35W
Columbia University, pt. of i., N.Y., U.S.	224	40.48N	73.58W
Columbretes, is., Spain (kô-lōōm-brĕ'tĕs)	152	39.54N	0.54E
Columbus, Ga., U.S. (kō-lŭm'bŭs)	90	32.29N	84.56W
Columbus, In., U.S.	92	39.15N	85.55W
Columbus, Ks., U.S.	104	37.10N	94.50W
Columbus, Ms., U.S.	108	33.30N	88.25W
Columbus, Mt., U.S.	98	45.39N	109.15W
Columbus, Ne., U.S.	96	41.25N	97.25W
Columbus, N.M., U.S.	102	31.50N	107.40W
Columbus, Oh., U.S.	90	40.00N	83.00W
Columbus, Tx., U.S.	106	29.44N	96.34W
Columbus, Wi., U.S.	96	43.20N	89.01W
Columbus Bank, bk. (kō-lŭm'bŭs)	116	22.05N	75.30W
Columbus Grove, Oh., U.S.	92	40.55N	84.05W
Columbus Point, c., Bah.	116	24.10N	75.15W
Colusa, Ca., U.S. (kō-lū'sȧ)	102	39.12N	122.01W
Colville, Wa., U.S. (kŏl'vĭl)	98	48.33N	117.53W
Colville, r., Ak., U.S.	89	69.00N	156.25W
Colville Indian Reservation, I.R., Wa., U.S.	98	48.15N	119.00W
Colville R, Wa., U.S.	98	48.25N	117.58W
Colvos Passage, strt., Wa., U.S. (kŏl'vōs)	100a	47.24N	122.32W
Colwood, Can. (kŏl'wo̊od)	100a	48.26N	123.30W
Colwyn, Pa., U.S.	225b	39.55N	75.15W
Comacchio, Italy (kō-mäk'kyō)	154	44.42N	12.12E
Comala, Mex. (kō-mä-lä')	112	19.22N	103.47W
Comalapa, Guat. (kō-mä-lä'-pä)	114	14.43N	90.56W
Comalcalco, Mex. (kō-mäl-käl'kō)	112	18.16N	93.13W
Comanche, Ok., U.S. (kō-măn'chē)	104	34.20N	97.58W
Comanche, Tx., U.S.	106	31.54N	98.37W
Comanche Creek, r., Tx., U.S.	106	31.02N	102.47W
Comayagua, Hond. (kō-mä-yä'gwä)	110	14.24N	87.36W
Combahee, r., S.C., U.S. (kŏm-bȧ-hē')	108	32.42N	80.40W
Comer, Ga., U.S. (kŭm'ẽr)	108	34.02N	83.07W
Comete, Cape, c., T./C. Is. (kō-mā'tȧ)	116	21.45N	71.25W
Comilla, Bngl. (kō-mĭl'ä)	174	23.33N	91.17E
Comino, Cape, c., Italy (kō-mē'nō)	154	40.30N	9.48E
Comitán, Mex. (kō-mē-tän')	110	16.16N	92.09W
Commencement Bay, b., Wa., U.S. (kŏ-mĕns'mĕnt bā)	100a	47.17N	122.21W
Commentry, Fr. (kō-män-trē')	150	46.16N	2.44E
Commerce, Ga., U.S. (kŏm'ẽrs)	108	34.10N	83.27W
Commerce, Ok., U.S.	104	36.57N	94.54W
Commerce, Tx., U.S.	104	33.15N	95.52W
Como, Austl.	239a	34.00S	151.04E
Como, Italy (kō'mō)	142	45.48N	9.03E
Como, Lago di, l., Italy (lä'gō-dē-kō'mō)	142	46.00N	9.30E
Comodoro Rivadavia, Arg.	126	45.47S	67.31W
Como-Est, Can.	77a	45.27N	74.08W
Comonfort, Mex. (kō-mōn-fō'rt)	112	20.43N	100.47W
Comorin, Cape, c., India (kŏ'mō-rĭn)	175c	8.05N	78.05E
Comoros, nation, Afr.	206	12.30S	42.45E
Comox, Can. (kō'mŏks)	80	49.40N	124.55W
Companario, Cerro, mtn., S.A. (sĕ'r-rō-kôm-pä-nä'ryō)	123b	35.54S	70.23W
Compans, Fr.	233c	49.00N	2.40E
Compiègne, Fr. (kôn-pyĕn'y')	140	49.25N	2.49E
Comporta, Port. (kōm-pôr'tȧ)	153b	38.24N	8.48W
Compostela, Mex. (kōm-pō-stā'lä)	112	21.14N	104.54W
Compton, Ca., U.S. (kŏmpt'tŭn)	101a	33.54N	118.14W
Conakry, Gui. (kō-nȧ-krē')	204	9.31N	13.43W
Conanicut, i., R.I., U.S. (kŏn'ȧ-nĭ-kŭt)	94b	41.34N	71.20W
Conasauga, r., Ga., U.S. (kō-nȧ)	108	34.40N	84.51W
Concarneau, Fr. (kôn-kär-nō')	150	47.54N	3.52W
Concepción, Bol. (kōn-sĕp'syōn')	124	15.47S	61.08W
Concepción, Chile	126	36.51S	72.59W
Concepción, Pan.	114	8.31N	82.38W
Concepción, Para.	126	23.29S	57.18W
Concepcion, Phil.	189a	15.19N	120.40E
Concepción, vol., Nic.	114	11.36N	85.43W
Concepción, r., Mex.	110	30.25N	112.20W
Concepción del Mar, Guat. (kōn-sĕp-syōn'dĕl mär')	114	14.07N	91.23W
Concepción del Oro, Mex. (kōn-sĕp-syōn' dĕl ō'rō)	110	24.39N	101.24W
Concepción del Uruguay, Arg. (kōn-sĕp-syô'n-dĕl-ōō-rōō-gwī')	126	32.31S	58.10W
Conception, i., Bah.	116	23.50N	75.05W
Conception, Point, c., Ca., U.S.	90	34.27N	120.28W
Conception Bay, b., Can. (kŏn-sĕp'shŭn)	86	47.50N	52.50W
Conchalí, Chile	230b	33.24S	70.39W
Concho, r., Tx., U.S. (kŏn'chō)	106	31.34N	100.00W
Conchos, r., Mex. (kōn'chōs)	106	25.03N	99.00W
Conchos, r., Mex.	110	29.30N	105.00W
Concord, Austl.	239a	33.52S	151.06E
Concord, Can.	223c	43.48N	79.29W
Concord, Ca., U.S. (kŏŋ'kŏrd)	100b	37.58N	122.02W
Concord, Ma., U.S.	87a	42.28N	71.21W
Concord, N.H., U.S.	90	43.10N	71.30W
Concord, N.C., U.S.	108	35.23N	80.11W
Concordia, Arg. (kōn-kôr'dĭ-ȧ)	126	31.18S	57.59W
Concordia, Col.	124a	6.04N	75.54W
Concordia, Mex. (kōn-kô'r-dyä)	112	23.17N	106.06W
Concordia, Ks., U.S.	104	39.32N	97.39W
Concord West, Austl.	239a	33.51S	151.05E
Concrete, Wa., U.S. (kŏn-'krēt)	98	48.33N	121.44W
Conde, Fr.	150	48.50N	0.36W
Conde, S.D., U.S. (kŏn-dē')	96	45.10N	98.06W
Condega, Nic. (kŏn-dĕ'gä)	114	13.20N	86.27W
Condeúba, Braz. (kōn-dā-ōō'bä)	124	14.47S	41.44W
Condom, Fr.	150	43.58N	0.22E
Condon, Or., U.S. (kŏn'dŭn)	98	45.14N	120.10W
Conecun, r., Al., U.S. (kō-nē'kŭ)	108	31.05N	86.52W
Conegliano, Italy (kō-nâl-yä'nō)	154	45.59N	12.17E
Conejos, r., Co., U.S. (kō-nā'hōs)	102	37.07N	106.19W
Conemaugh, Pa., U.S. (kŏn'ē-mô)	92	40.25N	78.50W
Coney Island, neigh., N.Y., U.S.	224	40.34N	74.00W
Coney Island, i., N.Y., U.S. (kō'nĭ)	94a	40.34N	73.27W
Conflans-Sainte-Honorine, Fr.	233c	48.59N	2.06E
Confolens, Fr. (kôn-fā-län')	150	46.01N	0.41E
Congaree, r., S.C., U.S. (kŏŋ-gȧ-rē')	108	33.53N	80.55W
Conghua, China (tsōŋ-hwä)	184	23.30N	113.40E
Congleton, Eng., U.K. (kŏŋ'g'l-tŭn)	138a	53.10N	2.13W
Congo, nation, Afr. (kŏn'gō)	206	3.00S	13.48E
Congo (Zaire), r., Afr. (kŏn'gō)	203	2.00S	17.00E
Congo, Serra do, mts., Ang.	210	6.25S	13.30E
Congo, The, see Zaire, nation, Afr.	206	1.00S	22.15E
Congo Basin, basin, Zaire	203	2.47N	20.58E
Congress Heights, neigh., D.C., U.S.	225d	38.51N	77.00W
Conisbrough, Eng., U.K. (kŏn'ĭs-bŭr-ō)	138a	53.29N	1.13W
Coniston, Can.	84	46.29N	80.51W
Conklin, Can. (kŏŋk'lĭn)	80	55.38N	111.05W
Conley, Ga., U.S. (kŏn'lĭ)	94c	33.38N	84.19W
Conn, Lough, l., Ire. (lŏk kŏn)	144	53.56N	9.25W
Connacht, hist. reg., Ire. (cŏn'ât)	144	53.50N	8.45W
Connaughton, Pa., U.S.	225b	40.05N	75.19W
Conneaut, Oh., U.S. (kŏn-ē-ôt')	92	41.55N	80.35W
Connecticut, state, U.S. (kŏ-nĕt'ĭ-kŭt)	90	41.40N	73.10W
Connecticut, r., U.S.	90	43.55N	72.15W
Connellsville, Pa., U.S. (kŏn'nĕlz-vĭl)	92	40.00N	79.40W
Connemara, mts., Ire. (kŏn-nē-mȧ'rȧ)	144	53.30N	9.54W
Connersville, In., U.S. (kŏn'ẽrz-vĭl)	92	39.35N	85.10W
Connors Range, mts., Austl. (kŏn'nŏrs)	196	22.15S	149.00E
Conrad, Mt., U.S. (kŏn'răd)	98	48.11N	111.56W
Conrich, Can. (kŏn'rĭch)	77e	51.06N	113.51W
Conroe, Tx., U.S. (kŏn'rō)	106	30.18N	95.23W
Conselheiro Lafaiete, Braz.	124	20.40S	43.46W
Conshohocken, Pa., U.S. (kŏn-shō-hŏk'ĕn)	94f	40.04N	75.18W
Consolação, neigh., Braz.	230d	23.33S	46.39W
Consolación del Sur, Cuba (kōn-sō-lä-syōn')	116	22.30N	83.55W
Consolidated Main Reef Mines, quarry, S. Afr.	240b	26.11S	27.56E
Con Son, is., Viet.	188	8.30N	106.28E
Constance, Mount, mtn., Wa., U.S. (kŏn'stăns)	100a	47.46N	123.08W
Constanţa, Rom. (kōn-stán'tsȧ)	136	44.12N	28.36E
Constantina, Spain (kŏn-stän-tē'nä)	152	37.52N	5.39W
Constantine, Alg. (kôn-stän'tēn')	204	36.28N	6.38E
Constantine, Mi., U.S. (kŏn'stăn-tēn)	92	41.50N	85.40W
Constitución, Chile (kōn'stĭ-tōō-syōn')	126	35.24S	72.25W
Constitución, neigh., Arg.	229d	34.37S	58.23W
Constitution, Ga., U.S. (kŏn-stĭ-tū'shŭn)	94c	33.41N	84.20W
Contagem, Braz. (kōn-tà'zhĕm)	123a	19.54S	44.05W
Contepec, Mex. (kōn-tĕ-pĕk')	112	20.04N	100.07W
Contreras, Mex. (kôn-trĕ'räs)	113a	19.18N	99.14W
Contwoyto, l., Can.	78	65.42N	110.50W
Converse, Tx., U.S. (kŏn'vẽrs)	101d	29.31N	98.17W
Conway, Ar., U.S. (kŏn'wā)	104	35.06N	92.27W
Conway, N.H., U.S.	92	44.00N	71.10W
Conway, S.C., U.S.	108	33.49N	79.01W
Conway, Wa., U.S.	100a	48.20N	122.20W
Conyers, Ga., U.S. (kŏn'yŏrz)	108	33.41N	84.01W
Cooch Behār, India (ko̊och bē-här')	174	26.25N	89.34E
Coogee, Austl.	239a	33.55S	151.16E
Cook, Cape, c., Can. (ko̊ok)	80	50.08N	127.55W
Cook, Mount, mtn., N.Z.	197a	43.27S	170.13E
Cook, Point, c., Austl.	239b	37.55S	144.48E
Cookeville, Tn., U.S. (ko̊ok'vĭl)	108	36.07N	85.30W
Cooking Lake, Can. (ko̊ok'ĭng)	77g	53.25N	113.08W
Cooking Lake, l., Can.	77g	53.25N	113.02W
Cook Inlet, b., Ak., U.S.	89	60.50N	151.38W
Cook Islands, dep., Oc.	2	20.00S	158.00W
Cooksmill Green, Eng., U.K.	231	51.44N	0.22E
Cook Strait, strt., N.Z.	197a	40.37S	174.15E
Cooktown, Austl. (ko̊ok'toun)	196	15.40S	145.20E
Cooleemee, N.C., U.S. (kōō-lē'mē)	108	35.50N	80.32W
Coolgardie, Austl. (kōōl-gär'dē)	196	31.00S	121.25E
Cooma, Austl. (kōō'mȧ)	196	36.22S	149.10E
Coonamble, Austl. (kōō-năm'b'l)	196	31.00S	148.30E
Coonoor, India	178	10.22N	76.15E
Coon Rapids, Mn., U.S. (kōōn)	101g	45.09N	93.17W
Cooper, Tx., U.S. (kōōp'ẽr)	104	33.23N	95.40W
Cooper Center, Ak., U.S.	89	61.54N	15.30W
Coopersale Common, Eng., U.K.	231	51.42N	0.08E
Coopers Creek, r., Austl. (kōō'pẽrz)	196	27.32N	141.19E
Cooperstown, N.Y., U.S. (kōōp'ẽrs-toun)	92	42.45N	74.55W
Cooperstown, N.D., U.S.	96	47.26N	98.07W
Coosa, Al., U.S. (kōō'sȧ)	108	32.43N	86.25W
Coosa, r., U.S.	90	34.00N	86.00W
Coosawattee, r., Ga., U.S.	108	34.37N	84.45W
Coos Bay, Or., U.S. (kōōs)	98	43.21N	124.12W
Coos Bay, b., Or., U.S.	98	43.19N	124.40W
Cootamundra, Austl. (ko̊otȧ-mŭnd'rȧ)	198	34.25S	148.00E
Copacabana, Braz. (kô'pä-kȧ-bä'nä)	126b	22.57S	43.11W
Copalita, r., Mex. (kō-pä-lē'tä)	112	15.55N	96.06W
Copán, hist., Hond. (kō-pän')	114	14.50N	89.10W
Copano Bay, b., Tx., U.S. (kō-pän'ō)	106	28.08N	97.25W
Copenhagen (København), Den.	136	55.43N	12.27E
Copiapó, Chile (kō-pyä-pō')	126	27.16S	70.28W
Copley, Oh., U.S. (kŏp'lē)	95d	41.06N	81.38W
Copparo, Italy (kōp-pä'rō)	154	44.53N	11.50E
Coppell, Tx., U.S. (kŏp'pĕl)	101c	32.57N	97.00W
Copper, r., Ak., U.S. (kŏp'ẽr)	89	62.38N	145.00W
Copper Cliff, Can.	84	46.28N	81.04W
Copper Harbor, Mi., U.S.	96	47.27N	87.53W
Copperhill, Tn., U.S. (kŏp'ẽr hĭl)	108	35.00N	84.22W
Coppermine, Can. (kŏp'ẽr-mīn)	78	67.46N	115.19W
Coppermine, r., Can.	78	66.48N	114.59W
Copper Mountain, mtn., Ak., U.S.	80	55.14N	132.36W
Copperton, Ut., U.S. (kŏp'ẽr-tŭn)	101b	40.34N	112.06W
Coquilee, Or., U.S. (kō-kēl')	98	43.11N	124.11W
Coquilhatville, see Mbandaka, Zaire	206	0.04N	18.16E
Coquimbo, Chile (kō-kēm'bō)	126	29.58S	71.31W
Coquimbo, prov., Chile	123b	31.50S	71.05W
Coquitlam Lake, l., Can. (kō-kwĭt-lȧm)	100d	49.23N	122.44W
Corabia, Rom. (kō-rä'bĭ-ȧ)	142	43.45N	24.29E
Coracora, Peru (kō'rä-kō'rä)	124	15.12S	73.42W
Coral Gables, Fl., U.S.	109a	25.43N	80.14W
Coral Rapids, Can. (kŏr'ăl)	78	50.18N	81.49W
Coral Sea, sea, Oc. (kŏr'ăl)	196	13.30S	150.00E
Coralville Reservoir, res., Ia., U.S.	96	41.45N	91.50W
Corangamite, Lake, l., Austl. (cōr-ăng'ȧ-mīt)	198	38.05S	142.55E
Coraopolis, Pa., U.S. (kō-rä-ŏp'ō-lĭs)	95e	40.30N	80.09W
Corato, Italy (kô'rä-tō)	154	41.08N	16.28E
Corbeil-Essonnes, Fr. (kôr-bā'yĕ-sŏn')	150	48.31N	2.29E
Corbett, Or., U.S. (kôr'bĕt)	100c	45.31N	122.17W
Corbie, Fr. (kôr-bē')	150	49.55N	2.27E
Corbin, Ky., U.S. (kôr'bĭn)	108	36.55N	84.06W
Corby, Eng., U.K. (kôr'bĭ)	138a	52.29N	0.38W
Corcovado, mtn., Braz. (kôr-kō-vä'dō)	126b	22.57S	43.13W
Corcovado, Golfo, b., Chile (kôr-kō-vä'dhō)	126	43.40S	75.00W
Cordeiro, Braz. (kôr-dā'rō)	123a	22.03S	42.22W
Cordele, Ga., U.S. (kôr-dēl')	108	31.55N	83.50W
Cordell, Ok., U.S. (kôr-dĕl')	104	35.19N	98.58W
Córdoba, Arg. (kôr'dō-vä)	126	30.20S	64.03W
Córdoba, Mex. (kô'r-dō-bä)	110	18.53N	96.54W
Córdoba, Spain (kô'r-dō-bä)	152	37.55N	4.45W
Córdoba, prov., Arg. (kôr'dō-vä)	126	32.00S	64.00W
Córdoba, Sierra de, mts., Arg.	126	31.15S	64.30W
Cordova, Al., U.S. (kôr'dō-ȧ)	108	33.45N	86.22W
Cordova, Ak., U.S. (kôr'dō-vä)	90a	60.34N	145.38W
Cordova Bay, b., Ak., U.S.	80	54.55N	132.35W
Corfu, see Kérkira, i., Grc.	136	39.33N	19.36E
Corigliano, Italy (kō-rē-lyä'nō)	154	39.35N	16.30E
Corinth, Ms., U.S. (kŏr'ĭnth)	108	34.55N	88.30W
Corinth, see Kórinthos, Grc.	136	37.56N	22.54E
Corinto, Braz. (kō-rē'n-tō)	124	18.20S	44.16W
Corinto, Col.	124a	3.09N	76.12W
Corinto, Nic. (kōr-ĭn'to)	114	12.30N	87.12W
Corio, Austl.	195a	38.05S	144.22E
Corio Bay, b., Austl.	195a	38.07S	144.25E
Corisco, Isla de, i., Eq. Gui.	210	0.50N	8.40E
Cork, Ire. (kôrk)	136	51.54N	8.25W
Cork Harbour, b., Ire.	144	51.44N	8.15W
Corleone, Italy (kôr-lå-ō'nä)	154	37.48N	13.18E
Cormano, Italy	234c	45.33N	9.10E
Cormeilles-en-Parisis, Fr.	233c	48.59N	2.12E
Cormorant Lake, l., Can.	82	54.13N	100.47W
Cornelia, Ga., U.S. (kôr-nē'lyȧ)	108	34.31N	83.30W
Cornelis, r., S. Afr. (kôr-nē'lĭs)	212d	27.48S	29.15E
Cornell, Ca., U.S. (kôr-nĕl')	101a	34.06N	118.46W
Cornell, Wi., U.S.	96	45.10N	91.10W
Cornellá, Spain	234e	41.21N	2.05E
Corner Brook, Can. (kôr'nẽr)	78	48.57N	57.57W
Corner Inlet, b., Austl.	198	38.55S	146.45E
Corning, Ar., U.S. (kôr'nĭng)	104	36.26N	90.35W
Corning, Ia., U.S.	96	40.58N	94.40W
Corning, N.Y., U.S.	92	42.10N	77.05W
Corno, Monte, mtn., Italy (kôr'nō)	142	42.28N	13.37E
Cornwall, Bah.	116	25.55N	77.15W
Cornwall, Can. (kôrn'wôl)	84	45.05N	74.35W
Coro, Ven. (kō'rō)	124	11.22N	69.43W
Corocoro, Bol. (kō-rō-kō'rō)	124	17.15S	68.21W
Coromandel Coast, cst., India (kŏr-ō-man'dĕl)	174	13.30N	80.30E
Coromandel Peninsula, pen., N.Z.	199	36.50S	176.00E
Corona, Al., U.S. (kō-rō'nȧ)	108	33.42N	87.28W
Corona, Ca., U.S.	101a	33.52N	117.34W
Coronada, Bahía de, b., C.R. (bä-ē'ä-dē-kō-rō-nä'dō)	114	8.47N	84.04W
Corona del Mar, Ca., U.S. (kô-rō'nȧ dĕl mär)	101a	33.36N	117.53W
Coronado, Ca., U.S. (kŏr-ō-nä'dō)	102a	32.42N	117.12W
Coronation Gulf, b., Can. (kŏr-ō-nā'shŭn)	78	68.07N	112.50W
Coronel, Chile (kō-rō-nĕl')	126	37.00S	73.10W
Coronel Brandsen, Arg. (kŏ-rō-nĕl-brȧ'nd-sĕn)	123c	35.09S	58.15W
Coronel Dorrego, Arg. (kŏ-rō-nĕl-dŏr-rĕ'gō)	126	38.43S	61.16W
Coronel Oviedo, Para. (kŏ-rō-nĕl-ō-vēē'dō)	126	25.28S	56.22W
Coronel Pringles, Arg. (kŏ-rō-nĕl-prĕn'glĕs)	126	37.54S	61.22W
Coronel Suárez, Arg. (kŏ-rō-nĕl-swä'räs)	126	37.27S	61.49W
Corowa, Austl. (cōr-ŏwȧ)	198	36.02S	146.23E
Corozal, Belize (cōr-ŏth-äl')	114a	18.25N	88.23W
Corpus Christi, Tx., U.S. (kôr'pŭs krĭstē)	90	27.48N	97.24W
Corpus Christi Bay, b., Tx., U.S.	106	27.47N	97.14W
Corpus Christi Lake, l., Tx., U.S.	106	28.08N	98.20W
Corral, Chile (kō-räl')	126	39.57S	73.15W
Corral de Almaguer, Spain (kō-räl'dā äl-mä-gâr')	152	39.45N	3.10W
Corralillo, Cuba (kō-rä-lē-yō)	116	23.00N	80.40W
Corregidor Island, i., Phil. (kō-rā-hē-dōr')	189a	14.21N	120.25E
Correntina, Braz. (kō-rĕn-tē-nȧ)	124	13.18S	44.33W
Corrib, Lough, l., Ire. (lŏk kŏr'ĭb)	144	53.25N	9.19W
Corrientes, Arg. (kō-ryĕn'tās)	126	27.25S	58.39W
Corrientes, prov., Arg.	126	28.45S	58.00W
Corrientes, Cabo, c., Col. (kȧ'bō-kō-ryĕn'tās)	124	5.34N	77.35W
Corrientes, Cabo, c., Cuba (kȧ'bō-kôr-rē-ĕn'tĕs)	116	21.50N	84.25W

ng-sing; ŋ-baŋk; N-nasalized n; nŏd; cŏmmit; ōld; ôbey; ôrder; oi-boil; fōōd; o̊-as oo in foot; ou-out; s-soft; sh-dish; th-thin; pūre; ůnite; ûrn; stŭd; circŭs; ü-as in French tu; '-indeterminate vowel.

PLACE (Pronunciation)	PAGE	Lat. °′	Long. °′
Corrientes, Cabo, c., Mex.	110	20.25N	105.41W
Corringham, Eng., U.K.	231	51.31N	0.28E
Corroios, Port.	234d	38.38N	9.09W
Corry, Pa., U.S. (kŏr'ĭ)	92	41.55N	79.40W
Corse, Cap, c., Fr. (kôrs)	140	42.59N	9.19E
Corsica, i., Fr. (kôr'sĭ-kä)	136	42.10N	8.55E
Corsicana, Tx., U.S. (kôr-sĭ-kăn'ȧ)	90	32.06N	96.28W
Corsico, Italy	234c	45.26N	9.07E
Cortazar, Mex. (kôr-tä-zär)	112	20.30N	100.57W
Corte, Fr. (kôr'tā)	154	42.18N	9.10E
Cortegana, Spain (kôr-tā-gä'nä)	152	37.54N	6.48W
Corte Madera, Ca., U.S.	227b	37.55N	122.31W
Cortes, bldg., Spain	234b	40.25N	3.41W
Cortés, Ensendada de, b., Cuba (ĕn-sĕ-nä-dä-dĕ-kôr-tās')	116	22.05N	83.45W
Cortez, Co., U.S.	102	37.21N	108.35W
Cortland, N.Y., U.S. (kôrt'lănd)	92	42.35N	76.10W
Cortona, Italy (kôr-tō'nä)	154	43.16N	12.00E
Corubal, r., Gui.-B.	208	11.43N	14.40W
Coruche, Port. (kō-rōō'she)	152	38.58N	8.34W
Çoruh, r., Asia (chō-rōōk')	160	40.30N	41.10E
Çorum, Tur. (chō-rōōm')	174	40.34N	34.45E
Corunna, Mi., U.S. (kō-rŭn'ȧ)	92	43.00N	84.05W
Coruripe, Braz. (kō-rō-rē'pĭ)	124	10.09S	36.13W
Corvallis, Or., U.S. (kŏr-văl'ĭs)	90	44.34N	123.17W
Corve, r., Eng., U.K. (kôr'vē)	138a	52.28N	2.43W
Corviale, neigh., Italy	235c	41.52N	12.25E
Corydon, In., U.S. (kŏr'ĭ-dŭn)	92	38.10N	86.05W
Corydon, Ia., U.S.	96	40.45N	93.20W
Corydon, Ky., U.S.	92	37.45N	87.40W
Cosamaloápan, Mex. (kō-sä-mä-lwä'pän)	112	18.21N	95.48W
Coscomatepec, Mex. (kôs'kōmä-tĕ-pĕk')	112	19.04N	97.03W
Cosenza, Italy (kō-zĕnt'sä)	142	39.18N	16.15E
Cosfanero, Canal de, strt., Arg.	229d	34.34S	58.22W
Coshocton, Oh., U.S. (kō-shŏk'tŭn)	92	40.15N	81.55W
Cosigüina, vol., Nic.	114	12.59N	87.35W
Cosmoledo Group, is., Sey. (kŏs-mō-lā'dō)	206	9.42S	47.45E
Cosmopolis, Wa., U.S. (kŏz-mŏp'ō-lĭs)	98	46.58N	123.47W
Cosne-sur-Loire, Fr. (kōn-sür-lwär')	150	47.25N	2.57E
Cosoleacaque, Mex. (kō sō lä-ä-kä'kē)	112	18.01N	94.38W
Costa de Caparica, Port.	153b	38.40N	9.12W
Costa Mesa, Ca., U.S. (kŏs'tȧ mā'sȧ)	101a	33.39N	118.54W
Costa Rica, nation, N.A. (kŏs'tȧ rē'kȧ)	110	10.30N	84.30W
Cosumnes, r., Ca., U.S. (kō-sŭm'nēz)	102	38.21N	121.17W
Cotabambas, Peru (kō-tä-bäm'bäs)	124	13.49S	72.17W
Cotabato, Phil. (kō-tä-bä'tō)	188	7.06N	124.13E
Cotaxtla, Mex. (kō-täs'tlä)	112	18.49N	96.22W
Cotaxtla, r., Mex.	112	18.54N	96.21W
Coteau-du-Lac, Can. (cō-tō'dü-läk)	77a	45.17N	74.11W
Coteau-Landing, Can.	77a	45.15N	74.13W
Coteaux, Haiti	116	18.15N	74.05W
Côte d'Or, reg., Fr.	150	47.02N	4.35E
Côte-Saint-Luc, Can.	223b	45.28N	73.40W
Côte Visitation, neigh., Can.	223b	45.33N	73.36W
Cotija de la Paz, Mex. (kō-tē'-ĸä-dĕ-lä-pȧ'z)	112	19.46N	102.43W
Cotonou, Benin (kō-tō-nōō')	204	6.21N	2.26E
Cotopaxi, mtn., Ec. (kō-tō-păk'sē)	124	0.40S	78.26W
Cotorro, Cuba (kō-tôr-rō)	117a	23.03N	82.17W
Cotswold Hills, hills, Eng., U.K. (kŭtz'wōld)	144	51.35N	2.16W
Cottage City, Md., U.S.	225d	38.56N	76.57W
Cottage Grove, Mn., U.S. (kŏt'āj grōv)	101g	44.50N	92.52W
Cottage Grove, Or., U.S.	98	43.48N	123.04W
Cottbus, Ger. (kōt'bōōs)	140	51.47N	14.20E
Cottonwood, r., Mn., U.S. (kŏt'ŭn-wŏŏd)	96	44.25N	95.35W
Cotulla, Tx., U.S. (kō-tŭl'lȧ)	106	28.26N	99.14W
Coubert, Fr. (kōō-bâr')	151b	48.40N	2.43E
Coudersport, Pa., U.S. (kou'dērz-pōrt)	92	41.45N	78.00W
Coudres, Île aux, i., Can.	86	47.17N	70.12W
Coulommiers, Fr. (kōō-lô-myā')	151b	48.49N	3.05E
Coulsdon, neigh., Eng., U.K.	231	51.19N	0.08W
Coulto, Serra do, mts., Braz. (sĕ'r-rä-dō-kō-ō'tō)	126b	22.33S	43.27W
Council Bluffs, Ia., U.S. (koun'sĭl blŭf)	90	41.16N	95.53W
Council Grove, Ks., U.S. (koun'sĭl grōv)	104	38.39N	96.30W
Coupeville, Wa., U.S. (kōōp'vĭl)	100a	48.13N	122.41W
Courantyne, r., S.A. (kôr'ăntīn)	124	4.28N	57.42W
Courbevoie, Fr.	233c	48.54N	2.15E
Courcelle, Fr.	233c	48.42N	2.06E
Courtenay, Can. (cōōrt-nā')	78	49.41N	125.00W
Courtleigh, Md., U.S.	225c	39.22N	76.46W
Courtry, Fr.	233c	48.55N	2.36E
Coushatta, La., U.S. (kou-shăt'ȧ)	106	32.02N	93.21W
Coutras, Fr. (kōō-trä')	150	45.02N	0.07W
Cova da Piedade, Port.	234d	38.40N	9.10W
Covelo, Ang.	210	12.06S	13.55E
Cove Neck, N.Y., U.S.	224	40.53N	73.31W
Coventry, Eng., U.K. (kŭv'ĕn-trĭ)	144	52.25N	1.29W
Covina, Ca., U.S. (kō-vē'nȧ)	101a	34.06N	117.54W
Covington, Ga., U.S. (kŭv'ĭng-tŭn)	108	33.36N	83.50W
Covington, In., U.S.	92	40.10N	87.15W
Covington, Ky., U.S.	90	39.05N	84.31W
Covington, La., U.S.	106	30.30N	90.06W
Covington, Oh., U.S.	92	40.10N	84.20W
Covington, Ok., U.S.	104	36.18N	97.32W
Covington, Tn., U.S.	108	35.33N	89.40W
Covington, Va., U.S.	92	37.50N	80.00W
Cowal, Lake, l., Austl. (kou'ăl)	198	33.30S	147.10E
Cowan, l., Austl. (kou'ăn)	196	32.00S	122.30E
Cowan Heights, Ca., U.S.	228	33.47N	117.47W
Cowansville, Can.	84	45.13N	72.47W
Cow Creek, r., Or., U.S. (kou)	98	42.45N	123.35W
Cowes, Eng., U.K. (kouz)	144	50.43N	1.25W
Cowichan Lake, l., Can.	80	48.54N	124.20W
Cowley, neigh., Eng., U.K.	231	51.32N	0.29W
Cowlitz, r., Wa., U.S. (kou'lĭts)	98	46.30N	122.45W
Cowra, Austl. (kou'rȧ)	198	33.50S	148.33E
Coxim, Braz. (kō-shēɴ')	124	18.32S	54.43W
Coxquihui, Mex. (kōz-kē-wē')	112	20.10N	97.34W
Cox's Bāzār, Bngl.	178	21.32N	92.00E
Coyaima, Col. (kō-yäē'mä)	124a	3.48N	75.11W
Coyame, Mex. (kō-yä'mä)	106	29.26N	105.05W
Coyanosa Draw, Tx., U.S. (kŏ yȧ-nō'sä)	106	30.55N	103.07W
Coyoacán, Mex. (kō-yō-ȧ-kän')	112	19.21N	99.10W
Coyote, r., Ca., U.S. (kī'ōt)	100b	37.37N	121.57W
Coyuca de Benítez, Mex. (kō-yōō'kä dā bā-nē'tāz)	112	17.04N	100.06W
Coyuca de Catalán, Mex. (kō-yōō'kä dā kä-tä-län')	112	18.19N	100.41W
Coyutla, Mex. (kō-yōō'tlä)	112	20.13N	97.40W
Cozad, Ne., U.S. (kō'zăd)	104	40.53N	99.59W
Cozaddale, Oh., U.S. (kō-zăd-dāl)	95f	39.16N	84.09W
Cozoyoapan, Mex. (kō-zō-yō-ä-pȧ'n)	112	16.45N	98.17W
Cozumel, Mex. (kŏ-zōō-mĕ'l)	114a	20.31N	86.55W
Cozumel, Isla de, i., Mex. (ē's-lä-dĕ-kŏ-zōō-mĕ'l)	110	20.26N	87.10W
Crab Creek, r., Wa., U.S.	98	47.21N	119.09W
Crab Creek, r., Wa., U.S. (krăb)	98	46.47N	119.43W
Cradock, S. Afr. (kră'dŭk)	206	32.12S	25.38E
Crafton, Pa., U.S. (krăf'tŭn)	95e	40.26N	80.04W
Craig, Co., U.S. (krāg)	98	40.32N	107.31W
Craighall Park, neigh., S. Afr.	240b	26.08S	28.01E
Craiova, Rom. (krȧ-yō'vȧ)	142	44.18N	23.50E
Cranberry, l., N.Y., U.S. (krăn'bĕr-ĭ)	92	44.10N	74.50W
Cranbourne, Austl.	195a	38.07S	145.16E
Cranbrook, Can. (krăn'brŏŏk)	78	49.31N	115.46W
Cranbury, N.J., U.S. (krăn'bē-rĭ)	94a	40.19N	74.31W
Crandon, Wi., U.S. (krăn'dŭn)	96	45.35N	88.55W
Crane Prairie Reservoir, res., Or., U.S.	98	43.50N	121.55W
Cranford, N.J., U.S.	224	40.39N	74.19W
Crank, Eng., U.K.	233a	53.29N	2.45W
Cranston, R.I., U.S. (krăns'tŭn)	94b	41.46N	71.25W
Crater Lake, l., Or., U.S. (krā'tēr)	98	43.00N	122.08W
Crater Lake National Park, rec., Or., U.S.	98	42.58N	122.40W
Craters of the Moon National Monument, rec., Id., U.S. (krā'tērs)	98	43.28N	113.15W
Crateús, Braz. (krä-tȧ-ōōzh')	124	5.09S	40.35W
Crato, Braz. (krä'tō)	124	7.19S	39.13W
Crawford, Ne., U.S. (krô'fērd)	96	42.41N	103.25W
Crawford, Wa., U.S.	100c	45.49N	122.24W
Crawfordsville, In., U.S. (krô'fērdz-vĭl)	92	40.00N	86.55W
Crazy Mountains, mts., Mt., U.S. (krā'zĭ)	98	46.11N	110.25W
Crazy Woman Creek, r., Wy., U.S.	98	44.08N	106.40W
Crecy, S. Afr. (krē-sē)	212d	24.38S	28.52E
Crécy-en-Brie, Fr. (krā-sē'-ĕɴ-brē')	151b	48.52N	2.55E
Crécy-en-Ponthieu, Fr.	150	50.13N	1.48E
Credit, r., Can.	77d	43.41N	79.55W
Cree, l., Can. (krē)	78	57.35N	107.52W
Creekmouth, neigh., Eng., U.K.	231	51.31N	0.06E
Creighton, S. Afr. (cre-tŏn)	207c	30.02S	29.52E
Creighton, Ne., U.S. (krā'tŭn)	96	42.27N	97.54W
Creil, Fr. (krĕ'y')	150	49.18N	2.28E
Crema, Italy (krā'mä)	154	45.21N	9.53E
Cremona, Italy (krā-mō'nä)	142	45.09N	10.02E
Crépy-en-Valois, Fr. (krā-pē'ĕɴ-vä-lwä')	151b	49.14N	2.53E
Cres, Cro. (tsrĕs)	154	44.58N	14.21E
Cres, i., Yugo.	154	44.50N	14.31E
Crescent Beach, Can.	100d	49.03N	122.58W
Crescent City, Ca., U.S. (krĕs'ĕnt)	98	41.46N	124.13W
Crescent City, Fl., U.S.	108	29.26N	81.35W
Crescent Lake, l., Fl., U.S. (krĕs'ĕnt)	108	29.33N	81.30W
Crescent Lake, l., Or., U.S.	98	43.25N	121.58W
Crescentville, neigh., Pa., U.S.	225b	40.02N	75.05W
Cresco, Ia., U.S. (krĕs'kō)	96	43.23N	92.07W
Cresskill, N.J., U.S.	224	40.57N	73.57W
Crested Butte, Co., U.S. (krĕst'ĕd būt)	102	38.50N	107.00W
Crest Haven, Md., U.S.	225d	39.02N	76.59W
Crestline, Ca., U.S. (krĕst-līn)	101a	34.15N	117.17W
Crestline, Oh., U.S.	92	40.50N	82.40W
Crestmore, Ca., U.S. (krĕst'môr)	101a	34.02N	117.23W
Creston, Can. (krĕs'tŭn)	78	49.06N	116.31W
Creston, Ia., U.S.	96	41.04N	94.22W
Creston, Oh., U.S.	95d	40.59N	81.54W
Crestview, Fl., U.S. (krĕst'vū)	108	30.44N	86.35W
Crestwood, Il., U.S.	227a	41.39N	87.44W
Crestwood, Ky., U.S. (krĕst'wŏŏd)	95h	38.20N	85.28W
Crestwood, Mo., U.S.	101e	38.33N	90.23W
Crete, Il., U.S. (krēt)	95a	41.26N	87.38W
Crete, Ne., U.S.	104	40.38N	96.56W
Crete, i., Grc.	136	35.15N	24.30E
Créteil, Fr.	233c	48.48N	2.28E
Creus, Cabo de, c., Spain (kȧ'-bō-dĕ-krĕ-ōōs)	152	42.16N	3.18E
Creuse, r., Fr. (krûz)	150	46.51N	0.49E
Creve Coeur, Mo., U.S. (krēv kôr)	101e	38.40N	90.27W
Crevillente, Spain (krā-vē-lyĕn'tā)	152	38.12N	0.48W
Crewe, Eng., U.K. (krōō)	144	53.06N	2.27W
Crewe, Va., U.S.	108	37.09N	78.08W
Crimea, see Krymskiy Poluostrov, pen., Ukr.	160	45.18N	33.30E
Crimmitschau, Ger. (krĭm'ĭt-shou)	148	50.49N	12.22E
Cripple Creek, Co., U.S. (krĭp''l)	104	38.44N	105.12W
Crisfield, Md., U.S. (krĭs-fēld)	92	38.00N	75.50W
Cristal, Monts de, mts., Gabon	210	0.50N	10.30E
Cristina, Braz. (krēs-tē'-nä)	123a	22.13S	45.15W
Cristóbal Colón, Pico, mtn., Col. (pē'kō-krēs-tô'bäl-kō-lôn')	124	11.00N	74.00W
Cristo Redentor, Estatua do, hist., Braz.	230c	22.57S	43.13W
Crişul Alb, r., Rom. (krē'shōōl älb)	148	46.20N	22.15E
Crna, r., Yugo. (ts'r'nȧ)	154	41.03N	21.46E
Crna Gora (Montenegro), hist. reg., Yugo.	154	42.55N	18.52E
Črnomelj, Slo. (ch'r'nō-māl')	154	45.35N	15.11E
Croatia, nation, Eur.	154	45.24N	15.18E
Crockenhill, Eng., U.K.	231	51.23N	0.10E
Crockett, Ca., U.S. (krŏk'ĕt)	100b	38.03N	122.14W
Crockett, Tx., U.S.	106	31.19N	95.28W
Crofton, Md., U.S.	94e	39.01N	76.43W
Crofton, Ne., U.S.	96	42.44N	97.32W
Croissy-Beaubourg, Fr.	233c	48.50N	2.40E
Croissy-sur-Seine, Fr.	233c	48.53N	2.09E
Croix, Lac la, l., N.A. (läk lä krōō-ä')	96	48.19N	91.53W
Croker, i., Austl. (krô'kȧ)	196	10.45S	132.25E
Cromer, Austl.	239a	33.44S	151.17E
Cronenberg, neigh., Ger.	232	51.12N	7.08E
Cronton, Eng., U.K.	233a	53.23N	2.46W
Cronulla, Austl. (krō-nŭl'ȧ)	195b	34.03S	151.09E
Crooked, i., Bah.	116	22.45N	74.10W
Crooked, l., Can.	86	48.25N	56.05W
Crooked, r., Can.	80	54.30N	122.55W
Crooked, r., Or., U.S.	98	44.07N	120.30W
Crooked Creek, r., Il., U.S. (krōōk'ĕd)	104	40.21N	90.49W
Crooked Island Passage, strt., Bah.	116	22.40N	74.50W
Crookston, Mn., U.S. (krŏŏks'tŭn)	96	47.44N	96.35W
Crooksville, Oh., U.S. (krŏŏks'vĭl)	92	39.45N	82.05W
Crosby, Eng., U.K.	138a	53.30N	3.02W
Crosby, Mn., U.S. (krôz'bĭ)	96	46.29N	93.58W
Crosby, N.D., U.S.	96	48.55N	103.18W
Crosby, Tx., U.S.	107a	29.55N	95.04W
Crosby, neigh., S. Afr.	240b	26.12S	27.59E
Crosne, Fr.	233c	48.43N	2.28E
Cross, l., La., U.S.	106	32.33N	93.58W
Cross, r., Nig.	208	5.35N	8.05E
Cross City, Fl., U.S.	108	29.55N	83.25W
Crossett, Ar., U.S. (krôs'ĕt)	104	33.08N	92.00W
Cross Lake, l., Can.	78	54.45N	97.30W
Cross River Reservoir, res., N.Y., U.S. (krôs)	94a	41.14N	73.34W
Cross Sound, strt., Ak., U.S. (krŏs)	89	58.12N	137.20W
Crosswell, Mi., U.S. (krŏz'wĕl)	92	43.15N	82.35W
Crotch, l., Can.	84	44.55N	76.55W
Crotone, Italy (krō-tô'nĕ)	154	39.05N	17.08E
Croton Falls Reservoir, res., N.Y., U.S. (krōtŭn)	94a	41.22N	73.44W
Croton-on-Hudson, N.Y., U.S. (krō'tŭn-ŏn hŭd'sŭn)	94a	41.12N	73.53W
Crouse Run, r., Pa., U.S.	226b	40.35N	79.58W
Crow, l., Can.	96	49.13N	93.29W
Crow Agency, Mt., U.S.	98	45.36N	107.27W
Crow Creek, r., Co., U.S.	104	41.08N	104.25W
Crow Creek Indian Reservation, I.R., S.D., U.S.	96	44.17N	99.17W
Crow Indian Reservation, I.R., Mt., U.S. (krō)	98	45.26N	108.12W
Crowle, Eng., U.K. (kroul)	138a	53.36N	0.49W
Crowley, La., U.S. (krou'lē)	106	30.13N	92.22W
Crown Mountain, mtn., Can. (kroun)	100d	49.24N	123.05W
Crown Mountain, mtn., V.I.U.S.	111c	18.22N	64.58W
Crown Point, In., U.S. (kroun point')	95a	41.25N	87.22W
Crown Point, N.Y., U.S.	92	44.00N	73.25W
Crows Nest, Austl.	239a	33.50S	151.12E
Crowsnest Pass, p., Can.	80	49.39N	114.45W
Crow Wing, r., Mn., U.S.	96	46.42N	94.48W
Crow Wing, r., Mn., U.S. (krō)	96	44.50N	94.01W
Crow Wing, North Fork, r., Mn., U.S.	96	45.16N	94.28W
Crow Wing, South Fork, r., Mn., U.S.	96	44.59N	94.42W
Croxley Green, Eng., U.K.	231	51.39N	0.27W
Croydon, Austl.	195a	37.48S	145.17E
Croydon, Austl. (kroi'dŭn)	196	18.15S	142.15E
Croydon, Eng., U.K.	140	51.22N	0.06W
Croydon, Pa., U.S.	94f	40.05N	74.55W
Crozet, Îles, is., F.S.A.T. (krô-zĕ')	2	46.20S	51.30E
Cruces, Cuba (krōō'sås)	116	22.20N	80.20W
Cruces, Arroyo de, r., Mex. (är-rō'yō-dĕ-krōō'sĕs)	106	26.17N	104.32W
Cruillas, Mex. (krōō-ēl'yäs)	106	24.45N	98.31W
Crum Lynne, Pa., U.S.	225b	39.52N	75.20W
Cruz, Cabo, c., Cuba (kȧ'-bō-krōōz)	110	19.50N	77.45W
Cruz, Cayo, i., Cuba (kä'yō-krōōz)	116	22.15N	77.50W
Cruz Alta, Braz. (krōōz äl'tä)	126	28.41S	54.02W
Cruz del Eje, Arg. (krōō's-dĕl-ĕ-kĕ)	126	30.46S	64.45W
Cruzeiro, Braz. (krōō-zā'rō)	123a	22.36S	44.57W
Cruzeiro do Sul, Braz. (krōō-zā'rō dō sōōl)	124	7.34S	72.40W
Crysler, Can.	77c	45.13N	75.09W
Crystal Beach, Can.	226a	42.52N	79.04W
Crystal City, Tx., U.S. (krĭs'tăl sĭ'tĭ)	106	28.40N	99.50W
Crystal Falls, Mi., U.S. (krĭs'tăl fôls)	96	46.06N	88.21W
Crystal Lake, Il., U.S. (krĭs'tăl lāk)	95a	42.15N	88.18W
Crystal Springs, Ms., U.S. (krĭs'tăl sprĭngz)	108	31.58N	90.20W
Crystal Springs, oasis, Ca., U.S.	100b	37.31N	122.26W
Csömör, Hung.	235g	47.33N	19.14E
Csongrád, Hung. (chôn'gräd)	148	46.42N	20.09E
Csorna, Hung. (chôr'nä)	148	47.39N	17.11E
Cúa, Ven. (kōō'ä)	125b	10.10N	66.54W
Cuajimalpa, Mex. (kwä-hē-mäl'pä)	113a	19.21N	99.18W
Cuale, Sierra del, mts., Mex. (sē-ĕ'r-rä-dĕl-kwä'lē)	112	20.20N	104.58W
Cuamato, Ang. (kwä-mä'tō)	210	17.05S	15.09E
Cuamba, Moz.	210	14.49S	36.33E
Cuando, Ang. (kwän'dō)	210	16.32S	22.07E
Cuando, r., Afr.	206	14.30S	20.00E
Cuangar, Ang.	210	17.36S	18.39E
Cuango, r., Afr.	206	9.00S	18.00E
Cuanza, r., Ang. (kwän'zä)	206	9.45S	15.00E
Cuarto, r., Arg.	126	33.00S	63.25W

PLACE (Pronunciation)	PAGE	Lat. °′	Long. °′
Cuatro Caminos, Cuba (kwä'trô-kä-mē'nôs)	117a	23.01N	82.13W
Cuatro Ciénegas, Mex. (kwä'trō syā'nā-gäs)	106	26.59N	102.03W
Cuauhtemoc, Mex. (kwä-ōō-tē-mŏk')	112	15.43N	91.57W
Cuautepec, Mex. (kwä-ōō-tĕ-pĕk)	112	16.41N	99.04W
Cuautepec, Mex.	112	20.01N	98.19W
Cuautepec el Alto, Mex.	229a	19.34N	99.08W
Cuautitlán, Mex. (kwä-ōō-tēt-län')	113a	19.40N	99.12W
Cuautla, Mex. (kwä-ōō'tlà)	112	18.47N	98.57W
Cuba, Port. (kōō'bà)	152	38.10N	7.55W
Cuba, nation, N.A. (kū'bȧ)	110	22.00N	79.00W
Cubagua, Isla, i., Ven. (ē's-lä-kōō-bä'gwä)	125b	10.48N	64.10W
Cubango (Okavango), r., Afr. (kōō-bäŋ'gō)	206	17.10S	18.20E
Cub Hills, hills, Can. (kŭb)	82	54.20N	104.30W
Cucamonga, Ca., U.S. (kōō-kȧ-mŏŋ'gȧ)	101a	34.05N	117.35W
Cuchi, Ang.	206	14.40S	16.50E
Cuchillo Parado, Mex. (kōō-chē'lyō pä-rä'dō)	106	29.26N	104.52W
Cuchumatanes, Sierra de los, mts., Guat.	114	15.35N	91.10W
Cúcuta, Col. (kōō'kōō-tä)	124	7.56N	72.30W
Cudahy, Wi., U.S. (kŭd'ȧ-hī)	95a	42.57N	87.52W
Cuddalore, India (kŭd ȧ-lōr')	174	11.49N	79.46E
Cuddapah, India (kŭd'ȧ-pä)	174	14.31N	78.52E
Cudham, neigh., Eng., U.K.	231	51.19N	0.05E
Cue, Austl. (kū)	196	27.30S	118.10E
Cuéllar, Spain (kwā'lyär')	152	41.24N	4.15W
Cuenca, Ec. (kwĕn'kä)	124	2.52S	78.54W
Cuenca, Spain	142	40.05N	2.07W
Cuenca, Sierra de, mts., Spain (sē-ĕ'r-rä-dĕ-kwĕ'n-kä)	152	40.02N	1.50W
Cuencame, Mex. (kwĕn-kä-mā')	106	24.52N	103.42W
Cuerámaro, Mex. (kwā-rä'mä-rō)	112	20.39N	101.44W
Cuernavaca, Mex. (kwĕr-nä-vä'kä)	110	18.55N	99.15W
Cuero, Tx., U.S. (kwā'rō)	106	29.05N	97.16W
Cuetzalá del Progreso, Mex. (kwĕt-zä-lä dĕl prō-grā'sō)	112	18.07N	99.51W
Cuetzalan del Progreso, Mex.	112	20.02N	97.33W
Cuevas del Almanzora, Spain (kwĕ'väs-dĕl-äl-män-zō-rä)	142	37.19N	1.54W
Cuffley, Eng., U.K.	231	51.42N	0.07W
Cuglieri, Italy (kōō-lyâ'rĕ)	154	40.11N	8.37E
Cuicatlán, Mex. (kwē-kä-tlän')	112	17.46N	96.57W
Cuigezhuang, China	236b	40.01N	116.28E
Cuilapa, Guat. (kò-ē-lä'pä)	114	14.16N	90.20W
Cuilo (Kwilu), r., Afr.	210	9.15S	19.30E
Cuito, r., Ang. (kōō-ē'-tō)	206	14.45S	19.00E
Cuitzeo, Mex. (kwēt'zā-ō)	112	19.57N	101.11W
Cuitzeo, Laguna de, l., Mex. (lä-ò'nä-dĕ-kwēt'zā-ō)	112	19.58N	101.05W
Cul de Sac, pl., Haiti (kōō'l-dĕ-sä'k)	116	18.35N	72.05W
Culebra, i., P.R. (kōō-lā'brä)	111b	18.19N	65.32W
Culebra, Sierra de la, mts., Spain (sē-ĕ'r-rä-dĕ-lä-kōō-lĕ-brä)	152	41.52N	6.21W
Culemborg, Neth.	139a	51.57N	5.14E
Culgoa, r., Austl. (kŭl-gō'ȧ)	196	29.21S	147.00E
Culiacán, Mex. (kōō-lyä-ká'n)	110	24.45N	107.30W
Culion, Phil. (kōō-lē-ōn')	188	11.43N	119.58E
Cúllar de Baza, Spain (kōō'l-yär-dĕ-bä'zä)	152	37.36N	2.35W
Cullera, Spain (kōō-lyā'rä)	142	39.12N	0.15W
Cullinan, S. Afr. (kŏ'lĭ-nán)	212d	25.41S	28.32E
Cullman, Al., U.S. (kŭl'mȧn)	108	34.10N	86.50W
Culmore, Va., U.S.	225d	38.51N	77.08W
Culpeper, Va., U.S. (kŭl'pĕp-ĕr)	92	38.30N	77.55W
Culross, Can. (kŭl'rôs)	77f	49.43N	97.54W
Culver, In., U.S. (kŭl'vēr)	92	41.15N	86.25W
Culver City, Ca., U.S.	101a	34.00N	118.23W
Culverstone Green, Eng., U.K.	231	51.20N	0.21E
Cumaná, Ven.	124	10.28N	64.10W
Cumberland, Can. (kŭm'bēr-lȧnd)	77c	45.31N	75.25W
Cumberland, Md., U.S.	90	39.40N	78.40W
Cumberland, Wa., U.S.	100a	47.17N	121.55W
Cumberland, Wi., U.S.	96	45.31N	92.01W
Cumberland, r., U.S.	108	36.45N	85.33W
Cumberland, Lake, res., Ky., U.S.	90	36.55N	85.20W
Cumberland Islands, is., Austl.	196	20.20S	149.46E
Cumberland Peninsula, pen., Can.	78	65.59N	64.05W
Cumberland Plateau, plat., U.S.	108	35.25N	85.30W
Cumberland Sound, strt., Can.	78	65.27N	65.44W
Cundinamarca, dept., Col. (kōōn-dē-nä-mä'r-ká)	124a	4.57N	74.27W
Cunduacán, Mex. (kòn-dōō-á-kän')	112	18.04N	93.23W
Cunene (Kunene), r., Afr.	206	17.05S	12.35E
Cuneo, Italy (kōō'nā-ō)	154	44.24N	7.31E
Cunha, Braz. (kōō'nyá)	123a	23.05S	44.56W
Cunnamulla, Austl. (kŭn-ȧ-mŭl-ȧ)	196	28.00S	145.55E
Cupula, Pico, mtn., Mex. (pē'kō-kōō'pōō-lä)	110	24.45N	111.10W
Cuquío, Mex. (kōō-kē'ō)	112	20.55N	103.03W
Curaçao, i., Neth. Ant. (kōō-rä-sä'ō)	124	12.12N	68.58W
Curacautín, Chile (kä-rä-käōō-tē'n)	126	38.25S	71.53W
Curaumilla, Punta, c., Chile (kōō-rou-mē'lyä)	123b	33.05S	71.44W
Curepto, Chile (kōō-rĕp-tō)	123b	35.06S	72.02W
Curitiba, Braz. (kōō-rē-tē'bá)	124	25.20S	49.15W
Curly Cut Cays, is., Bah.	116	23.40N	77.40W
Currais Novos, Braz. (kōōr-rä'ēs nō-vōs)	124	6.02S	36.39W
Curran, Can. (kü-rän')	77c	45.30N	74.59W
Current, i., Bah. (kŭ-rĕnt)	116	25.20N	76.50W
Current, r., Mo., U.S. (kûr'ĕnt)	104	37.18N	91.21W
Currie, Mount, mtn., S. Afr. (kŭ-rē)	207c	30.28S	29.23E
Currituck Sound, strt., N.C., U.S. (kûr'ĭ-tŭk)	108	36.27N	75.42W

PLACE (Pronunciation)	PAGE	Lat. °′	Long. °′
Curtis, Ne., U.S. (kûr'tĭs)	104	40.36N	100.29W
Curtis, i., Austl.	196	23.38S	151.43E
Curtis B, Md., U.S.	225c	39.13N	76.35W
Curtisville, Pa., U.S. (kûr'tĭs-vĭl)	95e	40.38N	79.50W
Čurug, Yugo. (chōō'rōg)	154	45.27N	20.03E
Curunga, Ang.	210	12.51S	21.12E
Curupira, Serra, mts., S.A. (sĕr'rȧ kōō-rōō-pē'rȧ)	124	1.00N	65.30W
Cururupu, Braz. (kōō-rò-rò-pōō')	124	1.40S	44.56W
Curvelo, Braz. (kòr-vĕl'ò)	124	18.47S	44.14W
Cusano Milanino, Italy	234c	45.33N	9.11E
Cushing, Ok., U.S. (kŭsh'ĭng)	104	35.58N	96.46W
Custer, S.D., U.S. (kŭs'tēr)	96	43.46N	103.36W
Custer, Wa., U.S.	100d	48.55N	122.39W
Custer Battlefield National Monument, rec., Mt., U.S. (kŭs'tēr băt''l-fēld)	98	45.44N	107.15W
Cut Bank, Mt., U.S. (kŭt bănk)	98	48.38N	112.19W
Cuthbert, Ga., U.S. (kŭth'bērt)	108	31.47N	84.48W
Cuttack, India (kŭ-tăk')	174	20.38N	85.53E
Cutzamala, r., Mex. (kōō-tzä-mä-lä')	112	18.57N	100.41W
Cutzamalá de Pinzón, Mex. (kōō-tzä-mä-lä'dĕ-pēn-zō'n)	112	18.28N	100.36W
Cuvo, r., Ang. (kōō'vō)	206	11.00S	14.30E
Cuxhaven, Ger. (kòks'hä-fĕn)	140	53.51N	8.43E
Cuxton, Eng., U.K.	231	51.22N	0.27E
Cuyahoga, r., Oh., U.S. (kī-ȧ-hō'gȧ)	95d	41.22N	81.38W
Cuyahoga Falls, Oh., U.S.	95d	41.08N	81.29W
Cuyahoga Heights, Oh., U.S.	225a	41.26N	81.39W
Cuyapaire Indian Reservation, I.R., Ca., U.S. (kū-yá-pâr)	102	32.46N	116.20W
Cuyo Islands, is., Phil. (kōō'yō)	188	10.54N	120.08E
Cuyotenango, Guat. (kōō-yò-tĕ-näŋ'gò)	114	14.30N	91.35W
Cuyuni, r., S.A. (kōō-yōō'nē)	124	6.40N	60.44W
Cuyutlán, Mex. (kōō-yōō-tlän')	112	18.54N	104.04W
Cuzco, Peru	124	13.36S	71.52W
Cyclades, see Kikládhes, is., Grc.	136	37.30N	24.45E
Cynthiana, Ky., U.S. (sĭn-thĭ-ăn'ȧ)	92	38.20N	84.20W
Cypress, Ca., U.S. (sī'prēs)	101a	33.50N	118.03W
Cypress Hills, hills, Can.	82	49.40N	110.20W
Cypress Lake, l., Can.	82	49.28N	109.43W
Cyprus, nation, Asia (sī'prŭs)	174	35.00N	31.00E
Cyprus, North, nation, Asia	174	35.15N	33.40E
Cyrenaica, see Barqah, hist. reg., Libya	204	31.09N	21.45E
Cyrildene, neigh., S. Afr.	240b	26.11S	28.06E
Czechoslovakia, nation, Eur. (chĕk'ô-slô-vä'kĭ-ȧ)	136	49.28N	16.00E
Czersk, Pol. (chĕrsk)	148	53.47N	17.58E
Częstochowa, Pol. (chăN-stô kô'vá)	140	50.49N	19.10E

D

PLACE (Pronunciation)	PAGE	Lat. °′	Long. °′
Da'an, China (dä-än)	184	45.25N	124.22E
Dabakala, I.C. (dä-bä-kä'lä)	204	8.16N	4.36W
Daba Shan, mts., China (dä-bä shän)	180	32.25N	108.20E
Dabeiba, Col. (dä-bā'bä)	124a	7.01N	76.16W
Dabie Shan, mts., China (dä-bĭē shän)	180	31.40N	114.50E
Dabnou, Niger	208	14.09N	5.22E
Dabob Bay, b., Wa., U.S. (dā'bŏb)	100a	47.50N	122.50W
Dabola, Gui.	208	10.45N	11.07W
Dąbrowa Białostocka, Pol.	148	53.37N	23.18E
Dachang, China (dä-chäŋ)	183b	31.18N	121.25E
Dachangshan Dao, i., China (dä-chäŋ-shän dou)	182	39.21N	122.31E
Dachau, Ger. (dä'κou)	148	48.16N	11.26E
Dacotah, Can. (dȧ-kō'tá)	77f	49.52N	97.38W
Dadar, neigh., India	236e	19.01N	72.50E
Dade City, Fl., U.S. (dād)	109a	28.22N	82.09W
Dadeville, Al., U.S. (dād'vĭl)	108	32.48N	85.44W
Dādra & Nagar Haveli, India	174	20.00N	73.00E
Dadu, r., China (dä-dōō)	184	29.20N	103.03E
Daet, mtn., Phil. (dä'ät)	189a	14.07N	122.59E
Dafoe, r., Can.	82	55.50N	95.50W
Dafter, Mi., U.S. (dăf'tēr)	101k	46.21N	84.26W
Dagana, Sen. (dä-gä'nä)	204	16.31N	15.30W
Dagana, reg., Chad	208	12.20N	15.15E
Dagang, China (dä-gäŋ)	183a	22.48N	113.24E
Dagda, Lat. (dág'dá)	146	56.04N	27.30E
Dagenham, Eng., U.K. (dăg'ĕn-ăm)	138b	51.32N	0.09E
Dagestan, hist. reg., Russia (dä-gĕs-tän')	160	43.40N	46.10E
Daggafontein, S. Afr.	240b	26.18S	28.28E
Daggett, Ca., U.S. (dăg'ĕt)	102	34.50N	116.52W
Dagu, China (dä-gōō)	184	39.00N	117.42E
Dagu, r., China	182	36.29N	120.06W
Dagupan, Phil. (dä-gōō'pän)	189a	16.02N	120.20E
Daheishan Dao, i., China (dä-hā-shän dou)	182	37.57N	120.37E
Dahīrpur, neigh., India	236d	28.43N	77.12E
Dahl, Ger. (däl)	151c	51.18N	7.33E
Dahlak Archipelago, is., Eth.	204	15.45N	40.30E
Dahlem, neigh., Ger.	234a	52.28N	13.17E
Dahlerau, Ger.	232	51.13N	7.19E
Dahlwitz, Ger.	234a	52.30N	13.38E
Dahomey, see Benin, nation, Afr.	204	8.00N	2.00E
Dahra, Libya	176	29.34N	17.50E
Daibu, China (dī-bōō)	182	31.22N	119.29E
Daigo, Japan (dī-gō)	187b	34.57N	135.49E

PLACE (Pronunciation)	PAGE	Lat. °′	Long. °′
Daimiel Manzanares, Spain (dī-myĕl'män-zä-nä'rĕs)	152	39.05N	3.36W
Dairy, r., Or., U.S. (dâr'ĭ)	100c	45.33N	123.04W
Dai-Sen, mtn., Japan (dī'sĕn')	187	35.22N	133.35E
Dai-Tenjo-dake, mtn., Japan (dī-tĕn'jō dä-κä)	187	36.21N	137.38E
Daiyun Shan, mtn., China (dī-yòn shän)	184	25.40N	118.08E
Dajabón, Dom. Rep. (dä-κä-bō'n)	116	19.35N	71.40W
Dajarra, Austl. (dȧ-jăr'ȧ)	196	21.45S	139.30E
Dakar, Sen. (dà-kär')	204	14.40N	17.26W
Dakhla, W. Sah.	204	23.45N	16.04W
Dakouraoua, Niger	208	13.58N	6.15E
Dakovica, Yugo.	154	42.33N	20.28E
Dalälven, r., Swe.	136	60.26N	15.50E
Dalby, Austl. (dôl'bē)	196	27.10S	151.15E
Dalcour, La., U.S. (dăl-kour)	94d	29.49N	89.59W
Dale, Nor. (dä'lē)	146	60.35N	5.55E
Dale Hollow Lake, res., Tn., U.S. (dāl hŏl'ō)	90	36.33N	85.03W
Dalemead, Can. (dä'lē-mēd)	77e	50.53N	113.38W
Dalen, Nor. (dä'lĕn)	146	59.28N	8.01E
Daleside, S. Afr. (dāl'sīd)	212d	26.30S	28.03E
Dalesville, Can. (dālz'vĭl)	77a	45.42N	74.23W
Daley Waters, Austl. (dā lē)	196	16.15N	133.30E
Dalhart, Tx., U.S. (dăl härt)	104	36.04N	102.32W
Dalhousie, Can. (dăl-hōō'zē)	86	48.04N	66.23W
Dali, China	180	35.00N	109.38E
Dali, China	180	26.00N	100.08E
Dali, China (dä-lē)	183a	23.07N	113.06E
Dalian, China (lü-dä)	180	38.54N	121.35E
Dalian Wan, b., China (dä-lĭĕn wän)	182	38.55N	121.50E
Dalías, Spain (dä-lē'ás)	152	36.49N	2.50W
Dall, i., Ak., U.S. (dăl)	89	54.50N	133.10W
Dallas, Or., U.S. (dăl'lás)	98	44.55N	123.20W
Dallas, S.D., U.S.	96	43.13N	99.34W
Dallas, Tx., U.S.	90	32.45N	96.48W
Dalles Dam, Or., U.S.	98	45.36N	121.08W
Dallgow, Ger.	234a	52.32N	13.05E
Dall Island, i., Ak., U.S.	80	54.50N	132.55W
Dalmacija, hist. reg., Yugo. (däl-mä'tsē-yä)	154	43.25N	16.37E
Dalnerechensk, Russia	158	46.07N	133.21E
Daloa, I.C.	208	6.53N	6.27W
Dalroy, Can. (dăl'roi)	77e	51.07N	113.39W
Dalrymple, Mount, mtn., Austl. (dăl'rĭm-p'l)	196	21.14S	148.46E
Dalton, S. Afr. (dôl'tŏn)	207c	29.21S	30.41E
Dalton, Eng., U.K.	233a	53.34N	2.46W
Dalton, Ga., U.S. (dôl'tŭn)	108	34.46N	84.58W
Daly, r., Austl. (dā'lĭ)	196	14.15S	131.15E
Daly City, Ca., U.S. (dā'lē)	100b	37.42N	122.27W
Damān, India	174	20.32N	72.53E
Damanhūr, Egypt (dä-män-hōōr')	204	30.59N	30.31E
Damar, Pulau, i., Indon.	188	7.15S	129.15E
Damara, Cen. Afr. Rep.	208	4.58N	18.42E
Damaraland, hist. reg., Nmb. (dă'nȧ-rȧ-lănd)	206	22.15S	16.15E
Damas Cays, is., Bah. (dä'mäs)	116	23.50N	79.50W
Damascus, Syria	174	33.30N	36.18E
Damāvand, Qolleh-ye, mtn., Iran	174	36.05N	52.05E
Damba, Ang. (däm'bä)	206	6.41S	15.08E
Dame Marie, Cap, c., Haiti (dām mȧrē')	116	18.35N	74.50W
Dāmghān, Iran (dām-gän')	174	35.50N	54.15E
Daming, China (dä-mĭŋ)	184	36.15N	115.09E
Dammartin-en-Goële, Fr. (däN-mär-tăN-äN-gô-ĕl')	151b	49.03N	2.40E
Dampier, Selat, strt., Indon. (dăm'pēr)	188	0.40S	131.15E
Dampier Archipielago, is., Austl.	196	20.15S	116.25E
Dampier Land, reg., Austl.	196	17.30S	122.25E
Dan, r., N.C., U.S. (dăn)	108	36.26N	79.40W
Dana, Mount, mtn., Ca., U.S.	102	37.54N	119.13W
Da Nang, Viet.	188	16.08N	108.22E
Danbury, Eng., U.K.	138b	51.42N	0.34E
Danbury, Ct., U.S. (dăn'bēr-ĭ)	94a	41.23N	73.27W
Danbury, Tx., U.S.	107a	29.14N	95.22W
Dandenong, Austl. (dăn'dē-nông)	198	37.59S	145.13E
Dandong, China (dän-dôŋ)	180	40.10N	124.30E
Dane, r., Eng., U.K. (dān)	138a	53.11N	2.14W
Danea, Gui.	208	11.27N	13.12W
Danforth, Me., U.S.	86	45.38N	67.53W
Dan Gora, Nig.	208	11.30N	8.09E
Dangtu, China (däŋ-tōō)	184	31.35N	118.28E
Dani, Burkina	204	13.43N	0.10W
Dania, Fl., U.S. (dā'nĭ-à)	109a	26.01N	80.10W
Daniels, Md., U.S.	225c	39.26N	77.03W
Danilov, Russia (dä'nē-lôf)	160	58.12N	40.08E
Danissa Hills, hills, Kenya	210	3.20N	40.55E
Dankov, Russia (däŋ'kôf)	160	53.17N	39.09E
Dannemora, N.Y., U.S. (dăn-ē-mō'rȧ)	92	44.45N	73.45W
Dannhauser, S. Afr. (dän'hou-zēr)	207c	28.07S	30.04E
Dansville, N.Y., U.S. (dănz'vĭl)	92	42.30N	77.40W
Danube, r., Eur.	136	43.00N	24.00E
Danube, Mouths of the, mth., Rom. (dăn'ūb)	156	45.13N	29.37E
Danvers, Ma., U.S. (dăn'vērz)	87a	42.34N	70.57W
Danville, Ca., U.S. (dăn'vĭl)	100b	37.49N	122.00W
Danville, Il., U.S.	92	40.10N	87.35W
Danville, In., U.S.	92	39.45N	86.30W
Danville, Ky., U.S.	92	37.35N	84.50W
Danville, Pa., U.S.	92	41.00N	76.35W
Danville, Va., U.S.	90	36.35N	79.24W
Danxian, China (dän shyĕn)	184	19.30N	109.38E
Danyang, China (dän-yäŋ)	182	32.01N	119.32E
Danzig, Gulf of, b., Eur. (dán'tsĭk)	140	54.41N	19.01E
Daoxian, China (dou shyĕn)	184	25.35N	111.27E
Dapango, Togo	208	10.52N	0.12E
Daphnae, hist., Egypt	173a	30.43N	32.12E

PLACE (Pronunciation)	PAGE	Lat. °'	Long. °'
Daqin Dao, i., China (dä-chyĭn dou)	182	38.18N	120.50E
Darabani, Rom. (dă-ră-băn'ĭ)	148	48.13N	26.38E
Daraj, Libya	204	30.12N	10.14E
Dār as-Salām, Egypt	240a	29.59N	31.13E
Darāw, Egypt (dȧ-rä'ōō)	212b	24.24N	32.56E
Darbhanga, India (dŭr-bŭŋ'gä)	174	26.03N	85.09E
Darby, Pa., U.S. (där'bĭ)	94f	39.55N	75.16W
Darby, i., Bah.	116	23.50N	76.20W
Dardanelles, see Çanakkale Boğazi, strt., Tur.	142	40.05N	25.50E
Dar es Salaam, Tan. (där ĕs sȧ-läm')	206	6.48S	39.17E
Dārfūr, hist. reg., Sudan (där-fōōr')	204	13.21N	23.46E
Dargai, Pak. (dŭr-gä'ē)	178	34.35N	72.00E
Darien, Col. (dā-rĭ-ĕn')	124a	3.56N	76.30W
Darien, Ct., U.S. (dâ-rē-ĕn')	94a	41.04N	73.28W
Darién, Cordillera de, mts., Nic.	114	13.00N	85.42W
Darien, Serranía del, mts.	114	8.13N	77.28W
Darjeeling, India (dŭr-jē'lĭng)	174	27.05N	88.16E
Darling, r., Austl.	196	31.50S	143.20E
Darling Downs, reg., Austl.	196	27.22S	150.00E
Darling Range, mts., Austl.	196	30.30S	115.45E
Darlington, Eng., U.K. (där'lĭng-tŭn)	144	54.32N	1.35W
Darlington, S.C., U.S.	108	34.15N	79.52W
Darlington, Wi., U.S.	96	42.41N	90.06W
Darłowo, Pol. (där-lô'vô)	148	54.26N	16.23E
Darmstadt, Ger. (därm'shtät)	140	49.53N	8.40E
Darnah, Libya	204	32.44N	22.41E
Darnley Bay, b., Ak., U.S. (därn'lē)	89	70.00N	124.00W
Daroca, Spain (dä-rō-kä)	152	41.08N	1.24W
Dartford, Eng., U.K.	138b	51.27N	0.14E
Dartmoor, for., Eng., U.K. (därt'mōōr)	144	50.35N	4.05W
Dartmouth, Can. (därt'mŭth)	78	44.40N	63.34W
Dartmouth, Eng., U.K.	144	50.33N	3.28W
Daru, Pap. N. Gui. (dä'rōō)	188	9.04S	143.21E
Daruvar, Cro. (där'rōō-vär)	154	45.37N	17.16E
Darwen, Eng., U.K. (där'wĕn)	138a	53.42N	2.28W
Darwin, Austl. (där'wĭn)	196	12.25S	131.00E
Darwin, Cordillera, mts., Chile (kôr-dēl-yĕ'rä-där'wĕn)	126	54.40S	69.30W
Dash Point, Wa., U.S. (dăsh)	100a	47.19N	122.25W
Dasht, r., Pak. (dŭsht)	174	25.30N	62.30E
Dasol Bay, b., Phil. (dä-sōl')	189a	15.53N	119.40E
Datchet, Eng., U.K.	231	51.29N	0.34W
Datian Ding, mtn., China (dä-tĭĕn dĭŋ)	184	22.25N	111.20E
Datong, China (dä-tôŋ)	184	40.00N	113.30E
Dattapukur, India	178a	22.45N	88.32E
Datteln, Ger. (dät'tĕln)	151c	51.39N	7.20E
Datu, Tandjung, c., Asia	188	2.08N	110.15E
Datuan, China (dä-tůän)	183b	30.57N	121.43E
Daugava (Zapadnaya Dvina), r., Eur.	146	56.40N	24.40E
Daugavpils, Lat. (dä'ŏŏ-gäv-pēls)	160	55.52N	26.32E
Dauphin, Can. (dô'fĭn)	78	51.09N	100.00W
Dauphin Lake, l., Can.	82	51.17N	99.48W
Dāvangere, India	178	14.30N	75.55E
Davao, Phil. (dä'vä-ô)	188	7.05N	125.30E
Davao Gulf, b., Phil.	188	6.30N	125.45E
Davenport, Ia., U.S. (dăv'ĕn-pōrt)	90	41.34N	90.38W
Davenport, Wa., U.S.	98	47.39N	118.07W
Daveyton Location, S. Afr.	240b	26.09S	28.25E
David, Pan. (dȧ-vēdh')	110	8.27N	82.27W
David City, Ne., U.S. (dā'vĭd)	96	41.15N	97.10W
David-Gorodok, Bela. (dȧ-vēt' gô-rō'dôk)	160	52.02N	27.14E
Davis, Ok., U.S. (dā'vĭs)	104	34.34N	97.08W
Davis, W.V., U.S.	92	39.15N	79.25W
Davis Lake, l., Or., U.S.	98	43.38N	121.43W
Davis Mountains, mts., Tx., U.S.	106	30.45N	104.17W
Davis Strait, strt., N.A.	76	66.00N	60.00W
Davlekanovo, Russia	160	54.15N	55.05E
Davos, Switz. (dä'vōs)	148	46.47N	9.50E
Davyhulme, Eng., U.K.	233b	53.27N	2.22W
Dawa, r., Afr.	204	4.30N	40.30E
Dawāsir, Wādī ad, val., Sau. Ar.	174	20.48N	44.07E
Dawei, Burma	188	14.04N	98.19E
Dawen, r., China (dä-wŭn)	182	35.58N	116.53E
Dawley, Eng., U.K. (dô'lĭ)	138a	52.38N	2.28W
Dawna Range, mts., Burma (dô'nȧ)	188	17.02N	98.01E
Dawson, Can. (dô'sŭn)	78	64.04N	139.22W
Dawson, Ga., U.S.	108	31.45N	84.29W
Dawson, Mn., U.S.	96	44.54N	96.03W
Dawson, r., Austl.	196	24.20S	149.45E
Dawson Bay, b., Can.	82	52.55N	100.50W
Dawson Creek, Can.	78	55.46N	120.14W
Dawson Range, mts., Can.	89	62.15N	138.10W
Dawson Springs, Ky., U.S.	108	37.10N	87.40W
Dawu, China (dä-wōō)	182	31.33N	114.07E
Dawuji, China	236b	39.51N	116.30E
Dax, Fr. (dȧks)	140	43.42N	1.06W
Daxian, China (dä-shyĕn)	180	31.12N	107.30E
Daxing, China (dä-shyĭŋ)	184a	39.44N	116.19E
Dayiqiao, China (dä-yē-chyou)	182	31.43N	120.40E
Dayr az Zawr, Syria (dȧ-ērĕz-zôr')	174	35.15N	40.01E
Dayton, Ky., U.S. (dā'tŭn)	95f	39.07N	84.28W
Dayton, N.M., U.S.	104	32.44N	104.23W
Dayton, Oh., U.S.	90	39.54N	84.15W
Dayton, Tn., U.S.	108	35.30N	85.00W
Dayton, Tx., U.S.	106	30.03N	94.53W
Dayton, Wa., U.S.	98	46.18N	117.59W
Daytona Beach, Fl., U.S. (dā-tō'nȧ)	90	29.11N	81.02W
Dayu, China (dä-yōō)	184	25.20N	114.20E
Da Yunhe (Grand Canal), can., China (dä yön-hŭ)	180	35.00N	117.00E
Dayville, Ct., U.S. (dā'vĭl)	92	41.50N	71.55W
De Aar, S. Afr. (dē-är')	206	30.45S	24.05E
Dead, l., Mn., U.S. (dĕd)	96	46.28N	96.00W
Dead Sea, l., Asia	174	31.30N	35.30E
Deadwood, S.D., U.S. (dĕd'wŏŏd)	90	44.23N	103.43W
Deal Island, Md., U.S. (dēl-ī'lănd)	92	38.10N	75.55W
Dean, r., Can. (dēn)	80	52.45N	125.30W
Dean Channel, strt., Can.	80	52.33N	127.13W
Deán Funes, Arg. (dĕ-ȧ'n-fōō-nĕs)	126	30.26S	64.12W
Dean Row, Eng., U.K.	233b	53.20N	2.11W
Dearborn, Mi., U.S. (dēr'bŭrn)	95b	42.18N	83.15W
Dearborn Heights, Mi., U.S.	226c	42.19N	83.14W
Dearg, Ben, mtn., Scot., U.K. (bĕn dŭrg)	144	57.48N	4.59W
Dease Strait, strt., Can. (dēz)	78	68.50N	108.20W
Death Valley, Ca., U.S.	102	36.18N	116.26W
Death Valley, val., Ca., U.S.	90	36.30N	117.00W
Death Valley National Monument, rec., Ca., U.S.	102	36.34N	117.00W
Debal'tsevo, Ukr. (dyĕb'ál-tsyĕ'vô)	156	48.23N	38.29E
Debao, China (dŭ-bou)	180	23.18N	106.40E
Debar, Mac. (dĕ'bär) (dä'brä)	154	41.31N	20.32E
Dęblin, Pol. (dăɴ'blĭn)	148	51.34N	21.49E
Dębno, Pol. (dĕb-nô')	148	52.47N	13.43E
Debo, Lac, l., Mali	208	15.15N	4.40W
Debrecen, Hung. (dĕ'brĕ-tsĕn)	136	47.32N	21.40E
Debre Markos, Eth.	204	10.15N	37.45E
Debre Tabor, Eth.	204	11.57N	38.09E
Decatur, Al., U.S. (dē-kā'tŭr)	108	34.35N	87.00W
Decatur, Ga., U.S.	94c	33.47N	84.18W
Decatur, Il., U.S.	90	39.50N	88.59W
Decatur, In., U.S.	92	40.50N	84.55W
Decatur, Mi., U.S.	92	42.10N	86.00W
Decatur, Tx., U.S.	104	33.14N	97.33W
Decazeville, Fr. (dē-käz'vēl')	140	44.33N	2.16E
Deccan, plat., India (dĕk'ăn)	174	19.05N	76.40E
Deception Lake, l., Can.	82	56.33N	104.15W
Deception Pass, p., Wa., U.S. (dē-sĕp'shŭn)	100a	48.24N	122.44W
Děčín, Czech. (dyĕ'chēn)	148	50.47N	14.14E
Decorah, Ia., U.S. (dē-kō'rȧ)	96	43.18N	91.48W
Dedenevo, Russia (dyĕ-dyĕ'nyĕ-vô)	164b	56.14N	37.31E
Dedham, Ma., U.S. (dĕd'ăm)	87a	42.15N	71.11W
Dedo do Deus, mtn., Braz. (dĕ-dô-dô-dĕ'ōōs)	126b	22.30S	43.02W
Dédougou, Burkina (dā-dō-gōō')	204	12.38N	3.28W
Dee, r., U.K.	138a	53.15N	3.05E
Dee, r., Scot., U.K.	144	57.05N	2.25W
Deep, r., N.C., U.S. (dēp)	108	35.36N	79.32W
Deep Fork, r., Ok., U.S.	104	35.35N	96.42W
Deep River, Can.	84	46.06N	77.20W
Deepwater, Mo., U.S. (dep-wô-tēr)	104	38.15N	93.46W
Deer, i., Me., U.S.	86	44.07N	68.38W
Deerfield, Il., U.S. (dēr'fēld)	95a	42.10N	87.51W
Deer Island, Or., U.S.	100c	45.56N	122.51W
Deer Lake, Can.	79a	49.10N	57.25W
Deer Lake, l., Can.	82	52.40N	94.30W
Deer Lodge, Mt., U.S. (dēr lŏj)	98	46.23N	112.42W
Deer Park, Oh., U.S.	95f	39.12N	84.24W
Deer Park, Wa., U.S.	98	47.58N	117.28W
Deer River, Mn., U.S.	96	47.20N	93.49W
Dee Why, Austl.	239a	33.45S	151.17E
Dee Why Head, c., Austl.	239a	33.46S	151.19E
Dee Why Lagoon, b., Austl.	239a	33.45S	151.18E
Defiance, Oh., U.S. (dē-fī'ăns)	92	41.15N	84.20W
DeFuniak Springs, Fl., U.S. (dē fū'nĭ-ăk)	108	30.42N	86.06W
Deganga, India	178a	22.41N	88.41E
Degeh Bur, Eth.	212a	8.10N	43.25E
Deggendorf, Ger. (dĕ'ghĕn-dôrf)	148	48.50N	12.59E
Degollado, Mex. (dā-gô-lyä'dō)	112	20.27N	102.11W
DeGrey, r., Austl. (dē grā')	196	20.20S	119.25E
Degtyarsk, Russia (dĕg-ty'arsk)	164a	56.42N	60.05E
Dehiwala-Mount Lavinia, Sri L.	178	6.47N	79.55E
Dehra Dūn, India (dā'rŭ)	174	30.09N	78.07E
Dehua, China (dŭ-hwä)	184	25.30N	118.15E
Dej, Rom. (dāzh)	142	47.09N	23.53E
De Kalb, Il., U.S. (dē kălb')	92	41.54N	88.46W
Dekese, Zaire	210	3.27S	21.24E
Delacour, Can. (dĕ-lä-kōōr')	77e	51.09N	113.45W
Delagua, Co., U.S. (dĕl-ä'gwä)	104	37.19N	104.42W
Delair, N.J., U.S.	225b	39.59N	75.03W
De Land, Fl., U.S. (dē lănd')	108	29.00N	81.19W
Delano, Ca., U.S. (dĕl'ȧ-nō)	102	35.47N	119.15W
Delano Peak, mtn., Ut., U.S.	90	38.25N	112.25W
Delavan, Wi., U.S. (dĕl'ȧ-văn)	96	42.39N	88.38W
Delaware, Oh., U.S. (dĕl'ȧ-wâr)	92	40.15N	83.05W
Delaware, state, U.S.	90	38.40N	75.30W
Delaware, r., U.S.	92	41.50N	75.20W
Delaware, r., Ks., U.S.	104	39.45N	95.47W
Delaware Bay, b., U.S.	90	39.05N	75.10W
Delaware Reservoir, res., Oh., U.S.	92	40.30N	83.05E
Delémont, Switz. (dē-lä-môɴ')	148	47.21N	7.18E
De Leon, Tx., U.S. (dē lē-ŏn')	106	32.06N	98.33W
Delft, Neth. (dĕlft)	144	52.01N	4.20E
Delfzijl, Neth.	144	53.20N	6.50E
Delgada, Punta, c., Arg. (pōō'n-tä-dĕl-gä'dä)	126	43.46S	63.46W
Delgado, Cabo, c., Moz. (kȧ'bô-dĕl-gä'dō)	206	10.40S	40.35E
Delhi, India	174	28.54N	77.13E
Delhi, Il., U.S. (dĕl'hī)	101e	39.03N	90.16W
Delhi, La., U.S.	106	32.26N	91.29W
Delhi, state, India	174	28.30N	76.50E
Delhi Cantonment, India	236d	28.36N	77.08E
Delitzsch, Ger. (dā'lĭch)	148	51.32N	12.18E
Dellansjöarna, l., Swe.	146	61.57N	16.25E
Delles, Alg. (dĕ'lĕs')	204	36.59N	3.40E
Dell Rapids, S.D., U.S. (dĕl)	96	43.50N	96.43W
Dellwig, neigh., Ger.	232	51.29N	6.56E
Dellwood, Mn., U.S. (dĕl'wŏŏd)	101g	45.05N	92.58W
Del Mar, Ca., U.S. (dĕl mär')	102a	32.57N	117.16W
Delmas, S. Afr. (dĕl'mȧs)	212d	26.08S	28.43E
Delmenhorst, Ger. (dĕl'mĕn-hôrst)	148	53.03N	8.38E
Del Norte, Co., U.S. (dĕl nôrt')	102	37.40N	106.25W
De-Longa, i., Russia	158	76.21N	148.56E
De Long Mountains, mts., Ak., U.S. (dē'lŏng)	89	68.38N	162.30W
Deloraine, Austl. (dĕ-lŭ-rān)	198	41.30S	146.40E
Delphi, In., U.S. (dĕl'fī)	92	40.35N	86.40W
Delphos, Oh., U.S. (dĕl'fŏs)	92	40.50N	84.20W
Delran, N.J., U.S.	225b	40.02N	74.58W
Delray Beach, Fl., U.S. (dĕl-rā')	109a	26.27N	80.05W
Del Rio, Tx., U.S. (dĕl rē'ō)	90	29.21N	100.52W
Delson, Can. (dĕl'sŭn)	77a	45.24N	73.32W
Delta, Co., U.S.	102	38.45N	108.05W
Delta, Ut., U.S.	102	39.20N	112.35W
Delta Beach, Can.	77f	50.10N	98.20W
Delvine, Alb. (dĕl'vē-nȧ)	154	39.58N	20.10E
Del Viso, Arg.	229d	34.26S	58.46W
Dëma, r., Russia (dyĕm'ä)	160	53.40N	54.30E
Demarest, N.J., U.S.	224	40.57N	73.58W
Demba, Zaire	210	5.30S	22.16E
Dembi Dolo, Eth.	204	8.46N	34.46E
Demidov, Russia (dzyĕ'mē-dô'f)	156	55.16N	31.32E
Deming, N.M., U.S. (dĕm'ĭng)	90	32.15N	107.45W
Demmeltrath, neigh., Ger.	232	51.11N	7.03E
Demmin, Ger. (dĕm'mēn)	148	53.54N	13.04E
Demnat, Mor. (dĕm-nät)	204	31.58N	7.03W
Demopolis, Al., U.S. (dē-mŏp'ō-lĭs)	108	32.30N	87.50W
Demotte, In., U.S. (dē'mŏt)	95a	41.12N	87.13W
Dempo, Gunung, mtn., Indon. (dĕm'pô)	188	4.04S	103.11E
Dem'yanka, r., Russia (dyĕm-yän'kä)	162	59.07N	72.58E
Demyansk, Russia (dyĕm-yänsk')	156	57.39N	32.26E
Denain, Fr. (dē-năɴ')	150	50.23N	3.21E
Denakil Plain, pl., Eth.	204	12.45N	41.01E
Denali National Park, rec., Ak., U.S.	90a	63.48N	153.02W
Denbigh, Wales, U.K. (dĕn'bĭ)	144	53.15N	3.25W
Dendermonde, Bel.	139a	51.02N	4.04E
Dendron, Va., U.S. (dĕn'drŭn)	108	37.02N	76.53W
Denenchōfu, neigh., Japan	238a	35.35N	139.41E
Denezhkin Kamen, Gora, mtn., Russia (dzyĕ-ŋĕ'zhkĕn kămēŋ)	164a	60.26N	59.35E
Denham, Mount, mtn., Jam.	110	18.20N	77.30W
Den Helder, Neth. (dĕn hĕl'dĕr)	144	52.55N	5.45E
Denia, Spain (dā'nyä)	152	38.48N	0.06E
Deniliquin, Austl. (dĕ-nĭl'ĭ-kwĭn)	196	35.20S	144.52E
Denison, Ia., U.S. (dĕn'ĭ-sŭn)	96	42.01N	95.22W
Denison, Tx., U.S.	90	33.45N	97.02W
Denisovka, Kaz. (dĕ-nē'sof-kȧ)	164a	52.26N	61.45E
Denizli, Tur. (dĕn-ĭz-lē')	142	37.40N	29.10E
Denklingen, Ger. (dĕn'klĕn-gĕn)	151c	50.54N	7.40E
Denmark, S.C., U.S. (dĕn'märk)	108	33.18N	81.09W
Denmark, nation, Eur.	136	56.14N	8.30E
Denmark Strait, strt., Eur.	76	66.30N	27.00W
Dennilton, S. Afr. (dĕn-ĭl-tŭn)	212d	25.18S	29.13E
Dennison, Oh., U.S. (dĕn'ĭ-sŭn)	92	40.25N	81.20W
Denpasar, Indon.	188	8.35S	115.10E
Denshaw, Eng., U.K.	233b	53.35N	2.02W
Denton, Eng., U.K. (dĕn'tŭn)	138a	53.27N	2.07W
Denton, Md., U.S.	92	38.55N	75.50W
Denton, Tx., U.S.	104	33.12N	97.06W
D'Entrecasteaux, Point, c., Austl. (däɴ-tr'kȧs-tō')	196	34.50S	114.45E
D'Entrecasteaux Islands, is., Pap. N. Gui. (däɴ-tr'-lȧs-tō')	188	9.45S	152.00E
Denver, Co., U.S. (dĕn'vĕr)	90	39.44N	104.59W
Deoli, India	178	25.52N	75.23E
De Pere, Wi., U.S. (dē pēr')	96	44.25N	88.04W
Depew, N.Y., U.S. (dē-pū')	95c	42.55N	78.43W
Deping, China (dŭ-pĭŋ)	182	37.28N	116.57E
Deptford, neigh., Eng., U.K.	231	51.28N	0.02W
Depue, Il., U.S. (dē pū)	92	41.15N	89.55W
De Queen, Ar., U.S. (dē kwēn')	104	34.02N	94.21W
De Quincy, La., U.S. (dē kwĭn'sĭ)	106	30.27N	93.27W
Dera, Lach, r., Afr. (läk dä'rä)	212a	0.45N	41.26E
Dera, Lak, r., Afr.	204	0.45N	41.30E
Dera Ghāzi Khān, Pak. (dä'rŭ gä-zē' ĸan')	174	30.09N	70.39E
Dera Ismāīl Khān, Pak. (dä'rŭ ĭs-mä-ēl' ĸăn')	178	31.55N	70.51E
Derbent, Russia (dĕr-bĕnt')	160	42.00N	48.10E
Derby, Austl. (där'bē) (dûr'bē)	196	17.20S	123.40E
Derby, S. Afr. (där'bĭ)	212d	25.55S	27.02E
Derby, Eng., U.K. (där'bē)	140	52.55N	1.29W
Derby, Ct., U.S. (dûr'bē)	92	41.20N	73.05W
Derbyshire, co., Eng., U.K.	138a	53.11N	1.30W
Derdepoort, S. Afr.	212d	24.39S	26.21E
Derendorf, neigh., Ger.	232	51.15N	6.48E
Derg, Lough, l., Ire. (lŏk dĕrg)	144	53.00N	8.09W
De Ridder, La., U.S. (dē rĭd'ēr)	106	30.50N	93.18W
Dermott, Ar., U.S. (dûr'mŏt)	104	33.32N	91.24W
Derne, neigh., Ger.	232	51.34N	7.31E
Derry, N.H., U.S. (dâr'ĭ)	87a	42.53N	71.22W
Derventa, Bos. (dĕr'ven-tȧ)	154	44.58N	17.58E
Derwent, r., Austl. (dĕr'wĕnt)	198	42.21S	146.30E
Derwent, r., Eng., U.K.	138a	52.54N	1.24W
Desagüe, Gran Canal del, can., Mex.	229a	19.29N	99.05W
Des Arc, Ar., U.S. (dāz ärk')	104	34.59N	91.31W
Descalvado, Braz. (dĕs-käl-vȧ-dô)	123a	21.55S	47.37W
Descartes, Fr.	150	46.58N	0.42E
Deschambault Lake, l., Can.	82	54.40N	103.35W
Deschênes, Can.	77c	45.23N	75.47W
Deschenes, Lake, l., Can.	77c	45.25N	75.53W
Deschutes, r., Or., U.S. (dā-shōōt')	98	44.25N	121.21W
Desdemona, Tx., U.S. (dĕz-dē-mō'nȧ)	106	32.16N	98.33W
Dese, Eth.	204	11.00N	39.51E
Deseado, Río, r., Arg. (rē-ō-dā-sä-ä'dhō)	126	46.50S	67.45W
Desirade Island, i., Guad. (dā-zē-räs')	115b	16.21N	60.51W
De Smet, S.D., U.S. (dē smĕt')	96	44.23N	97.33W
Des Moines, Ia., U.S. (dē moin')	90	41.35N	93.37W
Des Moines, N.M., U.S.	104	36.42N	103.48W

ăt; finăl; rāte; senāte; ärm; ásk; sofȧ; fâre; ch-choose; dh-as th in other; bē; ēvent; bĕt; recĕnt; cratẽr; g-gō; gh-guttural g; bĭt; ĭ-short neutral; rīde; ᴋ-guttural k as ch in German ich;

PLACE (Pronunciation)	PAGE	Lat. °'	Long. °'
Des Moines, Wa., U.S.	100a	46.24N	122.20W
Des Moines, r., U.S.	90	42.30N	94.20W
Desna, r., Eur. (dyĕs-ná')	160	51.55N	31.45E
Desolación, i., Chile (dĕ-sô-lä-syō'n)	126	53.05S	74.00W
De Soto, Mo., U.S. (dē sō'tō)	104	38.07N	90.32W
Des Peres, Mo., U.S. (dĕs pĕr'ĕs)	101e	38.36N	90.26W
Des Plaines, Il., U.S. (dĕs plānz')	95a	42.02N	87.54W
Des Plaines, r., U.S.	95a	41.39N	87.56W
Dessau, Ger. (dĕsou)	140	51.50N	12.15E
Detmold, Ger. (dĕt'mōld)	148	51.57N	8.55E
Detroit, Mi., U.S. (dē-troit')	90	42.22N	83.10W
Detroit, Tx., U.S.	104	33.41N	95.16W
Detroit, r., Mi., U.S.	226c	42.06N	83.08W
Detroit Lake, res., Or., U.S.	98	44.42N	122.10W
Detroit Lakes, Mn., U.S. (dē-troit'lăkz)	96	46.48N	95.51W
Detroit Metropolitan-Wayne County Airport, arpt., Mi., U.S.	226c	42.13N	83.22W
Detva, Czech. (dyĕt'vȧ)	148	48.32N	19.21E
Deuil-la-Barre, Fr.	233c	48.59N	2.20E
Deurne, Bel.	139a	51.13N	4.27E
Deusen, neigh., Ger.	232	51.33N	7.26E
Deutsch Wagram, Aus.	139e	48.19N	16.34E
Deux-Montagnes, Can.	77a	45.33N	73.53W
Deux Montagnes, Lac des, l., Can.	77a	45.28N	74.00W
Deva, Rom. (dā'vä)	142	45.52N	22.52E
Dévaványa, Hung. (dā'vô-vän-yô)	148	47.01N	20.58E
Develi, Tur. (dĕ'vȧ-lē)	160	38.20N	35.10E
Deventer, Neth. (dĕv'ĕn-tēr)	144	52.14N	6.07E
Devils, r., Tx., U.S.	106	29.55N	101.10W
Devils Island, see Diable, Île du, i., Fr. Gu.	124	5.15N	52.40W
Devils Lake, N.D., U.S.	90	48.10N	98.55W
Devils Lake, l., N.D., U.S. (dĕv''lz)	96	47.57N	99.04W
Devils Lake Indian Reservation, I.R., N.D., U.S.	96	48.08N	99.40W
Devils Postpile National Monument, rec., Ca., U.S.	102	37.42N	119.12W
Devils Tower National Monument, rec., Wy., U.S.	98	44.38N	105.07W
Devoll, r., Alb.	154	40.55N	20.10E
Devon, Can.	77g	53.23N	113.43W
Devon, S. Afr. (dĕv'ŭn)	212d	26.23S	28.47E
Devonport, Austl. (dĕv'ŭn-pôrt)	196	41.20S	146.30E
Devonport, N.Z.	197a	36.50S	174.45E
Devore, Ca., U.S. (dē-vôr')	101a	34.13N	117.24W
Dewatto, Wa., U.S. (dē-wăt'ō)	100a	47.27N	123.04W
Dewey, Ok., U.S. (dū'ĭ)	104	36.48N	95.55W
De Witt, Ar., U.S. (dē wĭt')	104	34.17N	91.22W
De Witt, Ia., U.S.	96	41.46N	90.34W
Dewsbury, Eng., U.K. (dūz'bēr-ĭ)	138a	53.42N	1.39W
Dexter, Me., U.S. (dĕks'tēr)	86	45.01N	69.19W
Dexter, Mo., U.S.	104	36.46N	89.56W
Dezfūl, Iran	174	32.14N	48.37E
Dezhnëva, Mys, c., Russia (dyĕzh'nyĭf)	172	68.00N	172.00W
Dezhou, China (dŭ-jō)	184	37.28N	116.17E
Dháfni, Grc.	235d	38.01N	23.39E
Dhahran, see Az Zahrān, Sau. Ar.	174	26.13N	50.00E
Dhaka, Bngl. (dä'kä) (dăk'ȧ)	174	23.45N	90.29E
Dharamtar Creek, r., India	179b	18.49N	72.54E
Dharmavaram, India	178	14.32N	77.43E
Dhaulāgiri, mtn., Nepal (dou-lȧ-gē'rē)	174	28.42N	83.31E
Dhenoúsa, i., Grc.	154	37.09N	25.53E
Dhībān, Jord.	173a	31.30N	35.46E
Dhidhimótikhon, Grc.	154	41.20N	26.27E
Dhodhekánisos (Dodecanese), is., Grc.	154	38.00N	26.10E
Dhule, India	174	20.58N	74.43E
Día, i., Grc. (dē'ä)	154a	35.27N	25.17E
Diable, Île du, i., Fr. Gu.	124	5.15N	52.40W
Diablo, Mount, mtn., Ca., U.S. (dyä'blŏ)	100b	37.52N	121.55W
Diablo Heights, Pan. (dyá'blŏ)	110a	8.58N	79.34W
Diablo Range, mts., Ca., U.S.	100b	37.47N	121.50W
Diaca, Moz.	210	11.30S	39.59E
Diaka, r., Mali	208	14.40N	5.00E
Diamantina, Braz.	124	18.14S	43.32W
Diamantina, r., Austl. (dī'man-tē'nȧ)	196	25.38S	139.53E
Diamantino, Braz. (dē-á-män-tē'no)	124	14.22S	56.23W
Diamond Creek, Austl.	239b	37.41S	145.09E
Diamond Peak, mtn., Or., U.S.	98	43.32N	122.08W
Diana Bank, bk. (dī'ăn'ȧ)	116	22.30N	74.45W
Dianbai, China (dĭĕn-bī)	184	21.30N	111.20E
Dian Chi, l., China (dĭĕn chē)	180	24.58N	103.18E
Diancun, China	236b	39.55N	116.14E
Dickinson, N.D., U.S. (dĭk'ĭn-sŭn)	90	46.52N	102.49W
Dickinson, Tx., U.S. (dĭk'ĭn-sŭn)	107a	29.28N	95.02W
Dickinson Bayou, Tx., U.S.	107a	29.26N	95.08W
Dickson, Tn., U.S. (dĭk'sŭn)	108	36.03N	87.24W
Dickson City, Pa., U.S.	92	41.25N	75.40W
Didcot, Eng., U.K. (dĭd'cŏt)	138b	51.35N	1.15W
Didiéni, Mali	208	13.53N	8.06W
Didsbury, neigh., Eng., U.K.	233b	53.25N	2.14W
Die, Fr. (dē)	150	44.45N	5.22E
Diefenbaker, res., Can.	78	51.20N	108.10W
Diego de Ocampo, Pico, mtn., Dom. Rep. (pē'-kô-dyĕ'gô-dĕ-ô-kä'm-pô)	116	19.40N	70.45W
Diego Ramirez, Islas, is., Chile (dē ä'gō rä-mē'rāz)	126	56.15S	70.15W
Diéma, Mali	208	14.32N	9.12W
Dien Bien Phu, Viet.	180	21.38N	102.49E
Diepensee, Ger.	234a	52.22N	13.31E
Dieppe, Can. (dē-ĕp')	86	46.06N	64.45W
Dieppe, Fr.	140	49.54N	1.05E
Dierks, Ar., U.S. (dērks)	104	34.06N	94.02W
Diessem, neigh., Ger.	232	51.20N	6.35E
Diessen, Ger. (dēs'sĕn)	139d	47.57N	11.06E
Diest, Bel.	139a	50.59N	5.05E
Digby, Can. (dĭg'bĭ)	78	44.37N	65.46W
Dighton, Ma., U.S. (dī-tŭn)	94b	41.49N	71.05W

PLACE (Pronunciation)	PAGE	Lat. °'	Long. °'
Digmoor, Eng., U.K.	233a	53.32N	2.45W
Digne, Fr. (dēn'y')	150	44.07N	6.16E
Digoin, Fr. (dē-gwăn')	150	46.28N	4.06E
Digra, India	236a	22.50N	88.20E
Digul, r., Indon.	188	7.00S	140.27E
Dijohan Point, c., Phil. (dē-kô-än)	189a	16.24N	122.25E
Dijon, Fr. (dē-zhôn')	136	47.21N	5.02E
Dikson, Russia (dĭk'sŏn)	158	73.30N	80.35E
Dikwa, Nig. (dē'kwȧ)	204	12.06N	13.53E
Dili, Indon. (dĭl'ē)	188	8.35S	125.35E
Di Linosa Island, i., Italy (dē-lē-nô'sä)	142	36.01N	12.43E
Dilizhan, Arm.	160	40.45N	45.00E
Dillingham, Ak., U.S. (dĭl'ĕng-hăm)	90a	59.10N	158.38W
Dillon, Mt., U.S. (dĭl'ŭn)	98	45.12N	112.40W
Dillon, S.C., U.S.	108	34.24N	79.28W
Dillon Park, Md., U.S.	225d	38.52N	76.56W
Dillon Reservoir, res., Oh., U.S.	92	40.05N	82.05W
Dilolo, Zaire (dē-lō'lō)	206	10.19S	22.23E
Dimashq, see Damascus, Syria	174	33.31N	36.18E
Dimbokro, I.C.	208	6.39N	4.42W
Dimbovița, r., Rom.	154	44.43N	25.41E
Dimitrovo, see Pernik, Bul.	142	42.36N	23.04E
Dimlang, mtn., Nig.	208	8.24N	11.47E
Dimona, Isr.	173a	31.03N	35.01E
Dinagat Island, i., Phil.	188	10.15N	126.15E
Dinājpur, Bngl.	178	25.38N	87.39E
Dinan, Fr. (dē-nän')	150	48.27N	2.03W
Dinant, Bel. (dē-nän')	144	50.17N	4.50E
Dinara, mts., Yugo. (dē'nä-rä)	142	43.50N	16.15E
Dinard, Fr.	150	48.38N	2.04W
Dindigul, India	178	10.25N	78.03E
Dingalan Bay, b., Phil. (dĭŋ-gä'län)	189a	15.19N	121.33E
Dingle, Ire. (dĭng''l)	144	52.10N	10.13W
Dingle, neigh., Eng., U.K.	233a	53.23N	2.57W
Dingle Bay, b., Ire.	140	52.02N	10.15W
Dingo, Austl. (dĭŋ'gō)	196	23.45S	149.26E
Dinguiraye, Gui.	208	11.18N	10.43W
Dingwall, Scot., U.K. (dĭng'wôl)	144	57.37N	4.23W
Dingxian, China (dĭŋ shyĕn)	184	38.30N	115.00E
Dingxing, China (dĭŋ-shyĭŋ)	184	39.18N	115.50E
Dingyuan, China (dĭŋ-yüän)	182	32.32N	117.40E
Dingzi Wan, b., China	182	36.33N	121.06E
Dinosaur National Monument, rec., Co., U.S. (dī'nô-sôr)	98	40.45N	109.17W
Dinslaken, Ger. (dēns'lä-kĕn)	151c	51.33N	6.44E
Dinslakener Bruch, Ger.	232	51.35N	6.43E
Dinteloord, Neth.	139a	51.38N	4.21E
Dinuba, Ca., U.S. (dĭ-nū'bȧ)	102	36.33N	119.29W
Dinwiddie, S. Afr.	240b	26.16S	28.10E
Dios, Cayo de, i., Cuba (kä'yō-dĕ-dē-ōs')	116	22.05N	83.05W
Diourbel, Sen. (dē-o͞or-bĕl')	204	14.40N	16.15W
Diphu Pass, p., Asia (dĭ-po͞o)	180	28.15N	96.45E
Diquis, r., C.R. (dē-kēs')	114	8.59N	83.24W
Dire Dawa, Eth.	204	9.40N	41.47E
Diriamba, Nic. (dēr-yäm'bä)	114	11.52N	86.15W
Dirk Hartog, i., Austl.	196	26.25S	113.15E
Dirksland, Neth.	139a	51.45N	4.04E
Dirranbandi, Austl. (dĭ-rȧ-băn'dē)	196	28.24S	148.29E
Dirty Devil, r., Ut., U.S. (dûr'tĭ dĕv''l)	102	38.20N	110.30W
Disappointment, l., Austl.	196	23.20S	123.00E
Disappointment, Cape, c., Wa., U.S. (dĭs'ȧ-point'ment)	100c	46.16N	124.11W
Discovery, S. Afr. (dĭs-kŭv'ēr-ĭ)	207b	26.10S	27.53E
Discovery, is., Can. (dĭs-kŭv'ēr-ē)	100a	48.25N	123.13W
Disko, i., Grnld. (dĭs'kō)	76	70.00N	54.00W
Disna, Bela. (dēs'nȧ)	160	55.34N	28.15E
Disneyland, pt. of i., Ca., U.S.	228	33.48N	117.55W
Dispur, India	178	26.00N	91.50E
Disraëli, Can. (dĭs-rā'lĭ)	84	45.53N	71.23W
Disteln, Ger.	232	51.36N	7.09E
District Heights, Md., U.S.	225d	38.51N	76.53W
District of Columbia, state, U.S.	90	38.50N	77.00W
Distrito Federal, dept., Braz. (dēs-trē'tô-fĕ-dĕ-rä'l)	124	15.49S	47.39W
Distrito Federal, dept., Mex.	112	19.14N	99.08W
Disūq, Egypt (dē-so͞ok')	212b	31.07N	30.41E
Ditton, Eng., U.K.	231	51.18N	0.27E
Diu, India (dē'o͞o)	174	20.48N	70.58E
Divilacan Bay, b., Phil. (dē-vē-lä'kän)	189a	17.26N	122.25E
Divinópolis, Braz. (dē-vē-nô'pô-lēs)	124	20.10S	44.53W
Divo, I.C.	208	5.50N	5.22W
Dixon, Il., U.S. (dĭks'ŭn)	96	41.50N	89.30W
Dixon Entrance, strt., N.A.	78	54.25N	132.00W
Diyarbakir, Tur. (dē-yär-bĕk'ĭr)	174	38.00N	40.10E
Dja, r., Afr.	204	2.30N	14.00E
Djakovo, neigh., Russia	235b	55.39N	37.40E
Djambala, Congo	210	2.33S	14.45E
Djanet, Alg.	204	24.29N	9.26E
Djebobo, mtn., Ghana	208	8.20N	0.37E
Djedi, Oued, r., Alg.	142	34.18N	4.39E
Djelo-Binza, Zaire	240c	4.23S	15.16E
Djember, Chad	208	10.25N	17.50E
Djerba, Île de, i., Tun.	142	33.53N	11.26E
Djerid, Chott, l., Tun. (jĕr'ĭd)	204	33.15N	8.29E
Djibasso, Burkina	208	13.07N	4.10W
Djibo, Burkina	208	14.06N	1.38W
Djibouti, Dji. (jē-bo͞o-tē')	212a	11.34N	43.00E
Djibouti, nation, Afr.	212a	11.35N	48.08E
Djokoumatombi, Congo	210	0.47N	15.22E
Djokupunda, Zaire	206	5.27S	20.58E
Djoua, r., Afr.	210	1.25N	13.40E
Djursholm, Swe. (djo͞ors'hōlm)	146	59.26N	18.01E
Dmitriyevka, Ukr. (d'mē-trē-yĕf'kȧ)	156	47.57N	38.56E
Dmitriyev-L'govskiy, Russia (d'mē'trĭ-yĕf l'gôf'skĭ)	156	52.07N	35.05E
Dmitrov, Russia (d'mē'trôf)	156	56.21N	37.32E
Dmitrovsk, Russia (d'mē'trôfsk)	156	52.30N	35.10E

PLACE (Pronunciation)	PAGE	Lat. °'	Long. °'
Dnepr (Dnieper), r., Eur.	160	46.45N	33.40E
Dneprodzerzhinsk, Ukr. (d'nyĕp'rô-zēr-shĭnsk)	160	48.32N	34.38E
Dneprodzerzhinskoye Vodokhranilishche, res., Ukr.	158	49.00N	34.10E
Dnepropetrovsk, Ukr.	158	48.15N	34.08E
Dnepropetrovsk, prov., Ukr. (d'nyĕp'rô-pā-trôfsk)	156	48.15N	34.10E
Dnepr Zaliv, b., Ukr. (dnyĕp'r zá'lĭf)	156	46.33N	31.45E
Dnestr (Dniester), r., Eur.	160	48.21N	28.10E
Dnestrovskiy Liman, l., Ukr.	156	46.13N	29.50E
Dniester, see Dnestr, r., Eur.	160	48.21N	28.10E
Dno, Russia (d'nô')	156	57.49N	29.59E
Do, Lac, l., Mali	208	15.50N	2.20W
Doba, Chad	208	8.39N	16.51E
Dobbs Ferry, N.Y., U.S. (dŏbz'fĕ'rē)	94a	41.01N	73.53W
Dobbyn, Austl. (dôb'ĭn)	196	19.45S	140.02E
Dobele, Lat. (dô'bĕ-lĕ)	146	56.37N	23.18E
Doberai, Jazirah, pen., Indon.	188	1.25S	133.15E
Döbling, neigh., Aus.	235e	48.15N	16.22E
Dobo, Indon.	188	6.00S	134.18E
Doboj, Bos. (dō'boi)	154	44.42N	18.04E
Dobrich, Bul.	142	43.33N	27.52E
Dobryanka, Russia (dôb-ryän'kȧ)	164a	58.27N	56.26E
Dobšina, Czech. (dôp'shē-nä)	148	48.48N	20.25E
Doce, r., Braz. (dō'sȧ)	124	19.01S	42.14W
Doce, Canal Numero, can., Arg.	123c	36.47S	59.00W
Doce Leguas, Cayos de las, is., Cuba	116	20.55N	79.05W
Doctor Arroyo, Mex. (dôk-tōr' är-rō'yō)	112	23.41N	100.10W
Doddinghurst, Eng., U.K.	231	51.40N	0.18E
Doddington, Eng., U.K. (dŏd'dĭng-tŏn)	138b	51.17N	0.47E
Dodecanese, see Dhodhekánisos, is., Grc.	154	38.00N	26.10E
Dodge City, Ks., U.S. (dŏj)	90	37.44N	100.01W
Dodgeville, Wi., U.S. (dŏj'vĭl)	96	42.58N	90.07W
Dodoma, Tan. (dō'dô-mȧ)	206	6.11S	35.45E
Dog, l., Can. (dŏg)	84	48.42N	89.24W
Dogger Bank, bk. (dŏg'gēr)	144	55.07N	2.25E
Dogubayazit, Tur.	160	39.35N	44.00E
Doha, see Ad Dawhah, Qatar	174	25.02N	51.28E
Dohad, India	178	22.52N	74.18E
Doiran, l., Grc.	154	41.10N	23.00E
Dokshitsy, Bela. (dôk-shē'tsē)	156	54.53N	27.49E
Dolbeau, Can.	78	48.52N	72.16W
Dole, Fr. (dōl)	140	47.07N	5.28E
Dolgaya, Kosa, c., Russia (kô'sȧ dôl-gä'yä)	156	46.42N	37.42E
Dolgeville, N.Y., U.S.	92	43.10N	74.45W
Dolgiy, i., Russia	160	69.20N	59.20E
Dolgoprudnyy, Russia	164b	55.57N	37.33E
Dolina, Ukr. (dô-lyē'nä)	148	48.57N	24.01E
Dolinsk, Russia (dá-lēnsk')	162	47.29N	142.31E
Dollard-des-Ormeaux, Can.	223b	45.29N	73.49W
Dollar Harbor, b., Bah.	116	25.30N	79.15W
Dolomite, Al., U.S. (dŏl'ô-mĭt)	94h	33.28N	86.57W
Dolomiti, mts., Italy	154	46.16N	11.43E
Dolores, Arg. (dô-lō'rĕs)	126	36.20S	57.42W
Dolores, Col.	124a	3.33N	74.54W
Dolores, Tx., U.S. (dô-lō'rĕs)	106	27.42N	99.47W
Dolores, Ur.	123c	33.32S	58.15W
Dolores, r., Co., U.S.	102	38.35N	108.50W
Dolores Hidalgo, Mex. (dô-lô'rĕs-ē-däl'gō)	112	21.09N	100.56W
Dolphin and Union Strait, strt., Can. (dŏl'fĭn ūn'yŭn)	78	69.22N	117.10W
Dolton, Il., U.S.	227a	41.39N	87.37W
Domažlice, Czech. (dō'mäzh-lē-tsĕ)	148	49.27N	12.55E
Dombasle-sur-Meurthe, Fr. (dôn-bäl')	150	48.38N	6.18E
Dombóvár, Hung. (dŏm'bō-vär)	148	46.22N	18.08E
Domeyko, Cordillera, mts., Chile (kôr-dēl-yĕ'rä-dô-mā'kô)	124	20.50S	69.02W
Dominguez, Ca., U.S.	228	33.50N	118.31W
Dominica, nation, N.A. (dŏ-mĭ-nē'kȧ)	110	15.30N	60.45W
Dominica Channel, strt., N.A.	115b	15.00N	61.30W
Dominican Republic, nation, N.A. (dô-mĭn'ĭ-kăn)	110	19.00N	70.45W
Dominion, Can. (dô-mĭn'yŭn)	86	46.13N	60.01W
Domiongo, Zaire	210	4.37S	21.15E
Domitilla, Catacombe di, pt. of i., Italy	235c	41.52N	12.31E
Domodedovo, Russia (dô-mô-dyĕ'do-vô)	164b	55.27N	37.45E
Dom Silvério, Braz. (dôn-sĕl-vĕ'ryō)	123a	20.09S	42.57W
Don, r., Can.	223c	43.39N	79.21W
Don, r., Russia	158	49.50N	41.30E
Don, r., Eng., U.K.	138a	53.39N	0.58W
Don, r., Scot., U.K.	144	57.19N	2.39W
Donaldson, Mi., U.S. (dŏn'ăl-sŭn)	101k	46.19N	84.22W
Donaldsonville, La., U.S. (dŏn'ăld-sŭn-vĭl)	106	30.05N	90.58W
Donalsonville, Ga., U.S.	108	31.02N	84.50W
Donaufeld, neigh., Italy	235e	48.15N	16.25E
Donaustadt, neigh., Aus.	235e	48.13N	16.30E
Donauturm, pt. of i., Aus.	235e	48.14N	16.25E
Donawitz, Aus. (dō'nȧ-vĭts)	148	47.23N	15.05E
Don Benito, Spain (dōn'bȧ-nē'tō)	152	38.55N	5.52W
Dönberg, Ger.	232	51.18N	7.10E
Don Bosco, neigh., Arg.	229d	34.42S	58.19W
Doncaster, Austl. (doŋ'kăs-tēr)	195a	37.47S	145.08E
Doncaster, Can.	223c	43.48N	79.25W
Doncaster, Eng., U.K. (doŋ'kăs-tēr)	144	53.32N	1.07W
Doncaster East, Austl.	239b	37.47S	145.10E
Dondo, Ang. (dōn'dō)	206	9.38S	14.25E
Dondo, Moz.	206	19.33S	34.47E
Dondra Head, c., Sri L.	175c	5.52N	80.52E
Donegal, Ire. (dŏn-ē-gôl')	144	54.44N	8.05W
Donegal Bay, Ire. (dŏn-ĕ-gôl')	140	54.35N	8.36W
Donets, r., Eur. (dō-nyĕts')	156	48.48N	38.42E
Donets Coal Basin, reg., Ukr. (dō-nyĕts')	156	48.15N	38.50E

ng-sing; ŋ-baŋk; ɴ-nasalized n; nŏd; cŏmmit; ōld; ôbey; ôrder; oi-boil; fo͞od; ȯ-as oo in foot; ou-out; s-soft; sh-dish; th-thin; pūre; ûnite; ûrn; stŭd; circŭs; ü-as in French tu; '-indeterminate vowel.

PLACE (Pronunciation)	PAGE	Lat. °′	Long. °′
Donetsk, Ukr. (dō-nyĕts′k)	158	48.00N	37.35E
Donetsk, prov., Ukr.	156	47.55N	37.40E
Dong, r., China (dôŋ)	180	24.13N	115.08E
Dongara, Austl. (dôn-gă′rȧ)	196	29.15S	115.00E
Dongba, China (dôŋ-bä)	182	31.40N	119.02E
Dongba, China	236b	39.58N	116.32E
Dongbahe, China	236b	39.58N	116.27E
Dong'e, China (dôŋ-ŭ)	182	36.21N	116.14E
Dong'ezhen, China	184	36.11N	116.16E
Dongfang, China (dôŋ-fäŋ)	184	19.08N	108.42E
Donggala, Indon. (dôn-gä′lä)	188	0.45S	119.32E
Dongguan, China (dôŋ-gůän)	183a	23.03N	113.46E
Dongguang, China (dôŋ-gůäŋ)	182	37.54N	116.33E
Donghai, China (dôŋ-hī)	184	34.35N	119.05E
Dong Hoi, Viet. (dông-hō-ē′)	188	17.25N	106.42E
Dongila, Eth.	204	11.17N	37.00E
Dongming, China (dôŋ-mĭŋ)	182	35.16N	115.06E
Dongo, Ang. (dôŋ′gō)	206	14.45S	15.30E
Dongon Point, c., Phil. (dông-ôn′)	189a	12.43N	120.35E
Dongou, Congo (dôŋ-gōō′)	204	2.02N	18.04E
Dongping, China (dôŋ-pĭŋ)	184	35.50N	116.24E
Dongping Hu, l., China (dôŋ-pĭŋ hōō)	182	36.06N	116.24E
Dongshan, China (doŋ-shän)	182	31.05N	120.24E
Dongshi, China	236b	39.49N	116.34E
Dongtai, China	182	32.51N	120.20E
Dongting Hu, l., China (dôŋ-tĭŋ hōō)	180	29.10N	112.30E
Dongxiang, China (dôŋ-shyän)	184	28.18N	116.38E
Doniphan, Mo., U.S. (dŏn′ĭ-făn)	104	36.37N	90.50W
Donji Vakuf, Bos. (dōn′yĭ väk′ŏf)	154	44.08N	17.25E
Don Martin, Presa de, res., Mex. (prĕ′sä-dĕ-dôn-mär-tē′n)	106	27.35N	100.38W
Donnacona, Can.	84	46.40N	71.46W
Donnemarie-en-Montois, Fr. (dôn-mä-rē′ĕɴ-môɴ-twä′)	151b	48.29N	3.09E
Donner und Blitzen, r., Or., U.S. (dŏn′ẽr ŏnt′blĭt′sĕn)	98	42.45N	118.57W
Donnybrook, S. Afr. (dŏ-nĭ-brŏŏk)	207c	29.56S	29.54E
Donora, Pa., U.S. (dŏ-nō′rȧ)	95e	40.10N	79.51W
Don Torcuato, Arg.	229d	34.29S	58.37W
Doolow, Som.	212a	4.10N	42.05E
Doonerak, Mount, mtn., Ak., U.S. (dōō′nē-răk)	89	68.00N	150.34W
Doorn, Neth.	139a	52.02N	5.21E
Door Peninsula, pen., Wi., U.S. (dōr)	96	44.40N	87.36W
Dora Baltea, r., Italy (dō′rä bäl′tä-ä)	154	45.40N	7.34E
Doraville, Ga., U.S. (dō′rȧ-vĭl)	94c	33.54N	84.17W
Dorchester, Eng., U.K. (dôr′chĕs-tẽr)	144	50.45N	2.34W
Dorchester Heights National Historic Site, hist., Ma., U.S.	223a	42.20N	71.03W
Dordogne, r., Fr. (dôr-dôn′yĕ)	136	44.53N	0.16E
Dordrecht, Neth. (dôr′drĕĸt)	144	51.48N	4.39E
Dordrecht, S. Afr. (dô′drĕĸt)	207c	31.24S	27.06E
Doré Lake, l., Can.	82	54.31N	107.06W
Dorgali, Italy (dôr′gä-lē)	154	40.18N	9.37E
Dörgön Nuur, l., Mong.	180	47.47N	94.01E
Dorion-Vaudreuil, Can. (dôr-yō)	77a	45.23N	74.01W
Dorking, Eng., U.K. (dôr′kĭng)	138b	51.12N	0.20W
Dormont, Pa., U.S. (dôr′mŏnt)	95e	40.24N	80.02W
Dornap, Ger.	232	51.15N	7.04E
Dornbirn, Aus. (dôrn′bĕrn)	148	47.24N	9.45E
Dornoch, Scot., U.K. (dôr′nŏĸ)	140	57.55N	4.01W
Dornoch Firth, b., Scot., U.K. (dôr′nŏĸ fûrth)	144	57.55N	3.55W
Dorogobuzh, Russia (dôrôgô′-bōō′zh)	156	54.57N	33.18E
Dorohoi, Rom. (dō-rō-hoi′)	148	47.57N	26.28E
Dorre Island, i., Austl. (dôr)	196	25.19S	113.10E
Dorseyville, Pa., U.S.	226b	40.35N	79.53W
Dorstfeld, neigh., Ger.	232	51.31N	7.25E
Dorstsen, Ger.	151c	51.40N	6.58E
Dortmund, Ger. (dôrt′mŏont)	140	51.31N	7.28E
Dortmund-Ems-Kanal, can., Ger. (dōrt′mōōnd-ĕms′kä-näl′)	151c	51.50N	7.25E
Dörtyol, Tur. (dûrt′yōl)	142	36.50N	36.20E
Dorval, Can. (dôr-vál′)	77a	45.26N	73.44W
Dos Bahías, Cabo, c., Arg. (kȧ′bō-dôs-bä-ē′äs)	126	44.55S	65.35W
Dos Caminos, Ven. (dôs-kä-mē′nôs)	125b	9.38N	67.17W
Dosewallips, r., Wa., U.S. (dō′sē-wäl′lĭps)	100a	47.45N	123.04W
Dos Hermanas, Spain (dōsĕr-mä′näs)	152	37.17N	5.56W
Dosso, Niger (dôs-ō′)	204	13.03N	3.12E
Dothan, Al., U.S. (dō′thȧn)	90	31.13N	85.23W
Douai, Fr. (dōō-å′)	140	50.23N	3.04E
Douala, Cam. (dōō-ä′lä)	204	4.03N	9.42E
Douarnenez, Fr. (dōō-ár nĕ-nĕs′)	150	48.06N	4.18W
Double Bayou, Tx., U.S. (dŭb′'l bī′yōō)	107a	29.40N	94.38W
Doubs, r., Eur.	150	46.15N	5.50E
Douentza, Mali	208	15.00N	2.57W
Douglas, I. of Man (dŭg′lȧs)	144	54.10N	4.24W
Douglas, Ak., U.S. (dŭg′lȧs)	89	58.18N	134.35W
Douglas, Az., U.S.	90	31.20N	109.30W
Douglas, Ga., U.S.	108	31.30N	82.53W
Douglas, Wy., U.S. (dŭg′lȧs)	98	42.45N	105.21W
Douglas, r., Eng., U.K. (dŭg′lȧs)	138a	53.38N	2.48W
Douglas Channel, strt., Can.	80	53.30N	129.12W
Douglas Lake, res., Tn., U.S. (dŭg′lȧs)	108	36.00N	83.35W
Douglas Lake Indian Reserve, I.R., Can.	80	50.10N	120.49W
Douglasville, Ga., U.S. (dŭg′lȧs-vĭl)	108	33.45N	84.47W
Dourada, Serra, mts., Braz. (sĕ′r-rä-dôōō-rá′dă)	124	15.11S	49.57W
Dourdan, Fr. (dōōr-däɴ′)	151b	48.32N	2.01E
Douro, r., Eur. (dwĕ′rō)	136	41.30N	4.30W
Douro, r., Port. (dô′ō-rō)	152	41.03N	8.12W
Dove, r., Eng., U.K. (dŭv)	138a	52.53N	1.47W
Dover, S. Afr.	212d	27.05S	27.44E
Dover, Eng., U.K.	136	51.08N	1.19E
Dover, De., U.S. (dō vẽr)	90	39.10N	75.30W
Dover, N.H., U.S.	92	43.15N	71.00W
Dover, N.J., U.S.	94a	40.53N	74.33W
Dover, Oh., U.S.	92	40.35N	81.30W
Dover, Strait of, strt., Eur.	136	50.50N	1.15W
Dover-Foxcroft, Me., U.S. (dō′vẽr fôks′krôft)	86	45.10N	69.15W
Dover Heights, Austl.	239a	33.53S	151.17E
Doveton, Austl.	239b	38.00S	145.14E
Dovre Fjell, mts., Nor. (dŏv′rĕ fyĕl′)	136	62.03N	8.36E
Dow, Il., U.S. (dou)	101e	39.01N	90.20W
Dowagiac, Mi., U.S. (dō-wô′jăk)	92	42.00N	86.05W
Dowlatābād, Iran	237h	35.37N	51.27E
Downers Grove, Il., U.S. (dou′nẽrz grōv)	95a	41.48N	88.00W
Downey, Ca., U.S. (dou′nĭ)	101a	33.56N	118.08W
Downieville, Ca., U.S. (dou′nĭ-nĭl)	102	39.35N	120.48W
Downs, Ks., U.S. (dounz)	104	39.29N	98.32W
Doylestown, Oh., U.S. (doilz′toun)	95d	40.58N	81.43W
Drâa, Cap, c., Mor. (drȧ)	204	28.39N	12.15W
Drâa, Oued, r., Afr.	204	28.00N	9.31W
Drabov, Ukr. (drä′bôf)	156	49.57N	32.14E
Drac, r., Fr. (dräĸ)	150	44.50N	5.47E
Dracut, Ma., U.S. (dră′kŭt)	87a	42.40N	71.19W
Draganovo, Bul. (drä-gä-nō′vŏ)	154	43.13N	25.45E
Drăgăşani, Rom. (drä-gá-shän′ĭ)	154	44.39N	24.18E
Draguignan, Fr. (drä-gēn-yäɴ′)	150	43.35N	6.28E
Drakensberg, mts., Afr. (drä′kĕnz-bĕrgh)	206	29.15S	29.07E
Drake Passage, strt. (drāk păs′ĭj)	122	57.00S	65.00W
Dráma, Grc. (drä′mä)	154	41.09N	24.10E
Drammen, Nor. (dräm′ĕn)	140	59.45N	10.15E
Drancy, Fr.	233c	48.56N	2.27E
Drau (Drava), r., Eur. (drou)	148	46.44N	13.45E
Drava, r., Eur. (drä′vä)	136	45.45N	17.30E
Draveil, Fr.	233c	48.41N	2.25E
Dravograd, Slo. (drä′vô-gräd′)	154	46.37N	15.01E
Dravosburg, Pa., U.S.	226b	40.21N	79.51W
Drawsko Pomorskie, Pol. (dräv′skō pō-mōr′skyĕ)	148	53.31N	15.50E
Drayton Harbor, b., Wa., U.S. (drā′tŭn)	100d	48.58N	122.40W
Drayton Plains, Mi., U.S.	95b	42.41N	83.23W
Drayton Valley, Can.	80	53.13N	114.59W
Drensteinfurt, Ger. (drĕn′shtīn-fōōrt)	151c	51.47N	7.44E
Dresden, Ger. (drās′dĕn)	136	51.05N	13.45E
Dreux, Fr. (drû)	150	48.44N	1.24E
Drewitz, neigh., Ger.	234a	52.22N	13.08E
Drexel Hill, Pa., U.S.	225b	39.57N	75.19W
Driefontein, S. Afr.	212d	25.53S	29.10E
Drin, r., Alb. (drēn)	154	42.13N	20.13E
Drina, r., Yugo. (drē′nä)	142	44.09N	19.30E
Drinit, Pellg i, b., Alb.	154	41.42N	19.17E
Dr. Ir. W. J. van Blommestein Meer, res., Sur.	124	4.45N	55.05W
Drissa, Bela. (drĭs′sä)	156	55.48N	27.59E
Drissa, r., Eur.	156	55.44N	28.58E
Driver, Va., U.S.	94g	36.50N	76.30W
Dröbak, Nor. (drû′bāk)	146	59.40N	10.35E
Drobeta-Turnu-Severin, Rom. (sĕ-vĕ-rēn′)	142	43.54N	24.49E
Drogheda, Ire. (drŏ′hĕ-dȧ)	140	53.43N	6.15W
Drogichin, Bela. (drō-gē′chĭn)	148	52.10N	25.11E
Drogobych, Ukr. (drō-hô′bĭch)	148	49.21N	23.31E
Drôme, r., Fr. (drōm)	150	44.42N	4.53E
Dronfield, Eng., U.K. (drŏn′fēld)	138a	53.18N	1.28W
Droylsden, Eng., U.K.	233b	53.29N	2.10W
Drumheller, Can. (drŭm-hĕl-ẽr)	78	51.28N	112.42W
Drummond, i., Mi., U.S. (drŭm′ŭnd)	92	46.00N	83.50W
Drummondville, Can. (drŭm′ŭnd-vĭl)	78	45.53N	72.33W
Drummoyne, Austl.	239a	33.51S	151.09E
Drumright, Ok., U.S. (drŭm′rīt)	104	35.59N	96.37W
Drunen, Neth.	139a	51.41N	5.10E
Drut′, r., Bela. (drōōt)	156	53.40N	29.45E
Druya, Bela. (drō′yȧ)	156	55.45N	27.26E
Družba, Russia	235b	55.53N	37.45E
Drwęca, r., Pol. (d′r-vän′tsȧ)	148	53.06N	19.13E
Dryden, Can. (drī-dĕn)	78	49.47N	92.50W
Drysdale, Austl.	195a	38.11S	144.34E
Dry Tortugas, is., Fl., U.S. (tôr-tōō′gäz)	109a	24.37N	82.45W
Dschang, Cam. (dshäng)	204	5.34N	10.09E
Duabo, Lib.	208	5.40N	8.05W
Duagh, Can.	77g	53.43N	113.24W
Duarte, Ca., U.S.	228	34.08N	117.58W
Duarte, Pico, mtn., Dom. Rep. (dŭŭ′ärtĕh pēcô)	110	19.00N	71.00W
Duas Barras, Braz. (dōō′äs-bá′r-räs)	123a	22.03S	42.30W
Dubai, *see* Dubayy, U.A.E.	174	25.18N	55.26E
Dubawnt, l., Can. (dōō-bônt′)	78	63.27N	103.30W
Dubawnt, r., Can.	78	61.30N	103.49W
Dubayy, U.A.E.	174	25.18N	55.26E
Dubbo, Austl. (dŭb′ō)	196	32.20S	148.42E
Dubesar', Mol.	156	47.16N	29.11E
Dubie, Zaire	210	8.33S	28.32E
Dublin, Ire.	136	53.20N	6.15W
Dublin, Ca., U.S. (dŭb′lĭn)	100b	37.42N	121.56W
Dublin, Ga., U.S.	108	32.33N	82.55W
Dublin, Tx., U.S.	106	32.05N	98.20W
Dubno, Ukr. (dōō′b-nô)	148	50.24N	25.44E
Du Bois, Pa., U.S. (dŏ-bois′)	92	41.10N	78.45W
Dubovka, Russia (dŏ-bôf′kȧ)	160	49.00N	44.50E
Dubrovka, Russia (dōō-brôf′kȧ)	164c	59.51N	30.56E
Dubrovnik, Cro. (dō′brôv-nĕk) (rä-gōō′sä)	136	42.40N	18.10E
Dubrovno, Bela. (dōō-brôf′nō)	156	54.39N	30.54E
Dubuque, Ia., U.S. (dŏ-būk′)	90	42.30N	90.43W
Duchesne, Ut., U.S. (dŏ-shān′)	102	40.12N	110.23W
Duchesne, r., Ut., U.S.	102	40.20N	110.50W
Duchess, Austl. (dŭch′ĕs)	196	21.30S	139.55E
Ducie Island, i., Pit. (dü-sē′)	2	25.30S	126.20W
Duck, r., Tn., U.S.	108	35.55N	87.40W
Duckabush, r., Wa., U.S. (dŭk′ȧ-bŏsh)	100a	47.41N	123.09W
Duck Lake, Can.	82	52.47N	106.13W
Duck Mountain, mtn., Can.	82	51.35N	101.00W
Ducktown, Tn., U.S. (dŭk′toun)	108	35.03N	84.20W
Duck Valley Indian Reservation, I.R., Id., U.S.	98	42.02N	115.49W
Duckwater Peak, mtn., Nv., U.S. (dŭk-wô-tẽr)	102	39.00N	115.31W
Duda, r., Col. (dōō′dä)	124a	3.25N	74.23W
Dudinka, Russia (dōō-dĭn′kȧ)	158	69.15N	85.42E
Dudley, Eng., U.K. (dŭd′lĭ)	140	52.28N	2.07E
Dugger, In., U.S. (dŭg′ẽr)	92	39.00N	87.10W
Dugi Otok, i., Yugo. (dōō′gē o′tôk)	154	44.03N	14.40E
Dugny, Fr.	233c	48.57N	2.25E
Duisburg, Ger. (dōō′ĭs-bŏrgh)	140	51.26N	6.46E
Duissern, neigh., Ger.	232	51.26N	6.47E
Dukhān, Qatar	176	25.25N	50.48E
Dukhovshchina, Russia (dōō-ĸôfsh-′chēnȧ)	156	55.13N	32.26E
Dukinfield, Eng., U.K. (dŭk′ĭn-fēld)	138a	53.28N	2.05W
Dukla Pass, p., Eur. (dŏ′klä)	140	49.25N	21.44E
Dulce, Golfo, b., C.R. (gōl′fō dōōl′sā)	110	8.25N	83.13W
Dülken, Ger. (dül′kĕn)	151c	51.15N	6.21E
Dülmen, Ger. (dül′mĕn)	151c	51.50N	7.17E
Duluth, Mn., U.S. (dŏ-lōōth′)	90	46.50N	92.07W
Dulwich, neigh., Eng., U.K.	231	51.26N	0.05W
Dumai, Indon.	173b	1.39N	101.30E
Dumali Point, c., Phil. (dōō-mä′lē)	189a	13.07N	121.42E
Dumas, Tx., U.S.	104	35.52N	101.58W
Dumbarton, Scot., U.K. (dŭm′bȧr-tŭn)	144	56.00N	4.35W
Dum-Dum, India	178a	22.37N	88.25E
Dumfries, Scot., U.K. (dŭm-frēs′)	144	55.05N	3.40W
Dumjor, India	178a	22.37N	88.14E
Dumont, N.J., U.S. (dōō′mŏnt)	94a	40.56N	74.00W
Dümpten, neigh., Ger.	232	51.27N	6.54E
Dumyāt, Egypt	204	31.22N	31.50E
Dunaföldvár, Hung. (dŏ′nô-fūld′vär)	148	46.48N	18.55E
Dunajec, r., Pol. (dŏ-nä′yĕts)	148	49.52N	20.53E
Dunaújváros, Hung.	148	46.57N	18.55E
Dunay, Russia (dōō′nī)	164c	59.59N	30.57E
Dunayevtsy, Ukr. (dŏ-nä′yĕf-tsĭ)	156	48.52N	26.51E
Dunbar, W.V., U.S.	92	38.20N	81.45W
Duncan, Can. (dŭŋ′kȧn)	78	48.47N	123.42W
Duncan, Ok., U.S.	104	34.29N	97.56W
Duncan, r., Can.	80	50.30N	116.45W
Duncan Dam, dam, Can.	80	50.15N	116.55W
Duncan Lake, l., Can.	80	50.20N	117.00W
Duncansby Head, c., Scot., U.K. (dŭn′kănz-bĭ)	144	58.40N	3.01W
Duncanville, Tx., U.S. (dŭn′kȧn-vĭl)	101c	32.39N	96.55W
Dundalk, Ire. (dŭn′kôk)	140	54.00N	6.18W
Dundalk, Md., U.S.	94e	39.16N	76.31W
Dundalk Bay, b., Ire. (dŭn′dôk)	144	53.55N	6.15W
Dundas, Austl.	239a	33.48S	151.02E
Dundas, Can. (dŭn-dăs′)	84	43.16N	79.58W
Dundas, l., Austl. (dŭn-dȧs)	196	32.15S	122.00E
Dundas Island, i., Can.	80	54.33N	130.55W
Dundas Strait, strt., Austl.	196	10.35S	131.15E
Dundedin, Fl., U.S. (dŭn-ē′dĭn)	109a	28.00N	82.43W
Dundee, S. Afr.	207c	28.14S	30.16E
Dundee, Scot., U.K.	136	56.30N	2.55W
Dundee, Il., U.S. (dŭn-dē)	95a	42.06N	88.17W
Dundrum Bay, b., N. Ire., U.K. (dŭn-drŭm′)	144	54.13N	5.47W
Dunedin, N.Z.	197a	45.48S	170.32E
Dunellen, N.J., U.S. (dŭn-ĕl′ĕn)	94a	40.36N	74.28W
Dunfermline, Scot., U.K. (dŭn-fẽrm′lĭn)	144	56.05N	3.30W
Dungarvan, Ire. (dŭn-gȧr′vȧn)	144	52.06N	7.50W
Dungeness, Wa., U.S. (dŭnj-nĕs′)	100a	48.09N	123.07W
Dungeness, r., Wa., U.S.	100a	48.03N	123.10W
Dungeness Spit, Wa., U.S.	100a	48.11N	123.03W
Dunham Town, Eng., U.K.	233b	53.23N	2.24W
Dunheved, Austl.	239a	33.45S	150.47E
Dunhua, China (dōn-hwä)	180	43.18N	128.10E
Dunkerque, Fr. (dŭɴ-kĕrk′)	140	51.02N	2.37E
Dunkirk, In., U.S. (dŭn′kûrk)	92	40.20N	85.25W
Dunkwa, Ghana	208	5.22N	1.12W
Dun Laoghaire, Ire. (dŭn-lä′rē)	140	53.16N	6.09W
Dunlap, Ia., U.S. (dŭn′lăp)	96	41.53N	95.33W
Dunlap, Tn., U.S.	108	35.23N	85.23W
Dunmore, Pa., U.S. (dŭn′mōr)	92	41.25N	75.30W
Dunn, N.C., U.S. (dŭn)	108	35.18N	78.37W
Dunnellon, Fl., U.S. (dŭn-ĕl′ŏn)	108	29.02N	82.28W
Dunn Loring, Va., U.S.	225d	38.53N	77.14W
Dunnville, Can. (dŭn′vĭl)	84	42.55N	79.40W
Dunqulah, Sudan	204	19.21N	30.19E
Dunsmuir, Ca., U.S. (dŭnz′mūr)	98	41.08N	122.17W
Dunton Green, Eng., U.K.	231	51.18N	0.11E
Dunton Wayletts, Eng., U.K.	231	51.35N	0.24E
Dunvegan, S. Afr.	240b	26.09S	28.09E
Dunwoody, Ga., U.S. (dŭn-wŏd′ĭ)	94c	33.57N	84.20W
Duolun, China (dwŏ-lōōn)	180	42.12N	116.15E
Duomo, rel., Italy	234c	45.27N	9.11E
Du Page, r., Il., U.S. (dōō pāj)	95a	41.41N	88.11W
Du Page, East Branch, r., Il., U.S.	95a	41.42N	88.09W
Du Page, West Branch, r., Il., U.S.	95a	41.42N	88.09W
Dupax, Phil. (dōō′päks)	189a	16.16N	121.06E
Dupo, Il., U.S. (dū′pō)	101e	38.31N	90.12W
Duque de Caxias, Braz. (dōō′kĕ-dĕ-kȧ′shyás)	123a	22.46S	43.18W
Duquesne, Pa., U.S. (dŏ-kān′)	95e	40.22N	79.51W
Du Quoin, Il., U.S. (dŏ-kwoin′)	104	38.01N	89.14W
Durance, r., Fr. (dü-räɴs′)	140	43.46N	5.52E
Durand, Mi., U.S. (dŭ-rănd′)	92	42.50N	84.00W
Durand, Wi., U.S.	96	44.37N	91.58W
Durango, Mex. (dōō-rä′n-gō)	110	24.02N	104.42W
Durango, Co., U.S. (dŏ-räŋ′gō)	102	37.15N	107.55W

PLACE (Pronunciation)	PAGE	Lat. °′	Long. °′
Durango, state, Mex.	110	25.00N	106.00W
Durant, Ms., U.S. (dů-rănt′)	108	33.05N	89.50W
Durant, Ok., U.S.	104	33.59N	96.23W
Duratón, r., Spain (doo-rä-tōn′)	152	41.30N	3.55W
Durazno, Ur. (doo-räz′nō)	126	33.21S	56.31W
Durazno, dept., Ur.	123c	33.00S	56.35W
Durban, S. Afr. (dûr′bǎn)	206	29.48S	31.00E
Durbanville, S. Afr. (dûr-bǎn′vĭl)	206a	33.50S	18.39E
Durbe, Lat. (door′bĕ)	146	56.36N	21.24E
Durchholz, Ger.	232	51.23N	7.17E
Đurđevac, Cro.	142	46.03N	17.03E
Düren, Ger. (dü′rĕn)	151c	50.48N	6.30E
Durham, Eng., U.K. (dûr′ăm)	144	54.47N	1.46W
Durham, N.C., U.S.	90	36.00N	78.55W
Durham Downs, Austl.	198	27.30S	141.55E
Durrës, Alb. (dor′ĕs)	136	41.19N	19.27E
Duryea, Pa., U.S. (door-yā′)	92	41.20N	75.50W
Dushan, China	182	31.38N	116.16E
Dushan, China (doo-shän)	184	25.50N	107.42E
Dushanbe, Taj.	158	38.30N	68.45E
Düssel, Ger.	232	51.16N	7.03E
Düsseldorf, Ger. (düs′ĕl-dôrf)	140	51.14N	6.47E
Dussen, Neth.	139a	51.43N	4.58E
Dutalan Ula, mts., Mong.	184	49.25N	112.40E
Dutch Harbor, Ak., U.S. (dŭch här′bẽr)	90a	53.58N	166.30W
Duvall, Wa., U.S. (doo′vâl)	100a	47.44N	121.59W
Duwamish, r., Wa., U.S. (doo-wäm′ĭsh)	100a	47.24N	122.18W
Duyun, China (doo-yon)	180	26.18N	107.40E
Dvinskaya Guba, b., Russia	160	65.10N	38.40E
Dwārka, India	178	22.18N	68.59E
Dwight, Il., U.S. (dwīt)	92	41.00N	88.20W
Dworshak Res, Id., U.S.	98	46.45N	115.50W
Dyat′kovo, Russia (dyät′kō-vō)	156	53.36N	34.19E
Dyer, In., U.S. (dī′ẽr)	95a	41.30N	87.31W
Dyersburg, Tn., U.S. (dī′ẽrz-bûrg)	108	36.02N	89.23W
Dyersville, Ia., U.S. (dī′ẽrz-vĭl)	96	42.28N	91.09W
Dyes Inlet, Wa., U.S. (dīz)	100a	47.37N	122.45W
Dyment, Can. (dī′mĕnt)	82	49.37N	92.19W
Dzamïn Üüd, Mong.	180	44.38N	111.32E
Dzaoudzi, May. (dzou′dzĭ)	206	12.44S	45.15E
Dzavhan, r., Mong.	180	48.19N	94.08E
Dzerzhinsk, Bela.	156	53.41N	27.14E
Dzerzhinsk, Russia	160	56.20N	43.50E
Dzerzhinsk, Ukr. (dzhĕr-zhĭnsk′)	156	48.26N	37.50E
Dzeržinskij, Russia	235b	55.38N	37.50E
Dzhalal-Abad, Kyrg. (jǎ-läl′ǎ-bät′)	158	40.56N	73.00E
Dzhambul, Kaz. (dzhäm-bool′)	158	42.51N	71.29E
Dzhankoy, Ukr. (dzhän′koi)	160	45.43N	34.22E
Dzhetygara, Kaz. (dzhĕt′-gä′rá)	164a	52.12N	61.18E
Dzhizak, Uzb. (dzhĕ′zäk)	162	40.13N	67.58E
Dzhugdzhur Khrebet, mts., Russia (jŏg-joor′)	158	56.15N	137.00E
Działoszyce, Pol. (jyä-wō-shē′tsĕ)	148	50.21N	20.22E
Dzibalchén, Mex. (zē-bäl-chĕ′n)	114a	19.25N	89.39W
Dzidzantún, Mex. (zēd-zän-too′n)	114a	21.18N	89.00W
Dzierżoniów, Pol. (dzyĕr-zhōn′yŭf)	148	50.44N	16.38E
Dzilam González, Mex. (zē-lä′m-gôn-zä′lĕz)	114a	21.21N	88.53W
Dzitás, Mex. (zē-tá′s)	114a	20.47N	88.32W
Dzungaria, reg., China (dzŏŋ-gä′rĭ-á)	180	44.39N	86.13E
Dzungarian Gate, p., Asia	180	45.00N	88.00E

E

PLACE (Pronunciation)	PAGE	Lat. °′	Long. °′
Eagle, W.V., U.S.	92	38.10N	81.20W
Eagle, r., Co., U.S.	102	39.32N	106.28W
Eaglecliff, Wa., U.S. (ē′gl-klĭf)	100c	46.10N	123.13W
Eagle Creek, r., In., U.S.	95g	39.54N	86.17W
Eagle Grove, Ia., U.S.	96	42.39N	93.55W
Eagle Lake, Me., U.S.	86	47.03N	68.38W
Eagle Lake, Tx., U.S.	106	29.37N	96.20W
Eagle Lake, l., Ca., U.S.	98	40.45N	120.52W
Eagle Mountain, Ca., U.S.	102	33.49N	115.27W
Eagle Mountain L, Tx., U.S.	101c	32.56N	97.27W
Eagle Pass, Tx., U.S.	90	28.49N	100.30W
Eagle Pk, Ca., U.S.	98	41.18N	120.11W
Eagle Rock, neigh., Ca., U.S.	228	34.09N	118.12W
Ealing, Eng., U.K. (ē′lĭng)	138b	51.29N	0.19W
Earle, Ar., U.S. (ûrl)	104	35.14N	90.28W
Earlington, Ky., U.S. (ûr′lĭng-tǔn)	108	37.15N	87.31W
Easley, S.C., U.S. (ēz′lĭ)	108	34.48N	82.37W
East, r., N.Y., U.S.	224	40.48N	73.48W
East, Mount, mtn., Pan.	110a	9.09N	79.46W
East Alton, Il., U.S. (ôl′tŭn)	101e	38.53N	90.08W
East Angus, Can. (ăŋ′gǔs)	84	45.35N	71.40W
East Arlington, Ma., U.S.	223a	42.25N	71.08W
East Aurora, N.Y., U.S. (ô-rō′rá)	95c	42.46N	78.38W
East Barnet, neigh., Eng., U.K.	231	51.38N	0.09W
East Bay, b., Tx., U.S.	107a	29.30N	94.41W
East Bedfont, neigh., Eng., U.K.	231	51.27N	0.26W
East Bernstadt, Ky., U.S. (bûrn′stát)	108	37.09N	84.08W
Eastbourne, Eng., U.K. (ēst′bôrn)	144	50.48N	0.16E
East Braintree, Ma., U.S.	223a	42.13N	70.58W
East Burwood, Austl.	239b	37.51S	145.09E
Eastbury, Eng., U.K.	231	51.37N	0.25W
East Caicos, i., T./C. Is. (kī′kōs)	116	21.40N	71.35W
East Cape, c., N.Z.	197a	37.37S	178.33E
East Cape, see Dezhnëva, Mys, c., Russia	172	68.00N	172.00W
East Carondelet, Il., U.S. (kǎ-rŏn′dĕ-lĕt)	101e	38.33N	90.14W
East Cherokee Indian Reservation, I.R., N.C., U.S.	108	35.33N	83.12W
Eastchester, N.Y., U.S.	224	40.57N	73.49W
East Chicago, In., U.S. (shĭ-kô′gō)	95a	41.39N	87.29W
East China Sea, sea, Asia	180	30.28N	125.52E
East Cleveland, Oh., U.S. (klēv′lǎnd)	95d	41.33N	81.35W
Eastcote, neigh., Eng., U.K.	231	51.35N	0.24W
East Cote Blanche Bay, b., La., U.S. (kōt blänsh′)	106	29.30N	92.07W
East Des Moines, r., Ia., U.S. (dē moin′)	96	42.57N	94.17W
East Detroit, Mi., U.S. (dē-troit′)	95b	42.28N	82.57W
Easter Island, see Rapa Nui, i., Chile	190	26.50S	109.00W
Eastern Ghāts, mts., India	174	13.50N	78.45E
Eastern Native, neigh., S. Afr.	240b	26.13S	28.05E
Eastern Turkestan, hist. reg., China (tŏr-kĕ-stän′)(tûr-kĕ-stăn′)	180	39.40N	78.20E
East Falls, neigh., Pa., U.S.	225b	40.01N	75.11W
East Grand Forks, Mn., U.S. (grănd fôrks)	96	47.56N	97.02W
East Greenwich, R.I., U.S (grĭn′ĭj)	94b	41.40N	71.27W
Eastham, Eng., U.K.	233a	53.19N	2.58W
East Ham, neigh., Eng., U.K.	231	51.32N	0.03E
Easthampton, Ma., U.S. (ēst-hămp′tǔn)	92	42.15N	72.45W
East Hartford, Ct., U.S. (härt′fẽrd)	92	41.45N	72.35W
East Helena, Mt., U.S. (hĕ-hĕ′ná)	98	46.31N	111.50W
East Hills, Austl.	239a	33.58S	150.59E
East Hills, N.Y., U.S.	224	40.47N	73.38W
East Ilsley, Eng., U.K. (ĭl′slē)	138b	51.30N	1.18W
East Jordan, Mi., U.S. (jôr′dǎn)	92	45.05N	85.05W
East Kansas City, Mo., U.S. (kăn′zás)	101f	39.09N	94.30W
East Lamma Channel, strt., H.K.	237c	22.15N	114.07E
Eastland, Tx., U.S. (ēst′lǎnd)	106	32.24N	98.47W
East Lansdowne, Pa., U.S.	225b	39.56N	75.16W
East Lansing, Mi., U.S. (lăn′sĭng)	92	42.45N	84.30W
Eastlawn, Mi., U.S.	95b	42.15N	83.35W
East Leavenworth, Mo., U.S. (lĕv′ĕn-wûrth)	101f	39.18N	94.50W
East Liberty, neigh., Pa., U.S.	226b	40.27N	79.55W
East Lindfield, Austl.	239a	33.46S	151.11E
East Liverpool, Oh., U.S. (lĭv′ẽr-pool)	92	40.40N	80.35W
East London, S. Afr. (lŭn′dǔn)	206	33.02S	27.54E
East Los Angeles, Ca., U.S. (lŏs ăŋ′hå-lăs)	101a	34.01N	118.09W
Eastmain, r., Can. (ēst′mān)	78	52.12N	73.19W
East Malling, Eng., U.K.	231	51.17N	0.26E
Eastman, Ga., U.S. (ēst′mǎn)	108	32.10N	83.11W
East Meadow, N.Y., U.S.	224	40.43N	73.34W
East Millstone, N.J., U.S. (mĭl′stōn)	94a	40.30N	74.35W
East Molesey, Eng., U.K.	231	51.24N	0.21W
East Moline, Il., U.S. (mō-lēn′)	96	41.31N	90.28W
East Newark, N.J., U.S.	224	40.45N	74.10W
East New York, neigh., N.Y., U.S.	224	40.40N	73.53W
East Nishnabotna, r., Ia., U.S. (nĭsh-ná-bŏt′ná)	96	40.53N	95.23W
East Norwich, N.Y., U.S.	224	40.50N	73.32W
Easton, Md., U.S. (ēs′tǔn)	92	38.45N	76.05W
Easton, Pa., U.S.	92	40.45N	75.15W
Easton L, Ct., U.S.	94a	41.18N	73.17W
East Orange, N.J., U.S. (ŏr′ĕnj)	94a	40.46N	74.12W
East Pakistan, see Bangladesh, nation, Asia	174	24.15N	90.00E
East Palo Alto, Ca., U.S.	100b	37.27N	122.07W
East Peoria, Il., U.S. (pē-ō′rĭ-á)	92	40.40N	89.30W
East Pittsburgh, Pa., U.S. (pĭts′bûrg)	95e	40.24N	79.50W
East Point, Ga., U.S.	94c	33.41N	84.27W
Eastport, Me., U.S. (ēst′pōrt)	86	44.53N	67.01W
East Providence, R.I., U.S. (prŏv′ĭ-dĕns)	94b	41.49N	71.22W
East Retford, Eng., U.K. (rĕt′fẽrd)	138a	53.19N	0.56W
East Richmond, Ca., U.S.	227b	37.57N	122.19W
East Rochester, N.Y., U.S. (rŏch′ĕs-tẽr)	92	43.10N	77.30W
East Rockaway, N.Y., U.S.	224	40.39N	73.40W
East Saint Louis, Il., U.S.	90	38.38N	90.10W
East Siberian Sea, sea, Russia (sī-bĭr′y′n)	158	73.00N	153.28E
Eastsound, Wa., U.S. (ēst-sound)	100d	48.42N	122.42W
East Stroudsburg, Pa., U.S. (stroudz′bûrg)	92	41.00N	75.10W
East Syracuse, N.Y., U.S. (sĭr′á-kūs)	92	43.05N	76.00W
East Tavaputs Plateau, plat., Ut., U.S. (tă-vă′-pŭts)	102	39.25N	109.45W
East Tawas, Mi., U.S. (tô′wǎs)	92	44.15N	83.30W
East Tilbury, Eng., U.K.	231	51.28N	0.26E
East Tustin, Ca., U.S.	228	33.46N	117.49W
East Walker, r., U.S. (wôk′ẽr)	102	38.36N	119.02W
East Walpole, Ma., U.S.	223a	42.10N	71.13W
East Watertown, Ma., U.S.	223a	42.22N	71.10W
East Weymouth, Ma., U.S.	223a	42.13N	70.55W
Eastwick, neigh., Pa., U.S.	225b	39.55N	75.14W
East Wickham, neigh., Eng., U.K.	231	51.28N	0.07E
Eastwood, Austl.	239a	33.48S	151.05E
East York, Can.	77d	43.41S	79.20W
Eaton, Co., U.S. (ē′tǔn)	104	40.31N	104.42W
Eaton, Oh., U.S.	92	39.45N	84.40W
Eaton Estates, Oh., U.S.	95d	41.19N	82.01W
Eaton Rapids, Mi., U.S. (răp′ĭdz)	92	42.30N	84.40W
Eatonton, Ga., U.S. (ē′tǔn-tǔn)	108	33.20N	83.24W
Eatontown, N.J., U.S. (ē′tǔn-toun)	94a	40.18N	74.04W
Eaubonne, Fr.	233c	49.00N	2.17E
Eau Claire, Wi., U.S. (ō klâr′)	90	44.47N	91.32W
Ebeltoft, Den. (ĕ′bĕl-tŭft)	146	56.11N	10.39E
Ebensburg, Pa., U.S. (ĕ′bĕnz-bûrg)	92	40.29N	78.44W
Ebersberg, Ger. (ĕ′bĕrs-bĕrgh)	139d	48.05N	11.58E
Ebina, Japan	238a	35.26N	139.25E
Ebingen, Ger. (ā′bĭng-ĕn)	148	48.13N	9.04E
Eboli, Italy (ĕb′ō-lē)	154	40.38N	15.04E
Ebolowa, Cam.	204	2.54N	11.09E
Ebreichsdorf, Aus.	139e	47.58N	16.24E
Ebrié, Lagune, b., I.C.	208	5.20N	4.50W
Ebro, r., Spain (ā′brō)	136	42.00N	2.00W
Ebute-Ikorodu, Nig.	240d	6.37N	3.30E
Eccles, Eng., U.K. (ĕk′'lz)	138a	53.29N	2.20W
Eccles, W.V., U.S.	92	37.45N	81.10W
Eccleshall, Eng., U.K.	138a	52.51N	2.15W
Eccleston, Eng., U.K.	233a	53.27N	2.47W
Eccleston, Md., U.S.	225c	39.24N	76.44W
Eceabat, Tur.	154	40.10N	26.21E
Echague, Phil. (ā-chä′gwä)	189a	16.43N	121.40E
Echandi, Cerro, mtn., N.A. (sĕ′r-rô-ĕ-chä′nd)	114	9.05N	82.51W
Ech Cheliff, Alg.	204	36.14N	1.32E
Echimamish, r., Can.	82	54.15N	97.30W
Echo Bay, Can. (ĕk′ō)	101k	46.29N	84.04W
Echoing, r., Can. (ĕk′ō-ĭng)	82	55.15N	91.30W
Echternach, Lux. (ĕk′tẽr-näk)	150	49.48N	6.25E
Echuca, Austl. (ĕ-chŏ′ká)	196	36.10S	144.47E
Écija, Spain (ā′thē-hä)	142	37.20N	5.07W
Eckernförde, Ger.	148	54.27N	9.51E
Eclipse, Va., U.S. (ē-klĭps′)	94g	36.55N	76.29W
Ecorse, Mi., U.S. (ē-kôrs′)	95b	42.15N	83.09W
Ecuador, nation, S.A. (ĕk′wá-dôr)	124	0.00N	78.30W
Ed, Eth.	204	13.57N	41.37E
Eda, neigh., Japan	238a	35.34N	139.34E
Eddyville, Ky., U.S. (ĕd′ĭ-vĭl)	108	37.03N	88.03W
Ede, Nig.	208	7.44N	4.27E
Edéa, Cam. (ĕ-dā′ä)	204	3.48N	10.08E
Éden, Braz.	230c	22.48S	43.24W
Eden, Tx., U.S.	106	31.13N	99.51W
Eden, Ut., U.S.	101b	41.18N	111.49W
Eden, r., Eng., U.K. (ē′dĕn)	144	54.40N	2.35W
Edenbridge, Eng., U.K. (ē′dĕn-brĭj)	138b	51.11N	0.05E
Edendale, S. Afr.	240b	26.09S	28.09E
Edenham, Eng., U.K. (ē′d'n-ǎm)	138a	52.46N	0.25W
Eden Prairie, Mn., U.S. (prâr′ĭ)	101g	44.51N	93.29W
Edenton, N.C., U.S. (ē′dĕn-tǔn)	108	36.02N	76.37W
Edenton, Oh., U.S.	95f	39.14N	84.02W
Edenvale, S. Afr. (ĕd′ĕn-văl)	207b	26.09S	28.10E
Edenvale Location, S. Afr.	240b	26.08S	28.11E
Edenville, S. Afr. (ē′d'n-vĭl)	212d	27.33S	27.42E
Eder, r., Ger. (ā′dẽr)	148	51.05N	8.52E
Edgefield, S.C., U.S. (ĕj′fēld)	108	33.52N	81.55W
Edge Hill, neigh., Eng., U.K.	233a	53.24N	2.57W
Edgeley, N.D., U.S. (ĕj′lĭ)	96	46.24N	98.43W
Edgemere, Md., U.S.	225c	39.14N	76.27W
Edgemont, S.D., U.S. (ĕj′mŏnt)	96	43.19N	103.50W
Edgerton, Wi., U.S. (ĕj′ẽr-tǔn)	96	42.49N	89.06W
Edgewater, Al., U.S. (ĕj-wô-tẽr)	94h	33.31N	86.52W
Edgewater, Md., U.S.	94e	38.58N	76.35W
Edgewater, N.J., U.S.	224	40.50N	73.58W
Edgewood, Can. (ĕj′wŏd)	80	49.47N	118.08W
Edgware, neigh., Eng., U.K.	231	51.37N	0.17W
Edgwater, N.Y., U.S.	226a	43.03N	78.55W
Edgworth, Eng., U.K.	233b	53.39N	2.24W
Édhessa, Grc.	142	40.48N	22.04E
Edina, Mn., U.S. (ē-dī′ná)	101g	44.55N	93.20W
Edina, Mo., U.S.	104	40.10N	92.11W
Edinburg, In., U.S. (ĕd′'n-bûrg)	92	39.20N	85.55W
Edinburg, Tx., U.S.	106	26.18N	98.08W
Edinburgh, Scot., U.K. (ĕd′'n-bŭr-ō)	136	55.57N	3.10W
Edirne, Tur.	154	41.41N	26.35E
Edison Park, neigh., Il., U.S.	227a	42.01N	87.49W
Edisto, r., S.C., U.S. (ĕd′ĭs-tō)	108	33.10N	80.50W
Edisto, North Fork, r., S.C., U.S.	108	33.42N	81.24W
Edisto, South Fork, r., S.C., U.S.	108	33.43N	81.35W
Edisto Island, S.C., U.S.	108	32.32N	80.20W
Edmond, Ok., U.S. (ĕd′mǔnd)	104	35.39N	97.29W
Edmonds, Wa., U.S. (ĕd′mǔndz)	100a	47.49N	122.23W
Edmonston, Md., U.S.	225d	38.57N	76.56W
Edmonton, Can.	78	53.33N	113.28W
Edmonton, neigh., Eng., U.K.	231	51.37N	0.04W
Edmundston, Can. (ĕd′mǔn-stǔn)	78	47.22N	68.20W
Edna, Tx., U.S. (ĕd′ná)	106	28.59N	96.39W
Edo, r., Japan	238a	35.41N	139.53E
Edogawa, neigh., Japan	238a	35.42N	139.52E
Edremit, Tur. (ĕd-rĕ-mēt′)	142	39.35N	27.00E
Edremit Körfezi, b., Tur.	154	39.28N	26.35E
Edson, Can. (ĕd′sǔn)	78	53.35N	116.26W
Edward, i., Can. (ĕd′wẽrd)	84	48.21N	88.29W
Edward, l., Afr.	206	0.25S	29.40E
Edwardsville, Il., U.S. (ĕd′wẽrdz-vĭl)	101e	38.49N	89.58W
Edwardsville, In., U.S.	95h	38.17N	85.53W
Edwardsville, Ks., U.S.	101f	39.04N	94.49W
Eel, r., Ca., U.S. (ēl)	98	40.39N	124.15W
Eel, r., In., U.S.	92	40.50N	85.55W
Efate, i., Vanuatu (ā-fä′tä)	196	18.02S	168.29E
Effigy Mounds National Monument, rec., la., U.S. (ĕf′ĭ-jŭ mounds)	96	43.04N	91.15W
Effingham, Il., U.S. (ĕf′ĭng-hăm)	92	39.05N	88.30W
Ega, r., Spain (ā′gä)	152	42.40N	2.20W
Egadi, Isole, is., Italy (ĕ′sō-lĕ-ĕ′gä-dē)	142	38.01N	12.00E
Egea de los Caballeros, Spain	152	42.07N	1.05W
Egegik, Ak., U.S. (ĕg′ĕ-jĭt)	89	58.10N	157.22W
Eger, Hung. (ĕ gĕr)	148	47.53N	20.24E
Egersund, Nor. (ĕ′ghĕr-sŏn′)	140	58.29N	6.01E
Egg Harbor, N.J., U.S. (ĕg här′bẽr)	92	39.30N	74.35W
Egham, Eng., U.K. (ĕg′ǔm)	138b	51.24N	0.33W
Egiyn, r., Mong.	180	49.41N	100.40E
Egmont, Cape, c., N.Z. (ĕg′mŏnt)	197a	39.18S	173.49E
Egmont, Mount, mtn., N.Z.	199	39.18S	174.04E
Egota, neigh., Japan	238a	35.43N	139.40E
Egypt, nation, Afr. (ē′jĭpt)	204	26.58N	27.01E
Eha-Amufu, Nig.	208	6.40N	7.46E

ng-sing; ŋ-baŋk; N-nasalized n; nŏd; cŏmmit; ōld; ōbey; ôrder; oi-boil; food; ŏ-as oo in foot; ou-out; s-soft; sh-dish; th-thin; pūre; ůnite; ûrn; stŭd; circǔs; ü-as in French tu; ′-indeterminate vowel.

PLACE (Pronunciation)	PAGE	Lat. °′	Long. °′
Ehingen, neigh., Ger.	232	51.22N	6.42E
Ehringhausen, Ger.	232	51.11N	7.33E
Ehringhausen, neigh., Ger.	232	51.09N	7.11E
Eibar, Spain (ā'ē-bär)	152	43.12N	2.20W
Eiche, Ger.	234a	52.34N	13.36E
Eichlinghofen, neigh., Ger.	232	51.29N	7.24E
Eichstätt, Ger. (īk'shtät)	148	48.54N	11.14E
Eichwalde, Ger. (īĸ'väl-dē)	139b	52.22N	13.37E
Eickerend, Ger.	232	51.13N	6.34E
Eidfjord, Nor. (ĕĭd'fyōr)	146	60.28N	7.04E
Eidsvoll, Nor. (ĭdhs'vôl)	140	60.19N	11.15E
Eifel, mts., Ger. (ī'fĕl)	148	50.08N	6.30E
Eiffel, Tour, pt. of i., Fr.	233c	48.51N	2.18E
Eigen, neigh., Ger.	232	51.33N	6.57E
Eighty Mile Beach, cst., Austl.	196	19.00S	121.00E
Eilenburg, Ger. (ī'lĕn-bŏorgh)	148	51.27N	12.38E
Einbeck, Ger. (īn'bĕk)	148	51.49N	9.52E
Eindhoven, Neth. (īnd'hō-vĕn)	144	51.29N	5.20E
Eisenach, Ger. (ī'zĕn-äĸ)	140	50.58N	10.18E
Eisenhüttenstadt, Ger.	148	52.08N	14.40E
Ejura, Ghana	208	7.23N	1.22W
Ejutla de Crespo, Mex. (å-hōōt'lä dā krās'pō)	112	16.34N	96.44W
Ekanga, Zaire	210	2.23S	23.14E
Ekenäs, Fin. (ĕ'kĕ-nâs)	146	59.59N	23.25E
Ekeren, Bel.	139a	51.17N	4.27E
Ekoli, Zaire	210	0.23S	24.16E
Eksāra, India	236a	22.38N	88.17E
El Aaiún, W. Sah.	204	26.45N	13.15W
El Affroun, Alg. (ĕl ȧf-froun')	152	36.28N	2.38E
El Aguacate, Ven.	230a	10.28N	66.59W
Elands, r., S. Afr. (ėlånds)	207c	31.48S	26.09E
Elands, r., S. Afr.	212d	25.11S	28.52E
Elandsfontein, S. Afr.	240b	26.10S	28.12E
El Arahal, Spain (ĕl ä-rä-äl')	152	37.17N	5.32W
El Arba, Alg.	152	36.35N	3.10E
Elat, Isr.	174	29.34N	34.57E
Elâziğ, Tur. (ĕl-ä'zēz)	174	38.40N	39.00E
Elba, Al., U.S. (ĕl'bȧ)	108	31.25N	86.01W
Elba, Isola d', i., Italy (ê-sō lä-d-ĕl'bȧ)	142	42.42N	10.25E
El Banco, Col. (ĕl băn'cō)	124	8.58N	74.01W
Elbansan, Alb. (ĕl-bä-sän')	142	41.08N	20.05E
El Barco de Valdeorras, Spain (ĕl bär'kō)	152	42.26N	6.58W
Elbe (Labe), r., Eur. (ĕl'bĕ)(lä'bĕ)	136	52.30N	11.30E
Elberfeld, neigh., Ger.	232	51.16N	7.08E
Elbert, Mount, mtn., Co., U.S. (ĕl'bērt)	90	39.05N	106.25W
Elberton, Ga., U.S. (ĕl'bēr-tŭn)	108	34.05N	82.53W
Elbeuf, Fr. (ĕl-bûf')	140	49.16N	0.59E
El Beyadh, Alg.	142	33.42N	1.06E
Elbistan, Tur. (ĕl-bē-stän')	142	38.20N	37.10E
Elblag, Pol. (ĕl'blăng)	140	54.11N	19.25E
El Bonillo, Spain (ĕl bō-nēl'yō)	152	38.56N	2.31W
El Boulaïda, Alg.	204	36.33N	2.45E
Elbow, r., Can. (ĕl'bō)	77e	51.03N	114.24W
Elbow Cay, i., Bah.	116	26.25N	76.55W
Elbow Lake, Mn., U.S.	96	46.00N	95.59W
El'brus, Gora, mtn., Russia (ĕl'brŏos')	158	43.20N	42.25E
El Burgo de Osma, Spain	152	41.35N	3.02W
Elburz Mountains, mts., Iran (ĕl'bŏorz')	174	36.30N	51.00E
El Cajon, Col. (ĕl-kä-kō'n)	124a	4.50N	76.35W
El Cajon, Ca., U.S.	102a	32.48N	116.58W
El Calvario, neigh., Cuba	229b	23.05N	82.20W
El Cambur, Ven. (käm-bōōr')	125b	10.24N	68.06W
El Campamento, neigh., Spain	234b	40.24N	3.46W
El Campo, Tx., U.S. (kăm'pō)	106	29.13N	96.17W
El Caribe, Ven.	230a	10.37N	66.49W
El Carmen, Chile (kå'r-mĕn)	123b	34.14S	71.23W
El Carmen, Col. (kå'r-mĕn)	124	9.54N	75.12W
El Casco, Ca., U.S. (kăs'kō)	101a	33.59N	117.08W
El Centro, Ca., U.S. (sĕn'trō)	102	32.47N	115.33W
El Cerrito, Ca., U.S. (sĕr-rē'tō)	100b	37.55N	122.19W
Elche, Spain (ĕl'chā)	152	38.15N	0.42W
El Cojo, Ven.	230a	10.37N	66.53W
El Corozo, Ven.	230a	10.35N	66.58W
El Cotorro, Cuba	229b	23.03N	82.16W
El Cuyo, Mex.	114a	21.30N	87.42W
Elda, Spain (ĕl'dä)	152	38.28N	0.44W
Elder Mills, Can.	223c	43.49N	79.38W
El Djelfa, Alg.	204	34.40N	3.17E
El Djouf, des., Afr. (ĕl djōōf)	204	21.45N	7.05W
Eldon, Ia., U.S. (ĕl-dŭn)	96	40.55N	92.15W
Eldon, Mo., U.S.	104	38.21N	92.36W
Eldora, Ia., U.S. (ĕl-dō'rȧ)	96	42.21N	93.08W
El Dorado, Ar., U.S. (ĕl dō-rä'dō)	90	33.13N	92.39W
Eldorado, Il., U.S.	92	37.50N	88.30W
El Dorado, Ks., U.S.	104	37.49N	96.51W
Eldorado Springs, Mo., U.S. (sprĭngz)	104	37.51N	94.02W
Eldoret, Kenya (ĕl-dō-rĕt')	210	0.31N	35.17E
El Ebano, Mex. (ā-bä'nō)	112	22.13N	98.26W
Electra, Tx., U.S. (ē-lĕk'trȧ)	104	34.02N	98.54W
Electric Peak, mtn., Mt., U.S. (ē-lĕk'trĭk)	98	45.03N	110.52W
Elektrogorsk, Russia (ĕl-yĕk'trô-gôrsk)	164b	55.53N	38.48E
Elektrostal', Russia (ĕl-yĕk'trō-stål)	164b	55.47N	38.27E
Elektrougli, Russia	164b	55.43N	38.13E
El Encantado, Ven.	230a	10.27N	66.47W
Elephanta Island (Ghārāpuri), i., India	236e	18.57N	72.55E
Elephant Butte Reservoir, res., N.M., U.S. (ĕl'ē-fănt būt)	90	33.25N	107.10W
El Escorial, Spain (ĕl-ĕs-kō-ryä'l)	153a	40.38N	4.08W
El Espino, Nic. (ĕl-ĕs-pē'nō)	114	13.26N	86.48W
Eleuthera, i., Bah. (ē-lū'thēr-ȧ)	110	25.05N	76.10W
Eleuthera Point, c., Bah.	116	24.35N	76.05W
Eleven Point, r., Mo., U.S. (ē-lĕv'ĕn)	104	36.53N	91.39W
El Ferrol, Spain (fā-rōl')	136	43.30N	8.12W
Elgin, Scot., U.K.	144	57.40N	3.30W
Elgin, Il., U.S. (ĕl'jĭn)	95a	42.03N	88.16W

PLACE (Pronunciation)	PAGE	Lat. °′	Long. °′
Elgin, Ne., U.S.	96	41.58N	98.04W
Elgin, Or., U.S.	98	45.34N	117.58W
Elgin, Tx., U.S.	106	30.21N	97.22W
Elgin, Wa., U.S.	100a	47.23N	122.42W
Elgon, Mount, mtn., Afr. (ĕl'gŏn)	204	1.00N	34.25E
El Granada, Ca., U.S.	227b	37.30N	122.28W
El Grara, Alg.	142	32.50N	4.26E
El Grullo, Mex. (grōōl-yō)	112	19.46N	104.10W
El Guapo, Ven. (gwȧ'pō)	125b	10.07N	66.00W
El Guarapo, Ven.	230a	10.36N	66.58W
El Hank, reg., Afr.	204	23.44N	6.45W
El Hatillo, Ven. (ä-tē'l-yō)	125b	10.08N	65.13W
Elie, Can. (ē'lē)	77f	49.55N	97.45W
Elila, r., Zaire (ĕ-lē'lȧ)	206	3.30S	28.00E
Elisa, i., Wa., U.S. (ĕ-lĭ'sȧ)	100d	48.43N	122.37W
Élisabethville, see Lubumbashi, Zaire	206	11.40S	27.28E
Elisenvaara, Russia (ā-lē'sĕn-vä'rȧ)	146	61.25N	29.46E
Elizabeth, La., U.S. (ē-lĭz'ȧ-bĕth)	106	30.50N	92.47W
Elizabeth, N.J., U.S.	94a	40.40N	74.13W
Elizabeth, Pa., U.S.	95e	40.16N	79.53W
Elizabeth City, N.C., U.S.	108	36.15N	76.15W
Elizabethton, Tn., U.S. (ē-lĭz-ȧ-bĕth'tŭn)	108	36.19N	82.12W
Elizabethtown, Ky., U.S. (ē-lĭz'ȧ-bĕth-toun)	92	37.40N	85.55W
El Jadida, Mor.	204	33.14N	8.34W
Elk, Pol.	140	53.53N	22.23E
Elk, r., Can.	80	50.00N	115.00W
Elk, r., Tn., U.S.	108	35.05N	86.36W
Elk, r., W.V., U.S.	92	38.30N	81.05W
El Kairouan, Tun. (kĕr-ō-än)	204	35.46N	10.04E
Elk City, Ok., U.S. (ĕlk)	104	35.23N	99.23W
El Kef, Tun. (xĕf')	142	36.14N	8.42E
Elkhart, In., U.S. (ĕlk'härt)	92	41.40N	86.00W
Elkhart, Ks., U.S.	104	37.00N	101.54W
Elkhart, Tx., U.S.	106	31.38N	95.35W
Elkhorn, Wi., U.S. (ĕlk'hôrn)	96	42.39N	88.32W
Elkhorn, r., Ne., U.S.	96	42.06N	97.46W
Elkin, N.C., U.S. (ĕl'kĭn)	108	36.15N	80.50W
Elkins Park, Pa., U.S.	225b	40.05N	75.08W
Elk Island, i., Can.	82	50.45N	96.32W
Elk Island National Park, rec., Can. (ĕlk ī'lănd)	78	53.37N	112.45W
Elko, Nv., U.S. (ĕl'kō)	90	40.51N	115.46W
Elk Point, S.D., U.S.	96	42.41N	96.41W
Elk Rapids, Mi., U.S. (răp'ĭdz)	92	44.55N	85.25W
Elkridge, Md., U.S.	225c	39.13N	76.42W
Elk River, Id., U.S. (rĭv'ēr)	98	46.47N	116.11W
Elk River, Mn., U.S.	96	45.17N	93.33W
Elkton, Ky., U.S. (ĕlk'tŭn)	108	36.47N	87.08W
Elkton, Md., U.S.	92	39.35N	75.50W
Elkton, S.D., U.S.	96	44.15N	96.28W
Elland, Eng., U.K. (el'ănd)	138a	53.41N	1.50W
Ellen, Mount, mtn., Ut., U.S. (ĕl'ĕn)	102	38.05N	110.50W
Ellendale, N.D., U.S. (ĕl'ĕn-dāl)	96	46.01N	98.33W
Ellensburg, Wa., U.S. (ĕl'ĕnz-bûrg)	98	47.00N	120.31W
Ellenville, N.Y., U.S. (ĕl'ĕn-vĭl)	92	41.40N	74.25W
Ellerslie, Can. (ĕl'ērz-lē)	77g	53.25N	113.30W
Ellesmere, Eng., U.K. (ĕlz'mēr)	138a	52.55N	2.54W
Ellesmere Island, i., Can.	76	81.00N	80.00W
Ellesmere Park, Eng., U.K.	233b	53.29N	2.20W
Ellesmere Port, Eng., U.K.	138a	53.17N	2.54W
Ellice Islands, see Tuvalu, nation, Oc.	2	5.20S	174.00E
Ellicott City, is., Md., U.S. (ĕl'ĭ-kŏt sĭ'tē)	94e	39.16N	76.48W
Ellicott Creek, r., N.Y., U.S.	95c	43.00N	78.46W
El Limoncito, Ven.	230a	10.29N	66.47W
Ellinghorst, neigh., Ger.	232	51.34N	6.57E
Elliot, S. Afr.	207c	31.19S	27.52E
Elliot, Wa., U.S. (ĕl'ĭ-ŭt)	100a	47.28N	122.08W
Elliotdale, Transkei (ĕl-ĭ-ŏt'dāl)	207c	31.58S	28.42E
Elliot Lake, Can.	84	46.23N	82.39W
Ellis, Ks., U.S. (ĕl'ĭs)	104	38.56N	99.34W
Ellisville, Ms., U.S. (ĕl'ĭs-vĭl)	108	31.37N	89.10W
Ellisville, Mo., U.S.	101e	38.35N	90.35W
Ellsworth, Ks., U.S. (ĕlz'wûrth)	104	38.43N	98.14W
Ellsworth, Me., U.S.	86	44.33N	68.26W
Ellsworth Mountains, mts., Ant.	213	77.00S	90.00W
Ellwangen, Ger. (ĕl'văn-gĕn)	148	48.47N	10.08E
Elm, Ger. (ĕlm)	139c	53.31N	9.13E
Elm, r., S.D., U.S.	96	45.47N	98.28W
Elm, r., W.V., U.S.	92	38.30N	81.05W
Elma, Wa., U.S. (ĕl'mȧ)	98	47.02N	123.20W
El Mahdia, Tun. (mä-dēȧ)(mä'dē-ȧ)	142	35.30N	11.09E
Elmendorf, Tx., U.S. (ĕl'mĕn-dôrf)	101d	29.16N	98.20W
El Menia, Alg.	204	30.39N	2.52E
Elm Fork, Tx., U.S. (ĕlm fŏrk)	101c	32.55N	96.56W
Elmhurst, Il., U.S. (ĕlm'hûrst)	95a	41.54N	87.56W
Elmhurst, neigh., N.Y., U.S.	224	40.44N	73.53W
El Miliyya, Alg. (mē'ä)	204	36.30N	6.16E
Elmira, N.Y., U.S. (ĕl-mī'rȧ)	92	42.05N	76.50W
Elmira Heights, N.Y., U.S.	92	42.10N	76.50W
El Modena, Ca., U.S. (mō-dē'nō)	101a	33.47N	117.48W
El Mohammadia, Alg.	152	35.35N	0.05E
El Molinito, Mex.	229a	19.27N	99.15W
Elmont, N.Y., U.S.	224	40.42N	73.42W
El Monte, Ca., U.S. (mŏn'tā)	101a	34.04N	118.02W
El Morro National Monument, rec., N.M., U.S.	102	35.05N	108.20W
Elmshorn, Ger. (ĕlms'hôrn)	148	53.45N	9.39E
Elmwood, neigh., Pa., U.S.	225b	39.56N	75.14W
Elmwood Park, Il., U.S.	227a	41.55N	87.49W
Elmwood Place, Oh., U.S. (ĕlm'wŏŏd plās)	95f	39.11N	84.30W
Elokomin, r., Wa., U.S. (ē-lō'kō-mĭn)	100c	46.16N	123.16W
El Oro, Mex. (ō-rō)	112	19.49N	100.04W
El Palmar, Ven.	230a	10.38N	66.52W
El Pao, Ven. (ĕl pȧ'ō)	124	8.08N	62.37W
El Paraíso, Hond. (pä-rä-ē'sō)	114	13.55N	86.35W

PLACE (Pronunciation)	PAGE	Lat. °′	Long. °′
El Pardo, Spain (pä'r-dō)	153a	40.31N	3.47W
El Paso, Tx., U.S. (pas'ō)	90	31.47N	106.27W
El Pedregal, neigh., Ven.	230a	10.30N	66.51W
El Pilar, Ven. (pē-lä'r)	125b	9.56N	64.48W
El Plantío, neigh., Spain	234b	40.28N	3.49W
El Porvenir, Pan. (pŏr-vä-nēr')	114	9.34N	78.55W
El Puerto de Santa María, Spain	152	36.36N	6.18W
El Qala, Alg.	142	36.52N	8.23E
El Qoll, Alg.	204	37.02N	6.29E
El Real, Pan. (rā-äl)	114	8.07N	77.43W
El Recreo, neigh., Ven.	230a	10.30N	66.53W
El Reloj, Mex.	229a	19.18N	99.08W
El Reno, Ok., U.S. (rē'nō)	104	35.31N	97.57W
El Rincón de la Florida, Chile	230b	33.33S	70.34W
Elroy, Wi., U.S. (ĕl'roi)	96	43.44N	90.17W
Elsa, Can.	89	63.55N	135.25W
Elsah, Il., U.S. (ĕl'zȧ)	101e	38.57N	90.22W
El Salto, Mex. (säl'tō)	112	23.48N	105.22W
El Salvador, nation, N.A.	110	14.00N	89.30W
El Sauce, Nic. (ĕl-sȧ'ŏ-sĕ)	114	13.00N	86.40W
Elsberry, Mo., U.S. (ĕlz'bĕr-ĭ)	104	39.09N	90.44W
Elsburg, S. Afr.	240b	26.15S	28.12E
Elsdorf, Ger. (ĕls'dŏrf)	151c	50.56N	6.35E
El Segundo, Ca., U.S. (sĕgŭn'dō)	101a	33.55N	118.24W
Elsinore, Ca., U.S. (ĕl'sĭ-nôr)	101a	33.40N	117.19W
Elsinore Lake, l., Ca., U.S.	101a	33.38N	117.21W
Elstorf, Ger. (ĕls'tŏrf)	139c	53.25N	9.48E
Elstree, Eng., U.K.	231	51.39N	0.16W
Eltham, Austl. (ĕl'thȧm)	195a	37.43S	145.08E
Eltham, neigh., Eng., U.K.	231	51.27N	0.04E
El Tigre, Ven. (tē'grĕ)	124	8.49N	64.15W
Elton, Eng., U.K.	233a	53.16N	2.49W
El'ton, l., Russia	160	49.10N	47.00E
El Toreo, pt. of i., Mex.	229a	19.27N	99.13W
El Toro, Ca., U.S. (tō'rō)	101a	33.37N	117.42W
El Triunfo, El Sal.	114	13.17N	88.32W
El Triunfo, Hond. (ĕl-trē-ōō'n-fō)	114	13.06N	87.00W
Elūru, India	174	16.44N	80.09E
El Vado Res, N.M., U.S.	102	36.37N	106.30W
El Valle, neigh., Ven.	230a	10.27N	66.55W
Elvas, Port. (ĕl'väzh)	142	38.53N	7.11W
Elverum, Nor. (ĕl'vĕ-rŏŏm)	146	60.53N	11.33E
El Viejo, Nic. (ĕl-vyĕ'kŏ)	114	12.10N	87.10W
El Viejo, vol., Nic.	114	12.44N	87.03W
Elvins, Mo., U.S. (ĕl'vĭnz)	104	37.49N	90.31W
El Wad, Alg.	204	33.23N	6.49E
El Wak, Kenya (wäk')	204	3.00N	41.00E
Elwell, Lake, res., Mt., U.S.	98	48.22N	111.17W
Elwood, Il., U.S. (ĕ'wŏŏd)	95a	41.24N	88.07W
Elwood, In., U.S.	92	40.15N	85.50W
Ely, Eng., U.K. (ē'lĭ)	144	52.25N	0.17E
Ely, Mn., U.S.	96	47.54N	91.53W
Ely, Nv., U.S.	90	39.16N	114.53W
Elyria, Oh., U.S. (ē-lĭr'ĭ-ȧ)	95d	41.22N	82.07W
El Zamural, Ven.	230a	10.27N	67.00W
El Zig-Zag, Ven.	230a	10.33N	66.58W
Ema, r., Est. (å'mȧ)	146	58.25N	27.00E
Emāmshahr, Iran	174	36.25N	55.01E
Emån, r., Swe.	146	57.15N	15.46E
Emba, r., Kaz. (yĕm'bȧ)	160	46.50N	54.10E
Embarrass, r., Il., U.S. (ĕm-băr'ăs)	92	39.15N	88.05W
Embrun, Can. (ĕm'brŭn)	77c	45.16N	75.17W
Embrun, Fr. (äɴ-brûɴ')	150	44.35N	6.32E
Embu, Braz.	230d	23.39S	46.51W
Embu, Kenya	210	0.32S	37.27E
Emden, Ger. (ĕm'dĕn)	148	53.21N	7.15E
Émerainville, Fr.	233c	48.49N	2.37E
Emerson, Can. (ĕm'ēr-sŭn)	78	49.00N	97.12W
Emerson, N.J., U.S.	224	40.58N	74.02W
Emeryville, Ca., U.S. (ĕm'ēr-ĭ-vĭl)	100b	37.50N	122.17W
Emi Koussi, mtn., Chad (ā'mē kōō-sē')	204	19.50N	18.30E
Emiliano Zapata, Mex. (ē-mē-lyȧ'nō-zä-pȧ'tȧ)	112	17.45N	91.46W
Emilia-Romagna, hist. reg., Italy (ē-mēl'yä rō-mȧ'n-yä)	154	44.35N	10.48E
Eminence, Ky., U.S. (ĕm'ĭ-nĕns)	92	38.25N	85.15W
Emira Island, i., Pap. N. Gui. (ā-mē-rä')	188	1.40S	150.28E
Emmen, Neth. (ĕm'ĕn)	144	52.48N	6.55E
Emmerich, Ger. (ĕm'ēr-ĭk)	151c	51.51N	6.16E
Emmetsburg, Ia., U.S. (ĕm'ĕts-bûrg)	96	43.07N	94.41W
Emmett, Id., U.S. (ĕm'ĕt)	98	43.53N	116.30W
Emmons, Mount, mtn., Ut., U.S. (ĕm'ŭnz)	90	40.43N	110.20W
Emory Peak, mtn., Tx., U.S. (ĕ'mō-rē pēk)	106	29.13N	103.20W
Empoli, Italy (ām'pō-lē)	154	43.43N	10.55E
Emporia, Ks., U.S. (ĕm-pō'rĭ-ȧ)	90	38.24N	96.11W
Emporia, Va., U.S.	108	37.40N	77.34W
Emporium, Pa., U.S. (ĕm-pō'rĭ-ŭm)	92	41.30N	78.15W
Empty Quarter, see Ar Rub' al Khālī, des., Asia	174	20.00N	51.00E
Ems, r., Ger. (ĕms)	148	52.52N	7.16E
Emst, neigh., Ger.	232	51.21N	7.30E
Ems-Weser Kanal, can., Ger.	148	52.23N	8.11E
Emsworth, Pa., U.S.	226b	40.30N	80.04W
Enånger, Swe. (ĕn-ôn'gēr)	146	61.36N	16.55E
Encantada, Cerro de la, mtn., Mex. (sĕ'r-rô-dĕ-lä-ĕn-kän-tä'dȧ)	110	31.58N	115.15W
Encanto, Cape, c., Phil. (ĕn-kän'tō)	189a	15.44N	121.46E
Encarnação, neigh., Port.	234d	38.47N	9.06W
Encarnación, Para. (ĕn-kär-nä-syōn')	126	27.26S	55.52W
Encarnación de Díaz, Mex. (ĕn-kär-nä-syōn dä dē'äz)	112	21.34N	102.15W
Encinal, Tx., U.S. (ĕn'sĭ-nôl)	106	28.02N	99.22W
Encino, neigh., Ca., U.S.	228	34.09N	118.30W
Encontrados, Ven. (ĕn-kōn-trä'dōs)	124	9.01N	72.10W
Encounter Bay, b., Austl. (ĕn-koun'tēr)	196	35.50S	138.45E

ăt; finăl; rāte; senāte; ärm; ȧsk; sofȧ; fâre; ch-choose; dh-as th in other; bē; ėvent; bĕt; recĕnt; cratēr; g-gō; gh-guttural g; bĭt; ĭ-short neutral; rīde; ĸ-guttural k as ch in German ich;

PLACE (Pronunciation)	PAGE	Lat. °′	Long. °′
Endako, r., Can.	80	54.05N	125.30W
Endau, r., Malay.	173b	2.29N	103.40E
Enderbury, i., Kir. (ĕn'dẽr-bûrĭ)	190	2.00S	171.00W
Enderby Land, reg., Ant. (ĕn'dẽr bĭĭ)	213	72.00S	52.00E
Enderlin, N.D., U.S. (ĕn'dẽr-lĭn)	96	46.38N	97.37W
Endicott, N.Y., U.S. (ĕn'dĭ-kŏt)	92	42.05N	76.00W
Endicott Mountains, mts., Ak., U.S.	89	67.30N	153.45W
Enez, Tur.	154	40.42N	26.05E
Enfer, Pointe d', c., Mart.	115b	14.21N	60.48W
Enfield, Austl.	239a	33.53S	151.06E
Enfield, Eng., U.K.	138b	51.38N	0.06W
Enfield, Ct., U.S. (ĕn'fēld)	92	41.55N	72.35W
Enfield, N.C., U.S.	108	36.10N	77.41W
Engaño, Cabo, c., Dom. Rep. (kä'-bô- ĕn-gä-nô)	110	18.40N	68.30W
Engcobo, Transkei (ĕŋg-cô-bô)	207c	31.41S	27.59E
Engel's, Russia (ĕn'gĕls)	160	51.20N	45.40E
Engelskirchen, Ger. (ĕn'gĕls-kĕr'kĕn)	151c	50.59N	7.25E
Engenho de Dentro, neigh., Braz.	230c	22.54S	43.18W
Engenho do Mato, Braz.	230c	22.57S	43.01W
Engenho Nofrvo, neigh., Braz.	230c	22.55S	43.17W
Enggano, Pulau, i., Indon. (ĕng-gä'nō)	188	5.22S	102.18E
Enghien-les-Bains, Fr.	233c	48.58N	2.19E
England, Ar., U.S. (ĭŋ'glănd)	104	34.33N	91.58W
England, reg., U.K. (ĭŋ'glănd)	136	51.35N	1.40W
Englefield Green, Eng., U.K.	231	51.26N	0.35W
Englewood, Co., U.S. (ĕn'g'l-wŏŏd)	104	39.39N	105.00W
Englewood, N.J., U.S.	94a	40.54N	73.59W
Englewood, neigh., Il., U.S.	227a	41.47N	87.39W
Englewood Cliffs, N.J., U.S.	224	40.53N	73.57W
English, In., U.S. (ĭn'glĭsh)	92	38.15N	86.25W
English, r., Can.	78	50.31N	94.12W
English Channel, strt., Eur.	136	49.45N	3.06W
Énguera, Spain (ān'gārä)	152	38.58N	0.42W
Enid, Ok., U.S. (ē'nĭd)	90	36.25N	97.52W
Enid Lake, res., Ms., U.S.	108	34.13N	89.47W
Enkeldoring, S. Afr. (ĕŋ'k'l-dôr-ĭng)	212d	25.24S	28.43E
Enköping, Swe. (ĕn'kû-pĭng)	146	59.39N	17.05E
Ennedi, mts., Chad (ĕn-nĕd'ē)	204	16.45N	22.45E
Ennepetal, Ger.	232	51.18N	7.22E
Ennis, Ire. (ĕn'ĭs)	144	52.54N	9.05W
Ennis, Tx., U.S.	106	32.20N	96.38W
Enniscorthy, Ire. (ĕn-ĭs-kôr'thĭ)	144	52.33N	6.27W
Enniskillen, N. Ire., U.K. (ĕn-ĭs-kĭl'ĕn)	144	54.20N	7.25W
Ennis Lake, res., Mt., U.S.	98	45.15N	111.30W
Enns, r., Aus. (ĕns)	140	47.37N	14.35E
Enoree, S.C., U.S. (ē-nō'rē)	108	34.43N	81.58W
Enoree, r., S.C., U.S.	108	34.35N	81.55W
Enriquillo, Dom. Rep. (ĕn-rē-kē'l-yō)	116	17.55N	71.15W
Enriquillo, Lago, l., Dom. Rep. (lä'gô-ĕn-rē-kē'l-yô)	116	18.35N	71.35W
Enschede, Neth. (ĕns'κā-dĕ)	140	52.10N	6.50E
Enseñada, Arg.	123c	34.50S	57.55W
Ensenada, Mex. (ĕn-sĕ-nä'dä)	110	32.00N	116.30W
Enshi, China (ŭn-shr)	180	30.18N	109.25E
Enshū-Nada, b., Japan (ĕn'shōō nä-dä)	187	34.25N	137.14E
Entebbe, Ug.	204	0.04N	32.28E
Enterprise, Al., U.S. (ĕn'tẽr-prīz)	108	31.20N	85.50W
Enterprise, Or., U.S.	98	45.25N	117.16W
Entiat, L, Wa., U.S.	98	45.43N	120.11W
Entraygues, Fr. (ĕN-trĕg')	150	44.39N	2.33E
Entre Ríos, prov., Arg.	126	31.30S	59.00W
Enugu, Nig. (ĕ-nōō'gōō)	204	6.27N	7.27E
Enumclaw, Wa., U.S. (ĕn'ŭm-klô)	100a	47.12N	121.59W
Envigado, Col. (ĕn-vē-gá'dō)	124a	6.10N	75.34W
Eolie, Isole, is., Italy (ĕ'ô-lē-ĕ-ō'lyĕ)	142	38.43N	14.43E
Epe, Nig.	208	6.37N	3.59E
Épernay, Fr. (ā-pĕr-nĕ')	140	49.02N	3.54E
Épernon, Fr. (ā-pĕr-nôN')	151b	48.36N	1.41E
Ephraim, Ut., U.S. (ē'frā-ĭm)	102	39.20N	111.40W
Ephrata, Wa., U.S. (ēfrā'tá)	98	47.18N	119.35W
Epi, Vanuatu (ā'pē)	196	16.59S	168.29E
Épila, Spain (ā'pē-lä)	152	41.38N	1.15W
Épinal, Fr. (ā-pē-nàl')	140	48.11N	6.27E
Épinay-sous-Sénart, Fr.	233c	48.42N	2.31E
Épinay-sur-Seine, Fr.	233c	48.57N	2.19E
Episkopi, Cyp.	173a	34.38N	32.55E
Eppendorf, neigh., Ger.	232	51.27N	7.11E
Eppenhausen, neigh., Ger.	232	51.21N	7.31E
Epping, Austl.	239a	33.46S	151.05E
Epping, Eng., U.K. (ĕp'ĭng)	138b	51.41N	0.06E
Epping Green, Eng., U.K.	231	51.44N	0.05E
Epping Upland, Eng., U.K.	231	51.43N	0.06E
Epsom, Eng., U.K.	138b	51.20N	0.16W
Epupa Falls, wtfl., Afr.	210	17.00S	13.05E
Epworth, Eng., U.K. (ĕp'wûrth)	138a	53.31N	0.50W
Equatorial Guinea, nation, Afr.	204	2.00N	7.15E
Équilles, Fr.	150a	43.34N	5.21E
Eramosa, r., Can. (ĕr-á-mō'sá)	77d	43.39N	80.08W
Erba, Jabal, mtn., Sudan (ĕr-bá)	204	20.53N	36.45E
Erciyeş Daği, mtn., Tur.	142	38.30N	35.36E
Erding, Ger. (ĕr'dēng)	139d	48.19N	11.54E
Erechim, Braz. (ĕ-rĕ-shē'N)	126	27.43S	52.11W
Ereğli, Tur. (ĕ-rā'ĭ-le)	142	37.40N	34.00E
Ereğli, Tur.	142	41.15N	31.25E
Erenköy, neigh., Tur.	235f	40.58N	29.04E
Erfurt, Ger. (ĕr'fŏŏrt)	140	50.59N	11.04E
Ergene, r., Tur. (ĕr'gĕ-nĕ)	154	41.17N	26.50E
Erges, r., Eur. (ĕr'-zhĕs)	152	39.45N	7.01W
Ērgļi, Lat.	146	56.54N	25.38E
Ergste, Ger.	232	51.25N	7.34E
Eria, r., Spain (ā-rē'ä)	152	42.10N	6.08W
Erick, Ok., U.S. (âr'ĭk)	104	35.14N	99.51W
Erie, Ks., U.S. (ē'rĭ)	104	37.35N	95.17W
Erie, Pa., U.S.	90	42.05N	80.05W
Erie, Lake, l., N.A.	90	42.15N	81.25W
Erimo Saki, c., Japan (ā'rē-mō sä-kē)	180	41.53N	143.20E

PLACE (Pronunciation)	PAGE	Lat. °′	Long. °′
Erin, Can. (ĕ'rĭn)	77d	43.46N	80.04W
Erith, neigh., Eng., U.K.	231	51.29N	0.10E
Eritrea, hist. reg., Eth. (ā-rē-trā'á)	204	16.15N	38.30E
Erkrath, Ger.	232	51.13N	6.55E
Erlangen, Ger. (ĕr'läng-ĕn)	148	49.36N	11.03E
Erlanger, Ky., U.S. (ẽr'lăng-ẽr)	95f	39.01N	84.36W
Erle, neigh., Ger.	232	51.33N	7.05E
Ermont, Fr.	233c	48.59N	2.16E
Ermoúpolis, Grc.	154	37.30N	24.56E
Ernākulam, India	174	9.58N	76.23E
Erne, Lower Lough, l., N. Ire., U.K.	144	54.30N	7.40W
Erne, Upper Lough, l., N. Ire., U.K. (lŏk ûrn)	144	54.20N	7.24W
Erode, India	178	11.20N	77.45E
Eromanga, i., Vanuatu	196	18.58S	169.18E
Eros, La., U.S. (ē'rōs)	106	32.23N	92.22W
Errego, Moz.	210	16.02S	37.14E
Errigal, mtn., Ire. (ĕr-ĭ-gôl')	144	55.02N	8.07W
Errol Heights, Or., U.S.	100c	45.29N	122.38W
Erskine Park, Austl.	239a	33.49S	150.47E
Erstein, Fr. (ĕr'shtīn)	150	48.27N	7.40E
Erwin, N.C., U.S. (ûr'wĭn)	108	35.16N	78.40W
Erwin, Tn., U.S.	108	36.07N	82.25W
Erzgebirge, mts., Eur. (ĕrts'gĕ-bē'gĕ)	136	50.29N	12.40E
Erzincan, Tur. (ĕr-zĭn-jän')	174	39.50N	39.30E
Erzurum, Tur. (ĕrz'rōōm')	174	39.55N	41.10E
Esambo, Zaire	210	3.40S	23.24E
Esashi, Japan (ĕs'ä-shē)	180	41.50N	140.10E
Esbjerg, Den. (ĕs'byĕrgh)	140	55.29N	8.25E
Esborn, Ger.	232	51.23N	7.20E
Escalante, Ut., U.S. (ĕs-kà-lăn'tē)	102	37.50N	111.40W
Escalante, r., Ut., U.S.	102	37.40N	111.20W
Escalón, Mex.	106	26.45N	104.20W
Escambia, r., Fl., U.S. (ĕs-kăm'bĭ-á)	108	30.38N	87.20W
Escanaba, Mi., U.S. (ĕs-ká-nô'bá)	90	45.44N	87.05W
Escanaba, r., Mi., U.S.	96	46.10N	87.22W
Escarpada Point, Phil.	188	18.40N	122.45E
Esch-sur-Alzette, Lux.	150	49.32N	6.21E
Eschwege, Ger. (ĕsh'vā-gĕ)	148	51.11N	10.02E
Eschweiler, Ger. (ĕsh'vī-lẽr)	151c	50.49N	6.15E
Escondido, Ca., U.S. (ĕs-kŏn-dē'dō)	102	33.07N	117.00W
Escondido, r., Nic.	114	12.04N	84.09W
Escondido, Río, r., Mex. (rē'ō-ĕs-kōn-dē'dô)	106	28.30N	100.45W
Escuadrón 020001, Mex.	229a	19.22N	99.06W
Escudo de Veraguas, i., Pan. (ĕs-kōō'dä dā vā-rä'gwäs)	114	9.07N	81.25W
Escuinapa, Mex. (ĕs-kwē-nä'pä)	110	22.49N	105.44W
Escuintla, Guat. (ĕs-kwēn'tlä)	114	14.16N	90.47W
Ese, Cayos de, i., Col.	114	12.24N	81.07W
Eşfahān, Iran	174	32.38N	51.30E
Esgueva, r., Spain (ĕs-gĕ'vä)	152	41.48N	4.10W
Esher, Eng., U.K.	138b	51.23N	0.22W
Eshowe, S. Afr. (ĕsh'ô-wē)	207c	28.54S	31.28E
Esiama, Ghana	208	4.56N	2.21W
Eskdale, W.V., U.S. (ĕsk'dāl)	92	38.05N	81.25W
Eskifjördur, Ice. (ĕs'kē-fyŭr'dōōr)	136	65.04N	14.01W
Eskilstuna, Swe. (ā'shĕl-stü-na)	140	59.23N	16.28E
Eskimo Lakes, l., Can. (es'kĭ-mō)	78	69.40N	130.10W
Eskişehir, Tur. (ĕs-kē-shĕ'h'r)	174	39.40N	30.20E
Esko, Mn., U.S. (ĕs'kô)	101h	46.27N	92.22W
Esla, r., Spain (ĕs-lä)	152	41.50N	5.48W
Eslöv, Swe. (ĕs'lûv)	146	55.50N	13.17E
Esmeraldas, Ec. (ĕs-mā-räl'däs)	124	0.58N	79.45W
Espanola, Can. (ĕs-pá-nō'lá)	78	46.11N	81.59W
Esparta, C.R. (ĕs-pär'tä)	114	9.59N	84.40W
Esperance, Austl. (ĕs'pē-răns)	196	33.45S	122.07E
Esperanza, Cuba (ĕs-pĕ-rä'n-zä)	116	22.30N	80.10W
Espichel, Cabo, c., Port. (ká'bō-ĕs-pē-shĕl')	152	38.25N	9.13W
Espinal, Col. (ĕs-pē-näl')	124	4.10N	74.53W
Espinhaço, Serra do, mts., Braz. (sĕ'r-rä-dô-ĕs-pē-nä-sō)	124	16.00S	44.00W
Espinillo, Punta, c., Ur. (pōō'n-tä-ĕs-pē-nē'l-yō)	123c	34.49S	56.27W
Espírito Santo, Braz. (ĕs-pē'rē-tō-sän'tō)	124	20.27S	40.18W
Espírito Santo, state, Braz.	124	19.57S	40.58W
Espiritu Santo, i., Vanuatu (ĕs-pē'rē-tōō sän'tō)	196	15.45S	166.50E
Espíritu Santo, Bahía del, b., Mex.	114a	19.25N	87.28W
Espita, Mex. (ĕs-pē'tä)	114a	20.57N	88.22W
Esplugas, Spain	234e	41.23N	2.06E
Espoo, Fin.	146	60.13N	24.41E
Esposende, Port. (ĕs-pō-zĕn'dā)	152	41.33N	8.45W
Esquel, Arg. (ĕs-kĕ'l)	126	42.47S	71.22W
Esquimalt, Can. (ĕs-kwī'mŏlt)	80	48.26N	123.24W
Essaouira, Mor.	204	31.34N	9.44W
Essel, neigh., Ger.	232	51.37N	7.15E
Essen, Bel.	139a	51.28N	4.27E
Essen, Ger. (ĕs'sĕn)	136	51.26N	6.59E
Essenberg, Ger.	232	51.26N	6.42E
Essendon, Austl.	195a	37.46S	144.55E
Essequibo, r., Guy. (ĕs-ā-kē'bō)	124	4.26N	58.17W
Essex, Il., U.S.	95a	41.11N	88.11W
Essex, Md., U.S.	94e	39.19N	76.29W
Essex, Ma., U.S.	87a	42.38N	70.47W
Essex, Vt., U.S.	92	44.30N	73.05W
Essex Fells, N.J., U.S. (ĕs'ĕks fĕlz)	94a	40.50N	74.16W
Essexville, Mi., U.S. (ĕs'ĕks-vĭl)	92	43.35N	83.50W
Essington, Pa., U.S.	225b	39.52N	75.18W
Essling, neigh., Aus.	235e	48.13N	16.32E
Esslingen, Ger. (ĕs'slĕn-gĕn)	148	48.45N	9.19E
Estacado, Llano, pl., U.S. (yä-nō ĕs-tá-cá-dō')	90	33.50N	103.20W
Estância, Braz. (ĕs-tän'sĭ-ä)	124	11.17S	37.18W
Estarreja, Port. (ĕ-tär-rā'zhä)	152	40.44N	8.39W
Estats, Pique d', mtn., Eur.	152	42.43N	1.30E

PLACE (Pronunciation)	PAGE	Lat. °′	Long. °′
Estcourt, S. Afr. (ĕst-cōōrt)	207c	29.04S	29.53E
Este, Italy (ĕs'tā)	154	45.13N	11.40E
Estella, Spain (ĕs-tāl'yä)	152	42.40N	2.01W
Estepa, Spain (ĕs-tā'pä)	152	37.18N	4.54W
Estepona, Spain (ĕs-tā-pō'nä)	152	36.26N	5.08W
Esterhazy, Can. (ĕs'tẽr-hā-zē)	82	50.40N	102.08W
Estero Bay, b., Ca., U.S. (ĕs-tā'rōs)	102	35.22N	121.04W
Estevan, Can. (ĕ-stē'văn)	78	49.07N	103.05W
Estevan Group, is., Can.	80	53.05N	129.40W
Estherville, Ia., U.S. (ĕs'tẽr-vĭl)	96	43.24N	94.49W
Estill, S.C., U.S. (ĕs'tĭl)	108	32.46N	81.15W
Eston, Can.	82	51.10N	108.45W
Estonia, nation, Eur.	158	59.10N	25.00E
Estoril, Port. (ĕs-tô-rĕl')	153b	38.45N	9.24W
Estrêla, mtn., Port. (mäl-you'N-dä-ĕs-trĕ'lä)	152	40.20N	7.38W
Estrêla, r., Braz. (ĕs-trĕ'lá)	126b	22.39S	43.16W
Estrêla, Serra da, mts., Port. (sĕr'rá dä ĕs-trā'lá)	152	40.25N	7.45W
Estrella, Cerro de la, mtn., Mex.	229a	19.21N	99.05W
Estremadura, hist. reg., Port. (ĕs-trā-mä-dōō'rá)	152	39.00N	8.36W
Estremoz, Port. (ĕs-trā-mōzh')	152	38.50N	7.35W
Estrondo, Serra do, mts., Braz. (sĕr'rá dô ĕs-trôn'dó)	124	9.52S	48.56W
Esumba, Île, i., Zaire	210	2.00N	21.12E
Esztergom, Hung. (ĕs'tĕr-gŏm)	148	47.46N	18.45E
Etah, Grnld. (ē'tá)	76	78.20N	72.42W
Étampes, Fr. (ā-tänp')	150	48.26N	2.09E
Étaples, Fr. (ā-täp'l')	150	50.32N	1.38E
Etchemin, r., Can. (ĕch'ĕ-mĭn)	77b	46.39N	71.03W
Ethiopia, nation, Afr. (ē-thē-ō'pē-á)	204	7.53N	37.55E
Eticoga, Gui.-B.	208	11.09N	16.08W
Etiwanda, Ca., U.S. (ē-tĭ-wän'dá)	101a	34.07N	117.31W
Etna, Pa., U.S. (ĕt'ná)	95e	40.30N	79.55W
Etna, Mount, vol., Italy	136	37.48N	15.00E
Etobicoke, Can.	84	43.39N	79.34W
Etobicoke Creek, r., Can.	77d	43.44N	79.48W
Etolin Strait, strt., Ak., U.S. (ĕt ō lĭn)	89	60.35S	165.40W
Eton, Eng., U.K.	231	51.31N	0.37W
Eton College, educ., Eng., U.K.	231	51.30N	0.36W
Etoshapan, pl., Nmb. (ĕtō'shä)	206	19.07S	15.30E
Etowah, Tn., U.S. (ĕt'ô-wä)	108	35.18N	84.31W
Etowah, r., Ga., U.S.	108	34.23N	84.19W
Étréchy, Fr. (ā-trā-shē')	151b	48.29N	2.12E
Etten-Leur, Neth.	139a	51.34N	4.38E
Etterbeek, Bel. (ĕt'ĕr-bāk)	139a	50.51N	4.24E
Etzatlán, Mex. (ĕt-zä-tlän')	112	20.44N	104.04W
Eucla, Austl. (ū'klá)	196	31.45S	128.50E
Euclid, Oh., U.S. (ū'klĭd)	95d	41.34N	81.32W
Eudora, Ar., U.S. (u-dō'rá)	104	33.07N	91.16W
Eufaula, Al., U.S. (û-fô'lá)	108	31.53N	85.09W
Eufaula, Ok., U.S.	104	35.16N	95.35W
Eufaula Reservoir, res., Ok., U.S.	104	35.00N	94.45W
Eugene, Or., U.S. (û-jēn')	90	44.02N	123.06W
Euless, Tx., U.S. (ū'lĕs)	101c	32.50N	97.05W
Eunice, La., U.S. (ū'nĭs)	106	30.30N	92.25W
Eupen, Bel. (oi'pĕn)	144	50.39N	6.05E
Euphrates, r., Asia (û-frā'tēz)	174	36.00N	40.00E
Eure, r., Fr. (ûr)	150	49.03N	1.22E
Eureka, Ca., U.S. (û-rē'ká)	90	40.45N	124.10W
Eureka, Ks., U.S.	104	37.48N	96.17W
Eureka, Mt., U.S.	98	48.53N	115.07W
Eureka, Nv., U.S.	102	39.33N	115.58W
Eureka, S.D., U.S.	96	45.46N	99.38W
Eureka, Ut., U.S.	102	39.55N	112.10W
Eureka Springs, Ar., U.S.	104	36.24N	93.43W
Europe, cont. (ū'rŭp)	136	50.00N	15.00E
Eustis, Fl., U.S. (ūs'tĭs)	108	28.50N	81.41W
Eutaw, Al., U.S. (ū-tâ)	108	32.48N	87.50W
Eutsuk Lake, l., Can. (ōōt'sŭk)	80	53.20N	126.44W
Evanston, Il., U.S. (ĕv'ăn-stŭn)	90	42.03N	87.41W
Evanston, Wy., U.S.	98	41.17N	111.02W
Evansville, In., U.S. (ĕv'ănz-vĭl)	90	38.00N	87.30W
Evansville, Wi., U.S.	96	42.46N	89.19W
Evart, Mi., U.S. (ĕv'ẽrt)	92	43.55N	85.10W
Evaton, S. Afr. (ĕv'á-tŏn)	212d	26.32S	27.53E
Eveleth, Mn., U.S. (ĕv'ē-lĕth)	96	47.27N	92.35W
Everard, l., Austl. (ĕv'ẽr-ărd)	196	31.20S	134.10E
Everard Ranges, mts., Austl.	196	27.15S	132.00E
Everest, Mount, mtn., Asia (ĕv'ẽr-ĕst)	174	28.00N	86.57E
Everett, Ma., U.S. (ĕv'ẽr-ĕt)	87a	42.24N	71.03W
Everett, Wa., U.S. (ĕv'ẽr-ĕt)	90	47.59N	122.11W
Everett Mountains, mts., Can.	78	62.34N	68.00W
Everglades, The, sw., Fl., U.S.	109a	25.35N	80.55W
Everglades City, Fl., U.S. (ĕv'ẽr-glādz)	109a	25.50N	81.25W
Everglades National Park, rec., Fl., U.S.	90	25.39N	80.57W
Evergreen, Al., U.S. (ĕv'ẽr-grēn)	108	31.25N	87.56W
Evergreen Park, Il., U.S.	95a	41.44N	87.42W
Everman, Tx., U.S. (ĕv'ẽr-măn)	101c	32.38N	97.17W
Everson, Wa., U.S. (ĕv'ẽr-sŭn)	100d	48.55N	122.21W
Everton, neigh., Eng., U.K.	233a	53.25N	2.58W
Eving, neigh., Ger.	232	51.33N	7.29E
Évora, Port. (ĕv'ô-rä)	142	38.35N	7.54W
Évreux, Fr. (ā-vrû')	140	49.02N	1.11E
Evrótas, r., Grc. (ĕv-rō'täs)	154	37.15N	22.17E
Évvoia, i., Grc.	142	38.38N	23.45E
Ewa Beach, Hi., U.S. (ē'wä)	88a	21.17N	158.03E
Ewaso Ng'iro, r., Kenya	204	0.59N	37.47E
Ewell, Eng., U.K.	231	51.21N	0.15W
Ewu, Nig.	240d	6.33N	3.19E
Excelsior, Mn., U.S. (ĕk-sel'sĭ-ŏr)	101g	44.54N	93.35W
Excelsior Springs, Mo., U.S.	104	39.20N	94.13W
Exe, r., Eng., U.K. (ĕks)	144	50.57N	3.37W
Exeter, Eng., U.K.	140	50.45N	3.33W
Exeter, Ca., U.S. (ĕk'sē-tẽr)	102	36.18N	119.09W
Exeter, N.H., U.S.	92	43.00N	71.00W

PLACE (Pronunciation)	PAGE	Lat. °′	Long. °′
Exmoor, for., Eng., U.K. (ĕks′mòr)	144	51.10N	3.55W
Exmouth, Eng., U.K. (ĕks′mŭth)	144	50.40N	3.20W
Exmouth Gulf, b., Austl.	196	21.45S	114.30E
Exploits, r., Can. (ĕks-ploits′)	86	48.50N	56.15W
Extórrax, r., Mex. (ĕx-tó′ràx)	112	21.04N	99.39W
Extrema, Braz. (ĕsh-trĕ′mä)	123a	22.52S	46.19W
Extremadura, hist. reg., Spain (ĕks-trä-mä-doo′rä)	152	38.43N	6.30W
Exuma Sound, strt., Bah. (ĕk-sōō′mä)	116	24.20N	76.20W
Eyasi, Lake, l., Tan. (å-yä′sė)	206	3.25S	34.55E
Eyjafjördur, b., Ice.	140	66.21N	18.20W
Eyl, Som.	212a	7.53N	49.45E
Eynsford, Eng., U.K.	231	51.22N	0.13E
Eyrarbakki, Ice.	140	63.51N	20.52W
Eyre, Austl. (âr)	196	32.15S	126.20E
Eyre, l., Austl.	196	28.43S	137.50E
Eyre Peninsula, pen., Austl.	196	33.30S	136.00E
Eyüp, neigh., Tur.	235f	41.03N	28.55E
Ezbekīyah, neigh., Egypt	240a	30.03N	31.15E
Ezeiza, Arg. (ĕ-zā′zä)	126a	34.52S	58.31W
Ezine, Tur. (å′zĭ-nå)	154	39.47N	26.18E

F

PLACE (Pronunciation)	PAGE	Lat. °′	Long. °′
Fabens, Tx., U.S. (fā′bĕnz)	106	31.30N	106.07W
Fåborg, Den. (fô′bòrg)	146	55.06N	10.19E
Fabreville, neigh., Can.	223b	45.34N	73.50W
Fabriano, Italy (fä-brē-ä′nô)	154	43.20N	12.55E
Fada, Chad (fä′dä)	204	17.06N	21.18E
Fada Ngourma, Burkina (fä′dä′n gōōr′mä)	204	12.04N	0.21E
Faddeya, i., Russia (fȧd-yä′)	158	76.12N	145.00E
Faenza, Italy (fä-ĕnd′zä)	154	44.16N	11.53E
Faeroe Islands, is., Eur. (fâ′rō)	136	62.00N	5.45W
Fafe, Port. (fä′fā)	152	41.30N	8.10W
Fafen, r., Eth.	212a	8.15N	42.40E
Făgăras, Rom. (fă-gă′răsh)	154	45.50N	24.55E
Fagerness, Nor. (fä′ghĕr-nĕs)	140	61.00N	9.10E
Fagnano, l., S.A. (fäk-nä′nô)	126	54.35S	68.20W
Faguibine, Lac, l., Mali	208	16.50N	4.20W
Fahrland, Ger.	234a	52.28N	13.01E
Faial, i., Port. (fä-yä′l)	204a	38.40N	29.19W
Fā'id, Egypt (fä-yēd′)	212c	30.19N	32.18E
Failsworth, Eng., U.K.	233b	53.31N	2.09W
Fairbanks, Ak., U.S. (fâr′bănks)	90a	64.50N	147.48W
Fairbury, Il., U.S. (fâr′bĕr-ĭ)	92	40.45N	88.25W
Fairbury, Ne., U.S.	104	40.09N	97.11W
Fairchild Creek, r., Can. (fâr′chīld)	77d	43.18N	80.10W
Fairfax, Mn., U.S. (fâr′făks)	96	44.29N	94.44W
Fairfax, S.C., U.S.	108	32.29N	81.13W
Fairfax, Va., U.S.	94e	38.51N	77.20W
Fairfield, Austl.	195b	33.52S	150.57E
Fairfield, Al., U.S. (fâr′fēld)	94h	33.30N	86.50W
Fairfield, Ct., U.S.	94a	41.08N	73.22W
Fairfield, Il., U.S.	92	38.25N	88.20W
Fairfield, Ia., U.S.	96	41.00N	91.59W
Fairfield, Me., U.S.	86	44.35N	69.38W
Fairfield, N.J., U.S.	224	40.53N	74.17W
Fairhaven, Md., U.S.	225d	38.47N	77.05W
Fairhaven, Ma., U.S. (fâr-hā′vĕn)	92	41.35N	70.55W
Fair Haven, Vt., U.S.	92	43.35N	73.15W
Fair Island, i., Scot., U.K. (fâr)	144a	59.34N	1.41W
Fair Lawn, N.J., U.S.	224	40.56N	74.07W
Fairlee, Md., U.S.	225d	38.52N	77.16W
Fairmont, Mn., U.S. (fâr′mŏnt)	96	43.39N	94.26W
Fairmont, W.V., U.S.	92	39.30N	80.10W
Fairmont City, Il., U.S.	101e	38.39N	90.05W
Fairmount, In., U.S.	92	40.25N	85.45W
Fairmount, Ks., U.S.	101f	39.12N	95.55W
Fairmount Heights, Md., U.S.	225d	38.54N	76.55W
Fair Oaks, Ga., U.S. (fâr ōks)	94c	33.56N	84.33W
Fairport, N.Y., U.S. (fâr′pōrt)	92	43.05N	77.30W
Fairport Harbor, Oh., U.S.	92	41.45N	81.15W
Fairseat, Eng., U.K.	231	51.20N	0.20E
Fairview, N.J., U.S.	224	40.49N	74.00W
Fairview, Ok., U.S. (fâr′vū)	104	36.16N	98.28W
Fairview, Or., U.S.	100c	45.32N	112.26W
Fairview, Ut., U.S.	102	39.35N	111.30W
Fairview Park, Oh., U.S.	95d	41.27N	81.52W
Fairweather, Mount, mtn., N.A. (fâr-wĕdh′ẽr)	89	59.12N	137.22W
Faisalabad, Pak.	174	31.29N	73.06E
Faith, S.D., U.S. (fāth)	96	45.02N	120.02W
Faizābād, India	174	26.50N	82.17E
Fajardo, P.R.	111b	18.20N	65.40W
Fakfak, Indon.	188	2.56S	132.25E
Faku, China (fä-kōō)	184	42.28N	123.20E
Falcón, dept., Ven. (fäl-kô′n)	125b	11.00N	68.28W
Falconer, N.Y., U.S. (fô′k′n-ẽr)	92	42.10N	79.10W
Falcon Heights, Mn., U.S. (fô′k′n)	101g	44.59N	93.10W
Falcon Reservoir, res., N.A. (fôk′n)	106	26.47N	99.03W
Faleshty, Mol. (fä-lâsh′tĭ)	156	47.33N	27.46E
Falfurrias, Tx., U.S. (făl′fōō-rē′ȧs)	106	27.15N	98.08W
Falher, Can. (făl′ẽr)	80	55.44N	117.12W
Falkenberg, Swe. (fäl′kĕn-bĕrgh)	146	56.54N	12.25E
Falkensee, Ger. (fäl′kĕn-zā)	139b	52.34N	13.05E
Falkenthal, Ger. (fäl′kĕn-täl)	139b	52.54N	13.18E
Falkirk, Scot., U.K. (fôl′kûrk)	144	55.59N	3.55W
Falkland Islands, dep., S.A. (fôk′lȧnd)	126	50.45S	61.00W
Falköping, Swe. (fäl′chûp-ĭng)	146	58.09N	13.30E
Fall City, Wa., U.S.	100a	47.34N	121.53W
Fall Creek, r., In., U.S. (fôl)	95g	39.52N	86.04W
Fallon, Nv., U.S. (făl′ŭn)	102	39.30N	118.48W
Fall River, Ma., U.S.	90	41.42N	71.07W
Falls Church, Va., U.S. (fălz chûrch)	94e	38.53N	77.10W
Falls City, Ne., U.S.	104	40.04N	95.37W
Fallston, Md., U.S. (fâls′ton)	94e	39.32N	76.26W
Falmouth, Jam.	116	18.30N	77.40W
Falmouth, Eng., U.K. (făl′mŭth)	144	50.08N	5.04W
Falmouth, Ky., U.S.	92	38.40N	84.20W
False Divi Point, c., India	178	15.45N	80.50E
Falster, i., Den. (fäls′tĕr)	146	54.48N	11.58E
Fălticeni, Rom. (fŭl-tē-chân′y′)	148	47.27N	26.17E
Falun, Swe. (fä-lōōn′)	140	60.38N	15.35E
Famadas, Spain	234e	41.21N	2.05E
Famagusta, N. Cyp. (fä-mä-gōōs′tä)	142	35.08N	33.59E
Famatina, Sierra de, mts., Arg.	126	29.00S	67.50W
Fangxian, China (fäŋ-shyĕn)	184	32.05N	110.45E
Fanning, i., Can.	77f	49 45N	97.46W
Fano, Italy (fä′nō)	154	43.49N	13.01E
Fanø, i., Den. (fän′û)	146	55.24N	8.10E
Fan Si Pan, mtn., Viet.	184	22.25N	103.50E
Farafangana, Madag. (fä-rä-fäŋ-gä′nä)	206	23.18S	47.59E
Farāh, Afg. (fä-rä′)	174	32.15N	62.13E
Farallón, Punta, c., Mex. (pò′n-tä-fä-rä-lōn)	112	19.21N	105.03W
Faranah, Gui. (fä-rä′nä)	204	10.02N	10.44W
Farasān, Jaza'ir, is., Sau. Ar.	174	16.45N	41.08E
Faregh, Wadi al, r., Libya (wädė ĕl fä-rĕg′)	142	30.10N	19.34E
Farewell, Cape, c., N.Z. (fâr-wĕl′)	197a	40.37S	172.40E
Fargo, N.D., U.S. (fär′gō)	90	46.53N	96.48W
Far Hills, N.J., U.S. (fär hĭlz)	94a	40.41N	74.38W
Faribault, Mn., U.S. (fâ′rĭ-bō)	96	44.19N	93.16W
Farilhões, is., Port. (fä-rė-lyŏnzh′)	152	39.28N	9.32W
Faringdon, Eng., U.K. (fă′rĭng-dŏn)	138b	51.38N	1.35W
Fāriskūr, Egypt (fä-rės-kōōr′)	212b	31.19N	31.46E
Farit, Amba, mtn., Eth.	204	10.51N	37.52E
Farley, Mo., U.S. (fär′lē)	101f	39.16N	94.49W
Farmers Branch, Tx., U.S.	101c	32.56N	96.53W
Farmersburg, In., U.S. (fär′mẽrz-bûrg)	92	39.15N	87.25W
Farmersville, Tx., U.S. (fär′mẽrz-vĭl)	104	33.11N	96.22W
Farmingdale, N.J., U.S. (färm′ĕng-dāl)	94a	40.11N	74.10W
Farmingdale, N.Y., U.S.	94a	40.44N	73.26W
Farmingham, Ma., U.S. (färm-ĭng-hăm)	87a	42.17N	71.25W
Farmington, Il., U.S. (färm-ĭng-tŭn)	104	40.42N	90.01W
Farmington, Me., U.S.	86	44.40N	70.10W
Farmington, Mi., U.S.	95b	42.28N	83.23W
Farmington, Mo., U.S.	104	37.46N	90.26W
Farmington, N.M., U.S.	102	36.40N	108.10W
Farmington, Ut., U.S.	101b	40.59N	111.53W
Farmington Hills, Mi., U.S.	226c	42.28N	83.23W
Farmville, N.C., U.S. (färm-vĭl)	108	35.35N	77.35W
Farmville, Va., U.S.	108	37.15N	78.23W
Farnborough, Eng., U.K. (färn′bŭr-ô)	138b	51.15N	0.45W
Farnborough, neigh., Eng., U.K.	231	51.21N	0.04E
Farne Islands, is., Eng., U.K. (färn)	144	55.40N	1.32W
Farnham, Can. (fär′năm)	92	45.15N	72.55W
Farningham, Eng., U.K. (fär′nĭng-ŭm)	138b	51.22N	0.14E
Farnworth, Eng., U.K. (färn′wŭrth)	138a	53.34N	2.24W
Faro, Braz. (fä′rò)	124	2.05S	56.32W
Faro, Port.	142	37.01N	7.57W
Farodofay, Madag.	206	24.59S	46.58E
Fårön, i., Swe.	146	57.57N	19.10E
Farquhar, Cape, c., Austl. (fär′kwȧr)	196	23.50S	112.55E
Farrell, Pa., U.S. (făr′ĕl)	92	41.10N	80.30W
Far Rockaway, neigh., N.Y., U.S.	224	40.36N	73.45W
Farrukhābād, India (fŭ-ròk-hä-băd′)	174	27.29N	79.35E
Fársala, Grc.	154	39.18N	22.25E
Farsund, Nor. (fär′sòn)	146	58.05N	6.47E
Fartak, Ra's, c., Yemen	174	15.43N	52.17E
Fartura, Serra da, mts., Braz. (sĕ′r-rä-dȧ-fär-tōō′rä)	126	26.40S	53.15W
Farvel, Kap, c., Grnld.	76	60.00N	44.00W
Farwell, Tx., U.S. (fär′wĕl)	104	34.24N	103.03W
Fasano, Italy (fä-zä′nō)	154	40.50N	17.22E
Fastov, Ukr. (fäs′tôf)	156	50.04N	29.57E
Fatëzh, Russia	156	52.06N	35.51E
Fatima, Port.	152	39.36N	9.36E
Fatsa, Tur. (fät′sä)	142	40.50N	37.30E
Faucilles, Monts, mts., Fr. (môn′ fō-sēl′)	150	48.07N	6.13E
Fauske, Nor.	140	67.15N	15.24E
Faust, Can. (foust)	80	55.19N	115.38W
Faustovo, Russia	164b	55.27N	38.29E
Faversham, Eng., U.K. (fă′vẽr-sh′m)	138b	51.19N	0.54E
Favoriten, neigh., Aus.	235e	48.11N	16.23E
Fawkham Green, Eng., U.K.	231	51.22N	0.17E
Fawkner, Austl.	239b	37.43S	144.58E
Fawsett Farms, Md., U.S.	225d	38.59N	77.14W
Faxaflói, b., Ice.	140	64.33N	22.40W
Fayette, Al., U.S. (fā-yĕt′)	108	33.40N	87.54W
Fayette, Ia., U.S.	96	42.49N	91.49W
Fayette, Ms., U.S.	108	31.43N	91.00W
Fayette, Mo., U.S.	104	39.09N	92.41W
Fayetteville, Ar., U.S. (fā-yĕt′vĭl)	104	36.03N	94.08W
Fayetteville, N.C., U.S.	108	35.02N	78.54W
Fayetteville, Tn., U.S.	108	35.10N	86.33W
Fazao, Forêt Classée du, for., Togo	208	8.50N	0.40E
Fazilka, India	178	30.30N	74.02E
Fazzān (Fezzan), hist. reg., Libya	204	26.45N	13.01E
Fdérik, Maur.	204	22.45N	12.38W
Fear, Cape, c., N.C., U.S. (fēr)	108	33.52N	77.48W
Feather, r., Ca., U.S. (fĕth′ẽr)	102	38.56N	121.41W
Feather, Middle Fork of, r., Ca., U.S.	102	39.49N	121.10W
Feather, North Fork of, r., Ca., U.S.	102	40.00N	121.20W
Featherstone, Eng., U.K. (fĕdh′ẽr stŭn)	138a	53.39N	1.21W
Fécamp, Fr. (fā-kän′)	140	49.45N	0.20E
Federal, Distrito, dept., Ven. (dēs-trē′tō-fĕ-dĕ-rä′l)	125b	10.34N	66.55W
Federal Way, Wa., U.S.	100a	47.20N	122.20W
Fëdorovka, Russia (fyô′dō-rôf-kȧ)	164b	56.15N	37.14E
Fehmarn, i., Ger. (fā′märn)	148	54.28N	11.15E
Fehrbellin, Ger. (fĕr′bĕl-lēn)	139b	52.49N	12.46E
Feia, Logoa, l., Braz. (lô-gôä-fĕ′yä)	123a	21.54S	41.15W
Feicheng, China (fā-chŭŋ)	182	36.18N	116.45E
Feidong, China (fā-dôŋ)	182	31.53N	117.28E
Feira de Santana, Braz. (fĕ′ê-rä dä sänt-än′ä)	124	12.16S	38.46W
Feixian, China (fā-shyĕn)	182	35.17N	117.59E
Felanitx, Spain (fā-lä-nēch′)	142	39.29N	3.09E
Feldkirch, Aus. (fĕlt′kĭrk)	148	47.15N	9.36E
Feldkirchen, Ger. (fĕld′kĕr-κĕn)	139d	48.09N	11.44E
Felipe Carrillo Puerto, Mex.	114a	19.36N	88.04W
Feltre, Italy (fĕl′trā)	154	46.02N	11.56E
Femunden, l., Nor.	140	62.17N	11.40E
Fengcheng, China	183b	30.55N	121.38E
Fengcheng, China (fŭŋ-chŭŋ)	184	40.28N	124.03E
Fengdu, China (fŭŋ-dōō)	180	29.58N	107.50E
Fengjie, China (fŭŋ-jyĕ)	180	31.02N	109.30E
Fengming Dao, i., China (fŭŋ-mĭŋ dou)	182	39.19N	121.15E
Fengrun, China (fŭŋ-rōn)	182	39.51N	118.06E
Fengtai, China (fŭŋ-tī)	184a	39.51N	116.19E
Fengxian, China	182	34.41N	116.36E
Fengxian, China (fŭŋ-shyĕn)	183b	30.55N	121.26E
Fengxiang, China (fŭŋ-shyäŋ)	180	34.25N	107.20E
Fengyang, China (fŭng′yăng′)	184	32.55N	117.32E
Fengzhen, China (fŭŋ-jŭn)	180	40.28N	113.20E
Fennimore Pass, strt., Ak., U.S. (fĕn-ĭ-mōr)	89a	51.40N	175.38W
Fenoarivo Atsinanana, Madag.	206	17.30S	49.31E
Fenton, Mi., U.S. (fĕn-tŭn)	92	42.50N	83.40W
Fenton, Mo., U.S.	101e	38.31N	90.27W
Fenyang, China	180	37.20N	111.48E
Feodosiya, Ukr.	160	45.02N	35.21E
Ferbitz, Ger.	234a	52.30N	13.01E
Ferdows, Iran	174	34.00N	58.13E
Ferencváros, neigh., Hung.	235g	47.28N	19.06E
Ferentino, Italy (fā-rĕn-tē′nō)	154	41.42N	13.18E
Fergana, Uzb.	158	40.23N	71.46E
Fergus Falls, Mn., U.S. (fûr′gŭs)	90	46.17N	96.03W
Ferguson, Mo., U.S. (fûr-gŭ-sŭn)	101e	38.45N	90.18W
Ferkéssédougou, I.C.	208	9.36N	5.12W
Fermo, Italy (fĕr′mō)	154	43.10N	13.43E
Fermoselle, Spain (fĕr-mō-săl′yā)	152	41.20N	6.23W
Fermoy, Ire. (fûr-moi′)	144	52.05N	8.06W
Fernandina Beach, Fl., U.S. (fûr-năn-dē′nȧ)	108	30.38N	81.29W
Fernando de Noronha, , Braz.	124	3.51S	32.25W
Fernando Póo, see Bioko, i., Eq. Gui.	204	3.35N	7.45E
Fernán-Núñez, Spain (fĕr-nän′nōōn′yâth)	152	37.42N	4.43W
Fernão Veloso, Baia de, b., Moz.	210	14.20S	40.55E
Ferndale, Ca., U.S. (fûrn′dāl)	98	40.34N	124.18W
Ferndale, Md., U.S.	225c	39.11N	76.38W
Ferndale, Mi., U.S.	95b	42.27N	83.08W
Ferndale, Mi., U.S.	226c	42.28N	83.08W
Ferndale, Wa., U.S.	100d	48.51N	122.36W
Fernie, Can. (fûr′nĭ)	78	49.30N	115.03W
Fern Prairie, Wa., U.S. (fûrn prâr′ĭ)	100c	45.38N	122.25W
Ferny Creek, Austl.	239b	37.53S	145.21E
Ferrara, Italy (fĕr-rä′rä)	142	44.50N	11.37E
Ferrat, Cap, c., Alg. (kăp fĕr-răt)	152	35.49N	0.29W
Ferraz de Vasconcelos, Braz.	230d	23.32S	46.22W
Ferreira do Alentejo, Port.	152	38.03N	8.06W
Ferreira do Zezere, Port. (fĕr-rĕ′ê-rä dò zā-zā′rĕ)	152	39.49N	8.17W
Ferrelview, Mo., U.S. (fĕr′rĕl-vū)	101f	39.18N	94.40W
Ferreñafe, Peru (fĕr-rĕn-yȧ′fĕ)	124	6.38S	79.48W
Ferriday, La., U.S. (fĕr′ĭ-dā)	106	31.38N	91.33W
Ferrieres, Fr.	233c	48.49N	2.42E
Ferry Village, N.Y., U.S.	226a	43.58N	78.57W
Fershampenuaz, Russia (fĕr-shàm′pĕn-wäz)	164a	53.32N	59.50E
Fertile, Mn., U.S. (fur′tĭl)	96	47.33N	96.18W
Fès, Mor. (fĕs)	204	34.08N	5.00W
Fessenden, N.D., U.S. (fĕs′ĕn-dĕn)	96	47.39N	99.40W
Festus, Mo., U.S. (fĕst′ŭs)	104	38.12N	90.22W
Fetcham, Eng., U.K.	231	51.17N	0.22W
Fethiye, Tur. (fĕt-hē′yĕ)	142	36.40N	29.05E
Feuilles, Rivière aux, r., Can.	78	58.30N	70.50W
Ffestiniog, Wales, U.K.	144	52.59N	3.58W
Fianarantsoa, Madag. (fyȧ-nä′rȧn-tsō′ȧ)	206	21.21S	47.15E
Fichtenau, Ger.	234a	52.27N	13.42E
Ficksburg, S. Afr. (fĭks′bûrg)	212d	28.53S	27.53E
Fidalgo Island, i., Wa., U.S. (fĭ-dăl′gō)	100a	48.28N	122.39W
Fiddlers Hamlet, Eng., U.K.	231	51.41N	0.08E
Fieldbrook, Ca., U.S. (fēld′bròk)	98	40.59N	124.02W
Fier, Alb. (fyĕr)	154	40.43N	19.34E
Fife Ness, c., Scot., U.K. (fĭf′nes′)	144	56.15N	2.19W
Fifth Cataract, wtfl., Sudan	204	18.27N	33.38E
Figeac, Fr. (fē-zhák′)	150	44.37N	2.02E
Figeholm, Swe. (fē-ghĕ-hōlm)	146	57.24N	16.33E
Figueira da Foz, Port. (fē-gwĕy-rä-dȧ-fô′z)	152	40.10N	8.50W
Figuig, Mor.	204	32.20N	1.30W
Fiji, nation, Oc. (fē′jē)	2	18.40S	175.00E
Filadelfia, C.R. (fĭl-ȧ-dĕl′fĭ-ȧ)	114	10.26N	85.37W
Filatovskoye, Russia (fĭ-lä′tôf-skô-yĕ)	164a	56.49N	62.20E
Filchner Ice Shelf, ice., Ant. (fĭlk′nẽr)	213	80.00S	35.00W
Fili, neigh., Russia	235b	55.45N	37.31E
Filicudi, i., Italy (fē′le-kōō′dē)	154	38.34N	14.39E

ăt; finăl; rāte; senâte; ärm; ȧsk; sofȧ; fâre; ch-choose; dh-as th in other; bē; ėvent; bĕt; recĕnt; cratẽr; g-gō; gh-guttural g; bĭt; ĭ-short neutral; rīde; κ-guttural k as ch in German ich;

PLACE (Pronunciation)	PAGE	Lat. °′	Long. °′
Filippovskoye, Russia (fĭ-lĭ-pôf′skô-yĕ)	164b	56.06N	38.38E
Filipstad, Swe. (fĭl′ĭps-städh)	146	59.44N	14.09E
Fillmore, Ut., U.S. (fĭl′môr)	102	39.00N	112.20W
Filsa, Nor.	146	60.35N	12.03E
Fimi, r., Zaire	206	2.43S	17.50E
Finaalspan, S. Afr.	240b	26.17S	28.15E
Finch, Can. (fĭnch)	77c	45.09N	75.06W
Finchley, neigh., Eng., U.K.	231	51.36N	0.10W
Findlay, Oh., U.S. (fĭnd′là)	92	41.05N	83.40W
Fingoe, Moz.	210	15.12S	31.50E
Finisterre, Cabo de, c., Spain (kå′bô-dĕ-fĭn-ĭs-târ′)	136	42.52N	9.48W
Finke, r., Austl. (fĭŋ′kė)	196	25.25S	134.30E
Finkenkrug, Ger.	234a	52.34N	13.03E
Finland, nation, Eur. (fĭn′l*ă*nd)	136	62.45N	26.13E
Finland, Gulf of, b., Eur. (fĭn′l*ă*nd)	136	59.35N	23.35E
Finlandia, Col. (fēn-lä′n-dēä)	124a	4.38N	75.39W
Finlay, r., Can. (fĭn′lå)	78	57.45N	125.30W
Finow, Ger. (fē′nōv)	139b	52.50N	13.44E
Finowfurt, Ger. (fē′nō-fo͞ort)	139b	52.50N	13.41E
Fircrest, Wa., U.S. (fûr′krĕst)	100a	47.14N	122.31W
Firenze, *see* Florence, Italy	136	43.47N	11.15E
Firenzuola, Italy (fē-rĕnt-swô′lä)	154	44.08N	11.21E
Firgrove, Eng., U.K.	233b	53.37N	2.08W
Firozpur, India	174	30.58N	74.39E
Fischa, r., Aus.	139e	48.04N	16.33E
Fischamend Markt, Aus.	139e	48.07N	16.37E
Fischeln, neigh., Ger.	232	51.18N	6.35E
Fish, r., Nmb. (fĭsh)	206	28.00S	17.30E
Fish Cay, i., Bah.	116	22.30N	74.20W
Fish Creek, r., Can. (fĭsh)	77e	50.52N	114.21W
Fisher, La., U.S. (fĭsh′ẽr)	106	31.28N	93.30W
Fisher Bay, b., Can.	82	51.30N	97.16W
Fisher Channel, strt., Can.	80	52.10N	127.42W
Fisherman's Wharf, pt. of i., Ca., U.S.	227b	37.48N	122.25W
Fisher Strait, strt., Can.	78	62.43N	84.28W
Fisherville, Can.	223c	43.47N	79.28W
Fishpool, Eng., U.K.	233b	53.35N	2.17W
Fitchburg, Ma., U.S. (fĭch′bûrg)	92	42.35N	71.48W
Fitri, Lac, l., Chad	208	12.50N	17.28E
Fitzgerald, Ga., U.S. (fĭts-jĕr′*ă*ld)	108	31.42N	83.17W
Fitz Hugh Sound, strt., Can. (fĭts hū)	80	51.40N	127.57W
Fitzroy, Austl.	239b	37.48S	144.59E
Fitzroy, r., Austl. (fĭts-roi′)	196	18.00S	124.05E
Fitzroy, r., Austl.	196	23.45S	150.02E
Fitzroy Crossing, Austl.	196	18.08S	126.00E
Fitzwilliam, i., Can. (fĭts-wĭl′y*ŭ*m)	84	45.30N	81.45W
Fiume, *see* Rijeka, Cro.	142	45.22N	14.24E
Fiumicino, Italy (fyo͞o-mē-chē′nô)	153d	41.47N	12.19E
Five Dock, Austl.	239a	33.52S	151.08E
Fjällbacka, Swe. (fyĕl′băk-å)	146	58.37N	11.17E
Flagstaff, Transkei (flăg′stăf)	207c	31.06S	29.31E
Flagstaff, Az., U.S. (flăg-stàf)	90	35.15N	111.40W
Flagstaff, l., Me., U.S. (flăg-stàf)	92	45.05N	70.30W
Flåm, Nor. (flôm)	146	60.50N	7.00E
Flambeau, r., Wi., U.S. (flăm-bō′)	96	45.32N	91.05W
Flaming Gorge Reservoir, res., U.S.	90	41.13N	109.30W
Flamingo, Fl., U.S. (fl*ȧ*-mĭŋ′gō)	108	25.10N	80.55W
Flamingo Cay, i., Bah. (fl*ȧ*-mĭŋ′gō)	116	22.50N	75.50W
Flamingo Point, c., V.I.U.S.	111c	18.19N	65.00W
Flanders, hist. reg., Fr. (flăn′dẽrz)	144	50.53N	2.29E
Flandreau, S.D., U.S. (flăn′drō)	96	44.02N	96.35W
Flatbush, neigh., N.Y., U.S.	224	40.39N	73.56W
Flathead, r., N.A.	80	49.30N	114.30W
Flathead, Middle Fork, r., Mt., U.S.	98	48.30N	113.47W
Flathead, North Fork, r., N.A.	98	48.45N	114.20W
Flathead, South Fork, r., Mt., U.S.	98	48.05N	113.45W
Flathead Indian Reservation, I.R., Mt., U.S.	98	47.30N	114.25W
Flathead Lake, l., Mt., U.S. (flăt′hĕd)	90	47.57N	114.20W
Flatow, Ger.	139b	52.44N	12.58E
Flat Rock, Mi., U.S. (flăt rŏk)	95b	42.06N	83.17W
Flattery, Cape, c., Wa., U.S. (flăt′ẽr-ĭ)	98	48.22N	124.45W
Flatwillow Creek, r., Mt., U.S. (flat wĭl′ō)	98	46.45N	108.47W
Flaunden, Eng., U.K.	231	51.42N	0.32W
Flehe, neigh., Ger.	232	51.12N	6.47E
Flekkefjord, Nor. (flăk′kĕ-fyôr)	146	58.19N	6.38E
Flemingsburg, Ky., U.S. (flĕm′ĭngz-bûrg)	92	38.25N	83.45W
Flensburg, Ger. (flĕns′bôrgh)	140	54.48N	9.27E
Flers, Fr. (flĕr)	140	48.43N	0.37W
Fletcher, N.C., U.S.	108	35.26N	82.30W
Fley, neigh., Ger.	232	51.23N	7.30E
Flinders, i., Austl.	196	39.35S	148.10E
Flinders, r., Austl.	196	18.48S	141.07E
Flinders, reg., Austl. (flĭn′dẽrz)	196	32.15S	138.45E
Flinders Reefs, rf., Austl.	196	17.30S	149.02E
Flin Flon, Can. (flĭn flŏn)	78	54.46N	101.53W
Flingern, neigh., Ger.	232	51.14N	6.49E
Flint, Wales, U.K.	138a	53.15N	3.07W
Flint, Mi., U.S.	90	43.00N	83.45W
Flint, r., Ga., U.S. (flĭnt)	90	31.25N	84.15W
Flora, Il., U.S. (flō′r*ȧ*)	92	38.40N	88.25W
Flora, In., U.S.	92	40.25N	86.30W
Florala, Al., U.S. (flŏr-ăl′*ȧ*)	108	31.01N	86.19W
Floral Park, N.Y., U.S. (flôr′*ă*l pärk)	94a	40.42N	73.42W
Florence, Italy	136	43.47N	11.15E
Florence, Al., U.S. (flŏr′*ĕ*ns)	90	34.46N	87.40W
Florence, Az., U.S.	102	33.00N	111.25W
Florence, Ca., U.S.	228	33.58N	118.15W
Florence, Co., U.S.	104	38.23N	105.08W
Florence, Ks., U.S.	104	38.14N	96.56W
Florence, S.C., U.S.	108	34.10N	79.45W
Florence, Wa., U.S.	100a	48.13N	122.21W
Florencia, Col. (flō-rĕn′sē-*ȧ*)	124	1.31N	75.13W
Florencio Sánchez, Ur. (flō-rĕn-sēō-sá′n-chĕz)	123c	33.52S	57.24W
Florencio Varela, Arg. (flō-rĕn′sē-ō vä-rā′lä)	126a	34.50S	58.16W
Florentia, S. Afr.	240b	26.16S	28.08E
Flores, Braz. (flō′rĕzh)	124	7.57S	37.48W
Flores, Guat.	114a	16.53N	89.54W
Flores, dept., Ur.	123c	33.33S	57.00W
Flores, neigh., Arg.	229d	34.38S	58.28W
Flores, i., Indon.	188	8.14S	121.08E
Flores, r., Arg.	123c	36.13S	60.28W
Flores, Laut (Flores Sea), sea, Indon.	188	7.09S	120.30E
Floresta, neigh., Arg.	229d	34.38S	58.29W
Floresville, Tx., U.S. (flō′rĕs-vĭl)	106	29.10N	98.08W
Floriano, Braz. (flō-rå-ä′nō)	124	6.17S	42.58W
Florianópolis, Braz. (flō-rē-ä-nō′pō-lēs)	126	27.30S	48.30W
Florida, Col. (flō-rē′dä)	124a	3.20N	76.12W
Florida, Cuba	116	22.10N	79.50W
Florida, S. Afr.	207b	26.11S	27.56E
Florida, N.Y., U.S. (flŏr′ĭ-d*ȧ*)	94a	41.20N	74.21W
Florida, Ur. (flō-rē-dhä)	126	34.06S	56.14W
Florida, dept., Ur. (flō-rē′dhä)	123c	33.48S	56.15W
Florida, state, U.S. (flŏr′ĭ-d*ȧ*)	90	30.30N	84.40W
Florida, i., Sol.Is.	196	8.56S	159.45E
Florida, Straits of, strt., N.A.	110	24.10N	81.00W
Florida Bay, b., Fl., U.S. (flŏr′ĭ-d*ȧ*)	109a	24.55N	80.55W
Florida Keys, is., Fl., U.S.	90	24.33N	81.20W
Florida Mountains, mts., N.M., U.S.	102	32.10N	107.35W
Florido, Río, r., Mex. (flō-rē′dō)	106	27.21N	104.48W
Floridsdorf, Aus. (flō′rĭds-dôrf)	139e	48.16N	16.25E
Florina, Grc. (flō-rē′nä)	142	40.48N	21.24E
Florissant, Mo., U.S. (flŏr′ĭ-s*ă*nt)	101e	38.47N	90.20W
Flotantes, Jardines, rec., Mex.	229a	19.16N	99.06W
Flourtown, Pa., U.S.	225b	40.07N	75.13W
Flower Hill, N.Y., U.S.	224	40.49N	73.41W
Floyd, r., Ia., U.S. (floid)	96	42.38N	96.15W
Floydada, Tx., U.S. (floi-dā′d*ȧ*)	104	33.59N	101.19W
Floyds Fork, r., Ky., U.S. (floi-dz)	95h	38.08N	85.30W
Flumendosa, r., Italy	154	39.45N	9.18E
Flushing, Mi., U.S. (flûsh′ĭng)	92	43.05N	83.50W
Flushing, neigh., N.Y., U.S.	224	40.45N	73.49W
Fly, r. (flī)	188	8.00S	141.45E
Foča, Bos. (fō′chä)	154	43.29N	18.48E
Fochville, S. Afr. (fōk′vĭl)	212d	26.29S	27.29E
Focşani, Rom. (fōk-shä′nė)	148	45.41N	27.17E
Fogang, China (fwo-gäŋ)	184	23.50N	113.35E
Foggia, Italy (fôd′jä)	142	41.30N	15.34E
Fogo, Can. (fō′gō)	86	49.43N	54.17W
Fogo, i., Can.	84	49.40N	54.13W
Fogo, i., C.V.	204b	14.46N	24.51W
Fohnsdorf, Aus. (fōns′dôrf)	148	47.13N	14.40E
Föhr, i., Ger. (fûr)	148	54.47N	8.30E
Foix, Fr. (fwä)	150	42.58N	1.34E
Fokku, Nig.	208	11.40N	4.31E
Folcroft, Pa., U.S.	225b	39.54N	75.17W
Folgares, Ang.	210	14.54S	15.08E
Foligno, Italy (fō-lēn′yō)	154	42.58N	12.41E
Folkeston, Eng., U.K.	144	51.05N	1.18E
Folkingham, Eng., U.K. (fō′kĭng-*ă*m)	138a	52.53N	0.24W
Folkston, Ga., U.S.	108	30.50N	82.01W
Folsom, Ca., U.S.	102	38.40N	121.10W
Folsom, N.M., U.S. (fōl′s*ŭ*m)	104	36.47N	103.56W
Folsom, Pa., U.S.	225b	39.54N	75.19W
Fomento, Cuba (fō-mĕ′n-tō)	116	21.35N	78.20W
Fómeque, Col. (fō′mē-kĕ)	124a	4.29N	73.52W
Fonda, Ia., U.S. (fŏn′d*ȧ*)	96	42.33N	94.51W
Fond du Lac, Wi., U.S. (fŏn dū lăk′)	90	43.47N	88.29W
Fond du Lac Indian Reservation, I.R., Mn., U.S.	96	46.44N	93.04W
Fondi, Italy (fōn′dē)	154	41.23N	13.25E
Fonsagrada, Spain (fōn-sä-grä′dhä)	152	43.08N	7.07W
Fonseca, Golfo de, b., N.A. (gôl-fô-dĕ-fōn-sā′kä)	110	13.09N	87.55W
Fontainebleau, Fr. (fôɴ-tĕn-blō′)	140	48.24N	2.42E
Fontainebleau, S. Afr.	240b	26.07S	27.59E
Fontana, Ca., U.S. (fŏn-tă′n*ȧ*)	101a	34.06N	117.27W
Fonte Boa, Braz. (fōn′tå bō′*ă*)	124	2.32S	66.05W
Fontenay-aux-Roses, Fr.	233c	48.47N	2.17E
Fontenay-le-Comte, Fr. (fôɴt-nĕ′lĕ-kôɴt′)	150	46.28N	0.53W
Fontenay-le-Fleury, Fr.	233c	48.49N	2.03E
Fontenay-sous-Bois, Fr.	233c	48.51N	2.29E
Fontenay-Trésigny, Fr. (fôɴ-te-hā′ tra-sēn-yē′)	151b	48.43N	2.53E
Fontenelle Reservoir, res., Wy., U.S.	98	42.05N	110.05W
Fontera, Punta, c., Mex. (po͞o′n-tä-fōn-tĕ′rä)	112	18.36N	92.43W
Fontibón, Col. (fōn-tē-bôn′)	124a	4.42N	74.09W
Fontur, c., Ice.	136	66.21N	14.02W
Foothills, S. Afr. (fōt-hĭls)	207b	25.55S	27.36E
Footscray, Austl.	195a	37.48S	144.54E
Fora, Ponta de, c., Braz.	230c	22.57S	43.07W
Foraker, Mount, mtn., Ak., U.S. (fŏr′*ȧ*-kẽr)	89	62.40N	152.40W
Forbach, Fr. (fōr′bäĸ)	150	49.12N	6.54E
Forbes, Austl. (fôrbz)	196	33.24S	148.05E
Forbes, Mount, mtn., Can.	80	51.52N	116.56W
Forbidden City, bldg., China	236b	39.55N	116.23E
Forchheim, Ger. (fôrĸ′hīm)	148	49.43N	11.05E
Fordham University, pt. of i., N.Y., U.S.	224	40.51N	73.53W
Fords, N.J., U.S.	224	40.32N	74.19W
Fordsburg, neigh., S. Afr.	240b	26.13S	28.02E
Fordyce, Ar., U.S. (fôr′dīs)	104	33.48N	92.24W
Forécariah, Gui. (fōr-kå-rē′ä′)	204	9.26N	13.06W
Forel, Mont, mtn., Grnld.	76	65.50N	37.41W
Forest, Ms., U.S. (fŏr′ĕst)	108	32.22N	89.29W
Forest, r., N.D., U.S.	96	48.08N	97.45W
Forest City, Ia., U.S.	96	43.14N	93.40W
Forest City, N.C., U.S.	108	35.20N	81.52W
Forest City, Pa., U.S.	92	41.35N	75.30W
Forest Gate, neigh., Eng., U.K.	231	51.33N	0.02E
Forest Grove, Or., U.S. (grōv)	100c	45.31N	123.07W
Forest Heights, Md., U.S.	225d	38.49N	77.00W
Forest Hill, Austl.	239b	37.50S	145.11E
Forest Hill, Md., U.S.	94e	39.35N	76.26W
Forest Hill, Tx., U.S.	101c	32.40N	97.16W
Forest Hill, neigh., Can.	223c	43.42N	79.24W
Forest Hills, Pa., U.S.	226b	40.26N	79.52W
Forest Hills, neigh., N.Y., U.S.	224	40.42N	73.51W
Forest Park, Il., U.S.	227a	41.53N	87.50W
Forest Park, neigh., Md., U.S.	225c	39.19N	76.41W
Forestville, Austl.	239a	33.46S	151.13E
Forestville, Can. (fŏr′ĕst-vĭl)	86	48.45N	69.06W
Forestville, Md., U.S.	94e	38.51N	76.55W
Forez, Monts du, mts., Fr. (môɴ dü fō-rā′)	150	44.55N	3.43E
Forfar, Scot., U.K. (fôr′f*ȧ*r)	144	57.10N	2.55W
Forillon, Parc National, rec., Can.	86	48.50N	64.05W
Forio, mtn., Italy (fô′ryō)	153c	40.29N	13.55E
Forked Creek, r., Il., U.S. (fôrk′d)	95a	41.16N	88.01W
Forked Deer, r., Tn., U.S.	108	35.53N	89.29W
Forli, Italy (fôr-lē′)	142	44.13N	12.03E
Formby, Eng., U.K. (fôrm′bė)	138a	53.34N	3.04W
Formby Point, c., Eng., U.K.	138a	53.33N	3.06W
Formentera, Isla de, i., Spain (ē′s-lä-dĕ-fōr-mĕn-tā′rä)	142	38.43N	1.25E
Formiga, Braz. (fōr-mē′gȧ)	124	20.27S	45.25W
Formigas Bank, bk. (fōr-mē′gäs)	116	18.30N	75.40W
Formosa, Arg. (fōr-mō′sä)	126	27.25S	58.12W
Formosa, Braz.	124	15.32S	47.10W
Formosa, prov., Arg.	126	24.30S	60.45W
Formosa, Serra, mts., Braz. (sĕ′r-rä)	124	12.59S	55.11W
Formosa Bay, b., Kenya	210	2.45S	40.30E
Formosa Strait, *see* Taiwan Strait, strt., Asia	180	24.30N	120.00E
Fornosovo, Russia (fōr-nô′sô vô)	164c	59.35N	30.34E
Forrest City, Ar., U.S. (for′ĕst sĭ′tĭ)	104	35.00N	90.46W
Forsayth, Austl. (fôr-sīth′)	196	18.33S	143.42E
Forshaga, Swe. (fôrs′hä′gä)	146	59.34N	13.25E
Forst, Ger. (fôrst)	140	51.45N	14.38E
Forsyth, Ga., U.S. (fôr-sīth′)	108	33.02N	83.56W
Forsyth, Mt., U.S.	98	46.15N	106.41W
Fort, neigh., India	236e	18.56N	72.50E
Fort Albany, Can. (fôrt ôl′b*ȧ* nĭ)	78	52.20N	81.30W
Fort Alexander Indian Reserve, I.R., Can.	82	50.27N	96.15W
Fortaleza, Braz. (fôr′tä-lā′zȧ) (sä-ä-rä′)	124	3.35S	38.31W
Fort Atkinson, Wi., U.S. (ăt′kĭn-s*ŭ*n)	96	42.55N	88.46W
Fort Beaufort, S. Afr. (bō′fôrt)	207c	32.47S	26.39E
Fort Belknap Indian Reservation, I.R., Mt., U.S.	98	48.16N	108.38W
Fort Bellefontaine, Mo., U.S. (bĕl-fōn-tān′)	101f	38.50N	90.15W
Fort Benton, Mt., U.S. (bĕn′t*ŭ*n)	98	47.51N	110.40W
Fort Berthold Indian Reservation, I.R., N.D., U.S. (bẽrth′ôld)	96	47.47N	103.28W
Fort Bragg, Ca., U.S.	102	39.26N	123.48W
Fort Branch, In., U.S. (brănch)	92	38.15N	87.35W
Fort Chipewyan, Can.	78	58.46N	111.15W
Fort Cobb Reservoir, res., Ok., U.S.	104	35.12N	98.28W
Fort Collins, Co., U.S. (kŏl′ĭns)	90	40.36N	105.04W
Fort Crampel, Cen. Afr. Rep. (kråm-pĕl′)	204	6.59N	19.11E
Fort-de-France, Mart. (dĕ fräɴs)	110	14.37N	61.06W
Fort Deposit, Al., U.S. (dē-pŏz′ĭt)	108	31.58N	86.35W
Fort-de-Possel, Cen. Afr. Rep. (dĕ pô-sĕl′)	204	5.03N	19.11E
Fort Dodge, Ia., U.S. (dŏj)	90	42.31N	94.10W
Fort Edward, N.Y., U.S. (wẽrd)	92	43.15N	73.30W
Fort Erie, Can. (ē′rĭ)	95c	42.55N	78.56W
Fortescue, r., Austl. (fôr′tĕs-kū)	196	21.25S	116.50E
Fort Fairfield, Me., U.S. (fâr′fēld)	86	46.46N	67.53W
Fort Fitzgerald, Can. (fĭts-jĕr′*ă*ld)	78	59.48N	111.50W
Fort Frances, Can. (frăn′s*ĕ*s)	78	48.36N	93.24W
Fort Frederica National Monument, rec., Ga., U.S. (frĕd′ĕ-rī-kȧ)	108	31.13N	85.25W
Fort Gaines, Ga., U.S. (gānz)	108	31.35N	85.03W
Fort Gibson, Ok., U.S. (gĭb′s*ŭ*n)	104	35.50N	95.13W
Fort Good Hope, Can. (go͝od hōp)	78	66.19N	128.52W
Forth, Firth of, b., Scot., U.K. (fûrth ŏv fôrth)	136	56.04N	3.03W
Fort Hall, Kenya (hôl)	206	0.47S	37.13E
Fort Hall Indian Reservation, I.R., Id., U.S.	98	43.02N	112.21W
Fort Howard, Md., U.S.	225c	39.12N	76.27W
Fort Huachuca, Az., U.S. (wä-cho͞o′kä)	102	31.30N	110.25W
Fortier, Can. (fôr′tyā′)	77f	49.56N	97.55W
Fort Jefferson National Monument, rec., Fl., U.S. (jĕf′ẽr-s*ŭ*n)	109a	24.42N	83.02W
Fort Kent, Me., U.S. (kĕnt)	86	47.14N	68.37W
Fort Langley, Can. (lăng′lĭ)	100d	49.10N	122.35W
Fort Lauderdale, Fl., U.S. (lô′dẽr-dāl)	109a	26.07N	80.09W
Fort Lee, N.J., U.S.	94a	40.50N	73.58W
Fort Liard, Can.	78	60.16N	123.34W
Fort Loudoun Lake, res., Tn., U.S. (fôrt lou′dĕn)	108	35.52N	84.10W
Fort Lupton, Co., U.S. (lŭp′t*ŭ*n)	104	40.04N	104.54W
Fort Macleod, Can. (m*ȧ*-ĸloud′)	78	49.43N	113.25W
Fort Madison, Ia., U.S. (măd′ĭ-s*ŭ*n)	96	40.40N	91.17W
Fort Matanzas, Fl., U.S. (mä-tän′zäs)	108	29.39N	81.17W
Fort McDermitt Indian Reservation, I.R., Or., U.S. (m*ă*k dẽr′mĭt)	98	42.04N	118.07W
Fort McHenry National Monument, pt. of i., Md., U.S.	225c	39.16N	76.35W
Fort McMurray, Can. (m*ȧ*k-mŭr′ĭ)	78	56.44N	111.23W
Fort McPherson, Can. (m*ȧ*k-fŭr′s′n)	78	67.37N	134.59W
Fort Meade, Fl., U.S. (mēd)	109a	27.45N	81.48W
Fort Mill, S.C., U.S. (mĭl)	108	35.03N	80.57W

ng-sing; ŋ-baŋk; ɴ-nasalized n; nŏd; c*ŏ*mmit; ōld; ôbey; ôrder; oi-boil; fo͞od; ŏ-as oo in foot; ou-out; s-soft; sh-dish; th-thin; pūre; ûnite; ûrn; stŭd; circ*ŭ*s; ü-as in French tu; ′-indeterminate vowel.

PLACE (Pronunciation)	PAGE	Lat. °′	Long. °′
Fort Mojave Indian Reservation, I.R., Ca., U.S. (mō-hä'vâ)	102	34.59N	115.02W
Fort Morgan, Co., U.S. (môr'găn)	104	40.14N	103.49W
Fort Myers, Fl., U.S. (mī'ĕrz)	109a	26.36N	81.45W
Fort Nelson, Can. (nĕl'sŭn)	78	58.57N	122.30W
Fort Nelson, r., Can. (nĕl'sŭn)	78	58.44N	122.20W
Fort Payne, Al., U.S. (pān)	108	34.26N	85.41W
Fort Peck, Mt., U.S. (pĕk)	98	47.58N	106.30W
Fort Peck Indian Reservation, I.R., Mt., U.S.	96	48.22N	105.40W
Fort Peck Lake, res., Mt., U.S.	90	47.52N	106.59W
Fort Pierce, Fl., U.S. (pērs)	109a	27.25N	80.20W
Fort Portal, Ug. (pôr'tȧl)	204	0.40N	30.16E
Fort Providence, Can. (prŏv'ĭ-dĕns)	78	61.27N	117.59W
Fort Pulaski National Monument, rec., Ga., U.S. (pu-lăs'kĭ)	108	31.59N	80.56W
Fort Qu'Appelle, Can.	82	50.46N	103.55W
Fort Randall Dam, dam, S.D., U.S.	96	42.48N	98.35W
Fort Resolution, Can. (rĕz'ō-lū'shŭn)	78	61.08N	113.42W
Fort Riley, Ks., U.S. (rī'lĭ)	104	39.05N	96.46W
Fort Saint James, Can. (fôrt sānt jāmz)	78	54.26N	124.15W
Fort Saint John, Can. (sānt jŏn)	78	56.15N	120.51W
Fort Sandeman, Pak. (săn'da-măn)	174	31.28N	69.29E
Fort Saskatchewan, Can. (săs-kăt'choo-ân)	77g	53.43N	113.13W
Fort Scott, Ks., U.S. (skŏt)	90	37.50N	94.43W
Fort Severn, Can. (sĕv'ērn)	78	55.58N	87.50W
Fort Shevchenko, Kaz. (shĕv-chĕn'kō)	160	44.30N	50.18E
Fort Sibut, Cen. Afr. Rep. (fôr sē-bü')	204	5.44N	19.05E
Fort Sill, Ok., U.S. (fôrt sĭl)	104	34.41N	98.25W
Fort Simpson, Can. (sĭmp'sŭn)	78	61.52N	121.48W
Fort Smith, Can.	78	60.09N	112.08W
Fort Smith, Ar., U.S. (smĭth)	90	35.23N	94.24W
Fort Stockton, Tx., U.S. (stŏk'tŭn)	106	30.54N	102.51W
Fort Sumner, N.M., U.S. (sŭm'nēr)	104	34.30N	104.17W
Fort Sumter National Monument, rec., S.C., U.S. (sŭm'tēr)	108	32.43N	79.54W
Fort Thomas, Ky., U.S. (tŏm'ăs)	95f	39.05N	84.27W
Fortuna, Ca., U.S. (fŏr-tū'nȧ)	98	40.36N	124.10W
Fortune, Can. (fôr'tůn)	86	47.04N	55.51W
Fortune, i., Bah.	116	22.35N	74.20W
Fortune Bay, b., Can.	79a	47.25N	55.25W
Fort Union National Monument, rec., N.M., U.S. (ūn'yŭn)	104	35.51N	104.57W
Fort Valley, Ga., U.S. (văl'ĭ)	108	32.33N	83.53W
Fort Vermilion, Can. (vēr-mĭl'yŭn)	78	58.23N	115.50W
Fort Victoria, *see* Masvingo, Zimb.	206	20.07S	30.47E
Fort Wayne, In., U.S. (wān)	90	41.00N	85.10W
Fort Wayne Military Museum, pt. of i., Mi., U.S.	226c	42.18N	83.06W
Fort William, Scot., U.K. (wĭl'yăm)	144	56.50N	3.00W
Fort William, hist., India	236a	22.33N	88.20E
Fort William, Mount, mtn., Austl. (wĭ'ĭ-ăm)	198	24.45S	151.15E
Fort Worth, Tx., U.S. (wûrth)	90	32.45N	97.20W
Fort Yukon, Ak., U.S. (yoo'kŏn)	90a	66.30N	145.00W
Fort Yuma Indian Reservation, I.R., Ca., U.S. (yoo'mä)	102	32.54N	114.47W
Foshan, China	180	23.02N	113.07E
Fossano, Italy (fôs-sä'nō)	154	44.34N	7.42E
Fossil Creek, r., Tx., U.S. (fŏs-ĭl)	101c	32.53N	97.19W
Fossombrone, Italy (fôs-sôm-brō'nä)	154	43.41N	12.48E
Foss Res, Ok., U.S.	104	35.38N	99.11W
Fosston, Mn., U.S. (fôs'tŭn)	96	47.34N	95.44W
Fosterburg, Il., U.S. (fŏs'tēr-bûrg)	101e	38.58N	90.04W
Foster City, Ca., U.S.	227b	37.34N	122.16W
Fostoria, Oh., U.S. (fŏs-tō'rĭ-ȧ)	92	41.10N	83.20W
Fougéres, Fr. (foo-zhâr')	140	48.23N	1.14W
Foula, i., Scot., U.K. (fou'lȧ)	144a	60.08N	2.04W
Foulwind, Cape, c., N.Z. (foul'wĭnd)	197a	41.45S	171.00E
Foumban, Cam. (foom-bän')	204	5.43N	10.55E
Fountain Creek, r., Co., U.S. (foun'tĭn)	104	38.36N	104.37W
Fountain Valley, Ca., U.S.	101a	33.42N	117.57W
Fourche la Fave, r., Ar., U.S. (foorsh lä fāv')	104	34.46N	93.45W
Fouriesburg, S. Afr. (fō'rēz-bûrg)	212d	28.38S	28.13E
Fourmies, Fr. (foor-mē')	150	50.01N	4.01E
Four Mountains, Islands of the, is., Ak., U.S.	89a	52.58N	170.40W
Fourqueux, Fr.	233c	48.53N	2.04E
Fourth Cataract, wtfl., Sudan	204	18.52N	32.07E
Fouta Djallon, mts., Gui. (foo'tä jä-lôN)	204	11.37N	12.29W
Foveaux Strait, strt., N.Z. (fō-vō')	197a	46.30S	167.43E
Fowler, Co., U.S. (foul'ēr)	104	38.04N	104.02W
Fowler, In., U.S.	92	40.35N	87.20W
Fowler, Point, c., Austl.	196	32.05S	132.30E
Fowlerton, Tx., U.S. (foul'ēr-tŭn)	106	28.26N	98.48W
Fox, i., Wa., U.S. (fŏks)	100a	47.15N	122.08W
Fox, r., Il., U.S.	96	41.35N	88.43W
Fox, r., Wi., U.S.	96	44.18N	88.23W
Foxboro, Ma., U.S. (fŏks'bŭrō)	87a	42.04N	71.15W
Fox Chapel, Pa., U.S.	226b	40.30N	79.55W
Foxe Basin, b., Can. (fŏks)	78	67.35N	79.21W
Foxe Channel, strt., Can.	78	64.30N	79.23W
Foxe Peninsula, pen., Can.	78	64.57N	77.26W
Fox Islands, is., Ak., U.S. (fŏks)	89a	53.04N	167.30W
Fox Lake, Il., U.S. (lăk)	95a	42.24N	88.11W
Fox Lake, l., Il., U.S.	95a	42.24N	88.07W
Fox Point, Wi., U.S.	95a	43.10N	87.54W
Fox Valley, Austl.	239a	33.45S	151.06E
Foyle, Lough, b., Eur. (lŏk foil')	144	55.07N	7.08W
Foz do Cunene, Ang.	210	17.16S	11.50E
Fraga, Spain (frä'gä)	152	41.31N	0.20E
Fragoso, Cayo, i., Cuba (kä'yō-frä-gō'sō)	116	22.45N	79.30W
Franca, Braz. (frä'n-kä)	124	20.28S	47.20W
Francavilla, Italy (fräŋ-kä-vēl'lä)	154	40.32N	17.37E
France, nation, Eur. (fråns)	136	46.39N	0.47E
Frances, l., Can. (frăn'sĭs)	78	61.27N	128.28W
Frances, Cabo, c., Cuba (kä'bō-frän-sĕ's)	116	21.55N	84.05W
Frances, Punta, c., Cuba (poo'n-tä-frän-sĕ's)	116	21.45N	83.10W
Francés Viejo, Cabo, c., Dom. Rep. (kȧ'bō-frän'sås vyā'hō)	116	19.40N	69.35W
Franceville, Gabon (fräns-vēl')	206	1.38S	13.35E
Francis Case, Lake, res., S.D., U.S. (från'sĭs)	90	43.15N	99.00W
Francisco Sales, Braz. (frän-sē's-kō-sȧ'lĕs)	123a	21.42S	44.26W
Francistown, Bots. (från'sis-toun)	206	21.17S	27.28E
Franconville, Fr.	233c	48.59N	2.14E
Frank, Pa., U.S.	226b	40.16N	79.48W
Frankby, Eng., U.K.	233a	53.22N	3.08W
Frankford, neigh., Pa., U.S.	225b	40.01N	75.05W
Frankfort, S. Afr. (frănk'fŏrt)	207c	32.43S	27.28E
Frankfort, S. Afr.	212d	27.17S	28.30E
Frankfort, Il., U.S. (frăŋk'fŭrt)	95a	41.30N	87.51W
Frankfort, In., U.S.	92	40.15N	86.30W
Frankfort, Ks., U.S.	104	39.42N	96.27W
Frankfort, Ky., U.S.	90	38.10N	84.55W
Frankfort, Mi., U.S.	92	44.40N	86.15W
Frankfort, N.Y., U.S.	92	43.05N	75.05W
Frankfurt am Main, Ger.	136	50.07N	8.40E
Frankfurt an der Oder, Ger.	140	52.20N	14.31E
Franklin, S. Afr.	207c	30.19S	29.28E
Franklin, In., U.S. (frănk'lĭn)	92	39.25N	86.00W
Franklin, Ky., U.S.	108	36.42N	86.34W
Franklin, La., U.S.	106	29.47N	91.31W
Franklin, Ma., U.S.	87a	42.05N	71.24W
Franklin, Mi., U.S.	226c	42.31N	83.18W
Franklin, Ne., U.S.	104	40.06N	99.01W
Franklin, N.H., U.S.	92	43.25N	71.40W
Franklin, N.J., U.S.	94a	41.08N	74.35W
Franklin, Oh., U.S.	92	39.30N	84.20W
Franklin, Pa., U.S.	92	41.25N	79.50W
Franklin, Tn., U.S.	108	35.54N	86.54W
Franklin, Va., U.S.	108	36.41N	76.57W
Franklin, l., Nv., U.S.	102	40.23N	115.10W
Franklin, District of, dept., Can.	78	70.46N	105.22W
Franklin D. Roosevelt Lake, res., Wa., U.S.	98	48.12N	118.43W
Franklin Mountains, mts., Can.	78	65.36N	125.55W
Franklin Park, Il., U.S.	95a	41.56N	87.53W
Franklin Park, Pa., U.S.	226b	40.35N	80.06W
Franklin Park, Va., U.S.	225d	38.55N	77.09W
Franklin Roosevelt Park, neigh., S. Afr.	240b	26.09S	27.59E
Franklin Square, N.Y., U.S.	94a	40.43N	73.40W
Franklinton, La., U.S. (frăŋk'lĭn-tŭn)	106	30.49N	90.09W
Frankston, Austl.	195a	38.09S	145.08E
Franksville, Wi., U.S. (frănkz'vĭl)	95a	42.46N	87.55W
Fransta, Swe.	146	62.30N	16.04E
Franz Josef Land, *see* Zemlya Frantsa-Iosifa, is., Russia	158	81.32N	40.00E
Frascati, Italy (fräs-kä'tē)	154	41.49N	12.45E
Fraser, Mi., U.S. (frā'zēr)	95b	42.32N	82.57W
Fraser, i., Austl.	196	25.12S	153.00E
Fraser, r., Can.	78	51.30N	122.00W
Fraserburgh, Scot., U.K. (frā'zēr-bûrg)	144	57.40N	2.01W
Fraser Plateau, plat., Can.	80	51.30N	122.00W
Frattamaggiore, Italy (frät-tä-mäg-zhyō'rē)	153c	40.41N	14.16E
Fray Bentos, Ur. (frī bĕn'tōs)	126	33.10S	58.19W
Frazee, Mn., U.S. (frā-zē')	96	46.42N	95.43W
Fraziers Hog Cay, i., Bah.	116	25.25N	77.55W
Frechen, Ger. (frĕ'kĕn)	151c	50.54N	6.49E
Fredericia, Den. (frĕdh-ĕ-rē'tsē-ȧ)	146	55.35N	9.45E
Frederick, Md., U.S. (frĕd'ēr-ĭk)	90	39.25N	77.25W
Frederick, Ok., U.S.	104	34.23N	99.01W
Frederick House, r., Can.	84	49.05N	81.20W
Fredericksburg, Tx., U.S. (frĕd'ēr-ĭkz-bûrg)	106	30.16N	98.52W
Fredericksburg, Va., U.S.	92	38.20N	77.30W
Fredericktown, Mo., U.S. (frĕd'ēr-ĭk-toun)	104	37.32N	90.16W
Fredericton, Can. (frĕd'ēr-ĭk-tn)	78	45.48N	66.39W
Frederikshavn, Den. (frĕdh'ĕ-rēks-houn)	140	57.27N	10.31E
Frederikssund, Den. (frĕdh'ĕ-rēks-sōn)	146	55.51N	12.04E
Fredersdorf bei Berlin, Ger.	234a	52.31N	13.44E
Fredonia, Col. (frē-dō'nyȧ)	124a	5.55N	75.40W
Fredonia, Ks., U.S. (frē-dō'nĭ-ȧ)	104	36.31N	95.50W
Fredonia, N.Y., U.S.	92	42.25N	79.20W
Fredrikstad, Nor. (frådh'rēks-städ)	140	59.14N	10.58E
Freeburg, Il., U.S. (frē'bûrg)	101e	38.26N	89.59W
Freehold, N.J., U.S. (frē'hōld)	94a	40.15N	74.16W
Freeland, Pa., U.S. (frē'lănd)	92	41.00N	75.50W
Freeland, Wa., U.S.	100a	48.01N	122.32W
Freels, Cape, c., Can. (frēlz)	86	46.37N	53.45W
Freelton, Can. (frēl'tŭn)	77d	43.24N	80.02W
Freeport, Bah.	116	26.30N	78.45W
Freeport, Il., U.S. (frē'pōrt)	90	42.19N	89.30W
Freeport, N.Y., U.S.	94a	40.39N	73.35W
Freeport, Tx., U.S.	106	28.56N	95.21W
Freetown, S.L. (frē'toun)	204	8.30N	13.15W
Fregenal de la Sierra, Spain (frā-hȧ-näl' dā lä syĕr'rä)	152	38.09N	6.40W
Fregene, Italy (frĕ-zhĕ'-nĕ)	153d	41.52N	12.12E
Freiberg, Ger. (frī'bĕrgh)	140	50.54N	13.18E
Freiburg, Ger.	140	48.00N	7.50E
Freienried, Ger. (frī'ĕn-rēd)	139d	48.20N	11.08E
Freirina, Chile (frå-ĭ-rē'nä)	126	28.35S	71.26W
Freisenbruch, neigh., Ger.	232	51.27N	7.06E
Freising, Ger. (frī'zĭng)	148	48.25N	11.45E
Fréjus, Fr. (frā-zhüs')	150	43.28N	6.46E
Fremantle, Austl. (frē'măn-t'l)	196	32.03S	116.05E
Fremont, Ca., U.S. (frē-mŏnt')	100b	37.33N	122.00W
Fremont, Mi., U.S.	92	43.25N	85.55W
Fremont, Ne., U.S.	96	41.26N	96.30W
Fremont, Oh., U.S.	92	41.20N	83.05W
Fremont, r., Ut., U.S.	102	38.20N	111.30W
Fremont Peak, mtn., Wy., U.S.	98	43.05N	109.35W
French Broad, r., Tn., U.S. (frĕnch brôd)	108	35.59N	83.01W
French Frigate Shoals, Hi., U.S.	88b	23.30N	167.10W
French Guiana, dep., S.A. (gē-ä'nä)	124	4.20N	53.00W
French Lick, In., U.S. (frĕnch lĭk)	92	38.35N	86.35W
Frenchman, r., N.A.	82	49.25N	108.30W
Frenchman Creek, r., Mt., U.S. (frĕnch-măn)	98	48.51N	107.20W
Frenchman Creek, r., Ne., U.S.	104	40.24N	101.50W
Frenchman Flat, Nv., U.S.	102	36.55N	116.11W
French Polynesia, dep., Oc.	2	15.00S	140.00W
French River, Mn., U.S.	101h	46.54N	91.54W
French's Forest, Austl.	239a	33.45S	151.14E
Freshfield, Eng., U.K.	233a	53.34N	3.04W
Freshfield, Mount, mtn., Can. (frĕsh'fēld)	80	51.44N	116.57W
Fresh Meadows, neigh., N.Y., U.S.	224	40.44N	73.48W
Fresnes, Fr.	233c	48.45N	2.19E
Fresnillo, Mex. (frås-nēl'yō)	110	23.10N	102.52W
Fresno, Col. (frĕs'nō)	124a	5.10N	75.01W
Fresno, Ca., U.S.	90	36.44N	119.46W
Fresno, r., Ca., U.S. (frĕz'nō)	102	37.00N	120.24W
Fresno Slough, Ca., U.S.	102	36.39N	120.12W
Freudenstadt, Ger. (froi'dĕn-shtät)	148	48.28N	8.26E
Freycinet Peninsula, pen., Austl. (frā-sē-nĕ')	198	42.13S	148.56E
Fria, Gui.	208	10.05N	13.32W
Fria, r., Az., U.S. (frē-ä)	102	34.03N	112.12W
Fria, Cape, c., Nmb. (frīȧ)	206	18.15S	12.10E
Friant-Kern Canal, can., Ca., U.S. (kûrn)	102	36.57N	119.37W
Frias, Arg. (frē-äs)	126	28.43S	65.03W
Fribourg, Switz. (frē-boor')	140	46.48N	7.07E
Fridley, Mn., U.S. (frĭd'lĭ)	101g	45.05N	93.16W
Friedberg, Ger. (frēd'bĕrgh)	139d	48.22N	11.00E
Friedenau, neigh., Ger.	234a	52.28N	13.20E
Friedland, Ger. (frēt'länt)	148	53.39N	13.34E
Friedrichsfeld, Ger.	232	51.38N	6.39E
Friedrichsfelde, neigh., Ger.	234a	52.31N	13.31E
Friedrichshafen, Ger. (frē-drĕks-häf'ĕn)	148	47.39N	9.28E
Friedrichshagen, neigh., Ger.	234a	52.27N	13.38E
Friedrichshain, neigh., Ger.	234a	52.31N	13.27E
Friemersheim, Ger.	232	51.23N	6.42E
Friend, Ne., U.S. (frĕnd)	104	40.40N	97.16W
Friends Colony, neigh., India	236d	28.34N	77.16E
Friendship International Airport, arpt., Md., U.S.	225c	39.11N	76.40W
Friendswood, Tx., U.S. (frĕnds'wŏd)	107a	29.31N	95.11W
Friern Barnet, neigh., Eng., U.K.	231	51.37N	0.10W
Fries, Va., U.S. (frēz)	108	36.42N	80.59W
Friesack, Ger. (frē'säk)	139b	52.44N	12.35E
Frillendorf, neigh., Ger.	232	51.28N	7.05E
Frio, Cabo, c., Braz. (kä'bō-frē'ō)	124	22.58S	42.08W
Frio R, Tx., U.S.	106	29.00N	99.15W
Frisian Islands, is., Neth. (frē'zhăn)	140	53.30N	5.20E
Friuli-Venezia Giulia, hist. reg., Italy	154	46.20N	13.20E
Frobisher Bay, b., Can.	78	62.49N	66.41W
Frobisher Lake, l., Can. (frŏb'ĭsh'ēr)	78	56.25N	108.20W
Frodsham, Eng., U.K. (frŏdz'ăm)	138a	53.18N	2.48W
Frohavet, b., Nor.	140	63.49N	9.12E
Frohnau, neigh., Ger.	234a	52.38N	13.18E
Frohnhausen, neigh., Ger.	232	51.27N	6.58E
Frome, Lake, l., Austl. (froom)	196	30.40S	140.13E
Frontenac, Ks., U.S. (frŏn'tē-năk)	104	37.27N	94.41W
Frontera, Mex. (frōn-tā'rä)	112	18.34N	92.38W
Front Range, mts., Co., U.S. (frŭnt)	104	40.59N	105.29W
Front Royal, Va., U.S. (frŭnt)	92	38.55N	78.10W
Frosinone, Italy (frō-zē-nō'nå)	154	41.38N	13.22E
Frostburg, Md., U.S. (frôst'bûrg)	92	39.40N	78.55W
Fruita, Co., U.S. (froot-ȧ)	102	39.10N	108.45W
Fryanovo, Russia (f'ryä'nô-vô)	164b	56.08N	38.28E
Fryazino, Russia (f'ryä'zĭ-nô)	164b	55.58N	38.05E
Frydlant, Czech. (frēd'länt)	148	50.56N	15.05E
Fryerning, Eng., U.K.	231	51.41N	0.22E
Fucheng, China (foo-chŭŋ)	182	37.53N	116.08E
Fuchu, Japan (foo'choo)	187a	35.41N	139.29E
Fuchun, r., China (foo-chon)	184	29.50N	120.00E
Fuego, vol., Guat. (fwā'gō)	114	14.29N	90.52W
Fuencarral, Spain (fuān-kär-räl')	153a	40.29N	3.42W
Fuensalida, Spain (fwān-sä-lē'dä)	152	40.04N	4.15W
Fuente, Mex. (fwĕ'n-tĕ')	106	28.39N	100.34W
Fuente de Cantos, Spain (fwĕn'tå dā kän'tōs)	152	38.15N	6.18W
Fuente el Saz, Spain (fwĕn'tå ĕl säth')	153a	40.39N	3.30W
Fuenteobejuna, Spain	152	38.15N	5.30W
Fuentesaúco, Spain (fwĕn-tå-sä-oo'kō)	152	41.18N	5.25W
Fuerte, Río del, r., Mex. (rē'ō-dĕl-foo-ĕ'r-tĕ)	110	26.15N	108.50W
Fuerte Olimpo, Para. (fwĕr'tå ō-lēm-pō)	126	21.10S	57.49W
Fuerteventura Island, i., Spain (fwĕr'tå-vĕn-too'rä)	204	28.24N	13.21W
Fuhai, China	180	47.01N	87.07E
Fuhlenbrock, neigh., Ger.	232	51.32N	6.54E
Fuji, Japan (joo'jē)	187	35.11N	138.44E
Fuji, r., Japan	187	35.20N	138.23E
Fujian, prov., China (foo-jyĕn)	180	25.40N	117.30E
Fujidera, Japan	187b	34.34N	135.37E
Fujiidera, Japan	238b	34.34N	135.36E
Fujin, China (foo-jyĭn)	180	47.13N	132.11E
Fuji San, mtn., Japan (foo'jē sän)	180	35.23N	138.44E
Fujisawa, Japan (foo'jē-sä'wa)	187a	35.20N	139.29E
Fujiyama, *see* Fuji San, mtn., Japan	180	35.23N	138.44E
Fukagawa, neigh., Japan	238a	35.40N	139.48E
Fukiai, neigh., Japan	238b	34.42N	135.12E

ăt; fīnăl; rāte; senåte; ärm; åsk; sofȧ; fâre; ch-choose; dh-as th in other; bē; ėvent; bĕt; recĕnt; cratēr; g-gō; gh-guttural g; bĭt; ĭ-short neutral; rīde; K-guttural k as ch in German ich;

PLACE (Pronunciation)	PAGE	Lat. °'	Long. °'
Fukuchiyama, Japan (fo͝o'kō-chē-yä'mȧ)	187	35.18N	135.07E
Fukue, i., Japan (fō-ko͞o'ā)	186	32.40N	129.02E
Fukui, Japan (fo͞o'ko͞o-ē)	180	36.05N	136.14E
Fukuoka, Japan (fo͞o'kō-ō'kȧ)	180	33.35N	130.23E
Fukuoka, Japan	187a	35.52N	139.31E
Fukushima, Japan (fo͞o'kō-shē'mȧ)	186	37.45N	140.29E
Fukushima, neigh., Japan	238b	34.42N	135.29E
Fukuyama, Japan (fo͞o'kō-yä'mȧ)	186	34.31N	133.21E
Fulda, Ger.	140	50.33N	9.41E
Fulda, r., Ger. (fo͝ol'dä)	148	51.05N	9.40E
Fulerum, neigh., Ger.	232	51.26N	6.57E
Fuling, China (fo͞o-lĭŋ)	180	29.40N	107.30E
Fullerton, Ca., U.S. (fo͝ol'ẽr-tŭn)	101a	33.53N	117.56W
Fullerton, La., U.S.	106	31.00N	93.00W
Fullerton, Ne., U.S.	96	41.21N	97.59W
Fulmer, Eng., U.K.	231	51.33N	0.34W
Fulton, Ky., U.S. (fŭl'tŭn)	108	36.30N	88.53W
Fulton, Mo., U.S.	104	38.51N	91.56W
Fulton, N.Y., U.S.	92	43.20N	76.25W
Fultondale, Al., U.S. (fŭl'tŭn-dāl)	94h	33.37N	86.48W
Funabashi, Japan (fo͞o'nȧ-bä'shē)	187	35.43N	139.59E
Funasaka, Japan	238b	34.49N	135.17E
Funaya, Japan (fo͞o-nä'yä)	187b	34.45N	135.52E
Funchal, Port. (fo͝on-shäl')	204	32.41N	16.15W
Fundación, Col. (fo͞on-dä-syō'n)	124	10.43N	74.13W
Fundão, Port. (fo͝on-douN')	152	40.08N	7.32W
Fundão, Ilha do, i., Braz.	230c	22.51S	43.14W
Funde, India	236e	18.54N	72.58E
Fundy, Bay of, b., Can. (fŭn'dĭ)	78	45.00N	66.00W
Fundy National Park, rec., Can.	78	45.38N	65.00W
Funing, China	182	39.55N	119.16E
Funing, China (fo͞o-nĭŋ)	184	33.55N	119.54E
Funing Wan, b., China	184	26.48N	120.35E
Funtua, Nig.	208	11.31N	7.17E
Furancungo, Moz.	210	14.55S	33.35E
Furbero, Mex. (fo͞or-bĕ'rô)	112	20.21N	97.32W
Furgun, mtn., Iran	174	28.47N	57.00E
Furmanov, Russia (fûr-mä'nôf)	160	57.14N	41.11E
Furnas, Represa de, res., Braz.	124	21.00S	46.00W
Furneaux Group, is., Austl. (fûr'nō)	196	40.15S	146.27E
Fürstenfeld, Aus. (für'stĕn-fĕlt)	148	47.02N	16.03E
Fürstenfeldbruck, Ger. (fur'stĕn-fĕld'bro͝ok)	139d	48.11N	11.16E
Fürstenwalde, Ger. (für'stĕn-väl-dĕ)	148	52.21N	14.04E
Fürth, Ger. (fürt)	140	49.28N	11.03E
Furuichi, Japan (fo͞o'rō-ē'chē)	187b	34.33N	135.37E
Fusa, Japan (fo͞o'sä)	187a	35.52N	140.08E
Fuse, Japan	187b	34.40N	135.33E
Fushimi, Japan (fo͞o'shē-mē)	187b	34.57N	135.47E
Fushun, China (fo͞o'sho͞on')	180	41.50N	124.00E
Fusong, China (fo͞o-soŋ)	184	42.12N	127.12E
Futatsubashi, Japan	238a	35.29N	139.30E
Futtsu, Japan (fo͞ot'so͞o')	187a	35.19N	139.49E
Futtsu Misaki, c., Japan (fo͞ot'tso͞o' mē-sä'kē)	187a	35.19N	139.46E
Fuwah, Egypt (fo͞o'wȧ)	212b	31.13N	30.35E
Fuxian, China (fo͞o shyĕn)	182	39.36N	121.59E
Fuxin, China (fo͞o-shyĭn)	184	42.05N	121.40E
Fuyang, China (fo͞o-yäŋ)	180	32.53N	115.48E
Fuyang, China	184	30.10N	119.58E
Fuyang, r., China (fo͞o-yäŋ)	182	36.59N	114.48E
Fuyu, China (fo͞o-yo͞o)	180	45.20N	125.00E
Fuzhou, China (fo͞o-jō)	180	26.02N	119.18E
Fuzhou, r., China	182	39.38N	121.43E
Fuzhoucheng, China (fo͞o-jō-chŭŋ)	182	39.46N	121.44E
Fyfield, Eng., U.K.	231	51.45N	0.16E
Fyn, i., Den. (fü''n)	146	55.24N	10.33E
Fyne, Loch, l., Scot., U.K. (fīn)	144	56.14N	5.10W
Fyresvatn, l., Nor.	146	59.04N	7.55E

G

PLACE (Pronunciation)	PAGE	Lat. °'	Long. °'
Gaalkacyo, Som.	212a	7.00N	47.30E
Gabela, Ang.	210	10.48S	14.20E
Gabès, Tun. (gä'bĕs)	204	33.51N	10.04E
Gabès, Golfe de, b., Tun.	204	32.22N	10.59E
Gabil, Chad	208	11.09N	18.12E
Gąbin, Pol. (gôN'bēn)	148	52.23N	19.47E
Gabon, nation, Afr. (gȧ-bôN')	206	0.30S	10.45E
Gaborone, Bots.	206	24.28S	25.59E
Gabriel, r., Tx., U.S. (gā'brĭ-ĕl)	106	30.38N	97.15W
Gabrovo, Bul. (gäb'rô-vō)	154	42.52N	25.19E
Gachsārān, Iran	176	30.12N	50.47E
Gacko, Bos. (gäts'kô)	154	43.10N	18.34E
Gadsden, Al., U.S. (gădz'dĕn)	90	34.00N	86.00W
Gadyach, Ukr. (gäd-yäch')	160	50.22N	33.59E
Găeşti, Rom. (gă-yĕsh'tē)	154	44.43N	25.21E
Gaeta, Italy (gä-å'tä)	154	41.18N	13.34E
Gaffney, S.C., U.S. (găf'nĭ)	108	35.04N	81.47W
Gafsa, Tun. (gäf'sä)	204	34.16N	8.37E
Gagarin, Russia	156	55.32N	34.58E
Gagnoa, I.C.	208	6.08N	5.56W
Gagny, Fr.	233c	48.53N	2.32E
Gahmen, neigh., Ger.	232	51.36N	7.32E
Gaillac-sur-Tarn, Fr. (gȧ-yäk'sür-tärn')	150	43.54N	1.52E
Gaillard Cut, reg., Pan. (gä-ēl-yä'rd)	110a	9.03N	79.42W
Gainesville, Fl., U.S. (gānz'vĭl)	90	29.40N	82.20W
Gainesville, Ga., U.S.	108	34.16N	83.48W
Gainesville, Tx., U.S.	104	33.38N	97.08W
Gainsborough, Eng., U.K. (gānz'bŭr-ô)	138a	53.23N	0.46W
Gairdner, Lake, l., Austl. (gârd'nẽr)	196	32.20S	136.30E
Gaithersburg, Md., U.S. (gā'thẽrs'bûrg)	94e	39.08N	77.13W
Gaixian, China (gī-shyĕn)	184	40.25N	122.20E
Galana, r., Kenya	210	3.00S	39.30E
Galapagar, Spain (gä-lä-pä-gär')	153a	40.36N	4.00W
Galapagos Islands, *see* Colón, Archipiélago de, is., Ec.	124	0.10S	87.45W
Galaria, r., Italy	153d	41.58N	12.21E
Galashiels, Scot., U.K. (găl-ȧ-shēlz)	144	55.40N	2.57W
Galata, neigh., Tur.	235f	41.01N	28.58E
Galati, Rom. (gȧ-lätz'ĭ)	136	45.25N	28.05E
Galatina, Italy (gä-lä-tē'nä)	154	40.10N	18.12E
Galátsion, Grc.	235d	38.01N	23.45E
Galaxídhion, Grc.	154	38.26N	22.22E
Galdhopiggen, mtn., Nor.	146	61.37N	8.17E
Galeana, Mex. (gä-lå-ä'nä)	106	24.50N	100.04W
Galena, Il., U.S. (gȧ-lē'nȧ)	96	42.26N	90.27W
Galena, In., U.S.	95h	38.21N	85.55W
Galena Peak, mtn., Tx., U.S.	107a	29.44N	95.14W
Galera, Cerro, mtn., Pan. (sĕ'r-rô-gä-lĕ'rä)	110a	8.55N	79.38W
Galeras, vol., Col. (gä-lĕ'räs)	124	0.57N	77.27W
Gales, r., Or., U.S. (gālz)	100c	45.33N	123.11W
Galesburg, Il., U.S. (gālz'bûrg)	90	40.56N	90.21W
Galesville, Wi., U.S. (gālz'vĭl)	96	44.04N	91.22W
Galeton, Pa., U.S. (gāl'tŭn)	92	41.45N	77.40W
Galich, Russia (gȧl'ĭch)	160	58.20N	42.38E
Galicia, hist. reg., Pol. (gȧ-lĭsh'ĭ-ȧ)	148	49.48N	21.05E
Galicia, hist. reg., Spain (gä-lē'thyä)	152	43.35N	8.03W
Galilee, l., Austl. (găl'ĭ-lē)	196	22.23S	145.09E
Galilee, Sea of, l., Isr.	173a	32.53N	35.45E
Galina Point, c., Jam. (gä-lē'nä)	116	18.25N	76.50W
Galion, Oh., U.S. (găl'ĭ-ŭn)	92	40.45N	82.50W
Galisteo, N.M., U.S. (gä-lĭs-tā'ō)	104	35.20N	106.00W
Gallarate, Italy (gäl-lä-rä'tä)	154	45.37N	8.48E
Gallardon, Fr. (gä-lär-dôN')	151b	48.31N	1.40E
Gallatin, Mo., U.S. (găl'ȧ-tĭn)	104	39.55N	93.58W
Gallatin, Tn., U.S.	108	36.23N	86.28W
Gallatin, r., Mt., U.S.	98	45.12N	111.10W
Galle, Sri L. (gäl)	175c	6.13N	80.10E
Gállego, r., Spain (gäl-yā'gō)	152	42.27N	0.37W
Gallinas, Punta de, c., Col. (gä-lyē'näs)	124	12.10N	72.10W
Gallipoli, Italy (gäl-lē'pô-lē)	154	40.03N	17.58E
Gallipoli, *see* Gelibolu, Tur.	142	40.25N	26.40E
Gallipoli Peninsula, pen., Tur.	154	40.23N	25.10E
Gallipolis, Oh., U.S. (găl-ĭ-pô-lēs)	92	38.50N	82.10W
Gällivare, Swe. (yĕl-ĭ-vär'ĕ)	140	68.06N	20.29E
Gallo, r., Spain (gäl'yō)	152	40.43N	1.42W
Gallup, N.M., U.S. (găl'ŭp)	90	35.30N	108.45W
Galty Mountains, mts., Ire.	144	52.19N	8.20W
Galva, Il., U.S. (găl'vȧ)	104	41.11N	90.02W
Galveston, Tx., U.S. (găl'vĕs-tŭn)	90	29.18N	94.48W
Galveston Bay, b., Tx., U.S.	90	29.39N	94.45W
Galveston I, Tx., U.S.	107a	29.12N	94.53W
Galvin, Austl.	239b	37.51S	144.49E
Galway, Ire.	136	53.16N	9.05W
Galway Bay, b., Ire. (gôl'wā)	144	53.10N	9.47W
Gamba, China (gäm-bä)	178	28.23N	89.42E
Gambaga, Ghana (gäm-bä'gä)	204	10.32N	0.26W
Gambela, Eth. (găm-bā'lȧ)	204	8.15N	34.33E
Gambia, nation, Afr. (găm'bē-ȧ)	204	13.38N	19.38W
Gambia (Gambie), r., Afr.	208	13.20N	15.55W
Gambie, r., Afr.	204	12.30N	13.00W
Gamboma, Congo (gäm-bō'mä)	206	1.53S	15.51E
Gamleby, Swe. (gäm'lĕ-bü)	146	57.54N	16.20E
Gan, r., China (gän)	184	26.50N	115.00E
Gandak, r., India	178	26.37N	84.22E
Gander, Can. (găn'dẽr)	78	48.57N	54.34W
Gander, r., Can.	86	49.10N	54.35W
Gander Lake, l., Can.	86	48.55N	55.40W
Gandhinagar, India	178	23.30N	72.47E
Gandi, Nig.	208	12.55N	5.49E
Gandía, Spain (gän-dē'ä)	152	38.56N	0.10W
Gangdisê Shan (Trans Himalayas), mts., China	180	30.25N	83.43E
Ganges, r., Asia (găn'jēz)	174	24.00N	89.30E
Ganges, Mouths of the, mth., Asia (găn'jēz)	174	21.18N	88.40E
Gangi, Italy (gän'jē)	154	37.48N	14.15E
Gangtok, India	174	27.15N	88.30E
Gannan, China (gän-nän)	184	47.50N	123.30E
Gannett Peak, mtn., Wy., U.S. (găn'ĕt)	90	43.10N	109.38W
Gano, Oh., U.S. (g'nō)	95f	39.18N	84.24W
Gänserndorf, Aus.	139e	48.21N	16.43E
Gansu, prov., China (gän-so͞o)	180	38.50N	101.10E
Ganwo, Nig.	208	11.13N	4.42E
Ganyu, China (gän-yo͞o)	182	34.52N	119.07E
Ganzhou, China (gän-jō)	180	25.50N	114.30E
Gao, Mali (gä'ō)	204	16.16N	0.03W
Gao'an, China (gou-än)	184	28.30N	115.02E
Gaobaita, China	236b	39.53N	116.30E
Gaobeidian, China	236b	39.54N	116.33E
Gaomi, China (gou-mē)	182	36.23N	119.46E
Gaoqiao, China (gou-chyou)	183b	31.21N	121.35E
Gaoshun, China (gou-shōn)	182	31.22N	118.50E
Gaotang, China (gou-täŋ)	182	36.52N	116.12E
Gaoyao, China (gou-you)	184	23.08N	112.25E
Gaoyi, China (gou-yē)	182	37.37N	114.39E
Gaoyou, China (gou-yō)	184	32.46N	119.26E
Gaoyou Hu, l., China (kä'ō-yo͞o'ho͞o)	182	32.42N	118.40E
Gap, Fr. (gȧp)	140	44.34N	6.08E
Gapan, Phil. (gä-pän)	189a	15.18N	120.56E
Gar, China	180	31.11N	80.35E
Garanhuns, Braz. (gä-rän-yo͞oNsh')	124	8.49S	36.28W
Garbagnate Milanese, Italy	234c	45.35N	9.05E
Garbatella, neigh., Italy	235c	41.52N	12.29E
Garber, Ok., U.S. (gär'bẽr)	104	36.28N	97.35W
Garches, Fr.	233c	48.51N	2.11E
Garching, Ger. (gär'kĕng)	139d	48.15N	11.39E
Garcia, Mex. (gär-sē'ä)	106	25.50N	100.37W
García de la Cadena, Mex.	112	21.14N	103.26W
Garda, Lago di, l., Italy (lä-gō-dē-gär'dä)	142	45.43N	10.26E
Gardanne, Fr. (gȧr-dȧn')	150a	43.28N	5.29E
Gardelegen, Ger. (gär-dĕ-lå'ghĕn)	148	52.32N	11.22E
Garden, i., Mi., U.S. (gär'd'n)	92	45.50N	85.50W
Gardena, Ca., U.S. (gär-dē'nȧ)	101a	33.53N	118.19W
Garden City, Ks., U.S.	104	37.58N	100.52W
Garden City, Mi., U.S.	95b	42.20N	83.21W
Garden City, N.Y., U.S.	224	40.43N	73.37W
Garden City Park, N.Y., U.S.	224	40.44N	73.40W
Garden Grove, Ca., U.S. (gär'd'n grōv)	101a	33.47N	117.56W
Garden Reach, India	178a	22.33N	88.17E
Garden River, Can.	101k	46.33N	84.10W
Gardēz, Afg.	178	33.43N	69.09E
Gardiner, Me., U.S. (gärd'nẽr)	86	44.12N	69.46W
Gardiner, Mt., U.S.	98	45.03N	110.43W
Gardiner, Wa., U.S.	100a	48.03N	122.55W
Gardiner Dam, dam, Can.	82	51.17N	106.51W
Gardner, Ma., U.S.	92	42.35N	72.00W
Gardner Canal, strt., Can.	80	53.28N	128.15W
Gardner Pinnacles, Hi., U.S.	88b	25.10N	167.00W
Gareloi, i., Ak., U.S. (gär-lo͞o-ä')	89a	51.40N	178.48W
Garenfeld, Ger.	232	51.24N	7.31E
Garfield, N.J., U.S. (gär'fēld)	94a	40.53N	74.06W
Garfield, N.J., U.S.	224	40.53N	74.07W
Garfield, Ut., U.S.	101b	40.45N	112.10W
Garfield Heights, Oh., U.S.	95d	41.25N	81.36W
Gargaliánoi, Grc. (gȧr-gä-lyä'nē)	154	37.07N	21.50E
Garges-lès-Gonesse, Fr.	233c	48.58N	2.25E
Gargždai, Lith. (gärgzh'dī)	146	55.43N	20.09E
Garibaldi, Mount, mtn., Can. (gâr-ĭ-băl'dē)	80	49.51N	123.01W
Garin, Arg. (gä-rē'n)	126a	34.25S	58.44W
Garissa, Kenya	210	0.28S	39.38E
Garland, Md., U.S.	225c	39.11N	76.39W
Garland, Tx., U.S. (gär'lănd)	101c	32.55N	96.39W
Garland, Ut., U.S.	98	41.45N	112.10W
Garm, Taj.	158	39.12N	70.28E
Garmisch-Partenkirchen, Ger. (gär'mēsh pär'tĕn-kĕr'kĕn)	148	47.38N	11.10E
Garnett, Ks., U.S. (gär'nĕt)	104	38.16N	95.15W
Garonne, r., Fr. (gȧ-rôn)	136	44.00N	1.00E
Garoua, Cam. (gär'wä)	204	9.18N	13.24E
Garrett, In., U.S. (găr'ĕt)	92	41.20N	85.10W
Garrison, Md., U.S.	225c	39.24N	76.45W
Garrison, N.Y., U.S. (găr'ĭ-sŭn)	94a	41.23N	73.57W
Garrison, N.D., U.S.	96	47.38N	101.24W
Garrovillas, Spain (gä-rô-vēl'yäs)	152	39.42N	6.30W
Garry, l., Can. (găr'ĭ)	78	66.16N	99.23W
Garsen, Kenya	210	2.16S	40.07E
Garson, Can.	84	46.34N	80.52W
Garstedt, Ger. (gär'shtĕt)	139c	53.40N	9.58E
Garston, Eng., U.K.	231	51.41N	0.23W
Garston, neigh., Eng., U.K.	233a	53.21N	2.53W
Gartenstadt, neigh., Ger.	232	51.30N	7.26E
Garulia, India	178a	22.48N	88.23E
Garwolin, Pol. (gär-vō'lēn)	148	51.54N	21.40E
Garwood, N.J., U.S.	224	40.39N	74.19W
Gary, In., U.S. (gā'rĭ)	90	41.35N	87.21W
Gary, W.V., U.S.	108	37.21N	81.33W
Garzón, Col. (gär-thōn')	124	2.13N	75.44W
Gasan, Phil. (gä-sän')	189a	13.19N	121.52E
Gasan-Kuli, Turk.	160	37.25N	53.55E
Gas City, In., U.S. (găs)	92	40.30N	85.40W
Gascogne, reg., Fr. (găs-kôn'yĕ)	150	43.45N	1.49W
Gasconade, r., Mo., U.S. (găs-kô-nād')	104	37.46N	92.15W
Gascoyne, r., Austl. (găs-koin')	196	25.15S	117.00E
Gashland, Mo., U.S. (găsh'-lănd)	101f	39.15N	94.35W
Gashua, Nig.	208	12.54N	11.00E
Gasny, Fr. (gäs-nē')	151b	49.05N	1.36E
Gaspé, Can.	78	48.50N	64.29W
Gaspé, Péninsule de, pen., Can.	78	48.30N	65.00W
Gasper Hernández, Dom. Rep. (gäs-pär' ĕr-nän'dāth)	116	19.40N	70.15W
Gassaway, W.V., U.S. (găs'ȧ-wā)	92	38.40N	80.45W
Gaston, Or., U.S. (găs'tŭn)	100c	45.26N	123.08W
Gastonia, N.C., U.S. (găs-tō'nĭ-ȧ)	108	35.15N	81.14W
Gastre, Arg. (gäs-trĕ)	126	42.12S	68.50W
Gata, Cabo de, c., Spain (kä'bô-dĕ-gä'tä)	142	36.42N	2.00W
Gata, Sierra de, mts., Spain (syĕr'rȧ dā gä'tä)	142	40.12N	6.39W
Gatchina, Russia (gä-chē'nȧ)	160	59.33N	30.08E
Gateacre, neigh., Eng., U.K.	233a	53.23N	2.51W
Gátes, Akrotírion, c., Cyp.	173a	34.30N	33.15E
Gateshead, Eng., U.K. (gāts'hĕd)	144	54.56N	1.38W
Gates of the Arctic National Park, rec., Ak., U.S.	89	67.45N	153.30W
Gatesville, Tx., U.S. (gāts'vĭl)	106	31.26N	97.34W
Gateway of India, hist., India	236e	18.55N	72.50E
Gâtine, Hauteurs de, hills, Fr.	150	46.40N	0.50W
Gatineau, Can. (gȧ'tē-nō)	77c	45.29N	75.38W
Gatineau, r., Can.	84	45.45N	75.50W
Gatineau, Parc de la, rec., Can.	84	45.32N	75.53W
Gatley, Eng., U.K.	233b	53.23N	2.14W
Gato Negro, Ven.	230a	10.33N	66.57W
Gattendorf, Aus.	139e	48.01N	17.00E
Gatun, Pan. (gä-to͞on')	114	9.16N	79.25W
Gatun, r., Pan.	110a	9.21N	79.40W
Gatún, Lago, l., Pan.	114	9.13N	79.24W
Gatun Locks, trans., Pan.	110a	9.16N	79.57W

PLACE (Pronunciation)	PAGE	Lat. °′	Long. °′
Gauhāti, India	174	26.09N	91.51E
Gauja, r., Lat. (gå′ò-yà)	146	57.10N	24.30E
Gaula, r., Nor.	146	62.55N	10.45E
Gāvanpāda, India	236e	18.57N	73.01E
Gávdhos, i., Grc. (gäv′dôs)	142	34.48N	24.08E
Gavins Point Dam, Ne., U.S. (gă′-vĭns)	96	42.47N	97.47W
Gāvkhūnī, Bātlāq-e, l., Iran	174	31.40N	52.48E
Gävle, Swe. (yĕv′lĕ)	136	60.40N	17.07E
Gävlebukten, b., Swe.	146	60.45N	17.30E
Gavrilov Posad, Russia (gá′vrê-lôf′ka po-sát)	156	56.34N	40.09E
Gavrilov-Yam, Russia (gá′vrê-lôf yäm′)	156	57.17N	39.49E
Gawler, Austl. (gô′lẽr)	196	34.35S	138.47E
Gawler Ranges, mts., Austl.	198	32.35S	136.30E
Gaya, India (gŭ′yä)(gī′á)	174	24.53N	85.00E
Gaya, Nig. (gä′yä)	204	11.58N	9.05E
Gaylord, Mi., U.S. (gā′lôrd)	92	45.00N	84.35W
Gayndah, Austl. (gān′däh)	198	25.43S	151.33E
Gaysin, Ukr.	160	48.46N	29.22E
Gayton, Eng., U.K.	233a	53.19N	3.06W
Gaza, Isr. Occ.	174	31.30N	34.29E
Gaziantep, Tur. (gä-zē-än′tĕp)	174	37.10N	37.30E
Gbarnga, Lib.	208	7.00N	9.29W
Gdańsk, Pol. (g′dänsk)	136	54.20N	18.40E
Gdov, Russia (g′dôf′)	160	58.44N	27.51E
Gdynia, Pol. (g′dĕn′yà)	140	54.29N	18.30E
Geary, Ok., U.S. (gē′rĭ)	104	35.36N	98.19W
Géba, r., Gui.-B.	208	12.25N	14.35W
Gebo, Wy., U.S. (gĕb′ō)	98	43.49N	108.13W
Ged, La., U.S. (gĕd)	106	30.07N	93.36W
Gediz, r., Tur.	142	38.44N	28.45E
Gedney, i., Wa., U.S. (gĕd-nê)	100a	48.01N	122.18W
Gedser, Den.	146	54.35N	12.08E
Gee Cross, Eng., U.K.	233b	53.26N	2.04W
Geel, Bel.	139a	51.09N	5.01E
Geelong, Austl. (jē-lông′)	196	38.06S	144.13E
Gegu, China (gŭ-gōō)	182	39.00N	117.30E
Ge Hu, l., China (gŭ hōō)	182	31.37N	119.57E
Geidam, Nig.	204	12.57N	11.57E
Geikie Range, mts., Austl. (gē′kê)	196	17.35S	125.32E
Geislingen, Ger. (gĭs′lĭng-ĕn)	148	48.37N	9.52E
Geist Reservoir, res., In., U.S. (gēst)	95g	39.57N	85.59W
Geita, Tan.	210	2.52S	32.10E
Gejiu, China (gŭ-jĭo)	184	23.32N	102.50E
Geldermalsen, Neth.	139a	51.53N	5.18E
Geldern, Ger. (gĕl′dĕrn)	151c	51.31N	6.20E
Gelibolu, Tur. (gĕl-lē′pô-lē)(gĕ-lĭb′ō-lò)	142	40.25N	26.40E
Gellep-Stratum, neigh., Ger.	232	51.20N	6.41E
Gellibrand, Point, c., Austl.	239b	37.52S	144.54E
Gel′myazov, Ukr.	156	49.49N	31.54E
Gelsenkirchen, Ger. (gĕl-zĕn-kĭrk-ĕn)	148	51.31N	7.05E
Gemas, Malay. (jĕm′ás)	173b	2.35N	102.37E
Gemena, Zaire	204	3.15N	19.46E
Gemlik, Tur. (gĕm′lĭk)	142	40.30N	29.10E
Genale (Jubba), r., Afr.	212a	5.15N	41.00E
General Alvear, Arg. (gĕ-nĕ-rál′ál-vĕ-á′r)	123c	36.04S	60.02W
General Arenales, Arg. (ä-rĕ-nä′lĕs)	123c	34.19S	61.16W
General Belgrano, Arg. (bĕl-grá′nò)	123c	35.45S	58.32W
General Cepeda, Mex. (sĕ-pĕ′dä)	106	25.24N	101.29W
General Conesa, Arg. (kô-nĕ′sä)	123c	36.30S	57.19W
General Guido, Arg. (gē′dô)	123c	36.41S	57.48W
General Lavalle, Arg. (lá-vá′l-yĕ)	123c	36.25S	56.55W
General Madariaga, Arg. (män-dá-rêä′gä)	126	36.59S	57.14W
General Pacheco, Arg.	229d	34.28S	58.37W
General Paz, Arg. (pá′z)	123c	35.30S	58.20W
General Pedro Antonio Santos, Mex.	112	21.37N	98.58W
General Pico, Arg. (pē′kô)	126	36.46S	63.44W
General Roca, Arg. (rô-kä)	126	39.01S	67.31W
General San Martin, Arg. (sän-már-tē′n)	126a	34.35S	58.32W
General Sarmiento (San Miguel), Arg.	126a	34.33S	58.43W
General Urquiza, neigh., Arg.	229d	34.34S	58.29W
General Viamonte, Arg. (vēá′môn-tĕ)	123c	35.01S	60.59W
General Zuazua, Mex. (zwä′zwä)	106	25.54N	100.07W
Genesee, r., N.Y., U.S. (jĕn-ê-sē′)	92	42.25N	78.10W
Geneseo, Il., U.S. (jē-nĕsêō)	92	41.28N	90.11W
Geneva (Genève), Switz.	136	46.14N	6.04E
Geneva, Al., U.S. (jē-nē′và)	108	31.03N	85.50W
Geneva, Il., U.S.	95a	41.53N	88.18W
Geneva, Ne., U.S.	104	40.32N	97.37W
Geneva, N.Y., U.S.	92	42.50N	77.00W
Geneva, Oh., U.S.	92	41.45N	80.55W
Geneva, Lake, l., Switz.	140	46.28N	6.30E
Genève, *see* Geneva, Switz.	136	46.14N	6.04E
Genichesk, Ukr. (gånê-chyĕsk′)	160	46.11N	34.47E
Genil, r., Spain (hå-nēl′)	152	37.15N	4.05W
Gennebreck, Ger.	232	51.19N	7.12E
Gennevilliers, Fr.	233c	48.56N	2.18E
Genoa, Italy	136	44.23N	9.52E
Genoa, Ne., U.S. (jen′ô-à)	104	41.26N	97.43W
Genoa City, Wi., U.S.	95a	42.31N	88.19W
Genova, Golfo di, b., Italy (gôl-fô-dē-jĕn′ō-vä)	136	44.10N	8.45E
Genovesa, i., Ec. (ĕ′s-lä-gĕ-nō-vĕ-sä)	124	0.08N	90.15W
Gent, Bel.	140	51.05N	3.40E
Genthin, Ger. (gĕn-tēn′)	148	52.24N	12.10E
Gentilly, Fr.	233c	48.49N	2.21E
Genzano di Roma, Italy (gzhĕnt-zá′-nô-dē-rō′mä)	153d	41.43N	12.49E
Geographe Bay, b., Austl. (jē-ô-graf′)	196	33.00S	114.00E
Geographe Channel, strt., Austl. (jēô′gră-fĭk)	196	24.15S	112.50E
Geokchay, Azer. (gĕ-ôk′chī)	160	40.40N	47.40E
George, l., N.Y., U.S. (jôrj)	92	43.40N	73.30W
George, Lake, l., N.A. (jôrg)	101k	46.26N	84.09W
George, Lake, l., Ug.	210	0.02N	30.25E
George, Lake, l., Fl., U.S. (jôr-ĭj)	108	29.10N	81.50W
George, Lake, l., In., U.S.	95a	41.31N	87.17W

PLACE (Pronunciation)	PAGE	Lat. °′	Long. °′
Georges, r., Austl.	195b	33.57S	151.00E
Georges Hall, Austl.	239a	33.55S	150.59E
George Town, Bah.	116	23.30N	75.50W
Georgetown, Can. (jôrg-toun)	77d	43.39N	79.56W
Georgetown, Can. (jôr-ĭj-toun)	86	46.11N	62.32W
Georgetown, Cay. Is.	116	19.20N	81.20W
Georgetown, Guy. (jôrj′toun)	124	7.45N	58.04W
George Town, Malay.	188	5.21N	100.09E
Georgetown, Ct., U.S.	94a	41.15N	73.25W
Georgetown, De., U.S.	92	38.40N	75.20W
Georgetown, Il., U.S.	92	40.00N	87.40W
Georgetown, Ky., U.S.	92	38.10N	84.35W
Georgetown, Md., U.S.	92	39.25N	75.55W
Georgetown, Ma., U.S. (jôrg-toun)	87a	42.43N	71.00W
Georgetown, S.C., U.S. (jôr-ĭj-toun)	108	33.22N	79.17W
Georgetown, Tx., U.S. (jôrg-toun)	106	30.37N	97.40W
Georgetown, neigh., D.C., U.S.	225d	38.54N	77.03W
Georgetown University, pt. of i., D.C., U.S.	225d	38.54N	77.04W
George Washington Birthplace National Monument, rec., Va., U.S. (jôrj wŏsh′ĭng-tŭn)	92	38.10N	77.00W
George Washington Carver National Monument, rec., Mo., U.S. (jôrg wăsh-ĭng-tŭn kär′vẽr)	104	36.58N	94.21W
George West, Tx., U.S.	106	28.20N	98.07W
Georgia, nation, Asia	158	42.17N	43.00E
Georgia, state, U.S. (jôr′ji-ä)	90	32.40N	83.50W
Georgia, Strait of, strt., N.A.	80	49.20N	124.00W
Georgiana, Al., U.S. (jôr-jē-ăn′à)	108	31.39N	86.44W
Georgian Bay, b., Can.	78	45.15N	80.50W
Georgian Bay Islands National Park, rec., Can.	84	45.20N	81.40W
Georgina, r., Austl. (jôr-jē′nà)	196	22.00S	138.15E
Georgiyevsk, Russia (gyôr-gyĕfsk′)	160	44.05N	43.30E
Gera, Ger. (gā′rä)	140	50.52N	12.06E
Geral, Serra, mts., Braz. (sĕr′rà zhå-räl′)	126	28.30S	51.00W
Geral de Goiás, Serra, mts., Braz. (zhå-räl′-dĕ-gô-yá′s)	124	14.22S	45.40W
Geraldton, Austl. (jĕr′ăld-tŭn)	196	28.40S	114.35E
Geraldton, Can.	78	49.43N	87.00W
Gerdview, S. Afr.	240b	26.10S	28.11E
Gérgal, Spain (gĕr′gäl)	152	37.08N	2.29W
Gering, Ne., U.S. (gē′rĭng)	96	41.49N	103.41W
Gerlachovský Štít, mtn., Czech.	148	49.12N	20.08E
Gerli, neigh., Arg.	229d	34.41S	58.23W
Germantown, Oh., U.S. (jûr′măn-toun)	92	39.35N	84.25W
Germantown, neigh., Pa., U.S.	225b	40.03N	75.11W
Germany, nation, Eur. (jûr′mà-nĭ)	136	51.00N	10.00E
Germiston, S. Afr. (jûr′mĭs-tŭn)	206	26.19S	28.11E
Gerona, Phil. (hā-rō′nä)	189a	15.36N	120.36E
Gerona, Spain (hĕ-rō′nä)	142	41.55N	2.48E
Gerrards Cross, Eng., U.K. (jĕrărds krŏs)	138b	51.34N	0.33W
Gers, r., Fr. (zhĕr)	152	43.25N	0.30E
Gersthofen, Ger. (gĕrst-hō′fĕn)	139d	48.26N	10.54E
Getafe, Spain (hä-tä′fā)	152	40.19N	3.44W
Gettysburg, Pa., U.S. (gĕt′ĭs-bûrg)	92	39.50N	77.15W
Gettysburg, S.D., U.S.	96	45.01N	99.59W
Getzville, N.Y., U.S.	226a	43.01N	78.46W
Gevelsberg, Ger. (gĕ-fĕls′bĕrgh)	151c	51.18N	7.20E
Geweke, neigh., Ger.	232	51.22N	7.25E
Ghāghra, r., India	174	26.00N	83.00E
Ghana, nation, Afr. (gän′ä)	204	8.00N	2.00W
Ghanzi, Bots. (gän′zē)	206	21.30S	22.00E
Ghārāpuri, India	236e	18.57N	72.56E
Ghardaïa, Alg. (gär-dä′ê-ä)	204	32.29N	3.38E
Gharo, Pak.	178	24.50N	68.35E
Ghāt, Libya	204	24.52N	10.16E
Ghātkopar, neigh., India	236e	19.05N	72.54E
Ghazāl, Bahr al-, r., Sudan	204	9.30N	30.00E
Ghazal, Bahr el, r., Chad (bär ĕl ghä-zäl′)	208	14.30N	17.00E
Ghāzipur, neigh., India	236d	28.38N	77.19E
Ghazzah, *see* Gaza, Isr. Occ.	174	31.30N	34.29E
Gheorgheni, Rom.	142	46.48N	25.30E
Gherla, Rom. (gĕr′lä)	148	47.01N	23.55E
Ghilizane, Alg.	204	35.43N	0.43E
Ghonda, neigh., India	236d	28.41N	77.16E
Ghondi, neigh., India	236d	28.42N	77.16E
Ghost Lake, Can.	77e	51.15N	114.46W
Ghudāmis, Libya	204	30.07N	9.26E
Ghūrīān, Afg.	176	34.21N	61.30E
Ghushuri, India	236a	22.37N	88.22E
Gia-dinh, Viet.	237m	10.48N	106.42E
Giannutri, Isola di, i., Italy (jän-nōō′trē)	154	42.15N	11.06E
Gibara, Cuba (hē-bä′rä)	116	21.05N	76.10W
Gibbsboro, N.J., U.S.	225b	39.50N	74.58W
Gibeon, Nmb. (gĭb′ê-ŭn)	206	25.15S	17.30E
Gibraleón, Spain (hē-brä-lå-ōn′)	152	37.24N	7.00W
Gibraltar, dep., Eur. (gĭ-bräl-tä′r)	136	36.08N	5.22W
Gibraltar, Strait of, strt.	136	35.55N	5.45W
Gibraltar Point, c., Can.	223c	43.36N	79.23W
Gibson City, Il., U.S. (gĭb′sŭn)	92	40.25N	88.20W
Gibson Desert, des., Austl.	196	24.45S	123.15E
Gibson Island, Md., U.S.	94e	39.05N	76.26W
Gibson Reservoir, res., Ok., U.S.	104	36.07N	95.08W
Giddings, Tx., U.S. (gĭd′ĭngz)	106	30.11N	96.55W
Gidea Park, neigh., Eng., U.K.	231	51.35N	0.12E
Gideon, Mo., U.S. (gĭd′ê-ŭn)	104	36.27N	89.56W
Gien, Fr. (zhē-äɴ′)	140	47.43N	2.37E
Giessen, Ger. (gēs′sĕn)	148	50.35N	8.40E
Gif-sur-Yvette, Fr.	233c	48.42N	2.08E
Gifu, Japan (gē′fōō)	180	35.25N	136.45E
Gig Harbor, Wa., U.S. (gĭg)	100a	47.20N	122.36W
Giglio, Isola del, i., Italy (jĕl′yō)	154	42.23N	10.55E
Gijón, Spain (hê-hōn′)	136	43.33N	5.37W
Gila, r., U.S. (hē′là)	90	33.00N	110.00W

PLACE (Pronunciation)	PAGE	Lat. °′	Long. °′
Gila Bend, Az., U.S.	102	32.59N	112.41W
Gila Cliff Dwellings National Monument, rec., N.M., U.S.	102	33.15N	108.20W
Gila River Indian Reservation, I.R., Az., U.S.	102	33.11N	112.38W
Gilbert, Mn., U.S. (gĭl′bẽrt)	96	47.27N	92.29W
Gilbert, r., Austl. (gĭl-bẽrt)	196	17.15S	142.09E
Gilbert, Mount, mtn., Can.	80	50.51N	124.20W
Gilbert Islands, is., Kir.	190	0.30S	174.00E
Gilboa, Mount, mtn., S. Afr. (gĭl-bô*a*)	207c	29.13N	30.17W
Gilford Island, i., Can. (gĭl′fẽrd)	80	50.45N	126.25W
Gilgit, Pak. (gĭl′gĭt)	174	35.58N	73.48E
Gil Island, i., Can. (gĭl)	80	53.13N	129.15W
Gillen, l., Austl. (jĭl′ĕn)	196	26.15S	125.15E
Gillett, Ar., U.S. (jĭ-lĕt′)	104	34.07N	91.22W
Gillette, Wy., U.S.	98	44.17N	105.30W
Gillingham, Eng., U.K. (gĭl′ĭng ăm)	144	51.23N	0.33E
Gilman, Il., U.S. (gĭl′măn)	92	40.45N	87.55W
Gilman Hot Springs, Ca., U.S.	101a	33.49N	116.57W
Gilmer, Tx., U.S. (gĭl′mẽr)	106	32.43N	94.57W
Gilmore, Ga., U.S. (gĭl′môr)	94c	33.51N	84.29W
Gilo, r., Eth.	204	7.40N	34.17E
Gilroy, Ca., U.S. (gĭl-roi′)	102	37.00N	121.34W
Giluwe, Mount, mtn., Pap. N. Gui.	188	6.04S	144.00E
Gimli, Can. (gĭm′lē)	82	50.39N	97.00W
Gimone, r., Fr. (zhē-mōn′)	150	43.26N	0.36E
Ginir, Eth.	204	7.13N	40.44E
Ginosa, Italy (jê-nō′zä)	154	40.35N	16.48E
Ginza, neigh., Japan	238a	35.40N	139.47E
Ginzo, Spain (hēn-thō′)	152	42.03N	7.43W
Gioia del Colle, Italy (jô′yä dĕl kôl′lā)	154	40.48N	16.55E
Girard, Ks., U.S. (jĭ-rärd′)	104	37.30N	94.50W
Girardot, Col. (hē-rär-dōt′)	124	4.19N	74.47W
Giresun, Tur. (ghĕr′ĕ-sòn′)	174	40.55N	38.20E
Girgaum, neigh., India	236e	18.57N	72.48E
Giridih, India (jē-rê-dê)	174	24.12N	86.18E
Gironde, r., Fr. (zhē-rōɴd′)	136	45.31N	1.00W
Girvan, Scot., U.K. (gûr′văn)	144	55.15N	5.01W
Gisborne, N.Z. (gĭz′bŭrn)	197a	38.40S	178.08E
Gisenyi, Rw.	206	1.43S	29.15E
Gisors, Fr. (zhē-zôr′)	150	49.19N	1.47E
Gitambo, Zaire	210	4.21N	24.45E
Gitega, Bdi.	206	3.39S	30.05E
Giurgiu, Rom. (jòr′jò)	154	43.53N	25.58E
Givet, Fr. (zhē-vĕ′)	150	50.08N	4.47E
Givors, Fr. (zhē-vôr′)	150	45.35N	4.46E
Giza, *see* Al Jīzah, Egypt	212b	30.01N	31.12E
Gizhiga, Russia (gē′zhi-gà)	158	61.59N	160.46E
Gizo, Sol.Is.	192e	8.06S	156.51E
Gizycko, Pol. (gĭ′zhĭ-ko)	140	54.03N	21.48E
Gjirokastër, Alb.	142	40.04N	20.10E
Gjøvik, Nor. (gyû′vêk)	140	60.47N	10.36E
Glabeek-Zuurbemde, Bel.	139a	50.52N	4.59E
Glace Bay, Can. (gläs bā)	86	46.12N	59.57W
Glacier Bay National Park, rec., Ak., U.S. (glā′shẽr)	90a	58.40N	136.50W
Glacier National Park, rec., Can.	78	51.45N	117.35W
Glacier Peak, mtn., Wa., U.S.	98	48.07N	121.10W
Glacier Point, c., Can.	100a	48.24N	123.59W
Gladbeck, Ger. (gläd′bĕk)	148	51.35N	6.59E
Gladdeklipkop, S. Afr.	212d	24.17S	29.36E
Gladesville, Austl.	239a	33.50S	151.08E
Gladstone, Austl. (glăd′stōn)	196	23.45S	152.00E
Gladstone, Austl.	196	33.15S	138.20E
Gladstone, Mi., U.S.	96	45.50N	87.04W
Gladstone, N.J., U.S.	94a	40.43N	74.39W
Gladstone, Or., U.S.	100c	45.23N	122.36W
Gladwin, Mi., U.S. (glăd′wĭn)	92	44.00N	84.25W
Gladwyne, Pa., U.S.	225b	40.02N	75.17W
Glåma, r., Nor.	136	61.30N	10.30E
Glarus, Switz. (glä′ròs)	148	47.02N	9.03E
Glasgow, Scot., U.K. (glás′gō)	136	55.54N	4.25W
Glasgow, Ky., U.S.	108	37.00N	85.55W
Glasgow, Mo., U.S.	104	39.14N	92.48W
Glasgow, Mt., U.S.	98	48.14N	106.39W
Glashütte, neigh., Ger.	232	51.13N	6.52E
Glassmanor, Md., U.S.	225d	38.49N	76.59W
Glassport, Pa., U.S. (glás′pōrt)	95e	40.19N	79.54W
Glassport, Pa., U.S.	226b	40.19N	79.54W
Glauchau, Ger. (glou′kou)	148	50.51N	12.28E
Glazov, Russia (glä′zôf)	158	58.05N	52.52E
Glehn, Ger.	232	51.10N	6.35E
Glen, r., Eng., U.K. (glĕn)	138a	52.44N	0.18W
Glénan, Îles de, is., Fr. (ĕl-dĕ-glā-näɴ′)	150	47.43N	4.42W
Glenarden, Md., U.S.	225d	38.56N	76.52W
Glen Burnie, Md., U.S. (bûr′nê)	94e	39.10N	76.38W
Glen Canyon, val., Ut., U.S.	102	37.10N	110.50W
Glen Canyon Dam, dam, Az., U.S. (glĕn kăn′yŭn)	90	36.57N	111.25W
Glen Canyon National Recreation Area, rec., U.S.	102	37.00N	111.20W
Glen Carbon, Il., U.S. (kär′bŏn)	101e	38.45N	89.59W
Glencoe, S. Afr. (glĕn-cô)	207c	28.14S	30.09E
Glencoe, Il., U.S.	95a	42.08N	87.45W
Glencoe, Mn., U.S. (glĕn′kō)	96	44.44N	94.07W
Glen Cove, N.Y., U.S. (kōv)	94a	40.51N	73.38W
Glendale, Az., U.S. (glĕn′dāl)	102	33.30N	112.15W
Glendale, Ca., U.S.	90	34.09N	118.15W
Glendale, Oh., U.S.	95f	31.16N	84.22W
Glendive, Mt., U.S. (glĕn′dīv)	90	47.08N	104.41W
Glendo, Wy., U.S.	98	42.32N	104.54W
Glendora, Ca., U.S. (glĕn-dō′rà)	101a	34.08N	117.52W
Glendora, N.J., U.S.	225b	39.50N	75.04W
Glen Echo, Md., U.S.	225d	38.58N	77.08W
Glenelg, r., Austl.	198	37.20S	141.30E
Glen Ellyn, Il., U.S. (glĕn ĕl′-lĕn)	95a	41.53N	88.04W
Glenfield, Austl.	239a	33.58S	150.54E

ăt; finăl; rāte; senåte; ärm; åsk; sof*a*; fâre; ch-choose; dh-as th in other; bē; êvent; bĕt; recĕnt; cratẽr; g-gō; gh-guttural g; bĭt; ĭ-short neutral; rīde; ĸ-guttural k as ch in German ich;

PLACE (Pronunciation)	PAGE	Lat. °′	Long. °′
Glen Head, N.Y., U.S.	224	40.50N	73.37W
Glenhuntly, Austl.	239b	37.54S	145.03E
Glen Innes, Austl. (ĭn′ĕs)	196	29.45S	152.02E
Glenmore, Md., U.S.	225c	39.11N	76.36W
Glenns Ferry, Id., U.S. (fĕr′ĭ)	98	42.58N	115.21W
Glen Olden, Pa., U.S. (ōl′d′n)	94f	39.54N	75.17W
Glenomra, La., U.S. (glĕn-mō′rȧ)	106	30.58N	92.36W
Glen Ridge, N.J., U.S.	224	40.49N	74.13W
Glen Rock, N.J., U.S.	224	40.58N	74.08W
Glenrock, Wy., U.S. (glĕn′rŏk)	98	42.50N	105.53W
Glenroy, Austl.	239b	37.42S	144.55E
Glens Falls, N.Y., U.S. (glĕnz fôlz)	92	43.20N	73.40W
Glenshaw, Pa., U.S. (glĕn′shô)	95e	40.33N	79.57W
Glenside, Pa., U.S.	225b	40.06N	75.09W
Glen Valley, Can.	100d	49.09N	122.30W
Glenview, Il., U.S. (glĕn′vū)	95a	42.04N	87.48W
Glenville, Ga., U.S. (glĕn′vĭl)	108	31.55N	81.56W
Glen Waverley, Austl.	239b	37.53S	145.10E
Glenwood, Ia., U.S.	96	41.03N	95.44W
Glenwood, Mn., U.S.	96	45.39N	95.23W
Glenwood, N.M., U.S.	102	33.19N	108.52W
Glenwood Landing, N.Y., U.S.	224	40.50N	73.39W
Glenwood Springs, Co., U.S.	102	39.35N	107.20W
Glienicke, Ger. (glē′nē-kē)	139b	52.38N	13.19E
Glinde, Ger. (glĕn′dĕ)	139c	53.32N	10.13E
Glittertinden, mtn., Nor.	146	61.39N	8.12E
Gliwice, Pol. (gwĭ-wĭt′sĕ)	140	50.18N	18.40E
Globe, Az., U.S. (glōb)	90	33.20N	110.50W
Globino, Ukr. (glô′bē-nô)	156	49.22N	33.17E
Głogów, Pol. (gwō′go͞ov)	140	51.40N	16.04E
Glommen, r., Nor. (glôm′ĕn)	146	60.03N	11.15E
Glonn, Ger. (glônn)	139d	47.59N	11.52E
Glorieuses, Îles, is., Reu.	206	11.28S	47.50E
Glossop, Eng., U.K. (glŏs′ŭp)	138a	53.26N	1.57W
Gloster, Ms., U.S. (glŏs′tēr)	108	31.10N	91.00W
Gloucester, Eng., U.K. (glŏs′tēr)	140	51.54N	2.11W
Gloucester, Ma., U.S.	87a	42.37N	70.40W
Gloucester City, N.J., U.S.	94f	39.53N	75.08W
Glouster, Oh., U.S. (glŏs′tēr)	92	39.35N	82.05W
Glover Island, i., Can. (glŭv′ēr)	86	48.44N	57.45W
Gloversville, N.Y., U.S. (glŭv′ērz-vĭl)	92	43.05N	74.20W
Glovertown, Can. (glŭv′ēr-toun)	86	48.41N	54.02W
Glubokoye, Bela. (glo͞o-bô-kō′yĕ)	160	55.08N	27.44E
Glückstadt, Ger. (glük-shtät)	139c	53.47N	9.25E
Glukhov, Ukr. (glo͞o′κôf′)	160	51.42N	33.52E
Glushkovo, Russia (glôsh′kô-vô)	156	51.21N	34.43E
Gmünden, Aus. (g′mün′dĕn)	148	47.57N	13.47E
Gniezno, Pol. (g′nyâz′nô)	140	52.32N	17.34E
Gnjilane, Yugo. (gnyē′lá-nĕ)	154	42.28N	21.27E
Goa, , India (gō′á)	174	15.45N	74.00E
Goascorán, Hond. (gō-äs′kō-rän′)	114	13.37N	87.43W
Goba, Eth. (gō′bä)	204	7.17N	39.58E
Gobabis, Nmb. (gō-bä′bĭs)	206	22.25S	18.50E
Gobi (Shamo), des., Asia (gō′bē)	180	43.29N	103.15E
Goble, Or., U.S. (gō′b'l)	100c	46.01N	122.53W
Goch, Ger. (gōk)	151c	51.35N	6.10E
Godāvari, r., India (gō-dä′vŭ-rē)	174	19.00N	78.30E
Goddards Soak, sw., Austl. (gŏd′ȧrdz)	196	31.20S	123.30E
Goderich, Can. (gōd′rĭch)	84	43.45N	81.45W
Godfrey, Il., U.S. (gŏd′frē)	101e	38.57N	90.12W
Godhavn, Grnld. (gōdh′håvn)	76	69.15N	53.30W
Gods, r., Can. (gŏdz)	82	55.17N	93.35W
Gods Lake, Can.	78	54.40N	94.09W
Godthåb, Grnld. (gŏt′hŏb)	76	64.10N	51.32W
Goéland, Lac au, l., Can.	84	49.47N	76.41W
Goffs, Ca., U.S. (gôfs)	102	34.57N	115.06W
Goff's Oak, Eng., U.K.	231	51.43N	0.05W
Gogebic, l., Mi., U.S. (gô-gē′bĭk)	96	46.24N	89.25W
Gogebic Range, mts., Mi., U.S.	96	46.37N	89.48W
Göggingen, Ger. (gûg′gĕn-gĕn)	139d	48.21N	10.53E
Gogland, i., Russia	146	60.04N	26.55E
Gogonou, Benin	208	10.50N	2.50E
Gogorrón, Mex. (gō-gô-rōn′)	112	21.51N	100.54W
Goiânia, Braz. (gō-yá′nyä)	124	16.41S	48.57W
Goiás, Braz. (gō-yá′s)	124	15.57S	50.10W
Goiás, state, Braz.	124	16.00S	48.00W
Goirle, Neth.	139a	51.31N	5.06E
Gökçeada, i., Tur.	154	40.10N	25.27E
Göksu, r., Tur. (gûk′so͞o′)	160	36.40N	33.30E
Gol, Nor. (gûl)	146	60.58N	8.54E
Golabāri, India	236a	22.36N	88.20E
Golax, Va., U.S. (gō′lăks)	108	36.41N	80.56W
Golcar, Eng., U.K. (gŏl′kȧr)	138a	53.38N	1.52W
Golconda, Il., U.S. (gŏl-kŏn′dȧ)	104	37.21N	88.32W
Gołdap, Pol. (gôl′dăp)	148	54.17N	22.17E
Golden, Can.	80	51.18N	116.58W
Golden, Co., U.S.	104	39.44N	105.15W
Goldendale, Wa., U.S. (gōl′dĕn-dāl)	98	45.49N	120.48W
Golden Gate, strt., Ca., U.S. (gōl′dĕn gāt)	100b	37.48N	122.32W
Golden Hinde, mtn., Can. (hīnd)	80	49.40N	125.45W
Golden's Bridge, N.Y., U.S.	94a	41.17N	73.41W
Golden Valley, Mn., U.S.	101g	44.58N	93.23W
Golders Green, neigh., Eng., U.K.	231	51.35N	0.12W
Goldfield, Nv., U.S. (gōld′fēld)	102	37.42N	117.15W
Gold Hill, mtn., Pan.	110a	9.03N	79.08W
Gold Mountain, mtn., Wa., U.S. (gōld)	100a	47.33N	122.48W
Goldsboro, N.C., U.S. (gōldz-bûr′ô)	108	35.23N	77.59W
Goldthwaite, Tx., U.S. (gōld′thwāt)	106	31.27N	98.34W
Goleniów, Pol. (gô-lĕ-nyŭf′)	148	53.33N	14.51E
Golets-Purpula, Gora, mtn., Russia	158	59.08N	115.22E
Golf, Il., U.S.	227a	42.03N	87.48W
Golfito, C.R. (gôl-fē′tō)	114	8.40N	83.12W
Golf Park Terrace, Il., U.S.	227a	42.03N	87.51W
Goliad, Tx., U.S. (gō-lĭ-ăd′)	106	28.40N	97.12W
Golo, r., Fr.	154	42.28N	9.18E
Golo Island, i., Phil. (gō′lō)	189a	13.38N	120.17E
Golovchino, Russia (gō-lôf′chē-nō)	156	50.34N	35.52E
Golyamo Konare, Bul. (gō′lȧ-mō-kō′nä-rĕ)	154	42.16N	24.33E
Golzow, Ger. (gōl′tsōv)	139b	52.17N	12.36E
Gombe, Nig.	204	10.19N	11.02E
Gomel', Bela. (go′mĕl′)	158	52.20N	31.03E
Gomel', prov., Bela. (Oblast)	156	52.18N	29.00E
Gomera Island, i., Spain (gô-mä′rä)	204	28.00N	18.01W
Gomez Farias, Mex. (gō′măz fä-rē′ás)	106	24.59N	101.02W
Gómez Palacio, Mex. (pä-lä′syō)	110	25.35N	103.30W
Gonaïves, Haiti (gō-nȧ-ēv′)	110	19.25N	72.45W
Gonaïves, Golfe des, b., Haiti (gō-nȧ-ēv′)	116	19.20N	73.20W
Gonâve, Île de la, i., Haiti (gô-nȧv′)	110	18.50N	73.30W
Gonda, India	178	27.13N	82.00E
Gondal, India	178	22.02N	70.47E
Gonder, Eth.	204	12.39N	37.30E
Gonesse, Fr. (gô-nĕs′)	151b	48.59N	2.28E
Gongga Shan, mtn., China (gôŋ-gä shän)	180	29.16N	101.46E
Goniri, Nig.	208	11.30N	12.20E
Gonō, r., Japan (gō′nō)	187	35.00N	132.25E
Gonor, Can. (gō′nŏr)	77f	50.04N	96.57W
Gonubie, S. Afr. (gŏn′o͞o-bē)	207c	32.56S	28.02E
Gonzales, Mex. (gôn-zá′lĕs)	112	22.47N	98.26W
Gonzales, Tx., U.S. (gŏn-zä′lĕz)	106	29.31N	97.25W
González Catán, Arg. (gôn-zá′lĕz-kä-tá′n)	126a	34.47S	58.39W
Good Hope, Cape of, c., S. Afr. (kăp ov go͝od hōp)	206	34.21S	18.29E
Good Hope Mountain, mtn., Can.	80	51.09N	124.10W
Gooding, Id., U.S. (go͝od′ĭng)	98	42.55N	114.43W
Goodland, In., U.S. (go͝od′lănd)	92	40.50N	87.15W
Goodland, Ks., U.S.	104	39.19N	101.43W
Goodwood, S. Afr. (go͝od′wo͝od)	206a	33.54S	18.33E
Goole, Eng., U.K. (go͞ol)	138a	53.42N	0.52W
Goose, r., N.D., U.S.	96	47.40N	97.41W
Gooseberry Creek, r., Wy., U.S. (go͞os-bĕr′ĭ)	98	44.04N	108.35W
Goose Creek, r., Id., U.S. (go͞os)	98	42.07N	113.53W
Goose Lake, l., Ca., U.S.	98	41.56N	120.35W
Gorakhpur, India (gō′rŭk-po͞or)	174	26.45N	82.39E
Gorda, Punta, c., Cuba (po͞o′n-tä-gôr-dä)	116	22.25N	82.10W
Gorda Cay, i., Bah. (gôr′dä)	116	26.05N	77.30W
Gordon, Can. (gôr′dŭn)	77f	50.00N	97.20W
Gordon, Ne., U.S.	96	42.47N	102.14W
Gordons Corner, Md., U.S.	225d	39.50N	76.57W
Gore, Eth. (gō′rĕ)	204	8.12N	35.34E
Gore Hill, Austl.	239a	33.49S	151.11E
Gorgān, Iran	174	36.44N	54.30E
Gorgona, Isola di, Italy (gôr-gō′nä)	142	43.27N	9.55E
Gori, Geor. (gō′rē)	160	42.00N	44.08E
Gorinchem, Neth. (gō′rĭn-kĕm)	139a	51.50N	4.59E
Goring, Eng., U.K. (gôr′ĭng)	138b	51.30N	1.08W
Gorizia, Italy (gō-rē′tsē-yä)	154	45.56N	13.40E
Gor'kiy, see Nizhniy Novgorod, Russia	158	56.15N	44.05E
Gor'kovskoye, res., Russia	158	56.38N	43.40E
Gor'kovskoye, res., Russia	160	57.00N	43.55E
Gorlice, Pol. (gôr-lē′tsĕ)	148	49.38N	21.11E
Görlitz, Ger. (gûr′lĭts)	140	51.10N	15.01E
Gorlovka, Ukr. (gôr′lôf-ká)	160	48.17N	38.03E
Gorman, Tx., U.S. (gôr′măn)	106	32.13N	98.40W
Gorna Oryakhovitsa, Bul. (gôr′nä-ôr-yĕk′ô-vē-tsá)	154	43.08N	25.40E
Gornji Milanovac, Yugo. (gôrn′yē-mē′la-nô-väts)	154	44.02N	20.29E
Gorno-Altay Autonomous Oblast, prov., Russia	162	51.00N	86.00E
Gorno-Altaysk, Russia (gôr′nŭ′ŭl-tīsk′)	158	51.58N	85.58E
Gorodēnka, Ukr. (gō-rô-deŋ′kä)	148	48.40N	25.30E
Gorodishche, Russia (gô-rô′dĭsh-chĕ)	164a	57.57N	57.03E
Gorodnya, Ukr. (gô-rŏd′′nyä)	156	51.54N	31.31E
Gorodok, Bela.	156	55.27N	29.58E
Gorodok, Russia	158	50.30N	103.58E
Gorodok, Ukr. (gô-rô-dôk′)	148	49.47N	23.39E
Gorontalo, Indon. (gō-rōn-tä′lo)	188	0.40N	123.04E
Gorton, neigh., Eng., U.K.	233b	53.27N	2.10W
Goryn', r., Eur. (gō′rĕn′)	148	50.55N	26.07E
Gorzów Wielkopolski, Pol. (gô-zho͞ov′vyĕl-ko-pōl′skē)	140	53.44N	15.15E
Gosely, Eng., U.K.	138a	52.33N	2.10W
Gosen, Ger.	234a	52.24N	13.43E
Goshen, In., U.S. (gō′shĕn)	92	41.35N	85.50W
Goshen, Ky., U.S.	95h	38.24N	85.34W
Goshen, N.Y., U.S.	94a	41.24N	74.19W
Goshen, Oh., U.S.	95f	39.14N	84.09W
Goshute Indian Reservation, I.R., Ut., U.S. (gō-sho͞ot′)	102	39.50N	114.00W
Goslar, Ger. (gôs′lär)	148	51.55N	10.25E
Gospa, r., Ven. (gôs-pä)	125b	9.43N	64.23W
Gostivar, Mac. (gos′tē-vär)	154	41.46N	20.58E
Gostynin, Pol. (gôs-tē′nĭn)	148	52.24N	19.30E
Göta, r., Swe. (gõëtä)	146	58.11N	12.03E
Göta Kanal, can., Swe. (yû′tȧ)	146	58.35N	15.24E
Gotanno, neigh., Japan	238a	35.46N	139.49E
Göteborg, Swe. (yû′tĕ-bôrgh)	136	57.39N	11.56E
Gotel Mountains, mts., Afr.	208	7.05N	11.20E
Gotera, El Sal. (gō-tä′rä)	114	13.41N	88.06W
Gotha, Ger. (gō′tȧ)	140	50.47N	10.43E
Gothenburg, Ne., U.S. (gŏth′ĕn-bûrg)	104	40.57N	100.08W
Gotland, i., Swe.	136	57.35N	17.35E
Gotska Sandön, i., Swe.	146	58.24N	19.15E
Götterswickerhamm, Ger.	232	51.35N	6.40E
Göttingen, Ger. (gŭt′ĭng-ĕn)	148	51.32N	9.57E
Gouda, Neth. (gou′dä)	139a	52.00N	4.42E
Gough, i., St. Hel. (gŏf)	2	40.00S	10.00W
Gouin, Réservoir, res., Can.	78	48.15N	74.15W
Goukou, China (gō-kō)	180	48.45N	121.42E
Goulais, r., Can.	84	46.45N	84.10W
Goulburn, Austl. (gōl′bŭrn)	196	34.47S	149.40E
Goumbati, mtn., Sen.	208	13.08N	12.06W
Goumbou, Mali (go͞om-bo͞o′)	204	14.59N	7.27W
Gouna, Cam.	208	8.32N	13.34E
Goundam, Mali (go͞on-däɴ′)	204	16.29N	3.37W
Gournay-sur-Marne, Fr.	233c	48.52N	2.34E
Goussainville, Fr.	233c	49.01N	2.28E
Gouverneur, N.Y., U.S. (gŭv-ēr-no͞or′)	92	44.20N	75.25W
Go-vap, Viet.	237m	10.49N	106.42E
Govenlock, Can. (gŭvĕn-lŏk)	78	49.15N	109.48W
Governador, Ilha do, i., Braz. (gô-vĕr-nä-dō-′r-ē-lä′dō)	126b	22.48S	43.13W
Governador Portela, Braz. (pōr-tĕ′lȧ)	126b	22.28S	43.30W
Governador Valadares, Braz. (vä-lä-dä′rĕs)	124	18.47S	41.45W
Governor's Harbour, Bah.	116	25.15N	76.15W
Gowanda, N.Y., U.S. (gô-wŏn′dȧ)	92	42.30N	78.55W
Goya, Arg. (gō′yä)	126	29.06S	59.12W
Goyt, r., Eng., U.K. (goit)	138a	53.19N	2.03W
Graaff-Reinet, S. Afr. (gräf′rī′nĕt)	206	32.10S	24.40E
Gračac, Cro. (grä′chäts)	154	44.16N	15.50E
Gračanica, Bos.	154	44.42N	18.18E
Graceville, Fl., U.S. (grās′vĭl)	108	30.57N	85.30W
Graceville, Mn., U.S.	96	45.33N	96.25W
Gracias, Hond. (grä′sē-äs)	114	14.35N	88.37W
Graciosa Island, i., Port. (grä-syō′sä)	204a	39.07N	27.30W
Gradačac, Bos. (gra-dä′chats)	142	44.50N	18.28E
Gradizhsk, Ukr. (grä-dēzhsk′)	156	49.12N	33.06E
Grado, Spain (grä′dō)	152	43.24N	6.04W
Gräfelfing, Ger. (grä′fĕl-fĕng)	139d	48.07N	11.27E
Grafenberg, neigh., Ger.	232	51.14N	6.50E
Grafing bei München, Ger. (grä′fĕng)	139d	48.03N	11.58E
Grafton, Austl. (graf′tŭn)	196	29.38S	153.05E
Grafton, Il., U.S.	101e	38.58N	90.26W
Grafton, Ma., U.S.	87a	42.13N	71.41W
Grafton, N.D., U.S.	96	48.24N	97.25W
Grafton, Oh., U.S.	95d	41.16N	82.04W
Grafton, W.V., U.S.	92	39.20N	80.00W
Gragnano, Italy (grän-yä′nô)	153c	40.27N	14.32E
Graham, N.C., U.S. (grā′ăm)	108	36.03N	79.23W
Graham, Tx., U.S.	104	33.07N	98.34W
Graham, Wa., U.S.	100a	47.03N	122.18W
Graham, i., Can.	78	53.50N	132.40W
Grahamstown, S. Afr. (grā′ăms′toun)	207c	33.19S	26.33E
Grajewo, Pol. (grä-yä′vo)	148	53.38N	22.28E
Grama, Serra de, mtn., Braz. (sĕ′r-rä-dĕ-grá′mȧ)	123a	20.42S	42.28W
Gramada, Bul. (grä′mä-dä)	154	43.46N	22.41E
Gramatneusiedl, Aus.	139e	48.02N	16.29E
Grampian Mountains, mts., Scot., U.K. (grăm′pĭ-ăn)	136	56.30N	4.55W
Granada, Nic. (grä-nä′dhä)	110	11.55N	85.58W
Granada, Spain (grä-nä′dä)	142	37.13N	3.37W
Gran Bajo, reg., Arg. (grȧn′bȧ′kō)	126	47.35S	68.45W
Granbury, Tx., U.S. (grăn′bĕr-ĭ)	106	32.26N	97.45W
Granby, Can. (grăn′bĭ)	78	45.30N	72.40W
Granby, Mo., U.S.	104	36.54N	94.15W
Granby, l., Co., U.S.	104	40.07N	105.40W
Gran Canaria Island, i., Spain (grän′kä-nä′rē-ä)	204	27.39N	15.39W
Gran Chaco, reg., S.A. (grán′chá′kō)	126	25.30S	62.15W
Grand, i., Mi., U.S.	96	46.37N	86.38W
Grand, l., Can.	86	45.59N	66.15W
Grand, l., Me., U.S.	86	45.17N	67.42W
Grand, r., Can.	84	43.45N	80.20W
Grand, r., Mi., U.S.	92	42.58N	85.13W
Grand, r., Mo., U.S.	104	39.50N	93.52W
Grand, r., S.D., U.S.	96	45.40N	101.55W
Grand, North Fork, r., U.S.	96	45.52N	102.49W
Grand, South Fork, r., S.D., U.S.	96	45.38N	102.56W
Grand Bahama, i., Bah.	110	26.35N	78.30W
Grand Bank, Can. (grănd băngk)	79a	47.06N	55.47W
Grand Bassam, I.C. (gräɴ bȧ-säɴ′)	204	5.12N	3.44W
Grand Bourg, Guad. (gräɴ bo͞or′)	115b	15.54N	61.20W
Grand Caicos, i., T./C. Is. (grănd kä-ē′kōs)	116	21.45N	71.50W
Grand Canal, can., Ire.	144	53.21N	7.15W
Grand Canal, see Da Yunhe, can., China	180	35.00N	117.00E
Grand Canyon, Az., U.S.	102	36.05N	112.10W
Grand Canyon, val., Az., U.S.	90	35.50N	113.16W
Grand Canyon National Park, rec., Az., U.S.	90	36.15N	112.20W
Grand Cayman, i., Cay. Is. (kā′măn)	110	19.15N	81.15W
Grand Coulee Dam, dam, Wa., U.S. (ko͞o′lē)	90	47.58N	119.28W
Grande, r., Arg.	123b	35.25S	70.14W
Grande, r., Mex.	112	17.37N	96.41W
Grande, r., Nic. (grän′dĕ)	114	13.01N	84.21W
Grande, r., Ur.	123c	33.19S	57.15W
Grande, Arroyo, r., Mex. (är-rō′yō-grä′n-dĕ)	112	23.30N	98.45W
Grande, Bahía, b., Arg. (bä-ē′ä-grán′dĕ)	126	50.45S	68.00W
Grande, Boca, mth., Ven. (bŏ′kä-grä′n-dĕ)	124	8.46N	60.17W
Grande, Cuchilla, mts., Ur. (ko͞o-chē′l-yä)	126	33.00S	55.15W
Grande, Ilha, i., Braz. (grän′dĕ)	123a	23.11S	44.14W
Grande, Río, r., Bol.	124	16.49S	63.19W
Grande, Rio, r., Braz.	124	19.48S	49.54W
Grande, Rio, r., N.A. (grăn′dā)	90	26.50N	99.10W
Grande, Salinas, l., Arg. (sä-lē′näs)	126	29.45S	65.00W
Grande, Salto, wtfl., Braz. (säl-tō)	124	16.18S	39.38W
Grande Cayemite, Île, i., Haiti	116	18.45N	73.45W
Grande de Otoro, r., Hond. (grä′dą dā ô-tō′rô)	114	14.42N	88.21W
Grande de Santiago, Río, r., Mex. (rēō-grä′n-dĕ-dĕ-sän-tyá′gō)	110	20.30N	104.00W

ng-sing; ŋ-baŋk; ɴ-nasalized n; nŏd; cŏmmit; ōld; ôbey; ôrder; oi-boil; fo͞od; ŏ-as oo in foot; ou-out; s-soft; sh-dish; th-thin; pūre; ûnite; ûrn; stŭd; circŭs; ü-as in French tu; ′-indeterminate vowel.

PLACE (Pronunciation)	PAGE	Lat. °′	Long. °′
Grande Pointe, Can. (grănd point′)	77f	49.47N	97.03W
Grande Prairie, Can. (prâr′ĭ)	78	55.10N	118.48W
Grand Erg Occidental, des., Alg.	204	30.00N	1.00E
Grand Erg Oriental, des., Alg.	204	30.00N	7.00E
Grande Rivière du Nord, Haiti (rē-vyâr′ dü nôr′)	116	19.35N	72.10W
Grande Ronde, r., Or., U.S. (rônd′)	98	45.32N	117.52W
Gran Desierto, des., Mex. (grän-dĕ-syĕ′r-tô)	102	32.14N	114.28W
Grande Terre, i., Guad.	115b	16.28N	61.13W
Grande Vigie, Pointe de la, c., Guad. (grăɴd vē-gē′)	115b	16.32N	61.25W
Grand Falls, Can. (fôlz)	79a	48.56N	55.40W
Grandfather Mountain, mtn., N.C., U.S. (grănd-fä-thẽr)	108	36.07N	81.48W
Grandfield, Ok., U.S. (grănd′fēld)	104	34.13N	98.39W
Grand Forks, Can. (fôrks)	78	49.02N	118.27W
Grand Forks, N.D., U.S.	90	47.55N	97.05W
Grand Haven, Mi., U.S. (hā′v′n)	92	43.05N	86.15W
Grand I, N.Y., U.S.	95c	43.03N	78.58W
Grand Island, Ne., U.S. (ī′lănd)	90	40.56N	98.20W
Grand Island, N.Y., U.S.	226a	42.49N	78.58W
Grand Junction, Co., U.S. (jŭngk′shŭn)	90	39.05N	108.35W
Grand Lake, l., Can. (lāk)	79a	49.00N	57.10W
Grand Lake, l., La., U.S.	106	29.57N	91.25W
Grand Lake, l., Mn., U.S.	101h	46.54N	92.26W
Grand Ledge, Mi., U.S. (lĕj)	92	42.45N	84.50W
Grand Lieu, Lac de, l., Fr. (grăɴ′-lyû)	150	47.00N	1.45W
Grand Manan, i., Can. (mă-năn)	86	44.40N	66.50W
Grand Mère, Can. (grăɴ mâr′)	78	46.36N	72.43W
Grândola, Port. (grăɴ′dô-lă)	152	38.10N	8.36W
Grand Portage Indian Reservation, I.R., Mn., U.S. (pōr′tĭj)	96	47.54N	89.34W
Grand Portage National Monument, rec., Mi., U.S.	96	47.59N	89.47W
Grand Prairie, Tx., U.S. (prē′rē)	101c	32.45N	97.00W
Grand Rapids, Can.	82	53.08N	99.20W
Grand Rapids, Mi., U.S. (răp′ĭdz)	90	43.00N	85.45W
Grand Rapids, Mn., U.S.	96	47.16N	93.33W
Grand-Riviere, Can.	86	48.26N	64.30W
Grand Teton, mtn., Wy., U.S.	90	43.46N	110.50W
Grand Teton National Park, Wy., U.S. (tē′tŏn)	98	43.54N	110.15W
Grand Traverse Bay, b., Mi., U.S. (trăv′ẽrs)	92	45.00N	85.30W
Grand Turk, T./C. Is. (tûrk)	116	21.30N	71.10W
Grand Turk, i., T./C. Is.	116	21.30N	71.10W
Grandview, Mo., U.S. (grănd′vyōō)	101f	38.53N	94.32W
Grandyle, N.Y., U.S.	226a	43.00N	78.57W
Grange Hill, Eng., U.K.	231	51.37N	0.05E
Granger, Wy., U.S. (grān′jẽr)	98	41.37N	109.58W
Grangeville, Id., U.S. (grānj′vĭl)	98	45.56N	116.08W
Granite, Md., U.S.	225c	39.21N	76.51W
Granite City, Il., U.S. (grăn′ĭt sĭt′ĭ)	101e	38.42N	90.09W
Granite Falls, Mn., U.S. (fôlz)	96	44.46N	95.34W
Granite Falls, N.C., U.S.	108	35.49N	81.25W
Granite Falls, Wa., U.S.	100a	48.05N	121.59W
Granite Lake, l., Can.	86	48.01N	57.00W
Granite Peak, mtn., Mt., U.S.	90	45.13N	109.48W
Graniteville, S.C., U.S. (grăn′ĭt-vĭl)	108	33.35N	81.50W
Granito, Braz. (grä-nē′tô)	124	7.39S	39.34W
Granma, prov., Cuba	116	20.10N	76.50W
Gränna, Swe. (grĕn′ȧ)	146	58.02N	14.38E
Granollers, Spain (grä-nôl-yĕrs′)	152	41.36N	2.19E
Gran Pajonal, reg., Peru (grä′n-pä-ĸô-näl′)	124	11.14S	71.45W
Gran Paradiso, mtn., Italy	154	45.32N	7.16E
Gran Piedra, mtn., Cuba (grän-pyĕ′drä)	116	20.00N	75.40W
Grantham, Eng., U.K. (grăn′tăm)	144	52.54N	0.38W
Grant Park, Il., U.S. (grȧnt pärk)	95a	41.14N	87.39W
Grant Park, pt. of i., Il., U.S.	227a	41.52N	87.37W
Grants Pass, Or., U.S. (grȧnts pȧs)	98	42.26N	123.20W
Granville, Austl.	239a	33.50S	151.01E
Granville, Fr. (grăɴ-vēl′)	140	48.52N	1.35W
Granville, N.Y., U.S. (grăn′vĭl)	92	43.25N	73.15W
Granville, l., Can.	78	56.18N	100.30W
Grão Mogol, Braz. (grouɴ′ mô-gôl′)	124	16.34S	42.35W
Grapevine, Tx., U.S. (grāp′vīn)	101c	32.56N	97.05W
Gräso, i., Swe.	146	60.30N	18.35E
Grass, r., N.Y., U.S.	92	44.45N	75.10W
Grass Cay, i., V.I.U.S.	111c	18.22N	64.50W
Grasse, Fr. (gräs)	150	43.39N	6.57E
Grassendale, neigh., Eng., U.K.	233a	53.21N	2.54W
Grass Mountain, mtn., Wa., U.S. (grȧs)	100a	47.13N	121.48W
Grates Point, c., Can. (grāts)	86	48.09N	52.57W
Gravelbourg, Can. (grăv′ĕl-bôrg)	78	49.53N	106.34W
Gravesend, Eng., U.K. (grāvz′ĕnd′)	138b	51.26N	0.22E
Gravina, Italy (grä-vē′nä)	154	40.48N	16.27E
Gravois, Pointe à, c., Haiti (grȧ-vwä′)	116	18.00N	74.20W
Gray, Fr. (grå)	150	47.26N	5.35E
Grayling, Mi., U.S. (grā′lĭng)	92	44.40N	84.40W
Grays, Eng., U.K.	231	51.29N	0.20E
Grays Harbor, b., Wa., U.S. (grās)	90	46.55N	124.23W
Grayslake, Il., U.S. (grāz′lāk)	95a	42.20N	88.20W
Grays Peak, mtn., Co., U.S. (grāz)	104	39.29N	105.52W
Grays Thurrock, Eng., U.K. (thŭ′rŏk)	138b	51.28N	0.19E
Grayvoron, Russia (grȧ-ē′vô-rôn)	156	50.28N	35.41E
Graz, Aus. (gräts)	136	47.05N	15.26E
Greasby, Eng., U.K.	233a	53.23N	3.07W
Great Abaco, i., Bah. (ä′bä-kō)	110	26.30N	77.05W
Great Altcar, Eng., U.K.	233a	53.33N	3.01W
Great Artesian Basin, basin, Austl. (är-tēzh-ăn bā-sĭn)	196	23.16S	143.37E
Great Australian Bight, bt., Austl. (ôs-trā′lĭ-ăn bīt)	196	33.30S	127.00E
Great Bahama Bank, bk. (bă-hā′mă)	116	25.00N	78.50W
Great Barrier, i., N.Z. (băr′ĭ-ẽr)	197a	36.10S	175.30E

PLACE (Pronunciation)	PAGE	Lat. °′	Long. °′
Great Barrier Reef, rf., Austl. (bă-rĭ-ẽr rēf)	196	16.43S	146.34E
Great Basin, basin, U.S. (grāt bā′s′n)	90	40.08N	117.10W
Great Bear Lake, l., Can. (bâr)	78	66.10N	119.53W
Great Bend, Ks., U.S. (bĕnd)	104	38.41N	98.46W
Great Bitter Lake, l., Egypt	212b	30.24N	32.27E
Great Blasket Island, i., Ire. (blăs′kĕt)	144	52.05N	10.55W
Great Bookham, Eng., U.K.	231	51.16N	0.22W
Great Burstead, Eng., U.K.	231	51.36N	0.25E
Great Corn Island, i., Nic.	114	12.10N	82.54W
Great Crosby, Eng., U.K.	233a	53.29N	3.01W
Great Dismal Swamp, sw., U.S. (dĭz′măl)	108	36.35N	76.34W
Great Divide Basin, basin, Wy., U.S. (dĭ-vīd′ bā′s′n)	98	42.10N	108.10W
Great Dividing Range, mts., Austl. (dĭ-vī-dĭng rānj)	196	35.16S	146.38E
Great Duck, i., Can. (dŭk)	84	45.40N	83.22W
Greater Antilles, is., N.A.	110	20.30N	79.15W
Greater Khingan Range, mts., China (dä hĭŋ-gän lĭŋ)	180	46.30N	120.00E
Greater Leech Indian Reservation, I.R., Mn., U.S. (grāt′ẽr lēch)	96	47.39N	94.27W
Greater Manchester, co., Eng., U.K.	138a	53.34N	2.41W
Greater Sunda Islands, is., Asia	188	4.00S	108.00E
Great Exuma, i., Bah. (ĕk-sōō′mä)	116	23.35N	76.00W
Great Falls, Mt., U.S. (fôlz)	90	47.30N	111.15W
Great Falls, S.C., U.S.	108	34.32N	80.53W
Great Falls, Va., U.S.	225d	39.00N	77.17W
Great Guana Cay, i., Bah. (gwä′nä)	116	24.00N	76.20W
Great Harbor Cay, i., Bah. (kē)	116	25.45N	77.50W
Great Inagua, i., Bah. (ē-nä′gwä)	110	21.00N	73.15W
Great Indian Desert, des., Asia	174	27.35N	71.37E
Great Isaac, i., Bah. (ī′zȧk)	116	26.05N	79.05W
Great Karroo, plat., S. Afr. (grāt kă′rōō)	206	32.45S	22.00E
Great Kills, neigh., N.Y., U.S.	224	40.33N	74.10W
Great Namaland, hist. reg., Nmb.	206	25.45S	16.15E
Great Neck, N.Y., U.S. (nĕk)	94a	40.48N	73.44W
Great Nicobar Island, i., India (nĭk-ô-bär′)	188	7.00N	94.18E
Great Oxney Green, Eng., U.K.	231	51.44N	0.25E
Great Parndon, Eng., U.K.	231	51.45N	0.05E
Great Pedro Bluff, c., Jam.	116	17.50N	78.05W
Great Pee Dee, r., S.C., U.S. (pē-dē′)	90	34.01N	79.26W
Great Plains, The, pl., N.A. (plāns)	76	45.00N	104.00W
Great Ragged, i., Bah.	116	22.10N	75.45W
Great Ruaha, r., Tan.	206	7.30S	37.00E
Great Salt Lake, l., Ut., U.S. (sôlt lāk)	90	41.19N	112.48W
Great Salt Lake Desert, des., Ut., U.S.	90	41.00N	113.30W
Great Salt Plains Reservoir, res., Ok., U.S.	104	36.56N	98.14W
Great Sand Dunes National Monument, rec., Co., U.S.	104	37.56N	105.25W
Great Sand Hills, hills, Can. (sănd)	82	50.35N	109.05W
Great Sandy Desert, des., Austl. (săn′dē)	196	21.50S	123.10E
Great Sandy Desert, des., Or., U.S. (săn′dĭ)	98	43.43N	120.44W
Great Sitkin, i., Ak., U.S. (sĭt-kĭn)	89a	52.18N	176.22W
Great Slave Lake, l., Can. (slāv)	78	61.37N	114.58W
Great Smoky Mountains National Park, rec., U.S. (smōk-ē)	90	35.43N	83.20W
Great Stirrup Cay, i., Bah. (stĭr-ŭp)	116	25.50N	77.55W
Great Sutton, Eng., U.K.	233a	53.17N	2.56W
Great Victoria Desert, des., Austl. (vĭk-tō′rĭ-ă)	196	29.45S	124.30E
Great Wall, hist., China	180	38.00N	109.00E
Great Waltham, Eng., U.K. (wôl′thŭm)	138b	51.47N	0.27E
Great Warley, Eng., U.K.	231	51.35N	0.17E
Great Yarmouth, Eng., U.K. (yär-mŭth)	140	52.35N	1.45E
Grebbestad, Swe. (grĕb-bĕ-städh)	146	58.42N	11.15E
Gréboun, Mont, mtn., Niger	204	20.00N	8.35E
Greco, neigh., Italy	234c	45.30N	9.13E
Gredos, Sierra de, mts., Spain (syĕr′rä dā grā′dōs)	152	40.13N	5.30W
Greece, nation, Eur. (grēs)	136	39.00N	21.30E
Greeley, Co., U.S. (grē′lĭ)	90	40.25N	104.41W
Green, r., U.S.	90	38.30N	110.10W
Green, r., Ky., U.S. (grēn)	108	37.13N	86.30W
Green, r., N.D., U.S.	96	47.05N	103.05W
Green, r., Ut., U.S.	102	38.30N	110.05W
Green, r., Wa., U.S.	100a	47.17N	121.57W
Green, r., Wy., U.S.	98	41.08N	110.27W
Greenbank, Wa., U.S. (grēn′bănk)	100a	48.06N	122.35W
Green Bay, Wi., U.S.	90	44.30N	88.04W
Green Bay, b., U.S.	90	44.55N	87.40W
Green Bayou, Tx., U.S.	107a	29.53N	95.13W
Greenbelt, Md., U.S. (grēn′bĕlt)	94e	38.59N	76.53W
Greenbrae, Ca., U.S.	227b	37.57N	122.31W
Greencastle, In., U.S. (grēn-kȧs′'l)	92	39.40N	86.50W
Green Cay, i., Bah.	116	24.05N	77.10W
Green Cove Springs, Fl., U.S. (kōv)	108	29.56N	81.42W
Greendale, Wi., U.S. (grēn′dāl)	95a	42.56N	87.59W
Greenfield, In., U.S. (grēn′fēld)	92	39.45N	85.40W
Greenfield, Ia., U.S.	96	41.16N	94.30W
Greenfield, Ma., U.S.	92	42.35N	72.35W
Greenfield, Mo., U.S.	104	37.23N	93.48W
Greenfield, Oh., U.S.	92	39.15N	83.25W
Greenfield, Tn., U.S.	108	36.08N	88.45W
Greenfield Park, Can.	77a	45.29N	73.29W
Greenhills, Oh., U.S. (grēn-hĭls)	95f	39.16N	84.31W
Greenhithe, Eng., U.K.	231	51.27N	0.17E
Greenland, dep., N.A. (grēn′lănd)	76	74.00N	40.00W
Greenland Sea, sea	56	77.00N	1.00W
Green Meadows, Md., U.S.	225d	38.58N	76.57W
Greenmount, Eng., U.K.	233b	53.37N	2.20W
Green Mountain, mtn., Or., U.S.	100c	45.52N	123.24W

PLACE (Pronunciation)	PAGE	Lat. °′	Long. °′
Green Mountain Reservoir, res., Co., U.S.	102	39.50N	106.20W
Green Mountains, mts., N.A.	90	43.10N	73.05W
Greenock, Scot., U.K. (grēn′ŭk)	140	55.55N	4.45W
Green Peter Lake, res., Or., U.S.	98	44.28N	122.30W
Green Pond Mountain, mtn., N.J., U.S. (pŏnd)	94a	41.00N	74.32W
Greenport, N.Y., U.S.	92	41.06N	72.22W
Green River, Ut., U.S. (grēn rĭv′ẽr)	102	39.00N	110.05W
Green River, Wy., U.S.	98	41.32N	109.26W
Green River Lake, res., Ky., U.S.	108	37.15N	85.15W
Greensboro, Al., U.S. (grēnz′bŭro)	108	32.42N	87.36W
Greensboro, Ga., U.S. (grēns-bûr′ô)	108	33.34N	83.11W
Greensboro, N.C., U.S.	90	36.04N	79.45W
Greensborough, Austl.	239b	37.42S	145.06E
Greensburg, In., U.S. (grēnz′bûrg)	92	39.20N	85.30W
Greensburg, Ks., U.S. (grēns-bûrg)	104	37.36N	99.17W
Greensburg, Pa., U.S.	92	40.20N	79.30W
Greenside, neigh., S. Afr.	240b	26.09S	28.01E
Greenstead, Eng., U.K.	231	51.42N	0.14E
Green Street, Eng., U.K.	231	51.40N	0.16W
Green Street Green, neigh., Eng., U.K.	231	51.21N	0.04E
Greenvale, N.Y., U.S.	224	40.49N	73.38W
Greenville, Lib.	204	5.01N	9.03W
Greenville, Al., U.S. (grēn′vĭl)	108	31.49N	86.39W
Greenville, Il., U.S.	104	38.52N	89.22W
Greenville, Ky., U.S.	108	37.11N	87.11W
Greenville, Me., U.S.	86	45.26N	69.35W
Greenville, Mi., U.S.	92	43.10N	85.25W
Greenville, Ms., U.S.	90	33.25N	91.00W
Greenville, N.C., U.S.	108	35.35N	77.22W
Greenville, Oh., U.S.	92	40.05N	84.35W
Greenville, Pa., U.S.	92	41.20N	80.25W
Greenville, S.C., U.S.	90	34.50N	82.25W
Greenville, Tn., U.S.	108	36.08N	82.50W
Greenville, Tx., U.S.	106	33.09N	96.07W
Greenwich, Eng., U.K.	138b	51.28N	0.00
Greenwich, Ct., U.S.	94a	41.01N	73.37W
Greenwich Observatory, pt. of i., Eng., U.K.	231	51.28N	0.00
Greenwich Village, neigh., N.Y., U.S.	224	40.44N	74.00W
Greenwood, Ar., U.S. (grēn-wŏŏd)	104	35.13N	94.15W
Greenwood, In., U.S.	95g	39.37N	86.07W
Greenwood, Ma., U.S.	223a	42.29N	71.04W
Greenwood, Ms., U.S.	108	33.30N	90.09W
Greenwood, S.C., U.S.	108	34.10N	82.10W
Greenwood, Lake, res., S.C., U.S.	108	34.17N	81.55W
Greenwood Lake, l., N.Y., U.S.	94a	41.13N	74.20W
Greer, S.C., U.S. (grēr)	108	34.55N	81.56W
Grefrath, Ger. (grĕf′rät)	151c	51.20N	6.21E
Gregory, S.D., U.S. (grĕg′ô-rĭ)	96	43.12N	99.27W
Gregory, Lake, l., Austl. (grĕg′ô-rē)	196	28.47S	139.15E
Gregory Range, mts., Austl.	196	19.23S	143.45E
Greifenberg, Ger. (grī′fĕn-bĕrgh)	139d	48.04N	11.06E
Greiffenburg, hist., Ger.	232	51.20N	6.38E
Greifswald, Ger. (grīfs′vält)	148	54.05N	13.24E
Greiz, Ger. (grīts)	148	50.39N	12.14E
Gremyachinsk, Russia (grâ′myȧ-chĭnsk)	164a	58.35N	57.53E
Grenada, Ms., U.S. (grē-nā′dȧ)	108	33.45N	89.47W
Grenada, nation, N.A.	110	12.02N	61.15W
Grenada Lake, res., Ms., U.S.	108	33.52N	89.30W
Grenadines, The, is., N.A. (grĕn′ȧ-dēnz)	115b	12.37N	61.35W
Grenen, c., Den.	140	57.43N	10.31E
Grenoble, Fr. (grē-nô′bl′)	140	45.14N	5.45E
Grenora, N.D., U.S. (grē-nō′rȧ)	96	48.38N	103.55W
Grenville, Can. (grĕn′vĭl)	92	45.40N	74.35W
Grenville, Gren.	115b	12.07N	61.38W
Gresham, Or., U.S. (grĕsh′ăm)	100c	45.30N	122.25W
Gretna, La., U.S. (grĕt′nȧ)	94d	29.56N	90.03W
Grevel, neigh., Ger.	232	51.34N	7.33E
Grevelingen Krammer, r., Neth.	139a	51.42N	4.03E
Grevenbroich, Ger. (grĕ′fĕn-broik)	151c	51.05N	6.36E
Grey, r., Can. (grā)	86	47.53N	57.00W
Grey, Point, c., Can.	100d	49.22N	123.16W
Greybull, Wy., U.S. (grā′bŏŏl)	98	44.28N	108.05W
Greybull, r., Wy., U.S.	98	44.13N	108.43W
Greylingstad, S. Afr. (grā-lĭng′shtȧt)	212d	26.40S	29.13E
Greymouth, N.Z. (grā′mouth)	197a	42.27S	171.17E
Grey Range, mts., Austl.	196	28.40S	142.05E
Greystanes, Austl.	239a	33.49S	150.58E
Greytown, S. Afr. (grā′toun)	207c	29.07S	30.38E
Grey Wolf Peak, mtn., Wa., U.S. (grā wŏŏlf)	100a	48.53N	123.12W
Gridley, Ca., U.S. (grĭd′lĭ)	102	39.22N	121.43W
Griffin, Ga., U.S. (grĭf′ĭn)	108	33.15N	84.16W
Griffith, Austl. (grĭf-ĭth)	198	34.16S	146.10E
Griffith, In., U.S.	95a	41.31N	87.26W
Grigoriopol′, Mol. (grĭ′gor-i-ô′pôl)	156	47.09N	29.18E
Grijalva, r., Mex. (grē-häl′vä)	112	17.25N	93.23W
Grim, Cape, c., Austl. (grĭm)	198	40.43S	144.30E
Grimma, Ger. (grĭm′ȧ)	148	51.14N	12.43E
Grimsby, Can. (grĭmz′bĭ)	77d	43.11N	79.33W
Grimsby, Eng., U.K.	140	53.35N	0.05W
Grímsey, i., Ice. (grĭms′ȧ)	140	66.30N	17.50W
Grimstad, Nor. (grĭm-städh)	140	58.21N	8.30E
Grindstone Island, Can.	86	47.25N	61.51W
Grinnel, Ia., U.S. (grĭ-nĕl′)	96	41.44N	92.44W
Grinzing, neigh., Aus.	235e	48.15N	16.21E
Griswold, Ia., U.S. (grĭz′wŭld)	96	41.11N	95.05W
Groais Island, i., Can.	86	50.57N	55.35W
Grobina, Lat. (grō′bĭnĭȧ)	146	56.35N	21.10E
Groblersdal, S. Afr.	212d	25.11S	29.25E
Grodno, Bela. (grôd′nô)	160	53.40N	23.49E
Grodzisk, Pol. (grō′jēsk)	148	52.14N	16.22E
Grodzisk Masowiecki, Pol. (grō′jēsk mä-zō-vyĕts′ke)	148	52.06N	20.40E
Groesbeck, Tx., U.S. (grōs′bĕk)	106	31.32N	96.31W

ăt; finăl; rāte; senåte; ärm; ȧsk; sofă; fâre; ch-choose; dh-as th in other; bē; ėvent; bĕt; recĕnt; cratẽr; g-gō; gh-guttural g; bĭt; ĭ-short neutral; rīde; ĸ-guttural k as ch in German ich;

PLACE (Pronunciation)	PAGE	Lat. °'	Long. °'
Groix, Île de, i., Fr. (ēl dē grwä')	150	47.39N	3.28W
Grójec, Pol. (gró'yĕts)	148	51.53N	20.52E
Gronau, Ger. (grō'nou)	148	52.12N	7.05E
Groningen, Neth. (grō'nĭng-ĕn)	140	53.13N	6.30E
Groote Eylandt, i., Austl. (grō'tē ī'länt)	196	13.50S	137.30E
Grootfontein, Nmb. (grōt'fōn-tān')	206	19.30S	18.15E
Groot-Kei, r., Afr. (kē)	207c	32.17S	27.30E
Grootkop, mtn., S. Afr.	206a	34.11S	18.23E
Groot Marico, S. Afr.	212d	25.36S	26.23E
Groot Marico, r., Afr.	212d	25.13S	26.20E
Groot-Vis, r., S. Afr.	207c	33.04S	26.08E
Groot Vloer, pl., S. Afr. (grōt' vlōr')	206	30.00S	21.00E
Gros-Mécatina, i., Can.	86	50.50N	58.33W
Gros Morne, mtn., Can. (grō môrn')	86	49.36N	57.48W
Gros Morne National Park, rec., Can.	79a	49.45N	59.15W
Gros Pate, mtn., Can.	86	50.16N	57.25W
Grossbeeren, Ger.	234a	52.21N	13.18E
Grosse Island, i., Mi., U.S. (grōs)	95b	42.08N	83.09W
Grosse Isle, Can. (īl')	77f	50.04N	97.27W
Grossenbaum, neigh., Ger.	232	51.22N	6.47E
Grossenhain, Ger. (grōs'ĕn-hīn)	148	51.17N	13.33E
Gross-Enzersdorf, Aus.	139e	48.13N	16.33E
Grosse Pointe, Mi., U.S. (point')	95b	42.23N	82.54W
Grosse Pointe Farms, Mi., U.S. (färm)	95b	42.25N	82.53W
Grosse Pointe Park, Mi., U.S. (pärk)	95b	42.23N	82.55W
Grosse Pointe Woods, Mi., U.S.	226c	42.27N	82.55W
Grosseto, Italy (grōs-sā'tō)	154	42.46N	11.09E
Grossglockner, mtn., Aus.	140	47.06N	12.45E
Gross Höbach, Ger. (hû'bäk)	139d	48.21N	11.36E
Grossjedlersdorf, neigh., Aus.	235e	48.17N	16.25E
Gross Kreutz, Ger. (kroitz)	139b	52.24N	12.47E
Gross Schönebeck, Ger. (shō'nē-bĕk)	139b	52.54N	13.32E
Gross Ziethen, Ger.	234a	52.24N	13.27E
Gros Ventre, r., Wy., U.S. (grōvĕn't'r)	98	43.38N	110.34W
Groton, Ct., U.S. (grŏt'ŭn)	92	41.20N	72.00W
Groton, Ma., U.S.	87a	42.37N	71.34W
Groton, S.D., U.S.	96	45.25N	98.04W
Grottaglie, Italy (grōt-täl'yā)	154	40.32N	17.26E
Grouard Mission, Can.	78	55.31N	116.09W
Groveland, Ma., U.S. (grōv'land)	87a	42.25N	71.02W
Groveton, N.H., U.S. (grōv'tŭn)	92	44.35N	71.30W
Groveton, Tx., U.S.	106	31.04N	95.07W
Groznyy, Russia (grŏz'nĭ)	158	43.20N	45.40E
Grudziądz, Pol. (grŏ'jyŏnts)	140	53.30N	18.48E
Grues, Île aux, i., Can. (ō grü)	77b	47.05N	70.32W
Gruiten, Ger.	232	51.14N	7.01E
Grumme, neigh., Ger.	232	51.30N	7.14E
Grünau, neigh., Ger.	234a	52.25N	13.34E
Grundy Center, Ia., U.S. (grŭn'dĭ sĕn'tĕr)	96	42.22N	92.45W
Grünewald, Ger.	232	51.13N	7.37E
Grunewald, neigh., Ger.	234a	52.30N	13.17E
Gruñidora, Mex. (grōō-nyē-dō'rō)	112	24.10N	101.49W
Grünwald, Ger. (grōōn'väld)	139d	48.04N	11.34E
Gryazi, Russia (gryä'zĭ)	156	52.31N	39.59E
Gryazovets, Russia (gryä'zō-vĕts)	160	58.52N	40.14E
Gryfice, Pol. (grĭ'fĭ-tsĕ)	148	53.55N	15.11E
Gryfino, Pol. (grĭ'fē-nō)	148	53.16N	14.30E
Guabito, Pan. (gwä-bē'tō)	114	9.30N	82.33W
Guacanayabo, Golfo de, b., Cuba (gōl-fō-dĕ-gwä-kä-nä-yä'bō)	116	20.30N	77.40W
Guacara, Ven. (gwá'kä-rä)	125b	10.16N	67.48W
Guadalajara, Mex. (gwä-dhä-lä-hä'rä)	110	20.41N	103.21W
Guadalajara, Spain (gwä-dä-lä-kä'rä)	142	40.37N	3.10W
Guadalcanal, Spain (gwä-dhäl-kä-näl')	152	38.05N	5.48W
Guadalcanal, i., Sol.Is.	196	9.48S	158.43E
Guadalcázar, Mex. (gwä-dhäl-kä'zär)	112	22.38N	100.24W
Guadalete, r., Spain (gwä-dhä-lā'tä)	152	36.53N	5.38W
Guadalhorce, r., Spain (gwä-dhäl-ôr'thā)	152	37.05N	4.50W
Guadalimar, r., Spain (gwä-dhä-lē-mär')	152	38.29N	2.53W
Guadalope, r., Spain (gwä-dä-lō-pā)	152	40.48N	0.10W
Guadalquivir, Río, r., Spain (rē'ō-gwä-dhäl-kē-vēr')	136	37.30N	5.00W
Guadalupe, Mex.	106	31.23N	106.06W
Guadalupe, i., Mex.	110	29.00N	118.45W
Guadalupe, r., Tx., U.S. (gwä-dhä-lōō'pā)	106	29.54N	99.03W
Guadalupe, Basílica de, rel., Mex.	229a	19.29N	99.07W
Guadalupe, Sierra de, mts., Spain (syĕr'rä dä gwä-dhä-lōō'pä)	142	39.30N	5.25W
Guadalupe Mountains, mts., N.M., U.S.	106	32.00N	104.55W
Guadalupe Peak, mtn., Tx., U.S.	106	31.55N	104.55W
Guadarrama, r., Spain (gwä-dhär-rä'mä)	153a	40.34N	3.58W
Guadarrama, Sierra de, mts., Spain (gwä-dhär-rä'mä)	136	41.00N	3.40W
Guadatentin, r., Spain	152	37.43N	1.58W
Guadeloupe, dep., N.A. (gwä-dē-lōōp)	110	16.40N	61.10W
Guadeloupe Passage, strt., N.A.	115b	16.26N	62.00W
Guadiana, r., Eur. (gwä-dvä'nä)	136	39.00N	6.00W
Guadiana, Bahía de, b., Cuba (bä-ē'ä-dē-gwä-dhē-ä'nä)	116	22.10N	84.35W
Guadiana Alto, r., Spain (äl'tō)	152	39.02N	2.52W
Guadiana Menor, r., Spain (mä'nôr)	152	37.43N	2.45W
Guadiaro, r., Spain (gwä-dhē-ä rō)	152	36.38N	5.25W
Guadiela, r., Spain (gwä-dhē-ā'lä)	152	40.27N	2.05W
Guadix, Spain (gwä-dēsh')	152	37.18N	3.09W
Guaianazes, neigh., Braz.	230d	23.33S	46.25W
Guaira, Braz. (gwä-ē-rä)	124	24.03S	54.02W
Guaire, r., Ven. (gwī'rĕ)	125b	10.25N	66.43W
Guajaba, Cayo, i., Cuba (kä'yō-gwä-hä'bä)	116	21.50N	77.35W
Guajará Mirim, Braz. (gwä-zhä-rä'mē-rēN')	124	10.58S	65.12W
Guajira, Península de, pen., S.A.	124	12.35N	73.00W
Gualán, Guat. (gwä-län')	114	15.08N	89.21W
Gualeguay, Arg. (gwä-lĕ-gwä'y)	126	33.10S	59.20W

PLACE (Pronunciation)	PAGE	Lat. °'	Long. °'
Gualeguay, r., Arg.	126	32.49S	59.05W
Gualicho, Salina, l., Arg. (sä-lē'nä-gwä-lē'chō)	126	40.20S	65.15W
Guam, i., Oc. (gwäm)	2	14.00N	143.20E
Guamo, Col. (gwá'mō)	124a	4.02N	74.58W
Gu'an, China (gōō-än)	184a	39.25N	116.18E
Guan, r., China (gůän)	182	31.56N	115.19E
Guanabacoa, Cuba (gwä-nä-bä-kō'ä)	110	23.08N	82.19W
Guanabara, Baía de, b., Braz.	123a	22.44S	43.09W
Guanacaste, Cordillera, mts., C.R.	114	10.54N	85.27W
Guanacevi, Mex. (gwä-nä-sē-vē')	110	25.30N	105.45W
Guanahacabibes, Península de, pen., Cuba	116	21.55N	84.35W
Guanajay, Cuba (gwäŋ-ä-hī')	116	22.55N	82.40W
Guanajuato, Mex. (gwä-nä-hwä'tō)	110	21.01N	101.16W
Guanajuato, state, Mex.	110	21.00N	101.00W
Guanape, Ven. (gwä-nä'pē)	125b	9.55N	65.32W
Guanape, r., Ven.	125b	9.52N	65.20W
Guanare, Ven. (gwä-nä'rā)	124	8.57N	69.47W
Guanduçu, r., Braz. (gwä'n-dōō'sōō)	126b	22.50S	43.40W
Guane, Cuba (gwä'nā)	116	22.10N	84.05W
Guangchang, China (gůäŋ-chäŋ)	184	26.50N	116.18E
Guangde, China (gůäŋ-dŭ)	184	30.40N	119.20E
Guangdong, prov., China (gůäŋ-dōŋ)	180	23.45N	113.15E
Guanglu Dao, i., China (gůäŋ-lōō dou)	182	39.13N	122.21E
Guangping, China (gůäŋ-pĭŋ)	182	36.30N	114.57E
Guangrao, China (gůäŋ-rou)	182	37.04N	118.24E
Guangshan, China (gůäŋ-shän)	182	32.02N	114.53E
Guangxi Zhuangzu, prov., China (gůäŋ-shyē)	180	24.00N	108.30E
Guangzhou, China	180	23.07N	113.15W
Guanhu, China (gůän-hōō)	182	34.26N	117.59E
Guannan, China (gůän-nän)	182	34.17N	119.17E
Guanta, Ven. (gwän'tä)	125b	10.15N	64.35W
Guantánamo, Cuba (gwän-tä'nä-mō)	116	20.10N	75.10W
Guantánamo, prov., Cuba	116	20.10N	75.05W
Guantánamo, Bahía de, b., Cuba	116	19.35N	75.35W
Guantao, China (gůän-tou)	182	36.39N	115.25E
Guanxian, China (gůän-shyĕn)	182	36.30N	115.28E
Guanyao, China (gůän-you)	183a	23.13N	113.04E
Guanyintang, China	236b	39.52N	116.31E
Guanyun, China (gůän-yōn)	182	34.28N	119.16E
Guapiles, C.R. (gwä-pē-lĕs)	114	10.05N	83.54W
Guapimirim, Braz. (gwä-pē-mē-rē'N)	126b	22.31S	42.59W
Guaporé, r., S.A. (gwä-pō-rā')	124	12.11S	63.47W
Guaqui, Bol. (guä'kē)	124	16.42S	68.47W
Guara, Sierra de, mts., Spain (sē-ĕ'r-rä-dē-gwä'rä)	152	42.24N	0.15W
Guarabira, Braz. (gwä-rä-bē'rá)	124	6.49S	35.27W
Guaracarumbo, Ven.	230a	10.34N	66.59W
Guaranda, Ec. (gwä-rán'dä)	124	1.39S	78.57W
Guarapari, Braz. (gwä-rä-pä'rē)	124	20.34S	40.31W
Guarapiranga, Represa do, res., Braz.	123a	23.45S	46.44W
Guarapuava, Braz. (gwä-rä-pwä'vá)	126	25.29S	51.26W
Guarda, Port. (gwär'dä)	152	40.32N	7.17W
Guardiato, r., Spain	152	38.10N	5.05W
Guarena, Spain (gwä-rā'nyä)	152	38.52N	6.08W
Guaribe, r., Ven. (gwä-rē'bē)	125b	9.48N	65.17W
Guárico, dept., Ven.	125b	9.42N	67.25W
Guarulhos, Braz. (gwá-rō'l-yôs)	123a	23.28S	46.30W
Guarus, Braz. (gwä'rōōs)	123a	21.44S	41.19W
Guasca, Col. (gwäs'kä)	124a	4.52N	73.52W
Guasipati, Ven. (gwä-sē-pä'tē)	124	7.26N	61.57W
Guastalla, Italy (gwäs-täl'lä)	154	44.53N	10.39E
Guasti, Ca., U.S. (gwäs'tĭ)	101a	34.04N	117.35W
Guatemala, Guat. (guä-tå-mä'lä)	110	14.37N	90.32W
Guatemala, nation, N.A.	110	15.45N	91.45W
Guatire, Ven. (gwä-tē'rē)	125b	10.28N	66.34W
Guaviare, r., Col.	124	3.35N	69.28W
Guayabal, Cuba (gwä-yä-bä'l)	116	20.40N	77.40W
Guayalejo, r., Mex. (gwä-yä-lē'hō)	112	23.24N	99.09W
Guayama, P.R. (gwä-yä'mä)	111b	18.00N	66.08W
Guayamouc, r., Haiti	116	19.05N	72.00W
Guayaquil, Ec. (gwī-ä-kēl')	124	2.16S	79.53W
Guayaquil, Golfo de, b., Ec. (gôl-fô-dē)	124	3.03S	82.12W
Guaymas, Mex. (gwá'y-mäs)	110	27.49N	110.58W
Guayubin, Dom. Rep. (gwá-yōō-bē'n)	116	19.40N	71.25W
Guazacapán, Guat. (gwä-zä-kä-pän')	114	14.04N	90.26W
Gubakha, Russia (gōō-bä'kå)	158	58.53N	57.35E
Gubbio, Italy (gōōb'byô)	154	43.23N	12.36E
Guben, Ger.	148	51.57N	14.43E
Gucheng, China (gōō-chŭŋ)	182	39.09N	115.43E
Gudar, Sierra de, mts., Spain (syĕr'rä dä gōō'dhär)	152	40.28N	0.47W
Gudena, r., Den.	146	56.20N	9.47E
Gudvangen, Nor. (gōōdh'väŋ-gĕn)	146	60.52N	6.45E
Guebwiller, Fr. (gĕb-vē-lâr')	150	47.53N	7.10E
Guédi, Mont, mtn., Chad	208	12.14N	18.58E
Guelma, Alg. (gwĕl'mä)	204	36.32N	7.17E
Guelph, Can. (gwĕlf)	84	43.33N	80.15W
Güere, r., Ven. (gwĕ'rē)	125b	9.39N	65.00W
Guéret, Fr. (gā-rĕ')	150	46.09N	1.52E
Guermantes, Fr.	233c	48.51N	2.42E
Guernsey, dep., Guernsey	150	49.28N	2.35W
Guernsey, i., Guernsey (gûrn'zĭ)	140	49.27N	2.36W
Guerrero, Mex. (gĕr-rā'rō)	106	26.47N	99.20W
Guerrero, Mex.	106	28.20N	100.24W
Guerrero, state, Mex.	110	17.45N	100.15W
Gueydan, La., U.S. (gā'dăn)	106	30.01N	92.31W
Guia de Pacobaíba, Braz. (gwē'ä-dĕ-pä'kō-bī'bä)	126b	22.42S	43.10W
Guiana Highlands, mts., S.A.	122	3.20N	60.00W
Guichi, China (gwä-chr)	184	30.35N	117.28E
Guichicovi, Mex. (gwē-chē-kō'vē)	112	16.58N	95.10W

PLACE (Pronunciation)	PAGE	Lat. °'	Long. °'
Guidonia, Italy (gwē-dō'nyä)	154	42.00N	12.45E
Guiglo, I.C.	208	6.33N	7.29W
Guignes-Rabutin, Fr. (gēN'yĕ)	151b	48.38N	2.48E
Güigüe, Ven. (gwĕ'gwĕ)	125b	10.05N	67.48W
Guija, Lago, l., N.A. (gē'hä)	114	14.16N	89.21W
Guildford, Austl.	239a	33.51S	150.59E
Guildford, Eng., U.K. (gĭl'fērd)	144	51.13N	0.34W
Guilford, In., U.S. (gĭl'fērd)	95f	39.10N	84.55W
Guilin, China (gwā-lĭn)	180	25.18N	110.22E
Guimarães, Port. (gē-mä-räNsh')	152	41.27N	8.22W
Guinea, nation, Afr. (gĭn'ē)	204	10.48N	12.28W
Guinea, Gulf of, b., Afr.	204	2.00N	1.00E
Guinea-Bissau, nation, Afr. (gĭn'ē)	204	12.00N	20.00W
Guingamp, Fr. (găN-gäN')	150	48.35N	3.10W
Guir, r., Mor.	142	31.55N	2.48W
Güira de Melena, Cuba (gwē'rä dā må-lā'nä)	116	22.45N	82.30W
Güiria, Ven. (gwê-rē'ä)	124	10.43N	62.16W
Guise, Fr. (guēz)	150	49.54N	3.37E
Guisisil, vol., Nic. (gē-sē-sēl')	114	12.40N	86.11W
Guiyang, China (gwā-yäŋ)	180	26.45N	107.00E
Guizhou, China (gwā-jō)	183a	22.46N	113.15E
Guizhou, prov., China	180	27.00N	106.10E
Gujānwāla, Pak. (gōj-rän'va-lá)	174	32.08N	74.14E
Gujarat, India	174	22.54N	72.00E
Gulbarga, India (gōl-bûr'gá)	174	17.25N	76.52E
Gulbene, Lat. (gōl-bă'nē)	146	57.09N	26.49E
Gulfport, Ms., U.S. (gŭlf'pōrt)	108	30.24N	89.05W
Gulja, see Yining, China	180	43.58N	80.40E
Gull Lake, Can.	82	50.10N	108.25W
Gull Lake, l., Can.	80	52.35N	114.00W
Gulph Mills, Pa., U.S.	225b	40.04N	75.21W
Gulu, Ug.	210	2.47N	32.18E
Gulyay Pole, Ukr.	156	47.39N	36.12E
Gumaca, Phil. (gōō-mä-kä')	189a	13.55N	122.06E
Gumbeyka, r., Russia (gōm-bĕy'kå)	164a	53.20N	59.42E
Gumel, Nig.	204	12.39N	9.22E
Gummersbach, Ger. (gŏm'ĕrs-bäk)	148	51.02N	7.34E
Gummi, Nig.	208	12.09N	5.09E
Gumpoldskirchen, Aus.	139e	48.04N	16.15E
Guna, India	178	24.44N	77.17E
Gunisao, r., Can. (gŭn-ĭ-sā'ō)	82	53.40N	97.35W
Gunisao Lake, l., Can.	82	53.35N	96.10W
Gunnedah, Austl. (gŭ'nē-dä)	198	31.00S	150.10E
Gunnison, Co., U.S. (gŭn'ĭ-sŭn)	102	38.33N	106.56W
Gunnison, Ut., U.S.	102	39.10N	111.50W
Gunnison, r., Co., U.S.	102	38.45N	108.20W
Guntersville, Al., U.S. (gŭn'tērz-vĭl)	108	34.20N	86.19W
Guntersville Lake, res., Al., U.S.	108	34.30N	86.20W
Guntramsdorf, Aus.	139e	48.04N	16.19E
Guntūr, India (gōn'tōōr)	174	16.22N	80.29E
Guoyang, China (gwō-yäŋ)	182	33.32N	116.10E
Gurdon, Ar., U.S. (gûr'dŭn)	104	33.56N	93.10W
Gurgueia, r., Braz.	124	8.12S	43.49W
Guri, Embalse, res., Ven.	124	7.30N	63.00W
Gurnee, Il., U.S. (gûr'nē)	95a	42.22N	87.55W
Gurskøy, i., Nor. (gōōrskûê)	146	62.18N	5.20E
Gurupi, Serra do, mts., Braz. (sĕ'r-rä-dō-gōō-rōō-pē')	124	5.32S	47.02W
Guru Sikhar, mtn., India	178	29.42N	72.50E
Gur'yev, Kaz. (gōōr'yĕf)	158	47.10N	51.50E
Gur'yevsk, Russia (gōōr-yĭfsk')	158	54.17N	85.56E
Gusau, Nig. (gōō-zä'ōō)	204	12.12N	6.40E
Gusev, Russia (gōō'sĕf)	146	54.35N	22.15E
Gushi, China (gōō-shr)	182	32.11N	115.39E
Gushiago, Ghana	208	9.55N	0.12W
Gusinje, Yugo. (gōō-sēn'yĕ)	154	42.34N	19.54E
Gus'-Khrustal'nyy, Russia (gōōs-kroō-stäl'ny')	160	55.39N	40.41E
Gustavo A. Madero, Mex. (gōōs-tä'vô-ä-mä-dĕ'rô)	112	19.29N	99.07W
Güstrow, Ger. (güs'trō)	148	53.48N	12.12E
Gütersloh, Ger. (gü'tērs-lō)	148	51.54N	8.22E
Guthrie, Ok., U.S. (gŭth'rĭ)	104	35.52N	97.26W
Guthrie Center, Ia., U.S.	96	41.41N	94.33W
Gutiérrez Zamora, Mex. (gōō-tĭ-ăr'räz zä-mō'rä)	112	20.27N	97.17W
Guttenberg, Ia., U.S. (gŭt'ĕn-bûrg)	96	42.48N	91.09W
Guttenberg, N.J., U.S.	224	40.48N	74.01W
Guyana, nation, S.A. (gŭy'ănä)	124	7.45N	59.00W
Guyancourt, Fr.	233c	48.46N	2.04E
Guyang, China (gōō-yäŋ)	182	34.56N	114.57E
Guye, China (gōō-yü)	182	39.46N	118.23E
Guymon, Ok., U.S. (gī'mŏn)	104	36.41N	101.29W
Guysborough, Can. (gīz'bŭr-ô)	86	45.23N	61.30W
Guzhen, China (gōō-jŭn)	184	33.20N	117.18E
Gvardeysk, Russia (gvăr-dĕysk')	146	54.39N	21.11E
Gwadabawa, Nig.	208	13.20N	5.15E
Gwādar, Pak. (gwä'dŭr)	174	25.15N	62.29E
Gwalior, India	174	26.13N	78.10E
Gwane, Zaire (gwän)	204	4.43N	25.50E
Gwda, r., Pol.	148	53.27N	16.52E
Gwembe, Zam.	210	16.30S	27.35E
Gweru, Zimb.	206	19.15S	29.48E
Gwinn, Mi., U.S. (gwĭn)	96	46.15N	87.30W
Gyaring Co, l., China	178	30.37N	88.33E
Gydan, Khrebet (Kolymskiy), mts., Russia	158	61.45N	155.00E
Gydanskiy Poluostrov, pen., Russia	158	70.42N	76.03E
Gympie, Austl. (gĭm'pē)	196	26.20S	152.50E
Gyöngyös, Hung. (dyûn'dyûsh)	142	47.47N	19.55E
Györ, Hung. (dyûr)	142	47.40N	17.37E
Gyōtoku, Japan (gyō'tō-kōō')	187a	35.42N	139.56E
Gypsumville, Can. (jĭp'sŭm-vĭl)	78	51.45N	98.35W

ng-sing; ŋ-baŋk; N-nasalized n; nŏd; cŏmmit; ōld; ôbey; ôrder; oi-boil; fōōd; ŏ-as oo in foot; ou-out; s-soft; sh-dish; th-thin; pūre; ûnite; ûrn; stŭd; circŭs; ü-as in French tu; '-indeterminate vowel.

PLACE (Pronunciation)	PAGE	Lat. °'	Long. °'
Gyula, Hung. (dyò'lä)	148	46.38N	21.18E

H

PLACE (Pronunciation)	PAGE	Lat. °'	Long. °'
Haan, Ger. (hän)	151c	51.12N	7.00E
Haapamäki, Fin. (häp'ȧ-mĕ-kē)	146	62.16N	24.20E
Haapsalu, Est. (häp'sä-lò)	146	58.56N	23.33E
Haar, Ger. (här)	139d	48.06N	11.44E
Haar, neigh., Ger.	232	51.26N	7.13E
Ha'Arava (Wādī al Jayb), val., Asia	173a	30.33N	35.10E
Haarlem, Neth. (här'lĕm)	144	52.22N	4.37E
Habana, prov., Cuba (hä-vä'nä)	116	22.45N	82.25W
Haberfield, Austl.	239a	33.53S	151.08E
Hābra, India	178a	22.49N	88.38E
Hachinohe, Japan (hä'chē-nō'hå)	186	40.29N	141.40E
Hachiōji, Japan (hä'chē-ō'jē)	186	35.39N	139.18E
Hacienda Heights, Ca., U.S.	228	33.58N	117.58W
Hackensack, N.J., U.S. (hăk'ĕn-săk)	94a	40.54N	74.03W
Hacketts, Eng., U.K.	231	51.45N	0.05W
Hackney, neigh., Eng., U.K.	231	51.33N	0.03W
Ḥadd, Ra's al, c., Oman	174	22.29N	59.46E
Haddonfield, N.J., U.S. (hăd'ŭn-fēld)	94f	39.53N	75.02W
Haddon Heights, N.J., U.S. (hăd'ŭn hīts)	94f	39.53N	75.03W
Hadejia, Nig. (hä-dā'jä)	204	12.30N	9.59E
Hadejia, r., Nig.	204	12.15N	10.00E
Ḥadera, Isr. (кȧ-dĕ'rȧ)	173a	32.26N	34.55E
Hadersdorf, neigh., Aus.	235e	48.13N	16.14E
Haderslev, Den. (hä'dhĕrs-lĕv)	146	55.17N	9.28E
Hadfield, Austl.	239b	37.42S	144.56E
Ḥadīdū, Yemen	174	12.40N	53.50E
Hadlock, Wa., U.S. (hăd'lŏk)	100a	48.02N	122.46W
Ḥaḍramawt, reg., Yemen	174	15.22N	48.40E
Ḥadūr Shu'ayb, mtn., Yemen	174	15.45N	43.45E
Haeju, N. Kor. (hä'ĕ-jŭ)	186	38.03N	125.42E
Hafnarfjörður, Ice.	140	64.02N	21.32W
Haft Gel, Iran	176	31.27N	49.27E
Hafun, Ras, c., Som. (hä-fōōn')	212a	10.15N	51.35E
Hageland, Mt., U.S. (hăge'lând)	98	48.53N	108.43W
Hagen, Ger. (hä'gĕn)	148	51.21N	7.29E
Hagerstown, In., U.S. (hā'gĕrz-toun)	92	39.55N	85.10W
Hagerstown, Md., U.S.	90	39.40N	77.45W
Hagi, Japan (hä'gĭ)	187	34.25N	131.25E
Hague, Cap de la, c., Fr. (dē lȧ äg')	150	49.44N	1.55W
Haguenau, Fr. (ȧg'nō')	150	48.47N	7.48E
Hahnenberg, Ger.	232	51.12N	7.24E
Hai'an, China (hī-än)	182	32.35N	120.25E
Haibara, Japan (hä'ē-bä'rä)	187	34.29N	135.57E
Haicheng, China (hī-chŭŋ)	184	40.58N	122.45E
Haidārpur, neigh., India	236d	28.43N	77.09E
Haidian, China (hī-dĭĕn)	182	39.59N	116.17E
Haifa, Isr. (hä'ē-fȧ)	174	32.48N	35.00E
Haifeng, China (hä'ē-fĕng')	184	23.00N	115.20E
Haifuzhen, China (hī-fōō-jŭn)	182	31.57N	121.48E
Haijima, Japan	238a	35.42N	139.21E
Haikou, China	180	20.03N	110.19E
Haikou, China (hī-kō)	184	20.00N	110.20E
Ḥā'il, Sau. Ar.	174	27.30N	41.47E
Hailar, China	180	49.10N	118.40E
Hailey, Id., U.S. (hā'lĭ)	98	43.31N	114.19W
Haileybury, Can.	84	47.27N	79.38W
Haileyville, Ok., U.S. (hā'lĭ-vĭl)	104	34.51N	95.34W
Hailing Dao, i., China (hī-lĭŋ dou)	184	21.30N	112.15E
Hailong, China (hī-loŋ)	184	42.32N	125.52E
Hailun, China (hä'ē-lōōn')	180	47.18N	126.50E
Hainan, prov., China	180	19.00N	109.30E
Hainan Dao, i., China (hī-nän dou)	180	19.00N	111.10E
Hainault, neigh., Eng., U.K.	231	51.36N	0.06E
Hainburg, Aus.	148	48.09N	16.57E
Haines, Ak., U.S. (hānz)	89	59.10N	135.38W
Haines City, Fl., U.S.	109a	28.05N	81.38W
Hai Phong, Viet. (hī'fông')(hä'ēp-hŏng)	188	20.52N	106.40E
Haiti, nation, N.A. (hā'tĭ)	110	19.00N	72.15W
Haizhou, China	182	34.34N	119.11E
Haizhou Wan, b., China	184	34.49N	120.35E
Hajdúböszormény, Hung. (hô'dò-bû'sûr-män')	148	47.41N	21.30E
Hajdúhadház, Hung. (hô'ĭ-dò-hôd'häz)	148	47.32N	21.32E
Hajdúnánás, Hung. (hô'ĭ-dò-nä'näsh)	148	47.52N	21.27E
Hakodate, Japan (hä-kō-dä't å)	180	41.46N	140.42E
Haku-San, mtn., Japan (hä'kōō-sän')	186	36.11N	136.45E
Halā'ib, Egypt (hä-lä'ēb)	204	22.10N	36.40E
Halbe, Ger. (häl'bē)	139b	52.07N	13.43E
Halberstadt, Ger. (häl'bĕr-shtät)	148	51.54N	11.07E
Halcon, Mount, mtn., Phil. (häl-kōn')	189a	13.19N	120.55E
Halden, Nor. (häl'dĕn)	140	59.10N	11.21E
Halden, neigh., Ger.	232	51.23N	7.31E
Haldensleben, Ger.	148	52.18N	11.23E
Hale, Eng., U.K. (hāl)	138a	53.22N	2.20W
Haleakala Crater, Hi., U.S. (hä'lā-ä'kä-lä)	88a	20.44N	156.15W
Haleakala National Park, Hi., U.S.	88a	20.46N	156.00W
Halebarns, Eng., U.K.	233b	53.22N	2.19W
Haledon, N.J., U.S.	224	40.56N	74.11W
Hales Corners, Wi., U.S. (hālz kôr'nērz)	95a	42.56N	88.03W
Halesowen, Eng., U.K. (hālz'ô-wĕn)	138a	52.26N	2.03W
Halethorpe, Md., U.S. (hāl-thôrp)	94e	39.15N	76.40W
Halewood, Eng., U.K.	233a	53.22N	2.49W
Haleyville, Al., U.S. (hā'lĭ-vĭl)	108	34.11N	87.36W
Half Moon Bay, Ca., U.S. (hăf'mōōn)	100b	37.28N	122.26W
Halfway House, S. Afr. (häf-wā hous)	207b	26.00S	28.08E
Halfweg, Neth.	139a	52.23N	4.45E
Halifax, Can. (hăl'ĭ-făks)	78	44.39N	63.36W
Halifax, Eng., U.K.	144	53.44N	1.52W
Halifax Bay, b., Austl. (hăl'ĭ-făx)	196	18.56S	147.07E
Halifax Harbour, b., Can.	86	44.35N	63.31W
Halkett, Cape, c., Ak., U.S.	89	70.50N	151.15W
Hallam, Austl.	239b	38.01S	145.16E
Hallam Peak, mtn., Can.	80	52.11N	118.46E
Halla San, mtn., S. Kor. (häl'lȧ-sän)	186	33.20N	126.37E
Halle, Bel. (häl'lĕ)	139a	50.45N	4.13E
Halle, Ger.	140	51.30N	11.59E
Hallettsville, Tx., U.S. (hăl'ĕts-vĭl)	106	29.26N	96.55W
Hallock, Mn., U.S. (hăl'ŭk)	96	48.46N	96.57W
Hall Peninsula, pen., Can. (hôl)	78	63.14N	65.40W
Halls Bayou, Tx., U.S.	107a	29.55N	95.23W
Hallsberg, Swe. (häls'bĕrgh)	146	59.04N	15.04E
Halls Creek, Austl. (hôlz)	196	18.15S	127.45E
Halmahera, i., Indon. (häl-mä-hā'rȧ)	188	0.45N	128.45E
Halmahera, Laut, Indon.	188	1.00S	129.00E
Halmstad, Swe. (hälm'städ)	140	56.40N	12.46E
Halsafjorden, fj., Nor. (häl'sĕ fyôrd)	146	63.03N	8.23E
Halstead, Eng., U.K.	231	51.20N	0.08E
Halstead, Ks., U.S. (hôl'stĕd)	104	38.02N	97.36W
Haltern, Ger. (häl'tĕrn)	151c	51.45N	7.10E
Haltom City, Tx., U.S. (hôl'tŏm)	101c	32.48N	97.13W
Halver, Ger.	151c	51.11N	7.30E
Ham, neigh., Eng., U.K.	231	51.26N	0.19W
Hamada, Japan	186	34.53N	132.05E
Hamadān, Iran (hŭ-mŭ-dän')	174	34.45N	48.07E
Ḥamāh, Syria (hä'mä)	174	35.08N	36.53E
Hamamatsu, Japan (hä'mä-mät'sò)	186	34.41N	137.43E
Hamar, Nor. (hä'mär)	140	60.49N	11.05E
Hamasaka, Japan (hä'mȧ-sä'kȧ)	187	35.57N	134.27E
Hamberg, S. Afr.	240b	26.11S	27.53E
Hamborn, Ger. (häm'bōrn)	151c	51.30N	6.43E
Hamburg, Ciskei (hăm'bûrg)	207c	33.18S	27.28E
Hamburg, Ger. (häm'bōōrgh)	136	53.34N	10.02E
Hamburg, Ar., U.S. (hăm'bûrg)	104	33.15N	91.49W
Hamburg, N.J., U.S.	94a	41.09N	74.35W
Hamburg, N.Y., U.S.	95c	42.44N	78.51W
Hamburg, state, Ger.	139c	53.35N	10.00E
Hamden, Ct., U.S. (hăm'dĕn)	92	41.20N	72.55W
Hämeenlinna, Fin. (hĕ'mån-lĭn-nȧ)	140	61.00N	24.29E
Hameln, Ger. (hä'mĕln)	148	52.06N	9.23E
Hamelwörden, Ger. (hä'mĕl-vûr-dĕn)	139c	53.47N	9.19E
Hamersley Range, mts., Austl. (hăm'ērz-lē)	196	22.15S	117.50E
Hamhŭng, N. Kor. (häm'hòng')	180	39.57N	127.35E
Hamhŭng, N. Kor.	186	39.54N	127.32E
Hami, China (hä-mē)(kò-mōōl')	180	42.58N	93.14E
Hamilton, Austl. (hăm'ĭl-tŭn)	196	37.50S	142.10E
Hamilton, Can.	78	43.15N	79.52W
Hamilton, N.Z.	197a	37.45S	175.28E
Hamilton, Al., U.S.	108	34.09N	88.01W
Hamilton, Ma., U.S.	87a	42.37N	70.52W
Hamilton, Mo., U.S.	104	39.43N	93.59W
Hamilton, Mt., U.S.	98	46.15N	114.09W
Hamilton, Oh., U.S.	90	39.22N	84.33W
Hamilton, Tx., U.S.	106	31.42N	98.07W
Hamilton, Lake, l., Ar., U.S.	104	34.25N	93.32W
Hamilton Harbour, b., Can.	77d	43.17N	79.50W
Hamilton Inlet, b., Can.	78	54.20N	56.57W
Hamina, Fin. (hȧ'mē-nȧ)	146	60.34N	27.15E
Hamlet, N.C., U.S. (hăm'lĕt)	108	35.52N	79.46W
Hamlin, Tx., U.S. (hăm'lĭn)	104	32.54N	100.08W
Hamm, Ger. (häm)	148	51.40N	7.48E
Hamm, neigh., Ger.	232	51.12N	6.44E
Hammanskraal, S. Afr. (hä-mȧns-kräl')	212d	25.24S	28.17E
Hamme, Bel.	139a	51.06N	4.07E
Hamme-Oste Kanal, can., Ger. (hä'mĕ-ōs'tĕ kä-näl)	139c	53.20N	8.59E
Hammerfest, Nor. (häm'mĕr-fĕst)	136	70.38N	23.59E
Hammersmith, neigh., Eng., U.K.	231	51.30N	0.14W
Hammond, In., U.S. (hăm'ŭnd)	90	41.37N	87.31W
Hammond, La., U.S.	106	30.30N	90.28W
Hammond, Or., U.S.	100c	46.12N	123.57W
Hammondville, Austl.	239a	33.57S	150.57E
Hammonton, N.J., U.S. (hăm'ŭn-tŭn)	92	39.40N	74.45W
Hampden, Me., U.S. (hăm'dĕn)	86	44.44N	68.51W
Hampstead, Md., U.S.	94e	39.36N	76.54W
Hampstead, neigh., Eng., U.K.	231	51.33N	0.11W
Hampstead Heath, pt. of i., Eng., U.K.	231	51.34N	0.10W
Hampstead Norris, Eng., U.K. (hămp-stĕd nŏ'rĭs)	138b	51.27N	1.14W
Hampton, Austl.	239b	37.56S	145.00E
Hampton, Can. (hămp'tŭn)	86	45.32N	65.51W
Hampton, Ia., U.S.	96	42.43N	93.15W
Hampton, Va., U.S.	92	37.02N	76.21W
Hampton, neigh., Eng., U.K.	231	51.25N	0.22W
Hampton National Historic Site, pt. of i., Md., U.S.	225c	39.25N	76.35W
Hampton Roads, b., Va., U.S.	94g	36.56N	76.23W
Hams Fork, r., Wy., U.S.	98	41.55N	110.40W
Hamtramck, Mi., U.S. (hăm-trăm'ĭk)	95b	42.24N	83.03W
Han, r., China	180	31.40N	112.04E
Han, r., China (hän)	184	25.00N	116.35E
Han, r., S. Kor.	186	37.10N	127.40E
Hana, Hi., U.S. (hä'nä)	88a	20.43N	155.59W
Hanábana, r., Cuba (hä-nä-bä'nä)	116	22.30N	80.55W
Hanalei Bay, b., Hi., U.S. (hä-nä-lā'ē)	88a	22.15N	159.40W
Hanang, mtn., Tan.	210	4.26S	35.24E
Hanau, Ger. (hä'nou)	148	50.08N	8.56E
Hancock, Mi., U.S. (hăn'kŏk)	90	47.08N	88.37W
Handan, China (hän-dän)	182	36.37N	114.30E
Handforth, Eng., U.K.	233b	53.21N	2.13W
Haney, Can. (hā-nē)	80	49.13N	122.36W
Hanford, Ca., U.S. (hăn'fērd)	102	36.20N	119.38W
Hangayn Nuruu, mts., Mong.	180	48.03N	99.45E
Hang Hau Town, H.K.	237c	22.19N	114.16E
Hango, Fin. (häŋ'gû)	136	59.49N	22.56E
Hangzhou, China (häng'chō')	180	30.17N	120.12E
Hangzhou Wan, b., China (häŋ-jō wän)	184	30.20N	121.25E
Hankamer, Tx., U.S. (hăn'kȧ-mēr)	107a	29.52N	94.42W
Hankinson, N.D., U.S. (häŋ'kĭn-sŭn)	96	46.04N	96.54W
Hankou, China (hän-kō)	184	30.42N	114.22E
Hann, Mount, mtn., Austl. (hän)	196	16.05S	126.07E
Hanna, Can. (hăn'ȧ)	78	51.38N	111.54W
Hanna, Wy., U.S.	98	41.51N	106.34W
Hannah, N.D., U.S.	96	48.58N	98.42W
Hannibal, Mo., U.S. (hăn'ĭ bȧl)	90	39.42N	91.22W
Hannover, Ger. (hän-ō'vēr)	136	52.22N	9.45E
Hanöbukten, b., Swe.	146	55.54N	14.55E
Hanoi, Viet. (hä-noi')	188	21.04N	105.50E
Hanover, Can. (hăn'ô-vēr)	84	44.10N	81.05W
Hanover, Md., U.S.	225c	39.11N	76.42W
Hanover, Ma., U.S.	87a	42.07N	70.49W
Hanover, N.H., U.S.	92	43.45N	72.15W
Hanover, Pa., U.S.	92	39.50N	77.00W
Hanover, i., Chile	126	51.00S	74.45W
Hanshan, China (hän'shän')	182	31.43N	118.06E
Hans Lollick, i., V.I.U.S. (häns'lôl'ĭk)	111c	18.24N	64.55W
Hanson, Ma., U.S. (hăn'sŭn)	87a	42.04N	70.53W
Hansville, Wa., U.S. (hăns'-vĭl)	100a	47.55N	122.33W
Hantengri Feng, mtn., Asia (hän-tŭŋ-rē fŭŋ)	180	42.10N	80.20E
Hantsport, Can. (hănts'pōrt)	86	45.04N	64.11W
Hanworth, neigh., Eng., U.K.	231	51.26N	0.23W
Hanyang, China (han'yäng')	180	30.30N	114.10E
Hanzhong, China (hän-jôŋ)	184	33.02N	107.00E
Haocheng, China (hou-chŭŋ)	182	33.19N	117.33E
Haparanda, Swe. (hä-pä-rän'dä)	140	65.54N	23.57E
Hapeville, Ga., U.S. (hāp'vĭl)	94c	33.39N	84.25W
Happy Camp, Ca., U.S.	98	41.47N	123.22W
Happy Valley-Goose Bay, Can.	78	53.19N	60.33W
Hapsford, Eng., U.K.	233a	53.16N	2.48W
Ḥaql, Sau. Ar.	173a	29.15N	34.57E
Ḥar, Laga, r., Kenya	210	2.15N	39.30E
Haramachida, Japan	238a	35.33N	139.27E
Harare, Zimb.	206	17.50S	31.03E
Harbin, China	180	45.40N	126.30E
Harbor Beach, Mi., U.S. (här'bēr bēch)	92	43.50N	82.40W
Harbor City, neigh., Ca., U.S.	228	33.48N	118.17W
Harbord, Austl.	239a	33.47S	151.17E
Harbor Isle, N.Y., U.S.	224	40.36N	73.40W
Harbor Springs, Mi., U.S.	92	45.25N	85.05W
Harbour Breton, Can. (brĕt'ŭn) (brē-tôn')	86	47.29N	55.48W
Harbour Grace, Can. (grās)	86	47.32N	53.13W
Harburg, Ger. (här-bòrgh)	139c	53.28N	9.58E
Hardangerfjorden, Nor. (här-däng'ēr fyôrd)	140	59.58N	6.30E
Hardin, Mt., U.S. (här'dĭn)	98	45.44N	107.36W
Harding, S. Afr. (här'dĭng)	206	30.34S	29.54E
Harding, Lake, res., U.S.	108	32.43N	85.00W
Hardwār, India (hŭr'dwär)	174	29.56N	78.06E
Hardy, r., Mex. (här'dĭ)	102	32.04N	115.10W
Hare Bay, b., Can. (hâr)	86	51.18N	55.50W
Harefield, neigh., Eng., U.K.	231	51.36N	0.29W
Harer, Eth.	204	9.43N	42.10E
Harerge, hist. reg., Eth.	204	8.15N	41.00E
Hargeysa, Som. (här-gä'ē-sȧ)	212a	9.20N	43.57E
Harghita, Munţii, mts., Rom.	148	46.25N	25.40E
Harima-Nada, b., Japan (hä'rē-mä nä-dä)	187	34.34N	134.37E
Haringey, neigh., Eng., U.K.	231	51.35N	0.07W
Haringvliet, r., Neth.	139a	51.49N	4.03E
Hari Rud, r., Asia	174	34.29N	61.16E
Harker Village, N.J., U.S.	225b	39.51N	75.09W
Harlan, Ia., U.S. (här'lăn)	104	41.40N	95.10W
Harlan, Ky., U.S.	108	36.50N	83.19W
Harlan County Reservoir, res., Ne., U.S.	104	40.03N	99.51W
Harlem, Mt., U.S. (hȧr'lĕm)	98	48.33N	108.50W
Harlem, neigh., N.Y., U.S.	224	40.49N	73.56W
Harlesden, neigh., Eng., U.K.	231	51.32N	0.15W
Harlingen, Neth. (här'lĭng-ĕn)	144	53.10N	5.24E
Harlingen, Tx., U.S.	90	26.12N	97.42W
Harlington, neigh., Eng., U.K.	231	51.29N	0.26W
Harlow, Eng., U.K. (här'lō)	138b	51.46N	0.08E
Harlowton, Mt., U.S. (hȧr'lô-tun)	98	46.26N	109.50W
Harmar Heights, Pa., U.S.	226b	40.33N	79.49W
Harmarville, Pa., U.S.	226b	40.32N	79.51W
Harmony, In., U.S. (här'mô-nĭ)	92	39.35N	87.00W
Harney Basin, Or., U.S. (här'nĭ)	98	43.26N	120.19W
Harney Lake, l., Or., U.S.	98	43.11N	119.23W
Harney Peak, mtn., S.D., U.S.	90	43.52N	103.32W
Härnosand, Swe. (hĕr-nû-sänd)	140	62.37N	17.54E
Haro, Spain (ä'rō)	152	42.35N	2.49W
Harola, India	236d	28.36N	77.19E
Harold Hill, neigh., Eng., U.K.	231	51.36N	0.13E
Harold Wood, neigh., Eng., U.K.	231	51.36N	0.14E
Haro Strait, strt., N.A. (hä'rō)	100a	48.27N	123.11W
Harpen, neigh., Ger.	232	51.29N	7.16E
Harpenden, Eng., U.K. (här'pĕn-d'n)	138b	51.48N	0.22W
Harper, Lib.	204	4.25N	7.43W
Harper, Ks., U.S. (här'pēr)	104	37.17N	98.02W
Harper, Wa., U.S.	100a	47.31N	122.32W
Harpers Ferry, W.V., U.S. (här'pērz)	92	39.20N	77.45W

ăt; finȧl; rāte; senāte; ärm; åsk; sofȧ; fâre; ch-choose; dh-as th in other; bē; ēvent; bĕt; recĕnt; cratēr; g-gō; gh-guttural g; bĭt; ĭ-short neutral; rīde; ĸ-guttural k as ch in German ich;

PLACE (Pronunciation)	PAGE	Lat. °'	Long. °'
Harper Woods, Mi., U.S.	226c	42.24N	82.55W
Harpurhey, neigh., Eng., U.K.	233b	53.31N	2.13W
Harricana, r., Can.	84	50.10N	78.50W
Harriman, Tn., U.S. (hă′ĭ-măn)	108	35.55N	84.34W
Harrington, De., U.S. (hăr′ĭng-tŭn)	92	38.55N	75.35W
Harris, i., Scot., U.K. (hăr′ĭs)	144	57.55N	6.40W
Harris, Lake, l., Fl., U.S.	109a	28.43N	81.40W
Harrisburg, Il., U.S. (hăr′ĭs-bûrg)	92	37.45N	88.35W
Harrisburg, Pa., U.S.	90	40.15N	76.50W
Harrismith, S. Afr. (hă-rĭs′mĭth)	212d	28.17S	29.08E
Harrison, Ar., U.S. (hăr′ĭ-sŭn)	104	36.13N	93.06W
Harrison, N.J., U.S.	224	40.45N	74.10W
Harrison, N.Y., U.S.	224	40.58N	73.43W
Harrison, Oh., U.S.	95f	39.16N	84.45W
Harrisonburg, Va., U.S. (hăr′ĭ-sŭn-bûrg)	92	38.30N	78.50W
Harrison Lake, l., Can.	80	49.31N	121.59W
Harrisonville, Md., U.S.	225c	39.23N	77.50W
Harrisonville, Mo., U.S. (hăr-ĭ-sŭn-vĭl)	104	38.39N	94.21W
Harris Park, Austl.	239a	33.49S	151.01E
Harrisville, Ut., U.S. (hăr′ĭs-vĭl)	101b	41.17N	112.00W
Harrisville, W.V., U.S.	92	39.10N	81.05W
Harrodsburg, Ky., U.S. (hăr′ŭdz-bûrg)	92	37.45N	84.50W
Harrods Creek, r., Ky., U.S. (hăr′ŭdz)	95h	38.24N	35.33W
Harrow, Eng., U.K. (hăr′ō)	138b	51.34N	0.21W
Harrow on the Hill, neigh., Eng., U.K.	231	51.34N	0.20W
Harsefeld, Ger. (här′zĕ-fĕld′)	139c	53.27N	9.30E
Harstad, Nor. (här′städh)	140	68.49N	16.10E
Hart, Mi., U.S. (härt)	92	43.40N	86.25W
Hartbeesfontein, S. Afr.	212d	26.46S	26.25E
Hartbeespoortdam, res., S. Afr.	207b	25.47S	27.43E
Hartford, Al., U.S. (härt′fērd)	108	31.05N	85.42W
Hartford, Ar., U.S.	104	35.01N	94.21W
Hartford, Ct., U.S.	90	41.45N	72.40W
Hartford, Il., U.S.	101e	38.50N	90.06W
Hartford, Ky., U.S.	108	37.25N	86.50W
Hartford, Mi., U.S.	92	42.15N	86.15W
Hartford, Wi., U.S.	96	43.19N	88.25W
Hartford City, In., U.S.	92	40.35N	85.25W
Hartington, Eng., U.K. (härt′ĭng-tŭn)	138a	53.08N	1.48W
Hartington, Ne., U.S.	96	42.37N	97.18W
Hartland Point, c., Eng., U.K.	144	51.03N	4.40W
Hartlepool, Eng., U.K. (här′t′l-pōōl)	140	54.40N	1.12W
Hartley, Eng., U.K.	231	51.23N	0.19E
Hartley, Ia., U.S. (härt′lĭ)	96	43.12N	95.29W
Hartley Bay, Can.	80	53.25N	129.15W
Hart Mountain, mtn., Can. (härt)	82	52.25N	101.30W
Hartsbeespoort, S. Afr.	207b	25.44S	27.51E
Hartselle, Al., U.S. (härt′sĕl)	108	34.24N	86.55W
Hartshorne, Ok., U.S. (härts′hôrn)	104	34.49N	95.34W
Hartsville, S.C., U.S. (härts′vĭl)	108	34.20N	80.04W
Hartwell, Ga., U.S. (härt′wĕl)	108	34.21N	82.56W
Hartwell Lake, res., U.S.	90	34.30N	83.00W
Hārua, India	178a	22.36N	88.40E
Harvard, Il., U.S. (här′vȧrd)	96	42.25N	88.39W
Harvard, Ma., U.S.	87a	42.30N	71.35W
Harvard, Ne., U.S.	104	40.36N	98.08W
Harvard, Mount, mtn., Co., U.S.	102	38.55N	106.20W
Harvel, Eng., U.K.	231	51.21N	0.22E
Harvey, Can.	86	45.44N	64.46W
Harvey, Il., U.S.	95a	41.37N	87.39W
Harvey, La., U.S.	94d	29.54N	90.05W
Harvey, N.D., U.S.	96	47.46N	99.55W
Harwich, Eng., U.K. (hăr′wĭch)	144	51.53N	1.13E
Harwick, Pa., U.S.	226b	40.34N	79.48W
Harwood, Eng., U.K.	233b	53.35N	2.23W
Harwood, Md., U.S.	225c	38.52N	76.37W
Harwood Heights, Il., U.S.	227a	41.59N	87.48W
Harwood Park, Md., U.S.	225c	39.12N	76.44W
Haryana, state, India	174	29.00N	75.45E
Harz Mountains, mts., Ger. (härts)	148	51.42N	10.50E
Ḥasanābād, Iran	237h	35.44N	51.19E
Hasbrouck Heights, N.J., U.S.	224	40.52N	74.04W
Hashimoto, Japan (hä′shē-mō′tō)	187	34.19N	135.37E
Haskayne, Eng., U.K.	233a	53.34N	2.58W
Haskell, Ok., U.S. (hăs′kĕl)	104	35.49N	95.41W
Haskell, Tx., U.S.	104	33.09N	99.43W
Hasköy, neigh., Tur.	235f	41.02N	28.58E
Haslingden, Eng., U.K. (hăz′lĭng dĕn)	138a	53.43N	2.19W
Hasselbeck-Schwarzbach, Ger.	232	51.16N	6.53E
Hassels, neigh., Ger.	232	51.10N	6.53E
Hassi Messaoud, Alg.	204	31.17N	6.13E
Hässleholm, Swe. (häs′lĕ-hōlm)	146	56.10N	13.44E
Hasslinghausen, Ger.	232	51.20N	7.17E
Hästen, neigh., Ger.	232	51.09N	7.06E
Hasten, neigh., Ger.	232	51.12N	7.09E
Hastings, N.Z.	197a	39.33S	176.53E
Hastings, Eng., U.K. (hās′tĭngz)	140	50.52N	0.28E
Hastings, Mi., U.S.	92	42.40N	85.20W
Hastings, Mn., U.S.	101g	44.44N	92.51W
Hastings, Ne., U.S.	90	40.34N	98.42W
Hastings-on-Hudson, N.Y., U.S. (ŏn-hŭd′sŭn)	94a	40.59N	75.53W
Hastingwood, Eng., U.K.	231	51.45N	0.09E
Hatchie, r., Tn., U.S. (hăch′ē)	108	35.28N	89.14W
Haţeg, Rom. (kät-säg′)	154	45.35N	22.57E
Hatfield Broad Oak, Eng., U.K. (hăt-fēld brôd ōk)	138b	51.50N	0.14E
Hatogaya, Japan (hä′tō-gä-yä)	187a	35.50N	139.45E
Hatsukaichi, Japan (hät′sōō-kȧ′ē-chē)	187	34.22N	132.19E
Hatteras, Cape, c., N.C., U.S. (hăt′ēr-ȧs)	90	35.15N	75.24W
Hattiesburg, Ms., U.S. (hăt′ĭz-bûrg)	90	31.20N	89.18W
Hattingen, Ger. (hä′tĕn-gĕn)	151c	51.24N	7.11E
Hatton, neigh., Eng., U.K.	231	51.28N	0.25W
Hattori, Japan	238b	34.46N	135.27E
Hatvan, Hung. (hôt′vôn)	148	47.39N	19.44E

PLACE (Pronunciation)	PAGE	Lat. °'	Long. °'
Hatzfeld, neigh., Ger.	232	51.17N	7.11E
Haugesund, Nor. (hou′gĕ-soon′)	140	59.26N	5.20E
Haughton Green, Eng., U.K.	233b	53.27N	2.06W
Haukivesi, l., Fin. (hou′kē-vĕ′sē)	146	62.02N	29.02E
Haultain, r., Can.	82	56.15N	106.35W
Hauptsrus, S. Afr.	212d	26.35S	26.16E
Hauraki Gulf, b., N.Z. (hä-ōō-rä′kē)	197a	36.30S	175.00E
Haut, Isle au, Me., U.S. (hō)	86	44.03N	68.13W
Haut Atlas, mts., Mor.	142	32.10N	5.49W
Hauterive, Can.	86	49.11N	68.16W
Hauula, Hi., U.S.	88a	21.37N	157.45W
Hauz Rāni, neigh., India	236d	28.32N	77.13E
Havana, Cuba	110	23.08N	82.23W
Havana, Il., U.S. (hȧ-vă′nȧ)	104	40.17N	90.02W
Havasu, Lake, res., U.S. (hăv′ȧ-sōō)	102	34.26N	114.09W
Havel, r., Ger. (hä′fĕl)	148	53.09N	13.10E
Havel-Kanal, can., Ger.	139b	52.36N	13.12E
Haverford, Pa., U.S.	225b	40.01N	75.18W
Haverhill, Ma., U.S. (hā′vēr-hĭl)	87a	42.46N	71.05W
Haverhill, N.H., U.S.	92	44.00N	72.05W
Havering, neigh., Eng., U.K.	231	51.34N	0.14E
Havering's Grove, Eng., U.K.	231	51.38N	0.23E
Haverstraw, N.Y., U.S. (hā′vēr-strô)	94a	41.11N	73.58W
Havertown, Pa., U.S.	225b	39.59N	75.18W
Havlíckuv Brod, Czech.	140	49.38N	15.34E
Havre, Mt., U.S. (hăv′ēr)	90	48.34N	109.42W
Havre-Boucher, Can. (hăv′rȧ-bōō-shā′)	86	45.42N	61.30W
Havre de Grace, Md., U.S. (hăv′ēr dē gräs′)	92	39.35N	76.05W
Havre-Saint Pierre, Can.	86	50.15N	63.36W
Haw, r., N.C., U.S. (hô)	108	36.17N	79.46W
Hawaii, state, U.S.	90c	20.00N	157.40W
Hawaii, i., Hi., U.S. (häw wī′ē)	90c	19.50N	157.15W
Hawaiian Gardens, Ca., U.S.	228	33.50N	118.04W
Hawaiian Islands, is., Hi., U.S. (hä-wī′ȧn)	90c	22.00N	158.00W
Hawaii Volcanoes National Park, rec., Hi., U.S.	90c	19.30N	155.25W
Hawarden, Ia., U.S. (hā′wȧr-dĕn)	96	43.00N	96.28W
Ḥawf, Jabal, hills, Egypt	240a	29.55N	31.21E
Hawi, Hi., U.S. (hä′wē)	88a	20.16N	155.48W
Hawick, Scot., U.K. (hô′ĭk)	144	55.25N	2.55W
Hawke Bay, b., N.Z. (hôk)	197a	39.17S	177.20E
Hawker, Austl. (hô′kēr)	198	31.58S	138.12E
Hawkesbury, Can. (hôks′bēr-ĭ)	84	45.35N	74.35W
Hawkinsville, Ga., U.S. (hô′kĭnz-vĭl)	108	32.15N	83.30W
Hawks Nest Point, c., Bah.	116	24.05N	75.30W
Hawley, Eng., U.K.	231	51.25N	0.14E
Hawley, Mn., U.S. (hô′lĭ)	96	46.52N	96.18W
Haworth, Eng., U.K. (hä′wûrth)	138a	53.50N	1.57W
Haworth, N.J., U.S.	224	40.58N	73.59W
Hawthorn, Austl.	239b	37.49S	145.02E
Hawthorne, Ca., U.S. (hô′thôrn)	101a	33.55N	118.22W
Hawthorne, Nv., U.S.	102	38.33N	118.39W
Hawthorne, N.J., U.S.	224	40.57N	74.09W
Haxtun, Co., U.S. (hăks′tŭn)	104	40.39N	102.38W
Hay, r., Austl. (hā)	196	23.00S	136.45E
Hay, r., Can.	78	60.21N	117.14W
Hayama, Japan (hä-yä′mä)	187a	35.16N	139.35E
Hayashi, Japan (hä-yä′shē)	187a	35.13N	139.38E
Hayden, Az., U.S. (hā′dĕn)	102	33.00N	110.50W
Hayes, neigh., Eng., U.K.	231	51.23N	0.01E
Hayes, r., Can.	78	55.25N	93.55W
Hayes, Mount, mtn., Ak., U.S. (hāz)	89	63.32N	146.40W
Haynesville, La., U.S. (hānz′vĭl)	106	32.55N	93.08W
Hayrabolu, Tur.	154	41.14N	27.05E
Hay River, Can.	78	60.50N	115.53W
Hays, Ks., U.S. (hāz)	104	38.51N	99.20W
Haystack Mountain, mtn., Wa., U.S. (hā-stăk′)	100a	48.26N	122.07W
Hayward, Ca., U.S. (hā′wērd)	100b	37.40N	122.06W
Hayward, Wi., U.S.	96	46.01N	91.31W
Hazard, Ky., U.S. (hăz′ȧrd)	108	37.13N	83.10W
Hazel Grove, Eng., U.K.	233b	53.23N	2.08W
Hazelhurst, Ga., U.S. (hā′z′l-hûrst)	108	31.50N	82.36W
Hazelhurst, Ms., U.S.	108	31.52N	90.23W
Hazel Park, Mi., U.S.	95b	42.28N	83.06W
Hazelton, Can. (hā′z′l-tŭn)	78	55.15N	127.40W
Hazelton Mountains, mts., Can.	80	55.00N	128.00W
Hazleton, Pa., U.S.	92	41.00N	76.00W
Headland, Al., U.S. (hĕd′lănd)	108	31.22N	85.20W
Headley, Eng., U.K.	231	51.17N	0.16W
Heald Green, Eng., U.K.	233b	53.22N	2.14W
Healdsburg, Ca., U.S. (hēldz′bûrg)	102	38.37N	122.52W
Healdton, Ok., U.S. (hēld′tŭn)	104	34.13N	97.28W
Heanor, Eng., U.K. (hĕn′ōr)	138a	53.01N	1.22W
Heard Island, i., Austl. (hûrd)	2	53.10S	74.35E
Hearne, Tx., U.S. (hûrn)	106	30.53N	96.35W
Hearst, Can. (hûrst)	78	49.36N	83.40W
Heart, r., N.D., U.S. (härt)	96	46.46N	102.34W
Heart Lake Indian Reserve, I.R., Can.	80	55.02N	111.30W
Heart's Content, Can. (härts kŏn′tĕnt)	86	47.52N	53.22W
Heathmont, Austl.	239b	37.49S	145.15E
Heaton Moor, Eng., U.K.	233b	53.25N	2.11W
Heavener, Ok., U.S. (hĕv′nēr)	104	34.52N	94.36W
Heaverham, Eng., U.K.	231	51.18N	0.15E
Heaviley, Eng., U.K.	233b	53.24N	2.09W
Hebbronville, Tx., U.S. (hē′brŭn-vĭl)	106	27.18N	98.40W
Hebbville, Md., U.S.	225c	39.20N	77.46W
Hebei, prov., China (hŭ-bā)	180	39.15N	115.40E
Heber City, Ut., U.S. (hē′bēr)	102	40.30N	111.25W
Heber Springs, Ar., U.S.	104	35.28N	91.59W
Hebgen Lake, res., Mt., U.S. (hĕb′gĕn)	98	44.47N	111.38W
Hebrides, is., Scot., U.K.	136	57.00N	6.30W
Hebrides, Sea of the, sea, Scot., U.K.	144	57.00N	7.00W
Hebron, Can. (hĕb′rŭn)	78	58.11N	62.56W

PLACE (Pronunciation)	PAGE	Lat. °'	Long. °'
Hebron, In., U.S.	95a	41.19N	87.13W
Hebron, Ky., U.S.	95f	39.04N	84.43W
Hebron, Ne., U.S.	104	40.11N	97.36W
Hebron, N.D., U.S.	96	46.54N	102.04W
Hebron, *see* Al Khalīl, Isr. Occ.	173a	31.31N	35.07E
Heby, Swe. (hĭ′bü)	146	59.56N	16.48E
Hecate Strait, strt., Can. (hĕk′ȧ-tē)	78	53.00N	131.00W
Hecelchakán, Mex. (ā-sĕl-chä-kän′)	112	20.10N	90.09W
Hechi, China (hŭ-chr)	184	24.50N	108.18E
Hechuan, China (hŭ-chyuän)	180	30.00N	106.20E
Hecla Island, i., Can.	82	51.08N	96.45W
Hedemora, Swe. (hĭ-dĕ-mō′rä)	146	60.16N	15.55E
Hedon, Eng., U.K. (hĕ-dŭn)	138a	53.44N	0.12W
Heemstede, Neth.	139a	52.20N	4.36E
Heerdt, neigh., Ger.	232	51.13N	6.43E
Heerlen, Neth.	144	50.55N	5.58E
Hefei, China (hŭ-fā)	180	31.51N	117.15E
Heflin, Al., U.S. (hĕf′lĭn)	108	33.40N	85.33W
Heide, Ger. (hī′dē)	148	54.13N	9.06E
Heide, neigh., Ger.	232	51.31N	6.52E
Heidelberg, Austl. (hī′dĕl-bûrg)	195a	37.45S	145.04E
Heidelberg, Ger. (hīdĕl-bĕrgh)	140	49.24N	8.43E
Heidelberg, S. Afr.	212d	26.32S	28.22E
Heidelberg, Pa., U.S.	226b	40.23N	80.05W
Heidenheim, Ger. (hī′dĕn-hīm)	148	48.41N	10.09E
Heil, Ger.	232	51.38N	7.35E
Heilbron, S. Afr. (hīl′brōn)	212d	27.17S	27.58E
Heilbronn, Ger. (hīl′brōn)	140	49.09N	9.16E
Heiligenhaus, Ger. (hī′lē-gĕn-houz)	151c	51.19N	6.58E
Heiligensee, neigh., Ger.	234a	52.36N	13.13E
Heiligenstadt, Ger. (hī′lē-gĕn-shtät)	148	51.21N	10.10E
Heilongjiang, prov., China (hā-lôŋ-jyäŋ)	180	46.36N	128.07E
Heinersdorf, Ger.	234a	52.23N	13.20E
Heinersdorf, neigh., Ger.	234a	52.34N	13.27E
Heinola, Fin. (hā-nō′lȧ)	146	61.13N	26.03E
Heinsberg, Ger. (hīnz′bĕrgh)	151c	51.04N	6.07E
Heisingen, neigh., Ger.	232	51.25N	7.04E
Heist-op-den-Berg, Bel.	139a	51.05N	4.14E
Hejaz, *see* Al Ḥijāz, reg., Sau. Ar.	174	23.45N	39.08E
Hejian, China (hŭ-jyĕn)	184	38.28N	116.05E
Hekla, vol., Ice.	136	63.53N	19.37W
Hel, Pol. (hāl)	148	54.37N	18.53E
Helagsfjället, mtn., Swe.	140	62.54N	12.24E
Helan Shan, mts., China (hŭ-län shän)	180	38.02N	105.20E
Helena, Ar., U.S. (hē-lē′nȧ)	90	34.33N	90.35W
Helena, Mt., U.S. (hĕ-lē′nȧ)	90	46.35N	112.01W
Helensburgh, Austl. (hĕl′ĕnz-bŭr-ō)	195b	34.11S	150.59E
Helensburgh, Scot., U.K.	144	56.01N	4.53W
Helgoland, i., Ger. (hĕl′gō-länd)	148	54.13N	7.30E
Heliopolis, hist., Egypt	240a	30.08N	31.17E
Hellier, Ky., U.S. (hĕl′yēr)	108	37.16N	82.27W
Hellín, Spain (ĕl-yĕn′)	142	38.30N	1.40W
Hells Canyon, val., U.S.	98	45.20N	116.45W
Helmand, r., Afg. (hĕl′mŭnd)	174	31.00N	63.48E
Helmond, Neth. (hĕl′mōnt) (ĕl′mōɴ′)	144	51.35N	5.04E
Helmstedt, Ger. (hĕlm′shtĕt)	148	52.14N	11.03E
Helotes, Tx., U.S. (hē′lōts)	101d	29.35N	98.41W
Helper, Ut., U.S. (hĕlp′ēr)	102	39.40N	110.55W
Helsby, Eng., U.K.	233a	53.16N	2.46W
Helsingborg, Swe. (hĕl′sĭng-bôrgh)	140	56.04N	12.40E
Helsingfors, *see* Helsinki, Fin.	136	60.10N	24.53E
Helsingør, Den. (hĕl-sĭng-ŭr′)	140	56.03N	12.33E
Helsinki, Fin. (hĕl′sĕn-kē) (hĕl′sĭng-fôrs′)	136	60.10N	24.53E
Hemel Hempstead, Eng., U.K. (hĕm′ĕl hĕmp′stĕd)	138b	51.43N	0.29W
Hemer, Ger.	151c	51.22N	7.46E
Hemet, Ca., U.S. (hĕm′ĕt)	101a	33.45N	116.57W
Hemingford, Ne., U.S. (hĕm′ĭng-fērd)	96	42.21N	103.30W
Hemphill, Tx., U.S. (hĕmp′hĭl)	106	31.20N	93.48W
Hempstead, N.Y., U.S. (hĕmp′stĕd)	94a	40.42N	73.37W
Hempstead, Tx., U.S.	106	30.07N	96.05W
Hemse, Swe. (hĕm′sē)	146	57.15N	18.25E
Hemsön, i., Swe.	146	62.43N	18.22E
Henan, prov., China (hŭ-nän)	180	33.58N	112.33E
Henares, r., Spain (ā-nä′räs)	152	40.50N	2.55W
Henderson, Ky., U.S. (hĕn′dēr-sŭn)	92	37.50N	87.30W
Henderson, Nv., U.S.	102	36.09N	115.04W
Henderson, N.C., U.S.	108	36.18N	78.24W
Henderson, Tn., U.S.	108	35.25N	88.40W
Henderson, Tx., U.S.	106	32.09N	94.48W
Hendersonville, N.C., U.S. (hĕn′dēr-sŭn-vĭl)	108	35.17N	82.28W
Hendersonville, Tn., U.S.	108	36.18N	86.37W
Hendon, Eng., U.K. (hĕn′dŭn)	138b	51.34N	0.13W
Hendrina, S. Afr. (hĕn-drē′nȧ)	212d	26.10S	29.44E
Hengch'un, Tai. (hĕng′chŭn′)	184	22.00N	120.42E
Hengelo, Neth. (hĕŋgĕ-lō)	144	52.20N	6.45E
Hengshan, China (hĕng′shän′)	184	27.20N	112.40E
Hengshui, China (hĕng′shōō-ē′)	182	37.43N	115.42E
Hengxian, China (hŭŋ shyĕn)	184	22.40N	109.20E
Hengyang, China	180	26.58N	112.30E
Henley on Thames, Eng., U.K. (hĕn′lē ŏn tĕmz)	138b	51.31N	0.54W
Henlopen, Cape, c., De., U.S. (hĕn-lō′pĕn)	92	38.45N	75.05W
Hennebont, Fr. (ĕn-bôɴ′)	150	47.47N	3.16W
Hennenman, S. Afr.	212d	27.59S	27.03E
Hennessey, Ok., U.S. (hĕn′ĕ-sĭ)	104	36.04N	97.53W
Hennigsdorf, Ger. (hĕ′nĕngz-dōrf)	139b	52.39N	13.12E
Hennops, r., S. Afr. (hĕn′ŏps)	207b	25.51S	27.57E
Hennopsrivier, S. Afr.	207b	25.50S	27.59E
Henrietta, Ok., U.S. (hĕn-rĭ-ĕt′ȧ)	104	35.25N	95.58W
Henrietta, Tx., U.S. (hen-rĭ-ĕ′tȧ)	104	33.47N	98.11W
Henrietta Maria, Cape, c., Can. (hĕn-rĭ-ĕt′ȧ)	78	55.10N	82.20W

ng-sing; ŋ-baŋk; ɴ-nasalized n; nŏd; cŏmmit; ōld; ōbey; ôrder; oi-boil; fōōd; ò-as oo in foot; ou-out; s-soft; sh-dish; th-thin; pūre; ûnite; ûrn; stŭd; circŭs; ü-as in French tu; ′-indeterminate vowel.

PLACE (Pronunciation)	PAGE	Lat. °'	Long. °'
Henry Mountains, mts., Ut., U.S. (hĕn'rĭ)	90	37.55N	110.45W
Henrys Fork, r., Id., U.S.	98	43.52N	111.55W
Henteyn Nuruu, mtn., Russia	184	49.40N	111.00E
Hentiyn Nuruu, mts., Mong.	180	49.25N	107.51E
Henzada, Burma	174	17.38N	95.28E
Heppner, Or., U.S. (hĕp'nẽr)	98	45.21N	119.33W
Hepu, China (hŭ-pōō)	184	21.28N	109.10E
Herāt, Afg. (hĕ-rät')	174	34.28N	62.13E
Herbede, Ger.	232	51.25N	7.16E
Hercules, Can.	77g	53.27N	113.20W
Herdecke, Ger. (hĕr'dĕ-kĕ)	151c	51.24N	7.26E
Heredia, C.R. (ā-rā'dhē-ä)	114	10.04N	84.06W
Hereford, Eng., U.K. (hĕrĕ'fẽrd)	144	52.05N	2.44W
Hereford, Md., U.S.	94e	39.35N	76.42W
Hereford, Tx., U.S. (hĕr'ĕ-fẽrd)	104	34.47N	102.25W
Hereford and Worcester, co., Eng., U.K.	138a	52.24N	2.15W
Herencia, Spain (å-rān'thē-ä)	152	39.23N	3.22W
Herentals, Bel.	139a	51.10N	4.51E
Herford, Ger. (hĕr'fôrt)	148	52.06N	8.42E
Herington, Ks., U.S. (hĕr'ĭng-tŭn)	104	38.41N	96.57W
Herisau, Switz. (hā'rē-zou)	148	47.23N	9.18E
Herk-de-Stad, Bel.	139a	50.56N	5.13E
Herkimer, N.Y., U.S. (hûr'kĭ-mẽr)	92	43.05N	75.00W
Hermannskogel, mtn., Aus.	235e	48.16N	16.18E
Hermansville, Mi., U.S. (hûr'măns-vĭl)	92	45.40N	87.35W
Hermantown, Mn., U.S. (hẽr'mȧn-toun)	101h	46.46N	92.12W
Hermanusdorings, S. Afr.	212d	24.08S	27.46E
Herminie, Pa., U.S. (hûr-mĭ'nē)	95e	40.16N	79.45W
Hermitage Bay, b., Can. (hûr'mĭ-tĕj)	86	47.35N	56.05W
Hermit Islands, is., Pap. N. Gui. (hûr'mĭt)	188	1.48S	144.55E
Hermosa Beach, Ca., U.S. (hẽr-mō'sȧ)	101a	33.51N	118.24W
Hermosillo, Mex. (ĕr-mô-sē'l-yō)	110	29.00N	110.57W
Hermsdorf, neigh., Ger.	234a	52.37N	13.18E
Hernals, neigh., Aus.	235e	48.13N	16.20E
Herndon, Va., U.S. (hĕrn'don)	94e	38.58N	77.22W
Herne, Ger. (hĕr'nĕ)	151c	51.32N	7.13E
Herning, Den. (hĕr'nĭng)	140	56.08N	8.55E
Hernwood Heights, Md., U.S.	225c	39.22N	77.50W
Héroes Chapultepec, Mex.	229a	19.28N	99.04W
Héroes de Churubusco, Mex.	229a	19.22N	99.06W
Heron, l., Mn., U.S. (hĕr'ŭn)	96	43.42N	95.23W
Herongate, Eng., U.K.	231	51.36N	0.21E
Heron Lake, Mn., U.S.	96	43.48N	95.20W
Heronsgate, Eng., U.K.	231	51.38N	0.31W
Herrero, Punta, Mex. (pô'n-tä-ĕr-rĕ'rô)	114a	19.18N	87.24W
Herrin, Il., U.S. (hĕr'ĭn)	92	37.50N	89.00W
Herschel, Transkei (hẽr'-shĕl)	207c	30.37S	27.12E
Herscher, Il., U.S. (hẽr'shẽr)	95a	41.03N	88.06W
Hersham, Eng., U.K.	231	51.22N	0.23W
Herstal, Bel. (hĕr'stäl)	144	50.42N	5.32E
Herten, Ger.	232	51.35N	7.07E
Hertford, Eng., U.K.	144	51.48N	0.05W
Hertford, N.C., U.S. (hûrt'fẽrd)	108	36.10N	76.30W
Hertfordshire, co., Eng., U.K.	138b	51.46N	0.05W
Hertzberg, Ger. (hĕrtz'bĕrgh)	139b	52.54N	12.58E
Hervás, Spain	152	40.16N	5.51W
Herzliyya, Isr.	173a	32.10N	34.49E
Hessen, hist. reg., Ger. (hĕs'ĕn)	148	50.42N	9.00E
Heswall, Eng., U.K.	233a	53.20N	3.06W
Hetch Hetchy Aqueduct, Ca., U.S. (hĕtch hĕt'chĭ ȧk'wē-dŭkt)	102	37.27N	120.54W
Hettinger, N.D., U.S. (hĕt'ĭn-jẽr)	96	45.58N	102.36W
Hetzendorf, neigh., Aus.	235e	48.10N	16.18E
Heuningspruit, S. Afr.	212d	27.28S	27.26E
Heven, neigh., Ger.	232	51.26N	7.17E
Hewlett, N.Y., U.S.	224	40.38N	73.42W
Hewlett Harbor, N.Y., U.S.	224	40.38N	73.41W
Hexian, China	182	31.44N	118.20E
Hexian, China (hŭ shyĕn)	184	24.20N	111.28E
Hextable, Eng., U.K.	231	51.25N	0.11E
Heyang, China (hŭ-yäŋ)	184	35.18N	110.18E
Heystekrand, S. Afr.	212d	25.16S	27.14E
Heyuan, China (hŭ-yůän)	184	23.48N	114.45E
Heywood, Eng., U.K. (hā'wŏŏd)	138a	53.36N	2.12W
Heze, China (hŭ-dzŭ)	182	35.13N	115.28E
Hialeah, Fl., U.S. (hī-å-lē'äh)	109a	25.49N	80.18W
Hiawatha, Ks., U.S. (hī-ȧ-wô'thȧ)	104	39.50N	95.33W
Hiawatha, Ut., U.S.	102	39.25N	111.05W
Hibbing, Mn., U.S. (hĭb'ĭng)	90	47.26N	92.58W
Hickman, Ky., U.S. (hĭk'mȧn)	108	34.33N	89.10W
Hickory, N.C., U.S. (hĭk'ô-rĭ)	108	35.43N	81.21W
Hickory Hills, Il., U.S.	227a	41.43N	87.49W
Hicksville, N.Y., U.S.	92	41.15N	84.45W
Hicksville, N.Y., U.S. (hĭks'vĭl)	94a	40.47N	73.25W
Hico, Tx., U.S. (hī'kō)	106	32.00N	98.02W
Hidalgo, Mex.	106	27.49N	99.53W
Hidalgo, Mex. (ē-dhäl'gō)	112	24.14N	99.25W
Hidalgo, state, Mex.	110	20.45N	99.30W
Hidalgo del Parral, Mex. (ē-dä'l-gō-dĕl-pär-rä'l)	110	26.55N	105.40W
Hidalgo Yalalag, Mex. (ē-dhäl'gō-yä-lä-läg)	112	17.12N	96.11W
Hiddinghausen, Ger.	232	51.22N	7.17E
Hierro Island, i., Spain (yĕ'r-rô)	204	27.37N	18.29W
Hiesfeld, Ger.	232	51.33N	6.46E
Hietzing, neigh., Aus.	235e	48.11N	16.18E
Higashi, neigh., Japan	238b	34.41N	135.31E
Higashimurayama, Japan	187a	35.46N	139.28E
Higashinada, neigh., Japan	238b	34.43N	135.16E
Higashinakano, Japan	238a	35.38N	139.25E
Higashinari, neigh., Japan	238b	34.40N	135.33E
Higashiōizumi, neigh., Japan	238a	35.45N	139.36E
Higashiōsaka, Japan	187b	34.40N	135.44E
Higashisumiyoshi, neigh., Japan	238b	34.37N	135.32E
Higashiyama, neigh., Japan	237e	35.00N	135.48E
Higashiyodogawa, neigh., Japan	238b	34.44N	135.29E
Higgins, l., Mi., U.S. (hĭg'ĭnz)	92	44.20N	84.45W
Higginsville, Mo., U.S. (hĭg'ĭnz-vĭl)	104	39.05N	93.44W
High, i., Mi., U.S.	92	45.45N	85.45W
Higham, Eng., U.K.	231	51.26N	0.28E
High Beach, Eng., U.K.	231	51.39N	0.02E
High Bluff, Can.	77f	50.01N	98.08W
Highborne Cay, i., Bah. (hī'bôrn kē)	116	24.45N	76.50W
Highcliff, Pa., U.S.	226b	40.32N	80.03W
Higher Broughton, neigh., Eng., U.K.	233b	53.30N	2.15W
Highgrove, Ca., U.S. (hī'grōv)	101a	34.01N	117.20W
High Island, Tx., U.S.	107a	29.34N	94.24W
Highland, Ca., U.S. (hī'lănd)	101a	34.08N	117.13W
Highland, Il., U.S.	104	38.44N	89.41W
Highland, In., U.S.	95a	41.33N	87.28W
Highland, Mi., U.S.	95b	42.38N	83.37W
Highland, Pa., U.S.	226b	40.33N	80.04W
Highland Park, Il., U.S.	95a	42.11N	87.47W
Highland Park, Md., U.S.	225d	38.54N	76.54W
Highland Park, Mi., U.S.	95b	42.24N	83.06W
Highland Park, N.J., U.S.	94a	40.30N	74.25W
Highland Park, Tx., U.S.	101c	32.49N	96.48W
Highlands, N.J., U.S. (hī-lăndz)	94a	40.24N	73.59W
Highlands, Tx., U.S.	107a	29.49N	95.01W
High Laver, Eng., U.K.	231	51.45N	0.13E
Highmore, S.D., U.S. (hī'mōr)	96	44.30N	99.26W
High Ongar, Eng., U.K. (on'gẽr)	138b	51.43N	0.15E
High Peak, mtn., Phil.	189a	15.38N	120.05E
High Point, N.C., U.S.	108	35.55N	80.00W
High Prairie, Can.	78	55.26N	116.29W
High Ridge, Mo., U.S.	101e	38.27N	90.32W
High River, Can.	78	50.35N	113.52W
High Rock Lake, res., N.C., U.S. (hī'-rŏk)	108	35.40N	80.15W
High Springs, Fl., U.S.	108	29.48N	82.38W
High Tatra Mountains, mts., Eur.	148	49.15N	19.40E
Hightown, Eng., U.K.	233a	53.32N	3.04W
Hightstown, N.J., U.S. (hīts-toun)	94a	40.16N	74.32W
High Wycombe, Eng., U.K. (wĭ-kŭm)	144	51.36N	0.45W
Higuero, Punta, c., P.R.	111b	18.21N	67.11W
Higuerote, Ven. (ē-gĕ-rô'tĕ)	125b	10.29N	66.06W
Higüey, Dom. Rep. (ē-gwĕ'y)	116	18.40N	68.45W
Hiiumaa, i., Est. (hē'ŏŏm-ô)	160	58.47N	22.05E
Hikone, Japan (hē'kô-nĕ)	187	35.15N	136.15E
Hildburghausen, Ger. (hĭld'bŏŏrg hou-zĕn)	148	50.26N	10.45E
Hilden, Ger. (hēl'dĕn)	151c	51.10N	6.56E
Hildesheim, Ger. (hĭl'dĕs-hīm)	140	52.08N	9.56E
Hillaby, Mount, mtn., Barb. (hĭl'ȧ-bĭ)	115b	13.15N	59.35W
Hill City, Ks., U.S. (hĭl)	104	39.22N	99.54W
Hill City, Mn., U.S.	96	46.58N	93.38W
Hill Crest, Pa., U.S.	225b	40.05N	75.11W
Hillcrest Heights, Md., U.S.	225d	38.52N	76.57W
Hillegersberg, Neth.	139a	51.57N	4.29E
Hillen, neigh., Ger.	232	51.37N	7.13E
Hillerød, Den. (hē'lĕ-rûdh)	146	55.56N	12.17E
Hillingdon, neigh., Eng., U.K.	231	51.32N	0.27W
Hillsboro, Il., U.S. (hĭlz'bŭr-ō)	104	39.09N	89.28W
Hillsboro, Ks., U.S.	104	38.22N	97.11W
Hillsboro, N.H., U.S.	92	43.05N	71.55W
Hillsboro, N.D., U.S.	96	47.23N	97.05W
Hillsboro, Oh., U.S.	92	39.10N	83.40W
Hillsboro, Or., U.S.	100c	45.31N	122.59W
Hillsboro, Tx., U.S.	106	32.01N	97.06W
Hillsboro, Wi., U.S.	96	43.39N	90.20W
Hillsburgh, Can. (hĭlz'bûrg)	77d	43.48N	80.09W
Hills Creek Lake, res., Or., U.S.	98	43.41N	122.26W
Hillsdale, Mi., U.S. (hĭls-dāl)	102	41.55N	84.35W
Hillside, Md., U.S.	225d	38.52N	76.55W
Hillside, neigh., N.Y., U.S.	224	40.42N	73.47W
Hillwood, Va., U.S.	225d	38.52N	77.10W
Hilo, Hi., U.S. (hē'lō)	90c	19.44N	155.01W
Hiltrop, neigh., Ger.	232	51.30N	7.15E
Hilvarenbeek, Neth.	139a	51.29N	5.10E
Hilversum, Neth. (hĭl'vēr-sŭm)	139a	52.13N	5.10E
Himachal Pradesh, India	174	32.00N	77.30E
Himalayas, mts., Asia	174	29.30N	85.02E
Himeji, Japan (hē'må-jė)	186	34.50N	134.42E
Himmelgeist, neigh., Ger.	232	51.10N	6.49E
Himmelpforten, Ger. (hē'mĕl-pfōr-tĕn)	139c	53.37N	9.19E
Ḩimş, Syria	174	34.44N	36.43E
Hinche, Haiti (hēn'chå) (ăNsh)	116	19.10N	72.05W
Hinchinbrook, i., Austl. (hĭn-chĭn-brŏŏk)	196	18.23S	146.57W
Hinckley, Eng., U.K. (hĭnk'lĭ)	138a	52.32N	1.21W
Hindley, Eng., U.K. (hĭnd'lĭ)	138a	53.32N	2.35W
Hindu Kush, mts., Asia (hĭn'dōō kōōsh')	174	35.15N	68.44E
Hindupur, India (hĭn'dōō-pōōr)	178	13.52N	77.34E
Hingham, Ma., U.S. (hĭng'ăm)	87a	42.14N	70.53W
Hinkley, Oh., U.S. (hĭnk'-lĭ)	95d	41.14N	81.45W
Hino, Japan	238a	35.41N	139.24E
Hinojosa del Duque, Spain (ē-nô-kō'sä)	152	38.30N	5.09W
Hinsdale, Il., U.S. (hĭnz'dāl)	95a	41.48N	87.56W
Hinsel, neigh., Ger.	232	51.26N	7.05E
Hinton, Can. (hĭn'tŭn)	80	53.25N	117.34W
Hinton, W.V., U.S. (hĭn'tŭn)	92	37.40N	80.55W
Hirado, i., Japan (hē'rä-dō)	186	33.19N	129.18E
Hirakata, Japan (hē'rä-kä'tä)	187b	34.49N	135.40E
Hirara, Japan	192d	24.48N	125.17E
Hiratsuka, Japan (hē-rät-sōō'kå)	187	35.20N	139.19E
Hirosaki, Japan (hē'rô-sä'kē)	180	40.31N	140.38E
Hirose, Japan (hē'rô-sä)	187	35.20N	133.11E
Hiroshima, Japan (hē-rô-shē'må)	180	34.22N	132.25E
Hirota, Japan	238b	34.45N	135.21E
Hirschstetten, neigh., Aus.	235e	48.14N	16.29E
Hirson, Fr. (ēr-sôN')	150	49.54N	4.00E
Hisar, India	178	29.15N	75.47E
Hispaniola, i., N.A. (hĭ'spăn-ĭ-ō-lå)	110	17.30N	73.15W
Hitachi, Japan (hē-tä'chē)	186	36.42N	140.47E
Hitchcock, Tx., U.S. (hĭch'kŏk)	107a	29.21N	95.01W
Hither Green, neigh., Eng., U.K.	231	51.27N	0.01W
Hitoyoshi, Japan (hē'tô-yō'shė)	187	32.13N	130.45E
Hitra, i., Nor. (hĭtrå)	140	63.34N	7.37E
Hittefeld, Ger. (hē'tĕ-fĕld)	139c	53.23N	9.59E
Hiwasa, Japan (hē'wå-sä)	187	33.44N	134.31E
Hiwassee, r., Tn., U.S. (hī-wôs'sē)	108	35.10N	84.35W
Hjälmaren, l., Swe.	140	59.07N	16.05E
Hjo, Swe. (yō)	146	58.19N	14.11E
Hjørring, Den. (jûr'ĭng)	140	57.27N	9.59E
Hlohovec, Czech. (hlō'ho-vĕts)	148	48.24N	17.49E
Hobart, Austl. (hō'bȧrt)	196	43.00S	147.30E
Hobart, In., U.S.	95a	41.31N	87.15W
Hobart, Ok., U.S.	104	35.02N	99.06W
Hobart, Wa., U.S.	100a	47.25N	121.58W
Hobbs, N.M., U.S. (hŏbs)	104	32.41N	103.15W
Hoboken, Bel. (hō'bō-kĕn)	139a	51.11N	4.20E
Hoboken, N.J., U.S.	94a	40.43N	74.03W
Hobro, Den. (hô-brô')	146	56.38N	9.47E
Hobson, Va., U.S. (hŏb'sŭn)	94g	36.54N	76.31W
Hobson's Bay, b., Austl. (hŏb'sŭnz)	195a	37.54S	144.45E
Hobyo, Som.	212a	5.24N	48.28E
Hochdahl, Ger.	232	51.13N	6.56E
Hochheide, Ger.	232	51.27N	6.41E
Ho Chi Minh City, Viet.	188	10.46N	106.34E
Hochlar, neigh., Ger.	232	51.36N	7.10E
Höchsten, Ger.	232	51.27N	7.29E
Hockinson, Wa., U.S. (hŏk'ĭn-sŭn)	100c	45.44N	122.29W
Hoctún, Mex. (ôk-tōō'n)	114a	20.52N	89.10W
Hodgenville, Ky., U.S. (hŏj'ĕn-vĭl)	92	37.35N	85.45W
Hodges Hill, mtn., Can. (hŏj'ĕz)	86	49.04N	55.53W
Hodgkins, Il., U.S.	227a	41.46N	87.51W
Hódmezővásárhely, Hung. (hōd'mĕ-zû-vô'shôr-hĕl-y')	148	46.24N	20.21E
Hodna, Chott el, l., Alg.	142	35.20N	3.27E
Hodonín, Czech. (hē'dô-nén)	148	48.50N	17.06E
Hoegaarden, Bel.	139a	50.46N	4.55E
Hoek van Holland, Neth.	139a	51.59N	4.05E
Hoeryŏng, N. Kor. (hwĕr'yŭng)	186	42.28N	129.39E
Hof, Ger. (hōf)	148	50.19N	11.55E
Hofburg, pt. of i., Aus.	235e	48.12N	16.22E
Hofsjökull, ice., Ice. (hôfs'yü'kōōl)	140	64.55N	18.40W
Hog, i., Mi., U.S.	92	45.50N	85.20W
Hogansville, Ga., U.S. (hō'gănz-vĭl)	108	33.10N	84.54W
Hogar y Redención, Mex.	229a	19.22N	99.13W
Hog Cay, i., Bah.	116	23.35N	75.30W
Hogsty Reef, rf., Bah.	116	21.45N	73.50W
Hohenbrunn, Ger. (hō'hĕn-brōōn)	139d	48.03N	11.42E
Hohenlimburg, Ger. (hō'hĕn lĕm'bōōrg)	151c	51.20N	7.35E
Hohen Neuendorf, Ger. (hō'hĕn noi'ĕn-dōrf)	139b	52.40N	13.22E
Hohenschönhausen, neigh., Ger.	234a	52.33N	13.30E
Hohensyburg, hist., Ger.	232	51.25N	7.29E
Hohe Tauern, mts., Aus. (hō'ĕ tou'ĕrn)	148	47.11N	12.12E
Hohhot, China (hŭ-hōō-tŭ)	180	41.05N	111.50E
Hohoe, Ghana	208	7.09N	0.28E
Hohokus, N.J., U.S. (hō-hō-kŭs)	94a	41.01N	74.08W
Höhscheid, neigh., Ger.	232	51.09N	7.04E
Hoi An, Viet.	184	15.48N	108.30E
Hoisington, Ks., U.S. (hoi'zĭng-tŭn)	104	38.30N	98.46W
Hoisten, Ger.	232	51.08N	6.42E
Hojo, Japan (hō'jō)	187	33.58N	132.50E
Hokitika, N.Z. (hō-kĭ-tē'kä)	197a	42.43S	170.59E
Hokkaidō, i., Japan (hôk'kī-dō)	186	43.30N	142.45E
Holbaek, Den. (hôl'bĕk)	146	55.42N	11.40E
Holborn, neigh., Eng., U.K.	231	51.31N	0.07W
Holbox, Mex. (ôl-bō'x)	114a	21.33N	87.19W
Holbox, Isla, i., Mex. (ē's-lä-ôl-bō'x)	114a	21.40N	87.21W
Holbrook, Az., U.S. (hōl'brŏŏk)	102	34.55N	110.15W
Holbrook, Ma., U.S.	87a	42.10N	71.01W
Holden, Ma., U.S. (hōl'dĕn)	87a	42.21N	71.51W
Holden, Mo., U.S.	104	38.42N	94.00W
Holden, W.V., U.S.	92	37.45N	82.05W
Holdenville, Ok., U.S. (hōl'dĕn-vĭl)	104	35.05N	96.25W
Holdrege, Ne., U.S. (hōl'drĕj)	104	40.25N	99.28W
Holguín, Cuba (ôl-gēn')	110	20.55N	76.15W
Holguín, prov., Cuba	116	20.40N	76.15W
Holidaysburg, Pa., U.S. (hŏl'ĭ-dāz-bûrg)	92	40.30N	78.30W
Hollabrunn, Aus.	148	48.33N	16.04E
Holland, Mi., U.S. (hŏl'ănd)	92	42.45N	86.10W
Hollands Diep, strt., Neth.	139a	51.43N	4.25E
Hollenstedt, Ger. (hō'lĕn-shtĕt)	139c	53.22N	9.43E
Hollins, Eng., U.K.	233b	53.34N	2.17W
Hollis, N.H., U.S. (hŏl'ĭs)	87a	42.30N	71.29W
Hollis, Ok., U.S.	104	34.39N	99.56W
Hollis, neigh., N.Y., U.S.	224	40.43N	73.46W
Hollister, Ca., U.S. (hŏl'ĭs-tẽr)	102	36.50N	121.25W
Holliston, Ma., U.S. (hŏl'ĭs-tŭn)	87a	42.12N	71.25W
Holly, Mi., U.S. (hŏl'ĭ)	92	42.45N	83.30W
Holly, Wa., U.S.	100a	47.34N	122.58W
Holly Springs, Ms., U.S. (hŏl'ĭ sprĭngz)	108	34.45N	89.28W
Hollywood, Ca., U.S. (hŏl'ē-wŏŏd)	101a	34.06N	118.20W
Hollywood, Fl., U.S.	109a	26.00N	80.11W
Hollywood Bowl, pt. of i., Ca., U.S.	228	34.07N	118.20W
Holmes, Pa., U.S.	225b	39.54N	75.19W
Holmes Reefs, rf., Austl. (hōmz)	196	16.33S	148.43E
Holmes Run Acres, Va., U.S.	225d	38.51N	77.13W
Holmestrand, Nor. (hŏl'mĕ-strän)	146	59.29N	10.17E
Holmsbu, Nor. (hŏlms'bōō)	146	59.36N	10.26E
Holmsjön, l., Swe.	146	62.23N	15.43E
Holroyd, Austl.	239a	33.50S	150.58E

ăt; fĭnăl; rāte; senāte; ärm; åsk; sofȧ; fâre; ch-choose; dh-as th in other; bē; ēvent; bĕt; recĕnt; cratẽr; g-gō; gh-guttural g; bĭt; ĭ-short neutral; rīde; ĸ-guttural k as ch in German ich;

PLACE (Pronunciation)	PAGE	Lat. °'	Long. °'
Holstebro, Den. (hôl'stĕ-brô)	140	56.22N	8.39E
Holston, r., Tn., U.S. (hōl'stŭn)	108	36.02N	83.42W
Holt, Eng., U.K. (hōlt)	138a	53.05N	2.53W
Holten, neigh., Ger.	232	51.31N	6.48E
Holthausen, neigh., Ger.	232	51.34N	7.26E
Holton, Ks., U.S. (hōl'tŭn)	104	39.27N	95.43W
Holy Cross, Ak., U.S. (hō'lĭ krôs)	89	62.10N	159.40W
Holyhead, Wales, U.K. (hŏl'ê-hĕd)	144	53.18N	4.45W
Holy Island, i., Eng., U.K.	144	55.43N	1.48W
Holy Island, i., Wales, U.K. (hō'lĭ)	144	53.15N	4.45W
Holyoke, Co., U.S. (hōl'yōk)	104	40.36N	102.18W
Holyoke, Ma., U.S.	92	42.10N	72.40W
Holzen, Ger.	232	51.26N	7.31E
Holzheim, Ger.	232	51.09N	6.39E
Holzwickede, Ger.	232	51.30N	7.36E
Homano, Japan (hō-mä'nō)	187a	35.33N	140.08E
Homberg, Ger. (hōm'bĕrgh)	151c	51.27N	6.42E
Hombori, Mali	208	15.17N	1.42W
Home Gardens, Ca., U.S. (hōm gär'd'nz)	101a	33.53N	117.32W
Homeland, Ca., U.S. (hōm'lănd)	101a	33.44N	117.07W
Homer, Ak., U.S. (hō'mēr)	89	59.42N	151.30W
Homer, La., U.S.	106	32.46N	93.05W
Homer Youngs Peak, mtn., Mt., U.S.	98	45.19N	113.41W
Homestead, Fl., U.S. (hōm'stĕd)	109a	25.27N	80.28W
Homestead, Mi., U.S.	101k	46.20N	84.07W
Homestead, Pa., U.S.	95e	40.29N	79.55W
Homestead National Monument of America, rec., Ne., U.S.	104	40.16N	96.51W
Hometown, Il., U.S.	227a	41.44N	87.44W
Homewood, Al., U.S. (hōm'wŏod)	94h	33.28N	86.48W
Homewood, Il., U.S.	95a	41.34N	87.40W
Homewood, neigh., Pa., U.S.	226b	40.27N	79.54W
Hominy, Ok., U.S. (hŏm'ĭ-nĭ)	104	36.25N	96.24W
Homochitto, r., Ms., U.S. (hō-mō-chĭt'ō)	108	31.23N	91.15W
Honda, Col. (hōn'dȧ)	124	5.13N	74.45W
Honda, Bahía, b., Cuba (bä-ē'ä-ô'n-dä)	116	23.10N	83.20W
Hondo, Tx., U.S.	106	29.20N	99.08W
Hondo, r., N.M., U.S.	104	33.22N	105.06W
Hondo, Río, r., N.A. (hon-dō')	114a	18.16N	88.32W
Honduras, nation, N.A. (hŏn-dōō'ràs)	110	14.30N	88.00W
Honduras, Gulf of, b., N.A.	110	16.30N	87.30W
Honea Path, S.C., U.S. (hŭn'ĭ păth)	108	34.25N	82.16W
Hönefoss, Nor. (hē'nĕ-fôs)	140	60.10N	10.15E
Honesdale, Pa., U.S. (hōnz'dāl)	92	41.30N	75.15W
Honey Grove, Tx., U.S. (hŭn'ĭ grōv)	104	33.35N	95.54W
Honey Lake, l., Ca., U.S. (hŭn'ĭ)	102	40.11N	120.34W
Honfleur, Can. (ôɴ-flûr')	77b	46.39N	70.53W
Honfleur, Fr. (ôɴ-flûr')	150	49.26N	0.13E
Hon Gay, Viet.	184	20.58N	107.10E
Hong Kong, dep., Asia (hŏng' kŏng')	180	21.45N	115.00E
Hongshui, r., China (hôŋ-shwā)	180	24.30N	105.00E
Honguedo, Détroit d', strt., Can.	86	49.08N	63.45W
Hongze Hu, l., China	180	33.17N	118.37E
Honiara, Sol.Is.	196	9.26S	159.57E
Honiton, Eng., U.K. (hŏn'ĭ-tŏn)	144	50.49N	3.10W
Honolulu, Hi., U.S. (hŏn-ô-lōō'lōō)	90c	21.18N	157.50W
Honomu, Hi., U.S. (hŏn'ô-mōō)	88a	19.50N	155.04W
Honshū, i., Japan	180	36.00N	138.00E
Höntrop, neigh., Ger.	232	51.27N	7.08E
Hood, Mount, mtn., Or., U.S.	90	45.20N	121.43W
Hood Canal, b., Wa., U.S. (hŏŏd)	100a	47.45N	122.45W
Hood River, Or., U.S.	90	45.42N	121.30W
Hoodsport, Wa., U.S. (hŏŏdz'pōrt)	100a	47.25N	123.09W
Hooghly-Chinsura, India	236a	22.54N	88.24E
Hoogly, r., India (hōōg'lĭ)	174	21.35N	87.50E
Hoogstraten, Bel.	139a	51.24N	4.46E
Hooker, Ok., U.S. (hŏŏk'ēr)	104	36.49N	101.13W
Hool, Mex. (ōō'l)	114a	19.32N	90.22W
Hoonah, Ak., U.S. (hōō'nä)	89	58.05N	135.25W
Hoopa Valley Indian Reservation, I.R., Ca., U.S.	98	41.18N	123.35W
Hooper, Ne., U.S. (hŏŏp'ēr)	104	41.37N	96.31W
Hooper, Ut., U.S.	101b	41.10N	112.08W
Hooper Bay, Ak., U.S.	89	61.32N	166.02W
Hoopeston, Il., U.S. (hōōps'tŭn)	92	40.35N	87.40W
Hoosick Falls, N.Y., U.S. (hōō'sĭk)	92	42.55N	73.15W
Hooton, Eng., U.K.	233a	53.18N	2.57W
Hoover Dam, Nv., U.S. (hōō'vēr)	102	36.00N	115.06W
Hoover Dam, dam, U.S.	90	36.00N	114.27W
Hopatcong, Lake, l., N.J., U.S. (hō-păt'kong)	94a	40.57N	74.38W
Hope, Ak., U.S. (hōp)	89	60.54N	149.48W
Hope, Ar., U.S.	104	33.41N	93.35W
Hope, N.D., U.S.	96	47.17N	97.45W
Hope, Ben, mtn., Scot., U.K. (bĕn hōp)	144	58.25N	4.25W
Hopedale, Can. (hōp'dāl)	78	55.26N	60.11W
Hopedale, Ma., U.S. (hōp'dāl)	87a	42.08N	71.33W
Hopelchén, Mex. (o-pĕl-chĕ'n)	114a	19.47N	89.51W
Hopes Advance, Cap, c., Can. (hōps ăd-vans')	78	61.05N	69.35W
Hopetoun, Austl. (hōp'toun)	196	33.50S	120.15E
Hopetown, S. Afr. (hōp'toun)	206	29.35S	24.10E
Hopewell, Va., U.S. (hōp'wĕl)	108	37.14N	77.15W
Hopi Indian Reservation, I.R., Az., U.S. (hō'pê)	102	36.20N	110.30W
Hopkins, Mn., U.S. (hŏp'kĭns)	101g	44.55N	93.24W
Hopkinsville, Ky., U.S. (hŏp'kĭns-vĭl)	90	36.50N	87.28W
Hopkinton, Ma., U.S. (hŏp'kĭn-tŭn)	87a	42.14N	71.31W
Hoppegarten, Ger.	234a	52.31N	13.40E
Hoquiam, Wa., U.S. (hō'kwĭ-ăm)	90	47.00N	123.53W
Horconcitos, Pan. (ŏr-kôn-sē'-tôs)	114	8.18N	82.11W
Hörde, neigh., Ger.	232	51.29N	7.30E
Horgen, Switz. (hôr'gĕn)	148	47.16N	8.35E
Horicon, Wi., U.S. (hŏr'ĭ-kŏn)	96	43.26N	88.40W

PLACE (Pronunciation)	PAGE	Lat. °'	Long. °'
Horinouchi, neigh., Japan	238a	35.41N	139.40E
Hormuz, Strait of, strt., Asia (hôr'mŭz')	174	26.30N	56.30E
Horn, i., Austl. (hôrn)	196	10.30S	143.30E
Horn, Cape, see Hornos, Cabo de, c., Chile	126	56.00S	67.00W
Hornavan, l., Swe.	140	65.54N	16.17E
Hornchurch, neigh., Eng., U.K.	231	51.34N	0.12E
Horndon on the Hill, Eng., U.K.	231	51.31N	0.25E
Horneburg, Ger. (hōr'nĕ-bòrgh)	139c	53.30N	9.35E
Horneburg, Ger.	232	51.38N	7.18E
Hornell, N.Y., U.S. (hôr-nĕl')	92	42.20N	77.40W
Horn Hill, Eng., U.K.	231	51.37N	0.32W
Hornos, Cabo de, c., Chile	126	56.00S	67.00W
Horn Plateau, plat., Can.	78	62.12N	120.29W
Hornsby, Austl. (hôrnz'bĭ)	195b	33.43S	151.06E
Hornsey, neigh., Eng., U.K.	231	51.35N	0.07W
Horqueta, Para. (ŏr-kĕ'tä)	126	23.20S	57.00W
Horse Creek, r., Co., U.S. (hôrs)	104	38.49N	103.48W
Horse Creek, r., Wy., U.S.	96	41.33N	104.39W
Horse Islands, is., Can.	86	50.11N	55.45W
Horsell, Eng., U.K.	231	51.19N	0.34W
Horsens, Den. (hôrs'ĕns)	146	55.50N	9.49E
Horseshoe Bay, Can. (hôrs-shōō)	100d	49.23N	123.16W
Horsforth, Eng., U.K. (hôrs'fŭrth)	138a	53.50N	1.38W
Horsham, Austl. (hôr'shăm) (hôrs'ăm)	196	36.42S	142.17E
Horsley, Austl.	239a	33.51S	150.51E
Horst, Ger. (hôrst)	139c	53.49N	9.37E
Horst, neigh., Ger.	232	51.32N	7.02E
Horsthausen, neigh., Ger.	232	51.33N	7.13E
Horstmar, neigh., Ger.	232	51.36N	7.33E
Hortaleza, neigh., Spain	234b	40.28N	3.39W
Horten, Nor. (hòr'tĕn)	146	59.26N	10.27E
Horton, Ks., U.S. (hôr'tŭn)	104	39.38N	95.32W
Horton, r., Ak., U.S. (hôr'tŭn)	89	68.38N	122.00W
Horton Kirby, Eng., U.K.	231	51.23N	0.15E
Horwich, Eng., U.K. (hŏr'ĭch)	138a	53.36N	2.33W
Hösel, Ger.	232	51.19N	6.54E
Hososhima, Japan (hō'sô-shē'mä)	186	32.25N	131.40E
Hospitalet, Spain	234e	41.22N	2.08E
Hoste, i., Chile (ôs'tä)	126	55.20S	70.45W
Hostotipaquillo, Mex. (ôs-tō'tĭ-pä-kēl'yō)	112	21.09N	104.05W
Hota, Japan (hō'tä)	187a	35.08N	139.50E
Hotan, China (hwô-tän)	180	37.11N	79.50E
Hotan, r., China	180	39.09N	81.08E
Hoto Mayor, Dom. Rep. (ô-tô-mä-yô'r)	116	18.45N	69.10W
Hot Springs, Ak., U.S. (hŏt sprĭngs)	89	65.00N	150.20W
Hot Springs, Ar., U.S.	90	34.29N	93.02W
Hot Springs, S.D., U.S.	96	43.28N	103.32W
Hot Springs, Va., U.S.	92	38.00N	79.55W
Hot Springs National Park, rec., Ar., U.S.	90	34.30N	93.00W
Hotte, Massif de la, mts., Haiti	116	18.25N	74.00W
Hotville, Ca., U.S. (hŏt'vĭl)	102	32.50N	115.24W
Houdan, Fr. (ōō-däɴ')	151b	48.47N	1.36E
Hough Green, Eng., U.K.	233a	53.23N	2.47W
Houghton, Mi., U.S. (hō'tŭn)	96	47.06N	88.36W
Houghton, l., Mi., U.S.	92	44.20N	84.45W
Houilles, Fr. (ōō-yēs')	151b	48.55N	2.11E
Houjie, China (hwō-jyĕ)	183a	22.58N	113.39E
Houlton, Me., U.S. (hōl'tŭn)	86	46.07N	67.50W
Houma, La., U.S. (hōō'mȧ)	106	29.36N	90.43W
Hounslow, neigh., Eng., U.K.	231	51.29N	0.22W
Housatonic, r., U.S. (hōō-sȧ-tŏn'ĭk)	92	41.50N	73.25W
House Springs, Mo., U.S. (hous sprĭngs)	101e	38.24N	90.34W
Houston, Ms., U.S. (hūs'tŭn)	108	33.53N	89.00W
Houston, Tx., U.S.	90	29.46N	95.21W
Houston Ship Channel, strt., Tx., U.S.	107a	29.38N	94.57W
Houtbaai, S. Afr.	206a	34.03S	18.22E
Houtman Rocks, is., Austl. (hout'män)	196	28.15S	112.45E
Houzhen, China (hwō-jŭn)	182	36.59N	118.59E
Hovd, Mong.	180	48.08N	91.40E
Hovd Gol, r., Mong.	180	49.06N	91.16E
Hove, Eng., U.K. (hōv)	144	50.50N	0.09W
Hövsgöl Nuur, l., Mong.	180	51.11N	99.11E
Howard, Ks., U.S. (hou'ărd)	104	37.27N	96.10W
Howard, S.D., U.S.	96	44.01N	97.31W
Howard Beach, neigh., N.Y., U.S.	224	40.40N	73.51W
Howden, Eng., U.K. (hou'dĕn)	138a	53.44N	0.52W
Howe, Cape, c., Austl. (hou)	196	37.30S	150.40E
Howell, Mi., U.S. (hou'ĕl)	92	42.40N	84.00W
Howe Sound, strt., Can.	80	49.22N	123.18W
Howick, Can. (hou'ĭk)	77a	45.11N	73.51W
Howick, S. Afr.	207c	29.29S	30.16E
Howland, i., Oc. (hou'lănd)	2	1.00N	176.00W
Howrah, India (hou'rä)	174	22.33N	88.20E
Howrah Bridge, trans., India	236a	22.35N	88.21E
Howse Peak, mtn., Can.	80	51.30N	116.40W
Howson Peak, mtn., Can.	80	54.25N	127.45W
Hoxie, Ar., U.S. (kŏh'sĭ)	104	36.03N	91.00W
Hoxton Park, Austl.	239a	33.55S	150.51E
Hoy, i., Scot., U.K. (hoi)	144a	58.53N	3.10W
Hōya, Japan	187a	35.45N	139.35E
Hoylake, Eng., U.K. (hoi-lāk')	138a	53.23N	3.11W
Hoyo, Sierra del, mts., Spain (sē-ĕ'r-rä-dĕl-ô'yô)	153a	40.39N	3.56W
Hradec Králové, Czech.	140	50.12N	15.50E
Hranice, Czech. (hrän'yĕ-tsĕ)	148	49.33N	17.45E
Hröby, Swe. (hûr'bü)	146	55.50N	13.41E
Hron, r., Czech.	148	48.22N	18.42E
Hrubieszów, Pol. (hrōō-byä'shōōf)	148	50.48N	23.54E
Hsawnhsup, Burma	180	24.29N	94.45E
Hsinchu, Tai. (hsĭn'chōō')	184	24.48N	121.00E
Hsinchuang, Tai.	237d	25.02N	121.26E
Hsinkao Shan, mtn., Tai.	180	23.38N	121.05E
Huadian, China (hwä-dĭĕn)	184	42.38N	126.45E

PLACE (Pronunciation)	PAGE	Lat. °'	Long. °'
Huai, r., China (hwī)	180	32.07N	114.38E
Huai'an, China (hwī-än)	184	33.31N	119.11E
Huailai, China	184	40.20N	115.45E
Huailin, China (hwī-lĭn)	182	31.27N	117.36E
Huainan, China	182	32.38N	117.02E
Huaiyang, China (hōōäï'yang)	184	33.45N	114.54E
Huaiyuan, China (hwī-yûän)	184	32.53N	117.13E
Huajicori, Mex. (wä-jê-kō'rê)	112	22.41N	105.24W
Huajuapan de León, Mex. (wäj-wä'päm dā lā-ón')	112	17.46N	97.45W
Hualapai Indian Reservation, I.R., Az., U.S. (wälåpī)	102	35.41N	113.38W
Hualapai Mountains, mts., Az., U.S.	102	34.53N	113.54W
Hualien, Tai. (hwä'lyĕn')	184	23.58N	121.58E
Huallaga, r., Peru (wäl-yä'gä)	124	8.12S	76.34W
Huamachuco, Peru (wä-mä-chōō'kō)	124	7.52S	78.11W
Huamantla, Mex. (wä-män'tlå)	112	19.18N	97.54W
Huambo, Ang.	206	12.44S	15.47E
Huamuxtitlán, Mex. (wä-mōōs-tē-tlän')	112	17.49N	98.38W
Huancavelica, Peru (wän'kä-vä-lē'kä)	124	12.47S	75.02W
Huancayo, Peru (wän-kä'yô)	124	12.09S	75.04W
Huanchaca, Bol. (wän-chä'kä)	124	20.09S	66.40W
Huang (Yellow), r., China (hůäŋ)	180	35.06N	113.39E
Huang, Old Beds of the, mth., China	180	40.28N	106.34E
Huang, Old Course of the, r., China	182	34.28N	116.59E
Huangchuan, China (hůäŋ-chůän)	184	32.07N	115.01E
Huangcun, China	236b	39.56N	116.11E
Huanghua, China (hůäŋ-hwä)	182	38.28N	117.18E
Huanghuadian, China (hůäŋ-hwä-dĭĕn)	182	39.22N	116.53E
Huangli, China (hōōäɴg'lē)	182	31.39N	119.42E
Huangpu, China (hůäŋ-pōō)	183a	22.44N	113.20E
Huangpu, r., China	183b	30.56N	121.16E
Huangqiao, China (hůän-chyou)	182	32.15N	120.13E
Huangxian, China (hůäŋ shyĕn)	182	37.39N	120.32E
Huangyuan, China (hůäŋ-yůän)	180	37.00N	101.01E
Huanren, China (hůän-rŭn)	184	41.10N	125.30E
Huánuco, Peru (wä-nōō'kô)	124	9.50S	76.17W
Huanuni, Bol. (wä-nōō'nē)	124	18.11S	66.43W
Huaquechula, Mex. (wä-kĕ-chōō'lä)	112	18.44N	98.37W
Huaral, Peru (wä-räl')	124	11.28S	77.11W
Huarás, Peru (öä'rá's)	124	9.32S	77.29W
Huascarán, Nevados, mts., Peru (wäs-kä-rän')	124	9.05S	77.50W
Huasco, Chile (wäs'kō)	126	28.32S	71.16W
Huatla de Jiménez, Mex. (wä'tlä-dĕ-ĸē-mĕ'nĕz)	112	18.08N	96.49W
Huatlatlauch, Mex. (wä'tlä-tlä-ōō'ch)	112	18.40N	98.04W
Huatusco, Mex. (wä-tōōs'kô)	112	19.09N	96.57W
Huauchinango, Mex. (wä-ōō-chê-näŋ'gô)	112	20.09N	98.03W
Huaunta, Nic. (wä-ô'n-tä)	114	13.30N	83.32W
Huaunta, Laguna, l., Nic. (lä-gö'nä-wä-ô'n-tä)	114	13.35N	83.46W
Huautla, Mex. (wä-ōō'tlä)	112	21.04N	98.13W
Huaxian, China (hwä shyĕn)	184	35.34N	114.32E
Huaynamota, Río de, r., Mex. (rē'ō-dĕ-wāy-nä-mō'tä)	112	22.10N	104.36W
Huazolotitlán, Mex. (wäzô-lô-tlē-tlän')	112	16.18N	97.55W
Hubbard, N.H., U.S. (hŭb'ērd)	87a	42.53N	71.12W
Hubbard, Tx., U.S.	106	31.53N	96.46W
Hubbard, l., Mi., U.S.	92	44.45N	83.30W
Hubbard Creek Reservoir, res., Tx., U.S.	106	32.50N	98.55W
Hubbelrath, Ger.	232	51.16N	6.55E
Hubei, prov., China (hōō-bā)	180	31.20N	111.58E
Hubli, India (hŏŏ'blê)	174	15.25N	75.09E
Hückeswagen, Ger. (hü'kĕs-vä'gĕn)	151c	51.09N	7.20E
Hucknall, Eng., U.K. (hŭk'năl)	138a	53.02N	1.12W
Huddersfield, Eng., U.K. (hŭd'ērz-fēld)	144	53.39N	1.47W
Hudiksvall, Swe. (hōō'dĭks-väl)	140	61.44N	17.05E
Hudson, Can. (hŭd'sŭn)	77a	45.26N	74.08W
Hudson, Ma., U.S.	87a	42.24N	71.34W
Hudson, Mi., U.S.	92	41.50N	84.15W
Hudson, N.Y., U.S.	92	42.15N	73.45W
Hudson, Oh., U.S.	95d	41.15N	81.27W
Hudson, Wi., U.S.	101g	44.59N	92.45W
Hudson, r., U.S.	90	42.30N	73.55W
Hudson Bay, Can.	82	52.52N	102.25W
Hudson Bay, b., Can.	78	60.15N	85.30W
Hudson Falls, N.Y., U.S.	92	43.20N	73.30W
Hudson Heights, Can.	77a	45.28N	74.09W
Hudson Strait, strt., Can.	78	63.25N	74.05W
Hue, Viet. (ü-ā')	188	16.28N	107.42E
Huebra, r., Spain (wĕ'brä)	152	40.44N	6.17W
Huehuetenango, Guat. (wä-wå-tå-näŋ'gô)	114	15.19N	91.26W
Huejotzingo, Mex. (wā-hō-tzĭŋ'gō)	112	19.09N	98.24W
Huejúcar, Mex. (wā-hōō'kär)	112	22.26N	103.12W
Huejuquilla el Alto, Mex. (wā-hōō-kēl'yä ĕl äl'tō)	112	22.42N	103.54W
Huejutla, Mex. (wā-hōō'tlä)	112	21.08N	98.26W
Huelma, Spain (wĕl'mä)	152	37.39N	3.36W
Huelva, Spain (wĕl'vä)	142	37.16N	6.58W
Huércal-Overa, Spain (wĕr-käl' ō-vä'rä)	152	37.12N	1.58W
Huerfano, r., Co., U.S. (wâr'fȧ-nō)	104	37.41N	105.13W
Huésca, Spain (wĕs-kä)	142	42.07N	0.25W
Huéscar, Spain (wās'kär)	152	37.50N	2.34W
Huetamo de Núñez, Mex.	112	18.34N	100.53W
Huete, Spain (wā'tå)	152	40.09N	2.42W
Hueycatenango, Mex. (wĕy-kȧ-tĕ-nä'n-gô)	112	17.31N	99.10W
Hueytlalpan, Mex. (wā'ĭ-tläl'păn)	112	20.03N	97.41W
Hueytown, Al., U.S.	94h	33.28N	86.59W
Huffman, Al., U.S. (hŭf'măn)	94h	33.36N	86.42W
Hügel, Villa, pt. of i., Ger.	232	51.25N	7.01E
Hugh Butler, l., Ne., U.S.	104	40.21N	100.40W

PLACE (Pronunciation)	PAGE	Lat. °′	Long. °′
Hughenden, Austl. (hū'ĕn-dĕn)	196	20.58S	144.13E
Hughes, Austl. (hūz)	196	30.45S	129.30E
Hughesville, Md., U.S.	94e	38.32N	76.48W
Hugo, Mn., U.S. (hū'gō)	101g	45.10N	93.00W
Hugo, Ok., U.S.	104	34.01N	95.32W
Hugoton, Ks., U.S. (hū'gō-tŭn)	104	37.10N	101.28W
Hugou, China (hōō-gō)	182	33.22N	117.07E
Huichapan, Mex. (wē-chä-pän')	112	20.22N	99.39W
Huila, dept., Col. (wē'lä)	124a	3.10N	75.20W
Huila, Nevado de, mtn., Col. (nĕ-vä-dô-de-wē'lä)	124a	2.59N	76.01W
Huilai, China	184	23.02N	116.18E
Huili, China	180	26.48N	102.20E
Huimanguillo, Mex. (wē-män-gēl'yō)	112	17.50N	93.16W
Huimin, China (hōōĭ mĭn)	180	37.29N	117.32E
Huipulco, Mex.	229a	19.17N	99.09W
Huitzilac, Mex. (ōē't-zē-lä'k)	113a	19.01N	99.16W
Huitzitzilingo, Mex. (wē-tzē-tzē-lē'n-go)	112	21.11N	98.42W
Huitzuco, Mex. (wē-tzōō'kō)	112	18.16N	99.20W
Huixquilucan, Mex. (ōē'x-kē-lōō-kä'n)	113a	19.21N	99.22W
Huiyang, China	184	23.05N	114.25E
Hukou, China (hōō-kō)	180	29.58N	116.20E
Hulan, China (hōō'län')	180	45.58N	126.32E
Hulan, r., China	184	47.20N	126.30E
Hulin, China (hōō'lĭn')	186	45.45N	133.25E
Hull, Can. (hŭl)	78	45.26N	75.43W
Hull, Ma., U.S.	87a	42.18N	70.54W
Hull, r., Eng., U.K.	138a	53.47N	0.20W
Hülscheid, Ger.	232	51.16N	7.34E
Hulst, Neth. (hōlst)	139a	51.17N	4.01E
Huludao, China (hōō-lōō-dou)	180	40.40N	120.55E
Hulun Nur, l., China (hōō-lòn nòr)	180	48.50N	116.45E
Humacao, P.R. (ōō-mä-kä'ō)	111b	18.09N	65.49W
Humansdorp, S. Afr. (hōō'mäns-dôrp)	206	33.57S	24.45E
Humbe, Ang. (hòm'bâ)	206	16.50S	14.55E
Humber, r., Can.	77d	43.53N	79.40W
Humber, r., Eng., U.K. (hŭm'bẽr)	140	53.30N	0.30E
Humbermouth, Can. (hŭm'bẽr-mŭth)	86	48.58N	57.55W
Humberside, co., Eng., U.K.	138a	53.47N	0.36W
Humble, Tx., U.S. (hŭm'b'l)	106	29.58N	95.15W
Humboldt, Can. (hŭm'bōlt)	78	52.12N	105.07W
Humboldt, Ia., U.S.	96	42.43N	94.11W
Humboldt, Ks., U.S.	104	37.48N	95.26W
Humboldt, Ne., U.S.	104	40.10N	95.57W
Humboldt, r., Nv., U.S.	90	40.30N	116.50W
Humboldt, East Fork, r., Nv., U.S.	98	40.59N	115.21W
Humboldt, North Fork, r., Nv., U.S.	98	41.25N	115.45W
Humboldt, Planetario, bldg., Ven.	230a	10.30N	66.50W
Humboldt Bay, b., Ca., U.S.	98	40.48N	124.25W
Humboldt Range, mts., Nv., U.S.	102	40.12N	118.16W
Humbolt, Tn., U.S.	108	35.47N	88.55W
Humbolt Salt Marsh, Nv., U.S.	102	39.49N	117.41W
Humbolt Sink, Nv., U.S.	102	39.58N	118.54W
Humen, China (hōō-mŭn)	183a	22.49N	113.39E
Humphreys Peak, mtn., Az., U.S. (hŭm'frĭs)	90	35.20N	111.40W
Humpolec, Czech. (hòm'pò-lĕts)	148	49.33N	15.21E
Humuya, r., Hond. (ōō-mōō'yä)	114	14.38N	87.36W
Hunaflói, b., Ice. (hōō'nä-flō'ĭ)	140	65.41N	20.44W
Hunan, prov., China (hōō'nän')	180	28.08N	111.25E
Hunchun, China (hòn-chûn)	180	42.53N	130.34E
Hunedoara, Rom. (κōō'nĕd-wä'rȧ)	154	45.45N	22.54E
Hungary, nation, Eur. (hŭŋ'gȧ-rĭ)	136	46.44N	17.55E
Hungerford, Austl. (hŭn'gẽr-fẽrd)	196	28.50S	144.32E
Hungry Horse Reservoir, res., Mt., U.S. (hŭŋ'gȧ-rĭ hôrs)	98	48.11N	113.30W
Hunsrück, mts., Ger. (hōōns'rûk)	148	49.43N	7.12E
Hunte, r., Ger. (hòn'tĕ)	148	52.45N	8.26E
Hunter Islands, is., Austl. (hŭn-tẽr)	196	40.33S	143.36E
Hunters Hill, Austl.	239a	33.50S	151.09E
Huntingburg, In., U.S. (hŭnt'ĭng-bûrg)	92	38.15N	86.55W
Huntingdon, Can. (hŭnt'ĭng-dŭn)	84	45.10N	74.05W
Huntingdon, Can.	100d	49.00N	122.16W
Huntingdon, Tn., U.S.	108	36.00N	88.23W
Huntington, In., U.S.	92	40.55N	85.30W
Huntington, Pa., U.S.	92	40.30N	78.00W
Huntington, Va., U.S.	225d	38.48N	77.15W
Huntington, W.V., U.S.	90	38.25N	82.25W
Huntington Beach, Ca., U.S.	101a	33.39N	118.00W
Huntington Park, Ca., U.S.	101a	33.59N	118.14W
Huntington Station, N.Y., U.S.	94a	40.51N	73.25W
Huntington Woods, Mi., U.S.	226c	42.29N	83.10W
Huntley, Mt., U.S.	98	45.54N	108.01W
Hunt's Cross, neigh., Eng., U.K.	233a	53.21N	2.51W
Huntsville, Can.	78	45.20N	79.15W
Huntsville, Al., U.S. (hŭnts'vĭl)	108	34.44N	86.36W
Huntsville, Md., U.S.	225d	38.55N	76.54W
Huntsville, Mo., U.S.	104	39.24N	92.32W
Huntsville, Tx., U.S.	106	30.44N	95.34W
Huntsville, Ut., U.S.	101b	41.16N	111.46W
Huolu, China (hòŭ lōō)	182	38.05N	114.20E
Huon Gulf, b., Pap. N. Gui.	188	7.15S	147.45E
Huoqiu, China (hwô-chyō)	182	32.19N	116.17E
Huoshan, China (hwô-shän)	184	31.30N	116.25E
Huraydin, Wādī, r., Egypt	173a	30.55N	34.12E
Hurd, Cape, c., Can. (hûrd)	84	45.15N	81.45W
Hurdiyo, Som.	212a	10.43N	51.05E
Hurley, Wi., U.S. (hûr'lĭ)	96	46.26N	90.11W
Hurlingham, Arg. (ōō'r-lēn-gäm)	126a	34.36S	58.38W
Huron, Oh., U.S. (hū'rŏn)	92	41.20N	82.35W
Huron, S.D., U.S.	90	44.22N	98.15W
Huron, r., Mi., U.S.	95b	42.12N	83.26W
Huron, Lake, l., N.A. (hū'rŏn)	90	45.15N	82.40W
Huron Mountains, mts., Mi., U.S. (hū'rŏn)	96	46.47N	87.52W
Hurricane, Ak., U.S. (hŭr'ĭ-kān)	89	63.00N	149.30W
Hurricane, Ut., U.S.	102	37.10N	113.20W
Hurricane Flats, bk. (hŭ-rĭ-kȧn flăts)	116	23.35N	78.30W
Hurst, Tx., U.S.	101c	32.48N	97.12W
Hurstville, Austl.	239a	33.58S	151.06E
Húsavik, Ice.	140	66.00N	17.10W
Husen, neigh., Ger.	232	51.33N	7.36E
Huşi, Rom. (kòsh')	156	46.52N	28.04E
Huskvarna, Swe. (hòsk-vär'nȧ)	146	57.48N	14.16E
Husum, Ger. (hōō'zòm)	148	54.29N	9.04E
Hutchins, Tx., U.S. (hŭch'ĭnz)	101c	32.38N	96.43W
Hutchinson, Ks., U.S. (hŭch'ĭn-sŭn)	90	38.02N	97.56W
Hutchinson, Mn., U.S.	96	44.53N	94.23W
Hütteldorf, neigh., Aus.	235e	48.12N	16.16E
Hüttenheim, neigh., Ger.	232	51.22N	6.43E
Hutton, Eng., U.K.	231	51.38N	0.22E
Huttrop, neigh., Ger.	232	51.27N	7.03E
Hutuo, r., China	184	38.10N	114.00E
Huy, Bel. (û-ē') (hû'ē)	144	50.33N	5.14E
Huyton, Eng., U.K.	233a	53.24N	2.50W
Hvannadalshnúkur, mtn., Ice.	140	64.09N	16.46W
Hvar, i., Yugo. (κhvär)	154	43.08N	16.28E
Hwange, Zimb.	206	18.22S	26.29E
Hwangju, N. Kor. (hwäng'jōō')	186	38.39N	125.49E
Hyargas Nuur, l., Mong.	180	48.00N	92.32E
Hyattsville, Md., U.S. (hī'ăt's-vĭl)	94e	38.57N	76.58W
Hyco Lake, res., N.C., U.S. (rōks' bŭr-ō)	108	36.22N	78.58W
Hydaburg, Ak., U.S. (hī-dă'bûrg)	89	55.12N	132.49W
Hyde, Eng., U.K. (hīd)	138a	53.27N	2.05W
Hyde Park, neigh., Il., U.S.	227a	41.48N	87.36W
Hyderābād, India (hī-dẽr-ȧ-băd')	174	17.29N	78.28E
Hyderabad, India	174	18.30N	76.50E
Hyderābād, Pak.	174	25.29N	68.28E
Hyéres, Fr. (ē-âr')	140	43.09N	6.08E
Hyéres, Îles d', is., Fr. (ēl'dyâr')	140	42.57N	6.17E
Hyesanjin, N. Kor. (hyĕ'sän-jĭn')	186	41.11N	128.12E
Hymera, In., U.S. (hī-mē'rȧ)	92	39.10N	87.20W
Hyndman Peak, mtn., Id., U.S. (hīnd'mȧn)	90	43.38N	114.04W
Hyōgo, dept., Japan (hĭyō'gō)	187b	34.54N	135.15E
Hyōgo, neigh., Japan	238b	34.47N	135.10E
Hythe End, Eng., U.K.	231	51.27N	0.32W

I

PLACE (Pronunciation)	PAGE	Lat. °′	Long. °′
Ia, r., Japan (ē'ä)	187b	34.54N	135.34E
Ialomiţa, r., Rom.	154	44.37N	26.42E
Iaşi, Rom. (yä'shē)	136	47.10N	27.40E
Iba, Phil. (ē'bä)	189a	15.20N	119.59E
Ibadan, Nig. (ē-bä'dän)	204	7.17N	3.30E
Ibagué, Col.	124	4.27N	75.14W
Ibar, r., Yugo. (ē'bär)	154	43.22N	20.35E
Ibaraki, Japan (ē-bä'rä-gē)	187b	34.49N	135.35E
Ibarra, Ec. (ē-bär'rä)	124	0.19N	78.08W
Ibb, Yemen	176	14.01N	44.10E
Iberoamericana, Universidad, educ., Mex.	229a	19.21N	99.08W
Iberville, Can. (ē-bår-vēl') (ī'bẽr-vĭl)	84	45.14N	73.01W
Ibese, Nig.	240d	6.33N	3.29E
Ibi, Nig. (ē'bē)	204	8.12N	9.45E
Ibiapaba, Serra da, mts., Braz. (sĕ'r-rä-dä-ē-byä-pá'bä)	124	3.30S	40.55W
Ibirapuera, neigh., Braz.	230d	23.37S	46.40W
Ibiza, Spain (ē-bē'thä)	152	38.55N	1.24E
Ibiza (Iviza), i., Spain (ē-bē'zä)	136	39.07N	1.05E
Ibo, Moz. (ē'bō)	206	12.20S	40.35E
Ibrāhīm, Būr, b., Egypt	212c	29.57N	32.33E
Ibrahim, Jabal, mtn., Sau. Ar.	174	20.31N	41.17E
Ibwe Munyama, Zam.	210	16.09S	28.34E
Ica, Peru (ē'kä)	124	14.09S	75.42W
Icá (Putumayo), r., S.A.	124	3.00S	69.00W
Içana, Braz. (ē-sä'nä)	124	0.15N	67.19W
Ice Harbor Dam, Wa., U.S.	98	46.15N	118.54W
İçel, Tur.	174	37.00N	34.40E
Iceland, nation, Eur. (īs'lȧnd)	136	65.12N	19.45W
Ichāpur, India	236a	22.50N	88.24E
Ichibusayama, mtn., Japan (ē'chē-bōō'sȧ-yä'mä)	187	32.19N	131.08E
Ichihara, Japan	187a	35.31N	140.05E
Ichikawa, Japan (ē'chē-kä'wä)	187a	35.44N	139.54E
Ichinomiya, Japan (ē'chē-nō-mē'yȧ)	187	35.19N	136.49E
Ichinomoto, Japan (ē-chē'nō-mō-tō)	187b	34.37N	135.50E
Ichnya, Ukr. (ĭch'nyä)	160	50.47N	32.23E
Ickenham, neigh., Eng., U.K.	231	51.34N	0.27W
Ickern, neigh., Ger.	232	51.36N	7.21E
Icy Cape, c., Ak., U.S. (ī'sĭ)	89	70.20N	161.40W
Idabel, Ok., U.S. (ī'dȧ-bĕl)	104	33.52N	94.47W
Idagrove, Ia., U.S. (ī'dȧ-grōv)	96	42.22N	95.29W
Idah, Nig. (ē'dä)	204	7.07N	6.43E
Idaho, state, U.S. (ī'dȧ-hō)	90	44.00N	115.10W
Idaho Falls, Id., U.S.	90	43.30N	112.01W
Idaho Springs, Co., U.S.	104	39.43N	105.32W
Idanha-a-Nova, Port. (ē-dän'yȧ-ä-nō'vȧ)	152	39.58N	7.13W
Iddo, neigh., Nig.	240d	6.28N	3.23E
Ider, r., Mong.	180	48.58N	98.38E
Idhra, i., Grc.	154	37.20N	23.30E
Idi, Indon. (ē'dē)	188	4.58N	97.47E
Idkū Lake, l., Egypt	212b	31.13N	30.22E
Idle, r., Eng., U.K. (īd''l)	138a	53.22N	0.56W
Idlib, Syria	176	35.55N	36.38E
Idriaj, Slo. (ē'drē-ä)	154	46.01N	14.01E
Idutywa, Transkei (ē-dò-tī'wȧ)	207c	32.06S	28.18E
Idylwood, Va., U.S.	225d	38.54N	77.12W
Ieper, Bel.	144	50.50N	2.53E
Ierápetra, Grc.	154a	35.01N	25.48E
Iesi, Italy (yā'sē)	154	43.37N	13.20E
Ife, Nig.	204	7.30N	4.30E
Iferouâne, Niger (ēf'rōō-än')	204	19.04N	8.24E
Ifôghas, Adrar des, plat., Afr.	204	19.55N	2.00E
Igalula, Tan.	210	5.14S	33.00E
Iganmu, neigh., Nig.	240d	6.29N	3.22E
Igarka, Russia (ē-gär'kȧ)	158	67.22N	86.16E
Igbobi, Nig.	240d	6.32N	3.22E
Ightham, Eng., U.K.	231	51.17N	0.17E
Iglesias, Italy (ē-lĕ'syôs)	142	39.20N	8.34E
Igli, Alg. (ē-glē')	204	30.32N	2.15W
Igloolik, Can.	78	69.33N	81.18W
Ignacio, Ca., U.S. (ĭg-nä'cĭ-ō)	100b	38.05N	122.32W
Iguaçu, r., Braz. (ē-gwä-sōō')	126b	22.42S	43.19W
Iguala, Mex. (ē-gwä'lä)	112	18.18N	99.34W
Igualada, Spain (ē-gwä-lä'dä)	152	41.35N	1.38E
Iguassu, r., S.A. (ē-gwä-sōō')	126	25.45S	52.30W
Iguassu Falls, wtfl., S.A.	124	25.40S	54.16W
Iguatama, Braz. (ē-gwä-tȧ'mä)	123a	20.13S	45.40W
Iguatu, Braz. (ē-gwä-tōō')	124	6.22S	39.17W
Iguidi, Erg, Afr.	204	26.22N	6.53W
Iguig, Phil. (ē-gēg')	189a	17.46N	121.44E
Iharana, Madag.	206	13.35S	50.05E
Ihiala, Nig.	208	5.51N	6.51E
Iida, Japan (ē'ē-dȧ)	187	35.39N	137.53E
Iijoki, r., Fin. (ē'yō'kĭ)	160	65.28N	27.00E
Iizuka, Japan (ē'ē-zò-kȧ)	187	33.39N	130.39E
Ijebu-Ode, Nig. (ē-jĕ'bōō ōdȧ)	204	6.50N	3.56E
IJmuiden, Neth.	139a	52.27N	4.36E
IJsselmeer, l., Neth. (ī'sĕl-mâr)	144	52.46N	5.14E
Ikaalinen, Fin. (ē'kä-lĭ-nĕn)	146	61.47N	22.55E
Ikaría, i., Grc. (ē-kä'ryȧ)	154	37.43N	26.07E
Ikeda, Japan (ē'kĕ-dä)	187b	34.49N	135.26E
Ikeja, Nig.	240d	6.36N	3.21E
Ikerre, Nig.	208	7.31N	5.14E
Ikhtiman, Bul. (ēk'tē-män)	154	42.26N	23.49E
Iki, i., Japan (ē'kē)	186	33.46N	129.44E
Ikoma, Japan	187b	34.41N	135.43E
Ikoma, Tan. (ē-kō'mä)	206	2.08S	34.47E
Ikorodu, Nig.	240d	6.37N	3.31E
Ikoyi, neigh., Nig.	240d	6.27N	3.26E
Ikoyi Island, i., Nig.	240d	6.27N	3.26E
Iksha, Russia (ĭk'shȧ)	164b	56.10N	37.30E
Ikuno, neigh., Japan	238b	34.39N	135.33E
Ila, Nig.	208	8.01N	4.55E
Ilagan, Phil.	189a	17.09N	121.52E
Ilan, Tai. (ē'län')	184	24.50N	121.42E
Iława, Pol. (ē-lä'vȧ)	148	53.35N	19.36E
Ilchester, Md., U.S.	225c	39.15N	76.46W
Île-á-la-Crosse, Can.	82	55.34N	108.00W
Ilebo, Zaire	206	4.19S	20.35E
Ilek, Russia (ē'lyĕk)	160	51.30N	53.10E
Ilek, r.	160	51.20N	53.10E
Île-Perrot, Can. (yl-pĕ-rōt')	77a	45.21N	73.54W
Ilesha, Nig.	204	7.38N	4.45E
Ilford, Eng., U.K. (ĭl'fẽrd)	138b	51.33N	0.06E
Ilfracombe, Eng., U.K. (ĭl-frȧ-kōōm')	144	51.13N	4.08W
Ilhabela, Braz. (ē'lä-bĕ'lä)	123a	23.47S	45.21W
Ilha Grande, Baía de, b., Braz. (ēl'yȧ grän'dĕ)	123a	23.17S	44.25W
Ílhavo, Port. (ēl'yȧ-vò)	142	40.36N	8.41W
Ilhéus, Braz. (ē-lĕ'ōōs)	124	14.52S	39.00W
Ili, r., Asia (ē'lē)	162	44.30N	76.45E
Iliamna, Ak., U.S.	89	60.18N	153.25W
Iliamna, Ak., U.S. (ē-lē-ăm'nȧ)	89	59.45N	155.05W
Iliamna, l., Ak., U.S.	89	59.25N	155.30W
Ilim, r., Russia (ē-lyēm')	162	57.28N	103.00E
Ilimsk, Russia (ē-lyēmsk')	158	56.47N	103.43E
Ilin Island, i., Phil. (ē-lyēn')	189a	12.16N	120.57E
Il'intsiy, Ukr.	156	49.07N	29.13E
Ilion, N.Y., U.S. (ĭl'ĭ-ŭn)	92	43.00N	75.05W
Ilioúpolis, Grc.	235d	37.56N	23.45E
Ilkeston, Eng., U.K. (ĭl'kĕs-tŭn)	138a	52.58N	1.19W
Illampu, Nevado, mtn., Bol. (nĕ-vá'dô-ēl-yäm-pōō')	124	15.50S	68.15W
Illapel, Chile (ē-zhä-pĕ'l)	126	31.37S	71.10W
Iller, r., Ger. (ĭlẽr)	148	47.52N	10.06E
Illimani, Nevado, mtn., Bol. (nĕ-vä'dô-ēl-yē-mä'nē)	124	16.50S	67.38W
Illinois, state, U.S. (ĭl-ĭ-noi') (ĭl-ĭ-noiz')	90	40.25N	90.40W
Illinois, r., Il., U.S.	90	39.00N	90.30W
Illizi, Alg.	204	26.35N	8.24E
Illovo, S. Afr.	240b	26.08S	28.03E
Il'men, l., Russia (ô'zĕ-rô el''men'') (ĭl'mĕn)	160	58.18N	32.00E
Ilo, Peru	124	17.46S	71.13W
Ilobasco, El Sal. (ē-lò-bäs'kô)	114	13.57N	88.46W
Iloilo, Phil. (ē-lō-ē'lō)	188	10.49N	122.33E
Ilopango, Lago, l., El Sal. (ē-lô-päŋ'gō)	114	13.48N	88.50W
Ilorin, Nig. (ē-lò-rēn')	204	8.30N	4.32E
Ilūkste, Lat.	146	55.59N	26.20E
Ilverich, Ger.	232	51.17N	6.42E
Ilwaco, Wa., U.S. (ĭl-wä'kò)	100c	46.19N	124.02W
Ilych, r., Russia (ē'lĭch)	160	62.30N	57.30E
Imabari, Japan (ē'mä-bä'rē)	186	34.05N	132.58E

ăt; finȧl; rāte; senāte; ärm; ȧsk; sofȧ; fâre; ch-choose; dh-as th in other; bē; ēvent; bĕt; recĕnt; cratẽr; g-gō; gh-guttural g; bĭt; ĭ-short neutral; rīde; κ-guttural k as ch in German ich;

PLACE (Pronunciation)	PAGE	Lat. °′	Long. °′
Imai, Japan (ė-mī′)	187b	34.30N	135.47E
Iman, r., Russia (ė-män′)	186	45.40N	134.31E
Imandra, l., Russia (ē-män′drȧ)	160	67.40N	32.30E
Imbābah, Egypt (ēm-bä′bȧ)	212b	30.06N	31.09E
Imeni Morozova, Russia (ĭm-yĕ′nyĭ mô rô′zô vȧ)	164c	59.58N	31.02E
Imeni Moskvy, Kanal (Moscow Canal), can., Russia (kȧ-näl′ĭm-yă′nĭ mŏs-kvĭ)	156	56.33N	37.15E
Imeni Tsyurupy, Russia	164b	55.30N	38.39E
Imeni Vorovskogo, Russia	164b	55.43N	38.21E
Imlay City, Mi., U S. (ĭm′lā)	92	43.00N	83.15W
Immenstadt, Ger. (ĭm′*ĕ*n-shtät)	148	47.34N	10.12E
Immerpan, S. Afr. (ĭmĕr-pän)	212d	24.29S	29.14E
Imola, Italy (ē′mȯ-lä)	154	44.19N	11.43E
Imotski, Cro. (ė-môts′kė)	154	43.25N	17.15E
Impameri, Braz.	124	17.44S	48.03W
Impendle, S. Afr. (ĭm-pĕnd′lȧ)	207c	29.38S	29.54E
Imperia, Italy (ėm-pä′rė-ä)	142	43.52N	8.00E
Imperial, Pa., U.S. (ĭm-pē′rĭ-*ă*l)	95e	40.27N	80.15W
Imperial Beach, Ca., U.S.	102a	32.34N	117.08W
Imperial Valley, Ca., U.S.	102	33.00N	115.22W
Impfondo, Congo (ĭmp-fōn′dȯ)	204	1.37N	18.04E
Imphāl, India (ĭmp′hŭl)	174	24.42N	94.00E
Ina, r., Japan (ė-nä′)	187b	34.56N	135.21E
Inagi, Japan	238a	35.38N	139.30E
Inaja Indian Reservation, I.R., Ca., U.S. (ė-nä′hȧ)	102	32.56N	116.37W
Inari, l., Fin.	140	69.02N	26.22E
Inatsuke, neigh., Japan	238a	35.46N	139.43E
Inca, Spain (ėŋ′kä)	152	39.43N	2.53E
Ince, Eng., U.K.	233a	53.17N	2.49W
Ince Blundell, Eng., U.K.	233a	53.31N	3.02W
Ince Burun, c., Tur. (ĭn′jȧ)	142	42.00N	35.00E
Inch'ŏn, S. Kor. (ĭn′chŭn)	180	37.26N	126.46E
Incudine, Monte, mtn., Fr. (ēn-ko͞o-dē′nȧ) (ăN-kü-dēn′)	154	41.53N	9.17E
Indalsälven, r., Swe.	140	62.50N	16.50E
Independence, Ks., U.S. (ĭn-dė-pĕn′dĕns)	104	37.14N	95.42W
Independence, Mo., U.S.	101f	39.06N	94.26W
Independence, Oh., U.S.	95d	41.23N	81.39W
Independence, Or., U.S.	98	44.49N	123.13W
Independence Mountains, mts., Nv., U.S.	98	41.15N	116.02W
Independence National Historical Park, rec., N.J., U.S.	225b	39.57N	75.09W
Inder, l., Kaz.	160	48.20N	52.10E
In der Bredde, Ger.	232	51.20N	7.23E
India, nation, Asia (ĭn′dĭ-*ȧ*)	174	23.00N	77.30E
India Gate, hist., India	236d	28.37N	77.12E
Indian, l., Mi., U.S. (ĭn′dĭ-*ă*n)	96	46.04N	86.34W
Indian, r., N.Y., U.S.	92	44.05N	75.45W
Indiana, Pa., U.S. (ĭn-dĭ-än′*ȧ*)	92	40.40N	79.10W
Indiana, state, U.S.	90	39.50N	86.45W
Indianapolis, In., U.S. (ĭn-dĭ-*ă*n-ăp′ȯ-lĭs)	90	39.45N	86.08W
Indian Arm, b., Can. (ĭn′dĭ-*ă*n ärm)	100d	49.21N	122.55W
Indian Head, Can.	78	50.29N	103.44W
Indian Head Park, Il., U.S.	227a	41.47N	87.54W
Indian Lake, l., Can.	84	47.00N	82.00W
Indian Ocean, o.	4	10.00S	70.00E
Indianola, Ia., U.S. (ĭn-dĭ-*ă*n-ō′l*ȧ*)	96	41.22N	93.33W
Indianola, Ms., U.S.	108	33.29N	90.35W
Indianola, Pa., U.S.	226b	40.34N	79.51W
Indianópolis, neigh., Braz.	230d	23.36S	46.38W
Indian Springs, Va., U.S.	225d	38.49N	77.10W
Indigirka, r., Russia (ėn-dė-gēr′kȧ)	162	67.45N	145.45E
Indio, r., Pan. (ē′n-dyô)	110a	9.13N	79.28W
Indochina, reg., Asia (ĭn-dȯ-chī′nȧ)	188	17.22N	105.18E
Indonesia, nation, Asia (ĭn′dȯ-nė-zh*ȧ*)	188	4.38S	118.45E
Indonesian Culture, Museum of, bldg., Indon.	237k	6.11S	106.49E
Indore, India (ĭn-dōr′)	174	22.48N	76.51E
Indragiri, r., Indon. (ĭn-drȧ-jē′rė)	188	0.27S	102.05E
Indrāvati, r., India (ĭn-drŭ-vä′tė)	174	19.00N	82.00E
Indre, r., Fr. (ăN′dr′)	150	47.13N	0.29E
Indus, Can. (ĭn′dŭs)	77e	50.55N	113.45W
Indus, r., Asia	174	26.43N	67.41E
Industria, neigh., S. Afr.	240b	26.12S	27.59E
Indwe, S. Afr. (ĭnd′wȧ)	207c	31.30S	27.21E
Inebolu, Tur. (ė-nȧ-bō′lo͞o)	142	41.50N	33.40E
Inego, Tur. (ė′nȧ-gŭ)	160	40.05N	29.20E
Infanta, Phil. (ėn-făn′tä)	189a	14.44N	121.39E
Infanta, Phil.	189a	15.50N	119.53E
Inferror, Laguna, l., Mex. (lä-gȯ′nä-ėn-fĕr-rôr)	112	16.18N	94.40W
Infiernillo, Presa de, res., Mex.	112	18.50N	101.50W
Infiesto, Spain (ēn-fyĕ′s-tȯ)	152	43.21N	5.24W
I-n-Gall, Niger	208	16.47N	6.56E
Ingatestone, Eng., U.K.	231	51.41N	0.22E
Ingeniero Budge, neigh., Arg.	229d	34.43S	58.28W
Ingersoll, Can. (ĭn′gĕr-s*ŏ*l)	84	43.05N	81.00W
Ingham, Austl. (ĭng′*ă*m)	196	18.45S	146.14E
Ingleburn, Austl.	239a	34.00S	150.52E
Ingles, Cayos, is., Cuba (kä-yōs-ė′n-glĕ′s)	116	21.55N	82.35W
Ingleside, neigh., Ca., U.S.	227b	37.43N	122.28W
Inglewood, Can.	77d	43.48N	79.56W
Inglewood, Ca., U.S. (ĭn′g′l-wȯd)	101a	33.57N	118.22W
Ingoda, r., Russia (ėn-gō′d*ȧ*)	162	51.29N	112.32E
Ingolstadt, Ger. (ĭŋ′gȯl-shtät)	148	48.46N	11.27E
Ingomar, Pa., U.S.	226b	40.35N	80.05W
Ingram, Pa., U.S.	226b	40.26N	80.04W
Ingrave, Eng., U.K.	231	51.36N	0.21E
Ingul, r., Ukr. (ėn-gȯl′)	156	47.22N	32.52E
Ingulets, r., Ukr. (ėn-go͞ol′yĕts′)	156	47.12N	33.12E
Ingur, r., Geor. (ėn-gȯr′)	160	42.30N	42.00E
Inhambane, Moz. (ėn-äm-bä′-nĕ)	206	23.47S	35.28E
Inhambupe, Braz. (ėn-yäm-bo͞o′pä)	124	11.47S	38.13W
Inharrime, Moz. (ėn-yär-rē′mä)	206	24.17S	35.07E
Inhomirim, Braz. (ē-nô-mė-rē′N)	126b	22.34S	43.11W
Inírida, r., Col. (ē-nė-rē′dä)	124	2.25N	70.38W
Injune, Austl. (ĭn′jȯn)	198	25.52S	148.30E
Inkeroinem, Fin. (ĭn′kĕr-oi-nĕn)	146	60.42N	26.50E
Inkster, Mi., U.S. (ĭngk′stĕr)	95b	42.18N	83.19W
Inn, r., Eur. (ĭn)	140	48.00N	12.00E
Innamincka, Austl. (ĭnn-*á*′mĭn-k*á*)	198	27.50S	140.48E
Inner Brass, i., V.I.U.S. (bräs)	111c	18.23N	64.58W
Inner Hebrides, is., Scot., U.K.	144	57.20N	6.20W
Inner Mongolia, *see* Nei Monggol, China	180	40.15N	105.00E
Innisfail, Can.	78	52.02N	113.57W
Innsbruck, Aus. (ĭns′brȯk)	140	47.15N	11.25E
Ino, Japan (ē′nȯ)	187	33.34N	133.23E
Inongo, Zaire (ė-nôŋ′gō)	206	1.57S	18.16E
Inowrocław, Pol. (ē-nô-vrŏts′läf)	148	52.48N	18.16E
In Salah, Alg.	204	27.13N	2.22E
Inscription House Ruin, Az., U.S. (ĭn′skrĭp-shŭn hous ro͞o′ĭn)	102	36.45N	110.47W
International Falls, Mn., U.S. (ĭn′tĕr-năsh′*ŭ*n-*ă*l fôlz)	90	48.34N	93.26W
Inuvik, Can.	78	68.40N	134.10W
Inuyama, Japan (ē′no͞o-yä′mä)	187	35.24N	137.01E
Invercargil, N.Z. (ĭn-vĕr-kär′gĭl)	199	46.25S	168.27E
Inverel, Austl. (ĭn-vĕr-el′)	196	29.50S	151.32E
Invergrove Heights, Mn., U.S. (ĭn′vĕr-grōv)	101g	44.51N	93.01W
Inverness, Can. (ĭn-vĕr-nĕs′)	86	46.14N	61.18W
Inverness, Scot., U.K.	140	57.30N	4.07W
Inverness, Fl., U.S.	108	28.48N	82.22W
Investigator Strait, strt., Austl. (ĭn-vĕst′*ĭ*′gā-tôr)	198	35.33S	137.00E
Inwood, N.Y., U.S.	224	40.37N	73.45W
Inyangani, mtn., Zimb. (ėn-yän-gä′nė)	206	18.06S	32.37E
Inyokern, Ca., U.S.	102	35.39N	117.51W
Inyo Mountains, mts., Ca., U.S. (ĭn′yō)	90	36.55N	118.04W
Inzer, r., Russia (ĭn′zĕr)	164a	54.24N	57.17E
Inzersdorf, neigh., Aus.	235e	48.09N	16.21E
Inzia, r., Zaire	210	5.55S	17.50E
Ioánnina, Grc. (yȯ-ä′nė-nȧ)	142	39.39N	20.52E
Ioco, Can.	100d	49.18N	122.53W
Iola, Ks., U.S. (ī-ō′l*ȧ*)	104	37.55N	95.23W
Iôna, Parque Nacional do, rec., Ang.	210	16.35S	12.00E
Ionia, Mi., U.S. (ī-ō′nĭ-ȧ)	92	43.00N	85.10W
Ionian Islands, is., Grc. (ī-ō′nĭ-*ă*n)	142	39.10N	20.05E
Ionian Sea, sea, Eur.	136	38.59N	18.48E
Íos, i., Grc. (ī′ŏs)	154	36.48N	25.25E
Iowa, state, U.S. (ī′ȯ-w*ȧ*)	90	42.05N	94.20W
Iowa, r., Ia., U.S.	96	41.55N	92.20W
Iowa City, Ia., U.S.	90	41.39N	91.31W
Iowa Falls, Ia., U.S.	96	42.32N	93.16W
Iowa Park, Tx., U.S.	104	33.57N	98.39W
Ipala, Tan.	210	4.30S	32.53E
Ipanema, neigh., Braz.	230c	22.59S	43.12W
Ípeirus, hist. reg., Grc.	154	39.35N	20.45E
Ipel', r., Eur. (ė′pĕl)	148	48.08N	19.00E
Ipiales, Col. (ē-pė-ä′lȧs)	124	0.48N	77.45W
Ipoh, Malay.	188	4.45N	101.05E
Ipswich, Austl. (ĭps′wĭch)	196	27.40S	152.50E
Ipswich, Eng., U.K.	140	52.05N	1.05E
Ipswich, Ma., U.S.	87a	42.41N	70.50W
Ipswich, S.D., U.S.	96	45.26N	99.01W
Ipu, Braz. (ē-po͞o)	124	4.11S	40.45W
Iput', r., Eur. (ė-pȯt′)	160	52.53N	31.57E
Iqaluit, Can.	78	63.48N	68.31W
Iquique, Chile (ē-kė′kĕ)	124	20.16S	70.07W
Iquitos, Peru (ė-kē′tōs)	124	3.39S	73.18W
Iráklion, Grc.	136	35.20N	25.10E
Iran, nation, Asia (ē-rän′)	174	31.15N	53.30E
Iran, Plateau of, plat., Iran	174	32.28N	58.00E
Iran Mountains, mts., Asia	188	2.30N	114.30E
Irapuato, Mex. (ē-rä-pwä′tō)	112	20.41N	101.24W
Iraq, nation, Asia (ē-räk′)	174	32.00N	42.30E
Irazú, vol., C.R. (ē-rä-zo͞o′)	114	9.58N	83.54W
Irbid, Jord. (ėr-bēd′)	176	32.33N	35.51E
Irbīl, Iraq	174	36.10N	44.00E
Irbit, Russia (ėr-bėt′)	158	57.40N	63.10E
Irby, Eng., U.K.	233a	53.21N	3.07W
Irébou, Zaire (ē-rā′bo͞o)	206	0.40S	17.48E
Ireland, nation, Eur. (īr-l*ă*nd)	136	53.33N	8.00W
Iremel', Gora, mtn., Russia (gȧ-rä′ĭ-rĕ′mĕl)	164a	54.32N	58.52E
Irene, S. Afr. (ĭ-rē-nē)	207b	25.53S	28.13E
Irgiz, Kaz. (ĭr-gēz′)	158	48.30N	61.17E
Irgiz, r., Kaz.	162	49.30N	60.32E
Irîgui, reg., Mali	208	16.45N	5.35W
Iriklinskoye Vodokhranilishche, res., Russia	160	52.20N	58.50E
Iringa, Tan. (ė-rĭŋ′gä)	206	7.46S	35.42E
Iriomote Jima, i., Japan (ērē′-ō-mō-tā)	180	24.20N	123.30E
Iriona, Hond. (ė-rė-ō′nä)	114	15.53N	85.12W
Irish Sea, sea, Eur. (ī′rĭsh)	136	53.55N	5.25W
Irkutsk, Russia (ĭr-kȯtsk′)	158	52.16N	104.00E
Irlam, Eng., U.K. (ûr′l*ă*m)	138a	53.26N	2.26W
Irois, Cap des, c., Haiti	116	18.25N	74.50W
Iron Bottom Sound, strt., Sol.Is.	192e	9.15S	160.00E
Iron Cove, b., Austl.	239a	33.52S	151.10E
Irondale, Al., U.S. (ī′ĕrn-dăl)	94h	33.32N	86.43W
Iron Gate, val., Eur.	154	44.43N	22.32E
Iron Knob, Austl. (ī-*ă*n nŏb)	198	32.47S	137.10E
Iron Mountain, Mi., U.S. (ī′ĕrn)	96	45.49N	88.04W
Iron River, Mi., U.S.	96	46.09N	88.39W
Ironton, Oh., U.S. (ī′ĕrn-tŭn)	92	38.30N	82.45W
Ironwood, Mi., U.S. (ī′ĕrn-wȯd)	96	46.28N	90.10W
Iroquois, r., Il., U.S. (ĭr′ȯ-kwoi)	92	40.55N	87.20W
Iroquois Falls, Can.	78	48.41N	80.39W
Irō-Saki, c., Japan (ē′rō sä′kē)	186	34.35N	138.54E
Irpen', r., Ukr. (ĭr-pĕn′)	156	50.13N	29.55E
Irrawaddy, r., Burma (ĭr-*ȧ*-wäd′ė)	174	23.27N	96.25E
Irtysh, r., Asia (ĭr-tĭsh′)	158	59.00N	69.00E
Irumu, Zaire (ė-rȯ′mo͞o)	204	1.30N	29.52E
Irun, Spain (ė-ro͞on′)	152	43.20N	1.47W
Irvine, Scot., U.K.	144	55.39N	4.40W
Irvine, Ca., U.S. (ûr′vĭn)	101a	33.40N	117.45W
Irvine, Ky., U.S.	92	37.40N	84.00W
Irving, Tx., U.S. (ûr′vēng)	101c	32.49N	96.57W
Irving Park, neigh., Il., U.S.	227a	41.57N	87.43W
Irvington, N.J., U.S. (ûr′vēng-t*ŭ*n)	94a	40.43N	74.15W
Irvington, neigh., Md., U.S.	225c	39.17N	76.41W
Irwin, Pa., U.S. (ûr′wĭn)	95e	40.19N	79.42W
Is, Russia (ēs)	164a	58.48N	59.44E
Isa, Nig.	208	13.14N	6.24E
Isaacs, Mount, mtn., Pan. (ē-sä-ȧ′ks)	110a	9.22N	79.31W
Isabela, i., Ec. (ē-sä-bā′lä)	124	0.47S	91.35W
Isabela, Cabo, c., Dom. Rep. (kȧ′bȯ-ė-sä-bĕ′lä)	116	20.00N	71.00W
Isabella, Cordillera, mts., Nic. (kȯr-dēl-yĕ′rä-ē-sä-bĕlä)	114	13.20N	85.37W
Isabella Indian Reservation, I.R., Mi., U.S. (ĭs-ȧ-bĕl′-lȧ)	92	43.35N	84.55W
Isaccea, Rom. (ė-säk′chä)	156	45.16N	28.26E
Ísafjördur, Ice. (ēs′ȧ-fŷr-dȯr)	140	66.09N	22.39W
Isando, S. Afr.	240b	26.09S	28.12E
Isangi, Zaire (ė-säŋ′gē)	180	0.46N	24.15E
Isar, r., Ger. (ē′zär)	140	48.30N	12.30E
Isarco, r., Italy (ė-sär′kō)	154	46.37N	11.25E
Isarog, Mount, mtn., Phil. (ė-sä-rȯ-g)	189a	13.40N	123.23E
Ischia, Italy (ēs′kyä)	153c	40.29N	13.58E
Ischia, Isola d', i., Italy (dė′sh-kyä)	142	40.26N	13.55E
Ise, Japan (ĭs′hĕ) (û′gē-yă′mă′dȧ)	186	34.30N	136.43E
Iselin, N.J., U.S.	224	40.34N	74.19W
Iseo, Lago d', l., Italy (lä-′gō-dē-ė-zĕ′ō)	154	45.50N	9.55E
Isére, r., Fr. (ė-zâr′)	140	45.15N	5.15E
Iserlohn, Ger. (ē′zĕr-lōn)	151c	51.22N	7.42E
Isernia, Italy (ė-zĕr′nyä)	154	41.35N	14.14E
Ise-Wan, b., Japan (ē′sĕ wän)	186	34.49N	136.44E
Iseyin, Nig.	204	7.58N	3.36E
Ishigaki, Japan	192d	24.20N	124.09E
Ishikari Wan, b., Japan (ē′shē-kä-rē wän)	186	43.30N	141.05E
Ishim, Russia (ĭsh-ėm′)	158	56.07N	69.13E
Ishim, r., Asia	158	53.17N	67.45E
Ishimbay, Russia (ē-shēm-bī′)	164a	53.28N	56.02E
Ishinomaki, Japan (ĭsh-nō-mä′kē)	180	38.22N	141.22E
Ishinomaki Wan, b., Japan (ē-shē-nō-mä′kē wän)	186	38.10N	141.40E
Ishly, Russia (ĭsh′lĭ)	164a	54.13N	55.55E
Ishlya, Russia (ĭsh′lyȧ)	164a	53.54N	57.48E
Ishmant, Egypt	212b	29.17N	31.15E
Ishpeming, Mi., U.S. (ĭsh′pė-mĭng)	96	46.28N	87.42W
Isidro Casanova, Arg.	229d	34.42S	58.35W
Isipingo, S. Afr. (ĭs-ĭ-pĭŋ-gȯ)	207c	29.59S	30.58E
Isiro, Zaire	204	2.47N	27.37E
İskenderun, Tur. (ĭs-kĕn′dĕr-o͞on)	174	36.45N	36.15E
İskenderun Körfezi, b., Tur.	142	36.22N	35.25E
İskilip, Tur. (ės′kĭ-lėp′)	142	40.40N	34.30E
Iskŭr, r., Bul. (ĭs′k'r)	154	43.05N	23.37E
Isla-Cristina, Spain (ī′lä-krė-stē′nä)	152	37.13N	7.20W
Islāmābād, Pak.	174	33.55N	73.05E
Isla Mujeres, Mex. (ė′s-lä-mo͞o-kĕ′rĕs)	114a	21.25N	86.53W
Island Lake, l., Can.	78	53.47N	94.25W
Island Park, N.Y., U.S.	224	40.36N	73.40W
Islands, Bay of, b., Can. (ī′l*ă*ndz)	86	49.10N	58.15W
Islay, i., Scot., U.K. (ī′lā)	140	55.55N	6.35W
Isle, r., Fr. (ēl)	150	45.02N	0.29E
Isle of Axholme, reg., Eng., U.K. (ăks′-hȯm)	138a	53.33N	0.48W
Isle of Man, dep., Eur. (măn)	144	54.26N	4.21W
Isle Royale National Park, rec., Mi., U.S. (īl′roi-*ă*l′)	90	47.57N	88.37W
Isleta, N.M., U.S. (ės-lā′t*ȧ*) (ī-lē′t*ȧ*)	102	34.55N	106.45W
Isleta Indian Reservation, I.R., N.M., U.S.	102	34.55N	106.45W
Isleworth, neigh., Eng., U.K.	231	51.28N	0.20W
Islington, neigh., Can.	223c	43.39N	79.32W
Islington, neigh., Eng., U.K.	231	51.34N	0.06W
Ismailia, Egypt (ēs-mā-ēl′ėȧ)	212b	30.35N	32.17E
Ismā'īlīyah, neigh., Egypt	240a	30.03N	31.14E
Ismā'īlīyah Canal, can., Egypt	212b	30.25N	31.45E
Ismaning, Ger. (ēz′mä-nēng)	139d	48.14N	11.41E
Isparta, Tur. (ė-spär′tȧ)	174	37.50N	30.40E
Israel, nation, Asia	174	32.40N	34.00E
Issaquah, Wa., U.S. (ĭz′să-kwăh)	100a	47.32N	122.02W
Isselburg, Ger. (ē′sĕl-bo͞org)	151c	51.50N	6.28E
Issoire, Fr. (ē-swȧr′)	150	45.32N	3.13E
Issoudun, Fr. (ē-so͞o-dăN′)	150	46.56N	2.00E
Issum, Ger. (ē′so͞om)	151c	51.32N	6.24E
Issyk-Kul, Ozero, l., Kyrg.	158	42.13N	76.12E
Issy-les-Moulineaux, Fr.	233c	48.49N	2.17E
Īstādeh-ye Moqor, Āb-e, l., Afg.	178	32.35N	68.00E
İstanbul, Tur. (ė-stän-bo͞ol′)	174	41.02N	29.00E
İstanbul Boğazi (Bosporus), strt., Tur.	174	41.10N	29.10E
Istead Rise, Eng., U.K.	231	51.24N	0.22E
Istiaía, Grc. (ĭs-tyī′yä)	154	38.58N	23.11E
Istmina, Col. (ēst-mė′nä)	124a	5.10N	76.40W
Istokpoga, Lake, l., Fl., U.S. (īs-tŏk-pō′gȧ)	109a	27.20N	81.33W
Istra, pen., Yugo. (ė-strä)	154	45.18N	13.48E

ng-sing; ŋ-baŋk; N-nasalized n; nŏd; c*ŏ*mmit; ōld; ȯbey; ôrder; oi-boil; fo͞od; ȯ-as oo in foot; ou-out; s-soft; sh-dish; th-thin; pūre; ůnite; ûrn; stŭd; circ*ŭ*s; ü-as in French tu; '-indeterminate vowel.

PLACE (Pronunciation)	PAGE	Lat. °′	Long. °′
Istranca Dağlari, mts., Eur. (ĭ-strän'jȧ)	154	41.50N	27.25E
Istres, Fr. (ēs'tr')	150a	43.30N	5.00E
Itabaiana, Braz. (ē-tä-bä-yȧ-nä)	124	10.42S	37.17W
Itabapoana, Braz. (ē-tä'-bä-pôä'nä)	123a	21.19S	40.58W
Itabapoana, r., Braz.	123a	21.11S	41.18W
Itabirito, Braz. (ē-tä-bē-rē'tô)	123a	20.15S	43.46W
Itabuna, Braz. (ē-tä-bo͞o'nȧ)	124	14.47S	39.17W
Itacoara, Braz. (ē-tä-kô'ä-rä)	123a	21.41S	42.04W
Itacoatiara, Braz. (ē-tȧ-kwȧ-tyä'rȧ)	124	3.03S	58.18W
Itagüí, Col. (ē-tä'gwē)	124a	6.11N	75.36W
Itagui, r., Braz.	126b	22.53S	43.43W
Itaipava, Braz. (ē-tī-pá'-vä)	126b	22.23S	43.09W
Itaipu, Braz. (ē-tī'po͞o)	126b	22.58S	43.02W
Itaipu, Ponta de, c., Braz.	230c	22.59S	43.03W
Itaituba, Braz. (ē-tä'ī-to͞o'bȧ)	124	4.12S	56.00W
Itajái, Braz. (ē-tä-zhī')	126	26.52S	48.39W
Italy, Tx., U.S.	106	32.11N	96.51W
Italy, nation, Eur. (ĭt'ȧ-lē)	136	43.58N	11.14E
Itambi, Braz. (ē-tä'm-bē)	126b	22.44S	42.57W
Itami, Japan (ē'tä'mē')	187b	34.47N	135.25E
Itapecerica, Braz. (ē-tä-pĕ-sĕ-rē'kȧ)	123a	20.29S	45.08W
Itapecuru-Mirim, Braz. (ē-tä-pĕ'ko͞o-ro͞o-mē-rēɴ')	124	3.17S	44.15W
Itaperuna, Braz. (ē-tȧ'pâ-ro͞o'nä)	124	21.12S	41.53W
Itapetininga, Braz. (ē-tä-pĕ-tē-nē'ɴ-gä)	124	23.37S	48.03W
Itapira, Braz.	123a	22.27S	46.47W
Itapira, Braz. (ē-tȧ-pē'rȧ)	124	20.42S	51.19W
Itaquaquecetuba, Braz.	230d	23.29S	46.21W
Itarsi, India	178	22.43N	77.45E
Itasca, Tx., U.S. (ī-täs'kȧ)	106	32.09N	97.08W
Itasca, l., Mn., U.S.	96	47.13N	95.14W
Itatiaia, Pico da, mtn., Braz. (pē'-kô-dȧ-ē-tä-tyȧ'ēä)	124	22.18S	44.41W
Itatiba, Braz. (ē-tä-tē'bä)	123a	23.01S	46.48W
Itaúna, Braz. (ē-tä-o͞o'nä)	123a	20.05S	44.35W
Ithaca, Mi., U.S. (ĭth'ȧ-kȧ)	92	43.20N	84.35W
Ithaca, N.Y., U.S.	90	42.25N	76.30W
Itháka, i., Grc. (ē'thä-kē)	154	38.27N	20.48E
Itigi, Tan.	210	5.42S	34.29E
Itimbiri, r., Zaire	210	2.40N	23.30E
Itire, Nig.	240d	6.31N	3.21E
Itoko, Zaire (ē-tō'kō)	206	1.13S	22.07E
Itu, Braz. (ē-to͞o')	123a	23.16S	47.16W
Ituango, Col. (ē-twäŋ'gō)	124	7.07N	75.44W
Ituiutaba, Braz. (ē-to͞o-ē͞oo-tä'bä)	124	18.56S	49.17W
Itumirim, Braz. (ē-to͞o-mē-rē'ɴ)	123a	21.20S	44.51W
Itundujia Santa Cruz, Mex. (ē-to͞on-do͞o-hē'ä sä'n-tä kro͞o'z)	112	16.50N	97.43W
Iturbide, Mex. (ē'to͞or-bē'dhā)	114a	19.38N	89.31W
Iturup, i., Russia (ē-to͞o-ro͞op')	162	45.35N	147.15E
Ituzaingo, Arg. (ē-to͞o-zä-ē'n-gō)	126a	34.40S	58.40W
Itzehoe, Ger. (ē'tzĕ-hō)	148	53.55N	9.31E
Iuka, Ms., U.S. (ī-ū'kȧ)	108	34.47N	88.10W
Iúna, Braz. (ē-o͞o'-nä)	123a	20.22S	41.32W
Iupeba, Braz.	230d	23.41S	46.22W
Ivanhoe, Austl. (ĭv'ăn-hō)	198	32.53S	144.10E
Ivanhoe, Austl.	239b	37.46S	145.03E
Ivano-Frankovsk, Ukr. (ē-vä'nō frän-kôvsk')	160	48.53N	24.46E
Ivanovo, Russia (ē-vä'nô-vō)	158	57.02N	41.54E
Ivanovo, prov., Russia	156	56.55N	40.30E
Ivanpol', Ukr. (ē-vän'pôl)	156	49.51N	28.11E
Ivanteyevka, Russia (ē-vȧn-tyĕ'yĕf-kȧ)	164b	55.58N	37.56E
Ivdel', Russia (ĭv'dyĕl)	164a	60.42N	60.27E
Iver, Eng., U.K.	231	51.31N	0.30W
Iver Heath, Eng., U.K.	231	51.32N	0.31W
Iviza, see Ibiza, i., Spain	136	38.55N	1.24E
Ivohibé, Madag. (ē-vō-hē-bā')	206	22.28S	46.59E
Ivory Coast, nation, Afr.	204	7.43N	6.30W
Ivrea, Italy (ē-vrĕ'ä)	142	45.25N	7.54E
Ivry-sur-Seine, Fr.	151b	48.49N	2.23E
Ivujivik, Can.	78	62.17N	77.52W
Iwaki, Japan	186	37.03N	140.57E
Iwate Yama, mtn., Japan (ē-wä-tē-yä'mä)	186	39.50N	140.56E
Iwatsuki, Japan	187a	35.48N	139.43E
Iwaya, Japan (ē'wȧ-yȧ)	187b	34.35N	135.01E
Iwo, Nig.	204	7.38N	4.11E
Ixcateopán, Mex. (ēs-kä-tä-ō-pän')	112	18.29N	99.49W
Ixelles, Bel.	139a	50.49N	4.23E
Ixhautlán, Mex. (ēs-wȧt-län')	112	20.41N	98.01W
Ixhuatán, Mex. (ēs-hwä-tän')	112	16.19N	94.30W
Ixmiquilpan, Mex. (ēs-mē-kēl'pän)	112	20.30N	99.12W
Ixopo, S. Afr.	207c	30.10S	30.04E
Ixtacalco, Mex. (ēs-tȧ-käl'kō)	113a	19.23N	99.07W
Ixtaltepec, Mex. (ēs-täl-tĕ-pĕk')	112	16.33N	95.04W
Ixtapalapa, Mex. (ēs'tä-pä-lä'pä)	113a	19.21N	99.06W
Ixtapaluca, Mex. (ēs'tä-pä-lo͞o'kä)	113a	19.18N	98.53W
Ixtepec, Mex. (ēks-tĕ'pĕk)	112	16.37N	95.09W
Ixtlahuaca, Mex. (ēs-tlä-wä'kä)	112	19.34N	99.46W
Ixtlán de Juárez, Mex. (ēs-tlän' dā hwä'râz)	112	17.20N	96.29W
Ixtlán del Río, Mex. (ēs-tlän'dĕl rē'ō)	112	21.05N	104.22W
Iya, r., Russia	162	53.45N	99.30E
Iyo-Nada, b., Japan (ē'yō nä-dä)	187	33.33N	132.07E
Izabal, Guat. (ē'zä-bäl')	114	15.23N	89.10W
Izabal, Lago, l., Guat.	114	15.30N	89.04W
Izalco, El Sal. (ē-zäl'kō)	114	13.50N	89.40W
Izamal, Mex. (ē-zä-mä'l)	114a	20.55N	89.00W
Izhevsk, Russia (ē-zhyĕfsk')	158	56.50N	53.15E
Izhma, Russia (ĭzh'mȧ)	160	65.00N	54.05E
Izhma, r., Russia	160	64.00N	53.00E
Izhora, r., Russia (ēz'hô-rȧ)	164c	59.36N	30.20E
Izmail, Ukr. (ēz-mȧ-ēl)	160	45.00N	28.49E
İzmir, Tur. (ĭz-mēr')	174	38.25N	27.05E

PLACE (Pronunciation)	PAGE	Lat. °′	Long. °′
Izmit, Tur. (ĭz-mēt')	142	40.45N	29.45E
Iznajar, Embalse de, res., Spain	152	37.15N	4.30W
Iztaccíhuatl, mtn., Mex.	112	19.10N	98.38W
Izuhara, Japan (ē'zo͞o-hä'rä)	187	34.11N	129.18E
Izumi-Ōtsu, Japan (ē'zo͞o-mo͞o ō'tso͞o)	187b	34.30N	135.24E
Izumo, Japan (ē'zo͞o-mō)	187	35.22N	132.45E
Izu Shichitō, is., Japan	180	34.32N	139.25E

J

PLACE (Pronunciation)	PAGE	Lat. °′	Long. °′
Jabal, Bahr al, r., Sudan	204	7.30N	31.00E
Jabalpur, India	174	23.18N	79.59E
Jabavu, S. Afr.	240b	26.15S	27.53E
Jablonec nad Nisou, Czech. (yäb'lô-nyĕts)	148	50.43N	15.12E
Jablunkov Pass, p., Czech. (yäb'lòn-kôf)	148	49.31N	18.35E
Jaboatão, Braz. (zhä-bô-ȧ-touɴ)	124	8.14S	35.08W
Jaca, Spain (hä'kä)	152	42.35N	0.30W
Jacala, Mex. (hä-kȧ'lä)	112	21.01N	99.11W
Jacaltenango, Guat. (hä-kȧl-tĕ-näŋ'gō)	114	15.39N	91.41W
Jacarézinho, Braz. (zhä-kä-rĕ'zē-nyō)	124	23.13S	49.58W
Jachymov, Czech. (yä'chĭ-môf)	148	50.22N	12.51E
Jacinto City, Tx., U.S. (hä-sĕn'tō) (jȧ-sĭn'tō)	107a	29.45N	95.14W
Jacksboro, Tx., U.S. (jăks'bŭr-ō)	104	33.13N	98.11W
Jackson, Al., U.S. (jăk'sŭn)	108	31.31N	87.52W
Jackson, Ca., U.S.	102	38.22N	120.47W
Jackson, Ga., U.S.	108	33.19N	83.55W
Jackson, Ky., U.S.	108	37.32N	83.17W
Jackson, La., U.S.	106	30.50N	91.13W
Jackson, Mi., U.S.	90	42.15N	84.25W
Jackson, Mn., U.S.	96	43.37N	95.00W
Jackson, Ms., U.S.	90	32.17N	90.10W
Jackson, Mo., U.S.	104	37.23N	89.40W
Jackson, Oh., U.S.	92	39.00N	82.40W
Jackson, Tn., U.S.	90	35.37N	88.49W
Jackson, Port, b., Austl.	195b	33.50S	151.18E
Jackson Heights, neigh., N.Y., U.S.	224	40.45N	73.53W
Jackson Lake, l., Wy., U.S.	98	43.57N	110.28W
Jacksonville, Al., U.S. (jăk'sŭn-vĭl)	108	33.52N	85.45W
Jacksonville, Fl., U.S.	90	30.20N	81.40W
Jacksonville, Il., U.S.	90	39.43N	90.12W
Jacksonville, Tx., U.S.	106	31.58N	95.18W
Jacksonville Beach, Fl., U.S.	108	31.18N	81.25W
Jacmel, Haiti (zhȧk-mĕl')	116	18.15N	72.30W
Jaco, l., Mex. (hä'kō)	106	27.51N	103.50W
Jacobābād, Pak.	178	28.22N	68.30E
Jacobina, Braz. (zhä-kô-bē'nȧ)	124	11.13S	40.30W
Jacomino, Cuba	229b	23.06N	82.20W
Jacques-Cartier, r., Can.	77b	47.04N	71.28W
Jacques Cartier, Détroit de, strt., Can.	86	50.07S	63.58W
Jacques-Cartier, Mont, mtn., Can.	86	48.59N	66.00W
Jacquet River, Can. (zhȧ-kĕ') (jăk'ĕt)	86	47.55N	66.00W
Jacutinga, Braz. (zhȧ-ko͞o-tēn'gä)	123a	22.17S	46.36W
Jade Buddha, Temple of the (Yufosi), rel., China	237a	31.14N	121.26E
Jadebusen, b., Ger.	148	53.28N	8.17E
Jadotville, see Likasi, Zaire	206	10.59S	26.44E
Jaén, Peru (ĸä-ĕ'n)	124	5.38S	78.49W
Jaen, Spain	142	37.45N	3.48W
Jaffa, Cape, c., Austl. (jăf'ȧ)	196	36.58S	139.29E
Jaffna, Sri L. (jäf'nȧ)	175c	9.44N	80.09E
Jagüey Grande, Cuba (hä'gwā grän'dā)	116	22.35N	81.05W
Jahore Strait, strt., Asia	173b	1.22N	103.37E
Jahrom, Iran	174	28.30N	53.28E
Jaibo, r., Cuba (hä-ē'bō)	116	20.10N	75.20W
Jaipur, India	174	27.00N	75.50E
Jaisalmer, India	178	27.00N	70.54E
Jajce, Bos. (yī'tsĕ)	154	44.20N	17.19E
Jajpur, India	178	20.49N	86.37E
Jakarta, Indon. (yä-kär'tä)	188	6.17S	106.45E
Jakobstad, Fin. (yȧ'kôb-städh)	140	63.33N	22.31E
Jalacingo, Mex. (hä-lä-sĭŋ'gō)	112	19.47N	97.16W
Jalālābād, Afg. (jŭ-lä-lȧ-bäd)	175a	34.25N	70.27E
Jalālah al Baḩrīyah, Jabal, mts., Egypt	212b	29.20N	32.00E
Jalapa, Guat. (hä-lä'pȧ)	114	14.38N	89.58W
Jalapa de Díaz, Mex.	112	18.06N	96.33W
Jalapa del Marqués, Mex. (dĕl mär-kās')	112	16.30N	95.29W
Jalapa Enríquez, Mex. (ĕn-rē'käz)	110	19.32N	96.53W
Jaleswar, Nepal	178	26.50N	85.55E
Jalgaon, India	178	21.08N	75.33E
Jalisco, Mex. (hä-lēs'kō)	112	21.27N	104.54W
Jalisco, state, Mex.	110	20.07N	104.45W
Jalón, r., Spain (hä-lōn')	152	41.22N	1.46W
Jalostotitlán, Mex. (hä-lòs-tē-tlän')	112	21.09N	102.30W
Jalpa, Mex. (häl'pä)	112	21.40N	103.04W
Jalpa, Mex. (häl'pä)	112	18.12N	93.06W
Jalpan, Mex. (häl'pän)	112	21.13N	99.31W
Jaltepec, Mex. (häl-tȧ-pĕk')	112	17.20N	95.15W
Jaltipan, Mex. (häl-tȧ-pän')	112	17.59N	94.42W
Jaltocan, Mex. (häl-tô-kän')	112	21.08N	98.32W
Jamaare, r., Nig.	208	11.50N	10.10E
Jamaica, nation, N.A.	110	17.45N	78.00W
Jamaica Bay, b., N.Y., U.S.	224	40.36N	73.51W
Jamaica Cay, i., Bah.	116	22.45N	75.55W

PLACE (Pronunciation)	PAGE	Lat. °′	Long. °′
Jamālīyah, neigh., Egypt	240a	30.03N	31.16E
Jamālpur, Bngl.	178	24.56N	89.58E
Jamay, Mex. (hä-mī')	112	20.16N	102.43W
Jambi, Indon. (mäm'bē)	188	1.45S	103.28E
James, r., U.S.	90	46.25N	98.55W
James, r., Mo., U.S.	104	36.51N	93.22W
James, r., Va., U.S.	90	37.35N	77.50W
James, Lake, res., N.C., U.S.	108	36.07N	81.48W
James Bay, b., Can. (jāmz)	78	53.53N	80.40W
Jamesburg, N.J., U.S. (jāmz'bûrg)	94a	40.21N	74.26W
Jameson Raid Memorial, hist., S. Afr.	240b	26.11S	27.49E
James Point, c., Bah.	116	25.20N	76.30W
James Range, mts., Austl.	196	24.15S	133.30E
James Ross, i., B.A.T.	122	64.20S	58.20W
Jamestown, S. Afr.	207c	31.07S	26.49E
Jamestown, N.Y., U.S. (jāmz'toun)	90	42.05N	79.15W
Jamestown, N.D., U.S.	90	46.54N	98.42W
Jamestown, R.I., U.S.	94b	41.30N	71.21W
Jamestown Reservoir, res., N.D., U.S.	96	47.16N	98.40W
Jamiltepec, Mex. (hä-mēl-tȧ-pĕk)	112	16.16N	97.54W
Jammerbugten, b., Den.	146	57.20N	9.28E
Jammu, India	174	32.50N	74.52E
Jammu and Kashmīr, hist. reg., Asia (kȧsh-mēr')	174	39.10N	75.05E
Jāmnagar, India (jäm-nŭ'gŭr)	174	22.33N	70.03E
Jamshedpur, India (jäm'shād-po͞or)	174	22.52N	86.11E
Jándula, r., Spain (hän'do͞o-lȧ)	152	38.28N	3.52W
Janesville, Wi., U.S. (jānz'vĭl)	96	42.41N	89.03W
Janin, Isr. Occ.	173a	32.27N	35.19E
Jan Mayen, i., Sval. (yän mī'ĕn)	140	70.59N	8.05W
Jánoshalma, Hung. (yä'nôsh-hôl-mô)	148	46.17N	19.18E
Janów Lubelski, Pol. (yä'no͞of lū-bĕl'skĭ)	148	50.40N	22.25E
Januária, Braz. (zhä-nwä'rē-ä)	124	15.31S	44.17W
Japan, nation, Asia (jȧ-pän')	180	36.30N	133.30E
Japan, Sea of, sea, Asia (jȧ-pän')	180	40.08N	132.55E
Japeri, Braz. (zhȧ-pĕ'rē)	126b	22.38S	43.40W
Japurá (Caquetá), r., S.A.	124	2.00S	68.00W
Jarabacoa, Dom. Rep. (ĸä-rä-bä-kô'ä)	116	19.05N	70.40W
Jaral del Progreso, Mex. (hä-räl dĕl prô-grā'sō)	112	20.21N	101.05W
Jarama, r., Spain (hä-rä'mä)	152	40.33N	3.30W
Jarash, Jord.	173a	32.17N	35.53E
Jardim Paulista, neigh., Braz.	230d	23.35S	46.40W
Jardines, Banco, bk., Cuba (bä'n-kō-här-dē'nȧs)	116	21.45N	81.40W
Jargalant, Mong.	184	46.28N	115.10E
Jari, r., Braz. (zhä-rē)	124	0.28N	53.00W
Jarocin, Pol. (yä-rō'tsyēn)	148	51.58N	17.31E
Jarosław, Pol. (yȧ-rôs-wäf)	140	50.01N	22.41E
Jarud Qi, China (jya-lo͞o-tŭ shyē)	180	44.35N	120.40E
Jasenevo, neigh., Russia	235b	55.36N	37.33E
Jasin, Malay.	173b	2.19N	102.26E
Jašiūnai, Lith. (dzȧ-sho͞o-nȧ'yē)	146	54.27N	25.25E
Jāsk, Iran (jäsk)	174	25.46N	57.48E
Jasło, Pol. (yȧs'wō)	148	49.44N	21.28E
Jason Bay, b., Malay.	173b	1.53N	104.14E
Jasonville, In., U.S. (jā'sŭn-vĭl)	92	39.10N	87.15W
Jasper, Can.	78	52.53N	118.05W
Jasper, Al., U.S. (jăs'pēr)	108	33.50N	87.17W
Jasper, Fl., U.S.	108	30.30N	82.56W
Jasper, In., U.S.	92	38.20N	86.55W
Jasper, Mn., U.S.	96	43.51N	96.22W
Jasper, Tx., U.S.	106	30.55N	93.59W
Jasper National Park, rec., Can.	78	53.09N	117.45W
Jászapáti, Hung. (yäs'ô-pä-tē)	148	47.29N	20.10E
Jászberény, Hung.	148	47.30N	19.56E
Jatibonico, Cuba (hä-tē-bô-nē'kô)	116	22.00N	79.15W
Játiva, Spain (hä'tē-vä)	142	38.58N	0.31W
Jauja, Peru (ĸä-ō'ĸ)	124	11.43S	75.32W
Jaumave, Mex. (hou-mä'vȧ)	112	23.23N	99.24W
Jaunjelgava, Lat. (youn'yĕl'gȧ-vȧ)	160	56.37N	25.06E
Java (Jawa), i., Indon.	188	8.35S	111.11E
Javari, r., S.A. (kȧ-vä-rē)	124	4.25S	72.07W
Java Trench, deep	188	9.45S	107.30E
Jávea, Spain (hȧ-vä'ä)	152	38.45N	0.07E
Jawa, Laut (Java Sea), sea, Indon.	188	5.10S	110.30E
Jawor, Pol. (yä'vôr)	148	51.04N	16.12E
Jaworzno, Pol. (yä-vôzh'nô)	148	50.11N	19.18E
Jaya, Puncak, mtn., Indon.	188	4.00S	137.00E
Jayapura, Indon.	188	2.30S	140.45W
Jayb, Wādī al (Ha'Arava), val., Asia	173a	30.33N	35.10E
Jazīrat Muhammad, Egypt	240a	30.07N	31.12E
Jazzīn, Leb.	173a	33.34N	35.37E
Jeanerette, La., U.S. (jĕn-ēr-et') (zhän-rĕt')	106	29.54N	91.41W
Jebba, Nig. (jĕb'ȧ)	204	9.07N	4.46E
Jeddore Lake, l., Can.	86	48.07N	55.35W
Jedlesee, neigh., Aus.	235e	48.16N	16.23E
Jędrzejów, Pol. (yäɴ-dzhā'yôf)	148	50.38N	20.18E
Jefferson, Ga., U.S. (jĕf'ēr-sŭn)	108	34.05N	83.35W
Jefferson, Ia., U.S.	96	42.10N	94.22W
Jefferson, La., U.S.	94d	29.57N	90.04W
Jefferson, Pa., U.S.	226b	39.56N	80.04W
Jefferson, Tx., U.S.	106	32.47N	94.21W
Jefferson, Wi., U.S.	96	42.59N	88.45W
Jefferson, r., Mt., U.S.	98	45.37N	112.22W
Jefferson, Mount, mtn., Or., U.S.	98	44.41N	121.50W
Jefferson City, Mo., U.S.	90	38.34N	92.10W
Jefferson Park, neigh., Il., U.S.	227a	41.59N	87.46W
Jeffersontown, Ky., U.S. (jĕf'ēr-sŭn-toun)	95h	38.11N	85.34W
Jeffersonville, In., U.S. (jĕf'ēr-sŭn-vĭl)	95h	38.17N	85.44W
Jega, Nig.	208	12.15N	4.23E
Jehol, hist. reg., China (jĕ-hŏl)	180	42.31N	118.12E
Jēkabpils, Lat. (yĕk'ȧb-pĭls)	160	56.29N	25.50E

ăt; finăl; rāte; senȧte; ärm; ȧsk; sofȧ; fâre; ch-choose; dh-as th in other; bē; ēvent; bĕt; recĕnt; cratēr; g-gō; gh-guttural g; bĭt; ĭ-short neutral; rīde; ĸ-guttural k as ch in German ich;

PLACE (Pronunciation)	PAGE	Lat. °′	Long. °′
Jelenia Góra, Pol. (yĕ-lĕn′yȧ gö′rȧ)	148	50.53N	15.43E
Jelgava, Lat.	146	56.39N	23.42E
Jellico, Tn., U.S. (jĕl′ĭ-kō)	108	36.34N	84.06W
Jemez Indian Reservation, I.R., N.M., U.S.	102	35.35N	106.45W
Jena, Ger. (yā′nä)	140	50.55N	11.37E
Jenkins, Ky., U.S. (jĕŋ′kĭnz)	108	37.09N	82.38W
Jenkintown, Pa., U.S. (jĕŋ′kĭn-toun)	94f	40.06N	75.08W
Jennings, La., U.S. (jĕn′ĭngz)	106	30.14N	92.40W
Jennings, Mi., U.S.	92	44.20N	85.20W
Jennings, Mo., U.S.	101e	38.43N	90.16W
Jequitinhonha, r., Braz. (zhĕ-kē-tĕŋ-ō′n-yä)	124	16.47S	41.19W
Jérémie, Haiti (zhā-rā-mē′)	116	18.40N	74.10W
Jeremoabo, Braz. (zhĕ-rä-mō-ȧ′bō)	124	10.03S	38.13W
Jerez, Punta, c., Mex. (pōō′n-tä-kĕ-räz′)	112	23.04N	97.44W
Jerez de la Frontera, Spain	142	36.42N	6.09W
Jerez de los Caballeros, Spain	152	38.20N	6.45W
Jericho, Austl. (jĕr′ĭ-kō)	196	23.38S	146.24E
Jericho, S. Afr. (jĕr-ĭkō)	212d	25.16N	27.47E
Jericho, N.Y., U.S.	224	40.48N	73.32W
Jericho, *see* Arīḥā, Isr. Occ.	173a	31.51N	35.28E
Jerome, Az., U.S. (jė-rōm′)	90	34.45N	112.10W
Jerome, Id., U.S.	98	42.44N	114.31W
Jersey, dep., Jersey	150	49.15N	2.10W
Jersey, i., Jersey (jûr′zĭ)	140	49.13N	2.07W
Jersey City, N.J., U.S.	90	40.43N	74.05W
Jersey Shore, Pa., U.S.	92	41.10N	77.15W
Jerseyville, Il., U.S. (jĕr′zė-vĭl)	104	39.07N	90.18W
Jerusalem, Isr. (jė-rōō′sȧ-lĕm)	174	31.46N	35.14E
Jesup, Ga., U.S. (jĕs′ŭp)	108	31.36N	81.53W
Jésus, Île, i., Can.	223b	45.35N	73.45W
Jesús Carranza, Mex. (hĕ-sōō′s-kär-rä′n-zä)	112	17.26N	95.01W
Jesús del Monte, neigh., Cuba	229b	23.06N	82.22W
Jesús María, Peru	229c	12.04S	77.04W
Jewel, Or., U.S. (jū′ĕl)	100c	45.56N	123.30W
Jewel Cave National Monument, rec., S.D., U.S.	96	43.44N	103.52W
Jhālawār, India	174	24.30N	76.00E
Jhang Maghiāna, Pak.	178	31.21N	72.19E
Jhānsi, India (jän′sė)	174	25.29N	78.32E
Jhārsuguda, India	178	22.51N	84.13E
Jhelum, Pak.	174	32.59N	73.43E
Jhelum, r., Asia (jā′lŭm)	174	31.40N	71.51E
Jhenkāri, India	236a	22.46N	88.18E
Jhil Kuranga, neigh., India	236d	28.40N	77.17E
Jiading, China (jyä-dĭŋ)	182	31.23N	121.15E
Jialing, r., China (jyä-lĭŋ)	180	32.30N	105.30E
Jiamusi, China	186	46.50N	130.21E
Ji'an, China (jyē-än)	180	27.15N	115.10E
Ji'an, China	184	41.00N	126.04E
Jianchangying, China (jyĕn-chäŋ-yĭŋ)	182	40.09N	118.47E
Jiangcun, China (jyän-tsòn)	183a	23.16N	113.14E
Jiangling, China (jyäŋ-lĭŋ)	180	30.30N	112.10E
Jiangshanzhen, China (jyäŋ-shän-jŭn)	182	36.39N	120.31E
Jiangsu, prov., China (jyäŋ-sōō)	180	33.45N	120.30E
Jiangwan, China (jyäŋ-wän)	183b	31.18N	121.29E
Jiangxi, prov., China (jyäŋ-shyē)	180	28.15N	116.00E
Jiangyin, China (jyäŋ-yĭn)	184	31.54N	120.15E
Jianli, China (jyĕn-lē)	184	29.50N	112.52E
Jianning, China (jyĕn-nĭŋ)	184	26.50N	116.55E
Jian'ou, China (jyĕn-ō)	184	27.10N	118.18E
Jianshi, China (jyĕn-shr)	184	30.40N	109.45E
Jiaohe, China	182	38.03N	116.18E
Jiaohe, China (jyou-hŭ)	184	43.40N	127.20E
Jiaoxian, China (jyou shyĕn)	180	36.18N	120.01E
Jiaozuo, China (jyou-dzwô)	182	35.15N	113.18E
Jiashan, China (jyä-shän)	182	32.41N	118.00E
Jiaxing, China (jyä-shyĭŋ)	180	30.45N	120.50E
Jiayu, China (jyä-yōō)	184	30.00N	114.00E
Jiazhou Wan, b., China (jyä-jō wän)	180	36.10N	119.55E
Jicarilla Apache Indian Reservation, I.R., N.M., U.S. (kē-kȧ-rēl′yȧ)	102	36.45N	107.00W
Jicarón, Isla, i., Pan. (kē-kä-rōn′)	114	7.14N	81.41W
Jiddah, Sau. Ar.	174	21.30N	39.15E
Jieshou, China	182	33.17N	115.20E
Jieyang, China (jyĕ-yäŋ)	180	23.38N	116.20E
Jiggalong, Austl. (jĭg′ȧ-lông)	196	23.20S	120.45E
Jiguani, Cuba (kē-gwä-nē′)	116	20.20N	76.30W
Jigüey, Bahía, b., Cuba (bä-ē′ä-kē′gwä)	116	22.15N	78.10W
Jihlava, Czech. (yē′hlȧ-vȧ)	140	49.23N	15.33E
Jijel, Alg.	140	36.49N	5.47E
Jijia, r., Rom.	148	47.35N	27.02E
Jijiashi, China (jyē-jyä-shr)	182	32.10N	120.17E
Jijiga, Eth.	212a	9.15N	42.48E
Jijona, Spain (kē-hō′nä)	152	38.31N	0.29W
Jilin, China (jyē-lĭn)	180	43.58N	126.40E
Jilin, prov., China	180	44.20N	124.50E
Jiloca, r., Spain (kē-lō′kȧ)	152	41.13N	1.30W
Jilotepeque, Guat. (kē-lô-tĕ-pĕ′kĕ)	114	14.39N	89.36W
Jima, Eth.	204	7.41N	36.52E
Jimbolia, Rom. (zhĭm-bô′lyä)	154	45.45N	20.44E
Jiménez, Mex.	106	27.09N	104.55W
Jiménez, Mex.	106	29.03N	100.42W
Jiménez, Mex. (kė-mä′nāz)	112	24.12N	98.29W
Jiménez del Téul, Mex. (tĕ-ōō′l)	112	21.28N	103.51W
Jimo, China (jyē-mwo)	184	36.22N	120.28E
Jim Thorpe, Pa., U.S. (jĭm′ thôrp′)	92	40.50N	75.45W
Jinan, China (jyē-nän)	180	36.40N	117.01E
Jincheng, China (jyĭn-chŭŋ)	184	35.30N	112.50E
Jindřichův Hradec, Czech. (yĕn′d′r-zhĭ-kōōf hrä′dĕts)	148	49.09N	15.02E
Jing, r., China (jyĭŋ)	184	34.40N	108.20E
Jing'anji, China (jyĭŋ-än-jē)	182	34.30N	116.55E

PLACE (Pronunciation)	PAGE	Lat. °′	Long. °′
Jingdezhen, China (jyĭn-dŭ-jŭn)	184	29.18N	117.18E
Jingjiang, China (jyĭŋ-jyäŋ)	182	32.02N	120.15E
Jingning, China (jyĭŋ-nĭŋ)	184	35.28N	105.50E
Jingpo Hu, l., China (jyĭŋ-pwo hōō)	184	44.10N	129.00E
Jingxian, China	182	37.43N	116.17E
Jingxian, China (jyĭŋ shyĕn)	184	26.32N	109.45E
Jingxing, China (jyĭŋ-shyĭŋ)	184	47.00N	123.00E
Jingzhi, China (jyĭŋ-jr)	182	36.19N	119.23E
Jinhua, China (jyĭn-hwä)	180	29.10N	119.42E
Jining, China (jyē-nĭŋ)	180	35.26N	116.34E
Jining, China	184	41.00N	113.10E
Jinja, Ug. (jĭn′jä)	204	0.26N	33.12E
Jinotega, Nic. (kē-nō-tā′gä)	114	13.07N	86.00W
Jinotepe, Nic. (kē-nō-tā′pā)	114	11.52N	86.12W
Jinqiao, China (jyĭn-chyou)	182	31.46N	116.46E
Jinshan, China (jyĭn-shän)	183b	30.53N	121.09E
Jinta, China (jyĭn-tä)	180	40.11N	98.45E
Jintan, China (jyĭn-tän)	182	31.47N	119.34E
Jin Xian, China (jyĭn shyĕn)	184	39.04N	121.40E
Jinxiang, China (jyĭn-shyäŋ)	182	35.03N	116.20E
Jinyun, China (jyĭn-yòn)	184	28.40N	120.08E
Jinzhai, China (jyĭn-jī)	182	31.41N	115.51E
Jinzhou, China (jyĭn-jō)	180	41.00N	121.00E
Jinzhou Wan, b., China (jyĭn-jō wän)	182	39.07N	121.17E
Jinzū-Gawa, r., Japan (jĕn′zōō gä′wä)	187	36.26N	137.18E
Jipijapa, Ec. (kē-pē-hä′pä)	124	1.36S	80.52W
Jiquilisco, El Sal. (kē-kē-lē′s-kô)	114	13.18N	88.32W
Jiquilpan de Juárez, Mex. (kē-kēl′pän dā hwä′räz)	112	20.00N	102.43W
Jiquipilco, Mex. (hē-kē-pē′l-kô)	113a	19.32N	99.37W
Jitotol, Mex. (kē-tô-tōl′)	112	17.03N	92.54W
Jiu, r., Rom.	154	44.45N	23.17E
Jiugang, China	236b	39.49N	116.27E
Jiujiang, China	180	29.43N	116.00E
Jiujiang, China (jyô-jyän)	183a	22.50N	113.02E
Jiuquan, China (jyô-chyän)	180	39.46N	98.26E
Jiurongcheng, China (jyô-rôŋ-chŭŋ)	182	37.23N	122.31E
Jiushouzhang, China (jyô-shō-jäŋ)	182	35.59N	115.52E
Jiuwuqing, China (jyô-wōō-chyĭŋ)	184a	32.31N	116.51E
Jiuyongnian, China (jyô-yôŋ-nĭĕn)	182	36.41N	114.46E
Jixian, China (jyē shyĕn)	182	35.25N	114.03E
Jixian, China	182	37.37N	115.33E
Jixian, China	182	40.03N	117.25E
Jiyun, r., China (jyē-yōōm)	182	39.35N	117.34E
Joachimsthal, Ger.	139b	52.58N	13.45E
João Pessoa, Braz.	124	7.09S	34.45W
João Ribeiro, Braz. (zhô-un-rē-bä′rō)	123a	20.42S	44.03W
Jobabo, r., Cuba (hō-bä′bä)	116	20.50N	77.15W
Jock, r., Can. (jŏk)	77c	45.08N	75.51W
Jocotepec, Mex. (jô-kō-tȧ-pĕk′)	112	20.17N	103.26W
Jodar, Spain (hō′där)	152	37.54N	3.20W
Jodhpur, India (hōd′pōōr)	174	26.23N	73.00E
Joensuu, Fin. (yô-ĕn′sōō)	146	62.35N	29.46E
Joffre, Mount, mtn., Can. (jŏ′f′r)	80	50.32N	115.13W
Jõgeva, Est. (yû′gĕ-vȧ)	146	58.45N	26.23E
Joggins, Can. (jŏ′gĭnz)	86	45.42N	64.27W
Johannesburg, S. Afr. (yô-hän′ĕs-bôrgh)	206	26.08S	27.54E
Johannisthal, neigh., Ger.	234a	52.26N	13.30E
John Carroll University, pt. of i., Oh., U.S.	225a	41.29N	81.32W
John Day, r., Or., U.S. (jŏn′dā)	98	44.46N	120.15W
John Day, Middle Fork, r., Or., U.S.	98	44.53N	119.04W
John Day, North Fork, r., Or., U.S.	98	45.03N	118.50W
John Day Dam, Or., U.S.	98	45.40N	120.15W
John F. Kennedy International Airport, arpt., N.Y., U.S.	224	40.38N	73.47W
John H. Kerr Reservoir, res., U.S.	90	36.30N	78.38W
John Martin Reservoir, res., Co., U.S. (jŏn mär′tĭn)	104	37.57N	103.04W
Johns Hopkins University, pt. of i., Md., U.S.	225c	39.20N	76.37W
Johnson, r., Or., U.S. (jŏn′sŭn)	100c	45.27N	122.20W
Johnsonburg, Pa., U.S. (jŏn′sŭn-bûrg)	92	41.30N	78.40W
Johnson City, Il., U.S. (jŏn′sŭn)	92	37.50N	88.55W
Johnson City, N.Y., U.S.	92	42.10N	76.00W
Johnson City, Tn., U.S.	90	36.17N	82.23W
Johnston, i., Oc. (jŏn′stŭn)	2	17.00N	168.00W
Johnstone Strait, strt., Can.	80	50.25N	126.00W
Johnston Falls, wtfl., Afr.	210	10.35S	28.50E
Johnstown, N.Y., U.S. (jonz′toun)	92	43.00N	74.20W
Johnstown, Pa., U.S.	90	40.20N	78.50W
Johor, r., Malay. (jŭ-hŏr′)	173b	1.39N	103.52E
Johor Baharu, Malay.	188	1.28N	103.46E
Jõhvi, Est. (yû′vĭ)	146	59.21N	27.21E
Joigny, Fr. (zhwàn-yē′)	150	47.58N	3.26E
Joinville, Braz. (zhwăn-vēl′)	126	26.18S	48.47W
Joinville, Fr.	150	48.28N	5.05E
Joinville, i., B.A.T.	122	63.00S	53.30W
Joinville-le-Pont, Fr.	233c	48.49N	2.28E
Jojutla, Mex. (hō-hōō′tlä)	112	18.39N	99.11W
Jola, Mex. (kô′lä)	112	21.08N	104.26W
Joliet, Il., U.S. (jō-lĭ-ĕt′)	95a	41.32N	88.05W
Joliette, Can. (zhō-lyĕt′)	78	46.01N	73.30W
Jolo, Phil. (hō-lō)	188	5.59N	121.05E
Jolo Island, i., Phil.	188	5.55N	121.15E
Jomalig, i., Phil. (hô-mä′lēg)	189a	14.44N	122.34E
Jomulco, Mex. (hô-mōōl′kō)	112	21.08N	104.24W
Jonacatepec, Mex.	112	18.39N	98.46W
Jonava, Lith. (yō-nä′vȧ)	146	55.05N	24.15E
Jones, Phil. (jōnz)	189a	12.56N	122.05E
Jones, Phil.	189a	16.35N	121.39E
Jonesboro, Ar., U.S. (jōnz′bŭro)	90	35.49N	90.42W
Jonesboro, La., U.S.	106	32.14N	92.43W
Jonesville, La., U.S. (jōnz′vĭl)	106	31.35N	91.50W
Jonesville, Mi., U.S.	92	42.00N	84.45W

PLACE (Pronunciation)	PAGE	Lat. °′	Long. °′
Jong, r., S.L.	208	8.10N	12.10W
Joniškis, Lith. (yô′nĭsh-kĭs)	146	56.14N	23.36E
Jönköping, Swe. (yûn′chû-pĭng)	140	57.47N	14.10E
Jonquiere, Can. (zhôn-kyâr′)	78	48.25N	71.15W
Jonuta, Mex. (hô-nōō′tä)	112	18.07N	92.09W
Jonzac, Fr. (zhôn-zȧk′)	150	45.27N	0.27W
Joplin, Mo., U.S. (jŏp′lĭn)	90	37.05N	94.31W
Jordan, nation, Asia (jôr′dăn)	174	30.15N	38.00E
Jordan, r., Asia	173a	32.05N	35.35E
Jordan, r., Ut., U.S.	101b	40.42N	111.56W
Jorhāt, India (jôr-hät′)	174	26.43N	94.16E
Jorullo, Volcán de, vol., Mex. (vôl-kä′n-dĕ-hō-rōōl′yō)	112	18.54N	101.38W
José C. Paz, Arg.	126a	34.32S	58.44W
Joseph Bonaparte Gulf, b., Austl. (jô′sĕf bô′nȧ-pärt)	196	13.30S	128.40E
Josephburg, Can.	77g	53.45N	113.06W
Joseph Lake, l., Can. (jô′sĕf lăk)	77g	53.18N	113.06W
Joshua Tree National Monument, rec., Ca., U.S. (jô′shū-ȧ trē)	102	34.02N	115.53W
Jos Plateau, plat., Nig. (jôs)	208	9.53N	9.05E
Jostedalsbreen, ice., Nor. (yôstĕ-däls-brĕĕn)	140	61.40N	6.55E
Jotunheimen, mts., Nor.	140	61.44N	8.11E
Joulter's Cays, is., Bah. (jōl′tẽrz)	116	25.20N	78.10W
Jouy-en-Josas, Fr.	233c	48.46N	2.10E
Jouy-le-Chatel, Fr. (zhwē-lĕ-shä-tĕl′)	151b	48.40N	3.07E
Jovellanos, Cuba (hō-vĕl-yä′nōs)	116	22.50N	81.10W
J. Percy Priest Lake, res., Tn., U.S.	108	36.00N	86.45W
Juan Aldama, Mex. (kòȧ′n-äl-dȧ′mä)	112	24.16N	103.21W
Juan Anchorena, neigh., Arg.	229d	34.29S	58.30W
Juan de Fuca, Strait of, strt., N.A. (hwän′ dā fōō′kä)	78	48.25N	124.37W
Juan de Nova, Île, i., Reu.	206	17.18S	43.07E
Juan Diaz, r., Pan. (kōōä′n-dē′äz)	110a	9.05N	79.30W
Juan Fernández, Islas de, is., Chile	122	33.30S	79.00W
Juan González Romero, Mex.	229a	19.30N	99.04W
Juan L. Lacaze, Ur. (hōōȧ′n-ĕ′lĕ-lä-kä′zĕ)	123c	34.25S	57.28W
Juan Luis, Cayos de, is., Cuba (ka-yōs-dĕ-hwän lōō-ēs′)	116	22.15N	82.00W
Juárez, Arg. (hōōä′rĕz)	126	37.42S	59.46W
Juázeiro, Braz. (zhōōȧ′zā′rô)	124	9.27S	40.28W
Juazeiro do Norte, Braz. (zhōōȧ′zā′rô-dô-nôr-tĕ)	124	7.16S	38.57W
Jubayl, Leb. (jōō-bĭl′)	173a	34.07N	35.38E
Jubba (Genale), r., Afr.	212a	1.30N	42.25E
Juby, Cap, c., Mor. (yōō′bė)	204	28.01N	13.21W
Júcar, r., Spain (hōō′kär)	142	39.10N	1.22W
Júcaro, Cuba (hōō′kȧ-rō)	116	21.40N	78.50W
Juchipila, Mex. (hōō-chē-pē′lȧ)	112	21.26N	103.09W
Juchitán, Mex. (hōō-chē-tän′)	110	16.15N	95.00W
Juchitlán, Mex. (hōō-chē-tlän)	112	20.05N	104.07W
Jucuapa, El Sal. (kōō-kwä′pä)	114	13.30N	88.24W
Judenburg, Aus. (jōō′dĕn-bûrg)	148	47.10N	14.40E
Judith, r., Mt., U.S. (jōō′dĭth)	98	47.20N	109.36W
Jugo-Zapad, neigh., Russia	235b	55.40N	37.32E
Juhua Dao, i., China (jyōō-hwä dou)	182	40.30N	120.47E
Juigalpa, Nic. (hwė-gäl′pä)	114	12.02N	85.24W
Juilly, Fr.	233c	49.01N	2.42E
Juiz de Fora, Braz. (zhò-ēzh′ dā fō′rä)	124	21.47S	43.20W
Jujuy, Arg. (hōō-hwē′)	126	24.14S	65.15W
Jujuy, prov., Arg. (hōō-hwē′)	126	23.00S	65.45W
Jukskei, r., S. Afr.	207b	25.58S	27.58E
Julesburg, Co., U.S. (jōōlz′bûrg)	104	40.59N	102.16W
Juliaca, Peru (hōō-lē-ä′kä)	124	15.26S	70.12W
Julian Alps, mts., Yugo.	142	46.05N	14.05E
Julianehåb, Grnld.	76	60.07N	46.20W
Jülich, Ger. (yü′lĕk)	151c	50.55N	6.22E
Jullundur, India	174	31.29N	75.39E
Julpaiguri, India	178	26.35N	88.48E
Jumento Cays, is., Bah. (hōō-mĕn′tō)	116	23.05N	75.40W
Jumilla, Spain (hōō-mēl′yä)	152	38.28N	1.20W
Jump, r., Wi., U.S. (jŭmp)	96	45.18N	90.53W
Jumpingpound Creek, r., Can. (jŭmp-ĭng-pound)	77e	51.01N	114.34W
Jumrah, Indon.	173b	1.48N	101.04E
Junagādh, India (jò-nä′gŭd)	174	21.33N	70.25E
Junayfah, Egypt	212c	30.11N	32.26E
Junaynah, Ra's al, mtn., Egypt	173a	29.02N	33.58E
Junction, Tx., U.S. (jŭŋk′shŭn)	106	30.29N	99.48W
Junction City, Ks., U.S.	104	39.01N	96.49W
Jundiaí, Braz.	124	23.11S	46.52W
Juneau, Ak., U.S. (jōō′nō)	90a	58.25N	134.30W
Jungfrau, mtn., Switz. (yòng′frou)	148	46.30N	7.59E
Juniata, neigh., Pa., U.S.	225b	40.01N	75.07W
Junín, Arg. (hōō-nē′n)	126	34.35S	60.56W
Junín, Col.	124a	4.47N	73.39W
Juniyah, Leb. (jōō-nē′ē)	173a	33.59N	35.38E
Jupiter, r., Can.	86	49.40N	63.20W
Jupiter, Mount, mtn., Wa., U.S.	100a	47.42N	123.04W
Jur, r., Sudan (jòr)	204	6.38N	27.52E
Jura, mts., Eur. (zhü-rȧ′)	140	46.55N	6.49E
Jura, i., Scot., U.K. (jōō′rȧ)	144	56.09N	6.45W
Jura, Sound of, strt., Scot., U.K. (jōō′rȧ)	144	55.45N	5.55W
Jurbarkas, Lith. (yōōr-bär′käs)	146	55.06N	22.50E
Jūrmala, Lat.	146	56.57N	23.37E
Jurong, China (jyōō-roŋ)	182	31.58N	119.12E
Jurong, Sing.	236c	1.21N	103.42E
Juruá, r., S.A.	124	5.30S	67.30W
Juruena, r., Braz. (zhōō-rōōĕ′nä)	124	12.22S	58.34W
Justice, Il., U.S.	227a	41.45N	87.50W
Jutiapa, Guat. (hōō-tē-ä′pä)	114	14.16N	89.55W
Juticalpa, Hond. (hōō-tē-käl′pä)	110	14.35N	86.17W
Jutland, *see* Jylland, reg., Den.	140	56.04N	9.00E

PLACE (Pronunciation)	PAGE	Lat. °′	Long. °′
Juventino Rosas, Mex.	112	20.38N	101.02W
Juventud, Isla de la, i., Cuba	110	21.40N	82.45W
Juvisy-sur-Orge, Fr.	233c	48.41N	2.23E
Juxian, China (jyōō shyĕn)	184	35.35N	118.50E
Juxtlahuaca, Mex. (hōōs-tlä-hwä'kä)	112	17.20N	98.02W
Juye, China (jyōō-yŭ)	182	35.25N	116.05E
Južna Morava, r., Yugo. (ū'zhnä mô'rä-vä)	154	42.30N	22.00E
Jwālahari, neigh., India	236d	28.40N	77.06E
Jylland, reg., Den.	140	56.04N	9.00E

K

PLACE (Pronunciation)	PAGE	Lat. °′	Long. °′
K2, mtn., Asia	174	36.06N	76.38E
Kaabong, Ug.	210	3.31N	34.08E
Kaalfontein, S. Afr. (kärl-fōn-tān)	207b	26.02S	28.16E
Kaappunt, c., S. Afr.	206a	34.21S	18.30E
Kaarst, Ger.	232	51.14N	6.37E
Kabaena, Pulau, i., Indon. (kä-bä-ā'nå)	188	5.35S	121.07E
Kabala, S.L. (kå-bå'lå)	204	9.43N	11.39W
Kabale, Ug.	210	1.15S	29.59E
Kabalega Falls, wtfl., Ug.	204	2.15N	31.41E
Kabalo, Zaire (kä-bä'lō)	206	6.03S	26.55E
Kabambare, Zaire (kä-bäm-bä'rå)	206	4.47S	27.45E
Kabba, Nig.	208	7.50N	6.03E
Kabe, Japan (kä'bā)	187	34.32N	132.30E
Kabel, neigh., Ger.	232	51.24N	7.29E
Kabinakagami, r., Can.	84	49.00N	84.15W
Kabinda, Zaire (kä-bēn'dä)	206	6.08S	24.29E
Kabompo, r., Zam. (kå-bôm'pō)	206	14.00S	23.40E
Kabongo, Zaire (kå-bông'ō)	206	7.58S	25.10E
Kabot, Gui.	208	10.48N	14.57W
Kaboudia, Ra's, c., Tun.	142	35.17N	11.28E
Kābul, Afg. (kä'bŏol)	174	34.39N	69.14E
Kabul, r., Asia (kä'bŏol)	174	34.44N	69.43E
Kabunda, Zaire	210	12.25S	29.22E
Kabwe, Zam.	206	14.27S	28.27E
Kachuga, Russia (kå-chōō-gå)	158	54.09N	105.43E
Kadei, r., Afr.	208	4.00N	15.10E
Kadıköy, neigh., Tur.	235f	40.59N	29.01E
Kadiyevka, Ukr. (kå-dĭ-yĕf'kå)	160	48.34N	38.37E
Kadnikov, Russia (käd'nē-kôf)	160	59.30N	40.10E
Kadoma, Japan	187b	34.43N	135.36E
Kadoma, Zimb.	206	18.21S	29.55E
Kaduna, Nig. (kä-dōō'nä)	204	10.33N	7.27E
Kaduna, r., Nig.	208	9.30N	6.00E
Kaédi, Maur. (kä-ā-dē')	204	16.09N	13.30W
Kaena Point, c., Hi., U.S. (kä'å-nä)	90d	21.33N	158.19W
Kaesŏng, N. Kor. (kä'ĕ-sŭng) (kĭ'jō)	180	38.00N	126.35E
Kafanchan, Nig.	208	9.36N	8.17E
Kafia Kingi, Sudan (kä'fē-å kĭŋ'gē)	204	9.17N	24.28E
Kafue, Zam. (kä'fōō)	206	15.45S	28.17E
Kafue, r., Zam.	206	15.45S	26.30E
Kafue Flats, sw., Zam.	210	16.15S	26.30E
Kafue National Park, rec., Zam.	210	15.00S	25.35E
Kafwira, Zaire	210	12.10S	27.33E
Kagal'nik, r., Russia (kä-gäl''nēk)	156	46.58N	39.25E
Kagera, r., Afr. (kä-gā'rå)	206	1.10S	31.10E
Kagoshima, Japan (kä'gō-shē'mä)	180	31.35N	130.31E
Kagoshima-Wan, b., Japan (kä'gō-shē'mä wän)	186	31.24N	130.39E
Kagran, neigh., Aus.	235e	48.15N	16.27E
Kahayan, r., Indon.	188	1.45S	113.40E
Kahemba, Zaire	210	7.17S	19.00E
Kahia, Zaire	210	6.21S	28.24E
Kahoka, Mo., U.S. (kå-hō'kå)	104	40.26N	91.42W
Kahoolawe, Hi., U.S. (kä-hōō-lä'wē)	88a	20.28N	156.48W
Kahramanmaraş, Tur.	174	37.40N	36.50W
Kahshahpiwi, r., Can.	96	48.24N	90.56W
Kahuku Point, c., Hi., U.S. (kä-hōō'kōō)	90d	21.50N	157.50W
Kahului, Hi., U.S.	90c	20.53N	156.28W
Kai, Kepulauan, is., Indon.	188	5.35S	132.45E
Kaiang, Malay.	173b	3.00N	101.47E
Kaiashk, r., Can.	84	49.40N	89.30W
Kaibab Indian Reservation, I.R., Az., U.S. (kä'ē-băb)	102	36.55N	112.45W
Kaibab Plat, Az., U.S.	102	36.30N	112.10W
Kaidori, Japan	238a	35.37N	139.27E
Kaidu, r., China (kī-dōō)	180	42.35N	84.04E
Kaieteur Fall, wtfl., Guy. (kī-ĕ-tōōr')	124	4.48N	59.24W
Kaifeng, China (kī-fŭŋ)	180	34.48N	114.22E
Kai Kecil, i., Indon.	188	5.45S	132.40E
Kailua, Hi., U.S. (kä'ē-lōō'ä)	90c	21.18N	157.43W
Kailua Kona, Hi., U.S.	88a	19.49N	155.59W
Kaimana, Indon.	188	3.32S	133.47E
Kaimanawa Mountains, mts., N.Z.	199	39.10S	176.00E
Kainan, Japan (kä'ē-nän')	187	34.09N	135.14E
Kainji Lake, res., Nig.	204	10.25N	4.50E
Kaisermühlen, neigh., Aus.	235e	48.14N	16.26E
Kaiserslautern, Ger. (kī-zĕrs-lou'tĕrn)	140	49.26N	7.46E
Kaiserwerth, neigh., Ger.	232	51.18N	6.44E
Kaitaia, N.Z. (kä-ē-tä'ē-å)	197a	35.30S	173.28E
Kaiwi Channel, strt., Hi., U.S. (kä'ē-wē)	90c	21.10N	157.38W
Kaiyuan, China (kī-yuän)	184	23.42N	103.20E
Kaiyuan, China	184	42.30N	124.00E
Kaiyuh Mountains, mts., Ak., U.S. (kī-yōō')	89	64.25N	157.38W
Kajaani, Fin. (kä'yå-nē)	140	64.15N	27.16E
Kajang, Gunong, mtn., Malay.	173b	2.47N	104.05E
Kajiki, Japan (kä'jē-kē)	186	31.44N	130.41E
Kakhovka, Ukr. (kä-kôf'kå)	156	46.46N	33.32E
Kakhovskoye, res., Ukr. (kå-kôf'skô-yĕ)	158	47.21N	33.33E
Kakhul, Mol.	156	45.49N	28.17E
Kākināda, India	174	16.58N	82.18E
Kaktovik, Ak., U.S. (kăk-tō'vĭk)	89	70.08N	143.51W
Kakwa, r., Can. (kăk'wå)	80	54.00N	118.55W
Kalach, Russia (kå-låch')	160	50.15N	40.55E
Kaladan, r., Asia	180	21.07N	93.04E
Kalahari Desert, des., Afr. (kä-lä-hä'rē)	206	23.00S	22.03E
Kalama, Wa., U.S. (kå-lăm'å)	100c	46.01N	122.50W
Kalama, r., Wa., U.S.	100c	46.03N	122.47W
Kalámai, Grc. (kä-lä-mī')	136	37.04N	22.08E
Kalamákion, Grc.	235d	37.55N	23.43E
Kalamazoo, Mi., U.S. (kăl-å-må-zōō')	90	42.20N	85.40W
Kalamazoo, r., Mi., U.S.	92	42.35N	86.00W
Kalanchak, Ukr. (kä-län-chäk')	156	46.17N	33.14E
Kalandula, Ang. (dōō'kå då brä-gäɴ'sä)	206	9.06S	15.57E
Kalaotoa, Pulau, i., Indon.	188	7.22S	122.30E
Kalapana, Hi., U.S. (kä-lä-pä'nä)	88a	19.25N	155.00W
Kalar, mtn., Iran	174	31.43N	51.41E
Kalāt, Pak. (kŭ-lät')	174	29.05N	66.36E
Kalemie, Zaire	206	5.56S	29.12E
Kalgan, see Zhangjiakou, China	180	40.45N	114.58E
Kalgoorlie, Austl. (kăl-gōōr'lē)	196	30.45S	121.35E
Kaliakra, Nos, c., Bul.	142	43.25N	28.42E
Kalima, Zaire	210	2.34S	26.37E
Kalina, neigh., Zaire	240c	4.18S	15.16E
Kaliningrad, Russia	158	54.42N	20.32E
Kaliningrad, Russia (kä-lē-nēn'grät)	164b	55.55N	37.49E
Kalinkovichi, Bela. (kä-lēn-ko-vē'chē)	156	52.07N	29.19E
Kalispel Indian Reservation, I.R., Wa., U.S. (kăl-ĭ-spĕl')	98	48.25N	117.30W
Kalispell, Mt., U.S. (kăl'ĭ-spĕl)	90	48.12N	114.18W
Kalisz, Pol. (kä'lēsh)	140	51.45N	18.05E
Kaliua, Tan.	210	5.04S	31.48E
Kalixälven, r., Swe.	140	67.12N	22.00E
Kālkāji, neigh., India	236d	28.33N	77.16E
Kalksburg, neigh., Aus.	235e	48.08N	16.15E
Kalkum, Ger.	232	51.18N	6.46E
Kallithéa, Grc.	235d	37.57N	23.42E
Kalmar, Swe. (käl'mär)	140	56.40N	16.19E
Kalmarsund, strt., Swe. (käl'mär)	146	56.30N	16.17E
Kal'mius, r., Ukr. (käl''myōōs)	156	47.15N	37.38E
Kalmyk Autonomous Soviet Socialist Republic, Russia (kål'mĭk)	160	46.56N	46.00E
Kalocsa, Hung. (kä'lō-chä)	148	46.32N	19.00E
Kalohi Channel, strt., Hi., U.S. (kä-lō'hĭ)	88a	20.55N	157.15W
Kaloko, Zaire	210	6.47S	25.48E
Kalomo, Zam. (kä-lō'mō)	206	17.02S	26.30E
Kalsubai Mount, mtn., India	178	19.43N	73.47E
Kaltenkirchen, Ger. (käl'tĕn-kēr-kĕn)	139c	53.50N	9.57E
Kālu, r., India	179b	19.18N	73.14E
Kaluga, Russia (kå-lō'gä)	158	54.29N	36.12E
Kaluga, prov., Russia	156	54.10N	35.00E
Kalundborg, Den. (kä-lōn''bôr')	146	55.42N	11.07E
Kalush, Ukr. (kä'lōsh)	148	49.02N	24.24E
Kalvarija, Lith. (käl-vä-rē'yå)	146	54.24N	23.17E
Kalwa, India	179b	19.12N	72.59E
Kal'ya, Russia (käl'yå)	164a	60.17N	59.58E
Kalyān, India	178	19.16N	73.07E
Kalyazin, Russia (käl-yå'zēn)	156	57.13N	37.55E
Kama, r., Russia (kä'mä)	158	56.10N	53.50E
Kamaishi, Japan (kä'mä-ē'shē)	186	39.16N	142.03E
Kamakura, Japan (kä'mä-kōō'rä)	187	35.19N	139.33E
Kamarān, i., Yemen	174	15.19N	41.47E
Kāmārhāti, India	178a	22.41N	88.23E
Kamata, neigh., Japan	238a	35.33N	139.43E
Kambove, Zaire (käm-bō'vē)	206	10.58S	26.43E
Kamchatka, r., Russia	162	54.15N	158.38E
Kamchatka, Poluostrov, pen., Russia	162	55.19N	157.45E
Kāmdebpur, India	236a	22.54N	88.20E
Kameari, neigh., Japan	238a	35.46N	139.51E
Kameido, neigh., Japan	238a	35.42N	139.50E
Kamen, Ger. (kä'mĕn)	151c	51.35N	7.40E
Kamenets-Podol'skiy, Ukr. (kå-mä'nĕts pô-dôl'skĭ)	160	48.41N	26.34E
Kamenjak, Rt, c., Cro. (κä'mĕ-nyäk)	154	44.45N	13.57E
Kamenka, Mol. (kä-mĕŋ'kå)	156	48.02N	28.43E
Kamenka, Ukr.	148	50.06N	24.20E
Kamen'-na-Obi, Russia (kå-mĭny'nŭ ô'bĕ)	158	53.43N	81.28E
Kamensk-Shakhtinskiy, Russia (kä'mĕnsk shäk'tĭn-skĭ)	156	48.17N	40.16E
Kamensk-Ural'skiy, Russia (kä'mĕnsk ōō-räl'skĭ)	160	56.27N	61.55E
Kamenz, Ger. (kä'mĕnts)	148	51.16N	14.05E
Kameoka, Japan (kä'mä-ōkä)	187b	35.01N	135.35E
Kāmet, mtn., Asia	178	30.50N	79.42E
Kamiakatsuka, neigh., Japan	238a	35.46N	139.39E
Kamiasao, Japan	238a	35.35N	139.30E
Kamień Pomorski, Pol.	148	53.57N	14.48E
Kamiishihara, Japan	238a	35.39N	139.32E
Kamikitazawa, neigh., Japan	238a	35.40N	139.38E
Kamikoma, Japan (kä'mē-kō'mä)	187b	34.45N	135.50E
Kamina, Zaire	206	8.44S	25.00E
Kaministikwia, r., Can. (kå-mĭ-nĭ-stĭk'wĭ-å)	96	48.40N	89.41W
Kamioyamada, Japan	238a	35.35N	139.24E
Kamitsuruma, Japan	238a	35.31N	139.25E
Kamituga, Zaire	210	3.04S	28.11E
Kamloops, Can. (kăm'lōōps)	78	50.40N	120.20W
Kamoshida, neigh., Japan	238a	35.34N	139.30E
Kamp, r., Aus. (kämp)	148	48.30N	15.45E
Kampala, Ug. (käm-pä'lä)	204	0.19N	32.25E
Kampar, r., Indon. (käm'pär)	188	0.30N	101.30E
Kampene, Zaire	210	3.36S	26.40E
Kampenhout, Bel.	139a	50.56N	4.33E
Kamp-Lintfort, Ger. (kämp-lĕnt'fōrt)	151c	51.30N	6.34E
Kampong Kranji, Sing.	236c	1.26N	103.46E
Kampong Loyang, Sing.	236c	1.22N	103.58E
Kâmpóng Saôm, Kam.	188	10.40N	103.50E
Kampong Tanjong Keling, Sing.	236c	1.18N	103.42E
Kâmpóng Thum, Kam. (kŏm'pŏng-tŏm)	188	12.41N	104.29E
Kâmpôt, Kam. (käm'pōt)	188	10.41N	104.07E
Kampuchea, see Cambodia, nation, Asia	188	12.15N	104.00E
Kamsack, Can. (kăm'săk)	78	51.34N	101.54W
Kamskoye, res., Russia	158	59.08N	56.30E
Kamudilo, Zaire	210	7.42S	27.18E
Kamuela, Hi., U.S.	88a	20.01N	155.40W
Kamui Misaki, c., Japan	186	43.25N	139.35E
Kámuk, Cerro, mtn., C.R. (sĕ'r-rō-kä-mōō'k)	114	9.18N	83.02W
Kamyshevatskaya, Russia	156	46.24N	37.58E
Kamyshin, Russia (kä-mwēsh'ĭn)	158	50.08N	45.20E
Kamyshlov, Russia (kä-mēsh'lôf)	158	56.50N	62.32E
Kan, r., Russia (kän)	162	56.30N	94.17E
Kanab, Ut., U.S. (kăn'ăb)	102	37.00N	112.30W
Kanabeki, Russia (kå-nä'byĕ-kĭ)	164a	57.48N	57.16E
Kanab Plateau, plat., Az., U.S.	102	36.31N	112.55W
Kanaga, i., Ak., U.S. (kă-nă'gă)	89a	52.02N	177.38W
Kanagawa, dept., Japan (kä'nä-gä'wä)	187a	35.29N	139.32E
Kanai, Japan	238a	35.35N	139.28E
Kanā'is, Ra's al, c., Egypt	142	31.14N	28.08E
Kanamachi, Japan (kä-nä-mä'chē)	187a	35.46N	139.52E
Kanamori, Japan	238a	35.32N	139.28E
Kananga, Zaire	206	6.14S	22.17E
Kananikol'skoye, Russia	164a	52.48N	57.29E
Kanasín, Mex. (kä-nä-sē'n)	114a	20.54N	89.31W
Kanatak, Ak., U.S. (kă-nă'tŏk)	89	57.35N	155.48W
Kanawha, r., W.V., U.S. (kå-nô'wå)	90	37.55N	81.50W
Kanaya, Japan (kä-nä'yä)	187a	35.10N	139.49E
Kanazawa, Japan (kä'nä-zä'wå)	180	36.34N	136.38E
Kānchenjunga, mtn., Asia (kĭn-chĭn-jôn'gå)	174	27.30N	88.18E
Kānchipuram, India	174	12.55N	79.43E
Kanda Kanda, Zaire (kän'då kän'då)	206	6.56S	23.36E
Kandalaksha, Russia (kån-då-låk'shå)	158	67.10N	33.05E
Kandalakshskiy Zaliv, b., Russia	160	66.20N	35.00E
Kandava, Lat. (kän'dä-vå)	146	57.03N	22.45E
Kandi, Benin (käɴ-dē')	204	11.08N	2.56E
Kandiāro, Pak.	178	27.09N	68.12E
Kandla, India (kŭnd'lŭ)	178	23.00N	70.20E
Kandy, Sri L. (kän'dē)	175c	7.18N	80.42E
Kane, Pa., U.S. (kān)	92	41.40N	78.50W
Kaneohe, Hi., U.S. (kä-nä-ō'hä)	88a	21.25N	157.47W
Kaneohe Bay, b., Hi., U.S.	90d	21.32N	157.40W
Kanëv, Ukr. (kä-nyôf')	156	49.46N	31.27E
Kanevskaya, Russia (kå-nyĕf'skå)	156	46.07N	38.58E
Kanevskoye Vodokhranilishche, res., Ukr.	158	50.10N	30.40E
Kangaroo, i., Austl. (kăŋ-gå-rōō')	196	36.05S	137.05E
Kangaroo Ground, Austl.	239b	37.41S	145.13E
Kangāvar, Iran (kŭŋ'gä-vär)	174	34.37N	46.45E
Kangean, Kepulauan, is., Indon. (käŋ'gē-än)	188	6.50S	116.22E
Kanggye, N. Kor. (käng'gyĕ)	180	40.55N	126.40E
Kanghwa, i., S. Kor. (käng'hwä)	186	37.38N	126.00E
Kangnŭng, S. Kor. (käng'nō ng)	186	37.42N	128.50E
Kango, Gabon (käɴ-gō)	206	0.09N	10.08E
Kangowa, Zaire	210	9.55S	22.48E
Kanin, Poluostrov, pen., Russia	158	68.00N	45.00E
Kaningo, Kenya	210	0.49S	38.32E
Kanin Nos, Mys, c., Russia	160	68.40N	44.00E
Kanjiža, Yugo. (kä'nyē-zhä)	154	46.05N	20.02E
Kankakee, Il., U.S. (kăŋ-kå kē')	92	41.07N	87.53W
Kankakee, r., Il., U.S.	92	41.15N	88.15W
Kankan, Gui. (käɴ-käɴ) (kän-kän')	204	10.23N	9.18W
Kannapolis, N.C., U.S. (kăn-ăp'ō-lĭs)	108	35.30N	80.38W
Kannoura, Japan (kä'nō-ōō'rä)	187	33.34N	134.18E
Kano, Nig. (kä'nō)	204	12.00N	8.30E
Kanonkop, mtn., S. Afr.	206a	33.49S	18.37E
Kanopolis Reservoir, res., Ks., U.S. (kăn-ŏp'ō-lĭs)	104	38.44N	98.01W
Kānpur, India (kän'pûr)	178	26.30N	80.10E
Kansas, state, U.S. (kăn'zås)	90	38.30N	99.40W
Kansas, r., Ks., U.S.	104	39.08N	95.52W
Kansas City, Ks., U.S.	90	39.06N	94.39W
Kansas City, Mo., U.S.	90	39.05N	94.35W
Kansk, Russia	158	56.14N	95.43E
Kansŏng, S. Kor.	186	38.09N	128.29E
Kantang, Thai. (kän'täng')	188	7.26N	99.28E
Kantchari, Burkina	208	12.29N	1.31E
Kanton, i., Kir.	190	3.50S	174.00W
Kantunilkin, Mex. (kän-tōō-nēl-kē'n)	114a	21.07N	87.30W
Kanzaki, r., Japan	238b	34.42N	135.25E
Kanzhakovskiy Kamen, Gora, mtn., Russia (kån-zhä'kôvs-kēē kämĭen)	164a	59.38N	59.12E
Kaohsiung, Tai. (kä-ô-syông')	180	22.35N	120.25E
Kaolack, Sen.	204	14.09N	16.04W
Kaouar, oasis, Niger	204	19.16N	13.09E
Kapaa, Hi., U.S.	88a	22.06N	159.20W
Kapal, Kaz. (kå-päl')	158	45.13N	79.08E
Kapanga, Zaire	210	8.21S	22.35E
Kapellen, Ger.	232	51.25N	6.35E
Kapfenberg, Aus. (kåp'fĕn-bĕrgh)	148	47.27N	15.16E

PLACE (Pronunciation)	PAGE	Lat. °'	Long. °'
Kapiri Mposhi, Zam.	210	13.58S	28.41E
Kapoeta, Sudan	204	4.45N	33.35E
Kaposvár, Hung. (kô′pôsh-vär)	148	46.21N	17.45E
Kapotn'a, neigh., Russia	235b	55.38N	37.48E
Kapsan, N. Kor. (käp′sän′)	186	40.59N	128.22E
Kapuskasing, Can.	78	49.28N	82.22W
Kapuskasing, r., Can.	84	48.55N	82.55W
Kapustin Yar, Russia (kä′pòs-tėn yär′)	160	48.30N	45.40E
Kaputar, Mount, mtn., Austl. (kă-pû-tăr)	198	30.11S	150.11E
Kapuvár, Hung. (kô′po͞o-vär)	148	47.35N	17.02E
Kara, Russia (kärȧ)	158	68.42N	65.30E
Kara, r., Russia	160	68.30N	65.20E
Karabalā', Iraq (kŭr′bȧ-lä)	174	32.31N	43.58E
Karabanovo, Russia (kä′rȧ-bȧ-nō-vô)	156	56.19N	38.43E
Karabash, Russia (kó-rȧ-bàsh′)	164a	55.27N	60.14E
Kara-Bogaz-Gol, Zaliv, b., Turk. (kȧ-rä′ bŭ-gäs′)	158	41.30N	53.40E
Karachev, Russia (kȧ-rȧ-chôf′)	160	53.08N	34.54E
Karāchi, Pak.	174	24.59N	68.56E
Karaganda, Kaz. (kȧ-rȧ-găn′dä)	158	49.42N	73.18E
Karaidel', Russia (kä′rī-dĕl)	164a	55.52N	56.54E
Kara-Khobda, r., Kaz. (kä-rȧ kôb′dȧ)	160	50.40N	55.00E
Karakoram Pass, p., Asia	174	35.35N	77.45E
Karakoram Range, mts., India (kä′rä kō′rŏm)	174	35.24N	76.38E
Karakorum, hist., Mong.	180	47.25N	102.22E
Karakumy, des., Turk. (kara-kum)	158	40.00N	57.00E
Karaman, Tur. (kä-rä-män′)	142	37.10N	33.00E
Karamay, China (kär-äm-ā)	180	45.37N	84.53E
Karamea Bight, bt., N.Z. (kȧ-rȧ-mē′ȧ bīt)	197a	41.20S	171.30E
Kara Sea, *see* Karskoye More, sea, Russia	158	74.00N	68.00E
Karashahr (Yanqui), China (kä-rä-shä-är) (yän-chyě)	180	42.14N	86.28E
Karatsu, Japan (kä′rȧ-tso͞o)	187	33.28N	129.59E
Karaul, Russia (kä-rä-ōl′)	162	70.13N	83.46E
Karave, India	236e	19.01N	73.01E
Karawanken, mts., Eur.	148	46.32N	14.07E
Karcag, Hung. (kär′tsäg)	148	47.18N	20.58E
Kardhítsa, Grc.	154	39.23N	21.57E
Kärdla, Est. (kĕrd′lȧ)	146	58.59N	22.44E
Karelian Autonomous Soviet Socialist Republic, Russia	158	62.30N	32.35E
Karema, Tan.	206	6.49S	30.26E
Kargat, Russia (kär-gät′)	158	55.17N	80.07E
Karghalik, *see* Yecheng, China	180	37.54N	77.25E
Kargopol', Russia (kär-gō-pōl″)	158	61.30N	38.50E
Kariba, Lake, res., Afr.	206	17.15S	27.55E
Karibib, Nmb. (kȧr′ȧ-bĭb)	206	21.55S	15.50E
Kārikāl, India (kä-rē-käl′)	178	10.58N	79.49E
Karimata, Kepulauan, is., Indon. (kä-rē-mä′tȧ)	188	1.08S	108.10E
Karimata, Selat, strt., Indon.	188	1.00S	107.10E
Karimun Besar, i., Indon.	173b	1.10N	103.28E
Karimunjawa, Kepulauan, is., Indon. (kä′rē-mo͞on-yä′vä)	188	5.36S	110.15E
Karin, Som. (kȧr′ĭn)	212a	10.43N	45.50E
Karkaralinsk, Kaz. (kär-kär-ä-lĕnsk′)	158	49.18N	75.28E
Karkar Dūmān, neigh., India	236d	28.39N	77.18E
Karkar Island, i., Pap. N. Gui. (kär′kär)	188	4.50S	146.45E
Karkheh, r., Iran	174	32.45N	47.50E
Karkinitskiy Zaliv, b., Ukr. (kär-kė-net′skĭ-ē zä′lĭf)	156	45.50N	32.45E
Karlobag, Cro. (kär-lō-bäg′)	154	44.30N	15.03E
Karlovac, Cro. (kär′lō-vȧts)	142	45.29N	15.16E
Karlovka, Ukr. (kȧr′lôv-kȧ)	156	49.26N	35.08E
Karlovo, Bul. (kär′lō-vō)	154	42.39N	24.48E
Karlovy Vary, Czech. (kär′lō-vė vä′rė)	140	50.13N	12.53E
Karlshamn, Swe. (kärls′häm)	146	56.11N	14.50E
Karlskrona, Swe. (kärls′krō-nä)	140	56.10N	15.33E
Karlsruhe, Ger. (kärls′ro͞o-ĕ)	140	49.00N	8.23E
Karlstad, Swe. (kärl′städ)	136	59.25N	13.28E
Karluk, Ak., U.S. (kär′lŭk)	89	57.30N	154.22W
Karmøy, i., Nor. (kärm-ûe)	146	59.14N	5.00E
Karnataka, state, India	174	14.55N	75.00E
Karnobat, Bul. (kär-nô′bät)	154	42.39N	26.59E
Kärnten (Carinthia), prov., Aus. (kĕrn′tĕn)	148	46.55N	13.42E
Karolinenhof, neigh., Ger.	234a	52.23N	13.38E
Karonga, Mwi. (kȧ-rōŋ′gȧ)	206	9.52S	33.57E
Kárpathos, i., Grc.	142	35.34N	27.26E
Karpinsk, Russia (kär′pĭnsk)	164a	59.46N	60.00E
Kars, Tur. (kärs)	174	40.35N	43.00E
Karsakpay, Kaz. (kär-säk-pī′)	162	47.47N	67.07E
Kārsava, Lat. (kär′sä-vä)	146	56.46N	27.39E
Karshi, Uzb. (kär′shē)	158	38.30N	66.08E
Karskiye Vorota, Proliv, strt., Russia	158	70.30N	58.07E
Karskoye More (Kara Sea), sea, Russia	158	74.00N	68.00E
Kartaly, Russia (kȧr′tȧ lė)	158	53.05N	60.40E
Karunagapalli, India	178	9.09N	76.34E
Karvina, Czech.	148	49.50N	18.30E
Kasaan, Ak., U.S.	80	55.32N	132.24E
Kasai, neigh., Japan	238a	35.39N	139.53E
Kasai (Cassai), r., Afr.	206	3.45S	19.10E
Kasama, Zam. (kȧ-sä′mȧ)	206	10.13S	31.12E
Kasanga, Tan. (kȧ-säŋ′gȧ)	206	8.28S	31.09E
Kasaoka, Japan (kä′sȧ-ō′kȧ)	187	34.33N	133.29E
Kasba-Tadla, Mor. (käs′bȧ-täd′lȧ)	204	32.37N	5.57W
Kasempa, Zam. (kȧ-sĕm′pȧ)	206	13.27S	25.50E
Kasenga, Zaire (kȧ-seŋ′gȧ)	206	10.22S	28.38E
Kasese, Ug.	210	0.10N	30.05E
Kasese, Zaire	210	1.38S	27.07E
Kāshān, Iran (kä-shän′)	174	33.52N	51.15E
Kashgar, *see* Kashi, China	180	39.29N	76.00E
Kashi (Kashgar), China (kä-shr) (käsh-gär)	180	39.29N	76.00E
Kashihara, Japan (kä′shė-hä′rä)	187b	34.31N	135.48E
Kashiji Plain, pl., Zam.	210	13.25S	22.30E
Kashin, Russia (kä-shēn′)	156	57.20N	37.38E
Kashira, Russia (kä-shē′rȧ)	156	54.49N	38.11E
Kashiwa, Japan (kä′shė-wä)	187a	35.51N	139.58E
Kashiwara, Japan	187b	34.35N	135.38E
Kashiwazaki, Japan (kä′shē-wä-zä′kė)	186	37.06N	138.17E
Kāshmar, Iran	176	35.12N	58.27E
Kashmir, *see* Jammu and Kashmir, hist. reg., Asia	174	39.10N	75.05E
Kashmor, Pak.	178	28.33N	69.34E
Kashtak, Russia (käsh′ták)	164a	55.18N	61.25E
Kasimov, Russia (kȧ-sē′môf)	160	54.56N	41.23E
Kaskanak, Ak., U.S. (käs-kă′năk)	89	60.00N	158.00W
Kaskaskia, r., Il., U.S. (kăs-kăs′kĭ-ȧ)	92	39.10N	88.50W
Kaskattama, r., Can. (kăs-kă-tä′mȧ)	82	56.28N	90.55W
Kaskö (Kaskinen), Fin. (kås′kû) (käs′kē-nĕn)	146	62.24N	21.18E
Kasli, Russia (käs′lĭ)	160	55.53N	60.46E
Kasongo, Zaire (kä-sôŋ′gō)	206	4.31S	26.42E
Kásos, i., Grc.	142	35.20N	26.55E
Kassándras, Kólpos, b., Grc.	154	40.10N	23.35E
Kassel, Ger. (käs′ĕl)	140	51.19N	9.30E
Kasslerfeld, neigh., Ger.	232	51.26N	6.45E
Kasson, Mn., U.S. (kăs′ŭn)	96	44.01N	92.45W
Kastamonu, Tur. (kä-stȧ-mō′no͞o)	174	41.20N	33.50E
Kastoría, Grc. (kȧs-tō′rĭ-ȧ)	142	40.28N	21.17E
Kasūr, Pak.	178	31.10N	74.29E
Kataba, Zam.	210	16.05S	25.10E
Katahdin, Mount, mtn., Me., U.S. (kȧ-tä′dĭn)	86	45.56N	68.57W
Katanga, hist. reg., Zaire (kȧ-täŋ′gȧ)	206	8.30S	25.00E
Katanning, Austl. (kȧ-tăn′ĭng)	196	33.45S	117.45E
Katano, Japan	238b	34.48N	135.42E
Katav-Ivanovsk, Russia (kä′tăf ĭ-vä′nôfsk)	164a	54.46N	58.13E
Katayama, neigh., Japan	238a	35.46N	139.34E
Kateninskiy, Russia (kátyĕ′nĭs-kĭ)	164a	53.12N	61.05E
Kateríni, Grc.	154	40.18N	22.36E
Katernberg, neigh., Ger.	232	51.29N	7.04E
Katete, Zam.	210	14.05S	32.07E
Katherine, Austl. (kăth′ēr-ĭn)	196	14.15S	132.20E
Kāthiāwār, pen., India (kä′tyȧ-wär′)	174	22.10N	70.20E
Kathmandu, Nepal (kăt-män-do͞o′)	174	27.49N	85.21E
Kathryn, Can. (kăth′rĭn)	77e	51.13N	113.42W
Kathryn, Ca., U.S.	101a	33.42N	117.45W
Katihār, India	178	25.39N	87.39E
Katiola, I.C.	208	8.08N	5.06W
Katmai National Park, rec., Ak., U.S. (kăt′mī)	90a	58.38N	155.00W
Katompi, Zaire	210	6.11S	26.20E
Katopa, Zaire	210	2.45S	25.06E
Katowice, Pol.	136	50.15N	19.00E
Katrineholm, Swe. (kȧ-trē′nĕ-hōlm)	146	59.01N	16.10E
Katsbakhskiy, Russia (kȧts-băk′skĭ)	164a	52.57N	59.37E
Katsina, Nig. (kăt′sė-nȧ)	204	13.00N	7.32E
Katsina Ala, Nig.	204	7.10N	9.17E
Katsura, r., Japan (kä′tsō-rä)	187b	34.55N	135.43E
Katsushika, neigh., Japan	238a	35.43N	139.51E
Katta-Kurgan, Uzb. (kȧ-tȧ-kòr-găn′)	162	39.45N	66.42E
Kattegat, strt., Eur. (kăt′ĕ-găt)	136	56.57N	11.25E
Katternberg, neigh., Ger.	232	51.09N	7.02E
Katumba, Zaire	210	7.45S	25.18E
Katun', r., Russia (kȧ-tōn′)	162	51.30N	86.18E
Katwijk aan Zee, Neth.	139a	52.12N	4.23E
Kauai, i., Hi., U.S.	90c	22.09N	159.15W
Kauai Channel, strt., Hi., U.S. (kä-o͞o-ä′ė)	90c	21.35N	158.52W
Kaufbeuren, Ger. (kouf′boi-rĕn)	148	47.52N	10.38E
Kaufman, Tx., U.S. (kôf′măn)	106	32.36N	96.18W
Kaukauna, Wi., U.S. (kô-kô′nȧ)	96	44.17N	88.15W
Kaulakahi Channel, strt., Hi., U.S. (kä′o͞o-lȧ-kä′hė)	88a	22.00N	159.55W
Kaulsdorf-Süd, neigh., Ger.	234a	52.29N	13.34E
Kaunakakai, Hi., U.S. (kä′o͞o-nȧ-kä′kĭ)	88a	21.06N	156.59W
Kaunas, Lith. (kou′nȧs) (kôv′nô)	158	54.42N	23.54E
Kaura Namoda, Nig.	204	12.35N	6.35E
Kavála, Grc. (kä-vä′lä)	142	40.55N	24.24E
Kavieng, Pap. N. Gui. (kä-vė-ĕng′)	188	2.44S	151.02E
Kavīr, Dasht-e, des., Iran (dŭsht-ė-ka-vēr′)	174	34.41N	53.30E
Kawagoe, Japan (kä-wă-gō′ȧ)	187	35.55N	139.29E
Kawaguchi, Japan (kä-wä-go͞o-chė)	187a	35.48N	139.44E
Kawaikini, mtn., Hi., U.S. (kä-wä′ė-kĭ-nĭ)	88a	22.05N	159.33W
Kawanishi, Japan (kä-wä′nė-shē)	187b	34.49N	135.26E
Kawasaki, Japan (kä-wä-sä′kė)	186	35.32N	139.43E
Kawashima, neigh., Japan	238a	35.28N	139.35E
Kaxgar, r., China	180	39.30N	75.00E
Kaya, Burkina (kä′yä)	204	13.05N	1.05W
Kayan, r., Indon.	188	1.45N	115.38E
Kaycee, Wy., U.S. (kā-sē′)	98	43.43N	106.38W
Kayes, Mali (kāz)	204	14.27N	11.26W
Kayseri, Tur. (kī′sĕ-rē)	174	38.45N	35.20E
Kazach'ye, Russia	158	70.46N	135.47E
Kazakhstan, nation, Asia	158	48.45N	59.00E
Kazan', Russia (kȧ-zän′)	158	55.50N	49.18E
Kazanka, Ukr. (kä-zän′kȧ)	156	47.49N	32.50E
Kazanlŭk, Bul. (kȧ′zȧn-lĕk)	154	42.47N	25.23E
Kazatin, Ukr.	160	49.43N	28.50E
Kazbek, Gora, mtn. (kȧz-bĕk′)	160	42.42N	44.31E
Kāzerūn, Iran	174	29.37N	51.44E
Kazincbarcika, Hung. (kô′zĭnts-bôr-tsĭ-ko)	148	48.15N	20.39E
Kazungula, Zam.	210	17.45S	25.20E
Kazusa Kameyama, Japan (kä-zo͞o-sä kä-mȧ′yä-mä)	187a	35.14N	140.06E
Kazym, r., Russia (kä-zēm′)	162	63.30N	67.41E
Kéa, i., Grc.	154	37.36N	24.13E
Kealaikahiki Channel, strt., Hi., U.S. (kā-ä′lä-ė-kä-hē′kē)	88a	20.38N	157.00W
Keansburg, N.J., U.S. (kēnz′bûrg)	94a	40.26N	74.08W
Kearney, Ne., U.S. (kär′nĭ)	96	40.42N	99.05W
Kearny, N.J., U.S.	94a	40.46N	74.09W
Kearsley, Eng., U.K.	233b	53.32N	2.23W
Keasey, Or., U.S. (kēz′ĭ)	100c	45.51N	123.20W
Kebayoram, neigh., Indon.	237k	6.14S	106.46E
Kebnekaise, mtn., Swe. (kĕp′nĕ-kȧ-ēs′ĕ)	136	67.53N	18.10E
Kecskemét, Hung. (kĕch′kĕ-māt)	142	46.52N	19.42E
Kedah, hist. reg., Malay. (kä′dä)	188	6.00N	100.31E
Kédainiai, Lith. (kē-dī′nĭ-ī)	146	55.16N	23.58E
Kedgwick, Can. (kĕdj′wĭk)	86	47.39N	67.21W
Keenbrook, Ca., U.S. (kēn′bròk)	101a	34.16N	117.29W
Keene, N.H., U.S. (kēn)	92	42.55N	72.15W
Keetmanshoop, Nmb. (kāt′mȧns-hōp)	206	26.30S	18.05E
Keet Seel Ruin, Az., U.S. (kēt sēl)	102	36.46N	110.32W
Keewatin, Mn., U.S. (kē-wä′tĭn)	96	47.24N	93.03W
Keewatin, District of, dept., Can.	78	61.26N	97.54W
Kefallinía, i., Grc.	142	38.08N	20.58E
Keffi, Nig. (kĕf′ė)	204	8.51N	7.52E
Ke Ga, Mui, c., Viet.	188	12.58N	109.50E
Kei, r., Afr. (kā)	207c	32.57S	26.50E
Keila, Est. (kā′lȧ)	146	59.19N	24.25E
Keilor, Austl.	195a	37.43S	144.50E
Kei Mouth, S. Afr.	207c	32.40S	28.23E
Keiskammahoek, Ciskei (kās′kämä-ho͞ok′)	207c	32.42S	27.11E
Kéita, Bahr, r., Chad	208	9.30N	19.17E
Keitele, l., Fin. (kā′tĕ-lĕ)	146	62.50N	25.40E
Kekaha, Hi., U.S.	88a	21.57N	159.42W
Kelafo, Eth.	212a	5.40N	44.00E
Kelang, Malay.	188	3.20N	101.27E
Kelang, r., Malay.	173b	3.00N	101.40E
Kelenföld, neigh., Hung.	235g	47.28N	19.03E
Kelkit, r., Tur.	142	40.38N	37.03E
Keller, Tx., U.S. (kĕl′ēr)	101c	32.56N	97.15W
Kellinghusen, Ger. (kĕ′lĕng-ho͞o-zĕn)	139c	53.57N	9.43E
Kellogg, Id., U.S. (kĕl′ŏg)	98	47.32N	116.07W
Kellyville, Austl.	239a	33.43S	150.57E
Kelme', Lith. (kĕl-mȧ)	146	55.36N	22.53E
Kélo, Chad	208	9.19N	15.48E
Kelowna, Can.	78	49.53N	119.29W
Kelsey Bay, Can. (kĕl′sė)	80	50.24N	125.57W
Kelso, Wa., U.S.	100c	46.09N	122.54W
Keluang, Malay.	173b	2.01N	103.19E
Kelvedon Hatch, Eng., U.K.	231	51.40N	0.16E
Kem', Russia (kĕm)	158	65.00N	34.48E
Kemah, Tx., U.S. (kē′mȧ)	107a	29.32N	95.01W
Kemerovo, Russia	158	55.31N	86.05E
Kemi, Fin. (kā′mė)	140	65.48N	24.38E
Kemi, r., Fin.	140	67.02N	27.50E
Kemigawa, Japan (kĕ′mė-gä′wä)	187a	35.38N	140.07E
Kemijarvi, Fin. (kā′mė-yĕr-vē)	140	66.48N	27.21E
Kemi-joki, l., Fin.	140	66.37N	28.13E
Kemmerer, Wy., U.S. (kĕm′ēr-ēr)	98	41.48N	110.36W
Kemp, l., Tx., U.S. (kĕmp)	104	33.55N	99.22W
Kempen, Ger. (kĕm′pĕn)	151c	51.22N	6.25E
Kempsey, Austl. (kĕmp′sė)	196	30.59S	152.50E
Kempt, l., Can. (kĕmpt)	84	47.28N	74.00W
Kempten, Ger. (kĕmp′tĕn)	140	47.44N	10.17E
Kempton Park, S. Afr. (kĕmp′tŏn pärk)	212d	26.07S	28.29E
Kemsing, Eng., U.K.	231	51.18N	0.14E
Ken, r., India	178	25.00N	79.55E
Kenai, Ak., U.S. (kĕ-nī′)	89	60.38N	151.18W
Kenai Fjords National Park, rec., Ak., U.S.	89	59.45N	150.00W
Kenai Mountains, mts., Ak., U.S.	89	60.00N	150.00W
Kenai Pen, Ak., U.S.	89	64.40N	150.18W
Kenberma, Ma., U.S.	223a	42.17N	70.52W
Kendal, S. Afr.	212d	26.03S	28.58E
Kendal, Eng., U.K. (kĕn′dȧl)	144	54.20N	1.48W
Kendallville, In., U.S. (kĕn′dȧl-vĭl)	92	41.25N	85.20W
Kenedy, Tx., U.S. (kĕn′ĕ-dĭ)	106	28.49N	97.50W
Kenema, S.L.	208	7.52N	11.12W
Kenilworth, Il., U.S.	227a	42.05N	87.43W
Kenilworth, N.J., U.S.	224	40.41N	74.18W
Kenitra, Mor. (kĕ-nē′trȧ)	142	34.21N	6.34W
Kenley, neigh., Eng., U.K.	231	51.19N	0.06W
Kenmare, N.D., U.S. (kĕn-mâr′)	96	48.41N	102.05W
Kenmore, N.Y., U.S. (kĕn′mōr)	95c	42.58N	78.53W
Kennebec, r., Me., U.S. (kĕn-ė-bĕk′)	86	44.23N	69.48W
Kennebunk, Me., U.S. (kĕn-ė-buŋk′)	86	43.24N	70.33W
Kennedale, Tx., U.S. (kĕn′-ė-dāl)	101c	32.38N	97.13W
Kennedy, Cape, *see* Canaveral, Cape, c., Fl., U.S.	90	28.30N	80.23W
Kennedy, Mount, mtn., Can.	89	60.25N	138.50W
Kenner, La., U.S. (kĕn′ēr)	106	29.58N	90.15W
Kennett, Mo., U.S. (kĕn′ĕt)	104	36.14N	90.01W
Kennewick, Wa., U.S. (kĕn′ė-wĭk)	98	46.12N	119.06W
Kenney Dam, dam, Can.	80	53.37N	124.58W
Kennydale, Wa., U.S. (kĕn-nė′dāl)	100a	47.31N	122.12W
Kénogami, Can. (kĕn-ŏ′gä-mė)	78	48.26N	71.14W
Kenogamissi Lake, l., Can.	84	48.15N	81.31W
Keno Hill, Can.	89	63.58N	135.18W
Kenora, Can. (kē-nō′rȧ)	78	49.47N	94.29W
Kenosha, Wi., U.S. (kē-nō′shȧ)	90	42.34N	87.50W
Kenova, W.V., U.S. (kē-nō′vȧ)	92	38.20N	82.35W
Kensico Reservoir, res., N.Y., U.S. (kĕn′sĭ-kō)	94a	41.08N	73.45W
Kensington, Austl.	239a	33.55S	151.14E

PLACE (Pronunciation)	PAGE	Lat. °'	Long. °'
Kensington, Ca., U.S.	227b	37.54N	122.16W
Kensington, Md., U.S.	225d	39.02N	77.03W
Kensington, neigh., S. Afr.	240b	26.12S	28.06E
Kensington, neigh., N.Y., U.S.	224	40.39N	73.58W
Kensington, neigh., Pa., U.S.	225b	39.58N	75.08W
Kensington and Chelsea, neigh., Eng., U.K.	231	51.29N	0.11W
Kent, Oh., U.S. (kĕnt)	92	41.05N	81.20W
Kent, Wa., U.S.	100a	47.23N	122.14W
Kentani, Transkei (kĕnt-änĭ′)	207c	32.31S	28.19E
Kentland, In., U.S. (kĕnt′lănd)	92	40.50N	87.25W
Kentland, Md., U.S.	225d	38.55N	76.53W
Kenton, Oh., U.S. (kĕn′tŭn)	92	40.40N	83.35W
Kent Peninsula, pen., Can.	78	68.28N	108.10W
Kentucky, state, U.S. (kĕn-tŭk′ĭ)	90	37.30N	87.35W
Kentucky, res., U.S.	90	36.20N	88.50W
Kentucky, r., Ky., U.S.	90	38.15N	85.01W
Kentwood, La., U.S. (kĕnt′wo͝od)	106	30.56N	90.31W
Kenya, nation, Afr. (kēn′yȧ)	206	1.00N	36.53E
Kenya, Mount (Kirinyaga), mtn., Kenya	206	0.10S	37.20E
Kenyon, Mn., U.S. (kĕn′yŭn)	96	44.15N	92.58W
Keokuk, Ia., U.S. (kē′ō-kŭk)	90	40.24N	91.34W
Keoma, Can. (kē-ō′mȧ)	77e	51.13N	113.39W
Keon Park, Austl.	239b	37.42S	145.01E
Kepenkeck Lake, l., Can.	86	48.13N	54.45W
Kępno, Pol. (kăŋ′pnō)	148	51.17N	17.59E
Kerala, state, India	174	16.38N	76.00E
Kerang, Austl. (kē-răng′)	196	35.32S	143.58E
Keratsinion, Grc.	235d	37.58N	23.37E
Kerch', Ukr. (kĕrch)	158	45.20N	36.26E
Kerchenskiy Proliv, strt., Eur. (kĕr-chĕn′skĭ prô′lĭf)	156	45.08N	36.35E
Kerempe Burun, c., Tur.	142	42.00N	33.20E
Keren, Eth.	204	15.46N	38.28E
Kerguélen, Îles, is., F.S.A.T. (kĕr′gȧ-lĕn)	2	49.50S	69.30E
Kericho, Kenya	210	0.22S	35.17E
Kerinci, Gunung, mtn., Indon.	188	1.45S	101.18E
Keriya, r., China (kē′rē-yä)	180	37.13N	81.59E
Keriya, *see* Yutian, China	180	36.55N	81.39E
Kerkebet, Eth.	176	16.18N	37.24E
Kerkenna, Îles, i., Tun. (kĕr′kĕn-nä)	204	34.49N	11.37E
Kerki, Turk. (kĕr′kē)	174	37.52N	65.15E
Kérkira, Grc.	142	39.36N	19.56E
Kérkira, i., Grc.	136	39.33N	19.36E
Kermadec Islands, is., N.Z. (kĕr-măd′ĕk)	2	30.30S	177.00E
Kermān, Iran (kĕr-män′)	174	30.23N	57.08E
Kermānshāh, *see* Bakhtarān, Iran	174	34.01N	47.00E
Kern, r., Ca., U.S.	102	35.31N	118.37W
Kern, South Fork, r., Ca., U.S.	102	35.40N	118.15W
Kerpen, Ger. (kĕr′pĕn)	151c	50.52N	6.42E
Kerrobert, Can.	82	51.53N	109.13W
Kerrville, Tx., U.S. (kûr′vĭl)	106	30.02N	99.07W
Kerulen, r., Asia (kĕr′o͞o-lĕn)	180	47.52N	113.22E
Kesagami Lake, l., Can.	84	50.23N	80.15W
Keşan, Tur. (kĕ′shȧn)	154	40.50N	26.37E
Keshan, China (kŭ-shän)	180	48.00N	126.30E
Kesour, Monts des, mts., Alg.	142	32.51N	0.30W
Kestell, S. Afr. (kĕs′tĕl)	212d	28.19N	28.43E
Keszthely, Hung. (kĕst′hĕl-lĭ)	148	46.46N	17.12E
Ket', r., Russia (kyĕt)	162	58.30N	84.15E
Keta, Ghana	204	6.00N	1.00E
Ketamputih, Indon.	173b	1.25N	102.19E
Ketapang, Indon. (kĕ-tȧ-päng′)	188	2.00S	109.57E
Ketchikan, Ak., U.S. (kĕch-ĭ-kăn′)	90a	55.21N	131.35W
Kętrzyn, Pol. (kăŋ′t′r-zĭn)	148	54.04N	21.24E
Kettering, Eng., U.K. (kĕt′ĕr-ĭng)	138a	52.23N	0.43W
Kettering, Oh., U.S.	92	39.40N	84.15W
Kettle, r., Can.	80	49.40N	119.00W
Kettle, r., Mn., U.S. (kĕt′'l)	96	46.20N	92.57W
Kettwig, Ger. (kĕt′vēg)	151c	51.22N	6.56E
Kęty, Pol. (kăŋ tĭ)	148	49.54N	19.16E
Ketzin, Ger. (kĕ′tzēn)	139b	52.29N	12.51E
Keuka, l., N.Y., U.S. (kē-ū′kȧ)	92	42.30N	77.10W
Kevelaer, Ger. (kĕ′fĕ-lăr)	151c	51.35N	6.15E
Kew, Austl.	195a	37.49S	145.02E
Kew, S. Afr.	240b	26.08S	28.06E
Kewanee, Il., U.S. (kē-wä′nē)	96	41.15N	89.55W
Kewaunee, Wi., U.S. (kē-wô′nē)	96	44.27N	87.33W
Keweenaw Bay, b., Mi., U.S. (kē′wē-nô)	96	46.59N	88.15W
Keweenaw Peninsula, pen., Mi., U.S.	96	47.28N	88.12W
Kew Gardens, pt. of i., Eng., U.K.	231	51.28N	0.18W
Keya Paha, r., S.D., U.S. (kē-yȧ pä′hä)	96	43.11N	100.10W
Key Largo, i., Fl., U.S.	109a	25.11N	80.15W
Keyport, N.J., U.S. (kē′pôrt)	94a	40.26N	74.12W
Keyport, Wa., U.S.	100a	47.42N	122.38W
Keyser, W.V., U.S. (kī′sēr)	92	39.25N	79.00W
Key West, Fl., U.S. (kē wĕst′)	90	24.31N	81.47W
Kežmarok, Czech. (kĕzh′mȧ-rôk)	148	49.10N	20.27E
Khabarovo, Russia (kŭ-bȧr-ôvô)	158	69.31N	60.41E
Khabarovsk, Russia (kä-bä′rôfsk)	158	48.35N	135.12E
Khaïdhárion, Grc.	235d	38.01N	23.39E
Khajuri, neigh., India	236d	28.43N	77.16E
Khakass Autonomous Oblast, prov., Russia	162	52.32N	89.33E
Khalándrion, Grc.	235d	38.01N	23.48E
Khālāpur, India	179b	18.48N	73.17E
Khalkidhiki, pen., Grc.	154	40.30N	23.18E
Khalkís, Grc. (käl′kĭs)	142	38.28N	23.38E
Khal'mer-Yu, Russia (kŭl-myĕr′-yo͞o′)	158	67.52N	64.25E
Khalturin, Russia (käl′to͞o-rēn)	160	58.28N	49.00E
Khambhāt, Gulf of, b., India	174	21.20N	72.27E
Khammam, India	178	17.09N	80.13E
Khānābād, Afg.	178	36.43N	69.11E
Khānaqīn, Iraq	176	34.21N	45.22E
Khandwa, India	178	21.53N	76.22E

PLACE (Pronunciation)	PAGE	Lat. °'	Long. °'
Khaníon, Kólpos, b., Grc.	154a	35.35N	23.55E
Khanka, l., Asia (ĸän′kȧ)	158	45.09N	133.28E
Khānpur, Pak.	178	28.42N	70.42E
Khanty-Mansiysk, Russia (kŭn-te′mŭn-sēsk′)	158	61.02N	69.01E
Khān Yūnus, Isr. Occ.	173a	31.21N	34.19E
Kharagpur, India (kŭ-rŭg′po͝or)	174	22.26N	87.21E
Khardah, India	236a	22.44N	88.22E
Khar'kov, Ukr. (ĸär′kôf)	158	50.00N	36.10E
Khar'kov, prov., Ukr.	156	49.33N	35.55E
Kharlovka, Russia	160	68.47N	37.20E
Kharmanli, Bul. (ĸȧr-män′lē)	154	41.54N	25.55E
Khartoum, Sudan	204	15.34N	32.36E
Khāsh, Iran	174	28.08N	61.08E
Khāsh, r., Afg.	174	32.30N	64.27E
Khasi Hills, hills, India	174	25.38N	91.55E
Khaskovo, Bul. (ĸȧs′kô-vô)	142	41.56N	25.32E
Khatanga, Russia (ĸȧ-tän′gȧ)	158	71.48N	101.47E
Khatangskiy Zaliv, b., Russia (kä-täŋ′g-skē)	158	73.45N	108.30E
Khayāla, neigh., India	236d	28.40N	77.06E
Khaybār, Sau. Ar.	174	25.45N	39.28E
Kherson, Ukr. (ĸĕr-sôn′)	160	46.38N	32.34E
Kherson, prov., Ukr.	156	46.32N	32.55E
Khichripur, neigh., India	236d	28.37N	77.19E
Khiitola, Russia (khē′tō-lȧ)	146	61.14N	29.40E
Khimki, Russia (ĸēm′kĭ)	164b	55.54N	37.27E
Khíos, Grc. (kē′ōs)	142	38.23N	26.09E
Khíos, i., Grc.	142	38.20N	25.45E
Khmel'nik, Ukr.	156	49.34N	27.58E
Khmel'nitskiy, Ukr. (kmiĕ′lnē′ts-kēē)	160	49.29N	26.54E
Khmel'nitskiy, prov., Ukr. (ĸmĕl-nēt′skĭ ôb′lȧst′)	156	49.27N	26.30E
Kholargós, Grc.	235d	38.00N	23.48E
Kholm, Russia (ĸôlm)	156	57.09N	31.07E
Kholmsk, Russia (ĸŭlmsk)	158	47.09N	142.33E
Khomeynīshahr, Iran	176	32.41N	51.31E
Khon Kaen, Thai.	188	16.37N	102.41E
Khopër, r., Russia (ĸô′pĕr)	160	52.00N	43.00E
Khor, Russia (ĸôr′)	186	47.50N	134.52E
Khor, r., Russia	186	47.23N	135.20E
Khóra Sfakión, Grc.	154a	35.12N	24.10E
Khorel, India	236a	22.42N	88.19E
Khorog, Taj.	178	37.30N	71.36E
Khorol, Ukr. (ĸô′rôl)	156	49.48N	33.17E
Khorol, r., Ukr.	156	49.50N	33.21E
Khorramābād, Iran	176	33.30N	48.20E
Khorramshahr, Iran (kô-ram′shär)	174	30.36N	48.15E
Khotin, Ukr. (ĸô′tēn)	160	48.29N	26.32E
Khot'kovo, Russia	164b	56.15N	38.00E
Khoyniki, Bela.	156	51.54N	30.00E
Khudzhand, Taj.	162	40.17N	69.37E
Khulna, Bngl.	174	22.50N	89.38E
Khūryān Mūryān, is., Oman	174	17.27N	56.02E
Khust, Ukr. (ĸo͝ost)	148	48.10N	23.18E
Khvalynsk, Russia (ĸvä-lĭnsk′)	160	52.30N	48.00E
Khvoy, Iran	174	38.32N	45.01E
Khyber Pass, p., Asia (kī′bĕr)	174	34.28N	71.18E
Kialwe, Zaire	210	9.22S	27.08E
Kiambi, Zaire (kyăm′bē)	206	7.20S	28.01E
Kiamichi, r., Ok., U.S. (kyȧ-mē′chē)	104	34.31N	95.34W
Kianta, l., Fin. (kyăn′tȧ)	160	65.00N	28.15E
Kibenga, Zaire	210	7.55S	17.35E
Kibiti, Tan.	210	7.44S	38.57E
Kibombo, Zaire	210	3.54S	25.55E
Kibondo, Tan.	210	3.35S	30.42E
Kičevo, Mac. (kē′chĕ-vô)	154	41.30N	20.59E
Kichijōji, Japan	238a	35.42N	139.35E
Kickapoo, r., Wi., U.S. (kĭk′ȧ-po͞o)	96	43.20N	90.55W
Kicking Horse Pass, p., Can.	80	51.25N	116.10W
Kidal, Mali (kē-däl′)	204	18.33N	1.00E
Kidderminster, Eng., U.K. (kĭd′ĕr-mĭn-stēr)	138a	52.23N	2.14W
Kidderpore, neigh., India	236a	22.31N	88.19E
Kidd's Beach, S. Afr. (kĭdz)	207c	33.09S	27.43E
Kidsgrove, Eng., U.K. (kĭdz′grōv)	138a	53.05N	2.15W
Kiel, Ger. (kēl)	136	54.19N	10.08E
Kiel, Wi., U.S.	96	43.52N	88.04W
Kiel Bay, b., Ger.	148	54.33N	10.19E
Kiel Canal, *see* Nord-Ostsee Kanal, can., Ger.	148	54.03N	9.23E
Kielce, Pol. (kyĕl′tsĕ)	148	50.50N	20.41E
Kieldrecht, Bel. (kēl′drĕĸt)	139a	51.17N	4.09E
Kierspe, Ger.	232	51.08N	7.35E
Kiev (Kiyev), Ukr. (kē′yĕf)	158	50.27N	30.30E
Kiev, prov., Ukr. (kē′yĕf)	156	50.05N	30.40E
Kievskoye Vodokhranilishche, res., Ukr.	158	51.00N	30.20E
Kiffa, Maur. (kēf′ȧ)	204	16.37N	11.24W
Kigali, Rw. (kē-gä′lē)	206	1.59S	30.05E
Kigoma, Tan. (kē-gō′mä)	206	4.57S	29.38E
Kii-Suido, strt., Japan (kē so͞o-ē′dō)	186	33.53N	134.55E
Kikaiga, i., Japan	186	28.25N	130.10E
Kikinda, Yugo. (ĸē′kēn-dä)	154	45.49N	20.30E
Kikládhes, is., Grc.	136	37.30N	24.45E
Kikwit, Zaire (kē′kwēt)	206	5.02S	18.49E
Kil, Swe. (kēl)	146	59.30N	13.15E
Kilauea, Hi., U.S. (kē-lä-o͞o-ā′ä)	88a	22.12N	159.25W
Kilauea Crater, Hi., U.S.	88a	19.28N	155.18W
Kilbuck Mountains, mts., Ak., U.S. (kĭl-bŭk)	89	60.05N	160.00W
Kilchu, N. Kor. (kĭl′cho͞o)	186	40.59N	129.23E
Kildare, Ire. (kĭl-dār′)	144	53.09N	7.05W
Kilembe, Zaire	210	5.42S	19.55E
Kilgore, Tx., U.S.	106	32.23N	94.53W
Kilifi, Kenya	210	3.38S	39.51E

PLACE (Pronunciation)	PAGE	Lat. °'	Long. °'
Kilimanjaro, mtn., Tan. (kyl-ē-măn-jä′rô)	206	3.09S	37.19E
Kilimatinde, Tan. (kĭl-ē-mä-tĭn′dā)	206	5.48S	34.58E
Kilindoni, Tan.	210	7.55S	39.39E
Kilingi-Nõmme, Est. (kē′lĭn-gē-nôm′mē)	146	58.08N	25.03E
Kilis, Tur. (kē′lēs)	142	36.50N	37.20E
Kiliya, Ukr. (kē′lyȧ)	156	45.28N	29.17E
Kilkenny, Ire. (kĭl-kĕn-ĭ)	140	52.40N	7.30W
Kilkis, Grc. (kĭl′kĭs)	154	40.59N	22.51E
Killala, Ire. (kĭ-lä′lȧ)	144	54.11N	9.10W
Killara, Austl.	239a	33.46S	151.09E
Killarney, Ire.	144	52.03N	9.05W
Killarney Heights, Austl.	239a	33.46S	151.13E
Killdeer, N.D., U.S. (kĭl′dēr)	96	47.22N	102.45W
Killiniq Island, i., Can.	78	60.32N	63.56W
Kilmarnock, Scot., U.K. (kĭl-mär′nŭk)	144	55.38N	4.25W
Kilrush, Ire. (kĭl′rŭsh)	144	52.40N	9.16W
Kilwa Kisiwani, Tan.	210	8.58S	39.30E
Kilwa Kivinje, Tan.	206	8.43S	39.18E
Kim, r., Cam.	208	5.40N	11.17E
Kimamba, Tan.	210	6.47S	37.08E
Kimba, Austl. (kĭm′bȧ)	198	33.08S	136.25E
Kimball, Ne., U.S. (kĭm-bȧl)	96	41.14N	103.41W
Kimball, S.D., U.S.	96	43.44N	98.58W
Kimberley, Can. (kĭm′bĕr-lĭ)	78	49.41N	115.59W
Kimberley, S. Afr.	206	28.40S	24.50E
Kimi, Cam.	208	6.05N	11.30E
Kími, Grc.	154	38.38N	24.05E
Kímolos, i., Grc. (kē′mô-lôs)	154	36.52N	24.20E
Kimry, Russia (kĭm′rē)	160	56.53N	37.24E
Kimvula, Zaire	210	5.44S	15.58E
Kinabalu, Gunong, mtn., Malay.	188	5.45N	115.26E
Kincardine, Can. (kĭn-kär′dĭn)	78	44.10N	81.15W
Kinda, Zaire	210	9.18S	25.04E
Kindanba, Congo	210	3.44S	14.31E
Kinder, La., U.S. (kĭn′dēr)	106	30.30N	92.50W
Kindersley, Can. (kĭn′dērz-lē)	78	51.27N	109.10W
Kindia, Gui. (kĭn′dē-ȧ)	204	10.04N	12.51W
Kindu, Zaire	206	2.57S	25.56E
Kinel'-Cherkassy, Russia	160	53.32N	51.32E
Kineshma, Russia (kē-nĕsh′mȧ)	160	57.27N	41.02E
King, i., Austl. (kĭng)	196	39.35S	143.40E
Kingaroy, Austl. (kĭŋ′gă-roi)	198	26.37S	151.50E
King City, Can.	77d	43.56N	79.32W
King City, Ca., U.S. (kĭng sĭ′tĭ)	102	36.12N	121.08W
Kingcome Inlet, b., Can. (kĭng′kŭm)	80	50.50N	126.10W
Kingfisher, Ok., U.S. (kĭng′fĭsh-ĕr)	104	35.51N	97.55W
King George Sound, strt., Austl. (jôrj)	196	35.17S	118.30E
King George's Reservoir, res., Eng., U.K.	231	51.39N	0.01W
Kingisepp, Russia (kĭŋ-gē-sep′)	160	59.22N	28.38E
King Leopold Ranges, mts., Austl. (lē′ô-pōld)	196	16.25S	125.00E
Kingman, Az., U.S. (kĭng′mǎn)	102	35.10N	114.05W
Kingman, Ks., U.S. (kĭng′mǎn)	104	37.38N	98.07W
King of Prussia, Pa., U.S.	225b	40.05N	75.23W
Kings, r., Ca., U.S.	102	36.28N	119.43W
Kingsbury, neigh., Eng., U.K.	231	51.35N	0.17W
Kings Canyon National Park, rec., Ca., U.S. (kăn′yŭn)	90	36.52N	118.53W
Kingsclere, Eng., U.K. (kĭngs-clēr)	138b	51.18N	1.15W
Kingscote, Austl. (kĭngz′kŭt)	198	35.45S	137.32E
Kingsdown, Eng., U.K.	231	51.21N	0.17E
Kingsford, Austl.	239a	33.56S	151.14E
Kingsgrove, Austl.	239a	33.57S	151.06E
Kings Langley, Eng., U.K.	231	51.43N	0.28W
King's Lynn, Eng., U.K. (kĭngz lĭn′)	144	52.45N	0.20E
Kings Mountain, N.C., U.S.	108	35.13N	81.30W
Kings Norton, Eng., U.K. (nôr′tŭn)	138a	52.25N	1.54W
King Sound, strt., Austl.	196	16.50S	123.35E
Kings Park, N.Y., U.S. (kĭngz pärk)	94a	40.53N	73.16W
Kings Park, Va., U.S.	225d	38.48N	77.15W
Kings Peak, mtn., Ut., U.S.	90	40.46N	110.20W
Kings Point, N.Y., U.S.	224	40.49N	73.45W
Kingsport, Tn., U.S. (kĭngz′pôrt)	108	36.33N	82.36W
Kingston, Austl. (kĭngz′tŭn)	196	37.52S	139.52E
Kingston, Can.	78	44.15N	76.30W
Kingston, Jam.	110	18.00N	76.45W
Kingston, N.Y., U.S.	90	42.00N	74.00W
Kingston, Pa., U.S.	92	41.15N	75.50W
Kingston, Wa., U.S.	100a	47.04N	122.29W
Kingston upon Hull, Eng., U.K.	136	53.45N	0.25W
Kingston upon Thames, neigh., Eng., U.K.	231	51.25N	0.19W
Kingstown, St. Vin. (kĭngz′toun)	110	13.10N	61.14W
Kingstree, S.C., U.S. (kĭngz′trē)	108	33.30N	79.50W
Kingsville, Tx., U.S. (kĭngz′vĭl)	106	27.32N	97.52W
King William Island, i., Can. (kĭng wĭl′yǎm)	78	69.25N	97.00W
King William's Town, S. Afr. (kĭng-wĭl′-yŭmz-toun)	207c	32.53S	27.24E
Kinira, r., Transkei	207c	30.37S	28.52E
Kinloch, Mo., U.S. (kĭn-lŏk)	101e	38.44N	90.19W
Kinnaird, Can. (kĭn-ärd′)	80	49.17N	117.39W
Kinnairds Head, c., Scot., U.K. (kĭn-ârds′hĕd)	140	57.42N	3.55W
Kinomoto, Japan (kē′nō-mōtō)	187	33.53N	136.07E
Kinosaki, Japan (kē′nō-sä′kē)	187	35.38N	134.47E
Kinshasa, Zaire	206	4.18S	15.18E
Kinshasa-Est, neigh., Zaire	240c	4.18S	15.18E
Kinshasa-Ouest, neigh., Zaire	240c	4.20S	15.15E
Kinsley, Ks., U.S. (kĭnz′lĭ)	104	37.55N	99.24W
Kinston, N.C., U.S. (kĭnz′tŭn)	108	35.15N	77.35W
Kintampo, Rapides de, wtfl., Afr.	206	4.19S	15.15E
Kintampo, Ghana (kēn-täm′pō)	204	8.03N	1.43W
Kintsana, Congo	240c	4.19S	15.10E

PLACE (Pronunciation)	PAGE	Lat. °′	Long. °′
Kintyre, pen., Scot., U.K.	144	55.50N	5.40W
Kiowa, Ks., U.S. (kī'ō-wa)	104	37.01N	98.30W
Kiowa, Ok., U.S.	104	34.42N	95.53W
Kiparissía, Grc.	142	37.17N	21.43E
Kiparissiakós Kólpos, b., Grc.	154	37.28N	21.15E
Kipawa, Lac, l., Can.	84	46.55N	79.00W
Kipembawe, Tan. (kē-pĕm-bä'wā)	206	7.39S	33.24E
Kipengere Range, mts., Tan.	210	9.10S	34.00E
Kipili, Tan.	210	7.26S	30.36E
Kipushi, Zaire	210	11.46S	27.14E
Kirakira, Sol.Is.	192e	10.27S	161.55E
Kirby, Tx., U.S. (kûr'bĭ)	101d	29.29N	98.23W
Kirbyville, Tx., U.S. (kûr'bĭ-vĭl)	106	30.39N	93.54W
Kirchderne, neigh., Ger.	232	51.33N	7.30E
Kirchende, Ger.	232	51.25N	7.26E
Kirchhellen, Ger.	232	51.36N	6.55E
Kirchheller Heide, for., Ger.	232	51.36N	6.53E
Kirchhörde, neigh., Ger.	232	51.27N	7.27E
Kirchlinde, neigh., Ger.	232	51.32N	7.22E
Kirdāsah, Egypt	240a	30.02N	31.07E
Kirenga, r., Russia (kē-rĕŋ'gȧ)	162	56.30N	108.18E
Kirensk, Russia (kē-rĕnsk')	158	57.47N	108.22E
Kirghizia, nation, Asia	158	41.45N	74.38E
Kirghiz Steppe, plat., Kyrg.	158	49.28N	57.07E
Kirgizskiy Khrebet, mts., Asia	174	37.58N	72.23E
Kiri, Zaire	210	1.27S	19.00E
Kiribati, nation, Oc.	2	1.30S	173.00E
Kirin, *see* Chilung, Tai.	180	25.02N	121.48E
Kiritimati, i., Kir.	2	2.20N	157.40W
Kirkby, Eng., U.K.	138a	53.29N	2.54W
Kirkby-in-Ashfield, Eng., U.K. (kûrk'bē-ĭn-ăsh'fēld)	138a	53.06N	1.16W
Kirkcaldy, Scot., U.K. (kĕr-kô'dĭ)	144	56.06N	3.15W
Kirkdale, neigh., Eng., U.K.	233a	53.26N	2.59W
Kirkenes, Nor.	140	69.40N	30.03E
Kirkham, Eng., U.K. (kûrk'ăm)	138a	53.47N	2.53W
Kirkland, Can.	223b	45.27N	73.52W
Kirkland, Wa., U.S. (kûrk'lănd)	100a	47.41N	122.12W
Kirklareli, Tur. (kèrk'lár-ĕ'lè)	142	41.44N	27.15E
Kirksville, Mo., U.S. (kûrks'vĭl)	90	40.12N	92.35W
Kirkūk, Iraq (kĭr-ko͝ok')	174	35.28N	44.22E
Kirkwall, Scot., U.K. (kûrk'wôl)	140	58.58N	2.59W
Kirkwood, S. Afr.	207c	33.26S	25.24E
Kirkwood, Md., U.S.	225d	38.57N	76.58W
Kirkwood, Mo., U.S. (kûrk'wo͝od)	101e	38.35N	90.24W
Kirn, Ger. (kērn)	148	49.47N	7.23E
Kirov, Russia	156	54.04N	34.19E
Kirov, Russia	158	58.35N	49.35E
Kirovabad, Azer.	158	40.40N	46.20E
Kirovgrad, Russia (kē'rŭ-vŭ-grad)	164a	57.26N	60.03E
Kirovograd, Ukr. (kē-rŭ-vŭ-grät')	160	48.33N	32.17E
Kirovograd, prov., Ukr.	156	48.23N	31.10E
Kirovsk, Russia	158	67.40N	33.58E
Kirovsk, Russia (kē-rôfsk')	164c	59.52N	30.59E
Kirsanov, Russia (kēr-sä'nôf)	160	52.40N	42.40E
Kirşehir, Tur. (kēr-shĕ'hēr)	174	39.10N	34.00E
Kirtachi Seybou, Niger	208	12.48N	2.29E
Kīrthar Range, mts., Pak. (kĭr-tŭr)	174	27.00N	67.10E
Kirton, Eng., U.K. (kûr'tŭn)	138a	53.29N	0.35W
Kiruna, Swe. (kē-ro͞o'nä)	140	67.49N	20.08E
Kirundu, Zaire	210	0.44S	25.32E
Kirwan Heights, Pa., U.S.	226b	40.22N	80.06W
Kirwin Reservoir, res., Ks., U.S. (kûr'wĭn)	104	39.34N	99.04W
Kiryū, Japan	186	36.24N	139.20E
Kirzhach, Russia (kēr-zhák')	156	56.08N	38.53E
Kisaki, Tan. (kē-sä'kē)	206	7.37S	37.43E
Kisangani, Zaire	204	0.30N	25.12E
Kisarazu, Japan (kē'sä-rä'zo͞o)	187a	35.23N	139.55E
Kiselëvsk, Russia (kē-sĭ-lyôfsk')	158	54.00N	86.39E
Kishinëv, Mol. (ke-shė-nyôf')	158	47.02N	28.52E
Kishiwada, Japan (kē'shė-wä'dä)	186	34.25N	135.18E
Kishkino, Russia (kĕsh'kĭ-nô)	164b	55.15N	38.04E
Kisiwani, Tan.	210	4.08S	37.57E
Kiska, i., Ak., U.S. (kĭs'kä)	90b	52.08N	177.10E
Kiskatinaw, r., Can.	80	55.10N	120.20W
Kiskittogisu Lake, l., Can.	82	54.05N	99.00W
Kiskitto Lake, l., Can. (kĭs-kĭ'tō)	82	54.16N	98.34W
Kiskunfélegyháza, Hung. (kĭsh'ko͝on-fā'lĕd-y'hä'zô)	148	46.42N	19.52E
Kiskunhalas, Hung. (kĭsh'ko͝on-hô'lŏsh)	148	46.24N	19.26E
Kiskunmajsa, Hung. (kĭsh'ko͝on-mī'shô)	148	46.29N	19.42E
Kismaayo, Som.	206	0.18S	42.30E
Kiso, Japan	238a	35.34N	139.26E
Kiso-Gawa, r., Japan (kē'sō-gä'wä)	187	35.29N	137.12E
Kiso-Sammyaku, mts., Japan (kē'sō säm'myä-ko͞o)	187	35.47N	137.39E
Kissamos, Grc.	154a	35.13N	23.35E
Kissidougou, Gui. (kē'sē-do͞o'go͞o)	204	9.11N	10.06W
Kissimmee, Fl., U.S. (kĭ-sĭm'ė)	109a	28.17N	81.25W
Kissimmee, r., Fl., U.S.	109a	27.45N	81.07W
Kissimmee, Lake, l., Fl., U.S.	109a	27.58N	81.17W
Kistarcsa, Hung.	235g	47.33N	19.16E
Kisujszallás, Hung.	148	47.12N	20.47E
Kisumu, Kenya (kē'so͞o-mo͞o)	206	0.06S	34.45E
Kita, Mali (kē'tà)	204	13.03N	9.29W
Kita, neigh., Japan	238a	35.45N	139.44E
Kitakami Gawa, r., Japan	186	39.20N	141.10E
Kitakyūshū, Japan	180	33.53N	130.50E
Kitale, Kenya	210	1.01N	35.00E
Kitamachi, neigh., Japan	238a	35.46N	139.39E
Kitamba, neigh., Zaire	240c	4.19S	15.14E
Kitatawara, Japan	238b	34.44N	135.42E
Kit Carson, Co., U.S.	104	38.46N	102.48W
Kitchener, Can. (kĭch'ĕ-nĕr)	78	43.25N	80.35W

PLACE (Pronunciation)	PAGE	Lat. °′	Long. °′
Kitenda, Zaire	210	6.53S	17.21E
Kitgum, Ug. (kĭt'gòm)	204	3.29N	33.04E
Kíthira, i., Grc.	142	36.15N	22.56E
Kíthnos, i., Grc.	154	37.24N	24.10E
Kitimat, Can. (kĭ'tĭ-măt)	78	54.03N	128.33W
Kitimat, r., Can.	80	53.50N	129.00W
Kitimat Ranges, mts., Can.	80	53.30N	128.50W
Kitlope, r., Can. (kĭt'lōp)	80	53.00N	128.00W
Kitsuki, Japan (kēt'sō-kė)	187	33.24N	131.35E
Kittanning, Pa., U.S. (kĭ-tăn'ĭng)	92	40.50N	79.30W
Kittatinny Mountains, mts., N.J., U.S. (kĭ-tă-tĭ'nė)	94a	41.16N	74.44W
Kittery, Me., U.S. (kĭt'ĕr-ĭ)	86	43.07N	70.45W
Kittsee, Aus.	139e	48.05N	17.05E
Kitty Hawk, N.C., U.S. (kĭt'ė hôk)	108	36.04N	75.42W
Kitunda, Tan.	210	6.48S	33.13E
Kitwe, Zam.	210	12.49S	28.13E
Kitzingen, Ger. (kĭt'zĭng-ĕn)	148	49.44N	10.08E
Kiunga, Kenya	210	1.45S	41.29E
Kivu, Lac, l., Afr.	206	1.45S	28.55E
Kiyev, *see* Kiev, Ukr.	158	50.27N	30.30E
Kiyose, Japan	187a	35.47N	139.32E
Kizel, Russia (kē'zĕl)	160	59.05N	57.42E
Kızıl, r., Tur.	174	40.00N	34.00E
Kizil'skoye, Russia (kĭz'ĭl-skô-yĕ)	164a	52.43N	58.53E
Kizlyar, Russia (kĭz-lyär')	160	44.00N	46.50E
Kizu, Japan (kē'zo͞o)	187	34.43N	135.49E
Kizuki, Japan	238a	35.34N	139.40E
Kizuri, Japan	238b	34.39N	135.34E
Kizyl-Arvat, Turk. (kē'zĭl-ŭr-vät')	158	38.55N	56.33E
Klaas Smits, r., S. Afr.	207c	31.45S	26.33E
Klaaswaal, Neth.	139a	51.46N	4.25E
Kladno, Czech. (kläd'nō)	148	50.10N	14.05E
Klagenfurt, Aus. (klä'gĕn-fòrt)	140	46.38N	14.19E
Klaipėda, Lith. (klī'pȧ-dȧ)	160	55.43N	21.10E
Klamath, r., U.S.	98	41.40N	123.25W
Klamath Falls, Or., U.S.	90	42.13N	121.49W
Klamath Mountains, mts., Ca., U.S.	98	42.00N	123.25W
Klarälven, r., Swe.	140	60.40N	13.00E
Klaskanine, r., Or., U.S. (klăs'kȧ-nīn)	100c	46.02N	123.43W
Klatovy, Czech. (klä'tò-vė)	140	49.23N	13.18E
Klawock, Ak., U.S. (klä'wăk)	89	55.32N	133.10W
Kleef, Ger.	232	51.11N	6.56E
Kleinebroich, Ger.	232	51.12N	6.35E
Kleinmachnow, Ger. (klīn-măk'nō)	139b	52.22N	13.12E
Klein Ziethen, Ger.	234a	52.23N	13.27E
Klerksdorp, S. Afr. (klĕrks'dôrp)	212d	26.52S	26.40E
Klerksraal, S. Afr. (klĕrks'räl)	212d	26.15S	27.10E
Kletnya, Russia (klyĕt'nyȧ)	156	53.19N	33.14E
Kletsk, Bela. (klĕtsk)	156	53.04N	26.43E
Kleve, Ger. (klĕ'fĕ)	148	51.47N	6.09E
Kley, neigh., Ger.	232	51.30N	7.22E
Klickitat, r., Wa., U.S.	98	46.01N	121.07W
Klimovichi, Bela. (klē-mô-vē'chė)	156	53.37N	31.21E
Klimovsk, Russia (klĭ'môfsk)	164b	55.21N	37.32E
Klin, Russia (klēn)	156	56.18N	36.43E
Klintehamn, Swe. (klĕn'tē-häm)	146	57.24N	18.14E
Klintsy, Russia (klĭn'tsĭ)	160	52.46N	32.14E
Klip, r., S. Afr. (klĭp)	212d	27.18S	29.25E
Klipgat, S. Afr.	212d	25.26S	27.57E
Klippan, Swe. (klyp'pȧn)	146	56.08N	13.09E
Klippoortje, S. Afr.	240b	26.17S	28.14E
Kliptown, S. Afr.	240b	26.17S	27.53E
Kłodzko, Pol. (klôd'skô)	148	50.26N	16.38E
Klondike Region, hist. reg., N.A. (klŏn'dīk)	78	64.12N	142.38W
Klosterfelde, Ger. (klōs'tĕr-fĕl-dĕ)	139b	52.47N	13.29E
Klosterneuburg, Aus. (klōs-tĕr-noi'bo͝orgh)	139e	48.19N	16.20E
Kluane, l., Can.	78	61.15N	138.40W
Kluane National Park, rec., Can.	78	60.25N	137.53W
Kluczbork, Pol. (klo͞och'bòrk)	148	50.59N	18.15E
Klyaz'ma, r., Russia (klyäz'mȧ)	156	55.49N	39.19E
Klyuchevskaya, vol., Russia (klyo͞o-chĕfskä'yä)	158	56.13N	160.00E
Klyuchi, Russia (klyo͞o'chĭ)	164a	57.03N	57.20E
Knezha, Bul. (knyä'zhȧ)	142	43.27N	24.03E
Knife, r., N.D., U.S. (nīf)	96	47.06N	102.33W
Knight Inlet, b., Can. (nīt)	80	50.41N	125.40W
Knightstown, In., U.S. (nīts'toun)	92	39.45N	85.30W
Knin, Cro. (knēn)	154	44.02N	16.14E
Knittelfeld, Aus.	140	47.13N	14.50E
Knob Peak, mtn., Phil. (nŏb)	189a	12.30N	121.20E
Knockholt, Eng., U.K.	231	51.18N	0.06E
Knockholt Pound, Eng., U.K.	231	51.19N	0.08E
Knoppiesfontein, S. Afr.	240b	26.05S	28.25E
Knottingley, Eng., U.K. (nŏt'ĭng-lĭ)	138a	53.42N	1.14W
Knott's Berry Farm, pt. of i., Ca., U.S.	228	33.50N	118.00W
Knotty Ash, neigh., Eng., U.K.	233a	53.25N	2.54W
Knowsley, Eng., U.K.	233a	53.27N	2.51W
Knox, Austl.	239b	37.53S	145.18E
Knox, In., U.S. (nŏks)	92	41.15N	86.40W
Knox, Cape, c., Can.	80	54.12N	133.20W
Knoxville, Ia., U.S. (nŏks'vĭl)	96	41.19N	93.05W
Knoxville, Tn., U.S.	90	35.58N	83.55W
Knutsford, Eng., U.K. (nŭts'fērd)	138a	53.18N	2.22W
Knyszyn, Pol. (knĭ'shĭn)	148	53.16N	22.59E
Kobayashi, Japan (kō'bȧ-yä'shė)	187	31.58N	130.59E
Kōbe, Japan (kō'bĕ)	180	34.30N	135.10E
Kobelyaki, Ukr. (kō-bĕl-yä'kė)	160	49.11N	34.12E
København, *see* Copenhagen, Den.	136	55.43N	12.27E
Koblenz, Ger. (kō'blĕntz)	140	50.18N	7.36E
Kobozha, r., Russia (kô-bō'zhȧ)	156	58.55N	35.18E
Kobrin, Bela. (kō'brēn')	160	52.13N	24.23E
Kobrinskoye, Russia (kô-brĭn'skô-yĕ)	164c	59.25N	30.07E

PLACE (Pronunciation)	PAGE	Lat. °′	Long. °′
Kobuk, r., Ak., U.S. (kō'bŭk)	89	66.58N	158.48W
Kobuk Valley National Park, rec., Ak., U.S.	89	67.20N	159.00W
Kobuleti, Geor. (kō-bò-lyā'tė)	160	41.50N	41.40E
Kočani, Mac. (kô'chä-nĕ)	154	41.54N	22.25E
Kočevje, Slo. (kô'chăv-ye)	154	45.38N	14.51E
Kocher, r., Ger. (kôк'ĕr)	148	49.00N	9.52E
Kōchi, Japan (kō'chė)	180	33.35N	133.32E
Kodaira, Japan	187a	35.43N	139.29E
Kodiak, Ak., U.S. (kō'dyăk)	90a	57.50N	152.30W
Kodiak Island, i., Ak., U.S.	89	57.24N	153.32W
Kodok, Sudan (ko'dŏk)	204	9.57N	32.08E
Koforidua, Ghana (kō fō-rĭ-do͞o'ȧ)	204	6.03N	0.17W
Kōfu, Japan (kō'fo͞o')	186	35.41N	138.34E
Koga, Japan (kō'gȧ)	187	36.13N	139.40E
Kogan, r., Gui.	208	11.30N	14.05W
Kogane, Japan (kō'gä-nȧ)	187a	35.50N	139.56E
Koganei, Japan (kō'gä-nā)	187a	35.42N	139.31E
Kogarah, Austl.	239a	33.58S	151.08E
Køge, Den. (kû'gĕ)	146	55.27N	12.09E
Køge Bugt, b., Den.	146	55.30N	12.25E
Kogil'nik, r., Eur. (kō-gēl-nēk')	156	46.08N	29.10E
Kogoni, Mali	208	14.44N	6.02W
Kohīma, India (kō-ē'mȧ)	174	25.45N	94.41E
Koito, r., Japan (kô'ē-tō)	187a	35.19N	139.58E
Kōje, i., S. Kor. (kû'jĕ)	186	34.53N	129.00E
Kokand, Uzb. (kō-känt')	158	40.27N	71.07E
Kokchetav, Kaz. (kôk'chĕ-täf)	162	53.15N	69.13E
Kokemäenjoki, r., Fin.	146	61.23N	22.03E
Kokhma, Russia (kôк'mȧ)	156	56.57N	41.08E
Kokkola, Fin. (kô'kô-lȧ)	140	63.47N	22.58E
Kokomo, In., U.S. (kō'kō-mō)	92	40.30N	86.20W
Koko Nor (Qinghai Hu), l., China (kō'kō nor) (chyĭŋ-hī ho͞o)	180	37.26N	98.30E
Kokopo, Pap. N. Gui. (kō-kō'pō)	188	4.25S	152.27E
Koksoak, r., Can. (kōk'sō-ăk)	78	57.42N	69.50W
Kokstad, S. Afr. (kōk'shtät)	207c	30.33S	29.27E
Kokubu, Japan (kō'ko͞o-bo͞o)	187	31.42N	130.46E
Kokubunji, Japan	238a	35.42N	139.29E
Kokuou, Japan (kō'ko͞o-ō'o͞o)	187b	34.34N	135.39E
Kola Peninsula, *see* Kol'skiy Poluostrov, pen., Russia	158	67.15N	37.40E
Kolār (Kolār Gold Fields), India (kōl-är')	174	13.39N	78.33E
Kolárovo, Czech. (kōl-ārōvō)	148	47.54N	17.59E
Kolbio, Kenya	210	1.10S	41.15E
Kol'chugino, Russia (kôl-chó'gē-nō)	156	56.19N	39.29E
Kolda, Sen.	208	12.53N	14.57W
Kolding, Den. (kŭl'dĭng)	146	55.29N	9.24E
Kole, Zaire (kō'lȧ)	206	3.19S	22.46E
Kolguyev, i., Russia (kôl-gò'yĕf)	158	69.00N	49.00E
Kolhāpur, India	178	16.48N	74.15E
Kolín, Czech. (kō'lēn)	148	50.01N	15.11E
Kolkasrags, c., Lat. (kôl-käs'rágz)	146	57.46N	22.39E
Köln, *see* Cologne, Ger.	151c	50.56N	6.57E
Kolno, Pol. (kôw'nō)	148	53.23N	21.56E
Koło, Pol. (kô'wô)	148	52.11N	18.37E
Kołobrzeg, Pol. (kō-lô'b'zhĕk)	140	54.10N	15.35E
Kolomenskoje, neigh., Russia	235b	55.40N	37.41E
Kolomna, Russia (kål-ôm'nȧ)	160	55.06N	38.47E
Kolomyya, Ukr. (kō'lô-mē'yȧ)	148	48.32N	25.04E
Kolonie Stolp, Ger.	234a	52.28N	13.46E
Kolp', r., Russia (kôlp)	156	59.18N	35.32E
Kolpashevo, Russia (kŭl pȧ shô'vȧ)	158	58.16N	82.43E
Kolpino, Russia (kôl'pē-nō)	160	59.45N	30.37E
Kolpny, Russia (kôlp'nyė)	156	52.14N	36.54E
Kol'skiy Poluostrov, pen., Russia	158	67.15N	37.40E
Kolva, r., Russia	160	61.00N	57.00E
Kolwezi, Zaire (kōl-wĕ'zē)	206	10.43S	25.28E
Kolyberovo, Russia (kō-lĭ-byā'rô-vô)	164b	55.16N	38.45E
Kolyma, r., Russia	158	66.30N	151.45E
Kolymskiy Mountains, *see* Gydan, Khrebet, mts., Russia	158	61.45N	155.00E
Kom, r., Afr.	210	2.15N	12.05E
Komadugu Gana, r., Nig.	208	12.15N	11.10E
Komae, Japan	187a	35.37N	139.35E
Komagome, neigh., Japan	238a	35.44N	139.45E
Komandorskiye Ostrova, is., Russia	172	55.40N	167.13E
Komárno, Czech. (kô'mär-nô)	148	47.46N	18.08E
Komarno, Ukr.	148	49.38N	23.42E
Komárom, Hung. (kô'mä-rôm)	148	47.45N	18.06E
Komatipoort, S. Afr. (kō-mä'tē-pōrt)	206	25.21S	32.00E
Komatsu, Japan (kō-mät'so͞o)	186	36.23N	136.26E
Komatsushima, Japan (kō-mät'so͞o-shė'mä)	187	34.04N	134.32E
Komeshia, Zaire	210	8.01S	27.07E
Komga, S. Afr. (kōm'gȧ)	207c	32.36S	27.54E
Komi Autonomous Soviet Socialist Republic, Russia (kômė)	158	63.00N	55.00E
Kommetjie, S. Afr.	206a	34.09S	18.19E
Kommunizma, Pik, mtn., Taj.	158	38.57N	72.01E
Komoé, r., I.C.	208	5.40N	3.40W
Komrat, Mol. (kòm-rät')	160	46.17N	28.38E
Komsomolets, Kaz. (kôm-sô-mô'lĕts)	164a	53.45N	62.04E
Komsomolets Zaliv, b., Kaz.	160	45.40N	52.00E
Komsomol'sk-na-Amure, Russia	158	50.46N	137.14E
Komsomol'skoye, Ukr. (kôm-sô-môl'skô-yĕ)	156	49.42N	28.44E
Kona, Mali	208	14.57N	3.53W
Konda, r., Russia (kôn'dȧ)	160	60.50N	64.00E
Kondas, r., Russia (kôn'dȧs)	164a	59.30N	56.28E
Kondli, neigh., India	236d	28.37N	77.19E
Kondoa, Tan. (kôn-dō'ȧ)	206	4.52S	36.00E
Kondolole, Zaire	210	1.20N	25.58E
Koné, N. Cal.	192f	21.04S	164.52E
Kong, I.C. (kông)	204	9.05N	4.41W

ng-sing; ŋ-baŋk; ɴ-nasalized n; nŏd; cŏmmit; ōld; ôbey; ôrder; oi-boil; fo͞od; ò-as oo in foot; ou-out; s-soft; sh-dish; th-thin; pūre; ůnite; ûrn; stŭd; circŭs; ü-as in French tu; '-indeterminate vowel.

PLACE (Pronunciation)	PAGE	Lat. °′	Long. °′
Kongbo, Cen. Afr. Rep.	210	4.44N	21.23E
Kongolo, Zaire (kôŋ'gō'lō)	206	5.23S	27.00E
Kongsberg, Nor. (küngs'bĕrg)	146	59.40N	9.36E
Kongsvinger, Nor. (küngs'viŋ-gĕr)	146	60.12N	12.00E
Koni, Zaire (kō'nē)	206	10.32S	27.27E
Königsberg, *see* Kaliningrad, Russia	158	54.42N	20.32E
Königsbrunn, Ger. (kû'nĕgs-brōōn)	139d	48.16N	10.53E
Königshardt, neigh., Ger.	232	51.33N	6.51E
Königs Wusterhausen, Ger. (kû'nĕgs vōōs'tĕr-hou-zĕn)	139b	52.18N	13.38E
Konin, Pol. (kô'nyĕn)	140	52.11N	18.17E
Kónitsa, Grc. (kô'nyē'tsà)	154	40.03N	20.46E
Konjic, Bos. (kôn'yēts)	154	43.38N	17.59E
Konju, S. Kor.	186	36.21N	127.05E
Konnagar, India	178a	22.41N	88.22E
Konohana, neigh., Japan	238b	34.41N	135.26E
Kōnoike, Japan	238b	34.42N	135.37E
Konotop, Ukr. (kô-nô-tôp')	160	51.13N	33.14E
Konpienga, r., Burkina	208	11.15N	0.35E
Konqi, r., China (kôn-chyē)	180	41.09N	87.46E
Końskie, Pol. (koin''skyĕ)	148	51.12N	20.26E
Konstantinovka, Ukr. (kôn-stán-tē'nôf-kà)	156	48.33N	37.42E
Konstanz, Ger. (kôn'shtänts)	148	47.39N	9.10E
Kontagora, Nig. (kōn-tá-gō'rä)	204	10.24N	5.28E
Konya, Tur. (kōn'yá)	174	36.55N	32.25E
Koocanusa, Lake, res., N.A.	98	49.00N	115.10W
Kootenay (Kootenai), r., N.A.	80	49.45N	117.05W
Kootenay Lake, l., Can.	80	49.35N	116.50W
Kootenay National Park, Can. (kōō'tē-nā)	78	51.06N	117.02W
Kooyong, Austl.	239b	37.50S	145.02E
Kōō-zan, mtn., Japan (kōō'zän)	187b	34.53N	135.32E
Kopervik, Nor. (kô'pĕr-vēk)	146	59.18N	5.20E
Kopeysk, Russia (kô-pāsk')	162	55.07N	61.37E
Köping, Swe. (chû'pĭng)	146	59.32N	15.58E
Kopparberg, Swe. (kŏp'pár-bĕrgh)	146	59.53N	15.00E
Koppeh Dāgh, mts., Asia	174	37.28N	58.29E
Koppies, S. Afr.	212d	27.15S	27.35E
Koprivnica, Cro. (kô'prēv-nē'tsá)	154	46.10N	16.48E
Kopychintsy, Ukr. (kô-pē-chēn'tsē)	148	49.06N	25.55E
Korčula, i., Yugo. (kôr'chōō-lá)	154	42.50N	17.05E
Korea, North, nation, Asia	180	40.00N	127.00E
Korea, South, nation, Asia	180	36.30N	128.00E
Korea Bay, b., Asia	184	39.18N	123.50E
Korean Archipelago, is., S. Kor.	180	34.05N	125.35E
Korea Strait, strt., Asia	180	33.30N	128.30E
Korets, Ukr. (kô-rēts')	148	50.35N	27.13E
Korhogo, I.C. (kôr-hō'gō)	204	9.27N	5.38W
Kōri, Japan	238b	34.47N	135.39E
Koridhallós, Grc.	235d	37.59N	23.39E
Korinthiakós Kólpos, b., Grc.	142	38.15N	22.33E
Kórinthos, Grc. (kô-rēn'thôs) (kŏr'ĭnth)	136	37.56N	22.54E
Kōriyama, Japan (kō'rē-yä'mä)	186	37.18N	140.25E
Korkino, Russia (kôr'kē-nŭ)	164a	54.53N	61.25E
Korla, China (kōr-lä)	180	41.37N	86.03E
Körmend, Hung. (kûr'mĕnt)	148	47.02N	16.36E
Kornat, i., Yugo. (kôr-nät')	154	43.46N	15.10E
Korneuburg, Aus. (kôr'noi-bôrgh)	139e	48.22N	16.21E
Koro, Mali	208	14.04N	3.05W
Korocha, Russia (kô-rō'chá)	156	50.50N	37.13E
Korop, Ukr. (kō'rôp)	156	51.33N	32.54E
Koro Sea, sea, Fiji	192g	18.00S	179.50E
Korosten', Ukr. (kô'rôs-tĕn)	160	50.51N	28.39E
Korostyshev, Ukr. (kô-rôs'tē-shôf)	156	50.19N	29.05E
Koro Toro, Chad	208	16.05N	18.30E
Korotoyak, Russia (kô'rô-tô-yák')	156	51.00N	39.06E
Korsakov, Russia (kôr'sá-kôf')	158	46.42N	143.16E
Korsnäs, Fin. (kôrs'nĕs)	146	62.51N	21.17E
Korsør, Den. (kôrs'ûr')	146	55.19N	11.08E
Kortrijk, Bel.	144	50.49N	3.10E
Koryakskiy Khrebet, mts., Russia	158	62.00N	168.45E
Koryukovka, Ukr. (kôr-yōō-kôf'kà)	156	51.44N	32.24E
Kościan, Pol. (kŭsh'tsyàn)	148	52.05N	16.38E
Kościerzyna, Pol. (kŭsh-tsyĕ-zhĕ'ná)	148	54.08N	17.59E
Kosciusko, Ms., U.S. (kŏs-ĭ-ŭs'kō)	108	33.04N	89.35W
Kosciusko, Mount, mtn., Austl.	196	36.26S	148.20E
Kosha, Sudan	204	20.49N	30.27E
Koshigaya, Japan (kō'shē-gä'yä)	187a	35.53N	139.48E
Kosi, r., India (kô'sē)	178	26.00N	86.20E
Košice, Czech. (kō'shē-tsĕ')	140	48.43N	21.17E
Kosino, Russia	235b	55.43N	37.52E
Kosmos, S. Afr. (kŏz'mŏs)	207b	25.45S	27.51E
Kosmosa, Monument, hist., Russia	235b	55.49N	37.38E
Kosobrodskiy, Russia (kä-sō'brôd-skĭ)	164a	54.14N	60.53E
Kosovska Mitrovica, Yugo. (kô'sôv-skä' mē'trô-vē-tsä ')	154	42.51N	20.50E
Kostajnica, Cro. (kôs'tä-ē-nē'tsá)	154	45.14N	16.32E
Koster, S. Afr.	212d	25.52S	26.52E
Kostino, Russia (kôs'tĭ-nô)	164b	55.54N	37.51E
Kostroma, Russia (kôs-trô-má')	158	57.46N	40.55E
Kostroma, prov., Russia	156	57.50N	41.10E
Kostrzyn, Pol. (kôst'chĕn)	140	52.35N	14.38E
Kos'va, r., Russia (kôs'vá)	164a	58.44N	57.08E
Koszalin, Pol. (kô-shä'lĭn)	140	54.12N	16.10E
Kőszeg, Hung. (kû'sĕg)	148	47.21N	16.32E
Kota, India	174	25.17N	75.49E
Kota Baharu, Malay. (kō'tä bä'rōō)	188	6.15N	102.23E
Kotabaru, Indon.	188	3.22S	116.15E
Kota Kinabalu, Malay.	188	5.55N	116.05E
Kota Tinggi, Malay.	173b	1.43N	103.54E
Kotel, Bul. (kō-tĕl')	154	42.54N	26.28E
Kotel'nich, Russia (kô-tyĕl'nēch)	160	58.15N	48.20E
Kotel'nyy, i., Russia (kô-tyĕl'nē)	158	74.51N	134.09E
Kotka, Fin. (kŏt'kà)	140	60.28N	26.56E
Kotlas, Russia (kôt'lás)	160	61.10N	46.50E
Kotlin, Ostrov, i., Russia (ôs-trôf' kôt'lĭn)	164c	60.02N	29.49E
Kōtō, neigh., Japan	238a	35.41N	139.48E
Kotor, Yugo.	154	42.25N	18.46E
Kotorosl', r., Russia (kô-tô'rôsl)	156	57.18N	39.08E
Kotovsk, Ukr. (kô-tôfsk')	156	47.49N	29.31E
Kotte, Sri L.	178	6.50N	80.05E
Kotto, r., Cen. Afr. Rep.	204	5.17N	22.04E
Kotuy, r., Russia (kô-tōō')	162	71.00N	103.15E
Kotzebue, Ak., U.S. (kŏt'sē-bōō)	90a	66.48N	162.42W
Kotzebue Sound, strt., Ak., U.S.	89	67.00N	164.28W
Kouchibouguac National Park, rec., Can.	86	46.53N	65.35W
Koudougou, Burkina (kōō-dōō'gōō)	204	12.15N	2.22W
Kouilou, r., Congo	206	4.30S	12.00E
Koula-Moutou, Gabon	210	1.08S	12.29E
Koulikoro, Mali (kōō-lē-kō'rō)	204	12.53N	7.33W
Koulouguidi, Mali	208	13.27N	17.33E
Koumac, N. Cal.	192f	20.33S	164.17E
Koumra, Chad	208	8.55N	17.33E
Koundara, Gui.	208	12.29N	13.18W
Kounradskiy, Kaz. (kŭ-ōōn-rät'skē)	158	47.25N	75.10E
Kouroussa, Gui. (kōō-rōō'sä)	204	10.39N	9.53W
Koutiala, Mali (kōō-tē-ä'lä)	204	12.29N	5.29W
Kouvola, Fin. (kō'ŏ-vô-lä)	146	60.51N	26.40E
Kouzhen, China (kō-jŭn)	182	36.19N	117.37E
Kovda, l., Russia (kôv'dá)	160	66.45N	32.00E
Kovel', Ukr. (kō'vĕl)	160	51.13N	24.45E
Kovno, *see* Kaunas, Lith.	158	54.42N	23.54E
Kovrov, Russia (kôv-rôf')	160	56.23N	41.21E
Kowloon (Jiulong), H.K.	180	22.18N	114.10E
Kowloon City, H.K.	237c	22.19N	114.11E
Koyuk, Ak., U.S. (kô-yŏŏk')	89	65.00N	161.18W
Koyukuk, r., Ak., U.S. (kô-yōō'kôk)	89	66.25N	153.50W
Kozáni, Grc.	142	40.16N	21.51E
Kozelets, Ukr. (kôzĕ-lyĕts)	156	50.53N	31.07E
Kozel'sk, Russia (kô-zĕlsk')	156	54.01N	35.49E
Kozienice, Pol. (kō-zyĕ-nē'tsĕ)	148	51.34N	21.35E
Koźle, Pol. (kôzh'lĕ)	148	50.19N	18.10E
Kozloduy, Bul. (kŭz'lô-dwĕ)	154	43.45N	23.42E
Kōzu, i., Japan (kō'zōō)	187	34.16N	139.03E
Kra, Isthmus of, isth., Asia	188	9.30S	99.45E
Kraai, r., S. Afr. (krä'ē)	207c	30.50S	27.03E
Krabbendijke, Neth.	139a	51.26N	4.05E
Krâchéh, Kam.	188	12.28N	106.06E
Kragujevac, Yugo. (krä'gōō'yĕ-vàts)	142	44.01N	20.55E
Krahenhöhe, neigh., Ger.	232	51.10N	7.06E
Kraków, Pol. (krä'kôf)	136	50.05N	20.00E
Kraljevo, Yugo. (kräl'ye-vô)	142	43.39N	20.48E
Kramatorsk, Ukr. (krá-mä'tôrsk)	156	48.43N	37.32E
Kramfors, Swe. (kräm'fôrs)	146	62.54N	17.49E
Krampnitz, Ger.	234a	52.28N	13.04E
Kranj, Slo. (krän')	142	46.16N	14.23E
Kranskop, S. Afr. (kränz'kŏp)	207c	28.57S	30.54E
Krāslava, Lat. (kräs'lä-vä)	146	55.53N	27.12E
Kraslice, Czech. (kräs'lē-tsĕ)	148	50.19N	12.30E
Krasnaya Gorka, Russia	164a	55.12N	56.40E
Krasnaya Sloboda, Russia	160	48.25N	44.35E
Kraśnik, Pol. (kräsh'nĭk)	148	50.53N	22.15E
Krasnoarmeysk, Russia (kràs'nô-ár-maśk')	164b	56.06N	38.09E
Krasnoarmeyskoye, Ukr.	156	48.19N	37.04E
Krasnodar, Russia (kräs'nô-dár)	158	45.03N	38.55E
Krasnodarskiy, prov., Russia (kràs-nô-där'skĭ ôb'lást)	156	45.25N	38.10E
Krasnogorsk, Russia	164b	55.49N	37.20E
Krasnogorskiy, Russia (kràs-nô-gôr'skĭ)	164a	54.36N	61.15E
Krasnograd, Ukr. (kräs'nô-grät)	156	49.23N	35.26E
Krasnogvardeyskiy, Russia (krá'sno-gvär-dzyĕ ĕs-kēē)	164a	57.17N	62.05E
Krasnokamsk, Russia (kräs-nô-kämsk')	160	58.00N	55.45E
Krasnokutsk, Ukr. (kràs-nô-kōōtsk')	156	50.03N	35.05E
Krasnosel'ye, Ukr. (kräs'nô-sĕl'yĕ)	156	48.44N	32.24E
Krasnoslobodsk, Russia (kräs'nô-slôbôtsk')	160	54.20N	43.50E
Krasnotur'insk, Russia (krŭs-nŭ-tōō-rensk')	158	59.47N	60.15E
Krasnoufimsk, Russia (krŭs-nŭ-ōō-fēmsk')	158	56.38N	57.46E
Krasnoural'sk, Russia (kräs'nô-ōō-rälsk')	160	58.21N	60.05E
Krasnousol'skiy, Russia (kräs-nô-ô-sôl'skĭ)	164a	53.54N	56.27E
Krasnovishersk, Russia (kräs-nô-vēshersk')	160	60.22N	57.20E
Krasnoyarsk, Russia (kräs-nô-yársk')	158	56.13N	93.12E
Krasnoye Selo, Russia (kräs'nŭ-yŭ sâ'lō)	164c	59.44N	30.06E
Krasnyj Stroitel', neigh., Russia	235b	55.35N	37.37E
Krasny Kholm, Russia (kräs'nē ĸôlm)	156	58.03N	37.11E
Krasnystaw, Pol. (kräs-nē-stáf')	148	50.59N	23.11E
Krasnyy Bor, Russia (kräs'nē bôr)	164c	59.41N	30.40E
Krasnyy Klyuch, Russia (kräs'nē'klyûch')	164a	55.24N	56.43E
Krasnyy Kut, Russia (krás-nē kōōt')	160	50.50N	47.00E
Kratovo, Mac. (krä'tô-vô)	154	42.04N	22.12E
Kratovo, Russia (krä'tô-vô)	164b	55.35N	38.10E
Kray, neigh., Ger.	232	51.28N	7.05E
Krefeld, Ger. (krā'fĕlt)	151c	51.20N	6.34E
Kremenchug, Ukr. (krĕm'ĕn-chōōgh')	160	49.04N	33.26E
Kremenchugskoye, res., Ukr. (krĕm-ĕn-chōōgh'skô-ye)	160	49.20N	32.45E
Kremenets, Ukr. (krĕ-mĕn-yĕts')	148	50.06N	25.43E
Kreml', bldg., Russia	235b	55.45N	37.37E
Kremmen, Ger. (krĕ'mĕn)	139b	52.45N	13.02E
Krempe, Ger. (krĕm'pĕ)	139c	53.50N	9.29E
Krems, Aus. (krĕms)	148	48.25N	15.36E
Kresttsy, Russia (krâst'sĕ)	156	58.16N	32.25E
Kretinga, Lith. (krĕ-tĭŋ'gá)	146	55.55N	21.17E
Kreuzberg, Ger.	232	51.09N	7.27E
Kreuzberg, neigh., Ger.	234a	52.30N	13.23E
Kribi, Cam. (krē'bē)	204	2.57N	9.55E
Krichëv, Bela. (krē'chôf)	156	53.44N	31.39E
Krilon, Mys, c., Russia (mĭs krĭl'ôn)	186	45.58N	142.00E
Krimpen aan de IJssel, Neth.	139a	51.55N	4.34E
Krishna, r., India	174	16.00N	79.00E
Krishnanagar, India	178	23.29N	88.33E
Krishnapur, India	236a	22.36N	88.26E
Kristiansand, Nor. (krĭs-tyán-sän'')	136	58.09N	7.59E
Kristianstad, Swe. (krĭs-tyán-städ')	140	56.02N	14.09E
Kristiansund, Nor. (krĭs-tyán-sòn'')	140	63.07N	7.49E
Kristinehamn, Swe. (krēs-tē'nē-häm')	140	59.20N	14.05E
Kristinestad, Fin. (krĭs-tē'nē-städh)	146	62.16N	21.28E
Kriva-Palanka, Mac. (krē-vá-pá-läŋ'ká)	154	42.12N	22.21E
Krivoye Ozero, Ukr.	156	47.57N	30.21E
Krivoy Rog, Ukr. (krê-voi' rôgh')	158	47.54N	33.22E
Križevci, Cro. (krē'zhĕv-tsĭ)	154	46.02N	16.30E
Krk, i., Yugo. (k'rk)	154	45.06N	14.33E
Krnov, Czech. (k'r'nôf)	148	50.05N	17.41E
Krokodil, r., S. Afr. (krŏ'kō-dĭl)	212d	24.25S	27.08E
Krolevets, Ukr. (krô-lĕ'vyĕts)	160	51.33N	33.21E
Kromy, Russia (krô'mē)	156	52.44N	35.41E
Kronshtadt, Russia (krōn'shtät)	160	59.59N	29.47E
Kroonstad, S. Afr. (krōn'shtät)	206	27.40S	27.15E
Kropotkin, Russia (krá-pôt'kĭn)	160	45.25N	40.30E
Krosno, Pol. (krôs'nô)	148	49.41N	21.46E
Krotoszyn, Pol. (krô-tō'shĭn)	148	51.41N	17.25E
Krško, Slo. (k'rsh'kô)	154	45.58N	15.30E
Kruger National Park, rec., S. Afr. (krōō'gĕr) (krü'gĕr)	206	23.22S	30.18E
Krugersdorp, S. Afr. (krōō'gĕrz-dôrp)	206	26.06S	27.46E
Krugersdorp West, S. Afr.	240b	26.06S	27.45E
Krummensee, Ger.	234a	52.36N	13.42E
Krung Thep, *see* Bangkok, Thai.	188	13.50N	100.29E
Kruševac, Yugo. (krŏ'shĕ-vàts)	154	43.34N	21.21E
Kruševo, Mac.	154	41.20N	21.15E
Krylatskoje, neigh., Russia	235b	55.45N	37.26E
Krylbo, Swe. (krŭl'bô)	146	60.07N	16.14E
Krymskaya, Russia (krĭm'skà-yà)	156	44.58N	38.01E
Krymskaya, prov., Ukr.	156	45.08N	34.05E
Krymskiy Poluostrov (Crimea), pen., Ukr. (krēm-skĭ pô-lô-ôs'trôf)	160	45.18N	33.30E
Krynki, Pol. (krĭn'kē)	148	53.15N	23.47E
Kryukov, Ukr. (k'r'yōō-kôf')	156	49.02N	33.26E
Ksar Chellala, Alg.	152	35.12N	2.20E
Ksar-el-Kebir, Mor.	142	35.01N	5.48W
Ksar-es-Souk, Mor.	142	31.58N	4.25W
Kuai, r., China (kōō-ī)	182	33.30N	116.56E
Kuala Klawang, Malay.	173b	2.57N	102.04E
Kuala Lumpur, Malay. (kwä'lä lōm-pōōr')	188	3.08N	101.42E
Kuandian, China (kùän-dĭĕn)	184	40.40N	124.50E
Kuba, Azer. (kōō'bä)	160	41.05N	48.30E
Kuban, r., Russia	160	45.20N	40.05E
Kubenskoye, l., Russia	160	59.40N	39.40E
Kuching, Malay. (kōō'chĭng)	188	1.30N	110.26E
Kuchinoerabo, i., Japan (kōō'chē nō ĕr'á-bō)	187	30.31N	129.53E
Kudamatsu, Japan (kōō'dá-mä'tsōō)	187	34.00N	131.51E
Kudap, Indon.	173b	1.14N	102.30E
Kudat, Malay. (kōō-dät')	188	6.56N	116.48E
Kudbrooke, neigh., Eng., U.K.	231	51.28N	0.03E
Kudirkos Naumietis, Lith. (kōōdĭr-kôs ná'ô-mē'tĭs)	146	54.51N	23.00E
Kudymkar, Russia (kōō-dĭm-kär')	158	58.43N	54.52E
Kufstein, Aus. (kōōf'shtīn)	148	47.34N	12.11E
Kuhstedt, Ger. (kōō'shtĕ)	139c	53.23N	8.58E
Kuibyshev, *see* Kuybyshev, Russia	158	53.10N	50.05E
Kuilsrivier, S. Afr.	206a	33.56S	18.41E
Kuito, Ang.	206	12.22S	16.56E
Kuji, Japan	180	40.11N	141.46E
Kujū-san, mtn., Japan (kōō'jō-sän')	187	33.07N	131.14E
Kukës, Alb. (kōō'kĕs)	154	42.03N	20.25E
Kula, Bul. (kōō'lá)	154	43.52N	23.13E
Kula, Tur.	142	38.32N	28.30E
Kula Kangri, mtn., Bhu.	174	33.11N	90.36E
Kular, Khrebet, mts., Russia (kô-lär')	162	69.00N	131.45E
Kuldīga, Lat. (kòl'dē-gá)	146	56.59N	21.59E
Kulebaki, Russia (kōō-lē-bäk'ĭ)	160	55.22N	42.30E
Küllenhahn, neigh., Ger.	232	51.14N	7.08E
Kulmbach, Ger. (klòlm'bäĸ)	148	50.07N	11.28E
Kulunda, Russia (kô-lòn'dá)	158	52.38N	79.00E
Kulundinskoye, l., Russia	162	52.45N	77.18E
Kum, r., S. Kor. (kòm)	186	36.50N	127.30E
Kuma, r., Russia (kōō'mä)	160	44.50N	45.10E
Kumamoto, Japan (kōō'mä-mō'tô)	180	32.49N	130.40E
Kumano-Nada, b., Japan (kōō-mä'nō nä-dä)	187	34.03N	136.36E
Kumanovo, Mac. (kò-mä'nô-vô)	154	42.10N	21.41E
Kumasi, Ghana (kōō-mä'sē)	204	6.41N	1.35W
Kumayri, Arm.	160	40.40N	43.50E
Kumba, Cam. (kòm'bà)	204	4.38N	9.25E
Kumbakonam, India (kòm'bŭ-kō'nŭm)	174	10.59N	79.25E
Kumkale, Tur.	154	39.59N	26.10E
Kumo, Nig.	208	10.03N	11.13E
Kumta, India	178	14.19N	75.28E
Kumul, *see* Hami, China	180	42.58N	93.14E
Kunashak, Russia (kû-nä'shák)	164a	55.43N	61.35E
Kunashir (Kunashiri), i., Russia (kōō-nŭ-shĕr')	180	44.00N	145.45E
Kunda, Est.	146	59.30N	26.28E
Kundravy, Russia (kōōn'drá-vĭ)	164a	54.50N	60.14E
Kundur, i., Indon.	173b	0.49N	103.20E

ăt; finăl; rāte; senāte; ärm; åsk; sofá; fâre; ch-choose; dh-as th in other; bē; ēvent; bĕt; recĕnt; cratĕr; g-gō; gh-guttural g; bĭt; ĭ-short neutral; rīde; ĸ-guttural k as ch in German ich;

PLACE (Pronunciation)	PAGE	Lat. °′	Long. °′
Kunene (Cunene), r., Afr.	206	17.05S	12.35E
Kungälv, Swe. (küng'ĕlf)	146	57.53N	12.01E
Kungsbacka, Swe. (küngs'bä-kȧ)	146	57.31N	12.04E
Kungur, Russia (kȯn-go͞or')	158	57.27N	56.53E
Kunitachi, Japan	238a	35.41N	139.26E
Kunlun Shan, mts., China (ko͞on-lo͞on shän)	180	35.26N	83.09E
Kunming, China (ko͞on-mĭŋ)	180	25.10N	102.50E
Kunsan, S. Kor. (kȯn'sän')	180	35.54N	126.46E
Kunshan, China (ko͞onshän)	183b	31.23N	120.57E
Kuntsëvo, Russia (kȯn-tsyô'vô)	156	55.43N	37.27E
Kun'ya, Russia	164a	58.42N	56.47E
Kun'ya, r., Russia (kȯn'yȧ)	156	56.45N	30.53E
Kuopio, Fin. (kȯ-ô'pē-ŏ)	140	62.48N	28.30E
Kupa, r., Yugo.	154	45.32N	14.50E
Kupang, Indon.	188	10.14S	123.37E
Kupavna, Russia	164b	55.49N	38.11E
Kupferdreh, neigh., Ger.	232	51.23N	7.05E
Kupino, Russia (ko͞o-pĭ'nô)	158	54.00N	77.47E
Kupiškis, Lith. (kȯ-pĭsh'kĭs)	146	55.50N	24.55E
Kupyansk, Ukr. (kȯp-yänsk')	160	49.44N	37.38E
Kuqa, China (ko͞o-chyä)	180	41.34N	82.44E
Kura, r., Asia (ko͞o'rȧ)	160	41.10N	45.40E
Kurashiki, Japan (ko͞o'rä-shē'kē)	187	34.37N	133.44E
Kuraymah, Sudan	204	18.34N	31.49E
Kurayoshi, Japan (ko͞o'rȧ-yō'shē)	187	35.25N	133.49E
Kurdistan, hist. reg., Asia (kûrd'ĭ-stăn)	174	37.40N	43.30E
Kurdufān, hist. reg., Sudan (kôr-dô-fän')	204	14.08N	28.39E
Kürdzhali, Bul.	154	41.39N	25.21E
Kure, Japan (ko͞o'rĕ)	180	34.17N	132.35E
Kuressaare, Est. (kŏ'rĕ-sä'rĕ)	146	58.15N	22.26E
Kurgan, Russia (kȯr-găn')	158	55.28N	65.14E
Kurgan-Tyube, Taj. (kȯr-gän' tyȯ'bĕ)	162	38.00N	68.49E
Kurihama, Japan (ko͞o-rē-hä'mä)	187a	35.14N	139.42E
Kuril Islands, is., Russia (ko͞o'rĭl)	162	46.20N	149.30E
Ku-ring-gai, Austl.	239a	33.45S	151.08E
Kurisches Haff, b., Eur.	146	55.10N	21.08E
Kurl, neigh., Ger.	232	51.35N	7.35E
Kurla, neigh., India	179b	19.03N	72.53E
Kurmuk, Sudan (kȯr'mo͝ok)	204	10.40N	34.13E
Kurnell, Austl.	239a	34.01S	151.13E
Kurnool, India (kȯr-no͞ol')	174	16.00N	78.04E
Kurrajong, Austl.	195b	33.33S	150.40E
Kuršėnai, Lith. (kȯr'shȧ-nī)	146	56.01N	22.56E
Kursk, Russia (ko͝orsk)	158	51.44N	36.08E
Kuršumlija, Yugo. (kȯr'shȯm'lĭ-yȧ)	154	43.08N	21.18E
Kuruçeşme, neigh., Tur.	235f	41.03N	29.02E
Kuruman, S. Afr. (ko͞o-ro͞o-män')	206	27.25S	23.30E
Kurume, Japan (ko͞o'rȯ-mĕ)	180	33.10N	130.30E
Kurume, Japan	238a	35.45N	139.32E
Kururi, Japan (ko͞o'rȯ-rē)	187a	35.17N	140.05E
Kusa, Russia (ko͞o'sȧ)	164a	55.19N	59.27E
Kushchëvskaya, Russia	156	46.34N	39.40E
Kushikino, Japan (ko͞o'shĭ-kē'nō)	187	31.44N	130.19E
Kushimoto, Japan (ko͞o'shĭ-mō'tō)	187	33.29N	135.47E
Kushiro, Japan (ko͞o'shē-rō)	180	43.00N	144.22E
Kush-Murun, l., Kaz. (ko͞osh-mȯ-ro͞on')	162	52.30N	64.15E
Kushum, r., Kaz. (kȯ-shȯm')	160	50.30N	50.40E
Kushva, Russia (ko͞osh'vȧ)	158	58.18N	59.51E
Kuskokwim, r., Ak., U.S.	89	61.32N	160.36W
Kuskokwim Bay, b., Ak., U.S. (kŭs'kô-kwĭm)	89	59.25N	163.14W
Kuskokwim Mountains, mts., Ak., U.S.	89	62.08N	158.00W
Kuskovak, Ak., U.S. (kŭs-kō'văk)	89	60.10N	162.50W
Kuskovo, neigh., Russia	235b	55.44N	37.49E
Kustanay, Kaz. (kȯs-tȧ-nī')	158	53.10N	63.39E
Kütahya, Tur. (kû-tä'hyȧ)	174	39.20N	29.50E
Kutaisi, Geor. (ko͞o-tŭ-ē'sē)	160	42.15N	42.40E
Kutch, Gulf of, b., India	174	22.45N	68.33E
Kutch, Rann of, sw., Asia	174	23.59N	69.13E
Kutenholz, Ger. (ko͞o'tĕn-hōlts)	139c	53.29N	9.20E
Kutim, Russia (ko͞o'tĭm)	164a	60.22N	58.51E
Kutina, Cro. (ko͞o'tē-nȧ)	154	45.29N	16.48E
Kutno, Pol. (kȯt'nô)	140	52.14N	19.22E
Kutno, l., Russia	160	65.15N	31.30E
Kutulik, Russia (kȯ to͞o'lyĭk)	158	53.12N	102.51E
Kuty, Ukr. (ko͞o'tē)	148	48.16N	25.12E
Kuujjuaq, Can.	78	58.06N	68.25W
Kuusamo, Fin. (ko͞o'sȧ-mȯ)	140	65.59N	29.10E
Kuvshinovo, Russia (kȯv-shē'nô-vô)	156	57.01N	34.09E
Kuwait, nation, Asia	174	29.00N	48.45E
Kuwana, Japan (ko͞o'wȧ-nȧ)	187	35.02N	136.40E
Kuybyshev, *see* Samara, Russia	160	53.10N	50.05E
Kuybyshevskoye, res., Russia	158	53.40N	49.00E
Kuz'minki, neigh., Russia	235b	55.42N	37.48E
Kuzneckovo, Russia	164b	55.29N	38.22E
Kuznetsk, Russia (ko͞oz-nyĕtsk')	160	53.00N	46.30E
Kuznetsk Basin, basin, Russia	158	56.30N	86.15E
Kuznetsovka, Russia (kȯz-nyĕt'sôf-kȧ)	164a	54.41N	56.40E
Kuznetsovo, Russia (kȯz-nyĕt-sô'vô)	156	56.39N	36.55E
Kuznetsy, Russia	164b	55.50N	38.39E
Kvarner Zaliv, b., Yugo. (kvär'nĕr)	154	44.41N	14.05E
Kvichak, Ak., U.S. (vĭc'-hăk)	89	59.00N	156.48W
Kwa, r., Zaire	210	3.00S	16.45E
Kwahu Plateau, plat., Ghana	208	7.00N	1.35W
Kwando (Cuando), r., Afr.	210	16.50S	22.40E
Kwangju, S. Kor.	186	35.09N	126.54E
Kwango (Cuango), r., Afr. (kwäng'ō')	210	6.35S	16.50E
Kwangwazi, Tan.	210	7.47S	38.15E
Kwa-Thema, S. Afr.	240b	26.18S	28.23E
Kwekwe, Zimb.	206	18.49S	29.45E
Kwenge, r., Afr. (kwĕŋ'gē)	206	6.45S	18.23E
Kwilu, r., Afr. (kwē'lo͞o)	206	4.00S	18.00E
Kyakhta, Russia (kyäk'ta)	158	51.00N	107.30E
Kyaukpyu, Burma (chouk'pyoo')	174	19.19N	93.33E
Kybartai, Lith. (kē'bär-tī')	146	54.40N	22.46E
Kyn, Russia (kĭn')	164a	57.52N	58.42E
Kynuna, Austl. (kī-no͞o'nȧ)	196	21.30S	142.12E
Kyoga, Lake, l., Ug.	204	1.30N	32.45E
Kyōga-Saki, c., Japan (kyō'gä sa'kē)	187	35.46N	135.14E
Kyŏngju, S. Kor. (kyŭng'yo͞o)	180	35.48N	129.12E
Kyŏngju, S. Kor.	186	35.51N	129.14E
Kyōto, Japan (kyō'tō')	180	35.00N	135.46E
Kyōto, dept., Japan	187b	34.56N	135.42E
Kyren, Russia (kĭ-rĕn')	158	51.46N	102.13E
Kyrönjoki, r., Fin.	146	63.03N	22.20E
Kyrya, Russia (kĕr'yȧ)	164a	59.18N	59.03E
Kyshtym, Russia (kĭsh-tĭm')	160	55.42N	60.34E
Kytlym, Russia (kĭt'lĭm)	164a	59.30N	59.15E
Kyūhōji, neigh., Japan	238b	34.38N	135.35E
Kyūshū, i., Japan	180	33.00N	131.00E
Kyustendil, Bul. (kyȯs-tĕn-dĭl')	142	42.16N	22.39E
Kyzyl, Russia (kĭ zĭl)	158	51.37N	93.38E
Kyzyl Kum, Peski, des., Asia (kĭ zĭl ko͞om)	158	42.47N	64.45E
Kzyl-Orda, Kaz. (kzĕl-ôr'dȧ)	158	44.58N	65.45E

L

PLACE (Pronunciation)	PAGE	Lat. °′	Long. °′
Laa, Aus.	148	48.42N	16.23E
Laab im Walde, Aus.	235e	48.09N	16.11E
La Almunia de Doña Godina, Spain	152	41.29N	1.22W
Laas Caanood, Som.	212a	8.24N	47.20E
La Asunción, Ven. (lä ä-so͞on-syōn')	124	11.02N	63.57W
La Baie, Can.	84	48.21N	70.53W
La Banda, Arg. (lä bän'dä)	126	27.48S	64.12W
La Bandera, Chile	230b	33.34S	70.39W
La Barca, Mex. (lä bär'kȧ)	112	20.17N	102.33W
Laberge, Lake, l., Can. (lȧ-bĕrzh')	78	61.08N	136.42W
Laberinto de las Doce Leguas, is., Cuba	116	20.40N	78.35W
Labinsk, Russia	160	44.30N	40.40E
Labis, Malay. (läb'ĭs)	173b	2.23N	103.01E
La Bisbal, Spain (lä bēs-bäl')	152	41.55N	3.00E
Labo, Phil. (lä'bō)	189a	14.11N	122.49E
Labo, Mount, mtn., Phil.	189a	14.00N	122.47E
Labouheyre, Fr. (lȧ-bo͞o-âr')	150	44.14N	0.58W
Laboulaye, Arg. (lȧ-bō'o͞o-lȧ-yĕ)	126	34.01S	63.10W
Labrador, reg., Can. (lăb'rȧ-dôr)	78	53.05N	63.30W
Labrador Sea, sea, Can.	86	50.38N	55.00W
Lábrea, Braz. (lä-brā'ȧ)	124	7.28S	64.39W
Labuan, Pulau, i., Malay. (lä-bȯ-än')	188	5.28N	115.11E
Labuha, Indon.	188	0.43S	127.35E
L'Acadie, Can. (lȧ-kȧ-dē')	77a	45.18N	73.22W
L'Acadie, r., Can.	77a	45.24N	73.21W
La Calera, Chile (lä-kä-lĕ-rä)	123b	32.47S	71.11W
La Calera, Col.	124a	4.43N	73.58W
Lac Allard, Can.	86	50.38N	63.28W
La Canada, Ca., U.S. (lä kän-yä'dä)	101a	34.13N	118.12W
La Candelaria, Mex.	229a	19.20N	99.09W
Lacantum, r., Mex. (lä-kän-to͞o'm)	112	16.13N	90.52W
La Carolina, Spain (lä kä-rō-lē'nä)	152	38.16N	3.48W
La Catedral, Cerro, mtn., Mex. (sĕ'r-rô-lä-kä-tĕ-drá'l)	113a	19.32N	99.31W
Lac-Beauport, Can. (lăk-bō-pōr')	77b	46.58N	71.17W
Laccadive Islands, *see* Lakshadweep, is., India	174	11.00N	73.02E
Laccadive Sea, sea, Asia	178	9.10N	75.17E
Lac Court Oreille Indian Reservation, I.R., Wi., U.S.	96	46.04N	91.18W
Lac du Flambeau Indian Reservation, I.R., Wi., U.S.	96	46.12N	89.50W
La Ceiba, Hond. (lä sēbä)	110	15.45N	86.52W
La Ceja, Col. (lä-sĕ-kä)	124a	6.02N	75.25W
Lac-Frontière, Can.	78	46.42N	70.00W
Lacha, l., Russia (lá'chä)	160	61.15N	39.05E
La Chaux de Fonds, Switz. (lȧ shō dē-fôN')	148	47.07N	6.47E
L'Achigan, r., Can. (lä-shē-gäN)	77a	45.49N	73.48W
Lachine, Can. (lȧ-shēn')	77a	45.26N	73.40W
Lachlan, r., Austl. (läk'lăn)	196	34.00S	145.00E
La Chorrera, Pan. (làchȯr-rā'rä)	114	8.54N	79.47W
Lachta, neigh., Russia	235a	60.00N	30.10E
Lachute, Can. (lȧ-sho͞ot')	84	45.39N	74.20W
La Ciotat, Fr. (lȧ syō-tá')	150	43.13N	5.35E
La Cisterna, Chile	230b	33.33S	70.41W
Lackawanna, N.Y., U.S. (lak-ȧ-wŏn'ȧ)	95c	42.49N	78.50W
Lac la Biche, Can.	78	54.46N	112.58W
Lacombe, Can.	78	52.28N	113.44W
Laconia, N.H., U.S. (lȧ-kō'nĭ-ȧ)	92	43.30N	71.30W
La Conner, Wa., U.S. (lȧ kŏn'ẽr)	100a	48.23N	122.30W
La Coruña, Spain (lä kō-ro͞on'yä)	136	43.20N	8.20W
La Courneuve, Fr.	233c	48.56N	2.23E
Lacreek, l., S.D., U.S. (lă'krēk)	96	43.04N	101.46W
La Cresenta, Ca., U.S. (lȧ krĕs'ĕnt-ȧ)	101a	34.14N	118.13W
La Cross, Ks., U.S. (lȧ-krôs')	104	38.30N	99.20W
La Crosse, Wi., U.S.	90	43.48N	91.14W
La Cruz, Col. (lȧ kro͞oz')	124	1.37N	77.00W
La Cruz, C.R. (lä-kro͞o'z)	114	11.05N	85.37W
Lacs, Riviere des, r., N.D., U.S. (rē-vyĕr' de läk)	96	48.30N	101.45W
La Cuesta, C.R. (lä-kwĕ's-tä)	114	8.32N	82.51W
La Cygne, Ks., U.S. (lȧ-sēn'y') (lȧ-sēn')	104	38.20N	94.45W
Ladd, Il., U.S. (lăd)	92	41.25N	89.25W
Ladíspoli, Italy (lȧ-dē's-pô-lē)	153d	41.57N	12.05E
Lādīz, Iran	176	28.56N	61.19E
Ladner, Can. (lăd'nẽr)	80	49.05N	123.05W
Lādnun, India (läd'nōn)	178	27.45N	74.20E
Ladoga, Lake, *see* Ladozhskoye Ozero, l., Russia	158	60.59N	31.30E
La Dolorita, Ven.	230a	10.29N	66.47W
La Dorado, Col. (lä dô-rä'dȧ)	124	5.28N	74.42W
Ladozhskoye Ozero, Russia (lȧ-dôsh'skô-yĕ ô'zĕ-rô)	158	60.59N	31.30E
La Durantaye, Can. (lä dü-räN-tā')	77b	46.51N	70.51W
Lady Frere, S. Afr. (lā-dē frâ'r')	207c	31.48S	27.16E
Lady Grey, S. Afr.	207c	30.44S	27.17E
Ladysmith, Can. (lā'dĭ-smĭth)	80	48.58N	123.49W
Ladysmith, S. Afr.	206	28.38S	29.48E
Ladysmith, Wi., U.S.	96	45.27N	91.07W
Lae, Pap. N. Gui. (lä'ȧ)	188	6.15S	146.57E
Laerdalsøyri, Nor.	146	61.08N	7.26E
La Esperanza, Hond. (lä ĕs-pȧ-rän'zä)	114	14.20N	88.21W
La Estrada, Spain (lä ĕs-trä'dä)	152	42.42N	8.29W
Lafayette, Al., U.S.	108	32.52N	85.25W
Lafayette, Ca., U.S.	100b	37.53N	122.07W
Lafayette, Ga., U.S. (lă-fā-yĕt')	108	34.41N	85.19W
Lafayette, In., U.S.	90	40.25N	86.55W
Lafayette, La., U.S.	90	30.15N	92.02W
La Fayette, R.I., U.S.	94b	41.34N	71.29W
Lafayette Hill, Pa., U.S.	225b	40.05N	75.15W
Laferrere, Arg.	229d	34.45S	58.35W
La Ferté-Alais, Fr. (lä-fĕr-tā'ä-lā')	151b	48.29N	2.19E
La Ferté-sous-Jouarre, Fr. (lȧ fĕr-tā'so͞o-zho͞o-är')	151b	48.56N	3.07E
Lafia, Nig.	208	8.30N	8.30E
Lafiagi, Nig.	208	8.52N	5.25E
Laflèche, Can.	223b	45.30N	73.28W
La Flèche, Fr. (lȧ flāsh')	150	47.43N	0.03W
La Floresta, Spain	234e	41.27N	2.04E
La Florida, Chile	230b	33.32S	70.33W
La Follete, Tn., U.S. (lă-fŏl'ĕt)	108	36.23N	84.07W
Lafourche, Bayou, r., La., U.S. (bȧ-yo͞o'lȧ-fo͞orsh')	106	29.25N	90.15W
La Frette-sur-Seine, Fr.	233c	48.58N	2.11E
La Gaiba, Braz. (lä-gī'bä)	124	17.54S	57.32W
La Galite, i., Tun. (gä-lēt)	142	37.36N	8.03E
Lågan, r., Nor. (lô'ghĕn)	136	61.00N	10.00E
Lagan, r., Swe.	146	56.34N	13.25E
Lagan, r., N. Ire., U.K. (lā'găn)	144	54.30N	6.00W
La Garenne-Colombes, Fr.	233c	48.55N	2.15E
Lagarto, r., Pan. (lä-gä'r-tô)	110a	9.08N	80.05W
Lagartos, l., Mex. (lä-gä'r-tôs)	114a	21.32N	88.15W
Laghouat, Alg. (lä-gwät')	204	33.45N	2.49E
Lagny, Fr. (län-yē')	151b	48.53N	2.41E
Lagoa da Prata, Braz. (lȧ-gô'ä-dȧ-prä'tȧ)	123a	20.04S	45.33W
Lagoa Dourada, Braz. (lȧ-gô'ä-dō-rä'dä)	123a	20.55S	44.03W
Lagogne, Fr. (laN-gōn'y')	150	44.43N	3.50E
Lagonay, Phil.	189a	13.44N	123.31E
Lagos, Nig. (lä'gōs)	204	6.27N	3.24E
Lagos, Port. (lä'gōzh)	152	37.08N	8.43W
Lagos de Moreno, Mex. (lä'gōs dā mō-rā'nō)	110	21.21N	101.55W
La Grand' Combe, Fr. (lȧ gräN kaNb')	150	44.12N	4.03E
La Grande, Or., U.S. (lȧ grănd')	90	45.20N	118.06W
La Grande, r., Can.	78	53.55N	77.30W
La Grange, Austl. (lä grānj)	196	18.40S	122.00E
La Grange, Ga., U.S. (lȧ-grānj')	90	33.01N	85.00W
La Grange, Il., U.S.	95a	41.49N	87.53W
Lagrange, In., U.S.	92	41.40N	85.25W
La Grange, Ky., U.S.	92	38.20N	85.25W
La Grange, Mo., U.S.	104	40.04N	91.30W
Lagrange, Oh., U.S.	95d	41.14N	82.07W
Lagrange, Tx., U.S.	106	29.55N	96.50W
La Grange Highlands, Il., U.S.	227a	41.48N	87.53W
La Grange Park, Il., U.S.	227a	41.50N	87.52W
La Granja, Chile	230b	33.32S	70.39W
La Grita, Ven. (lä grē'tȧ)	124	8.02N	71.59W
La Guaira, Ven. (lä gwä'ē-rä)	124	10.36N	66.54W
La Guardia, Spain (lä gwär'dē-ȧ)	152	41.55N	8.48W
La Guardia Airport, arpt., N.Y., U.S.	224	40.46N	73.53W
Laguna, Braz. (lä-go͞o'nä)	126	28.19S	48.42W
Laguna, Cayos, is., Cuba (kä'yōs-lä-gō'nä)	116	22.15N	82.45W
Laguna Indian Reservation, I.R., N.M., U.S.	102	35.00N	107.30W
Lagunillas, Bol. (lä-go͞o-nēl'yäs)	124	19.42S	63.38W
Lagunillas, Mex. (lä-go͞o-nē'l-yäs)	112	21.34N	99.41W
La Habana, *see* Havana, Cuba	110	23.08N	82.23W
La Habra, Ca., U.S. (lȧ hăb'rȧ)	101a	34.56N	117.57W
La Habra Heights, Ca., U.S.	228	33.57N	117.57W
Lahaina, Hi., U.S. (lä-hä'ē-nä)	88a	20.52N	156.39W
La Häy-les-Roses, Fr.	233c	48.47N	2.21E
Lāhījān, Iran	176	37.12N	50.01E
Laholm, Swe. (lä'hōlm)	146	56.30N	13.00E
La Honda, Ca., U.S. (lȧ hŏn'dȧ)	100b	37.20N	122.16W
Lahore, Pak. (lȧ-hōr')	174	32.00N	74.18E
Lahr, Ger. (lär)	148	48.19N	7.52E
Lahti, Fin. (lä'tē)	140	60.59N	27.39E
Laï, Chad	204	9.29N	16.18E
Lai'an, China (lī-än)	182	32.27N	118.25E
Laibin, China (lī-bĭn)	184	23.42N	109.20E
L'Aigle, Fr. (lĕ'gl')	150	48.45N	0.37E
Lainate, Italy	234c	45.34N	9.02E
Lainz, neigh., Aus.	235e	48.11N	16.17E
Laisamis, Kenya	210	1.36N	37.48E

ng-sing; ŋ-baŋk; N-nasalized n; nŏd; cŏmmit; ōld; ôbey; ôrder; oi-boil; fo͞od; ȯ-as oo in foot; ou-out; s-soft; sh-dish; th-thin; pūre; ůnite; ûrn; stŭd; circŭs; ü-as in French tu; '-indeterminate vowel.

PLACE (Pronunciation)	PAGE	Lat. °′	Long. °′
Laiyang, China (lāī'yäng)	184	36.59N	120.42E
Laizhou Wan, b., China (lī-jō wän)	180	37.22N	119.19E
Laja, Río de la, r., Mex. (rē'ō-dĕ-lä-lä'ĸä)	112	21.17N	100.57W
Lajas, Cuba (lä'häs)	116	22.25N	80.20W
Laje, Ponta da, c., Port.	234d	38.40N	9.19W
Lajeado, Braz. (lä-zhĕä'dô)	126	29.24S	51.46W
Lajeado Velho, neigh., Braz.	230d	23.32S	46.23W
Lajes, Braz. (là'zhĕs)	126	27.47S	50.17W
Lajinha, Braz. (lä-zhē'nyä)	123a	20.08S	41.36W
La Jolla, Ca., U.S. (là hoi'yà)	102a	32.51N	117.16W
La Jolla Indian Reservation, I.R., Ca., U.S.	102	33.19N	116.21W
La Junta, Co., U.S. (là hōōn'tà)	104	37.59N	103.35W
Lake Arrowhead, Ca., U.S.	228	33.52N	118.05W
Lake Arthur, La., U.S. (är'thŭr)	106	30.06N	92.40W
Lake Barcroft, Va., U.S.	225d	38.51N	77.09W
Lake Barkley, res., U.S.	108	36.45N	88.00W
Lake Benton, Mn., U.S. (bĕn'tŭn)	96	44.15N	96.17W
Lake Bluff, Il., U.S. (blŭf)	95a	42.17N	87.50W
Lake Brown, Austl. (broun)	196	31.03S	118.30E
Lake Charles, La., U.S. (chärlz')	90	30.15N	93.14W
Lake City, Fl., U.S.	108	30.09N	82.40W
Lake City, Ia., U.S.	96	42.14N	94.43W
Lake City, Mn., U.S.	96	44.28N	92.19W
Lake City, S.C., U.S.	108	33.57N	79.45W
Lake Clark National Park, rec., Ak., U.S.	89	60.30N	153.15W
Lake Cowichan, Can. (kou'ĭ-chăn)	80	48.50N	124.03W
Lake Crystal, Mn., U.S. (krĭs'tăl)	96	44.05N	94.12W
Lake District, reg., Eng., U.K. (lāk)	144	54.25N	3.20W
Lake Elmo, Mn., U.S. (ĕlmō)	101g	45.00N	92.53W
Lake Forest, Il., U.S. (fŏr'ĕst)	95a	42.16N	87.50W
Lake Fork, r., Ut., U.S.	102	40.30N	110.25W
Lake Geneva, Wi., U.S. (jĕ-nē'và)	96	42.36N	88.28W
Lake Harbour, Can. (här'bēr)	78	62.43N	69.40W
Lake Havasu City, Az., U.S.	102	34.27N	114.22W
Lake June, Tx., U.S. (jōōn)	101c	32.43N	96.45W
Lakeland, Fl., U.S. (lāk'lănd)	90	28.02N	81.58W
Lakeland, Ga., U.S.	108	31.02N	83.02W
Lakeland, Mn., U.S.	101g	44.57N	92.47W
Lake Linden, Mi., U.S. (lĭn'dĕn)	96	47.11N	88.26W
Lake Louise, Can. (lōō-ēz')	80	51.26N	116.11W
Lakemba, Austl.	239a	33.55S	151.05E
Lake Mead National Recreation Area, rec., U.S.	102	36.00N	114.30W
Lake Mills, Ia., U.S. (mĭlz')	96	43.25N	93.32W
Lakemore, Oh., U.S. (lāk-mōr)	95d	41.01N	81.24W
Lake Odessa, Mi., U.S.	92	42.50N	85.15W
Lake Oswego, Or., U.S. (ŏs-wē'go)	100c	45.25N	122.40W
Lake Placid, N.Y., U.S.	92	44.17N	73.59W
Lake Point, Ut., U.S.	101b	40.41N	112.16W
Lakeport, Ca., U.S. (lāk'pōrt)	102	39.03N	122.54W
Lake Preston, S.D., U.S. (prēs'tŭn)	96	44.21N	97.23W
Lake Providence, La., U.S. (prŏv'ĭ-dĕns)	106	32.48N	91.12W
Lake Red Rock, res., Ia., U.S.	96	41.30N	93.15W
Lake Sharpe, res., S.D., U.S.	96	44.30N	100.00W
Lakeside, S. Afr.	240b	26.06S	28.09E
Lakeside, Ca., U.S. (lāk'sīd)	102a	32.52N	116.55W
Lake Station, In., U.S.	95a	41.34N	87.15W
Lake Stevens, Wa., U.S.	100a	48.01N	122.04W
Lake Success, N.Y., U.S. (sŭk-sĕs')	94a	40.46N	73.43W
Lakeview, Or., U.S.	98	42.11N	120.21W
Lakeview, neigh., Il., U.S.	227a	41.57N	87.39W
Lake Village, Ar., U.S.	104	33.20N	91.17W
Lake Wales, Fl., U.S. (wālz')	109a	27.54N	81.35W
Lakewood, Ca., U.S. (lāk'wŏŏd)	101a	33.50N	118.09W
Lakewood, Co., U.S.	104	39.44N	105.06W
Lakewood, Oh., U.S.	90	41.29N	81.48W
Lakewood, Pa., U.S.	92	40.05N	74.10W
Lakewood, Wa., U.S.	100a	48.09N	122.13W
Lakewood Center, Wa., U.S.	100a	47.10N	122.31W
Lake Worth, Fl., U.S. (wûrth')	109a	26.37N	80.04W
Lake Worth Village, Tx., U.S.	101c	32.49N	97.26W
Lake Zurich, Il., U.S. (tsü'rĭk)	95a	42.11N	88.05W
Lakhdenpokh'ya, Russia (l'äk-dīe'npŏkyà)	146	61.33N	30.10E
Lakhtinskiy, Russia (làk-tĭn'skĭ)	164c	59.59N	30.10E
Lakota, N.D., U.S. (là-kō'tà)	96	48.04N	98.21W
Lakshadweep, state, India	174	10.10N	72.50E
Lakshadweep, is., India	174	11.00N	73.02E
Laleham, Eng., U.K.	231	51.25N	0.30W
La Libertad, El Sal.	114	13.29N	89.20W
La Libertad, Guat. (lä lē-bĕr-tädh')	114	15.31N	91.44W
La Libertad, Guat.	114a	16.46N	90.12W
La Ligua, Chile (lä lē'gwä)	123b	32.21S	71.13W
Lalín, Spain (lä-lē'n)	152	42.40N	8.05W
La Línea, Spain (lä lē'nā-ä)	142	36.11N	5.22W
La Lisa, Cuba	229b	23.04N	82.26W
Lalitpur, Nepal	174	27.23N	85.24E
La Louviere, Bel. (là lōō-vyâr')	144	50.30N	4.10E
La Luz, Mex. (lä lōōz')	112	21.04N	101.19W
Lama-Kara, Togo	208	9.33N	1.12E
La Malbaie, Can. (là mäl-bâ')	78	47.39N	70.10W
La Mancha, reg., Spain (lä män'chä)	152	38.55N	4.20W
Lamar, Co., U.S. (là-mär')	104	38.04N	102.44W
Lamar, Mo., U.S.	104	37.28N	94.15W
La Marmora, Punta, mtn., Italy (lä-mä'r-mô-rä)	142	40.00N	9.28E
La Marque, Tx., U.S. (là-märk)	107a	29.23N	94.58W
Lamas, Peru (lä'màs)	124	6.24S	76.41W
Lamballe, Fr. (län-bäl')	150	48.29N	2.36W
Lambari, Braz. (läm-bà'rē)	123a	21.58S	45.22W
Lambasa, Fiji	192g	16.26S	179.24E
Lambayeque, Peru (läm-bä-yä'kå)	124	6.41S	79.58W
Lambert, Ms., U.S. (lăm'bērt)	108	34.10N	90.16W
Lambertville, N.J., U.S. (lăm'bērt-vĭl)	92	40.20N	75.00W
Lambeth, neigh., Eng., U.K.	231	51.28N	0.07W
Lambourne End, Eng., U.K.	231	51.38N	0.08E
Lambrate, neigh., Italy	234c	45.29N	9.15E
Lambro, r., Italy	234c	45.26N	9.16E
Lambton, S. Afr.	240b	26.15S	28.10E
Lame Deer, Mt., U.S. (lām dēr')	98	45.36N	106.40W
Lamego, Port. (lä-mā'gō)	152	41.07N	7.47W
La Mesa, Col.	124a	4.38N	74.27W
La Mesa, Ca., U.S. (lä mā'sä)	102a	32.46N	117.01W
Lamesa, Tx., U.S.	104	32.44N	101.54W
Lamía, Grc. (là-mē'à)	142	38.54N	22.25E
La Mirada, Ca., U.S.	228	33.54N	118.01W
Lamon Bay, b., Phil. (lä-mōn')	188	14.35N	121.52E
La Mora, Chile (lä-mō'rä)	123b	32.28S	70.56W
La Mott, Pa., U.S.	225b	40.04N	75.08W
La Moure, N.D., U.S. (là mōōr')	96	46.23N	98.17W
Lampa, r., Chile (là'm-pä)	123b	33.15S	70.55W
Lampasas, Tx., U.S. (lăm-păs'às)	106	31.06N	98.10W
Lampasas, r., Tx., U.S.	106	31.18N	98.08W
Lampazos, Mex. (läm-pä'zōs)	110	27.03N	100.30W
Lampedusa, i., Italy (läm-pâ-dōō'sä)	142	35.29N	12.58E
Lamstedt, Ger. (läm'shtĕt)	139c	53.38N	9.06E
Lamu, Kenya (lä'mōō)	206	2.16S	40.54E
Lamu Island, i., Kenya	210	2.25S	40.50E
La Mure, Fr. (là mür')	150	44.55N	5.50E
Lan', r., Bela. (làn')	156	52.38N	27.05E
Lanai, i., Hi., U.S. (lä-nä'ē)	90c	20.48N	157.06W
Lanai City, Hi., U.S.	88a	20.50N	156.56W
Lanak La, p., China	180	34.40N	79.50E
Lanark, Scot., U.K. (lăn'ărk)	144	55.40N	3.50W
Lancashire, co., Eng., U.K. (lăŋ'kà-shĭr)	138a	53.49N	2.42W
Lancaster, Eng., U.K.	140	54.04N	2.55W
Lancaster, Ky., U.S.	92	37.35N	84.30W
Lancaster, Ma., U.S.	87a	42.28N	71.40W
Lancaster, N.H., U.S.	92	44.25N	71.30W
Lancaster, N.Y., U.S.	95c	42.54N	78.42W
Lancaster, Oh., U.S.	92	39.40N	82.35W
Lancaster, Pa., U.S.	90	40.05N	76.20W
Lancaster, Tx., U.S.	101c	32.36N	96.45W
Lancaster, Wi., U.S.	96	42.51N	90.44W
Lândana, Ang. (län-dä'nä)	206	5.15S	12.07E
Landau, Ger. (län'dou)	148	49.13N	8.07E
Lander, Wy., U.S. (lăn'dēr)	98	42.49N	108.24W
Landerneau, Fr. (län-dĕr-nō')	150	48.28N	4.14W
Landes, reg., Fr. (länd)	150	44.22N	0.52W
Landover, Md., U.S.	225d	38.56N	76.54W
Landsberg, Ger. (länds'bōōrgh)	148	48.03N	10.53E
Lands End, c., Eng., U.K.	136	50.03N	5.45W
Landshut, Ger. (länts'hōōt)	140	48.32N	12.09E
Landskrona, Swe. (làns-krō'nà)	146	55.51N	12.47E
Lane Cove, Austl.	239a	33.49S	151.10E
Lanett, Al., U.S. (là-nĕt')	108	32.52N	85.13W
Langadhás, Grc.	154	40.44N	23.10E
Langat, r., Malay.	173b	2.46N	101.33E
Langdon, Can. (lăng'dŭn)	77e	50.58N	113.40W
Langdon, Mn., U.S.	101g	44.49N	92.56W
Langdon Hills, Eng., U.K.	231	51.34N	0.25E
L'Ange-Gardien, Can. (länzh gàr-dyăn')	77b	46.55N	71.06W
Langeland, i., Den.	146	54.52N	10.46E
Langenberg, Ger.	232	51.21N	7.09E
Langenbochum, Ger.	232	51.37N	7.07E
Langendreer, neigh., Ger.	232	51.28N	7.19E
Langenhorst, Ger.	232	51.22N	7.02E
Langenzersdorf, Aus.	139e	48.30N	16.22E
Langesund, Nor. (läng'ĕ-sōn')	146	58.59N	9.38E
Langfjorden, fj., Nor.	146	62.40N	7.45E
Langhorne, Pa., U.S. (lăng'hôrn)	94f	40.10N	74.55W
Langhorne Acres, Md., U.S.	225d	38.51N	77.16W
Langia Mountains, mts., Ug.	210	3.35N	33.35E
Langjökoll, ice., Ice. (läng-yû'kōōl)	140	64.40N	20.31W
Langla Co, l., China (läŋ-lä tswo)	178	30.42N	80.40E
Langley, Can. (lăng'lĭ)	80	49.06N	122.39W
Langley, Md., U.S.	225d	38.57N	77.10W
Langley, S.C., U.S.	108	33.32N	81.52W
Langley, Wa., U.S.	100a	48.02N	122.25W
Langley Indian Reserve, I.R., Can.	100d	49.12N	122.31W
Langley Park, Md., U.S.	225d	38.59N	76.59W
Langnau, Switz. (läng'nou)	148	46.56N	7.46E
Langon, Fr. (län-gôn')	150	44.34N	0.16W
Langres, Fr. (län'gr')	150	47.53N	5.20E
Langres, Plateau de, plat., Fr. (plä-tō'dĕ-län'grĕ)	150	47.39N	5.00E
Langsa, Indon. (läng'sà)	188	4.33N	97.52E
Lang Son, Viet. (läng'sŏn')	188	21.52N	106.42E
Langst-Kierst, Ger.	232	51.18N	6.43E
L'Anguille, r., Ar., U.S. (län-gē'y')	104	35.23N	90.52W
Langxi, China (läŋ-shyē)	182	31.10N	119.09E
Langzhong, China (läŋ-jōŋ)	180	31.40N	106.05E
Lanham, Md., U.S. (lăn'ăm)	94e	38.58N	76.54W
Lanigan, Can. (lăn'ĭ-găn)	78	51.52N	105.02W
Lank-Latum, Ger.	232	51.18N	6.41E
Lankoviri, Nig.	208	9.00N	11.25E
Lankwitz, neigh., Ger.	234a	52.26N	13.21E
Lansdale, Pa., U.S. (lănz'dāl)	92	40.20N	75.15W
Lansdowne, Austl.	239a	33.54S	150.59E
Lansdowne, Md., U.S.	225c	39.15N	76.40W
Lansdowne, Pa., U.S.	94f	39.57N	75.17W
L'Anse, Mi., U.S. (làns)	96	46.43N	88.28W
L'Anse and Vieux Desert Indian Reservation, I.R., Mi., U.S.	96	46.41N	88.12W
Lansford, Pa., U.S. (lănz'fērd)	92	40.50N	75.50W
Lansing, Il., U.S.	95a	41.34N	87.33W
Lansing, Ia., U.S.	96	43.22N	91.16W
Lansing, Ks., U.S.	101f	39.15N	94.53W
Lansing, Mi., U.S.	90	42.45N	84.35W
Lansing, neigh., Can.	223c	43.45N	79.25W
Lantianchang, China	236b	39.58N	116.17E
Lanús, Arg. (lä-nōōs')	126a	34.42S	58.24W
Lanusei, Italy (lä-nōō-sĕ'y)	154	39.51N	9.34E
Lanúvio, Italy (lä-nōō'vyô)	153d	41.41N	12.42E
Lanzarote Island, i., Spain (län-zà-rō'tā)	204	29.04N	13.03W
Lanzhou, China (län-jō)	180	35.55N	103.55E
Laoag, Phil. (lä-wäg')	188	18.13N	120.38E
Laohumiao, China	236b	39.58N	116.20E
Laon, Fr. (län)	150	49.36N	3.35E
La Oroya, Peru (lä-ô-rō'yä)	124	11.30S	76.00W
Laos, nation, Asia (lä-ōs) (là-ōs')	188	20.15N	102.00E
Laoshan Wan, b., China (lou-shän wän)	182	36.21N	120.48E
Lapa, neigh., Braz.	230c	22.55S	43.11W
La Palma, Pan. (lä-päl'mä)	114	8.25N	78.07W
La Palma, Spain	152	37.24N	6.36W
La Palma Island, i., Spain	204	28.42N	19.03W
La Pampa, prov., Arg.	126	37.25S	67.00W
Lapa Rio Negro, Braz. (lä-pä-rē'ō-nĕ'grô)	126	26.12S	49.56W
La Paternal, neigh., Arg.	229d	34.36S	58.28W
La Paz, Arg. (lä päz')	126	30.48S	59.47W
La Paz, Bol.	124	16.31S	68.03W
La Paz, Hond.	114	14.15N	87.40W
La Paz, Mex.	110	24.00N	110.15W
La Paz, Mex. (lä-pá'z)	112	23.39N	100.44W
Lapeer, Mi., U.S. (là-pēr')	92	43.05N	83.15W
La-Penne-sur-Huveaune, Fr. (la-pĕn'sür-ü-vōn')	150a	43.18N	5.33E
La Perouse, Austl.	195b	33.59S	151.14E
La Piedad Cabadas, Mex. (lä pyā-dhädh' kä-bä'dhäs)	112	20.20N	102.04W
Lapland, hist. reg., Eur. (lăp'lănd)	136	68.20N	22.00E
La Plata, Arg. (lä plä'tä)	126	34.54S	57.57W
La Plata, Mo., U.S. (là plà'tà)	104	40.03N	92.28W
La Plata Peak, mtn., Co., U.S.	102	39.00N	106.25W
La Playa, Cuba	229b	23.06N	82.27W
La Pocatière, Can. (là pô-kà-tyâr')	84	47.24N	70.01W
La Poile Bay, b., Can. (là pwäl')	86	47.38N	58.20W
La Porte, In., U.S. (là pōrt')	92	41.35N	86.45W
Laporte, Oh., U.S.	95d	41.19N	82.05W
La Porte, Tx., U.S.	107a	29.40N	95.01W
La Porte City, Ia., U.S.	96	42.20N	92.10W
Lappeenranta, Fin. (lä'pēn-rän'tä)	146	61.04N	28.08E
La Prairie, Can. (là-prâ-rē')	77a	45.24N	73.30W
Lâpseki, Tur. (läp'sà-kē)	154	40.20N	26.41E
Laptev Sea, sea, Russia (läp'tyĭf)	158	75.39N	120.00E
La Puebla, Spain (lä pwā'blä)	152	39.46N	3.02E
La Puebla de Montalbán, Spain	152	39.54N	4.21W
La Puente, Ca., U.S. (pwĕn'tē)	101a	34.01N	117.57W
La Punta, Peru	229c	12.05S	77.10W
Lapuşul, r., Rom. (lä'pōō-shōōl)	148	47.29N	23.46E
La Queue-en-Brie, Fr.	233c	48.47N	2.35E
La Quiaca, Arg. (lä kē-ä'kä)	126	22.15S	65.44W
L'Aquila, Italy (là'kē-lä)	142	42.22N	13.24E
Lār, Iran (lär)	174	27.31N	54.12E
Lara, Austl.	195a	38.02S	144.24E
Larache, Mor. (lä-räsh')	204	35.15N	6.09W
Laramie, Wy., U.S. (lăr'à-mĭ)	90	41.20N	105.40W
Laramie, r., Co., U.S.	104	40.56N	105.55W
Laranjeiras, neigh., Braz.	230c	22.56S	43.11W
Larchmont, N.Y., U.S. (lärch'mŏnt)	94a	40.56N	73.46W
Larch Mountain, mtn., Or., U.S. (lärch)	100c	45.32N	122.06W
Laredo, Spain (lä-rā'dhō)	152	43.24N	3.24W
Laredo, Tx., U.S.	90	27.31N	99.29W
La Reina, Chile	230b	33.27S	70.33W
La Réole, Fr. (là rà-ōl')	150	44.37N	0.03W
Largeau, Chad (lär-zhō')	204	17.55N	19.07E
Largo, Cayo, Cuba (kä'yō-lär'gō)	116	21.40N	81.30W
Larimore, N.D., U.S. (lăr'ĭ-môr)	96	47.53N	97.38W
Larino, Italy (lä-rē'nō)	154	41.48N	14.54E
La Rioja, Arg. (lä rē-ōhä)	126	29.18S	67.42W
La Rioja, prov., Arg. (lä-rē-ô'kä)	126	28.45S	68.00W
Lárisa, Grc. (lä'rē-sà)	142	39.38N	22.25E
Lārkāna, Pak.	178	27.40N	68.12E
Larkspur, Ca., U.S.	227b	37.56N	122.32W
Larnaca, Cyp.	142	34.55N	33.37E
Lárnakos, Kólpos, b., Cyp.	173a	36.50N	33.45E
Larned, Ks., U.S. (lär'nĕd)	104	38.09N	99.07W
La Robla, Spain (lä rōb'lä)	152	42.48N	5.36W
La Rochelle, Fr. (là rô-shĕl')	136	46.10N	1.09W
La Roche-sur-Yon, Fr. (là rôsh'sûr-yôn')	140	46.39N	1.27W
La Roda, Spain (lä rō'dä)	152	39.13N	2.08W
La Romona, Dom. Rep. (lä-rä-mô'nä)	116	18.25N	69.00W
Larrey Point, c., Austl. (lăr'ē)	196	19.15S	118.15E
Laruns, Fr. (là-räns')	150	42.58N	0.28W
Larvik, Nor. (lär'vĕk)	140	59.06N	10.03E
La Sabana, Ven. (lä-sä-bà'nä)	125b	10.38N	66.24W
La Sabina, Cuba (lä-sä-bē'nä)	117a	22.51N	82.05W
La Sagra, mtn., Spain (lä sä'grä)	142	37.56N	2.35W
La Sal, Ut., U.S. (là sàl')	102	38.10N	109.20W
La Salle, Can.	77a	45.26N	73.39W
La Salle, Can.	77f	49.41N	97.16W
La Salle, Can. (là sàl')	95b	42.14N	83.06W
La Salle, Il., U.S.	92	41.20N	89.05W
Las Animas, Co., U.S. (làs ă'nĭ-măs)	104	38.03N	103.16W
La Sarre, Can.	78	48.43N	79.12W
Lascahobas, Haiti (läs-kä-ō'bàs)	116	19.00N	71.55W
Las Cruces, Mex. (läs-krōō'sĕs)	112	16.37N	93.54W
Las Cruces, N.M., U.S.	90	32.20N	106.50W
La Selle, Massif de, mtn., Haiti (lä'sĕl')	116	18.25N	72.05W
La Serena, Chile (lä-sĕ-rĕ'nä)	126	29.55S	71.24W
La Seyne, Fr. (lä-sân')	140	43.07N	5.52E
Las Flores, Arg. (läs flo'rĕs)	126	36.01S	59.07W
Las Flores, Ven.	230a	10.34N	66.56W

ăt; finăl; rāte; senâte; ärm; àsk; sofà; fâre; ch-choose; dh-as th in other; bē; ēvent; bĕt; recĕnt; cratẽr; g-gō; gh-guttural g; bĭt; ĭ-short neutral; rīde; ĸ-guttural k as ch in German ich;

PLACE (Pronunciation)	PAGE	Lat. °′	Long. °′
Lashio, Burma (lăsh′ē-ō)	180	22.58N	98.03E
Las Juntas, C.R. (läs-kōō′n-täs)	114	10.15N	85.00W
Las Maismas, sw., Spain (läs-mī′s-mäs)	152	37.05N	6.25W
Las Minas, Ven.	230a	10.27N	66.52W
La Solana, Spain (lä-sö-lä-nä)	152	38.56N	3.13W
Las Palmas, Pan.	114	8.08N	81.30W
Las Palmas de Gran Canaria, Spain (läs päl′mäs)	204	28.07N	15.28W
La Spezia, Italy (lä-spě′zyä)	136	44.07N	9.48E
Las Piedras, Ur. (läs-pyě′drås)	123c	34.42S	56.08W
Las Pilas, vol., Nic. (läs-pē′läs)	114	12.32N	86.43W
Las Rejas, Chile	230b	33.28S	70.44W
Las Rosas, Mex. (läs rō thäs)	112	16.24N	92.23W
Las Rozas de Madrid, Spain (läs rō′thas dā mä-dhrēd′)	153a	40.29N	3.53W
Lassee, Aus.	139e	48.14N	16.50E
Lassen Peak, mtn., Ca., U.S. (lăs′ĕn)	90	40.30N	121.32W
Lassen Volcanic National Park, rec., Ca., U.S.	90	40.43N	121.35W
L'Assomption, Can. (lås-sôm-syôN)	77a	45.50N	73.25W
Lass Qoray, Som.	212a	11.13N	48.19E
Las Tablas, Pan. (läs tä′bläs)	114	7.48N	80.16W
Last Mountain, l., Can. (låst moun′tĭn)	78	51.05N	105.10W
Lastoursville, Gabon (lås-tōōr-vēl′)	206	1.00S	12.49E
Las Tres Vírgenes, Volcán, vol., Mex. (vē′r-hĕ-nĕs)	110	26.00N	111.45W
Las Tunas, prov., Cuba	116	21.05N	77.00W
Las Vacas, Mex. (läs-vå′käs)	112	16.24N	95.48W
Las Vegas, Chile (läs-vĕ′gäs)	123b	32.50S	70.59W
Las Vegas, Nv., U.S. (läs vā′gäs)	90	36.12N	115.10W
Las Vegas, N.M., U.S.	90	35.36N	105.13W
Las Vegas, Ven. (läs-vĕ′gäs)	125b	10.26N	64.08W
Las Vigas, Mex.	112	19.38N	97.03W
Las Vizcachas, Meseta de, plat., Arg.	126	49.35S	71.00W
Latacunga, Ec. (lä-tä-köŋ′gä)	124	1.02S	78.33W
Latakia, *see* Al Lādhiqīyah, Syria	174	35.32N	35.51E
La Teste-de-Buch, Fr. (lä-tĕst-dĕ-büsh)	150	44.38N	1.11W
Lathrop, Mo., U.S. (lā′thrŭp)	104	39.32N	94.21W
Latimer, Eng., U.K.	231	51.41N	0.33W
Latoritsa, r., Eur. (lå-tô′rĭ-tså)	148	48.27N	22.30E
La Tortuga, Isla, i., Ven. (ē′s-lä-lä-tôr-tōō′gä)	124	10.55N	65.18W
Latourell, Or., U.S. (lå-tou′rĕl)	100c	45.32N	122.13W
La Tremblade, Fr. (lä-trĕN-bläd′)	150	45.45N	1.12W
Latrobe, Pa., U.S. (lå-trōb′)	92	40.25N	79.15W
Lattingtown, N.Y., U.S.	224	40.54N	73.36W
La Tuque, Can. (lå′tük′)	78	47.27N	72.49W
Lātūr, India (lä-tōōr′)	178	18.20N	76.35E
Latvia, nation, Eur.	158	57.28N	24.29E
Lau Group, is., Fiji	192g	18.20S	178.30W
Launceston, Austl. (lôn′sĕs-tŭn)	196	41.35S	147.22E
Launceston, Eng., U.K. (lôrn′stŏn)	144	50.38N	4.26W
La Unión, Chile (lä-ōō-nyô′n)	126	40.15S	73.04W
La Unión, El Sal.	114	13.18N	87.51W
La Unión, Mex. (lä ōōn-nyōn′)	112	17.59N	101.48W
La Unión, Spain	142	37.38N	0.50W
Laupendahl, Ger.	232	51.21N	6.56E
Laura, Austl. (lôr*á*)	196	15.40S	144.45E
Laurel, De., U.S. (lô′rĕl)	92	38.30N	75.40W
Laurel, Md., U.S.	94e	39.06N	76.51W
Laurel, Ms., U.S.	90	31.42N	89.07W
Laurel, Mt., U.S.	98	45.41N	108.45W
Laurel, Wa., U.S.	100d	48.52N	122.29W
Laurel Gardens, Pa., U.S.	226b	40.31N	80.01W
Laurel Hollow, N.Y., U.S.	224	40.52N	73.28W
Laurelwood, Or., U.S. (lô′rĕl-wöd)	100c	45.25N	123.05W
Laurens, S.C., U.S. (lô′rĕnz)	108	34.29N	82.03W
Laurentian Highlands, hills, Can. (lô′rĕn-tĭ-ån)	76	49.00N	74.50W
Laurentides, Can. (lô′rĕn-tīdz)	77a	45.51N	73.46W
Lauria, Italy (lou′rē-ä)	142	40.03N	15.02E
Laurinburg, N.C., U.S. (lô′rĭn-bûrg)	108	34.45N	79.27W
Laurium, Mi., U.S. (lô′rĭ-ŭm)	96	47.13N	88.28W
Lausanne, Switz. (lō-zån′)	136	46.32N	6.35E
Laut, Pulau, i., Indon.	188	3.39S	116.07E
Lautaro, Chile (lou-tä′rō)	126	38.40S	72.24W
Laut Kecil, Kepulauan, is., Indon.	188	4.44S	115.43E
Lautoka, Fiji	192g	17.37S	177.27E
Lauzon, Can. (lō-zôN′)	77b	46.50N	71.10W
Lava Beds National Monument, rec., Ca., U.S. (lä′v*á* bĕds)	98	41.38N	121.44W
Lavaca, r., Tx., U.S. (lå-våk′*á*)	106	29.05N	96.50W
Lava Hot Springs, Id., U.S.	98	42.37N	111.58W
Laval, Can.	78	45.31N	73.44W
Laval, Fr. (lä-väl′)	140	48.05N	0.47W
Laval-des-Rapides, neigh., Can.	223b	45.33N	73.42W
Laval-Ouest, neigh., Can.	223b	45.33N	73.52W
La Vecilla de Curueno, Spain	152	42.53N	5.18W
La Vega, Dom. Rep. (lä-vĕ′gä)	116	19.15N	70.35W
La Vega, neigh., Ven.	230a	10.28N	66.57W
Lavello, Italy (lä-vĕl′lō)	154	41.05N	15.50E
La Verne, Ca., U.S. (lå vûrn′)	101a	34.06N	117.46W
Laverton, Austl. (lā′vĕr-tŭn)	196	28.45S	122.30E
La Victoria, Peru	229c	12.04S	77.02W
La Victoria, Ven. (lä vēk-tō′rē-ä)	124	10.14N	67.20W
Lavonia, Ga., U.S. (l*á*-vō′nĭ-*á*)	108	34.26N	83.05W
Lavon Reservoir, res., Tx., U.S.	106	33.06N	96.20W
Lavras, Braz. (lä′vräzh)	123a	21.15S	44.59W
Lávrion, Grc. (läv′rĭ-ôn)	154	37.44N	24.05E
Lavry, Russia (lou′rå)	156	57.35N	27.28E
Lawndale, Ca., U.S. (lôn′dāl)	101a	33.54N	118.22W
Lawndale, neigh., Il., U.S.	227a	41.51N	87.43W
Lawndale, neigh., Pa., U.S.	225b	40.03N	75.05W
Lawnside, N.J., U.S.	225b	39.52N	75.03W
Lawra, Ghana	208	10.39N	2.52W

PLACE (Pronunciation)	PAGE	Lat. °′	Long. °′
Lawrence, In., U.S. (lô′rĕns)	95g	39.59N	86.01W
Lawrence, Ks., U.S.	90	38.57N	95.13W
Lawrence, Ma., U.S.	87a	42.42N	71.09W
Lawrence, Pa., U.S.	95e	40.18N	80.07W
Lawrenceburg, In., U.S. (lô′rĕns-bûrg)	95f	39.06N	84.47W
Lawrenceburg, Ky., U.S.	92	38.00N	85.00W
Lawrenceburg, Tn., U.S.	108	35.13N	87.20W
Lawrenceville, Ga., U.S. (lô-rĕns-vĭl)	108	33.56N	83.57W
Lawrenceville, Il., U.S.	92	38.45N	87.45W
Lawrenceville, N.J., U.S.	94a	40.17N	74.44W
Lawrenceville, Va., U.S.	108	36.43N	77.52W
Lawrenceville, neigh., Pa., U.S.	226b	40.28N	79.57W
Lawsonia, Md., U.S. (lô-sō′nĭ-*á*)	92	38.00N	75.50W
Lawton, Ok., U.S. (lô′tŭn)	90	34.36N	98.25W
Lawz, Jabal al, mtn., Sau. Ar.	174	28.46N	35.37E
Layang Layang, Malay. (lä-yäng′ lä-yäng′)	173b	1.49N	103.28E
Laysan, i., Hi., U.S.	88b	26.00N	171.00W
Layton, Ut., U.S. (lā′tŭn)	101b	41.04N	111.58W
Lazdijai, Lith. (läzh′dē-yī′)	146	54.12N	23.35E
Lazio (Latium), hist. reg., Italy	154	42.05N	12.25E
Lead, S.D., U.S. (lēd)	90	44.22N	103.47W
Leader, Can.	82	50.55N	109.32W
Leadville, Co., U.S. (lĕd′vĭl)	104	39.14N	106.18W
Leaf, r., Ms., U.S. (lēf)	108	31.43N	89.20W
League City, Tx., U.S. (lēg)	107a	29.31N	95.05W
Leamington, Can. (lĕm′ĭng-tŭn)	84	42.05N	82.35W
Leamington, Eng., U.K. (lĕ′mĭng-tŭn)	144	52.17N	1.25W
Leatherhead, Eng., U.K. (lĕdh′ēr-hĕd′)	138b	51.17N	0.20W
Leavenworth, Ks., U.S. (lĕv′ĕn-wûrth)	90	39.19N	94.54W
Leavenworth, Wa., U.S.	98	47.35N	120.39W
Leawood, Ks., U.S. (lē′wöd)	101f	38.58N	94.37W
Łeba, Pol. (lā′bä)	148	54.45N	17.34E
Lebam, r., Malay.	173b	1.35N	104.09E
Lebango, Congo	210	0.22N	14.49E
Lebanon, Il., U.S. (lĕb′*á*-nŭn)	101e	38.36N	89.49W
Lebanon, In., U.S.	92	40.00N	86.30W
Lebanon, Ky., U.S.	108	37.32N	85.15W
Lebanon, Mo., U.S.	104	37.40N	92.43W
Lebanon, N.H., U.S.	92	43.40N	72.15W
Lebanon, Oh., U.S.	92	39.25N	84.10W
Lebanon, Or., U.S.	98	44.31N	122.53W
Lebanon, Pa., U.S.	92	40.20N	76.20W
Lebanon, Tn., U.S.	108	36.10N	86.16W
Lebanon, nation, Asia	174	34.00N	34.00E
Lebedin, Ukr. (lyĕ′bĕ-dėn)	156	48.56N	31.35E
Lebedin, Ukr.	160	50.34N	34.27E
Lebedyan', Russia (lyĕ′bĕ-dyän′)	160	53.03N	39.08E
Le Blanc, Fr. (lĕ-blän′)	150	46.38N	0.59E
Le Blanc-Mesnil, Fr.	233c	48.56N	2.28E
Leblon, neigh., Braz.	230c	22.59S	43.13W
Le Borgne, Haiti (lĕ bōrn′y′)	116	19.50N	72.30W
Lębork, Pol. (lăN-börk′)	148	54.33N	17.46E
Le Bourget, Fr.	233c	48.56N	2.26E
Lebrija, Spain (lå-brē′hä)	152	36.55N	6.06W
Lecce, Italy (lĕt′chā)	142	40.22N	18.11E
Lecco, Italy (lĕk′kō)	154	45.52N	9.28E
Lech, r., Ger. (lĕk)	148	47.41N	10.52E
Le Châtelet-en-Brie, Fr. (lĕ-shä-tĕ-lä′ĕN-brē′)	151b	48.29N	2.50E
Leche, Laguna de, l., Cuba (lä-gö′nä-dĕ-lĕ′chĕ)	116	22.10N	78.30W
Leche, Laguna de la, l., Mex.	106	27.16N	102.45W
Lecompte, La., U.S.	106	31.06N	92.25W
Le Creusot, Fr. (lĕkrû-zō)	140	46.48N	4.23E
Ledesma, Spain (lå-dĕs′mä)	152	41.05N	5.59W
Ledsham, Eng., U.K.	233a	53.16N	2.58W
Leduc, Can. (lĕ-dōōk′)	80	53.16N	113.33W
Leech, l., Mn., U.S. (lēch)	96	47.06N	94.16W
Leeds, Eng., U.K.	136	53.48N	1.33W
Leeds, Al., U.S. (lēdz)	94h	33.33N	86.33W
Leeds, N.D., U.S.	96	48.18N	99.24W
Leeds and Liverpool Canal, can., Eng., U.K. (lĭv′ēr-pōōl)	138a	53.36N	2.38W
Leegebruch, Ger. (lĕh′gĕn-brōōk)	139b	52.43N	13.12E
Leek, Eng., U.K. (lēk)	138a	53.06N	2.01W
Lee Manor, Va., U.S.	225d	38.52N	77.15W
Leer, Ger. (lār)	148	53.14N	7.27E
Lees, Eng., U.K.	233b	53.32N	2.04W
Leesburg, Fl., U.S. (lēz′bûrg)	108	28.49N	81.53W
Leesburg, Va., U.S.	92	39.10N	77.30W
Lees Ferry, Az., U.S.	102	36.55N	111.45W
Lees Summit, Mo., U.S.	101f	38.55N	94.23W
Lee Stocking, i., Bah.	116	23.45N	76.05W
Leesville, La., U.S. (lēz′vĭl)	106	31.09N	93.17W
Leetonia, Oh., U.S. (lē-tō′nĭ-*á*)	92	40.50N	80.45W
Leeuwarden, Neth. (lā′wär-dĕn)	140	52.12N	5.50E
Leeuwin, Cape, c., Austl. (lōō′wĭn)	196	34.15S	114.30E
Leeward Islands, is., N.A. (lē′wērd)	106	17.00N	62.15W
Le François, Mart.	115b	14.37N	60.55W
Lefroy, l., Austl. (lē-froi′)	196	31.30S	122.00E
Leganés, Spain (lå-gä′nås)	153a	40.20N	3.46W
Legazpi, Phil. (lå-gäs′pē)	188	13.09N	123.44E
Legge Peak, mtn., Austl. (lĕg)	198	41.33S	148.10E
Leggett, Ca., U.S.	102	39.51N	123.42W
Leghorn, *see* Livorno, Italy	136	43.32N	11.18E
Legnano, Italy (lå-nyä′nō)	154	45.35N	8.53E
Legnica, Pol. (lĕk-nĭt′så)	140	51.13N	16.10E
Leh, India (lā)	178	34.10N	77.40E
Le Havre, Fr. (lĕ åv′r′)	136	49.31N	0.07E
Lehi, Ut., U.S. (lē′hī)	102	40.25N	111.55W
Lehman Caves National Monument, rec., Nv., U.S. (lē′m*ă*n)	102	38.54N	114.08W
Lehnin, Ger. (lĕh′nēn)	139b	52.19N	12.45E
Leião, Port.	234d	38.44N	9.18W

PLACE (Pronunciation)	PAGE	Lat. °′	Long. °′
Leicester, Eng., U.K. (lĕs′tēr)	136	52.37N	1.08W
Leicestershire, co., Eng., U.K.	138a	52.40N	1.12W
Leichhardt, Austl.	239a	33.53S	151.09E
Leichhardt, r., Austl. (līk′härt)	196	18.30S	139.45E
Leiden, Neth. (lī′dĕn)	144	52.09N	4.29E
Leigh Creek, Austl. (lē krēk)	198	30.33S	138.30E
Leikanger, Nor. (lī′käŋ′gēr)	146	61.11N	6.51E
Leimuiden, Neth.	139a	52.13N	4.40E
Leine, r., Ger. (lī′nĕ)	148	51.58N	9.56E
Leinster, hist. reg., Ire. (lĕn-stēr)	144	52.45N	7.19W
Leipsic, Oh., U.S. (līp′sĭk)	92	41.05N	84.00W
Leipzig, Ger. (līp′tsĭk)	136	51.20N	12.24E
Leiria, Port. (lā-rē′ä)	152	39.45N	8.50W
Leitchfield, Ky., U.S. (lēch′fēld)	108	37.28N	86.20W
Leitha, r., Aus.	139e	48.04N	16.57E
Leithe, neigh., Ger.	232	51.29N	7.06E
Leitrim, Can.	77c	45.20N	75.36W
Leizhou Bandao, pen., China (lā-jō bän-dou)	180	20.42N	109.10E
Le Kremlin-Bicêtre, Fr.	233c	48.49N	2.21E
Leksand, Swe. (lĕk′sänd)	146	60.45N	14.56E
Leland, Wa., U.S. (lē′l*ă*nd)	100a	47.54N	122.53W
Leliu, China (lŭ-lĭō)	183a	22.52N	113.09E
Le Locle, Switz. (lĕ lō′kl′)	148	47.03N	6.43E
Le Maire, Estrecho de, strt., Arg. (ĕs-trĕ′chō-dĕ-lĕ-mī′rĕ)	126	55.15S	65.30W
Le Mans, Fr. (lĕ mäN′)	140	48.01N	0.12E
Le Marin, Mart.	115b	14.28N	60.55W
Le Mars, Ia., U.S. (lē märz′)	96	42.46N	96.09W
Lemay, Mo., U.S.	101e	38.32N	90.17W
Lemdiyya, Alg.	204	36.18N	2.40E
Leme, Morro do, mtn., Braz.	230c	22.58S	43.10W
Lemery, Phil. (lā-mā-rē′)	189a	13.51S	120.55E
Le Mesnil-Amelot, Fr.	233c	49.01N	2.36E
Le Mesnil-le-Roi, Fr.	233c	48.56N	2.08E
Lemhi, r., Id., U.S.	98	44.40N	113.27W
Lemhi Range, mts., Id., U.S. (lĕm′hī)	98	44.35N	113.33W
Lemmon, S.D., U.S. (lĕm′ŭn)	96	45.55N	102.10W
Le Môle, Haiti (lĕ mōl′)	116	19.50N	73.20W
Lemon Grove, Ca., U.S. (lĕm′ŭn-grōv)	102a	32.44N	117.02W
Lemon Heights, Ca., U.S.	228	33.46N	117.48W
Le Moule, Guad. (lĕ mōōl′)	115b	16.19N	61.22W
LeMoyne, Can.	223b	45.31N	73.29W
Lempa, r., N.A. (lĕm′pä)	114	13.20N	88.46W
Lemvig, Den. (lĕm′vēgh)	146	56.33N	8.16E
Lena, r., Russia	158	68.00N	123.00E
Lençóes Paulista, Braz. (lĕN-sôNs′ pou-lēs′tå)	126	22.30S	48.45W
Lençóis, Braz. (lĕn-sóis)	124	12.38S	41.28W
Lenexa, Ks., U.S. (lē′nĕx-*ă*)	101f	38.58N	99.44W
Lengyandong, China (lŭŋ-yän-dōŋ)	183a	23.12N	113.21E
Lenik, r., Malay.	173b	1.59N	102.51E
Lenina, Gora, hill, Russia	235b	55.42N	37.31E
Leningrad, prov., Russia	156	59.15N	30.30E
Leningrad, *see* Saint Petersburg, Russia	158	59.57N	30.20E
Leningradskaya, Russia (lyĕ-nĭn-gräd′skå-yå)	156	46.19N	39.23E
Lenino, Russia (lyĕ′nĭ-nô)	164b	55.37N	37.41E
Leninogorsk, Kaz. (lyĕ-nĭn ŭ gôrsk′)	158	50.29N	83.25E
Leninsk, Russia (lyĕ-nēnsk′)	160	48.40N	45.10E
Leninsk-Kuznetski, Russia (lyĕ-nėnsk′kōōz-nyĕt′skĭ)	158	54.28N	86.48E
Lenkoran', Azer. (lĕn-kō-rän′)	158	38.52N	48.58E
Lennox, Ca., U.S.	228	33.56N	118.21W
Lennox, S.D., U.S. (lĕn′ŭks)	96	43.22N	96.53W
Lenoir, N.C., U.S. (lē-nōr′)	108	35.54N	81.35W
Lenoir City, Tn., U.S.	108	35.47N	84.16W
Lenox, Ia., U.S.	96	40.51N	94.29W
Lenz, S. Afr.	240b	26.19S	27.49E
Léo, Burkina	208	11.06N	2.06W
Leoben, Aus. (lå-ō′bĕn)	148	47.22N	15.09E
Léogane, Haiti (lā-ō-gan′)	116	18.30N	72.35W
Leola, S.D., U.S. (lē-ō′l*á*)	96	45.43N	99.55W
Leominster, Ma., U.S. (lĕm′ĭn-stēr)	92	42.32N	71.45W
León, Mex. (lå-ōn′)	110	21.08N	101.41W
León, Nic. (lĕ-ô′n)	110	12.28N	86.53W
León, Spain (lĕ-ô′n)	142	42.38N	5.33W
Leon, Ia., U.S. (lē′ŏn)	96	40.43N	93.44W
Leon, hist. reg., Spain (lĕ-ô′n)	152	41.18N	5.50W
Leon, r., Tx., U.S. (lē′ŏn)	106	31.54N	98.20W
Leonforte, Italy (la-ōn-fōr′tä)	154	37.40N	14.27E
Leonia, N.J., U.S.	224	40.52N	73.59W
Léopold, Mont, Zaire	240c	4.19S	15.15E
Leopoldau, neigh., Aus.	235e	48.16N	16.27E
Leopold II, Lac, *see* Mai-Ndombe, Lac, l., Zaire	206	2.16S	19.00E
Leopoldina, Braz. (lā-ō-pōl-dē′nä)	123a	21.32S	42.38W
Leopoldsburg, Bel.	139a	51.07N	5.18E
Leopoldsdorf im Marchfelde, Aus. (lā′ō-pōlts-dōrf′)	139e	48.14N	16.42E
Leopoldstadt, neigh., Aus.	235e	48.13N	16.23E
Léopoldville, *see* Kinshasa, Zaire	206	4.18S	15.18E
Leovo, Mol. (lå-ō′vō)	156	46.30N	28.16E
Lepe, Spain (lā′pā)	152	37.15N	7.12W
Le Pecq, Fr.	233c	48.54N	2.07E
Lepel', Bela. (lyĕ-pĕl′)	156	54.52N	28.41E
Le Perreux-sur-Marne, Fr.	233c	48.51N	2.30E
Leping, China (lŭ-pĭŋ)	184	29.02N	117.12E
L'Épiphanie, Can. (lā-pē-fä-nē′)	77a	45.51N	73.29W
Le Plessis-Belleville, Fr. (lĕ-plĕ-sē′bĕl-vēl′)	151b	49.05N	2.46E
Le Plessis-Bouchard, Fr.	233c	49.00N	2.14E
Le Plessis-Trévise, Fr.	233c	48.49N	2.34E
Le Port-Marly, Fr.	233c	48.53N	2.06E
Lepreau, Can. (lē-prō′)	86	45.10N	66.28W

ng-sing; ŋ-baŋk; N-nasalized n; nŏd; cŏmmit; ōld; ōbey; ôrder; oi-boil; fōōd; ö-as oo in foot; ou-out; s-soft; sh-dish; th-thin; pūre; ůnite; ûrn; stŭd; circŭs; ü-as in French tu; ′-indeterminate vowel.

PLACE (Pronunciation)	PAGE	Lat. °'	Long. °'
Le Pré-Saint-Gervais, Fr.	233c	48.53N	2.25E
Lepsinsk, Kaz.	158	45.32N	80.47E
Le Puy, Fr. (lē pwē')	140	45.02N	3.54E
Le Raincy, Fr.	233c	48.54N	2.31E
Lercara Friddi, Italy (lĕr-kä'rä)	154	37.47N	13.36E
Lerdo, Mex. (lĕr'dō)	110	25.31N	103.30W
Leribe, Leso.	207c	28.53S	28.02E
Lérida, Spain (lā'rē-dhä)	142	41.38N	0.37E
Lerma, Mex. (lĕr'mä)	112	19.49N	90.34W
Lerma, Mex.	113a	19.17N	99.30W
Lerma, Spain (lĕ'r-mä)	152	42.03N	3.45W
Lerma, r., Mex.	112	20.14N	101.50W
Le Roy, N.Y., U.S. (lē roi')	92	43.00N	78.00W
Lerwick, Scot., U.K. (lĕr'ĭk) (lûr'wĭk)	136	60.08N	1.27W
Léry, Can. (lā-rī')	77a	45.21N	73.49W
Lery, Lake, l., La., U.S. (lĕ'rē)	94d	29.48N	89.45W
Les Andelys, Fr. (lā-zäN-dē-lē')	151b	49.15N	1.25E
Les Cayes, Haiti	116	18.15N	73.45W
Les Cèdres, Can. (lā-sĕdr'')	77a	45.18N	74.03W
Les Clayes-sous-Bois, Fr.	233c	48.49N	1.59E
Les Grésillons, Fr.	233c	48.56N	2.01E
Lesh, Alb. (lĕshĕ) (ä-lā'sē-ō)	154	41.47N	19.40E
Leshan, China (lŭ-shän)	180	29.40N	103.40E
Lésigny, Fr.	233c	48.45N	2.37E
Lésina, Lago di, l., Italy (lā'gō dē lā'zē-nä)	154	41.48N	15.12E
Leskovac, Yugo. (lĕs'kō-váts)	142	43.00N	21.58E
Leslie, S. Afr.	212d	26.23S	28.57E
Leslie, Ar., U.S. (lĕz'lĭ)	104	35.49N	92.32W
Les Lilas, Fr.	233c	48.53N	2.25E
Les Loges-en-Josas, Fr.	233c	48.46N	2.09E
Lesnoj, neigh., Russia	235a	60.00N	30.20E
Lesnoy, Russia (lĕs'noi)	160	66.45N	34.45E
Lesogorsk, Russia (lyĕs'ō-gôrsk)	186	49.28N	141.59E
Lesotho, nation, Afr. (lĕsō'thō)	206	29.45S	28.07E
Lesozavodsk, Russia (lyĕ-sô-zá-vôdsk')	186	45.21N	133.19E
Les Pavillons-sous-Bois, Fr.	233c	48.55N	2.30E
Les Sables-d'Olonne, Fr. (lā sá'bl'dô-lŭn')	140	46.30N	1.47W
Les Saintes Islands, is., Guad. (lā-sănt')	115b	15.50N	61.40W
Lesser Antilles, is.	110	12.15N	65.00W
Lesser Khingan Range, mts., China	180	49.50N	129.26E
Lesser Slave, r., Can.	80	55.15N	114.30W
Lesser Slave Lake, l., Can. (lĕs'ĕr slāv)	78	55.25N	115.30W
Lesser Sunda Islands, is., Indon.	188	9.00S	120.00E
L'Estaque, Fr. (lĕs-täl)	150a	43.22N	5.20E
Lester, Pa., U.S.	225b	39.52N	75.17W
Les Thilliers-en-Vexin, Fr. (lā-tē-yā'ĕN-vĕ-săN')	151b	49.19N	1.36E
Le Sueur, Mn., U.S. (lē sōōr')	96	44.27N	93.53W
Lésvos, i., Grc.	136	39.15N	25.40E
Leszno, Pol. (lĕsh'nô)	140	51.51N	16.35E
L'Étang-la-Ville, Fr.	233c	48.52N	2.05E
Letchmore Heath, Eng., U.K.	231	51.40N	0.20W
Le Teil, Fr. (lē tā'y')	150	44.34N	4.39E
Lethbridge, Austl.	239a	33.44S	150.48E
Lethbridge, Can. (lĕth'brĭj)	78	49.42N	112.50W
Le Thillay, Fr.	233c	49.00N	2.28E
Letichev, Ukr. (lyĕ-tē-chĕf')	156	49.22N	27.29E
Leticia, Col. (lĕ-tē'syä)	124	4.04S	69.57W
Leting, China (lŭ-tĭŋ)	182	39.26N	118.53E
Le Tréport, Fr. (lĕ-trā'pôr')	150	50.03N	1.21E
Leuven, Bel.	144	50.53N	4.42E
Levack, Can.	84	46.38N	81.23W
Levádhia, Grc.	154	38.25N	22.51E
Le Val-d'Albian, Fr.	233c	48.45N	2.11E
Levallois-Perret, Fr. (lē-vál-wä'pĕ-rĕ')	151b	48.53N	2.17E
Levanger, Nor. (lĕ-väng'ĕr)	140	63.42N	11.01E
Levanna, mtn., Eur. (lå-vä'nä)	154	45.25N	7.14E
Levenshulme, neigh., Eng., U.K.	233b	53.27N	2.10W
Leveque, Cape, c., Austl. (lē-vĕk')	196	16.26S	123.08E
Leverkusen, Ger. (lĕ'fĕr-kōō-zĕn)	151c	51.01N	6.59E
Le Vésinet, Fr.	233c	48.54N	2.08E
Levice, Czech. (lā'vĕt-sĕ)	148	48.13N	18.37E
Levico, Italy (lā'vē-kō)	154	46.02N	11.20E
Le Vigan, Fr. (lē vē-gäN')	150	43.59N	3.36E
Lévis, Can. (lā-vē') (lē'vĭs)	78	46.49N	71.11W
Levittown, N.Y., U.S.	224	40.41N	73.31W
Levittown, Pa., U.S. (lĕ'vĭt-toun)	94f	40.08N	74.50W
Levkás, Grc. (lyĕfkäs')	154	38.49N	20.43E
Levkás, i., Grc.	142	38.42N	20.22E
Levoča, Czech. (lā'vō-chá)	148	49.03N	20.38E
Levuka, Fiji	192g	17.41S	178.50E
Lewes, Eng., U.K.	144	50.51N	0.01E
Lewes, De., U.S. (lōō'ĭs)	92	38.45N	75.10W
Lewinsville, Va., U.S.	225d	38.54N	77.12W
Lewinsville Heights, Va., U.S.	225d	38.53N	77.12W
Lewis, r., Wa., U.S.	98	46.05N	122.09W
Lewis, East Fork, r., Wa., U.S.	100c	45.52N	122.40W
Lewis, Island of, i., Scot., U.K. (lōō'ĭs)	144	58.05N	6.07W
Lewisburg, Tn., U.S. (lū'ĭs-bûrg)	108	35.27N	86.47W
Lewisburg, W.V., U.S.	92	37.50N	80.20W
Lewisdale, Md., U.S.	225d	38.58N	76.58W
Lewisham, S. Afr.	240b	26.07S	27.49E
Lewisham, neigh., Eng., U.K.	231	51.27N	0.01E
Lewis Hills, hills, Can.	86	48.48N	58.30W
Lewisporte, Can. (lū'ĭs-pōrt)	86	49.15N	55.04W
Lewis Range, mts., Mt., U.S. (lū'ĭs)	98	48.15N	113.20W
Lewis Smith Lake, res., Al., U.S.	108	34.05N	87.07W
Lewiston, Id., U.S. (lū'ĭs-tŭn)	90	46.24N	116.59W
Lewiston, Me., U.S.	90	44.05N	70.14W
Lewiston, N.Y., U.S.	95c	43.11N	79.02W
Lewiston, Ut., U.S.	98	41.58N	111.51W
Lewistown, Il., U.S. (lū'ĭs-toun)	104	40.23N	90.06W
Lewistown, Mt., U.S.	90	47.05N	109.25W
Lewistown, Pa., U.S.	92	40.35N	77.30W
Lexington, Ky., U.S. (lĕk'sĭng-tŭn)	90	38.05N	84.30W
Lexington, Ma., U.S.	87a	42.27N	71.14W
Lexington, Ms., U.S.	108	33.08N	90.02W
Lexington, Mo., U.S.	104	39.11N	93.52W
Lexington, Ne., U.S.	104	40.46N	99.44W
Lexington, N.C., U.S.	108	35.47N	80.15W
Lexington, Tn., U.S.	108	35.37N	88.24W
Lexington, Va., U.S.	92	37.45N	79.20W
Leybourne, Eng., U.K.	231	51.18N	0.25E
Leyte, i., Phil. (lā'tā)	188	10.35N	125.35E
Leżajsk, Pol. (lĕ'zhä-ĭsk)	148	50.14N	22.25E
Lezha, r., Russia (lĕ-zhä')	156	58.59N	40.27E
L'gov, Russia (lgôf)	156	51.42N	35.15E
Lhasa, China (läs'ä)	180	29.41N	91.12E
L'Hautil, Fr.	233c	49.00N	2.01E
Liangxiangzhen, China (lĭäŋ-shyäŋ-jŭn)	184a	39.43N	116.08E
Lianjiang, China (lĭĕn-jyäŋ)	184	21.38N	110.15E
Lianozovo, Russia (lĭ-a-nô'zô-vô)	164b	55.54N	37.36E
Lianshui, China (lĭĕn-shwā)	182	33.46N	119.15E
Lianyungang, China (lĭĕn-yón-gäŋ)	180	34.35N	119.09E
Liao, r., China	180	43.37N	120.05E
Liaocheng, China (lĭou-chŭŋ)	184	36.27N	115.56E
Liaodong Bandao, pen., China (lĭou-dôŋ bän-dou)	180	39.45N	122.22E
Liaodong Wan, b., China (lĭou-dôŋ wäŋ)	184	40.25N	121.15E
Liaoning, prov., China	180	41.31N	122.11E
Liaoyang, China (lyä'ō-yäng')	180	41.18N	123.10E
Liaoyuan, China (lĭou-yůän)	184	43.00N	124.59E
Liard, r., Can. (lē-är')	78	59.43N	126.42W
Libano, Col. (lē'bä-nō)	124a	4.55N	75.05W
Libby, Mt., U.S. (lĭb'ē)	98	48.27N	115.35W
Libenge, Zaire (lē-bĕŋ'gä)	204	3.39N	18.40E
Liberal, Ks., U.S. (lĭb'ĕr-ăl)	104	37.01N	100.56W
Liberdade, neigh., Braz.	230d	23.35S	46.37W
Liberec, Czech. (lē'bĕr-ĕts)	140	50.45N	15.06E
Liberia, C.R.	114	10.38N	85.28W
Liberia, nation, Afr. (lī-bē'rĭ-ă)	204	6.30N	9.55W
Libertad, Arg.	126a	34.42S	58.42W
Libertad de Orituco, Ven. (lē-bĕr-tä'd-dĕ-ō-rē-tōō'kō)	125b	9.32N	66.24W
Liberty, In., U.S. (lĭb'ĕr-tĭ)	92	39.35N	84.55W
Liberty, Mo., U.S.	101f	39.15N	94.25W
Liberty, Pa., U.S.	226b	40.20N	79.51W
Liberty, S.C., U.S.	108	34.47N	82.41W
Liberty, Tx., U.S.	106	30.03N	94.46W
Liberty, Ut., U.S.	101b	41.20N	111.52W
Liberty Bay, b., Wa., U.S.	100a	47.43N	122.41W
Liberty Lake, l., Md., U.S.	94e	39.25N	76.56W
Liberty Manor, Md., U.S.	225c	39.21N	76.47W
Libertyville, Il., U.S. (lĭb'ĕr-tĭ-vĭl)	95a	42.17N	87.57W
Libode, Transkei (lĭ-bō'dĕ)	207c	31.33S	29.03E
Libón, r., N.A.	116	19.30N	71.45W
Libourne, Fr. (lē-bōōrn')	140	44.55N	0.12W
Library, Pa., U.S.	226b	40.18N	80.02W
Libres, Mex. (lē'brās)	112	19.26N	97.41W
Libreville, Gabon (lē-br'vēl')	206	0.23N	9.27E
Liburn, Ga., U.S. (lĭb'ûrn)	94c	33.53N	84.09W
Libya, nation, Afr. (lĭb'ē-ä)	204	27.38N	15.00E
Libyan Desert, des., Afr. (lĭb'ē-ăn)	204	28.23N	23.34E
Libyan Plateau, plat., Afr.	176	30.58N	26.20E
Licancábur, Cerro, mtn., S.A. (sĕ'r-rô-lē-kán-ká'bōōr)	126	22.45S	67.45W
Licanten, Chile (lē-kän-tĕ'n)	123b	34.58S	72.00W
Lichfield, Eng., U.K. (lĭch'fēld)	138a	52.41N	1.49W
Lichinga, Moz.	210	13.18S	35.14E
Lichtenberg, neigh., Ger.	234a	52.31N	13.29E
Lichtenburg, S. Afr. (lĭk'tĕn-bĕrgh)	212d	26.09S	26.10E
Lichtendorf, Ger.	232	51.28N	7.37E
Lichtenplatz, neigh., Ger.	232	51.15N	7.12E
Lichtenrade, neigh., Ger.	234a	52.23N	13.25E
Lichterfelde, neigh., Ger.	234a	52.26N	13.19E
Lick Creek, r., In., U.S. (lĭk)	95g	39.43N	86.06W
Licking, r., Ky., U.S. (lĭk'ĭng)	92	38.30N	84.10W
Lida, Bela. (lē'dá)	148	53.53N	25.19E
Lidcombe, Austl.	239a	33.52S	151.03E
Lidgerwood, N.D., U.S. (lĭj'ĕr-wood)	96	46.04N	97.10W
Lidköping, Swe. (lēt'chû-pĭng)	146	58.31N	13.06E
Lido Beach, N.Y., U.S.	224	40.35N	73.38W
Lido di Roma, Italy (lē'dô-dē-rô'mä)	153d	41.19N	12.17E
Lidzbark, Pol. (lĭts'bärk)	148	54.07N	20.36E
Liebenbergsvlei, r., S. Afr.	212d	27.35S	28.25E
Liebenwalde, Ger. (lē'bĕn-väl-dĕ)	139b	52.52N	13.24E
Liechtenstein, nation, Eur. (lēk'tĕn-shtīn)	140	47.10N	10.00E
Liège, Bel.	140	50.38N	5.34E
Lienz, Aus. (lē-ĕnts')	148	46.49N	12.45E
Liepāja, Lat. (le'pä-yä')	160	56.31N	20.59E
Lier, Bel.	139a	51.08N	4.34E
Lierenfeld, neigh., Ger.	232	51.13N	6.51E
Liesing, Aus. (lē'sĭng)	139e	48.09N	16.17E
Liestal, Switz. (lēs'täl)	148	47.28N	7.44E
Lifanga, Zaire	210	0.19N	21.57E
Lifou, i., N. Cal.	196	21.15S	167.32E
Ligao, Phil. (lē-gä'ō)	189a	13.14N	123.33E
Lightning Ridge, Austl.	198	29.23S	147.50E
Ligonha, r., Moz. (lē-gō'nyă)	206	16.14S	39.00E
Ligonier, In., U.S. (lĭg-ô-nēr)	92	41.30N	85.35W
Ligovo, Russia (lē'gô-vô)	164c	59.51N	30.13E
Liguria, hist. reg., Italy (lē-gōō-rē-ä)	154	44.24N	8.27E
Ligurian Sea, sea, Eur. (lĭ-gū'rĭ-ăn)	142	43.42N	8.32E
Lihou Reefs, rf., Austl. (lē-hōō')	196	17.23S	152.43E
Lihuang, China (lē'hōōäng)	182	31.32N	115.46E
Lihue, Hi., U.S. (lē-hōō'ā)	90c	21.59N	159.23W
Lihula, Est. (lē'hò-lá)	146	58.41N	23.50E
Liji, China (lē-jyē)	182	33.47N	117.47E
Lijiang, China (lē-jyäŋ)	180	27.00N	100.08E
Lijin, China (lē-jyĭn)	184	37.30N	118.15E
Likasi, Zaire	206	10.59S	26.44E
Likhoslavl', Russia (lyē-kôsläv''l)	156	57.07N	35.27E
Likhovka, Ukr. (lyē-kôf'ká)	156	48.52N	33.57E
Likouala, r., Congo	210	0.10S	16.30E
Lille, Fr. (lēl)	136	50.38N	3.01E
Lille Baelt, strt., Den.	146	55.09N	9.53E
Lillehammer, Nor. (lēl'ĕ-häm'mĕr)	140	61.07N	10.25E
Lillesand, Nor. (lēl'ĕ-sän')	146	58.16N	8.19E
Lilleström, Nor. (lēl'ĕ-strûm)	146	59.56N	11.04E
Lilliwaup, Wa., U.S. (lĭl'ĭ-wŏp)	100a	47.28N	123.07W
Lillooet, Can. (lĭ'lōō-ĕt)	78	50.30N	121.55W
Lillooet, r., Can.	80	49.50N	122.10W
Lilongwe, Mwi. (lē-lō-än)	206	13.59S	33.44E
Liluāh, India	236a	22.37N	88.20E
Lilydale, Austl.	239b	37.45S	145.21E
Lilyfield, Austl.	239a	33.52S	151.10E
Lima, Peru (lē'mä)	124	12.06S	76.55W
Lima, Swe.	146	60.54N	13.24E
Lima, Oh., U.S. (lī'mă)	90	40.40N	84.05W
Lima, r., Eur.	152	41.45N	8.22W
Lima Duarte, Braz. (dwä'r-tĕ)	123a	21.52S	43.47W
Limão, neigh., Braz.	230d	23.30S	46.40W
Lima Reservoir, res., Mt., U.S.	98	44.45N	112.15W
Limassol, Cyp.	142	34.39N	33.02E
Limay, r., Arg. (lē-mä'ē)	126	39.50S	69.15W
Limbazi, Lat. (lēm'bä-zĭ)	146	57.32N	24.44E
Limbdi, India	178	22.37N	71.52E
Limburg an der Lahn, Ger. (lem-bòrg')	148	50.22N	8.03E
Limefield, Eng., U.K.	233b	53.37N	2.18W
Limeira, Braz. (lē-mā'rä)	123a	22.34S	47.24W
Limerick, Ire. (lĭm'nák)	140	52.39N	8.35W
Limestone Bay, b., Can. (līm'stōn)	82	53.50N	98.50W
Limfjorden, Den.	140	56.55N	8.56E
Limmen Bight, bt., Austl. (lĭm'ĕn)	196	14.45S	136.00E
Limni, Grc. (lēm'nē)	154	38.47N	23.22E
Limnos, i., Grc.	142	39.58N	24.48E
Limoges, Can. (lē-môzh')	77c	45.20N	75.15W
Límoges, Fr.	140	45.50N	1.15E
Limón, C.R. (lē-mōn')	110	10.01N	83.02W
Limón, Hond. (lē-mô'n)	114	15.53N	85.34W
Limon, Co., U.S. (lī'mŏn)	104	39.15N	103.41W
Limon, r., Dom. Rep.	116	18.20N	71.40W
Limón, Bahía, b., Pan.	110a	9.21N	79.58W
Limours, Fr. (lē-mōōr')	151b	48.39N	2.05E
Limousin, Plateaux du, plat., Fr. (plä-tō' dü lē-mōō-zăN')	150	45.44N	1.09E
Limoux, Fr. (lē-mōō')	150	43.03N	2.14E
Limpopo, r., Afr. (lĭm-pō'pō)	206	23.15S	27.46E
Linares, Chile (lē-nä'rās)	126	35.51S	71.35W
Linares, Mex.	110	24.53N	99.34W
Linares, Spain (lē-nä'rĕs)	142	38.07N	3.38W
Linares, prov., Chile	123b	35.53S	71.30W
Linaro, Cape, c., Italy (lē-nä'rä)	154	42.02N	11.53E
Lince, Peru	229c	12.05S	77.03W
Linchuan, China (lĭn-chůän)	180	27.58N	116.18E
Lincoln, Arg. (lĭŋ'kŭn)	126	34.51S	61.29W
Lincoln, Can.	77d	43.10N	79.29W
Lincoln, Eng., U.K.	140	53.14N	0.33W
Lincoln, Ca., U.S.	102	38.51N	121.19W
Lincoln, Il., U.S.	104	40.09N	89.21W
Lincoln, Ks., U.S.	104	39.02N	98.08W
Lincoln, Me., U.S.	86	45.23N	68.31W
Lincoln, Ma., U.S.	87a	42.25N	71.19W
Lincoln, Ne., U.S.	90	40.49N	96.43W
Lincoln, Pa., U.S.	226b	40.18N	79.51W
Lincoln, Mount, mtn., Co., U.S.	104	39.20N	106.19W
Lincoln Center, pt. of i., N.Y., U.S.	224	40.46N	73.59W
Lincoln Heath, reg., Eng., U.K.	138a	53.23N	0.39W
Lincolnia Heights, Va., U.S.	225d	38.50N	77.09W
Lincoln Park, Mi., U.S.	95b	42.14N	83.11W
Lincoln Park, N.J., U.S.	94a	40.56N	74.18W
Lincoln Park, pt. of i., Il., U.S.	227a	41.56N	87.38W
Lincoln Place, neigh., Pa., U.S.	226b	40.22N	79.55W
Lincolnshire, co., Eng., U.K.	138a	53.12N	0.29W
Lincolnshire Wolds, Eng., U.K. (woldz')	144	53.25N	0.23W
Lincolnton, N.C., U.S. (lĭŋ'kŭn-tŭn)	108	35.27N	81.15W
Lincolnwood, Il., U.S.	227a	42.00N	87.46W
Linda-a-Velha, Port.	234d	38.43N	9.14W
Lindale, Ga., U.S. (lĭn'dāl)	108	34.10N	85.10W
Lindau, Ger. (lĭn'dou)	148	47.33N	9.40E
Linden, Al., U.S. (lĭn'dĕn)	108	32.16N	87.47W
Linden, Ma., U.S.	223a	42.26N	71.02W
Linden, Mo., U.S.	101f	39.13N	94.35W
Linden, N.J., U.S.	94a	40.39N	74.14W
Linden, neigh., S. Afr.	240b	26.08S	28.00E
Lindenberg, Ger.	234a	52.36N	13.31E
Linden-Dahlhausen, neigh., Ger.	232	51.26N	7.09E
Lindenhorst, neigh., Ger.	232	51.33N	7.27E
Lindenhurst, N.Y., U.S. (lĭn'dĕn-hûrst)	94a	40.41N	73.23W
Lindenwold, N.J., U.S. (lĭn'dĕn-wôld)	94f	39.50N	75.00W
Linderhausen, Ger.	232	51.18N	7.17E
Lindesberg, Swe. (lĭn'dĕs-bĕrgh)	146	59.37N	15.14E
Lindesnes, c., Nor. (lĭn'ĕs-nĕs)	136	58.00N	7.05E
Lindfield, Austl.	239a	33.47S	151.10E
Lindi, Tan. (lĭn'dē)	206	10.00S	39.43E
Lindi, r., Zaire	204	1.00N	27.13E
Lindian, China (lĭn-dĭĕn)	184	47.08N	124.59E
Lindley, S. Afr. (lĭnd'lē)	212d	27.52S	27.55E
Lindow, Ger. (lēn'dōv)	139b	52.58N	12.59E
Lindsay, Can. (lĭn'zē)	84	44.20N	78.45W
Lindsay, Ok., U.S.	104	34.50N	97.38W
Lindsborg, Ks., U.S. (lĭnz'bôrg)	104	38.34N	97.42W
Lineville, Al., U.S. (līn'vīl)	108	33.18N	85.45W

ăt; finăl; rāte; senāte; ärm; åsk; sofă; fåre; ch-choose; dh-as th in other; bē; ēvent; bĕt; recĕnt; cratĕr; g-gō; gh-guttural g; bĭt; ĭ-short neutral; rīde; ĸ-guttural k as ch in German ich;

PLACE (Pronunciation)	PAGE	Lat. °′	Long. °′
Linfen, China	180	36.00N	111.38E
Linga, Kepulauan, is., Indon.	188	0.35S	105.05E
Lingao, China (lĭn-gou)	184	19.58N	109.40E
Lingayen, Phil. (lĭŋ′gä-yän′)	188	16.01N	120.13E
Lingayen Gulf, b., Phil.	189a	16.18N	120.11E
Lingdianzhen, China	182	31.52N	121.28E
Lingen, Ger. (lĭŋ′gĕn)	148	52.32N	7.20E
Lingling, China (lĭŋ-lĭŋ)	184	26.10N	111.40E
Lingshou, China (lĭŋ-shō)	182	38.21N	114.41E
Linguère, Sen. (lĭŋ-gĕr′)	204	15.24N	15.07W
Lingwu, China	184	38.05N	106.18E
Lingyuan, China (lĭŋ-yůän)	184	41.12N	119.20E
Linhai, China	184	28.52N	121.08E
Linhe, China (lĭn-hŭ)	184	40.49N	107.45E
Linhuaiguan, China (lĭn-hwī-gůän)	182	32.55N	117.38E
Linhuanji, China	182	33.42N	116.33E
Linjiang, China (lĭn-jyäŋ)	184	41.45N	127.00E
Linköping, Swe. (lĭn′chû-pĭng)	140	58.25N	15.35E
Linksfield, neigh., S. Afr.	240b	26.10S	28.06E
Linmeyer, S. Afr.	240b	26.16S	28.04E
Linn, neigh., Ger.	232	51.20N	6.38E
Linnhe, Loch, b., Scot., U.K. (lĭn′ė)	144	56.35N	4.30W
Linqing, China (lĭn-chyĭŋ)	180	36.49N	115.42E
Linqu, China (lĭn-chyo͞o)	182	36.31N	118.33E
Lins, Braz. (lė′ɴs)	124	21.42S	49.41W
Linthicum Heights, Md., U.S. (lĭn′thĭ-kŭm)	94e	39.12N	76.39W
Linton, In., U.S. (lĭn′tŭn)	92	39.05N	87.15W
Linton, N.D., U.S.	96	46.16N	100.15W
Lintorf, Ger.	232	51.20N	6.49E
Linwu, China (lĭn′wo͞o′)	184	25.20N	112.30E
Linxi, China (lĭn-shyē)	184	43.30N	118.02E
Linyi, China (lĭn-yē)	180	35.04N	118.21E
Linying, China (lĭn′yĭng′)	182	33.48N	113.56E
Linz, Aus. (lĭnts)	140	48.18N	14.18E
Linzhang, China (lĭn-jäŋ)	182	36.19N	114.40E
Lion, Golfe du, b., Fin.	136	43.00N	4.00E
Lipa, Phil. (lė-pä′)	188	13.55N	121.10E
Lipari, Italy (lē′pä-rė)	154	38.29N	15.00E
Lipari, i., Italy	154	38.32N	15.04E
Lipetsk, Russia (lyē′pĕtsk)	158	52.26N	39.34E
Lipetsk, prov., Russia	156	52.18N	38.30E
Liping, China (lē-pĭŋ)	180	26.18N	109.00E
Lipno, Pol. (lēp′nô)	148	52.50N	19.12E
Lippe, r., Ger. (lĭp′ĕ)	151b	51.36N	6.45E
Lippolthausen, neigh., Ger.	232	51.37N	7.29E
Lippstadt, Ger. (lĭp′shtät)	148	51.39N	8.20E
Lipscomb, Al., U.S. (lĭp′skŭm)	94h	33.26N	86.56W
Liptsy, Ukr. (lyēp′tsė)	156	50.11N	36.25E
Lipu, China (lē-po͞o)	184	24.38N	110.35E
Lira, Ug.	210	2.15N	32.54E
Liri, r., Italy (lē′rē)	154	41.49N	13.30E
Liria, Spain (lė′ryä)	152	39.35N	0.34W
Lisala, Zaire (lė-sä′lä)	204	2.09N	21.31E
Lisboa, *see* Lisbon, Port.	136	38.42N	9.05W
Lisbon (Lisboa), Port.	136	38.42N	9.05W
Lisbon, N.D., U.S.	96	46.21N	97.43W
Lisbon, Oh., U.S.	92	40.45NC.50	W
Lisbon Falls, Me., U.S.	86	43.59N	70.03W
Lisburn, N. Ire., U.K. (lĭs′bŭrn)	144	54.35N	6.05W
Lisburne, Cape, c., Ak., U.S.	90a	68.20N	165.40W
Lishi, China (lē-shr)	184	37.32N	111.12E
Lishu, China	184	43.12N	124.18E
Lishui, China	180	28.28N	120.00E
Lishui, China (lĭ′shwĭ′)	182	31.41N	119.01E
Lisianski Island, i., Hi., U.S.	88b	25.30N	174.00W
Lisieux, Fr. (lē-zyû′)	150	49.10N	0.13E
Lisiy Nos, Russia (lĭ′sĭy-nôs)	164c	60.01N	30.00E
Liski, Russia (lyēs′kė)	156	50.56N	39.28E
Lisle, Il., U.S. (līl)	95a	41.48N	88.04W
L'Isle-Adam, Fr. (lēl-ädäɴ′)	151b	49.05N	2.13E
Lismore, Austl. (lĭz′môr)	196	28.48S	153.18E
Litani, r., Leb.	173a	33.28N	35.42E
Litchfield, Il., U.S. (lĭch′fēld)	104	39.10N	89.38W
Litchfield, Mn., U.S.	96	45.08N	94.34W
Litchfield, Oh., U.S.	95d	41.10N	82.01W
Litherland, Eng., U.K.	233a	53.28N	2.59W
Lithgow, Austl. (lĭth′gō)	196	33.23S	149.31E
Lithinon, Akra, c., Grc.	154a	34.59N	24.35E
Lithonia, Ga., U.S. (lĭ-thō′nĭ-*ȧ*)	94c	33.43N	84.07W
Lithuania, nation, Eur. (lĭth-ů-ā-′nĭ-*ȧ*)	158	55.42N	23.30E
Litin, Ukr. (lė-tēn)	156	49.16N	28.11E
Litókhoron, Grc. (lē′tô-ᴋō′rôn)	154	40.05N	22.29E
Litoko, Zaire	210	1.13S	24.47E
Litoměřice, Czech. (lē′tô-myĕr′zhĭ-tsĕ)	148	50.33N	14.10E
Litomyšl, Czech. (lē′tô-mėsh′l)	148	49.52N	16.14E
Litoo, Tan.	210	9.45S	38.24E
Little, r., Austl.	195a	37.54S	144.27E
Little, r., Tn., U.S.	108	36.28N	89.39W
Little, r., Tx., U.S.	106	30.48N	96.50W
Little Abaco, i., Bah. (ä′bä-kō)	116	26.55N	77.45W
Little Abitibi, r., Can.	84	50.15N	81.30W
Little America, sci., Ant.	213	78.30S	161.30W
Little Andaman, i., India (ăn-d*ȧ*-măn′)	188	10.39N	93.08E
Little Bahama Bank, bk. (b*ȧ*-hä′m*ȧ*)	116	26.55N	78.40W
Little Belt Mountains, mts., Mt., U.S. (bĕlt)	90	47.00N	110.50W
Little Berkhamsted, Eng., U.K.	231	51.45N	0.08W
Little Bighorn, r., Mt., U.S. (bĭg-hôrn)	98	45.08N	107.30W
Little Bitter Lake, l., Egypt	212b	30.10N	32.36E
Little Bitterroot, r., Mt., U.S. (bĭt′ẽr-o͞ot)	98	47.45N	114.45W
Little Blue, r., Ia., U.S. (blo͞o)	101f	38.52N	94.25W
Little Blue, r., Ne., U.S.	104	40.15N	98.01W
Littleborough, Eng., U.K. (lĭt′′l-bŭr-ô)	138a	53.39N	2.06W
Little Burstead, Eng., U.K.	231	51.36N	0.24E
Little Calumet, r., Il., U.S. (kăl-ů-mĕt′)	95a	41.38N	87.38W
Little Cayman, i., Cay. Is. (kā′m*ȧ*n)	116	19.40N	80.05W
Little Chalfont, Eng., U.K.	231	51.40N	0.34W
Little Colorado, r., Az., U.S. (kŏl-ô-rä′dō)	90	36.05N	111.35W
Little Compton, R.I., U.S. (kŏmp′t*ŏ*n)	94b	41.31N	71.07W
Little Corn Island, i., Nic.	114	12.19N	82.50W
Little End, Eng., U.K.	231	51.41N	0.14E
Little Exuma, i., Bah. (ĕk-so͞o′mä)	116	23.25N	75.40W
Little Falls, Mn., U.S. (fôlz)	96	45.58N	94.23W
Little Falls, N.J., U.S.	224	40.53N	74.14W
Little Falls, N.Y., U.S.	92	43.05N	74.55W
Little Ferry, N.J., U.S.	224	40.51N	74.03W
Littlefield, Tx., U.S. (lĭt′′l-fēld)	104	33.55N	102.17W
Little Fork, r., Mn., U.S. (fôrk)	96	48.24N	93.30W
Little Goose Dam, dam, Wa., U.S.	98	46.35N	118.02W
Little Hans Lollick, i., V.I.U.S. (häns lôl′lĭk)	111c	18.25N	64.54W
Little Hulton, Eng., U.K.	233b	53.32N	2.25W
Little Humboldt, r., Nv., U.S. (hŭm′bōlt)	98	41.10N	117.40W
Little Inagua, i., Bah. (ė-nä′gwä)	116	21.30N	73.00W
Little Isaac, i., Bah. (ī′z*ȧ*k)	116	25.55N	79.00W
Little Kanawha, r., W.V., U.S. (k*ȧ*-nô′w*ȧ*)	92	39.05N	81.30W
Little Karroo, plat., S. Afr. (kä-ro͞o)	206	33.50S	21.02E
Little Lever, Eng., U.K.	233b	53.34N	2.22W
Little Mecatina, r., Can. (mĕ c*ȧ* tī nå)	78	52.40N	62.21W
Little Miami, r., Oh., U.S. (mī-ăm′ĭ)	95f	39.19N	84.15W
Little Minch, strt., Scot., U.K.	144	57.35N	6.45W
Little Missouri, r., U.S.	90	46.00N	104.00W
Little Missouri, r., Ar., U.S. (mĭ-so͞o′rĭ)	104	34.15N	93.54W
Little Nahant, Ma., U.S.	223a	42.25N	70.56W
Little Neck, neigh., N.Y., U.S.	224	40.46N	73.44W
Little Pee Dee, r., S.C., U.S. (pē-dē′)	108	34.35N	79.21W
Little Powder, r., Wy., U.S. (pou′dẽr)	98	44.51N	105.20W
Little Red, r., Ar., U.S. (rĕd)	104	35.25N	91.55W
Little Red, r., Ok., U.S.	104	33.53N	94.38W
Little Rock, Ar., U.S. (rôk)	90	34.42N	92.16W
Little Sachigo Lake, l., Can. (să′chĭ-gō)	82	54.09N	92.11W
Little Salt Lake, l., Ut., U.S.	102	37.55N	112.53W
Little San Salvador, i., Bah. (săn săl′vȧ-dôr)	116	24.35N	75.55W
Little Satilla, r., Ga., U.S. (sȧ-tĭl′*ȧ*)	108	31.43N	82.47W
Little Sioux, r., Ia., U.S. (so͞o)	96	42.22N	95.47W
Little Smoky, r., Can. (smōk′ĭ)	80	55.10N	116.55W
Little Snake, r., Co., U.S. (snāk)	98	40.40N	108.21W
Little Stanney, Eng., U.K.	233a	53.15N	2.53W
Little Sutton, Eng., U.K.	233a	53.17N	2.57W
Little Tallapoosa, r., Al., U.S. (tăl-ȧ-pô′să)	108	32.25N	85.28W
Little Tennessee, r., Tn., U.S. (tĕn-*ĕ*-sē′)	108	35.36N	84.05W
Little Thurrock, Eng., U.K.	231	51.28N	0.21E
Littleton, Eng., U.K.	231	51.24N	0.28W
Littleton, Co., U.S. (lĭt′′l-tŭn)	104	39.34N	105.01W
Littleton, Ma., U.S.	87a	42.32N	71.29W
Littleton, N.H., U.S.	92	44.15N	71.45W
Little Wabash, r., Il., U.S. (wô′băsh)	92	38.50N	88.30W
Little Warley, Eng., U.K.	231	51.35N	0.19E
Little Wood, r., Id., U.S. (wŏŏd)	98	43.00N	114.08W
Liuhe, China	184	42.10N	125.38E
Liuli, Tan.	210	11.05S	34.38E
Liulicun, China	236b	39.56N	116.28E
Liupan Shan, mts., China	184	36.20N	105.30E
Liuwa Plain, pl., Zam.	210	14.30S	22.40E
Liuyang, China (lyo͞o′yäng′)	184	28.10N	113.35E
Liuyuan, China (lĭô-yůän)	182	36.09N	114.37E
Liuzhou, China (lĭô-jō)	180	24.25N	109.30E
Līvāni, Lat. (lē′vȧ-nė)	146	56.24N	26.12E
Lively, Can.	84	46.26N	81.09W
Livengood, Ak., U.S. (lĭv′*ĕ*n-gŏŏd)	89	65.30N	148.35W
Live Oak, Fl., U.S. (lĭv′ōk)	108	30.15N	83.00W
Livermore, Ca., U.S. (lĭv′ẽr-mōr)	100b	37.41N	121.46W
Livermore, Ky., U.S.	92	37.30N	87.05W
Liverpool, Austl. (lĭv′ẽr-po͞ol)	195b	33.55S	150.56E
Liverpool, Can.	78	44.02N	64.41W
Liverpool, Eng., U.K.	136	53.25N	2.52W
Liverpool, Tx., U.S.	107a	29.18N	95.17W
Liverpool Bay, b., Can.	89	69.45N	130.00W
Liverpool Range, mts., Austl.	196	31.47S	151.00E
Livindo, r., Afr.	204	1.09N	13.30E
Livingston, Guat.	114	15.50N	88.45W
Livingston, Al., U.S. (lĭv′ĭng-stŭn)	108	32.35N	88.09W
Livingston, Il., U.S.	101e	38.58N	89.51W
Livingston, Mt., U.S.	90	45.40N	110.35W
Livingston, N.J., U.S.	94a	40.47N	74.20W
Livingston, Tn., U.S.	108	36.23N	85.20W
Livingstone, Zam. (lĭv-ĭng-stôn)	206	17.50S	25.53E
Livingstone, Chutes de, wtfl., Afr.	210	4.50S	14.30E
Livingstonia, Mwi. (lĭv-ĭng-stō′nĭ-*ȧ*)	206	10.36S	34.07E
Livno, Bos. (lēv′nô)	142	43.50N	17.03E
Livny, Russia (lēv′nė)	160	52.28N	37.36E
Livonia, Mi., U.S. (lĭ-vō-nĭ-*ȧ*)	95b	42.25N	83.23W
Livorno, Italy (lė-vôr′nō) (lĕg′hôrn)	136	43.32N	11.18E
Livramento, Braz. (lē-vrȧ-mĕ′n-tô)	126	30.46S	55.21W
Livry-Gargan, Fr.	233c	48.56N	2.33E
Lixian, China	182	38.30N	115.38E
Lixian, China (lē shyĕn)	184	29.42N	111.40E
Liyang, China (lē′yäng′)	184	31.30N	119.29E
Lizard Point, c., Eng., U.K. (lĭz′*ȧ*rd)	140	49.55N	5.09W
Lizy-sur-Ourcq, Fr. (lēk-sē′sür-o͞ork′)	151b	49.01N	3.02E
Ljubljana, Slo. (lyo͞o′blyä′na)	136	46.04N	14.29E
Ljubuški, Bos. (lyo͞o′bôsh-kė)	154	43.11N	17.29E
Ljungan, r., Swe.	146	62.50N	13.45E
Ljungby, Swe. (lyông′bü)	146	56.49N	13.56E
Ljusdal, Swe. (lyo͞os′däl)	146	61.50N	16.11E
Ljusnan, r., Swe.	140	61.55N	15.33E
Llandudno, Wales, U.K. (lăn-dŭd′nō)	144	53.20N	3.46W
Llanelli, Wales, U.K. (lȧ-nĕl′ĭ)	140	51.44N	4.09W
Llanes, Spain (lyä′nås)	142	43.25N	4.41W
Llano, Tx., U.S. (lă′nō) (lyä′nō)	106	30.45N	98.41W
Llano, r., Tx., U.S.	106	30.38N	99.04W
Llanos, reg., S.A. (lyȧ′nŏs)	124	4.00N	71.15W
Llera, Mex. (lyā′rä)	112	23.16N	99.03W
Llerena, Spain (lyā-rā′nä)	152	38.14N	6.02W
Llobregat, r., Spain (lyô-brĕ-gät′)	152	41.55N	1.55E
Lloyd Lake, l., Can. (loid)	77e	50.52N	114.13W
Lloydminster, Can.	78	53.17N	110.00W
Lluchmayor, Spain (lyo͞och-mä-yôr′)	152	39.28N	2.53E
Llullaillaco, Volcán, vol., S.A. (lyo͞o-lyī-lyä′kō)	126	24.50S	68.30W
Loange, r., Afr. (lô-äŋ′gä)	206	5.00S	20.15E
Lo Aranguiz, Chile	230b	33.23S	70.40W
Lobatse, Bots. (lō-bä′tsē)	206	25.13S	25.35E
Lobau, reg., Aus.	235e	48.10N	16.32E
Lobería, Arg. (lô-bĕ′rē′ä)	126	38.13S	58.48W
Lobito, Ang. (lô-bē′tō)	206	12.30S	13.34E
Lobnya, Russia (lôb′nyȧ)	164b	56.01N	37.29E
Lobo, Phil.	189a	13.39N	121.14E
Lobos, Arg. (lō′bôs)	123c	35.10S	59.08W
Lobos, Cayo, i., Bah. (lō′bôs)	116	22.25N	77.40W
Lobos, Isla de, i., Mex. (ė′s-lä-dĕ-lô′bōs)	112	21.24N	97.11W
Lobos de Tierra, i., Peru (lô′bō-dĕ-tyĕ′r-rä)	124	6.29S	80.55W
Lobva, Russia (lôb′vȧ)	164a	59.12N	60.28E
Lobva, r., Russia	164a	59.14N	60.17E
Locarno, Switz. (lô-kär′nō)	148	46.10N	8.43E
Lochearn, Md., U.S.	225c	39.21N	76.43W
Loches, Fr. (lôsh)	150	47.08N	0.56E
Loch Raven Reservoir, res., Md., U.S.	94e	39.28N	76.38W
Lockeport, Can.	86	43.42N	65.07W
Lockhart, S.C., U.S. (lŏk′hårt)	108	34.47N	81.30W
Lockhart, Tx., U.S.	106	29.54N	97.40W
Lock Haven, Pa., U.S. (lŏk′hā-v*ĕ*n)	92	41.05N	77.30W
Lockland, Oh., U.S. (lŏk′lănd)	95f	39.14N	84.27W
Lockport, Il., U.S.	95a	41.35N	88.04W
Lockport, N.Y., U.S.	92	43.11N	78.43W
Lockwillow, S. Afr.	240b	26.17S	27.50E
Loc Ninh, Viet. (lōk′nĭng′)	188	12.00N	106.30E
Locust Grove, N.Y., U.S.	224	40.48N	73.30W
Locust Valley, N.Y., U.S.	224	40.53N	73.36W
Lod, Isr. (lôd)	173a	31.57N	34.55E
Lodève, Fr. (lô-dĕv′)	150	43.43N	3.18E
Lodeynoye Pole, Russia (lô-dĕy-nô′yĕ)	160	60.43N	33.24E
Lodge Creek, r., N.A. (lŏj)	98	49.20N	110.20W
Lodge Creek, r., Mt., U.S.	98	48.51N	109.30W
Lodgepole Creek, r., Wy., U.S. (lŏj′pōl)	96	41.22N	104.48W
Lodhran, Pak.	178	29.40N	71.39E
Lodi, Italy (lô′dē)	154	45.18N	9.30E
Lodi, Ca., U.S. (lō′dī)	102	38.07N	121.17W
Lodi, N.J., U.S.	224	40.53N	74.05W
Lodi, Oh., U.S. (lō′dī)	95d	41.02N	82.01W
Lodosa, Spain (lô-dô′sä)	152	42.27N	2.04W
Lodwar, Kenya	210	3.07N	35.36E
Łódź, Pol.	136	51.46N	19.30E
Loeches, Spain (lô-āch′ĕs)	153a	40.22N	3.25W
Loffa, r., Afr.	208	7.10N	10.35W
Lofoten, is., Nor. (lô′fō-t*ĕ*n)	136	68.26N	13.42E
Logan, Oh., U.S. (lō′g*ȧ*n)	92	39.35N	82.25W
Logan, Ut., U.S.	90	41.46N	111.51W
Logan, W.V., U.S.	92	37.50N	82.00W
Logan, Mount, mtn., Can.	78	60.54N	140.33W
Logansport, In., U.S. (lō′g*ă*nz-pōrt)	90	40.45N	86.25W
Logan Square, neigh., Il., U.S.	227a	41.56N	87.42W
Lognes, Fr.	233c	48.50N	2.38E
Logone, r., Afr. (lō-gō′nä) (lô-gôn′)	204	10.20N	15.30E
Logroño, Spain (lô-grō′nyō)	142	42.28N	2.25W
Logrosán, Spain (lô-grô-sän′)	152	39.22N	5.29W
Løgstør, Den. (lügh-stûr′)	146	56.56N	9.15E
Lohausen, neigh., Ger.	232	51.16N	6.44E
Lohberg, Ger.	232	51.35N	6.46E
Lo Hermida, Chile	230b	33.29S	70.33W
Lohheide, Ger.	232	51.30N	6.40E
Löhme, Ger.	234a	52.37N	13.40E
Lohmühle, Ger.	232	51.31N	6.40E
Löhnen, Ger.	232	51.36N	6.39E
Loir, r., Fr. (lwår)	150	47.40N	0.07E
Loire, r., Fr.	136	47.30N	2.00E
Loja, Ec. (lō′hä)	124	3.49S	79.13W
Loja, Spain (lô′-kä)	152	37.10N	4.11W
Loka, Zaire	210	0.20N	17.57E
Lokala Drift, Bots. (lô′kä-l*ȧ* drĭft)	212d	24.00S	26.38E
Lokandu, Zaire	210	2.31S	25.47E
Lokhvitsa, Ukr. (lôᴋ-vėt′sȧ)	160	50.21N	33.16E
Lokichar, Kenya	210	2.23N	35.39E
Lokitaung, Kenya	210	4.16N	35.45E
Lokofa-Bokolongo, Zaire	210	0.12N	19.22E
Lokoja, Nig. (lô-kō′yä)	204	7.47N	6.45E
Lokolama, Zaire	210	2.34S	19.53E
Lokosso, Burkina	208	10.19N	3.40W
Lol, r., Sudan (lōl)	204	9.06N	28.09E
Loliondo, Tan.	210	2.03S	35.37E
Lolland, i., Den. (lôl′än′)	146	54.41N	11.00E
Lolo, Mt., U.S.	98	46.45N	114.05W
Lom, Bul. (lōm)	142	43.48N	23.15E
Loma Linda, Ca., U.S. (lō′m*ȧ* lĭn′d*ȧ*)	101a	34.04N	117.16W
Lomami, r., Zaire	206	0.50S	24.40E
Lomas Chapultepec, neigh., Mex.	229a	19.26N	99.13W
Lomas de Zamora, Arg. (lō′mäs dā zä-mō′rä)	123c	34.46S	58.24W
Lombard, Il., U.S. (lŏm-bärd)	95a	41.53N	88.01W

ng-sing; ŋ-baŋk; ɴ-nasalized n; nŏd; cŏmmit; ōld; ôbey; ôrder; oi-boil; fo͞od; ŏŏ-as oo in foot; ou-out; s-soft; sh-dish; th-thin; pūre; ůnite; ûrn; stŭd; circ*ŭ*s; ü-as in French tu; ′-indeterminate vowel.

PLACE (Pronunciation)	PAGE	Lat. °′	Long. °′
Lombardia, hist. reg., Italy (lòm-bär-dē'ä)	154	45.20N	9.30E
Lombardy, S. Afr.	240b	26.07S	28.08E
Lomblen, Pulau, i., Indon. (lŏm-blĕn')	188	8.08S	123.45E
Lombok, i., Indon. (lŏm-bŏk')	188	9.15S	116.15E
Lomé, Togo	204	6.08N	1.13E
Lomela, Zaire (lô-mā'lä)	206	2.19S	23.33E
Lomela, r., Zaire	206	0.35S	21.20E
Lometa, Tx., U.S. (lô-mē'tȧ)	106	31.10N	98.25W
Lomié, Cam. (lô-mē-ā')	208	3.10N	13.37E
Lomita, Ca., U.S. (lō-mē'tȧ)	101a	33.48N	118.20W
Lommel, Bel.	139a	51.14N	5.21E
Lommond, Loch, l., Scot., U.K. (lŏk lō'mŭnd)	144	56.15N	4.40W
Lomonosov, Russia (lô-mô'nô-sof)	164c	59.54N	29.47E
Lompoc, Ca., U.S. (lŏm-pōk')	102	34.39N	120.30W
Łomża, Pol. (lôm'zhȧ)	148	53.11N	22.04E
Lonaconing, Md., U.S. (lō-nȧ-kō'nĭng)	92	39.35N	78.55W
London, Can. (lŭn'dŭn)	78	43.00N	81.20W
London, Eng., U.K.	136	51.30N	0.07W
London, Ky., U.S.	108	37.07N	84.06W
London, Oh., U.S.	92	39.50N	83.30W
London (Heathrow) Airport, arpt., Eng., U.K.	231	51.27N	0.28W
London Colney, Eng., U.K.	231	51.43N	0.18W
Londonderry, Can. (lŭn'dŭn-dĕr-ĭ)	86	45.29N	63.36W
Londonderry, N. Ire., U.K.	140	55.00N	7.19W
Londonderry, Cape, c., Austl.	196	13.30S	127.00E
London Zoo, pt. of i., Eng., U.K.	231	51.32N	0.09W
Londrina, Braz. (lôn-drē'nä)	124	21.53S	51.17W
Lonely, i., Can. (lōn'lĭ)	78	45.35N	81.30W
Lone Pine, Ca., U.S.	102	36.36N	118.03W
Lone Star, Nic.	114	13.58N	84.25W
Long, i., Bah.	110	23.25N	75.10W
Long, i., Can.	86	44.21S	66.25W
Long, l., N.D., U.S.	96	46.47N	100.14W
Long, l., Wa., U.S.	100a	47.29N	122.36W
Longa, r., Ang. (lôŋ'gȧ)	206	10.20S	15.15E
Long Bay, b., S.C., U.S.	108	33.30N	78.54W
Long Beach, Ca., U.S. (lông bēch)	90	33.46N	118.12W
Long Beach, N.Y., U.S.	94a	40.35N	73.38W
Long Branch, N.J., U.S. (lông brȧnch)	94a	40.18N	73.59W
Long Ditton, Eng., U.K.	231	51.23N	0.20W
Longdon, N.D., U.S. (lông'-dŭn)	96	48.45N	98.23W
Long Eaton, Eng., U.K. (ē'tŭn)	138a	52.54N	1.16W
Longfield, Eng., U.K.	231	51.24N	0.18E
Longford, Ire. (lŏng'fērd)	144	53.43N	7.40W
Longgu, China (lôŋ-gōō)	182	34.52N	116.48E
Longhorn, Tx., U.S. (lông-hôrn)	101d	29.33N	98.23W
Longhua, China	237a	31.09N	121.26E
Longido, Tan.	210	2.44S	36.41E
Long Island, i., Pap. N. Gui.	188	5.10S	147.30E
Long Island, i., Ak., U.S.	80	54.54N	132.45W
Long Island, i., N.Y., U.S. (lông)	90	40.50N	72.50W
Long Island City, neigh., N.Y., U.S.	224	40.45N	73.56W
Long Island Sound, strt., U.S. (lông ī'lănd)	90	41.05N	72.45W
Longjumeau, Fr. (lôN-zhü-mō')	151b	48.42N	2.17E
Longkou, China (lôŋ-kō)	182	37.39N	120.21E
Longlac, Can. (lông'lăk)	78	49.41N	86.28W
Longlake, S.D., U.S. (lông-lāk)	96	45.52N	99.06W
Long Lake, l., Can.	84	49.10N	86.45W
Longmont, Co., U.S. (lông'mŏnt)	104	40.11N	105.07W
Longnor, Eng., U.K. (lông'nôr)	138a	53.11N	1.52W
Long Pine, Ne., U.S. (lông pīn)	96	42.31N	99.42W
Long Point, Austl.	239a	34.01S	150.54E
Long Point, c., Can.	82	53.02N	98.40W
Long Point, c., Can.	84	42.35N	80.05W
Long Point, c., Can.	86	48.48N	58.46W
Long Point Bay, b., Can.	84	42.40N	80.10W
Long Range Mountains, mts., Can.	79a	48.00N	58.30W
Longreach, Austl. (lông'rēch)	196	23.32S	144.17E
Long Reach, r., Can.	86	45.26N	66.05W
Long Reef, c., Austl.	195b	33.45S	151.22E
Longridge, Eng., U.K. (lông'rĭj)	138a	53.51N	2.37W
Longs Peak, mtn., Co., U.S. (lôngz)	90	40.17N	105.37W
Longtansi, China (lôŋ-tä-sz)	182	32.12N	115.53E
Longton, Eng., U.K. (lông'tŭn)	138a	52.59N	2.08W
Longueuil, Can. (lôN-gû'y')	84	45.32N	73.30W
Longueville, Austl.	239a	33.50S	151.10E
Longview, Tx., U.S.	106	32.29N	94.44W
Longview, Wa., U.S. (lông-vū)	98	46.06N	123.02W
Longville, La., U.S. (lông'vĭl)	106	30.36N	93.14W
Longwy, Fr. (lôN-wē')	150	49.32N	6.14E
Longxi, China (lôŋ-shyē)	180	35.00N	104.40E
Long Xuyen, Viet. (loung' sōō'yĕn)	188	10.31N	105.28E
Longzhou, China (lôŋ-jō)	180	22.20N	107.02E
Lonoke, Ar., U.S. (lō'nōk)	104	34.48N	91.52W
Lons-le-Saunier, Fr. (lôN-lē-sō-nyā')	150	46.40N	5.33E
Lontue, r., Chile (lōn-tōĕ')	123b	35.20S	70.45W
Looc, Phil. (lō-ōk')	189a	12.16N	121.59E
Loogootee, In., U.S.	92	38.40N	86.55W
Lookout, Cape, c., N.C., U.S. (lòk'out)	108	34.34N	76.38W
Lookout Point Lake, res., Or., U.S.	98	43.51N	122.38W
Loolmalasin, mtn., Tan.	210	3.03S	35.46E
Looma, Can. (ō'mä)	77g	53.22N	113.15W
Loop, neigh., Il., U.S.	227a	41.53N	87.38W
Loop Head, c., Ire. (lōōp)	144	52.32N	9.59W
Loosahatchie, r., Tn., U.S. (lōz-ȧ-hă'chē)	108	35.20N	89.45W
Loosdrechtsche Plassen, l., Neth.	139a	52.11N	5.09E
Lopatka, Mys, c., Russia (lō-pät'kȧ)	172	51.00N	156.52E
Lopez, Cap, c., Gabon	210	0.37N	8.43E
Lopez Bay, b., Phil. (lō'pāz)	189a	14.04N	122.00E
Lopez I, Wa., U.S.	100a	48.25N	122.53W
Lopori, r., Zaire (lō-pō'rē)	204	1.35N	20.43E

PLACE (Pronunciation)	PAGE	Lat. °′	Long. °′
Lo Prado Arriba, Chile	230b	33.26S	70.45W
Lora, Spain (lō'rä)	152	37.40N	5.31W
Lorain, Oh., U.S. (lō-rān')	95d	41.28N	82.10W
Loralai, Pak. (lō-rŭ-lī')	174	30.31N	68.35E
Lorca, Spain (lôr'kä)	142	37.39N	1.40W
Lord Howe, i., Austl. (lôrd hou)	196	31.44S	157.56W
Lordsburg, N.M., U.S. (lôrdz'bûrg)	102	32.20N	108.45W
Lorena, Braz. (lō-rā'nȧ)	123a	22.45S	45.07W
Loreto, Braz. (lō-rā'tō)	124	7.09S	45.10W
Loretteville, Can. (lō-rĕt-vĕl')	77b	46.51N	71.21W
Lorica, Col. (lō-rē'kä)	124	9.14N	75.54W
Lorient, Fr. (lō-rē'äN')	140	47.45N	3.22W
Lorn, Firth of, b., Scot., U.K. (fûrth ŏv lôrn')	144	56.10N	6.09W
Lörrach, Ger. (lûr'äκ)	148	47.36N	7.38E
Los Alamitos, Ca., U.S. (lōs ăl-ȧ-mē'tōs)	101a	33.48N	118.04W
Los Alamos, N.M., U.S. (ăl-ȧ-mōs')	102	35.53N	106.20W
Los Altos, Ca., U.S. (ăl-tôs')	100b	37.23N	122.06W
Los Andes, Chile (ăn'dēs)	123b	32.44S	70.36W
Los Angeles, Chile (äŋ'hȧ-lās)	126	37.27S	72.15W
Los Angeles, Ca., U.S.	102	34.03N	118.14W
Los Angeles, r., Ca., U.S.	101a	33.50N	118.13W
Los Angeles Aqueduct, Ca., U.S.	102	35.12N	118.02W
Los Angeles International Airport, arpt., Ca., U.S.	228	33.56N	118.24W
Los Bronces, Chile (lōs brō'n-sĕs)	123b	33.09S	70.18W
Loscha, r., Id., U.S. (lōs'chȧ)	98	46.20N	115.11W
Los Cuatro Álamos, Chile	230b	33.32S	70.44W
Los Dos Caminos, Ven.	230a	10.31N	66.50W
Los Estados, Isla de, i., Arg. (ē's-lä dē lōs ĕs-dōs)	126	54.45S	64.25W
Los Gatos, Ca., U.S. (gă'tōs)	102	37.13N	121.59W
Los Herreras, Mex. (ĕr-rā-räs)	106	25.55N	99.23W
Los llanos, Dom. Rep. (lōs ē-lă'nōs)	116	18.35N	69.30W
Los Indios, Cayos de, is., Cuba (kä'yōs dĕ lōs ē'n-dyō's)	116	21.50N	83.10W
Lošinj, i., Yugo.	154	44.35N	14.34E
Losino Petrovskiy, Russia	164b	55.52N	38.12E
Los Nietos, Ca., U.S. (nyā'tōs)	101a	33.57N	118.05W
Los Palacios, Cuba	116	22.35N	83.15W
Los Pinos, r., Co., U.S. (pē'nōs)	102	36.58N	107.35W
Los Reyes, Mex.	110	19.35N	102.29W
Los Reyes, Mex.	113a	19.21N	98.58W
Los Santos, Pan. (săn'tōs)	114	7.57N	80.24W
Los Santos de Maimona, Spain (săn'tōs)	152	38.38N	6.30W
Lost, r., Or., U.S.	98	42.07N	121.30W
Los Teques, Ven. (tĕ'kĕs)	124	10.22N	67.04W
Lost River Range, mts., Id., U.S. (rĭ'vēr)	98	44.23N	113.48W
Los Vilos, Chile (vē'lōs)	126	31.56S	71.29W
Lot, r., Fr. (lôt)	140	44.30N	1.30E
Lota, Chile (lō'tä)	126	37.11S	73.14W
Lothian, Md., U.S. (lōth'ĭăn)	94e	38.50N	76.38W
Lotikipi Plain, pl., Afr.	210	4.25N	34.55E
Lötschberg Tunnel, trans., Switz.	148	46.26N	7.54E
Louangphrabang, Laos (lōō-ang'prä-bäng')	188	19.47N	102.15E
Loudon, Tn., U.S. (lou'dŭn)	108	35.43N	84.20W
Loudonville, Oh., U.S. (lou'dŭn-vĭl)	92	40.40N	82.15W
Loudun, Fr.	150	47.03N	0.00
Loughborough, Eng., U.K. (lŭf'bŭr-ō)	138a	52.46N	1.12W
Loughton, Eng., U.K.	231	51.39N	0.03E
Louisa, Ky., U.S. (lōō'ēz-ȧ)	92	38.05N	82.40W
Louisade Archipelago, is., Pap. N. Gui.	196	10.44S	153.58E
Louisberg, N.C., U.S. (lōō'ĭs-bûrg)	108	36.05N	79.19W
Louisburg, Can. (lōō'ĭs-bourg)	86	45.55N	59.58W
Louiseville, Can.	84	46.17N	72.58W
Louisiana, Mo., U.S. (lōō-ē-zē-ăn'ȧ)	104	39.24N	91.03W
Louisiana, state, U.S.	90	30.50N	92.50W
Louis Trichardt, S. Afr. (lōō'ĭs trĭchărt)	206	22.52S	29.53E
Louisville, Co., U.S. (lōō'ĭs-vĭl) (lōō'ē-vĭl)	104	39.58N	105.08W
Louisville, Ga., U.S.	108	33.00N	82.25W
Louisville, Ky., U.S.	90	38.15N	85.45W
Louisville, Ms., U.S.	108	33.07N	89.02W
Louis XIV, Pointe, c., Can.	78	54.35N	79.51W
Louny, Czech. (lō'nē)	148	50.20N	13.47E
Loup, r., Ne., U.S. (lōōp)	96	41.17N	97.58W
Loup City, Ne., U.S.	96	41.15N	98.59W
Lourdes, Fr. (lōōrd)	140	43.06N	0.03W
Lourenço Marques, see Maputo, Moz.	206	26.50S	32.30E
Loures, Port. (lō'rĕzh)	153b	38.49N	9.10W
Lousa, Port. (lō'zȧ)	152	40.05N	8.12W
Louth, Eng., U.K. (louth)	144	53.27N	0.02W
Louvain, see Leuven, Bel.	144	50.53N	4.42E
Louveciennes, Fr.	233c	48.52N	2.07E
Louviers, Fr. (lōō-vyā')	150	49.13N	1.11E
Louvre, bldg., Fr.	233c	48.52N	2.20E
Lovech, Bul. (lō'vĕts)	154	43.10N	24.40E
Lovedale, Pa., U.S.	226b	40.17N	79.52W
Loveland, Co., U.S. (lŭv'lănd)	104	40.24N	105.04W
Loveland, Oh., U.S.	95f	39.16N	84.15W
Lovell, Wy., U.S. (lŭv'ĕl)	98	44.50N	108.23W
Lovelock, Nv., U.S. (lŭv'lŏk)	102	40.10N	118.37W
Loves Green, Eng., U.K.	231	51.43N	0.24E
Lovick, Al., U.S. (lŭ'vĭk)	94h	33.34N	86.38W
Loviisa, Fin. (lō'vē-sȧ)	146	60.28N	26.10E
Low, Cape, c., Can. (lō)	78	62.58N	86.50W
Lowa, r., Zaire (lō'wȧ)	206	1.30S	27.18E
Lowell, In., U.S.	95a	41.17N	87.26W
Lowell, Ma., U.S.	90	42.38N	71.18W
Lowell, Mi., U.S.	92	42.55N	85.20W
Löwenberg, Ger. (lû'vĕn-bĕrgh)	139b	52.53N	13.09E
Lower Broughton, neigh., Eng., U.K.	233b	53.29N	2.15W
Lower Brule Indian Reservation, I.R., S.D., U.S. (brü'lā)	96	44.15N	100.21W
Lower Granite Dam, dam, Wa., U.S.	98	46.40N	117.26W

PLACE (Pronunciation)	PAGE	Lat. °′	Long. °′
Lower Higham, Eng., U.K.	231	51.26N	0.28E
Lower Hutt, N.Z. (hŭt)	197a	41.10S	174.55E
Lower Klamath Lake, l., Ca., U.S. (klăm'ȧth)	98	41.55N	121.50W
Lower Lake, l., Ca., U.S.	98	41.21N	119.53W
Lower Marlboro, Md., U.S. (lō'ēr märl'bōrō)	94e	38.40N	76.42W
Lower Monumental Dam, dam, Wa., U.S.	98	46.34N	118.32W
Lower Nazeing, Eng., U.K.	231	51.44N	0.01E
Lower New York Bay, b., N.Y., U.S.	224	40.33N	74.02W
Lower Otay Lake, res., Ca., U.S. (ō'tā)	102a	32.37N	116.46W
Lower Place, Eng., U.K.	233b	53.36N	2.09W
Lower Red Lake, l., Mn., U.S.	96	47.58N	94.31W
Lowestoft, Eng., U.K. (lō'stŏf)	144	52.31N	1.45E
Łowicz, Pol. (lô'vĭch)	148	52.06N	19.57E
Lowville, N.Y., U.S. (lou'vĭl)	92	43.45N	75.30W
Loxicha, Mex.	112	16.03N	96.46W
Loxton, Austl. (lōks'tŭn)	198	34.25S	140.38E
Loyauté, Îles, is., N. Cal.	196	21.00S	167.00E
Loznica, Yugo. (lōz'nē-tsȧ)	142	44.31N	19.16E
Lozorno, Czech.	139e	48.21N	17.03E
Lozovatka, Ukr. (lō-zō-văt'kä)	156	48.03N	33.19E
Lozovaya, Ukr.	160	48.53N	36.23E
Lozovaya Pavlovka, Ukr.	156	48.27N	38.37E
Luama, r., Zaire (lōō'ä-mȧ)	206	4.17S	27.45E
Lu'an, China (lōō-än)	184	31.45N	116.29E
Luan, r., China	180	41.25N	117.15E
Luanda, Ang. (lōō-än'dä)	206	8.48S	13.14E
Luanguinga, r., Afr. (lōō-ä-gĭŋ'gȧ)	206	14.00S	20.45E
Luanshya, Zam.	210	13.08S	28.24E
Luanxian, China (luän shyĕn)	182	39.47N	118.40E
Luao, Ang.	210	10.42S	22.12E
Luarca, Spain (lwä'kä)	142	43.33N	6.30W
Lubaczów, Pol. (lōō-bä'chōf)	148	50.08N	23.10E
Lubań, Pol. (lōō'băn')	148	51.08N	15.17E
Lubānas Ezers, l., Lat. (lōō-bä'nȧs ā'zĕrs)	146	56.48N	26.30E
Lubang, Phil. (lōō-băng')	189a	13.49N	120.07E
Lubang Islands, is., Phil.	188	13.47N	119.56E
Lubango, Ang.	206	14.55S	13.30E
Lubartów, Pol. (lōō-bär'tōf)	148	51.27N	22.37E
Lubawa, Pol. (lōō-bä'vä)	148	53.31N	19.47E
Lübben, Ger. (lüb'ĕn)	148	51.56N	13.53E
Lubbock, Tx., U.S.	90	33.35N	101.50E
Lubec, Me., U.S. (lū'bĕk)	86	44.49N	67.01W
Lübeck, Ger. (lü'bĕk)	136	53.53N	10.42E
Lübecker Bucht, b., Ger. (lü'bĕ-kĕr bōōκt)	140	54.10N	11.20E
Lubilash, r., Zaire (lōō-bē-lȧsh')	206	7.35S	23.55E
Lubin, Pol. (lyō'bĭn)	148	51.24N	16.14E
Lublin, Pol. (lyō'blēn')	136	51.14N	22.33E
Lubny, Ukr. (lōōb'nē)	160	50.01N	33.02E
Lubuagan, Phil. (lō-bwä-gä'n)	189a	17.24N	121.11E
Lubudi, Zaire	210	9.57S	25.58E
Lubudi, r., Zaire (lō-bō'dē)	206	10.00S	24.30E
Lubumbashi, Zaire	206	11.40S	27.28E
Lucano, Ang.	210	11.16S	21.38E
Lucca, Italy (lōōk'kä)	142	43.51N	10.29E
Lucea, Jam.	116	18.25N	78.10W
Luce Bay, b., Scot., U.K. (lūs)	144	54.45N	4.45W
Lucena, Phil. (lōō-sā'nä)	189a	13.55N	121.36E
Lucena, Spain (lōō-thā'nä)	142	37.25N	4.28W
Lucena del Cid, Spain	152	40.08N	0.18W
Lučenec, Czech. (lōō'chā-nyĕts)	140	48.19N	19.41E
Lucera, Italy (lōō-châ'rä)	142	41.31N	15.22E
Luchi, China	184	28.18N	110.10E
Luchou, Tai.	237d	25.05N	121.28E
Lucin, Ut., U.S. (lū-sēn')	98	41.23N	113.59W
Lucipara, Kepulauan, is., Indon.	188	5.45S	128.15E
Luckenwalde, Ger.	148	52.05N	13.10E
Lucknow, India (lŭk'nou)	174	26.54N	80.58E
Lucky Peak Lake, res., Id., U.S.	98	43.33N	116.00W
Luçon, Fr. (lü-sôN')	150	46.27N	1.12W
Lucrecia, Cabo, c., Cuba	116	21.05N	75.30W
Luda Kamchiya, r., Bul.	154	42.46N	27.13E
Luddesdown, Eng., U.K.	231	51.22N	0.24E
Lüdenscheid, Ger. (lü'dĕn-shīt)	151c	51.13N	7.38E
Lüderitz, Nmb. (lü'dĕr-ĭts) (lü'dĕ-rĭts)	206	26.35S	15.15E
Lüderitz Bucht, b., Nmb.	206	26.35S	14.30E
Ludhiāna, India	174	31.00N	75.52E
Lüdinghausen, Ger.	151c	51.46N	7.27E
Ludington, Mi., U.S. (lŭd'ĭng-tŭn)	92	44.00N	86.25W
Ludlow, Eng., U.K. (lŭd'lō)	138a	52.22N	2.43W
Ludlow, Ky., U.S.	95f	39.05N	84.33W
Ludvika, Swe. (loodh-vē'kȧ)	146	60.10N	15.09E
Ludwigsburg, Ger.	148	48.53N	9.14E
Ludwigsfelde, Ger.	139b	52.18N	13.16E
Ludwigshafen, Ger.	148	49.29N	8.26E
Ludwigslust, Ger.	148	53.18N	11.31E
Ludza, Lat. (lōōd'zȧ)	146	56.33N	27.45E
Luebo, Zaire (lōō-ā'bō)	206	5.15S	21.22E
Luena, Ang.	206	11.45S	19.55E
Luena, Zaire	210	9.27S	25.47E
Lufira, r., Zaire (lōō-fē'rȧ)	206	9.32S	27.15E
Lufkin, Tx., U.S. (lŭf'kĭn)	106	31.21N	94.43W
Luga, Russia (lōō'gȧ)	160	58.43N	29.52E
Luga, r., Russia	156	59.00N	29.25E
Lugano, Switz. (lōō-gä'nō)	148	46.01N	8.52E
Lugansk, Ukr.	158	48.34N	39.18E
Lugansk, prov., Ukr.	156	49.30N	38.35E
Lugarno, Austl.	239a	33.59S	151.03E
Lugenda, r., Moz.	206	12.05S	38.15E
Lugo, Italy (lōō'gō)	154	44.28N	11.57E
Lugo, Spain (lōō'gō)	142	43.01N	7.32W

ăt; finȧl; rāte; senāte; ärm; ȧsk; sofȧ; fâre; ch-choose; dh-as th in other; bē; ėvent; bĕt; recĕnt; cratẽr; g-gō; gh-guttural g; bĭt; ĭ-short neutral; rīde; κ-guttural k as ch in German ich;

PLACE (Pronunciation)	PAGE	Lat. °'	Long. °'
Lugoj, Rom.	142	45.51N	21.56E
Lugouqiao, China	236b	39.51N	116.13E
Luhe, China (lo͞o-hŭ)	182	32.22N	118.50E
Luiana, Ang.	210	17.23S	23.03E
Luilaka, r., Zaire (lo͞o-ē-lä'kȧ)	206	2.18S	21.15E
Luis Moya, Mex. (lo͞oē's-mô-yä)	112	22.26N	102.14W
Luján, Arg. (lo͞o'hän')	123c	34.36S	59.07W
Luján, r., Arg.	123c	34.33S	58.59W
Lujia, China (lo͞o-jyä)	182	31.17N	120.54W
Lukanga Swamp, sw., Zam. (lo͞o-kăŋ'gȧ)	206	14.30S	27.25E
Lukenie, r., Zaire (lo͞o-kā'ynȧ)	206	3.10S	19.05E
Lukolela, Zaire	206	1.03S	17.01E
Lukovit, Bul. (lo͞o'kō-vêt')	154	43.13N	24.07E
Łuków, Pol. (wō'kôf)	148	51.57N	22.25E
Lukuga, r., Zaire (lo͞o-ko͞o'gȧ)	206	5.50S	27.35E
Lüleburgaz, Tur. (lü'lē-bòr-gäs')	154	41.25N	27.23E
Luling, Tx., U.S. (lū'lĭng)	106	29.41N	97.38W
Lulong, China (lo͞o-lôŋ)	180	39.54N	118.53E
Lulonga, r., Zaire	210	1.00N	18.37E
Luluabourg, *see* Kananga, Zaire	206	6.14S	22.17E
Lulu Island, i., Can.	100d	49.09N	123.05W
Lulu Island, i., Ak., U.S.	78	55.28N	133.30W
Lumajangdong Co, l., China	178	34.00N	81.47E
Lumber, r., N.C., U.S. (lŭm'bẽr)	108	34.45N	79.10W
Lumberton, Ms., U.S. (lŭm'bẽr-tŭn)	108	31.00N	89.25W
Lumberton, N.C., U.S.	108	34.47N	79.00W
Luminárias, Braz. (lo͞o-mē-ná'ryäs)	123a	21.32S	44.53W
Lummi, i., Wa., U.S.	100d	48.42N	122.43W
Lummi Bay, b., Wa., U.S. (lŭm'ĭ)	100d	48.47N	122.44W
Lummi Island, Wa., U.S.	100d	48.44N	122.42W
Lumwana, Zam.	210	11.50S	25.10E
Lün, Mong.	180	47.58N	104.52E
Luna, Phil. (lo͞o'nȧ)	189a	16.51N	120.22E
Lund, Swe. (lŭnd)	140	55.42N	13.10E
Lundy, i., Eng., U.K. (lŭn'dē)dep)	144	51.12N	4.50W
Lüneburg, Ger. (lü'nē-bòrgh)	148	53.16N	10.25E
Lunel, Fr. (lü-nĕl')	150	43.41N	4.07E
Lünen, Ger. (lü'nĕn)	151c	51.36N	7.30E
Lunenburg, Can. (lo͞o'nĕn-bûrg)	78	44.23N	64.19W
Lunenburg, Ma., U.S.	87a	42.36N	71.44W
Lunéville, Fr. (lü-nȧ-vel')	150	48.37N	6.29E
Lunga, Ang.	210	14.42S	18.32E
Lungué-Bungo, r., Afr.	206	13.00S	20.30E
Lunsar, S.L.	208	8.41N	12.32W
Lunt, Eng., U.K.	233a	53.31N	2.59W
Luodian, China (lwô-dĭĕn)	182	31.25N	121.20E
Luoding, China (lwô-dĭŋ)	184	23.42N	111.35E
Luohe, China (lwô-hŭ)	182	33.35N	114.02E
Luoyang, China (lwô-yäŋ)	180	34.45N	112.32E
Luozhen, China (lwô-jŭn)	182	37.45N	118.29E
Luque, Para. (loo'kā)	126	25.18S	57.17W
Luray, Va., U.S. (lū-rā')	92	38.40N	78.25W
Lurgan, N. Ire., U.K. (lûr'găn)	140	54.27N	6.28W
Lurigancho, Peru	229c	12.02S	77.01W
Lúrio, Moz. (lo͞o'rē-ō)	206	13.17S	40.29E
Lúrio, Moz.	206	14.00S	38.45E
Lurnea, Austl.	239a	33.56S	150.54E
Lusaka, Zaire	210	7.10S	29.27E
Lusaka, Zam. (lō-sä'kȧ)	206	15.25S	28.17E
Lusambo, Zaire (lo͞o-säm'bō)	206	4.58S	23.27E
Lusanga, Zaire	206	5.13S	18.43E
Lusangi, Zaire	210	4.37S	27.08E
Lushan, China	184	33.45N	113.00E
Lushiko, r., Afr.	210	6.35S	19.45E
Lushoto, Tan. (lo͞o-shō'tō)	206	4.47S	38.17E
Lüshun, China (lü-shŭn)	180	38.49N	121.15E
Lusikisiki, Transkei (lo͞o-sē-kē-sē'kē)	207c	31.22S	29.37E
Lusk, Wy., U.S. (lŭsk)	96	42.46N	104.27W
Lūt, Dasht-e, des., Iran (dă'sht-ē-lo͞ot)	174	31.47N	58.38E
Lutcher, La., U.S. (lŭch'ẽr)	106	30.03N	90.43W
Lütgendortmund, neigh., Ger.	232	51.30N	7.21E
Luton, Eng., U.K. (lū'tŭn)	144	51.55N	0.28W
Lutsk, Ukr. (lo͞otsk)	160	50.45N	25.20E
Lüttringhausen, neigh., Ger.	232	51.13N	7.14E
Luuq, Som.	212a	3.38N	42.35E
Luverne, Al., U.S. (lū-vûn')	108	31.42N	86.15W
Luverne, Mn., U.S.	96	43.40N	96.13W
Luwingu, Zam.	210	10.15S	29.55E
Luxapallila Creek, r., U.S. (lŭk-sȧ-pŏl'ĭ-lȧ)	108	33.36N	88.08W
Luxembourg, Lux.	136	49.38N	6.30E
Luxembourg, nation, Eur.	136	49.30N	6.22E
Luxeuil-les-Baines, Fr.	150	47.49N	6.19E
Luxomni, Ga., U.S. (lŭx'ŏm-nī)	94c	33.54N	84.07W
Luxor, *see* Al Uqṣur, Egypt	204	25.38N	32.59E
Lu Xun Museum, bldg., China	237a	31.16N	121.28E
Luya Shan, mtn., China	184	38.50N	111.40E
Luyi, China (lo͞o-yē)	182	33.52N	115.32E
Luyuan, China	236b	39.54N	116.27E
Luz, Braz.	230c	22.48S	43.05W
Luz, neigh., Port.	234d	38.46N	9.10W
Luzern, Switz. (lō-tsĕrn)	140	47.03N	8.18E
Luzhou, China (lo͞o-jō)	180	28.58N	105.25E
Luziânia, Braz. (lo͞o-zyȧ'nēȧ)	124	16.17S	47.44W
Lužniki, neigh., Russia	235b	55.43N	37.33E
Luzon, i., Phil. (lo͞o-zŏn')	188	17.10N	119.45E
Luzon Strait, strt., Asia	184	20.40N	121.00E
L'vov, Ukr.	158	49.50N	24.00E
Lyalta, Can.	77e	51.07N	113.36W
Lyalya, r., Russia (lyȧ'lyȧ)	164a	58.58N	60.17E
Lyaskovets, Bul.	154	43.07N	25.41E
Lydenburg, S. Afr. (lī'dĕn-bûrg)	206	25.06S	30.21E
Lydiate, Eng., U.K.	233a	53.32N	2.57W
Lye Green, Eng., U.K.	231	51.43N	0.35W
Lyell, Mount, mtn., Ca., U.S. (lī'ĕl)	102	37.44N	119.22W
Lykens, Pa., U.S. (lī'kĕnz)	92	40.35N	76.45W
Lyna, r., Eur. (lĭn'ȧ)	148	53.56N	20.30E
Lynbrook, N.Y., U.S.	224	40.39N	73.41W
Lynch, Ky., U.S. (lĭnch)	108	36.56N	82.55W
Lynchburg, Va., U.S. (lĭnch'bûrg)	90	37.23N	79.08W
Lynch Cove, Wa., Wa., U.S. (lĭnch)	100a	47.26N	122.54W
Lynden, Can. (lĭn'dĕn)	77d	43.14N	80.08W
Lynden, Wa., U.S.	100d	48.56N	122.27W
Lyndhurst, Austl.	195a	38.03S	145.14E
Lyndhurst, N.J., U.S.	224	40.49N	74.07W
Lyndhurst, Oh., U.S.	225a	41.31N	81.30W
Lyndon, Ky., U.S. (lĭn'dŭn)	95h	38.15N	85.36W
Lyndonville, Vt., U.S. (lĭn'dŭn-vĭl)	92	44.35N	72.00W
Lyne, Eng., U.K.	231	51.23N	0.33W
Lynn, Ma., U.S. (lĭn)	90	42.28N	70.57W
Lynnewood Gardens, Pa., U.S.	225b	40.04N	75.09W
Lynnfield, Ma., U.S.	223a	42.32N	71.03W
Lynn Lake, Can. (lăk)	78	56.51N	101.05W
Lynwood, Ca., U.S. (lĭn'wŏd)	101a	33.56N	118.13W
Lyon, Fr. (lē-ôN')	136	45.44N	4.52E
Lyons, Ga., U.S. (lī'ŭnz)	108	32.08N	82.19W
Lyons, Il., U.S.	227a	41.49N	87.50W
Lyons, Ks., U.S.	104	38.20N	98.11W
Lyons, Ne., U.S.	96	41.57N	96.28W
Lyons, N.J., U.S.	94a	40.41N	74.33W
Lyons, N.Y., U.S.	92	43.05N	77.00W
Lysefjorden, fj., Nor.	146	58.59N	6.35E
Lysekil, Swe. (lü'sĕ-kĕl)	146	58.17N	11.22E
Lysterfield, Austl.	239b	37.56S	145.18E
Lys'va, Russia (lĭs'vȧ)	160	58.07N	57.47E
Lytham, Eng., U.K. (lĭth'ăm)	138a	53.44N	2.58W
Lytkarino, Russia	164b	55.35N	37.55E
Lyttelton, S. Afr. (lĭt'l'ton)	207b	25.51S	28.13E
Lyuban', Russia (lyo͞o'bán)	156	59.21N	31.15E
Lyubar, Ukr. (lyo͞o'bär)	156	49.56N	27.44E
Lyubertsy, Russia (lyo͞o'bĕr-tsē)	156	55.40N	37.55E
Lyubim, Russia (lyo͞o-bēm')	156	58.24N	40.39E
Lyublino, Russia (lyo͞ob'lĭ-nō)	164b	55.41N	37.45E
Lyudinovo, Russia (lū-dē'novō)	156	53.52N	34.28E

M

PLACE (Pronunciation)	PAGE	Lat. °'	Long. °'
Ma'ān, Jord. (mä-än')	174	30.12N	35.45E
Maartensdijk, Neth.	139a	52.09N	5.10E
Maas (Meuse), r., Eur.	144	51.50N	5.40E
Maastricht, Neth. (mäs'trĭkt)	144	50.51N	5.35E
Mabaia, Ang.	210	7.13S	14.03E
Mabana, Wa., U.S. (mä-bä-nä)	100a	48.06N	122.25W
Mabank, Tx., U.S. (mă'bănk)	106	32.21N	96.05W
Mabeskraal, S. Afr.	212d	25.12S	26.47E
Mableton, Ga., U.S. (mā'b'l-tŭn)	94c	33.49N	84.34W
Mabrouk, Mali	204	19.27N	1.16W
Mabula, S. Afr. (mă'bo͞o-la)	212d	24.49S	27.59E
Macalelon, Phil. (mä-kä-lä-lōn')	189a	13.46N	122.09E
Macao, dep., Asia	180	22.00N	113.00E
Macau, Braz. (mä-kà'ò)	124	5.12S	36.34W
Macaya, Pico de, mtn., Haiti	116	18.25N	74.00W
Macclesfield, Eng., U.K. (măk''lz-fēld)	138a	53.15N	2.07W
Macclesfield Canal, can., Eng., U.K. (măk''lz-fēld)	138a	53.14N	2.07W
Macdona, Tx., U.S. (măk-dō'nȧ)	101d	29.20N	98.42W
Macdonald, l., Austl. (măk-dŏn'ăld)	196	23.40S	127.40E
Macdonnell Ranges, mts., Austl. (măk-dŏn'ĕl)	196	23.40S	131.30E
MacDowell Lake, l., Can. (măk-dou ĕl)	82	52.15N	92.45W
Macdui, Ben, mtn., Scot., U.K. (bĕn măk-do͞o'ē)	140	57.06N	3.45W
Macedonia, Oh., U.S. (măs-ē-dō'nĭ-ȧ)	95d	41.19N	81.30E
Macedonia, ctry., Eur.	155	41.50N	22.00E
Macedonia, hist. reg., Eur. (măs-ē-dō'nĭ-ȧ)	142	41.05N	22.15E
Maceió, Braz.	124	9.40S	35.43W
Macerata, Italy (mä-chā-rä'tä)	154	43.18N	13.28E
Macfarlane, Lake, l., Austl. (măc'fär-lān)	198	32.10S	137.00E
Machache, mtn., Leso.	207c	29.22S	27.53E
Machado, Braz. (mä-shá-dô)	123a	21.42S	45.55W
Machakos, Kenya	210	1.31S	37.16E
Machala, Ec. (mä-chá'lä)	124	3.18S	78.54W
Machens, Mo., U.S. (măk'ĕns)	101e	38.54N	90.20W
Machias, Me., U.S. (mȧ-chī'ȧs)	86	44.22N	67.29W
Machida, Japan (mä-chē'dä)	187a	35.32N	139.28E
Machilīpatnam, India	174	16.22N	81.10E
Machu Picchu, Peru (má'chò-pē'k-chò)	124	13.07S	72.34W
Măcin, Rom. (mȧ-chēn')	156	45.15N	28.09E
Macina, reg., Mali	208	14.50N	4.40W
Mackay, Austl. (mȧ-kī')	196	21.15S	149.08E
Mackay, Id., U.S. (măk-kā')	98	43.55N	113.38W
Mackay, l., Austl. (mȧ-kī')	196	22.30S	127.45E
MacKay, l., Can. (măk-kā')	78	64.10N	112.35W
Mackenzie, r., Can.	78	63.38N	124.23W
Mackenzie, District of, dept., Can.	78	63.48N	125.25W
Mackenzie Bay, b., Can.	89	69.20N	137.10W
Mackenzie Mountains, mts., Can. (mȧ-kĕn'zĭ)	78	63.41N	129.27W
Mackinaw, r., Il., U.S.	92	40.35N	89.25W
Mackinaw City, Mi., U.S. (măk'ĭ-nô)	92	45.45N	84.45W
Mackinnon Road, Kenya	210	3.44S	39.03E
Macleantown, S. Afr. (măk-lăn'toun)	207c	32.48S	27.48E
Maclear, S. Afr. (mȧ-klēr')	206	31.06S	28.23E
Macleod, Austl.	239b	37.43S	145.04E
Macomb, Il., U.S. (mȧ-ko͞om')	104	40.27N	90.40W
Mâcon, Fr. (mä-kôN)	140	46.19N	4.51E
Macon, Ga., U.S. (mā'kŏn)	90	32.49N	83.39W
Macon, Ms., U.S.	108	32.07N	88.31W
Macon, Mo., U.S.	104	39.42N	92.29W
Macquarie, r., Austl.	196	31.43S	148.04E
Macquarie Fields, Austl.	239a	33.59S	150.53E
Macquarie Islands, is., Austl. (mȧ-kwŏr'ē)	2	54.36S	158.45E
Macquarie University, educ., Austl.	239a	33.46S	151.06E
Macritchie Reservoir, res., Sing.	236c	1.21N	103.50E
Macuelizo, Hond. (mä-kwē-lē'zô)	114	15.22N	88.32W
Macuto, Ven.	230a	10.37N	66.53W
Mad, r., Ca., U.S. (măd)	98	40.38N	123.37W
Madagascar, nation, Afr. (măd-ȧ-găs'kȧr)	206	18.05S	43.12E
Madame, i., Can. (mȧ-dȧm')	86	45.33N	61.02W
Madanapalle, India	178	13.06N	78.09E
Madang, Pap. N. Gui. (mä-däng')	188	5.15S	145.45E
Madaoua, Niger (mȧ-dou'ȧ)	204	14.04N	6.03E
Madawaska, r., Can. (măd-ȧ-wôs'kȧ)	84	45.20N	77.25W
Madeira, r., S.A.	124	6.48S	62.43W
Madeira, Arquipélago da, is., Port.	203	33.26N	16.44W
Madeira, Ilha da, i., Port. (mä-dā'rä)	204	32.41N	16.15W
Madelia, Mn., U.S. (mȧ-dē'lĭ-ȧ)	96	44.03N	94.23W
Madeline, i., Wi., U.S. (măd'ē-lĭn)	96	46.47N	91.30W
Madera, Ca., U.S. (mȧ-dā'rȧ)	102	36.57N	120.04W
Madera, vol., Nic.	114	11.27N	85.30W
Madgaon, India	178	15.09N	73.58E
Madhya Pradesh, state, India (mŭd'vŭ prŭ-dāsh')	174	22.04N	77.48E
Madill, Ok., U.S. (mȧ-dĭl')	104	34.04N	96.45W
Madīnat ash Sha'b, Yemen	174	12.45N	44.00E
Madingo, Congo	210	4.07S	11.22E
Madingou, Congo	210	4.09S	13.34E
Madison, Fl., U.S. (măd'ĭ-sŭn)	108	30.28N	83.25W
Madison, Ga., U.S.	108	33.34N	83.29W
Madison, Il., U.S.	101e	38.40N	90.09W
Madison, In., U.S.	92	38.45N	85.25W
Madison, Ks., U.S.	104	38.08N	96.07W
Madison, Me., U.S.	86	44.47N	69.52W
Madison, Mn., U.S.	96	44.59N	96.13W
Madison, Ne., U.S.	96	41.49N	97.27W
Madison, N.J., U.S.	94a	40.46N	74.25W
Madison, N.C., U.S.	108	36.22N	79.59W
Madison, S.D., U.S.	96	44.01N	97.08W
Madison, Wi., U.S.	90	43.05N	89.23W
Madison Heights, Mi., U.S.	226c	42.30N	83.06W
Madison Res, Mt., U.S.	98	45.25N	111.28W
Madisonville, Ky., U.S. (măd'ĭ-sŭn-vĭl)	92	37.20N	87.30W
Madisonville, La., U.S.	106	30.22N	90.10W
Madisonville, Tx., U.S.	106	30.57N	95.55W
Madjori, Burkina	208	11.26N	1.15E
Mado Gashi, Kenya	210	0.44N	39.10E
Madona, Lat. (mȧ'dō'nȧ)	146	56.50N	26.14E
Madrakah, Ra's al, c., Oman	174	18.53N	57.48E
Madras, India (mȧ-dräs') (mŭ-drŭs')	174	13.08N	80.15E
Madre, Laguna, l., Mex. (lä-go͞o'nä mä'drā)	106	25.08N	97.41W
Madre, Sierra, mts., N.A. (sē-ĕ'r-rä-mä'drē)	112	15.55N	92.40W
Madre, Sierra, mts., Phil.	189a	16.40N	122.10E
Madre de Dios, Archipiélago, is., Chile (mä'drā dā dē-ōs')	126	50.40S	76.30W
Madre de Dios, Río, r., S.A. (rē'ō-mä'drā dā dē-ōs')	124	12.07S	68.02W
Madre del Sur, Sierra, mts., Mex. (sē-ĕ'r-rä-mä'drā dĕlso͞or')	110	17.35N	100.35W
Madre Occidental, Sierra, mts., Mex.	110	29.30N	107.30W
Madre Oriental, Sierra, mts., Mex.	110	25.30N	100.45W
Madrid, Spain (mä-drē'd)	136	40.26N	3.42W
Madrid, Ia., U.S. (măd'rĭd)	96	41.51N	93.48W
Madridejos, Spain (mä-dhrē-dhä'hōs)	152	39.29N	3.32W
Madrillon, Va., U.S.	225d	38.55N	77.14W
Madura, i., Indon. (mȧ-do͞o'rä)	188	6.45S	113.30E
Madurai, India (mä-do͞o'rä)	174	9.57N	78.04E
Madureira, neigh., Braz.	230c	22.53S	43.21W
Madureira, Serra do, mtn., Braz. (sĕ'r-rä-dō-mä-do͞o-rā'rȧ)	126b	22.49S	43.30W
Maebashi, Japan (mä-ē-bä'shē)	180	36.26N	139.04E
Maeno, neigh., Japan	238a	35.46N	139.42E
Maestra, Sierra, mts., Cuba (sē-ĕ'r-rä-mä-ās'trä)	110	20.05N	77.05W
Maewo, i., Vanuatu	196	15.17S	168.16E
Mafeking, Boph. (mȧf'ē'kĭng)	206	25.46S	24.45E
Mafra, Braz. (mä'frä)	126	26.21N	49.59W
Mafra, Port. (mäf'rȧ)	153b	38.56N	9.20W
Magadan, Russia (mȧ-gȧ-dän')	158	59.39N	150.43E
Magadan Oblast, Russia	162	65.00N	160.00E
Magadi, Kenya	210	1.54S	36.17E
Magalhães Bastos, neigh., Braz.	230c	22.53S	43.23W
Magalies, r., S. Afr. (mä-gä'lyĕs)	207b	25.51S	27.42E
Magaliesberg, mts., S. Afr.	207b	25.45S	27.43E
Magaliesburg, S. Afr.	212d	26.01S	27.32E
Magallanes, Estrecho de, strt., S.A.	126	52.30S	68.45W
Magat, r., Phil. (mä-gät')	189a	16.45N	121.16E
Magdalena, Arg. (mäg-dä-lā'nä)	123c	35.05S	57.32W
Magdalena, Bol.	124	13.17S	63.57W
Magdalena, Mex.	90	30.34N	110.50W
Magdalena, N.M., U.S.	102	34.10N	107.45W

ng-sing; ŋ-baŋk; N-nasalized n; nŏd; cŏmmit; ōld; ōbey; ôrder; oi-boil; fo͞od; ŏ-as oo in foot; ou-out; s-soft; sh-dish; th-thin; pūre; ůnite; ûrn; stŭd; circŭs; ü-as in French tu; '-indeterminate vowel.

PLACE (Pronunciation)	PAGE	Lat. °'	Long. °'
Magdalena, i., Chile	126	44.45S	73.15W
Magdalena, Bahía, b., Mex. (bä-ē'ä-mäg-dä-lä'nä)	110	24.30N	114.00W
Magdalena, Río, r., Col.	124	7.45N	74.04W
Magdalena del Mar, Peru	229c	12.06S	77.05W
Magdalen Laver, Eng., U.K.	231	51.45N	0.11E
Magdeburg, Ger. (mäg'dē-bo̤rgh)	136	52.07N	11.39E
Magenta, Italy (mȧ-jĕn'tȧ)	154	45.26N	8.53E
Magerøya, i., Nor.	140	71.10N	24.11E
Maggiore, Lago, l., Italy	142	46.03N	8.25E
Maghāghah, Egypt	212b	28.38N	30.50W
Maghniyya, Alg.	142	34.52N	1.40W
Maghull, Eng., U.K.	233a	53.32N	2.57W
Maginu, Japan	238a	35.35N	139.36E
Magiscatzin, Mex. (mä-kēs-kät-zēn')	112	22.48N	98.42W
Maglaj, Bos. (mȧ'glä-ē)	154	44.34N	18.12E
Magliana, neigh., Italy	235c	41.50N	12.25E
Maglie, Italy (mäl'yā)	154	40.06N	18.20E
Magna, Ut., U.S. (măg'nȧ)	101b	40.43N	112.06W
Magnitogorsk, Russia (mȧg-nyē'tô-gôrsk)	158	53.26N	59.05E
Magnolia, Ar., U.S. (măg-nō'lĭ-ȧ)	104	33.16N	93.13W
Magnolia, Ms., U.S.	108	31.08N	90.27W
Magnolia, N.J., U.S.	225b	39.51N	75.02W
Magny-en-Vexin, Fr. (mä-nyē'ĕN-vĕ-sȧN')	151b	49.09N	1.45E
Magny-les-Hameaux, Fr.	233c	48.44N	2.04E
Magog, Can. (mȧ-gŏg')	84	45.15N	72.10W
Magome, neigh., Japan	238a	35.35N	139.43E
Magpie, r., Can.	84	48.13N	84.50W
Magpie, r., Can.	86	50.40N	64.30W
Magpie, Lac, l., Can.	86	50.55N	64.39W
Magrath, Can.	78	49.25N	112.52W
Maguanying, China	236b	39.52N	116.17E
Magude, Moz. (mä-go͞o'dȧ)	206	24.58S	32.39E
Magwe, Burma (mŭg-wā')	174	20.19N	94.57E
Mahābād, Iran	176	36.55N	45.50E
Mahahi Port, Zaire (mä-hä'gē)	204	2.14N	31.12E
Mahajanga, Madag.	206	15.12S	46.26E
Mahakam, r., Indon.	188	0.30S	116.15E
Mahali Mountains, mts., Tan.	210	6.20S	30.00E
Mahaly, Madag. (mȧ-hȧl-ē')	206	24.09S	46.20E
Mahanoro, Madag. (mȧ-hȧ-nô'rō)	206	19.57S	48.47E
Mahanoy City, Pa., U.S. (mä-hȧ-noi')	92	40.50N	76.10W
Mahaṭṭat al-Hilmīyah, neigh., Egypt	240a	30.07N	31.19E
Maḥaṭṭat al Qaṭrānah, Jord.	173a	31.15N	36.04E
Maḥaṭṭat 'Aqabat al Ḥijāzīyah, Jord.	173a	29.45N	35.55E
Maḥaṭṭat ar Ramlah, Jord.	173a	29.31N	35.57E
Maḥaṭṭat Jurf ad Darāwīsh, Jord.	173a	30.41N	35.51E
Mahd adh-Dhahab, Sau. Ar.	176	23.30N	40.52E
Mahe, India (mä-ā')	174	11.42N	75.39E
Mahenge, Tan. (mä-hĕŋ'gȧ)	206	7.38S	36.16E
Mahi, r., India	178	23.16N	73.20E
Māhīm, neigh., India	236e	19.03N	72.49E
Māhīm Bay, b., India	179b	19.03N	72.45E
Mahlabatini, S. Afr. (mä'lȧ-bȧ-tē'nē)	207c	28.15S	31.29E
Mahlow, Ger. (mä'lōv)	139b	52.23N	13.24E
Mahlsdorf, neigh., Ger.	234a	52.31N	13.37E
Mahlsdorf-Süd, neigh., Ger.	234a	52.29N	13.36E
Mahnomen, Mn., U.S. (mô-nō'mĕn)	96	47.18N	95.58W
Mahón, Spain (mä-ōn')	142	39.52N	4.15E
Mahone Bay, Can. (mȧ-hōn')	86	44.27N	64.23W
Mahone Bay, b., Can.	86	44.30N	64.15W
Mahopac, Lake, l., N.Y., U.S. (mā-hō'păk)	94a	41.24N	73.45W
Mahrauli, neigh., India	236d	28.31N	77.11E
Māhul, neigh., India	236e	19.01N	72.53E
Mahwah, N.J., U.S. (mȧ-wä')	94a	41.05N	74.09W
Maidenhead, Eng., U.K. (mād'ĕn-hĕd)	138b	51.30N	0.44W
Maidstone, Austl.	239b	37.47S	144.52E
Maidstone, Eng., U.K.	144	51.17N	0.32E
Maiduguri, Nig. (mä'ē-dȧ-go͞o'rē)	204	11.51N	13.10E
Maigualida, Sierra, mts., Ven. (sē-ĕ'r-rȧ-mī-gwä'lē-dĕ)	124	6.30N	65.50W
Maijdi, Bngl.	178	22.59N	91.08E
Maikop, see Maykop, Russia	158	44.35N	40.07E
Main, r., Ger. (mīn)	148	49.49N	9.20E
Main Barrier Range, mts., Austl. (băr'ĭ-ēr)	196	31.25S	141.40E
Mai-Ndombe, Lac, l., Zaire	206	2.16S	19.00E
Maine, state, U.S. (mān)	90	45.25N	69.50W
Mainland, i., Scot., U.K. (mān-lănd)	140	60.19N	2.40W
Maintenon, Fr. (mäN-tē-nôN')	151b	48.35N	1.35E
Maintirano, Madag. (mä'ēn-tē-rä'nō)	206	18.05S	44.08E
Mainz, Ger. (mīnts)	136	49.59N	8.16E
Maio, i., C.V. (mä'yo)	204b	15.15N	22.50W
Maipo, S.A.	126	34.08S	69.51W
Maipo, r., Chile (mī'pô)	123b	33.45S	71.08W
Maiquetía, Ven. (mī-kē-tē'ä)	124	10.37N	66.56W
Maison-Rouge, Fr. (mā-zôN-ro͞ozh')	151b	48.34N	3.09E
Maisons-Alfort, Fr.	233c	48.48N	2.26E
Maisons-Laffitte, Fr.	151b	48.57N	2.09E
Maitani, Japan	238b	34.49N	135.22E
Maitland, Austl. (māt'lănd)	196	32.45S	151.40E
Maizuru, Japan (mä-ĭ'zo͞o-ro͞o)	187	35.26N	135.15E
Majene, Indon.	188	3.34S	119.00E
Maji, Eth.	204	6.14N	35.34E
Majorca, see Mallorca, i., Spain	136	39.18N	2.22E
Makah Indian Reservation, I.R., Wa., U.S.	98	48.17N	124.52W
Makala, Zaire	240c	4.25S	15.15E
Makanya, Tan. (mä-kän'yä)	206	4.15S	37.49E
Makanza, Zaire	204	1.42N	19.08E
Makarakomburu, Mount, mtn., Sol.Is.	192e	9.43S	160.02E
Makarska, Cro. (mȧ'kär-skȧ)	154	43.17N	17.05E
Makar'yev, Russia	160	57.50N	43.48E
Makasar, Selat (Makassar Strait), strt., Indon.	188	2.00S	118.07E
Makasar, see Ujung Pandang, Indon.	188	5.08S	119.28E
Makati, Phil.	237g	14.34N	121.01E
Makaw, Zaire	210	3.29S	18.19E
Make, i., Japan (mä'kȧ)	187	30.43N	130.49E
Makeni, S.L.	204	8.53N	12.03W
Makeyevka, Ukr. (mŭk-yā'ŭf-kŭ)	160	48.03N	38.00E
Makgadikgadi Pans, pl., Bots.	206	20.38S	21.31E
Makhachkala, Russia (mäk'äch-kä'lä)	160	43.00N	47.40E
Makhaleng, r., Leso.	207c	29.53S	27.33E
Makindu, Kenya	210	2.17S	37.49E
M'akino, Russia	235b	55.48N	37.22E
Makkah, see Mecca, Sau. Ar.	174	21.27N	39.45E
Makkovik, Can.	78	55.01N	59.10W
Makokou, Gabon (mȧ-kô-ko͞o')	204	0.34N	12.52E
Maków Mazowiecki, Pol. (mä'kōov mä-zō-vyĕts'kē)	148	52.51N	21.07E
Makuhari, Japan (mä-ko͞o-hä'rē)	187a	35.39N	140.04E
Makurazaki, Japan (mä'ko̤-rä-zä'kē)	187	31.16N	130.18E
Makurdi, Nig.	204	7.45N	8.32E
Makushin, Ak., U.S. (mȧ-ko̤'shĭn)	89	53.57N	166.28W
Makushino, Russia (mȧ-kô-shēn'ô)	158	55.03N	67.43E
Mala, Punta, c., Pan. (po͞o'n-tä-mä'lä)	114	7.32N	79.44W
Malabar Coast, cst., India (măl'ȧ-bär)	178	11.19N	75.33E
Malabar Point, c., India	179b	18.57N	72.47E
Malabo, Eq. Gui.	204	3.45N	8.47E
Malabon, Phil.	189a	14.39N	120.57E
Malacca, Strait of, strt., Asia (mȧ-lăk'ȧ)	188	4.15N	99.44E
Malad City, Id., U.S. (mȧ-lăd')	98	42.11N	112.15W
Málaga, Col. (mȧ'lä-gȧ)	124	6.41N	72.46W
Málaga, Spain	136	36.45N	4.25W
Malagón, Spain (mä-lä-gōn')	152	39.12N	3.52W
Malaita, i., Sol.Is. (mȧ-lä'ē-tȧ)	196	8.38S	161.15E
Malakāl, Sudan (mȧ-lȧ-käl')	204	9.46N	31.54E
Malakhovka, Russia (mȧ-lăk'ôf-kȧ)	164b	55.38N	38.01E
Malakoff, Fr.	233c	48.49N	2.19E
Malakpur, neigh., India	236d	28.42N	77.12E
Malang, Indon.	188	8.06S	112.50E
Malanje, Ang. (mä-läŋ-gȧ)	206	9.32S	16.20E
Malanville, Benin	204	12.04N	3.09E
Mälaren, l., Swe.	140	59.38N	16.55E
Malartic, Can.	78	48.07N	78.11W
Malatya, Tur. (mȧ-lä'tyȧ)	174	38.30N	38.15E
Malawi, nation, Afr.	206	11.15S	33.45E
Malawi, Lake, see Nyasa, Lake, l., Afr.	206	10.45S	34.30E
Malaya Vishera, Russia (vē-shä'rä)	158	58.51N	32.13E
Malay Peninsula, pen., Asia (mȧ-lā') (mā'lā)	188	6.00N	101.00E
Malaysia, nation, Asia (mȧ-lā'zhȧ)	188	4.10N	101.22E
Malbon, Austl. (măl'bŭn)	196	21.15S	140.30E
Malbork, Pol. (mäl'bôrk)	140	54.02N	19.04E
Malcabran, r., Port. (mäl-kä-brän')	153b	38.47N	8.46W
Malden, Ma., U.S. (môl'dĕn)	87a	42.26N	71.04W
Malden, Mo., U.S.	104	36.32N	89.56W
Malden, i., Kir.	2	4.20S	154.30W
Maldives, nation, Asia	172	4.30N	71.30E
Maldon, Eng., U.K. (môrl'dŏn)	138b	51.44N	0.39E
Maldonado, Ur. (mäl-dŏ-nȧ'dô)	126	34.54S	54.57W
Maldonado, Punta, c., Mex. (po͞o'n-tä)	112	16.18N	98.34W
Maléa, Ákra, c., Grc.	142	36.31N	23.13E
Mālegaon, India	178	20.35N	74.30E
Malé Karpaty, mts., Czech.	148	48.31N	17.15E
Malekula, i., Vanuatu (mä-lā-ko͞o'lä)	196	16.44S	167.45E
Malema, Moz.	210	14.57S	37.20E
Malheur, r., Or., U.S. (mȧ-lo͞or')	98	43.45N	117.41W
Malheur Lake, l., Or., U.S. (mȧ-lo͞or')	98	43.16N	118.37W
Mali, nation, Afr.	204	15.45N	0.15W
Malibu, Ca., U.S. (măl'ĭ-bo͞o)	101a	34.03N	118.38W
Malik, Wādī al, r., Sudan	204	16.48N	29.30E
Malimba, Monts, mts., Zaire	210	7.45S	29.15E
Malin, Ukr. (mȧ-lēn')	156	50.44N	29.15E
Malinalco, Mex. (mä-lē-näl'kō)	112	18.54N	99.31W
Malinaltepec, Mex. (mä-lē-näl-tȧ-pĕk')	112	17.01N	98.41W
Malindi, Kenya (mä-lēn'dē)	206	3.14S	40.04E
Malin Head, c., Ire.	140	55.23N	7.24W
Malino, Russia (mä'lĭ-nô)	164b	55.07N	38.12E
Malinovka, Ukr. (mȧ-lē-nôf'kȧ)	156	49.50N	36.43E
Malkara, Tur. (mäl'kȧ-rȧ)	154	40.51N	26.52E
Malko Tŭrnovo, Bul. (mäl'kō-t'r'nô-vȧ)	154	41.59N	27.28E
Mallaig, Scot., U.K.	144	56.59N	5.55W
Mallet Creek, Oh., U.S. (măl'ĕt)	95d	41.10N	81.55W
Mallorca, i., Spain	136	39.30N	3.00E
Mallorquinas, Spain	234e	41.28N	2.16E
Mallow, Ire. (măl'ō)	144	52.07N	9.04W
Malmédy, Bel. (mȧl-mā-dē')	144	50.25N	6.01E
Malmesbury, S. Afr. (mämz'bēr-ĭ)	206	33.30S	18.35E
Malmköping, Swe. (mälm'chû'pĭng)	146	59.09N	16.39E
Malmö, Swe.	136	55.36N	13.00E
Malmyzh, Russia (mȧl-mēzh')	158	49.58N	137.07E
Malmyzh, Russia	160	56.30N	50.48E
Malnoue, Fr.	233c	48.50N	2.36E
Maloarkhangelsk, Russia (mä'lô-ȧr-kän'gĕlsk)	156	52.26N	36.29E
Malolos, Phil. (mä-lô'lôs)	189a	14.51N	120.49E
Malomal'sk, Russia (mȧ-lô-mälsk')	164a	58.47N	59.55E
Malone, N.Y., U.S. (mȧ-lōn')	92	44.50N	74.20W
Malonga, Zaire	210	10.24S	23.10E
Maloti Mountains, mts., Leso.	207c	29.00S	28.29E
Maloyaroslavets, Russia (mä'lô-yä-rô-slä-vyĕts)	156	55.01N	36.25E
Malozemel'skaya Tundra, reg., Russia	160	67.30N	50.00E
Malpas, Eng., U.K. (môl'pȧz)	138a	53.01N	2.46W
Malpelo, Isla de, i., Col. (mäl-pā'lō)	124	3.55N	81.30W
Malpeque Bay, b., Can. (môl-pĕk')	86	46.30N	63.47W
Malta, Mt., U.S. (môl'tȧ)	98	48.20N	107.50W
Malta, nation, Eur.	136	35.52N	13.30E
Maltahöhe, Nmb. (mäl'tä-hō'ĕ)	206	24.45S	16.45E
Maltrata, Mex. (mäl-trä'tä)	112	18.48N	97.16W
Maluku (Moluccas), is., Indon.	188	2.22S	128.25E
Maluku, Laut (Molucca Sea), sea, Indon.	188	0.15N	125.41E
Malūṭ, Sudan	204	10.30N	32.17E
Mālvan, India	178	16.08N	73.32E
Malvern, Austl.	239b	37.52S	145.02E
Malvern, Ar., U.S. (măl'vērn)	104	34.21N	92.47W
Malvern, neigh., S. Afr.	240b	26.12S	28.06E
Malverne, N.Y., U.S.	224	40.40N	73.40W
Malvern East, S. Afr.	240b	26.12S	28.08E
Malyy Anyuy, r., Russia	162	67.52N	164.30E
Malyy Tamir, i., Russia	162	78.10N	107.30E
Mamantel, Mex. (mä-mȧn-tĕl')	112	18.36N	91.06W
Mamaroneck, N.Y., U.S. (măm'ȧ-rō-nĕk)	94a	40.57N	73.44W
Mambasa, Zaire	210	1.21N	29.03E
Mamburao, Phil. (mäm-bo͞o'rä-ō)	189a	13.14N	120.35E
Mamera, Ven.	230a	10.27N	66.59W
Mamfe, Cam. (mäm'fĕ)	204	5.46N	9.17E
Mamihara, Japan (mä'mē-hä-rä)	187	32.41N	131.12E
Mammoth Cave, Ky., U.S. (măm'ŏth)	108	37.10N	86.04W
Mammoth Cave National Park, rec., Ky., U.S.	90	37.20N	86.21W
Mammoth Hot Springs, Wy., U.S. (măm'ŭth hôt sprĭngz)	98	44.55N	110.50W
Mamnoli, India	179b	19.17N	73.15E
Mamoré, r., S.A.	124	13.00S	65.20W
Mamou, Gui.	204	10.26N	12.07W
Mampong, Ghana	208	7.04N	1.24W
Mamry, Jezioro, l., Pol. (mäm'rĭ)	148	54.10N	21.28E
Man, I.C.	208	7.24N	7.33W
Manacor, Spain (mä-nä-kôr')	152	39.35N	3.15E
Manado, Indon.	188	1.29N	124.50E
Managua, Cuba (mä-nä'gwä)	117a	22.58N	82.17W
Managua, Nic.	110	12.10N	86.16W
Managua, Lago de, l., Nic. (lä'gô-dĕ)	114	12.28N	86.10W
Manakara, Madag. (mä-nä-kä'rŭ)	206	22.17S	48.06E
Mananara, r., Madag. (mä-nä-nä'rŭ)	206	23.15S	48.15E
Mananjary, Madag. (mä-nän-zhä'rē)	206	20.16S	48.13E
Manas, China	180	44.30N	86.00E
Manassas, Va., U.S. (mȧ-năs'ȧs)	92	38.45N	77.30W
Manaus, Braz. (mä-nä'o͞ozh)	124	3.01S	60.00W
Manayunk, neigh., Pa., U.S.	225b	40.01N	75.13W
Mancelona, Mi., U.S. (măn-sē-lō'nȧ)	92	44.50N	85.05W
Mancha Real, Spain (män'chä rā-äl')	152	37.48N	3.37W
Manchazh, Russia (män'chȧsh)	164a	56.30N	58.10E
Manchester, Eng., U.K.	136	53.28N	2.14W
Manchester, Ct., U.S. (măn'chĕs-tēr)	92	41.45N	72.30W
Manchester, Ga., U.S.	108	32.50N	84.37W
Manchester, Ia., U.S.	96	42.30N	91.30W
Manchester, Ma., U.S.	87a	42.35N	70.47W
Manchester, Mo., U.S.	101e	38.36N	90.31W
Manchester, N.H., U.S.	90	43.00N	71.30W
Manchester, Oh., U.S.	92	38.40N	83.35W
Manchester Docks, pt. of i., Eng., U.K.	233b	53.28N	2.17W
Manchester Ship Canal, Eng., U.K.	138a	53.20N	2.40W
Manchuria, hist. reg., China (măn-cho͞o'rē-ȧ)	180	48.00N	124.58E
Mandal, Nor. (män'däl)	146	58.03N	7.28E
Mandalay, Burma (măn'dȧ-lā)	174	22.00N	96.08E
Mandalselva, r., Nor.	146	58.25N	7.30E
Mandaluyong, Phil.	237g	14.35N	121.02E
Mandan, N.D., U.S. (măn'dăn)	90	46.49N	100.54W
Mandāoli, neigh., India	236d	28.38N	77.18E
Mandara Mountains, mts., Afr. (män-dä'rä)	204	10.15N	13.23E
Mandau Siak, r., Indon.	173b	1.03N	101.25E
Mandimba, Moz.	210	14.21S	35.39E
Mandinga, Pan. (män-dĭŋ'gä)	114	9.32N	79.04W
Mandla, India	178	22.43N	80.23E
Mándra, Grc. (män'drä)	154	38.06N	23.32E
Mandres-les-Roses, Fr.	233c	48.42N	2.33E
Mandritsara, Madag. (män-drēt-sä'rȧ)	206	15.49S	48.47E
Manduria, Italy (män-do͞o'rē-ä)	154	40.23N	17.41E
Mandve, India	179b	18.47N	72.52E
Māndvi, India (mŭnd'vē)	174	22.54N	69.23E
Māndvi, India (mŭnd'vē)	179b	19.29N	72.53E
Mandvi, neigh., India	236e	18.57N	72.50E
Mandya, India	178	12.40N	77.00E
Manfredonia, Italy (män-frȧ-dô'nyä)	154	41.39N	15.55E
Manfredónia, Golfo di, b., Italy (gôl-fô-dē)	154	41.34N	16.05E
Mangabeiras, Chapada das, pl., Braz.	124	8.05S	47.32W
Mangalore, India (mŭŋ-gŭ-lōr')	174	12.53N	74.52E
Manganji, Japan	238a	35.40N	139.26E
Mangaratiba, Braz. (män-gä-rä-tē'bȧ)	123a	22.56S	44.03W
Mangatarem, Phil. (mäŋ'gȧ-tä'rĕm)	189a	15.48N	120.18E
Mange, Zaire	210	0.54N	20.30E
Mangkalihat, Tanjung, c., Indon.	188	1.25N	119.55E
Mangles, Islas de, Cuba (ē's-läs-dē-mäŋ'gläs) (măn'g'lz)	116	22.05N	82.50W
Mangoche, Mwi.	206	14.16S	35.14E
Mangoky, r., Madag. (män-gō'kē)	206	22.02S	44.11E
Mangole, Pulau, i., Indon.	188	1.35S	126.22E
Mangualde, Port. (män-gwäl'dĕ)	152	40.38N	7.44W
Mangueira, Lagoa da, l., Braz.	126	33.15S	52.45W
Mangum, Ok., U.S. (măŋ'gŭm)	104	34.52N	99.31W
Mangyshlak, Poluostrov, pen., Kaz.	160	44.30N	50.40E
Mangzhangdian, China (mäŋ-jäŋ-dĭĕn)	182	32.07N	114.44E
Manhasset, N.Y., U.S.	224	40.48N	73.42W
Manhattan, Il., U.S.	95a	41.25N	87.29W
Manhattan, Ks., U.S. (măn-hăt'ăn)	90	39.11N	96.34W
Manhattan Beach, Ca., U.S.	101a	33.53N	118.24W

ăt; finăl; rāte; senȧte; ärm; ȧsk; sofȧ; fâre; ch-choose; dh-as th in other; bē; ėvent; bĕt; recĕnt; cratēr; g-gō; gh-guttural g; bĭt; ĭ-short neutral; rīde; K-guttural k as ch in German ich;

PLACE (Pronunciation)	PAGE	Lat. °′	Long. °′
Manhuaçu, Braz. (män-ȯá'sōō)	123a	20.17S	42.01W
Manhumirim, Braz. (män-ōō-mē-rē'n)	123a	22.30S	41.57W
Manicouagane, r., Can.	78	50.00N	68.35W
Manicouagane, Lac, res., Can.	78	51.30N	68.19W
Manicuare, Ven. (mä-nē-kwä'rē)	125b	10.35N	64.10W
Manihiki Islands, is., Cook Is. (mä'nē-hē'kē)	190	9.40S	158.00W
Manila, Phil.	188	14.37N	121.00E
Manila Bay, b., Phil. (mȧ-nĭl'ȧ)	189a	14.38N	120.46E
Manique de Baixo, Port.	234d	38.44N	9.22W
Manisa, Tur. (mä'nē-sȧ)	142	38.40N	27.30E
Manistee, Mi., U.S. (măn-ĭs-tē')	92	44.15N	86.20W
Manistee, r., Mi., U.S.	92	44.25N	85.45W
Manistique, Mi., U.S. (măn-ĭs-tēk')	96	45.58N	86.16W
Manistique, l., Mi., U.S.	96	46.14N	85.30W
Manistique, r., Mi., U.S.	96	46.05N	86.09W
Manitoba, prov., Can. (măn-ĭ-tō'bȧ)	78	55.12N	97.29W
Manitoba, Lake, l., Can.	78	51.00N	98.45W
Manito Lake, l., Can. (măn'ĭ-tō)	82	52.45N	109.45W
Manitou, i., Mi., U.S. (măn'ĭ-tōō)	96	47.21N	87.33W
Manitou, l., Can.	96	49.21N	93.01W
Manitou Islands, is., Mi., U.S.	92	45.05N	86.00W
Manitoulin Island, i., Can. (măn-ĭ-tōō'lĭn)	78	45.45N	81.30W
Manitou Springs, Co., U.S.	104	38.51N	104.58W
Manitowoc, Wi., U.S. (măn-ĭ-tô-wŏk')	96	44.05N	87.42W
Manitqueira, Serra da, mts., Braz.	123a	22.40S	45.12W
Maniwaki, Can.	84	46.23N	76.00W
Manizales, Col. (mä-nē-zä'lȧs)	124	5.05N	75.31W
Manjacaze, Moz. (man'yä-kä'zĕ)	206	24.37S	33.49E
Mankato, Ks., U.S. (măn-kā'tō)	104	39.45N	98.12W
Mankato, Mn., U.S.	90	44.10N	93.59W
Mankim, Cam.	208	5.01N	12.00E
Manlléu, Spain (män-lyā'ōō)	152	42.00N	2.16E
Manly, Austl.	239a	33.48S	151.17E
Mannar, Sri L. (mȧ-när')	175c	9.48N	80.03E
Mannar, Gulf of, b., Asia	174	8.47N	78.33E
Mannheim, Ger. (män'hīm)	140	49.30N	8.31E
Manning, Ia., U.S. (măn'ĭng)	96	41.53N	95.04W
Manning, S.C., U.S.	108	33.41N	80.12W
Mannington, W.V., U.S. (măn'ĭng-tŭn)	92	39.30N	80.55W
Mannswörth, neigh., Aus.	235e	48.09N	16.31E
Mano, r., Afr.	208	7.00N	11.25W
Man of War Bay, b., Bah.	116	21.05N	74.05W
Man of War Channel, strt., Bah.	116	22.45N	76.10W
Manokwari, Indon. (mȧ-nŏk-wä'rē)	188	0.56S	134.10E
Manono, Zaire	210	7.18S	27.25E
Manor, Can. (măn'ẽr)	82	49.36N	102.05W
Manor, Wa., U.S.	100c	45.45N	122.36W
Manorhaven, N.Y., U.S.	224	40.50N	73.42W
Manori, neigh., India	179b	19.13N	72.43E
Manosque, Fr. (mȧ-nōsh')	150	43.51N	5.48E
Manotick, Can.	77c	45.13N	75.41W
Manouane, r., Can.	84	50.15N	70.30W
Manouane, Lac, l., Can. (mȧ-nōō'án)	86	50.36N	70.50W
Manresa, Spain (män-rā'sä)	142	41.44N	1.52E
Mansa, Zam.	206	11.12S	28.53E
Mansel, i., Can. (măn'sĕl)	78	61.56N	81.10W
Manseriche, Pongo de, reg., Peru (pŏ'n-gô-dĕ-män-sĕ-rē'chĕ)	124	4.15S	77.45W
Mansfield, Eng., U.K. (mănz'fēld)	138a	53.08N	1.12W
Mansfield, La., U.S.	106	32.02N	93.43W
Mansfield, Oh., U.S.	92	40.45N	82.30W
Mansfield, Wa., U.S.	98	47.48N	119.39W
Mansfield, Mount, mtn., Vt., U.S.	92	44.30N	72.45W
Mansfield Woodhouse, Eng., U.K. (wŏd-hous)	138a	53.08N	1.12W
Manta, Ec. (män'tä)	124	1.03S	80.16W
Manteno, Il., U.S. (măn-tē-nō)	95a	41.15N	87.50W
Manteo, N.C., U.S.	108	35.55N	75.40W
Mantes-la-Jolie, Fr. (mänt-ĕ-lä-zhō-lē')	150	48.59N	1.42E
Manti, Ut., U.S. (măn'tī)	102	39.15N	11.40W
Mantilla, neigh., Cuba	229b	23.04N	82.20W
Mantova, Italy (män'tô-vä) (măn'tụ-ȧ)	142	45.09N	10.47E
Mantua, Cuba (män-tōō'ȧ)	116	22.20N	84.15W
Mantua, Md., U.S.	225d	38.51N	77.15W
Mantua, Ut., U.S. (măn'tụ-ȧ)	101b	41.30N	111.57W
Mantua, *see* Mantova, Italy	142	45.09N	10.47E
Manua Islands, is., Am. Sam.	192a	14.13S	169.35W
Manui, Pulau, i., Indon. (mä-nōō'ē)	188	3.35S	123.38E
Manus Island, i., Pap. N. Gui. (mä'nōōs)	188	2.22S	146.22E
Manvel, Tx., U.S. (măn'vel)	107a	29.28N	95.22W
Manville, N.J., U.S. (măn'vĭl)	94a	40.33N	74.36W
Manville, R.I., U.S.	94b	41.57N	71.27W
Manyal Shīhah, Egypt	240a	29.57N	31.14E
Manzala Lake, l., Egypt	212b	31.14N	32.04E
Manzanares, Col. (män-sä-nä'rĕs)	124a	5.15N	75.09W
Manzanares, r., Spain (mänz-nä'rĕs)	153a	40.36N	3.48W
Manzanares, Canal del, Spain (kä-nä'l-dĕl-män-thä-nä'rĕs)	153a	40.20N	3.38W
Manzanillo, Cuba (män'zä-nēl'yō)	110	20.20N	77.05W
Manzanillo, Mex.	110	19.02N	104.21W
Manzanillo, Bahía de, b., Mex. (bä-ē'ä-dĕ-män-zä-nē'l-yō)	112	19.00N	104.38W
Manzanillo, Bahía de, b., N.A.	116	19.55N	71.50W
Manzanillo, Punta, c., Pan.	114	9.40N	79.33W
Manzhouli, China (män-jō-lē)	180	49.25N	117.15E
Manzovka, Russia (mȧn-zhō'f-kȧ)	186	44.16N	132.13E
Mao, Chad (mä'ō)	204	14.07N	15.19E
Mao, Dom. Rep.	116	19.35N	71.10W
Maoke, Pegunungan, mts., Indon.	188	4.00S	138.00E
Maoming, China	180	21.55N	110.40E
Maoniu Shan, mtn., China (mou-niō shän)	184	32.45N	104.09E
Mapastepec, Mex. (ma-päs-tȧ-pĕk')	112	15.24N	92.52W
Mapia, Kepulauan, i., Indon.	188	0.57N	134.22E
Mapimí, Mex. (mä-pē-mē')	106	25.50N	103.50W
Mapimí, Bolsón de, des., Mex. (bôl-sŏ'n-dĕ-mä-pē'mē)	106	27.27N	103.20W
Maple Creek, Can. (mā'p'l) (crēk)	78	49.55N	109.27W
Maple Cross, Eng., U.K.	231	51.37N	0.30W
Maple Grove, Can. (grōv)	77a	45.19N	73.51W
Maple Heights, Oh., U.S.	95d	41.25N	81.34W
Maple Leaf Gardens, rec., Can.	223c	43.40N	79.23W
Maple Shade, N.J., U.S. (shād)	94f	39.57N	75.01W
Maple Valley, Wa., U.S. (văl'ē)	100a	47.24N	122.02W
Maplewood, Mn., U.S. (wŏd)	101g	45.00N	93.03W
Maplewood, Mo., U.S.	101e	38.37N	90.20W
Maplewood, N.J., U.S.	224	40.44N	74.17W
Mapocho, r., Chile	230b	33.25S	70.47W
Mapumulo, S. Afr. (mä-pä-mōō'lō)	207c	29.12S	31.05E
Maputo, Moz.	206	26.50S	32.30E
Maquela do Zombo, Ang. (mȧ-kā'lȧ dò zôm'bò)	206	6.08S	15.15E
Maquoketa, Ia., U.S. (mȧ-kō-kē-tȧ)	96	42.04N	90.42W
Maquoketa, r., Ia., U.S.	96	42.08N	90.40W
Mar, Serra do, mts., Braz. (sĕr'rȧ dò mär')	126	26.30S	49.15W
Maracaibo, Ven. (mä-rä-kī'bō)	124	10.38N	71.45W
Maracaibo, Lago de, l., Ven. (lä'gô-dĕ-mä-rä-kī'bō)	124	9.55N	72.13W
Maracay, Ven. (mä-rä-käy')	124	10.15N	67.35W
Marādah, Libya	204	29.10N	19.07E
Maradi, Niger (mȧ-rȧ-dē')	204	13.29N	7.06E
Marāgheh, Iran	176	37.20N	46.10E
Maraisburg, S. Afr.	207b	26.12S	27.57E
Marais des Cygnes, r., Ks., U.S.	104	38.30N	95.30W
Marajó, Ilha de, i., Braz.	124	1.00S	49.30W
Maralal, Kenya	210	1.06N	36.42E
Marali, Cen. Afr. Rep.	208	6.01N	18.24E
Marand, Iran	176	38.26N	45.46E
Maranguape, Braz. (mä-räŋ-gwä'pĕ)	124	3.48S	38.38W
Maranhão, state, Braz. (mä-rän-youn)	124	5.15S	45.52W
Maranoa, r., Austl. (mä-rä-nō'ä)	196	27.01S	148.03E
Marano di Napoli, Italy (mä-rä'nō-dē-nä'pō-lē)	153c	40.39N	14.12E
Marañón, Río, r., Peru (rē'ō-mä-rä-nyōn')	124	4.26S	75.08W
Maraoli, neigh., India	236e	19.03N	72.54E
Marapanim, Braz. (mä-rä-pä-nē'n)	124	0.45S	47.42W
Marathon, Can.	78	48.50N	86.10W
Marathon, Fl., U.S. (măr'ȧ-thŏn)	109a	24.41N	81.06W
Marathon, Oh., U.S.	95f	39.09N	83.59W
Maravatio, Mex. (mä-rä-vä'tē-ō)	112	19.54N	100.25W
Marawi, Sudan	204	18.07N	31.57E
Marayong, Austl.	239a	33.45S	150.54E
Marble Bar, Austl. (märb'l bär)	196	21.15S	119.15E
Marble Canal, can., Az., U.S. (mär'b'l)	102	36.21N	111.48W
Marblehead, Ma., U.S. (mär'b'l-hĕd)	87a	42.30N	70.51W
Marburg an der Lahn, Ger.	148	50.49N	8.46E
Marca, Ponta da, c., Ang.	210	16.31S	11.42E
Marcala, Hond. (mär-kä-lä)	114	14.08N	88.01W
Marceline, Mo., U.S. (mär-sē-lēn')	104	39.42N	92.56W
Marche, hist. reg., Italy (mär'kā)	154	43.35N	12.33E
Marchegg, Aus.	139e	48.18N	16.55E
Marchena, Spain (mär-chā'nä)	142	37.20N	5.25W
Marchena, i., Ec. (ĕ's-lä-mär-chĕ'nä)	124	0.29N	90.31W
Marchfeld, reg., Aus.	139e	48.14N	16.37E
Mar Chiquíta, Laguna, l., Arg. (lä-gōō'nä-mär-chē-kē'tä)	123c	34.25S	61.10W
Marco Polo Bridge, trans., China	236b	39.52N	116.12E
Marcos Paz, Arg. (mär-kōs' päz)	123c	34.49S	58.51W
Marcus, i., Japan (mär'kŭs)	190	24.00N	155.00E
Marcus Hook, Pa., U.S. (mär'kŭs hŏk)	94f	39.49N	75.25W
Marcy, Mount, mtn., N.Y., U.S. (mär'sē)	92	44.10N	73.55W
Mar de Espanha, Braz. (mär-dĕ-ĕs-pȧ'nyȧ)	123a	21.53S	43.00W
Mar del Plata, Arg. (mär dĕl- plä'ta)	126	37.59S	57.35W
Mardin, Tur. (mär-dēn')	174	37.25N	40.40E
Maré, i., N. Cal. (mȧ-rā')	196	21.53S	168.30E
Maree, Loch, b., Scot., U.K. (mä-rē')	144	57.40N	5.44W
Mareil-Marly, Fr.	233c	48.53N	2.05E
Marengo, Ia., U.S. (mȧ-rĕŋ'gō)	96	41.47N	92.04W
Marennes, Fr. (mȧ-rĕn')	150	45.49N	1.08W
Marfa, Tx., U.S. (mär'fȧ)	106	30.19N	104.01W
Marganets, Ukr.	156	47.41N	34.33E
Margarethenhöhe, neigh., Ger.	232	51.26N	6.58E
Margaretting, Eng., U.K.	231	51.41N	0.25E
Margarita, Pan. (mär-gōō-rē'tä)	110a	9.20N	79.55W
Margarita, Isla de, i., Ven. (mä-gȧ-rē'tȧ)	124	11.00N	64.15W
Margate, S. Afr. (mä-gāt')	207c	30.52S	30.21E
Margate, Eng., U.K. (mär'gāt)	144	51.21N	1.17E
Margherita Peak, mtn., Afr.	204	0.22N	29.51E
Marguerite, r., Can.	86	50.39N	66.42W
Maria, Can. (mȧ-rē'ȧ)	86	48.10N	66.04W
Mariager, Den. (mä-rē-ägh'ẽr)	146	56.38N	10.00E
Mariana, Braz. (mä-ryä'nä)	123a	20.23S	43.24W
Mariana Islands, is., Oc.	4	16.00N	145.30E
Marianao, Cuba (mä-rē-ä-nä'ō)	110	23.05N	82.26W
Mariana Trench, deep	190	12.00N	144.00E
Marianna, Ar., U.S. (mā-rĭ-ăn'ȧ)	104	34.45N	90.45W
Marianna, Fl., U.S.	108	30.46N	85.14W
Marianna, Pa., U.S.	95e	40.01N	80.05W
Mariano Acosta, Arg. (mä-rēä'nō-ȧ-kōs'tä)	126a	34.28S	58.48W
Mariano J. Haedo, Arg.	229d	34.39S	58.36W
Mariánské Lázně, Czech. (mär'yȧn-skĕ'läz'nyĕ)	148	49.58N	12.42E
Maria Paula, Braz.	230c	22.54S	43.02W
Marias, r., Mt., U.S. (mȧ-rī'ȧz)	98	48.15N	110.50W
Marias, Islas, is., Mex. (mä-rē'äs)	110	21.30N	106.40W
Mariato, Punta, c., Pan.	114	7.17N	81.09W
Maribo, Den. (mä'rē-bô)	146	54.46N	11.29E
Maribor, Slo. (mä're-bôr)	136	46.33N	15.37E
Maribyrnong, Austl.	239b	37.46S	144.54E
Maricaban, i., Phil. (mä-rē-kä-bän')	189a	13.40N	120.44E
Mariefred, Swe. (mä-rē'ĕ-frĭd)	146	59.17N	17.09E
Marie Galante, i., Guad. (mȧ-rē' gȧ-länt')	115b	15.58N	61.05W
Mariehamn, Fin. (mȧ-rē'ĕ-häm''n)	146	60.07N	19.57E
Mariendorf, neigh., Ger.	234a	52.26N	13.23E
Marienfelde, neigh., Ger.	234a	52.25N	13.22E
Mariestad, Swe. (mä-rē'ĕ-städ')	146	58.43N	13.45E
Marietta, Ga., U.S. (mā-rĭ-ĕt'ȧ)	94c	33.57N	84.33W
Marietta, Oh., U.S.	92	39.25N	81.30W
Marietta, Ok., U.S.	104	33.53N	97.07W
Marietta, Wa., U.S.	100d	48.48N	122.35W
Mariinsk, Russia (mȧ-re'ĭnsk)	162	56.15N	87.28E
Marijampole, Lith. (mä-rē-yäm-pô'lĕ)	146	54.33N	23.26E
Marikana, S. Afr. (mä'-rĭ-kä-nȧ)	212d	25.40S	27.28E
Marikina, Phil.	237g	14.37N	121.06E
Marília, Braz. (mä-rē'lyȧ)	124	22.02S	49.48W
Marimba, Ang.	210	8.28S	17.08E
Marín, Spain	152	42.24N	8.40W
Marina del Rey, Ca., U.S.	228	33.59N	118.28W
Marina del Rey, b., Ca., U.S.	228	33.58N	118.27W
Marin City, Ca., U.S.	227b	37.52N	122.21W
Marinduque Island, i., Phil. (mä-rēn-dōō'kä)	189a	13.14N	121.45E
Marine, Il., U.S. (mȧ-rēn')	101e	38.48N	89.47W
Marine City, Mi., U.S.	92	42.45N	82.30W
Marine Lake, l., Mn., U.S.	101g	45.13N	92.55W
Marineland of the Pacific, pt. of i., Ca., U.S.	228	33.44N	118.24W
Marine on Saint Croix, Mn., U.S.	101g	45.11N	92.47W
Marinette, Wi., U.S. (măr-ĭ-nĕt')	90	45.04N	87.40W
Maringa, r., Zaire (mȧ-riŋ'gä)	204	0.30N	21.00E
Marinha Grande, Port. (mä-rēn'yȧ grän'dĕ)	152	39.49N	8.53W
Marion, Al., U.S. (măr'ĭ-ŭn)	108	32.36N	87.19W
Marion, Il., U.S.	92	37.40N	88.55W
Marion, In., U.S.	90	40.35N	85.45W
Marion, Ia., U.S.	96	42.01N	91.39W
Marion, Ks., U.S.	104	38.21N	97.02W
Marion, Ky., U.S.	108	37.19N	88.05W
Marion, N.C., U.S.	108	35.40N	82.00W
Marion, N.D., U.S.	96	46.37N	98.20W
Marion, Oh., U.S.	92	40.35N	83.10W
Marion, S.C., U.S.	108	34.08N	79.23W
Marion, Va., U.S.	108	36.48N	81.33W
Marion, Lake, res., S.C., U.S.	108	33.25N	80.35W
Marion Reef, rf., Austl.	196	18.57S	151.31E
Mariposa, Chile (mä-rē-pō'sä)	123b	35.33S	71.21W
Mariposa Creek, r., Ca., U.S.	102	37.14N	120.30W
Mariquita, Col. (mä-rē-kē'tä)	124a	5.13N	74.52W
Mariscal Estigarribia, Para.	126	22.03S	60.28W
Marisco, Ponta do, c., Braz. (pô'n-tä-dō-mä-rē's-kō)	126b	23.01S	43.17W
Maritime Alps, mts., Eur. (mȧ'rĭ-tīm ălps)	140	44.20N	7.02E
Mariupol', Ukr. (zhdä'nôf)	158	47.07N	37.32E
Mariveles, Phil.	189a	14.27N	120.29E
Marj Uyan, Leb.	173a	33.21N	35.36E
Marka, Som.	212a	1.45N	44.47E
Markaryd, Swe. (mär'kä-rüd)	146	56.30N	13.34E
Marked Tree, Ar., U.S. (märkt trē)	104	35.31N	90.26W
Marken, i., Neth.	139a	52.26N	5.08E
Market Bosworth, Eng., U.K. (bŏz'wûrth)	138a	52.37N	1.23W
Market Deeping, Eng., U.K. (dēp'ĭng)	138a	52.40N	0.19W
Market Drayton, Eng., U.K. (drā'tŭn)	138a	52.54N	2.29W
Market Harborough, Eng., U.K. (här'bŭr-ō)	138a	52.28N	0.55W
Market Rasen, Eng., U.K. (rā'zĕn)	138a	53.23N	0.21W
Markham, Can. (märk'ȧm)	84	43.53N	79.15W
Markham, Mount, mtn., Ant.	213	82.59S	159.30E
Markovka, Ukr. (mȧr-kôf'kȧ)	156	49.32N	39.34E
Markovo, Russia (mär'kô-vô)	158	64.46N	170.48E
Markrāna, India	178	27.08N	74.43E
Marks, Russia	160	51.42N	46.46E
Marksville, La., U.S. (märks'vĭl)	106	31.09N	92.05W
Markt Indersdorf, Ger. (märkt ēn'dĕrs-dōrf)	139d	48.22N	11.23E
Marktredwitz, Ger. (märk-rĕd'vĕts)	148	50.02N	12.05E
Markt Schwaben, Ger. (märkt shvä'bĕn)	139d	48.12N	11.52E
Marl, Ger. (märl)	151c	51.40N	7.05E
Marlboro, N.J., U.S.	94a	40.18N	74.15W
Marlborough, Ma., U.S.	87a	42.21N	71.33W
Marlette, Mi., U.S. (mär-lĕt')	92	43.25N	83.05W
Marlin, Tx., U.S. (mär'lĭn)	106	31.18N	96.52W
Marlinton, W.V., U.S. (mär'lĭn-tŭn)	92	38.15N	80.10W
Marlow, Eng., U.K. (mär'lō)	138b	51.33N	0.46W
Marlow, Ok., U.S.	104	34.38N	97.56W
Marls, The, b., Bah. (märls)	116	26.30N	77.15W
Marly-le-Roi, Fr.	233c	48.52N	2.05E
Marmande, Fr. (mȧr-mänd')	150	44.30N	0.10E
Marmara Denizi, sea, Tur.	174	40.40N	28.00E
Marmarth, N.D., U.S. (mär'mȧrth)	96	46.19N	103.57W
Mar Muerto, l., Mex. (mär-mòĕ'r-tô)	112	16.13N	94.22W
Marne, Ger. (mär'nĕ)	139c	53.57N	9.01E
Marne, r., Fr. (märn)	140	49.00N	4.30E
Maroa, Ven. (mä-rō'ä)	124	2.43N	67.37W
Maroantsetra, Madag. (mȧ-rō-äŋ-tsä'trȧ)	206	15.18S	49.48E
Maro Jarapeto, mtn., Col. (mȧ-rō-hä-rä-pĕ'tō)	124a	6.29N	76.39W
Marolles-en-Brie, Fr.	233c	48.44N	2.33E
Maromokotro, mtn., Madag.	206	14.00S	49.11E

ng-sing; ŋ-baŋk; n-nasalized n; nŏd; cŏmmit; ōld; ôbey; ôrder; oi-boil; fōōd; ŏ-as oo in foot; ou-out; s-soft; sh-dish; th-thin; pūre; ûnite; ûrn; stŭd; circŭs; ü-as in French tu; '-indeterminate vowel.

PLACE (Pronunciation)	PAGE	Lat. °′	Long. °′
Marondera, Zimb.	206	18.10S	31.36E
Maroni, r., S.A. (mȧ-rō'nē)	124	3.02N	53.54W
Maro Reef, rf., Hi., U.S.	88b	25.15N	170.00W
Maroua, Cam. (mär'wä)	204	10.36N	14.20E
Maroubra, Austl.	239a	33.57S	151.16E
Marple, Eng., U.K. (mär'p'l)	138a	53.24N	2.04W
Marquard, S. Afr.	212d	28.41S	27.26E
Marquesas Islands, is., Fr. Poly. (mär-kĕ'säs)	2	8.50S	141.00W
Marquesas Keys, is., Fl., U.S. (mȧr-kē'zȧs)	109a	24.37N	82.15W
Marquês de Valença, Braz. (mȧr-kĕ's-dĕ-vä-lĕ'n-sȧ)	123a	22.16S	43.42W
Marquette, Can. (mȧr-kĕt')	77f	50.04N	97.43W
Marquette, Mi., U.S.	90	46.32N	87.25W
Marquez, Tx., U.S. (mär-kāz')	106	31.14N	96.15W
Marra, Jabal, mtn., Sudan (jĕb'ĕl mär'ä)	204	13.00N	23.47E
Marrakech, Mor. (mȧr-rä'kĕsh)	204	31.38N	8.00W
Marree, Austl. (mär'rē)	196	29.38S	137.55E
Marrero, La., U.S.	94d	29.55N	90.06W
Marrickville, Austl.	239a	33.55S	151.09E
Marrupa, Moz.	210	13.08S	37.30E
Mars, Pa., U.S. (märz)	95e	40.42N	80.01W
Marsabit, Kenya	210	2.20N	37.59E
Marsala, Italy (mär-sä'lä)	142	37.48N	12.28E
Marscheid, neigh., Ger.	232	51.14N	7.14E
Marsden, Eng., U.K. (märz'dĕn)	138a	53.36N	1.55W
Marseille, Fr. (mȧr-sâ'y')	136	43.18N	5.25E
Marseilles, Il., U.S. (mär-sĕlz')	92	41.20N	88.40W
Marsfield, Austl.	239a	33.47S	151.07E
Marshall, Il., U.S. (mär'shăl)	92	39.20N	87.40W
Marshall, Mi., U.S.	92	42.20N	84.55W
Marshall, Mn., U.S.	96	44.28N	95.49W
Marshall, Mo., U.S.	104	39.07N	93.12W
Marshall, Tx., U.S.	90	32.33N	94.22W
Marshall Islands, nation, Oc.	2	10.00N	165.00E
Marshalltown, Ia., U.S. (mär'shȧl-toun)	96	42.02N	92.55W
Marshallville, Ga., U.S. (mär'shȧl-vĭl)	108	32.29N	83.55W
Marshfield, Ma., U.S. (märsh'fēld)	87a	42.06N	70.43W
Marshfield, Mo., U.S.	104	37.20N	92.53W
Marshfield, Wi., U.S.	96	44.40N	90.10W
Marsh Harbour, Bah.	116	26.30N	77.00W
Mars Hill, In., U.S. (märz'hĭl')	95g	39.43N	86.15W
Mars Hill, Me., U.S.	86	46.34N	67.54W
Marstrand, Swe. (mär'stränd)	146	57.54N	11.33E
Marsyaty, Russia (märs'yȧ-tĭ)	164a	60.03N	60.28E
Mart, Tx., U.S. (märt)	106	31.32N	96.49W
Martaban, Gulf of, b., Burma (mär-tŭ-bän')	188	16.34N	96.58E
Martapura, Indon.	188	3.19S	114.45E
Marten, neigh., Ger.	232	51.31N	7.23E
Martha's Vineyard, i., Ma., U.S. (mär'thȧz vĭn'yȧrd)	92	41.25N	70.35W
Martigny, Switz. (mȧr-tē-nyē')	148	46.06N	7.00E
Martigues, Fr.	150	43.24N	5.05E
Martin, Tn., U.S. (mär'tĭn)	108	36.20N	88.45W
Martina Franca, Italy (mär-tē'nä frăŋ'kä)	154	40.43N	17.21E
Martinez, Ca., U.S. (mär-tē'nĕz)	100b	38.01N	122.08W
Martinez, Tx., U.S.	101d	29.25N	98.20W
Martínez, neigh., Arg.	229d	34.29S	58.30W
Martinique, dep., N.A. (mȧr-tē-nēk')	110	14.50N	60.40W
Martin Lake, res., Al., U.S.	108	32.40N	86.05W
Martin Point, c., Ak., U.S.	89	70.10N	142.00W
Martinsburg, W.V., U.S. (mär'tĭnz-bûrg)	92	39.30N	78.00W
Martins Ferry, Oh., U.S. (mär'tĭnz)	92	40.05N	80.45W
Martinsville, In., U.S. (mär'tĭnz-vĭl)	92	39.25N	86.25W
Martinsville, Va., U.S.	108	36.40N	79.53W
Martos, Spain (mär'tōs)	152	37.43N	3.58W
Martre, Lac la, l., Can. (läk la märtr)	78	63.24N	119.58W
Marugame, Japan (mä'rōō-gä'mä)	187	34.19N	133.48E
Marungu, mts., Zaire	210	7.50S	29.50E
Marve, neigh., India	179b	19.12N	72.43E
Marwitz, Ger.	234a	52.41N	13.09E
Mary, Turk. (mä'rē)	158	37.45N	61.47E
Mar'yanskaya, Russia (mȧr-yän'skȧ-yȧ)	156	45.04N	38.39E
Maryborough, Austl. (mä'rĭ-bŭr-ō)	196	25.35S	152.40E
Maryborough, Austl.	196	37.00S	143.50E
Maryland, state, U.S. (mĕr'ĭ-lănd)	90	39.10N	76.25W
Maryland Park, Md., U.S.	225d	38.53N	76.54W
Marys, r., Nv., U.S. (mā'rĭz)	98	41.25N	115.10W
Marystown, Can. (mâr'ĭz-toun)	86	47.11N	55.10W
Marysville, Can.	86	45.59N	66.35W
Marysville, Ca., U.S.	102	39.09N	121.37W
Marysville, Oh., U.S.	92	40.15N	83.25W
Marysville, Wa., U.S.	100a	48.03N	122.11W
Maryville, Il., U.S. (mā'rĭ-vĭl)	101e	38.44N	89.57W
Maryville, Mo., U.S.	104	40.21N	94.51W
Maryville, Tn., U.S.	108	35.44N	83.59W
Marzahn, neigh., Ger.	234a	52.33N	13.33E
Mārzuq, Libya	204	26.00N	14.09E
Marzūq, Idehan, des., Libya	204	24.30N	13.00E
Masai Steppe, plat., Tan.	210	4.30S	36.40E
Masaka, Ug.	210	0.20S	31.44E
Masalasef, Chad	208	11.43N	17.08E
Masalembo-Besar, i., Indon.	188	5.40S	114.28E
Masan, S. Kor. (mä-sän')	180	35.10N	128.31E
Masangwe, Tan.	210	5.28S	30.05E
Masasi, Tan. (mä-sä'sē)	206	10.43S	38.48E
Masatepe, Nic. (mä-sä-tĕ'pĕ)	114	11.57N	86.10W
Masaya, Nic. (mä-sä'yä)	114	11.58N	86.05W
Masbate, Phil. (mäs-bä'tä)	189a	12.21N	123.38E
Masbate, i., Phil.	188	12.19N	123.03E
Mascarene Islands, is., Afr.	4	20.20S	56.40E
Mascot, Austl.	239a	33.56S	151.12E
Mascot, Tn., U.S. (măs'kŏt)	108	36.04N	83.45W

PLACE (Pronunciation)	PAGE	Lat. °′	Long. °′
Mascota, Mex. (mäs-kō'tä)	112	20.33N	104.45W
Mascota, r., Mex.	112	20.33N	104.52W
Mascouche, Can. (mȧs-kōōsh')	77a	45.45N	73.36W
Mascouche, r., Can.	77a	45.44N	73.45W
Mascoutah, Il., U.S. (mäs-kū'tä)	101e	38.29N	89.48W
Maseru, Leso. (măz'ēr-ōō)	206	29.09S	27.11E
Mashhad, Iran	174	36.17N	59.30E
Māshkel, Hāmūn-i-, l., Asia (hä-mōōn'ē mäsh-kĕl')	174	28.28N	64.13E
Mashra'ar Raqq, Sudan	204	8.28N	29.15E
Masi-Manimba, Zaire	210	4.46S	17.55E
Masindi, Ug. (mä-sēn'dē)	204	1.44N	31.43E
Masjed Soleymān, Iran	174	31.45N	49.17E
Mask, Lough, b., Ire. (lŏk mȧsk)	144	53.35N	9.23W
Maslovo, Russia (mäs'lô-vô)	164a	60.08N	60.28E
Mason, Mi., U.S. (mā'sŭn)	92	42.35N	84.25W
Mason, Oh., U.S.	95f	39.22N	84.18W
Mason, Tx., U.S.	106	30.46N	99.14W
Mason City, Ia., U.S.	90	43.08N	93.14W
Masonville, Va., U.S.	225d	38.51N	77.12W
Maspeth, neigh., N.Y., U.S.	224	40.43N	73.55W
Massa, Italy (mäs'sä)	154	44.02N	10.08E
Massachusetts, state, U.S. (măs-ȧ-chōō'sĕts)	90	42.20N	72.30W
Massachusetts Bay, b., Ma., U.S.	86	42.26N	70.20W
Massafra, Italy (mäs-sä'frä)	154	40.35N	17.05E
Massa Marittima, Italy	154	43.03N	10.55E
Massapequa, N.Y., U.S.	94a	40.41N	73.28W
Massaua, *see* Mitsiwa, Eth.	204	15.40N	39.19E
Massena, N.Y., U.S. (mă-sē'nȧ)	92	44.55N	74.55W
Masset, Can. (măs'ĕt)	78	54.02N	132.09W
Masset Inlet, b., Can.	80	53.42N	132.20W
Massif Central, Fr. (mȧ-sēf' säN-trȧl')	136	45.12N	3.02E
Massillon, Oh., U.S. (măs'ĭ-lŏn)	92	40.50N	81.35W
Massinga, Moz. (mä-sĭn'gä)	206	23.18S	35.18E
Massive, Mount, mtn., Co., U.S. (măs'ĭv)	90	39.05N	106.30W
Masson, Can. (mäs-sŭn)	77c	45.33N	75.25W
Massy, Fr.	233c	48.44N	2.17E
Masuda, Japan (mä-sōō'dȧ)	187	34.42N	131.53E
Masuria, reg., Pol.	148	53.40N	21.10E
Masvingo, Zimb.	206	20.07S	30.47E
Matadi, Zaire (mȧ-tä'dē)	206	5.49S	13.27E
Matagalpa, Nic. (mä-tä-gäl'pä)	110	12.52N	85.57W
Matagami, l., Can. (mȧ-tä-gä'mē)	78	50.10N	78.28W
Matagorda Bay, b., Tx., U.S. (măt-ȧ-gôr'dȧ)	106	28.32N	96.13W
Matagorda Island, i., Tx., U.S.	106	28.13N	96.27W
Matam, Sen. (mä-täm')	204	15.40N	13.15W
Matamoros, Mex. (mä-tä-mō'rôs)	106	25.32N	103.13W
Matamoros, Mex.	110	25.52N	97.30W
Matane, Can. (mȧ-tȧn')	78	48.51N	67.32W
Matanzas, Cuba (mä-tän'zäs)	110	23.05N	81.35W
Matanzas, prov., Cuba	116	22.45N	81.20W
Matanzas, Bahía, b., Cuba (bä-ē'ä)	116	23.10N	81.30W
Matapalo, Cabo, c., C.R. (kä'bô-mä-tä-pä'lō)	114	8.22N	83.25W
Matapédia, Can. (mă-tȧ-pā'dē-ȧ)	86	47.58N	66.56W
Matapédia, l., Can.	86	48.33N	67.32W
Matapédia, r., Can.	86	48.10N	67.10W
Mataquito, r., Chile (mä-tä-kē'tô)	123b	35.08S	71.35W
Matara, Sri L. (mä-tä'rä)	175c	5.59N	80.35E
Mataram, Indon.	188	8.45S	116.15E
Matatiele, S. Afr. (mä-tä-tyā'lā)	207c	30.21S	28.49E
Matawan, N.J., U.S.	94a	40.24N	74.13W
Matehuala, Mex. (mä-tĕ-wä'lä)	110	23.38N	100.39W
Matera, Italy (mä-tâ'rä)	154	40.42N	16.37E
Mateur, Tun. (mȧ-tûr')	142	37.09N	9.43E
Mātherān, India	179b	18.58N	73.16E
Matheson, Can.	84	48.35N	80.33W
Mathews, Lake, l., Ca., U.S. (măth ūz)	101a	33.50N	117.24W
Mathura, India (mu-tŏ'rŭ)	174	27.39N	77.39E
Matias Barbosa, Braz. (mä-tē'äs-bȧr-bô-sä)	123a	21.53S	43.19W
Matillas, Laguna, l., Mex. (lä-gŏ'nä-mä-tē'l-yäs)	112	18.02N	92.36W
Matina, C.R. (mä-tē'nä)	114	10.06N	83.20W
Matiši, Lat. (mä'tē-sē)	146	57.43N	25.09E
Matlalcueyetl, Cerro, mtn., Mex. (sĕ'r-rä-mä-tläl-kwĕ'yĕtl)	112	19.13N	98.02W
Matlock, Eng., U.K. (măt'lŏk)	138a	53.08N	1.33W
Matochkin Shar, Russia (mä'tŏch-kĭn)	158	73.57N	56.16E
Mato Grosso, Braz. (măt'ŏ grōs'ŏ)	124	15.04S	59.58W
Mato Grosso, state, Braz.	124	14.38S	55.36W
Mato Grosso, Chapada de, hills, Braz. (shä-pä'dä-dē)	124	13.39S	55.42W
Mato Grosso do Sul, state, Braz.	124	20.00S	56.00W
Matosinhos, Port.	152	41.10N	8.48W
Maţraḩ, Oman (mȧ-trä')	174	23.36N	58.27E
Matsubara, Japan	187b	34.34N	135.34E
Matsudo, Japan (mät'sō-dō)	187a	35.48N	139.55E
Matsue, Japan (mät'sō-ĕ)	180	35.29N	133.04E
Matsumoto, Japan (mät'sō-mō'tō)	186	36.15N	137.59E
Matsuyama, Japan (mät'sō-yä'mä)	180	33.48N	132.45E
Matsuzaka, Japan (mät'sō-zä'kä)	187	34.35N	136.34E
Mattamuskeet, Lake, l., N.C., U.S. (măt-tȧ-mŭs'kēt)	108	35.34N	76.03W
Mattaponi, r., Va., U.S. (măt'ȧ-pon-ī')	92	37.45N	77.00W
Mattawa, Can. (măt'ȧ-wȧ)	78	46.15N	78.49W
Matterhorn, mtn., Switz. (măt'ēr-hôrn)	148	45.57N	7.36E
Matteson, Il., U.S. (mătt'ē-sŭn)	95a	41.30N	87.42W
Matthew Town, Bah. (măth'ū toun)	116	21.00N	73.40W
Mattoon, Il., U.S. (mă-tōōn')	90	39.30N	88.20W
Maturín, Ven. (mä-tōō-rēn')	124	9.48N	63.16W
Mátyásföld, neigh., Hung.	235g	47.31N	19.13E
Mátyas-Templom, rel., Hung.	235g	47.30N	19.02E

PLACE (Pronunciation)	PAGE	Lat. °′	Long. °′
Maúa, Moz.	210	13.51S	37.10E
Mauban, Phil. (mä'ōō-bän')	189a	14.11N	121.44E
Maubeuge, Fr. (mô-bûzh')	150	50.18N	3.57E
Maud, Oh., U.S. (môd)	95f	39.21N	84.23W
Mauer, Aus. (mou'ēr)	139e	48.09N	16.16E
Maués, Braz. (mȧ-wĕ's)	124	3.34S	57.30W
Mau Escarpment, cliff, Kenya	210	0.45S	35.50E
Maui, i., Hi., U.S. (mä'ōō-ē)	90c	20.52N	156.02W
Maule, r., Chile (mà'ŏ-lĕ)	123b	35.45S	70.50W
Maumee, Oh., U.S. (mô-mē')	92	41.30N	83.40W
Maumee, r., In., U.S.	92	41.10N	84.50W
Maumee Bay, b., Oh., U.S.	92	41.50N	83.20W
Maun, Bots. (mä-ōn')	206	19.52S	23.40E
Mauna Kea, mtn., Hi., U.S. (mä'ŏ-näkä'ä)	90c	19.52N	155.30W
Mauna Loa, mtn., Hi., U.S. (mä'ŏ-nälō'ä)	90c	19.28N	155.38W
Maurecourt, Fr.	233c	49.00N	2.04E
Maurepas Lake, l., La., U.S. (mō-rē-pä')	106	30.18N	90.40W
Mauricie, Parc National de la, rec., Can.	84	46.46N	73.00W
Mauritania, nation, Afr. (mô-rē-tā'nĭ-ȧ)	204	19.38N	13.30W
Mauritius, nation, Afr. (mô-rĭsh'ĭ-ŭs)	2	20.18S	57.36E
Maury, Wa., U.S. (mô'rĭ)	100a	47.22N	122.23W
Mauston, Wi., U.S. (môs'tŭn)	96	43.46N	90.05W
Maverick, r., Az., U.S. (mā-vûr'ĭk)	102	33.40N	109.30W
Mavinga, Ang.	210	15.50S	20.21E
Mawlamyine, Burma	188	16.30N	97.39E
Maxville, Can. (măks'vĭl)	77c	45.17N	74.52W
Maxville, Mo., U.S.	101e	38.26N	90.24W
Maya, r., Russia (mä'yä)	162	58.00N	135.45E
Mayaguana, i., Bah.	116	22.25N	73.00W
Mayaguana Passage, strt., Bah.	116	22.20N	73.25W
Mayagüez, P.R. (mä-yä-gwāz')	110	18.12N	67.10W
Mayari, r., Cuba	116	20.25N	75.35W
Mayas, Montañas, mts., N.A. (mŏntăn'äs mä'äs)	114a	16.43N	89.00W
Mayd, i., Som.	212a	11.24N	46.38E
Mayen, Ger. (mī'ĕn)	148	50.19N	7.14E
Mayenne, r., Fr. (mȧ-yĕn)	150	48.14N	0.45W
Mayfair, neigh., S. Afr.	240b	26.12S	28.01E
Mayfair, neigh., Pa., U.S.	225b	40.02N	75.03W
Mayfield, Ky., U.S. (mā'fēld)	108	36.44N	88.19W
Mayfield Creek, r., Ky., U.S.	108	36.54N	88.47W
Mayfield Heights, Oh., U.S.	95d	41.31N	81.26W
Mayfield Lake, res., Wa., U.S.	98	46.31N	122.34W
Maykop, Russia	158	44.35N	40.07E
Maykor, Russia (mī-kôr')	164a	59.01N	55.52E
Maymyo, Burma (mī'myō)	180	22.14N	96.32E
Maynard, Ma., U.S. (mā'nȧrd)	87a	42.25N	71.27W
Mayne, Can. (mān)	100d	48.51N	123.18W
Mayne, i., Can.	100d	48.52N	123.14W
Mayo, Can. (mä-yō')	78	63.40N	135.51W
Mayo, Fl., U.S.	108	30.02N	83.08W
Mayo, Md., U.S.	94e	38.54N	76.31W
Mayodan, N.C., U.S. (mā-yō'dăn)	108	36.25N	79.59W
Mayon Volcano, vol., Phil. (mä-yōn')	189a	13.21N	123.43E
Mayotte, dep., Afr. (mȧ-yôt')	206	13.07S	45.32E
May Pen, Jam.	116	18.00N	77.25W
Mayraira Point, c., Phil.	184	18.40N	120.45E
Mayran, Laguna de, l., Mex. (lä-ŏ'nä-dĕ-mī-rän')	110	25.40N	102.35W
Maysville, Ky., U.S. (māz'vĭl)	92	38.35N	83.45W
Mayumba, Gabon	206	3.25S	10.39E
Mayville, N.Y., U.S. (mā'vĭl)	92	42.15N	79.30W
Mayville, N.D., U.S.	96	47.30N	97.20W
Mayville, Wi., U.S.	96	43.30N	88.45W
Maywood, Ca., U.S. (mā'wŏd)	101a	33.59N	118.11W
Maywood, Il., U.S.	95a	41.53N	87.51W
Maywood, N.J., U.S.	224	40.56N	74.04W
Mazabuka, Zam. (mä-zä-bōō'kä)	206	15.51S	27.46E
Mazagão, Braz. (mä-zȧ-gou'N)	124	0.05S	51.27W
Mazapil, Mex. (mä-zä-pēl')	106	24.40N	101.30W
Mazara del Vallo, Italy (mät-sä'rä dĕl väl'lō)	154	37.40N	12.37E
Mazār-i-Sharīf, Afg. (mȧ-zär'-ē-shȧ-rēf')	174	36.48N	67.12E
Mazarrón, Spain (mä-zär-rō'n)	152	37.37N	1.29W
Mazatenango, Guat. (mä-zä-tā-näŋ'gō)	110	14.30N	91.30W
Mazatla, Mex.	113a	19.30N	99.24W
Mazatlán, Mex.	110	23.14N	106.27W
Mazatlán (San Juan), Mex. (mä-zä-tlän') (säN hwän')	112	17.05N	95.26W
Mažeikiai, Lith. (mä-zhā'kē-ī)	146	56.19N	22.24E
Mazhafah, Jabal, mtn., Sau. Ar.	173a	28.56N	35.05E
Mazilovo, neigh., Russia	235b	55.44N	37.26E
Mazorra, Cuba	229b	23.01N	82.24W
Mbabane, Swaz. (m'bä-bä'nē)	206	26.18S	31.14E
Mbaiki, Cen. Afr. Rep. (m'bȧ-ē'kē)	204	3.53N	18.00E
Mbakana, Montagne de, mts., Cam.	208	7.55N	14.40E
Mbakaou, Barrage de, dam, Cam.	208	6.10N	12.55E
Mbala, Zam.	206	8.50S	31.22E
Mbale, Ug.	210	1.05N	34.10E
Mbamba Bay, Tan.	210	11.17S	34.46E
Mbandaka, Zaire	206	0.04N	18.16E
M'banza Congo, Ang.	206	6.30S	14.10E
Mbanza-Ngungu, Zaire	206	5.20S	10.55E
Mbarara, Ug.	210	0.37S	30.39E
Mbasay, Chad	208	7.39N	15.40E
Mbigou, Gabon (m-bē-gōō')	206	2.07S	11.30E
Mbinda, Congo	210	2.00S	12.55E
Mbogo, Tan.	210	7.26S	33.26E
Mbomou (Bomu), r., Afr. (m'bō'mōō)	204	4.50N	24.00E
Mbout, Maur. (m'bōō')	204	16.03N	12.31W
Mbuji-Mayi, Zaire	210	6.09S	23.38E
McAdam, Can. (măk-ăd'ăm)	86	45.36N	67.20W
McAfee, N.J., U.S. (măk-ȧ'fē)	94a	41.10N	74.32W
McAlester, Ok., U.S. (măk ăl'ĕs-tēr)	90	34.55N	95.45W

ăt; finăl; rāte; senāte; ärm; åsk; sofȧ; fâre; ch-choose; dh-as th in other; bē; ēvent; bĕt; recĕnt; cratēr; g-gō; gh-guttural g; bĭt; ĭ-short neutral; rīde; K-guttural k as ch in German ich;

PLACE (Pronunciation)	PAGE	Lat. °′	Long. °′
McAllen, Tx., U.S. (măk-ăl'ĕn)	106	26.12N	98.14W
McBride, Can. (măk-brīd')	78	53.18N	120.10W
McCalla, Al., U.S. (măk-kăl'là)	94h	33.20N	87.00W
McCamey, Tx., U.S. (mă-kā'mĭ)	106	31.08N	102.13W
McColl, S.C., U.S. (mȧ-kōl')	108	34.40N	79.34W
McComb, Ms., U.S. (mȧ-kōm')	108	31.14N	90.27W
McConaughy, Lake, l., Ne., U.S. (măk kŏ'nō ĭ')	96	41.24N	101.40W
McCook, Il., U.S.	227a	41.48N	87.50W
McCook, Ne., U.S. (mȧ-kŏŏk')	104	40.13N	100.37W
McCormick, S.C., U.S. (mȧ-kôr'mĭk)	108	33.56N	82.20W
McCormick Place, pt. of i., Il., U.S.	227a	41.51N	87.37W
McDonald, Pa., U.S. (măk-dŏn'ăld)	95e	40.22N	80.13W
McDonald Island, i., Austl.	213	53.00S	72.45E
McDonald Lake, l., Can. (măk-dŏn-ăld)	77e	51.12N	113.53W
McGehee, Ar., U.S. (mȧ-gē')	104	33.39N	91.22W
McGill, Nv., U.S. (mȧ-gĭl')	102	39.25N	114.47W
McGill University, educ., Can.	223b	45.30N	73.35W
McGowan, Wa., U.S. (măk-gou'ăn)	100c	46.15N	123.55W
McGrath, Ak., U.S. (măk'gràth)	90a	62.58N	155.20W
McGregor, Can. (măk-grĕg'ẽr)	95b	42.08N	82.58W
McGregor, Ia., U.S.	96	42.58N	91.12W
McGregor, Tx., U.S.	106	31.26N	97.23W
McGregor, r., Can.	80	54.10N	121.00W
McGregor Lake, l., Can. (măk-grĕg'ẽr)	77c	45.38N	75.44W
McHenry, Il., U.S. (măk-hĕn'rĭ)	95a	42.21N	88.16W
Mchinji, Mwi.	206	13.42S	32.50E
McIntosh, S.D., U.S. (măk'ĭn-tŏsh)	96	45.54N	101.22W
McKay, r., Or., U.S.	100c	45.43N	123.00W
McKeesport, Pa., U.S. (mȧ-kēz'pōrt)	95e	40.21N	79.51W
McKees Rocks, Pa., U.S. (mȧ-kēz' rŏks)	95e	40.29N	80.05W
McKenzie, Tn., U.S. (mȧ-kĕn'zĭ)	108	36.07N	88.30W
McKenzie, r., Or., U.S.	98	44.07N	122.20W
McKinley, Mount, mtn., Ak., U.S. (mȧ-kĭn'lĭ)	90a	63.00N	151.02W
McKinney, Tx., U.S. (mȧ-kĭn'ĭ)	104	33.12N	96.35W
McKnight Village, Pa., U.S.	226b	40.31N	80.00W
McLaughlin, S.D., U.S. (măk-lŏf'lĭn)	96	45.48N	100.45W
McLean, Va., U.S. (măc'lān)	94e	38.56N	77.11W
McLeansboro, Il., U.S. (mȧ-klānz'bŭr-ō)	92	38.10N	88.35W
McLennan, Can. (măk-lĕn'năn)	78	55.42N	116.54W
McLeod, r., Can.	80	53.45N	115.55W
McLeod Lake, Can.	80	54.59N	123.02W
McLoughlin, Mount, mtn., Or., U.S. (măk-lŏk'lĭn)	98	42.27N	122.20W
McMillan Lake, l., Tx., U.S. (măk-mĭl'ăn)	106	32.40N	104.09W
McMillin, Wa., U.S. (măk-mĭl'ĭn)	100a	47.08N	122.14W
McMinnville, Or., U.S. (măk-mĭn'vĭl)	98	45.13N	123.13W
McMinnville, Tn., U.S.	108	35.41N	85.47W
McMurray, Pa., U.S.	226b	40.17N	80.05W
McMurray, Wa., U.S. (măk-mŭr'ĭ)	100a	48.19N	122.15W
McNary, Az., U.S. (măk-nâr'ē)	102	34.10N	109.55W
McNary, La., U.S.	106	30.58N	92.32W
McNary Dam, Or., U.S.	98	45.57N	119.15W
McPherson, Ks., U.S. (măk-fŭr's'n)	104	38.21N	97.41W
McRae, Ga., U.S. (măk-rā')	108	32.02N	82.55W
McRoberts, Ky., U.S. (măk-rŏb'ẽrts)	108	37.12N	82.40W
Mead, Ks., U.S. (mēd)	104	37.17N	100.21W
Mead, Lake, l., U.S.	90	36.20N	114.14W
Meade Peak, mtn., Id., U.S.	98	42.19N	111.16W
Meadow Lake, Can. (mĕd'ō lāk)	78	54.08N	108.26W
Meadowlands, S. Afr.	240b	26.13S	27.54E
Meadows, Can. (mĕd'ōz)	77f	50.02N	97.35W
Meadville, Pa., U.S. (mēd'vĭl)	92	41.40N	80.10W
Meaford, Can. (mē'fẽrd)	84	44.35N	80.40W
Mealy Mountains, mts., Can. (mē'lē)	78	53.32N	57.58W
Meandarra, Austl. (mē-ăn-dă'rȧ)	198	27.47S	149.40E
Meaux, Fr. (mō)	150	48.58N	2.53E
Mecapalapa, Mex. (mā-kä-pä-lä'pä)	112	20.32N	97.52W
Mecatina, r., Can. (mā-kȧ-tē'nȧ)	86	50.50N	59.45W
Mecca (Makkah), Sau. Ar. (mĕk'ȧ)	174	21.27N	39.45E
Mechanic Falls, Me., U.S. (mē-kăn'ĭk)	86	44.05N	70.23W
Mechanicsburg, Pa., U.S. (mē-kăn'ĭks-bûrg)	92	40.15N	77.00W
Mechanicsville, Md., U.S. (mē-kăn'ĭks-vĭl)	94e	38.27N	76.45W
Mechanicville, N.Y., U.S. (mē-kăn'ĭk-vĭl)	92	42.55N	73.45W
Mechelen, Bel.	144	51.01N	4.28E
Mechriyya, Alg.	142	33.30N	0.13W
Mecicine Bow Range, mts., Co., U.S. (mĕd'ĭ-sĭn bō)	104	40.55N	106.02W
Meckinghoven, Ger.	232	51.37N	7.19E
Mecklenburg, hist. reg., Ger.	148	53.30N	13.00E
Medan, Indon. (mā-dän')	188	3.35N	98.35E
Medanosa, Punta, c., Arg. (pōō'n-tä-mĕ-dä-nô'sä)	126	47.50S	65.53W
Medden, r., Eng., U.K. (mĕd'ĕn)	138a	53.14N	1.05W
Medellín, Col. (mā-dhĕl-yēn')	124	6.15N	75.34W
Medellín, Mex. (mĕ-dĕl-yĕ'n)	112	19.03N	96.08W
Medenine, Tun. (mā-dĕ-nēn')	142	33.22N	10.33E
Medfeld, Ma., U.S. (mĕd'fēld)	87a	42.11N	71.19W
Medford, Ma., U.S. (mĕd'fẽrd)	87a	42.25N	71.07W
Medford, N.J., U.S.	94f	39.54N	74.50W
Medford, Ok., U.S.	104	36.47N	97.44W
Medford, Or., U.S.	90	42.19N	122.52W
Medford, Wi., U.S.	96	45.09N	90.22W
Medford Hillside, Ma., U.S.	223a	42.24N	71.07W
Media, Pa., U.S. (mē'dĭ-ȧ)	94f	39.55N	75.24W
Mediaş, Rom. (mĕd-yäsh')	148	46.09N	24.21E
Medical Lake, Wa., U.S. (mĕd'ĭ-kăl)	98	47.34N	117.40W
Medicine Bow, r., Wy., U.S.	98	41.58N	106.30W
Medicine Hat, Can. (mĕd'ĭ-sĭn hăt)	78	50.03N	110.40W
Medicine Lake, l., Mt., U.S. (mĕd'ĭ-sĭn)	98	48.24N	104.15W
Medicine Lodge, Ks., U.S.	104	37.17N	98.37W

PLACE (Pronunciation)	PAGE	Lat. °′	Long. °′
Medicine Lodge, r., Ks., U.S.	104	37.20N	98.57W
Medina, N.Y., U.S. (mē-dī'nȧ)	92	43.15N	78.20W
Medina, Oh., U.S.	95d	41.08N	81.52W
Medina, r., Tx., U.S.	106	29.45N	99.13W
Medina, see Al Madīnah, Sau. Ar.	174	24.26N	39.42E
Medina del Campo, Spain (mā-dē'nä dĕl käm'pō)	142	41.18N	4.54W
Medina de Ríoseco, Spain (mā-dē'nä dā rē-ō-sā'kō)	152	41.53N	5.05W
Medina Lake, l., Tx., U.S.	106	29.36N	98.47W
Medina Sidonia, Spain	152	36.28N	5.58W
Mediterranean Sea, sea (mĕd-ĭ-tẽr-ā'nē-ăn)	142	36.22N	13.25E
Medjerda, Oued, r., Afr.	142	36.43N	9.54E
Mednogorsk, Russia	158	51.27N	57.22E
Medveditsa, r., Russia (mĕd-vyĕ'dē tsȧ)	160	50.10N	43.40E
Medvedkovo, neigh., Russia	235b	55.53N	37.38E
Medvezhegorsk, Russia (mĕd-vyĕzh'yĕ-gôrsk')	160	63.00N	34.20E
Medway, Ma., U.S. (mĕd'wā)	87a	42.08N	71.23W
Medyn', Russia (mĕ-dēn')	156	54.58N	35.53E
Medzhibozh, Ukr. (mĕd-zhē-bōzh')	156	49.23N	27.29E
Meekatharra, Austl. (mē-kȧ-thăr'ȧ)	196	26.30S	118.38E
Meeker, Co., U.S. (mēk'ẽr)	102	40.00N	107.55W
Meelpaeg Lake, l., Can. (mēl'pȧ-ĕg)	86	48.22N	56.52W
Meerane, Ger. (mā-rä'nē)	148	50.51N	12.27E
Meerbusch, Ger.	151c	51.15N	6.41E
Meerut, India (mē'rŭt)	174	28.59N	77.43E
Megalópolis, Grc. (mĕg-ȧ lŏ'pō-lĭs)	154	37.22N	22.08E
Meganom, Mys, c., Ukr.	156	44.48N	35.17E
Mégara, Grc. (mĕg'ȧ-rȧ)	154	37.59N	23.21E
Megget, S.C., U.S. (mĕg'ĕt)	108	32.44N	80.15W
Megler, Wa., U.S. (mĕg'lẽr)	100c	46.15N	123.52W
Meguro, neigh., Japan	238a	35.38N	139.42E
Meherrin, r., Va., U.S. (mē-hĕr'ĭn)	108	36.40N	77.49W
Mehlville, Mo., U.S.	101e	38.30N	90.19W
Mehpālpur, neigh., India	236d	28.33N	77.08E
Mehrābād, Iran	237h	35.40N	51.20E
Mehram Nagar, neigh., India	236d	28.34N	77.07E
Mehrow, Ger.	234a	52.34N	13.37E
Mehrum, Ger.	232	51.35N	6.37E
Mehsāna, India	178	23.42N	72.23E
Mehun-sur-Yévre, Fr. (mē-ŭN-sür-yĕvr')	150	47.11N	2.14E
Meide, Ger.	232	51.11N	6.55E
Meiderich, neigh., Ger.	232	51.28N	6.46E
Meidling, neigh., Aus.	235e	48.11N	16.20E
Meiersberg, Ger.	232	51.17N	6.57E
Meiji Shrine, rel., Japan	238a	35.41N	139.42E
Meiling Pass, p., China (mā'lĭng')	180	25.22N	115.00E
Meinerzhagen, Ger. (mī'nĕrts-hä-gĕn)	151c	51.06N	7.39E
Meiningen, Ger. (mī'nĭng-ĕn)	148	50.35N	10.25E
Meiringen, Switz.	148	46.45N	8.11E
Meissen, Ger.	148	51.11N	13.28E
Meizhu, China (mā-jōō)	182	31.17N	119.12E
Mejillones, Chile (mā-kē-lyō'nās)	126	23.07S	70.31W
Mekambo, Gabon	210	1.01N	13.56E
Mekele, Eth.	204	13.31N	39.19E
Meknés, Mor. (mĕk'nĕs) (mĕk-nĕs')	204	33.56N	5.44W
Mekong, r., Asia	188	18.00N	104.30E
Melaka, Malay.	188	2.11N	102.15E
Melaka, state, Malay.	173b	2.19N	102.09E
Melbourne, Austl. (mĕl'bŭrn)	196	37.52S	145.08E
Melbourne, Eng., U.K.	138a	52.49N	1.26W
Melbourne, Fl., U.S.	109a	28.05N	80.37W
Melbourne, Ky., U.S.	95f	39.02N	84.22W
Melcher, Ia., U.S. (mĕl'chẽr)	96	41.13N	93.11W
Melekess, Russia (mĕl-yĕk-ĕs)	160	54.14N	49.39E
Melenki, Russia (mĕ-lyĕŋ'kē)	160	55.25N	41.34E
Melfort, Can. (mĕl'fŏrt)	78	52.52N	104.36W
Melghir, Chott, l., Alg.	204	33.52N	5.22E
Melilla, Sp. N. Afr. (mā-lēl'yä)	204	35.24N	3.30W
Melipilla, Chile (mā-lē-pē'lyä)	126	33.40S	71.12W
Melita, Can.	82	49.11N	101.09W
Melitopol', Ukr. (mā-lē-tô'pōl-y')	160	46.49N	35.19E
Melívoia, Grc.	154	39.42N	22.47E
Melkrivier, S. Afr.	212d	24.01S	28.23E
Mellen, Wi., U.S. (mĕl'ĕn)	96	46.20N	90.40W
Mellerud, Swe. (mål'ĕ-rōōdh)	146	58.43N	12.25E
Melling, Eng., U.K.	233a	53.30N	2.56W
Melmoth, S. Afr.	207c	28.38S	31.26E
Melo, Ur. (mā'lō)	126	32.18S	54.07W
Melocheville, Can. (mĕ-lôsh-vĕl')	77a	45.24N	73.56W
Melozha, r., Russia (myĕ'lô-zhȧ)	164b	56.06N	38.34E
Melrose, Ma., U.S. (mĕl'rōz)	87a	42.29N	71.06W
Melrose, Mn., U.S.	96	45.39N	94.49W
Melrose Highlands, Ma., U.S.	223a	42.28N	71.04W
Melrose Park, Il., U.S.	95a	41.54N	87.52W
Meltham, Eng., U.K. (mĕl'thăm)	138a	53.35N	1.51W
Melton, Austl. (mĕl'tŭn)	195a	37.41S	144.35E
Melton Mowbray, Eng., U.K. (mō'brâ)	138a	52.45N	0.52W
Melúli, r., Moz.	210	16.10S	39.30E
Melun, Fr. (mĕ-lŭN')	140	48.32N	2.40E
Melunga, Ang.	210	17.16S	16.24E
Melville, Can. (mĕl'vĭl)	78	50.55N	102.48W
Melville, La., U.S.	106	30.39N	91.45W
Melville, i., Austl.	196	11.30S	131.12E
Melville, l., Can.	78	53.46N	59.31W
Melville, Cape, c., Austl.	196	14.15S	145.50E
Melville Hills, hills, Can.	78	69.18N	124.57W
Melville Peninsula, pen., Can.	78	67.44N	84.09W
Melvindale, Mi., U.S. (mĕl'vĭn-dāl)	95b	42.17N	83.11W
Melyana, Alg.	140	36.19N	1.56E
Mélykút, Hung. (mā'l'kōōt)	148	46.14N	19.21E
Memba, Moz. (mĕm'bȧ)	206	14.12N	40.35E
Memel, S. Afr. (mĕ'mĕl)	212d	27.42S	29.35E

PLACE (Pronunciation)	PAGE	Lat. °′	Long. °′
Memel, see Klaipėda, Lith.	160	55.43N	21.10E
Memmingen, Ger. (mĕm'ĭng-ĕn)	148	47.59N	10.10E
Memo, r., Ven. (mĕ'mō)	125b	9.32N	66.30W
Memphis, Mo., U.S. (mĕm'fĭs)	104	40.27N	92.11W
Memphis, Tn., U.S. (mĕm'fĭs)	90	35.07N	90.03W
Memphis, Tx., U.S.	104	34.42N	100.33W
Memphis, hist., Egypt	212b	29.50N	31.12E
Mena, Ukr. (mē-nà')	156	51.31N	32.14E
Mena, Ar., U.S. (mē'nȧ)	104	34.35N	94.09W
Menangle, Austl.	195b	34.08S	150.48E
Menard, Tx., U.S. (mē-närd')	106	30.56N	99.48W
Menasha, Wi., U.S. (mē-năsh'ȧ)	96	44.12N	88.29W
Mende, Fr. (mäNd)	150	44.31N	3.30E
Menden, Ger. (mĕn'dĕn)	151c	51.26N	7.47E
Menden, neigh., Ger.	232	51.24N	6.54E
Mendes, Braz. (mĕ'n-dĕs)	126b	22.32S	43.44W
Mendocino, Ca., U.S.	102	39.18N	123.47W
Mendocino, Cape, c., Ca., U.S. (mĕn'dō-sē'nō)	90	40.25N	12.42W
Mendota, Il., U.S. (mĕn-dō'tȧ)	96	41.34N	89.06W
Mendota, l., Wi., U.S.	96	43.09N	89.41W
Mendoza, Arg. (mĕn-dō'sä)	126	32.48S	68.45W
Mendoza, prov., Arg.	126	35.10S	69.00W
Mengcheng, China (mŭŋ-chŭŋ)	182	33.15N	116.34E
Mengede, neigh., Ger.	232	51.34N	7.23E
Menglinghausen, neigh., Ger.	232	51.28N	7.25E
Meng Shan, mts., China (mŭŋ shän)	182	35.47N	117.23E
Mengzi, China	180	23.22N	103.20E
Menindee, Austl. (mĕ-nĭn-dē)	198	32.23S	142.30E
Menlo Park, Ca., U.S. (mĕn'lō pärk)	100b	37.27N	122.11W
Menlo Park Terrace, N.J., U.S.	224	40.32N	74.20W
Menno, S.D., U.S. (mĕn'ō)	96	43.14N	97.34W
Menominee, Mi., U.S. (mē-nŏm'ĭ-nē)	96	45.08N	87.40W
Menominee, r., Mi., U.S.	96	45.37N	87.54W
Menominee Falls, Wi., U.S. (fôls)	95a	43.11N	88.06W
Menominee Ra, Mi., U.S.	96	46.07N	88.53W
Menomonee, r., Wi., U.S.	95a	43.09N	88.06W
Menomonie, Wi., U.S.	96	44.53N	91.55W
Menongue, Ang.	210	14.36S	17.48E
Menorca (Minorca), i., Spain (mĕ-nō'r-kä)	136	40.05N	3.58E
Mentana, Italy (mĕn-tà'nä)	153d	42.02N	12.40E
Mentawai, Kepulauan, is., Indon. (mĕn-tä-vī')	188	1.08S	98.10E
Menton, Fr. (mäN-tôN')	150	43.46N	7.37E
Mentone, Austl.	239b	37.59S	145.05E
Mentone, Ca., U.S. (mĕn'tōne)	101a	34.05N	117.08W
Mentz, l., S. Afr. (mĕnts)	207c	33.13S	25.15E
Menzel Bourguiba, Tun.	142	37.12N	9.51E
Menzelinsk, Russia (mĕn'zyĕ-lĕnsk')	160	55.40N	53.15E
Menzies, Austl. (mĕn'zēz)	196	29.45S	122.15E
Meogui, Mex. (mā-ō'gē)	106	28.17N	105.28W
Meopham, Eng., U.K.	231	51.22N	0.22E
Meopham Station, Eng., U.K.	231	51.23N	0.21E
Meppel, Neth. (mĕp'ĕl)	144	52.41N	6.08E
Meppen, Ger. (mĕp'ĕn)	148	52.40N	7.18E
Merabéllou, Kólpos, b., Grc.	154a	35.16N	25.55E
Meramec, r., Mo., U.S. (mĕr'ȧ-mĕk)	104	38.06N	91.06W
Merano, Italy (mā-rä'nō)	142	46.39N	11.10E
Merasheen, i., Can. (mē'rȧ-shēn)	86	47.30N	54.15W
Merauke, Indon. (mā-rou'kā)	188	8.32S	140.17E
Meraux, La., U.S. (mē-ro')	94d	29.56N	89.56W
Mercader y Millás, Spain	234e	41.21N	2.05E
Mercato San Severino, Italy	153c	40.34N	14.38E
Merced, Ca., U.S.	102	37.25N	120.31W
Merced, Ca., U.S. (mẽr-sĕd')	102	37.17N	120.30W
Mercedario, Cerro, mtn., Arg. (mĕr-sȧ-dhä'rē-ō)	126	31.58S	70.07W
Mercedes, Arg.	123c	34.41S	59.26W
Mercedes, Arg. (mĕr-sā'dhās)	126	29.04S	58.01W
Mercedes, Tx., U.S.	106	26.09N	97.55W
Mercedes, Ur.	126	33.17S	58.04W
Mercedita, Chile (mĕr-sĕ-dē'tä)	123b	33.51S	71.10W
Mercer Island, Wa., U.S. (mûr'sẽr)	100a	47.35N	122.15W
Mercês, Braz. (mĕ-sĕ's)	123a	21.13S	43.20W
Mercês, Port.	234d	38.47N	9.19W
Merchtem, Bel.	139a	50.57N	4.13E
Mercier, Can.	77a	45.19N	73.45W
Mercy, Cape, c., Can.	78	64.48N	63.22W
Merdeka Palace, bldg., Indon.	237k	6.10S	106.49E
Mere, Eng., U.K.	233b	53.20N	2.25W
Meredale, S. Afr.	240b	26.17S	27.59E
Meredith, N.H., U.S. (mĕr'ē-dĭth)	92	43.35N	71.35W
Merefa, Ukr. (mā-rĕf'ȧ)	156	49.49N	36.04E
Merendón, Serranía de, mts., Hond.	114	15.01N	89.05W
Mereworth, Eng., U.K. (mĕ-rĕ wûrth)	138b	51.15N	0.23E
Mergui, Burma (mẽr-gē')	188	12.29N	98.39E
Mergui Archipelago, is., Burma	188	12.04N	97.02E
Meric (Maritsa), r., Eur.	146	40.43N	26.19E
Mérida, Mex.	110	20.58N	89.37W
Mérida, Ven.	124	8.30N	71.15W
Mérida, Cordillera de, mts., Ven. (mĕ'rē-dhä)	124	8.30N	70.45W
Meriden, Ct., U.S. (mĕr'ĭ-dĕn)	92	41.30N	72.50W
Meridian, Ms., U.S. (mē-rĭd-ĭ-ăn)	90	32.21N	88.41W
Meridian, Tx., U.S.	106	31.56N	97.37W
Mérignac, Fr.	150	44.50N	0.40W
Merikarvia, Fin. (mā'rē-kàr'vē-ȧ)	146	61.51N	21.30E
Mering, Ger. (mĕ'rĕng)	139d	48.16N	11.00E
Merion Station, Pa., U.S.	225b	40.00N	75.15W
Merkel, Tx., U.S. (mûr'kĕl)	106	32.26N	100.02W
Merkinė, Lith.	146	54.10N	24.10E
Merksem, Bel.	139a	51.15N	4.27E
Merkys, r., Lith. (mär'kĭs)	148	54.23N	25.00E
Merlo, Arg. (mĕr-lō)	126a	34.40S	58.44W

ng-sing; ŋ-baŋk; N-nasalized n; nŏd; cŏmmit; ōld; ôbey; ôrder; oi-boil; fōōd; ŏŏ-as oo in foot; ou-out; s-soft; sh-dish; th-thin; pūre; ůnite; ûrn; stŭd; circŭs; ü-as in French tu; '-indeterminate vowel.

PLACE (Pronunciation)	PAGE	Lat. °′	Long. °′
Merlynston, Austl.	239b	37.43S	144.58E
Meron, Hare, mtn., Isr.	173a	32.58N	35.25E
Merriam, Ks., U.S. (mĕr-rĭ-yăm)	101f	39.01N	94.42W
Merriam, Mn., U.S.	101g	44.44N	93.36W
Merrick, N.Y., U.S. (mĕr'ĭk)	94a	40.40N	73.33W
Merri Creek, r., Austl.	239b	37.48S	144.59E
Merrifield, Va., U.S. (mĕr'ĭ-fēld)	94e	38.50N	77.12W
Merrill, Wi., U.S. (mĕr'ĭl)	96	45.11N	89.42W
Merrimac, Ma., U.S. (mĕr'ĭ-măk)	87a	45.20N	71.00W
Merrimack, N.H., U.S.	87a	42.51N	71.25W
Merrimack, r., Ma., U.S. (mĕr'ĭ-măk)	92	43.10N	71.30W
Merrionette Park, Il., U.S.	227a	41.41N	87.42W
Merritt, Can. (mĕr'ĭt)	78	50.07N	120.47W
Merrylands, Austl.	239a	33.50S	150.59E
Merryville, La., U.S. (mĕr'ĭ-vĭl)	106	30.46N	93.34W
Mersa Fatma, Eth.	204	14.54N	40.14E
Merscheid, neigh., Ger.	232	51.10N	7.01E
Merseburg, Ger. (mĕr'zĕ-bŏŏrgh)	148	51.21N	11.59E
Mersey, r., Eng., U.K. (mûr'zē)	138a	53.20N	2.55W
Merseyside, co., Eng., U.K.	138a	53.29N	2.59W
Mersing, Malay.	173b	2.25N	103.51E
Merta Road, India (mār'tŭ rōd)	178	26.50N	73.54E
Merthyr Tydfil, Wales, U.K. (mûr'thĕr tĭd'vĭl)	144	51.46N	3.30W
Mértola Almodóvar, Port. (mĕr-tô-lá-äl-mô-dô'vär)	152	37.39N	8.04W
Merton, neigh., Eng., U.K.	231	51.25N	0.12W
Méru, Fr. (mā-rü')	150	49.14N	2.08E
Meru, Kenya (mā'rōō)	204	0.01N	37.45E
Meru, Mount, mtn., Tan.	210	3.15S	36.43E
Merume Mountains, mts., Guy. (mĕr-ü'mĕ)	124	5.45N	60.15W
Merwede Kanaal, can., Neth.	139a	52.15N	5.01E
Merwin, l., Wa., U.S. (mĕr'wĭn)	100c	45.58N	122.27W
Merzifon, Tur. (mĕr'ze-fōn)	174	40.50N	35.30E
Mesa, Az., U.S. (mā'sá)	102	33.25N	111.50W
Mesabi Range, mts., Mn., U.S. (mā-sŏb'bē)	96	47.17N	93.04W
Mesagne, Italy (mā-sän'yå)	154	40.34N	17.51E
Mesa Verde National Park, rec., Co., U.S. (vĕr'dē)	90	37.22N	108.27W
Mescalero Apache Indian Reservation, I.R., N.M., U.S. (mĕs-kä-lā'rō)	102	33.10N	105.45W
Meščerskij, Russia	235b	55.40N	37.25E
Meshchovsk, Russia (myĕsh'chĕfsk)	156	54.17N	35.19E
Mesilla, N.M., U.S. (må-sē'yä)	102	32.15N	106.45W
Meskine, Chad	208	11.25N	15.21E
Mesolóngion, Grc. (mĕ-sô-lôŋ'gē-ôn)	154	38.23N	21.28E
Mesquita, Braz.	126b	22.48S	43.26W
Messina, Italy (mĕ-sē'ná)	136	38.11N	15.34E
Messina, S. Afr.	206	22.17S	30.13E
Messina, Stretto di, strt., Italy (strĕ't-tô dē)	142	38.10N	15.34E
Messíni, Grc.	154	37.05N	22.00E
Messy, Fr.	233c	48.58N	2.42E
Mestaganem, Alg.	204	36.04N	0.11E
Mestre, Italy (mĕs'trā)	154	45.29N	12.15E
Meta, dept., Col. (mĕ'tä)	124a	3.28N	74.07W
Meta, r., S.A.	124	4.33N	72.09W
Métabetchouane, r., Can. (mĕ-tá-bĕt-chōō-än')	84	47.45N	72.00W
Metairie, La., U.S.	106	30.00N	90.11W
Metán, Arg. (mĕ-tá'n)	126	25.32S	64.51W
Metangula, Moz.	206	12.42S	34.48E
Metapán, El Sal. (må-täpän')	114	14.21N	89.26W
Metcalfe, Can. (mĕt-käf)	77c	45.14N	75.27W
Metchosin, Can.	100a	48.22N	123.33W
Metepec, Mex.	112	19.15N	99.36W
Metepec, Mex. (må-tĕ-pĕk')	112	18.56N	98.31W
Methow, r., Wa., U.S. (mĕt'hou) (mĕt hou')	98	48.26N	120.15W
Methuen, Ma., U.S. (mē-thū'ĕn)	87a	42.44N	71.11W
Metković, Cro. (mĕt'kô-vĭch)	154	43.02N	17.40E
Metlakatla, Ak., U.S. (mĕt-lá-kăt'lá)	89	55.08N	131.35W
Metropolis, Il., U.S. (mē-trŏp'ô-lĭs)	104	37.09N	88.46W
Metropolitan Museum of Art, pt. of i., N.Y., U.S.	224	40.47N	73.58W
Metter, Ga., U.S. (mĕt'ēr)	108	32.21N	82.05W
Mettmann, Ger. (mĕt'män)	151c	51.15N	6.58E
Metuchen, N.J., U.S. (mĕ-tŭ'chĕn)	94a	40.32N	74.21W
Metz, Fr. (mĕtz)	140	49.08N	6.10E
Metztitlán, Mex. (mĕtz-têt-län)	112	20.36N	98.45W
Meuban, Cam.	208	2.27N	12.41E
Meudon, Fr.	233c	48.48N	2.14E
Meuse (Maas), r., Eur. (mûz) (müz)	144	50.32N	5.22E
Mexborough, Eng., U.K. (mĕks'bŭr-ô)	138a	53.30N	1.17W
Mexia, Tx., U.S. (må-hē'ä)	106	31.32N	96.29W
Mexian, China	180	24.20N	116.10E
Mexicalcingo, Mex. (mĕ-kē-käl-sēn'go)	113a	19.13N	99.34W
Mexicali, Mex. (mák-sē-kä'lē)	110	32.28N	115.29W
Mexicana, Altiplanicie, plat., Mex.	112	22.38N	102.33W
Mexican Hat, Ut., U.S. (mĕk'sĭ-kăn hăt)	102	37.10N	109.55W
Mexico, Me., U.S. (mĕk'sĭ-kō)	86	44.34N	70.33W
Mexico, Mo., U.S.	104	39.09N	91.51W
Mexico, nation, N.A.	110	23.45N	104.00W
Mexico, Gulf of, b., N.A.	110	25.15N	93.45W
Mexico City, Mex. (mĕk'sĭ-kō)	110	19.28N	99.09W
Mexticacán, Mex. (mĕs'tē-kä-kän')	112	21.12N	102.43W
Meyers Chuck, Ak., U.S.	80	55.44N	132.15W
Meyersdale, Pa., U.S. (mī'ĕrz-dāl)	92	39.55N	79.00W
Meyerton, S. Afr. (mī'ĕr-tŭn)	212d	26.35S	28.01E
Meymaneh, Afg.	174	35.53N	64.38E
Mezen', Russia	158	65.50N	44.05E
Mezen', r., Russia	160	65.20N	44.45E
Mézenc, Mont, mtn., Fr. (mōN-mä-zĕN')	150	44.55N	4.12E
Mezha, r., Eur. (myā'zhá)	156	55.53N	31.44E
Mézieres-sur-Seine, Fr. (mā-zyâr'sür-sân')	151b	48.58N	1.49E
Mezőkövesd, Hung. (mĕ'zû-kû'vĕsht)	148	47.49N	20.36E
Mezötur, Hung. (mĕ'zû-tōōr)	148	47.00N	20.36E
Mezquital, Mex. (máz-kē-täl')	112	23.30N	104.20W
Mezquitic, Mex. (máz-kē-tēk')	112	22.25N	103.43W
Mezquitic, r., Mex.	112	22.25N	103.45W
Mfangano Island, i., Kenya	210	0.28S	33.35E
Mga, Russia (m'gá)	164c	59.45N	31.04E
Mglin, Russia (m'glĕn')	156	53.03N	32.52W
Mia, Oued, r., Alg.	142	29.26N	3.15E
Miacatlán, Mex. (mē'ā-kä-tlän')	112	18.42N	99.17W
Mia-dong, neigh., S. Kor.	237b	37.37N	127.01E
Miahuatlán, Mex. (mē'ā-wä-tlän')	112	16.20N	96.38W
Miajadas, Spain (mē-ā-hā'däs)	152	39.10N	5.53W
Miami, Az., U.S.	90	33.20N	110.55W
Miami, Fl., U.S.	90	25.45N	80.11W
Miami, Ok., U.S.	104	36.51N	94.51W
Miami, Tx., U.S.	104	35.41N	100.39W
Miami Beach, Fl., U.S.	109a	25.47N	80.07W
Miamisburg, Oh., U.S. (mī-ăm'iz-bûrg)	92	39.40N	84.20W
Miamitown, Oh., U.S. (mī-ăm'ĭ-toun)	95f	39.13N	84.43W
Mīāneh, Iran	174	37.15N	47.13E
Miangas, Pulau, i., Indon.	188	5.30N	127.00E
Miaoli, Tai. (mē-ou'lĭ)	184	24.30N	120.48E
Miaozhen, China (miou-jŭn)	182	31.44N	121.28E
Miass, Russia (mī-äs')	162	54.59N	60.06E
Miastko, Pol. (myäst'kô)	148	54.01N	17.00E
Miccosukee Indian Reservation, I.R., Fl., U.S.	109a	26.10N	80.50W
Michajlovskoje, Russia	235b	55.35N	37.35E
Michalovce, Czech. (mē'ĸä-lôf'tsĕ)	148	48.44N	21.56E
Michel Peak, mtn., Can.	80	53.35N	126.25W
Michelson, Mount, mtn., Ak., U.S. (mĭch'ĕl-sŭn)	89	69.11N	144.12W
Michendorf, Ger. (mē'ĸĕn-dōrf)	139b	52.19N	13.02E
Miches, Dom. Rep. (mē'chĕs)	116	19.00N	69.05W
Michigan, state, U.S. (mĭsh-'ĭ-găn)	90	45.55N	87.00W
Michigan, Lake, l., U.S.	90	43.20N	87.10W
Michigan City, In., U.S.	92	41.40N	86.55W
Michillinda, Ca., U.S.	228	34.07N	118.05W
Michipicoten, r., Can.	96	47.56N	84.42W
Michipicoten Harbour, Can.	96	47.58N	84.58W
Michurinsk, Russia (mĭ-chōō-rĭnsk')	160	52.53N	40.32E
Mico, Punta, c., Nic. (pōō'n-tä-mē'kô)	114	11.38N	83.24W
Micronesia, Federated States Of, nation, Oc.	2	5.00N	152.00E
Micronesia, Federated States of, dep., T.T.P.I.	2	9.30N	143.00E
Midas, Nv., U.S. (mī'dás)	98	41.15N	116.50W
Middelfart, Den. (mēd''l-färt)	146	55.30N	9.45E
Middle, r., Can.	80	55.00N	125.50W
Middle Andaman, i., India (ăn-dá-măn')	188	12.44N	93.21E
Middle Bayou, Tx., U.S.	107a	29.38N	95.06W
Middleburg, S. Afr. (mĭd'ĕl-bûrg)	206	31.30S	25.00E
Middleburg, S. Afr.	212d	25.47S	29.30E
Middleburgh Heights, Oh., U.S.	225a	41.22N	81.48W
Middlebury, Vt., U.S. (mĭd''l-bĕr-ĭ)	92	44.00N	73.10W
Middle Concho, Tx., U.S. (kōn'chō)	106	31.21N	100.50W
Middle River, Md., U.S.	94e	39.20N	76.27W
Middlesboro, Ky., U.S. (mĭd''lz-bŭr-ô)	108	36.36N	83.42W
Middlesbrough, Eng., U.K. (mĭd''lz-brŭ)	140	54.35N	1.18W
Middlesex, N.J., U.S. (mĭd''l-sĕks)	94a	40.34N	74.30W
Middleton, Can. (mĭd''l-tŭn)	86	44.57N	65.04W
Middleton, Eng., U.K.	138a	53.34N	2.12W
Middletown, Ct., U.S.	92	41.35N	72.40W
Middletown, De., U.S.	92	39.30N	75.40W
Middletown, Ma., U.S.	87a	42.35N	71.01W
Middletown, N.Y., U.S.	92	41.26N	74.25W
Middletown, Oh., U.S.	92	39.30N	84.25W
Middlewich, Eng., U.K. (mĭd''l-wĭch)	138a	53.11N	2.27W
Middlewit, S. Afr. (mĭd'l'wĭt)	212d	24.50S	27.00E
Midfield, Al., U.S.	94h	33.28N	86.54W
Midi, Canal du, Fr. (kä-näl-dü-mē-dē')	140	43.22N	1.35E
Mid Illovo, S. Afr. (mĭd ĭl'ô-vō)	207c	29.59S	30.32E
Midland, Can. (mĭd'lănd)	78	44.45N	79.50W
Midland, Mi., U.S.	92	43.40N	84.20W
Midland, Tx., U.S.	106	32.05N	102.05W
Midland Beach, neigh., N.Y., U.S.	224	40.34N	74.05W
Midlothian, Il., U.S.	227a	41.38N	87.42W
Midvale, Ut., U.S. (mĭd'vāl)	101b	40.37N	111.54W
Midway, S. Afr.	240b	26.18S	27.51E
Midway, Al., U.S. (mĭd'wā)	108	32.03N	85.30W
Midway City, Ca., U.S.	228	33.45N	118.00W
Midway Islands, is., Oc.	2	28.00N	179.00W
Midwest, Wy., U.S. (mĭd-wĕst')	98	43.25N	106.15W
Midye, Tur. (mēd'yĕ)	160	41.35N	28.10E
Międzyrzecz, Pol. (myăn-dzŭ'zhĕch)	148	52.26N	15.35E
Mielec, Pol. (myĕ'lĕts)	148	50.17N	21.27E
Mier, Mex. (myâr)	106	26.26N	99.08W
Mieres, Spain (myā'rās)	152	43.14N	5.45W
Mier y Noriega, Mex. (myâr'ē nō-rē-ā'gä)	112	23.28N	100.08W
Miguel Auza, Mex.	112	24.17N	103.27W
Miguel Pereira, Braz.	126b	22.27S	43.28W
Mijares, r., Spain	152	39.55N	0.01W
Mikage, Japan (mē'ká-gå)	187b	34.42N	135.15E
Mikawa-Wan, b., Japan (mē'kä-wä wän)	187	34.43N	137.09E
Mikhaylov, Russia (mē-ĸäy'lôf)	160	54.14N	39.03E
Mikhaylovka, Russia	160	50.05N	43.10E
Mikhaylovka, Russia	164a	55.35N	57.57E
Mikhaylovka, Russia	164c	59.20N	30.21E
Mikhaylovka, Ukr. (mē-kä'ē-laf-ká)	156	47.16N	35.12E
Mikhnëvo, Russia (mĭk-nyô'vô)	164b	55.08N	37.57E
Miki, Japan (mē'kē)	187b	34.47N	134.59E
Mikindani, Tan. (mē-kēn-dä'nē)	206	10.17S	40.07E
Mikkeli, Fin. (mēk'ĕ-lĭ)	140	61.42N	27.14E
Míkonos, i., Grc.	154	37.26N	25.30E
Mikulov, Czech. (mĭ'kōō-lôf)	148	48.47N	16.39E
Mikumi, Tan.	210	7.24S	36.59E
Mikuni, Japan (mē'kōō-nē)	187	36.09N	136.14E
Mikuni-Sammyaku, mts., Japan (säm'myä-kōō)	187	36.51N	138.38E
Mikura, i., Japan (mē'kōō-rá)	187	33.53N	139.26E
Milaca, Milaca, Mn., U.S. (mē-lăk'á)	96	45.45N	93.41W
Milan, Italy	136	38.13N	15.17E
Milan (Milano), Italy	154	45.29N	9.12E
Milan, Mi., U.S. (mĭ'lăn)	92	42.05N	83.40W
Milan, Mo., U.S.	104	40.13N	93.07W
Milan, Tn., U.S.	108	35.54N	88.47W
Milano, *see* Milan, Italy	136	45.29N	9.12E
Milâs, Tur. (mē'läs)	142	37.10N	27.25E
Milbank, S.D., U.S. (mĭl'băŋĸ)	96	45.13N	96.38W
Mildura, Austl. (mĭl-dū'rá)	196	34.10S	142.18E
Miles City, Mt., U.S. (mīlz)	90	46.24N	105.50W
Milford, Ct., U.S. (mĭl'fērd)	92	41.15N	73.05W
Milford, De., U.S.	92	38.55N	75.25W
Milford, Md., U.S.	225c	39.21N	76.44W
Milford, Ma., U.S.	87a	42.09N	71.31W
Milford, Mi., U.S.	95b	42.35N	83.36W
Milford, N.H., U.S.	92	42.50N	71.40W
Milford, Oh., U.S.	95f	39.11N	84.18W
Milford, Ut., U.S.	102	38.20N	113.05W
Milford Sound, strt., N.Z.	199	44.35S	167.47E
Miling, Austl. (mĭl''ng)	196	30.30S	116.25E
Milipitas, Ca., U.S. (mĭl-ĭ-pĭ'tăs)	100b	37.26N	121.54W
Milk, r., N.A.	90	48.30N	107.00W
Millau, Fr. (mē-yō')	140	44.06N	3.04E
Millbourne, Pa., U.S.	225b	39.58N	75.15W
Millbrae, Ca., U.S. (mĭl'brā)	100b	37.36N	122.23W
Millburn, N.J., U.S.	224	40.44N	74.20W
Millbury, Ma., U.S. (mĭl'bēr-ĭ)	87a	42.12N	71.46W
Mill Creek, r., Can. (mĭl)	77g	53.28N	113.25W
Mill Creek, r., Ca., U.S.	102	40.07N	121.55W
Milledgeville, Ga., U.S. (mĭl'ĕj-vĭl)	108	33.05N	83.15W
Mille Îles, Rivière des, r., Can. (rē-vyâr' dā mĭl'ĭl')	77a	45.41N	73.40W
Mille Lac Indian Reservation, I.R., Mn., U.S. (mĭl lăk')	96	46.14N	94.13W
Mille Lacs, l., Mn., U.S.	96	46.25N	93.22W
Mille Lacs, Lac des, l., Can. (lăk dē mēl lăks)	84	48.52N	90.53W
Millen, Ga., U.S. (mĭl'ĕn)	108	32.47N	81.55W
Miller, S.D., U.S. (mĭl'ēr)	96	44.31N	99.00W
Millerovo, Russia (mĭl'ĕ-rô-vô)	160	48.58N	40.27E
Millersburg, Ky., U.S. (mĭl'ērz-bûrg)	92	38.15N	84.10W
Millersburg, Oh., U.S.	92	40.35N	81.55W
Millersburg, Pa., U.S.	92	40.35N	76.55W
Millerton, Can. (mĭl'ēr-tŭn)	86	46.56N	65.40W
Millertown, Can. (mĭl'ēr-toun)	86	48.49N	56.32W
Mill Green, Eng., U.K.	231	51.41N	0.22E
Mill Hill, neigh., Eng., U.K.	231	51.37N	0.13W
Millicent, Austl. (mĭl-ĭ-sĕnt)	198	37.30S	140.20E
Millinocket, Me., U.S. (mĭl-ĭ-nŏk'ĕt)	86	45.40N	68.44W
Millis, Ma., U.S. (mĭl-ĭs)	87a	42.10N	71.22W
Mill Neck, N.Y., U.S.	224	40.52N	73.34W
Millstadt, Il., U.S. (mĭl'stăt)	101e	38.27N	90.06W
Millstone, r., N.J., U.S. (mĭl'stōn)	94a	40.27N	74.38W
Millstream, Austl. (mĭl'strēm)	196	21.45S	117.10E
Milltown, Can. (mĭl'toun)	86	45.13N	67.19W
Millvale, Pa., U.S.	226b	40.29N	79.58W
Mill Valley, Ca., U.S. (mĭl)	100b	37.54N	122.32W
Millwood Reservoir, res., Ar., U.S.	104	33.00N	94.00W
Milly-la-Forêt, Fr. (mē-yē'-la-fō-rĕ')	151b	48.24N	2.28E
Milmont Park, Pa., U.S.	225b	39.53N	75.20W
Milnerton, S. Afr. (mĭl'nĕr-tŭn)	206a	33.52S	18.30E
Milnor, N.D., U.S. (mĭl'nēr)	96	46.17N	97.29W
Milnrow, Eng., U.K.	233b	53.37N	2.06W
Milo, Me., U.S.	86	44.16N	69.01W
Milon-la-Chapelle, Fr.	233c	48.44N	2.03E
Milos, i., Grc. (mē'lŏs)	142	36.45N	24.35E
Milpa Alta, Mex. (mē'l-pä-á'l-tä)	113a	19.11N	99.01W
Milspe, Ger.	232	51.18N	7.21E
Milton, Can.	77d	43.31N	79.53W
Milton, Fl., U.S. (mĭl'tŭn)	108	30.37N	87.02W
Milton, Pa., U.S.	92	41.00N	76.50W
Milton, Ut., U.S.	101b	41.04N	111.44W
Milton, Wa., U.S.	100a	47.15N	122.20W
Milton, Wi., U.S.	96	42.45N	89.00W
Milton-Freewater, Or., U.S.	98	45.57N	118.25W
Milvale, Pa., U.S. (mĭl'văl)	95e	40.29N	79.58W
Milville, N.J., U.S. (mĭl'vĭl)	92	39.25N	75.00W
Milwaukee, Wi., U.S.	90	43.03N	87.55W
Milwaukee, r., Wi., U.S.	95a	43.10N	87.56W
Milwaukie, Or., U.S. (mĭl-wô'kē)	98	45.27N	122.38W
Mimiapan, Mex. (mē-myä-pán')	113a	19.26N	99.28W
Mimoso do Sul, Braz. (mē-mō'sō-dô-sōō'l)	123a	21.03S	41.21W
Min, r., China (mēn)	180	26.03N	118.30E
Min, r., China	184	29.30N	104.00E
Mina, r., Alg. (mē'ná)	152	35.24N	0.51E
Minago, r., Can. (mĭ-nä'gō)	82	54.25N	98.45W
Minakuchi, Japan (mē'ná-kōō'chē)	187	34.59N	136.06E
Minami, neigh., Japan	237e	34.58N	135.45E
Minamisenju, neigh., Japan	238a	35.44N	139.48E
Minas, Cuba (mē'näs)	116	21.30N	77.35W
Minas, Indon.	173b	0.52N	101.29E
Minas, Ur. (mē'näs)	126	34.18S	55.12W
Minas, Sierra de las, mts., Guat. (syĕr'rá dā läs mē'näs)	114	15.08N	90.25W

ăt; finăl; rāte; senāte; ärm; ásk; sofá; fâre; ch-choose; dh-as th in other; bē; ēvent; bĕt; recĕnt; cratēr; g-gō; gh-guttural g; bĭt; ĭ-short neutral; rīde; ĸ-guttural k as ch in German ich;

PLACE (Pronunciation)	PAGE	Lat. °'	Long. °'
Minas Basin, b., Can. (mī'năs)	86	45.20N	64.00W
Minas Channel, strt., Can.	86	45.15N	64.45W
Minas de Oro, Hond. (mē'näs-dĕ-dĕ-ō-rô)	114	14.52N	87.19W
Minas de Riotinto, Spain (mē'näs dā rē-ō-tēn'tō)	152	37.43N	6.35W
Minas Novas, Braz. (mē'näzh nō'väzh)	124	17.20S	42.19W
Minatare, l., Ne., U.S. (mĭn'à-târ)	96	41.56N	103.07W
Minatitlán, Mex. (mē-nä-tē-tlän')	110	17.59N	94.33W
Minatitlán, Mex.	112	19.21N	104.02W
Minato, Japan (mē'nà-tô)	187	35.13N	139.52E
Minato, neigh., Japan	238a	35.39N	139.45E
Minato, neigh., Japan	238b	34.39N	135.26E
Minch, The, strt., Scot., U.K.	136	58.04N	6.04W
Mindanao, i., Phil.	188	8.00N	125.00E
Mindanao Sea, sea, Phil.	188	8.55N	124.00E
Minden, Ger. (mĭn'dĕn)	148	52.17N	8.58E
Minden, La., U.S.	106	32.36N	93.19W
Minden, Ne., U.S.	104	40.30N	98.54W
Mindoro, i., Phil.	188	12.50N	121.05E
Mindoro Strait, strt., Phil.	189a	12.28N	120.33E
Mindyak, Russia (mēn'dyák)	164a	54.01N	58.48E
Mineola, N.Y., U.S. (mĭn-ē-ō'là)	94a	40.43N	73.38W
Mineola, Tx., U.S.	106	32.39N	95.31W
Mineral del Chico, Mex. (mė-nä-räl'dĕl chē'kô)	112	20.13N	98.46W
Mineral del Monte, Mex. (mė-nä-räl dĕl mōn'tå)	112	20.18N	98.39W
Mineral'nyye Vody, Russia	160	44.10N	43.15E
Mineral Point, Wi., U.S. (mĭn'ẽr-ăl)	96	42.50N	90.10W
Minerál Wells, Tx., U.S. (mĭn'ẽr-ăl wĕlz)	106	32.48N	98.06W
Minerva, Oh., U.S. (mĭ-nur'và)	92	40.45N	81.10W
Minervino, Italy (mē-nĕr-vē'nô)	154	41.07N	16.05E
Mineyama, Japan (mē-nĕ-yä'mä)	187	35.38N	135.05E
Mingan, Can.	78	50.18N	64.02W
Mingenew, Austl. (mĭn'gĕ-nů)	196	29.15S	115.45E
Mingo Junction, Oh., U.S. (mĭŋ'gō)	92	40.15N	80.40W
Minho, hist. reg., Port. (mēn yò)	152	41.32N	8.13W
Minho (Miño), r., Eur. (mē'n-yô)	152	41.28N	9.05W
Ministik Lake, l., Can. (mĭ-nĭs'tĭk)	77g	53.23N	113.05W
Minna, Nig. (mĭn'à)	204	9.37N	6.33E
Minneapolis, Ks., U.S. (mĭn-ē-ăp'ô-lĭs)	104	39.07N	97.41W
Minneapolis, Mn., U.S.	90	44.58N	93.15W
Minnedosa, Can. (mĭn-ē-dō'så)	78	50.14N	99.51W
Minneota, Mn., U.S. (mĭn-ē-ō'tà)	96	44.34N	95.59W
Minnesota, state, U.S. (mĭn-ē-sō'tă)	90	46.10N	90.20W
Minnesota, r., Mn., U.S.	90	44.30N	95.00W
Minnetonka, l., Mn., U.S. (mĭn-ē-tôŋ'kà)	96	44.52N	93.34W
Minnitaki Lake, l., Can. (mĭ'nĭ-tä'kē)	82	49.58N	92.00W
Mino, r., Japan	187b	34.56N	135.06E
Minonk, Il., U.S. (mī'nŏnk)	92	40.55N	89.00W
Minooka, Il., U.S. (mĭ-nōō'kà)	95a	41.27N	88.15W
Minot, N.D., U.S.	90	48.13N	101.17W
Minsk, Bela. (mėnsk)	158	53.54N	27.35E
Minsk, prov., Bela.	156	53.50N	27.43E
Mińsk Mazowiecki, Pol. (mēn'sk mä-zô-vyĕt'skĭ)	148	52.10N	21.35E
Minsterley, Eng., U.K. (mĭnstẽr-lē)	138a	52.38N	2.55W
Mintard, Ger.	232	51.22N	6.54E
Minto, Austl.	239a	34.01S	150.51E
Minto, Can.	86	46.05N	66.05W
Minto, l., Can.	78	57.18N	75.50W
Minturno, Italy (mėn-tōōr'nō)	154	41.17N	13.44E
Minūf, Egypt (mė-nōōf')	212b	30.26N	30.55E
Minusinsk, Russia (mē-nò-sėnsk')	158	53.47N	91.45E
Min'yar, Russia	164a	55.06N	57.33E
Miquelon Lake, l., Can. (mĭ'kė-lôn)	77g	53.16N	112.55W
Miquihuana, Mex. (mė-kė-wä'nä)	112	23.36N	99.45W
Miquon, Pa., U.S.	225b	40.04N	75.16W
Mir, Bela. (mēr)	148	53.27N	26.25E
Miracema, Braz. (mē-rä-sĕ'mä)	123a	21.24S	42.10W
Miracema do Norte, Braz.	124	9.34S	48.24W
Mirador, Braz. (mė-rá-dōr')	124	6.19S	44.12W
Miraflores, Col. (mē-rä-flō'räs)	124	5.10N	73.13W
Miraflores, Peru	124	16.19S	71.20W
Miraflores, Peru	229c	12.08S	77.03W
Miraflores Locks, trans., Pan.	110a	9.00N	79.35W
Miragoâne, Haiti (mė-rá-gwän')	116	18.25N	73.05W
Mira Loma, Ca., U.S. (mĭ'rà lō'mà)	101a	34.01N	117.32W
Miramar, Ca., U.S. (mĭr'ă-mär)	102a	32.53N	117.08W
Miramar, neigh., Cuba	229b	23.07N	82.25W
Miramas, Fr.	150	43.35N	5.00E
Miramichi Bay, b., Can. (mĭr'à-mė'shē)	86	47.08N	65.08W
Miranda, Austl.	239a	34.02S	151.06E
Miranda, Col. (mē-rä'n-dä)	124a	3.14N	76.11W
Miranda, Ca., U.S.	102	40.14N	123.49W
Miranda, Ven.	125b	10.09N	68.24W
Miranda, dept., Ven.	125b	10.17N	66.41W
Miranda de Ebro, Spain (mē-rá'n-dä-dĕ-ĕ'brō)	152	42.42N	2.59W
Miranda do Douro, Port. (mė-rän'dä dô-dwĕ'rô)	152	41.30N	6.17W
Mirandela, Port. (mė-rän-dā'là)	152	41.28N	7.10W
Mirando City, Tx., U.S. (mĭr-án'dō)	106	27.25N	99.03W
Mira Por Vos Islets, is., Bah. (mē'rä pôr vōs)	116	22.05N	74.30W
Mira Por Vos Pass, strt., Bah.	116	22.10N	74.35W
Mirbāṭ, Oman	174	16.58N	54.42E
Mirebalais, Haiti (mēr-bá-lĕ')	116	18.50N	72.05W
Mirecourt, Fr. (mēr-kōōr')	150	48.20N	6.08E
Mirfield, Eng., U.K. (mûr'fēld)	138a	53.41N	1.42W
Mirgorod, Ukr.	160	49.56N	33.36E
Miri, Malay. (mē'rē)	188	4.13N	113.56E
Mirim, Lagoa, l., S.A. (mė-rėɴ')	126	33.00S	53.15W
Mírina, Grc.	154	39.52N	25.01E
Miropol'ye, Ukr. (mē-rô-pôl'yĕ)	156	51.02N	35.13E
Mīrpur Khās, Pak. (mēr'pōōr ĸäs)	178	25.36N	69.10E
Mirzāpur, India (mēr'zä-pōōr)	174	25.12N	82.38E
Mirzāpur, India	236a	22.50N	88.24E
Misailovo, Russia	235b	55.34N	37.49E
Misantla, Mex. (mė-sän'tlä)	112	19.55N	96.49W
Miscou, i., Can. (mĭs'kō)	86	47.58N	64.35W
Miscou Point, c., Can.	86	48.04N	64.32W
Miseno, Cape, c., Italy (mė-zĕ'nō)	153c	40.33N	14.12E
Misery, Mount, mtn., St. K./N. (mĭz'rĕ-ĭ)	115b	17.28N	62.47W
Mishan, China (mĭ'shäɴ)	186	45.32N	132.19E
Mishawaka, In., U.S. (mĭsh-à-wôk'à)	92	41.45N	86.15W
Mishina, Japan (mė'shė-mä)	187	35.09N	138.56E
Misiones, prov., Arg. (mė-syō'nās)	126	27.00S	54.30W
Miskito, Cayos, is., Nic.	114	14.34N	82.30W
Miskolc, Hung. (mĭsh'kōlts)	136	48.07N	20.50E
Misool, Pulau, i., Indon. (mė-sól')	188	2.00S	130.05E
Misquah Hills, Mn., U.S. (mĭs-kwä' hĭlz)	96	47.50N	90.30W
Miṣr al Jadīdah, Egypt	212b	30.06N	31.35E
Miṣr al-Qadīmah (Old Cairo), neigh., Egypt	240a	30.00N	31.14E
Misrātah, Libya	204	32.23N	14.58E
Missinaibi, r., Can. (mĭs'ĭn-ä'ē-bė)	78	50.27N	83.01W
Missinaibi Lake, l., Can.	84	48.23N	83.40W
Mission, Ks., U.S. (mĭsh'ŭn)	101f	39.02N	94.39W
Mission, Tx., U.S.	106	26.14N	98.19W
Mission City, Can. (sĭ'tĭ)	80	49.08N	112.18W
Mississagi, r., Can.	84	46.35N	83.30W
Mississauga, Can.	84	43.34N	79.37W
Mississippi, state, U.S. (mĭs-ĭ-sĭp'ė)	90	32.30N	89.45W
Mississippi, l., Can.	84	45.05N	76.15W
Mississippi, r., U.S.	90	32.00N	91.30W
Mississippi Sound, strt., Ms., U.S.	108	34.16N	89.10W
Missoula, Mt., U.S. (mĭ-zōō'là)	90	46.55N	114.00W
Missouri, state, U.S. (mĭ-sōō'rė)	90	38.00N	93.40W
Missouri, r., U.S.	90	40.40N	96.00W
Missouri City, Tx., U.S.	107a	29.37N	95.32W
Missouri Coteau, hills, U.S.	90	47.30N	101.00W
Missouri Valley, Ia., U.S.	96	41.35N	95.53W
Mist, Or., U.S. (mĭst)	100c	46.00N	123.15W
Mistassini, Can. (mĭs-tá-sĭ'nė)	84	48.56N	71.55W
Mistassini, l., Can. (mĭs-tá-sĭ'nė)	78	50.48N	73.30W
Mistelbach, Aus. (mĭs'tĕl-bäk)	148	48.34N	16.33E
Misteriosa, Lago, l., Mex. (mēs-tĕ-ryô'sä)	114a	18.05N	90.15W
Misti, Volcán, vol., Peru	124	16.04S	71.20W
Mistretta, Italy (mė-strĕt'tä)	154	37.54N	14.22E
Misty Fjords National Monument, rec., Ak., U.S.	89	51.00N	131.00W
Mita, Punta de, c., Mex. (pōō'n-tä-dĕ-mē'tä)	112	20.44N	105.34W
Mitaka, Japan (mė'tä-kä)	187a	35.42N	139.34E
Mitcham, Austl.	239b	37.49S	145.12E
Mitcham, neigh., Eng., U.K.	231	51.24N	0.10W
Mitchell, Il., U.S. (mĭch'ĕl)	101e	38.46N	90.05W
Mitchell, In., U.S.	92	38.45N	86.25W
Mitchell, Ne., U.S.	96	41.56N	103.49W
Mitchell, S.D., U.S.	96	43.42N	98.01W
Mitchell, Mount, mtn., N.C., U.S.	90	35.47N	82.15W
Mīt Ghamr, Egypt	212b	30.43N	31.20E
Mitilíni, Grc.	142	39.09N	26.35E
Mitla Pass, p., Egypt	173a	30.03N	32.40E
Mito, Japan (mē'tō)	186	36.20N	140.23E
Mitry-Mory, Fr.	233c	48.59N	2.37E
Mitsiwa, Eth.	204	15.40N	39.19E
Mitsu, Japan (mēt'sò)	187	34.21N	132.49E
Mitte, neigh., Ger.	234a	52.31N	13.24E
Mittelland Kanal, can., Ger. (mĭt'ĕl-länd)	148	52.18N	10.42E
Mittenwalde, Ger. (mē'tĕn-väl-dĕ)	139b	52.16N	13.33E
Mittweida, Ger. (mĭt-vī'dä)	148	50.59N	12.58E
Mitumba, Monts, mts., Zaire	210	10.50S	27.00E
Mityayevo, Russia (mĭt-yä'yĕ-vô)	164a	60.17N	61.02E
Miura, Japan	187a	35.08N	139.37E
Miwa, Japan (mē'wä)	187b	34.32N	135.51E
Mixcoac, neigh., Mex.	229a	19.23N	99.12W
Mixico, Guat. (mēs'kô)	114	14.37N	90.37W
Mixquiahuala, Mex. (mēs-kė-wä'lä)	112	20.12N	99.13W
Mixteco, r., Mex. (mės-tā'kō)	112	17.45N	98.10W
Miyake, Japan (mē'yä-kå)	187b	34.35N	135.34E
Miyake, i., Japan (mē'yä-kå)	187	34.06N	139.21E
Miyakojima, neigh., Japan	238b	34.43N	135.33E
Miyakonojō, Japan	186	31.44N	131.04E
Miyazaki, Japan (mē'yä-zä'kė)	186	31.55N	131.27E
Miyoshi, Japan (mė-yō'shė')	186	34.48N	132.49E
Mizdah, Libya (mēz'dä)	176	31.29N	13.09E
Mizil, Rom. (mē'zėl)	154	45.01N	26.30E
Mizonuma, Japan	238a	35.48N	139.36E
Mizoram, state, India	174	23.25N	92.45E
Mizue, neigh., Japan	238a	35.41N	139.54E
Mizuho, Japan	238a	35.46N	139.21E
Mjölby, Swe. (myûl'bü)	146	58.20N	15.09E
Mjörn, l., Swe.	146	57.55N	12.22E
Mjösa, l., Nor. (myûsä)	140	60.41N	11.25E
Mkalama, Tan.	206	4.07S	34.38E
Mkushi, Zam.	210	13.40S	29.20E
Mkwaja, Tan.	210	5.47S	38.51E
Mladá Boleslav, Czech. (mlä'dä bô'lĕ-släf)	148	50.26N	14.52E
Mlala Hills, hills, Tan.	210	6.47S	31.45E
Mlanje Mountains, mts., Mwi.	210	15.55S	35.30E
Mława, Pol. (mwä'vá)	140	53.07N	20.25E
Mmabatho, Boph.	206	25.42S	25.43E
Mnevniki, neigh., Russia	235b	55.45N	37.28E
Moa, r., Afr.	208	7.40N	11.15W
Moa, Pulau, i., Indon.	188	8.30S	128.30E
Moab, Ut., U.S. (mō'ăb)	102	38.35N	109.35W
Moanda, Gabon	206	1.37S	13.09E
Moar Lake, l., Can. (môr)	82	52.00N	95.09W
Moba, Nig.	240d	6.27N	3.28E
Moba, Zaire	206	7.12S	29.39E
Mobaye, Cen. Afr. Rep. (mô-bä'y')	204	4.19N	21.11E
Mobayi-Mbongo, Zaire	204	4.14N	21.11E
Moberly, Mo., U.S. (mō'bẽr-lĭ)	90	39.24N	92.25W
Mobile, Al., U.S. (mô-bēl')	90	30.42N	88.03W
Mobile, r., Al., U.S.	108	31.15N	88.00W
Mobile Bay, b., Al., U.S.	90	30.26N	87.56W
Mobridge, S.D., U.S. (mō'brĭj)	96	45.32N	100.26W
Moca, Dom. Rep. (mô'kä)	116	19.25N	70.35W
Moçambique, Moz. (mō-säɴ-bē'kĕ)	210	15.03S	40.42E
Moçâmedes, Ang. (mô-zá-mĕ-dĕs)	206	15.10S	12.09E
Moçâmedes, hist. reg., Ang.	206	16.00S	12.15E
Mochitlán, Mex. (mō-chė-tlän')	112	17.10N	99.19W
Mochudi, Bots. (mō-chōō'dė)	206	24.13S	26.07E
Mocímboa da Praia, Moz. (mô-sē'ēm-bô-à prä'ēá)	206	11.20S	40.21E
Moclips, Wa., U.S.	98	47.14N	124.13W
Môco, Serra do, mtn., Ang.	210	12.25S	15.10E
Mococa, Braz. (mô-kô'kà)	123a	21.29S	46.58W
Moctezuma, Mex. (mōk'tå-zōō'mä)	112	22.44N	101.06W
Mocuba, Moz.	210	16.50S	36.59E
Modderbee, S. Afr.	240b	26.10S	28.24E
Modderfontein, S. Afr.	207b	26.06S	28.10E
Modena, Italy (mô'dĕ-nä)	142	44.38N	10.54E
Modesto, Ca., U.S. (mô-dĕs'tō)	102	37.39N	121.00W
Modjeska, Ca., U.S.	228	33.43N	117.37W
Mödling, Aus. (mûd'lĭng)	139e	48.06N	16.17E
Moelv, Nor.	146	60.55N	10.40E
Moengo, Sur.	124	5.43N	54.19W
Moenkopi, Az., U.S.	102	36.07N	111.13W
Moers, Ger. (mûrs)	151c	51.27N	6.38E
Moffat Tunnel, trans., Co., U.S. (môf'ăt)	104	39.52N	106.20W
Mofolo, S. Afr.	240b	26.14S	27.53E
Mogadishu, see Muqdisho, Som.	212a	2.08N	45.22E
Mogadore, Oh., U.S. (mŏg-á-dōr')	95d	41.04N	81.23E
Mogaung, Burma (mō-gä'ông)	174	25.30N	96.52E
Mogi das Cruzes, Braz. (mô-gė-däs-krōō'sĕs)	124	23.33S	46.10W
Mogi-Guaçu, r., Braz. (mô-gē-gwá'sōō)	123a	22.06S	47.12W
Mogilëv, Bela. (mô-gē-lyôf')	158	53.53N	30.22E
Mogilëv, prov., Bela. (mô-gė-lyôf')	156	53.28N	30.15E
Mogilëv-Poldol'skiy, Ukr. (mô-gė-lyôf) (pô-dôl'skĭ)	160	48.27N	27.51E
Mogilno, Pol. (mô-gēl'nô)	148	52.38N	17.58W
Mogi-Mirim, Braz. (mô-gė-mē-rē'ɴ)	123a	22.26S	46.57W
Mogok, Burma (mô-gōk')	174	23.14N	96.38E
Mogol, r., S. Afr. (mô-gŏl)	212d	24.12S	27.55E
Mogollon Plateau, plat., Az., U.S.	90	34.15N	110.45W
Mogollon Rim, cliff, Az., U.S. (mō-gô-yōn')	102	34.26N	111.17W
Moguer, Spain (mô-gĕr')	152	37.15N	6.50W
Mohács, Hung. (mô'häch)	148	45.59N	18.38E
Mohale's Hoek, Leso.	207c	30.09S	27.28E
Mohall, N.D., U.S. (mō'hôl)	96	48.46N	101.29W
Mohave, l., Nv., U.S. (mô-hä'vä)	102	35.23N	114.40W
Mohe, China (mwo-hŭ)	180	53.33N	122.30E
Mohenjo-Dero, hist., Pak.	174	27.20N	68.10E
Mohili, neigh., India	236e	19.06N	72.53E
Mõisaküla, Est. (mẽẽ'sá-kü'lä)	146	58.07N	25.12E
Moissac, Fr. (mwä-sák')	150	44.07N	1.05E
Moita, Port. (mô-ē'tà)	153b	38.39N	9.00W
Mojave, Ca., U.S.	102	35.06N	118.09W
Mojave, r., Ca., U.S. (mô-hä'vä)	102	34.46N	117.24W
Mojave Desert, Ca., U.S.	102	35.05N	117.30W
Mojave Desert, des., Ca., U.S.	90	35.00N	117.00W
Mokhotlong, Leso.	207c	29.18S	29.06E
Mokp'o, S. Kor. (môk'pô')	180	34.50N	126.30E
Mol, Bel.	139a	51.21N	5.09E
Moldavia, hist. reg., Rom.	148	47.20N	27.12E
Moldavia, see Moldova	158	48.00N	28.00E
Molde, Nor. (môl'dĕ)	140	62.44N	7.15E
Moldova, r., Rom.	148	47.17N	26.27E
Moldova, nation, Eur.	158	48.00N	28.00E
Moldoveanu, mtn., Rom.	154	45.33N	24.38E
Molepolole, Bots. (mō-lā-pô-lō'lå)	206	24.15S	25.33W
Molfetta, Italy (môl-fĕt'tä)	142	41.11N	16.38E
Molina, Chile (mô-lē'nä)	123b	35.07S	71.17W
Molina de Aragón, Spain (mô-lē'nä dĕ ä-rä-gô'n)	152	40.40N	1.54W
Molina de Segura, Spain (mô-lē'nä dĕ sĕ-gōō'rä)	152	38.03N	1.07W
Moline, Il., U.S. (mô-lēn')	104	41.31N	90.34W
Molino de Rosas, Mex.	229a	19.22N	99.13W
Molíns de Rey, Spain	234e	41.25N	2.01E
Moliro, Zaire	206	8.13S	30.34E
Moliterno, Italy (mōl-ē-tĕr'nō)	154	40.13N	15.54W
Möllen, Ger.	232	51.35N	6.42E
Mollendo, Peru (mô-lyĕn'dō)	124	17.02S	71.59W
Moller, Port, Ak., U.S. (pōrt mōl'ẽr)	89	56.18N	161.30W
Mölndal, Swe. (mûln'däl)	146	57.39N	12.01E
Molochnaya, r., Ukr. (mô-lôch'ná-yá) (rĕ-kä')	156	47.05N	35.22E
Molochnoye, Ozero, l., Ukr. (ô'zĕ-rô mô-lôch'nô-yĕ)	156	46.35N	35.32E
Molodechno, Bela. (mô-lô-dĕch'nô)	160	54.18N	26.57E
Molody Tud, Russia (mō-lô-dô'ĕ tōō'd)	164b	55.17N	37.31E
Molokai, i., Hi., U.S. (mō-lô kä'ē)	90c	21.15N	157.05E
Molokcha, r., Russia (mô'lôk-chä)	164b	56.15N	38.29E
Molopo, r., Afr. (mō-lō-pô)	206	27.45S	20.45E
Molson Lake, l., Can. (mōl'sŭn)	82	54.12N	96.45W
Molteno, S. Afr. (môl-tā'nō)	207c	31.24S	26.23E
Moluccas, see Maluku, is., Indon.	188	2.22S	128.25E

PLACE (Pronunciation)	PAGE	Lat. °′	Long. °′
Moma, Moz.	210	16.44S	39.14E
Mombasa, Kenya (mōm-bä′sä)	206	4.03S	39.40E
Mombetsu, Japan (mȯm′bĕt-so͞o′)	186	44.21N	142.48E
Momence, Il., U.S. (mȯ-mĕns′)	95a	41.09N	87.40W
Momostenango, Guat. (mȯ-mȯs-tā-näŋ′gȯ)	114	15.02N	91.25W
Momotombo, Nic.	114	12.25N	86.43W
Mompog Pass, strt., Phil. (mōm-pōg′)	189a	13.35N	122.09E
Mompos, Col. (mōm-pōs′)	124	9.05N	74.30W
Møn, i., Den. (mûn)	146	54.54N	12.30E
Monaca, Pa., U.S. (mŏ-nȧ′kō)	95e	40.41N	80.17W
Monaco, nation, Eur. (mŏn′ȧ-kō)	136	43.43N	7.47E
Monaghan, Ire. (mŏ′ȧ-găn)	144	54.16N	7.20W
Mona Passage, strt., N.A. (mō′nă)	110	18.00N	68.10W
Monarch Mountain, mtn., Can. (mŏn′ẽrk)	80	51.41N	125.53W
Monashee Mountains, mts., Can. (mŏ-nă′shē)	80	50.30N	118.30W
Monastir, Tun. (mȯn-ȧs-tēr′)	142	35.49N	10.56E
Monastir, *see* Bitola, Mac.	136	41.02N	21.22E
Monastyrishche, Ukr. (mȯ-nȧs-tē-rēsh′chȧ)	156	48.57N	29.53E
Monastyrshchina, Russia (mȯ-nȧs-tērsh′chĭ-nȧ)	156	54.19N	31.49E
Moncada, Spain	234e	41.29N	2.11E
Monção, Braz. (mon-souɴ′)	124	3.39S	45.23W
Moncayo, mtn., Spain (mȯn-kä′yō)	152	41.44N	1.48W
Monchegorsk, Russia (mōn′chĕ-gôrsk)	160	69.00N	33.35E
Mönchengladbach, Ger. (mûn′ᴋĕn gläd′bäᴋ)	148	51.12N	6.28E
Moncique, Serra de, mts., Port. (sĕr′rä dä mȯn-chē′kĕ)	152	37.22N	8.37W
Monclova, Mex. (mȯn-klō′vä)	110	26.53N	101.25W
Moncton, Can. (mŭŋk′tŭn)	78	46.06N	64.47W
Mondêgo, r., Port. (mōn-dĕ′gō)	152	40.10N	8.36W
Mondego, Cabo, c., Port. (kȧ′bō mȯn-dā′gȯ)	152	40.12N	8.55W
Mondeor, S. Afr.	240b	26.17S	28.00E
Mondombe, Zaire (mȯn-dôm′bȧ)	206	0.45S	23.06E
Mondoñedo, Spain (mȯn-dȯ-nyā′dō)	152	43.35N	7.18W
Mondovi, Wi., U.S. (mŏn-dō′vĭ)	96	44.35N	91.42W
Monee, Il., U.S. (mŏ-nĭ)	95a	41.25N	87.45W
Monessen, Pa., U.S. (mŏ′nĕs′sĕn)	95e	40.09N	79.53W
Monett, Mo., U.S. (mȯ-nĕt′)	104	36.55N	93.55W
Monfalcone, Italy	154	45.49N	13.30E
Monforte de Lemos, Spain (mȯn-fôr′tā dĕ lĕ′mȯs)	152	42.30N	7.30W
Mongala, r., Zaire (mŏn-gȧl′ȧ)	204	3.20N	21.30E
Mongalla, Sudan	204	5.11N	31.46E
Mongat, Spain	234e	41.28N	2.17E
Monghyr, India (mŏn-gēr′)	174	25.23N	86.34E
Mongo, r., Afr.	208	9.50N	11.50W
Mongolia, nation, Asia (mŏŋ-gō′lĭ-ȧ)	180	46.00N	100.00E
Mongos, Chaîne des, mts., Cen. Afr. Rep.	204	8.04N	21.59E
Mongoumba, Cen. Afr. Rep. (mŏŋ-go͞om′bȧ)	204	3.38N	18.36E
Mongu, Zam. (mŏŋ-go͞o′)	206	15.15S	23.09E
Monken Hadley, neigh., Eng., U.K.	231	51.40N	0.11W
Monkey Bay, Mwi.	210	14.05S	34.55E
Monkey River, Belize (mŭŋ′kĭ)	114a	16.22N	88.33W
Monkland, Can. (mŭngk-lănd)	77c	45.12N	74.52W
Monkoto, Zaire (mȯn-kō′tȯ)	206	1.38S	20.39E
Monmouth, Il., U.S. (mŏn′mŭth)(mŏn′mouth)	104	40.54N	90.38W
Monmouth Junction, N.J., U.S. (mŏn′mouth jŭngk′shŭn)	94a	40.23N	74.33W
Monmouth Mountain, mtn., Can. (mŏn′mŭth)	80	51.00N	123.47W
Mono, r., Afr.	208	7.20N	1.25E
Mono Lake, l., Ca., U.S. (mō′nō)	102	38.04N	119.00W
Monon, In., U.S. (mō′nŏn)	92	40.55N	86.55W
Monongah, W.V., U.S. (mȯ-nŏŋ′gȧ)	92	39.25N	80.10W
Monongahela, Pa., U.S. (mȯ-nŏn-gȧ-hē′lȧ)	95a	40.11N	79.55W
Monongahela, r., W.V., U.S.	92	39.30N	80.10W
Monopoli, Italy (mȯ-nô′pȯ-lê)	154	40.55N	17.17E
Monóvar, Spain (mȯ-nō′vär)	152	38.26N	0.50W
Monreale, Italy (mōn-rȧ-ä′lā)	154	38.04N	13.15E
Monroe, Ga., U.S. (mŭn-rō′)	108	33.47N	83.43W
Monroe, La., U.S.	90	32.30N	92.06W
Monroe, Mi., U.S.	92	41.55N	83.25W
Monroe, N.Y., U.S.	94a	41.19N	74.11W
Monroe, N.C., U.S.	108	34.58N	80.34W
Monroe, Ut., U.S.	102	38.35N	112.10W
Monroe, Wa., U.S.	100a	47.52N	121.58W
Monroe, Wi., U.S.	96	42.35N	89.40W
Monroe, Lake, l., Fl., U.S.	108	28.50N	81.15W
Monroe City, Mo., U.S.	104	39.38N	91.41W
Monroeville, Al., U.S. (mŭn-rō′vĭl)	108	31.33N	87.19W
Monrovia, Lib.	204	6.18N	10.47W
Monrovia, Ca., U.S. (mŏn-rō′vĭ-ȧ)	101a	34.09N	118.00W
Mons, Bel. (môɴ′)	140	50.29N	3.55E
Monson, Me., U.S. (mŏn′sŭn)	86	45.17N	69.28W
Mönsterås, Swe. (mŭn′stĕr-ȯs)	146	57.04N	16.24E
Montagne Tremblant Provincial Park, rec., Can.	90	46.30N	75.51W
Montague, Can. (mŏn′tȧ-gū)	86	46.10N	62.39W
Montague, Mi., U.S.	92	43.30N	86.25W
Montague, i., Ak., U.S.	89	60.10N	147.00W
Montalbán, Ven. (mōnt-äl-bän)	125b	10.14N	68.19W
Montalbancito, Ven.	230a	10.28N	66.59W
Montalegre, Port. (mōn-tä-lā′grė)	152	41.49N	7.48W
Montana, state, U.S. (mŏn-tăn′ȧ)	90	47.10N	111.50W
Montánchez, Spain (mȯn-tän′chȧth)	152	39.18N	6.09W
Montara, Ca., U.S.	227b	37.33N	122.31W

PLACE (Pronunciation)	PAGE	Lat. °′	Long. °′
Montargis, Fr. (môɴ-tȧr-zhē′)	140	47.59N	2.42E
Montataire, Fr. (mȯɴ-tȧ-târ)	151b	49.15N	2.26E
Montauban, Fr. (môɴ-tȯ-bäɴ′)	140	44.01N	1.22E
Montauk, N.Y., U.S.	92	41.03N	71.57W
Montauk Point, c., N.Y., U.S. (mŏn-tôk′)	92	41.05N	71.55W
Montbanch, Spain (mȯnt-bän′ch)	152	41.20N	1.08E
Montbard, Fr. (môɴ-bȧr′)	150	47.40N	4.19E
Montbéliard, Fr. (môɴ-bā-lyȧr′)	150	47.32N	6.45E
Mont Belvieu, Tx., U.S. (mŏnt bĕl′vū)	107a	29.51N	94.53W
Montbrison, Fr. (môɴ-brė-zoɴ′)	150	45.38N	4.06E
Montceau, Fr. (môɴ-sō′)	150	46.39N	4.22E
Montclair, Ca., U.S.	228	34.06N	117.41W
Montclair, N.J., U.S. (mŏnt-klâr′)	94a	40.49N	74.13W
Mont-de-Marsan, Fr. (mȯɴ-dē-mȧr-säɴ′)	140	43.54N	0.32W
Montdidier, Fr. (môɴ-dē-dyā′)	150	49.42N	2.33E
Monte, Arg. (mŏ′n-tĕ)	123c	35.25S	58.49W
Monteagudo, Bol. (mōn′tȧ-ä-go͞o′dhō)	124	19.49S	63.48W
Montebello, Can.	77c	45.40N	74.56W
Montebello, Ca., U.S. (mŏn-tė-bĕl′ō)	101a	34.01N	118.06W
Monte Bello Islands, is., Austl.	196	20.30S	114.10E
Monte Caseros, Arg. (mŏ′n-tĕ-kä-sĕ′rȯs)	126	30.16S	57.39W
Monte Chingolo, neigh., Arg.	229d	34.45S	58.20W
Montecillos, Cordillera de, mts., Hond.	114	14.19N	87.52W
Monte Cristi, Dom. Rep. (mȯ′n-tĕ-krė′s-tē)	116	19.50N	71.40W
Montecristo, Isola di, i., Italy (mōn′tȧ-krēs′tō)	154	42.20N	10.19E
Monte Escobedo, Mex. (mōn′tȧ ĕs-kȯ-bā′dhō)	112	22.18N	103.34W
Monteforte Irpino, Italy (mȯn-tĕ-fō′r-tĕ ē′r-pē′nō)	153c	40.39N	14.42E
Montefrío, Spain (mōn-tȧ-frē′ō)	152	37.20N	4.02W
Montego Bay, Jam. (mŏn-tē′gō)	110	18.30N	77.55W
Montelavar, Port. (mōn-tĕ-lȧ-vär′)	153b	38.51N	9.20W
Montélimar, Fr. (môɴ-tā-lē-mär′)	140	44.33N	4.47E
Montellano, Spain (mōn-tȧ-lyä′nō)	152	37.00N	5.34W
Montello, Wi., U.S. (mŏn-tĕl′ō)	96	43.47N	89.20W
Montemorelos, Mex. (mōn′tȧ-mō-rā′lōs)	110	25.14N	99.50W
Montemor-o-Novo, Port. (mōɴ-tĕ-mȯr′ȯ-nȯ′vȯ)	152	38.39N	8.11W
Montenegro, reg., Moz.	210	13.07S	39.00E
Montepulciano, Italy (mȯn′tȧ-po͞ol-chä′nō)	154	43.05N	11.48E
Montereau-faut-Yonne, Fr. (môɴ-t'rō′fō-yȯn′)	150	48.24N	2.57E
Monterey, Ca., U.S. (mŏn-tĕ-rā′)	90	36.36N	121.53W
Monterey, Tn., U.S.	108	36.06N	85.15W
Monterey Bay, b., Ca., U.S.	90	36.48N	122.01W
Monterey Park, Ca., U.S.	101a	34.04N	118.08W
Montería, Col. (mōn-tā-rā′ä)	124	8.47N	75.57W
Monteros, Arg. (mȯn-tĕ′rȯs)	126	27.14S	65.29W
Monterotondo, Italy (mȯn-tĕ-rȯ-tô′n-dō)	153d	42.03N	12.39E
Monterrey, Mex. (mōn-tĕr-rā′)	110	25.43N	100.19W
Montesano, Wa., U.S. (mŏn-tė-sä′nō)	98	46.59N	123.35W
Monte Sant'Angelo, Italy (mô′n-tĕ sän ä′n-gzhĕ-lȯ)	142	41.43N	15.59E
Montes Claros, Braz. (môn-tĕs-klä′rȯs)	124	16.44S	43.41W
Montespaccato, neigh., Italy	235c	41.54N	12.23E
Montevallo, Al., U.S. (môn-tė-văl′ō)	108	33.05N	86.49W
Montevarchi, Italy (mōn-tȧ-vär′kē)	154	43.30N	11.45E
Monteverde Nuovo, neigh., Italy	235c	41.51N	12.27E
Montevideo, Mn., U.S. (mōn′tȧ-vė-dhā′ō)	96	44.56N	95.42W
Montevideo, Ur. (mōn′tȧ-vė-dhā′ō)	126	34.50S	56.10W
Monte Vista, Co., U.S. (mŏn′tė vĭs′tȧ)	102	37.35N	106.10W
Montezuma, Ga., U.S. (mŏn-tė-zo͞o′mȧ)	108	32.17N	84.00W
Montezuma Castle National Monument, rec., Az., U.S.	102	34.38N	111.50W
Montfermeil, Fr.	233c	48.54N	2.34E
Montflorit, Spain	234e	41.29N	2.08E
Montfoort, Neth.	139a	52.02N	4.56E
Montfor-l'Amaury, Fr. (mŏɴ-fōr′lä-mō-rē′)	151b	48.47N	1.49E
Montfort, Fr. (mŏn-fōr)	150	48.09N	1.58W
Montgeron, Fr.	233c	48.42N	2.27E
Montgomery, Al., U.S. (mŏnt-gŭm′ẽr-ĭ)	90	32.23N	86.17W
Montgomery, W.V., U.S.	92	38.10N	81.25W
Montgomery City, Mo., U.S.	104	38.58N	91.29W
Montgomery Knolls, Md., U.S.	225c	39.14N	76.48W
Monticello, Ar., U.S. (mŏn-tĭ-sĕl′ō)	104	33.38N	91.47W
Monticello, Fl., U.S.	108	30.32N	83.53W
Monticello, Ga., U.S.	108	33.00N	83.11W
Monticello, Il., U.S.	92	40.05N	88.35W
Monticello, In., U.S.	92	40.40N	86.50W
Monticello, Ia., U.S.	96	42.14N	91.13W
Monticello, Ky., U.S.	108	36.47N	84.50W
Monticello, Me., U.S.	86	46.19N	67.53W
Monticello, Mn., U.S.	96	45.18N	93.48W
Monticello, N.Y., U.S.	92	41.35N	74.40W
Monticello, Ut., U.S.	102	37.55N	109.25W
Montigny-le-Bretonneux, Fr.	233c	48.46N	2.02E
Montigny-lés-Cormeilles, Fr.	233c	48.59N	2.12E
Montijo, Port. (mȯn-tė′zhō)	153b	38.42N	8.58W
Montijo, Spain (mȯn-tē′hō)	152	38.55N	6.35W
Montijo, Bahía, b., Pan. (bä-ē′ä mȯn-tē′hō)	110	7.36N	81.11W
Mont-Joli, Can. (môɴ zhȯ-lē′)	78	48.35N	68.11W
Montjuich, Castillo de, hist., Spain	234e	41.22N	2.10E
Montluçon, Fr. (môɴ-lü-sôɴ′)	140	46.20N	2.35E
Montmagny, Can. (môɴ-mȧn-yē′)	84	46.59N	70.33W
Montmagny, Fr.	233c	48.58N	2.21E
Montmartre, neigh., Fr.	233c	48.53N	2.21E
Montmorency, Austl.	239b	37.43S	145.07E
Montmorency, Fr. (môɴ′mȯ-räɴ-sē′)	151b	48.59N	2.19E
Montmorency, r., Can. (mŏnt-mȯ-rĕn′sĭ)	77b	47.03N	71.10W

PLACE (Pronunciation)	PAGE	Lat. °′	Long. °′
Montmorillon, Fr. (môɴ′mȯ-rė-yôɴ′)	150	46.26N	0.50E
Montone, r., Italy (mȯn-tȯ′nĕ)	154	44.03N	11.45E
Montoro, Spain (mȯn-tō′rȯ)	152	38.01N	4.22W
Montpelier, Id., U.S.	98	42.19N	111.19W
Montpelier, In., U.S. (mŏnt-pēl′yẽr)	92	40.35N	85.20W
Montpelier, Oh., U.S.	92	41.35N	84.35W
Montpelier, Vt., U.S.	90	44.20N	72.35W
Montpellier, Fr. (môɴ-pĕ-lyā′)	140	43.38N	3.53E
Montréal, Can. (mŏn-trė-ôl′)	78	45.30N	73.35W
Montreal, r., Can.	84	47.50N	80.30W
Montreal, r., Can.	84	47.15N	84.20W
Montreal Lake, l., Can.	82	54.20N	105.40W
Montréal-Nord, Can.	77a	45.36N	73.38W
Montréal-Ouest, Can.	223b	45.27N	73.39W
Montreuil, Fr.	151b	48.52N	2.27E
Montreux, Switz. (môn-trû′)	148	46.26N	6.52E
Montrose, Austl.	239b	37.49S	145.21E
Montrose, Scot., U.K.	144	56.45N	2.25W
Montrose, Ca., U.S. (mŏnt-rōz)	101a	34.13N	118.13W
Montrose, Co., U.S. (mŏn-trōz′)	102	38.30N	107.55W
Montrose, Oh., U.S.	95d	41.08N	81.38W
Montrose, Pa., U.S. (mŏnt-rōz′)	92	41.50N	75.50W
Montrose Hill, Pa., U.S.	226b	40.30N	79.51W
Montrouge, Fr.	151b	48.49N	2.19E
Mont-Royal, Can.	77a	47.31N	73.39W
Monts, Pointe des, c., Can. (pwăɴt′ dā môɴ′)	86	49.19N	67.22W
Mont Saint Martin, Fr. (mŏɴ sȧɴ mär-tȧɴ′)	150	49.34N	6.13E
Montserrat, dep., N.A. (mŏnt-sĕ-răt′)	110	16.48N	63.15W
Montvale, N.J., U.S. (mŏnt-vāl′)	94a	41.02N	74.01W
Monywa, Burma (mŏn′yo͞o-wȧ)	174	22.02N	95.16E
Monza, Italy (mōn′tsä)	154	45.34N	9.17E
Monzón, Spain (mōn-thōn′)	152	41.54N	0.09E
Moóca, neigh., Braz.	230d	23.33S	46.35W
Moody, Tx., U.S. (mo͞o′dĭ)	106	31.18N	97.20W
Mooi, r., S. Afr.	207c	29.00S	30.15E
Mooi, r., S. Afr. (mo͞o′ĭ)	212d	26.34S	27.03E
Mooirivier, S. Afr.	207c	29.14S	29.59E
Moolap, Austl.	195a	38.11S	144.26E
Moonachie, N.J., U.S.	224	40.50N	74.03W
Moonta, Austl. (mo͞on′tȧ)	196	34.05S	137.42E
Moora, Austl. (mȯr′ȧ)	196	30.35S	116.12E
Moorabbin, Austl.	195a	37.56S	145.02E
Moore, l., Austl. (mōr)	196	29.50S	118.12E
Moorebank, Austl.	239a	33.56S	150.56E
Moorenweis, Ger. (mō′rĕn-vīz)	139d	48.10N	11.05E
Moore Reservoir, res., Vt., U.S.	92	44.20N	72.10W
Moorestown, N.J., U.S. (morz′toun)	94f	39.58N	74.56W
Mooresville, In., U.S. (mōrz′vĭl)	95g	39.37N	86.22W
Mooresville, N.C., U.S.	108	35.34N	80.48W
Moorhead, Mn., U.S. (mōr′hĕd)	96	46.52N	96.44W
Moorhead, Ms., U.S.	108	33.25N	90.30W
Mooroolbark, Austl.	239b	37.47S	145.19E
Moorside, Eng., U.K.	233b	53.34N	2.04W
Moose, r., Can.	78	51.01N	80.42W
Moose Creek, Can.	77c	45.16N	74.58W
Moosehead, Me., U.S. (mo͞os′hĕd)	86	45.37N	69.15W
Moose Island, i., Can.	82	51.50N	97.09W
Moose Jaw, Can. (mo͞os jô)	78	50.23N	105.32W
Moose Jaw, r., Can.	82	50.34N	105.17W
Moose Lake, Can.	82	53.40N	100.28W
Moose Mountain, mtn., Can.	82	49.45N	102.37W
Moose Mountain Creek, r., Can.	82	49.12N	102.10W
Moosilauke, mtn., N.H., U.S. (mo͞o-sĭ-lȧ′kē)	92	44.00N	71.50W
Moosinning, Ger. (mō′zē-nēng)	139d	48.17N	11.51E
Moosomin, Can. (mo͞o′sȯ-mĭn)	82	50.07N	101.40W
Moosonee, Can. (mo͞o′sȯ-nė)	78	51.20N	80.44W
Mopti, Mali (mŏp′tė)	204	14.30N	4.12W
Moquegua, Peru (mȯ-kā′gwä)	124	17.15S	70.54W
Mór, Hung. (mōr)	148	47.25N	18.14E
Mora, India	179b	18.54N	72.56E
Mora, Spain (mȯ-rä)	152	39.42N	3.45W
Mora, Swe. (mō′rä)	146	61.00N	14.29E
Mora, Mn., U.S. (mō′rȧ)	96	45.52N	93.18W
Mora, N.M., U.S.	104	35.58N	105.17W
Morādābād, India (mȯ-rä-dä-bäd′)	174	28.57N	78.48E
Morales, Guat. (mȯ-rä′lĕs)	114	15.29N	88.46W
Moramanga, Madag. (mō-rä-mäŋ′gä)	206	18.48S	48.09E
Morangis, Fr.	233c	48.42N	2.20E
Morant Point, c., Jam. (mȯ-rănt′)	116	17.55N	76.10W
Morata de Tajuña, Spain (mȯ-rä′tä dā tä-ho͞o′nyä)	153a	40.14N	3.27W
Moratuwa, Sri L.	178	6.35N	79.59E
Morava (Moravia), hist. reg., Czech.	148	49.21N	16.57E
Morava, r., Czech.	140	49.00N	17.30E
Moravia, *see* Morava, hist. reg., Czech.	148	49.21N	16.57E
Morawhanna, Guy. (mȯ-rȧ-hwä′nȧ)	124	8.12N	59.33W
Moray Firth, b., Scot., U.K. (mŭr′ȧ)	136	57.41N	3.55W
Mörbylånga, Swe. (mûr′bü-lȯŋ′gȧ)	146	56.32N	16.23E
Morden, Can. (môr′dĕn)	78	49.11N	98.05W
Mordialloc, Austl. (mȯr-dĭ-ăl′ŏk)	195a	38.00S	145.05E
Mordvin Autonomous Soviet Socialist Republic, Russia	160	54.18N	43.50E
More, Ben, mtn., Scot., U.K. (bĕn môr)	144	58.09N	5.01W
Moreau, r., S.D., U.S. (mȯ-rō′)	96	45.13N	102.22W
Moree, Austl. (mō′rē)	196	29.20S	149.50E
Morehead, Ky., U.S.	92	38.10N	83.25W
Morehead City, N.C., U.S. (mōr′hĕd)	108	34.43N	76.43W
Morehouse, Mo., U.S. (mōr′hous)	104	36.49N	89.41W
Morelia, Mex. (mȯ-rā′lyä)	110	19.43N	101.12W
Morella, Spain (mȯ-rāl′yä)	152	40.38N	0.07W
Morelos, Mex.	106	28.24N	100.51W
Morelos, Mex. (mȯ-rā′lōs)	112	22.46N	102.36W

ăt; finăl; rāte; senȧte; ärm; ȧsk; sofȧ; fâre; ch-choose; dh-as th in other; bē; ėvent; bĕt; recĕnt; cratẽr; g-gō; gh-guttural g; bĭt; ĭ-short neutral; rīde; ᴋ-guttural k as ch in German ich;

PLACE (Pronunciation)	PAGE	Lat. °′	Long. °′
Morelos, Mex.	113a	19.41N	99.29W
Morelos, neigh., Mex.	229a	19.27N	99.07W
Morelos, r., Mex.	106	25.27N	99.35W
Morena, Sierra, mtn., Ca., U.S. (syĕr'rä mō-rā'nä)	100b	37.24N	122.19W
Morena, Sierra, mts., Spain (syĕr'rä mō-rā'nä)	136	38.15N	5.45W
Morenci, Az., U.S. (mō-rĕn'sĭ)	102	33.05N	109.25W
Morenci, Mi., U.S.	92	41.50N	84.50W
Moreno, Arg. (mō-rĕ'nō)	126a	34.39S	58.47W
Moreno, Ca., U.S.	101a	33.55N	117.09W
Mores, i., Bah. (mōrz)	116	26.20N	77.35W
Moresby, i., Can. (mōrz'bĭ)	100d	48.43N	123.15W
Moresby Island, i., Can.	78	52.50N	131.55W
Moreton, Eng., U.K.	233a	53.24N	3.07W
Moreton, i., Austl. (môr'tŭn)	198	26.53S	152.42E
Moreton Bay, b., Austl. (môr'tŭn)	198	27.12S	153.10E
Morewood, Can. (mōr'wŏd)	77c	45.11N	75.17W
Morgan, Mt., U.S. (môr'găn)	98	48.55N	107.56W
Morgan, Ut., U.S.	98	41.04N	111.42W
Morgan City, La., U.S.	106	29.41N	91.11W
Morganfield, Ky., U.S. (môr'găn-fēld)	92	37.40N	87.55W
Morgan's Bay, S. Afr.	207c	32.42S	28.19E
Morganton, N.C., U.S. (môr'găn-tŭn)	108	35.44N	81.42W
Morgantown, W.V., U.S. (môr'găn-toun)	92	39.40N	79.55W
Morga Range, mts., Afg.	175a	34.02N	70.38E
Morgenzon, S. Afr. (môr'gănt-sŏn)	212d	26.44S	29.39E
Moriac, Austl.	195a	38.15S	144.20E
Morice Lake, l., Can.	80	54.00N	127.37W
Moriguchi, Japan (mō'rē-gōō'chē)	187b	34.44N	135.34E
Morinville, Can. (mō'rĭn-vĭl)	77g	53.48N	113.39W
Morioka, Japan (mō'rē-ō'kà)	180	39.40N	141.21E
Morivione, neigh., Italy	234c	45.26N	9.12E
Morkoka, r., Russia (môr-kô'kà)	162	65.35N	111.00E
Morlaix, Fr. (mŏr-lĕ')	140	48.36N	3.48W
Morley, Can. (mŏr'lē)	77e	51.10N	114.51W
Morley Green, Eng., U.K.	233b	53.20N	2.16W
Mormant, Fr.	151b	48.35N	2.54E
Morne Diablotin, Dom.	115b	15.31N	61.24W
Morne Gimie, St. Luc. (môrn' zhē-mē')	115b	13.53N	61.03W
Morningside, Md., U.S.	225d	38.50N	76.53W
Mornington, Austl.	195a	38.13S	145.02E
Morobe, Pap. N. Gui.	188	8.03S	147.45E
Morocco, nation, Afr. (mō-rŏk'ō)	204	32.00N	7.00W
Morogoro, Tan. (mō-rō-gō'rō)	206	6.49S	37.40E
Moroleón, Mex. (mō-rō-lā-ōn')	112	20.07N	101.15W
Morombe, Madag. (mōō-rōōm'bā)	206	21.39S	43.34E
Morón, Arg. (mo-rō'n)	123c	34.39S	58.37W
Morón, Cuba (mō-rōn')	116	22.05N	78.35W
Morón, Ven. (mō-rō'n)	125b	10.29N	68.11W
Morondava, Madag. (mō-rōn-dä'và)	206	20.17S	44.18E
Morón de la Frontera, Spain (mō-rōn'dā lāf rōn-tā'rä)	152	37.08N	5.20W
Morongo Indian Reservation, I.R., Ca., U.S. (mō-rôŋ'gō)	102	33.54N	116.47W
Moroni, Com.	206	11.41S	43.16E
Moroni, Ut., U.S. (mō-rō'nĭ)	102	39.30N	111.40W
Morotai, i., Indon. (mō-rō-tä'ē)	188	2.12N	128.30E
Moroto, Ug.	210	2.32N	34.39E
Morozovsk, Russia	160	48.20N	41.50E
Morrill, Ne., U.S. (mŏr'ĭl)	96	41.59N	103.54W
Morrilton, Ar., U.S. (mŏr'ĭl-tŭn)	104	35.09N	92.42W
Morrinhos, Braz. (mō-rēn'yōzh)	124	17.45S	48.56W
Morris, Can. (mŏr'ĭs)	78	49.21N	97.22W
Morris, Il., U.S.	92	41.20N	88.25W
Morris, Mn., U.S.	96	45.35N	95.53W
Morris, r., Can.	82	49.30N	97.30W
Morrison, Il., U.S. (mŏr'ĭ-sŭn)	96	41.48N	89.58W
Morris Reservoir, res., Ca., U.S.	101a	34.11N	117.49W
Morristown, N.J., U.S. (mŏr'rĭs-toun)	94a	40.48N	74.29W
Morristown, Tn., U.S.	108	36.10N	83.18W
Morrisville, Pa., U.S. (mŏr'ĭs-vĭl)	94f	40.12N	74.46W
Morro, Castillo del, hist., Cuba	229b	23.09N	82.21W
Morro do Chapéu, Braz. (môr-ō dō-shä-pĕ'ōō)	124	11.34S	41.03W
Morrow, Oh., U.S. (mŏr'ō)	95f	39.21N	84.07W
Mors, i., Den.	146	56.46N	8.38E
Mörsenbroich, neigh., Ger.	232	51.15N	6.48E
Morshansk, Russia (môr-shánsk')	160	53.25N	41.35E
Mortara, Italy (môr-tä'rä)	154	45.13N	8.47E
Morteros, Arg. (môr-tĕ'tôs)	126	30.47S	62.00W
Mortes, Rio das, r., Braz. (rēō-däs-mô'r-tĕs)	123a	21.04S	44.29W
Mortlake, Austl.	239a	33.51S	151.07E
Mortlake, neigh., Eng., U.K.	231	51.28N	0.16W
Morton, Pa., U.S.	225b	39.55N	75.20W
Morton Grove, Il., U.S.	227a	42.02N	87.47W
Morton Indian Reservation, I.R., Mn., U.S. (mŏr'tŭn)	96	44.35N	94.48W
Mortsel, Bel. (mór-sĕl')	139a	51.10N	4.28E
Morvan, mts., Fr. (mōr-văn')	150	47.11N	4.10E
Morzhovets, i., Russia (môr'zhō-vyĕts')	160	66.40N	42.30E
Mosal'sk, Russia (mō-zálsk')	156	54.27N	34.57E
Moscavide, Port.	153b	38.47N	9.06W
Moscow (Moskva), Russia	158	55.45N	37.37E
Moscow, Id., U.S. (mŏs'kō)	90	46.44N	116.57W
Mosel (Moselle), r., Eur. (mō'sĕl) (mō-zĕl)	148	49.49N	7.00E
Moses, r., S. Afr.	212d	25.17S	29.04E
Moses Lake, Wa., U.S.	98	47.08N	119.15W
Moses Lake, l., Wa., U.S. (mō'zĕz)	98	47.09N	119.30W
Moshchnyy, is., Russia (môsh'chnĭ)	146	59.56N	28.07E
Moshi, Tan. (mō'shē)	206	3.21S	37.20E
Mosjøen, Nor.	140	65.50N	13.10E
Moskháton, Grc.	235d	37.57N	23.41E
Moskva, prov., Russia	156	55.38N	36.48E
Moskva, r., Russia	160	55.30N	37.05E
Moskva, *see* Moscow, Russia	158	55.45N	37.37E
Mosman, Austl.	239a	33.49S	151.14E
Mosonmagyaróvár, Hung.	148	47.51N	17.16E
Mosquitos, Costa de, cst., Nic. (kôs-tä-dĕ-mŏs-kē'tō)	114	12.05N	83.49W
Mosquitos, Gulfo de los, b., Pan. (gōō'l-fō-dĕ-lôs-mŏs-kē'tōs)	110	9.17N	80.59W
Moss, Nor. (môs)	140	59.29N	10.39E
Moss Bank, Eng., U.K.	233a	53.29N	2.44W
Moss Beach, Ca., U.S. (môs bēch)	100b	37.32N	122.31W
Moss Crest, mtn., Va., U.S.	225d	38.55N	77.15W
Mosselbaai, S. Afr. (mô'sŭl bā)	206	34.06S	22.23E
Mossendjo, Congo	210	2.57S	12.44E
Mossley, Eng., U.K. (môs'lĭ)	138a	53.31N	2.02W
Mossley Hill, neigh., Eng., U.K.	233a	53.23N	2.55W
Moss Point, Ms., U.S. (môs)	108	30.25N	88.32W
Most, Czech. (môst)	148	50.32N	13.37E
Mostar, Bos. (môs'tär)	142	43.20N	17.51E
Móstoles, Spain (mōs-tō'lās)	153a	40.19N	3.52W
Mostoos Hills, hills, Can. (mŏs'tōōs)	82	54.50N	108.45W
Mosvatnet, l., Nor.	146	59.55N	7.50E
Motagua, r., N.A. (mō-tä'gwä)	114	15.29N	88.39W
Motala, Swe. (mō-tô'lä)	146	58.34N	15.00E
Motherwell, Scot., U.K. (mŭdh'ĕr-wĕl)	140	55.45N	4.05W
Motril, Spain (mō-trēl')	142	36.44N	3.32W
Mottingham, neigh., Eng., U.K.	231	51.26N	0.03E
Motul, Mex. (mō-tōō'l)	114a	21.07N	89.14W
Mouaskar, Alg.	204	35.25N	0.08E
Mouchoir Bank, bk. (mōō-shwär')	116	21.35N	70.40W
Mouchoir Passage, strt., T./C. Is.	116	21.05N	71.05W
Moudjéria, Maur.	208	17.53N	12.20W
Mouila, Gabon	210	1.52S	11.01E
Mouille Point, c., S. Afr.	206a	33.54S	18.19E
Moulins, Fr. (mōō-lăN')	140	46.34N	3.19E
Moulouya, Oued, r., Mor. (mōō-lōō'yà)	204	34.00N	4.00W
Moultrie, Ga., U.S. (mōl'trĭ)	108	31.10N	83.48W
Moultrie, Lake, l., S.C., U.S.	108	33.12N	80.00W
Mound City, Il., U.S.	104	37.06N	89.13W
Mound City, Mo., U.S.	104	40.08N	95.13W
Mound City Group National Monument, rec., Oh., U.S.	92	39.25N	83.00W
Moundou, Chad	208	8.34N	16.05E
Moundsville, W.V., U.S. (moundz'vĭl)	92	39.50N	80.50W
Mount, Cape, c., Lib.	208	6.47N	11.20W
Mountain Brook, Al., U.S. (moun'tĭn brŏk)	94h	33.30N	86.45W
Mountain Creek Lake, l., Tx., U.S.	101c	32.43N	97.03W
Mountain Grove, Mo., U.S. (grōv)	104	37.07N	92.16W
Mountain Home, Id., U.S. (hōm)	98	43.08N	115.43W
Mountain Park, Can. (pärk)	78	52.55N	117.14W
Mountain View, Ca., U.S. (moun'tĭn vū)	100b	37.25N	122.07W
Mountain View, Mo., U.S.	104	36.59N	91.46W
Mount Airy, N.C., U.S. (âr'ĭ)	108	36.28N	80.37W
Mount Ayliff, Transkei (â'lĭf)	207c	30.48S	29.24E
Mount Ayr, Ia., U.S. (âr)	96	40.43N	94.06W
Mount Baldy, Ca., U.S.	228	34.14N	117.40W
Mount Carmel, Il., U.S. (kär'mĕl)	92	38.25N	87.45W
Mount Carmel, Pa., U.S.	92	40.50N	76.25W
Mount Carooll, Il., U.S.	96	42.05N	89.55W
Mount Clemens, Mi., U.S. (klĕm'ĕnz)	95b	42.36N	82.52W
Mount Dennis, neigh., Can.	223c	43.42N	79.30W
Mount Desert, i., Me., U.S. (dē-zûrt')	86	44.15N	68.08W
Mount Dora, Fl., U.S. (dō'rà)	109a	28.45N	81.38W
Mount Druitt, Austl.	239a	33.46S	150.49E
Mount Duneed, Austl.	195a	38.15S	144.20E
Mount Eliza, Austl.	195a	38.11S	145.05E
Mount Ephraim, N.J., U.S.	225b	39.53N	75.06W
Mount Fletcher, Transkei (flĕ'chĕr)	207c	30.42S	28.32E
Mount Forest, Can. (fŏr'ĕst)	84	44.00N	80.45W
Mount Frere, Transkei (frâr')	207c	30.54S	29.02E
Mount Gambier, Austl. (găm'bēr)	196	37.30S	140.53E
Mount Gilead, Oh., U.S. (gĭl'ēăd)	92	40.30N	82.50W
Mount Greenwood, neigh., Il., U.S.	227a	41.42N	87.43W
Mount Healthy, Oh., U.S. (hĕlth'ē)	95f	39.14N	84.32W
Mount Hebron, Md., U.S.	225c	39.18N	76.50W
Mount Holly, N.J., U.S. (hŏl'ĭ)	94f	39.59N	74.47W
Mount Hope, Can.	77d	43.09N	79.55W
Mount Hope, N.J., U.S. (hōp)	94a	40.55N	74.32W
Mount Hope, W.V., U.S.	92	37.55N	81.10W
Mount Isa, Austl. (ī'zà)	196	21.00S	139.45E
Mount Kisco, N.Y., U.S. (kĭs'ko)	94a	41.12N	73.44W
Mountlake Terrace, Wa., U.S. (mount lāk tĕr'ĭs)	100a	47.48N	122.19W
Mount Lebanon, Pa., U.S. (lĕb'á-nŭn)	95e	40.22N	80.03W
Mount Magnet, Austl. (măg-nĕt)	196	28.00S	118.00E
Mount Martha, Austl.	195a	38.17S	145.01E
Mount Morgan, Austl. (môr-găn)	196	23.42S	150.45E
Mount Moriac, Austl.	195a	38.13S	144.12E
Mount Morris, Mi., U.S. (mŏr'ĭs)	92	43.10N	83.45W
Mount Morris, N.Y., U.S.	92	42.45N	77.50W
Mountnessing, Eng., U.K.	231	51.39N	0.21E
Mount Nimba National Park, rec., I.C.	208	7.35N	8.10W
Mount Olive, N.C., U.S. (ŏl'ĭv)	108	35.11N	78.05W
Mount Oliver, Pa., U.S.	226b	40.28N	79.59W
Mount Peale, Ut., U.S.	102	38.26N	109.16W
Mount Pleasant, Ia., U.S. (plĕz'ănt)	96	40.59N	91.34W
Mount Pleasant, Mi., U.S.	92	43.35N	84.45W
Mount Pleasant, S.C., U.S.	108	32.46N	79.51W
Mount Pleasant, Tn., U.S.	108	35.31N	87.12W
Mount Pleasant, Tx., U.S.	106	33.10N	94.56W
Mount Pleasant, Ut., U.S.	102	39.35N	111.20W
Mount Pritchard, Austl.	239a	33.54S	150.54E
Mount Prospect, Il., U.S. (prŏs'pĕkt)	95a	42.03N	87.56W
Mount Rainier, Md., U.S.	225d	38.56N	76.58W
Mount Rainier National Park, rec., Wa., U.S. (rā-nēr')	90	46.47N	121.17W
Mount Revelstoke National Park, Can. (rĕv'ĕl-stōk)	78	51.22N	120.15W
Mount Savage, Md., U.S. (săv'āj)	92	39.45N	78.55W
Mount Shasta, Ca., U.S. (shăs'tȧ)	98	41.18N	122.17W
Mount Sterling, Il., U.S. (stûr'lĭng)	104	39.59N	90.44W
Mount Sterling, Ky., U.S.	92	38.05N	84.00W
Mount Stewart, Can. (stū'ărt)	86	46.22N	62.52W
Mount Union, Pa., U.S. (ūn'yŭn)	92	40.25N	77.50W
Mount Vernon, Il., U.S. (vûr'nŭn)	92	38.20N	88.50W
Mount Vernon, In., U.S.	92	37.55N	87.50W
Mount Vernon, Mo., U.S.	104	37.09N	93.48W
Mount Vernon, N.Y., U.S.	94a	40.55N	73.51W
Mount Vernon, Oh., U.S.	92	40.25N	82.30W
Mount Vernon, Pa., U.S.	226b	40.17N	79.48W
Mount Vernon, Va., U.S.	94e	38.43N	77.06W
Mount Vernon, Wa., U.S.	98	48.25N	122.20W
Mount Washington, neigh., Md., U.S.	225c	39.22N	76.40W
Mount Washington Summit, Md., U.S.	225c	39.23N	76.40W
Mount Waverley, Austl.	239b	37.53S	145.08E
Moura, Braz. (mō'rȧ)	124	1.33S	61.38W
Moura, Port.	152	38.08N	7.28W
Mourne Mountains, mts., N. Ire., U.K. (môrn)	144	54.10N	6.09W
Moussoro, Chad	208	13.39N	16.29E
Moûtiers, Fr. (mōō-tyâr')	150	45.31N	6.34E
Mowbullan, Mount, mtn., Austl.	198	26.50S	151.34E
Moyahua, Mex. (mō-yä'wä)	112	21.16N	103.10W
Moyale, Kenya (mō-yä'lä)	204	3.28N	39.04E
Moyamba, S.L. (mō-yăm'bä)	204	8.10N	12.26W
Moyen Atlas, mts., Mor.	142	32.49N	5.28W
Moyeuvre-Grande, Fr.	150	49.15N	6.26E
Moyie, r., Id., U.S. (moi'yē)	98	38.50N	116.10W
Moylan, Pa., U.S.	225b	39.54N	75.23W
Moyobamba, Peru (mō-yō-bäm'bä)	124	6.12S	76.56W
Moyuta, Guat. (mō-ē-ōō'tä)	114	14.01N	90.05W
Moyyero, r., Russia	162	67.15N	104.10E
Mozambique, nation, Afr. (mō-zăm-bēk')	206	20.15S	33.53E
Mozambique Channel, strt., Afr. (mō-zăm-bek')	206	24.00S	38.00E
Mozdok, Russia (môz-dôk')	160	43.45N	44.35E
Mozhaysk, Russia (mô-zhäysk')	156	55.31N	36.02E
Mozhayskiy, Russia (mô-zhäy'skĭ)	164c	59.42N	30.08E
Mozyr', Bela. (mō-zür')	160	52.03N	29.14E
Mpanda, Tan.	210	6.22S	31.02E
Mpika, Zam.	210	11.54S	31.26E
Mpimbe, Mwi.	210	15.18S	35.04E
Mporokoso, Zam. ('m-pō-rō-kō'sō)	206	9.23S	30.05E
Mpwapwa, Tan. ('m-pwä'pwä)	206	6.21S	36.29E
Mqanduli, Transkei ('m-kän'dōō-lē)	207c	31.50S	28.42E
Mrągowo, Pol. (mrăŋ'gô-vô)	148	53.52N	21.18E
M'Sila, Alg. (m'sē'là)	204	35.47N	4.34E
Msta, r., Russia (m'stá')	160	58.30N	33.00E
Mstislavl', Bela. (m'stē-slävl')	156	54.01N	31.42E
Mtakataka, Mwi.	210	14.12S	34.32E
Mtamvuna, r., Afr.	207c	30.43S	29.53E
Mtata, r., Transkei	207c	31.48S	29.03E
Mtsensk, Russia (m'tsĕnsk)	160	53.17N	36.33E
Mtwara, Tan.	210	10.16S	40.11E
Muar, r., Malay.	173b	2.18N	102.43E
Mubende, Ug.	210	0.35N	31.23E
Mubi, Nig.	208	10.18N	13.20E
Mucacata, Moz.	210	13.20S	39.59E
Much, Ger. (mōōk)	151c	50.54N	7.24E
Muchinga Mountains, mts., Zam.	210	12.40S	30.50E
Much Wenlock, Eng., U.K. (mŭch wĕn'lŏk)	138a	52.35N	2.33W
Muckalee Creek, r., Ga., U.S. (mŭk'ă lē)	108	31.55N	84.10W
Mucking, Eng., U.K.	231	51.30N	0.26E
Muckleshoot Indian Reservation, I.R., Wa., U.S. (mŭck'’l-shōōt)	100a	47.21N	122.04W
Mucubela, Moz.	210	16.55S	37.52E
Mud, l., Mi., U.S. (mŭd)	96	46.12N	84.32W
Mudan, r., China (mōō-dän)	184	45.30N	129.40E
Mudanjiang, China (mōō-dän-jyäŋ)	184	44.28N	129.38E
Muddy, r., Nv., U.S. (mŭd'ĭ)	102	36.56N	114.42W
Muddy Boggy Creek, r., Ok., U.S. (mud'ĭ bŏg'ĭ)	104	34.42N	96.11W
Muddy Creek, r., Ut., U.S. (mŭd'ĭ)	102	38.45N	111.10W
Mudgee, Austl. (mŭ-jē)	198	32.47S	149.10E
Mudjatik, r., Can.	82	56.23N	107.40W
Mufulira, Zam.	210	12.33S	28.14E
Muğla, Tur. (mōōg'lä)	174	37.10N	28.20E
Mühileiten, Aus.	235e	48.10N	16.34E
Mühldorf, Ger. (mül-dôrf)	148	48.15N	12.33E
Mühlenbeck, Ger.	234a	52.40N	13.22E
Mühlhausen, Ger. (mül'hou-zĕn)	148	51.13N	10.25E
Muhu, i., Est. (mōō'hōō)	146	58.41N	22.55E
Muir Woods National Monument, rec., Ca., U.S. (mūr)	102	37.54N	123.22W
Muizenberg, S. Afr. (mwĭz-ĕn-bûrg')	206a	34.07S	18.28E
Mujāhidpur, neigh., India	236d	28.34N	77.13E
Mukachëvo, Ukr. (mŏ-kà-chyô'vô)	148	48.25N	22.43E
Mukhtuya, Russia (mōk-tōō'yà)	158	61.00N	113.00E
Mukilteo, Wa., U.S. (mū-kĭl-tā'ō)	100a	47.57N	122.18W
Muko, Japan (mōō'kō)	187b	34.57N	135.43E
Muko, r., Japan (mōō'kō)	187b	34.52N	135.17E
Mukutawa, r., Can.	82	53.10N	97.28W
Mukwonago, Wi., U.S. (mū-kwō-nȧ'gō)	95a	42.52N	88.19W
Mula, Spain (mōō'lä)	152	38.05N	1.12W
Mula, Al., U.S. (mūl'gȧ)	94h	33.33N	86.59W
Mulde, r., Ger. (mŏl'dĕ)	148	50.30N	12.30E
Muleros, Mex. (mōō-lä'rōs)	112	23.44N	104.00W

ng-sing; ŋ-baŋk; N-nasalized n; nŏd; cŏmmit; ōld; ôbey; ôrder; oi-boil; fōōd; ŏ-as oo in foot; ou-out; s-soft; sh-dish; th-thin; pūre; ûnite; ûrn; stŭd; circŭs; ü-as in French tu; '-indeterminate vowel.

PLACE (Pronunciation)	PAGE	Lat. °'	Long. °'
Muleshoe, Tx., U.S.	104	34.13N	102.43W
Mulgrave, Can. (mŭl'grāv)	86	45.37N	61.23W
Mulhacén, mtn., Spain	142	37.04N	3.18W
Mülheim, Ger. (mül'hīm)	151c	51.25N	6.53E
Mulhouse, Fr. (mü-lo͞oz')	140	47.46N	7.20E
Muling, China (mo͞o-lĭŋ)	184	44.32N	130.18E
Muling, r., China	184	44.40N	130.30E
Mull, Island of, i., Scot., U.K. (mŭl)	144	56.40N	6.19W
Mullan, Id., U.S. (mŭl'ăn)	98	47.26N	115.50W
Müller, Pegunungan, mts., Indon. (mül'ēr)	188	0.22N	113.05E
Mullingar, Ire. (mŭl-ĭn-gär)	144	53.31N	7.26W
Mullins, S.C., U.S. (mŭl'ĭnz)	108	34.11N	79.13W
Mullins River, Belize	114a	17.08N	88.18W
Multān, Pak. (mo̤-tän')	174	30.17N	71.13E
Multnomah Channel, strt., Or., U.S. (mŭl nō mȧ)	100c	45.41N	122.53W
Mulumbe, Monts, mts., Zaire	210	8.47S	27.20E
Mulvane, Ks., U.S. (mŭl-vān')	104	37.30N	97.13W
Mumbwa, Zam. (mo̤m'bwä)	206	14.59S	27.04E
Mumias, Kenya	210	0.20N	34.29E
Muna, Mex. (mo͞o'nȧ)	114a	20.28N	89.42W
Münchehofe, Ger.	234a	52.30N	13.40E
München, see Munich, Ger.	136	48.08N	11.35E
Muncie, In., U.S. (mŭn'sĭ)	90	40.10N	85.30W
Mundelein, Il., U.S. (mŭn-dė-lĭn')	95a	42.16N	88.00W
Mündelheim, neigh., Ger.	232	51.21N	6.41E
Mundonueva, Pico de, mtn., Col. (pē'kô-dě-mo͞o'n-dô-nwě'vä)	124a	4.18N	74.12W
Muneco, Cerro, mtn., Mex. (sě'r-rô-mo͞o-ně'kō)	113a	19.13N	99.20W
Mungana, Austl. (mŭn-găn'ȧ)	196	17.15S	144.18E
Mungbere, Zaire	210	2.38N	28.30E
Munger, Mn., U.S. (mŭn'gẽr)	101h	46.48N	92.20W
Mungindi, Austl. (mŭn-gĭn'dė)	196	29.00S	148.45E
Munhall, Pa., U.S. (mŭn'hôl)	95e	40.24N	79.53W
Munhango, Ang. (mo̤n-häŋ'gȧ)	206	12.15S	18.55E
Munich, Ger.	136	48.08N	11.35E
Munirka, neigh., India	236d	28.34N	77.10E
Munising, Mi., U.S. (mū'nĭ-sĭng)	96	46.24N	86.41W
Muniz Freire, Braz.	123a	20.29S	41.25W
Munku Sardyk, mtn., Asia (mo̤n'ko̤ sär-dĭk')	158	51.45N	100.30E
Muñoz, Phil. (mo͞on-nyōth')	189a	15.44N	120.53E
Munro, neigh., Arg.	229d	34.32S	58.31W
Münster, Ger. (mün'stẽr)	140	51.57N	7.38E
Munster, In., U.S. (mŭn'stẽr)	95a	41.34N	87.31W
Munster, hist. reg., Ire. (mŭn-stẽr)	144	52.30N	9.24W
Muntok, Indon. (mo̤n-tŏk')	188	2.05S	105.11E
Muong Sing, Laos (mo͞o'ông-sĭng')	188	21.06N	101.17E
Muping, China (mo͞o-pĭŋ)	182	37.23N	121.36E
Muqdisho, Som.	212a	2.08N	45.22E
Muqui, Braz. (mo͞o-kòė)	123a	20.56S	41.20W
Mur, r., Eur. (mo͞or)	140	47.00N	15.00E
Muradiye, Tur. (mo͞o-rä'dė-yě)	160	39.00N	43.40E
Murat, Fr. (mü-rä')	150	45.05N	2.56E
Murat, r., Tur. (mo͞o-rät')	174	39.00N	42.00E
Murayama, Japan	238a	35.45N	139.23E
Murchison, r., Austl. (mûr'chĭ-sŭn)	196	26.45S	116.15E
Murcia, Spain (mo͞or'thyä)	136	38.00N	1.10W
Murcia, hist. reg., Spain	152	38.35N	1.51W
Murdo, S.D., U.S. (mûr'dȯ)	96	43.53N	100.42W
Mureș, r., Rom. (mo͞o'rěsh)	142	46.02N	21.50E
Muret, Fr. (mü-rě')	150	43.28N	1.17E
Murfreesboro, Tn., U.S. (mûr'frėz-bŭr-ô)	108	35.50N	86.19W
Murgab, r., Asia (mo͞or-gäb')	174	37.07N	62.32E
Muriaé, r., Braz.	123a	21.20S	41.40W
Murino, Russia (mo͞o'rĭ-nô)	164c	60.03N	30.28E
Müritz, l., Ger. (mür'its)	148	53.20N	12.33E
Murmansk, Russia (mo͞or-mänsk')	158	69.00N	33.20E
Murom, Russia (mo͞o'rôm)	158	55.30N	42.00W
Muroran, Japan (mo͞o'rô-rän)	180	42.21N	141.05E
Muros, Spain (mo͞o'rōs)	152	42.48N	9.00W
Muroto-Zaki, c., Japan (mo͞o'rô-tō zä'kė)	186	33.14N	134.12E
Murphy, Mo., U.S. (mŭr'fĭ)	101e	38.29N	90.29W
Murphy, N.C., U.S.	108	35.05N	84.00W
Murphysboro, Il., U.S. (mŭr'fĭz-bŭr-ô)	104	37.46N	89.21W
Murray, Ky., U.S. (mŭr'ĭ)	108	36.39N	88.17W
Murray, Ut., U.S.	101b	40.40N	111.53W
Murray, r., Austl.	196	34.20S	140.00E
Murray, r., Can.	80	55.00N	121.00W
Murray, Lake, res., S.C., U.S. (mŭr'ĭ)	108	34.07N	81.18W
Murray Bridge, Austl.	196	35.10S	139.35E
Murray Harbour, Can.	86	46.00N	62.31W
Murray Region, reg., Austl. (mŭ'rē)	196	33.20S	142.30E
Murrumbidgee, r., Austl. (mŭr-ŭm-bĭd'jė)	196	34.30S	145.20E
Murrupula, Moz.	210	15.27S	38.47E
Murshidābād, India (mo̤r'shė-dä-bäd')	178	24.08N	88.11E
Murska Sobota, Slo. (mo͞or'skä sô'bô-tä)	154	46.40N	16.14E
Murtal, Port.	234d	38.42N	9.22W
Muruasigar, mtn., Kenya	210	3.08N	35.02E
Murwāra, India	174	23.54N	80.23E
Murwillumbah, Austl. (mŭr-wĭl'lŭm-bŭ)	198	28.15S	153.30E
Mürz, r., Aus. (mürts)	148	47.30N	15.21E
Mürzzuschlag, Aus. (mürts'tso͞o-shlägh)	148	47.37N	15.41E
Mus, Tur. (mo͞osh)	160	38.55N	41.30E
Musala, mtn., Bul.	154	42.05N	23.24E
Musan, N. Kor. (mo̤'sän)	180	41.11N	129.10E
Musashino, Japan (mo͞o-sä'shė-nō)	187a	35.43N	139.35E
Muscat, Oman (mŭs-kăt')	174	23.23N	58.30E
Muscat and Oman, see Oman, nation, Asia	174	20.00N	57.45E
Muscatine, Ia., U.S. (mŭs-kȧ-tēn)	96	41.26N	91.00W
Muscle Shoals, Al., U.S. (mŭs''l shōlz)	108	34.44N	87.38W

PLACE (Pronunciation)	PAGE	Lat. °'	Long. °'
Musgrave Ranges, mts., Austl. (mŭs'grāv)	196	26.15S	131.15E
Mushie, Zaire (mŭsh'ė)	206	3.04S	16.50E
Mushin, Nig.	208	6.32N	3.22E
Musi, r., Indon. (mo͞o'sė)	188	2.40S	103.42E
Musinga, Alto, mtn., Col. (ä'l-tô-mo͞o-sė'n-gä)	124a	6.40N	76.13W
Muskego Lake, l., Wi., U.S. (mŭs-kē'gō)	95a	42.53N	88.10W
Muskegon, Mi., U.S. (mŭs-kē'gŭn)	90	43.15N	86.20W
Muskegon, r., Mi., U.S.	92	43.20N	85.55W
Muskegon Heights, Mi., U.S.	92	43.10N	86.20W
Muskingum, r., Oh., U.S. (mŭs-kĭŋ'gŭm)	92	39.45N	81.55W
Muskogee, Ok., U.S. (mŭs-kō'gė)	90	35.44N	95.21W
Muskoka, l., Can. (mŭs-kō'kȧ)	84	45.00N	79.30W
Musoma, Tan.	210	1.30S	33.48E
Mussau Island, i., Pap. N. Gui. (mo͞o-sä'o͞o)	188	1.30S	149.32E
Musselshell, r., Mt., U.S. (mŭs''l-shĕl)	98	46.25N	108.20W
Mussende, Ang.	210	10.32S	16.05E
Mussuma, Ang.	210	14.14S	21.59E
Mustafakemalpaşa, Tur.	142	40.05N	28.30E
Mustang Bayou, Tx., U.S.	107a	29.22N	95.12W
Mustang Creek, r., Tx., U.S. (mŭs'tăng)	104	36.22N	102.46W
Mustang Island, i., Tx., U.S.	106	27.43N	97.00W
Mustique, i., St. Vin. (müs-tēk')	115b	12.53N	61.03W
Musturud, Egypt	240a	30.08N	31.17E
Mustvee, Est. (mo͞ost'vě-ě)	146	58.50N	26.54E
Musu Dan, c., N. Kor. (mo̤'so̤ dän)	180	40.51N	130.00E
Muswellbrook, Austl. (mŭs'wŭnl-bro̤k)	198	32.15S	150.50E
Mutare, Zimb.	206	18.49S	32.39E
Mutombo Mukulu, Zaire (mo͞o-tôm'bō mo͞o-ko͞o'lo͞o)	206	8.12S	23.56E
Mutsu Wan, b., Japan (mo͞ot'so͞o wän)	186	41.20N	140.55E
Mutton Bay, Can. (mŭt''n)	86	50.48N	59.02W
Mutum, Braz. (mo͞o-to͞o'm)	123a	19.48S	41.24W
Muyun-Kum, Peski, des., Kaz. (mo͞o-yo͞on'ko͞om')	158	44.30N	70.00E
Muzaffargarh, Pak.	178	30.09N	71.15E
Muzaffarpur, India	178	26.13N	85.20E
Muzon, Cape, c., Ak., U.S.	80	54.41N	132.44W
Muzquiz, Mex. (mo͞oz'kēz)	106	27.53N	101.31W
Muztagata, mtn., China	180	38.20N	75.28E
Mvomero, Tan.	210	6.20S	37.25E
Mvoti, r., S. Afr.	207c	29.18S	30.52E
Mwali, i., Com.	206	12.15S	43.45E
Mwanza, Tan. (mwän'zä)	206	2.31S	32.54E
Mwaya, Tan. (mwä'yä)	206	9.19S	33.51E
Mwenga, Zaire	210	3.02S	28.26E
Mweru, l., Afr.	206	8.50S	28.50E
Mwingi, Kenya	210	0.56S	38.04E
Myanmar, see Burma, nation, Asia	172	21.00N	95.15E
Myingyan, Burma (myĭng-yŭn')	174	21.37N	95.26E
Myitkyina, Burma (myĭ'chē-nȧ)	174	25.33N	97.25E
Myjava, Czech. (mûė'yȧ-vä)	148	48.45N	17.33E
Mymensingh, Bngl.	174	24.48N	90.28E
Mynämäki, Fin.	146	60.41N	21.58E
Myohyang San, mtn., N. Kor. (myō'hyang)	186	40.00N	126.12E
Mýrdalsjökull, ice., Ice. (mür'däls-yû'kôl)	140	63.34N	18.04W
Myrtle Beach, S.C., U.S. (mûr't'l)	108	33.42N	78.53W
Myrtle Point, Or., U.S.	98	43.04N	124.08W
Mysen, Nor.	146	59.32N	11.16E
Myshikino, Russia (mėsh'kė-nô)	156	57.48N	38.21E
Mysore, India (mī-sōr')	174	12.31N	76.42E
Mysovka, Russia (mė' sôf-kȧ)	146	55.11N	21.17E
Mystic, Ia., U.S. (mĭs'tĭk)	96	40.47N	92.54W
Mytishchi, Russia (mė-tēsh'chi)	164b	55.55N	37.46E
Mziha, Tan.	210	5.54S	37.47E
Mzimba, Mwi. ('m-zĭm'bä)	206	11.52S	33.34E
Mzimkulu, r., Afr.	207c	30.12S	29.57E
Mzimvubu, r., Transkei	207c	31.22S	29.20E
Mzuzu, Mwi.	210	11.30S	34.10E

N

PLACE (Pronunciation)	PAGE	Lat. °'	Long. °'
Naab, r., Ger. (näp)	148	49.38N	12.15E
Naaldwijk, Neth.	139a	52.00N	4.11E
Naalehu, Hi., U.S.	88a	19.00N	155.35W
Naantali, Fin. (nän'tá-lė)	146	60.29N	22.03E
Nabberu, l., Austl. (năb'ēr-o͞o)	196	26.05S	120.35E
Naberezhnyye Chelny, Russia	158	55.42N	52.19E
Nabeul, Tun. (nā-bûl')	204	36.34N	10.45E
Nabiswera, Ug.	210	1.28N	32.16E
Naboomspruit, S. Afr.	212d	24.32S	28.43E
Nābulus, Isr. Occ.	173a	32.13N	35.16E
Nacala, Moz. (nä-kä'lȧ)	206	14.34S	40.41E
Nacaome, Hond. (nä-kä-ō'mȧ)	114	13.32N	87.28W
Na Cham, Viet. (nä chäm')	184	22.02N	106.30E
Naches, r., Wa., U.S. (năch'ĕz)	98	46.51N	121.03W
Náchod, Czech. (näк'ôt)	148	50.25N	16.08E
Nächstebreck, neigh., Ger.	232	51.18N	7.14E
Nacimiento, Lake, res., Ca., U.S. (nȧ-sĭ-myĕn'tô)	102	35.50N	121.00W
Nacogdoches, Tx., U.S. (năk'ô-dō'chĕz)	106	31.36N	94.40W
Nadadores, Mex. (nä-dä-dō'räs)	106	27.04N	101.36W

PLACE (Pronunciation)	PAGE	Lat. °'	Long. °'
Nadiād, India	178	22.45N	72.51E
Nadir, V.I.U.S.	111c	18.19N	64.53W
Nădlac, Rom.	154	46.09N	20.52E
Nadvornaya, Ukr. (näd-vôr'nȧ-yȧ)	148	48.37N	24.35E
Nadym, r., Russia (nȧ'dĭm)	162	64.30N	72.48E
Naestved, Den. (nĕst'vĭdh)	140	55.14N	11.46E
Nafada, Nig.	208	11.08N	11.20E
Nafishah, Egypt	212c	30.34N	32.15E
Nafūd ad Dahy, des., Sau. Ar.	174	22.15N	44.15E
Nag, Co, l., China	178	31.38N	91.18E
Naga, Phil. (nä'gä)	188	13.37N	123.12E
Naga, i., Japan	187	32.09N	130.16E
Nagahama, Japan (nä'gä-hä'mä)	187	33.32N	132.29E
Nagahama, Japan	187	35.23N	136.16E
Nagaland, India	174	25.47N	94.15E
Nagano, Japan (nä'gä-nô)	180	36.42N	138.12E
Nagao, Japan	238b	34.50N	135.43E
Nagaoka, Japan (nä'gȧ-ō'kȧ)	180	37.22N	138.49E
Nagaoka, Japan	187b	34.54N	135.42E
Nāgappattinam, India	174	10.48N	79.51E
Nagarote, Nic. (nä-gä-rō'tě)	114	12.17N	86.35W
Nagasaki, Japan (nä'gȧ-sä'kė)	180	32.48N	129.53E
Nagata, neigh., Japan	238b	34.40N	135.09E
Nagatino, neigh., Russia	235b	55.41N	37.41E
Nagatsuta, neigh., Japan	238a	35.32N	139.30E
Nāgaur, India	178	27.19N	73.41E
Nagaybakskiy, Russia (nȧ-gáy-bäk'skĭ)	164a	53.33N	59.33E
Nagcarlan, Phil. (näg-kär-län')	189a	14.07N	121.24E
Nāgercoil, India	178	8.15N	77.29E
Nagorno Karabakh, hist. reg., Azer. (nu-gôr'nŭ-kŭ-rŭ-bäk')	160	40.10N	46.50E
Nagoya, Japan	180	35.09N	136.53E
Nāgpur, India (näg'po͞or)	174	21.12N	79.09E
Nagua, Dom. Rep. (nä'gwä)	116	19.20N	69.40W
Nagykanizsa, Hung. (nôd'y'kô'nė-shô)	142	46.27N	17.00E
Nagykōrōs, Hung. (nôd'y'kŭ-rŭsh)	148	47.02N	19.46E
Nagytarcsa, Hung.	235g	47.32N	19.17E
Naha, Japan (nä'hä)	180	26.02N	127.43E
Nahanni National Park, rec., Can.	78	62.10N	125.15W
Nahant, Ma., U.S. (nȧ-hănt)	87a	42.26N	70.55W
Nahant Bay, b., Ma., U.S.	223a	42.27N	70.55W
Nahariyya, Isr.	173a	33.01N	35.06E
Nahaut, Ma., U.S.	223a	42.25N	70.55W
Nahmer, Ger.	232	51.20N	7.35E
Nahuel Huapi, l., Arg. (nä'wĕl wä'pė)	126	41.00S	71.30W
Nahuizalco, El Sal. (nä-wė-zäl'kō)	114	13.50N	89.43W
Naic, Phil. (nä-ēk)	189a	14.20N	120.46E
Naica, Mex. (nä-ē'kä)	106	27.53N	105.30W
Naiguata, Pico, mtn., Ven. (pē'kô)	125b	10.32N	66.44W
Naihāti, India	236a	22.54N	88.25E
Nain, Can. (nīn)	78	56.29N	61.52W
Nā'īn, Iran	176	32.52N	53.05E
Nairn, Scot., U.K. (nârn)	144	57.35N	3.54W
Nairobi, Kenya (nī-rō'bė)	206	1.17S	36.49E
Naivasha, Kenya (nī-vä'shȧ)	206	0.47S	36.29E
Najd, hist. reg., Sau. Ar.	174	25.18N	42.38E
Najin, N. Kor. (nä'jĭn)	180	42.04N	130.35E
Najran, des., Sau. Ar. (nŭj-rän')	174	17.29N	45.30E
Naju, S. Kor. (nä'jo͞o')	186	35.02N	126.42E
Najusa, r., Cuba (nä-ho͞o'sä)	116	20.55N	77.55W
Naka, r., Japan	238a	35.39N	139.51E
Nakajima, Japan	238a	35.26N	139.56E
Nakanobu, neigh., Japan	238a	35.36N	139.43E
Nakatsu, Japan (nä'käts-o͞o)	186	33.34N	131.10E
Nakhichevan, Azer. (nȧ-kē-chě-vän')	160	39.10N	45.30E
Nakhodka, Russia (nŭ-kôt'kŭ)	158	43.03N	133.08E
Nakhon Ratchasima, Thai.	188	14.56N	102.14E
Nakhon Sawan, Thai.	188	15.42N	100.06E
Nakhon Si Thammarat, Thai.	188	8.27N	99.58E
Nakło nad Notecia, Pol.	148	53.10N	17.35E
Nakskov, Den. (näk'skou)	140	54.51N	11.06E
Naktong, r., S. Kor. (näk'tŭng)	186	36.10N	128.30E
Nal'chik, Russia (nȧl-chĕk')	160	43.30N	43.35E
Nalón, r., Spain (nä-lōn')	152	43.15N	5.38W
Nālūt, Libya (nä-lo͞ot')	204	31.51N	10.49E
Namak, Daryacheh-ye, l., Iran	174	34.58N	51.33E
Namakan, l., Mn., U.S. (nă'mȧ-kȧn)	96	48.20N	92.43W
Namamugi, neigh., Japan	238a	35.29N	139.41E
Namangan, Uzb. (nȧ-män-gän')	162	41.08N	71.59E
Namao, Can.	77g	53.43N	113.30W
Namatanai, Pap. N. Gui. (nä'mä-tȧ-nä'ė)	188	3.43S	152.26E
Nambour, Austl. (năm'bòr)	198	26.48S	153.00E
Nam Co, l., China (näm tswo)	180	30.30N	91.10E
Nam Dinh, Viet. (näm dēnк')	188	20.30N	106.10E
Nametil, Moz.	210	15.43S	39.21E
Namhae, i., S. Kor. (näm'hī')	186	34.23N	128.05E
Namib Desert, des., Nmb. (nä-mēb')	206	18.45S	12.45E
Namibia, nation, Afr.	206	19.30S	16.13E
Namoi, r., Austl. (nămoi)	196	30.10S	148.43E
Namous, Oued en, r., Alg. (nȧ-mo͞os')	142	31.48N	0.19W
Nampa, Id., U.S. (năm'pȧ)	90	43.35N	116.35W
Namp'o, N. Kor.	180	38.47N	125.28E
Nampuecha, Moz.	210	13.59S	40.18E
Nampula, Moz.	210	15.07S	39.15E
Namsos, Nor. (näm'sôs)	140	64.28N	11.14E
Namu, Can.	80	51.53N	127.50W
Namuli, Serra, mts., Moz.	210	15.05S	37.05E
Namur, Bel. (nȧ-mür')	140	50.29N	4.55E
Namutoni, Nmb. (nȧ-mo͞o-tō'nė)	206	18.45S	17.00E
Nan, r., Thai.	188	18.11N	100.29E
Nanacamilpa, Mex. (nä-nä-kä-mē'l-pä)	113a	19.30N	98.33W
Nanaimo, Can. (nȧ-nī'mō)	78	49.10N	123.56W
Nanam, N. Kor. (nä'nän')	186	41.38N	129.37E
Nanao, Japan (nä'nä-ō)	186	37.03N	136.59E
Nan'ao Dao, i., China (nän-ou dou)	184	23.30N	117.30E

PLACE (Pronunciation)	PAGE	Lat. °'	Long. °'
Nancefield, S. Afr.	240b	26.17S	27.53E
Nanchang, China (nän'chäng')	180	28.38N	115.48E
Nanchangshan Dao, i., China (nän-chäŋ-shän dou)	182	37.56N	120.42E
Nancheng, China (nän-chäŋ)	180	26.50N	116.40E
Nanchong, China (nän-chôŋ)	180	30.45N	106.05E
Nancy, Fr. (näN-sē')	140	48.42N	6.11E
Nancy Creek, r., Ga., U.S. (năn'cē)	94c	33.51N	84.25W
Nanda Devi, mtn., India (nän'dä dā'vē)	174	30.30N	80.25E
Nānded, India	178	19.13N	77.21E
Nandurbār, India	178	21.29N	74.13E
Nandyāl, India	178	15.54N	78.09E
Nanga Parbat, mtn., Pak.	178	35.20N	74.35E
Nangi, India	178a	22.30N	88.14E
Nangis, Fr. (näN-zhē')	151b	48.33N	3.01E
Nangong, China (nän-gôŋ)	184	37.22N	115.22E
Nangweshi, Zam.	210	16.26S	23.17E
Nanhuangcheng Dao, i., China (nän-hüäŋ-chüŋ dou)	182	38.22N	120.54E
Nanhui, China	182	31.03N	121.45E
Naniwa, neigh., Japan	238b	34.39N	135.30E
Nanjing, China (nän-jyĭŋ)	180	32.04N	118.46E
Nanjuma, r., China (nän-jyōō-mä)	182	39.37N	115.45E
Nanle, China (nän-lŭ)	182	36.03N	115.13E
Nan Ling, mts., China	180	25.15N	111.40E
Nanliu, r., China (nän-lĭô)	184	22.00N	109.18E
Nannine, Austl. (nă-nēn')	196	25.50S	118.30E
Nanning, China (nän'nĭng')	180	22.56N	108.10E
Nānole, neigh., India	236e	19.01N	72.55E
Nanpan, r., China (nän-pän)	184	24.50N	105.30E
Nanping, China (nän-pĭŋ)	180	26.40N	118.05E
Nansei-shotō, is., Japan	180	27.30N	127.00E
Nansemond, Va., U.S. (năn'sē-mŭnd)	94g	36.46N	76.32W
Nantai Zan, mtn., Japan (nän-täē zän)	186	36.47N	139.28E
Nanterre, Fr.	233c	48.53N	2.12E
Nantes, Fr. (näNt')	136	47.13N	1.37W
Nanteuil-le-Haudouin, Fr. (näN-tû-lĕ-ō-dwăN')	151b	49.08N	2.49E
Nanticoke, Pa., U.S. (năn'tĭ-kōk)	92	41.10N	76.00W
Nantong, China	182	32.08N	121.06E
Nantong, China (nän-tôŋ)	182	32.02N	120.51E
Nantouillet, Fr.	233c	49.00N	2.42E
Nantucket, i., Ma., U.S. (năn-tŭk'ĕt)	90	41.15N	70.05W
Nantwich, Eng., U.K. (nănt'wĭch)	138a	53.04N	2.31W
Nanxiang, China (nän-shyäŋ)	182	31.17N	121.17E
Nanxiong, China (nän-shôŋ)	184	25.10N	114.20E
Nanyang, China	180	33.00N	112.42E
Nanyang Hu, l., China (nän-yäŋ hōō)	182	35.14N	116.24E
Nanyuan, China (nän-yůän)	184a	39.48N	116.24E
Nao, Cabo de la, c., Spain (kå'bô-dĕ-lä-nä'ō)	136	38.43N	0.14E
Naoābād, India	236a	22.28N	88.27E
Naolinco, Mex. (nä-o-lēŋ'kō)	112	19.39N	96.50W
Naopukuria, India	236a	22.55N	88.16E
Náousa, Grc. (nä'ōō-så)	154	40.38N	22.05E
Naozhou Dao, i., China (nou-jō dou)	184	20.58N	110.58E
Napa, Ca., U.S. (năp'ȧ)	90	38.20N	122.17W
Napanee, Can. (năp'ȧ-nē)	84	44.15N	77.00W
Naperville, Il., U.S. (nā'pēr-vĭl)	95a	41.46N	88.09W
Napier, N.Z. (nā'pĭ-ēr)	197a	39.30S	177.00E
Napierville, Can. (nā'pĭ-ē-vĭl)	77a	45.11N	73.24W
Naples (Napoli), Italy	136	40.37N	14.12E
Naples, Fl., U.S. (nā'p'lz)	109a	26.07N	81.46W
Napo, r., S.A. (nä'pō)	124	1.49S	74.20W
Napoleon, Oh., U.S. (nȧ-pō'lē-ŭn)	92	41.20N	84.10W
Napoleonville, La., U.S. (nȧ-pō'lē-ŭn-vĭl)	106	29.56N	91.03W
Napoli, Golfo di, b., Italy	142	40.29N	14.08E
Napoli, see Naples, Italy	136	40.37N	14.12E
Nappanee, In., U.S. (năp'ȧ-nē)	92	41.30N	86.00W
Nara, Japan (nä'rä)	180	34.41N	135.50E
Nara, Mali	204	15.09N	7.27W
Nara, dept., Japan	187b	34.36N	135.49E
Nara, r., Russia	156	55.05N	37.16E
Naracoorte, Austl. (nȧ-rȧ-kōōn'tē)	196	36.50S	140.50E
Narashino, Japan	187a	35.41N	140.01E
Naraspur, India	178	16.32N	81.43E
Nārāyanpāra, India	236a	22.54N	88.19E
Narberth, Pa., U.S. (när'bûrth)	94f	40.01N	75.17W
Narbonne, Fr. (nȧr-bôn')	140	43.12N	3.00E
Nare, Col. (nä'rē)	124a	6.12N	74.37W
Narew, r., Pol. (när'ĕf)	148	52.43N	21.19E
Narmada, r., India	174	22.30N	75.30E
Naroch', l., Bela. (nä'rôch)	156	54.51N	27.00E
Narodnaya, Gora, mtn., Russia (nȧ-rôd'nȧ-yȧ)	158	65.10N	60.10E
Naro-Fominsk, Russia (nä'rô-mēnsk')	160	55.23N	36.43E
Narrabeen, Austl. (năr-ȧ-bĭn)	195b	33.44S	151.18E
Narragansett, R.I., U.S. (năr-ă-găn'sĕt)	94b	41.26N	71.27W
Narragansett Bay, b., R.I., U.S.	92	41.20N	71.15W
Narrandera, Austl. (nȧ-rȧn-dē'rȧ)	196	34.40S	146.40E
Narraweena, Austl.	239a	33.45S	151.16E
Narre Warren North, Austl.	239b	37.59S	145.19E
Narrogin, Austl. (năr'ō-gĭn)	196	33.00S	117.15E
Naruo, Japan	238b	34.43N	135.23E
Narva, Est. (nȧr'vȧ)	160	59.24N	28.12E
Narvacan, Phil. (när-vä-kän')	189a	17.27N	120.29E
Narva Jõesuu, Est. (nȧr'vȧ ô-ô-ă'sōō-ô)	146	59.26N	28.02E
Narvik, Nor. (när'vēk)	136	68.21N	17.18E
Narvskiy Zaliv, b., Eur. (nȧr'vskĭ zä'lĭf)	146	59.35N	27.25E
Narvskoye, res., Eur.	146	59.18N	28.14E
Nar'yan-Mar, Russia (när'yȧn mär')	158	67.42N	53.30E
Naryilco, Austl. (năr-ĭl'kō)	198	28.40S	141.50E
Narym, Russia (nä-rēm')	158	58.47N	82.05E
Naryn, r., Asia (nŭ-rĭn')	162	41.20N	76.00E
Naseby, Eng., U.K. (nāz'bĭ)	138a	52.23N	0.59W
Nashua, Mo., U.S. (năsh'ŭ-ȧ)	101f	39.18N	94.34W
Nashua, N.H., U.S.	90	42.47N	71.23W
Nashville, Ar., U.S. (năsh'vĭl)	104	33.56N	93.50W
Nashville, Ga., U.S.	108	31.12N	83.15W
Nashville, Il., U.S.	104	38.21N	89.42W
Nashville, Mi., U.S.	92	42.35N	85.50W
Nashville, Tn., U.S.	90	36.10N	86.48W
Nashwauk, Mn., U.S. (năsh'wôk)	96	47.21N	93.12W
Näsi, l., Fin.	140	61.42N	24.05E
Našice, Cro. (nä'shē-tsĕ)	142	45.29N	18.06E
Nasielsk, Pol. (nä'syĕlsk)	148	52.35N	20.50E
Nāsik, India (nä'sĭk)	174	20.02N	73.49E
Nāşir, Sudan (nä-zēr')	204	8.30N	33.06E
Nasirabād, India	178	26.13N	74.48E
Naskaupi, r., Can. (năs'kô-pĭ)	78	53.59N	61.10W
Nasondoye, Zaire	210	10.22S	25.06E
Nass, r., Can. (năs)	80	55.00N	129.30W
Nassau, Bah. (năs'ô)	110	25.05N	77.20W
Nassenheide, Ger. (nä'sĕn-hī-dĕ)	139b	52.49N	13.13E
Nasser, Lake, res., Egypt	204	23.50N	32.50E
Nasugbu, Phil. (nȧ-sòg-bōō')	189a	14.05N	120.37E
Nasworthy Lake, l., Tx., U.S. (năz'wûr-thē)	106	31.17N	100.30W
Natagaima, Col. (nä-tä-gī'mä)	124a	3.38N	75.07W
Nātāgarh, India	236a	22.42N	88.25E
Natal, Braz. (nä-täl')	124	6.00S	35.13W
Natal, prov., S. Afr. (nȧ-täl')	206	28.50S	30.07E
Natalspruit, S. Afr.	240b	26.19S	28.09E
Natashquan, Can. (nä-tăsh'kwän)	78	50.11N	61.49W
Natashquan, r., Can.	86	50.35N	61.35W
Natchez, Ms., U.S. (năch'ĕz)	90	31.35N	91.20W
Natchitoches, La., U.S. (năk'ĭ-tŏsh)(năch-ĭ-tŏsh')	106	31.46N	93.06W
Natick, Ma., U.S. (nā'tĭk)	87a	42.17N	71.21W
National Bison Range, I.R., Mt., U.S. (năsh'ŭn-ăl bī's'n)	98	47.18N	113.58W
National City, Ca., U.S.	102a	32.38N	117.01W
National Park, Pa., U.S.	225b	39.51N	75.12W
Natitingou, Benin	204	10.19N	1.22E
Natividade, Braz. (nä-tē-vē-dä'dē)	124	11.43S	47.34W
Natron, Lake, l., Tan. (nā'trŏn)	206	2.17S	36.10E
Natrona Heights, Pa., U.S. (nā'trō nȧ)	95e	40.38N	79.43W
Naṭrūn, Wādī an, val., Egypt	212b	30.33N	30.12E
Natuna Besar, i., Indon.	188	4.00N	106.50E
Natural Bridges National Monument, rec., Ut., U.S. (năt'ū-răl brĭj'ĕs)	102	37.20N	110.20W
Naturaliste, Cape, c., Austl. (năt-ū-rȧ-lĭst')	196	33.30S	115.10E
Naucalpan, Mex. (nä'ōō-käl-pá'n)	113a	19.28N	99.14W
Nauchampatepetl, mtn., Mex. (näōō-chäm-pä-tĕ'pĕtl)	112	19.32N	97.09W
Nauen, Ger. (nou'ĕn)	139b	52.36N	12.53E
Naugatuck, Ct., U.S. (nô'gȧ-tŭk)	92	41.25N	73.05W
Naujan, Phil. (nä-ō-hän')	189a	13.19N	121.17E
Naumburg, Ger. (noum'bòrgh)	148	51.10N	11.50E
Naupada, neigh., India	236e	19.04N	72.50E
Nauru, nation, Oc.	2	0.30S	167.00E
Nautla, Mex. (nä-ōōt'lä)	110	20.14N	96.44W
Nava, Mex. (nä'vä)	106	28.25N	100.44W
Nava del Rey, Spain (nä-vä dĕl rā'ē)	152	41.22N	5.04W
Navahermosa, Spain (nä-vä-ĕr-mō'sä)	152	39.39N	4.28W
Navajas, Cuba (nä-vä-häs')	116	22.40N	81.20W
Navajo Hopi Joint Use Area, I.R., Az., U.S.	102	36.15N	110.30W
Navajo Indian Reservation, I.R., U.S. (năv'ȧ-hō)	102	36.31N	109.24W
Navajo National Monument, rec., Az., U.S.	102	36.43N	110.39W
Navajo Reservoir, res., N.M., U.S.	102	36.57N	107.26W
Navalcarnero, Spain (nä-väl-kär-nā'rō)	153a	40.17N	4.05W
Navalmoral de la Mata, Spain	152	39.53N	5.32W
Navan, Can. (nă'vȧn)	77c	45.25N	75.26W
Navarino, i., Chile (nȧ-vä-rē'nō)	126	55.30S	68.15W
Navarra, hist. reg., Spain (nä-vär'rä)	152	42.40N	1.35W
Navarro, Arg. (nä-vá'r-rō)	123c	35.00S	59.16W
Navasota, Tx., U.S. (năv-ȧ-sō'tȧ)	106	30.24N	96.05W
Navasota, r., Tx., U.S.	106	31.03N	96.11W
Navassa, i., N.A. (nȧ-văs'ȧ)	116	18.25N	75.15W
Navestock, Eng., U.K.	231	51.39N	0.13E
Navestock Side, Eng., U.K.	231	51.39N	0.16E
Navia, r., Spain (nä-vē'ä)	152	43.10N	6.45W
Navidad, Chile (nä-vē-dä'd)	123b	33.57S	71.51W
Navidad Bank, bk. (nä-vē-dädh')	116	20.05N	69.00W
Navidade do Carangola, Braz. (nä-vē-dä'dō-kȧ-rän-gô'la)	123a	21.04S	41.58W
Navojoa, Mex. (nä-vō-kô'ä)	110	27.00N	109.40W
Navotas, Phil.	237g	14.40N	120.57E
Návplion, Grc.	154	37.33N	22.46E
Nawābshāh, Pak. (nȧ-wäb'shä)	178	26.20N	68.30E
Náxos, i., Grc. (nȧk'sôs)	142	37.15N	25.20E
Nayābās, India	236d	28.35N	77.19E
Nayarit, state, Mex. (nä-yä-rēt')	110	22.00N	105.15W
Nayarit, Sierra de, mts., Mex. (sē-ĕ'r-rä-dĕ)	112	23.20N	105.07W
Naye, Sen.	208	14.25N	12.12W
Naylor, Md., U.S. (nā'lōr)	94e	38.43N	76.46W
Nazaré da Mata, Braz. (dä-mä-tä)	124	7.46S	35.13W
Nazas, Mex. (nä'zäs)	106	25.14N	104.08W
Nazas, r., Mex.	110	25.30N	104.40W
Nazerat, Isr.	173a	32.43N	35.19E
Nazilli, Tur. (nȧ-zĭ-lē')	160	37.40N	28.10E
Naziya, r., Russia (nȧ-zē'yȧ)	164c	59.48N	31.18E
Nazko, r., Can.	80	52.35N	123.10W
Nazlat as-Sammān, Egypt	240a	29.59N	31.08E
Nazlat Khalīfah, Egypt	240a	30.01N	31.10E
N'dalatando, Ang.	210	9.18S	14.54E
Ndali, Benin	208	9.51N	2.43E
Ndikiniméki, Cam.	208	4.46N	10.50E
N'Djamena, Chad	204	12.07N	15.03E
Ndjili, neigh., Zaire	240c	4.21S	15.19E
Ndola, Zam. (n'dō'lä)	206	12.58S	28.38E
Ndoto Mountains, mts., Kenya	210	1.55N	37.05E
Ndrhamcha, Sebkha de, l., Maur.	208	18.50N	15.15W
Nduye, Zaire	210	1.50N	29.01E
Neagh, Lough, l., N. Ire., U.K. (lŏk nā)	140	54.40N	6.47W
Néa Ionía, Grc.	235d	38.02N	23.45E
Néa Liósia, Grc.	235d	38.02N	23.42E
Néa Páfos, Cyp.	173a	34.46N	32.27E
Neapean, r., Austl.	195b	33.40S	150.39E
Neápolis, Grc. (nȧ-ŏp' ô-lĭs)	154	36.35N	23.08E
Neápolis, Grc.	154a	35.17N	25.37E
Near Islands, is., Ak., U.S. (nēr)	89a	52.20N	172.40E
Near North Side, neigh., Il., U.S.	227a	41.54N	87.38W
Néa Smírni, Grc.	235d	37.57N	23.43E
Neath, Wales, U.K. (nēth)	144	51.41N	3.50W
Nebine Creek, r., Austl. (nĕ-bēne')	198	27.50S	147.00E
Nebit-Dag (Krasnovodsk), Turk.	158	40.00N	52.50E
Nebit-Dag, Turk. (nyĕ-bĕt'dăg')	160	39.30N	54.20E
Nebraska, state, U.S. (nē-brăs'kȧ)	90	41.45N	101.30W
Nebraska City, Ne., U.S.	104	40.40N	95.50W
Nechako, r., Can.	80	53.45N	124.55W
Nechako Plateau, plat., Can. (nĭ-chă'kō)	80	54.00N	124.30W
Nechako Range, mts., Can.	80	53.20N	124.30W
Nechako Reservoir, res., Can.	80	53.25N	125.10W
Neches, r., Tx., U.S. (nĕch'ĕz)	106	31.03N	94.40W
Neckar, r., Ger. (nĕk'är)	148	49.16N	9.06E
Necker Island, i., Hi., U.S.	88b	24.00N	164.00W
Necochea, Arg. (nā-kô-chā'ä)	126	38.30S	58.45W
Nedlitz, neigh., Ger.	234a	52.26N	13.03E
Nedrigaylov, Ukr. (nĕ-drĭ-gī'lôf)	156	50.49N	33.52E
Needham, Ma., U.S. (nēd'ăm)	87a	42.17N	71.14W
Needham Heights, Ma., U.S.	223a	41.28N	71.14W
Needles, Ca., U.S. (nē'd'lz)	102	34.51N	114.39W
Neenah, Wi., U.S. (nē'nȧ)	96	44.10N	88.30W
Neepawa, Can.	78	50.13N	99.29W
Nee Reservoir, res., Co., U.S. (nee)	104	38.26N	102.56W
Nee Soon, Sing.	236c	1.24N	103.49E
Negareyama, Japan (nā'gä-rȧ-yä'mä)	187a	35.52N	139.54E
Negaunee, Mi., U.S. (nē-gô'nē)	96	46.30N	87.37W
Negeri Sembilan, state, Malay. (nā'grē-sĕm-bē-län')	173b	2.46N	101.54E
Negev, des., Isr. (nĕ'gĕv)	173a	30.34N	34.43E
Negombo, Sri L.	178	7.39N	79.49E
Negotin, Yugo. (nĕ'gō-tēn)	154	44.13N	22.33E
Negro, r., Arg.	126	39.50S	65.00W
Negro, r., N.A.	114	13.01N	87.10W
Negro, r., S.A.	123c	33.17S	58.18W
Negro, Cerro, mtn., Pan. (sĕ'-rrô-nā'grō)	114	8.44N	80.37W
Negro, Rio, r., S.A. (rē'ō nā'grō)	124	0.18S	63.21W
Negros, i., Phil. (nā'grōs)	188	9.50N	121.45E
Nehalem, r., Or., U.S. (nē-hăl'ĕm)	98	45.52N	123.37W
Nehaus an der Oste, Ger. (noi'houz)(ōz'tē)	139c	53.48N	9.02E
Nehbandān, Iran	176	31.32N	60.02E
Nehe, China (nŭ-hŭ)	184	48.23N	124.58E
Neheim-Hüsten, Ger. (nĕ'hīm)	151c	51.28N	7.58E
Neiba, Dom. Rep. (nȧ-ē'bä)	116	18.30N	71.20W
Neiba, Bahía de, b., Dom. Rep.	116	18.10N	71.00W
Neiba, Sierra de, mts., Dom. Rep. (sē-ĕr'rä-dē)	116	18.40N	71.40W
Neihart, Mt., U.S. (nī'hȧrt)	98	46.54N	110.39W
Neijiang, China (nā-jyäŋ)	184	29.38N	105.01E
Neillsville, Wi., U.S. (nēlz'vĭl)	96	44.35N	90.37W
Neiqiu, China (nā-chyō)	182	37.17N	114.32E
Neira, Col. (nā'rä)	124a	5.10N	75.32W
Neisse, r., Eur. (nēs)	148	51.30N	15.00E
Neiva, Col. (nȧ-ē'vä)(nā'vä)	124	2.55N	75.16W
Neixiang, China (nā-shyäŋ)	184	33.00N	111.38E
Nekemte, Eth.	204	9.09N	36.29E
Nekoosa, Wi., U.S. (nē-kōō'sȧ)	96	44.19N	89.54W
Neligh, Ne., U.S. (nē'lĭg)	96	42.06N	98.02W
Nel'kan, Russia (nĕl-kän')	158	57.45N	136.36E
Nellore, India (nĕl-lōr')	174	14.28N	79.59E
Nel'ma, Russia (nĕl-mä')	186	47.34N	139.05E
Nelson, Can. (nĕl'sŭn)	78	49.29N	117.17W
Nelson, N.Z.	197a	41.15S	173.22E
Nelson, Eng., U.K.	138a	53.50N	2.13W
Nelson, i., Ak., U.S.	89	60.38N	164.42W
Nelson, r., Can.	82	56.50N	93.40W
Nelson, Cape, c., Austl.	198	38.29S	141.20E
Nelsonville, Oh., U.S. (nĕl'sŭn-vĭl)	92	39.30N	82.15W
Néma, Maur. (nā'mä)	204	16.37N	7.15W
Nemadji, r., Wi., U.S. (nē-măd'jē)	101h	46.33N	92.16W
Neman, Russia (nĕ'-mȧn)	146	55.02N	22.01E
Neman, r., Eur.	160	53.28N	24.45E
Nematābād, Iran	237h	35.38N	51.21E
Nembe, Nig.	208	4.35N	6.26E
Nemčinovka, Russia	235b	55.43N	37.23E
Nemeiben Lake, l., Can. (nĕ-mē'bȧn)	82	55.20N	105.20W
Nemirov, Ukr. (nyȧ-mē'rôf)	156	48.56N	28.51E
Nemours, Fr.	150	48.16N	2.41E
Nemuro, Japan (nā'mô-rō)	180	43.13N	145.10E
Nemuro Strait, strt., Asia	186	43.07N	145.10E
Nen, r., China (nŭn)	180	47.07N	123.28E
Nen, r., Eng., U.K. (nĕn)	138a	52.32N	0.19W
Nenagh, Ire. (nē'nȧ)	144	52.50N	8.05W
Nenana, Ak., U.S. (nā-nä'nȧ)	89	64.28N	149.18W
Nenikyul', Russia (nĕ-nyĕ'kyûl)	164c	59.26N	30.40E
Nenjiang, China (nŭn-jyäŋ)	180	49.02N	125.15E
Neodesha, Ks., U.S. (nē-ô-dĕ-shô')	104	37.24N	95.41W

PLACE (Pronunciation)	PAGE	Lat. °'	Long. °'
Neosho, Mo., U.S.	104	36.51N	94.22W
Neosho, r., Ks., U.S. (nē-ō'shō)	104	38.07N	95.40W
Nepal, nation, Asia (nĕ-pôl')	174	28.45N	83.00E
Nephi, Ut., U.S. (nē'fī)	102	39.40N	111.50W
Nepomuceno, Braz. (nĕ-pô-mōō-sĕ'no)	123a	21.15S	45.13W
Nera, r., Italy (nā'rä)	154	42.45N	12.54E
Nérac, Fr. (nā-räk')	150	44.08N	0.19E
Nerchinsk, Russia (nyĕr' chĕnsk)	158	51.47N	116.17E
Nerchinskiy Khrebet, mts., Russia	158	50.30N	118.30E
Nerchinskiy Zavod, Russia (nyĕr'chĕn-skĭzá-vôt')	158	51.35N	119.46E
Nerekhta, Russia (nyĕ-rĕĸ'tá)	156	57.29N	40.34E
Neretva, r., Yugo. (nĕ'rĕt-vá)	154	43.08N	17.50E
Nerja, Spain (nĕr'hä)	152	36.45N	3.53W
Nerl', r., Russia (nyĕrl)	156	56.59N	37.57E
Nerskaya, r., Russia (nyĕr'ská-yá)	164b	55.31N	38.46E
Nerussa, r., Russia (nyå-rōō'så)	156	52.24N	34.20E
Ness, Eng., U.K.	233a	53.17N	3.03W
Ness, Loch, l., Scot., U.K. (lŏĸ nĕs)	144	57.23N	4.20W
Ness City, Ks., U.S. (nĕs)	104	38.27N	99.55W
Nesterov, Russia (nyĕs-tă'rôf)	146	54.39N	22.38E
Nesterov, Ukr. (ŋĕs'-tzhyĕ-rôf)	148	50.03N	23.58E
Neston, Eng., U.K.	233a	53.18N	3.04W
Néstos (Mesta), r., Eur. (nās'tōs)	154	41.25N	24.12E
Nesvizh, Bela. (nyĕs'vēsh)	156	53.13N	26.44E
Netanya, Isr.	173a	32.19N	34.52E
Netcong, N.J., U.S. (nĕt'cŏnj)	94a	40.54N	74.42W
Netherlands, nation, Eur. (nĕdh'ĕr-lăndz)	136	53.01N	3.57E
Netherlands Guiana, *see* Suriname, nation, S.A.	124	4.00N	56.00W
Netherton, Eng., U.K.	233a	53.30N	2.58W
Nette, neigh., Ger.	232	51.33N	7.25E
Nettilling, l., Can.	78	66.30N	70.40W
Nett Lake Indian Reservation, I.R., Mn., U.S. (nĕt lāk)	96	48.23N	93.19W
Nettuno, Italy (nĕt-tōō'nô)	153d	41.28N	12.40E
Neubeckum, Ger. (noi'bĕ-kōōm)	151c	51.48N	8.01E
Neubrandenburg, Ger. (noi-brän'dĕn-bŏrgh)	148	53.33N	13.16E
Neuburg, Ger. (noi'bŏrgh)	148	48.43N	11.12E
Neuchâtel, Switz. (nû-shá-tĕl')	140	47.00N	6.52E
Neuchâtel, Lac de, l., Switz.	148	46.48N	6.53E
Neudorf, neigh., Ger.	232	51.25N	6.47E
Neuenhagen, Ger. (noi'ĕn-hä-gĕn)	139b	52.31N	13.41E
Neuenhof, neigh., Ger.	232	51.10N	7.13E
Neuenkamp, neigh., Ger.	232	51.26N	6.44E
Neuenrade, Ger. (noi'ĕn-rä-dĕ)	151c	51.17N	7.47E
Neu-Erlaa, neigh., Aus.	235e	48.08N	16.19E
Neu Fahrland, Ger.	234a	52.26N	13.03E
Neufchâtel-en-Bray, Fr. (nû-shä-tĕl'ĕɴ-brā')	150	49.43N	1.25E
Neuilly-sur-Marne, Fr.	233c	48.51N	2.32E
Neuilly-sur-Seine, Fr.	233c	48.53N	2.16E
Neukirchen, Ger.	232	51.27N	6.33E
Neulengbach, Aus.	139e	48.13N	15.55E
Neumarkt, Ger. (noi'märkt)	148	49.17N	11.30E
Neumünster, Ger. (noi'münstĕr)	140	54.04N	10.00E
Neunkirchen, Aus. (noin'kĭrĸ-ĕn)	148	47.43N	16.05E
Neuquén, Arg. (nĕ-ò-kān')	126	38.52S	68.12W
Neuquén, prov., Arg.	126	39.40S	70.45W
Neuquén, r., Arg.	126	38.45S	69.00W
Neuruppin, Ger. (noi'rōō-pēn)	148	52.55N	12.48E
Neuse, r., N.C., U.S. (nūz)	108	36.12N	78.50W
Neusiedler See, l., Eur. (noi-zēd'lĕr)	148	47.54N	16.31E
Neuss, Ger. (nois)	151c	51.12N	6.41E
Neusserweyhe, neigh., Ger.	232	51.13N	6.39E
Neustadt, Ger. (noi'shtät)	148	49.21N	8.08E
Neustadt bei Coburg, Ger. (bī kō'bōōrgh)	148	50.20N	11.09E
Neustadt in Holstein, Ger.	148	54.06N	10.50E
Neustift am Walde, neigh., Aus.	235e	48.15N	16.18E
Neustrelitz, Ger. (noi-strā'lĭts)	148	53.21N	13.05E
Neutral Hills, hills, Can. (nū'trăl)	82	52.10N	110.50W
Neu Ulm, Ger. (noi ŏ lm')	148	48.23N	10.01E
Neuva Pompeya, neigh., Arg.	229d	34.39S	58.25W
Neuville, Can. (nū'vĭl)	77b	46.39N	71.35W
Neuville-sur-Oise, Fr.	233c	49.01N	2.04E
Neuwaldegg, neigh., Aus.	235e	48.14N	16.17E
Neuwied, Ger. (noi'vēdt)	148	50.26N	7.28E
Neva, r., Russia (nyĕ-vä')	156	59.49N	30.54E
Nevada, Ia., U.S. (nē-vā'dȧ)	96	42.01N	93.27W
Nevada, Mo., U.S.	104	37.49N	94.21W
Nevada, state, U.S. (nĕ vá'dá)	90	39.30N	117.00W
Nevada, Sierra, mts., Spain (syĕr'rä nā-vä'dhä)	136	37.01N	3.28W
Nevada, Sierra, mts., U.S. (sē-ĕ'r-rä nĕ-vä'dá)	90	39.20N	120.05W
Nevado, Cerro el, mtn., Col. (sĕ'r-rô-ĕl-nĕ-vä'dō)	124a	4.02N	74.08W
Neva Stantsiya, Russia (nyĕ-vä' stän'tsĭ-yá)	164c	59.53N	30.30E
Neve, Serra da, mts., Ang.	210	13.40S	13.20E
Nevel', Russia (nyĕ'vĕl)	160	56.03N	29.57E
Neveri, r., Ven. (nĕ-vĕ-rē)	125b	10.13N	64.18W
Nevers, Fr. (nē-vár')	140	46.59N	3.10E
Neves, Braz.	126b	22.51S	43.06W
Nevesinje, Bos. (nĕ-vĕ'sên-yĕ)	154	43.15N	18.08E
Neviges, Ger.	232	51.19N	7.05E
Neville Island, i., Pa., U.S.	226b	40.31N	80.08W
Nevis, i., St. K./N. (nē'vĭs)	110	17.05N	62.38W
Nevis, Ben, mtn., Scot., U.K. (bĕn)	140	56.47N	5.00W
Nevis Peak, mtn., St. K./N.	115b	17.11N	62.33W
Nevşehir, Tur. (nĕv-shĕ'hĕr)	142	38.40N	34.35E
Nev'yansk, Russia (nĕv-yänsk')	158	57.29N	60.14E
New, r., Va., U.S. (nū)	108	37.20N	80.35W
Newabāgam, India	236a	22.48N	88.24E
New Addington, neigh., Eng., U.K.	231	51.21N	0.01W
Newala, Tan.	210	10.56S	39.18E
New Albany, In., U.S. (nû ôl'bȧ-nĭ)	95h	38.17N	85.49W
New Albany, Ms., U.S.	108	34.28N	39.00W
New Amsterdam, Guy. (ăm'stĕr-dăm)	124	6.14N	57.30W
Newark, Eng., U.K. (nū'ērk)	138a	53.04N	0.49W
Newark, Ca., U.S. (nū'ērk)	100b	37.32N	122.02W
Newark, De., U.S. (nōō'ärk)	92	39.40N	75.45W
Newark, N.J., U.S. (nōō'ûrk)	90	40.44N	74.10W
Newark, N.Y., U.S. (nū'ērk)	92	43.05N	77.10W
Newark, Oh., U.S.	92	40.05N	82.25W
Newaygo, Mi., U.S. (nū'wā-go)	92	43.25N	85.50W
New Bedford, Ma., U.S. (bĕd'fĕrd)	90	41.35N	70.55W
Newberg, Or., U.S. (nū'bûrg)	92	45.17N	122.58W
New Bern, N.C., U.S. (bûrn)	90	35.05N	77.05W
Newbern, Tn., U.S.	108	36.05N	89.12W
Newberry, Mi., U.S. (nū'bĕr-ĭ)	96	46.22N	85.31W
Newberry, S.C., U.S.	108	34.15N	81.40W
New Boston, Mi., U.S. (bôs'tŭn)	95b	42.10N	83.24W
New Boston, Oh., U.S.	92	38.45N	82.55W
New Braunfels, Tx., U.S. (nū broun'fĕls)	106	29.43N	98.07W
New Brighton, Eng., U.K.	233a	53.26N	3.03W
New Brighton, Mn., U.S. (brī'tŭn)	101g	45.04N	93.12W
New Brighton, Pa., U.S.	95e	40.34N	80.18W
New Brighton, neigh., N.Y., U.S.	224	40.38N	74.06W
New Britain, Ct., U.S. (brĭt''n)	92	41.40N	72.45W
New Britain, i., Pap. N. Gui.	188	6.45S	149.38E
New Brunswick, N.J., U.S. (brŭnz'wĭk)	94a	40.29N	74.27W
New Brunswick, prov., Can.	78	47.14N	66.30W
Newburg, In., U.S.	92	38.00N	87.25W
Newburg, Mo., U.S.	104	37.54N	91.53W
Newburgh, N.Y., U.S.	92	41.30N	74.00W
Newburgh Heights, Oh., U.S.	95d	41.27N	81.40W
Newbury, Eng., U.K. (nū'bĕr-ĭ)	144	51.24N	1.26W
Newbury, Ma., U.S.	87a	42.48N	70.52W
Newburyport, Ma., U.S. (nū'bĕr-ĭ-pōrt)	87a	42.48N	70.53W
New Caledonia, dep., Oc.	196	21.28S	164.40E
New Canaan, Ct., U.S. (kā-nȧn)	94a	41.06N	73.30W
New Carlisle, Can. (kär-līl')	78	48.01N	65.20W
New Carrollton, Md., U.S.	225d	38.58N	76.53W
Newcastle, Austl. (nū-kás''l)	198	33.00S	151.55E
Newcastle, Can.	78	47.00N	65.34W
New Castle, De., U.S.	92	39.40N	75.35W
New Castle, In., U.S.	92	39.55N	85.25W
New Castle, Oh., U.S.	92	40.20N	82.10W
New Castle, Pa., U.S.	92	41.00N	80.25W
Newcastle, Tx., U.S.	104	33.13N	98.44W
Newcastle, Wy., U.S.	96	43.51N	104.11W
Newcastle under Lyme, Eng., U.K. (nû-kás''l) (nû-kăs''l)	138a	53.01N	2.14W
Newcastle upon Tyne, Eng., U.K.	136	55.00N	1.45W
Newcastle Waters, Austl. (wô'tērz)	196	17.10S	133.25E
Newclare, neigh., S. Afr.	240b	26.11S	27.58E
Newcomerstown, Oh., U.S. (nū'kŭm-ērz-toun)	92	40.15N	81.40W
New Croton Reservoir, res., N.Y., U.S. (krŏ'tôn)	94a	41.15N	73.47W
New Delhi, India (dĕl'hī)	174	28.43N	77.18E
Newell, S.D., U.S. (nū'ĕl)	96	44.43N	103.26W
New Eltham, neigh., Eng., U.K.	231	51.26N	0.04E
New England Range, mts., Austl. (nû ĭŋ'glănd)	196	29.32S	152.30E
Newenham, Cape, c., Ak., U.S. (nū-ĕn-hăm)	89	58.40N	162.32W
Newfane, N.Y., U.S. (nū-fān)	95c	43.17N	78.44W
New Ferry, Eng., U.K.	233a	53.22N	2.59W
Newfoundland, prov., Can.	79a	48.15N	56.53W
Newgate, Can. (nū'gāt)	80	49.01N	115.10W
Newgate Street, Eng., U.K.	231	51.44N	0.07W
New Georgia, i., Sol.Is. (jôr'jĭ-ȧ)	196	8.08S	158.00E
New Georgia Group, is., Sol.Is.	192e	8.30S	157.20E
New Georgia Sound, strt., Sol.Is.	192e	8.00S	158.10E
New Glasgow, Can. (glás'gō)	78	45.35N	62.36W
New Guinea, i. (gĭne)	188	5.45S	140.00E
Newhalem, Wa., U.S. (nū hā'lŭm)	98	48.44N	121.11W
Newham, neigh., Eng., U.K.	231	51.32N	0.03E
New Hampshire, state, U.S. (hămp'shĭr)	90	43.55N	71.40W
New Hampton, Ia., U.S. (hămp'tŭn)	96	43.03N	92.20W
New Hanover, S. Afr. (hăn'ōvĕr)	207c	29.23S	30.32E
New Hanover, i., Pap. N. Gui.	188	2.37S	150.15E
New Harmony, In., U.S. (nū här'mô-nĭ)	92	38.10N	87.55W
New Haven, Ct., U.S. (hā'vĕn)	90	41.20N	72.55W
New Haven, In., U.S. (nū hāv''n)	92	41.05N	85.00W
New Hebrides, is., Vanuatu	196	16.00S	167.00E
New Hey, Eng., U.K.	233b	53.36N	2.06W
New Holland, Eng., U.K. (hŏl'ănd)	138a	53.42N	0.21W
New Holland, N.C., U.S.	108	35.27N	76.14W
New Hope Mountain, mtn., Al., U.S. (hōp)	94h	33.23N	86.45W
New Hudson, Mi., U.S. (hŭd'sŭn)	95b	42.30N	83.36W
New Hyde Park, N.Y., U.S.	224	40.44N	73.41W
New Hythe, Eng., U.K.	231	51.19N	0.27E
New Iberia, La., U.S. (ī-bē'rĭ-ȧ)	106	30.00N	91.50W
Newington, Can. (nū'ĕng-tŏn)	77c	45.07N	75.00W
New Ireland, i., Pap. N. Gui. (īr'lănd)	188	3.15S	152.30E
New Jersey, state, U.S. (jûr'zĭ)	90	40.30N	74.50W
New Kensington, Pa., U.S. (kĕn'zĭng-tŭn)	95e	40.34N	79.35W
Newkirk, Ok., U.S. (nū'kûrk)	104	36.52N	97.03W
New Kowloon (Xinjiulong), H.K.	237c	22.20N	114.10E
New Lagos, neigh., Nig.	240d	6.30N	3.22E
New Lenox, Il., U.S. (lĕn'ŭk)	95a	41.31N	87.58W
New Lexington, Oh., U.S. (lĕk'sĭng-tŭn)	92	39.40N	82.10W
New Lisbon, Wi., U.S. (lĭz'bŭn)	96	43.52N	90.11W
New Liskeard, Can.	84	47.30N	79.40W
New London, Ct., U.S. (lŭn'dŭn)	92	41.20N	72.05W
New London, Wi., U.S.	96	44.24N	88.45W
New Madrid, Mo., U.S. (măd'rĭd)	104	36.34N	89.31W
Newman's Grove, Ne., U.S. (nū'măn grōv)	96	41.46N	97.44W
Newmarket, Can. (nū'mär-kĕt)	84	44.00N	79.30W
Newmarket, S. Afr.	240b	26.17S	28.08E
New Martinsville, W.V., U.S. (mär'tĭnz-vĭl)	92	39.35N	80.50W
New Meadows, Id., U.S.	98	44.58N	116.20W
New Mexico, state, U.S. (mĕk'sĭ-kō)	90	34.30N	107.10W
New Milford, N.J., U.S.	224	40.56N	74.01W
New Mills, Eng., U.K. (mĭlz)	138a	53.22N	2.00W
New Munster, Wi., U.S. (mŭn'stĕr)	95a	42.35N	88.13W
Newnan, Ga., U.S. (nū'năn)	108	33.22N	84.47W
New Norfolk, Austl. (nôr'fŏk)	196	42.50S	147.17E
New Orleans, La., U.S. (ôr'lē-ănz)	90	30.00N	90.05W
New Philadelphia, Oh., U.S. (fĭl-ȧ-dĕl'fĭ-ȧ)	92	40.30N	81.30W
New Plymouth, N.Z. (plĭm'ŭth)	197a	39.04S	174.13E
Newport, Austl.	195b	33.39S	151.19E
Newport, Austl.	239b	37.51S	144.53E
Newport, Eng., U.K.	138a	52.46N	2.22W
Newport, Eng., U.K. (nū-pôrt)	144	50.41N	1.25W
Newport, Wales, U.K.	140	51.36N	3.05W
Newport, Ar., U.S. (nū'pōrt)	104	35.35N	91.16W
Newport, Ky., U.S.	90	39.05N	84.30W
Newport, Me., U.S.	86	44.49N	69.20W
Newport, Mn., U.S.	101g	44.52N	92.59W
Newport, N.H., U.S.	92	43.20N	72.10W
Newport, Or., U.S.	98	44.39N	124.02W
Newport, R.I., U.S.	92	41.29N	71.16W
Newport, Tn., U.S.	108	35.55N	83.12W
Newport, Vt., U.S.	92	44.55N	72.15W
Newport, Wa., U.S.	98	48.12N	117.01W
Newport Beach, Ca., U.S. (bēch)	101a	33.36N	117.55W
Newport News, Va., U.S.	90	36.59N	76.24W
New Prague, Mn., U.S. (nū prāg)	96	44.33N	93.35W
New Providence, i., Bah. (prŏv'ĭ-dĕns)	116	25.00N	77.25W
New Redruth, S. Afr.	240b	26.16S	28.07E
New Richmond, Oh., U.S. (rĭch'mŭnd)	92	38.55N	84.15W
New Richmond, Wi., U.S.	96	45.07N	92.34W
New Roads, La., U.S. (rōds)	106	30.42N	91.26W
New Rochelle, N.Y., U.S. (rū-shĕl')	94a	40.55N	73.47W
New Rockford, N.D., U.S. (rŏk'fōrd)	96	47.40N	99.08W
New Ross, Ire. (rôs)	144	52.25N	6.55W
New Sarepta, Can.	77g	53.17N	113.09W
New Siberian Islands, *see* Novosibirskiye Ostrova, is., Russia	158	74.00N	140.30E
New Smyrna Beach, Fl., U.S. (smûr'nȧ)	108	29.00N	80.57W
New South Wales, state, Austl. (wālz)	196	32.45S	146.14E
Newton, Can. (nū'tŭn)	77f	49.56N	98.04W
Newton, Eng., U.K.	138a	53.27N	2.37W
Newton, Il., U.S.	92	39.00N	88.10W
Newton, Ia., U.S.	96	41.42N	93.04W
Newton, Ks., U.S.	104	38.03N	97.22W
Newton, Ma., U.S.	87a	42.21N	71.13W
Newton, Ms., U.S.	108	32.18N	89.10W
Newton, N.J., U.S.	94a	41.03N	74.45W
Newton, N.C., U.S.	108	35.40N	81.19W
Newton, Tx., U.S.	106	30.47N	93.45W
Newton Brook, neigh., Can.	223c	43.48N	79.24W
Newton Highlands, Ma., U.S.	223a	41.19N	71.13W
Newton Lower Falls, Ma., U.S.	223a	42.19N	71.23W
Newtonsville, Oh., U.S. (nū'tŭnz-vĭl)	95f	39.11N	84.04W
Newton Upper Falls, Ma., U.S.	223a	42.19N	71.13W
Newtonville, Ma., U.S.	223a	42.21N	71.13W
Newtown, N.D., U.S. (nū'toun)	96	47.57N	102.25W
Newtown, Oh., U.S.	95f	39.08N	84.22W
Newtown, Pa., U.S.	94f	40.13N	74.56W
Newtown, neigh., Austl.	239a	33.54S	151.11E
Newtownards, N. Ire., U.K. (nu-t'n-ardz')	144	54.35N	5.39W
New Ulm, Mn., U.S. (ŭlm)	96	44.18N	94.27W
New Utrecht, neigh., N.Y., U.S.	224	40.36N	73.59W
New Waterford, Can. (wô'tĕr-fĕrd)	78	46.15N	60.05W
New Westminster, Can. (wĕst'mĭn-stĕr)	80	49.12N	122.55W
New York, N.Y., U.S. (yôrk)	90	40.40N	73.58W
New York, state, U.S.	90	42.45N	78.05W
New Zealand, nation, Oc. (zē'lánd)	197a	42.00S	175.00E
Nexapa, r., Mex. (nĕks-ä'pä)	112	18.32N	98.29W
Neya-gawa, Japan (nā'yä gä'wä)	187b	34.47N	135.38E
Neyshābūr, Iran	174	36.06N	58.45E
Neyva, r., Russia (nĕy'vá)	164a	57.39N	60.37E
Nezhin, Ukr. (nyĕzh'ĕn)	160	51.03N	31.52E
Nez Perce, Id., U.S. (nĕz' pûrs')	98	46.16N	116.15W
Nez Perce Indian Reservation, I.R., Id., U.S.	98	46.20N	116.30W
Ngami, l., Bots. (n'gä'mē)	206	20.56S	22.31E
Ngamouéri, Congo	240c	4.14S	15.14E
Ngangerabeli Plain, pl., Kenya	210	1.20S	40.10E
Ngangla Ringco, l., China (ŋäŋ-lä rĭŋ-tswo)	178	31.42N	82.53E
Ngarimbi, Tan.	210	8.28S	38.36E
Ngoko, r., Afr.	210	1.55N	15.53E
Ngol-Kedju Hill, mtn., Cam.	208	6.20N	9.45E
Ngombe, Zaire	240c	4.24S	15.11E
Ngong, Kenya ('n-gông)	206	1.27S	36.39E
Ngounié, r., Gabon	210	1.15S	10.43E
Ngoywa, Tan.	210	5.56S	32.48E
Ngqeleni, Transkei ('ng-kĕ-lā'nĕ)	207c	31.41S	29.04E
Nguigmi, Niger ('n-gĕg'mē)	204	14.15N	13.07E
Ngurore, Nig.	208	9.18N	12.14E
Nguru, Nig. ('n-gōō'rōō)	204	12.53N	10.26E
Nguru Mountains, mts., Tan.	210	6.10S	37.35E

ăt; finăl; rāte; senåte; ärm; åsk; sofȧ; fâre; ch-choose; dh-as th in other; bē; ėvent; bĕt; recĕnt; cratĕr; g-gō; gh-guttural g; bĭt; ĭ-short neutral; rīde; ĸ-guttural k as ch in German ich;

PLACE (Pronunciation)	PAGE	Lat. °'	Long. °'
Nha Trang, Viet. (nyä-träng')	188	12.08N	108.56E
Niafounke, Mali	204	16.03N	4.17W
Niagara, Wi., U.S. (nī-ăg'á-rá)	96	45.45N	88.05W
Niagara, r., N.A.	95c	43.12N	79.03W
Niagara Falls, Can.	95c	43.05N	79.05W
Niagara Falls, N.Y., U.S.	90	43.06N	79.02W
Niagara-on-the-Lake, Can.	77d	43.16N	79.05W
Niakaramandougou, I.C.	208	8.40N	5.17W
Niamey, Niger (nē-ä-mā')	204	13.31N	2.07E
Niamtougou, Togo	208	9.46N	1.06E
Niangara, Zaire (nē-äŋ-gá'rá)	204	3.42N	27.52E
Niangua, r., Mo., U.S. (nī-ăŋ'gwá)	104	37.30N	93.05W
Nias, Pulau, i., Indon. (nē'äs')	188	0.58N	97.43E
Nibe, Den. (nē'bĕ)	146	56.57N	9.36E
Nicaragua, nation, N.A. (nĭk-á-rä'gwá)	110	12.45N	86.15W
Nicaragua, Lago de, l., Nic. (lä'gô dĕ)	110	11.45N	85.28W
Nicastro, Italy (nē-käs'trō)	142	38.39N	16.15E
Nicchehabin, Punta, c., Mex. (pōō'n-tä-nĕk-chĕ-ä-bē'n)	114a	19.50N	87.20W
Nice, Fr. (nēs)	136	43.42N	7.21E
Nicheng, China (nē-chŭŋ)	183b	30.54N	121.48E
Nichicun, l., Can. (nĭch'ĭ-kŭn)	78	53.07N	72.10W
Nicholas Channel, strt., N.A. (nĭk'ô-lás)	116	23.30N	80.20W
Nicholasville, Ky., U.S. (nĭk'ô-lás-vĭl)	92	37.55N	84.35W
Nicobar Islands, is., India (nĭk-ô-bär')	188	8.28N	94.04E
Nicolai Mountain, mtn., Or., U.S. (nē-cō lī')	100c	46.05N	123.27W
Nicolás Romero, Mex. (nē-kô-lä's rô-mĕ'rô)	113a	19.38N	99.20W
Nicolet, Lake, l., Mi., U.S. (nĭ'kŏ-lĕt)	101k	46.22N	84.14W
Nicolls Town, Bah.	116	25.10N	78.00W
Nicols, Mn., U.S. (nĭk'ĕls)	101g	44.50N	93.12W
Nicomeki, r., Can.	100d	49.04N	122.47W
Nicosia, Cyp. (nē-kô-sē'á)	174	35.10N	33.22E
Nicoya, C.R. (nē-kō'yä)	114	10.08N	85.27W
Nicoya, Golfo de, b., C.R. (gôl-fô-dĕ)	114	10.03N	85.04W
Nicoya, Península de, pen., C.R.	114	10.05N	86.00W
Nidzica, Pol. (nē-jĕt'sá)	148	53.21N	20.30E
Niederaden, neigh., Ger.	232	51.36N	7.34E
Niederbonsfeld, Ger.	232	51.23N	7.08E
Niederdonk, Ger.	232	51.14N	6.41E
Niederelfringhausen, Ger.	232	51.21N	7.10E
Niedere Tauern, mts., Aus.	148	47.15N	13.41E
Niederkrüchten, Ger. (nē'dĕr-krük-tĕn)	151c	51.12N	6.14E
Nieder-Neuendorf, Ger.	234a	52.37N	13.12E
Niederösterreich, prov., Aus.	139e	48.24N	16.20E
Niedersachsen (Lower Saxony), hist. reg., Ger. (nē'dĕr-zäk-sĕn)	148	52.52N	8.27E
Niederschöneweide, neigh., Ger.	234a	52.27N	13.31E
Niederschönhausen, neigh., Ger.	234a	52.35N	13.23E
Niellim, Chad	208	9.42N	17.49E
Niemeyer, neigh., Braz.	230c	23.00S	43.15W
Nienburg, Ger. (nē'ĕn-bòrgh)	148	52.40N	9.15E
Nierst, Ger.	232	51.19N	6.43E
Nietverdiend, S. Afr.	212d	25.02S	26.10E
Nieuw Nickerie, Sur. (nē-nē'kĕ-rē')	124	5.51N	57.00W
Nieves, Mex. (nyā'vâs)	112	24.00N	102.57W
Niğde, Tur. (nĭg'dĕ)	142	37.55N	34.40E
Nigel, S. Afr. (nī'jĕl)	212d	26.26S	28.27E
Niger, nation, Afr. (nī'jĕr)	204	18.02N	8.30E
Niger, r., Afr.	204	8.00N	6.00E
Niger Delta, d., Nig.	208	4.45N	5.20E
Nigeria, nation, Afr. (nī-jē'rĭ-á)	204	8.57N	6.30E
Nihoa, i., Hi., U.S.	88b	23.15N	161.30W
Nihonbashi, neigh., Japan	238a	35.41N	139.47E
Nii, i., Japan (nē)	187	34.26N	139.23E
Niigata, Japan (nē'ē-gä'tá)	180	37.47N	139.04E
Niihau, i., Hi., U.S. (nē'ē-ha'ōō)	90c	21.50N	160.05W
Niimi, Japan (nē'mē)	187	34.59N	133.28E
Niiza, Japan	187a	35.48N	139.34E
Nijmegen, Neth. (nī'mā-gĕn)	144	51.50N	5.52E
Nikaia, Grc.	235d	37.58N	23.39E
Nikitinka, Russia (nē-kĭ'tĭn-ká)	156	55.33N	33.19E
Nikolayev, Ukr. (nē-kô-lä'yĕf)	158	46.58N	32.02E
Nikolayev, prov., Ukr.	156	47.27N	31.25E
Nikolayevka, Russia (nē-kô-lä'yĕf-ká)	164c	59.29N	29.48E
Nikolayevka, Russia	186	48.37N	134.09E
Nikolayevskiy, Russia	160	50.00N	45.30E
Nikolayevsk-na-Amure, Russia	158	53.18N	140.49E
Nikolo-Chovanskoje, Russia	235b	55.36N	37.27E
Nikol'sk, Russia (nē-kôlsk')	158	59.30N	45.40E
Nikol'skoye, Russia (nē-kôl'skô-yĕ)	164c	59.27N	30.00E
Nikopol, Bul. (nē'kô-pŏl')	142	43.41N	24.52E
Nikopol', Ukr.	160	47.36N	34.24E
Nilahue, r., Chile (nē-lá'wĕ)	123b	34.36S	71.50W
Nile, r., Afr. (nīl)	204	27.30N	31.00E
Niles, Il., U.S.	227a	42.01N	87.49W
Niles, Mi., U.S. (nīlz)	92	41.50N	86.15W
Niles, Oh., U.S.	92	41.15N	80.45W
Nileshwar, India	178	12.08N	74.14E
Nilgani, India	236a	22.46N	88.26E
Nilgiri Hills, hills, India	178	12.05N	76.22E
Nilópolis, Braz. (nē-lô'pō-lēs)	123a	22.48S	43.25W
Nīmach, India	178	24.32N	74.51E
Nimba, Mont, mtn., Afr. (nĭm'bá)	204	7.40N	8.33W
Nimba Mountains, mts., Afr.	208	7.30N	8.35W
Nîmes, Fr. (nēm)	136	43.49N	4.22E
Nimrod Reservoir, res., Ar., U.S. (nĭm'rŏd)	104	34.58N	93.46W
Nimule, Sudan (nē-mōō'lā)	204	3.38N	32.12E
Ninda, Ang.	210	14.47S	21.24E
Nine Ashes, Eng., U.K.	231	51.42N	0.18E
Nine Mile Creek, r., Ut., U.S. (mīn'īmôd')	102	39.50N	110.30W
Ninety Mile Beach, cst., Austl.	196	38.20S	147.30E
Nineveh, Iraq (nĭn'ē-vá)	174	36.30N	43.10E
Ning'an, China (nĭŋ-än)	180	44.20N	129.20E
Ningbo, China (nĭŋ-bwo)	180	29.56N	121.30E
Ningde, China (nĭŋ-dŭ)	180	26.38N	119.33E
Ninghai, China (nĭng'hī')	184	29.20N	121.20E
Ninghe, China (nĭŋ-hŭ)	182	39.20N	117.50E
Ningjin, China (nĭŋ-jyĭn)	182	37.39N	116.47E
Ningjin, China	182	37.37N	114.55E
Ningming, China	184	22.22N	107.06E
Ningwu, China (nĭng'wōō')	180	39.00N	112.12E
Ningxia Huizu, prov., China (nĭŋ-shyä)	180	37.10N	106.00E
Ningyang, China (nĭng'yäng')	182	35.46N	116.48E
Ninh Binh, Viet. (nēn bēnk')	188	20.22N	106.00E
Ninigo Group, is., Pap. N. Gui.	188	1.15S	143.30E
Ninnescah, r., Ks., U.S. (nĭn'ĕs-kä)	104	37.37N	98.31W
Nioaque, Braz. (nēō-á'-kĕ)	124	21.14S	55.41W
Niobrara, r., U.S. (nī-ô-brâr'á)	90	42.46N	98.46W
Niokolo Koba, Parc National du, rec., Sen.	208	13.05N	13.00W
Nioro du Sahel, Mali (nē-ō'rō)	204	15.15N	9.35W
Nipawin, Can.	78	53.22N	104.00W
Nipe, Bahía de, b., Cuba (bä-ē'ä-dĕ-nē'pä)	116	20.50N	75.30W
Nipe, Sierra de, mts., Cuba (sē-ĕ'r-rá-dĕ)	116	20.20N	75.50W
Nipigon, Can. (nĭp'ĭ-gŏn)	78	48.58N	88.17W
Nipigon, l., Can.	78	49.37N	89.55W
Nipigon Bay, b., Can.	84	48.56N	88.00W
Nipisiguit, r., Can. (nĭ-pĭ'sĭ-kwĭt)	86	47.26N	66.15W
Nipissing, l., Can. (nĭp'ĭ-sĭng)	78	45.59N	80.19W
Niquero, Cuba (nē-kā'rō)	116	20.00N	77.35W
Nirmali, India	178	26.30N	86.43E
Niš, Yugo.	136	43.19N	21.54E
Nisa, Port. (nē'sá)	152	39.32N	7.41W
Nišava, r., Eur. (nē'shá-vá)	154	43.17N	22.17E
Nishi, Japan	238b	34.41N	135.30E
Nishinari, neigh., Japan	238b	34.38N	135.28E
Nishino, i., Japan (nēsh'ē-nō)	187	36.06N	132.49E
Nishinomiya, Japan (nēsh'ē-nō-mē'yá)	187b	34.44N	135.21E
Nishio, Japan (nēsh'ē-ō)	187	34.50N	137.01E
Nishiyodogawa, neigh., Japan	238b	34.42N	135.27E
Niska Lake, l., Can. (nĭs'ká)	82	55.35N	108.38W
Nisko, Pol. (nēs'kô)	148	50.30N	22.07E
Nisku, Can. (nĭs-kū')	77g	53.21N	113.33W
Nisqually, r., Wa., U.S. (nĭs-kwôl'ĭ)	98	46.51N	122.33W
Nissan, r., Swe.	146	57.06N	13.22E
Nisser, l., Nor. (nĭs'ĕr)	146	59.14N	8.35E
Nissum Fjord, fj., Den.	146	56.24N	7.35E
Niterói, Braz. (nē-tĕ-rô'ĭ)	124	22.53S	43.07W
Nith, r., Scot., U.K. (nĭth)	144	55.13N	3.55W
Nitra, Czech. (nē'trá)	148	48.18N	18.04E
Nitra, r., Czech.	148	48.13N	18.14E
Nitro, W.V., U.S. (nī'trō)	92	38.25N	81.50W
Niue, dep., Oc. (nĭ'ò)	190	19.50S	167.00W
Nivelles, Bel. (nē'vĕl')	144	50.33N	4.17E
Nixon, Tx., U.S. (nĭk'sŭn)	106	29.16N	97.48W
Nizāmābād, India	174	18.48N	78.07E
Nizhne-Angarsk, Russia (nyĕzh'nyĭ-ŭngärsk')	158	55.49N	108.46E
Nizhne-Chirskaya, Russia	160	48.20N	42.50E
Nizhne-Kolymsk, Russia (kô-lĕmsk')	158	68.32N	160.56E
Nizhneudinsk, Russia (nĕzh'nyĭ-ōōdĕnsk')	158	54.58N	99.15E
Nizhniye Sergi, Russia (nyĕzh' nyĕ sĕr'gĕ)	160	56.41N	59.19E
Nizhniye Serogozy, Ukr. (nyĕzh'nyĭ sĕ-rô-gô'zĭ)	156	46.51N	34.25E
Nizhniy Novgorod (Gor'kiy), Russia	158	56.15N	44.05E
Nizhniy Tagil, Russia (tŭgēl')	158	57.54N	59.59E
Nizhnyaya Kur'ya, Russia (nyĕ'zhnyá-yá koor'yá)	164a	58.01N	56.00E
Nizhnyaya Salda, Russia (nyĕ'zhnya'ya säl'da')	164a	58.05N	60.43E
Nizhnyaya Taymyra, r., Russia	162	72.30N	95.18E
Nizhnyaya Tunguska, r., Russia	158	64.13N	91.30E
Nizhnyaya Tura, Russia (tōō'rá)	164a	58.38N	59.50E
Nizhnyaya Us'va, Russia (ŏ'vá)	164a	59.05N	58.53E
Nízke Tatry, mts., Czech.	148	48.57N	19.18E
Njazidja, i., Com.	206	11.44S	42.38E
Njombe, Tan.	210	9.20S	34.46E
Njurunda, Swe. (nyōō-rôn'dá)	146	62.15N	17.24E
Nkala Mission, Zam.	210	15.55S	26.00E
Nkandla, S. Afr. ('n-känd'lä)	207c	28.40S	31.06E
Nkawkaw, Ghana	208	6.33N	0.47W
Nkhota, Mwi. (kō-tá kō-tá)	206	12.52S	34.16E
Noākhāli, Bngl.	174	22.52N	91.08E
Noatak, Ak., U.S. (nô-á'ták)	89	67.22N	163.28W
Noatak, r., Ak., U.S.	89	67.58N	162.15W
Nobeoka, Japan (nō-bá-ō'ká)	186	32.36N	131.41E
Noblesville, In., U.S. (nō'bl'z-vĭl)	92	40.00N	86.00W
Nobleton, Can. (nō'bl'tŭn)	77d	43.54N	79.39W
Noborito, Japan	238a	35.37N	139.34E
Nocera Inferiore, Italy (ēn-fĕ-ryō'rĕ)	153c	40.30N	14.38E
Nochistlán, Mex. (nô-chēs-tlän')	112	21.23N	102.52W
Nochixtlón, Mex. (ä-sòn-syōn')	112	17.28N	97.12W
Nogales, Mex.	110	31.15N	111.00W
Nogales, Mex. (nō-gä'lĕs)	112	18.49N	97.09W
Nogales, Az., U.S. (nô-gä'lĕs)	90	31.20N	110.55W
Nogal Valley, val., Som. (nō'gäl)	212a	8.30N	47.50E
Nogaysk, Ukr. (nô-gīsk')	156	46.43N	36.21E
Nogent-le-Roi, Fr. (nŏ-zhŏɴ-lē-rwä')	151b	48.39N	1.32E
Nogent-le-Rotrou, Fr. (rō-trōō')	150	48.22N	0.47E
Nogent-sur-Marne, Fr.	233c	48.50N	2.29E
Noginsk, Russia (nô-gēnsk')	160	55.52N	38.28E
Noguera Pallares, r., Spain	152	42.18N	1.03E
Noirmoutier, Île de, i., Fr. (nwár-mōō-tyā')	140	47.03N	3.08W
Noisy-le-Grand, Fr.	233c	48.51N	2.33E
Noisy-le-Roi, Fr.	233c	48.51N	2.04E
Noisy-le-Sec, Fr.	233c	48.53N	2.28E
Nojima-Zaki, c., Japan (nō'jē-mä zä-kē)	187	34.54N	139.48E
Nokomis, Il., U.S. (nô-kō'mĭs)	92	39.15N	89.10W
Nola, Italy (nô'lä)	154	40.41N	14.32E
Nolinsk, Russia (nô-lēnsk')	160	57.32N	49.50E
Noma Misaki, c., Japan (nō'mä mē'sä-kē)	187	31.25N	130.09E
Nombre de Dios, Mex. (nôm-brē-dĕ-dyō's)	112	23.50N	104.14W
Nombre de Dios, Pan. (nô'm-brĕ)	114	9.34N	79.28W
Nome, Ak., U.S. (nōm)	90a	64.30N	165.20W
Nonacho, l., Can.	78	61.48N	111.20W
Nonantum, Ma., U.S.	223a	42.20N	71.12W
Nong'an, China (nôŋ-än)	184	44.25N	125.10E
Nongoma, S. Afr. (nōn-gō'má)	206	27.48S	31.45E
Nooksack, Wa., U.S. (nòk'săk)	100d	48.55N	122.19W
Nooksack, r., Wa., U.S.	100d	48.54N	122.31W
Noordwijk aan Zee, Neth.	139a	52.14N	4.25E
Noordzee Kanaal, can., Neth.	139a	52.27N	4.42E
Nootka, i., Can. (nōōt'ká)	78	49.32N	126.42W
Nootka Sound, strt., Can.	80	49.33N	126.38W
Nóqui, Ang. (nô-kē')	206	5.51S	13.25E
Nor, r., China (nou')	186	46.55N	132.45E
Nora, Swe.	146	59.32N	14.56E
Nora, In., U.S. (nō'rä)	95g	39.54N	86.08W
Noranda, Can.	84	48.15N	79.01W
Norbeck, Md., U.S. (nôr'bĕk)	94e	39.06N	77.05W
Norborne, Mo., U.S. (nôr'bôrn)	104	39.17N	93.39W
Norco, Ca., U.S. (nôr'kô)	101a	33.57N	117.33W
Norcross, Ga., U.S. (nôr'krôs)	94c	33.56N	84.13W
Nord, Riviere du, Can. (rēv-yĕr' dü nōr)	77a	45.45N	74.02W
Nordegg, Can. (nûr'dĕg)	80	52.28N	116.04W
Norden, Ger. (nôr'dĕn)	148	53.35N	7.14E
Norden, Eng., U.K.	233b	53.38N	2.13W
Norderney, i., Ger. (nōr'dĕr-nĕy)	148	53.45N	6.58E
Nordfjord, fj., Nor. (nô'fyôr)	146	61.50N	5.35E
Nordhausen, Ger. (nôrt'hau-zĕn)	140	51.30N	10.48E
Nordhorn, Ger. (nôrt'hôrn)	148	52.26N	7.05E
Nordland, Wa., U.S. (nôrd'lănd)	100a	48.03N	122.41W
Nördlingen, Ger. (nûrt'lĭng-ĕn)	148	48.51N	10.30E
Nord-Ostsee Kanal (Kiel Canal), can., Ger. (nôrd-ōzt-zā) (kēl)	148	54.03N	9.23E
Nordrhein-Westfalen (North Rhine-Westphalia), hist. reg., Ger. (nôrd'hīn-vĕst-fä-lĕn)	148	50.50N	6.53E
Nordvik, Russia (nôrd'vĕk)	158	73.57N	111.15E
Nore, r., Ire. (nōr)	144	52.34N	7.15W
Norf, Ger.	232	51.09N	6.43E
Norfolk, Ma., U.S. (nôr'fŏk)	87a	42.07N	71.19W
Norfolk, Ne., U.S.	90	42.10N	97.25W
Norfolk, Va., U.S.	90	36.55N	76.15W
Norfolk, i., Oc.	190	27.10S	166.50E
Norfork, Lake, l., Ar., U.S.	104	36.25N	92.09W
Noril'sk, Russia (nô rēlsk')	158	69.00N	87.11E
Normal, Il., U.S. (nôr'măl)	92	40.35N	89.00W
Norman, r., Austl.	196	18.27S	141.29E
Norman, Lake, res., N.C., U.S.	90	35.30N	80.53W
Normandie, hist. reg., Fr. (nŏr-mäɴ-dē')	150	49.02N	0.17E
Normandie, Collines de, hills, Fr. (kô-lēn'dĕ-nŏr-män-dē')	150	48.46N	0.50W
Normandy Heights, Md., U.S.	225c	39.17N	76.48W
Normanhurst, Austl.	239a	33.43S	151.06E
Normanton, Austl. (nôr'mán-tŭn)	196	17.45S	141.10E
Normanton, Eng., U.K.	138a	53.40N	1.21W
Norman Wells, Can.	78	65.26N	127.00W
Nornalup, Austl. (nôr-năl'ŭp)	196	35.00S	117.00E
Nørresundby, Den. (nû-rĕ-sòn'bü)	146	57.04N	9.55E
Norridge, Il., U.S.	227a	41.57N	87.49W
Norris, Tn., U.S. (nŏr'ĭs)	108	36.09N	84.05W
Norris Lake, res., Tn., U.S.	90	36.17N	84.10W
Norristown, Pa., U.S. (nŏr'ĭs-town)	94f	40.07N	75.21W
Norrköping, Swe. (nôr'chûp'ĭng)	136	58.37N	16.10E
Norrtälje, Swe. (nôr-tĕl'yĕ)	140	59.47N	18.39E
Norseman, Austl. (nôrs'mán)	196	32.15S	122.00E
Norte, Punta, c., Arg. (pōō'n-tä-nôr'tĕ)	123c	36.17S	56.46W
Norte, Serra do, mts., Braz. (sĕ'r-rä-dô-nôr'te)	124	12.04S	59.08W
North, Cape, c., Can.	86	47.02N	60.25W
North Abington, Ma., U.S.	223a	42.08N	70.57W
North Adams, Ma., U.S. (ăd'ămz)	92	42.40N	73.05W
Northam, Austl. (nôr-dhăm)	196	31.50S	116.45E
Northam, S. Afr. (nôr'thăm)	212d	24.52S	27.16E
North America, cont.	76	45.00N	100.00W
North American Basin, deep (á-mĕr'ĭ-kán)	4	23.45N	62.45W
Northampton, Austl. (nôr-thămp'tŭn)	196	28.22S	114.45E
Northampton, Eng., U.K. (nôrth-ămp'tŭn)	140	52.14N	0.56W
Northampton, Ma., U.S.	92	42.20N	72.45W
Northampton, Pa., U.S.	92	40.45N	75.30W
Northamptonshire, co., Eng., U.K.	138a	52.25N	0.47W
North Andaman Island, i., India (ăn-dá-măn')	188	13.15N	93.30E
North Andover, Ma., U.S. (ăn'dô-vĕr)	87a	42.42N	71.07W
North Arlington, N.J., U.S.	224	40.47N	74.08W
North Arm, mth., Can. (ärm)	100d	49.13N	123.01W
North Atlanta, Ga., U.S. (ăt-lăn'tá)	94c	33.52N	84.20W
North Attleboro, Ma., U.S. (ăt''l-bŭr-ô)	94b	41.59N	71.18W
North Auburn, Austl.	239a	33.50S	151.02E
North Baltimore, Oh., U.S. (bôl'tĭ-mōr)	92	41.10N	83.40W
North Balwyn, Austl.	239b	37.48S	145.05E

PLACE (Pronunciation)	PAGE	Lat. °′	Long. °′
North Barnaby, Md., U.S.	225d	38.49N	76.57W
North Barrackpore, India	236a	22.46N	88.22E
North Basque, Tx., U.S. (băsk)	106	31.56N	98.01W
North Battleford, Can. (băt''l-fērd)	78	52.47N	108.17W
North Bay, Can.	78	46.13N	79.26W
North Beach, neigh., Ca., U.S.	227b	37.48N	122.25W
North Bellmore, N.Y., U.S.	224	40.41N	73.32W
North Bend, Or., U.S. (bĕnd)	98	43.23N	124.13W
North Bergen, N.J., U.S.	224	40.48N	74.01W
North Berwick, Me., U.S. (bûr'wĭk)	86	43.18N	70.46W
North Bight, bt., Bah. (bīt)	116	24.30N	77.40W
North Bimini, i., Bah. (bĭ'mĭ-nē)	116	25.45N	79.20W
North Borneo, see Sabah, hist. reg., Malay.	188	5.10N	116.25E
Northborough, Ma., U.S.	87a	42.19N	71.39W
North Box Hill, Austl.	239b	37.48S	145.07E
North Braddock, Pa., U.S.	226b	40.24N	79.52W
Northbridge, Austl.	239a	33.49S	151.13E
Northbridge, Ma., U.S. (nôrth'brĭj)	87a	42.09N	71.39W
North Caicos, i., T./C. Is. (kī'kōs)	116	21.55N	72.00W
North Caldwell, N.J., U.S.	224	40.52N	74.16W
North Cape, c., N.Z.	197a	34.31S	173.02E
North Carolina, state, U.S. (kăr-ō-lī'nȧ)	90	35.40N	81.30W
North Cascades National Park, rec., Wa., U.S.	80	48.50N	120.50W
North Cat Cay, i., Bah.	116	25.35N	79.20W
North Channel, strt., Can.	84	46.10N	83.20W
North Channel, strt., U.K.	136	55.15N	7.56W
North Charleston, S.C., U.S. (chärlz'tŭn)	108	32.49N	79.57W
North Chicago, Il., U.S. (shĭ-kô'gō)	95a	42.19N	87.51W
Northcliff, neigh., S. Afr.	240b	26.09S	27.58E
North College Hill, Oh., U.S. (kŏl'ĕj hĭl)	95f	39.13N	84.33W
North Concho, Tx., U.S. (kŏn'chō)	106	31.40N	100.48W
North Cooking Lake, Can. (kŏok'ĭng lāk)	77g	53.28N	112.57W
Northcote, Austl.	239b	37.46S	145.00E
North Cyprus, nation, Asia	174	35.15N	33.40E
North Dakota, state, U.S. (dȧ-kō'tȧ)	90	47.20N	101.55W
North Downs, Eng., U.K. (dounz)	144	51.11N	0.01W
North Dum-Dum, India	178a	22.38N	88.23E
Northeast Cape, c., Ak., U.S. (nôrth-ēst)	89	63.15N	169.04W
Northeast Point, c., Bah.	116	22.45N	73.50W
Northeast Point, c., Bah.	116	21.25N	73.00W
Northeast Providence Channel, strt., Bah. (prŏv'ĭ-dĕns)	116	25.45N	77.00W
Northeim, Ger. (nôrt'hīm)	148	51.42N	9.59E
North Elbow Cays, is., Bah.	116	23.55N	80.30W
North Englewood, Md., U.S.	225d	38.55N	76.55W
Northern Cheyenne Indian Reservation, I.R., Mt., U.S.	98	45.32N	106.43W
Northern Dvina, see Severnaya Dvina, r., Russia	158	63.00N	42.40E
Northern Ireland, , U.K. (īr'lănd)	136	54.48N	7.00W
Northern Land, see Severnaya Zemlya, is., Russia	158	79.33N	101.15E
Northern Mariana Islands, dep., Oc. (mä-rē-ä'nȧ)	2	17.20N	145.00E
Northern Territory, , Austl.	196	18.15S	133.00E
Northern Yukon National Park, rec., Can.	89	69.00N	140.00W
North Essendon, Austl.	239b	37.45S	144.54E
Northfield, Il., U.S.	227a	42.06N	87.46W
Northfield, Mn., U.S. (nôrth'fēld)	96	44.28N	93.11W
North Fitzroy, Austl.	239b	37.47S	144.59E
Northfleet, Eng., U.K.	231	51.27N	0.21E
North Flinders Ranges, mts., Austl. (flĭn'dērz)	198	31.55S	138.45E
North Foreland, Eng., U.K. (fōr'lănd)	144	51.20N	1.30E
North Franklin Mountain, mtn., Tx., U.S. (frăŋ'klĭn)	106	31.55N	106.30W
North Frisian Islands, is., Eur.	140	55.16N	8.15E
North Gamboa, Pan. (gäm-bô'ä)	114	9.07N	79.40W
North Germiston, S. Afr.	240b	26.14S	28.09E
North Gower, Can. (gŏw'ēr)	77c	45.08N	75.43W
North Haledon, N.J., U.S.	224	40.58N	74.11W
North Hanover, Ma., U.S.	223a	42.09N	70.52W
North Hills, N.Y., U.S.	224	40.47N	73.41W
North Hollywood, Ca., U.S. (hŏl'ē-wŏod)	101a	34.10N	118.23W
North Island, i., N.Z.	197a	37.20S	173.30E
North Island, i., Ca., U.S.	102a	32.39N	117.14W
North Judson, In., U.S. (jŭd'sŭn)	92	41.15N	86.50W
North Kansas City, Mo., U.S. (kăn'zȧs)	101f	39.08N	94.34W
North Kingstown, R.I., U.S.	94b	41.34N	71.26W
Northlake, Il., U.S.	227a	41.55N	87.54W
North Little Rock, Ar., U.S. (lĭt''l rŏk)	104	34.46N	92.13W
North Loup, r., Ne., U.S. (lōōp)	96	42.05N	100.10W
North Manchester, In., U.S. (măn'chĕs-tēr)	92	41.00N	85.45W
North Manly, Austl.	239a	33.46S	151.16E
Northmead, Austl.	239a	33.47S	151.00E
Northmead, S. Afr.	240b	26.10S	28.20E
North Merrick, N.Y., U.S.	224	40.41N	73.34W
Northmoor, Mo., U.S. (nôth'mōōr)	101f	39.10N	94.37W
North Moose Lake, l., Can.	82	54.09N	100.20W
North Mount Lofty Ranges, mts., Austl.	198	33.50S	138.30E
North Ockendon, neigh., Eng., U.K.	231	51.32N	0.18E
North Ogden, Ut., U.S. (ŏg'dĕn)	101b	41.18N	111.58W
North Ogden Peak, mtn., Ut., U.S.	101b	41.23N	111.59W
North Olmsted, Oh., U.S. (ōlm-stĕd)	95d	41.25N	81.55W
North Parramatta, Austl.	239a	33.48S	151.00E
North Pease, r., Tx., U.S. (pēz)	104	34.19N	100.58W
North Pender, i., Can. (pĕn'dēr)	100d	48.48N	123.16W
North Philadelphia, neigh., Pa., U.S.	225b	39.58N	75.09W
North Plains, Or., U.S. (plānz)	100c	45.36N	123.00W
North Platte, Ne., U.S. (plăt)	90	41.08N	100.45W
North Platte, r., U.S.	90	41.20N	102.40W

PLACE (Pronunciation)	PAGE	Lat. °′	Long. °′
North Point, H.K.	237c	22.17N	114.12E
North Point, c., Barb.	115b	13.22N	59.36W
North Point, c., Mi., U.S.	92	45.00N	83.20W
Northport, Al., U.S. (nôrth'pōrt)	108	33.12N	87.35W
Northport, N.Y., U.S.	94a	40.53N	73.20W
Northport, Wa., U.S.	98	48.53N	117.47W
North Quincy, Ma., U.S.	223a	42.17N	71.01W
North Randolph, Ma., U.S.	223a	42.12N	71.04W
North Reading, Ma., U.S. (rĕd'ĭng)	87a	42.34N	71.04W
North Richland Hills, Tx., U.S.	101c	32.50N	97.13W
North Richmond, Ca., U.S.	227b	37.57N	122.22W
Northridge, Ca., U.S. (nôrth'rĭdj)	101a	34.14N	118.32W
North Ridgeville, Oh., U.S. (rĭj-vĭl)	95d	41.23N	82.01W
North Riverside, Il., U.S.	227a	41.51N	87.49W
North Ronaldsay, i., Scot., U.K.	144a	59.21N	2.23W
North Royalton, Oh., U.S. (roi'ăl-tŭn)	95d	41.19N	81.44W
North Ryde, Austl.	239a	33.48S	151.07E
North Saint Paul, Mn., U.S. (sånt pôl')	96	45.01N	92.59W
North Santiam, r., Or., U.S. (săn'tyăm)	98	44.42N	122.50W
North Saskatchewan, r., Can. (săn-kăch'ē-wän)	78	54.00N	111.30W
North Sea, Eur.	136	56.09N	3.16E
North Side, neigh., Pa., U.S.	226b	40.28N	80.01W
North Skunk, r., Ia., U.S. (skŭnk)	96	41.39N	92.46W
North Springfield, Va., U.S.	225d	38.48N	77.13W
North Stradbroke Island, i., Austl. (străd'brōk)	196	27.45S	154.18E
North Sydney, Austl.	239a	33.50S	151.13E
North Sydney, Can. (sĭd'nē)	86	46.13N	60.15W
North Taranaki Bight, N.Z. (tá-rȧ-nä'kĭ bīt)	197a	38.40S	174.00E
North Tarrytown, N.Y., U.S. (tăr'ĭ-toun)	94a	41.05N	73.52W
North Thompson, r., Can.	80	50.50N	120.10W
North Tonawanda, N.Y., U.S. (tŏn-ȧ-wŏn'dȧ)	95c	43.02N	78.53W
North Truchas Peaks, mtn., N.M., U.S. (trōō'chäs)	90	35.58N	105.40W
North Twillingate, i., Can. (twĭl'ĭn-gāt)	86	35.58N	105.37W
North Uist, i., Scot., U.K. (û'ĭst)	144	57.37N	7.22W
Northumberland, N.H., U.S.	92	44.30N	71.30W
Northumberland Islands, is., Austl.	196	21.42S	151.30E
Northumberland Strait, strt., Can. (nôr thŭm'bēr-lȧnd)	86	46.25N	64.20W
North Umpqua, r., Or., U.S. (ŭmp'kwȧ)	98	43.20N	122.50W
North Valley Stream, N.Y., U.S.	224	40.41N	73.41W
North Vancouver, Can. (văn-kōō'vēr)	78	49.19N	123.04W
North Vernon, In., U.S. (vûr'nŭn)	92	39.05N	85.45W
North Versailles, Pa., U.S.	226b	40.22N	79.48W
Northville, Mi., U.S. (nôrth-vĭl)	95b	42.26N	83.28W
North Wales, Pa., U.S. (wālz)	94f	40.12N	75.16W
North Weald Bassett, Eng., U.K.	231	51.43N	0.10E
North West Cape, c., Austl. (nôrth'wĕst)	196	21.50S	112.25E
Northwest Cape Fear, r., N.C., U.S. (căp fēr)	108	34.34N	79.46W
Northwestern University, pt. of i., Il., U.S.	227a	42.04N	87.40W
North West Gander, r., Can. (găn'dēr)	86	48.40N	55.15W
Northwest Harbor, b., Md., U.S.	225c	39.16N	76.35W
Northwest Providence Channel, strt., Bah. (prŏv'ĭ-dĕns)	116	26.15N	78.45W
Northwest Territories, , Can. (tĕr'ĭ-tō'rĭs)	78	64.42N	119.09W
North Weymouth, Ma., U.S.	223a	42.15N	70.57W
Northwich, Eng., U.K. (nôrth'wĭch)	138a	53.15N	2.31W
North Wilkesboro, N.C., U.S. (wĭlks'bûrô)	108	36.08N	81.10W
North Wilmington, Ma., U.S.	223a	42.34N	71.10W
Northwood, Ia., U.S. (nôrth'wŏod)	96	43.26N	93.13W
Northwood, N.D., U.S.	96	47.44N	97.36W
Northwood, neigh., Eng., U.K.	231	51.37N	0.25W
North Yamhill, r., Or., U.S. (yăm' hĭl)	100c	45.22N	123.21W
North York, Can.	84	43.47N	79.25W
North York Moors, for., Eng., U.K. (yôrk mōorz')	144	54.20N	0.40W
North Yorkshire, co., Eng., U.K.	138a	53.50N	1.10W
Norton, Ks., U.S. (nôr'tŭn)	104	39.40N	99.54W
Norton, Ma., U.S.	94b	41.58N	71.08W
Norton, Va., U.S.	108	36.54N	82.36W
Norton Bay, b., Ak., U.S.	89	64.22N	162.18W
Norton Heath, Eng., U.K.	231	51.43N	0.19E
Norton Reservoir, res., Ma., U.S.	94b	42.01N	71.07W
Norton Sound, strt., Ak., U.S.	89	63.48N	164.50W
Norval, Can. (nôr'vål)	77d	43.39N	79.52W
Norwalk, Ca., U.S. (nôr'wôk)	101a	33.54N	118.05W
Norwalk, Ct., U.S.	94a	41.06N	73.25W
Norwalk, Oh., U.S.	92	41.15N	82.35W
Norway, Me., U.S.	86	44.11N	70.35W
Norway, Mi., U.S.	96	45.47N	87.55W
Norway, nation, Eur. (nôr'wā)	136	63.48N	11.17E
Norway House, Can.	78	53.59N	97.50W
Norwegian Sea, sea, Eur. (nôr-wē'jăn)	140	66.54N	1.43E
Norwell, Ma., U.S. (nôr'wĕl)	87a	42.10N	70.47W
Norwich, Eng., U.K.	140	52.40N	1.15E
Norwich, Ct., U.S. (nôr'wĭch)	92	41.20N	72.00W
Norwich, N.Y., U.S.	92	42.35N	75.30W
Norwood, Ma., U.S. (nôr'wŏod)	87a	42.11N	71.13W
Norwood, N.C., U.S.	108	35.15N	80.08W
Norwood, Oh., U.S.	95f	39.10N	84.27W
Norwood, Pa., U.S.	225b	39.53N	75.18W
Norwood Park, neigh., Il., U.S.	227a	41.59N	87.48W
Nose, neigh., Japan	238b	34.49N	135.09E
Nose Creek, r., Can. (nōz)	77e	51.09N	114.02W
Noshiro, Japan (nō'shē-rō)	186	40.09N	140.02E
Nosovka, Ukr. (nō'sôf-kȧ)	156	50.54N	31.35E
Nossob, r., Afr. (nō'sŏb)	206	24.15S	19.10E
Noteć, r., Pol. (nō'tĕch)	148	52.50N	16.19E

PLACE (Pronunciation)	PAGE	Lat. °′	Long. °′
Notodden, Nor. (nōt'ôd'n)	146	59.35N	9.15E
Notre-Dame, rel., Fr.	233c	48.51N	2.21E
Notre Dame, Monts, mts., Can.	86	46.35N	70.35W
Notre Dame Bay, b., Can. (nō't'r dȧm')	79a	49.45N	55.15W
Notre-Dame-des-Victoires, neigh., Can.	223b	45.35N	73.34W
Notre-Dame-du-Lac, Can.	86	47.37N	68.51W
Nottawasaga Bay, b., Can. (nŏt'ȧ-wȧ-sä'gȧ)	84	44.45N	80.35W
Nottaway, r., Can. (nôt'ȧ-wā)	78	50.58N	78.02W
Nottingham, Eng., U.K. (nŏt'ĭng-ăm)	140	52.58N	1.09W
Nottingham, Pa., U.S.	225b	40.07N	74.58W
Nottingham Island, i., Can.	78	62.58N	78.53W
Nottingham Park, Il., U.S.	227a	41.46N	87.48W
Nottinghamshire, co., Eng., U.K.	138a	53.03N	1.05W
Notting Hill, Austl.	239b	37.54S	145.08E
Nottoway, r., Va., U.S. (nôt'ȧ-wā)	108	36.53N	77.47W
Notukeu Creek, r., Can.	82	49.55N	106.30W
Nouadhibou, Maur.	204	21.02N	17.09W
Nouakchott, Maur.	204	18.06N	15.57W
Nouamrhar, Maur.	204	19.22N	16.31W
Nouméa, N. Cal. (nōō-mā'ä)	196	22.16S	166.27E
Nouvelle, Can. (nōō-vĕl')	86	48.09N	66.22W
Nouvelle-France, Cap de, c., Can.	78	62.03N	74.00W
Nouzonville, Fr. (nōō-zôɴ-vēl')	150	49.51N	4.43E
Nova Cachoeirinha, neigh., Braz.	230d	23.28S	46.40W
Nova Cruz, Braz. (nō'vȧ-krōō'z)	124	6.22S	35.20W
Nova Friburgo, Braz. (frē-bōōr'gō)	124	22.18S	42.31W
Nova Iguaçu, Braz. (nō'vä-ē-gwä-sōō')	124	22.45S	43.27W
Nova Lima, Braz. (lē'mä)	123a	19.59S	43.51W
Nova Lisboa, see Huambo, Ang.	206	12.44S	15.47E
Nova Mambone, Moz. (nō'vȧ-mȧm-bō'nē)	206	21.04S	35.13E
Novara, Italy (nō-vä'rä)	142	45.24N	8.38E
Nova Resende, Braz.	123a	21.12S	46.25W
Nova Scotia, prov., Can. (skō'shȧ)	78	44.28N	65.00W
Novate Milanese, Italy	234c	45.32N	9.08E
Novaya Ladoga, Russia (nô'vá-ya lá-dô-gá)	146	60.06N	32.16E
Novaya Lyalya, Russia (lyá'lyá)	164a	59.03N	60.36E
Novaya Odessa, Ukr. (ô-dĕs'ä)	156	47.18N	31.48E
Novaya Praga, Ukr. (prä'gȧ)	156	48.34N	32.54E
Novaya Sibir, i., Russia (sē-bēr')	158	75.00N	149.00E
Novaya Vodolaga, Ukr. (vō-dôl'á-gá)	156	49.43N	35.51E
Novaya Zemlya, i., Russia (zĕm-lyá')	158	72.00N	54.46E
Nova Zagora, Bul. (zä'gō-rȧ)	154	42.30N	26.01E
Novelda, Spain (nō-vĕl'dȧ)	152	38.22N	0.46W
Nové Mesto nad Váhom, Czech. (nô'vĕ myĕs'tō)	148	48.44N	17.47E
Nové Zámky, Czech. (zäm'kē)	140	47.58N	18.10E
Novgorod, Russia (nôv'gô-rŏt)	160	58.32N	31.16E
Novgorod, prov., Russia	156	58.27N	31.55E
Novgorod-Severskiy, Ukr.	160	52.01N	33.14E
Novi, Mi., U.S. (nō'vĭ)	95b	42.29N	83.28W
Novigrad, Cro. (nō'vĭ gràd)	154	44.09N	15.34E
Novi Ligure, Italy (nô'vē)	154	44.43N	8.48E
Novinger, Mo., U.S. (nŏv'ĭn-jēr)	104	40.14N	92.43W
Novi Pazar, Bul. (pä-zär')	154	43.22N	27.26E
Novi Pazar, Yugo. (pȧ-zär')	142	43.08N	20.30E
Novi Sad, Yugo. (säd')	136	45.15N	19.53E
Novoarchangel'skoje, Russia	235b	55.55N	37.33E
Novoasbest, Russia (nô-vô-äs-bĕst')	164a	57.43N	60.14E
Novoaydar, Ukr. (nô'vô-ī-där')	156	48.57N	39.01E
Novocherkassk, Russia (nô'vô-chĕr-kåsk')	160	47.25N	40.04E
Novochovrino, neigh., Russia	235b	55.52N	37.30E
Novogirejevo, neigh., Russia	235b	55.45N	37.49E
Novo-Kazalinsk, Kaz. (nô-vŭ-kŭ-zȧ-lyĕnsk')	158	45.47N	62.00E
Novokuznetsk, Russia (nô'vô-kô'z-nyĕ'tsk) (stä'lĕnsk)	158	53.43N	86.59E
Novo-Ladozhskiy Kanal, can., Russia (nô-vô-lä'dôzh-skĭ kȧ-näl')	146	59.54N	31.19E
Novo Mesto, Slo. (nôvô mås'tô)	154	45.48N	15.13E
Novomirgorod, Ukr. (nô'vô-mēr'gô-rôt)	156	48.46N	31.44E
Novomoskovsk, Russia (nô'vô-môs-kôfsk')	158	54.06N	38.08E
Novomoskovsk, Ukr.	160	48.37N	35.12E
Novonikol'skiy, Russia (nô'vô-nyĭ-kôl'skĭ)	164a	52.28N	57.12E
Novorossiysk, Russia (nô'vô-rô-sēsk')	158	44.43N	37.48E
Novorzhev, Russia (nô'vô-rzhĕv')	156	57.01N	29.17E
Novo-Selo, Bul. (nô'vô-sĕ'lô)	154	44.09N	22.46E
Novosibirsk, Russia (nô'vô-sē-bērsk')	158	55.09N	82.58E
Novosibirskiye Ostrova (New Siberian Islands), is., Russia	158	74.00N	140.30E
Novosil', Russia (nô'vô-sĭl)	156	52.58N	37.03E
Novosokol'niki, Russia (nô'vô-sô-kôl'nē-kē)	156	56.18N	30.07E
Novotatishchevskiy, Russia (nô'vô-tá-tyĭsh'chĕv-skĭ)	164a	53.22N	60.24E
Novoukrainka, Ukr.	160	48.18N	31.33E
Novouzensk, Russia (nô-vô-ô-zĕnsk')	160	50.40N	48.08E
Novozybkov, Russia (nô'vô-zĕp'kôf)	160	52.31N	31.54E
Nový Jičín, Czech. (nô'vē yē'chēn)	148	49.36N	18.02E
Novyy Bug, Ukr. (bōōk)	156	47.43N	32.33E
Novyy Oskol, Russia (ôs-kôl')	156	50.46N	37.53E
Novyy Port, Russia (nô'vē)	158	67.19N	72.28E
Nowa Sól, Pol. (nô'vá sŭl')	148	51.49N	15.41E
Nowata, Ok., U.S. (nô-wä'tȧ)	104	36.42N	95.38W
Nowood Creek, r., Wy., U.S.	98	44.02N	107.37W
Nowra, Austl. (nou'rȧ)	198	34.55S	150.45E
Nowy Dwór Mazowiecki, Pol. (nô'vĭ dvōōr mä-zo-vyĕts'ke)	148	52.26N	20.46E
Nowy Sącz, Pol. (nô'vē sônch')	148	49.36N	20.42E
Nowy Targ, Pol. (tärk')	148	49.29N	20.02E

ăt; finȧl; rāte; senåte; ärm; åsk; sofȧ; fâre; ch-choose; dh-as th in other; bē; ēvent; bĕt; recĕnt; cratēr; g-gō; gh-guttural g; bĭt; ĭ-short neutral; rīde; ĸ-guttural k as ch in German ich;

PLACE (Pronunciation)	PAGE	Lat. °′	Long. °′
Noxon Reservoir, res., Mt., U.S.	98	47.50N	115.40W
Noxubee, r., Ms., U.S. (nŏks′ū-bē)	108	33.20N	88.55W
Noya, Spain (no′yä)	152	42.46N	8.50W
Noyes Island, i., Ak., U.S. (noiz)	80	55.30N	133.40W
Nozaki, Japan (nō′zä-kė)	187b	34.43N	135.39E
Nozuta, Japan	238a	35.35N	139.27E
Nqamakwe, Transkei ('n-gä-mä′kwȧ)	207c	32.13S	27.57E
Nqutu, S. Afr. ('n-kōō′tōō)	207c	28.17S	30.41E
Nsawam, Ghana	208	5.50N	0.20W
Ntshoni, mtn., S. Afr.	207c	29.34S	30.03E
Ntwetwe Pan, pl., Bots.	206	20.00S	24.18E
Nubah, Jibāl an, mts., Sudan	204	12.22N	30.39E
Nubian Desert, des., Sudan (nōō′bĭ-ăn)	204	21.13N	33.09E
Nudo Coropuna, mtn., Peru (nōō′dô kō-rō-pōō′nä)	124	15.53S	72.04W
Nudo de Pasco, mtn., Peru (dě pás′kô)	124	10.34S	76.12W
Nueces, r., Tx., U.S. (nū-ā′sås)	90	28.20N	98.08W
Nueltin, l., Can. (nwĕl′tin)	78	60.14N	101.00W
Nueva Armenia, Hond. (nwā′vä är-mä′nė-à)	114	15.47N	86.32W
Nueva Atzacoalco, Mex.	229a	19.29N	99.05W
Nueva Chicago, neigh., Arg.	229d	34.40S	58.30W
Nueva Coronela, Cuba	229b	23.04N	82.28W
Nueva Esparta, dept., Ven. (nwě′vä ěs-pä′r-tä)	125b	10.50N	64.35W
Nueva Gerona, Cuba (kĕ-rō′nä)	116	21.55N	82.45W
Nueva Palmira, Ur. (päl-mē′rä)	123c	33.53S	58.23W
Nueva Rosita, Mex. (nòĕ′vä rô-sė′tä)	90	27.55N	101.10W
Nueva San Salvador, El Sal.	114	13.41N	89.16W
Nueve, Canal Numero, can., Arg.	123c	36.22S	58.19W
Nueve de Julio, Arg. (nwā′vå dā hōō′lyô)	126	35.26S	60.51W
Nuevitas, Cuba (nwā-vē′tās)	110	21.35N	77.15W
Nuevitas, Bahía de, b., Cuba (bä-ē′ä dě nwä-vē′täs)	116	21.30N	77.05W
Nuevo, Ca., U.S. (nwā′vō)	101a	33.48N	117.09W
Nuevo Laredo, Mex. (lä-rā′dhō)	110	27.29N	99.30W
Nuevo Leon, state, Mex. (lå-ōn′)	110	26.00N	100.00W
Nuevo San Juan, Pan. (nwě′vô sän kōō-ä′n)	110a	9.14N	79.43W
Nugumanovo, Russia (nû-gû-mä′nô-vô)	164a	55.28N	61.50E
Nulato, Ak., U.S. (nōō-lä′tō)	89	64.40N	158.18W
Nullagine, Austl. (nŭ-lă′jēn)	196	22.00S	120.07E
Nullarbor Plain, pl., Austl. (nŭ-lär′bôr)	196	31.45S	126.30E
Numabin Bay, b., Can. (nōō-mä′bĭn)	82	56.30N	103.08W
Numansdorp, Neth.	139a	51.43N	4.25E
Numazu, Japan (nōō′mä-zōō)	186	35.06N	138.55E
Numfoor, Pulau, i., Indon.	188	1.20S	134.48E
Nun, r., Nig.	208	5.05N	6.10E
Nunawading, Austl.	195a	37.49S	145.10E
Nuneaton, Eng., U.K. (nŭn′ē-tŭn)	144	52.31N	1.28W
Nunivak, i., Ak., U.S. (nōō′nĭ-văk)	90a	60.25N	167.42W
Ñuñoa, Chile	230b	33.28S	70.36W
Nunyama, Russia (nûn-yä′mȧ)	89	65.49N	170.32W
Nuoro, Italy (nwô′rō)	154	40.29N	9.20E
Nura, r., Kaz. (nōō′rä)	162	49.48N	73.54E
Nurata, Uzb. (nōōr′ät′á)	158	40.33N	65.28E
Nuremberg, see Nürnberg, Ger.	136	49.28N	11.07E
Nürnberg, Ger. (nürn′bĕrgh)	136	49.28N	11.07E
Nurse Cay, i., Bah.	116	22.30N	75.50W
Nusabyin, Tur. (nōō′sĭ-bėn)	160	37.05N	41.10E
Nushagak, r., Ak., U.S. (nū-shă-găk′)	89	59.28N	157.40W
Nushan Hu, l., China	182	32.50N	117.59E
Nushki, Pak. (nŭsh′kė)	174	29.30N	66.02E
Nussdorf, neigh., Aus.	235e	48.15N	16.22E
Nuthe, r., Ger. (nōō′tė)	139b	52.15N	13.11E
Nutley, N.J., U.S. (nŭt′lė)	94a	40.49N	74.09W
Nutter Fort, W.V., U.S. (nŭt′ēr fôrt)	92	39.15N	80.15W
Nutwood, Il., U.S. (nŭt′wŏod)	101e	39.05N	90.34W
Nuwaybi 'al Muzayyinah, Egypt	173a	28.59N	34.40E
Nuweland, S. Afr.	206a	33.58S	18.28E
Nyack, N.Y., U.S. (nī′ăk)	94a	41.05N	73.55W
Nyainqêntanglha Shan, mts., China (nyä-ĭn-chyŭn-täŋ-lä shän)	180	29.55N	88.08E
Nyakanazi, Tan.	210	3.00S	31.15E
Nyala, Sudan	204	12.00N	24.52E
Nyanga, r., Gabon	210	2.45S	10.30E
Nyanza, Rw.	210	2.21S	29.45E
Nyasa, Lake, l., Afr. (nyä′sä)	206	10.45S	34.30E
Nyazepetrovsk, Russia (nyä′zĕ-pĕ-trôvsk′)	164a	56.04N	59.38E
Nyborg, Den. (nü′bôr″)	146	55.20N	10.45E
Nybro, Swe. (nü′brô)	146	56.44N	15.56E
Nyeri, Kenya	210	0.25S	36.57E
Nyika Plateau, plat., Mwi.	210	10.30S	35.50E
Nyíregyháza, Hung. (nyē′rĕd-y′hä′zä)	142	47.58N	21.45E
Nykøbing, Den. (nü′kû-bĭng)	140	56.46N	8.47E
Nykøbing, Den.	146	54.45N	11.54E
Nykøbing Sjaelland, Den.	146	55.55N	11.37E
Nyköping, Swe. (nü′chû-pĭng)	140	58.46N	16.58E
Nylstroom, S. Afr. (nĭl′strōm)	206	24.42S	28.25E
Nymagee, Austl. (nī-mä-gē′)	196	32.17S	146.18E
Nymburk, Czech. (nėm′bŏŏrk)	140	50.12N	15.03E
Nynäshamn, Swe. (nü-nĕs-hȧm′n)	146	58.53N	17.55E
Nyngan, Austl. (nĭŋ′gȧn)	196	31.31S	147.25E
Nyong, r., Cam. (nyông)	204	4.00N	12.00E
Nyou, Burkina	208	12.46N	1.56W
Nýřany, Czech. (nėr-zhä′nė)	148	49.43N	13.13E
Nysa, Pol. (nē′sȧ)	148	50.29N	17.20E
Nytva, Russia	160	58.00N	55.10E
Nyungwe, Mwi.	210	10.16S	34.07E
Nyunzu, Zaire	210	5.57S	28.01E
Nyuya, r., Russia (nyōō′yȧ)	162	60.30N	111.45E
Nzega, Tan.	210	4.13S	33.11E
N'zeto, Ang.	206	7.14S	12.52E
Nzi, r., I.C.	208	7.00N	4.27W
Nzwani, i., Com. (äɴ-zhwä′ɴ)	206	12.14S	44.47E

O

PLACE (Pronunciation)	PAGE	Lat. °′	Long. °′
Oahe, Lake, res., U.S.	90	45.20N	100.00W
Oahu, i., Hi., U.S. (ō-ä′hōō) (ō-ä′hū)	90c	21.38N	157.48W
Oak Bay, Can.	80	48.27N	123.18W
Oak Bluff, Can. (ōk blŭf)	77f	49.47N	97.21W
Oak Creek, Co., U.S. (ōk krēk′)	98	40.20N	106.50W
Oakdale, Ca., U.S. (ōk′dāl)	102	37.45N	120.52W
Oakdale, Ky., U.S.	92	38.15N	85.50W
Oakdale, La., U.S.	106	30.49N	92.40W
Oakdale, Pa., U.S.	95e	40.24N	80.11W
Oakengates, Eng., U.K. (ōk′ĕn-gāts)	138a	52.41N	2.27W
Oakes, N.D., U.S. (ōks)	96	46.10N	98.50W
Oakfield, Me., U.S. (ōk′fēld)	86	46.08N	68.10W
Oakford, Pa., U.S. (ōk′fōrd)	94f	40.08N	74.58W
Oak Forest, Il., U.S.	227a	41.36N	87.45W
Oak Grove, Or., U.S. (grōv)	100c	45.25N	122.38W
Oakham, Eng., U.K. (ōk′ăm)	138a	52.40N	0.38W
Oakharbor, Oh., U.S. (ōk′här′bēr)	92	41.30N	83.05W
Oak Harbor, Wa., U.S.	100a	48.18N	122.39W
Oakland, Ca., U.S. (ōk′lănd)	90	37.48N	122.16W
Oakland, Md., U.S.	225d	38.52N	76.55W
Oakland, Ne., U.S.	96	41.50N	96.28W
Oakland, neigh., Pa., U.S.	226b	40.26N	79.58W
Oakland City, In., U.S.	92	38.20N	87.20W
Oakland Gardens, neigh., N.Y., U.S.	224	40.45N	73.45W
Oaklawn, Il., U.S. (ōk′lôn)	95a	41.43N	87.45W
Oakleigh, Austl. (ōk′lȧ)	195a	37.54S	145.05E
Oakleigh South, Austl.	239b	37.56S	145.05E
Oakley, Id., U.S. (ōk′lĭ)	98	42.15N	135.53W
Oakley, Ks., U.S.	104	39.08N	100.49W
Oakman, Al., U.S. (ōk′măn)	108	33.42N	87.20W
Oakmont, Pa., U.S. (ōk′mŏnt)	95e	40.31N	79.50W
Oak Mountain, mtn., Al., U.S.	94h	33.22N	86.42W
Oak Park, Il., U.S. (pärk)	95a	41.53N	87.48W
Oak Park, Mi., U.S.	226c	42.28N	83.11W
Oak Point, Wa., U.S.	100c	46.11N	123.11W
Oak Ridge, Tn., U.S. (rĭj)	108	36.01N	84.15W
Oak View, Md., U.S.	225d	39.01N	76.59W
Oakview, N.J., U.S.	225b	39.51N	75.09W
Oakville, Can.	77f	49.56N	97.58W
Oakville, Can. (ōk′vĭl)	84	43.27N	79.40W
Oakville, Mo., U.S.	101e	38.27N	90.18W
Oakville Creek, r., Can.	77d	43.34N	79.54W
Oakwood, Oh., U.S.	225a	41.06N	84.23W
Oakwood, Tx., U.S. (ōk′wŏod)	106	31.36N	95.48W
Oatley, Austl.	239a	33.59S	151.05E
Oatman, Az., U.S. (ōt′măn)	102	34.00N	114.25W
Oaxaca, state, Mex. (wä-hä′kä)	110	16.45N	97.00W
Oaxaca, Sierra de, mts., Mex. (sē-ĕ′r-rä dě)	112	16.15N	97.25W
Oaxaca de Juárez, Mex. (kōōá′rĕz)	110	17.03N	96.42W
Ob', r., Russia	158	62.15N	67.00E
Oba, Can. (ō′bȧ)	78	48.58N	84.09W
Obama, Japan (ō′bá-mä)	187	35.29N	135.44E
Oban, Scot., U.K. (ō′băn)	144	56.25N	5.35W
Oban Hills, hills, Nig.	208	5.35N	8.30E
O'Bannon, Ky., U.S. (ō-băn′nŏn)	95h	38.17N	85.30W
Obatogamau, l., Can. (ō-bȧ-tō′găm-ô)	84	49.38N	74.10W
Oberbauer, Ger.	232	51.17N	7.26E
Oberbonsfeld, Ger.	232	51.22N	7.08E
Oberelfringhausen, Ger.	232	51.20N	7.11E
Oberhaan, Ger.	232	51.13N	7.02E
Oberhausen, Ger. (ō′bĕr-hou′zĕn)	151c	51.27N	6.51E
Oberkassel, neigh., Ger.	232	51.14N	6.46E
Ober-kirchbach, Aus.	235e	48.17N	16.12E
Oberlaa, neigh., Aus.	235e	48.08N	16.24E
Oberlin, Ks., U.S. (o′bēr-lĭn)	104	39.49N	100.30W
Oberlin, Oh., U.S.	92	41.15N	82.15W
Oberösterreich, prov., Aus.	148	48.05N	13.15E
Oberroth, Ger. (ō′bĕr-rōt)	139d	48.19N	11.20E
Ober Sankt Veit, neigh., Aus.	235e	48.11N	16.16E
Oberschöneweide, neigh., Ger.	234a	52.28N	13.31E
Oberwengern, Ger.	232	51.23N	7.22E
Obgruiten, Ger.	232	51.13N	7.01E
Obi, Kepulauan, is., Indon. (ō′bė)	188	1.25S	128.15E
Obi, Pulau, i., Indon.	188	1.30S	127.45E
Óbidos, Braz. (ō′bė-dòzh)	124	1.57S	55.32W
Obihiro, Japan (ō′bē-hē′rō)	186	42.55N	142.50E
Obion, r., Tn., U.S.	108	36.10N	89.25W
Obion, North Fork, r., Tn., U.S. (ō-bī′ŏn)	108	35.49N	89.06W
Obitochnaya, Kosa, spit, Ukr. (kô-sä′ ô-bē-tôch′nȧ-yȧ)	156	46.32N	36.07E
Obitsu, r., Japan (ō′bēt′sōō)	187a	35.19N	140.03E
Obock, Dji. (ō-bŏk′)	212a	11.55N	43.15E
Obol', r., Bela. (ô-bŏl′)	156	55.24N	29.24E
Oboyan', Russia (ô-bô-yän′)	160	51.14N	36.16E
Obskaya Guba, b., Russia	158	67.13N	73.45E
Obu, neigh., Japan	238b	34.44N	135.09E
Obuasi, Ghana	208	6.14N	1.39W
Óbuda, neigh., Hung.	235g	47.33N	19.02E
Obukhov, Ukr. (ô′bōō-kôf)	156	50.07N	30.36E
Obukhovo, Russia	164b	55.50N	38.17E
Očakovo, neigh., Russia	235b	55.41N	37.27E
Ocala, Fl., U.S. (ô-kä′lȧ)	108	29.11N	82.09W
Ocampo, Mex. (ō-käm′pō)	112	22.49N	99.23W
Ocaña, Col. (ō-kän′yä)	124	8.15N	73.37W
Ocaña, Spain (ō-kä′n-yä)	152	39.58N	3.31W
Occidental, Cordillera, mts., Col.	124a	5.05N	76.04W
Occidental, Cordillera, mts., Peru	124	10.12S	76.58W
Ocean Beach, Ca., U.S. (ō′shăn bēch)	102a	32.44N	117.14W
Ocean Bight, bt., Bah.	116	21.15N	73.15W
Ocean City, Md., U.S.	92	38.20N	75.10W
Ocean City, N.J., U.S.	92	39.15N	74.35W
Ocean Falls, Can. (Fôls)	78	52.21N	127.40W
Ocean Grove, Austl.	195a	38.16S	144.32E
Ocean Grove, N.J., U.S. (grōv)	92	40.10N	74.00W
Oceanside, Ca., U.S. (ō′shăn-sīd)	102	33.11N	117.22W
Oceanside, N.Y., U.S.	94a	40.38N	73.39W
Ocean Springs, Ms., U.S. (sprĭngs)	108	30.25N	88.49W
Ochakov, Ukr. (ô-chä′kôf)	156	46.38N	31.33E
Ochiai, neigh., Japan	238a	35.43N	139.42E
Ochlockonee, r., Fl., U.S. (ŏk-lô-kō′nē)	108	30.10N	84.38W
Ocilla, Ga., U.S. (ô-sĭl′ȧ)	108	31.36N	83.15W
Ockelbo, Swe. (ôk′ĕl-bô)	146	60.54N	16.35E
Ockham, Eng., U.K.	231	51.18N	0.27W
Ocklawaha, Lake, res., Fl., U.S.	108	29.30N	81.50W
Ocmulgee, r., Ga., U.S.	108	32.25N	83.30W
Ocmulgee National Monument, rec., Ga., U.S. (ôk-mŭl′gē)	108	32.45N	83.28W
Ocna-Sibiului, Rom. (ōck′nà-sė-byōō-lōō-ė)	154	45.52N	24.04E
Ocnele Mari, Rom.	154	45.05N	24.17E
Ocoa, Bahía de, b., Dom. Rep.	116	18.20N	70.40W
Ococingo, Mex. (ô-kô-sē′n-gô)	112	17.03N	92.18W
Ocom, Lago, l., Mex. (ô-kô′m)	114a	19.26N	88.18W
Oconee, r., Ga., U.S. (ô-kō′nē)	90	32.45N	83.00W
Oconee, Lake, res., Ga., U.S.	108	33.30N	83.15W
Oconomowoc, Wi., U.S. (ô-kŏn′ô-mô-wŏk′)	96	43.06N	88.24W
Oconto, Wi., U.S. (ô-kŏn′tō)	96	44.54N	87.55W
Oconto, r., Wi., U.S.	96	45.08N	88.24W
Oconto Falls, Wi., U.S.	96	44.53N	88.11W
Ocós, Guat. (ô-kōs′)	114	14.31N	92.12W
Ocotal, Nic. (ō-kô-täl′)	114	13.36N	86.31W
Ocotepeque, Hond. (ô-kō-tā-pā′kå)	114	14.25N	89.13W
Ocotlán, Mex. (ō-kô-tlän′)	112	20.19N	102.44W
Ocotlán de Morelos, Mex. (dā mô-rā′lôs)	112	16.46N	96.41W
Ocozocoautla, Mex. (ô-kō′zô-kwä-ōō′tlä)	112	16.44N	93.22W
Ocumare del Tuy, Ven. (ô-kōō-mä′ra del twē′)	124	10.07N	66.47W
Oda, Ghana	208	5.55N	0.59W
Odawara, Japan (ō′dȧ-wä′rä)	187	35.15N	139.10E
Odda, Nor. (ôdh-ȧ)	146	60.04N	6.30E
Odebolt, Ia., U.S. (ō′dē-bōlt)	96	42.20N	95.14W
Odemira, Port. (ō-dȧ-mē′rȧ)	152	37.35N	8.40W
Ödemiş, Tur. (û′dĕ-mēsh)	142	38.12N	28.00E
Odendaalsrus, S. Afr. (ō′dĕn-däls-rûs′)	212d	27.52S	26.41E
Odense, Den. (ō′dhĕn-sĕ)	140	55.24N	10.20E
Odenton, Md., U.S. (ō′dĕn-tŭn)	94e	39.05N	76.43W
Odenwald, for., Ger. (ō′dĕn-väld)	148	49.39N	8.55E
Oder, r., Eur. (ō′dēr)	136	52.40N	14.19E
Oderhaff, l., Eur.	148	53.47N	14.02E
Odessa, Ukr. (ô-dĕs′sä)	158	46.28N	30.44E
Odessa, Tx., U.S. (ô-dĕs′á)	106	31.52N	102.21W
Odessa, Wa., U.S.	98	47.20N	118.42W
Odessa, prov., Ukr.	156	46.05N	29.48E
Odiel, r., Spain (ō-dė-ĕl′)	152	37.47N	6.42W
Odiham, Eng., U.K. (ŏd′ē-ăm)	138b	51.14N	0.56W
Odintsovo, Russia (ô-dēn′tsô-vô)	164b	55.40N	37.16E
Odiongan, Phil. (ō-dė-ōŋ′gän)	189a	12.24N	121.59E
Odivelas, Port. (ō-dė-vä′lyäs)	153b	38.47N	9.11W
Odobeşti, Rom. (ō-dô-bĕsh′t′)	148	45.46N	27.08E
O'Donnell, Tx., U.S. (ō-dŏn′ĕl)	104	32.59N	101.51W
Odorhei, Rom. (ō-dôr-hā′)	148	46.18N	25.17E
Odra, see Oder, r., Eur. (ô′drȧ)	136	52.40N	14.19E
Oeiras, Braz. (wȧ-ē-räzh′)	124	7.05S	42.01W
Oeirás, Port. (ō-ĕ′y-rá′s)	153b	38.42N	9.18W
Oella, Md., U.S.	225c	39.16N	76.47W
Oelwein, Ia., U.S. (ōl′wīn)	96	42.40N	91.56W
Oespel, neigh., Ger.	232	51.30N	7.23E
Oestrich, Ger.	232	51.22N	7.38E
Oestrich, neigh., Ger.	232	51.34N	7.22E
Oestrum, Ger.	232	51.25N	6.40E
O'Fallon, Il., U.S. (ō-făl′ŭn)	101e	38.36N	89.55W
O'Fallon Creek, r., Mt., U.S.	98	46.25N	104.47W
Ofanto, r., Italy (ô-fän′tō)	154	41.08N	15.33E
Offa, Nig.	208	8.09N	4.44E
Offenbach, Ger. (ôf′ĕn-bäk)	148	50.06N	8.50E
Offenburg, Ger. (ôf′ĕn-bŏorgh)	148	48.28N	7.57E
Ofin, Nig.	240d	6.33N	3.30E
Ofomori, neigh., Japan	238a	35.34N	139.44E
Ofuna, Japan (ō′fōō-nä)	187a	35.21N	139.32E
Ogaden Plateau, plat., Eth.	212a	6.45N	44.53E
Ogaki, Japan	186	35.21N	136.36E
Ogallala, Ne., U.S. (ō-gä-lä′lä)	96	41.08N	101.44W
Ogawa, Japan	238a	35.44N	139.28E
Ogbomosho, Nig. (ŏg-bô-mō′shō)	204	8.08N	4.15E
Ogden, Ia., U.S. (ŏg′dĕn)	96	42.10N	94.20W
Ogden, Ut., U.S.	90	41.14N	111.58W
Ogden, r., Ut., U.S.	101b	41.16N	111.54W
Ogden Peak, mtn., Ut., U.S.	101b	41.11N	111.51W
Ogdensburg, N.J., U.S. (ŏg′dĕnz-bûrg)	94a	41.05N	74.36W
Ogdensburg, N.Y., U.S.	90	44.40N	75.30W
Ogeechee, r., Ga., U.S. (ô-gē′chė)	108	32.35N	81.50W
Ogies, S. Afr.	212d	26.03S	29.04E
Ogilvie Mountains, mts., Can. (ō′g'l-vĭ)	78	64.45N	138.10W

PLACE (Pronunciation)	PAGE	Lat. °'	Long. °'
Oglesby, Il., U.S. (ō'g'lz-bĭ)	92	41.20N	89.00W
Oglio, r., Italy (ōl'yō)	154	45.15N	10.19E
Ōgo, Japan (ō'gō)	187b	34.49N	135.06E
Ogou, r., Togo	208	8.05N	1.30E
Ogoyo, Nig.	240d	6.26N	3.29E
Ogudnëvo, Russia (ôg-ôd-nyô'vô)	164b	56.04N	38.17E
Ogudu, Nig.	240d	6.34N	3.24E
Ogulin, Cro. (ō-gōō-lēn')	154	45.17N	15.11E
Ogwashi-Uku, Nig.	208	6.10N	6.31E
O'Higgins, prov., Chile (ô-kē'gēns)	123b	34.17S	70.52W
Ohio, state, U.S. (ô'hī'ō)	90	40.30N	83.15W
Ohio, r., U.S.	90	37.25N	88.05W
Ohoopee, r., Ga., U.S. (ô-hōō'pe-mc)	108	32.32N	82.38W
Ohře, r., Eur. (ŏr'zhĕ)	148	50.08N	12.45E
Ohrid, Mac. (ō'krēd)	154	41.08N	20.46E
Ohrid, Lake, l., Eur.	154	40.58N	20.35E
Ōi, Japan (oi')	187a	35.51N	139.31E
Oi-Gawa, r., Japan (ō'ē-gä'wȧ)	187	35.09N	138.05E
Oil City, Pa., U.S. (oil sĭ'tĭ)	92	41.25N	79.40W
Oirschot, Neth.	139a	51.30N	5.20E
Oise, r., Fr. (wäz)	140	49.30N	2.56E
Oisterwijk, Neth.	139a	51.34N	5.13E
Oita, Japan (ō'ē-tä)	186	33.14N	131.38E
Oji, Japan (ō'jē)	187b	34.36N	135.43E
Ojinaga, Mex. (ō-kē-nä'gä)	110	29.34N	104.26W
Ojitlán, Mex. (ōkē-tlän') (sän-lōō'käs)	112	18.04N	96.23W
Ojocaliente, Mex. (ô-kô-kä-lyĕ'n-tĕ)	112	22.39N	102.15W
Ojo Caliente, Mex. (ōkō käl-yĕn'tȧ)	112	21.50N	100.43W
Ojo del Toro, Pico, mtn., Cuba (pē'kô-ô-kō-dĕl-tô'rô)	116	19.55N	77.25W
Oka, Can. (ō-kä)	77a	45.28N	74.05W
Oka, r., Russia (ô-kȧ')	160	55.10N	42.10E
Oka, r., Russia (ô-kȧ')	160	52.10N	35.20E
Oka, r., Russia (ō-kä')	162	53.28N	101.09E
Okahandja, Nmb.	206	21.50S	16.45E
Okanagan (Okanogan), r., N.A. (ō'kȧ-näg'ǎn)	80	49.06N	119.43W
Okanagan Lake, l., Can.	78	50.00N	119.28W
Okano, r., Gabon (ō'kä'nō)	204	0.15N	11.08E
Okanogan, Wa., U.S.	98	48.20N	119.34W
Okanogan, r., Wa., U.S.	98	48.36N	119.33W
Okatibbee, r., Ms., U.S. (ō'kä-tĭb'ē)	108	32.37N	88.54W
Okatoma Creek, r., Ms., U.S. (ô-kȧ-tō'mä)	108	31.43N	89.34W
Okavango (Cubango), r., Afr.	206	18.00S	20.00E
Okavango Swamp, sw., Bots.	206	19.30S	23.02E
Okaya, Japan (ō'kȧ-yȧ)	187	36.04N	138.01E
Okayama, Japan (ō'kȧ-yä'mȧ)	180	34.39N	133.54E
Okazaki, Japan (ō'kȧ-zä'kē)	186	34.58N	137.09E
Okeechobee, Fl., U.S. (ō-kē-chō'bē)	108	27.15N	80.50W
Okeechobee, Lake, l., Fl., U.S.	90	27.00N	80.49W
O'Keefe Centre, bldg., Can.	223c	43.37N	79.22W
Okeene, Ok., U.S. (ō-kēn')	104	36.06N	98.19W
Okefenokee Swamp, sw., U.S. (ō'kē-fē-nō'kē)	108	30.54N	82.20W
Okemah, Ok., U.S. (ō-kē'mä)	104	35.26N	96.18W
Okene, Nig.	208	7.33N	6.15E
Oke Ogbe, Nig.	240d	6.24N	3.23E
Okha, Russia (ŭ-kä')	158	53.44N	143.12E
Okhotino, Russia (ô-kō'tĭ-nô)	164b	56.14N	38.24E
Okhotsk, Russia (ô-kôtsk')	158	59.28N	143.32E
Okhotsk, Sea of, sea, Asia (ô-kôtsk')	158	56.45N	146.00E
Okinawa, i., Japan	180	26.30N	128.00E
Okino, i., Japan (ō'kē-nō)	187	36.22N	133.27E
Ōkino Erabu, i., Japan (ō-kē'nō-ȧ-rä'bōō)	186	27.18N	129.00E
Oklahoma, state, U.S. (ō-klȧ-hō'mȧ)	90	36.00N	98.20W
Oklahoma City, Ok., U.S.	90	35.27N	97.32W
Oklawaha, r., Fl., U.S. (ŏk-lȧ-wô'hô)	108	29.13N	82.00W
Okmulgee, Ok., U.S. (ôk-mŭl'gē)	104	35.37N	95.58W
Okolona, Ky., U.S. (ō-kô-lō'nȧ)	95h	38.08N	85.41W
Okolona, Ms., U.S.	108	33.59N	88.43W
Okushiri, i., Japan (ō'koo-shē'rē)	186	42.12N	139.30E
Okuta, Nig.	208	9.14N	3.15E
Olalla, Wa., U.S. (ō-lä'lȧ)	100a	47.26N	122.33W
Olanchito, Hond. (ō'län-chē'tô)	114	15.28N	86.35W
Öland, i., Swe. (û-länd')	136	57.03N	17.15E
Olathe, Ks., U.S. (ō-lā'thē)	101f	38.53N	94.49W
Olavarría, Arg. (ō-lä-vär-rē'ä)	126	36.49N	60.15W
Oława, Pol. (ô-lä'vȧ)	148	50.57N	17.18E
Olazoago, Arg. (ô-läz-kôä'gô)	123c	35.14S	60.37W
Olbia, Italy (ô'l-byä)	154	40.55N	9.28E
Olching, Ger. (ōl'kēng)	139d	48.13N	11.21E
Old Bahama Channel, strt., N.A. (bȧ-hā'mȧ)	116	22.45N	78.30W
Old Bight, Bah.	116	24.15N	75.20W
Old Bridge, N.J., U.S. (brĭj)	94a	40.24N	74.22W
Old Brookville, N.Y., U.S.	224	40.49N	73.36W
Old Crow, Can. (crō)	78	67.51N	139.58W
Oldenburg, Ger. (ôl'dĕn-bōrgh)	140	53.09N	8.13E
Old Forge, Pa., U.S. (fôrj)	92	41.20N	75.50W
Oldham, Eng., U.K. (ōld'ǎm)	144	53.32N	2.07W
Oldham Pond, l., Ma., U.S.	223a	42.03N	70.51W
Old Harbor, Ak., U.S. (här'bĕr)	89	57.18N	153.20W
Old Head of Kinsale, c., Ire. (ōld hĕd ŏv kĭn-sāl)	144	51.35N	8.35W
Old Malden, neigh., Eng., U.K.	231	51.23N	0.15W
Old North Church, pt. of i., Ma., U.S.	223a	42.22N	71.03W
Old R, Tx., U.S.	107a	29.54N	94.52W
Olds, Can. (ōldz)	78	51.47N	114.06W
Old Tate, Bots.	206	21.18S	27.43E
Old Town, Me., U.S. (toun)	86	44.55N	68.42W
Old Westbury, N.Y., U.S.	224	40.47N	73.37W
Old Windsor, Eng., U.K.	231	51.28N	0.35W
Old Wives Lake, l., Can. (wīvz)	82	50.05N	106.00W
Olean, N.Y., U.S. (ō-lē-ăn')	90	42.05N	78.25W

PLACE (Pronunciation)	PAGE	Lat. °'	Long. °'
Olecko, Pol. (ô-lĕt'skô)	148	54.02N	22.29E
Olekma, r., Russia (ô-lyĕk-mȧ')	162	55.41N	120.33E
Olëkminsk, Russia (ô-lyĕk-mênsk')	158	60.39N	120.40E
Olenëk, r., Russia (ô-lyĕ-nyôk')	158	68.00N	113.00E
Oléron Île, d', i., Fr. (ēl' dō lā-rôN')	140	45.52N	1.58W
Oleśnica, Pol. (ô-lĕsh-nĭ'tsȧ)	140	51.13N	17.24E
Olfen, Ger. (ōl'fĕn)	151c	51.43N	7.22E
Ol'ga, Russia (ôl'gȧ)	158	43.48N	135.44E
Ol'gi, Zaliv, b., Russia (zä'lĭf ôl'gĭ)	186	43.43N	135.25E
Ol'gopol', Ukr. (ôl-gô-pôl'y')	156	48.11N	29.28E
Olhão, Port. (ôl-youN')	142	37.02N	7.54W
Olievenhoutpoort, S. Afr.	207b	25.58S	27.55E
Ólimbos, Grc.	142	40.03N	22.22E
Ólimbos, mtn., Cyp.	173a	34.56N	32.52E
Olinda, Austl.	239b	37.51S	145.22E
Olinda, Braz. (ô-lē'n-dä)	124	8.00S	34.58W
Olinda, Braz.	126b	22.49S	43.25W
Oliva, Spain (ô-lē'vä)	152	38.54N	0.07W
Oliva de la Frontera, Spain (ô-lē'vä dā)	152	38.33N	6.55W
Olivais, neigh., Port.	234d	34.46N	9.06W
Olive Hill, Ky., U.S. (ŏl'ĭv)	92	38.15N	83.10W
Olivelra, Braz. (ô-lē-vā'rä)	123a	20.42S	44.49W
Olive Mount, neigh., Eng., U.K.	233a	53.24N	2.55W
Olivenza, Spain (ō-lē-vĕn'thä)	152	38.42N	7.06W
Oliver, Can.	77g	53.38N	113.21W
Oliver, Can. (ŏ'lĭ-vĕr)	78	49.11N	119.33W
Oliver, Wi., U.S. (ŏ'lĭvĕr)	101h	46.39N	92.12W
Oliver Lake, l., Can.	77g	53.19N	113.00W
Olivia, Mn., U.S. (ō-lĭv'ē-ȧ)	96	44.46N	95.00W
Olivos, Arg. (ōlē'vōs)	126a	34.30S	58.29W
Ollagüe, Chile (ô-lyä'gȧ)	124	21.17S	68.17W
Ollerton, Eng., U.K. (ôl'ēr-tŭn)	138a	53.12N	1.02W
Olmos Park, Tx., U.S. (ōl'mŭs pärk')	101d	29.27N	98.32W
Olmsted, Oh., U.S.	225a	41.24N	81.44W
Olmsted Falls, Oh., U.S.	225a	41.22N	81.55W
Olney, Il., U.S. (ŏl'nĭ)	92	38.45N	88.05W
Olney, Or., U.S. (ŏl'nē)	100c	46.06N	123.45W
Olney, Tx., U.S.	104	33.24N	98.43W
Olney, neigh., Pa., U.S.	225b	40.02N	75.08W
Olomane, r., Can. (ō'lô mȧ'nē)	86	51.05N	60.50W
Olomouc, Czech. (ō'lô-mōts)	140	49.37N	17.15E
Olonets, Russia (ô-lô'nĕts)	146	60.58N	32.54E
Olongapo, Phil.	188	14.49S	120.17E
Oloron, Gave d', r., Fr. (gäv-dŏ-lō-rŏN')	150	43.21N	0.44W
Oloron-Sainte Marie, Fr. (ō-lô-rôNt'sǎNt mȧ-rē')	150	43.11N	1.37W
Olot, Spain (ô-lōt')	142	42.09N	2.30E
Olpe, Ger. (ōl'pē)	151c	51.02N	7.51E
Ol'shanka, Ukr. (ôl'shäŋ-kȧ)	156	48.14N	30.52E
Ol'shany, Ukr. (ôl'shȧn-ē)	156	50.02N	35.54E
Olsnitz, Ger. (ōlz'nĕtz)	148	50.25N	12.11E
Olsztyn, Pol. (ōl'shtĭn)	140	53.47N	20.28E
Olt, r., Rom.	142	44.09N	24.40E
Olten, Switz. (ōl'tĕn)	148	47.20N	7.53E
Oltenița, Rom. (ôl-tā'nĭ-tsȧ)	154	44.05N	26.39E
Olvera, Spain (ôl-vĕ'rä)	152	36.55N	5.16W
Olympia, Wa., U.S. (ō-lĭm'pĭ-ȧ)	90	47.02N	122.52W
Olympic Mountains, mts., Wa., U.S.	98	47.54N	123.58W
Olympic National Park, rec., Wa., U.S. (ō-lĭm'pĭk)	90	47.54N	123.00W
Olympieion, pt. of i., Grc.	235d	37.58N	23.44E
Olympus, Mount, mtn., Wa., U.S. (ō-lĭm'pŭs)	98	47.43N	123.30W
Olyphant, Pa., U.S. (ŏl'ĭ-fǎnt)	92	41.30N	75.40W
Olyutorskiy, Mys, c., Russia (ŭl-yōō'tŏr-skē)	158	59.49N	167.16E
Omae-Zaki, c., Japan (ō'mä-ȧ zä'kē)	187	34.37N	138.15E
Omagh, N. Ire., U.K. (ō'mä)	144	54.35N	7.25W
Omaha, Ne., U.S. (ō'mȧ-hä)	90	41.18N	95.57W
Omaha Indian Reservation, I.R., Ne., U.S.	96	42.09N	96.08W
Oman, nation, Asia	174	20.00N	57.45E
Oman, Gulf of, b., Asia	174	24.24N	58.58E
Omaruru, Nmb. (ō-mä-rōō'rōō)	206	21.25S	16.50E
Ombrone, r., Italy (ôm-brō'nä)	154	42.48N	11.18E
Omdurman, Sudan	204	15.45N	32.30E
Omealca, Mex. (ōmȧ-äl'kō)	112	18.44N	96.45W
Ometepec, Mex. (ō-mä-tȧ-pĕk')	112	16.41N	98.27W
Om Hajer, Eth.	204	14.06N	36.46E
Omineca, r., Can. (ō-mĭ-nĕk'ȧ)	80	55.50N	125.45W
Omineca Mountains, mts., Can.	80	56.00N	125.00W
Ōmiya, Japan (ō'mē-yȧ)	187	35.54S	139.38E
Omo, r., Eth. (ō'mō)	204	5.54N	36.09E
Omoa, Hond. (ō-mō'rä)	114	15.43N	88.03W
Omoko, Nig.	208	5.20N	6.39E
Omolon, r., Russia (ō'mō)	162	67.43N	159.15E
Ōmori, Japan (ō'mô-rē)	187a	35.50N	140.09E
Omotepe, Isla de, i., Nic. (ē's-lä-dĕ-ō-mô-tā'pȧ)	114	11.32N	85.30W
Omro, Wi., U.S. (ŏm'rō)	96	44.01N	89.46W
Omsk, Russia (ômsk)	158	55.12N	73.19E
Ōmura, Japan (ō'mōō-rȧ)	187	32.56N	129.57E
Ōmuta, Japan (ō'mô-tȧ)	187	33.02N	130.28E
Omutninsk, Russia (ō'mōō-tnēnsk)	160	58.38N	52.10E
Onawa, Ia., U.S. (ŏn-ȧ-wȧ)	96	42.02N	96.05W
Onaway, Mi., U.S.	92	45.25N	84.10W
Once, neigh., Arg.	229d	34.36S	58.24W
Oncócua, Ang.	210	16.34S	13.28E
Onda, Spain (ōn'dä)	152	39.58N	0.13W
Ondava, r., Czech. (ōn'dȧ-vȧ)	148	48.51N	21.40E
Ondo, Nig.	208	7.04N	4.47E
Öndörhaan, Mong.	180	47.20N	110.40E
Onega, Russia (ô-nyĕ'gȧ)	158	63.50N	38.08E
Onega, r., Russia	160	63.20N	39.20E

PLACE (Pronunciation)	PAGE	Lat. °'	Long. °'
Onega, Lake, *see* Onezhskoye Ozero, l., Russia	160	62.02N	34.35E
Oneida, N.Y., U.S. (ō-nī'dȧ)	92	43.05N	75.40W
Oneida, l., N.Y., U.S.	92	43.10N	76.00W
O'Neill, Ne., U.S. (ō-nēl')	96	42.28N	98.38W
Oneonta, N.Y., U.S. (ō-nē-ŏn'tȧ)	92	42.25N	75.05W
Onezhskaja Guba, b., Russia	160	64.30N	36.00E
Onezhskiy, Poluostrov, pen., Russia	160	64.30N	37.40E
Onezhskoye Ozero, Russia (ô-năsh'skô-yĕ ô'zĕ-rô)	160	62.02N	34.35E
Ongiin Hiid, Mong.	180	46.00N	102.46E
Ongole, India	178	15.36N	80.03E
Onilahy, r., Madag.	206	23.41S	45.00E
Onitsha, Nig. (ô-nĭt'shȧ)	204	6.09N	6.47W
Onomichi, Japan (ō'nô-mē'chē)	186	34.27N	133.12E
Onon, r., Asia (ô'nôn)	158	49.00N	112.00E
Onoto, Ven. (ô-nŏ'tô)	125b	9.38N	65.03W
Onslow, Austl. (ŏnz'lō)	196	21.53S	115.00E
Onslow B, N.C., U.S. (ônz'lō)	108	34.22N	77.35W
Ontake San, mtn., Japan (ôn'tä-kȧ sän)	186	35.55N	137.29E
Ontario, Ca., U.S. (ŏn-tā'rĭ-ō)	101a	34.04N	117.39E
Ontario, Or., U.S.	98	44.02N	116.57W
Ontario, prov., Can.	78	50.47N	88.50W
Ontario, Lake, l., N.A.	90	43.35N	79.05W
Ontario Science Centre, bldg., Can.	223c	43.43N	79.21W
Onteniente, Spain (ōn-tȧ-nyĕn'tā)	152	38.48N	0.35W
Ontonagon, Mi., U.S. (ŏn-tô-năg'ŏn)	96	46.50N	89.20W
Ōnuki, Japan (ō'nōō-kē)	187a	35.17N	139.51E
Oodnadatta, Austl. (ōōd'nȧ-dȧ'tȧ)	196	27.38S	135.40E
Ooldea Station, Austl. (ōōl-dā'ä)	196	30.35S	132.08E
Oologah Reservoir, res., Ok., U.S.	90	36.43N	95.32W
Ooltgensplaat, Neth.	139a	51.41N	4.19E
Oostanaula, r., Ga., U.S. (ōō-stȧ-nô'lȧ)	108	34.25N	85.10W
Oostende, Bel. (ōst-ĕn'dē)	140	51.14N	2.55E
Oosterhout, Neth.	139a	51.38N	4.52E
Ooster Schelde, r., Neth.	139a	51.40N	3.40E
Ootsa Lake, l., Can.	80	53.49N	126.18W
Opalaca, Sierra de, mts., Hond. (sē-sē'r-rä-dĕ-ô-pä-lä'kä)	114	14.30N	88.29W
Opasquia, Can. (ô-päs'kwē-ȧ)	82	53.16N	93.53W
Opatów, Pol. (ô-pä'tôf)	148	50.47N	21.25E
Opava, Czech. (ō'pä-vä)	148	49.56N	17.52E
Opelika, Al., U.S. (ŏp-ē-lī'kȧ)	108	32.39N	85.23W
Opelousas, La., U.S. (ŏp-ē-lōō'sȧs)	106	30.33N	92.04W
Opeongo, l., Can. (ŏp-ē-ôŋ'gō)	84	45.40N	78.20W
Opheim, Mt., U.S. (ō-fīm')	98	48.51N	106.19W
Ophir, Ak., U.S. (ō'fēr)	89	63.10N	156.28W
Ophir, Mount, mtn., Malay.	173b	2.22N	102.37E
Ophirton, neigh., S. Afr.	240b	26.14S	28.01E
Opico, El Sal. (ô-pē'kō)	114	13.50N	89.23W
Opinaca, r., Can. (ŏp-ĭ-nä'kȧ)	78	52.28N	77.40W
Opladen, Ger. (ōp'lä-dĕn)	151c	51.04N	7.00E
Opobo, Nig.	208	4.34N	7.27E
Opochka, Russia (ō-pôch'kȧ)	160	56.43N	28.39E
Opoczno, Pol. (ô-pôch'nô)	148	51.22N	20.18E
Opole, Pol. (ô-pôl'ȧ)	140	50.42N	17.55E
Opole Lubelskie, Pol. (ô-pō'lă lōō-bĕl'skyĕ)	148	51.09N	21.58E
Oposhnya, Ukr. (ô-pôsh'nyȧ)	156	49.57N	34.34E
Opp, Al., U.S. (ŏp)	108	31.18N	86.15W
Oppdal, Nor. (ôp'däl)	146	62.37N	9.41E
Opportunity, Wa., U.S. (ŏp-ŏr tū'nĭ tĭ)	98	47.37N	117.20W
Oppum, neigh., Ger.	232	51.19N	6.37E
Oquirrh Mountains, mts., Ut., U.S. (ō'kwēr)	101b	40.38N	112.11W
Oradea, Rom. (ô-räd'yä)	136	47.02N	21.55E
Oradell, N.J., U.S.	224	40.57N	74.02W
Oran, Alg. (ō-rän)(ō-räN')	204	35.46N	0.45W
Orán, Arg. (ō-rá'n)	126	23.13S	64.17W
Oran, Mo., U.S. (ôr'ǎn)	104	37.05N	89.39W
Oran, Sebkha d', l., Alg.	152	35.28N	0.28W
Orange, Austl. (ŏr'ĕnj)	196	33.15S	149.08E
Orange, Fr. (ô-ränzh')	140	44.08N	4.48E
Orange, Ca., U.S.	101a	33.48N	117.51W
Orange, Ct., U.S.	92	41.15N	73.00W
Orange, N.J., U.S.	94a	40.46N	74.14W
Orange, Tx., U.S.	104	30.07N	93.44W
Orange, r., Afr.	206	29.15S	17.30E
Orange, Cabo, c., Braz. (kȧ-bô-rȧ'n-zhĕ)	124	4.25N	51.30W
Orangeburg, S.C., U.S. (ŏr'ĕnj-bûrg)	108	33.30N	80.50W
Orange Cay, i., Bah. (ŏr-ĕnj kē)	116	24.55N	79.05W
Orange City, Ia., U.S.	96	43.01N	96.06W
Orange Free State, prov., S. Afr.	206	28.15S	26.00E
Orange Grove, neigh., S. Afr.	240b	26.10S	28.05E
Orange Lake, l., Fl., U.S.	108	29.30N	82.12W
Orangeville, Can. (ŏr'ĕnj-vĭl)	84	43.55N	80.06W
Orangeville, S. Afr.	212d	27.05S	28.13E
Orange Walk, Belize (wôl'k)	114a	18.09N	88.32W
Orani, Phil. (ō-rä'nē)	189a	14.47N	120.32E
Oranienburg, Ger. (ō-rä'nē-ĕn-bōrgh)	148	52.45N	13.14E
Oranjemund, Nmb.	206	28.33S	16.20E
Orăştie, Rom. (ô-rŭsh'tyȧ)	154	45.50N	23.14E
Orbetello, Italy (ôr-bȧ-tĕl'lō)	154	42.27N	11.15E
Orbigo, r., Spain (ôr-bē'gō)	152	42.30N	5.55W
Orbost, Austl. (ôr'bŭst)	198	37.43S	148.20E
Orcas, i., Wa., U.S. (ôr'kȧs)	100d	48.43N	122.52W
Orchard Farm, Mo., U.S. (ôr'chĕrd färm)	101e	38.53N	90.27W
Orchard Park, N.Y., U.S.	95c	42.46N	78.46W
Orchards, Wa., U.S. (ôr'chĕdz)	100c	45.40N	122.33W
Orchila, Isla, i., Ven.	124	11.47N	66.34W
Ord, Ne., U.S. (ôrd)	96	41.36N	98.57W
Ord, r., Austl.	196	17.30S	128.40E
Ord, Mount, mtn., Az., U.S.	102	33.55N	109.40W
Orda, Russia (ôr'dȧ)	164a	57.10N	57.12E
Órdenes, Spain (ôr'dȧ-nās)	152	43.00N	8.24W

ăt; finǎl; rāte; senāte; ärm; ȧsk; sofȧ; fâre; ch-choose; dh-as th in other; bē; ēvent; bĕt; recĕnt; cratēr; g-gō; gh-guttural g; bĭt; ĭ-short neutral; rīde; κ-guttural k as ch in German ich;

PLACE (Pronunciation)	PAGE	Lat. °′	Long. °′
Ordos Desert, des., China	180	39.12N	108.10E
Ordu, Tur. (ôr′dò)	142	41.00N	37.50E
Ordway, Co., U.S. (ôrd′wā)	104	38.11N	103.46W
Örebro, Swe. (û′rē-brō)	140	59.16N	15.11E
Oredezh, r., Russia (ô′rĕ-dězh)	164c	59.23N	30.21E
Oregon, Il., U.S.	96	42.01N	89.21W
Oregon, state, U.S.	90	43.40N	121.50W
Oregon Caves National Monument, rec., Or., U.S. (cāvz)	98	42.05N	123.13W
Oregon City, Or., U.S.	100c	45.21N	122.36W
Öregrund, Swe. (û-rĕ-grònd)	146	60.20N	18.26E
Orekhov, Ukr. (ôr-yĕ′ĸôf)	156	47.34N	35.51E
Orekhovo, Bul.	154	43.43N	23.59E
Orekhovo-Zuyevo, Russia (ôr-yĕ′ĸô-vô zò′yĕ-vô)	158	55.46N	39.00E
Orël, Russia (ôr-yôl′)	158	52.59N	36.05E
Orël, prov., Russia	156	52.35N	36.08E
Orel′, r., Ukr.	156	49.08N	34.55E
Oreland, Pa., U.S.	225b	40.07N	75.11W
Orem, Ut., U.S. (ŏ′rĕm)	102	40.15N	111.50W
Ore Mountains, *see* Erzgebirge, mts., Eur.	136	50.29N	12.40E
Orenburg, Russia (ô′rĕn-bōōrg)	158	51.50N	55.05E
Orense, Spain (ô-rĕn′sā)	152	42.20N	7.52W
Øresund, strt., Eur.	146	55.50N	12.40E
Órganos, Sierra de los, mts., Cuba (sē-ĕ′r-rá-dĕ-lôs-ŏ′r-gä-nôs)	116	22.20N	84.10W
Organ Pipe Cactus National Monument, rec., Az., U.S. (ôr′găn pīp kăk′tŭs)	102	32.14N	113.05W
Orgãos, Serra das, mtn., Braz. (sĕ′r-rä-däs-ôr-gouɴ′s)	123a	22.30S	43.01W
Orhon, r., Mong.	180	48.33N	103.07E
Oriental, Cordillera, mts., Col. (kôr-dēl-yĕ′rä)	124a	3.30N	74.27W
Oriental, Cordillera, mts., Dom. Rep. (kôr-dēl-yĕ′rä-ô-ryĕ′n-täl)	116	18.55N	69.40W
Oriental, Cordillera, mts., S.A. (kôr-dēl-yĕ′rä ō-rē-ĕn-täl′)	124	14.00S	68.33W
Orihuela, Spain (ō′rê-wā′lä)	152	38.04N	0.55W
Orillia, Can. (ô-rĭl′ĭ-*á*)	78	44.35N	79.25W
Orin, Wy., U.S.	98	42.40N	105.10W
Orinda, Ca., U.S.	100b	37.53N	122.11W
Orinoco, Río, r., Ven. (rē′ō-ô-rĭ-nō′kō)	124	8.32N	63.13W
Orion, Phil. (ō-rē-ōn′)	189a	14.37N	120.34E
Orissa, state, India (ō-rĭs′*á*)	174	25.09N	83.50E
Oristano, Italy (ô-rês-tä′nō)	142	39.53N	8.38E
Oristano, Golfo di, b., Italy (gôl-fô-dē-ô-rês-tä′nō)	154	39.53N	8.12E
Orituco, r., Ven. (ô-rē-tōō′kō)	125b	9.37N	66.25W
Oriuco, r., Ven. (ô-rēōō′kō)	125b	9.36N	66.25W
Orivesi, l., Fin.	146	62.15N	29.55E
Orizaba, Mex. (ô-rê-zä′bä)	110	18.52N	97.05E
Orizaba, Pico de, vol., Mex.	110	19.04N	97.14W
Orkanger, Nor.	146	63.19N	9.54W
Orkhey, Mol.	160	47.27N	28.49E
Orkla, r., Nor. (ôr′klȧ)	146	62.55N	9.50E
Orkney, S. Afr. (ôrk′nĭ)	212d	26.58S	26.39E
Orkney Islands, is., Scot., U.K.	136	59.01N	2.08W
Orlando, S. Afr. (ôr-lăn-dô)	207b	26.15S	27.56E
Orlando, Fl., U.S. (ôr-lăn′dō)	90	28.32N	81.22W
Orlando West Extension, S. Afr.	240b	26.15S	27.54E
Orland Park, Il., U.S. (ôr-lăn′)	95a	41.38N	87.52W
Orleans, Can. (ôr-lȧ-äɴ′)	77c	45.28N	75.31W
Orléans, Fr. (ôr-lā-äɴ′)	136	47.55N	1.56E
Orleans, In., U.S. (ôr-lēnz′)	92	38.40N	86.25W
Orléans, Île d′, i., Can.	84	46.56N	70.57W
Orly, Fr.	151b	48.45N	2.24E
Ormond, Austl.	239b	37.54S	145.03E
Ormond Beach, Fl., U.S. (ôr′mŏnd)	108	29.15N	81.05W
Ormskirk, Eng., U.K. (ôrms′kĕrk)	138a	53.34N	2.53W
Ormstown, Can. (ôrms′toun)	77a	45.07N	74.00W
Orneta, Pol. (ôr-nyĕ′tä)	148	54.07N	20.10E
Örnsköldsvik, Swe. (ûrn′skôlts-vēk)	140	63.10N	18.32E
Oro, Río del, r., Mex.	102	26.04N	105.40W
Oro, Río del, r., Mex. (rē′ō dĕl ō′rō)	112	18.04N	100.59W
Orobie, Alpi, mts., Italy (äl′pē-ô-rō′byĕ)	154	46.05N	9.47E
Oron, Nig.	208	4.48N	8.14E
Orosei, Golfo di, b., Italy (gôl-fô-dē-ō-rô-sā′ē)	154	40.12N	9.45E
Orosháza, Hung. (ô-rôsh-hä′sô)	148	46.33N	20.31E
Orosi, vol., C.R. (ō-rō′sē)	114	11.00N	85.30W
Oroville, Ca., U.S. (ŏr′ô-vĭl)	102	39.29N	121.34W
Oroville, Wa., U.S.	98	48.55N	119.25W
Oroville, Lake, res., Ca., U.S.	102	39.32N	121.25W
Orpington, neigh., Eng., U.K.	231	51.23N	0.06E
Orrville, Oh., U.S. (ôr′vĭl)	92	40.45N	81.50W
Orsa, Swe. (ōr′sä)	146	61.08N	14.35E
Orsay, Fr.	233c	48.42N	2.11E
Orsett, Eng., U.K.	231	51.31N	0.22E
Orsha, Bela. (ôr′shȧ)	160	54.29N	30.28E
Orsk, Russia (ôrsk)	158	51.15N	58.50E
Orşova, Rom. (ôr′shô-vä)	154	44.43N	22.26E
Orsoy, Ger.	232	51.31N	6.41E
Ortega, Col. (ôr-tĕ′gä)	124a	3.56N	75.12W
Ortegal, Cabo, c., Spain (kä′bô-ôr-tä-gäl′)	142	43.46N	8.15W
Orth, Aus.	139e	48.09N	16.42E
Orthez, Fr. (ôr-tĕz′)	152	43.29N	0.43W
Ortigueira, Spain (ôr-tê-gā′ê-rä)	142	43.40N	7.50W
Orting, Wa., U.S. (ôrt′ĭng)	100a	47.06N	122.12W
Ortona, Italy (ôr-tō′nä)	154	42.22N	14.22E
Ortonville, Mn., U.S. (ôr-t*ŭ*n-vĭl)	96	45.18N	96.26W
Oruba, Nig.	240d	6.35N	3.25E
Orūmīyeh, Iran	174	37.30N	45.15E
Orūmīyeh, Daryacheh-ye, l., Iran	174	38.01N	45.17E

PLACE (Pronunciation)	PAGE	Lat. °′	Long. °′
Oruro, Bol. (ô-rōō′rō)	124	17.57S	66.59W
Orvieto, Italy (ôr-vyâ′tō)	154	42.43N	12.08E
Oryu-dong, neigh., S. Kor.	237b	37.29N	126.51E
Osa, Russia (ô′sȧ)	160	57.18N	55.25E
Osa, Península de, pen., C.R. (ō′sä)	114	8.30N	83.25W
Osage, Ia., U.S. (ō′sāj)	96	43.16N	92.49W
Osage, N.J., U.S.	225b	39.51N	75.01W
Osage, r., Mo., U.S.	104	38.10N	93.12W
Osage City, Ks., U.S. (ō′sāj sĭ′tĭ)	104	38.28N	95.53W
Ōsaka, Japan (ō′sä-kä)	180	34.40N	135.27E
Ōsaka, dept., Japan	187b	34.45N	135.36E
Osaka Castle, hist., Japan	238b	34.41N	135.32E
Ōsaka-Wan, b., Japan (wän)	186	34.34N	135.16E
Osakis, Mn., U.S. (ô-sā′kĭs)	96	45.51N	95.09W
Osakis, l., Mn., U.S.	96	45.55N	94.55W
Osasco, Braz.	230d	23.32S	46.46W
Osawatomie, Ks., U.S. (ŏs-*á*-wăt′ô-mê)	104	38.29N	94.57W
Osborne, Ks., U.S. (ŏz′b*ŭ*rn)	104	39.25N	98.42W
Osceola, Ar., U.S. (ŏs-ē-ō′lȧ)	104	35.42N	89.58W
Osceola, Ia., U.S.	96	41.04N	93.45W
Osceola, Mo., U.S.	104	38.02N	93.41W
Osceola, Ne., U.S.	96	41.11N	97.34W
Oscoda, Mi., U.S. (ŏs-kō′d*á*)	92	44.25N	83.20W
Osëtr, r., Russia (ô′sĕt′r)	156	54.27N	38.15E
Osgood, In., U.S. (ŏz′gòd)	92	39.10N	85.20W
Osgoode, Can.	77c	45.09N	75.37W
Osh, Kyrg. (ôsh)	158	40.33N	72.48E
Oshawa, Can. (ŏsh′*á*-w*á*)	78	43.50N	78.50W
Ōshima, i., Japan (ō′shē′mä)	187	34.47N	139.35E
Oshkosh, Ne., U.S. (ŏsh′kŏsh)	96	41.24N	102.22W
Oshkosh, Wi., U.S.	90	44.01N	88.35W
Oshmyany, Bela. (ôsh-myä′nĭ)	146	54.27N	25.55E
Oshodi, Nig.	240d	6.34N	3.21E
Oshogbo, Nig.	204	7.47N	4.34E
Osijek, Cro. (ôs′ĭ-yĕk)	142	45.33N	18.48E
Osinniki, Russia (ŭ-sē′nyĭ-kē)	162	53.37N	87.21E
Oskaloosa, Ia., U.S. (ŏs-k*á*-lōō′s*á*)	96	41.16N	92.40W
Oskarshamm, Swe. (ôs′kärs-häm′n)	146	57.16N	16.24E
Oskarström, Swe. (ôs′kärs-strûm)	146	56.48N	12.55E
Oskol, r., Eur. (ôs-kôl′)	160	51.00N	37.41E
Oslo, Nor. (ôs′lō)	136	59.56N	10.41E
Oslofjorden, fj., Nor.	146	59.03N	10.35E
Osmaniye, Tur.	142	37.10N	36.30E
Osnabrück, Ger. (ôs-nä-brük′)	148	52.16N	8.05E
Osorno, Chile (ô-sō′r-nō)	126	40.42S	73.13W
Osorun, Nig.	240d	6.33N	3.29E
Osøyra, Nor.	146	60.24N	5.22E
Osprey Reef, rf., Austl. (ŏs′prå)	196	14.00S	146.45E
Ossa, Mount, mtn., Austl. (ŏs*á*)	196	41.45S	146.05E
Ossenberg, Ger.	232	51.34N	6.35E
Osseo, Mn., U.S. (ŏs′sē-ō)	101g	45.07N	93.24W
Ossining, N.Y., U.S. (ŏs′ĭ-nĭng)	94a	41.09N	73.51W
Ossipee, N.H., U.S. (ŏs′ĭ-pê)	86	43.42N	71.08W
Ossjøen, l., Nor. (ôs-syûēn)	146	61.20N	12.00E
Ossum-Bösinghoven, Ger.	232	51.18N	6.39E
Ostankino, neigh., Russia	235b	55.49N	37.37E
Ostashkov, Russia (ôs-täsh′kôf)	160	57.07N	33.04E
Oster, Ukr. (ōs′tĕr)	156	50.55N	30.52E
Osterdalälven, r., Swe.	140	61.40N	13.00E
Osterfeld, neigh., Ger.	232	51.30N	6.53E
Østerfjord, fj., Nor. (ûs′tĕr fyôr′)	146	60.40N	5.25E
Östersund, Swe. (ûs′tĕr-sōōnd)	140	63.09N	14.49E
Östhammar, Swe. (ûst′häm′är)	146	60.16N	18.21E
Ostrava, Czech.	136	49.51N	18.18E
Ostróda, Pol. (ôs′trôt-ä)	148	53.41N	19.58E
Ostrog, Ukr. (ŏs-trôk′)	160	50.21N	26.40E
Ostrogozhsk, Russia (ôs-tr-gôzhk′)	160	50.53N	39.03E
Ostrołęka, Pol. (ôs-trô-wóɴ′kà)	148	53.04N	21.35E
Ostropol′, Ukr. (ôs-trô-pôl′)	156	49.48N	27.32E
Ostrov, Russia (ôs-trôf′)	160	57.21N	28.22E
Ostrov, Russia	235b	55.35N	37.51E
Ostrowiec Świętokrzyski, Pol. (ôs-trō′vyĕts shvyĕɴ-tō-kzhĭ′ske)	140	50.55N	21.24E
Ostrów Lubelski, Pol. (ôs′trôf lōō′bĕl-skĭ)	148	51.32N	22.49E
Ostrów Mazowiecka, Pol. (mä-zô-vyĕt′skä)	140	52.47N	21.54E
Ostrów Wielkopolski, Pol. (ôs′trōōf vyĕl-kō-pōl′skē)	140	51.38N	17.49E
Ostrzeszów, Pol. (ôs-tzhā′shôf)	148	51.26N	17.56E
Ostuni, Italy (ôs-tōō′nē)	154	40.44N	17.35E
Osum, r., Alb. (ō′sòm)	154	40.37N	20.00E
Osuna, Spain (ô-sōō′nä)	152	37.18N	5.05W
Osveya, Bela. (ôs′vĕ-yȧ)	156	56.00N	28.08E
Oswaldtwistle, Eng., U.K. (ŏz-w*ă*ld-twĭs′'l)	138a	53.44N	2.23W
Oswegatchie, r., N.Y., U.S. (ŏs-wê-găch′ĭ)	92	44.15N	75.20W
Oswego, Ks., U.S. (ŏs-wē′gō)	104	37.10N	95.08W
Oswego, N.Y., U.S.	90	43.25N	76.30W
Oświęcim, Pol. (ôsh-vyăɴ′tsyĭm)	148	50.02N	19.17E
Otaru, Japan (ō′tȧ-rò)	180	43.07N	141.00E
Otavalo, Ec. (ōtä-vä′lō)	124	0.14N	78.16W
Otavi, Nmb. (ô-tä′vê)	206	19.35S	17.20E
Otay, Ca., U.S. (ō′tä)	102a	32.36N	117.04W
Otepää, Est.	146	58.03N	26.30E
Otford, Eng., U.K.	231	51.19N	0.12E
Óthris, Óros, mtn., Grc.	154	39.00N	22.15E
Oti, r., Afr.	208	9.00N	0.10E
Otish, Monts, mts., Can. (ô-tĭsh′)	78	52.15N	70.20W
Otjiwarongo, Nmb. (ŏt-jê-wȧ-rôn′gō)	206	20.20S	16.25E
Otočac, Cro. (ō′tô-chàts)	154	44.53N	15.15E
Otra, r., Nor.	146	59.13N	7.20E
Otra, r., Russia (ôt′rȧ)	164b	55.22N	38.20E
Otradnoye, Russia (ô-trȧ′d-nôyĕ)	164c	59.46N	30.50E

PLACE (Pronunciation)	PAGE	Lat. °′	Long. °′
Otranto, Italy (ô′trän-tô) (ô-trăn′tō)	154	40.07N	18.30E
Otranto, Strait of, strt., Eur.	136	40.30N	18.45E
Otsego, Mi., U.S. (ŏt-sē′gō)	92	42.25N	85.45W
Otsu, Japan (ō′tsò)	186	35.00N	135.54E
Otta, l., Nor. (ôt′tȧ)	146	61.53N	8.40E
Ottakring, neigh., Aus.	235e	48.12N	16.19E
Ottavia, neigh., Italy	235c	41.58N	12.24E
Ottawa, Can. (ŏt′*á*-w*á*)	78	45.25N	75.43W
Ottawa, Il., U.S.	92	41.20N	88.50W
Ottawa, Ks., U.S.	104	38.37N	95.16W
Ottawa, Oh., U.S.	92	41.00N	84.00W
Ottawa, r., Can.	78	46.05N	77.20W
Otter Creek, r., Ut., U.S. (ŏt′ẽr)	102	38.20N	111.55W
Otter Creek, r., Vt., U.S.	92	44.05N	73.15W
Otter Point, c., Can.	100a	48.21N	123.50W
Ottershaw, Eng., U.K.	231	51.22N	0.32W
Otter Tail, l., Mn., U.S.	96	46.21N	95.52W
Otterville, Il., U.S. (ŏt′ẽr-vĭl)	101e	39.03N	90.24W
Ottery, S. Afr. (ŏt′ẽr-ĭ)	206a	34.02S	18.31E
Ottumwa, Ia., U.S. (ô-tŭm′w*á*)	90	41.00N	92.26W
Otukpa, Nig.	208	7.09N	7.41E
Otumba, Mex. (ô-tŭm′bä)	112	19.41N	98.46W
Otway, Cape, c., Austl. (ŏt′wā)	196	38.55S	153.40E
Otway, Seno, b., Chile (sĕ′nō-ô′t-wä′y)	126	53.00S	73.00W
Otwock, Pol. (ôt′vôtsk)	148	52.05N	21.18E
Ouachita, r., U.S.	90	33.25N	92.30W
Ouachita Mountains, mts., U.S. (wŏsh′ĭ-tô)	90	34.29N	95.01W
Ouagadougou, Burkina (wä′gȧ-dōō′gōō)	204	12.22N	1.31W
Ouahigouya, Burkina (wä-ê-gōō′yä)	204	13.35N	2.25W
Oualâta, Maur. (wä-lä′tä)	204	17.11N	6.50W
Ouallene, Alg. (wäl-lân′)	204	24.43N	1.15E
Ouanaminthe, Haiti	116	19.35N	71.45W
Ouarane, reg., Maur.	204	20.44N	10.27W
Ouarkoye, Burkina	208	12.05N	3.40W
Ouassel, r., Alg.	152	35.30N	1.55E
Oubangui (Ubangi), r., Afr. (ōō-băŋ′gē)	210	4.30N	20.35E
Oude Rijn, r., Neth.	139a	52.09N	4.33E
Oudewater, Neth.	139a	52.01N	4.52E
Oud-Gastel, Neth.	139a	51.35N	4.27E
Oudtshoorn, S. Afr. (outs′hōrn)	206	33.33S	23.36E
Oued Rhiou, Alg.	152	35.55N	0.57E
Oued Tlelat, Alg.	152	35.33N	0.28W
Oued-Zem, Mor. (wĕd-zĕm′)	204	33.05N	5.49W
Ouessant, Island d′, i., Fr. (ēl-dwĕ-säɴ′)	140	48.28N	5.00W
Ouesso, Congo	204	1.37N	16.04E
Ouest, Point, c., Haiti	116	19.00N	73.25W
Ouezzane, Mor. (wĕ-zan′)	204	34.48N	5.40W
Ouham, r., Afr.	208	8.30N	17.50E
Ouidah, Benin (wē-dä′)	204	6.25N	2.05E
Oujda, Mor.	204	34.41N	1.45W
Oulins, Fr. (ōō-lăɴ′)	151b	48.52N	1.27E
Oullins, Fr. (ōō-lăɴ′)	150	45.44N	4.46E
Oulu, Fin. (ō′lò)	136	64.58N	25.43E
Oulujärvi, l., Fin.	140	64.20N	25.48E
Oum Chalouba, Chad (ōōm shä-lōō′bä)	204	15.48N	20.30E
Oum Hadjer, Chad	208	13.18N	19.41E
Ounas, r., Fin. (ō′nȧs)	140	67.46N	24.40E
Oundle, Eng., U.K. (ôn′d'l)	138a	52.28N	0.28W
Ounianga Kébir, Chad (ōō-nê-äŋ′gȧ kē-bēr′)	204	19.04N	20.22E
Ouray, Co., U.S. (ōō-rā′)	104	38.00N	107.40W
Ourinhos, Braz. (ôò-rē′nyôs)	124	23.04S	49.45W
Ourique, Port. (ō-rē′kĕ)	152	37.39N	8.10W
Ouro Fino, Braz. (ōŭ-rō-fē′nō)	123a	22.18S	46.21W
Ouro Prêto, Braz. (ō′rò prā′tò)	126	20.24S	43.30W
Outardes, Rivière aux, r., Can.	78	50.53N	68.50W
Outer, i., Wi., U.S. (out′ẽr)	96	47.03N	90.20W
Outer Brass, i., V.I.U.S. (bräs)	111c	18.24N	64.58W
Outer Hebrides, is., Scot., U.K.	144	57.20N	7.50W
Outjo, Nmb. (ōt′yō)	206	20.05S	17.10E
Outlook, Can.	82	51.31N	107.05W
Outremont, Can. (ōō-trē-môɴ′)	77a	45.31N	73.36W
Ouvéa, i., N. Cal.	196	20.43S	166.48E
Ouyen, Austl. (ōō-*ĕ*n)	198	35.05S	142.10E
Ovalle, Chile (ō-väl′yä)	126	30.43S	71.16W
Ovando, Bahía de, b., Cuba (bä-ē′ä-dĕ-ô-vä′n-dō)	116	20.10N	74.05W
Ovar, Port. (ô-vär′)	152	40.52N	8.38W
Overbrook, neigh., Pa., U.S.	225b	39.58N	75.16W
Overbrook, neigh., Pa., U.S.	226b	40.24N	79.59W
Overijse, Bel.	139a	50.46N	4.32E
Overland, Mo., U.S. (ō-vẽr-l*ă*nd)	101e	38.42N	90.22W
Overland Park, Ks., U.S.	101f	38.59N	94.40W
Overlea, Md., U.S. (ō′vẽr-lā)(ō′vẽr-lē)	94e	39.21N	76.31W
Övertornea, Swe.	140	66.19N	23.31E
Ovidiopol′, Ukr.	156	46.15N	30.28E
Oviedo, Dom. Rep. (ô-vyĕ′dō)	116	17.50N	71.25W
Oviedo, Spain (ō-vē-ā′dhō)	136	43.22N	5.50W
Ovruch, Ukr. (ôv′ròch)	156	51.19N	28.51E
Owada, Japan (ō′wä-dȧ)	187a	35.49N	139.33E
Owambo, hist. reg., Nmb.	206	18.10S	15.00E
Owando, Congo	206	0.29S	15.55E
Owasco, l., N.Y., U.S. (ō-wăsk′kō)	92	42.50N	76.30W
Owase, Japan (ō′wä-shê)	187	34.03N	136.12E
Owego, N.Y., U.S. (ō-wē′gō)	92	42.05N	76.15W
Owen, Wi., U.S. (ō′ĕn)	96	44.56N	90.35W
Owensboro, Ky., U.S. (ō′ĕnz-bŭr-ô)	90	37.45N	87.05W
Owens Lake, l., Ca., U.S.	102	37.13N	118.20W
Owen Sound, Can. (ō′ĕn)	78	44.30N	80.55W
Owen Stanley Range, mts., Pap. N. Gui. (stăn′lê)	188	9.00S	147.30E
Owensville, In., U.S. (ō′ĕnz-vĭl)	92	38.15N	87.40W
Owensville, Mo., U.S.	104	38.20N	91.29W
Owensville, Oh., U.S.	95f	39.08N	84.07W

PLACE (Pronunciation)	PAGE	Lat. °′	Long. °′
Owenton, Ky., U.S. (ō'ĕn-tŭn)	92	38.35N	84.55W
Owerri, Nig. (ō-wĕr'ē)	204	5.26N	7.04E
Owings Mill, Md., U.S. (ōwĭngz mĭl)	94e	39.25N	76.50W
Owl Creek, r., Wy., U.S. (oul)	98	43.45N	108.46W
Owo, Nig.	208	7.15N	5.37E
Oworonsoki, Nig.	240d	6.33N	3.24E
Owosso, Mi., U.S. (ō-wŏs'ō)	92	43.00N	84.15W
Owyhee, r., U.S.	90	43.04N	117.45W
Owyhee, Lake, res., Or., U.S.	90	43.27N	117.30W
Owyhee, South Fork, r., Id., U.S.	98	42.07N	116.43W
Owyhee Mountains, mts., Id., U.S. (ō-wī'hē)	90	43.15N	116.48W
Oxbow, Can.	82	49.12N	102.11W
Oxchuc, Mex. (ôs-chōōk')	112	16.47N	92.24W
Oxford, Can. (ŏks'fẽrd)	86	45.44N	63.52W
Oxford, Eng., U.K.	140	51.43N	1.16W
Oxford, Al., U.S. (ŏks'fẽrd)	108	33.38N	80.46W
Oxford, Ma., U.S.	87a	42.07N	71.52W
Oxford, Mi., U.S.	92	42.50N	83.15W
Oxford, Ms., U.S.	108	34.22N	89.30W
Oxford, N.C., U.S.	108	36.17N	78.35W
Oxford, Oh., U.S.	92	39.30N	84.45W
Oxford Falls, Austl.	239a	33.44S	151.15E
Oxford Lake, l., Can.	82	54.51N	95.37W
Oxfordshire, co., Eng., U.K.	138b	51.36N	1.30W
Oxkutzcab, Mex. (ôx-kōō'tz-käb)	114a	20.18N	89.22W
Oxmoor, Al., U.S. (ŏks'mŏr)	94h	33.25N	86.52W
Oxnard, Ca., U.S. (ŏks'närd)	102	34.08N	119.12W
Oxon Hill, Md., U.S. (ŏks'ŏn hĭl)	94e	38.48N	77.00W
Oxshott, Eng., U.K.	231	51.20N	0.21W
Oyama, Japan	238a	35.36N	139.22E
Oyapock, r., S.A. (ō-yȧ-pŏk')	124	2.45N	52.15W
Oyem, Gabon	204	1.37N	11.35E
Øyeren, l., Nor. (ûĭĕrĕn)	146	59.50N	11.25E
Oymyakon, Russia (oi-myŭ-kôn')	158	63.14N	142.58E
Oyo, Nig. (ō'yō)	204	7.51N	3.56E
Oyodo, neigh., Japan	238b	34.43N	135.30E
Oyonnax, Fr. (ō-yō-näks')	150	46.16N	5.40E
Oyster Bay, N.Y., U.S.	94a	40.52N	73.32W
Oyster Bay Cove, N.Y., U.S.	224	40.52N	73.31W
Oyster Bayou, Tx., U.S.	107a	29.41N	94.33W
Oyster Creek, r., Tx., U.S. (ois'tẽr)	107a	29.13N	95.29W
Ozama, r., Dom. Rep. (ō-zä'mä)	116	18.45N	69.55W
Ozamiz, Phil. (ō-zä'mēz)	188	8.06N	123.43E
Ozark, Al., U.S. (ō'zärk)	108	31.28N	85.28W
Ozark, Ar., U.S.	104	35.29N	93.49W
Ozark Plateau, plat., U.S.	90	36.37N	93.56W
Ozarks, Lake of the, l., Mo., U.S. (ō'zärksz)	90	38.06N	93.26W
Ozëry, Russia (ô-zyô'rē)	156	54.53N	38.31E
Ozieri, Italy	142	40.38N	8.53E
Ozoir-la-Ferrière, Fr.	233c	48.46N	2.40E
Ozone Park, neigh., N.Y., U.S.	224	40.40N	73.51W
Ozorków, Pol. (ô-zôr'kôf)	148	51.58N	19.20E
Ozuluama, Mex.	112	21.34N	97.52W
Ozumba, Mex.	113a	19.02N	98.48W

P

PLACE (Pronunciation)	PAGE	Lat. °′	Long. °′
Paarl, S. Afr. (pärl)	206	33.45S	18.55E
Paarlshoop, neigh., S. Afr.	240b	26.13S	27.59E
Paauilo, Hi., U.S. (pä-ä-ōō'ē-lō)	88a	20.03N	155.25W
Pabianice, Pol. (pä-byȧ-nē'tsĕ)	148	51.40N	19.29E
Pacaás Novos, Massiço de, mts., Braz.	124	11.03S	64.02W
Pacaraima, Serra, mts., S.A. (sĕr'rȧ pä-kä-rä-ē'mȧ)	124	3.45N	62.30W
Pacasmayo, Peru (pä-käs-mä'yō)	124	7.24S	79.30W
Pachuca, Mex. (pä-chōō'kä)	110	20.07N	98.43W
Pacific, Wa., U.S. (pȧ-sĭf'ĭk)	100a	47.16N	122.15W
Pacifica, Ca., U.S. (pȧ-sĭf'ĭ-kä)	100b	37.38N	122.29W
Pacific Beach, Ca., U.S.	102a	32.47N	117.22W
Pacific Grove, Ca., U.S.	102	36.37N	121.54W
Pacific Ocean, o.	2	0.00	170.00W
Pacific Palisades, neigh., Ca., U.S.	228	34.03N	118.32W
Pacific Ranges, mts., Can.	80	51.00N	125.30W
Pacific Rim National Park, rec., Can.	80	49.00N	126.00W
Paço de Arcos, Port.	234d	38.42N	9.17W
Pacolet, r., S.C., U.S. (pă'cō-lĕt)	108	34.55N	81.49W
Pacy-sur-Eure, Fr. (pä-sē-sür-ûr')	151b	49.01N	1.24E
Padang, Indon. (pä-däng')	188	1.01S	100.28E
Padang, i., Indon.	173b	1.12N	102.21E
Padang Endau, Malay.	173b	2.39N	103.38E
Paddington, neigh., Eng., U.K.	231	51.31N	0.10W
Paden City, W.V., U.S. (pā'dĕn)	92	39.30N	80.55W
Paderborn, Ger. (pä-dĕr-bôrn')	148	51.43N	8.46E
Paderno Dugnano, Italy	234c	45.34N	9.10E
Padibe, Ug.	210	3.28N	32.50E
Padiham, Eng., U.K. (păd'ĭ-hăm)	138a	53.48N	2.19W
Padilla, Mex. (pä-dēl'yä)	112	24.00N	98.45W
Padilla Bay, b., Wa., U.S. (pä-dēl'lá)	100a	48.31N	122.34W
Padova, Italy (pä'dō-vä)(păd'ū-ȧ)	142	45.24N	11.53E
Padre Island, i., Tx., U.S. (pä'drā)	106	27.09N	97.15W
Padre Miguel, neigh., Braz.	230c	22.53S	43.26W
Padua, *see* Padova, Italy	142	45.24N	11.53E
Paducah, Ky., U.S.	90	37.05N	88.36W
Paducah, Tx., U.S.	104	34.01N	100.18W
Paektu-san, mtn., Asia (pâk'tōō-sän')	186	42.00N	128.03E
Pag, i., Yugo. (päg)	154	44.30N	14.48E
Pagai Selatan, Pulau, i., Indon.	188	2.48S	100.22E
Pagai Utara, Pulau, i., Indon.	188	2.45S	100.02E
Pagasitikós Kólpos, b., Grc.	154	39.15N	23.00E
Page, Az., U.S.	102	36.57N	111.27W
Pago Pago, Am. Sam.	192a	14.16S	170.42W
Pagosa Springs, Co., U.S. (pȧ-gō'sȧ)	104	37.15N	107.05W
Pagote, India	236e	18.54N	72.59E
Pahala, Hi., U.S. (pä-hä'lä)	88a	19.11N	155.28W
Pahang, state, Malay.	173b	3.02N	102.57E
Pahang, r., Malay.	188	3.39N	102.41E
Pahokee, Fl., U.S. (pȧ-hō'kē)	109a	26.45N	80.40W
Paide, Est. (pī'dĕ)	146	58.54N	25.30E
Päijänne, l., Fin. (pĕ'ē-yĕn-nĕ)	140	61.38N	25.05E
Pailolo Channel, strt., Hi., U.S. (pä-ē-lō'lō)	88a	21.05N	156.41W
Paine, Chile (pī'nĕ)	123b	33.49S	70.44W
Painesville, Oh., U.S. (pānz'vĭl)	92	41.40N	81.15W
Painted Desert, des., Az., U.S. (pānt'ĕd)	104	36.15N	111.35W
Painted Rock Reservoir, res., Az., U.S.	102	33.00N	113.05W
Paintsville, Ky., U.S. (pānts'vĭl)	92	37.50N	82.50W
Paisley, Austl.	239b	37.51S	144.51E
Paisley, Scot., U.K. (pāz'lĭ)	140	55.50N	4.30W
Paita, Peru (pä-ē'tä)	124	5.11S	81.12W
Pai T'ou Shan, mts., N. Kor.	180	40.30N	127.20E
Paiute Indian Reservation, I.R., Ut., U.S.	102	38.17N	113.50W
Pajápan, Mex. (pä-hä'pän)	112	18.16N	94.41W
Pakanbaru, Indon.	188	0.43N	101.15E
Pakhra, r., Russia (päĸ'rá)	164b	55.29N	37.51E
Pakistan, nation, Asia	174	28.00N	67.30E
Pakokku, Burma (pȧ-kŏk'kò)	180	21.29N	95.00E
Paks, Hung. (pôksh)	148	46.38N	18.53E
Pala, Chad	208	9.22N	14.54E
Palacios, Tx., U.S. (pä-lä'syōs)	106	28.42N	96.12W
Palagruža, Otoci, is., Yugo.	154	42.20N	16.23E
Palaión Fáliron, Grc.	235d	37.55N	23.41E
Palaiseau, Fr. (pȧ-lĕ-zō')	151b	48.44N	2.16E
Palana, Russia	158	59.07N	159.58E
Palanan Bay, b., Phil. (pä-lä'nän)	189a	17.14N	122.35E
Palanan Point, c., Phil.	189a	17.12N	122.40E
Pālanpur, India (pä'lŭn-pōōr)	174	24.08N	73.29E
Palapye, Bots. (pȧ-läp'yĕ)	206	22.34S	27.28E
Palatine, Il., U.S. (păl'ȧ-tīn)	95a	42.07N	88.03W
Palatka, Fl., U.S. (pȧ-lăt'kȧ)	108	29.39N	81.40W
Palau (Belau), dep., Oc. (pä-lä'ō)	2	7.15N	134.30E
Palauig, Phil. (pä-lou'ēg)	189a	15.27N	119.54E
Palawan, i., Phil. (pä-lä'wán)	188	9.50N	117.38E
Pālayankottai, India	178	8.50N	77.50E
Paldiski, Est. (päl'dĭ-skĭ)	146	59.22N	24.04E
Palembang, Indon. (pä-lĕm-bäng')	188	2.57S	104.40E
Palencia, Guat. (pä-lĕn'sē-á)	114	14.40N	90.22W
Palencia, Spain (pä-lĕ'n-syä)	142	42.02N	4.32W
Palenque, Mex. (pä-lĕŋ'kā)	112	17.34N	91.58W
Palenque, Punta, c., Dom. Rep. (pōō'n-tä)	116	18.10N	70.10W
Palermo, Col. (pä-lĕr'mô)	124a	2.53N	75.26W
Palermo, Italy	136	38.08N	13.24E
Palermo, neigh., Arg.	229d	34.35S	58.25W
Palestine, Tx., U.S.	90	31.46N	95.38W
Palestine, hist. reg., Asia (păl'ĕs-tīn)	173a	31.33N	35.00E
Paletwa, Burma (pŭ-lĕt'wä)	174	21.19N	92.52E
Palghāt, India	178	10.49N	76.40E
Pāli, India	178	25.53N	73.18E
Palín, Guat. (pä-lēn')	114	14.42N	90.42W
Palisades Park, N.J., U.S.	224	40.51N	74.00W
Palizada, Mex. (pä-lē-zä'dä)	112	18.17N	92.04W
Palk Strait, strt., Asia (pôk)	174	10.00N	79.23E
Palma, Braz. (päl'mä)	123a	21.23S	42.18W
Palma, Spain	136	39.35N	2.38E
Palma, Bahía de, b., Spain	152	39.24N	2.37E
Palma del Río, Spain	152	37.43N	5.19W
Palmar de Cariaco, Ven.	230a	10.34N	66.55W
Palmares, Braz. (päl-má'rĕs)	124	8.46S	35.28W
Palmas, Braz. (päl'mäs)	126	26.20S	51.56W
Palmas, Cape, c., Lib.	204	4.22N	7.44W
Palma Soriano, Cuba (sō-ré-ä'nō)	116	20.15N	76.00W
Palm Beach, Fl., U.S. (päm bēch')	109a	26.43N	80.03W
Palmeira dos Índios, Braz. (pä-mā'rä-dōs-ē'n-dyōs)	124	9.26S	36.33W
Palmeirinhas, Ponta das, c., Ang.	210	9.05S	13.00E
Palmela, Port. (päl-mä'lä)	152	38.34N	8.54W
Palmer, Ak., U.S. (päm'ẽr)	89	61.38N	149.15W
Palmer, Wa., U.S.	100a	47.19N	121.53W
Palmer Park, Md., U.S.	225d	38.55N	76.52W
Palmerston North, N.Z. (päm'ẽr-stŭn)	197a	40.20N	175.35W
Palmerville, Austl. (päm'ẽr-vĭl)	196	16.08S	144.15E
Palmetto, Fl., U.S. (pál-mĕt'ō)	109a	27.32N	82.34W
Palmetto Point, c., Bah.	116	21.15N	73.25W
Palmi, Italy (päl'mē)	154	38.21N	15.54E
Palmira, Col. (päl-mē'rä)	124	3.33N	76.17W
Palmira, Cuba	116	22.15N	80.25W
Palmyra, Mo., U.S. (păl-mī'rȧ)	104	39.45N	91.32W
Palmyra, N.J., U.S.	94f	40.01N	75.00W
Palmyra, i., Oc.	2	6.00N	162.20W
Palmyra, hist., Syria	174	34.25N	38.28E
Palmyras Point, c., India	178	20.42N	87.45E
Palo Alto, Ca., U.S. (pä'lō äl'tō)	100b	37.27N	122.09W
Paloduro Creek, r., Tx., U.S. (pā-lō-dōō'rō)	104	36.16N	101.12W
Paloh, Malay.	173b	2.11N	103.12E
Paloma, l., Mex. (pä-lō'mä)	106	26.53N	104.02W
Palomar Park, Ca., U.S.	227b	37.29N	122.16W
Palomo, Cerro el, mtn., Chile (sĕ'r-rō-ĕl-pä-lô'mô)	123b	34.36S	70.20W
Palos, Cabo de, c., Spain (kå'bô-dĕ-pä'lôs)	142	39.38N	0.43W
Palos Heights, Il., U.S.	227a	41.40N	87.48W
Palos Hills, Il., U.S.	227a	41.41N	87.49W
Palos Park, Il., U.S.	227a	41.40N	87.50W
Palos Verdes Estates, Ca., U.S. (pă'lŭs vûr'dĭs)	101a	33.48N	118.24W
Palouse, Wa., U.S. (pȧ-lōōz')	98	46.54N	117.04W
Palouse, r., Wa., U.S.	98	47.02N	117.35W
Palu, Tur. (pä-lōō')	160	38.55N	40.10E
Paluan, Phil. (pä-lōō'än)	189a	13.25N	120.29E
Pamiers, Fr. (pȧ-myā')	140	43.07N	1.34E
Pamirs, mts., Asia	174	38.14N	72.27E
Pamlico, r., N.C., U.S. (păm'lĭ-kō)	108	35.25N	76.59W
Pamlico Sound, strt., N.C., U.S.	90	35.10N	76.10W
Pampa, Tx., U.S. (păm'pȧ)	90	35.32N	100.56W
Pampa de Castillo, pl., Arg. (pä'm-pä-dĕ-käs-tē'l-yō)	126	45.30S	67.30W
Pampana, r., S.L.	208	8.35N	11.55W
Pampanga, r., Phil. (päm-päŋ'gä)	189a	15.20N	120.48E
Pampas, reg., Arg. (päm'päs)	126	37.00S	64.30W
Pampilhosa do Botão, Port. (päm-pē-lyō'sȧ-dō-bō-touɴ)	152	40.21N	8.32W
Pamplona, Col. (päm-plō'nä)	124	7.19N	72.41W
Pamplona, Spain (päm-plō'nä)	142	42.49N	1.39W
Pamunkey, r., Va., U.S. (pȧ-mŭŋ'kĭ)	92	37.40N	77.20W
Pana, Il., U.S. (pā'nȧ)	92	39.25N	89.05W
Panagyurishte, Bul. (pȧ-nȧ-gyōō'rēsh-tĕ)	154	42.30N	24.11E
Panaji (Panjim), India	174	15.33N	73.52E
Panamá, Pan.	110	8.58N	79.32W
Panama, nation, N.A.	110	9.00N	80.00W
Panamá, Istmo de, isth., Pan.	110	9.00N	80.00W
Panama City, Fl., U.S. (păn-ȧ mä' sĭ'tĭ)	108	30.08N	85.39W
Panamint Range, mts., Ca., U.S. (păn-ȧ-mĭnt')	102	36.40N	117.30W
Panarea, i., Italy (pä-nä'rĕ-ä)	154	38.37N	15.05E
Panaro, r., Italy (pä-nä'rō)	154	44.47N	11.06E
Panay, i., Phil. (pä-nī')	188	11.15N	121.38E
Pančevo, Yugo. (pán'chĕ-vô)	142	44.52N	20.42E
Pānchghara, India	236a	22.44N	88.16E
Panch'iao, Tai.	237d	25.01N	121.27E
Panchor, Malay.	173b	2.11N	102.43E
Pānchur, India	178a	22.31N	88.17E
Panda, Zaire (pän'dä')	206	10.59S	27.24E
Pan de Guajaibon, mtn., Cuba (pän dā gwä-jä-bōn')	116	22.50N	83.20W
Panevėžys, Lith. (pä'nyĕ-vāzh'ēs)	160	55.44N	24.21E
Panfilov, Kaz. (pŭn-fē'lôf)	158	44.12N	79.58E
Panga, Zaire (päŋ'gä)	204	1.51N	26.25E
Pangani, Tan. (pän-gä'nē)	206	5.28S	38.58E
Pangani, r., Tan.	210	4.40S	37.45E
Pangkalpinang, Indon. (päng-käl'pē-näng')	188	2.11S	106.04E
Pangnirtung, Can.	78	66.08N	65.26W
Panguitch, Ut., U.S. (păn'gwĭch)	102	37.50N	112.30W
Panié, Mont, mtn., N. Cal.	192f	20.36S	164.46E
Pānihāti, India	178a	22.42N	88.23E
Panimávida, Chile (pä-nē-má'vē-dä)	123b	35.44S	71.26W
Panje, India	236e	18.54N	72.57E
Pankow, neigh., Ger.	234a	52.34N	13.24E
Panshi, China (pän-shē)	184	42.50N	126.48E
Pantar, Pulau, i., Indon. (pän'tär)	188	8.40N	123.45E
Pantelleria, i., Italy (pän-tĕl-lå-rē'ä)	142	36.43N	11.59E
Pantepec, Mex. (pän-tå-pĕk')	112	17.11N	93.04W
Pantheon, hist., Italy	235c	41.54N	12.29E
Pantin, Fr.	233c	48.54N	2.24E
Pantitlán, Mex.	229a	19.25N	99.05W
Pánuco, Mex. (pä'nōō-kō)	112	23.25N	105.55W
Panuco, Mex. (pä'nōō-kō)	112	22.04N	98.11W
Panuco, r., Mex.	110	21.59N	98.20W
Pánuco de Coronado, Mex. (pä'nōō-kō dā kō-rō-nä'dhō)	106	24.33N	104.20W
Panvel, India	179b	18.59N	73.06E
Panyu, China (pä-yōō)	183a	22.56N	113.22E
Panzós, Guat. (pän-zós')	114	15.26N	89.40W
Pao, r., Ven. (pá'ō)	125b	9.52N	67.57W
Paola, Ks., U.S. (pā-ō'lȧ)	104	38.34N	94.51W
Paoli, In., U.S. (pā-ō'lĭ)	92	38.35N	86.30W
Paoli, Pa., U.S.	94f	40.03N	75.29W
Paonia, Co., U.S. (pā-ō'nyȧ)	102	38.50N	107.40W
Pápa, Hung. (pä'pô)	142	47.18N	17.27E
Papagayo, r., Mex. (pä-pä-gä'yō)	112	16.52NE99.41	W
Papagayo, Golfo del, b., C.R. (gôl-fô-dĕl-pä-pä-gá'yō)	114	10.44N	85.56W
Papagayo, Laguna, l., Mex. (lä-ō-nä)	112	16.44N	99.44W
Papago Indian Reservation, I.R., Az., U.S. (pá'pá'gō)	102	32.33N	112.12W
Papantla de Olarte, Mex. (pä-pän'tlä dā-ō-lä'r-tĕ)	110	20.30N	97.15W
Papatoapan, r., Mex. (pä-pä-tô-ä-pä'n)	112	18.00N	96.22W
Papelón, Ven.	230a	10.27N	66.47W
Papenburg, Ger. (päp'ĕn-bôrgh)	148	53.05N	7.23E
Papinas, Arg. (pä-pē'näs)	123c	35.30S	57.19W
Papineauville, Can. (pä-pē-nō'vĕl)	77c	45.38N	75.01W
Papua, Gulf of, b., Pap. N. Gui. (păp-ōō-ȧ)	188	8.20S	144.45E
Papua New Guinea, nation, Oc. (păp-ōō-ȧ)(gĭnē)	188	7.00S	142.15E
Papudo, Chile (pä-pōō'dō)	123b	32.30S	71.25W
Paquequer Pequeno, Braz. (pä-kĕ-kĕ'r-pĕ-kĕ'nō)	126b	22.19S	43.02W
Para, r., Russia	156	53.45N	40.58E
Paracale, Phil. (pä-rä-kä'lä)	189a	14.17N	122.47E

PLACE (Pronunciation)	PAGE	Lat. °′	Long. °′
Paracambi, Braz.	126b	22.36S	43.43W
Paracatu, Braz. (pä-rä-kä-tōō′)	124	17.17S	46.43W
Paracel Islands, is., Asia	188	16.40N	113.00E
Paraćin, Yugo. (pȧ′rä-chėn)	142	43.51N	21.26E
Para de Minas, Braz. (pä-rä-dě-mē′näs)	124	19.52S	44.37W
Paradise, i., Bah.	116	25.05N	77.20W
Paradise Valley, Nv., U.S. (păr′ȧ-dīs)	98	41.28N	117.32W
Parados, Cerro de los, mtn., Col. (sĕ′r-rô-dě-lôs-pä-rä′dōs)	124a	5.44N	75.13W
Paragould, Ar., U.S. (păr′ȧ-gōōld)	104	36.03N	90.29W
Paraguaçu, r., Braz. (pä-rä-gwä-zōō′)	124	12.25S	39.46W
Paraguay, nation, S.A. (păr′ȧ-gwā)	126	24.00S	57.00W
Paraguay, Río, r., S.A. (rē′ô-pä-rä-gwä′y)	126	21.12S	57.31W
Paraíba, state, Braz. (pä-rä-ē′bä)	124	7.11S	37.05W
Paraíba, r., Braz.	123a	23.02S	45.43W
Paraíba do Sul, Braz. (dô-sōō′l)	123a	22.10S	43.18W
Paraibuna, Braz. (pä-räē-bōō′nä)	123a	23.23S	45.38W
Paraíso, C.R.	114	9.50N	83.53W
Paraíso, Mex.	112	18.24N	93.11W
Paraiso, Pan. (pä-rä-ē′sō)	110a	9.02N	79.38W
Paraisópolis, Braz. (pä-räē-sô′pō-lēs)	123a	22.35S	45.45W
Paraitinga, r., Braz. (pä-rä-ē-tē′n-gä)	123a	23.15S	45.24W
Parakou, Benin (pȧ-rȧ-kōō′)	204	9.21N	2.37E
Paramaribo, Sur. (pȧ-rȧ-mȧ′rē-bō)	124	5.50N	55.15W
Paramatta, Austl. (păr-ȧ-măt′ȧ)	195b	33.49S	150.59E
Paramillo, mtn., Col. (pä-rä-mē′l-yō)	124a	7.06N	75.55W
Paramount, Ca., U.S.	228	33.53N	118.09W
Paramus, N.J., U.S.	94a	40.56N	74.04W
Paran, r., Asia	173a	30.05N	34.50E
Paraná, Arg.	126	31.44S	60.32W
Paraná, Río, r., S.A.	126	24.00S	54.00W
Paranaíba, Braz. (pä-rä-nä-ē′bȧ)	124	19.43S	51.13W
Paranaíba, r., Braz.	124	18.58S	50.44W
Paraná Ibicuy, r., Arg.	123c	33.27S	59.26W
Paranam, Sur.	124	5.39N	55.13W
Paranápanema, r., Braz. (pä-rä′nȧ′pä-nĕ-mä)	124	22.28S	52.15W
Parañaque, Phil.	237g	14.30N	120.59E
Paraopeda, r., Braz. (pä-rä-o-pĕ′dä)	123a	20.09S	44.14W
Parapara, Ven. (pä-rä-pä-rä)	125b	9.44N	67.17W
Parati, Braz. (pä-rätē)	123a	23.14S	44.43W
Paray-le-Monial, Fr. (pȧ-rĕ′lē-mô-nyäl′)	150	46.27N	4.14E
Pārbati, r., India	178	24.50N	76.44E
Parchim, Ger. (par′kĭm)	148	53.25N	11.52E
Parczew, Pol. (pär′chĕf)	148	51.38N	22.53E
Pardo, r., Braz.	123a	21.32S	46.40W
Pardo, r., Braz. (pär′dō)	124	15.25S	39.40W
Pardubice, Czech. (pär′dô-bĭt-sĕ)	148	50.02N	15.47E
Parecis, Serra dos, mts., Braz. (sĕr′rȧ dōs pä-rȧ-sēzh′)	124	13.45S	59.28W
Paredes de Nava, Spain (pä-rā′dås dä nä′vä)	152	42.10N	4.41W
Paredón, Mex.	106	25.56N	100.58W
Parent, Can.	78	47.59N	74.30W
Parent, Lac, l., Can.	84	48.40N	77.00W
Parepare, Indon.	188	4.01S	119.38E
Pargolovo, Russia (pȧr-gô′lô vô)	164c	60.04N	30.18E
Pari, neigh., Braz.	230d	23.32S	46.37W
Paria, r., Az., U.S.	102	37.07N	111.51W
Paria, Golfo de, b. (gôl-fô-dĕ-br-pä-rē-ä)	124	10.33N	62.14W
Paricutín, Volcán, vol., Mex.	112	19.27N	102.14W
Parida, Río de la, r., Mex. (rē′ō-dĕ-lä-pä-rē′dä)	106	26.23N	104.40W
Parima, Serra, mts., S.A. (sĕr′rȧ pä-rē′mȧ)	124	3.45N	64.00W
Pariñas, Punta, c., Peru (pōō′n-tä-pä-rē′n-yäs)	124	4.30S	81.23W
Parintins, Braz. (pä-rĭn-tĭnzh′)	124	2.34S	56.30W
Paris, Can.	84	43.15N	80.23W
Paris, Fr. (pȧ-rē′)	136	48.51N	2.20E
Paris, Ar., U.S. (păr′ĭs)	104	35.17N	93.43W
Paris, Il., U.S.	92	39.35N	87.40W
Paris, Ky., U.S.	92	38.15N	84.15W
Paris, Mo., U.S.	104	39.27N	91.59W
Paris, Tn., U.S.	108	36.16N	88.20W
Paris, Tx., U.S.	90	33.39N	95.33W
Paris-le-Bourget, Aéroport de, arpt., Fr.	233c	48.57N	2.25E
Paris-Orly, Aéroport de, arpt., Fr.	233c	48.45N	2.25E
Parita, Golfo de, b., Pan. (gôl-fô-dĕ-pä-rē′tä)	114	8.06N	80.10W
Park City, Ut., U.S.	98	40.39N	111.33W
Parkdene, S. Afr.	240b	26.14S	28.16E
Parker, S.D., U.S. (pär′kẽr)	96	43.24N	97.10W
Parker Dam, dam, U.S.	90	34.20N	114.00W
Parkersburg, W.V., U.S. (pär′kẽrz-bûrg)	90	39.15N	81.35W
Parkes, Austl. (pärks)	198	33.10S	148.10E
Park Falls, Wi., U.S. (pärk)	96	45.55N	90.29W
Park Forest, Il., U.S.	95a	41.29N	87.41W
Parkgate, Eng., U.K.	233a	53.18N	3.05W
Parkhill Gardens, S. Afr.	240b	26.14S	28.11E
Parkland, Wa., U.S. (pärk′lănd)	100a	47.09N	122.26W
Parklawn, Va., U.S.	225d	38.50N	77.09W
Parklea, Austl.	239a	33.44S	150.57E
Park Orchards, Austl.	239b	37.46S	145.13E
Park Range, mts., Co., U.S.	98	40.54N	106.40W
Park Rapids, Mn., U.S.	96	46.53N	95.05W
Park Ridge, Il., U.S.	95a	42.00N	87.50W
Park Ridge Manor, Il., U.S.	227a	42.02N	87.50W
Park River, N.D., U.S.	96	48.22N	97.43W
Parkrose, Or., U.S. (pärk′rōz)	100c	45.33N	122.33W
Park Rynie, S. Afr.	207c	30.22S	30.43E
Parkston, S.D., U.S. (pärks′tŭn)	96	43.22N	97.59W
Park Town, neigh., S. Afr.	240b	26.11S	28.03E
Parktown North, neigh., S. Afr.	240b	26.09S	28.02E
Parkview, Pa., U.S.	226b	40.30N	79.56W
Parkville, Md., U.S.	94e	39.22N	76.32W
Parkville, Mo., U.S.	101f	39.12N	94.41W
Parkwood, Md., U.S.	225d	39.01N	77.05W
Parla, Spain (pär′lä)	153a	40.14N	3.46W
Parliament, Houses of, pt. of i., Eng., U.K.	231	51.30N	0.07W
Parma, Italy (pär′mä)	142	44.48N	10.20E
Parma, Oh., U.S.	95d	41.23N	81.44W
Parma Heights, Oh., U.S.	95d	41.23N	81.36W
Parnaíba, Braz. (pär-nä-ē′bä)	124	3.00S	41.42W
Parnaíba, r., Braz.	124	3.57S	42.30W
Parnassós, mtn., Grc.	154	38.36N	22.35E
Parndorf, Aus.	139e	48.00N	16.52E
Pärnu, Est. (pĕr′nōō)	160	58.24N	24.29E
Pärnu, r., Est.	146	58.40N	25.05E
Pärnu Laht, b., Est. (läĸt)	146	58.15N	24.17E
Paro, Bhu. (pä′rô)	178	27.30N	89.30E
Paroo, r., Austl. (pä′rōō)	196	30.00S	144.00E
Paropamisus, mts., Afg.	174	34.45N	63.58E
Páros, Grc. (pä′rôs) (pā′rōs)	154	37.05N	25.14E
Páros, i., Grc.	142	37.11N	25.00E
Parow, S. Afr. (pă′rô)	206a	33.54S	18.36E
Parowan, Ut., U.S. (păr′ô-wăn)	102	37.50N	112.50W
Parral, Chile (pär-rä′l)	126	36.07S	71.47W
Parral, r., Mex.	106	27.25N	105.08W
Parramatta, r., Austl. (păr-ȧ-măt′ȧ)	195b	33.42S	150.58E
Parras, Mex. (pär-räs′)	106	25.28N	102.08W
Parrita, C.R. (pär-rē′tä)	114	9.32N	84.17W
Parrsboro, Can. (pärz′bŭr-ô)	86	45.24N	64.20W
Parry, i., Can. (păr′ĭ)	84	45.15N	80.00W
Parry, Mount, mtn., Can.	80	52.53N	128.45W
Parry Islands, is., Can.	76	75.30N	110.00W
Parry Sound, Can.	78	45.20N	80.00W
Parsnip, r., Can. (pärs′nĭp)	80	54.45N	122.20W
Parsons, Ks., U.S. (pär′s′nz)	90	37.20N	95.16W
Parsons, W.V., U.S.	92	39.05N	79.40W
Parthenay, Fr. (pȧr-t′nĕ′)	150	46.39N	0.16W
Partington, Eng., U.K.	233b	53.25N	2.26W
Partinico, Italy (pär-tē′nē-kô)	154	38.02N	13.11E
Partizansk, Russia	158	43.15N	133.19E
Parys, S. Afr. (pȧ-rīs′)	212d	26.53S	27.28E
Pasadena, Ca., U.S. (păs-ȧ-dē′nȧ)	90	34.09N	118.09W
Pasadena, Md., U.S.	94e	39.06N	76.35W
Pasadena, Tx., U.S.	107a	29.43N	95.13W
Pasay, Phil.	237g	14.33N	121.00E
Pascagoula, Ms., U.S. (păs-kȧ-gōō′lȧ)	108	30.22N	88.33W
Pascagoula, r., Ms., U.S.	108	30.52N	88.48W
Paşcani, Rom. (päsh-kän′)	148	47.46N	26.42E
Pasco, Wa., U.S. (păs′kō)	98	46.13N	119.04W
Pascoe Vale, Austl.	239b	37.44S	144.56E
Pasewalk, Ger. (pä′zē-välk)	148	53.31N	14.01E
Pashiya, Russia (pä′shĭ-yȧ)	164a	58.27N	58.17E
Pashkovo, Russia (pȧsh-kô′vô)	186	48.52N	131.09E
Pashkovskaya, Russia (pȧsh-kôf′skȧ-yȧ)	156	45.00N	39.04E
Pasig, Phil.	189a	14.34N	121.05E
Pasión, Río de la, r., Guat. (rē′ō-dĕ-lä-pä-syōn′)	114a	16.31N	90.11W
Pasir Gudang, Malay.	236c	1.27N	103.53E
Pasir Panjang, Sing.	236c	1.17N	103.47E
Pasir Puteh, Malay.	236c	1.26N	103.56E
Paso de los Libres, Arg. (pä-sô-dĕ-lôs-lē′brēs)	126	29.33S	57.05W
Paso de los Toros, Ur. (tŏ′rôs)	123c	32.43S	56.33W
Paso del Rey, Arg.	229d	34.39S	58.45W
Paso Robles, Ca., U.S. (pă′sō rō′blĕs)	102	35.38N	120.44W
Pasquia Hills, hills, Can. (păs′kwē-ȧ)	82	53.13N	102.37W
Passaic, N.J., U.S. (pă-sā′ĭk)	94a	40.52N	74.08W
Passaic, r., N.J., U.S.	94a	40.42N	74.26W
Passamaquoddy Bay, b., N.A. (păs′ȧ-mȧ-kwŏd′ĭ)	86	45.06N	66.59W
Passa Tempo, Braz. (pä′s-sä-tĕ′m-pô)	123a	20.40S	44.29W
Passau, Ger. (päsou)	140	48.34N	13.27E
Pass Christian, Ms., U.S. (pȧs krĭs′tyĕn)	108	30.20N	89.15W
Passero, Cape, c., Italy (päs-sĕ′rô)	136	36.34N	15.13E
Passo Fundo, Braz. (pä′sō fōn′dô)	126	28.16S	52.13W
Passos, Braz. (pä′s-sōs)	124	20.45S	46.37W
Pastaza, r., S.A. (päs-tä′zä)	124	3.05S	76.18W
Pasto, Col. (päs′tō)	124	1.15N	77.19W
Pastora, Mex. (päs-tô-rä)	112	22.08N	100.04W
Pasuruan, Indon.	188	7.45S	112.50E
Pasvalys, Lith. (päs-vä-lēs′)	146	56.04N	24.23E
Patagonia, reg., Arg. (păt-ȧ-gō′nĭ-ȧ)	126	46.45S	69.30W
Pātālganga, r., India	179b	18.52N	73.08E
Patapsco, r., Md., U.S. (pȧ-tăps′kō)	94e	39.12N	76.30W
Pateros, Lake, res., Wa., U.S.	98	48.05N	119.45W
Paterson, N.J., U.S. (păt′ẽr-sŭn)	94a	40.55N	74.10W
Pathein, Burma	174	16.46N	94.47E
Pathfinder Reservoir, res., Wy., U.S. (păth′fīn-dẽr)	98	42.22N	107.10W
Patiāla, India (pŭt-ē-ä′lŭ)	174	30.25N	76.28E
Pati do Alferes, Braz. (pä-tē-dô-ȧl-fĕ′rĕs)	126b	22.25S	43.25W
Patna, India (pŭt′nŭ)	174	25.33N	85.18E
Patnanongan, i., Phil. (pät-nä-nôŋ′gän)	189a	14.50N	122.25E
Patoka, r., In., U.S. (pȧ-tō′kȧ)	92	38.25N	87.25W
Patom Plateau, plat., Russia	158	59.30N	115.00E
Patos, Braz. (pä′tōzh)	124	7.03S	37.14W
Patos, Wa., U.S. (pä′tōs)	100d	48.47N	122.57W
Patos, Lagoa dos, l., Braz. (lä′gō-ȧ dozh pä′tōzh)	126	31.15S	51.30W
Patos de Minas, Braz. (dĕ-mē′nȧzh)	124	18.39S	46.31W
Pátrai, Grc. (pä-trī′) (pä-träs′)	142	38.15N	21.48E
Patraïkós Kólpos, b., Grc.	154	38.16N	21.19E
Patras, *see* Pátrai, Grc.	142	38.15N	21.48E
Patrocínio, Braz. (pä-trō-sē′nē-ō)	124	18.48S	46.47W
Pattani, Thai. (păt′ȧ-nē)	188	6.56N	101.13E
Patten, Me., U.S. (păt′′n)	86	45.59N	68.27W
Patterson, La., U.S. (păt′ẽr-sŭn)	106	29.41N	91.20W
Patterson, i., Can.	84	48.38N	87.14W
Patton, Pa., U.S.	92	40.40N	78.45W
Patuca, r., Hond.	114	15.22N	84.31W
Patuca, Punta, c., Hond. (pōō′n-tä-pä-tōō′kä)	114	15.55N	84.05W
Patuxent, r., Md., U.S. (pȧ-tŭk′sĕnt)	92	39.10N	77.10W
Pátzcuaro, Mex. (päts′kwä-rô)	112	19.30N	101.36W
Pátzcuaro, Lago de, l., Mex. (lä′gô-dĕ)	112	19.36N	101.38W
Patzicia, Guat. (pät-zē′syä)	114	14.36N	90.57W
Patzún, Guat. (pät-zōōn′)	114	14.40N	91.00W
Pau, Fr. (pō)	140	43.18N	0.23W
Pau, Gave de, r., Fr. (gäv-dē)	150	43.33N	0.51W
Paulding, Oh., U.S. (pôl′dĭng)	92	41.05N	84.35W
Paulinenaue, Ger. (pou′lē-nĕ-nou-ĕ)	139b	52.40N	12.43E
Paulistano, Braz. (pá′ô-lēs-tá-nä)	124	8.13S	41.06W
Paulo Afonso, Salto, wtfl., Braz. (säl-tô-pou′lô äf-fôɴ′sô)	124	9.33S	38.32W
Paul Roux, S. Afr. (pôrl rōō)	212d	28.18S	27.57E
Paulsboro, N.J., U.S. (pôlz′bē-rô)	94f	39.50N	75.16W
Pauls Valley, Ok., U.S. (pôlz văl′ē)	104	34.43N	97.13W
Pavarandocito, Col. (pä-vä-rän-dô-sē′tô)	124a	7.18N	76.32W
Pavda, Russia (päv′da)	164a	59.16N	59.32E
Pavia, Italy (pä-vē′ä)	142	45.12N	9.11E
Pavlodar, Kaz. (päv-lô-där′)	158	52.17N	77.23E
Pavlof Bay, b., Ak., U.S. (păv-lŏf)	89	55.20N	161.20W
Pavlograd, Ukr. (päv-lô-grȧt′)	160	48.32N	35.52E
Pavlovsk, Russia (päv-lôfsk′)	156	50.28N	40.05E
Pavlovsk, Russia	164c	59.41N	30.27E
Pavlovskiy Posad, Russia (päv-lôf′skĭ pô-sȧt′)	160	55.47N	38.39E
Pavuna, Braz. (pä-vōō′nȧ)	126b	22.48S	43.21W
Päwesin, Ger. (pă′vĕ-zĕn)	139b	52.31N	12.44E
Pawhuska, Ok., U.S. (pô-hŭs′kȧ)	104	36.41N	96.20W
Pawnee, Ok., U.S. (pô-nē′)	104	36.20N	96.47W
Pawnee, r., Ks., U.S.	104	38.18N	99.42W
Pawnee City, Ne., U.S.	104	40.08N	96.09W
Paw Paw, Mi., U.S. (pô′pô)	92	42.15N	85.55W
Paw Paw, r., Mi., U.S.	96	42.14N	86.21W
Pawtucket, R.I., U.S. (pô-tŭk′ĕt)	92	41.53N	71.23W
Paxoi, i., Grc.	154	39.14N	20.15E
Paxton, Il., U.S. (păks′tŭn)	92	40.35N	88.00W
Paya Lebar, Sing.	236c	1.22N	103.53E
Payette, Id., U.S. (pȧ-ĕt′)	98	44.05N	116.55W
Payette, r., Id., U.S.	98	43.57N	116.26W
Payette, North Fork, r., Id., U.S.	98	44.10N	116.10W
Payette, South Fork, r., Id., U.S.	98	44.07N	115.43W
Pay-Khoy, Khrebet, mts., Russia	160	68.08N	63.04E
Payne, l., Can. (pān)	78	59.22N	73.16W
Paynesville, S. Afr.	240b	26.14S	28.28E
Paynesville, Mn., U.S. (pānz′vĭl)	96	45.23N	94.43W
Paysandú, Ur. (pī-sän-dōō′)	126	32.16S	57.55W
Payson, Ut., U.S. (pā′s′n)	102	40.05N	111.45W
Pazardzhik, Bul. (pä-zȧr-dzhek′)	142	42.10N	24.22E
Pazin, Cro. (pä′zēn)	154	45.14N	13.57E
Peabody, Ks., U.S. (pē′bŏd-ĭ)	104	38.09N	97.09W
Peabody, Ma., U.S.	87a	42.32N	70.56W
Peabody Institute, pt. of i., Md., U.S.	225c	39.18N	76.37W
Peace, r., Can.	78	57.30N	117.30W
Peace Creek, r., Fl., U.S. (pēs)	109a	27.16N	81.53W
Peace Dale, R.I., U.S. (dāl)	94b	41.27N	71.30W
Peace River, Can. (rĭv′ẽr)	78	56.14N	117.17W
Peacock Hills, hills, Can. (pē-kŏk′ hĭlz)	78	66.08N	109.55W
Peak Hill, Austl.	196	25.38S	118.50E
Peakhurst, Austl.	239a	33.58S	151.04E
Pearl, r., U.S. (pûrl)	90	30.30N	89.45W
Pearland, Tx., U.S. (pûrl′ănd)	107a	29.34N	95.17W
Pearl Harbor, Hi., U.S.	88a	21.20N	157.53W
Pearl Harbor, b., Hi., U.S.	90d	21.22N	157.58W
Pearsall, Tx., U.S. (pēr′sôl)	106	28.53N	99.06W
Pearse Island, i., Can. (pērs)	80	54.51N	130.21W
Pearston, S. Afr. (pē′ẽrstŏn)	207c	32.36S	25.09E
Peary Land, reg., Grnld. (pēr′ĭ)	56	82.00N	40.00W
Pease, r., Tx., U.S. (pēz)	104	34.07N	99.53W
Peason, La., U.S. (pēz′′n)	106	31.25N	93.19W
Pebane, Moz. (pĕ-bá′nĕ)	206	17.10S	38.08E
Pecan Bay, Tx., U.S. (pē-kăn′)	106	32.04N	99.15W
Peçanha, Braz. (pā-kän′yȧ)	124	18.37S	42.26W
Pecatonica, r., Il., U.S. (pĕk-ȧ-tŏn-ĭ-kȧ)	96	42.21N	89.28W
Pechenga, Russia (pyĕ′chĕŋ-gȧ)	160	69.30N	31.10E
Pechincha, neigh., Braz.	230c	22.56S	43.21W
Pechora, r., Russia	158	66.00N	54.00E
Pechora Basin, Russia (pyĕ-chô′rȧ)	158	67.55N	58.37E
Pechori, Russia (pĕt′sĕ-rĕ)	156	57.48N	27.33E
Pecos, N.M., U.S. (pā′kôs)	102	35.29N	105.41W
Pecos, Tx., U.S.	106	31.26N	103.30W
Pecos, r., U.S.	90	31.10N	103.10W
Pécs, Hung. (pāch)	142	46.04N	18.15E
Peddie, Ciskei	207c	33.13S	27.09E
Pedley, Ca., U.S. (pĕd′lē)	101a	33.59N	117.29W
Pedra Azul, Braz. (pā′drä-zōō′l)	124	16.03S	41.13W
Pedreiras, Braz. (pĕ-drā′räs)	124	4.30S	44.31W
Pedro, Point, c., Sri L. (pē′drô)	178	9.50N	80.14E
Pedro Antonio Santos, Mex.	114a	18.55N	88.13W
Pedro Betancourt, Cuba (bā-täŋ-kōrt′)	116	22.40N	81.15W
Pedro de Valdivia, Chile (pĕ′drô-dĕ-väl-dē′vē-ä)	126	22.32S	69.55W
Pedro do Rio, Braz. (dô-rē′rô)	126b	22.20S	43.09W
Pedro II, Braz. (pā′drô sȧ-gôn′dô)	124	4.20S	41.27W
Pedro Juan Caballero, Para. (hōȧ′n-kä-bäl-yĕ′rō)	126	22.40S	55.42W
Pedro Miguel, Pan. (mĕ-gāl′)	110a	9.01N	79.36W
Pedro Miguel Locks, trans., Pan. (mĕ-gāl′)	110a	9.01N	79.36W

PLACE (Pronunciation)	PAGE	Lat. °′	Long. °′
Peebinga, Austl. (pē-bĭng'á)	196	34.43S	140.55E
Peebles, Scot., U.K. (pē'b'lz)	144	55.40N	3.15W
Peekskill, N.Y., U.S. (pēks'kĭl)	94a	41.17N	73.55W
Pegasus Bay, b., N.Z. (pĕg'á-sŭs)	197a	43.18S	173.25E
Pegnitz, r., Ger. (pĕgh-nēts)	148	49.38N	11.40E
Pego, Spain (pā'gō)	152	38.50N	0.09W
Peguis Indian Reserve, I.R., Can.	82	51.20N	97.35W
Pegu Yoma, mts., Burma (pĕ-gōō'yō'mä)	174	19.16N	95.59E
Pehčevo, Mac. (pĕĸ'chĕ-vō)	154	41.42N	22.57E
Pehladpur, neigh., India	236d	28.35N	77.06E
Peigan Indian Reserve, I.R., Can.	80	49.35N	113.40W
Peipus, Lake, see Chudskoye Ozero, l., Eur.	160	58.43N	26.45E
Peit'ou, Tai.	237d	25.08N	121.29E
Pekin, Il., U.S. (pē'kĭn)	92	40.35N	89.30W
Peking, see Beijing, China	180	39.55N	116.23E
Pelagie, Isole, is., Italy	142	35.46N	12.32E
Pélagos, i., Grc.	154	39.17N	24.05E
Pelahatchie, Ms., U.S. (pĕl-á-hăch'ē)	108	32.17N	89.48W
Pelat, Mont, mtn., Fr. (pē-lá')	140	44.16N	6.43E
Peleduy, Russia (pyĕl-yĭ-dōō'ē)	158	59.50N	112.47E
Pelée, Mont, mtn., Mart. (pē-lā')	115b	14.49N	61.10W
Pelee, Point, c., Can.	84	41.55N	82.30W
Pelee Island, i., Can. (pē'lē)	84	41.45N	82.30W
Pelequén, Chile (pĕ-lĕ-kĕ'n)	123b	34.26S	71.52W
Pelham, Ga., U.S. (pĕl'hăm)	108	31.07N	84.10W
Pelham, N.H., U.S.	87a	42.43N	71.22W
Pelham, N.Y., U.S.	224	40.55N	73.49W
Pelham Manor, N.Y., U.S.	224	40.54N	73.48W
Pelican, l., Mn., U.S.	96	46.36N	94.00W
Pelican Bay, b., Can.	82	52.45N	100.20W
Pelican Harbor, b., Bah. (pĕl'ĭ-kăn)	116	26.20N	76.45W
Pelican Rapids, Mn., U.S. (pĕl'ĭ-kăn)	96	46.34N	96.05W
Pella, Ia., U.S. (pĕl'á)	96	41.25N	92.50W
Pellworm, i., Ger. (pĕl'vōrm)	148	54.33N	8.25E
Pelly, l., Can.	78	66.08N	102.57W
Pelly, r., Can.	78	62.20N	133.00W
Pelly Bay, b., Can. (pĕl'ĭ)	78	68.57N	91.05W
Pelly Crossing, Can.	89	62.50N	136.50W
Pelly Mountains, mts., Can.	78	61.50N	133.05W
Peloncillo Mountains, mts., Az., U.S. (pĕl-ŏn-sĭl'lō)	102	32.40N	109.20W
Peloponnisos, pen., Grc.	154	37.28N	22.14E
Pelotas, Braz. (pā-lō'tăzh)	126	31.45S	52.18W
Pelton, Can. (pĕl'tŭn)	95b	42.15N	82.57W
Pelym, r., Russia	160	60.20N	63.05E
Pelzer, S.C., U.S. (pĕl'zēr)	108	34.38N	82.30W
Pemanggil, i., Malay.	173b	2.37N	104.41E
Pematangsiantar, Indon.	188	2.58N	99.03E
Pemba, Moz. (pĕm'bá)	206	12.58S	40.30E
Pemba, Zam.	206	15.29S	27.22E
Pemba Channel, strt., Afr.	210	5.10S	39.30E
Pemba Island, i., Tan.	210	5.20S	39.57E
Pembina, N.D., U.S. (pĕm'bĭ-ná)	96	48.58N	97.15W
Pembina, r., Can.	80	53.05N	114.30W
Pembina, r., N.A.	82	49.08N	98.20W
Pembroke, Can. (pĕm' brŏk)	78	45.50N	77.00W
Pembroke, Wales, U.K.	144	51.40N	5.00W
Pembroke, Ma., U.S. (pĕm'brŏk)	87a	42.05N	70.49W
Pen, India	179b	18.44N	73.06E
Penafiel, Port. (pā-ná-fyĕl')	152	41.12N	8.19W
Peñafiel, Spain (pā-nyá-fyĕl')	152	41.38N	4.08W
Peña Grande, neigh., Spain	234b	40.23N	3.44W
Peñalara, mtn., Spain (pā-nyä-lä'rä)	142	40.52N	3.57W
Pena Nevada, Cerro, Mex.	112	23.47N	99.52W
Peñaranda de Bracamonte, Spain	152	40.54N	5.11W
Peñarroya-Pueblonuevo, Spain (pĕn-yär-rō'yä-pwĕ'blŏ-nwĕ'vō)	152	38.18N	5.18W
Peñas, Cabo de, c., Spain (ká'bŏ-dĕ-pā'nyās)	152	43.42N	6.12W
Penas, Golfo de, b., Chile (gōl-fō-dĕ-pĕ'n-äs)	126	47.15S	77.30W
Penasco, r., Tx., U.S. (pā-nás'kō)	106	32.50N	104.45W
Pendembu, S.L. (pĕn-dĕm'bōō)	204	8.06N	10.42W
Pender, Ne., U.S. (pĕn'dēr)	96	42.08N	96.43W
Penderisco, r., Col. (pĕn-dĕ-rē's-kō)	124a	6.30N	76.21W
Pendjari, Parc National de la, rec., Benin	208	11.25N	1.30E
Pendlebury, Eng., U.K.	233b	53.31N	2.20W
Pendleton, Or., U.S. (pĕn'd'l-tŭn)	90	45.41N	118.47W
Pend Oreille, r., Wa., U.S.	98	48.44N	117.20W
Pend Oreille, Lake, l., Id., U.S. (pŏn-dō-rā') (pĕn-dŏ-rĕl')	90	48.09N	116.38W
Penedo, Braz. (pā-nā'dō)	124	10.17S	36.28W
Penetanguishene, Can. (pĕn'ē-tăŋ-gĭ-shēn')	84	44.45N	79.55W
Pengcheng, China (pŭŋ-chŭŋ)	182	36.24N	114.11E
Penglai, China (pŭŋ-lī)	184	37.49N	120.45E
Penha, neigh., Braz.	230c	22.49S	43.17W
Penha de França, neigh., Braz.	230d	23.32S	46.32W
Peniche, Port. (pĕ-nē'chá)	152	39.22N	9.24W
Peninsula, Oh., U.S. (pĕn-ĭn'sū-lá)	95d	41.14N	81.32W
Penistone, Eng., U.K. (pĕn'ĭ-stŭn)	138a	53.31N	1.38W
Penjamillo, Mex. (pĕn-hä-mēl'yō)	112	20.06N	101.56W
Pénjamo, Mex. (pān'hä-mō)	112	20.27N	101.43W
Penk, r., Eng., U.K. (pĕnk)	138a	52.41N	2.10W
Penkridge, Eng., U.K. (pĕnk'rĭj)	138a	52.43N	2.07W
Pennant Hills, Austl.	239a	33.44S	151.04E
Penne, Italy (pĕn'nā)	154	42.28N	13.57E
Penner, r., India (pĕn'ēr)	174	14.43N	79.09E
Penn Hills, Pa., U.S.	226b	40.28N	79.53W
Pennines, hills, Eng., U.K. (pĕn-īn')	144	54.30N	2.10W
Pennines, Alpes, mts., Eur.	148	46.02N	7.07E
Pennsauken, N.J., U.S.	225b	39.58N	75.04W
Pennsboro, W.V., U.S. (pĕnz'bŭr-ō)	92	39.10N	81.00W
Penns Grove, N.J., U.S. (pĕnz grōv)	94f	39.44N	75.28W

PLACE (Pronunciation)	PAGE	Lat. °′	Long. °′
Pennsylvania, state, U.S. (pĕn-sĭl-vā'nĭ-á)	90	41.00N	78.10W
Penn Valley, Pa., U.S.	225b	40.01N	75.16W
Penn Wynne, Pa., U.S.	225b	39.59N	75.16W
Penn Yan, N.Y., U.S. (pĕn yăn')	92	42.40N	77.00W
Pennycutaway, r., Can.	82	56.10N	93.25W
Peno, l., Russia (pā'nō)	156	56.55N	32.28E
Penobscot, r., Me., U.S.	90	45.00N	68.36W
Penobscot Bay, b., Me., U.S. (pē-nŏb'skŏt)	86	44.20N	69.00W
Penong, Austl. (pē-nông')	196	32.00S	133.00E
Penrith, Austl.	195b	33.45S	150.42E
Pensacola, Fl., U.S. (pĕn-sá-kō'lá)	90	30.25N	87.13W
Pensacola Dam, Ok., U.S.	104	36.27N	95.02W
Pensby, Eng., U.K.	233a	53.21N	3.06W
Pensilvania, Col. (pĕn-sĕl-vá'nyä)	124a	5.31N	75.05W
Pentagon, pt. of i., Va., U.S.	225d	38.52N	77.03W
Pentecost, i., Vanuatu (pĕn'tē-kŏst)	196	16.05S	168.28E
Penticton, Can.	78	49.30N	119.35W
Pentland Firth, strt., Scot., U.K. (pĕnt'lănd)	144	58.44N	3.25W
Penza, Russia (pĕn'zá)	158	53.10N	45.00E
Penzance, Eng., U.K. (pĕn-zăns')	144	50.07N	5.40W
Penzberg, Ger. (pĕnts'bĕrgh)	148	47.43N	11.21E
Penzhina, r., Russia (pyĭn-zē-nŭ)	162	62.15N	166.30E
Penzhino, Russia	158	63.42N	168.00E
Penzhinskaya Guba, b., Russia	162	60.30N	161.30E
Penzing, neigh., Aus.	235e	48.12N	16.18E
Peoria, Il., U.S. (pē-ō'rĭ-á)	90	40.45N	89.35W
Peotillos, Mex. (pā-ō-tel'yōs)	112	22.30N	100.39W
Peotone, Il., U.S. (pē'ō-tōn)	95a	41.20N	87.47W
Pepacton Reservoir, res., N.Y., U.S. (pĕp-ăc'tŭn)	92	42.05N	74.40W
Pepe, Cabo, c., Cuba (kä'bō-pĕ'pĕ)	116	21.30N	83.10W
Pepperell, Ma., U.S. (pĕp'ēr-ĕl)	87a	42.40N	71.36W
Peqin, Alb. (pĕ-kēn')	154	41.03N	19.48E
Pequannock, N.J., U.S.	224	40.57N	74.18W
Perales, r., Spain (pā-rä'lās)	153a	40.24N	4.07W
Perales de Tajuña, Spain (dā tä-hōō'nyä)	153a	40.14N	3.22W
Perche, Collines du, hills, Fr.	150	48.25N	0.40E
Perchtoldsdorf, Aus. (pĕrk'tōlts-dôrf)	139e	48.07N	16.17E
Perdekop, S. Afr.	212d	27.11S	29.38E
Perdido, r., Al., U.S. (pĕr-dī'dō)	108	30.45N	87.38W
Perdido, Monte, mtn., Spain (pĕr-dē'dō)	152	42.40N	0.00
Perdões, Braz. (pĕr-dō'ĕs)	123a	21.05S	45.05W
Pereira, Col. (pā-rā'rä)	124	4.49N	75.42W
Perekop, Ukr. (pĕr-ā-kŏp')	160	46.08N	33.39E
Pere Marquette, Mi., U.S.	92	43.55N	86.10W
Pereshchepino, Ukr. (pā'rāsh-chĕ'pē-nō)	156	49.02N	35.19E
Pereslavl'-Zalesskiy, Russia (pâ-rå-slav''l zá-lyĕs'kĭ)	160	56.43N	38.52E
Pereyaslav, Ukr. (pĕ-rá-yäs'läv)	160	50.05N	31.25E
Pergamino, Arg. (pĕr-gä-mē'nō)	126	33.53S	60.36W
Perham, Mn., U.S. (pĕr'hăm)	96	46.37N	95.35W
Peribonca, r., Can. (pĕr-ĭ-bŏŋ'ká)	78	50.30N	71.00W
Périgueux, Fr. (pā-rē-gû')	140	45.12N	0.43E
Perija, Sierra de, mts., Col. (sē-ĕ'r-rä-dĕ-pĕ-rē'ĸä)	124	9.25N	73.30W
Peristérion, Grc.	235d	38.01N	23.42E
Perivale, neigh., Eng., U.K.	231	51.32N	0.19W
Perkam, Tanjung, c., Indon.	188	1.20S	138.45E
Perkins, Can. (pĕr'kĕns)	77c	45.37N	75.37W
Perlas, Archipiélago de las, is., Pan.	114	8.29N	79.15W
Perlas, Laguna las, l., Nic. (lä-gō'nä-dĕ-läs)	114	12.34N	83.19W
Perleberg, Ger. (pĕr'lē-bĕrg)	148	53.06N	11.51E
Perm', Russia (pĕrm)	158	58.00N	56.15E
Pernambuco, state, Braz. (pĕr-näm-bōō'kō)	124	8.08S	38.54W
Pernambuco, see Recife, Braz.	124	8.09S	34.59W
Pernik, Bul. (pĕr-nēk')	142	42.36N	23.04E
Péronne, Fr. (pā-rôn')	150	49.57N	2.49E
Perote, Mex. (pĕ-rō'tē)	112	19.33N	97.13W
Perovo, Russia (pâ'rô-vô)	164b	55.43N	37.47E
Perpignan, Fr. (pĕr-pē-nyäɴ')	140	42.42N	2.48E
Perris, Ca., U.S. (pĕr'ĭs)	101a	33.46N	117.14W
Perros, Bahía, b., Cuba (bä-ē'ä-pā'rōs)	116	22.25N	78.35W
Perrot, Île, i., Can.	77a	45.23N	73.57W
Perry, Fl., U.S. (pĕr'ĭ)	108	30.06N	83.35W
Perry, Ga., U.S.	108	32.27N	83.44W
Perry, Ia., U.S.	96	41.49N	94.40W
Perry, N.Y., U.S.	92	42.45N	78.00W
Perry, Ok., U.S.	104	36.17N	97.18W
Perry, Ut., U.S.	101b	41.27N	112.02W
Perry Hall, Md., U.S.	94e	39.24N	76.29W
Perrymont, Pa., U.S.	226b	40.33N	80.02W
Perryopolis, Pa., U.S. (pĕr-ē-ŏ'pō-lĭs)	95e	40.05N	79.45W
Perrysburg, Oh., U.S. (pĕr ĭz-bûrg)	92	41.35N	83.35W
Perryton, Tx., U.S. (pĕr'ĭ-tŭn)	104	36.23N	100.48W
Perryville, Ak., U.S. (pĕr-ĭ-vĭl)	89	55.58N	159.28W
Perryville, Mo., U.S.	104	37.41N	89.52W
Persan, Fr. (pĕr-säɴ')	151b	49.09N	2.15E
Persepolis, hist., Iran (pĕr-sĕpō-lĭs)	174	30.15N	53.08E
Persian Gulf, b., Asia (pûr'zhăn)	174	27.38N	50.30E
Perth, Austl. (pûrth)	196	31.50S	116.10E
Perth, Can.	84	44.40N	76.15W
Perth, Scot., U.K.	140	56.24N	3.25W
Perth Amboy, N.J., U.S. (ăm'boi)	94a	40.31N	74.16W
Pertuis, Fr. (pĕr-tüē')	150	43.43N	5.29E
Peru, Il., U.S. (pē-rōō')	92	41.20N	89.10W
Peru, In., U.S.	92	40.45N	86.00W
Peru, nation, S.A.	124	10.00S	75.00W
Perugia, Italy (pā-rōō'jä)	142	43.08N	12.24E
Peruque, Mo., U.S. (pĕ rō'kē)	101e	38.52N	90.36W

PLACE (Pronunciation)	PAGE	Lat. °′	Long. °′
Pervomaysk, Ukr. (pĕr-vô-mīsk')	160	48.04N	30.52E
Pervoural'sk, Russia (pĕr-vô-ō-rálsk')	164a	56.54N	59.58E
Perwenitz, Ger.	234a	52.40N	13.01E
Pesaro, Italy (pā'zä-rō)	142	43.54N	12.55E
Pescado, r., Ven. (pĕs-kä'dō)	125b	9.33N	65.32W
Pescara, Italy (pās-kä'rä)	154	42.26N	14.15E
Pescara, r., Italy	154	42.18N	13.22E
Peschanyy, Mys, c., Kaz.	160	43.10N	51.20E
Pescia, Italy (pā'shä)	154	43.53N	11.42E
Peshāwar, Pak. (pĕ-shä'wŭr)	174	34.01N	71.34E
Peshtera, Bul.	154	42.03N	24.19E
Peshtigo, Wi., U.S. (pĕsh'tē-gō)	96	45.03N	87.46W
Peshtigo, r., Wi., U.S.	96	45.15N	88.14W
Peski, Russia (pyâs'kĭ)	164b	55.13N	38.48E
Pêso da Régua, Port. (pā-sō-dä-rā'gwä)	152	41.09N	7.47W
Pespire, Hond. (pås-pē'rå)	114	13.35N	87.20W
Pesqueria, r., Mex. (pås-kå-rē'á)	106	25.55N	100.25W
Pessac, Fr.	150	44.48N	0.38W
Pesterzsébet, neigh., Hung.	235g	47.26N	19.07E
Pestlorinc, neigh., Hung.	235g	47.26N	19.12E
Pestújhely, neigh., Hung.	235g	47.32N	19.07E
Petacalco, Bahía de, b., Mex. (bä-ē'ä-dĕ-pĕ-tä-käl'kō)	112	17.55N	102.00W
Petah Tiqwa, Isr.	173a	32.05N	34.53E
Petaluma, Ca., U.S. (pĕt-á-lō'má)	102	38.15N	122.38W
Petare, Ven. (pĕ-tä'rĕ)	125b	10.28N	66.48W
Petatlán, Mex. (pā-tä-tlän')	112	17.31N	101.17W
Petawawa, Can.	84	45.54N	77.17W
Petén, Laguna de, l., Guat. (lä-gō'nä-dĕ-pā-tān')	114a	17.05N	89.54W
Petenwell Reservoir, res., Wi., U.S.	96	44.10N	89.55W
Peterborough, Austl.	196	32.53S	138.58E
Peterborough, Can. (pē'tēr-bŭr-ō)	78	44.20N	78.20W
Peterborough, Eng., U.K.	144	52.35N	0.14W
Peterhead, Scot., U.K. (pē-tēr-hĕd')	144	57.36N	3.47W
Peter Pond Lake, l., Can. (pŏnd)	78	55.55N	108.44W
Petersburg, Ak., U.S. (pē'tērz-bûrg)	89	56.52N	133.10W
Petersburg, Il., U.S.	104	40.01N	89.51W
Petersburg, In., U.S.	92	38.30N	87.15W
Petersburg, Ky., U.S.	95f	39.04N	84.52W
Petersburg, Va., U.S.	90	37.12N	77.30W
Peters Creek, r., Pa., U.S.	226b	40.18N	79.52W
Petershagen, Ger. (pĕ'tĕrs-hä-gĕn)	139b	52.32N	13.46E
Petersham, Austl.	239a	33.54S	151.09E
Petershausen, Ger. (pĕ'tĕrs-hou-zĕn)	139d	48.25N	11.29E
Pétionville, Haiti	116	18.30N	72.20W
Petit, S. Afr.	240b	26.06S	28.22E
Petitcodiac, Can. (pē-tē-kō-dyák')	86	45.56N	65.10W
Petite Terre, i., Guad. (pē-tēt'târ')	115b	16.12N	61.00W
Petit Goâve, Haiti (pē-tē' gō-áv')	116	18.25N	72.50W
Petit Jean Creek, r., Ar., U.S. (pē-tē'zhäɴ')	104	35.05N	93.55W
Petit Loango, Gabon	210	2.16S	9.35E
Petlalcingo, Mex. (pĕ-tläl-sĕŋ'gō)	112	18.05N	97.53W
Peto, Mex. (pĕ'tō)	114a	20.07N	88.49W
Petorca, Chile (pā-tōr'ká)	123b	32.14S	70.55W
Petoskey, Mi., U.S. (pē-tŏs-kĭ)	92	45.25N	84.55W
Petra, hist., Jord.	173a	30.21N	35.25E
Petra Velikogo, Zaliv, b., Russia	186	42.40N	131.50E
Petre, Point, c., Can.	84	43.50N	77.00W
Petrich, Bul. (pā'trĭch)	142	41.24N	23.13E
Petrified Forest National Park, rec., Az., U.S. (pĕt'rĭ-fīd fôr'ĕst)	102	34.58N	109.35W
Petrikov, Bela. (pyĕ'trē-kō-v)	156	52.09N	28.30E
Petrikovka, Ukr. (pyĕ'trē-kôf-kä)	156	48.43N	34.29E
Petrinja, Cro. (pā'trēn-yá)	154	45.25N	16.17E
Petrodvorets, Russia (pyĕ-trō-dvô-ryĕts')	164c	59.53N	29.55E
Petrokrepost', Russia (pyĕ'trô-krĕ-pôst)	160	59.56N	31.03E
Petrolia, Can. (pē-trō'lĭ-á)	84	42.50N	82.10W
Petrolina, Braz. (pĕ-trō-lē'ná)	124	9.18S	40.28W
Petronell, Aus.	139e	48.07N	16.52E
Petropavlovka, Russia	164a	54.10N	59.50E
Petropavlovka, Ukr. (pyĕ'trô-päv'lôf-ká)	156	48.24N	36.23E
Petropavlovsk, Kaz. (pyĕ-trō-päv'lôfsk)	158	54.44N	69.07E
Petropavlovsk-Kamchatskiy, Russia (kăm-chät'skĭ)	158	53.13N	158.56E
Petrópolis, Braz. (på-trō-pō-lēzh')	124	22.31S	43.10W
Petroşani, Rom.	154	45.24N	23.24E
Petrovsk, Russia (pyĕ-trôfsk')	160	52.20N	45.15E
Petrovskaya, Russia (pyĕ-trôf'ská-yá)	156	45.25N	37.50E
Petrovsko-Razumovskoje, neigh., Russia	235b	55.50N	37.34E
Petrovskoye, Russia	160	45.20N	43.00E
Petrovsk-Zabaykal'skiy, Russia (pyĕ-trôfskză-bī-käl'skĭ)	158	51.13N	109.08E
Petrozavodsk, Russia (pyă'trō-zá-vôtsk')	158	61.46N	34.25E
Petrus Steyn, S. Afr.	212d	27.40S	28.09E
Pewaukee, Wi., U.S. (pĭ-wô'kē)	95a	43.05N	88.15W
Pewaukee Lake, l., Wi., U.S.	95a	43.03N	88.18W
Pewee Valley, Ky., U.S. (pe wē)	95h	38.19N	85.29W
Peza, r., Russia (pyâ'zá)	160	65.35N	46.50E
Pézenas, Fr. (pā-zĕ-nä')	150	43.26N	3.24E
Pforzheim, Ger. (pfôrts'hīm)	140	48.52N	8.43E
Phalodi, India	178	27.13N	72.22E
Phan Thiet, Viet. (p'hän')	188	11.30N	108.43E
Phelps Corner, Md., U.S.	225d	38.48N	76.58W
Phelps Lake, l., N.C., U.S.	108	35.46N	76.27W
Phenix City, Al., U.S. (fē'nĭks)	108	32.29N	85.00W
Philadelphia, Ms., U.S. (fĭl-á-dĕl'phĭ-á)	108	32.45N	89.07W
Philadelphia, Pa., U.S.	90	40.00N	75.13W
Philip, S.D., U.S. (fĭl'ĭp)	96	44.03N	101.35W
Philippeville, see Skikda, Alg.	204	36.58N	6.51E
Philippines, nation, Asia (fĭl'ĭ-pēnz)	188	14.25N	125.00E
Philippine Sea, sea (fĭl'ĭ-pēn)	190	16.00N	133.00E
Philippine Trench, deep	188	10.30N	127.15E

PLACE (Pronunciation)	PAGE	Lat. °′	Long. °′
Philipsburg, Pa., U.S. (fĭl'ĭps-bĕrg)	92	40.55N	78.10W
Philipsburg, Wy., U.S.	98	46.19N	113.19W
Phillip, i., Austl. (fĭl'ĭp)	198	38.32S	145.10E
Phillip Channel, strt., Indon.	173b	1.04N	103.40E
Phillipi, W.V., U.S. (fĭ-lĭp'ī)	92	39.10N	80.00W
Phillips, Wi., U.S. (fĭl'ĭps)	96	45.41N	90.24W
Phillipsburg, Ks., U.S. (fĭl'ĭps-bĕrg)	104	39.44N	99.19W
Phillipsburg, N.J., U.S.	92	40.45N	75.10W
Phinga, India	236a	22.41N	88.25E
Phitsanulok, Thai.	188	16.51N	100.15E
Phnum Pénh, Kam. (nŏm'pĕn')	188	11.39N	104.53E
Phoenix, Az., U.S. (fē'nĭks)	90	33.30N	112.00W
Phoenix, Md., U.S.	94e	39.31N	76.40W
Phoenix Islands, is., Kir.	2	4.00S	174.00W
Phoenixville, Pa., U.S. (fē'nĭks-vĭl)	94f	40.08N	75.31W
Phou Bia, mtn., Laos	188	19.36N	103.00E
Phra Nakhon Si Ayutthaya, Thai.	188	14.16N	100.37E
Phuket, Thai.	188	7.57N	98.19E
Phu Quoc, Dao, i., Viet.	188	10.13N	104.00E
Phu-tho-hoa, Viet.	237m	10.46N	106.39E
Pi, r., China (bē)	182	32.06N	116.31E
Piacenza, Italy (pyä-chĕnt'sä)	142	45.02N	9.42E
Pianosa, i., Italy (pyä-nō'sä)	154	42.13N	15.45E
Piave, r., Italy (pyä'vā)	154	45.45N	12.15E
Piazza Armerina, Italy (pyät'sä är-mȧ-rē'nä)	154	37.23N	14.26E
Pibor, r., Sudan (pē'bôr)	204	7.21N	32.54E
Pic, r., Can. (pĕk)	84	48.48N	86.28W
Picara Point, c., V.I.U.S. (pē-kä'rä)	111c	18.23N	64.57W
Picayune, Ms., U.S. (pĭk'ȧ yōōn)	108	30.32N	89.41W
Picher, Ok., U.S. (pĭch'ẽr)	104	36.58N	94.49W
Pichilemu, Chile (pē-chē-lĕ'mōō)	123b	34.22S	72.01W
Pichucalco, Mex. (pē-chōō-käl'kō)	112	17.34N	93.06W
Pickerel, l., Can. (pĭk'ẽr-ĕl)	84	48.35N	91.10W
Pickwick Lake, res., U.S. (pĭk'wĭck)	108	35.04N	88.05W
Pico, Ca., U.S. (pē'kō)	101a	34.01N	118.05W
Pico Island, i., Port. (pē'kō)	204a	38.16N	28.49W
Pico Riveria, Ca., U.S.	101a	34.01N	118.05W
Picos, Braz. (pē'kōzh)	124	7.13S	41.23W
Picton, Austl. (pĭk'tŭn)	195b	34.11S	150.37E
Picton, Can.	84	44.00N	77.15W
Pictou, Can. (pĭk-tōō')	86	45.41N	62.43W
Pidálion, Akrotírion, c., Cyp.	173a	34.50N	34.05E
Pidurutalagala, mtn., Sri L. (pē'dō-rō-tä'lȧ-gä'lȧ)	174	7.00N	80.46E
Pie, i., Can. (pī)	84	48.10N	89.07W
Piedade, Braz. (pyä-dä'dĕ)	123a	23.42S	47.25W
Piedade do Baruel, Braz.	230d	23.37S	46.18W
Piedmont, Al., U.S. (pēd'mŏnt)	108	33.54N	85.36W
Piedmont, Ca., U.S.	100b	37.50N	122.14W
Piedmont, Mo., U.S.	104	37.09N	90.42W
Piedmont, S.C., U.S.	108	34.40N	82.27W
Piedmont, W.V., U.S.	92	39.30N	79.05W
Piedrabuena, Spain (pyā-drä-bwä'nä)	152	39.01N	4.10W
Piedras, Punta, c., Arg. (pōō'n-tä-pyĕ'dräs)	123c	35.25S	57.10W
Piedras Negras, Mex. (pyā'dräs nā'gräs)	110	28.41N	100.33W
Pieksämäki, Fin. (pyĕk'sĕ-mĕ-kĕ)	146	62.18N	27.14E
Piemonte, hist. reg., Italy (pyĕ-mô'n-tĕ)	154	44.30N	7.42E
Pienaars, r., S. Afr.	212d	25.13S	28.05E
Pienaarsrivier, S. Afr.	212d	25.12S	28.18E
Pierce, Ne., U.S. (pērs)	96	42.11N	97.33W
Pierce, W.V., U.S.	92	39.15N	79.30W
Piermont, N.Y., U.S. (pēr'mŏnt)	94a	41.03N	73.55W
Pierre, S.D., U.S. (pēr)	90	44.22N	100.20W
Pierrefitte-sur-Seine, Fr.	233c	48.58N	2.22E
Pierrefonds, Can.	77a	45.29N	73.52W
Piešt'any, Czech.	148	48.36N	17.48E
Pietermaritzburg, S. Afr. (pē-tẽr-mȧ-rĭts-bûrg)	206	29.36S	30.23E
Pietersburg, S. Afr. (pē'tẽrz-bûrg)	206	23.56S	29.30E
Pietersfield, S. Afr.	240b	26.14S	28.26E
Piet Retief, S. Afr. (pēt rĕ-tēf')	206	27.00S	30.58E
Pietrosul Peak, mtn., Rom.	148	47.35N	24.49E
Pieve di Cadore, Italy (pyā'vȧ dē kä-dō'rȧ)	142	46.26N	12.22E
Pigeon, r., N.A. (pĭj'ŭn)	96	48.05N	90.13W
Pigeon Lake, Can.	77f	49.57N	97.36W
Pigeon Lake, l., Can.	80	53.00N	114.00W
Piggott, Ar., U.S. (pĭg-ŭt)	104	36.22N	90.10W
Pijijiapan, Mex. (pēke-kē-ä'pän)	112	15.40N	93.12W
Pijnacker, Neth.	139a	52.01N	4.25E
Pikes Peak, mtn., Co., U.S. (pīks)	90	38.49N	105.03W
Pikesville, Md., U.S.	225c	39.23N	76.44W
Pikeville, Ky., U.S. (pīk'vĭl)	92	37.28N	82.31W
Pikou, China (pē-kō)	184	39.25N	122.19E
Pikwitonei, Can. (pĭk'wĭ-tōn)	82	55.35N	97.09W
Piła, Pol. (pē'lȧ)	148	53.09N	16.44E
Pilansberg, mtn., S. Afr. (pē'ăns'bûrg)	212d	25.08S	26.55E
Pilar, Arg. (pē'lär)	123c	34.27S	58.55W
Pilar, Para.	126	27.00S	58.15W
Pilar de Goiás, Braz. (dĕ-gô'yȧ's)	124	14.47S	49.33W
Pilchuck, r., Wa., U.S.	100a	48.03N	121.58W
Pilchuck Creek, r., Wa., U.S. (pĭl'chŭck)	100a	48.19N	122.11W
Pilchuck Mountain, mtn., Wa., U.S.	100a	48.03N	121.48W
Pilcomayo, r., S.A. (pēl-cō-mī'ō)	126	24.45S	59.15W
Pilgrim Gardens, N.J., U.S.	225b	39.57N	75.19W
Pilgrims Hatch, Eng., U.K.	231	51.38N	0.17E
Pili, Phil. (pē'lē)	189a	13.34N	123.17E
Pilica, r., Pol. (pē-lēt'sä)	148	51.00N	19.48E
Pillar Point, c., Wa., U.S. (pĭl'ȧr)	100a	48.14N	124.06W
Pillar Rocks, Wa., U.S.	100c	46.16N	123.35W
Pilón, r., Mex. (pē-lōn')	112	24.13N	99.03W
Pilot Point, Tx., U.S. (pī'lŭt)	104	33.24N	97.00W
Pilsen, see Plzeň, Czech.	136	49.46N	13.25E
Piltene, Lat. (pĭl'tĕ-nĕ)	146	57.17N	21.40E
Pimal, Cerra, mtn., Mex. (sĕ'r-rä-pē-mäl')	112	22.58N	104.19W
Pimba, Austl. (pĭm'bȧ)	196	31.15S	137.50E
Pimville, neigh., S. Afr. (pĭm'vĭl)	207b	26.17S	27.54E
Pinacate, Cerro, mtn., Mex. (sĕ'r-rō-pē-nä-kä'tĕ)	110	31.45N	113.30W
Pinamalayan, Phil. (pē-nä-mä-lä'yän)	189a	13.04N	121.31E
Pinang, see George Town, Malay.	188	5.21N	100.09E
Pinarbaşi, Tur. (pē'när-bä'shĭ)	142	38.50N	36.10E
Pinar del Río, Cuba (pē-när' dĕl rē'ō)	110	22.25N	83.35W
Pinar del Río, prov., Cuba	116	22.45N	83.25W
Pinatubo, mtn., Phil. (pē-nä-tōō'bō)	189a	15.09N	120.19E
Pincher Creek, Can. (pĭn'chẽr krēk)	80	49.29N	113.57W
Pinckneyville, Il., U.S. (pĭnk'nĭ-vĭl)	104	38.06N	89.22W
Pińczów, Pol. (pēn''chōf)	148	50.32N	20.33E
Pindamonhangaba, Braz. (pē'n-dä-mōnyä'n-gä-bä)	123a	22.56S	45.26W
Pinder Point, c., Bah.	116	26.35N	78.35W
Píndhos Oros, mts., Grc.	136	39.48N	21.19E
Pindiga, Nig.	208	9.59N	10.54E
Pine, r., Can. (pīn)	80	55.30N	122.20W
Pine, r., Wi., U.S.	96	45.50N	88.37W
Pine Bluff, Ar., U.S. (pīn blŭf)	90	34.13N	92.01W
Pine Brook, N.J., U.S.	224	40.52N	74.20W
Pine City, Mn., U.S. (pīn)	96	45.50N	93.01W
Pine Creek, Austl.	196	13.45S	132.00E
Pine Creek, r., Nv., U.S.	102	40.15N	116.17W
Pinecrest, Va., U.S.	225d	38.50N	77.09W
Pine Falls, Can.	82	50.35N	96.15W
Pine Flat Lake, res., Ca., U.S.	102	36.52N	119.18W
Pine Forest Range, mts., Nv., U.S.	98	41.35N	118.45W
Pinega, Russia (pē-nyĕ'gȧ)	158	64.40N	43.30E
Pinega, r., Russia	160	64.10N	42.30E
Pine Grove, Can.	223c	43.48N	79.35W
Pine Hill, N.J., U.S. (pīn hĭl)	94f	39.47N	74.59W
Pinehurst, Ma., U.S.	223a	42.32N	71.14W
Pine Island Sound, strt., Fl., U.S.	109a	26.32N	82.30W
Pine Lake Estates, Ga., U.S. (lāk ĕs-tāts')	94c	33.47N	84.13W
Pinelands, S. Afr. (pīn'lănds)	206a	33.57S	18.30E
Pine Lawn, Mo., U.S. (lôn)	101e	38.42N	90.17W
Pine Pass, p., Can.	80	55.22N	122.40W
Pine Ridge, Va., U.S.	225d	38.52N	77.14W
Pinerolo, Italy (pē-nȧ-rô'lō)	154	44.47N	7.18E
Pines, Lake o' the, Tx., U.S.	106	32.50N	94.40W
Pinetown, S. Afr. (pīn'toun)	207c	29.47S	30.52E
Pine View Reservoir, res., Ut., U.S. (vū)	101b	41.17N	111.54W
Pineville, Ky., U.S. (pīn'vĭl)	106	36.48N	83.43W
Pineville, La., U.S.	106	31.20N	92.25W
Ping, r., Thai.	188	17.54N	98.29E
Pingding, China (pĭŋ-dĭŋ)	184	37.50N	113.30E
Pingdu, China (pĭŋ-dōō)	184	36.46N	119.57E
Pingfang, China	236b	39.56N	116.33E
Pinggir, Indon.	173b	1.05N	101.12E
Pinghe, China (pĭŋ-hŭ)	184	24.30N	117.02E
Pingle, China (pĭŋ-lŭ)	184	24.30N	110.22E
Pingliang, China (pĭng'lyăng')	180	35.12N	106.50E
Pingquan, China (pĭŋ-chyůän)	184	40.58N	118.40E
Pingtan, China (pĭŋ-tän)	184	25.30N	119.45E
Pingtan Dao, i., China (pĭŋ-tän dou)	184	25.40N	119.45E
P'ingtung, Tai.	184	22.40N	120.35E
Pingwu, China (pĭŋ-wōō)	184	32.20N	104.40E
Pingxiang, China (pĭŋ-shyäŋ)	184	27.40N	113.50E
Pingyi, China (pĭŋ-yē)	182	35.30N	117.38E
Pingyuan, China (pĭŋ-yůän)	182	37.11N	116.26E
Pingzhou, China (pĭŋ-jō)	183a	23.01N	113.11E
Pinhal, Braz. (pē-nyá'l)	123a	22.11S	46.43W
Pinhal Novo, Port. (nō vō)	153b	38.38N	8.54W
Pinheiros, r., Braz.	230d	23.38S	46.43W
Pinhel, Port. (pēn-yĕl')	152	40.45N	7.03W
Pinhel, Port.	152	40.46N	7.04W
Pini, Pulau, i., Indon.	188	0.07S	98.38E
Piniós, r., Grc.	154	39.30N	21.40E
Pinnacles National Monument, rec., Ca., U.S. (pĭn'ȧ-k'lz)	102	36.30N	121.00W
Pinneberg, Ger. (pĭn'ĕ-bĕrg)	139c	53.40N	9.48E
Pinner, neigh., Eng., U.K.	231	51.36N	0.23W
Pinole, Ca., U.S. (pĭ-nō'lē)	100b	38.01N	122.17W
Pinos-Puente, Spain (pwān'tȧ)	152	37.15N	3.43W
Pinotepa Nacional, Mex. (pē-nō-tā'pä nä-syō-näl')	112	16.21N	98.04W
Pins, Île des, i., N. Cal.	196	22.44S	167.44E
Pinsk, Bela. (pēn'sk)	158	52.07N	26.05E
Pinta, i., Ec.	124	0.41N	90.47W
Pintendre, Can. (pĕN-tăNdr')	77b	46.45N	71.07W
Pinto, Spain (pēn'tō)	153a	40.14N	3.42W
Pinto Butte, Can. (pĭn'tō)	82	49.22N	107.25W
Pioche, Nv., U.S. (pī-ō'chē)	102	37.56N	114.28W
Piombino, Italy (pyōm-bē'nō)	142	42.56N	10.33E
Pioneer Mountains, mts., Mt., U.S. (pī'ō-nēr')	98	45.23N	112.51W
Piotrków Trybunalski, Pol. (pyōtr'kōōv trĭ-bōō-nal'skē)	140	51.23N	19.44E
Piper, Al., U.S. (pī'pẽr)	108	33.04N	87.00W
Piper, Ks., U.S.	101f	39.09N	94.51W
Pipéri, i., Grc. (pē'per-ē)	154	39.19N	24.20E
Pipe Spring National Monument, rec., Az., U.S. (pīp spring)	102	36.50N	112.45W
Pipestone, Mn., U.S. (pīp'stōn)	96	44.00N	96.19W
Pipestone National Monument, rec., Mn., U.S.	96	44.03N	96.24W
Pipmuacan, Réservoir, res., Can. (pĭp-mä-kän')	84	49.45N	70.00W
Piqua, Oh., U.S. (pĭk'wȧ)	92	40.10N	84.15W
Piracaia, Braz. (pē-rä-kȧ'yä)	123a	23.04S	46.20W
Piracicaba, Braz. (pē-rä-sē-kä'bä)	124	22.43S	47.39W
Piraíba, r., Braz. (pä-rä-ē'bȧ)	123a	21.38S	41.29W
Piraiévs, Grc.	142	37.57N	23.38E
Piramida, mtn., Russia	158	54.00N	96.00E
Pirámide de Cuicuilco, hist., Mex.	229a	19.18N	99.11W
Piran, Slo. (pē-rä'n)	154	45.31N	13.34E
Piranga, Braz. (pē-rä'n-gä)	123a	20.41S	43.17W
Pirapetinga, Braz. (pē-rä-pē-tē'n-gä)	123a	21.40S	42.20W
Pirapora, Braz. (pē-rȧ-pō'rȧ)	124	17.39S	44.54W
Pirassununga, Braz. (pē-rä-sōō-nōō'n-gä)	123a	22.00S	47.24W
Pirenópolis, Braz. (pē-rē-nô'pō-lēs)	124	15.56S	48.49W
Pírgos, Grc.	142	37.51N	21.28E
Piritu, Laguna de, l., Ven. (lä-gō'nä-dē-pē-rē'tōō)	125b	10.00N	64.57W
Pirmasens, Ger. (pĭr-mä-zĕns')	148	49.12N	7.34E
Pirna, Ger. (pĭr'nä)	148	50.57N	13.56E
Pirot, Yugo. (pē'rōt)	142	43.09N	22.35E
Pirtleville, Az., U.S. (pûr't'l-vĭl)	102	31.25N	109.35W
Piru, Indon. (pē-rōō')	188	3.15S	128.25E
Piryatin, Ukr. (pēr-yä-tēn')	160	50.13N	32.31E
Pisa, Italy (pē'sä)	142	43.52N	10.24E
Pisagua, Chile (pē-sä'gwä)	124	19.43S	70.12W
Piscataway, Md., U.S. (pĭs-kȧ-tȧ-wā)	94e	38.42N	76.59W
Piscataway, N.J., U.S.	94a	40.35N	74.27W
Pisco, Peru (pēs'kō)	124	13.43S	76.07W
Pisco, Bahía de, b., Peru	124	13.43S	77.48W
Piseco, l., N.Y., U.S. (pĭ-sā'kō)	92	43.25N	74.35W
Pisek, Czech. (pē'sĕk)	140	49.18N	14.08E
Pisticci, Italy (pēs-tē'chē)	154	40.24N	16.34E
Pistoia, Italy (pēs-tô'yä)	142	43.57N	11.54E
Pisuerga, r., Spain (pē-swĕr'gä)	152	41.48N	4.28W
Pit, r., Ca., U.S. (pĭt)	98	40.58N	121.42W
Pitalito, Col. (pē-tä-lē'tō)	124	1.45N	75.09W
Pitampura Kālan, neigh., India	236d	28.42N	77.08E
Pitcairn, Pa., U.S. (pĭt'kârn)	95e	40.29N	79.47W
Pitcairn, dep., Oc.	2	25.04S	130.05W
Piteälven, r., Swe.	140	66.08N	18.51E
Piteşti, Rom. (pē-tĕsht'')	154	44.51N	24.51E
Pithara, Austl. (pĭt'ărȧ)	196	30.27S	116.45E
Pithiviers, Fr. (pē-tē-vyā')	150	48.12N	2.14E
Pitman, N.J., U.S. (pĭt'mȧn)	94f	39.44N	75.08W
Pitseng, Leso.	207c	29.03S	28.13E
Pitt, r., Can.	100d	49.19N	122.39W
Pitt Island, i., Can.	80	53.35N	129.45W
Pittsburg, Ca., U.S. (pĭts'bûrg)	100b	38.01N	121.52W
Pittsburg, Ks., U.S.	90	37.25N	94.43W
Pittsburg, Tx., U.S.	104	32.00N	94.57W
Pittsburgh, Pa., U.S.	90	40.26N	80.01W
Pittsfield, Il., U.S. (pĭts'fēld)	104	39.37N	90.47W
Pittsfield, Me., U.S.	86	44.45N	69.44W
Pittsfield, Ma., U.S.	92	42.25N	73.15W
Pittston, Pa., U.S. (pĭts'tŭn)	92	41.20N	75.50W
Piũi, Braz. (pē-ōō'ē)	123a	20.27S	45.57W
Piura, Peru (pē-ōō'rä)	124	5.13S	80.46W
Piya, Russia (pē'yȧ)	164a	58.34N	61.12E
Placentia, Can.	86	47.15N	53.58W
Placentia, Ca., U.S. (plă-sĕn'shĭ-ȧ)	101a	33.52N	117.50W
Placentia Bay, b., Can.	79a	47.14N	54.30W
Placerville, Ca., U.S. (plăs'ẽr-vĭl)	102	38.43N	120.47W
Placetas, Cuba (plä-thā'täs)	116	22.10N	79.40W
Placid, l., N.Y., U.S. (plăs'ĭd)	92	44.20N	74.00W
Plain City, Ut., U.S. (plān)	101b	41.18N	112.06W
Plainfield, Il., U.S. (plān'fēld)	95a	41.37N	88.12W
Plainfield, In., U.S.	95g	39.42N	86.23W
Plainfield, N.J., U.S.	94a	40.38N	74.25W
Plainview, Ar., U.S. (plān'vū)	104	34.59N	93.15W
Plainview, Mn., U.S.	96	44.09N	93.12W
Plainview, Ne., U.S.	96	42.20N	97.47W
Plainview, Tx., U.S.	104	34.11N	101.42W
Plainwell, Mi., U.S. (plan'wĕl)	92	42.25N	85.40W
Plaisance, Can. (plĕ-zäNs')	77c	45.37N	75.07W
Plana or Flat Cays, is., Bah. (plä'nä)	116	22.35N	73.35W
Plandome Manor, N.Y., U.S.	224	40.49N	73.42W
Planegg, Ger. (plä'nĕg)	139d	48.06N	11.27E
Plano, Tx., U.S. (plā'nō)	104	33.01N	96.42W
Plantagenet, Can. (plăN-tȧzh-nĕ')	77c	45.33N	75.00W
Plant City, Fl., U.S. (plȧnt sĭ'tĭ)	109a	28.00N	82.07W
Plaquemine, La., U.S. (plăk'mēn')	106	30.17N	91.14W
Plasencia, Spain (plä-sĕn'thē-ä)	152	40.02N	6.07W
Plast, Russia (plást)	160	54.22N	60.48E
Plaster Rock, Can. (plȧs'tẽr rŏk)	86	46.54N	67.24W
Plastun, Russia (plȧs-tōōn')	186	44.41N	136.08E
Plata, Río de la, est., S.A. (dălȧ plä'tä)	126	34.35S	58.15W
Platani, r., Italy (plä-tä'nē)	154	37.26N	13.28E
Plateforme, Pointe, c., Haiti	116	19.35N	73.50W
Platinum, Ak., U.S. (plăt'ĭ-nŭm)	89	59.00N	161.27W
Plato, Col. (plä'tō)	124	9.49N	74.48W
Platón Sánchez, Mex. (plä-tōn' sän'chĕz)	112	21.14N	98.20W
Platt, Eng., U.K.	231	51.17N	0.20E
Platte, S.D., U.S. (plăt)	96	43.22N	98.51W
Platte, r., Mo., U.S.	104	40.09N	94.40W
Platte, r., Ne., U.S.	90	40.50N	100.40W
Platteville, Wi., U.S. (plăt'vĭl)	96	42.44N	90.31W
Plattsburg, Mo., U.S. (plăts'bûrg)	104	39.33N	94.26W
Plattsburg, N.Y., U.S.	92	44.40N	73.30W
Plattsmouth, Ne., U.S. (plăts'mŭth)	96	41.00N	95.53W
Plauen, Ger. (plou'ĕn)	140	50.30N	12.08E
Playa de Guanabo, Cuba (plä-yä-dĕ-gwä-nä'bō)	117a	23.10N	82.07W
Playa del Rey, neigh., Ca., U.S.	228	33.58N	118.26W
Playa de Santa Fé, Cuba	117a	23.05N	82.31W
Playas Lake, l., N.M., U.S. (plä'yȧs)	102	31.50N	108.30W
Playa Vicente, Mex. (vē-sĕn'tā)	112	17.49N	95.49W

PLACE (Pronunciation)	PAGE	Lat. °'	Long. °'
Playa Vicente, r., Mex.	112	17.36N	96.13W
Playgreen Lake, l., Can. (plā'grēn)	82	54.00N	98.10W
Plaza de Toros Monumental, rec., Spain	234e	41.24N	2.11E
Pleasant, l., N.Y., U.S. (plĕz'ănt)	92	43.25N	74.25W
Pleasant Grove, Al., U.S.	94h	33.29N	86.57W
Pleasant Hill, Ca., U.S.	100b	37.57N	122.04W
Pleasant Hill, Mo., U.S.	104	38.46N	94.18W
Pleasant Hills, Pa., U.S.	226b	40.20N	79.58W
Pleasanton, Ca., U.S. (plĕz'ăn-tŭn)	100b	37.40N	121.53W
Pleasanton, Ks., U.S.	104	38.10N	94.41W
Pleasanton, Tx., U.S.	106	28.58N	98.30W
Pleasant Plain, Oh., U.S. (plĕz'ănt)	95f	39.17N	84.06W
Pleasant Ridge, Mi., U.S.	95b	42.28N	83.09W
Pleasant View, Ut., U.S. (plĕz'ănt vū)	101b	41.20N	112.02W
Pleasantville, Md., U.S.	225c	39.11N	76.38W
Pleasantville, N.Y., U.S. (plĕz'ănt-vĭl)	94a	41.08N	73.47W
Pleasure Ridge Park, Ky., U.S. (plĕzh'ēr rĭj)	95h	38.09N	85.49W
Plenty, Bay of, b., N.Z. (plĕn'tē)	197a	37.30S	177.10E
Plentywood, Mt., U.S. (plĕn'tē-wo͝od)	98	48.47N	104.38W
Ples, Russia (plyĕs)	156	57.26N	41.29E
Pleshcheyevo, l., Russia (plĕsh-chă'yĕ-vô)	156	56.50N	38.22E
Plessisville, Can. (plĕ-sē'vēl')	84	46.12N	71.47W
Pleszew, Pol. (plĕ'zhĕf)	148	51.54N	17.48E
Plettenberg, Ger. (plĕ'tĕn-bĕrgh)	151c	51.13N	7.53E
Pleven, Bul. (plĕ'vĕn)	142	43.24N	24.26E
Pljevlja, Yugo. (plĕv'lyä)	142	43.20N	19.21E
Płock, Pol. (pwôtsk)	140	52.32N	19.44E
Ploërmel, Fr. (plô-ĕr-mĕl')	150	47.56N	2.25W
Ploieşti, Rom. (plô-yĕsht'')	136	44.56N	26.01E
Plomārion, Grc. (plô-mä'rĭ-ŏn)	154	38.51N	26.24E
Plomb du Cantal, mtn., Fr. (plôɴ'dükäɴ-tăl')	140	45.30N	2.49E
Plonge, Lac la, l., Can. (plōɴzh)	82	55.08N	107.25W
Plovdiv, Bul. (plôv'dĭf) (fĭl-ĭp-ŏp'ô-lĭs)	136	42.09N	24.43E
Pluma Hidalgo, Mex. (plo͞o'mä ē-däl'gō)	112	15.54N	96.23W
Plumpton, Austl.	239a	33.45S	150.50E
Plunge, Lith. (plòn'gā)	146	55.56N	21.45E
Plymouth, Monts.	115b	16.43N	62.12W
Plymouth, Eng., U.K. (plĭm'ŭth)	140	50.25N	4.14W
Plymouth, In., U.S.	92	41.20N	86.20W
Plymouth, Ma., U.S.	92	42.00N	70.45W
Plymouth, Mi., U.S.	95b	42.23N	83.27W
Plymouth, N.H., U.S.	92	43.50N	71.40W
Plymouth, N.C., U.S.	108	35.50N	76.44W
Plymouth, Pa., U.S.	92	41.15N	75.55W
Plymouth, Wi., U.S.	96	43.45N	87.59W
Plyussa, r., Russia (plyo͞o'sà)	156	58.33N	28.30E
Plzeň, Czech.	136	49.45N	13.23E
Po, r., Italy	136	45.10N	11.00E
Pocahontas, Ar., U.S. (pō-kȧ-hŏn'tȧs)	104	36.15N	91.01W
Pocahontas, Ia., U.S.	96	42.43N	94.41W
Pocatello, Id., U.S. (pō-kȧ-tĕl'ō)	90	42.54N	112.30W
Pochëp, Russia (pô-chĕp')	160	52.56N	33.27E
Pochinok, Russia (pô-chē'nôk)	156	54.14N	32.27E
Pochinski, Russia	160	54.40N	44.50E
Pochotitán, Mex. (pô-chô-tē-tá'n)	112	21.37N	104.33W
Pochutla, Mex.	112	15.46N	96.28W
Pocomoke City, Md., U.S. (pō-kō-mōk')	92	38.05N	75.35W
Pocono Mountains, mts., Pa., U.S. (pō-cō'nō)	92	41.10N	75.30W
Poços de Caldas, Braz. (pō-sôs-dĕ-käl'dás)	124	21.48S	46.34W
Poder, Sen. (pô-dôr')	204	16.35N	15.04W
Podkamennaya Tunguska, r., Russia	158	61.43N	93.45E
Podol'sk, Russia (pô-dôl''sk)	160	55.26N	37.33E
Podvolochisk, Ukr.	156	49.32N	26.16E
Poggibonsi, Italy (pôd-jē-bôn'sē)	154	43.27N	11.12E
Pogodino, Bela. (pô-gô'dē-nô)	160	54.17N	31.00E
P'ohangdong, S. Kor.	186	35.57N	129.23E
Point Cook, Austl.	239b	37.56S	144.45E
Pointe-à-Pitre, Guad. (pwăɴt' á pē-tr')	110	16.15N	61.32W
Pointe-aux-Trembles, Can. (po͞o-ănt' ō-trăɴbl)	77a	45.39N	73.30W
Pointe Claire, Can. (po͞o-ăɴt' klĕr)	77a	45.27N	73.48W
Pointe-des-Cascades, Can. (kăs-kādz')	77a	45.19N	73.58W
Pointe Fortune, Can. (fŏr'tün)	77a	45.34N	74.23W
Pointe-Gatineau, Can. (po͞o-ăɴt'gä-tē-nō')	77c	45.28N	75.42W
Pointe Noire, Congo	206	4.48S	11.51E
Point Hope, Ak., U.S. (hōp)	89	68.18N	166.38W
Point Pleasant, Md., U.S.	225c	39.11N	76.35W
Point Pleasant, W.V., U.S. (plĕz'ănt)	92	38.50N	82.10W
Point Roberts, Wa., U.S. (rŏb'ērts)	100d	48.59N	123.04W
Poissy, Fr. (pwá-sē')	151b	48.55N	2.02E
Poitiers, Fr. (pwá-tyā')	140	46.35N	0.18E
Pokaran, India (pō'kŭr-ŭn)	178	27.00N	72.05E
Pokrov, Russia (pô-krôf)	156	55.56N	39.09E
Pokrovsko-Strešnevo, neigh., Russia	235b	55.49N	37.29E
Pokrovskoye, Russia (pô-krôf'skô-yĕ)	156	47.27N	38.54E
Pola, r., Russia (pō'lä)	156	57.44N	31.53E
Pola de Laviana, Spain (dĕ-lä-vyä'nä)	152	43.15N	5.29W
Pola de Siero, Spain	152	43.24N	5.39W
Poland, nation, Eur. (pō'lănd)	136	52.37N	17.01E
Polangui, Phil. (pô-läŋ'gē)	189a	13.18N	123.29E
Polazna, Russia (pô'láz-ná)	164a	58.18N	56.25E
Polessk, Russia (pô'lĕsk)	146	54.50N	21.14E
Poles'ye (Pripyat Marshes), sw., Eur.	160	52.10N	27.30E
Polevskoy, Russia (pô-lĕ'vs-kô'ĕ)	164a	56.28N	60.14E
Polgár, Hung. (pôl'gär)	148	47.54N	21.10E
Policastro, Golfo di, b., Italy	154	40.00N	13.23E
Poligny, Fr. (pō-lē-nyē')	150	46.48N	5.42E
Polikhnitos, Grc.	154	39.05N	26.11E
Polillo, Phil. (pô-lēl'yō)	189a	14.42N	121.56W
Polillo Islands, is., Phil.	174	15.05N	122.15E
Polillo Strait, strt., Phil.	189a	15.02N	121.40E
Polist', r., Russia (pô'lĭst)	156	57.42N	31.02E
Polistena, Italy (pō-lēs-tā'nä)	154	38.25N	16.05E
Políyiros, Grc.	154	40.23N	23.27E
Polkan, Gora, mtn., Russia	158	60.18N	92.08E
Pollensa, Spain (pōl-yĕn'sä)	152	39.50N	3.00E
Polochic, r., Guat. (pō-lô-chēk')	114	15.19N	89.45W
Polonnoye, Ukr. (pô'lô-nô-yĕ)	156	50.07N	27.31E
Polotsk, Bela. (pô'lôtsk)	160	55.30N	28.48E
Polpaico, Chile (pôl-pá'y-kô)	123b	33.10S	70.53W
Polson, Mt., U.S. (pōl'sŭn)	98	47.40N	114.10W
Polsum, Ger.	232	51.37N	7.03E
Poltava, Ukr. (pôl-tä'vä)	158	49.35N	34.33E
Poltava, prov., Ukr.	156	49.53N	32.58E
Põltsamaa, Est. (pōlt'sá-mä)	146	58.39N	26.00E
Polunochnoye, Russia (pô-lo͞o-nô'ch-nô'yĕ)	164a	60.52N	60.27E
Poluy, r., Russia (pôl'wē)	162	65.45N	68.15E
Polyakovka, Russia (pŭl-yä'kôv-kȧ)	164a	54.38N	59.42E
Polyarnyy, Russia (pŭl-yär'nē)	158	69.10N	33.30E
Pomba, r., Braz. (pô'm-bȧ)	123a	21.28S	42.28W
Pomerania, hist. reg., Pol. (pŏm-ē-rā'nĭ-ȧ)	148	53.50N	15.20E
Pomeroy, S. Afr. (pŏm'ēr-roi)	207c	28.36S	30.26E
Pomeroy, Wa., U.S. (pŏm'ēr-oi)	98	46.28N	117.35W
Pomezia, Italy (pô-mĕ't-zyä)	153d	41.41N	12.31E
Pomigliano d'Arco, Italy (pô-mē-lyä'nô-d-ä'r-kô)	153c	40.39N	14.23E
Pomme de Terre, Mn., U.S. (pôm dē tĕr')	96	45.22N	95.52W
Pomona, Ca., U.S. (pô-mō'nȧ)	90	34.04N	117.45W
Pomona Estates, S. Afr.	240b	26.06S	28.15E
Pomorie, Bul.	142	42.24N	27.41E
Pompano Beach, Fl., U.S. (pŏm'pȧ-nō)	109a	26.12N	80.07W
Pompeii Ruins, hist., Italy	153c	40.31N	14.29E
Pomponne, Fr.	233c	48.53N	2.41E
Pompton Lakes, N.J., U.S. (pŏmp'tŏn)	94a	41.01N	74.16W
Pompton Plains, N.J., U.S.	224	40.58N	74.18W
Pomuch, Mex. (pô-mo͞o'ch)	114a	20.12N	90.10W
Ponca, Ne., U.S. (pŏn'kȧ)	96	42.34N	96.43W
Ponca City, Ok., U.S.	104	36.42N	97.07W
Ponce, P.R. (pōn'sä)	110	18.01N	66.43W
Ponders End, neigh., Eng., U.K.	231	51.39N	0.03W
Pondicherry, India	174	11.58N	79.48E
Pondicherry, state, India	174	11.50N	74.50E
Ponferrada, Spain (pôn-fĕr-rä'dhä)	142	42.33N	6.38W
Ponoka, Can. (pŏ-nō'kȧ)	78	52.42N	113.35W
Ponoy, Russia	160	66.58N	41.00E
Ponoy, r., Russia	160	67.00N	39.00E
Ponta Delgada, Port. (pōn'tȧ dĕl-gä'dȧ)	204a	37.40N	25.45W
Ponta Grossa, Braz. (grō'sȧ)	124	25.09S	50.05W
Pont-à-Mousson, Fr. (pôɴ'tá-mo͞osôɴ')	150	48.55N	6.02E
Pontarlier, Fr. (pôɴ'tár-lyā')	150	46.53N	6.22E
Pont-Audemer, Fr. (pôɴ'tōd'mâr')	150	49.23N	0.28E
Pontault-Combault, Fr.	233c	48.47N	2.36E
Pontchartrain Lake, l., La., U.S. (pôɴ-shȧr-trăn')	106	30.10N	90.10W
Pontedera, Italy (pōn-tā-dā'rä)	154	43.37N	10.37E
Ponte de Sor, Port.	152	39.14N	8.03W
Pontefract, Eng., U.K. (pŏn'tē-frăkt)	138a	53.41N	1.18W
Ponte Nova, Braz. (pô'n-tē-nô'vȧ)	124	20.26S	42.52W
Pontevedra, Arg.	229d	34.46S	58.43W
Pontevedra, Spain (pôn-tĕ-vĕ-drä)	142	42.28N	8.38W
Ponthierville, see Ubundi, Zaire	206	0.21S	25.29E
Pontiac, Il., U.S. (pŏn'tĭ-ăk)	92	40.55N	88.35W
Pontiac, Mi., U.S.	90	42.37N	83.17W
Pontianak, Indon. (pôn-tē-ä'nȧk)	188	0.04S	109.20E
Pontian Kechil, Malay.	173b	1.29N	103.24E
Pontic Mountains, mts., Tur.	160	41.20N	34.30E
Pontinha, neigh., Port.	234d	38.46N	9.11W
Pontivy, Fr. (pôɴ-tē-vē')	150	48.05N	2.57W
Pontoise, Fr. (pôɴ-twȧz')	150	49.03N	2.05E
Pontonnyy, Russia (pôn'tôn-nyĭ)	164c	59.47N	30.39E
Pontotoc, Ms., U.S. (pŏn-tô-tŏk')	108	34.11N	88.59W
Pontremoli, Italy (pôn-trĕm'ô-lē)	154	44.21N	9.50E
Ponziane, Isole, i., Italy (ē'sō-lĕ)	142	40.55N	12.58E
Poole, Eng., U.K. (po͞ol)	144	50.43N	2.00W
Poolesville, Md., U.S. (po͞oles-vĭl)	94e	39.08N	77.26W
Pooley Island, i., Can. (po͞o'lē)	80	52.44N	128.16W
Poopó, Lago de, l., Bol.	124	18.45S	67.07W
Popayán, Col. (pō-pä-yän')	124	2.21N	76.43W
Poplar, Mt., U.S. (pŏp'lēr)	98	48.08N	105.10W
Poplar, neigh., Eng., U.K.	231	51.31N	0.01W
Poplar, r., Mt., U.S.	98	48.34N	105.20W
Poplar, West Fork, r., Mt., U.S.	98	48.59N	106.06W
Poplar Bluff, Mo., U.S. (blŭf)	104	36.43N	90.22W
Poplar Heights, Va., U.S.	225d	38.53N	77.12W
Poplar Plains, Ky., U.S. (plāns)	92	38.20N	83.40W
Poplar Point, Can.	77f	50.04N	97.57W
Poplarville, Ms., U.S. (pŏp'lēr-vĭl)	108	30.50N	89.33W
Popocatépetl Volcán, Mex. (pô-pô-kä-tā'pĕ't'l)	110	19.01N	98.38W
Popokabaka, Zaire (pō'pō-kȧ-bä'kȧ)	206	5.42S	16.35E
Popovka, Ukr. (pô'pôf-kȧ)	156	50.03N	33.41E
Popovka, Ukr.	156	51.13N	33.08E
Popovo, Bul. (pô'pō-vō)	154	43.23N	26.17E
Porbandar, India (pōr-bŭn'dŭr)	174	21.44N	69.40E
Porce, r., Col. (pôr-sē)	124a	7.11N	74.55W
Porcher Island, i., Can. (pôr'kēr)	80	53.57N	130.30W
Porcuna, Spain (pôr-ko͞o'nä)	152	37.54N	4.10W
Porcupine, r., N.A.	89	67.38N	140.07W
Porcupine Creek, r., Mt., U.S.	98	48.27N	106.24W
Porcupine Hills, hills, Can.	82	52.30N	101.45W
Pordenone, Italy (pōr-dȧ-nō'nȧ)	154	45.58N	12.38E
Pori, Fin. (pô'rē)	140	61.29N	21.45E
Poriúncula, Braz.	123a	20.58S	42.02W
Porkhov, Russia (pôr'kôf)	160	57.46N	29.33E
Porlamar, Ven. (pôr-lä-mär')	124	11.00N	63.55W
Pornic, Fr. (pôr-nēk')	150	47.08N	2.07W
Poronaysk, Russia (pô'rô-nīsk)	158	49.21N	143.23E
Porrentruy, Switz. (pô-räɴ-trüē')	148	47.25N	7.02E
Porsgrunn, Nor. (pôrs'grôn')	146	59.09N	9.36E
Portachuelo, Bol. (pôrt-ä-chwā'lô)	124	17.20S	63.12W
Portage, Pa., U.S. (pôr'tāj)	92	40.25N	78.35W
Portage, Wi., U.S.	96	43.33N	89.29W
Portage Des Sioux, Mo., U.S. (dē so͞o)	101e	38.56N	90.21W
Portage-la-Prairie, Can. (lä-prā'rĭ)	78	49.57N	98.25W
Port Alberni, Can. (pōr äl-bĕr-nē')	78	49.14N	124.48W
Portalegre, Port. (pôr-tä-lā'grĕ)	142	39.18N	7.26W
Portales, N.M., U.S. (pôr-tä'lĕs)	104	34.10N	103.11W
Port Alfred, S. Afr. (kou'ĭ)	206	33.36S	26.55E
Port Alice, Can. (ăl'ĭs)	78	50.23N	127.27W
Port Allegany, Pa., U.S. (ăl-ē-gā'nĭ)	92	41.50N	78.10W
Port Angeles, Wa., U.S. (ăn'jē-lĕs)	90	48.07N	123.26W
Port Antonio, Jam.	110	18.10N	76.25W
Portarlington, Austl.	195a	38.07S	144.39E
Port Arthur, Tx., U.S.	90	29.52N	93.59W
Port Augusta, Austl. (ô-gŭs'tȧ)	198	32.28S	137.50E
Port au Port Bay, b., Can. (pôr'tō pōr')	86	48.41N	58.45W
Port-au-Prince, Haiti (prăɴs')	110	18.35N	72.20W
Port Austin, Mi., U.S. (ôs'tĭn)	92	44.00N	83.00W
Port Blair, India (blâr)	188	12.07N	92.45E
Port Bolivar, Tx., U.S. (bŏl'ĭ-vȧr)	107a	29.22N	94.46W
Port Borden, Can. (bôr'dĕn)	86	46.15N	63.42W
Port-Bouët, I.C.	204	5.24N	3.56W
Port-Cartier, Can.	86	50.01N	66.53W
Port Chester, N.Y., U.S. (chĕs'tēr)	94a	40.59N	73.40W
Port Chicago, Ca., U.S. (shĭ-kô'gō)	100b	38.03N	122.01W
Port Clinton, Oh., U.S. (klĭn'tŭn)	92	41.30N	83.00W
Port Colborne, Can.	84	42.53N	79.13W
Port Coquitlam, Can. (kô-kwĭt'lȧm)	80	49.16N	122.46W
Port Credit, Can. (krĕd'ĭt)	77d	43.33N	79.35W
Port-de-Bouc, Fr. (pôr-dē-bo͞ok')	150a	43.24N	5.00E
Port de Paix, Haiti (pĕ)	116	19.55N	72.50W
Port Dickson, Malay. (dĭk'sŭn)	173b	2.33N	101.49E
Port Discovery, b., Wa., U.S. (dĭs-kŭv'ēr-ĭ)	100a	48.05N	122.55W
Port Edward, S. Afr. (ĕd'wērd)	207c	31.04S	30.14E
Port Elgin, Can. (ĕl'jĭn)	86	46.03N	64.05W
Port Elizabeth, S. Afr. (ē-lĭz'ȧ-bĕth)	206	33.57S	25.37E
Porterdale, Ga., U.S. (pōr'tēr-dāl)	108	33.34N	83.53W
Porterville, Ca., U.S. (pōr'tēr-vĭl)	102	36.03N	119.05W
Portezuelo de Tupungato, vol., S.A.	126	33.30S	69.52W
Port Francqui, see Ilebo, Zaire	206	4.19S	20.35E
Port Gamble, Wa., U.S. (găm'bŭl)	100a	47.52N	122.36W
Port Gamble Indian Reservation, I.R., Wa., U.S.	100a	47.54N	122.33W
Port-Gentil, Gabon (zhäɴ-tē')	206	0.43S	8.47E
Port Gibson, Ms., U.S.	108	31.56N	90.57W
Port Harcourt, Nig. (här'kŭrt)	204	4.43N	7.05E
Port Hardy, Can. (här'dĭ)	80	50.43N	127.29W
Port Hawkesbury, Can.	86	45.37N	61.21W
Port Hedland, Austl. (hĕd'lănd)	196	20.30S	118.30E
Porthill, Id., U.S.	98	49.00N	116.30W
Port Hood, Can. (hŏd)	86	46.01N	61.32W
Port Hope, Can. (hōp)	84	43.55N	78.10W
Port Huron, Mi., U.S. (hū'rŏn)	90	43.00N	82.30W
Portici, Italy (pôr'tē-chē)	153c	40.34N	14.20E
Portillo, Chile (pôr-tē'l-yô)	123b	32.51S	70.09W
Portimão, Port. (pôr-tē-mouɴ)	152	37.09N	8.34W
Port Jervis, N.Y., U.S. (jûr'vĭs)	94a	41.22N	74.41W
Portland, Austl. (pōrt'lănd)	196	38.20S	142.40E
Portland, In., U.S.	92	40.25N	85.00W
Portland, Me., U.S.	90	43.40N	70.16W
Portland, Mi., U.S.	92	42.50N	85.00W
Portland, Or., U.S.	90	45.31N	122.41W
Portland, Tx., U.S.	106	27.53N	97.20W
Portland Bight, bt., Jam.	116	17.45N	77.05W
Portland Canal, can., Ak., U.S.	80	55.10N	130.08W
Portland Inlet, b., Can.	80	54.50N	130.15W
Portland Point, c., Jam.	116	17.40N	77.20W
Port Lavaca, Tx., U.S. (lȧ-vä'kȧ)	106	28.36N	96.38W
Port Lincoln, Austl. (lĭŋ-kŭn)	196	34.39S	135.50E
Port Ludlow, Wa., U.S. (lŭd'lō)	100a	47.26N	122.41W
Port Macquarie, Austl. (mȧ-kwŏ'rĭ)	196	31.25S	152.45E
Port Madison Indian Reservation, I.R., Wa., U.S. (măd'ĭ-sŭn)	100a	47.46N	122.38W
Port Maria, Jam. (mȧ-rī'ȧ)	116	18.20N	76.55W
Port Melbourne, Austl.	239b	37.51S	144.56E
Port Moody, Can. (mo͞od'ĭ)	80	49.17N	122.51W
Port Moresby, Pap. N. Gui. (mōrz'bē)	188	9.34S	147.20E
Port Neches, Tx., U.S. (nĕch'ĕz)	106	29.59N	93.57W
Port Nelson, Can. (nĕl'sŭn)	82	57.03N	92.36W
Portneuf-Sur-Mer, Can. (pôr-nûf'sür mĕr)	86	48.36N	69.06W
Port Nolloth, S. Afr. (nŏl'ŏth)	206	29.10S	17.00E
Porto (Oporto), Port. (pōr'tō)	136	41.10N	8.38W
Porto Acre, Braz. (ä'krĕ)	124	9.38S	67.34W
Porto Alegre, Braz. (ä-lā'grĕ)	126	29.58S	51.11W
Porto Amboim, Ang.	206	11.01S	13.45E
Portobelo, Pan. (pôr'tô-bā'lô)	110	9.32N	79.40W
Pôrto de Pedras, Braz. (pā'dräzh)	124	9.09S	35.20W
Pôrto Feliz, Braz. (fē-lē's)	123a	23.12S	47.30W
Portoferraio, Italy (pōr'tō-fĕr-rä'yō)	154	42.47N	10.20E
Port of Spain, Trin. (spān)	124	10.44N	61.24W
Portogruaro, Italy (pōr'tō-grô-ä'rō)	154	45.48N	12.49E
Portola, Ca., U.S. (pôr'tō-lȧ)	102	39.47N	120.29W
Porto Mendes, Braz. (mĕ'n-dĕs)	124	24.41S	54.13W
Porto Murtinho, Braz. (mōr-tēn'yō)	124	21.43S	57.43W

ăt; finăl; rāte; senāte; ärm; åsk; sofȧ; fâre; ch-choose; dh-as th in other; bē; ēvent; bĕt; recĕnt; cratēr; g-gō; gh-guttural g; bĭt; ĭ-short neutral; rīde; ĸ-guttural k as ch in German ich;

PLACE (Pronunciation)	PAGE	Lat. °'	Long. °'
Porto Nacional, Braz. (ná-syô-näl')	124	10.43S	48.14W
Porto Novo, Benin (pōr'tô-nō'vō)	204	6.29N	2.37E
Port Orchard, Wa., U.S. (ôr'chērd)	100a	47.32N	122.38W
Port Orchard, b., Wa., U.S.	100a	47.40N	122.39W
Porto Salvo, Port.	234d	38.43N	9.18W
Porto Santo, Ilha de, i., Port. (säN'tò)	204	32.41N	16.15W
Porto Seguro, Braz. (sā-gōō'rò)	124	16.26S	38.59W
Porto Torres, Italy (tôr'rĕs)	154	40.49N	8.25E
Porto-Vecchio, Fr. (vĕk'ē-ô)	154	41.36N	9.17E
Porto Velho, Braz. (väl'yò)	124	8.45S	63.43W
Portoviejo, Ec. (pôr-tō-vyā'hō)	124	1.11S	80.28W
Port Phillip Bay, b., Austl. (fĭl'ĭp)	196	37.57S	144.50E
Port Pirie, Austl. (pĭ'rē)	196	33.10S	138.00E
Port Radium, Can. (rā'dē-ŭm)	78	66.06N	118.03W
Port Reading, N.J., U.S.	224	40.34N	74.16W
Port Royal, b., Jam. (roi'ăl)	116	17.50N	76.45W
Port Said, Egypt	212c	31.15N	32.19E
Port Saint Johns, Transkei (sânt jŏnz)	206	31.37S	29.32E
Port Shepstone, S. Afr. (shĕps'tŭn)	206	30.45S	30.23E
Portsmouth, Dom.	115b	15.33N	61.28W
Portsmouth, Eng., U.K. (pôrts'mŭth)	136	50.45N	1.03W
Portsmouth, N.H., U.S.	90	43.05N	70.50W
Portsmouth, Oh., U.S.	90	38.45N	83.00W
Portsmouth, Va., U.S.	90	36.50N	76.19W
Port Sulphur, La., U.S. (sŭl'fēr)	108	29.28N	89.41W
Port Sunlight, Eng., U.K.	233a	53.21N	2.59W
Port Susan, b., Wa., U.S. (sū-zán')	100a	48.11N	122.25W
Port Townsend, Wa., U.S. (tounz'ĕnd)	100a	48.07N	122.46W
Port Townsend, b., Wa., U.S.	100a	48.05N	122.47W
Portugal, nation, Eur. (pōr'tu-găl)	136	38.15N	8.08W
Portugalete, Spain (pōr-tōō-gä-lā'tā)	152	43.18N	3.05W
Portuguese West Africa, see Angola, nation, Ang.	206	14.15S	16.00E
Port Vendres, Fr.	150	42.32N	3.07E
Port Vila, Vanuatu	196	17.44S	168.19E
Port Vue, Pa., U.S.	226b	40.20N	79.52W
Port Wakefield, Austl. (wāk'fēld)	196	34.12S	138.10E
Port Washington, N.Y., U.S. (wôsh'ĭng-tŭn)	94a	40.49N	73.42W
Port Washington, Wi., U.S.	96	43.24N	87.52W
Posadas, Arg. (pō-sä'dhäs)	126	27.32S	55.56W
Posadas, Spain (pô-sä-däs)	152	37.48N	5.09W
Poshekhon'ye Volodarsk, Russia (pô-shyĕ'kŏn-yĕ vôl'ô-dársk)	156	58.31N	39.07E
Poso, Danau, l., Indon. (pō'sō)	188	2.00S	119.40E
Pospelokova, Russia (pôs-pyĕl'kô-vá)	164a	59.25N	60.50E
Possession Sound, strt., Wa., U.S. (pŏ-zĕsh-ŭn)	100a	47.59N	122.17W
Possum Kingdom Reservoir, res., Tx., U.S. (pŏs'ŭm kĭng'dŭm)	106	32.58N	98.12W
Post, Tx., U.S. (pōst)	104	33.12N	101.21W
Postojna, Slo. (pōs-tōyná)	154	45.45N	14.13E
Pos'yet, Russia (pos-yĕt')	186	42.27N	130.47E
Potawatomi Indian Reservation, I.R., Ks., U.S. (pŏt-å-wä'tō mē)	104	39.30N	96.11W
Potchefstroom, S. Afr. (pŏch'ĕf-strōm)	206	26.42S	27.06E
Poteau, Ok., U.S. (pō-tō')	104	35.03N	94.37W
Poteet, Tx., U.S. (pō-tēt)	106	29.05N	98.35W
Potenza, Italy (pō-tĕnt'sä)	142	40.39N	15.49E
Potenza, r., Italy	154	43.09N	13.00E
Potgietersrus, S. Afr. (pŏt-кē'tērs-rûs)	206	24.09S	29.04E
Potholes Reservoir, res., Wa., U.S.	98	47.00N	119.20W
Poti, Geor. (pô'tē)	160	42.10N	41.40E
Potiskum, Nig.	204	11.43N	11.05E
Potomac, Md., U.S. (pō-tō'măk)	94e	39.01N	77.13W
Potomac, r., U.S. (pō-tō'măk)	90	38.15N	76.55W
Poto Poto, neigh., Congo	240c	4.15S	15.18E
Potosí, Bol.	124	19.35S	65.45W
Potosi, Mo., U.S. (pō-tō'sĭ)	104	37.56N	90.46W
Potosí, r., Mex. (pō-tô-sē')	106	25.04N	99.36W
Potrerillos, Hond. (pō-trâ-rēl'yōs)	114	15.13N	87.58W
Potsdam, Ger. (pôts'däm)	140	52.24N	13.04E
Potsdam, N.Y., U.S. (pŏts'dăm)	92	44.40N	75.00W
Pottenstein, Aus.	139e	47.58N	16.06E
Potters Bar, Eng., U.K. (pŏt'ĕz bär)	138b	51.41N	0.12W
Potter Street, Eng., U.K.	231	51.46N	0.08E
Pottstown, Pa., U.S. (pŏts'toun)	92	40.15N	75.40W
Pottsville, Pa., U.S. (pôts'vĭl)	92	40.40N	76.15W
Poughkeepsie, N.Y., U.S. (pŏ-kĭp'sē)	90	41.45N	73.55W
Poulsbo, Wa., U.S. (pōlz'bò)	100a	47.44N	122.38W
Poulton-le-Fylde, Eng., U.K. (pōl'tŭn-lē-fīld')	138a	53.52N	2.59W
Pouso Alegre, Braz. (pō'zò ä-lā'grĕ)	124	22.13S	45.56W
Póvoa de Varzim, Port. (pō-vō'á dā vär'zēN)	142	41.23N	8.44W
Powder, r., U.S. (pou'dēr)	90	45.18N	105.37W
Powder, r., Or., U.S.	98	44.55N	117.35W
Powder, South Fork, r., Wy., U.S.	98	43.13N	106.54W
Powder River, Wy., U.S.	98	43.06N	106.55W
Powell, Wy., U.S. (pou'ĕl)	98	44.44N	108.44W
Powell, Lake, res., U.S.	90	37.26N	110.25W
Powell Lake, l., Can.	80	50.10N	124.13W
Powell Point, c., Bah.	116	24.50N	76.20W
Powell Reservoir, res., Ky., U.S.	108	36.30N	83.35W
Powell River, Can.	78	49.52N	124.33W
Poyang Hu, l., China	180	29.20N	116.28E
Poygan, r., Wi., U.S. (poi'gán)	96	44.10N	89.05W
Poyle, Eng., U.K.	231	51.28N	0.31W
Poynton, Eng., U.K.	233b	53.21N	2.07W
Požarevac, Yugo. (pō'zhá'rĕ-váts)	154	44.38N	21.12E
Poza Rica, Mex. (pō-zō-rē'kä)	112	20.32N	97.25W
Poznań, Pol.	136	52.25N	16.55E
Pozoblanco, Spain (pō-thō-bläŋ'kō)	152	38.23N	4.50W
Pozos, Mex. (pō'zōs)	112	22.05N	100.50W
Pozuelo de Alarcón, Spain (pô-thwā'lō dā ä-lär-kōn')	153a	40.27N	3.49W
Pozzuoli, Italy (pôt-swô'lē)	154	40.34N	14.08E
Pra, r., Ghana (prá)	208	5.45N	1.35W
Pra, r., Russia	156	55.00N	40.13E
Prachin Buri, Thai. (prä'chēn)	188	13.59N	101.15E
Pradera, Col. (prä-dĕ'rä)	124a	3.24N	76.13W
Prades, Fr. (prád)	150	42.37N	2.23E
Prado, Col. (prädô)	124a	3.44N	74.55W
Prado, Museo del, bldg., Spain	234b	40.25N	3.41W
Prado Churubusco, Mex.	229a	19.21N	99.07W
Prado Reservoir, res., Ca., U.S. (prä'dō)	101a	33.45N	117.40W
Prados, Braz. (prá'dôs)	123a	21.05S	44.04W
Prague, Czech.	148	50.05N	14.26E
Praha, see Prague, Czech.	136	50.05N	14.26E
Prahran, Austl.	239b	37.51S	144.59E
Praia, C.V. (prä'yá)	204b	15.00N	23.30W
Praia Funda, Ponta da, c., Braz. (pôn'tä-dá-prä'yá-fōō'n-dä)	126b	23.04S	43.34W
Prairie du Chien, Wi., U.S. (prā'rĭ dò shēn')	96	43.02N	91.10W
Prairie Grove, Can. (prâ'rĭ grōv)	77f	49.48N	96.57W
Prairie Island Indian Reservation, I.R., Mn., U.S.	96	44.42N	92.32W
Prairies, Rivière des, r., Can. (rē-vyâr' dā prâ-rē')	77a	45.40N	73.34W
Pratas Island, i., Asia	184	20.40N	116.30E
Prat del Llobregat, Spain	234e	41.20N	2.06E
Prato, Italy (prä'tō)	154	43.53N	11.03E
Pratt, Ks., U.S. (prăt)	104	37.37N	98.43W
Pratt's Bottom, neigh., Eng., U.K.	231	51.20N	0.07E
Prattville, Al., U.S. (prăt'vĭl)	108	32.28N	86.27W
Pravdinsk, Russia	146	54.26N	21.00E
Pravdinskiy, Russia (práv-dĕn'skĭ)	164b	56.03N	37.52E
Pravia, Spain (prä'vē-ä)	152	43.30N	6.08W
Pregolya, r., Russia (prĕ-gô'lä)	146	54.37N	20.50E
Premont, Tx., U.S. (prē-mŏnt')	106	27.20N	98.07W
Prenton, Eng., U.K.	233a	53.22N	3.03W
Prenzlau, Ger. (prĕnts'lou)	148	53.19N	13.52E
Prenzlauer Berg, neigh., Ger.	234a	52.32N	13.26E
Přerov, Czech. (przhĕ'rôf)	140	49.28N	17.28E
Prescot, Eng., U.K. (prĕs'kŭt)	138a	53.25N	2.48W
Prescott, Can. (prĕs'kŭt)	92	44.45N	75.35W
Prescott, Az., U.S. (prĕs'kŏt)	90	34.30N	112.30W
Prescott, Ar., U.S.	104	33.47N	93.23W
Prescott, Wi., U.S. (prĕs'kŏt)	101g	44.45N	92.48W
Presho, S.D., U.S. (prĕsh'ô)	96	43.56N	100.04W
Presidencia Rogue Sáenz Peña, Arg.	126	26.52S	60.15W
Presidente Epitácio, Braz. (prā-sē-dĕn'tĕ å-pē-tä'syò)	124	21.56S	52.01W
Presidente Roosevelt, Estação, trans., Braz.	230d	23.33S	46.36W
Presidio, Tx., U.S. (prĕ-sĭ'dĭ-ô)	106	29.33N	104.23W
Presidio, Río del, r., Mex. (rē'ō-dĕl-prĕ-sē'dyô)	112	23.54N	105.44W
Presidio of San Francisco, pt. of i., Ca., U.S.	227b	37.48N	122.28W
Prešov, Czech. (prĕ'shôf)	140	49.00N	21.18E
Prespa, Lake, l., Eur. (prĕs'pä)	154	40.49N	20.50E
Prespuntal, r., Ven.	125b	9.55N	64.32W
Presque Isle, Me., U.S. (prĕsk'ēl')	86	46.41N	68.03W
Pressbaum, Aus.	139e	48.12N	16.06E
Prestea, Ghana	208	5.27N	2.08W
Preston, Austl.	195a	37.45S	145.01E
Preston, Eng., U.K. (prĕs'tŭn)	144	53.46N	2.42W
Preston, Id., U.S. (pres'tŭn)	98	42.05N	111.54W
Preston, Mn., U.S. (prĕs'tŭn)	96	43.42N	92.06W
Preston, Wa., U.S.	100a	47.31N	121.56W
Prestonburg, Ky., U.S. (prĕs'tŭn-bûrg)	92	37.35N	82.50W
Prestwich, Eng., U.K. (prĕst'wĭch)	138a	53.32N	2.17W
Pretoria, S. Afr. (prē-tō'rĭ-á)	206	25.43S	28.16E
Pretoria North, S. Afr. (prē-tô'rĭ-á nōōrd)	212d	25.41S	28.11E
Préveza, Grc. (prĕ'vĕ-zä)	154	38.58N	20.44E
Pribilof Islands, is., Ak., U.S. (prĭ'bĭ-lof)	89	57.00N	169.20W
Priboj, Yugo. (prē'boi)	154	43.33N	19.33E
Price, Ut., U.S. (prīs)	102	39.35N	110.50W
Price, r., Ut., U.S.	102	39.21N	110.35W
Prichard, Al., U.S. (prĭt'chârd)	108	30.44N	88.04W
Priddis, Can. (prĭd'dĭs)	77e	50.53N	114.20W
Priddis Creek, r., Can.	77e	50.56N	114.32W
Priego, Spain (prē-ā'gō)	152	37.27N	4.13W
Prienai, Lith. (prē-ĕn'ī)	146	54.38N	23.56E
Prieska, S. Afr. (prē-ĕs'ká)	206	29.40S	22.50E
Priest Lake, l., Id., U.S. (prēst)	98	48.30N	116.43W
Priest Rapids Dam, Wa., U.S.	98	46.39N	119.55W
Priest Rapids Lake, res., Wa., U.S.	98	46.42N	119.58W
Priiskovaya, Russia (prĭ-ĕs'kô-vá-yá)	164a	60.50N	58.55E
Prijedor, Bos. (prē'yĕ-dôr)	154	44.58N	16.43E
Prijepolje, Yugo. (prĕ'yĕ-pô'lyĕ)	154	43.22N	19.41E
Prilep, Mac. (prē'lĕp)	142	41.20N	21.35E
Priluki, Ukr. (prē-lōō'kē)	160	50.36N	32.21E
Primorsk, Russia (prē-môrsk')	146	60.24N	28.35E
Primorsko-Akhtarskaya, Russia (prē-môr'skô äκ-tär'skĭ-ê)	160	46.03N	38.09E
Primos, Pa., U.S.	225b	39.55N	75.18W
Primrose, S. Afr.	207b	26.11S	28.11E
Primrose Lake, l., Can.	82	54.55N	109.45W
Prince Albert, Can. (prĭns ăl'bērt)	78	53.12N	105.46W
Prince Albert National Park, rec., Can.	78	54.10N	105.25W
Prince Albert Sound, strt., Can.	78	70.23N	116.57W
Prince Charles Island, i., Can. (chärlz)	78	67.41N	74.10W
Prince Edward Island, prov., Can.	78	46.45N	63.10W
Prince Edward Islands, is., S. Afr.	213	46.36S	37.57E
Prince Edward National Park, rec., Can. (ĕd'wērd)	78	46.33N	63.35W
Prince Edward Peninsula, pen., Can.	92	44.00N	77.15W
Prince Frederick, Md., U.S. (prĭnce frĕdĕrĭk)	94e	38.33N	76.35W
Prince George, Can. (jôrj)	78	53.51N	122.57W
Prince of Wales, i., Austl.	196	10.47S	142.15E
Prince of Wales, i., Ak., U.S.	89	55.47N	132.50W
Prince of Wales, Cape, c., Ak., U.S. (wālz)	89	65.48N	169.08W
Prince Rupert, Can. (roo'pērt)	78	54.19N	130.19W
Princes Risborough, Eng., U.K. (prĭns'ĕz rĭz'brŭ)	138b	51.41N	0.51W
Princess Charlotte Bay, b., Austl. (shär'lŏt)	196	13.45S	144.15E
Princess Royal Channel, strt., Can. (roi'ăl)	80	53.10N	128.37W
Princess Royal Island, i., Can.	80	52.57N	128.49W
Princeton, Can. (prĭns'tŭn)	78	49.27N	120.31W
Princeton, Il., U.S.	92	41.20N	89.25W
Princeton, In., U.S.	92	38.20N	87.35W
Princeton, Ky., U.S.	108	37.07N	87.52W
Princeton, Mi., U.S.	96	46.16N	87.33W
Princeton, Mn., U.S.	96	45.34N	93.36W
Princeton, Mo., U.S.	104	40.23N	93.34W
Princeton, N.J., U.S.	92	40.21N	74.40W
Princeton, W.V., U.S.	108	37.21N	81.05W
Princeton, Wi., U.S.	96	43.50N	89.09W
Prince William Sound, strt., Ak., U.S. (wĭl'yăm)	89	60.40N	147.10W
Príncipe, i., S. Tom./P. (prēn'sē-pē)	204	1.37N	7.25E
Principe Channel, strt., Can. (prĭn'sĭ-pē)	80	53.28N	129.45W
Prineville, Or., U.S. (prīn'vĭl)	98	44.17N	120.48W
Prineville Reservoir, res., Or., U.S.	98	44.07N	120.45W
Prinzapolca, Nic. (prēn-zä-pōl'kä)	114	13.18N	83.35W
Prinzapolca, r., Nic.	114	13.23N	84.23W
Prior Lake, Mn., U.S. (prī'ēr)	101g	44.43N	93.26W
Priozërsk, Russia (prĭ-ô'zērsk)	146	61.03N	30.08E
Pripyat, r., Eur. (prē'pyät)	160	51.50N	29.45E
Pripyat Marshes, see Poles'ye, sw., Eur.	160	52.10N	27.30E
Priština, Yugo. (prēsh'tĭ-nä)	142	42.39N	21.12E
Pritzwalk, Ger. (prĭts'välk)	148	53.09N	12.12E
Privas, Fr. (prē-väs')	150	44.44N	4.37E
Privol'noye, Ukr. (prē'vôl-nô-yĕ)	156	47.30N	32.21E
Prizren, Yugo. (prē'zrĕn)	142	42.11N	20.45E
Procida, Italy (prô'chē-dä)	153c	40.31N	14.02E
Procida, Isola di, i., Italy	153c	40.32N	13.57E
Proctor, Mn., U.S. (prŏk'tēr)	101h	46.45N	92.14W
Proctor, Vt., U.S.	92	43.40N	73.00W
Proebstel, Wa., U.S. (prŏb'stĕl)	100c	45.40N	122.29W
Proenca-a-Nova, Port. (prô-ān'sá-ä-nō'vá)	152	39.44N	7.55W
Progreso, Hond. (prô-grĕ'sô)	114	15.28N	87.49W
Progreso, Mex.	106	27.29N	101.05W
Progreso, Mex. (prô-grā'sō)	110	21.14N	89.39W
Prokop'yevsk, Russia	162	53.53N	86.45E
Prokuplje, Yugo. (prô'kôp'l-yĕ)	154	43.16N	21.40E
Prome, Burma	188	18.46N	95.15E
Pronya, r., Bela. (prô'nyä)	156	54.08N	30.58E
Pronya, r., Russia	156	54.08N	39.30E
Prospect, Austl.	239a	33.48S	150.56E
Prospect, Ky., U.S. (prŏs'pĕkt)	95h	38.21N	85.36W
Prospect Heights, Il., U.S.	227a	42.06N	87.56W
Prospect Park, N.J., U.S.	224	40.56N	74.10W
Prospect Park, Pa., U.S. (prŏs'pĕkt pärk)	94f	39.53N	75.18W
Prosser, Wa., U.S. (prŏs'ēr)	98	46.10N	119.46W
Prostějov, Czech. (prôs'tyĕ-yôf)	148	49.28N	17.08E
Protea, S. Afr.	240b	26.17S	27.51E
Protection, i., Wa., U.S. (prô-tĕk'shŭn)	100a	48.07N	122.56W
Protoka, r., Russia (prôt'ô-kä)	156	55.00N	36.42E
Provadiya, Bul. (prō-väd'ē-yá)	154	43.13N	27.28E
Providence, Ky., U.S. (prŏv'ĭ-dĕns)	92	37.25N	87.45W
Providence, R.I., U.S.	90	41.50N	71.23W
Providence, Ut., U.S.	98	41.42N	111.50W
Providencia, Chile	230b	33.26S	70.37W
Providencia, Isla de, i., Col.	114	13.21N	80.55W
Providenciales, i., T./C. Is.	116	21.50N	72.15W
Provideniya, Russia (prô-vĭ-dă'nĭ-yá)	89	64.30N	172.54W
Provincetown, Ma., U.S.	92	42.03N	70.11W
Provo, Ut., U.S. (prō'vō)	90	40.15N	111.40W
Prozor, Bos. (prô'zôr)	154	43.48N	17.59E
Prudence Island, i., R.I., U.S. (prōō'dĕns)	94b	41.38N	71.20W
Prudhoe Bay, b., Ak., U.S.	89	70.40N	147.25W
Prudnik, Pol. (prôd'nĭk)	148	50.19N	17.34E
Prussia, hist. reg., Eur. (prŭsh'á)	148	50.43N	8.35E
Pruszków, Pol. (prôsh'kôf)	148	52.09N	20.50E
Prut, r., Eur. (prōōt)	136	48.05N	27.07E
Pryor, Ok., U.S. (prī'ēr)	104	36.16N	95.19W
Przedbórz, Pol.	148	51.05N	19.53E
Przemyśl, Pol. (pzhĕ'mĭsh'l)	136	49.47N	22.45E
Przheval'sk, Kyrg. (p'r-zhĭ-välsk')	158	42.29N	78.24E
Psël, r., Eur. (psĕl)	160	49.45N	33.42E
Psikhikón, Grc.	235d	38.00N	23.47E
Pskov, Russia (pskôf)	158	57.48N	28.19E
Pskov, prov., Russia	156	57.33N	29.05E
Pskovskoye Ozero, l., Eur. (p'skôv'skô'yĕ ôzē-rō)	160	58.05N	28.15E
Ptich', r., Bela. (p'tēch)	160	53.17N	28.16E
Ptuj, Slo. (ptōō'ē)	154	46.24N	15.54E
Pucheng, China (pōō-chŭŋ)	182	35.43N	115.22E
Pucheng, China (pōō'chĕng')	184	28.02N	118.25E
Puck, Pol. (pòtsk)	148	54.43N	18.23E
Puddington, Eng., U.K.	233a	53.15N	3.00W

PLACE (Pronunciation)	PAGE	Lat. °'	Long. °'
Pudozh, Russia (po͞o'dôzh)	160	61.50N	36.50E
Puebla, Mex. (pwā'blä)	110	19.02N	98.11W
Puebla, state, Mex.	112	19.00N	97.45W
Puebla de Don Fadrique, Spain	152	37.55N	2.55W
Pueblo, Co., U.S. (pwā'blō)	90	38.15N	104.36W
Pueblo Libre, Peru	229c	12.05S	77.05W
Pueblo Nuevo, Mex. (nwā'vō)	112	23.23N	105.21W
Pueblo Nuevo, neigh., Spain	234b	40.26N	3.39W
Pueblo Viejo, Mex. (vyā'hō)	112	17.23N	93.46W
Puente Alto, Chile (pwĕ'n-tĕ ál'tô)	123b	33.36S	70.34W
Puenteareas, Spain (pwĕn-tä-ä-rä'äs)	152	42.09N	8.23W
Puentedeume, Spain (pwĕn-tå-dhå-o͞o'må)	152	43.28N	8.09W
Puente-Genil, Spain (pwĕn'tå-hå-nēl')	152	37.25N	4.18W
Puerco, Rio, r., N.M., U.S. (pwĕr'kō)	102	35.15N	107.05W
Puerto Aisén, Chile (pwĕ'r-tō ä'y-sĕ'n)	126	45.28S	72.44W
Puerto Angel, Mex. (pwĕ'r-tō äŋ'hål)	112	15.42N	96.32W
Puerto Armuelles, Pan. (pwe'r-tō är-mo͞o-ā'lyās)	114	8.18N	82.52W
Puerto Barrios, Guat. (pwĕ'r-tō bär'rē-ōs)	110	15.43N	88.36W
Puerto Bermúdez, Peru (pwĕ'r-tō bĕr-mo͞o'dāz)	124	10.17S	74.57W
Puerto Berrío, Col. (pwĕ'r-tō bĕr-rē'ō)	124	6.29N	74.27W
Puerto Cabello, Ven. (pwĕ'r-tō kä-bĕl'yō)	124	10.28N	68.01W
Puerto Cabezas, Nic. (pwĕ'r-tō kä-bā'zäs)	114	14.01N	83.26W
Puerto Casado, Para. (pwĕ'r-tō kä-sä'dō)	126	22.16S	57.57W
Puerto Castilla, Hond. (pwĕ'r-tō käs-tēl'yō)	114	16.01N	86.01W
Puerto Chicama, Peru (pwĕ'r-tō chē-kä'mä)	124	7.46S	79.18W
Puerto Colombia, Col. (pwĕr'tō kō-lôm'bē-å)	124	11.08N	75.09W
Puerto Cortés, C.R. (pwĕ'r-tō kôr-tās')	114	9.00N	83.37W
Puerto Cortés, Hond. (pwĕ'r-tō kôr-tās')	110	15.48N	87.57W
Puerto Cumarebo, Ven. (pwĕ'r-tō ko͞o-mä-rĕ'bō)	124	11.25N	69.17W
Puerto de Luna, N.M., U.S. (pwĕr'tō då lo͞o'nä)	104	34.49N	104.36W
Puerto de Nutrias, Ven. (pwĕ'r-tō dĕ no͞o-trē-äs')	124	8.02N	69.19W
Puerto Deseado, Arg. (pwĕ'r-tō dā-så-ä'dhō)	126	47.38S	66.00W
Puerto de Somport, p., Eur.	152	42.51N	0.25W
Puerto Eten, Peru (pwĕ'r-tō ĕ-tĕ'n)	124	6.59S	79.51W
Puerto Jiménez, C.R. (pwĕ'r-tō κē-mĕ'nĕz)	114	8.35N	83.23W
Puerto La Cruz, Ven. (pwĕ'r-tō lä kro͞o'z)	124	10.14N	64.38W
Puertollano, Spain (pwĕ-tôl-yä'nō)	142	38.41N	4.05W
Puerto Madryn, Arg. (pwĕ'r-tō mä-drĕn')	126	42.45S	65.01W
Puerto Maldonado, Peru (pwĕr-tō mäl-dō-nä'dō)	124	12.43S	69.01W
Puerto Miniso, Mex. (pwĕ'r-tō mē-nē'sō)	112	16.06N	98.02W
Puerto Montt, Chile (pwĕ'r-tō mô'nt)	126	41.29S	73.00W
Puerto Natales, Chile (pwĕ'r-tō nä-tá'lĕs)	126	51.48S	72.01W
Puerto Niño, Col. (pwĕ'r-tō nē'n-yō)	124a	5.57N	74.36W
Puerto Padre, Cuba (pwĕ'r-tō pä'drā)	116	21.10N	76.40W
Puerto Peñasco, Mex. (pwĕ'r-tō pĕn-yä's-kō)	110	31.39N	113.15W
Puerto Pinasco, Para. (pwĕ'r-tō pē-nå's-kō)	126	22.31S	57.50W
Puerto Píritu, Ven. (pwĕ'r-tō pē'rē-to͞o)	125b	10.05N	65.04W
Puerto Plata, Dom. Rep. (pwĕ'r-tō plä'tä)	110	19.50N	70.40W
Puerto Princesa, Phil. (pwĕr-tō prēn-sā'sä)	188	9.45N	118.41E
Puerto Rico, dep., N.A. (pwĕr'tō rē'kō)	110	18.16N	66.50W
Puerto Rico Trench, deep	110	19.45N	66.30W
Puerto Salgar, Col. (pwĕ'r-tō säl-gär')	124a	5.30N	74.39W
Puerto Santa Cruz, Arg. (pwĕ'r-tō sän'tä kro͞oz')	126	50.04S	68.32W
Puerto Suárez, Bol. (pwĕ'r-tō swä'rāz)	124	18.55S	57.39W
Puerto Tejada, Col. (pwĕ'r-tō tĕ-κä'dä)	124	3.13N	76.23W
Puerto Vallarta, Mex. (pwĕ'r-tō väl-yär'tä)	112	20.36N	105.13W
Puerto Varas, Chile (pwĕ'r-tō vä'räs)	126	41.16S	73.03W
Puerto Wilches, Col. (pwĕ'r-tō vēl'c-hĕs)	124	7.19N	73.54W
Pugachëv, Russia (po͞o'gå-chyôf)	160	52.00N	48.40E
Puget, Wa., U.S. (pū'jĕt)	100c	46.10N	123.23W
Puget Sound, strt., Wa., U.S.	98	47.49N	122.26W
Puglia (Apulia), hist. reg., Italy (po͞o'lyä) (ä-po͞o'lyä)	154	41.13N	16.10E
Pukaskwa National Park, rec., Can.	78	48.22N	85.55W
Pukeashun Mountain, mtn., Can.	80	51.12N	119.14W
Pukin, r., Malay.	173b	2.53N	102.54E
Pula, Cro. (po͞o'lä)	142	44.52N	13.55E
Pulacayo, Bol. (po͞o-lä-kä'yō)	124	20.12N	66.33W
Pulaski, Tn., U.S. (pū-lăs'kĭ)	108	35.11N	87.03W
Pulaski, Va., U.S.	108	37.00N	81.45W
Puławy, Pol. (pō-wä'vĕ)	148	51.24N	21.59E
Pulicat, r., India	178	13.58N	79.52E
Pullman, Wa., U.S. (pōol'măn)	98	46.44N	117.10W
Pullman, neigh., Il., U.S.	227a	41.43N	87.36W
Pulog, mtn., Phil. (po͞o'lôg)	189a	16.38N	120.53E
Puma Yumco, l., China (po͞o-mä yo͞om-tswo)	178	28.30N	90.10E
Pumphrey, Md., U.S.	225c	39.13N	76.38W
Pumpkin Creek, r., Mt., U.S. (pŭmp'kĭn)	98	45.47N	105.35W
Punakha, Bhu. (po͞o-nŭk'ŭ)	174	27.45N	89.59E
Punata, Bol. (po͞o-nä'tä)	124	17.43S	65.43W
Punchbowl, Austl.	239a	33.56S	151.03E
Pune, India	174	18.38N	73.53E
Punggol, Sing.	236c	1.25N	103.55E
Punjab, state, India (pŭn'jäb')	174	31.00N	75.30E
Puno, Peru (po͞o'nō)	124	15.58S	70.02W
Punta Arenas, Chile (po͞o'n-tä-rĕ'näs)	126	53.09S	70.48W
Punta Brava, Cuba	229b	23.01N	82.30W
Punta de Piedras, Ven. (po͞o'n-tä dĕ pyĕ'dräs)	125b	10.54N	64.06W
Punta Gorda, Belize (pōn'tä gôr'dä)	114	16.07N	88.50W
Punta Gorda, Fl., U.S. (pŭn'tå gôr'då)	109a	26.55N	82.02W
Punta Gorda, Río, r., Nic. (po͞o'n-tä gô'r-dä)	114	11.34N	84.13W
Punta Indio, Canal, strt., Arg. (po͞o'n-tä- ē'n-dyō)	123c	34.56S	57.20W
Puntarenas, C.R. (pōnt-ä-rā'näs)	110	9.59N	84.49W
Punto Fijo, Ven. (po͞o'n-tō fē'κō)	124	11.48N	70.14W
Punxsutawney, Pa., U.S. (pŭnk-sŭ-tô'nē)	92	40.55N	79.00W
Puquio, Peru (po͞o'kyō)	124	14.43S	74.02W
Pur, r., Russia	162	65.30N	77.30E
Purcell, Ok., U.S. (pûr-sĕl')	104	35.01N	97.22W
Purcell Mountains, mts., N.A. (pûr-sĕl')	80	50.00N	116.30W
Purdy, Wa., U.S. (pûr'dē)	100a	47.23N	122.37W
Purépero, Mex. (po͞o-rā'pā-rō)	112	19.56N	102.02W
Purfleet, Eng., U.K.	231	51.29N	0.15E
Purgatoire, r., Co., U.S. (pûr-gå-twär')	104	37.25N	103.53W
Puri, India (pō'rē)	174	19.52N	85.51E
Purial, Sierra de, mts., Cuba (sē-ĕ'r-rå-dē-po͞o-rē-äl')	116	20.15N	74.40W
Purificación, Col. (po͞o-rē-fē-kä-syōn')	124	3.52N	74.54W
Purificación, Mex. (po͞o-rē-fē-kä-syō'n)	112	19.44N	104.38W
Purificación, r., Mex.	112	19.30N	104.54W
Purkersdorf, Aus.	139e	48.13N	16.11E
Purley, neigh., Eng., U.K.	231	51.20N	0.07W
Puruandiro, Mex. (pō-ro͞o-än'dē-rō)	112	20.04N	101.33W
Purús, r., S.A. (po͞o-ro͞o's)	124	6.45S	64.34W
Pusan, S. Kor.	180	35.08N	129.05E
Pushkin, Russia (pōsh'kĭn)	160	59.43N	30.25E
Pushkino, Russia (po͞osh'kē-nō)	156	56.01N	37.51E
Pustoshka, Russia (pûs-tôsh'kå)	156	56.20N	29.33E
Pustunich, Mex. (po͞os-to͞o'nēch)	112	19.10N	90.29W
Putaendo, Chile (po͞o-tä-ĕn-dō)	123b	32.37S	70.42W
Puteaux, Fr. (pü-tō')	151b	48.52N	2.12E
Putfontein, S. Afr. (pōt'fōn-tān)	207b	26.08S	28.24E
Puth Kalān, neigh., India	236d	28.43N	77.05E
Putian, China (po͞o-tĭĕn)	184	25.40N	119.02E
Putilkovo, Russia	235b	55.52N	37.23E
Putivl', Ukr. (po͞o-tēv'l')	156	51.21N	33.52E
Putla de Guerrero, Mex. (po͞o'tlä-dĕ-gĕr-rĕ'rō)	112	17.03N	97.55W
Putnam, Ct., U.S. (pŭt'năm)	92	41.55N	71.55W
Putney, neigh., Eng., U.K.	231	51.28N	0.13W
Putorana, Gory, mts., Russia	158	68.45N	93.15E
Pütt, Ger.	232	51.11N	6.59E
Puttalam, Sri L.	175c	8.02N	79.44E
Putumayo, r., S.A. (po͞o-to͞o-mä'yō)	124	1.02S	73.50W
Putung, Tanjung, c., Indon.	188	3.35S	111.50E
Puulavesi, l., Fin.	146	61.49N	27.10E
Puyallup, Wa., U.S. (pū-ăl'ŭp)	100a	47.12N	122.18W
Puyang, China (po͞o-yäŋ)	184	35.42N	114.58E
Pweto, Zaire (pwä'tō)	206	8.29S	28.58E
Pyasina, r., Russia (pyä-sē'nå)	162	72.45N	87.37E
Pyatigorsk, Russia (pyå-tē-gôrsk')	160	44.00N	43.00E
Pyhäjärvi, l., Fin.	146	60.57N	21.50E
Pyinmana, Burma (pyēn-mä'nŭ)	174	19.47N	96.15E
Pymatuning Reservoir, res., Pa., U.S. (pī-må-tŭn'ĭng)	92	41.40N	80.30W
Pymble, Austl.	239a	33.45S	151.09E
Pyŏnggang, N. Kor. (pyŭng'gäng')	186	38.21N	127.18E
P'yŏngyang, N. Kor.	180	39.03N	125.48E
Pyramid, l., Nv., U.S. (pĭ'rå-mĭd)	102	40.02N	119.50W
Pyramid Lake Indian Reservation, I.R., Nv., U.S.	102	40.17N	119.52W
Pyramids, hist., Egypt	212b	29.53N	31.10E
Pyrenees, mts., Eur. (pĭr-e-nēz')	136	43.00N	0.05E
Pyrford, Eng., U.K.	231	51.19N	0.30W
Pyrzyce, Pol. (pĕzhĭ'tsĕ)	148	53.09N	14.53E

Q

PLACE (Pronunciation)	PAGE	Lat. °'	Long. °'
Qal'at Bishah, Sau. Ar.	174	20.01N	42.30E
Qamdo, China (chyäm-dwō)	180	31.06N	96.30E
Qandahār, Afg.	174	31.43N	65.58E
Qandala, Som.	176	11.28N	49.52E
Qarqan, r., China	180	38.55N	87.15E
Qarqan, see Qiemo, China	180	38.02N	85.16E
Qārūn, Birket, l., Egypt	204	29.34N	30.34E
Qaṣr al Burayqah, Libya	204	30.25N	19.20E
Qasr al-Farāfirah, Egypt	204	27.04N	28.13E
Qaṣr Banī Walīd, Libya	204	31.45N	14.04E
Qasr-e Fīrūzeh, Iran	237h	35.40N	51.32E
Qasr el Boukhari, Alg.	142	35.50N	2.48E
Qatar, nation, Asia (kä'tår)	174	25.00N	52.45E
Qaṭārah, Munkhafaḍ al, depr., Egypt	204	30.07N	27.30E
Qāyen, Iran	174	33.45N	59.08E
Qazvīn, Iran	174	36.10N	49.59E
Qeshm, Iran	174	26.51N	56.10E
Qeshm, i., Iran	174	26.52N	56.15E
Qezel Owzan, r., Iran	174	36.30N	49.00E
Qezi'ot, Isr.	173a	30.53N	34.28E
Qianwei, China (chyĕn-wā)	182	40.11N	120.05E
Qi'anzhen, China (chyē-än-jŭn)	182	32.16N	120.59E
Qibao, China (chyē-bou)	183b	31.06N	121.16E
Qiblīyah, Jabal al Jalālat al, mts., Egypt	173a	28.49N	32.21E
Qieshikou, China	236b	39.59N	116.24E
Qijiang, China (chyē-jyäŋ)	184	29.05N	106.40E
Qikou, China (chyē-kō)	182	38.37N	117.33E
Qilian Shan, mts., China (chyē-lĭĕn shän)	180	38.43N	98.00E
Qiliping, China (chyē-lē-pĭŋ)	182	31.28N	114.41E
Qindao, China (chyĭn-dou)	180	36.05N	120.10E
Qing'an, China (chyĭŋ-än)	184	46.50N	127.30E
Qingcheng, China (chyĭŋ-chŭŋ)	182	37.12N	117.43E
Qingfeng, China (chyĭŋ-fŭŋ)	182	35.52N	115.05E
Qinghai, prov., China (chyĭŋ-hī)	180	36.14N	95.30E
Qinghai Hu, see Koko Nor, l., China	180	37.26N	98.30E
Qinghe, China (chyĭŋ-hŭ)	184a	40.08N	116.16E
Qinghuayuan, China	236b	40.00N	116.19E
Qingjiang, China	182	33.34N	118.58E
Qingjiang, China (chyĭŋ-jyäŋ)	184	28.00N	115.30E
Qingliu, China (chyĭŋ-lĭō)	184	26.15N	116.50E
Qingningsi, China (chyĭŋ-nĭŋ-sz)	183b	31.16N	121.33E
Qingping, China (chyĭŋ-pĭŋ)	182	36.46N	116.03E
Qingpu, China (chyĭŋ-po͞o)	184	31.08N	121.06E
Qingxian, China (chyĭŋ shyĕn)	182	38.37N	116.48E
Qingyang, China (chyĭŋ-yäŋ)	180	36.02N	107.42E
Qingyuan, China (chyĭŋ-yōän)	184	23.43N	113.10E
Qingyuan, China	184	42.05N	125.00E
Qingyun, China (chyĭŋ-yōn)	182	37.52N	117.26E
Qingyundian, China (chĭŋ-yōn-dĭĕn)	184a	39.41N	116.31E
Qinhuangdao, China (chyĭn-huaŋ-dou)	180	39.57N	119.34E
Qin Ling, mts., China (chyĭn lĭŋ)	180	33.25N	108.58E
Qinyang, China (chyĭn-yäŋ)	184	35.00N	112.55E
Qinzhou, China (chyĭn-jō)	184	22.00N	108.35E
Qionghai, China (chyôŋ-hī)	184	19.10N	110.28E
Qiqian, China (chyē-chyĕn)	180	52.23N	121.04E
Qiqihar, China	180	47.18N	124.00E
Qiryat Gat, Isr.	173a	31.38N	34.36E
Qiryat Shemona, Isr.	173a	33.12N	35.34E
Qitai, China (chyē-tī)	180	44.07N	89.04E
Qiuxian, China (chyō shyĕn)	182	36.43N	115.13E
Qixian, China (chyē-shyĕn)	182	34.33N	114.47E
Qixian, China	184	35.36N	114.13E
Qiyang, China (chyē-yäŋ)	184	26.40N	112.00E
Qom, Iran	174	34.28N	50.53E
Quabbin Reservoir, res., Ma., U.S. (kwā'bĭn)	92	42.20N	72.10W
Quachita, Lake, l., Ar., U.S. (kwä shĭ'tô)	104	34.47N	93.37W
Quadra Island, i., Can.	80	50.08N	125.16W
Quadraro, neigh., Italy	235c	41.51N	12.33E
Quakers Hill, Austl.	239a	33.43S	150.53E
Quakertown, Pa., U.S. (kwā'kĕr-toun)	92	40.30N	75.20W
Quanah, Tx., U.S. (kwä'nå)	104	34.19N	99.43W
Quang Ngai, Viet. (kwäng n'gä'ē)	188	15.05N	108.58E
Quang Ngai, mtn., Viet.	188	15.10N	108.20E
Quanjiao, China (chyuän-jyou)	182	32.06N	118.17E
Quanzhou, China (chyuän-jō)	180	24.58N	118.40E
Quanzhou, China	184	25.58N	111.02E
Qu'Appelle, r., Can.	78	50.30N	104.00W
Qu'Appelle Dam, dam, Can.	82	51.00N	106.25W
Quartu Sant'Elena, Italy (kwär-to͞o' sänt ä'lå-nä)	154	39.16N	9.12E
Quartzsite, Az., U.S.	102	33.40N	114.13W
Quatsino Sound, strt., Can. (kwŏt-sē'nō)	80	50.25N	128.10W
Qūchān, Iran	176	37.06N	58.30E
Qudi, China	182	37.06N	117.15E
Québec, Can. (kwē-bĕk') (kå-bĕk')	77b	46.49N	71.13W
Quebec, prov., Can.	78	51.07N	70.25W
Quedlinburg, Ger. (kvĕd'lĕn-bo͞orgh)	148	51.45N	11.10E
Queen Bess, Can.	80	51.16N	124.34W
Queen Charlotte Islands, is., Can. (kwēn shär'lŏt)	78	53.30N	132.25W
Queen Charlotte Ranges, mts., Can.	80	53.00N	132.00W
Queen Charlotte Sound, strt., Can.	80	51.30N	129.30W
Queen Charlotte Strait, strt., Can. (strāt)	78	50.40N	127.25W
Queen Elizabeth Islands, is., Can. (ē-lĭz'å-bĕth)	76	78.20N	110.00W
Queen Maud Gulf, b., Can. (măd)	78	68.27N	102.55W
Queen Maud Land, reg., Ant.	213	75.00S	10.00E
Queen Maud Mountains, mts., Ant.	213	85.00S	179.00W
Queens Channel, strt., Austl. (kwēnz)	196	14.25S	129.10E
Queenscliff, Austl.	195a	38.16S	144.39E
Queensland, state, Austl. (kwēnz'lănd)	196	22.45S	141.01E
Queenstown, Austl. (kwēnz'toun)	198	42.00S	145.40E
Queenstown, S. Afr.	207c	31.54S	26.53E
Queimados, Braz. (kä-må'dôs)	126b	22.42S	43.34W
Quela, Ang.	210	9.16S	17.02E
Quelimane, Moz. (kä-lē-mä'nĕ)	206	17.48S	37.05E
Queluz, Port.	153b	38.45N	9.15W
Quemado de Güines, Cuba (kä-mä'dhä-dĕ-gwĕ'nĕs)	116	22.45N	80.20W
Quemoy, Tai.	184	24.30N	118.20E
Quemoy, i., Tai.	184	24.27N	118.23E
Quepos, C.R. (kā'pôs)	114	9.26N	84.10W
Quepos, Punta, c., C.R. (po͞o'n-tä)	114	9.23N	84.20W
Querenburg, neigh., Ger.	232	51.27N	7.16E
Querétaro, Mex. (kå-rā'tä-rō)	110	20.37N	100.25W
Querétaro, state, Mex.	112	21.00N	100.00W
Quesada, Spain (kå-sä'dhä)	152	37.51N	3.04W
Quesnel, Can. (kā-nĕl')	78	52.59N	122.30W
Quesnel, r., Can.	80	52.15N	122.00W
Quesnel Lake, l., Can.	78	52.32N	121.05W

ăt; finăl; rāte; senåte; ärm; åsk; sofå; fâre; ch-choose; dh-as th in other; bē; ēvent; bĕt; recĕnt; cratẽr; g-gō; gh-guttural g; bĭt; ĭ-short neutral; rīde; κ-guttural k as ch in German ich;

PLACE (Pronunciation)	PAGE	Lat. °'	Long. °'
Quetame, Col. (kĕ-tä′mĕ)	124a	4.20N	73.50W
Quetta, Pak. (kwĕt′ä)	174	30.19N	67.01E
Quezaltenango, Guat. (kå-zäl′tå-näŋ′gō)	110	14.50N	91.30W
Quezaltepeque, El Sal. (kĕ-zäl′tĕ′pĕ-kĕ)	114	13.50N	89.17W
Quezaltepeque, Guat. (kå-zäl′tå-pä′kå)	114	14.39N	89.26W
Quezon City, Phil. (kā-zōn)	188	14.40N	121.02E
Qufu, China (chyōō-fōō)	182	35.37N	116.54E
Quibdo, Col. (kēb′dō)	124	5.42N	76.41W
Quiberon, Fr. (kē-bē-rôn′)	150	47.29N	3.08W
Quiçama, Parque Nacional de, rec., Ang.	210	10.00S	13.25E
Quicksborn, Ger. (kvēks′bōrn)	139c	53.44N	9.54E
Quilcene, Wa., U.S. (kwĭl-sēn′)	100a	47.50N	122.53W
Quilimari, Chile (kē-lē-mä′rē)	123b	32.06S	71.28W
Quillan, Fr. (kē-yäN′)	150	42.53N	2.13E
Quillota, Chile (kēl-yō′tä)	126	32.52S	71.14W
Quilmes, Arg. (kēl′mās)	123c	34.43S	58.16W
Quilon, India (kwē-lōn′)	175c	8.58N	76.16E
Quilpie, Austl. (kwĭl′pē)	196	26.34S	149.20E
Quimbaya, Col. (kēm-bä′yä)	124a	4.38N	75.46W
Quimbele, Ang.	210	6.28S	16.13E
Quimbonge, Ang.	210	8.36S	18.30E
Quimper, Fr. (kăN-pĕr′)	140	47.59N	4.04W
Quinalt, r., Wa., U.S.	98	47.23N	124.10W
Quinault Indian Reservation, I.R., Wa., U.S.	98	47.27N	124.34W
Quincy, Fl., U.S. (kwĭn′sē)	108	30.35N	84.35W
Quincy, Il., U.S.	90	39.55N	91.23W
Quincy, Ma., U.S.	87a	42.15N	71.00W
Quincy, Mi., U.S.	92	42.00N	84.50W
Quincy, Or., U.S.	100c	46.08N	123.10W
Quincy Bay, b., Ma., U.S.	223a	42.17N	70.58W
Qui Nhon, Viet. (kwĭnyôn)	188	13.51N	109.03E
Quinn, r., Nv., U.S. (kwĭn)	98	41.42N	117.45W
Quintanar de la Orden, Spain (kēn-tä-när′)	152	39.36N	3.02W
Quintana Roo, state, Mex. (rô′ô)	110	19.30N	88.30W
Quinta Normal, Chile	230b	33.27S	70.42W
Quintero, Chile (kēn-tĕ′rô)	123b	32.48S	71.30W
Quinto Romano, neigh., Italy	234c	45.29N	9.05E
Quionga, Moz.	210	10.37S	40.30E
Quiroga, Mex. (kē-rō′gä)	112	19.39N	101.30W
Quiroga, Spain (kē-rô′gä)	152	42.28N	7.18W
Quitaúna, Braz.	230d	23.31S	46.47W
Quitman, Ga., U.S. (kwĭt′măn)	108	30.46N	83.35W
Quitman, Ms., U.S.	108	33.02N	88.43W
Quito, Ec. (kē′tō)	124	0.17S	78.32W
Qumbu, Transkei (kòm′bōō)	207c	31.10S	28.48E
Quorn, Austl. (kwôrn)	198	32.20S	138.00E
Qurayyah, Wādī, r., Egypt	173a	30.08N	34.27E
Qutang, China (chyōō-täŋ)	182	32.33N	120.07E
Quthing, Leso.	207c	30.35S	27.42E
Quxian, China (chyōō-shyĕn)	180	28.58N	118.58E
Quxian, China	184	30.40N	106.48E
Quzhou, China (chyoō-jō)	182	36.47N	114.58E

R

PLACE (Pronunciation)	PAGE	Lat. °'	Long. °'
Raab (Raba), r., Eur. (räp)	148	46.55N	15.55E
Raadt, neigh., Ger.	232	51.24N	6.56E
Raahe, Fin. (rä′ĕ)	140	64.39N	24.22E
Raasdorf, Aus.	235e	48.15N	16.34E
Rab, i., Yugo. (räb)	154	44.45N	14.40E
Raba, Indon.	188	8.32S	118.49E
Raba (Raab), r., Eur.	148	47.28N	17.12E
Rabat, Mor. (rá-bät′)	204	33.59N	6.47W
Rabaul, Pap. N. Gui. (rä′boul)	188	4.15S	152.19E
Rābigh, Sau. Ar.	176	22.48N	39.01E
Raby, Eng., U.K.	233a	53.19N	3.02W
Raccoon, r., Ia., U.S. (ră-kōōn′)	96	42.07N	94.45W
Raccoon Cay, i., Bah.	116	22.25N	75.50W
Race, Cape, c., Can. (rās)	86	46.40N	53.10W
Raceview, S. Afr.	240b	26.17S	28.08E
Rachado, Cape, c., Malay.	173b	2.26N	101.29E
Racibórz, Pol. (rä-chē′bōōzh)	148	50.06N	18.14E
Racine, Wi., U.S. (rȧ-sēn′)	90	42.43N	87.49W
Raco, Mi., U.S. (rȧ cō)	101k	46.22N	84.43W
Rădăuti, Rom.	142	47.53N	25.55E
Radcliffe, Eng., U.K. (răd′klĭf)	138a	53.34N	2.20W
Radevormwald, Ger. (rä′dĕ-fōrm-väld)	151c	51.12N	7.22E
Radford, Va., U.S. (răd′fĕrd)	108	37.06N	81.33W
Rādhanpur, India	178	23.57N	71.38E
Radium, S. Afr. (rā′dĭ-ŭm)	212d	25.06S	28.18E
Radlett, Eng., U.K.	231	51.42N	0.20W
Radnor, Pa., U.S.	225b	40.02N	75.21W
Radom, Pol. (rä′dôm)	140	51.24N	21.11E
Radomir, Bul. (rä′dô-mēr)	154	42.33N	22.58E
Radomsko, Pol. (rä-dôm′skô)	140	51.04N	19.27E
Radomyshl, Ukr. (rä-dô-mēsh″l)	160	50.30N	29.13E
Radul′, Ukr. (rá′dōōl)	156	51.52N	30.46E
Radviliškis, Lith. (räd′vē-lēsh′kēs)	146	55.49N	23.31E
Radwah, Jabal, mtn., Sau. Ar.	174	24.44N	38.14E
Radzyń Podlaski, Pol. (räd′zēn-y′ pŭd-lä′skĭ)	148	51.49N	22.40E
Raeford, N.C., U.S. (rā′fĕrd)	108	34.57N	79.15W
Raesfeld, Ger. (rāz′fĕld)	151c	51.46N	6.50E
Raeside, l., Austl. (rā′sīd)	196	29.20S	122.30E
Rae Strait, strt., Can. (rā)	78	68.40N	95.03W
Rafaela, Arg. (rä-fä-ā′lä)	126	31.15S	61.21W
Rafael Castillo, Arg.	229d	34.42S	58.37W
Rafah, Pak. (rä′fä)	173a	31.14N	34.12E
Rafsanjān, Iran	174	30.45N	56.30E
Raft, r., Id., U.S. (răft)	98	42.20N	113.17W
Ragay, Phil. (rä-gī′)	189a	13.49N	122.45E
Ragay Gulf, b., Phil.	189a	13.44N	122.38E
Ragunda, Swe. (rä-gòn′dä)	146	63.07N	16.24E
Ragusa, Italy (rä-gōō′sä)	142	36.58N	14.41E
Rahm, neigh., Ger.	232	51.21N	6.47E
Rahnsdorf, neigh., Ger.	234a	52.26N	13.42E
Rahway, N.J., U.S. (rô′wā)	94a	40.37N	74.16W
Rāichūr, India (rä′ē-chōōr′)	174	16.23N	77.18E
Raigarh, India (rī′gŭr)	174	21.57N	83.32E
Rainbow Bridge National Monument, rec., Ut., U.S. (rān′bō)	102	37.05N	111.00W
Rainbow City, Pan.	110a	9.20N	79.53W
Rainford, Eng., U.K.	233a	53.30N	2.48W
Rainhill, Eng., U.K.	233a	53.26N	2.46W
Rainhill Stoops, Eng., U.K.	233a	53.24N	2.45W
Rainier, Or., U.S.	100c	46.05N	122.56W
Rainier, Mount, mtn., Wa., U.S. (rā-nēr′)	90	46.52N	121.46W
Rainy, r., N.A.	90	48.50N	94.41W
Rainy Lake, l., N.A. (rān′ē)	78	48.43N	94.29W
Rainy River, Can.	78	48.43N	94.29W
Raipur, India (rä′jŭ-bōō-rē′)	178	21.25N	81.37E
Raisin, r., Mi., U.S. (rā′zĭn)	92	42.00N	83.35W
Raitan, N.J., U.S. (rā-tăn)	94a	40.34N	74.40W
Rājahmundry, India (räj-ŭ-mŭn′drē)	174	17.03N	81.51E
Rajang, r., Malay.	188	2.10N	113.30E
Rājapālaiyam, India	178	9.30N	77.33E
Rājasthān, state, India (rä′jŭs-tän)	174	26.00N	72.00E
Rājkot, India (räj′kōt)	174	22.20N	70.48E
Rājpur, India	178a	22.24N	88.25E
Rājpur, neigh., India	236d	28.41N	77.12E
Rājshāhi, Bngl.	174	24.26S	88.39E
Rakhov, Ukr. (rä′kôf)	148	48.02N	24.13E
Rakh′oya, Russia (räk′yȧ)	164c	60.06N	30.50E
Rakitnoye, Russia (rá-kēt′nô-yĕ)	160	50.51N	35.53E
Rákoscsaba, neigh., Hung.	235g	47.29N	19.17E
Rákoshegy, neigh., Hung.	235g	47.28N	19.14E
Rákoskeresztúr, neigh., Hung.	235g	47.29N	19.15E
Rákosliget, neigh., Hung.	235g	47.30N	19.16E
Rákospalota, neigh., Hung.	235g	47.34N	19.08E
Rákosszentmihály, neigh., Hung.	235g	47.32N	19.11E
Rakovník, Czech.	148	50.07N	13.45E
Rakvere, Est. (rák′vĕ-rĕ)	160	59.22N	26.14E
Raleigh, N.C., U.S.	90	35.45N	78.39W
Ram, r., Can.	80	52.10N	115.05W
Rama, Nic. (rä′mä)	114	12.11N	84.14W
Ramallo, Arg. (rä-mä′l-yô)	123c	33.28S	60.02W
Ramanāthapuram, India	178	9.13N	78.52E
Rambouillet, Fr. (räN-bōō-yĕ′)	150	48.39N	1.49E
Rame Head, c., Transkei	207c	31.48S	29.22E
Ramenka, neigh., Russia	235b	55.41N	37.30E
Ramenskoye, Russia (rá′mĕn-skô-yĕ)	156	55.34N	38.15E
Ramlat as Sab′atayn, reg., Asia	174	16.08N	45.15E
Ramm, Jabal, mtn., Jord.	173a	29.37N	35.32E
Ramos, Mex. (rä′mōs)	112	22.46N	101.52W
Ramos, r., Nig.	208	5.10N	5.40E
Ramos Arizpe, Mex. (ä-rēz′pā)	106	25.33N	100.57W
Rampart, Ak., U.S. (răm′pärt)	89	65.28N	150.18W
Rampo Mountains, mts., N.J., U.S. (răm′pō)	94a	41.06N	72.12W
Rāmpur, India (räm′pōōr)	174	28.53N	79.03E
Ramree Island, i., Burma (răm′rē′)	188	19.01N	93.23E
Ramsayville, Can. (răm′zē vĭl)	77c	45.23N	75.34W
Ramsbottom, Eng., U.K. (rămz′bŏt-ŭm)	138a	53.39N	2.20W
Ramsden Heath, Eng., U.K.	231	51.38N	0.28E
Ramsey, I. of Man (răm′zē)	144	54.20N	4.25W
Ramsey, N.J., U.S.	94a	41.03N	74.09W
Ramsey Lake, l., Can.	84	47.15N	82.16W
Ramsgate, Austl.	239a	33.59S	151.08E
Ramsgate, Eng., U.K. (rămz′gāt)	144	51.19N	1.20E
Ramu, r., Pap. N. Gui. (rä′mōō)	188	5.35S	145.16E
Rancagua, Chile (rän-kä′gwä)	126	34.10S	70.43W
Rance, r., Fr. (räNs)	150	48.17N	2.30W
Rānchī, India	174	23.21N	85.20E
Ranchleigh, Md., U.S.	225c	39.22N	76.40W
Rancho Boyeros, Cuba (rä′n-chô-bô-yĕ′rôs)	117a	23.00N	82.23W
Rancho Palos Verdes, Ca., U.S.	228	33.45N	118.24W
Randallstown, Md., U.S. (răn′dălz-toun)	94e	39.22N	76.48W
Randburg, S. Afr.	240b	26.06S	27.59E
Randers, Den. (rän′ĕrs)	140	56.28N	10.03E
Randfontein, S. Afr. (ränt′fŏn-tān)	207b	26.10S	27.42E
Randleman, N.C., U.S. (răn′d′l-măn)	108	35.49N	79.50W
Randolph, Ma., U.S. (răn′dôlf)	87a	42.10N	71.03W
Randolph, Ne., U.S.	96	42.22N	97.22W
Randolph, Vt., U.S.	92	43.55N	72.40W
Random Island, i., Can. (răn′dŭm)	86	48.12N	53.25W
Randsfjorden, Nor.	146	60.35N	10.10E
Randwick, Austl.	195b	33.55S	151.15E
Ranérou, Sen.	208	15.18N	13.58W
Rangeley, Me., U.S. (rānj′lē)	86	44.56N	70.38W
Rangeley, l., Me., U.S.	86	45.00N	70.25W
Ranger, Tx., U.S. (rān′jĕr)	90	32.26N	98.41W
Rangia, India	178	26.32N	91.39E
Rangoon (Yangon), Burma (răŋ-gōōn′)	174	16.46N	96.09E
Rangpur, Bngl. (rŭng′pōōr)	174	25.48N	89.19E
Rangsang, i., Indon. (räng′säng′)	173b	0.53N	103.05E
Rangsdorf, Ger. (rängs′dōrf)	139b	52.17N	13.25E
Ranholas, Port.	234d	38.47N	9.22W
Rānīganj, India (rä-nē-gŭnj′)	178	23.40N	87.08E
Rankin, Pa., U.S.	226b	40.25N	79.53W
Rankin Inlet, b., Can. (răŋ′kĕn)	78	62.45N	94.27W
Ranova, r., Russia (rä′nô-vȧ)	156	53.55N	40.03E
Rantau, Malay.	173b	2.35N	101.58E
Rantekombola, Bulu, mtn., Indon.	188	3.22S	119.50E
Rantoul, Il., U.S. (răn-tōōl′)	92	40.25N	88.05W
Raoyang, China (rou-yäŋ)	182	38.16N	115.45E
Rapallo, Italy (rä-päl′lô)	154	44.21N	9.14E
Rapa Nui (Easter Island), i., Chile	190	26.50S	109.00W
Rapel, r., Chile (rä-pål′)	123b	34.05S	71.30W
Rapid, r., Mn., U.S. (răp′ĭd)	96	48.21N	94.50W
Rapid City, S.D., U.S.	90	44.06N	103.14W
Rapla, Est. (räp′lȧ)	146	59.02N	24.46E
Rappahannock, r., Va., U.S. (răp′ȧ-hăn′ŭk)	92	38.20N	75.25W
Raquette, l., N.Y., U.S. (răk′ĕt)	92	43.50N	74.35W
Raritan, r., N.J., U.S. (răr′ĭ-tăn)	94a	40.32N	74.27W
Rarotonga, Cook Is. (rä′rô-tŏŋ′gȧ)	2	20.40S	163.00W
Ra′s an Naqb, Jord.	173a	30.00N	35.29E
Ras Dashen Terara, mtn., Eth. (räs dä-shän′)	204	12.49N	38.14E
Raseiniai, Lith. (rä-syā′nyĭ)	146	55.23N	23.04E
Rashayya, Leb.	173a	33.30N	35.50E
Rashīd, Egypt (rȧ-shēd′) (rô-zĕt′ȧ)	176	31.22N	30.25E
Rashīd, Masabb, mth., Egypt	212b	31.30N	29.58E
Rashkina, Russia (ràsh′kĭ-nȧ)	164a	59.57N	61.30E
Rashkov, Mol. (räsh′kôf)	156	47.55N	28.51E
Rasht, Iran	174	37.13N	49.45E
Raška, Yugo. (räsh′kȧ)	154	43.16N	20.40E
Rasskazovo, Russia (räs-kä′sô-vô)	160	52.40N	41.40E
Rastatt, Ger. (rä-shtät)	148	48.51N	8.12E
Rastes, Russia (rás′tĕs)	164a	59.24N	58.49E
Rastunovo, Russia (ràs-tōō′nô-vô)	164b	55.15N	37.50E
Ratangarh, India (rŭ-tŭn′gŭr)	178	28.10N	74.30E
Ratcliff, Tx., U.S. (răt′klĭf)	106	31.22N	95.09W
Rath, neigh., Ger.	232	51.17N	6.49E
Rathenow, Ger. (rä′tĕ-nō)	148	52.36N	12.20E
Rathlin Island, i., N. Ire., U.K. (răth-lĭn)	144	55.18N	6.13W
Rathmecke, Ger.	232	51.15N	7.38E
Ratingen, Ger. (rä′tēn-gĕn)	151c	51.18N	6.51E
Rat Islands, is., Ak., U.S. (răt)	89a	51.35N	176.48E
Ratlām, India	178	23.19N	75.05E
Ratnāgiri, India	178	17.04N	73.24E
Raton, N.M., U.S. (rȧ-tōn′)	90	36.52N	104.26W
Rattlesnake Creek, r., Or., U.S. (răt″l snāk)	98	42.38N	117.39W
Rättvik, Swe. (rĕt′vēk)	146	60.54N	15.07E
Rauch, Arg. (rá′ōōch)	126	36.47S	59.05W
Raufoss, Nor. (rou′fôs)	146	60.44N	10.30E
Raúl Soares, Braz. (rä-ōō′l-sôä′rĕs)	123a	20.05S	42.28W
Rauma, Fin. (rä′ô-mȧ)	140	61.07N	21.31E
Rauna, Lat. (rȧŭ′nȧ)	146	57.21N	25.31E
Raurkela, India	174	22.15N	84.53E
Rautalampi, Fin. (rä′ōō-tē-läm′pô)	146	62.39N	26.25E
Rava-Russkaya, Ukr. (rä′vȧ rōs′kä-yȧ)	148	50.14N	23.40E
Ravenna, Italy (rä-vĕn′nä)	142	44.27N	12.13E
Ravenna, Ne., U.S. (rȧ-vĕn′ȧ)	96	41.20N	98.50W
Ravenna, Oh., U.S.	92	41.10N	81.20W
Ravensburg, Ger. (rä′vĕns-bōōrgh)	148	47.48N	9.35E
Ravensdale, Wa., U.S. (rā′vĕnz-dāl)	100a	47.22N	121.58W
Ravensthorpe, Austl. (rā′vĕns-thôrp)	196	33.30S	120.20E
Ravenswood, S. Afr.	240b	26.11S	28.15E
Ravenswood, W.V., U.S. (rā′vĕnz-wòd)	92	38.55N	81.50W
Ravensworth, Va., U.S.	225d	38.48N	77.13W
Ravenwood, Va., U.S.	225d	38.52N	77.09W
Rāwalpindi, Pak. (rä-wŭl-pēn′dē)	174	33.40N	73.10E
Rawa Mazowiecka, Pol.	148	51.46N	20.17E
Rawāndūz, Iraq	174	36.37N	44.30E
Rawicz, Pol. (rä′vēch)	148	51.36N	16.51E
Rawlina, Austl. (rôr-lēnȧ)	196	31.13S	125.45E
Rawlins, Wy., U.S. (rô′lĭnz)	90	41.46N	107.15W
Rawson, Arg.	123c	34.36S	60.03W
Rawson, Arg. (rô′sŭn)	126	43.16S	65.09W
Rawtenstall, Eng., U.K. (rô′tĕn-stôl)	138a	53.42N	2.17W
Ray, Cape, c., Can. (rā)	79a	47.40N	59.18W
Raya, Bukit, mtn., Indon.	188	0.45S	112.11E
Raychikinsk, Russia (rī′chĭ-kēnsk)	162	49.52N	129.17E
Rayleigh, Eng., U.K. (rā′lē)	138b	51.35N	0.36E
Raymond, Can. (rā′mŭnd)	80	49.27N	112.39W
Raymond, Wa., U.S.	98	46.41N	123.42W
Raymondville, Tx., U.S. (rā′mŭnd-vĭl)	104	26.30N	97.46W
Ray Mountains, mts., Ak., U.S.	89a	65.40N	151.45W
Rayne, La., U.S. (rān)	106	30.12N	92.15W
Rayón, Mex. (rä-yōn′)	112	21.49N	99.39W
Rayton, S. Afr. (rā′tŭn)	207b	25.45S	28.33E
Raytown, Mo., U.S. (rā′toun)	101f	39.01N	94.48W
Rayville, La., U.S. (rā-vĭl)	106	32.28N	91.46W
Raz, Pointe du, c., Fr. (pwăNt dü rä)	140	48.02N	4.43W
Razdel′naya, Ukr. (räz-dĕl′nä-yȧ)	156	46.47N	30.08E
Razdol′noye, Russia (räz-dôl′nô-yĕ)	186	43.38N	131.58E
Razgrad, Bul.	142	43.32N	26.32E
Razlog, Bul. (räz′lôk)	154	41.54N	23.32E
Razorback Mountain, mtn., Can. (rā′zĕr-băk)	80	51.35N	124.42W
Rea, r., Eng., U.K. (rē)	138a	52.25N	2.31W
Reaburn, Can. (rā′bûrn)	77f	50.06N	97.53W
Reading, Eng., U.K. (rĕd′ĭng)	140	51.25N	0.58W
Reading, Ma., U.S.	87a	42.32N	71.07W
Reading, Mi., U.S.	92	41.45N	84.45W
Reading, Oh., U.S.	95f	39.14N	84.26W
Reading, Pa., U.S.	90	40.20N	75.55W
Readville, neigh., Ma., U.S.	223a	42.14N	71.08W
Realengo, Braz. (rē-ä-län-gô)	123a	23.50S	43.25W

PLACE (Pronunciation)	PAGE	Lat. °′	Long. °′
Real Felipe, Castillo, hist., Peru	229c	12.04S	77.09W
Rebel Hill, Pa., U.S.	225b	40.04N	75.20W
Rebiana, Libya	204	24.10N	22.03E
Rebun, i., Japan (rē′bo͞on)	186	45.25N	140.54E
Recanati, Italy (rā-kä-nä′tė)	154	43.25N	13.35E
Recherche, Archipelago of the, is., Austl. (rẽ-shârsh′)	196	34.17S	122.30E
Rechitsa, Bela. (ryĕ′chėt-sȧ)	160	52.22N	30.24E
Recife, Braz. (rå-sē′fẽ)	124	8.09S	34.59W
Recife, Kapp, c., S. Afr. (rå-sē′fẽ)	207c	34.03S	25.43E
Recklinghausen, Ger. (rĕk′lĭng-hou-zĕn)	151c	51.36N	7.13E
Recklinghausen Süd, neigh., Ger.	232	51.34N	7.13E
Reconquista, Arg. (rā-kȯn-kēs′tä)	126	29.01S	59.41W
Reconquista, r., Arg.	229d	34.39S	58.45W
Rector, Ar., U.S. (rĕk′tẽr)	104	36.16N	90.21W
Red, r., Asia	188	21.00N	103.00E
Red, r., N.A. (rĕd)	90	48.00N	97.00W
Red, r., U.S.	90	31.40N	92.55W
Red, r., Tn., U.S.	108	36.35N	86.55W
Red, North Fork, r., U.S.	104	35.20N	100.08W
Red, Prairie Dog Town Fork, r., U.S. (prā′rĭ)	104	34.54N	101.31W
Red, Salt Fork, r., U.S.	104	35.04N	100.31W
Redan, Ga., U.S. (rė-dăn′) (rĕd′ăn)	94c	33.44N	84.09W
Red Bank, N.J., U.S. (băngk)	94a	40.21N	74.06W
Red Bank National Park, N.J., U.S.	225b	39.52N	75.10W
Red Bluff Reservoir, res., Tx., U.S.	106	32.03N	103.52W
Redbridge, neigh., Eng., U.K.	231	51.34N	0.05E
Redby, Mn., Mn., U.S. (rĕd′bė)	96	47.52N	94.55W
Red Cedar, r., Wi., U.S. (sē′dẽr)	96	45.03N	91.48W
Redcliff, Can. (rĕd′clĭf)	78	50.05N	110.47W
Redcliffe, Austl. (rĕd′clĭf)	198	27.20S	153.12E
Red Cliff Indian Reservation, I.R., Wi., U.S.	96	46.48N	91.22W
Red Cloud, Ne., U.S. (kloud)	104	40.06N	98.32W
Red Deer, Can. (dēr)	78	52.16N	113.48W
Red Deer, r., Can.	78	51.00N	111.00W
Red Deer, r., Can.	82	52.55N	102.10W
Red Deer Lake, l., Can.	82	52.58N	101.28W
Reddick, Il., U.S. (rĕd′dĭk)	95a	41.06N	88.16W
Redding, Ca., U.S. (rĕd′ĭng)	98	40.36N	122.25W
Reddish, Eng., U.K.	233b	53.26N	2.09W
Redenção da Serra, Braz. (rĕ-dĕn-souɴ-dä-sĕ′r-rä)	123a	23.17S	45.31W
Redfield, S.D., U.S. (rĕd′fēld)	96	44.53N	98.30W
Red Fish Bar, Tx., U.S.	107a	29.29N	94.53W
Redford, neigh., Mi., U.S.	226c	42.25N	83.16W
Redford Township, Mi., U.S.	226c	42.25N	83.16W
Red Hill, Ca., U.S.	228	33.45N	117.48W
Red Indian Lake, l., Can. (ĭn′dĭ-ăn)	79a	48.40N	56.50W
Red Lake, Can. (lāk)	78	51.02N	93.49W
Red Lake, r., Mn., U.S.	96	48.02N	96.04W
Red Lake Falls, Mn., U.S. (lāk fôls)	96	47.52N	96.17W
Red Lake Indian Reservation, I.R., Mn., U.S.	96	48.09N	95.55W
Redlands, Ca., U.S. (rĕd′lăndz)	101a	34.04N	117.11W
Red Lion, Pa., U.S. (lī′ŭn)	92	39.55N	76.30W
Red Lodge, Mt., U.S.	98	45.13N	107.16W
Redmond, Wa., U.S. (rĕd′mŭnd)	100a	47.40N	122.07W
Rednitz, r., Ger. (rĕd′nētz)	148	49.10N	11.00E
Red Oak, Ia., U.S. (ōk)	96	41.00N	95.12W
Redon, Fr. (rẽ-dôɴ′)	150	47.42N	2.03W
Redonda, Isla, i., Braz. (ē′s-lä-rĕ-dȯ′n-dä)	126b	23.05S	43.11W
Redonda Island, i., Antig. (rĕ-dŏn′dȧ)	115b	16.55N	62.28W
Redondela, Spain (rā-dhȯn-dā′lä)	152	42.16N	8.34W
Redondo, Port. (rå-dȯn′dȯ)	152	38.40N	7.32W
Redondo, Wa., U.S. (rė-dŏn′dō)	100a	47.21N	122.19W
Redondo Beach, Ca., U.S.	101a	33.50N	118.23W
Red Pass, Can. (pȧs)	80	52.59N	118.59W
Red Rock, r., Mt., U.S.	98	44.54N	112.44W
Red Sea, sea	174	23.15N	37.00E
Redstone, Can. (rĕd′stōn)	80	52.08N	123.42W
Red Sucker Lake, l., Can. (sŭk′ẽr)	82	54.09N	93.40W
Redwater, r., Mt., U.S.	98	47.37N	105.25W
Red Willow Creek, r., Ne., U.S.	104	40.34N	100.48W
Red Wing, Mn., U.S.	96	44.34N	92.35W
Redwood City, Ca., U.S. (rĕd′ wȯd)	100b	37.29N	122.13W
Redwood Falls, Mn., U.S.	96	44.32N	95.06W
Redwood Valley, Ca., U.S.	102	39.15N	123.12W
Ree, Lough, l., Ire. (lŏĸ′rē′)	140	53.30N	7.45W
Reed City, Mi., U.S. (rēd)	92	43.50N	85.35W
Reed Lake, l., Can.	82	54.37N	100.30W
Reedley, Ca., U.S. (rēd′lė)	102	36.37N	119.27W
Reedsburg, Wi., U.S. (rēdz′bûrg)	96	43.32N	90.01W
Reedsport, Or., U.S. (rēdz′pȯrt)	98	43.42N	124.08W
Reelfoot Lake, res., Tn., U.S. (rēl′fȯt)	108	36.18N	89.20W
Rees, Ger. (rĕz)	151c	51.46N	6.25E
Reeves, Mount, mtn., Austl. (rēv′s)	198	33.50S	149.56E
Reform, Al., U.S. (rė-fôrm′)	108	33.23N	88.00W
Refugio, Tx., U.S. (rå-fo͞o′hyȯ) (rĕ-fū′jō)	106	28.18N	97.15W
Rega, r., Pol. (rĕ-gä)	148	53.48N	15.30E
Regen, r., Ger. (rā′ghĕn)	148	49.09N	12.21E
Regensburg, Ger. (rā′ghĕns-bȯrgh)	140	49.02N	12.06E
Regents Park, Austl.	239a	33.53S	151.02E
Regent's Park, pt. of i., Eng., U.K.	231	51.32N	0.09W
Reggio, La., U.S. (rĕg′jĭ-ō)	94d	29.50N	89.46W
Reggio di Calabria, Italy (rĕ′jȯ dē kä-lä′brė-ä)	142	38.07N	15.42E
Reggio nell' Emilia, Italy	142	44.43N	10.34E
Reghin, Rom. (rå-gēn′)	148	46.47N	24.44E
Regina, Can. (rė-jī′nȧ)	82	50.25N	104.39W
Regla, Cuba (rāg′lä)	116	23.08N	82.20W
Regnitz, r., Ger. (rĕg′nētz)	148	49.50N	10.55E
Rego Park, neigh., N.Y., U.S.	224	40.44N	73.52W
Reguengos de Monsaraz, Port.	152	38.26N	7.30W
Rehoboth, Nmb.	206	23.10S	17.15E
Rehovot, Isr.	173a	31.53N	34.49E
Reichenbach, Ger. (rī′ĸĕn-bäĸ)	148	50.36N	12.18E
Reidsville, N.C., U.S. (rēdz′vĭl)	108	36.20N	79.37W
Reigate, Eng., U.K. (rī′gāt)	144	51.12N	0.12W
Reims, Fr. (răɴs)	136	49.16N	4.00E
Reina Adelaida, Archipiélago, is., Chile	126	52.00S	74.15W
Reinbeck, Ia., U.S. (rīn′bĕk)	96	42.22N	92.34W
Reindeer, l., Can. (rān′dēr)	78	57.36N	101.23W
Reindeer, r., Can.	82	55.45N	103.30W
Reindeer Island, i., Can.	82	52.25N	98.00W
Reinosa, Spain (rå-ė-nō′sä)	152	43.01N	4.08W
Reisholz, neigh., Ger.	232	51.11N	6.52E
Reistertown, Md., U.S. (rēs′tẽr-toun)	94e	39.28N	76.50W
Reitz, S. Afr.	212d	27.48S	28.25E
Rema, Jabal, mtn., Yemen	174	14.13N	44.38E
Rembau, Malay.	173b	2.36N	102.06E
Remedios, Col. (rĕ-mĕ′dyȯs)	124a	7.03N	74.42W
Remedios, Cuba (rā-mā′dhė-ōs)	116	22.30N	79.35W
Remedios, Pan. (rĕ-mĕ′dyōs)	114	8.14N	81.46W
Remedios de Escalada, neigh., Arg.	229d	34.43S	58.23W
Remiremont, Fr. (rẽ-mēr-môɴ′)	150	48.01N	6.35E
Rempang, i., Indon.	173b	0.51N	104.04E
Remscheid, Ger. (rĕm′shīt)	151c	51.10N	7.11E
Rena, Nor.	146	61.08N	11.17E
Renca, Chile	230b	33.24S	70.44W
Renca, Cerro, mtn., Chile	230b	33.23S	70.43W
Rendova, i., Sol.Is. (rĕn′dȯ-vȧ)	196	8.38S	156.26E
Rendsburg, Ger. (rĕnts′bȯrgh)	148	54.19N	9.39E
Renfrew, Can. (rĕn′fro͞o)	78	45.30N	76.30W
Rengam, Malay. (rĕn′gäm′)	173b	1.53N	103.24E
Rengo, Chile (rĕn′gō)	123b	34.22S	70.50W
Reni, Ukr. (ran′)	156	45.26N	28.18E
Renmark, Austl. (rĕn′märk)	196	34.10S	140.50E
Rennel, i., Sol.Is. (rĕn-nĕl′)	196	11.50S	160.38E
Rennes, Fr. (rĕn)	136	48.07N	1.02W
Reno, Nv., U.S. (rē′nō)	90	39.32N	119.49W
Reno, r., Italy (rā′nȯ)	154	44.10N	10.55E
Renovo, Pa., U.S. (rė-nō′vō)	92	41.20N	77.50W
Renqiu, China (rŭn-chyȯ)	182	38.44N	116.05E
Rensselaer, In., U.S. (rĕn′sẽ-lâr)	92	41.00N	87.10W
Rensselaer, N.Y., U.S. (rĕn′sẽ-lâr)	92	42.40N	73.45W
Rentchler, Il., U.S. (rĕnt′chlẽr)	101e	38.30N	89.52W
Renton, Wa., U.S. (rĕn′tŭn)	100a	47.29N	122.13W
Repentigny, Can.	77a	45.47N	73.26W
Republic, Al., U.S. (rė-pŭb′lĭk)	94h	33.37N	86.54W
Republic, Wa., U.S.	98	48.38N	118.44W
Republican, r., U.S.	90	40.15N	100.00W
Republican, South Fork, r., Co., U.S. (rė-pŭb′lĭ-kăn)	104	39.35N	102.28W
Repulse Bay, b., Austl. (rė-pŭls′)	196	20.56S	149.22E
Requena, Spain (rå-kā′nä)	142	39.29N	1.03W
Reseda, neigh., Ca., U.S.	228	34.12N	118.31W
Resende, Braz. (rĕ-sĕ′n-dĕ)	123a	22.30S	44.26W
Resende Costa, Braz. (kôs-tä)	123a	20.55S	44.12W
Reservoir, Austl.	239b	37.43S	145.00E
Reshetilovka, Ukr. (ryĕ′ shĕ-tė-lôf-kȧ)	156	49.34N	34.04E
Resistencia, Arg. (rā-sės-tĕn′syä)	126	27.24S	58.54W
Reşiţa, Rom. (rå′shė-tȧ)	154	45.18N	21.56E
Resolute, Can. (rĕz-ȯ-lūt′)	76	74.41N	95.00W
Resolution, i., Can. (rĕz-ȯ-lū′shŭn)	78	61.30N	63.58W
Resolution Island, i., N.Z. (rĕz-ŏl-ûshûn)	197a	45.43S	166.20E
Resse, neigh., Ger.	232	51.34N	7.07E
Restigouche, r., Can.	86	47.35N	67.35W
Restrepo, Col. (rĕs-trĕ′pȯ)	124a	3.49N	76.31W
Restrepo, Col.	124a	4.16N	73.32W
Retalhuleu, Guat. (rā-täl-o͞o-lān′)	114	14.31N	91.41W
Rethel, Fr. (r-tl′)	150	49.34N	4.20E
Réthimnon, Grc.	154a	35.21N	24.30E
Retie, Bel.	139a	51.16N	5.08E
Retiro, Parque del, rec., Spain	234b	40.25N	3.41W
Retsil, Wa., U.S. (rĕt′sĭl)	100a	47.33N	122.37W
Reunion, dep., Afr. (rā-ü-nyôn′)	2	21.06S	55.36E
Reus, Spain (rā′o͞os)	142	41.08N	1.05E
Reutlingen, Ger. (roit′lĭng-ĕn)	148	48.29N	9.14E
Reutov, Russia (rĕ-o͞o′ôf)	164b	55.45N	37.52E
Revda, Russia (ryâv′dȧ)	164a	56.48N	59.57E
Revelstoke, Can. (rĕv′ĕl-stōk)	78	51.00N	118.12W
Reventazón, Río, r., C.R. (rå-vĕn-tä-zōn′)	114	10.10N	83.30W
Revere, Ma., U.S. (rė-vēr′)	87a	42.24N	71.01W
Revesby, Austl.	239a	33.57S	151.01E
Revillagigedo, Islas, is., Mex. (ė′s-läs-rĕ-vėl-yä-hė′gĕ-dȯ)	110	18.45N	111.00W
Revillagigedo Chan, Ak., U.S. (rĕ-vĭl′ȧ-gĭ-gē′dō)	80	55.10N	131.13W
Revillagigedo Island, i., Ak., U.S.	80	55.35N	131.23W
Revin, Fr. (rẽ-văɴ)	150	49.56N	4.34E
Rewa, India (rā′wä)	174	24.41N	81.11E
Rewāri, India	178	28.19N	76.39E
Rexburg, Id., U.S. (rĕks′bûrg)	98	43.50N	111.48W
Rey, Iran	176	35.35N	51.25E
Rey, l., Mex. (rā)	106	27.00N	103.33W
Rey, Isla del, i., Pan. (ė′s-lä-dĕl-rā′ė)	114	8.20N	78.40W
Reyes, Bol. (rā′yĕs)	124	14.19S	67.16W
Reyes, Point, c., Ca., U.S.	102	38.00N	123.00W
Reykjanes, c., Ice. (rā′kyȧ-nĕs)	136	63.37N	24.33W
Reykjavík, Ice. (rā′kyȧ-vēk)	136	64.09N	21.39W
Reynosa, Mex. (rā-ė-nō′sä)	106	26.05N	98.21W
Rēzekne, Lat. (rå′zĕk-nĕ)	160	56.31N	27.19E
Rezh, Russia (rĕzh′)	164a	57.22N	61.23E
Rezina, Mol. (ryĕzh′ĕ-nĭ)	156	47.44N	28.56E
Rhaetian Alps, mts., Eur.	148	46.30N	10.00E
Rhaetien Alps, mts., Eur.	154	46.22N	10.33E
Rheinberg, Ger. (rīn′bĕrgh)	151c	51.33N	6.37E
Rheine, Ger. (rī′nĕ)	148	52.16N	7.26E
Rheinen, Ger.	232	51.27N	7.38E
Rheinhausen, Ger.	232	51.24N	6.44E
Rhein-Herne-Kanal, can., Ger.	232	51.27N	6.47E
Rheinkamp, Ger.	151c	51.30N	6.37E
Rheinland-Pfalz (Rhineland-Palatinate), hist. reg., Ger.	148	50.05N	6.40E
Rheydt, Ger. (rĕ′yt)	151c	51.10N	6.28E
Rhin, r., Ger. (rēn)	139b	52.52N	12.49E
Rhine, r., Eur.	136	50.34N	7.21E
Rhinelander, Wi., U.S. (rīn′lăn-dẽr)	96	45.39N	89.25W
Rhin Kanal, can., Ger. (rēn kä-näl′)	139b	52.47N	12.40E
Rhiou, r., Alg.	152	35.45N	1.18E
Rho, Italy	234c	45.32N	9.02E
Rhode Island, state, U.S. (rōd ī′lȧnd)	90	41.35N	71.40W
Rhode Island, i., R.I., U.S.	94b	41.31N	71.14W
Rhodes, Austl.	239a	33.50S	151.05E
Rhodes, S. Afr. (rȯdz)	207c	30.48S	27.56E
Rhodes, Eng., U.K.	233b	53.33N	2.14W
Rhodes, *see* Ródhos, i., Grc.	136	36.00N	28.29E
Rhodon, Fr.	233c	48.43N	2.04E
Rhodope Mountains, mts., Eur. (rô′dȯ-pĕ)	136	42.00N	24.08E
Rhondda, Wales, U.K. (rŏn′dhȧ)	144	51.40N	3.40W
Rhône, r., Fr. (rōn)	136	44.30N	4.45E
Rhoon, Neth.	139a	51.52N	4.24E
Rhum, i., Scot., U.K. (rŭm)	144	57.00N	6.20W
Riachão, Braz. (rė-ä-chouɴ′)	124	7.15S	46.30W
Rialto, Ca., U.S. (rē-ăl′tō)	101a	34.06N	117.23W
Riau, prov., Indon.	173b	0.56N	101.25E
Riau, Kepulauan, i., Indon.	188	0.30N	104.55E
Riau, Selat, strt., Indon.	173b	0.40N	104.27E
Riaza, r., Spain (rė-ä′thä)	152	41.25N	3.25W
Ribadavia, Spain (rē-bä-dhä′vė-ä)	152	42.18N	8.06W
Ribadeo, Spain (rē-bä-dhā′ō)	152	43.32N	7.05W
Ribadesella, Spain (rē′bä-dā-sāl′yä)	152	43.30N	5.02W
Ribe, Den. (rē′bĕ)	146	55.20N	8.45E
Ribeirão Prêto, Braz. (rė-bā-rouɴ-prĕ′tô)	124	21.11S	47.47W
Ribera, N.M., U.S. (rē-bĕ′rä)	104	35.23N	105.27W
Riberalta, Bol. (rē-bå-räl′tä)	124	11.06S	66.02W
Rib Lake, Wi., U.S. (rĭb lāk)	96	45.20N	90.11W
Rice, l., Can.	84	44.05N	78.10W
Rice Lake, Wi., U.S.	96	45.30N	91.44W
Rice Lake, l., Mn., U.S.	101g	45.10N	93.09W
Richards Island, i., Can. (rĭch′ẽrds)	89	69.45N	135.30W
Richards Landing, Can. (lănd′ĭng)	101k	46.18N	84.02W
Richardson, Tx., U.S. (rĭch′ẽrd-sŭn)	101c	32.56N	96.44W
Richardson, Wa., U.S.	100a	48.27N	122.54W
Richardson Mountains, mts., Can.	78	66.58N	136.19W
Richardson Mountains, mts., N.Z.	199	44.50S	168.30E
Richardson Park, De., U.S. (pärk)	92	39.45N	75.35W
Richelieu, r., Can. (rēsh′lyû′)	84	45.05N	73.25W
Richfield, Mn., U.S.	101g	44.53N	93.17W
Richfield, Oh., U.S.	95d	41.14N	81.38W
Richfield, Ut., U.S.	102	38.45N	112.05W
Richford, Vt., U.S. (rĭch′fẽrd)	92	45.00N	72.35W
Rich Hill, Mo., U.S. (rĭch hĭl)	104	38.05N	94.21W
Richibucto, Can. (rĭ-chĭ-bŭk′tō)	78	46.41N	64.52W
Richland, Ga., U.S. (rĭch′lănd)	108	32.05N	84.40W
Richland, Wa., U.S.	98	46.17N	119.19W
Richland Center, Wi., U.S. (sĕn′tẽr)	96	43.20N	90.25W
Richmond, Austl.	195b	33.36S	150.45E
Richmond, Austl. (rĭch′mŭnd)	196	20.47S	143.14E
Richmond, Austl.	239b	37.49S	145.00E
Richmond, Can.	77c	45.12N	75.49W
Richmond, Can.	84	45.40N	72.07W
Richmond, S. Afr.	207c	29.52S	30.17E
Richmond, Il., U.S.	95a	42.29N	88.18W
Richmond, In., U.S.	92	39.50N	85.00W
Richmond, Ky., U.S.	92	37.45N	84.20W
Richmond, Mo., U.S.	104	39.16N	93.58W
Richmond, Tx., U.S.	106	29.35N	95.45W
Richmond, Ut., U.S.	98	41.55N	111.50W
Richmond, Va., U.S.	90	37.35N	77.30W
Richmond, neigh., Eng., U.K.	231	51.28N	0.18W
Richmond, neigh., N.J., U.S.	225b	39.59N	75.06W
Richmond Beach, Wa., U.S.	100a	47.47N	122.23W
Richmond Heights, Mo., U.S.	101e	38.38N	90.20W
Richmond Heights, Oh., U.S.	225a	41.33N	81.29W
Richmond Highlands, Wa., U.S.	100a	47.46N	122.22W
Richmond Hill, Can. (hĭl)	84	43.53N	79.26W
Richmondtown Restoration, pt. of i., N.Y., U.S.	224	40.34N	74.09W
Richmond Valley, neigh., N.Y., U.S.	224	40.31N	74.13W
Richton, Ms., U.S. (rĭch′tŭn)	108	31.20N	89.54W
Richwood, W.V., U.S. (rĭch′wȯd)	92	38.10N	80.30W
Ricketts Point, c., Austl.	239b	38.00S	145.02E
Rickmansworth, Eng., U.K.	231	51.39N	0.29W
Ridderkerk, Neth.	139a	51.52N	4.35E
Rideau, r., Can.	77c	45.17N	75.41W
Rideau Lake, l., Can. (rė-dō′)	84	44.40N	76.20W
Ridge, Eng., U.K.	231	51.41N	0.15W
Ridgefield, Ct., U.S. (rij′fēld)	94a	41.16N	73.30W
Ridgefield, N.J., U.S.	224	40.50N	74.00W
Ridgefield, Wa., U.S.	100c	45.49N	122.40W
Ridgefield Park, N.J., U.S.	224	40.51N	74.01W
Ridgeway, Can. (rĭj′wā)	95c	42.53N	79.02W
Ridgewood, N.J., U.S. (ridj′wȯd)	94a	40.59N	74.08W
Ridgewood, neigh., N.Y., U.S.	224	40.42N	73.53W
Ridgway, Pa., U.S.	92	41.25N	78.40W
Riding Mountain, mtn., Can. (rīd′ĭng)	82	50.37N	99.37W
Riding Mountain National Park, rec., Can. (rīd′ĭng)	78	50.59N	99.19W
Riding Rocks, is., Bah.	116	25.20N	79.10W

ăt; finăl; rāte; senåte; ärm; åsk; sofȧ; fâre; ch-choose; dh-as th in other; bē; ėvent; bĕt; recĕnt; cratẽr; g-gō; gh-guttural g; bĭt; ĭ-short neutral; rīde; ĸ-guttural k as ch in German ich;

PLACE (Pronunciation)	PAGE	Lat. °′	Long. °′
Ridley Park, Pa., U.S.	225b	39.53N	75.19W
Riebeek-Oos, S. Afr.	207c	33.14S	26.09E
Ried, Aus. (rēd)	148	48.13N	13.30E
Riemke, neigh., Ger.	232	51.30N	7.13E
Riesa, Ger. (rē'zȧ)	148	51.17N	13.17E
Rieti, Italy (rē-ā'tē)	142	42.25N	12.51E
Rietvlei, S. Afr.	240b	26.18S	28.03E
Rievleidam, res., S. Afr.	207b	25.52S	28.18E
Riffe Lake, res., Wa., U.S.	98	46.20N	122.10W
Rifle, Co., U.S. (rī'f'l)	102	39.35N	107.50W
Rīga, Lat. (rē'gȧ)	158	56.55N	24.05E
Riga, Gulf of, b., Eur.	160	57.56N	23.05E
Rīgān, Iran	174	28.45N	58.55E
Rigaud, Can. (rē-gō')	77a	45.29N	74.18W
Rigby, Id., U.S. (rĭg'bē)	98	43.40N	111.55W
Rigeley, W.V., U.S. (rĭj'lē)	92	39.40N	78.45W
Rīgestān, des., Afg.	174	30.53N	64.42E
Rigolet, Can. (rĭg-ō-lā')	78	54.10N	58.40W
Riihimäki, Fin.	146	60.44N	24.44E
Rijeka, Cro. (rĭ-yĕ'kä)	142	45.22N	14.24E
Rijkevorsel, Bel.	139a	51.21N	4.46E
Rijswijk, Neth.	139a	52.03N	4.19E
Rika, r., Ukr. (rē'kȧ)	148	48.21N	23.37E
Rima, r., Nig.	208	13.30N	5.50E
Rímac, Peru	229c	12.02S	77.03W
Rímac, r., Peru	229c	12.02S	77.09W
Rimavska Sobota, Czech. (rē'mȧf-skȧ sô'bô-tȧ)	148	48.25N	20.01E
Rimbo, Swe. (rēm'bô)	146	59.45N	18.22E
Rimini, Italy (rē'mē-nē)	142	44.03N	12.33E
Rîmnicu-Sărat, Rom.	142	45.24N	27.06E
Rîmnicu-Vilcea, Rom.	154	45.07N	24.22E
Rimouski, Can. (rē-mo͞os'kē)	78	48.27N	68.32W
Rincón de Romos, Mex. (rēn-kōn dā rô-mōs')	112	22.13N	102.21W
Ringkøbing, Den. (rĭng'kûb-ĭng)	140	56.06N	8.14E
Ringkøbing Fjord, fj., Den.	146	55.55N	8.04E
Ringsted, Den. (rĭng'stĕdh)	146	55.27N	11.49E
Ringvassøya, i., Nor. (rĭng'väs-ûē)	140	69.58N	16.43E
Ringwood, Austl.	195a	37.49S	145.14E
Ringwood North, Austl.	239b	37.48S	145.14E
Rinjani, Gunung, mtn., Indon.	188	8.39S	116.22E
Río Abajo, Pan. (rē'ō-ä-bä'ĸō)	110a	9.01N	78.30W
Río Balsas, Mex. (rē'ō-bäl-säs)	112	17.59N	99.45W
Riobamba, Ec. (rē'ō-bäm-bä)	124	1.45S	78.37W
Rio Bonito, Braz. (rē'ô bō-nē'tô)	123a	22.44S	42.38W
Rio Branco, Braz. (rē'ô brăŋ'kô)	124	9.57S	67.50W
Rio Branco, Ur. (rĭō brăncô)	126	32.33S	53.29W
Rio Casca, Braz. (rē'ō-kà's-kä)	123a	20.15S	42.39W
Río Chico, Ven. (rē'ō chē'kŏ)	125b	10.20N	65.58W
Río Claro, Braz. (rē'ō klä'rô)	124	22.25S	47.33W
Rio Comprido, neigh., Braz.	230c	22.55S	43.12W
Río Cuarto, Arg. (rē'ō kwär'tō)	126	33.05S	64.15W
Rio das Flores, Braz. (rē'ō-däs-flô-rĕs)	123a	22.10S	43.35W
Rio de Janeiro, Braz. (rē'ō dā zhä-nâ'ê-rô)	126b	22.50S	43.20W
Rio de Janeiro, state, Braz.	124	22.27S	42.43W
Río de Jesús, Pan.	114	7.54N	80.59W
Rio de Mouro, Port.	234d	38.46N	9.20W
Río Frío, Mex. (rē'ō-frē'ō)	113a	19.21N	98.40W
Río Gallegos, Arg. (rē'ō gä-lā'gōs)	126	51.43S	69.15W
Rio Grande, Braz. (rē'ŏ grän'dĕ)	126	31.04S	52.14W
Río Grande, Mex. (rē'ō grän'dā)	112	23.51N	102.59W
Riogrande, Tx., U.S. (rē'ō grȧn-dā)	106	26.23N	98.48W
Río Grande, Ven.	230a	10.35N	66.57W
Rio Grande do Norte, state, Braz.	124	5.26S	37.20W
Rio Grande do Sul, state, Braz. (rē'ŏ grän'dĕ-dô-so͞o'l)	126	29.00S	54.00W
Ríohacha, Col. (rē'ō-ä'chä)	124	11.30N	72.54W
Río Hato, Pan. (rē'ō-ä'tô)	114	8.19N	80.11W
Riom, Fr. (rē-ôɴ')	150	45.54N	3.08E
Rio Muni, hist. reg., Eq. Gui. (rē'ō mo͞o'nē)	204	1.47N	8.33E
Ríonegro, Col. (rē'ō-nĕ'grō)	124a	6.09N	75.22W
Río Negro, prov., Arg. (rē'ō nā'grō)	126	40.15S	68.15W
Río Negro, dept., Ur. (rē'ō-nĕ'grō)	123c	32.48S	57.45W
Río Negro, Embalse del, res., Ur.	126	32.45S	55.50W
Rionero, Italy (rē-ō-nā'rô)	154	40.55N	15.42E
Rio Novo, Braz. (rē'ō-nô'vô)	123a	21.30S	43.08W
Rio Pardo de Minas, Braz. (rē'ō pär'dō-dĕ-mē'näs)	124	15.43S	42.24W
Rio Pombo, Braz. (rē'ō pôm'bä)	123a	21.17S	43.09W
Rio Sorocaba, Represa do, res., Braz.	123a	23.37S	47.19W
Ríosucio, Col. (rē'ō-so͞o'syô)	124a	5.25N	75.41W
Río Tercero, Arg. (rē'ō dĕr-sĕ'rô)	126	32.12S	63.59W
Rio Verde, Braz. (vĕr'dĕ)	124	17.47S	50.49W
Ríoverde, Mex. (rē'ō-vĕr'dā)	110	21.54N	99.59W
Ripley, Eng., U.K. (rĭp'lē)	138a	53.03N	1.24W
Ripley, Eng., U.K.	231	51.18N	0.29W
Ripley, Ms., U.S.	108	34.44N	88.55W
Ripley, Tn., U.S.	108	35.44N	89.34W
Ripoll, Spain (rē-pōl'')	152	42.10N	2.10E
Ripon, Wi., U.S. (rĭp'ŏn)	96	43.49N	88.50W
Ripon, i., Austl.	196	20.05S	118.10E
Ripon Falls, wtfl., Ug.	206	0.38N	33.02E
Risaralda, dept., Col.	124a	5.15N	76.00W
Risdon, Austl. (rĭz'dŭn)	196	42.37S	147.32E
Rishiri, i., Japan (rē-shē'rē)	186	45.10N	141.08E
Rishon le Ziyyon, Isr.	173a	31.57N	34.48E
Rishra, India	178a	22.42N	88.22E
Rising Sun, In., U.S. (rīz'ĭng sŭn)	92	38.55N	84.55W
Risor, Nor. (rēs'ûr)	140	58.44N	9.10E
Ritacuva, Alto, mtn., Col. (ä'l-tô-rē-tä-ko͞o'vä)	124	6.22N	72.13W
Ritchie, Va., U.S.	225d	38.52N	76.52W
Rithāla, neigh., India	236d	28.43N	77.06E
Rittman, Oh., U.S. (rĭt'năn)	95d	40.58N	81.47W
Ritzville, Wa., U.S. (rĭts'vĭl)	98	47.08N	118.23W
Riva, Dom. Rep. (rē'vä)	116	19.10N	69.55W
Riva, Italy (rē'vä)	154	45.54N	10.49E
Riva, Md., U.S. (rĭ'vȧ)	94e	38.57N	76.36W
Rivas, Nic. (rē'väs)	114	11.25N	85.51W
Rive-de-Gier, Fr. (rēv-dē-zhē-ā')	150	45.32N	4.37E
Rivera, Ur. (rē-vā'rä)	126	30.52S	55.32W
River Cess, Lib. (rĭv'ēr sĕs)	204	5.46N	9.52W
Riverdale, Il., U.S. (rĭv'ēr dāl)	95a	41.38N	87.36W
Riverdale, Md., U.S.	225d	38.58N	76.55W
Riverdale, Ut., U.S.	101b	41.11N	112.00W
Riverdale, neigh., N.Y., U.S.	224	40.54N	73.54W
River Edge, N.J., U.S.	224	40.56N	74.02W
River Falls, Al., U.S.	108	31.20N	86.25W
River Falls, Wi., U.S.	96	44.48N	92.38W
River Forest, Il., U.S.	227a	41.53N	87.49W
River Grove, Il., U.S.	227a	41.56N	87.50W
Riverhead, Eng., U.K.	231	51.17N	0.10E
Riverhead, N.Y., U.S. (rĭv'ēr hĕd)	92	40.55N	72.40W
Riverina, reg., Austl. (rĭv-ēr-ē'nä)	196	34.55S	144.30E
River Jordan, Can. (jôr'dăn)	100a	48.25N	124.03W
River Oaks, Tx., U.S. (ōkz)	101c	32.47N	97.24W
River Rouge, Mi., U.S. (ro͞ozh)	95b	42.16N	83.09W
Rivers, Can.	82	50.01N	100.15W
Riverside, Ca., U.S. (rĭv'ēr-sīd)	90	33.59N	117.21W
Riverside, Il., U.S.	227a	41.50N	87.49W
Riverside, N.J., U.S.	94f	40.02N	74.58W
Rivers Inlet, Can.	80	51.45N	127.15W
Riverstone, Austl.	195b	33.41S	150.52E
Riverton, Va., U.S.	92	39.00N	78.15W
Riverton, Wy., U.S.	98	43.02N	108.24W
Rivesaltes, Fr. (rēv'zält')	150	42.48N	2.48E
Riviera Beach, Fl., U.S. (rĭv-ĭ-ēr'ȧ bēch)	109a	26.46N	80.04W
Riviera Beach, Md., U.S.	94e	39.10N	76.32W
Rivière-Beaudette, Can.	77a	45.14N	74.20W
Rivière-du-Loup, Can. (rē-vyâr' dü lo͞o')	78	47.50N	69.32W
Rivière Qui Barre, Can. (rēv-yĕr' kē-bär)	77g	53.47N	113.51W
Rivière-Trois-Pistoles, Can. (trwä'pēs-tôl')	86	48.07N	69.10W
Riyadh, Sau. Ar.	174	24.31N	46.47E
Rize, Tur. (rē'zĕ)	142	41.00N	40.30E
Rizhao, China (rē-jou)	184	35.27N	119.28E
Rizzuto, Cape, c., Italy (rēt-so͞o'tô)	154	38.53N	17.05E
Rjukan, Nor. (ryo͞o'kän)	140	59.53N	8.30E
Roanne, Fr. (rō-än')	140	46.02N	4.04E
Roanoke, Al., U.S. (rō'ȧ-nōk)	108	33.08N	85.21W
Roanoke, Va., U.S.	90	37.16N	79.55W
Roanoke, r., U.S.	90	36.17N	77.22W
Roanoke Rapids, N.C., U.S.	108	36.25N	77.40W
Roanoke Rapids Lake, res., N.C., U.S.	108	36.28N	77.37W
Roan Plateau, plat., Co., U.S. (rōn)	102	39.25N	110.00W
Roatan, Hond. (rō-ä-tän')	114	16.18N	86.33W
Roatán, i., Hond.	114	16.19N	86.46W
Robbeneiland, i., S. Afr.	206a	33.48S	18.22E
Robbins, Il., U.S. (rŏb'ĭnz)	95a	41.39N	87.42W
Robbinsdale, Mn., U.S. (rŏb'ĭnz-dāl)	101g	45.03N	93.22W
Robe, Wa., U.S. (rōb)	100a	48.06N	121.50W
Roberts, Mount, mtn., Austl. (rŏb'ērts)	196	28.05S	152.30E
Roberts, Point, c., Wa., U.S. (rŏb'ērts)	100d	48.58N	123.05W
Robertsham, neigh., S. Afr.	240b	26.15S	28.00E
Robertson, Lac, l., Can.	86	51.00N	59.10W
Robertsport, Lib. (rŏb'ērts-pōrt)	204	6.45N	11.22W
Roberval, Can. (rŏb'ēr-văl) (rō-bĕr-vȧl')	78	48.32N	72.15W
Robinson, Can.	86	48.16N	58.50W
Robinson, S. Afr.	240b	26.09S	27.43E
Robinson, Il., U.S. (rŏb'ĭn-sŭn)	92	39.00N	87.45W
Robinvale, Austl. (rŏb-ĭn'văl)	198	34.45S	142.45E
Roblin, Can.	82	51.15N	101.25W
Robson, Mount, mtn., Can. (rŏb'sŭn)	80	53.07N	119.09W
Robstown, Tx., U.S. (rŏbz'toun)	106	27.46N	97.41W
Roby, Eng., U.K.	233a	53.25N	2.51W
Roca, Cabo da, c., Port. (kȧ'bō-dä-rô'kä)	152	38.47N	9.30W
Rocas, Atol das, atoll, Braz. (ä-tôl-däs-rō'kȧs)	124	3.50S	33.46W
Rocha, Ur. (rō'chȧs)	126	34.26S	54.14W
Rocha Miranda, neigh., Braz.	230c	22.52S	43.22W
Rocha Sobrinho, Braz.	230c	22.47S	43.25W
Rochdale, Eng., U.K. (rŏch'dāl)	144	53.37N	2.09W
Roche à Bateau, Haiti (rôsh ȧ bȧ-tō')	116	18.10N	74.00W
Rochefort, Fr. (rôsh-fōr')	140	45.55N	0.57W
Rochelle, Il., U.S. (rō-shĕl')	96	41.53N	89.06W
Rochelle Park, N.J., U.S.	224	40.55N	74.04W
Rochester, Eng., U.K.	138a	51.24N	0.30E
Rochester, In., U.S. (rŏch'ĕs-tēr)	92	41.05N	86.20W
Rochester, Mi., U.S.	95b	42.41N	83.09W
Rochester, Mn., U.S.	90	44.01N	92.30W
Rochester, N.H., U.S.	92	43.20N	71.00W
Rochester, N.Y., U.S.	90	43.15N	77.35W
Rochester, Pa., U.S.	95e	40.42N	80.16W
Rock, r., U.S.	90	41.40N	90.00W
Rock, r., Ia., U.S.	96	43.17N	96.13W
Rock, r., Or., U.S.	100c	45.34N	122.52W
Rock, r., Or., U.S.	100c	45.52N	123.14W
Rockaway, N.J., U.S. (rŏck'ȧ-wā)	94a	40.54N	74.30W
Rockaway Park, neigh., N.Y., U.S.	224	40.35N	73.50W
Rockaway Point, neigh., N.Y., U.S.	224	40.33N	73.55W
Rockbank, Austl.	195a	37.44S	144.40E
Rockcliffe Park, Can. (rok'klĭf pärk)	77c	45.27N	75.40W
Rock Creek, r., Can. (rŏk)	98	49.01N	107.00W
Rock Creek, r., Il., U.S.	95a	41.16N	87.54W
Rock Creek, r., Mt., U.S.	98	46.25N	113.40W
Rock Creek, r., Or., U.S.	98	45.30N	120.06W
Rock Creek, r., Wa., U.S.	98	47.09N	117.50W
Rock Creek Park, pt. of i., D.C., U.S.	225d	38.58N	77.03W
Rockdale, Austl.	195b	33.57S	151.08E
Rockdale, Md., U.S.	94e	39.22N	76.49W
Rockdale, Tx., U.S. (rŏk'dāl)	106	30.39N	97.00W
Rockefeller Center, pt. of i., N.Y., U.S.	224	40.45N	74.00W
Rock Falls, Il., U.S. (rŏk fôlz)	96	41.45N	89.42W
Rock Ferry, Eng., U.K.	233a	53.22N	3.00W
Rockford, Il., U.S. (rŏk'fērd)	90	42.16N	89.07W
Rockhampton, Austl. (rŏk-hămp'tŭn)	196	23.26S	150.29E
Rock Hill, S.C., U.S. (rŏk'hĭl)	90	34.55N	81.01W
Rockingham, N.C., U.S. (rŏk'ĭng-hăm)	108	34.54N	79.45W
Rockingham Forest, for., Eng., U.K. (rok'ĭng-hăm)	138a	52.29N	0.43W
Rock Island, Il., U.S.	90	41.31N	90.37W
Rock Island Dam, Wa., U.S. (ī lănd)	98	47.17N	120.33W
Rockland, Can. (rŏk'lănd)	77c	45.33N	75.17W
Rockland, Me., U.S.	86	44.06N	69.09W
Rockland, Ma., U.S.	87a	42.07N	70.55W
Rockland Reservoir, res., Austl.	198	36.55S	142.20E
Rockledge, Pa., U.S.	225b	40.03N	75.05W
Rockmart, Ga., U.S. (rŏk'märt)	108	33.58N	85.00W
Rockmont, Wi., U.S. (rŏk'mŏnt)	101h	46.34N	91.54W
Rockport, In., U.S. (rŏk'pōrt)	92	38.20N	87.00W
Rockport, Ma., U.S.	87a	42.39N	70.37W
Rockport, Mo., U.S.	104	40.25N	95.30W
Rockport, Tx., U.S.	106	28.03N	97.03W
Rock Rapids, Ia., U.S. (răp'ĭdz)	96	43.26N	96.10W
Rock Sound, strt., Bah.	116	24.50N	76.05W
Rocksprings, Tx., U.S. (rŏk sprĭngs)	106	30.02N	100.12W
Rock Springs, Wy., U.S.	90	41.35N	109.13W
Rockstone, Guy. (rŏk'stôn)	124	5.55N	57.27W
Rock Valley, Ia., U.S. (văl'ĭ)	96	43.13N	96.17W
Rockville, In., U.S. (rŏk'vĭl)	92	39.45N	87.15W
Rockville, Md., U.S.	94e	39.05N	77.11W
Rockville Centre, N.Y., U.S. (sĕn'tēr)	94a	40.39N	73.39W
Rockwall, Tx., U.S. (rŏk'wôl)	104	32.55N	96.23W
Rockwell City, Ia., U.S. (rŏk'wĕl)	96	42.22N	94.37W
Rockwood, Can. (rŏk-wo͝od)	77d	43.37N	80.08W
Rockwood, Me., U.S.	86	45.39N	69.45W
Rockwood, Tn., U.S.	108	35.51N	84.41W
Rocky, r., Oh., U.S.	225a	41.30N	81.49W
Rocky, East Branch, r., Oh., U.S.	95d	41.13N	81.43W
Rocky, West Branch, r., Oh., U.S.	95d	41.17N	81.54W
Rocky Boys Indian Reservation, I.R., Mt., U.S.	98	48.08N	109.34W
Rocky Ford, Co., U.S.	104	38.02N	103.43W
Rocky Hill, N.J., U.S. (hĭl)	94a	40.24N	74.38W
Rocky Island Lake, l., Can.	84	46.56N	83.04W
Rocky Mount, N.C., U.S.	108	35.55N	77.47W
Rocky Mountain House, Can.	80	52.22N	114.55W
Rocky Mountain National Park, rec., Co., U.S.	90	40.29N	106.06W
Rocky Mountains, mts., N.A.	76	50.00N	114.00W
Rocky River, Oh., U.S.	95d	41.29N	81.51W
Rocky River, Oh., U.S.	225a	41.30N	81.40W
Rocquencourt, Fr.	233c	48.50N	2.07E
Rodas, Cuba (rō'dhȧs)	116	22.20N	80.35W
Roden, r., Eng., U.K. (rō'dĕn)	138a	52.49N	2.38W
Rodeo, Mex. (rō-dā'ō)	106	25.12N	104.34W
Rodeo, Ca., U.S. (rō'dēō)	100b	38.02N	122.16W
Roderick Island, i., Can. (rŏd'ē-rĭk)	80	52.40N	128.22W
Rodez, Fr. (rō-dĕz')	140	44.22N	2.34E
Rōdhos, Grc.	142	36.24N	28.15E
Ródhos, i., Grc.	136	36.00N	28.29E
Rodniki, Russia (rôd'nē-kē)	160	57.08N	41.48E
Rodonit, Kep I, c., Alb.	154	41.38N	19.01E
Roebling, N.J., U.S. (rōb'lĭng)	94f	40.07N	74.48W
Roebourne, Austl. (rō'bŭrn)	196	20.50S	117.15E
Roebuck Bay, b., Austl. (rō'bŭck)	196	18.15S	121.10E
Roedtan, S. Afr.	212d	24.37S	29.08E
Roehampton, neigh., Eng., U.K.	231	51.27N	0.14W
Roeselare, Bel.	144	50.55N	3.05E
Roesiger, l., Wa., U.S. (rōz'ĭ-gēr)	100a	47.59N	121.56W
Roes Welcome Sound, strt., Can. (rōz)	78	64.10N	87.23W
Rogachëv, Bela. (rôg'á-chyôf)	160	53.07N	30.04E
Rogans Hill, Austl.	239a	33.44S	151.01E
Rogatica, Bos. (rō-gä'tē-tsä)	154	43.46N	19.00E
Rogatin, Ukr. (rō-gä'tĭn)	148	49.22N	24.37E
Rogers, Ar., U.S. (rŏj-ērz)	104	36.19N	94.07W
Rogers City, Mi., U.S.	92	45.30N	83.50W
Rogers Park, neigh., Il., U.S.	227a	42.01N	87.40W
Rogersville, Tn., U.S.	108	36.21N	83.00W
Rognac, Fr. (rōn-yäk')	150a	43.29N	5.15E
Rogoaguado, l., Bol. (rō'gō-ä-gwä-dō)	124	12.42S	66.46W
Rogovskaya, Russia (rô-gôf'skȧ-yȧ)	156	45.43N	38.42E
Rogózno, Pol. (rō'gôzh-nō)	148	52.44N	16.53E
Rogue, r., Or., U.S. (rōg)	98	42.32N	124.13W
Rohdenhaus, Ger.	232	51.18N	7.01E
Röhlinghausen, neigh., Ger.	232	51.31N	7.08E
Rohrbeck, Ger.	234a	52.32N	13.02E
Roissy, Fr.	233c	48.47N	2.39E
Roissy-en-France, Fr.	233c	49.00N	2.31E
Rojas, Arg. (rō'häs)	123c	34.11S	60.42W
Rojo, Cabo, c., Mex. (rō'hō)	112	21.35N	97.16W
Rojo, Cabo, c., P.R. (rō'hō)	111b	17.55N	67.14W
Rokel, r., S.L.	208	9.00N	11.55W
Rokkō-Zan, mtn., Japan (rôk'kō zän)	187b	34.46N	135.16E
Roksana, S. Afr.	240b	26.07S	28.24E
Rokycany, Czech. (rô'kĭ'tsȧ-nĭ)	148	49.44N	13.37E
Roldanillo, Col. (rôl-dä-nē'l-yō)	124a	4.24N	76.09W
Rolla, Mo., U.S.	104	37.56N	91.45W
Rolla, N.D., U.S.	96	48.52N	99.32W
Rolleville, Bah.	116	23.40N	76.00W
Rolling Acres, Md., U.S.	225c	39.17N	76.52W

ng-sing; ŋ-baŋk; ɴ-nasalized n; nŏd; cŏmmit; ōld; ôbey; ôrder; oi-boil; fo͞od; o͝o-as oo in foot; ou-out; s-soft; sh-dish; th-thin; pūre; ûnite; ûrn; stŭd; circŭs; ü-as in French tu; '-indeterminate vowel.

PLACE (Pronunciation)	PAGE	Lat. °'	Long. °'
Röllinghausen, neigh., Ger.	232	51.36N	7.14E
Rolling Hills, Ca., U.S.	228	33.46N	118.21W
Roma, Austl. (rō'mȧ)	196	26.30S	148.48E
Roma, Leso.	207c	29.28S	27.43E
Romaine, r., Can. (rō-mĕn')	78	51.22N	63.23W
Romainville, Fr.	233c	48.53N	2.26E
Roman, Rom. (rō'män)	148	46.56N	26.57E
Romania, nation, Eur. (rō-mā'nē-ȧ)	136	46.18N	22.53E
Romano, Cape, c., Fl., U.S. (rō-mä'nō)	109a	25.48N	82.00W
Romano, Cayo, i., Cuba (kä'yō-rô-mä'nô)	116	22.15N	78.00W
Romanovo, Russia (rô-mä'nô-vô)	164a	59.09N	61.24E
Romans, Fr. (rô-mäN')	150	45.04N	4.49E
Roma, see Rome, Italy	136	41.52N	12.37E
Romblon, Phil. (rōm-blōn')	189a	12.34N	122.16E
Romblon Island, i., Phil.	189a	12.33N	122.17E
Rome (Roma), Italy	136	41.52N	12.37E
Rome, Ga., U.S. (rōm)	90	34.14N	85.10W
Rome, N.Y., U.S.	92	43.15N	75.25W
Romeo, Mi., U.S. (rō'mē-ō)	92	42.50N	83.00W
Romford, Eng., U.K. (rŭm'fērd)	138b	51.35N	0.11E
Romiley, Eng., U.K.	233b	53.25N	2.05W
Romilly-sur-Seine, Fr. (rō-mē-yē'sür-sān')	150	48.32N	3.41E
Romita, Mex. (rō-mē'tä)	112	20.53N	101.32W
Romny, Ukr. (rôm'nĭ)	160	50.46N	33.31E
Rømø, i., Den. (rûm'û)	146	55.08N	8.17E
Romoland, Ca., U.S. (rō'mō'lănd)	101a	33.44N	117.11W
Romorantin-Lanthenay, Fr. (rô-mô-räN-täN')	150	47.24N	1.46E
Rompin, Malay.	173b	2.42N	102.30E
Rompin, r., Malay.	173b	2.54N	103.10E
Romsdalsfjorden, Nor.	146	62.40N	7.05W
Romulus, Mi., U.S. (rom'ū lŭs)	95b	42.14N	83.24W
Ron, Mui, c., Viet.	184	18.05N	106.45E
Ronan, Mt., U.S. (rō'năn)	98	47.28N	114.03W
Roncador, Serra do, mts., Braz. (sĕr'rȧ dô rôn-kä-dôr')	124	12.44S	52.19W
Roncesvalles, Spain (rôn-sĕs-vä'l-yĕs)	152	43.00N	1.17W
Ronceverte, W.V., U.S. (rŏn'sē-vûrt)	92	37.45N	80.30W
Ronda, Spain (rōn'dä)	160	36.45N	5.10W
Ronda, Sierra de, mts., Spain	152	36.35N	5.03W
Rondebult, S. Afr.	240b	26.18S	28.14E
Rondônia, , Braz.	124	10.15S	63.07W
Ronge, Lac la, l., Can. (rōnzh)	78	55.10N	105.00W
Rongjiang, China (rôŋ-jyäŋ)	184	25.52N	108.45E
Rongxian, China	184	22.50N	110.32E
Rønne, Den. (rûn'ĕ)	140	55.08N	14.46E
Ronneby, Swe. (rōn'ĕ-bü)	146	56.13N	15.17E
Ronne Ice Shelf, ice., Ant.	213	77.30S	38.00W
Ronsdorf, neigh., Ger.	232	51.14N	7.12E
Roodepoort, S. Afr. (rō'dē-pōrt)	207b	26.10S	27.52E
Roodhouse, Il., U.S. (ro͞od'hous)	104	39.29N	90.21W
Rooiberg, S. Afr.	212d	24.46S	27.42E
Roosendaal, Neth. (rō'zĕn-däl)	139a	51.32N	4.27E
Roosevelt, N.Y., U.S.	224	40.41N	73.36W
Roosevelt, Ut., U.S. (rōz''vĕlt)	102	40.20N	110.00W
Roosevelt, r., Braz. (rō'sē-vĕlt)	124	9.22S	60.28W
Roosevelt Island, i., Ant.	213	79.30S	168.00W
Root, r., Wi., U.S.	95a	42.49N	87.54W
Rooty Hill, Austl.	239a	33.46S	150.50E
Roper, r., Austl. (rōp'ēr)	196	14.50S	134.00E
Ropsha, Russia (rôp'shȧ)	164c	59.44N	29.53E
Roque Pérez, Arg. (rô'kĕ-pĕ'rĕz)	123c	35.23S	59.22W
Roques, Islas los, is., Ven.	124	12.25N	67.40W
Roraima, , Braz. (rō'rīy-mă)	124	2.00N	62.15W
Roraima, Mount, mtn., S.A. (rō-rä-ē'mä)	124	5.12N	60.52W
Røros, Nor. (rûr'ôs)	140	62.36N	11.25E
Ros', r., Ukr. (rôs)	156	49.40N	30.22E
Rosa, Monte, mtn., Italy (mōn'tä rō'zä)	142	45.56N	7.51E
Rosales, Mex. (rō-zä'läs)	106	28.15N	100.43W
Rosales, Phil. (rō-sä'lĕs)	189a	15.54N	120.38E
Rosamorada, Mex. (rō'zä-mō-rä'dhä)	112	22.06N	105.16W
Rosanna, Austl.	239b	37.45S	145.04E
Rosaria, Laguna, l., Mex. (lä-gô'nä-rō-sä'ryä)	112	17.50N	93.51W
Rosario, Arg. (rō-zä'rē-ō)	126	32.58S	60.42W
Rosario, Braz. (rō-zä'rē-ō)	124	2.49S	44.15W
Rosario, Mex.	106	26.31N	105.40W
Rosario, Mex.	112	22.58N	105.54W
Rosario, Phil.	189a	13.49N	121.13W
Rosario, Ur.	123c	34.19S	57.24E
Rosario, Cayo, i., Cuba (kä'yō-rō-sä'ryō)	116	21.40N	81.55W
Rosário do Sul, Braz. (rō-zä'rē-ō-dō-so͞o'l)	126	30.17S	54.52W
Rosário Oeste, Braz. (ō'ĕst'ĕ)	124	14.47S	56.20W
Rosario Strait, strt., Wa., U.S.	100a	48.27N	122.45W
Rosas, Golfo de, b., Spain (gôl-fô-dĕ-rō'zäs)	152	42.10N	3.20E
Rosbach, Ger. (rōz'bäK)	151c	50.47N	7.38E
Roscoe, Tx., U.S. (rôs'kō)	106	32.26N	100.38W
Roseau, Dom.	115b	15.17N	61.23W
Roseau, Mn., U.S. (rō-zō')	96	48.52N	95.47W
Roseau, r., Mn., U.S.	96	48.52N	96.11W
Rosebank, neigh., S. Afr.	240b	26.09S	28.02E
Roseberg, Or., U.S. (rōz'bûrg)	90	43.13N	123.30W
Rosebery, neigh., Austl.	239a	33.55S	151.12E
Rosebud, r., Can. (rōz'bŭd)	80	51.20N	112.20W
Rosebud Creek, r., Mt., U.S.	98	45.48N	106.34W
Rosebud Indian Reservation, I.R., S.D., U.S.	96	43.13N	100.42W
Rosedale, Ms., U.S.	108	33.49N	90.56W
Rosedale, Wa., U.S.	100a	47.20N	122.39W
Rosedale, neigh., Can.	223c	43.41N	79.22W
Rosedale, neigh., N.Y., U.S.	224	40.39N	73.45W
Roseires Reservoir, res., Sudan	204	11.15N	34.45E
Roseland, neigh., Il., U.S.	227a	41.42N	87.38W
Roselle, Il., U.S. (rō-zĕl')	95a	41.59N	88.05W
Roselle, N.J., U.S.	224	40.40N	74.16W
Rosemead, Ca., U.S.	228	34.04N	118.03W
Rosemère, Can. (rōz'mēr)	77a	45.38N	73.48W
Rosemont, Il., U.S.	227a	41.59N	87.52W
Rosemont, Pa., U.S.	225b	40.01N	75.19W
Rosemount, Mn., U.S. (rōz'mount)	101g	44.44N	93.08W
Rosendal, S. Afr. (rō-sĕn'täl)	212d	28.32S	27.56E
Roseneath, S. Afr.	240b	26.17S	28.11E
Rosenheim, Ger. (rō'zĕn-hīm)	140	47.52N	12.06E
Rosenthal, neigh., Ger.	234a	52.36N	13.23E
Rosetown, Can. (rōz'toun)	78	51.33N	108.00W
Rose Tree, Pa., U.S.	225b	39.56N	75.23W
Rosetta, see Rashīd, Egypt	176	31.22N	30.25E
Rosettenville, neigh., S. Afr.	207b	26.15S	28.04E
Roseville, Austl.	239a	33.47S	151.11E
Roseville, Ca., U.S. (rōz'vĭl)	102	38.44N	121.19W
Roseville, Mi., U.S.	95b	42.30N	82.55W
Roseville, Mn., U.S.	101g	45.01N	93.10W
Rosiclare, Il., U.S. (rōz'y-klâr)	92	37.30N	88.15W
Rosignol, Guy. (rŏs-ĭg-nól)	124	6.16N	57.37W
Roșiori-de-Vede, Rom. (rō-shôr'ē dĕ vĕ-dĕ)	154	44.06N	25.00E
Roskilde, Den. (rôs'kēl-dĕ)	146	55.39N	12.04E
Roslavl', Russia (rôs'läv'l)	160	53.56N	32.52E
Roslyn, N.Y., U.S.	224	40.48N	73.39W
Roslyn, Wa., U.S. (rŏz'lĭn)	98	47.14N	121.00W
Roslyn Estates, N.Y., U.S.	224	40.47N	73.40W
Roslyn Heights, N.Y., U.S.	224	40.47N	73.39W
Rosny-sous-Bois, Fr.	233c	48.53N	2.29E
Rosovka, Ukr.	156	47.14N	36.35E
Rösrath, Ger. (rûz'rät)	151c	50.53N	7.11E
Ross, Oh., U.S. (rôs)	95f	39.19N	84.39W
Rossano, Italy (rô-sä'nō)	142	39.34N	16.38E
Rossan Point, c., Ire.	144	54.45N	8.30W
Ross Creek, r., Can.	77g	53.40N	113.08W
Rosseau, l., Can. (rōs-sō')	84	45.15N	79.30W
Rossel, i., Pap. N. Gui. (rō-sĕl')	196	11.31S	154.00E
Rosser, Can. (rôs'sēr)	77f	49.59N	97.27W
Ross Ice Shelf, ice., Ant.	213	81.30S	175.00W
Rossignol, Lake, l., Can.	86	44.10N	65.10W
Ross Island, i., Can.	82	54.14N	97.45W
Ross Lake, res., Wa., U.S.	98	48.40N	121.07W
Rossland, Can. (rôs'lănd)	78	49.05N	118.48W
Rossmore, Austl.	239a	33.57S	150.46E
Rossosh', Russia (rôs'sŭsh)	160	50.12N	39.32E
Rossouw, S. Afr.	207c	31.12S	27.18E
Ross Sea, sea, Ant.	213	76.00S	178.00W
Rossvatnet, l., Nor.	140	65.36N	13.08E
Rossville, Ga., U.S. (rôs'vĭl)	108	34.57N	85.22W
Rossville, Md., U.S.	225c	39.20N	76.29W
Rosthern, Can.	82	52.41N	106.25W
Rostherne, Eng., U.K.	233b	53.21N	2.23W
Rostock, Ger. (rôs'tŭk)	140	54.04N	12.06E
Rostov, Russia	160	57.13N	39.23E
Rostov, prov., Russia	156	47.38N	39.15E
Rostov-na-Donu, Russia (rôstôv-nȧ-dô-no͞o)	158	47.16N	39.47E
Roswell, Ga., U.S. (rôz'wĕl)	108	34.02N	84.21W
Roswell, N.M., U.S.	90	33.23N	104.32W
Rosyln, Pa., U.S.	225b	40.07N	75.08W
Rotan, Tx., U.S. (rō-tăn')	104	32.51N	100.27W
Rothenburg, Ger.	148	49.20N	10.10E
Rotherham, Eng., U.K. (rŏdh'ēr-ăm)	138a	53.26N	1.21W
Rothesay, Can. (rôth'sȧ)	86	45.23N	66.00W
Rothesay, Scot., U.K.	144	55.50N	3.14W
Rothneusiedl, neigh., Aus.	235e	48.08N	16.23E
Rothwell, Eng., U.K.	138a	53.44N	1.30W
Roti, Pulau, i., Indon. (rō'tē)	188	10.30S	122.52E
Roto, Austl. (rō'tô)	198	33.07S	145.30E
Rotorua, N.Z.	199	38.07S	176.17E
Rotterdam, Neth. (rôt'ēr-däm')	136	51.55N	4.27E
Rottweil, Ger. (rōt'vīl)	148	48.10N	8.36E
Roubaix, Fr. (ro͞o-bĕ')	150	50.42N	3.10E
Rouen, Fr. (ro͞o-äN')	136	49.25N	1.05E
Rouge, r., Can. (ro͞ozh)	77d	43.53N	79.21W
Rouge, r., Can.	84	46.40N	74.50W
Rouge, r., Mi., U.S.	95b	42.30N	83.15W
Rough River Reservoir, res., Ky., U.S.	92	37.45N	86.10W
Round Lake, Il., U.S.	95a	42.21N	88.05W
Round Pond, l., Can.	86	48.15N	55.57W
Round Rock, Tx., U.S.	106	30.31N	97.41W
Round Top, mtn., Or., U.S. (tŏp)	100c	45.41N	123.22W
Roundup, Mt., U.S. (round'ŭp)	98	46.25N	108.35W
Rousay, i., Scot., U.K. (ro͞o'zȧ)	144a	59.10N	3.04W
Rouyn, Can. (ro͞on)	78	48.22N	79.03W
Rovaniemi, Fin. (rô'vȧ-nyĕ'mĭ)	140	66.29N	25.45E
Rovato, Italy (rō-vä'tō)	154	45.33N	10.00E
Roven'ki, Russia	156	49.54N	38.54E
Roven'ki, Ukr. (rō-vĕn'kĭ')	156	48.06N	39.44E
Rovereto, Italy (rō-vā-rā'tō)	154	45.53N	11.05E
Rovigo, Italy (rō-vē'gô)	154	45.05N	11.48E
Rovinj, Cro. (rō'ēn')	154	45.05N	13.40E
Rovira, Col. (rō-vē'rä)	124a	4.14N	75.13W
Rovno, Ukr. (rôv'nō)	160	50.37N	26.17E
Rovno, prov., Ukr.	156	50.55N	27.00E
Rovnoye, Ukr. (rôv'nō-yĕ)	156	48.11N	31.46E
Rovuma (Ruvuma), r., Afr.	210	10.50S	39.50E
Rowland Heights, Ca., U.S.	228	33.59N	117.54W
Rowley, Ma., U.S. (rou'lē)	87a	42.43N	70.53W
Rowville, Austl.	239b	37.56S	145.14E
Roxana, Il., U.S. (rŏks'ăn-nȧ)	101e	38.51N	90.05W
Roxas, Phil. (rô-xäs)	188	11.30N	122.47E
Roxboro, Can.	223b	45.31N	73.48W
Roxborough, neigh., Pa., U.S.	225b	40.02N	75.13W
Roxbury, neigh., N.Y., U.S.	224	40.34N	73.54W
Roxo, Cap, c., Sen.	208	12.20N	16.43W
Roy, N.M., U.S. (roi)	104	35.54N	104.09W
Roy, Ut., U.S.	101b	41.10N	112.02W
Royal, i., Bah.	116	25.30N	76.50W
Royal Albert Hall, pt. of i., Eng., U.K.	231	51.30N	0.11W
Royal Canal, can., Ire. (roi-ăl)	144	53.28N	6.45W
Royal Natal National Park, rec., S. Afr.	207c	28.35S	28.54E
Royal Naval College, pt. of i., Eng., U.K.	231	51.29N	0.01W
Royal Oak, Can. (roi'ăl ōk)	100a	48.30N	123.24W
Royal Oak, Mi., U.S.	95b	42.29N	83.09W
Royal Oak Township, Mi., U.S.	226c	42.27N	83.10W
Royal Ontario Museum, bldg., Can.	223c	43.40N	79.24W
Royalton, Mi., U.S. (roi'ăl-tŭn)	92	42.00N	86.25W
Royan, Fr. (rwä-yäN')	150	45.40N	1.02W
Roye, Fr. (rwä)	150	49.43N	2.40E
Royersford, Pa., U.S. (rô' yērz-fērd)	94f	40.11N	75.32W
Royston, Ga., U.S. (roiz'tŭn)	108	34.15N	83.06W
Royton, Eng., U.K. (roi'tŭn)	138a	53.34N	2.07W
Rozay-en-Brie, Fr. (rô-zā-ĕN-brē')	151b	48.41N	2.57E
Rozelle, Austl.	239a	33.52S	151.10E
Rozhaya, r., Russia (rô'zhȧ-yȧ)	164b	55.20N	37.37E
Rožňava, Czech. (rôzh'nyȧ-vȧ)	148	48.39N	20.32E
Rtishchevo, Russia ('r-tĭsh'chĕ-vô)	160	52.15N	43.40E
Ru, r., China (ro͞o)	182	33.07N	114.18E
Ruacana Falls, wtfl., Afr.	206	17.15S	14.45E
Ruaha National Park, rec., Tan.	210	7.15S	34.50E
Ruapehu, vol., N.Z. (rō-ȧ-pā'ho͞o)	197a	39.15S	175.37E
Rubeho Mountains, mts., Tan.	210	6.45S	36.15E
Rubidoux, Ca., U.S.	101a	33.59N	117.24W
Rubondo Island, i., Tan.	210	2.10S	31.55E
Rubtsovsk, Russia	158	51.31N	81.17E
Ruby, Ak., U.S. (ro͞o'bē)	90a	64.38N	155.22W
Ruby, l., Nv., U.S.	102	40.11N	115.20W
Ruby, r., Mt., U.S.	98	45.06N	112.10W
Ruby Mountains, mts., Nv., U.S.	102	40.11N	115.36W
Rüdersdorf, Ger.	234a	52.29N	13.47E
Rudge Ramos, Braz.	230d	23.41S	46.34W
Rüdinghausen, neigh., Ger.	232	51.27N	7.25E
Rudkøbing, Den. (ro͞odh'kûb-ĭng)	146	54.56N	10.44E
Rüdnitz, Ger. (rüd'nētz)	139b	52.44N	13.38E
Rudolf, Lake, l., Afr. (ro͞o'dôlf)	204	3.30N	36.05E
Rudow, neigh., Ger.	234a	52.25N	13.30E
Rueil-Malmaison, Fr.	233c	48.53N	2.11E
Rufā'ah, Sudan (ro͞o-fä'ä)	204	14.52N	33.30E
Ruffec, Fr. (rü-fĕk')	150	46.03N	0.11E
Rufiji, r., Tan. (rō-fē'jē)	206	8.00S	38.00E
Rufisque, Sen. (rü-fēsk')	204	14.43N	17.17W
Rufunsa, Zam.	210	15.05S	29.40E
Rufus Woods, Wa., U.S.	98	48.02N	119.33W
Rugao, China (ro͞o-gou)	184	32.24N	120.33E
Rugby, Eng., U.K. (rŭg'bē)	138a	52.22N	1.15W
Rugby, N.D., U.S.	96	48.22N	100.00W
Rugeley, Eng., U.K. (ro͞oj'lē)	138a	52.46N	1.56W
Rügen, i., Ger. (rü'ghĕn)	136	54.28N	13.47E
Rüggeberg, Ger.	232	51.16N	7.22E
Ruhlsdorf, Ger.	234a	52.23N	13.16E
Ruhnu-Saar, i., Est. (ro͞onō-sȧ'ȧr)	146	57.46N	23.15E
Ruhr, r., Ger. (rōr)	148	51.18N	8.17E
Ruhrort, neigh., Ger.	232	51.26N	6.45E
Rui'an, China (rwā-än)	184	27.48N	120.40E
Ruislip, neigh., Eng., U.K.	231	51.34N	0.25W
Ruiz, Mex. (rōē'z)	112	21.55N	105.09W
Ruiz, Nevado del, vol., Col. (nĕ-vȧ'dō-dĕl-ro͞oē'z)	124a	4.52N	75.20W
Rūjiena, Lat. (rō'yĭ-ā-nȧ)	146	57.54N	25.19E
Ruki, r., Zaire	210	0.05S	18.55E
Rukwa, Lake, l., Tan. (ro͞ok-wä')	206	8.00S	32.25E
Rum, r., Mn., U.S. (rŭm)	96	45.52N	93.45W
Ruma, Yugo. (ro͞o'mȧ)	154	45.00N	19.53E
Rum'ancevo, Russia	235b	55.38N	37.26E
Rumbek, Sudan (rŭm'bĕk)	204	6.52N	29.43E
Rum Cay, i., Bah.	116	23.40N	74.50W
Rumelihisari, neigh., Tur.	235f	41.05N	29.03E
Rumford, Me., U.S. (rŭm'fērd)	86	44.32N	70.35W
Rummah, Wādī ar, val., Sau. Ar.	174	26.17N	41.45E
Rummānah, Egypt	173a	31.01N	32.39E
Rummelsburg, neigh., Ger.	234a	52.30N	13.29E
Rummenohl, Ger.	232	51.17N	7.32E
Runan, China (ro͞o-nän)	184	32.59N	114.22E
Runcorn, Eng., U.K. (rŭŋ'kôrn)	138a	53.20N	2.44W
Runnemede, N.J., U.S.	225b	39.51N	75.04W
Runnymede, pt. of i., Eng., U.K.	231	51.26N	0.34W
Ruo, r., China (rwō)	180	41.15N	100.46E
Rupat, i., Indon. (ro͞o'pät)	173b	1.55N	101.35E
Rupat, Selat, strt., Indon.	173b	1.55N	101.17E
Rupert, Id., U.S. (ro͞o'pērt)	98	42.36N	113.41W
Rupert, Rivière de, r., Can.	78	51.35N	76.30W
Rural Ridge, Pa., U.S.	226b	40.35N	79.50W
Ruse, Bul. (ro͞o'sĕ) (rō'sĕ)	136	43.50N	25.59E
Rushan, China (ro͞o-shän)	182	36.54N	121.31E
Rush City, Mn., U.S.	96	45.40N	92.59W
Rusholme, neigh., Eng., U.K.	233b	53.27N	2.12W
Rushville, Il., U.S. (rŭsh'vĭl)	104	40.08N	90.34W
Rushville, In., U.S.	92	39.35N	85.30W
Rushville, Ne., U.S.	96	42.43N	102.27W
Rusizi, r., Afr.	210	3.00S	29.05E
Rusk, Tx., U.S. (rŭsk)	106	31.49N	95.09W
Ruskin, Can. (rŭs'kĭn)	100d	49.10N	122.25W
Russ, r., Aus.	139e	48.12N	16.55E
Russas, Braz. (ro͞o's-säs)	124	4.48S	37.50W
Russell, Can.	77c	45.15N	75.22W
Russell, Can. (rŭs'ĕl)	78	50.47N	101.15W
Russell, Ca., U.S.	100b	37.39N	122.08W

ăt; finăl; rāte; senāte; ärm; ȧsk; sofȧ; fâre; ch-choose; dh-as th in other; bē; ēvent; bĕt; recĕnt; cratēr; g-gō; gh-guttural g; bĭt; ĭ-short neutral; rīde; K-guttural k as ch in German ich;

PLACE (Pronunciation)	PAGE	Lat. °′	Long. °′
Russell, Ks., U.S.	104	38.51N	98.51W
Russell, Ky., U.S.	92	38.30N	82.45W
Russel Lake, l., Can.	82	56.15N	101.30W
Russell Gardens, N.Y., U.S.	224	40.47N	73.43W
Russell Islands, is., Sol.Is.	196	9.16S	158.30E
Russellville, Al., U.S. (rŭs'ĕl-vĭl)	108	34.29N	87.44W
Russellville, Ar., U.S.	104	35.16N	93.08W
Russelville, Ky., U.S.	108	36.48N	86.51W
Russia, nation, Russia	158	61.00N	60.00E
Russian, r., Ca., U.S. (rŭsh'ăn)	102	38.59N	123.10W
Rustenburg, S. Afr. (rŭs'tĕn-bûrg)	212d	25.40S	27.15E
Ruston, La., U.S. (rŭs'tŭn)	106	32.32N	92.39W
Ruston, Wa., U.S.	100a	47.18N	122.30W
Rusville, S. Afr.	240b	26.10S	28.18E
Rutchenkovo, Ukr. (rŏ-chĕn'kô-vô)	156	47.54N	37.36E
Rute, Spain (rōō'tā)	152	38.20N	4.34W
Ruth, Nv., U.S. (rōōth)	102	39.17N	115.00W
Ruthenia, hist. reg., Ukr.	148	48.25N	23.00E
Rutherford, N.J., U.S.	224	40.49N	74.07W
Rutherfordton, N.C., U.S. (rŭdh'ẽr-fẽrd-tŭn)	108	35.23N	81.58W
Rutland, Vt., U.S.	92	43.35N	72.55W
Rutledge, Md., U.S. (rŭt'lĕdj)	94e	39.34N	76.33W
Rutledge, Pa., U.S.	225b	39.54N	75.20W
Rutog, China	180	33.29N	79.26E
Rutshuru, Zaire (rōōt-shōō'rōō)	206	1.11S	29.27E
Rüttenscheid, neigh., Ger.	232	51.26N	7.00E
Ruvo, Italy (rōō'vô)	154	41.07N	16.32E
Ruvuma, r., Afr.	206	11.30S	37.00E
Ruza, Russia (rōō'zȧ)	156	55.42N	36.12E
Ruzhany, Bela. (rŏ-zhän'ĭ)	148	52.49N	24.54E
Rwanda, nation, Afr.	206	2.10S	29.37E
Ryabovo, Russia (ryä'bô-vô)	164c	59.24N	31.08E
Ryarsh, Eng., U.K.	231	51.19N	0.24E
Ryazan', Russia (ryä-zän'')	158	54.37N	39.43E
Ryazan', prov., Russia	156	54.10N	39.37E
Ryazhsk, Russia (ryäzh'sk')	160	53.43N	40.04E
Rybachiy, Poluostrov, pen., Russia	160	69.50N	33.20E
Rybatskoye, Russia	164c	59.50N	30.31E
Rybinsk, Russia	158	58.02N	38.52E
Rybinskoye, res., Russia	158	58.23N	38.15E
Rybnik, Pol. (rĭb'nêk)	148	50.06N	18.37E
Rybnitsa, Mol. (rĭb'nêt-sȧ)	156	47.45N	29.02E
Rydal, Pa., U.S.	225b	40.06N	75.06W
Rydalmere, Austl.	239a	33.49S	151.02E
Ryde, Austl.	239a	33.49S	151.06E
Ryde, Eng., U.K. (rīd)	144	50.43N	1.16W
Rye, N.Y., U.S. (rī)	94a	40.58N	73.42W
Ryl'sk, Russia (rêl''sk)	160	51.33N	34.42E
Rynfield, S. Afr.	240b	26.09S	28.20E
Ryōtsu, Japan (ryōt'sōō)	186	38.02N	138.23E
Rypin, Pol. (rĭ'pên)	148	53.04N	19.25E
Rysy, mtn., Eur.	148	49.12N	20.04E
Ryukyu Islands, *see* Nansei-shotō, is., Japan	180	27.30N	127.00E
Rzeszów, Pol. (zhå-shoof)	140	50.02N	22.00E
Rzhev, Russia ('r-zhĕf)	158	56.16N	34.17E
Rzhishchĕv, Ukr. ('r-zhĭsh'chĕf)	156	49.58N	31.05E

S

PLACE (Pronunciation)	PAGE	Lat. °′	Long. °′
Saale, r., Ger. (sä-lĕ)	148	51.14N	11.52E
Saalfeld, Ger. (säl'fĕlt)	148	50.38N	11.20E
Saarbrücken, Ger. (zähr'brü-kĕn)	140	49.15N	7.01E
Saaremaa, i., Est.	160	58.25N	22.30E
Saarland, state, Ger.	148	49.25N	6.50E
Saarn, neigh., Ger.	232	51.24N	6.53E
Saarnberg, neigh., Ger.	232	51.25N	6.53E
Saavedra, Arg. (sä-ä-vä'drä)	126	37.45S	62.23W
Saba, i., Neth. Ant. (sä'bä)	115b	17.39N	63.20W
Šabac, Yugo. (shä'bats)	142	44.45N	19.49E
Sabadell, Spain (sä-bä-dhål')	142	41.32N	2.07E
Sabah, hist. reg., Malay.	188	5.10N	116.25E
Sabana, Archipiélago de, is., Cuba	116	23.05N	80.00W
Sabana, Río, r., Pan. (sä-bä'nä)	114	8.40N	78.02W
Sabana de la Mar, Dom. Rep. (sä-bä'nä dā lä mär')	116	19.05N	69.30W
Sabana de Uchire, Ven. (sä-bä'nä dĕ ōō-chē'rĕ)	125b	10.02N	65.32W
Sabanagrande, Hond. (sä-bä'nä-grä'n-dĕ)	114	13.47N	87.16W
Sabanalarga, Col. (sä-bá'nä-lär'gä)	124	10.38N	75.02W
Sabanas Páramo, mtn., Col. (sä-bá'näs pá'rä-mô)	124a	6.28N	76.08W
Sabancuy, Mex. (sä-bäŋ-kwē')	112	18.58N	91.09W
Sabang, Indon. (sä'bäng)	188	5.52N	95.26E
Sabaudia, Italy (sȧ-bou'dē-ä)	154	41.19N	13.00E
Sabetha, Ks., U.S. (sȧ-bĕth'ȧ)	104	39.54N	95.49W
Sabi (Rio Save), r., Afr. (sä'bē)	206	20.18S	32.07E
Sabile, Lat. (sä'bē-lĕ)	146	57.03N	22.34E
Sabinal, Tx., U.S. (sȧ-bī'nȧl)	106	29.19N	99.27W
Sabinal, Cayo, i., Cuba (kä'yō sä-bē-näl')	116	21.40N	77.20W
Sabinas, Mex.	110	28.05N	101.30W
Sabinas, r., Mex. (sä-bē'näs)	106	26.37N	99.52W
Sabinas, Río, r., Mex. (rê'ō sä-bē'näs)	106	27.25N	100.33W
Sabinas Hidalgo, Mex. (ê-däl'gō)	106	26.30N	100.10W
Sabine, Tx., U.S. (sȧ-bēn')	106	29.44N	93.54W
Sabine, r., U.S.	90	32.00N	94.30W
Sabine, Mount, mtn., Ant.	213	72.05S	169.10E
Sabine Lake, l., La., U.S.	106	29.53N	93.41W
Sablayan, Phil. (säb-lä-yän')	189a	12.49N	120.47E
Sable, Cape, c., Can. (sā'b'l)	78	43.25N	65.24W
Sable, Cape, c., Fl., U.S.	90	25.12N	81.10W
Sables, Rivière aux, r., Can.	84	49.00N	70.20W
Sablé-sur-Sarthe, Fr. (säb-lā-sür-särt')	150	47.50N	0.17W
Sablya, Gora, mtn., Russia	160	64.50N	59.00E
Sàbor, r., Port. (sä-bōr')	152	41.18N	6.54W
Saburovo, neigh., Russia	235b	55.38N	37.42E
Sabzevār, Iran	176	36.13N	57.42E
Sac, r., Mo., U.S. (sôk)	104	38.11N	93.45W
Sacandaga Reservoir, res., N.Y., U.S. (să-kăn-dâ'gȧ)	92	43.10N	74.15W
Sacavém, Port. (sä-kä-vĕn')	153b	38.47N	9.06W
Sacavém, r., Port.	153b	38.52N	9.06W
Sac City, Ia., U.S. (sŏk)	96	42.25N	95.00W
Sachigo Lake, l., Can. (săch'ĭ-gō)	82	53.49N	92.08W
Sachsen, hist. reg., Ger. (zäk'sĕn)	148	50.45N	12.17E
Sacketts Harbor, N.Y., U.S. (săk'ĕts)	92	43.55N	76.05W
Sackville, Can. (săk'vĭl)	86	45.54N	64.22W
Saco, Me., U.S. (sô'kô)	86	43.30N	70.28W
Saco, r., Braz. (sä'kô)	126b	22.20S	43.26W
Saco, r., Me., U.S.	86	43.53N	70.46W
Sacramento, Mex.	106	27.05N	101.45W
Sacramento, Mex.	106	25.45N	103.22W
Sacramento, Ca., U.S. (săk-rȧ-mĕn'tō)	90	38.35N	121.30W
Sacramento, r., Ca., U.S.	102	40.20N	122.07W
Sacrow, neigh., Ger.	234a	52.26N	13.06E
Şa'dah, Yemen	174	16.50N	43.45E
Saddle Brook, N.J., U.S.	224	40.54N	74.06W
Saddle Lake Indian Reserve, I.R., Can.	80	54.00N	111.40W
Saddle Mountain, mtn., Or., U.S. (săd''l)	100c	45.58N	123.40W
Saddle Rock, N.Y., U.S.	224	40.48N	73.45W
Sadiya, India (sŭ-dē'yä)	174	27.53N	95.35E
Sado, i., Japan (sä'dō)	180	38.05N	138.26E
Sado, r., Port. (sä'dò)	152	38.15N	8.20W
Saeby, Den. (sĕ'bü)	146	57.21N	10.29E
Saeki, Japan (sä'ā-kē)	186	32.56N	131.51E
Safdar Jang's Tomb, rel., India	236d	28.36N	77.13E
Säffle, Swe.	146	59.10N	12.55E
Safford, Az., U.S. (săf'fẽrd)	102	32.50N	109.45W
Safi, Mor. (sä'fē) (äs'fē)	204	32.24N	9.09W
Saga, Japan (sä'gä)	187	33.15N	130.18E
Sagamihara, Japan	238a	35.34N	139.23E
Sagami-Nada, b., Japan (sä'gä'mē nä-dä)	187	35.06N	139.24E
Sagamore Hills, Oh., U.S. (săg'ȧ-môr hĭlz)	95d	41.19N	81.34W
Saganaga, l., N.A. (sä-gȧ-nä'gȧ)	96	48.13N	91.17W
Sāgar, India	174	23.55N	78.45E
Saginaw, Mi., U.S. (săg'ĭ-nô)	90	43.25N	84.00W
Saginaw, Mn., U.S.	101h	46.51N	92.26W
Saginaw, Tx., U.S.	101c	32.52N	97.22W
Saginaw Bay, b., Mi., U.S.	90	43.50N	83.40W
Sagiz, r., Kaz. (sä'gĕz)	160	48.30N	56.10E
Saguache, Co., U.S. (sȧ-wăch') (sȧ-gwä'chē)	102	38.05N	106.10W
Saguache Creek, r., Co., U.S.	92	38.05N	106.40W
Sagua de Tánamo, Cuba (sä-gwä dĕ tá'nä-mō)	116	20.40N	75.15W
Sagua la Grande, Cuba (sä-gwä lä grä'n-dĕ)	116	22.45N	80.05W
Saguaro National Monument, rec., Az., U.S. (säg-wä'rō)	102	32.12N	110.40W
Saguenay, r., Can. (săg-ĕ-nā')	78	48.20N	70.15W
Sagunto, Spain (sä-gōōn'tō)	142	39.40N	0.17W
Sahara, des., Afr. (sȧ-hä'rȧ)	204	23.44N	1.40W
Saharan Atlas, mts., Afr.	142	32.51N	1.02W
Sahāranpur, India (sŭ-hä'rŭn-pōōr')	174	29.58N	77.41E
Sahara Village, Ut., U.S. (sȧ-hä'rȧ)	101b	41.06N	111.58W
Sāhīwāl, Pak.	178	30.43N	73.04E
Sahuayo de Dias, Mex.	112	20.03N	102.43W
Saigon, *see* Ho Chi Minh City, Viet.	188	10.46N	106.34E
Saijō, Japan (sä'ē-jō)	187	33.55N	133.13E
Saimaa, l., Fin. (sä'ĭ-mä)	140	61.24N	28.45E
Sain Alto, Mex. (sä-ēn' äl'tō)	112	23.35N	103.13W
Saint Adolphe, Can. (sånt a'dŏlf) (săN' tá-dôlf')	77f	49.40N	97.07W
Saint Afrique, Fr. (săN' tá-frēk')	150	43.58N	2.52E
Saint Albans, Austl. (sånt ôl'bȧnz)	195a	37.44S	144.47E
Saint Albans, Eng., U.K.	144	51.44N	0.20W
Saint Albans, Vt., U.S.	92	44.50N	73.05W
Saint Albans, W.V., U.S.	92	38.20N	81.50W
Saint Albans, neigh., N.Y., U.S.	224	40.42N	73.46W
Saint Albans Cathedral, pt. of i., Eng., U.K.	231	51.45N	0.20W
Saint Albert, Can. (sånt ăl'bẽrt)	80	53.38N	113.38W
Saint Amand-Mont Rond, Fr. (săN't a-mäN' môn-rôN')	150	46.44N	2.28E
Saint André-Est, Can.	77a	45.33N	74.19W
Saint Andrews, Can.	78	45.05N	67.03W
Saint Andrews, Scot., U.K.	144	56.20N	2.40W
Saint Andrew's Channel, strt., Can.	86	46.06N	60.28W
Saint Anicet, Can. (sĕNt ä-nē-sĕ')	77a	45.07N	74.23W
Saint Ann, Mo., U.S. (sånt ăn')	101e	38.44N	90.23W
Sainte Anne, Guad.	115b	16.15N	61.23W
Saint Anne, Il., U.S.	95a	41.01N	87.44W
Sainte-Anne, r., Can.	77b	47.07N	70.50W
Sainte Anne, r., Can. (săNt ȧn') (sånt ăn')	84	46.55N	71.46W
Sainte Anne-des-Plaines, Can. (dā plĕN)	77a	45.46N	73.49W
Saint Anne of the Congo, rel., Congo	240c	4.16S	15.17E
Saint Ann's Bay, Jam.	116	18.25N	77.15W
Saint Anns Bay, b., Can. (ănz)	86	46.20N	60.30W
Saint Anselme, Can. (săN' tăN-sĕlm')	77b	46.37N	70.58W
Saint Anthony, Can. (săN ăn'thô-nē)	78	51.24N	55.35W
Saint Anthony, Id., U.S. (sånt ăn'thô-nē)	98	43.59N	111.42W
Saint Antoine-de-Tilly, Can.	77b	46.40N	71.31W
Saint Apollinaire, Can. (săN' tȧ-pôl-ē-nâr')	77b	46.36N	71.30W
Saint Arnoult-en-Yvelines, Fr. (săN-tär-nōō'ĕN-nēv-lēn')	151b	48.33N	1.55E
Saint Augustin-de-Québec, Can. (sĕn tō-gŭs-tēn')	77b	46.45N	71.27W
Saint Augustin-Deux-Montagnes, Can.	77a	45.38N	73.59W
Saint Augustine, Fl., U.S. (sånt ô'gŭs-tēn)	90	29.53N	81.21W
Sainte Barbe, Can. (sånt bärb')	77a	45.14N	74.12W
Saint Barthélemy, i., Guad.	115b	17.55N	62.32W
Saint Bees Head, c., Eng., U.K. (sånt bēz' hĕd)	144	54.30N	3.40W
Saint Benoit, Can. (sĕN bē-nōō-ä')	77a	45.34N	74.05W
Saint Bernard, La., U.S. (bẽr-närd')	94d	29.52N	89.52W
Saint Bernard, Oh., U.S.	95f	39.10N	84.30W
Saint Bride, Mount, mtn., Can. (sånt brīd)	80	51.30N	115.57W
Saint Brieuc, Fr. (săN' brēs')	140	48.32N	2.47W
Saint Bruno, Can. (brū'nō)	77a	45.31N	73.20W
Saint Canut, Can. (săN' kȧ-nü')	77a	45.43N	74.04W
Saint Casimir, Can. (kȧ-zē-mēr')	84	46.45N	72.34W
Saint Catharines, Can. (kăth'ȧ-rĭnz)	78	43.10N	79.14W
Saint Catherine, Mount, mtn., Gren.	115b	12.10N	61.42W
Saint Chamas, Fr. (săN-shä-mä')	150a	43.32N	5.03E
Saint Chamond, Fr. (săN' shȧ-môN')	140	45.30N	4.17E
Saint Charles, Can. (săN' shärlz')	77b	46.47N	70.57W
Saint Charles, Il., U.S. (sånt chärlz')	95a	41.55N	88.19W
Saint Charles, Mi., U.S.	92	43.20N	84.10W
Saint Charles, Mn., U.S.	96	43.56N	92.05W
Saint Charles, Mo., U.S.	101e	38.47N	90.29W
Saint Charles, Lac, l., Can.	77b	46.56N	71.21W
Saint Clair, Mi., U.S. (sånt klâr)	92	42.55N	82.30W
Saint Clair, l., Can.	90	42.25N	82.30W
Saint Clair, r., Can.	84	42.45N	82.25W
Sainte Claire, Can.	77b	46.36N	70.52W
Saint Clair Shores, Mi., U.S.	95b	42.30N	82.54W
Saint Claude, Fr. (săN' klōd')	150	46.24N	5.53E
Saint Clet, Can. (săNt' klā')	77a	45.22N	74.21W
Saint-Cloud, Fr.	233c	48.51N	2.13E
Saint Cloud, Fl., U.S. (sånt kloud')	109a	28.13N	81.17W
Saint Cloud, Mn., U.S.	90	45.33N	94.08W
Saint Constant, Can. (kŏn'stănt)	77a	45.23N	73.34W
Saint Croix, i., V.I.U.S. (sånt kroi')	110	17.40N	64.43W
Saint Croix, r., N.A. (kroi')	86	45.28N	67.32W
Saint Croix, r., U.S. (sånt kroi')	90	45.45N	93.00W
Saint Croix Indian Reservation, I.R., Wi., U.S.	96	45.40N	92.21W
Saint Croix Island, i., S. Afr. (săN krwä)	207c	33.48S	25.45E
Saint-Cyr-l'Ecole, Fr.	233c	48.48N	2.04E
Saint Damien-de-Buckland, Can. (sånt dä'mē-ĕn)	77b	46.37N	70.39W
Saint David, Can. (dā'vĭd)	77b	46.47N	71.11W
Saint Davids, Pa., U.S.	225b	40.02N	75.22W
Saint David's Head, c., Wales, U.K.	144	51.54N	5.25W
Saint-Denis, Fr. (săN'dē-nē')	140	48.26N	2.22E
Saint Dizier, Fr. (dē-zyā')	140	48.49N	4.55E
Saint Dominique, Can. (sĕN dō-mē-nēk')	77a	45.19N	74.09W
Sainte-Dorothée, neigh., Can.	223b	45.32N	73.49W
Saint Edouard-de-Napierville, Can. (sĕN-tē-dōō-är')	77a	45.14N	73.31W
Saint Elias, Mount, mtn., N.A. (sånt ē-lī'ăs)	78	60.25N	141.00W
Saint Étienne, Fr.	140	45.26N	4.22E
Saint Etienne-de-Lauzon, Can. (săN' tā-tyĕn')	77b	46.39N	71.19W
Sainte Euphémie, Can. (sĕNt û-fē-mē')	77b	46.47N	70.27W
Saint Eustache, Can. (săN' tû-stȧsh')	77a	45.34N	73.54W
Saint Eustache, Can.	77f	49.58N	97.47W
Sainte Famille, Can. (săN't fȧ-mē'y')	77b	46.58N	70.58W
Saint Félicien, Can. (săN fā-lē-syăN')	78	48.39N	72.28W
Sainte Felicite, Can.	86	48.54N	67.20W
Saint Féréol, Can. (fa-rā-ōl')	77b	47.07N	70.52W
Saint Florent-sur-Cher, Fr. (săN' flô-răN'sür-shâr')	150	46.58N	2.15E
Saint Flour, Fr. (săN flōōr')	150	45.02N	3.09E
Sainte Foy, Can. (sånt fwä)	84	46.47N	71.18W
Saint Francis, r., Ar., U.S.	104	35.56N	90.27W
Saint Francis Lake, l., Can. (săN frăn'sĭs)	84	45.00N	74.20W
Saint François, Can. (săN'frăN-swä')	77b	47.01N	70.49W
Saint François de Boundji, Congo	210	1.03S	15.22E
Saint Francois Xavier, Can.	77f	49.55N	97.32W
Saint Gaudens, Fr. (gō-dăNs')	150	43.07N	0.43E
Sainte-Geneviève, Can.	223b	45.29N	73.52W
Sainte Genevieve, Mo., U.S. (sånt jĕn'ĕ-vēv)	104	37.58N	90.02W
Saint George, Austl. (sånt jôrj')	196	28.02S	148.40E
Saint George, Can. (săN'zhôrzh')	77d	43.14N	80.15W
Saint George, Can. (săN jôrj')	78	45.08N	66.49W
Saint George, S.C., U.S. (sånt jôrj')	108	33.11N	80.35W
Saint George, Ut., U.S.	102	37.05N	113.40W
Saint George, neigh., N.Y., U.S.	224	40.39N	74.05W
Saint George, i., Ak., U.S.	89	56.30N	169.40W
Saint George, Cape, c., Can.	79a	48.28N	59.15W
Saint George, Cape, c., Fl., U.S.	108	29.30N	85.20W
Saint George's, Can. (jôrj'ĕs)	78	48.26N	58.29W
Saint Georges, Fr. Gu.	124	3.48N	51.47W
Saint George's, Gren.	115b	12.02N	61.57W

PLACE (Pronunciation)	PAGE	Lat. °'	Long. °'
Saint George's Bay, b., Can.	79a	48.20N	59.00W
Saint Georges Bay, b., Can.	86	45.49N	61.45W
Saint George's Channel, strt., Eur. (jôr-jĕz)	136	51.45N	6.30W
Saint Germain-en-Laye, Fr. (săn' zhĕr-măn-än-lā')	150	48.53N	2.05E
Saint Gervais, Can. (zhĕr-vĕ')	77b	46.43N	70.53W
Saint Girons, Fr. (zhē-rôn')	150	42.58N	1.08E
Saint-Gratien, Fr.	233c	48.58N	2.17E
Saint Gregory, Mount, mtn., Can. (sånt grĕg'ēr-ē)	86	49.19N	58.13W
Saint Helena, i., St. Hel.	203	16.01S	5.16W
Saint Helenabaai, b., S. Afr.	206	32.25S	17.15E
Sainte-Hélène, Île, i., Can.	223b	45.31N	73.32W
Saint Helens, Eng., U.K. (sånt hĕl'ĕnz)	138a	53.27N	2.44W
Saint Helens, Or., U.S. (hĕl'ĕnz)	100c	45.52N	122.49W
Saint Helens, Mount, vol., Wa., U.S.	98	46.13N	122.10W
Saint Helier, Jersey (hyĕl'yĕr)	150	49.12N	2.06W
Saint Henri, Can. (săn' hĕn'rē)	77b	46.41N	71.04W
Saint Hubert, Can.	77a	45.29N	73.24W
Saint Hyacinthe, Can.	78	45.35N	72.55W
Saint Ignace, Mi., U.S. (sånt ĭg'nås)	96	45.51N	84.39W
Saint Ignace, i., Can. (săn' ĭg'nås)	84	48.47N	88.14W
Saint Irenee, Can. (săn' tē-rā-nā')	84	47.34N	70.15W
Saint Isidore-de-Laprairie, Can.	77a	45.18N	73.41W
Saint Isidore-de-Prescott, Can. (săn' ĭz'ĭ-dôr-prĕs-kŏt)	77c	45.23N	74.54W
Saint Isidore-Dorchester, Can. (dŏr-chĕs'tĕr)	77b	46.35N	71.05W
Saint Ives, Austl.	239a	33.44S	151.10E
Saint Jacob, Il., U.S. (jā-kŏb)	101e	38.43N	89.46W
Saint James, Mn., U.S. (sånt jāmz')	96	43.58N	94.37W
Saint James, Mo., U.S.	104	37.59N	91.37W
Saint James, Cape, c., Can.	80	51.58N	131.00W
Saint Janvier, Can. (săn' zhän-vyā')	77a	45.43N	73.56W
Saint Jean, Can.	77b	46.55N	70.54W
Saint Jean, Can. (săn' zhän')	78	45.20N	73.15W
Saint Jean, Lac, l., Can.	78	48.35N	72.00W
Saint Jean-Chrysostome, Can. (krĭ-zōs-tōm')	77b	46.43N	71.12W
Saint Jean-d'Angely, Fr. (dän-zhā-lē')	150	45.56N	0.33W
Saint Jean-de-Luz, Fr. (dē lüz')	150	43.23N	1.40W
Saint Jérôme, Can. (sånt jĕ-rōm') (săn zhā-rōm')	77a	45.47N	74.00W
Saint Joachim-de-Montmorency, Can. (sånt jō'á-kĭm)	77b	47.04N	70.51W
Saint John, Can. (sånt jŏn)	78	45.16N	66.03W
Saint John, In., U.S.	95a	41.27N	87.29W
Saint John, Ks., U.S.	104	37.59N	98.44W
Saint John, N.D., U.S.	96	48.57N	99.42W
Saint John, i., V.I.U.S.	111b	18.16N	64.48W
Saint John, r., N.A.	78	47.00N	68.00W
Saint John, Cape, c., Can.	86	50.00N	55.32W
Saint Johns, Antig.	115b	17.07N	61.50W
Saint John's, Can. (jŏns)	79a	47.34N	52.43W
Saint Johns, Az., U.S. (jŏnz)	102	34.30N	109.25W
Saint Johns, Mi., U.S.	92	43.05N	84.35W
Saint Johns, r., Fl., U.S.	90	29.54N	81.32W
Saint Johnsburg, N.Y., U.S.	226a	43.05N	78.53W
Saint Johnsbury, Vt., U.S. (jŏnz'bĕr-ē)	92	44.25N	72.00W
Saint John's University, pt. of i., N.Y., U.S.	224	40.43N	73.48W
Saint Joseph, Dom.	115b	15.25N	61.26W
Saint Joseph, Mi., U.S.	92	42.05N	86.30W
Saint Joseph, Mo., U.S. (sånt jô-sĕf)	90	39.44N	94.49W
Saint Joseph, i., Can.	92	46.15N	83.55W
Saint Joseph, l., Can. (jō'zhŭf)	78	51.31N	90.40W
Saint Joseph, r., Mi., U.S. (sånt jō'sĕf)	92	41.45N	85.50W
Saint Joseph Bay, b., Fl., U.S. (jō'zhŭf)	108	29.48N	85.26W
Saint Joseph-de-Beauce, Can. (sĕn zhō-zĕf' dē bōs)	84	46.18N	70.52W
Saint Joseph-du-Lac, Can. (sĕn zhō-zĕf' dü läk)	77a	45.32N	74.00W
Saint Joseph Island, i., Tx., U.S. (sånt jô-sĕf)	106	27.58N	96.50W
Saint Junien, Fr. (săn'zhü-nyăn')	150	45.53N	0.54E
Sainte Justine-de-Newton, Can. (sånt jŭs-tēn')	77a	45.22N	74.22W
Saint Kilda, Austl.	195a	37.52S	144.59E
Saint Kilda, i., Scot., U.K. (kĭl'dá)	144	57.50N	8.32W
Saint Kitts, i., St. K./N. (sånt kĭtts)	110	17.24N	63.30W
Saint Kitts and Nevis, nation, N.A.	110	17.24N	63.30W
Saint Lambert, Can.	92	45.29N	73.29W
Saint Lambert-de-Lévis, Can.	77b	46.35N	71.12W
Saint Laurent, Can. (săn'lō-rän)	77a	45.31N	73.41W
Saint Laurent, Fr. Gu.	124	5.27N	53.56W
Saint Laurent-d'Orleans, Can.	77b	46.52N	71.00W
Saint Lawrence, Can. (sānt lô'rĕns)	86	46.55N	55.23W
Saint Lawrence, i., Ak., U.S. (sånt lô'rĕns)	90a	63.10N	172.12W
Saint Lawrence, r., N.A.	78	48.24N	69.30W
Saint Lawrence, Gulf of, b., Can.	78	48.00N	62.00W
Saint Lazare, Can. (săn'lá-zár')	77b	46.39N	70.48W
Saint Lazare-de-Vaudreuil, Can.	77a	45.24N	74.08W
Saint Léger-en-Yvelines, Fr. (săn-lā-zhĕ'ĕn-nēv-lēn')	151b	48.43N	1.45E
Saint Léonard, Can.	77a	45.36N	73.35W
Saint Leonard, Can. (sånt lĕn'árd)	86	47.10N	67.56W
Saint Leonard, Md., U.S.	94e	38.29N	76.31W
Saint Lô, Fr.	140	49.07N	1.05W
Saint-Louis, Sen.	204	16.02N	16.30W
Saint Louis, Mi., U.S. (sånt lōō'ĭs)	92	43.25N	84.35W
Saint Louis, Mo., U.S. (sånt lōō'ĭs) (lōō'ē)	90	38.39N	90.15W
Saint Louis, r., Mn., U.S. (sånt lōō'ĭs)	96	46.57N	92.58W
Saint Louis, Lac, l., Can. (săn' lōō-ē')	77a	45.24N	73.51W
Saint Louis-de-Gonzague, Can. (săn' lōō ē')	77a	45.13N	74.00W
Saint Louis Park, Mn., U.S.	101g	44.56N	93.21W
Saint Lucia, nation, N.A.	110	13.54N	60.40W
Saint Lucia Channel, strt., N.A. (lū'shĭ-á)	115b	14.15N	61.00W
Saint Lucie Canal, can., Fl., U.S. (lū'sē)	109a	26.57N	80.25W
Saint Magnus Bay, b., Scot., U.K. (măg'nŭs)	144a	60.25N	2.09W
Saint Malo, Fr. (săn' má-lō')	140	48.40N	2.02W
Saint Malo, Golfe de, b., Fr. (gôlf-dē-săn-mä-lō')	140	48.50N	2.49W
Saint Marc, Haiti (săn' márk')	116	19.10N	72.40W
Saint-Marc, Canal de, strt., Haiti	116	19.05N	73.15W
Saint Marcellin, Fr. (mär-sē-lăn')	150	45.08N	5.15E
Saint Margarets, Md., U.S.	94e	39.02N	76.30W
Sainte Marie, Cap, c., Madag.	206	25.31S	45.00E
Sainte-Marie-aux-Mines, Fr. (săn'tē-mä-rē'ō-mēn')	150	48.14N	7.08E
Sainte Marie-Beauce, Can. (sănt'má-rē')	84	46.27N	71.03W
Saint Maries, Id., U.S. (sånt mā'rēs)	98	47.18N	116.34W
Saint Martin, i., N.A. (mär'tĭn)	115b	18.06N	62.54W
Sainte Martine, Can.	77a	45.14N	73.37W
Saint Martins, Can. (mär'tĭnz)	86	45.21N	65.32W
Saint Martinville, La., U.S. (mär'tĭn-vĭl)	106	30.08N	91.50W
Saint Mary, r., Can. (mā'rē)	80	49.25N	113.00W
Saint Mary, Cape, c., Gam.	208	13.28N	16.40W
Saint Mary Cray, neigh., Eng., U.K.	231	51.23N	0.07E
Saint Marylebone, neigh., Eng., U.K.	231	51.31N	0.10W
Saint Mary Reservoir, res., Can.	80	49.30N	113.00W
Saint Marys, Austl. (mā'rēz)	198	41.40S	148.10E
Saint Marys, Austl.	239a	33.47S	150.47E
Saint Marys, Can.	84	43.15N	81.10W
Saint Marys, Ga., U.S.	108	30.43N	81.35W
Saint Mary's, Ks., U.S.	104	39.12N	96.03W
Saint Mary's, Oh., U.S.	92	40.30N	84.25W
Saint Marys, Pa., U.S.	92	41.25N	78.30W
Saint Marys, W.V., U.S.	92	39.20N	81.15W
Saint Marys, r., N.A.	101k	46.27N	84.33W
Saint Marys, r., U.S.	108	30.37N	82.05W
Saint Mary's Bay, b., Can.	86	44.20N	66.10W
Saint Mary's Bay, b., Can.	86	46.50N	53.47W
Saint Mathew, S.C., U.S. (măth'ū)	108	33.40N	80.46W
Saint Matthew, i., Ak., U.S.	89	60.25N	172.10W
Saint Matthews, Ky., U.S. (măth'ūz)	95h	38.15N	85.39W
Saint Maur-des-Fossés, Fr.	151b	48.48N	2.29E
Saint-Maurice, Fr.	233c	48.49N	2.25E
Saint Maurice, r., Can. (săn' mō-rēs') (sånt mô'rĭs)	78	47.20N	72.55W
Saint-Mesmes, Fr.	233c	48.59N	2.42E
Saint Michael, Ak., U.S. (sånt mī'kĕl)	89	63.22N	162.20W
Saint Michel, Can. (săn'mē-shĕl')	77b	46.52N	70.54W
Saint-Michel, neigh., Can.	223b	45.35N	73.35W
Saint Michel, Bras, r., Can.	77b	46.47N	70.51W
Saint Michel-de-l'Atalaye, Haiti	116	19.25N	72.20W
Saint Michel-de-Napierville, Can.	77a	45.14N	73.34W
Saint Mihiel, Fr. (săn' mē-yĕl')	150	48.53N	5.30E
Saint Nazaire, Fr. (săn'ná-zâr')	136	47.18N	2.13W
Saint Nérée, Can. (nā-rā')	77b	46.43N	70.43W
Saint Nicolas, Can. (ne-kō-lä')	77b	46.42N	71.22W
Saint Nicolas, Cap, c., Haiti	116	19.45N	73.35W
Saint Omer, Fr. (săn'tō-mâr')	150	50.44N	2.16E
Saint-Ouen, Fr.	233c	48.54N	2.20E
Saint Pancras, neigh., Eng., U.K.	231	51.32N	0.07W
Saint Pascal, Can. (sĕn pă-skăl')	86	47.32N	69.48W
Saint Paul, Can. (sånt pôl')	78	53.59N	111.17W
Saint Paul, Mn., U.S.	90	44.57N	93.05W
Saint Paul, Ne., U.S.	96	41.13N	98.28W
Saint Paul, i., Can.	86	47.15N	60.10W
Saint Paul, i., Ak., U.S.	89	57.10N	170.20W
Saint Paul, r., Lib.	208	7.10N	10.00W
Saint Paul, Île, i., F.S.A.T.	2	38.43S	77.31E
Saint Paul Park, Mn., U.S. (pārk)	101g	44.51N	93.00W
Saint Pauls, N.C., U.S. (pôls)	108	34.47N	78.57W
Saint Paul's Cathedral, pt. of i., Eng., U.K.	231	51.31N	0.06W
Saint Paul's Cray, neigh., Eng., U.K.	231	51.24N	0.07E
Saint Peter, Mn., U.S. (pē tĕr)	96	44.20N	93.56W
Saint Peter Port, Guernsey	150	49.27N	2.35W
Saint Petersburg (Sankt-Peterburg) (Leningrad), Russia	158	59.57N	30.20E
Saint Petersburg, Fl., U.S. (pē'tĕrz-bûrg)	90	27.47N	82.38W
Sainte Pétronille, Can. (sĕnt pĕt-rō-nēl')	77b	46.51N	71.08W
Saint Philémon, Can. (sĕn fēl-mōn')	77b	46.41N	70.28W
Saint Philippe-d'Argenteuil, Can. (săn'fe-lēp')	77a	45.38N	74.25W
Saint Philippe-de-Lapairie, Can.	77a	45.20N	73.28W
Saint-Pierre, Can.	223b	45.27N	73.39W
Saint Pierre, Mart. (săn'pyâr')	115b	14.45N	61.12W
Saint Pierre, i., St. P./M.	86	46.47N	56.11W
Saint Pierre, Lac, l., Can.	84	46.07N	72.45W
Saint Pierre and Miquelon, dep., N.A.	79a	46.53N	56.40W
Saint Pierre-d'Orléans, Can.	77b	46.53N	71.04W
Saint Pierre-Montmagny, Can.	77b	46.55N	70.37W
Saint Placide, Can. (pläs'ĭd)	77a	45.32N	74.11W
Saint Pol-de-Léon, Fr. (săn-pô'dē-lā-ôn')	150	48.41N	4.00W
Saint-Prix, Fr.	233c	49.01N	2.16E
Saint Quentin, Fr. (săn'kän-tăn')	140	49.52N	3.16E
Saint Raphaël, Can. (rä-fä-ĕl')	77b	46.48N	70.46W
Saint Raymond, Can.	84	46.50N	71.51W
Saint Rédempteur, Can. (săn rā-dänp-tûr')	77b	46.42N	71.18W
Saint Rémi, Can. (sĕn rĕ-mē')	77a	45.15N	73.36W
Saint-Rémy-lès-Chevreuse, Fr.	233c	48.42N	2.04E
Saint Romuald-d'Etchemin, Can. (sĕn rō'mōō-äl)	84	46.45N	71.14W
Sainte Rose, Guad.	115b	16.19N	61.45W
Sainte-Rose, neigh., Can.	223b	45.36N	73.47W
Saintes, Fr.	150	45.44N	0.41W
Sainte Scholastique, Can. (skô-lás-tēk')	77a	45.39N	74.05W
Saint Siméon, Can.	84	47.51N	69.55W
Saint Stanislas-de-Kostka, Can.	77a	45.11N	74.08W
Saint Stephen, Can. (stē'vĕn)	78	45.12N	66.17W
Saint Sulpice, Can.	77a	45.50N	73.21W
Saint Thérèse-de-Blainville, Can. (tē-rĕz' dē blĕn-vēl')	84	45.38N	73.51W
Saint-Thibault-des-Vignes, Fr.	233c	48.52N	2.41E
Saint Thomas, Can. (tŏm'ás)	78	42.45N	81.15W
Saint Thomas, i., V.I.U.S.	110	18.22N	64.57W
Saint Thomas Harbor, b., V.I.U.S. (tŏm'ás)	111c	18.19N	64.56W
Saint Timothée, Can. (tē-mô-tā')	77a	45.17N	74.03W
Saint Tropez, Fr. (trô-pē')	150	43.15N	6.42E
Saint Valentin, Can. (văl-ĕn-tīn)	77a	45.07N	73.19W
Saint Valéry-sur-Somme, Fr. (vá-lā-rē')	150	50.10N	1.39E
Saint Vallier, Can. (väl-yā')	77b	46.54N	70.49W
Saint Victor, Can. (vĭk'tĕr)	84	46.09N	70.56W
Saint Vincent, Gulf, b., Austl. (vĭn'sĕnt)	198	34.55S	138.00E
Saint Vincent and the Grenadines, nation, N.A.	110	13.20N	60.50W
Saint-Vincent-de-Paul, neigh., Can.	223b	45.37N	73.39W
Saint Vincent Passage, strt., N.A.	115b	13.35N	61.10W
Saint Walburg, Can.	78	53.39N	109.12W
Saint Yrieix-la-Perche, Fr. (ē-rē-ē)	150	45.30N	1.08E
Saitama, dept., Japan (sī'tä-mä)	187a	35.52N	139.40E
Saitbaba, Russia (sá-ĕt'bá-bá)	164a	54.06N	56.42E
Sajama, Nevada, mtn., Bol. (nĕ-vá'dä-sä-há'mä)	124	18.13S	68.53W
Sakai, Japan (sä'kä-ē)	186	34.34N	135.28E
Sakaiminato, Japan	187	35.33N	133.15E
Sakākah, Sau. Ar.	174	29.58N	40.03E
Sakakawea, Lake, res., N.D., U.S.	90	47.49N	101.58W
Sakania, Zaire (sá-kä'nĭ-á)	206	12.45S	28.34E
Sakarya, r., Tur. (sá-kär'yá)	174	40.10N	31.00E
Sakata, Japan (sä'kä-tä)	180	38.56N	139.57E
Sakchu, N. Kor. (säk'chō)	186	40.29N	125.09E
Sakhalin, i., Russia (sá-ká-lēn')	158	52.00N	143.00E
Šakiai, Lith. (shä'kĭ-ī)	146	54.59N	23.05E
Sakishima-guntō, is., Japan (sä'kē-shē'ma gón'tō')	180	24.25N	125.00E
Sakmara, r., Russia	160	52.00N	56.10E
Sakomet, r., R.I., U.S. (sä-kō'mĕt)	94b	41.32N	71.11W
Sakurai, Japan	187b	34.31N	135.51E
Sakwaso Lake, l., Can. (sá-kwá'sō)	82	53.01N	91.55W
Sal, i., C.V. (säal)	204b	16.45N	22.39W
Sal, r., Russia (sál)	160	47.30N	43.00E
Sal, Cay, i., Bah. (kē sāl)	116	23.45N	80.25W
Sala, Swe. (sô'lä)	146	59.56N	16.34E
Sala Consilina, Italy (sä'lä kôn-sē-lē'nä)	154	40.24N	15.38E
Salada, Laguna, l., Mex. (lä-gò'nä-sä-lä'dä)	102	32.34N	115.45W
Saladillo, Arg. (sä-lä-dēl'yō)	126	35.38S	59.48W
Salado, Hond. (sä-lä'dhō)	114	15.44N	87.03W
Salado, r., Arg.	123c	35.53S	58.12W
Salado, r., Arg. (sä-lä'dō)	126	26.05S	63.35W
Salado, r., Arg.	126	37.00S	67.00W
Salado, r., Mex.	110	28.00N	102.00W
Salado, r., Mex. (sä-lä'dō)	112	18.30N	97.29W
Salado Creek, r., Tx., U.S.	101d	29.23N	98.25W
Salado de los Nadadores, Río, r., Mex. (dē-lōs-nä-dä-dō'rĕs)	106	27.26N	101.35W
Salal, Chad	208	14.51N	17.13E
Salamanca, Chile (sä-lä-mä'n-kä)	123b	31.48S	70.57W
Salamanca, Mex.	110	20.36N	101.10W
Salamanca, Spain (sä-lä-mä'n-ká)	136	40.54N	5.42W
Salamanca, N.Y., U.S. (săl-á-măŋ'ká)	92	42.10N	78.45W
Salamat, Bahr, r., Chad (bär sä-lä-mät')	204	10.06N	19.16E
Salamina, Col. (sä-lä-mē'-nä)	124a	5.25N	75.29W
Salamis, Grc. (săl'á-mĭs)	154	37.58N	23.30E
Salat-la-Canada, Fr.	150	44.52N	1.13E
Salaverry, Peru (sä-lä-vā'rē)	124	8.16S	78.54W
Salawati, i., Indon. (sä-lä-wä'tē)	188	1.07S	130.52E
Salawe, Tan.	210	3.19S	32.52E
Sala y Gómez, Isla, i., Chile	190	26.50S	105.50W
Salcedo, Dom. Rep. (säl-sä'dō)	116	19.25N	70.30W
Saldaña, r., Col. (säl-dá'n-yä)	124a	3.42N	75.16W
Saldanha, S. Afr.	206	32.55S	18.05E
Saldus, Lat. (sál'dòs)	146	56.39N	22.30E
Sale, Austl. (sāl)	198	38.10S	147.07E
Sale, Eng., U.K.	138a	53.24N	2.20W
Sale, r., Can. (sál'rē-vyâr')	77f	49.44N	97.11W
Salekhard, Russia (sŭ-lyĭ-kärt)	160	66.35N	66.50E
Salem, India	174	11.39N	78.11E
Salem, S. Afr.	207c	33.29S	26.30E
Salem, Il., U.S. (sā'lĕm)	92	38.40N	89.00W
Salem, In., U.S.	92	38.35N	86.00W
Salem, Ma., U.S.	87a	42.31N	70.54W
Salem, Mo., U.S.	104	37.36N	91.33W
Salem, N.H., U.S.	87a	42.46N	71.16W
Salem, N.J., U.S.	92	39.35N	75.30W
Salem, Oh., U.S.	92	40.55N	80.50W
Salem, Or., U.S.	90	44.55N	123.03W
Salem, S.D., U.S.	96	43.43N	97.23W
Salem, Va., U.S.	108	37.16N	80.05W
Salem, W.V., U.S.	92	39.15N	80.35W
Salemi, Italy (sä-lā'mē)	154	37.49N	12.48E
Salerno, Italy (sä-lĕr'nō)	142	40.27N	14.46E
Salerno, Golfo di, b., Italy (gòl-fō-dē)	142	40.30N	14.40E
Salford, Eng., U.K. (săl'fĕrd)	144	53.26N	2.19W

ăt; finăl; rāte; senåte; ärm; ásk; sofá; fâre; ch-choose; dh-as th in other; bē; ēvent; bĕt; recĕnt; cratēr; g-gō; gh-guttural g; bĭt; ĭ-short neutral; rīde; K-guttural k as ch in German ich;

PLACE (Pronunciation)	PAGE	Lat. °'	Long. °'
Salgir, r., Ukr. (sál'gẽr)	156	45.25N	34.22E
Salgótarján, Hung. (shôl'gô-tôr-yän)	148	48.06N	19.50E
Salida, Co., U.S. (sȧ-lī'dȧ)	104	38.31N	106.01W
Salies-de-Béan, Fr.	150	43.27N	0.58W
Salima, Mwi.	210	13.47S	34.26E
Salina, Ks., U.S. (sȧ-lī'nȧ)	90	38.50N	97.37W
Salina, Ut., U.S.	102	39.00N	111.55W
Salina, i., Italy (sä-lē'nä)	154	38.35N	14.48E
Salina Cruz, Mex. (sä-lē'nä krōōz')	110	16.10N	95.12W
Salina Point, c., Bah.	116	22.10N	74.20W
Salinas, Mex.	110	22.38N	101.42W
Salinas, P.R.	111b	17.58N	66.16W
Salinas, Ca., U.S. (sȧ-lē'nȧs)	102	36.41N	121.40W
Salinas, r., Mex. (sä-lē'näs)	112	16.15N	90.31W
Salinas, r., Ca., U.S.	102	36.33N	121.29W
Salinas, Bahía de, b., N.A. (bä-ē'ä-dě-sȧ-lē'nȧs)	114	11.05N	85.55W
Salinas, Cape, c., Spain (sä-lênäs)	152	39.14N	1.02E
Salinas National Monument, rec., N.M., U.S.	102	34.10N	106.05W
Salinas Victoria, Mex. (sä-lē'näs vėk-tō'rē-ä)	106	25.59N	100.19W
Saline, r., Ar., U.S. (sȧ-lēn')	104	34.06N	92.30W
Saline, r., Ks., U.S.	104	39.05N	99.43W
Salins-les-Bains, Fr. (sȧ-lăN'-lā-băN')	150	46.55N	5.54E
Salisbury, Can.	86	46.03N	65.05W
Salisbury, Eng., U.K. (sôlz'bẽ-rė)	140	50.35N	1.51W
Salisbury, Md., U.S.	92	38.20N	75.40W
Salisbury, Mo., U.S.	104	39.24N	92.47W
Salisbury, N.C., U.S.	108	35.40N	80.29W
Salisbury, *see* Harare, Zimb.	206	17.50S	31.03E
Salisbury Island, i., Can.	78	63.36N	76.20W
Salisbury Plain, pl., Eng., U.K.	144	51.15N	1.52W
Salkehatchie, r., S.C., U.S. (sô-kė-hăch'ė)	108	33.09N	81.10W
Salkhia, India	236a	22.35N	88.21E
Sallisaw, Ok., U.S. (săl'ĭ-sô)	104	35.27N	94.48W
Salmon, Id., U.S. (săm'ŭn)	98	45.11N	113.54W
Salmon, r., Can.	80	54.00N	123.50W
Salmon, r., Can.	86	46.19N	65.36W
Salmon, r., Id., U.S.	90	45.30N	115.45W
Salmon, r., Id., U.S.	98	44.54N	114.50W
Salmon, r., Id., U.S.	98	44.51N	115.47W
Salmon, r., N.Y., U.S.	92	44.35N	74.15W
Salmon, r., Wa., U.S.	100c	45.44N	122.36W
Salmon Arm, Can.	80	50.42N	119.16W
Salmon Falls Creek, r., Id., U.S.	98	42.22N	114.53W
Salmon Gums, Austl. (gŭmz)	196	33.00S	122.00E
Salmon River Mountains, mts., Id., U.S.	90	44.15N	115.44W
Salon-de-Provence, Fr. (sȧ-lôN-dē-prô-văNs')	150	43.48N	5.09E
Salonta, Rom. (sä-lôn'tä)	148	46.46N	21.38E
Salop, co., Eng., U.K.	138a	52.36N	2.45W
Saloum, r., Sen.	208	14.10N	15.45W
Salsette Island, i., India	179b	19.12N	72.52E
Sal'sk, Russia (sälsk)	160	46.30N	41.20E
Salt, r., Az., U.S. (sôlt)	90	33.28N	111.35W
Salt, r., Mo., U.S.	104	39.54N	92.11W
Salta, Arg. (säl'tä)	126	24.50S	65.16W
Salta, prov., Arg.	126	25.15S	65.00W
Saltair, Ut., U.S. (sôlt'âr)	101b	40.46N	112.09W
Salt Cay, i., T./C. Is.	116	21.20N	71.15W
Salt Creek, r., Il., U.S. (sôlt)	95a	42.01N	88.01W
Saltillo, Mex. (säl-tēl'yō)	110	25.24N	100.59W
Salt Lake City, Ut., U.S. (sôlt lāk sĭ'tĭ)	90	40.45N	111.52W
Salto, Arg. (säl'tō)	123c	34.17S	60.15W
Salto, Ur.	126	31.18S	57.45W
Salto, r., Mex.	112	22.16N	99.18W
Salto, Serra do, mtn., Braz. (sĕ'r-rä-dô)	123a	20.26S	43.28W
Salto Grande, Braz. (grän'dā)	124	22.57S	49.58W
Salton Sea, Ca., U.S. (sôlt'ŭn)	102	33.28N	115.43W
Salton Sea, l., Ca., U.S.	90	33.19N	115.50W
Saltpond, Ghana	204	5.16N	1.07W
Salt River Indian Reservation, I.R., Az., U.S. (sôlt rĭv'ẽr)	102	33.40N	112.01W
Saltsjöbaden, Swe. (sält'shû-bäd'ĕn)	146	59.15N	18.20E
Saltspring Island, i., Can. (sălt'sprĭng)	80	48.47N	123.30W
Saltville, Va., U.S. (sôlt'vĭl)	108	36.50N	81.45W
Saltykovka, Russia (sál-tē'kôf-kȧ)	164b	55.45N	37.56E
Salud, Mount, mtn., Pan. (sä-lōō'th)	110a	9.14N	79.42W
Saluda, S.C., U.S. (sȧ-lōō'dȧ)	108	34.02N	81.46W
Saluda, r., S.C., U.S.	108	34.07N	81.48W
Saluzzo, Italy (sä-lōōt'sō)	154	44.39N	7.31E
Salvador, Braz. (säl-vä-dōr') (bä-ē'ȧ)	124	12.59S	38.27W
Salvador Lake, l., La., U.S.	106	29.45N	90.20W
Salvador Point, c., Bah.	116	24.30N	77.45W
Salvatierra, Mex. (säl-vä-tyĕr'rä)	112	20.13N	100.52W
Salween, r., Asia	172	21.00N	98.00E
Sal'yany, Azer.	160	39.40N	49.10E
Salzburg, Aus. (sälts'bŏŏrgh)	140	47.48N	13.04E
Salzburg, state, Aus.	148	47.30N	13.18E
Salzwedel, Ger. (sälts-vā'dĕl)	148	52.51N	11.10E
Samāika, neigh., India	236d	28.32N	77.05E
Samālūt, Egypt (sä-mä-lōōt')	176	28.17N	30.43E
Samana, Cabo, c., Dom. Rep.	110	19.20N	69.00W
Samana or Atwood Cay, i., Bah.	116	23.05N	73.45W
Samar, i., Phil. (sä'mär)	188	11.30N	126.07E
Samara (Kuybyshev), Russia	160	53.10N	50.05E
Samara, r., Russia	160	52.50N	50.35E
Samara, r., Ukr. (sȧ-mä'rȧ)	156	48.47N	35.30E
Samarai, Pap. N. Gui. (sä-mä-rä'ē)	188	10.45S	150.49E
Samarinda, Indon.	188	0.30S	117.10E
Samarkand, Uzb. (sȧ-mȧr-känt')	158	39.42N	67.00E
Samba, Zaire	210	4.38S	26.22E
Sambalpur, India (sŭm'bŭl-pŏŏr)	174	21.30N	84.05E

PLACE (Pronunciation)	PAGE	Lat. °'	Long. °'
Sāmbhar, r., India	178	27.00N	74.58E
Sambor, Ukr. (säm'bôr)	148	49.31N	23.12E
Samborombón, r., Arg.	123c	35.20S	57.52W
Samborombón, Bahía, b., Arg. (bä-ē'ä-säm-bô-rôm-bô'n)	123c	35.57S	57.05W
Sambre, r., Eur. (säN'br')	144	50.20N	4.15E
Sambungo, Ang.	210	8.39S	20.43E
Sammamish, r., Wa., U.S.	100a	47.43N	122.08W
Sammamish, Lake, l., Wa., U.S. (sȧ-măm'ĭsh)	100a	47.35N	122.02W
Samoa Islands, is., Oc.	192a	14.00S	171.00W
Samokov, Bul. (sä'mô-kôf)	154	42.20N	23.33E
Samora Correia, Port. (sä-mô'rä-kôr-rĕ'yä)	153b	38.55N	8.52W
Samorovo, Russia (sȧ-mȧ-rô'vô)	162	60.47N	69.13E
Sámos, i., Grc. (sä'mŏs)	142	37.53N	26.35E
Samothráki, i., Grc.	142	40.23N	25.10E
Sampaloc Point, c., Phil. (säm-pä'lôk)	189a	14.43N	119.56E
Sam Rayburn Reservoir, res., Tx., U.S.	106	31.10N	94.15W
Samson, Al., U.S. (săm'sŭn)	108	31.06N	86.02W
Samsu, N. Kor. (säm'sōō')	186	41.12N	128.00E
Samsun, Tur. (sȧm'sōōn')	174	41.20N	36.05E
Samtredia, Geor. (sȧm'trĕ-dē)	160	42.18N	42.25E
Samuel, i., Can. (săm'ū-ĕl)	100d	48.50N	123.10W
Samur, r. (sä-mōōr')	160	41.40N	47.20E
San, Mali (sän)	204	13.18N	4.54W
San, r., Eur.	140	50.33N	22.12E
Şan'ā', Yemen (sän'ä)	174	15.17N	44.05E
Sanaga, r., Cam. (sä-nä'gä)	204	4.30N	12.00E
San Ambrosio, Isla, i., Chile (ē's-lä-dĕ-sän äm-brō'zē-ō)	122	26.40S	80.00W
Sanana, Pulau, i., Indon.	188	2.15S	126.38E
Sanandaj, Iran	174	36.44N	46.43E
San Andreas, Ca., U.S. (săn ăn'drē-ăs)	102	38.10N	120.42W
San Andreas, l., Ca., U.S.	100b	37.36N	122.26W
San Andrés, Col. (sän-än-drĕ's)	124a	6.57N	75.41W
San Andrés, Mex. (sän än-drās')	113a	19.15N	99.10W
San Andrés, i., Col.	114	12.32N	81.34W
San Andres, Laguna de, l., Mex.	112	22.40N	97.50W
San Andres Mountains, mts., N.M., U.S. (săn ăn'drē-ăs)	90	33.00N	106.40W
San Andrés Tuxtla, Mex. (sän-än-drā's-tōōs'tlä)	110	18.27N	95.12W
San Angelo, Tx., U.S. (săn ăn-jĕ-lō)	90	31.28N	100.22W
San Antioco, Isola di, i., Italy (ē'sō-lä-dē-sän-än-tyŏ'kô)	154	39.00N	8.25E
San Antonio, Chile (sän-ȧn-tō'nyō)	126	33.34S	71.36W
San Antonio, Col.	124a	2.57N	75.06W
San Antonio, Col.	124a	3.55N	75.28W
San Antonio, Phil.	189a	14.57N	120.05E
San Antonio, Tx., U.S. (săn ăn-tō'nē-ō)	90	29.25N	98.30W
San Antonio, r., Tx., U.S.	106	29.00N	97.58W
San Antonio, Cabo, c., Cuba (ká'bô-sän-än-tō'nyô)	110	21.55N	84.55W
San Antonio, Lake, res., Ca., U.S.	102	36.00N	121.13W
San Antonio Abad, Spain (sän än-tō'nyô ä-bädh')	152	38.59N	1.17E
San Antonio Bay, b., Tx., U.S.	106	28.20N	97.08W
San Antonio de Areco, Arg. (dā ä-rä'kô)	123c	34.16S	59.30W
San Antonio de Galipán, Ven.	230a	10.33N	66.53W
San Antonio de las Vegas, Cuba	117a	22.51N	82.23W
San Antonio de los Baños, Cuba (dā lōs băn'yōs)	116	22.54N	82.30W
San Antonio de los Cobres, Arg. (dā lōs kō'brās)	126	24.15S	66.29W
San Antônio de Pádua, Braz. (dĕ-pá'dwä)	123a	21.32S	42.09W
San Antonio de Tamanaco, Ven.	125b	9.42N	66.03W
San Antonio Heights, Ca., U.S.	228	34.10N	117.40W
San Antonio Oeste, Arg. (sän-nä-tō'nyô ô-ĕs'tå)	126	40.49S	64.56W
San Antonio Peak, mtn., Ca., U.S. (săn ăn-tō'nĭ-ō)	101a	34.17N	117.39W
Sanarate, Guat. (sä-nä-rä'tĕ)	114	14.47N	90.12W
San Augustine, Tx., U.S. (săn ô'gŭs-tēn)	106	31.33N	94.08W
San Bartolo, Mex.	106	24.43N	103.12W
San Bartolo, Mex. (sän bär-tō'lô)	113a	19.36N	99.43W
San Bartolomé de la Cuadra, Spain	234e	41.26N	2.02E
San Bartolomeo, Italy (bär-tô-lô-mā'ô)	154	41.25N	15.04E
San Baudilio de Llobregat, Spain	234e	41.21N	2.03E
San Benedetto del Tronto, Italy (bā'nȧ-dĕt'tô dĕl trōn'tô)	154	42.58N	13.54E
San Benito, Tx., U.S. (săn bĕ-nē'tô)	106	26.07N	97.37W
San Benito, r., Ca., U.S.	102	36.40N	121.20W
San Bernardino, Ca., U.S. (bûr-när-dē'nô)	90	34.07N	117.19W
San Bernardino Mountains, mts., Ca., U.S.	102	34.05N	116.23W
San Bernardo, Chile (sän bĕr-när'dô)	123b	33.35S	70.42W
San Blas, Mex. (sän bläs')	110	21.33N	105.19W
San Blas, Cape, c., Fl., U.S.	90	29.38N	85.38W
San Blas, Cordillera de, mts., Pan.	114	9.17N	78.20W
San Blas, Golfo de, b., Pan.	114	9.33N	78.42W
San Blas, Punta, c., Pan.	114	9.35N	78.55W
San Bruno, Ca., U.S. (săn brū-nô)	100b	37.38N	122.25W
San Buenaventura, Mex. (bwā'nȧ-vĕn-tōō'rá)	106	27.07N	101.30W
San Carlos, Chile (sän-kä'r-lôs)	126	36.23S	71.58W
San Carlos, Col.	124a	6.11N	74.58W
San Carlos, Eq. Gui.	210	3.27N	8.33E
San Carlos, Mex.	106	24.36N	98.52W
San Carlos, Mex. (sän kär'lōs)	112	17.49N	92.33W
San Carlos, Nic. (sän-kä'r-lôs)	114	11.08N	84.48W
San Carlos, Phil.	189a	15.56N	120.20E
San Carlos, Ca., U.S. (săn kär'lōs)	100b	37.30N	122.15W

PLACE (Pronunciation)	PAGE	Lat. °'	Long. °'
San Carlos, Ven.	124	9.36N	68.35W
San Carlos, r., C.R.	114	10.36N	84.18W
San Carlos de Bariloche, Arg.	126	41.15S	71.26W
San Carlos Indian Reservation, I.R., Az., U.S. (săn kär'lōs)	102	33.27N	110.15W
San Carlos Lake, res., Az., U.S.	102	33.05N	110.29W
San Casimiro, Ven. (kä-sē-mē'rō)	125b	10.01N	67.02W
San Cataldo, Italy (kä-täl'dō)	154	37.30N	13.59E
Sánchez, Dom. Rep. (sän'chĕz)	110	19.15N	69.40W
Sanchez, Río de los, r., Mex. (rē'ō-dĕ-lôs)	112	20.31N	102.29W
Sánchez Román, Mex. (rô-má'n)	112	21.48N	103.20W
Sanchung, Tai.	237d	25.04N	121.29E
San Clemente, Spain (sän klå-mĕn'tå)	152	39.25N	2.24W
San Clemente de Llobregat, Spain	234e	41.20N	2.00E
San Clemente Island, i., Ca., U.S.	90	32.54N	118.29W
San Cristóbal, Dom. Rep. (krēs-tō'bäl)	116	18.25N	70.05W
San Cristóbal, Guat.	114	15.22N	90.26W
San Cristóbal, Ven.	124	7.43N	72.15W
San Cristobal, i., Sol.Is.	196	10.47S	162.17E
Sancti Spíritus, Cuba (säŋk'tē spē'rē-tōōs)	110	21.55N	79.25W
Sancti Spiritus, prov., Cuba	116	22.05N	79.20W
San Cugat del Vallés, Spain	234e	41.28N	2.05E
Sancy, Puy de, mtn., Fr. (pwē-dē-sȧN-sē')	140	45.30N	2.53E
Sand, i., Or., U.S. (sănd)	100c	46.16N	124.01W
Sand, i., Wi., U.S.	96	46.03N	91.09W
Sand, r., S. Afr.	207c	28.30S	29.30E
Sand, r., S. Afr.	212d	28.09S	26.46E
Sanda, Japan (sän'dä)	187	34.53N	135.14E
Sandakan, Malay. (sȧn-dä'kȧn)	188	5.51N	118.03E
Sanday, i., Scot., U.K. (sănd'ā)	144a	59.17N	2.25W
Sandbach, Eng., U.K. (sănd'băch)	138a	53.08N	2.22W
Sandefjord, Nor. (sän'dĕ-fyôr')	146	59.09N	10.14E
San de Fuca, Wa., U.S. (de-fōō-cä)	100a	48.14N	122.44W
Sanders, Az., U.S.	102	35.13N	109.20W
Sanderson, Tx., U.S. (săn'dẽr-sŭn)	106	30.09N	102.24W
Sanderstead, neigh., Eng., U.K.	231	51.20N	0.05W
Sandersville, Ga., U.S. (săn'dẽrz-vĭl)	108	32.57N	82.50W
Sandhammaren, c., Swe. (sänt'hăm-mår)	140	55.24N	14.37E
Sand Hills, reg., Ne., U.S. (sănd)	96	41.57N	101.29W
Sand Hook, N.J., U.S. (sănd hŏŏk)	94a	40.29N	74.05W
Sandhurst, Eng., U.K. (sănd'hûrst)	138b	51.20N	0.48W
Sandia Indian Reservation, I.R., N.M., U.S.	102	35.15N	106.30W
San Diego, Ca., U.S. (săn dē-ā'gô)	90	32.43N	117.10W
San Diego, Tx., U.S.	104	27.47N	98.13W
San Diego, r., Ca., U.S.	102	32.53N	116.57W
San Diego de la Unión, Mex. (săn dē-ā-gô dā lä ōō-nyōn')	112	21.27N	100.52W
Sandies Creek, r., Tx., U.S. (sănd'ēz)	106	29.13N	97.34W
San Dimas, Mex. (dē-mäs')	112	24.08N	105.57W
San Dimas, Ca., U.S. (săn dē-mȧs)	101a	34.07N	117.49W
Sandnes, Nor. (sänd'nĕs)	146	58.52N	5.44E
Sandoa, Zaire (sän-dō'ȧ)	206	9.39S	23.00E
Sandomierz, Pol. (sȧn-dô'myĕzh)	148	50.39N	21.45E
San Doná di Piave, Italy (sän dô nà' dē pyä'vē)	154	45.38N	12.34E
Sandoway, Burma (sän-dô-wī')	174	18.24N	94.28E
Sandpoint, Id., U.S. (sănd point)	98	48.17N	116.34W
Sandringham, Austl. (săn'drĭng-ăm)	195a	37.57S	145.01E
Sandringham, neigh., S. Afr.	240b	26.09S	28.07E
Sandrio, Italy (sä'n-dryô)	154	46.11N	9.53E
Sands Point, N.Y., U.S.	224	40.51N	73.43W
Sand Springs, Ok., U.S. (sănd sprĭnz)	104	36.08N	96.06W
Sandstone, Austl. (sănd'stōn)	196	28.00S	119.25E
Sandstone, Mn., U.S.	96	46.08N	92.53W
Sanduo, China (sän-dwô)	182	32.49N	119.39E
Sandusky, Al., U.S. (săn-dŭs'kē)	94h	33.32N	86.50W
Sandusky, Mi., U.S.	92	43.25N	82.50W
Sandusky, Oh., U.S.	90	41.25N	82.45W
Sandusky, r., Oh., U.S.	92	41.10N	83.20W
Sandwich, Il., U.S. (sănd'wĭch)	92	42.35N	88.53W
Sandy, Or., U.S. (sănd'ē)	100c	45.24N	122.16W
Sandy, Ut., U.S.	101b	40.36N	111.53W
Sandy, r., Or., U.S.	100c	45.28N	122.17W
Sandy Cape, c., Austl.	196	24.25S	153.10E
Sandy Hook, Ct., U.S. (hŏŏk)	94a	41.25N	73.17W
Sandy Lake, l., Can.	77g	53.46N	113.58W
Sandy Lake, l., Can.	82	53.00N	93.07W
Sandy Lake, l., Can.	86	49.16N	57.00W
Sandy Point, Tx., U.S.	107a	29.22N	95.27W
Sandy Point, c., Wa., U.S.	100d	48.48N	122.42W
Sandy Springs, Ga., U.S. (springz)	94c	33.55N	84.23W
San Estanislao, Para. (ĕs-tä-nēs-lá'ô)	126	24.38S	56.20W
San Esteban, Hond. (ĕs-tĕ'bän)	114	15.13N	85.53W
San Fabian, Phil. (fä-byä'n)	189a	16.14N	120.28E
San Felipe, Chile (fĕ-lē'pȧ)	126	32.45S	70.43W
San Felipe, Mex.	112	22.21N	105.26W
San Felipe, Mex. (fĕ-lē'pĕ)	112	21.29N	101.13W
San Felipe, Ven. (fĕ-lē'pĕ)	124	10.13N	68.45W
San Felipe, Cayos de, is., Cuba (kä'yōs-dĕ-sän-fĕ-lē'pĕ)	116	22.00N	83.30W
San Felipe Creek, r., Ca., U.S. (săn fĕ-lēp'ȧ)	102	33.10N	116.03W
San Felipe Indian Reservation, I.R., N.M., U.S.	102	35.26N	106.26W
San Feliu de Guixols, Spain (sän fā-lē'ōō dā gē-hôls)	152	41.45N	3.01E
San Félix, Isla, i., Chile (ē's-lä-dĕ-sän fā-lēks')	122	26.20S	80.10W
San Fernanda, Spain (fĕr-nä'n-dä)	152	36.28N	6.13W
San Fernando, Arg. (fĕr-ná'n-dô)	126a	34.26S	58.34W

ng-sing; ŋ-baŋk; N-nasalized n; nŏd; cŏmmit; ōld; ôbey; ôrder; oi-boil; fōōd; ŏŏ-as oo in foot; ou-out; s-soft; sh-dish; th-thin; pūre; ûnite; ûrn; stŭd; circŭs; ü-as in French tu; '-indeterminate vowel.

PLACE (Pronunciation)	PAGE	Lat. °′	Long. °′
San Fernando, Chile	123b	35.36S	70.58W
San Fernando, Mex. (fĕr-nän′dō)	106	24.52N	98.10W
San Fernando, Phil. (sän fĕr-nä′n-dō)	188	16.38N	120.19E
San Fernando, Ca., U.S. (fĕr-nän′dō)	101a	34.17N	118.27W
San Fernando, r., Mex. (sän fĕr-nän′dō)	106	25.07N	98.25W
San Fernando de Apure, Ven. (sän-fĕr-nä′n-dō-dĕ-ä-po͞o′rå)	124	7.46N	67.29W
San Fernando de Atabapo, Ven. (dĕ-ä-tä-bä′pō)	124	3.58N	67.41W
San Fernando de Henares, Spain (dĕ-ā-nä′rås)	153a	40.23N	3.31W
Sånfjället, mtn., Swe.	140	62.19N	13.30E
Sanford, Can. (săn′fẽrd)	77f	49.41N	97.27W
Sanford, Fl., U.S. (săn′fôrd)	90	28.46N	81.18W
Sanford, Me., U.S. (săn′fẽrd)	86	43.26N	70.47W
Sanford, N.C., U.S.	108	35.26N	79.10W
San Francisco, Arg. (săn frăn′sĭs′kō)	126	31.23S	62.09W
San Francisco, El Sal.	114	13.48N	88.11W
San Francisco, Ca., U.S.	90	37.45N	122.26W
San Francisco, r., N.M., U.S.	102	33.35N	108.55W
San Francisco Bay, b., Ca., U.S. (săn frăn′sĭs′kō)	102	37.45N	122.21W
San Francisco Culhuacán, Mex.	229a	19.20N	99.06W
San Francisco del Oro, Mex. (dĕl ō′rō)	110	27.00N	106.37W
San Francisco del Rincón, Mex. (dĕl rēn-kōn′)	112	21.01N	101.51W
San Francisco de Macaira, Ven. (dĕ-mä-kī′rä)	125b	9.58N	66.17W
San Francisco de Macoris, Dom. Rep. (dā-mä-kō′rēs)	116	19.20N	70.15W
San Francisco de Paula, Cuba (dā pou′lå)	117a	23.04N	82.18W
San Francisco el Grande, Iglesia de, rel., Spain	234b	40.25N	3.43W
San Gabriel, Ca., U.S. (săn gä-brē-ĕl′) (gā′brē-ĕl)	101a	34.06N	118.06W
San Gabriel, r., Ca., U.S.	101a	33.47N	118.06W
San Gabriel Chilac, Mex. (sän-gä-brē-ĕl-chē-läk′)	112	18.19N	97.22W
San Gabriel Mts, Ca., U.S.	101a	34.17N	118.03W
San Gabriel Reservoir, res., Ca., U.S.	101a	34.14N	117.48W
Sangamon, r., Il., U.S. (săn′gå-msion)	104	40.08N	90.08W
Sangenjaya, neigh., Japan	238a	35.38N	139.40E
Sanger, Ca., U.S. (săng′ẽr)	102	36.42N	119.33W
Sangerhausen, Ger. (säng′ĕr-hou-zĕn)	148	51.28N	11.17E
Sangha, r., Afr.	204	2.40N	16.10E
Sangihe, Pulau, i., Indon.	188	3.30N	125.30E
San Gil, Col. (sän-κē′l)	124	6.32N	73.13W
San Giovanni in Fiore, Italy (sän jō-vän′nē ēn fyō′rå)	154	39.15N	16.40E
San Giuseppe Vesuviano, Italy	153c	40.36N	14.31E
Sangju, S. Kor. (säng′jo͞o′)	186	36.20N	128.07E
Sāngli, India	174	16.56N	74.38E
Sangmélima, Cam.	208	2.56N	11.59E
San Gorgonio Mountain, mtn., Ca., U.S. (săn gôr-gō′nī-ō)	101a	34.06N	116.50W
Sangre de Cristo Mountains, mts., U.S.	90	37.45N	105.50W
San Gregoria, Ca., U.S. (săn grĕ-gôr′ă)	100b	37.20N	122.23W
San Gregorio Atlapulco, Mex.	229a	19.15N	99.03W
Sangro, r., Italy (säŋ′grō)	154	41.38N	13.56E
Sangüesa, Spain (sän-gwĕ′sä)	152	42.36N	1.15W
Sanhe, China (sän-hŭ)	182	39.59N	117.06E
Sanibel Island, i., Fl., U.S. (săn′ĭ-bĕl)	109a	26.26N	82.15W
San Ignacio, Belize	114a	17.11N	89.04W
San Ildefonso, Cape, c., Phil. (sän-ēl-dĕ-fōn-sō)	189a	16.03N	122.10E
San Ildefonso o la Granja, Spain (ō lä grän′khä)	152	40.54N	4.02W
San Isidro, Arg. (ē-sē′drō)	123c	34.28S	58.31W
San Isidro, C.R.	114	9.24N	83.43W
San Isidro, Peru	229c	12.07S	77.03W
San Jacinto, Phil. (sän hä-sēn′tō)	189a	12.33N	123.43E
San Jacinto, Ca., U.S. (săn jȧ-sĭn′tō)	101a	33.47N	116.57W
San Jacinto, r., Ca., U.S. (săn jȧ-sĭn′tō)	101a	33.44N	117.14W
San Jacinto, r., Tx., U.S.	106	30.25N	95.05W
San Jacinto, West Fork, r., Tx., U.S.	106	30.35N	95.37W
San Javier, Chile (sän-hå-vē′ĕr)	123b	35.35S	71.43W
San Jerónimo, Mex.	113a	19.31N	98.46W
San Jerónimo de Juárez, Mex. (hå-rō′nē-mō dā hwä′råz)	112	17.08N	100.30W
San Jerónimo Lídice, Mex.	229a	19.20N	99.13W
San Joaquin, Ven.	125b	10.16N	67.47W
San Joaquin, r., Ca., U.S. (săn hwä-kēn′)	102	37.10N	120.51W
San Joaquin Valley, Ca., U.S.	102	36.45N	120.30W
San Jorge, Golfo, b., Arg. (gōl-fō-sän-κō′r-κĕ)	126	46.15S	66.45W
San José, C.R. (sän hō-sā′)	110	9.57N	84.05W
San Jose, Phil.	189a	15.49N	120.57E
San Jose, Phil.	189a	12.22N	121.04E
San Jose, Ca., U.S. (săn hō-zā′)	90	37.20N	121.54W
San José, i., Mex. (κô-sĕ′)	110	25.00N	110.35W
San José, Isla de, i., Pan. (ē′s-lä-dĕ-sän hō-sā′)	114	8.17N	79.20W
San Jose, Rio, r., N.M., U.S. (săn hō-zā′)	102	35.15N	108.10W
San José de Feliciano, Arg. (dā lä ĕs-kē′nå)	126	30.26S	58.44W
San José de Galipán, Ven.	230a	10.35N	66.54W
San José de Gauribe, Ven. (sän-hô-sĕ′dĕ-gåo͞o-rē′bĕ)	125b	9.51N	65.49W
San José de las Lajas, Cuba (sän-κō-sĕ′dĕ-läs-lå′käs)	117a	22.58N	82.10W
San José Iturbide, Mex. (ē-to͞or-bē′dĕ)	112	21.00N	100.24W
San Juan, Arg. (hwän′)	126	31.36S	68.29W
San Juan, Col. (hōå′n)	124a	3.23N	73.48W
San Juan, Dom. Rep. (sän hwän′)	116	18.50N	71.15W
San Juan, Phil.	189a	16.41N	120.20E
San Juan, P.R. (sän hwän′)	110	18.30N	66.10W
San Juan, prov., Arg.	126	31.00S	69.30W
San Juan, r., Mex. (sän-ho͞o-än′)	112	18.10N	95.23W
San Juan, r., N.A.	110	10.58N	84.18W
San Juan, r., U.S.	90	36.30N	109.00W
San Juan, Cabezas de, c., P.R.	111b	18.29N	65.30W
San Juan, Cabo, c., Eq. Gui.	210	1.08N	9.23E
San Juan, Pico, mtn., Cuba (pē′kō-sän-kōå′n)	116	21.55N	80.00W
San Juan, Río, r., Mex. (rē′ō-sän-hwän)	106	25.35N	99.15W
San Juan Bautista, Para. (sän hwän′ bou-tēs′tä)	126	26.48S	57.09W
San Juan Capistrano, Mex. (sän-ho͞o-än′ kä-pēs-trä′nō)	112	22.41N	104.07W
San Juan Creek, r., Ca., U.S. (săn hwän′)	102	35.24N	120.12W
San Juan de Aragón, Mex.	229a	19.28N	99.05W
San Juan de Aragón, Bosque, rec., Mex.	229a	19.28N	99.04W
San Juan de Aragón, Zoológico de, rec., Mex.	229a	19.28N	99.05W
San Juan de Dios, Ven.	230a	10.35N	66.57W
San Juan de Guadalupe, Mex. (sän hwan dā gwä-dhä-lo͞o′på)	106	24.37N	102.43W
San Juan del Monte, Phil.	237g	14.36N	121.02E
San Juan del Norte, Nic.	114	10.55N	83.44W
San Juan del Norte, Bahía de, b., Nic.	114	11.12N	83.40W
San Juan de los Lagos, Mex. (sän-ho͞o-än′dā los lä′gōs)	112	21.15N	102.18W
San Juan de los Lagos, r., Mex. (dā lōs lä′gōs)	112	21.13N	102.12W
San Juan de los Morros, Ven. (dĕ-lōs-mô′r-rôs)	125b	9.54N	67.22W
San Juan del Río, Mex. (sän hwän del rē′ō)	106	24.47N	104.29W
San Juan del Río, Mex.	112	20.21N	99.59W
San Juan del Sur, Nic. (dĕl so͞or)	110	11.15N	85.53W
San Juan Evangelista, Mex. (sän-ho͞o-ä′n-å-väŋ-kå-lĕs′ta′)	112	17.57N	95.08W
San Juan Island, i., Wa., U.S.	100a	48.28N	123.08W
San Juan Islands, is., Can. (sän hwän)	80	48.49N	123.14W
San Juan Islands, is., Wa., U.S.	164a	48.36N	122.50W
San Juan Ixtenco, Mex. (ēx-tĕ′n-kô)	112	19.14N	97.52W
San Juan Martínez, Cuba	116	22.15N	83.50W
San Juan Mountains, mts., Co., U.S. (san hwán′)	90	37.50N	107.30W
San Julián, Arg. (sän ho͞o-lyå′n)	126	49.17S	68.02W
San Justo, Arg. (ho͞os′tō)	126a	34.40S	58.33W
San Justo Desvern, Spain	234e	41.23N	2.05E
Sankanbiriwa, mtn., S.L.	208	8.56N	10.48W
Sankarani, r., Afr. (sän′kä-rä′nē)	204	11.10N	8.35W
Sankt Gallen, Switz.	140	47.25N	9.22E
Sankt Moritz, Switz. (sånt mō′rĭts) (zäŋkt mō′rēts)	148	46.31N	9.50E
Sankt Pölten, Aus. (zäŋkt-pûl′tĕn)	148	48.12N	15.38E
Sankt Veit, Aus. (zäŋκt vīt′)	148	46.46N	14.20E
Sankuru, r., Zaire (sän-ko͞o′ro͞o)	206	4.00S	22.35E
San Lázaro, Cabo, c., Mex. (sän-lå′zä-rō)	110	24.58N	113.30W
San Leandro, Ca., U.S. (săn lē-ăn′drō)	100b	37.43N	122.10W
San Lorenzo, Arg. (sän lô-rĕn′zō)	126	32.46S	60.44W
San Lorenzo, Hond. (sän lō-rĕn′zō)	114	13.24N	87.24W
San Lorenzo, Ca., U.S. (săn lō-rĕn′zō)	100b	37.41N	122.08W
San Lorenzo de El Escorial, Spain	152	40.36N	4.09W
San Lorenzo Tezonco, Mex.	229a	19.18N	99.04W
Sanlúcar de Barrameda, Spain (sän-lo͞o′kär)	142	36.46N	6.21W
San Lucas, Bol. (lo͞o′kås)	124	20.12S	65.06W
San Lucas, Cabo, c., Mex.	110	22.45N	109.45W
San Luis, Arg. (lō-ēs′)	126	33.16S	66.15W
San Luis, Col. (lōē′s)	124a	6.03N	74.57W
San Luis, Cuba	116	20.15N	75.50W
San Luis, Guat.	114	14.38N	89.42W
San Luis, prov., Arg.	126	32.45S	66.00W
San Luis, neigh., Cuba	229b	23.05N	82.20W
San Luis de la Paz, Mex. (dā lä päz′)	112	21.17N	100.32W
San Luis del Cordero, Mex. (dĕl kōr-dā′rō)	106	25.25N	104.20W
San Luis Obispo, Ca., U.S. (ō-bĭs′pō)	90	35.18N	120.40W
San Luis Obispo Bay, b., Ca., U.S.	102	35.07N	121.05W
San Luis Potosí, Mex.	110	22.08N	100.58W
San Luis Potosí, state, Mex.	110	22.45N	101.45W
San Luis Rey, r., Ca., U.S. (rā′ē)	102	33.22N	117.06W
San Luis Tlaxialtemalco, Mex.	229a	19.15N	99.03W
San Manuel, Az., U.S. (sän măn′ū-ĕl)	102	32.30N	110.45W
San Marcial, N.M., U.S. (săn mår-shäl′)	102	33.40N	107.00W
San Marco, Italy (sän mär′kô)	154	41.53N	15.50E
San Marcos, Guat. (mär′kōs)	114	14.57N	91.49W
San Marcos, Mex.	112	16.46N	99.23W
San Marcos, Tx., U.S. (săn mär′kōs)	106	29.53N	97.56W
San Marcos, r., Tx., U.S.	106	30.08N	98.15W
San Marcos, Universidad de, educ., Peru	229c	12.03S	77.05W
San Marcos de Colón, Hond. (sän-må′r-kōs-dĕ-kō-lô′n)	114	13.17N	86.50W
San Maria di Léuca, Cape, c., Italy (dē-lĕ′o͞o-kä)	142	39.47N	18.20E
San Marino, S. Mar. (sän mä-rē′nō)	154	44.55N	12.26E
San Marino, Ca., U.S. (săn mẽr-ē′nō)	101a	34.07N	118.06W
San Marino, nation, Eur.	136	43.40N	13.00E
San Martín, Col. (sän mär-tē′n)	124a	3.42N	73.44W
San Martín, vol., Mex. (mär-tē′n)	112	18.36N	95.11W
San Martín, I., S.A.	126	48.15S	72.30W
San Martín Chalchicuautla, Mex.	112	21.22N	98.39W
San Martin de la Vega, Spain (sän mär ten′ dā lä vā′gä)	153a	40.12N	3.34W
San Martín Hidalgo, Mex. (sän mär-tē′n-ē-däl′gō)	112	20.27N	103.55W
San Mateo, Mex.	112	16.59N	97.04W
San Mateo, Spain (sän mä-tā′ō)	152	40.26N	0.09E
San Mateo, Ca., U.S. (săn mä-tā′ō)	100b	37.34N	122.20W
San Mateo, Ven. (sän må-tĕ′ō)	125b	9.45N	64.34W
San Matías, Golfo, b., Arg. (sän mä-tē′äs)	126	41.30S	63.45W
Sanmen Wan, b., China	184	29.00N	122.15E
San Miguel, Chile	230b	33.30S	70.40W
San Miguel, El Sal. (sän mē-gål′)	110	13.28N	88.11W
San Miguel, Mex. (sän mē-gål′)	112	18.18N	97.09W
San Miguel, Pan.	114	8.26N	78.55W
San Miguel, Peru	229c	12.06S	77.06W
San Miguel, Phil. (sän mē-gĕ′l)	189a	15.09N	120.56E
San Miguel, Ven. (sän mē-gĕ′l)	125b	9.56N	64.58W
San Miguel, vol., El Sal.	114	13.27N	88.17W
San Miguel, i., Ca., U.S.	102	34.03N	120.23W
San Miguel, r., Bol. (sän-mē-gĕl′)	124	13.34S	63.58W
San Miguel, r., N.A. (sän mē-gål′)	112	15.27N	92.00W
San Miguel, r., Co., U.S. (săn mē-gĕl′)	102	38.15N	108.40W
San Miguel, Bahía, b., Pan. (bä-ē′ä-sän mē-gål′)	114	8.17N	78.26W
San Miguel Bay, b., Phil.	189a	13.55N	123.12E
San Miguel de Allende, Mex. (dā ä-lyĕn′dā)	112	20.54N	100.44W
San Miguel del Padrón, Cuba	229b	23.05N	82.19W
San Miguel el Alto, Mex. (ĕl äl′tō)	112	21.03N	102.26W
Sannār, Sudan	204	14.25N	33.30E
San Narcisco, Phil. (sän när-sē′sō)	189a	15.01N	120.05E
San Narcisco, Phil.	189a	13.34N	122.33E
San Nicolás, Arg. (sän nē-kô-lå′s)	126	33.20S	60.14W
San Nicolas, Phil. (nē-kō-läs′)	189a	16.05N	120.45E
San Nicolas, i., Ca., U.S. (săn nĭ′kō-lå)	102	33.14N	119.10W
San Nicolás, r., Mex.	112	19.40N	105.08W
Sanniquellie, Lib.	208	7.22N	8.43W
Sannois, Fr.	233c	48.58N	2.15E
Sannūr, Wādī, Egypt	212b	28.48N	31.12E
Sanok, Pol. (sä′nōk)	148	49.31N	22.13E
San Pablo, Phil. (sän-pä-blō)	189a	14.05N	121.20E
San Pablo, Ca., U.S. (săn păb′lō)	100b	37.58N	122.21W
San Pablo, Ven. (sän-på′blô)	125b	9.46N	65.04W
San Pablo, r., Pan. (sän päb′lō)	114	8.12N	81.12W
San Pablo Bay, b., Ca., U.S. (săn păb′lō)	100b	38.04N	122.25W
San Pablo Res, Ca., U.S.	100b	37.55N	122.12W
San Pascual, Phil. (päs-kwäl′)	189a	13.08N	122.59E
San Pedro, Arg.	123c	33.41S	59.42W
San Pedro, Arg. (sän pā′drō)	126	24.15S	64.15W
San Pedro, Chile (sän pĕ′drō)	123b	33.54S	71.27W
San Pedro, El Sal. (sän pā′drō)	114	13.49N	88.58W
San Pedro, Mex. (sän pā′drō)	112	18.38N	92.25W
San Pedro, Para. (sän-pĕ′drō)	126	24.13S	57.00W
San Pedro, Ca., U.S. (săn pē′drō)	101a	33.44N	118.17W
San Pedro, r., Cuba (sän-pĕ′drō)	116	21.05N	78.15W
San Pedro, r., Mex.	106	27.56N	105.50W
San Pedro, r., Mex. (sän pā′drō)	112	22.08N	104.59W
San Pedro, r., Az., U.S.	102	32.48N	110.37W
San Pedro, Río de, r., Mex.	112	21.51N	102.24W
San Pedro, Río de, r., N.A.	112	18.23N	92.13W
San Pedro Bay, b., Ca., U.S. (săn pē′drō)	101a	33.42N	118.12W
San Pedro de las Colonias, Mex. (dĕ-läs-kō-lô′nyäs)	106	25.47N	102.58W
San Pedro de Macorís, Dom. Rep. (sän-pĕ′drō-dā mä-kō-rēs′)	116	18.30N	69.30W
San Pedro Lagunillas, Mex. (sän pā′drō lä-go͞o-nēl′yäs)	112	21.12N	104.47W
San Pedro Sula, Hond. (sän pā′drō so͞o′lä)	114	15.29N	88.01W
San Pedro Xalostoc, Mex.	229a	19.32N	99.05W
San Pedro Zacatenco, Mex.	229a	19.31N	99.08W
San Pietro, Isola di, i., Italy (ē′sō-lä-dē-sän pyā′trō)	154	39.09N	8.15E
San Pietro in Vaticano, rel., Vat.	235c	41.54N	12.28E
San Quentin, Ca., U.S. (sän kwēn-tēn′)	100b	37.57N	122.29W
San Quintin, Phil. (sän kēn-tēn′)	189a	15.59N	120.47E
San Rafael, Arg. (sän rä-fä-āl′)	126	34.30S	68.13W
San Rafael, Col. (sän-rä-fä-ĕ′l)	124a	6.18N	75.02W
San Rafael, Ca., U.S. (săn rå-fĕl)	100b	37.58N	122.31W
San Rafael, r., Ut., U.S. (săn rå-fĕl′)	102	39.05N	110.50W
San Rafael, Cabo, c., Dom. Rep. (kå′bō)	116	19.00N	68.50W
San Ramón, C.R.	114	10.07N	84.30W
San Ramon, Ca., U.S. (sän rä-mōn′)	100b	37.47N	122.59W
San Remo, Italy (sän rā′mō)	154	43.48N	7.46E
San Roque, Col. (sän-rô′kĕ)	124a	6.29N	75.00W
San Roque, Spain	152	36.13N	5.23W
San Saba, Tx., U.S. (săn sä′bå)	106	31.12N	98.43W
San Saba, r., Tx., U.S.	106	30.58N	99.12W
San Salvador, El Sal. (sän säl-vä-dōr′)	110	13.45N	89.11W
San Salvador (Watling), i., Bah. (săn săl′vå-dôr)	116	24.05N	74.30W
San Salvador, i., Ec.	124	0.14S	90.50W
San Salvador, r., Ur. (sän-säl-vä-dô′r)	123c	33.42S	58.04W
Sansanné-Mango, Togo (sän-så-nā′ mäɴ′gō)	204	10.21N	0.28E
San Sebastián, Spain	136	43.19N	1.59W
San Sebastian, Spain (sän så-bås-tyän′)	204	28.09N	17.11W
San Sebastián, Ven. (sän-sĕ-bäs-tyå′n)	125b	9.58N	67.11W
San Sebastiàn de los Reyes, Spain	153a	40.33N	3.38W
San Severo, Italy (sän sĕ-vå′rō)	142	41.43N	15.24E
Sanshui, China (sän-shwā)	180	23.14N	112.51E

ăt; finăl; rāte; senåte; ärm; åsk; sofȧ; fâre; ch-choose; dh-as th in other; bē; ēvent; bĕt; recĕnt; cratẽr; g-gō; gh-guttural g; bĭt; ĭ-short neutral; rīde; κ-guttural k as ch in German ich;

PLACE (Pronunciation)	PAGE	Lat. °′	Long. °′
San Simon Creek, r., Az., U.S. (săn sī-mōn′)	102	32.45N	109.30W
San Siro, neigh., Italy	234c	45.29S	9.07E
Sanssouci, Schloss, hist., Ger.	234a	52.24N	13.02E
Santa Ana, El Sal.	110	14.02N	89.35W
Santa Ana, Mex. (sän′tä ä′nä)	112	19.18N	98.10W
Santa Ana, Ca., U.S. (săn′tȧ ăn′ȧ)	90	33.45N	117.52W
Santa Ana, r., Ca., U.S.	101a	33.41N	117.57W
Santa Ana Mountains, mts., Ca., U.S.	101a	33.44N	117.36W
Santa Anna, Tx., U.S.	106	31.44N	99.18W
Santa Antão, i., C.V. (sä-tä-ä′n-zhē-lò)	204b	17.20N	26.05W
Santa Bárbara, Braz. (sän-tä-bá′r-bä-rä)	124	19.57S	43.25W
Santa Bárbara, Hond.	114	14.52N	88.20W
Santa Barbara, Mex.	106	26.48N	105.50W
Santa Barbara, Ca., U.S.	90	34.26N	119.43W
Santa Barbara, i., Ca., U.S.	102	33.30N	118.44W
Santa Barbara Channel, strt., Ca., U.S.	102	34.15N	120.00W
Santa Branca, Braz. (sän-tä-brä′N-kä)	123a	23.25S	45.52W
Santa Catalina, i., Ca., U.S.	90	33.29N	118.37W
Santa Catalina, Cerro de, mtn., Pan.	114	8.39N	81.36W
Santa Catalina, Gulf of, b., Ca., U.S. (săn′tȧ kă-tȧ-lē′nȧ)	102	33.00N	117.58W
Santa Catarina, Mex. (sän′tá kä-tä-rē′nä)	106	25.41N	100.27W
Santa Catarina, state, Braz. (sän-tä-kä-tä-rê′nà)	126	27.15S	50.30W
Santa Catarina, r., Mex.	112	16.31N	98.39W
Santa Clara, Cuba (sän′t klä′rá)	110	22.25N	80.00W
Santa Clara, Mex.	106	24.29N	103.22W
Santa Clara, Ca., U.S. (săn′tȧ klârȧ)	98	37.21N	121.56W
Santa Clara, Ur.	126	32.46S	54.51W
Santa Clara, vol., Nic.	114	12.44N	87.00W
Santa Clara, r., Ca., U.S. (săn′tȧ klä′rȧ)	102	34.22N	118.53W
Santa Clara, Bahía de, b., Cuba (bä-ē′ä-dĕ-sän-tä-klä-rä)	116	23.05N	80.50W
Santa Clara, Sierra, mts., Mex. (sē-ĕ′r-rä-sän′tá klä′rá)	110	27.30N	113.50W
Santa Clara Indian Reservation, I.R., N.M., U.S.	102	35.59N	106.10W
Santa Coloma de Gramanet, Spain	234e	41.27N	2.13E
Santa Cruz, Bol. (sän′tá krōōz′)	124	17.45S	63.03W
Santa Cruz, Braz. (sän-tä-krōō′s)	126	29.43S	52.15W
Santa Cruz, Braz.	126b	22.55S	43.41W
Santa Cruz, Chile	123b	34.38S	71.21W
Santa Cruz, C.R.	114	10.16N	85.37W
Santa Cruz, Mex.	106	25.50N	105.25W
Santa Cruz, Phil.	189a	13.28N	122.02E
Santa Cruz, Phil.	189a	14.17N	121.25E
Santa Cruz, Phil.	189a	15.46N	119.53E
Santa Cruz, Ca., U.S.	90	36.59N	122.02W
Santa Cruz, prov., Arg.	126	48.00S	70.00W
Santa Cruz, i., Ec. (sän-tä-krōō′z)	124	0.38S	90.20W
Santa Cruz, r., Arg. (sän′tá krōōz)	126	50.05S	71.00W
Santa Cruz, r., Az., U.S. (săn′tȧ krōōz′)	102	32.30N	111.30W
Santa Cruz Barillas, Guat. (sän-tä-krōō′z-bä-rē′l-yäs)	114	15.47N	91.22W
Santa Cruz del Sur, Cuba (sän-tä-krōō′s-dĕl-sōō′r)	116	20.45N	78.00W
Santa Cruz de Tenerife, Spain (sän′tä krōōz dä tā-nå-rē′få)	203	28.07N	15.27W
Santa Cruz Islands, is., Sol.Is.	196	10.58S	166.47E
Santa Cruz Meyehualco, Mex.	229a	19.20N	99.03W
Santa Cruz Mountains, mts., Ca., U.S. (săn′tȧ krōōz′)	100b	37.30N	122.19W
Santa Domingo, Cay, i., Bah.	116	21.50N	75.45W
Santa Eduviges, Chile	230b	33.33S	70.39W
Santa Elena del Gomero, Chile	230b	33.29S	70.46W
Santa Eugenia de Ribeira, Spain	152	42.34N	8.55W
Santa Eulalia del Río, Spain	152	38.58N	1.29E
Santa Fe, Arg. (sän′tä fā′)	126	31.33S	60.45W
Santa Fé, Cuba (sän-tä-fē′)	116	21.45N	82.40W
Santa Fe, Mex.	229a	19.23N	99.14W
Santa Fe, Spain (sän′tä-fā′)	152	37.12N	3.43W
Santa Fe, N.M., U.S. (săn′tȧ fā′)	90	35.40N	106.00W
Santa Fe, prov., Arg. (sän′tä fā′)	126	32.00S	61.15W
Santa Fe de Bogotá, Col.	124	4.36N	74.05W
Santa Filomena, Braz. (sän-tä-fē-lò-mĕ′nä)	124	9.09S	44.45W
Santa Genoveva, mtn., Mex. (sän-tä-hĕ-nō-vĕ′vä)	110	23.30N	110.00W
Santai, China (san-tī)	180	31.02N	105.02E
Santa Inés, Ven. (sän′tä ē-nĕ′s)	125b	9.54N	64.21W
Santa Inés, i., Chile (sän′tä ē-nās′)	126	53.45S	74.15W
Santa Isabel, i., Sol.Is.	196	7.57S	159.28E
Santa Isabel, Pico de, mtn., Eq. Gui.	208	3.35N	8.46E
Santa Lucia, Cuba (sän′tá lōō-sē′á)	116	21.15N	77.30W
Santa Lucia, Ur. (sän-tä-lōō-sē′ä)	126	34.27S	56.23W
Santa Lucia, Ven.	125b	10.18N	66.40W
Santa Lucia, r., Ur.	123c	34.19S	56.13W
Santa Lucia Bay, b., Cuba (sän′tá lōō-sē′á)	116	22.55N	84.20W
Santa Margarita, i., Mex. (sän′tá mär-gä-rē′tá)	110	24.15N	112.00W
Santa Maria, Braz. (sän′tá mä-rē′á)	126	29.40S	54.00W
Santa Maria, Italy (sän-tä mä-rē′ä)	154	41.05N	14.15E
Santa Maria, Phil. (sän-tä-mä-rē′ä)	189a	14.48N	120.57E
Santa Maria, Ca., U.S. (săn-tȧ mȧ-rē′ȧ)	102	34.57N	120.28W
Santa María, vol., Guat.	114	14.45N	91.33W
Santa Maria, r., Mex. (sän′tä mä-rē′ä)	112	21.33N	100.17W
Santa Maria, Cabo de, c., Port. (ká′bō-dĕ-sän-tä-mä-rē′ä)	152	36.58N	7.54W
Santa Maria, Cape, c., Bah.	116	23.45N	75.30W
Santa Maria, Cayo, i., Cuba	116	22.40N	79.00W
Santa Maria del Oro, Mex. (sän′tä-mä-rē′ä-dĕl-ô-rô)	112	21.21N	104.35W
Santa Maria de los Angeles, Mex. (dĕ-lôs-á′n-hĕ-lĕs)	112	22.10N	103.34W
Santa María del Río, Mex.	112	21.46N	100.43W
Santa María del Rosario, Cuba	229b	23.04N	82.15W
Santa María de Ocotán, Mex.	112	22.56N	104.30W
Santa Maria Island, i., Port. (sän-tä-mä-rē′ä)	204a	37.09N	26.02W
Santa Maria Madalena, Braz.	123a	22.00S	42.00W
Santa Marta, Col. (sän′tá mär′tá)	124	11.15N	74.13W
Santa Marta, Peru	229c	12.02S	76.56W
Santa Marta, Cabo de, c., Ang.	210	13.52S	12.25E
Santa Martha Acatitla, Mex.	229a	19.22N	99.01W
Santa Monica, Ca., U.S. (săn′tȧ mŏn′ĭ-kȧ)	90	34.01N	118.29W
Santa Mónica, neigh., Ven.	230a	10.29N	66.53W
Santa Monica Bay, b., Ca., U.S.	228	33.54N	118.25W
Santa Monica Mountains, mts., Ca., U.S.	101a	34.08N	118.38W
Santana, r., Braz. (sän-tä′nä)	126b	22.33S	43.37W
Santander, Col. (sän-tän-dĕr′)	124a	3.00N	76.25W
Santander, Spain (sän-tän-dâr′)	136	43.27N	3.50W
Santa Paula, Ca., U.S. (săn′tȧ pô′lȧ)	102	34.24N	119.05W
Santarém, Braz. (sän-tä-rĕN′)	124	2.28S	54.37W
Santarém, Port.	152	39.18N	8.48W
Santaren Channel, strt., Bah. (sän-tȧ-rĕn′)	116	24.15N	79.30W
Santa Rita do Sapucai, Braz. (sä-pò-kà′ē)	123a	22.15S	45.41W
Santa Rosa, Arg. (sän-tä-rô-sä)	126	36.45S	64.10W
Santa Rosa, Col. (sän-tä-rô-sä)	124a	6.38N	75.26W
Santa Rosa, Ec.	124	3.29S	79.55W
Santa Rosa, Guat. (sän′tá rō′sȧ)	114	14.21N	90.16W
Santa Rosa, Hond.	114	14.45N	88.51W
Santa Rosa, Ca., U.S. (săn′tȧ rō′zȧ)	90	38.27N	122.42W
Santa Rosa, N.M., U.S. (săn′tȧ rō′sȧ)	104	34.55N	104.41W
Santa Rosa, Ven. (sän-tä-rô-sä)	125b	9.37N	64.10W
Santa Rosa de Cabal, Col. (sän-tä-rô-sä-dĕ-kä-bä′l)	124a	4.53N	75.38W
Santa Rosa de Huechuraba, Chile	230b	33.21S	70.41W
Santa Rosa de Viterbo, Braz. (sän-tä-rô-sá-dĕ-vē-tĕr′-bô)	123a	21.30S	47.21W
Santa Rosa Indian Reservation, I.R., Ca., U.S. (săn′tȧ rō′zȧ′)	102	33.28N	116.50W
Santa Rosalía, Mex. (sän′tá rô-zä′lē-á)	110	27.13N	112.15W
Santa Rosa Range, mts., Nv., U.S. (săn′tȧ rō′zȧ)	98	41.33N	117.50W
Santa Susana, Ca., U.S. (săn′tȧ sōō-zä′nȧ)	101a	34.16N	118.42W
Santa Teresa, Arg. (sän-tä-tĕ-rĕ′sä)	123c	33.27S	60.47W
Santa Teresa, Ven.	125b	10.14N	66.40W
Santa Teresa de lo Ovalle, Chile	230b	33.23S	70.47W
Santa Úrsula Coapa, Mex.	229a	19.17N	99.11W
Santa Vitória do Palmar, Braz. (sän-tä-vē-tō′ryä-dô-päl-már)	126	33.30S	53.16W
Santa Ynez, r., Ca., U.S. (săn′tȧ ē-nĕz′)	102	34.40N	120.20W
Santa Ysabel Indian Reservation, I.R., Ca., U.S. (săn-tȧ ĭ-zȧ-bĕl′)	102	33.05N	116.46W
Santee, Ca., U.S. (săn tē′)	102a	32.50N	116.58W
Santee, r., S.C., U.S.	90	33.00N	79.45W
Santeny, Fr.	233c	48.43N	2.34E
Sant' Eufemia, Golfo di, b., Italy (gôl-fô-dē-sän-tĕ′ô-fĕ′myä)	154	38.53N	15.53E
Santiago, Braz. (sän-tyá′gô)	126	29.05S	54.46W
Santiago, Chile (sän-tē-ä′gô)	126	33.26S	70.40W
Santiago, Pan.	110	8.07N	80.58W
Santiago, Phil. (sän-tyä′gô)	189a	16.42N	121.33E
Santiago, prov., Chile (sän-tyá′gô)	123b	33.28S	70.55W
Santiago, i., Phil.	189a	16.29N	120.03E
Santiago de Compostela, Spain	142	42.52N	8.32W
Santiago de Cuba, Cuba (sän-tyá′gô-dā kōō′bá)	110	20.00N	75.50W
Santiago de Cuba, prov., Cuba	116	20.20N	76.05W
Santiago de las Vegas, Cuba (sän-tyá′gô-dĕ-läs-vĕ′gäs)	117a	22.58N	82.23W
Santiago del Estero, Arg.	126	27.50S	64.14W
Santiago del Estero, prov., Arg. (sän-tē-á′gō-dĕl ĕs-tā-rô)	126	27.15S	63.30W
Santiago de los Cabelleros, Dom. Rep.	110	19.30N	70.45W
Santiago Mountains, mts., Tx., U.S. (sän-tē-ä′gô)	90	30.00N	103.30W
Santiago Reservoir, res., Ca., U.S.	101a	33.47N	117.42W
Santiago Rodriguez, Dom. Rep. (sän-tyá′gô-rô-drē′gĕz)	116	19.30N	71.25W
Santiago Tepalcatlalpan, Mex.	229a	19.15N	99.08W
Santiago Tuxtla, Mex. (sän-tyá′gô-tōō′x-tlä)	112	18.28N	95.18W
Santiaguillo, Laguna de, l., Mex. (lä-oō′nä-dĕ-sän-tē-a-gēl′yô)	106	24.51N	104.43W
Santissimo, neigh., Braz.	230c	22.53S	43.31W
Santisteban del Puerto, Spain (sän′tē stá-bän′dĕl pwĕr′tô)	152	38.15N	3.12W
Santo Amaro, Braz. (sän′tò ä-mä′rò)	124	12.32S	38.33W
Santo Amaro, neigh., Braz.	230d	23.39S	46.42W
Santo Amaro de Campos, Braz.	123a	22.01S	41.05W
Santo André, Braz.	123a	23.40S	46.31W
Santo Angelo, Braz. (sän-tô-ä′n-zhĕ-lô)	126	28.16S	53.59W
Santo Antônio do Monte, Braz. (sän-tô-än-tô′nyô-dô-môn′tĕ)	123a	20.06S	45.18W
Santo Domingo, Cuba (sän′tô-dōmĭŋ′gô)	116	22.35N	80.20W
Santo Domingo, Dom. Rep. (sän′tô dô-mĭn′gô)	110	18.30N	69.55W
Santo Domingo, Nic. (sän-tô-dô-mē′n-gō)	114	12.15N	84.56W
Santo Domingo de la Caizada, Spain (dä lä käl-thä′dä)	152	42.27N	2.55W
Santoña, Spain (sän-tō′nyä)	152	43.25N	3.27W
Sant' Onofrio, neigh., Italy	235c	41.56N	12.25E
Santos, Braz. (sän′tozh)	124	23.58S	46.20W
Santos Dumont, Braz. (sän′tôs-dò-mô′nt)	124	21.28S	43.33W
Sanuki, Japan (sä′nōō-kê)	187a	35.16N	139.53E
San Urbano, Arg. (sän-òr-bä′nô)	123c	33.39S	61.28W
San Valentin, Monte, mtn., Chile (sän-vä-lĕn-tē′n)	126	46.41S	73.30W
San Vicente, Arg. (sän-vē-sĕn′tĕ)	123c	35.00S	58.26W
San Vicente, Chile	123b	34.25S	71.06W
San Vicente, El Sal. (sän vē-sĕn′tá)	114	13.41N	88.43W
San Vicente de Alcántara, Spain	152	39.24N	7.08W
San Vicente dels Horts, Spain	234e	41.24N	2.01E
San Vito al Tagliamento, Italy (san vē′tô)	154	45.53N	12.52E
San Xavier Indian Reservation, I.R., Az., U.S. (x-ā′vĭēr)	102	32.07N	111.12W
San Ysidro, Ca., U.S. (săn ysĭ-drō′)	102a	32.33N	117.02W
Sanyuanli, China (sän-yûän-lē)	183a	23.11N	113.16E
São Bernardo do Campo, Braz. (souN-bĕr-nár′dô-dô-ká′m-pô)	123a	23.44S	46.33W
São Borja, Braz. (souN-bôr-zhä)	126	28.44S	55.59W
São Caetano do Sul, Braz.	230d	23.37S	46.34W
São Carlos, Braz. (souN kär′lōzh)	124	22.02S	47.54W
São Cristovão, Braz. (souN-krēs-tō-vouN)	124	11.04S	37.11W
São Cristóvão, neigh., Braz.	230c	22.54S	43.14W
São Fidélis, Braz. (souN-fē-dĕ′lēs)	123a	21.41S	41.45W
São Francisco, Braz. (souN frän-sēsh′kò)	124	15.59S	44.42W
São Francisco, Rio, r., Braz. (rē′ō-sän-frän-sē′s-kō)	124	8.56S	40.20W
São Francisco do Sul, Braz. (souN frän-sēsh′kò-dô-sōō′l)	126	26.15S	48.42W
São Gabriel, Braz. (souN′gä-brē-ĕl′)	126	30.28S	54.11W
São Geraldo, Braz. (souN-zhĕ-rä′l-dô)	123a	21.01S	42.49W
São Gonçalo, Braz. (souN′gōŋ-sä′lò)	123a	22.55S	43.04W
Sao Hill, Tan.	210	8.20S	35.12E
São João, Gui.-B.	208	11.32N	15.26W
São João da Barra, Braz. (souN-zhôuN-dä-bà′rä)	123a	21.40S	41.03W
São João da Boa Vista, Braz. (souN-zhôuN-dä-bôä-vē′s-tä)	123a	21.58S	46.45W
São João del Rei, Braz. (souN zhô-ouN′dĕl-rā)	126	21.08S	44.14W
São João de Meriti, Braz. (souN-zhôuN-dĕ-mĕ-rē-tē)	126b	22.47S	43.22W
São João do Araguaia, Braz. (souN zhô-ouN′dô-ä-rä-gwä′yä)	124	5.29S	48.44W
São João dos Lampas, Port. (souN′ zhô-ouN′ dōzh län-päzh′)	153b	38.52N	9.24W
São João Nepomuceno, Braz. (souN-zhôuN-nĕ-pô-mōō-sĕ-nō)	123a	21.33S	43.00W
São Jorge Island, i., Port. (souN zhôr′zhĕ)	204a	38.28N	27.34W
São José do Rio Pardo, Braz. (souN-zhô-sĕ′dô-rē′ō-pá′r-d . . . . . . ō)	123a	21.36S	46.50W
São José do Rio Prêto, Braz. (souN zhô-zĕ′dô-re′ō-prĕ-tô)	124	20.57S	49.12W
São José dos Campos, Braz. (souN-zhô-zā′dōzh kän pōzh′)	123a	23.12S	45.53W
São Julião da Barra, Port.	234d	38.40N	9.21W
São Leopoldo, Braz. (souN-lĕ-ô-pôl′dô)	126	29.46S	51.09W
São Luis, Braz.	124	2.31S	43.14W
São Luis do Paraitinga, Braz. (souN-lōōē′s-dô-pä-rä-ē-tē′n-g . . . . ä)	123a	23.15S	45.18W
São Manuel, r., Braz.	124	8.28S	57.07E
São Mateus, Braz. (souN mä-tā′ōzh)	124	18.44S	39.45W
São Mateus, Braz.	126b	22.49S	43.23W
São Miguel Arcanjo, Braz. (souN-mē-gĕ′l-ár-kän-zhō)	123a	23.54S	47.59W
São Miguel Island, i., Port.	204a	37.59N	26.38W
Saona, i., Dom. Rep. (sä-ô′nä)	116	18.10N	68.55W
Saône, r., Fr. (sōn)	136	47.00N	5.30E
São Nicolau, i., C.V. (souN′ nĕ-kô-louN′)	204b	16.19N	25.19W
São Paulo, Braz. (souN′ pou′lò)	124	23.34S	46.38W
São Paulo, state, Braz. (souN pou′lò)	124	21.45S	50.47W
São Paulo de Olivença, Braz. (souN′pou′lòdä ô-lē-vĕn′sȧ)	124	3.32S	68.46W
São Pedro, Braz. (souN-pĕ′drô)	123a	22.34S	47.54W
São Pedro de Aldeia, Braz. (souN-pĕ′drô-dĕ-äl-dĕ′yä)	123a	22.50S	42.04W
São Pedro e São Paulo, Rocedos, rocks, Braz.	122	1.50N	30.00W
São Raimundo Nonato, Braz. (souN′ rī-mô′n-do nô-nä′tò)	124	9.09S	42.32W
São Roque, Braz. (souN′ rō′kĕ)	123a	23.32S	47.08W
São Roque, Cabo de, c., Braz. (kä′bō-dĕ-souN′ rō′kĕ)	124	5.06S	35.11W
São Sebastião, Braz. (souN sá-bäs-tē-ouN′)	123a	23.48S	45.25W
São Sebastião, Ilha de, i., Braz.	123a	23.52S	45.22W
São Sebastião do Paraiso, Braz.	123a	20.54S	46.58W
São Simão, Braz. (souN-sē-mouN)	123a	21.30S	47.33W
São Tiago, i., C.V. (souN tê-ä′gô)	204b	15.09N	24.45W
São Tomé, S. Tom./P.	204	0.20N	6.44E
Sao Tome and Principe, nation, Afr. (prēn′sē-pĕ)	204	1.00N	6.00E
Saoura, Oued, r., Alg.	204	29.39N	1.42W
São Vicente, Braz. (souN ve-se′n-tĕ)	124	23.57S	46.25W
São Vicente, i., C.V. (souN vê-sĕn′tä)	204b	16.51N	24.35W
São Vicente, Cabo de, c., Port. (ká′bō-dĕ-sän-vē-sĕ′n-tĕ)	136	37.03N	9.31W
Sapele, Nig. (sä-pā′lā)	204	5.54N	5.41E
Sapitwa, mtn., Mwi.	210	15.58S	35.38E
Sapozhok, Russia (sä-pô-zhôk′)	156	53.58N	40.44E
Sapporo, Japan (säp-pô′rô)	180	43.02N	141.29E

ng-sing; ŋ-baŋk; N-nasalized n; nŏd; cŏmmit; ōld; ôbey; ôrder; oi-boil; fōōd; ŏŏ-as oo in foot; ou-out; s-soft; sh-dish; th-thin; pūre; ûnite; ûrn; stŭd; circŭs; ü-as in French tu; ′-indeterminate vowel.

PLACE (Pronunciation)	PAGE	Lat.	Long.
Sapronovo, Russia (sáp-rô′nô-vô) . . .	164b	55.13N	38.25E
Sapucaí, r., Braz. (sä-pōō-ká-ē′)	123a	22.20S	45.53W
Sapucaia, Braz. (sä-pōō-kä′yá)	123a	22.01S	42.54W
Sapucaí Mirim, r., Braz. (sä-pōō-ká-ē′mē-rēn)	123a	21.06S	47.03W
Sapulpa, Ok., U.S. (sá-pŭl′pá)	104	36.01N	96.05W
Saqqez, Iran	176	36.14N	46.16E
Saquarema, Braz. (sä-kwä-rĕ-mä)	123a	22.56S	42.32W
Sara, Wa., U.S. (sä′rä)	100c	45.45N	122.42W
Sara, Bahr, r., Chad (bär)	204	8.19N	17.44E
Sarajevo, Bos. (sä-rá-yĕv′ô) (sä-rä′ya-vô)	136	43.50N	18.26E
Sarakhs, Iran	176	36.32N	61.11E
Sarana, Russia (sä-rá′nä)	164a	56.31N	57.44E
Saranac Lake, N.Y., U.S.	92	44.20N	74.05W
Saranac Lake, l., N.Y., U.S. (săr′á-năk)	92	44.15N	74.20W
Sarandi, Arg. (sä-rän′dĕ)	126a	34.41S	58.21W
Sarandí Grande, Ur. (sä-rän′dĕ-grän′dĕ)	123c	33.42S	56.21W
Saranley, Som.	212a	2.28N	42.15E
Saransk, Russia (sä-ränsk′)	158	54.10N	45.10E
Sarany, Russia (sä-rá′nĭ)	164a	58.33N	58.48E
Sara Peak, mtn., Nig.	208	9.37N	9.25E
Sarapul, Russia (sä-räpŏl′)	160	56.28N	53.50E
Sarasota, Fl., U.S. (săr-á-sōtá)	109a	27.27N	82.30W
Saratoga, Tx., U.S. (săr-á-tō′gá)	106	30.17N	94.31W
Saratoga, Wa., U.S.	100a	48.04N	122.29W
Saratoga Pass, Wa., U.S.	100a	48.09N	122.33W
Saratoga Springs, N.Y., U.S. (springz)	92	43.05N	74.50W
Saratov, Russia (sá rä′tôf)	158	51.30N	45.30E
Saravane, Laos	184	15.48N	106.40E
Sarawak, hist. reg., Malay. (sä-rä′wäk)	188	2.30N	112.45E
Sárbogárd, Hung. (shär′bô-gärd)	148	46.53N	18.38E
Sarcee Indian Reserve, I.R., Can. (sär′sĕ)	77e	50.58N	114.23W
Sarcelles, Fr.	151b	49.00N	2.23E
Sardalas, Libya	204	25.59N	10.33E
Sardinia, i., Italy (sär-dĭn′ĭá)	136	40.08N	9.05E
Sardis, Ms., U.S. (sär′dĭs)	108	34.26N	89.55W
Sardis Lake, res., Ms., U.S.	108	34.27N	89.43W
Sargent, Ne., U.S. (sär′jĕnt)	96	41.40N	99.38W
Sarh, Chad (är-chän-bô′)	204	9.09N	18.23E
Sarikamis, Tur.	160	40.30N	42.40E
Sariñena, Spain (sä-rēn-yĕ′nä)	152	41.46N	0.11W
Sark, i., Guernsey (särk)	150	49.28N	2.22W
Şarköy, Tur. (shär′kû-ĕ)	154	40.39N	27.07E
Sarmiento, Monte, mtn., Chile (mô′n-tĕ-sär-myĕn′tô)	126	54.28S	70.40W
Sarnia, Can. (sär′nĭ-á)	78	43.00N	82.25W
Sarno, Italy (sä′r-nô)	153c	40.35N	14.38E
Sarny, Ukr. (sär′nĕ)	160	51.17N	26.39E
Saronikós Kólpos, b., Grc.	154	37.51N	23.30E
Sárospatak, Hung. (shä′rôsh-pô′tôk)	148	48.19N	21.35E
Šar Planina, mts., Yugo. (shär plä′nĕ-na)	154	42.07N	21.54E
Sarpsborg, Nor. (särps′bôrg)	146	59.17N	11.07E
Sarratt, Eng.	231	51.41N	0.29W
Sarrebourg, Fr. (sär-bōōr′)	150	48.44N	7.02E
Sarreguemines, Fr. (sär-gĕ-mēn′)	140	49.06N	7.05E
Sarria, Spain (sär′ĕ-ä)	142	42.14N	7.17W
Sarstun, r., N.A. (särs-tōō′n)	114	15.50N	89.26W
Sartène, Fr. (sär-tĕn′)	154	41.36N	8.59E
Sarthe, r., Fr. (särt)	140	47.44N	0.32W
Sartrouville, Fr.	233c	48.57N	2.10E
Sárvár, Hung. (shär′vär)	148	47.14N	16.55E
Sarych, Mys, c., Ukr. (mĭs sä-rēch′)	160	44.25N	33.00E
Sary-Ishikotrau, Peski, des., Kyrg. (sä′rĕ ĕ′ shĕk-ō′trou)	158	46.12N	75.30E
Sarysu, r., Kaz. (sä′rĕ-sōō)	162	47.47N	69.14E
Sasarãm, India (sŭs-ŭ-räm′)	174	25.00N	84.00E
Sasayama, Japan (sä′sä-yä′mä)	187	35.05N	135.14E
Sasebo, Japan (sä′sä-bô)	180	33.12N	129.43E
Sashalom, neigh., Hung.	235g	47.31N	19.11E
Saskatchewan, prov., Can.	78	54.46N	107.40W
Saskatchewan, r., Can. (săs-kăch′ĕ-wän)	78	53.45N	103.20W
Saskatoon, Can. (săs-ká-tōōn′)	78	52.07N	106.38W
Sasolburg, S. Afr.	212d	26.52S	27.47E
Sasovo, Russia (sás′ô-vô)	160	54.20N	42.00E
Saspamco, Tx., U.S. (săs-păm′cô)	101d	29.13N	98.18W
Sassafras, Austl.	239b	37.52S	145.21E
Sassandra, I.C.	208	4.58N	6.05W
Sassandra, r., I.C. (säs-sän′drá)	204	5.35N	6.25W
Sassari, Italy (säs′sä-rĕ)	142	40.44N	8.33E
Sassnitz, Ger. (säs′nĕts)	148	54.31N	13.37E
Satadougou, Mali (sä-tá-dōō-goó′)	208	12.21N	12.07W
Säter, Swe. (sē′tĕr)	146	60.21N	15.50E
Sãtghara, India	236a	22.44N	88.21E
Satilla, r., Ga., U.S. (sá-tĭl′á)	108	31.15N	82.13W
Satka, Russia (sät′kä)	160	55.03N	59.02E
Sátoraljaujhely, Hung. (shä′tô-rô-lyô-ōō′yĕl′)	148	48.24N	21.40E
Satu-Mare, Rom. (sä′tōō-má′rĕ)	142	47.50N	22.53E
Saturna, Can. (sä-tûr′nä)	100d	48.48N	123.12W
Saturna, i., Can.	100d	48.47N	123.03W
Sauda, Nor.	146	59.40N	6.21E
Saudárkrókur, Ice.	136	65.41N	19.38W
Saudi Arabia, nation, Asia (sä-ô′dĭ ä-rä′bĭ-á)	174	22.40N	46.00E
Sauerlach, Ger. (zou′ĕr-läk)	139d	47.58N	11.39E
Saugatuck, Mi., U.S. (sô′gá-tŭk)	92	42.40N	86.10W
Saugeen, r., Can.	84	44.20N	81.20W
Saugerties, N.Y., U.S. (sô′gĕr-tēz)	92	42.05N	73.55W
Saugus, Ma., U.S. (sô′gŭs)	87a	42.28N	71.01W
Sauk, r., Mn., U.S. (sôk)	96	45.30N	94.45W
Sauk Centre, Mn., U.S.	96	45.30N	94.57W
Sauk City, Wi., U.S.	96	43.16N	89.45W
Sauk Rapids, Mn., U.S. (răp′ĭd)	96	45.35N	94.08W
Sault Sainte Marie, Can.	78	46.31N	84.20W
Sault Sainte Marie, Mi., U.S. (sōō sänt má-rē′)	90	46.29N	84.21W
Saumatre, Étang, l., Haiti	116	18.40N	72.10W
Saunders Lake, l., Can. (săn′dĕrs)	77g	53.18N	113.25W
Saurimo, Ang.	206	9.39S	20.24E
Sausalito, Ca., U.S. (sô-sá-lē′tô)	100b	37.51N	122.29W
Sausset-les-Pins, Fr. (sō-sĕ′lä-pán′)	150a	43.20N	5.08E
Saútar, Ang.	210	11.06S	18.27E
Sauvie Island, i., Or., U.S. (sô′vē)	100c	45.43N	123.49W
Sava, r., Yugo. (sä′vä)	136	44.50N	18.30E
Savage, Md., U.S. (sä′vĕj)	94e	39.07N	76.49W
Savage, Mn., U.S.	101g	44.47N	93.20W
Savaiʻi, i., W. Sam.	192a	13.35S	172.25W
Savalen, l., Nor.	146	62.19N	10.15E
Savalou, Benin	204	7.56N	1.58E
Savanna, Il., U.S. (sá-văn′á)	96	42.05N	90.09W
Savannah, Ga., U.S. (sá-văn′á)	90	32.04N	81.07W
Savannah, Mo., U.S.	104	39.58N	94.49W
Savannah, Tn., U.S.	108	35.13N	88.14W
Savannah, r., U.S.	90	33.11N	81.51W
Savannakhét, Laos	188	16.33N	104.45E
Savanna la Mar, Jam. (sá-văn′á lä mär′)	116	18.10N	78.10W
Save, r., Fr.	150	43.32N	0.50E
Save, Rio (Sabi), r., Afr. (rē′ō-sä′vĕ)	206	21.28S	34.14E
Sãveh, Iran	176	35.01N	50.20E
Saverne, Fr. (sä-vĕrn′)	150	48.40N	7.22E
Savigliano, Italy (sä-vēl-yä′nô)	154	44.38N	7.42E
Savigny-sur-Orge, Fr.	151b	48.41N	2.22E
Savona, Italy (sä-nō′nä)	142	44.19N	8.28E
Savonlinna, Fin. (sá′vôn-lēn′nä)	146	61.53N	28.49E
Savran', Ukr. (säv-rän′)	156	48.07N	30.09E
Sawahlunto, Indon.	188	0.37S	100.50E
Sawãkin, Sudan	204	19.02N	37.19E
Sawda, Jabal as, mts., Libya	204	28.14N	13.46E
Sawhãj, Egypt	204	26.34N	31.40E
Sawknah, Libya	204	29.04N	15.53E
Sawu, Laut (Savu Sea), sea, Indon.	188	9.15S	122.15E
Sawyer, I., Wa., U.S. (sô′yĕr)	100a	47.20N	122.02W
Say, Niger (sä′ē)	204	13.09N	2.16E
Sayan Khrebet, mts., Russia (sŭ-yän′)	158	51.30N	90.00E
Sayhūt, Yemen	174	15.23N	51.28E
Sayre, Ok., U.S. (sä′ĕr)	104	35.19N	99.40W
Sayre, Pa., U.S.	92	41.55N	76.30W
Sayreton, Al., U.S. (sä′ĕr-tŭn)	94h	33.34N	86.51W
Sayreville, N.J., U.S. (sär′vil)	94a	40.28N	74.21W
Sayr Usa, Mong.	180	44.15N	107.00E
Sayula, Mex. (sä-yōō′lä)	112	17.51N	94.56W
Sayula, Mex.	112	19.50N	103.33W
Sayula, Laguna de, l., Mex. (lä-gô′nä-dĕ)	112	20.00N	103.33W
Sayʻun, Yemen	174	16.00N	48.59E
Sayville, N.Y., U.S. (sä′vil)	92	40.45N	73.10W
Sazanit, i., Alb.	142	40.30N	19.17E
Sázava, r., Czech.	148	49.36N	15.24E
Sazhino, Russia (säz-hē′nô)	164a	56.20N	58.15E
Scala, Teatro alla, bldg., Italy	234c	45.28N	9.11E
Scandinavian Peninsula, pen., Eur.	172	62.00N	14.00E
Scanlon, Mn., U.S. (skän′lŏn)	101h	46.27N	92.26W
Scappoose, Or., U.S. (skä-pōōs′)	100c	45.46N	122.53W
Scappoose, r., Or., U.S.	100c	45.47N	122.57W
Scarborough, Can. (skär′bĕr-ô)	84	43.45N	79.12W
Scarborough, Eng., U.K. (skär′bŭr-ô)	144	54.16N	0.19W
Scarsdale, N.Y., U.S. (skärz′dál)	94a	41.01N	73.47W
Scarth Hill, Eng., U.K.	233a	53.33N	2.52W
Scatari I, Can. (skät′á-rē)	86	46.00N	59.44W
Sceaux, Fr.	233c	48.47N	2.17E
Schaerbeek, Bel. (skär′bäk)	139a	50.50N	4.23E
Schaffhausen, Switz. (shäf′hou-zĕn)	140	47.42N	8.38E
Schalksmühle, Ger.	232	51.14N	7.31E
Schapenrust, S. Afr.	240b	26.16S	28.22E
Scharnhorst, neigh., Ger.	232	51.32N	7.32E
Schaumburg, Il., U.S.	227a	41.58N	87.52W
Schefferville, Can.	78	54.52N	67.01W
Scheibbs, Aus.	148	48.16N	16.13E
Scheiblingstein, Aus.	235e	48.16N	16.13E
Schelde, r., Eur.	144	51.04N	3.55E
Schenectady, N.Y., U.S. (skĕ-nĕk′tá-dĕ)	90	42.50N	73.55W
Scheveningen, Neth.	139a	52.06N	4.15E
Schiedam, Neth.	139a	51.55N	4.23E
Schildow, Ger.	234a	52.38N	13.23E
Schiller Park, Il., U.S.	227a	41.58N	87.52W
Schiltigheim, Fr. (shĕl′tegh-hīm)	150	48.48N	7.47E
Schio, Italy (skē′ô)	154	45.43N	11.23E
Schleswig, Ger. (shĕls′vĕgh)	140	54.32N	9.32E
Schleswig-Holstein, hist. reg., Ger. (shlĕs′vĕgh-hōl′shtīn)	148	54.40N	9.10E
Schmalkalden, Ger. (shmäl′käl-dĕn)	148	50.41N	10.25E
Schneider, In., U.S. (shnīd′ĕr)	95a	41.12N	87.26W
Schofield, Wi., U.S. (skō′fĕld)	96	44.52N	89.37W
Schöller, Ger.	232	51.14N	7.01E
Schönbrunn, Schloss, pt. of i., Aus.	235e	48.11N	16.19E
Schönebeck, Ger. (shū′nĕ-bergh)	148	52.01N	11.44E
Schönebeck, neigh., Ger.	232	51.28N	6.56E
Schönebeck, neigh., Ger.	234a	52.29N	13.21E
Schönefeld, Ger.	234a	52.23N	13.30E
Schöneiche, Ger.	234a	52.28N	13.41E
Schönerlinde, Ger.	234a	52.39N	13.27E
Schönow, Ger.	234a	52.40N	13.32E
Schönwalde, Ger.	234a	52.37N	13.07E
Schoonhoven, Neth.	139a	51.56N	4.51E
Schramberg, Ger. (shräm′bĕrgh)	148	48.14N	8.24E
Schreiber, Can.	84	48.50N	87.10W
Schroon, l., N.Y., U.S. (skrōōn)	92	43.50N	73.50W
Schultzendorf, Ger. (shōōl′tzĕn-dôrf)	139b	52.21N	13.55E
Schumacher, Can.	84	48.30N	81.30W
Schüren, neigh., Ger.	232	51.30N	7.32E
Schuyler, Ne., U.S. (slī′ler)	96	41.28N	97.05W
Schuylkill, r., Pa., U.S. (skōōl′kĭl)	94f	40.10N	75.31W
Schuylkill-Haven, Pa., U.S. (skōōl′kĭl hä-vĕn)	92	40.35N	76.10W
Schwabach, Ger. (shvä′bäk)	148	49.19N	11.02E
Schwäbische Alb, mts., Ger. (shvĕ′bĕ-shĕ älb)	148	48.11N	9.09E
Schwäbisch Gmünd, Ger. (shvĕ′bĕsh gmünd)	148	48.47N	9.49E
Schwäbisch Hall, Ger. (häl)	148	49.08N	9.44E
Schwafheim, Ger.	232	51.25N	6.39E
Schwandorf, Ger. (shvän′dôrf)	148	49.19N	12.08E
Schwanebeck, Ger.	234a	52.37N	13.32E
Schwanenwerder, neigh., Ger.	234a	52.27N	13.10E
Schwaner, Pegunungan, mts., Indon. (sкvän′ĕr)	188	1.05S	112.30E
Schwarzenberg, Ger.	232	51.24N	6.42E
Schwarzwald, for., Ger. (shvärts′väld)	148	47.54N	7.57E
Schwaz, Aus.	148	47.20N	11.45E
Schwechat, Aus. (shvĕ′át)	148	48.09N	16.29E
Schwedt, Ger. (shvĕt)	148	53.04N	14.17E
Schweflinghausen, Ger.	232	51.16N	7.25E
Schweinfurt, Ger. (shvīn′fôrt)	148	50.03N	10.14E
Schwelm, Ger. (shvĕlm)	151c	51.17N	7.18E
Schwenke, Ger.	232	51.11N	7.26E
Schwerin, Ger. (shvĕ-rēn′)	148	53.36N	11.25E
Schwerin, neigh., Ger.	232	51.33N	7.20E
Schweriner See, l., Ger. (shvĕ′rē-nĕr zä)	148	53.40N	11.06E
Schwerte, Ger. (shvĕr′tĕ)	151c	51.26N	7.34E
Schwielowsee, l., Ger. (shvē′lôv zä)	139b	52.20N	12.52E
Schwyz, Switz. (schĕts)	148	47.01N	8.38E
Sciacca, Italy (shĕ-äk′kä)	154	37.30N	13.09E
Science and Industry, Museum of, pt. of i., Il., U.S.	227a	41.47N	87.35W
Scilly, Isles of, is., Eng., U.K. (sĭl′ĕ)	136	49.56N	6.50W
Scioto, r., Oh., U.S. (sī-ō′tō)	90	39.10N	82.55W
Scituate, Ma., U.S. (sĭt′ū-āt)	87a	42.12N	70.45W
Scobey, Mt., U.S. (skō′bē)	98	48.48N	105.29W
Scoggin, Or., U.S. (skō′gĭn)	100c	45.28N	123.14W
Scoresby, Austl.	239b	37.54S	145.14E
Scotch, r., Can. (skōch)	77c	45.21N	74.58W
Scotia, Ca., U.S. (skō′shá)	98	40.29N	124.06W
Scotland, neigh., U.K. (skōt′lánd)	136	57.05N	5.10W
Scotland, S.D., U.S.	96	43.08N	97.43W
Scotland Neck, N.C., U.S. (nĕk)	108	36.06N	77.25W
Scotstown, Can. (skŏts′toun)	92	45.35N	71.15W
Scott, r., Ca., U.S.	98	41.20N	122.55W
Scott, Cape, c., Can. (skŏt)	78	50.47N	128.26W
Scott, Mount, mtn., Or., U.S.	98	42.55N	122.00W
Scott Air Force Base, Il., U.S.	101e	38.33N	89.52W
Scottburgh, S. Afr. (skŏt′bûr-ô)	206	30.18S	30.42E
Scott City, Ks., U.S.	104	38.28N	100.54W
Scottdale, Ga., U.S. (skŏt′dál)	94c	33.47N	84.16W
Scott Islands, is., Ant.	213	67.00S	178.00E
Scottsbluff, Ne., U.S. (skŏts′blŭf)	96	41.52N	103.40W
Scottsboro, Al., U.S. (skŏts′bŭro)	108	34.40N	86.03W
Scottsburg, In., U.S. (skŏts′bûrg)	92	38.40N	85.50W
Scottsdale, Austl. (skŏts′dal)	198	41.25S	147.37E
Scottsville, Ky., U.S. (skŏts′vil)	108	36.45N	86.10W
Scott Township, Pa., U.S.	226b	40.24N	80.06W
Scottville, Mi., U.S.	92	44.00N	86.20W
Scranton, Pa., U.S. (skrăn′tŭn)	90	41.15N	75.45W
Scugog, l., Can. (skē′gŏg)	84	44.05N	78.55W
Scunthorpe, Eng., U.K. (skŭn′thôrp)	138a	53.36N	0.38W
Scutari, Lake, l., Eur. (skōō′tä-rē)	142	42.14N	19.33E
Scutari, see Shkodër, Alb.	136	42.04N	19.30E
Seabeck, Wa., U.S. (sē′bĕck)	100a	47.38N	122.50W
Sea Bright, N.J., U.S. (sē brĭt)	94a	40.22N	73.58W
Seabrook, Md., U.S.	225d	38.58N	76.51W
Seabrook, Tx., U.S. (sē′brŏk)	106	29.34N	95.01W
Sea Cliff, N.Y., U.S.	224	40.51N	73.38W
Seacombe, Eng., U.K.	233a	53.25N	3.01W
Seaford, De., U.S. (sē′fĕrd)	92	38.35N	75.40W
Seaford, N.Y., U.S.	224	40.40N	73.30W
Seaforth, Austl.	239a	33.48S	151.15E
Seaforth, Eng., U.K.	233a	53.28N	3.01W
Seagraves, Tx., U.S. (sē′grāvs)	104	32.51N	102.38W
Sea Islands, is., Ga., U.S. (sē)	108	31.21N	81.05W
Seal, Eng., U.K.	231	51.17N	0.14E
Seal, r., Can.	78	59.08N	96.37W
Seal Beach, Ca., U.S.	101a	33.44N	118.06W
Seal Cays, is., Bah.	116	22.40N	75.55W
Seal Cays, is., T./C. Is.	116	21.10N	71.45W
Seal Island, i., S. Afr. (sēl)	206a	34.07S	18.36E
Seal Rocks, Ca., U.S.	227b	37.47N	122.31W
Sealy, Tx., U.S. (sē′lē)	106	29.46N	96.10W
Searcy, Ar., U.S. (sûr′sē)	104	35.13N	91.43W
Searles, I., Ca., U.S. (sûrl′s)	102	35.44N	117.22W
Searsport, Me., U.S. (sē′rz′pôrt)	86	44.28N	68.55W
Seaside, Or., U.S. (sē′sīd)	98	45.59N	123.55W
Seat Pleasant, Md., U.S.	225d	38.53N	76.52W
Seattle, Wa., U.S. (sē-ăt″l)	98	47.36N	122.20W
Sebaco, Nic. (sē-bä′kô)	114	12.50N	86.03W
Sebago, Me., U.S. (sē-bā′gô)	86	43.52N	70.20W
Sebastián Vizcaíno, Bahía, b., Mex.	110	28.45N	115.15W
Sebastopol, Ca., U.S. (sē-bás′tô-pôl)	102	38.37N	122.50W
Sebderat, Eth.	204	15.30N	36.45E
Sebewaing, Mi., U.S. (sē′bē-wăng)	92	43.45N	83.25W
Sebezh, Russia (syĕ′bĕzh)	156	56.16N	28.29E
Sebinkarahisar, Tur.	142	40.15N	38.10E
Sebnitz, Ger. (zĕb′nĕts)	148	51.01N	14.16E
Sebou, Oued, r., Mor.	204	34.23N	5.18W
Sebree, Ky., U.S. (sē-brē′)	92	37.35N	87.30W
Sebring, Fl., U.S. (sē′brĭng)	109a	27.30N	81.26W

ăt; fĭnăl; rāte; senāte; ärm; ásk; sofá; fâre;   ch-choose;   dh-as th in other;   bē; ĕvent; bĕt; recĕnt; cratĕr;   g-gō; gh-guttural g;   bĭt; ĭ-short neutral; rīde;   к-guttural k as ch in German ich;

PLACE (Pronunciation)	PAGE	Lat. °'	Long. °'
Sebring, Oh., U.S.	92	40.55N	81.05W
Secane, Pa., U.S.	225b	39.55N	75.18W
Secaucus, N.J., U.S.	224	40.47N	74.04W
Secchia, r., Italy (sĕ'kyä)	154	44.25N	10.25E
Seco, r., Mex. (sĕ'kô)	112	18.11N	93.18W
Sedalia, Mo., U.S.	90	38.42N	93.12W
Sedan, Fr. (sē-däN)	140	49.49N	4.55E
Sedan, Ks., U.S. (sē-dăn')	104	37.07N	96.08W
Sedom, Isr.	173a	31.04N	35.24E
Sedro Woolley, Wa., U.S. (sē'drō-wŏŏl'ē)	100a	48.30N	122.14W
Šeduva, Lith. (shĕ'dŏŏ-vå)	146	55.46N	23.45E
Seeberg, Ger.	234a	52.33N	13.41E
Seeburg, Ger.	234a	52.31N	13.07E
Seefeld, Ger.	234a	52.37N	13.40E
Seer Green, Eng., U.K.	231	51.37N	0.36W
Seestall, Ger. (zā'shtäl)	139d	47.58N	10.52E
Sefrou, Mor. (sē-frōō')	142	33.49N	4.46W
Sefton, Eng., U.K.	233a	53.30N	2.58W
Seg, l., Russia (syĕgh)	160	63.20N	33.30E
Segamat, Malay. (sā'gà-màt)	173b	2.30N	102.49E
Segang, China (sŭ-gäŋ)	182	31.59N	114.13E
Segbana, Benin	208	10.56N	3.42E
Segorbe, Spain (sĕ-gôr-bĕ)	152	39.50N	0.30W
Ségou, Mali (sā-gōō')	204	13.27N	6.16W
Segovia, Col. (sĕ-gô'vēä)	124a	7.08N	74.42W
Segovia, Spain (så-gō'vē-ä)	142	40.58N	4.05W
Segre, r., Spain (så'grā)	152	41.54N	1.10E
Seguam, i., Ak., U.S. (sē'gwäm)	89a	52.16N	172.10W
Seguam Passage, strt., Ak., U.S.	89a	52.20N	173.00W
Séguédine, Niger	208	20.12N	12.59E
Séguéla, I.C. (sā-gā-lä')	204	7.57N	6.40W
Seguin, Tx., U.S. (sĕ-gēn')	106	29.35N	97.58W
Segula, i., Ak., U.S. (sē-gū'lå)	89a	52.08N	178.35E
Segura, r., Spain	142	38.24N	2.12W
Segura, Sierra de, mts., Spain (sē-ĕ'r-rä-dĕ)	152	38.05N	2.45W
Sehwān, Pak.	178	26.33N	67.51E
Seibeeshiden, Japan	238a	35.34N	139.22E
Seibo, Dom. Rep. (sĕ'y-bō)	116	18.45N	69.05W
Seiling, Ok., U.S.	104	36.09N	98.56W
Seinäjoki, Fin. (sâ'ē-nĕ-yô'kē)	146	62.47N	22.50E
Seine, r., Can. (sån)	77f	49.48N	97.03W
Seine, r., Can. (sån)	84	49.04N	91.00W
Seine, r., Fr.	136	48.00N	4.30E
Seine, Baie de la, b., Fr. (bī dĕ lä sån)	150	49.37N	0.53W
Seio do Venus, mtn., Braz. (sĕ-yō-dō-vĕ'nōōs)	126b	22.28S	43.12W
Seixal, Port. (så-ē-shäl')	153b	38.38N	9.06W
Sekenke, Tan.	210	4.16S	34.10E
Sekondi-Takoradi, Ghana (sē-kôn'dē tä-kō-rä'dē)	204	4.59N	1.43W
Sekota, Eth.	204	12.47N	38.59E
Selangor, state, Malay. (så-län'gŏr)	173b	2.53N	101.29E
Selanovtsi, Bul. (sĕl'å-nôv-tsĭ)	154	43.42N	24.05E
Selaru, Pulau, i., Indon.	188	8.30S	130.30E
Selatan, Tanjung, c., Indon. (så-lä'tän)	188	4.09S	114.40E
Selawik, Ak., U.S. (sē-lå-wĭk)	89	66.30N	160.09W
Selayar, Pulau, i., Indon.	188	6.15S	121.15E
Selbecke, neigh., Ger.	232	51.20N	7.28E
Selbusjøen, l., Nor. (sĕl'bōō)	146	63.18N	11.55E
Selby, Eng., U.K. (sĕl'bē)	138a	53.47N	1.03W
Selby, neigh., S. Afr.	240b	26.13S	28.02E
Seldovia, Ak., U.S. (sĕl-dō'vē-ȧ)	89	59.26N	151.42W
Selection Park, S. Afr.	240b	26.18S	28.27E
Selemdzha, r., Russia (sâ-lĕmt-zhä')	162	52.28N	131.50E
Selenga (Selenge), r., Asia (sĕ lĕŋ gä')	158	49.00N	102.00E
Selenge, r., Asia	180	49.04N	102.23E
Selennyakh, r., Russia (sĕl-yĭn-yäk)	162	67.42N	141.45E
Sélestat, Fr. (sē-lē-stä')	150	48.16N	7.27E
Seletar, Sing.	236c	1.25N	103.53E
Sélibaby, Maur. (sâ-lē-bå-bē')	204	15.21N	12.11W
Seliger, l., Russia (sĕl'lē-gĕr)	160	57.14N	33.18E
Selizharovo, Russia (så'lē-zhä'rô-vô)	156	56.51N	33.28E
Selkirk, Can. (sĕl'kûrk)	78	50.09N	96.52W
Selkirk Mountains, mts., Can.	78	51.00N	117.40W
Selleck, Wa., U.S. (sĕl'ĕck)	100a	47.22N	121.52W
Sellersburg, In., U.S. (sĕl'ērs-bûrg)	95h	38.25N	85.45W
Sellya Khskaya, Guba, b., Russia (sĕl-yäk'skå-yå)	162	72.30N	136.00E
Selma, Al., U.S. (sĕl'mȧ)	90	32.25N	87.00W
Selma, Ca., U.S.	102	36.34N	119.37W
Selma, N.C., U.S.	108	35.33N	78.16W
Selma, Tx., U.S.	101d	29.33N	98.19W
Selmer, Tn., U.S.	108	35.11N	88.36W
Selsingen, Ger. (zĕl'zēn-gĕn)	139c	53.22N	9.13E
Selway, r., Id., U.S. (sĕl'wå)	98	46.07N	115.12W
Selwyn, l., Can. (sĕl'wĭn)	78	59.41N	104.30W
Seman, r., Alb.	154	40.48N	19.53E
Semarang, Indon. (sĕ-mä'räng)	188	7.03S	110.27E
Sembawang, Sing.	236c	1.27N	103.50E
Semënovka, Ukr. (sĕ-myôn'ôf-kå)	160	52.10N	32.34E
Semeru, Gunung, mtn., Indon.	188	8.06S	112.55E
Semiahmoo Indian Reserve, I.R., Can.	100d	49.01N	122.43W
Semiahmoo Spit, Wa., U.S. (sĕm'ĭ-å-mōō)	100d	48.59N	122.52W
Semichi Islands, is., Ak., U.S. (sē-mē'chī)	89a	52.40N	174.50E
Seminoe Reservoir, res., Wy., U.S. (sĕm'ĭ nō)	98	42.08N	107.10W
Seminole, Ok., U.S. (sĕm'ĭ-nōl)	104	35.13N	96.41W
Seminole, Tx., U.S.	106	32.43N	102.39W
Seminole, Lake, res., U.S.	108	30.57N	84.46W
Semipalatinsk, Kaz. (sĕ'mē-pá-lå-tyēnsk')	158	50.28N	80.29E
Semisopochnoi, i., Ak., U.S. (sĕ-mē-så-pôsh' noi)	89a	51.45N	179.25E
Semiyarskoye, Kaz. (sĕ'mē-yär'skô-yĕ)	158	51.03N	78.28E

PLACE (Pronunciation)	PAGE	Lat. °'	Long. °'
Semliki, r., Afr. (sĕm'lē-kē)	204	0.45N	29.36E
Semmering Pass, p., Aus. (sĕm'ĕr-ĭng)	148	47.39N	15.50E
Senador Pompeu, Braz. (sĕ-nä-dōr-pôm-pĕ'ŏ)	124	5.34S	39.18W
Senatobia, Ms., U.S. (sĕ-nå-tō'bē-ȧ)	108	34.36N	89.56W
Send, Eng., U.K.	231	51.17N	0.31W
Sendai, Japan (sĕn-dī')	180	38.18N	141.02E
Seneca, Ks., U.S. (sĕn'ē-kȧ)	104	39.49N	96.03W
Seneca, Md., U.S.	94e	39.04N	77.20W
Seneca, S.C., U.S.	108	34.40N	82.58W
Seneca, l., N.Y., U.S.	92	42.30N	76.55W
Seneca Falls, N.Y., U.S.	92	42.55N	76.55W
Senegal, nation, Afr. (sĕn-ĕ-gôl')	204	14.53N	14.58W
Sénégal, r., Afr.	204	16.00N	14.00W
Senekal, S. Afr. (sĕn'ĕ-kȧl)	212d	28.20S	27.37E
Senftenberg, Ger. (zĕnf'tĕn-bĕrgh)	148	51.32N	14.00E
Sengunyane, r., Leso.	207c	29.35S	28.08E
Senhor do Bonfim, Braz. (sĕn-yôr dō bôn-fē'N)	124	10.21S	40.09W
Senigallia, Italy (så-nē-gäl'lyä)	154	43.42N	13.16E
Senj, Cro. (sĕn')	154	44.58N	14.55E
Senja, i., Nor. (sĕnyä)	140	69.28N	16.10E
Senlis, Fr. (säN-lēs')	151b	49.13N	2.35E
Sennar Dam, dam, Sudan	204	13.38N	33.38E
Senneterre, Can.	78	48.20N	77.22W
Senno, Bela. (syĕ'nō)	156	54.48N	29.43E
Senriyama, Japan	238b	34.47N	135.30E
Sens, Fr. (säNs)	150	48.05N	3.18E
Sensuntepeque, El Sal. (sĕn-sōōn-tå-pā'kå)	114	13.53N	88.34W
Senta, Yugo. (sĕn'tä)	142	45.54N	20.05E
Sentosa, i., Sing.	236c	1.15N	103.50E
Senzaki, Japan (sĕn'zä-kē)	187	34.22N	131.09E
Seoul (Sŏul), S. Kor.	180	37.35N	127.03E
Sepang, Malay.	173b	2.43N	101.45E
Sepetiba, Baía de, b., Braz. (bäē'ä dĕ sā-pā-tē'bȧ)	126b	23.01S	43.42W
Sepik, r. (sĕp-ĕk')	188	4.07S	142.40E
Septentrional, Cordillera, mts., Dom. Rep.	116	19.50N	71.15W
Septeuil, Fr. (sĕ-tû')	151b	48.53N	1.40E
Sept-Îles, Can. (sĕ-tēl')	86	50.12N	66.23W
Sequatchie, r., Tn., U.S. (sē-kwăch'ē)	108	35.33N	85.14W
Sequim, Wa., U.S. (sē'kwĭm)	100a	48.05N	123.07W
Sequim Bay, b., Wa., U.S.	100a	48.04N	122.58W
Sequoia National Park, rec., Ca., U.S. (sē-kwoi'ȧ)	90	36.34N	118.37W
Seraing, Bel. (sē-răN')	144	50.38N	5.28E
Serāmpore, India	178a	22.44N	88.21E
Serang, Indon. (så-räng')	188	6.13S	106.10E
Seranggung, Indon.	173b	0.49N	104.11E
Serangoon, Sing.	236c	1.22N	103.54E
Serangoon Harbour, b., Sing.	236c	1.23N	103.57E
Serbia, see Srbija, hist. reg., Yugo.	154	44.05N	20.35E
Serdobsk, Russia (sĕr-dôpsk')	160	52.30N	44.20E
Serebr'anyj Bor, neigh., Russia	235b	55.47N	37.25E
Sered', Czech.	148	48.17N	17.43E
Seredina-Buda, Ukr. (sĕ-rå-dē'nå-bōō'dȧ)	156	52.11N	34.03E
Seremban, Malay. (sĕr-ĕm-băn')	173b	2.44N	101.57E
Serengeti National Park, rec., Tan.	210	2.20S	34.50E
Serengeti Plain, pl., Tan.	210	2.40S	34.55E
Serenje, Zam. (sē-rĕn'yē)	206	13.12S	30.49E
Seret, r., Ukr. (sĕr'ĕt)	148	49.45N	25.30E
Sergeya Kirova, i., Russia (sĕr-gyē'yȧ kē'rô-vå)	162	77.30N	86.10E
Sergipe, state, Braz. (sĕr-zhē'pĕ)	124	10.27S	37.04W
Sergiyev Posad, Russia	164b	56.18N	38.08E
Sergiyevsk, Russia	160	53.58N	51.00E
Sérifos, Grc.	154	37.10N	24.32E
Sérifos, i., Grc.	154	37.42N	24.17E
Serodino, Arg. (sĕ-rō-dē'nō)	123c	32.36S	60.56W
Seropédica, Braz. (sĕ-rō-pĕ'dē-kä)	126b	22.44S	43.43W
Serov, Russia (syĕ-rôf')	162	59.36N	60.30E
Serowe, Bots. (sĕ-rō'wĕ)	206	22.18S	26.39E
Serpa, Port. (sĕr-pä)	152	37.56N	7.38W
Serpukhov, Russia (syĕr'pŏŏ-kôf)	158	54.53N	37.27E
Sérrai, Grc. (sĕr'rĕ) (sĕr'ĕs)	142	41.06N	23.36E
Serrinha, Braz. (sĕr-rēn'yȧ)	124	11.43S	38.49W
Serta, Port. (sĕr'tȧ)	152	39.48N	8.01W
Sertânia, Braz. (sĕr-tȧ'nyä)	124	8.28S	37.13W
Sertãozinho, Braz. (sĕr-touN-zê'n-yō)	123a	21.10S	47.58W
Serting, r., Malay.	173b	3.01N	102.32E
Servon, Fr.	233c	48.43N	2.35E
Sese Islands, is., Ug.	210	0.30S	32.30E
Sesia, r., Italy (sâz'yä)	154	45.33N	8.25E
Sesimbra, Port. (sĕ-sē'm-brä)	153b	38.27N	9.06W
Sesmyl, r., S. Afr.	207b	25.51S	28.06E
Sesto San Giovanni, Italy	234c	45.32N	9.14E
Sestri Levante, Italy (sĕs'trē lå-vän'tå)	154	44.15N	9.24E
Sestroretsk, Russia (sĕs-trô-rĕtsk)	160	60.06N	29.58E
Sestroretskiy Razliv, Ozero, l., Russia	164c	60.05N	30.07E
Seta, Japan (sĕ'tä)	187b	34.58N	135.56W
Setagaya, neigh., Japan	238a	35.39N	139.40E
Sète, Fr. (sĕt)	140	43.24N	3.42E
Sete Lagoas, Braz. (sĕ-tĕ lä-gô'äs)	124	19.23S	43.58W
Sete Pontes, Braz.	126b	22.51S	43.05W
Seto, Japan (sĕ'tō)	187	35.11N	137.07E
Seto-Naikai, sea, Japan (sĕ'tō nī'kī)	187	33.50N	132.25E
Seton Hall University, pt. of i., N.Y., U.S.	224	40.45N	74.15W
Settat, Mor. (sĕt-ät') (sĕ-tà')	204	33.02N	7.30W
Sette-Cama, Gabon (sĕ-tĕ-kä-mä')	206	2.29S	9.40E
Settecamini, neigh., Italy	235c	41.56N	12.37E
Settimo Milanese, Italy	234c	45.29N	9.03E

PLACE (Pronunciation)	PAGE	Lat. °'	Long. °'
Settlement Point, c., Bah. (sĕt'l-mĕnt)	116	26.40N	79.00W
Settlers, S. Afr. (sĕt'lērs)	212d	24.57S	28.33E
Settsu, Japan	187b	34.46N	135.33E
Setúbal, Port. (så-tōō'bäl)	142	38.32N	8.54W
Setúbal, Baía de, b., Port.	152	38.27N	9.08W
Seul, Lac, l., Can. (låk sûl)	78	50.20N	92.30W
Sevan, l., Arm. (syĭ-vän')	160	40.10N	45.20E
Sevastopol', Ukr. (syĕ-vås-tô'pôl'')	158	44.34N	33.34E
Seven Hills, Austl.	239a	33.46S	150.57E
Seven Hills, Oh., U.S.	225a	41.22N	81.41W
Seven Kings, neigh., Eng., U.K.	231	51.34N	0.05E
Sevenoaks, Eng., U.K. (sĕ-vĕn-ôks')	138b	51.16N	0.12E
Severka, r., Russia (sâ'vĕr-kå)	164b	55.11N	38.41E
Severn, r., Can. (sĕv'ērn)	78	55.21N	88.42W
Severn, r., U.K.	144	51.50N	2.25W
Severna Park, Md., U.S. (sĕv'ērn-å)	94e	39.04N	76.33W
Severnaya Dvina, r., Russia	158	63.00N	42.40E
Severnaya Zemlya (Northern Land), is., Russia (sĕ-vyĭr-nīŭ zĭ-m'lyä')	158	79.33N	101.15E
Severoural'sk, Russia (sĕ-vyĭ-rŭ-ōō-rälsk')	162	60.08N	59.53E
Sevier, r., Ut., U.S.	90	39.25N	112.20W
Sevier, East Fork, r., Ut., U.S.	102	37.45N	112.10W
Sevier Lake, l., Ut., U.S. (sē-vēr')	102	38.55N	113.10W
Sevilla, Col. (sĕ-vē'l-yä)	124a	4.16N	75.56W
Sevilla, Spain (så-vēl'yä)	136	37.29N	5.58W
Seville, Oh., U.S. (sĕ'vĭl)	95d	41.01N	81.45W
Sevlievo, Bul. (sĕv'lyĕ-vô)	142	43.02N	25.05E
Sevran, Fr.	233c	48.56N	2.32E
Sèvres, Fr.	233c	48.49N	2.12E
Sevsk, Russia (syĕfsk)	156	52.08N	34.28E
Seward, Ak., U.S. (sū'ård)	90a	60.18N	149.28W
Seward, Ne., U.S.	104	40.55N	97.06W
Seward Peninsula, pen., Ak., U.S.	89	65.40N	164.00W
Sewell, Chile (sĕ'ō-ĕl)	126	34.01S	70.18W
Sewickley, Pa., U.S. (sē-wĭk'lē)	95e	40.33N	80.11W
Seybaplaya, Mex. (sä-ē-bä-plä'yä)	112	19.38N	90.40W
Seychelles, nation, Afr. (sā-shĕl')	2	5.20S	55.10E
Seydisfjördur, Ice. (sā'dēs-fyûr-dŏr)	140	65.21N	14.08W
Seyhan, r., Tur.	142	37.28N	35.40E
Seylac, Som.	212a	11.19N	43.20E
Seym, r., Eur. (sĕym)	160	51.23N	33.22E
Seymour, Ciskei (sē'môr)	207c	32.33S	26.48E
Seymour, In., U.S. (sē'mōr)	92	38.55N	85.55W
Seymour, Ia., U.S.	96	40.41N	93.03W
Seymour, Tx., U.S.	104	33.35N	99.16W
Sezela, S. Afr.	207c	30.33S	30.37W
Sezze, Italy (sĕt'så)	154	41.32N	13.00E
Sfax, Tun. (sfäks)	204	34.51N	10.45E
Sfîntu-Gheorghe, Rom.	142	45.53N	25.49E
's-Gravenhage, see The Hague, Neth. ('s krä'vĕn-hä'kĕ) (hāg)	136	52.05N	4.16E
Sha, r., China (shä)	180	33.33N	114.30E
Shaanxi, prov., China (shän-shyē)	180	35.30N	109.10E
Shabeelle (Shebele), r., Afr.	212a	1.38N	43.50E
Shache, China (shä-chŭ)	180	38.15N	77.15E
Shackleton Ice Shelf, ice., Ant. (shăk''l-tŭn)	213	65.00S	100.00E
Shades Creek, r., Al., U.S. (shādz)	94h	33.20N	86.55W
Shades Mountain, mtn., Al., U.S.	94h	33.22N	86.51W
Shagamu, Nig.	208	6.51N	3.39E
Shāhdād, Namakzār-e, l., Iran (nŭ-mŭk-zär')	174	31.00N	58.30E
Shāhdara, neigh., India	236d	28.40N	77.18E
Shāhjahānpur, India (shä-jŭ-hän'pōōr)	174	27.58N	79.58E
Shah Mosque, rel., Iran	237h	35.40N	51.25E
Shajing, China (shä-jyĭŋ)	183a	22.44N	113.48E
Shakarpur Khās, neigh., India	236d	28.38N	77.17E
Shaker Heights, Oh., U.S. (shā'kĕr)	95d	41.28N	81.34W
Shakhty, Russia (shäk'tē)	158	47.41N	40.11E
Shaki, Nig.	208	8.39N	3.25E
Shakopee, Mn., U.S. (shăk'ō-pe)	101g	44.48N	93.31W
Shakūrpur, neigh., India	236d	28.41N	77.09E
Shala Lake, l., Eth. (shä'lå)	204	7.34N	39.00E
Shām, Jabal ash, mtn., Oman	174	23.01N	57.45E
Shambe, Sudan (shäm'bå)	204	7.08N	30.46E
Shammar, Jabal, mts., Sau. Ar. (jĕb'ĕl shŭm'ár)	174	27.13N	40.16E
Shamokin, Pa., U.S. (shȧ-mō'kĭn)	92	40.45N	76.30W
Shamrock, Tx., U.S. (shăm'rŏk)	104	35.14N	100.12W
Shamva, Zimb. (shäm'vȧ)	206	17.18S	31.35E
Shandon, Oh., U.S. (shăn-dŭn)	95f	39.20N	84.13W
Shandong, prov., China (shän-dôŋ)	180	36.08N	117.09E
Shandong Bandao, pen., China (shän-dôŋ bän-dou)	180	37.00N	120.10E
Shangcai, China (shäŋ-tsī)	182	33.16N	114.16E
Shangcheng, China (shäŋ-chŭŋ)	182	31.47N	115.22E
Shangdu, China (shäŋ-dōō)	184	41.38N	113.22E
Shanghai, China (shäng'hī')	180	31.14N	121.27E
Shanghai-Shi, prov., China (shäŋ-hī shr)	180	31.30N	121.45E
Shanghe, China (shäŋ-hŭ)	182	37.18N	117.10E
Shanglin, China (shäŋ-lĭn)	182	38.20N	116.05E
Shangqiu, China (shäŋ-chyō)	184	34.24N	115.39E
Shangrao, China (shäŋ-rou)	184	28.25N	117.58E
Shangzhi, China (shäŋ-jr)	184	45.18N	127.52E
Shanhaiguan, China	184	40.01N	119.45E
Shannon, Al., U.S. (shăn'ŭn)	94h	33.23N	86.52W
Shannon, r., Ire. (shăn'ŏn)	140	52.30N	10.15W
Shanshan, China (shän'shån')	180	42.51N	89.53E
Shantar, i., Russia (shän'tär)	162	55.13N	138.42E
Shantou, China (shän-tō)	180	23.20N	116.40E
Shanxi, prov., China (shän-shyē)	180	37.30N	112.00E
Shan Xian, China (shän shyĕn)	182	34.47N	116.04E
Shaobo, China (shou-bwo)	184	32.33N	119.30E
Shaobo Hu, l., China (shou-bwo hōō)	182	32.47N	119.13E

PLACE (Pronunciation)	PAGE	Lat. °'	Long. °'
Shaoguan, China (shou-gůän)	180	24.58N	113.42E
Shaoxing, China (shou-shyĭŋ)	180	30.00N	120.40E
Shaoyang, China	180	27.15N	111.28E
Shapki, Russia (shäp'kĭ)	164c	59.36N	31.11E
Shark Bay, b., Austl. (shärk)	196	25.30S	113.00E
Sharon, Ma., U.S. (shăr'ŏn)	87a	42.07N	71.11W
Sharon, Pa., U.S.	92	41.15N	80.30W
Sharon Hill, Pa., U.S.	225b	39.55N	75.16W
Sharon Springs, Ks., U.S.	104	38.51N	101.45W
Sharonville, Oh., U.S. (shăr'ŏn vĭl)	95f	39.16N	84.24W
Sharpsburg, Pa., U.S. (shärps'bûrg)	95e	40.30N	79.54W
Sharps Hill, Pa., U.S.	226b	40.30N	79.56W
Sharr, Jabal, mtn., Sau. Ar.	174	28.00N	36.07E
Shashi, China (shä-shē)	180	30.20N	112.18E
Shasta, Mount, mtn., Ca., U.S.	90	41.35N	122.12W
Shasta Lake, res., Ca., U.S. (shăs'tȧ)	90	40.51N	122.32W
Shatsk, Russia (shȧtsk)	160	54.00N	41.40E
Shattuck, Ok., U.S. (shăt'ŭk)	104	36.16N	99.53W
Shaunavon, Can.	78	49.40N	108.25W
Shaw, Eng., U.K.	233b	53.35N	2.06W
Shaw, Ms., U.S. (shô)	108	33.36N	90.44W
Shawano, Wi., U.S. (shȧ-wô'nō)	96	44.41N	88.13W
Shawinigan, Can.	78	46.32N	72.46W
Shawnee, Ks., U.S. (shô-nē')	101f	39.01N	94.43W
Shawnee, Ok., U.S.	90	35.20N	96.54W
Shawneetown, Il., U.S. (shô'nē-toun)	92	37.40N	88.05W
Shayang, China	184	31.00N	112.38E
Shchara, r., Bela. (sh-chä'rȧ)	148	53.17N	25.12E
Shchëlkovo, Russia (shchĕl'kô-vô)	156	55.55N	38.00E
Shchëtovo, Ukr. (shchĕ'tô-vô)	156	48.11N	39.13E
Shchigry, Russia (shchē'grē)	156	51.52N	36.54E
Shchors, Ukr. (shchôrs)	156	51.38N	31.58E
Shchuch'ye Ozero, Russia (shchōōch'yĕ ô'zĕ-rō)	164a	56.31N	56.35E
Sheakhala, India	178a	22.47N	88.10E
Shebele (Shabeelle), r., Afr. (shā'bā-lē)	212a	6.07N	43.10E
Sheboygan, Wi., U.S. (shē-boi'gȧn)	90	43.45N	87.44W
Sheboygan Falls, Wi., U.S.	96	43.43N	87.51W
Shechem, hist., Isr. Occ.	173a	32.15N	35.22E
Shedandoah, Pa., U.S.	92	40.50N	76.15W
Shediac, Can. (shĕ'dē-ăk)	86	46.13N	64.32W
Shedin Peak, mtn., Can. (shĕd'ĭn)	80	55.55N	127.32W
Sheepshead Bay, neigh., N.Y., U.S.	224	40.35N	73.56W
Sheerness, Eng., U.K. (shēr'nĕs)	138b	51.26N	0.46E
Sheffield, Can.	77d	43.20N	80.13W
Sheffield, Eng., U.K.	140	53.23N	1.28W
Sheffield, Al., U.S. (shĕf'fēld)	108	35.42N	87.42W
Sheffield, Oh., U.S.	95d	41.26N	82.05W
Sheffield Lake, Oh., U.S.	95d	41.30N	82.03W
Sheksna, r., Russia (shĕks'nȧ)	160	59.50N	38.40E
Shelagskiy, Mys, c., Russia (shĭ-läg'skē)	158	70.08N	170.52E
Shelbina, Ar., U.S. (shĕl-bī'nȧ)	104	39.41N	92.03W
Shelburn, In., U.S. (shĕl'bŭrn)	92	39.10N	87.30W
Shelburne, Can.	78	43.46N	65.19W
Shelburne, Can.	84	44.04N	80.12W
Shelby, In., U.S. (shĕl'bē)	95a	41.12N	87.21W
Shelby, Mi., U.S.	92	43.35N	86.20W
Shelby, Ms., U.S.	108	33.56N	90.44W
Shelby, Mt., U.S.	98	48.35N	111.55W
Shelby, N.C., U.S.	108	35.16N	81.35W
Shelby, Oh., U.S.	92	40.50N	82.40W
Shelbyville, Il., U.S. (shĕl'bē-vĭl)	92	39.20N	88.45W
Shelbyville, In., U.S.	92	39.30N	85.45W
Shelbyville, Ky., U.S.	92	38.10N	85.15W
Shelbyville, Tn., U.S.	108	35.30N	86.28W
Shelbyville Reservoir, res., Il., U.S.	92	39.30N	88.45W
Sheldon, Ia., U.S. (shĕl'dŭn)	96	43.10N	95.50W
Sheldon, Tx., U.S.	107a	29.52N	95.07W
Shelekhova, Zaliv, b., Russia	158	60.00N	156.00E
Shelikof Strait, strt., Ak., U.S. (shĕ'lē-kôf)	89	57.56N	154.20W
Shellbrook, Can.	82	53.15N	106.22W
Shelley, Id., U.S. (shĕl'lē)	98	43.24N	112.06W
Shellow Bowells, Eng., U.K.	231	51.45N	0.20E
Shellrock, r., Ia., U.S. (shĕl'rŏk)	96	43.25N	93.19W
Shelon', r., Russia (shȧ'lôn)	156	57.50N	29.40E
Shelter, Port, b., H.K.	237c	22.21N	114.17E
Shelton, Ct., U.S. (shĕl'tŭn)	92	41.15N	73.05W
Shelton, Ne., U.S.	104	40.46N	98.41W
Shelton, Wa., U.S.	98	47.14N	123.05W
Shemakha, Azer.	160	40.35N	48.40E
Shemakha, Russia (shĕ-mȧ-kä')	164a	56.16N	59.19E
Shenandoah, Ia., U.S. (shĕn-ăn-dō'ȧ)	104	40.46N	95.23W
Shenandoah, Va., U.S.	92	38.30N	78.30W
Shenandoah, r., Va., U.S.	92	38.55N	78.05W
Shenandoah National Park, rec., Va., U.S.	90	38.35N	78.25W
Shendam, Nig.	208	8.53N	9.32E
Shenfield, Eng., U.K.	231	51.38N	0.19E
Shengfang, China (shengfäng)	182	39.05N	116.40E
Shenkursk, Russia (shĕn-kōōrsk')	158	62.10N	43.08E
Shenmu, China	184	38.55N	110.35E
Shenqiu, China	184	33.11N	115.06E
Shenxian, China (shŭn shyĕn)	182	36.14N	115.38E
Shenxian, China (shŭn shyän)	182	38.02N	115.33E
Shenyang, China (shŭn-yäŋ)	180	41.45N	123.22E
Shenze, China (shŭn-dzŭ)	182	38.12N	115.12E
Sheopur, India	174	25.37N	77.10E
Shepard, Can. (shĕ'pärd)	77e	50.57N	113.55W
Shepetovka, Ukr. (shĕ-pĕ-tôf'kȧ)	160	50.10N	27.01E
Shepparton, Austl. (shĕp'ăr-tŭn)	198	36.15S	145.25E
Shepperton, Eng., U.K.	231	51.24N	0.27W
Sherborn, Ma., U.S. (shûr'bŭrn)	87a	42.15N	71.22W
Sherbrooke, Can.	78	45.24N	71.54W
Sherburn, Eng., U.K. (shûr'bŭrn)	138a	53.47N	1.15W

PLACE (Pronunciation)	PAGE	Lat. °'	Long. °'
Shereshevo, Bela. (shĕ-rĕ-shĕ-vô)	148	52.31N	24.08E
Sheridan, Ar., U.S. (shĕr'ĭ-dȧn)	104	34.19N	92.21W
Sheridan, Or., U.S.	98	45.06N	123.22W
Sheridan, Wy., U.S.	90	44.48N	106.56W
Sherman, Tx., U.S. (shĕr'măn)	90	33.39N	96.37W
Sherman Oaks, neigh., Ca., U.S.	228	34.09N	118.26W
Sherna, r., Russia (shĕr'nȧ)	164b	56.08N	38.45E
Sherridon, Can.	82	55.10N	101.10W
's Hertogenbosch, Neth. (sĕr-tō'ghĕn-bôs)	144	51.41N	5.19E
Sherwood, Or., U.S.	100c	45.21N	122.50W
Sherwood Forest, for., Eng., U.K.	138a	53.11N	1.07W
Sherwood Park, Can.	80	53.31N	113.19W
Shetland Islands, is., Scot., U.K. (shĕt'lănd)	136	60.35N	2.10W
Sheva, India	236e	18.56N	72.57E
Shevchenko, Kaz.	174	43.35N	51.05E
Shewa Gimira, Eth.	204	7.13N	35.49E
Shexian, China (shŭ shyĕn)	182	36.34N	113.42E
Sheyang, r., China (she-yäŋ)	182	33.42N	119.40E
Sheyenne, r., N.D., U.S. (shī-ĕn')	96	46.42N	97.52W
Shi, r., China	182	32.09N	114.11E
Shi, r., China (shr)	182	31.58N	115.50E
Shiawassee, r., Mi., U.S. (shī-ȧ-wôs'ē)	92	43.15N	84.05W
Shibām, Yemen (shē'bäm)	174	16.02N	48.40E
Shibīn al Kawn, Egypt (shē-bēn'ĕl kōm')	212b	30.31N	31.01E
Shibīn al Qanāṭir, Egypt (kȧ-nä'tēr)	212b	30.18N	31.21E
Shibuya, neigh., Japan	238a	35.40N	139.42E
Shicun, China (shr-tsòn)	182	33.47N	117.18E
Shields, r., Mt., U.S. (shēldz)	98	45.54N	110.40W
Shifnal, Eng., U.K. (shĭf'năl)	138a	52.40N	2.22W
Shihlin, Tai.	237d	25.05N	121.31E
Shijian, China (shr-jyĕn)	182	31.27N	117.51E
Shijiazhuang, China (shr-jyä-jůäŋ)	180	38.04N	114.31E
Shijiu Hu, l., China (shr-jyō hōō)	182	31.29N	119.07E
Shijōnawate, Japan	238b	34.45N	135.39E
Shikārpur, Pak.	174	27.51N	68.52E
Shiki, Japan (shē'kē)	187a	35.50N	139.35E
Shikoku, i., Japan (shē'kō'kōō)	180	33.43N	133.33E
Shilibao, China	236b	39.55N	116.29E
Shilka, r., Russia (shĭl'kȧ)	162	53.00N	118.45E
Shilla, mtn., India	178	32.18N	78.17E
Shillong, India (shēl-lông')	174	25.39N	91.58E
Shiloh, Il., U.S. (shī'lō)	101e	38.34N	89.54W
Shilong, China (shr-lòŋ)	184	23.05N	113.58E
Shilou, China	183a	22.58N	113.29E
Shimabara, Japan (shē'mä-bä'rä)	187	32.46N	130.22E
Shimada, Japan (shē'mä-dä)	187	34.49N	138.13E
Shimber Berris, mtn., Som.	212a	10.40N	47.23E
Shimizu, Japan (shē'mē-zōō)	186	35.00N	138.29E
Shimminato, Japan (shēm'mē'nä-tô)	187	36.47N	137.05E
Shimoda, Japan (shē'mô-dȧ)	187	34.41N	138.58E
Shimoga, India	178	13.59N	75.38E
Shimohōya, Japan	238a	35.45N	139.34E
Shimoigusa, neigh., Japan	238a	35.43N	139.37E
Shimomizo, Japan	238a	35.31N	139.23E
Shimoni, Kenya	210	4.39S	39.23E
Shimonoseki, Japan	180	33.58N	130.55E
Shimo-Saga, Japan (shē'mô sä'gä)	187b	35.01N	135.41E
Shimo-shakujii, neigh., Japan	238a	35.45N	139.37E
Shimotsuruma, Japan	238a	35.29N	139.28E
Shimoyugi, Japan	238a	35.38N	139.23E
Shin, Loch, l., Scot., U.K. (lŏĸ shĭn)	144	58.08N	4.02W
Shinagawa-Wan, b., Japan (shē'nä-gä'wä wän)	187a	35.37N	139.49E
Shinano-Gawa, r., Japan (shē-nä'nô gä'wä)	187	36.43N	138.22E
Shīndand, Afg.	176	33.18N	62.08E
Shinji, l., Japan (shĭn'jē)	187	35.23N	133.05E
Shinjuku, neigh., Japan	238a	35.41N	139.42E
Shinkolobwe, Zaire	210	11.02S	26.35E
Shinyanga, Tan. (shĭn-yäŋ'gä)	206	3.40S	33.26E
Shiono Misaki, c., Japan (shē-ô'nô mē'sä-kē)	186	33.20N	136.10E
Shipai, China (shr-pī)	183a	23.07N	113.23E
Ship Channel Cay, i., Bah. (shĭp chă-nĕl kē)	116	24.50N	76.50W
Shipley, Eng., U.K. (shĭp'lē)	138a	53.50N	1.47W
Shippegan, Can. (shĭ'pē-găn)	86	47.45N	64.42W
Shippegan Island, i., Can.	86	47.50N	64.38W
Shippenburg, Pa., U.S. (shĭp'ĕn bûrg)	92	40.00N	77.30W
Shipshaw, r., Can. (shĭp'shô)	84	48.50N	71.03W
Shiqma, r., Isr.	173a	31.31N	34.40E
Shirane-san, mtn., Japan (shē'rä'nȧ-sän')	187	35.44N	138.14E
Shirati, Tan. (shē-rä'tē)	206	1.15S	34.02E
Shīrāz, Iran (shē-räz')	174	29.32N	52.27E
Shire, r., Afr. (shē'rȧ)	206	15.00S	35.00E
Shiriya Saki, c., Japan (shē'rē-yä sä'kē)	186	41.25N	142.10E
Shirley, Ma., U.S. (shûr'lē)	87a	42.33N	71.39W
Shirokoye, Ukr. (shē'rô-kô-yĕ)	156	47.40N	33.18E
Shishaldin Volcano, vol., Ak., U.S. (shī-shăl'dĭn)	89a	54.48N	164.00W
Shively, Ky., U.S. (shīv'lē)	95h	38.11N	85.47W
Shivpuri, India	174	25.31N	77.46E
Shivta, Horvot, hist., Isr.	173a	30.54N	34.36E
Shivwits Plateau, plat., Az., U.S.	102	36.13N	113.42W
Shiwan, China (shr-wän)	183a	23.01N	113.04E
Shiwan Dashan, mts., China (shr-wän dä-shän)	184	22.10N	107.30E
Shizuki, Japan (shĭ'zōō-kē)	187	34.29N	134.51E
Shizuoka, Japan (shē'zōō'ôkä)	186	34.58N	138.24E
Shklov, Bela. (shklôf)	156	54.11N	30.23E
Shkodër, Alb. (shkô'dûr) (skōō'tárē)	136	42.04N	19.30E
Shkotovo, Russia (shkô'tô-vô)	186	43.15N	132.21E
Shoal Creek, r., Il., U.S. (shōl)	104	38.37N	89.25W

PLACE (Pronunciation)	PAGE	Lat. °'	Long. °'
Shoal Lake, l., Can.	82	49.32N	95.00W
Shoals, In., U.S. (shōlz)	92	38.40N	86.45W
Shōdai, Japan	238b	34.51N	135.42E
Shōdo, i., Japan (shō'dō)	187	34.27N	134.27E
Shogunle, Nig.	240d	6.35N	3.21E
Sholāpur, India (shō'lä-pōōr)	174	17.42N	75.51E
Shomolu, Nig.	240d	6.32N	3.23E
Shoreham, Eng., U.K.	231	51.20N	0.11E
Shorewood, Wi., U.S. (shōr'wŏŏd)	95a	43.05N	87.54W
Shoshone, Id., U.S. (shō-shōn'tē)	98	42.56N	114.24W
Shoshone, r., Wy., U.S.	98	44.35N	108.50W
Shoshone Lake, l., Wy., U.S.	98	44.17N	110.50W
Shoshoni, Wy., U.S.	98	43.14N	108.05W
Shostka, Ukr. (shôst'kȧ)	156	51.51N	33.31E
Shouguang, China (shō-gůäŋ)	182	36.53N	118.45E
Shouxian, China (shō shyĕn)	182	32.36N	116.45E
Shpola, Ukr. (shpô'lȧ)	160	49.01N	31.36E
Shreveport, La., U.S. (shrēv'pōrt)	90	32.30N	93.46W
Shrewsbury, Eng., U.K. (shrōōz'bēr-ĭ)	144	52.43N	2.44W
Shrewsbury, Ma., U.S.	87a	42.18N	71.43W
Shroud Cay, i., Bah.	116	24.20N	76.40W
Shuangcheng, China (shůäŋ-chŭŋ)	184	45.18N	126.18E
Shuanghe, China (shůäŋ-hŭ)	182	31.33N	116.48E
Shuangliao, China	180	43.37N	123.30E
Shuangyang, China	184	43.28N	125.45E
Shubrā al-Khaymah, Egypt	240a	30.06N	31.15E
Shuhedun, China (shōō-hŭ-dòn)	182	31.33N	117.01E
Shuiye, China (shwā-yŭ)	182	36.08N	114.07E
Shule, r., China (shōō-lŭ)	180	40.53N	94.55E
Shullsburg, Wi., U.S. (shŭlz'bûrg)	96	42.35N	90.16W
Shumagin, is., Ak., U.S. (shōō'mȧ-gĕn)	89	55.22N	159.20W
Shumen, Bul.	142	43.15N	26.54E
Shunde, China (shòn-dŭ)	183a	22.50N	113.15E
Shungnak, Ak., U.S. (shŭng'nȧk)	89	66.55N	157.20W
Shunut, Gora, mtn., Russia (gȧ-rä shōō'nôt)	164a	56.33N	59.45E
Shunyi, China (shòn-yē)	182	40.09N	116.38E
Shuqrah, Yemen	174	13.32N	46.02E
Shūrāb, r., Iran (shōō räb)	174	31.08N	55.30E
Shuri, Japan (shōō'rē)	186	26.10N	127.48E
Shurugwi, Zimb.	206	19.34S	30.03E
Shūshtar, Iran (shōōsh'tŭr)	174	31.50N	48.46E
Shuswap Lake, l., Can. (shōōs'wŏp)	80	50.57N	119.15W
Shuya, Russia (shōō'yȧ)	158	56.52N	41.23E
Shuyang, China (shōō yäng)	182	34.09N	118.47E
Shweba, Burma	174	22.23N	96.13E
Siak Kecil, r., Indon.	173b	1.01N	101.45E
Siaksriinderapura, Indon. (sē-äks'rĭ ĕn'drȧ-pōō'rä)	173b	0.48N	102.05E
Siālkot, Pak. (sē-äl'kōt)	174	32.39N	74.30E
Siátista, Grc. (syä'tĭs-ta)	154	40.15N	21.32E
Siau, Pulau, i., Indon.	188	2.40N	126.00E
Šiauliai, Lith. (shē-ou'lē-ī)	160	55.57N	23.19E
Sibay, Russia (sē'bȧy)	164a	52.41N	58.40E
Šibenik, Cro. (shē-bā'nĕk)	142	43.44N	15.55E
Siberia, reg., Russia	172	57.00N	97.00E
Siberut, Pulau, i., Indon. (sē'bȧ-rōōt)	188	1.22S	99.45E
Sibiti, Congo (sē-bē-tē')	206	3.41S	13.21E
Sibiu, Rom. (sē-bĭ-ōō')	142	45.47N	24.09E
Sibley, Ia., U.S. (sĭb'lē)	96	43.24N	95.33W
Sibolga, Indon. (sē-bō'gä)	188	1.45N	98.45E
Sibpur, India	236a	22.34N	88.19E
Sibsāgar, India (sēb-sŭ'gŭr)	174	26.47N	94.45E
Sibutu Island, i., Phil.	188	4.40N	119.30E
Sibuyan, i., Phil. (sē-bōō-yän')	189a	12.19N	122.25E
Sibuyan Sea, sea, Phil.	188	12.43N	122.38E
Sichuan, prov., China (sz-chůän)	180	31.20N	103.00E
Sicily, i., Italy (sĭs'ĭ-lē)	136	37.38N	13.30E
Sico, r., Hond. (sē-kō)	114	15.32N	85.42W
Sidamo, hist. reg., Eth. (sē-dä'mō)	204	5.08N	37.45E
Sidao, China	236b	39.51N	116.26E
Sidcup, neigh., Eng., U.K.	231	51.25N	0.06E
Siderno Marina, Italy (sē-dĕr'nô mä-rē'nä)	154	38.18N	16.19E
Sídheros, Ákra, c., Grc.	154a	35.19N	26.20E
Sidhirókastron, Grc.	154	41.13N	23.27E
Sidi Aïssa, Alg.	152	35.53N	3.44E
Sidi bel Abbès, Alg. (sē'dē-bĕl ȧ-bĕs')	204	35.15N	0.43W
Sidi Ifni, Mor. (ēf'nē)	204	29.22N	10.15W
Sidley, Mount, mtn., Ant. (sĭd'lē)	213	77.25S	129.00W
Sidney, Can.	80	48.39N	123.24W
Sidney, Mt., U.S. (sĭd'nē)	98	47.43N	104.07W
Sidney, Ne., U.S.	96	41.10N	103.00W
Sidney, Oh., U.S.	92	40.20N	84.10W
Sidney Lanier, Lake, res., Ga., U.S. (lăn'yēr)	90	34.27N	83.56W
Sido, Mali	208	11.40N	7.36W
Sidon, *see* Saydā, Leb.	174	33.34N	35.23E
Sidr, Wādī, r., Egypt	173a	29.43N	32.58E
Sidra, Gulf of, *see* Surt, Khalīj, b., Libya	204	31.30N	18.28E
Siedlce, Pol. (syĕd''l-tsĕ)	148	52.09N	22.20E
Siegburg, Ger. (zēg'bōōrgh)	148	50.48N	7.13E
Siegen, Ger. (zē'ghĕn)	148	50.52N	8.01E
Sieghartskirchen, Aus.	139e	48.16N	16.00E
Siemensstadt, neigh., Ger.	234a	52.32N	13.17E
Siemiatycze, Pol. (syĕm'yä'tē-chĕ)	148	52.26N	22.52E
Siemionówka, Pol. (sĕĕ-mēō'nôf-kä)	148	52.53N	23.50E
Siem Reap, Kam. (syĕm'rä'äp)	188	13.32N	103.54E
Siena, Italy (sē-ĕn'ä)	142	43.19N	11.21E
Sieradz, Pol. (syĕ'rädz)	148	51.35N	18.45E
Sierpc, Pol. (syĕrpts)	148	52.51N	19.42E
Sierra Blanca, Tx., U.S. (sē-ĕ'rȧ blaŋ-kä)	106	31.10N	105.20W
Sierra Blanca Peak, mtn., N.M., U.S. (blăn'kȧ)	90	33.25N	105.50W

PLACE (Pronunciation)	PAGE	Lat. °′	Long. °′
Sierra Leone, nation, Afr. (sê-ĕr'rä lå-ō'nå)	204	8.48N	12.30W
Sierra Madre, Ca., U.S. (mă'drê)	101a	34.10N	118.03W
Sierra Mojada, Mex. (sē-ĕ'r-rä-mô-кä'dä)	106	27.22N	103.42W
Sífnos, i., Grc.	154	36.58N	24.30E
Sigean, Fr. (sē-zhōN')	150	43.02N	2.56E
Sigeurney, Ia., U.S. (sē-gûr-nĭ)	96	41.16N	92.10W
Sighetu Marmatiei, Rom.	148	47.57N	23.55E
Sighişoara, Rom. (sē-gē-shwä'rå)	148	46.11N	24.48E
Siglufjördur, Ice.	140	66.06N	18.45W
Signakhi, Geor.	160	41.45N	45.50E
Signal Hill, Ca., U.S. (sĭg'năl hĭl)	101a	33.48N	118.11W
Sigsig, Ec. (sēg-sēg')	124	3.04S	78.44W
Sigtuna, Swe. (sēgh-tōō'nå)	146	59.40N	17.39E
Siguanea, Ensenada de la, b., Cuba	116	21.45N	83.15W
Siguatepeque, Hond. (sē-gwå'tĕ-pĕ-kĕ)	114	14.33N	87.51W
Sigüenza, Spain (sē-gwĕ'n-zä)	142	41.03N	2.38W
Siguiri, Gui. (sê-gê-rē')	204	11.25N	9.10W
Sihong, China (sz-hôŋ)	182	33.25N	118.13E
Siirt, Tur. (sĭ-ērt')	160	38.00N	42.00E
Sikalongo, Zam.	210	16.46S	27.07E
Sikasso, Mali (sê-käs'sō)	204	11.19N	5.40W
Sikeston, Mo., U.S. (sīks'tŭn)	104	36.50N	89.35W
Sikhote Alin', Khrebet, mts., Russia (se-кô'ta a-lēn')	158	45.00N	135.45E
Síkinos, i., Grc. (sĭ'kĭ-nōs)	154	36.45N	24.55E
Sikkim, state, India	174	27.42N	88.25E
Siklós, Hung. (sĭ'klōsh)	148	45.51N	18.18E
Sil, r., Spain (sēl)	152	42.20N	7.13W
Silāmpur, neigh., India	236d	28.40N	77.16E
Silang, Phil. (sê-läng')	189a	14.14N	120.58E
Silao, Mex. (sê-lä'ō)	112	20.56N	101.25W
Silchar, India (sĭl-chär')	174	24.52N	92.50E
Silent Valley, S. Afr. (sī'lĕnt vă'lē)	212d	24.32S	26.40E
Siler City, N.C., U.S. (sī'lēr)	108	35.45N	79.29W
Silesia, hist. reg., Pol. (sĭ-lē'shå)	148	50.58N	16.53E
Silifke, Tur.	142	36.20N	34.00E
Siling Co, l., China	180	32.05N	89.10E
Silistra, Bul. (sê-lēs'trå)	142	44.01N	27.13E
Siljan, l., Swe. (sēl'yän)	140	60.48N	14.28E
Silkeborg, Den. (sĭl'kĕ-bôr')	146	56.10N	9.33E
Sillery, Can. (sēl'-re')	77b	46.46N	71.15W
Siloam Springs, Ar., U.S. (sī-lōm)	104	36.10N	94.32W
Siloana Plains, pl., Zam.	210	16.55S	23.10E
Silocayoápan, Mex. (sē-lô-kä-yô-ä'pän)	112	17.29N	98.09W
Silsbee, Tx., U.S. (sĭlz' bê)	106	30.19N	94.09W
Silschede, Ger.	232	51.21N	7.19E
Šilutė, Lith.	146	55.21N	21.29E
Silva Jardim, Braz. (sê'l-vä-zhär-dēN)	123a	22.40N	42.24W
Silvana, Wa., U.S. (sĭ-văn'ă)	100a	48.12N	122.16W
Silvânia, Braz. (sēl-vá'nyä)	124	16.43S	48.33W
Silvassa, India	178	20.10N	73.00E
Silver, l., Mo., U.S.	104	39.38N	93.12W
Silverado, Ca., U.S. (sĭl-vĕr-ä'dō)	101a	33.45N	117.40W
Silver Bank, bk.	116	20.40N	69.40W
Silver Bank Passage, strt., N.A.	116	20.40N	70.20W
Silver Bay, Mn., U.S.	96	47.24N	91.07W
Silver City, Pan.	114	9.20N	79.54W
Silver City, N.M., U.S. (sĭl'vĕr sĭ'tĭ)	102	32.45N	108.20W
Silver Creek, N.Y., U.S. (crēk)	92	42.35N	79.10W
Silver Creek, r., Az., U.S.	102	34.30N	110.05W
Silver Creek, r., In., U.S.	95h	38.20N	85.45W
Silver Creek, Muddy Fork, r., In., U.S.	95h	38.26N	85.52W
Silverdale, Wa., U.S. (sĭl'vĕr-dāl)	100a	49.39N	122.42W
Silver Hill, Md., U.S.	225d	38.51N	76.57W
Silver Lake, Ma., U.S.	223a	42.00N	70.48W
Silver Lake, Wi., U.S. (lāk)	95a	42.33N	88.10W
Silver Lake, l., Wi., U.S.	95a	42.35N	88.08W
Silver Spring, Md., U.S. (sprĭng)	94e	39.00N	77.00W
Silver Star Mountain, mtn., Wa., U.S.	100c	45.45N	122.15W
Silverthrone Mountain, mtn., Can. (sĭl'vĕr-thrōn)	80	51.31N	126.06W
Silverton, S. Afr.	212d	25.45S	28.13E
Silverton, Co., U.S. (sĭl'vĕr-tŭn)	102	37.50N	107.40W
Silverton, Oh., U.S.	95f	39.12N	84.24W
Silverton, Or., U.S.	98	45.02N	122.46W
Silves, Port. (sēl'vĕzh)	142	37.15N	8.24W
Silvies, r., Or., U.S. (sĭl'vēz)	98	43.44N	119.15W
Sim, Russia (sĭm)	164a	55.00N	57.42E
Sim, r., Russia	164a	54.50N	56.50E
Simao, China (sz-mou)	180	22.56N	101.07E
Simard, Lac, l., Can.	84	47.38N	78.40W
Simba, Zaire	210	0.36N	22.55E
Simcoe, Can. (sĭm'kō)	144	42.50N	80.20W
Simcoe, l., Can.	78	44.30N	79.20W
Simeulue, Pulau, i., Indon.	188	2.27N	95.30E
Simferopol', Ukr.	158	44.58N	34.04E
Simi, i., Grc.	142	36.27N	27.41E
Similk Beach, Wa., U.S. (sē'mĭlk)	100a	48.27N	122.35W
Simla, India (sĭm'lå)	174	31.09N	77.15E
Simla, neigh., India	236a	22.35N	88.22E
Simleul-Silvaniei, Rom. (shē-mlā'ōōl-sēl-vä'nyē-ē)	142	47.14N	22.46E
Simms Point, c., Bah.	116	25.00N	77.40W
Simojovel, Mex. (sê-mō-hô-vĕl')	112	17.12N	92.43W
Simonésia, Braz. (sē-mô-nĕ'syä)	123a	20.04S	41.53W
Simonette, r., Can. (sī-mŏn-ĕt')	80	54.15N	118.00W
Simonstad, S. Afr.	206a	34.11S	18.25E
Simood Sound, Can.	80	50.45N	126.25W
Simplon Pass, p., Switz. (sĭm'plŏn) (săN-plōN')	148	46.13N	7.53E
Simpson, i., Can.	96	48.43N	87.44W
Simpson Desert, des., Austl. (sĭmp-sŭn)	196	24.40S	136.40E
Simrishamn, Swe. (sēm'rês-häm'n)	146	55.35N	14.19E
Sims Bayou, Tx., U.S. (sĭmz bī-yōō')	107a	29.37N	95.23W
Simushir, i., Russia (se-mōō'shēr)	180	47.15N	150.47E
Sinaia, Rom. (sĭ-nä'yå)	154	45.20N	25.30E
Sinai Peninsula, pen., Egypt (sī'nī)	204	29.24N	33.29E
Sinaloa, state, Mex. (sē-nä-lô-ä)	110	25.15N	107.45W
Sinan, China (sz-nän)	180	27.50N	108.30E
Sinanju, N. Kor. (sĭ'nän-jŏ')	186	39.39N	125.41E
Sincelejo, Col. (sēn-så-lā'hō)	124	9.12N	75.30W
Sinclair Inlet, Wa., U.S. (sĭn-klâr')	100a	47.31N	122.41W
Sinclair Mills, Can.	80	54.02N	121.41W
Sindi, Est. (sēn'dê)	146	58.20N	24.40E
Sinel'nikovo, Ukr. (sē'nye-brl-nė'kô'vô)	160	48.19N	35.33E
Sines, Port. (sē'nåzh)	152	37.57N	8.50W
Singapore, Sing. (sĭn'gå-pōr')	188	1.18N	103.52E
Singapore, nation, Asia	188	1.22N	103.45E
Singapore Strait, strt., Asia	173b	1.14N	104.20E
Singlewell or Ifield, Eng., U.K.	231	51.25N	0.23E
Singu, Burma (sĭn'gŭ)	180	22.37N	96.04E
Siniye Lipyagi, Russia (sēn'ê lēp'yä-gê)	156	51.24N	38.29E
Sinj, Cro. (sēn')	154	43.42N	16.39E
Sinjah, Sudan	204	13.09N	33.52E
Sinkāt, Sudan	176	18.50N	36.50E
Sinkiang, see Xinjiang Uygur, , China	180	40.15N	82.15E
Sin'kovo, Russia (sĭn-kô'vô)	164b	56.23N	37.19E
Sinnamary, Fr. Gu.	124	5.15N	52.52W
Sinni, r., Italy (sēn'nē)	154	40.05N	16.15E
Sinnūris, Egypt	212b	29.25N	30.52E
Sino, Pedra de, mtn., Braz. (pĕ'drä-dô-sê'nô)	126b	22.27S	43.02W
Sinop, Tur.	174	42.00N	35.05E
Sint Eustatius, i., Neth. Ant.	115b	17.32N	62.45W
Sint Niklaas, Bel.	139a	51.10N	4.07E
Sinton, Tx., U.S. (sĭn'tŭn)	106	28.03N	97.30W
Sintra, Port. (sēn'trå)	152	38.48N	9.23W
Sint Truiden, Bel.	139a	50.49N	5.14E
Sinŭiju, N. Kor. (sĭ'noĭ-jōō)	180	40.04N	124.33E
Sinyavino, Russia (sĭn-yä'vĭ-nô)	164c	59.50N	31.07E
Sinyaya, r., Eur. (sēn'yá-yá)	156	56.40N	28.20E
Sinyukha, r., Ukr. (sē'nyô-кȧ)	156	48.34N	30.49E
Sion, Switz. (sē'ôN')	148	46.15N	7.17E
Sioux City, Ia., U.S. (sōō sĭ'tĭ)	90	42.30N	96.25W
Sioux Falls, S.D., U.S. (fôlz)	90	43.33N	96.43W
Sioux Lookout, Can.	78	50.06N	91.55W
Siping, China (sz-pĭŋ)	180	43.05N	124.24E
Sipiwesk, Can.	78	55.27N	97.24W
Sipsey, r., Al., U.S. (sĭp'sê)	108	33.26N	87.42W
Sipura, Pulau, i., Indon.	188	2.15S	99.33E
Siqueros, Mex. (sê-kā'rōs)	112	23.19N	106.14W
Siquia, Río, r., Nic. (sê-kē'ä)	114	12.23N	84.36W
Siracusa, Italy (sē-rä-koo'sä)	142	37.02N	15.19E
Sirājganj, Bngl. (sĭ-räj'gŭnj)	174	24.23N	89.43E
Sirama, El Sal. (Sē-rä-mä)	114	13.23N	87.55W
Sir Douglas, Mount, mtn., Can. (sûr dŭg'lăs)	80	50.44N	115.20W
Sir Edward Pellew Group, is., Austl. (pĕl'ū)	196	15.15S	137.15E
Siret, Rom.	148	47.58N	26.01E
Siret, r., Rom.	142	47.00N	27.00E
Sirhān, Wadi, depr., Sau. Ar.	174	31.02N	37.16E
Síros, i., Grc.	142	37.23N	24.55E
Sirsa, India	178	29.39N	75.02E
Sir Sandford, Mount, mtn., Can. (sûr sănd'fērd)	80	51.40N	117.52W
Sirvintos, Lith. (shēr'vĭn-tôs)	146	55.02N	24.59E
Sir Wilfrid Laurier, Mount, mtn., Can. (sûr wĭl'frĭd lôr'yēr)	80	52.47N	119.45W
Sisak, Cro. (sê'såk)	142	45.29N	16.20E
Sisal, Mex. (sê-säl')	110	21.09N	90.03W
Sishui, China (sz-shwā)	182	35.40N	117.17E
Sisquoc, r., Ca., U.S. (sĭs'kwŏk)	102	34.47N	120.13W
Sisseton, S.D., U.S. (sĭs'tŭn)	96	45.39N	97.04W
Sistān, Daryacheh-ye, l., Asia	174	31.45N	61.15E
Sisteron, Fr. (sēst'rôN')	150	44.10N	5.55E
Sisterville, W.V., U.S. (sĭs'tēr-vĭl)	92	39.30N	81.00W
Sitía, Grc. (sē'tĭ-å)	154a	35.09N	26.10E
Sitka, Ak., U.S. (sĭt'kȧ)	90a	57.08N	135.18W
Sittingbourne, Eng., U.K. (sĭt-ĭng-bôrn)	138b	51.20N	0.44E
Sittwe, Burma	174	20.09N	92.54E
Sivas, Tur. (sē'väs)	174	39.50N	36.50E
Sivash, l., Ukr. (sē'våsh)	156	45.55N	34.42E
Siverek, Tur. (sē'vĕ-rĕk)	174	37.50N	39.20E
Siverskaya, Russia (sē'vĕr-skå-yå)	146	59.17N	30.03E
Sīwah, Egypt	176	29.12N	25.31E
Siwah, oasis, Egypt (sē'wä)	204	29.33N	25.11E
Sixaola, r., C.R.	114	9.31N	83.07W
Sixian, China (sz shyĕn)	182	33.37N	117.51E
Sixth Cataract, wtfl., Sudan	204	16.26N	32.44E
Siyang, China (sz-yäŋ)	182	33.43N	118.42E
Sjaelland, i., Den. (shĕl'lán')	146	55.34N	11.35E
Sjenica, Yugo. (syĕ'nē-tså)	154	43.15N	20.02E
Skadovsk, Ukr. (skä'dôfsk)	156	46.08N	32.54E
Skagen, Den. (skä'ghĕn)	146	57.43N	10.32E
Skagerrak, strt., Eur. (skä-ghĕ-räk')	136	57.43N	8.28E
Skagit, r., Wa., U.S.	98	48.29N	121.52W
Skagit Bay, b., Wa., U.S. (skăg'ĭt)	100a	48.20N	122.32W
Skagway, Ak., U.S. (skăg-wā)	90a	59.30N	135.28W
Skälderviken, b., Swe.	146	56.20N	12.25E
Skalistyy, Golets, mtn., Russia	158	57.28N	119.48E
Skamania, Wa., U.S. (skȧ-mā'nĭ-ȧ)	100c	45.37N	112.03W
Skamokawa, Wa., U.S.	100c	46.16N	123.27W
Skanderborg, Den. (skän-ĕr-bôr')	146	56.04N	9.55E
Skaneateles, N.Y., U.S. (skăn-ĕ-ăt'lĕs)	92	42.55N	76.25W
Skaneateles, l., N.Y., U.S.	92	42.50N	76.20W
Skänninge, Swe. (shĕn'ĭng-ĕ)	146	58.24N	15.02E
Skanör-Falsterbo, Swe. (skän'ûr)	146	55.24N	12.49E
Skara, Swe. (skä'rå)	146	58.25N	13.24E
Skeena, r., Can. (skē'nä)	78	54.30N	129.00W
Skeena Mountains, mts., Can.	80	56.00N	128.00W
Skeerpoort, S. Afr.	207b	25.49S	27.45E
Skeerpoort, r., S. Afr.	207b	25.58S	27.41E
Skeldon, Guy. (skĕl'dŭn)	124	5.49N	57.15W
Skellefteå, Swe. (shĕl'ĕf-tē-a')	140	64.47N	20.48E
Skellefteälven, r., Swe.	140	65.15N	19.30E
Skelmersdale, Eng., U.K.	233a	53.33N	2.48W
Skhodnya, Russia (skôd'nyȧ)	164b	55.57N	37.21E
Skhodnya, r., Russia	164b	55.55N	37.16E
Skíathos, i., Grc. (skē'á-thôs)	154	39.15N	23.25E
Skibbereen, Ire. (skĭb'ēr-ēn)	144	51.32N	9.25W
Skidegate, b., Can. (skĭ'-dē-gāt')	80	53.15N	132.00W
Skidmore, Tx., U.S. (skĭd'môr)	106	28.16N	97.40W
Skien, Nor. (skē'ĕn)	140	59.13N	9.35E
Skierniewice, Pol. (skyĕr-nyē-vēt'sĕ)	148	51.58N	20.13E
Skihist Mountain, mtn., Can.	80	50.11N	121.54W
Skikda, Alg.	204	36.58N	6.51E
Skilpadfontein, S. Afr.	212d	25.02S	28.50E
Skíros, Grc.	154	38.53N	24.32E
Skiros, i., Grc.	142	38.50N	24.43E
Skive, Den. (skē'vĕ)	146	56.34N	8.56E
Skjálfandafljót, r., Ice. (skyäl'fänd-ô)	140	65.24N	16.40W
Skjerstad, Nor. (skyĕr-städ)	140	67.12N	15.37E
Škofja Loka, Slo. (shkôf'yá lō'ká)	154	46.10N	14.20E
Skokie, Il., U.S. (skō'kê)	95a	42.02N	87.45W
Skokomish Indian Reservation, I.R., Wa., U.S. (Skŏ-kō'mĭsh)	100a	47.22N	123.07W
Skole, Ukr. (skô'lĕ)	148	49.03N	23.32E
Skópelos, i., Grc. (skô'pä-lôs)	154	39.04N	23.31E
Skopin, Russia (skô'pĕn)	160	53.49N	39.35E
Skopje, Mac. (skôp'yĕ)	136	42.02N	21.26E
Skövde, Swe. (shûv'dĕ)	140	58.25N	13.48E
Skovorodino, Russia (skô'vô-rô'dĭ-nô)	158	53.53N	123.56E
Skowhegan, Me., U.S. (skou-hē'găn)	86	44.45N	69.27W
Skradin, Cro. (skrä'dĕn)	154	43.49N	17.58E
Skreia, Nor. (skrĭ'å)	146	60.40N	10.55E
Skudeneshavn, Nor. (skōō'dĕ-nes-houn')	146	59.10N	5.19E
Skuilte, S. Afr.	240b	26.07S	28.19E
Skull Valley Indian Reservation, I.R., Ut., U.S. (skŭl)	102	40.25N	112.50W
Skuna, r., Ms., U.S. (skû'nȧ)	108	33.57N	89.36W
Skunk, r., Ia., U.S. (skŭnk)	96	41.12N	92.14W
Skuodas, Lith. (skwô'dás)	146	56.16N	21.32E
Skurup, Swe. (skû'rôp)	146	55.29N	13.27E
Skvira, Ukr. (skvē'rȧ)	160	49.43N	29.41E
Skwierzyna, Pol. (skvê-ĕr'zhĭ-ná)	148	52.35N	15.30E
Skye, Island of, i., Scot., U.K. (skī)	140	57.25N	6.17W
Skykomish, r., Wa., U.S. (skī'kō-mĭsh)	100a	47.50N	121.55W
Skyring, Seno de, b., Chile (sĕ'nô-s-krē'ng)	126	52.35S	72.30W
Slade Green, neigh., Eng., U.K.	231	51.28N	0.12E
Slagese, Den.	146	55.25N	11.19E
Slamet, Gunung, mtn., Indon. (slä'mĕt)	188	7.15S	109.15E
Slănic, Rom. (slŭ'nĕk)	154	45.13N	25.56E
Slater, Mo., U.S. (slāt'ēr)	104	39.13N	93.03W
Slatina, Rom. (slä'tē-nä)	154	44.26N	24.21E
Slaton, Tx., U.S. (slā'tŭn)	104	33.26N	101.38W
Slattocks, Eng., U.K.	233b	53.35N	2.10W
Slave, r., Can. (slāv)	78	59.40N	111.21W
Slavgorod, Russia (sláf'gô-rôt)	158	52.58N	78.43E
Slavonija, hist. reg., Yugo. (slä-vô'nē-yä)	154	45.29N	17.31E
Slavonska Požega, Cro. (slä-vôn'skä pô'zhĕ-gä)	154	45.18N	17.42E
Slavonski Brod, Cro. (slä-vôn'skê brôd)	142	45.10N	18.01E
Slavuta, Ukr. (slá-vōō'tá)	156	50.18N	27.01E
Slavyansk, Ukr. (sláv'yänsk')	160	48.52N	37.34E
Slavyanskaya, Russia (sláv-yán'ská-yá)	156	45.14N	38.09E
Sławno, Pol. (swav'nō)	148	54.21N	16.38E
Slayton, Mn., U.S. (slā'tŭn)	96	44.00N	95.44W
Sleaford, Eng., U.K. (slē'fērd)	138a	53.00N	0.25W
Sleepy Eye, Mn., U.S. (slēp'ĭ ī)	96	44.17N	94.44W
Sleepy Hollow, Ca., U.S.	228	33.57N	117.47W
Slidell, La., U.S. (slī-dĕl')	106	30.17N	89.47W
Sliedrecht, Neth.	139a	51.49N	4.46E
Sligo, Ire. (slī'gō)	140	54.17N	8.19W
Slite, Swe. (slē'tĕ)	146	57.41N	18.47E
Sliven, Bul. (slē'vĕn)	142	42.41N	26.20E
Sloan, N.Y., U.S.	226a	42.54N	78.47W
Sloatsburg, N.Y., U.S. (slōts'bŭrg)	94a	41.09N	74.11W
Slobodka, Bela. (slô'bôd-kȧ)	146	54.34N	26.12E
Slonim, Bela. (swô'nĭm)	148	53.05N	25.19E
Slough, Eng., U.K. (slou)	138b	51.29N	0.36W
Slovakia, see Slovensko, hist. reg., Czech.	148	48.50N	20.00E
Slovenia, hist. reg., Eur.	154	45.58N	14.43E
Slovenia, ctry., Eur.	154	46.15N	15.10E
Slovensko (Slovakia), hist. reg., Czech.	148	48.50N	20.00E
Sluch', r., Ukr.	160	50.56N	26.48E
Slunj, Cro. (slòn')	154	45.08N	15.46E
Słupsk, Pol. (swópsk)	140	54.28N	17.02E
Slutsk, Bela. (slótsk)	160	53.02N	27.34E
Slyne Head, c., Ire. (slīn)	140	53.25N	10.05W
Smackover, Ar., U.S. (smăk'ô-vēr)	104	33.22N	92.42W
Smederevo, Yugo.	154	44.39N	20.54E
Smederevska Palanka, Yugo. (smĕ-dĕ-rĕv'skä pä-län'kä)	154	44.21N	21.00E
Smedjebacken, Swe. (smĭ'tyĕ-bä-kĕn)	146	60.09N	15.19E
Smela, Ukr. (smyā'lȧ)	160	49.14N	31.52E
Smeloye, Ukr. (smyā'lô-ĕ)	156	50.55N	33.36E
Smethport, Pa., U.S. (smĕth'pōrt)	92	41.50N	78.25W
Smethwick, Eng., U.K.	144	52.31N	2.04W
Smiltene, Lat. (smĕl'tĕ-nĕ)	146	57.26N	25.57E
Smith, Can. (smĭth)	78	55.10N	114.02W
Smith, i., Wa., U.S.	100a	48.20N	122.53W

ng-sing; ŋ-baŋk; N-nasalized n; nŏd; cŏmmit; ōld; ôbey; ôrder; oi-boil; fōōd; ó-as oo in foot; ou-out; s-soft; sh-dish; th-thin; pūre; ûnite; ûrn; stŭd; circŭs; ü-as in French tu; '-indeterminate vowel.

PLACE (Pronunciation)	PAGE	Lat. °′	Long. °′
Smith, r., Mt., U.S.	98	47.00N	111.20W
Smith Center, Ks., U.S. (sĕn'tĕr)	104	39.45N	98.46W
Smithers, Can. (smĭth'ērs)	78	54.47N	127.10W
Smithfield, Austl.	239a	33.51S	150.57E
Smithfield, N.C., U.S. (smĭth'fēld)	108	35.30N	78.21W
Smithfield, Ut., U.S.	98	41.50N	111.49W
Smithland, Ky., U.S. (smĭth'lănd)	92	37.10N	88.25W
Smith Mountain Lake, res., Va., U.S.	108	37.00N	79.45W
Smith Point, Tx., U.S.	107a	29.32N	94.45W
Smiths Falls, Can. (smĭths)	78	44.55N	76.05W
Smithton, Austl. (smĭth'tŭn)	198	40.55S	145.12E
Smithton, Il., U.S.	101e	38.24N	89.59W
Smithville, Tx., U.S. (smĭth'vĭl)	106	30.00N	97.08W
Smitswinkelvlakte, pl., S. Afr.	206a	34.16S	18.25E
Smoke Creek Desert, des., Nv., U.S. (smōk crēk)	102	40.28N	119.40W
Smoky, r., Can. (smōk'ĭ)	80	55.30N	117.30W
Smoky Hill, r., U.S. (smōk'ĭ hĭl)	90	38.40N	100.00W
Smøla, i., Nor. (smûlä)	140	63.16N	7.40E
Smolensk, Russia (smô-lyĕnsk')	158	54.46N	32.03E
Smolensk, prov., Russia	156	55.00N	32.18E
Smyadovo, Bul.	154	43.04N	27.00E
Smyrna, De., U.S. (smûr'nȧ)	92	39.20N	75.35W
Smyrna, Ga., U.S.	94c	33.53N	84.31W
Smyrna, see İzmir, Tur.	174	38.25N	27.05E
Snag, Can. (snăg)	89	62.18N	140.30W
Snake, r., U.S.	90	45.30N	117.00W
Snake, r., Mn., U.S. (snāk)	96	45.58N	93.20W
Snake Range, mts., Nv., U.S.	102	39.20N	114.15W
Snake River Plain, pl., Id., U.S.	98	43.08N	114.46W
Snap Point, c., Bah.	116	23.45N	77.30W
Sneffels, Mount, mtn., Co., U.S. (snĕf'ĕlz)	102	38.00N	107.50W
Snelgrove, Can. (snĕl'grōv)	77d	43.44N	79.50W
Sniardwy, Jezioro, l., Pol. (snyärt'vĭ)	148	53.46N	21.59E
Snodland, Eng., U.K.	231	51.20N	0.27E
Snöhetta, mtn., Nor. (snû-hĕttä)	140	62.18N	9.12E
Snohomish, Wa., U.S. (snô-hō'mĭsh)	100a	47.55N	122.05W
Snohomish, r., Wa., U.S.	100a	47.53N	122.04W
Snoqualmie, Wa., U.S. (snō qwäl'mē)	100a	47.32N	121.50W
Snoqualmie, r., Wa., U.S.	98	47.32N	121.53W
Snov, r., Eur. (snôf)	156	51.38N	31.38E
Snowden, Pa., U.S.	226b	40.16N	79.58W
Snowdon, mtn., Wales, U.K.	144	53.05N	4.04W
Snow Hill, Md., U.S. (hĭl)	92	38.15N	75.20W
Snow Lake, Can.	82	54.50N	100.10W
Snowy Mountains, mts., Austl. (snō'ē)	196	36.17S	148.30E
Snyder, Ok., U.S. (snī'dēr)	104	34.40N	98.57W
Snyder, Tx., U.S.	106	32.48N	100.53W
Soar, r., Eng., U.K. (sōr)	138a	52.44N	1.09W
Sobat, r., Sudan (sō'bȧt)	204	9.04N	32.02E
Sobinka, Russia (sô-bĭŋ'kȧ)	156	55.59N	40.02E
Sobo Zan, mtn., Japan (sô'bô zän)	186	32.47N	131.27E
Sobral, Braz. (sô-brä'l)	124	3.39S	40.16W
Sochaczew, Pol. (sô-Kä'chĕf)	148	52.14N	20.18E
Sochi, Russia (sôch'ĭ)	158	43.35N	39.50E
Society Islands, is., Fr. Poly. (sō-sī'ĕ-tē)	190	15.00S	157.30W
Socoltenango, Mex. (sô-kôl-tĕ-näŋ'gō)	112	16.17N	92.20W
Socorro, Braz. (sŏ-kô'r-rō)	123a	22.35S	46.32W
Socorro, Col. (sô-kôr'rō)	124	6.23N	73.19W
Socorro, N.M., U.S.	102	34.05N	106.55W
Socúellamos, Spain (sô-kōō-äl'yä-mōs)	152	39.18N	2.48W
Soda, l., Ca., U.S. (sō'dȧ)	102	35.12N	116.25W
Soda Peak, mtn., Wa., U.S.	100c	45.53N	122.04W
Soda Springs, Id., U.S. (sprĭngz)	98	42.39N	111.37W
Söderhamn, Swe. (sû-dĕr-häm''n)	140	61.20N	17.00E
Söderköping, Swe.	146	58.30N	16.14E
Södertälje, Swe. (sû-dĕr-tĕl'yĕ)	140	59.12N	17.35E
Sodingen, neigh., Ger.	232	51.32N	7.15E
Sodo, Eth.	204	7.03N	37.46E
Sodpur, India	236a	22.42N	88.23E
Soest, Ger. (zōst)	148	51.35N	8.05E
Soeurs, Île des, i., Can.	223b	45.28N	73.33W
Sofia (Sofiya), Bul. (sô'fē-yȧ) (sô'fē-ȧ)	136	42.43N	23.20E
Sofiya, see Sofia, Bul.	136	42.43N	23.20E
Sofiyevka, Ukr. (sô-fē'yĕf-kȧ)	156	48.03N	33.53E
Soga, Japan (sō'gä)	187a	35.35N	140.08E
Sogamoso, Col. (sô-gä-mō'sō)	124	5.42N	72.51W
Sognafjorden, fj., Nor.	136	61.09N	5.30E
Sogozha, r., Russia (sô'gô-zhȧ)	156	58.35N	39.08E
Sohano, Pap. N. Gui.	192e	5.27S	154.40E
Soissons, Fr. (swä-sôN')	150	49.23N	3.17E
Soisy-sous-Montmorency, Fr.	233c	48.59N	2.18E
Sōka, Japan (sō'kä)	187a	35.50N	139.49E
Sokal', Ukr. (sô'käl')	148	50.28N	24.20E
Söke, Tur. (sû'kĕ)	142	37.40N	27.10E
Sokółka, Pol. (sô-kōl'kȧ)	148	53.23N	23.30E
Sokol'niki, neigh., Russia	235b	55.48N	37.41E
Sokolo, Mali (sô-kô-lō')	204	14.51N	6.09W
Sokołów Podlaski, Pol. (sô-kô-wôf' pŭd-lä'skĭ)	148	52.24N	22.15E
Sokone, Sen.	208	13.53N	16.22W
Sokoto, Nig. (sō'kô-tō)	204	13.04N	5.16E
Sola de Vega, Mex.	112	16.31N	96.58W
Solander, Cape, c., Austl.	195b	34.03S	151.16E
Solano, Phil. (sō-lä'nō)	189a	16.31N	121.11E
Sölderholz, neigh., Ger.	232	51.29N	7.35E
Soledad, Col. (sŏ-lĕ-dä'd)	124	10.47N	75.00W
Soledad Díez Gutiérrez, Mex.	112	22.19N	100.54W
Soleduck, r., Wa., U.S. (sōl'dŭk)	98	47.59N	124.28W
Solentiname, Islas de, is., Nic. (ē's-läs-dĕ-sô-lĕn-tē-nä'mȧ)	114	11.15N	85.16W
Solheim, S. Afr.	240b	26.11S	28.10E
Solihull, Eng., U.K. (sō'lĭ-hŭl)	138a	52.25N	1.46W
Solikamsk, Russia (sô-lē-kȧmsk')	160	59.38N	56.48E
Sol'-Iletsk, Russia	158	51.10N	55.05E
Solimões, Rio, r., Braz. (rē'ō-sô-lē-mô'ĕs)	124	2.45S	67.44W
Solingen, Ger. (zō'lĭng-ĕn)	148	51.10N	7.05E
Sóller, Spain (sō'lyĕr)	152	39.45N	2.40E
Solncevo, Russia	235b	55.39N	37.24E
Sologne, reg., Fr. (sō-lŏn'yĕ)	150	47.36N	1.53E
Solola, Guat. (sô-lô'lä)	114	14.45N	91.12W
Solomon, r., Ks., U.S.	104	39.24N	98.19W
Solomon, North Fork, r., Ks., U.S.	104	39.34N	99.52W
Solomon, South Fork, r., Ks., U.S.	104	39.19N	99.52W
Solomon Islands, nation, Oc. (sŏ'lō-mūn)	2	7.00S	160.00E
Solon, China (swo-lōōn)	180	46.32N	121.18E
Solon, Oh., U.S. (sō'lŭn)	95d	41.23N	81.26W
Solothurn, Switz. (zō'lō-thōōrn)	148	47.13N	7.30E
Solovetskiye Ostrova, is., Russia	160	65.10N	35.40E
Šolta, i., Yugo. (shôl'tä)	154	43.20N	16.15E
Soltau, Ger. (sōl'tou)	148	53.00N	9.50E
Sol'tsy, Russia (sôl'tsē)	156	58.04N	30.13E
Solvay, N.Y., U.S. (sŏl'vā)	92	43.05N	76.10W
Sölvesborg, Swe. (sûl'vĕs-bôrg)	146	56.04N	14.35E
Sol'vychegodsk, Russia (sôl'vē-chĕ-gôtsk')	160	61.18N	46.58E
Solway Firth, b., U.K. (sŏl'wā fûrth')	140	54.42N	3.55W
Solwezi, Zam.	210	12.11S	26.25E
Somalia, nation, Afr. (sō-mä'lē-ȧ)	212a	3.28N	44.47E
Somanga, Tan.	210	8.24S	39.17E
Sombor, Yugo. (sôm'bôr)	142	45.45N	19.10E
Sombrerete, Mex. (sôm-brå-rā'tå)	112	23.38N	103.37W
Sombrero, Cayo, i., Ven. (kä-yô-sôm-brĕ'rô)	125b	10.52N	68.12W
Somerdale, N.J., U.S.	225b	39.51N	75.01W
Somerset, Ky., U.S. (sŭm'ĕr-sĕt)	108	37.05N	84.35W
Somerset, Md., U.S.	225d	38.58N	77.05W
Somerset, Ma., U.S.	94b	41.46N	71.05W
Somerset, Pa., U.S.	92	40.00N	79.05W
Somerset, Tx., U.S.	101d	29.13N	98.39W
Somerset East, S. Afr.	207c	32.44S	25.36E
Somersworth, N.H., U.S. (sŭm'ērz-wûrth)	86	43.16N	70.53W
Somerton, Az., U.S. (sŭm'ēr-tŭn)	102	32.36N	114.43W
Somerton, neigh., Pa., U.S.	225b	40.06N	75.01W
Somerville, Ma., U.S. (sŭm'ēr-vĭl)	87a	42.23N	71.06W
Somerville, N.J., U.S.	94a	40.34N	74.37W
Somerville, Tn., U.S.	108	35.14N	89.21W
Somerville, Tx., U.S.	106	30.21N	96.31W
Someşul, r., Eur. (sô-mȧ'shôl)	148	47.43N	23.09E
Somma Vesuviana, Italy (sôm'mä vä-zōō-vē-ä'nä)	153c	40.38N	14.27E
Somme, r., Fr. (sŏm)	150	50.02N	2.04E
Sommerberg, Ger.	232	51.27N	7.32E
Sommerfeld, Ger. (zō'mĕr-fĕld)	139b	52.48N	13.02E
Sommerville, Austl.	195a	38.14S	145.10E
Somoto, Nic. (sô-mō'tō)	114	13.28N	86.37W
Son, r., India (sōn)	174	24.40N	82.35E
Sonari, India	236e	18.52N	72.59E
Sŏnchŏn, N. Kor. (sŭn'shŭn)	186	39.49N	124.56E
Sondags, r., S. Afr.	207c	33.17S	25.14E
Sønderborg, Den. (sûn''er-bôrgh)	140	54.55N	9.47E
Sondershausen, Ger. (zôn'dĕrz-hou'zĕn)	148	51.17N	10.45E
Song Ca, r., Viet.	184	19.15N	105.00E
Songea, Tan. (sôn-gā'ä)	206	10.41S	35.39E
Songjiang, China	180	31.01N	121.14E
Sŏngjin, N. Kor. (sŭng'jĭn')	186	40.38N	129.10E
Songkhla, Thai. (sông'Klä')	188	7.09N	100.34E
Songwe, Zaire	210	12.25S	29.40E
Sonneberg, Ger. (sôn'ĕ-bĕrgh)	148	50.20N	11.14E
Sonora, Ca., U.S. (sô-nō'rȧ)	102	37.58N	120.22W
Sonora, Tx., U.S.	106	30.33N	100.38W
Sonora, state, Mex.	110	29.45N	111.15W
Sonora, r., Mex.	110	28.45N	111.35W
Sonora Peak, mtn., Ca., U.S.	90	38.22N	119.39W
Sonseca, Spain (sôn-sā'kä)	152	39.41N	3.56W
Sonsón, Col. (sôn-sôn')	124	5.42N	75.28W
Sonsonate, El Sal. (sōn-sō-nä'tå)	114	13.46N	89.43W
Sonsorol Islands, is., T.T.P.I. (sŏn-sō-rōl')	188	5.03N	132.33E
Sooke Basin, b., Can. (sŏŏk)	100a	48.21N	123.47W
Soo Locks, trans., Mi., U.S. (sōō lŏks)	101a	46.30N	84.30W
Sopetrán, Col. (sō-pĕ-trä'n)	124a	6.30N	75.44W
Sopot, Pol. (sô'pôt)	148	54.26N	18.25E
Sopron, Hung. (shŏp'rôn)	142	47.41N	16.36E
Sora, Italy (sō'rä)	154	41.43N	13.37E
Sorbas, Spain (sôr'bäs)	152	37.05N	2.07W
Sorbonne, educ., Fr.	233c	48.51N	2.21E
Sordo, r., Mex. (sō'r-dō)	112	16.39N	97.33W
Sorel, Can. (sō-rĕl')	78	46.01N	73.07W
Sorell, Cape, c., Austl.	198	42.10S	144.50E
Soresina, Italy (sō-rå-zē'nä)	154	45.17N	9.51E
Soria, Spain (sō'rē-ä)	142	41.46N	2.28W
Soriano, dept., Ur. (sō-rēä'nō)	123c	33.25S	58.00W
Sorocaba, Braz. (sō-rō-kä'bȧ)	124	23.29S	47.27W
Soroka, Mol.	160	48.09N	28.17E
Sorong, Indon. (sō-rông')	188	1.00S	131.20E
Sorot', r., Russia (sō-rō'tzh)	156	57.08N	29.23E
Soroti, Ug. (sō-rō'tē)	204	1.43N	33.37E
Sørøya, i., Nor.	140	70.37N	20.58E
Sorraia, r., Port. (sōr-rī'ȧ)	152	38.55N	8.42W
Sorrento, Italy (sōr-rĕn'tō)	154	40.23N	14.23E
Sorsogon, Phil. (sōr-sōgōn')	188	12.51N	124.02E
Sortavala, Russia (sôr'tä-vä-lä)	158	61.43N	30.40E
Sosenki, Russia	235b	55.34N	37.26E
Sosna, r., Russia (sôs'nȧ)	156	50.33N	38.15E
Sosnitsa, Ukr. (sôs-nē'tsȧ)	156	51.30N	32.29E
Sosnogorsk, Russia	158	63.13N	54.09E
Sosnowiec, Pol. (sôs-nô'vyĕts)	148	50.17N	19.10E
Sosunova, Mys, c., Russia (mĭs sô'sô-nôf'ȧ)	186	46.28N	138.06E
Sos'va, r., Russia (sôs'vȧ)	160	63.10N	63.30E
Sos'va, r., Russia (sôs'vȧ)	164a	59.55N	60.40E
Sota, r., Benin	208	11.10N	3.20E
Sota la Marina, Mex. (sô-tä-lä-mä-rē'nä)	112	23.45N	98.11W
Soteapan, Mex. (sō-tå-ä'pän)	112	18.14N	94.51W
Soto la Marina, Río, r., Mex. (rē'ō-so'tō lä mä-rē'nä)	112	23.55N	98.30W
Sotuta, Mex. (sô-tōō'tä)	114a	20.35N	89.00W
Soublette, Ven. (sō-ōō-blĕ'tĕ)	125b	9.55N	66.06W
Souflíon, Grc.	154	41.12N	26.17E
Soufrière, St. Luc. (sōō-frē-âr')	115b	13.50N	61.03W
Soufrière, vol., Guad. (sōō-frē-âr')	115b	16.06N	61.42W
Soufrière, vol., Monts.	115b	16.43N	62.10W
Soufrière, Mount, mtn., St. Vin.	115b	13.19N	61.12W
Sŏul, see Seoul, S. Kor.	180	37.35N	127.03E
Sounding Creek, r., Can. (soun'dĭng)	82	51.35N	111.00W
Souq Ahras, Alg.	140	36.23N	8.00E
Sources, Mount aux, mtn., Afr. (môN'tō sôrs')	206	28.47S	29.04E
Soure, Port. (sōr-ĕ)	152	40.04N	8.37W
Souris, Can.	78	49.38N	100.15W
Souris, Can. (sōō'rē')	86	46.20N	62.17W
Souris, r., N.A.	78	48.30N	101.30W
Sourlake, Tx., U.S. (sour'lāk)	106	30.09N	94.24W
Sousse, Tun. (sōōs)	204	36.00N	10.39E
South, r., Ga., U.S.	94c	33.40N	84.15W
South, r., N.C., U.S.	108	34.49N	78.33W
South Africa, nation, Afr.	206	28.00S	24.50E
Southall, neigh., Eng., U.K.	231	51.31N	0.23W
South Amboy, N.J., U.S. (south'ăm'boi)	94a	40.28N	74.17W
South America, cont.	122	15.00S	60.00W
Southampton, Eng., U.K. (south-ămp'tŭn)	136	50.54N	1.30W
Southampton, N.Y., U.S.	92	40.53N	72.24W
Southampton Island, i., Can.	78	64.38N	84.00W
South Andaman Island, i., India (ăn-dȧ-măn')	188	11.57N	93.24E
South Australia, state, Austl. (ôs-trā'lĭ-ȧ)	196	29.45S	132.00E
South Bay, b., Bah.	116	20.55N	73.35W
South Bend, In., U.S. (bĕnd)	90	41.40N	86.20W
South Bend, Wa., U.S. (bĕnd)	98	46.39N	123.48W
South Bight, bt., Bah.	116	24.20N	77.35W
South Bimini, i., Bah. (bē'mē-nē)	116	25.40N	79.20W
Southborough, Ma., U.S. (south'bŭr-ô)	87a	42.18N	71.33W
South Boston, Va., U.S. (bôs'tŭn)	108	36.41N	78.55W
South Boston, neigh., Ma., U.S.	223a	42.20N	71.03W
Southbridge, Ma., U.S. (south'brĭj)	92	42.05N	72.00W
South Brooklyn, neigh., N.Y., U.S.	224	40.41N	73.59W
South Caicos, i., T./C. Is. (kī'kōs)	116	21.30N	71.35W
South Carolina, state, U.S. (kăr-ô-lī'nȧ)	90	34.15N	81.10W
South Cave, Eng., U.K. (cāv)	138a	53.45N	0.35W
South Charleston, W.V., U.S.	92	38.20N	81.40W
South Chicago, neigh., Il., U.S.	227a	41.44N	87.33W
South China Sea, sea, Asia (chī'nȧ)	188	15.23N	114.12E
South Creek, r., Austl.	195b	33.43S	150.50E
Southcrest, S. Afr.	240b	26.15S	28.07E
South Dakota, state, U.S. (dȧ-kō'tȧ)	90	44.20N	101.55W
South Darenth, Eng., U.K.	231	51.24N	0.15E
South Downs, Eng., U.K. (dounz)	144	50.55N	1.13W
South Dum-Dum, India	178a	22.36N	88.25E
South East Cape, c., Austl.	196	43.47S	146.03E
Southend-on-Sea, Eng., U.K. (south-ĕnd')	144	51.33N	0.41E
Southern Alps, mts., N.Z. (sŭ-thûrn ălps)	197a	43.35S	170.00E
Southern California, University of, pt. of i., Ca., U.S.	228	34.02N	118.17W
Southern Cross, Austl.	196	31.13S	119.30E
Southern Indian, l., Can. (sŭth'ērn ĭn'dĭ-ăn)	78	56.46N	98.57W
Southern Pines, N.C., U.S. (sŭth'ērn pīnz)	108	35.10N	79.23W
Southern Ute Indian Reservation, I.R., Co., U.S. (ūt)	102	37.05N	108.23W
South Euclid, Oh., U.S. (ū'klĭd)	95d	41.30N	81.34W
Southfield, Mi., U.S.	226c	42.29N	83.17W
Southfleet, Eng., U.K.	231	51.25N	0.19E
South Fox, i., Mi., U.S. (fŏks)	92	45.25N	85.55W
South Gate, Ca., U.S. (gāt)	101a	33.57N	118.13W
Southgate, neigh., Eng., U.K.	231	51.38N	0.08W
South Georgia, i., Falk. Is. (jôr'jȧ)	122	54.00S	37.00W
South Germiston, S. Afr.	240b	26.15S	28.10E
South Green, Eng., U.K.	231	51.37N	0.26E
South Haven, Mi., U.S. (hāv''n)	92	42.25N	86.15W
South Head, c., Austl.	239a	33.50S	151.17E
South Hempstead, N.Y., U.S.	224	40.41N	73.37W
South Hill, Va., U.S.	108	36.44N	78.08W
South Hills, neigh., S. Afr.	240b	26.15S	28.05E
South Holston Lake, res., U.S.	108	36.35N	82.00W
South Indian Lake, Can.	82	56.50N	99.00W
Southington, Ct., U.S. (sŭdh'ĭng-tŭn)	92	41.35N	72.55W
South Island, i., N.Z.	197a	42.40S	169.00E
South Loup, r., Ne., U.S. (lōōp)	96	41.21N	100.08W
South Lynnfield, Ma., U.S.	223a	42.31N	71.00W
South Media, Pa., U.S.	225b	39.54N	75.23W
South Melbourne, Austl.	239b	37.50S	144.57E
South Merrimack, N.H., U.S. (mĕr'ĭ-măk)	87a	42.47N	71.36W
South Milwaukee, Wi., U.S. (mĭl-wô'kē)	95a	42.55N	87.52W
South Mimms, Eng., U.K.	231	51.42N	0.14W
South Moose Lake, l., Can.	82	53.51N	100.20W
South Nation, r., Can.	84	45.00N	75.25W
South Negril Point, c., Jam. (nå-grēl')	116	18.15N	78.25W

PLACE (Pronunciation)	PAGE	Lat. °′	Long. °′
South Ockendon, Eng., U.K.	231	51.32N	0.18E
South Ogden, Ut., U.S. (ŏg′dĕn)	101b	41.12N	111.58W
South Orange, N.J., U.S.	224	40.45N	74.15W
South Orkney Islands, is., B.A.T.	122	57.00S	45.00W
South Oxhey, Eng., U.K.	231	51.38N	0.23W
South Paris, Me., U.S. (păr′ĭs)	86	44.13N	70.32W
South Park, Ky., U.S. (pärk)	95h	38.06N	85.43W
South Pasadena, Ca., U.S. (păs-à-dē′nȧ)	101a	34.06N	118.08W
South Pease, r., Tx., U.S. (pēz)	104	33.54N	100.45W
South Pender, i., Can. (pĕn′dĕr)	100d	48.45N	123.09W
South Philadelphia, neigh., Pa., U.S.	225b	39.56N	75.10W
South Pittsburg, Tn., U.S. (pĭs′bûrg)	108	35.00N	85.42W
South Platte, r., U.S. (plăt)	90	40.40N	102.40W
South Point, c., Barb.	115b	13.00N	59.43W
South Point, c., Mi., U.S.	92	44.50N	83.20W
South Porcupine, Can.	84	48.28N	81.13W
Southport, Austl. (south′pōrt)	196	27.57S	153.27E
Southport, Eng., U.K. (south′pôrt)	144	53.38N	3.00W
Southport, In., U.S.	95g	39.40N	86.07W
Southport, N.C., U.S.	108	35.55N	78.02W
South Portland, Me., U.S. (pōrt-lănd)	86	43.37N	70.15W
South Prairie, Wa., U.S. (prâ′rĭ)	100a	47.08N	122.06W
South Range, Wi., U.S. (rānj)	101h	46.37N	91.59W
South River, N.J., U.S. (rĭv′ẽr)	94a	40.27N	74.23W
South Ronaldsay, i., Scot., U.K. (rŏn′ăld-s′ā)	144a	58.48N	2.55W
South Saint Paul, Mn., U.S.	101g	44.54N	93.02W
South Salt Lake, Ut., U.S. (sôlt lāk)	101b	40.44N	111.53W
South Sandwich Islands, is., Falk. Is. (sănd′wĭch)	122	58.00S	27.00W
South Sandwich Trench, deep	122	55.00S	27.00W
South San Francisco, Ca., U.S. (săn frăn-sĭs′kō)	100b	37.39N	122.24W
South San Jose Hills, Ca., U.S.	228	34.01N	117.55W
South Saskatchewan, r., Can. (sȧs-kach′ē-wăn)	78	50.30N	110.30W
South Shetland Islands, is., B.A.T.	122	62.00S	70.00W
South Shields, Eng., U.K. (shēldz)	140	55.00N	1.22W
South Shore, neigh., Il., U.S.	227a	41.46N	87.35W
South Side, neigh., Pa., U.S.	226b	40.26N	79.58W
South Sioux City, Ne., U.S. (so͞o sĭt′ē)	96	42.48N	96.26W
South Taranaki Bight, bt., N.Z. (tä-rä-nä′kē)	197a	39.35S	173.50E
South Thompson, r., Can. (tŏmp′sŭn)	80	50.41N	120.21W
Southton, Tx., U.S. (south′tŭn)	101d	29.18N	98.26W
South Uist, i., Scot., U.K. (ū′ĭst)	144	57.15N	7.24W
South Umpqua, r., Or., U.S. (ŭmp′kwȧ)	98	43.00N	122.54W
South Walpole, Ma., U.S.	223a	42.06N	71.16W
South Waltham, Ma., U.S.	223a	42.22N	71.15W
Southwark, neigh., Eng., U.K.	231	51.30N	0.06W
South Weald, Eng., U.K.	231	51.37N	0.16E
Southwell, Eng., U.K. (south′wĕl)	138a	53.04N	0.56W
South West Africa, see Namibia, nation, Afr.	206	19.30S	16.13E
South Westbury, N.Y., U.S.	224	40.45N	73.35W
Southwest Miramichi, r., Can. (mĭr ȧ-mē′shē)	86	46.35N	66.17W
Southwest Point, c., Bah.	116	23.55N	74.30W
Southwest Point, c., Bah.	116	25.50N	77.10W
South Weymouth, Ma., U.S.	223a	42.10N	70.57W
South Whittier, Ca., U.S.	228	33.56N	118.03W
South Yorkshire, co., Eng., U.K.	138a	53.29N	1.35W
Sovetsk, Russia (sô-vyĕtsk′)	160	55.04N	21.54E
Sovetskaya Gavan′, Russia (sŭ-vyĕt′skī-u gä′vŭn′)	158	48.59N	140.14E
Sow, r., Eng., U.K. (sou)	138a	52.45N	2.12W
Soweto, neigh., S. Afr.	240b	26.14S	27.54E
Soya Kaikyō, strt., Asia	186	45.45N	141.38E
Sōya Misaki, c., Japan (sō′yȧ mē′sä-kē)	186	45.35N	141.25E
Soyo, Ang.	206	6.10S	12.25E
Sozh, r., Eur. (sôzh)	160	52.50N	31.00E
Sozopol, Bul. (sôz′ō-pôl′)	154	42.18N	27.50E
Spa, Bel. (spä)	144	50.30N	5.50E
Spain, nation, Eur. (spān)	136	40.15N	4.30W
Spalding, Ne., U.S. (spôl′dĭng)	96	41.43N	98.23W
Spanaway, Wa., U.S. (spăn′ȧ-wā)	100a	47.06N	122.26W
Spandau, neigh., Ger.	234a	52.32N	13.12E
Spangler, Pa., U.S. (spăng′lẽr)	92	40.40N	78.50W
Spanish Fork, Ut., U.S. (spăn′ĭsh fôrk)	102	40.10N	111.40W
Spanish Town, Jam.	110	18.00N	76.55W
Sparks, Nv., U.S. (spärks)	102	39.34N	119.45W
Sparrows Point, Md., U.S. (spăr′ōz)	94e	39.13N	76.29W
Sparta, Ga., U.S. (spär′tȧ)	108	33.16N	82.59W
Sparta, Il., U.S.	104	38.07N	89.42W
Sparta, Mi., U.S.	92	43.10N	85.45W
Sparta, Tn., U.S.	108	35.54N	85.26W
Sparta, Wi., U.S.	96	43.56N	90.50W
Sparta Mountains, mts., N.J., U.S.	94a	41.00N	74.38W
Spartanburg, S.C., U.S. (spär′tăn-bûrg)	90	34.57N	82.13W
Sparta, see Spárti, Grc.	142	37.07N	22.28E
Spartel, Cap, c., Mor. (spär-tĕl′)	152	35.48N	5.50W
Spárti, Grc. (Sparta)	142	37.07N	22.28E
Spartivento, Cape, c., Italy	136	38.54N	8.52E
Spartivento, Cape, c., Italy (spär-tē-vĕn′tô)	154	37.55N	16.09E
Spas-Demensk, Russia (spȧs dyē-mĕnsk′)	156	54.24N	34.02E
Spas-Klepiki, Russia (spȧs klĕp′ē-kē)	156	55.09N	40.11E
Spassk-Ryazanskiy, Russia (ryä-zän′skĭ)	156	54.24N	40.21E
Spassk-Dal′niy, Russia (spŭsk′däl′nyē)	158	44.30N	133.00E
Spátha, Ákra, c., Grc.	154a	35.42N	23.45E
Spaulding, Al., U.S. (spôl′dĭng)	94h	33.27N	86.50W
Spear, Cape, c., Can. (spēr)	86	47.32N	52.32W
Spearfish, S.D., U.S. (spēr′fĭsh)	96	44.28N	103.52W
Speed, In., U.S. (spēd)	95h	38.25N	85.45W

PLACE (Pronunciation)	PAGE	Lat. °′	Long. °′
Speedway, In., U.S. (spēd′wā)	95g	39.47N	86.14W
Speichersee, l., Ger.	139d	48.12N	11.47E
Speke, neigh., Eng., U.K.	233a	53.21N	2.51W
Speldorf, neigh., Ger.	232	51.25N	6.52E
Spellen, Ger.	232	51.37N	6.37E
Spencer, In., U.S. (spĕn′sẽr)	92	39.15N	86.45W
Spencer, Ia., U.S.	96	43.09N	95.08W
Spencer, N.C., U.S.	108	35.43N	80.25W
Spencer, W.V., U.S.	92	38.55N	81.20W
Spencer Gulf, b., Austl. (spĕn′sẽr)	196	34.20S	136.55E
Sperenberg, Ger. (shpĕ′rĕn-bĕrgh)	139b	52.09N	13.22E
Sperkhiós, r., Grc.	154	38.54N	22.02E
Spey, l., Scot., U.K. (spā)	144	57.25N	3.29W
Speyer, Ger. (shpī′ẽr)	148	49.18N	8.26E
Sphinx, hist., Egypt (sfĭnks)	212b	29.57N	31.08E
Spijkenisse, Neth.	139a	51.51N	4.18E
Spinazzola, Italy (spē-nät′zō-lä)	154	40.58N	16.05E
Spirit Lake, Id., U.S. (spĭr′ĭt)	98	47.58N	116.51W
Spirit Lake, Ia., U.S. (lāk)	96	43.25N	95.08W
Spišská Nová Ves, Czech. (spĕsh′skä nō′vä vĕs)	140	48.56N	20.35E
Spitsbergen, see Svalbard, dep., Eur.	158	77.00N	20.00E
Split, Cro. (splēt)	136	43.30N	16.28E
Split Lake, l., Can.	82	56.08N	96.15W
Spokane, Wa., U.S. (spōkăn′)	90	47.39N	117.25W
Spokane, r., Wa., U.S.	98	47.47N	118.00W
Spokane Indian Reservation, I.R., Wa., U.S.	98	47.55N	118.00W
Spoleto, Italy (spô-lā′tō)	154	42.44N	12.44E
Spoon, r., Il., U.S. (spo͞on)	104	40.36N	90.22W
Spooner, Wi., U.S. (spo͞on′ẽr)	96	45.50N	91.53W
Sportswood, Austl.	239b	37.50S	144.53E
Spotswood, N.J., U.S. (spŏtz′wo͝od)	94a	40.23N	74.22W
Sprague, r., Or., U.S. (sprāg)	98	42.30N	121.42W
Spratly, i., Asia (sprăt′lē)	188	8.38N	11.54E
Spray, N.C., U.S. (sprā)	108	36.30N	79.44W
Spree, r., Ger. (shprā)	148	51.53N	14.08E
Spremberg, Ger. (shprĕm′bĕrgh)	148	51.35N	14.23E
Spring, r., Ar., U.S.	104	36.25N	91.35W
Springbok, S. Afr. (sprĭng′bŏk)	206	29.35S	17.55E
Spring Creek, r., Nv., U.S. (sprĭng)	102	40.18N	117.45W
Spring Creek, r., Tx., U.S.	106	30.03N	95.43W
Spring Creek, r., Tx., U.S.	106	31.08N	100.50W
Springdale, Can.	86	49.30N	56.05W
Springdale, Ar., U.S. (sprĭng′dāl)	104	36.10N	94.07W
Springdale, Pa., U.S.	95e	40.33N	79.46W
Springer, N.M., U.S. (sprĭng′ẽr)	104	36.21N	104.37W
Springerville, Az., U.S.	102	34.08N	109.17W
Springfield, Co., U.S. (sprĭng′fēld)	104	37.24N	102.04W
Springfield, Il., U.S.	90	39.46N	89.37W
Springfield, Ky., U.S.	92	37.35N	85.10W
Springfield, Ma., U.S.	90	42.05N	72.35W
Springfield, Mn., U.S.	96	44.14N	94.59W
Springfield, Mo., U.S.	90	37.13N	93.17W
Springfield, Oh., U.S.	90	39.55N	83.50W
Springfield, Or., U.S.	98	44.01N	123.02W
Springfield, Pa., U.S.	225b	39.55N	75.24W
Springfield, Tn., U.S.	108	36.30N	86.53W
Springfield, Vt., U.S.	92	43.20N	72.35W
Springfield, Va., U.S.	225d	38.45N	77.13W
Springfontein, S. Afr. (sprĭng′fôn-tīn)	206	30.16S	25.45E
Springhill, Can. (sprĭng-hĭl′)	78	45.39N	64.03W
Spring Mill, Pa., U.S.	225b	40.04N	75.17W
Spring Mountains, mts., Nv., U.S.	102	36.18N	115.49W
Springs, S. Afr. (sprĭngs)	212d	26.16S	28.27E
Springstein, Can. (sprĭng′stīn)	77f	49.49N	97.29W
Springton Reservoir, res., Pa., U.S. (sprĭng-tŭn)	94f	39.57N	75.26W
Springvale, Austl.	195a	37.57S	145.09E
Springvale South, Austl.	239b	37.58S	145.09E
Spring Valley, Ca., U.S.	102a	32.46N	117.01W
Springvalley, Il., U.S. (sprĭng-văl′ĭ)	92	41.20N	89.15W
Spring Valley, Mn., U.S.	96	43.41N	92.26W
Spring Valley, N.Y., U.S.	94a	41.07N	74.03W
Springville, Ut., U.S. (sprĭng-vĭl)	102	40.10N	111.40W
Springwood, Austl.	195b	33.42S	150.34E
Sprockhövel, Ger.	232	51.22N	7.15E
Spruce Grove, Can. (spro͞os grōv)	77g	53.32N	113.55W
Spur, Tx., U.S. (spûr)	104	33.29N	100.51W
Squam, l., N.H., U.S. (skwôm)	92	43.45N	71.30W
Squamish, Can. (skwŏ′mĭsh)	80	49.42N	123.09W
Squamish, r., Can.	80	50.10N	123.30W
Squillace, Golfo di, b., Italy (go͞o′l-fô-dē skwēl-lä′chā)	154	38.44N	16.47E
Squirrel Hill, neigh., Pa., U.S.	226b	40.26N	79.55W
Squirrel's Heath, neigh., Eng., U.K.	231	51.35N	0.13E
Srbija (Serbia), hist. reg., Yugo. (sr bē-yä) (sẽr′bē-ä)	154	44.05N	20.35E
Srbobran, Yugo. (s′r′bō-brän′)	154	45.32N	19.50E
Sredne-Kolymsk, Russia (s′rĕd′nyē kō-lêmsk′)	158	67.49N	154.55E
Sredne Rogatka, Russia (s′red′nȧ-ya) (rō gär′tkȧ)	164c	59.49N	30.20E
Sredniy Ik, r., Russia (srĕd′nĭ ĭk)	164a	55.46N	58.50E
Sredniy Ural, mts., Russia (ō′rál)	164a	57.47N	59.00E
Śrem, Pol. (shrĕm)	148	52.06N	17.01E
Sremska Karlovci, Yugo. (srĕm′skē kär′lov-tsē)	154	45.10N	19.57E
Sremska Mitrovica, Yugo. (srĕm′skä mē′trō-vē-tsä′)	154	44.59N	19.39E
Sretensk, Russia (s′rĕ′tĕnsk)	158	52.13N	117.39E
Sri Lanka, nation, Asia	175c	8.45N	82.30E
Srīnagar, India (srē-nŭg′ŭr)	174	34.11N	74.49E
Środa, Pol. (shrō′dȧ)	148	52.14N	17.17E
Staaken, neigh., Ger.	234a	52.32N	13.08E

PLACE (Pronunciation)	PAGE	Lat. °′	Long. °′
Stabroek, Bel.	139a	51.20N	4.21E
Stade, Ger. (shtä′dē)	148	53.36N	9.28E
Städjan, mtn., Swe. (stĕd′yän)	146	61.53N	12.50E
Stadlau, neigh., Aus.	235e	48.14N	16.28E
Stafford, Eng., U.K. (stăf′fẽrd)	144	52.48N	2.06W
Stafford, Ks., U.S.	104	37.58N	98.37W
Staffordshire, co., Eng., U.K.	138a	52.45N	2.00W
Stahnsdorf, Ger. (shtäns′dôrf)	139b	52.22N	13.10E
Staines, Eng., U.K.	138b	51.26N	0.13W
Stains, Fr.	233c	48.57N	2.23E
Stalingrad, see Volgograd, Russia	158	48.40N	42.20E
Stalybridge, Eng., U.K.	138a	53.29N	2.03W
Stambaugh, Mi., U.S. (stăm′bô)	96	46.03N	88.38W
Stamford, Eng., U.K.	138a	52.39N	0.28W
Stamford, Ct., U.S. (stăm′fẽrd)	94a	41.03N	73.32W
Stamford, Tx., U.S.	104	32.57N	99.48W
Stammersdorf, Aus. (shtäm′ẽrs-dôrf)	139e	48.19N	16.25E
Stamps, Ar., U.S. (stămps)	104	33.22N	93.31W
Stanberry, Mo., U.S. (stan′bĕr-ē)	104	40.12N	94.34W
Standerton, S. Afr. (stăn′dẽr-tŭn)	206	26.57S	29.17E
Standing Rock Indian Reservation, I.R., N.D., U.S. (stănd′ĭng rŏk)	96	47.07N	101.05W
Standish, Eng., U.K. (stăn′dĭsh)	138a	53.36N	2.39W
Stanford, Ky., U.S. (stăn′fẽrd)	108	37.29N	84.40W
Stanford le Hope, Eng., U.K.	231	51.31N	0.26E
Stanford Rivers, Eng., U.K.	231	51.41N	0.13E
Stanger, S. Afr. (stăŋ-ger)	207c	29.22S	31.18E
Staniard Creek, Bah.	116	24.50N	77.55W
Stanislaus, r., Ca., U.S. (stăn′ĭs-lô)	102	38.10N	120.16W
Stanley, Can. (stăn′lē)	86	46.17N	66.44W
Stanley, Falk. Is.	126	51.46S	57.59W
Stanley, H.K.	237c	22.13N	114.12E
Stanley, N.D., U.S.	96	48.20N	102.25W
Stanley, Wi., U.S.	96	44.56N	90.56W
Stanley Mound, hill, H.K.	237c	22.14N	114.12E
Stanley Pool, l., Afr.	206	4.07S	15.40E
Stanley Reservoir, res., India (stăn′lē)	178	12.07N	77.27E
Stanleyville, see Kisangani, Zaire	204	0.30S	25.12E
Stanlow, Eng., U.K.	233a	53.17N	2.52W
Stanmore, neigh., Eng., U.K.	231	51.37N	0.19W
Stann Creek, Belize (stăn krēk)	114a	17.01N	88.14W
Stanovoy Khrebet, mts., Russia (stŭn-ȧ-voi′)	158	56.12N	127.12E
Stansted, Eng., U.K.	231	51.20N	0.18E
Stanton, Ca., U.S. (stăn′tŭn)	101a	33.48N	118.00W
Stanton, Ne., U.S.	96	41.57N	97.15W
Stanton, Tx., U.S.	106	32.08N	101.46W
Stanwell, Eng., U.K.	231	51.27N	0.29W
Stanwell Moor, Eng., U.K.	231	51.28N	0.30W
Stanwood, Wa., U.S. (stăn′wŏd)	100a	48.14N	122.23W
Stapleford Abbots, Eng., U.K.	231	51.38N	0.10E
Stapleford Tawney, Eng., U.K.	231	51.40N	0.11E
Staples, Mn., U.S. (stā′p′lz)	96	46.21N	94.48W
Stapleton, Al., U.S.	108	30.45N	87.48W
Stara Planina, mts., Bul.	136	42.50N	24.45E
Staraya Kupavna, Russia (stä′rȧ-yȧ kū-päf′nȧ)	164b	55.48N	38.10E
Staraya Russa, Russia (stä′rȧ-yȧ ro͞os′ȧ)	160	57.58N	31.21E
Stara Zagora, Bul. (zä′gô-rȧ)	142	42.26N	25.37E
Starbuck, Can. (stär′bŭk)	77f	49.46N	97.36W
Stargard Szczeciński, Pol. (shtär′gärt shchĕ-chyn′skē)	140	53.19N	15.03E
Staritsa, Russia (stä′rē-tsȧ)	156	56.29N	34.58E
Starke, Fl., U.S. (stärk)	108	29.55N	82.07W
Starkville, Co., U.S. (stärk′vĭl)	104	37.06N	104.34W
Starkville, Ms., U.S.	108	33.27N	88.47W
Starnberg, Ger. (shtärn-bĕrgh)	139d	47.59N	11.20E
Starnberger See, l., Ger.	148	47.58N	11.30E
Starobel′sk, Ukr. (stä-rô-byĕlsk′)	160	49.19N	38.57E
Starodub, Russia (stä-rô-drŏp′)	156	52.25N	32.49E
Starogard Gdański, Pol. (stä′rô-grad gdĕn′skē)	140	53.58N	18.33E
Staro-Konstantinov, Ukr. (stä′rô kôn-stȧn-tē′nôf)	160	49.45N	27.12E
Staro-Minskaya, Russia (stä′rô mĭn′skȧ-yȧ)	160	46.19N	38.51E
Staro-Shcherbinovskaya, Russia	156	46.38N	38.38E
Staro-Subkhangulovo, Russia (stäro-so͞ob-kan-go͞o′lōvō)	164a	53.08N	57.24E
Staroutkinsk, Russia (stȧ-rô-o͞ot′kĭnsk)	164a	57.14N	59.21E
Staroverovka, Ukr.	156	49.31N	35.48E
Start Point, c., Eng., U.K. (stärt)	140	50.14N	3.34W
Stary Sącz, Pol. (stä-rē sŏnch′)	148	49.32N	20.36E
Staryy Oskol, Russia (stä′rē ôs-kôl′)	160	51.18N	37.51E
Stassfurt, Ger. (shtäs′fo͞ort)	148	51.52N	11.35E
Staszów, Pol. (stä′shŏf)	148	50.32N	21.13E
State College, Pa., U.S. (stāt kŏl′ĕj)	92	40.50N	77.55W
State Line, Mn., U.S. (līn)	101h	46.36N	92.18W
Staten Island, i., N.Y., U.S. (stăt′ĕn)	94a	40.35N	74.10W
Statesboro, Ga., U.S. (stāts′bŭr-ō)	108	32.26N	81.47W
Statesville, N.C., U.S. (stās′vĭl)	108	34.45N	80.54W
Statue of Liberty National Monument, rec., N.Y., U.S.	224	40.41N	74.03W
Staunton, Il., U.S. (stôn′tŭn)	101e	39.01N	89.47W
Staunton, Va., U.S.	92	38.10N	79.05W
Stavanger, Nor. (stä′väng′ẽr)	136	58.59N	5.44E
Stave, r., Can. (stāv)	100d	49.12N	122.24W
Staveley, Eng., U.K. (stāv′lē)	138a	53.17N	1.21W
Stavenisse, Neth.	139a	51.35N	3.59E
Stavropol′, Russia	158	45.05N	41.50E
Steamboat Springs, Co., U.S. (stēm′bōt′)	104	40.30N	106.48W
Steblëv, Ukr. (styĕp′lyôf)	156	49.23N	31.03E
Steel, r., Can. (stēl)	84	49.08N	86.55W
Steelton, Pa., U.S. (stēl′tŭn)	92	40.15N	76.45W

PLACE (Pronunciation)	PAGE	Lat. °'	Long. °'
Steenbergen, Neth.	139a	51.35N	4.18E
Steens Mountain, mts., Or., U.S. (stēnz)	98	42.15N	118.52W
Steep Point, c., Austl. (stēp)	196	26.15N	112.05E
Stefanie, Lake, *see* Chew Bahir, l., Afr.	204	4.46N	37.31E
Steglitz, neigh., Ger.	234a	52.28N	13.19E
Steiermark (Styria), prov., Aus. (shtī'ēr-märk)	148	47.22N	14.40E
Steinbach, Can.	78	49.32N	96.41W
Steinkjer, Nor. (stěīn-kyěr)	140	64.00N	11.19E
Steinstücken, neigh., Ger.	234a	52.23N	13.08E
Stella, Wa., U.S. (stěl'*à*)	100c	46.11N	123.12W
Stellarton, Can. (stěl'*ár*-t*ŭn*)	78	45.34N	62.40W
Stendal, Ger. (shtěn'däl)	148	52.37N	11.51E
Stepanakert, Azer. (styě'pän-á-kěrt)	160	39.50N	46.40E
Stephens, Port, b., Austl. (stē'fěns)	198	32.43N	152.55E
Stephenville, Can. (stē'věn-vĭl)	79a	48.33N	58.35W
Stepney, neigh., Eng., U.K.	231	51.31N	0.02W
Stepnyak, Kaz. (styĭp-nyäk')	158	52.50N	70.50E
Sterkrade, Ger. (shtěr'krädě)	151c	51.31N	6.51E
Sterkstroom, S. Afr.	207c	31.33S	26.36E
Sterling, Co., U.S. (stûr'lĭng)	90	40.38N	103.14W
Sterling, Il., U.S.	92	41.48N	89.42W
Sterling, Ks., U.S.	104	38.11N	98.11W
Sterling, Ma., U.S.	87a	42.26N	71.41W
Sterling, Tx., U.S.	106	31.53N	100.58W
Sterling Park, Ca., U.S.	227b	37.41N	122.26W
Sterlitamak, Russia (styěr'lê-ta-mák')	158	53.38N	55.56E
Šternberk, Czech. (shtěrn'běrk)	148	49.44N	17.18E
Stettin, *see* Szczecin, Pol.	136	53.25N	14.35E
Stettler, Can.	78	52.19N	112.43W
Steubenville, Oh., U.S. (stū'běn-vĭl)	92	40.20N	80.40W
Stevens, l., Wa., U.S. (stē'věnz)	100a	47.59N	122.06W
Stevens Point, Wi., U.S.	96	44.30N	89.35W
Stevensville, Mt., U.S. (stē'věnz-vĭl)	98	46.31N	114.03E
Stewart, r., Can. (stū'ērt)	78	63.27N	138.48W
Stewart Island, i., N.Z.	197a	46.56S	167.40E
Stewart Manor, N.Y., U.S.	224	40.43N	73.41W
Stewiacke, Can. (stū'wê-ăk)	86	45.08N	63.21W
Steynsrus, S. Afr. (stīns'rōōs)	212d	27.58S	27.33E
Steyr, Aus. (shtīr)	140	48.03N	14.24E
Stickney, Il., U.S.	227a	41.49N	87.47W
Stiepel, neigh., Ger.	232	51.25N	7.15E
Stif, Alg.	204	36.18N	5.21E
Stikine, r., Can. (stĭ-kēn')	78	58.17N	130.10W
Stikine Ranges, Can.	78	59.05N	130.00W
Stillaguamish, r., Wa., U.S.	100a	48.11N	122.18W
Stillaguamish, South Fork, r., Wa., U.S. (stĭl-*à*-gwä'mĭsh)	100a	48.05N	121.59W
Stillwater, Mn., U.S. (stĭl'wô-tēr)	101g	45.04N	92.48W
Stillwater, Mt., U.S.	98	45.23N	109.45W
Stillwater, Ok., U.S.	104	36.06N	97.03W
Stillwater, r., Mt., U.S.	98	48.47N	114.40W
Stillwater Range, mts., Nv., U.S.	102	39.43N	118.11W
Stintonville, S. Afr.	240b	26.14S	28.13E
Štip, Mac. (shtĭp)	154	41.43N	22.07E
Stirling, Scot., U.K. (stûr'lĭng)	144	56.05N	3.59W
Stittsville, Can. (stĭts'vĭl)	77c	45.15N	75.54W
Stizef, Alg. (měr-syä' lá-kôNb)	152	35.18N	0.11W
Stjördalshalsen, Nor. (styûr-däls-hälsěn)	146	63.26N	11.00E
Stockbridge Munsee Indian Reservation, I.R., Wi., U.S. (stŏk'brĭdj mŭn-sē)	96	44.49N	89.00W
Stockerau, Aus. (shtō'kě-rou)	148	48.24N	16.13E
Stockholm, Swe. (stŏk'hōlm)	136	59.23N	18.00E
Stockholm, Me., U.S. (stŏk'hōlm)	86	47.05N	68.08W
Stockport, Eng., U.K. (stŏk'pôrt)	144	53.24N	2.09W
Stockton, Eng., U.K.	144	54.35N	1.25W
Stockton, Ca., U.S. (stŏk't*ŭn*)	90	37.56N	121.16W
Stockton, Ks., U.S.	104	39.26N	99.16W
Stockton, i., Wi., U.S.	96	46.56N	90.25W
Stockton Plateau, plat., Tx., U.S.	90	30.34N	102.35W
Stockton Reservoir, res., Mo., U.S.	104	37.40N	93.45W
Stockum, neigh., Ger.	232	51.28N	7.22E
Stöde, Swe. (stû'dě)	146	62.26N	16.35E
Stoeng Trêng, Kam. (stông'trěng')	188	13.36N	106.00E
Stoke d'Abernon, Eng., U.K.	231	51.19N	0.23W
Stoke Newington, neigh., Eng., U.K.	231	51.34N	0.05W
Stoke-on-Trent, Eng., U.K. (stōk-ŏn-trěnt)	140	53.01N	2.12W
Stoke Poges, Eng., U.K.	231	51.33N	0.35W
Stokhod, r., Ukr. (stō-kōd)	148	51.24N	25.20E
Stolac, Bos. (stô'láts)	154	43.03N	17.59E
Stolbovoy, is., Russia (stôl-bô-voi')	162	74.05N	136.00E
Stolin, Ukr. (stô'lēn)	148	51.54N	26.52E
Stolpe, Ger.	234a	52.40N	13.16E
Stömstad, Swe.	146	58.58N	11.09E
Stondon Massey, Eng., U.K.	231	51.41N	0.18E
Stone, Eng., U.K.	138a	52.54N	2.09W
Stone, Eng., U.K.	231	51.27N	0.16E
Stoneham, Can. (stōn'*à*m)	77b	46.59N	71.22W
Stoneham, Ma., U.S.	87a	42.30N	71.05W
Stonehaven, Scot., U.K. (stōn'hā-v'n)	144	56.57N	2.09W
Stone Mountain, Ga., U.S. (stōn)	94c	33.49N	84.10W
Stone Park, Il., U.S.	227a	41.45N	87.53W
Stonewall, Can. (stōn'wôl)	77f	50.09N	97.21W
Stonewall, Ms., U.S.	108	32.08N	88.44W
Stoney Creek, Can. (stō'nê)	77d	43.13N	79.45W
Stonington, Ct., U.S. (stōn'ĭng-t*ŭn*)	92	41.20N	71.55W
Stony Indian Reserve, I.R., Can.	77e	51.10N	114.45W
Stony Mountain, Can.	77f	50.05N	97.13W
Stony Plain, Can. (stō'nê plān)	77g	53.32N	114.00W
Stony Plain Indian Reserve, I.R., Can.	77g	53.29N	113.48W
Stony Point, N.Y., U.S.	94a	41.13N	73.58W
Stony Run, Md., U.S.	225c	39.11N	76.42W
Stora Sotra, i., Nor.	146	60.24N	4.35E
Stord, i., Nor. (stôrd)	146	59.54N	5.15E
Store Baelt, strt., Den.	146	55.25N	10.50E
Storeton, Eng., U.K.	233a	53.21N	3.03W
Storfjorden, fj., Nor.	146	62.17N	6.19E
Stormberg, mts., S. Afr. (stôrm'bûrg)	207c	31.28S	26.35E
Storm Lake, Ia., U.S.	96	42.39N	95.12W
Stormy Point, c., V.I.U.S. (stôr'mē)	111c	18.22N	65.01W
Stornoway, Scot., U.K. (stôr'nô-wā)	140	58.13N	6.21W
Storozhinets, Ukr. (stô-rô'zhěn-yěts)	148	48.10N	25.44E
Störsjo, Swe. (stôr'shû)	146	62.49N	13.08E
Störsjoen, l., Nor. (stôr-syûěn)	146	61.32N	11.30E
Störsjon, l., Swe.	140	63.06N	14.00E
Storvik, Swe.	146	60.37N	16.31E
Stoughton, Wi., U.S.	96	42.54N	89.15W
Stour, r., Eng., U.K. (stour)	144	52.09N	0.29E
Stourbridge, Eng., U.K. (stour'brĭj)	138a	52.27N	2.08W
Stow, Ma., U.S. (stō)	87a	42.56N	71.31W
Stow, Oh., U.S.	95d	41.09N	81.26W
Stowe Township, Pa., U.S.	226b	40.29N	80.04W
Straatsdrif, S. Afr.	212d	25.19S	26.22E
Strabane, N. Ire., U.K. (stră-băn')	144	54.59N	7.27W
Straelen, Ger. (shtrā'lěn)	151c	51.26N	6.16E
Strahan, Austl. (strā'*ă*n)	196	42.08S	145.28E
Strakonice, Czech. (strä'kô-nyê-tsě)	148	49.18N	13.52E
Straldzha, Bul. (sträl'dzhá)	154	42.37N	26.44E
Stralsund, Ger. (shräl'sŏont)	140	54.18N	13.04E
Strangford Lough, l., N. Ire., U.K.	144	54.30N	5.34W
Strängnäs, Swe. (strěng'nĕs)	146	59.23N	16.59E
Stranraer, Scot., U.K. (străn-rär')	144	54.55N	5.05W
Strasbourg, Fr. (strás-bōōr')	136	48.36N	7.49E
Stratford, Can. (străt'fērd)	84	43.20N	81.05W
Stratford, Ct., U.S.	92	41.10N	73.05W
Stratford, Wi., U.S.	96	44.16N	90.02W
Stratford-upon-Avon, Eng., U.K.	144	52.13N	1.41W
Strathfield, Austl.	239a	33.52S	151.06E
Strathmoor, neigh., Mi., U.S.	226c	42.23N	83.11W
Straubing, Ger. (strou'bĭng)	148	48.52N	12.36E
Strauch, Ger.	232	51.09N	6.56E
Strausberg, Ger. (strous'běrgh)	148	52.35N	13.50E
Strawberry, r., Ut., U.S.	102	40.05N	110.55W
Strawberry Point, Ca., U.S.	227b	37.54N	122.31W
Strawn, Tx., U.S. (strôn)	106	32.38N	98.28W
Streatham, neigh., Eng., U.K.	231	51.26N	0.08W
Streator, Il., U.S. (strē'tēr)	92	41.05N	88.50W
Streeter, N.D., U.S.	96	46.40N	99.22W
Streetsville, Can. (strētz'vĭl)	77d	43.34N	79.43W
Strehaia, Rom. (strě-kä'yá)	154	44.37N	23.13E
Strel'na, Russia (strěl'ná)	164c	59.52N	30.01E
Stretford, Eng., U.K. (strět'fērd)	138a	53.25N	2.19W
Strickland, r., Pap. N. Gui. (strĭk'l*ă*nd)	188	6.15S	142.00E
Strijen, Neth.	139a	51.44N	4.32E
Stromboli, Italy (strôm'bô-lē)	142	38.46N	15.16E
Stromyn, Russia (strô'mĭn)	164b	56.02N	38.29E
Strong, r., Ms., U.S. (strông)	108	32.03N	89.42W
Strongsville, Oh., U.S. (strŏngz'vĭl)	95d	41.19N	81.50W
Stronsay, i., Scot., U.K. (strŏn'sā)	144a	59.09N	2.35W
Stroudsburg, Pa., U.S. (stroudz'bûrg)	92	41.00N	75.15W
Strubenvale, S. Afr.	240b	26.16S	28.28E
Struer, Den.	146	56.29N	8.34E
Strugi Krasnyye, Russia (strōō'gĭ krä's-ny'yě)	156	58.14N	29.10E
Struisbelt, S. Afr.	240b	26.19S	28.29E
Struma, r., Eur. (strōō'ma)	154	41.55N	23.05E
Strumica, Mac. (strōō'mĭ-tsá)	154	41.26N	22.38E
Strümp, Ger.	232	51.17N	6.40E
Strunino, Russia	164b	56.23N	38.34E
Struthers, Oh., U.S. (strŭdh'ērz)	92	41.00N	80.35W
Struvenhütten, Ger. (shtrōō'věn-hü-těn)	139c	53.52N	10.04E
Strydpoortberge, mts., S. Afr.	212d	24.08S	29.18E
Stryy, Ukr. (strē')	148	49.16N	23.51E
Strzelce Opolskie, Pol. (stzhěl'tsě o-pŏl'skyě)	148	50.31N	18.20E
Strzelin, Pol. (stzhě-lĭn)	148	50.48N	17.06E
Strzelno, Pol. (stzhál'nô)	148	52.37N	18.10E
Stuart, Fl., U.S. (stū'ērt)	109a	27.10N	80.14W
Stuart, Ia., U.S.	96	41.31N	94.20W
Stuart, i., Ak., U.S.	89	63.25N	162.45W
Stuart, i., Wa., U.S.	100d	48.42N	123.10W
Stuart Lake, l., Can.	80	54.32N	124.35W
Stuart Range, mts., Austl.	196	29.00S	134.30E
Stupava, Czech.	139e	48.17N	17.02E
Sturgeon, r., Can.	77g	53.41N	113.46W
Sturgeon, r., Mi., U.S.	96	46.43N	88.43W
Sturgeon Bay, Wi., U.S.	96	44.50N	87.22W
Sturgeon Bay, b., Can.	82	52.00N	98.00W
Sturgeon Falls, Can.	78	46.19N	79.49W
Sturgis, Ky., U.S.	92	37.35N	88.00W
Sturgis, Mi., U.S.	92	41.45N	85.25W
Sturgis, S.D., U.S.	96	44.25N	103.31W
Sturt Creek, r., Austl.	196	19.40S	127.40E
Sturtevant, Wi., U.S. (stŭr'tē-vănt)	95a	42.42N	87.54W
Stutterheim, S. Afr. (stŭrt'ēr-hīm)	207c	32.34S	27.27E
Stuttgart, Ger. (shtōōt'gärt)	136	48.48N	9.15E
Stuttgart, Ar., U.S. (stŭt'gärt)	104	34.30N	91.33W
Styal, Eng., U.K.	233b	53.21N	2.15W
Stykkishólmur, Ice.	140	65.00N	21.48W
Styr', r., Eur. (stēr)	148	51.44N	26.07E
Styria, *see* Steiermark, prov., Aus.	148	47.22N	14.40E
Styrum, neigh., Ger.	232	51.27N	6.51E
Suao, Tai. (sōōóu)	184	24.35N	121.45E
Subarnarekha, r., India	178	22.38N	86.26E
Subata, Lat. (sŏŏ'bá-tá)	146	56.02N	25.54E
Subic, Phil. (sōō'bĭk)	189a	14.52N	120.15E
Subic Bay, b., Phil.	189a	14.41N	120.11E
Subotica, Yugo. (sōō'bô'tê-tsá)	136	46.06N	19.41E
Subugo, mtn., Kenya	210	1.40S	35.49E
Succasunna, N.J., U.S. (s*ŭ*k'k*à*-sŭn'n*à*)	94a	40.52N	74.37W
Suceava, Rom. (sōō-chá-ä'vá)	148	47.39N	26.17E
Suceava, r., Rom.	148	47.45N	26.10E
Sucha, Pol. (sōō'kȧ)	148	49.44N	19.40E
Suchiapa, Mex. (sōō-chê-ä'pä)	112	16.38N	93.08W
Suchiapa, r., Mex.	112	16.27N	93.26W
Suchitoto, El Sal. (sōō-chê-tō'tō)	114	13.58N	89.03W
Sucio, r., Col. (sōō'syô)	124a	6.55N	76.15W
Suck, r., Ire. (sŭk)	144	53.34N	8.16W
Sucre, Bol. (sōō'krā)	124	19.06S	65.16W
Sucre, dept., Ven. (sōō'krě)	125b	10.18N	64.12W
Sucy-en-Brie, Fr.	233c	48.46N	2.32E
Sud, Canal du, strt., Haiti	116	18.40N	73.15W
Sud, Rivière du, r., Can. (rê-vyâr'dü süd')	77b	46.56N	70.35W
Suda, Russia (sô'dá)	164a	56.58N	56.45E
Suda, r., Russia (sô'dá)	156	59.24N	36.40E
Sudair, Sau. Ar. (sŭ-dä'ĕr)	174	25.48N	46.28E
Sudalsvatnet, l., Nor.	146	59.35N	6.59E
Sudan, nation, Afr.	204	14.00N	28.00E
Sudan, reg., Afr. (sōō-dän')	204	15.00N	7.00E
Sudberg, neigh., Ger.	232	51.11N	7.08E
Sudbury, Can. (sŭd'běr-ê)	78	46.28N	81.00W
Sudbury, Ma., U.S.	87a	42.23N	71.25W
Suderwich, neigh., Ger.	232	51.37N	7.15E
Sudetes, mts., Eur.	136	50.41N	15.37E
Sudogda, Russia (sô'dôk-dá)	156	55.57N	40.29E
Sudost', r., Eur. (sô-dôst')	156	52.43N	33.13E
Sudzha, Russia (sŏd'zhá)	156	51.14N	35.11E
Sueca, Spain (swā'kä)	152	39.12N	0.18W
Suez, Egypt	204	29.58N	32.34E
Suez, Gulf of, b., Egypt (sōō-ěz')	204	29.53N	32.33E
Suez Canal, can., Egypt	204	30.53N	32.21E
Suffern, N.Y., U.S. (sŭf'fērn)	94a	41.07N	74.09W
Suffolk, Va., U.S. (sŭf'*ŭ*k)	94g	36.43N	76.35W
Sugandha, India	236a	22.54N	88.20E
Sugar City, Co., U.S.	104	38.12N	103.42W
Sugar Creek, Mo., U.S.	101f	39.07N	94.27W
Sugar Creek, r., Il., U.S. (shóg'ēr)	104	40.14N	89.28W
Sugar Creek, r., In., U.S.	92	39.55N	87.10W
Sugar Island, i., Mi., U.S.	101k	46.31N	84.12W
Sugarloaf Point, c., Austl. (sóg*ẽ*r'lôf)	198	32.19S	153.04E
Suggi Lake, l., Can.	82	54.22N	102.47W
Suginami, neigh., Japan	238a	35.42N	139.38E
Sühbaatar, Mong.	180	50.18N	106.31E
Suhl, Ger. (zōōl)	148	50.37N	10.41E
Suichuan, mtn., China	184	26.25N	114.10E
Suide, China (swā-dü)	184	37.32N	110.12E
Suifenhe, China (swā-fŭn-hŭ)	180	44.47N	131.13E
Suihua, China	180	46.38N	126.50E
Suining, China (sōō'ê-nĭng')	182	33.54N	117.57E
Suipacha, Arg. (swê-pä'chä)	123c	34.45S	59.43W
Suiping, China (swā-pĭŋ)	182	33.09N	113.58E
Suir, r., Ire. (sūr)	144	52.20N	7.32W
Suisun Bay, b., Ca., U.S. (sōōê-sōōn')	100b	38.07N	122.02W
Suita, Japan (sô'ê-tä)	187b	34.45N	135.32E
Suitland, Md., U.S. (sōt'lănd)	94e	38.51N	76.57W
Suixian, China (swā shyěn)	184	31.42N	113.20E
Suiyüan, hist. reg., China (swā-yüěn)	180	41.31N	107.04E
Suizhong, China (swā-jôŋ)	184	40.22N	120.20E
Sukabumi, Indon.	188	6.52S	106.56E
Sukadana, Indon.	188	1.15S	110.30E
Sukagawa, Japan (sōō'kä-gä'wä)	187	37.08N	140.07E
Sukhinichi, Russia (sōō'ĸē'nê-chê)	160	54.07N	35.18E
Sukhona, r., Russia (sô-kô'ná)	160	59.30N	42.20E
Sukhoy Log, Russia (sōō'kôy lôg)	164a	56.55N	62.03E
Sukhumi, Geor. (sô-kôm')	160	43.00N	41.00E
Sukkur, Pak. (sŭk'ŭr)	174	27.49N	68.50E
Sukkwan Island, i., Ak., U.S.	80	55.05N	132.45W
Suksun, Russia (sôk'sôn)	164a	57.08N	57.22E
Sukumo, Japan (sōō'kô-mô)	187	32.58N	132.45E
Sukunka, r., Can.	80	55.00N	121.50W
Sula, r., Ukr. (sōō-lá')	156	50.36N	33.13E
Sula, Kepulauan, is., Indon.	188	2.20S	125.20E
Sulaco, r., Hond. (sōō-lä'kō)	114	14.55N	87.31W
Sulaimān Range, mts., Pak. (sô-lä-ê-män')	174	29.47N	69.10E
Sulak, r., Russia (sōō-lák')	160	43.30N	47.00E
Sulfeld, Ger. (zōō'fěld)	139c	53.48N	10.13E
Sulina, Rom. (sōō-lē'ná)	142	45.08N	29.38E
Sulitelma, mtn., Eur. (sōō-lê-tyěl'má)	140	67.03N	16.35E
Sullana, Peru (sōō-lyä'ná)	124	4.57S	80.47W
Sulligent, Al., U.S. (sŭl'ĭ-jěnt)	108	33.52N	88.06W
Sullivan, Il., U.S. (sŭl'ĭ-v*ă*n)	92	41.35N	88.35W
Sullivan, In., U.S.	92	39.05N	87.20W
Sullivan, Mo., U.S.	104	38.13N	91.09W
Sulmona, Italy (sōōl-mō'ná)	154	42.02N	13.58E
Sulphur, Ok., U.S. (sŭl'f*ŭ*r)	104	34.31N	96.58W
Sulphur, r., Tx., U.S.	104	33.26N	95.06W
Sulphur Springs, Tx., U.S. (sprĭngz)	104	33.09N	95.36W
Sultan, Wa., U.S. (sŭl't*ă*n)	100a	47.52N	121.49W
Sultan, r., Wa., U.S.	100a	47.55N	121.49W
Sultepec, Mex. (sōōl-tá-pěk')	112	18.50N	99.51W
Sulu Archipelago, is., Phil. (sōō'lōō)	188	5.52N	122.00E
Suluntah, Libya	142	32.39N	21.49E
Sulūq, Libya	204	31.39N	20.15E
Sulu Sea, sea, Asia	188	8.25N	119.00E
Suma, Japan (sōō'mä)	187b	34.39N	135.08E
Sumas, Wa., U.S. (sū'm*à*s)	100d	49.00N	122.16W
Sumatera, i., Indon. (sô-mä-trá)	188	2.06N	99.40E
Sumatra, *see* Sumatera, i., Indon.	188	2.06N	99.40E
Sumba, i., Indon. (sŭm'bá)	188	9.52S	119.00E
Sumba, Île, i., Zaire	210	1.44N	19.32E
Sumbawa, i., Indon. (sôm-bä'wä)	188	9.00S	118.18E
Sumbawa-Besar, Indon.	188	8.32S	117.20E

ăt; finăl; rāte; senāte; ärm; ȧsk; sof*ȧ*; fâre; ch-choose; dh-as th in other; bē; ėvent; bĕt; recĕnt; cratẽr; g-gō; gh-guttural g; bĭt; ĭ-short neutral; rīde; ĸ-guttural k as ch in German ich;

PLACE (Pronunciation)	PAGE	Lat. °′	Long. °′
Sumbawanga, Tan.	210	7.58S	31.37E
Sumbe, Ang.	206	11.13S	13.50E
Sümeg, Hung. (shü'mĕg)	148	46.59N	17.19E
Sumida, r., Japan (so͞o'mē-dä)	187	36.01N	139.24E
Sumidouro, Braz. (so͞o-mē-dō'rŏ)	123a	22.04S	42.41W
Sumiyoshi, Japan (so͞o'mē-yō'shē)	187b	34.43N	135.16E
Sumiyoshi, neigh., Japan	238b	34.36N	135.31E
Summer Lake, l., Or., U.S. (sŭm'ẽr)	98	42.50N	120.35W
Summerland, Can. (sŭ'mẽr-lănd)	80	49.39N	119.40W
Summerseat, Eng., U.K.	233b	53.38N	2.19W
Summerside, Can. (sŭm'ẽr-sīd)	78	46.25N	63.47W
Summerton, S.C., U.S. (sŭm'ẽr-tŭn)	108	33.37N	80.22W
Summerville, S.C., U.S. (sŭm'ẽr-vĭl)	108	33.00N	80.10W
Summit, Il., U.S. (sŭm'mĭt)	95a	41.47N	87.48W
Summit, N.J., U.S.	94a	40.43N	74.21W
Summit Lake Indian Reservation, I.R., Nv., U.S.	98	41.35N	119.30W
Summit Park, Md., U.S.	225c	39.23N	76.41W
Summit Peak, mtn., Co., U.S.	102	37.20N	106.40W
Sumner, Wa., U.S. (sŭm'nẽr)	100a	47.12N	122.14W
Šumperk, Czech. (shòm'pĕrk)	148	49.57N	17.02E
Sumrall, Ms., U.S. (sŭm'rôl)	108	31.25N	89.34W
Sumter, S.C., U.S. (sŭm'tẽr)	108	33.55N	80.21W
Sumy, Ukr. (so͞o'mĭ)	158	50.54N	34.47E
Sumy, prov., Ukr.	156	51.02N	34.05E
Sun, r., Mt., U.S. (sŭn)	98	47.34N	111.53W
Sunburst, Mt., U.S.	98	48.53N	111.55W
Sunbury, Eng., U.K.	231	51.25N	0.26W
Sunda, Selat, strt., Indon.	188	5.45S	106.15E
Sundance, Wy., U.S. (sŭn'dăns)	98	44.24N	104.27W
Sundarbans, sw., Asia (sòn'dẽr-bŭns)	174	21.50N	89.00E
Sunday Strait, strt., Austl. (sŭn'dā)	196	15.50S	122.45E
Sundbyberg, Swe. (sòn'bü-bĕrgh)	146	59.24N	17.56E
Sunderland, Eng., U.K. (sŭn'dẽr-lănd)	140	54.55N	1.25W
Sunderland, Md., U.S.	94e	38.41N	76.36W
Sundridge, Eng., U.K.	231	51.17N	0.08E
Sundsvall, Swe. (sònds'väl)	136	62.24N	19.19E
Sungari (Songhua), r., China	180	46.09N	127.53E
Sungari Reservoir, res., China	184	42.55N	127.50E
Sungurlu, Tur. (so͝on'gòr-lò')	142	40.08N	34.20E
Sun Kosi, r., Nepal	178	27.13N	85.52E
Sunland, Ca., U.S. (sŭn-lănd)	101a	34.16N	118.18W
Sunne, Swe. (so͝on'ĕ)	146	59.51N	13.07E
Sunninghill, Eng., U.K. (sŭnĭng'hĭl)	138b	51.23N	0.40W
Sunnymead, Ca., U.S. (sŭn'ĭ-mēd)	101a	33.56N	117.15W
Sunnyside, Ut., U.S.	102	39.35N	110.20W
Sunnyside, Wa., U.S.	98	46.19N	120.00W
Sunnyvale, Ca., U.S. (sŭn-nē-vāl)	100b	37.23N	122.02W
Sunol, Ca., U.S. (so͞o'nŭl)	100b	37.36N	122.53W
Sunset, Ut., U.S. (sŭn-sĕt)	101b	41.08N	112.02W
Sunset Beach, Ca., U.S.	228	33.43N	118.04W
Sunset Crater National Monument, rec., Az., U.S. (krā'tẽr)	102	35.20N	111.30W
Sunshine, Austl.	195a	37.47S	144.50E
Suntar, Russia (sòn-tàr')	158	62.14N	117.49E
Sunyani, Ghana	208	7.20N	2.20W
Suoyarvi, Russia (so͞o'ô-yĕr'vē)	160	62.12N	32.29E
Superior, Az., U.S. (su-pē'rĭ-ẽr)	102	33.15N	111.10W
Superior, Ne., U.S.	104	40.04N	98.05W
Superior, Wi., U.S.	90	46.44N	92.06W
Superior, Wy., U.S.	98	41.45N	108.57W
Superior, Laguna, l., Mex. (lä-go͞o'nä so͞o-pā-rē-ōr')	112	16.20N	94.55W
Superior, Lake, l., N.A.	90	47.38N	89.20W
Superior Village, Wi., U.S.	101h	46.38N	92.07W
Sup'ung Reservoir, res., Asia (so͞o'po͝ong)	186	40.35N	126.00E
Suqian, China (so͞o-chyĕn)	182	33.57N	118.17E
Suquamish, Wa., U.S. (so͞o-gwä'mĭsh)	100a	47.44N	122.34W
Suquṭrā (Socotra), i., Yemen (sô-kō'trȧ)	174	13.00N	52.30E
Şūr, Leb. (so͞or) (tīr)	173a	33.16N	35.13E
Şūr, Oman	174	22.23N	59.28E
Šura, neigh., India	236a	22.33N	88.25E
Surabaya, Indon.	188	7.23S	112.45E
Surakarta, Indon.	188	7.35S	110.45E
Šurany, Czech. (shōo'rȧ-nû')	148	48.05N	18.11E
Surat, Austl. (sū-răt)	198	27.18S	149.00E
Surat, India (sò'rŭt)	174	21.08N	73.22E
Surat Thani, Thai.	188	8.59N	99.14E
Surazh, Bela.	156	55.24N	30.46E
Surazh, Russia (so͞o-räzh')	156	53.02N	32.27E
Surbiton, neigh., Eng., U.K.	231	51.24N	0.18W
Surco, Peru	229c	12.09S	77.01W
Suresnes, Fr.	233c	48.52N	2.14E
Surgères, Fr. (sür-zhâr')	150	46.06N	0.51W
Surgut, Russia (sòr-gòt')	158	61.18N	73.38E
Suriname, nation, S.A. (so͞o-rē-näm')	124	4.00N	56.00W
Sūrmaq, Iran	176	31.03N	52.48E
Surquillo, Peru	229c	12.07S	77.02W
Surt, Libya	204	31.14N	16.37E
Surt, Khalīj, b., Libya	204	31.30N	18.28E
Suruga-Wan, b., Japan (so͞o'ro͞o-gä wän)	186	34.52N	138.36E
Suru-Lere, neigh., Nig.	240d	6.31N	3.22E
Susa, Japan	187	34.40N	131.39E
Sušak, i., Yugo.	154	42.45N	16.30E
Susak, Otok, i., Yugo.	154	44.31N	14.15E
Susaki, Japan (so͞o'sä-kē)	187	33.23N	133.16E
Sušice, Czech.	148	49.14N	13.31E
Susitna, Ak., U.S. (so͞o-sĭt'nȧ)	89	61.28N	150.28W
Susitna, r., Ak., U.S.	89	62.00N	150.28W
Susong, China (so͞o-sòŋ)	184	30.18N	116.08E
Susquehanna, Pa., U.S. (sŭs'kwē-hăn'ȧ)	92	41.55N	73.55W
Susquehanna, r., U.S.	92	39.50N	76.20W
Sussex, Can. (sŭs'ĕks)	78	45.43N	65.31W
Sussex, N.J., U.S.	94a	41.12N	74.36W
Sussex, Wi., U.S.	95a	43.08N	88.12W
Sutherland, Austl. (sŭdh'ẽr-lănd)	195b	34.02S	151.04E
Sutherland, S. Afr. (sŭ'thẽr-lănd)	206	32.25S	20.40E
Sutlej, r., Asia (sŭt'lĕj)	174	30.15N	73.00E
Sutton, Eng., U.K. (sut''n)	138b	51.21N	0.12W
Sutton, Ma., U.S.	87a	42.09N	71.46W
Sutton-at-Hone, Eng., U.K.	231	51.25N	0.14E
Sutton Coldfield, Eng., U.K. (kōld'fēld)	138a	52.34N	1.49W
Sutton-in-Ashfield, Eng., U.K. (ĭn-ăsh'fēld)	138a	53.07N	1.15W
Suurbekom, S. Afr.	240b	26.19S	27.44E
Suurberge, mts., S. Afr.	207c	33.15S	25.32E
Suva, Fiji	192g	18.08S	178.25E
Suwa, Japan (so͞o'wä)	187	36.03N	138.08E
Suwałki, Pol. (sò-vou'kē)	148	54.05N	22.58E
Suwanee Lake, l., Can.	82	56.08N	100.10W
Suwannee, r., U.S. (sò-wô'nē)	90	29.42N	83.00W
Suways al Ḩulwah, Tur'at as, can., Egypt	212c	30.15N	32.20E
Suxian, China (so͞o shyĕn)	184	33.29N	117.51E
Suzdal', Russia (so͞oz'dȧl)	156	56.26N	40.29E
Suzhou, China (so͞o-jō)	180	31.19N	120.37E
Suzuki-shinden, Japan	238a	35.43N	139.31E
Suzu Misaki, c., Japan (so͞o'zo͞o mē'sä-kē)	186	37.30N	137.35E
Svalbard (Spitsbergen), dep., Eur. (svăl'bărt) (spĭts'bûr-gĕn)	158	77.00N	20.00E
Svaneke, Den. (svä'nĕ-kĕ)	146	55.08N	15.07E
Svatovo, Ukr. (svä'tō-vō)	160	49.23N	38.10E
Svedala, Swe. (svĕ'dä-lä)	146	55.29N	13.11E
Sveg, Swe.	146	62.03N	14.22E
Svelvik, Nor. (svĕl'vēk)	146	59.37N	10.18E
Svenčionys, Lith.	146	55.09N	26.09E
Svendborg, Den. (svĕn-bôrgh)	146	55.05N	10.35E
Svensen, Or., U.S. (svĕn'sĕn)	100c	46.10N	123.39W
Sverdlovsk, *see* Yekaterinburg, Russia	158	56.51N	60.36E
Svetlaya, Russia (svyĕt'lá-yȧ)	186	46.09N	137.53E
Svilajnac, Yugo. (svē'lá-ē-náts)	154	44.12N	21.14E
Svilengrad, Bul. (svĕl'ĕn-grát)	154	41.44N	26.11E
Svir', r., Russia	160	60.55N	33.40E
Svir Kanal, can., Russia (kȧ-näl')	146	60.10N	32.40E
Svishtov, Bul. (svĕsh'tôf)	142	43.36N	25.21E
Svisloch', r., Bela. (svēs'lôk)	156	53.38N	28.10E
Svitavy, Czech.	148	49.46N	16.28E
Svitsa, r., Ukr. (svĭ-tsä)	148	49.09N	24.10E
Svobodnyy, Russia (svŏ-bôd'nĭ)	158	51.28N	128.28E
Svolvaer, Nor. (svôl'vĕr)	140	68.15N	14.29E
Svyatoy Nos, Mys, c., Russia (svyŭ'toi nôs)	158	72.18N	139.28E
Swadlincote, Eng., U.K. (swŏd'lĭn-kōt)	138a	52.46N	1.33W
Swain Reefs, rf., Austl. (swān)	196	22.12S	152.08E
Swainsboro, Ga., U.S. (swānz'bŭr-ō)	108	32.37N	82.21W
Swakopmund, Nmb. (svä'kōp-mònt) (swȧ'kŏp-mŏnd)	206	22.40S	14.30E
Swallowfield, Eng., U.K. (swŏl'ō-fēld)	138b	51.21N	0.58W
Swampscott, Ma., U.S. (swŏmp'skŏt)	87a	42.28N	70.55W
Swan, r., Austl.	196	31.30S	116.30E
Swan, r., Can.	82	51.58N	101.45W
Swan, r., Mt., U.S.	98	47.50N	113.40W
Swan Acres, Pa., U.S.	226b	40.33N	80.02W
Swan Hill, Austl.	196	35.20S	143.30E
Swan Hills, Can. (hĭlz)	78	54.52N	115.45W
Swan Island, i., Austl. (swŏn)	195a	38.15S	144.41E
Swan Lake, l., Can.	82	52.30N	100.45W
Swanland, reg., Austl. (swŏn'lănd)	196	31.45S	119.15E
Swanley, Eng., U.K.	231	51.24N	0.12E
Swan Range, mts., Mt., U.S.	98	47.50N	113.40W
Swan River, Can. (swŏn rĭv'ẽr)	78	52.06N	101.16W
Swanscombe, Eng., U.K.	231	51.26N	0.18E
Swansea, Wales, U.K.	140	51.37N	3.59W
Swansea, Il., U.S. (swŏn'sē)	101e	38.32N	89.59W
Swansea, Ma., U.S.	94b	41.45N	71.09W
Swansea, neigh., Can.	223c	43.38N	79.28W
Swanson Reservoir, res., Ne., U.S. (swŏn'sŭn)	104	40.13N	101.30W
Swartberg, mtn., Afr.	207c	30.08S	29.34E
Swarthmore, Pa., U.S.	225b	39.54N	75.21W
Swartkop, mtn., S. Afr.	206a	34.13S	18.27E
Swartruggens, S. Afr.	212d	25.40S	26.40E
Swartspruit, S. Afr.	207b	25.44S	28.01E
Swatow, *see* Shantou, China	180	23.20N	116.40E
Swaziland, nation, Afr. (swä'zē-lănd)	206	26.45S	31.30E
Sweden, nation, Eur. (swē'dĕn)	136	60.10N	14.10E
Swedesboro, N.J., U.S. (swēdz'bē-rô)	94f	39.45N	75.22W
Sweetwater, Tn., U.S. (swēt'wô-tẽr)	108	35.36N	84.29W
Sweetwater, Tx., U.S.	90	32.28N	100.25W
Sweetwater, l., N.D., U.S.	96	48.15N	98.35W
Sweetwater, r., Wy., U.S.	98	42.19N	108.35W
Sweetwater Reservoir, res., Ca., U.S.	102a	32.42N	116.54W
Świdnica, Pol. (shvĭd-nē'tsȧ)	148	50.50N	16.30E
Świdwin, Pol. (shvĭd'vĭn)	148	53.46N	15.48E
Świebodzice, Pol.	148	50.51N	16.17E
Świebodzin, Pol. (shvyĕn-bo'jĕts)	148	52.16N	15.36E
Świecie, Pol. (shvyăn'tsyĕ)	148	53.23N	18.26E
Świętokrzyskie, Góry, mts., Pol. (shvyĕn-tō-kzhĭ'skyĕ go͞o'rĭ)	148	50.57N	21.02E
Swift, r., Eng., U.K.	138a	52.26N	1.08W
Swift, r., Me., U.S. (swĭft)	86	44.42N	70.40E
Swift Creek Reservoir, res., Wa., U.S.	98	46.03N	122.10W
Swift Current, Can. (swĭft kûr'ĕnt)	78	50.17N	107.50W
Swindle Island, i., Can.	80	52.32N	128.35W
Swindon, Eng., U.K. (swĭn'dŭn)	144	51.35N	1.55W
Swinomish Indian Reservation, I.R., Wa., U.S. (swĭ-nō'mĭsh)	100a	48.25N	122.27W
Świnoujście, Pol. (shvĭ-nĭ-ô-wĕsh'chyĕ)	148	53.56N	14.14E
Swinton, Eng., U.K. (swĭn'tŭn)	138a	53.30N	1.19W
Swinton, Eng., U.K.	233b	53.31N	2.20W
Swissvale, Pa., U.S. (swĭs'vāl)	95e	40.25N	79.53W
Switzerland, nation, Eur. (swĭt'zẽr-lănd)	136	46.30N	7.43E
Syas', r., Russia (syäs)	156	59.28N	33.24E
Sycamore, Il., U.S. (sĭk'ȧ-mōr)	96	42.00N	88.42W
Sycan, r., Or., U.S.	98	42.45N	121.00W
Sychëvka, Russia (sē-chôf'kȧ)	156	55.52N	34.18E
Sydenham, Austl.	239b	37.42S	144.46E
Sydenham, neigh., S. Afr.	240b	26.09S	28.06E
Sydenham, neigh., Eng., U.K.	231	51.26N	0.03W
Sydney, Austl. (sĭd'nē)	196	33.55S	151.17E
Sydney, Can.	78	46.09N	60.11W
Sydney Mines, Can.	78	46.14N	60.14W
Syktyvkar, Russia (sük-tüf'kär)	158	61.35N	50.40E
Sylacauga, Al., U.S. (sĭl-ȧ-kô'gȧ)	108	33.10N	86.15W
Sylarna, mtn., Eur.	146	63.00N	12.10E
Sylt, i., Ger. (sĭlt)	148	54.55N	8.30E
Sylvania, Austl.	239a	34.01S	151.07E
Sylvania, Ga., U.S. (sĭl-vā'nĭ-ȧ)	108	32.44N	81.40W
Sylvania Heights, Austl.	239a	34.02S	151.06E
Sylvester, Ga., U.S. (sĭl-vĕs'tẽr)	108	31.32N	83.50W
Syndal, Austl.	239b	37.53S	145.09E
Syosset, N.Y., U.S.	224	40.50N	73.30W
Syracuse, Ks., U.S. (sĭr'ȧ-kūs)	104	37.59N	101.44W
Syracuse, N.Y., U.S.	90	43.05N	76.10W
Syracuse, Ut., U.S.	101b	41.06N	112.04W
Syr Darya, r., Asia	158	44.15N	65.45E
Syria, nation, Asia (sĭr'ĭ-ȧ)	174	35.00N	37.15E
Syrian Desert, des., Asia	174	32.00N	40.00E
Sysert', Russia (sĕ'sĕrt)	164a	56.30N	60.48E
Sysola, r., Russia	160	60.50N	50.40E
Syukunosho, Japan	238b	34.50N	135.32E
Syzran', Russia (sĕz-rän')	158	53.09N	48.27E
Szamotuły, Pol. (shȧ-mō-to͞o'wē)	148	52.36N	16.34E
Szarvas, Hung. (sôr'vôsh)	148	46.51N	20.36E
Szczebrzeszyn, Pol. (shchĕ-bzhā'shĕn)	148	50.41N	22.58E
Szczecin, Pol. (shchĕ'tsĭn)	136	53.25N	14.35E
Szczecinek, Pol. (shchĕ'tsĭ-nĕk)	140	53.41N	16.42E
Szczuczyn, Pol. (shcho͞o'chĕn)	148	53.32N	22.17E
Szczytno, Pol. (shchĭt'nô)	148	53.33N	21.00E
Szechwan Basin, basin, China	180	30.45N	104.40E
Szeged, Hung. (sĕ'gĕd)	136	46.15N	20.12E
Székesfehérvár, Hung. (sā'kĕsh-fĕ'hār-vär)	142	47.12N	18.26E
Szekszárd, Hung. (sĕk'särd)	142	46.19N	18.42E
Szentendre, Hung. (sĕnt'ĕn-drĕ)	148	47.40N	19.07E
Szentes, Hung. (sĕn'tĕsh)	148	46.38N	20.18E
Szigetvar, Hung. (sē'gĕt-vär)	148	46.05N	17.50E
Szolnok, Hung.	148	47.11N	20.12E
Szombathely, Hung. (sôm'bôt-hĕl')	142	47.13N	16.35E
Szprotawa, Pol. (shprō-tä'vä)	148	51.34N	15.29E
Szydłowiec, Pol. (shid-wô'vyets)	148	51.13N	20.53E

T

PLACE (Pronunciation)	PAGE	Lat. °′	Long. °′
Taal, l., Phil. (tä-äl')	189a	13.58N	121.06E
Tabaco, Phil. (tä-bä'kō)	189a	13.27N	123.40E
Tabankulu, Transkei (tä-bän-ko͞o'la)	207c	30.56S	29.19E
Tabasará, Serranía de, mts., Pan.	114	8.29N	81.22W
Tabasco, Mex. (tä-bäs'kō)	112	21.47N	103.04W
Tabasco, state, Mex.	110	18.10N	93.00W
Taber, Can.	78	49.47N	112.08W
Tablas, i., Phil. (tä'bläs)	189a	12.26N	122.00E
Tablas Strait, strt., Phil.	189a	12.17N	121.41E
Table Bay, b., S. Afr. (tā'b'l)	206a	33.41S	18.27E
Table Mountain, mtn., S. Afr.	206a	33.58S	18.26E
Table Rock Lake, Mo., U.S.	104	36.37N	93.29W
Tabligbo, Togo	208	6.35N	1.30E
Taboão da Serra, Braz.	230d	23.38S	46.46W
Taboga, i., Pan. (tä-bō'gä)	110a	8.48N	79.35W
Taboguilla, i., Pan. (tä-bō-gē'l-yä)	110a	8.48N	79.31W
Tábor, Czech. (tä'bôr)	148	49.25N	14.40E
Tabora, Tan. (tä-bō'rä)	206	5.01S	32.48E
Tabou, I.C. (tȧ-bo͞o')	204	4.25N	7.21W
Tabrīz, Iran (tȧ-brēz')	174	38.00N	46.13E
Tabuaeran, i., Kir.	2	3.52N	159.20W
Tabwémasana, Mont, mtn., Vanuatu	192f	15.20S	166.44E
Tacámbaro, r., Mex. (tä-käm'bä-rō)	112	18.55N	101.25W
Tacámbaro de Codallos, Mex.	112	19.12N	101.28W
Tacarigua, Laguna de la, l., Ven.	125b	10.18N	65.43W
Tacheng, China (tä-chŭŋ)	180	46.50N	83.24E
Tachie, r., Can.	80	54.30N	125.00W
Tachikawa, Japan	238a	35.42N	139.25E
Tacloban, Phil. (tä-klō'bän)	188	11.06N	124.58E
Tacna, Peru (täk'nä)	124	18.34S	70.16W
Tacoma, Wa., U.S. (tȧ-kō'mȧ)	90	47.14N	122.27W
Taconic Range, mts., N.Y., U.S. (tȧ-kŏn'ĭk)	92	41.55N	73.40W
Tacony, neigh., Pa., U.S.	225b	40.02N	75.03W
Tacotalpa, Mex. (tä-kō-täl'pä)	112	17.37N	92.51W
Tacotalpa, r., Mex.	112	17.24N	92.38W
Tacuba, neigh., Mex.	229a	19.28N	99.12W
Tacubaya, neigh., Mex.	229a	19.25N	99.12W

PLACE (Pronunciation)	PAGE	Lat. °′	Long. °′
Tademaït, Plateau du, plat., Alg. (tä-dē-mä'ēt)	204	28.00N	2.15E
Tadio, Lagune, b., I.C.	208	5.20N	5.25W
Tadjoura, Dji. (tȧd-zhōō'rȧ)	212a	11.48N	42.54E
Tadley, Eng., U.K. (tăd'lē)	138b	51.19N	1.08W
Tadotsu, Japan (tä'dô-tsō)	187	34.14N	133.43E
Tadoussac, Can. (tȧ-dōō-sȧk')	84	48.09N	69.43W
Tadworth, Eng., U.K.	231	51.17N	0.14W
Taebaek Sanmaek, mts., Asia (tī-bīk' sän-mīk')	186	37.20N	128.50E
Taedong, r., N. Kor. (tī-dŏng)	186	38.38N	124.32E
Taegu, S. Kor. (tī'gōō')	180	35.49N	128.41E
Taejŏn, S. Kor.	186	36.20N	127.26E
Tafalla, Spain (tä-fäl'yä)	152	42.30N	1.42W
Tafna, r., Alg. (täf'nä)	152	35.28N	1.00W
Taft, Ca., U.S. (tȧft)	102	35.09N	119.27W
Tagama, reg., Niger	208	15.50N	6.30E
Taganrog, Russia (tȧ-gȧn-rôk')	160	47.12N	38.56E
Taganrogskiy Zaliv, b., Eur. (tȧ-gȧn-rôk'skĭ zä'lĭf)	160	46.55N	38.17E
Tagula, i., Pap. N. Gui. (tä'gōō-lȧ)	196	11.45S	153.46E
Tagus (Tajo), r., Eur. (tā'gŭs)	136	39.40N	5.07W
Tahan, Gunong, mtn., Malay.	188	4.33N	101.52E
Tahat, mtn., Alg. (tä-hät')	204	23.22N	5.21E
Tahiti, i., Fr. Poly. (tä-hē'tē) (tä'ē-tē')	2	17.30S	149.30W
Tahkuna Nina, c., Est. (tȧh-kōō'nȧ nē'nȧ)	146	59.08N	22.03E
Tahlequah, Ok., U.S. (tä-lĕ-kwä')	104	35.54N	94.58W
Tahoe, l., U.S. (tä'hō)	90	39.09N	120.18W
Tahoua, Niger (tä'ōō-ä)	204	14.54N	5.16E
Tahtsa Lake, l., Can.	80	53.33N	127.47W
Tahuya, Wa., U.S. (tȧ-hū-yä')	100a	47.23N	123.03W
Tahuya, r., Wa., U.S.	100a	47.28N	122.55W
Tai'an, China (tī-än)	184	36.13N	117.08E
Taibai Shan, mtn., China (tī-bī shän)	184	33.42N	107.25E
Taibus Qi, China (tī-bōō-sz chyē)	184	41.52N	115.25E
Taicang, China (tī-tsäŋ)	182	31.26N	121.06E
T'aichung, Tai. (tī'chŏng)	180	24.10N	120.42E
Tai'erzhuang, China (tī-är-jůäŋ)	182	34.34N	117.44E
Taigu, China (tī-gōō)	184	37.25N	112.35E
Taihang Shan, mts., China (tī-häŋ shän)	184	35.45N	112.00E
Taihe, China (tī-hŭ)	182	33.10N	115.38E
Tai Hu, l., China (tī hōō)	180	31.13N	120.00E
Tailagoin, reg., Mong. (tī'lȧ-găn' kä'rä)	180	43.39N	105.54E
Tailai, China (tī-lī)	184	46.20N	123.10E
Tailem Bend, Austl. (tā-lĕm)	198	35.15S	139.30E
T'ainan, Tai. (tī'nan')	180	23.08N	120.18E
Taínaron, Ákra, c., Grc.	136	37.45N	22.00E
Taining, China (tī'nĭng')	184	26.58N	117.15E
T'aipei, Tai. (tī'pā')	180	25.02N	121.38E
Taipei Institute of Technology, educ., Tai.	237d	25.02N	121.32E
Taiping, pt. of i., Malay.	188	4.56N	100.39E
Taiping Ling, mtn., China	184	47.03N	120.30E
Tai Po Tsai, H.K.	237c	22.21N	114.15E
Taisha, Japan (tī'shä)	187	35.23N	132.40E
Taishan, China (tī-shän)	184	22.15N	112.50E
Tai Shan, mts., China (tī shän)	184	36.16N	117.05E
Taitao, Península de, pen., Chile	126	46.20S	77.15W
Taitō, neigh., Japan	238a	35.43N	139.47E
T'aitung, Tai. (tī'tōōng')	184	22.45N	121.02E
Taiwan, nation, Asia (tī-wän) (fŏr-mō'sȧ)	180	23.30N	122.20E
Taiwan Normal University, educ., Tai.	237d	25.02N	121.31E
Taiwan Strait, strt., Asia	180	24.30N	120.00E
Tai Wan Tau, H.K.	237c	22.18N	114.17E
Tai Wan Tsun, H.K.	237c	22.19N	114.12E
Taixian, China (tī shyĕn)	182	32.31N	119.54E
Taixing, China (tī-shyĭŋ)	182	32.12N	119.58E
Taiyanggong, China	236b	39.58N	116.25E
Taiyuan, China (tī-yůän)	180	37.32N	112.38E
Taizhou, China (tī-jō)	182	32.23N	119.41E
Ta'izz, Yemen	176	13.38N	44.04E
Tajano de Morais, Braz. (tē-zhä'nō-dĕ-mô-rä'ēs)	123a	22.05S	42.04W
Tajikistan, nation, Asia	158	39.22N	69.30E
Tajninka, Russia	235b	55.54N	37.45E
Tajumulco, vol., Guat. (tä-hōō-mōōl'kō)	114	15.03N	91.53W
Tajuña, r., Spain (tä-κōō'n-yä)	152	40.23N	2.36W
Tājūrā', Libya	142	32.56N	13.24W
Tak, Thai.	188	16.57N	99.12E
Taka, i., Japan (tä'kä)	187	30.47N	130.23E
Takada, Japan (tä'kȧ-dä)	186	37.08N	138.30E
Takahashi, Japan (tä'kä'hä-shĭ)	187	34.47N	133.35E
Takaishi, Japan	187b	34.32N	135.27E
Takamatsu, Japan (tä'kä'mä-tsōō')	180	34.20N	134.02E
Takamori, Japan (tä'kä'mō-rē')	187	32.50N	131.08E
Takaoka, Japan (tä'kä'ō-kä')	186	36.45N	136.59E
Takapuna, N.Z.	199	36.48S	174.47E
Takarazuka, Japan (tä'kä-rä-zōō'kä)	187b	34.48N	135.22E
Takasaki, Japan (tä'kät'sōō-kē')	186	36.20N	139.00E
Takatsu, Japan (tä-kät'sōō) (mē'zō-nô-kô'chê)	187a	35.36N	139.37E
Takatsuki, Japan (tä'kät'sōō-kē')	187b	34.51N	135.38E
Takayama, Japan (tä'kä'yä'mä)	187	36.11N	137.16E
Takefu, Japan (tä'kē-fōō)	186	35.57N	136.09E
Takenotsuka, neigh., Japan	238a	35.48N	139.48E
Takla Lake, l., Can.	78	55.25N	125.53W
Takla Makan, des., China (mä-kȧn')	180	39.22N	82.34E
Takoma Park, Md., U.S. (tȧ'kōmȧ pȧrk)	94e	38.59N	77.00W
Takum, Nig.	208	7.17N	9.59E
Tala, Mex. (tä'lä)	112	20.39N	103.42W
Talagante, Chile (tä-lä-gȧ'n-tē)	123b	33.39S	70.54W
Talamanca, Cordillera de, mts., C.R.	114	9.37N	83.55W
Talanga, Hond. (tä-lä'n-gä)	114	14.21N	87.09W
Talara, Peru (tä-lä'rä)	124	4.32S	81.17W
Talasea, Pap. N. Gui. (tä-lä-sā'ä)	188	5.20S	150.00E
Talata Mafara, Nig.	208	12.35N	6.04E
Talaud, Kepulauan, is., Indon. (tä-lout')	188	4.17N	127.30E
Talavera de la Reina, Spain	142	39.58N	4.51W
Talca, Chile (täl'kä)	126	35.25S	71.39W
Talca, prov., Chile	123b	35.23S	71.15W
Talca, Punta, c., Chile (pōō'n-tä-täl'kä)	123b	33.25S	71.42W
Talcahuano, Chile (täl-kä-wä'nō)	126	36.41S	73.05W
Taldom, Russia (täl-dôm)	156	56.44N	37.33E
Taldy-Kurgan, Kaz. (tál'dĭ-kôr-gän')	158	45.03N	77.18E
Talea de Castro, Mex. (tä'lā-ä dā käs'trō)	112	17.22N	96.14W
Talibu, Pulau, i., Indon.	188	1.30S	125.00E
Talim, i., Phil. (tä-lēm')	189a	14.21N	121.14E
Talisay, Phil. (tä-lē'sī)	189a	14.08N	122.56E
Talkeetna, Ak., U.S. (tȧl-kēt'nȧ)	89	62.18N	150.02W
Talladega, Al., U.S. (tăl-ȧ-dē'gȧ)	108	33.25N	86.06W
Tallahassee, Fl., U.S. (tăl-ȧ-hăs'ē)	90	30.25N	84.17W
Tallahatchie, r., Ms., U.S. (tal-ȧ hăch'ē)	108	34.21N	90.03W
Tallapoosa, Ga., U.S. (tăl-ȧ-pōō'sȧ)	108	33.44N	85.15W
Tallapoosa, r., Al., U.S.	108	32.22N	86.08W
Tallassee, Al., U.S. (tăl'ȧ-sē)	108	32.30N	85.54W
Tallinn, Est. (tȧl'lĕn) (rä'väl)	158	59.26N	24.44E
Tallmadge, Oh., U.S. (tăl'mĭj)	95d	41.06N	81.26W
Tallulah, La., U.S. (tă-lōō'lȧ)	106	32.25N	91.13W
Tally Ho, Austl.	239b	37.52S	145.09E
Tal'noye, Ukr. (tȧl'nô-yĕ)	156	48.52N	30.43E
Talo, mtn., Eth.	204	10.45N	37.55E
Taloje Budrukh, India	179b	19.05N	73.05E
Talpa de Allende, Mex. (täl'pä dā äl-yĕn'dȧ)	112	20.25N	104.48W
Talquin, Lake, res., Fl., U.S.	108	30.26N	84.33W
Talsi, Lat. (tal'sĭ)	146	57.16N	22.35E
Taltal, Chile (täl-täl')	126	25.26S	70.32W
Taly, Russia (tä'lĭ)	156	49.51N	40.07E
Tama, Ia., U.S. (tā'mȧ)	96	41.57N	92.36W
Tama, r., Japan	187a	35.38N	139.35E
Tamagawa, neigh., Japan	238a	35.37N	139.39E
Tama-kyūryō, mts., Japan	238a	35.35N	139.30E
Tamale, Ghana (tä-mä'lȧ)	204	9.25N	0.50W
Taman', Russia (tȧ-män'')	156	45.13N	36.46E
Tamanaco, r., Ven. (tä-mä-nä'kō)	125b	9.32N	66.00W
Tamaqua, Pa., U.S. (tȧ-mô'kwȧ)	92	40.45N	75.50W
Tamar, r., Eng., U.K. (tā'mär)	144	50.35N	4.15W
Tamarite de Litera, Spain (tä-mä-rē'tä)	152	41.52N	0.24E
Tamaulipas, state, Mex. (tä-mä-ōō-lē'päs')	110	23.45N	98.30W
Tamazula de Gordiano, Mex.	112	19.44N	103.09W
Tamazulapan del Progreso, Mex.	112	17.41N	97.34W
Tamazunchale, Mex. (tä-mä-zōn-chä'lȧ)	112	21.16N	98.46W
Tambacounda, Sen. (täm-bä-kōōn'dä)	204	13.47N	13.40W
Tambador, Serra do, mts., Braz. (sĕ'r-rä-dô-täm'bä-dōr)	124	10.33S	41.16W
Tambelan, Kepulauan, is., Indon. (täm-bȧ-län')	188	0.38N	107.38E
Tambo, Austl. (tăm'bō)	196	24.50S	146.15E
Tambov, Russia (täm-bôf')	158	52.45N	41.10E
Tambov, prov., Russia	156	52.50N	40.42E
Tambre, r., Spain (täm'brā)	152	42.59N	8.33W
Tambura, Sudan (täm-bōō'rä)	204	5.34N	27.30E
Tame, r., Eng., U.K. (tām)	138a	52.41N	1.42W
Tâmega, r., Port. (tȧ-mā'gȧ)	152	41.30N	7.45W
Tamenghest, Alg.	204	22.34N	5.34E
Tamenghest, Oued, r., Alg.	204	22.15N	2.51E
Tamgak, Monts, mtn., Niger (tam-gäk')	204	18.40N	8.40E
Tamgué, Massif du, mtn., Gui.	204	12.15N	12.35W
Tamiahua, Mex. (tä-myä-wä)	112	21.17N	97.26W
Tamiahua, Laguna, l., Mex. (lä-gō'nä-tä-myä-wä)	112	21.38N	97.33W
Tamiami Canal, can., Fl., U.S. (tă-mī-ăm'ĭ)	109a	25.52N	80.08W
Tamil Nadu, state, India	174	11.30N	78.00E
Tampa, Fl., U.S. (tăm'pȧ)	90	27.57N	82.25W
Tampa Bay, b., Fl., U.S.	90	27.35N	82.38W
Tampere, Fin. (tȧm'pĕ-rĕ)	140	61.21N	23.39E
Tampico, Mex. (täm-pē'kō)	110	22.14N	97.51W
Tampico Alto, Mex. (täm-pē'kō äl'tō)	112	22.07N	97.48W
Tampin, Malay.	173b	2.28N	102.15E
Tam Quan, Viet.	184	14.20N	109.10E
Tamuín, Mex. (tä-mōō-ē'n)	112	22.04N	98.47W
Tamworth, Austl. (tăm'wûrth)	196	31.01S	151.00E
Tamworth, Eng., U.K.	138a	52.38N	1.41W
Tana, i., Vanuatu	196	19.32S	169.27E
Tana, r., Kenya (tä'nä)	206	0.30S	39.30E
Tanabe, Japan (tä-nä'bā)	186	33.45N	135.21E
Tanabe, Japan	187b	34.49N	135.46E
Tanacross, Ak., U.S. (tă'nȧ-crōs)	89	63.20N	143.30W
Tanaga, i., Ak., U.S. (tä-nä'gä)	89a	51.28N	178.10W
Tanahbala, Pulau, i., Indon. (tȧ-nä-bä'lȧ)	188	0.30S	98.22E
Tanahmasa, Pulau, i., Indon. (tȧ-nä-mä'sä)	188	0.03S	97.30E
Tanakpur, India (tăn'ăk-pôr)	178	29.10N	80.07E
Tana Lake, l., Eth.	204	12.09N	36.41E
Tanami, Austl. (tȧ-nä'mē)	196	19.45S	129.50E
Tanana, Ak., U.S. (tă'nȧ-nô)	89	65.18N	152.20W
Tanana, r., Ak., U.S.	89	64.26N	148.40W
Tanaro, r., Italy (tä-nä'rô)	154	44.45N	8.02E
Tanashi, Japan	187a	35.44N	139.34E
Tan-binh, Viet.	237m	10.48N	106.40E
Tanbu, China (tän-bōō)	183a	23.20N	113.06E
Tancheng, China (tän-chŭŋ)	184	34.37N	118.22E
Tanchŏn, N. Kor. (tän'chŭn)	186	40.29N	128.50E
Tancítaro, Mex. (tän-sē'tä-rō)	112	19.16N	102.24W
Tancítaro, Cerro de, mtn., Mex. (sĕ'r-rô-dĕ)	112	19.24N	102.19W
Tancoco, Mex. (tän-kō'kō)	112	21.16N	97.45W
Tandil, Arg. (tän-dēl')	126	36.16S	59.01W
Tandil, Sierra del, mts., Arg.	126	38.40S	59.40W
Tanega, i., Japan (tä'nȧ-gä')	180	30.36N	131.11E
Tanezrouft, reg., Alg. (tä'nĕz-rôft)	204	24.17N	0.30W
Tang, r., China (täŋ)	182	33.38N	117.29E
Tang, r., China	182	39.13N	114.45E
Tanga, Tan. (tăŋ'gȧ)	206	5.04S	39.06E
Tangancícuaro, Mex. (täŋ-gän-sē'kwa-rô)	112	19.52N	102.13W
Tanganyika, Lake, l., Afr.	206	5.15S	29.40E
Tanger, Mor. (tän-jēr')	204	35.52N	5.55W
Tangermünde, Ger. (täŋ'ĕr-mün'de)	148	52.33N	11.58E
Tanggu, China (täŋ-gōō)	182	39.04N	117.41E
Tanggula Shan, mts., China (täŋ-gōō-lä shän)	180	33.15N	89.07E
Tanghe, China	184	32.40N	112.50E
Tangier, *see* Tanger, Mor.	204	35.52N	5.55W
Tangipahoa, r., La., U.S. (tăn'jē-pȧ-hō'ȧ)	106	30.48N	90.28W
Tangra Yumco, l., China (täŋ-rä yōōm-tswo)	178	30.50N	85.40E
T'angshan, China	184	39.38N	118.11E
Tangxian, China (täŋ shyĕn)	182	38.49N	115.00E
Tangzha, China (täŋ-jä)	182	32.06N	120.48E
Tanimbar, Kepulauan, is., Indon.	188	8.00S	132.00E
Tanjong Piai, c., Malay.	173b	1.16N	103.11E
Tanjong Ramunia, c., Malay.	173b	1.27N	104.44E
Tanjungbalai, Indon. (tän'jông-bä'lȧ)	173b	1.00N	103.26E
Tanjungkarang-Telukbetung, Indon.	188	5.16S	105.06E
Tanjungpandan, Indon.	188	2.47S	107.51E
Tanjungpinang, Indon. (tän'jông-pē'näng)	173b	0.55N	104.29E
Tanjungpriok, neigh., Indon.	237k	6.06S	106.53E
Tannu-Ola, mts., Asia	158	51.00N	94.00E
Tannūrah, Ra's at, c., Sau. Ar.	174	26.45N	49.59E
Tano, r., Afr.	208	5.40N	2.30W
Tan-qui-dong, Viet.	237m	10.44N	106.43E
Tanquijo, Arrecife, i., Mex. (är-rē-sē'fē-tän-kē'kô)	112	21.07N	97.16W
Tanshui Ho, r., Tai.	237d	25.08N	121.27E
Tan Son Nhut Airport, arpt., Viet.	237m	10.49N	106.40E
Ţanţā, Egypt	204	30.47N	31.00E
Tan-thuan-dong, Viet.	237m	10.45N	106.44E
Tantoyuca, Mex. (tän-tō-yōō'kä)	112	21.22N	98.13W
Tanyang, S. Kor.	186	36.53N	128.20E
Tanzania, nation, Afr.	206	6.48S	33.58E
Tao, r., China (tou)	184	35.30N	103.40E
Tao'an, China (tou-än)	180	45.15N	122.45E
Tao'er, r., China (tou-är)	180	45.40N	122.00E
Taormina, Italy (tä-ôr-mē'nä)	154	37.53N	15.18E
Taos, N.M., U.S. (tä'ōs)	102	36.25N	105.35W
Taoudenni, Mali (tä'ōō-dĕ-nē')	204	22.57N	3.37W
Taoussa, Mali	208	16.55N	0.35W
Taoyuan, China (tou-yüän)	184	29.00N	111.15E
Tapa, Est. (tȧ'pȧ)	146	59.16N	25.56E
Tapachula, Mex.	114	14.55N	92.20W
Tapajós, r., Braz. (tä-pä-zhô's)	124	3.27S	55.33W
Tapalque, Arg. (tä-päl-kĕ')	123c	36.22S	60.05W
Tapanatepec, Mex. (tä-pä-nä-tĕ-pĕk)	112	16.22N	94.19W
Tāpi, r., India	174	21.00N	76.30E
Tapiales, Arg.	229d	34.42S	58.30W
Tappi Saki, c., Japan (täp'pē sä'kē)	186	41.05N	139.40E
Tapps, l., Wa., U.S. (tăpz)	100a	47.20N	122.12W
Taquara, neigh., Braz.	230c	22.55S	43.21W
Taquara, Serra de, mts., Braz. (sĕ'r-rä-dĕ-tä-kwä'rä)	124	15.28S	54.33W
Taquari, r., Braz. (tä-kwä'rĭ)	124	18.35S	56.50W
Tar, r., N.C., U.S. (tär)	108	35.58N	78.06W
Tara, Russia (tä'rȧ)	158	56.58N	74.13E
Tara, i., Phil. (tä'rä)	189a	12.18N	120.28E
Tara, r., Russia (tä'rȧ)	162	56.32N	76.13E
Ţarābulus, Leb. (tȧ-rä'bô-lōōs)	174	34.25N	35.50E
Ţarābulus, Libya	204	32.50N	13.13E
Ţarābulus (Tripolitania), hist. reg., Libya	204	31.00N	12.26E
Tarakan, Indon.	188	3.17N	118.04E
Tarancón, Spain (tä-rän-kōn')	152	40.01N	3.00W
Taranto, Italy (tä'rän-tô)	142	40.30N	17.15E
Taranto, Golfo di, b., Italy (gôl-fô-dē tä'rän-tô)	136	40.03N	17.10E
Tarapoto, Peru (tä-rä-pô'tō)	124	6.29S	76.26W
Tarare, Fr. (tȧ-rär')	150	45.55N	4.23E
Tarascon, Fr. (tȧ-räs-kôN')	150	42.53N	1.35E
Tarascon, Fr. (tä-räs-kôn)	150	43.47N	4.41E
Tarashcha, Ukr. (tä'rȧsh-chȧ)	156	49.34N	30.52E
Tarasht, Iran	237h	35.42N	51.21E
Tarata, Bol. (tä-rä'tä)	124	17.43S	66.00W
Taravo, r., Fr.	154	41.54N	8.58E
Tarazit, Massif de, mts., Niger	208	20.05N	7.35E
Tarazona, Spain (tä-rä-thō'nä)	152	41.54N	1.45W
Tarazona de la Mancha, Spain (tä-rä-zō'nä-dĕ-lä-mä'n-chä)	152	39.13N	1.50W
Tarbes, Fr. (tȧrb)	140	43.04N	0.05E
Tarbock Green, Eng., U.K.	233a	53.23N	2.49W
Tarboro, N.C., U.S. (tär'bŭr-ô)	108	35.53N	77.34W
Taredo, neigh., India	236e	19.58N	72.49E
Taree, Austl. (tȧ-rē')	198	31.52S	152.21E
Tarentum, Pa., U.S. (tȧ-rĕn'tŭm)	95e	40.36N	79.44W
Tarfa, Wādī at, val., Egypt	212b	28.14N	31.00E
Tarhūnah, Libya	176	32.26N	13.38E
Tarija, Bol. (tär-rē'hä)	124	21.42S	64.52W
Tarīm, Yemen (tä-rīm')	174	16.13N	49.08E
Tarim, r., China (tȧ-rĭm')	180	40.45N	85.39E
Tarim Basin, basin, China (tȧ-rĭm')	180	39.52N	82.34E
Tarka, r., S. Afr. (tär'kȧ)	207c	32.15S	26.00E
Tarkastad, S. Afr.	207c	32.01S	26.18E

ăt; finȧl; rāte; senȧte; ärm; ȧsk; sofȧ; fâre; ch-choose; dh-as th in other; bē; ēvent; bĕt; recĕnt; cratẽr; g-gō; gh-guttural g; bĭt; ĭ-short neutral; rīde; κ-guttural k as ch in German ich;

PLACE (Pronunciation)	PAGE	Lat. °'	Long. °'
Tarkhankut, Mys, c., Ukr. (mĭs tår-kän'kòt)	160	45.21N	32.30E
Tarkio, Mo., U.S. (tär'kĭ-ō)	104	40.27N	95.22W
Tarkwa, Ghana (tärk'wä)	204	5.19N	1.59W
Tarlac, Phil. (tär'läk)	188	15.29N	120.36E
Tarlton, S. Afr. (tärl'tŭn)	207b	26.05S	27.38E
Tarma, Peru (tär'mä)	124	11.26S	75.40W
Tarn, r., Fr. (tärn)	140	43.45N	2.00E
Tarnów, Pol. (tär'nòf)	140	50.02N	21.00E
Taro, r., Italy (tä'rō)	154	44.41N	10.03E
Taroudant, Mor. (tå-rōō-dänt')	204	30.39N	8.52W
Tarpon Springs, Fl., U.S. (tär'pŏn)	109a	28.07N	82.44W
Tarporley, Eng., U.K. (tär'pēr-lė)	138a	53.09N	2.40W
Tarpum Bay, b., Bah. (tär'pŭm)	116	25.05N	76.20W
Tarquinia, Italy (tär-kwē'nē-ä)	154	42.16N	11.46E
Tarragona, Spain (tär-rä-gō'nä)	136	41.05N	1.15E
Tarrant, Al., U.S. (tăr'ănt)	94h	33.35N	86.46W
Tarrasa, Spain (tär-rä'sä)	152	41.34N	2.01E
Tárrega, Spain (tä rå-gä)	152	41.40N	1.09E
Tarrejón de Ardoz, Spain (tär-rĕ-κō'n-dĕ-är-dōz)	153a	40.28N	3.29W
Tarrytown, N.Y., U.S. (tăr'ĭ-toun)	94a	41.04N	73.52W
Tarsus, Tur. (tar'sòs) (tär'sŭs)	174	37.00N	34.50E
Tartagal, Arg. (tär-tä-gá'l)	126	23.31S	63.47W
Tartu, Est. (tär'tōō) (dôr'pät)	158	58.23N	26.44E
Ţarţūs, Syria	176	34.54N	35.59E
Tarumi, Japan (tä'rōō-mê)	187b	34.38N	135.04E
Tarusa, Russia (tä-rōōs'á)	156	54.43N	37.11E
Tarzana, Ca., U.S. (tär-zä'ă)	101a	34.10N	118.32W
Tashauz, Turk. (tŭ-shŭ-ōōs')	158	41.50N	59.45E
Tashkent, Uzb. (tásh'kĕnt)	158	41.23N	69.04E
Tasman Bay, b., N.Z. (tăz'măn)	197a	40.50S	173.20E
Tasmania, state, Austl.	196	41.28S	142.30E
Tasman Peninsula, pen., Austl.	198	43.00S	148.30E
Tasman Sea, sea, Oc.	190	29.30S	155.00E
Tasquillo, Mex. (täs-kē'lyō)	112	20.34N	99.21W
Tatarsk, Russia (tá-tärsk')	158	55.13N	75.58E
Tatar Strait, strt., Russia	158	51.00N	141.45E
Tate Gallery, pt. of i., Eng., U.K.	231	51.29N	0.08W
Tater Hill, mtn., Or., U.S. (tāt'ēr hĭl)	100c	45.47N	123.02W
Tateyama, Japan (tä'tė-yä'mä)	187	35.04N	139.52E
Tathong Channel, strt., H.K.	237c	22.15N	114.15E
Tatlow, Mount, mtn., Can.	80	51.23N	123.52W
Tatsfield, Eng., U.K.	231	51.18N	0.02E
Tau, Nor.	146	59.05N	5.59E
Tauern Tunnel, trans., Aus.	148	47.12N	13.17E
Taung, Boph. (tä'òng)	206	27.25S	24.47E
Taunton, Ma., U.S. (tän'tŭn)	92	41.54N	71.03W
Taunton, r., R.I., U.S.	94b	41.50N	71.02W
Taupo, Lake, l., N.Z. (tä'ōō-pō)	197a	38.42S	175.55E
Taurage, Lith. (tou'rá-gā)	146	55.15N	22.18E
Taurus Mountains, *see* Toros Dağlari, mts., Tur.	174	37.00N	32.40E
Tauste, Spain (tä-ōōs'tå)	152	41.55N	1.15W
Tavda, Russia (táv-dá')	158	58.00N	64.44E
Tavda, r., Russia	162	58.30N	64.15E
Taverny, Fr. (tá-vĕr-nē')	151b	49.02N	2.13E
Taviche, Mex. (tä-vē'chĕ)	112	16.43N	96.35W
Tavira, Port. (tä-vē'ră)	152	37.09N	7.42W
Tavistock, N.J., U.S.	225b	39.53N	75.02W
Tavşanlı, Tur. (táv'shän-lĭ)	160	39.30N	29.30E
Tawakoni, l., Tx., U.S.	106	32.51N	95.59W
Tawaramoto, Japan (tä'wä-rä-mô-tô)	187b	34.33N	135.48E
Tawas City, Mi., U.S.	92	44.15N	83.30W
Tawas Point, c., Mi., U.S. (tô'wăs)	92	44.15N	83.25W
Tawitawi Group, is., Phil. (tä'wē-tä'wē)	188	4.52N	120.35E
Tawkar, Sudan	204	18.28N	37.46E
Taxco de Alarcón, Mex. (täs'kō dĕ ä-lär-kō'n)	112	18.34N	99.37W
Tay, r., Scot., U.K.	144	56.35N	3.37W
Tay, Loch, l., Scot., U.K.	144	56.25N	4.07W
Tayabas Bay, b., Phil. (tä-yä'bäs)	189a	13.44N	121.40E
Tayga, Russia (tī'gä)	162	56.12N	85.47E
Taygonos, Mys, c., Russia	158	60.37N	160.17E
Taylor, Mi., U.S.	226c	42.13N	83.16W
Taylor, Tx., U.S.	106	30.35N	97.25W
Taylor, Mount, mtn., N.M., U.S.	90	35.20N	107.40W
Taylorville, Il., U.S. (tā'lēr-vĭl)	92	39.30N	89.20W
Taymyr, l., Russia (tī-mĭr')	158	74.13N	100.45E
Taymyr, Poluostrov, pen., Russia	158	75.15N	95.00E
Táyros, Grc.	235d	37.58N	23.42E
Tayshet, Russia (tī-shĕt')	158	56.09N	97.49E
Taytay, Phil.	237g	14.34N	121.08E
Tayug, Phil.	189a	16.01N	120.45E
Taz, r., Russia (táz)	162	67.15N	80.45E
Taza, Mor. (tä'zä)	204	34.08N	4.00W
Tazovskoye, Russia	158	66.58N	78.28E
Tbessa, Alg.	204	35.27N	8.13E
Tbilisi, Geor. ('tbĭl-yē'sē)	160	41.40N	44.45E
Tchentlo Lake, l., Can.	80	55.11N	125.00W
Tchibanga, Gabon (chē-bäŋ'gä)	206	2.51S	11.02E
Tchien, Lib.	208	6.04N	8.08W
Tchigai, Plateau du, plat., Afr.	208	21.20N	14.50E
Tczew, Pol. (t'chĕf')	140	54.06N	18.48E
Teabo, Mex. (tĕ-ä'bô)	114a	20.25N	89.14W
Teague, Tx., U.S.	106	31.39N	96.16W
Teaneck, N.J., U.S.	224	40.53N	74.01W
Teapa, Mex. (tā-ä'pä)	112	17.35N	92.56W
Tebing Tinggi, i., Indon. (teb'ĭng-tĭng'gä)	173b	0.54N	102.39E
Tecalitlán, Mex. (tā-kä-lē-tlän')	112	19.28N	103.17W
Techiman, Ghana	208	7.35N	1.56W
Tecoanapa, Mex. (tāk-wä-nä-pä')	112	16.33N	98.46W
Tecoh, Mex. (tĕ-kô)	114a	20.46N	89.27W
Tecolotlán, Mex. (tā-kō-lō-tlän')	112	20.13N	103.57W
Tecolutla, Mex. (tā-kō-lōō'tlä)	112	20.33N	97.00W
Tecolutla, r., Mex.	112	20.16N	97.14W
Tecomán, Mex. (tā-kō-män')	112	18.53N	103.53W
Tecómitl, Mex. (tĕ-kŏ'mētl)	113a	19.13N	98.59W
Tecozautla, Mex. (tā'kō-zä-ōō'tlä)	112	20.33N	99.38W
Tecpan de Galeana, Mex. (tĕk-pän' dā gä-lā-ä'nä)	112	17.13N	100.41W
Tecpatán, Mex. (tĕk-pä-tá'n)	112	17.08N	93.18W
Tecuala, Mex. (tĕ-kwä-lä)	112	22.24N	105.29W
Tecuci, Rom. (ta-kòch')	142	45.51N	27.30E
Tecumseh, Can. (tė-kŭm'sĕ)	95b	42.19N	82.53W
Tecumseh, Mi., U.S.	92	42.00N	84.00W
Tecumseh, Ne., U.S.	104	40.21N	96.09W
Tecumseh, Ok., U.S.	104	35.18N	96.55W
Teddington, neigh., Eng., U.K.	231	51.25N	0.20W
Tees, r., Eng., U.K. (tēz)	144	54.40N	2.10W
Teganuna, l., Japan (tā'gä-nōō'nä)	187a	35.50N	140.02E
Tegel, neigh., Ger.	234a	52.35N	13.17E
Tegeler See, l., Ger.	234a	52.35N	13.15E
Tegucigalpa, Hond. (tå-gōō-sē-gäl'pä)	110	14.08N	87.15W
Tehachapi Mountains, mts., Ca., U.S. (tē-hă-shă'pĭ)	102	34.50N	118.55W
Tehar, neigh., India	236d	28.38N	77.07E
Tehrān, Iran (tĕ-hrän')	174	35.45N	51.30E
Tehuacan, Mex. (tā-wä-kän')	110	18.27N	97.23W
Tehuantepec, Mex.	110	16.20N	95.14W
Tehuantepec, r., Mex.	112	16.30N	95.23W
Tehuantepec, Golfo de, b., Mex. (gôl-fô dĕ)	110	15.45N	95.00W
Tehuantepec, Istmo de, isth., Mex. (ē'st-mô dĕ)	112	17.55N	94.35W
Tehuehuetla, Arroyo, r., Mex. (tĕ-wĕ-wĕ'tlä är-rô-yô)	112	17.54N	100.26W
Tehuitzingo, Mex. (tā-wē-tzĭŋ'gō)	112	18.21N	98.16W
Tejeda, Sierra de, mts., Spain (sē-ĕ'r-rä dĕ tĕ-kĕ'dä)	152	36.55N	4.00W
Tejúpan, Mex. (tĕ-κōō-pä'n) (sän-tyá'gô)	112	17.39N	97.34W
Tejúpan, Punta, c., Mex.	112	18.19N	103.30W
Tejupilco de Hidalgo, Mex. (tå-hōō-pēl'kō dā ē-dhäl'gō)	112	18.52N	100.07W
Tekamah, Ne., U.S. (tė-kā'mă)	96	41.46N	96.13W
Tekax de Alvaro Obregon, Mex.	114a	20.12N	89.11W
Tekeze, r., Afr.	204	13.38N	38.00E
Tekit, Mex. (tĕ-kē't)	114a	20.35N	89.18W
Tekoa, Wa., U.S. (tė-kō'ă)	98	47.15N	117.03W
Tekstil'ščiki, neigh., Russia	235b	55.42N	37.44E
Tela, Hond. (tā'lä)	110	15.45N	87.25W
Tela, India	236d	28.44N	77.20E
Tela, Bahía de, b., Hond.	114	15.53N	87.29W
Telapa Burok, Gunong, mtn., Malay.	173b	2.51N	102.04E
Telavi, Geor.	160	42.00N	45.20E
Tel Aviv-Yafo, Isr. (tĕl-ä-vēv'já'fă)	174	32.03N	34.46E
Telegraph Creek, Can. (tĕl'ē-gráf)	78	57.59N	131.22W
Teleneshty, Mol. (tyĕ-le-nĕsht'ĭ)	156	47.31N	28.22E
Telescope Peak, mtn., Ca., U.S. (tĕl'ē skōp)	90	36.12N	117.05W
Telesung, Indon.	173b	1.07N	102.53E
Telica, vol., Nic. (tå-lē'kä)	114	12.38N	86.52W
Tell City, In., U.S. (tĕl)	92	38.00N	86.45W
Teller, Ak., U.S. (tĕl'ēr)	89	65.17N	166.28W
Tello, Col. (tĕ'l-yô)	124a	3.05N	75.08W
Telluride, Co., U.S. (tĕl'ū-rīd)	102	37.55N	107.50W
Telok Datok, Malay.	173b	2.51N	101.33E
Teloloapan, Mex. (tā'lô-lô-ä'pän)	112	18.19N	99.54W
Tel'pos-Iz, Gora, mtn., Russia (tyĕl'pôs-ēz')	158	63.50N	59.20E
Telšiai, Lith. (tĕl'sha'ē)	146	55.59N	22.17E
Teltow, Ger. (tĕl'tō)	139b	52.24N	13.12E
Teltower Hochfläche, reg., Ger.	234a	52.22N	13.20E
Teluklecak, Indon.	173b	1.53N	101.45E
Tema, Ghana	208	5.38N	0.01E
Temascalcingo, Mex. (tā'mäs-käl-sĭŋ'gō)	112	19.55N	100.00W
Temascaltepec, Mex. (tā'mäs-käl-tå pĕk)	112	19.00N	100.03W
Temax, Mex. (tĕ'mäx)	110	21.10N	88.51W
Temir, Kaz. (tyĕ'mēr)	158	49.10N	57.15E
Temir-Tau, Kaz.	158	50.08N	73.13E
Temiscouata, l., Can. (tĕ'mĭs-kō-ä'tä)	86	47.40N	68.50W
Témiskaming, Can. (tė-mĭs'kă-mĭng)	78	46.41N	79.01W
Temoaya, Mex. (tĕ-mô-a-um-yä)	113a	19.28N	99.36W
Tempe, Az., U.S. (tĕm-pē')	102	33.24N	111.54W
Tempelhof, neigh., Ger.	234a	52.28N	13.23E
Temperley, Arg. (tĕ'm-pĕr-lā)	126a	34.47S	58.24W
Tempio Pausania, Italy (tĕm'pė-ō pou-sä'nē-ä)	154	40.55N	9.05E
Temple, Tx., U.S. (tĕm'p'l)	106	31.06N	97.20W
Temple City, Ca., U.S.	101a	34.07N	118.02W
Temple Hills, Md., U.S.	225d	38.49N	76.57W
Temple of Heaven, rel., China	236b	39.53N	116.25E
Templestowe, Austl.	239b	37.45S	145.07E
Templeton, Can. (tĕm'p'l-tŭn)	77c	45.29N	75.37W
Temple University, pt. of i., Pa., U.S.	225b	39.59N	75.09W
Templin, Ger. (tĕm-plēn')	148	53.08N	13.30E
Tempoal, r., Mex. (tĕm-pô-ä'l)	112	21.38N	98.23W
Temryuk, Russia (tyĕm-ryòk')	160	45.17N	37.21E
Temuco, Chile (tå-mōō'kō)	126	38.46S	72.38W
Temyasovo, Russia (tĕm-yä'sô-vô)	164a	53.00N	58.06E
Tenafly, N.J., U.S.	224	40.56N	73.58W
Tenāli, India	178	16.10N	80.32E
Tenamaxtlán, Mex. (tā'nä-mäs-tlän')	112	20.13N	104.06W
Tenancingo, Mex. (tå-nän-sēŋ'gō)	112	18.54N	99.36W
Tenango, Mex. (tå-näŋ'gō)	113a	19.09N	98.51W
Tenasserim, Burma (tĕn-ăs'ēr-ĭm)	188	12.09N	99.01E
Tenderovskaya Kosa, spit, Ukr. (tĕn-dĕ-fôf'ská-yá kô-sä')	156	46.12N	31.17E
Tenerife Island, i., Spain (tå-nå-rē'fä) (tĕn-ĕr-ĭf')	204	28.41N	17.02W
Tènès, Alg. (tā-nĕs')	140	36.28N	1.22E
Tengiz, l., Kaz. (tyĭn-gēz')	162	50.45N	68.39E
Tengxian, China (tŭŋ shyĕn)	184	35.07N	117.08E
Tenjin, Japan (tĕn'jĕn)	187b	34.54N	135.04E
Tenke, Zaire (tĕŋ'kå)	206	11.26S	26.45E
Tenkiller Ferry Reservoir, res., Ok., U.S. (tĕn-kĭl'ēr)	104	35.42N	94.47W
Tenkodogo, Burkina (tĕŋ-kô-dō'gô)	204	11.47N	0.22W
Tenmile, r., Wa., U.S. (tĕn mīl)	100d	48.52N	122.32W
Tennant Creek, Austl. (tĕn'ănt)	196	19.45S	134.00E
Tennessee, state, U.S. (tĕn-ĕ-sē')	90	35.50N	88.00W
Tennessee, r., U.S.	90	35.35N	88.20W
Tennille, Ga., U.S. (tĕn'ĭl)	108	32.55N	86.50W
Tennōji, neigh., Japan	238b	34.39N	135.31E
Teno, r., Chile (tĕ'nô)	123b	34.55S	71.00W
Tenora, Austl. (tĕn-ôr'ă)	198	34.23S	147.33E
Tenosique, Mex. (tā-nô-sē'kå)	112	17.27N	91.25W
Tenri, Japan	187b	34.36N	135.50E
Tenryū-Gawa, r., Japan (tĕn'ryōō'gä'wä)	187	35.16N	137.54E
Tensas, r., La., U.S. (tĕn'sô)	106	31.54N	91.30W
Tensaw, r., Al., U.S. (tĕn'sô)	108	30.45N	87.52W
Tenterfield, Austl. (tĕn'tĕr-fēld)	196	29.00S	152.06E
Ten Thousand, Islands, is., Fl., U.S. (tĕn thou'zănd)	109a	25.45N	81.35W
Teocaltiche, Mex. (tā'ô-käl-tē'chå)	112	21.27N	102.38W
Teocelo, Mex. (tā-ô-sā'lō)	112	19.22N	96.57W
Teocuitatlán de Corona, Mex.	112	20.06N	103.22W
Teófilo Otoni, Braz. (tĕ-ô'fē-lō-tô'nē)	124	17.49S	41.18W
Teoloyucan, Mex. (tā'ô-lô-yōō'kän)	112	19.43N	99.12W
Teopisca, Mex. (tā-ô-pēs'kä)	112	16.30N	92.33W
Teotihuacán, Mex. (tĕ-ô-tē-wà-kà'n)	113a	19.40N	98.52W
Teotitlán del Camino, Mex. (tā-ô-tė-tlän' dĕl kä-mē'nô)	112	18.07N	97.04W
Tepalcatepec, Mex. (tā'päl-kä-tā'pĕk)	112	19.11N	102.51W
Tepalcatepec, r., Mex.	112	18.54N	102.25W
Tepalcates, Mex.	229a	19.23N	99.04W
Tepalcingo, Mex. (tā-päl-sēŋ'gô)	112	18.34N	98.49W
Tepatitlán de Morelos, Mex. (tā-pä-tē-tlän' dā mô-rā'los)	110	20.55N	102.47W
Tepeaca, Mex. (tā-på-ä'kä)	112	18.57N	97.54W
Tepecoacuilco de Trujano, Mex.	112	18.15N	99.29W
Tepeji del Río, Mex. (tā-på-κe' dĕl rē'ô)	112	19.55N	99.22W
Tepelmeme, Mex. (tā'pĕl-mā'må)	112	17.51N	97.23W
Tepepan, Mex.	229a	19.16N	99.08W
Tepetlaoxtoc, Mex. (tā'på-tlä'ôs-tōk')	112	19.34N	98.49W
Tepezala, Mex. (tā-på-zä-lä')	112	22.12N	102.12W
Tepic, Mex. (tā-pēk')	110	21.32N	104.53W
Tëplaya Gora, Russia (tyôp'lá-yá gô-rá)	164a	58.32N	59.08W
Teplice, Czech.	140	50.39N	13.50E
Teposcolula, Mex.	112	17.33N	97.29W
Tequendama, Salto de, wtfl., Col. (sä'l-tô dĕ tĕ-kĕn-dä'mä)	124	4.34N	74.18W
Tequila, Mex. (tå-kē'lä)	112	20.53N	103.48W
Tequisistlán, r., Mex. (tĕ-kē-sės-tlá'n)	112	16.20N	95.40W
Tequisquiapan, Mex. (tå-kēs-kė-ä'pän)	112	20.33N	99.57W
Ter, r., Spain (tĕr)	152	42.04N	2.52E
Téra, Niger	208	14.01N	0.45E
Tera, r., Spain (tā'rä)	152	42.05N	6.24W
Teramo, Italy (tā'rä-mô)	154	42.40N	13.41E
Terborg, Neth. (tĕr-bōrg)	151c	51.55N	6.23E
Tercan, Tur. (tĕr'jän)	160	39.40N	40.12E
Terceira Island, i., Port. (tĕr-sā'rä)	204a	38.49N	26.36W
Terebovlya, Ukr. (tĕ-rä'bôv-lyá)	148	49.18N	25.43E
Terek, r., Russia	160	43.30N	45.10E
Terenkul', Russia (tĕ-rĕn'kôl)	164a	55.38N	62.18E
Teresina, Braz. (tĕr-å-sē'nă)	124	5.04S	42.42W
Teresópolis, Braz. (tĕr-ā-sô'pō-lēzh)	123a	22.25S	42.59W
Teriberka, Russia (tyĕr-ē-byôr'kå)	160	69.00N	35.15E
Terme, Tur. (tĕr'mĕ)	160	41.05N	37.00E
Termez, Uzb. (tyĕr'mĕz)	174	37.19N	67.20E
Terminal, Ca., U.S.	228	33.45N	118.15W
Termini, Italy (tĕr'mē-nē)	154	37.58N	13.39E
Términos, Laguna de, l., Mex. (lä-gò'nä dĕ ĕ'r-mē-nôs)	110	18.37N	91.32W
Termoli, Italy (tĕr'mô-lē)	154	42.00N	15.01E
Tern, r., Eng., U.K. (tûrn)	138a	52.49N	2.31W
Ternate, Indon. (tĕr-nä'tā)	188	0.52N	127.25E
Terni, Italy (tĕr'nē)	142	42.38N	12.41E
Ternopol', Ukr. (tĕr-nō-pōl')	160	49.32N	25.36E
Terpeniya, Mys, c., Russia	158	48.44N	144.42E
Terpeniya, Zaliv, b., Russia (zä'lĭf tĕr-pā'nĭ-yá)	186	49.10N	143.05E
Terrace, Can. (tĕr'ĭs)	78	54.31N	128.35W
Terracina, Italy (tĕr-rä-chē'nä)	142	41.18N	13.14E
Terra Nova National Park, rec., Can.	79a	48.37N	54.15W
Terrebonne, Can. (tĕr-bŏn')	92	45.42N	73.38W
Terrebonne Bay, b., La., U.S.	106	28.55N	90.30W
Terre Haute, In., U.S. (tĕr-ē hōt')	90	39.25N	87.25W
Terrell, Tx., U.S. (tĕr'ĕl)	106	32.44N	96.15W
Terrell, Wa., U.S.	100d	48.53N	122.44W
Terrell Hills, Tx., U.S. (tĕr'ĕl hĭlz)	101d	29.28N	98.27W
Terschelling, i., Neth. (tĕr-skĕl'ĭng)	144	53.25N	5.12E
Teruel, Spain (tå-rōō-ĕl')	142	40.20N	1.05W
Tešanj, Bos. (tĕ'shän')	154	44.36N	17.59E
Teschendorf, Ger. (tĕ'shĕn-dōrf)	139b	52.51N	13.10E
Tesecheacan, Mex. (tĕ-sĕ-chĕ-ä-kà'n)	112	18.10N	95.41W
Teshekpuk, l., Ak., U.S. (tē-shĕk'pŭk)	89	70.18N	152.36W
Teshio Dake, mtn., Japan (tĕsh'ē-ō-dä'kä)	186	44.00N	142.50E
Teshio Gawa, r., Japan (tĕsh'ē-ō gä'wä)	186	44.53N	144.55E
Tesiyn, r., Asia	180	49.45N	96.00E
Teslin, Can. (tĕs-lĭn)	89	60.10N	132.30W
Teslin, l., Can.	78	60.12N	132.08W
Teslin, r., Can.	78	61.18N	134.14W
Tessaoua, Niger (tĕs-sä'ō-ä)	204	13.53N	7.53E

PLACE (Pronunciation)	PAGE	Lat. °′	Long. °′
Tessenderlo, Bel.	139a	51.04N	5.08E
Test, r., Eng., U.K. (tĕst)	144	51.10N	1.30W
Testa del Gargano, c., Italy (täs′tä dĕl gär-gä′nō)	154	41.48N	16.13E
Tetachuck Lake, l., Can.	80	53.20N	125.50W
Tete, Moz. (tā′tĕ)	206	16.13S	33.35E
Tête Jaune Cache, Can. (tĕt′zhōn-kăsh)	80	52.57N	119.26W
Teterboro, N.J., U.S.	224	40.52N	74.03W
Teterev, r., Ukr. (tyĕ′tyĕ-rĕf)	160	51.05N	29.30E
Teterow, Ger. (tā′tĕ-rō)	148	53.46N	12.33E
Teteven, Bul. (tĕt′ĕ-ven′)	154	42.57N	24.15E
Teton, r., Mt., U.S. (tē′tŏn)	98	47.54N	111.37W
Tétouan, Mor.	204	35.42N	5.34W
Tetovo, Mac. (tā′tô-vô)	142	42.01N	21.00E
Tetyukhe-Pristan, Russia (tĕt-yōō′κĕ prĭ-stän′)	186	44.21N	135.44E
Tetyushi, Russia (tyĕt-yó′shĭ)	160	54.57N	48.50E
Teupitz, Ger. (toi′pētz)	139b	42.08N	13.37E
Tevere, r., Italy	142	42.30N	12.14E
Teverya, Isr.	173a	32.48N	35.32E
Tewksbury, Ma., U.S. (tūks′bĕr-ĭ)	87a	42.37N	71.14W
Texada Island, i., Can.	80	49.40N	124.24W
Texarkana, Ar., U.S. (tĕk-sär-kăn′ă)	90	33.26N	94.02W
Texarkana, Tx., U.S.	90	33.26N	94.04W
Texas, state, U.S.	90	31.00N	101.00W
Texas City, Tx., U.S.	106	29.23N	94.54W
Texcaltitlán, Mex. (tās-käl′tē-tlän′)	112	18.54N	99.51W
Texcoco, Mex. (tās-kō′kō)	112	19.31N	98.53W
Texcoco, Lago de, l., Mex.	113a	19.30N	99.00W
Texel, i., Neth. (tĕk′sĕl)	144	53.10N	4.45E
Texistepec, Mex. (tĕk-sēs-tā-pĕk′)	112	17.51N	94.46W
Texmelucan, Mex.	112	19.17N	98.26W
Texoma, Lake, res., U.S. (tĕk′ō-mă)	90	34.03N	96.28W
Texontepec, Mex. (tå-zōn-tå-pĕk′)	112	19.52N	98.48W
Texontepec de Aldama, Mex. (dā äl-dä′mä)	112	20.19N	99.19W
Teyateyaneng, Leso.	207c	29.11S	27.43E
Teykovo, Russia (tĕy-kô-vô)	160	56.52N	40.34E
Teziutlán, Mex. (tå-zē-ōō-tlän′)	112	19.48N	97.21W
Tezpur, India	178	26.42N	92.52E
Tha-anne, r., Can.	78	60.50N	96.56W
Thabana Ntlenyana, mtn., Leso.	207c	29.28S	29.17E
Thabazimbi, S. Afr.	212d	24.36S	27.22E
Thailand, nation, Asia	188	16.30N	101.00E
Thailand, Gulf of, b., Asia	188	11.37N	100.46E
Thākurpukur, India	236a	22.28N	88.19E
Thale Luang, l., Thai.	188	7.51N	99.39E
Thame, Eng., U.K. (tām)	138b	51.43N	0.59W
Thames, r., Can. (tĕmz)	84	42.40N	81.45W
Thames, r., Eng., U.K.	136	51.30N	1.30W
Thames Ditton, Eng., U.K.	231	51.23N	0.21W
Thāmit, Wadi, r., Libya	142	30.39N	16.23E
Thāna, India (thä′nŭ)	178	19.13N	72.58E
Thāna Creek, r., India	179b	19.03N	72.58E
Thanh Hoa, Viet. (tän′hō′á)	188	19.46N	105.42E
Thanjāvūr, India	174	10.51N	79.11E
Thann, Fr. (tän)	150	47.49N	7.05E
Thaon-les-Vosges, Fr. (tä-ŏN-lā-vōzh′)	150	48.16N	6.24E
Thargomindah, Austl. (thär′gō-mĭn′dá)	196	27.58S	143.57E
Thásos, i., Grc. (thä′sôs)	142	40.41N	24.53E
Thatch Cay, i., V.I.U.S. (thăch)	111c	18.22N	64.53W
Thatto Heath, Eng., U.K.	233a	53.26N	2.45W
Thaya, r., Eur. (tä′yá)	148	48.48N	15.40E
Thayer, Mo., U.S. (thâ′ĕr)	104	36.30N	91.34W
The Basin, Austl.	239b	37.51S	145.19E
Thebes, hist., Egypt (thēbz)	204	25.47N	32.39E
Thebes, see Thívai, Grc.	142	38.20N	23.18E
The Brothers, mtn., Wa., U.S.	100a	47.39N	123.08W
The Capital, pt. of i., D.C., U.S.	225d	38.53N	77.00W
The Coorong, l., Austl. (kô′rŏng)	198	36.07S	139.45E
The Coteau, hills, Can.	82	51.10N	107.30W
The Dalles, Or., U.S. (dălz)	90	45.36N	121.10W
The Father, mtn., Pap. N. Gui.	188	5.05S	151.30E
The Hague ('s-Gravenhage), Neth.	136	52.05N	4.16E
The Narrows, strt., N.Y., U.S.	224	40.37N	74.03W
The Oaks, Austl.	195b	34.04S	150.36E
Theodore, Austl. (thēō′dôr)	198	24.51S	150.09E
Theodore Roosevelt Dam, dam, Az., U.S. (thē-ô-dōr rōō-sĕ-vĕlt)	102	33.46N	111.25W
Theodore Roosevelt Lake, res., Az., U.S.	102	33.45N	111.00W
Theodore Roosevelt National Park, N.D., U.S.	96	47.20N	103.42W
Theológos, Grc.	154	40.37N	24.41E
The Oval, pt. of i., Eng., U.K.	231	51.29N	0.07W
The Pas, Can. (pä)	78	53.50N	101.15W
Thermopolis, Wy., U.S. (thĕr-mŏp′ō-lĭs)	98	43.38N	108.11W
The Round Mountain, mtn., Austl.	198	30.17S	152.19E
The Sound, strt., Austl.	239a	33.49S	151.17E
Thessalía, hist. reg., Grc.	154	39.50N	22.09E
Thessalon, Can.	78	46.11N	83.37W
Thessaloníki, Grc. (thĕs-sä-lô-nē′kē)	136	40.38N	22.59E
Thetford Mines, Can. (thĕt′fĕrd mīns)	84	46.05N	71.20W
The Twins, mtn., Afr. (twĭnz)	207c	30.09S	28.29E
Theunissen, S. Afr.	212d	28.25S	26.44E
Theydon Bois, Eng., U.K.	231	51.40N	0.06E
Thiais, Fr.	233c	48.46N	2.23E
Thibaudeau, Can. (tĭ′bō-dō′)	82	57.05N	94.08W
Thibodaux, La., U.S. (tē-bō-dō′)	106	29.48N	90.48W
Thief, l., Mn., U.S. (thēf)	96	48.32N	95.46W
Thief, r., Mn., U.S.	96	48.18N	96.07E
Thief Rivers Falls, Mn., U.S. (thēf rĭv′ĕr fôlz)	96	48.07N	96.11W
Thiers, Fr. (tyâr)	150	45.51N	3.32E
Thiès, Sen. (tē-ĕs′)	204	14.48N	16.56W
Thika, Kenya	210	1.03S	37.05E
Thimphu, Bhu.	174	27.33N	89.42E
Thingvallavatn, l., Ice.	140	64.12N	20.22W
Thio, N. Cal.	192f	21.37S	166.14E
Thionville, Fr. (tyôN-vēl′)	140	49.23N	6.31E
Third Cataract, wtfl., Sudan	204	19.53N	30.11E
Thisted, Den. (tēs′tĕdh)	146	56.57N	8.38E
Thistilfjördur, b., Ice.	140	66.29N	14.59W
Thistle, i., Austl. (thĭs′'l)	198	34.55S	136.11E
Thistletown, neigh., Can.	223c	43.44N	79.33W
Thjórsá, r., Ice. (tyûr′sá)	140	64.23N	19.18W
Thohoyandou, Venda	206	23.00S	30.29E
Tholen, Neth.	139a	51.32N	4.11E
Thomas, Ok., U.S. (tŏm′ăs)	104	35.44N	98.43W
Thomas, W.V., U.S.	92	39.15N	79.30W
Thomaston, Ga., U.S. (tŏm′ăs-tŭn)	108	32.51N	84.17W
Thomaston, N.Y., U.S.	224	40.47N	73.43W
Thomastown, Austl.	239b	37.41S	145.01E
Thomasville, Al., U.S. (tŏm′ăs-vĭl)	108	31.55N	87.43W
Thomasville, N.C., U.S.	108	35.52N	80.05W
Thomlinson, Mount, mtn., Can.	80	55.33N	127.29W
Thompson, Can.	78	55.48N	97.59W
Thompson, r., Can.	80	50.15N	121.20W
Thompson, r., Mo., U.S.	104	40.32N	93.49W
Thompson Falls, Mt., U.S.	98	47.35N	115.20W
Thomson, r., Austl. (tŏm-sŏn)	196	24.30S	143.07E
Thomson's Falls, Kenya	210	0.02N	36.22E
Thon Buri, neigh., Thai.	237f	13.43N	100.29E
Thong, Eng., U.K.	231	51.24N	0.24E
Thong Hoe, Sing.	236c	1.25N	103.42E
Thong-tay-hoi, Viet.	237m	10.50N	106.39E
Thonon-les-Bains, Fr. (tô-nôN′lā-băN′)	150	46.22N	6.27E
Thorigny-sur-Marne, Fr.	233c	48.53N	2.42E
Thornbury, Austl.	239b	37.45S	145.00E
Thorne, Eng., U.K. (thôrn)	138a	53.37N	0.58W
Thornhill, S. Afr.	240b	26.07S	28.09E
Thornleigh, Austl.	239a	33.44S	151.05E
Thornton, Eng., U.K.	233a	53.30N	3.00W
Thornton Hough, Eng., U.K.	233a	53.19N	3.03W
Thornton-le-Moors, Eng., U.K.	233a	53.16N	2.50W
Thorntown, In., U.S. (thôrn′tŭn)	92	40.05N	86.35W
Thornwood Common, Eng., U.K.	231	51.43N	0.08E
Thorold, Can. (thō′rōld)	84	43.13N	79.12W
Thouars, Fr. (tōō-är′)	150	47.00N	0.17W
Thousand Islands, is., N.Y., U.S. (thou′zănd)	92	44.15N	76.10W
Thrace, hist. reg. (thrās)	154	41.20N	26.07E
Thrapston, Eng., U.K. (thrăp′stŭn)	138a	52.23N	0.32W
Three Forks, Mt., U.S. (thrē fôrks)	98	45.56N	111.35W
Three Oaks, Mi., U.S. (thrē ōks)	92	41.50N	86.40W
Three Points, Cape, c., Ghana	204	4.45N	2.06W
Three Rivers, Mi., U.S.	92	42.00N	83.40W
Thule, Grnld.	76	76.34N	68.47W
Thun, Switz. (tōōn)	148	46.46N	7.34E
Thunder Bay, Can.	84	48.28N	89.12W
Thunder Bay, b., Can. (thŭn′dĕr)	84	48.29N	88.52W
Thunder Hills, hills, Can.	82	54.30N	106.00W
Thunersee, l., Switz.	148	46.40N	7.30E
Thurber, Tx., U.S. (thûr′bĕr)	106	32.30N	98.23W
Thüringen (Thuringia), hist. reg., Ger. (tü′rĭng-ĕn)	148	51.07N	10.45E
Thurles, Ire. (thûrlz)	144	52.44N	7.45W
Thursday, i., Austl. (thûrz-dā)	196	10.17S	142.23E
Thurso, Can. (thŭn′sô)	77c	45.36N	75.15W
Thurso, Scot., U.K.	144	58.35N	3.40W
Thurston Island, i., Ant. (thûrs′tŭn)	213	71.20S	98.00W
Tiananmen, hist., China	236b	39.55N	116.23E
Tiandong, China (tĭĕn-dôŋ)	184	23.32N	107.10E
Tianjin, China	180	39.08N	117.14E
Tianjin Shi, China (tĭĕn-jyĭn shr)	184	39.30N	117.13E
Tianmen, China (tĭĕn-mŭn)	184	30.40N	113.10E
Tianshui, China (tĭĕn-shwā)	184	34.25N	105.40E
Tibagi, Braz. (tē′bá-zhē)	124	24.40S	50.35W
Tibasti, Sarir, des., Libya	204	24.00N	16.30E
Tibati, Cam.	208	6.27N	12.38E
Tibesti, mts., Chad	204	20.40N	17.48E
Tibet, see Xizang, prov., China (tĭ-bĕt′)	180	32.22N	83.30E
Țibleșului, Munții, mts., Rom.	148	47.41N	24.05E
Tibnīn, Leb.	173a	33.12N	35.23E
Tiburon, Haiti	116	18.35N	74.25W
Tiburon, Ca., U.S. (tē-bōō-rōn′)	100b	37.53N	122.27W
Tiburon, Ca., U.S.	227b	36.04N	119.19W
Tiburón, i., Mex.	110	28.45N	113.10W
Tiburón, Cabo, c. (ká′bô)	114	8.42N	77.19W
Tiburon Island, i., Ca., U.S.	100b	37.52N	122.26W
Ticao Island, i., Phil. (tē-kä′ō)	189a	12.40N	123.30E
Tickhill, Eng., U.K. (tĭk′ĭl)	138a	53.26N	1.06W
Ticonderoga, N.Y., U.S. (tī-kŏn-dĕr-ō′gă)	92	43.50N	73.30W
Ticul, Mex. (tē-kōō′l)	114a	20.22N	89.32W
Tidaholm, Swe. (tē′dá-hōlm)	146	58.11N	13.53E
Tideswell, Eng., U.K. (tīdz′wĕl)	138a	53.17N	1.47W
Tidikelt, reg., Alg. (tē-dē-kĕlt′)	204	25.53N	2.11E
Tidjikdja, Maur. (tē-jĭk′jä)	204	18.33N	11.25W
Tidra, Île, i., Maur.	208	19.50N	16.45W
Tiefenbroich, Ger.	232	51.18N	6.49E
Tieling, China (tĭĕ-lĭŋ)	180	42.18N	123.50E
Tielmes, Spain (tyâl-màs′)	153a	40.15N	3.20W
Tienen, Bel.	139a	50.49N	4.58E
Tien Shan, mts., Asia	180	42.00N	78.46E
Tientsin, see Tianjin, China	180	39.08N	117.14E
Tiergarten, neigh., Ger.	234a	52.31N	13.21E
Tierp, Swe. (tyĕrp)	146	60.21N	17.28E
Tierpoort, S. Afr.	207b	25.53S	28.26E
Tierra Blanca, Mex. (tyĕ′r-rä-blä′n-kä)	112	18.28N	96.19W
Tierra del Fuego, i., S.A. (tyĕr′rä dĕl fwā′gō)	126	53.50S	68.45W
Tiétar, r., Spain (tē-ā′tär)	152	39.56N	5.44W
Tiffin, Oh., U.S. (tĭf′ĭn)	92	41.10N	83.15W
Tifton, Ga., U.S. (tĭf′tŭn)	108	31.25N	83.34W
Tigard, Or., U.S. (tī′gärd)	100c	45.25N	122.46W
Tignish, Can. (tĭg′nĭsh)	86	46.57N	64.02W
Tigoda, r., Russia (tē′gô-dá)	164c	59.29N	31.15E
Tigre, r., Peru	124	2.20S	75.41W
Tigres, Península dos, pen., Ang. (pĕ-nē′ŋ-sōō-lä-dôs-tē′grĕs)	206	16.30S	11.45E
Tigris, r., Asia	174	34.45N	44.10E
Tīh, Jabal at, mts., Egypt	173a	29.23N	34.05E
Tihert, Alg.	204	35.28N	1.15E
Tihuatlán, Mex. (tē-wä-tlän′)	112	20.43N	97.34W
Tijuana, Mex. (tē-hwä′nä)	110	32.32N	117.02W
Tijuca, Pico da, mtn., Braz. (pē′kō-dä-tē-zhōō′kå)	126b	22.56S	43.17W
Tikal, hist., Guat. (tē-käl′)	114a	17.16N	89.49W
Tikhoretsk, Russia (tē-kôr-yĕtsk′)	160	45.55N	40.05E
Tikhvin, Russia (tēκ-vēn′)	158	59.36N	33.38E
Tikrīt, Iraq	174	34.36N	43.31E
Tiksi, Russia (tĕk-sē′)	158	71.42N	128.32E
Tilburg, Neth. (tĭl′bûrg)	140	51.33N	5.05E
Tilbury, Eng., U.K.	138b	51.28N	0.23E
Tilemsi, Vallée du, val., Mali	208	17.50N	0.25E
Tilichiki, Russia (tyĭ-le-chĭ-kē)	158	60.49N	166.14E
Tiligul, r., Ukr. (tē′lĭ-gûl)	156	47.25N	30.27E
Tilimsen, Alg.	204	34.53N	1.21W
Tillabéry, Niger (tē-yá-bā-rē′)	204	14.14N	1.30E
Tillamook, Or., U.S. (tĭl′á-mök)	98	45.27N	123.50W
Tillamook Bay, b., Or., U.S.	98	45.32N	124.26W
Tillberga, Swe. (tĕl-bĕr′ghă)	146	59.40N	16.34E
Tillsonburg, Can. (tĭl′sŭn-bûrg)	84	42.50N	80.50W
Tim, Russia (têm)	156	51.39N	37.07E
Timaru, N.Z. (tĭm′á-rōō)	197a	44.26S	171.17E
Timashevskaya, Russia (tēmä-shĕfs-kä′yä)	160	45.47N	38.57E
Timbalier Bay, b., La., U.S. (tĭm′bá-lĕr)	106	28.55N	90.14W
Timber, Or., U.S. (tĭm′bĕr)	100c	45.43N	123.17W
Timberview, Md., U.S.	225c	39.13N	76.45W
Timbo, Gui. (tĭm′bō)	204	10.41N	11.51W
Timbuktu, see Tombouctou, Mali	204	16.46N	3.01W
Times Square, pt. of i., N.Y., U.S.	224	40.45N	74.00W
Timétrine Monts, mts., Mali	208	19.50N	0.30W
Timimoun, Alg. (tē-mē-mōōn′)	204	29.14N	0.22E
Timiris, Cap, c., Maur.	204	19.23N	16.32W
Timiș, r., Eur.	154	45.28N	21.06E
Timișoara, Rom.	142	45.44N	21.21E
Timmins, Can. (tĭm′ĭnz)	78	48.25N	81.22W
Timmonsville, S.C., U.S. (tĭm′ŭnz-vĭl)	108	34.09N	79.55W
Timok, r., Eur.	154	43.35N	22.13E
Timor, i., Indon. (tē-mōr′)	188	10.08S	125.00E
Timor Sea, sea	196	12.40S	125.00E
Timpanogos Cave National Monument, rec., Ut., U.S. (tĭ-măn′ō-gŏz)	102	40.25N	111.45W
Timperley, Eng., U.K.	233b	53.24N	2.19W
Timpson, Tx., U.S. (tĭmp′sŭn)	106	31.55N	94.24W
Timsāh, l., Egypt (tĭm′sä)	212b	30.34N	32.22E
Tina, r., Transkei (tē′nă)	207c	30.50S	28.44E
Tina, Monte, mtn., Dom. Rep. (mô′n-tē-tē′nä)	116	18.50N	70.40W
Tinaguillo, Ven. (tē-nä-gē′l-yô)	125b	9.55N	68.18W
Tīnah, Khalīj at, b., Egypt	173a	31.06N	32.42E
Tindouf, Alg. (tēn-dōōf′)	204	27.43N	7.44W
Tinggi, i., Malay.	173b	2.16N	104.16E
Tinghert, Plateau du, plat., Alg.	204	27.30N	7.30E
Tingi Mountains, mts., S.L.	208	9.00N	10.50W
Ting Kau, H.K.	237c	22.23N	114.04E
Tinglin, China	183b	30.53N	121.18E
Tingo María, Peru (tē′ngô-mä-rē′ä)	124	9.15S	76.04W
Tingréla, I.C.	208	10.29N	6.24W
Tingsryd, Swe. (tĭngs′rüd)	146	56.32N	14.58E
Tinguindio, Mex.	112	19.38N	102.02W
Tinguiririca, r., Chile (tē′n-gē-rē-rē′kä)	123b	34.48S	70.45W
Tinley Park, Il., U.S. (tĭn′lē)	95a	41.34N	87.47W
Tinnoset, Nor. (tĕn′nôs′sĕt)	146	59.44N	9.00E
Tinogasta, Arg. (tē-nô-gäs′tä)	126	28.07S	67.30W
Tínos, i., Grc.	142	37.45N	25.12E
Tinsukia, India (tin-sōō′kĭ-á)	174	27.18N	95.29W
Tintic, Ut., U.S. (tĭn′tĭk)	102	39.55N	112.15W
Tio, Pic de, mtn., Gui.	208	8.55N	8.55W
Tioga, neigh., Pa., U.S.	225b	40.00N	75.10W
Tioman, i., Malay.	173b	2.50N	104.15E
Tipitapa, Nic. (tē-pē-tä′pä)	114	12.14N	86.05W
Tipitapa, r., Nic.	114	12.13N	85.57W
Tippah Creek, r., Ms., U.S. (tĭp′pă)	108	34.43N	88.15W
Tippecanoe, r., In., U.S. (tĭp-ē-kă-nōō′)	92	40.55N	86.45W
Tipperary, Ire. (tĭ-pē-râ′rē)	140	52.28N	8.13W
Tippo Bay, Ms., U.S. (tĭp′ō bīōō′)	104	33.35N	90.06W
Tipton, In., U.S.	92	40.15N	86.00W
Tipton, Ia., U.S.	96	41.46N	91.10W
Tiranë, Alb. (tē-rä′nä)	136	41.48N	19.50E
Tirano, Italy (tē-rä′nō)	154	46.12N	10.09E
Tiraspol′, Mol. (tē-räs′pôl′)	160	46.52N	29.38E
Tire, Tur. (tē′rĕ)	142	38.05N	27.48E
Tiree, i., Scot., U.K. (tī-rē′)	140	56.34N	6.30W
Tires, Port.	234d	38.43N	9.21W
Tîrgoviște, Rom.	142	44.54N	25.29E
Tîrgu-Jiu, Rom.	142	45.02N	23.17E
Tîrgu-Mureș, Rom.	142	46.33N	24.33E
Tîrgu Neamt, Rom.	148	47.14N	26.23E
Tîrgu-Ocna, Rom.	148	46.18N	26.38E
Tîrgu-Secuiesc, Rom.	148	46.04N	26.06E
Tirlyanskiy, Russia (tĭr-lyän′skĭ)	164a	54.13N	58.37E

PLACE (Pronunciation)	PAGE	Lat. °′	Long. °′
Tîrnăveni, Rom.	148	46.19N	24.18E
Tírnavos, Grc.	154	39.50N	22.14E
Tirol, prov., Aus. (tē-rōl′)	148	47.13N	11.10E
Tiruchchirāppalli, India (tĭr′ŏ-chĭ-rä′pȧ-lĭ)	174	10.49N	78.48E
Tirunelveli, India	175c	8.53N	77.43E
Tiruppur, India	178	11.11N	77.08E
Tisdale, Can. (tĭz′dāl)	78	52.51N	104.04W
Tista, r., Asia	178	26.00N	89.30E
Tisza, r., Eur. (tē′sä)	136	47.30N	21.00E
Titāgarh, India	178a	22.44N	88.23E
Titicaca, Lago, l., S.A. (lä′gô-tē-tē-kä′kä)	124	16.12S	70.33W
Titiribi, Col. (tē-tē-rē-bē′)	124a	6.05N	75.47W
Tito, Lagh, r., Kenya	210	2.25N	39.05E
Titograd, Yugo.	154	42.25N	19.15E
Titovo Užice, Yugo. (tē′tô-vô o͞o′zhĕ-tsĕ)	154	43.51N	19.53E
Titov Veles, Mac. (tē′tôv vĕ′lĕs)	154	41.42N	21.50E
Titterstone Clee Hill, hill, Eng., U.K. (klē)	138a	52.24N	2.37W
Titule, Zaire	210	3.17N	25.32E
Titusville, Fl., U.S. (tī′tŭs-vĭl)	109a	28.37N	80.44W
Titusville, Pa., U.S.	92	40.40N	79.40W
Titz, Ger. (tētz)	151c	51.00N	6.26E
Tiu Keng Wan, H.K.	237c	22.18N	114.15E
Tiverton, R.I., U.S. (tĭv′ẽr-tun)	94b	41.38N	71.11W
Tivoli, Italy (tē′vô-lē)	142	41.38N	12.48E
Tixkokob, Mex. (tēx-kō-kō′b)	114a	21.01N	89.23W
Tixtla de Guerrero, Mex. (tē′x-tlä-dĕ-gĕr-rĕ′rô)	112	17.36N	99.24W
Tizapán, Mex.	229a	19.20N	99.13W
Tizard Bank and Reef, rf., Asia (tĭz′ȧrd)	188	10.51N	113.20E
Tizimín, Mex. (tē-zē-mē′n)	114a	21.08N	88.10W
Tizi-Ouzou, Alg. (tē′zē-o͞o-zo͞o′)	204	36.44N	4.04E
Tiznados, r., Ven. (tēz-nä′dôs)	125b	9.53N	67.49W
Tiznit, Mor. (tēz-nēt)	204	29.52N	9.39W
Tlacolula de Matamoros, Mex.	112	16.56N	96.29W
Tlacotálpan, Mex. (tlä-kô-täl′pän)	112	18.39N	95.40W
Tlacotepec, Mex. (tlä-kô-tä-pĕ′k)	112	17.46N	99.57W
Tlacotepec, Mex.	112	19.11N	99.41W
Tlacotepec, Mex.	112	18.41N	97.40W
Tláhuac, Mex. (tlä-wäk′)	113a	19.16N	99.00W
Tlajomulco de Zúñiga, Mex. (tlä-hô-mo͞ol′-ko-dĕ-zo͞o′n-yē-gä)	112	20.30N	103.27W
Tlalchapa, Mex. (tläl-chä′pä)	112	18.26N	100.29W
Tlalixcoyan, Mex. (tlä-lēs′kô-yän′)	112	18.53N	96.04W
Tlalmanalco, Mex. (tläl-mä-nä′l-kô)	113a	19.12N	98.48W
Tlalnepantla, Mex.	113a	19.32N	99.13W
Tlalnepantla, Mex. (tläl-nå-pån′tlä)	113a	18.59N	99.01W
Tlalpan, Mex. (tläl-pä′n)	112	19.17N	99.10W
Tlalpujahua, Mex. (tläl-po͞o-κä′wä)	112	19.50N	100.10W
Tlaltenco, Mex.	229a	19.17N	99.01W
Tlapa, Mex. (tlä′pä)	112	17.30N	98.30W
Tlapacoyan, Mex. (tlä-pä-kô-yä′n)	112	19.57N	97.11W
Tlapehuala, Mex. (tlä-på-wä′lä)	112	18.17N	100.30W
Tlaquepaque, Mex. (tlä-kĕ-pä′kĕ)	112	20.39N	103.17W
Tlatlaya, Mex. (tlä-tlä′yä)	112	18.36N	100.14W
Tlaxcala, Mex. (tläs-kä′lä)	110	19.16N	98.14W
Tlaxcala, state, Mex.	112	19.30N	98.15W
Tlaxco, Mex. (tläs′kō)	112	19.37N	98.06W
Tlaxiaco Santa María Asunción, Mex.	112	17.16N	97.41W
Tlayacapan, Mex. (tlä-yä-kä-pä′n)	113a	18.57N	99.00W
Tlevak Strait, strt., Ak., U.S.	80	53.03N	132.58W
Tlumach, Ukr. (t′lŭ-mäch′)	148	48.47N	25.00E
Toa, r., Cuba (tō′ä)	116	20.25N	74.35W
Toamasina, Madag.	206	18.14S	49.25E
Toar, Cuchillas de, mts., Cuba (ko͞o-chē′l-lyäs-dĕ-tô-ä′r)	116	20.20N	74.50W
Tobago, i., Trin. (tô-bā′gō)	110	11.15N	60.30W
Toba Inlet, b., Can.	80	50.20N	124.50W
Tobarra, Spain (tô-bär′rä)	152	38.37N	1.42W
Tobol, r., Asia	158	52.00N	62.00E
Tobol'sk, Russia (tô-bôlsk′)	162	58.09N	68.28E
Tocaima, Col. (tô-kä′y-mä)	124a	4.28N	74.38W
Tocantinópolis, Braz. (tô-kän-tē-nŏ′pō-lēs)	124	6.27S	47.18W
Tocantins, state, Braz.	124	10.00S	48.00W
Tocantins, r., Braz. (tō-kän-tēɴs′)	124	3.28S	49.22W
Toccoa, Ga., U.S. (tŏk′ô-ȧ)	108	34.35N	83.20W
Toccoa, r., Ga., U.S.	108	34.53N	84.24W
Tochigi, Japan (tō′chē-gĭ)	187	36.25N	139.45E
Tocoa, Hond. (tō-kō′ä)	114	15.37N	86.01W
Tocopilla, Chile (tō-kô-pēl′yä)	126	22.03S	70.08W
Tocuyo de la Costa, Ven. (tô-ko͞o′yō-dĕ-lä-kôs′tä)	125b	11.03N	68.24W
Toda, Japan	187a	35.48N	139.42E
Todmorden, Eng., U.K. (tŏd′môr-dĕn)	138a	53.43N	2.05W
Tofino, Can. (tō-fē′nō)	80	49.09N	125.54W
Töfsingdalens National Park, rec., Swe.	146	62.09N	13.05E
Tōgane, Japan (tō′gä-nä)	187	35.29N	140.16E
Togian, Kepulauan, is., Indon.	188	0.20S	122.00E
Togo, nation, Afr. (tō′gō)	204	8.00N	0.52E
Toguzak, r., Russia (tō′gô-zák)	164a	53.40N	61.42E
Tohopekaliga, Lake, l., Fl., U.S. (tō′hō-pē′kȧ-lī′gȧ)	109a	28.16N	81.09W
Tohor, Tanjong, c., Malay.	173b	1.53N	102.29E
Toijala, Fin. (toi′yȧ-lȧ)	146	61.11N	23.46E
Toi-Misaki, c., Japan (toi mē′sä-kē)	186	31.20N	131.20E
Toiyabe, Nv., U.S. (toi′yă-bē)	102	38.59N	117.22W
Tokachi Gawa, r., Japan (tō-kä′chē gä′wä)	186	43.10N	142.30E
Tokaj, Hung. (tô′kô-ē)	148	48.06N	21.24E
Tokat, Tur. (tō-κät′)	174	40.20N	36.30E
Tokelau Islands, dep., Oc. (tō-kē-lä′ō)	2	8.00S	176.00W
Tokmak, Kyrg. (tôk′måk)	158	42.44N	75.41E
Tokorozawa, Japan (tô′kô-rô-zä′wä)	187a	35.47N	139.29E
Toksu Palace, bldg., S. Kor.	237b	37.35N	126.58E
Tokuno, i., Japan (tô-ko͞o′nō)	180	27.42N	129.25E
Tokushima, Japan (tō′kô′shē-mä)	180	34.06N	134.31E
Tokuyama, Japan (tō′kô′yä-mä)	187	34.04N	131.49E
Tōkyō, Japan	180	35.42N	139.46E
Tōkyō-Wan, b., Japan (tō′kyō wän)	187	35.56N	139.56E
Tolcayuca, Mex. (tôl-kä-yo͞o′kä)	112	19.55N	98.54W
Toledo, Spain (tô-lĕ′dô)	142	39.53N	4.02W
Toledo, Ia., U.S. (tô-lē′dō)	96	41.59N	92.35W
Toledo, Oh., U.S.	90	41.40N	83.35W
Toledo, Or., U.S.	98	44.37N	123.58W
Toledo, Montes de, mts., Spain (mô′n-tĕs-dĕ-tô-lĕ′dô)	152	39.33N	4.40W
Toledo Bend Reservoir, res., U.S.	90	31.30N	93.30W
Toliara, Madag.	206	23.16S	43.44E
Tolima, dept., Col. (tô-lē′mä)	124a	4.07N	75.20W
Tolima, Nevado del, mtn., Col. (nĕ-vä-dô-dĕl-tô-lē′mä)	124a	4.40N	75.20W
Tolimán, Mex. (tô-lê-män′)	112	20.54N	99.54W
Tollesbury, Eng., U.K. (tōl′z-bĕrĭ)	138b	51.46N	0.49E
Tollygunge, neigh., India	236a	22.30N	88.21E
Tolmezzo, Italy (tôl-mĕt′zô)	154	46.25N	13.03E
Tolmin, Slo. (tôl′mēn)	154	46.12N	13.45E
Tolna, Hung. (tôl′nô)	148	46.25N	18.47E
Tolo, Teluk, b., Indon. (tō′lō)	188	2.00S	122.06E
Tolosa, Spain (tô-lō′sä)	142	43.10N	2.05W
Tolt, r., Wa., U.S. (tōlt)	100a	47.13N	121.49W
Toluca, Mex. (tô-lo͞o′kȧ)	110	19.17N	99.40W
Toluca, Il., U.S. (tô-lo͞o′kȧ)	92	41.00N	89.10W
Toluca, Nevado de, mtn., Mex. (nĕ-vä-dô-dĕ-tô-lo͞o′kä)	110	19.09N	99.42W
Tolworth, neigh., Eng., U.K.	231	51.23N	0.17W
Tolyatti, Russia	160	53.30N	49.10E
Tom', r., Russia	162	55.33N	85.00E
Tomah, Wi., U.S. (tō′mȧ)	96	43.58N	90.31W
Tomahawk, Wi., U.S. (tŏm′ȧ-hôk)	96	45.27N	89.44W
Tomakovka, Ukr. (tô-mä′kôf-kȧ)	156	47.49N	34.43E
Tomanivi, mtn., Fiji	192g	17.37S	178.01E
Tomar, Port. (tō-mär′)	152	39.36N	8.26W
Tomashevka, Bela. (tô-mȧ′shĕf-kȧ)	148	51.34N	23.37E
Tomaszów Lubelski, Pol. (tô-mä′shôf lo͞o-bĕl′skĭ)	148	50.20N	23.27E
Tomaszów Mazowiecki, Pol. (tô-mä′shôf mä-zô′vyĕt-skĭ)	148	51.33N	20.00E
Tomatlán, Mex. (tô-mä-tlä′n)	112	19.54N	105.14W
Tombadonkéa, Gui.	208	11.00N	14.23W
Tombador, Serra do, mts., Braz. (sĕr′rȧ dô tôm-bä-dôr′)	124	11.31S	57.33W
Tombigbee, r., U.S. (tŏm-bĭg′bē)	90	33.00N	88.30W
Tombos, Braz. (tô′m-bōs)	123a	20.53S	42.00W
Tombouctou, Mali	204	16.46N	3.01W
Tombs of the Caliphs, pt. of i., Egypt	240a	30.03N	31.17E
Tombstone, Az., U.S. (to͞om′stōn)	102	31.40N	110.00W
Tombua, Ang. (ȧ-lē-zhän′drĕ)	206	15.49S	11.53E
Tomelilla, Swe. (tô′mĕ-lēl-lä)	146	55.34N	13.55E
Tomelloso, Spain (tō-mål-lyō′sō)	152	39.09N	3.02W
Tommot, Russia (tŏm-mŏt′)	158	59.13N	126.22E
Tomsk, Russia (tŏmsk)	158	56.29N	84.57E
Tonala, Mex.	112	20.38N	103.14W
Tonalá, r., Mex.	112	18.05N	94.08W
Tonawanda, N.Y., U.S. (tôn-ȧ-wŏn′dȧ)	95c	43.01N	78.53W
Tonawanda, Town of, N.Y., U.S.	226a	42.59N	78.52W
Tonawanda Creek, r., N.Y., U.S.	95c	43.05N	78.43W
Tonbridge, Eng., U.K. (tŭn-brĭj)	138b	51.11N	0.17E
Tonda, Japan (tôn′dä)	187b	34.51N	135.38E
Tondabayashi, Japan (tôn-dä-bä′yä-shē)	187b	34.29N	135.36E
Tondano, Indon. (tôn-dä′nō)	188	1.15N	124.50E
Tønder, Den. (tûn′nẽr)	146	54.47N	8.49E
Tone-Gawa, r., Japan (tô′nĕ gä′wa)	187	36.12N	139.19E
Tonga, nation, Oc. (tŏŋ′gȧ)	190	18.50S	175.20W
Tong'an, China (tôŋ-än)	184	24.48N	118.02E
Tonga Trench, deep	190	23.00S	172.30W
Tongbei, China (tôŋ-bā)	180	48.00N	126.48E
Tongguan, China (tôŋ-gūän)	180	34.48N	110.25E
Tonghe, China (tôŋ-hŭ)	184	45.58N	128.40E
Tonghua, China (tôŋ-hwä)	180	41.43N	125.50E
Tongjiang, China (tôŋ-jyäŋ)	180	47.38N	132.54E
Tongliao, China (tôŋ-lĭou)	184	43.30N	122.15E
Tongo, Cam.	208	5.11N	14.00E
Tongoy, Chile (tōn-goi′)	126	30.16S	71.29W
Tongren, China (tôŋ-rŭn)	180	27.45N	109.12E
Tongshan, China (tôŋ-shän)	182	34.27N	116.27E
Tongtian, r., China (tôŋ-tĭĕn)	180	33.00N	97.00E
Tongue, r., Mt., U.S. (tŭng)	98	45.08N	106.40W
Tongxian, China (tôŋ shyĕn)	182	39.55N	116.40E
Tonj, r., Sudan (tônj)	204	6.18N	28.33E
Tonk, India (Tŏŋk)	174	26.13N	75.45E
Tonkawa, Ok., U.S. (tŏŋ kȧ-wô)	104	36.42N	97.19W
Tonkin, Gulf of, b., Asia (tôn-kăn′)	188	20.30N	108.10E
Tonle Sap, l., Kam. (tôn′lā säp′)	188	13.03N	102.49E
Tonneins, Fr. (tô-näɴ′)	150	44.24N	0.18E
Tönning, Ger. (tû′nēng)	148	54.20N	8.55E
Tonopah, Nv., U.S. (tō-nô-pä′)	90	38.04N	117.15W
Tönsberg, Nor. (tûns′bĕrgh)	140	59.19N	10.25E
Tönsholt, Ger.	232	51.38N	6.58E
Tonto, r., Mex. (tōn′tō)	112	18.15N	96.13W
Tonto Creek, r., Az., U.S.	102	34.05N	111.15W
Tonto National Monument, rec., Az., U.S. (tôn′tô)	102	33.33N	111.08W
Tooele, Ut., U.S. (tô-ĕl ē)	101b	40.33N	112.17W
Toongabbie, Austl.	239a	33.47S	150.57E
Toot Hill, Eng., U.K.	231	51.42N	0.12E
Toowoomba, Austl. (tô wo͝om′bȧ)	196	27.32S	152.10E
Topanga, Ca., U.S. (tō′păn-gȧ)	101a	34.05N	118.36W
Topeka, Ks., U.S. (tô-pē′kȧ)	90	39.02N	95.41W
Topilejo, Mex. (tô-pē-lĕ′hô)	113a	19.12N	99.09W
Topkapi, neigh., Tur.	235f	41.02N	28.54E
Topkapi Müzesi, bldg., Tur.	235f	41.00N	28.59E
T'oplyj Stan, neigh., Russia	235b	55.37N	37.30E
Topock, Az., U.S.	102	34.40N	114.20W
Top of Hebers, Eng., U.K.	233b	53.34N	2.12W
Topol'čany, Czech. (tô-pôl′chä-nü)	148	48.38N	18.10E
Topolobampo, Mex. (tō-pō-lô-bä′m-pô)	110	25.45N	109.00W
Topolovgrad, Bul.	154	42.05N	26.19E
Toppenish, Wa., U.S. (tôp′ĕn-ĭsh)	98	46.22N	120.00W
Toppings, Eng., U.K.	233b	53.37N	2.25W
Torbat-e Ḩeydarīyeh, Iran	176	35.16N	59.13E
Torbat-e Jām, Iran	176	35.14N	60.36E
Torbay, Can. (tôr-bā′)	86	47.40N	52.43W
Torbay, see Torquay, Eng., U.K.	144	50.30N	3.26W
Torbreck, Mount, mtn., Austl. (tōr-brĕk)	198	37.05S	146.55E
Torch, l., Mi., U.S. (tôrch)	92	45.00N	85.30W
Torcy, Fr.	233c	48.51N	2.39E
Tor di Quinto, neigh., Italy	235c	41.56N	12.28E
Töreboda, Swe. (tü′rĕ-bō′dä)	146	58.44N	14.04E
Torhout, Bel.	144	51.01N	3.04E
Toribío, Col. (tô-rē-bē′ô)	124a	2.58N	76.14W
Toride, Japan (tô′rē-dä)	187a	35.54N	104.04E
Torino, see Turin, Italy	136	45.05N	7.44E
Tormes, r., Spain (tōr′mās)	152	41.12N	6.15W
Torneälven, r., Eur.	136	67.00N	22.30E
Torneträsk, l., Swe. (tôr′nĕ trĕsk)	140	68.10N	20.36E
Torngat Mountains, mts., Can.	78	59.18N	64.35W
Tornio, Fin. (tôr′nĭ-ô)	136	65.55N	24.09E
Toro, Lac, l., Can.	84	46.53N	73.46W
Toronto, Can. (tô-rŏn′tō)	78	43.40N	79.23W
Toronto, Oh., U.S.	92	40.30N	80.35W
Toronto, res., Mex.	106	27.35N	105.37W
Toropets, Russia (tô′rô-pyĕts)	160	56.31N	31.37E
Toros Dağlari, Tur. (tô′rŭs)	174	37.00N	32.40E
Torote, r., Spain (tô-rō′tä)	153a	40.36N	3.24W
Tor Pignatara, neigh., Italy	235c	41.52N	12.32E
Torquay, Eng., U.K. (tôr-kē′)	144	50.30N	3.26W
Torra, Cerro, mtn., Col. (sĕ′r-rô-tō′r-rä)	124a	4.41N	76.22W
Torrance, Ca., U.S. (tŏr′rănc)	101a	33.50N	118.20W
Torre Annunziata, Italy (tôr′rä ä-no͞on-tsē-ä′tä)	153c	40.31N	14.27E
Torreblanca, Spain	152	40.18N	0.12E
Torre del Greco, Italy (tôr′rā dĕl grā′kō)	154	40.32N	14.23E
Torrejoncillo, Spain (tôr′rā-hôn-thē′lyō)	152	39.54N	6.26W
Torrelavega, Spain (tôr-rā′lä-vä′gä)	152	43.22N	4.02W
Torrellas de Llobregat, Spain	234e	41.21N	1.59E
Torre Maggiore, Italy (tôr′rā mäd-jō′rā)	154	41.41N	15.18E
Torrens, Lake, l., Austl. (tŏr-ĕns)	196	30.07S	137.40E
Torrente, Spain (tôr-rĕn′tä)	152	39.25N	0.28W
Torreón, Mex. (tôr-rå-ōn′)	110	25.32N	103.26W
Torres Islands, is., Vanuatu (tôr′rĕs) (tŏr′ĕz)	196	13.18N	165.59E
Torres Martinez Indian Reservation, I.R., Ca., U.S. (tôr′ĕz mär-tē′nĕz)	102	33.33N	116.21W
Torres Novas, Port. (tôr′rĕzh nō′väzh)	152	39.28N	8.37W
Torres Strait, strt., Austl. (tôr′rĕs)	196	10.30S	141.30E
Torres Vedras, Port. (tôr′rĕsh vā′dräzh)	152	39.08N	9.18W
Torrevieja, Spain (tôr-rā-vyā′hä)	152	37.58N	0.40W
Torrijos, Phil. (tôr-rē′hōs)	189a	13.19N	122.06E
Torrington, Ct., U.S. (tŏr′ĭng-tŭn)	92	41.50N	73.10W
Torrington, Wy., U.S.	96	42.04N	104.11W
Torro, Spain (tô′r-rō)	152	41.27N	5.23W
Tor Sapienza, neigh., Italy	235c	41.54N	12.35E
Torsby, Swe. (tôrs′bü)	146	60.07N	12.56E
Torshälla, Swe. (tôrs′hĕl-ä)	146	59.26N	16.21E
Tórshavn, Faer. Is. (tôrs-houn′)	136	62.00N	6.55W
Tortola, i., V.I., Br. (tôr-tō′lä)	111b	18.34N	64.40W
Tortona, Italy (tôr-tō′nä)	154	44.52N	8.52W
Tortosa, Spain (tôr-tō′sä)	136	40.59N	0.33E
Tortosa, Cabo de, c., Spain (kà′bô-dĕ-tôr-tō-sä)	152	40.42N	0.55E
Tortue, Canal de la, strt., Haiti (tôr-tü′)	116	20.05N	73.20W
Tortue, Île de la, i., Haiti	116	20.10N	73.00W
Tortue, Rivière de la, r., Can. (lä tōr-tü′)	77a	45.12N	73.32W
Tortuguitas, Arg.	229d	34.28S	58.45W
Toruń, Pol.	136	53.02N	18.35E
Tõrva, Est. (t′r′vȧ)	146	58.02N	25.56E
Torzhok, Russia (tôr′zhôk)	160	57.03N	34.53E
Toscana, hist. reg., Italy (tôs-kä′nä)	154	43.23N	11.08E
Toshima, neigh., Japan	238a	35.44N	139.43E
Tosna, r., Russia	164c	59.28N	30.53E
Tosno, Russia (tôs′nô)	156	59.32N	30.52E
Tostado, Arg. (tôs-tä′dô)	126	29.10S	61.43W
Tosya, Tur. (tôz′yȧ)	142	41.00N	34.00E
Totana, Spain (tō-tä-nä)	152	37.45N	1.28W
Tot'ma, Russia (tôt′mȧ)	160	60.00N	42.20E
Totness, Sur.	124	5.51N	56.17W
Totonicapán, Guat. (tôtō-nē-kä′pän)	110	14.55N	91.20W
Totoras, Arg. (tô-tô′räs)	123c	32.33S	61.13W
Totowa, N.J., U.S.	224	40.54N	74.13W
Totsuka, Japan (tōt′so͞o-kä)	187a	35.24N	139.32E
Tottenham, Eng., U.K. (tŏt′ĕn-ȧm)	138b	51.35N	0.06W
Tottenville, neigh., N.Y., U.S.	224	40.31N	74.15W
Totteridge, neigh., Eng., U.K.	231	51.38N	0.12W
Tottington, Eng., U.K.	233b	53.37N	2.20W
Tottori, Japan (tô′tô-rē)	180	35.30N	134.15E
Touba, I.C.	208	8.17N	7.41W
Touba, Sen.	208	14.51N	15.53W
Toubkal, Jebel, mtn., Mor.	204	31.15N	7.46W
Tougan, Burkina	208	13.04N	3.04W
Touggourt, Alg. (to͞o-go͞ort′) (to͞o-go͞or′)	204	33.09N	6.07E
Touil, Oued, r., Alg. (to͞o-ēl′)	142	34.42N	2.16E
Toul, Fr. (to͞ol)	140	48.39N	5.51E
Toulon, Fr. (to͞o-lôɴ′)	136	43.09N	5.54E
Toulouse, Fr. (to͞o-lo͞oz′)	136	43.37N	1.27E
Toungoo, Burma (tō-ôŋ-go͞o′)	188	19.00N	96.29E

ng-sing; ŋ-baŋk; ɴ-nasalized n; nŏd; cŏmmit; ōld; ôbey; ôrder; oi-boil; fo͞od; ŏ-as oo in foot; ou-out; s-soft; sh-dish; th-thin; pūre; ûnite; ûrn; stŭd; circŭs; ü-as in French tu; ′-indeterminate vowel.

PLACE (Pronunciation)	PAGE	Lat. °′	Long. °′
Tourcoing, Fr. (tòr-kwan')	140	50.44N	3.06E
Tournan-en-Brie, Fr. (to͞or-nän-ĕn-brē')	151b	48.45N	2.47E
Tours, Fr. (to͞or)	136	47.23N	0.39E
Touside, Pic, mtn., Chad (to͞o-sē-dā')	204	21.10N	16.30E
Toussus-le-Noble, Fr.	233c	48.45N	2.07E
Tovdalselva, r., Nor. (tôv-däls-ĕlvå)	146	58.23N	8.16E
Towaco, N.J., U.S.	224	40.56N	74.21W
Towanda, Pa., U.S. (tō-wän'dȧ)	92	41.45N	76.30W
Tower Hamlets, neigh., Eng., U.K.	231	51.32N	0.03W
Tower of London, pt. of i., Eng., U.K.	231	51.30N	0.05W
Towers of Silence, rel., India	236e	18.58N	72.48E
Town Bluff Lake, l., Tx., U.S.	106	30.52N	94.30W
Towner, N.D., U.S. (tou'nẽr)	96	48.21N	100.24W
Town Reach, strt., Asia	236c	1.28N	103.44E
Townsend, Ma., U.S. (toun'zĕnd)	87a	42.41N	71.42W
Townsend, Mt., U.S.	98	46.19N	111.35W
Townsend, Mount, mtn., Wa., U.S.	100a	47.52N	123.03W
Townsville, Austl. (tounz'vĭl)	196	19.18S	146.50E
Towson, Md., U.S. (tou'sŭn)	94e	39.24N	76.36W
Towuti, Danau, l., Indon. (tō-wo͞o'tē)	188	3.00S	121.45E
Toxkan, r., China	180	40.34N	77.15E
Toyah, Tx., U.S. (tô'yȧ)	106	31.19N	103.46W
Toyama, Japan (tō'yä-mä)	180	36.42N	137.14E
Toyama-Wan, b., Japan	187	36.58N	137.16E
Toyoda, Japan	238a	35.39N	139.23E
Toyohashi, Japan (tō'yō-hä'shē)	186	34.44N	137.21E
Toyonaka, Japan (tō'yō-nä'kå)	187b	34.47N	135.28E
Tozeur, Tun. (tō-zûr')	142	33.59N	8.11E
Traar, neigh., Ger.	232	51.23N	6.36E
Trabzon, Tur. (tráb'zōn)	174	41.00N	39.45E
Tracy, Can.	84	46.00N	73.13W
Tracy, Ca., U.S. (trā'sē)	102	37.45N	121.27W
Tracy, Mn., U.S.	96	44.13N	95.37W
Tracy City, Tn., U.S.	108	35.15N	85.44W
Trafalgar, Cabo, c., Spain (kä'bō-trä-fäl-gä'r)	152	36.10N	6.02W
Trafaria, Port.	234d	38.40N	9.14W
Trafford Park, Eng., U.K.	233b	53.28N	2.20W
Trafonomby, mtn., Madag.	206	24.32S	46.35E
Trail, Can. (trāl)	78	49.06N	117.42W
Traisen, r., Aus.	139e	48.15N	15.55E
Traiskirchen, Aus.	139e	48.01N	16.18E
Trakai, Lith. (trá-káy)	146	54.38N	24.59E
Trakiszki, Pol. (trá-kē'-sh-kē)	148	54.16N	23.07E
Tralee, Ire. (trȧ-lē')	140	52.16N	9.20W
Tranås, Swe. (trän'ôs)	146	58.03N	14.56E
Trancoso, Port. (träṇ-kō'sō)	152	40.46N	7.23W
Trangan, Pulau, i., Indon. (träṇ'gän)	188	6.52S	133.30E
Trani, Italy (trä'nē)	154	41.15N	16.25E
Tranmere, Eng., U.K.	233a	53.23N	3.01W
Transkei, nation, Afr.	206	31.20S	29.00E
Transvaal, prov., S. Afr.	206	25.00S	29.00E
Transylvania, hist. reg., Rom. (trăn-sĭl-vā'nĭ-ȧ)	148	46.30N	22.35E
Trapani, Italy	142	38.01N	12.31E
Trappes, Fr. (tráp)	151b	48.47N	2.01E
Traralgon, Austl. (trā'răl-gŏn)	198	38.15S	146.33E
Trarza, reg., Maur.	208	17.35N	15.15W
Trasimeno, Lago, l., Italy (lä'gō trä-sē-mā'nō)	154	43.00N	12.12E
Trás-os-Montes, hist. reg., Port. (träzh'ōzh mōn'täzh)	142	41.33N	7.13W
Traun, r., Aus. (troun)	148	48.10N	14.15E
Traunstein, Ger. (troun'stīn)	148	47.52N	12.38E
Traverse, Lake, l., Mn., U.S. (trăv'ẽrs)	96	45.46N	96.53W
Traverse City, Mi., U.S.	92	44.45N	85.40W
Travnik, Bos. (träv'nēk)	154	44.13N	17.43E
Treasure Island, i., Ca., U.S. (trĕzh'ẽr)	100b	37.49N	122.22W
Trebbin, Ger. (trĕ'bēn)	139b	52.13N	13.13E
Trebinje, Bos. (trå'bēn-yĕ)	154	42.43N	18.21E
Trebišov, Czech. (trĕ'bē-shôf)	148	48.36N	21.32E
Tregrosse Islands, is., Austl. (trē-grōs')	196	18.08S	150.53E
Treinta y Tres, Ur. (trå-ēn'tä ē träs')	126	33.14S	54.17W
Trelew, Arg. (trē'lū)	126	43.15S	65.25W
Trelleborg, Swe.	146	55.24N	13.07E
Tremblay-lès-Gonesse, Fr.	233c	48.59N	2.34E
Tremiti, Isole, is., Italy (ē'sō-lē trä-mē'tē)	154	42.07N	16.33E
Tremont, neigh., N.Y., U.S.	224	40.51N	73.55W
Trenčín, Czech. (trĕn'chēn)	140	48.52N	18.02E
Trenque Lauquén, Arg. (trĕn'kĕ-lä'ō-kĕ'n)	126	35.50S	62.44W
Trent, r., Can. (trĕnt)	84	44.15N	77.55W
Trent, r., Eng., U.K.	138a	53.25N	0.45W
Trent and Mersey Canal, can., Eng., U.K. (trĕnt) (mûr zē)	138a	53.11N	2.24W
Trentino-Alto Adige, hist. reg., Italy	154	46.16N	10.47E
Trento, Italy (trĕn'tô)	142	46.04N	11.07E
Trenton, Can. (trĕn'tŭn)	78	44.05N	77.35W
Trenton, Can.	86	45.37N	62.38W
Trenton, Mi., U.S.	95b	42.08N	83.12W
Trenton, Mo., U.S.	104	40.05N	93.36W
Trenton, N.J., U.S.	90	40.13N	74.46W
Trenton, Tn., U.S.	108	35.57N	88.55W
Trepassey, Can. (trē-pás'ē)	86	46.44N	53.22W
Trepassey Bay, b., Can.	86	46.40N	53.20W
Treptow, neigh., Ger.	234a	52.29N	13.29E
Tres Arroyos, Arg. (träs'är-rō'yōs)	126	38.18S	60.16W
Três Corações, Braz. (trĕ's kō-rä-zō'ĕs)	123a	21.41S	45.14W
Tres Cumbres, Mex. (trĕ's ko͞o'm-brĕs)	113a	19.03N	99.14W
Três Lagoas, Braz. (trĕ's lä-gô'äs)	124	20.48S	51.42W
Três Marias, Represa, res., Braz.	124	18.15S	45.30W
Tres Morros, Alto de, mtn., Col. (ä'l-tō dĕ trĕ's mô'r-rôs)	124a	7.08N	76.10W
Três Pontas, Braz. (trĕ'pô'n-täs)	123a	21.22S	45.30W
Três Pontas, Cabo das, c., Ang.	210	10.23S	13.32E
Três Rios, Braz. (trĕ's rē'ōs)	123a	22.07S	43.13W
Très-Saint Rédempteur, Can. (săn rā-dänp-tûr')	77a	45.26N	74.23W
Tressancourt, Fr.	233c	48.55N	2.00E
Treuenbrietzen, Ger. (troi'ĕn-brē-tzĕn)	139b	52.06N	12.52E
Treviglio, Italy (trā-vē'lyô)	154	45.30N	9.34E
Treviso, Italy (trĕ-vē'sō)	142	45.39N	12.15E
Trichardt, S. Afr. (trĭ-kärt')	212d	26.32N	29.16E
Triel-sur-Seine, Fr.	233c	48.59N	2.00E
Trier, Ger.	140	49.45N	6.38E
Trieste, Italy (trē-ĕs'tä)	136	45.39N	13.48E
Trigueros, Spain (trē-gā'rōs)	152	37.23N	6.50W
Tríkala, Grc.	142	39.33N	21.49E
Trikora, Puncak, mtn., Indon.	188	4.15S	138.45E
Trim Creek, r., Il., U.S. (trĭm)	95a	41.19N	87.39W
Trincomalee, Sri L. (trĭṇ-kō-mȧ-lē')	175c	8.39N	81.12E
Tring, Eng., U.K. (trĭng)	138b	51.46N	0.40W
Trinidad, Bol. (trē-nē-dhädh')	124	14.48S	64.43W
Trinidad, Cuba (trē-nē-dhädh')	110	21.50N	80.00W
Trinidad, Co., U.S. (trĭn'ĭdăd)	90	37.11N	104.31W
Trinidad, Ur.	126	33.29S	56.55W
Trinidad, i., Trin. (trĭn'ĭ-dăd)	124	10.00N	61.00W
Trinidad, r., Pan.	110a	8.55N	80.01W
Trinidad, Sierra de, mts., Cuba (sē-ĕ'r-rä dĕ trē-nē-dä'd)	116	21.50N	79.55W
Trinidad and Tobago, nation, N.A. (trĭn'ĭ-dăd) (tō-bā'gō)	110	11.00N	61.00W
Trinitaria, Mex. (trē-nē-tä'ryä)	112	16.09N	92.04W
Trinity, Can. (trĭn'ĭ-tē)	86	48.59N	53.55W
Trinity, Tx., U.S.	106	30.52N	95.27W
Trinity, is., Ak., U.S.	89	56.25N	153.15W
Trinity, r., Ca., U.S.	98	40.50N	123.20W
Trinity, r., Tx., U.S.	90	30.50N	95.09W
Trinity, East Fork, r., Tx., U.S.	104	33.24N	96.42W
Trinity, West Fork, r., Tx., U.S.	104	33.22N	98.26W
Trinity Bay, b., Can.	78	48.00N	53.40W
Trino, Italy (trē'nô)	154	45.11N	8.16E
Trion, Ga., U.S. (trī'ŏn)	108	34.32N	85.18W
Tripoli (Tarābulus), Libya	204	32.50N	13.13E
Trípolis, Grc. (trĭ'pō-lĭs)	142	37.32N	22.32E
Tripolitania, see Tarābulus, hist. reg., Libya	204	31.00N	12.26E
Tripura, state, India	174	24.00N	92.00E
Tristan da Cunha Islands, is., St. Hel. (trēs-tän'dä ko͞on'yà)	2	35.30S	12.15W
Triste, Golfo, b., Ven. (gôl-fô trĕ's-tĕ)	125b	10.40N	68.05W
Triticus Reservoir, res., N.Y., U.S. (trī tĭ-cŭs)	94a	41.20N	73.36W
Trivandrum, India (trē-vŭn'drŭm)	175c	8.34N	76.58E
Trnava, Czech. (t'r'nà-và)	148	48.22N	17.34E
Trobriand Islands, is., Pap. N. Gui. (trō-brē-ănd')	188	8.25S	151.45E
Trogir, Cro. (trō'gēr)	154	43.32N	16.17E
Troice-Lykovo, neigh., Russia	235b	55.47N	37.24E
Trois Fourches, Cap des, c., Mor.	152	35.28N	2.58W
Trois-Rivières, Can. (trwä'rē-vyâ')	78	46.21N	72.35W
Troitsk, Russia (trô'ĭtsk)	162	54.06N	61.35E
Troitsko-Pechorsk, Russia (trô'ĭtsk-ô-pyĕ-chôrsk')	158	62.18N	56.07E
Troitskoye, Ukr.	156	47.39N	30.16E
Trollhättan, Swe. (trôl'hĕt-ĕn)	140	58.17N	12.17E
Trollheimen, mts., Nor. (trôll-hĕīm)	146	62.48N	9.05E
Trombay, neigh., India	236e	19.02N	72.57E
Trona, Ca., U.S. (trō'nȧ)	102	35.49N	117.20W
Tronador, Cerro, mtn., S.A. (sĕ'r-rō trō-nä'dōr)	126	41.17S	71.56W
Troncoso, Mex. (trôn-kô'sō)	112	22.43N	102.22W
Trondheim, Nor. (trôn'hȧm)	136	63.25N	11.35E
Tropar'ovo, neigh., Russia	235b	55.39N	37.29E
Trosa, Swe. (trō'sä)	146	58.54N	17.25E
Trottiscliffe, Eng., U.K.	231	51.19N	0.21E
Trout, l., Can.	78	61.10N	121.30W
Trout, l., Can.	78	51.16N	92.46W
Trout Creek, r., Or., U.S.	98	42.18N	118.31W
Troutdale, Or., U.S. (trout'dāl)	100c	45.32N	122.23W
Trout Lake, Mi., U.S.	96	46.20N	85.02W
Trouville, Fr. (tro͞o-vēl')	150	49.23N	0.05E
Troy, Al., U.S. (troi)	108	31.47N	85.46W
Troy, Il., U.S.	101e	38.44N	89.53W
Troy, Ks., U.S.	104	39.46N	95.07W
Troy, Mo., U.S.	104	38.56N	99.57W
Troy, Mt., U.S.	98	48.28N	115.56W
Troy, N.Y., U.S.	90	42.45N	73.45W
Troy, N.C., U.S.	108	35.21N	79.58W
Troy, Oh., U.S.	92	40.00N	84.10W
Troy, hist., Tur.	174	39.59N	26.14E
Troyes, Fr. (trwä)	140	48.18N	4.03E
Trstenik, Yugo. (t'r'stē-nēk)	142	43.36N	21.00E
Trubchëvsk, Russia (tróp'chĕfsk)	160	52.36N	33.46E
Trucial States, see United Arab Emirates, nation, Asia	174	24.00N	54.00E
Truckee, Ca., U.S. (trŭk'ē)	102	39.20N	120.12W
Truckee, r., Ca., U.S.	102	39.25N	120.07W
Truganina, Austl.	195a	37.49S	144.44E
Trujillo, Col. (tró-kē'l-yō)	124a	4.10N	76.20W
Trujillo, Peru	124	8.08S	79.00W
Trujillo, Spain (tro͞o-kē'l-yō)	142	39.27N	5.50W
Trujillo, Ven.	124	9.15N	70.28W
Trujillo, r., Mex.	112	23.12N	103.10W
Trujin, Lago, l., Dom. Rep. (tro͞o-kēn')	116	17.45N	71.25W
Truk Islands, is., Micron.	192c	7.25N	151.47E
Trumann, Ar., U.S. (tro͞o'măn)	104	35.41N	90.31W
Trŭn, Bul. (trŭn)	154	42.49N	22.39E
Truro, Can. (tro͞o'rō)	78	45.22N	63.16W
Truro, Eng., U.K.	144	50.17N	5.05W
Trussville, Al., U.S. (trŭs'vĭl)	94h	33.37N	86.37W
Truth or Consequences, N.M., U.S. (tro͞oth ŏr kŏn'sē-kwĕn-sĭs)	102	33.10N	107.20W
Trutnov, Czech. (tròt'nôf)	148	50.36N	15.36E
Trzcianka, Pol. (tchyän'kà)	148	53.02N	16.27E
Trzebiatów, Pol. (tchĕ-byä'tò-v)	148	54.03N	15.16E
Tsaidam Basin, basin, China (tsī-däm)	180	37.19N	94.08E
Tsala Apopka Lake, r., Fl., U.S. (tsä'lȧ ă-pŏp'kȧ)	108	28.57N	82.11W
Tsast Bogd, mtn., Mong.	180	46.44N	92.34E
Tsavo National Park, rec., Kenya	210	2.35S	38.45E
Tsawwassen Indian Reserve, I.R., Can.	100d	49.03N	123.11W
Tselinograd, Kaz. (tsĕ'lē-nō-grä'd)	158	51.10N	71.43E
Tsentral'nyy-Kospashskiy, Russia (tsĕn-träl'nyĭ-kôs-pash'skĭ)	164a	59.03N	57.48E
Tshela, Zaire (tshā'lȧ)	206	4.59S	12.56E
Tshikapa, Zaire (tshē-kä'pä)	206	6.25S	20.48E
Tshofa, Zaire	210	5.14S	25.15E
Tshuapa, r., Zaire	206	0.30S	22.00E
Tsiafajovona, mtn., Madag.	206	19.17S	47.27E
Tsing Island, i., H.K.	237c	22.21N	114.05E
Tsin Shui Wan, b., H.K.	237c	22.13N	114.10E
Tsiribihina, r., Madag. (tsē'rē-bē-hē-nä')	206	19.45S	43.30E
Tsitsa, r., Transkei (tsē'tsá)	207c	31.28S	28.53E
Tsolo, Transkei (tsō'lō)	207c	31.19S	28.47E
Tsomo, Transkei	207c	32.03S	27.49E
Tsomo, r., Transkei	207c	31.53S	27.48E
Tsu, Japan (tso͞o)	186	34.42N	136.31E
Tsuchiura, Japan (tso͞o'chē-o͞o-rä)	187	36.04N	140.09E
Tsuda, Japan (tso͞o'dä)	187b	34.48N	135.43E
Tsugaru Kaikyō, strt., Japan	180	41.25N	140.20E
Tsukumono, neigh., Japan	238b	34.50N	135.11E
Tsumeb, Nmb. (tso͞o'mĕb)	206	19.10S	17.45E
Tsunashima, Japan (tso͞o'nä-shē'mä)	187a	35.32N	139.37E
Tsuruga, Japan (tso͞o'rò-gä)	186	35.39N	136.04E
Tsurugi San, mtn., Japan (tso͞o'rò-gē sän)	186	33.52N	134.07E
Tsurumi, r., Japan	238a	35.29N	139.41E
Tsuruoka, Japan (tso͞o'rò-ō'kä)	186	38.43N	139.51E
Tsurusaki, Japan (tso͞o'rò-sä'kē)	187	33.15N	131.42E
Tsu Shima, is., Japan (tso͞o shē'mä)	180	34.28N	129.30E
Tsushima Strait, strt., Asia	180	34.00N	129.00E
Tsu Wan (Quanwan), H.K.	237c	22.22N	114.07E
Tsuwano, Japan (tso͞o'wá-nō')	187	34.28N	131.47E
Tsuyama, Japan (tso͞o'yä-mä')	186	35.05N	134.00E
Tua, r., Port. (to͞o'ä)	152	41.23N	7.18W
Tualatin, r., Or., U.S. (to͞o'á-lä-tĭn)	100c	45.25N	122.54W
Tuamoto, Îles, Fr. Poly. (to͞o-ä-mō'to͞o)	190	19.00S	141.20W
Tuapse, Russia (tò'áp-sĕ)	160	44.00N	39.10E
Tuareg, hist. reg., Alg.	204	21.26N	2.51E
Tubarão, Braz. (to͞o-bä-roun')	126	28.23N	48.56W
Tübingen, Ger. (tü'bĭng-ĕn)	148	48.33N	9.05E
Tubinskiy, Russia (tû bĭn'skĭ)	164a	52.53N	58.15E
Tubruq, Libya	204	32.03N	24.04E
Tucacas, Ven. (to͞o-kä'käs)	124	10.48N	68.20W
Tuckahoe, N.Y., U.S.	224	40.57N	73.50W
Tucker, Ga., U.S. (tŭk'ẽr)	94c	33.51N	84.13W
Tucson, Az., U.S. (to͞o-sŏn')	90	32.15N	111.00W
Tucumán, Arg. (to͞o-ko͞o-män')	126	26.52S	65.08W
Tucumán, prov., Arg.	126	26.30S	65.30W
Tucumcari, N.M., U.S. (tū'kŭm-kâr-ē)	104	35.11N	103.43W
Tucupita, Ven. (to͞o-ko͞o-pē'tä)	124	9.00N	62.09W
Tudela, Spain (to͞o-dhā'lä)	142	42.03N	1.37W
Tugaloo, r., Ga., U.S. (tŭg'ȧ-lo͞o)	108	34.35N	83.05W
Tugela, r., S. Afr. (to͞o-gel'ȧ)	207c	28.50S	30.52E
Tugela Ferry, S. Afr.	207c	28.44S	30.27E
Tug Fork, r., U.S. (tŭg)	92	37.50N	82.30W
Tuguegarao, Phil. (to͞o-gā-gȧ-rä'ō)	188	17.37N	121.44E
Tuhai, r., China (to͞o-hī)	182	37.05N	116.56E
Tuinplaas, S. Afr.	212d	24.54S	28.46E
Tujunga, Ca., U.S. (to͞o-jŭṇ'gȧ)	101a	34.15N	118.16W
Tukan, Russia (to͞o'kȧn)	164a	53.52N	57.25E
Tukangbesi, Kepulauan, is., Indon.	188	6.00S	124.15E
Tūkrah, Libya	204	32.34N	20.47E
Tuktoyaktuk, Can.	78	69.32N	132.37W
Tukums, Lat. (tò'kòms)	160	56.57N	23.09E
Tukuyu, Tan. (to͞o-ko͞o'yȧ)	206	9.13S	33.43E
Tukwila, Wa., U.S. (tŭk'wĭ-lȧ)	100a	47.28N	122.16W
Tula, Mex. (to͞o'lä)	112	20.04N	99.22W
Tula, Russia (to͞o'lȧ)	160	54.12N	37.37E
Tula, prov., Russia	156	53.45N	37.19E
Tula, r., Mex. (to͞o'lä)	112	20.40N	99.27W
Tulagai, i., Sol.Is. (to͞o-lä'gē)	196	9.15S	160.17E
Tulaghi, Sol.Is.	192e	9.06S	160.09E
Tulalip, Wa., U.S. (tū-lă'lĭp)	100a	48.04N	122.18W
Tulalip Indian Reservation, I.R., Wa., U.S.	100a	48.06N	122.16W
Tulancingo, Mex. (to͞o-län-sĭṇ'gō)	110	20.04N	98.24W
Tulangbawang, r., Indon.	188	4.17S	105.00E
Tulare, Ca., U.S. (to͞o-lä'rā) (tul-âr')	102	36.12N	119.22W
Tulare Lake Bed, l., Ca., U.S.	102	35.57N	120.18W
Tularosa, N.M., U.S. (to͞o-lȧ-rō'zȧ)	102	33.05N	106.05W
Tulcán, Ec. (to͞ol-kän')	124	0.44N	77.52W
Tulcea, Rom. (tòl'chȧ)	142	45.10N	28.47E
Tul'chin, Ukr. (to͞ol'chĕn)	160	48.42N	28.53E
Tulcingo, Mex. (to͞ol-sĭṇ'gō)	112	18.03N	98.27W
Tule, r., Ca., U.S. (to͞ol'lȧ)	102	36.08N	118.50W
Tule River Indian Reservation, I.R., Ca., U.S. (to͞o'lȧ)	102	36.05N	118.35W
Tuli, Zimb. (to͞o'lē)	206	20.58S	29.12E
Tulia, Tx., U.S. (to͞o'lĭ-ȧ)	104	34.32N	101.46W
Tulik Volcano, vol., Ak., U.S. (tò'lĭk)	89a	53.28N	168.10W
Tülkarm, Isr. Occ. (to͞ol kärm)	173a	32.19N	35.02E
Tullahoma, Tn., U.S. (tŭl-ȧ-hō'mȧ)	108	35.21N	86.12W
Tullamarine, Austl.	239b	37.41S	144.52E

PLACE (Pronunciation)	PAGE	Lat. °′	Long. °′
Tullamore, Ire. (tŭl-*ȧ*-mōr′)	144	53.15N	7.29W
Tulle, Fr. (tül)	150	45.15N	1.45E
Tulln, Aus. (tòln)	148	48.21N	16.04E
Tullner Feld, reg., Aus.	139e	48.20N	15.59E
Tulpetlac, Mex. (to͞ol-på-tlåk′)	113a	19.33N	99.04W
Tulsa, Ok., U.S. (tŭl′s*ȧ*)	90	36.08N	95.58W
Tulum, Mex. (to͞o-lò′m)	114a	20.17N	87.26W
Tulun, Russia (tò-lo͞on′)	158	54.29N	100.43E
Tuma, r., Nic. (to͞o′mä)	114	13.07N	85.32W
Tumba, Lac, l., Zaire (tòm′bä)	206	0.50S	17.45E
Tumbes, Peru (to͞o′m-bĕs)	124	3.39S	80.27W
Tumbiscatío, Mex. (to͞om-bė-skȧ-tē′ō)	112	18.32N	102.23W
Tumbo, i., Can.	100d	48.49N	123.04W
Tumen, China (to͞o-mŭn)	184	43.00N	129.50E
Tumen, r., Asia	186	42.08N	128.40E
Tumeremo, Ven. (to͞o-må-rā′mō)	124	7.15N	61.28W
Tumkūr, India	178	13.22N	77.05E
Tumuacacori National Monument, rec., Az., U.S. (to͞o-mä-kä′kå-rē)	102	31.36N	110.20W
Tumuc-Humac Mountains, mts., S.A. (to͞o-mòk′o͞o-mäk′)	124	2.15N	54.50W
Tunas de Zaza, Cuba (to͞o′näs dā zä′zä)	116	21.40N	79.35W
Tunbridge Wells, Eng., U.K. (tŭn′brĭj welz′)	144	51.05N	0.09E
Tunduru, Tan.	210	11.07S	37.21E
Tungabhadra Reservoir, res., India	178	15.26N	75.57E
Tuni, India	178	17.29N	82.38E
Tunica, Ms., U.S. (tū′nĭ-kȧ)	108	34.41N	90.23W
Tunis, Tun. (tū′nĭs)	204	36.59N	10.06E
Tunis, Golfe de, b., Tun.	142	37.06N	10.43E
Tunisia, nation, Afr. (tu-nĭzh′ė-ȧ)	204	35.00N	10.11E
Tunja, Col. (to͞o′n-hȧ)	124	5.32N	73.19W
Tunkhannock, Pa., U.S. (tŭnk-hăn′*ŭ*k)	92	41.35N	75.55W
Tunnel, r., Wa., U.S. (tŭn′*ĕ*l)	100a	47.48N	123.04W
Tuoji Dao, i., China (twȯ-jyē dou)	182	38.11N	120.45E
Tuolumne, r., Ca., U.S. (twô-lŭm′nė)	102	37.35N	120.37W
Tuostakh, r., Russia	162	67.09N	137.30E
Tupelo, Ms., U.S. (tū′pė-lō)	108	34.14N	88.43W
Tupinambaranas, Ilha, i., Braz.	124	3.04S	58.09W
Tupiza, Bol. (to͞o-pē′zä)	124	21.26S	65.43W
Tupper Lake, N.Y., U.S. (tŭp′ẽr)	92	44.15N	74.25W
Tuquerres, Col. (to͞o-kĕ′r-rĕs)	124	1.12N	77.44W
Tura, Russia (tòr′*ȧ*)	158	64.08N	99.58E
Turbio, r., Mex. (to͞or-byȯ)	112	20.28N	101.40W
Turbo, Col. (to͞o′bō)	124	8.02N	76.43W
Turda, Rom. (tòr′dȧ)	148	46.35N	23.47E
Turfan Depression, depr., China	180	42.16N	90.00E
Turffontein, neigh., S. Afr.	207b	26.15S	28.02E
Tŭrgovishte, Bul.	154	43.14N	26.36E
Turgutlu, Tur.	160	38.30N	27.20E
Türi, Est. (tü′rĭ)	146	58.49N	25.29E
Turia, r., Spain (to͞o′ryä)	152	40.12N	1.18W
Turicato, Mex. (to͞o-rė-kä′tō)	112	19.03N	101.24W
Turiguano, i., Cuba (to͞o-rė-gwä′nō)	116	22.20N	78.35W
Turin, Italy	136	45.05N	7.44E
Turka, Ukr. (tòr′kȧ)	148	49.10N	23.02E
Turkestan, Kaz. (tûr-kĕ-stăn′) (tòr-kĕ-stan′)	158	44.00N	68.00E
Turkestan, hist. reg., Asia	158	43.27N	62.14E
Turkey, nation, Asia	136	38.45N	32.00E
Turkey, r., Ia., U.S. (tûrk′ė)	96	43.20N	92.16W
Turkmenistan, nation, Asia	158	40.46N	56.01E
Turks, is., T./C. Is. (tûrks)	110	21.40N	71.45W
Turks Island Passage, strt., T./C. Is.	116	21.15N	71.25W
Turku, Fin. (tòrgokò)	136	60.28N	22.12E
Turlock, Ca., U.S. (tûr′lŏk)	102	37.30N	120.51W
Turneffe, i., Belize	110	17.25N	87.43W
Turner, Ks., U.S. (tûr′nẽr)	101f	39.05N	94.42W
Turner Sound, strt., Bah.	116	24.20N	78.05W
Turners Peninsula, pen., S.L.	208	7.20N	12.40W
Turnhout, Bel. (tŭrn-hout′)	144	51.19N	4.58E
Turnov, Czech. (tòr′nôf)	148	50.36N	15.12E
Turnu-Măgurele, Rom.	142	43.54N	24.49E
Turpan, China (to͞o-är-pän)	180	43.06N	88.41E
Turquino, Pico de, mtn., Cuba (pē′kō dā to͞or-kē′nō)	116	20.00N	76.50W
Turramurra, Austl.	239a	33.44S	151.08E
Turrialba, C.R. (to͞or-ryä′l-bä)	114	9.54N	83.41W
Turtkul′, Uzb. (tòrt-kòl′)	158	41.28N	61.02E
Turtle, r., Can.	82	49.20N	92.30W
Turtle Bay, b., Tx., U.S.	107a	29.48N	94.38W
Turtle Creek, Pa., U.S.	226b	40.25N	79.49W
Turtle Creek, r., S.D., U.S.	96	44.40N	98.53W
Turtle Mountain Indian Reservation, I.R., N.D., U.S.	96	48.45N	99.57W
Turtle Mountains, mts., N.D., U.S.	96	48.57N	100.11W
Turukhansk, Russia (to͞o-ro͞o-ᴋänsk′)	158	66.03N	88.39E
Tur′ya, r., Ukr. (to͞or′yȧ)	148	51.18N	24.55E
Tuscaloosa, Al., U.S. (tŭs-kȧ-lo͞o′s*ȧ*)	90	33.10N	87.35W
Tuscarora, Nv., U.S. (tŭs-k*ȧ*-rō′r*ȧ*)	98	41.18N	116.15W
Tuscarora Indian Reservation, I.R., N.Y., U.S.	95c	43.10N	78.51W
Tuscola, Il., U.S. (tŭs-kō-l*ȧ*)	92	39.50N	88.20W
Tuscumbia, Al., U.S. (tŭs-kŭm′bĭ-*ȧ*)	108	34.41N	87.42W
Tushino, Russia (to͞o′shĭ-nô)	164b	55.51N	37.24E
Tuskegee, Al., U.S. (tŭs-kē′gė)	108	32.25N	85.40W
Tustin, Ca., U.S. (tŭs′tĭn)	101a	33.44N	117.49W
Tutayev, Russia (to͞o-tȧ-yĕf′)	160	57.53N	39.34E
Tutbury, Eng., U.K. (tŭt′bẽr-ė)	138a	52.52N	1.51W
Tuticorin, India (to͞o-tė-kȯ-rĭn′)	175c	8.51N	78.09E
Tutitlan, Mex. (to͞o-tē-tlä′n)	113a	19.38N	99.10W
Tutóia, Braz. (to͞o-tō′y*ȧ*)	124	2.42S	42.21W
Tutrakan, Bul.	142	44.02N	26.36E
Tuttle Creek Reservoir, res., Ks., U.S.	104	39.30N	96.38W
Tuttlingen, Ger. (tòt′lĭng-ĕn)	148	47.58N	8.50E

PLACE (Pronunciation)	PAGE	Lat. °′	Long. °′
Tutuila, i., Am. Sam.	192a	14.18S	170.42W
Tutwiler, Ms., U.S. (tŭt′wĭ-lẽr)	108	34.01N	90.25W
Tuva A.S.S.R., prov., Russia	162	51.15N	90.45E
Tuvalu, nation, Oc.	2	5.20S	174.00E
Tuwayq, Jabal, mts., Sau. Ar.	174	20.45N	46.30E
Tuxedo, Md., U.S.	225d	38.55N	76.55W
Tuxedo Park, N.Y., U.S. (tŭk-sē′dō pärk)	94a	41.11N	74.11W
Tuxford, Eng., U.K. (tŭks′fẽrd)	138a	53.14N	0.54W
Túxpan, Mex.	110	20.57N	97.26W
Tuxpan, Mex. (to͞os′pän)	112	19.34N	103.22W
Túxpan, r., Mex. (to͞os′pän)	112	20.55N	97.52W
Túxpan, Arrecife, i., Mex. (är-rĕ-sė′fē-to͞o′x-pä′n)	112	21.01N	97.12W
Tuxtepec, Mex. (tòs-tå-pĕk′)	112	18.06N	96.09W
Tuxtla Gutiérrez, Mex. (tòs′tlä go͞o-tyår′rĕs)	110	16.44N	93.08W
Tuy, r., Ven. (to͞o′ė)	125b	10.15N	66.03W
Tuyra, r., Pan. (to͞o-ē′rȧ)	114	7.55N	77.37W
Tuzlgoot National Monument, rec., Az., U.S.	102	34.40N	111.52W
Tuzla, Bos. (tòz′lȧ)	142	44.33N	18.46E
Tvedestrand, Nor. (tvĭ′dhĕ-stränd)	146	58.39N	8.54E
Tveitsund, Nor. (tvåt′sònd)	146	59.03N	8.29E
Tver′, Russia	158	56.52N	35.57E
Tver′, prov., Russia	156	56.50N	33.08E
Tvertsa, r., Russia (tvĕr′tsȧ)	156	56.58N	35.22E
Tweed, r., U.K. (twēd)	144	55.32N	2.35W
Tweeling, S. Afr. (twē′lĭng)	212d	27.34S	28.31E
Twenty Mile Creek, r., Can. (twĕn′tĭ mīl)	77d	43.09N	79.49W
Twickenham, Eng., U.K. (twĭk″n-*ă*m)	138b	51.26N	0.20W
Twillingate, Can. (twĭl′ĭn-gāt)	79a	49.39N	54.46W
Twin Bridges, Mt., U.S. (twĭn brĭ-jėz)	98	45.34N	112.17W
Twin Falls, Id., U.S. (fôls)	90	42.33N	114.29W
Twinsburg, Oh., U.S. (twĭnz′bŭrg)	95d	41.19N	81.26W
Twitchell Reservoir, res., Ca., U.S.	102	34.50N	120.10W
Two Butte Creek, r., Co., U.S. (to͞o būt)	104	37.39N	102.45W
Two Harbors, Mn., U.S.	96	47.00N	91.42W
Two Prairie Bay, Ar., U.S. (prā′rĭ bī o͞o′)	104	34.48N	92.07W
Two Rivers, Wi., U.S. (rĭv′ẽrz)	96	44.09N	87.36W
Tyabb, Austl.	195a	38.16S	145.11E
Tyachev, Ukr. (tyä′chĕf)	148	48.01N	23.42E
Tyasmin, r., Ukr. (tyås-mĭn′)	156	49.14N	32.23E
Tylden, S. Afr. (tĭl-d*ĕ*n)	207c	32.08S	27.06E
Tyldesley, Eng., U.K. (tĭldz′lė)	138a	53.32N	2.28W
Tyler, Mn., U.S. (tī′lẽr)	96	44.18N	96.08W
Tyler, Tx., U.S.	90	32.21N	95.19W
Tyler Park, Va., U.S.	225d	38.52N	77.12W
Tylertown, Ms., U.S. (tī′lẽr-toun)	108	31.08N	90.06W
Tyndall, S.D., U.S. (tĭn′dȧl)	96	42.58N	97.52W
Tyndinskiy, Russia	158	55.22N	124.45E
Tyne, r., Eng., U.K. (tīn)	144	54.59N	1.56W
Tynemouth, Eng., U.K. (tīn′mŭth)	140	55.04N	1.39W
Tyngsboro, Ma., U.S. (tĭnj-bûr′ȯ)	87a	42.40N	71.27W
Tynset, Nor. (tün′sĕt)	140	62.17N	10.45E
Tyre, *see* Şūr, Leb.	173a	33.16N	35.13E
Tyrifjorden, l., Nor.	146	60.03N	10.25E
Tyrone, Pa., U.S.	92	40.40N	78.15W
Tyrrell, Lake, l., Austl. (tir′ĕll)	198	35.12S	143.00E
Tyrrhenian Sea, sea, Italy (tĭr-rē′nĭ-*ȧ*n)	136	40.10N	12.15E
Tysons Corner, Va., U.S.	225d	38.55N	77.14W
Tyub-Karagan, Mys, c., Kaz.	160	44.30N	50.10E
Tyukalinsk, Russia (työ-kȧ-lĭnsk′)	158	56.03N	71.43E
Tyukyan, r., Russia (työk′yȧn)	162	65.42N	116.09E
Tyuleniy, i., Russia	160	44.30N	48.00E
Tyumen′, Russia (tyo͞o-mĕn′)	158	57.02N	65.28E
Tyura-Tam, Kaz.	158	46.00N	63.15E
Tzucacab, Mex. (tzo͞o-kä-kä′b)	114a	20.06N	89.03W

U

PLACE (Pronunciation)	PAGE	Lat. °′	Long. °′
Uaupés, Braz. (wä-o͞o′pās)	124	0.02S	67.03W
Ubangi, r., Afr. (o͞o-bäŋ′gė)	204	3.00N	18.00E
Ubatuba, Braz. (o͞o-bå-to͞o′bȧ)	123a	23.25S	45.06W
Ubeda, Spain (o͞o′bå-dä)	152	38.01N	3.23W
Uberaba, Braz. (o͞o-bå-rä′b*ȧ*)	124	19.47S	47.47W
Uberlândia, Braz. (o͞o-bĕr-lá′n-dyä)	124	18.54S	48.11W
Ubombo, S. Afr. (o͞o-bôm′bȯ)	206	27.33S	32.13E
Ubon Ratchathani, Thai. (o͞o′bŭn rä′chätá-nē)	188	15.15N	104.52E
Ubort′, r., Eur. (o͞o-bôrt′)	156	51.18N	27.43E
Ubrique, Spain (o͞o-brē′kå)	152	36.43N	5.36W
Ubundu, Zaire	206	0.21S	25.29E
Ucayali, r., Peru (o͞o′kä-yä′lē)	124	8.58S	74.13W
Uccle, Bel. (ū′kl′)	139a	50.48N	4.17E
Uchaly, Russia (û-chä′lĭ)	164a	54.22N	59.28E
Uch-Aral, Kaz. (òch′ȧ-ral′)	158	46.14N	80.58E
Uchiko, Japan (o͞o′chė-kō)	187	33.30N	132.39E
Uchinoura, Japan (o͞o′chė-nȯ-o͞o′rȧ)	187	31.16N	131.03E
Uchinskoye Vodokhranilishche, res., Russia	164b	56.08N	37.44E
Uchiura-Wan, b., Japan (o͞o′chė-o͞o′rä wän)	186	42.20N	140.44E
Uchur, r., Russia (ò-chòr′)	162	57.25N	130.35E
Ückendorf, neigh., Ger.	232	51.30N	7.07E
Uda, r., Russia	162	53.54N	131.29E

PLACE (Pronunciation)	PAGE	Lat. °′	Long. °′
Uda, r., Russia (ò′dȧ)	162	52.28N	110.51E
Udaipur, India (ò-dŭ′ė-po͞or)	178	24.41N	73.41E
Uday, r., Ukr. (ò-dī′)	156	50.45N	32.13E
Uddevalla, Swe. (o͞od′dĕ-väl-ȧ)	140	58.21N	11.55E
Udine, Italy (o͞o′dė-nå)	142	46.05N	13.14E
Udmurt Autonomous Soviet Socialist Republic, Russia	160	57.00N	53.00E
Udon Thani, Thai.	188	17.31N	102.51E
Udskaya Guba, b., Russia	158	55.00N	136.30E
Ueda, Japan (wä′dä)	186	36.26N	138.16E
Uedesheim, neigh., Ger.	232	51.10N	6.48E
Uekermünde, Ger. (ü′kĕr-mün-dĕ)	148	53.43N	14.01E
Uele, r., Zaire (wä′lå)	204	3.55N	23.30E
Uelzen, Ger. (ült′sĕn)	148	52.58N	10.34E
Uerdingen, neigh., Ger.	232	51.21N	6.39E
Ufa, Russia (ò′fa)	158	54.45N	55.57E
Ufa, r., Russia	160	56.00N	57.05E
Ugab, r., Nmb. (o͞o′gäb)	206	21.10S	14.00E
Ugalla, r., Tan. (o͞o-gä′lä)	206	6.15S	32.30E
Uganda, nation, Afr. (o͞o-gän′dä) (û-găn′d*ȧ*)	204	2.00N	32.28E
Ugashik Lake, l., Ak., U.S. (o͞o′gȧ-shėk)	89	57.36N	157.10W
Ugie, S. Afr. (ò′jē)	207c	31.13S	28.14E
Uglegorsk, Russia (o͞o-glĭ-gôrsk)	158	49.00N	142.31E
Ugleural′sk, Russia (òg-lĕ-ò-rálsk′)	164a	58.58N	57.35E
Uglich, Russia (o͞og-lėch′)	156	57.33N	38.19E
Uglitskiy, Russia (òg-lĭt′skĭ)	164a	53.50N	60.18E
Uglovka, Russia (o͞og-lôf′kȧ)	156	58.14N	33.24E
Ugra, r., Russia (o͞og′rȧ)	160	54.43N	34.20E
Ugŭrchin, Bul.	154	43.06N	24.23E
Uhrichsville, Oh., U.S. (ū′rĭks-vĭl)	92	40.25N	81.20W
Uíge, Ang.	206	7.37S	15.03E
Uiju, N. Kor. (ò′ėjo͞o)	180	40.09N	124.33E
Uil, r., Kaz. (ò-ēl′)	160	49.30N	55.10E
Uinkaret Plateau, plat., Az., U.S. (ů-ĭn′kâr-ĕt)	102	36.43N	113.15W
Uinskoye, Russia (ò-ĭn′skô-yĕ)	164a	56.53N	56.25E
Uinta, r., Ut., U.S. (ů-ĭn′tȧ)	102	40.25N	109.55W
Uintah and Ouray Indian Reservation, I.R., Ut., U.S.	102	40.20N	110.20W
Uinta Mountains, mts., Ut., U.S.	90	40.35N	111.00W
Uitenhage, S. Afr.	206	33.46S	25.26E
Uithoorn, Neth.	139a	52.13N	4.49E
Uji, Japan (o͞o′jē)	187b	34.53N	135.49E
Ujiji, Tan. (o͞o-jē′jė)	206	4.55S	29.41E
Ujjain, India (o͞o-jŭėn)	174	23.18N	75.37E
Ujungpandang, Indon.	188	5.08S	119.28E
Ukerewe Island, i., Tan.	210	2.00S	32.40E
Ukhta, Russia (o͞ok′tȧ)	160	65.22N	31.30E
Ukhta, Russia	160	63.08N	53.42E
Ukiah, Ca., U.S. (ū-kī′ȧ)	102	39.09N	122.12W
Ukita, neigh., Japan	238a	35.40N	139.52E
Ukmerge, Lith. (òk′mĕr-ghå)	160	55.16N	24.45E
Ukraine, nation, Eur.	158	49.15N	30.15E
Uku, i., Japan (o͞ok′o͞o)	187	33.18N	129.02E
Ulaangom, Mong.	180	50.23N	92.14E
Ulan Bator (Ulaanbaatar), Mong.	180	47.56N	107.00E
Ulan-Ude, Russia (o͞o′län o͞o′då)	158	51.59N	107.41E
Ulchin, S. Kor. (o͞ol′chėn′)	186	36.57N	129.26E
Ulcinj, Yugo. (o͞ol′tsėn′)	142	41.56N	19.15E
Ulhās, r., India	179b	19.13N	73.03E
Ulhāsnagar, India	178	19.10N	73.07E
Uliastay, Mong.	180	47.49N	97.00E
Ulindi, r., Zaire (o͞o-lĭn′dė)	206	1.55S	26.17E
Ulla, Bela. (òl′ȧ)	156	55.14N	29.15E
Ulla, r., Bela.	156	54.58N	29.03E
Ulla, r., Spain (o͞o′lä)	152	42.45N	8.33W
Ullŭng, i., S. Kor. (o͞ol′lòng′)	186	37.29N	130.50E
Ulm, Ger. (òlm)	140	48.24N	9.59E
Ulmer, Mount, mtn., Ant. (ŭl′mûr′)	213	77.30S	86.00W
Ulricehamn, Swe. (òl-rē′sĕ-häm)	146	57.49N	13.23E
Ulsan, S. Kor. (o͞ol′sän′)	186	35.35N	129.22E
Ulster, hist. reg., Eur. (ŭl′stẽr)	144	54.41N	7.10W
Ulua, r., Hond. (o͞o-lo͞o′ȧ)	114	15.49N	87.45W
Ulubāria, India	178a	22.27N	88.09E
Ulukişla, Tur. (o͞o-lo͞o-kēsh′lȧ)	142	36.40N	34.30E
Ulunga, Russia (ò-lo͞on′gȧ)	186	46.16N	136.29E
Ulungur, r., China (o͞o-lo͞on-gůr)	180	46.31N	88.00E
Ulu-Telyak, Russia (o͞o lò′tĕlyăk)	164a	54.54N	57.01E
Ulverstone, Austl. (ŭl′vẽr-st*ŭ*n)	196	41.20S	146.22E
Ul′yanovka, Russia	164c	59.38N	30.47E
Ul′yanovsk, Russia (o͞o-lyä′nôfsk)	158	54.20N	48.24E
Ulysses, Ks., U.S. (ū-lĭs′ēz)	104	37.34N	101.25W
Umán, Mex. (o͞o-män′)	114a	20.52N	89.44W
Uman′, Ukr. (ò-mȧn′)	160	48.44N	30.13E
Umatilla Indian Reservation, I.R., Or., U.S. (ū-mȧ-tĭl′ȧ)	98	45.38N	118.35W
Umberpāda, India	179b	19.28N	73.04E
Umbria, hist. reg., Italy (ŭm′brĭ-*ȧ*)	154	42.53N	12.22E
Umeälven, r., Swe.	136	64.57N	18.51E
Umhlatuzi, r., S. Afr. (òm′hlȧ-to͞o′zĭ)	207c	28.47S	31.17E
Umiat, Ak., U.S. (o͞o′mĭ-ăt)	90a	69.20N	152.28W
Umkomaas, S. Afr. (òm-kō′mäs)	207c	30.12S	30.48E
Umnak, i., Ak., U.S. (o͞om′nȧk)	90b	53.10N	169.08W
Umnak Pass, Ak., U.S.	89a	53.10N	168.04W
Umniati, r., Zimb.	206	17.08S	29.11E
Umpqua, r., Or., U.S. (ŭmp′kwȧ)	98	43.42N	123.50W
Umtata, Transkei (òm-tä′tä)	206	31.36S	28.47E
Umtentweni, S. Afr.	207c	30.41S	30.29E
Umzimkulu, Transkei (òm-zėm-ko͞o′lo͞o)	207c	30.12S	29.53E
Umzinto, S. Afr. (òm-zĭn′tȯ)	207c	30.19S	30.41E
Una, r., Yugo. (o͞o′nȧ)	154	44.38N	16.10E
Unalakleet, Ak., U.S. (ū-nȧ-lȧk′lēt)	89	63.50N	160.42W
Unalaska, Ak., U.S. (ū-nȧ-lȧs′kȧ)	89a	53.30N	166.20W
Unare, r., Ven.	125b	9.45N	65.12W

ng-sing; ŋ-baŋk; ɴ-nasalized n; nŏd; c*ŏ*mmit; ōld; ȯbey; ôrder; oi-boil; fo͞od; ò-as oo in foot; ou-out; s-soft; sh-dish; th-thin; pūre; ůnite; ûrn; stŭd; circ*ŭ*s; ü-as in French tu; ′-indeterminate vowel.

PLACE (Pronunciation)	PAGE	Lat. °'	Long. °'
Unare, Laguna de, l., Ven. (lä-gò'nä-de-ōō-nä'rĕ)	125b	10.07N	65.23W
Unayzah, Sau. Ar.	174	25.50N	44.02E
Uncas, Can. (ŭŋ'kȧs)	77g	53.30N	113.02W
Uncia, Bol. (ōōn'sē-ä)	124	18.28S	66.32W
Uncompahgre, r., Co., U.S.	102	38.20N	107.45W
Uncompahgre Peak, mtn., Co., U.S. (ŭn-kŭm-pä'grê)	102	38.00N	107.30W
Uncompahgre Plateau, plat., Co., U.S.	102	38.40N	108.40W
Underberg, S. Afr. (ŭn'dẽr-bûrg)	207c	29.51S	29.32E
Unecha, Russia (ò-nĕ'chá)	156	52.51N	32.44E
Ungava, Péninsule d', pen., Can.	78	59.55N	74.00W
Ungava Bay, b., Can. (ŭŋ-gā'vȧ)	78	59.46N	67.18W
União da Vitória, Braz. (ōō-nê-ouN' dä vē-tô'ryä)	126	26.17S	51.13W
Unidad Sante Fe, Mex.	229a	19.23N	99.15W
Unije, i., Yugo. (ōō'nê-yĕ)	154	44.39N	14.10E
Unimak, i., Ak., U.S. (ōō-nê-mȧk')	89	54.30N	163.35W
Unimak Pass, Ak., U.S.	89a	54.22N	165.22W
Union, Ms., U.S. (ūn'yŭn)	108	32.35N	89.07W
Union, Mo., U.S.	104	38.28N	90.59W
Union, N.J., U.S.	224	40.42N	74.16W
Union, N.C., U.S.	108	34.42N	81.40W
Union, Or., U.S.	98	45.13N	117.52W
Union City, Ca., U.S.	100b	37.36N	122.01W
Union City, In., U.S.	92	40.10N	85.00W
Union City, Mi., U.S.	92	42.00N	85.10W
Union City, N.J., U.S.	224	40.46N	74.02W
Union City, Pa., U.S.	92	41.50N	79.50W
Union City, Tn., U.S.	108	36.25N	89.04W
Uniondale, N.Y., U.S.	224	40.43N	73.36W
Unión de Reyes, Cuba	116	22.45N	81.30W
Unión de San Antonio, Mex.	112	21.07N	101.56W
Unión de Tula, Mex.	112	19.57N	104.14W
Union Grove, Wi., U.S. (ūn-yŭn grōv)	95a	42.41N	88.03W
Unión Hidalgo, Mex. (ê-dä'lgô)	112	16.29N	94.51W
Union Point, Ga., U.S.	108	33.37N	83.08W
Union Springs, Al., U.S. (sprĭngz)	108	32.08N	85.43W
Uniontown, Al., U.S. (ūn'yŭn-toun)	108	32.26N	87.30W
Uniontown, Oh., U.S.	95d	40.58N	81.25W
Uniontown, Pa., U.S.	92	39.55N	79.45W
Unionville, Mo., U.S. (ūn'yŭn-vĭl)	104	40.28N	92.58W
Unisan, Phil. (ōō-nē'sän)	189a	13.50N	121.59E
United Arab Emirates, nation, Asia	174	24.00N	54.00E
United Kingdom, nation, Eur.	136	56.30N	1.40W
United Nations Headquarters, pt. of i., N.Y., U.S.	224	40.45N	73.58W
United States, nation, N.A.	90	38.00N	110.00W
Unity, Can.	82	52.27N	109.10W
Universal, In., U.S. (ū-nĭ-vûr'sȧl)	92	39.35N	87.30W
University City, Mo., U.S. (ū'nĭ-vûr'sĭ-tĭ)	101e	38.40N	90.19W
University Heights, Oh., U.S.	225a	41.30N	81.32W
University Park, Md., U.S.	225d	38.58N	76.57W
University Park, Tx., U.S.	101c	32.51N	96.48W
Unna, Ger. (ōō'nä)	151c	51.32N	7.41E
Uno, Canal Numero, can., Arg.	123c	36.43S	58.14W
Unterhaching, Ger. (ōōn'tĕr-hä-kĕng)	139d	48.03N	11.38E
Untermauerbach, Aus.	235e	48.14N	16.12E
Ünye, Tur. (ün'yĕ)	142	41.00N	37.10E
Unzha, r., Russia (ōn'zhá)	160	57.45N	44.10E
Upa, r., Russia (ò'pȧ)	156	53.54N	36.48E
Upata, Ven. (ōō-pä'tä)	124	7.58N	62.27W
Upemba, Parc National de l', rec., Zaire	210	9.10S	26.15E
Up Holland, Eng., U.K.	233a	53.33N	2.44W
Upington, S. Afr. (ŭp'ĭng-tŭn)	206	28.25S	21.15E
Upland, Ca., U.S. (ŭp'lănd)	101a	34.06N	117.38W
Upland, Pa., U.S.	225b	39.51N	75.23W
Upolu, i., W. Sam.	192a	13.55S	171.45W
Upolu Point, c., Hi., U.S. (ōō-pô'lōō)	88a	20.15N	155.48W
Upper Arrow Lake, l., Can. (ăr'ō)	80	50.30N	117.55W
Upper Brookville, N.Y., U.S.	224	40.51N	73.34W
Upper Darby, Pa., U.S. (där'bĭ)	94f	39.58N	75.16W
Upper des Lacs, l., N.A. (dĕ läk)	96	48.58N	101.55W
Upper Ferntree Gully, Austl.	239b	37.54S	145.19E
Upper Kapuas Mountains, mts., Asia	188	1.45N	112.06E
Upper Klamath Lake, l., Or., U.S.	98	42.23N	122.55W
Upper Lake, l., Nv., U.S. (ŭp'ẽr)	98	41.42N	119.59W
Upper Marlboro, Md., U.S. (ûpẽr märl'bōrō)	94e	38.49N	76.46W
Upper Mill, Wa., U.S. (mĭl)	100a	47.11N	121.55W
Upper New York Bay, b., N.Y., U.S.	224	40.41N	74.03W
Upper Red Lake, l., Mn., U.S. (rĕd)	96	48.14N	94.53W
Upper Saint Clair, Pa., U.S.	226b	40.21N	80.05W
Upper Sandusky, Oh., U.S. (săn-dŭs'kê)	92	40.50N	83.20W
Upper San Leandro Reservoir, res., Ca., U.S. (ŭp'ẽr săn lê-ăn'drō)	100b	37.47N	122.04W
Upper Tooting, neigh., Eng., U.K.	231	51.26N	0.10W
Upper Volta, *see* Burkina Faso, nation, Afr.	204	13.00N	2.00W
Uppingham, Eng., U.K. (ŭp'ĭng-ăm)	138a	52.35N	0.43W
Uppsala, Swe. (ōōp'sȧ-lä)	136	59.53N	17.39E
Upton, Eng., U.K.	231	51.30N	0.35W
Uptown, Ma., U.S. (ŭp'toun)	87a	42.10N	71.36W
Uptown, neigh., Il., U.S.	227a	41.58N	87.40W
Upwey, Austl.	239b	37.54S	145.20E
Uraga, Japan (ōō'rȧ-gȧ')	187a	35.15N	139.43E
Ural, r. (ò-räl'') (ū-rôl)	158	48.00N	51.00E
Urals, mts., Russia	158	56.28N	58.13E
Ural'sk, Kaz. (ò-rálsk')	158	51.14N	51.22E
Uran, India (ōō-rän')	179b	18.53N	72.46E
Uranium City, Can.	78	59.34N	108.59W
Urawa, Japan (ōō'rä-wä')	186	35.52N	139.39E
Urayasu, Japan (ōō'rä-yä'sōō)	187a	35.40N	139.54E
Urazovo, Russia (ò-rá'zô-vô)	156	50.08N	38.03E
Urbana, Il., U.S. (ûr-băn'ȧ)	92	40.10N	88.15W
Urbana, Oh., U.S.	92	40.05N	83.50W
Urbino, Italy (ōōr-bē'nô)	154	43.43N	12.37E
Urda, Kaz. (òr'dȧ)	160	48.50N	47.30E
Urdaneta, Phil. (ōōr-dä-nä'tä)	189a	15.59N	120.34E
Urdinarrain, Arg. (ōōr-dē-när-rȧē'n)	123c	32.43S	58.53W
Urdzhar, Kaz. (òrd-zhär')	158	47.28N	82.00E
Urfa, Tur. (òr'fȧ)	174	37.20N	38.45E
Uritsk, Russia (ōō'rĭtsk)	164c	59.50N	30.11E
Urla, Tur. (òr'lȧ)	154	38.20N	26.44E
Urman, Russia (òr'mán)	164a	54.53N	56.52E
Urmi, r., Russia (òr'mê)	186	48.50N	134.00E
Urmston, Eng., U.K.	233b	53.27N	2.21W
Uromi, Nig.	208	6.44N	6.18E
Urrao, Col. (ōōr-rá'ô)	124	6.19N	76.11W
Urshel'skiy, Russia (ōōr-shĕl'skêê)	156	55.50N	40.11E
Ursus, Pol.	148	52.12N	20.53E
Urubamba, r., Peru (ōō-rōō-bäm'bä)	124	11.48S	72.34W
Uruguaiana, Braz.	126	29.45S	57.00W
Uruguay, nation, S.A. (ōō-rōō-gwä) (ū'rōō-gwī)	126	32.45S	56.00W
Uruguay, Rio, r., S.A. (rē'ō-ò-rōō-gwī)	126	27.05S	55.15W
Ürümqi, China (ů-rům-chyē)	180	43.49N	87.43E
Urup, i., Russia (ò'ròp')	180	46.00N	150.00E
Uryupinsk, Russia (òr'yò-pēn-sk')	160	50.50N	42.00E
Urziceni, Rom. (ò-zē-chĕn'')	154	44.45N	26.42E
Usa, Japan	186	33.31N	131.22E
Usa, r., Russia (ò'sȧ)	160	66.00N	58.20E
Uşak, Tur. (ōō'shȧk)	142	38.45N	29.15E
Usakos, Nmb. (ōō-sä'kōs)	206	22.00S	15.40E
Usambara Mountains, mts., Tan.	210	4.40S	38.25E
Usangu Flats, sw., Tan.	210	8.10S	34.00E
Ushaki, Russia (ōō'shá-kĭ)	164c	59.28N	31.00E
Ushakovskoye, Russia (ò-shá-kôv'skô-yĕ)	164a	56.18N	62.23E
Ushashi, Tan.	210	2.00S	33.57E
Ushiku, Japan (ōō'shê-kōō)	187a	35.24N	140.09E
Ushimado, Japan (ōō'shê-mä'dō)	187	34.37N	134.09E
Ushuaia, Arg. (ōō-shōō-ī'ä)	126	54.46S	68.24W
Usman', Russia (ōōs-mán')	160	52.03N	39.40E
Usmānpur, neigh., India	236d	28.41N	77.15E
Usol'ye, Russia (ò-sô'lyĕ)	164a	59.24N	56.40E
Usol'ye-Sibirskoye, Russia (ò-sô'lyĕsĭ' bĕr'skô-yĕ)	162	52.44N	103.46E
Uspallata Pass, p., S.A. (ōōs-pä-lyä'tä)	126	32.47S	70.08W
Uspanapa, r., Mex. (ōōs-pä-nä'pä)	112	17.43N	94.14W
Ussel, Fr. (üs'ĕl)	150	45.33N	2.17E
Ussuri, r., Asia (ōō-sōō'rê)	162	47.30N	134.00E
Ussuriysk, Russia	158	43.48N	132.09E
Ust'-Bol'sheretsk, Russia	158	52.41N	157.00E
Ustica, Isola di, i., Italy	154	38.43N	12.11E
Ústí nad Labem, Czech.	148	50.40N	14.02E
Ustinovka, Ukr. (òs-tē'nôf-kȧ)	156	47.59N	32.31E
Ust'-Izhora, Russia (òst-ēz'hô-rȧ)	164c	59.49N	30.35E
Ustka, Pol. (ōōst'kȧ)	148	54.34N	16.52E
Ust'-Kamchatsk, Russia	158	56.13N	162.18E
Ust'-Kamenogorsk, Kaz.	162	49.58N	82.38E
Ust'-Katav, Russia (òst kȧ'tȧf)	164a	54.55N	58.12E
Ust'-Kishert', Russia (òst kē'shĕrt)	164a	57.21N	57.13E
Ust'-Kulom, Russia (kò'lŭm)	158	61.38N	54.00E
Ust'-Maya, Russia (má'yȧ)	158	60.33N	134.43E
Ust' Olenëk, Russia	158	72.52N	120.15E
Ust-Ordynskiy, Russia (òst-ôr-dyēnsk'ĭ)	162	52.47N	104.39E
Ust' Penzhino, Russia	162	63.00N	165.10E
Ust' Port, Russia (òst'pôrt')	158	69.20N	83.41E
Ust'-Tsil'ma, Russia (tsĭl'má)	158	65.25N	52.10E
Ust'-Tyrma, Russia (tur'má)	158	50.27N	131.17E
Ust' Uls, Russia	164a	60.35N	58.32E
Ust'-Urt, Plato, plat., Asia	158	44.03N	54.58E
Ustyuzhna, Russia (yōōzh'ná)	160	58.49N	36.19E
Usu, China (ů-sōō)	180	44.28N	84.07E
Usuki, Japan (ōō'sōō-kê')	187	33.06N	131.47E
Usulutan, El Sal. (ōō-sōō-lä-tän')	114	13.22N	88.25W
Usumacinta, r., N.A. (ōō'sōō-mä-sēn'tō)	112	18.24N	92.30W
Us'va, Russia (ōōs'vȧ)	164a	58.41N	57.38E
Utah, state, U.S. (ū'tô)	90	39.25N	112.40W
Utah Lake, l., Ut., U.S.	102	40.10N	111.55W
Utan, India	179b	19.17N	72.43E
Ute Mountain Indian Reservation, I.R., N.M., U.S.	102	36.57N	108.34W
Utena, Lith. (ōō'tā-nä)	146	55.32N	25.40E
Utete, Tan. (ōō-tā'tā)	206	8.05S	38.47E
Utfort, Ger.	232	51.28N	6.38E
Utica, In., U.S. (ū'tĭ-kȧ)	95h	38.20N	85.39W
Utica, N.Y., U.S.	92	43.05N	75.10W
Utiel, Spain (ōō-tyâl')	152	39.34N	1.13W
Utika, Mi., U.S. (ū'tĭ-kȧ)	95b	42.37N	83.02W
Utik Lake, l., Can.	82	55.16N	96.00W
Utikuma Lake, l., Can.	80	55.50N	115.25W
Utila, i., Hond. (ōō-tē'lä)	114	16.07N	87.05W
Utinga, Braz.	230d	23.38S	46.32W
Uto, Japan (ōō'tō')	186	32.43N	130.39E
Utrecht, Neth. (ū'trĕkt) (ū'trĕkt)	140	52.05N	5.06E
Utrera, Spain (ōō-trā'rä)	142	37.12N	5.48W
Utsunomiya, Japan (ōōt'sò-nò-mē-yȧ')	180	36.35N	139.52E
Uttaradit, Thai.	188	17.47N	100.10E
Uttarpara-Kotrung, India	178a	22.40N	88.21E
Uttar Pradesh, state, India (òt-tär-prä-dĕsh)	174	27.00N	80.00E
Uttoxeter, Eng., U.K. (ŭt-tôk'sē-tẽr)	138a	52.54N	1.52W
Utuado, P.R. (ōō-tōō-ä'dhō)	111b	18.16N	66.40W
Uusikaupunki, Fin.	146	60.48N	21.24E
Uvalde, Tx., U.S. (ū-văl'dê)	106	29.14N	99.47W
Uvel'skiy, Russia (ò-vyĕl'skĭ)	164a	54.27N	61.22E
Uvinza, Tan.	210	5.06S	30.22E
Uvira, Zaire (ōō-vē'rä)	206	3.28S	29.03E
Uvod', r., Russia (ò-vôd')	156	56.40N	41.10E
Uvongo Beach, S. Afr.	207c	30.49S	30.23E
Uvs Nuur, l., Asia	180	50.29N	93.32E
Uwajima, Japan (ōō-wä'jê-mä)	186	33.12N	132.35E
Uxbridge, Ma., U.S. (ŭks'brĭj)	87a	42.05N	71.38W
Uxbridge, neigh., Eng., U.K.	231	51.33N	0.29W
Uxmal, hist., Mex. (ōō'x-mä'l)	114a	20.22N	89.44W
Uy, r., Russia (ōōy)	164a	54.05N	62.11E
Uyama, Japan	238b	34.50N	135.41E
Uyskoye, Russia (ûy'skô-yĕ)	164a	54.22N	60.01E
Uyuni, Bol. (ōō-yōō'nê)	124	20.28S	66.45W
Uyuni, Salar de, pl., Bol. (sä-lär-dĕ)	124	20.58S	67.09W
Uzbekistan, nation, Asia	158	42.42N	60.00E
Uzh, r., Ukr. (ôzh)	156	51.07N	29.05E
Uzhgorod, Ukr. (ôzh'gô-rôt)	148	48.38N	22.18E
Uzunköprü, Tur.	154	41.17N	26.42E

V

PLACE (Pronunciation)	PAGE	Lat. °'	Long. °'
Vaal, r., S. Afr. (väl)	206	28.15S	24.30E
Vaaldam, res., S. Afr.	212d	26.58S	28.37E
Vaalplaas, S. Afr.	212d	25.39S	28.56E
Vaalwater, S. Afr.	212d	24.17S	28.08E
Vaasa, Fin. (vä'sȧ)	136	63.06N	21.39E
Vác, Hung. (väts)	148	47.46N	19.10E
Vache, Île à, i., Haiti	116	18.05N	73.40W
Vadstena, Swe. (väd'stĭ'nȧ)	146	58.27N	14.53E
Vaduz, Liech. (vä'dòts)	148	47.10N	9.32E
Vaga, r., Russia (va'gȧ)	160	61.55N	42.30E
Vah, r., Czech. (väĸ)	140	48.07N	17.52E
Vaigai, r., India	178	10.20N	78.13E
Vaires-sur-Marne, Fr.	233c	48.52N	2.39E
Vakh, r., Russia (vȧĸ)	162	61.30N	81.33E
Valachia, hist. reg., Rom.	154	44.45N	24.17E
Valcanuta, neigh., Italy	235c	41.53N	12.25E
Valcartier-Village, Can. (väl-kärt-yĕ'vē-läzh')	77b	46.56N	71.28W
Valdai Hills, hills, Russia (vȧl-dī' gô'rĭ)	160	57.50N	32.35E
Valday, Russia (vȧl-dī')	160	57.58N	33.13E
Valdecañas, Embalse de, res., Spain	152	39.45N	5.30W
Valdemārpils, Lat.	146	57.22N	22.34E
Valdemorillo, Spain (väl-då-mò-rēl'yō)	153a	40.30N	4.04W
Valdepeñas, Spain (väl-då-pān'yäs)	142	38.46N	3.22W
Valderaduey, r., Spain (väl-dĕ-rä-dwĕ'y)	152	41.39N	5.35W
Valdés, Peninsula, pen., Arg. (vȧl-dĕ's)	126	42.15S	63.15W
Valdez, Ak., U.S. (văl'dĕz)	89	61.10N	146.18W
Valdilecha, Spain (väl-dê-lā'chä)	153a	40.17N	3.19W
Valdivia, Chile (väl-dē'vä)	126	39.47S	73.13W
Valdivia, Col. (väl-dê'vēä)	124a	7.10N	75.26W
Val-d'Or, Can.	78	48.03N	77.50W
Valdosta, Ga., U.S. (văl-dŏs'tȧ)	90	30.50N	83.18W
Valdoviño, Spain (väl-dō-vē'nō)	152	43.36N	8.05W
Vale, Or., U.S. (vāl)	98	43.59N	117.14W
Valença, Braz. (vä-lĕN'sȧ)	124	13.43S	38.58W
Valença, Port.	152	42.03N	8.36W
Valence, Fr. (vä-lĕnNs)	140	44.56N	4.54E
Valencia, Spain (vä-lĕn'thê-ä)	136	39.26N	0.23W
Valencia, Ven. (vä-lĕn'syä)	124	10.11N	68.00W
Valencia, hist. reg., Spain (vä-lĕn'thê-ä)	152	39.08N	0.43W
Valencia, Golfo de, b., Spain	152	39.50N	0.30E
Valencia, Lago de, l., Ven.	125b	10.11N	67.45W
Valencia de Alcántara, Spain	152	39.34N	7.13W
Valenciennes, Fr. (vȧ-läN-syĕn')	150	50.24N	3.36E
Valentín Alsina, neigh., Arg.	229d	34.40S	58.25W
Valentine, Ne., U.S. (vȧ lăN-tê-nyē')	90	42.52N	100.34W
Valera, Ven. (vä-lĕ'rä)	124	9.12N	70.45W
Valerianovsk, Russia (vȧ-lĕ-rĭ-ä'nôvsk)	164a	58.47N	59.34E
Valérien, Mont, hill, Fr.	233c	48.53N	2.13E
Valga, Est. (väl'gȧ)	160	57.47N	26.03E
Valhalla, S. Afr. (văl-hăl-ȧ)	207b	25.49S	28.09E
Valier, Mt., U.S. (vȧ-lēr')	98	48.17N	112.14W
Valjevo, Yugo. (väl'yȧ-vō)	154	44.17N	19.57E
Valki, Ukr. (väl'kê)	156	49.49N	35.40E
Valladolid, Mex. (väl-yä-dhō-lēdh')	110	20.39N	88.13W
Valladolid, Spain (väl-yä-dhō-lēdh')	136	41.41N	4.41W
Valldoreix, Spain	234e	41.28N	2.04E
Valle, Arroyo del, Ca., U.S. (ä-rō'yō dĕl väl'yȧ)	102	37.36N	121.43W
Vallecas, Spain (väl-yä'käs)	153a	40.23N	3.37W
Valle de Allende, Mex. (väl'yä dä äl-yĕn'då)	106	26.55N	105.25W
Valle de Bravo, Mex. (brä'vō)	112	19.12N	100.07W
Valle de Guanape, Ven. (vä'l-yĕ-dĕ-gwä-nä'pĕ)	125b	9.54N	65.41W
Valle de la Pascua, Ven. (lä-pä's-kōōä)	124	9.12N	65.08W
Valle del Cauca, dept., Col. (vä'l-yĕ dĕl kou'kä)	124a	4.03N	76.13W
Valle de Santiago, Mex. (sän-tê-ä'gō)	112	20.23N	101.11W
Valledupar, Col. (dōō-pär')	124	10.13N	73.39W
Valle Grande, Bol. (grän'dä)	124	18.27S	64.03W
Vallejo, Ca., U.S. (vȧ-yä'hō) (vȧ-lā'hō)	90	38.06N	122.15W
Vallejo, Sierra de, mts., Mex. (sē-ĕ'r-rä-dĕ-väl-yĕ'ĸō)	112	21.00N	105.10W
Vallenar, Chile (väl-yȧ-när')	126	28.39S	70.52W
Valles, Mex.	110	21.59N	99.02W

ăt; finăl; rāte; senāte; ärm; ȧsk; sofȧ; fâre; ch-choose; dh-as th in other; bē; ēvent; bĕt; recĕnt; cratẽr; g-gō; gh-guttural g; bĭt; ĭ-short neutral; rīde; ĸ-guttural k as ch in German ich;

PLACE (Pronunciation)	PAGE	Lat. °'	Long. °'
Valletta, Malta (väl-lĕt'ä)	142	35.50N	14.29E
Valle Vista, Ca., U.S. (väl'yă vĭs'tȧ)	101a	33.45N	116.53W
Valley City, N.D., U.S.	90	46.55N	97.59W
Valley City, Oh., U.S. (văl'ĭ)	95d	41.14N	81.56W
Valleydale, Ca., U.S.	228	34.06N	117.56W
Valley Falls, Ks., U.S.	104	39.25N	95.26W
Valleyfield, Can. (văl'ē-fēld)	78	45.16N	74.09W
Valley Mede, Md., U.S.	225c	39.17N	76.50W
Valley Park, Mo., U.S. (văl'ē pärk)	101e	38.33N	90.30W
Valley Stream, N.Y., U.S. (văl'ĭ strēm)	94a	40.39N	73.42W
Valli di Comácchio, l., Italy (vä'lē-dē-kô-mä'chyô)	154	44.38N	12.15E
Vallière, Haiti (väl-yâr')	116	19.30N	71.55W
Vallimanca, r., Arg. (väl-yē-mä'n-kä)	123c	36.21S	60.55W
Valls, Spain (väls)	142	41.15N	1.15E
Valmiera, Lat. (vål'myĕ-rȧ)	160	57.34N	25.54E
Valognes, Fr. (vȧ-lôn'y')	150	49.32N	1.30W
Valona, see Vlorë, Alb.	142	40.28N	19.31E
Valparaíso, Chile (väl'pä-rä-ē'sô)	126	33.02S	71.32W
Valparaíso, Mex.	112	22.49N	103.33W
Valparaiso, In., U.S. (văl-pȧ-rā'zō)	92	41.25N	87.05W
Valpariso, prov., Chile	123b	32.58S	71.23W
Valréas, Fr. (väl-rà-ä')	150	44.25N	4.56E
Vals, r., S. Afr.	212d	27.32S	26.51E
Vals, Tanjung, c., Indon.	188	8.30S	137.15E
Valsbaai, b., S. Afr.	206a	34.14S	18.35E
Valuyevo, Russia (vȧ-lo͞o'yĕ-vô)	164b	55.34N	37.21E
Valuyki, Russia (vȧ-lò-ē'kē)	160	50.14N	38.04E
Valverde del Camino, Spain (väl-vĕr-dĕ-dĕl-kä-mē'nō)	152	37.34N	6.44W
Vammala, Fin.	146	61.19N	22.51E
Van, Tur. (vȧn)	174	38.04N	43.10E
Van Buren, Ar., U.S. (văn bū'rĕn)	104	35.26N	94.20W
Van Buren, Me., U.S.	86	47.09N	67.58W
Vanceburg, Ky., U.S. (văns'bûrg)	92	38.35N	83.20W
Vancouver, Can. (văn-ko͞o'vẽr)	78	49.16N	123.06W
Vancouver, Wa., U.S.	90	45.37N	122.40W
Vancouver Island, i., Can.	78	49.50N	125.05W
Vancouver Island Ranges, mts., Can.	80	49.25N	125.25W
Vandalia, Il., U.S. (văn-dā'lĭ-ȧ)	92	39.00N	89.00W
Vandalia, Mo., U.S.	104	39.19N	91.30W
Vanderbijlpark, S. Afr.	212d	26.43S	27.50E
Vanderhoof, Can.	78	54.01N	124.01W
Van Diemen, Cape, c., Austl. (văndē'mĕn)	196	11.05S	130.15E
Van Diemen Gulf, b., Austl.	196	11.50S	131.30E
Vanegas, Mex. (vä-nĕ'gäs)	110	23.54N	100.54W
Vänern, l., Swe.	136	58.52N	13.17E
Vänersborg, Swe. (vĕ'nĕrs-bôr')	140	58.24N	12.15E
Vanga, Kenya (väŋ'gä)	206	4.38S	39.10E
Vangani, India	179b	19.07N	73.15E
Van Horn, Tx., U.S.	106	31.03N	104.50W
Vanier, Can.	77c	45.27N	75.39W
Vaniköy, neigh., Tur.	235f	41.04N	29.04E
Van Lear, Ky., U.S. (văn lēr')	92	37.45N	82.50W
Vannes, Fr. (vȧn)	140	47.42N	2.46W
Van Nuys, Ca., U.S. (văn nīz')	101a	34.11N	118.27W
Van Rees, Pegunungan, mts., Indon.	188	2.30S	138.45E
Vantaan, r., Fin.	146	60.25N	24.43E
Vanua Levu, i., Fiji	192g	16.33S	179.15E
Vanuatu, nation, Oc.	196	16.02S	169.15E
Vanves, Fr.	233c	48.50N	2.18E
Van Wert, Oh., U.S. (văn wûrt')	92	40.50N	84.35W
Vanzago, Italy	234c	45.32N	9.00E
Vara, Swe. (vä'rä)	146	58.17N	12.55E
Varaklāni, Lat.	146	56.38N	26.46E
Varallo, Italy (vä-räl'lô)	154	45.44N	8.14E
Vārānasi (Benares), India	174	25.25N	83.00E
Varangerfjorden, b., Nor.	136	70.05N	30.20E
Varano, Lago di, l., Italy (lä'gō-dē-vä-rä'nō)	154	41.52N	15.55E
Varaždin, Cro. (vä'räzh'dēn)	142	46.17N	16.20E
Varazze, Italy (vä-rät'sā)	154	44.23N	8.34E
Varberg, Swe. (vär'bĕrg)	146	57.06N	12.16E
Vardar, r., Yugo. (vär'där)	154	41.40N	21.50E
Varėna, Lith. (vä-rā'nȧ)	146	54.16N	24.35E
Varennes, Can. (vȧ-rĕn')	77a	45.41N	73.27W
Vareš, Bos. (vä'rĕsh)	154	44.10N	18.20E
Varese, Italy (vä-rā'sā)	154	45.45N	8.49E
Vargem Grande, neigh., Braz.	230c	22.59S	43.29W
Varginha, Braz. (vär-zhē'n-yä)	124	21.33S	45.25W
Varkaus, Fin. (vär'kous)	146	62.19N	27.51E
Varlamovo, Russia (vár-lá'mô-vô)	164a	54.37N	60.41E
Varna, Bul. (vär'nȧ)	136	43.14N	27.58E
Varna, Russia	164a	53.22N	60.59E
Värnamo, Swe. (vĕr'ná-mô)	146	57.11N	13.45E
Varnsdorf, Czech. (värns'dôrf)	148	50.54N	14.36E
Varnville, S.C., U.S. (värn'vĭl)	108	32.49N	81.05W
Várpalota, pt. of i., Hung.	235g	47.30N	19.02E
Varvaropolye, Ukr. (vár'vár'ô-pô-lyĕ)	156	48.38N	38.37E
Vasa, India	179b	19.20N	72.47E
Vascongadas, hist. reg., Spain (väs-kôn-gä'däs)	152	43.00N	2.46W
Vashka, r., Russia	160	64.00N	48.00E
Vashon, Wa., U.S. (văsh'ŭn)	100a	47.27N	122.28W
Vashon Heights, Wa., U.S. (hītz)	100a	47.30N	122.28W
Vashon Island, i., Wa., U.S.	100a	47.27N	122.27W
Vasiljevskij, Ostrov, i., Russia	235a	59.56N	30.15E
Vasil'kov, Ukr. (vȧ-sēl'-kôf')	160	50.10N	30.22E
Vaslui, Rom. (vȧs-lo͞o'ē)	148	46.39N	27.49E
Vassar, Mi., U.S. (văs'ẽr)	92	43.25N	83.35W
Vassouras, Braz. (väs-sō'räzh)	123a	22.25S	43.40W
Västerås, Swe. (vĕs'tĕr-ôs)	140	59.39N	16.30E
Västerdalälven, r., Swe.	140	61.06N	13.10E
Västervik, Swe. (vĕs'tĕr-vēk)	140	57.45N	16.35E
Vasto, Italy (väs'tô)	142	42.06N	12.42E
Vasyugan, r., Russia (vȧs-yo͞o-gȧn')	162	58.52N	77.30E
Vatican City, nation, Eur.	154	41.54N	12.22E
Vaticano, Cape, c., Italy (vä-tē-kä'nô)	154	38.38N	15.52E
Vatnajökull, ice., Ice. (vät'nȧ-yû-kôl)	140	64.34N	16.41W
Vatomandry, Madag.	206	18.53S	48.13E
Vatra Dornei, Rom. (vät'rȧ dôr'nā')	148	47.22N	25.20E
Vättern, l., Swe.	136	58.15N	14.24E
Vattholma, Swe.	146	60.01N	17.40E
Vaucluse, Austl.	239a	33.51S	151.17E
Vaudreuil, Can. (vô-drû'y')	77a	45.24N	74.02W
Vaugh, Wa., U.S. (vôn)	100a	47.21N	122.47W
Vaughan, Can.	77d	43.47N	79.36W
Vaughn, N.M., U.S.	104	34.37N	105.13W
Vauhallan, Fr.	233c	48.44N	2.12E
Vaujours, Fr.	233c	48.56N	2.35E
Vaupés, r., S.A. (vá'o͞o-pĕ's)	124	1.18N	71.14W
Vaxholm, Swe. (väks'hôlm)	146	59.26N	18.19E
Växjo, Swe. (vĕks'shû)	140	56.53N	14.46E
Vaygach, i., Russia (vī-gách')	158	70.00N	59.00E
Veadeiros, Chapadas dos, hills, Braz. (shä-pä'däs-dôs-vĕ-á-dā'rōs)	124	14.00S	47.00W
Vedea, r., Rom. (vá'dyȧ)	154	44.25N	24.45E
Vedia, Arg. (vĕ'dyä)	123c	34.29S	61.30W
Veedersburg, In., U.S. (vē'dẽrz-bûrg)	92	40.05N	87.15W
Vega, i., Nor.	140	65.38N	10.51E
Vega de Alatorre, Mex. (vä'gä dä ä-lä-tōr'rȧ)	112	20.02N	96.39W
Vega Real, reg., Dom. Rep. (vĕ'gä-rĕ-ä'l)	116	19.30N	71.05W
Vegreville, Can.	78	53.30N	112.03W
Vehār Lake, l., India	179b	19.11N	72.52E
Veinticinco de Mayo, Arg.	123c	35.26S	60.09W
Vejer de la Frontera, Spain	152	36.15N	5.58W
Vejle, Den. (vī'lĕ)	140	55.41N	9.29E
Velbert, Ger. (fĕl'bĕrt)	151c	51.20N	7.03E
Velebit, mts., Yugo. (vā'lĕ-bēt)	142	44.25N	15.23E
Velen, Ger. (fĕ'lĕn)	151c	51.54N	7.00E
Vélez-Málaga, Spain (vā'läth-mä'lä-gä)	152	36.48N	4.05W
Vélez-Rubio, Spain (ro͞o'bē-ô)	152	37.38N	2.05W
Velika Kapela, mts., Yugo. (vĕ'lē-kä kä-pĕ'lä)	142	45.03N	15.20E
Velika Morava, r., Yugo. (mô'rä-vä)	142	44.00N	21.30E
Velikaya, r., Russia (vá-lē'ká-yá)	156	57.25N	28.07E
Velikiy Bychkov, Ukr. (vĕ-lē'kē bòch-kôf')	148	47.59N	24.01E
Velikiye Luki, Russia (vyē-lē'-kyē lo͞o'ke)	158	56.19N	30.32E
Velikiy Ustyug, Russia (vȧ-lē'kĭ o͞os-tyôg')	158	60.45N	46.38E
Veliko Tŭrnovo, Bul.	142	43.06N	25.38E
Velikoye, Russia (vȧ-lē'kô-yĕ)	156	57.21N	39.45E
Velikoye, l., Russia	156	57.00N	36.53E
Veli Lošinj, Cro. (lō'shēn')	154	44.30N	14.29E
Velizh, Russia (vâ'lēzh)	160	55.37N	31.11E
Vella Lavella, i., Sol.Is.	196	8.00S	156.42E
Velletri, Italy (vĕl-lā'trē)	154	41.42N	12.48E
Vellore, India (vĕl-lōr')	174	12.57N	79.09E
Vels, Russia (vĕls)	164a	60.35N	58.47E
Vel'sk, Russia (vĕlsk)	158	61.00N	42.18E
Velten, Ger. (fel'tĕn)	139b	52.41N	13.11E
Velya, r., Russia (vĕl'yȧ)	164b	56.23N	37.54E
Venadillo, Col. (vĕ-nä-dē'l-yō)	124a	4.43N	74.55W
Venado, Mex. (vā-mä'dō)	112	22.54N	101.07W
Venado Tuerto, Arg. (vĕ-nä'dô-to͞oĕ'r-tô)	126	33.28S	61.47W
Venda, nation, Afr.	206	23.00S	30.30E
Vendôme, Fr. (väN-dōm')	150	47.46N	1.05E
Veneto, hist. reg., Italy (vĕ-nĕ'tô)	154	45.58N	11.24E
Venëv, Russia (vĕn-ĕf')	160	54.19N	38.14E
Venezia, see Venice, Italy	136	45.25N	12.18E
Venezuela, nation, S.A. (vĕn-ē-zwē'lȧ)	124	8.00N	65.00W
Venezuela, Golfo de, b., S.A. (gôl-fô-dĕ)	124	11.34N	71.02W
Veniaminof, Mount, mtn., Ak., U.S.	89	56.12N	159.20W
Venice, Italy	136	45.25N	12.18E
Venice, Ca., U.S. (vĕn'ĭs)	101a	33.59N	118.28W
Venice, Il., U.S.	101e	38.40N	90.10W
Venice, neigh., Ca., U.S.	228	34.00N	118.29W
Venice, Gulf of, b., Italy	142	45.23N	13.00E
Venlo, Neth.	151c	51.22N	6.11E
Vennhausen, neigh., Ger.	232	51.13N	6.51E
Venta, r., Eur. (vĕn'tá)	146	57.05N	21.45E
Ventana, Sierra de la, mts., Arg. (sē-ĕ-rä-dĕ-lä-vĕn-tá'nä)	126	38.00S	63.00W
Ventersburg, S. Afr. (vĕn-tĕrs'bûrg)	212d	28.06S	27.10E
Ventersdorp, S. Afr. (vĕn-tĕrs'dôrp)	212d	26.20S	26.48E
Ventimiglia, Italy (vĕn-tē-mēl'yä)	154	43.46N	7.37E
Ventnor, N.J., U.S. (vĕnt'nẽr)	92	39.20N	74.25W
Ventspils, Lat. (vĕnt'spĕls)	160	57.24N	21.41E
Ventuari, r., Ven. (vĕn-to͞oá'rē)	124	4.47N	65.56W
Ventura, Ca., U.S. (vĕn-to͞o'rȧ)	102	34.18N	119.18W
Venukovsky, Russia (vĕ-no͞o'kôv-skĭ)	164b	55.10N	37.26E
Venustiano Carranza, Mex. (vĕ-no͞os-tyä'nō-kär-rä'n-zä)	112	19.44N	103.48W
Venustiano Carranzo, Mex. (kär-rä'n-zô)	112	16.21N	92.36W
Vera, Arg. (vĕ-rä)	126	29.22S	60.09W
Vera, Spain (vā'rä)	152	37.18N	1.53W
Veracruz, Mex.	110	19.13N	96.07W
Vera Cruz, state, Mex. (vā-rä-kro͞oz')	110	20.30N	97.15W
Verāval, India (vĕr'vŭ-väl)	174	20.59N	70.49E
Verberg, neigh., Ger.	232	51.22N	6.36E
Vercelli, Italy (vĕr-chĕl'lē)	154	45.18N	8.27E
Verchères, Can. (vĕr-shâr')	77a	45.46N	73.21W
Verde, i., Phil. (vĕr'dē)	189a	13.34N	121.11E
Verde, r., Mex.	112	21.48N	99.50W
Verde, r., Mex.	112	16.05N	97.44W
Verde, r., Mex.	112	20.50N	103.00W
Verde, r., Az., U.S. (vûrd)	102	34.04N	111.40W
Verde, Cap, c., Bah.	116	22.50N	75.00W
Verde, Cay, i., Bah.	116	22.00N	75.05W
Verde Island Passage, strt., Phil. (vĕr'dē)	189a	13.36N	120.39E
Verdemont, Ca., U.S. (vûr'dē-mŏnt)	101a	34.12N	117.22W
Verden, Ger. (fĕr'dĕn)	148	52.55N	9.15E
Verdigris, r., Ok., U.S. (vûr'dē-grēs)	104	36.50N	95.29W
Verdun, Can. (vĕr'dŭN')	84	45.27N	73.34W
Verdun, Fr. (vâr-dûN')	140	49.09N	5.21E
Verdun, Fr.	152	43.48N	1.10E
Vereeniging, S. Afr. (vĕ-rā'nĭ-gĭng)	212d	26.40S	27.56E
Verena, S. Afr. (vĕr-ĕn ȧ)	212d	25.30S	29.02E
Vereya, Russia (vĕ-rå'yȧ)	156	55.21N	36.08E
Verga, N.J., U.S.	225b	39.52N	75.10W
Vergara, Spain (vĕr-gä'rä)	152	43.08N	2.23W
Verín, Spain (vå-rēn')	152	41.56N	7.26W
Verkhne-Kamchatsk, Russia (vyĕrk'nyĕ kȧm-chatsk')	158	54.42N	158.41E
Verkhne Neyvinskiy, Russia (nā-vĭn'skĭ)	164a	57.17N	60.10E
Verkhne Ural'sk, Russia (ò-ralsk')	158	53.53N	59.13E
Verkhneye, Ukr. (vyĕrk'nĕ-yĕ)	156	48.53N	38.29E
Verkhniy Avzyan, Russia (vyĕrk'nyĕ ȧv-zyȧn')	164a	53.32N	57.30E
Verkhniye Kigi, Russia (vyĕrk'nĭ-yĕ kĭ'gĭ)	164a	55.23N	58.37E
Verkhniy Ufaley, Russia (ò-fä'lā)	164a	56.04N	60.15E
Verkhnyaya Pyshma, Russia (vyĕrk'nyä-yä po͞osh'mȧ)	164a	56.57N	60.37E
Verkhnyaya Salda, Russia (säl'dȧ)	164a	58.03N	60.33E
Verkhnyaya Tunguska (Angara), r., Russia (tòn-gòs'kȧ)	162	58.13N	97.00E
Verkhnyaya Tura, Russia (tò'rȧ)	164a	58.22N	59.51E
Verkhnyaya Yayva, Russia (yäy'vȧ)	164a	59.28N	57.38E
Verkhotur'ye, Russia (vyĕr-kô-to͞or'yĕ)	164a	58.52N	60.47E
Verkhoyansk, Russia (vyĕr-kô-yänsk')	158	67.43N	133.33E
Verkhoyanskiy Khrebet, mts., Russia (vyĕr-kô-yänskĭ)	158	67.45N	128.00E
Vermilion, Can. (vẽr-mĭl'yŭn)	78	53.22N	110.51W
Vermilion, l., Mn., U.S.	96	47.49N	92.35W
Vermilion, r., Can.	82	53.30N	111.00W
Vermilion, r., Can.	84	47.30N	73.15W
Vermilion, r., Il., U.S.	92	41.05N	89.00W
Vermilion, r., Mn., U.S.	96	48.09N	92.31W
Vermilion Hills, hills, Can.	82	50.43N	106.50W
Vermilion Range, mts., Mn., U.S.	96	47.55N	91.59W
Vermillion, S.D., U.S.	96	42.46N	96.56W
Vermillion, r., S.D., U.S.	96	43.54N	97.14W
Vermillion Bay, b., La., U.S.	106	29.47N	92.00W
Vermont, Austl.	239b	37.50S	145.12E
Vermont, state, U.S. (vẽr-mŏnt')	90	43.50N	72.50W
Vernal, Ut., U.S. (vûr'nȧl)	98	40.29N	109.40W
Verneuk Pan, pl., S. Afr. (vĕr-nŭk')	206	30.10S	21.46E
Vernon, Can.	77c	45.10N	75.27W
Vernon, Can. (vĕr-nôN')	78	50.18N	119.15W
Vernon, Ca., U.S. (vûr'nŭn)	101a	34.01N	118.12W
Vernon, In., U.S. (vûr'nŭn)	92	39.00N	85.40W
Vernon, N.J., U.S.	94a	39.00N	85.40W
Vernon, Tx., U.S.	104	34.09N	99.16W
Vernonia, Or., U.S. (vûr-nō'nyȧ)	100c	45.52N	123.12W
Vero Beach, Fl., U.S. (vē'rô)	109a	27.36N	80.25W
Véroia, Grc.	154	40.30N	22.13E
Verona, Italy (vä-rō'nä)	142	45.28N	11.02E
Verona, N.J., U.S.	224	40.50N	74.12W
Verona, Pa., U.S.	226b	40.30N	79.50W
Verrières-le-Buisson, Fr.	233c	48.45N	2.16E
Versailles, Fr. (vĕr-sī'y')	140	48.48N	2.07E
Versailles, Ky., U.S. (vẽr-sālz')	92	38.05N	84.45W
Versailles, Mo., U.S.	104	38.27N	92.52W
Versailles, Pa., U.S.	226b	40.21N	79.51W
Versailles, neigh., Arg.	229d	34.38S	58.31W
Versailles, Château de, hist., Fr.	233c	48.48N	2.07E
Vert, Cap, c., Sen.	204	14.43N	17.30W
Verulam, S. Afr. (vĕ-ro͞o-lăm)	207c	29.39S	31.08E
Verulamium, pt. of i., Eng., U.K.	231	51.45N	0.22W
Verviers, Bel. (vĕr-vyā')	144	50.35N	5.57E
Vesëloye, Ukr. (vĕ-syô'lô-yĕ)	156	46.59N	34.56E
Vesijärvi, l., Fin.	146	61.09N	25.10E
Vešn'aki, neigh., Russia	235b	55.44N	37.49E
Vesoul, Fr. (vĕ-so͞ol')	150	47.38N	6.11E
Vestavia Hills, Al., U.S.	94h	33.26N	86.46W
Vesterålen, is., Nor. (vĕs'tĕr ô'lĕn)	140	68.54N	14.03E
Vestfjord, fj., Nor.	136	67.33N	12.59E
Vestmannaeyjar, Ice. (vĕst'män-ä-ā'yär)	140	63.12N	20.17W
Vesuvio, vol., Italy (vĕ-so͞o'vyä)	136	40.35N	14.26E
Ves'yegonsk, Russia (vĕ-syĕ-gônsk')	156	58.42N	37.09E
Veszprem, Hung. (vĕs'prām)	148	47.05N	17.53E
Vészto, Hung. (vĕs'tû)	148	46.55N	21.18E
Vet, r., S. Afr. (vĕt)	212d	28.25S	26.37E
Vetka, Bela. (vyĕt'kȧ)	156	52.36N	31.05E
Vetlanda, Swe. (vĕt-län'dä)	146	57.26N	15.05E
Vetluga, Russia (vyĕt-lo͞o'gȧ)	160	57.50N	45.42E
Vetluga, r., Russia	160	56.50N	45.50E
Vetovo, Bul. (vā'tô-vô)	154	43.42N	26.18E
Vetren, Bul. (vĕt'rĕn')	154	42.16N	24.04E
Vevay, In., U.S. (vē'vā)	92	38.45N	85.05W
Veynes, Fr. (vān'')	150	44.31N	5.47E
Vézère, r., Fr. (vā-zer')	150	45.01N	1.00E
Viacha, Bol. (vēá'chä)	124	16.43S	68.16W
Viadana, Italy (vē-ä-dä'nä)	154	44.55N	10.30E
Vian, Ok., U.S. (vī'ăn)	105	35.30N	95.00W
Viana, Braz. (vē-ä'nä)	124	3.09S	44.44W
Viana del Bollo, Spain (vē-ä'nä dĕl bôl'yô)	152	42.10N	7.07W
Viana do Alentejo, Port. (vē-ä'nȧ dò ä-lĕN-tā'hò)	152	38.20N	8.02W
Viana do Castelo, Port. (dò käs-tā'lò)	142	41.41N	8.45W
Viangchan, Laos	188	18.07N	102.33E

PLACE (Pronunciation)	PAGE	Lat. °′	Long. °′
Viar, r., Spain (vē-ä'rä)	152	38.15N	6.08W
Viareggio, Italy (vē-ä-rĕd'jô)	154	43.52N	10.14E
Viborg, Den. (vē'bôr)	146	56.27N	9.22E
Vibo Valentia, Italy (vē'bô-vä-lĕ'n-tyä)	154	38.47N	16.06E
Vicálvaro, Spain	153a	40.25N	3.37W
Vicente López, Arg. (vē-sĕ'n-tĕ-lŏ'pĕz)	126a	34.31S	58.29W
Vicenza, Italy (vē-chĕnt'sä)	142	45.33N	11.33E
Vich, Spain (vēch)	152	41.55N	2.14E
Vichuga, Russia (vē-chōō'gȧ)	160	57.13N	41.58E
Vichy, Fr. (vē-shē')	140	46.06N	3.28E
Vickersund, Nor.	146	60.00N	9.59E
Vicksburg, Mi., U.S. (vĭks'bûrg)	92	42.10N	85.30W
Vicksburg, Ms., U.S.	90	32.20N	90.50W
Viçosa, Braz. (vē-sô'sä)	123a	20.46S	42.51W
Victoria, Arg. (vēk-tô'rēä)	126	32.36S	60.09W
Victoria, Cam. (vĭk-tō'rĭ-ȧ)	204	4.01N	9.12E
Victoria, Can. (vĭk-tō'rĭ-ȧ)	78	48.26N	123.23W
Victoria, Chile (vēk-tô-rēä)	126	38.15S	72.16W
Victoria, Col. (vēk-tô'rēä)	124a	5.19N	74.54W
Victoria, H.K.	237c	22.17N	114.09E
Victoria, Phil. (vēk-tô-ryä)	189a	15.34N	120.41E
Victoria, Tx., U.S. (vĭk-tō'rĭ-ȧ)	106	28.48N	97.00W
Victoria, Va., U.S.	108	36.57N	78.13W
Victoria, state, Austl.	196	36.46S	143.15E
Victoria, neigh., Arg.	229d	34.28S	58.31W
Victoria, l., Afr.	206	0.50S	32.50E
Victoria, r., Austl.	196	17.25S	130.50E
Victoria, Mount, mtn., Burma	174	21.26N	93.59E
Victoria, Mount, mtn., Pap. N. Gui.	188	9.35S	147.45E
Victoria de las Tunas, Cuba (vēk-tō'rē-ä dä läs tōō'näs)	116	20.55N	77.05W
Victoria Falls, wtfl., Afr.	206	17.55S	25.51E
Victoria Island, i., Can.	76	70.13N	107.45W
Victoria Island, i., Nig.	240d	6.26N	3.26E
Victoria Lake, l., Can.	86	48.20N	57.40W
Victoria Land, reg., Ant.	213	75.00S	160.00E
Victoria Nile, r., Ug.	210	2.20N	31.35E
Victoria Peak, mtn., Belize (vēk-tōri'ȧ)	114a	16.47N	88.40W
Victoria Peak, mtn., Can.	80	50.03N	126.06W
Victoria Peak, mtn., H.K.	237c	22.17N	114.08E
Victoria River Downs, Austl. (vĭc-tôr'ĭȧ)	196	16.30S	131.10E
Victoria Station, pt. of i., Eng., U.K.	233b	53.29N	2.15W
Victoria Strait, strt., Can. (vĭk-tō'rĭ-ȧ)	78	69.10N	100.58W
Victoriaville, Can. (vĭk-tō'rĭ-ȧ-vĭl)	78	46.04N	71.59W
Victoria West, S. Afr. (wĕst)	206	31.25S	23.10E
Vidalia, Ga., U.S. (vĭ-dā'lĭ-ȧ)	108	32.10N	82.26W
Vidalia, La., U.S.	106	31.33N	91.28W
Vidin, Bul. (vĭ'dĭn)	142	44.00N	22.53E
Vidnoye, Russia	164b	55.33N	37.41E
Vidzy, Bela. (vē'dzĭ)	156	55.23N	26.46E
Viedma, Arg. (vyād'mä)	126	40.55S	63.03W
Viedma, l., Arg.	126	49.40S	72.35W
Viejo, r., Nic. (vyā'hō)	114	12.45N	86.19W
Vienna (Wien), Aus.	136	48.13N	16.22E
Vienna, Ga., U.S. (vē-ĕn'ȧ)	108	32.03N	83.50W
Vienna, Il., U.S.	104	37.24N	88.50W
Vienna, Va., U.S.	94e	38.54N	77.16W
Vienne, Fr. (vyĕn')	140	45.31N	4.54E
Vienne, r., Fr.	150	47.06N	0.20E
Vieques, P.R. (vyā'kås)	111b	18.09N	65.27W
Vieques, i., P.R. (vyā'kås)	111b	18.05N	65.28W
Vierfontein, S. Afr. (vēr'fōn-tān)	212d	27.06S	26.45E
Vieringhausen, neigh., Ger.	232	51.11N	7.10E
Viersen, Ger. (fēr'zĕn)	151c	51.15N	6.24E
Vierwaldstätter See, l., Switz.	148	46.54N	8.36E
Vierzon, Fr. (vyâr-zôn')	140	47.14N	2.04E
Viesca, Mex. (vē-äs'kä)	106	25.21N	102.47W
Viesca, Laguna de, l., Mex. (lä-ō'nä-dĕ)	106	25.30N	102.40W
Vieste, Italy (vyĕs'tå)	154	41.52N	16.10E
Vietnam, nation, Asia (vyĕt'näm')	188	18.00N	107.00E
View Park, Ca., U.S.	228	34.00N	118.21W
Vigan, Phil. (vēgän)	188	17.36N	120.22E
Vigentino, neigh., Italy	234c	45.25N	9.11E
Vigevano, Italy (vē-jå-vä'nô)	154	45.18N	8.52E
Vigny, Fr. (vēn-y'ē')	151b	49.05N	1.54E
Vigo, Spain (vē'gō)	136	42.18N	8.42W
Vihti, Fin. (vē'tĭ)	146	60.27N	24.18E
Vijayawāda, India	174	16.31N	80.37E
Viksøyri, Nor.	146	61.06N	6.35E
Vila Augusta, Braz.	230d	23.28S	46.32W
Vila Boacaya, neigh., Braz.	230d	23.29S	46.44W
Vila Caldas Xavier, Moz.	210	15.59S	34.12E
Vila de Manica, Moz. (vē'lä dä mä-nē'kå)	206	18.48S	32.49E
Vila de Rei, Port. (vē'lȧ dä rā'ĭ)	152	39.42N	8.03W
Vila do Conde, Port. (vē'lä dò kôn'dĕ)	152	41.21N	8.44W
Vilafranca de Xira, Port. (fräŋ'kȧ dä shē'rä)	152	38.58N	8.59W
Vila Guilherme, neigh., Braz.	230d	23.30S	46.36W
Vilaine, r., Fr. (vē-lân')	150	47.34N	2.15W
Vila Isabel, neigh., Braz.	230c	22.55S	43.15W
Vila Jaguára, neigh., Braz.	230d	23.31S	46.45W
Vila Madalena, neigh., Braz.	230d	23.33S	46.42W
Vila Mariana, neigh., Braz.	230d	23.35S	46.38W
Vilanculos, Moz. (vē-län-kōō'lôs)	206	22.03S	35.13E
Vilāni, Lat. (vē'lä-nĭ)	146	56.31N	27.00E
Vila Nova de Foz Côa, Port. (nō'vȧ dä fôz-kō'ȧ)	152	41.08N	7.11W
Vila Nova de Gaia, Port. (vē'lä nō'vȧ dä gä'yä)	152	41.08N	8.40W
Vila Nova de Milfontes, Port. (nō'vȧ dä mēl-fôn'tāzh)	152	37.44N	8.48W
Vila Progresso, Braz.	230c	22.55S	43.03W
Vila Prudente, neigh., Braz.	230d	23.35S	46.33W
Vila Real, Port. (rä-äl')	142	41.18N	7.48W
Vila Real de Santo Antonio, Port.	152	37.14N	7.25W
Vila Viçosa, Port. (vē-sō'zȧ)	152	38.47N	7.24W
Vileyka, Bela. (vē-lā'ē-kȧ)	156	54.19N	26.58E
Vilhelmina, Swe.	140	64.37N	16.30E
Viljandi, Est. (vēl'yän-dē)	160	58.24N	25.34E
Viljoenskroon, S. Afr.	212d	27.13S	26.58E
Vilkaviškis, Lith. (vēl-kȧ-vēsh'kēs)	146	54.40N	23.08E
Vil'kitskogo, i., Russia (vyl-kēts-kōgō)	162	73.25N	76.00E
Vilkovo, Ukr. (vĭl-kō-vō)	160	45.24N	29.36E
Villa Acuña, Mex. (vēl'yä-kōō'n-yä)	106	29.20N	100.56W
Villa Adelina, neigh., Arg.	229d	34.31S	58.32W
Villa Ahumada, Mex. (ä-ōō-mä'dä)	106	30.43N	106.30W
Villa Alta, Mex. (äl'tä)(sän ēl-dä-fōn'sō)	112	17.20N	96.08W
Villa Angela, Arg. (vē'l-yä ȧ'n-κē-lä)	126	27.31S	60.42W
Villa Ballester, Arg. (vē'l-yä-bäl-yĕs-tĕr)	126a	34.33S	58.33W
Villa Bella, Bol. (bĕ'l-yä)	124	10.25S	65.22W
Villablino, Spain (vēl-yä-blē'nō)	152	42.58N	6.18W
Villa Borghese, pt. of i., Italy	235c	41.55N	12.29E
Villa Bosch, neigh., Arg.	229d	34.36S	58.34W
Villacañas, Spain (vēl-yä-kän'yäs)	152	39.39N	3.20W
Villacarrillo, Spain (vēl-yä-kä-rēl'yō)	152	38.09N	3.07W
Villach, Aus. (fē'läκ)	140	46.38N	13.50E
Villacidro, Italy (vē-lä-chē'drō)	154	39.28N	8.41E
Villa Ciudadela, neigh., Arg.	229d	34.38S	58.34W
Villa Clara, prov., Cuba	116	22.40N	80.10W
Villa Constitución, Arg. (kōn-stē-tōō-syōn')	123c	33.15S	60.19W
Villa Coronado, Mex. (kō-rō-nä'dhō)	106	26.45N	105.10W
Villa Cuauhtémoc, Mex. (vēl'yä-kōō-äō-tē'mōk)	112	22.11N	97.50W
Villa de Allende, Mex. (vēl'yä'dä äl-yĕn'dȧ)	106	25.18N	100.01W
Villa de Alvarez, Mex. (vēl'yä-dĕ-ä'l-vä-rĕz)	112	19.17N	103.44W
Villa de Cura, Ven. (dĕ-kōō'rä)	125b	10.03N	67.29W
Villa de Guadalupe, Mex. (dĕ-gwä-dhä-lōō'pä)	112	23.22N	100.44W
Villa de Mayo, Arg.	126a	34.31S	58.41W
Villa Devoto, neigh., Arg.	229d	34.36S	58.31W
Villa Diamante, neigh., Arg.	229d	34.41S	58.26W
Villa Dolores, Arg. (vēl'yä dō-lō'räs)	126	31.50S	65.05W
Villa Domínico, neigh., Arg.	229d	34.41S	58.20W
Villa Escalante, Mex. (vēl'yä-ĕs-kä-lȧn'tĕ)	112	19.24N	101.36W
Villa Flores, Mex. (vēl'yä-flō'räs)	112	16.13N	93.17W
Villafranca, Italy (vēl-lä-fräŋ'kä)	154	45.22N	10.53E
Villafranca del Bierzo, Spain	152	42.37N	6.49W
Villafranca de los Barros, Spain	152	38.34N	6.22W
Villafranca del Panadés, Spain	152	41.20N	1.40E
Villafranche-de-Rouergue, Fr. (dē-rōō-ĕrg')	150	44.21N	2.02E
Villa García, Mex. (gär-sē'ä)	112	22.07N	101.55W
Villagarcia, Spain (vēl'yä-gär-thē'ä)	152	42.38N	8.43W
Villagrán, Mex.	106	24.28N	99.30W
Villa Grove, Il., U.S. (vĭl'ȧ grōv')	92	39.55N	88.15W
Villaguay, Arg. (vē'l-yä-gwī)	126	31.47S	58.53W
Villa Hayes, Para. (vēl'yä äyås)(hāz)	126	25.07S	57.31W
Villahermosa, Mex. (vēl'yä-ĕr-mō'sä)	110	17.59N	92.56W
Villa Hidalgo, Mex. (vēl'yäē-dăl'gō)	112	21.39N	102.41W
Villa José L. Suárez, neigh., Arg.	229d	34.32S	58.34W
Villajoyosa, Spain (vēl'yä-hō-yō'sä)	152	38.30N	0.14W
Villalba, Spain	152	43.18N	7.43W
Villaldama, Mex. (vēl-yäl-dä'mä)	110	26.30N	100.26W
Villa Lopez, Mex. (vēl'yä lō'pĕz)	106	27.00N	105.02W
Villalpando, Spain (vēl-yäl-pän'dō)	152	41.54N	5.24W
Villa Lugano, neigh., Arg.	229d	34.41S	58.28W
Villa Lynch, neigh., Arg.	229d	34.36S	58.32W
Villa Madero, Arg.	229d	34.41S	58.30W
Villa María, Arg. (vē'l-yä-mä-rē'ä)	126	32.17S	63.08W
Villamatín, Spain (vēl-yä-mä-tē'n)	152	36.50N	5.38W
Villa Mercedes, Arg. (mĕr-sā'dås)	126	33.38S	65.16W
Villa Montes, Bol. (vē'l-yä-mô'n-tĕs)	124	21.13S	63.26W
Villa Morelos, Mex. (mō-rē'lomcs)	112	20.01N	101.24W
Villa Nova, Md., U.S.	225c	39.21N	76.44W
Villanova, Pa., U.S.	225b	40.02N	75.21W
Villanueva, Col. (vē'l-yä-nōē'vä)	124	10.44N	73.08W
Villanueva, Hond. (vēl'yä-nwä'vä)	114	15.19N	88.02W
Villanueva, Mex. (vēl'yä-nōē'vä)	112	22.25N	102.53W
Villanueva de Córdoba, Spain (vēl-yä-nwĕ'vä-dä kôr'dō-bä)	152	38.18N	4.38W
Villanueva de la Serena, Spain (lä sā-rā'nä)	152	38.59N	5.56W
Villa Obregón, Mex. (vē'l-yä-ô-brē-gô'n)	113a	19.21N	99.11W
Villa Ocampo, Mex. (ō-käm'pō)	106	26.26N	105.30W
Villa Pedro Montoya, Mex. (vēl'yä-pĕ'drō-mōn-tō'yȧ)	112	21.38N	99.51W
Villard-Bonnot, Fr. (vēl-yär'bōn-nō')	150	45.15N	5.53E
Villa Real, neigh., Arg.	229d	34.37S	58.31W
Villarreal, Spain (vēl-yär-rē-äl)	152	39.55N	0.07W
Villarrica, Para. (vēl-yä-rē'kä)	126	25.55S	56.23W
Villarrobledo, Spain (vēl-yär-rō-blā'dhō)	142	39.15N	2.37W
Villa Sáenz Peña, neigh., Arg.	229d	34.36S	58.31W
Villa San Andrés, neigh., Arg.	229d	34.33S	58.30W
Villa Santos Lugares, neigh., Arg.	229d	34.36S	58.32W
Villa Unión, Mex. (vēl'yä-ōō-nyōn')	112	23.10N	106.14W
Villaverde, neigh., Spain	234b	40.21N	3.42W
Villavicencio, Col. (vē'l-yä-vē-sĕ'n-syō)	124	4.09N	73.38W
Villaviciosa de Odón, Spain	153a	40.22N	3.38W
Villavieja, Col. (vēl-yä-vē-ĕ'κä)	124a	3.13N	75.13W
Villazón, Bol. (vē'l-yä-zô'n)	124	22.02S	65.42W
Villecresnes, Fr.	233c	48.43N	2.32E
Ville-d'Avray, Fr.	233c	48.50N	2.11E
Villefranche, Fr.	140	45.59N	4.43E
Villejuif, Fr. (vēl'zhüst')	151b	48.48N	2.22E
Ville-Marie, Can.	78	47.18N	79.22W
Villemomble, Fr.	233c	48.53N	2.31E
Villena, Spain (vē-lyā'nȧ)	142	38.37N	0.52W
Villenbon-sur-Yvette, Fr.	233c	48.42N	2.15E
Villeneuve, Can. (vēl'nûv')	77g	53.40N	113.49W
Villeneuve-le-Roi, Fr.	233c	48.44N	2.25E
Villeneuve-Saint Georges, Fr. (săN-zhôrzh')	151b	48.43N	2.27E
Villeneuve-sur-Lot, Fr. (sür-lō')	150	44.25N	0.41E
Villeparisis, Fr.	233c	48.56N	2.37E
Ville Platte, La., U.S. (vēl plát')	106	30.41N	92.17W
Villers Cotterêts, Fr. (vē-ār'kō-trā')	151b	49.15N	3.05E
Villers-sur-Marne, Fr.	233c	48.50N	2.33E
Villerupt, Fr. (vēl'rüp')	150	49.28N	6.16E
Ville-Saint Georges, Can. (vĭl-sĕN-zhôrzh')	84	46.07N	70.40W
Villeta, Col. (vē'l-yĕ'tȧ)	124a	5.02N	74.29W
Villeurbanne, Fr. (vēl-ûr-bän')	140	45.43N	4.55E
Villiers, S. Afr. (vĭl'ĭ-ērs)	212d	27.03S	28.38E
Villiers-le-Bâcle, Fr.	233c	48.44N	2.08E
Villiers-le-Bel, Fr.	233c	49.00N	2.23E
Villingen-Schwenningen, Ger.	148	48.04N	8.33E
Villisca, Ia., U.S. (vĭ'lĭs'kȧ)	96	40.56N	94.56W
Villupuram, India	178	11.59N	79.33E
Vilnius, Lith. (vĭl'nē-ōs)	158	54.40N	25.26E
Vilppula, Fin. (vĭl'pŭ-lȧ)	146	62.01N	24.24E
Vilvoorde, Bel.	139a	50.56N	4.25E
Vilyuy, r., Russia (vēl'yĭ)	158	63.00N	121.00E
Vilyuysk, Russia (vē-lyōō'ĭsk')	158	63.41N	121.47E
Vimmerby, Swe. (vĭm'ĕr-bü)	146	57.41N	15.51E
Vimperk, Czech. (vĭm-pĕrk')	148	49.04N	13.41E
Viña del Mar, Chile (vē'nyä dĕl mär')	126	33.00S	71.33W
Vinalhaven, Me., U.S. (vī-năl-hā'vĕn)	86	44.03N	68.49W
Vinaroz, Spain (vē-nä'rōth)	152	40.29N	0.27E
Vincennes, Fr. (văN-sĕn')	151b	48.51N	2.27E
Vincennes, In., U.S. (vĭn-zĕnz')	90	38.40N	87.30W
Vincennes, Château de, hist., Fr.	233c	48.51N	2.26E
Vincent, Al., U.S. (vĭn'sĕnt)	108	33.21N	86.25W
Vindelälven, r., Swe.	140	65.02N	18.30E
Vindeln, Swe. (vĭn'dĕln)	140	64.10N	19.52E
Vindhya Range, mts., India (vĭnd'yä)	174	22.30N	75.50E
Vineland, N.J., U.S. (vīn'lănd)	92	39.30N	75.00W
Vinh, Viet. (vēn'y')	188	18.38N	105.42E
Vinhais, Port. (vēn-yä'ēzh)	152	41.51N	7.00W
Vinings, Ga., U.S. (vī'nĭngz)	94c	33.52N	84.28W
Vinita, Ok., U.S. (vĭ-nē'tȧ)	104	36.38N	95.09W
Vinkovci, Cro. (vēn'kōv-tsē)	154	45.17N	18.47E
Vinnitsa, Ukr. (vē'nēt-sȧ)	158	49.13N	28.31E
Vinnitsa, prov., Ukr.	156	48.45N	28.01E
Vinogradovo, Russia (vĭ-nō-grä'do-vō)	164b	55.25N	38.33E
Vinson Massif, mtn., Ant.	213	77.40S	87.00W
Vinton, Ia., U.S. (vĭn'tŭn)	96	42.08N	92.01W
Vinton, La., U.S.	106	30.12N	93.35W
Violet, La., U.S. (vī'ō-lĕt)	94d	29.54N	89.54W
Virac, Phil. (vē-räk')	184	13.38N	124.20E
Virbalis, Lith. (vēr'bȧ-lēs)	146	54.38N	22.55E
Virden, Can. (vûr'dĕn)	78	49.51N	101.55W
Virden, Il., U.S.	104	39.28N	89.46W
Vírgen del San Cristóbal, rel., Chile	230b	33.26S	70.39W
Virgin, r., U.S.	102	36.51N	113.50W
Virginia, S. Afr.	212d	28.07S	26.54E
Virginia, Mn., U.S. (vĕr-jĭn'yȧ)	90	47.32N	92.36W
Virginia, state, U.S.	90	37.00N	80.45W
Virginia Beach, Va., U.S.	92	36.50N	75.58W
Virginia City, Nv., U.S.	102	39.18N	119.40W
Virginia Hills, Va., U.S.	225d	38.47N	77.06W
Virginia Water, Eng., U.K.	231	51.24N	0.34W
Virgin Islands, is., N.A. (vûr'jĭn)	110	18.15N	64.00W
Viroflay, Fr.	233c	48.48N	2.10E
Víron, Grc.	235d	37.57N	23.45E
Viroqua, Wi., U.S. (vĭ-rō'kwȧ)	96	43.33N	90.54W
Virovitica, Cro. (vē-rō-vē'tē-tsȧ)	154	45.50N	17.24E
Virpazar, Yugo. (vêr'pä-zär')	154	42.16N	19.06E
Virrat, Fin. (vĭr'ăt)	146	62.15N	23.45E
Virserum, Swe. (vĭr'sē-rōm)	146	57.22N	15.35E
Vis, Cro. (vēs)	154	43.03N	16.11E
Vis, i., Yugo.	142	43.00N	16.10E
Visalia, Ca., U.S. (vĭ-sā'lĭ-ȧ)	102	36.20N	119.18W
Visby, Swe. (vĭs'bü)	136	57.39N	18.19E
Viscount Melville Sound, strt., Can.	76	74.00N	110.00W
Višegrad, Bos. (vē'shĕ-gräd)	154	43.48N	19.17E
Vishākhapatnam, India	174	17.48N	83.21E
Vishera, r., Russia (vĭ'shĕ-rȧ)	164a	60.40N	58.46E
Vishnyakovo, Russia	164b	55.44N	38.10E
Vishoek, S. Afr.	206a	34.13S	18.26E
Visim, Russia (vē'sĭm)	164a	57.38N	59.32E
Viskan, r., Swe.	146	57.20N	12.25E
Viški, Lat. (vēs'kĭ)	146	56.02N	26.47E
Visoko, Bos. (vē'sô-kô)	154	43.59N	18.10E
Vistula, r., Chile	230b	33.24S	70.36W
Vistula, see Wisła, r., Pol.	136	52.30N	20.00E
Vitarte, Peru	229c	12.02S	76.54W
Vitebsk, Bela. (vē'tyĕpsk)	158	55.12N	30.16E
Vitebsk, prov., Bela.	156	55.05N	29.18E
Viterbo, Italy (vē-tĕr'bō)	142	42.24N	12.08E
Viti Levu, i., Fiji	192g	18.00S	178.00E
Vitim, Russia (vē'tĕm)	158	59.22N	112.43E
Vitim, r., Russia (vē'tĕm)	158	54.00N	115.00E
Vitino, Russia (vē'tĭ-nō)	164c	59.40N	29.51E
Vitória, Braz. (vē-tō'rē-ä)	124	20.09S	40.17W
Vitoria, Spain (vē-tô-ryä)	142	42.43N	2.43W
Vitória de Conquista, Braz. (vē-tō'rē-ä-dä-kōn-kwē's-tä)	124	14.51S	40.44W
Vitry-le-François, Fr. (vē-trē'lĕ-fräN-swá')	150	48.44N	4.34E
Vitry-sur-Seine, Fr.	233c	48.48N	2.24E
Vittorio, Italy (vē-tô'rē-ô)	154	45.59N	12.17E
Vivero, Spain (vē-vä'rō)	152	43.39N	7.37W

PLACE (Pronunciation)	PAGE	Lat. °'	Long. °'
Vivian, La., U.S. (vĭv'ĭ-ăn)	106	32.51N	93.59W
Vizianagaram, India	174	18.10N	83.29E
Vlaardingen, Neth. (vlär'dĭng-ĕn)	144	51.54N	4.20E
Vladikavkaz, Russia	160	43.05N	44.35E
Vladimir, Russia (vlá-dyē'mēr)	158	56.08N	40.24E
Vladimir, prov., Russia (vlä-dyē'mēr)	156	56.08N	39.53E
Vladimiro-Aleksandrovskoye, Russia	186	42.50N	133.00E
Vladimir-Volynskiy, Ukr. (vlá-dyē'mēr vô-lēn'skĭ)	148	50.50N	24.20E
Vladivostok, Russia (vlá-dē-vôs-tŏk')	158	43.06N	131.47E
Vladykino, neigh., Russia	235b	55.52N	37.36E
Vlasenica, Bos. (vlä'sĕ-nēt'sá)	154	44.11N	18.58E
Vlasotince, Yugo. (vlä'sô-tēn-tsĕ)	154	42.58N	22.08E
Vlieland, i., Neth. (vlē'länt)	144	53.19N	4.55E
Vlissingen, Neth. (vlĭs'sĭng-ĕn)	144	51.30N	3.34E
Vlorë, Alb.	142	40.27N	19.30E
Vltava, r., Czech.	148	49.24N	14.18E
Vodl, l., Russia (vôd''l)	160	62.20N	37.20E
Voerde, Ger.	151c	51.35N	6.41E
Vogelheim, neigh., Ger.	232	51.29N	6.59E
Voghera, Italy (vô-gā'rä)	154	44.58N	9.02E
Vohwinkel, neigh., Ger.	232	51.14N	7.09E
Voight, r., Wa., U.S.	100a	47.03N	122.08W
Voinjama, Lib.	208	8.25N	9.45W
Voiron, Fr. (vwá-rôN')	150	45.23N	5.48E
Voisin, Lac, l., Can. (vwŏ'-zĭn)	82	54.13N	107.15W
Volchansk, Ukr. (vôl-chänsk')	160	50.18N	36.56E
Volchonka-Zil, neigh., Russia	235b	55.40N	37.37E
Volga, r., Russia (vôl'gä)	158	47.30N	46.20E
Volga, Mouths of the, mth.	160	46.00N	49.10E
Volgograd, Russia (vŏl-gō-grä't)	158	48.40N	42.20E
Volgogradskoye, res., Russia (vôl-gô-grad'skô-yĕ)	158	51.10N	45.10E
Volkhov, Russia (vôl'kôf)	146	59.54N	32.21E
Volkhov, r., Russia	160	58.45N	31.40E
Volkovysk, Bela. (vôl-kô-vēsk')	148	53.11N	24.29E
Vollme, Ger.	232	51.10N	7.36E
Volmarstein, Ger.	232	51.22N	7.23E
Volmerswerth, neigh., Ger.	232	51.11N	6.46E
Volodarskiy, Russia (vô-lô-där'skĭ)	164c	59.49N	30.06E
Vologda, Russia (vô'lôg-dá)	158	59.12N	39.52E
Vologda, prov., Russia	156	59.00N	37.26E
Volokolamsk, Russia (vô-lô-kô-lamsk)	156	56.02N	35.58E
Volokonovka, Russia (vô-lô-kô'nôf-ká)	156	50.28N	37.52E
Volozhin, Bela. (vô'lô-shēn)	156	54.04N	26.38E
Vol'sk, Russia (vôl'sk)	160	52.02N	47.23E
Volta, r., Ghana	208	6.05N	0.30E
Volta, Lake, res., Ghana (vôl'tá)	204	7.10N	0.30W
Volta Blanche (White Volta), r., Afr.	208	11.30N	0.40W
Volta Noire, *see* Black Volta, r., Afr.	204	11.30N	4.00W
Volta Redonda, Braz. (vōl'tä-rā-dôn'dä)	124	22.32S	44.05W
Volterra, Italy (vôl-tĕr'rä)	154	43.22N	10.51E
Voltri, Italy (vōl'trē)	154	44.25N	8.45E
Volturno, r., Italy (vôl-tōōr'nô)	154	41.12N	14.20E
Vólvi, Límni, l., Grc.	154	40.41N	23.23E
Volzhskoye, l., Russia (vôl'sh-skô-yĕ)	156	56.43N	36.18E
Von Ormy, Tx., U.S. (vŏn ôr'mē)	101d	29.18N	98.36W
Vōōpsu, Est. (vōōp'sŏ)	146	58.06N	27.30E
Voorburg, Neth.	139a	52.04N	4.21E
Voortrekkerhoogte, S. Afr.	207b	25.48S	28.10E
Vop', r., Russia (vôp)	156	55.20N	32.55E
Vopnafjördur, Ice.	140	65.43N	14.58W
Vorarlberg, prov., Aus.	148	47.20N	9.55E
Vordingborg, Den. (vôr'dĭng-bôr)	146	55.10N	11.55E
Vorhalle, neigh., Ger.	232	51.23N	7.28E
Voríai Sporádhes, is., Grc.	154	38.55N	24.05E
Vorkuta, Russia (vôr-kōō'tá)	158	67.28N	63.40E
Vormholz, Ger.	232	51.24N	7.18E
Vormsi, i., Est. (vôrm'sĭ)	146	59.06N	23.05E
Vórois Evvoïkós Kólpos, b., Grc.	154	38.48N	23.02E
Vorona, r., Russia (vô-rô'na)	160	51.50N	42.00E
Voronezh, Russia (vô-rô'nyĕzh)	158	51.39N	39.11E
Voronezh, prov., Russia	156	51.10N	39.13E
Voronezh, r., Russia	160	52.17N	39.32E
Voronovo, Bela. (vô'rô-nô-vô)	148	54.07N	25.16E
Vorontsovka, Russia (vô-rônt'sôv-ká)	164a	59.40N	60.14E
Voron'ya, r., Russia (vô-rôn'yá)	160	68.20N	35.20E
Võrts-Järv, l., Est. (vôrts yärv)	146	58.15N	26.12E
Võru, Est. (vô'rû)	160	57.50N	26.58E
Vorya, r., Russia (vôr'yá)	164b	55.55N	38.15E
Vosges, mts., Fr. (vōzh)	140	48.09N	6.57E
Voskresensk, Russia (vôs-krĕ-sĕnsk')	164b	55.20N	38.42E
Voss, Nor. (vôs)	140	60.40N	6.24E
Vostryakovo, Russia	164b	55.23N	37.49E
Votkinsk, Russia (vôt-kēnsk')	160	57.00N	54.00E
Votkinskoye Vodokhranilishche, res., Russia	160	57.30N	55.00E
Vouga, r., Port. (vō'gá)	152	40.43N	7.51W
Vouziers, Fr. (vōō-zyā')	150	49.25N	4.40E
Voxnan, r., Swe.	146	61.30N	15.24E
Voyageurs National Park, Mn., U.S.	96	48.30N	92.40W
Vozhe, l., Russia (vôzh'yĕ)	160	60.40N	39.00E
Voznesensk, Ukr. (vôz-nyĕ-sĕnsk')	160	47.34N	31.22E
Vrangelya (Wrangel), i., Russia	158	71.25N	178.30W
Vranje, Yugo. (vrän'yĕ)	154	42.33N	21.55E
Vratsa, Bul. (vrät'tsá)	142	43.12N	23.31E
Vrbas, Yugo. (v'r'bäs)	154	45.34N	19.43E
Vrbas, r., Yugo.	154	44.25N	17.17E
Vrchlabi, Czech. (v'r'chlä-bē)	148	50.32N	15.51E
Vrede, S. Afr. (vrĭ'dĕ)(vrĕd)	212d	27.25S	29.11E
Vredefort, S. Afr. (vrĭ'dĕ-fôrt)(vrĕd'fōrt)	212d	27.00S	27.21E
Vreeswijk, Neth.	139a	52.00N	5.06E
Vršac, Yugo. (v'r'shàts)	142	45.08N	21.18E
Vrutky, Czech. (vrōōt'kē)	148	49.09N	18.55E
Vryburg, S. Afr. (vrī'bûrg)	206	26.55S	24.45E
Vryheid, S. Afr. (vrī'hīt)	206	27.43S	30.58E
Vsetín, Czech. (fsĕt'yēn)	148	49.21N	18.01E
Vsevolozhskiy, Russia (vsyĕ'vôlô'zh-skĕĕ)	164c	60.01N	30.41E
Vuelta Abajo, reg., Cuba (vwĕl'tä ä-bä'hō)	116	22.20N	83.45W
Vught, Neth.	139a	51.38N	5.18E
Vukovar, Cro. (vŏ'kô-vär)	154	45.20N	19.00E
Vulcan, Mi., U.S. (vŭl'kăn)	92	45.45N	87.50W
Vulcano, i., Italy (vōōl-kä'nô)	154	38.23N	15.00E
Vŭlchedrŭma, Bul.	154	43.43N	23.29E
Vyartsilya, Russia (vyár-tsē'lyá)	146	62.10N	30.40E
Vyatka, r., Russia (vyát'ká)	160	59.20N	51.25E
Vyazemskiy, Russia (vyá-zĕm'skĭ)	186	47.29N	134.39E
Vyaz'ma, Russia (vyáz'má)	160	55.12N	34.17E
Vyazniki, Russia (vyáz'nē-kē)	160	56.10N	42.10E
Vyborg, Russia (vwē'bôrk)	158	60.43N	28.46E
Vychegda, r., Russia (vē'chĕg-dá)	160	61.40N	48.00E
Vym, r., Russia (vwĕm)	160	63.15N	51.20E
Vyritsa, Russia (vē'rĭ-tsá)	164c	59.24N	30.20E
Vyshnevolotskoye, l., Russia (vŭy'sh-ŋĕ'vôlôt's-kô'yĕ)	156	57.30N	34.27E
Vyshniy Volochëk, Russia (vêsh'nyĭ vôl-ô-chĕk')	158	57.34N	34.35E
Vyškov, Czech. (vêsh'kôf)	148	49.17N	16.58E
Vysoké Mýto, Czech. (vû'sô-kā mû'tô)	148	49.58N	16.07E
Vysokovsk, Russia (vĭ-sô'kôfsk)	156	56.16N	36.32E
Vytegra, Russia (vû'tĕg-rá)	158	61.00N	36.20E

W

PLACE (Pronunciation)	PAGE	Lat. °'	Long. °'
W, Parcs Nationaux du, rec., Niger	208	12.20N	2.40E
Waal, r., Neth. (väl)	144	51.46N	5.00E
Waalwijk, Neth.	139a	51.41N	5.05E
Wabamun, Grc.	142	39.23N	22.56E
Wabamuno, Can. (wŏ'bă-mŭn)	80	53.33N	114.28W
Wabasca, Can. (wŏ-bás'kă)	80	56.00N	113.53W
Wabash, In., U.S. (wô'băsh)	92	40.45N	85.50W
Wabash, r., U.S.	90	38.00N	88.00W
Wabasha, Mn., U.S. (wä'bá-shô)	96	44.24N	92.04W
Wabe Gestro, r., Eth.	204	6.25N	41.21E
Wabowden, Can. (wä-bō'd'n)	82	54.55N	98.38W
Wąbrzeźno, Pol. (vôŋ-bzĕzh'nô)	148	53.17N	18.59E
Wabu Hu, l., China (wä-bōō hōō)	182	32.25N	116.35E
W. A. C. Bennett Dam, dam, Can.	80	56.01N	122.10W
Waccamaw, r., S.C., U.S. (wăk'á-mô)	108	33.47N	78.55W
Waccasassa Bay, b., Fl., U.S. (wă-ká-să'sá)	108	29.02N	83.10W
Wachow, Ger. (vä'kōv)	139b	53.32N	12.46E
Waco, Tx., U.S. (wā'kō)	90	31.35N	97.06W
Waconda Lake, res., Ks., U.S.	104	39.45N	98.15W
Wadayama, Japan (wä'dä'yä-mä)	187	35.19N	134.49E
Waddenzee, sea, Neth.	144	53.00N	4.50E
Waddington, Mount, mtn., Can. (wŏd'dĭng-tŭn)	78	51.23N	125.15W
Wadena, Can.	82	51.57N	103.50W
Wadena, Mn., U.S. (wŏ-dē'ná)	96	46.26N	95.09W
Wadesboro, N.C., U.S. (wādz'bŭr-ô)	108	34.57N	80.05W
Wadeville, S. Afr.	240b	26.16S	28.11E
Wadley, Ga., U.S. (wŭd'lē)	108	32.54N	82.25W
Wad Madani, Sudan (wäd mē-dä'nē)	204	14.27N	33.31E
Wadowice, Pol. (vá-dô'vēt-sĕ)	148	49.53N	19.31E
Wadsworth, Oh., U.S. (wŏdz'wŭrth)	95d	41.01N	81.44W
Wager Bay, b., Can. (wā'jēr)	78	65.48N	88.19W
Wagga Wagga, Austl. (wôg'á wôg'á)	196	35.10S	147.30E
Wagoner, Ok., U.S. (wăg'ŭn-ēr)	104	35.58N	95.22W
Wagon Mound, N.M., U.S. (wăg'ŭn mound)	104	35.59N	104.45W
Wągrowiec, Pol. (vôŋ-grô'vyĕts)	148	52.47N	17.14E
Waha, Libya	176	28.16N	19.54E
Wahiawa, Hi., U.S.	90d	21.30N	158.03W
Wahoo, Ne., U.S. (wä-hōō')	96	41.14N	96.39W
Wahpeton, N.D., U.S. (wô'pē-tŭn)	96	46.17N	96.38W
Währing, neigh., Aus.	235e	48.14N	16.21E
Wahroonga, Austl.	239a	33.43S	151.07E
Waialua, Hi., U.S. (wä'ē-ä-lōō'ä)	88a	21.33N	158.08W
Waianae, Hi., U.S. (wä'ē-á-nä'ā)	88a	21.25N	158.11W
Waidhofen, Aus. (vīd'hôf-ĕn)	148	47.58N	14.46E
Waidmannslust, neigh., Ger.	234a	52.36N	13.20E
Waigeo, Pulau, i., Indon. (wä-ē-gā'ō)	188	0.07N	131.00E
Waikato, r., N.Z. (wä'ē-kä'to)	197a	38.10S	175.35E
Waikerie, Austl. (wā'kēr-ē)	198	34.15S	140.00E
Wailuku, Hi., U.S. (wä'ē-lōō'kōō)	90c	20.55N	156.30W
Waimanalo, Hi., U.S. (wä-ē-mä'nä-lo)	88a	21.19N	157.53W
Waimea, Hi., U.S. (wä-ē-mā'ä)	88a	21.56N	159.38W
Wainganga, r., India (wä-ēn-gŭŋ'gä)	174	20.30N	80.15E
Waingapu, Indon.	188	9.32S	120.00E
Wainwright, Can.	78	52.49N	110.52W
Wainwright, Ak., U.S. (wān-rīt)	89	74.40N	159.00W
Waipahu, Hi., U.S. (wä'ē-pä'hōō)	90d	21.20N	158.02W
Waiska, r., Mi., U.S. (wá-ĭz-ká)	101k	46.20N	84.38W
Waitara, Austl.	239a	33.43S	150.06E
Waitsburg, Wa., U.S. (wāts'bûrg)	98	46.17N	118.08W
Wajima, Japan (wä'jē-má)	187	37.23N	136.56E
Wajir, Kenya	210	1.45N	40.04E
Wakami, r., Can.	84	47.43N	82.22W
Wakasa-Wan, b., Japan (wä'kä-sä wän)	186	35.43N	135.39E
Wakatipu, l., N.Z. (wä-kä-tē'pōō)	197a	45.04S	168.30E
Wakayama, Japan (wä-kä'yä-mä)	180	34.14N	135.11E
Wake, i., Oc. (wāk)	2	19.25N	167.00E
Wa Keeney, Ks., U.S. (wô-kē'nē)	104	39.01N	99.53W
Wakefield, Can. (wāk-fēld)	77c	45.39N	75.55W
Wakefield, Eng., U.K.	144	53.41N	1.25W
Wakefield, Ma., U.S.	87a	42.31N	71.05W
Wakefield, Mi., U.S.	96	46.28N	89.55W
Wakefield, Ne., U.S.	96	42.15N	96.52W
Wakefield, R.I., U.S.	94b	41.26N	71.30W
Wake Forest, N.C., U.S. (wāk fŏr'ĕst)	108	35.58N	78.31W
Waki, Japan (wä'kē)	187	34.05N	134.10E
Wakkanai, Japan (wä'kä-nä'ē)	180	45.19N	141.43E
Wakkerstroom, S. Afr. (vák'ĕr-strōm)(wăk'ĕr-strōōm)	206	27.19S	30.04E
Wakonassin, r., Can.	84	46.35N	82.10W
Waku Kundo, Ang.	206	11.25S	15.07E
Wałbrzych, Pol. (väl'bzhûk)	148	50.46N	16.16E
Walcott, Lake, res., Id., U.S.	98	42.40N	113.23W
Wałcz, Pol. (välch)	148	53.11N	16.30E
Waldbauer, neigh., Ger.	232	51.18N	7.28E
Waldoboro, Me., U.S. (wôl'dô-bŭr-ô)	86	44.06N	69.22W
Waldo Lake, l., Or., U.S. (wôl'dō)	98	43.46N	122.10W
Waldorf, Md., U.S. (wăl'dôrf)	94e	38.37N	76.57W
Waldron, Mo., U.S.	101f	39.14N	94.47W
Waldron, i., Wa., U.S.	100d	48.42N	123.02W
Wales, reg., U.K.	136	52.12N	3.40W
Wales, Ak., U.S. (wālz)	89	65.35N	168.14W
Walewale, Ghana	208	10.21N	0.48W
Walgett, Austl. (wôl'gĕt)	196	30.00S	148.10E
Walhalla, S.C., U.S. (wŭl-hăl'á)	108	34.45N	83.04W
Walikale, Zaire	210	1.25S	28.03E
Walkden, Eng., U.K.	138a	53.32N	2.24W
Walker, Mn., U.S. (wôk'ēr)	96	47.06N	94.37W
Walker, r., Nv., U.S.	102	39.07N	119.10W
Walker, Mount, mtn., Wa., U.S.	100a	47.47N	122.54W
Walker Lake, l., Can.	82	54.42N	96.57W
Walker Lake, l., Nv., U.S.	102	38.46N	118.30W
Walker River Indian Reservation, I.R., Nv., U.S.	102	39.06N	118.20W
Walkerville, Mt., U.S. (wôk'ēr-vĭl)	98	46.20N	112.32W
Wallace, Id., U.S. (wŏl'ås)	98	47.27N	115.55W
Wallaceburg, Can.	84	42.39N	82.25W
Wallach, Ger.	232	51.35N	6.34E
Wallacia, Austl.	195b	33.52S	150.40E
Wallaroo, Austl. (wŏl-á-rōō)	196	33.52S	137.45E
Wallasey, Eng., U.K. (wŏl'á-sē)	138a	53.25N	3.03W
Walla Walla, Wa., U.S. (wŏl'á wŏl'á)	90	46.03N	118.20W
Walled Lake, Mi., U.S. (wôl'd lāk)	95b	42.32N	83.29W
Wallel, Tulu, mtn., Eth.	204	9.00N	34.52E
Wallgrove, Austl.	239a	33.47S	150.51E
Wallingford, Eng., U.K. (wŏl'ĭng-fērd)	138b	51.34N	1.08W
Wallingford, Pa., U.S.	225b	39.54N	75.22W
Wallingford, Vt., U.S.	92	43.30N	72.55W
Wallington, N.J., U.S.	224	40.51N	74.07W
Wallington, neigh., Eng., U.K.	231	51.21N	0.09W
Wallis and Futuna Islands, dep., Oc.	190	13.00S	176.10E
Wallisville, Tx., U.S. (wŏl'ĭs-vĭl)	107a	29.50N	94.44W
Wallowa, Or., U.S. (wôl'ô-wá)	98	45.34N	117.32W
Wallowa, r., Or., U.S.	98	45.28N	117.28W
Wallowa Mountains, mts., Or., U.S.	98	45.10N	117.22W
Wallula, Wa., U.S.	98	46.08N	118.55W
Walmersley, Eng., U.K.	233b	53.37N	2.18W
Walnut, Ca., U.S. (wôl'nŭt)	101a	34.00N	117.51W
Walnut, r., Ks., U.S.	104	37.28N	97.06W
Walnut Canyon National Mon, rec., Az., U.S.	102	35.10N	111.30W
Walnut Creek, Ca., U.S.	100b	37.54N	122.04W
Walnut Creek, r., Tx., U.S.	101c	32.37N	97.03W
Walnut Ridge, Ar., U.S. (rĭj)	104	36.04N	90.56W
Walpole, Ma., U.S. (wôl'pōl)	87a	42.09N	71.15W
Walpole, N.H., U.S.	92	43.05N	72.25W
Walsall, Eng., U.K. (wôl-sôl)	144	52.35N	1.58W
Walsenburg, Co., U.S. (wôl'sĕn-bûrg)	104	37.38N	104.46W
Walsum, Ger.	151c	51.32N	6.41E
Walter F. George Reservoir, res., U.S.	108	32.00N	85.00W
Walter Reed Army Medical Center, pt. of i., D.C., U.S.	225d	38.58N	77.02W
Walters, Ok., U.S. (wôl'tērz)	104	34.21N	98.19W
Waltersdorf, Ger.	234a	52.22N	13.35E
Waltham, Ma., U.S. (wôl'thăm)	87a	42.22N	71.14W
Waltham Forest, neigh., Eng., U.K.	231	51.35N	0.01W
Walthamstow, Eng., U.K. (wôl'tăm-stō)	138b	51.34N	0.01W
Walton, Eng., U.K.	231	51.24N	0.25W
Walton, N.Y., U.S.	92	42.10N	75.05W
Walton-le-Dale, Eng., U.K. (lē-dāl')	138a	53.44N	2.40W
Walton on the Hill, Eng., U.K.	231	51.17N	0.15W
Waltrop, Ger.	232	51.37N	7.23E
Walt Whitman Homes, N.J., U.S.	225b	39.52N	75.11W
Walvis Bay, S. Afr. (wôl'vĭs)	206	22.50S	14.30E
Walworth, Wi., U.S. (wôl'wŭrth)	96	42.33N	88.39W
Walze, Ger.	232	51.16N	7.31E
Wama, Ang.	210	12.14S	15.33E
Wamba, r., Zaire	206	7.00S	18.00E
Wambel, neigh., Ger.	232	51.32N	7.32E
Wamego, Ks., U.S. (wŏ-mē'gō)	104	39.13N	96.17W
Wami, r., Tan. (wä'mē)	206	6.31S	37.17E
Wanapitei Lake, l., Can.	84	46.45N	80.45W
Wanaque, N.J., U.S. (wŏn'á-kū)	94a	41.03N	74.16W
Wanaque Reservoir, res., N.J., U.S.	94a	41.06N	74.20W
Wanda Shan, mts., China (wän-dä shän)	180	45.54N	131.45E
Wandhofen, Ger.	232	51.26N	7.33E
Wandoan, Austl.	198	26.09S	149.51E

ng-sing; ŋ-baŋk; N-nasalized n; nŏd; cŏmmit; ōld; ôbey; ôrder; oi-boil; fōōd; ŏ-as oo in foot; ou-out; s-soft; sh-dish; th-thin; pūre; ůnite; ûrn; stŭd; circŭs; ü-as in French tu; '-indeterminate vowel.

PLACE (Pronunciation)	PAGE	Lat. °′	Long. °′
Wandsbek, Ger. (vänds'bĕk)	139c	53.34N	10.07E
Wandsworth, Eng., U.K. (wôndz'wûrth)	138b	51.26N	0.12W
Wanganui, N.Z. (wôŋ'gȧ-nōō'ė)	197a	39.53S	175.01E
Wangaratta, Austl. (wŏŋ'gȧ-răt'ȧ)	198	36.23S	146.18E
Wangeroog, i., Ger. (vän'gĕ-rōg)	148	53.49N	7.57E
Wangqingtuo, China (wäŋ-chyĭŋ-twò)	182	39.14N	116.56E
Wangsi, China (wäŋ-sē)	182	37.59N	116.57E
Wangsim-ni, neigh., S. Kor.	237b	37.36N	127.03E
Wanheimerort, neigh., Ger.	232	51.24N	6.46E
Wanne-Eickel, Ger.	232	51.32N	7.09E
Wannsee, neigh., Ger.	234a	52.25N	13.09E
Wansdorf, Ger.	234a	52.38N	13.05E
Wanstead, neigh., Eng., U.K.	231	51.34N	0.02E
Wantage, Eng., U.K. (wŏn'tȧj)	138b	51.33N	1.26W
Wantagh, N.Y., U.S.	94a	40.41N	73.30W
Wantirna, Austl.	239b	37.51S	145.14E
Wantirna South, Austl.	239b	37.52S	145.14E
Wanxian, China (wän-shyĕn)	180	30.48N	108.22E
Wanxian, China (wän shyĕn)	182	38.51N	115.10E
Wanzai, China (wän-dzī)	184	28.05N	114.25E
Wanzhi, China (wän-jr)	182	31.11N	118.31E
Wapakoneta, Oh., U.S. (wä'pȧ-kò-nĕt'ȧ)	92	40.35N	84.10W
Wapawekka Hills, hills, Can. (wŏ'pă-wĕ'kă-hĭlz)	82	54.45N	104.20W
Wapawekka Lake, l., Can.	82	54.55N	104.40W
Wapello, Ia., U.S. (wŏ-pĕl'ō)	96	41.10N	91.11W
Wappapello Reservoir, res., Mo., U.S. (wă'pȧ-pĕl-lō)	90	37.07N	90.10W
Wappingers Falls, N.Y., U.S. (wŏp'ĭn-jẽrz)	92	41.35N	73.55W
Wapsipinicon, r., Ia., U.S. (wŏp'sĭ-pĭn'ĭ-kŏn)	96	42.16N	91.35W
Warabi, Japan (wä'rä-bė)	187a	35.50N	139.41E
Warangal, India (wŭ'rȧŋ-gȧl)	174	18.03N	79.45E
Warburton, The, r., Austl. (wŏr'bûr-tŭn)	196	27.30S	138.45E
Wardān, Wādī, r., Egypt	173a	29.22N	33.00E
Ward Cove, Ak., U.S.	80	55.24N	131.43W
Warden, S. Afr. (wôr'dĕn)	212d	27.52N	28.59E
Wardha, India (wŭr'dä)	174	20.46N	78.42E
Wardle, Eng., U.K.	233b	53.39N	2.08W
War Eagle, W.V., U.S. (wôr ē'g'l)	92	37.30N	81.50W
Waren, Ger. (vä'rĕn)	148	53.32N	12.43E
Warendorf, Ger. (vä'rĕn-dōrf)	151c	51.57N	7.59E
Wargla, Alg.	204	32.00N	5.18E
Warialda, Austl.	198	29.32S	150.34E
Warlingham, Eng., U.K.	231	51.19N	0.04W
Warmbad, Nmb. (värm'bäd) (wôrm'băd)	206	28.25S	18.45E
Warmbad, S. Afr.	212d	24.52S	28.18E
Warm Beach, Wa., U.S. (wôrm)	100a	48.10N	122.22W
War Memorial Stadium, pt. of i., N.Y., U.S.	226a	42.54N	78.52W
Warm Springs Indian Reservation, I.R., Or., U.S. (wôrm sprĭnz)	98	44.55N	121.30W
Warm Springs Reservoir, res., Or., U.S.	98	43.42N	118.40W
Warner Mountains, mts., Ca., U.S.	90	41.30N	120.17W
Warner Robins, Ga., U.S.	108	32.37N	83.36W
Warnow, r., Ger. (vär'nō)	148	53.51N	11.55E
Warracknabeal, Austl.	198	36.20S	142.28E
Warragamba Reservoir, res., Austl.	198	33.40S	150.00E
Warrandyte, Austl.	239b	37.45S	145.13E
Warrandyte South, Austl.	239b	37.46S	145.14E
Warrāq al-'Arab, Egypt	240a	30.06N	31.12E
Warrāq al-Hadar, Egypt	240a	30.06N	31.13E
Warrawee, Austl.	239a	33.44S	151.07E
Warrego, r., Austl. (wôr'ē-gò)	196	27.13S	145.58E
Warren, Can.	77f	50.08N	97.32W
Warren, Ar., U.S. (wŏr'ĕn)	104	33.37N	92.03W
Warren, In., U.S.	92	40.40N	85.25W
Warren, Mi., U.S.	95b	42.33N	83.03W
Warren, Mn., U.S.	96	48.11N	96.44W
Warren, Oh., U.S.	92	41.15N	80.50W
Warren, Or., U.S.	100c	45.49N	122.51W
Warren, Pa., U.S.	92	41.50N	79.10W
Warren, R.I., U.S.	94b	41.44N	71.14W
Warrendale, Pa., U.S. (wŏr'ĕn-dāl)	95e	40.39N	80.04W
Warrensburg, Mo., U.S. (wŏr'ĕnz-bûrg)	104	38.45N	93.42W
Warrensville Heights, Oh., U.S.	225a	41.26N	81.29W
Warrenton, Ga., U.S. (wŏr'ĕn-tŭn)	108	33.26N	82.37W
Warrenton, Or., U.S.	100c	46.10N	123.56W
Warrenton, Va., U.S.	92	38.45N	77.50W
Warri, Nig. (wär'ė)	204	5.33N	5.43E
Warrington, Eng., U.K.	138a	53.22N	2.30W
Warrington, Fl., U.S. (wŏ'ĭng-tŭn)	108	30.21N	87.15W
Warrnambool, Austl. (wôr'năm-bōōl)	196	38.20S	142.28E
Warroad, Mn., U.S. (wôr'rōd)	96	48.55N	95.20W
Warrumbungle Range, mts., Austl. (wôr'ŭm-bŭŋ-g'l)	196	31.18S	150.00E
Warsaw, Pol.	136	52.15N	21.05E
Warsaw, Il., U.S. (wôr'sô)	104	40.21N	91.26W
Warsaw, In., U.S.	92	41.15N	85.50W
Warsaw, N.Y., U.S.	92	42.45N	78.10W
Warsaw, NC, N.C., U.S.	108	35.00N	78.07W
Warsop, Eng., U.K. (wôr'sŭp)	138a	53.13N	1.05W
Warszawa, *see* Warsaw, Pol.	136	52.15N	21.05E
Warta, r., Pol. (vär'tȧ)	140	52.30N	16.00E
Wartburg, S. Afr.	207c	29.26S	30.39E
Wartenberg, neigh., Ger.	234a	52.34N	13.31E
Warwick, Austl. (wŏr'ĭk)	196	28.05S	152.10E
Warwick, Can.	84	45.58N	71.57W
Warwick, Eng., U.K.	144	52.19N	1.46W
Warwick, N.Y., U.S.	94a	41.15N	74.22W
Warwick, R.I., U.S.	92	41.42N	71.27W
Warwickshire, co., Eng., U.K.	138a	52.30N	1.35W
Wasatch Mountains, mts., Ut., U.S. (wô'săch)	101b	40.45N	111.46W

PLACE (Pronunciation)	PAGE	Lat. °′	Long. °′
Wasatch Plateau, plat., Ut., U.S.	102	38.55N	111.40W
Wasatch Range, mts., U.S.	90	39.10N	111.30W
Wasbank, S. Afr.	207c	28.27S	30.09E
Wasco, Or., U.S. (wăs'kō)	98	45.36N	120.42W
Waseca, Mn., U.S. (wŏ-sē'kȧ)	96	44.04N	93.31W
Waseda University, educ., Japan	238a	35.42N	139.43E
Wash, The, Eng., U.K. (wŏsh)	140	53.00N	0.20E
Washburn, Me., U.S. (wŏsh'bŭrn)	86	46.46N	68.10W
Washburn, Wi., U.S.	96	46.41N	90.55W
Washburn, Mount, mtn., Wy., U.S.	98	44.55N	110.10W
Washington, D.C., U.S. (wŏsh'ĭng-tŭn)	90	38.50N	77.00W
Washington, Ga., U.S.	108	33.43N	82.46W
Washington, In., U.S.	92	38.40N	87.10W
Washington, Ia., U.S.	96	41.17N	91.42W
Washington, Ks., U.S.	104	39.48N	97.04W
Washington, Mo., U.S.	104	38.33N	91.00W
Washington, N.C., U.S.	108	35.32N	77.01W
Washington, Pa., U.S.	92	40.10N	80.14W
Washington, state, U.S.	90	47.30N	121.10W
Washington, i., Wi., U.S.	96	45.18N	86.42W
Washington, Lake, l., Wa., U.S.	100a	47.34N	122.12W
Washington, Mount, mtn., N.H., U.S.	90	44.15N	71.15W
Washington Court House, Oh., U.S.	92	39.30N	83.25W
Washington Monument, pt. of i., D.C., U.S.	225d	38.53N	77.03W
Washington National Airport, arpt., Va., U.S.	225d	38.51N	77.02W
Washington Park, Il., U.S.	101e	38.38N	90.06W
Washita, r., Ok., U.S. (wŏsh'ĭ-tô)	104	35.33N	99.16W
Washougal, Wa., U.S. (wŏ-shōō'gȧl)	100c	45.35N	122.21W
Washougal, r., Wa., U.S.	100c	45.38N	122.17W
Wasilków, Pol. (vȧ-sēl'kóf)	148	53.12N	23.13E
Waskaiowaka Lake, l., Can. (wŏ'skă-yŏ'wŏ-kă)	82	56.30N	96.20W
Wassenberg, Ger. (vä'sĕn-bĕrgh)	151c	51.06N	6.07E
Wassmannsdorf, Ger.	234a	52.22N	13.28E
Wassuk Range, mts., Nv., U.S. (wȧs'sŭk)	102	38.58N	119.00W
Waswanipi, Lac, l., Can.	84	49.35N	76.15W
Water, i., V.I.U.S. (wô'tẽr)	111c	18.20N	64.57W
Waterberge, mts., S. Afr. (wôrtẽr'bûrg)	212d	24.25S	27.53E
Waterboro, S.C., U.S. (wô'tẽr-bûr-ō)	108	32.50N	80.40W
Waterbury, Ct., U.S. (wô'tẽr-bĕr-ė)	92	41.30N	73.00W
Water Cay, i., Bah.	116	22.55N	75.50W
Waterdown, Can. (wô'tẽr-doun)	77d	43.20N	79.54W
Wateree Lake, res., S.C., U.S. (wô'tẽr-ē)	108	34.40N	80.48W
Waterford, Ire. (wô'tẽr-fẽrd)	140	52.20N	7.03W
Waterford, Wi., U.S.	95a	42.46N	88.13W
Waterloo, Bel.	139a	50.44N	4.24E
Waterloo, Can. (wô-tẽr-lōō')	84	43.30N	80.40W
Waterloo, Can.	84	45.25N	72.30W
Waterloo, Eng., U.K.	233a	53.28N	3.02W
Waterloo, Il., U.S.	104	38.19N	90.08W
Waterloo, Ia., U.S.	90	42.30N	92.22W
Waterloo, Md., U.S.	94e	39.11N	76.50W
Waterloo, N.Y., U.S.	92	42.55N	76.50W
Waterton-Glacier International Peace Park, rec., N.A. (wô'ter-tŭn-glā'shûr)	90	48.55N	114.10W
Waterton Lakes National Park, rec., Can.	80	49.05N	113.50W
Watertown, Ma., U.S. (wô'tẽr-toun)	87a	42.22N	71.11W
Watertown, N.Y., U.S.	90	44.00N	75.55W
Watertown, S.D., U.S.	90	44.53N	97.07W
Watertown, Wi., U.S.	96	43.13N	88.40W
Water Valley, Ms., U.S. (văl'ė)	108	34.08N	89.38W
Waterville, Me., U.S.	86	44.34N	69.37W
Waterville, Mn., U.S.	96	44.10N	93.35W
Waterville, Wa., U.S.	98	47.38N	120.04W
Watervliet, N.Y., U.S. (wô'tẽr-vlēt')	92	42.45N	73.54W
Watford, Eng., U.K. (wŏt'fŏrd)	144	51.38N	0.24W
Wathaman Lake, l., Can.	82	56.55N	103.43W
Watlington, Eng., U.K.	138b	51.37N	1.01W
Watonga, Ok., U.S. (wŏ-tôŋ'gȧ)	104	35.50N	98.26W
Watsa, Zaire (wät'sä)	204	3.03N	29.32E
Watseka, Il., U.S. (wŏt-sē'kȧ)	92	40.45N	87.45W
Watson, In., U.S. (wŏt'sŭn)	95h	38.21N	85.42W
Watsonia, Austl.	239b	37.43S	145.05E
Watson Lake, Can.	78	60.18N	128.50W
Watsons Bay, Austl.	239a	33.51S	151.17E
Watsonville, Ca., U.S. (wŏt'sŭn-vĭl)	102	36.55N	121.46W
Wattenscheid, Ger. (vä'tĕn-shīd)	151c	51.30N	7.07E
Watts, Ca., U.S. (wŏts)	101a	33.56N	118.15W
Watts Bar Lake, res., Tn., U.S. (bär)	108	35.45N	84.49W
Wattville, S. Afr.	240b	26.13S	28.18E
Waubay, S.D., U.S. (wô'bā)	96	45.19N	97.18W
Wauchula, Fl., U.S. (wô-chōō'lȧ)	109a	27.32N	81.48W
Wauconda, Il., U.S. (wô-kŏn'dȧ)	95a	42.15N	88.08W
Waukegan, Il., U.S. (wô-kē'gȧn)	90	42.22N	87.51W
Waukesha, Wi., U.S. (wô'kė-shô)	95a	43.01N	88.13W
Waukon, Ia., U.S. (wô kŏn)	96	43.15N	91.30W
Waupaca, Wi., U.S. (wô-păk'ȧ)	96	44.22N	89.06W
Waupun, Wi., U.S. (wô-pŭn')	96	43.37N	88.45W
Waurika, Ok., U.S. (wô-rē'kȧ)	104	34.09N	97.59W
Wausau, Wi., U.S. (wô'sô)	90	44.58N	89.40W
Wausaukee, Wi., U.S. (wô-sô'kė)	96	45.22N	87.58W
Wauseon, Oh., U.S. (wô'sė-ŏn)	92	41.30N	84.10W
Wautoma, Wi., U.S. (wô-tō'mȧ)	96	44.04N	89.11W
Wauwatosa, Wi., U.S. (wô-wȧ-t'ŏ'sȧ)	95a	43.03N	88.00W
Waveland, Ma., U.S.	223a	42.17N	70.53W
Waveney, r., Eng., U.K. (wăv'nė)	144	52.27N	1.17E
Waverley, Austl.	239a	33.54S	151.16E
Waverly, S. Afr.	207c	31.54S	26.29E
Waverly, Ia., U.S. (wā'vẽr-lė)	96	42.43N	92.29W
Waverly, Ma., U.S.	223a	42.23N	71.11W
Waverly, Tn., U.S.	108	36.04N	87.46W

PLACE (Pronunciation)	PAGE	Lat. °′	Long. °′
Wāw, Sudan	204	7.41N	28.00E
Wawa, Can.	84	47.59N	84.47W
Wāw al-Kabīr, Libya	204	25.23N	16.52E
Wawanesa, Can. (wŏ'wŏ-nē'să)	82	49.36N	99.41W
Wawasee, l., In., U.S. (wô-wô-sē')	92	41.25N	85.45W
Waxahachie, Tx., U.S. (wăk-sȧ-hăch'ė)	106	32.23N	96.50W
Wayland, Ky., U.S. (wā'lănd)	108	37.25N	82.47W
Wayland, Ma., U.S.	87a	42.23N	71.22W
Wayne, Mi., U.S.	95b	42.17N	83.23W
Wayne, Ne., U.S.	96	42.13N	97.03W
Wayne, N.J., U.S.	94a	40.56N	74.16W
Wayne, Pa., U.S.	94f	40.03N	75.22W
Waynesboro, Ga., U.S. (wānz'bŭr-ō)	108	33.05N	82.02W
Waynesboro, Pa., U.S.	92	39.45N	77.35W
Waynesboro, Va., U.S.	92	38.05N	78.50W
Waynesburg, Pa., U.S. (wānz'bûrg)	92	39.55N	80.10W
Waynesville, N.C., U.S. (wānz'vĭl)	108	35.28N	82.58W
Waynoka, Ok., U.S. (wā-nō'kȧ)	104	36.34N	98.52W
Wayzata, Mn., U.S. (wā-zä-tȧ)	101g	44.58N	93.31W
Wazīrābād, neigh., India	236d	28.43N	77.14E
Wazirbad, Pak.	178	32.39N	74.11E
Wāzīrpur, neigh., India	236d	28.41N	77.10E
Weagamow Lake, l., Can. (wē'ăg-ă-mou)	82	52.53N	91.22W
Weald, The, reg., Eng., U.K. (wēld)	144	50.58N	0.15W
Wealdstone, neigh., Eng., U.K.	231	51.36N	0.20W
Weatherford, Ok., U.S. (wĕ-dhẽr-fẽrd)	104	85.32N	98.41W
Weatherford, Tx., U.S.	106	32.45N	97.46W
Weaver, r., Eng., U.K. (wē'vẽr)	138a	53.09N	2.31W
Weaverville, Ca., U.S. (wē'vẽr-vĭl)	98	40.44N	122.55W
Webb City, Mo., U.S.	104	37.10N	94.26W
Weber, r., Ut., U.S.	101b	41.13N	112.07W
Webster, Ma., U.S.	87a	42.04N	71.52W
Webster, S.D., U.S.	96	45.19N	97.30W
Webster City, Ia., U.S.	96	42.28N	93.49W
Webster Groves, Mo., U.S. (grōvz)	101e	38.36N	90.22W
Webster Springs, W.V., U.S. (sprĭngz)	92	38.30N	80.20W
Wedau, neigh., Ger.	232	51.24N	6.48E
Weddell Sea, sea, Ant. (wĕd'ĕl)	213	73.00S	45.00W
Wedding, neigh., Ger.	234a	52.33N	13.22E
Weddinghofen, Ger.	232	51.36N	7.37E
Wedel, Ger. (vā'dĕl)	139c	53.35N	9.42E
Wedge Mountain, mtn., Can. (wĕj)	80	50.10N	122.50W
Wedgeport, Can. (wĕj'pōrt)	86	43.44N	65.59W
Wednesfield, Eng., U.K. (wĕd''nz-fēld)	138a	52.36N	2.04W
Weed, Ca., U.S. (wēd)	98	41.35N	122.21W
Weehawken, N.J., U.S.	224	40.46N	74.01W
Weenen, S. Afr. (vā'nĕn)	207c	28.52S	30.05E
Weert, Neth.	144	51.16N	5.39E
Weesow, Ger.	234a	52.39N	13.43E
Weesp, Neth.	139a	52.18N	5.01E
Wegendorf, Ger.	234a	52.36N	13.45E
Węgorzewo, Pol. (vôŋ-gô'zhĕ-vò)	148	54.14N	21.46E
Węgrow, Pol. (vôŋ'gròf)	148	52.23N	22.02E
Wehofen, neigh., Ger.	232	51.32N	6.46E
Wehringhausen, neigh., Ger.	232	51.21N	7.27E
Wei, r., China (wā)	180	34.00N	108.10E
Wei, r., China (wā)	182	35.47N	114.27E
Weichang, China (wā-chäŋ)	180	41.50N	118.00E
Weiden, Ger.	148	49.41N	12.09E
Weidling, Aus.	235e	48.17N	16.19E
Weidlingau, neigh., Aus.	235e	48.13N	16.13E
Weidlingbach, Aus.	235e	48.16N	16.15E
Weifang, China	180	36.43N	119.08E
Weihai, China (wa'hāī')	180	37.30N	122.05E
Weilheim, Ger. (vīl'hīm')	148	47.50N	11.06E
Weimar, Ger. (vī'mȧr)	140	50.59N	11.20E
Weinan, China	184	34.32N	109.40E
Weipa, Austl.	196	12.25S	141.54E
Weir, r., Can. (wẽr-rĭv-ẽr)	82	56.49N	94.04W
Weirton, W.V., U.S.	92	40.25N	80.35W
Weiser, Id., U.S. (wē'zẽr)	98	44.15N	116.58W
Weiser, r., Id., U.S.	98	44.26N	116.40W
Weishi, China (wā-shr)	184	34.23N	114.12E
Weissenburg, Ger.	148	49.04N	11.20E
Weissenfels, Ger. (vī'sĕn-fĕlz)	148	51.13N	11.58E
Weiss Lake, res., Al., U.S.	108	34.15N	85.35W
Weitmar, neigh., Ger.	232	51.27N	7.12E
Weixi, China (wā-shyē)	180	27.27N	99.30E
Weixian, China (wā shyĕn)	182	36.59N	115.17E
Wejherowo, Pol. (vā-hĕ-rô'vò)	148	54.36N	18.15E
Welch, W.V., U.S. (wĕlch)	108	37.24N	81.28W
Welcome Monument, hist., Indon.	237k	6.11S	106.49E
Weldon, N.C., U.S. (wĕl'dŭn)	108	36.24N	77.36W
Weldon, r., Mo., U.S.	104	40.22N	93.39W
Weleetka, Ok., U.S. (wė-lēt'kȧ)	104	35.19N	96.08W
Welford, Austl. (wĕl'fẽrd)	198	25.08S	144.43E
Welhamgreen, Eng., U.K.	231	51.44N	0.13W
Welheim, neigh., Ger.	232	51.32N	6.59E
Welkom, S. Afr. (wĕl'kŏm)	206	27.57S	26.45E
Welland, Can. (wĕl'ănd)	84	42.59N	79.13W
Wellesley, Ma., U.S. (wĕlz'lė)	87a	42.18N	71.17W
Wellesley Hills, Ma., U.S.	223a	42.19N	71.17W
Wellesley Islands, is., Austl.	196	16.15S	139.25E
Well Hill, Eng., U.K.	231	51.21N	0.09E
Wellinghofen, neigh., Ger.	232	51.28N	7.29E
Wellington, Austl. (wĕl'lĭng-tŭn)	198	32.40S	148.50E
Wellington, N.Z.	197a	41.15S	174.45E
Wellington, Eng., U.K.	138a	52.42N	2.30W
Wellington, Ks., U.S.	104	37.16N	97.24W
Wellington, Oh., U.S.	92	41.10N	82.10W
Wellington, Tx., U.S.	104	34.51N	100.12W
Wellington, i., Chile (ŏĕ'lĕng-tŏn)	126	49.30S	76.30W
Wells, Can.	78	53.06N	121.34W
Wells, Mi., U.S.	92	45.50N	87.00W
Wells, Mn., U.S.	96	43.44N	93.43W

ăt; finȧl; rāte; senȧte; ärm; ȧsk; sofȧ; fâre; ch-choose; dh-as th in other; bē; ėvent; bĕt; recĕnt; cratẽr; g-gō; gh-guttural g; bĭt; ĭ-short neutral; rīde; K-guttural k as ch in German ich;

PLACE (Pronunciation)	PAGE	Lat. °'	Long. °'
Wells, Nv., U.S.	98	41.07N	115.04W
Wells, l., Austl. (wĕlz)	196	26.35S	123.40E
Wellsboro, Pa., U.S. (wĕlz'bŭ-rô)	92	41.45N	77.15W
Wellsburg, W.V., U.S. (wĕlz'bûrg)	92	40.10N	80.40W
Wells Dam, dam, Wa., U.S.	98	48.00N	119.39W
Wellston, Oh., U.S. (wĕlz'tŭn)	92	39.05N	82.30W
Wellsville, Mo., U.S. (wĕlz'vĭl)	104	39.04N	91.33W
Wellsville, N.Y., U.S.	92	42.10N	78.00W
Wellsville, Oh., U.S.	92	40.35N	80.40W
Wellsville, Ut., U.S.	98	41.38N	111.57W
Welper, Ger.	232	51.25N	7.12E
Wels, Aus. (vĕls)	140	48.10N	14.01E
Welshpool, Wales, U.K. (wĕlsh'po͞ol)	144	52.44N	3.10W
Welverdiend, S. Afr. (vĕl-vĕr-dēnd')	212d	26.23S	27.16E
Welwyn Garden City, Eng., U.K. (wĕlĭn)	138b	51.46N	0.17W
Wem, Eng., U.K. (wĕm)	138a	52.51N	2.44W
Wembere, r., Tan.	210	4.35S	33.55E
Wembley, neigh., Eng., U.K.	231	51.33N	0.18W
Wen, r., China (wŭn)	182	36.24N	119.00E
Wenan Wa, sw., China (wĕn'ăn' wä)	182	38.56N	116.29E
Wenatchee, Wa., U.S. (wê-năch'ê)	98	47.24N	120.18W
Wenatchee Mountains, mts., Wa., U.S.	98	47.28N	121.10W
Wenchang, China (wŭn-chäŋ)	184	19.32N	110.42E
Wenchi, Ghana	208	7.42N	2.07W
Wendelville, N.Y., U.S.	226a	43.04N	78.47W
Wendeng, China (wŭn-dŭŋ)	182	37.14N	122.03E
Wendo, Eth.	204	6.37N	38.29E
Wendorer, Ut., U.S.	98	40.47N	114.01W
Wendover, Can. (wĕn-dōv'ẽr)	77c	45.34N	75.07W
Wendover, Eng., U.K.	138b	51.44N	0.45W
Wengern, Ger.	232	51.24N	7.21E
Wenham, Ma., U.S. (wĕn'ăm)	87a	42.36N	70.53W
Wennington, neigh., Eng., U.K.	231	51.30N	0.13E
Wenquan, China (wŭn-chyůän)	180	47.10N	120.00E
Wenshan, China	180	23.20N	104.15E
Wenshang, China (wĕn'shäng)	182	35.43N	116.31E
Wensu, China (wĕn-sò)	180	41.45N	80.30E
Wentworth, Austl. (wĕnt'wûrth)	196	34.03S	141.53E
Wentworthville, Austl.	239a	33.49S	150.58E
Wenzhou, China (wŭn-jō)	180	28.00N	120.40E
Wepener, S. Afr. (wē'pĕn-ĕr) (vā'pĕn-ĕr)	206	29.43S	27.04E
Werden, neigh., Ger.	232	51.23N	7.00E
Werder, Ger. (vĕr'dĕr)	139b	52.23N	12.56E
Were Ilu, Eth.	204	10.39N	39.21E
Werl, Ger. (vĕrl)	151c	51.33N	7.55E
Wermelskirchen, Ger.	151c	51.08N	7.13E
Werne, neigh., Ger.	232	51.29N	7.18E
Werneuchen, Ger. (vĕr'hoi-ĸĕn)	139b	52.38N	13.44E
Wernsdorf, Ger.	234a	52.22N	13.43E
Werra, r., Ger. (vĕr'ä)	148	51.16N	9.54E
Werribee, Austl.	195a	37.54S	144.40E
Werribee, r., Austl.	195a	37.40S	144.37E
Wersten, neigh., Ger.	232	51.11N	6.49E
Wertach, r., Ger. (vĕr'täk)	148	48.12N	10.40E
Weseke, Ger. (vĕ'zĕ-kĕ)	151c	51.54N	6.51E
Wesel, Ger. (vā'zĕl)	151c	51.39N	6.37E
Weser, r., Ger. (vā'zĕr)	136	51.00N	10.30E
Weslaco, Tx., U.S. (wĕs-lā'kō)	106	26.10N	97.59W
Weslemkoon, l., Can.	84	45.02N	77.25W
Wesleyville, Can. (wĕs'lē-vĭl)	86	49.09N	53.34W
Wessel Islands, is., Austl. (wĕs'ĕl)	196	11.45S	136.25E
Wesselsbron, S. Afr. (wĕs'ĕl-brŏn)	212d	27.51S	26.22E
Wessington Springs, S.D., U.S. (wĕs'ĭng-tŭn)	96	44.06N	98.35W
West, Mount, mtn., Pan.	110a	9.10N	79.52W
West Abington, Ma., U.S.	223a	42.08N	70.59W
West Allis, Wi., U.S. (wĕst-ăl'ĭs)	95a	43.01N	88.01W
West Alton, Mo., U.S. (ôl'tŭn)	101e	38.52N	90.13W
West Athens, Ca., U.S.	228	33.55N	118.18W
West Bay, b., Fl., U.S.	108	30.20N	85.45W
West Bay, b., Tx., U.S.	107a	29.11N	95.03W
West Bend, Wi., U.S. (wĕst bĕnd)	96	43.25N	88.13W
West Bengal, state, India (bĕn-gôl')	174	23.30N	87.30E
West Blocton, Al., U.S. (blŏk'tŭn)	108	33.05N	87.05W
Westborough, Ma., U.S. (wĕst'bŭr-ô)	87a	42.17N	71.37W
West Boylston, Ma., U.S. (boil'stŭn)	87a	42.22N	71.46W
West Branch, Mi., U.S. (wĕst brȧnch)	92	44.15N	84.10W
West Bridgford, Eng., U.K. (brĭj'fĕrd)	138a	52.55N	1.08W
West Bromwich, Eng., U.K. (wĕst brŭm'ĭj)	138a	52.32N	1.59W
Westbrook, Me., U.S. (wĕst'bro͝ok)	86	43.41N	70.23W
Westbury, N.Y., U.S.	224	40.45N	73.35W
Westby, Wi., U.S. (wĕst'bē)	96	43.40N	90.52W
West Caicos, i., T./C. Is. (kä'ē'kō) (kī'kōs)	116	21.40N	72.30W
West Caldwell, N.J., U.S.	224	40.51N	74.17W
West Cape Howe, c., Austl.	196	35.15S	117.30E
West Carson, Ca., U.S.	228	33.50N	118.18W
Westchester, Il., U.S.	227a	41.51N	87.53W
West Chester, Oh., U.S. (chĕs'tĕr)	95f	39.20N	84.24W
West Chester, Pa., U.S.	94f	39.57N	75.36W
Westchester, neigh., Ca., U.S.	228	33.55N	118.25W
Westchester, neigh., N.Y., U.S.	224	40.51N	73.52W
West Chicago, Il., U.S. (chĭ-kȧ'gō)	95a	41.53N	88.12W
West Collingswood, N.J., U.S.	225b	39.54N	75.06W
West Columbia, S.C., U.S. (cŏl'ŭm-bē-ȧ)	108	33.58N	81.05W
West Columbia, Tx., U.S.	106	29.08N	95.39W
West Conshohocken, N.J., U.S.	225b	40.04N	75.19W
West Cote Blanche Bay, b., La., U.S.	106	29.30N	92.17W
West Covina, Ca., U.S. (wĕst kō-vē'nȧ)	101a	34.04N	117.55W
Westdale, Il., U.S.	227a	41.56N	87.55W
West Derby, neigh., Eng., U.K.	233a	53.26N	2.54W
West Des Moines, Ia., U.S. (dē moin')	96	41.35N	93.42W
West Des Moines, r., Ia., U.S.	96	42.52N	94.32W
West Drayton, neigh., Eng., U.K.	231	51.30N	0.29W
West Elizabeth, Pa., U.S.	226b	40.17N	79.54W
West End, Bah.	116	26.40N	78.55W
West End, Eng., U.K.	231	51.44N	0.04W
West End, neigh., Eng., U.K.	231	51.32N	0.24W
West End, neigh., Pa., U.S.	226b	40.27N	80.02W
Westende, Ger.	232	51.25N	7.24E
Westenfeld, neigh., Ger.	232	51.28N	7.09E
Westerbauer, neigh., Ger.	232	51.20N	7.23E
Westerham, Eng., U.K. (wĕ'stẽr'ŭm)	138b	51.15N	0.05E
Westerholt, Ger.	232	51.36N	7.05E
Westerhörn, Ger. (vĕs'tĕr-hōrn)	139c	53.52N	9.41E
Westerlo, Bel.	139a	51.05N	4.57E
Westerly, R.I., U.S. (wĕs'tĕr-lē)	92	41.25N	71.50W
Western Australia, state, Austl. (ôs-trā'lĭ-ȧ)	196	24.15S	121.30E
Western Dvina, see Zapadnaya Dvina, r., Eur.	146	55.30N	28.27E
Western Ghāts, mts., India	174	17.35N	74.00E
Western Port, Md., U.S. (wĕs'tĕrn pōrt)	92	39.30N	79.00W
Western Sahara, dep., Afr. (sȧ-hä'rȧ)	204	23.05N	15.33W
Western Samoa, nation, Oc.	2	14.30S	172.00W
Western Siberian Lowland, depr., Russia	158	63.37N	72.45E
Western Springs, Il., U.S.	227a	41.47N	87.53W
Westerville, Oh., U.S. (wĕs'tĕr-vĭl)	92	40.10N	83.00W
Westerwald, for., Ger. (vĕs'tĕr-väld)	148	50.35N	7.45E
Westfalenhalle, pt. of i., Ger.	232	51.30N	7.27E
Westfield, Ma., U.S. (wĕst'fēld)	92	42.05N	72.45W
Westfield, N.J., U.S.	94a	40.39N	74.21W
Westfield, N.Y., U.S. (wĕst'fēld)	94a	42.20N	79.40W
Westford, Ma., U.S. (wĕst'fĕrd)	87a	42.35N	71.26W
West Frankfort, Il., U.S. (frăŋk'fŭrt)	92	37.55N	88.55W
West Ham, Eng., U.K.	138b	51.30N	0.00W
West Hanover, Ma., U.S.	223a	42.07N	70.53W
West Hartford, Ct., U.S. (härt'fĕrd)	92	41.45N	72.45W
Westhead, Eng., U.K.	233a	53.34N	2.51W
West Heidelberg, Austl.	239b	37.45S	145.02E
West Helena, Ar., U.S. (hĕl'ĕn-ȧ)	104	34.32N	90.39W
West Hempstead, N.Y., U.S.	224	40.42N	73.39W
Westhofen, Ger.	232	51.25N	7.31E
West Hollywood, Ca., U.S.	228	34.05N	118.24W
West Homestead, Pa., U.S.	226b	40.24N	79.55W
West Horndon, Eng., U.K.	231	51.34N	0.21E
West Hoxton, Austl.	239a	33.55S	150.50E
West Hyde, Eng., U.K.	231	51.37N	0.30W
Westick, Ger.	232	51.35N	7.38E
West Indies, is. (ĭn'dēz)	110	19.00N	78.30W
West Jordon, Ut., U.S. (jôr'dŭn)	101b	40.37N	111.56W
West Kirby, Eng., U.K. (kûr'bē)	138a	53.22N	3.11W
West Lafayette, In., U.S. (lä-fā-yĕt')	92	40.25N	86.55W
Westlake, Oh., U.S.	95d	41.27N	81.55W
Westland, Mi., U.S.	226c	42.19N	83.23W
West Lawn, Va., U.S.	225d	38.52N	77.11W
Westleigh, S. Afr. (wĕst-lē)	212d	27.39S	27.18E
West Liberty, Ia., U.S. (wĕst lĭb'ĕr-tĭ)	96	41.34N	91.15W
West Liberty, neigh., Pa., U.S.	226b	40.24N	80.01W
West Linn, Or., U.S. (lĭn)	100c	45.22N	122.37W
Westlock, Can. (wĕst'lŏk)	80	54.09N	113.52W
West Los Angeles, neigh., Ca., U.S.	228	34.03N	118.28W
West Malling, Eng., U.K.	231	51.18N	0.25E
West Manayunk, Pa., U.S.	225b	40.01N	75.14W
West Memphis, Ar., U.S.	104	35.08N	90.11W
West Midlands, co., Eng., U.K.	138a	52.26N	1.50W
West Mifflin, Pa., U.S.	226b	40.22N	79.52W
Westminster, Ca., U.S. (wĕst'min-stẽr)	101a	33.45N	117.59W
Westminster, Md., U.S.	92	39.40N	76.55W
Westminster, S.C., U.S.	108	34.38N	83.10W
Westminster Abbey, pt. of i., Eng., U.K.	231	51.30N	0.07W
Westmont, Ca., U.S.	228	33.56N	118.18W
Westmount, Can. (wĕst'mount)	77a	45.29N	73.36W
West Newbury, Ma., U.S. (nū'bĕr-ē)	87a	42.47N	70.57W
West Newton, Ma., U.S.	223a	42.21N	71.14W
West Newton, Pa., U.S. (nū'tŭn)	95e	40.12N	79.45W
West New York, N.J., U.S. (nů yôrk)	94a	40.47N	74.01W
West Nishnabotna, r., Ia., U.S. (nĭsh-nȧ-bŏt'nȧ)	96	40.56N	95.37W
West Norwood, neigh., Eng., U.K.	231	51.26N	0.06W
Weston, Ma., U.S. (wĕs'tŭn)	87a	42.22N	71.18W
Weston, W.V., U.S.	92	39.00N	80.30W
Westonaria, S. Afr.	212d	26.19S	27.38E
Weston-super-Mare, Eng., U.K. (wĕs'tŭn sū'pẽr-mā'rē)	144	51.23N	3.00W
West Orange, N.J., U.S. (wĕst ŏr'ĕnj)	94a	40.46N	74.14W
West Palm Beach, Fl., U.S. (päm bēch)	90	26.44N	80.04W
West Peabody, Ma., U.S.	223a	42.30N	70.57W
West Pensacola, Fl., U.S. (pĕn-sȧ-kō'lȧ)	108	30.24N	87.18W
West Pittsburg, Ca., U.S. (pĭts'bûrg)	100b	38.02N	121.56W
Westplains, Mo., U.S. (wĕst-plānz')	104	36.42N	91.51W
West Point, Ga., U.S.	108	32.52N	85.10W
West Point, Ms., U.S.	108	33.36N	88.39W
Westpoint, Ne., U.S.	96	41.50N	96.00W
West Point, N.Y., U.S.	94a	41.23N	73.58W
West Point, Ut., U.S.	101b	41.07N	112.05W
West Point, Va., U.S.	92	37.25N	76.50W
West Point Lake, res., U.S.	108	33.00N	85.10W
Westport, Ire.	144	53.44N	9.36W
Westport, Ct., U.S. (wĕst'pōrt)	94a	41.07N	73.22W
Westport, Or., U.S. (wĕst'pōrt)	100c	46.08N	123.22W
West Puente Valley, Ca., U.S.	228	34.04N	117.59W
West Pymble, Austl.	239a	33.46S	151.08E
Westray, i., Scot., U.K. (wĕs'trā)	144a	59.19N	3.05W
West Road, r., Can. (rōd)	80	53.00N	124.00W
West Ryde, Austl.	239a	33.48S	151.05E
West Saint Paul, Mn., U.S. (sånt pôl')	101g	44.55N	93.05W
West Sand Spit, i., T./C. Is.	116	21.25N	72.10W
West Seneca, N.Y., U.S.	226a	42.50N	78.45W
West Slope, Or., U.S.	100c	45.30N	122.46W
West Somerville, Ma., U.S.	223a	42.24N	71.07W
West Tavaputs Plateau, plat., Ut., U.S. (wĕst tăv'ȧ-pŏts)	102	39.45N	110.35W
West Terre Haute, In., U.S. (tĕr-ê hōt')	92	39.30N	87.30W
West Thurrock, Eng., U.K.	231	51.29N	0.16E
West Tilbury, Eng., U.K.	231	51.29N	0.24E
West Turffontein, neigh., S. Afr.	240b	26.16S	28.02E
West Union, Ia., U.S. (ūn'yŭn)	96	42.58N	91.48W
West University Place, Tx., U.S.	107a	29.43N	95.26W
Westview, Oh., U.S. (wĕst'vů)	95d	41.21N	81.54W
West View, Pa., U.S.	95e	40.31N	80.02W
Westville, Can. (wĕst'vĭl)	86	45.35N	62.43W
Westville, Il., U.S.	92	40.00N	87.40W
Westville, N.J., U.S.	225b	39.52N	75.08W
Westville Grove, N.J., U.S.	225b	39.51N	75.07W
West Virginia, state, U.S. (wĕst vẽr-jĭn'ĭ-ȧ)	90	39.00N	80.50W
West Walker, r., Ca., U.S. (wôk'ẽr)	102	38.25N	119.25W
West Warwick, R.I., U.S. (wŏr'ĭk)	94b	41.42N	71.31W
Westwego, La., U.S. (wĕst-wē'gō)	94d	29.55N	90.09W
West Whittier, Ca., U.S.	228	33.59N	118.04W
West Wickham, neigh., Eng., U.K.	231	51.22N	0.01W
Westwood, Ca., U.S. (wĕst'wo͝od)	102	40.18N	121.00W
Westwood, Ks., U.S.	101f	39.03N	94.37W
Westwood, Ma., U.S.	87a	42.13N	71.14W
Westwood, N.J., U.S.	94a	40.59N	74.02W
Westwood, neigh., Ca., U.S.	228	34.04N	118.27W
West Wyalong, Austl. (wī'ălông)	196	34.00S	147.20E
West Yorkshire, co., Eng., U.K.	138a	53.37N	1.48W
Wetar, Pulau, i., Indon. (wĕt'ár)	188	7.34S	126.00E
Wetaskiwin, Can. (wĕ-tăs'kê-wŏn)	78	52.58N	113.22W
Wetherill Park, Austl.	239a	33.51S	150.54E
Wethmar, Ger.	232	51.37N	7.33E
Wetmore, Tx., U.S. (wĕt'mōr)	101d	29.34N	98.25W
Wetter, Ger.	151c	51.23N	7.23E
Wetumpka, Al., U.S. (wê-tŭmp'kȧ)	108	32.33N	86.12W
Wetzlar, Ger. (vets'lär)	148	50.35N	8.30E
Wewak, Pap. N. Gui. (wȧ-wäk')	188	3.19S	143.30E
Wewoka, Ok., U.S. (wê-wō'kȧ)	104	35.09N	96.30W
Wexford, Ire. (wĕks'fĕrd)	140	52.20N	6.30W
Weybridge, Eng., U.K. (wā'brĭj)	138b	51.20N	0.26W
Weyburn, Can. (wā'bûrn)	78	49.41N	103.52W
Weyer, neigh., Ger.	232	51.10N	7.01E
Weymouth, Eng., U.K. (wā'mŭth)	144	50.37N	2.34W
Weymouth, Ma., U.S.	87a	42.44N	70.57W
Weymouth, Oh., U.S.	95d	41.11N	81.48W
Whalan, Austl.	239a	33.45S	150.49E
Whale Cay, i., Bah.	116	25.20N	77.45W
Whale Cay Channels, strt., Bah.	116	26.45N	77.10W
Wharton, N.J., U.S. (hwôr'tŭn)	94a	40.54N	74.35W
Wharton, Tx., U.S.	106	29.19N	96.06W
What Cheer, Ia., U.S. (hwŏt chēr)	96	41.23N	92.24W
Whatcom, Lake, l., Wa., U.S. (hwät'kŭm)	100c	48.44N	123.34W
Whatshan Lake, l., Can. (wŏt'shăn)	80	50.00N	118.03W
Wheatland, Wy., U.S. (hwēt'lănd)	98	42.04N	104.52W
Wheatland Reservoir Number 2, res., Wy., U.S.	98	41.52N	105.36W
Wheaton, Il., U.S. (hwē'tŭn)	95a	41.52N	88.06W
Wheaton, Md., U.S.	94e	39.05N	77.05W
Wheaton, Mn., U.S.	96	45.48N	96.29W
Wheeler Peak, mtn., Nv., U.S.	90	38.58N	114.15W
Wheeling, Il., U.S. (hwēl'ĭng)	95a	42.08N	87.54W
Wheeling, W.V., U.S.	92	40.05N	80.45W
Wheelwright, Arg. (ôē'l-rē'gt)	123c	33.46S	61.14W
Whelpleyhill, Eng., U.K.	231	51.44N	0.33W
Whidbey Island, i., Wa., U.S. (hwĭd'bē)	100a	48.13N	122.50W
Whippany, N.J., U.S. (hwĭp'ȧ-nē)	94a	40.49N	74.25W
Whiston, Eng., U.K.	233a	53.25N	2.50W
Whitaker, Pa., U.S.	226b	40.24N	79.53W
Whitby, Can. (hwĭt'bē)	78	43.50N	79.00W
Whitby, Eng., U.K.	233a	53.17N	2.54W
Whitchurch, Eng., U.K. (hwĭt'chûrch)	138a	52.58N	2.49W
White, l., Can.	84	45.15N	76.35W
White, l., Can.	84	48.47N	85.50W
White, r., Can.	84	48.34N	85.46W
White, r., U.S.	90	35.30N	92.00W
White, r., U.S.	96	43.41N	99.48W
White, r., U.S.	102	40.10N	108.55W
White, r., In., U.S.	92	39.15N	86.45W
White, r., S.D., U.S.	96	43.13N	101.04W
White, r., Tx., U.S.	104	36.25N	102.20W
White, r., Vt., U.S.	92	43.45N	72.35W
White, r., Wa., U.S.	98	47.07N	121.48W
White, East Fork, r., In., U.S.	92	38.45N	86.20W
White Bay, b., Can.	79a	50.00N	56.30W
White Bear Indian Reserve, I.R., Can.	82	49.50N	102.15W
White Bear Lake, l., Mn., U.S.	101g	45.04N	92.58W
White Castle, La., U.S.	106	30.10N	91.09W
White Center, Wa., U.S.	100a	47.31N	122.21W
White Cloud, Mi., U.S.	92	43.35N	85.45W
Whitecourt, Can. (wĭt'cōrt)	78	54.09N	115.41W
White Earth, r., N.D., U.S.	96	48.30N	102.44W
White Earth Indian Reservation, I.R., Mn., U.S.	96	47.18N	95.42W
Whiteface, r., Mn., U.S. (whīt'fās)	96	47.12N	92.13W
Whitefield, Eng., U.K.	233b	53.33N	2.18W
Whitefield, N.H., U.S. (hwĭt'fēld)	92	44.20N	71.35W
Whitefish Bay, Wi., U.S.	95a	43.07N	77.54W
Whitefish Bay, b., Can.	82	49.26N	94.14W
Whitefish Bay, b., N.A.	96	46.36N	84.50W
White Hall, Il., U.S.	104	39.26N	90.23W
Whitehall, Mi., U.S. (hwĭt'hôl)	92	43.20N	86.20W

ng-sing; ŋ-baŋk; ɴ-nasalized n; nŏd; cŏmmit; ōld; ôbey; ôrder; oi-boil; fo͞od; ŏŏ-as oo in foot; ou-out; s-soft; sh-dish; th-thin; pūre; ûnite; ûrn; stŭd; circŭs; ü-as in French tu; '-indeterminate vowel.

PLACE (Pronunciation)	PAGE	Lat. °′	Long. °′
Whitehall, N.Y., U.S.	92	43.30N	73.25W
Whitehall, Pa., U.S.	226b	40.22N	79.59W
Whitehaven, Eng., U.K. (hwīt'hā-vĕn)	144	54.35N	3.30W
Whitehead, Ma., U.S.	223a	42.17N	70.52W
Whitehorn, Point, c., Wa., U.S. (hwīt'hôrn)	100d	48.54N	122.48W
Whitehorse, Can. (whīt'hôrs)	78	60.39N	135.01W
White House, pt. of i., D.C., U.S.	225d	38.54N	77.02W
White Lake, l., La., U.S.	106	29.40N	92.35W
Whiteley Village, Eng., U.K.	231	51.21N	0.26W
Whiteman, Ma., U.S.	223a	42.05N	70.56W
Whitemarsh, Pa., U.S.	225b	40.07N	75.13W
White Mountain Peak, mtn., Ca., U.S.	102	37.38N	118.13W
White Mountains, mts., Me., U.S.	86	44.22N	71.15W
White Mountains, mts., N.H., U.S.	92	42.20N	71.05W
Whitemouth, l., Can.	82	49.14N	95.40W
White Nile (Al Bahr al Abyad), r., Sudan	204	12.30N	32.30E
White Oak, Pa., U.S.	226b	40.21N	79.48W
White Otter, l., Can.	84	49.15N	91.48W
White Pass, p., N.A.	89	59.35N	135.03W
White Plains, N.Y., U.S.	94a	41.02N	73.47W
White River, Can.	84	48.38N	85.23W
White Rock, Can.	80	49.01N	122.49W
Whiterock Reservoir, res., Tx., U.S. (hwīt'rŏk)	101c	32.51N	96.40W
Whitesail Lake, l., Can. (whīt'sāl)	80	53.30N	127.00W
White Sands National Monument, rec., N.M., U.S.	102	32.50N	106.20W
White Sea, sea, Russia	158	66.00N	40.00E
White Settlement, Tx., U.S.	101c	32.45N	97.28W
Whitestone, neigh., N.Y., U.S.	224	40.47N	73.49W
White Sulphur Springs, Mt., U.S.	98	46.32N	110.49W
White Umfolzi, r., S. Afr. (ŭm-fō-lō'zē)	207c	28.12S	30.55E
Whiteville, N.C., U.S. (hwīt'vĭl)	108	34.18N	78.45W
White Volta (Volta Blanche), r., Afr.	208	9.40N	1.10W
Whitewater, Wi., U.S. (whīt-wŏt'ēr)	96	42.49N	88.40W
Whitewater, l., Can.	82	49.14N	100.39W
Whitewater, r., In., U.S.	95f	39.19N	84.55W
Whitewater Bay, b., Fl., U.S.	109a	25.16N	80.21W
Whitewater Creek, r., Mt., U.S.	98	48.50N	107.50W
Whitewell, Tn., U.S. (hwĭt'wĕl)	108	35.11N	85.31W
Whitewright, Tx., U.S. (hwīt'rīt)	104	33.33N	96.25W
Whitham, r., Eng., U.K. (wĭth'ŭm)	138a	53.08N	0.15W
Whiting, In., U.S. (hwīt'ĭng)	95a	41.41N	87.30W
Whitinsville, Ma., U.S. (hwīt'ĕns-vĭl)	87a	42.06N	71.40W
Whitman, Ma., U.S. (hwĭt'măn)	87a	42.05N	70.57W
Whitmire, S.C., U.S. (hwĭt'mīr)	108	34.30N	81.40W
Whitney, Mount, mtn., Ca., U.S.	90	36.34N	118.18W
Whitney Lake, l., Tx., U.S. (hwĭt'nē)	106	32.02N	97.36W
Whitstable, Eng., U.K. (wĭt'stăb'l)	138b	51.22N	1.03E
Whitsunday, i., Austl. (hwĭt's'n-dā)	196	20.16S	149.00E
Whittier, Ca., U.S. (hwĭt'ĭ-ēr)	101a	33.58N	118.02W
Whittier South, Ca., U.S.	228	33.57N	118.01W
Whittlesea, Ciskei (wĭt'l'sē)	207c	32.11S	26.51E
Whitworth, Eng., U.K. (hwĭt'wŭrth)	138a	53.40N	2.10W
Whyalla, Austl. (hwī-ăl'ȧ)	196	33.00S	137.32E
Whymper, Mount, mtn., Can. (wĭm'pēr)	80	48.57N	124.10W
Wiarton, Can. (wī'ăr-tŭn)	78	44.45N	80.45W
Wichita, Ks., U.S. (wĭch'ĭ-tô)	90	37.42N	97.21W
Wichita, r., Tx., U.S.	104	33.50N	99.38W
Wichita Falls, Tx., U.S. (fôls)	90	33.54N	98.29W
Wichita Mountains, mts., Ok., U.S.	90	34.48N	98.43W
Wichlinghofen, neigh., Ger.	232	51.27N	7.30E
Wick, Scot., U.K. (wĭk)	140	58.25N	3.05W
Wickatunk, N.J., U.S. (wĭk'á-tŭnk)	94a	40.21N	74.15W
Wickede, neigh., Ger.	232	51.32N	7.37E
Wickenburg, Az., U.S.	102	33.58N	112.44W
Wickiup Reservoir, res., Or., U.S.	98	43.40N	121.43W
Wickliffe, Oh., U.S. (wĭk'klĭf)	95d	41.37N	81.29W
Wicklow, Ire.	144	52.59N	6.06W
Wicklow Mountains, mts., Ire. (wĭk'lō)	144	52.49N	6.20W
Wickup Mountain, mtn., Or., U.S. (wĭk'ŭp)	100c	46.06N	123.35W
Wiconisco, Pa., U.S. (wĭ-kon'ĭs-kō)	92	43.35N	76.45W
Widen, W.V., U.S. (wī'dĕn)	92	38.25N	80.55W
Widnes, Eng., U.K. (wĭd'nĕs)	138a	53.21N	2.44W
Wieliczka, Pol. (vyĕ-lēch'kȧ)	148	49.58N	20.06E
Wiemelhausen, neigh., Ger.	232	51.28N	7.13E
Wien, prov., Aus.	139e	48.11N	16.23E
Wiener Berg, Aus.	235e	48.10N	16.22E
Wiener Neustadt, Aus. (vē'nĕr noi'shtät)	140	47.48N	16.15E
Wiener Wald, for., Aus.	139e	48.09N	16.05E
Wien, *see* Vienna, Aus.	136	48.13N	16.22E
Wieprz, r., Pol. (vyĕpzh)	148	51.25N	22.45E
Wiergate, Tx., U.S. (wēr'gāt)	106	31.00N	93.42W
Wiesbaden, Ger. (vēs'bä-dĕn)	140	50.05N	8.15E
Wigan, Eng., U.K. (wĭg'ăn)	144	53.33N	2.37W
Wiggins, Ms., U.S. (wĭg'ĭnz)	108	30.51N	89.05W
Wight, Isle of, i., Eng., U.K. (wīt)	144	50.44N	1.17W
Wilber, Ne., U.S. (wĭl'bēr)	104	40.29N	96.57W
Wilburton, Ok., U.S. (wĭl'bēr-tŭn)	104	34.54N	95.18W
Wilcannia, Austl. (wĭl-cān-ĭȧ)	196	31.30S	143.30E
Wildau, Ger. (vēl'dou)	139b	52.20N	13.39E
Wildberg, Ger. (vēl'bĕrgh)	139b	52.52N	12.39E
Wildcat Hill, hill, Can. (wīld'kăt)	82	53.17N	102.30W
Wildercroft, Md., U.S.	225d	38.58N	76.53W
Wildhay, r., Can. (wīld'hā)	80	53.15N	117.20W
Wildomar, Ca., U.S. (wĭl'dō-mär)	101a	33.35N	117.17W
Wild Rice, r., Mn., U.S.	96	47.10N	96.40W
Wild Rice, r., N.D., U.S.	96	46.10N	97.12W
Wild Rice Lake, l., Mn., U.S.	101h	46.54N	92.10W
Wildspitze, mtn., Aus.	148	46.55N	10.50E
Wildwood, N.J., U.S.	92	39.00N	74.50W
Wildwood Manor, Md., U.S.	225d	39.01N	77.07W
Wiley, Co., U.S. (wī'lē)	104	38.08N	102.41W

PLACE (Pronunciation)	PAGE	Lat. °′	Long. °′
Wilge, r., S. Afr. (wĭl'jĕ)	212d	25.38S	29.09E
Wilge, r., S. Afr.	212d	27.27S	28.46E
Wilhelm, Mount, mtn., Pap. N. Gui.	188	5.58S	144.58E
Wilhelmina Gebergte, mts., Sur.	124	4.30N	57.00W
Wilhelmina Kanaal, can., Neth.	139a	51.37N	4.55E
Wilhelmshaven, Ger. (vēl-hĕlms-hä'fĕn)	140	53.30N	8.10E
Wilhelmstadt, neigh., Ger.	234a	52.31N	13.11E
Wilkes-Barre, Pa., U.S. (wĭlks'băr-ē)	90	41.15N	75.50W
Wilkes Land, reg., Ant.	213	71.00S	126.00E
Wilkeson, Wa., U.S. (wĭl-kē'sŭn)	100a	47.06N	122.03W
Wilkie, Can. (wĭlk'ē)	78	52.25N	108.43W
Wilkinsburg, Pa., U.S. (wĭl'kĭnz-bûrg)	95e	40.26N	79.53W
Wilkins Township, Pa., U.S.	226b	40.25N	79.50W
Willamette, r., Or., U.S.	90	45.00N	123.00W
Willapa Bay, b., Wa., U.S.	98	46.37N	124.00W
Willard, Oh., U.S. (wĭl'ȧrd)	92	41.00N	82.50W
Willard, Ut., U.S.	101b	41.24N	112.02W
Willaston, Eng., U.K.	233a	53.18N	3.00W
Willcox, Az., U.S. (wĭl'kŏks)	102	32.15N	109.50W
Willcox Playa, l., Az., U.S.	102	32.08N	109.51W
Willemstad, Neth. Ant.	124	12.12N	68.58W
Willesden, Eng., U.K. (wĭlz'dĕn)	138b	51.31N	0.17W
William "Bill" Dannelly Reservoir, res., Al., U.S.	108	32.10N	87.15W
William Creek, Austl. (wĭl'yăm)	196	28.45S	136.20E
Williams, Az., U.S. (wĭl'yămz)	102	35.15N	112.15W
Williams, i., Bah.	116	24.30N	78.30W
Williamsburg, Ky., U.S. (wĭl'yămz-bûrg)	108	36.42N	84.09W
Williamsburg, Oh., U.S.	95f	39.04N	84.02W
Williamsburg, Va., U.S.	108	37.15N	76.41W
Williamsburg, neigh., N.Y., U.S.	224	40.42N	73.57W
Williams Lake, Can.	80	52.08N	122.09W
Williamson, W.V., U.S. (wĭl'yăm-sŭn)	92	37.40N	82.15W
Williamsport, Md., U.S.	92	39.35N	77.45W
Williamsport, Pa., U.S.	92	41.15N	77.05W
Williamston, N.C., U.S. (wĭl'yămz-tŭn)	108	35.50N	77.04W
Williamston, S.C., U.S.	108	34.36N	82.30W
Williamstown, Austl.	195a	37.52S	144.54E
Williamstown, W.V., U.S. (wĭl'yămz-toun)	92	39.20N	81.30W
Williamsville, N.Y., U.S. (wĭl'yăm-vĭl)	95c	42.58N	78.46W
Willich, Ger.	232	51.16N	6.33E
Willimantic, Ct., U.S. (wĭl-ĭ-măn'tĭk)	92	41.40N	72.10W
Willingale, Eng., U.K.	231	51.44N	0.19E
Willis, Tx., U.S. (wĭl'ĭs)	106	30.24N	95.29W
Willis Islands, is., Austl.	196	16.15S	150.30E
Williston, N.D., U.S. (wĭl'ĭs-tŭn)	90	48.08N	103.38W
Williston, Lake, l., Can.	78	55.40N	123.40W
Williston Park, N.Y., U.S.	224	40.45N	73.39W
Willmar, Mn., U.S. (wĭl'mär)	96	45.07N	95.05W
Willmersdorf, Ger.	234a	52.40N	13.41E
Willoughby, Austl.	239a	33.48S	151.12E
Willoughby, Oh., U.S. (wĭl'ō-bē)	95d	41.39N	81.25W
Willow, Ak., U.S.	89	61.50N	150.00W
Willow Brook, Ca., U.S.	228	33.55N	118.14W
Willow Creek, r., Or., U.S.	98	44.21N	117.34W
Willow Grove, Pa., U.S.	94f	40.07N	75.07W
Willowick, Oh., U.S. (wĭl'ō-wĭk)	95d	41.39N	81.28W
Willowmore, S. Afr. (wĭl'ō-môr)	206	33.15S	23.37E
Willow Run, Mi., U.S. (wĭl'ō rŭn)	95b	42.16N	83.34W
Willow Run, Va., U.S.	225d	38.49N	77.10W
Willows, Ca., U.S. (wĭl'ōz)	102	39.32N	122.11W
Willow Springs, Il., U.S.	227a	41.44N	87.52W
Willow Springs, Mo., U.S. (sprĭngz)	104	36.59N	91.56W
Willowvale, Transkei (wĭ-lō'vāl)	207c	32.17S	28.32E
Wills Point, Tx., U.S. (wĭlz point)	106	32.42N	96.02W
Wilmer, Tx., U.S. (wĭl'mēr)	101c	32.35N	96.40W
Wilmette, Il., U.S. (wĭl-mĕt')	95a	42.04N	87.42W
Wilmington, Austl.	198	32.39S	138.07E
Wilmington, Eng., U.K.	231	51.26N	0.12E
Wilmington, Ca., U.S. (wĭl'mĭng-tŭn)	101a	33.46N	118.16W
Wilmington, De., U.S.	90	39.45N	75.33W
Wilmington, Il., U.S.	95a	41.19N	88.09W
Wilmington, Ma., U.S.	87a	42.34N	71.10W
Wilmington, N.C., U.S.	90	34.12N	77.56W
Wilmington, Oh., U.S.	92	39.20N	83.50W
Wilmore, Ky., U.S. (wĭl'mōr)	92	37.50N	84.35W
Wilmslow, Eng., U.K. (wĭlmz'lō)	138a	53.19N	2.14W
Wilno, *see* Vilnius, Lith.	158	54.40N	25.26E
Wilpoort, S. Afr.	212d	26.57S	26.17E
Wilson, Ar., U.S. (wĭl'sŭn)	104	35.35N	90.02W
Wilson, N.C., U.S.	108	35.42N	77.55W
Wilson, Ok., U.S.	104	34.09N	97.27W
Wilson, r., Al., U.S.	108	34.53N	87.28W
Wilson, Mount, mtn., Ca., U.S.	101a	34.15N	118.06W
Wilson, Point, c., Austl.	195a	38.05S	144.31E
Wilson Lake, res., Al., U.S.	90	34.45N	87.30W
Wilson's Promontory, pen., Austl. (wĭl'sŭnz)	196	39.05S	146.50E
Wilsonville, Il., U.S. (wĭl'sŭn-vĭl)	101e	39.04N	89.52W
Wilstedt, Ger. (vēl'shtĕt)	139c	53.45N	10.04E
Wilster, Ger. (vēl'stĕr)	139c	53.55N	9.23E
Wilton, Ct., U.S. (wĭl'tŭn)	94a	41.11N	73.25W
Wilton, N.D., U.S.	96	47.09N	100.47W
Wilton Woods, Va., U.S.	225d	38.47N	77.06W
Wiluna, Austl. (wĭ-lōō'nȧ)	196	26.35S	120.25E
Wimbledon, neigh., Eng., U.K.	231	51.25N	0.12W
Wimbledon Common, pt. of i., Eng., U.K.	231	51.26N	0.14W
Winamac, In., U.S. (wĭn'ȧ măk)	92	41.05N	86.40W
Winburg, S. Afr. (wĭm-bûrg)	212d	28.31S	27.02E
Winchester, Eng., U.K.	144	51.04N	1.20W
Winchester, Ca., U.S. (wĭn'chĕs-tēr)	101a	33.41N	117.06W
Winchester, Id., U.S.	98	46.14N	116.39W
Winchester, In., U.S.	92	40.10N	84.50W

PLACE (Pronunciation)	PAGE	Lat. °′	Long. °′
Winchester, Ky., U.S.	92	38.00N	84.15W
Winchester, Ma., U.S.	87a	42.28N	71.09W
Winchester, N.H., U.S.	92	42.45N	72.25W
Winchester, Tn., U.S.	108	35.11N	86.06W
Winchester, Va., U.S.	92	39.10N	78.10W
Wind, r., Wy., U.S.	98	43.17N	109.02W
Windber, Pa., U.S. (wĭnd'bēr)	92	40.15N	78.45W
Wind Cave National Park, rec., S.D., U.S.	96	43.36N	103.53W
Winder, Ga., U.S. (wīn'dēr)	108	33.58N	83.43W
Windermere, Eng., U.K. (wĭn'dēr-mēr)	144	54.25N	2.59W
Windham, Ct., U.S. (wĭnd'ăm)	92	41.45N	72.05W
Windham, N.H., U.S.	87a	42.49N	71.21W
Windhoek, Nmb. (vĭnt'hŏk)	206	22.05S	17.10E
Wind Lake, l., Wi., U.S.	95a	42.49N	88.06W
Wind Mountain, mtn., N.M., U.S.	106	32.02N	105.30W
Windom, Mn., U.S. (wĭn'dŭm)	96	43.50N	95.04W
Windora, Austl. (wĭn-dō'rȧ)	196	25.15S	142.50E
Wind River Indian Reservation, I.R., Wy., U.S.	98	43.07N	109.08W
Wind River Indian Reservation, I.R., Wy., U.S.	98	43.26N	109.00W
Wind River Range, mts., Wy., U.S.	90	43.19N	109.47W
Windsor, Austl. (wĭn'zēr)	195b	33.37S	150.49E
Windsor, Can.	78	42.19N	83.00W
Windsor, Can.	78	44.59N	64.08W
Windsor, Can.	79a	48.57N	55.40W
Windsor, Eng., U.K.	144	51.27N	0.37W
Windsor, Co., U.S.	104	40.27N	104.51W
Windsor, Mo., U.S.	104	38.32N	93.31W
Windsor, N.C., U.S.	108	35.58N	76.57W
Windsor, Vt., U.S.	92	43.30N	72.25W
Windsor, University of, educ., Can.	226c	42.18N	83.04W
Windsor Airport, arpt., Can.	226c	42.17N	82.58W
Windsor Castle, hist., Eng., U.K.	231	51.29N	0.36W
Windsor Hills, Ca., U.S.	228	33.59N	118.21W
Windward Islands, is., N.A. (wĭnd'wērd)	110	12.45N	61.40W
Windward Passage, strt., N.A.	110	19.30N	74.20W
Winefred Lake, l., Can.	82	55.30N	110.35W
Winfield, Ks., U.S.	104	37.14N	97.00W
Wing Lake Shores, Mi., U.S.	226c	42.33N	83.17W
Winifred, Mt., U.S. (wĭn ĭ frĕd)	98	47.35N	109.20W
Winisk, r., Can.	78	54.30N	86.30W
Wink, Tx., U.S. (wĭŋk)	106	31.48N	103.06W
Winkler, Can. (wĭnk'lēr)	82	49.11N	97.56W
Winneba, Ghana (wĭn'ē-bȧ)	208	5.25N	0.36W
Winnebago, Mn., U.S. (wĭn'ē-bā'gō)	96	43.45N	94.08W
Winnebago, Lake, l., Wi., U.S.	96	44.09N	88.10W
Winnebago Indian Reservation, I.R., Ne., U.S.	96	42.15N	96.06W
Winnemucca, Nv., U.S. (wĭn-ē-mŭk'ȧ)	90	40.59N	117.43W
Winnemucca, l., Nv., U.S.	102	40.06N	119.07W
Winner, S.D., U.S. (wĭn'ēr)	96	43.22N	99.50W
Winnetka, Il., U.S. (wĭ-nĕtkȧ)	95a	42.07N	87.44W
Winnett, Mt., U.S. (wĭn'ĕt)	98	47.01N	108.20W
Winnfield, La., U.S. (wĭn'fēld)	106	31.56N	92.39W
Winnibigoshish, l., Mn., U.S. (wĭn'ĭ-bĭ-gō'shĭsh)	96	47.30N	93.45W
Winnipeg, Can. (wĭn'ĭ-pĕg)	78	49.53N	97.09W
Winnipeg, r., Can.	78	50.30N	95.00W
Winnipeg, Lake, l., Can.	78	52.00N	97.00W
Winnipegosis, Can. (wĭn'ĭ-pē-gō'sĭs)	78	51.39N	99.56W
Winnipegosis, l., Can.	78	52.30N	100.00W
Winnipesaukee, l., N.H., U.S. (wĭn'ē-pē-sô'kē)	92	43.40N	71.20W
Winnsboro, La., U.S. (wĭnz'bŭr'ō)	106	32.09N	91.42W
Winnsboro, S.C., U.S.	108	34.29N	81.05W
Winnsboro, Tx., U.S.	104	32.56N	95.15W
Winona, Can. (wĭ-nō'nȧ)	77d	43.13N	79.39W
Winona, Mn., U.S.	90	44.03N	91.40W
Winona, Ms., U.S.	108	33.29N	89.43W
Winooski, Vt., U.S. (wĭ-nōōs-kē)	92	44.30N	73.10W
Winsen, Ger. (vēn'zĕn)	139c	53.22N	10.13E
Winsford, Eng., U.K. (wĭnz'fērd)	138a	53.11N	2.30W
Winslow, Az., U.S. (wĭnz'lō)	102	35.00N	110.45W
Winslow, Wa., U.S.	100a	47.38N	122.31W
Winsted, Ct., U.S. (wĭn'stĕd)	92	41.55N	73.05W
Winster, Eng., U.K. (wĭn'stēr)	138a	53.08N	1.38W
Winston-Salem, N.C., U.S. (wĭn stŭn-sā'lĕm)	90	36.05N	80.15W
Winterberg, Ger.	232	51.17N	7.18E
Winterberge, mts., Afr.	207c	32.18S	26.25E
Winter Garden, Fl., U.S. (wĭn'tēr gär'd'n)	109a	28.32N	81.35W
Winter Haven, Fl., U.S. (hā'vĕn)	109a	28.01N	81.38W
Winter Park, Fl., U.S. (pärk)	109a	28.35N	81.21W
Winters, Tx., U.S. (wĭn'tērz)	106	31.59N	99.58W
Winterset, Ia., U.S. (wĭn'tēr-sĕt)	96	41.19N	94.03W
Winterswijk, Neth.	151c	51.58N	6.44E
Winterthur, Switz. (vĭn'tēr-tōōr)	148	47.30N	8.32E
Winterton, S. Afr.	207c	28.51S	29.33E
Winthrop, Me., U.S. (wĭn'thrŭp)	86	44.19N	70.00W
Winthrop, Ma., U.S.	87a	42.23N	70.59W
Winthrop, Mn., U.S.	96	44.31N	94.20W
Winton, Austl. (wĭn-tŭn)	196	22.17S	143.08E
Winz, Ger.	232	51.23N	7.09E
Wipperfürth, Ger. (vĕ'pēr-fürt)	151c	51.07N	7.23E
Wirksworth, Eng., U.K. (wûrks'wûrth)	138a	53.05N	1.35W
Wisconsin, state, U.S. (wĭs-kŏn'sĭn)	90	44.30N	91.00W
Wisconsin, r., Wi., U.S.	90	43.14N	90.34W
Wisconsin Dells, Wi., U.S.	96	43.38N	89.46W
Wisconsin Rapids, Wi., U.S.	96	44.24N	89.50W
Wishek, N.D., U.S. (wĭsh'ĕk)	96	46.15N	99.34W
Wisła, r., Pol. (vēs'wȧ)	136	52.30N	20.00E
Wisłoka, r., Pol. (vēs-wō'kȧ)	148	49.55N	21.26E
Wismar, Ger. (vĭs'mär)	140	53.53N	11.28E

ăt; finăl; rāte; senâte; ärm; ȧsk; sofȧ; fâre; ch-choose; dh-as th in other; bē; ėvent; bĕt; recĕnt; cratēr; g-gō; gh-guttural g; bĭt; ĭ-short neutral; rīde; ĸ-guttural k as ch in German ich;

PLACE (Pronunciation)	PAGE	Lat. °′	Long. °′
Wismar, Guy. (wĭs′mȧr)	124	5.58N	58.15W
Wisner, Ne., U.S. (wĭz′nẽr)	96	42.00N	96.55W
Wissembourg, Fr. (vē-säɴ-bōōr′)	150	49.03N	7.58E
Wissinoming, neigh., Pa., U.S.	225b	40.01N	75.04W
Wissous, Fr.	233c	48.44N	2.20E
Wister, Lake, l., Ok., U.S. (vĭs′tẽr)	104	35.02N	94.52W
Witbank, S. Afr. (wĭt-băŋk)	212d	25.53S	29.14E
Witberg, mtn., Afr.	207c	30.32S	27.18E
Witfield, S. Afr.	240b	26.11S	28.12E
Witham, Eng., U.K. (wĭdh′ăm)	138b	51.48N	0.37E
Witham, r., Eng., U.K.	138a	53.11N	0.20W
Withamsville, Oh., U.S. (wĭdh′ămz-vĭl)	95f	39.04N	84.16W
Withington, neigh., Eng., U.K.	233b	53.26N	2.14W
Withlacoochee, r., Fl., U.S.			
(wĭth-lȧ-kōō′chē)	109a	28.58N	82.30W
Withlacoochee, r., Ga., U.S.	108	31.15N	83.30W
Withrow, Mn., U.S. (wĭdh′rō)	101g	45.08N	92.54W
Witney, Eng., U.K. (wĭt′nē)	138b	51.45N	1.30W
Witpoortje, S. Afr.	240b	26.08S	27.50E
Witt, Il., U.S. (vĭt)	92	39.10N	89.15W
Witten, Ger. (vē′tĕn)	151c	51.26N	7.19E
Wittenau, neigh., Ger.	234a	52.35N	13.20E
Wittenberg, Ger. (vē′tĕn-bĕrgh)	148	51.53N	12.40E
Wittenberge, Ger. (vĭt-ĕn-bĕr′gĕ)	148	52.59N	11.45E
Wittlaer, Ger.	232	51.19N	6.44E
Wittlich, Ger. (vĭt′lĭk)	148	49.58N	6.54E
Witu, Kenya (wē′tōō)	206	2.18S	40.28E
Witu Islands, is., Pap. N. Gui.	188	4.45S	149.50E
Witwatersberg, mts., S. Afr.			
(wĭt-wôr-tẽrz-bûrg)	207b	25.58S	27.53E
Witwatersrand, mtn., S. Afr.			
(wĭt-wôr′tẽrs-rănd)	212d	25.55S	26.27E
Witwatersrand, University of, educ., S. Afr.	240b	26.12S	28.02E
Witwatersrand Gold Mines, quarry, S. Afr.	240b	26.12S	28.10E
Wkra, r., Pol. (f′krȧ)	148	52.40N	20.35E
Włocławek, Pol. (vwô-tswä′vĕk)	148	52.38N	19.08E
Włodawa, Pol. (vwô-dä′vä)	148	51.33N	23.33E
Włoszczowa, Pol. (vwôsh-chō′vä)	148	50.51N	19.58E
Woburn, Ma., U.S. (wō′bŭrn) (wō′bŭrn)	87a	42.29N	71.10W
Woburn, neigh., Can.	223c	43.46N	79.13W
Woerden, Neth.	139a	52.05N	4.52E
Woking, Eng., U.K.	138b	51.18N	0.33W
Wokingham, Eng., U.K. (wō′kĭng-hăm)	138b	51.23N	0.50W
Wolcott, Ks., U.S. (wōl′kŏt)	101f	39.12N	94.47W
Woldingham, Eng., U.K.	231	51.17N	0.02W
Wolf, i., Can. (wŏolf)	84	44.10N	76.25W
Wolf, r., Ms., U.S.	108	30.45N	89.36W
Wolf, r., Wi., U.S.	96	45.14N	88.45W
Wolfenbüttel, Ger. (vôl′fĕn-büt-ĕl)	148	52.10N	10.32E
Wolf Lake, l., Il., U.S.	95a	41.39N	87.33W
Wolf Point, Mt., U.S. (wŏolf point)	98	48.07N	105.40W
Wolfratshausen, Ger. (vōlf′räts-hou-zĕn)	139d	47.55N	11.25E
Wolfsburg, Ger. (vōlfs′bōōrgh)	148	52.30N	10.37E
Wolfville, Can. (wŏolf′vĭl)	86	45.05N	64.22W
Wolgast, Ger. (vôl′gäst)	148	54.04N	13.46E
Wolhuterskop, S. Afr.	207b	25.41S	27.40E
Wolkersdorf, Aus.	139e	48.24N	16.31E
Wollaston, Ma., U.S.	223a	42.16N	71.01W
Wollaston, l., Can. (wŏol′ȧs-tŭn)	78	58.15N	103.20W
Wollaston Peninsula, pen., Can.	78	70.00N	115.00W
Wollongong, Austl. (wŏol′ŭn-gŏng)	196	34.26S	151.05E
Wołomin, Pol. (vô-wō′mēn)	148	52.19N	21.17E
Wolseley, Can.	82	50.25N	103.15W
Woltersdorf, Ger. (vōl′tĕs-dōrf)	139b	52.07N	13.13E
Woltersdorf, Ger.	234a	52.26N	13.45E
Wolverhampton, Eng., U.K.			
(wŏol′vẽr-hămp-tŭn)	140	52.35N	2.07W
Wolverine, Mi., U.S.	226c	42.33N	83.29W
Wolwehoek, S. Afr.	212d	26.55S	27.50E
Wonga Park, Austl.	239b	37.44S	145.16E
Wŏnsan, N. Kor. (wŭn′sän′)	180	39.08N	127.24E
Wonthaggi, Austl. (wŏnt-hăg′ē)	196	38.45S	145.42E
Wood, S.D., U.S. (wŏod)	96	43.26N	100.25W
Woodbine, Ia., U.S. (wŏod′bīn)	96	41.44N	95.42W
Woodbridge, N.J., U.S. (wŏod′brĭj′)	94a	40.33N	74.18W
Woodbrook, Md., U.S.	225c	39.23N	76.37W
Wood Buffalo National Park, rec., Can.	78	59.50N	118.53W
Woodburn, Il., U.S. (wŏod′bûrn)	101e	39.03N	90.01W
Woodburn, Or., U.S.	98	45.10N	122.51W
Woodbury, N.J., U.S. (wŏod′bĕr-ē)	94f	39.50N	75.14W
Woodbury, N.Y., U.S.	224	40.49N	73.28W
Woodbury Terrace, N.J., U.S.	225b	39.51N	75.08W
Woodcrest, Ca., U.S. (wŏod′krĕst)	101a	33.53N	117.18W
Woodford, Eng., U.K.	233b	53.21N	2.10W
Woodford Bridge, neigh., Eng., U.K.	231	51.36N	0.04E
Wood Green, neigh., Eng., U.K.	231	51.36N	0.07W
Woodhaven, neigh., N.Y., U.S.	224	40.41N	73.51W
Woodinville, Wa., U.S. (wŏod′ĭn-vĭl)	100a	47.46N	122.09W
Woodland, Ca., U.S. (wŏod′lănd)	102	38.41N	121.47W
Woodland, Wa., U.S.	100c	45.54N	122.45W
Woodland Hills, Ca., U.S.	101a	34.10N	118.36W
Woodlands, Sing.	236c	1.27N	103.46E
Woodlark Island, i., Pap. N. Gui.			
(wŏod′lärk)	188	9.07S	152.00E
Woodlawn, Md., U.S.	225c	39.19N	76.43W
Woodlawn, Md., U.S.	225d	38.57N	76.53W
Woodlawn, neigh., Il., U.S.	227a	41.47N	87.36W
Woodlawn Beach, N.Y., U.S.			
(wŏod′lôn bēch)	95c	42.48N	78.51W
Woodlawn Heights, Md., U.S.	225c	39.11N	76.39W
Woodlyn, Pa., U.S.	225b	39.52N	75.21W
Woodlynne, N.J., U.S.	225b	39.55N	75.05W
Woodmansterne, Eng., U.K.	231	51.19N	0.10W
Woodmere, N.Y., U.S.	224	40.38N	73.43W
Woodmoor, Md., U.S.	225c	39.20N	76.44W
Wood Mountain, mtn., Can.	82	49.14N	106.20W
Wood Ridge, N.J., U.S.	224	40.51N	74.05W
Wood River, Il., U.S.	101e	38.52N	90.06W
Woodroffe, Mount, mtn., Austl.			
(wŏod′rŭf)	196	26.05S	132.00E
Woodruff, S.C., U.S. (wŏod′rŭf)	108	34.43N	82.03W
Woods, l., Austl. (wŏodz)	196	18.00S	133.18E
Woods, Lake of the, l., N.A.	78	49.25N	93.25W
Woodsburgh, N.Y., U.S.	224	40.37N	73.42W
Woods Cross, Ut., U.S. (krôs)	101b	40.53N	111.54W
Woodsfield, Oh., U.S. (wŏodz-fēld)	92	39.45N	81.10W
Woodside, neigh., N.Y., U.S.	224	40.45N	73.55W
Woodson, Or., U.S. (wŏod-sŭn)	100c	46.07N	123.20W
Woodstock, Can.	78	46.09N	67.34W
Woodstock, Can. (wŏod′stŏk)	84	43.10N	80.50W
Woodstock, Eng., U.K.	138b	51.48N	1.22W
Woodstock, Il., U.S.	96	42.20N	88.29W
Woodstock, Va., U.S.	92	38.55N	78.25W
Woodsville, N.H., U.S. (wŏodz′vĭl)	92	44.10N	72.00W
Woodville, Ms., U.S. (wŏod′vĭl)	108	31.06N	91.11W
Woodville, Tx., U.S.	106	30.48N	94.25W
Woodward, Ok., U.S. (wŏod′wôrd)	104	36.25N	99.24W
Woollahra, Austl.	239a	33.53S	151.15E
Woolton, neigh., Eng., U.K.	233a	53.23N	2.52W
Woolwich, Eng., U.K. (wŏol′ĭj)	138b	51.28N	0.05E
Woomera, Austl. (wōōm′ẽrȧ)	196	31.15S	136.43E
Woonsocket, R.I., U.S. (wōōn-sŏk′ĕt)	94b	42.00N	71.30W
Woonsocket, S.D., U.S.	96	44.03N	98.17W
Wooster, Oh., U.S. (wŏos′tẽr)	92	40.50N	81.55W
Worcester, S. Afr. (wōōs′tẽr)	206	33.35S	19.31E
Worcester, Eng., U.K. (wŏo′stẽr)	140	52.09N	2.14W
Worcester, Ma., U.S. (wŏos′tẽr)	90	42.16N	71.49W
Worden, Il., U.S. (wôr′dĕn)	101e	38.56N	89.50W
Workington, Eng., U.K. (wûr′kĭng-tŭn)	144	54.40N	3.30W
Worksop, Eng., U.K.			
(wûrk′sŏp) (wûr′sŭp)	138a	53.18N	1.07W
Worland, Wy., U.S. (wûr′lănd)	98	44.02N	107.56W
Wormley, Eng., U.K.	231	51.44N	0.01W
Worms, Ger. (vōrms)	140	49.37N	8.22E
Worona Reservoir, res., Austl.	195b	34.12S	150.55E
Woronora, Austl.	239a	34.01S	151.03E
Worsley, Eng., U.K.	233b	53.30N	2.23W
Worth, Il., U.S. (wûrth)	95a	41.42N	87.47W
Wortham, Tx., U.S. (wûr′dhăm)	106	31.46N	96.22W
Worthing, Eng., U.K. (wûr′dhĭng)	144	50.48N	0.29W
Worthington, In., U.S. (wûr′dhĭng-tŭn)	92	39.05N	87.00W
Worthington, Md., U.S.	225c	39.14N	76.47W
Worthington, Mn., U.S.	96	43.38N	95.36W
Worth Lake, l., Tx., U.S.	101c	32.48N	97.32W
Wowoni, Pulau, i., Indon. (wō-wō′nē)	188	4.05S	123.45E
Wragby, Eng., U.K. (răg′bē)	138a	53.17N	0.19W
Wrangell, Ak., U.S. (răn′gĕl)	90a	56.28N	132.25W
Wrangell, Mount, mtn., Ak., U.S.	89	61.58N	143.50W
Wrangell Mountains, mts., Ak., U.S.	89	62.28N	142.40W
Wrangell-Saint Elias National Park, rec.,			
Ak., U.S.	89	61.00N	142.00W
Wrath, Cape, c., Scot., U.K. (răth)	144	58.34N	5.01W
Wray, Co., U.S. (rā)	104	40.06N	102.14W
Wraysbury, Eng., U.K.	231	51.27N	0.33W
Wreak, r., Eng., U.K. (rēk)	138a	52.45N	0.59W
Wreck Reefs, rf., Austl. (rĕk)	196	22.00S	155.52E
Wrekin, The, mtn., Eng., U.K. (rĕk′ĭn)	138a	52.40N	2.33W
Wrens, Ga., U.S. (rĕnz)	108	33.15N	82.25W
Wrentham, Ma., U.S.	87a	42.04N	71.20W
Wrexham, Wales, U.K. (rĕk′săm)	144	53.03N	3.00W
Wrights Corners, N.Y., U.S.			
(rīts kôr′nẽrz)	95c	43.14N	78.42W
Wrightsville, Ga., U.S. (rīts′vĭl)	108	32.44N	82.44W
Writtle, Eng., U.K.	231	51.44N	0.26E
Wrocław, Pol. (vrôtsläv) (brĕs′lou)	148	51.07N	17.10E
Wrotham, Eng., U.K. (rōōt′ŭm)	138b	51.18N	0.19E
Wrotham Heath, Eng., U.K.	231	51.18N	0.21E
Września, Pol. (vzhāsh′nyȧ)	148	52.19N	17.33E
Wu, r., China (wōō′)	180	27.30N	107.00E
Wuchang, China (wōō-chäŋ)	180	30.32N	114.25E
Wuchang, China	184	44.59N	127.00E
Wucheng, China (wōō-chŭŋ)	182	37.14N	116.03E
Wuhan, China	180	30.30N	114.15E
Wuhu, China (wōō′hōō)	184	31.22N	118.22E
Wuji, China (wōō-jyē)	184	38.12N	114.57E
Wujiang, China (wōō-jyäŋ)	182	31.10N	120.38E
Wuleidao Wan, b., China			
(wōō-lā-dou wän)	182	36.55N	122.00E
Wülfrath, Ger.	232	51.17N	7.02E
Wulidian, China (wōō-lē-dĭĕn)	182	32.09N	114.17E
Wünsdorf, Ger. (vüns′dorf)	139b	52.10N	13.29E
Wupatki National Monument, rec., Az.,			
U.S.	102	35.35N	111.45W
Wuping, China (wōō-pĭŋ)	184	25.05N	116.01E
Wupper, r., Ger.	232	51.14N	7.06E
Wuppertal, Ger. (vŏŏp′ẽr-täl)	140	51.16N	7.14E
Wuqiao, China (wōō-chyou)	182	37.37N	116.29E
Würm, r., Ger. (vürm)	139d	48.07N	11.20E
Würselen, Ger. (vür′zē-lĕn)	151c	50.49N	6.09E
Würzburg, Ger. (vürts′bŏrgh)	140	49.48N	9.57E
Wurzen, Ger. (vŏrt′sĕn)	140	51.22N	12.45E
Wushi, China (wōō-shr)	180	41.13N	79.08E
Wusong, China (wōō-sôŋ)	182	31.23N	121.29E
Wustermark, Ger. (vōōs′tẽr-märk)	139b	52.33N	12.57E
Wustrau, Ger. (vōost′rou)	139b	52.40N	12.51E
Wuustwezel, Bel.	139a	51.23N	4.36E
Wuwei, China (wōō′wā′)	184	31.19N	117.53E
Wuxi, China (wōō-shyē)	180	31.36N	120.17E
Wuxing, China (wōō-shyĭŋ)	180	30.38N	120.10E
Wuyi Shan, mts., China (wōō-yē shän)	184	26.38N	116.35E
Wuyou, China (wōō-yō)	182	33.18N	120.15E
Wuzhi Shan, mtn., China (wōō-jr shän)	184	18.48N	109.30E
Wuzhou, China (wōō-jō)	180	23.32N	111.25E
Wyandotte, Mi., U.S. (wī′ăn-dŏt)	95b	42.12N	83.10W
Wye, Eng., U.K. (wī)	138b	51.12N	0.57E
Wye, r., Eng., U.K.	138a	53.14N	1.46W
Wylie, Lake, res., S.C., U.S.	108	35.02N	81.21W
Wymore, Ne., U.S. (wī′mōr)	104	40.09N	96.41W
Wynberg, S. Afr. (wĭn′bĕrg)	206a	34.00S	18.28E
Wyncote, Pa., U.S.	225b	40.05N	75.09W
Wyndham, Austl. (wīnd′ăm)	196	15.30S	128.15E
Wyndmoor, Pa., U.S.	225b	40.05N	75.12W
Wynne, Ar., U.S. (wĭn)	104	35.12N	90.46W
Wynnewood, Ok., U.S. (wĭn′wŏod)	104	34.39N	97.10W
Wynnewood, Pa., U.S.	225b	40.01N	75.17W
Wynona, Ok., U.S. (wī-nō′nȧ)	104	36.33N	96.19W
Wynyard, Can. (wīn′yẽrd)	78	51.47N	104.10W
Wyoming, Oh., U.S. (wī-ō′mĭng)	95f	39.14N	84.28W
Wyoming, state, U.S.	90	42.50N	108.30W
Wyoming Range, mts., Wy., U.S.	90	42.43N	110.35W
Wyre Forest, for., Eng., U.K. (wīr)	138a	52.24N	2.24W
Wysokie Mazowieckie, Pol.			
(vē-sô′kyĕ mä-zô-vyĕts′kyĕ)	148	52.55N	22.42E
Wyszków, Pol. (vēsh′kôf)	148	52.35N	21.29E
Wythenshawe, neigh., Eng., U.K.	233b	53.24N	2.17W
Wytheville, Va., U.S. (wĭth′vĭl)	108	36.55N	81.06W

X

PLACE (Pronunciation)	PAGE	Lat. °′	Long. °′
Xabregas, neigh., Port.	234d	38.44N	9.07W
Xagua, Banco, bk., Cuba			
(bä′n-kō-sä′gwä)	116	21.35N	80.50W
Xai Xai, Moz.	206	25.00S	33.45E
Xangongo, Ang.	206	16.50S	15.05E
Xanten, Ger. (ksän′tĕn)	151c	51.40N	6.28E
Xánthi, Grc.	142	41.08N	24.53E
Xau, Lake, l., Bots.	206	21.15S	24.38E
Xcalak, Mex. (sä-lä′k)	114a	18.15N	87.50W
Xenia, Oh., U.S. (zē′nĭ-ȧ)	92	39.40N	83.55W
Xi, r., China (shyē)	184	23.15N	112.10E
Xiajin, China (shyä-jyĭn)	184	36.58N	115.59E
Xiamen, China	180	24.30N	118.10E
Xiamen, i., Tai. (shyä-mŭn)	184	24.28N	118.20E
Xi'an, China (shyē-än)	180	34.20N	109.00E
Xiang, r., China (shyäŋ)	180	27.30N	112.30E
Xianghe, China (shyäŋ-hŭ)	182	39.46N	116.59E
Xiangtan, China (shyäŋ-tän)	180	27.55N	112.45E
Xianyang, China (shyĕn-yäŋ)	184	34.20N	108.40E
Xiaoxingkai Hu, l., China			
(shyou-shyĭŋ-kī hōō)	186	42.25N	132.45E
Xiaoxintian, China	236b	39.58N	116.22E
Xiapu, China (shyä-pōō)	180	27.00N	120.00E
Xiayi, China (shyä-yē)	182	34.15N	116.07E
Xicotencatl, Mex. (sē-kō-tĕn-kät′'l)	112	23.00N	98.58W
Xifeng, China (shyē-fŭŋ)	184	42.40N	124.40E
Xiheying, China (shyē-hŭ-yĭŋ)	182	39.58N	114.50E
Xiliao, r., China (shyē-lĭou)	184	41.40N	122.40E
Xiliao, r., China	184	43.23N	121.40E
Xilitla, Mex. (sē-lē′tlä)	112	21.24N	98.59W
Xinchang, China (shўn-chäŋ)	183b	31.02N	121.38E
Xing'an, China (shyĭŋ-än)	184	25.44N	110.32E
Xingcheng, China (shyĭŋ-chŭŋ)	182	40.38N	120.41E
Xinghua, China (shyĭŋ-hwä)	182	32.58N	119.48E
Xingjiawan, China (shyĭŋ-jyä-wän)	182	37.16N	114.54E
Xingtai, China (shyĭŋ-tī)	184	37.04N	114.33E
Xingu, r., Braz. (zhĕŋ-gō′)	124	6.20S	52.34W
Xinhai, China (shyĭn-hī)	182	36.59N	117.33E
Xinhua, China (shyĭn-hwä)	184	27.45N	111.20E
Xinhuai, r., China (shyĭn-hwī)	182	33.48N	119.39E
Xinhui, China (shyn-hwā)	184	22.40N	113.08E
Xining, China (shyē-nĭŋ)	180	36.52N	101.36E
Xinjiang Uygur (Sinkiang), prov., China			
(shyĭn-jyäŋ)	180	40.15N	82.15E
Xinjin, China (shyĭn-jyĭn)	184	39.23N	121.57E
Xinmin, China (shyĭn-mĭn)	184	42.00N	122.42E
Xintai, China (shyĭn-tī)	182	35.55N	117.44E
Xintang, China (shyĭn-täŋ)	183a	23.08N	113.36E
Xinxian, China (shyĭn shyĕn)	182	31.47N	114.50E
Xinxian, China	184	38.20N	112.45E
Xinxiang, China (shyĭn-shyäŋ)	184	35.17N	113.49E
Xinyang, China (shyĭn-yäŋ)	180	32.08N	114.04E
Xinye, China (shyĭn-yŭ)	184	32.40N	112.20E
Xinzao, China (shyĭn-dzou)	183a	23.01N	113.25E
Xinzheng, China (shyĭn-jŭŋ)	182	34.24N	113.43E
Xinzhuang, China	236b	39.56N	116.31E
Xiongyuecheng, China (shyôŋ-yŭĕ-chŭŋ)	182	40.10N	122.08E
Xiping, China (shyē-pĭŋ)	182	33.21N	114.01E
Xishui, China (shyē-shwā)	184	30.30N	115.10E
Xixian, China (shyē shyĕn)	182	32.20N	114.42E
Xiyang, China (shyē-yäŋ)	182	37.37N	113.42E
Xiyou, China (shyē-yō)	182	37.21N	119.59E
Xizang (Tibet), prov., China (shyē-dzäŋ)	180	31.15N	87.30E
Xizhong Dao, i., China (shyē-jôŋ dou)	182	39.27N	121.06E

ng-sing; ŋ-baŋk; ɴ-nasalized n; nŏd; cŏmmit; ōld; ōbey; ôrder; oi-boil; fōōd; ŏo-as oo in foot; ou-out; s-soft; sh-dish; th-thin; pūre; ûnite; ûrn; stŭd; circŭs; ü-as in French tu; ′-indeterminate vowel.

PLACE (Pronunciation)	PAGE	Lat. °′	Long. °′
Xochihuehuetlán, Mex. (sô-chē-wē-wē-tlä'n)	112	17.53N	98.29E
Xochimilco, Mex. (sō-chē-mēl'kō)	113a	19.15N	99.06W
Xochimilco, Lago de, l., Mex.	229a	19.16N	99.06W
Xuancheng, China (shyůän-chŭŋ)	184	30.52N	118.48E
Xuanhua, China (shyůän-hwä)	184	40.35N	115.05E
Xuanhuadian, China (shyůän-hwä-dĭĕn)	182	31.42N	114.29E
Xuchang, China (shyōō-chäŋ)	184	34.02N	113.49E
Xuddur, Som.	212a	3.55N	43.45E
Xun, r., China (shyòn)	184	23.28N	110.30E
Xuzhou, China	180	34.17N	117.10E
Y			
Ya'an, China (yä-än)	180	30.00N	103.20E
Yablonitskiy Pereval, p., Ukr. (yàb-lô'nĭt-skĭ pĕ-rĕ-väl')	148	48.20N	24.25E
Yablonovyy Khrebet, mts., Russia (yá-blô-nô-vē')	158	51.15N	111.30E
Yacheng, China (yä-chŭŋ)	184	18.20N	109.10E
Yachiyo, Japan	187a	35.43N	140.07E
Yacolt, Wa., U.S. (yă'kōlt)	100c	45.52N	122.24W
Yacolt Mountain, mtn., Wa., U.S.	100c	45.52N	122.27W
Yacona, r., Ms., U.S. (yă'cō nă)	108	34.13N	89.30W
Yacuiba, Bol. (yá-kōō-ē'bá)	124	22.02S	63.44W
Yadkin, r., N.C., U.S. (yăd'kĭn)	108	36.12N	80.40W
Yafran, Libya	204	31.57N	12.04E
Yagotin, Ukr. (yä'gô-tên)	156	50.18N	31.46E
Yaguajay, Cuba (yä-guä-hä'ē)	116	22.20N	79.20W
Yahagi-Gawa, r., Japan (yä'hä-gē gä'wä)	187	35.16N	137.22E
Yaho, Japan	238a	35.41N	139.27E
Yahongqiao, China (yä-hôŋ-chyou)	182	39.45N	117.52E
Yahualica, Mex. (yä-wä-lē'kä)	112	21.08N	102.53W
Yajalón, Mex. (yä-hä-lōn')	112	17.16N	92.20W
Yakhroma, Russia (yäl'rô-ma)	164b	56.17N	37.30E
Yakhroma, r., Russia	164b	56.15N	37.38E
Yakima, Wa., U.S. (yăk'ĭmȧ)	90	46.35N	120.30W
Yakima, r., Wa., U.S. (yăk'ĭ-mȧ)	98	46.48N	120.22W
Yakima Indian Reservation, I.R., Wa., U.S.	98	46.16N	121.03W
Yakō, neigh., Japan	238a	35.32N	139.41E
Yakoma, Zaire	210	4.05N	22.27E
Yaku, i., Japan (yä'kōō)	180	30.15N	130.41E
Yakutat, Ak., U.S. (yăk'ô-tăt)	89	59.32N	139.35W
Yakut Autonomous Soviet Socialist Republic, , Russia	158	65.21N	117.13E
Yakutsk, Russia (yá-kòtsk')	158	62.13N	129.49E
Yale, Mi., U.S.	92	43.05N	82.45W
Yale, Ok., U.S.	104	36.07N	96.42W
Yale Lake, res., Wa., U.S.	98	46.00N	122.20W
Yalinga, Cen. Afr. Rep. (yá-lĭŋ'gá)	204	6.56N	23.22E
Yalobusha, r., Ms., U.S. (yă-lô-bòsh'ȧ)	108	33.48N	90.02W
Yalong, r., China (yä-lôŋ)	180	32.29N	98.41E
Yalta, Ukr. (yäl'tá)	160	44.29N	34.12E
Yalu, r., Asia	180	41.20N	126.35E
Yalutorovsk, Russia (yä-lōō-tô'rôfsk)	158	56.42N	66.32E
Yamada, Japan (yä'má-dá)	187	33.37N	133.39E
Yamagata, Japan (yä-má'gä-tá)	180	38.12N	140.24E
Yamaguchi, Japan (yä-má'gōō-chē)	186	34.10N	131.30E
Yamaguchi, Japan	238b	34.50N	135.15E
Yamal, Poluostrov, pen., Russia (yä-mäl')	158	71.15N	70.00E
Yamantau, Gora, mtn., Russia (gá-rä' yä'man-tâw)	164a	54.16N	58.08E
Yamasaki, Japan (yä'má'sä-kē)	187	35.01N	134.33E
Yamasaki, Japan	187b	34.53N	135.41E
Yamashina, Japan (yä'mä-shē'nä)	187b	34.59N	135.50E
Yamashita, Japan (yä'mä-shē'tä)	187b	34.53N	135.25E
Yamato, Japan	187a	35.28N	139.28E
Yamato, Japan	238a	35.44N	139.26E
Yamato, Japan	238a	35.47N	139.37E
Yamato, r., Japan	238b	34.36N	135.26E
Yamato-Kōriyama, Japan	187b	34.39N	135.48E
Yamato-takada, Japan (yä'mä-tô tä'kä-dä)	187b	34.31N	135.45E
Yambi, Mesa de, mtn., Col. (mĕ'sä-dĕ-yà'm-bē)	124	1.55N	71.45W
Yambol, Bul. (yám'bôl)	142	42.28N	26.31E
Yamdena, i., Indon.	188	7.23S	130.30E
Yamenkou, China	236b	39.53N	116.12E
Yamethin, Burma (yŭ-mē'thĕn)	174	20.14N	96.27E
Yamhill, Or., U.S. (yăm'hĭl)	100c	45.20N	123.11W
Yamkino, Russia (yäm'kĭ-nô)	164b	55.56N	38.25E
Yamma Yamma, Lake, l., Austl. (yăm'á yăm'á)	196	26.15S	141.30E
Yamoussoukro, I.C.	204	6.49N	5.17W
Yamsk, Russia (yämsk)	158	59.41N	154.09E
Yamuna, r., India	174	25.30N	80.30E
Yamzho Yumco, l., China (yäm-jwo yōōm-tswo)	180	29.11N	91.26E
Yana, r., Russia (yä'ná)	158	71.00N	136.00E
Yanac, Austl. (yăn'ăk)	196	36.10S	141.30E
Yanagawa, Japan (yä-nä'gä-wä)	187	33.11N	130.24E
Yanam, India (yŭnŭm')	174	16.48N	82.15E
Yan'an, China (yän-än)	180	36.46N	109.15E
Yanbu', Sau. Ar.	174	23.57N	38.02E
Yancheng, China	184	33.38N	113.59E
Yancheng, China (yän-chŭŋ)	184	33.23N	120.11E
Yandongi, Zaire	210	2.51N	22.16E
Yangcheng Hu, l., China (yäŋ-chŭŋ hōō)	182	31.30N	120.31E
Yangchun, China (yäŋ-chòn)	184	22.08N	111.48E
Yang'erzhuang, China (yäŋ-är-jůäŋ)	182	38.18N	117.31E
Yanggezhuang, China (yäŋ-gŭ-jůäŋ)	184a	40.10N	116.48E
Yanggu, China (yäŋ-gōō)	182	36.06N	115.46E
Yanghe, China (yäŋ-hŭ)	182	33.48N	118.23E
Yangjiang, China (yäŋ-jyäŋ)	184	21.52N	111.58E
Yangjiaogou, China (yäŋ-jyou-gō)	182	37.17N	118.53E
Yangon, see Rangoon, Burma	174	16.46N	96.09E
Yangquan, China (yäŋ-chyůän)	182	37.52N	113.36E
Yangtze (Chang), r., China (yăng'tse) (chäŋ)	180	30.30N	117.25E
Yangxin, China (yäŋ-shyĭn)	182	37.39N	117.34E
Yangyang, S. Kor. (yäng'yäng')	186	38.02N	128.38E
Yangzhou, China (yäŋ-jō)	180	32.24N	119.24E
Yanji, China (yän-jyē)	180	42.55N	129.35E
Yanjiahe, China (yän-jyä-hŭ)	182	31.55N	114.47E
Yanjin, China (yän-jyĭn)	182	35.09N	114.13E
Yankton, S.D., U.S. (yănk'tŭn)	90	42.51N	97.24W
Yanling, China (yän-lĭŋ)	182	34.07N	114.12E
Yanshan, China (yän-shän)	184	38.05N	117.15E
Yanshou, China (yän-shō)	184	45.25N	128.43E
Yantai, China	180	37.32N	121.22E
Yanychi, Russia (yä'nĭ-chĭ)	164a	57.42N	56.24E
Yanzhou, China (yäŋ-jō)	180	35.35N	116.50E
Yanzhuang, China (yän-jůäŋ)	182	36.08N	117.47E
Yao, Chad (yä'ō)	196	13.00N	17.38E
Yao, Japan	187b	34.37N	135.37E
Yaoundé, Cam.	204	3.52N	11.31E
Yap, i., Micron. (yăp)	2	11.00N	138.00E
Yapen, Pulau, i., Indon.	188	1.30S	136.15E
Yaque del Norte, r., Dom. Rep. (yä'kå dĕl nôr'tå)	110	19.40N	71.25W
Yaque del Sur, r., Dom. Rep. (yä-kĕ-dĕl-sōō'r)	116	18.35N	71.05W
Yaqui, r., Mex. (yä'kē)	110	28.15N	109.40W
Yaracuy, dept., Ven. (yä-rä-kōō'ē)	125b	10.10N	68.31W
Yaraka, Austl. (yá-răk'ȧ)	196	24.50S	144.08E
Yaransk, Russia (yä-ränsk')	158	57.18N	48.05E
Yarda, oasis, Chad (yär'dȧ)	204	18.29N	19.13E
Yare, r., Eng., U.K.	144	52.40N	1.32E
Yarkand, see Shache, China (yär'mänth)	180	38.15N	77.15E
Yarkand, see Shache, China	180	38.15N	77.15E
Yaroslavka, Russia (yá-rô-släv'ká)	164a	55.52N	57.59E
Yaroslavl', Russia (yá-rô-släv''l)	158	57.37N	39.54E
Yaroslavl', prov., Russia	156	58.05N	38.05E
Yarra, r., Austl.	195a	37.51S	144.54E
Yarra Canal, can., Austl.	239b	37.49S	144.55E
Yarraville, Austl.	239b	37.49S	144.53E
Yarro-to, l., Russia (yá'rô-tô')	160	67.55N	71.35E
Yartsevo, Russia	158	60.13N	89.52E
Yartsevo, Russia (yär'tsyĕ-vô)	160	55.04N	32.38E
Yarumal, Col. (yä-rōō-mäl')	124	6.57N	75.24W
Yasawa Group, is., Fiji	192g	17.00S	177.23E
Yasel'da, r., Bela. (yä-syŭl'dá)	148	52.13N	25.53E
Yasinya, Ukr.	148	48.17N	24.21E
Yateras, Cuba (yä-tā'räs)	116	20.00N	75.00W
Yates Center, Ks., U.S. (yāts)	104	37.53N	95.44W
Yathkyed, l., Can. (yáth-kĭ-ĕd')	78	62.41N	98.00W
Yatsuga-take, mtn., Japan (yät'sōō-gä dä'kä)	187	36.01N	138.21W
Yatsushiro, Japan (yät'sōō'shē-rô)	187	32.30N	130.35E
Yatta Plateau, plat., Kenya	210	1.55S	38.10E
Yautepec, Mex. (yä-ōō-tå-pĕk')	112	18.53N	99.04W
Yavorov, Ukr.	148	49.56N	23.24E
Yawata, Japan (yä'wä-tä)	187	34.52N	135.43E
Yawatahama, Japan (yä'wä'tä'hä-mä)	187	33.24N	132.25E
Yaxian, China (yä shyĕn)	184	18.10N	109.32E
Yayama, Zaire	210	1.16S	23.07E
Yayao, China (yä-you)	183a	23.10N	113.40E
Yazd, Iran	174	31.59N	54.03E
Yazoo, r., Ms., U.S. (yă'zōō)	90	32.32N	90.40W
Yazoo City, Ms., U.S.	108	32.50N	90.18W
Ye, Burma (yā)	188	15.13N	97.52E
Yeading, neigh., Eng., U.K.	231	51.32N	0.24W
Yeadon, Pa., U.S. (yē'dŭn)	94f	39.56N	75.16W
Yecla, Spain (yā'klä)	152	38.35N	1.09W
Yedikule, neigh., Tur.	235f	40.59N	28.55E
Yefremov, Russia (yĕ-frä'môf)	156	53.08N	38.04E
Yegor'yevsk, Russia (yĕ-gôr'yĕfsk)	160	55.23N	38.59E
Yeji, China (yŭ-jyē)	182	31.52N	115.57E
Yekaterinburg, Russia	158	56.51N	60.36E
Yelabuga, Russia (yĕ-lä'bò-gá)	160	55.50N	52.18E
Yelan, Russia	160	50.50N	44.00E
Yelets, Russia (yĕ-lyĕts')	158	52.35N	38.28E
Yelizavetpol'skiy, Russia (yĕ'lĭ-za-vĕt-pôl-skĭ)	164a	52.51N	60.38E
Yelizavety, Mys, c., Russia (yĕ-lyĕ-sá-vyĕ'tĭ)	158	54.28N	142.59E
Yell, i., Scot., U.K. (yĕl)	144a	60.35N	1.27W
Yellow, r., Fl., U.S. (yĕl'ô)	108	30.33N	86.53W
Yellowhead Pass, p., Can. (yĕl'ô-hĕd)	80	52.52N	118.35W
Yellow, see Huang, r., China	180	35.06N	113.39E
Yellowknife, Can. (yĕl'ô-nīf)	78	62.29N	114.38W
Yellow Sea, sea, Asia	180	35.20N	122.15E
Yellowstone, r., U.S.	90	46.00N	108.00W
Yellowstone, Clarks Fork, r., U.S.	98	44.55N	109.05W
Yellowstone Lake, l., Wy., U.S.	90	44.27N	110.03W
Yellowstone National Park, rec., U.S. (yĕl'ô-stōn)	90	44.45N	110.35W
Yel'nya, Russia (yĕl'nyá)	156	54.34N	33.12E
Yemanzhelinsk, Russia (yĕ-mán-zhâ'lĭnsk)	164a	54.47N	61.24E
Yemen, nation, Asia (yĕm'ĕn)	174	15.00N	47.00E
Yemetsk, Russia	160	63.28N	41.28E
Yenakiyevo, Ukr. (yĕ-nä'kĭ-yĕ-vô)	156	48.14N	38.12E
Yenangyaung, Burma (yā'nän-d oung)	174	20.27N	94.59E
Yencheng, China	180	37.30N	79.26E
Yendi, Ghana (yĕn'dē)	204	9.26N	0.01W
Yengisar, China (yŭn-gĕ-sär)	180	39.01N	75.29E
Yenice, r., Tur.	160	41.10N	33.00E
Yenikapi, neigh., Tur.	235f	41.00N	28.57E
Yenisey, r., Russia (yĕ-nĕ-sĕ'ē)	158	71.00N	82.00E
Yeniseysk, Russia (yĕ-nĭĕsā'ĭsk)	158	58.27N	90.28E
Yeo, l., Austl. (yō)	196	28.15S	124.00E
Yerevan, Arm. (yĕ-rĕ-vän')	160	40.10N	44.30E
Yerington, Nv., U.S. (yē'rĭng-tŭn)	102	38.59N	119.10W
Yermak, i., Russia	160	66.45N	71.30E
Yeste, Spain (yĕs'tå)	152	38.23N	2.19W
Yeu, Île d', i., Fr. (ēl dyû)	140	46.43N	2.45W
Yevpatoriya, Ukr. (yĕf-pä'tô-rĭ-yá)	160	45.13N	33.22E
Yevrey Autonomous Oblast, prov., Russia	162	48.45N	132.00E
Yexian, China (yŭ-shyĕn)	182	37.09N	119.57E
Yeya, r., Russia (yă'yá)	156	46.25N	39.17E
Yeysk, Russia (yĕysk)	160	46.41N	38.13E
Yi, r., China	182	34.38N	118.07E
Yiannitsá, Grc.	154	40.47N	22.26E
Yiaros, i., Grc.	154	37.52N	24.42E
Yibin, China (yē-bĭn)	180	28.50N	104.40E
Yichang, China (yē-chäŋ)	180	30.38N	111.22E
Yidu, China (yē-dōō)	184	36.42N	118.30E
Yiewsley, neigh., Eng., U.K.	231	51.31N	0.28W
Yilan, China (yē-län)	180	46.10N	129.40E
Yinchuan, China (yĭn-chůän)	180	38.22N	106.22E
Yingkou, China (yĭŋ-kō)	180	40.35N	122.10E
Yining, China (yē-nĭŋ)	180	43.58N	80.40E
Yin Shan, mts., China (yĭng'shän')	184	40.50N	110.30E
Yio Chu Kang, Sing.	236c	1.23N	103.51E
Yishan, China (yē-shän)	180	24.32N	108.42E
Yishui, China (yē-shwā)	182	35.49N	118.40E
Yíthion, Grc.	154	36.50N	22.37E
Yitong, China (yē-tôŋ)	180	43.15N	125.10E
Yixian, China (yē shyĕn)	184	41.30N	121.15E
Yixing, China	182	31.26N	119.57E
Yiyang, China (yē-yäŋ)	184	28.52N	112.12E
Yoakum, Tx., U.S. (yō'kŭm)	106	29.18N	97.09W
Yockanookany, r., Ms., U.S. (yŏk'á-nōō-kä-nĭ)	108	32.47N	89.38W
Yodo-Gawa, strt., Japan (yō'dō'gä-wä)	187b	34.46N	135.35E
Yog Point, c., Phil. (yōg)	184	14.00N	124.30E
Yogyakarta, Indon. (yŏg-yá-kär'tá)	188	7.50S	110.20E
Yoho National Park, Can. (yō'hō)	78	51.26N	116.30W
Yojoa, Lago de, l., Hond. (lä'gô dĕ yô-hō'ä)	114	14.49N	87.53W
Yokkaichi, Japan (yō'kä'ē-chē)	186	34.58N	136.35E
Yokohama, Japan (yō'kô-hä'mą)	180	35.37N	139.40E
Yokosuka, Japan (yô-kō'sò-kä)	186	35.17N	139.40E
Yokota, Japan (yō-kō'tä)	187a	35.23N	140.02E
Yola, Nig. (yō'lä)	204	9.13N	12.27E
Yolaina, Cordillera de, mts., Nic.	114	11.34N	84.34W
Yomou, Gui.	208	7.34N	9.16W
Yonago, Japan (yō'nä-gō)	186	35.27N	133.19E
Yŏnch'on, neigh., S. Kor.	237b	37.38N	127.04E
Yonezawa, Japan (yō'nĕ'zá-wä)	186	37.50N	140.07E
Yong'an, China (yôŋ-än)	184	26.00N	117.22E
Yongding, r., China (yôŋ-dĭŋ)	184	40.25N	115.00E
Yŏngdŏk, S. Kor. (yŭng'dŭk')	186	36.28N	129.25E
Yongdŭngp'o, neigh., S. Kor.	237b	37.32N	126.54E
Yŏnghŭng, N. Kor. (yŭng'hòng')	186	39.31N	127.11E
Yŏnghŭng Man, b., N. Kor.	186	39.10N	128.00E
Yongnian, China (yôŋ-nĭĕn)	184	36.47N	114.32E
Yongqing, China (yôŋ-chyĭŋ)	184a	39.18N	116.27E
Yongshun, China (yôŋ-shòn)	180	29.05N	109.58E
Yonkers, N.Y., U.S. (yŏŋ'kĕrz)	94a	40.57N	73.54W
Yonne, r., Fr. (yôn)	150	48.18N	3.15E
Yono, Japan (yō'nō)	187a	35.53N	139.36E
Yorba Linda, Ca., U.S. (yôr'bȧ lĭn'dȧ)	101a	33.55N	117.51W
York, Austl.	196	32.00S	117.00E
York, Can.	77d	43.41N	79.29W
York, Eng., U.K.	140	53.58N	1.10W
York, Al., U.S. (yôrk)	108	32.33N	88.16W
York, Ne., U.S.	104	40.52N	97.36W
York, Pa., U.S.	90	40.00N	76.40W
York, S.C., U.S.	108	34.59N	81.14W
York, Cape, c., Austl.	196	10.45S	142.35E
York, Kap, c., Grnld.	76	75.30N	73.00W
Yorke Peninsula, pen., Austl.	198	34.24S	137.20E
Yorketown, Austl.	198	35.00S	137.28E
York Factory, Can.	82	57.05N	92.18W
Yorkfield, Il., U.S.	227a	41.52N	87.56W
Yorkshire Wolds, Eng., U.K. (yôrk'shĭr)	144	54.00N	0.35W
Yorkton, Can. (yôrk'tŭn)	78	51.13N	102.28W
Yorktown, Tx., U.S. (yôrk'toun)	106	28.57N	97.30W
Yorktown, Va., U.S.	108	37.12N	76.31W
Yorkville, neigh., Can.	223c	43.40N	79.24W
Yoro, Hond. (yō'rō)	114	15.09N	87.05W
Yoron, i., Japan	186	26.48N	128.40E
Yosemite National Park, rec., Ca., U.S. (yô-sĕm'ĭ-tē)	90	38.03N	119.36W
Yoshida, Japan (yō'shē-dá)	187	34.39N	132.41E
Yoshikawa, Japan (yō-shē'kä'wä')	187a	35.53N	139.51E
Yoshino, r., Japan (yō'shē-nō)	187	34.04N	133.57E
Yoshkar-Ola, Russia (yôsh-kär'ô-lä')	160	56.35N	48.05E
Yos Sudarsa, Pulau, i., Indon.	188	7.20S	138.30E
Yŏsu, S. Kor. (yŭ'sōō')	186	34.42N	127.42W

ăt; finăl; rāte; senåte; ärm; åsk; sofȧ; fâre; ch-choose; dh-as th in other; bē; ēvent; bĕt; recĕnt; cratẽr; g-gō; gh-guttural g; bĭt; ĭ-short neutral; rīde; ĸ-guttural k as ch in German ich;

PLACE (Pronunciation)	PAGE	Lat. °'	Long. °'
You, r., China (yō)	184	23.55N	106.50E
Youghal, Ire. (yōō'ôl) (yôl)	144	51.58N	7.57E
Youghal Bay, b., Ire.	144	51.52N	7.46W
Young, Austl. (yŭng)	198	34.15S	148.18E
Young, Ur. (yô-ōō'ng)	123c	32.42S	57.38W
Youngs, l., Wa., U.S. (yŭngz)	100a	47.25N	122.08W
Youngstown, N.Y., U.S.	95c	43.15N	79.02W
Youngstown, Oh., U.S.	92	41.05N	80.40W
Yozgat, Tur. (yôz'gȧd)	174	39.50N	34.50E
Ypsilanti, Mi., U.S. (ĭp-sĭ-lăn'tĭ)	95b	42.15N	83.37W
Yreka, Ca., U.S. (wī-rē'kȧ)	98	41.43N	122.36W
Ysleta, Tx., U.S. (ēz-lĕ'tȧ)	106	31.42N	106.18W
Yssingeaux, Fr. (ē-săN-zhō)	150	45.09N	4.08E
Ystad, Swe.	140	55.25N	13.49E
Yu'alliq, Jabal, mts., Egypt	173a	30.12N	33.42E
Yuan, r., China (yůän)	180	28.50N	110.50E
Yuan'an, China (yůän-än)	184	31.08N	111.28E
Yuan Huan, pt. of i., Tai.	237d	25.03N	121.31E
Yuanling, China (yůän-lĭŋ)	184	28.30N	110.18E
Yuanshi, China (yůän-shr)	184	37.45N	114.32E
Yuasa, Japan	187	34.02N	135.10E
Yuba City, Ca., U.S. (yōō'bȧ)	102	39.08N	121.38W
Yucaipa, Ca., Ca., U.S. (yŭ-kȧ-ē'pȧ)	101a	34.02N	117.02W
Yucatán, state, Mex. (yōō-kä-tän')	110	20.45N	89.00W
Yucatan Channel, strt., N.A.	110	22.30N	87.00W
Yucheng, China (yōō-chŭŋ)	182	34.31N	115.54E
Yucheng, China	184	36.55N	116.39E
Yuci, China (yōō-tsz)	184	37.32N	112.40E
Yudoma, r., Russia (yōō-dō'mȧ)	162	59.13N	137.00E
Yueqing, China (yůĕ-chyĭn)	184	28.02N	120.40E
Yueyang, China (yůĕ-yäŋ)	180	29.25N	113.05E
Yuezhuang, China (yůĕ-jůäŋ)	182	36.13N	118.17E
Yug, r., Russia (yòg)	160	59.50N	45.55E
Yugoslavia, nation, Eur. (yōō-gō-slä-vĭ-ȧ)	136	44.00N	21.00E
Yukhnov, Russia (yòk'nof)	156	54.44N	35.15E
Yukon, , Can. (yōō'kŏn)	78	63.16N	135.30W
Yukon, r., N.A.	90a	64.00N	159.30W
Yukutat Bay, b., Ak., U.S. (yōō-kū tät')	89	59.34N	140.50W
Yuldybayevo, Russia (yòld'bȧ'yĕ-vô)	164a	52.20N	57.52E
Yulin, China	180	38.18N	109.45E
Yulin, China (yōō-lĭn)	184	22.38N	110.10E
Yuma, Az., U.S. (yōō'mä)	90	32.40N	114.40W
Yuma, Co., U.S.	104	40.08N	102.50W
Yuma, r., Dom. Rep.	116	19.05N	70.05W
Yumbi, Zaire	210	1.14S	26.14E
Yumen, China (yōō-mŭn)	180	40.14N	96.56E
Yuncheng, China (yòn-chŭŋ)	184	35.00N	110.40E
Yungho, Tai.	237d	25.01N	121.31E
Yung Shu Wan, H.K.	237c	22.14N	114.06E
Yunnan, prov., China (yun'nän')	180	24.23N	101.03E
Yunnan Plat, plat., China (yò-nän)	180	26.03N	101.26E
Yunxian, China (yòn shyĕn)	180	32.50N	110.55E
Yunxiao, China (yòn-shyou)	184	24.00N	117.20E
Yura, Japan (yōō'rä)	187	34.18N	134.54E
Yurécuaro, Mex. (yōō-rā'kwä-rō)	112	20.21N	102.16W
Yurimaguas, Peru (yōō-rē-mä'gwäs)	124	5.59S	76.12W
Yuriria, Mex. (yōō'rē-rē'ä)	112	20.11N	101.08W
Yurovo, Russia	164b	55.30N	38.24E
Yur'yevets, Russia	160	57.15N	43.08E
Yuscarán, Hond. (yōōs-kä-rän')	114	13.57N	86.48W
Yushan, China (yōō-shän)	184	28.42N	118.20E
Yushu, China (yōō-shōō)	184	44.58N	126.32E
Yutian, China (yōō-tĭĕn) (kŭ-r-yä)	180	36.55N	81.39E
Yutian, China (yōō-tĭĕn)	184	39.54N	117.45E
Yuty, Para. (yōō-tē')	126	26.45S	56.13W
Yuwangcheng, China (yü'wäng'chĕng)	182	31.32N	114.26E
Yuxian, China (yōō shyĕn)	184	39.40N	114.38E
Yuzha, Russia (yōō'zhȧ)	160	56.38N	42.20E
Yuzhno-Sakhalinsk, Russia (yōōzh'nô-sä-κä-lĭnsk')	158	47.11N	143.04E
Yuzhnoural'skiy, Russia (yōōzh-nô-ò-rál'skĭ)	164a	54.26N	61.17E
Yuzhnyy Ural, mts., Russia (yōō'zhnĭ ò-räl')	164a	52.51N	57.48E
Yverdon, Switz. (ē-vĕr-dôn)	148	46.46N	6.35E
Yvetot, Fr. (ēv-tō')	150	49.39N	0.45E

Z

PLACE (Pronunciation)	PAGE	Lat. °'	Long. °'
Za, r., Mor.	142	34.19N	2.23W
Zaachila, Mex. (sä-ä-chē'lȧ)	112	16.56N	96.45W
Zaandam, Neth. (zän'dȧm)	144	52.25N	4.49E
Ząbkowice Śląskie, Pol.	148	50.35N	16.48E
Zabrze, Pol. (zäb'zhĕ)	140	50.18N	18.48E
Zacapa, Guat. (sä-kä'pä)	114	14.56N	89.30W
Zacapoaxtla, Mex. (sä-kä-pō-äs'tlä)	112	19.51N	97.34W
Zacatecas, Mex. (sä-kä-tā'käs)	110	22.44N	102.32W
Zacatecas, state, Mex.	110	24.00N	102.45W
Zacatecoluca, El Sal. (sä-kä-tȧ-kò-lōō'kä)	114	13.31N	88.50W
Zacatelco, Mex.	112	19.12N	98.12W
Zacatepec, Mex. (sä-kä-tȧ-pĕk') (sän-tē-ä'gō)	112	17.10N	95.53W
Zacatlán, Mex. (sä-kä-tlän')	112	19.55N	97.57W
Zacoalco de Torres, Mex. (sä-kō-äl'kō dä tōr'rĕs)	112	20.12N	103.33W
Zacualpan, Mex. (sä-kò-äl-pän')	112	18.43N	99.46W
Zacualtipan, Mex. (sȧ-kò-äl-tē-pän')	112	20.38N	98.39W
Zadar, Cro. (zä'där)	136	44.08N	15.16E
Zadonsk, Russia (zä-dônsk')	156	52.22N	38.55E
Žagare, Lat. (zhȧgȧrĕ)	146	56.21N	23.14E
Zagarolo, Italy (tzä-gä-rô'lô)	153d	41.51N	12.53E
Zaghouan, Tun. (zȧ-gwän')	204	36.30N	10.04E
Zagreb, Cro. (zä'grĕb)	136	45.50N	15.58E
Zagros Mountains, mts., Iran	174	33.30N	46.30E
Zāhedān, Iran (zä'hȧ-dän)	174	29.37N	60.31E
Zahlah, Leb. (zä'lä')	173a	33.50N	35.54E
Zahorska-Ves, Czech.	139e	48.24N	16.51E
Zaire, nation, Afr.	206	1.00S	22.15E
Zaječar, Yugo. (zä'yĕ-chär')	154	43.54N	22.16E
Zákinthos, Grc.	154	37.48N	20.55E
Zákinthos, i., Grc.	142	37.45N	20.32E
Zakopane, Pol. (zȧ-kô-pä'nĕ)	148	49.18N	19.57E
Zakouma, Parc National de, rec., Chad	208	10.50N	19.20E
Zalaegerszeg, Hung. (zŏ'lô-ĕ'gĕr-sĕg)	148	46.50N	16.50E
Zalău, Rom. (zȧ-lŭ'ò)	148	47.11N	23.06E
Zaltan, Libya	204	28.20N	19.40E
Zaltbommel, Neth.	139a	51.48N	5.15E
Zama, Japan	238a	35.29N	139.24E
Zambezi, r., Afr. (zȧm-bā'zē)	206	16.00S	29.45E
Zambia, nation, Afr. (zăm'bē-ȧ)	206	14.23S	24.15E
Zamboanga, Phil. (säm-bō-aŋ'gä)	188	6.58N	122.02E
Zambrów, Pol. (zäm'bróf)	148	52.29N	22.17E
Zamora, Mex. (sä-mō'rä)	110	19.59N	102.16W
Zamora, Spain (thä-mō'rä)	142	41.32N	5.43W
Zanatepec, Mex.	112	16.30N	94.22W
Zandvoort, Neth.	139a	52.22N	4.30E
Zanesville, Oh., U.S. (zānz'vĭl)	92	39.55N	82.00W
Zangasso, Mali	208	12.09N	5.37W
Zanjān, Iran	174	36.26N	48.24E
Zanzibar, Tan. (zăn'zĭ-bär)	206	6.10S	39.11E
Zanzibar, i., Tan.	206	6.20S	39.37E
Zanzibar Channel, strt., Tan.	210	6.05S	39.00E
Zaozhuang, China (dzou-jůäŋ)	182	34.51N	117.34E
Zapadnaya Dvina, r., Eur. (zä'pȧd-nȧ-yȧ dvē'nȧ)	146	55.30N	28.27E
Zapala, Arg. (zä-pä'lä)	126	38.53S	70.02W
Zapata, Tx., U.S. (sä-pä'tä)	106	26.52N	99.18W
Zapata, Ciénaga de, sw., Cuba (syĕ'nä-gä-dĕ-zä-pȧ'tä)	116	22.30N	81.20W
Zapata, Península de, pen., Cuba (pĕ-nĕ'n-sōō-lä-dĕ-zä-pȧ'tä)	116	22.20N	81.30W
Zapatera, Isla, i., Nic. (ē's-lä-sä-pä-tā'rō)	114	11.45N	85.45W
Zapopan, Mex. (sä-pō'pän)	112	20.42N	103.23W
Zaporoshskoye, Russia (zȧ-pô-rôsh'skô-yĕ)	146	60.36N	30.31E
Zaporozh'ye, Ukr. (zä-pô-rôzh'yĕ)	158	47.50N	35.10E
Zaporozh'ye, prov., Ukr. (zä-pô-rôzh'yĕ ôb'ást)	156	47.20N	35.05E
Zapotiltic, Mex. (sä-pô-tēl-tēk')	112	19.37N	103.25W
Zapotitlán, Mex. (sä-pô-tē-tlän')	112	17.13N	98.58W
Zapotitlán, Mex.	229a	19.18N	99.02W
Zapotitlán, Punta, c., Mex.	112	18.34N	94.48W
Zapotlanejo, Mex. (sä-pô-tlä-nä'hô)	112	20.38N	103.05W
Zaragoza, Mex. (sä-rä-gō'sä)	112	23.59N	99.45W
Zaragoza, Mex.	112	22.02N	100.45W
Zaragoza, Spain (thä-rä-gō'thä)	136	41.39N	0.53W
Zarand, Munții, mts., Rom.	148	46.07N	22.21E
Zaranda Hill, mtn., Nig.	208	10.15N	9.35E
Zaranj, Afg.	176	31.06N	61.53E
Zarasai, Lith. (zä-rä-sī')	146	55.45N	26.18E
Zárate, Arg. (zä-rä'tä)	126	34.05S	59.05W
Zaraysk, Russia (zä-rä'ēsk)	160	54.46N	38.53E
Zarečje, Russia	235b	55.41N	37.23E
Zaria, Nig. (zä'rē-ä)	204	11.07N	7.44E
Zarqā', r., Jord.	173a	32.13N	35.43E
Zarzal, Col. (zär-zá'l)	124a	4.23N	76.04W
Zashiversk, Russia (zá'shĭ-vĕrsk')	158	67.08N	144.02E
Zastavna, Ukr. (zás-täf'nȧ)	148	48.32N	25.50E
Zastron, S. Afr. (zȧs'trŭn)	207c	30.19S	27.07E
Žatec, Czech. (zhä'tĕts)	148	50.19N	13.32E
Zavitinsk, Russia	162	50.12N	129.44E
Zawiercie, Pol. (zȧ-vyĕr'tsyĕ)	148	50.28N	19.25E
Zāwiyat al-Baydā', Libya	204	32.49N	21.46E
Zāwiyat Nābit, Egypt	240a	30.07N	31.09E
Zāyandeh, r., Iran	174	32.15N	51.00E
Zaysan, Kaz. (zī'sȧn)	158	47.43N	84.44E
Zaysan, l., Kaz.	158	48.16N	84.05E
Zaza, r., Cuba (zá'zá)	116	21.40N	79.25W
Zbarazh, Ukr. (zbä-räzh')	148	49.39N	25.48E
Zbruch, r., Ukr. (zbròch)	148	48.56N	26.18E
Zdolbunov, Ukr.	148	50.31N	26.17E
Zduńska Wola, Pol. (zdōōn''skä vō'lä)	148	51.36N	18.27E
Zebediela, S. Afr.	212d	24.19S	29.21E
Zeeland, Mi., U.S. (zē'lȧnd)	92	42.50N	86.00W
Zefat, Isr.	173a	32.58N	35.30E
Zehdenick, Ger. (tsā'dē-nēk)	148	52.59N	13.20E
Zehlendorf, Ger. (tsā'lĕn-dôrf)	139b	52.47N	13.23E
Zehlendorf, neigh., Ger.	234a	52.26N	13.15E
Zeist, Neth.	139a	52.05N	5.14E
Zelenogorsk, Russia (zĕ-lă'nô-gôrsk)	146	60.13N	29.39E
Zella-Mehlis, Ger. (tsâl'á-mā'lēs)	148	50.40N	10.38E
Zémio, Cen. Afr. Rep. (za-myō')	204	5.03N	25.11E
Zemlya Frantsa-Iosifa (Franz Josef Land), is., Russia	158	81.32N	40.00E
Zempoala, Punta, c., Mex. (pōō'n-tä-sĕm-pô-ä'lä)	112	19.30N	96.18W
Zempoatlépetl, mtn., Mex. (sĕm-pô-ä-tlä'pĕt'l)	112	17.13N	95.59W
Zemun, Yugo. (zĕ'mōōn) (sĕm'lĭn)	142	44.50N	20.25E
Zengcheng, China (dzŭŋ-chŭŋ)	183a	23.18N	113.49E
Zenica, Bos. (zĕ'nēt-sä)	154	44.10N	17.54E
Zeni-Su, is., Japan (zĕ'nē sōō)	187	33.55N	138.55E
Zen'kov, Ukr. (zĕn-kôf')	156	50.13N	34.23E
Žepče, Bos. (zhĕp'chĕ)	156	44.26N	18.01E
Zepernick, Ger. (tsĕ'pĕr-nēk)	139b	52.39N	13.32E
Zerbst, Ger. (tsĕrbst)	148	51.58N	12.03E
Zerpenschleuse, Ger. (tsĕr'pĕn-shloi-zĕ)	139b	52.51N	13.30E
Zeuthen, Ger. (tsoi'tĕn)	139b	52.21N	13.38E
Zevenaar, Neth.	151c	51.56N	6.06E
Zevenbergen, Neth.	139a	51.38N	4.36E
Zeya, Russia (zâ'yȧ)	158	53.43N	127.29E
Zeya, r., Russia	162	52.31N	128.30E
Zeytinburnu, neigh., Tur.	235f	40.59N	28.54E
Zeytun, Tur. (zā-tōōn')	160	38.00N	36.40E
Zezere, r., Port. (zĕ'zȧ-rĕ)	152	39.54N	8.12W
Zgierz, Pol. (zgyĕzh)	148	51.51N	19.26E
Zgurovka, Ukr. (zgōō'rôf-kä)	156	50.31N	31.43E
Zhangbei, China (jäŋ-bā)	180	41.12N	114.50E
Zhanggezhuang, China (jäŋ-gŭ-jůäŋ)	182	40.09N	116.56E
Zhangguangcai Ling, mts., China (jäŋ-gůäŋ-tsī lĭŋ)	184	43.50N	127.55E
Zhangjiakou, China	180	40.45N	114.58E
Zhangqiu, China (jäŋ-chyô)	182	36.50N	117.29E
Zhangye, China (jäŋ-yu)	180	38.46N	101.00E
Zhangzhou, China (jäŋ-jō)	180	24.35N	117.45E
Zhangzi Dao, i., China (jäŋ-dz dou)	182	39.02N	122.44E
Zhanhua, China (jän-hwä)	182	37.42N	117.49E
Zhanjiang, China (jän-jyäŋ)	180	21.20N	110.28E
Zhanyu, China (jän-yōō)	184	44.30N	122.30E
Zhao'an, China (jou-än)	184	23.48N	117.10E
Zhaodong, China (jou-dôŋ)	184	45.58N	126.00E
Zhaotong, China (jou-tôŋ)	180	27.18N	103.50E
Zhaoxian, China (jou shyĕn)	182	37.46N	114.48E
Zhaoyuan, China (jou-yuän)	182	37.22N	120.23E
Zhecheng, China (jŭ-chŭŋ)	184	34.05N	115.19E
Zhegao, China (jŭ-gou)	182	31.47N	117.44E
Zhejiang, prov., China (jŭ-jyäŋ)	180	29.30N	120.00E
Zhelaniya, Mys, c., Russia (zhĕ'lä-nĭ-yȧ)	158	75.43N	69.10E
Zhengding, China (jŭŋ-dĭŋ)	184	38.10N	114.35E
Zhen'guosi, China	236b	39.51N	116.21E
Zhengyang, China (jŭŋ-yäŋ)	182	32.34N	114.22E
Zhengzhou, China (jŭŋ-jō)	180	34.46N	113.42E
Zhenjiang, China (jŭn-jyäŋ)	180	32.13N	119.24E
Zhenru, China	237a	31.15N	121.24E
Zhenyuan, China (jŭn-yůän)	184	27.08N	108.30E
Zhigalovo, Russia (zhē-gä'lô-vô)	158	54.52N	105.05E
Zhigansk, Russia (zhē-gánsk')	158	66.45N	123.20E
Zhijiang, China (jr-jyäŋ)	184	27.25N	109.45E
Zhitomir, Ukr. (zhē'tô'mêr)	158	50.15N	28.40E
Zhitomir, prov., Ukr.	156	50.40N	28.07E
Zhizdra, Russia (zhēz'drȧ)	156	53.47N	34.41E
Zhizhitskoye, l., Russia (zhē-zhēt'skô-yĕ)	156	56.08N	31.34E
Zhmerinka, Ukr. (zhmyĕ'rĕŋ-kȧ)	160	49.02N	28.09E
Zhongshan Park, rec., China	237a	31.13N	121.25E
Zhongwei, China (jôŋ-wā)	180	37.32N	105.10E
Zhongxian, China (jôŋ shyĕn)	180	30.20N	108.00E
Zhongxin, China (jôŋ-shyĭn)	183a	23.16N	113.38E
Zhoucun, China (jō-tsōōn)	184	36.49N	117.52E
Zhoukouzhen, China (jō-kō-jŭn)	182	33.39N	114.40E
Zhoupu, China (jō-pōō)	182	31.07N	121.33E
Zhoushan Qundao, is., China (jō-shän-chyòn-dou)	180	30.00N	123.00E
Zhouxian, China (jō shyĕn)	184	39.30N	115.59E
Zhu, r., China (jōō)	183a	22.48N	113.36E
Zhuanghe, China (jůäŋ-hŭ)	184	39.40N	123.00E
Zhuanqiao, China (jůäŋ-chyou)	183b	31.02N	121.24E
Zhucheng, China (jōō-chŭŋ)	184	36.01N	119.24E
Zhuji, China (jōō-jyē)	184	29.58N	120.10E
Zhujiang Kou, b., Asia (jōō-jyäŋ kō)	184	22.00N	114.00E
Zhukovskiy, Russia (zhò-kôf'skĭ)	164b	55.33N	38.09E
Zi, r., China (dzē)	184	26.50N	111.00E
Zia Indian Reservation, I.R., N.M., U.S.	102	35.30N	106.43W
Zibo, China (dzē-bwo)	182	36.48N	118.04E
Ziel, Mount, mtn., Austl. (zēl)	196	23.15S	132.45E
Zielona Góra, Pol. (zhyĕ-lô'nä gōō'rä)	148	51.56N	15.30E
Zigazinskiy, Russia (zĭ-gazinskēē)	164a	53.50N	57.18E
Ziguinchor, Sen.	204	12.35N	16.16W
Zile, Tur. (zē-lĕ')	142	40.20N	35.50E
Žilina, Czech. (zhē'lĭ-nä)	140	49.14N	18.45E
Zillah, Libya	204	28.26N	17.52E
Zima, Russia (zē'mȧ)	162	53.58N	102.08E
Zimapan, Mex. (sē-mä'pän)	112	20.43N	99.23W
Zimatlán de Alvarez, Mex.	112	16.52N	96.47W
Zimba, Zam.	210	17.19S	26.13E
Zimbabwe, nation, Afr. (rô-dē'zhĭ-ȧ)	206	17.50S	29.30E
Zimnicea, Rom. (zēm-nē'chȧ)	154	43.39N	25.22E
Zin, r., Isr.	173a	30.50N	35.12E
Zinacatepec, Mex. (zē-nä-kä-tē'pĕk)	112	18.19N	97.15W
Zinapécuaro, Mex. (sē-nä-pä'kwä-rô)	112	19.50N	100.49W
Zinder, Niger (zĭn'dĕr)	204	13.48N	8.59E
Zion, Il., U.S. (zī'ŭn)	95a	42.27N	87.50W
Zion National Park, rec., Ut., U.S.	90	37.20N	113.00W
Zionsville, In., U.S. (zīŭnz-vĭl)	95g	39.57N	86.15W
Zirandaro, Mex. (sē-rän-dä'rō)	112	18.28N	101.02W
Zitacuaro, Mex. (sē-tä-kwä'rō)	112	19.25N	100.22W
Zitlala, Mex. (sē-tlä'lä)	112	17.38N	99.09W
Zittau, Ger. (tsē'tou)	148	50.55N	14.48E
Ziway, l., Eth.	204	8.08N	39.11E
Ziya, r., China (dzē-yä)	182	38.38N	116.31E
Zlatograd, Bul.	154	41.24N	25.05E
Zlatoust, Russia (zlá-tô-ôst')	158	55.13N	59.39E
Zlītan, Libya	204	32.27N	14.33E
Złoczew, Pol. (zwô'chĕf)	148	51.23N	18.34E
Zlynka, Russia (zlĕŋ'kȧ)	156	52.28N	31.39E
Znamenka, Ukr. (znä'mĕn-kä)	156	48.43N	32.35E

ng-sing; ŋ-baŋk; N-nasalized n; nŏd; cŏmmit; ōld; ōbey; ôrder; oi-boil; fōōd; ò-as oo in foot; ou-out; s-soft; sh-dish; th-thin; pūre; ůnite; ûrn; stŭd; circŭs; ü-as in French tu; '-indeterminate vowel.

PLACE (Pronunciation)	PAGE	Lat. °	Long. °
Znamensk, Russia (znä′měnsk)	146	54.37N	21.13E
Znojmo, Czech. (znoi′mô)	140	48.52N	16.03E
Zoetermeer, Neth.	139a	52.08N	4.29E
Zoeterwoude, Neth.	139a	52.08N	4.29E
Zográfos, Grc.	235d	37.59N	23.46E
Zolochěv, Ukr. (zô′lô-chěf)	148	49.48N	24.55E
Zolotonosha, Ukr. (zô′lô-tô-nô′shá) . .	160	49.41N	32.03E
Zolotoy, Mys, c., Russia (mís zô-lô-tôy′)	186	47.24N	139.10E
Zomba, Mwi. (zôm′bá)	206	15.23S	35.18E
Zongo, Zaire (zöŋ′gô)	204	4.19N	18.36E
Zonguldak, Tur. (zŏn′gōōl′dák)	174	41.25N	31.50E
Zonhoven, Bel.	139a	50.59N	5.24E
Zoquitlán, Mex. (sô-kĕt-län′)	112	18.09N	97.02W
Zorita, Spain (thō-rē′tä)	152	39.18N	5.41W
Zossen, Ger. (tsô′sĕn)	139b	52.13N	13.27E
Zouar, Chad	208	20.27N	16.32E
Zouxian, China (dzô shyĕn)	184	35.24N	116.54E
Zubtsov, Russia (zŏp-tsôf′)	156	56.13N	34.34E
Zuera, Spain (thwä′rä)	152	41.40N	0.48W
Zuger See, I., Switz. (tsōōg)	148	47.10N	8.40E
Zugspitze, mtn., Eur.	148	47.25N	11.00E
Zuidelijk Flevoland, reg., Neth.	139a	52.22N	5.20E
Zújar, r., Spain (zōō′kär)	152	38.55N	5.05W
Zújar, Embalse del, res., Spain	152	38.50N	5.20W
Zulueta, Cuba (zōō-lô-ě′tä)	116	22.20N	79.35W
Zumbo, Moz. (zōōm′bò)	206	15.36S	30.25E
Zumbro, r., Mn., U.S. (zŭm′brô)	96	44.18N	92.14W
Zumbrota, Mn., U.S. (zŭm-brô′ta)	96	44.16N	92.39W
Zumpango, Mex. (sòm-päŋ-gò)	112	19.48N	99.06W
Zundert, Neth.	139a	51.28N	4.39E
Zungeru, Nig. (zóŋ-gä′rōō)	204	9.48N	6.09E
Zunhua, China (dzón-hwä)	184	40.12N	117.55E
Zuni, r., Az., U.S.	102	34.40N	109.30W
Zuni Indian Reservation, I.R., N.M., U.S. (zōō′ně)	102	35.10N	108.40W
Zuni Mountains, mts., N.M., U.S. . . .	102	35.10N	108.10W
Zunyi, China	180	27.58N	106.40E
Zürich, Switz. (tsü′rĭk)	136	47.22N	8.32E
Zürichsee, I., Switz.	148	47.18N	8.47E
Zushi, Japan (zōō′shě)	187a	35.17N	139.35E
Zuurbekom, S. Afr.	240b	26.19S	27.49E
Zuwārah, Libya	204	32.58N	12.07E
Zuwayzā, Jord.	173a	31.42N	35.55E
Zvenigorod, Russia (zvä-ně′gô-rôt) . . .	156	55.46N	36.54E
Zvenigorodka, Ukr.	160	49.07N	30.59E
Zvishavane, Zimb.	206	20.15S	30.28E
Zvolen, Czech. (zvô′lĕn)	148	48.35N	19.10E
Zvornik, Bos. (zvôr′nĕk)	154	44.24N	19.08E
Zweckel, neigh., Ger.	232	51.36N	6.59E
Zweibrücken, Ger. (tsvī-brük′ĕn)	148	49.16N	7.20E
Zwickau, Ger. (tsvĭkóu)	140	50.43N	12.30E
Zwolle, Neth. (zvôl′ě)	140	52.33N	6.05E
Żyradów, Pol. (zhě-rär′dóf)	148	52.04N	20.28E
Zyryanka, Russia (zě-ryän′ká)	158	65.45N	151.15E
Zyryanovsk, Kaz. (zě-ryä′nôfsk)	158	49.43N	84.20E

Listed below are major topics covered by the thematic maps, graphs and/or statistics.
Page citations are for world, continent and country maps and for world tables.

Abaca   38
Agricultural regions   30-31, 58, 74, 120, 165, 169,
   179, 183, 194, 201
Alliances   54
Aluminum   42
American Indian population   71
Apples   36
Aquifers   68, 194
Areas   2-3, 241-4
Bananas   36
Barley   34
Bauxite   42, 58, 120, 129, 165, 179, 194
Beef trade   39
Birth rate   22
Black population   71
Cacao   34
Calorie supply   26
Cancer   72
Cassava   35
Castor beans   37
Cattle   39
Cellulosic fibers   38
Chromite   44, 165, 169, 179, 201
Citrus fruit   36
Climate   8-9, 65
Coal   48-49, 57, 58, 69, 119, 120, 127, 129, 165,
   167, 169, 179, 183, 193, 194, 201
Cobalt   44, 201
Coffee   33, 179
Continental drift   215
Copper   42, 58, 120, 129, 165, 169, 179, 183, 194,
   201
Copra   37
Corn   33
Cotton   38, 179
Cottonseed   37
Currents   14-15, 190-191
Dates   36
Death rate   22
Deciduous fruit   36
Diamonds   201
Drift, continental   215
Earth-sun relationships   xvi
Economies   28-29
Education   71
Electricity   50
Energy   47, 50, 57, 119, 127, 167, 193
Energy production and consumption   47
Environments   59, 60-61, 88, 121, 130-131, 170,
   171, 195, 202
Eskimo and Aleut population   71
Ethnic groups   118, 119, 166, 200
Exports   51
Farming   74
Ferroalloys   44
Fertilizers   46
Fibers   38
Fisheries   36
Flax   38
Flaxseed   37
Fleets   53
Forest regions   40
Frost dates   65
Frost free period   65
Fruit   36
Fuels   48-49, 57, 119, 127, 167, 193
Gas, natural   48-49, 57, 69, 119, 127, 167, 193
GDP   24
Geothermal power   50, 57, 127, 167, 193
Glaciation   62-63, 64, 132-133
Gold   41, 165, 194, 201
Grain sorghum   34
Grapes   41

Gross domestic product   24
Ground nuts   37
Ground water   68, 194
Hazardous waste   72
Hazards, natural   57, 119, 127, 167, 193, 200
Historical   73
Heart disease   72
Hispanic population   71
Hospital beds   72
Hydroelectric power   50, 57, 119, 127, 167, 193
Imports   51
Income   72
Infant mortality   22
Inland waterways   52-53, 75
Iron ore   44, 58, 69, 120, 129, 165, 169, 179, 183,
   194, 201
Jute   38, 179
Kapok   38
Labor   73
Land areas   2-3, 241-4
Landforms   6-7, 57, 62-63, 119, 132-133, 200
Land transportation   52-53, 75, 194
Land use   28-29, 199
Languages   25, 134-135, 179, 200
Lead   43, 58, 120, 129, 165, 169, 183, 194
Life expectancy   22, 27, 71
Lignite   48-49, 57, 69, 119, 127, 129, 165, 167, 193
Linseed   37
Literacy   24
Lumber exports   40
Maize   33
Manganese   44, 165, 169, 179, 183, 194, 201
Manufacturing   45, 74
Map projections   x-xii
Merchant fleets   53
Millet   34
Mineral fertilizers   46
Minerals, see specific mineral
Minority population   71
Moisture regions   65
Molybdenum   44
Natural gas   48-49, 57, 69, 119, 127, 167, 193
Natural hazards   57, 119, 127, 167, 193, 200
Natural vegetation   16-17, 58, 66-67, 88, 120, 128,
   169, 194, 201
Newspaper circulation   24
Nickel   44, 58, 165, 169
Nitrogen, synthetic   46
Non-cellulosic fibers   38
Nuclear power   50, 57, 119, 127, 167
Nutrition   26
Nylon   38
Oats   33
Occupational structure   28-29, 73
Ocean currents   14-15, 190-191
Ocean transportation   52-53
Oil palm   37
Oil (petroleum)   48-49, 57, 58, 69, 119, 120, 127,
   129, 165, 167, 169, 193, 194, 201
Oils, vegetable   37
Olives   37
Peanuts   37
Peoples   118, 119, 166, 200
Petroleum   48-49, 57, 58, 69, 119, 120, 127, 129,
   165, 167, 169, 193, 194, 201
Phosphate   46, 165, 169, 183, 201
Physical world   4-5
Physicians   27, 72
Physiography   62-63, 132-133
Pig iron   45
Pigs (swine)   49
Pineapples   36
Pipelines   75

Plate tectonics   214
Platinum   41, 165
Political change (Africa)   200
Political world   2-3
Polyester   38
Population change   71
Population, countries   2-3, 241-4
Population density   20-21, 58, 70, 88, 120, 129,
   165, 168, 183, 194, 201
Population, major cities   247
Population, natural increase   1, 23
Population, urban-rural (graph)   21
Population, world total (graph, table)   3, 245
Potash   46
Potatoes   35
Poverty   72
Precious metals   41
Precipitation   12-13, 14-15, 58, 64, 88, 120, 128,
   168, 194, 201
Pressure, atmospheric   12-13, 65
Protein consumption   26
Pyrites   46
Railroads   52-53, 75, 194
Rapeseed   37
Religions   25
Rice   34
Roads   52-53, 75, 194
Rubber   41, 179
Rye   32
Sesame seed   37
Sheep   40
Silver   41, 194
Sisal   38
Soils   18-19
Solar power   50
Soybeans   37
Steel   45
Sugar   35, 179
Sulfur   46, 120
Sunflower seed   37
Sunshine, percentage   65
Swine   39
Tanker fleets   53
Tea   32, 179
Tectonics   214
Temperature   10-11
Territorial evolution (Canada)   73
Thermal efficiency   65
Time Zones   xvi, 75, 194
Tin   42, 120, 169, 183, 201
Tobacco   36
Trade   51
Trade routes   52-53
Transportation   52-53, 75, 194
Tung nuts   37
Tungsten   44, 120, 165, 169, 183, 194
Unemployment   72
Uranium   48-49, 57, 119, 127, 165, 167, 193, 201
Urbanization   23
Vanadium   44
Vegetable oils   37
Vegetation   16-17, 58, 66-67, 88, 120, 128, 169,
   194, 201
Waste, hazardous   72
Water power   50, 57, 119, 127, 167, 193
Water problems   68
Water resources   57, 68, 194
Westward expansion (United States)   73
Wheat   32
Winds   12-13
Wood   40
Wool   40
Zinc   43, 58, 120, 129, 165, 169, 183, 194

SOURCES

The sources listed below have been consulted during the process of creating and updating the thematic maps and statistics for the 18th edition.

Agricultural Statistics U.S. Dept. of Agriculture
Air Carrier Traffic at Canadian Airports Statistics Canada, Minister of Supply and Services
Alberta Energy Portfolio Energy Resources Conservation Board
Annual Abstract of Statistics Central Statistical Office (U.K.)
Annual Economic Review and Statistical Abstract Guam Dept. of Commerce, Economic Research Center
Annual Report on Alaska's Mineral Resources U.S. Dept. of the Interior, Geological Survey
Anuario Estatistico do Brasil Fundacao Instituto Brasileiro de Geografia e Estatistica
Area Handbook - East Germany U.S. Dept. of Defense
Atlas of Economic Mineral Deposits Cornell University Press
Atlas of Iran Sahab Geographic and Drafting Institute
Atlas Narodov Mira, Central Administration of Geodesy and Cartography of the U.S.S.R.
Atlas of Nuclear Energy Georgia State University, Dept. of Geography
Australian Demographic Statistics Australian Bureau of Statistics
Britain - An Official Handbook United Kingdom Central Office of Information
Canada Year Book Statistics Canada, Minister of Supplies and Services
China - A Geographical Survey Halsted Press
City and County Data Book U.S. Dept. of Commerce, Bureau of the Census
Coal Fields of the United States U.S. Dept. of the Interior, Geological Survey
Coal Production U.S. Dept. of Energy, Energy Information Administration
Coal Resources and Reserves of Canada Minister of Supply and Services (Canada)
COMECON Data Greenwood Press, Inc.
Commercial Nuclear Power Stations around the World Nuclear News, American Nuclear Society
Commercial Nuclear Power Stations in the United States Nuclear News, American Nuclear Society
Compendium of Human Settlements Statistics United Nations, Dept. of International Economic and Social Affairs
Concise Marine Almanac Van Nostrand Reinhold Co., Inc.
The Copper Industry of the U.S.S.R. U.S. Dept. of the Interior, Bureau of Mines
Demographic Yearbook United Nations, Dept. of International Economic and Social Affairs
East Germany - A Country Study U.S. Dept. of Defense
Energy Statistics Yearbook United Nations, Dept. of International Economic and Social Affairs
FAA Statistical Handbook of Aviation U.S. Dept. of Transportation, Federal Aviation Administration
FAO Atlas of the Living Resources of the Seas United Nations, Food and Agriculture Organization
FAO Fertilizer Yearbook United Nations, Food and Agriculture Organization
FAO Production Yearbook United Nations, Food and Agriculture Organization
FAO Trade Yearbook United Nations, Food and Agriculture Organization
FAO Yearbook of Fishery Statistics United Nations, Food and Agriculture Organization
FAO Yearbook of Forest Products United Nations, Food and Agriculture Organization
General Review of the Mineral Industries Statistics Canada, Industries Division
Geology and Economic Minerals of Canada Geological Survey of Canada, Dept. of Mines and Technical Surveys
Geothermal Resources Council Bulletin Geothermal Resources Council
Global Estimates and Projections of Populations by Sex and Age United Nations, Dept. of International Economic and Social Affairs
Handbook of Economic Statistics U.S. Central Intelligence Agency
Handbook of International Trade and Development Statistics United Nations, Conference on Trade and Development
India and Pakistan - Land, People and Economy Methuen and Co., Ltd.
Industrial Statistics Yearbook, Vols. 1 and 2 United Nations, Dept. of International Economic and Social Affairs
Information Please Almanac Houghton Mifflin Company
International Energy Annual U.S. Dept. of Energy, Energy Information Administration
International Petroleum Encyclopedia PennWell Publishing Co.
International Trade Statistics Yearbook, Vols. 1 and 2 United Nations, Dept. of International Economic and Social Affairs
International Water Power and Dam Construction Handbook Reed Business Publishing Ltd.
Jane's World Railways, Jane's Publishing Co., Inc.
Mapa Gospadarczaswiata - Rolnictwo Government of Poland
Maritime Transport Organization for Economic Co-operation and Development
Mineral Industries of Africa U.S. Dept. of the Interior, Bureau of Mines
Mineral Industries of Europe and the U.S.S.R. U.S. Dept. of the Interior, Bureau of Mines
Mineral Industries of the Far East and South Asia U.S. Dept. of the Interior, Bureau of Mines
Mineral Industries of Latin America U.S. Dept. of the Interior, Bureau of Mines
Mineral Industries of the Middle East U.S. Dept. of the Interior, Bureau of Mines
Mineral Production of Australia Australian Bureau of Statistics
Mineral Resources of the World Prentice-Hall, Inc.
Minerals Yearbook, Vols. 1, 2 and 3 U.S. Dept. of the Interior, Bureau of Mines
The Mining Industry of British Columbia and the Yukon British Columbia Hydro and Power Authority, Industrial Development Department

Mining Survey South Africa Chamber of Mines
Monthly Bulletin of Statistics United Nations, Dept. of International Economic and Social Affairs
MVMA Motor Vehicle Facts and Figures Motor Vehicle Manufacturers Assoc. of the U.S.
Namibia U.S. Dept. of the Interior, Bureau of Mines
National Atlas - Canada, Dept. of Energy, Mines, and Resources
National Atlas - Chile, Instituto Geografico Militar
National Atlas - China, Cartographic Publishing House
National Atlas - Greece (Economic and Social Atlas), National Statistical Service
National Atlas - Japan, Geographical Survey Institute
National Atlas - United States, U.S. Dept. of the Interior, Geological Survey
National Atlas - U.S.S.R., Central Administration of Geodesy and Cartography
National Economy of the U.S.S.R. Central Statistical Office (U.S.S.R.)
National Priorities List U.S. Environmental Protection Agency
New Zealand Official Yearbook New Zealand, Dept. of Statistics
Non-Ferrous Metal Data American Bureau of Metal Statistics
Nuclear Power Reactors in the World International Atomic Energy Agency
Oil and Gas Journal Data Book PennWell Publishing Co.
Oxford Economic Atlas of the World Oxford University Press
The People's Republic of China - A New Industrial Power U.S. Dept. of the Interior, Bureau of Mines
The Persian Gulf U.S. Central Intelligence Agency
Population and Vital Statistics Reports United Nations, Dept. of International Economic and Social Affairs
Primary Aluminum Plants Worldwide, Parts 1 and 2 U.S. Dept. of the Interior, Bureau of Mines
The Prospects of World Urbanization United Nations, Dept. of International Economic and Social Affairs
Railway Transport in Canada - Commodity Statistics Statistics Canada, Minister of Supply and Services
Rand McNally Road Atlas Rand McNally
Republic of China - A Reference Book Hilit Publishing Co., Ltd.
A Review of the Natural Resources of the African Continent United Nations, Educational, Scientific and Cultural Organization
Romania Yearbook Editura Stiintifica si Enciclopedica
Scandinavia - An Introductory Geography Praeger Publications
South Africa - Official Yearbook Bureau for Information (South Africa)
South America Hodder and Stoughton, Ltd.
Soviet Geography V. H. Winston and Sons, Inc.
Soviet Natural Resources in the World Economy Association of American Geographers
The Soviet Union - A Systematic Geography L. Symons et al.
Soviet Union - Coal and Major Minerals U.S. Central Intelligence Agency
Statistical Abstract Central Statistical Organisation, Ministry of Planning (India)
Statistical Abstract of the United States U.S. Dept. of the Interior, Bureau of the Census
Statistical Yearbook United Nations, Dept. of International Economic and Social Affairs
Statistical Yearbook of China Economic Information Agency
Statistical Yearbook of Denmark Danmarks Statistik
Statistics des Auslandes Statistisches Bundesamt
Sugar Yearbook International Sugar Organization
Survey of Energy Resources World Energy Conference
Textile Organon "World Man-made Fiber Survey" Textile Economics Bureau, Inc.
Tin Ore Resources of Asia and Australia United Nations, Economic Commission for Asia and the Far East
The United States Energy Atlas Macmillan Publishing Co., Inc.
Uranium Industry Annual U.S. Dept. of Energy, Energy Information Administration
Uranium Resources, Production and Demand Organization for Economic Co-operation and Development
U.S.S.R. Energy Atlas U.S. Central Intelligence Agency
U.S.S.R. in Maps Holmes and Meier Publishers, Inc.
World Atlas of Agriculture Istituto Geografico De Agostini
World Atlas of Geology and Mineral Deposits Mining Journal Books, Ltd.
World Coal Resources and Major Trade Routes Miller Freeman Publications, Inc.
World Development Report The World Bank
The World Factbook U.S. Central Intelligence Agency
World Metal Statistics Year Book World Bureau of Metal Statistics
World Mineral Statistics British Geological Survey
World Mining Porphyry Copper Miller Freeman Publications, Inc.
World Oil "International Outlook" Gulf Publishing Company
World Population Profile U.S. Dept. of Commerce, Bureau of the Census
World Population Prospects United Nations, Dept. of International Economic and Social Affairs
World Transport Data International Road Transport Union, Dept. of Economic Affairs
Year Book Australia Australian Bureau of Statistics
Year Book of Labour Statistics International Labour Organization
Year End Review South Africa Chamber of Mines
Zimbabwe U.S. Dept. of the Interior, Bureau of Mines